The Whole Genuine and Complete Works of Flavius Josephus Translated From the Original in the Greek Language And Diligently Revised and Compared With the Writings of Cotemporary Authors, of Different Nations

FRONTISPIECE

TO THE AMERICAN EDITION OF MAYNARDS JOSEPHUS

JOSEPHUS recounting the ANTIQUITIES and WARS of the JEWS at whose feet are the emblems that characterize him as a Warrior as well as an Historian. In the attitude of writing he is inspired by the HISTORIC MUSE who holds in one hand the MIRROR of TRUTH which she reflects on the MOSAIC WRITINGS and with the other points to the past. The statues of TITUS and his father VESPASIAN the Roman emperors. AARON and his Brother MOSES the great Lawgiver trampling on IDOLATRY. In the distance the Roman army destroying the City of JERUSALEM over which are THUNDER and LIGHTNING to denote the vengeance of heaven and behind the SETTING SUN an emblem of the total destruction of the JEWISH EMPIRE

THE

WHOLE GENUINE AND COMPLETE

WORKS

OF

FLAVIUS JOSEPHUS

THE LEARNED AND AUTHENTIC

JEWISH HISTORIAN,

AND

CELEBRATED WARRIOR.

CONTAINING

I The Antiquities of the Jews, in Twenty Books, with their Wars, memorable Transactions, remarkable Occurrences, their various Turns of Glory and Misery, Prosperity and Adversity, from the Creation of the World

II The Wars of the Jews with the Romans, from their Commencement to the final destruction of Jerusalem by Titus in the Reign of Vespasian In Seven Books

III The Book of Josephus against Apion in Defence of the Jewish Antiquities In Two Parts

IV The Martyrdoms of the Maccabees

V The Embassy of Philo from the Jews of Alexandria, to the Emperor Caius Caligula

VI The Life of Flavius Josephus, written by himself

VII Testimonies of Josephus concerning our Blessed Saviour, St John the Baptist, &c clearly vindicated

Translated from the Original in the Greek Language

And diligently revised and compared with the Writings of cotemporary Authors o[illegible] [illegible], on the Subject
All tending to prove the Authenticity of the Work

TO WHICH IS ADDED,

VARIOUS USEFUL INDEXES,

Particularly of the COUNTRIES, CITIES, TOWNS, VILLAGES, SEAS, RIVERS, MOUNTAINS, LAKES, &c which are related in the HISTORY

ALSO, A

CONTINUATION

OF THE

HISTORY of the JEWS,

From JOSEPHUS down to the present Time,

INCLUDING A PERIOD OF MORE THAN ONE THOUSAND SEVEN HUNDRED YEARS

CONTAINING

An Account of their Dispersion into the various Parts of Europe, Asia, Africa and America, their different Persecutions, Transactions, various Occurrences, and present State throughout the known World

WITH

a great variety of other interesting and authentic Particulars collected from various valuable Works, recording the principal Transactions of the Jews since the time of JOSEPHUS

By *GEORGE HENRY MAYNARD, L L D*

Illustrated with MARGINAL REFERENCES and NOTES, Historical, Biographical, Classical, Critical, Geographical, and Explanatory

By *the Rev EDWARD KIMPTON*

Author of the Complete UNIVERSAL HISTORY of the HOLY BIBLE

Embellished with Sixty beautiful Engravings, taken from original Drawings of Messrs [illegible], STOTHARD, and CORBOULD, Members of the Royal Academy, and engraved by AMERICAN ARTISTS

PHILADELPHIA

Printed and Sold by ARCHIBALD WOODRUFF and WILLIAM PECHIN, No [illegible], Market Street

MDCCXCV

THE

TRANSLATOR's

ADDRESS TO THE READER.

TO thoſe who are curious in ſearching into *ancient hiſtory*, whatever concerns ſo remarkable a people as the Jews muſt be extremely *intereſting* as well as *entertaining*, and perhaps many people, who would not look for their hiſtory in the Sacred Writings, might be irreſiſtibly inclined to hear what a learned man of their own nation, who was a ſoldier, a prieſt, and a politician, has delivered down to us concerning their origin and moſt remarkable tranſactions. Joſephus was not only a man of learning, but likewiſe well acquainted with the ſubject he treats of, and ſeems to have had almoſt as much connexion with the Roman people as with his own: for at twenty-ſix years of age, he went to Rome, lived there, and became intimately acquainted with Nicanor, (who was afterwards a colonel in Veſpaſian's army) and alſo with Aliturus, one of Nero's favourites. By him he was likewiſe introduced to Popæa the empreſs, from whom he received many honours.

Our Hiſtorian, therefore, cannot fail to give us much uſeful information as well as entertainment, when he treats of the manners and conduct of that enlightened and warlike people the Romans, by whom he was much reſpected and eſteemed. When he returned to Jeruſalem the war between the Jews and Romans was juſt breaking out, and he then appeared in defence of his countrymen, not only as a very able politician, but as an indefatigable and valiant commander: for being, at thirty years of age, appointed one of the governors of Galilee, he bravely reſiſted the Romans as long as courage and wiſdom could avail any thing againſt them. But alas! they were ſent as the tremendous ſcourge of Providence to an abandoned ungrateful people: they fought under the banner of an avenging God, and literally fulfilled our Saviour's prophecy, when they planted the Roman eagle in the heart of Judæa, "Whereſoever the carcaſs is, there will the Eagles be gathered together."—*Luke* xvii. 37.

Joſephus was happily ſpared from the dreadful deſtruction juſtly denounced againſt his countrymen: nor, indeed, can we wonder at God's kind preſervation of him, if we conſider attentively many circumſtances in his Life and Writings, which ſeem ſtrongly to indicate a liberal way of thinking, a mind ſtrongly biaſſed in favour of truth wherever he found it, and far above the obſtinate prejudices of Judaiſm.

His Sacred Hiſtory, though nearly correſpondent to the account of Moſes, is enriched with much Rabbinical learning, and adorned with many eloquent and nervous ſpeeches, highly expreſſive of the ſentiments of thoſe ancient men of renown who make ſo fair a figure in the hiſtoric page: but when he comes to relate the dreadful ſtruggle between the Jews and Romans, which ended in the death of 1,100,000 of the former, and the total overthrow of their ſtate and temple, ſo clear and circumſtantial is his account, that we follow him, as it were, ſtep by ſtep, ſympathize in all the various turns of fortune and ſhare the horrors of the war.

Joſephus appears moreover to have been ſingularly favoured by the Almighty in ſome particular revelations of his providential deſigns, for it is a known fact that he foretold to Veſpaſian that he ſhould be Emperor of the Romans when he was only a general in their armies, and he confeſſes, Chap. xiv. "That God ſhewed him, in a dream, the deſtruction of the Jews, and their conqueſt by "the Romans, and what ſhould happen to the Roman Emperors." Being a prieſt, he was well acquainted with the ſacred books of the Prophets, and knew how to explain them, and from his knowledge he frequently ſuggeſted to the Jews, that God had forſaken them, and gone over to the

Romans. He was even so bold and candid as to tell his obstinate countrymen, that in opposing the Romans, they fought not only against an incensed enemy, but against the decrees of God.

What may be expected then from so learned and impartial an Historian, writing in a manly, nervous style, and delivering to us a faithful account of those tremendous scenes he was witness to, and oftentimes actually engaged in? We cannot, perhaps, any where meet with a more interesting or entertaining history.

When the war was over, and all things he had foretold had exactly come to pass, he determined to publish this remarkable history, which we now offer in this new dress to the attention of the curious. He first wrote it in Hebrew, for the use of the eastern nations, which work is unfortunately lost to the world; but coming afterwards to Rome, with Titus, who greatly respected him, he then wrote that Greek copy which is now extant amongst us, and from whence many translations have deservedly been made into different languages.

It is not possible, in this short address, to give more than a faint idea of the curious information, and infinite entertainment, to be met with in this noble and impartial work; but it must certainly add to its value with every good christian, that there is good reason to believe that the author, at the time he wrote it, was more than "*almost persuaded to be a christian himself*." That famous passage, introduced in the 4th Chap. of the 18th Book of his antiquities, concerning our blessed Saviour, and which some superficial judges have pretended is spurious, will certainly appear, if fairly, and *even critically* examined, to be evidently such a plain and simple narration of an historical fact, as any Jew, in his situation, might have written to the Heathens, especially if we recollect that Josephus frequently tells his readers that he relates facts as he finds them; and, in his account of the opinions of the Pharisees, and the Sadducees or Essenes, he gives them as he found them in their books. Why then should he not be supposed to give us, with the same candor, though he does it in so respectful a manner, a plain relation of what he saw and heard concerning the Christians, and their opinion of their blessed master, especially as the Christians were then very numerous, and the general topic of discourse both among Jews and Romans?

Not to be tedious to our readers, we omit a very excellent criticism on the original Greek of this famous passage, sent us by a learned friend; but we take the liberty of assuring them, as far as we are able to judge, that it appears to us, from this criticism, equal to demonstration, that Josephus actually inserted, with his own hand, this fair and honorable testimony in favor of Christ and his followers. His defence against Apion, and his other writings, bear equal testimony both to his great abilities and integrity; each separate work has its intrinsic merit, and the whole forms a most useful, interesting, and amusing volume of real history; and it is sincerely hoped that our endeavours to maintain the sense and spirit of the original Greek, will be a considerable addition to the merit of the present translation.

To complete the work, we have annexed a supplement, collected from authentic manuscripts, bringing down the Jewish history to the present time, which, being an attempt entirely new, we flatter ourselves, will stamp an additional value upon our undertaking, and make it in every respect worthy the patronage of a judicious and candid public.

GEORGE HENRY MAYNARD.

THE

PREFACE OF JOSEPHUS

TO HIS

Hiftory of the Antiquities of the Jews.

VARIOUS are the motives by which Hiftorians are induced to tranfmit to pofterity their records of paft events. Some are incited to difplay their talents by the love of fame; others have exerted their utmoft abilities to conciliate the efteem of thofe whofe actions they relate; others are impelled by a defire of perpetuating the remembrance of thofe events in which they have been perfonally concerned; while others take up the pen to refcue from oblivion tranfactions worthy of knowledge, to vindicate truth, and prevent the perverfion of facts.

Of thefe motives the two laft prompted me to this undertaking: for having borne an active part in the Wars between the Jews and Romans, being witnefs of their rife and progrefs, and particularly concerned in the events, I was inclined to attempt an authentic narrative of the fame, to counteract the defigns of thofe who had fabricated falfehoods to impofe upon mankind.

The Work I have entered upon will, I doubt not, appear worthy the attention of the Greeks, as it will comprehend an account of the Antiquities, Policy and Government of our nation, faithfully tranflated from the Hebrew writings into their own tongue.

When I heretofore undertook the Hiftory of the Wars, it was my intention to explain the origin of the Jews, the viciffitudes of fortune they underwent, to delineate the character of the Legiflator by whom they had been taught the practice of piety and virtue, and to relate the feveral military tranfactions in which they had been fometimes neceffarily, and fometimes reluctantly concerned.

But finding the Antiquities a fubject too copious and prolix to be treated in connexion with any other, I determined to detach it from the Hiftory of the Wars, and direct my attention to the Antiquities previous to the Wars and other fucceeding events. Yet (as is frequently the cafe with thofe who engage in arduous purfuits) I found a difinclination to perfevere, as the work proved laborious, and my progrefs feemed retarded in proportion to its prolixity. Some, however, from a laudable defire of acquiring knowledge, encouraged me to proceed, and efpecially EPAPHRODITUS, a man who had a propenfity to literature in general, and hiftory in particular, and had himfelf held very confiderable employments, experienced many viciffitudes of fortune, and manifefted throughout the whole an integrity and magnanimity rarely to be equalled.

Thus prevailed on by the perfuafion of fo zealous a patron of whatever might conduce to the public good on the one hand, and difdaining to prefer an ignominious floth to the profecution of a laudable undertaking on the other, I refumed my tafk with a renewed defire of completing it, at the fame time reflecting, that our anceftors were ever difpofed to make ufeful communications, and that the Greeks were particularly defirous of obtaining an authentic hiftory of our nation.

When I alfo reflected that king Ptolomy II. (a fovereign who greatly favoured learning, and was defirous of obtaining literary information even at immenfe charge) procured a Greek tranflation of our code of laws, conftitution and government; and that Eleazar our high prieft, inferior to none of his predeceffors in knowledge or virtue, could not deny to that prince the participation of the inftruction and entertainment to be derived from fuch a work, as he knew it was the cuftom of our anceftors not to conceal that which might be ufeful to mankind in general; I held it my incumbent duty to imitate the liberality of our high-prieft, and the more fo as I am perfuaded there are now many perfons as much attached to literature, and as anxioufly defirous of obtaining knowledge as was that prince in his day.

King Ptolomy, indeed, did not obtain all our writings; thofe only which related to the Law were prefented to him by the interpreters at Alexandria; whereas the fubjects comprifed in the facred Writings are innumerable, fince they contain the hiftory of near four thousand years; an hiftory replete with furprifing events refpecting the various fortunes of war, the glorious atchievements of heroes, and the extraordinary revolutions of ftates.

In fine, thoſe who peruſe this Hiſtory will diſcover that actions piouſly deſigned will terminate proſperouſly, and that future bliſs will be the ultimate reward of preſent obedience to the Divine will, ſo on the contrary, ſuch who deviate from thoſe commands will be fruſtrated in their deſigns and expectations, which, though they may preſent to the view the moſt pleaſing proſpects, will end in irreparable calamities

Thoſe, therefore, who may be diſpoſed to read this Work are exhorted to raiſe their minds to the contemplation of the Deity, that they may be enabled to conform themſelves to his divine will, and examine whether our great Legiſlator has ſpoken of his nature, deſcribed his works in general, and the origin of things in particular, with a dignity becoming ſo exalted a theme, and whether he has in his narrative, avoided thoſe fictions evident in all other writings The antiquity of his Hiſtory might have ſecured him from detection, for he lived two thouſand years ago *(that is 2000 years before the time of Joſephus)* a period ſo diſtant that the poets dare not refer to it the genealogy of their gods, or trace from it the actions of any of the heroes they have laboured to perpetuate In the proſecution of my deſign I ſhall relate circumſtances minutely as to the order and time in which they occurred in a word, it ſhall be my undeviating plan to be genuine without prolixity, faithful without preciſion, and conciſe without retrenchment

As the principal ſubjects of our Work depend on the information we derive from Moſes our great Lawgiver, it appears neceſſary to premiſe ſome things concerning him, leſt any ſhould be ſurpriſed, that a work which promiſes an account of the religion, laws, conſtitution and hiſtorical events of the Jewiſh nation ſhould contain ſo much philoſophy and natural hiſtory

It is, therefore, to be underſtood, that Moſes lays it down, as eſſentially neceſſary for that man who would live virtuouſly himſelf, to preſcribe rules for regulating the conduct of others, to be well acquainted with the attributes of the Divine being, and having truly contemplated all his works both as to their operations and effects, and thereby traced his power and goodneſs, to endeavour, as far as in him lies, to imitate his perfections as the grand example in all things. Without this knowledge of the Divine Attributes, and the Divine Power and Goodneſs, as diſplayed in the works of Creation and Providence, as well as endeavour to imitate the Divine Perfection, neither can the Legiſlator be qualified in himſelf, nor can his writings conduce to the promotion of knowledge or virtue He wiſely conſidered that God, the common Parent and Lord of the univerſe, ſees all things, and diſtributes rewards and puniſhments according as men obey or deviate from his ſacred commands Moſes, therefore, in the eſtabliſhment of this grand and important doctrine, did not follow the example of other legiſlators, whoſe codes were mere contracts between man and man, but raiſed the minds of the people he was to inſtruct to the knowledge of God the Univerſal Creator He taught them that Man was the nobleſt of all his works, and that his true dignity and excellence conſiſted in imitating his perfections

Having thus wiſely rendered them ſubſervient to God, he ſoon inculcated in their minds thoſe ſocial obligations which reſpected one another They became obedient not from a principle of fear but piety, not from conſtraint but conviction Other legiſlators, under the influence of traditionary fables, aſcribe as attributes to their fictious deities the moſt enormous vices of which human creatures can be capable, and by that means, inſtead of ſuppreſſing, countenanced the moſt flagitious crimes But our excellent Lawgiver, having premiſed that the Divine Being is the center and perfection of virtue, infers, as a neceſſary conſequence, that it is the incumbent duty as well as the higheſt excellence of man as a rational creature, to aſpire to an imitation of his bright original, while he denounces on ſuch as reject theſe important doctrines the ſevereſt judgments

By this teſt it is my earneſt deſire that my works may be proved, conſcious that nothing will be found therein derogatory to the dignity of the Supreme Being, or contrary to his gracious deſigns towards men, but that, on the other hand, they will appear a diſplay of his perfections and a comment on his benevolence, as well as demonſtrate that all things are diſpoſed in exact conformity to the laws of univerſal nature, and principles of the ſublimeſt rectitude

Theſe grand points Moſes has amply diſcuſſed where it is requiſite his language is plain and explicit, in other parts his narrative abounds with allegorical figures, to inveſtigate which requires the aid of philoſophical diſquiſition But diſmiſſing this ſubject for the preſent, I ſhall apply myſelf to the Work I have undertaken, and begin with the Creation of the World.

FLAVIUS JOSEPHUS

The
SIX DAYS WORK
of the
CREATION.
GENESIS
CHAP I
2 the Firmament is made
5 The Creation of Bird & Fishes
6 The Creation of Man &c.

FLAVIUS JOSEPHUS

ON THE

ANTIQUITIES

OF THE

JEWS.

BOOK I.

FROM THE CREATION OF THE WORLD TO THE DEATH OF ISAAC.

[CONTAINING A PERIOD OF MORE THAN TWO THOUSAND YEARS.]

CHAP. I.

The Creation of the World in six days, with the distinct operations of each day. Man's superiority in the work of creation. The formation of woman, and her introduction as a companion to Adam. Subtlety of the serpent. Fall of our first parents. Denunciation of God's judgments. Their expulsion from Paradise.

IN the origin of the universe God, the omnipotent Jehovah, created the heaven and the earth; but the latter being enveloped in impenetrable darkness, God pronounced the Almighty *fiat*, light immediately shone forth, and, to distinguish the light from the darkness, he called the one *day*, and the other *night*. The first appearance of light he named *morning*, and the time of its departure *evening*. This was the first day, or this was the especial work of the first day, which, by Moses, is emphatically termed *one* day.

On the second day God formed the firmament, fixed it above all things, separated it from the grosser particles of earth, and endowed it with a quality moist and humid, that the earth might be rendered fruitful by showers.

On the third day he divided the land and waters from each other, and brought forth the vegetable system in all its beauty and variety.

On the fourth day he enlightened the heaven with the sun, the moon, and the stars, appointing their vicissitudes and regular courses, that the revolving seasons might be thereby distinguished.

On the fifth day he created and appointed to their respective elements, the inhabitants of the air and the waters, and endowed them with the faculty of propagation.

On the [illegible] he created [illegible] quadrupeds, or four-footed [illegible] male and female, [illegible] the noblest of all his works, M[illegible]

Thus we are to understand, according to the Mosaic account, that in these six days the world and all things therein were created, and that on the seventh day God rested, and ceased from his work. On that day, therefore, we desist from labour, and term it *sabbath*, which, in the Hebrew language, signifies *rest*.

Moses having thus given a general description of the creation, proceeds to a philosophical (a) disquisition of the formation of man in particular, in terms to this amount. God formed man of the slime or dust of the earth, and infused into him spirit, or life, or soul. This being, man, was called *Adam*, (b) implying in the Hebrew language, *red*, because he was formed of the purest and richest kind of earth, which is of that colour.

As the first instance of man's superiority in the rank of creation, the [illegible] presented to Adam all kinds of living creatures he had formed, both male and female, to which he gave distinct appellations, according to their respective species and natures.

But as the situation of Adam, contrary to that of the animal creation in general, was desolate and forlorn without an help-mate, whose society might contribute to his felicity, the beneficent Creator was pleased soon to throw him into a sound sleep, took out one of his ribs, and formed thence of a woman, who being presented to him, was gratefully acknowledged as a partner bountifully granted for his solace and comfort, and admitted as part of himself. In the Hebrew language the general word by which a woman is distinguished, is *Issa*, but this woman being the first, was termed *Eva*, i.e. *The Mother of* [illegible]

Moses then enters into account of the [illegible] garden in the east, which was called [illegible] abounding with all kinds of vegetables, and [illegible] [illegible] good and evil were [illegible] distinguished. In this P[illegible]

(a) [illegible]

(b) Adam [illegible]

the Almighty [illegible] Adam and Eve with orders to attend to the cultivation of the various plants. This garden was watered by [illegible] which surrounded its whole circumference, dividing itself into four channels. The first current called [illegible] (signifying abundance, or a multitude) flowing through India, falls into the ocean, and is by the Greeks called *Ganges*. The second called *Euphrates*, and in the Hebrew [illegible] (the [illegible]) and the third called Tigris or Diglath ([illegible], *rapid*,) both run into the Red Sea. *Geon* which in its course through Egypt, signifies in Hebrew, rising from the east, but is called by the Greeks *Nilus*.

The bountiful Parent of universal nature gave full permission to Adam and Eve to eat of the fruit of all the plants in this celestial spot, the *tree of knowledge* excepted, from which they were commanded to abstain on the severest penalty, inevitable death. Hitherto there was one common language(*b*) among animals in general, and they were social [illegible] their dispositions, but the serpent being in habits of [illegible] with Adam and Eve, and envying the felicity they enjoyed, while obedient to the divine command plotted to allure them from their innocence, and seduce them to disobedience of their Creator's command. To effect this infernal design, he first accosted the woman and urged his persuasions to taste the forbidden fruit, by assuring her that she should [illegible], be exempt from the penalty denounced, but (to tamper with her pride) telling her, that [illegible] the [illegible] of discerning between good and evil, by [illegible], both herself and her husband would become [illegible] Beings and [illegible] the Creator himself [illegible] and happiness.

[illegible] her curiosity, she [illegible] her [illegible] innocence, tasted, and being delighted with the fruit, [illegible] her husband to participate in the crime. No longer shielded by innocence from shame, they saw each others nakedness, were confounded at the sight and covered themselves with aprons made of fig-leaves, and fancied themselves happier in discovering that by their guilt, which innocence had veiled from their knowledge.

When the Almighty appeared in the garden, Adam who before was accustomed to familiar intercourse with his Creator, shrunk from his presence, appalled by conscious guilt: when demanded to assign the cause of his thus attempting to seclude himself from a presence which had hitherto constituted his supreme felicity, he stood confounded, mute and [illegible]. But the Almighty expressed [illegible] mind and will to the following effect: "[illegible] the [illegible] whereby you might have [illegible] your happiness, lived free from labour, [illegible] or pain: all bountiful nature, [illegible] the influence of my Providence should have supplied your every want, you would have been exempted [illegible] death, its rueful effect, even bliss eternal would have been your lot; but you have disobeyed my sacred command, and your silence is an argument, not of your reverence, but conscious guilt." [illegible] attempted to palliate his crime, and plead in excuse the persuasion of the woman, by which he had been induced thus flagrantly to offend. Eve also sought to exculpate herself, alledging that she had been beguiled by the subtlety of the serpent.

The Almighty included them all under the awful sentence of his just indignation. He declared to Adam, that as he had suffered himself to be prevailed on to transgress by the counsel of the woman, he was consigned to labour to procure those necessaries of life, which, in a state of innocence Nature would have spontaneously bestowed, nay, that his hardest toil and most sanguine expectation should be frequently frustrated. Eve was subjected to the pain and peril of child-bearing, for being allured by the temptation of the serpent, and then seducing and involving her husband in extreme calamity. The serpent was deprived of the power of speech, and for his malignity, sentenced to bear poison about him, as an emblem of that enmity which should subsist between him and the human race, for which the Almighty predicted they should bruise his head, because therein lay his power against them, and the [illegible] blows proved mortal. He was also deprived of his feet, and doomed to trail his body on the ground in the most abject manner, for having been the instrumental cause of that ground being accursed. Having thus denounced these several judgments on the delinquents, as respective objects of his distributive justice, the Almighty, as a confirmation of his awful displeasure, expelled the guilty pair from the terrestrial paradise, as they were no longer deemed inhabitants worthy the realms of pure and uncorruptible bliss.

CHAP. II.

Strife of Cain and Abel. Murder of Abel. Banishment of Cain. Cain the inventor of weights and measures, and the first divider of ground. Building of Enos the first city. Invention of music by Jubal. Of brass and iron-work, by Tubal Cain. Seth and sons the first astronomers. Pillars of Seth.

THE first children of our first parents were Cain and Abel. The name of the first implies possession, that of the latter, affliction or sorrow. They had also three daughters. The dispositions of the brothers were as different as their occupations and employments. Abel the younger, conscious of the Divine Omnipresence and Omniscience, was actuated by principles of inflexible justice, and steadily pursued the paths of virtue, in all the innocent simplicity of a shepherd's solitary life.

Cain, on the contrary, was wicked in the extreme, and wholly addicted to the acquisition of profit. He invented the use of the plough, but the advantages he reaped from the cultivation of the earth increased his avarice, and excited his jealousy and resentment to such a degree as to be productive of the first murder, even the murder of his brother.

Having mutually agreed to offer sacrifice to the Almighty, Cain, according to the nature of his avocation, offered the produce of agriculture, while Abel's oblation consisted of the milk of his herds and the firstlings of his flock. The Deity preferred the latter (*c*) sacrifice as the simple spontaneous production of nature, while the former appeared as the effect of laborious avarice, and the result of interested principle. This excited the indignation of Cain, who to glut his revenge, slew his brother, and having concealed his body, thought the murder would escape detection. But no scheme could evade the perception of Omniscience: the Almighty demanded of Cain the cause of his brother's absence for several days, as heretofore they had been constant associates. Sensible of the enormity of his crime, and being at a loss for a reply, after some hesitation, he said he had not seen him; but when God urged him to an explicit answer, he presumptuously replied, that he was neither his brother's keeper, nor bound to interest himself in his concerns. The murder was then brought home to the criminal, and his plea of ignorance totally obviated, by a positive charge of his having been the perpetrator of his brother's death.

This circumstance, heinous as it was in itself, afforded an opportunity for the display of what is justly termed the darling attribute of the Deity, *mercy*; for upon the offender's offering sacrifice, and imploring a mitigation of his punishment, he was permitted to enjoy that life of which he had deprived his brother. But to fix a stigma on the

---

(*a*) B[illegible] the [illegible] Sea [illegible] the Arabian Gulph [illegible] alone [illegible] Sea [illegible] the Red Sea [illegible] the Persian Gulph [illegible] the [illegible] Indies.

(*b*) It appears [illegible] Josephus [illegible] of [illegible] his part [illegible] the [illegible] could speak before the Fall [illegible] Sons, [illegible] than [illegible] that their present [illegible] been made greater than what we can at this time [illegible]

(*c*) St. John's reason why God accepted the sacrifice of Abel, and rejected that of Cain, and also why Cain slew Abel, is much better than this of Josephus. Because Cain was of that evil one, and slew his brother: and wherefore slew he him? Because his own works were evil, and his brother's righteous. 1 Epist. John [illegible]

ADAM and EVE in PARADISE

ADAM
Giving Names
And Adam gave names to all cattle,
and to the fowl of the air, and to every
beast of the field
Godwin Sculp.

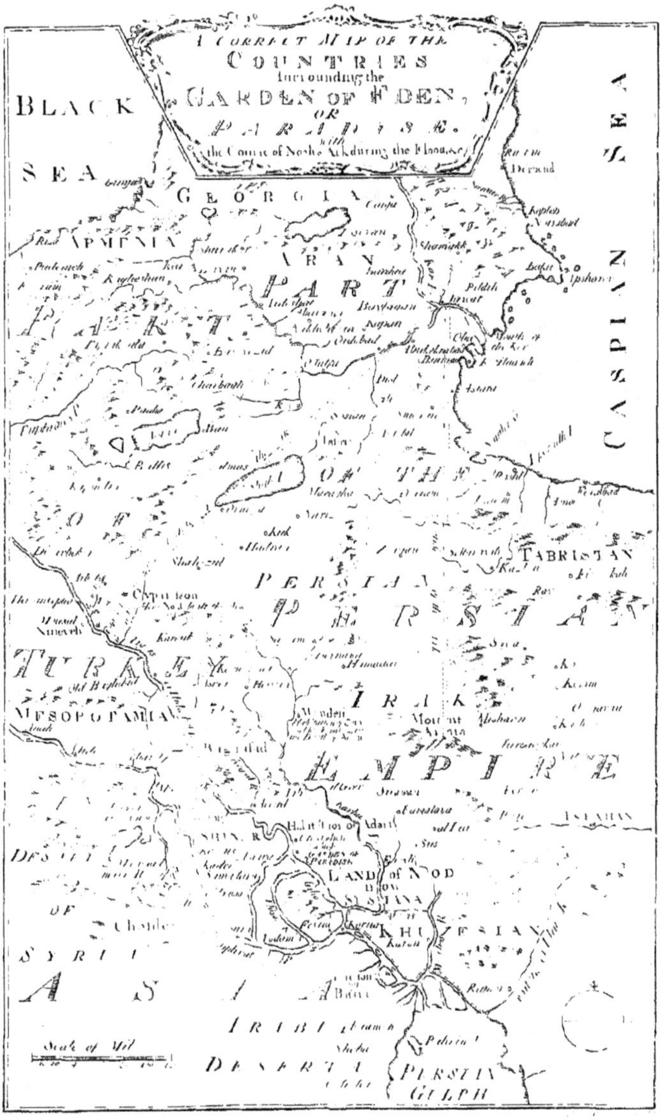
A CORRECT MAP OF THE
COUNTRIES
surrounding the
GARDEN OF EDEN,
OR
PARADISE.
with
the Course of Noah's Ark during the Flood, &c.
BLACK
SEA
CASPIAN SEA
GEORGIA
ARMENIA
ARAN
PART
PART
OF
TURKEY
MESOPOTAMIA
PERSIA
PERSIAN
EMPIRE
IRAK
TABRISTAN
ISPAHAN
LAND of NOD
KHUZESTAN
DESERT
OF
SYRIA
ASIA
ARABIA
DESERTA
PERSIAN
GULPH
Scale of Miles

moſt enormous of crimes, he and his poſterity (*a*) to the ſeventh generation, were pronounced accurſed, and both him and his wife were expelled from their native region; but expreſſing an apprehenſion that his criminality would expoſe him to the ravages of the brute creation, God was pleaſed to ſet a viſible mark upon him, as a token of protection, and then diſmiſſed him to wander on the face of the earth.

Cain, and his wife, having traverſed a vaſt ſpace of land, fixed their abode at Nais (by ſome called Naid and by others Nod) where his family conſiderably increaſed. Far from being reformed by the chaſtiſement of his Creator, his depravity became more apparent in the gratification of the moſt ſordid deſires, in acts of cruelty and rapine, and in ſetting an example which had the moſt baneful influence on the conduct of others.

He deſtroyed the honeſt ſimplicity which had prevailed in thoſe days in mutual concerns between man and man, by the invention of weights and meaſures, which opened an ample field for the practice of fraud to the excluſion of all ſincerity and plain dealing. As his ambition was equal to his avarice, he firſt encloſed lands, built the firſt city, and having ſurrounded it with walls, and fortified it with a rampart, obliged his family and dependants to dwell within its bounds.

This city he called Enos, or (Enoch) from the name of his eldeſt ſon. Irad was the ſon of Enoch, from whom deſcended Mahujael, whoſe ſon was Mathuſael, the father of Lamech, who had ſeventy-ſeven children by two wives, Zella and Adah. Jabel, the ſon of Adah, firſt erected tents, and followed the paſtoral life. Jubal his brother, applied himſelf to the ſtudy of ſound, and, upon organical or muſical principles, invented the pſaltery and harp.

Tubal, ſon of Lamech, by his other wife, Zillah, was celebrated for his ſtrength and ſkill in martial exerciſes. He firſt invented the art of forging, and by theſe qualifications united, acquired great riches. Lamech had alſo a daughter, called Naamah.

Lamech being a man of underſtanding, and ſenſible of the curſe entailed on the poſterity of Cain, for the heinous crime of fratricide, communicated the particulars of that fatal event to both his wives. During the life of Adam, the immediate deſcendants of Cain were notoriouſly profligate, and through force of example, inclined to cruelty and rapine. If any of them refrained from the enormous ſin of murder, they invaded the property of other men without the leaſt remorſe, and were continually offering outrages to all around them.

But Adam, our firſt parent (as we muſt recur to him) after the death of Abel, and the flight of Cain, was extremely ſolicitous for peopling the world, and therefore very deſirous of children. He was then one hundred and thirty years of age, to which having added eight hundred years, he paid the debt of human nature, as the penalty incurred by his firſt tranſgreſſion, having, in that interval, had a conſiderable progeny, (*b*) amongſt whom was a ſon called Seth.

This laſt mentioned of the immediate deſcendants of Adam was a character worthy of notice and imitation. Being trained by his father to the practice of virtue from his earlieſt years, he followed the example of his parent in the education of his own children, who ſo far profited thereby, as to paſs through life with tranquillity, (*c*) and render their memories revered by their ſurvivors. By contemplating the power of the Divine Being, as manifeſted in its various operations, they acquired the ſcience of aſtronomy, or knowledge of the heavenly bodies.

Leſt poſterity ſhould loſe the benefit of their invention (as Adam had predicted that the world ſhould be deſtroyed at two diſtinct periods, the firſt by water, the laſt by fire) they erected two ſtupendous pillars, the one of brick, and the other of ſtone, and engraved upon each a particular account of their diſcoveries, in order that, if that of brick ſhould be ſwept away by the violence of the waters, that of ſtone might remain, and thereby preſerve their obſervations for the information of poſterity. The former was [illegible] by the deluge, but the ſtone pillar is to be ſeen [illegible] of Syria to this day.

CHAP. III.

General depravity of mankind. Conſequences thereof. [illegible] perture of Noah into another land. [illegible] for the preſervation of Noah and his family. The deluge. Noah ſacrifices to the Almighty [illegible]. His oblation is accepted, and a covenant [illegible]. The rainbow fixed in the ſky as a token that the earth ſhall no more be deſtroyed by water. Noah's age, &c. &c.

DURING ſeven generations the deſcendants of Seth continued to imitate the virtuous example of their pious progenitors, influenced by a due veneration to the majeſty of their Supreme Creator, and a ſacred regard for his divine inſtitutions; but, in proceſs of time, they became degenerate and negligent of their duty to God, as well as of all ſocial and moral obligations. The profligacy of theſe people now became as notorious as their piety had been eminent, inſomuch, that they juſtly incurred the diſpleaſure of an incenſed Deity. Many of the angels (by Moſes called the ſons of God) ſo denominated for their ſingular piety and virtue, [illegible] promiſcuouſly, brought forth a [illegible] of their ſtrength bold in their crimes, and [illegible] of our age, the giants mentioned by the conſults of [illegible]. Noah, who retained his integrity, and was ſhocked to behold the general depravity, expoſtulated with them on the enormity of their crimes, and earneſtly recommended the neceſſity of a reformation; but finding all his admonitions ineffectual, and that they were determined to the moſt impious purſuits, he deemed it expedient to retire, with his family, from a place in which he had reaſon to imagine he ſhould be continually expoſed to the cruelty and rapine of its abandoned inhabitants.

The unexampled piety of Noah ſecured him the favour of an approving God, who now determined to wreak his vengeance on the whole human race, and exterminate from the face of the earth all creatures in general, in order to produce a virtuous generation, the period of whoſe lives ſhould be limited to the ſpace of 120 years.

Previous to the execution of this, which was to take place in a general inundation, God ſuggeſted to Noah the means of ſafety, ſo that in conformity to the divine intimation, he cauſed an ark to be built, conſiſting of four ſtories, three hundred cubits in length, fifty in breadth, and thirty in height.

Into this ark, or providential aſylum, Noah entered, together with his family, and having provided all things neceſſary for their ſubſiſtence, took with him ſeven couples of ſome kinds of animals, and at leaſt a male and female of all, in order to preſerve a remnant of each ſpecies for the uſe of future generations. This ark was conſtructed on ſuch a plan, as to be at once impenetrable and impregnable, and therefore ſecure from the attack of the moſt violent ſurge, or boiſterous ſtorm.

Thus was Noah (who may be termed the ſecond father of mankind) wonderfully preſerved with his family, by the interpoſition of Providence, from the ravages of a deluge, in which were involved a guilty race, as a memento of Divine indignation. Noah, by lineal deſcent, was the tenth from Adam; the regular ſucceſſion being Adam, Seth, Enos, Cainan, Mahalaleel, Jared, Enoch, Methuſelah, Lamech, and Noah.

The deluge (*d*) happened in the ſix hundredth year of Noah, and in the ſecond month, which by the Macedonians, is called Dius, and, by the Hebrews,

(*a*) Of the puniſhment of Cain in the ſeventh generation [illegible] his poſterity, the [illegible] accompliſhment of it will be fully ſhewn in a ſubſequent part of the work.

(*b*) The number of Adam's children, as ſays the old tradition, was thirty three ſons and twenty three daughters.

(*c*) What is here ſaid of Seth and his poſterity [illegible] happy [illegible] agreeable to that [illegible] world and the conduct of [illegible].

(*d*) Joſephus here [illegible] began about the autumnal equ[illegible]

(also followed the Egyptian chronology) Marſomane, or Murſuane. Moſes constituted Niſan, or as it is called by the Macedonians, Xanthicus, as the firſt month, and enjoined the obſervance of it in all religious matters, becauſe in that month he delivered the Iſraelites from Egyptian bondage; but with reſpect to civil concerns in general he obſerved the ancient calculation, beginning the year with December. According to the Moſaic account the deluge began the ſeventeenth day of the ſecond month, in the year 1656, from the creation of Adam, and the ſacred chronology is held moſt minute and authentic.

From thence it is deducible that, at the birth of Seth, Adam was 130 years old, and that he lived 930 years. Seth, about the age of 105, had Enos, who, after living 905 years, left the management of his affairs to his ſon Canan. He lived 910 years, leaving a ſon called Mahalaleel, to whom was born Jared. Jared was the father of Enoch, and lived 962 years. Enoch, when he had lived 365 years, was tranſlated, or taken up into heaven, by an exertion of Divine power: his death, therefore, hath not been recorded by any hiſtorian. Enoch had a ſon named Methuſelah, who left to his ſon Lamech the authority he had held during his life. Lamech, having governed 777 years, was ſucceeded by his ſon Noah.

In theſe ſucceſſions, the births, rather than the deaths, of theſe men, are to be adhered to, for they lived to ſee many ſucceeding generations.

The Almighty at the appointed time, cauſed torrents of water to fall upon the earth in ſuch rapid and ceaſeleſs ſucceſſion, for the ſpace of forty days, that the moſt elevated parts were overwhelmed to the depth of fifteen cubits; ſo that the guilty inhabitants were deprived of the power of flight, and of courſe involved in the general calamity; the rain ceaſing gradually, the waters decreaſed in proportion, and at the expiration of an hundred and fifty days, on the ſeventeenth day of the ſeventh month, the ark being lodged upon the ſummit of a mountain in Armenia, Noah opened a window, and perceiving certain ſpots of dry land, conſoled himſelf with a hope of a ſpeedy deliverance. On the gradual decreaſe of the waters, Noah ſent forth a raven, to diſcover if the inundation had ſo far ſubſided, that they might deſcend from the ark with ſecurity; but the winged meſſenger finding no place whereon to perch, ſoon returned to its aſylum, the ark.

After an interval of ſeven days, he let fly a dove, on the ſame embaſſy as the raven, but with different ſucceſs in the event, for ſhe returned with an olive branch, by which token Noah was happily aſſured that the inundation was no more. Deeming it expedient to wait ſtill ſeven days, he diſmiſſed all the living creatures, and followed with his wife and family, and having firſt offered oblations to their all-gracious deliverer, enjoyed thoſe ſocial bleſſings which they owed to his wonderful interpoſition.

The Armenians call the ſpot on which the ark reſted at the deſcent of Noah, *Apobaterion* (a) ſignifying an exit or coming out, and the inhabitants ſhew ſome remains of that ſtupendous fabrick, which they have preſerved to this day.

Various Pagan hiſtorians have left their teſtimonies of this general deluge, and the ark in which the ſelect few were ſecured from inundation. Beroſus, the Chaldean, writes, "That ſome fragments of this veſſel are ſtill to be "ſeen in the mountains of the Cordyeans, in Armenia, "and that many of them carry off pieces of the pitch, which "cloſed its ſeams, as charms againſt enchantment." Hieronymus, the Egyptian, in his Antiquities of the Phœnicians, ſpeaks to the ſame purport, as do many others. But Nicholaus, of Damaſcus, informs us more explicitly, "That "above the province of Minias, in Armenia, there is a "certain ſtupendous mountain named Paris, to which, it "is reported, that many flying at the time of the deluge, "by that means eſcaped, and that a man was borne on an "ark to the ſummit of that mountain, and ſome fragments "of the materials, of which the ark was compoſed, remain "there to this day." He adds, "This, probably "man alluded to by Moſes, the legiſlator of the

Noah, apprehenſive that the Almighty had deci utter extirpation of the human race, and therefore d in annual return of the flood, having offered ſacr the offended Deity, moſt humbly beſought him th after he would maintain the former order of thin again wreak his vengeance on mankind in the ſam ner, by devoting all things exiſting to one comm ſtruction; but that, having conſigned the diſobe due puniſhment, he would extend his benevolence t who had hitherto been the objects of his favoura gard, otherwiſe their ſtate would be more deſpera that of thoſe who had periſhed by one deluge, n reſerved as victims to another, after having ſhu at being witneſſes to ſo tremendous an event.

He then implored the Almighty to accept the o offered, and avert his judgments from the earth, and his poſterity, applying themſelves to the cultiv the ground, and building of cities, might be gra permitted to enjoy the fruits of their labours to a g age, as their progenitors had done before the de

Noah having thus preſented his ſupplications bountiful Father of the Univerſe, he was pleaſed, fr approbation of his integrity, to grant his requeſt, n ing, at the ſame time, that thoſe who periſhed [illegible] own diſobedience, and not through his will, as the of their deſtruction. He then conſoled him wi ſoothing expreſſions: "I gave not life with a deſig "ſtroy it, but their crimes were ſo atrocious, tha "compelled to exterminate them. I am not, howe "exorable: your interceſſion ſhall prevail with me t "of the rigor of their chaſtiſement, nor will I "them in another deluge; but it is my poſitive co "that ye abſtain from murder, and inflict the ſ "puniſhments on delinquents in that particular, a "ly offenſive to the Majeſty of heaven. All living "tures are at your own diſpoſal, as lords of the c "whether of the land, the water, or the air. I enjo "only to abſtain from their blood, for in that co "their life. It is therefore prohibited by my ſpecia "mand; and to free you from apprehenſion of a "deluge, I fix my bow in the ſkies, as a token t "world ſhall be no more deſtroyed by water." that time the rainbow has been conſidered as the bow of the Creator of the Univerſe.

Noah continued in a ſtate of tranquillity 350 yea the flood, and then concluded a life of which th was 950 years. In forming a compariſon between t gevity of the ancients, or antediluvians, and the narr of our preſent lives, there is no reaſonable argument validate what I have advanced on that ſubject, ſinc no means follows that, becauſe human life is now a ed, it was not protracted in the days of our proge Beſides, in thoſe early times a purer air, greater ſim of manners, and, above all, much greater temperanc eſſentially have contributed to its prolongation. It w neceſſary that the term of life ſhould be thus exten order to bring to perfection the ſciences of geomet aſtronomy, which could not be attained but by inte plication during a long ſeries of time, as the great or grand revolution of the planets, is accounted a ſ ſix hundred years. In confirmation of what I ha vanced concerning the longevity of the antediluv could produce the concurring teſtimonies of all the hiſtorians, whether Greeks or barbarians, as Mane his Egyptian, and Beroſus, in his Chaldean, Hiſtor Hieronymus, the Egyptian, who, as well as Mochu trus, wrote the Hiſtory of Phoenicia. Heſiod, H us, Hellanicus, Acuſilaus, Eporus, and Nicolaus, admit, that many of the ancients lived to the ag thouſand years. Nevertheleſs, I ſubmit what I h lated to the judgment of the reader.

(a) This [illegible] the proper [illegible] the Armenians [illegible] It is a laſting monument of the preſervation of Noah on the [illegible] upon the top of that mountain, [illegible] whoſe foot it was [illegible] where the firſt city or town was erected after the flood.

The BUILDING of the TOWER of BABEL

CHAP. IV.

The posterity of Noah commanded to people the earth, and form [illegible] different parts. They neglect the Divine injunction [illegible] the building of the tower of Babel [illegible] the [illegible] of Nimrod. The confusion of tongues. Sybil's description of the demolition of the tower.

THE first of the human race, who descended from the mountains to the plains after the tremendous inundation, were the three sons of Noah, Shem, Ham, and Japhet, born about one hundred years before that memorable event. The remainder of his family, who apprehensive of a second deluge, had staid behind, animated by their example, at length descended and joined them; and the spot on which they first fixed their abode was called Shinar, or Senaar.

From the vast increase of population, they were commanded by the Almighty to disperse themselves, and form distinct colonies in different parts of the earth, not only to prevent those dissentions which might arise from their continuance in a promiscuous body, but that they might extend the cultivation, and reap a more abundant harvest from their labours. Such, however, was their ignorance and obstinacy, that they neglected the mandate of the Almighty, and suffered condign punishment through the infliction of great calamities. Yet, as their numbers continued to increase, God was pleased to repeat and enforce his command as to their dispersion and formation of colonies; but these perverse mortals, vainly attributing their possessions to the acquisition of their combined strength, and not to the beneficence of an all-bountiful Creator, persisted in their disobedience, by not paying any attention to the divine command.

They were incited to this contumacious disobedience of the sacred injunction by Nimrod (or, as he is called in the Greek, Nabrod) the grandson of Ham, one of the sons of Noah. This Nimrod, who was remarkable for bodily strength, and intrepidity of mind, suggested to them, that their flourishing condition was not the effect of providential blessings, but of their own power and wisdom. By these means he introduced a tyrannical government, and to confirm himself in the same, by gaining their confidence as a supposed protector, persuaded them to a vain belief, that if they should be alarmed by the apprehension of a deluge, he would undertake to defend them from its ravages, by erecting a tower of such inaccessible height, as to brave the violence of the flood, and secure them from the possibility of danger.

Prevailed upon by the fallacious pretensions of this presumptuous demagogue, the credulous multitude were inclined to think that obedience to the Divine command was an instance of pusillanimity, and therefore applied themselves most assiduously to their new conceited project of building this tower. From the great numbers employed in the work, and the alacrity with which they pursued it, in a short time it was raised to a stupendous height; but such was the amazing thickness, that the elevation seemed diminished to the view of the spectator. The sides were composed of burnt brick, cemented with a bituminous mortar, to prevent the admission of water.

Though their madness and presumption were thus flagrantly offensive to the Almighty, such was his benevolence, notwithstanding his late example of vengeance, that he condemned them not to a general extirpation, but, by changing their tongues, caused such a diversity of language amongst them as to render them totally unintelligible to each other. The spot on which this tower was erected is now called Babylon, from the confusion of tongues which arose there, the word Babel, in Hebrew, signifying *confusion*. Of this tower, and the diversity or confusion of languages, the Sybil (*) speaks in the following terms: "When all "men spoke the same language, they attempted to build "a tower of stupendous height, as if from thence they "intended to ascend to heaven; but the Gods [illegible] "the winds upon them, overthrew the structure, con"founded the language of the builders, and thereby sub"verted the whole design: whence it came to pass, that "the city afterwards built upon that [illegible] spot, was called "*Babylon*." With respect to the plain of Senaar, [illegible] Babylonian, Hestiæus, the [illegible] that "The "priests, who escaped from the general calamity, took the sacred reliques of Jupiter [illegible] the conqueror, and carried them to Sinnar or Senaar in the country of Babylon."

CHAP. V.

Dispersion of the posterity of Noah [illegible]

THE confusion of tongues naturally occasioned the dispersion of the people, who formed themselves into distinct colonies, and occupied those parts of the earth to which they were providentially conducted; so that not only the shores, but the continent were amply filled with inhabitants. Some constructed vessels, and took possession of various islands. Several nations still retain the original names given them by the founders. Those of others are changed, and some are altered, in order that they [illegible] become the [illegible] intelligible. The latter are denominated by terms derived from the Greeks, for when that people maintained [illegible] among nations from the acquisition of power, [illegible] to themselves the glory of antiquity [illegible] such as [illegible] countries they vanquished, as in [illegible] that from them, and them only, they derived their origin.

CHAP. VI.

Descendants of Noah, [illegible] the several nations [illegible] Noah's [illegible] [illegible] the posterity of his son Ham, [illegible] The [illegible] Hebrews. [illegible] Genealogy of Abraham. [illegible]

THE descendants of Noah made it an invariable rule to affix their own names to the nations they severally founded. Thus the seven sons of Japhat the son of Noah, spreading themselves over Asia, from the mountains Taurus and Amanus, to the river Tanais, extending in Europe [illegible] Cades, and cultivating the various territories in that space, which were before uninhabited, called themselves severally [illegible] distinctly by their own names. Gomar was the founder of the Gomarians, whom the Greeks now call Gallatians. Magog planted that colony anciently called from his name Magoge, but now termed by the Greeks Scythians. Madai, the eldest son of Japhat, was the founder of the Medeans, by the Greeks called Medes; as was Javan, or Jovan, his other son, of the Ionians, from whom the other Greeks in general derive their origin. The Thobelians, now called Iberians took their names from their founder Thobelus; as did the Moschenians, now called Cappadocians, from Moscha. Indeed, they still retain the trace of this ancient title in the city of Mazaca, from whence it is probable that, in ancient times, the whole country was called by the same name. The Thiraeans, whom the Greeks call Thracians, sprang from Thiras. All these nations derived their origin, and consequently their appellations, from the names of their respective founders, the seven sons of Japhat.

The three sons of Gomer, Ascanaxes, Riphates, and Tygrames, founded the Ascanaxians, now called by the Greeks, Rhegmians; the Riphatheans, now called Paphlagonians; and the Tygramenians now styled Phrygians.

The three sons of Javan, or Jovan, Elisas, Tharsus, and Cethymus, gave name to three distinct people. The Alysians now called Æolians [illegible] the [illegible]

(*) [illegible] Chaldean historian, confirms this account [illegible] of the builders [illegible] [illegible] God overthrew the [illegible] by a terrible storm, and confounded the language [illegible] nation.

ſians, ſince called Cilicians, as appears from the name of their metropolis, Tharſus, and the inhabitants of Cethyma, now called Cyprus, and from which not only all iſlands, but all places on the ſea-coaſt were called, by the Hebrews, Chethim In Cyprus there is ſtill a town, which the Greeks call Citium Theſe nations were founded by, and derived their names from the immediate deſcendants of Japhet

Before I proceed, a particular circumſtance, perhaps unknown even to the Greeks, requires attention, which is, that I have frequently, in compliance with their manner, to facilitate and harmonize pronunciation, changed the termination of their proper names, an innovation of which we never admit

The deſcendants of Ham took poſſeſſion of Syria, from mount Amanus and Libanus into the ſea-coaſt, and gave names to all places within the limits of their dominions, but moſt of them are now either wholly obliterated, or ſo corrupted, that they cannot be traced to their originals The Ethiopians, however, have preſerved their ancient name, for having been founded by Chus, one of the ſons of Ham, they are called Chuſites, or Chuſeans, not only in their own country, but throughout all Aſia, to this day The Meſtreans alſo retain the ſame honor they derived their name from Meſtrce, by which Egypt is ſtill called, as are the Egyptians, Meſtrean.

Phut, who planted a colony in Lybia, gave denomination to the Phutians, in confirmation of which, divers Greek hiſtorians mention a diſtrict of Mauritania, called Phute, ſituate on the banks of a river of the ſame name but its modern appellation is derived from Libys, one of the ſons of Meſtraim

Canaan, the fourth ſon of Ham, gave the name of Canaanites to the inhabitants of the nation he eſtabliſhed, which is now called Judæa Chus, who was the eldeſt ſon of Ham, had ſeven ſons, Sabas, founder of the Sabæans, Evilas of the Evileans, or Getulians, Sabatees, of the Sabatheans, or Aſtabarians, Rammus, of the Ramæans, and Nimrod of the Babylonians

Meſtraim had eight ſons, who poſſeſſed the whole diſtrict between Gaza and Egypt, but one only, named Philiſtin, gave denomination to the colony he planted, now called, by the Greeks, Paleſtine The nations founded by the other ſons being deſolated, as will be hereafter ſhewn, in the Ethiopian war (*a*) no material circumſtance is retained concerning them, Labyn excepted, who planted a colony in Lybia, ſo called from his name

Canaan was the father of eleven ſons, of whom Sidonius called the city he founded Sidon, which it ſtill retains, not having been corrupted by the Greeks, as did Amath, to Amathe, or Amathine, which by the inhabitants, is ſtill ſo called, though the Macedonians, in honor of one of their princes, have changed it into Epiphania Aradæus planted the iſland of Aradus, as did Arcæus the colony of Arce, on mount Libanus Of the other ſeven ſons, Enæus, Chetæus, Jebuſæus, Ammorræus, Gergeſæus, Sinæus, and Samaræus, nothing more remains in ſacred hiſtory than their names, the Hebrews having deſtroyed their cities on the following account

When the earth was re-eſtabliſhed after the flood, Noah applied himſelf to agriculture, and particularly to the cultivation of vines When the fruit was ripe, he preſſed it, and made wine, of which, having firſt offered an oblation to the bountiful father of the Univerſe, he drank to ſuch exceſs, that intoxication enſuing, he fell into a ſtate of inſenſibility, and was expoſed in a ſituation highly indecent

His ſon Ham, perceiving his father in this condition, diſdainfully diſcovered it to his brothers, but they, touched with filial reverence, approached and veiled the ſhame of their aged parent Noah, therefore, coming to the knowledge of this circumſtance, pronounced his bleſſing on the dutiful ſons, Shem and Japhet, and though he did not curſe the perſon of Ham, he imprecated the direſt calamities on his poſterity

Shem had five ſons, who inhabited thoſe parts of Aſia which extend from the Euphrates to the Indian Ocean Elam was the founder of the Elamites, or Perſians, Aſſur of the city of Nineveh, and the Aſſyrian empire, Arphaxad, of the Arphaxadeans, or Chaldeans, Aram of the Armenians, or Syrians, and Ludis, of the Ludeans, or Lydians

Of Aram's four ſons, Uz eſtabliſhed the colony of the Traſhonites, and built the city of Damaſcus, between Paleſtine and Cœlo-Syria Ul founded Armenia, Gether, Bactria, and Meſanæa, now called the valley of Paſin Arphaxad was the father of Salas, whoſe ſon Heber (*b*) gave denomination to the Hebrews Heber had two ſons, Jucta, or Joctan, and Phalec, who was ſo called from having been born at ſuch time as lands were firſt divided, Phalec, in Hebrew, ſignifying *diviſion*.

The ſons of Jucta were Elmodad, Saleph, Azermoth, Eldrais, Edoram, Uzal, Dael, Ebal, Abimael, Sabæus, Ophir, Evilath, and Jobab Theſe occupied that country which is ſituated between Syria and the river Cophen, in India Having thus treated of the progeny of Shem, we ſhall now advert to the Hebrews

From Phalec, the ſon of Heber, deſcended Ragaus, from whence came Serug, whoſe name was Nachor, who begat Thares, the father of Abram, the tenth in ſucceſſion from Noah He was born 292 years after the deluge, in the ſeventieth year of his father's age Nachor was 120 years old when he had Thares, and Serug about 132 when he begat Nachor, Ragaus 130 when he had Serug, and Phalec about the ſame age when he had Ragaus, Heber 134 when he begat Phalec Salas was born in the 135th year of his father Arphaxad, who was begotten by Shem two years after the deluge

Abram had two brothers, Nachor and Aran The latter leaving behind him one ſon, Lot, and two daughters, Sarah and Melcha, died at Ur, in Chaldea, where his ſepulchre is yet to be ſeen His kinſmen eſpouſed his two daughters, Nachor taking Melcha, and Abram, Sarah Thares was ſo much affected by the death of his ſon Aran, that he removed, with his family, from Chaldea to Charan, a city in Meſopotamia, where he died with grief, and was buried in his 105th year About the time the Almighty was pleaſed to abbreviate the ſpace of man's life to the term of 120 years, preciſely the age to which Moſes attained

Nachor's wife, Melcha, bore him eight ſons, Uz, Baux, Cameul, Chazard, Azam, Phildas, Jadelphas, and Bethuel, and his concubine, Ruma, four, Tabeus, Gadam, Thavan, and Machan Bethuel, one of Nachor's legitimate ſons, had a ſon and a daughter, named Laban and Rebecca.

CHAP VII

Abram the founder of the Jewiſh nation Quits Chaldea, and dwells in Canaan, now called Judea His wiſdom He inſtructs the people in the nature and attributes of the Deity His memory perpetuated

ABRAM having little hope of legitimate iſſue, adopted Lot, the ſon of his brother Aran, and brother of his wife Sarah In obedience to the divine command, he departed from Chaldea in the 75th year of his age, and ſettled in the land of Canaan where he lived in tranquillity, and, at his death left it to his deſcendants Abram poſſeſſed a moſt ſolid judgment, great powers of oratory, and a general knowledge of men and things Eminent in all exemplary virtues, he was the firſt man who undertook to rectify the erroneous opinions men entertained of the Supreme Being, to inſtruct them in the nature of his attributes, and to inculcate, that there were but one God, the Creator of all things, to whoſe providence men were indebted for all the enjoyments of life, independent of any merit or power of their own Theſe doctrines he enforced by argument deduced from the operations of nature in general, and the planetary ſyſtem in particular, laying it down as a

(*a*) Th[illegible] only, [illegible] occaſion the removal of deſt[illegible] the [illegible] cities of Meſtraim, with their cities [illegible] Joſephus [illegible] been poſſeſſed of ancient records [illegible]

[illegible] (by ſome means or other) that records are now l[illegible]

(*b*) That the Jews were called Hebrews from their progenitor, Heber, Joſephus [illegible]

The PARTING of LOT and ABRAHAM,
after separating their Flocks &c.

maxim, that, as there is a certain predisposing power, by the influence of which all things are actuated, as all things are subject to the controul of Omnipotence, to that should be attributed man's every blessing, and to that should be gratefully ascribed honour and glory in the highest.

These doctrines, founded on the sublimest principles of religion and philosophy, were so averse to the contracted notions of the Chaldeans and Mesopotamians, as to excite a mutiny against him. Abram therefore, at the Divine injunction, removed into the land of Canaan, where he erected an altar, and offered sacrifice to the God of his deliverance. Berosus, the historian, evidently alludes to our father Abram, though he does not mention his name, when he writes, "In the tenth generation after the flood, "there lived amongst the Chaldeans a man of extraordi-"nary piety and probity, and remarkably versed in the "knowledge of the heavenly bodies." Hecatæus not only makes mention of him, but has recorded his actions in a select volume; and Nicolaus of Damascus, in the fourth book of his history, bears this positive testimony concerning him: "Abram (though a stranger) reigned in Damas-"cus, whither he arrived with a numerous train from a "country situate beyond Babylon, called Chaldea: but the "inhabitants in a short time rising against him, he retired "with his own people to the land of Canaan, now called "Judea, where he settled, and left a numerous progeny." The name of Abram is still held in honour at Damascus, and there is an adjacent villa called Abram's habitation.

CHAP. VIII.

A famine [illegible] Canaan, Abram [illegible] to Egypt. The [illegible] desires of the Egyptians [illegible] by their [illegible] [illegible] [illegible] knowledge of religion, as also in the sciences of arithmetic and astronomy. On his return to Canaan [illegible] the country between himself and his kinsman Lot.

A DREADFUL famine happening in Canaan, Abram having intelligence of the plenty which abounded in Egypt, determined to retire thither, not only on account of the fertility of the soil, but that he might have an opportunity of conferring with the Egyptian priests on the subject of religion; determined as a man of a liberal mind, open to conviction, to adhere to, or swerve, from their tenets and opinions, as they appeared founded on the invariable principles of reason and nature. As his wife Sarai accompanied him to Egypt, and he was apprized of the incontinency of the inhabitants, in order to obviate any dangerous effects that might arise from the king's attachment to her, being remarkably beautiful in person, it was mutually agreed between them that she should pass for his sister.

Abram's apprehension was confirmed, for they no sooner arrived in Egypt than the fame of his wife's beauty was spread around, which exciting the curiosity of Pharaoh to see her, was of course followed by an ardent desire to possess her; but the divine interposition frustrated his vicious design by means of a pestilence and insurrection prevailing at the same time among his subjects. Alarmed at these sudden strokes of adversity, he consulted his priests on the causes which had incurred, and the means of averting such tremendous judgments. They informed him, that the cause of his calamities was his intention of violence to the wife of a stranger. Impressed by the answer of the priests, he interrogated Sarai as to herself, and the man who accompanied her, and on her ingenuously declaring the truth, excused himself to Abram on pretence of his supposing her to have been his sister, and declaring, that he by no means intended to violate the laws of hospitality; then dismissing him with a sumptuous present, he gave him full permission to confer with the greatest and most learned men throughout his dominions.

This circumstance tended to display his virtues and enhance his character; for, as the Egyptians entertained a variety of opinions, and bigotted attachment produced schism and animosity, upon examining the grounds of their tenets in the course of his conferences with them, he demonstrated to them [illegible] difference [illegible] [illegible] their religious [illegible] and ceremonies, were vague, idle, and void of foundation or truth. He enforced these points with such perspicuity and eloquence as procured him the highest veneration, not only as a man of universal knowledge, but endued with the happiest faculty of conveying instruction to others. He was the first who taught the Egyptians the sciences of arithmetic and astronomy, of which they were, before his residence among them, totally ignorant: therefore, as he [illegible] introduced them from Chaldea into Egypt, and from thence they were afterwards transported into Greece, he may justly be said to have laid the foundation of attic literature.

Upon his return to Canaan, he divided the country with Lot, which affording cause for contention among their shepherds concerning the boundaries of their respective lands, he submitted the point to Lot's entire option, and that particular part which might appear to him most eligible, contenting himself with what his kinsman rejected. Abram then fixed his residence on the mountains near Hebron (a city founded seven years prior to Tanis in Egypt), while Lot chose the plain on the banks of the river Jordan, near Sodom, then a flourishing city, but afterwards laid in ruins, and extirpated even in name, as a token of the Almighty's vengeance for the enormous crimes of its inhabitants.

CHAP. IX.

The defeat of the Sodomites [illegible] [illegible] [illegible] Assyrians. The lake of Asphaltites. [illegible]

AS the Assyrians at this time held the empire of Asia, and they envied them in rivalling wealth and power, the Sodomites, whose country was divided into five provinces under the government of the same number of kings, viz. Ballas, Barsas, Senabar, Symobar, and the king of the Ballenians, they determined to make war upon them, and to that end entered their territories with a powerful army under the conduct of four able commanders. The contest being soon decided in favour of the Assyrians, who totally vanquished the Sodomites, these five kings from that time became tributaries to the conquerors. Having for twelve years duly paid the fine imposed, they refused to continue it on the thirteenth, and revolted from their obligation; upon which the Assyrians again mustered their forces under their commanders Amraphel, Arioch, Chedorlaomer, and Thadal, who ravaged all Syria, and overthrew the race of the giants. Penetrating into the country of Sodom, they encamped in a valley that derived its name from the bituminous pits with which that country abounded till the destruction of its chief city, when it became a lake, and was called Asphaltites, or bituminous. A battle ensued, and was maintained some time with equal valour on both sides; but at length victory declined for the Assyrians, great numbers of the Sodomites fell, and the rest were taken prisoners, amongst whom was Lot, who came to assist his countrymen in repelling the invasion of the enemy.

CHAP. X.

Abram pursues the victorious Assyrians, [illegible] [illegible] stores the captive Sodomites. Melchisedec [illegible] king of Solyma, afterwards called Jerusalem. [illegible] [illegible] Abram. Punishment of Hagar for [illegible] of [illegible] Sarai. Promise of Ishmael. Also [illegible].

WHEN Abram received intelligence of the success of the Assyrians, he was much affected by the captivity of his kinsman Lot, and the calamities entailed upon his neighbours the Sodomites. Revolving these [illegible] circumstances in his mind, he determined on [illegible] to their deliverance, and to that purpose [illegible] [illegible] his servants and dependents, pursued the Assyrians [illegible] [illegible] unawares [illegible] [illegible] [illegible] [illegible] night near Dan, at [illegible] of the [illegible] Jordan.

Being [illegible] prepared, and vigorously attacked [illegible] unexpected [illegible], when [illegible] [illegible] [illegible] [illegible] [illegible] [illegible] [illegible] [illegible] [illegible] [illegible] [illegible] [illegible] [illegible] [illegible] [illegible] [illegible] [illegible] who killed great numbers and put the reſt to flight

Abram effectually proſecuted the advantages he had gained, and purſued with ſuch fury, that on the ſecond day he drove the enemy into Hoba of Damaſcus, demonſtrating thereby, that genuine courage is more conducive to victory than numbers, as with about three hundred and eighteen of his houſehold, and the aid of three leading friends, he totally defeated ſo formidable an army that the few who eſcaped ſlaughter returned to their own country branded with eternal diſgrace

Having accompliſhed the ends of his undertaking in the reſcue of his kinſman, and the captive Sodomites, from the thraldom of the Aſſyrians, Abram ſet forth on his return, and was met on his way at a place called the King's Field, or Valley Ro[illegible]l, by the King of Sodom, and *Melchizedeck*, king of Solyma, ſince called Jeruſalem Melchizedeck ſignifies *juſt* or *righteous*, a name more pertinently applicable to this monarch, who was not only choſen to rule the civil affairs by the unanimous ſuffrages of the people, but for his inflexible integrity appointed to the ſacred office of prieſt unto the moſt High

This excellent perſonage liberally entertained Abram and his followers, ſupplied them with every thing neceſſary for their comfort and ſupport, applauded the prowels of the Patriarch, and glorified God for the important victory he had obtained Abram in return preſented Melchizedeck with the tenths of the ſpoils he had taken from the Aſſyrians The king of Sodom entreated Abram to retain the booty, requiring only the reſtitution of his reſcued ſubjects But Abram refuſed theſe terms alledging that he would not avail himſelf of the advantages he had obtained, his utmoſt deſire being only to retain ſuch a ſhare of the ſpoils as might requite the ſervices of his houſehold, and his three faithful friends, Eſcol, Ennerus, and Mambre, who had bravely ſupported him in the heat of the action The Almighty pleaſed with the magnanimous conduct of Abram, declared that it ſhould be bountifully rewarded He ſignified with all humility, that a recompenſe would profit him little, ſince it could be but temporary, having no heir to inherit after him — Upon this his benevolent Creator promiſed to bleſs him with a ſon and an offspring numerous as the ſtars in the firmament This aſſurance occaſioned him to offer a ſacrifice conformable to the Divine command It conſiſted of an heifer, a goat, a ram, a turtle, and a pigeon each three years old The birds were to be offered entire, but the quadrupeds were to be cut aſunder, according to Divine direction During the preparation of the altar, as the birds hovered around, attracted by the ſteam of the blood of the beaſts, a voice from heaven was heard to predict, that the poſterity of Abram ſhould ſuffer bondage in Egypt for the ſpace of 400 years, at the expiration of which they ſhould vanquiſh their oppreſſors, expel the Canaanites, and take poſſeſſion of their country

Abram then reſided at the oak called Ogyges, in the land of Canaan, near the city of Hebron, and being much afflicted by the barrenneſs of his wife, offered up inceſſant prayers to God, that he would vouchſafe him a ſon The Almighty encouraged him to hope for a fulfilment of the promiſe made not only reſpecting a ſon, but all the bleſſings mentioned when he received the Divine command to leave Meſopotamia At this time Sarai, through a providential intimation, cauſed Hagar an Egyptian, one of her handmaids, to have intercourſe with her huſband, in order that by thoſe means he might have iſſue Hagar becoming pregnant behaved with arrogance and treated her miſtreſs with ſupercilious contempt, preſuming that her iſſue would ſucceed to the poſſeſſion of the father's domains But Abram, as a check to her inſolence delivered her up for condign puniſhment to his wife Dreading the vengeance of her incenſed miſtreſs, the handmaid determined on flight, recommending herſelf to the care of [illegible] protecting Providence

As ſhe wandered through a dreary deſart, ſhe was accoſted by an angel, who commanded her to return home, aſſuring her, that if ſhe deported herſelf with becoming humility, ſhe ſhould be treated with indulgence, and reminded her, that through pride and inſolence ſhe had brought upon herſelf the preſent calamities To enforce the injunction, the heavenly meſſenger added, that on failure of compliance immediate death would be her puniſhment, but on the other hand if ſhe obeyed and returned, ſhe ſhould bear a ſon who in proceſs of time ſhould become ruler of the whole country wherein ſhe dwelt Hagar with profoundeſt reverence obeyed the Divine command, and on her return and humiliation at the feet of her offended miſtreſs, not only obtained her pardon, but the accompliſhment of the promiſe made by the angel, for ſoon after ſhe bore a ſon, who was named Iſhmael, ſignifying *heard of the Lord*, becauſe God had vouchſafed to hear the prayer of the mother

At the birth of Iſhmael, Abram was eighty-ſix years old, and in his ninety-ninth year, the Almighty viſited him, aſſured him that he ſhould have a ſon by his wife Sarai commanded him to call him *Iſaac*, declaring at the ſame time, that from him ſhould deſcend powerful nations and mighty kings, who ſhould extend their conqueſts throughout the whole country of Canaan, from Sidon even unto Egypt. Abram was alſo enjoined to circumciſe every male of his houſehold on the eighth day after the birth, that his poſterity might not intermarry with other nations The good father anxious for the fate of Iſhmael, humbly inquired of the Lord, if he ſhould be permitted to live? He received the Divine promiſe, that he ſhould not only live, but flouriſh, and become the founder of many great and powerful nations Abram then offered moſt grateful acknowledgments to his benevolent Creator, and in compliance with his injunction, was himſelf circumciſed, together with his ſon Iſhmael, and all the males of his family

CHAP. XI

Flagrant impiety and enormous criminality of the inhabitants of Sodom Denunciation of the Divine vengeance Abram entertains the angels. Prediction and accompliſhment of the deſtruction of Sodom Puniſhment inflicted on Lot's wife for diſobedience.

THE extenſive power and immenſe opulence of the inhabitants of Sodom produced an univerſal profligacy of manners, inſomuch that they became devoted to acts of the moſt flagrant impiety towards God, and the commiſſion of the moſt horrid and atrocious crimes towards one another The Almighty, juſtly provoked with their enormities, denounced his Divine vengeance, not only againſt the people but the country, determining the demolition of their city and total deſolation of the ſurrounding plain

When this awful ſentence was paſſed, three angels appeared to Abraham (*a*) as he was ſitting under the oak of Mamre at the entrance of his tent Apprehending them to be travellers, he aroſe, ſaluted, and entreated them to accept an hoſpitable entertainment His invitation being received, he commanded his ſervants to make the neceſſary preparations for their repaſt, and ſome bread of the fineſt flour, together with a dreſſed calf, being produced accordingly, to all appearance they ſeemed to eat Inquiring after Sarah his wife, he told them ſhe was within the tent, to which as it riſing, they replied, that before their return, ſhe would be a mother Sarah being called in and informed of the declaration, indicated her diffidence by a ſmile, being now in her ninetieth and her huſband in his hundredth year This produced a diſcovery, the gueſts acknowledged themſelves the angels of God, opened their Divine commiſſions, and aſſured him that they were ſent, one as the meſſenger of the birth of a ſon, and the others to effect the deſtruction of Sodom

On hearing the fatal ſentence Abraham was greatly alarmed, and earneſtly implored the Almighty not to involve the juſt and impious in one common deſtruction But upon the declaration of God, that there was not even one juſt man in the whole country of Sodom, and that if

(*a*) About th[illegible] time God made a covenant with Abr[illegible] in which he changed [illegible] name to Abraham, and [illegible] his wife Sarai to Sarah, indicating th[illegible] ſhould be the [illegible] of [illegible] nations [illegible]

HAGAR in the WILDERNESS having laid her Son ISHMAEL under a TREE that she might not see him perish thro' want providentially relieved by an ANGEL who directs her where to find RELIEF

there had been but ten innocent perſons amongſt them, he would have remitted the general ſentence. Abraham deſiſted from his interceſſion.

The two angels entered Sodom, and were invited by Lot to partake of entertainment in his houſe, for Lot imitated the hoſpitable example of Abraham. Some of the moſt abandoned of the Sodomites obſerving the graceful appearance of theſe ſtrangers, began to offer outrage to their perſons. Lot uſed every argument to diſſuade them from ſo flagrant a violation of the laws of decency and hoſpitality, and even offered to ſacrifice the chaſtity of his two daughters, to prevent the commiſſion of a crime moſt deteſtable of all others in the eyes both of God and man.

But all his endeavours proving ineffectual, the Almighty was ſo incenſed at their moſt audacious profligacy that he ſtruck them with inſtant blindneſs, which prevented their finding the entrance into Lot's houſe, while he ſentenced the inhabitants to a general perdition. Previous to the execution of the awful ſentence, Lot was warned by God to depart the city, together with his wife, his two daughters, who were yet unmarried, and the two youths, to whom they were contracted; but the latter contemned the gracious intimation, and profanely ridiculed the impending devaſtation.

The Divine vengeance now burſt forth in all its horrors; the Almighty darted devouring flames on the city, which ſpread deſolation in every quarter, and rapidly involved the inhabitants, and ſurrounding confines, in one general and irreparable deſtruction.

Lot's wife allured by a fatal curioſity to behold the deſtruction of the city, on their retreat looked back, contrary to the expreſs command of the Almighty, and, for her diſobedience, was immediately transformed into a pillar, or ſtatue of ſalt, (*a*) which as I have been occular witneſs, remains unto this day.

After this dire cataſtrophe, Lot and his daughters took up their reſidence on a little ſpot which the flames had ſpared, called Zoar, which in the Hebrew, ſignifies *ſmall*. But in this place, deſtitute of inhabitants, and almoſt barren of proviſions, they ſuffered much both in body and in mind. Thus ſolitarily ſituated, the daughters of Lot imagining that the male part of the human race was totally extinct, concerted the means of having private intercourſe with their father.

The iſſue of this contrivance was, each of them brought forth a ſon: that born of the elder was called Moab, ſignifying *of my father*; that of the younger was named Ammon, which implies *the ſon of my race* [illegible]. The firſt of theſe was the founder of the Moabites, who at this day are a powerful nation, and the latter of the Ammonites, both of which inhabit Cœlo-Syria.

CHAP. XII.

Tranſactions between Abraham and Abimelech. Birth of Iſaac. [illegible] the Jews and the Arabians. Baniſhment of Iſhmael and Hagar. Hagar accoſted and [illegible] by an angel. Progeny of Iſhmael.

ABRAHAM now removed to Gerar in the country of Paleſtine, whither his wife Sarah accompanied him in quality of his ſiſter, for he entertained the ſame apprehenſions of Abimelech king of that country, as he had done of Pharaoh, king of Egypt. Nor were his ſuſpicions groundleſs, for this monarch conceiving a paſſion for Sarah, would have injured him in the tendereſt point, had he not been providentially afflicted by a dreadful diſeaſe, and warned in a dream from violating the laws of hoſpitality in offering outrage to the woman, who accompanied the ſtranger, as ſhe was not his ſiſter but his lawful wife. Upon his recovery, he related to his friends the particulars of his dream, acknowledging that he had been viſited with ſickneſs, for the preſervation of the chaſtity of the ſtranger's wife, and ſending for Abraham, gave him every encouraging aſſurance with the moſt ſolemn promiſes of his future favour and protection. He then, [illegible] his friends, careſſed Abraham, [illegible] manner, that his wife was and ſhould ſtill remain [illegible] having been under the immediate protection of Almighty power. In confirmation of what he declared [illegible] called God and the woman's conſcience to witneſs, adding, that had he known ſhe was his wife, he would not have indulged an unwarrantable deſire. He further begged Abraham to pardon the injury offered him, and intercede with God in his favour, promiſing him ample protection, if he continued in the country, and if he choſe to depart, every thing neceſſary for his journey.

Abraham exculpated himſelf from the deception in calling his wife a ſiſter, by adverting to their affinity, as ſhe was the daughter of his brother, and obſerving further, that without having recourſe to ſuch means, he could not proſecute his travels with ſafety. He avowed his concern for the diſeaſe with which the king had been afflicted, and accepted his offer of continuing in his dominion.

Abimelech then aſſigned over to Abraham an extenſive tract of land, and a proportionate ſum of money to ſtock it, entering at the ſame time with him into a mutual covenant of friendſhip and amity, which was ratified at a certain well called Berſebe, or the *well of the* [illegible] *covenant*, and it bears that name in the language of the inhabitants to this day.

Soon after theſe tranſactions, Abraham had a ſon by his wife Sarah, according to the Divine promiſe, and called his name Iſaac, ſignifying in Hebrew, *laughter*, alluding to his mother's ſmile of diffidence, when the angel aſſured her ſhe ſhould bear a ſon, ſhe being then in her ninetieth, and her huſband in his hundredth year. On the (*b*) eighth day after his birth the boy was circumciſed, at which time the Jews ſtill continue the obſervance of that rite.

The Arabians, however, do not perform it till the thirteenth year, becauſe Iſhmael, Abraham's ſon by the concubine, and friend of that people, did not undergo the operation till he arrived at that age. Sarah had been as affectionately attached to Iſhmael, the ſon of her handmaid Hagar, as if he had been her own, and even regarded him as preſumptive heir to the family; but when Iſaac was born, ſhe thought a ſeparation expedient, leſt Iſhmael the elder might, on the deceaſe of his father, uſurp authority, and lay claim to the ſucceſſion. She therefore propoſed to Abraham the immediate diſmiſſion of Iſhmael and his mother to ſome other place. Abraham at firſt rejected the propoſal, as unnatural and inhuman, but at length, [illegible] by tokens of the Divine approbation, he acquieſced, committed the child to the care of his mother, and having given her a portion of bread, and a pitcher of water, diſmiſſed them to purſue that courſe to which their neceſſity might direct them. When their proviſion of bread and water was exhauſted, and the child was almoſt ſpent with fatigue and famine, ſhe laid him down under an oak, and retired to a little diſtance, that ſhe might not be ſhocked with his expiring groans. Ruminating on her miſeries ſhe was addreſſed by a meſſenger from on high, who pointed out to her a neighbouring ſpring, and charged her to attend ſedulouſly to the nurture of her child, as her ultimate happineſs depended on his preſervation.

Animated by theſe Divine intimations, ſhe purſued her courſe till ſhe met with ſome ſhepherds, by whoſe bounty all her wants were moſt amply ſupplied.

When Iſhmael attained to years of maturity, he took to wife an Egyptian woman, by whom he had [illegible] ſons, Nabaioth, Kedar, [illegible] Maſma, Mema, Maſmes, Chodam, Theman, Jetur, Naphiſh, and Cadmas, whoſe poſterity ſpread themſelves over the whole country called Nabatene, which extended from the Red Sea to the river Euphrates. [illegible] Arabians [illegible] valour [illegible] of Abraham [illegible]

(*a*) The pillar of ſalt which had been ſtanding in the days of Joſephus [illegible] This it was ſtanding [illegible] Clement of [illegible] with Joſephus [illegible] that it was to [illegible] the next century [illegible] by [illegible]

(*b*) [illegible]

C H A P XIII.

Abraham enjoined by the Divine command to make a sacrifice of his son Isaac. His obedience. Address to his son previous to the intended oblation. Isaac's acquiescence. The Almighty [illegible] arrests the sacrifice of the youth, signifies his approbation of his obedience, and presents Abraham with a ram for the sacrifice as a substitute for Isaac.

ABRAHAM was most affectionately attached to Isaac as his only legitimate son, the child of his age, and the peculiar gift of God, according to his Divine promise.

On the other hand, Isaac, by his filial duty and obedience, his fervent piety and uniform practice of virtue, enhanced, if possible, the affection of his parents, insomuch that Abraham's earthly delight centering in his son, his safety and happiness became the chief objects of his concern, and he waited with resignation his dismission from a scene of transient existence, provided his possessions in general might devolve to him; a desire which, through the favour of the Almighty, he happily effected.

It now seemed meet to the wise Disposer of all events to put the pious man's faith to the severest test. He therefore appeared to him in an extraordinary manner, and having reminded him of the various benefits he had conferred upon him, and the singular felicity he now enjoyed, under his peculiar protection and favour, proposed to him the sacrifice of his son Isaac, *as an oblation, in token of his gratitude* and obedience to the God of all his mercies, commanding him at the same time to conduct him to the mountain of Moriah, and there make of him a Burnt Offering on an altar to be erected for that special purpose.

Abraham, duly impressed with duty towards the Father of all Mercies, and firmly persuaded that his Divine command was not to be dispensed with, or even delayed on any human pretence, determined on immediate submission. Without communicating God's injunction, or his own resolution, to his wife and household, lest they should divert him from his duty, he took his son Isaac, with two servants, and loading an ass with the necessary apparatus for the sacrifice, departed for the mountain. Descrying the destined spot on the third day, he left the servants in the valley, and, attended only by his son, ascended the mountain, upon which King David appointed the Temple to be afterwards built (*e*). They also carried with them every thing necessary for the sacrifice, the victim only excepted. Isaac, who was then five and twenty years old, having himself erected and prepared the altar, but observing no victim, intimated his surprise to his father, and inquired of him as to the manner in which they should proceed to the sacrifice. Abraham, in the fulness of his heart, replied to the innocent youth, that God, the omnipotent Jehovah, would provide a victim if he approved the oblation.

At length, when every necessary preparation was made, he addressed his son in words to the following import: "Child of my doating age, of my fervent prayers, I have "nurtured thee with the fondest affection, and most unremitting attention; all my delight centered in the expectation of leaving thee successor to my possessions, when I "should be directed to pay the debt of nature; but since it "pleaseth the Sovereign of the Universe, that the father "to whom thou wert given in mercy, should now be the "instrument of thy restitution to his Divine will, let silent "submission testify acquiescent obedience, and devoutly "consecrate thyself to that God who demands thee as a "victim. This we are enjoined as a token of grateful obedience for innumerous benefits conferred. Since therefore "as a descendant of Adam mortality is thy inevitable doom, "reflect that thy dismission from this life is not in the ordinary way of sickness, or any common calamity, but "through the immediate instrumentality of thine own "father, as a victim to the divine command; and let this "consideration dispose thee to give up thy spirit at the altar "with fervent supplication and pious resignation, that thou "mayest be translated to the realms of bliss, and be rendered supremely happy in the Fountain of the Divine "Presence. By these means thy remembrance will console me to my latest days, when I reflect that though I "have lost the aid and comfort of a son, I shall ever be "guarded by the shield of Omnipotence."

Isaac, animated by the same sense of duty as his pious father, listened to his address with fixed attention and glowing ardour, eagerly replying, that "he should deem "himself unworthy of birth, if he should hesitate to obey "the command of God, or murmur at the requisition of "his father; nay, that he would without reluctance, have "submitted to the sacrifice even at the command of his "father alone, from the immutable regard he had ever "entertained for filial duty and obedience." Having thus said, he approached the altar with alacrity, and placed himself thereon in a proper position; the father's arm was uplifted, and prepared for the decisive stroke, when, at the critical moment, that very voice from above that had given the command sounded the prohibition, and arrested the blow. The merciful Parent of the universe was pleased to declare, that his command arose not from a delight he took in human sacrifices, or depriving him of a son whom he had bestowed on him as a peculiar favour, but a desire of putting his faith and obedience to the severest test; that as he had given such singular proofs of his piety, his family should be the particular objects of his paternal regard; that his son should live to a good old age, leave his dominions to his posterity, who should increase the same, and possess domains to a vast extent. It was added, that they should expel the inhabitants of Canaan by force of arms, inhabit the land themselves, and become the wonder and envy of surrounding nations.

When the Divine voice ceased, a ram suddenly appeared, and presenting itself as a victim, Abraham and his son mutually embraced, as a token of joy at so signal a deliverance, and the promise of such inestimable blessings, proceeded to the oblation with most fervent devotion, and then returned to their house with all the complacency of an applauding conscience, and an approving God, to reap the benefits arising from their piety and obedience.

C H A P XIV.

Death of Sarah, Abraham's wife. Her sepulchral monument at Hebron.

SOON after this important event Sarah died, having attained to the age of 127 years, and was interred at Hebron. The inhabitants of Canaan freely offered him a burial-place for his wife, but he declined acceptance, and purchased a spot of ground of a private person for four hundred shekels of silver, where the sepulchral monuments of himself and posterity still remain.

C H A P. XV.

Origin of the Troglodytes. Abraham deputes a messenger to [illegible] Rebecca in marriage for his son Isaac. Manner of [illegible] amongst the Jews. Conference between the messenger and relatives of the [illegible]. Consummation of the marriage.

ABRAHAM, on the demise of Sarah, took to wife a woman called Chetura, by whom he had six children, endued with equal powers of body and mind. Their names were Zambran, Jazar, Madan, Madian, Josabac and Sous. The latter had two sons, Sabathan and Dadan, to whom were born Latusim, Assur and Luom. The sons of Madian were Ephas, Ophren, Anoch, Ebidas, and Eldas. All these and their successors [illegible] Abraham,

---

(*e*) Here is a plain [illegible] the [illegible] David [illegible] words built the temple on this mount Moriah, which it was certainly Solomon that built the temple. But if the word [illegible] is [illegible] used [illegible] that of the [illegible] error will be [illegible] was David and [illegible] Solomon who erected the [illegible] to [illegible] mount Moriah [illegible] Jewish [illegible]

founded colonies in the country of the Troglodytes, and that part of Arabia Felix which is bounded by the Red Sea Tradition reports that Ophir entered Lybia at the head of an army, took possession of it, and that his successors, taking up their residence in it, called it in process of time by the name of Africa. This report is, in some measure, confirmed by Alexander Polyphistor, who alludes to an history of the Jews, written in the style and manner of Moses, by the Prophet Cleodamus, or Malchus This writer relates, "that Abraham had several children by Chetura, of whom "he names three, Ophir, Surim, and Japher The Sy- "rians derive their appellation from Surim, as do the city "of Aphra and the country of Africa from the two others "He adds, that they fought under the command of Her- "cules, in his expedition in Lybia against Antæus, and "that Hercules taking to wife the daughter of Apher, she "bore him a son called Debor, or Deden, who was father "of Sopho, founder of a barbarous race, known by the "appellation of Sophaces"

Isaac having now almost attained to the age of forty years, his father became anxious to provide him a wife, and therefore deputed a trusty servant as messenger to demand in marriage Rebecca the daughter of Bethuel, his brother Nachor's son Having previously bound him to a faithful discharge of his commission by an oath (which ceremony was performed by the servant's putting his hand under his master's thigh) Abraham dismissed him with valuable presents to dispense at his discretion upon his arrival After a tedious and fatiguing journey through Mesopotamia, where the traveller is impeded in the winter by deep bogs, and by a scarcity of water in the summer, as well as constantly exposed to the depredations of robbers, he at length arrived at the city of Charan, and in the suburbs met several young maidens going to a well to draw water This induced him to offer up an ejaculation to God, that if the intended alliance had his sanction, Rebecca, whom his master had sent him to demand in marriage for his son, might come forth among the rest, and that the token by which he should distinguish her might be the immediate compliance with his request of some water to appease his thirst, after a general denial from the rest Possessed with this idea, he approached the well, and applying individually to each to give him to drink, was refused on different pretences by them all, one excepted, who reproaching her companions with their uncourteous behaviour to a stranger, as well as want of deference to the male character, with the greatest humanity presented him her pitcher

This propitious event encouraged the messenger to pave the way for the introduction of his commission therefore, after commending her humanity and generosity, in relieving a distressed traveller, even at the expense of her own labour, he proceeded to inquire concerning her parents, whom he pronounced happy in such a daughter, adding an earnest prayer to the Almighty that she might be blessed with a pious and affectionate husband, and become the mother of a numerous and virtuous offspring

The innocent maid, without reserve, ingenuously replied, "My name is Rebecca Bethuel, my father, is long "deceased, so that the concerns of our family are under "the direction of my mother and my uncle Laban, who "are the guardians of my youthful age"

Inferring from what had passed, that the negociation was avowed by the interposition of Providence, he presented the maid with several female ornaments, requesting her acceptance as a recompense for her singular courtesy on the most pressing occasion, and adding an earnest entreaty that he might be vouchsafed an asylum in her uncle's house as night coming on, he could not prosecute his journey without danger of sustaining the loss of jewels of immense value, which could not be in any place of such assurance of security as at the house of those whose benevolence and humanity he conceived so firm an opinion of from the open and ingenuous behaviour of their beauteous relative and concluded with declaring, that if her uncle and [illegible] would deign him reception, he would make them [illegible] recompense also for his entertainment

Rebecca returned for answer that his opinion of the humanity of her relations was well founded, but not his suspicion of their liberality, assuring him that if admitted he would be entertained without expense, and then entreated permission to acquaint her uncle with the circumstance, previous to his introduction Laban being thus apprized of the arrival of a stranger, received him with the frankest hospitality, giving orders to his servants to take care of his camels, while he was entertained at his own table Supper being removed, the messenger thus addressed the mother and uncle of Rebecca "I am deputed on a spe- "cial embassy from Abraham the son of Thares for Na- "chor (addressing himself to the woman) the grandfather "of your children, was brother to Abraham by the same "father and mother I am authorized by him to ask your "daughter in marriage to his legitimate son and heir "whom he hath refused to the most powerful and opulent "of his country, preferring an alliance with those of his "own kindred Frustrate not, therefore, his well found- "ed intentions, especially as the Divine interposition ap- "pears so evidently to have formed the design in direct- "ing me first to the maiden, and then to your habita- "tion, for when I entered the city, and perceived ma- "ny virgins approaching the well, I offered up a fervent "prayer that I might find the maiden of whom I was in "quest, which the Almighty was pleased to grant Rati- "fy, therefore, by your authority, an union so fruitful, "approved from on high, and render my master happy, in "acceding to the purport of my commission, by the volun- "tary resignation of your daughter to the possession of his "beloved son" The match appearing, on the shortest reflection, so conducive to the welfare of the virgin, the honor and dignity of the family, as well as conformable to the will of God, he obtained the consent of the parties concerned Rebecca was therefore consigned to the care of the trusty messenger, by whom she was conducted to Isaac, now become lord of his father's possessions, as all the sons of Abraham by Chetura, had departed and fixed their residence in remote countries

CHAP XVI

Death and Burial of Abraham

ABRAHAM, soon after the consummation of the marriage between his darling son Isaac and the beauteous Rebecca, which he had so devoutly wished, paid the debt of nature in the hundred and seventy-fifth year of his age His piety and virtue were so eminently conspicuous throughout the transactions of his whole life, that he was not only singularly favored by his God, but revered by his cotemporaries as an ornament to human nature, and a character worthy of universal imitation He was buried at Hebron, near his wife Sarah, the funeral rites being performed by his sons Ismael and Isaac

CHAP XVII

Births of Esau and Jacob Famine in the land of Canaan Isaac is restrained from going into Egypt [illegible] Repairs to Gerar [illegible] Abimelech [illegible] After [illegible] [illegible] by Jacob [illegible] father's blessing [illegible] [illegible]

SOON after Isaac had performed his last office of duty to his deceased parent, his wife Rebecca became pregnant and being of most extraordinary bulk, her husband, as the time of her delivery approached, was extremely anxious for her safety, and inquired of the Lord the cause of so singular an appearance He was informed that his wife should bear twins (a) who should give names to several nations and that in process of time he who at first seemed to be the less mighty should become the most important At length, according to the Divine intimation,

(a) The births of Esau and Jacob are by Josephus, said to be after Abraham's death but it should have been expressed after Sarah's death He[illegible] [illegible] to [illegible] [illegible]

C

Rebecca was delivered of twins, the elder of whom was covered with hair from head to feet and the younger came into the world holding his brother by the heel. The former called Esau (and by some Seir, from the hairiness of his body,) was the favourite of his father, but the latter, whose name was Jacob, engrossed the affection of his mother.

A dreadful famine raging at this time in Canaan, Isaac was inclined to retire into Egypt, but being diverted from his purpose, at the Divine command, he repaired to Gerar. King Abimelech at first gave him a kind reception, according to the league of friendship and amity which had subsisted between that monarch and his father Abraham. But soon perceiving the peculiar interposition of Divine Providence in favour of Isaac in all his concerns, his envy and jealousy were excited to such a degree, that he expelled him from his environs. Isaac withdrew to a place called Pharan, or the valley, not far distant from Gerar, where his servants, on attempting to dig, in order to discover a spring of water, were opposed by some of the king's shepherds, and as Isaac determined not to contend with them, they imagined they had carried their point. Removing to a more distant place, Isaac's servants renewed the attempt, and were annoyed in the same manner as before, but his prudence again inducing him to avoid extremities, he at length obtained permission from the king to dig, upon which he sunk a well and called it Rooboth, signifying, in Hebrew, *large* or *spacious*. One of the two former places he named Escon, and the other Siennes, words implying in the original, *contention* and *enmity*.

But the increasing power and riches of Isaac raised disquieting apprehensions in the mind of Abimelech, which added to reflections on the instances of his breach of friendship in the late circumstance of digging for the well, excited his fear lest Isaac should embrace the first opportunity of revenging the injuries he had done him. He had therefore recourse to dissimulation, and taking with him Picol, one of his principal officers, as arbiter, repaired to the place of Isaac's residence, and there proposed a renewal of the former league of friendship and amity. Isaac being of a most courteous disposition, readily complied. The ratification of the league put an end to all animosity, and Abimelech, having accomplished his purpose, returned home with perfect satisfaction.

Esau, Isaac's favourite son, having obtained to the age of forty years, took to himself two wives, Ada, the daughter of Elon and Alibama, the daughter of Esebion two of the most powerful persons amongst the Canaanites. In neither of these contracts did Esau consult the will and pleasure of his father, assured he should never obtain his consent, as Isaac was averse to any alliance with the people of the country. The error, however, being irremovable such was the good father's candour and moderation, that he did not command their expulsion, but only enjoined his son to conceal his marriage.

When Isaac was stricken in years and deprived of sight, he called his son Esau to him, and having lamented the infirmities of age and the loss of his eyes, which prevented him from serving God with his wonted alacrity, expressed an earnest desire of leaving him his blessing before his departure. To this purpose he ordered his son to proceed to the hunt, and to prepare him a repast (*a*) from whatever chance might throw in his way, adding, that upon such consideration, he would offer up his fervent prayer to the Almighty for his future protection and favour towards him, as the best manner he could employ the short interval between the present moment, and his entrance on an eternal world.

Esau immediately set forth, but (*b*) Rebecca over-hearing what passed, and desirous of transferring the promised blessing from Esau to her favourite son Jacob, though in direct opposition to her husband's mind and will, commanded him instantly to kill a kid, and prepare a repast for his father. Jacob, obsequious to his mother, obeyed her command, and having prepared every thing according to her direction, spread the skin of the kid over his neck and hands, that by those means he might elude the suspicion of his parent, aged and blind, and confirm him in the assurance of his being his brother Esau, as he resembled him in every other particular instance. In this disguise, therefore, lest he should be surprised before Isaac had finished his prayer, and through a detection of the imposition, incur a curse instead of procuring a blessing, he hastened to present what he had prepared to his sire. But the old man perceiving that his voice differed from that of his brother, desired his son to approach him. Jacob then putting forth his arms covered with the kid's skin, Isaac exclaimed, "Though thy voice be like unto Jacob, yet by the hairiness of thy arms thou seemest unto me to be Esau." Then without the least suspicion of deceit, as soon as he had eaten what was prepared, he thus invoked the God of heaven and earth: "Eternal, and supreme, and universal "Creator, who to my father hast been pleased to promise, "and on me to confer, many and important blessings with "assurance of continuing them to my posterity, let thy "mercies be still extended towards me, nor let them de"part from me in my present languid state, in which I most "need thy Divine support. Vouchsafe to preserve this my "son, protect him from evil, bless him according to thine "abundant goodness, render him formidable to his ene"mies, and the joy and delight of his family and friends." Thus did the good old Isaac prefer his prayer to the Almighty as he thought, in behalf of his favourite son Esau, but he had scarcely come to a conclusion when Esau returned from the hunt, which though the father perceived, as he knew his intention was frustrated, he passed unnoticed. The elder brother, thus disappointed, entreated a similar blessing with the younger, but his father denied him alledging, that he could neither recal nor transfer the blessing given to Jacob, so that Esau had only to lament the severity of his fate. Isaac, moved by his tears, in order to console, assured him, that he and his posterity should excel in, and acquire vast renown from, personal strength, activity in hunting, and martial exercises though he must ever act in subordination to his brother Jacob, apprehensive of his brother's resentment, for having by stratagem supplanted him in so important a concern as his aged father's blessing, was freed from his fears by means of his mother, who prevailed on his father to send him into Mesopotamia, to select a wife from amongst her kindred. Whilst Esau, conscious of having displeased his father in forming an alliance with the Canaanites determined to make some reparation for his errors by marrying Bassamath the daughter of Ishmael, to whom he was in future more affectionately attached than to either of his other wives.

CHAP. XVIII.

Jacob sets out for Mesopotamia. Vision of the ladder. He arrives at Haran, and enters into conversation with Rachael, is introduced to, and cordially received. Asks Rachael in marriage. Obtains Laban's consent. Deception practised by Laban. Jacob's servitude. Marriage with Rachael. Explication of the names of his sons. Jacob's flight. Is pursued and overtaken by Laban. His accusation against Jacob. Jacob's vindication. Laban's duplicity. The parties enter into a covenant of amity.

JACOB having received orders from his father, through the persuasion of his mother Rebecca, to set out for Mesopotamia, to form an union with the daughter of his uncle Laban, proceeded on his journey through the country of Canaan. But as the inhabitants maintained a most inveterate aversion to his

(*a*) This repast, or supper, to be caught by hunting, was intended for a festival on a sacrifice, and [illegible] expected that upon the prayers usual on those occasions, his son would be interested in the blessings supplicated for him. We find that after having, through deception, blessed Jacob, he attempts not to retract, conscious that the blessing came not from him but from God, and that an alteration was out of his power.

(*b*) Whether Jacob or his mother Rebecca were most to be censured for this imposition upon Isaac in his old age, is not easy to be determined. However the blessing being derived [illegible] prediction of future events and foretelling things to [illegible] power; [illegible] Jacob [illegible] certainly [illegible] family, he used the utmost precaution as indispensably necessary for his security, insomuch, that he would not take up even a temporary residence amongst them, choosing rather to repose upon stones, as a pillow, under the canopy of heaven. One night as he slept in this manner, a vision represented to his imagination a ladder fixed on the earth, and reaching with its summit to heaven. On the steps descended certain beings, surpassing in form the ordinary part of mankind. At the upper extremity appeared the Almighty, who calling Jacob by his name, addressed him in words to the following purport: "Descendant of a "pious father, and a grandfather eminent for his exalted "virtues, be not dismayed by dangers or difficulties that "may now present themselves, but be encouraged by the "prospect of my future favour and protection. I am He "who conducted Abraham hither, when he was expelled "Mesopotamia by his kindred, who crowned thy father "with blessings, nor shall they be wanting to thee. Prosecute, therefore, thy journey under my immediate direction. The event of thy intended marriage shall be prosperous in a numerous and virtuous offspring, to whom "and their descendants I will give not only the possession "of this land, but they shall increase the population of the "whole earth, throughout every part to which the "beams of the sun extend their genial influence. Proceed, then, with confident reliance on my guidance, "and be assured of my continual assistance."

Animated by these great and important promises, which the Almighty was pleased to communicate to him in the vision, Jacob anointed the stones on which he had rested his head, while he received the happy tidings, and vowed, if he returned in safety, to sacrifice to God on that very spot, which he accordingly performed, by offering up a tenth part of all his substance. To perpetuate the remembrance of the place where the vision appeared to him, he called it Bethel, signifying in the Hebrew, *House of God*.

Pursuing his journey, Jacob at length arrived at Haran, and meeting in the suburbs some shepherds and several young persons sitting on the bank of a fountain, joined, and requested them to let him drink. A conversation ensuing, he took an opportunity of making inquiry concerning one Laban, and was informed that the fame of Laban had long established his name, which was therefore well known throughout the country. They added that his daughter was expected there, being accustomed to feed her flock with them, and referred him to her for all the intelligence he wished to obtain.

Rachael at that instant appeared, and being made acquainted with the stranger's inquiries, indicated great complacency, asked him concerning his family and business, and discovered the utmost readiness to afford him her best information and assistance. Charmed by the beauty of her person, rather than attracted by the courtesy of her demeanour, or the alliance of kin, Jacob conceived the tenderest passion for the lovely maid, whom he thus addressed: "It "fair creature, thou art the daughter of Laban, our families were united by the ties, both of consanguinity and "friendship long previous to thine or my existence, Abraham, Arran, and Nachor, being the immediate offspring "of Thares. Bethuel, thy grandfather, was Nachor's son, "and Abraham, and Sarah, the daughter of Arran, were "the parents of my father Isaac. But there is yet a nearer "and dearer tie of affinity, for my mother, Rebecca, is thy "father Laban's sister, by one and the same father and mother. The object of my journey, therefore, is to renew "the ancient family league." The recital of these particulars calling to her memory many circumstances she had heard from her father in her earliest years, respecting Rebecca, of whom she was assured her parents would gladly receive intelligence, moved an affectionate tear, so that having saluted the young man, she informed him, that nothing would more conduce to the happiness of her father and the whole family, than to receive tidings of his sister, and therefore [illegible] desired him to accompany her [illegible], that the good old man might no longer be deprived of so exquisite a gratification.

Jacob being introduced by Rachael to her father Laban, was acknowledged, and saluted as his relation, passed [illegible] time in social tranquillity, and contributed much to the domestic felicity of the family. In process of time, Laban having expressed the utmost satisfaction in the society of Jacob, discovered a desire of learning the motive which induced him to leave his parents in their advanced age, when they required his most unremitting attention, assuring him at the same time that nothing should be wanting on his part to promote the design and intention of his journey. Jacob then frankly disclosed the whole matter, informing him, "that Isaac had twin sons, Esau and himself, that as, by his mother's contrivance and assistance, he had deprived his brother of their father's intended inheritance (a) Esau sought his life, as having wrested from him his legal possessions, as well as the blessings for which his father imagined he had interceded in his behalf." He confessed, that, with the advice of his mother, he had fled to him for refuge, and assured him that next to the care of Providence, he expected succour and assistance from one so nearly and dearly allied as himself.

Laban gave him the most solemn assurance of support and protection, not only on account of the alliance of their ancestors, but the cordial affection he entertained for his mother, in proof of which he appointed him overseer of his numerous flocks, and superintendant of all his shepherds, till such time as he should be desirous of returning home, when he would dismiss him with every token of respect, that could bespeak a regard for his alliance.

Jacob expressed the highest sense of such singular proofs of esteem, professed himself bound to the best services of his liberal patron, as his supreme delight, but intimated that the only compensation he desired, was the bestowal in marriage of the beauteous Rachael, whose person and virtues were the objects of his admiration, and the spring of all his words and actions.

Jacob's ingenuous behaviour was highly pleasing to Laban, who readily consented to the marriage, preferring him to any other man as a son-in-law, but requested him to continue his abode with him some time, as he was [illegible] disinclined to send his daughter amongst the Canaanites, having often repented his sister's forming an alliance in so remote a country.

Jacob readily acceded to the proposal, and entered into a covenant to serve his uncle seven years, expressing a satisfaction in having an opportunity of testifying his fidelity in such a manner as to prove himself worthy of the alliance.

The covenant was ratified, and being fulfilled, Laban prepared the nuptial feast, but night drawing on, he found means, without the suspicion of Jacob, to convey his other daughter, Leah, less beautiful and more advanced in years than Rachael, to the bridal bed. Jacob through the [illegible] of the night, and the [illegible] of intoxication, had intercourse with her, but the return of morning discovering the delusion, Jacob reproached his uncle with the treachery of his behaviour, when he exculpated himself from an evil intention, by urging necessity as a plea, as the custom of the country precluded the younger sister from marrying before the elder. He added that he should still possess Rachael, on condition that he would serve him the other seven years. Such was his passion, that he agreed to servitude for the same term as before, at the expiration of which his labours were compensated by receiving the object of his adoration as his own.

The father appointed two handmaids to attend his daughters: Zilpah waited on Leah, and Bilhah on Rachael; [illegible] [illegible] Rachael [illegible] with [illegible] she [illegible] herself [illegible] intervals with hopes that [illegible]

[illegible]

her children, ſhe might thereby conciliate his eſteem, and therefore put up inceſſant prayers to God, that he would grant her iſſue The event confirmed her hope, ſhe brought forth a ſon, who being the means of reſtoring her huſband's affection, was called REUBEN, or *The ſon of Viſion*, becauſe ſhe obtained him through the mercy of God

She afterwards brought him three other ſons, Simeon, implying that *God hath heard her*, Levy, meaning the *Band of Society*, and Judah, ſignifying *Thankſgiving* Rachael, apprehenſive that Leah's fruitfulneſs might ſupplant her in the eſteem of her huſband, cauſed her handmaid Billah to have intercourſe with Jacob, to whom ſhe conceived a ſon called Dan, or *The judgment of God*, and after him another, named Naphtali, or *Artifice* becauſe ſhe had recourſe to ſubtlety to requite her ſiſter's fruitfulneſs Leah in reſentment adopted the ſame ſtratagem againſt Rachael, and gave up her maid Zilpah to her huſband, who by her had two ſons, Gad, or *Son of Chance*, and Aſſer, or *Bleſſed*, becauſe Leah was preferred for her fruitfulneſs

Reuben, the eldeſt ſon of Leah, brought to his mother ſome apples of mandrake, which Rachael perceiving, ſhe expreſſed a longing deſire to taſte the fruit Leah churliſhly denied her, alledging, that ſhe ought to reſt contented with the aſcendency ſhe held in her huſband's affection To ſooth her ſiſter into compliance, and gratify her own inclination, Rachael told her ſhe would reſign Jacob to her that night, in conſequence of which he had again children by Leah, viz Iſſachar, or *gained by Hire* and Zebulon, or *Token of Good Will* and a daughter, called Dinah

Rachael at length brought forth a ſon, who was called Joſeph, or *Addition*. As Jacob had now ſerved his father-in-law for the ſpace of twenty years, he became deſirous of returning with his wives to his own inheritance, but as he could by no means obtain Laban's conſent, he determined to effect his flight by ſtratagem To this purpoſe he ſounded the diſpoſition of his wives, who both encouraged him in the attempt Jacob departed, and took with him privately half of Laban's flocks, while Rachael conveyed off her father's idols, not through any veneration, as ſhe had been taught by Jacob the wickedneſs and abſurdity of worſhipping images, but thinking if Laban ſhould purſue them, a reconciliation might be accompliſhed, by reſtoring them She was accompanied in her flight by her ſiſter, the four handmaids, and all their children

Laban, on the firſt notice of their eſcape, purſued them with a ſtrong party, intending to aſſault them, and in the evening of the ſeventh day overtook them as they were reſting themſelves on a riſing ground But Divine Providence interpoſing, he was forbidden in a viſion to uſe violence either againſt Jacob or his daughters, aſſuring him that if from a preſumption of the weakneſs of the inferior party he ſhould dare to aſſail them, the Almighty would eſpouſe their cauſe, and lift up his Omnipotent arm in their defence

Laban, duly impreſſed with the Divine command, appointed a conference with Jacob the enſuing day, and having mentioned the particular circumſtances of his dream, expoſtulated with him on the impropriety of his conduct in attempting to depart ſecretly from one, by whom, in a ſtate of indigence, he had been ſo liberally ſupplied with every thing of which he ſtood in need "I have (ſaid Laban) given "thee my daughters in marriage, hoping thereby to have "confirmed our friendſhip, but you, on the contrary, regardleſs of your duty to your mother, to me, to your "wives, or to your children, have treated me as an enemy, in ranſacking my property, ſeducing my daughters to abandon their father and carrying off my houſehold gods which I and my progenitors have held in ſuch "profound veneration This is the treatment I have received at the hand, not of a profeſſed enemy, but at "the hand of a nearly allied relative, the ſon of my "ſiſter, the huſband of my daughters, and the covenanted friend of my boſom"

Jacob urged, in vindication of himſelf, that the love of his country was a paſſion common to mankind, and ſtamped as it were with the Divine Image on his mind, that it was therefore natural for him, after ſo long an abſence, to feel a deſire of returning, that with reſpect to the robbery of which he was accuſed, he had a right to the effects he had taken, as a compenſation for his long ſervitude, and that his daughters had accompanied him in lawful obedience to the command of an huſband, and from motives of an affectionate regard for their children He proceeded to obſerve, by way of juſt reproach, that Laban, who was the brother of his mother, and who had given him his daughters in marriage, had ſubjected him by artifice to long and moſt laborious ſervitude, to toils, from which, had he borne him any reſentment, he might long ſince have delivered himſelf Laban had certainly dealt unjuſtly by Jacob, for perceiving that God was pleaſed to favour him with tokens of his protection and bleſſing, he promiſed him at one time all the whole cattle that ſhould be produced in the year, and at another all the flock, but at the expiration of the reſpective terms, he refuſed to fulfil the agreement Jacob gave him full liberty to ſearch for the images but Rachael had hidden them under her camel's ſaddle, and evaded the ſearching, by pretending to a periodical indiſpoſition A reconciliation now enſued, the terms of which were, that paſt injuries ſhould be buried in oblivion, and that Jacob ſhould love and cheriſh his daughters They then entered into a ſolemn covenant, which was ratified on a mountain, where they erected a pillar in the form of an altar, ſtyling that ſpot and the ſurrounding country Galead, or *The Hill of Witneſs*, which name it retains to this day The treaty was ſucceeded by a feſtival, after which the parties ſet out for their reſpective habitations

CHAP XIX

Jacob diſpatches meſſengers to Eſau, previous to his return. In a viſion wreſtles with an angel, and overcomes Amicable interview with Eſau

DURING his journey to the land of Canaan, Jacob had many propitious viſions, wherefore, he named the place where they occurred, *The Field of God* But ſtill apprehenſive of Eſau's reſentment, he diſpatched meſſengers to diſcover the ſituation of affairs at home, and charged one of them with this intimation to his brother, "That having, on a former occaſion, rouſed his indignation, he had choſen to abandon his country, and now hoped that time had eraſed former animoſities That he was upon his return, with his wives, his children, and the effects he had by his induſtry acquired, that he had ſent ſome of the moſt valuable as a token of his ſubmiſſion, and would eſteem it his greateſt happineſs to have the bleſſing God had imputed to him, with his beloved brother

This frank and ingenuous behaviour was highly pleaſing to Eſau, who ſet forth at the head of four hundred armed men to meet his brother Jacob was alarmed at the intelligence of the approach of a formidable body of men, yet fixing his confidence in the aid of Omnipotence, he determined to repel force by force, and dividing his company into two compact bodies, ordered one to advance, and act as occaſion might require, and the other to proceed ſlowly in the rear, in order to ſuſtain them in caſe of an aſſault.

Having taken ſuch neceſſary precaution, he again ſent meſſengers with preſents to his brother. Theſe conſiſted of curious animals, which marched in proceſſion, the better to diſplay their ſize, properties, and numbers, enhance their value, and thereby conciliate the eſteem of his brother, to whom the meſſengers were charged to ſhew every token of reſpect and ſubmiſſion The day being ſpent in making theſe diſpoſitions, he cauſed his company to march by night, and when they had paſſed a brook called Jabboch, Jacob, who brought up the rear, had a viſion, in which he ſeemed to wreſtle with an angel, and came off victorious The angel then addreſſed him, aſſuring him that his having atchieved ſo extraordinary a feat as that of overcoming an heavenly meſſenger, preſaged much future ſucceſs, that his poſterity ſhould be invincible and conquer in all their enterprizes He therefore enjoined him by the Divine direction to assume in future the name of Israel which, in the Hebrew, signifies *struggling* or *resisting*.

As Jacob had importuned a relation of his future fortune, he requested of the angel, when he became sensible of his divine commission, to be explicit in every circumstance, which done, the vision disappeared. Jacob animated by so joyful an event, named the place Phanuel, or *The face of God*. But one of the sinews of his thigh being strained in the contest, he ever after abstained from eating the hind part of any animal, a custom still observed by our nation.

On receiving intelligence of the approach of Esau and his company, Jacob ordered his wives and their attendants to keep at a distance from the main body, as a security for their persons, if there should be a necessity for coming to action.

When he perceived the pacific disposition of his brother, Jacob ran to him, and threw himself at his feet. Esau, on the other hand, cordially embraced him, kindly inquired after the welfare of his wives and children, and humanely offered to conduct them to his father. Jacob declined the offer, on pretence of the fatigues his cattle had sustained through a tedious journey, so that they separated for the present: his brother retiring to the town of Seir, so called from the thickness of Esau's hair, while Jacob removed to a place called at this day *The Tents*, and from thence to Shechem a city of the Canaanites.

CHAP. XX

Violation of Dinah's chastity. Discovery of Laban's idols. Death of Rachael, and afterwards of Isaac.

THE inhabitants of Shechem were at this time engaged in the celebration of a festival, and Dinah, Jacob's only daughter, repaired thither, to gratify her curiosity, by observing the female customs and fashions of the country. Shechem seeing Dinah, and becoming enamoured of her beauty, first violated her chastity, which the more inflaming his passion, he asked permission of his father to take her to wife. The king not only complied with the prince's request, but made application himself to Jacob for his concurrence. The overture threw Jacob into the greatest perplexity, not daring on the one hand, to dispute the authority of a monarch, nor deeming it lawful or expedient, on the other, to form an alliance with a stranger. He therefore evaded an explicit answer, and intreated time for mature deliberation. The king thereupon retired, hoping to obtain consent. Jacob immediately referred the matter to his sons, communicating to them, at the same time the rape of their sister, and the request of Dinah, that she might be given in marriage to the prince his son. Those of them who were not immediately interested, were silent upon the occasion, but Simeon and Levi, descended from the same mother with the injured female, vowed revenge. The present season, being entirely devoted to festivity, was very proper for the execution of their design, so that the brothers, in the dead of the night, having first fallen upon and slain the guards, entered the city and massacred all the males (the king and his son among the rest) but offered no violence to the women. Finding their sister, they conducted her home, and having discovered the transaction to their father, he was greatly displeased, and signified his disapprobation in the severest terms: but the Almighty was pleased to console him in a dream, and commanded him to perform the sacrifice which he had vowed at the time he saw the vision in his journey to Mesopotamia. In making the necessary preparation for these solemn rites, he casually discovered Laban's idols, which Rachael had stolen, and concealed under an oak tree in Shechem, without his knowledge.

Taking his departure from thence, he offered an oblation to the Almighty in Bethel, on the very spot where he had seen the vision, at the commencement of his journey into Mesopotamia. As he was pursuing his course into the land of Ephrata, Rachael, his wife died in child-bed, and was there interred, being the only one of the family who had not a place in the sepulchre at Hebron. Jacob having made great lamentation for the loss of his beloved wife Rachael, called the child she bare on that melancholy occasion Benjamin, or *the Son of Sorrow*, from the mortal pangs his birth had given his mother. The children of Jacob were twelve sons and one daughter, of whom eight were legitimate, six by Leah, and two by Rachael, and two by each of their handmaids, whose names have been already mentioned.

From Ephrata Jacob returned to Hebron, the residence of his father Isaac, by whom he was informed of the death of his mother Rebecca, a short time before his arrival. Nor did the good old Isaac long survive his beloved consort, but paid the debt of nature soon after his return, and was buried by Jacob and Esau, near his progenitors in the sepulchral tomb in Hebron. Isaac imitated the virtues of his pious father, and experienced the peculiar affection and favor of the Almighty on the demise of Abraham. After a life devoted to the honor of God, and the good of mankind, he closed a scene of transient existence, in the 185th year of his age, leaving an example worthy the imitation of posterity.

THE END OF THE FIRST BOOK.

FLAVIUS JOSEPHUS

ON THE

ANTIQUITIES

OF THE

JEWS.

BOOK II

FROM THE DEATH OF ISAAC TO THE DEPARTURE OF THE ISRAELITES OUT OF EGYPT

[CONTAINING A PERIOD OF ABOVE TWO HUNDRED AND TWENTY YEARS]

Eſau and Jacob divide their inheritance, and quit their former places of reſidence. Eſau ſells his birthright, and is therefore called Edom. His progeny

ON the demiſe of Iſaac, his ſons, Eſau and Jacob, divided his inheritance, and, in conſequence thereof, quitted their former habitations Eſau leaving the city of Hebron to his brother, took up his abode in Seir, and became chief of the country of Idumæa, called Edom from the name he himſelf acquired on the following ſingular occaſion

Returning on a certain time during his juvenile days, from hunting, much oppreſſed with fatigue and hunger, and finding his brother preparing for himſelf ſome lentil-pottage, the colour of which being red, the more created his appetite, he earneſtly requeſted that he might participate of his fare But Jacob availing himſelf of his brother's urgent neceſſity peremptorily refuſed him, unleſs he would reſign to him his birthright, to which Eſau being ſtimulated by hunger, was conſtrained to accede, and the covenant of aſſignment was confirmed by a ſolemn oath Hence his cotemporaries called him in deriſion Edom, from the red hue of the pottage, for, in the Hebrew language, Edom ſignifies *red* Hence alſo this country was denominated Edom, but the Greeks, for the ſake of rendering the ſound more agreeable to the ear, called it Idumæa

Eſau had five ſons, of whom he had three by his wife Alibama, Jaus, Jolam, and Chore, by Ada, Alipazes, of Aliphates; and Moſametha, or Baſemmatha, by Raguel Aliphates had five legitimate children, Theman, Omer, or Opher, Jotham, and Cenez, or Cenaz Amelech was illegitimate, being born of one of his concubines, whoſe name was Theſma These inhabited that track of Idumæa called Goboliteſ, and another part named, from Amelech, Amelechitis But Idumæa being a country of vaſt extent, retained its name in a general acceptation, though ſome particular provinces derived their appellations from their reſpective founders

CHAP II

To [illegible] [illegible] his brethren His [illegible] [illegible] of [illegible] [illegible], [illegible] [illegible] his [illegible] [illegible] againſt his life

JACOB having been peculiarly favoured by the Divine protection and bleſſing, and ſurpaſſing all the inhabitants of the country, not only in the number and virtue of his children, but alſo in opulence and dignity, became at once an object of reverential awe and rankling envy His progeny were endued with extraordinary mental and corporeal abilities, and equally adept in ſuch exercises as required their reſpective exertions Indeed the Almighty ſeemed ſo peculiarly to ſuperintend his concerns in general, that events to human wiſdom, apparently adverſe, were, by an overruling Providence, rendered ſubſervient to his benefit, and that of his poſterity, as is evident from our anceſtors quitting the land of Egypt on the following occaſion

Joſeph, the ſon of Rachael, from his mental and perſonal accompliſhments, became the peculiar favourite of his father Jacob This partiality, together with the dreams he had related, preſaging his future ſucceſs, naturally created the envy and hatred of his brethren, for it is a foible (*not to call it a vice*) too incidental to mankind to behold the proſperity of others with an eye of jealouſy. The viſions which rouſed ſuch malevolent paſſions were theſe

Being ſent by his father with the reſt of his brethren to work at the harveſt, a viſion appeared to him of ſo extraordinary a nature from dreams in general, that being induced to conſult them on the occaſion, he related to them the particulars "Behold (ſaid he) I ſaw laſt night "in my ſleep the ſheaf of corn which I had bound, "ſtanding firm on the very ſpot where I had fixed it, and "thoſe of your binding moving towards it, in an inclin-"ing reverential poſture" His brethren clearly inferred, from thence, that his future undertakings ſhould be crowned with ſucceſs, and that he ſhould acquire power and ſuperiority over them, and though they concealed their opinions from Joſeph, inwardly conceived the moſt inveterate averſion for him, and concerted the means of [illegible] events [illegible] to their own pride and ambition

But it pleaſed God to [illegible] all their [illegible] ſchemes, by cauſing a ſecond and more extraordinary viſion to appear unto Joſeph He beheld in his dream the ſun moon, and eleven of the ſtars, deſcend on the earth, and do him reverence [illegible]

in the presence of his brethren (without suspicion of incurring ill-will) who entreated him to explain the meaning. The dream afforded Jacob satisfaction, as from revolving the circumstances in his mind, he perceived they presaged much good to his son. He thence inferred that Joseph should be exalted to opulence and power, and should receive obedience from his father, mother, and brethren. The sun and moon seemed to him to represent the father and mother, because the latter nourishes and increases all things, and from the former all things derive their form and force. The stars seemed to refer to his brethren, who were in number eleven, and derive their power from the sun and moon.

Jacob's interpretation seemed founded on probability, and therefore had a deeper effect on the minds of Joseph's brethren, for with respect to the blessings foretold, they considered him in the light of a stranger, not as a brother in whose success they would participate, and therefore formed a resolution of compassing his death.

Having concerted the means of accomplishing their horrid design, when the harvest was gathered in, they retired with their flocks into Shechem, a part of the country adapted to grazing, without giving their father any notice of their departure. Jacob receiving no intelligence respecting the state and condition of his flocks, and being also anxious for the welfare of his sons, sent Joseph to make the necessary inquiries, with orders to transmit him immediate information.

CHAP III

Joseph's brother Reuben concerts a scheme to save his life. He is sold to some Arabian merchants. Artifice by his brethren to deceive their father, who bewails him as dead.

THE approach of Joseph was an event agreeable to his enraged brethren, not from motives of affection arising from the tie of consanguinity, but because they imagined it would afford them an opportunity of satiating their envy and malice by his immediate death, on which they had mutually resolved. But Reuben, the eldest, recoiling at so base a design, endeavoured to dissuade them from it, by representing its heinous and atrocious nature, and the universal detestation they would incur thereby. He enforced his advice, by observing, that if in the eye of God the murder even of a stranger in cool blood was a crime of the deepest dye, how aggravated and detestable must it be to embrue their hands in the blood of a brother, whose premature death would plant daggers in the breast of a doating father, and be to him a source of perpetual affliction. He proceeded to conjure them to desist from their wicked intention, to consider the consequences that must result from the murder of a person so justly admired for his mental and personal accomplishments, to dread the detection of such a crime, and the revenge of Omnipotence, and to remember that if they could be so abandoned as to perpetrate so horrid a deed, they would ever bear about them the intolerable load of conscious guilt, which would render them accursed beyond expression. He pleaded the innocence of the youth as an object of compassion, rather than malevolence, observed, that envy being the motive, would be an aggravation of the offence, and contended lastly, that they would tempt the justice of God, and render themselves objects of his vengeance, by attempting the death of one so manifestly honoured with tokens of the Divine favour and protection.

By these and many other arguments did Reuben endeavour to divert his brethren from shedding the blood of the innocent youth, but finding that all his entreaties had no effect, nay, that they rather incensed them [illegible], he had recourse to other means, and proposed, that as his death was [illegible] determined, they should [illegible] manner, and thereby in some degree extenuate [illegible], alledging that rather than [illegible] their hands [illegible] blood, it would be more advisable to cast him into a pit, and there leave him to the chance of death. This proposal being generally approved, Reuben took Joseph, and binding him with a cord, let him gently down into a pit, and then went in quest of better pasturage for his cattle.

After the departure of Reuben, Judah, one of Jacob's sons, perceiving the approach of some Arabian merchants, who from Gilead carry spices and other Syrian merchandize into Egypt, proposed to his brethren to sell Joseph to these adventurers, by which means they would be exempt from the imputation of being accessary to his death, which would then in all probability happen in a remote country. Having obtained their consent, Joseph was drawn out of the pit, and sold to these merchants for twenty pieces of silver, being at that time 17 years old.

Reuben, unacquainted with this circumstance, and determined at all events to preserve the life of his brother Joseph, came by night to the pit, and called upon him by name, but from his not answering, conjecturing that his brethren had put him to death, he reproached them bitterly, till he was appeased by their confession of the truth.

After these transactions, the brethren consulted on the means of evading their father's suspicion, and concluded first to tear the coat of which they had stripped Joseph when they cast him into the pit, and then having stained it with goat's blood, to present it to their father as a token of his having been slain by wild beasts. This point adjusted, they returned to the old man (who by this time had heard some tidings of his son being lost, or sold captive) and presenting the coat rent and bloody, confirmed him in the belief of what they wished him to entertain, especially as they assured him they had neither seen their brother, nor knew what had befallen him, more than from the token of the coat they had found rent and bloody, from which they conjectured he had been slain by wild beasts. Jacob, hereupon, became inconsolable, covered himself with sackcloth according to the custom of the country, and notwithstanding all that could be offered to mitigate his grief, lamented the death of his son, as if confirmed by the most indubitable testimony.

CHAP IV

Joseph is sold by the merchants [illegible] Potiphar, one of king Pharaoh's household. [illegible] the affections of his master's [illegible]. Rejects her [illegible]. Joseph [illegible] to prison.

THE persecuted Joseph was afterwards sold by the merchants to Potiphar, an Egyptian officer, steward of king Pharaoh's household, who [illegible] high estimation, caused him to be instructed in the liberal arts, and at length promoted him to the superintendance of the concerns of his family. In this elevated station he maintained his integrity, and, by a conduct uniformly just and virtuous, demonstrated, that his piety was genuine, equally proof against the allurements of prosperity, or the attacks of adversity. In a short time the graces of his person, and the affability of his disposition, captivated the affection of his master's wife, who, from the attraction of her charms, and her exalted rank, [illegible] his ready compliance with her desires as his highest honour and happiness. But herein she had respect to his station only, and not to his virtue, which so [illegible] shone [illegible] throughout the whole of his conduct.

At length [illegible] and [illegible] a [illegible] Joseph [illegible] times alledging, [illegible] from [illegible] to [illegible] elevation, [illegible] in the [illegible] the complete [illegible] according [illegible]

A ſolemn day of feſtivity approaching on which, according to the Egyptian cuſtom, the women were accuſtomed to deck themſelves in all their ſplendor, ſhe excuſed herſelf from appearing on that occaſion on pretence of indiſpoſition, that ſhe might have a convenient opportunity for a private aſſignation with Joſeph. Succeeding thus far in her deſign, ſhe accoſted him in the moſt endearing terms, obſerving, that he would have acted becoming his duty, and conſiſtently with his intereſt, in complying with her firſt ſolicitation: but that omiſſion could be amply atoned by his then obedience. She added, that ſhe now did him peculiar honor, as well as afforded him the moſt ſtriking proof of her affectionate regard, in foregoing the grandeur and pleaſures of a public feſtivity, for the enjoyment of his company and intercourſe. She enforced her addreſs by exhorting him to immediate compliance, and aſſuring him that if, to her favour, he preferred his own ſcrupulous delicacy, he would become the object of her moſt rancorous hatred, impelled by which, ſhe would accuſe him to Potiphar of an attempt upon her virtue, who would readily admit the truth of her allegation, and not fail of bringing him to the ſevereſt puniſhment.

But neither her careſſes, her vows, her tears, nor her threatenings, could prevail on Joſeph to violate his maſter's honor, by receding from his virtuous reſolve. Nay, he even took upon him to admoniſh his miſtreſs to a due obſervance of the ſolemn rites of the marriage bed, which ought to be held ſacred and inviolate, and ſhould not be diſpenſed with on any pretence whatſoever. Inordinate gratifications, he added, were followed by repentance and ſhame; whereas conjugal fidelity brought with it the reward of a good conſcience, and the approbation of the virtuous; and inferred, from the whole, that it was more praiſe-worthy in her to exerciſe command over him as a ſervant, than debaſe herſelf, by alluring him to the commiſſion of a crime, which would ſo flagrantly redound to their mutual diſgrace.

By theſe, and other arguments equally powerful, did Joſeph ſtill endeavour to abate the violence of his miſtreſs's paſſion, and reclaim her from her criminal intention; but they produced a contrary effect, for his perſuaſions to chaſtity ſerved only to inflame her deſire, till at length ſhe endeavoured to effect that compliance by force, which ſhe could not obtain by the moſt flattering blandiſhments.

Loſt to all ſenſe of ſhame, ſhe ſeized and held him by his garment, till the youth was under a neceſſity of leaving a part behind him, in order to extricate himſelf, and flee from her enchanting embraces. Fired by a repulſe on the one hand, and impelled by fear of detection on the other, ſhe determined to ſhield herſelf under a malicious accuſation, as well as by that means to revenge herſelf on Joſeph, for the ſuppoſed indignity he had offered her. She therefore aſſumed the guiſe of grief and indignation, excited by an attempt on her honor and chaſtity, which Potiphar perceiving on his return, afforded her an opportunity, on his inquiring into the cauſe, of addreſſing him in terms to the following purport: "Thou deſerveſt no longer from "me a return of conjugal affection, if thou doſt not ri-"gorouſly puniſh that audacious ſlave, who has attempt-"ed to violate the honor of thy bed; who, unmindful of "every tie of duty and of gratitude, has endeavoured "to injure thee in the tendereſt point; and that too in "thine abſence, and on a day of feſtivity. Hence it is "manifeſt, that his apparent modeſty is founded on the "deepeſt diſſimulation, and that the favours you have "conferred upon him have emboldened him to arrogate "a claim even to the poſſeſſion of thy wife."

To enforce this addreſs and confirm her huſband in the belief of it, ſhe produced the tattered remnant of his garment, which, as ſhe declared, he left behind him, after a ſtruggle to violate her chaſtity. Potiphar, affected by this declaration of his wife, accompanied with tears, and fired with reſentment againſt Joſeph, committed him, without inquiring into the merits of the cauſe, to priſon, amongſt the common malefactors; while he applauded the chaſtity of his wife, thus confirmed and approved, as he imagined, by the cleareſt evidence.

CHAP. V.

Joſeph conciliates eſteem in the priſon. Expounds the king's butler and baker's dreams. Explains Pharaoh's dream concerning the famine. Is releaſed from priſon, and promoted to the higheſt dignities.

SUPPORTED by conſcious innocence, Joſeph did not attempt to exculpate himſelf, but patiently ſubmitted himſelf to impriſonment, placing his ſole reliance on the interpoſition of Divine Providence. Nor was he fruſtrated in his dependence: for in a ſhort time the keeper of the priſon, attracted by the courteſy of his behaviour, not only freed him from fetters, but ſhewed him ſingular marks of indulgence, and thereby alleviated the puniſhment of being confined. The priſoners, as was common in their circumſtances, conferring together during their intervals of ſuſpenſion from labour, on the cauſes of their commitments, and other topics, Joſeph, by thoſe means, became familiar with one who had been king Pharaoh's butler, once high in favor, but now, from ſome particular diſguſt of that monarch, caſt into priſon. This perſon, obſerving, in the courſe of converſation, that Joſeph manifeſted uncommon penetration, related to him a dream, and requeſted an interpretation, lamenting as an aggravation of the misfortunes fallen upon him, from having incurred his ſovereign's diſpleaſure, his perplexity ariſing from dreams, which frequently diſturbed his repoſe. He informed Joſeph, that, in his ſleep, he ſaw three cluſters of grapes, perfectly ripe, hanging from as many vine branches; that having preſſed the juice of the fruit into a veſſel, which the king held for that purpoſe, his majeſty drank, and was abundantly ſatisfied.

The butler having thus related his dream, and repeated his deſire of an explanation, Joſeph bade him take courage, as within the ſpace of three days he ſhould be releaſed from priſon, and reſtored to the king's favor and ſervice. The juice of the vine (ſaid the interpreter) was given for the uſe and delight of mankind; the moderate and diſcreet uſe of it cements friendſhip, baniſhes anger, diſſipates care, and diſpoſes to complacency of mind. The king's receiving the wine favourably, which you had preſſed from the three cluſters, preſages good, and indicates your deliverance within the three days repreſented by thoſe diſtinct cluſters. When you find my prediction fulfilled in the obtaining your liberty, let not it (ſaid he) eraſe from your memory the bondage of your late fellow priſoners. It is not through guilt I thus ſuffer, but through an inflexible adherence to, and regard for, my maſter's honor, in preference to the gratification of my miſtreſs's deſires and my own emolument. Happy in this interpretation of his dream, the butler, with longing expectation, waited the event.

There happened to be at the ſame time in the priſon another of the king's ſervants, who had been the chief baker, till, like the butler, he had incurred his diſpleaſure, and became ſubject to the ſame puniſhment. Encouraged by Joſeph's late interpretation, this man requeſted of him the explanation of a dream he had the night paſt, which he thus related: "I imagined, in my ſleep (ſaid he,) I carried on my head three baſkets, two of which were filled with bread, and the other with the choiceſt viands, prepared for the king's table; but the birds of the air hovered round me as I paſſed in ſpite of all my endeavours, and devoured the contents of the whole." This ſaid, he expected a preſage favourable as the former: but Joſeph having attended to the particulars, and premiſed that he could have wiſhed to have been the harbinger of more welcome news, ingenuouſly aſſured him that he had only two days to live, ſo that on the third day he ſhould be hanged, and expoſed to the prey of thoſe birds he could not drive from the baſket of proviſion. Joſeph's predictions were fully verified; for the third day, from that time, being the anniverſary of Pharaoh's nativity, he ordered the baker to be hanged, and the butler to be reſtored to his former office.

Joſeph had now lain two years in priſon, unaſſiſted in any degree by the ungrateful butler, when the following ſingular interpoſition of Providence procured him his liberty.

King Pharaoh having in one night had two dreams, which he conceived imported him evil (though the interpretation that had been given of them at the same time had slipt his memory,) early in the morning summoned several of the Egyptian sages, and required of them an explanation. Their hesitation indicating doubt or inability, increased his anxiety, which the butler observing, and Joseph's expertness in such matters occurring to his mind, he immediately repaired to his master, and informed him of the singular manner in which his predictions, from the circumstances of his own dream, and that of the baker, had been respectively verified. He further represented to the king, that he had been formerly servant to Potiphar, treasurer of his household, and that, from his own account, he was an Hebrew, descended from honorable parents. Animated by this intelligence of the ability of Joseph, the king immediately sent for him into the royal presence, courteously took him by the hand, and thus addressed him: "I understand, by one of my attendants, that thou art remarkably expert in interpreting of dreams, of which thou hast given him a singular instance to reveal, therefore, unto me my dreams in the same manner that thou didst unto him, but do not exaggerate or extenuate any circumstance, from motives either of fear or flattery, but speak the truth plainly and impartially. In my sleep I fancied I was walking by the side of a river, (*a*) and that I saw seven large and fat oxen, which went from the river towards a pasture: after which I saw seven lean meagre oxen, which seemed to come from the pasture towards the river, and, meeting the fat cattle in the way, devoured them, without any apparent increase of their own bulk. Upon this I awoke, and, as I was reflecting on the nature and import of my dream, fell insensibly asleep again, and I saw a vision more extraordinary, and which affects me more than the former. I beheld as it were, seven ears of corn spring out of one stem, which were so weighty with the grain they bore, that their heads inclined to the earth. Afterwards there appeared seven other ears, scanty and bare of grain, which, to my astonishment, devoured the former."

Joseph then informed the king, that one interpretation would suffice for both dreams. "The fat and lean oxen, and the full and scanty ears of corn, portended, that seven years of plenty would be immediately succeeded by as many years of famine, so that the abundance of the first seven years would not be adequate to the demands of the ensuing dearth, represented by the lean cattle devouring the fat, and the scanty ears of grain swallowing the full." He added, "that the Almighty was pleased to afford such intimations, not to terrify his creatures, but in order that they might provide for extremities, and alleviate distresses through prudence and forecast," and requested the king to make a due application of his remarks, as the most effectual means of averting the calamities which would otherwise ensue from so long a series of famine." The king, charmed with the sagacity of Joseph in the exposition of his dreams, requested his advice with respect to the precaution necessary to be taken, in order to guard against the impending calamity. He immediately recommended the strictest parsimony, and the retrenchment of all superfluity, in order to furnish a reserve for future exigencies, also that a number of magazines should be amply stocked, out of which the people should be supplied with no more than was barely sufficient for present subsistence.

Pharaoh was so struck with admiration at the extraordinary wisdom of Joseph in these important concerns, that he made him superintendent of his stores, with full authority to proceed in such manner as might appear to him most conducive to promote the general good, observing that no man was so proper to put in execution a plan of public utility as the author. Being thus vested with authority, and all its splendid appendages, Joseph proceeded to the execution of his plan, making a tour in a chariot of state throughout Egypt, depositing the grain in the king's magazines, and distributing only what was necessary for a present supply, without assigning to any man the cause of his proceedings.

CHAP. VI.

Joseph forms an honorable alliance. The famine. His brethren arrive in Egypt. Are practised on by his brethren. Supplies them with grain, and dismisses them home for their brother Benjamin.

AT the time of this distinguished prosperity Joseph was about thirty years of age, when as a singular mark of his wisdom, the king called him by a name which, in the Egyptian language, signifies, *A Discoverer of Hidden Things.* He also at the instigation of his sovereign, formed an alliance equally honorable and advantageous, by marrying the daughter of Potiphar, (*b*) the priest of On (*c*) or Heliopolis, who brought him two children previous to the famine, Manasses, or *Oblivion*, alluding to his late miseries, and Ephraim, or *Restitution*, referring to his exalted situation at the time of his birth.

The years of plenty being expired according to Joseph's prediction, the famine began to rage, insomuch that the multitude, sorely oppressed, repaired in crowds to the stores and magazines of the king. Being referred to Joseph for redress, he supplied their wants with such discretion, and at the same time with such competency, that he acquired the venerable appellation of *Saviour of the People*. Indeed he had respect not only to natives, but foreigners, on the sublime principal of universal philanthropy, which naturally produces universal benevolence.

The famine not being confined to Egypt alone, but raging in Canaan, and, indeed throughout the greatest part of the continent, Jacob being informed that strangers were permitted to purchase grain in Egypt, deputed all his sons, Benjamin (who was born of Rachael, and brother on both sides to Joseph) excepted, with an especial commission to provide for his family. Upon their arrival in Egypt, the ten brethren applied, in the most submissive terms to Joseph, entreating permission to purchase grain, being informed that their reception at court depended on the deference shewn to the king's dignified favourite. Joseph recognized them at the first glance, though they had not the smallest recollection of him. He therefore determined to put them to a severe trial, in order to sound their dispositions and intentions. To effect this, he not only refused them his permission to purchase grain, but ordered them to be apprehended as spies, alledging, that they appeared to him to be of different births, though they pretended to be kindred, as it was highly improbable that an individual subject should have so numerous and comely a progeny, a blessing rarely accorded to kings. This insinuation was to draw from his brethren the precise situation of his family, and particularly of his brother Benjamin, as he was apprehensive that youth had been exposed to the same treatment from them with himself. They were much alarmed at this stern and distant reception, as

---

(*a*) The river here alluded to was the Nile, so much celebrated in ancient history. This river has its rise in Numidia, and after running many miles northward, through a country scorched with the violent heat of the sun, enters Upper Egypt with great force, and passes over a tract of broken rocks. From hence it continues its course full north [illegible] receiving the addition of many other rivers, falls over another cataract, and then continues its course to the Lower Egypt as far as Grand Cairo, after which [illegible] divides itself into three branches in the form of a triangle, and then empties itself into the Mediterranean Sea. Once every year it overflows the greater part of Lower Egypt, and from that proceeds either scarcity or plenty. If the water rises too high, scarcity ensues, because it lies too long on the ground; and if too low, then there is not a sufficiency to fertilize the soil.

(*b*) This is a different person from him who was captain of the guard, and was in a different quality, and therefore, as the learned Vossius justly observes, there is no reason from the similarity of names to think that Joseph married the daughter of him who [illegible] certainly have abhorred an alliance with one that was [illegible] mistress.

(*c*) On was a famous city in Egypt, situated between the Nile and the Arabian Gulph, about twenty miles from Memphis, the metropolis of the kingdom. He was celebrated [illegible] of the [illegible] afterward called [illegible]. The word [illegible] one who gave [illegible] Priests were [illegible] of the kingdom [illegible]

well as apprehensive that the design of their journey would be defeated, till at length Reuben, the eldest, undertook to plead the common cause, in terms to the following effect: "We come not hither (said he) as spies to annoy his majesty's subjects, but as constrained by dire necessity, to purchase corn for the subsistence of our family, at the hands of those who have signalized their humanity, not only in supplying natives, but opening a trade to strangers in general. That we are brothers, it is presumed, must appear from the similitude of our features. Our father Jacob, is an Hebrew by birth, and we were in all twelve sons, born to him by four women. While they all lived, prosperity attended our family, but when our brother Joseph was taken from us, our calamities accumulated. Our father still laments his loss, and his sorrows render us inconsolable, as we were when mischance first deprived us of our dearest brother. During our absence on this commission, the care of our aged parent devolves on our youngest brother Benjamin. If you are still dubious of our sincerity, you have only to dispatch a messenger to our father's house."

Joseph, being thus assured of the welfare both of his father and his brother Benjamin, committed them to close custody, for further examination. Summoning them before him at the expiration of three days, he thus addressed them: "Since ye affirm that ye came not hither as spies, or to annoy his majesty's subjects, and aver that ye are brethren, and the sons of Jacob, to convince me of the truth of your affertions let one remain here as a pledge of the integrity of all. The rest shall be supplied with corn, and permitted to go to Canaan, but under this positive injunction, that they bring back with them their youngest brother, Benjamin, as the surest test of their probity. You may be assured that the hostage who remains shall experience the kindest treatment."

Alarmed at this proposition, and dreading the extreme calamity approaching, as another instance of the Divine vengeance for their cruelty to their brother Joseph, they melted into tears; but Reuben reprehended their unseasonable repentance, and recommended to them a patient submission to the Divine will. This conversation passed in the Hebrew tongue, which they supposed none of the by-standers understood; but Joseph was so affected by the scene, that he thought it expedient to retire, lest he should be discovered by his sensibility. On his return, however, he selected Simeon (*a*) as his hostage, then gave them permission to purchase what grain they required, and having previously commanded his servants to put every man's money into the mouth of his sack, issued orders for their departure.

CHAP. VII.

The brethren arrive at Canaan. Relate the event of their journey to their father. Jacob delivers up Benjamin at the representation of Judah. Scheme of Joseph to prove the attachment of his brethren to Benjamin. Judah's oration offers, and is applauded by Joseph, who makes himself known to his brethren, and dispatches them for his father and family.

THE brethren proceeded to Canaan, and, on their arrival, related to their father the singular events which had befallen them in Egypt, particularly that they had been taken for spies, and impostors in their pretence to affinity of blood, insomuch, that, at the special requisition of the governor, Simeon was left behind as an hostage, till their return with their brother Benjamin, should confirm the truth of what they averred. They therefore entreated Jacob to consent to their younger brother's departure with them, as a matter of indispensible necessity. The old man was much dissatisfied with the conduct of his sons, and greatly affected by the loss of Simeon, but became inconsolable at the thought of resigning Benjamin, whom he prized dearer than life; nor could Reuben, with all his solicitations, enforced by offering his own children as pledges for the security of Benjamin, obtain his consent. In this state of confusion their anxiety was increased on discovering the money they had paid for the grain inclosed in their sacks. When their provision began to fail, and famine to stare them in the face, Jacob was induced to deliberate on the injunction his sons had received of bringing with them their brother Benjamin, without whom they dared not, on their peril, to return to Egypt; but still inclining to hesitate at parting with his best beloved, Judah, of a temper more vehement and resolute than the rest, thus addressed his father on the pressing occasion: "You are too anxiously, as well as partially, solicitous for the safety of Benjamin, whom nothing can befal, either at home or abroad, without the interference of Divine Providence. Do you not hazard the loss of your own and our lives through famine, and also leave our brother Simeon in a most perilous situation, in thus hesitating to comply with what is so indispensibly necessary for the preservation of us all? Resign, therefore, your son to the care and protection of the Almighty, and rest assured that I will either restore him to you in safety, or perish myself in the attempt."

Jacob, being at length wrought into compliance, delivered up Benjamin to his brethren, together with a double portion of money for the purchase of the grain, and the choicest produce of Canaan, such as balm, myrrh, turpentine, and honey, as presents for the governor. The separation was mutually affecting, the father being anxious for the welfare of his sons, and the sons apprehensive that their departure and absence might put a period to their father's existence before their return.

Upon their arrival in Egypt they repaired to Joseph, and lest they should be accused of having fraudulently conveyed away with them the purchase money for the former portion of grain, represented to the steward, that, without their privacy, the money had been put into their sacks, which, as bound in duty, they now brought back with them on their return. The steward disclaimed any knowledge of the matter, so that they were not only freed from anxious apprehension, but greatly encouraged in their expectations, by Simeon's being set at full liberty, and thereby having the opportunity of constant intercourse with them. As soon as Joseph returned from attending on the king, they presented their respective gifts, and he was made happy in hearing, on inquiry of the welfare of his father; but when he beheld Benjamin, and the brethren replied in the affirmative on his asking, Is this your youngest brother? he could not refrain from exclaiming, "The Providence of God directeth all things," which having pronounced, such was his agitation of mind, that he withdrew, lest his tears should betray him to his brethren. In the evening he invited them to a banquet, and causing them to be placed in the same order as they were wont to be at their father's table, treated them courteously, but discovered a particular attachment to Benjamin, in allotting him a double portion of whatever was served up. (*b*)

During the time of repose, after the banquet, he ordered every man's sack to be filled, and the money to be deposited as before; but the steward was directed to convey into Benjamin's sack the goblet, out of which the governor himself usually drank. This was done in order to put to the test the affection of his brethren for Benjamin, in standing by him in case of an accusation of theft, or to

(*a*) It is particularly assigned as a reason why Simeon was selected from the rest of his brethren as Joseph's prisoner, that he was one of the most inveterate of all his brethren against him.

(*b*) It was the custom among the ancients for all the provision to be placed on one table, and the master of the feast to distribute to every one his portion. Joseph certainly did this, not only to shew his particular regard to Benjamin, but also to observe whether they would look upon their younger brother with the same envious eye, as they had formerly done upon himself. The custom of allotting the largest portion at the banquets of the ancients to any particular person, by way of preference, was practised in Homer's time, [illegible] from Agamemnon's speech to Idomeneus:

> For this in banquets, when the generous bowls
> Restore our blood, and raise the warriors souls,
> Tho' all the rest with stated rules are bound,
> Unmix'd, unmeasur'd are thy goblets crown'd.

[illegible] hypocritical colour of [illegible] deserting, and leaving him to be punished as a malefactor, and returning to their father unconcerned at the event.

The necessary preparations being made, according to Joseph's orders, they set out on their journey early in the morning, rejoicing in the view of restoring both Simeon and Benjamin to the arms of their aged, doating parent: but their joy was soon damped, by being suddenly overtaken and assaulted by a troop of horsemen, amongst whom was the party who conveyed the goblet into Benjamin's sack. Reproaching the soldiers with violating the laws of hospitality, by so sudden a reverse of behaviour, they were loaded by them with the severest invectives for returning evil for good, and trespassing on the humanity of the governor, in the commission of a theft, which, however they might have concealed, from the observation of the officer who attended at table, they could not hide from God's all-seeing eye: and demanded how they could be so stupidly insensible, as to indulge a hope of escaping the punishment due to so flagrant a crime?

In this manner were they reviled and tormented by the Egyptians, whilst, armed with conscious innocence, they expressed the greatest surprise that even a suspicion should be entertained of their integrity, after having offered to restore the money formerly deposited in their sacks, without, at least, the concealed privacy of any person whatever, and this they repeatedly alledged to invalidate the accusation.

To give, however, their assailants ample satisfaction, they desired them to search their sacks, subjecting themselves individually to condign punishment, if any one of them was proved guilty of the theft with which they were charged. The proposal was agreed to, with this exception, that punishment should only be inflicted on the guilty. They then proceeded to the search, and making the scrutiny according to seniority, they at last came to Benjamin's sack, where, according to their previous knowledge, the goblet of course was found. The rest being exculpated, and assured of the integrity of Benjamin were upbraiding their pursuers for detaining them so long from their journey, at the very instant the goblet was found in his sack, a circumstance equally surprising and afflictive, from the consideration of their brother's being exposed to immediate death, and their consequent inability of producing him, according to solemn promise, to their father, on their return. To aggravate their grief, this calamity befel them when they least suspected it, nor could they but consider themselves, from their pressing importunity with their father to consent to Benjamin's departure, as the authors of these remediless evils.

The Egyptians having secured Benjamin, conducted him accompanied by his sorrowful brothers, unto Joseph, who, to carry on the design, thus sternly upbraided them: "Basest of men, (said he) is it thus you acknowledge the "bounty of Providence, or requite my hospitality, in so "glaring an instance of injustice and ingratitude?" They all mournfully replied, they were really ready to suffer in the place of Benjamin, reproaching themselves, at the same time, in their own language, with their treatment of Joseph, who was happy (if dead) in being exempt from the casualties incidental to human life, and inferring (if living) that the Almighty had inflicted this punishment on them for his sake. Reuben also awakend in their minds a most poignant sense of their cruel behaviour towards their virtuous and innocent brother.

Joseph then dismissed them all as exculpated, the convict Benjamin excepted, declaring, that as he could not conscientiously punish the innocent for the guilty, or release the guilty at the requisition of the innocent, he should therefore only detain Benjamin, and declared that the rest might depart in peace, [illegible] the [illegible] of safe conduct in their way. Equally alarmed and affected by these expressions, they [illegible] speechless. Judah, who had before signalized himself in the very occasion of prevailing with his father to send Benjamin with them, thus replied in the name of the rest.

"We acknowledge, my lord, that the crime of which "our youngest brother stands guilty, merits the severest punishment, and should absolutely despair of his life, were "it not for the proofs we have had of your clemency and "goodness. Suffer yourself, therefore, to be actuated in "this matter, not by the rigid maxims of distributive jus"tice, but by that god-like benevolence which so emi"nently adorns your character. Let not those persons who "throw themselves on your mercy, and as you have deli"vered us from the famine, the most horrid of deaths, by "a liberal supply of our wants, deign to extend your com"passion and spare the lives you vouchsafed to preserve. "By these means (as preserving and sparing life are equally "objects of mercy) your goodness will be enhanced: and "to you we shall stand indebted, not only for the means "of subsistence, but for existence itself. It seems that the "Wise Disposer of events has now afforded you a singular "opportunity for the display of that most amiable of vir"tues the pardon of an injury: let it be known then, that "you are as humane as liberal, as merciful as charitable. "It is praise-worthy to relieve the distresses of the indigent, "but exalted characters display a clemency almost divine, "when they remit punishment to offences committed a"gainst themselves. I am induced to be thus importunate, "from a consciousness of our father's inconsolable grief "for the fate of our brother Benjamin, as well as a desire of "your adding to the honors you have already acquired. "Our own lives we consider of little moment, and would "willingly resign them, were it not for the anxiety our "deaths would surely give an aged parent. For his sake, "not our own: for the sake of a father eminent for his "piety and virtue, and to avert the miseries our punishment "must inevitably entail on him, we are now your humble "supplicants. The tidings of our fate, with the infamy of "the cause, would put a period to his existence. Let lenity, "then, for our venerable parent plead in our favour. It is "yours either to take or spare our lives. Pronounce the par"don, and live long to reap the reward of conscious good"ness, of imitating the brightest of all the Divine perfec"tions: so shall the Almighty and Universal Father crown "you with numberless blessings, for compassionating the "case of the aged Jacob. In pardoning our brother, you "give life to us all, inasmuch as our lives depend upon his. "We cannot return to our father but with Benjamin. If "you remain inexorable, we only request to be included "in the punishment, as if we had been accomplices in the "guilt: a more eligible death than in consequence of the "loss of our brother, laying violent hands on ourselves. I "there might plead his youth and want of experience, but "these considerations your candor will suggest: so that I "will close the address I have the honor to prefer, with "shewing, that, whether we are condemned through the "inability of the advocate, or absolved through the spon"taneous clemency of the judge, the merit will be wholly "yours. If, after all, my lord, you adjudge him to death, "admit me as his substitute, and vicarious victim; but if "you are pleased to sentence him to slavery, I offer myself "in his place to bear the severest hardships. (a)"

Judah and his brethren now fell prostrate at the feet of Joseph, (b) whose feelings were so strongly impressed, that having dismissed his attendants, he thus disclosed himself: "I cannot but applaud the affection you have shewn for "your brother Benjamin, especially, as upon former occa"sions, you have been so much wanting in fraternal regard "for me. In this instance I have proved your disposition to "the test, and, from your present behaviour, am disposed "to impute the evils which, through your procurement, be"fel me to the will of God, for wise and gracious pur"poses. The information I receive of my father's wel"fare, together with the [illegible] proof of your [illegible] "dent affection for my youngest brother, hold me "the supremest pleasure, so that I [illegible] from [illegible]

(a) In all this speech of Judah we may observe that Joseph [illegible] [illegible] that this was the punishment of [illegible] in the [illegible] of Joseph, though [illegible] was [illegible] by the [illegible] of Moses.

(b) Here we see Joseph's dream [illegible] [illegible] the very [illegible] [illegible] shewn to him by his [illegible]

"memorance of former transactions, esteeming you the "agents of Providence, in raising me to my present exalted "situation, and convinced that it thus pleased God to bring "good out of evil Return home with these joyful tidings "to your father, and share with him the common blessing "a bountiful Providence has imparted lest he die with grief, "and I am deprived of the happiness of an interview Now "depart, and bring back as speedily as possible, your father, with all your respective families into Egypt, that "you may participate with me the blessings of plenty, "during the five years of the famine yet unexpired"

Stung with remorse at their former treatment of so affectionate a brother, tears suppressed their verbal acknowledgment of his extraordinary goodness Joseph, however, cordially embraced, and prepared for them a magnificent entertainment, after which they were honored with tokens of the royal munificence, as presents for themselves, their father and families, and then dismissed by Joseph, with many presents of fraternal regard, which was shewn to his youngest brother Benjamin, in a most distinguished manner

CHAP VIII

Divine appearance to Jacob upon an extraordinary occasion. He prosecutes his journey into Egypt with his family Their names Affecting interview between Joseph and his father, who is well received by Pharaoh The famine produces dreadful calamities, which at length ceases Joseph's policy increases the national revenue Death of Jacob, and afterwards of Joseph.

WHEN Jacob learnt from his sons, on their return, that Joseph was not only alive, but had attained to a degree of pre-eminence in Egypt next to the king himself, he returned unfeigned thanks to the Supreme Governor of the Universe for his infinite mercies towards him, after he had been tossed a long time to and fro on the billows of adversity and then made necessary preparations for paying him a visit

When he came near the Well of the Covenant he offered an oblation to God, but apprehensive that the fertility of the soil of Egypt might induce his posterity to fix their residence on that spot, by which means they would of course lose possession of the promised land of Canaan, he began to entertain doubts whether his proposed journey had the Divine sanction, and also whether his life should be prolonged to see his darling son Joseph, till it pleased the Almighty to give him an extraordinary manifestation of his Divine will

One night on the journey he fell into a profound sleep, and being twice distinctly called on by name, and asking who it was that called him, he received from the Divine voice the following intimation "Dost thou not know, O "Jacob, that I am the God who protected thee and thy ancestors, who appeared for thee in all thy exigencies? who, "contrary to thy father's intention, secured to thee thine "inheritance? who brought about thy marriage in Mesopotamia, and effected thy return into thine own country, "crowned with opulence and a numerous progeny? "When Joseph to all appearance, was lost, did I not raise "him in Egypt to a dignity exalted next to that of a "king? The design of my present appearance is, to direct "thee in thy journey, and to foretel that thou shalt depart this life in the arms of thy son Joseph, and that "your descendants shall become a mighty nation, and "possess the land which I have promised them."

Animated by this vision, he prosecuted his journey into Egypt with greater alacrity, having with him his sons with their families, amounting to threescore and ten persons Their names, on account of their harshness, I should have omitted, were it not necessary to mention them, in order to convince those to the contrary, who imagine that we are not Mesopotamians, but Egyptians

The sons of Jacob were twelve, of whom Joseph went long before the rest into Egypt The others are these, with their sons Reuben, who had four sons, Hanoch, Phallu, Assaron, and Charmi Simeon, who had six, Jamuel, Jamin, Ohad, Jachin, Zoar, and Shaul Levi, who had three, Garson, Chaath, and Merari Judah, who had also three, Salah, Pharez, and Zarah, and two grandsons by Pharez, Esron and Amyr Issachar, who had three, Thulas, Phuas, and Samaron Zebulon, who had three, Saran, Elon, and Jalel These were the children that Jacob had by Leah, who carried with her Dinah, her daughter, the number of whom, with their offspring and attendants, amounted to thirty-three persons Jacob had, by Rachael, two sons, Joseph and Benjamin From the former descended Manasses and Ephraim, from the latter Bolau, Baccharis, Asabel, Gera, Naaman, Ies, Ros, Momphis, Opphis, and Arad, who, added to the other thirty-three, amount to the number of forty-seven

These were the legitimate issue of Jacob By Bilhah, his concubine, he had two sons, Dan and Naphthali. The former had only one son, Usis, but the latter had four, Jesel, Guni, Issares, and Sellim, which, added to the above number, make fifty-four. By Zilpah, his other concubine, Jacob had two sons, Gad and Asar The former had seven sons, Sophonias, Augis, Sunis, Azabon Aerin, Eroed, and Ariel The latter had one daughter, Sarah, and six sons, Jomnes, Isus, Isuis, Baris, Abar, and Melchiel, which sixteen, added to the former, amount to seventy persons, without including Jacob himself

As they drew near their journey's end, Judah was dispatched to announce his father's approach unto Joseph, who immediately set out to meet him The interview happened at a place called Heros, or Heliopolis, and was of so affecting a nature, that both father and son almost sunk under mutual transport

Joseph desired his aged parent to proceed by slow and easy journies, while he himself, taking five of his brethren, hastened to the king to pay their devoirs, before the arrival of the rest of the family in his dominions

Pharaoh, pleased with the news, inquired of Joseph into the nature of their occupations, in order that he might assign them proper employment He replied, that they had, in general, been trained to rural pursuits, and that the pastoral life was what they mostly affected The design of this answer was, that, by living contiguously, they might be the better able to concur in their assiduities to their aged father, and also to suppress any envious emotions in the minds of the natives, that might arise from the family interfering with their professions, as the Egyptians had little or no knowledge of pasturage

When Jacob was introduced to the king, and had paid his obedience with the usual formalities, Pharaoh courteously raised him, and inquired his age Being answered one hundred and thirty, and expressing much surprise, Jacob gave him to understand, that the lives of his ancestors had been extended to a much greater length The king then gave permission to him and his family to reside at Heliopolis.

As the earth received no moisture, either from the kindly rain of heaven, or the usual overflowing of the Nile, the famine raged, of course, with more severity, and horrid were the calamities thereby entailed The situation of the poorer and common sort was piteous beyond description for, having laid in but a very scanty store, and not being able to obtain a supply without ready money, when that was exhausted, they were reduced to the necessity of exchanging their cattle, slaves, lands, nay their last little all, to procure grain from the king's granaries, to protract a needy, miserable life When, by these means they became totally destitute, they were abandoned to a desolate world, that the king might secure their bartered possessions, but the priests (a) were exempted from this rigorous treatment, and per-

(a) The Egyptian priests were the whole body of the nobility of the land They were the king's counsellors and (according to Diodorus Siculus) in some things his joint agents They were the most learned body of the nation particularly in astronomy They also acted as magistrates, and filled the chief offices of state, for the original word equally signifies prince and priest Hence we see the reason why Joseph did not purchase their lands, namely, from the greatness of their authority, which rendered their persons and consequently their estates, too sacred to be taxed or alienated to the crown The king, during the famine, distributed to them provisions sufficient for their subsistence so that they were not under the necessity of selling their lands

THE EGYPTIANS MURDERING

...ing the Male Children of the Hebrews

mitted to continue in the possession of their landed property. Such, however, was the general calamity of the nation, that the minds and bodies of the people were affected to the greatest degree, and equally embarrassed to devise means of subsistence.

But when, at length, the river overflowed, watered the earth, revived drooping nature, and produced a fertile aspect, Joseph made the tour of the kingdom, and summoning the respective landholders, restored to them such parts as they had sold to the king, on condition of their paying a fifth, as tribute to him, by virtue of his prerogative; and then enjoined them to the same diligence in their improvements, as if they were to derive the emoluments resulting from the whole.

Transported at the returning prospect of plenty, and the restitution of their landed property, the people applied themselves to agriculture with unremitting assiduity; so that, by this well-timed act of policy, Joseph established his own authority in Egypt, and increased the standing revenues of all its succeeding monarchs.

The good old Jacob, having resided with his family in Egypt seventeen years, at length expired in the presence of his sons, in the 147th year of his age. After commending them to the Divine blessing and protection, and prophesying that the posterity of each of them should hereafter possess a part of the land of Canaan, as well as bestowing the highest encomiums on Joseph, for his singular piety towards God, and paternal and fraternal affection towards [illegible] and his brethren, he enjoined them to receive Joseph's sons Ephraim and Manasses into their number, and admit them to a participation of the land of Canaan, when it should be divided according to the Divine prediction. His last request was that he might be interred in Hebron.

Jacob, in piety and virtue followed the example of his worthy progenitors, and was as eminently favoured by especial tokens of the Divine regard and protection. By the king's permission, Joseph caused his body to be conveyed to Hebron, and there interred him, with due honours in the sepulchral tomb of his ancestors. When the funeral rites were performed, his brethren expressed much reluctance at returning to Egypt, still apprehensive, from conscious guilt, of Joseph's resentment, especially as they had lost their advocate in the death of their father; but he quieted their suspicions, brought them back, endowed them with large possessions, and continued to show them every instance of brotherly kindness.

This eminent character paid the debt of nature when he had attained to the age of 110 years. Joseph possessed very singular and shining talents, equally adapted to acquire and maintain the highest preferments. The rest of the brethren lived with honour, and died in peace in Egypt, and were, at the respective periods of their demise, conveyed, by their surviving relatives, to Hebron, in order to be interred in the tomb of their ancestors. The bones of Joseph were afterwards conveyed by the Hebrews, on their departure out of Egypt, into Canaan, according to his own express injunction (*a*). But of this and other transactions relative to the Jewish nation, we shall treat in due order.

CHAP. IX.

The Hebrews incur the envy of the Egyptians. Are subjected to slavery for 400 years. Prophecy respecting Moses. Pharaoh's edict for the destruction of the male children of the Hebrews. Birth of Moses. His miraculous preservation. Adopted by Pharaoh's daughter.

THE Egyptians being addicted to luxury and effeminate pursuits, and of course averse to laborious exercises, it was natural for them to conceive an ill will and hatred towards the Hebrews, who, by diligence and industry, crowned with the Divine blessing, had rendered themselves a numerous and formidable people.

The advantages resulting from the politic [illegible] of Joseph [illegible] being [illegible] forgotten, and the [illegible] transferred to another line, it became the study and delight of the Egyptians to devise means for oppressing the Hebrews; such as cutting trenches for conveying off the river Nile in small streams, encompassing the city with walls, raising fortifications and banks, to prevent any damage that might arise from inundations. The [illegible] pyramids, monuments of Egyptian toil, and vanity, which remain to this day, were raised by the art and labour of our nation, which was subjected to Egyptian vassalage for the space of 400 years.

In process of time, an event occurred which exasperated them more against the Hebrews. For one of their scribes, or magi (to whose judgment and opinion the people in general paid a most implicit deference) informing the king, that, about that period, an Hebrew male child would be born, who should humble the power of the Egyptians, and exalt that of the Israelites to so great a degree, as to acquire immortal honour, Pharaoh, alarmed at such intimation, instantly issued his royal edict, commanding that all male children, henceforward born to the Israelites, should be immediately cast into the river and drowned. He likewise commanded the Egyptian (*b*) midwives, minutely to attend to the state of the pregnancy of the Hebrew women, and annexed the penalty of death to the whole family of such as should dare to attempt an evasion of the purpose of the edict, by concealing the birth of any child.

The calamity of the Hebrews on this occasion, was beyond description, not only as it subjected them to the loss of their children, and, in some degree rendered them accessary to their deaths, but as it must eventually have tended to the extirpation of their race. Human efforts, however, opposed to the Divine will, must at length prove abortive. The Hebrew child, alluded to by the scribe, was born, and brought up, notwithstanding the terror of the edict, and the scrupulous investigation of the king's spies, and lived to fulfil what was predicted concerning him, to the utmost extent.

Amram an Hebrew of noble birth, anxious, at the last stage of his wife's pregnancy, both from motives of natural affection and the loss the nation must sustain through want of male progeny, had recourse, by prayer, to the Father of Mercies, the all-wise God, that he would vouchsafe his protection to his long favoured people, and avert the impending ruin that threatened their nation.

The Almighty appeared to Amram in a dream, exhorting him to be of good courage, not despair as to future events, for the piety of his ancestors being ever before him, he would, in due time, accomplish the deliverance of their descendants, as he had formerly interposed in their favour. He was pleased to remind him, that he had brought up Abraham alone out of Mesopotamia into Canaan, and there placed him in a blessed situation, that he had favoured him with a son by his wife, who had long been barren; that he had rendered his children rich and powerful, bestowing Arabia on Ishmael, on the sons of Chetura the country of the Troglodytes, and upon Isaac, the land of Canaan; and that the name of Jacob had not only been rendered renowned amongst foreign nations, for his personal achievements, and the immense possessions of his descendants, but that, from the inconsiderable number of [illegible] persons in family, who accompanied their father into Egypt, they were now increased to upwards of 60,000. He then assured him, of his care and protection both as to the nation in general, and himself in particular; that the male child whose birth the Egyptians sought, should be born, elude their menaces, effect the deliverance of the Hebrews from their bondage, and obtain the [illegible] immortal fame, not only [illegible] amongst his own people, but throughout the world [illegible] and that this victorious [illegible] should [illegible] till the [illegible] with [illegible] perpetual in his family.

(*a*) [illegible] were [illegible] none of [illegible] till the [illegible]
(*b*) Josephus [illegible] that the [illegible] were Egyptian [illegible]

[illegible]

Amram revealed these particulars to his wife Jochabel, which, on the first reflection, rather increased their suspicions, not only with respect to the fate of the child in its infancy, but in advanced life. The manner of her delivery, however, soon confirmed the Divine intimation, for a gentle labour, unattended with the usual pains and exclamations, afforded an opportunity for eluding the vigilance of the spies, so that the infant was cherished at home three months without detection, till Amram, fearing the result of a discovery, determined to commit him to the care and protection of Divine Providence, rather than expose his life, and, indeed, the lives of the whole family, to continual danger.

Forming this resolution, they made a cradle (*a*) of wicker, and, after tempering it with pitch to keep out the water, placed the child therein, launched it into the stream, and committed him to the mercy of an over-ruling Providence. As it floated down the stream, Mariam, the child's sister, by command of the mother, walked on the opposite bank to watch the fate of its innocent, but precious inhabitant, when an event took place, that, amongst others, singularly manifested the superiority of Divine wisdom and power, and that the will of God must be accomplished in spite of all opposition.

It happened that Thermuthis, (*b*) the king's daughter, walking by the river side, observed the cradle floating with the stream, and ordered some of her attendants to bring it on shore. When it approached the bank, and the princess discovered the features of its beauteous inhabitant, she broke into a rhapsody of delight and complacency, for such were the personal attractions of this favourite of heaven, that even those, who at his birth, appeared determined on his destruction, were, on beholding the serenity of his countenance, disposed to shew him favour and protection.

A woman, at the command of the princess, being brought to suckle the child, he rejected her breast, as he had those of several other Egyptian women, on which Mariam, who had now mixed with her retinue, representing the cause of disgust as arising from their being of another nation, and recommending an Hebrew nurse, the princess committed that branch of his nurture to her care, declaring an acquiescence in her choice. She therefore introduced the mother, unknown to any of the attendants, who, with the permission of the princess, both suckled him, and took care of his education.

To perpetuate the memory of the accident which befel this extraordinary person at his birth, he was called Moses, or Mouses, which in the Egyptian language signifies *Water*, and *Preserved*. Indeed he became, according to the Divine prediction, the most shining character that ever adorned the Hebrew nation. According to lineal descent he was the seventh from Abraham, being the son of Amram, who sprang from Caath, whose father was Levi, the son of Jacob, who was born unto Isaac, the son of Abraham. In his childhood, he gave proofs of knowledge far superior to his years, and so eminent were his mental abilities and personal attractions, that he became an object of admiration to all who beheld him. Thermuthis, therefore, having no issue, adopted him as her heir, and presented him to the king her father, with this address: "I have trained up an infant, "as singular for his genius as the symmetry of his person, "and having miraculously received him from the river, to "which he was committed, am determined to adopt him "as my son, and establish him as thy successor on the throne "of Egypt." Having thus said, she conveyed him to the arms of her father, who, after many fond embraces, to conciliate the mind of his daughter, put the crown on the child's head, but Moses, with a look of contempt, snatched it from his head, cast it on the ground and spurned it with his feet, an act supposed ominous to the state. The scribe, who from his nativity, had predicted the decline of the Egyptian empire, recommended, from this event, his immediate destruction, observing, in most pointed terms, to the king, "that the presage concerning this child was amply confirmed by the insult offered his dignity in spurning the crown, and that nothing but his death could deliver the Egyptians from the direst apprehensions, as well as disappoint the Hebrews in their towering expectations of his mighty atchievements." But Thermuthis, to secure the life of her favourite, caused him to be conveyed off, nor did the king seem disposed to follow the advice of the scribe. Moses was therefore educated under the immediate care of the princess, and grew up the hope and glory of the Hebrews (*c*). Indeed the Egyptians themselves began to abate in their prejudices, and concluding, on mature reflection, that there was no apparent heir better qualified to promote the interest of the state, than the successor appointed by the king, desisted from their design on his life.

CHAP. X.

The Ethiopians make inroads on the Egyptians. Moses undertakes the conduct of the war. Obtains a victory over the Ethiopians. Invests Saba, their metropolis. Marries Tharbis the king's daughter, on condition of its being surrendered to the Egyptians.

AN opportunity soon offered for putting the wisdom as well as prowess of this extraordinary Hebrew to the severest test. The Ethiopians, who inhabited the lands that lie contiguous to Egypt, having made inroads into their country, committed depredations on the Egyptians, who, to retaliate the injuries they had sustained, levied an army, and marched against them, but victory declaring in favor of the plunderers, the Egyptians were under a necessity of making an ignominious retreat. Elated with success, the Ethiopians pursued their fortune, and determining to avail themselves of the advantages they had already obtained, entered the country, laid all waste before them, and meeting with no effectual opposition extended their victorious arms towards Memphis and the sea, still encouraged in their ravages by the pusillanimity of the inhabitants, who tamely submitted to the most flagrant injuries.

In this perilous situation the Egyptians had recourse to the oracle, in order to obtain intimations of the means to extricate themselves from their present calamities. Being given to understand, "that they should make choice of an Hebrew to conduct the war," the king immediately dispatched his mandate to his daughter to deliver up Moses, in order that he might vest in him the command of the Egyptian army (*d*). Having exacted an oath from her father to secure the identity of his person, the princess delivered him up, esteeming it a fortunate event for Moses to be thus singled out for the defence of the country, as well as a just reproach on those scribes, in calling for the assistance of one, whom they adjudged to death, as a common enemy. Moses, at the instance of the king and princess, chearfully undertook the command, which gave much satisfaction to the priests of both nations: to those of the Egyptians, as they cherished a hope, that the conquest he might obtain over their enemies, would facilitate the means for dispatching him by guile; to those of the Hebrews, as if he proved able and expert in the manoeuvres of the field, he might deliver them from their tedious bondage.

(*a*) Though the cradle, or boat, is said to have been made with rushes, it is [illegible] probable that it was formed with flags of the [illegible], of which the [illegible] made their paper, and which grew [illegible] on the banks of the Nile. Clemens Alexandrinus expressly says that the vessel was made of papyrus, the produce of the country, and this [illegible] is confirmed by several other [illegible].

(*b*) [illegible] this princess was the king's only daughter, and that [illegible] having [illegible], she pretended to be with child, [illegible] whom she owned as her son. That he was esteemed [illegible] the apostle to the [illegible] [illegible] was thought the son of [illegible].

(*c*) [illegible] excellent [illegible] Aaron, his brother, [illegible] [illegible] which [illegible] to [illegible] different persons, but they may each be [illegible] and [illegible] by the Lord of Hosts. Thus Polydamus, in Homer, Iliad [illegible], tells Hector, God gives to different men different accomplishment.

To some the powers of bloody war belong,
To some sweet music, and the charm of song;
To few, and wondrous few, has Jove assign'd
A wise, extensive, all considering mind.

Pope.

(*d*) The history of Moses, as General of the Egyptians against the Ethiopians, is not to be found in the sacred records, but is cited by Irenaeus, who says, "That when Moses was nourished in the king's palace, he was appointed general of the army against the Ethiopians, and conquered them, when he married the [illegible] daughter [illegible], because, out of her affection for him, she delivered the city up to him."

Moses, therefore, before the enemy was apprised of the appointment, mustered his forces, and led them, not along the banks of the river, but through the main land, in which he displayed a striking instance of military skill. Foreseeing that an inland march would expose the troops to great danger, from the multitude of serpents with which the country was infested, and which are of the most destructive and malignant kind, he had recourse, by way of prevention, to an admirable device. Having ordered some baskets to be prepared in the shape of coffers, he filled them with certain birds, called Ibis, [Storks,] and ordered them to be carried as part of the baggage. These birds being mortal enemies to serpents, those reptiles ever seek to avoid them, but are sometimes overtaken in flight, when they infallibly become their prey. In other instances the birds are harmless and tractable, but as the Greeks are acquainted with their species and instinct, a further description is unnecessary.

On arrival, therefore, in that part of the country infested with these serpents, he caused the birds to be dispersed, thereby totally obviating the annoyance, and coming up with the Ethiopians, lulled in security, suddenly charged, routed them, and not only blasted their hopes of conquering Egypt, but retaliated amply on the foe the depredations and slaughter they had so lately experienced from them.

Elated also with success, under the conduct of Moses, the Egyptians pursued their conquests, especially as the enemy seemed driven to a state of despair, till at length, having followed them to Saba, their metropolis (so called by Cambyses Meroe, in honour of his sister) they laid close siege to them in the garrison, whither they had betaken themselves for shelter. This place was deemed impregnable, being almost encompassed with the river Nile, and the rapid current of the rivers Astaphus and Astabora, on the other side, greatly stopping up the passage to it. Besides, it was environed with a very stout wall, between which and the rivers ramparts were erected, so that it seemed formed by nature and art to repel the most vigorous attack.

As the enemy would not face him in the open field, and his army was incompetent to the reduction of their city, Moses remained in a state of embarrassment, till relieved by an extraordinary incident. Tharbis, the daughter of the king of Ethiopia, struck with admiration of the military atchievements and personal accomplishments of Moses, who, in so short a time, had reversed the fortunes of the Ethiopians and the Egyptians, became passionately enamoured of the young hero, and sent some of her suite to offer him her hand. Moses acceded to the proposal, on condition of the surrender of the city, solemnly promising to consummate the marriage as soon as the terms should be fulfilled, so that this point being settled, without delay, he fully accomplished the purport of his commission, celebrated his nuptials, and sent back the Egyptians to their own country.

CHAP. XI.

The Egyptians seek the life of Moses, who flies to Midian. He is protected by Jethro, and marries his daughter.

THE Egyptians, notwithstanding the very important services they had so lately derived from Moses in the total defeat of their Ethiopian enemies, could not suppress the envy and hatred they had imbibed; insomuch, that, fearful he would assume too great a power, to the prejudice of their state, and the aggrandizement of his own people, they prosecuted their design of compassing his death. To this end, they accused him of murder before the king, who, indulging no former suspicions, and prevailed on by a jealousy he entertained from his late acts of valour, as well as the instigation of all present, took this as a pretence to issue his mandate for causing him to be apprehended.

But Moses, apprised of their design, withdrew, and to elude the vigilance of the soldiers who were posted in the road to intercept him, directed his flight through the desert, where he encountered the greatest difficulties with invincible fortitude and magnanimity. Arriving near a city of the Midianites, which is situated upon the shore of the Red sea, and takes its name from one of the sons of Abraham by Cheturah, he sat down near a well, to refresh himself after the fatigues of his journey, it being then about noon, and the city within sight. An incident it afforded an opportunity of displaying his courage, and the improvement of his fortune.

A drought often prevailing in these climates, the shepherds are extremely anxious to reach the wells, in order to procure a sufficient supply of water for their own herds, lest they should be anticipated and deprived of it by others. To this well repaired seven virgin daughters of Raguel, otherwise Jethro, the priest, a man of respectable character. These daughters, according to the custom of the Troglodytes, having the care of their father's flocks, were busily employed in serving them, when they were rudely interrupted, and driven from the well, by some shepherds, that they might engross the water. Moses, incensed at the behaviour so unbecoming the male character, espoused the cause of the virgins, protected them from the insult of the shepherds, whom he drove from the spot, and thereby left the well free and unincumbered.

On their return, the virgins, returning a grateful sense of this signal interposition in their favour, related the circumstance to their father, and entreated him to shew some token of regard for the brave and resolute stranger, who had thus vindicated their right, when invaded by a number of dastardly males. The father commending his daughters' gratitude for their intrepid deliverer, sent for Moses, in order to confer on him a reward due to his merit. He attended, and was assured of the grateful sense his daughters entertained, both of his humanity and his courage. After passing many encomiums on his virtues, he added, that his good offices had not been shewn to such as were insensible of them, or incapable of rewarding them, and that he should soon meet with an adequate compensation. Soon after he adopted Moses as his son, gave him in marriage to his daughter Zipporah, and made him superintendant of his flocks, an honourable station in those days, when pasturage was the general source of wealth.

CHAP. XII.

Divine appearance to Moses in the bush. His rod turned into a serpent. Divine command to [illegible] from the Israelites [illegible] their belief of God's promise.

MOSES, having received these honourable tokens at the hands of Jethro, resided with him as superintendant of his flocks. Happening to lead the cattle to a mountain, called Sinai, which, though abounding with the choicest herbage, and most commodiously situated for pasturage, had never been grazed upon, from an opinion which prevailed, that it was the peculiar residence of the Deity, an extraordinary prodigy appeared to him upon this spot. A flame of fire seemed to seize the whole substance of a bush, without affecting the verdure of the plant, the variegated colour of the flowers, or the fruit pendant from the branches. To add to his surprize and amazement, he heard a voice issuing from the fire, call him distinctly by name, reprehend his audacity in daring to tread upon ground hitherto inviolate, and admonish him to depart, nor stay to indulge a criminal curiosity, lest, though he was a good and virtuous man, awful consequences might ensue. The same voice also assured him that through the Divine protection, he should attain to the highest honour and dignity amongst men, and commanded him to go boldly into Egypt, where he should be the guide and deliverer of the Hebrew nation from the usurpation and bondage of the Egyptians. For (continued the voice) they shall possess that fertile country once inhabited by your father Abraham, and, through your direction, enjoy the most important and invaluable blessings. It further commanded him, that, having released the Hebrews from Egyptian bondage, an oblation should be offered on this very spot.

Such were the intimations communicated to Moses out of the fire, after which he thus expressed his [illegible] [illegible]: "God, thy power, [illegible] "and my anceſtors, would, O Father of mercies, be cul-"pable in the higheſt degree, yet may I preſume to expreſs "my doubts of my ability through want of power of ſpeech "to perſuade my countrymen to leave the place they now "inhabit, and follow me whither I am to conduct them; "alſo, of the poſſibility of prevailing with Pharaoh to "permit them to depart, as, through their toil and in-"duſtry, the Egyptians daily increaſe in opulence."

The Almighty was then pleaſed to animate him with the promiſe of every neceſſary aid, whether of ſpeech or action, for the accompliſhment of the great and important purpoſes of his will; and, to confirm the ſame, ordered him to drop his ſtaff upon the ground, which having done, a ſerpent crept upon the place, and winding itſelf into a circular figure, erected his creſt, as if in defiance of thoſe who ſhould aſſail him, and then reſumed its former figure of a ſtaff. He was then commanded to put his hand into his boſom, which having obeyed, he drew it out white as chalk, and ſoon after it recovered its natural colour. He was next commanded to draw water out of an adjoining well, and pour it on the ground, when it appeared of the colour of blood. Whilſt he was loſt in amazement at theſe wonders, he was exhorted to aſſume reſolution, and aſſured that he ſhould meet with ſuch aid as ſhould enable him to overcome every difficulty. He was alſo enjoined to diſplay theſe ſigns in the face of men, to eſtabliſh them in a belief that he executed the Divine commands at the Divine will, and by the Divine power and authority. The voice commanded him to haſten with all poſſible ſpeed into Egypt, to the relief of the Hebrews thus grievouſly oppreſſed.

Moſes, encouraged by theſe extraordinary revelations of the Divine will and pleaſure, entreated the exertion of the ſame power in Egypt, if it ſhould be neceſſary. He alſo ſupplicated, that the Divine Being would deign to communicate to him the appellation by which he ſhould invoke him, when he offered the oblations according to command, and this favour was moſt graciouſly vouchſafed. By this eſpecial power veſted in Moſes, and the ſigns which appeared to him in the burning buſh, he was confirmed in the truth of God's promiſes of his protection and rendered fully confident that he ſhould deliver his countrymen from the calamities they ſuffered in Egypt.

CHAP. XIII.

Moſes departs from Midian to go into Egypt. Entertained by the Hebrews. Diſplays his miracles. Solicits the king to diſmiſs the Iſraelites. Shews wonders to Pharaoh, who oppreſſes the Hebrews the more, and remains inflexible in his reſolution of detaining them.

HAVING received authentic intelligence of the death of Pharaoh, from whoſe tyranny he had fled, Moſes requeſted of Jethro permiſſion to go into Egypt, to attempt the deliverance of his countrymen, and taking with him his wife Zipporah, the daughter of Jethro, and the two children, Gerſhom and Eleazar, whom he had by her, ſet forward accordingly. Gerſhom in the Hebrew language, ſignifies *foreign*, and Eleazar *favoured by God*, and theſe names were given them as a token that Moſes had eſcaped from amongſt the Egyptians by the aſſiſtance of the God of his fathers.

As he approached the borders, he was met on ſpecial appointment, by his brother Aaron, to whom he communicated the revelation of the Divine will, as he had received it on the mountain. As they advanced, the principal men of their nation came forth to meet them; when it was found requiſite for Moſes to diſplay his power of working miracles, as the moſt effectual means of gaining their confidence in the Divine promiſe, that they ſhould be delivered from their oppreſſion. When he found that the Hebrews, animated by a ſpirit of liberty, were diſpoſed implicitly to obey whatever he ſhould enjoin them, he preſented himſelf before the king (who had lately ſucceeded to the throne) and having laid before him the ſignal ſervices he had rendered the Egyptians, at the very juncture of their ſuſtaining the moſt ignominious treatment from the Ethiopians, who had ravaged their country, and rendered them a by-word amongſt nations, recapitulated the dangers he had encountered for their deliverance, and recited the occurrences that had paſſed on Mount Sinai, together with the extraordinary revelations communicated to him there, he exhorted the king by no means to oppoſe the Divine will.

Pharaoh treated his repreſentation with raillery, whereupon Moſes proceeded to diſplay the miracles as wrought upon the mount; but this, inſtead of convincing, incenſed him the more, inſomuch that he reviled Moſes as a ſlave lately eſcaped from Egyptian bondage, who now endeavoured by the aid of magic, to impoſe himſelf on the credulity of the people, as a mighty man of wiſdom and valour. To confirm his opinion, the king ordered ſome magicians to be called in, and to demonſtrate that the Egyptians were ſkilled in thoſe arts, which, though Moſes declared them to be Divine operations, were, he affirmed, mere human devices to delude the vulgar. The magicians, at the royal command, caſting their rods on the ground, they became to appearance, ſerpents. Moſes, unaffected by this circumſtance, coolly aſſured the king, that though he by no means deſpiſed the learning or abilities of the Egyptians, the ſigns he had wrought as far ſurpaſſed their magic art, as the Divine power tranſcends the human. To demonſtrate this, he dropped his ſtaff on the ground, commanding that it ſhould change into a ſerpent. The transformation was inſtant, and that particular (a) ſerpent having devoured thoſe produced by the art of the magicians, Moſes took it up and it reaſſumed its form of a ſtaff.

But this effort on the part of Moſes, had the ſame effect with the king as the former; therefore, to retaliate what he judged an impoſition to reflect diſgrace on the Egyptians, he iſſued immediate orders to the ſuperintendants of the works to double their taſks, nor grant them the leaſt intermiſſion from the ſevereſt labour. To add to their toil, they were no longer indulged with ſtraw to make bricks, but reduced to the neceſſity of providing that material in the night time, after they had been fatigued with the exceſſive hardſhips of the day.

Moſes, however, was not in the leaſt diſmayed either at the menaces of the king, or the vexatious importunity of his countrymen; but bravely perſevered in the deſign he was determined to accompliſh. To this end he applied to the king for permiſſion for the Hebrews to go to Mount Sinai, to offer up a ſolemn oblation to God. He urged his importunity, by repreſenting the importance of the Divine favour on the one hand, and the indignation and conſequent calamities he would entail on himſelf, his children and people, on the other hand, ſhould he, by perſevering in his obſtinacy, render them objects of the Divine vengeance. He concluded, however, with declaring, that, at all events, the Hebrews would effect their deliverance, and the Egyptians meet with the puniſhment due to their obſtinacy and diſobedience.

CHAP. XIV.

The ten plagues of Egypt. Inſtitution of the paſſover.

AS Pharaoh ſtill continued obdurate, and deſpiſed both the menaces and admonitions of Moſes, the ſevereſt calamities ſoon befel the Egyptian nation. To theſe I ſhall circumſtantially attend for three diſtinct cauſes, viz. as they were puniſhments never inflicted on any nation before, as they confirmed the predictions of Moſes, and as they afford a leſſon to mankind, not to incur the Divine diſpleaſure, by an obſtinate perſeverance or diſobedience to his will.

The firſt calamity that befel the Egyptians, was the river Nile being turned into blood, ſo that the people were deprived of all means of quenching their thirſt, as they had no other fountain of water; beſides, the water was [illegible]

(a) This was a ſufficient demonſtration of the ſuperior power by which Moſes acted above them, which might have convinced Pharaoh, if his [illegible] had not perſuaded him that they would in time ſhew a power ſuperior to Moſes.

not only changed in colour, but in quality, and affected those, whose parching thirst compelled them to drink, with the severest pains. To the Hebrews its former taste remained, and it therefore answered its former purposes.

Prevailed on by this alarming incident, Pharaoh issued his licence for the departure of the Hebrews, but the cause no sooner ceased than he revoked it. The whole country was then infested with frogs (*a*) which abounded in the river to such a degree, that, dying and becoming putrified, the water was rendered nauseous and loathsome. They also corrupted their food of every kind, and caused a stench to exhale, deadly and poisonous in its effects. This calamity inclined the king to recoil again, and he no sooner consented that Moses should proceed on his journey with the Hebrews, than it ceased, and the face of nature re-assumed its wanted form. But this plague was no sooner removed, than the obstinacy of Pharaoh brought on a third, which was a swarm of lice, that corroded the bodies of the Egyptians in a most miraculous manner, nor could any means be found to counteract the malignity of these pestiferous vermin, or effect their extirpation. Pharaoh, again dreading the extermination of his subjects, in a manner of all others the most infamous, gave the Hebrews assurance of their departure, on condition that their wives and children should be left behind as hostages for their return. This incensed the Almighty the more as it carried with it a presumptuous hope of over-ruling his Divine will, and argued a belief that it was Moses, and not Providence, that interposed in behalf of the Hebrews. The land was therefore covered with a vast variety of flies and insects, which not only proved fatal to many persons, but totally suspended the pursuit of agriculture, for what they did not destroy, was killed by a distemper that was also baneful to the cattle. Notwithstanding these distresses, Pharaoh remained inflexible, nor would suffer the Hebrews to depart, but on the before mentioned conditions. The Almighty was therefore pleased to punish his contumacy with sorer afflictions. The bodies of the Egyptians were covered with ulcers, which proved mortal to many, but the king still persevering in his obstinacy, an extraordinary kind of hail, such as had never been seen before in Egypt, poured down in torrents, and instantaneously destroyed the fruits of the earth. This was followed by a swarm of locusts, (*b*) which nipped the rising grain, and blasted all their hopes of harvest.

Such judgments might be deemed sufficient to soften the most obdurate heart, and enforce acquiescence with the Divine will, but Pharaoh, instigated by malice, sacrificed his subjects to his obstinacy, and impiously set the Almighty at defiance. He at length enjoined Moses to lead away the Hebrews with their wives, but to leave their effects behind them as an equivalent for the loss the Egyptians had sustained on their account.

Whilst Moses was remonstrating with him on the injustice of this proposal, which, if complied with would take from them the means of offering an oblation to God, an impenetrable darkness, or fog, overspread the land of Egypt, which deprived many of their sight, and, by stopping respiration, proved mortal to others. The darkness having continued three days, and as many nights, without producing the due effect upon Pharaoh, Moses at length thus addressed him, "How long will you persist to trample on the counsel of the Most High? It is the Divine command that the Hebrews depart, nor can you be freed from the curses of the Almighty, but by obedience to his will." Incensed at this peremptory observation, the king threatened him with the loss of his head, if he even dared to renew his importunities in his presence. Moses replied, that he should urge him no further, but that, in a short time, both himself and the principal of his subjects, would entreat the Hebrews to depart; which said, he withdrew.

But the Almighty, being pleased to give another proof of his vengeance against the Egyptians, commanded Moses to enjoin the people to prepare the sacrifice by the tenth day of the month Xanthicus, that it might be celebrated on the fourteenth of the same month, and that he should then lead the Hebrews away, with all their effects. This month is called by the Egyptians Pharmuthi, by the Hebrews Nisan, and by the Macedonians Xanthicus. Moses accordingly caused the necessary preparations to be made; and on the dawn of the fourteenth day, the whole people (drawn up ready for a march) offered sacrifice, and, with small bundles of hyssop, purified their houses, sprinkling them with blood. Having supped, they burned the residue of the meat, as being on the point of departure. To this day we retain this custom, calling the festival *Pascha*, that is to say *Passage*, because, on that night, God having in mercy spared and passed by the Hebrews, struck the Egyptians with a terrible plague, which, in the course of a few hours, exterminated all their first-born, so that Pharaoh was harrassed with importunate solicitations to dismiss the Hebrews. Sending, therefore, for Moses, he gave immediate orders for their departure, supposing that their absence would exempt the country from its accumulated plagues. The Egyptians made them ample presents to hasten their journey, and as a token of the intercourse and familiarity which had so long subsisted between them.

CHAP. XV.

The Israelites leave Egypt under the conduct of Moses. Institution of the feast of the Azymes, or unleavened bread. The Israelites pursued by the Egyptians. Make to the Red Sea. Much perplexed. Exhorted by Moses to rely on the Divine protection.

THE Hebrews had no sooner taken their departure, than the Egyptians discovered much remorse for the cruelties they had exercised over them. Having taken their route towards Letopolis, at that time deserted, though the spot on which Babylon was afterwards built, about the time that Cambyses depopulated Egypt, they arrived on the third day at Beelzephon, near the Red Sea. In this desert they lived upon cakes, lightly kneaded, and prepared with small heat, for the space of thirty days, for they had brought no more provision out of Egypt, than what was barely sufficient to serve them for that time. In commemoration of this necessity, we still observe a feast for the space of eight days, called the feast of Azymes, or of (*c*) UNLEAVENED BREAD.

The number of the Israelites who came out of Egypt, including such only as were able to bear arms, are computed at six hundred thousand.

They took their departure from Egypt on the fifteenth day of the month Xanthicus, 415 years from our father Abraham's settling in Canaan, 230 years from Jacob's arrival in Egypt, and in the 80th year of the life of Moses, whose brother Aaron was three years older than

(*a*) This plague of the frogs, as well as that of the water being changed into blood, was excellently adapted to subvert the superstitions of Egypt, and to demonstrate the over ruling power of the Almighty. [illegible] the waters of the Nile was the grand scene of the magical operations of the Egyptians, in which [illegible] and frogs made a principal part of their [illegible], by common [illegible], that [illegible] to produce such an [illegible] of these creatures to annoy them [illegible] the Almighty adapted their chastisement to the nature of their crimes. For frogs were not only the instruments of their abominations, but likewise the emblems of those impure demons whom they invoked by their incantations.

(*b*) In the year 1748 great numbers of these insects visited different parts of England, but happily their stay was of short duration. Many of them were taken alive, in the months of August and September, of the length of two inches and an half, to that of four inches, some of which were taken and sent a [illegible] for three, four, five and six weeks. There are many accounts given of these devouring insects. Pliny says, that these creatures generally made their appearance while the strong east winds continued, and we read that [illegible] east wind was [illegible] were driven by an east wind out of Turkey into Poland, where they did much mischief. We read further that, in 1650, a prodigious swarm of locusts were driven from the Pontus to Poland, where they destroyed every thing that came [illegible] twenty miles round. In August 1747, a swarm of [illegible] so numerous as to darken the air settled in Transylvania, where they devoured the vegetable productions of the country to the very roots.

(*c*) The use of unleavened bread might be enjoined to remind them of their purity, leaven being a symbol of corruption. But others think it was ordered to commemorate their hasty deliverance, which did not allow them time to leaven their bread.

himself. They also carried with them the bones of Joseph, according to the injunction he had laid on his descendants.

The Egyptians soon began to repent them of the dismission of the Hebrews, and Pharaoh to conclude that all their calamities arose from the enchantment of Moses. Forming therefore, a resolution to pursue them, they provided the necessary implements of war, not doubting but to overtake and bring them back to their late bondage, especially as they were unprepared for an attack, and harrassed with the fatigues of their journey. Inquiring their route, they pursued them with alacrity, though the badness of the roads was such, as not only to obstruct the progress of an army, but incommodious to single passengers. Moses conducted them this way, in order to foil the Egyptians, if they should be maliciously disposed to follow them, as well as to evade the discovery of the Philistines, who had conceived an ancient grudge to the Hebrews, their country bordering upon Egypt. Travelling, therefore, through the desert, where he knew they must undergo many hardships, his intent was to bring them into Canaan, that he might afterwards lead them to Mount Sinai, there to offer up the oblation, according to the Divine command.

As soon as the Egyptians had overtaken the Israelites, they drew up in order of battle, amounting in number to fifty thousand horse, two hundred thousand foot, attended by six hundred chariots. They had obtained every advantage, blocked up the Hebrews between inaccessible rocks on the one side, and the sea on the other, and, by pitching their tents at the mouth of the aperture, cut off all possibility of their escape. In this embarrassed situation, unable to sustain a siege through want of provision, to effect their flight from being blockaded, or to maintain a battle through want of arms, they had no apparent resource but to surrender at mercy to the enemy. They now began to inveigh most severely against Moses, totally unmindful of the wonders performed by the Divine power through his agency; nay, they were driven to such despair, that notwithstanding his exhortation to rely on the arm of Omnipotence, they were ready to express their resentment by stoning him, and then voluntarily resigning themselves to the thraldom of the Egyptians. To this they were instigated by the piercing cries of the women and children, who had nothing in view but immediate destruction. Moses bore the invectives of the multitude with the calmest composure, nor discovered the least diffidence of the Divine promises. Assuring them that the Almighty would not suffer them to be subjected to their enemies, he thus addressed them, "If "your interest and concerns had been under the direction "of human prudence only, you would have been justified "in your doubts and suspicions of the event, but your dis-"trust of the Divine power, shews at once your impiety "and your folly, especially as you have had such convin-"cing tokens of his care, in your deliverance by me, at a "time most unexpected. This should encourage your "hope, that God will extricate you out of present diffi-"culties, as he has out of former, though they appear "both to you and your enemies insurmountable, in order "to display his goodness and power. Rely, then, on the "aid of Omnipotence, which can either elate or deject at "pleasure. Be not dismayed at the terrific numbers of the "Egyptians, nor despair of your lives, though escape "seems impracticable, but remember that the Almighty, "if consistent with his Divine will, can level the moun-"tains, and turn the sea into dry land."

CHAP. XVI.

The prayer of Moses. The Red Sea divides. The Hebrews safely pass through it. The Egyptians are drowned. Song of Moses. The arms of the Egyptians cast on shore in the camp of the Hebrews, who soon after go on Mount Sinai.

MOSES, having concluded his address, conducted the Hebrews towards the sea, in full view of the Egyptians, who, tired with the fatigues of the pursuit, declined the combat till the ensuing day. As soon as Moses arrived at the bank, he invoked the Divine assistance, to the following effect:

"Thou well knowest, Almighty Father, that human "force can never effect our escape from the calamities "impending. Thou alone, canst save this multitude, "who have forsaken Egypt at thine especial command. "We therefore commend ourselves to the protection of "thy Providence, assured that by that means alone we can "be delivered from the rage of the Egyptians. Manifest, "therefore, thy power in our weakness, relieve and ani-"mate thy people, though, through distrust they have "offended thee. Thou canst free us from the difficulties "with which we are surrounded. The sea is thine, the "dry land is thine, the expanse of the universe is thine. "The sea shall divide itself at thy command, the powers "of the air shall also obey."

Having thus invoked the Divine protection, he struck the sea with his rod, which, suddenly dividing (a) and retiring back, left a dry passage for the escape of the Hebrews. Moses immediately entered, and commanding the multitude to follow him, they boldly marched through the passage thus opened, congratulating one another on the danger of their enemies, and their own miraculous preservation, through the interposition of Divine Providence. The Egyptians at first thought, that, having with despair, they had precipitated themselves into perdition, but observing them make a considerable progress, without the least obstruction in their passage, they also determined to follow, and, ordering their cavalry to keep in front, marched with their whole army. While the Egyptians were employed in putting on their armour, the Hebrews had reached the opposite shore, which further animated the former to follow them without the least suspicion of danger or difficulty, ignorant that the passage was opened for the Hebrews alone, and impassible to any others. As the whole body of the Egyptians was proceeding up the channels, the sea again diffused itself, and with a force reverberated by the driving winds, overwhelmed them in the waves. Impetuous showers attended with roaring peals of thunder, and almost incessant flashes of lightning, added to the horrors of the scene, which exhibited the most tremendous tokens of the Divine vengeance, and, so total was their destruction, that not one escaped to carry back the tidings of this awful catastrophe.

The Hebrews were transported beyond degree at their own signal deliverance, and the overthrow of their enemies, and, as a testimony of their gratitude, passed the night in offering up praises and thanksgivings, and singing hymns, which Moses had composed and adapted to the occasion.

I have recited these occurrences as they stand recorded in holy writ, nor let any person suspect the credibility of them, since, not long ago, the sea of Pamphylia divided itself, and opened a passage for Alexander, king of Macedon, when the Almighty was pleased, by his means, to subvert the Persian empire. This fact is attested by the several historians who have recorded the memorable deeds of that renowned monarch.

The next day the arms and baggage of the Egyptians were carried, by the force of the waves, to the Hebrew camp, which Moses considering as a token of the Divine regard, he caused to be collected for future use, and then led the Hebrews to Mount Sinai, to offer up their oblations to the Almighty for their signal deliverance, according to his own especial command.

(a) There have been many objections made to this passage of the Israelites over the Red Sea in one night; but the most eminent geographers, and ablest mathematicians inform us that this sea, for about five days journey, is no where more than about 20 or 30 miles broad, and in one place but 4 or 5 miles, according to De Lisle's map, which is made from the best travellers themselves, and not copied from others. Dr. Calmet, and other learned men who surveyed this sea with great exactness, declares that there is no great flux or reflux in these parts. Vide Wall's Bible, and Josephus.

END OF THE SECOND BOOK.

PHARAOH and his Host of Egyptians DROWNED
in the Red Sea

FLAVIUS JOSEPHUS

ON THE

ANTIQUITIES

OF THE

JEWS.

BOOK III

[RECORDING A PERIOD OF ABOUT TWO YEARS]

CHAP. I.

The Israelites distressed for water in the desert The water purified at the intercession of Moses The people murmur for want of sustenance Moses enumerates the Divine favours to appease them Implores the Divine aid. They are relieved by a flight of quails Manna sent Command respecting the manner of gathering it Support of the Israelites for forty years Drought prevails Moses produces water.

THE joy resulting from the Israelites late deliverance was soon damped by a succession of difficulties in their progress to Mount Sinai (*a*), the country being desert and destitute of food, water, and provisions of every kind, for man and beast The water that, by command of their leader, they had brought with them from the places through which they lately passed, being now expended, they were under the necessity of sinking wells, at immense toil, through the hardness of the ground, and after all their labours the water was by no means adequate to their wants, either in quality or quantity Proceeding on their journey, they arrived, about dusk, at a certain spot, which, from the brackishness of its water, they called Marah, that is, *bitterness*, and, being fatigued with travel and fasting, resided there for some time To this they were induced on account of the well, which, though incompetent to the full supply of so numerous a body, afforded them considerable relief Besides, they were given to understand, by their scouts, that, in their progress, they would find the water wholly unfit for their own use, as well as that of their cattle

When Moses observed the general despair that prevailed amongst the multitude, and reflected that his people were not composed of a body of men possessed of fortitude to sustain hardships, but comprised a promiscuous collection of women and children, who could not suppress the feelings of nature, he was extremely concerned, as if he had been the author of this calamity, which, added to the entreaties of the women in behalf of their children, and of the men in behalf of their wives, he had recourse, by supplication, to the Father of Mercies, that he would graciously interfere in their present exigency His request being granted, he took a piece of wood, cleft, and cast it into the pit, assuring the people, that the Almighty was disposed to accord to their desires, provided they would with alacrity perform that which should be commanded On their expressing their conformity, he enjoined the strongest men amongst them to draw water assuring them by way of encouragement, that when the well was nearly exhausted, the residue would be potable The event justified his declaration, for the water, purged by agitation, became agreeable to the palate, and refreshed the parching multitude

They hence removed to Helim, or Elim, a region which at a distance, afforded a pleasing prospect, being adorned with palm-trees, but on a nearer survey, presented a barren aspect, for these palm-trees were but seventy

(*a*) There is now a convent at Mount Sinai, founded by the empress Helena, and dedicated to the celebrated St Catharine It stands at the bottom of the mountain, and is an irregular, awkward building of unburnt bricks walled round, and stopped at every entrance to prevent the incursions of the roving Arabs The principal entrance is by a window, that is upwards of thirty feet from the ground [illegible] and to which people are drawn up in a machine by a windlass Here is the shrine of St Catharine The relics are deposited in a marble chest whereon are carved several pieces of foliage in basso relievo Adjoining to the east end of the church wherein these relics are preserved, is the chapel of the Holy Bush, which the monks assert, grew on the same spot where now lies a flag of white marble, which Christians approach and [illegible] devoutly kiss [illegible] will [illegible] enter this chapel without [illegible] shoes on Here are two wells, one is called the Well of Moses which hath very fine cool water and [illegible] summer the other is called the Well of the Holy Bush and is of a warmer temperature The church containing the relics of St Catharine is called the great church of the transfiguration and is situated to the [illegible] end of the convent The Turks destroyed the pavement of this church by digging [illegible] in hopes of discovering treasures but it was elegantly repaired by [illegible] in the last century.

in number, and those reduced in growth and sap from the dry and gravelly quality of the soil. There were also twelve springs, but the avenues were so contracted, that, instead of flowing, they could only be said to drop, and, on removal of the clogging sand by digging, the water was so muddy as not to be potable. The trees too, from continued drought yielded no fruit.

The multitude again exclaimed against Moses, as the author of all their miseries, and their provision being exhausted, and no hope left of a supply, were reduced to their former state of despair, and threatened to vent their fury upon him in the same manner as before. But though he found the people thus wickedly incensed against him, he doubted not of the Divine assistance, for, conscious of his integrity, he presented himself in the midst of those who were most clamorous, and were preparing to stone him. Being well acquainted with human nature, and endeavouring to touch the passions by the prevailing force of his elocution, he found means to appease their indignation, by exhorting them not to suffer present ills to obliterate from their minds past blessings, but rather to expect deliverance from their woes by the providential interference of that God, who, to make trial of their resignation to his will, and to impress them with a just sense of former miracles wrought in their behalf, permitted them to labour under these adversities. He represented to them, that, to repine under their trials, argued at once the highest impiety and ingratitude, as well as contempt of the Divine will, in obedience to which they forsook Egypt; and added, that they were very culpable in persecuting, with unabated rigour, the agent employed in bringing about the Divine purposes, as he had ever acted with uprightness, and in strict conformity to the Divine command.

He then proceeded to enumerate these particulars. That the Egyptians were first tormented, and then exterminated, for endeavouring to detain them in opposition to the decree of the Almighty: that the water of the very river, to their enemies rendered noxious, to them remained sweet and refreshing: that the very sea, which retired and opened to them a passage, again diffused itself, and overwhelmed the Egyptians in one general inundation: that, being without arms, they were amply supplied: that they had been frequently delivered from imminent danger, nay, from death itself: that since the power of God was infinite, they should not despair of its effects, but sustain their ills, with patient resignation persuaded that their deliverance, though late, was certain: that the delay in redressing their grievance, was to make trial of their fortitude and constancy, in bearing the wants of natural refreshments as men, rather than have recourse to means, unbecoming the rank of creation in which they stood. And concluded with observing, that though he was less solicitous for his own life than their safety, he could not but dissuade them from rising against him, lest it should be deemed an impeachment of the Divine Wisdom and Government.

Having thus calmed their rage, and repressed their fury, he deemed it proper to address himself to the Father of Mercies: accordingly, therefore, ascending an eminence, he supplicated Him to shew compassion to the people in the relief of their exigencies, and implored his forgiveness of their repeated deviations from their duty, as they arose from a pungent sense of their calamities. The Almighty, having vouchsafed to promise his speedy aid, Moses came down to the multitude, who, observing a transport of joy on his countenance, no longer gave way to despair, but changed their former melancholy for a habit of cheerful complacency. Moses then informed them, that he came to bring them immediate remedy for their wants, when a vast number of quails (*a*) (birds that abound in the gulph of Arabia) rapidly flew across the sea, and being wearied with a long flight, fell in the centre of the camp of the Hebrews, who caught and devoured them as a repast sent by Providence to relieve their outrageous famine. Moses, as in duty bound, returned grateful acknowledgments to God for his present aid and future promises. This relief was succeeded by a supply of another sort, for while Moses stretched forth his hands in prayer, the dew fell, which adhering to them, he supposed to be a kind of food sent from heaven, and, on tasting, found it to be very pleasing to the palate. Addressing the people, who supposed it to be snow, as it was then the usual season for its descent, he informed them it was not the ordinary dew of heaven, but a substance providentially sent for their food and nourishment. Having eaten of it himself, he presented it to them, and they were greatly refreshed. In flavour it resembled honey, in odour bdellium, and in form the seed of coriander, so that it was gathered with the utmost care.

No individual was permitted to gather in one day more than the measure of an assaron (the tenth part of an ephah,) a precaution taken to prevent the stronger from encroaching on the weaker, in gathering more than sufficed them. Those, indeed, who sought to provide more than the limited quantity, were frustrated in their expectations, for that which remained till the next morning became bitter, and overrun with vermin. So nutrimental was this food, that it was of itself sufficient sustenance, nay, to this day, a flower is to be seen in that country bearing some resemblance of that with which Moses was so peculiarly favoured. The Hebrews called it *manna*, (*b*) for, in our language, the word *man* is an interrogation, signifying, *What is this or that?* Upon this food they lived forty years, that is, the whole space of time they were in the desert.

Upon their arrival at Rephidim they were much distressed for want of water, and again became incensed with Moses, who, as his never-failing resource, applied himself, in humble supplication, to the Giver of every good and perfect gift, beseeching him, that, as he had vouchsafed them food in the direst necessity, he would now be graciously pleased to afford them drink, without which they must inevitably perish. The Almighty was pleased to attend to his supplication, and assured him that a fountain should spring from a spot whence he least expected it. He then commanded him to strike, with his rod, an adjacent rock, in the presence of the people, and they should be supplied with water without the least pains or labour. Moses had no sooner obtained the promise, than he hastened to the multitude, who waited with the utmost impatience his descent from the rock, where he had addressed the Almighty in their behalf. He immediately communicated to them the Divine assurance of relief in their present calamity, by causing a fountain to flow from an adjacent rock. Whilst they were lost between doubt and expectation, Moses struck the rock (*c*) with his rod,

(*a*) It is to be observed that this extraordinary descent of quails was at that time of the year when those birds are known to fly from Egypt across the Red Sea in prodigious numbers: so that this miracle did not so much consist in the number of the birds, as in their direction to the camp of the Israelites, and on that very evening when they were promised food.

(*b*) This manna, in several parts of scripture, is called Angels food. See Psalm lxxviii. 95. John vi. 31.

(*c*) The rock from whence this water flowed in so miraculous a manner is particularly noticed by Dr. Shaw, who says, "After we had descended, with no small difficulty, down the other, or western side of Mount Sinai, we came into the plain or wilderness of Rephidim, where we saw that extraordinary antiquity the rock of Meribah, which has continued down to this day, without the least injury from time or accidents. [illegible] rightly called, from its hardness, Deut. viii. 15. *a rock of flint*, though [illegible] the purple, or reddish colour of it, it may be rather rendered [illegible], or *the granite rock*. It is about five yards square, lying tottering, as it were, and loose near the middle of the valley, and seems to have been formerly a part, or cliff, of Mount Sinai, which hangs in a variety of precipices all over this plain. *The waters which gushed out, and the streams which flowed withal*, Psal. lxxviii. 21. have hollowed across one corner of this rock a channel about two inches deep, and twenty wide, all over incrustated like the inside of a tea-kettle, which has been long used. Besides several mossy productions which are still preserved by the dew, we see all over this channel a great number of holes, some of them four or five inches deep, and one or two in diameter, the lively and demonstrative tokens of their having been formerly so many fountains. Neither could art or chance be concerned in the contrivance, inasmuch as every circumstance points out to us a miracle, and, in the same manner with the rent in the rock of mount Calvary at Jerusalem, never fails to produce the greatest seriousness and devotion in all who see it. The Arabs, who were our guards, were ready to stone me, for attempting to break off a corner of it.

and there issued forth a most copious and limpid stream, to their great surprise as well as consolation, for they soon found that the water was grateful to their taste, and a peculiar instance of the Divine power and bounty. Moses was now held in the greatest veneration, as highly favoured of God, whose miraculous interposition they gratefully acknowledged, by offering up oblations and solemn thanksgivings. The sacred records, which are deposited in the temple of Jerusalem, declare that Moses, at the especial command of the Most High, in this manner caused water to issue from the rock.

CHAP. II.

The Amalekites wage war against the Israelites, who are encouraged by Moses with assurance of victory. Joshua appointed their commander. Defeat of the Amalekites. Distribution of the spoil. The Israelites again repair to Sinai.

THE increasing numbers and power of the Hebrews now spread an alarm throughout the adjacent countries, insomuch, that embassies were sent from one to the other to concert the means of their expulsion and extirpation. The inhabitants of the country of Gobol and the city Petra, called Amalekites, the most warlike of all the neighbouring nations, were peculiarly active in this expedition. The kings of those districts stirred up each other, as well as those who lived contiguous, to wage war against the Hebrews, alleging that they were an army of aliens escaped from Egyptian bondage, and recommending it as a maxim of sound policy to make the attack in the desert, before their numbers and power increased, rather than, by delay, afford them an opportunity of possessing themselves of lands, and acquiring additional strength to sustain a conflict. These considerations having been duly weighed by the several combined parties, it was unanimously resolved to commence hostilities against the Hebrews. Moses, suspecting no hostile proceedings, was rather alarmed at receiving intimation of their design, but when the enemy was in sight, and there was an inevitable necessity for hazarding an engagement, a general panic and consternation prevailed throughout the Hebrew camp, from a dread of encountering a power with men well prepared, and trained to the exercise of arms. Moses, therefore, emboldened them to the conflict, by reminding them of former exertions of the Divine Power in their behalf, as a ground for reliance on future assistance, and observing, that however inferior they might be, in point of weapons and ammunition, to the enemy, as they had the arm of Omnipotence engaged for them, they need not doubt of success. This he enforced by adding, that, in the severest contests with famine and thirst, and the perils of blockade, they had been brought off more than conquerors, through the same irresistible power.

Having thus animated the multitude, he summoned the chiefs of the respective tribes, and enjoined the younger to [illegible] the elder, while he enforced an universal obedience to the command of the general. Spurning danger, and panting to enter upon action, which they hoped would terminate their calamities, they anxiously pressed to be led against the enemy, that their ardour might not be abated by an untimely delay.

For the whole multitude he selected Joshua, the son of Nun, of the tribe of Ephraim, as commander in chief, being an [illegible] patient of labour, and zealous for the honour of God, according to the instructions he had received from Moses his preceptor. A party was ordered to take [illegible] round the water, and another stationed to [illegible] guard the camp. They continued all night under arms, expecting the signal for a general attack. Moses [illegible] giving instructions to Joshua respecting the disposition of the army. At daybreak [illegible] the troops [illegible] Joshua [illegible] to equal [illegible] held, and [illegible] which [illegible] and the Hebrews in general, [illegible] to suffer the conflict [illegible] good [illegible]. Having given the necessary orders, he commended [illegible] to the protection of God, and delegating the command to Joshua, retired to a mountain.

The engagement was maintained [illegible] equal fury and doubtful success. While Moses extended his hands, the Hebrews had the advantage, but it was observed, that, when they dropped through fatigue, the enemy prevailed, perceiving which his brother Aaron, and Hur the husband of his sister Miriam, to support his hands in the erect posture. This being done, the Hebrews charged the Amalekites with such resolution, that had not night put an end to the contest a general slaughter must have ensued. Our ancestors, however, obtained a most glorious and [illegible] ble victory, for besides the renown they acquired by conquering so formidable an enemy, by [illegible] their camp they amassed immense riches, whereas, before they were deprived of the means of common subsistence. But this victory was attended with prosperous effects, future as well as present, as it not only reduced the enemy to submission, but afterwards rendered them the terror of surrounding nations. The spoils taken were very considerable, for besides a great quantity of gold and silver found in the camp, there were vessels and tables of brass, warlike implements, accoutrements for men and horse, with every requisite for the complete array of an army. The Hebrews elated by this conquest were ready to undertake the most arduous exploits.

The next day Moses ordered the bodies of the [illegible] to be stripped, and the scattered arms of those that fled to be collected. He conferred honours on those who had signalized their valour in the action, and, with the concurrence of the whole army, bestowed the highest eulogium on Joshua, their commander. Not one Hebrew fell upon the occasion. The hosts of the enemy were put to the sword. In token of their gratitude, an oblation was offered to the giver of all victory, and an altar erected with this inscription, TO GOD THE CONQUEROR. He denounced the extirpation of the Amalekites, for having assaulted the Hebrews in circumstances of singular distress, [illegible] from their [illegible] in a desert, and their want of all necessaries. A general festival was then prepared, and thus concluded their first engagement from the day of their deliverance out of Egypt. After the multitude had been refreshed, Moses caused them to be drawn up in array, in order to supply such as were deficient, with the arms and ammunition taken from the enemy. Proceeding by [illegible] they arrived, the third month after their departure from Egypt, at Mount Sinai, where Moses and the [illegible] extraordinary visions [illegible].

CHAP. III.

Jethro [illegible] Moses, at Mount Sinai [illegible] his [illegible]

JETHRO, the father-in-law of Moses, having received intelligence of his extraordinary success, came with his daughter Zipporah, and his two sons, to congratulate him upon the joyful occasion. Having offered sacrifice to God, Moses prepared a banquet for the people, near the [illegible] which withstood the [illegible], and there he took an opportunity for disposing them in ranks, according to the order of their respective tribes. Aaron, Jethro, and the multitude [illegible] in hymns of thanksgiving, ascribed to the Almighty the praises due for their mighty deliverance. He likewise, with united voice, extolled the wisdom and virtue of their leaders, which had brought events to [illegible] while Jethro passed equal commendation on the [illegible] and on Moses, as [illegible] the [illegible] at once honourable and serviceable to their country.

CHAP. [illegible]

Jethro [illegible]

JETHRO [illegible] that Moses was [illegible] [illegible] the people, who [illegible] [illegible] reserving to himself only those of moment, in which the national interest was essentially concerned, for there were many persons to be found amongst the Hebrews competent to determine in ordinary pleas, though he alone was adequate to the weightier concerns of the people, considered in a collective view "Persuaded, said he, of your virtues, and the rectitude of your conduct towards the people, as the vicegerent of God, I see them to submit their suits to the decision of others, whilst you are devoted to those matters which more immediately respect the service of God, and the defence and glory of the people committed to your care. It, therefore, you will listen to my advice in human affairs, muster the whole army and appoint chieftains to preside over parties, composed of ten thousands, thousands, five hundreds, and fifties over these, thus arranged, set judicial officers, who dividing them into thirties and tens, may determine their suits and controversies. Let their titles signify the number over which they have charge, and let these speak by the people, as men of sound judgment, and inflexible integrity, hear and decide their differences. If any intricate matter arises, let it be referred to those who are highest in authority, and if it then remains undecided, let the last appeal be to yourself. By these means right will be preserved inviolate to the people, and you will have opportunity of attending to the service of God, and to your supplications for the general good."

Moses, convinced of the propriety of Jethro's counsel, made the respective arrangements in exact conformity to his plan, nor did he arrogate to himself the merit of the service, but publicly ascribed it to the political talents of his father-in-law. Indeed, Jethro is recorded by him, in his writings, as the author of these regulations, esteeming it a duty to give merit its due praise, and thereby testifying a mind discerning, candid, and ingenious.

CHAP. V.

Moses ascends Mount Sinai. Tempest, attended with tremendous thunder and lightning. Moses addresses the multitude. The Ten Commandments issued from the Divine Voice. Moses fasts forty days and forty nights, the time of his continuance in the mountain. Descends and displays, in the presence of the people, the two tables, containing the Ten Commandments.

MOSES having convened the multitude, informed them, that he must ascend Mount Sinai, to receive the Divine Commands, which he would communicate to them. At the same time, he commanded them to pitch their tents at the foot of the mountain, that they might be the more ready to receive such intimation as the Almighty should be pleased to afford.

He then ascended the mountain, which is not only the highest in that country, but, by reason of its craggy precipices, inaccessible, and formidable to the view; hence, an opinion prevailed, that it was the peculiar residence of the Divine Being. The Hebrews, in obedience to Moses, took their stand at the foot of the mountain, in full expectation of the blessings he had promised to procure. During the space they expected the return of their guide, they observed strict temperance, abstaining from sensual gratifications, and purifying themselves for three days, according to command. They also besought the Almighty, that he would favour Moses with a gracious reception, and, through his means, vouchsafe to confer on them the promised blessings. For this, they held a sumptuous festival, and arrayed themselves, their wives and children, in their best attire. On the third day, before sunrise, a cloud (such as never been seen before) bore down upon their camp, and [illegible] the place where they had fixed their tents. Though the sky in every other part appeared serene, a sudden tempest arose in that quarter attended with boisterous winds, torrents of rain, peals of thunder, and flashes of lightning, which not only diffused universal horror, but indicated that the Almighty was there present in an especial manner. Let those who read what I have recited, judge for themselves whether it be lawful for us to deviate from the letter of Holy Writ.

The Hebrews were greatly agitated by this tremendous event, and as they gave into the common opinion repeatedly specified, it impressed their minds with an universal dread, so that they kept within their tents, concluding that Moses had fallen a victim to the Divine Displeasure, and momentarily expected their own extermination.

In this state of anxiety and consternation, Moses suddenly presenting himself to them, with a countenance full of joy and majesty, which dissipated their fears, and encouraged their hopes, especially as the late terrific appearances were vanished. Moses assembled the whole multitude, in order that he might recite in their hearing the Commandments he had received from the Almighty; to which purpose he ascended an eminence, that he might be the better seen and heard, and thus addressed them.

"The Almighty God, O Hebrews, who has never rejected my prayers, hath at this time received me with singular grace and favour, and vouchsafed to communicate to you, by my means, such rules and laws as, if obeyed, will equally conduce to your interest and happiness. Estimate not the importance of what I am about to deliver by the intrinsic merit of the agent but the respect you owe to him at whose command it is delivered. It is not Moses, the son of Amram and Jochabel, who is about to give you these admirable precepts, but that Almighty Being who caused the river Nile to overflow with blood, and overwhelmed the Egyptians in great calamities, for your deliverance. He who opened a passage for you in the midst of the ocean; He who supplied you with food from heaven in the direst extremity; He, who brought water from the rock to quench your thirst; He, who gave Adam and his posterity dominion over all things, both in earth and sea; He, by whom Noah was saved from the deluge; He, by whom our ancestor Abraham obtained the land of Canaan; He, by whose indulgence Isaac was born to his father and mother in an advanced age; by whom Jacob was blessed with a numerous and honourable progeny, and by whom Joseph attained to the first dignities amongst the Egyptians. Let these, his precepts, therefore, be held inviolate, and esteemed more precious than your wives and children."

This said, he led the promiscuous multitude (men, women, and children) to a spot from which they might hear the instructions from the Divine Voice, that their authority might not be invalidated by the weakness and insufficiency of an human tongue. *An audible voice was then heard to* proceed from the mountain, so that each individual distinctly comprehended the several precepts, which Moses has transmitted to us, in the two tables of laws. I shall not state them word for word, according to the precise form in which they were delivered to Moses, but endeavour to express the sense and meaning, which seem to be to the following purport.

1. There is but one God, who alone is to be worshipped (*c*).
2. No image of any living creature is to be worshipped (*b*).
3. We are not to swear rashly by the name of God (*c*).
4. The seventh day is to be kept holy, and not profaned by labour (*a*).

[illegible] the meaning of his command [illegible] that no object [illegible], at any time [illegible] in the service of the God, who is the universal [illegible] both of providence and grace.

(*b*) From the words of this precept it appears that the worship of idols was [illegible] the [illegible], and perhaps in more other [illegible].

The heathens were [illegible], on many occasions to speak in an irreverent manner of their idols [illegible] and lest the children of [illegible] have done so [illegible] respect the name of the true God, they are

here strictly prohibited from it [illegible] every person [illegible] guilty of a breach of this commandment who uses the name of God in an irreverent manner [illegible] most aggravated breach is that by swearing falsely, or [illegible] into a court of justice to commit perjury [illegible] of God [illegible] therefore let us never mention it [illegible] either in prayer, or to decide, by an oath, controversies among our fellow [illegible].

(*a*) Here God, by a written command, enjoins one day in seven for the most valuable purposes that could be [illegible]

5 Father and mother are to be honoured (*b*)
6 We must not commit murder (*c*)
7 We must abstain from adultery (*d*)
8 No man must steal (*e*)
9 False testimony must not be borne (*f*)
10 No man must covet any manner of thing that is his neighbour's (*g*)

The people having thus heard the declaration of God confirmed by the Divine Voice, were dismissed to their tents. But in a short time they importuned Moses to procure such laws as might serve for the better regulation of their government.

This he performed, but I pass them over at present, reserving them for the subject of a particular book.

Soon after these occurrences, Moses having given previous notice, re-ascended the mountain in the sight of the multitude, but being absent forty days, they became apprehensive that some ill had befallen him. Various were their conjectures concerning his fate. Some were of opinion that he was devoured by wild beasts, and others that he was translated to the Divine Presence; but the wiser party, who neither listened to, or were affected by, mere surmise, bore his absence with patient resignation, from a persuasion of his integrity and the favour of the Almighty so frequently displayed towards him, though they could not but regret even a temporary loss of so wise and virtuous a leader. They durst not decamp, because Moses had enjoined them there to fix their tents, and await his return.

At the expiration of the forty days he appeared, having, during that space of time, taken no human sustenance. His presence diffused a joy throughout the whole multitude, whom he assured of the Divine regard for their welfare, adding, that while he was absent, he had received intimation of the means of establishing their government on a happy and prosperous basis, and that it was the Almighty's especial command to them to erect a tabernacle, (*h*) into which he would occasionally descend, and which might be constructed on such a plan, as to be rendered portable from place to place, and thereby obviate the necessity of ascending Mount Sinai. He then displayed the two tables, including the Ten Commandments, as issued from the mount by the Divine Voice.

CHAP VI

Moses erects a tabernacle in the Desert. Form, and other particulars, of the structure, with their significations. Construction of the ark. Tables [illegible].

THE multitude, overjoyed with what Moses had communicated to them, applied themselves with the utmost assiduity, to the building of the tabernacle. They cheerfully contributed gold, silver, and brass, with store of wood of a durable nature, also goats hair, and sheeps skins, dyed of different colours, and variously ornamented, together with wool, precious stones, and every material requisite for the completion of the work proposed. The materials, thus liberally furnished, Moses appointed artificers, whose names are to be seen on the Sacred Records, as follows: Bazaleel the son of Uri, of the tribe of Judah, and Mariam, Moses's sister, and Aholiab, the son of A[illegible], of the tribe of Dan. The people were so zealous in promoting the undertaking, by contributing materially, that Moses was under the necessity of issuing a proclamation, that he was authorised by the artificers to declare that they had already sent in what was fully adequate to complete the undertaking. Moses, as he had been previously instructed, gave the necessary directions as to the model, and so zealous were the very women, as to emulate each other in preparing vestments for the priests, and every thing that could contribute to the honour and service of God.

The necessary preparations being made, a solemn festival and sacrifice were held at the particular institution of Moses, after which they proceeded to the accomplishment of their important undertaking.

The outward court was to be 50 cubits in breadth and 100 in length. On each side were to be 20 brazen pillars long-ways, and 10 across; every pillar was 5 cubits in height, with rings and borders to it of silver. The bases were of brass, curiously wrought and gilt, fastened to the earth with pins of a cubit length, pointed at the end like a spear, which, by means of cords, that passed through the rings, connected the whole and secured it against the most violent tempest. It was also encompassed by a veil of curiously wrought linen, that hung from the cornices to the bases, and subserved the purpose of a general enclosure.

These were the dimensions of three sides of the structure. It was fifty cubits in front, the space of twenty was left open for an entrance, with two columns on each side of the passage. These were covered with silver work, only the bases were of brass. To strengthen the work, six other planks, three on each hand, were conjoined, and a curtain curiously wrought drawn over them. The grand entrance being twenty cubits wide, and five in depth, was ornamented with an elegant embroidery of flowers and figures of variegated colours, but not one representing any living creature.

[illegible] minds of the people the remembrance of all those wonders that God had wrought for them, and [illegible], that their souls [illegible] [illegible] [illegible] day [illegible]. We read that when God had finished the work of creation, he rested on the seventh day, and there is no doubt but the same was observed by all those that feared him, to the time of Jacob's going down into Egypt, although not expressly mentioned. It seems, that while the children of Israel were in Egypt, they had either forgot the sabbath, or perhaps had been forced to work on that day by their cruel task-masters. This seems to have been the reason why God commanded Moses to revive that institution; and the greatest divines, both ancient and modern, are of opinion, that the sabbath kept by the children of Israel answered exactly to the weekly return of that day on which God finished the works of creation.

(*b*) Disobedience to parents is a crime of such a nature, that it leads to many others. How is it possible that we can ever be consistent with the nature of subordination in society, pay obedience to our civil superiors, while we refuse to honour our natural parents? As to the promise of long life, it must not be understood to extend any further than God thinks proper for his own glory and the good of the obedient person. God may, for wise reasons, see proper to remove by death a very obedient child; but in a natural sense, perhaps the greatest number of obedient children to their parents, both prosper well in the world, and also [illegible].

(*c*) As God is the sole giver and supporter of life, so none but he has a right to take it away, with respect to civil society, the power of taking it away is committed to the magistrate; but a private person is not to do it [illegible] consent. Murder is no less than high treason or open rebellion against God; [illegible] actually taking upon ourselves to exercise his regal power [illegible].

(*d*) Adultery, or the [illegible] of married women [illegible] [illegible] [illegible] ladies [illegible] [illegible], or the [illegible] of [illegible] bed [illegible] whatever. It [illegible] [illegible] [illegible], [illegible] [illegible] forbids the indulging [illegible] [illegible] of obscene expressions.

(*e*) [illegible] both, because they are generally the first [illegible] their own [illegible] what has been stolen [illegible] [illegible]. We [illegible] [illegible] [illegible] several manner, here would be an end of [illegible], and [illegible] of civil society would be totally destroyed.

(*f*) To speak ill of our neighbour, when he has done nothing to [illegible] makes us appear mean [illegible]. [illegible] while we know it to be [illegible] [illegible] [illegible] when either his [illegible] or his property [illegible], to go into a court of judicature and declare [illegible] commit [illegible] [illegible] guilty of [illegible].

(*g*) All the other commandments depend [illegible] this [illegible] [illegible] [illegible].

(*h*) The [illegible] [illegible] removed from one place to another [illegible] [illegible] of the Jews, [illegible] [illegible] [illegible] [illegible] dwell in tents [illegible] [illegible] [illegible] [illegible] law.

In the centre of this court stood the tabernacle, fronting the east, that it might receive the radiant beams of the rising sun. It was 30 cubits in length, and 12 in breadth. One side of it looked towards the south, another to the north, and the back part of it to the west. The two sides were composed of 40 wooden planks, 20 on each side. They were of a quadrangular form, a cubit and a half in breadth, and in thickness four fingers. They were plated with gold, two tenons to every plank, and two silver bases, with mortises to receive those tenons. On the west side were six other boards, likewise overlaid with gold, and connected in so masterly a manner, that they seemed one entire piece. These twenty boards being each of them a cubit and a half over, just amount to the length of thirty cubits. The six boards on the western side were no more than nine cubits, but then they were joined by two planks, one at each corner, in the same position, and of the same length and breadth with the other, but much thicker, the more effectually to secure that side of the tabernacle. There were golden rings or staples, driven into every plank, and disposed in such order, that they answered each other in [illegible]. Through these rings passed several bars five cubits long, and plated with gold, which reaching from end to end, kept the whole quarter firm and compact. At the lower end of this structure the boards were all arranged in the same manner, by passing a gilt bar through as many rings as there were plates, and accommodating one part to another. There were moreover, bolts and staples at the corners, to connect ends and sides, which, with the help of [illegible], to bind one piece to another, secured the tabernacle from the violence of wind and weather.

The inside of that tabernacle was divided into partitions of ten cubits in length. At ten cubits from the bottom there stood four pillars, across, of the same workmanship, the same materials, and the same bases as those already described, but standing at equal distances from each other. Within these pillars was the *most holy place*, which was inaccessible even to the priests, to whom the rest of the tabernacle was open. The division of the tabernacle into three parts, seems to have borne some resemblance to the universe. The first part, into which the priests were not permitted to enter, represented heaven, sacred to the Deity alone. The space of twenty cubits, to which the priests only had admittance, had some resemblance to the earth and sea.

At the entrance of the tabernacle were five gilded columns, fixed upon bases of brass, and covered with curtains of fine yarn, dyed of variegated colours, and interwoven. The first of these curtains was ten cubits square, and served as a covering to the partition between the *most holy place* and the *holy*, to veil the former.

The temple itself was called Holy, but the space between the four pillars bore the name of *Sanctum Sanctorum*. The curtain, or veil, was embellished with curious flowers and figures, living creatures only excepted. There was another veil in every respect equal to the former, which encompassed the five pillars at the entrance. It was fastened at the top with hooks and eyes, and so down to the middle of the five columns, leaving the rest open for the priests to enter. This veil had another over it of the same size, and almost contiguous, but of a woven ground. It had rings with a string through them to draw at pleasure, especially on festivals, to indulge the people with a view of the under curtain, curiously embellished with embroidery. At other times, and particularly in boisterous weather, the upper curtain served as a covert to secure the inner, being composed of a stuff that was proof against rain. This kind of curtain has been used at the door of the temple, from the building of it to the present day.

There were likewise ten pieces of hanging, in compass twenty-eight cubits, in depth four cubits, and so nicely connected with golden loops, as to seem one entire piece. These hangings covered the whole tabernacle, within one foot of the ground. There were also eleven hangings more of the same depth, but thirty cubits in length, woven, with the same art, of hair, as the others were of wool. These were a covering to the other ten, and, as they negligently flowed upon the ground, in some degree resembled a canopy. The eleventh served to cover the entrance. These were covered with divers skins as an outward tegument to preserve them from the effects of [illegible] or rains. The spectacle, indeed, was an object of admiration, as the columns shone with such lustre as to resemble the firmament of heaven.

The tabernacle, thus finished, they proceeded to the construction of the ark of God, which was framed of a particular wood, durable and impenetrable in its nature, called, by the Hebrews, *[illegible]*. The figure was as follows. It was two cubits and an half in length, one and an half in breadth, and as much in depth, and so covered with the purest gold, that no part of the wood was to be seen. The cover was cramped with golden hooks, so well finished, and so smooth in every part, that there was no danger of its sustaining any damage from rubbing. At the two ends were rivetted into the frame four golden rings, one at each corner. Through these rings were passed two gilded bars on each side, to remove the ark from place to place, as occasion might require, for it was never shifted but on the shoulders of the priests and Levites. On the cover were two figures, which the Hebrews call *cherubims*, having wings according to the description of what Moses saw about the Divine throne, and unseen by mortals before. In this ark were deposited the two tables of the decalogue. Each table comprised five of the commandments, two and a half in a column. The ark was laid up in the sanctuary.

In this holy place was a table not unlike that at Delphi, two cubits in length, one in breadth, and a cubit and an half in height. The feet, from the middle downwards, resembled those the Dorians make use of for their beds, but from thence upwards, they were square, with a border projecting about four fingers, and a crown of gold over it and under it on every side. Under this border were four rings of gold, fastened into the upper part of the four feet, one at each corner, and gilt bars of the finest wood passed through them, and served as handles on its removal from place to place. This table stood in the temple towards the north, not far from the sanctuary itself. There were placed on it twelve loaves of unleavened bread, in two rows, six on each side. They were made of the finest flour, two assarons in quantity, or seven attic cotylas, after the Hebrew measure, each cake containing two omers. Over these loaves were two golden dishes of incense. At the end of seven days these loaves were taken away, and others put in their places. The seventh day we call our sabbath. But of this hereafter.

Opposite this table, on the south side stood a golden candlestick, of hollow cast. It weighed an hundred moses, which the Hebrews call *chinchares*, and the Greeks talents. The candlestick was wrought with bowls, lillies, pomegranates, and small cups, all in pure gold, to the number of seventy pieces, which shot from the shank into seven branches, answering to the number of the planets, and they were ranged in uniform order. On the top of these seven branches were as many lamps, which, according to the position of the candlestick, faced towards the east and the south.

Between the candlestick and the table was a little altar for incense, made of the same durable wood with the ark. It was in length and breadth a cubit, and in height two. It had a golden fire-hearth, and a crown of the purest gold round about from corner to corner, with rings and staves through them for the conveniency of carriage.

There was also another altar before the tabernacle, of the same materials with the former, five cubits square, and three in height, and finished after the same design, except its being plated with brass, and its having in the middle a brazen grate for the ashes to fall through. There were [illegible] also funnels, [illegible], censers, cups and other vessels for the service of the altar, all of pure gold. Thus much for the tabernacle, and the vessels [illegible].

CHAP. VII.

Description of the vestments of the sacerdotal order. Signification of the structure of the Tabernacle, and the ornaments of the priests.

WE now proceed to treat of the vestments appointed both for the priests in ordinary, called Chaanaeans, and the Anarabaches, or High Priest, and shall begin with the former. No priest could officiate, according to law, without being first purified. His under garment was of fine twisted linen, made in the form of drawers. The Hebrews call it *manachasin*, or binder. The feet were put through it, and being drawn over the thighs, it was fastened at the waistband. Over this was a garment of very fine linen, which the Hebrews call *chethomene*, that is a linen cloth, as Chethem is taken from the flax of which it was made. It sat close, had narrow sleeves, and reached down to the heel. It was fastened with a girdle round the middle, about four fingers broad, and so curiously adorned with needle-work of different colours, that it bore some resemblance to the skin of a snake. It was ornamented with variegated flowers and figures, but the ground was linen. This girdle went twice about the body of the priest, and, for the sake of a graceful appearance, hung from the breast to the feet, except when in the exercise of his function, on which occasion he cast it over his left shoulder, that it might not encumber him. Moses calls this girdle *abaneth*, but we now call it *emian*, a word borrowed from the Babylonians. This garment was made without plaits or folds, wide in the neck, and buckled before and behind. The Hebrew name is *massabazanes*.

The priest wore a kind of mitre, or bonnet, resembling a small helmet, and covering rather more than half his head. It is called *masnaemphthes*, made of linen, and bound with a fillet to keep it steady. This was covered with a cap of curious fine linen, which came so low, that the smallest part of it could not be seen, and every part was so secured, as to prevent its falling or encumbering the priest in his office. Such were the vestments of the priests in ordinary.

The high priest, besides the ornaments already described, had others peculiar to his office. He wore a purple robe that reached down to his ancles, which we call *methir*, with a girdle, for colours and figures, resembling the before mentioned, excepting the addition of an intermixture of gold. The skirt of this vest was trimmed with a fringe, and hung round with pomegranates, and golden bells of curious workmanship, interchangeably placed at equal distances from each other. This garment was without seam, and had no opening, except lengthways, a little below the shoulders, behind and about the middle of the breast before, with two borders, one to cover the opening, and another as a kind of ornament to that part of it that was left for the arms to pass through the sleeves.

Over this vestment was a third, called the *ephod*, and much the same with the *epomis* of the Greeks. It was a cubit in length, embroidered with variegated colours, intermixed with gold, and covered the whole breast. It had likewise sleeves, and was, in effect, a kind of additional ornament.

Upon the fore part of this robe, and in the middle of the breast, was left a vacant space for the *essen*, which the Greeks call *logion*, and the Latins, *rationale*, that is, the oracle. This square piece exactly filled up the vacant space. There were golden rings at each corner, through which ran purple ribbons, to connect the ephod and the rationale. The high priest wore upon each shoulder, a sardonyx, set in gold, which served as buckles to clasp one part of the ephod to the other. They had golden ringlets to bind them and the rationale together. Upon these stones were engraved, in Hebrew characters, the names of Jacob's twelve sons, the six elder on the right shoulder, and the other six on the left. The essen, or rationale, was distinguished also by twelve stones, of such extraordinary magnitude and lustre, that, for value and ornament, were inestimable. They were disposed in four rows, three in a row, and so divided from each other by little partitions of gold as to secure them from falling out. In the first row was a sardonyx, a topaz, and an emerald; in the second a ruby, a jasper, and a sapphire; in the third, a ligurius, an amethyst, and an agate; and in the fourth, a chrysolite, an onyx, and a beryl. Upon these twelve precious stones were severally inscribed the names of Jacob's twelve sons, whom we deem the heads of our tribes, so that the names were inserted in the order of seniority. And as hooks were too weak to sustain the weight of these precious stones, stronger fastenings were fixed to the upper part of the rationale, that projected from the work of the garment. To this were annexed two wreathed golden chains, that were conveyed, by secret passages, up to the shoulder-piece. The upper end of these chains was carried about to the back, and hooked with a ring behind upon the border of the ephod; and by these means the whole was kept in a firm and uniform state. There was also fixed to the rationale a girdle, of the colours before-mentioned, but interwoven with gold. It went twice about the body, and being tied in a knot before, the two ends were left flowing, with a curious gold fringe as an ornament to each.

The high priest's *tiara*, or mitre, was the same with that of other priests, excepting that it was covered with another of a purple colour, and encircled with a triple crown of gold, on which was raised, in gold, the resemblance of a cup, in form like the bud of a plant by us called *saccharus*, and, by the Greeks, *hyoscyamus*.

For the information of those who may be ignorant of the nature of this plant, it may not be improper briefly to describe it. It commonly rises above three spans high: its root is like that of a turnip, and its leaf like mint. It branches out into a round bud, invested with a coat which it sheds as the fruit ripens.

The cup that was placed over the golden crown, was about the size of the joint of the smaller finger, round and hollow, like the inside of a goblet. In figure it was a kind of hemisphere, narrowing a little upwards, and then being dilated towards the brim into the form of a bason, like a pomegranate cut in two. To this there was annexed a round cover (a great natural curiosity) with sharp points, rising out of it like the prickles of a pomegranate. Within this cup and cover, the fruit was nourished and preserved. The seed is like that of the plant Sideritis, or Wall-sage; and the flower like plantane.

Thus was the mitre adorned from the back part of the head round to the temples: but the forehead had a golden plate over it, inscribed with the venerable name of the Deity. Such were the vestments of the high priest.

It is matter of wonder that other nations have imbibed a prejudice against us, as blasphemers of that Divine Being whom they profess to adore. Let any person attend to the structure of the tabernacle, the vestments of the priests, and the vessels used in the performance of our sacred rites, and he must be convinced that our lawgiver was a pious man, and that the clamours against us are mere calumny and slander. The particulars alluded to are a representation of the world, as will appear to every candid observer. The division of the tabernacle into three parts, that is, two for the priests in general, as a place common to all, and free of access, represents the earth and the sea; but the third place, accessible to no mortal, is like the heavens, the peculiar residence of the Deity. The twelve loaves of shew-bread upon the table, denote the twelve months of the year. The candlestick, composed of seventy pieces, refers to the twelve signs of the Zodiac, through which the seven planets take their course; and the seven lamps, on the top of the seven branches, bear an analogy to the planets themselves. The curtains, with the four colours of their materials, represent the four elements. The linen may signify the earth from whence it was derived; and the purple the sea, from the blood of a shell-fish, called *murex*, that gives it the tincture. The violet colour is a symbol of the air, and the scarlet of the fire. The linen garment of the high priest typifies the earth; and the violet colour the heavens. The pomegranate semble the lightning, as do the sound of the bells the thunder. The four coloured ephod bears resemblance to the four elements, and the intermixture weaving it with gold seems to refer to the rays from which we derive light. The middle of the ephod, or rationale, in the centre of the world, and the girdle about the body of the priest, the sea, which environs all things. The two stones of sardonyx signify the sun and moon; and the twelve other stones the twelve signs in the circle, which the Greeks call Zodiac. The purple coloured tiara, or mitre, hath an allusion to heaven; and the triple crown and plate may point out the glory of the majesty on high.

This shall suffice for the present: the sequel will furnish ample matter for the display of the piety and wisdom of our incomparable lawgiver.

CHAP. VIII.

Aaron elected high priest. Taxes, rites, and ceremonies. Dedication of the tabernacle and priests. Punishment of death inflicted on Nadab and Abihu, the sons of Aaron, for disobeying the injunction of Moses. Sacrifices and gifts of the heads of the tribes. Moses supplicates intimation of the Divine will in the tabernacle.

AFTER the tabernacle was completed, but before its consecration, Moses received the Divine command to appoint his brother Aaron high priest, being a man who, from his superior virtues, merited that dignity. To this end, having assembled the multitude, and, by expatiating on his virtues, his affections for them, and the dangers he had encountered in their behalf, obtained their unanimous applause and approbation of the choice of his brother, he thus addressed them:

"The work, O men of Israel, is now completed according to the will of God, through the means and abilities we have derived from his bounty; but as this tabernacle is the place which it pleaseth him to honour with his presence in an especial manner, the choice of a person to officiate in holy things, and make supplication for the people, becomes a main and principal concern. If this important matter had been committed to me, I might have deemed myself entitled to the office, not only from a principle of self-love, but a consciousness of the laborious tasks I have repeatedly performed to promote your interest: but it is the will of the Almighty, that Aaron be raised to the dignity of high priest, as a token of his approbation of his integrity. Let him therefore be invested with the sacred robes, the care of the altars, the performance of sacrifices, and the putting up supplications in behalf of the people. God will vouchsafe graciously to attend, from the singular regard he has shewn for your race, as well as the man appointed by his Divine command to the important office."

(a) The multitude, pleased with this address, unanimously acquiesced in the choice. Indeed, it must be admitted that Aaron, by reason of his descent, alliance to Moses, and many extraordinary qualifications, had superior claim to this honour. He had at this time four sons, Nadab, Abihu, Eleazer, and Ithamar.

Moses gave orders that the remainder of what had been collected for the building of the tabernacle, should be laid out in covers for the sacred vessels, and, indeed, for the general service of the tabernacle itself, to prevent the sustaining of any damage from rain or dust. Having once more convened the people, he levied, by way of impost, from each individual, half a shekel. The shekel is an Hebrew coin, equivalent to four Athenian drachms. They complied without the least reluctance. The number that offered amounted to six hundred and five thousand, five hundred and fifty. All these were persons of free condition, and from twenty to fifty years of age: and the money thus raised was appropriated to the service of the tabernacle.

Then followed the ceremony of the purification of the tabernacle and the priests in this manner. Having taken five hundred shekels worth of choice myrrh, and the like quantity of iris, cinnamon, and balsam (of most fragrant smell) half of the above weight, he caused them all to be pulverized; and being mixed in an hin of oil of olives (the Hebrew hin contains two Athenian choas) to be boiled up so as to compose an ointment. With this he anointed the priests, the tabernacle, and all the appurtenances, by way of purification. He also gave orders for the odours, and all necessary articles for the altar of incense: but these I shall not enumerate, lest I should be thought too prolix. It is necessary, however, to observe, that twice a day (that is before sun-rise and about sun-set) they were to burn incense, and supply the lamps with purified oil; three of which, in reverence to the Deity, were to remain burning every day upon the sacred candlestick, and the rest were to be lighted in the evening. The artificers, who acquired the greatest reputation in the performance of the various articles heretofore mentioned, were Bezaleel and Aholiab; for they improved and embellished the plans of others, as well as produced plans of their own; but Bezaleel, in the general opinion, had the preference. These grand and important works were finished in seven months; and this period completed a year from the time of their deliverance from out of Egypt.

In the beginning of the second year, in the month called by the Macedonians, Xanthicus, and by us Nisan, upon the new moon, they dedicated the tabernacle, with all its appurtenances, to the immediate service of God, who vouchsafed to signify his approbation of the same, by the manifestation of his presence in an especial manner. The rest of the sky being serene, a kind of (b) cloud overspread the tabernacle, not dark and gloomy, as precedes a winter storm, but almost penetrable to the human eye: from this distilled a dew giving intimation of the Divine presence.

Moses having recompensed the several artificers according to their respective merit, offered a sacrifice, at the Divine command, near the porch of the tabernacle, of a bull, a ram, and a kid, for the sins of the people. Of the particular ceremonies I shall speak hereafter. He then with the blood of the victims, sprinkled the vestment of Aaron, purifying both him and his sons with precious ointment and spring water, as priests of the Most High. This ceremony of purification, both of the tabernacle and the priests, was continued for seven successive days; but, on the eighth, a festival was appointed for the people, who, upon that occasion, vied with each other in shewing their liberality. No sooner were the victims placed on the altar, than a spontaneous fire issued from them, the flame of which resembled a flash of lightning which consumed all before it.

Aaron at the same time was visited with an affliction poignant as could befal a father; but he bore it with becoming patience and resignation, persuaded that nothing could happen without the Divine permission to accomplish the Divine purposes. His two eldest sons, Nadab and Abihu, bringing to the altar other victims than those appointed by Moses, were scorched by the violence of the flames: that immediate death ensued.

Moses gave orders for their funerals without the camp, and their sudden departure was universally regretted. Their relatives were strictly enjoined not to lament, as it would be unbecoming the sacerdotal office, by which they were solely devoted to the honour of God. Moses, rejecting all dignity as proffered him by the people, gave himself wholly up to the service of the Most High. He went no longer to Mount Sinai, but entering the tabernacle, there sought intimation of the Divine will. He appeared in every respect in a private capacity, nor distinguished himself in any instance, but in his care and concern for the common weal. He enacted such laws, for the regulation of the state, as tended to the honour of God, and the interest of the community. These laws, which he gave them in writing, will be particularized on a future occasion.

(a) It is worthy of observation, that the two principal qualifications of the high priest were, that he should have an excellent character for virtuous and good actions, and also that he should have the approbation of the people.

(b) This cloud was the usual signal to the Hebrews, by which they knew when to march, and when to [illegible] the tabernacle they continued where they [illegible] [illegible]

But here I muſt digreſs, a little, to make ſome remarks on the prieſts veſtments, which, in reality, afford no ſcope to falſe prophets, or the circulation of their impoſtures, as they can never adduce proofs of the Divine function, though the Hebrews had ſo many indubitable teſtimonies thereof.

The ſardonyx, which was fixed on the right ſhoulder of the high prieſt, ſhone remarkably bright, whilſt the Divine being was propitiouſly preſent at the ſacrifice, though the ſtone has no natural ſplendour, a circumſtance that muſt raiſe the admiration of all, but thoſe who affect to ridicule whatever is ſolemn and ſacred. Another more extraordinary inſtance was the indication of victory by the ſingular brilliancy of the twelve ſtones affixed to the eſſen upon the breaſt of the high prieſt, which had ſo powerful an effect as to aſſure the people of the Divine aid, upon the approach of a conflict with their enemies. The Greeks confirm, rather than diſpute this point, by terming the eſſen, in their language, *logion*, or oracle. But theſe extraordinary appearances ceaſing two hundred years before I undertook this work, as the Deity withdrew ſuch manifeſtations of his favor from a people who proved unworthy, I ſhall refer them to future conſideration, and revert to the former ſubject.

The concerns of the tabernacle and prieſts being fully ſettled, the people, elated with aſſurance of the Divine favour and protection, vied with each other in preſenting oblations, and ſhewing their gratitude to the Author of all mercies. The heads of the twelve tribes offered ſix waggons, with a yoke of oxen to each, to tranſport the tabernacle, as occaſion might require, beſides a ſilver charger, of an hundred and thirty ſhekels weight, and a ſilver bowl, of ſeventy ſhekels, both full of fine flour, mingled with oil, to be uſed in the ſacrifices, with an incenſe cup full of perfumes valued at ten daricks. They offered likewiſe a young bullock, a ram, and a lamb of a year old, for a burnt-offering, with a he-goat for a ſin offering. They brought, beſides, their peace-offerings, that is two bullocks a-day, five rams, with as many lambs and he-goats of a year old. Theſe ſacrifices continued for twelve ſucceſſive days.

As heretofore obſerved, Moſes ceaſed to aſcend the mountain, but received inſtructions for the formation of laws for regulating the government in the tabernacle. But this ſubject ſhall be diſcuſſed hereafter.

CHAP. IX.

Deſcriptions of ſacrifices, with their various forms and ceremonies.

SACRIFICES are of two kinds; one for private perſons, the other for the people in general, and they are performed in two diſtinct forms. In the one, all that is placed on the altar is conſumed, whence it is called *holocauſt*, or burned. The other is in token of thankſgiving, and made as a feaſt to thoſe who perform the ceremony.

With reſpect to the firſt, a private perſon brings an ox, a lamb, and a kid, each of the two laſt one year old, the former may be older, but they muſt all be males. Theſe being killed, the prieſts ſprinkle the altar with the blood, then having diſſected the victim and ſprinkled it with ſalt, they lay it on the altar, where a fire is already kindled, after which, having cleanſed the feet and inteſtines, they are laid with the reſt. The ſkins are the perquiſites of the prieſts. Such is the form of the burnt-offering or holocauſt.

In ſacrifices of peace-offering, or thankſgiving, the victims are of the ſame kind, but they may be more than a year old and of different genders. When theſe are offered, the altar is ſprinkled with blood, but the reins and caul, and all the fat, with the lobe of the liver, together with the tail of the lamb, are laid upon the altar. The breaſt, and right ſhoulder, are reſerved for the entertainment of the prieſts, but what remains may be eaten during two days by the offerers, and the reſt muſt be conſumed by fire. The ſame ceremony is obſerved in ſacrifices for ſins; but thoſe who cannot purchaſe large victims, may offer two young pigeons or turtles, one of which becomes the perquiſite of the prieſt, and the other is conſumed.

Thoſe who ſin through ignorance, offer a lamb and a female kid of the ſame age. The prieſt beſprinkles the altar with the blood, but not in the ſame manner as before, confining it to the extremities or horns of the altar. The perquiſites of the prieſts, in this caſe, are the ſkins, and the fleſh, which they muſt eat the ſame day in the tabernacle, as they are prohibited from reſerving any thing for the enſuing day. He who is conſcious of a ſin, though unknown to others, is to bring a ram to be eaten by the prieſts in the tabernacle the ſame day. Heads of tribes, making ſacrifice for their own ſins, offer in the ſame manner as private men, excepting that they bring a bull and a male kid.

In ſacrifices both private and public, the fineſt flour was to be uſed; to a lamb, the meaſure of an aſſaron, to a ram, two, to a bullock three. The flour is firſt mixed with oil, and then conſecrated upon the altar. Thoſe who ſacrifice bring with them oil in proportion to the victim, for an ox, the half of an hin, for a ram, a third, and for a lamb, a fourth. They preſent wine in the ſame proportion as oil, and ſprinkle it about the altar. If any perſon, without ſacrificing, and only to accompliſh a vow, brings fine flour, a ſmall handful is put upon the altar, and the reſt becomes the perquiſite of the prieſt, but whatever the prieſt offers muſt be burned. It is forbidden to ſacrifice the young of any beaſt with its dam, and alſo till it is eight days old. There are other ſacrifices for the cure of maladies, where cakes are eaten with the victims, but nothing muſt be reſerved till the next morning, after the prieſts have taken ſuch parts as law allots them.

CHAP. X.

Manner of celebrating feſtivals, with an account of their ſolemnities.

ACCORDING to poſitive command, a lamb of a year old muſt be daily offered at the public charge, one in the morning, and the other in the evening; but two were to be ſacrificed on the ſeventh or ſabbath-day, at the times ſtated above. Upon the ſolemnities of the new moons, beſides the daily offerings, they preſent ſeven lambs of a year's growth, a ram, and a kid, as an expiation of thoſe ſins of omiſſion, which happen through forgetfulneſs. Upon the ſeventh month (which the Macedonians call Hyperberetus) in addition to the above mentioned, we offered a bullock, one ſheep, ſeven lambs, and a kid. On the tenth of the ſame month they faſt till evening, and ſacrifice the ſame day a young bullock, two rams, ſeven lambs, and a goat for a ſin-offering. Beſides theſe, two kids are brought, one of which is ſent into the deſert, as a ſcape goat, or general expiation for ſin; the other is carried a ſhort ſpace from the tents, and by fire reduced to aſhes. In like manner they ſacrifice the bullock, which is not produced at the public charge, but at the expenſe of the high prieſt. After their death, the blood both of the bullock and kid, being conveyed into the tabernacle, the prieſt ſprinkles the cover with his fingers dipped in it ſeven times, upwards and downwards, and taking the remainder into the court, he pours it about the great altar. The high prieſt alſo preſents a ram for a burnt offering.

Upon the fifteenth day of the ſame month (winter then approaching) the people were commanded to pitch their tents contiguous to each other, as more convenient during the extremity of the inclement ſeaſon. On their arrival in the promiſed land, they were to repair to the metropolis as the ſeat of the holy temple, and there to celebrate a feſtival for the ſpace of eight days, and offer oblations of various kinds unto the Almighty, bearing in their hands a bundle, compoſed of myrtle, willow, palm, and citron.

On the firſt of theſe eight days they were to ſacrifice thirteen oxen, fourteen lambs, two rams, and a kid for a ſin-offering. The number of the lambs and rams with the goat, were to be the ſame for ſix days, but one bullock was to be abated daily till the number was reduced to ſeven. The eighth was to be a day of reſt, and obſerved as before deſcribed. This was the Feaſt of Tabernacles upon the Hebrews erecting their tents, and is conſtantly obſerved by our nation.

In the month of Xanthicus (which is Niſan) which commences the year on the fourteenth day [illegible] the sun being then in the first sign of the Zodiac, called Aries, we are commanded to solemnize an anniversary sacrifice called *pascha*, in commemoration of our deliverance out of Egypt. This feast is celebrated in tribes, without any reserve of what is offered. It is succeeded by that of the *azymes*, or unleavened bread, which commences the fifteenth and continues seven days, during which are diurnally sacrificed two bullocks, one ram, and seven lambs, for a burnt-offering, which are all consumed by fire; to which is added a kid as a sin-offering, as a donation to the priests.

On the second day of this festival they begin to taste of the fruits of the earth, which though gathered the preceding harvest season, remain till that time untouched. But previous to this, as a token of their gratitude to that Being from whom they derive every mercy, they offer the first fruits of the barley, in the following manner: having dried a handful of the ears, and by beating, cleansed it from the chaff, they offer an assaron of the same upon the altar, leaving the rest for the use of the priests. After this ceremony, they are allowed to avail themselves of the produce of the harvest at discretion. With these first fruits they likewise present a lamb for a holocaust.

Seven weeks (or forty-nine days) being elapsed after the passover, upon the fiftieth day, which the Hebrews call *asartha* (of the same signification as *pentecostos*, a fiftieth) they offered two assarons of leavened bread made of the finest flour, and two lambs as a sacrifice. These being solely oblations to the Deity, after the ceremony devolve to the priests, who make a reserve of them to the next day. The burnt-offerings consisted of three calves, two rams, and fourteen lambs, besides two kids for a sin-offering. No festival is celebrated without a burnt-offering, and desisting from manual labour, and all their forms and ceremonies are prescribed by laws. The unleavened bread, composed of twenty-four assarons of fine flour, was furnished at the public charge. The loaves are prepared the day before the sabbath, and in the morning are placed upon the sacred table, in the same order, and devoted in the same manner as before described. The incense being cast into the sacred fire in which the burnt-offerings were consumed, fresh was supplied upon fresh loaves. The high-priest, at his own charge, offered twice a-day of the finest flour, mixed with oil, and a little hardened by fire. The measure of the flour is an assaron. But of these ceremonies I shall treat more largely on a future occasion.

CHAP. XI.

Purification, with its particular laws, forms, and ceremonies.

MOSES, having separated the tribe of Levi, as selected to the immediate service of God, purified them with spring water and sacrifices adapted to the occasion. To their charge he committed the tabernacle with its appurtenances, and appointed them to minister to the priests, being consecrated and set apart to that office. An ordinance was likewise established, respecting abstinence from certain living creatures. The eating of blood was most solemnly prohibited, as containing the very life of the animal, as was also the flesh of beasts that died of themselves, together with the caul of goats, sheep, or oxen. Leprous persons were separated from society. Women, at certain temporary returns, were restricted from male intercourse for the space of seven days. Those who assisted at funerals were debarred from converse for the same space. In a word such as laboured under any infection, or had rendered themselves by any means unclean and obnoxious, were either subject to certain modes of purification, or secluded from society. Those who recovered from leprous, or any infectious diseases, were enjoined to testify their gratitude, by offering oblations according to the best of their abilities.

This proves the envy and fallacy of a fabulous report, that Moses fled out of Egypt, because he was infected with a leprosy, and that the Hebrews, whom he conducted towards the land of Canaan, laboured, in general, under that disease: for had that been the case, Moses would not have formed a law that reflected disgrace on himself, or countenanced such a law, if proposed by another. Besides, in many other nations, persons infected with that disease are not only exempt from the injunctions laid upon the Hebrews, but admitted to offices of the first dignity, both in the army and the state, as well as to religious privileges in general. Furthermore, admitting that Moses had been infected according to this report, he might have introduced clauses in particular statutes, to obviate the odium and penalty annexed to the same. It is therefore evident that malice is the source of this obloquy, and that the statutes were ordained from laudable motives. But let every man judge for himself.

Women, after delivery of a male child, were forbidden the temple for forty days. On their entrance they were to present their oblations, of which one part was consecrated, and the other belonged to the priests.

If any man suspected his wife of adultery, he was to bring an assaron of barley meal, and casting an handful upon the altar, the rest was reserved for the priests. Then one of the priests, placing the woman in the porch opposite the temple, and uncovering her head writes the sacred name of the Deity on a parchment, and causes her to swear with deadly imprecations on herself if perjured, that she has not violated her chastity: but if the suspicion arises through excess of love or jealousy, to implore that in ten months after she may bring forth a son. After this solemnity, the priest dips the parchment in water to erase the sacred name, pours it into a phial, and then taking some of the dust of the temple, and mingling it with the same, gives it to the woman to drink. If she has been unjustly accused she should prove pregnant, and bring forth a child, but if guilty, she should die an ignominious death. These are the laws prescribed by Moses, concerning sacrifices and purifications. Those respecting other particulars are as follow.

CHAP. XII.

Various laws respecting adultery, incest, and the marriage of priests. Cessation from tillage every seventh year. The year of jubilee. Customs of war. Disposition of the army. Use of the trumpets of silver.

ADULTERY was most solemnly prohibited, conjugal fidelity being justly deemed the basis of social happiness, as well as the most effectual security of the property and interest of the state in general, and of private families in particular. Incest, deviations from the laws of decency, and unnatural propensities in general, were likewise strictly forbidden, and those who transgressed were severely punished.

But the priests were enjoined to observe laws more rigid (a) than the people in common, being commanded to abstain not only from enormous crimes, but interdicted from marrying women cast off, or such as were prisoners, that had dwelt in any house of common reception, or had been divorced from any cause whatever. The high priest was not permitted even to marry a widow (though lawful for the other priests) but had liberty only to take a virgin to wife. He was also forbidden to approach a dead person, whilst other priests were allowed to see their deceased relatives.

Priests, in general, were to be men of integrity, of manners, and of sound body: if any one received an accidental blemish, he was allowed his portion with the other priests, but not permitted to minister in holy things. Purity was not only enjoined them in the performance of their sacred functions, but they were to preserve a rectitude of manners throughout their general conduct. Those therefore who entered on the sacred office were to be men chaste and abstemious. They were forbidden the use of wine in

(a) These words of Josephus are remarkable, that the Lawgiver of the Jews required of the priests a double degree of purity, in comparison of that required of the people, of which he gives several instances. This was also the case [illegible] among the [illegible] Christians, of the clergy in comparison of the laity, as the apostolical [illegible]

their vestments, and were also to offer up their sacrifices without any defect.

These laws were to be observed during their continuance in the desert, but there were others that were not to take place till they should enter into possession of the land of Canaan. Every seventh year, the earth was neither tilled nor planted, as people ceased from labour every seventh day. The spontaneous product was to be common without reservation, for the use of strangers as well as natives. The same decree was to take effect at the expiration of seven times seven years, and the year following, being the fiftieth, was called by the Hebrews jubilee, or liberty. All debtors, on this occasion, were to be released from imprisonment, bondmen, enjoined to servitude for transgressions of the laws, were to be set free, and all lands were to be restored to their first proprietors after this manner. Upon the approach of the jubilee, the seller and purchaser met together, and took a fair estimate of the profits and expenses that had been derived from and laid out on the land. If the former exceeded the latter, the seller immediately received possession, but if the contrary appeared, the purchaser, on satisfaction made him for the deficiencies, reinstated the seller in his property. If the profits and expenses were equal, restitution was made to the ancient possessor. The same law held good with respect to houses, for if the seller, within the space of the year, refunded the purchase money, the buyer restored him the premises, but if the year was expired, and the money not deposited, it became the legal property of the purchaser. These laws Moses received from the Divine intimation upon Mount Sinai, and they were by him communicated to the Hebrews for their due observation.

All matters relative to civil government being thus adjusted, Moses turned his thoughts to such concerns as respected the army. He issued a mandate to all the heads of tribes (that of Levi excepted) to muster, and make a report of all who were able to bear arms, in consequence of which they were found to amount to six hundred and three thousand and upwards, between the years of twenty and fifty. In the place of Levi (whose tribe was exempt from military engagements) he raised Manasses the son of Joseph as leader, and for Joseph substituted Ephraim [illegible] Jacob, as [illegible] Joseph brought to his sons by adoption.

While the army was encamped (a) the tabernacle was pitched in the centre, and guarded by three tribes, who took their respective stations. Between them were left spaces to pass and repass. They had likewise a market, and goods exposed to sale by artizans of the different occupations, so that it resembled a trading city. The priests were assigned their posts round about the tabernacle, and next to them the Levites (for of them there were, by computation, males exceeding the age of thirty, 23,880) as they officiated as assistants in holy concerns. During the time that the cloud hovered over the tabernacle, in token of the Divine presence, the people remained in the same places, and moved as they were directed by the cloud.

Moses invented a trumpet, made of silver, according to this model. In length it was almost a cubit, it was a little thicker than a flute, the pipe was strait, and the cavity, which was to convey and receive the wind, ended in the form of a bell, like trumpets in common. It is called, in the Hebrew language, a *sophra*. There were two of these trumpets made, one was to call the people to general assemblies, and the other to summon the heads of the tribes to hold consultation on the affairs of state, but at the sound of both, the princes, or heads, and the people, were to assemble in general.

The tabernacle was moved in this solemn order. On the first alarm of the trumpet, those who were encamped towards the east dislodged, on the next those to the southward, then the tabernacle was unfixed and carried in the centre, between six tribes in the front, and six in the rear, all the Levites officially attending. At the third alarm, those to the westward moved, and at the fourth, those on the north followed them. These trumpets were also used on sacred occasions, both on the sabbath and other days. Then also was the first passover celebrated by our ancestors after that in the desert, in commemoration of their deliverance from Egyptian bondage.

The whole form, order and mode of encampment of the Israelites, with the disposition of the twelve tribes, and the respective numbers of each, will be seen, at one view, by the following table.

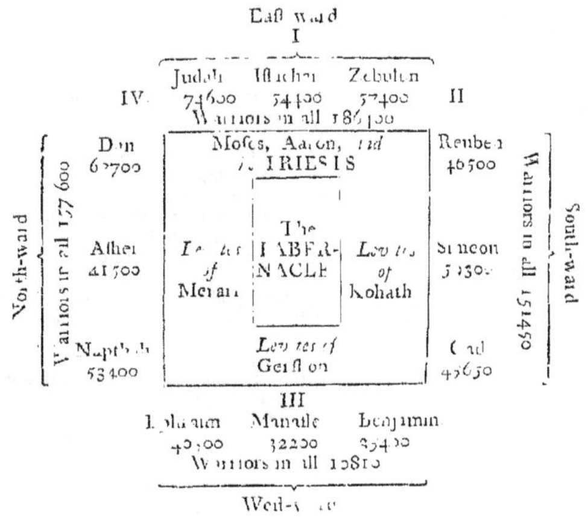

(a) Each of these camps had [illegible] Reuben [illegible] Judah [illegible] Ephraim, of [illegible] prophet [illegible] to shew his power [illegible] eagle, to shew his [illegible] in the execution of God's will [illegible] his Gospel [illegible] St. Luke [illegible] St. John [illegible]

CHAP. XIII.

Sedition against Moses. Hebrews obtain relief. Punished for mutiny.

SOON after the Hebrews left Mount Sinai, and, after a few stations by the way, they arrived at a place called Jeremoth. There the people again began to be mutinous, and to blame Moses for the hardships they had encountered in their travels, charging him with having persuaded them to leave a fertile country, and now reduced them to a necessity of wandering about in a state of misery and want, insomuch, that they had not water to drink, and should it happen that manna failed them, they must inevitably perish. Whilst they were loading him with the bitterest invectives, notwithstanding his consummate abilities, one of the multitude stepped forth, and exhorted them to regard him with gratitude for the wonders he had done for them, nor ever despair of the aid and assistance of the Almighty. But this friendly admonition incensed them the more, and increased their spleen against Moses, who, nevertheless, encouraged them in their despairing situation, and assured them that, notwithstanding the obloquy he had received at their hands, he would procure for them a store of provisions, not for one, but for many days. When they remained incredulous, and one of them asked whence he could raise provision for so numerous a body, he answered, "the great God and his servant, notwithstanding your reproaches, will never cease to be careful for you, as you will shortly perceive." Scarce had he spoken this, when the camp was covered with quails (*a*) of which they took great numbers. However, they were soon punished for their insolent reproaches, by so great a (*b*) plague amongst them, that the place retains the memory of their destruction to this day, and is called Cabrothaba, or Kibroth hattavah or, *The Sepulchres of concupiscence.*

CHAP. XIV.

Spies sent to Canaan. Multitude differently affected by their report. Mutiny against Moses. Appeased by Caleb and Joshua. Moses and Aaron intercede for the people. Their prayers heard.

WHEN Moses had conducted the Hebrews from thence to a place called Pharan, or the Straits, upon the confines of Canaan, he summoned the heads to a council, and thus addressed them. "Of the two great "benefits, liberty and the possession of an happy country, "promised you by the God of truth, you already enjoy the "one, and the other will speedily follow. We are now on "the borders of Canaan, nor can the force of united na-"tions, deprive us of the acquisition of it. Let us, there-"fore, prepare for a vigorous exertion, as we cannot ex-"pect that the inhabitants will resign their title without "resistance, or that we should obtain a conquest without "resolution. My counsel is, that certain spies be sent "out to survey the country, and the strength of the inha-"bitants. But above all things, let me recommend una-"nimity, and a firm reliance on the power and protection "of the Almighty."

The proposal of Moses met with general approbation, and twelve men of the first rank, one out of each tribe, were appointed as spies. Having surveyed the land of Canaan from the borders of Egypt, they came to mount Libanus, and having explored the nature of the soil, as well as the inhabitants, they returned after an absence of forty days. They brought with them samples of the fruits of the land, pointed out their excellence, and gave so pleasing an account of the country in general, as to inspire the people with resolution to engage in a contest. But they were dismayed, on the other hand, by the difficulty of the acquisition, being informed that the rivers were so wide and deep as to be impassable, and the mountains so steep as to be inaccessible; also that their cities were strongly fortified with walls and bulwarks. They also reported that, in Hebron, they had found the posterity of the giants. Upon the whole, the spies, intimidated themselves, represented the difficulties and horrors they had encountered in such a light, as struck the multitude with consternation: so that, giving up the conquest as impracticable, they dissolved the assembly, and returned home to their wives and children deploring their fate, as if the great Arbiter of all things had promised that which would never be effected. They also blamed Moses, and reviled both him and his brother Aaron, the high-priest. They passed the night in disquiet and reproaches, and in the morning re-assembled in a tumultuous manner, with an intention (*c*) to stone both Moses and Aaron, and then return to Egypt.

But two of the spies, Joshua, the son of Nun, of the tribe of Ephraim, and Caleb, of the tribe of Judah, fearful of the consequences of these tumults, rushed into the midst of the multitude, whom they endeavoured to appease, by desiring them not to despair of the accomplishment of the Divine promises, from any rumours that had been spread respecting the situation of affairs in Canaan, and exhorting them to attend to those who would be the principal agents in bringing about the expected event. "For (continued they) neither the height of mountains, nor the depth of rivers, can deter men of valour from the attempt, especially when they rely on the Divine aid. Let us, therefore, go forward without dismay, and in full confidence of victory, having the arm of Omnipotence to protect and defend us." Thus did they endeavour at once to appease the multitude, and inspire them with resolution, whilst Moses and Aaron, falling prostrate, humbly besought the Almighty, not for their own safety, but that he would be pleased to restore the despairing people to a quiet mind, who were now in such a state of tumult and disorder. The cloud then appeared, and resting upon the tabernacle, gave testimony of the Divine Presence.

CHAP. XV.

Moses foretells that the Israelites should wander in the desert forty years. They repent. Instances of the authority of Moses.

MOSES now boldly presented himself to the multitude, and informed them, that the Almighty, provoked at their outrages, was determined to punish them not indeed according to their deserts, but as tender parents chastised their children. For, that while he continued in the tabernacle, and besought Him in their behalf, he had recounted the benefits conferred upon them, and the many instances of their ingratitude and disobedience, particularly in giving more credit to the report of the spies than to his promise; for which cause, though he would not exterminate their whole race (whom he had preferred to the rest of mankind) yet he would not permit them to take possession of the land of Canaan, nor enjoy its abundance, but would cause them to wander in the desert forty years, promising, at the same time, to their children, the possession and enjoyment of those good things, which they had forfeited by their murmuring and disobedience."

(*a*) Commentators have differed in their opinions what this food was which we translate *quails*, some endeavouring to prove that our translation is right, whilst others attempt to shew, that, instead of *quails* the word should have been rendered *locusts*. The original term implies both, and perhaps both were sent at the same time. They complained for want of variety, and therefore God might give them the variety they lusted after. The Psalmist seems to favour this interpretation, when he says that God *rained flesh upon them as thick as dust, and feathered fowls like as the sand of the sea.* Psal. lxxviii. 27.

(*b*) Or, as some writers say, the leprosy, which proceeds from a precarious and [illegible] [illegible] which [illegible] upon the [illegible] [illegible] on the inner [illegible], it casts warts upon the extremities of the tendons and muscles, from whence arises a total corruption of the whole mass of blood.

(*c*) From this it [illegible] appears evident that the children of Israel were very obdurate and hardened wretches; for although God was daily working miracles, [illegible] [illegible] they would be [illegible] nor would they [illegible] [illegible]

When Moses had communicated these particulars, the people were greatly affected, and entreated him to procure their reconciliation with the offended Majesty of Heaven, that they might not continue to lead a wandering life, but be indulged with a permanent residence. But he replied, that this was inadmissible, for the Almighty was not incensed against them after the manner of men, but had, for his own wise ends, denounced that punishment which could not be averted. Nor is it improbable that Moses, though but a single individual, should pacify such multitudes, for he was assisted by power Divine, which now wrought the people into a persuasion, that all their calamities were the effect of their contumacy and disobedience.

But Moses was as admirable for his virtue and prevailing influence over the minds and conduct of men, not only during his natural life, but remains so, in these our days, as there is not one of the Hebrews but holds himself as much bound to obey his ordinances and institutions now, as if he were actually present with them. There are many reasons to suppose that his power was more than human. Amongst others, when certain strangers have travelled from parts beyond the Euphrates, at immense charge and great peril, to honor our temple and offer sacrifice, they were not permitted to partake of the victims, because Moses had forbidden it, from their being disqualified. Some have not sacrificed at all, while others have left their sacrifices unfinished, and many more have been forbidden access to the temple, choosing rather to adhere to the institutions of Moses, than in any one instance indulge their inclinations, and that from motives truly conscientious. Thus did the legislation of Moses appear to be truly Divine.

As another instance, a little before the wars of the Jews, when Claudius was emperor of the Romans, and Ismael was an high priest, so great a famine prevailed, that an assaron of meal was sold for four drachms, and there was brought to the festival of Azymes, the quantity of seventy *corus* (which are equal to thirty-one Sicilian, and forty-one Athenian *medimni*) yet not one of the priests would touch a grain of it, notwithstanding the general distress, and that from an awful dread of the Divine punishment of sin, whatever plea might be urged by the offender.

The singular events of former times, therefore, should not excite our wonder, when we consider that the writings of Moses are in such force even to this day, that our professed enemies acknowledge our government and laws were instituted by God himself, and that through the means of his chosen servant.

END OF THE THIRD BOOK

FLAVIUS JOSEPHUS

ON THE

ANTIQUITIES

OF THE

JEWS.

BOOK IV.

[RECORDING A PERIOD OF ABOUT THIRTY-EIGHT YEARS.]

CHAP. I.

The Hebrews wage war with the Canaanites without taking counsel from Moses, and are defeated.

THE troubles and afflictions both of body and mind to which the Hebrews were continually exposed in the desert, rendered them so desperate, that, notwithstanding the express prohibition of the Almighty, and the most powerful dissuasives of Moses, they determined on a war against the Canaanites, alledging that God would vouchsafe them his aid, not out of regard to the intercession of Moses, but the especial favour he had shewn their nation from the time of their forefathers, whose virtues he had [illegible] by singular interpositions of his providence. They had also a presumptuous reliance on their own strength and abilities, though Moses should endeavour to counteract their efforts. Indeed, they seemed to have imbibed a general opinion, that it would redound to their interest to establish a form of government amongst themselves, and that though Moses had been, in some degree, accessary to their deliverance from Egyptian bondage, it did not follow that they were under an obligation of submitting to his tyrannical imposition, [illegible] God had communicated his will [illegible] them from a partial attachment to him. The leaders of this design took care also to insinuate, that as they were all the posterity of Abraham, his vanity and [illegible] were highly censurable, in affecting [illegible] knowledge of events that should happen to him from Divine [illegible] peculiar to himself, and that therefore it would be prudent in them to oppose his arrogant pretences, [illegible] their sole confidence in the Almighty for obtaining possession of the country he had promised them, [illegible] continuation of the calamities [illegible] proceed to [illegible] of Omnipotence, [illegible] to

This proposal being universally approved, as the wisest expedient, they sallied forth against their enemies who not being the least intimidated, either by the attack, or the multitudinous body which made it, resisted so valiantly, that the Hebrews were routed with great slaughter, compelled to a most ignominious flight, and pursued even to their very camp. This unexpected overthrow reduced them to a state of desperation, as from thence they concluded it was inflicted as a punishment from the Almighty for embarking in an enterprize without his council and approbation.

When Moses observed the desponding situation of his countrymen, and that the enemy were elated with their victory, he deemed it proper to withdraw the army into the wilderness, to a farther distance from the Canaanites. The people now resigned themselves up to his guidance, conscious that without him their affairs could not prosper. They accordingly decamped, and [illegible] into the desert, resolving not to make a farther attempt against their enemies, before they were favoured with due intimation of the Divine will.

But as it often happens amongst promiscuous multitudes, especially upon ill success, that the [illegible] headstrong and disobedient to command, so it [illegible] with respect to the Hebrews upon this occasion, for [illegible] in number to six hundred thousand, [illegible] their fortunes, having been [illegible] were now more exasperated by their [illegible] occasioned a sedition, of which there [illegible] similar instance amongst the Greeks, or even [illegible]. It would have proved destructive, had not Moses, forgetting the [illegible] his life, interposed in their behalf. Nor were they totally abandoned [illegible] Almighty [illegible] which had so often protected them, [illegible] the indignities they [illegible] and their disobedience to the Divine commands [illegible] them from that danger into which they brought themselves by their mutiny and rebellion, [illegible] in the sequel.

CHAP II

Sedition of Corah and the multitude against Moses and his brother Aaron, concerning the priesthood Corah raises a mutiny, and accuses many of the leaders from Moses, who addresses them upon that occasion

CORAH, an Hebrew of great wealth and influence, and famous for his eloquence, becoming jealous of the dignity to which Moses had attained, raised a clamour against him amongst the Levites, who were of the same tribe, by suggesting to them, in an occasional harangue, "That it redounded to their dishonour, thus tamely to "suffer Moses, under pretence of the Divine command, "to retain unlimited authority, vest the priesthood in his "brother Aaron without their suffrages, and bestow places "of honour and profit at pleasure" He added, "that "these measures were the more oppressive and grievous, as "founded on the arts of sophistry and insinuation, that "those who are conscious of deserving posts of dignity, "endeavour to obtain them, not by force, but mild per-"suasion that it was the interest of a state to check the "ambition of such aspiring individuals, before they ac-"quired an influence that might prove destructive" He demanded by what authority Moses had conferred the priesthood on Aaron and his sons? enforced his own title as superior to theirs, both by descent and property, that if it was the will of God, it should be vested in the tribe of Levi, and concluded with observing, that if the honour appertained to the most ancient of the tribes, that of Reuben should enjoy it, in which case it would fall to the lot of Dathan, Abiram, or Peleth, as claimants from antiquity and opulence

This address of Corah might have had the semblance of public virtue, but it was dictated by interested principles, to raise a tumult, and obtrude himself into the office of the priesthood In a short time, indeed, it had, in some degree, the desired effect, for the opinions he advanced being industriously propagated by his party, as well as exaggerated by report, those who were averse to the interest of Aaron, raised a party of two hundred and fifty to join in this conspiracy, wrest the priesthood from him, and transfer it to Corah Nay, the multitude were so far prevailed on by these factious proceedings, that they attempted to stone Moses, and surrounded the tabernacle in tumultuous uproar, exclaiming, that the tyrant should be exterminated, who, under the pretext of the Divine command, had reduced them to a state of abject slavery, and adding, that if God had chosen one to the office of high priest, he would not have conferred it on a person who was far inferior to others, and also, if it had been so decreed, Aaron would undoubtedly have obtained it by the suffrages of the people, and not the usurped authority of his brother

Moses, conscious of his integrity, and that the appointment of his brother to the priesthood was pursuant to the Divine will, was by no means dismayed by the calumny of Corah, nor its effect upon the incensed multitude, in whose presence he thus addressed their factious leader

"I readily grant (said he) that you, Corah, and your "associates, are all worthy of honour, but I contemn not "the rest of the assembly, though inferior to you in riches, "and other endowments Aaron was not appointed to "the office of high priest for his wealth (for you are "more opulent) nor for his nobility, for in that we are "equal, as deriving our origin from the same progenitor "Nor have I deprived any man of his right in what I "conferred on my brother Nay, if I had not been ac-"tuated by becoming motives, I should have taken the "office upon myself Besides it would have been the "height of folly to expose myself to danger by an act of "injustice, from which another might reap benefit, ex-"clusive of myself, but far be from me such impiety "and injustice The Almighty would neither have suf-"fered his honour to be thus violated, or [illegible] have "remained in such ignorance of what was acceptable to "him It was God who chose the priest it is God who "absolves me from the charge of criminality But now "admitting that Aaron holds the office by Divine ap-"pointment, without any partiality on my part, he will "rest his cause on your suffrages, without insisting upon "the legality of what has passed, though with your ap-"probation This proposal is to convince you that am-"bition is not his motive and that he is ready to part "with his just right, provided it could be the means of "suppressing your sedition It would have been highly "impious to have refused an office of Divine appoint-"ment, so that the acceptance of it can be no just ground "of offence But as it is more reasonable that the donor "should confirm the gift, let the matter be once again "referred to the Divine appointment, and then you may "abide by the person so chosen to the sacred function "Surely Corah would not be so presumptuous as to ques-"tion the Divine right of appointing the office of high "priest. One day, without further controversy, will "bring this point to an issue Let all the claimants ap-"pear to-morrow with their censers in their hands, with "fire and incense in them You, Corah, must patiently "wait the Divine determination, without presuming to "arrogate a pre-eminence, but appear amongst the com-"petitors Nor do I see what should exclude Aaron from "putting in his claim, as he hath hitherto maintained an "unexceptionable character in the exercise of his func-"tion, and is also of the same tribe of yourself When "you are all together, you shall offer incense in the pre-"sence of the people, and let that person whose offerings "shall be most acceptable in the sight of God, be declared "and confirmed high priest This will decide the point "in dispute, and acquit me of the charge, as malevolent-"ly as falsely alledged against me."

CHAP III.

Tremendous judgment on the authors of the sedition The office of high priest confirmed to Aaron and his sons

THIS address of Moses not only appeased the clamour of the multitude, but disposed them in his favour as a person in every respect qualified to fill the character he represented, and thereupon the assembly separated

The next day the people re-assembled to attend the sacrifice, and wait the event of the election, for which they were in general, very solicitous, though attached to different interests Some were tumultuous, and for proceeding in a riotous manner against Moses but the wise and discreet part recommended peace and good order, persuaded that sedition and mutiny were subversive of all government, as the rabble are ever fond of novelty and ready to revile their superiors, as well as receive and propagate slander upon every occasion

Moses, however, summoned Dathan and Abiram to attend the issue of the sacrifice and prefer their respective claims, but they absolutely refused, avowing that they would no longer submit to his usurped authority Upon this answer, Moses took some of the elders with him, and notwithstanding his exalted station went in person to these revolters When Dathan and his associates heard of the approach of Moses and the elders they came out of their tents, with their wives and children resolutely to wait for him, having their attendants at hand, in order to repel force by force, if necessity should require it Moses proceeded directly till he came to Dathan, when, lifting up his hands to heaven, he invoked the Almighty in the hearing of the whole multitude, to the following effect

"Almighty God, thou who art [illegible] of the Universe, "the judge of all my actions, art witness that whatever I "have done has been in perfect [illegible] to thy will "thou, who, in compaſſion to the Hebrews, haſt been gracious to them, as well as my conſtant ſupport upon every occaſion, hear my prayer, thou, who knoweſt the ſecrets of all hearts, vouchſafe to bring the truth to light, and manifeſt the ingratitude of theſe men, thou from whom nothing can be hidden, and to whom is known every action of my life, do thou be pleaſed to bear teſtimony to my innocence, againſt thoſe who revile and ſlander me Thou knoweſt that I quitted a quiet and comfortable life, which I enjoyed through thy bleſſing upon my endeavours and the favour of my father-in-law, Jethro, for the exchange of hazardous enterprizes, for the liberty and ſecurity of theſe people But now, ſince I am become obnoxious to thoſe who, by my means have been delivered from the extremeſt difficulties and dangers, do thou, Lord, that didſt appear to me out of the fire upon mount Sinai, let me hear thy voice, and be witneſs of thy Divine directions Thou, that didſt honour me with an embaſſy into Egypt, humbling the pride of the Egyptians, and delivering the Hebrews out of their bondage, thou that laidſt the power of Pharaoh at my feet, turning the ſea into dry land, and that dry land into ſea again, for the ſafety of thy people, and the confuſion of their enemies, thou, who gaveſt us arms when we were defenceleſs, who madeſt the bitter waters ſweet and pleaſant, and didſt ſupply us with water in extremity out of the rock, as well with food out of the ſea, and meat from heaven, thou that didſt lay the foundation of our government, that art the judge of all things, avenge my cauſe, and witneſs for me, that I have not been corrupted to favour injuſtice, or eſpouſe the intereſt of a rich man to the oppreſſion of a poor one, yet I ſtand accuſed of partial adminiſtration as if I had confirmed the prieſthood on my brother, from motives of private affection and not at thy Divine command Be pleaſed, therefore, to make appear, that all things are diſpoſed by thy providence, and brought to paſs, not by chance, but thy ſpecial appointment Teſtify thy wonted kindneſs to the Hebrews, by inflicting condign puniſhment on Dathan and Abiram, for ſuggeſting that thy purpoſes are oppoſed by my arts Viſit theſe detractors from thy glory with exemplary vengeance Let the earth on which they tread ſwallow them up, with their families and ſubſtance, to the manifeſtation of thy power, and, as an example to poſterity not to think unworthily of the Majeſty of Heaven But if the charge alledged is proved againſt me, may theſe curſes light on mine own head, and my accuſers be perfectly happy After thou haſt puniſhed the diſobedient, keep the reſt in peace, concord, and the obſervance of thy commandments, ſince it is contrary to thy juſtice to confound the innocent with the guilty"

Moſes had ſcarcely uttered theſe words, intermixed with tears, when ſuddenly the earth was ſo convulſed, that the multitude were ſtruck with horror, and a diſmal outcry was heard throughout all their tents At length, with a dreadful noiſe, the ground opened, and ſwallowed up the ſeditious, with all their property, and immediately cloſed ſo exactly, that no ſign of the rupture was to be ſeen

Thus periſhed a ſeditious faction as examples of the power and vengeance of the Moſt High They fell unpitied by their own kindred nay, the whole multitude rejoiced at this ſignal diſplay of the Divine Juſtice, in the extermination of ſuch obnoxious members of the ſtate, ſuch peſts of their nation and ſociety in general

After the extinction of Dathan and his accomplices, Moſes ſummoned the candidates for the prieſthood, referring the people to the choice of that perſon whoſe ſacrifice ſhould be moſt acceptable unto God There aſſembled upon the occaſion two hundred and fifty perſons, who, for the virtues of their anceſtors, and their own merit were held in eſteem With theſe ſtood forth Aaron and Corah, offering, before the tabernacle, the incenſe they brought in their cenſers, when ſuddenly appeared ſo fierce a fire as to exceed that of burning mountains, or the conflagration of whole foreſts It was aſtoniſhingly bright and flaming, and beyond doubt, came from heaven, as no earthly materials could have produced ſuch a blaze. By the force of this fire, Corah, and his two hundred and fifty accomplices, were ſo totally conſumed, that the leaſt relic of their bodies was not to be found Aaron alone remained untouched, as a certain evidence that it was the work of a Divine Power Moſes, to perpetuate the memory of this awful judgment, commanded Eleazar, the ſon of Aaron, to conſecrate their cenſers, and faſten them to a brazen altar, as a warning to future generations not to preſume to counteract the deſigns of the Moſt High From theſe judgments it was evident beyond a doubt, that Aaron obtained not the prieſthood by ſiniſter means, but by Divine appointment, ſo that he held it ever after, but not without a diſpute concerning his title

CHAP IV

Various occurrences which befel the Hebrews in the deſert, during the ſpace of thirty-eight years Regulations reſpecting the ſacerdotal office, and other ſolemn concerns Death of Miriam, the ſiſter, and Aaron, the brother, of Moſes.

NOTWITHSTANDING the puniſhments inflicted upon the abettors of the former faction, a new ſedition aroſe, from an opinion which the people had imbibed, that the late judgments, admitted by them as the effects of a Divine Power, were brought to paſs merely for the ſake of Moſes To him, therefore, they imputed theſe calamities, ſuggeſting, that theſe men were not puniſhed for their ſins but through the ſolicitation of Moſes, as no crime could be alledged to their charge unleſs their zeal for the ſervice of God could be ſo called That Moſes availed himſelf of the deſtruction of the people, in confirming his brother in the prieſthood, and entailing it upon his line, ſince it was certain none of the former candidates would preſume to put themſelves in competition The kindred of the deceaſed embraced this opportunity of repreſenting to the multitude the neceſſity of reſtraining the exorbitant power of Moſes, which they might do eaſily and effectually

Moſes, to prevent the conſequences of another tumult, convened the multitude, heard their grievances and without making reply, leſt they ſhould be more incenſed, appointed the heads of the tribes to bring every one a rod, with the names of their tribes inſcribed upon them, promiſing that the prieſthood ſhould be veſted in him, upon whoſe rod God ſhould ſhew any particular ſign This propoſal being acceded to, they brought their rods, with the inſcriptions as directed Aaron brought his rod amongſt the reſt, on which was inſcribed the name of the tribe of Levi Moſes laid all their rods in the tabernacle, and the next day produced them, which were eaſily known by the reſpective marks that were ſet upon them. They were found all to remain in the ſame form, that of Aaron excepted, which ſprouted out with branches and buds, and what was more wonderful, bearing ripe almonds, the rod being of the wood of the almond tree The people, amazed at this extraordinary ſpectacle, abated in their animoſity towards Moſes and Aaron, acknowledged the Divine interpoſition in favour of the latter, admitted his right of election, thus confirmed a third time by the Divine approbation, an event that put a happy period to the factions and ſeditions which had prevailed amongſt the Hebrews

The tribe of Levi being dedicated to God's immediate ſervice, were already exempted from military concerns, but leſt worldly cares might divert them from due attention to the duties of their function, Moſes ordained that, after the land of Canaan ſhould, by the Divine aid, be conquered, forty-eight of the beſt cities ſhould be allotted for the maintenance of the Levites, with two thouſand cubits of land contiguous to the walls of the place He moreover enjoined a tenth part of the yearly profits ariſing from the fruits of the earth, and collected from the whole body of the people, to be paid as a duty to the prieſts and

Levites, which has been duly observed ever since. Having mentioned these matters we shall now state what exclusively belongs to the priests themselves.

It was ordained, that, of the forty-eight cities before mentioned, the Levites should yield thirteen of them to the priests, and the tenth part of the fifths, besides the first fruits of all the products of the earth, as an offering to God. The firstling of all four-footed beasts allowed for sacrifice, if a male, it was to be delivered to the priests to sacrifice, to be afterwards eaten in the city with their family. For those which, by the law, were forbidden to be eat, the owner was to present a shekel and a half, instead of a firstling, and for the first-born of a man, five shekels. There was a duty also imposed upon wool and corn, the one from sheep-shearing, the other from baking of bread.

When those who are called Nazareens, and are bound, by vow, neither to cut their hair, or to drink wine, have accomplished their vow, and present themselves to have their hair consecrated, whatever they offer in sacrifice belongs to the priests. Those that call themselves *corban*, that is, by interpretation, *a gift*, when they desire to be discharged of their obligation and voluntary vow, they pay a duty to the priest of fifty shekels for a man, and thirty for a woman, and those who have not the means, must refer themselves to the discretion of the priest. Those who kill a beast for private use, and not for sacrifice, were to allow the priest the breast and the right shoulder. This is the allotment by Moses to the priests, besides the sin-offering, as mentioned in the foregoing book. It was likewise ordained that the wives, children, and servants of the priests, should have a share in all contributions, except the sin-offering, of which only those priests who officiate were to partake, and that in the tabernacle in the very same day.

Affairs being thus settled, and the mutiny appeased, Moses removed the camp to the borders of Idumæa, having dispatched ambassadors to the king to grant his troops a free passage through his country, on condition of peaceable behaviour, and paying for whatever provision they might require. But the king refused to comply with the requisition, and drew up an army to oppose him, if he should offer to force his way. Moses sought Divine counsel, and being prohibited from making the first attack, took his way through the desert.

At this time died Mariam, (*a*) the sister of Moses, the fortieth year after their departure out of Egypt, and in the beginning of the month Xanthicus. She was magnificently interred, at the public charge, on a mountain called Sin, and, after thirty days mourning, Moses caused the people to be purified, in this manner: the high priest took a young red heifer, without blemish, into a very clean place, a little way from the camp, where he killed it, dipped his finger seven times in the blood, and therewith sprinkled the tabernacle. He then put the whole heifer into the fire, skin, entrails, and all, casting in a stick of cedar, a little hyssop and scarlet wool. A young man, of unspotted chastity, gathered up the ashes, and put them in a clean place. Those who stood in need of purification, either from having touched a dead body, or assisted at a funeral, had only to cast some of those ashes into spring water, dip a branch of hyssop in it and sprinkle themselves with it on the third and the seventh days. Moses ordained, that this ceremony of purification should be used when the Hebrews should be put in possession of the promised land.

These forms having been observed for the death of his sister, Moses led them through the desert into Arabia, and arrived at the metropolis formerly called Arce, now Petra, where there was a very high mountain. Aaron being foretold by his brother that his dissolution approached, ascended this mountain, divested himself of his priestly robes, which he delivered to his son Eleazar as his successor in office, and gave up the ghost there, in the sight of the whole multitude, in the 123d year of his age, and in the first moon of the month of August, called by the Athenians, Hecatombaeon, by the Macedonians, Lous, by the Hebrews, Sabba, and by the Romans, Augustus. His sister also departed this life in the same year.

CHAP. V.

Moses obtains a conquest over the kings, Sehon and Og, and distributes their possessions, by lot, to two tribes and a half of the Hebrews.

AFTER the funeral (*b*) obsequies for his brother were past (which continued thirty days) Moses decamped and pitched his tents near the river Arnon that springs from the mountains of Arabia, and running through the desert, empties itself into the lake Asphaltitis, dividing the country of the Moabites from that of the Amorites. This country is very fruitful.

Moses sent a very respectful message to Sehon, king of the Amorites, requesting permission to pass through his territories, with assurance that the inhabitants should not be molested, and that all expenses incurred should be duly discharged. Sehon refused him and marched his forces to the banks of the river, to oppose the passage of the Hebrews.

When Moses found the Amorites disposed to hostility and considered that the Hebrews, through idleness and want, might again relapse into their former seditious spirit, he sought the Divine will whether he should force his passage by the sword.

Having not only obtained permission, but assurance of victory, he animated the army to such a degree, that, without hesitation, they marched up and charged the enemy with the utmost resolution. Sehon and his troops, notwithstanding their former defiance of the Hebrews, were now struck with consternation. Their only hope was in flight, and the security of their fortified places, but this was vain, for, at the first onset, they were routed, fled in the greatest confusion before the Hebrews, who, being alert and light armed, as well as expert in the use of their slings and darts, reached those they could not otherwise overtake, and cut off vast numbers at the river where they stopped to quench their thirst, and amongst the rest Sehon the king. The victory in fine, was decisive. The Hebrews obtained a prodigious booty, as well as abundance of corn, as the harvest was not yet gathered in. Indeed they ransacked the country without controul, as they met with no resistance, and had only to enjoy the fruits of their conquest.

Thus were the Amorites destroyed, being destitute both of conduct and courage, either to prevent or oppose the fatal attack. The Hebrews, of course, became masters of their country, which is a kind of peninsula betwixt three rivers, Arnon on the south, Jaboc (that falls into the Jordan) on the north, and the Jordan itself on the west.

In their prosperous situation the Hebrews had yet another enemy to encounter. This was Og, king of Galadene, and of Gaulonitis, who was marching to the relief of Sehon, his ally. Though informed on his way of the attack and total defeat, he determined to put the matter to the issue of another effort, but he was fatally disappointed, for he fell himself and his army was totally cut off.

Moses after this victory, passed the river Jaboc, and entering Og's dominions, laid all waste before him. The inhabitants were opulent and powerful then king was brave and resolute, as well as of enormous bulk and stature, as appeared from the dimensions of his bed, found in his palace at Rabatne. The frame was of iron, was four cubits in breadth, and nine in length. This success was not only attended with present advantages to the Hebrews, but the

(*a*) Mariam was the eldest of the three, and was near an hundred and thirty years old. [illegible] assures us, that in his time her tomb was found at Kadesh, [illegible] distance from Petra, the capital of Arabia. Several [illegible] are of opinion, that she died a virgin, and that she was the legislatrix and governess of the Hebrew women, as Moses was the legislator of the [illegible]

(*b*) Aaron was buried on the spot where he died [illegible] to bury persons of eminence on high places. See Joshua [illegible]

foundation of future conqueſts; for they poſſeſſed themſelves of ſixty fortified places, that were under his government, as well as acquired immenſe booty.

CHAP. VI.

War between the Hebrews and Midianites. Transactions between Balaak, king of the Moabites, and Balaam, a prophet. The Hebrews seduced to idolatry. Fate of Zimri and Cozbi.

MOSES, after theſe repeated ſucceſſes, removed his camp to a ſpacious plain near Jericho, an opulent city, abounding with palm-trees and balm. The people being now elated with conqueſt, and diſpoſed to gratify their martial propenſity, their leader, after ſacrificing and feaſting, detached a party to lay waſte the country of the Midianites. This war originated from the following cauſes.

Balaak king of the Moabites, an ancient ally of the Midianites, from the increaſing power of the Hebrews, began to entertain apprehenſions for the ſecurity of his territories, not knowing that they were prohibited by the Divine injunction from attempting the (*a*) conqueſt of any country, but that of Canaan. Not deeming it by any means prudent to make war upon a people fluſhed with victory, but yet deſirous of ſtopping their progreſs, he ſent ambaſſadors to the Midianites, to conſult with them on the means of their common ſecurity. The Midianites diſpatched Balaak's ambaſſadors, with ſome leading men of their own, to one *Balaam beyond the Euphrates, a famous prophet*, and attached to them, requeſting him to come over to them, and curſe the Iſraelites. The prophet entertained the ambaſſadors hoſpitably, and ſought the Divine will as to the anſwer he ſhould give them. Being forbidden to comply with their requeſt, he told them that, though he had been diſpoſed to gratify them, he was ſtrictly enjoined to the contrary by that adorable Being to whom he owed the gift of prophecy: and added, that the people they deſired him to curſe were highly favoured of God. He therefore adviſed them to make peace with the Hebrews upon any conditions, and thus diſmiſſed the ambaſſadors. But the Midianites, urged by the importunity of Balaak, ſent back the ſame ambaſſadors upon the ſame errand; when Balaam again conſulted the Divine will, and anſwer was given, "That he might go with the ambaſſadors." Not conceiving that the terms in which the anſwer was uttered implied diſapprobation, although it was in the affirmative, he accordingly went with them. As he proceeded on his way, an angel met him in a narrow place betwixt two walls. The aſs on which he rode, at the ſight of the viſion, ſtopped, and, upon his ſtriking and preſſing her to go forward, cruſhed him againſt the wall, nor could he by any means ſtimulate her to proceed. While the angel kept his ſtation, and the prophet continued tormenting the beaſt, it pleaſed the Almighty to open her mouth in a complaint of the injuſtice and cruelty of her maſter in ſtimulating her to get forward, when the angel of the Lord ſtood in the paſſage to oppoſe his progreſs. As he ſtood amazed at the prodigy, the angel rebuked him for his conduct, telling him the beaſt was not in fault, but that he deſerved chaſtiſement, for preſuming to take a journey contrary to the declared will of God.

Balaam would have returned, but he was commanded by God, through means of the angel, to proceed, charging him to utter only that with which he ſhould be inſpired.

After this charge he went to Balaak, who entertained him with reſpect. The prophet deſired the king that he might be conducted to ſome high mountain to ſurvey the Hebrew camp. Balaak therefore, accompanied the prophet, royally attended, to the top of the mountain, which was about ſixty furlongs diſtant from the camp. The prophet, having made his obſervations, directed ſeven altars to be raiſed, and ſeven bulls, and as many rams, to be prepared for ſacrifices. This being done in order to form a judgment upon the point in queſtion, Balaam having digeſted his obſervations, with his face toward the Hebrews, ſpoke to the following purport:

"Happy people! Providence your guide, your ſupport, you ſhall enjoy abundance of all good things, acquire a reputation above all men for your exemplary virtues, and your fame ſhall excel that of your progenitors, as the Almighty will take you under his immediate protection, and render you, of all nations under the ſun, peculiarly bleſſed. You ſhall poſſeſs the rich land promiſed you, and your poſterity ſhall hold it for ever. Your fame ſhall be extended throughout the univerſe, and your iſſue ſo multiplied as to be diffuſed throughout every part of the earth. Wonderful body, thus compoſed of the deſcendants of one ſingle man! The land of Canaan muſt, at preſent, ſuffice you, though not adequate to your number or dignity; but hereafter you ſhall have the whole world for your habitation, ſo that both on the iſlands, and the continent, your progeny ſhall equal the ſtars in the firmament. Though ſo numerous, you ſhall lack nothing but enjoy plenty in peace, conqueſt in war, and you ſhall hold your enemies in ſubjection. May our adverſaries, therefore, be yours; for deſtruction ſhall attend thoſe who riſe againſt you, and their poſterity ſhall rue the conduct of their fathers, in daring to oppoſe you. For theſe extraordinary tokens of favour you are to adore the providence of God, who can exalt or deject, according to his ſovereign will."

Theſe words Balaam delivered as dictated by the ſpirit of prophecy, at which Balaak, being much incenſed, exclaimed, that he had violated his promiſe, having, with a view of great rewards, been brought there to curſe the Hebrews, and when it came to a criſis, pronounced a bleſſing inſtead of a curſe. In vindication of himſelf, the prophet thus replied:

"Can the king imagine that when prophets are called upon to ſpeak concerning future events, they can diſcover or conceal what they liſt? They are only paſſive inſtruments to convey Divine decrees. They ſpeak without knowledge or thought. I am conſcious that I came hither, at the earneſt ſolicitation both of yourſelf and the Midianites, with a deſire of giving you ſatiſfaction. But can I counteract the power and will of God? Nay, I was diſpoſed to do that, which I afterwards found I dared not preſume to do. When once under the direction of the Superior Power we are no longer under our own guidance. I entertained not a thought of uttering a word in favour of the Hebrews, or the bleſſing reſerved for them; but as it is the will of God to render them a great and happy people, I have been compelled to ſpeak, what you have heard, inſtead of what I had previouſly determined to ſay upon the ſubject. However, fully to comply with your deſire and that of the Midianites, let us erect other altars, and provide new ſacrifices, and once more make trial if it be the Divine will that I curſe theſe people."

Balaak highly approved of the propoſal and the ſacrifices were accordingly repeated; but the prophet could not obtain permiſſion to curſe the Hebrews. On the contrary, he fell on his face, and foretold the fate of thoſe kingdoms and cities which ſhould oppoſe them, of which ſome are not yet extant, whilſt others, to our knowledge, have fulfilled the prediction, both on the continent and in

(*a*) What Joſephus remarks here is worthy of obſervation, viz. that the Hebrews were never to meddle with the Moabites or any other people but thoſe belonging to the land of Canaan, and the countries of Sehon and Og beyond Jordan, and [illegible] the deſcendants of Lot [illegible] therefore no other people had reaſon to fear their conqueſt but that those countries given them by God, were their proper and peculiar portion among the nations, and [illegible] who endeavoured to diſturb them ſhould be [illegible] juſtly left or [illegible] islands, from whence we infer, upon good ground, that the remainder will, in due time take effect

Balaak being highly displeased with this disappointment of his hope and expectation, dismissed the prophet abruptly, but as he approached the Euphrates, on reflection, he desired to speak with the king and princes of the Midianites, whom he thus addressed

"To convince you, O king, and ye princes, of my "disposition to gratify you, though in some degree, con- "trary to the will of God, I have devised an expedient "that, perhaps, may answer the purpose Imagine not "that war, pestilence, or famine, can effect the extinction "of the Hebrews, as, by the superintending care of Pro- "vidence, they will ever be free from the destructive con- "sequences Some temporary afflictions they may under- "go, but these in the event, will turn to their advantage "But if the gaining some present trivial ascendency over "them will afford you pleasure, attend to my counsel "Send to their camp a number of the most beautiful vir- "gins you can select, decorated with all the ornaments of "nature and of art, to captivate and allure When their "young men become enamoured, let them threaten to de- "part immediately, unless they will renounce the laws "of their country, and the honour of God who preserved "them, and adore the gods of the Midianites and the "Moabites This (said he) will draw upon their heads "the Divine vengeance" (a)

The Midianites approving the counsel of Balaam, sent the virgins to the Hebrew camp, and the young men, falling into conversation with them, soon became enamoured The virgins, according to instructions given them before their departure, affected a desire immediately to depart, but by solicitations of the young men, and assurances of absolute devotion to their will and pleasure, they were prevailed on to stay, and one of them, in the name of the rest, spoke to the following purport

"Illustrious and valiant young men, we came not hi- "ther through want of fortune, credit, the love of our "parents, or the respect of our kindred, much less for "the prostitution of our persons we are influenced only "by motives of hospitality and courtesy, which as stran- "gers we wish to shew you As you profess so ardent "an affection for us, and seem troubled at our departure, "we are desirous of conciliating your esteem, which can "only be done by terms of conjugal alliance but you "must permit us to express an apprehension of being sent "back with scandal and reproach to our parents, should "your importunity overcome our resolves"

Finding the suitors compliant in every particular, she then proceeded

"Since we are thus far agreed, it will be necessary to "remind you of some customs peculiar to you, respecting "certain meats and drinks, and to assure you, that if we "intermarry, they must be dispensed with You must "worship our gods (b) as the most convincing proof "of your affection for us You can incur no blame by "conforming to the religion of the country from whence "we are come, and adoring our gods in common with "nations in general whereas, your God is solely the "object of your people's consideration

This was the alternative proposed to their consideration

The Hebrews, blinded and infatuated by their passions, consented to the requisition of the females, suffering themselves to be seduced to the renouncing of the religion of their forefathers, transgressing the most sacred ordinances, and lapsing into the idolatry of the country They admitted a plurality of gods, used meats in common and to gratify the women, trampled on every law which they before held solemn, obligatory, and binding This licentious and dissolute turn prevailed throughout the younger part of the army, and occasioned a more dangerous mutiny than any former, so far as to the total subversion of regularity and good order, and the introduction of whatever was impious and profane For when the religion and morals of youth are once perverted, they make a rapid progress in the paths of vice and immorality Indeed, high and low, great and small, became generally apostates

While this infatuation prevailed, Zimri, an Hebrew, one of the chiefs of the tribe of Simeon, married Cosbi a Midianite, the daughter of Zur, a man of rank and eminence in that country This Hebrew, at the instance of his wife, openly practised the most palpable idolatry, in flagrant violation of the rites, ceremonies, and constitution of the religion and laws of his forefathers During this disordered state of affairs, Moses, lest some fatal consequences should ensue, summoned the people, and remonstrated with them how unworthy it was of the character which they and their ancestors had sustained for their piety and virtue, to prefer the gratification of ignoble passions to the veneration of their God, and the observance of his sacred commandments. He pointed out the necessity of timely repentance, and shewed the merit of their character as men, and particularly as Hebrews, not by contemning the Divine laws, but [illegible] their immoderate passions He also [illegible] the inconsistency of their behaviour, in thus abandoning themselves to luxury and dissipation, in a plentiful country, after having seen such examples of moderation in the desert, and squandered in profusion that which they acquired by much toil, and in the time of distress.

He then endeavoured to bring the infatuated youth to a sense of shame, and an attention to the dictates of reason and conscience, but, in what he said, he reflected on no individual, judging that personal reproof would render them more incorrigible, and that his main object was not to expose, but reclaim them. These oblique hints, however, gave occasion to Zimri to rise, and thus speak in vindication of himself

"Moses, you are at liberty to contend for the use and "observance of your own laws, which have obtained a "sanction and authority by long custom alone, or you "would have been brought to merited disgrace and "punishment, and found, to your cost, that the Hebrews "were not to be deluded by your arts I will never sub- "ject myself to your tyrannical decrees, assured that, "under a pretext of regard to religion and law, you seek "to enslave us, and establish a supreme authority over "us, by denying us those liberties to which all free-born "men have an undoubted right Was there a more "grievous oppression, during the whole course of an "Egyptian bondage, than the power you usurped of "punishing every man by laws of your own invention? "You particularly deserve punishment for abrogating "and annulling those customs, laws, and privileges, "which are authorised and established by the common "consent of nations, and preferring the [illegible] of "your fancy to rules so generally followed [illegible] "ally founded Conscious that I have done nothing "wrong, I now frankly declare, [illegible] "I have married a strange woman [illegible] confess, "with an honest boldness, and would do the same in "the face of the world I also worship the gods whom "thou hast forbidden to be worshipped, as I do not hold "myself bound to submit to your arbitrary [illegible], either "in matters of law or religion, but may [illegible] the [illegible]

(a) This great maxim that God's people could never be hurt or destroyed but by drawing them to sin against God, [illegible] conspicuous by the entire history of that people both in the Bible and in Josephus, and is often taken notice of in them both

(b) What Josephus here puts into the mouths of the Midianite women who came to entice the Hebrews to lewdness and idolatry, viz. that their worship [illegible] the one God, in opposition to the plurality of gods implied in [illegible] [illegible] to the holy laws [illegible] the true God [illegible] Moses [illegible] [illegible] laws [illegible] were [illegible] consideration and [illegible] [illegible] the law of Moses [illegible] whereas God's people [illegible] laws [illegible]

"berty of inveſtigating the truth for myſelf, and direct-
"ing my own perſonal concerns."

Zimri, in this ſpeech, delivered the general ſentiments of the whole faction, while the multitude ſilently waited the iſſue of his preſumptuous conduct, for they apprehended much confuſion would enſue. As Moſes was not diſpoſed to contend any longer, leſt he might render a ſeditious man more outrageous, and leſt others incited by his example, ſhould riſe, and by that means the tumult become univerſal, he therefore, upon this conſideration, diſſolved the aſſembly, though the clamour moſt probably would have been productive of more miſchievous effects, had not Zimri the chief abettor of it, been ſuddenly cut off in the following manner.

His contumacy, and flagrantly inſolent behaviour to Moſes, raiſed the reſentment of one Phineas to the higheſt degree. He was a youth eminent for the dignity of his family, his ſingular proweſs, and his perſonal virtues. Eleazar, the high prieſt, being his father, he was nearly allied to the great law-giver. Senſible that to ſuffer ſuch indignity to paſs with impunity, would bring both the religion and laws of the Hebrews into contempt, he determined to make an example of the ringleader of the ſedition, as his exalted rank would cauſe that example to have a greater influence on the minds of the people. His reſolution being equal to his zeal, he repaired, without delay, to the tent of Zimri, and, at one ſtroke, ſlew both him and Coſbi, his wife. This reſolute act excited an emulation amongſt thoſe of his cotemporaries, who ſtill maintained a regard for the honour of their country, to avenge themſelves on thoſe who had done it violation, inſomuch, that they fell moſt furiouſly upon the faction, and put great numbers of them to the ſword. Thoſe who eſcaped the vengeance of the ſword, were cut off by a peſtilence that followed ſoon after, and ſwept away not only thoſe who took an active part in the ſedition, but alſo their kindred, and thoſe who, by their authority and influence, might have reſtrained, if not prevented it. There periſhed by this peſtilence fourteen thouſand of the Hebrews.

Moſes, incenſed againſt the Midianites for their foul practices, ſent out a powerful army to exterminate their nation. We ſhall ſhortly treat of that expedition, deeming it neceſſary, on this occaſion, firſt to advert to the wiſdom and candour of our great law-giver. Though Balaam, invited and allured, by preſents from the Midianites, to curſe the Hebrews, when he found from the Divine prohibition, that he could not effect their purpoſe, ſuggeſted ſuch an expedient to them, as tended to the ruin of the Hebrews, in miſleading and corrupting them in their religion and laws, yet Moſes did him great honour in inſerting his prophecies in his writings. He had it in his power to aſſume the credit himſelf, as there could be no witneſs againſt him, but he was too noble and ingenious to be guilty of a fallacy, or deviate from that principle of rectitude which ſo eminently adorned his character.

CHAP. VII.

Conqueſt of the Hebrews over the Midianites. Moſes appoints Joſhua his ſucceſſor. Law reſpecting the allocation of cities for manſlaughter.

MOSES, as before obſerved, ſent an army of twelve thouſand men againſt the Midianites, chooſing out of every tribe one thouſand, and appointed Phineas to the command, as a reward of his extraordinary merit, in aſſerting their religion and laws, and avenging the common cauſe on Zimri, the leader of a ſeditious faction. The Midianites on receiving intelligence of the approach of the enemy, collected their forces, lined the ſeveral paſſes through which they might break in upon them, and put themſelves in as good a poſture of defence as the time would permit. But no ſooner did Phineas charge them at the head of the Hebrews, than they were totally routed with incredible ſlaughter. Five kings, viz. Ochus, Sures, Robeus, Ures, and Recem, fell on the ſpot. The capital city of Arabia, built by the latter, is known by his name to this day. They call it Rekem, and the Grecians, Petra.

The Hebrews, having obtained an entire victory over their enemies, ravaged their whole country, putting all the inhabitants to the ſword, the virgins excepted, in conformity to the eſpecial command of Moſes to Phineas, who returned with the army in ſafety, and brought with him a memorable and glorious booty, conſiſting of fifty-two thouſand and ſixty-ſeven oxen, ſixty thouſand aſſes, houſehold plate, and veſſels of gold and ſilver to an immenſe value: ſuch were the opulence and luxury of the Midianites. They alſo brought with them above thirty thouſand captive virgins.

Moſes, in the diviſion of the booty, allotted one fiftieth part to Eleazar and the prieſts, another fiftieth to the Levites, and the reſt to the people, which enabled them to enjoy the fruits of their toils and hazards in plenty and peace. Our great legiſlator, being now advanced in years, appointed Joſhua to ſucceed him in the ſeveral offices of a prophet, a leader, and a governor, according to the Divine command, for he was moſt expert in the knowledge of their religion and laws, having been inſtructed therein by Moſes, his preceptor.

About this time the tribes of Gad and Reuben, with half that of Manaſſes, joined in a petition to Moſes, for a grant of the country of the Amorites, as a place lately conquered, abounding with rich paſturage, and therefore commodious for their herds and other cattle. Moſes imputed their requeſt to puſillanimity, and reproached them in words to this purport:

"You deſire to live in eaſe and luxury; and, by appro-
"priating to yourſelves the advantages of a common war,
"deprive others of their ſhare of what has been jointly
"acquired. It ſtill requires you together with the reſt
"of your brethren, to exert yourſelves in extending your
"victorious arms beyond Jordan, in order to obtain poſ-
"ſeſſion of the land that God hath promiſed them." The tribes which preferred the petition, in order to ſoothe Moſes, thus apparently incenſed againſt them, declared, that they neither wiſhed to avoid danger through fear, nor ſhun labour through ſloth, but were only deſirous of leaving their booty in a place of ſecurity, that they might be more at liberty to proſecute the war: therefore if Moſes would aſſign them towns for the reception of their wives, their children, and their property, they were ready to march whitherſoever they might be commanded, and venture their lives in the common cauſe. Moſes, ſatisfied with what they advanced in their own vindication, in the preſence of Eleazar, the high prieſt, Joſhua and the reſt of the magiſtrates, granted them the land of the Amorites, according to requeſt, but on condition that they ſhould join with their countrymen in a league, offenſive and defenſive, againſt their common enemies, nor lay down their arms till the cloſe of the war. Having acceded to theſe terms, they were put in poſſeſſion of ſtrong cities, where their wives, children, and ſubſtance were perfectly ſecure.

Moſes built ten cities in that country, which are to be reckoned amongſt the forty-eight heretofore mentioned. He appointed three of them ſanctuaries, or places of refuge, for thoſe that fled thither in caſe of caſual homicide. The refugee was to continue in exile during the life of the high prieſt, under whoſe juriſdiction the fact was committed, but, at his death, permitted to return. During the time of their exile, it was lawful for any of the kindred of the man that was ſlain to take revenge upon the homicide, if he ſhould be found without the walls of the city of refuge, but it was not permitted to any other. The names of the refuge cities were, Bezor on the border of Arabia; Ariman in the country of Ga-

Ludene, and Gaulanan, in the land of Batanæa. Moses also ordained, that, after the conquest of Canaan, three more cities of the Levites should be appointed as places of refuge, and with the same privileges as the former.

About this time an eminent person of the tribe of Manasses, called Salophades, leaving only three daughters, some of the heads of the tribes applied to Moses to consult him respecting the daughters' right of inheritance. The decree was, that, if they were married within their tribe, they should inherit, but if they chose to marry into another tribe, they should lose their patrimony in their own. Upon this occasion an ordinance was passed, that every tribe should keep its own inheritance, without alienating or transferring it.

CHAP. VIII.

The policy of Moses, and his departure from mankind.

As there now remained but thirty days to fulfil the number of forty years since the Hebrews came out of Egypt, Moses called a general assembly at a place known by the name of Abila, near the side of the river Jordan, and environed with palm-trees. When they were convened, he delivered to them a speech to the following effect:

"Hebrews, and companions in a long and tedious "journey, with whom I have been exposed to, and de-"livered from, so many dangers, since it is now the will "of God, in the hundred and twentieth year of a toil-"some life, to take me out of this world (the course of "nature also requiring it) and since it seemeth not good "in God's sight that I should be any further assistant to "you, either by arms or counsel, in what remains to be "brought to pass beyond Jordan, I have resolved to em-"ploy that little space of life which remains, to esta-"blish your felicity so far as in me lies, by stating to "you in what it consists, and pointing out the means of "attaining it, so that I may be remembered by you with "esteem, when you arrive at the possession of what is "promised you. I make no doubt but I shall find credit "with you, and I may presume to add, that I deserve it "too, for the indefatigable constancy of my endeavours to "serve you. Listen, therefore, and attend to my words.

"Ye sons of Israel, be sure there is but one source of "happiness to all mankind, the spring and fountain "from whence alone it can be derived, that is, the fa-"vour of God, (a) for he alone is able to confer blessings "on those who obey his commandments, and to deprive "those of them who transgress. Attend seriously and "constantly to your duty to God, according to the pre-"cepts and instructions which I have laid before you as "authorised by his Divine commission, and your piety "and virtue shall attract the admiration, while your "prosperity shall excite the envy, of surrounding nations. "You shall keep possession of your present blessings, and "obtain a plentiful store of all you want. Take heed to "be obedient to God's will and commandments, and you "may rest assured of all good. Never prefer any other "constitution of government to the laws now given you, "nor disregard the modes and ceremonies of religious "worship established amongst you, or change them for "any other form. If you follow my advice, you shall "be victorious and invincible; for if God is present with "you, what power or force can oppose you? The re-"wards of virtue are great, glorious, and certain; nay, "virtue is in itself the greatest of rewards, from the con-"scious bliss with which it is inseparably attended. By "it all other blessings are obtained. Practise it, there-"fore, towards one another, and you shall be perfectly "happy yourselves, and render others so, to the comfort "of your present state of existence [illegible] your [illegible] "honour in times to come.

"These things you have a right to expect, [illegible] "neither violate yourselves, nor [illegible] to be [illegible] "yourselves, the written law I received [illegible] by "God's especial direction, nor, in the [illegible], [illegible] "their wisdom and equity, the subjects of your constant "meditation and study. This will secure your happiness; "and I shall die in peace, if I see it promoted by these "means, commending to you the observance of these "precepts of piety and prudence that are laid down for "your instruction and practice, and to an obedient com-"pliance with the rules prescribed by your superiors, "who are appointed to superintend your civil concerns. "That God, under whose guidance you have hitherto "lived, to whose goodness alone you stand indebted for "all the benefits you have received by my means as his "instrument, that God will continue his care over you, "and vouchsafe you his constant protection, so long as "you worship him in the way and manner prescribed by "his Divine command. You will not want excellent "monitors in Eleazar, the high priest, and Joshua, [illegible] "the senate and principals of the tribes, who will go be-"fore you, and suggest the best advice, by following "which you will continue to be happy. Treat it with "due respect, follow their counsel without reluctance, "always bearing in mind, that he who is instructed to obey "well will, when he shall attain to that dignity, govern "well. Do not imagine that liberty consists in opposing "such directions as your superiors think it expedient to "give you for your practice, as you have formerly done "by mistaking anarchy for liberty. Beware of this error, "and your state will be more prosperous. I would to "God that you may never discover such perverseness and "contumacy towards any of my successors, as you have "repeatedly done towards me, for you forget that I have "been oftener in danger of death from you than from the "common enemy. I speak not this to reproach you, "for as I sustained the injuries with calmness and com-"posure, when they were offered, I would not bring to "your remembrance a circumstance that might affect "your minds, now I am about to take my last farewel. "Be advised in your future conduct, lest you become "haughty and refractory, when you are put in possession "of the land of Canaan. Consider it as your interest, as "well as duty, to behave with reverence towards those "who are in authority over you; for if through wealth "and luxury, you fall into contempt of religion, virtue "and authority, you will forfeit the favour of God, [illegible] "when you have made him your enemy, you will lose "that land with infamy, which you have obtained with "honour, and be scattered over the face of the earth, as "the most despicable of mankind. If you should ever "experience such a reverse of fortune [illegible] "represented, you will [illegible] "you have broken, [illegible] to [illegible] "avoid this danger [illegible] the [illegible] "God of your fathers, [illegible] "live after you have conquered them [illegible] "conducive to your interest to [illegible] all [illegible] "you permit them to live, you [illegible] infected [illegible] "manners, and thereby corrupt [illegible] "I do farther exhort you to [illegible] tem-"ples, groves, and, indeed, to exterminate [illegible] "with fire and sword. By [illegible] "ness of your happy constitution can be [illegible] "But lest any should [illegible] either [illegible] "I have written a body of laws and [illegible] "by the Divine command, [illegible] "form, you will be of all men happy."

When Moses had thus [illegible] delivered [illegible] the laws and [illegible] of government, [illegible]

(a) Josephus here in the [illegible] sentence [illegible] [illegible] the book of Deuteronomy [illegible] of such importance that they deserve to be held in constant remembrance [illegible] by Jews [illegible] upon which they were melted into tears, and appeared sensibly affected with the loss they should sustain of their great leader, calling to remembrance the many dangers he had passed through, and the anxious solicitude he had ever manifested for their preservation. They desponded of ever having a governor of equal worth, and feared, lest, on his departure, they should never meet with a mediator, who could so effectually intercede with the Almighty in their behalf. They also bitterly repented of their outrages against him in the desert; and such was their grief as to be productive of lamentations which the most consolatory words could not suppress. Moses at length, however, diverted their thoughts from the melancholy subject that thus engrossed them, by exhorting them to attend to the instruction he had given them, and then dissolved the assembly.

Before I proceed to other matters, I shall describe these laws fully, and particularly, in order to demonstrate the wisdom and virtue of their compiler, and their conformity to the usages and customs of our commonwealth from its first institution. As every thing which our lawgiver wrote is extant, I shall not add by way of ornament, nor introduce any thing by way of variation. I have, however, taken the liberty of altering the method, and digesting the several kinds of laws into a regular system, being left by him in writing, as they were accidentally scattered in the delivery, and as he, upon inquiry, received them from the Divine voice. I thought it necessary to premise this observation, to obviate any calumniating reflections of our people, that I had not faithfully handed down the writings and institutions of Moses. I shall, on the present occasion, confine myself to the public laws, which appertain peculiarly to the policy of our government. Those which Moses left concerning our common intercourse with one another, or with strangers, I have referred to a commentary, which I propose, with the Divine assistance, to write hereafter.

When you have conquered the land of Canaan, and have leisure to enjoy the good things of it; when you have afterward determined to build cities, if you do what is pleasing in the sight of God, and keep his commandments, your happiness will be complete and permanent.

Let there be then one holy city of the land of Canaan, and this situated in the most agreeable place, for beauty of prospect, and fertility of soil, and let it be that which God shall choose for himself by prophetic revelation. Let there be but one temple in it and one altar, and that reared of unhewn stones out of the quarry, gathered at random, but so put together, by the skill of the artificer, as to render the work agreeable to the sight. Let not the ascent be by steps, but by a gradual rising (a) of the ground, for the decency of the approach. But in the other city, let there be neither temple nor altar; for the Hebrew nation is but one, and worship but one God.

Whoever shall blaspheme the holy name of God, let him be stoned to death, his body exposed on a gibbet for a day, and then buried in an ignominious manner.

Let all the Hebrews, from their several quarters, repair to the holy city and temple thrice every year, to join in their adoration of the Supreme Being, offer up thanksgivings for benefits received, and implore future aid and protection; and let them, by this means, maintain a friendly correspondence with one another; for it is expedient that such intercourse should be held by people who are descended from the same stock, and governed by the same laws, and professedly of the same religion. If they do not hold this friendly intercourse, they will live as strangers to each other, and be deprived of the comforts and advantages of communication.

Let there be taken out of your fruits a tenth (besides that allotted to the priests and Levites) arising from the sale in the market, but to be appropriated to the particular charge of the sacrifices and festivals in the holy city; for it is but reasonable to dedicate the fruits of the earth to the honour and service of that liberal benefactor from whom we derive their possession.

You are not to offer sacrifices, out of the hire (b) of an harlot; for the Deity cannot be pleased with any thing that is wicked, of which nothing can be more so than prostitution, nor can any thing be acceptable to a pure and spotless Being, that appertains to, or is procured by, that which is indecent and unclean.

Let no man blaspheme the gods of other nations, or rifle their temples, or take any thing out of them that is dedicated to religious uses.

Let no Hebrew wear a garment of wool and linen, as it belongeth only to the priests.

When the multitude are assembled together every seventh year, in the holy city, to celebrate the festival of the tabernacles, let the high priest ascend a raised pulpit, where he may be heard by the whole congregation, read the whole law to all the people without exception, men, women, and children, nay, the very slaves to be admitted to the hearing. For when the laws are imprinted in the mind, and thus preserved in the memory, they not only facilitate obedience, but obviate every pretended plea of ignorance. The laws will also have more weight on the consciences of offenders, when they are informed before-hand of the penalty annexed to the breaking of them. What men receive by the ear, is communicated to the mind, so that, being convinced of the wisdom and excellent tendency of the laws, they stand self-condemned on their violation.

Let your children, in particular, be early instructed in these laws, as the best thing they can be taught, as soon as they are capable of discipline, and most conducive to their present and future happiness. Wherefore, twice a day, morning and evening, they are to be reminded of God's mercies in general, and his deliverance of their fathers from Egyptian bondage in particular; it being equally reasonable to acknowledge former blessings, as to implore the bestowal of future.

The principal of God's blessings are to be inscribed upon your doors, and the remembrance of them is to be shewn upon your arms and heads. These are to serve as memorials of the power of God, and his providential care and protection of his people.

Let there be chosen in every city seven magistrates, such as have been most exemplary in the practice of virtue and righteousness. Let each of these magistrates have two assistants of the tribe of Levi. Let those, who are thus chosen in every city, be held in great honour; so that no man, in their presence, may presume to utter irreverent or contumelious words; for the practice of awe and respect towards those set over us in high office by God's appointment, leads to the love of piety and virtue, and due veneration for the sacred Majesty of God himself. There must be no appeal from the sentence of the judge, whose decree must be held inviolable, unless it can be rendered apparent that they have taken bribes to the perversion of justice, or any other accusation can be alledged against them whereby it may be proved that they have passed an unjust sentence. They must also judge and give sentence without regard to power, interest or affection, and always prefer justice to every other consideration. It is a reproach to the Divine Power and Goodness, to fear human authority before God himself. Justice is the power of God. He, therefore, who gratifies the most dignified

(a) The reason why this ascent was to be on a declivity, and not by steps, is obvious; for before the invention of [illegible] such as are now used, decency could not otherwise be provided for in the loose garments which the priests wore, as the law required.

(b) The hire of public harlots was given to Venus in Syria, as Lucian informs us; and against such heathen practices of the old idolaters this law seems to have been made.

character to its perverſion, arrogantly preſumes to uſurp that power himſelf, and treats the Lord and Ruler of the Univerſe with manifeſt contempt. If their judges cannot determine on the point in queſtion, being either miſinformed, as to the particulars, or incompetent, as to the knowledge (which ſometimes happens) let the cauſe undetermined be ſent up to the holy city, and there let the high prieſt, the prophet, and the ſenate, finally decide the controverſy.

The teſtimony of a ſingle witneſs ſhall not be received, but of three, or at leaſt of two, and thoſe whoſe teſtimony is confirmed by their probity and unſpotted reputation.

The teſtimony of a woman cannot be admitted, on account of the levity and temerity of the ſex.

Nor is it lawful for a bondman to be admitted as a witneſs, by reaſon of his degenerate and ignoble mind: for it is to be ſuſpected that, either awed by fear, or allured by gain, he will not depoſe the truth.

If any witneſs ſhould be convicted of perjury, let him be ſubject to the ſame penalty which he, againſt whom he bore falſe teſtimony, was to have ſuffered.

If homicide be committed in any place, and the offender cannot be found out, and it appears, moreover, that the man was not ſlain out of malice prepenſe, let diligent inquiry be made after the man, and rewards propoſed for diſcovering him. If, after all this ſearch and diligence, no information can be procured, let the magiſtracy of the cities contiguous to the ſpot in which the fact was committed, aſſemble together, and meaſure the diſtance from the place where the dead body lies. Then let the inhabitants of the neareſt city thereunto purchaſe an heifer, and bring it to a valley, as to a place where there is no land ploughed, or trees planted, and let them cut the ſinews of the neck of the heifer. Then the prieſts and Levites, and ſenate of that city, ſhall take water, and waſh their hands over the head of the heifer, and they ſhall publicly declare, that their hands are innocent of this murder, and that they have neither done it themſelves, nor been aiding or aſſiſting to any that did it. The ceremony to be finiſhed with offering up prayers to Almighty God to preſerve that place and people from the guilt of blood for the time to come.

Ariſtocracy appears to be the beſt form of government, becauſe it veſts the authority in the hands of men of noble birth and dignified character. Therefore let the Hebrews deſire no other form, but always love that form, have the laws for their governors, and govern all their actions by the laws. But let them ever remember that God is their king and their ſupreme governor.

But if you ſhould deſire to have a king, ſee that you elect one of your own nation, who will ſteadily maintain juſtice, and all the other virtues, being guided by God and the laws, as his infallible directory, and higheſt wiſdom. Let him not undertake any thing without the authority of the high prieſt and the ſenate. Let not his mind be ſet upon a multitude of wives, nor the glare of treaſure, nor the pomp of houſes, leſt thereby he become inſolent, and diſdain to ſubmit to the laws. If he ſhould affect an unwarrantable power and magnificence, let him be reſtrained, that he may not become more important than is conſiſtent with the true intereſt of the ſtate.

It is not lawful to remove the boundaries or land-marks either of your own land or your neighbours, for they are the beſt ſecurity of the common peace. They ſhould remain firm and immoveable, as a Divine limitation of rights, as a removal may afford cauſe for great broils and conteſts, for thoſe whoſe avarice or ambition admit of no bounds, are eaſily led to violate the laws.

The firſt fruits of trees, that bear before the fourth year, from the time of their planting, are neither to be offered to God, nor eaten by man, becauſe, not being produced in proper ſeaſon, they are abortions, and contrary to nature. But all the fruit that ſhall grow in the fourth year, when it comes to maturity, ſhall be gathered, and brought into the holy city, and there expended during the feaſt, which the owner makes for his friends, together with widows and orphans: but in the fifth year he ſhall reſerve the whole product for his own uſe.

Sow not the ground that is planted with vines, for it is ſufficient it affords nouriſhment to that plant, nor doth it need to be nouriſhed by the plough.

The land is to be ploughed with oxen alone and no other kind of beaſts yoked with them, for the tillage muſt always be performed by beaſts of the ſame kind.

Let the ſeeds be ſown ſimple and unmixt, not two or three ſorts together, for nature doth not admit of a commixture of different things.

You are not to permit beaſts of different kinds to gender together, for there is reaſon to fear that this unnatural practice may have a corrupt effect on the human ſpecies, as the fouleſt extravagancies have taken their riſe from trivial cauſes. Wherefore nothing ought to be introduced in converſation, that, by a perverſe application, may tend to promote a depravity of manners. Nor ſhould the laws neglect ſmall matters, but provide for decency of conduct and behaviour in all things.

Let not thoſe that reap, and gather in the corn that is reaped, gather in the gleanings alſo, but let them rather leave ſome allowance for thoſe that are in want of the neceſſaries of life. In like manner, when they gather their grapes at the time of vintage, let them leave ſome ſmaller bunches on the vine for the poor, and let them paſs over ſome of the fruits of the olive-trees, when they gather them, and leave them for ſuch as have no kind of proviſion. For the advantage ariſing from the exact collection of all, will not be ſo conſiderable to the owners, as will ariſe from the prayers of the poor. God will bleſs the land with fertility, and the proprietor with plenty, if he is not ſolely attentive to his own gain, but has a regard to the wants of the indigent.

The ox is not to be muzzled when he treads out the corn, for it would be unreaſonable to deny any thing a part in the fruit of its own labours.

The traveller, on his journey, muſt not be denied to gather and taſte of the ripe fruits, but on the contrary, permitted to take the ſame freely, whether he be of the country, or a ſtranger. He ſhall depart ſatisfied with what he has eat, but he is prohibited from carrying any away with him. Thoſe likewiſe who gather grapes, ought not to refuſe a traveller to taſte of them, as they bear them to the preſs, for it would be very unjuſt, that the good things which God hath beſtowed upon mankind in ſuch abundance, ſhould be denied the needy in a ſmall proportion, eſpecially as the ſeaſon ſoon paſſes away. Nay, thoſe are to be invited, that, from a ſcrupulous modeſty, forbear touching, or even aſking for the ſame. If they are Hebrews, they are to be eſteemed friends and fellow-ſharers in what you have, being of the ſame race. If ſtrangers, we ſhould exerciſe hoſpitality towards them, not thinking we ſuſtain any loſs by the ſmall preſent we make them of the fruits we enjoy through God's bounty. Nor can that be ill beſtowed which is thus courteouſly given to another, ſince the bountiful Father of the Univerſe affordeth all things in rich abundance, not that any individuals ſhould engroſs them, but that they ſhould be rendered a common benefit to mankind. Nor can men more effectually acknowledge God's munificence towards themſelves, than by communicating a part of his bleſſings to others. Whoſoever ſhall preſume to act contrary to what is here preſcribed, let him be beaten with forty ſtripes ſave one, by the public executioner. Let him undergo this puniſhment (which is a moſt ignominious one for a freeman) becauſe he was ſuch a ſlave to gain, as to ſully his own dignity. It is by all means expedient (added Moſes) that you, who have had the experience of ſuch

upon which they burst into tears, and appeared sensibly affected with the loss they should sustain of their great leader, calling to memory the many dangers he had passed through, and the anxious solicitude he had ever manifested for their preservation. They desponded of ever having a governor of equal worth; and feared, lest, on his departure, they should never meet with a mediator, who could so successfully intercede with the Almighty in their behalf. They also bitterly repented of their outrages against him in the desert, and such was their grief as to be productive of lamentations which the most consolatory words could not suppress. Moses at length, however, diverted their thoughts from the melancholy subject that so engaged them, by exhorting them to attend to the instruction he had given them, and then dissolved the assembly.

Before I proceed to other matters, I shall describe these laws fully and particularly, in order to demonstrate the wisdom and virtue of their compiler, and their conformity to the usages and customs of our commonwealth from its first institution. As every thing which our lawgiver wrote is extant, I shall not add by way of ornament, nor omit or deduce any thing by way of variation. I have, however, taken the liberty of altering the method, and digesting the several kinds of laws into a regular system, being left by him in writing, as they were accidentally scattered in the delivery, and as he, upon inquiry, received them from the Divine voice. I thought it necessary to premise this observation, to obviate any calumniating reflections of our people, that I had not faithfully handed down the writings and institutions of Moses. I shall, on the present occasion, confine myself to the public laws, which appertain peculiarly to the policy of our government. Those which Moses left concerning our common intercourse with one another, or with strangers, I have referred to a commentary, which I propose, with the Divine assistance, to write hereafter.

When you have conquered the land of Canaan, and have leisure to enjoy the good things of it, when you have afterwards determined to build cities, if you do what is pleasing in the sight of God, and keep his commandments, your happiness will be complete and permanent.

Let there be then one holy city of the land of Canaan, and this situated in the most agreeable place, for beauty of prospect, and fertility of soil; and let it be that which God shall choose for himself by prophetic revelation. Let there be but one temple in it, and one altar, and that reared of unhewn stone, out of the quarry, gathered at random, but so put together, by the skill of the artificer, as to render the work agreeable to the sight. Let not the ascent be by steps, but by a gradual rising (*a*) of the ground, for the decency of the approach. But in the other city, let there be neither temple nor altar; for the Hebrew nation is but one, and worship but one God.

Whoever shall blaspheme the holy name of God, let him be stoned to death, his body exposed on a gibbet for a day, and then buried in an ignominious manner.

Let all the Hebrews, from their several quarters, repair to the holy city and temple thrice every year, to join in their adoration of the Supreme Being, offer up thanksgivings for benefits received, and implore future aid and protection; and let them, by this means, maintain a friendly correspondence with one another; for it is expedient that such intercourse should be held by people who are descended from the same stock, and governed by the same laws, and professedly of the same religion. If they do not hold this friendly intercourse, they will live as strangers to each other, and be deprived of the comforts and advantages of communication.

Let there be taken out of your fruits a tenth (besides that allotted to the priests and Levites) arising from the sale in the market, but to be appropriated to the particular charge of the sacrifices and festivals in the holy city; for it is but reasonable to dedicate the fruits of the earth to *the honour and service of that liberal benefactor from whom we derive their possession*.

You are not to offer sacrifices, out of the hire (*b*) of an harlot; for the Deity cannot be pleased with any thing that is wicked, of which nothing can be more so than prostitution; nor can any thing be acceptable to a pure and spotless Being, that appertains to, or is procured by, that which is indecent and unclean.

Let no man blaspheme the gods of other nations, or rifle their temples, or take any thing out of them that is dedicated to religious uses.

Let no Hebrew wear a garment of wool and linen, as it belongeth only to the priests.

When the multitude are assembled together every seventh year, in the holy city, to celebrate the festival of the tabernacles, let the high priest ascend a raised pulpit, *where he may be heard by the whole congregation*, read the whole law to all the people without exception, men, women, and children, nay, the very slaves to be admitted to the hearing. For when the laws are imprinted in the mind, and thus preserved in the memory, they not only facilitate obedience, but obviate every pretended plea of ignorance. The laws will also have more weight on the consciences of offenders, when they are informed before-hand of the penalty annexed to the breaking of them. What men receive by the ear, is communicated to the mind; so that, being convinced of the wisdom and excellent tendency of the laws, they stand self condemned on their violation.

Let your children, in particular, be early instructed in these laws, as the best thing they can be taught, as soon as they are capable of discipline, and most conducive to their present and future happiness. Wherefore, twice a day, morning and evening, they are to be reminded of God's mercies in general, and his deliverance of their fathers from Egyptian bondage in particular; it being equally reasonable to acknowledge former blessings, as to implore the bestowal of future.

The principal of God's blessings are to be inscribed upon your doors, and the remembrance of them is to be shewn upon your arms and heads. These are to serve as memorials of the power of God, and his providential care and protection of his people.

Let there be chosen in every city seven magistrates, such as have been most exemplary in the practice of virtue and righteousness. Let each of these magistrates have two assistants of the tribe of Levi. Let those, who are thus chosen in every city, be held in great honour, so that no man, in their presence, may presume to utter irreverent or contumelious words; for the practice of awe and respect towards those set over us in high office by God's appointment, leads to the love of piety and virtue, and due veneration for the sacred Majesty of God himself. There must be no appeal from the sentence of the judge, whose decree must be held inviolable, unless it can be rendered apparent that they have taken bribes to the perversion of justice, or any other accusation can be alledged against them whereby it may be proved that they have passed an unjust sentence. They must also judge and give sentence without regard to power, interest or affection, and always prefer justice to every other consideration. It is a reproach to the Divine Power and Goodness, to set human authority before God himself. Justice is the power of God. He, therefore, who gratifies the most dignified

(*a*) [illegible] of decency, and not by steps [illegible] the [illegible] are [illegible] decency would not [illegible] in the holy [illegible] the priests wore [illegible] law required.

(*b*) The [illegible] this law [illegible] the old [illegible] law seems to have been [illegible]

character to its perversion, arrogantly presumes to usurp that power himself, and treats the Lord and Ruler of the Universe with manifest contempt. If these judges cannot determine on the point in question, being either misinformed, as to the particulars, or incompetent, as to the knowledge (which sometimes happens) let the cause undetermined be sent up to the holy city, and there let the high priest, the prophet, and the senate, finally decide the controversy.

The testimony of a single witness shall not be received, but of three, or at least of two, and those whose testimony is confirmed by their probity and unspotted reputation.

The testimony of a woman cannot be admitted, on account of the levity and temerity of the sex.

Nor is it lawful for a bondman to be admitted as a witness, by reason of his degenerate and ignoble mind: for it is to be suspected that, either awed by fear, or allured by gain, he will not depose the truth.

If any witness should be convicted of perjury, let him be subject to the same penalty which he, against whom he bore false testimony, was to have suffered.

If homicide be committed in any place, and the offender cannot be found out, and it appears, moreover, that the man was not slain out of malice prepense, let diligent inquiry be made after the man, and rewards proposed for discovering him. If, after all this search and diligence, no information can be procured, let the magistracy of the cities contiguous to the spot in which the fact was committed, assemble together, and measure the distance from the place where the dead body lies. Then let the inhabitants of the nearest city thereunto purchase an heifer, and bring it to a valley, as to a place where there is no land ploughed, or trees planted, and let them cut the sinews of the neck of the heifer. Then the priests and Levites, and senate of that city, shall take water, and wash their hands over the head of the heifer, and they shall publicly declare, that their hands are innocent of this murder, and that they have neither done it themselves, nor been aiding or assisting to any that did it. The ceremony to be finished with offering up prayers to Almighty God to preserve that place and people from the guilt of blood for the time to come.

Aristocracy appears to be the best form of government, because it vests the authority in the hands of men of noble birth and dignified character. Therefore let the Hebrews desire no other form, but always love that form, have the laws for their governors, and govern all their actions by the laws. But let them ever remember that God is their king and their supreme governor.

But if you should desire to have a king, see that you elect one of your own nation, who will steadily maintain justice, and all the other virtues, being guided by God and the laws, as his infallible directory, and highest wisdom. Let him not undertake any thing without the authority of the high priest and the senate. Let not his mind be set upon a multitude of wives, nor the glare of treasure, nor the pomp of houses, lest thereby he become insolent, and disdain to submit to the laws. If he should affect an unwarrantable power and magnificence, let him be restrained, that he may not become more important than is consistent with the true interest of the state.

It is not lawful to remove the boundaries or land-marks either of your own land or your neighbours, for they are the best security of the common peace. They should remain firm and immoveable, as a Divine limitation of rights, as a removal may afford cause for great broils and contests, for those whose avarice or ambition admit of no bounds, are easily led to violate the laws.

The first fruits of trees, that bear before the fourth year, from the time of their planting, are neither to be offered to God, nor eaten by man, because, not being produced in proper season, they are abortions, and contrary to nature. But all the fruit that shall grow in the fourth year, when it comes to maturity, shall be gathered, and brought into the holy city, and there expended during the feast, which the owner makes for his friends, together with widows and orphans: but in the fifth year he shall reserve the whole product for his own use.

Sow not the ground that is planted with vines, for it is sufficient it affords nourishment to that plant, nor doth it need to be nourished by the plough.

The land is to be ploughed with oxen alone, and no other kind of beasts yoked with them, for the tillage must always be performed by beasts of the same kind.

Let the seeds be sown simple and unmixt, not two or three sorts together, for nature doth not admit of a commixture of different things.

You are not to permit beasts of different kinds to gender together, for there is reason to fear that this unnatural practice may have a corrupt effect on the human species, as the foulest extravagancies have taken their rise from trivial causes. Wherefore nothing ought to be introduced in conversation, that, by a perverse application, may tend to promote a depravity of manners. Nor should the laws neglect small matters, but provide for decency of conduct and behaviour in all things.

Let not those that reap, and gather in the corn that is reaped, gather in the gleanings also, but let them rather leave some allowance for those that are in want of the necessaries of life. In like manner, when they gather their grapes at the time of vintage, let them leave some smaller bunches on the vine for the poor, and let them pass over some of the fruits of the olive-trees, when they gather them, and leave them for such as have no kind of provision. For the advantage arising from the exact collection of all, will not be so considerable to the owners, as will arise from the prayers of the poor. God will bless the land with fertility, and the proprietor with plenty, if he is not solely attentive to his own gain, but has a regard to the wants of the indigent.

The ox is not to be muzzled when he treads out the corn, for it would be unreasonable to deny any thing a part in the fruit of its own labours.

The traveller, on his journey, must not be denied to gather and taste of the ripe fruits, but on the contrary, permitted to take the same freely, whether he be of the country, or a stranger. He shall depart satisfied with what he has eat, but he is prohibited from carrying any away with him. Those likewise who gather grapes, ought not to refuse a traveller to taste of them, as they bear them to the press, for it would be very unjust, that the good things which God hath bestowed upon mankind in such abundance, should be denied the needy in a small proportion, especially as the season soon passes away. Nay, those are to be invited, that, from a scrupulous modesty, forbear touching, or even asking for the same. If they are Hebrews, they are to be esteemed friends, and fellow-sharers in what you have, being of the same race. If strangers, we should exercise hospitality towards them, not thinking we sustain any loss by the small present we make them of the fruits we enjoy through God's bounty. Nor can that be ill bestowed which is thus courteously given to another, since the bountiful Father of the Universe affordeth all things in such abundance, not that any individuals should engross them, but that they should be rendered a common benefit to mankind. Nor can men more effectually acknowledge God's munificence toward themselves, than by communicating a part of his blessings to others. Whosoever shall presume to act contrary to what is here prescribed, let him be beaten with forty stripes save one, by the public executioner. Let him undergo this punishment (which is a most ignominious one for a freeman) because he was such a slave to gain, as to lessen his own dignity. It is by all means expedient (added Moses) that you who have had the experience of such afflictions in Egypt, and in the desert, should be affected with tenderness and compassion for others in like circumstances; and, as you have now obtained plenty yourselves, through the mercy and providence of God, that you should distribute of that plenty, by the like sympathy, to such as stand in need of it.

Besides the two yearly tenths already appointed to be paid (the one to the Levites, the other towards the charges of the holy festivals) you are to bring every third year a third (a) tythe, to be distributed to those that want, to widows and to orphans. But as to the ripe fruits let them carry that which first ripens unto the temple and after thanksgiving to God for the earth which brought them forth, and which he had given them for a possession, and having likewise offered those sacrifices which the law commanded them to bring, let them give the first fruits to the priests. But when any one hath done this, and has brought the tythe of all that he hath, together with those first fruits that are for the Levites, and for the festivals, let him, when he is ready to return home, stand before the holy temple, give thanks to God, that he has delivered them from their grievous treatment in Egypt, given them a goodly land, and permitted them to enjoy the fruits thereof; and when he has openly testified that he has fully paid the tythes, according to the law and appointment of Moses, let him entreat God that he will ever be merciful and gracious to him, and continue to be so to all the Hebrews, both by preserving the good things which he hath already given them, and by adding what is still in his power to bestow upon them.

When men are of years to marry, let them make choice of virgins, born of honest parents, and virtuously educated. And he that does not take a virgin to wife, let him not seduce the wife of another man to the disquiet and affliction of her husband. Let not a freeman marry a bond-woman, though his affection should strongly incline him so to do, for it is praise-worthy and honourable to govern our passions. Furthermore, let no man marry an harlot, for God will not receive her matrimonial oblations, because she hath dishonoured herself: besides, those children are more laudably and virtuously inclined, who are descended from honest parents, than those who spring from a shameful alliance contracted by impure desires.

If any one has espoused a woman as a virgin, and afterwards finds that she is not so, let him accuse her, and bring his action, adducing all the proofs he can to justify his suspicion. On the other hand, let the woman's cause be defended by her father, her brother, or the next of kin. If she be acquitted of the charge alledged against her, her accuser shall be bound to live in wedlock with her, nor shall the marriage hereafter be annulled, unless upon positive evidence. But he that shall rashly, and without cause, slander his wife, shall be punished with thirty-nine stripes, and stand condemned in a fine of fifty shekels to her father. If it be proved that the woman has been corrupted before her marriage, she shall be stoned to death for not having preserved her virginity till she was lawfully married; but if she be the daughter of a priest, she shall be burnt alive.

If any man hath two wives, and he is particularly attached to one of them, either from affection, beauty, or any other motive, while the other is of less esteem, and the son of her that is beloved be the younger, demands the prerogative of the elder, from the attachment of his father to his mother, and would thereby attain a double portion of his father's patrimony (for so much our ordinances import) let not this by any means be granted: for it is unjust that he, who is the elder by birth should be deprived of his right on the father's disposition of his estate, because his mother possessed not an equal share in his affection.

If any man shall have debauched a maiden contracted to another, and with her consent, they shall both be punished with death, as they are both equally guilty of sin, the man for corrupting the woman, and the woman for consenting: the one for seducing the woman into a preference of inordinate gratification, to an honourable marriage, the other for prostituting herself either from inclination or profit. If a man force a woman when she is alone, and has none to come to her assistance, let him openly be put to death. Let him that hath corrupted a virgin, not yet espoused, marry her. But if the father of the damsel approves not of her being his wife, let him pay fifty shekels as a reparation for the injury.

He that desires to be separated from his wife from any cause whatever (as many causes happen amongst men) let him confirm it in writing, that he will never more entertain her again; for, by this divorce, she may be at liberty to marry another husband, and refuse the former. But if it happens that she be ill used by the second, or that, he being dead, the first would take her again in marriage, it is not lawful for the wife to return to him.

If a woman's husband dies, and leaves her without children, let the brother of the deceased marry the widow, and let him call the son born to him by his brother's name, and educate him as the heir to his inheritance: for this procedure will be for the benefit of the public, as names and families should be preserved, and the possessions kept entire. This will also be for the solace of wives under their affliction, that they are to be married to the next relations of their former husbands. But if the brother refuse to marry her, let the woman come before the senate and protest, that, though she desired to continue in the family, and bear him children, her husband's brother had given her a repulse, and thereby cast a dishonour on his memory. The senate shall then demand of the brother the reasons of his refusal. Whatever cause he assigns, the point must come to this issue. The woman shall loose the sandals of the brother, and spit in his face, telling him, that he deserves this reproachful treatment from her, as having injured the memory of the deceased. After this he departs the court with a brand of infamy which he carries to his grave, and the widow is free to marry were she pleases.

If any man take captive a maid, wife, or widow, and is disposed to marry her, let him not be allowed to cohabit with her before she has shaved her head, put on her mourning habit, and lamented her relations and friends that were slain in the battle, that, by this means, she may give vent to her sorrow for them, and after that may betake herself to feasting and matrimony. It is reasonable for him who takes a woman to have children by her to gratify the inclinations of his wife, and not merely pursue his own will and pleasure, regardless of what is agreeable to her. But when thirty days are past, as the time of mourning (for so many are sufficient to prudent persons for lamenting the dearest friends) then let them proceed to the marriage. If the man be too fickle, or too proud, to retain her as his wife, let him not have it in his power to make her his slave again, but let her go whither she pleases, and have the privileges of a free woman, as by the marriage she hath purchased her liberty.

As to those young persons who despise their parents, and, instead of paying them honour, behave themselves undutifully and contemptuously, either because they are ashamed of them, or think themselves wiser than they, in the first place, let their parents (whom nature has constituted their judges) admonish them to this purport

(a) Josephus's plain and express interpretation of this law of Moses, that the Jews were bound every third year to pay three tythes, that to the Levites, that for sacrifices at Jerusalem, and this for the indigent, the widows and the orphans, is fully confirmed by the practice of good old Tobit, even when he was a captive in Assyria.

"That they cohabited together not for the ſake of pleaſure, or the augmentation of their wealth by uniting their ſtocks, but that they might have children to comfort them in their old age. That when they were born they took them up with joy and gladneſs, and rendered God the moſt unfeigned thanks for them, brought them up with the tendereſt care, and ſpared nothing that ſeemed neceſſary for their preſervation, and inſtruction in whatever was moſt excellent. That now, ſince it is reaſonable to pardon the errors of thoſe who are young, it ſhould ſuffice them to have given ſo many indications of contempt of their parents, and they ſhould therefore reform, and act more wiſely for the time to come. That they ſhould remember God is diſpleaſed with thoſe who are undutiful to their parents, becauſe he is himſelf the Father of the whole race of mankind, and ſeems to bear part of that diſhonor which falls upon earthly parents, when they do not meet with ſuitable returns from their children. And finally, that they ſhould bear in mind the ſeverity of the puniſhment which the laws inflict on the diſobedient, and which the affectionate parent hopes the child will never experience."

If the obſtinacy and perverſeneſs of children are removed by ſuch admonitions, let them be freed from the reproach which their former errors deſerved, as it will redound to the honour of the law-giver, and the happineſs of parents. But if it ſhould happen that neither authority or advice can effect a reformation of manners, and that rebellious children will ſtill perſiſt in incorrigible obſtinacy, the law muſt then be put in execution. Let ſuch, therefore, be brought by thoſe very parents, whom they have ſo flagrantly offended by their diſobedience, out of the city, with a multitude following, and let them be ſtoned to death, and there continue one whole day expoſed to public view, and at night be buried with infamy. All who are ſentenced to death by the laws are buried in the ſame manner. Public enemies are not to be denied burial, nor is any dead body to lie above ground. The law preſcribes the puniſhment, to which juſtice enjoins an exact adherence.

Let no Hebrew lend to another upon uſury, nor take uſury either upon meat or drink, for it is illiberal to take advantage of the misfortunes of our brethren. Count it ſufficient, when you have aſſiſted a brother in a caſe of extremity, that he acknowledges the kind office with gratitude. Charity brings with it its own reward, being ever attended with the conſolation of an approving conſcience, and an approving God.

Thoſe who borrow either money, or any kind of ſaleable commodity, let them cheerfully reſtore the ſame as ſoon as Providence ſhall enable them ſo to do, laying it up, as it were, in their own treaſuries, and juſtly expecting to receive it thence when occaſion ſhall require.

But if the debtor has neither ſhame or conſcience, to induce him to reſtore what he has borrowed, the creditor ſhall not enter his houſe and take a pledge before judgment be given concerning it; but let him demand it at the door, where the debtor himſelf is to deliver it, without the leaſt oppoſition to him that comes upon him under the protection of the law. If he who gave the pledge be in good circumſtances, let the creditor retain it till he has repaid his due; but if he be indigent, let it be returned before the going down of the ſun, eſpecially if the pledge be a garment, that the poor man may not want a covering in the night, for God himſelf ſhews mercy to the poor.

It is not lawful to take a mill, or any utenſil belonging thereunto, as a pledge, leſt the debtor be thereby deprived of inſtruments to obtain the means of a livelihood, and be expoſed to extreme want.

Let it be death to ſpirit away, or ſteal a man; and he that hath purloined gold or ſilver, let him pay double.

If any man ſlay a man that is in the act of ſtealing, or breaking into the houſe, he ſhall be held guiltleſs.

Let him that hath ſtolen cattle pay four-fold for what is loſt, unleſs it be an ox, in which caſe the thief is to pay five-fold. But if the offending party is ſo poor that he cannot pay the fine, let him be his ſervant to whom he was adjudged by the law to pay it.

If one Hebrew be ſold to another, let him ſerve him ſix years, and on the ſeventh let him go free. But if it ſhould ſo fall out that he hath children in his maſter's houſe by any female ſervant, and be diſpoſed, from good will to his maſter, and natural affection to his wife and children, to continue in ſervice, let him be ſet free only in the year of the jubilee, together with his wife and children.

If any man find gold or ſilver upon the highway, let him inquire after him that loſt it, and make proclamation of the place where he found it, in order to the reſtoring it, as not deeming it juſt to avail himſelf of the misfortune of another. The ſame rule is to be obſerved with reſpect to cattle ſtrayed and wandering in a deſert. If the owner be not preſently diſcovered, let the finder keep them to himſelf, and appeal to God that he has not purloined what belongs to another.

It is not lawful to paſs by any beaſt that is over-burdened, or bemired upon the way, but to help and preſerve it as if it was your own property.

It is alſo a duty to direct the ignorant traveller in his way, and give him the beſt direction and advice to ſet him forward on his journey. It is barbarous to ſport with him, or cauſe a delay in the proſecution of his buſineſs.

Let no man revile his fellow who is either deaf, blind, or dumb.

If any man ſtrikes another upon a ſudden quarrel, and it be not with a weapon, let him that is ſmitten be avenged on the aggreſſor immediately, by returning the ſame number of blows as he had received. But if he that was ſtruck be carried home, lie ſick many days, and then dies, there ſhall lie no action of murder in the caſe; but if he that is ſmitten recovers, the other party ſhall pay the whole expenſe he has been ſubject to during the whole time of his ſickneſs.

If any man ſhall kick a woman with child, ſo that ſhe miſcarries, the judges ſhall mulct him a ſum of money for the loſs of a ſubject, beſides another ſum of money by way of fine to the woman's huſband; but if ſhe die of the ſtroke, the man muſt die, according to the law of life for life.

If there ſhould be found in the poſſeſſion of any Hebrew, the preparation of any poiſon that may cauſe death, or any other harm, he ſhall ſuffer death, or undergo the ſame injury that he would have brought upon them for whom the preparation was made.

He that maimeth any man, let him undergo the ſame himſelf, and be deprived of the like member of which he hath deprived the other, unleſs he that is maimed ſhall think fit to compound for it with money; for the law admits of a man's being ſo far a judge in his own caſe as to moderate the rigour of a penalty for an injury done to himſelf.

Let him that is owner of an ox that is miſchievous and given to goring, kill him. If an ox gores any one, let him be immediately ſtoned to death, and no man preſume to eat of his fleſh; but if his owner be convicted as knowing the fierceneſs of the beaſt, and not keeping him up, he ſhall himſelf ſuffer death, as being acceſſary to the death of another man.

If the ox had killed a man-ſervant or maid-ſervant, let him be ſtoned, and the owner pay thirty ſhekels to the maſter of him that was ſlain. But if it be an ox that is thus ſmitten and killed, [illegible] that which ſmote [illegible] the other, and that which was killed, be sold, and let the price be divided between the two owners

Let those that dig a well or pit, be careful to lay planks over them, and so keep them shut as not to hinder the drawing of water, but to give notice of danger, and thereby prevent man or beast from falling into them In case any one's beast should fall into a well or pit thus digged, and not shut up, and perish, the owner of the ground shall make satisfaction to the value of the beast

Whoever has received any thing in trust for the use of another man, let him preserve it as sacred, and not on any consideration to be touched by man or woman, though immense profit was to accrue, and there was no possibility of bringing it to light It is fit that a man's conscience should direct him as the only judge and evidence of what we do, and whether we do well or ill Let his conscience bear inward testimony, and also induce him so to act, as to procure him commendation from others, but let him chiefly have regard to God, from whom no wicked man can be concealed But if he in whom the trust was reposed, without any fraud, lose what was deposited with him, let him come before the seven judges, and there make oath, in the presence of God, that nothing has been lost willingly, or with a fraudulent design, he shall then stand acquitted, and depart blameless, but if it shall be made appear, that he hath made use of the least part of what was committed to him, let him be condemned to make good the whole of the deposit

The same punctuality is to be observed with respect to paying the labourer his hire Be it ever remembered, that you are not to defraud a poor man of his wages, being sensible that Providence has allotted him those wages, instead of land and other possessions Nor is the payment to be delayed, but made to the full due upon the same day that his work is finished, for the labourer should not be deprived of the immediate use of that for which he has toiled

Children are not to be punished for the iniquity of their parents, but where they preserve a reputable character deserve pity for the misfortune of such alliances Nor are the sins of the children to be imputed to their fathers, while young persons indulge themselves in practices different from what they had been instructed in, and this through their proud refusal of such instruction

Let those who have made themselves eunuchs be held in detestation, and be secluded from the converse of society, as having deprived themselves of their manhood, to the disappointment of the main end of their creation The depravity of their minds, must lead them to make so unnatural an experiment on their bodies, for it is evident, that when the soul is effeminate, that effeminacy is diffused throughout the whole frame Wherefore let neither man, nor any living creature, be castrated, for it is a departure from the grand institution of nature

Let this be the constitution of your political laws in times of peace, and God will preserve this excellent settlement free from disturbance But as human affairs are precarious, and troubles and dangers will happen, either undesigned or intentional, it will be necessary to lay down some rules for obviating these contingencies, that so being apprised before-hand what ought to be done, you may have salutary counsels ready when you want them, and may not then be unprovided, and fall into disagreeable circumstances

May you continue in the quiet possession of the land, that God hath allotted you, and reap the fruit of your industry and patience, without the hazard of open enemies from abroad, or of worse enemies amongst professed friends A schism at home would endanger the laws, customs, discipline, and religion of your forefathers, which are the ordinances of God himself, being warranted by the authority of his divine approbation From these constitutions you are never to depart

Let all military operations, whether at present, or in future, be carried on out of your own boundaries Before you actually wage war, send ambassadors to those who are your voluntary enemies for it is expedient to expostulate with them, before you proceed to acts of hostility, and assure them that, although you have a numerous army, provided with horses, arms, and all warlike accoutrements, and moreover, a God, whose power has ever been exerted in your behalf, do you, however, desire them not to compel you to fight against them, nor to take from them what they have, which, indeed, would be your gain, though it would tend to their irreparable loss But if your competitors should think fit to put the cause upon a trial of war, lead your army against them, committing the government of the whole to God, and next, under him, to the bravest man of arms, policy, and courage, that you can pitch upon as vicegerent Do not have many principal officers, as, besides being an obstacle to action, through want of agreement, they frequently interrupt and impede execution and dispatch Look well to the choice of your levies, let them be of chosen men, endued with extraordinary strength of body, and hardiness of mind Dismiss the timid part, lest they desert in the hour of action, and so afford an advantage to your enemies

You shall exempt from obligation, those to serve who have lately built them houses, and have not occupied them a year, and those who have planted vine-yards, and have not yet reaped the fruits, as well as those who are betrothed, or have lately taken to themselves wives, lest having their minds set upon those objects, they fear to hazard their lives, and become dastardly and pusillanimous

When you have pitched your camp, take care to avoid whatever is cruel If engaged in a siege, you want timber for the making of warlike implements, do not cut down fruit-trees, but spare them, considering that they were planted and reared for the benefit of man If they could speak, they would expostulate with you on the impropriety of destroying that, which was no cause of the war, for the service of it

When you have the fortune to overcome in battle, give no quarter to those of your enemies who were obstinate and stood it out, but preserve the rest, and make them your tributaries, excepting the Canaanites, those you are to extirpate, even the whole nation, root and branch

Let no man assume the habit of a woman, nor woman that of a man, especially in a military action

This was the form of political government left us by Moses He had already delivered laws in writing, which he had compiled forty years before Of these we shall treat on a future occasion

After this he held assemblies for several successive days, awarding blessings to those who conformed to the laws, and denouncing curses against those who transgressed them He then recited a kind of poetic song, composed in hexameter verse, and containing a prediction of future events, in the very order in which they occurred, without variation, as to time or matter This song was inserted in the holy book

To the priests he delivered his books, with the ark, in which were deposited the ten commandments, written on two tables He left it in charge to the people as soon as they were in possession of the promised land, and had fixed their settlement, to avenge themselves on the Amalekites, for the injuries they had formerly done them in the desert

He also enjoined them, on the conquest of Canaan, and exterminating the inhabitants, to erect an altar to the eastward, near the city of Shechem, between the mountains, Garizim on the right hand, and Gebal on the left, and to divide the army in such a manner, that six tribes should be in each of the mountains, with the priests and Levites They were to offer up prayers alternately, imploring Divine blessings on those who kept the holy commandments, and observed the statutes of Moses, the Lawgiver At the close, the tribes upon Gebal, in acclamations, by way or reſponſe, ſignified an Amen, or, *be it ſo* Curſes were then denounced and ratified in the ſame manner as the bleſſings These benedictions and imprecations were committed to writing for future reference He alſo ordered them to be inſcribed on each ſide of the altar, the people at the ſame time ſacrificing and offering up burnt-offerings, though, after that day they never offered ſacrifice upon it, being deemed unlawful Theſe are the ordinances of Moſes, which, by the Hebrew nation, are moſt religiouſly obſerved to this day

The next day Moſes called a general aſſembly of the people, men, women and children, even ſlaves not excepted, and bound them, by a ſolemn oath, to the obſervance of the laws according to the will of God, from which they were not, in any point, to deviate, from motives of favour, fear, nor any other pretence whatſoever If any individual, even ſo near and dear to them, or any collective body, was to attempt an innovation, and thereby a diſſolution, of the form of government eſtabliſhed by them, the people were to take a general vengeance on him or them, and exterminate perſons and poſſeſſions from the face of the earth But if, by ſome means that might prevent, they could not avenge themſelves in this manner, they were to join in a proteſt againſt ſuch impious proceedings, as totally oppoſite to their conſent and approbation To theſe particulars the multitude bound themſelves by oath

Moſes added ſome inſtructions as to the form of ſacrifice, and the meaſures of proceeding in great enterprizes, referring them, for aſſurance of the Divine approbation, to the ſtones on the breaſt-plate of the high prieſt, as already deſcribed

While Moſes was preſent, Joſhua, by a prophetic impulſe, foretold what he was to do for the welfare of the people, either in the conduct of war abroad, or the adminiſtration of government at home, preparing them, by this introductory addreſs, for compliance with a new mode of diſcipline He ſaid, that by inſpiration of God, he was authorized to declare, that if they violated the ſacred inſtitutions of their religion and laws, they ſhould fall into the direſt calamities, their poſſeſſions ſhould become a prey to ſtrangers, their cities ſhould be ranſacked, their temples laid in aſhes, and themſelves ſold as ſlaves to a mercileſs people, till they came at laſt too late to repentance He added that God would, in time, reſtore their cities, with their temples alſo but yet they were to forfeit theſe bleſſings not once only, but often

Moſes then appointed Joſhua to lead the Hebrew army againſt the Canaanites, aſſuring him of the Divine aid and protection, and preſaging the choiceſt bleſſings to the people He then took his farewell in an addreſs to the following purport

"Since it is the will of God that I go to my fathers, "and that this be the day of my departure, it becomes "me, in your preſence, to acknowledge the providential "care he has exerciſed towards you and your affairs, not "only in your deliverance from the extremeſt miſeries, "but in conferring upon you innumerable and ineſtimable bleſſings nor can I but acknowledge, as in duty "bound, the Divine direction and aſſiſtance in all my endeavours for your advantage and proſperity, in the promotion of which I was but a mere inſtrument, whilſt "God himſelf was the grand author and finiſher For all "his mercies, I render him unfeigned praiſes and thankſgivings, and to his gracious protection, as a dying "man, I commend you Remember to ſerve and honour "that Supreme Being, who alone is entitled to your adoration and worſhip Eſteem his laws as the moſt valuable of all his bounties Call to mind that a human "lawgiver would think it the higheſt indignity to have "his ordinances contemned and his authority trampled "upon, and then reflect, what muſt be the awful conſequence of being ſummoned to appear before the tribunal of an incenſed God, for wilful contempt and "breach of his commandments"

This farewell addreſs was accompanied with ſeveral bleſſings on the tribes, preſages of their future deſtiny, and torrents of tears from the multitude, the women beating their breaſts, and the very children expreſſing extreme regret, at the approaching death of their great leader In ſhort, the lamentation was univerſal [illegible] in advanced life, grieved for the loſs of ſo conſtant and vigilant a protector, thoſe in early life, that they ſhould be deprived of ſo able a guide

But none were more ſenſibly affected upon this occaſion than the grand comforter himſelf, for notwithſtanding his profeſſed contempt of death, and reſignation to the will of God, and the law of nature, yet theſe teſtimonies of the affection of the people ſo overcame him, that he could not refrain from tears As he went to the place where he was to vaniſh from their ſight, they followed him weeping, but he beckoned with his hand to thoſe at a diſtance, to ſtop where they were, and deſired thoſe who were near, not to interrupt the peace of his laſt hours At his importunity they ſtood ſtill, but not without bewailing the calamity of ſo general a loſs He was accompanied only by the ſenate, Eleazar the high prieſt, and Joſhua, his ſucceſſor

As ſoon as they came to Abraham, (a) or Nebo a mountain over againſt Jericho, which affords a proſpect of the fair and fruitful land of Canaan, he diſmiſſed the ſenate, and, as he was embracing Eleazar and Joſhua, and diſcourſing with them, a cloud ſuddenly environed him, and he was tranſlated into a certain valley The ſacred records ſay that he died, leſt men ſhould imagine, from his extraordinary virtues, that he was yet alive and with God (b)

Moſes lived 120 years, a third part of which, within one month, he was ruler of the Hebrews He died on the laſt month of the year, and on the firſt day of the month, called, by the Macedonians, Dyſtrus, but by us, Adar

Moſes was a man of ſingular underſtanding, (c) which he applied to the wiſeſt purpoſes He was a perfect

(a) There were mountains ſituated in the country of the Moabites, between the two rivers Arnon and Jordan, and commanded a moſt extenſive proſpect of the land of Canaan One part of theſe mountains was diſtinguiſhed by the name of Nebo, as appears from Deut xxxii 49 but if we compare this with Deut xxxiv 1 we ſhall find that Nebo and Piſgah were one and the ſame mountain If therefore there was any diſtinction between the names, it was probably this, that the top of the mountain was more peculiarly called Piſgah which ſignifies to *elevate* or *raiſe up* and therefore may very properly denote the *top*, or *ſummit*, of any mountain Not far from Nebo was Bethpeor, which was probably ſo called from ſome deity of that name, worſhipped by the Moabites

(b) As the place of his interment was not known, ſo no public monument could be erected on the ſpot to his memory but that no particle of his great name might be loſt his ſucceſſor Joſhua (who, no doubt was the author of the laſt chapter of Deuteronomy) has there given him an honourable epitaph, which may be thus paraphraſed —See Deut xxxiv 10, 11,

What prophet by the ſacred breath inſpir'd,
What friend of God with holy raptures fir'd,
Whoſe deathleſs name can equal glories ſhare
Or with God's ſervant Moſes e'er compare?
With mortal eyes the Infinite he ſaw
On trembling Sinai's top receiv'd the law
From Egypt's fetters ranſom'd Iſrael brought
And in their ſight great ſigns and wonders wrought

(c) The character of Moſes has been celebrated by a variety of inſpired, as well as profane, writers, all of whom acknowledge him to have been the moſt excellent legiſlator, and [illegible] The [illegible] diſperſed through the courſe of this hiſtory ſufficiently convince us of the truth of this aſſertion, and that he was a moſt profound philoſopher, [illegible] general and [illegible] prophet [illegible]

The commendation which the author of Eccleſiaſticus gives Moſes is comprized in theſe words "Moſes (ſays he) was beloved of God and men [illegible] He made him like to the glorious ſaints, and magnified him, ſo that his enemies ſtood in fear of him By his words he cauſed the wonders to ceaſe, and he made him glorious in the ſight of kings, gave him a commandment for his people, and ſhewed him part of his glory He ſanctified him in his faithfulneſs and meekneſs, and choſe him out of all men He made him to hear his voice, and brought him into the dark cloud, and gave him commandments before his face, even the law of life and knowledge, that he might teach Jacob his covenants, and Iſrael his judgments" Chap xlv [illegible]

orator, capable of expressing, in the most striking light, his own feelings, and working most effectually upon the passions of others. He was moreover a skilful general, an eminent prophet, and a faithful guardian of the people. The people mourned for him thirty days, nor did ever any grief so deeply affect them, as upon the death of this great and holy man. He not only maintained an excellent character amongst his cotemporaries, but his writings have transmitted his fame to immortal ages. Thus much for the end of Moses.

The character St. Augustin gives of Moses is short, but at the same time very expressive. "He was, (says he) the most faithful servant of God; humble in wishing to decline so weighty a ministry, but dutiful in undertaking it; just in keeping, and resolute in executing it; vigilant in government, strict in justice, zealous in love, and patient in suffering."

The apostle St. Paul, in his epistle to the Hebrews, speaks of Moses as follows: "By faith (says he) Moses, when he was come to age, refused to be called the son of Pharaoh's daughter, choosing rather to suffer adversity with the people of God, than to enjoy the pleasures of sin for a season. By faith he forsook Egypt, not fearing the king's displeasure. Through faith he instituted the passover and effusion of blood, lest he that slew the first born should touch them. By faith he passed through the Red Sea, as on dry land, which when the Egyptians attempted to do, they were swallowed up."

St. Stephen, the Protomartyr, in speaking of Moses, says thus: "Moses was mighty in word and deed, to whom, in the wilderness of Mount Sinai, an angel appeared in a flame of fire in a bush. Him God sent for a prince and a deliverer of the people, by seeking them from a servile state of bondage, which he accomplished after doing wonders and miracles in the land of Egypt. This is he that was in the congregation (the church) in the wilderness, and conversed with our fathers, who received the lively oracles to give unto us."

The character given of Moses by St. Ambrose is as follows: "Moses (says he) was the figure of that Preceptor that was to come, who should preach the gospel, fulfil the Old Testament, build the New, and feed the people with celestial aliment. Hence the dignity of the human condition is so highly advanced, that he is called by the name of God, *I have made thee a God to Pharaoh*, Exod. vii. 1. that is, I have given thee authority to speak to him in my name. And, indeed, he became his character; for he was master of his passions, not inclined to worldly desires, but, in mind and body, endeavoured to conduct himself after the likeness of that perfection of his God, as far as nature would permit. And, therefore, we read quite differently of him, to what we do of others, who die through some defect of nature. With him it was otherwise; for notwithstanding his great age he retained the use of all his faculties to the last, his eyes not failing, nor his natural force abated, but died according to the word of the Lord."

END OF THE FOURTH BOOK.

FLAVIUS JOSEPHUS

ON THE

ANTIQUITIES

OF THE

JEWS.

BOOK V

[INCLUDING A PERIOD OF ABOUT THREE HUNDRED AND FIFTY-SEVEN YEARS.]

CHAP. I.

Joshua succeeds Moses. Sends spies into Canaan. They are protected by a woman called Rahab. Jericho besieged, and laid waste by the Hebrews. Joshua forms a league with the Gibeonites. Obtains a complete conquest over the Canaanites. Divides their lands among the different tribes. Lot of each tribe. Death and character of Joshua.

AFTER the accustomed ceremonies were over, and the last duty paid to the memory of Moses, Joshua ordered the people to get themselves in readiness for marching, and, in the mean time, dispatched certain persons to Jericho, in order to learn the strength of the place, and the disposition of the inhabitants. On this occasion he convened the leaders of the tribes of Reuben and Gad, and the half tribe of Manasseh, the latter of whom had been promised to settle in the country of the Amorites, which includes a seventh part of the land of Canaan.

When these leaders were assembled together, Joshua reminded them of the promises they had made to Moses, and earnestly entreated them, not only for his sake, but also for their own, to fulfil their engagement. They cheerfully complied with Joshua's request, and immediately joined his army with a body of 50,000 men.

Joshua having received this assistance, marched with his whole army about sixty furlongs towards the banks of the river Jordan. They had scarce pitched their tents, before the spies, who had been sent to Jericho, arrived, and gave the following account of what had happened to them during their stay in that city.

That the inhabitants considering them as strangers come to gratify their curiosity, permitted them to perambulate the city without interruption, in consequence of which they had the opportunity of viewing the walls, ramparts, and other fortifications raised for the defence of the city. That, towards the close of the day, they retired to a house, situated near the wall of the city, where they refreshed themselves, and intended leaving the place early the next morning. While they were at this house, information had been given the king, that there were spies in the city from the Hebrew camp, and that they were concealed in the house of a woman named Rahab, in consequence of which, an order was issued for apprehending them, and that, if they did not confess who they were, and on what business they came, they should be put to the torture. As soon as Rahab was informed of this, she communicated the intelligence to the spies, and taking them to a retired part of the house, concealed them, by covering them over with a large quantity of flax. That when the officers of justice came in search of them, Rahab told them, there had, indeed, been strangers there, but that, after supper, they departed, and as the time was but short since they went, if they were the dangerous people suspected, she did not doubt but, by immediate endeavours, they might be easily taken. The honesty of the woman's countenance, and the simple manner in which she expressed herself, satisfied the officers, and they immediately left the house to go in quest of the spies, but after travelling some way, and finding no likelihood of succeeding, they desisted from their pursuit, supposing they had effectually made their escape. That when the confusion which the alarm occasioned, had in some degree subsided, Rahab uncovered them, related what had passed, and pointed out the great danger to which she had exposed herself and family for their protection, in return for which she expected from them an oath, that when the city should be invested and rendered desolate by the Hebrews (for she told them it had been revealed to her by the Almighty that it should) they should preserve her and her relations from the general destruction. That they had faithfully promised the protection she requested, to effect which they had told her that, when she found the city attacked, to shut herself up, together with her relations, in her house, and that, in order to distinguish it from the rest, she must affix red strings to the door, which signal should be communicated to the general, who would no doubt, give such directions, as to secure her from all danger. That after this agreement was made between them, they departed, being assisted by Rahab, who, for that purpose, had got a rope, and fastened it to the top of one part of the house, by means of which they made their escape unperceived.

When the spies had given the relation to Joshua, and the principal officers of the army, a consultation was held with Eleazar, the high priest, and the elders, whether the promise made by the spies to Rahab ought to be strictly observed, which was agreed to by those sages, and the obligation ratified.

The Hebrews were on the opposite side of the river to that of Jericho, and the great difficulty was to pass the river, the current being exceeding rapid, and no method to be projected that could facilitate their design. These reflections gave great uneasiness to Joshua, but his troubles were soon removed by a Divine revelation from the Almighty, who assured him, that those obstacles should be removed, and that the river should be rendered so fordable, that the army might pass it with the greatest safety.

This Divine promise was fulfilled two days after it was made, and the whole army passed the river in the following order: first, the priests bearing the ark, who were followed by the Levites, carrying the tabernacle and the holy vessels. After these marched the whole army, divided into ranks, according to the order of their respective tribes. The women and children were placed in the centre of the army, that they might be the better secured from the violence of the current. When the priests entered the river the rapidity of the stream abated, and the water gradually sunk, till the bottom became quite dry, so that the whole multitude passed over without the least apprehension of danger. The priests were the last who quitted the bed of the river, which they had no sooner done, than the waters returned and resumed their natural course, and thus was the promise made by the Almighty amply fulfilled.

After passing the river, the whole army proceeded immediately on the march, and encamped within ten furlongs of the city of Jericho. On this spot Joshua erected an altar, consisting of twelve stones, which, by his order, had been brought by twelve princes of the several tribes from the bottom of the river. This altar was raised by Joshua, to perpetuate the remembrance of the miraculous separation of waters, and on it he offered sacrifices, and celebrated the feast of the passover. (*a*)

While the Israelites were on the other side the river Jordan, they had, for some time, laboured under great difficulties from the manna, which had been their principal subsistence during forty years in the wilderness, having failed them; but when they came on that side of the river next Jericho, these inconveniencies were removed. It happened to be at the time when the harvest of the Canaanites was ripe, and the country well stocked with cattle and other kinds of provision, all which they had the power of enjoying without interruption.

From the apparent pusillanimity of the Canaanites, in suffering the Israelites to ravage their country at discretion, and at the same time keeping themselves secured within the walls of the city, Joshua was convinced he should not be able to bring them to action, and therefore determined to lay siege to the place, and put all the inhabitants to the sword.

Having formed this resolution, on the first day of the Feast of the Passover he ordered a procession to be made round the wall of the city, the manner of which was this: first, a certain number of priests, carrying the ark surrounded by a considerable body of the troops; these were followed by seven other priests, each blowing a horn, or trumpet, to animate the soldiers; and the whole was closed by the elders. In this manner they marched round the walls of the city, and then returned to their camp.

This ceremony was repeated for six successive days, during which time, not a single person of the Canaanites was seen without the walls of the city. On the seventh day Joshua addressed himself not only to the army, but the people in general, told them, that, on that day the city of Jericho should be delivered into their hands, and that without any efforts being made on their parts to effect it, for that the very walls would fall of themselves, and the city would be rendered totally defenceless. He strictly charged them to confine attention to the destruction of the inhabitants, all of whom they should put to the sword, except Rahab and her family, that the oath might be strictly performed which had been given by the spies, when they were on the other side the river Jordan. He likewise told them that whatever gold or silver they should find, to lay it in a heap on the spot, for it should be dedicated to God as the first fruits of a victory obtained over the Canaanites.

Joshua, after delivering these instructions to the army and people, marched towards the city, and proceeded around the walls of it in the same manner, and with the same ceremonies, as before mentioned in the Feast of the Passover; but as they were passing the seventh time they made a halt, when the wall suddenly gave way, and the whole fell to the ground.

This surprising and unexpected event, threw the Canaanites into the utmost consternation, insomuch that they had not power to attempt the least resistance. In consequence of this, the Israelites immediately entered the city, and to obey the instructions previously given them by Joshua, put all to the sword, (*b*) except Rahab and her family, the former of whom being brought before Joshua, he rewarded her in the most ample manner for the services she had done him.

To make a final destruction of the city of Jericho, the Israelites, after murdering the inhabitants, set it on fire, and the whole was reduced to an heap of ashes. A prophetical curse (*c*) was likewise denounced against any person who should ever after attempt to rebuild it, that whoever should take upon him to lay the first stone might be punished by the loss of his eldest son, and whoever should finish the work, his youngest. In the city were found great quantities of gold, silver, and brass, the whole of which was of immense value, and being gathered together, as Joshua had ordered, he presented it to the priests to be deposited in the sacred treasury.

Notwithstanding the caution Joshua had taken to prevent private plunder, yet one Achar, the son of *Zebedee*, and of the tribe of Judah, made a breach on the injunction, by concealing the cloak of the king of the Canaanites, which was not only rich in itself, but had about it as much gold as weighed two hundred shekels. He argued with himself, that as he had hazarded his life to obtain it, he thought he had a right to enjoy it, and that it would

---

(*a*) This was the third time of their celebrating that festival. The first was at their departure out of Egypt, and the second at their erecting the tabernacle at the foot of Mount Sinai.

(*b*) Here we may observe that whenever any of the public enemies of the Jews, had been, for their wickedness, solemnly devoted to destruction according to the Divine command, as were generally the seven wicked nations of Canaan, and those sinners the Amalekites, it was utterly unlawful to permit those enemies to be redeemed; but they were to be all totally destroyed. Numb. xxi. 2, 3.

(*c*) The words of Joshua's execration, in the text, are as follow: "Cursed be the man before the Lord that riseth up and buildeth this city Jericho: he shall lay the foundation thereof in his firstborn, and in his youngest son shall he set up the gates of it." Josh. vi. 26.

The falling of the Walls of JERICHO, burning the City and destruction of the Inhabitants by the ISRAELITES

ACHAR *confessing his* SACRILEGIOUS THEFT *and delivering up his plunder in presence of the multitude previous to his being* STONED *to* DEATH

be ridiculous to offer that to God which was only designed for the use of man. He therefore dug a pit in his tent and there hid the cloak, supposing that it would be equally hidden from God, as it was from his companions.

The army of the Israelites was at this time encamped at a place called by them Galgal, which signifies *liberty*, intimating, that they now thought themselves secure from any future danger, and that they should never again be sensible of the like misfortunes they had experienced during their residence in the wilderness.

A short time after the destruction of Jericho, Joshua sent out a detachment of 3000 men to invest Ain, another city, situated at a small distance from the former. In this attack, the Israelites met with a warm repulse; thirty-six of them were slain, among whom were several persons the relations of distinguished characters, and the rest were obliged to seek their safety by flight. The news of this defeat, greatly dispirited the whole army of the Israelites, who, from the promises made them by Divine revelation, had set it down for granted, that whatever project they engaged in, it would infallibly prove successful. From this disappointment, and the reflection of its consequences, they cloathed themselves with sackcloth, and spent one day in fasting and prayer. The mind of Joshua was likewise particularly impressed with despair, and prostrating himself on the ground, in the most fervent manner addressed the Almighty in words to the following effect:

"Lord (said he) we came not hither rashly, or unadvisedly, to reduce this country under our power and dominion, but from a pure deference and respect to the persuasion of thy servant Moses, to whom thou didst promise the possession of this country, and that we should be victorious over all our enemies. The sudden change which has taken place, in the disappointment of our hopes and loss of our friends, greatly alarms us, and the more so, lest we should prove equally unsuccessful in any future attempts. Do thou therefore, O Lord, who alone art able to give us relief, help and preserve us. Vouchsafe unto us comfort and victory, and be graciously pleased to give us future hopes, by removing the despair under which we at present labour."

When Joshua had finished his prayer, God commanded him to rise, and to purge the army from a pollution it had acquired by a sacrilegious theft, and which was the real cause of the mischief that had befallen them. That there should be lots cast to find out the criminal, who should be made an example of for his perfidiousness; and that afterwards, whatever they undertook, should be attended with success.

Joshua immediately communicated these instructions and assurances to the people, and calling to him Eleazar the high priest, and the princes of the tribes, he ordered that lots should be first cast to discover the tribe to which the thief belonged. This was accordingly done, when it fell upon the tribe of Judah, in consequence of which lots were again cast among the several families of that tribe. On examination it appeared that the lot fell on Achar, who belonged to the family of Zacharias. He was accordingly taken into custody, and being conscious of his iniquity, confessed the fact, and delivered up the plunder in the presence of the multitude. Upon this he was immediately put to an ignominious death, and his body denied the accustomed ceremonies of interment.

When Joshua had purged his army, agreeable to the Divine command, he marched towards the city of Ain, and planting a body of men in ambuscade the preceding evening, he the next morning presented himself in sight of the enemy with his main body. The Ainites were so elated with their former success, that, as soon as they saw the Israelites they immediately advanced in the most furious manner to give them battle. On this Joshua feigned a retreat, till having drawn the Ainites a considerable distance from the city, he made a stop, and gave a signal (which had been previously agreed on) to the troops in ambush. Agreeable to this signal they immediately entered the city, where they met with little opposition, the greater part of the inhabitants having planted themselves on the walls to see the action, in full confidence, from the success they had met with before, that the Israelites would be totally overthrown. These detached troops made themselves masters of the city, and put the inhabitants to the sword, while the grand army engaged that of the Ainites, and totally defeated them. The greater part were killed in the action, and the remainder fled for protection to the city, not suspecting that it was already in the hands of their enemies; but when they discovered its situation, and the great danger they were in, they had immediate recourse to flight, and concealed themselves in the wilds and deserts. The booty taken on this occasion was of immense value, consisting of great quantities of plate, costly furniture, gold, silver, coined money, and other articles, all which were divided among the soldiers, as a reward for their past, and an encouragement for their future, conduct.

The great success of Joshua against the cities of Jericho and Ain, and the slaughter made among the inhabitants, had struck such a panic in the kings of the respective provinces on that side the river Jordan, that they confederated together, and entered into a league for their mutual defence. But the Gibeonites, foreseeing the destruction that awaited them, and being apprehensive that all resistance would be in vain, consulted with their neighbours, the inhabitants of Cephirah and Kiriathjearim, among whom it was agreed, that endeavours should be used to obtain a peace with the Israelites; but as they knew that could not be effected, should it be known they were Canaanites, they had recourse to the following stratagem. They selected a certain number of artful men, who were instructed to feign themselves ambassadors come from a very distant country, in order to obtain a league with the people of Israel. To make this story appear plausible, they were dressed in tattered garments, with worn out shoes on their feet, and the bread they took with them in their bags was so musty as to be entirely useless. In this situation they arrived at Galgal (c) the place where Joshua was encamped, to whom being introduced, they told him, that from the many miracles which God had wrought for them in the land of Egypt, and the wonderful successes wherewith he had blessed their arms, against every power that had opposed them in their coming to that place, their states and rulers had sent them from a very remote country to form a league of friendship with them, and that on such conditions as were customary with their forefathers. They then pointed to their garments, which they solemnly assured Joshua were quite new when they sat out on their journey, but that the great length of it had reduced them to the state in which they then appeared.

This plausible tale gained such credit with the Israelites, that they entered into an amicable alliance with them; and Eleazar the high priest, with the princes of the respective tribes, solemnly ratified the treaty, the whole multitude assenting to the oaths made by their leaders. When the business was over, the ambassadors took their leave, and hasted to the Gibeonites with the glad tidings of their distinguished success.

A few days after the departure of the ambassadors the whole was discovered, when it appeared that the Gibeonites were inhabitants of Canaan, and that they resided at a small distance from Jerusalem. This discovery

(c) This place was so called from the rite of circumcision, which was [illegible] It lay about two miles on the east side of Jericho [illegible] [illegible] greatly alarmed Joshua, who sent for the governors, and reproached them for having practised such a deception; to which they replied, that they were compelled to do it in their own defence, as they had reason to think they should otherwise share a similar fate with the inhabitants of Jericho and Ai. Joshua was desirous of having the league cancelled; but as it was confirmed by a solemn oath, this could not be done without incurring the Divine displeasure. It was therefore resolved, in order to appease the people, that, as a punishment for the imposition, the Gibeonites should ever after be kept in a state of bondage.

When the confederate princes (who were five in number, the principal of whom was the king of Jerusalem) heard of the separate treaty made by the Gibeonites, and the artful manner in which it was obtained, they resolved to be revenged on them for desertion of the common cause. Accordingly, they joined all their forces, and marched towards their city, with a determined resolution of laying siege to it. When they came within a small distance of the place they pitched their tents, intending to begin the attack early the next morning. In the mean time, the Gibeonites dispatched a messenger to Joshua, imploring his immediate assistance, as they must otherwise inevitably fall into the hands of the Canaanites. Joshua lost no time in complying with the request of the Gibeonites, and marching his army the whole night, he, the next morning, arrived at the spot where the enemy were encamped. He immediately led on his troops to action, and the Canaanites, finding all resistance was likely to prove ineffectual, fled, but were pursued by the Israelites to a place called Beth-hora. In this expedition God had all along encouraged Joshua, by promising him success; and, therefore, as the confederate forces were endeavouring to escape, and save themselves by flight, he suffered a violent storm of hail (*a*) to fall, the stones of which were so large that more people were destroyed by them than what fell by the sword. As a farther proof of Divine interposition a circumstance occurred on that day, the like of which never happened either before or since, namely, the sun itself stood still (*b*) in the firmament, that the Israelites might not want day-light to complete the victory. This last circumstance is most expressly attested in the Holy Scriptures, according to the copies preserved in the temple.

The confederate kings, finding themselves so closely pursued, and likely to be either slain or made captives, concealed themselves in a cave at a place called Makkedah, intelligence of which being given to Joshua, he ordered the cave to be blocked up, and a guard placed over it. After he returned from pursuing the enemy, he ordered the cave to be opened, and the kings being brought forth, they were hung upon trees till the evening, when their bodies were taken down, and thrown into the cave; so that the place they had pitched on for a sanctuary became their sepulchre.

After this defeat, Joshua proceeded to the southern parts of Canaan, where, having destroyed the inhabitants and seized their most valuable possessions, he returned with his army to the camp at Gilgal.

Though the great destruction made by the army of the Israelites had struck a terror in most parts of Canaan, yet it had not that effect on the princes of the north, who instead of being intimidated, formed the resolution of boldly attacking Joshua. They accordingly drew their forces together, and pitched their camp at Berotha, a city of the Upper Galilee, not far from the waters of Merom (*c*). Their army consisted of 300,000 foot, 10,000 horse, and 2000 chariots.

When the Israelites understood what a formidable army was raised against them by the Canaanites, they became greatly dispirited, and even Joshua himself was almost sunk into despair. But they were dispelled, on Joshua's receiving assurances from God that they should overcome their enemies, and, to make their conquest complete, he was commanded to kill their horses, and burn their chariots.

Encouraged by this Divine protection, Joshua immediately marched his army against that of the Canaanites. On the fifth day he came within sight of their camp, and ordering his troops to advance with all possible dispatch, they fell so suddenly on the enemy, that they were immediately thrown into disorder. Those who attempted resistance were all slain on the spot; and such as fled, being pursued, were overtaken and slain. Their horses were also all killed, and their chariots committed to the flames.

The success of this day made Joshua absolute master of the country. He pursued his rout to a considerable distance, plundering every town he came to, and putting all the inhabitants to the sword. In short, the whole country was one continued scene of desolation, and the inhabitants of it totally extirpated, except a small number who had accidentally escaped, and secured themselves in places of great strength. Such was the desolation made in the land of Canaan during a war of only five years.

Joshua having thus reduced the Canaanites, returned with his army to Gilgal; from whence, after a short time, he removed to the mountainous part of the country, and fixed the holy tabernacle in the city of Shiloh. The situation of this place was exceeding delightful; and here it was that Joshua intended, when circumstances would permit, to build a temple.

From Shiloh Joshua removed, with all his people, to Shechem, where he erected an altar, as had been long years before appointed by Moses. He then divided his army, one half of which was placed on Mount Gerizim, and the other half on Mount Gebal. At the latter place he erected another altar on which the priests offered sacrifices; and when they had denounced the maledictions before recited, and engraved them upon the altar, they returned to Shiloh.

At this place, a short time after, Joshua convened a general assembly of the people, and, after reminding them of the great success they had met with through the assistance of the Divine protection, he observed that the Canaanites had still many cities in their possession which were rendered so strong by nature and art together, as to be almost impregnable. That as it must

(*a*) The propriety and [illegible] of the miracles performed this day are thus explained by a learned Divine: "All nations had at that time their several tutelary deities, to whose protection they committed themselves and their country, and of whose power they judged by their successes in war. Now the three principal deities, whom the inhabitants of Canaan adored were the sun, the moon, and heavens or air. To convince them, therefore, in their own way, that the gods in whom they trusted were subject to the God of Israel, and to punish them at the same time, for the worship they paid them, the Lord showered down great hailstones from the heavens on them, which slew vast numbers of their people; and then stopped the sun and moon in their courses, which gave the Israelites time and opportunity to complete their victory over the remainder."

(*b*) The deists have greatly cavilled at this miracle, on account of its not being recorded by heathen writers. But that it should not be mentioned by them is not in the least to be wondered at, when we consider that Homer, who wrote above a thousand years after Joshua, is their oldest writer now extant. Letters were not then known among the heathens, and therefore [illegible] no wonder [illegible] such a circumstance should have been [illegible] written.

(*c*) Some of the learned are of opinion that by the Waters of Merom are meant the lake Semechon, which lies between the head of the river Jordan and the lake Genesareth. But others imagine that these waters were somewhere about the brook Kishon, there being [illegible] of that name [illegible] in the account of the battle against Sisera, Judges v. [illegible] more reasonable to think that the confederate kings advanced as far as the brook Kishon [illegible] led into the country to [illegible] penetrating it, [illegible] wanted to [illegible] in the [illegible] country, leaving all Galilee in his rear, and the [illegible] the brook Kishon to the lake Semechon. See Wells's Geography of the Old Testament.

ANATOLIA
OR
ASIA MINOR
CAPPADOCIA
ARMENIA
Erzerum
Tokat
PART OF THE
Tripoli
Balbec
IDUMEA
ARABIA
ARABIA
HOLY LAND
with the
By Thos Bowen

consequently be a work of time to subdue them, he thought it advisable, in the first place, that those tribes who came with them from the other side of Jordan, and had assisted them with such fidelity in destroying their enemies, should be dismissed, with suitable acknowledgments for their services. And, secondly, that a proper person should be chosen out for every tribe, who should act as commissioners for taking an exact survey of the captured land, a proper state of which should be laid before another assembly convened for the purpose.

These propositions being universally approved of by the people, commissioners (one out of each of the tribes, who were to partake of the division of the country) were accordingly chosen, and a certain number of men, distinguished for their superior knowledge in surveying, were appointed to assist them. As some parts of the country were remarkable for their richness and fertility of the soil, while others were almost barren, they had instructions to take the admeasurement agreeable to the quality, so that though one part might be much more extensive than another, yet the whole divisions might be, on an average, of equal value.

These commissioners, with their assistants, having executed the business on which they were sent, returned, at the expiration of seven months, to Shiloh, which was at that time the seat of the tabernacle. On their arrival, Joshua convened another assembly, consisting of Eleazar, the high-priest, together with the elders, and the princes of the respective tribes. When the state of the admeasurement was laid before them, Joshua divided the whole country (*a*) between the nine tribes and the half tribe of Manasses, proportioning the shares to the number of families in each tribe. The different allotments were as follow.

To the tribe of Judah was assigned all the Upper Judea, extending, in length, to the city of Jerusalem, and in breadth, to the lake of Sodom, in which compass were included the cities of Ascalon and Gaza.

The tribe of Simeon had that part of Idumæa which borders on Egypt and Arabia.

To the tribe of Benjamin was allotted all that part of the country, which extends, in length, from the river Jordan to the sea, and in breadth, from Jerusalem to Bethel. This district is exceeding small in proportion to the rest, but the quality makes amends for the quantity, more especially as it contains the two cities of Jericho and Jerusalem.

The tribe of Ephraim had, for their lot, that part of the country, which reaches, in length, from Jordan to Gad[illegible], and in breadth, from Bethel to the Great Plain.

To the half tribe of Manasses was allotted that track of land which reaches, in length, from the river Jordan to the city of Dora, and, in breadth, to the city of Bethsan, since known by the name of Scythopolis.

The tribe of Issachar had, for their lot, all that part of the country which reaches, in length, from the river Jordan to Mount Carmel, and, in breadth to Mount Itabyri.

To the tribe of Zebulon was assigned all that track of land which borders on Mount Carmel and the sea, and [illegible] as far as the lake Genesareth.

The tribe of Aser had for their lot, all the country behind Mount Carmel, opposite to Sidon, in which district was included the city of Arce, otherwise called Actipus.

To the tribe of Naphthali was allotted the Upper Galilee, and the eastern parts of the country, including the city of Damascus, Mount Libanus, and the head of the river Jordan, which takes its rise from that side of the mount belonging to the city of Arce.

The tribe of Dan had, for their own share, all the valleys lying to the west between Azotus and Doram, together with the cities of Jamnia and Gitta, with the whole country from Acron, where the portion allotted to the tribe of Judah commences.

Thus did Joshua divide, among the nine tribes and a half, the six provinces of the Canaanites, which received their names from so many of the sons of Canaan. The seventh province (named Amorinæa, from another of the sons of Canaan) was not at his disposal, it having been long before granted by Moses to the other half tribe of Manasses, and the two tribes of Reuben and Gad. Those parts of the country which belonged to the Sidonians, Arucæans, Amathæans, and Arithæans, being, at the time the above division was made, uninhabited, were totally excluded.

Joshua, being now far advanced in years, and fearful, from the natural infirmities of age, he should not be able, much longer, to hold the reins of government, called together the heads of the different tribes, to whom he gave a strict charge, that they would be particularly diligent in using their utmost endeavours to destroy the Canaanites, and not to suffer any to reside in the land they possessed, and which had been divided amongst them by lots. He told them that a strict attention to this request would be in conformity to the will of their late legislator Moses, and that it was fully consistent both with their laws and religion. He likewise strictly charged them to deliver up to the Levites the remaining thirty-eight, out of the forty-eight, cities assigned them by Moses, they being already in possession of the other ten, situated in Amorinæa, on the other side the river Jordan. Three of these cities he assigned as places of refuge, being earnestly solicitous that nothing should be neglected which Moses had ordained. The first of these cities was Hebron, belonging to the tribe of Judah, the second Shechem, belonging to the tribe of Ephraim, and the third, Ceden, in Upper Galilee, belonging to the tribe of Naphthali. These regulations were received by the people with universal applause, they being very willing to pay a strict attention and reverence to the ordinances of Moses.

After Joshua had laid these injunctions on the people, he proceeded to divide the plunder which had been taken from the Canaanites, among his soldiers. It consisted of cattle and flocks innumerable, together with great quantities of money, plate, furniture, and other articles, so that though the number of people was great, each person had a very considerable booty.

A few days after Joshua had made these regulations, he assembled together the auxiliaries (namely the tribes of Reuben and Gad, with the half tribe of Manasses, consisting of 50,000 men) who had come with him from the other side the river Jordan, and had assisted him with fidelity during the whole course of the war against the Canaanites. When these people were assembled together, Joshua addressed them in words to the following effect.

"Friends and Brethren,

"Seeing it hath pleased God not only to establish us "in this country, but to promise a perpetual possession "of it to our posterity, and since God has been likewise "pleased to accept your proffered service in assisting us to subdue our enemies, it is but reasonable "that you who have shared so great a part in the dangers "and difficulties of the war, should now share a part "also in the comforts and blessings of a common peace

(*a*) [illegible] the [illegible] Joshua took on this occasion were exactly conformable to the [illegible] which God had given to Moses. [illegible] [illegible] See Numb. xxvi. 5, &c.

"To this end we think it but juſtice to diſcharge you "from any farther attendance at preſent, not doubting "but, if occaſion ſhall require it, you will readily "contribute your aſſiſtance at any future period. For the "ſervices you have already done us, accept our moſt "grateful acknowledgments; and we hope that the ſenſe "of good offices gone and paſt, may be improved into "a mutual and inviolable league of friendſhip for the time "to come, remembering that we ſtand indebted for the "advantages already received, next under God, to the "force of this reciprocal alliance. Your ſervices have "not gone unrewarded, ſo far, at leaſt, as an ineſtima-"ble booty may be conſidered as a recompenſe. Be aſ-"ſured you will ever find in me a moſt ſincere friend, "being ſufficiently ſatisfied that you have paid a ſtrict "attention to the laſt will of Moſes, and that you "have done every thing in your power that was con-"ſiſtent with his ordinances. I now give you full li-"berty to depart to your reſpective homes, and moſt "ſincerely wiſh you to enjoy the advantages you have re-"ceived from our great ſucceſs in war. Let no diſtance "of place, no interpoſition of rivers, ſet limits to our "friendſhip, or divide our affections; for, however ſe-"parated, we are all Hebrews ſtill. It was from one "and the ſame God that Abraham, and all our forefa-"thers, received their being; and it is that God we are "all to worſhip, according to the ordinances and inſti-"tutions left us by Moſes. So long as we ſtand firm to "our religion, we may be aſſured of the favour and pro-"tection of that God for our comfort: but ſhould you "deviate from your religious principles, and embrace "idolatry, depend upon it the God of your fathers will "deſert and forſake you."

When Joſhua had finiſhed his ſpeech, he took a ſolemn and diſtinct leave, firſt of the princes, and then of the people; and they immediately departed for their own country. The other tribes accompanied them a conſiderable way; and when they parted, the latter teſtified their affection by tears and lamentation.

As ſoon as the diſbanded tribes arrived on the other ſide the river Jordan, they erected an altar near the place where they and their brethren miraculouſly paſſed over; not for any religious uſe, but as a memorial to ſucceeding generations, that, though they were parted by the river, they were of the ſame deſcent and religion, and held an equal right to the tabernacle at Shiloh, and to the worſhip of God performed there, as their brethren on the other ſide the river. The latter either from being miſinformed, or miſapprehending the intent of this altar being erected, fell into a violent rage againſt them, as apoſtates from the true religion; and immediately took up arms in vindication of the worſhip and religion of their forefathers, and to avenge the cauſe of God upon the heads and chief authors of this defection. But, before they proceeded to theſe extremities, their rulers adviſed them to ſuſpend the execution of their wrath till they had ſent a deputation, in order to know their reaſon for building ſuch an altar. This being agreed to by the people, they made choice of Phineas, the ſon of Eleazar, with ten other perſons of eminent diſtinction, to go on the embaſſy. As ſoon as theſe commiſſioners arrived on the other ſide the river Jordan they convened an aſſembly of the people, when Phineas addreſſed them as follows:

"We are very ſenſible that the crime charged on you at "preſent is of too heinous a nature to be puniſhed by "words only; but we have not raſhly taken up arms to "execute vengeance in proportion to the degree of iniqui-"ty committed. We have conſidered that you are in alli-"ance with us, and hope that on ſerious reflection, and "a proper admonition from us, you will be made ſenſi-"ble of your error, and brought to a proper ſenſe of your "duty. We deſire that you will frankly and honeſtly in-"form us, upon what motives, and with what deſign "you erected this altar. If it was from motives conſiſt-"ent with the religion of Moſes, we are not angry with "you; but if you are gone over to a falſe worſhip, we "muſt draw our ſwords in defence of that religion you "have ſo ſacrilegiouſly violated. We moſt ſincerely "hope the latter is not the caſe; for we cannot think it "poſſible that a people ſo well acquainted with the law "of God, our friends and allies, from whom we have "ſo lately parted, can be ſo inſenſible and ungrateful, as "to abandon the holy tabernacle, the ark and the altar, "and the worſhip of your forefathers, to join with our "enemies, the Canaanites, in the worſhip of falſe gods. "Should this unfortunately be the caſe, we entreat you to "repent, and return to that reverence you owe to the laws "of God and your country, and you ſhall be again re-"ceived: but if you obſtinately perſiſt in your error, we "muſt compel you to obedience by force of arms. Do "not imagine that, becauſe you are ſeparated from us by "a river, you are therefore out of the reach of God's "power; for you are under his juriſdiction wherever you "exiſt. If the temptations of the place in which you "live are too powerful for you to withſtand, remove to a "diſtant country; for depend on it, if you continue here, "and perſevere in your error, deſtruction will be the con-"ſequence. Take advice in time, relinquiſh your apoſ-"tacy, and adore the true God, who will ever protect "you, as he has hitherto done your forefathers. Conſider "well what is now ſaid to you, and do not put us to the "neceſſity of commencing a war that will be exceedingly "diſagreeable to us, and infallibly deſtructive to you. "You have ſtill your choice left, either to continue "friends, by returning to your duty, or otherwiſe to be-"come enemies; in the latter of which caſes no diſtinc-"tion will be made between apoſtate Iſraelites, and pro-"feſſed Canaanites."

When Phineas had finiſhed his ſpeech, one of the rulers of the aſſembly, in the name of the whole multitude, addreſſing himſelf to the deputies, returned the following anſwer:

"The accuſation you have laid againſt us is ill-found-"ed. We have not made the leaſt breach in the alliance "ſo happily formed with our brethren on the other ſide "Jordan, nor have we been guilty of any affection or "novelty in erecting this altar. We know but one God, "who is the God of all the Hebrews, and but one altar, "which is the brazen altar before the tabernacle. With "reſpect to the altar in queſtion, it was never intended "for any religious uſe, but only as a memorial to poſte-"rity of our mutual friendſhip and alliance, and rather "to keep us ſteady in our ancient religion, than to be any "ways inſtrumental to the violation of it. God is our "witneſs that this, and this only, was the occaſion of "the altar being erected; whence we entreat you to lay "aſide thoſe ſuſpicions you have entertained, and not "impute to us what would render any part of the poſte-"rity of Abraham, who ſhould be guilty of ſuch conduct, "deſerving of immediate death."

This anſwer gave great ſatisfaction to the deputies, who immediately returned to Joſhua, and an aſſembly being called, related to them the particulars of all that had paſſed. Not only Joſhua, but the princes of the tribes, and in ſhort, all the people, rejoiced at the reſult of this embaſſy; for which they offered ſacrifices of thankſgiving to God. When this was done, Joſhua diſmiſſed the people, and retired to Shechem.

No particular occurrence took place from this period till the death of Joſhua, which happened about twenty years after. He was at this time far advanced in years; and finding his diſſolution near at hand, he convened an aſſembly of the leaders of the tribes, the elders, magiſtrates, and as many of the common people as could be gathered together. When the whole appeared before him he harangued them in a pertinent diſcourſe on the great benefits and protection they had received from the hand of Providence. He pointed out to them in what manner he had preserved them even in the midst of dangers, and that he had not only relieved them in all their wants and distresses, but had raised them from the most abject to the most prosperous situation in life. For these great and distinguished benefits he strictly enjoined them to be always diligent and attentive to their religious duties, and, if they would wish to preserve the favour of their great benefactor, to live in the fear and love of him, and in the observance of his commandments. He told them, that as this would, in all probability, be the last time he should have the opportunity of addressing himself to them, he hoped what he had said would remain impressed on their minds, and that in remembrance of him, and their great legislator Moses, they would conduct themselves in such a manner, as to obtain happiness in this world, and everlasting felicity in the next.

When Joshua had finished his address, he dismissed the assembly, a short time after which he paid the debt of nature. At the time of his death he was in the 110th year of his age, 40 of which were spent under the direction of Moses, whom he succeeded in the administration, and in which office he continued 26 years.

He was a man who possessed great prudence, and had a manner of expressing his thoughts that gave pleasure to all who heard him. He was brave and indefatigable in war, and in times of peace he conducted himself in such a manner as to acquire the universal good-will and affection of the people. His remains were deposited at Tharnia, a city belonging to the tribe of Ephraim.

About the same time that Joshua died, Eleazar, the high-priest, also paid the debt of nature, and was succeeded in the priesthood by his son Phineas. His remains were deposited in the city of Gibatha.

CHAP. II.

The government of the Israelites vested in the tribe of Judah. Their success against the Canaanites. Jerusalem besieged. The people become disobedient. The Benjamites maltreat the wife of a Levite. A civil war between them and the other tribes. The Benjamites defeated, after which a peace is made and they are restored to their former privileges.

AFTER the death of Joshua the people had a consultation with Phineas, relative to the farther prosecution of the war against the Canaanites, when it was resolved that it should be carried on with the greatest vigour, and that the chief command and direction of it should be committed to the tribe of Judah, who should be assisted by the tribe of Simeon.

The Canaanites were at this time exceeding strong, and receiving intimation of the intentions of the Israelites, they gathered together a great army under the command of Adonibezec, and encamped themselves near the city of Bezec. Their principal expectations of success were built on the loss of Joshua, but they soon found themselves deceived, for when the two tribes of Israelites attacked them, they fell on with such resolution, that the Canaanites immediately gave way, and upwards of 10,000 were killed on the spot. Great numbers took to flight, but being close pursued by the Israelites, few of them escaped. Adonibezec, their leader, was taken prisoner, and being brought before the leaders of the two tribes, they ordered his thumbs and great toes to be cut off, in the manner as he had done to no less than seventy little kings or princes; so that the similitude of punishment made the tyrant reflect on his own cruel disposition, and acknowledge the justice of God in what he had brought upon him.

The two united tribes, after the conquest of Bezec, pushed their rout farther into the country, plundered the respective towns through which they passed, and put the inhabitants to the sword. They at length laid siege to Jerusalem, and soon made themselves masters of the suburbs, but finding the city itself too strongly fortified both by nature and art, they gave up all thoughts of attempting to reduce it.

From Jerusalem the Israelites proceeded to Hebron, which they entered by assault, and after plundering the inhabitants, put them all to the sword. This place was given to the Levites, with a part of the land round it to the amount of 2000 cubits. The other part which belonged to it was given to Caleb, who was one of the spies employed by Moses to make discoveries in the land of Canaan. A dividend was also given to the posterity of Jethro, Moses's father-in-law, because they had left their native country, and borne a part with the Hebrews in the war.

After the reduction of Hebron the two tribes proceeded in search of farther conquests, and took many cities, both on the mountains and on the plains, near the sea. They had some thoughts of laying siege to the two cities of Gaza and Ascalon, but as they were strongly fortified, and the inhabitants had great numbers of chariots, they thought proper to relinquish the design.

Having now amassed considerable wealth by the conquests already made, the two enterprising tribes of Judah and Simeon resolved, for the present, to lay aside all farther prosecution of the war against the Canaanites. They therefore broke up their camps, and returned to their respective habitations.

The tribe of Benjamin, to whose lot the city of Jerusalem fell, compounded with the inhabitants, and suffered them to live in peace, in consideration of their paying an annual tribute for the indulgence. The like measures were also taken by several of the other tribes.

While the united tribes of Judah and Simeon were at war with the Canaanites, the tribe of Ephraim undertook the conquest of Bethel. They laid before the place a considerable time without being able to make an attack, from the great strength of the walls, and the different fortifications. But at length, they effected by treachery what they could not obtain by force. Meeting with a native of the town, who had been to get provisions for his family, they seized him, and made an agreement with him, that if he would contrive to let them secretly into the city, both he and all his relations should be secured from any danger. The man strictly fulfilled the engagement, and the Ephraimites entering the city put all the inhabitants to the sword except the man and his family, whose lives they had promised to preserve.

The advantages obtained by the different tribes, from their great success against the Canaanites, threw them into a state of dissipation, and, instead of prosecuting the war, as they had been commanded, they indulged themselves in luxury. For this neglect they were chastised by the Almighty, who gave them to understand, that, for their disobedience, they should be persecuted by the very people they had been commanded to extirpate. They were, at first, greatly startled at this revelation, but they had become so depraved from the possessions they had already got, and even so elated at the annual tribute paid by the Canaanites that they suffered the enjoyment of the luxuries of life to take the pre-eminence of their duty to their maker. In fact, the whole system of government was overturned, and both civil and religious authority totally annihilated. During this course of dissipation, a circumstance occurred of a very singular nature, and which occasioned the breaking out of a civil war, the particulars of which were as follow.

In the tribe of Ephraim [illegible] exaction [illegible]

have equal success as before When the army of the Israelites had got that of the Benjamites at such a distance from the city, as to be within reach of those in ambuscade, they made a sudden stop, and fell on the front of the Benjamites with great impetuosity, while the ambuscades, by a proper signal given, fell on those in the rear The Benjamites were so surprised at this unexpected manœuvre, that they were immediately thrown into confusion A select body of 600, who were distinguished for their great courage and strength, broke their way through the enemy's troops, and escaped to a lofty mountain, while the rest fled with great precipitation to a deep valley, where, being closely surrounded by the Israelites, they all perished, the whole number amounted to 25,000 men After this the Israelites burnt the city, and put all the inhabitants to the sword They likewise destroyed several other cities belonging to the Benjamites, and particularly wreaked their vengeance on the inhabitants of Jabes, a city of Gilead, for having refused to assist them against the Benjamites They first burnt the city to the ground, and then put every creature to the sword, except four hundred virgins, whom they brought away with them Such were the dreadful consequences that took place from the ridiculous obstinacy of the Benjamites, in not delivering up the people who had committed so flagrant a violation on the person of the Levite's wife

When the Israelites began to reflect on the severity with which they had treated the Benjamites, and that the whole tribe were, in a manner, cut off from the main body they repented of what they had done, and heartily wished for a reconciliation To effect this they sent commissioners to invite back the six hundred men that had fled to the mountains, where they found them on the rock called Rhoa, or Rimmon These commissioners after condoling with them on the misfortunes that had befel them, not only in the loss of their relations and friends, but that of almost the whole tribe, advised them to return, and not suffer themselves to be totally extirpated, by withdrawing from the fellowship They likewise told them that all their lands, cattle, and every thing else that belonged to them, should be restored, and that they should be placed in the same situation as before the rupture broke out The Benjamites confessed they had acted very wrong, and acknowledged the righteous judgment of God in what they had suffered They thanked the commissioners for their advice, accepted the invitation, and immediately returned to their own tribe

When the commissioners informed the Israelites of the issue of their embassy they were greatly pleased and, in order to restore the tribe of Benjamin, they sent the four hundred virgins, brought from the city of Jabes as wives for that number out of the six hundred They then deliberated in what manner to provide for the remaining two hundred, the Israelites having bound themselves by oath, before the war, not to intermarry with the tribe of Benjamin It was the opinion of some that the oath might be rendered void, from its having been taken in the heat of passion, and that as it was to restore an almost lost tribe, it would not be displeasing to the Almighty This proposition was entirely objected to by the elders, who would not, upon any consideration whatever, listen to a matter that had in it the least appearance of perjury At length one of the senators [illegible] a proposition, in words to the following effect "We have (says he) a "public festival held three times a year in Shiloh, at "which it is customary for our wives and daughters to "be present On this occasion, let us permit the Benjamites to seize as many of the virgins as are wanted "for the two hundred men If the parents should appeal "for justice, they must be told, it was their own faults, "in not taking more care of their daughters, and that "it would be indiscreet to force them from the Benjamites as dissentions with those people had already produced the most direful consequences"

This proposition was highly approved of by the people, in consequence of which the plan was communicated to the Benjamites Accordingly, on the morning of the festival, the two hundred men, who wanted wives, concealed themselves in the most private places near the city, and, as the unsuspecting virgins passed by, each seized his mate, and fled with her to his home This, for some time, occasioned great confusion but when the elders told the parents the impropriety of attempting to regain their daughters by force, they were appeased

The six hundred Benjamites, being thus provided with wives, applied themselves diligently to their respective callings, and by their industry and prudence, from the most wretched and forlorn condition, they soon became again considerable, both in number, wealth and power Such was the conclusion of this war.

CHAP. III.

The Danites persecuted by the Canaanites The Israelites, being totally addicted to luxury and dissipation, their [illegible] disposition provoke the just vengeance of the Almighty Are reduced to slavery, and kept in a state of subjection by Cusharth, king of the Assyrians

THE Israelites having for some time laid aside martial discipline, and instead thereof, directed their attention only to husbandry, and other domestic occupations, the Canaanites took advantage of it, and entered into a conspiracy against them They accordingly raised a considerable army, built a great number of chariots, and trained up all the young people to martial discipline They were farther animated to prosecute their intentions, by having brought over to them Ascalon and Accaron, from the tribe of Judah, as also the inhabitants of several cities of the plains.

The first attack they made was on the tribe of Dan, whom they forced to leave their possessions, and retire into the mountainous parts of the country The Danites were so circumstanced that they could not think of revenging themselves by war, and in their then situation, there was not a sufficiency of land for them to subsist on in a state of peace They, therefore, sent five people into the inland parts of the country in order to find out a proper spot where they might fix their residence At [illegible] one day [illegible] the wide and open country about Sidon, not far from mount Libanus, [illegible] and the springs of [illegible]

[illegible] separates Syria from Palestine It consists of a kind of [illegible] length, beginning at three or four leagues distance from the Mediterranean [illegible] Smyrna and going from north to south towards Sidon from thence [illegible] to [illegible] Sidon towards Damascus [illegible] from the [illegible] southward from the heights [illegible] Damascus [illegible] [illegible] mountains [illegible] properly called [illegible] The other part, which [illegible] extends from south to north [illegible] by the Greeks [illegible] Between these two [illegible] is a long [illegible] called [illegible] Hollow Syria [illegible]

Josephus [illegible] Lebanon [illegible] [illegible] Mediterranean [illegible] [illegible] [illegible]

Bethlehem, belonging to the tribe of Judah (*a*). The woman was exceeding handsome, and her husband passionately fond of her; but, from some unknown cause, she slighted his affection, and, within four months after their marriage, left him, and returned to her parents. The husband no sooner missed his wife than he hasted to her father, by whom he was received with great tenderness; and the umbrage which the daughter had taken against her husband, was adjusted to the satisfaction of all parties. After staying five days, the man and his wife departed for their own home, attended by one servant, and taking with them an ass for the better convenience of the woman. When the servant advised them not to proceed any further till the next morning, as it would be dangerous travelling in the night through an enemy's country, and that, even among friends, those who travelled after daylight were considered as suspicious persons. The man refused to take this salutary advice from his servant, and prosecuting his journey, it was so late when they came to the city of Gibeah, belonging to the tribe of Benjamin, that they could not obtain a lodging (*b*) or find any place to get refreshment. While they were in this dilemma, they met with an ancient man belonging to the tribe of Ephraim, who asked them from whence they came, and what occasioned them to be out at so unseasonable an hour? The man replied, He was a Levite, that he belonged to the tribe of Ephraim, and that he was going home with his wife. As the old man belonged to the same tribe, and was naturally of an hospitable disposition, he took them with him to his house, and gave them every refreshment that lay in his power. It happened that in their way to the old man's house they had been observed by some young men belonging to the town, who, being captivated with the appearance of the woman, repaired to the house, knocked at the door, and demanded the woman to be delivered up to them. Both the old man and the husband expostulated with them on the impropriety of their conduct; but all the answer they received was, "Deliver up "the woman and no farther trouble shall ensue." Finding that all remonstrances were ineffectual, the old man, as the last effort, offered to deliver up his own daughter instead of the stranger; but this was of no avail, for they threatened that if he did not immediately deliver up the very woman they requested, death should be his portion. The old man, being impelled to give her up, they took her away to their own quarters, and after having, for the whole night, treated her with every degree of indecency, they dismissed her. The woman immediately returned to the old man's house, loaded with such confusion, between shame and indignation, that, when she saw her husband, she had not power to speak, but immediately fell on the ground, and died. The husband preserved great presence of mind on this alarming occasion. When his trouble had a little subsided, he placed the body of his dead wife on the ass, and after thanking the old man for the civility with which he had treated him, he departed. As soon as he arrived at his own house, he divided the body into twelve parts, and sent one to each of the twelve tribes, with a proper relation, by the respective bearers, of every particular that had attended this cruel and unprecedented transaction.

When the several tribes had investigated the heinousness of this action among themselves, they were fired with indignation, and the principals of each tribe immediately assembled together at Shiloh, with a determined resolution of laying siege to Gibeah. They would immediately have put their design into execution, but were restrained from their purpose by the interposition of one of the elders, who told them, that it would be very indiscreet to wage war with their allies, without first making a strict inquiry into the merits of the case. He therefore proposed that proper persons should be appointed to go to the principal people of Gibeah, and demand the criminals who had been guilty of such violence. If they readily delivered them up, they might punish them at discretion; but if they refused, he thought they had a right to do themselves justice by force of arms.

This advice being cordially received by the people, the messengers appointed went to Gibeah, and demanded the persons who had committed so flagrant a violence on the Levite's wife. The inhabitants of Gibeah absolutely refused to give them up, saying, they did not think it honourable to be directed by other people, that they wanted neither courage, skill, or numbers, and that they were determined to stand by each other in the cause of a common defence.

When the messengers returned with the answer, the Israelites were so enraged, that they all took an oath not to intermarry with any of the tribe of Benjamin; and it was resolved that a war should be carried on against them with the like vigour as had been done by their forefathers against the Canaanites. In consequence of this the Israelites took the field with an army of 400,000 men. The army of the Benjamites consisted only of 25,600, among whom were 500 slingers, particularly distinguished for their abilities as marksmen. The two armies met near Gibeah, when a dreadful encounter immediately took place; the Israelites were routed with the loss of 22,000 on the spot, and the slaughter would have been much more considerable, had not night parted them. The next morning each party renewed the action with equal violence, when the Israelites again proved unsuccessful, their loss, on the spot, amounting to at least 18,000 men. These two disasters so intimidated them, that they broke up their camp, and retired to Bethel, a city near Gibeah, where they spent the day in fasting and prayer, beseeching the Almighty that he would interpose in their behalf, and once more take them under his Divine protection.

Having received assurance by the mouth of Phineas (*c*) that their prayers were heard, and that their future attempts would be attended with success, they determined to make another attempt on the city of Gibeah. They accordingly divided their army into two bodies, one half of which was planted in ambuscade, near the city, late in the evening, and early the next morning the other part marched to attack the army of the Benjamites. On the first charge the Israelites gave way, and retreated a considerable distance, which step being considered by the Benjamites as a mark of timidity, not only the army, but the greater part of the inhabitants closely followed them, not doubting but they should

---

(*a*) Josephus's early date of this history before the beginning of the Judges or when there was no king in Israel (Judges xix. 1.) is strongly confirmed by the large number of Benjamites both in the days of Asa and Jehoshaphat, 2 Chron. xiv. 8. and xvii. 17. Commentators on sacred writ besides are generally of opinion, that this transaction happened between the death of Joshua and the appointment of the first judge. Some conceive that the reason why Samuel, or whoever was the author of the Book of Judges, places it at the end of [illegible], because he was unwilling to interrupt the thread of his story by intermixing these matters with it, but reserved them to be related apart by themselves.

(*b*) The laws of hospitality were in ancient times, held exceeding sacred; but the men of Gibeah, as they were grossly abandoned in vice, so were they wholly defective in this, [illegible] suffering these travellers to remain in the streets, without any invitation; which, at length, they received from [illegible] man, who was himself only a sojourner amongst them. It must be remembered that then, as well as at present, there were no such things as Inns in the countries, [illegible] travellers always took with them (especially on long journeys) not only provisions and other necessaries for [illegible], but [illegible] the Levite.

(*c*) This was the same Phineas who distinguished [illegible] God on a former occasion. [illegible] placed in the book of Judges) [illegible] of [illegible] old [illegible] before [illegible] death [illegible] appointment of the first Judge.

Jordan finding it a rich, fruitful foil, and in every refpect formed for the intended purpofe, they returned, and gave a particular defcription of it to their countrymen. In confequence of this, the whole tribe marched to the fpot, and being perfectly fatisfied with it, they built a city and called it Dan, from one of the fons of Jacob of that name, and from whom the whole tribe received their appellation.

The Ifraelites were at this time in a very depraved ftate. They had given a loofe to all the vices of the Canaanites, had neglected every religious duty, and purfued a life of debauchery and diffipation. This conduct greatly difpleafed the Almighty, who, as a punifhment, took from them, for a time, his Divine protection, and left them expofed to the power of their enemies.

The firft ftroke they received was from Chufarth, king of the Affyrians, who marched againft them with a confiderable army. This monarch was fo powerful that he drove all before him. Great numbers of the Ifraelites fell by the fword, and many of their towns and cities were feized by the conqueror. The captured Ifraelites were now fubject to a moft tyrannical monarch, who oppreffed them by heavy taxes, and treated them with the moft contemptible indignities.

CHAP. IV.

The Ifraelites are delivered from their fubjection to the Affyrians by Othniel, the fon of Kenaz.

IN this deplorable fituation did the Ifraelites remain for eight years, when they were delivered out of the hands of their oppreffors in the following manner. A perfon, named Othniel, the fon of Kenaz, of the tribe of Judah, a man of great courage and difcernment, having received a fecret impulfe from Heaven to interpofe in behalf of the wretched Ifraelites, he communicated the matter to fome of his particular friends, whom he knew to be men of courage and integrity, and who were greatly diffatisfied with the ftate of public affairs. After confidering what meafures were moft proper to take, it was at length refolved to make a fudden attack on the king's guards, and to put every man to the fword. This fcheme being attended with fuccefs, it brought over great numbers to the intereft of Othniel, who, in a fhort time, marched at the head of them to give the Affyrians battle. The encounter was at firft doubtful, but the Ifraelites foon became conquerors: great numbers of the Affyrians were flain, and the reft faved themfelves by paffing the Euphrates. Thus, at the inftigation of the brave and intrepid Othniel, were the Ifraelites again reftored to their liberty, in acknowledgment for which, they prefented him with the government, and in this fituation he continued during the remainder of his life, which was a courfe of forty years.

CHAP. V.

The Ifraelites are fubject to the Moabites during the term of eighteen years, and are delivered by one Ehud, who retained the government eighty years.

ON the death of Othniel, the Ifraelites, being without a leader, returned again to a diffolute way of living, neither paying refpect to the laws of their country, nor their duty to God. This confequently produced confufion in their public affairs, which being taken notice of by Eglon king of the Moabites, he marched againft them with a confiderable army. Several battles took place, in all which the Ifraelites were worfted, and their army being at length totally fubdued, they became tributary to their conqueror, who erected a palace at Jericho, and kept them in the moft abject ftate upwards of eighteen years.

At the expiration of this time, the Ifraelites were refcued from the hands of their oppreffor by the following fingular occurrences. In Jericho lived a young man named Ehud, the fon of Geron of the tribe of Benjamin. He was of an enterprifing difpofition, remarkably handfome in his perfon, and had great bodily ftrength. He had not only ingratiated himfelf into the favour of the king, by making him repeated prefents, but had alfo many friends at court, fo that he had free accefs at difcretion, and this gave him the opportunity of executing the project he had laid for relieving the diftreffed Ifraelites. Being one day to make a prefent to the king, he went in his ufual drefs, attended by two fervants, taking with him a dagger, which he fecreted on his right fide, having the greateft ftrength in his left arm. On his arrival at the palace, he was admitted, as ufual, to the prefence of the king, and, after complimenting him with the prefent, told him he had a matter to relate to him, that demanded privacy. On this the king ordered his attendants to withdraw, and feating himfelf on his throne, waited for the expected intelligence. Ehud told him he had a dream to impart to him by command of the Almighty, at the found of which the king, impatient to hear, fuddenly arofe from his feat, when Ehud drew the dagger from his fide, and plunged it into his heart. In this fituation he left the king, immediately quitted the palace, and haftened with all expedition to Jerufalem. The attendants of the palace fuppofing the king to have compofed himfelf to fleep, did not prefume to enter the room for a confiderable time after the departure of Ehud, till at length, fearing fomething particular was the occafion of not feeing or hearing him, they ventured to open the door of his apartment, where they found him laying in his gore. In the mean time, Ehud having related to his countrymen what had happened, and advifed them to take advantage of it, they immediately difpatched proper perfons to different parts of the country with horns (as was the cuftom on fuch occafions) to call together the people. They accordingly affembled in great bodies, and proceeding with the greateft expedition to the palace, fell on the guards, all of whom they killed on the fpot: the reft of the army, amounting to about 10,000 men, made for the river, towards the country of Moab; but the Ifraelites, having previoufly fecured all the paffes, intercepted their flight, and the whole body were cut to pieces. Thus were the Ifraelites extricated out of the hands of the Moabites, and as Ehud was the principal inftigator of their deliverance, they beftowed on him the government which he enjoyed upwards of eighty years. He was a perfon of the moft diftinguifhed merit, and conducted himfelf in fuch a manner, as to deferve what was univerfally beftowed on him, namely, the good-will and affection of the people he governed. He was fucceeded by Shamgar, the fon of Anath, who died in the firft year of his government.

CHAP. VI.

The Ifraelites are enflaved under different tyrannies by the Canaanites, and at length delivered by Barak and Deborah.

THE Ifraelites not in the leaft amending their lives, or taking warning from the calamities they had experienced, but ftill continuing not to worfhip God, or obey his laws, were again brought to fubjection by another monarch, namely, Jabin, king of the Canaanites. This prince originally came from the city of Azor, fituated near the lake Semachonitis. He kept an army confifting of 300,000 foot, 10,000 horfe, and 3000 chariots: the grand command of which was given to Sifera, who was next in dignity to the king. This general foon

GIDEON's SACRIFICE
consumed by Fire on being touched by the Staff of the Angel

reduced the Israelites, brought them to subjection, and made them pay tribute to his master.

In this state of servitude did the Israelites continue for twenty years, when they began to reflect that their miseries were certainly inflicted on them by God, as a just punishment for their contempt of the laws of their forefathers. In this state of contrition they went to a famous prophetess (*a*) named Deborah (which, in the Hebrew tongue, signifies a bee) and implored her to intercede in their behalf, that God would be pleased to forgive them their past faults, and rescue them out of the hands of their cruel persecutors. Deborah complied with their request, and the Almighty being pleased to promise them a deliverance, he made choice of Barak of the tribe of Naphtali, to effect it. Accordingly Deborah sent for Barak, (which, in the Hebrew language, signifies *lightning*) and ordered him immediately to raise an army of 10,000 men, and march with all expedition against the Canaanites. Barak, at first, objected to take the command of so small a number, against so large a body as that of the enemy; but Deborah informed him, that God had said the number was sufficient. Notwithstanding this, he still refused the command, unless she would go with him and take a part; at which Deborah replied with indignation, "Would you give to a woman part of that "honour which God hath assigned for thee alone? However, I will not refuse it." They accordingly drew out their army, and pitched their tents on Mount Tabor, while Sisera, general of the Canaanites, by the king's orders, marched to give them battle. When the two armies came within sight of each other, the Israelites were struck with horror at the great multitude of the enemy, and were inclined to make a precipitate retreat; but Deborah prevailed on them to stand a battle, assuring them it was the cause of God, and that he would assist them in conquering their enemies. The truth of this was soon manifested to the Israelites, for no sooner were the two armies engaged, than there fell a most dreadful shower of rain and hail, attended with a violent wind, which blowing full in the faces of the Canaanites, obliged them to shut their eyes, so that their bows and slings were rendered entirely useless; besides which, their nerves were so contracted by the cold, that they were not able to handle their arms. The Israelites seeing the disadvantages under which the Canaanites laboured, fell on them with great impetuosity, and their whole army was broken, dispersed, and cut to pieces. Great numbers fell by the sword, many were trampled to death by the horses, and the few that attempted to save themselves by flight, were made prisoners; so that this prodigious army was, in effect, totally destroyed. When Sisera, the Canaanitish general, saw the destruction of his army, he leapt from his chariot, and fled to the house of one Jael, a Kenite, (*b*) who received him with apparent hospitality. Being greatly fatigued, he asked her for some refreshment, which, having received, he laid himself on the ground, and soon fell fast asleep. While he was in this situation, Jael took a large iron nail, and suddenly driving it through his temple, fastened him to the floor, just at the time the Israelites arrived at her house in search of him. This fully completed the victory; after which Barak marched with his army to Azor, and laying siege to the place, slew the greater part of the inhabitants, together with Jabin, their king, and, in order totally to extirpate them, he burnt the city to the ground. After this victory, Barak kept possession of the government during the space of forty years.

CHAP. VII.

The Israelites are conquered by the Midianites, in conjunction with the Amalekites and Arabians, and held in vassalage.

ON the death of Barak, which happened about the same time with that of Deborah, the Midianites, Amalekites, and Arabians, entered into an alliance against the Israelites, and so powerful were their arms, that they conquered wherever they went, destroying the fruits of the ground, and carrying with them every thing that was valuable. They continued these hostilities with such violence, that the wretched Israelites were obliged to fly to the mountains for refuge, where they dug caverns, in which they hid themselves, and the little property they could save, from their merciless enemies. They remained in this state seven years, during which time their enemies permitted them to cultivate their land in the winter; but it was only to serve their own purposes, for they made themselves masters of the greater part of the produce when it was fit for removal. The small quantity, therefore, the Israelites could obtain for themselves, was scarce sufficient to enable them to preserve their existence; besides which they were in the most extreme distress, so that finding themselves likely to perish from want, they made their supplications to God, in the most fervent manner, desiring him that he would be pleased to deliver them from the wretched state into which they had fallen.

CHAP. VIII.

Gideon musters the tribes to advance against the Midianites. Receives an omen of success, chooses a select few for the expedition. Obtains a complete victory. Rules the people with integrity and justice for forty years.

WHILE they were in this deplorable situation, as one Gideon, the son of Joas, a leading man of the tribe of Manasseh, was threshing a little corn at a wine press, not daring to do it on the floor, for fear of being discovered by the enemy, an angel appeared to him in the likeness of a young man, who told him, "He "was a happy man and beloved of God." To which Gideon answered, "It is no great sign of favour, since I "am obliged to use my wine-press instead of a threshing "floor." The angel bade him be of good courage, and direct his attention to arms, whereby himself and his countrymen might be restored to their liberty. "Alas! "(says Gideon) it is impossible for me to undertake so "great a thing: we have not a sufficiency of men in our "tribe to make such an attempt; neither am I a proper "person, to conduct so important a design." The angel answered, that all his deficiencies would be supplied by the Almighty; and that if he would but take upon him the command of a body of men, the Israelites should obtain a complete victory over their enemies.

Gideon requested of the angel that he would not depart till he had prepared a sacrifice on the occasion: which being complied with, he made ready a kid, with unleavened cakes, and having brought them before the angel, he ordered Gideon to lay them on a rock. This was immediately complied with, when the angel touching it with a staff, fire issued out of the rock, and the whole was consumed; after which the angel disappeared.

(*a*) The words *prophet* and *prophetess* in the Old Testament, sometimes signify persons endued with special, though not miraculous, gifts or graces for the interpreting and explaining the word of God; and of this sort were the sons of the prophets, or such as were brought up in the schools of the prophets. As, therefore, we read of no miraculous action that Deborah did, she was perhaps only a woman of eminent holiness, prudence and knowledge of the Holy Scriptures, by which she was singularly qualified to judge the people, that is, to determine rules and controversies among them according to the word of God.

(*b*) The Kenites, though they were proselytes, and worshipped the true God, according to the Mosaic law, yet being strangers by birth, and therefore having no right or title to the land of Canaan, they lived [illegible] times to observe a neutrality, and maintain peace as well as they could, both with the Israelites and Canaanites. It was upon this account [illegible] there was peace between king Jabin and the family of Heber, the Kenite; and that gave confidence to Sisera in his distress, to fly to Heber's tent for protection.

When Gideon had a little recovered himself from the surprise into which he was thrown from this singular occurrence, he related the particulars to some of the most considerable of the Israelites, who had such faith in the revelation, that they immediately raised an army of 10,000 men, fully resolved to hazard a battle with the tyrannical Midianites. But, before they took the field, the Divine agent again appeared to Gideon, and spoke to him to this effect: "It is too common for mankind to claim "that merit to themselves which belongs to God alone; "and such is the disposition of the people you have gathered together, and are about to lead against the Midianites: but to shew you that victory is influenced from "above, and not to be obtained by the strength of man "without Divine assistance, take your army to the river "Jordan in the heat of the day, and observe the manner "in which the soldiers drink the water. Those who take it up with their hands and lap it, you may depend on "being men of courage; but such as lie down and drink "at leisure, are not to be trusted." Gideon obeyed the Divine command, and found only three hundred men that lapped the water from their hands, which he immediately detached from the rest. With this small number God commanded him to march against the enemy, and to attack them in the night. He accordingly advanced at the head of his chosen men, and encamped near the river Jordan, resolving to pass it the following day. But Gideon was still doubtful of success, and the more so, from being commanded to attack the enemy in the night. However, these fears were removed by the interposition of the Almighty, who, the preceding evening, told Gideon to take with him one of his soldiers, and go privately to the camp of the Midianites, from whom he should hear something that would animate and give him courage. In obedience to this injunction he went, taking with him a servant, named Phuran. They arrived at the camp unperceived, and approaching one of the tents, heard a soldier relating the following dream to his comrades: "Methought (said he) I saw a barley loaf (the "coarsest of all grains, and not fit for man to eat) come "rolling into the camp, and having passed through the "king's tent, and thrown it down, it afterwards entered "all the other tents and did the like." This dream was interpreted by one of the soldier's comrades, who said it denoted the total destruction of the army. "The barley (says he) is, as you say, the coarsest of grains, "and the Israelites are the vilest and most abject of all "the people in Asia. Gideon is now at the head of an "army against us; and, I am afraid, the barley loaf "overthrowing our tents implies, that we shall be totally destroyed by the Israelites."

When Gideon had heard this dream, and its interpretation, he was inspired with new courage, and immediately returning to his people, and acquainting them with it, he ordered them to prepare themselves, with all expedition, to march against the enemy. Accordingly, about the fourth watch (a) Gideon drew out his men, and divided them into three companies, of an hundred each. Every man had a burning torch secreted in a long pitcher, and in his right hand, a ram's horn, by way of trumpet. The enemy's camp took up a large space of ground, having in it a great number of camels; and the people were more dispersed than usual on account of their belonging to different nations. The Israelites had received instructions, that as soon as they came near the camp of the Midianites, on a signal given, they should break their pitchers, display their torches, sound their horns, and immediately begin the attack. These orders they strictly obeyed, when the Midianites were immediately thrown into the utmost confusion. A great slaughter ensued; but more were destroyed by the hands of their own people, than by the Israelites; for it being dark, and they of different nations, they could not understand each other, so that every man took the [illegible] for next him for an enemy. In short, the whole was one scene of confusion, of which the Israelites took proper advantages. A great number of the Midianites were slain on the spot, and the remainder for the present saved themselves by flight. The troops which Gideon had left behind, hearing of his success, immediately marched [illegible] all the difficult passes, in order to cut off the retreat of the enemy. They came up with a great body of them in a flat part of the country, when immediately surrounding them, they put every man to the sword, and, among them, two of their kings, named Oreb and Zeb. In the mean time Gideon marched with his three hundred men against the remainder of the enemy, amounting to about 10,000, who had fixed themselves on a spot at a considerable distance under the command of their proper officers. When Gideon came near them he was joined by the rest of his troops, and a general engagement ensued, in which the whole army of the Midianites were cut to pieces, and two of their princes, named Zebah and Halmunna, taken prisoners. The number of the enemy killed in these encounters amounted to 120,000. Thus did the Israelites gain a complete victory over their enemies, besides which, they greatly enriched themselves with plunder, consisting of gold, silver, rich stuffs, camels, asses, &c.

Gideon, having executed the business on which he was sent, by destroying the Midianites, returned to Ephraim, where he put to death the two captive kings. The tribe to which he belonged (through envy of his great success, and glorious atchievements) appeared displeased with him for engaging in a public act of hostility without their approbation; and their anger arose to such a pitch, that they were just on the point of making war with him. But this was prevented by the prudence of Gideon, who told them it was not his war but God's, by whom he was commanded to act as he had done, and that therefore he did not claim any merit to himself.

This answer perfectly satisfied the people, and they joined with the rest in desiring Gideon, as he had redeemed his countrymen from slavery, that he would accept the government. Gideon, at first, begged to be excused; but finding the people determined, he at length complied, and ruled them forty years, during the whole of which time his conduct was such as merited universal approbation. He lived to a very great age; and, when he died, his remains were deposited at Ophra, the place of his nativity.

CHAP. IX.

Abimelech obtains the government wickedly, and rules tyrannically, and is at length slain in an extraordinary manner. The Israelites apostatizing again, are oppressed and enslaved by the Philistines and the Ammonites. Jephtha entrusted with the government of Israel. Makes a peculiar vow. Defeats the Ammonites. Suppresses an insurrection among the Ephraimites. His death.

GIDEON, at the time of his death, had no less than seventy sons, all born in wedlock, besides one by Druma, his concubine, named Abimelech. This [illegible] immediately after his father's decease, made use of the most horrid means to obtain the government. He went to the relations of his mother at Shechem, and told them

(a) Though the Romans, in after ages, divided the night into four watches, (Matth. xiv. 25.) yet in the eastern parts, and in more ancient times, it consisted but of three; whereof the first began at six, and continued to ten. The second was therefore called the middle watch, and began at ten. So that [illegible] supposed it was some time after ten that Gideon alarmed the Midianites' camp; and the reason why he chose this part of the night [illegible] is obvious, because the trumpets would then seem to sound louder, and the lights to shine brighter, and thereby [illegible] and conceal the smallness of his own army.

that, as his father was dead, it would certainly be better for the people to be governed by one person than seventy, meaning his legitimate brothers. This was approved of by his relations, who furnishing him with a considerable sum of money, he returned to his father's house, bringing with him a set of men, whom he knew to be infamous in disposition, and willing to engage in any enterprize, however inconsistent with laws, either human or Divine.

The first step Abimelech took, after returning to his father's house, was, to murder all his brothers, except Jotham, who happily saved himself by flight, and, notwithstanding the cruelty of the action, it answered the wishes of Abimelech, no one objecting to his taking upon himself the government. The people, however, had soon reason to wish they had not been so pliant, for he ruled them with such tyranny, that they were little better situated than when in the hands of their enemies. He followed no other law than that of his own will, and even professed himself an enemy to common justice.

Some time after Abimelech had thus usurped the government, a day of solemnity was kept at Shechem, on which occasion a prodigious concourse of people were assembled. Before the festival began, Jotham, the brother of Abimelech, who had till now concealed himself, appeared on the top of Gerizim, which overlooks Shechem, and calling aloud to the people, he addressed them in words to the following effect.

"There was a time, says he, when the trees (a) had "meetings together in order to regulate the government "of the vegetable part of the creation, and to appoint "one to rule the whole. In a council held on this oc"casion, the major part of the plants were for having "the fig-tree to govern, but the fig-tree declined the "honour, being sufficiently satisfied for the esteem bore "for its fruit. On this the trees applied to the olive "and the vine, both of which likewise refused, for the "same reason as had been given by the fig-tree. At "length they applied to the bramble, who said, If you "are in earnest, I'll willingly take upon me the govern"ment, but remember, you most rest quietly under my "shadow. If you prove refractory, there shall come a "fire out of me that shall destroy you. This, said Jo"tham, is not a tale to divert you, but to make you "reflect on your absurd conduct, in violating your sa"cred obligations to Gideon, by suffering Abimelech, "the murderer of the children of your deliverer, to "usurp and tyrannize over you. This Abimelech is "the very fire I have told you in the fable." (b)

After Jotham had thus delivered himself to the people, he retired, and fled to the mountains, where he concealed himself till the death of his cruel brother Abimelech.

The speech made by Jotham opened the eyes of the Shechemites, who not only dethroned Abimelech, but forced him out of the city, upon which Abimelech, and those who accompanied him, vowed revenge on the inhabitants.

It happened at this time to be the season for gathering in the grapes, but the people had such terrible apprehensions of the cruelty of Abimelech, that they durst not go into the fields to reap their vintage. In this distressed situation they applied to one Gaal, a prince of the country, who had lately come to Shechem with a band of armed men, to protect them, who readily complying with their request, they strengthened his force by adding to them a troop of their own soldiers. Thus secured, they reaped their fruits, and carried them home in safety, and when elated with liquor, they took the freedom of aspersing the characters of Abimelech and his relations. They placed ambuscades in different parts round the city, and taking many of the guards belonging to Abimelech, put them all to the sword.

While matters were in this situation, one Zebul, a principal man among the Shechemites, and a great friend to Abimelech, sent him the particulars of Gaal's conduct, and the disposition of the people. He advised Abimelech to plant soldiers in ambush near the city, and told him, that he would persuade Gaal, to come out and engage him, whereby he would have an opportunity of getting his enemy into his own power, and that he did not doubt but he should soon be able to reinstate him in his regal dignity.

In consequence of this information, Abimelech, after the day was closed, placed a number of men in different parts at some distance from the city. Gaal and Zebul were parading the suburbs during the night as usual, but when the morning opened, and Gaal saw men in armour approaching, he called aloud to Zebul, telling him, that an army in battle array was marching towards the city. Zebul said he was mistaken, for that what he saw was nothing more than the shadow of the mountains. But Gaal, on their nearer approach, insisted they were not shadows, but a real company of armed men. To which Zebul answered, "Didst thou not say that Abimelech was "a slothful and cowardly prince? Now shew thyself "what a man thou art in engaging with him." Gaal accordingly marched against the enemy, and received the first shock, but finding himself too weak, and having lost several of his men, he retreated, and fled into the city.

Zebul took advantage of this, by prejudicing the minds of the people against Gaal, whom he represented as a coward, and, in consequence of Zebul's influence, Gaal was expelled the city.

In the mean time Abimelech, being informed by Zebul, that the citizens intended to prosecute the gathering of the vintage, placed several ambuscades near the city in order to surprise them. Accordingly, on their first coming out, he detached a third part of his army to take possession of the gates of the city, and by that means to cut off the retreat of those who had left it. When the ambuscaders thought it a proper time they made their appearance, which so terrified the defenceless Shechemites, that they attempted to save themselves by flight, but being closely pursued, the greater part fell by the sword. In the mean time the rest of Abimelech's army laid siege to the city, which they took on the first assault, the inhabitants immediately consulting their own safety by flight, though, in the attempt, many were slain. After Abimelech had thus routed the Shechemites, and made himself master of the city, he ordered it to be levelled with the ground, and, as the last insult of triumph, had salt (c) sown on those parts where the walls had stood.

(a) The Greeks pretend to have been the inventors of these [illegible] fables, but there is nothing more absurd than their vanity in this respect. A long time before Æsop, and every other author known to their nation, the Orientals, and particularly the Hebrews, made use of this ingenious manner, for the forming of which no reasons may be assigned. Because men would suffer themselves to be reprehended under this disguise, when they would not digest plain words. And also, because they heard them with delight and pleasure, and remembered them better than any grave or common discourse.

(b) The words of this fable carry a lively image of Abimelech's cruel spirit, and menaces to take severe vengeance on the nobles of Shechem who had been chiefly instrumental in his promotion, in case they should deter[illegible] The whole intent and meaning of [illegible] Shechemites [illegible] folly in choosing such a one for their king, who was no more able to protect them than a bramble was to cover other trees [illegible] under the shadow of its branches.

(c) The [illegible] Not that [illegible] be [illegible] under the [illegible] to shew [illegible] inhabitants were [illegible] conduct [illegible] should [illegible] rebuilt, but [illegible] and desolate.

The wretched Shechemites, who had escaped the rage of Abimelech by flight, gathered themselves into a body, and finding a place on a rock which was rendered strong by nature, they formed the resolution of fixing themselves on this spot, as a place of refuge, and to increase its natural strength, they fortified it in the best manner they could. Intimation of this being given to Abimelech, he marched against them with his army, and getting within the wall, he ordered his men to raise a pile of wood and faggots round the buildings, which was no sooner done, than fire was immediately set to it, and every soul perished in the flames. Such was the fate of the wretched Shechemites, who suffered unlamented, for their ungrateful treatment of the posterity of Gideon. It was a lesson to the Israelites to beware of falling into the same hands, lest they should share the same fate.

Abimelech, not yet satiated with revenge, marched with his army against Thebes, and took the outer town by assault. The garrison retreated into a strong castle, and Abimelech, pushing the attack up to the very gates, resolved either to take the city or destroy it by fire. But his cruel intentions were happily frustrated by means of a woman, who, while he was standing near the wall giving directions to his men, threw down a large piece of a millstone (*a*) which falling on Abimelech's head, struck him to the ground. When he came a little to himself, and found the wound was mortal, he called for his armour-bearer, whom he desired immediately to dispatch him, that it might not be said he fell by the hands of a woman. The officer performed his commands, and thus was Abimelech punished for his cruelty to his brethren, and his inhumanity to the Shechemites. When the soldiers found their leader was no more, they dispersed, every man returning to his own habitation.

After the death of Abimelech, and the re-establishment of the Shechemites, one Tolah, the son of Puah, an eminent man of the tribe of Issachar, was appointed leader of the people, in which office he continued for twenty-three years. He dwelt during the whole time of his government, on mount Ephraim, near the centre of the country, that the people might, with the greater convenience, resort to him for judgment (*b*).

On the death of Tolah the government fell into the hands of one Jair, a Gileadite, of the tribe of Manasseh. He was a man not only happy in his worldly acquisitions, but also in his family. He had no less than thirty sons, all of whom were men of courage, and with their father, universally esteemed by the people. Jair held the government twenty-two years, when he died at an advanced age, and was buried at Camon, a city of Gilead.

During the life of Jair, the Israelites payed a proper attention both to the civil and ecclesiastical laws of their country; but after his death they degenerated in their manners, giving themselves up to every kind of vice, and disregarding every religious duty.

The Ammonites and Philistines, understanding the manner in which the Israelites lived, determined to take advantage of their negligence. They accordingly raised a powerful army, with which they marched into their country, laying every thing waste wherever they came, and, not satisfied with this, they resolved to prosecute their ravages, till they should make a thorough conquest of the countries on both sides the river Jordan.

The Israelites began now to reflect on their past conduct, and to consider that the distressed situation in which they were again involved, arose from their disobedience to the laws of their great legislator Moses. They therefore offered up prayers and sacrifices to God, beseeching him to interpose in their behalf and to remove from them their present troubles. Their prayers were not offered in vain, the Almighty being pleased to promise them his Divine assistance.

The Ammonites having entered the country of Gilead with a large army, the inhabitants took up arms in order to oppose them, but they were at a loss how to act, for want of a leader. At length they bethought themselves of one *Jephtha*, *a man of singular courage and conduct*, who resided at a place called Tob, and maintained an army under him at his own expence. To this person the Gileadites sent messengers, with a promise, that if he should assist them against the Ammonites, they would confer the government on him during his life. Jephtha, at first, refused to comply with their request, but the Gileadites continuing to press him with repeated importunities, he at length complied, but not before he had made them take oaths of fidelity to him as their general.

This matter being adjusted, Jephtha joined his army with that of the Gileadites, and, after giving some necessary orders, marched with the whole body to Mispeh. From hence he sent ambassadors to the king of the Ammonites, to demand the reason of his invading the country of the Gileadites. His answer was, that the land was his, that the Israelites, in their passage from Egypt had taken it from his ancestors, and that he was now determined to recover it. In consequence of this Jephtha sent other ambassadors to tell the king of Ammon, that, if either conquest or prescription conferred a title they had a just right to the country they possessed, since they took it not from them, but the Ammonites, that they had quietly enjoyed it upwards of three hundred years, and that they were determined to oppose any monarch, however powerful, that should attempt to infringe on their property.

This peremptory declaration put an end to their treaty, and immediate preparations were made on both sides to determine the contest by the sword. But before Jephtha took the field, he prayed to God, in the most fervent manner, to grant him success, and made a solemn vow, that if he proved victorious, he would offer up to him, in sacrifice, the first living creature he should meet on his return to his family.

With this resolution Jephtha attacked the enemy, and, in a short time, obtained a complete victory, great numbers being slain and the rest put to flight. He pursued and killed the fugitives as far as the city Maniah, from whence he proceeded to the country of Ammon, where he destroyed many cities, and divided the spoil among his army. Thus did Jephtha totally subdue his enemies, and redeem the Israelites from a state of slavery, under which they had laboured upwards of eighteen years.

The war being over, Jephtha returned to his family when, lo! instead of receiving that satisfaction he expected after so long an absence, a circumstance occurred that pierced him to the heart. On approaching his house, the first object that presented itself, was his only daughter, who was flying with eager joy to receive and bid him welcome. When Jephtha saw his daughter, his soul almost sunk within him, and for some time, he was unable to speak. Having a little recovered himself, he looked at her with tears trickling from his cheeks and, after blaming her for her officiousness in coming to meet him, told her the vow he had made, by which he had obliged himself to offer her to God as a sacrifice. The innocent devotee did not appear the least alarmed at this melancholy intelligence, but with great coolness,

(*a*) It was common in that age, as well as in later times, before the invention of gun powder, to [illegible] large round stones kept within castles which were thrown over upon the enemies [illegible] approached the walls, and the stone [illegible] [illegible] down by this woman seems to have been one of them.

(*b*) Though there is not much recorded of this person, yet it may be reasonably supposed he was a prudent and peaceable man, that he removed [illegible] from among the people, endeavouring to suppress idolatry, appeased tumults, and healed those wounds which had been given to the state during the usurpation of Abimelech.

SAMPSON
Killing the Lion

And he rent him as he would have rent a kid and he had nothing in his hand

replied that, if the loss of her life would secure his honour, and the liberty of her country, she would willingly part with it. She only requested he would indulge her with two months, that she might have an opportunity of taking a proper farewell of all her acquaintance, and that, after that time was expired he might fulfil his vow. Her father granted her request, and, at the expiration of the two months, she was made a sacrifice, which was the consequence of the rash vow made by Jephtha, the fulfilment of which was neither conformable either to law or Justice.

The success of Jephtha against the Ammonites gave great umbrage to the Ephraimites, who told him he had engaged in the late expedition, without consulting them from ambitious motives, and that he might reserve not only the booty, but the glory of the action to himself. Jephtha told them, they were not insensible of the oppression under which their allies laboured, and that they had been applied to for their assistance, but refused to give it. That they had acted with great injustice, and that if they did not content themselves and be quiet, he would compel them to it by force.

Jephtha finding the Ephraimites paid no attention to his remonstrance, but, on the contrary, had raised an army to oppose him, he immediately marched against them, when a dreadful battle ensued, in which the Ephraimites were totally defeated, and 22,000 were killed on the spot.

Having thus reduced the refractory Ephraimites, Jephtha returned to Tob, where he died, and was buried at Sebeth, in Gilead, the place of his nativity.

After the death of Jephtha, the government was vested in the hands of Absan, a citizen of Bethlehem, and of the tribe of Judah. He ruled only seven years, when he died at an advanced age, and was buried at Bethlehem.

Absan was succeeded by Elon, of the tribe of Zebulon, who governed ten years, during which time nothing material occurred.

Elon was succeeded by Abdon, the son of Helel, of the tribe of Ephraim. He was universally beloved by the people, and died at a very advanced age, leaving behind him a numerous progeny. He was buried with great funeral pomp in the city of Pharathon, the place of his nativity.

CHAP. X.

The birth, life, exploits and death of Samson.

AFTER the death of Abdon, the Israelites, not having a proper leader, were greatly persecuted by the Philistines who subdued them in most parts of the country, and kept them in a very servile state upwards of forty years, when they were happily relieved by the following means.

There was a certain man, named Manoah, of the family of the Danites, who, without exception, was esteemed the best and principal person of his tribe. He had a most beautiful woman to his wife, and was exceedingly fond of her, but his happiness was greatly curtailed by her not bearing children. In consequence of his uneasiness on this account, he frequently walked with his wife to a retired spot near the suburbs of the city, when he offered up supplications to God, that he would grant him a lawful heir to succeed him. On one of the days Manoah went on this errand, he left his wife for a short time alone, when an angel appeared to her in the likeness of a tall, handsome man, telling her, "He brought her glad tidings, for that by the favour of God, she should bring forth a son, who should prove remarkable for his strength, and humble the pride of the Philistines, charging her not to cut his hair, nor suffer him to taste any drink stronger than water, for so God had enjoined." After saying this, the angel disappeared.

When Manoah returned to his wife, she related to him the particulars of all that had passed, and described the person of the messenger with such an apparent secret satisfaction, that Manoah was touched with jealousy, and intimated his suspicions, that an illegal intercourse had taken place between them. The woman, seeing the uneasiness of her husband, and desirous of removing his suspicions, fell on her knees and earnestly prayed to God, "That he would again vouchsafe to send his angel, that her husband might also behold him." Her prayers were heard and granted, the angel appeared a second time to her alone, whereupon she prevailed on him to stay till she should fetch her husband. When Manoah came, he asked the angel to repeat what he had before said to his wife in private. The angel replied, "It was sufficient that his wife had been made acquainted with the things he had told her." Manoah then asked the angel to tell him who he was, that he and his wife might make some return for the news he had brought them when the child should be born. The angel replied, "He did not stand in need of any reward, nor was it from any lucrative motive he had brought him the intelligence." Manoah then entreated the angel to stay and take some refreshment which he at first refused, but at length agreed to. Manoah then slew a kid, and ordered his wife to dress it with all expedition. When it was ready, the angel told the woman to put the flesh, together with the bread, on a rock. This being done, the angel touched the meat with a rod he had in his hand, when immediately a flame of fire burst from the rock, and consumed both meat and bread, and the angel in the sight of Manoah and his wife, ascended in the smoke.

When Manoah beheld this, he was struck with fear, thinking it portended some great evil to come; but his wife endeavoured to remove his apprehensions, by saying, "If God had been displeased with them, he would neither have accepted their sacrifice, nor imparted to them the knowledge of such good tidings."

A short time after this the woman became pregnant, and when the child was born, it proved to be a son, whom they named Samson, which signifies *robust*, or *strong*. The woman strictly observed the orders she had received from the angel, and as the child grew up he discovered the most manifest signs of his becoming what had been foretold previous to his birth.

When Samson was arrived to the age of maturity, he fell in love with the daughter of a Philistine, who lived at Timnath, and though his parents did not approve of the match, because she was sprung from an idolatrous family, yet such was their affection to their son, that they indulged his passion and went with him to Timnath to treat about the marriage. As they were on their journey, and Samson was straggling a small distance from the company, all on a sudden he discovered a young lion running towards him with open mouth. Samson was not in the least intimidated at this sight, and, when the lion approached, he seized him by the throat, and strangled him with as much ease as if he had been a kid, after which he threw the body into a thicket. A short time after, as he was travelling on the very same road, he went out of his way to look at the carcase of the lion, when, to his great surprise, he found a swarm of bees working in the breast of the beast. He took out three of the honey-combs, which he presented to his bride, [illegible] did not tell her in what manner he had obtained [illegible]

The nuptials being now to be solemnized (the ceremony and entertainment of which lasted seven days), the relations of the bride brought with [illegible] the [illegible] stoutest and handsomest young men [illegible] out of compliment and respect to Samson, as [illegible] pretended, but [illegible] a guard over him, lest [illegible] his great strength, he should, when in his cups, do [illegible] mischief. In the course of the [illegible] day, [illegible] mony universally approved among the company, S[illegible]

Killing the Lion

And he rent him as he would have rent a kid, and he had nothing in his hand

replied that, if the loss of her life would secure his honour, and the liberty of her country, she would willingly part with it. She only requested he would indulge her with two months, that she might have an opportunity of taking a proper farewell of all her acquaintance, and that, after that time was expired he might fulfil his vow. Her father granted her request, and, at the expiration of the two months, she was made a sacrifice, which was the consequence of the rash vow made by Jephtha, the fulfilment of which was neither conformable either to law or justice.

The success of Jephtha against the Ammonites gave great umbrage to the Ephraimites, who told him he had engaged in the late expedition, without consulting them from ambitious motives, and that he might receive not only the booty, but the glory of the action to himself. Jephtha told them, they were not insensible of the oppression under which their allies laboured, and that they had been applied to for their assistance, but refused to give it. That they had acted with great injustice, and that if they did not content themselves and be quiet, he would compel them to it by force.

Jephtha finding the Ephraimites paid no attention to his remonstrance, but, on the contrary, had raised an army to oppose him, he immediately marched against them, when a dreadful battle ensued, in which the Ephraimites were totally defeated, and 42,000 were killed on the spot.

Having thus reduced the refractory Ephraimites, Jephtha returned to Tob, where he died, and was buried at Sebeth, in Gilead, the place of his nativity.

After the death of Jephtha, the government was vested in the hands of Absan, a citizen of Bethlehem, and of the tribe of Judah. He ruled only seven years, when he died at an advanced age, and was buried at Bethlehem.

Absan was succeeded by Elon, of the tribe of Zebulon, who governed ten years, during which time nothing material occurred.

Elon was succeeded by Abdon, the son of Helel, of the tribe of Ephraim. He was universally beloved by the people, and died at a very advanced age, leaving behind him a numerous progeny. He was buried with great funeral pomp in the city of Pharathon, the place of his nativity.

CHAP. X.

The birth, life, exploits, and death of Samson.

AFTER the death of Abdon, the Israelites, not having a proper leader, were greatly persecuted by the Philistines who subdued them in most parts of the country, and kept them in a very servile state upwards of forty years, when they were happily relieved by the following means.

There was a certain man, named Manoah, of the family of the Danites, who, without exception, was esteemed the best and principal person of his tribe. He had a most beautiful woman to his wife, and was exceedingly fond of her, but his happiness was greatly embittered by her not bearing children. In consequence of his uneasiness on this account, he frequently walked with his wife to a retired spot near the suburbs of the city, when he offered up supplications to God, that he would give him a lawful heir to succeed him. On one of these days Manoah went out this errand he left his wife for a short time alone, when an angel appeared to her in the likeness of a tall, handsome man, telling her, "He brought her glad tidings, for that by the favour of God, she should bring forth a son, who should prove remarkable for his strength, and humble the pride of the Philistines, charging her not to cut his hair, nor suffer him to taste any drink stronger than water, for so God had enjoined." After saying this, the angel disappeared.

When Manoah returned to his house, she related to him the particulars of all that had passed, and described the person of the messenger with such an appearance of satisfaction, that Manoah was touched with jealousy, and intimated his suspicions, that an illegal intercourse had taken place between them. The woman, seeing the earnestness of her husband, and desirous of removing his suspicions, fell on her knees and earnestly prayed to God, "That he would again vouchsafe to send his angel, that her husband might also behold him." Her prayers were heard and granted, the angel appeared a second time to her alone, whereupon she prevailed on him to stay till she should fetch her husband. When Manoah came, he asked the angel to repeat what he had before said to his wife in private. The angel replied, "It was sufficient that his wife had been made acquainted with the things he had told her." Manoah then asked the angel to tell him who he was, that he and his wife might make some return for the news he had brought them when the child should be born. The angel replied, "He did not stand in need of any reward, nor was he from any lucrative motive he had brought them the intelligence." Manoah then entreated the angel to stay and take some refreshment, which he at first refused, but at length agreed to. Manoah then slew a kid, and ordered his wife to dress it with all expedition. When it was ready, the angel told the woman to put the flesh, together with the bread, on a rock. This being done, the angel touched the meat with a rod he had in his hand, when immediately a flame of fire burst from the rock, and consumed both meat and bread, and the angel, in the sight of Manoah and his wife, ascended in the smoke.

When Manoah beheld this, he was struck with fear, thinking it portended some great evil to come. But his wife endeavoured to remove his apprehensions, by saying, "If God had been displeased with them, he would not then have accepted their sacrifice, nor imparted to them the knowledge of such good things."

A short time after this the woman became pregnant, and when the child was born, it proved to be a son, whom they named Samson, which signifies *robust*, or *strong*. The woman strictly observed the orders she had received from the angel, and as the child grew up he discovered the most manifest signs of his becoming what had been foretold previous to his birth.

When Samson was arrived to the age of maturity, he fell in love with the daughter of a Philistine, who lived at Timnath, and though his parents did not approve of the match, because she was sprung from an idolatrous family, yet such was their affection for their son, that they indulged his passion and went with him to Timnath to treat about the marriage. As they were on their journey, and Samson was straggling a little distance from the company, all on a sudden he discovered a young lion running towards him with open mouth. Samson was not in the least intimidated at this sight, and, when the lion approached, he seized him by the throat, and strangled him with as much ease as if he had been a kid, after which he threw the body into a thicket. A short time after, as he was travelling on the very same road, he went out of his way to look at the carcase of the lion, when, to his great surprise, he found a swarm of bees working in the breast of the beast. He took out three [illegible] honey-combs, which he presented to his [illegible] [illegible] them in what manner he had come [illegible]

The nuptials being now to [illegible] [illegible] mony and entertainment of which [illegible] the relations of the bride brought [illegible] stoutest and handsomest young men [illegible] out of compliment and respect to Samson [illegible] [illegible], but [illegible] strength, [illegible] [illegible] [illegible] addressed himself to the thirty young men, telling them he had a (a) riddle to propound to them, and if they would explain it before the expiration of the seven days, he would give to each man a shirt and a coat. The Philistines accepted the proposal, and desired Samson to state the question, which he did as follows: "Out of the eater "came forth meat, and out of the strong came forth "sweetness." The Philistines laid their heads together to expound this riddle, but after three days, finding their endeavours fruitless, and despairing to accomplish it before the expiration of the time, they went to the new bride, and threatened her, if she did not get the secret from her husband, and reveal it to them, they would burn her to death. Intimidated at these threats, the woman sat about the business, and, after great difficulty, obtained from Samson, the particulars of his killing the lion, and of the honey-comb he had found in the carcase, and brought to her, all which she privately communicated to the Philistines. Towards the close of the seventh day, which was the time appointed for solving the riddle, the Philistines assembled, one of whom, addressing himself to Samson, said, "Nothing is stronger than a lion, or "sweeter than honey." "No," replied Samson, "nor "falser than the woman who has enabled you to expound "the riddle." Samson was greatly irritated at this imposition, but determined to fulfil his engagement with the thirty men. To do this, he went, in the heat of his passion, to the city of Askalon, (b) belonging to the Philistines, where having slain thirty men, he brought away their shirts and coats, and delivered them to those who expounded the riddle. Fired with resentment at the treachery of his wife, Samson left her, and she, in revenge, married a young man who had been one of Samson's principal companions during the wedding week.

Samson was so enraged at the treatment he had received from his wife, that he determined not only to wreak his vengeance on her, but the whole country of the Philistines, and an opportunity soon offered, which enabled him to put his design into execution. It happened to be near the time of harvest, and the corn being ripe on the ground, Samson hit upon a project for destroying it, and thereby distressing the Philistines by famine. He got together three hundred foxes, (c) and tying them two and two by their tails, with a lighted torch between each pair, he turned them loose, when running into the fields, they not only destroyed all the corn, but likewise the vines and olive trees, so that the whole country for a time appeared in one continued blaze.

When the Philistines understood that Samson was the author of this destruction, and that he had been induced to take such a step in revenge for the treatment he had received from his wife's family, they sent a number of people, with proper officers, to Timnath, who seized Samson's wife, with her father and relations, burnt them all alive, as being the special cause of so great a calamity.

Samson continued to commit various depredations in different parts of the country belonging to the Philistines, till at length, being apprehensive of danger, he retired for security, to a rock (d) near Etam, belonging to the tribe of Judah.

When the Philistines knew where Samson had secreted himself, they sent ambassadors to the inhabitants of Etam, with orders that they should deliver him into their hands. In consequence of this they went with an armed force to Samson's retreat, and, after expostulating with him on the danger to which they were exposed on his account, begged he would give himself quietly up to the Philistines.

Samson not only complied with their request, but submitted himself to be bound with cords, on condition that they would do him no farther hurt than delivering him into the hands of the enemy. Accordingly he came from the rock, and being brought to the ambassadors, they conducted him to the camp of the Philistines, who no sooner saw him at a distance, than they ran in considerable bodies to meet him, exulting at their conquest over so daring an invader. But Samson soon convinced them of the impropriety of their imaginations. As soon as they came near him, he suddenly snapped the cords with which he was bound, and seeing the jaw-bone (e) of an ass lying on the ground, he took it up, and falling on the Philistines he slew one thousand on the spot, which so intimidated the rest, that, instead of making any resistance, they betook themselves to flight. Samson exulted beyond bounds at this victory, instead of ascribing it, as he ought, to the assistance of the Divine Power.

Fatigued with this encounter, and being excessive thirsty, he sought for water, but found himself in a place where no such refreshment was to be had. In this distressed situation he made his application to God, who immediately caused a stream of delicious water to flow from an hollow rock adjoining to the spot where Samson had slain the Philistines, from which circumstance the place was ever after known by the name of the Jaw.

After this singular conquest Samson looked upon the Philistines with contempt, and not fearing any hurt they could do him, he went openly into one of the cities called Gaza, where he took up his residence in a house of public entertainment. The governor of the town being informed of Samson's situation, placed guards without the gates of the city, during the day, to prevent his leaving the place. But Samson having received intelligence of this, totally baffled the governor's intention. He rose about midnight, and taking the two gates, (f) to

---

(a) It was a very ancient custom for the masters of feasts to propose enigmas [illegible] other [illegible] exercise their wit, and enlivening conversation instead of passing their whole time in downright eating and drinking. The Greeks derived this custom from the Orientals, and they generally proposed a reward to those who expounded the riddle.

(b) This city was situated between Azoth and Gaza, on the coast of the Mediterranean [illegible] distant from Jerusalem. It is said to have been of great note among the Gentiles in ancient times, for a temple dedicated to [illegible], the mother of [illegible], here worshipped in the form of a mermaid, and for another temple of Apollo [illegible] Herod the father of [illegible] and grandfather of Herod the Great [illegible] priest. It [illegible], in the [illegible] times of Christianity, an episcopal see [illegible] of the only [illegible] beautified with a new wall and many fine buildings, by Richard I. King of England.

(c) Foxes, as is well known, [illegible] apt to do a great deal of mischief wherever they abound [illegible] therefore [illegible] might have this farther design [illegible] so many [illegible] that [illegible] his own country of such [illegible] at the same time, he very well knew [illegible] could be more convenient [illegible] and determining his enemies [illegible] very [illegible] of foot, [illegible] they [illegible] were [illegible] the burning [illegible] alive [illegible] and then as they were tied in couples [illegible] this would [illegible] the [illegible] retarded in their flight, and staying longer in a place, they would give the [illegible] to spread itself, and at length occasioned an universal conflagration.

(d) This rock was formed by nature as to be accessible only [illegible] that so narrow as not to admit two people to walk abreast [illegible] perhaps, one of the most defensible places that could be in [illegible].

(e) It may appear strange to some that a single person [illegible] no other weapon than the jaw-bone of an ass should be able to slay so many people [illegible] his feet [illegible] will cease, when [illegible] the word of the sacred text, that at the time [illegible] the Spirit of the Lord came mightily upon him. The Philistines, no doubt, were astonished to see the cords [illegible] from his hands, and he advancing with the greatest [illegible] against them [illegible] The whole must be ascribed to the power of God, who can increase our strength in all respects to what degree he pleases, and at the same time enfeeble [illegible] of those who oppose his designs [illegible] them [illegible] power to help themselves.

From this singular achievement [illegible] was afterwards called Ramath-lehi, which in the Hebrew language signifies [illegible].

(f) He did not stay to break open the gates [illegible] pluck [illegible] out of the ground with the doors [illegible] which extraordinary action so astonished the guards [illegible] they had not power to follow [illegible].

SAMSON slaying the PHILISTINES
with the jaw bone of an Ass.

DELILAH *after cutting off* SAMSON's HAIR *treacherously be-traying him into the hands of the Philistines*

RUTH.

gether with the poſts, bars, bolts, and chains, he laid them on his ſhoulders, and carrying them to a hill, called Mount Hebron, there left them.

Some time after this circumſtance happened, which, in the end, proved fatal to Samſon. Being naturally of an amorous diſpoſition, he fell in love with a common proſtitute of the Philiſtines, named Delilah, with whom he was ſo infatuated as not to pay the leaſt attention to his own ſafety. The principal leader of the Philiſtines obſerving Samſon's ungovernable paſſion for this woman, determined to take advantage of it. They accordingly ſent for her, and when ſhe came, they promiſed her, if ſhe would learn of Samſon, and diſcover to them, what was the cauſe of his wonderful ſtrength, and how he might be deprived of it, they would reward her with a conſiderable ſum of money.

The treacherous Delilah undertook the taſk, and uſed all the art ſhe was miſtreſs of, to obtain from Samſon the important ſecret. For ſome time he amuſed her with fictions, and made her believe his ſtrength conſiſted ſometimes in one thing, and ſometimes in another; firſt, that binding him with bands made of green withs; then, that tying him with ſeven ropes never before uſed; and again, weaving his hair into treſſes, and filleting them up, would deprive him of his ſtrength. Delilah tried all theſe maxims, but finding them of no effect, ſhe upbraided Samſon for his falſeneſs, and told him his apparent affection was all deceit, otherwiſe he would not heſitate to tell her a matter ſhe was ſo anxiouſly deſirous to know. At length, by daily importunities, did the treacherous Delilah prevail on Samſon to divulge the important ſecret, viz. "That in the preſervation of his "hair lay all his ſtrength and ſecurity." From the manner in which Samſon told this, Delilah believed he ſpoke truth; and ſoon after tried the experiment, by cutting off his hair as he lay ſleeping with his head in her lap. When ſhe found him diveſted of his ſtrength, and no longer able to defend himſelf, ſhe delivered him up to his enemies, who, after putting out his eyes, and leading him about the ſtreets as a public ſpectacle to the people, ſent him to priſon.

In proceſs of time Samſon's hair grew again, and with it returned his ſtrength. This, however, was not thought of by the Philiſtines; and Samſon, when an opportunity offered, took advantage of it, to the deſtruction of great numbers of his enemies. On a certain day was held a feaſt, at which were preſent the greater part of the princes and nobility among the Philiſtines. The feaſt was held in a very elegant and ſpacious building, the roof of which was ſupported by only two pillars. In the height of their jollity they ſent for blind Samſon, and for ſome time made him the ſport of the company. Samſon was vexed to the heart at this treatment, and knowing his ſtrength, reſolved to return it on his perſecutors. He complained of being greatly fatigued with ſtanding ſo long, and deſired the boy that led him to the place, to let him lean againſt one of the pillars to reſt himſelf. The boy complied with his requeſt, when Samſon, graſping the pillars with his arms (after a ſhort ejaculation to God for the reſtoration of his former ſtrength) gave it ſuch a ſhake that the whole building (a) immediately fell to the ground; and Samſon, with about three thouſand men, were buried in the ruins.

Such was the end of Samſon, after having held the government of Iſrael twenty years. He was remarkable not only for his great ſtrength, but his diſtinguiſhed magnanimity, and purſued, to the laſt moment of his life, his revenge on the enemies of his country. When his relations heard of his death, they took his body to Saraſa, the place of his nativity, and there buried it in the ſepulchre of his anceſtors.

CHAP. XI.

Eli ſucceeds Samſon in the government. Boaz marries Ruth, from whom came Obed, the grandfather of David. The birth of Samuel. The Iſraelites engage with the Philiſtines, are defeated, and their ark taken from them.

AFTER the death of Samſon the government of the Iſraelites fell to Eli, the high prieſt, during whoſe time there happened a moſt dreadful famine. To avoid the conſequences of this calamity, one Abimelech a citizen of Bethlehem, and of the tribe of Judah, removed, with Naomi, his wife, and his two ſons, named Mahlon and Chellion, to the land of Moab. After living very happily at this place for ſome time, Abimelech married his ſons to two women of the country, named Orpha and Ruth, the former being eſpouſed to Chellion, and the latter to Mahlon.

At the expiration of ten years, Abimelech and his two ſons died, within a ſhort time of each other. Naomi was inconſolable for the loſs of ſuch near relatives for whoſe ſake ſhe had quitted her native country. She therefore formed the reſolution of returning to Bethlehem; on which the wives of her two ſons, who had a great affection for her, and were unwilling to be ſeparated, importuned her to take them with her. Naomi adviſed them to continue in their native place, and wiſhed they might be happier with their next huſbands than they had been with her ſons. She told them it was not in her power to give them any aſſiſtance, and that it would be imprudent for them to riſque ſo long a journey, for no other purpoſe than that of condoling with a wretched mother-in-law. Orpha liſtened to Naomi's remonſtrance and ſtaid behind; but Ruth being reſolute, ſhe and her mother-in-law ſet out on their journey.

When they entered the city of Bethlehem, ſome of the people, who recollected the features of Naomi, with ſurpriſe ſaid, Art thou not Naomi, the wife of Abimelech? To which ſhe replied, Call me not Naomi, but rather Marah, (the former, in the Hebrew, ſignifying *happineſs*, and the latter *ſorrow*.)

It was now the time of harveſt, and Ruth, in order to obtain ſuſtenance for herſelf and mother-in-law, begged ſhe would let her go into the fields to glean. Naomi aſſenting, Ruth went on the buſineſs, and, after being ſome little time in the fields, was accoſted by a ſervant of Boaz (the maſter of the land, and a kinſman of Abimelech Naomi's deceaſed huſband) with whom ſhe had ſome converſation. Some time after Boaz came into the field

(a) [illegible]

[illegible] Pliny mentions [illegible] by Samſon.

himself, and seeing Ruth, inquired of his servant who she was, and from whence she came. The servant who had learned from her the particulars of her life and present situation, related the whole to Boaz, who was so pleased with her for the respect she shewed her mother-in-law, that he ordered his servant to tell her, she was not only at liberty to glean in the fields, but to gather what she thought proper, and that she should be allowed both food and drink in common with the reapers. Ruth reserved a part of her allowance for her mother-in-law, and in the evening, carried it home with her corn, when she related to Naomi the occurrences of the day.

When Naomi understood who was the person that had been so great a benefactor to Ruth, she told her he was a near kinsman, and being a man of a pious and liberal disposition he might probably extend his benevolence to their mutual advantage. She therefore advised Ruth to [illegible] her labours, and to attend in the fields with the servants of Boaz, during the remainder of the harvest.

The harvest being over, Boaz was very diligent in threshing his corn, and being one day greatly fatigued, he laid himself on the floor and fell asleep, in which situation he was left by the people who had attended him. Information of this being given to Naomi, she advised Ruth to go to the barn, and lay herself gently at his feet, imagining that when Boaz should wake and discover her, it might produce something to her advantage.

Ruth, thinking it her duty to comply with the orders of her mother-in-law, immediately went, and getting into the barn, laid herself at the feet of Boaz. About the middle of the night Boaz awoke, and perceiving a woman lying by him, asked who she was. Ruth immediately discovered herself, and begged he would permit her to lie by him as one of his handmaids, which Boaz granted, and again fell asleep. Early in the morning, before the servants were come to their work, Boaz desired Ruth to get up, and, after taking as much corn as she could carry, go immediately to her mother-in-law, that she might not be seen by any of the servants, for though nothing had taken place between them of a criminal nature, yet it was prudent to avoid calumny, which would certainly arise should she be found with him. "But (says Boaz) before you go, I have this to say to "you. There is a person of much nearer kin to you "than I am. I will ask him if he chooses to marry you: "if he consents, you must go with him, but if he refuses, I will marry you myself." Ruth then departed, and when she got home, related all that had passed to her mother-in-law, who was highly pleased with her success and the expectation of so profitable an alliance.

About the middle of the day Boaz went into the city, and convened an assembly of the elders. As soon as they were met, he sent for Ruth and the kinsman nearest allied to her, both of whom appearing, Boaz addressed himself to the man as follows: "If I am not mistaken, "you are at present in possession of the inheritance of "Abimelech and his sons." To which he replied, "I "am, and the law has put me in possession of it, and "being nearest of blood." Boaz answered, "The "same law that gives you one part obliges you to take "the other. Before you stands the widow of Mahlon, "and you are bound by the law (a) either to marry "her, or quit the inheritance." The man said he could not marry her, having already a wife and children. He therefore resigned the woman and estate to Boaz, who was the next in kindred to the deceased. In consequence of this declaration, Ruth was commanded to unloose the shoe (b) of the man, and spit in his face, agreeably to the custom used on such occasions.

A few days after Boaz took Ruth to wife, and at the expiration of a year she was delivered of a son. The boy was placed under the care of Naomi, who called him by the name of Obed, signifying in the Hebrew language, *servant* or *assistance*, which she expected from him in her more advanced years. From Obed came Jesse, the father of David, in whose family the government continued one and twenty generations. I have been thus particular in my account of Ruth, to shew the power and wise dispensations of Providence, who can raise characters to the most elevated dignity on earth, however insignificant the objects from whom they are descended.

The Israelites grew exceeding indolent under the government of Eli, which being observed by the Philistines, they determined to take advantage of it. The general dissipation of the people arose from the precedent set them by the two sons of Eli, named Hophni and Phineas, who were mere libertines. They domineered over the men, and violated the women at their devotions; and so far were they from being content with the portions which God had allotted them as priests, that they forced from the people (even before they had made their oblations) what part of the sacrifice they pleased, which gave so general a disgust, that religion grew into contempt, and the worship of God was almost totally disused.

The Almighty was pleased to chastise them for their remissness and to forewarn them of the event by the prophet Samuel, of whose birth the following are the particulars.

In the city of Ramah belonging to the tribe of Ephraim, lived a man named Elkanah, who had two wives, Hannah and Peninnah. He went three times a year to Shiloh, to offer up his usual sacrifice, and, as he was a pious and religious man, he generally took his two wives with him, that they, in like manner, might make their oblations. Hannah had not any children, notwithstanding which she was Elkanah's favourite; and at every feast, on the peace-offering, he usually sent her a separate mess, and of his choicest meat. Peninnah, being highly offended at the particular attention being paid to Hannah, vented her resentment by upbraiding her with sterility, or want of children. This greatly affected Hannah, insomuch that all her husband said could not assuage her grief. As soon as she rose from table, she hastened to the tabernacle, and there prayed to God, in most fervent manner, that he would be pleased to bless her with a son, for which favour she promised to make him a Nazarite, and solely to devote him to his service. Her prayers were heard, and in a proper time, she conceived and brought forth a son, whom she called Samuel, that is to say, *asked of God*. Hannah, as she had promised, went to the tabernacle at Shiloh, and after offering a sacrifice of thanksgiving for the birth of her son, and paying the tithes [illegible]

(a) The reason of this law is [illegible] grounded upon the law by which the first born of the second marriage was to bear the name of the woman's former husband, in order to keep up the name in Israel; so that if this kinsman had married Ruth, and should have had but one son by her, that son being to bear his name but the name of her former husband, he himself would have no son to keep his name in Israel; so that not being willing to run this hazard, he declined the marriage.

(b) There was a manner of confirming bargains, exchanges and [illegible] among the Israelites. It consisted of two forms, the first of which was [illegible] when a man refused to marry the wife of his brother, he died with[illegible] out issue. In this case the law commanded that the woman should [illegible] shoe, and spit in his face, at the same time using these words, [illegible] [illegible] [illegible] She [illegible] ceremony was a token of resignation, and [illegible] the compelling of the kinsman in the second [illegible] the widow, but he might transfer his right to another [illegible] [illegible] [illegible] vered [illegible] this [illegible] [illegible] elders.

-cording to cuſtom, ſhe delivered him to Eli, who clothed him with a proper habit, that he might attend on the ſervice of the tabernacle. After this Hannah had ſeveral other ſons, and three daughters, by her huſband Elkanah.

When Samuel had attained to his thirteenth year, God was pleaſed to make him his agent, by inſpiring him with the power of prophecy. As Samuel was one night aſleep, God called him by his name, which he taking for the voice of Eli, immediately ran to him to know his pleaſure, when he told him that he was miſtaken, for that he had not mentioned his name. On this Samuel retired and went again to reſt, when he was repeatedly diſturbed by the ſame voice, upon which he again went to Eli, and told him how diſtinctly he had been ſeveral times called, and that he thought it to be his voice. Eli ſaid it was not him, but the voice of God. He then told Samuel to retire again to reſt, and when he heard the voice again, to ſay, "Here I am, Lord, ſpeak, for thy "ſervant heareth, and is ready to obey thee." Samuel did as Eli had ordered, and, when he again heard the voice, anſwered, "Here I am, Lord, ready to do what- "ſoever thou ſhouldeſt command." The voice replied, "Know, then, that calamities hang over Iſrael, greater "than have been hitherto known. The two ſons of Eli "ſhall be cut off in one day, and the prieſthood ſhall be "taken from him, and given to the family of Eleazar "for Eli hath preferred his children to my honour and "worſhip."

Samuel was unwilling to relate theſe melancholy tidings to Eli, but being at length urged to it, he gave a particular account of the whole revelation, which Eli received with a mind apparently reſigned to the Divine will.

The time was now come when Samuel's prophecy was to be fulfilled, and the diſpleaſure of the Almighty manifeſted to the diſobedient Iſraelites. The Philiſtines had raiſed a powerful army, with which they marched againſt the Iſraelites, and encamped at Aphek, a city of Judah. Finding no oppoſition, they advanced farther, and, at length, meeting the army of the Iſraelites, a deſperate battle enſued, in which 4000 of the latter were ſlain, and the remainder put to flight.

This defeat greatly alarmed the Iſraelites, ſome of whom imputed it to ariſe from the want of the ark in the army, which, as the ſymbol of God's preſence, they ſaid would be a ſure means of ſucceſs. Accordingly a meſſenger was diſpatched to Hophni and Phineas, to bring the ark, which no ſooner arrived in the camp, than the people teſtified their joy by the loudeſt acclamations. When the Philiſtines firſt heard that the ark was brought to the camp of the Iſraelites, they were greatly diſpirited, but at length taking courage, and exhorting each other to perſeverance, they prepared themſelves to oppoſe the enemy. The Iſraelites, not doubting of ſucceſs, attacked the Philiſtines with great fury, but they were ſoon repulſed, with the loſs of [illegible]0,000 men, among whom were Hophni and Phineas. The reſt of the army were glad to ſave themſelves by flight, ſo that the ark of the Lord fell into the hands of the Philiſtines.

CHAP. XII.

The Iſraelites lament the loſs of the ark. Death of Eli, the high prieſt.

THE melancholy news of this defeat was carried to Shiloh on the ſame day it happened, by a ſoldier of the tribe of Benjamin, who had made his eſcape from the field of battle. As ſoon as it was known, an univerſal outcry and lamentation prevailed throughout the city, and when Eli came to underſtand what was the cauſe of it, he ſent for the man to know the particulars. The ſoldier told him, the Iſraelites were routed, his two ſons ſlain, and the ark of the Lord taken by the enemy. Eli heard the defeat of the army, and the death of his ſons, without appearing in the leaſt agitated, but when he was told the ark of the Lord had fallen into the enemy's hands, his ſpirits forſook him, he fell from his chair, and inſtantly expired, in the 98th year of his age, and 40th of his government.

When the wife of Phineas (who was at this time with child, and near her time) heard of the deaths of her huſband and father, and (what was worſt of all) of the captivity of the ark, ſhe immediately fell in labour, and being ſhortly delivered of a ſon, ſhe had juſt ſtrength enough to name him Ichabod, which ſignifies *ſhame* and *ignominy* before ſhe died, becauſe the ark, which was the glory of Iſrael, was departed from them.

Eli was the firſt of the family of Ithamar (another of the ſons of Aaron) that exerciſed the function of high prieſt, for the family of Eleazar officiated in that capacity firſt, the ſon ſtill receiving that honour from the father. Eleazar bequeathed it to his ſon Phineas, he to his ſon Abiezer, from whom it went to his ſon Bukkias and thence to his ſon Ozis. After, when Eli, of whom we have been ſpeaking, had the prieſthood, which was returned in his line until the reign of King Solomon when it reverted to the poſterity of Eleazar.

END OF THE FIFTH BOOK.

FLAVIUS JOSEPHUS

ON THE

ANTIQUITIES

OF THE

JEWS.

BOOK VI.

[INCLUDING A PERIOD OF ABOUT THREE HUNDRED AND FIFTY-SEVEN YEARS.]

CHAP. I.

Divers plagues and calamities befal the Philiſtines for detaining the ark. Reſolved in council to reſtore it. Manner in which it was brought back to the Iſraelites.

AFTER the Philiſtines had defeated the Iſraelites, and made themſelves maſters of the ark, they carried it in great triumph to one of their principal cities, called Aſhdod, or Azotus, and there placed it in the temple of their god Dagon, (*a*) near his image. The next morning when the people went to the temple to pay their devotions, they found Dagon fallen down upon his face before the ark; but ſuppoſing it to be an accident, they ſet him up again. When they went the following morning to the temple, they found him not only on the ground, but in an imperfect ſtate, his head and hands being broke off in the fall. They again repeatedly ſet him up, but as repeatedly found him the next day lying proſtrate before the ark.

The inhabitants of Aſhdod were greatly alarmed at this circumſtance, and began to think that their Dagon was far inferior to the God of Iſrael. They had farther reaſon to imagine this, when they found that a moſt dreadful epidemical diſtemper prevailed throughout the city, which carried off great numbers in a very ſhort time; and to add to this calamity, their fields were over-run with mice, which deſtroying all the fruits of the earth, diveſted them of the common neceſſaries of life. Thinking theſe calamities aroſe from their having in poſſeſſion the ark of the Iſraelites, they ſent a meſſenger to the people of Aſcalon, deſiring them to admit it into their city. This offer was readily accepted, and the ark immediately removed to Aſcalon; but when the people found that the ſame calamities, which had befallen the inhabitants of Aſhdod, attended them, they removed the ark to another city. The ſame calamities attended the people of that place, as alſo the other cities to which the ark was removed.

The Philiſtines began now ſeriouſly to think that all their troubles aroſe from having the ark in their poſſeſſion. They therefore determined to part with it, and for that purpoſe called together the prieſts of the different cities in which it had been placed, to conſult with them in what manner it ſhould be removed from their country. After different propoſitions it was at length reſolved that there ſhould be made five golden images (*b*) one for each of the

(*a*) Dagon was repreſented as a monſter, being half a man and half a fiſh; whence the Hebrews derive his name from the Hebrew word Dag, which ſignifies a fiſh. Milton enumerates this deity among the fallen angels, and thus deſcribes him:

————————Next came one
Who mourn'd in earneſt, when the captive ark
Maim'd his brute image, head and hands lopp'd off
In his own temple on the groundſel edge,
Where he fell flat and ſham'd his worſhippers:
Dagon his name, ſea monſter, upward man
And downward fiſh; yet had his temple high
Rear'd in Azotus, dreaded through the coaſt
Of Paleſtine, in Gath and Aſcalon,
And Accaron and Gaza's frontier bounds.

(*b*) It was an ancient cuſtom (ſays Mr. Locke) in caſe a city or country was infeſted with any plague of diſeaſes, or noxious creatures, to conſult the taliſman, who ordered an image to be erected of the plague under a certain influence of celeſtial configuration; and this was the cauſe why the Philiſtine prieſts gave counſel that golden images ſhould be made to repreſent the diſeaſe with which they had been afflicted, as alſo of thoſe vermin which had deſtroyed the fruits of the earth. Tavernier tells us, that ſomething ſimilar to this is ſtill practiſed among the Indians; for when a pilgrim there goes to a pagod for the cure of any diſeaſe, he brings the figure of the member affected, made either of gold, ſilver or copper, according to his circumſtances, which he offers to the idol, and then ſings and dances for joy in expectation of his malady being removed. It was alſo a cuſtom among the ancient heathens [illegible] their idols [illegible] of their deliverance.

DAGON the IDOL of the Philistines, falling before the ARK of GOD
in the Idolatrous Temple of the [illegible]

cities in which the ark had stood, to be dedicated to God, as also five golden mice (alluding to the vermin that had destroyed the fruits of the earth) That these should be enclosed in a box, and, with the ark put into a cart made for the purpose, to be drawn by two milch cows, who never had been yoked before, and their calves to be closely confined (a) That the waggon with the ark, should be conducted to a spot where three roads met, and the cattle left there at liberty to go whither they pleased If they took the Hebrew road, and went on, they might impute their calamities to the ark, but if they took another course, they might consider them only as common accidents

All things being adjusted, the kine were led to the spot fixed on, attended by a great number of the Philistines, where they were no sooner left to themselves than they immediately took the Hebrew road, and went lowing along till they came to Bethshemeth, a village belonging to the tribe of Judah, where they stood still by a great stone As soon as the ark was seen, and the news of its arrival spread about, the people flocked to it in great multitudes, and after taking out the ark and the box, they burnt the cart, and sacrificed the two kine as a burnt-offering to God, at the close of which ceremony the Philistines, who had attended the ark to this place, returned to their own country

CHAP II

Judgment inflicted for prophanation. Reformation amongst the Hebrews, who are assembled by Samuel, and admonished to recover their liberty Expedition against the Philistines under the conduct of Samuel The Hebrews are victorious

SOME of the Bethshemites (either from joy or curiosity) venturing to look into the ark (which was expressly against the Divine command) were immediately slain, to the number of seventy, which so terrified the rest, that they sent to the people of Kirjath-jearim, acquainting them that the Philistines had brought back the ark, and desiring them to come and fetch it, as they were not worthy to have it in their possession The inhabitants of Kirjath-jearim accordingly came, and taking with them the ark it was placed in the house of one Abinadab, a Levite, a man distinguished for his integrity, and religion, in whose charge, and that of his sons, it remained twenty years

When the ark was removed to Kirjath-jearim, the people applied themselves, with great diligence, to the performance of religious duties and gave ample testimony of their strict observance to the law The prophet Samuel (who succeeded to the government after the death of Eli) seeing this, and thinking it a proper opportunity, harangued the multitude as follows

"O ye men of Israel (said he) ye have fatally experienced the implacable hatred and malice of your "enemies, but ye have reason to be once more happy, "seeing that your earnest supplications to God have not "been in vain Let me therefore recommend it to you "to inure yourselves to the love and practice of justice, "purge your minds of all improper affections, turn to "God, adore him, and honour him in your lives and "conversation, as well as with your lips If you do "good things, good will come of it, that is to say, you "will be possessed of liberty and conquest But these "are the blessings not to be obtained by force of arms, "strength of body, or bands of soldiers [illegible] it is God "alone who can bestow these privileges, which he has "promised to you if ye adhere strictly to his word [illegible] "and you may depend upon it he will not disappoint "you."

This speech was universally approved of by the people, who promised Samuel, they would strictly conform to all he had said, and inviolably obey the Divine commands

A short time after this Samuel summoned an assembly of the people at Mispeh (that is to say, *conspicuous*) where they held a fast and humiliation to God. The Philistines, being informed of this meeting, marched with a great army towards Mispeh, intending to attack the Israelites by surprise As soon as the Philistines were seen, the whole multitude were struck with terror, and told Samuel, there was no possibility of escaping the fury of so inveterate an enemy unless he could prevail with God to grant them his Divine assistance Samuel told them not to fear, for God had promised them his protection, and would most certainly fulfil his word Samuel then sacrificed a suckling lamb to God, in the name of the people, imploring his aid against the power of the Philistines The Almighty was pleased to accept the sacrifice, and to promise Samuel, that the Israelites should obtain a complete victory over their enemies

While the sacrifice was yet on the altar, the Philistines drew out in order of battle, but they had no sooner begun the attack, than the earth shook under their feet with such violence as to prevent their standing, and in some places, it opened, and swallowed them up This was attended with a dreadful storm of thunder and lightning, which so affected them that they were totally unable to use their arms, and from the whole, were so frightened, that they betook themselves to flight The Israelites, seeing this, immediately pursued them as far as Bethear, (killing great numbers in their way) where Samuel set up a stone in memory of the victory He called it the *stone of assistance*, intimating that it was by the help of God they had conquered their enemies.

This defeat struck such a panic into the Philistines, that they did not presume to make any farther attempt on the Israelites On the contrary, Samuel, with his army, pursued them from one city to another, and at length retook the whole country that lies betwixt Gath and Ekron, which had formerly belonged to the Israelites, but was taken from them by the Philistines

CHAP III

Samuel being advanced in years, [illegible] the government [illegible] his two sons, who degenerate from the conduct and character of their father

AFTER Samuel had thus reduced the Philistines, and reinstated the people in the possession of their lands and cities, he appointed public meetings to be held at certain times, for the administration of justice, and took a circuit twice every year, to see that it was properly executed, making it his principal care to prevent any violation of the laws of his country

(a) The learned Dr Stackhouse, in speaking of this passage, says "It was no bad policy in the Philistines to take milch kine that had never been yoked before to draw the cart in order to know whether or not there was the hand of God in what had befallen them As those creatures were unacquainted with the yoke, it would be a wonder if they should go on the [illegible] and not [illegible] one another [illegible] it would be a wonder if their natural [illegible] would [illegible] the [illegible] while [illegible] left behind and it would be a greater wonder [illegible] at a different [illegible] to time, they should go directly forward towards Judea [illegible] of division [illegible] was [illegible] consequent [illegible] nothing [illegible] it was [illegible] amongst the heathens, that in the [illegible] heifer or cow [illegible] was [illegible] was something [illegible] the Divine will

Being now grown in years, and unable, from natural infirmities, to discharge the duties of his office, Samuel relinquished the government, and put it into the hands of his two sons, Joel and Abiah He appointed one of them to reside at Bethel, and the other at Beersheba, and ordered them to go different circuits to administer justice to the people

The two sons of Samuel acted diametrically opposite to the maxims of their father, and to the injunctions he had laid on them for the government of the people They prostituted justice for gain, and decided controversies by the value of the bribe They gave themselves up to every kind of vice, and seemed to bid defiance not only to the injunctions of their father, but to the commands of their Maker.

CHAP II.

The people, disgusted at the government of Samuel's sons, request to have a king set over them. A king is promised them by Samuel.

THE elders of the people, incensed at the mal-administration of the sons of Samuel, went in a body to their father, who then resided at Ramah, and, after representing the grievances they lay under, from his infirmities, and the mal-administration of his sons, demanded to have the form of their government changed, and that a king might be appointed over them as in other nations

This demand gave great uneasiness to Samuel, and, for some time, he knew not how to act At length he applied to God, who told him to comply with the request of the people, notwithstanding the affront was not so much on Samuel as on himself But, before they proceeded to the choice of a king, God ordered Samuel to acquaint them with what his prerogatives were, and what they might expect he would demand from them, and withal, to inform them, that slavery to them and their children, subjection to the meanest offices, loss of liberty, heavy taxes, constant war, and other inconveniencies, would be the consequence of a kingly power

Samuel, having received this intelligence from the Almighty, assembled the people together, and told them the various consequences that would follow, should they persist in subjecting themselves to the kingly power But all his remonstrances were of no effect The people were absolute in their demand, upon which Samuel broke up the assembly, telling the people, he would call them again together, as soon as he should receive directions from God who was to be their king

CHAP III.

Saul, by the appointment of God, anointed king. He acts against the Ammonites, and defeats them

NEVER was the interposition of Providence manifested in a greater degree, than in the election of Saul as king over the Israelites, the circumstances attending which cannot be read without distinguished admiration

Saul was the son of Kish, of the tribe of Benjamin He was remarkably handsome in his person, and had a mind answerable to the graces of his body It happened at this time that one of his father's asses had gone astray, and he and a servant were sent to look for them (a). They wandered a great way without gaining any intelligence, till coming to Ramah, (b) the place of Samuel's residence, Saul, at the instigation of the servant, went to consult with the prophet concerning his asses

Samuel had been all the preceding day employed in supplicating God to tell him what person to appoint king, and the Almighty was pleased to answer, that the next day he should receive his orders, for there should come to him a young man of the tribe of Benjamin at that same hour

The prophet staid at home the whole day, and when the precise period arrived, as he was going down to supper, he met Saul, whom he knew, by an immediate inspiration, to be the person designed for the government Saul, not knowing him, asked for the prophet, when Samuel answered, he had found him already He then told Saul, that not only the asses he sought for were safe, but that himself was on the point of being advanced to the highest pitch of sovereign power When supper was ready, Samuel placed Saul above the rest of the guests (who were seventy in number) and his servants next him and ordered the attendants to bring Saul a royal mess The time being come for the company to break up, they departed to their respective homes, except Saul and his servant, whom the prophet desired to remain with him for that night

Early in the morning Samuel called up his guests, and having accompanied them some way from the city, he desired Saul to order his servants to go forward, as he had something to say to him in private This being done, Samuel took out of his pocket a phial of oil, which having poured on Saul's head, he kissed him, and then spoke to the following effect "Be thou king, for "such thou art appointed to be by God, in order to revenge the injuries committed by the Philistines on the "Israelites In token of this observe what I am now "going to relate When thou art departed from me, "thou shalt find, in thy journey, three men going to "Bethel to worship God, the first carrying three loaves, "the second a kid, and the third a bottle of wine They "will all shew you great respect, and offer you two of "the loaves, which you are to receive When you have "advanced as far as the place called Rachel's Sepulchre, "you will meet a man, who will give you tidings of "your asses After this, on your arrival at Gabatha, you "will join with a company of prophets, and, by the assistance of the spirit of God, will prophecy with them, "to the great admiration of the multitude, who will exclaim, How comes the son of Kish to be found among "the prophets? When this shall come to pass, you may "be assured that God is with you Go then to your "father and kindred, and when I send for you, come to "me at Gilgal, that we may conjunctively offer up our "prayers to God, with sacrifices and thanksgiving" Having said this, Samuel parted with Saul who found every thing to happen as had been told him by the prophet

When Saul arrived at his father's house, his uncle Abner (for whom he had a particular esteem) asked him to relate the occurrences that had happened in the course of his journey Saul told him of his going to the prophet, but did not chuse to mention a syllable of his elevation to the throne, lest, if believed, it should produce the envy, if not the censure of the people

Thus was Saul appointed king, but then it was only between Samuel and himself To make, therefore, the appointment and inauguration more public, Samuel con-

---

(a) By this it appears that Saul's employment was in the manner of the patriarchs ... of a mean nature ... but it is to be observed that, in ... times ... it was deemed honour ... kings and princes kept flocks ... were ... the ... of the ... The ... prince descended from Esau, who kept the asses of his father, Gen. xxxvi. 24 Asses were considered ... all ... they ... of ... in Judea ... and princes ... commonly rode on them

(b) Ramah ... a city of Benjamin, situated ... miles to the north of Jerusalem It ... the time of ... but it was then only a poor village

[illegible] an assembly of the people at Mizpeh, and when they were gathered together, he addressed them in words to the following effect "I am commanded by God himself, to inform you that it was he who not only delivered you out of Egyptian bondage, but also repeatedly rescued you from the hands of your enemies In return for which you have been so ungrateful as to shake off his authority, by insisting to have a king of your own choice, a king who will rule over you with tyrannical sway, and treat you with such indignation and cruelty, as if himself did not belong to the same species But since ye are resolved to have a king, divide yourselves by your tribes and families and then cast lots who shall be the man" The Israelites did as Samuel directed, and the lot of the tribe fell upon Benjamin, that of the family upon Matri, and when they came to try it personally, the lot fell upon Saul, the son of Kish

Saul, knowing what business was in hand, had concealed himself from a sense of modesty, but being at length found, he was brought before the people, who [illegible] highly pleased with his majestic deportment and the graces of his person Samuel, addressing himself to the multitude, said, "This is he whom God hath appointed to be your king look at him, and behold in his person how well he is qualified for such an honour" On this the people universally shouted, "God save the king" Samuel hereupon (having previously written down every thing that was to happen) related the same to the people before Saul, after which he placed the book in the tabernacle of God, there to remain, as an undeniable evidence forever of what he had prophecied

This business being over Samuel went to Ramah, and Saul to Gibeah (*a*) the place of his nativity He was accompanied by the principal people of the different tribes, who congratulated him on his accession to the throne with the loudest acclamations Indeed, he had the good wishes of all the people except some few disorderly persons who disapproved of the choice, and, in pure contempt, refused to make him the usual presents, which Saul could not but perceive through, in point of prudence he thought proper, at that time, not to notice the circumstance

Saul had not been many days on the throne, when an opportunity offered for him to shew his regal authority Nahash, king of the Ammonites, heading a powerful army, had committed various outrages, in different parts on the other side the river Jordan He not only destroyed those cities and towns of the Israelites, but exercised the most cruel barbarities on the poor captives, ordering them to be punished with the loss of their right eye (*b*) At length he laid siege to Jabesh, the capital city of the Gileadites, and sent a summons to the inhabitants that if they did not deliver up the place and submit to the loss of their right eyes he would immediately reduce the whole to ashes After some consultation the inhabitants returned for answer, that they only desired seven days to send to their friends for relief, and if they did not receive any in that time, they would either surrender themselves up or stand a contest Nahash looked on the Israelites in so contemptible a light and thought himself so secure of reducing them at discretion, that he granted their request

In consequence of this the Gileadites dispatched messengers to Gibeah requesting of Saul to send them immediate succour that they might be enabled to defend themselves against the power of their enemies

CHAP VI

Saul [illegible] Advances [illegible] the Ammonites [illegible] Is a second time [illegible] king Samuel [illegible] his conduct [illegible] Delivers a [illegible] to the people

WHILE the affairs of the Israelites were in this critical situation, Saul was [illegible] the prophet [illegible], and dispatched the messengers to Jabesh, with a promise of assistance in three days, when they should overcome their enemies before the rising of the sun Being desirous of inflaming the minds of the people towards this war, (through fear of the losses they should otherwise sustain), he cut the sinews of his own oxen, and threatened to do the same to all such as did not the next day appear in arms at the river Jordan, and then follow him and Samuel wherever they should lead them By these means he raised an army of 700,000 men, besides 70,000 more of the tribe of Judah With this army he marched against the Ammonites, and dividing the whole into three companies they fell upon the besiegers before day-light After a short contest the Ammonites were totally routed, and the greater part slain among whom was Nahash their leader

This victory, and the deliverance it procured from a barbarous and insulting enemy, raised the reputation of Saul to so great a degree, that some of the people (recollecting the malignities passed [illegible] at his coronation) [illegible] the height of their zeal, [illegible] them immediately [illegible] death but Saul very prudently opposed the motion and [illegible] his aversion to having the glories of that day sullied with the blood of any of his subjects

From this victory however, Samuel took occasion to give those, who had hitherto withheld their allegiance, an opportunity of coming in, and recognizing the king For this purpose he convened a general assembly of the people at Gilgal, when Saul was again anointed king, and his right to the throne fully established Thus was the government of the Israelites changed to a monarchy, which, for a considerable time before, was lodged in magistrates under the name of Judges

Samuel was at this time to resign the government entirely into the hands of Saul He therefore made a speech to the people on the occasion, in which, after vindicating himself from any misconduct during his administration, he thus reminded them of their transgressions and disobedience to God "What (says he) should you choose another king for, after the experience of so many signal mercies and miraculous deliverances, while you were under God's protection, and owned him for your governor? You have forgot the circumstance of Jacob's coming into Egypt with only seventy men in his train and purely for want of bread, how God provided for them and in what manner, by his blessing they were relieved You have forgot the slavery to which [illegible] were subjected, till, from their cries and supplications, God relieved them by the hands of Moses and Aaron, and brought them into the land they now possess How can you be so ungrateful now, after so many distinguished benefits received, as to depart from your allegiance to your Divine protector? How often have you fallen into the hands of your enemies for your apostacy and disobedience, and as often restored to God's favour [illegible] your liberty, by humiliation and repentance? Who was it that gave you victory over all your enemies but God? It was not by the power of kings, but [illegible]

(*a*) [illegible] Jerusalem [illegible] Saul the first [illegible] Saul [illegible]

(*b*) [illegible]

Being now grown in years, and unable, from natural infirmities, to diſcharge the duties of his office, Samuel relinquiſhed the government, and put it into the hands of his two ſons, Joel and Abiah He appointed one of them to reſide at Bethel, and the other at Beerſheba, and ordered them to go different circuits to adminiſter juſtice to the people

The two ſons of Samuel acted diametrically oppoſite to the maxims of their father, and to the injunctions he had laid on them for the government of the people They proſtituted juſtice for gain, and decided controverſies by the value of the bribe They gave themſelves up to every kind of vice, and ſeemed to bid defiance not only to the injunctions of their father, but to the commands of their Maker

CHAP IV.

The people, diſguſted at the government of Samuel's ſons, require a king to rule over them A king is promiſed them by Samuel.

THE elders of the people, incenſed at the mal-adminiſtration of the ſons of Samuel, went in a body to their father, who then reſided at Ramah, and, after repreſenting the grievances they lay under, from his infirmities, and the mal-adminiſtration of his ſons, demanded to have the form of their government changed, and that a king might be appointed over them as in other nations

This demand gave great uneaſineſs to Samuel, and, for ſome time, he knew not how to act At length he applied to God, who told him to comply with the requeſt of the people, notwithſtanding the affront was not ſo much on Samuel as on himſelf But, before they proceeded to the choice of a king, God ordered Samuel to acquaint them with what his prerogatives were, and what they might expect he would demand from them, and withal, to inform them, that ſlavery to them and their children, ſubjection to the meaneſt offices, loſs of liberty, heavy taxes, conſtant war, and other inconveniencies, would be the conſequence of a kingly power

Samuel, having received this intelligence from the Almighty, aſſembled the people together, and told them the various conſequences that would follow, ſhould they perſiſt in ſubjecting themſelves to the kingly power But all his remonſtrances were of no effect The people were abſolute in their demand, upon which Samuel broke up the aſſembly, telling the people, he would call them again together, as ſoon as he ſhould receive directions from God who was to be their king

CHAP V

Saul, by the appointment of God, anointed king Heads an army againſt the Ammonites, and defeats them

NEVER was the interpoſition of Providence manifeſted in a greater degree, than in the election of Saul as king over the Iſraelites, the circumſtances attending which cannot be read without diſtinguiſhed admiration

Saul was the ſon of Kiſh, of the tribe of Benjamin He was remarkably handſome in his perſon, and had a mind anſwerable to the graces of his body It happened at this time that ſome of his father's aſſes had gone aſtray, and he and a ſervant were ſent to look for them (a). They wandered a great way without gaining any intelligence, till coming to Ramah, (b) the place of Samuel's reſidence, Saul, at the inſtigation of the ſervant, went to conſult with the prophet concerning his aſſes.

Samuel had been all the preceding day employed in ſupplicating God to tell him what perſon to appoint king, and the Almighty was pleaſed to anſwer, that the next day he ſhould receive his order, for there ſhould come to him a young man of the tribe of Benjamin at that ſame hour

The prophet ſtaid at home the whole day, and when the preciſe period arrived, as he was going down to ſupper, he met Saul, whom he knew, by an immediate inſpiration, to be the perſon deſigned for the government Saul, not knowing him, aſked for the prophet, when Samuel anſwered, he had found him already. He then told Saul, that not only the aſſes he ſought for were ſafe, but that himſelf was on the point of being advanced to the higheſt pitch of ſovereign power When ſupper was ready, Samuel placed Saul above the reſt of the gueſts (who were ſeventy in number) and his ſervants next him, and ordered the attendants to bring Saul a royal meſs The time being come for the company to break up, they departed to their reſpective homes, except Saul and his ſervant, whom the prophet deſired to remain with him for that night

Early in the morning Samuel called up his gueſts, and having accompanied them ſome way from the city, he deſired Saul to order his ſervants to go forward, as he had ſomething to ſay to him in private This being done, Samuel took out of his pocket a phial of oil, which having poured on Saul's head, he kiſſed him, and then ſpoke to the following effect "Be thou king, for "ſuch thou art appointed to be by God, in order to re-"venge the injuries committed by the Philiſtines on the "Iſraelites In token of this obſerve what I am now "going to relate When thou art departed from me, "thou ſhalt find, in thy journey, three men going to "Bethel to worſhip God, the firſt carrying three loaves, "the ſecond a kid, and the third a bottle of wine They "will all ſhew you great reſpect, and offer you two of "the loaves, which you are to receive When you have "advanced as far as the place called Rachel's Sepulchre, "you will meet a man, who will give you tidings of "your aſſes After this, on your arrival at Gabatha, you "will join with a company of prophets, and, by the aſ-"ſiſtance of the ſpirit of God, will prophecy with them, "to the great admiration of the multitude, who will ex-"claim, How comes the ſon of Kiſh to be found among "the prophets? When this ſhall come to paſs, you may "be aſſured that God is with you. Go then to your "father and kindred, and when I ſend for you, come to "me at Gilgal, that we may conjunctively offer up our "prayers to God, with ſacrifices and thankſgiving" Having ſaid this, Samuel parted with Saul who found every thing to happen as had been told him by the prophet

When Saul arrived at his father's houſe, his uncle Abner (for whom he had a particular eſteem) aſked him to relate the occurrences that had happened in the courſe of his journey Saul told him of his going to the prophet, but did not chooſe to mention a ſyllable of his elevation to the throne, leſt, if believed, it ſhould produce the envy, if not the cenſure of the people

Thus was Saul appointed king, but then it was only between Samuel and himſelf To make, therefore, his appointment and inauguration more public, Samuel con

(a) By [illegible] it appears that Saul's employment, according to the manners of the preſent age, was [illegible] of a mean nature but it is to be obſerved that, in ancient times every thing which pertained to a rural life was deemed honourable Even heroes and princes kept flocks and [illegible], indeed, were the occupations of the patriarchs The ſcripture ſpeaks of a prince deſcended from Eſau who kept the aſſes of his father, Gen xxxvi 2, Aſſes were a conſiderable part of the people's poſſeſſions in Judea, and perſons of the firſt diſtinction there commonly rode on them

(b) Ramah was a city of Benjamin, ſituated between Gaba and Bethel, ſix miles to the north of Jeruſalem It was in being in the time of St Jerome, but was then only a poor village

vened an assembly of the people at Mizpeh, and when they were gathered together, he addressed them in words to the following effect "I am commanded, by God himself, to inform you that it was he who not only delivered you out of Egyptian bondage, but also repeatedly rescued you from the hands of your enemies In return for which you have been so ungrateful as to shake off his authority, by insisting to have a king of your own choice, a king who will rule over you with tyrannical sway, and treat you with such indignation and cruelty, as if himself did not belong to the same species But since ye are resolved to have a king, divide yourselves by your tribes and families, and then cast lots who shall be the man" The Israelites did as Samuel directed, and the lot of the tribe fell upon Benjamin, that of the families upon Matri, and when they came to try it personally, the lot fell upon Saul, the son of Kish

Saul, knowing what business was in hand, had concealed himself from a sense of modesty but being at length found, he was brought before the people, who were highly pleased with his majestic deportment and the graces of his person Samuel, addressing himself to the multitude, said, "This is he whom God hath appointed to be your king look at him, and behold in his person how well he is qualified for such an honour" On this the people universally shouted, "God save the king" Samuel hereupon (having previously written down every thing that was to happen) related the same to the people before Saul, after which he placed the book in the tabernacle of God, there to remain, as an undeniable evidence forever of what he had prophesied

This business being over, Samuel went to Ramah, and Saul to Gibeah (*a*) the place of his nativity He was accompanied by the principal people of the different tribes, who congratulated him on his accession to the throne with the loudest acclamations Indeed, he had the good wishes of all the people, except some few disorderly persons, who disapproved of the choice, and, in pure contempt, refused to make him the usual presents; which Saul could not but perceive, though, in point of prudence, he thought proper, for that time, not to notice the circumstance

Saul had not been many days on the throne, when an opportunity offered for him to shew his regal authority Nahash, king of the Ammonites, heading a powerful army, had committed various outrages, in different parts on the other side the river Jordan He not only destroyed those cities and towns of the Israelites, but exercised the most cruel barbarities on the poor captives, ordering them to be punished with the loss of their right eye (*b*) At length he laid siege to Jabesh, the capital city of the Gileadites, and sent a summons to the inhabitants, that if they did not deliver up the place, and submit to the loss of their right eyes he would immediately reduce the whole to ashes After some consultation the inhabitants returned for answer, that they desired only seven days to send to their friends for relief, and if they did not receive any in that time, they would either surrender themselves up, or stand a contest Nahash looked on the Israelites in so contemptible a light, and thought himself so secure of reducing them at discretion, that he granted their request

In consequence of this the Gileadites dispatched messengers to Gibeah requesting of Saul to send them immediate succour, that they might be enabled to defend themselves against the power of their enemies

CHAP VI

Saul musters a powerful army Advances and obtains a complete victory over the Ammonites Acquires glory by his prowess Is a second time proclaimed king Samuel vindicates his conduct in a general appeal Delivers a charge to the people

WHILE the affairs of the Israelites were in this critical situation, Saul was seized with a prophetic spirit, and sent back the messengers to Jabesh, with a promise of assistance in three days, when they should overcome their enemies before the rising of the sun Being desirous of inclining the minds of the people towards this war, (through fear of the losses they should otherwise sustain), he cut the sinews of his own oxen, and threatened to do the same to all such as did not the next day appear in arms at the river Jordan, and then follow him and Samuel wherever they should lead them By these means he raised an army of 700,000 men, besides 70,000 more of the tribe of Judah With this army he marched against the Ammonites, and dividing the whole into three companies, they fell on the besiegers before day light After a short contest the Ammonites were totally routed, and the greater part slain, among whom was Nahash their leader

This victory, and the deliverance it procured from a barbarous and insulting enemy, raised the reputation of Saul to so great a degree, that some of the people (recollecting the indignities put on him at his coronation) were in the height of their zeal, for having them immediately punished with death, but Saul very prudently opposed the motion, and expressed his aversion at having the glories of that day sullied with the blood of any of his subjects

From this victory, however, Samuel took occasion to give those, who had hitherto refused their allegiance, an opportunity of coming in, and recognizing the king For this purpose he convened a general assembly of the people of Gilgal, when Saul was again anointed king, and his right to the throne fully established Thus was the government of the Israelites changed to a monarchy, which, for a considerable time before, was lodged in magistrates under the name of judges

Samuel was at this time to resign the government entirely into the hands of Saul He therefore made a speech to the people on the occasion, in which, after vindicating himself from any misconduct during his administration, he thus reminded them of their transgressions and disobedience to God "What (says he) should you choose another king for, after the experience of so many signal mercies, and miraculous deliverances, while you were under God's protection, and owned him for your governor? You have forgot the circumstance of Jacob's coming into Egypt with only seventy men in his train, and purely for want of bread, how God provided for them, and in what manner, by his blessing they were relieved You have forgot the slavery to which they were subjected, till, from their cries and supplications, God rescued them by the hands of Moses and Aaron, and brought them into the land they now possess How can you be so ungrateful now, after so many distinguished benefits received, as to depart from your allegiance to your Divine protector? How often have you fallen into the hands of your enemies for your apostacy and disobedience, and as often restored to God's favour and your liberty, by humiliation and repentance! Who was it that gave you victory over all your enemies but God? It was not by the power of kings, but under the

(*a*) Gibeah was a city of the tribe of Benjamin [illegible] north of Jerusalem [illegible] twenty or thirty furlongs [illegible] hill [illegible] importance [illegible] this city is celebrated [illegible] gave birth to Saul [illegible] of Israel for which reason it is frequently called Gibeah of Saul or Gibeah the native country of Saul

(*b*) [illegible] the manner of [illegible] days [illegible]

[illegible] the loss of the right eye would [illegible] their enemies [illegible] natural cruelty of [illegible] would have commanded the loss of both [illegible] had it not been for [illegible] reason [illegible] them [illegible] capable of [illegible] conduct of Jephtha and Gideon. What madness, then, has possessed you, to give up an heavenly government for an earthly one. However, you have taken for a king, and a king you have got: but to convince you now the Almighty is offended at your conduct, I do now beg from heaven, as a testimony of the truth of what I say, that such a tempest may at this instant fall as was never before seen by man."

No sooner had Samuel uttered these last words than there fell such a violent storm of thunder, lightning and hail, as almost to produce a general dissolution of nature. And so great terror [illegible] among the people they [illegible] acknowledged their transgressions, and entreated Samuel to intercede with the Almighty to pardon their sins. Samuel not only promised to comply with their request, but to assist them with his best instructions, so long as they adhered to the observation of God's laws; but at the same time told them, if they refused his instructions, not only they, but also their king, would be infallibly destroyed. Having said this, Samuel dismissed the assembly, and immediately retired.

CHAP. VII.

Jonathan [illegible] son [illegible], [illegible] the [illegible] the Philistines. Saul [illegible], [illegible] the [illegible] [illegible] progress.

AFTER [illegible] the [illegible] the Ammonites, he disbanded all his army, except only three thousand, two [illegible] which he kept for his body guard, and the other [illegible] he appointed to attend on his son Jonathan, who was a prince of great bravery, and had cut off a garrison of the Philistines at Gibeah. Whenever the Philistines gained an advantage over the Jews, they not only disarmed them, but forbade them the use of iron in any case whatever; so that they were under a necessity of applying to the Philistine artificers for all mechanical [illegible] [illegible].

The Philistines, resolving to oppose the [illegible], raised a powerful army consisting of [illegible], with which they marched against them, and encamped [illegible] a place called Michmash. The Hebrew army, which [illegible] appointed to rendezvous at Gilgal, came in but very slowly, and of those that did, many were so faint-hearted as to secrete themselves in rocks and caves; while others, from their apprehension of danger, retired beyond the river Jordan. In short, not only the people but even Saul himself, was greatly intimidated, and the more so on the account of Samuel, whom they expected, not being yet come. Saul, therefore, fearing the enemy should fall on him before he had addressed himself to God for success, ordered [illegible] to be made, and the burnt-offering was [illegible] sacrificed when Samuel arrived.

When Samuel found what Saul had done, he reprehended him for his conduct, in having offered a sacrifice to God in his absence. Saul endeavoured to excuse himself, by saying his people were so intimidated, on hearing the enemy had marched towards Gilgal, that he found it necessary to be expeditious in his motions, lest they should entirely desert him. To this the prophet replied, "it would have been better for you to have followed my "advice and not have acted in opposition to the will of "the Divine Being, who otherwise would have established the government in you and your posterity." After this Samuel departed, highly offended at what Saul had done.

The only alternative Saul now had, was, either to attempt defending himself against the Philistines, or openly submit to their superior power. After some deliberation he determined on the former, and, for that purpose, taking with him his son Jonathan, marched his army, consisting only of 600 men, towards the enemy. It is to be observed, that Saul's troops were badly armed, for the Philistines, having made themselves masters of various parts of the country, had prohibited the people from making any use of iron, as before observed.

When Saul's army came near that of the Philistines, he, together with his son Jonathan, and Ahiah, the high priest, ascended a steep rock, where they had a full view of the enemy unperceived. On this Jonathan, taking aside his armour-bearer, asked him how far he would assist him in a bold enterprize for the redemption of his country. To which the armour-bearer answered, with an oath, that he would, however dangerous the situation, stand by him to the last extremity. Jonathan then made a proposition, which was immediately agreed to, that he and his armour-bearer, should endeavour secretly to get into the enemy's camp, and, if they succeeded, fall violently on the Philistines, and thereby throw them into [illegible] confusion. This design was, with great difficulty carried into execution. They got into the camp of the Philistines at a time when they were all at rest [illegible] apprehensive of danger. Jonathan and his armour-bearer, took proper advantage of this favourable opportunity, and immediately falling on the Philistines, put [illegible] to the sword, which occasioned such an universal confusion, that the Philistines, mistaking [illegible] for foes, destroyed each other (*). Intimation of this being given to Saul, and the news circulated among the great body of the Israelites, those who had secreted themselves through fear immediately came from their [illegible], and Saul having soon mustered together his army, marched against the Philistines, and so fell on them with such fury, that they were totally defeated.

[illegible] this success [illegible] so fully determined, [illegible] to exterminate the Philistines, that he denounced [illegible] on every Hebrew who should [illegible] from pursuing the enemy, even to eat or drink [illegible] night should put a period to the slaughter. It happened that Jonathan, who was a stranger to the malediction, [illegible] passing through a wood, found a honey-comb, and being greatly fatigued, [illegible] a piece and sucked it. He soon [illegible] repeated this refreshment in the presence of several people, who reprehended him for his conduct, [illegible] his father's orders; upon which Jonathan immediately desisted, but said, that Saul had committed a [illegible] in prohibiting such a thing; for had the men been refreshed by eating, they would have pursued the enemy with more vigour, and took captive, or put to the sword, a much greater number.

After the Israelites had pursued the Philistines till night, and slain many thousands, they returned to seize their camp, in which they found abundance of spoil, and withal many sheep, which the soldiers slew and eat, together with the blood. This being an offence against the [illegible], the [illegible] complained of it to the king, who ordered a large stone to be placed in the middle of the camp, the beasts to be killed on that stone, and the flesh not to be eaten till the blood had been properly drained from it, being a thing contradictory to the express command of God. This decree was readily obeyed, and Saul erected an altar, on which he offered sacrifices to God for his late success.

(*) [illegible] Jonathan [illegible] [illegible] the Philistines [illegible] not improbable that God [illegible] the whole [illegible] [illegible]

Saul being desirous of improving this victory, thought it advisable to follow the blow by pursuing those who had escaped, and falling on them before they could have time to grow formidable by numbers. But previous to his making this attempt, he desired the high-priest to consult the will of God on his intentions. [illegible] accordingly done, when the high-priest returned for answer, "That God was unwilling to satisfy his [illegible] this time." Saul then said, "There is some cause why God doth not reveal his oracle to us [illegible] it, seeing that he has heretofore been so gracious as to prevent our requests by granting them [illegible]. There has been certainly some secret sin committed against him that occasions this silence, and I am determined if possible to find it out. Now I swear, by the Supreme Majesty of heaven, that [illegible] the transgressor, my son Jonathan, [illegible] excepted, his life shall answer for it."

When the people heard this, they unanimously agreed to undergo the examination, and, for that purpose, immediately assembled at one spot, Saul and [illegible] standing near [illegible]. In order to discover the [illegible] lots were drawn, when, behold [illegible] Jonathan, who was accordingly declared the guilty person. On this Saul asked him in the hearing of the people what [illegible] he had committed, and in [illegible] of his life he had been guilty of, what [illegible] impiety? To this Jonathan replied, "I have been guilty of no other crime than only tasting [illegible], [illegible] pursued the enemy, which however, [illegible] I did, not knowing your decree to be contrary." [illegible] answered, "Though my kindred and relations are [illegible], yet they are [illegible] the obligation [illegible] to fulfil the vow I have made. As you, therefore, [illegible] transgressor, you must make atonement [illegible] of your life." Jonathan, instead of being [illegible] dismayed at the [illegible] of [illegible] father, with a brave and generous [illegible], [illegible] he desired not to be forgiven. "[illegible] come to me [illegible] the [illegible] religious vow. I have lived long [illegible], I have lived to see the pride [illegible] the Philistines brought down by the Hebrews, [illegible] on will carry me in peace to my grave."

When the people heard Jonathan [illegible] they were greatly affected, and swore they would not suffer him to die who was the principal cause of their [illegible] victory. In consequence of this oath Jonathan's life was preserved, and the people unanimously [illegible] God in the most fervent manner, that he would be pleased to pardon the offence he had unintentionally committed.

After this victory Saul returned to Gilgal, [illegible] very happily acquitting himself with great reputation in all his military exploits against the Ammonites, the Moabites, the Philistines and the Edomites. He had, indeed, a very large and flourishing family. Ahinoam, the daughter of Ahimaaz, was his wife; Jonathan, Joshua, and Melchishua, were his sons. Michal and Merab his daughters, and Abner, his cousin-german, was general of his forces. He kept a great number of chariots and horsemen, and whatever enemy he attacked his endeavours were crowned with success. His body guards, of which he had great numbers, were the tallest and handsomest men that could be selected, and he kept his court in the most splendid manner. In short, he advanced the Israelites to the highest pitch of glory [illegible] martial exploits, and made them so formidable as to be a perpetual dread to their enemies.

CHAP. VII.

Saul is commanded by the prophet to [illegible]. Disobeys by [illegible] Agag, their king [illegible] for his disobedience.

WHILE the [illegible] were thus [illegible], Samuel [illegible] must go to deliver him by the special direction of God, and that as the Almighty had been pleased to make him king in preference to all others, it was his duty to obey his Divine commands, which [illegible]. "[illegible] whereas the Amalekites had treated the Hebrews with [illegible] when they were come out of Egypt into the land they then possessed, it was the will of God that he should immediately [illegible] them, and that, upon subduing them, he should [illegible] put to the sword every man, woman and child, and that he should also destroy [illegible], and that they should not take to themselves any part of the spoil, but that the whole should be devoted to God as one common sacrifice; that the very name of Amalek should be utterly extirpated, according to the command of Moses, and all the evils [illegible] brought on the Israelites."

Saul promised Samuel, that the [illegible] should be [illegible] obeyed, and that he would [illegible] bringing them into execution. He accordingly drew [illegible] forces, which he mustered at Gilgal, and found them to consist of 400,000, besides 30,000 belonging to the tribe of Judah.

With this army Saul marched into the country of the Amalekites, and placing several of his companies in ambuscade, they suddenly fell on the inhabitants and put every one to the sword. After this he marched against the main body of the enemy, which he [illegible] the enemies [illegible] of the Amalekites did [illegible] attacked and killed, so that not a single person was left to [illegible] the defeat.

Saul having thus far succeeded in executing the commission, proceeded to invest the cities of the Amalekites, some of which he took by storm, some by mining, and others [illegible]. At length he reduced the whole of the [illegible], and put all the inhabitants to the sword, except Agag, their king, whom he [illegible] to preserve on account of the comeliness of his person. [illegible] a force on the Divine commands, for the Amalekites had made themselves so abominable in the sight of heaven that God had ordered him to destroy all, and not suffer a single person to escape. The soldiers likewise [illegible] on the Divine commands, by driving away many of the cattle and sheep, and preserving, for their own use, the most valuable articles.

In this expedition Saul laid waste the whole country of the Amalekites, from Pelusium, on the borders of Egypt, to the Red Sea, leaving only the Shechemites in the [illegible] of Midian. Previous to the commencement of the war, he had sent orders to those people not to join with the Amalekites, but rather to retire, lest they should fall in the general destruction that was to take place. The reason of [illegible] these people was out of respect to Moses, whose father-in-law Jethro, was a Shechemite.

Saul, having ravaged the whole country of the Amalekites, returned with his army to Gilgal, highly pleased with what he had done, not reflecting that he was deficient in the injunctions laid on him before he went on the expedition. His sparing the life of Agag, and the people converting the spoil to their own use, being two articles expressly forbidden in his commission, gave great offence to the Almighty, who was pleased to declare to Samuel that he lamented having made Saul king, seeing, that instead of doing what he had been commanded, he was determined to take the power out of his hands, by doing as he pleased.

Samuel was so affected in his mind at this intelligence, that he spent the whole night in fervent prayers and intercessions to God, that he would pardon the crime Saul had committed. But the Almighty instead of granting his request, gave him an answer to this effect: "That it [illegible] "nature, as the pardoning of one offence would be only an encouragement for the commission of another."

When Samuel found his prayers ineffectual, and that God was so displeased as not to be moved in favour of Saul, he was greatly grieved, and went the next morning to Gilgal, to communicate the melancholy intelligence to the king. As soon as Saul saw Samuel, he ran to meet him, and embracing him in his arms, said, "I return "thanks to God for having given me the victory. More- "over I have performed all that he enjoined me to do." To this Samuel replied, "How comes it then, that I hear "the bleating of sheep, and the lowing of oxen?" Saul "answered, "Those were only some beasts the people "had reserved for sacrifices; and that he had destroyed "all the Amalekites, except Agag, their king, whom "he kept prisoner till he might have advice what should "be done with him." "God (says Samuel) delights "not in sacrifices, but in the righteousness of good and "just men, that study [illegible] to observe his holy will "and keep his commandments. He does not consider "the sacrifice but the obedience, without which all "other things are of no effect. Know then, Saul, that "thou art fallen under God's heavy displeasure, for the "neglect and contempt of his commandments. What can "you say for yourself when he calls you to account for "receiving those things for sacrifices which he expressly "ordered should be totally destroyed? For this disobe- "dience you are condemned to lose your kingdom, and "to be divested of that power which was providentially "bestowed upon you in preference to the rest of man- "kind."

When Saul heard this he made a frank confession of his guilt, but apologized for the conduct of his soldiers, by saying, "That he was fearful, had he prohibited them from taking some of the spoil, they might have revolted and himself been exposed to an enraged people. But (says Saul to Samuel) let me prevail on you to endeavour to obtain a pardon for me from God; and if you should succeed, and he will be pleased to grant your request, the future part of my life shall be spent in strict observance of every religious duty, and in inviolable attention to his most holy will." After saying this, Saul begged of Samuel, that before he left him, he would sacrifice to God in his behalf. But Samuel knowing it would be ineffectual, was going to retire, when Saul caught hold of his garment to detain him, and in the scuffle it was rent asunder. This circumstance was interpreted by Samuel as an omen, that Saul would lose his kingdom, and that it would be given to a man of piety and justice. "The sentence (says Samuel) is passed, and it is not with God as with men, for his decrees are unchangeable." Saul acknowledged his iniquity, and the justness of the punishment inflicted by Providence. He said, what he had committed could not be undone, and therefore begged Samuel to honour him before the elders of the people, and accompany him to worship God. The prophet yielded to the importunate request of Saul, and went with him to sacrifice, after which Samuel ordered Agag, the king of the Amalekites to be brought before him. As soon as Agag appeared he said, "Surely the bitterness of death is past." To which Samuel replied, "As thy sword has made women childless so shall thy mother be childless among women." He then slew Agag with his own hands, and leaving Gilgal went immediately to Ramah, the place of his residence.

This was the last interview between Samuel and Saul, the latter of whom, being sensible of his calamities, retired to his palace at Gibeah, and there spent his time in penitence and prayer.

CHAP. IX.

Saul having transgressed the Divine command, the kingdom is transferred, and David anointed and proclaimed prince.

SAMUEL was greatly afflicted for the fate of Saul, upon which God told him to grieve no longer, but to take an horn of oil, and go to Bethlehem to Jesse, the son of Obed, and anoint one of his sons, whom he had appointed, and would discover to him, to be king over the Israelites. Samuel expressed his fears, that, on executing his commission, Saul would seek his life; but the Almighty promising him security from all danger, he went to Bethlehem, where he was received by the people with the most expressive joy; and on being asked what was the cause of his coming thither, he answered, "To perform sacrifice."

The ceremony of the sacrifice being over, Samuel invited Jesse and his sons to partake of the feast; and as soon as he saw the eldest, who was remarkably handsome, he said within himself, "This is to be our king." But Samuel was mistaken, for on asking God whether he should anoint him, he received an answer to this effect. "God seeth not as man sees. Thou supposest "him to be worthy of a kingdom from his outward ap- "pearance only; but such honors are not to be bestowed "as due to the merit of a person's figure; they are to "be given as a reward for the virtuous qualifications of "the mind: wherefore look unto that man who is per- "fect in piety and justice, courage and meekness, vir- "tues which truly constitute the beauties of the mind." On this Samuel ordered the other sons, who were six in number, to pass him, one by one; and consulting God which was to be the person anointed, he was answered *none*. Samuel then asked Jesse if he had any more sons. He answered he had one more, whose name was David, and that he was then looking after his sheep. Samuel ordered Jesse immediately to send for him, as they could not sit down to the feast unless he was present. David was accordingly sent for, and immediately obeyed the summons. As he had a manly countenance, on the first sight of him Samuel argued with himself, this is the person God has appointed to be king. He then placed David next to himself, and Jesse, with the rest of his sons, in regular order after them. This being done, he took out the oil, and pouring it on David's head, said, "By "this thou art informed, that God has been pleased to "appoint thee king over the Israelites. I therefore strict- "ly charge thee to do justice to the people, and be par- "ticularly careful to observe God's commandments. In "doing this, thou shalt reign long and happy: thou "shalt triumph over the Philistines, and be victorious in "all encounters. You shall live great, and die memo- "rable." Having said this Samuel departed, and the spirit of God passed from Saul to David *(a)*, the latter was immediately possessed of the power of prophecy.

In the mean time Saul declined more and more in God's favour; and as he was naturally of a timorous and suspicious temper, an unhappy turn of mind grew upon him, which at length settled into a confirmed melancholy, of such a nature as to be frequently attended with violent perturbations, and sometimes with a phrenzy. To relieve him in this melancholy state, some of his courtiers advised music, as it would most likely lull his disturbed mind to rest. They recommended David, the son of Jesse, not only as a proper master of music, but likewise as a man possessed of the most distinguished accomplishments.

(a) That is God was no longer with him [illegible] and guided him [illegible] punishment for his disobedience to the [illegible] melancholy [illegible] spirit which [illegible] left him [illegible] nature of [illegible] ty [illegible] virtue and [illegible] into the min[d] [illegible] almost perpetual [illegible] dispos[e] those who [illegible] under the [illegible] influence [illegible] to the most unw[illegible] [illegible]

In consequence of this recommendation David was sent for to court; and as soon as Saul saw him, he was greatly pleased with the beauty of his person. When he heard him exercise his skill on the harp, he was perfectly transported, insomuch, that it banished from him all uneasy and melancholy thoughts. In short, Saul conceived such a kindness for David, for having cured him of his malady, that he made him one of his armour-bearers. When the king was better David returned to his brother and attended to his flocks.

CHAP. V.

The Philistines make another expedition against the Hebrews in the reign of Saul. A single combat between Goliath and David, in consequence of a challenge from the former.

THE Philistines, having gathered together a considerable army, marched against the Israelites, and pitched their tents between Shocoh and Azekah. In consequence of this Saul drew out his men, and placing them on a mountain, obliged the Philistines to remove, and encamp themselves on another mountain opposite the Israelites, the valley between dividing the two armies.

While they were in this situation, there came from the Philistine camp Goliath, a citizen of Gath, a man remarkable for his prodigious stature, being no less than six cubits and a span high. He was dressed in armour, and his coat of mail weighed 5000 shekels. The head of his spear was iron, weighing 600 shekels, and he carried it on his shoulder. Thus accoutred did this mighty man march down the hill attended by a troop of armed men, and placing himself in the middle of the valley, between the two armies, he thus addressed himself to the Israelites: "Ye men of Israel, I am come hither, to do an "office of humanity, by preventing the loss of many "lives. Why should so many persons perish, when the dis- "pute may be determined between only two people? I "offer myself as a champion for the Philistines: do "you choose another for my opponent; and whoever con- "quers, the people belonging to him vanquished, shall "be subject to those of the conqueror. It is better to "expose one than so many thousands." Having said this Goliath retired, but returned the next day, and repeated his challenge, which he continued to do forty days successively, the Israelites not knowing whom to choose for his antagonist.

In Saul's army were three of the sons of Jesse, to whom their father sent David then [illegible] with necessaries, and to bring him intelligence of the situation of the Hebrew [illegible]. Soon after David arrived at the camp Goliath again appeared, and reproached the Hebrews with cowardice, saying, they had not a man in their army, that dare look him in the face. David was so incensed at this, that he told his brother he would accept the challenge himself. But Eliab, the eldest, reproved him for his ridiculous presumption, and told him to go again to his father, and attend his sheep. Though David paid great respect to his brother, yet he could not help repeating what he had before said in the hearing of the soldiers, which being reported to the king, he sent for him, and asked him what he had to say relative to Goliath? David replied, "Great Prince, fear not. I am he who will "take down the pride of this mighty boaster, and make "your terrible enemy appear ridiculous when they shall "behold him fall by the hand of an inexperienced boy." Saul stood amazed at the intrepidity of the youth, but did not think it prudent to try the issue on so unequal a match. David, finding Saul's diffidence, told him, the combat [illegible] not to be considered as a trial of skill between Goliath and him, but Goliath and God. "It is not (says he) "my [illegible] that will decide the battle, but the power of "[illegible] God, who frequently makes the weakest ob- "[illegible] to be instruments of his divine purposes. In that "[illegible] put my trust, and doubt not but he will protect "me, however difficult the task in which I engage, hav- "ing already experienced, in two instances, his Divine "[illegible]. On a time, while I was attending my fa- "ther's sheep, a lion suddenly came among the flock "and ran away with a lamb. I pursued the [illegible] and "having come up with him, rescued the lamb [illegible] put "a period to the lion's existence. I had an encounter of "the like nature with a bear, which proved equally suc- "cessful. Now I doubt not but I [illegible] "listine as I did with the lion and bear, that he shall "no more add defiance to the [illegible] of the Israelites, or "reproach the living God, but [illegible] "tim by my means, through the Divine assistance, to his "daring presumption."

From the manner in which this speech was delivered Saul thought David's resolution arose not from presumptive courage, but Divine inspiration. He therefore said to him, "Go, and the Lord be with thee." After which he prepared David for the action, by dressing him in his own armour, and giving him his coat of mail, sword, and helmet. David, not having been accustomed to such arms, found them rather burdensome than useful, and told Saul they were much fitter for a prince than a shepherd, begging, at the same time, that he would permit him to throw them off, and take his own way. This being granted, David took his shepherd's staff, a sling, and five smooth stones, and with these only he advanced to meet his antagonist. When Goliath saw David he looked upon him with contempt, and in a deriding manner, said, "Comest "thou to fight a son as thou would a dog?" To which David replied, "I come to fight neither [illegible] "the [illegible], and much worse than a dog." This so exasperated Goliath that he swore, by his gods, that he would give David's flesh to the fowls of the air and the beasts of the field. David answered, "You come to me "with a sword, a spear and a coat of mail; but I come "to you in the name of the Lord of Hosts, the God of the "armies of Israel, whom you have defied. This day will "the Lord deliver you into my hand, and I will smite you "and take your head from you, and give your carcase to the "fowls of the air and to the wild beasts of the earth, that "all the world may know there is a God in Israel. The "whole assembly shall see that the Lord [illegible] not with "sword and spear. The battle is his, and he will deli- "ver you into our hands."

Goliath advanced toward David with as much expedition as the weight of his armour would permit, at the same time intimating by his gestures the contemptible light in which he considered this almost defenceless adversary. David, putting his trust in the Almighty, hastened to meet him, and, when he thought himself at a proper distance, he took one of the stones out of his bag, put it in his sling, and cast it at the Philistine. The stone went in such a direction as to strike him in the forehead, and that with such force, that he immediately fell prostrate on the ground. David seeing this ran directly to Goliath, and taking his sword from the sheath (not having any of his own) slew him, and cut off his head.

CHAP. VI.

Saul [illegible] victory, routs many of the Philistines. — Conceives [illegible] jealousy against David [illegible] except [illegible] Events thereto ensuing [illegible]

WHEN the Philistines saw the fate of their champion, they were so chagrined that they immediately betook themselves to flight. The Hebrews availed themselves of this circumstance, and pursuing the Philistines as far as the skirts of Gath, and the very gates of Ascalon, killed upwards of 30,000, besides wounding double the number. Saul in his return, rifled their camp, and then set fire to it, and David carried the head of Goliath to his tent, and dedicated his sword to his [illegible].

This distinguished conquest raised the reputation of David to the highest summit [illegible] the time [illegible] it [illegible] on him the [illegible] hatred of the king. On Saul's return from the victory, he was met by great numbers of women, [illegible] out of every city, who congratulated him on his success with dances [illegible] of musical instruments, [illegible] them singing, *Saul hath [illegible] his thousands, and David his ten thousands.*

Saul was so irritated at this superior compliment paid to David, that he gave [illegible] to [illegible] left, in time, he might become so popular among the people as to [illegible] him in the sovereignty. As the character David [illegible], [illegible] armour-bearer, obliged him to be near the king, Saul removed him from that office, and [illegible] him captain over a thousand men. This, indeed, was a more advantageous place than the [illegible] of armour-bearer; [illegible] Saul's bestowing it on David, did not [illegible] from [illegible] to him, on the contrary, it was from a design against his life, as he [illegible] to employ him in the most dangerous enterprizes.

David, however, escaped the malicious designs of Saul; for, having God [illegible] his side, he proved successful in all his undertakings. He became not only universally beloved by the people, but also by those about the court; and [illegible] the grace of his person, and so distinguished [illegible] that he particularly attracted the [illegible] of Saul's daughter, who gave evident signs of her [illegible] him, which [illegible] all [illegible]. Saul took no notice of his daughter's affection for David, but did not [illegible] in the least [illegible] to it, thinking to make this the means of producing an opportunity that might prove effectual to his designs against David's life.

After some consideration Saul hit upon a project for [illegible] his purposes, which was, to make a proclamation, that whoever brought him the heads of 600 Philistines, should have his daughter in marriage. He imagined that David, from his renowned courage, would not [illegible] to accept of this offer, and that the attempt would cost him his life. [illegible] the most decent means of obtaining revenge on David, as he would look [illegible] to have him [illegible] by the Philistines than by his [illegible] orders.

Having formed this plan, Saul [illegible] some of his domestics to sound David [illegible] his affection towards [illegible], and whether he would be willing to receive her in marriage. They told him he was beloved both by the king and people, and that it was Saul's desire he should become his son-in-law. "You [illegible] him, "(says David) [illegible] me, not think it a great matter to be [illegible] son-in-law [illegible] mighty prince; but, under the circumstances of [illegible] and extraction, I am not [illegible] to [illegible] such an honour."

When Saul's messengers told him what David had said, he [illegible] his intention. "Tell him "(says he) I desire neither money nor presents, when I "[illegible] with my daughter she shall be bestowed, not sold. "I am determined to give her to a man, who is renowned "for his valour, courage, and other virtuous accomplishments [illegible] bring me the heads of "600 Philistines, [illegible] be more acceptable to "me than all the [illegible] the world. Go tell [illegible] "man [illegible] freely bestow [illegible] together, which will be "an honour to me, and give me the most pleasing satisfaction."

David was so pleased with Saul's proposition, not suspecting but his intentions were honest, and only calculated to confirm a [illegible] tie of friendship, that he [illegible] consider the difficulty of the action, or [illegible] to be practicable. He immediately set out with his army to meet the enemy, in order to execute what was desired, and to obtain the king's daughter in marriage. By the assistance and protection of God he succeeded in the undertaking; and having killed 600 Philistines, he cut off their heads and brought them to the king, demanding him to perform the covenant made between them, [illegible] to his daughter. Saul would willingly have evaded the fulfilment of his promise, but thinking it might disclose the treachery of his heart, he at length complied, and gave David his daughter Michal to wife.

CHAP. XI.

Saul commands to lay [illegible] for the life of David, who [illegible] escapes through the friendly offices of Jonathan.

THE [illegible] alliance between Saul and David did not in the least mitigate the enmity of the former against the latter. He found that David grew daily more and more the favourite of the people, and [illegible] king himself in danger while he lived. He formed the resolution of having him dispatched, and ordered Jonathan his son, with some of his most trusty servants, to perpetrate the horrid deed.

Jonathan was thunderstruck when he received these orders from his father. He loved David as his soul, and determined to prevent the [illegible] designs of the king. He accordingly hastened to David, and told him Saul's intentions, [illegible] him, as he loved his life, immediately to [illegible] ("in the [illegible]" says he) "I will go to my "father, and [illegible] of the disgust he has [illegible] against you, will endeavour [illegible] in my "power to appease [illegible]." David, knowing the fidelity of Jonathan, took his advice, and immediately departed.

CHAP. XII.

Jonathan [illegible] with his father [illegible] behalf of David, [illegible] Saul's [illegible], and [illegible] offer.

EARLY the next morning Jonathan went to his father's apartment, and finding him in a pleasant humour, he took the opportunity of fulfilling the promise he had made to David. "Father (says he) I cannot "conceive by [illegible] of your having taken so great a "dislike to David, as to issue orders for his death. Has "he committed any offence for which thou thinkest "he deserves to die? Was not thy life, in a great "measure, preserved through his means, and [illegible] "not the Philistines [illegible] the force of his [illegible] "[illegible]? Did he not [illegible] the honour of [illegible]

[illegible]

The TRIUMPH *of* DAVID *after having slain the Giant* GOLIOTH
the great Champion of the Philistine Army

"[illegible] from the reward of [illegible] forty days amongst in the "challenge of the giant? Did he not purchase my sister "for his wife at your price, by bringing you the heads "of 600 Philistines? Surely, instead of your resentment, "he is entitled to your esteem and tenderness, not only "by his distinguished courage, but his close alliance "with your family. Consider with yourself what great "injury you will do your daughter, by making her feel "the miseries of a widow before she has tasted the en-"joyments of a mother. Let me beg of you, my dear "father, to reflect on these things, and to be more "moderate in your determination. Remember, it was "this person who relieved you from bodily complaints "of the most horrid nature, and remember it was he, "next under God, who delivered us from our most im-"placable enemies. That the benefits of the most dis-"tinguished nature, and, if forgot, will stain your cha-"racter with the [illegible] of ingratitude."

This forcible speech made such an impression on Saul, that he bound himself, by oath, never to do any thing more to the injury of David secretly.

Jonathan, as soon as possible, hasted with the wel-come news to David, told him the particulars of all that had passed, and assured him he need not be afraid, for his father had made a solemn vow never to do him the least injury. He then took David with him to court, and presenting him to the king, a seeming reconciliation took place, and David was reinstated in his office.

CHAP. XII.

Saul [illegible] of David, [illegible] [illegible] [illegible] he escapes, and flies to the [illegible] Samuel. Jonathan forms a league of friendship with David, [illegible] [illegible] [illegible] his [illegible] [illegible]. David goes to the city of Nob, and [illegible] [illegible] [illegible] Abimelech, the high-priest. [illegible] [illegible] [illegible] [illegible] [illegible] [illegible] David [illegible] [illegible] to [illegible] [illegible] David [illegible] the [illegible] [illegible] [illegible] [illegible], but [illegible] [illegible] [illegible] [illegible] [illegible] [illegible] [illegible] [illegible] [illegible] The death of Samuel. David's [illegible] [illegible] [illegible] [illegible], who [illegible] afterwards [illegible] [illegible] king of Gath, [illegible] David, and [illegible] [illegible] [illegible] of the [illegible] of Ziklag. [illegible] [illegible] [illegible] [illegible] [illegible] [illegible] [illegible].

THE Philistines, having again made war against the Israelites, and brought into the field a very considerable army, Saul ordered David to march with all expedition to give them battle. David obeyed the king's order, and meeting the Philistines he fell on them, and obtained a [illegible] victory, the greatest part being slain, and the remainder put to flight.

Pleased with this success, David hastened to communicate (as he thought) the agreeable news to the king. But Saul, instead of expressing his satisfaction at the victory, was highly jealous of David's increasing reputation, and imagined that what tended to his honour must be prejudicial to himself. He forgot the obligations he was under to David, and the vow he had formerly made not to injure him. Hatred and enmity proved predominant over reason, justice and gratitude, and he again determined to take away the life of David.

Saul being one day afflicted with a fit of his old disorder, the phrensy, he sent for David to play on the harp to him. David accordingly obeyed, but while he was tuning the instrument, Saul [illegible], arose, and taking up a javelin to cast it with all his might at David. The [illegible] [illegible] missed him, and stuck in the wall, upon which David hastily left the room, and ran to his own house, where he continued the remainder of the day.

In the mean time Saul sent messengers with a body of his [illegible] to watch [illegible] [illegible] [illegible] [illegible] taking his escape, ordering them, as soon as it was day-light, to seize and bring him with them, for that he should suffer death as a common criminal.

Michal, David's wife, being apprised of the king's intentions, told her husband the danger he was in, and that if he did not make his escape before morning, he would certainly be a dead man. David readily took his wife's advice, and, after embracing each other in the most tender manner, she let him down, by the assistance of a rope, from a back window of the house, in order to [illegible] [illegible] the guards, he might [illegible] escape.

As soon as David was departed, Michal [illegible] a [illegible] bed in such a manner, that it appeared to contain a sick person, and to make the deception [illegible], she put [illegible] beneath the covering the [illegible] [illegible] [illegible] for the purpose. [illegible] [illegible] [illegible] when the messengers asked for David, she told them he was sick, and had been restless all the night. The messengers [illegible] [illegible] her word she took them up stairs, and they [illegible] [illegible] ed by the motion [illegible] from the liver, [illegible] [illegible] [illegible] left her, and returned to relate the [illegible] [illegible] [illegible].

Saul, fired with indignation, ordered the messengers immediately to return, and bring David in whatever situation they found him, for he was determined he should be put to death. The messengers accordingly returned, and, on removing the bed-clothes in search of David, discovered the deception, and that the motion of the clothes which resembled the palpitation of the heart, was occasioned by the warm liver of the goat.

When the messengers returned [illegible] [illegible] [illegible] [illegible] the trick that had been played on them by Michal, he sent for her and upbraided her for her conduct; but she excused herself by saying, she did it through fear, as David had threatened her life; that it was not done from choice, but necessity, and that she thought he was not so anxious for the destruction of David as he was for the preservation of his daughter. [illegible] Saul [illegible] [illegible] this excuse, forgave Michal, and restored her to his favour.

In the mean time David [illegible] to the prophet [illegible] [illegible] Ramah, to whom he related the snares which had been laid for him by Saul, [illegible] [illegible] [illegible] [illegible] [illegible] made his escape. He told Samuel [illegible] [illegible] [illegible] of having committed the least offence [illegible] [illegible] [illegible] [illegible] behaved himself to the king as became a dutiful subject, that, by the assistance of God, he had repeatedly conquered his enemies, and this, he [illegible] was the only cause of the king's displeasure.

Samuel, being informed of the unjust proceedings of Saul, left Ramah, and taking David with him, went to a place called Galbaath (in the scripture Naioth), where they resided together for some time.

When Saul understood where David was, and with whom, he dispatched a body of men to Galbaath, with orders to seize David and bring him immediately to the palace. But when they came to Galbaath, [illegible] that Samuel was there, and [illegible] [illegible] the young prophets, they were seized with the spirit of prophecy [illegible] [illegible] could not refrain. In consequence of this Saul sent other messengers, and [illegible] [illegible] [illegible] again; but no sooner had they come near the place than they were all affected in the same manner. Saul, at length impatient of these delays, went himself; but as he drew near the place, the spirit of prophecy seized him also, and he went along prophesying, till he came to the place where Samuel and David were, and then, casting off his upper garment, he lay (as it were in [illegible]) on the ground all that day, and the following night.

David took the opportunity of making his escape to his friend Jonathan, [illegible] [illegible] [illegible] [illegible] [illegible] the [illegible] behaviour of his father, [illegible]

[illegible] him, and [illegible], with an oath, that he [illegible] told to [illegible] the [illegible] news [illegible] supposed that the [illegible] great [illegible] I [illegible]

[illegible] David [illegible] as [illegible] "[illegible] Now [illegible] here [illegible] At [illegible] I [illegible] with my [illegible] If he [illegible] his [illegible] the [illegible] the world [illegible] David [illegible] God [illegible] to heaven, [illegible] that God [illegible] for you [illegible] that [illegible] of my [illegible] a father [illegible]"

[illegible] Jonathan desired David to retire [illegible] and [illegible] soon [illegible] arrow [illegible] Saul [illegible] his right hand, [illegible] left, but the

[illegible] of David was [illegible] Saul took no notice of his absence [illegible], supposing he might not be present [illegible] circumstance [illegible] (a), but [illegible] the second [illegible] asked Jonathan what [illegible] the son of Jesse (b) was absent from the feast [illegible] Jonathan [illegible], he had given him leave to go to Bethlehem, [illegible] his own tribe on the [illegible], that David [illegible] his company, and, [illegible] knew the friendship he had for him, if he pleased he would follow him. This [illegible] confession touched Saul to the quick, and being no longer able to conceal his hatred against David, he fell into a violent passion, called Jonathan a traitor and an enemy, an abettor of, and confederate with David, and that he was a conspirator against his own family. "He must be [illegible] (said he) [illegible] who cannot see that my [illegible] and kingdom are in the most imminent danger while David lives. I command thee, therefore, immediately to send for him, "that he may be brought to justice." Jonathan, in a very cool and respectful manner, begged his father to tell him what capital crime David had committed, for that he had never known him guilty of the least [illegible]. This question threw Saul into such a rage, that he immediately snatched up a [illegible], and would certainly have [illegible] Jonathan to his resentment, had he not been prevented by some of the friends then present.

This violent outrage convinced Jonathan of his father's hatred to David, and that he was determined to put a period to his life. He quitted the company as soon as he was able, and retiring to his chamber, spent the whole night in [illegible] supplications for the safety of his friend. [illegible] morning he took his bow and arrows and [illegible] went into the fields under pretence of shooting, but, in reality, to discover to David the disposition of his father, as had been before agreed. He conveyed the intelligence by leaving the armour on the ground, after which he sent the lad back to the city, that he might have the opportunity of going to David [illegible] him all that had passed. As soon as Jonathan came near to David, the latter fell prostrate [illegible] his [illegible] mighty preserver. Jonathan [illegible], raised him from the ground, and after embracing him, with tears, he told him all that had passed between him and his father, that he was implacable, and determined to destroy him; and therefore he advised him to [illegible] his escape as fast as possible. They [illegible] their protestations to each other of perpetual friendship, and having again embraced, Jonathan left him with fervent prayers that the Divine protection might accompany him wherever he went.

David, knowing the necessity there was for attending to the advice of Jonathan, left the place of his retirement, and went to Nob (c), where, at that time stood the tabernacle, and where Abimelech was high-priest. Not having any attendants with him, Abimelech took notice of it, and asked him the reason (d). David told him, he was commissioned upon particular business by the express orders of the king, that as it was of a private nature, he had, for the present, discharged his train, but that they were to meet him at a certain time and place he had appointed. He then told Abimelech he was greatly distressed for necessaries to prosecute his journey, and that he should consider it as the most friendly office if he would supply him with such as he wanted. This request the high-priest readily granted; upon which David told him he would give him more in the obligation, if he would furnish him

(a) [illegible]

(b) [illegible]

(c) [illegible]

(d) [illegible]

[illegible] sword of Goliath [illegible] I have no other arms than the sword [illegible] Goliath, which was hung up, and dedicated to God, [illegible] vest. (A [illegible] conversation between David and Abimelech, [illegible] a servant of Saul's [illegible] Doeg, who was a Syrian by birth, and enjoyed the office of groom to the king.)

David, being provided with necessaries for a journey, and having with him the sword of Goliath, left Nob and went to the city of Gath, belonging to Achish, king of the Philistines. He had not been long here before he was discovered, and the king informed of his being the person who had so often defeated and destroyed the Philistines. In consequence of this information David was taken before Achish, when, to avoid the danger that threatened him, he feigned madness and an epilepsy, which he did in so artful a manner, that the king, after rebuking the officers, ordered him to be discharged.

The next day David left Gath, and took up his residence in a cave near Adullam, a town belonging to the tribe of Judah. His friends and relations, hearing where he was, came flocking to him, together with many malcontents, and men of desperate fortunes, the whole amounting to about four hundred.

This junction was very acceptable to David; but his mind was greatly distressed on account of his aged parents, whom he feared would fall victims to the rage of Saul. He therefore applied to the king of Moab, beseeching him to take them under his protection. The king readily complied with his request, received them with great cordiality, and treated them with distinguished respect.

David continued, with his little army, in the cave for some time, till at length he was advised, by the prophet Gad, who attended him, to return to the land of Judah; which he accordingly did, and took up his station in the forest of Hareth.

Saul, being informed of David's situation, and the number of people he had with him, was greatly alarmed. He knew his natural [illegible], and was fearful of the consequences. He therefore convened an assembly of his friends, captains, and the tribe to which he belonged, at Gibeah, whom he addressed as follows:

"Ye men of Benjamin (says he) ye cannot be insensible "of the many good offices I have done you; and that "through my means many of you have been advanced to "the highest posts of honour. Wherefore, I now ask "whether ye expect greater favours from the hands of "the son of Jesse than ye have received from me? I am "informed that ye are all ready to revolt to him, and "that ye are countenanced in your conduct by my son "Jonathan. I am no stranger to the solemn league and "confederacy between him and David, nor of his abetting the cause of my adversaries with his power [illegible] "[illegible] and council. Let me intreat you not to listen to "[illegible] nor to suffer any of his persuasions to direct "your conduct, but be good subjects, and [illegible] "[illegible] from [illegible]."

As soon as Saul had finished his speech, Doeg, the groom, who was one [illegible] that passed between David and Ahimelech (at Nob) [illegible] related the following particulars: "When (says he) I went to Ahimelech, the "high-priest, at the city of Nob, I saw David, who "had come thither to consult the oracle. Ahimelech "furnished him with the conveniencies for his journey, "and, as an instrument of defence, gave him the sword "with which he [illegible] Goliath."

In consequence of this declaration, Saul immediately sent for Ahimelech, and ordered that all his relations should be brought with him. When the high-priest arrived, Saul addressed him as follows: "What [illegible] "[illegible] of the son of Jesse, [illegible] and "[illegible] him [illegible] as [illegible] "[illegible] in my [illegible] kingdom [illegible] "[illegible] "[illegible] contrary [illegible]."

Ahimelech [illegible] then [illegible] "[illegible] mentioned [illegible] not to [illegible] "[illegible] to promote [illegible] "[illegible] officers [illegible] "[illegible] to [illegible] "[illegible] "[illegible] "[illegible] "[illegible] God, [illegible] "[illegible] "[illegible] "[illegible] "[illegible] "[illegible] "[illegible] believed "[illegible] it would have been an [illegible] to you "[illegible] "[illegible] and David [illegible] "[illegible] as your subject [illegible] "[illegible] respect [illegible] and the king's "[illegible] [illegible] of David."

The endeavours of Ahimelech to [illegible] his conduct [illegible] David availed little with Saul, who, as soon as he had finished, ordered him and all his family to be put to the sword. The guards, who stood by, and heard the high-priest's defence, [illegible] to execute the royal orders, thinking it an act of [illegible]. In consequence of this the king commanded Doeg, Ahimelech's accuser, to perform the bloody deed. He immediately, [illegible], to execute the royal commands, not [illegible] Ahimelech, slew him and his family, the whole amounting to 385 persons. Not satisfied with this, Saul dispatched a party to the city of Nob, with orders to put to the sword every [illegible], and afterwards to burn the city to the ground. This was fulfilled what had been foretold by God to Eli, the high-priest, namely, that his posterity should be destroyed for the abominable impieties of his two sons.

The enormous cruelty of Saul in extirpating the sacerdotal race, putting to death both old and young, without either pity for the one, or reverence for the other, [illegible] God himself had honoured with a peculiar privilege, [illegible] a [illegible] for priests and prophets [illegible] [illegible] the natural corruptness of Saul's heart, and point him out to us in his [illegible] colours. While men are low, poor, subject to laws and penalties, and, in truth, under the [illegible] of appearing honest for want of power to be otherwise, [illegible] they live [illegible] religious [illegible] the omnipresence of an all-seeing God; but no sooner do they come to an advanced station, than they become quite different creatures. Like actors on the stage, they [illegible] manner [illegible] and change both the scene and the person. They [illegible] proud and imperious, and [illegible] [illegible] Instead of being [illegible] [illegible] that [illegible] [illegible] neither God [illegible] [illegible] elevation [illegible] [illegible] the [illegible] of Divine [illegible]. What [illegible] arrogant [illegible] the [illegible] what [illegible] general [illegible], not reason [illegible] [illegible] and bestow their favours [illegible] to others. They endeavour to make the world believe their conduct is directed by the will of heaven, though, at the same time, they have not the least [illegible] [illegible] them [illegible] with [illegible]

[illegible] of their dignity [illegible] their lives [illegible] without trial or [illegible]. This [illegible] an instance [illegible] which [illegible] those who frequently [illegible] on the most erroneous a[illegible]tions (a).

The difference thus [illegible] between a low and elevated situation [illegible] evidently manifested in Saul, the son of [illegible], who was the first king of the Hebrews after the dissolution of the aristocracy, and taking the administration out of the hands of the judges. On a [illegible] suspicion of [illegible] done him by Ahimelech, he not only ordered him together with more than three hundred priests and prophets to be put to death, but also their city to be reduced to ashes, and the place, which contained the [illegible] of God, to be rendered desolate.

Saul's intentions were entirely to extirpate the family of Ahimelech, but it happened that one of his sons named Abiathar, fortunately escaped and fled to David, to whom he related all the particulars relative to his [illegible], and the destruction of his kindred. David was greatly [illegible] when he heard of Saul's cruelty, and the more so, as he considered himself in some measure as the [illegible] cause [illegible] of it. "I thought (said David) [illegible] Doeg at your father's house, he would have [illegible] before [illegible], and I am sorry to find my conjectures were too well founded. I lament that so [illegible] a circumstance should have taken place on my account, but [illegible] no. Abiathar [illegible] place yourself under my protection, and I will [illegible] from all danger."

While Saul was embruing his hands in the blood of his innocent subjects, David was employing his arms in the necessary defence of his country. For hearing the Philistines had made an incursion [illegible] Keilah, [illegible] Judah, he went and relieved the place, [illegible] the enemy with a great loss of men, and took from them a considerable booty in cattle.

The news of this action soon reached the ears of Saul, who, supposing David would fortify himself in the town, sent an army to [illegible] it. In the mean time David, having consulted the Divine Oracle (b) and being informed that the inhabitants of the place would prove perfidious to him, he left it before the arrival of Saul's army, and retired, with his men, to a wood in the desert of Ziph (c).

Saul, not knowing whither David had fled, could not pursue him; but Jonathan, his son, having received intelligence, immediately [illegible] to him, and gave him all the comfort and encouragement he could. He assured him his father's malice could never reach him, that he doubted not but the time would come when he should [illegible] him king of Israel, [illegible] that [illegible] such blessings were not to be obtained without [illegible] hazard. They then renewed the [illegible] of friendship between them, and, after embracing each other, parted.

The inhabitants of Ziph were very officious in sending intelligence to Saul where David was, and told him, if he would supply them with a proper force, they would engage to deliver him into his hands. Saul thanked them for the intelligence, and immediately sent a body of men to assist them in the execution of their intentions, resolving soon to follow with his whole army. David, being apprized of the conspiracy of the Ziphites, baffled all their schemes, by retiring, with great precipitation, to a rock in the wilderness of Maon.

Saul, having received intelligence whither David had retired, marched against him, and pressed him so close, that the two armies were only separated by a narrow valley. Saul's intention was, to encompass the army of David, in order to prevent their escape; but before he could carry his design into execution, news was brought that the Philistines had broken in upon the Hebrews, and were ravaging their country, so that Saul was forced to drop his private resentment for the public good, and to divert his arms another way. David, having thus escaped the danger that surrounded him, left the rock and took shelter, with his army, in the wilderness of Engedi.

In the mean time Saul, having defeated the Philistines, and received intelligence where David had retired, selected 3000 of his choicest men, and marched against him with the greatest expedition. David and his men had concealed themselves in a cave, which was very deep and wide, and extended a considerable distance in length. [illegible] happened that when Saul came to this cave he had occasion to give a loose to nature, and, not suspecting that the place was inhabited, [illegible] from his army and went [illegible] for that purpose. One of David's men seeing Saul, and knowing him, communicated the intelligence to David, telling him, he had now the opportunity of a glorious revenge, by cutting off the head of his mortal enemy, for that God had delivered Saul into his hands. But David rejected the proposition with abhorrence, saying, "God forbid I should stretch forth my hands against the Lord's anointed," and only (to shew Saul how much he was in his power) went forth, and cut off the skirt of his upper garment.

When Saul was gone out of the cave, David followed and called after him. The king, well knowing the voice, turned about, when David, with great reverence and respect, [illegible] him in [illegible] to this effect: "What an unhappy thing it is, when a great prince so listens to the tongues of calumniators and detractors as to suspect the integrity of his tried and most faithful friends! I certainly would be much more laudable to judge every man by his works. Words may be false as well as true, but demonstration [illegible] fact is infallible. Believe me, great king, when I tell you I am a well-wisher both to [illegible] and to your family, and yet you make it your continual business to endeavour to seek my life. How can you excuse yourself to God for committing so enormous a wickedness as to desire the death of a person, who this very day had it in his power to revenge himself by depriving you of your existence? I could as easily have taken your head from your shoulders, as this piece of stuff from your mantle, (shewing the skirt he had cut off); but I had not the heart to commit so villainous an act. While you, at the same time, without the least [illegible] of conscience, pursue me with a [illegible]

(a) [illegible] of Josephus [illegible] the generality of men in great authority [illegible] and humanity to [illegible] Divine Providence [illegible] God [illegible] to have [illegible] mankind.

(b) [illegible] were [illegible] most [illegible] extraordinary [illegible] place [illegible] both [illegible] and [illegible] God could [illegible] and [illegible] David [illegible] with an earnest desire to relieve [illegible] not [illegible] therefore [illegible] enquired of God, saying [illegible] question [illegible] God [illegible] David [illegible] Go [illegible] the Philistines and [illegible] Keilah.

(c) This mountainous wilderness was [illegible] the precincts of the tribe of [illegible] (Joshua) [illegible] It is supposed to have [illegible] the word Zepheth [illegible] fit [illegible].

[illegible] petition [illegible] But let God judge between us, and if I have done any thing either in thought or deed, to your detriment, let me be punished as I deserve."

The graceful and modest manner in which David delivered his speech, and the circumstance of his sparing the king's life when he had it in his power to take it away, made such an impression on Saul that he fetched a deep sigh, which being answered by David, the king said, "Such lamentations better become me than you. Thou hast been the author of many good things to me, but I of many calamities to thee. You have convinced me, by your conduct, that you are not degenerated from the good acts of your ancestors, who, when they had their enemies in their power, refused to take advantage of it, by giving them their lives and liberty. From the transactions of this day it appears manifestly evident that you are designed by God as the ruler of this kingdom, and that the whole nation of the Israelites will be subject to your government. Wherefore I have this request to make, that you will promise, on oath, to forgive all the injuries I have done you, and that when you come to be possessed of your government, you will be merciful to my family."

Saul having obtained this request, returned home; but David, not choosing to trust to his fair words, kept himself close in the fastnesses of the hills.

About this time died the prophet Samuel, a man universally respected by the Hebrews for his probity and virtue. He was buried at Ramah (a), and the people testified their respect to him by mourning more than the usual time, and celebrating his funeral rites with the most distinguished pomp. While he lived his actions declared him born to execute justice, which he adhered to in every circumstance of life, with an impartial hand; and on that account was particularly beloved of God (b). He died in the 98th year of his age, twelve of which he governed alone, and eighteen in conjunction with Saul.

During the time of lamentation for Samuel, David removed from Engedi, and retired farther into the wilderness of Paran, not far from Maon, where he had once before taken up his residence.

In the neighbourhood of this place lived a person named Nabal, a man naturally of a very savage and morose disposition. While David abode in this part of the country before, he had taken great care to restrain his men from doing any injury to Nabal's flocks; and it being now the time of sheep-shearing (which was always a season of great festivity and entertainment) he sent messengers to him, requesting that, in consideration of the many civilities he had shewn him, he would be pleased to send some provisions for the support of his army.

Nabal received the messengers in a very abrupt manner, and, with some opprobrious reflections on David himself, sent them away empty. This treatment so exasperated David, that in the heat of his resentment, he vowed he would destroy all Nabal's family before the next morning. But he was prevented from executing his design by means of Abigail, Nabal's wife (a very beautiful woman, and, in temper, quite the reverse of her husband) who, being informed of what had passed, took the following expedient to divert David's resentment against her husband. She ordered her servants to pack up two hundred loaves of bread, two bottles of wine (c), five sheep ready dressed, five measures of parched corn, an hundred clusters of raisins, and two hundred cakes of figs. With these articles, placed on asses, Abigail hastened to meet David, who was marching with all speed, accompanied by four hundred of his men, (the number being now increased to six hundred, two of which he left to take care of the baggage) to put in execution his rash vow. As soon as Abigail saw David she threw herself prostrate on the ground, and besought him to pass over the words of her husband, he being a man whose name was suited to his nature, (Nabal, in the Hebrew language, signifying a *fool*, or *madman*.) She said she saw not the messengers that came, begged pardon for what had happened, and desired David to give God thanks for rendering her as the instrument to keep his hands from being stained with blood. "Be pleased, Sir, (said she) I beseech you to accept of the good-will of your poor servant with these small presents, and, upon my humble request, to pass over the offence of my husband, who has so often incurred your displeasure; for there is nothing so well becoming the character of the person who is designed for a crown as clemency and compassion."

The very feeling manner in which Abigail addressed herself to David so wrought upon him, that he accepted the presents. His indignation was totally laid aside, and they both parted with mutual satisfaction; he, for being thus prevented from shedding of blood; and she, for having thus happily succeeded in her errand.

When Abigail arrived at her home she found her husband feasting and drinking, so that she deferred telling him what passed till the next morning. But when he came to understand the danger to which he had been exposed he was so terrified at the thoughts of it, that he suddenly became quite stupid, and continued in that state for ten days, when he gave up the ghost.

David, hearing of Nabal's decease, sent for Abigail, and married her, as he did also another woman, whose name was Ahinoam, a Jezreelite; for his first wife, Michal, had been some time given by Saul to Phalti, the son of Laish, or Gallim.

Some time after this the Ziphites (who were professed enemies to David) gave information to Saul of the place where he and his men were concealed; in consequence of which (notwithstanding the solemn promises Saul had made not to do any thing in future to the injury of David) he headed 3000 men, and, marching with all expedition against him, pitched his tents on the mountains of Hachilah.

David having received intelligence where Saul's army lay encamped, went first privately himself to reconnoitre it. On the evening of the same day he went again, taking with him his nephew, Abishai, and Ahimelech, the Hittite, who, on their arrival at the camp, found Saul in his tent, with his general Abner, and the guards about him all fast asleep. Abishai, seeing the king in his bed, and his spear by him, would willingly have dispatched him; but David restrained his hands, saying, "He is God's king, and therefore only accountable to him for his misdeeds. But, (says he), that he may be

(a) In the time of the emperor Arcadius [illegible] Constantinople and [illegible] St. Jerome informs us) removed [illegible]

(b) A late learned writer [illegible] describing the character of Samuel [illegible] He was indeed [illegible] an excellent [illegible] whole administration [illegible] corruption [illegible] his life may [illegible]

(c) It will at first view appear [illegible] could bear [illegible]

[illegible] David [illegible] they [illegible] understood of such bottles [illegible] continually [illegible] in these eastern countries [illegible] keep their wine and water in [illegible] vessels made of [illegible] goats [illegible] vessels they called [illegible] Such were the bottles [illegible] brought [illegible] Gibeonites to Joshua [illegible] pretended long journey. See Joshua ix. [illegible] And we [illegible] hollow [illegible] Savary [illegible] the explained by [illegible] one [illegible] And [illegible] two [illegible] a great quantity [illegible] Abigail [illegible]

"convinced how much he was in my power, I will take "with me his spear, and the pitcher of water from his "bed-side." Having done [illegible], left the [illegible], and when David had got at such a distance as to be distinctly heard, he called aloud unto Abner, who waking, and desiring to know who was the person that called, was answered, "It is David, the son of Jesse:" after which he thus ironically upbraided Abner: "Are not you (said "he) a very proper person to be the favourite of a great "prince, the general of [illegible], and the protector of "his royal person, [illegible] all these obligations, to "be stretching yourself at ease, when your master's life "is in danger? Can you tell what is become of the king's "spear, and the pitcher of water that were this night taken by the enemy, out of his tent, [illegible] from his very "bed-side without you or your guards knowing any "thing of the matter? Whether this [illegible] from neglect "or treachery is immaterial, for which ever it was, thou "deservest death."

Saul, hearing the voice of David, came out of his tent, and understanding the great danger he had been in, and that his life was in the hands of the very person he meant to destroy, he was so sensible of the goodness of David, that he gave him public thanks for his life. He accused himself of cruelty, applauded David's generosity, confessed his guilt, and promised, for the future never to make any farther attempts on his life.

When Saul had done speaking, David desired him to send some person for his spear and the pitcher of water, after which he called upon God to judge between them, and to bear him witness, that, when he took them from Saul's bed-side, he could with as much ease have destroyed him or [illegible].

Saul now returned home with his army, soon after which David knowing the instability of his temper, and how [illegible] it was for him to [illegible] in safety while he continued in his dominions, determined to go over to the Philistines. Accordingly, having [illegible] from Achish, king of Gath, [illegible] to conduct himself and [illegible] men, he lived for some time in the [illegible], but not liking his accommodation, and growing [illegible] more in favour of Achish, he obtained from him [illegible] town called Ziglag, which the king gave to him and his heirs for ever.

During David's stay at Ziglag, [illegible] he made several excursions into the territories of the Amal[illegible] and other nations, from whom he took very considerable booty, but was cautious in not [illegible] any [illegible], lest it might be known by Achish from whom he obtained the plunder. He made great presents to the king, who asked him from whence he had obtained them, to which David replied, from the southern [illegible] of Judah. This gave great satisfaction to Achish, who imagined, that whilst David abode in his territories, [illegible] to commit hostilities against his own nation he would become his most trusty and faithful servant.

CHAP. [illegible]

The Philistines make war against the Israelites. Saul consults the Witch of Endor. David follows the camp of the Philistines, [illegible] the Amalekites destroy Ziglag. [illegible] against [illegible], obtain a defeat, recover the spoil they had taken. Saul engages the army of the Philistines, is defeated, and his three sons slain, upon which he puts [illegible] to his own existence.

THE Philistines having determined to lead an army against the Israelites, they dispatched messengers to all their allies and territories, to prepare themselves on the occasion, and to [illegible] [illegible] [illegible] place being [illegible] for the general meeting of the army. In consequence of this [illegible] Achish acquainted David with his intentions of taking him and his men with him to assist him against the Israelites. This declaration was far from being displeasing to David, who answered, he was ready to perform all [illegible] [illegible] showed himself, and [illegible] then [illegible], he hoped the time was now come when he should be able, in some measure, to make a return for the great services he had received at his hands. [illegible] Achish replied, "If we succeed in this battle I promise "to invest thee with all the honours it is in my power to "bestow."

Saul, having received intelligence that the Philistines were advanced as far as Shunem, and had encamped [illegible] the plain there, marched with his forces against them and pitched his tents near the mountain of Gilboah, directly opposite the camp of the enemy. Having in this place a full view of the army of the Philistines, and [illegible] them much more numerous, and in better order than his own, Saul began to despair of success; but his heart quite [illegible] gave him, when he found, on application to God, that he would not be consulted by him, nor give him any instructions in what manner to act.

Some time before this Saul had banished all [illegible] and such as dealt with familiar spirits, out of the nation; but being now in the utmost perplexity, he was resolved to consult some person of this profession, in order to know what would be the issue of the war. At a place called Endor, about three leagues from Mount Gilboa, he was told there lived a witch, or sorceress, upon which disguising himself, and taking but two servants with him to avoid suspicion, he went to the woman by night, and desired her to use her skill in calling upon the ghost of such a person as he should name. The woman at first refused, [illegible] it [illegible] she should be [illegible] [illegible] But Saul assuring her, with the most bitter imprecations that no mortal should ever know [illegible] [illegible] between them, she at length consented [illegible] Saul desired her to raise up the ghost of Samuel, [illegible] her complying with this request [illegible] [illegible] immediately appeared [illegible] [illegible] woman learnt it was Saul who had employed her, [illegible] Saul, when he saw it, knowing it to be the figure of Samuel, bowed his face to the ground. The apparition spoke first, [illegible] the reason why he had raised him from the dead. Saul replied, that the Philistines, with a powerful army, had invaded him, and that in his distress, God had forsaken him, and would give no answer whatever way he consulted him. The spirit answered, that, for his disobedience in not destroying the Amalekites, God had [illegible] the kingdom from his family, and given it to David, and that as to the [illegible] of the war, the Philistines, the next day, should [illegible] his army, and he and his sons fall in the battle.

Saul was so affected at this information, that his [illegible] left him, he fainted, and fell to the ground. He was, indeed, at this time exceeding weak in body, not having taken any refreshment for a considerable time. When he had a little recovered himself, the woman entreated him to taste some kind of sustenance, [illegible] the [illegible] [illegible] other reward for the danger in which she had placed herself, than the opportunity of enabling him to [illegible] his army. After many importunities Saul was at length prevailed on to accept the woman's offer, upon which she immediately killed a young calf, the only companion of her solitary life, and having properly prepared the flesh, set it before Saul and his attendants, who, after eating thereof, returned that night to the camp.

[illegible] Ziglag [illegible] [illegible] of Judah [illegible] [illegible] [illegible] [illegible] first [illegible] of [illegible] Jour[illegible] But [illegible] seem [illegible] [illegible] [illegible]

The APPARITION of SAMUEL raised by the WITCH of ENDOR
at the request of King Saul

[illegible] is but just [illegible] his [illegible] woman, [illegible] to take [illegible] of her distinguished [illegible] towards Saul. She [illegible] being [illegible] accommodately [illegible] her as a [illegible] stranger, [illegible] himself [illegible] notwithstanding [illegible] was [illegible] complied with his request. She likewise treated him in the [illegible] hospitable manner [illegible] terms, and all this without the least expectation of any future reward, for she knew that Saul was on the point of losing both his kingdom [illegible] Such generous [illegible] lays to us the [illegible] humanity, of [illegible] the difference [illegible] we may be assured that [illegible] sincere and unaffected [illegible] virtue of [illegible] other [illegible] acceptable in the sight of God.

Some [illegible] Saul on this occasion. He was [illegible] told [illegible] the prophet, not [illegible] to his fate, and [illegible] at the expence of his people. He [illegible] to the fighting for the defence of his government, and [illegible] whole family, [illegible] the [illegible] at the disposal of the persons who should succeed him. Such conduct [illegible] to all [illegible] The [illegible] between [illegible] favourable circumstances, may [illegible] when he knows he [illegible] his destruction [illegible] of being able [illegible] This character [illegible] due to Saul [illegible] kind of reproach [illegible] this digression [illegible]

[illegible] Achish [illegible] David [illegible] his [illegible] among [illegible] from whence they came, and who brought them [illegible] To this question Achish replied, [illegible] young man (pointing to David) was one of Saul's servants, but [illegible] incurred his displeasure, he was obliged to [illegible] "He [illegible] me [illegible] and [illegible] for [illegible] protection for "himself and his people. I received him, and provided "for him, [illegible] promised, on this occasion, to "[illegible] against the Israelites, "[illegible] the services he has received [illegible]"

When the Philistines knew who David was, they [illegible] against accepting his assistance [illegible] confidence in a person [illegible] to their professed enemies. They therefore [illegible] Achish [illegible] told him the desire of the [illegible] agreeable to David, he [illegible] departed with his men to [illegible]

David, [illegible] his march, was joined by se[illegible] [illegible] of the [illegible] of Manasseh, that he [illegible] [illegible] This, indeed, was a [illegible] when he came to Ziklag, [illegible] (a) [illegible] during his [illegible] the [illegible] the occasion of [illegible]

In [illegible] David [illegible] the priest, [illegible] he should prove successful and [illegible] The high priest [illegible] David, [illegible] to take care of [illegible] the [illegible] the enemy. [illegible] which [illegible] took, he [illegible] and [illegible] in consequence [illegible] they [illegible] as to [illegible] He [illegible] opportunity [illegible] to the [illegible] few only [illegible] by [illegible] together the people [illegible] and [illegible] spoils they had not only [illegible] but [illegible] their [illegible] returned [illegible]

The [illegible] of this [illegible] one [illegible] soldiers who were left [illegible] the baggage and [illegible] part of the [illegible] the former, [illegible] wives and children [illegible] distribute [illegible] David [illegible] told them the victory was God's [illegible] the common cause [illegible] be [illegible] of the [illegible] camp and baggage, [illegible] this ceremony David established [illegible] ever [illegible] an equal division [illegible] among those who [illegible] to guard the camp, as those who were present in the battle.

During these transactions a desperate engagement took place [illegible] the Philistines and the Israelites. The former were so powerful that the [illegible] were obliged to give way, [illegible] mount Gilboa, [illegible] with [illegible] Saul and his sons did all that [illegible] the Philistines [illegible] them with [illegible] so that Jonathan [illegible] his brothers, Abinadab and Melchishua, were killed on the spot, and the whole army [illegible] into confusion.

Saul [illegible] but [illegible] being at length [illegible] broken [illegible] piercing him. He found himself so weakened [illegible] wounds and loss of blood, that, to prevent falling [illegible] hands of the Philistines, and being [illegible] he begged of his armour-bearer to [illegible] him [illegible] refused to perform the office, upon which Saul [illegible] the point of his sword to his breast and leaned upon it, but [illegible] weakness, to finish what he [illegible] he requested the assistance of a young [illegible] Amalekite, who stood near him. The young man readily complied, [illegible] the sword [illegible]

[illegible footnotes]

It is but justice due to this poor woman, that we should here take some notice of her distinguished liberality towards Saul. She had been greatly injured by the king, in being restrained from the practice of that art whereby she comfortably maintained herself and family. He came to her as a mere stranger, and requested her advice by a method himself had prohibited; yet, notwithstanding the danger she was in, she complied with his request. She likewise treated him in the most hospitable manner her circumstances would permit, and all this without the least expectation of any future reward, for she knew that Saul was on the point of losing both his kingdom and life. Such generous conduct finely displays to us the honour and humanity of relieving the distressed; and we may be assured that a sincere and unaffected charity is a virtue of all others the most acceptable in the sight of God.

Some encomiums are likewise due to Saul on this occasion. He was certain he should die in the combat, having been told so by the prophet; notwithstanding which he was determined to submit to his fate, and not save himself at the expence of his people. He esteemed it a glory, to die fighting for the defence of his government, and rather to have his sons, and his whole family, share with him in the conflict, than be left at the disposal of the person who should succeed him. Such conduct dignifies the man and the prince, and ought to be an example to all elevated characters. The man who hazards his life in the common course of war, acts between hope and fear, and by favourable circumstances, may escape; but the greatest fortitude is placed in him, who, when he knows he must unavoidably perish, boldly meets his destruction and encounters his fate without the least hope of being able to surmount it. This character is justly due to Saul, and his conduct should be an example to all future princes, to whom either a mediocrity of courage or virtue, is a kind of reproach. But I leave this digression and resume the history.

The Philistines having gathered their troops together from all quarters, according to their distribution into [illegible] kingdoms, and governments, Achish, the king of Gath, with his men, after the rest, and David with his little army after Achish. Some of the Philistine commanders observing there were many Israelites among them, asked who they were, from whence they came, and who brought them thither? To this question Achish replied, that the young man (pointing to David) was one of Saul's servants, but that having incurred his displeasure, he was obliged to have recourse to flight. "He came to me (says Achish) and solicited protection for himself and his people. I received him, and provided for him, and he has promised, on this occasion, to use his utmost efforts in assisting us against the Israelites, as an acknowledgment for the services he has received at my hands."

When the Philistines knew who David was, they strongly objected against accepting his assistance, saying it was certainly dangerous to place the least confidence in a person belonging to their professed enemies. They therefore insisted that he should be dismissed, upon which Achish called David aside, told him the desire of the people, which, though nothing could be more disagreeable to David, he immediately left the camp, and departed with his men to Ziklag.

David, in the course of his march, was joined by several of the tribe of Manasseh, that his army became considerably augmented. This, indeed, was a fortunate circumstance; for when he came to Ziklag, he found that the (*a*) Amalekites had, during his absence, pillaged and burnt the place, carried away his two wives, and all the inhabitants; but what added to this misfortune was, the soldiers accused him of being the occasion of it.

In consequence of this disaster, David consulted Abiathar the priest, whether, if he went against the Amalekites, he should prove successful, and recover the spoils they had taken? The high priest bid him follow them and prosper. On this encouragement David, leaving two hundred of his men to take care of the baggage, pursued the rest against the enemy. Having gained intelligence which way they took, he soon came up with them, and found them so intoxicated in consequence of the spoil they had taken, as to be totally insensible. He took advantage of this favourable opportunity, and immediately falling on them, put the greatest part to the sword, a very few only saving themselves by flight (*b*). He then gathered together the people whom they had made captives, and with the spoils they had not only taken from him, but from others, in their expedition, returned to Ziklag.

The issue of this battle occasioned a dispute between the soldiers who were left as guards over the baggage and those who attended David, the latter not agreeing to allow any part of the booty to the former, except their wives and children. After some altercation the dispute was settled by David, who told them, the victory was God's, and being all engaged in the common cause, it was but reasonable that the whole body should partake of the benefits; for that those who guarded the camp and baggage, did equally their duty as those who attended in the field. From this circumstance David established it as a law, (which has ever since been in force), that whatever plunder should be obtained in war, an equal division thereof should be made, as well among those who were ordered to guard the camp, as those who were present in the battle.

During these transactions a desperate engagement took place between the two armies of the Philistines and the Israelites. The former were so powerful that the latter were obliged to give way, and they maintained a running fight till they came to mount Gilboa, where taking advantage of the ground, they attempted again to rally, but with as little success as before. Saul and his sons did all that was possible for brave men to do, but the Philistines aiming wholly at them, in a short time overpowered them with numbers, so that Jonathan, with two of his brothers, Abinadab and Melchishua, were killed on the spot, and the whole army thrown into confusion.

Saul defended himself, for a time, with unparalleled resolution; but the small party that remained with him being at length entirely broken, and the enemies archers pressing hard, he found himself so weakened from the wounds and loss of blood, that, to prevent falling into the hands of the Philistines, and being insulted by them, he begged of his armour-bearer to dispatch him. The man refused to perform the office, upon which Saul fixed the point of his sword to his breast, and leaned upon it, but not being able, from weakness, to finish what he had begun, he requested the assistance of a young man, an Amalekite, who stood near him. The young man readily complied, the sword penetrated to the heart

(*a*) [illegible] who ram[illegible] [illegible] could [illegible] not have [illegible] spared [illegible] [illegible] the Natio[illegible]

(*b*) [illegible] David [illegible] [illegible] Amalekites were [illegible] prudence [illegible] of Saul, and he fell, and died; after which the Amalekite took the golden bracelets from his arms, and the royal crown from his head, and fled away. When the armour-bearer saw his master dead, he desperately followed his example, and, in the same manner, put a period to his existence. There was not a single person of the king's guards that escaped; the whole number, without distinction either of age or sex, being put to the sword.

No sooner did the Hebrews, who resided in the valley beyond Jordon, as also those who inhabited the cities in the plain, hear of the death of Saul and his sons with the destruction of the army, than they immediately withdrew themselves to fastnesses and strong holds; while the Philistines, in the mean time, quietly made themselves masters of the places they had quitted.

Early the next morning the Philistines went into the field of battle, to take a view of the general carnage, when finding the bodies of Saul and his sons among the slain, they stripped them of their armour, cut off their heads, and sent expresses to every place of their victory. They sent their armour to the temple of [illegible], [illegible] their bodies they hung on gibbets against the walls of Bethshan.

This barbarous outrage committed on the bodies of Saul and his sons, coming to the ears of the [illegible] Jabesh-Gilead (who retained a grateful sense of the services Saul had done them) they sent a party of [illegible] soldiers by night who took down their bodies and [illegible] them to Jabesh, where they first burnt their flesh, and afterwards honourably interred their bones and ashes [illegible] grove near the city. The people mourned on the occasion, seven successive days, during which time, men, women, and children, kept a strict fast, and continued to express their grief by the greatest lamentations.

Such was the end of Saul, according to the [illegible] of Samuel, (a) for his having disobeyed God, [illegible] stroying the race of the Amalekites, and for putting [illegible] melech and his whole family to the sword. He [illegible] forty years, eighteen of which were during the [illegible] Samuel, and twenty-two after his decease.

(a) But while we consider the obstinacy and fate of Saul, who can avoid dropping a tear over the faithful the amiable Jonathan? There are few characters among men more lovely, or more extraordinary. He was possessed of fortitude, fidelity and magnanimity. He had a soul susceptible of the most re[illegible] friendship, and superior to all the temptations [illegible] and all these good qualities [illegible] the [illegible] God.

END OF THE SIXTH BOOK.

The PHILISTINES depositing the Armour of Saul in the Temple of ASHTAROTH

The [illegible] acting of the [illegible] [illegible] [illegible]
after having de[illegible]ted the [illegible] [illegible]

FLAVIUS JOSEPHUS

ON THE

ANTIQUITIES

OF THE

JEWS.

BOOK VII

[INCLUDING A PERIOD OF ABOUT FORTY-ONE YEARS.]

CHAP I

David laments the death of Saul and Jonathan. Is appointed to the sovereignty by the tribe of Judah, but opposed by Abner, the late king's general, who proclaimeth Ishbosheth, the only remaining son of Saul, successor to the throne. Abner marches against the army of David, and is defeated by Joab, his general. He goes over to David, and is barbarously murdered by Joab. David laments his death, and pays the greatest respect to his funeral obsequies.

THE battle between the army of the Philistines and that of the Israelites happened on the very same day that David returned to Ziglag, after defeating the Amalekites. In the morning of the third day after this, the man who had slain Saul, having escaped out of the battle, come to Ziglag, and with his cloths rent, and ashes on his head, threw himself prostrate on the ground before David. Being asked from whence he came, and why he appeared so mournful, he answered, that he was an Amalekite, and came to inform him of the event of the battle between the Hebrews and Philistines. That the king and his sons were slain, and the greatest part of the army shared the same fate. He told him, that what he said might be depended on, for that he was a spectator of the whole scene. That he stood by Saul when he attempted to stab himself but not having strength enough, from the many wounds he had received, to force the point of his sword through his body, after he had leant upon it, he begged him to finish what himself was unable to perform, and that he readily obeyed the royal command. To confirm what he had related, he produced the golden bracelets and crown of Saul, and told David he took them away, after Saul was dead, with no other design than to make a present of them to him.

David being convinced of the truth of this relation, rent his cloths, and spent the whole day in fasting and lamentation. He was particularly afflicted for the loss of Jonathan, who had more than once been the preserver of his life. And such respect did he still shew to the memory of Saul, notwithstanding the repeated attempts he had made to take away his life, that, instead of rewarding the man for the presents he brought, he ordered him to be put to death, not only as an enemy, but a professed regicide.

When David had performed his last duties to the memory of Saul and his sons, and the time of mourning was expired, he consulted God, by the prophet, which of the cities of Judah should be allotted for his habitation. Being answered, the city of Hebron (a), he immediately left Ziglag, and removed thither with his family and forces, soon after which the princes of Judah came to Hebron to congratulate him on his return to his native country, and in a full assembly, convened for the purpose, elected him their king.

By this time David had been informed of the generous conduct of the people of Jabesh-Gilead, in rescuing the bodies of Saul and his sons, and giving them honourable interment. He was so pleased with this information, that he sent messengers to thank them for what they had done, and to assure them that they might ever depend on his favour and protection. He likewise desired the messengers to inform them, that he had been chosen, by the tribe of Judah, as successor to the sovereignty.

While the princes of Judah were interesting themselves in behalf of David, Abner, the late king's uncle, and general of the army, set up (b) Ishbosheth, the only

---

(a) The city of Hebron stood in [illegible] the [illegible] metropolis of the whole tribe [illegible] David [illegible] dence at this juncture for [illegible] people of that [illegible] influence the whole tribe.

(b) [illegible] was forty [illegible] properly [illegible] Hebrews [illegible] people [illegible] Judah [illegible]

remaining son of Saul, as successor to the throne. He appointed Mahanaim (a), on the other side of Jordan, as the place of his residence, and by his great interest and authority, Ishbosheth was recognized king by all the tribes except that of Judah.

Abner was so incensed against the tribe of Judah for choosing David their king, that he determined to make war against them, and accordingly dispatched a body of the best men he could select from his whole army for that purpose. In the mean time Joab (the general of David's forces) hearing that Abner was on his way, marched from Hebron with his army against him, taking with him his two brothers, Abishai, and Asahel. When the two armies came near each other, and were drawn up in order of battle, Abner proposed that the contest should be determined by twenty-four men, twelve to be chosen out of each army. This proposition being agreed to, the men were selected and engaged, when their skill was so equal on both sides, that every man killed his antagonist, and the whole twenty-four lay dead on the spot. In consequence of this a general engagement commenced between the two armies, which, for some time, was exceeding desperate on both sides, but at length Abner was totally routed, and put to flight. Joab, and his two brothers, pursued the fugitives, and Asahel, the younger brother of Joab, being much more active than the rest, got greatly a-head, and made the best of his way after Abner. As soon as he came up with him, Abner, who knew him, begged he would desist and not attempt to attack him, as he should be very unwilling, by defending himself, to rob him of his existence. Asahel paid no attention to this remonstrance but, ambitious of taking a general prisoner, made a stroke at Abner, who, with his spear, gave him a wound, of which he immediately died.

When the victorious army came to the spot where the body of Asahel lay, they were so shocked at the spectacle that they immediately ceased the pursuit. Abner availed himself of this opportunity to rally his scattered forces, and taking post on a rising ground where he could not be attacked, he sounded a trumpet, and calling aloud to Joab, thus addressed him: "This dangerous animosity (says he) has already cost too many "people of the same blood their lives. As to your "brother Asahel, I begged him to desist, but he was so "obstinate in his determination, that I was reduced to the "necessity of taking away his life for the security of my "own, otherwise I had no thing to his own rashness." Joab could not but admit the justness of Abner's argument, upon which he sounded a retreat, and the two armies separated. Abner immediately marched with his men to the palace of Ishbosheth, but Joab encamped on the spot that night. The next morning he took a view of the field, and found upon computation, that Abner had lost about 360 men, and himself nineteen, exclusive of Asahel, whose remains were carried, by Joab and Abishai to Bethlehem, and there interred in the sepulchre of their Ancestors. After this ceremony they returned to Hebron, whither David had retired with his army.

From this period a civil war continued between the families of Saul and David for some years, during which time the forces of the latter, in most rencounters, had the advantage, and the interest of David increased in the nation, as that of Ishbosheth sensibly declined.

While David reigned at Hebron he had six sons, born of as many wives, namely, Amnon, the son of Ahinoam, Chileab, the son of Abigail, Absalom the son of Maacah, the daughter of Talmai, king of Geshur, Adonijah, the son of Haggith, Shephatiah, the son of Abital, and Ithream, the son of Eglah.

While the civil war lasted between David and Ishbosheth, Abner was the grand support of the latter, and by his prudence and interest, the people were kept to their duty, but a circumstance at length occurred which produced a fatal difunion to both parties. Abner had for some time preserved a familiar intimacy with Rizpah, the daughter of Sibeth, one of Saul's concubines. Intimation of this coming to the ears of Ishbosheth, he severely rebuked Abner for his conduct, who, thinking himself treated with indignity, vowed no less revenge than converting his interest from Ishbosheth to David.

In consequence of this determination, Abner sent a commission to Hebron, with full power to form a league with David, on the following single condition: That from and after the time he should draw off the tribes from Ishbosheth, and place David upon the throne by the universal consent of the people, he should be received as his prime minister, and have the chief management (exclusive of himself) in all public affairs.

This proposition was very acceptable to David, who, in return, requested Abner, as an earnest of their future alliance, that he would restore to him his wife Michal, whom he had not only purchased with the heads of six hundred Philistines but also at the most imminent danger and hazard of his own life.

These matters being reciprocally agreed to, Abner immediately took Michal from Phaltiel (on whom she was bestowed by Saul with the privity and assistance of Ishbosheth) and sent her to David, after which calling together the elders and principal people both civil and military, he thus addressed them: "There was a time, (says "he) when you would willingly have renounced your "allegiance to Ishbosheth, and gone over to David. I "was then against it, but you are now at liberty to use "your own discretion. I am fully convinced that, as "God, by the prophet Samuel hath anointed and constituted him king over all the Hebrews, and hath foretold "that he should be the scourge of the Philistines, and should "subdue and bring them under his obedience, so he will "actually obtain the sovereignty over all Israel." When the elders and the officers of the army, found the sentiments of Abner corresponded with those they had themselves entertained, they unanimously agreed with him in opinion, and from that time acted openly in favour of David.

Abner, having thus far proved successful, summoned together the tribe of Benjamin, which included the guards of Ishbosheth, to whom he addressed himself in the same manner as he had done to the elders and officers. These likewise he found condescending and ready to favour his designs, upon which, selecting twenty of the choicest he took them with him and went to David, in order to ratify the treaty that had been agreed on between them. David received Abner and his company with the greatest affection, and entertained them, for some days, in the most sumptuous manner, at the expiration of which Abner desired to be dismissed for the present, that he might go and bring the army and people to Hebron, in order to make good what he had undertaken, by publicly delivering up the government into his hands.

Abner had hardly quitted the gates of the city when he met Joab, David's general, to whom he related the particulars of all that had passed relative to the treaty of alliance between him and David. Joab at this information, was immediately struck with an outrageous fit of jealousy, thinking, from the great ambition of Abner, that he would infallibly supplant him in his master's esteem. He therefore hastened to David with all expedition, and remonstrated with him on the impropriety of his conduct in listening to any terms proposed by Abner, whom he

(a) [illegible] so that he [illegible] ... [illegible]

[illegible] is a place [illegible] ... Gen. xxxii [illegible]

that side to Joab [illegible] ... the [illegible] ... David [illegible] ... his command [illegible] better opportunity [illegible] ...

[illegible] was to be [illegible] in no other light than a spy, [illegible] the protector and supporter of [illegible] That [illegible] he had done [illegible] he [illegible] probably gone home to take [illegible] of [illegible] his alleged credulity.

[illegible] forming [illegible] the observations [illegible] Joab [illegible] the latter [illegible] revenge on [illegible] formed a resolution of [illegible] by [illegible] away [illegible] accordingly [illegible] Abner, in the [illegible] of David, [illegible] to return, as some [illegible] that were exceed-[illegible] The messengers overtook Abner at a [illegible] Sirah, about twenty furlongs from Hebron [illegible] communicating their business he [illegible] they re-[illegible]

[illegible] Joab, attended only by his brother [illegible] himself in a private place [illegible] and when Abner came to the [illegible] he [illegible] telling him he had some business to re-[illegible] a private [illegible] Abner not suspecting [illegible] complied with Joab's request [illegible] then the latter, [illegible] his [illegible] stabbed him to the [illegible] was taken off by the perfidy of Joab [illegible] in revenge for the death of his brother Asahel, but, in reality, it [illegible] to gratify his jea-[illegible] and revenge, for fear of being supplanted in the [illegible] favour.

When David was informed of Abner's death, he was [illegible] affected, that he knew not how to contain himself [illegible] stretching out his hands and lifting up his eyes to heaven, he solemnly declared in the presence of all about [illegible] that he was [illegible] contrary to the murder, nor [illegible] previous to its being perpetrated. He denounced the most heavy curses on Joab and his fa-[illegible] wishing they might receive that punishment due to [illegible] crime. He ordered all his army to march before the [illegible] with tears and lamenta-[illegible] their clothes [illegible] and putting on sackcloth, to [illegible] his loss, and to perform all funeral rites to him [illegible] the most solemn manner. He attended himself [illegible] chief mourner, and the [illegible] his lamentations for the loss of Abner, [illegible] the people. In short, so [illegible] David at [illegible] that, notwithstanding the [illegible] of his friends, he could not be pre-vailed upon to take the least refreshment that day, [illegible] he would not take any thing till the sun was gone [illegible] The [illegible] of this religious [illegible] gained the [illegible] of the people, who were [illegible] satisfied that David was not only a total stranger to the mur-der of Abner, but that he held him in the highest esteem. Besides [illegible] greatly [illegible] the character and [illegible] of David [illegible] people naturally supposing [illegible] he [illegible] of [illegible] he paid to the memory of [illegible] he had done [illegible] of Abner.

When the funeral ceremonies were [illegible] David [illegible] in a very pathetic harangue, in which he [illegible] pointed out to them his own particular [illegible] being deprived of a friend to whom he had so great a value [illegible] then to [illegible] that his loss [illegible] by the whole nation [illegible] he was not only a brave soldier, but [illegible] and prudent counsellor. "But [illegible] God (says he) [illegible] governs all things, will not let this murder pass [illegible] my witness that my [illegible] will not [illegible] me to [illegible] Joab and Abishai [illegible] defence [illegible] probably a greater interest in the army than I [illegible] but I doubt not that, sooner or later [illegible] justice will [illegible] out and inflict on them that punishment they merit for so enormous a crime."

Thus did the great general [illegible] to the [illegible] envy [illegible] in [illegible]

CHAP. II.

The [illegible] murder of Ishbosheth [illegible] David [illegible] Hebron [illegible] city of Jerusalem [illegible] Joab [illegible] on this occasion.

WHEN Ishbosheth heard of the death of Abner, he was greatly afflicted in his mind, not only on account of having lost a relation but a person who had been the means of advancing him to the throne. He did not however long survive his friend, being soon after treacherously murdered by Baanah and Rechab, the sons of Rimmon. These two persons being Benjamites, and of the first rank, thought if they put Ishbosheth to death, it would be well received by David, and that, for their conduct, he would advance them to some honourable em-ployment. Having resolved on carrying their design in-to execution, they went into that apartment of the palace where Ishbosheth was accustomed to repose himself dur-ing the heat of the day. There being no guards about the place, and the servant appointed to watch the door absent, they stole into the chamber, where finding Ishbo-sheth alone, and fast asleep, they first stabbed him, and then cutting off his head, hasted with all expedition to Hebron, in order to present it as fresh as possible to Da-vid. They made not the least doubt of being amply re-warded for this singular atchievement. But they soon found themselves mistaken: for when they presented the head to David, he was so far from approving of what they had done, that he expressed his detestation of so im-pious an act in words to this effect: "Ye basest of "wretches, (says he) immediately prepare yourselves to "receive the just reward of your horrid villainy. What! "have ye so soon forgot the punishment I inflicted on "him who brought me the crown of gold belonging to "Saul after he had slain him, at his own desire, for fear "of falling into the hands of his enemy! Do you imagine "I am not the same person now I was then? Or can you "suppose me so abandoned a wretch as to countenance the "murder you have committed on your master, by taking "off his head in his own bed chamber, the head of "him who never did injury to any man, and who in an "especial manner, heaped his favours on you? Where-"fore I will avenge his death by taking away your lives, "and avenge myself on you for [illegible] him [illegible] under "pretence of doing me service. Your entertaining such "[illegible] sentiments of me is the greatest injury you could "have done to my honour and reputation." Having said this, he ordered their hands and feet to be cut off, and their bodies to be hung up in a public place as a ter-ror to all regicides, after which he ordered the head of Ish-bosheth to be honourably interred in the sepulchre of Abner.

As soon as the death of Ishbosheth was generally known, all the tribes sent deputies to David, acknow-ledging his right to the sovereignty and promising him their allegiance. David received them with the greatest respect, and assured them, that so long as they continued obedient and faithful subjects, they should not have reason to repent having chosen him as their king. He enter-tained the deputies for several days in the most hospitable and magnificent manner, after which he dismissed them, with orders to [illegible] the whole body of the people to repair immediately to his palace at Hebron.

The deputies having obeyed their orders, and the dif-ferent tribes being gathered together, the number [illegible] as follows:

Of the tribe of Judah, 6,800, armed with shields and lances [illegible] Saul's [illegible]

Of the tribe of Simeon, 7,100.

Of the tribe of Levi, [illegible] their [illegible] With these was Zadok the high-priest, to [illegible] twenty-two of his kindred, all captains.

Of the tribe of Benjamin, [illegible] this tribe [illegible] men that [illegible]

[illegible]

Of the tribe of Ephraim, 20,800, all stout and courageous men.

Of the half tribe of Manasses, 18,000.

Of the tribe of Issachar, 20,000 armed, besides 200, who were skilled in foretelling future events.

Of the tribe of Zebulon, 50,000 all well armed.

Of the tribe of Naphthali, 1,000 commanders, armed with shields and spears, and attended by an innumerable multitude of their followers.

Of the tribe of Dan, 27,000 choice men.

Of the tribe of Asher, 40,000.

Of the two tribes beyond Jordan, and the other half of the tribe of Manasses, 22,000 all armed with shields, spears, swords and helmets.

Each of these tribes brought with them great quantities of corn, wine, and other provisions, which were respectfully received by David; and in the presence of the whole multitude, he was anointed king over all Israel, after having reigned at Hebron, over the tribe of Judah only, for the space of seven years and six months.

David, being now invested with full regal power, and having a multitude of brave and gallant soldiers to attend him, formed the resolution of making an expedition against Jerusalem, which was at this time inhabited by the Jebusites, a people belonging to the race of the Canaanites. He accordingly marched with his army towards the place; and, when he came to the castle, or fort of Zion, which commanded the city, and was thought impregnable, he summoned the inhabitants to surrender. But they were so little intimidated, that they bid defiance to him, and, by way of derision, placed on the walls great numbers of people, who were lame and infirm, saying [illegible] wanted no other guard to protect them from [illegible] enemy. This insult so irritated David, that he resolved immediately to attack the city, reasonably imagining that if he made himself master of that, it would so terrify those in the castle, that they would readily submit. He accordingly besieged the place with the flower of his army, and making a general assault, soon entered the lower Town. The Jebusites made all the resistance they were able, but by the intrepidity of David's army, they were soon overpowered, the greater part of them killed on the spot, and the rest obliged to save themselves by a precipitate flight. Having thus made himself master of the lower city, he marched to the castle, but the inhabitants being still resolute, and the place so strong as to render the attack dangerous, he knew not, for some time, how to act, till at length, in order to encourage his men to undertake the arduous [illegible], he caused a proclamation to be made throughout the camp, that whoever first mounted the walls, and made good his station, should be made captain-general of all his forces. This had the desired effect, a general emulation immediately arising among the people; but Joab being more active than the rest, got before all, and having ascended the tower, called aloud to David to fulfil his promise. The rest of the troops immediately following Joab, the castle was [illegible] [illegible] at the same time [illegible] of the place. After this David expelled the Jebusites, enlarged the buildings of the Lower City, which he joined to the citadel, making it his place of residence, and gave it the name of *The City of David*. He erected many fortifications in different parts of it, surrounded the whole with a strong wall, and gave the command of it to Joab, who made repairs, [illegible] and enlarged the upper city, for the better accommodation of the people. From this time David kept his court at Jerusalem.

CHAP. III.

Hiram, king of Tyre, courts the friendship and alliance of David. [illegible]

ABOUT this time, Hiram, king of Tyre, hearing how prosperous David [illegible] in all his affairs, sent ambassadors to congratulate him on his accession to the throne, and to join with him in a treaty of alliance and friendship. He likewise sent him a present of cedar trees, [illegible] and other artificers [illegible] him in erecting a royal palace [illegible]

The city of Jerusalem (which received the name of David's city after subduing the Jebusites) was called, in the days of Abraham, Solyma, and was governed by [illegible]. Hierosolyma at this city, [illegible] the priests of the [illegible] of Solyma, [illegible] word, [illegible] *[illegible]*. From the time that Joshua [illegible] war with the inhabitants of Canaan, and, after subduing them, divided their country among the Hebrews, the Jebusites still kept possession of the city, nor could they be driven out of it till it was conquered by David, which was an interval of no less than 515 years.

There was left among the Jebusites one Orphan, who was not slain at the siege of Jerusalem, at the [illegible] instance of David, because of the good will he bore the Hebrews in general, and the king in particular [illegible] his name is worthy of record.

Soon after David had established himself in his new city, he took to him several new wives, as also many concubines. By these he had born to him eleven sons, named Amnon, [illegible], Nathan, Solomon, Jebar, Elia, Phalna, Ennaphen, Jenae and Eliphale, besides a daughter named Tamar, who was sister to Absalom. The first of the sons were by his lawful wives, but the two last by concubines.

CHAP. IV.

David totally routs the Philistines, [illegible] Removes the ark to Jerusalem [illegible] design of building [illegible] ple, and acknowledges the Divine favour.

IN the mean time the Philistines having heard of David's increasing greatness, and suspecting it [illegible] prove a refuge of their own downfall, determined to check his power as soon as possible; to effect which they raised a considerable army, and marching towards Jerusalem encamped in a place called *The Valley of the Giants*, not far from the city.

David, not choosing to engage in any enterprize without first consulting the Divine oracle, commanded the high-priest to signify to him the pleasure of the Almighty, and what issue he would vouchsafe to give shou'd he engage the Philistines. Having received an answer that he should obtain the victory, he immediately drew out his men, and marching with all expedition against the enemy, fell on them so suddenly, that they were thrown into the greatest confusion, and in a short time, totally routed. Great numbers were killed on the spot, many others desperately wounded, and the remainder saved themselves by flight.

But the Philistines were so far from being intimidated at this overthrow, that a short time after, they came again with an army consisting of thrice the number they had before, having been joined by the Syrians, Phoenicians and other warlike nations. On this occasion David again consulted the oracle, and received orders that he should march with his army to a certain place not far from the enemy, called *The Groves of Lamentation*, from whence he should not attempt to move, on any account whatever, till he saw the branches of the trees move without the blowing of the wind. That when this took place he might suppose the time was come that Providence had allotted for his encountering the enemy, and that he should immediately leave the place and begin the attack. David strictly attended to these directions, and, as soon as he discovered the providential signs, immediately marched out with his army, fully [illegible] the business he was about would prove successful. [illegible] Philistines gave way at the first onset, when they found themselves closely attacked, [illegible] betook themselves to flight. David pursued them as far as Gaza, a city on the [illegible] borders of their country, and killed great numbers in their way; after which he returned to their camp, took what valuables they had left behind, and destroyed their idols. This defeat so weakened the Philistines, that they did not attempt to attack the Hebrews for many succeeding years.

The war with the Philistines [illegible] and [illegible] things quiet, David thought it a very proper time for to remove the ark of God [illegible]

[illegible] had continued [illegible] the city. For this purpose he summoned the elders and principal men of the tribes [illegible] together with the priests and Levites, [illegible] with him a strong guard [illegible] grand [illegible] He [illegible] removed [illegible] head [illegible] upon their shoulders, they, in imitation of the Philistines, put it into a cart drawn by two oxen, and in this manner proceeded with it towards Jerusalem, the king going before it, and the multitude following after, singing praises to God, and dancing to various tunes played on different instruments, such as harps, psalteries, cornets and cymbals. When they came to a place called *Nachon's Threshing-floor*, the cart [illegible] overturned, [illegible] Uzzah, one of the drivers, in order to save [illegible] for [illegible] presumption [illegible] the Almighty was pleased to punish him [illegible] David, but the whole multitude, [illegible] called the place ever after by the name of Perez-Uzzah, that is *the breach of Uzzah*.

[illegible] the sudden death which the Almighty had inflicted on Uzzah for touching the ark, that he was afraid [illegible] should [illegible] presume to carry it to [illegible] Instead, therefore, of proceeding [illegible] he turned out of the way, and went to the house of a righteous man, a Levite, named Obed-Edom, into whose custody he left the ark, where it remained [illegible] three months. At the expiration of [illegible] David [illegible] heard of the [illegible] Obed-Edom [illegible] since the [illegible] delivered from the [illegible] concerned, [illegible] intentions of [illegible] with great form [illegible] the shoulders of the priests, [illegible] David [illegible] the [illegible] company [illegible] went before it, and the king [illegible] followed, dressed in [illegible] ephod (*a*), [illegible] his harp [illegible] being brought into the city, and properly seated in the place allotted to it, David [illegible] to God of considerable value, [illegible] the people, giving to each [illegible] of bread, a flaggon of wine, and a piece of [illegible]

When David returned home, he [illegible] his wife Michal (the daughter of the late king Saul), who, having seen him through [illegible] dancing before the ark, upbraided him for his conduct, [illegible] In reply to this, David told her that [illegible] done was in honour of that God who had ordained him to govern Israel, in preference to her own father, and to all other men; and that such condescension would never bring him under any just contempt. Michal had [illegible] by David, but she had five sons by her other husband, to whom Saul her father gave her [illegible] after he had forcibly taken her from David.

By this time the palace (which Hiram, king of Tyre, had furnished David with [illegible] materials to build) was finished, and as he was reflecting on the meanness of God's habitation compared with his own, he determined to build a temple for his reception, and to place in it the ark of the Lord. He communicated his design to the prophet Nathan, who [illegible] but that night the word [illegible] to Nathan (*b*) to this effect: "[illegible] of his people [illegible] building a temple to my service [illegible] many wars, and has [illegible] in the blood of his enemies [illegible] his son Solomon, over [illegible] father, [illegible] the [illegible] line of his family; and, if he should [illegible] or [illegible] I will not totally reject him as I did Saul, but only punish him with [illegible]"

The prophet Nathan, having communicated [illegible] to David, [illegible] rejoiced [illegible] the [illegible] succession being [illegible] his posterity so [illegible] provided for, that he [illegible] repaired to the [illegible] of God, and [illegible] addressed [illegible] "Blessed be thy name, for all [illegible] [illegible] the law [illegible] in life to the [illegible] and [illegible] for all [illegible] continued [illegible] [illegible] promises to my posterity [illegible] multiplied deliverances and protection [illegible] [illegible] united.

CHAP. V.

David [illegible]

AS the Almighty had thought proper to refuse David the privileges of building him a temple, and had reserved that work for his son Solomon, he thought it advisable to employ his time in [illegible] every side, that when his son came to the [illegible] affairs he might meet with as little interruption as possible.

In consequence of these thoughts he immediately gathered together his forces, and resolved first to attack the Philistines, who had twice [illegible] the [illegible] accordingly marched against the enemy, [illegible] part of their country, and [illegible] of his own people. He [illegible] Moabites, whom he totally subdued, and having destroyed two thirds of them [illegible] rendered them tributary. After this he gained a victorious action over Hadadezer, the son of Rehob, king of Sophene, whom he defeated near the Euphrates, 20,000 foot and 5000 horse, [illegible] in the action. [illegible] chariots taken he reserved but [illegible] ordering the rest to be consumed.

CHAP. VI.

David [illegible]

IN the mean time Hadad, king of [illegible] having heard of the ill success of Hadadezer, [illegible] his particular friend and ally, [illegible] body of [illegible] He came [illegible] near the river Euphrates, when [illegible] between his [illegible] army of David [illegible] men [illegible] the rest [illegible]

His kingdom [illegible]

(*a*) David [illegible] with [illegible] [illegible]

(*b*) [illegible]

Damascus, in the fifth book of his history, who says, "A certain valiant man, named Adad, reigned over Damascus and Syria, Phenicia only excepted. He having declared war against David several rencounters took place between them, but at last he was overcome near Euphrates, behaving himself with the resolution of a brave prince and a great commander." The same writer, in speaking of the posterity of Adad, says, "After his death his posterity, for the succeeding generations, possessed the sovereignty, each, at that men became king, taking upon him the name of Adad, as the kings of Egypt did that of Ptolemy. The third of these becoming very powerful resolved to renew the war his father had begun, upon which he made an inroad into Judea, and infested the country now called Samaria." This account of Nicholaus is authentic, for this is that Adad who invaded Samaria, when Ahab reigned over Israel.

David, having reduced the Syrians, and made himself master of that country, put garrisons into the fortified cities, and made the inhabitants tributary. Having done this he returned home, loaded with spoils and honours, but all the valuable articles, such as gold, silver, and a particular sort of brass, which was more esteemed than gold, was the metal Solomon afterwards used in making some of the vessels for the service of his temple.

The successes of David were enhanced by those which attended his deputies, several of whom he dispatched, with a proper number of forces, to engage the enemy in such parts as he had directed. Among these was Abishai, Joab's brother, who being sent out with an army against the Idumaeans, totally subdued them, killing 18,000 on the spot, and making the survivors tributary to David.

When Toi, the king of Hamath, heard of the great victories obtained by David, he sent his son Joram to congratulate him on the occasion, and made him a considerable present of vessels of gold, silver, &c. (all which he dedicated to God) as an acknowledgment for his having destroyed the power of his most inveterate enemies.

Though David's attention had been engaged in the prosecution of foreign wars, yet at the same time, he was not unmindful of administering justice to his subjects at home, for the effecting of which he had a certain number of very great men employed in the highest offices of trust. Joab was captain-general, Jehoshaphat, keeper of the records, Abiathar, high priest, Seraiah, secretary of state, Benaiah, captain of his guard, and his own sons, prime ministers of his household. To these David added one more, namely, Mephibosheth, the son of Jonathan, whom, with great difficulty, he found out, by means of one Ziba, who had for many years been a servant to Saul. He restored to him all his grandfather's estates, and though he was a cripple (a), and lame of both his feet, yet (from the great respect he had for his father) he entertained him with the most distinguished kindness, and ordered him to sit with his own sons at the royal table.

Some time after this, David hearing of the death of his good friend and ally Nahash king of the Ammonites, sent his compliments of condolence to his son and successor Hanun; but the great men who were about the young king made him believe that the sole intent of David's sending this embassy was, to spy out the weakness of the city, and in what place it might be most advantageously assaulted. In consequence of this, he ordered his ambassadors to be half shaved (b), and their cloaths cut short, even to the waist, and with this ignominious appearance they were dismissed.

David, fired with indignation at this treatment of his ambassadors as a violation of the law of nations as well as hospitality and honour, determined to assert his rights, and avenge the insult he had himself thought then received from their king. The principal men among the Ammonites, conscious that so flagrant a breach of friendship would excite the resentment of the king of Israel, no sooner heard of his determination, than they prepared for opposition, and dispatched ambassadors to Syrus king of Mesopotamia, as well as the kings of Zoba, Maachah and Ishtob, who, for valuable considerations, furnished them with a powerful armament.

CHAP. VII.

Joab's victories over the Ammonites. The history of David and Bathsheba, the wife of one of his military officers. Absalom takes away the life of Amnon for committing incest with his own sister.

DAVID, by no means intimidated by the preparations of the Ammonites in forming such powerful alliances, maintained his resolution, conscious of the justice of his cause, and depending therefore on the divine aid and protection. He appointed Joab commander of a select body of forces, and dispatched him against the enemy. He pitched his camp near Rabbath, their metropolis, whereupon they came out, and set themselves in array in two bodies, the auxiliaries being fixed on the plains by themselves, and the Ammonites before the port over against the Hebrews. Joab observing the disposition of the enemy, as an expert general opposed stratagem to stratagem, and selecting the choicest men, prepared to head them, and charge the confederates, while he gave his brother Abishai the command of the rest of the army, with orders to attack the Ammonites, and come to his relief, if he should find him oppressed by the confederates.

Having exhorted his brother, and the troops under his command, to a conduct becoming their country and cause, Joab began the action by an attack on the Syrians, who, for some time, withstood him with great bravery, till, dismayed by the slaughter around them, they betook themselves to flight, and the Ammonites, observing the confusion into which the confederates were thrown, followed their example, and with the utmost precipitation ran towards the city, before Abishai's detachment could come up with them. So that Joab returned to Jerusalem with honour.

This defeat, however, did not suppress the hostile designs of the Ammonites, who sent to Chalama, a king of the Syrians beyond Euphrates, and hired of him an army of auxiliaries. Shobach was his lieutenant-general, and had command of 80,000 foot and 7000 horse. When David received intelligence that the Ammonites were so powerfully reinforced he determined to take the command in person, so that passing the river Jordan with the whole army, he gave them battle, and routed them with great slaughter. Forty thousand foot, and seven thousand of their horse, fell in the action, and Shobach the general of the Syrians, received a wound which proved mortal. The Mesopotamians, awed by this victory, submitted to the king of Israel, and gratified him with presents by their ambassadors. After this glorious enterprize, David returned in safety to Jerusalem. As soon as the season would permit, he sent Joab

(a) Mephibosheth ... [illegible]

(b) The ... [illegible]

[illegible]

Damascus, mentions [illegible] of his history, [illegible] "[illegible] with him, [illegible] Adad, [illegible] Euphrates and Syria, [illegible] excepted. He [illegible] declared [illegible] David [illegible] accounts took [illegible] then, [illegible] he was [illegible] Euphrates, [illegible] since [illegible] . [illegible] in speaking of the posterity of Adad, [illegible] After his death his posterity, for the succeeding generations, possessed [illegible] sovereignty, each, [illegible] time he became king, [illegible] on him the [illegible] of Adad, as the kings of [illegible] that of [illegible] become [illegible] powerful [illegible] the war his [illegible] had begun upon which [illegible] an inroad into [illegible] [illegible] Samaria." This account of [illegible] is authentic, for this is that Adad who invaded [illegible], when Ahab reigned over Israel.

David having [illegible] the Syrians, and made himself master of that country, put garrisons into the fortified cities, and made the inhabitants tributary. Having done this he returned home, loaded with spoils and honours: but all the valuable articles, such as gold, silver, and particularly [illegible], which was more esteemed than gold, was that [illegible] Solomon afterwards used in [illegible] the vessels [illegible] the service of the temple.

The successes of David were enhanced by the [illegible] of his [illegible] several of whom he [illegible] with a proper number of forces, to engage the enemy [illegible] he had directed. Among these was Abishai, Joab's brother, [illegible] Idumeans, [illegible] subdued them, killing 18,000 on the spot, and [illegible] the survivors tributary to David.

When [illegible], the king of Hamath, heard of the great victories obtained by David, he sent his son [illegible] to congratulate him on the occasion, and made him a considerable present of vessels of gold, silver, &c. [illegible] which were dedicated to God, as an acknowledgement for his having destroyed the power of [illegible] enemies.

Though David's attention had been engaged in the prosecution of [illegible] at this time he was not unmindful of [illegible] to his [illegible] [illegible] for the [illegible] of which he [illegible] of [illegible] the highest offices [illegible] Joab was captain general, Jehoshaphat, keeper of the records, Abiathar, high-priest, Seraiah, secretary [illegible], Benaiah, captain of his guard, and his own sons, [illegible] [illegible]. [illegible] David [illegible] Mephibosheth the son of Jonathan, [illegible] with great difficulty, he found out, by means of one Ziba, who had for many years been a servant to Saul. He restored to him all his grandfather's estates; and though he was a cripple (a), and lame of [illegible] [illegible] (from the great respect he had for his [illegible]) he entertained him with the most distinguished kindness, and ordered him to sit with his own sons at the [illegible].

Soon after this, David hearing of the death of his good friend and ally Nahash, king of the Ammonites, [illegible] compliments of condolence to his son and successor Hanun; but the great men [illegible] the young [illegible] that the [illegible] intent of David's [illegible] was to spy out the weakness of the city, and in what place it might be taken with advantage. In consequence [illegible] ordered his [illegible] [illegible] beards to be [illegible] shaved (b), and their cloths [illegible] [illegible] to the [illegible] with [illegible] ignominious [illegible] they were dismissed.

[illegible], fired with indignation at the treatment of his [illegible] [illegible] and [illegible] perfidity, and [illegible] to [illegible] and avenge the insult he had [illegible] through them, received from their king. The principal men among the Ammonites, conscious that so [illegible] a breach of friendship would excite the resentment of the king of Israel, no sooner [illegible] of his determination, than they prepared for opposition, [illegible] and [illegible] Syrus, king of Mesopotamia, as well as the kings of [illegible], Maachah and [illegible], for valuable considerations, furnished them with a [illegible].

CHAP. VII.

Joab [illegible] the Ammonites. [illegible] [illegible] [illegible] [illegible] [illegible] be [illegible] to [illegible] [illegible]

DAVID [illegible] no means intimidated by the preparations of the Ammonites in forming such powerful alliances, maintained his resolution, conscious of the justice of his cause, and depending [illegible] on the divine protection. He appointed Joab commander of the [illegible] body of troops, and [illegible] him to [illegible] the [illegible]. He pitched his camp near Rabbath [illegible] [illegible] [illegible] set themselves in [illegible] bodies, the [illegible] being fixed on the plain [illegible] themselves, and the Ammonites before the [illegible] [illegible] the Hebrews. Joab observing the disposition of the enemy, [illegible] opposed himself to them, and selecting the bravest men, prepared to lead them, and charge the confederates, while he gave his brother Abishai the command of the rest of the army, [illegible] orders to attack the Ammonites, and come to his [illegible], if he should find [illegible] the confederates.

Having exhorted his brother and the troops under his command to a conduct becoming their country and [illegible], Joab began the action by an attack on the Syrians, who [illegible] some time [illegible] him with great bravery; till, dismayed [illegible] slaughter around them, they betook themselves to flight, and the Ammonites, [illegible] the confederates were [illegible] [illegible] [illegible], and, with the utmost precipitation [illegible] to the city before [illegible] detachment could come up with them. So that Joab returned to Jerusalem with honour.

This defeat, however, did not suppress the hostile designs of the Ammonites, who sent to Chalaman, a king of the Syrians, beyond Euphrates, and hired of him an army of auxiliaries. Shobach was his lieutenant-general, and had command of 80,000 foot and [illegible],000 horse. When David received intelligence that the Ammonites were so powerfully reinforced, he determined to take the command in person; so that passing the river Jordan with the whole army, he gave them battle, and [illegible] them with great slaughter. Forty thousand foot, and seven thousand of their horse, fell in the action, and Shobach the general of the Syrians received a wound which proved mortal. The Mesopotamians, awed by this victory, [illegible] to the king of Israel, and gratified him with presents by their ambassadors. [illegible] glorious [illegible] [illegible] David returned [illegible] to Jerusalem [illegible] [illegible] the season [illegible], [illegible] Joab

(a) [illegible]

(b) [illegible]

King DAVID presenting URIAH with the LETTER to JOAB,
wherein Uriah's fatal Commission was seal'd.

The PROPHET NATHAN rebuking KING DAVID and foretelling the Calamities that afterwards befel him

against the tarbi[illegible] [illegible] ters, or [illegible] their country, [illegible], drove t[illegible] to the [illegible] pous, [illegible] ed them in.

While Joab was carrying on the siege of [illegible] David [illegible] God, [illegible] the re[illegible] of [illegible] great [illegible] offence [illegible] as [illegible] prince, for the [illegible] of the air, he [illegible] or a [illegible] exquisite [illegible] He [illegible] predict [illegible] Bathsheba [illegible] the Hittite, [illegible] Joab at the siege of Rabbah. [illegible] informed [illegible] ordered [illegible] when [illegible] so wrought [illegible] to [illegible] his bed, [illegible] for [illegible] finding her [illegible] [illegible] her honour and [illegible] whereby it might be concealed. David [illegible] messenger to Joab [illegible] orders [illegible] [illegible] particular nature, [illegible] to give [illegible] [illegible] [illegible] [illegible] [illegible] [illegible]

[illegible] to [illegible] given to David [illegible] he [illegible] [illegible] wives. He [illegible] [illegible] [illegible] [illegible] [illegible] [illegible] Uriah [illegible] [illegible] wife, [illegible] [illegible] Uriah [illegible] [illegible] I know [illegible] "not [illegible]."

David [illegible] length [illegible] [illegible] Joab, commanding him on the first dangerous [illegible] [illegible] Ammonites [illegible] should [illegible] Uriah [illegible] Joab [illegible] Uriah [illegible] [illegible] [illegible] with the [illegible]

When the Ammonites [illegible] [illegible] [illegible] gates, [illegible] Hebrews [illegible] to the orders of Joab, [illegible] [illegible] the power of [illegible] after receiving several [illegible] [illegible] coming

[illegible] [illegible] [illegible] messenger to inform David [illegible] [illegible] [illegible] to carry on the siege [illegible] had made himself [illegible] of [illegible] to the ground, and [illegible] [illegible]

In the mean time Bathsheba, the wife of Uriah, being informed of her husband's death [illegible] for him some days, [illegible] for [illegible] that ceremony David [illegible] her [illegible] [illegible] she brought him a son.

This [illegible] [illegible] to Nathan, the prophet, [illegible] David [illegible] who [illegible] consulting with him [illegible] the kings, [illegible] [illegible] son [illegible] not to tell David [illegible] and the [illegible] of the Almighty, but [illegible] [illegible] manner, that he [illegible] [illegible] [illegible] [illegible] before the king, he [illegible] as follows: "[illegible] (says he) [illegible] "[illegible] was rich, and [illegible] and great "herds and flocks of oxen and sheep [illegible] "poor [illegible] had but one little ewe-lamb, which [illegible] "[illegible] brought up, and nourished with his [illegible] "[illegible] a stranger came to [illegible] "[illegible] was [illegible], by [illegible] to [illegible] "[illegible] not doing it at his own expence, [illegible] "[illegible] away [illegible] the poor man's [illegible] "[illegible] and set it before his guest." [illegible] [illegible] to [illegible] and [illegible] [illegible] [illegible] put to death. "Why [illegible] (says [illegible]) [illegible] "[illegible] no [illegible] judgment on himself." He [illegible] had greatly [illegible] the Divine [illegible] that God [illegible] [illegible] and [illegible] Saul. That the Almighty [illegible] [illegible] [illegible] to death, [illegible] that God would [illegible] [illegible] by causing his wives to be [illegible] [illegible] he [illegible] [illegible] [illegible] would be [illegible] He concluded with this [illegible]

David [illegible] received this [illegible] from God, by the mouth of Nathan, was thrown into the greatest [illegible] [illegible] confession of his [illegible] [illegible] [illegible] [illegible] [illegible] [illegible] the son of God [illegible] [illegible] [illegible] [illegible] [illegible] Nathan [illegible] [illegible] [illegible] [illegible] [illegible] [illegible] [illegible] [illegible] Bathsheba [illegible] David [illegible] [illegible] the Almighty [illegible] [illegible] [illegible] [illegible] [illegible] [illegible] [illegible] [illegible] [illegible] [illegible] David [illegible]

The PROPHET NATHAN *rebuking* KING DAVID *and foretelling the Calamities that afterwards befel him*

tion of the prophet Nathan, was named Solomon (*a*)

During these transactions Joab was carrying on the siege of Rabbah, and renewing his assaults every day He at length got possession of the works which supplied the city with water Having thus in distressed the enemy, he dispatched a messenger to acquaint the king, that the city was reduced to the utmost extremity, that it was in no condition to hold out much longer, and therefore he desired him to come in person, that he might have the honour of taking it David, agreeable to his general's desire, went with a strong reinforcement, took the place by storm, and divided the spoil among his soldiers, reserving only to himself such articles as belonged to the king, among which was the crown of inestimable value Having thus reduced the city, he put those who had held out against him, to the most exquisite torments, and the inhabitants of other places, who would not immediately surrender, he treated with the like severity Thus were the Ammonites totally subdued by David, who, returning with his army to Jerusalem, was received by the people with the loudest acclamations of joy

David had been but a short time at Jerusalem, after conquering the Ammonites before a circumstance occurred in his family that gave him great uneasiness He had several sons, but only one daughter, a virgin, named Tamar, who was sister to Absalom by the same mother She was most exquisitely beautiful in her person, and possessed of every female accomplishment Amnon, the eldest son of David, by another queen, fell desperately in love (*b*) with her, and, for some time pined away with an hopeless desire of obtaining her At length, by the advice and contrivance of Jonadab, his intimate friend and cousin-german, he found means to decoy her into his apartment, when notwithstanding all her entreaties and expostulations, he first ravished her, and, when his brutish passion was satisfied, in a sullen humour bid her be gone She for some time remonstrated with him on the ill-treatment she had received, and the ignominy to which she must be exposed, but all remonstrances were in vain, and Amnon finding her unwilling to go, at length ordered his servants to turn her out of the house

In this distressed situation Tamar immediately repaired to her brother Absalom, and related to him the whole particulars of what had passed Absalom, though a man naturally of a high spirit, advised her, as the most prudent method, to be silent on the occasion, because her ravisher was heir apparent to the crown and he so artfully concealed his own resentment, that the people doubted whether he ever knew of the transaction In the mean time David, having heard of the circumstance, was greatly afflicted, but as Amnon was his eldest and most beloved son, he did not think proper to expose him by punishment

About two years after this (during which time Tamar resided with her brother) Absalom took the opportunity of revenging the injury done by Amnon to his sister It being the time of sheep-shearing (which was usually attended with great mirth and jollity) he invited the king and all the princes of the blood, to come to his country seat at Hazor, to partake of the entertainment David excused himself, by saying he would not put him to so great a trouble as must consequently follow his attendance On this Absalom desired he would permit his brothers to come, to which the king readily complied They accordingly went to Hazor, where, while they were engaged in feasting and drinking, the servants of Absalom (who had received previous instructions how to act) suddenly fell on Amnon, and immediately dispatched him

CHAP VIII

To escape his father's resentment, Absalom flies to Geshur Joab reconciles him to David Absalom engages in rebellion, and is guilty of breaches of piety and filial duty through the persuasion of Ahithophel

THE unexpected violence on Amnon so alarmed the rest of the princes, that fearful of meeting the like fate, they precipitately left the place, and fled with all expedition to their father's house A messenger who was dispatched on the occasion, arriving first at the palace, with a relation of the event, David was thrown into the utmost consternation, supposing that Absalom had killed all his sons, but his fears were soon removed by the arrival of the princes, when a scene of the most affecting nature took place, the father and sons reciprocally greeting each other with tears, and all lamenting the cruel death of Amnon

In the mean time Absalom, knowing how highly his father would resent this treacherous murder, fled to his mother's relations, and was entertained by his grand-father Talmai, at Geshur Here he remained three years, at the expiration of which Joab perceiving that David had a secret desire to see Absalom, projected a scheme for facilitating the accomplishment of his wishes, without exposing him to censure for his conduct He procured an ancient and artful woman from Tekoah, and having dressed her in mourning, introduced her to the king, with a feigned petition for the life of one of her sons, who had killed the other She related her tale in so apparently an affecting manner, that the king was induced to comply with her request, upon which she told him that the case she had been stating was Absalom's, and that, if he was disposed to shew mercy to a private man, there was much more reason for his pardoning his own son, whose absence the people lamented, and for whom they had the greatest respect

David easily saw through this piece of artifice, and, on interrogating the woman, found it (as he suspected) to have been concerted by Joab He therefore sent for him, told him he had gained his point, and ordered him to recall Absalom Joab, highly pleased with the royal command, immediately went to Geshur, and without delay brought Absalom with him to Jerusalem When the king was informed of his arrival, he ordered him to go to his own house, and there live retired with his family, as he did not yet choose to admit him into his presence, nor would he, by any means, allow him to appear in public

In this recluse manner did Absalom live for two years with his family, (which consisted of three sons, and one daughter named Tamar) when, being tired of his situation, he sent to Joab, intreating him to intercede with his father for a free pardon Joab, not complying with his request, he sent to him again, but receiving no answer, he ordered some of his people to go to a field of corn belonging to Joab, and set it on fire As soon as Joab was informed of this he went to Absalom, and asked him why he treated him in that manner? Upon which he answered, "I had no other method of getting a sight of you I wrote to

(*a*) The word Solomon is properly derived from *Schalom*, which signifies peace, intimating that his reign should be *peaceable* but Nathan gave the name of *Jedidiah* which signifies *beloved of God* The scriptures however never call him by this name only by that of Solomon but for what reason we cannot tell unless we may suppose that the people being harrassed in wars during the [illegible] length of [illegible] his name, and use it rather than the other [illegible] their hope and longing desire of peace And for this reason among others it may be inferred that Solomon was born after the conclusion of the Ammonitish war [illegible] the sacred historian [illegible] from the [illegible] some [illegible] another [illegible] David called Nathan, and it is [illegible] that the [illegible] who on Joseph's side [illegible] from Solomon, and on Mary's from Nathan See Matt [illegible] 6 7 [illegible]

(*b*) [illegible] to [illegible] the passion of love is so [illegible] and [illegible] vexatious as where it is unlawful A quick sense of guilt especially when it is enormous, as in the present instance strikes the soul with horror and the impossibility of an innocent gratification loads that horror with desperation A conflict too cruel and too dreadful for human [illegible] Witness the two most remarkable instances of it found in history that of Antiochus for Stratonice his mother in law, and this of Amnon for Tamar his sister [illegible] it of Antiochus appears the less criminal of the two inasmuch as he seemed determined to conceal his [illegible] till death, and at the same time to hasten that death to prevent its publication had not the sagacity of his physician discovered it Though possibly Amnon had done the same had not the importunity of his false and subtle friend Jonadab the son of Shimeah David's brother drawn the secret from him It is [illegible] to think that the heart of royalty [illegible] vicissitudes of infinitely more consequence than that of meaner men, should yet be under not [illegible] to tell it

The ASSASSINATION *of* AMNON *by order of his Brother Absalom*

The ASSASSINATION *of* AMNON *by order of his* —
— *Brother Absalom* —

"you about interceding for me to my father, but you have "not taken the least notice of it. Let me beseech you to "try if you can pacify him; for the manner in which I "now live is a greater punishment to me than when I was "in exile." This had the desired effect. Joab immediately complied with his request, and so far succeeded, that Absalom was ordered into the king's presence. As soon as he saw his father he fell prostrate on the ground, and in the most humiliating manner, begged pardon for the offence he had committed. Upon this the king took him by the hand, raised him from the ground, and saluted him, as a token of his forgiveness and royal favour.

Absalom was, in person, one of the handsomest men in all Israel, nor was his beauty the least impaired by the punishment he had lately undergone. He was remarkable for having a prodigious head of hair, which he had cut once every year, and the quantity was usually so great, that in general, it weighed about two hundred shekels. This greatly added to the natural beauty of his person, and having a graceful air of address, he was particularly noticed by all ranks of people.

Some time after Absalom was restored to his father's favour (Amnon his elder brother, being slain, and his second brother dead) he considered himself as presumptive heir to the crown, and thereupon affected a state and equipage greater than usual. He provided himself with chariots and horses, and had a guard of fifty men to attend his person. But notwithstanding all this pomp, he was so obsequious and humble in his manner, as to stoop to the meanest people who had any thing to say to him. He offered his service to all who requested any favour at court, and at proper opportunities, took the advantage of instilling into the people's minds a bad opinion of his father's administration, intimating that the public affairs were neglected, and that, if he was at the helm, business should be conducted in a very different manner. By these arts and insinuations, which were advantageously seconded by the comeliness of his person, and the familiarity of his address, he gained the hearts of the people, and prepared them for becoming serviceable to his ambitious and treacherous designs.

In the fortieth year after the reconciliation took place between David and Absalom, the latter, thinking matters were properly ripe for his purpose, desired leave of his father to go to Hebron, pretending he had made a vow in his exile, that, whenever it should please God to bring him back to Jerusalem, he would offer in that place a solemn sacrifice of thanksgiving. The king little suspecting his hidden design, and being desirous that all religious services should be performed, gave him free permission to go, wishing him a good journey, and a safe return.

Absalom accordingly set out for Hebron, accompanied by a great multitude of people, exclusive of his own guards and attendants, who not knowing his design, went from a pure motive of attending the sacrifice. As soon as he came to Hebron, he sent for Ahithophel, David's counsellor, and dispatched emissaries into different parts to sound the inclination of the several tribes, and to exhort those, whom they should gain over to his party, to be ready to take up arms, as soon as they should hear that he was proclaimed king.

These emissaries proved [illegible] embassy. Absalom was the darling of the people, who on the summons, flocked to him from every part, and on his being proclaimed king in Hebron a general insurrection took place.

In the mean time David, having received intelligence of his son's treachery, and the great success he had met with among the people, thought it not safe to continue any longer in Jerusalem. Leaving the care of his palace to the care of ten of his concubines, he set out with a design of retiring beyond Jordan, taking with him the six hundred troops who had so closely stuck by him at the time he was persecuted by Saul, and also [illegible] a great number of his most intimate and sincere friends.

When Zadock and Abiathar, the high-priests, understood that David was about to leave Jerusalem, they [illegible] out the ark of the Lord to accompany him in his distress, but he desired them to carry it back and to continue in Jerusalem, as they might be useful in giving him intelligence of the enemy's motions and designs; while their own characters were too sacred to fear any violence from the usurper. Ahimaaz, the son of Zadock, and Jonathan the son of Abiathar, he left with their fathers, knowing them to be strictly devoted to his interest; but Ittai, the Gittite, who was no less his friend, would not leave him, notwithstanding David earnestly pressed him to continue in the city.

As David was ascending Mount Olivet, walking barefoot, and the company about him weeping, he received intelligence that Ahithophel was gone over to the faction of Absalom. This gave him great uneasiness, well knowing his distinguished abilities as a statesman; upon which he prayed to God so to infatuate Ahithophel, that he might be deprived of his powers, and thereby rendered useless to his rebellious son and rival.

When David had got to the top of the mount, he espied his faithful friend and counsellor Hushai, who had followed him unknown, and, with all expressions of sorrow at seeing him in such distress, earnestly intreated that he might share with him in his fortune. But David enjoined him to return, telling him he would be more serviceable to him in the city, by pretending to adhere to Absalom, and by defeating the counsels of Ahithophel, who was engaged in his son's measures, and from whose great abilities he thought himself in the utmost danger.

David had scarce passed over Mount Olivet, when Ziba, whom he had made steward to Mephibosheth his friend Jonathan's son, accosted him, and presented him with a considerable quantity of wine and other provisions. David asked him where his master was, to which the perfidious wretch replied, he had left him in Jerusalem, where he determined to remain, in hopes, from the present broils, of being himself chosen king. The too credulous David, in this general distraction of his affairs, believing the accusation to be true, made an hasty grant of all Mephibosheth's estate to the base and treacherous Ziba.

When David came near to Behurim, a city belonging to the tribe of Benjamin, one Shimei, a descendant of the family of Saul, who lived there, threw stones at him, and, in the hearing of the whole multitude, loaded him with the bitterest reproaches. This so irritated Abishai, that he begged permission to dispatch the rebel for his insolence, but David would not, by any means, suffer him to commit such a violence. He bore all with great patience and resignation to the Divine will, being conscious of his own guilt in the case of Uriah, and of the Divine justice in thus punishing him for his transgressions.

While David was at Behurim, Absalom, and his party entered Jerusalem, and were received with the general acclamations of the people. Hushai not forgetting the instructions given him by David, went to Absalom, complimented him on the occasion, and offered him his services. The latter, knowing that Hushai was his father's friend and counsellor, at first bantered him for pretending to desert his old master, but Hushai [illegible] himself in such a manner, and answered all his questions with such subtilties, that Absalom was perfectly convinced, and he admitted him a member of his privy-council.

Absalom, placing his dependence chiefly on the abilities of Ahithophel, sent for him to consult what measures were most proper to pursue, in order to establish him on his father's throne. The treacherous statesman advised him, first to lie publicly with David's concubines, "for, (says he) by so doing, you will convince the people that a reconciliation can never take place between "you and your father, in consequence of [illegible] "he, [illegible] the soldiers will exert their utmost [illegible] "vours in your behalf. They have [illegible] "[illegible], expecting you [illegible] "if a reconciliation should take place [illegible] "[illegible]

[illegible] ed to say, that if all his children should perish, that column would perpetuate his memory to future ages.

He had three sons, besides a daughter named Tamar, one of the most beautiful women of the age in which she lived. She was afterwards married to Rehoboam, the son of Solomon, by whom she bore a son who succeeded to the kingdom.

CHAP. X.

David laments the death of Absalom. He returns to Jerusalem, is reconciled to Shimei, and returns Mephibosheth his possessions. Sheba raises a [illegible], upon which David sends Amasa against him, who is treacherously murdered by Joab. Sheba's rebellion suppressed, and [illegible] brought to David. The Israelites afflicted with a famine, and [illegible] punished with a pestilence, on account of David['s] [illegible].

AS soon as the army of David had obtained a complete victory over that of Absalom, Ahimaaz, the son of Zadok the high priest, begged of Joab that he might be immediately dispatched with the glad tidings to the king. Joab, at first, did not think proper to comply with his request, but sent a person named Cushi, in his stead; Ahimaaz still soliciting Joab to let him go, he at length consented, when Ahimaaz knowing the nearest way, and being more alert than Cushi, got first to David's camp. He found the king sitting at the gate of the city, waiting, with anxious expectation to know the event of the battle. As soon as David saw him, he hastily asked, "What news from the army?" To which Ahimaaz replied, "Great success and victory!" David then asked, what was become of his son Absalom? to which the other replied, he could not inform him, having been dispatched in such haste, that his orders were only to carry the news of the victory, and that at his departure the name of his son was not even mentioned. By this time Cushi arrived, when the king asking him what was become of his son, he replied, "As to him, so may it be with all the enemies of my lord the king."

These words struck David to the heart, and all the joy of victory was immediately turned into sorrow. He withdrew himself to the room of [illegible] highest turrets in the city, where he gave vent to his grief by beating his breast, tearing his hair, and [illegible] crying, "O! my son Absalom! my son! my son! Would to God I could have died for thee!" [illegible] the army instead of returning in triumph, [illegible] the city, as if they had come and fled and instead of conquering, had lost the battle.

David was so affected at the loss of his son, that he gave himself up to the deepest melancholy. This was soon perceived by Joab who being sensible that such excessive grief, at this juncture of affairs would be of great prejudice to the king, went boldly to his apartment, and expostulated with him on his conduct in the following terms:

"My Lord (says he) you dishonour yourself by this "ridiculous and effeminate lamentation. It appears as if "you detested the very people, who have preserved your "life at the hazard of their own, and that you respected "those mortal enemies who have suffered [illegible] punishment "they justly deserved. If Absalom had overcome us, "and possessed himself of the kingdom he would have "begun his vengeance on you and your family, and the "whole of us should have fallen in an undistinguished "ruin. Both your contentment and your honour ought to "check you from this intemperate concern for the memo-"ry of so implacable an enemy. It is true, he was your "son, but he was certainly a [illegible] one; and "you cannot be [illegible] to God's providence, without [illegible]-"knowledging the [illegible] Let "me, therefore, beg that you will immediately shew "yourself cheerfully to your people, and tell them that "next under God, it is owing to their loyalty and cou-"rage, you are indebted for the honour of this day. If "you persist in your lamentations, your army and king-"dom will fall into other hands, and then you will have "just cause to weep and lament your absurd conduct."

This speech had the desired effect: the king was roused from his melancholy, and appeared in public, to the great satisfaction of his subjects. He was however greatly offended with Joab, for the blunt manner in which he had chastised him, and, as he had [illegible] many [illegible] created by him on several other occasions, he resolved, from this time, to take the first opportunity he could of dismissing him from his post [illegible].

Those of David's subjects, who had appeared in arms against him being now made fully sensible of [illegible], of their rebellion became [illegible] in shewing their loyalty: but what greatly afflicted David was, [illegible] (that of Judah), appearing very indifferent. In consequence of this he sent to Zadock and Abiathar, the high-priests, not only to remind them of their own duty, but to authorize them likewise to treat with Amasa, who had commanded Absalom's army, and was a man of great authority in the tribe. David told them to offer Amasa a free pardon, and to assure him, that if he would come fully into his interest, he should be placed in the same character that he had been in under Absalom. The high-priests strictly obeyed the king's orders, and Amasa, being satisfied with the promise made him, was readily brought over to the interest of David.

All things thus conspiring to David's happy restoration, he left Mahanaim and set forward on his journey towards Jerusalem. He was attended by the chiefs of the respective tribes, but those of Judah were now the most forward in shewing their [illegible]. They went before him to the banks of the river Jordan and assisted by some others belonging to the tribe of Benjamin laid a bridge over the river, for the better convenience of his passing it with his troops.

Among many others, who came to meet David on this occasion, was Shimei, the Benjamite who, a short time before, had loaded him with the most [illegible] reflections. He was attended by a thousand men of his own tribe whom he brought with him as witnesses of his humiliation for his past conduct. As soon as he saw David he threw himself at his feet, begged pardon for the indignities he had put upon him, and hoped that his early repentance, and return to his allegiance, would in some measure, atone for his past transgressions. Abishai would willingly have had him put to death, but David strongly objected to this proposition, saying, he would not eclipse the public joy with the blood of any one. He therefore gave him his royal word and oath that no harm whatever should come to him on his account; upon which assurance Shimei made his reverence, and departed.

The next distinguished person who appeared before David was Mephibosheth, the grandson of Saul. He was dressed in a very mean habit, with his hair dishevelled and his clothes rent, in which state he had remained ever since the king's departure from Jerusalem. Having prostrated himself before David, and done him reverence, the king asked him, "Why he did not follow him, and "make himself a companion of his flight and troubles?" Mephibosheth replied, that it was owing to the injustice of Ziba his servant, who, instead of getting things ready for his journey, as he had desired, totally neglected him, and [illegible] treated him as his [illegible] his master. That he [illegible] going [illegible] on, though he knew, from his [illegible] lameness [illegible] impossible for him to walk. "But [illegible] the injury that Ziba has done me, he has also [illegible] "[illegible] and forged lies to prevail [illegible]-

[illegible footnotes]

C.

"ter against me. But [illegible] thou art so righteously disposed, and such a lover of truth, that thou wilt not give "credit to unjust detractions." Having said this, David resolved neither to punish Mephibosheth, nor to condemn Ziba. He told him that, believing him to be negligent in his duty, he had given all his possessions to Ziba; but he now forgave him, and promised that one half (*) of his estate should be restored to him. Mephibosheth replied, "Let Ziba possess the whole; it is enough for me "that my lord has recovered his kingdom."

Another remarkable person who came to wait on David and pay his respects to him before he passed the river Jordan, was one Barzillai, who had been very kind to him in his exile, and constantly supplied him with provisions while he continued at Mahanaim. After he had paid the king reverence David, in gratitude for his kindness, invited him to go with him to Jerusalem. Barzillai modestly excused himself, saying, that from his great age, being near fourscore, he had lost the relish of the pleasures of a court, and rather desired that he might retire to his own estate, and spend the remainder of his days in preparing himself for a happy dissolution. David admitted his request, but desired that he would leave with him his son Chimham, on whom he would bestow some distinguished favours. This being agreed to, Barzillai left his son, and after paying reverence to the king, and wishing him success in his undertakings, departed to his own home.

David having passed the river Jordan, was desirous of making all possible haste to Jerusalem, and, as the tribe of Judah was the first that came to conduct him home, he (probably to gratify them) marched on without waiting for the great men of Israel, who were flocking from all parts in order to join him. This circumstance occasioned some dispute between the princes of Israel and those of Judah, and as the king was unwilling to displease either party, and therefore did not think proper to interfere in the controversy, several of the tribes of Israel took umbrage at it, and an insurrection ensued. Sheba, of the tribe of Benjamin (a man of a factious and turbulent spirit, and probably a descendant of Saul) made public proclamation by the sound of trumpet, that, "since the tribe of Judah had engrossed David to themselves, they might e'en take him, and since all the other tribes had visibly deserted, the wisest way would be to stand to their arms, and take such measures as were most proper for their own security." In consequence of this, many of the tribes followed Sheba, but the men of Judah persisted in their loyalty and conducted the king to Jerusalem.

The first thing David did, after his arrival in the city, was to clear his palace of his concubines, who had been defiled by Absalom. They were accordingly removed to a building appointed for the purpose, where they were supplied, by the king's especial command, with all things necessary for their subsistence. In this place they were kept during the remainder of their lives, the king never after having the least intercourse with them.

David, having appointed Amasa his general instead of Joab, ordered him to gather together what troops he could from the tribe of Judah, and bring them to him in three days, that he might give him the sole command of them, with orders to march against Sheba. Amasa found more difficulty in executing this order than was expected, and not having accomplished it at the time limited, David sent Joab, accompanied by his brother Abishai, with his guards and the company of six hundred men, in quest of Sheba, desiring him, as soon as possible, to join his army with that of Amasa, and engage the rebels, lest they should secure themselves in some fortified place, from whence it might be difficult to rout them.

Joab resolved to make no delay, but taking with him his brother, and the troops assigned him, marched in quest of Sheba. When they came to a village called Gibeon about forty furlongs from Jerusalem, they met with Amasa, who was marching with the expedition, at the head of a considerable army. As Amasa was to take upon him the sovereign command of the whole troops, Joab did it [illegible] with all [illegible], friendship [illegible] salute him on the occasion. In his way he designedly caused his sword to fall from the scabbard, which he took up and kept naked in his right hand till he closely approached to Amasa, when taking him by the beard with his left hand, as if going to salute him, he, with the other plunged the sword into his heart, and he immediately expired.

Joab then ordered a proclamation to be made throughout the army, that Amasa was a bad man, and that he had served him only according to his deserts. As the body of the deceased particularly attracted the notice of the people, Joab, fearful it might produce bad consequences, ordered it to be removed to a private place at some distance, after which he took the command of the troops, and marched with all expedition in pursuit of Sheba.

In the mean time Sheba had applied to all the tribes of Israel, to try if he could prevail with them to take up arms against David, but finding very few who were willing to engage in his measures, he was forced at last to shut himself up in Abel, a fortified town belonging to the tribe of Naphtali, in the northern part of Judea.

As soon as Joab received intelligence of Sheba's retreat, he immediately marched to the place, laid siege to it, and made the necessary preparations for an assault; but he was prevented from executing his design by the interposition of a woman, who, getting on the top of the walls, called to the besiegers, and desired that she might be permitted to speak to their general.

This being granted, Joab approached the walls within hearing, when the woman addressed him as follows: "It has (says she) been always a custom, founded on "the law of God, that whenever the Hebrews came be"fore any city, to offer peace in the first place, even "though the inhabitants were of another nation, much "more ought it to be done to a people who are of the "same blood, and the greatest part of them loyal sub"jects to the king." Joab replied, "He had not any "ill design against the people of the city; all he requir"ed was, that they would deliver up the rebel Sheba, "on doing which he would immediately raise the siege, "and draw off his army." The woman begged him to desist for a short time, and his request should be complied with; for that the head of Sheba should be thrown to him from the battlements. She then went to the principal people of the city, and expostulated with them to this effect: "Will ye (said she) like traitors, suffer your "wives and children to perish for the sake of a villain, "whom none of you know? What has Sheba done for "you that can balance the obligations you lie under to "David? Or, setting aside all other arguments, how can "you be so unreasonable as to suppose that you are able "to resist the force of so powerful an army as is even "now before you? Be quick in your determination, for "on that depends either your safety or immediate ruin."
This had the desired effect. Sheba was immediately seized, his head cut off, and thrown over the walls to the soldiers. Joab, according to his promise, immediately raised the siege, and taking with him the head of Sheba, returned with his troops to Jerusalem. David was so pleased with his services on this occasion, that he laid aside his former wrath, and reinstated him in his office of captain-general of his army.

Some time after this there happened a most dreadful famine throughout the whole country, and the [illegible]

* [illegible] by David's disposal of [illegible] to Ziba, one would [illegible] that he was [illegible] Nor [illegible] to deal with him [illegible] only forgave him [illegible] Nor [illegible] and a S. [illegible] wholly free from suspicion of hypocrisy. If Ziba neglected [illegible] to bring Mephibosheth [illegible] might [illegible] to David [illegible] unreasonable to suppose that so great a man [illegible] should not [illegible] or [illegible] the same purpose.

continuance of it (which [illegible] for three years) made David suspect it did not proceed from any common cause, but that it was inflicted by the immediate hand of God. He accordingly consulted the Divine oracle, to know the occasion of it, and received for answer, that it arose from Saul's cruelty to the Gibeonites, in having killed great numbers contrary to a treaty which had been sacrilegiously made between him and them. In consequence of this, David sent to the Gibeonites to know what satisfaction they desired, who returned for answer, that they expected he would deliver into their hands seven of Saul's posterity. David immediately complied with their demand, by sending two sons of Rizpah, Saul's concubine, and five of Michal [illegible] eldest daughter, choosing to preserve Mephibosheth from the great respect he had for his father (a). These seven being delivered to the Gibeonites, they put them to death by hanging them on gibbets (b), and soon after the Almighty sent down rain (the want of which had occasioned the famine) to nourish the earth. The ground was no longer parched, the country again flourished, and its accustomed productions appeared in abundance.

The calamity of the famine was no sooner removed, than David's attention was engaged in opposing the Philistines, who, though they had been greatly humbled in the beginning of his reign, having yet some gigantic men among them, again waged war against him. He accordingly marched out at the head of a considerable army, and engaging them obtained a complete victory. In this rencounter, however, he narrowly escaped with his life; for one of the Philistines (a man of so large a size, that his lance weighed three hundred shekels) seeing David alone, and quite spent, turned short, and suddenly struck him to the ground; but Abishai, the brother of Joab, coming at the precise moment to his relief, not only preserved the king, but killed the Philistine. The whole army were so sensible of the king's danger, and the interposition of Providence for his safety, that the officers bound him, by an oath, never from that time, personally to engage in battle, lest his undaunted courage should involve him in the like, or worse misfortunes, by means of which the nation would sustain an irreparable loss, and the people be deprived of those distinguished blessings they had continually experienced under his government (c).

Notwithstanding this defeat, the Philistines were still determined to disturb the peace of Israel. They rallied their forces and three other engagements took place between them and the army of David, in all which the Philistines were defeated, and among great numbers of others, four of their gigantic men were slain by David's officers. The last contest sickened the Philistines, and they relinquished all further thoughts of interrupting the Israelites.

David being now at leisure from the toils of war, employed his time in composing hymns and psalms, in different measures (such as trimeters and pentameters) to the glory of God. These he ordered to be sung by the Levites on their sabbaths and other festivals, accompanied with several musical instruments he had provided for the purpose.

The chief of these instruments were, a ten stringed harp, which was touched with a quill; a psaltery, of twelve strings, played upon with the fingers; and several large cymbals of brass.

The king had at this time about him great numbers of men of the most approved courage, thirty seven of whom he called his *Worthies*, they having performed exploits of the most dangerous and surprizing nature. Of these we shall only take notice of the actions of five, by which a tolerable idea may be formed of the achievements of the rest.

The first of these was I[illegible]m, the son of Achem, who, in one encounter, broke into the ranks of the enemy, and with his own hands, laid 800 dead at his feet.

The next was Eleazar, the son of Dodo, who distinguished himself for his great valour and strength in an engagement at which David was present. The Philistines were so numerous that the Israelites gave way and fled, but Eleazar maintained his ground, and encountering the enemy, made such a dreadful slaughter among them, that his sword in a manner stuck to his right hand with their blood. This example of bravery animated the whole army, who immediately returned, and falling vigorously on the Philistines, they were totally defeated, and the greater part slain.

The third was Seba, the son of I[illegible]. This chief also in an engagement with the Philistines, maintained his ground with such courage, after the Israelites had given way, that he put them to flight, and from his valour, obtained a complete conquest. These three heroes, besides the feats already mentioned, performed one of a very singular nature in conjunction. The camp of the Philistines lay in the valley of Rephaim, between David's camp and Bethlehem, where they had likewise a garrison. David intimated a desire of having some water from the well of Bethlehem, which being heard by these three chiefs, they found their way through the enemy's camp, and having drawn some water out of the well, returned uninterrupted (the Philistines staring at them with distinguished amazement as they passed) and presented it to the king. When David understood at what price it had been purchased, even at the most imminent hazard of their lives, he would not touch it, but giving God thanks for their safety, poured it on the ground as an offering to the Lord.

The fourth of these champions was Abishai, the brother of Joab, who, in one day, slew 300 of the Philistines with his own hands.

The fifth and last we shall mention was Benaiah, a man of a sacerdotal family. He was challenged by two brothers (Moabites) famous for their [illegible] exploits, whom he fought and slew. He likewise engaged with an Egyptian, a man of prodigious strength and size. His adversary was well provided with arms, and himself almost defenceless, but closing with him,

(a) David [illegible] Saul [illegible] that he would [illegible] seed after him [illegible] of [illegible] house. His [illegible] committed crimes worthy of death [illegible] punishing them [illegible] had [illegible] David [illegible] cut off his seed after him [illegible] to destroy the name [illegible] of his father's house [illegible] oath to Saul. Now David did not [illegible] of the [illegible] Saul [illegible] which had a tendency to destroy his name out of his father's house [illegible] reckoned by the male [illegible] females of [illegible] and he [illegible] father's house could only be [illegible] by the [illegible] David gave up only two bastard [illegible] the sons of Rizpah Saul's concubine, who were [illegible] of Saul [illegible] five of the sons of [illegible] eldest daughter by [illegible] (who could only keep up Adriel's name and not Saul's) and [illegible] without [illegible] least violation [illegible] oath to Saul. None of [illegible] persons [illegible] was capable of succeeding Saul [illegible] were alive. Now [illegible] Mephibosheth [illegible] Jonathan's eldest son [illegible] David [illegible] enough to [illegible] have children and indeed had [illegible] whom [illegible] numerous posterity [illegible] whole (sons and grandsons included) to not less than [illegible] This was undoubtedly [illegible] that [illegible] oath to Saul [illegible] with the Gibeonites but on the contrary [illegible] the [illegible] project [illegible] preserving it.

(b) The sacred [illegible] Rizpah knew of this [illegible] a tent [illegible] near the place in which she [illegible] kept watch [illegible] to prevent the birds and beasts from doing any [illegible] to the [illegible] David was informed of her pious care [illegible] removed [illegible] the bones of Saul and Jonathan his son (which had been [illegible] at Jabesh Gilead) and together with these seven [illegible] gave them an honourable interment in the sepulchre of [illegible] the father of Saul at Zelah in the country of Benjamin.

(c) The [illegible] of David [illegible] in the scripture [illegible] the light of Israel. 2 Sam. xxi. [illegible] Good kings are [illegible] call [illegible] light of the people [illegible] 39) because [illegible] the comfort and safety [illegible] of a people [illegible] good kings.

he wrested his spear from his hands, and killed him with his own weapon. But he performed another atchievement still more extraordinary than the former. A lion had fallen into a pit, from whence he could not extricate himself, and there being at the same time a deep snow, the mouth of the pit (being narrow) was almost closed, which occasioned the lion to set up a most hedious roar. Benaiah directed by the noise, went to the place, and immediately descended into the pit, struck the lion with his club, and killed him.

Such were the exploits performed by these five champions, and the other thirty-two were no less distinguished for their military prowess.

David, whatever was the occasion of it, suddenly took it into his head that he would know the number of his people, forgetting the command of Moses, who had said, that, on such occasions, there should be an oblation of half a shekel by the head offered to the Lord. He accordingly gave orders to his chief officers to go through the whole kingdom, and bring him an account of all the people. Joab endeavoured to remonstrate against it in a manner more modest than was customary with him; but the king's orders were positive, upon which Joab with other officers to assist him, began on the east side of the river Jordan, went round by the other parts of Canaan, and returned to Jerusalem at the end of nine months and twenty days. By the estimate he brought there appeared to be 800,000 men fit to bear arms, and 500,000 in the tribe of Judah only, exclusive of the tribes of Levi and Benjamin, whom he had not numbered.

David had no sooner received the account than his heart misgave him. He knew he had offended the Almighty in what he had done, and intreated pardon by the most fervent prayers and supplication. Soon after the Prophet Gad was sent to him with an offer of three things for his choice, namely, a seven years famine, a persecution from his enemies for three months, or a pestilence for three days. The choice of such great evils exceedingly perplexed and confounded David. "If (says he) I choose the famine, it will appear as if I had more "care for myself than my people, as it is very unlikely "I should be distressed for the want of bread. If I "choose a course of unsuccessful battles with the ene-"my, it will appear the same, having strong holds and "castles to which I can fly for safety. But for the last, "it is a calamity common as well to kings as subjects, "and which strikes terror into all without distinction. "I had rather fall into the hands of God, than those of "our enemies." David having made choice of the pestilence, God was pleased to send it immediately among the people, and it raged with such irresistible violence that in a very short time it took off no less than 70,000 souls. It began in the extreme part of the kingdom, and made hasty advances towards Jerusalem, which, when the king and the inhabitants heard, they cloathed themselves in sackcloth, and, with all humility, cried unto God for mercy.

A little before the offering up of the evening sacrifice, there appeared an angel (*a*) over Jerusalem, brandishing a flaming sword, as if going to destroy it, upon which David exclaimed, "Lord punish the shepherd but pre-"serve the sheep; pour down thy wrath on me and my "family, but let me beseech thee to spare the innocent "people, for 'tis I alone who have offended thee." The Almighty was pleased to listen to his prayers, by immediately putting a stop to the pestilence. He also ordered David by the mouth of the prophet Gad, to go, without delay to the thrashing floor of Araunah, the Jebusite, there to erect an altar and offer up sacrifices. David obeyed the Divine commands, and when he came to the place found Araunah thrashing his corn, who no sooner saw David than he ran to meet him, and after paying reverence, asked him why he came there, and what commands he had for his servant. "I came (says "David) to purchase your thrashing floor, in order to "raise an altar on it, and to offer sacrifices to God." Araunah replied, "Not only my thrashing floor, but all "that I have is at my lord's service gratis; and I humbly "beseech God, that he will be pleased to accept your sa-"crifice." David thanked him for his generous offers, but told him he could not accept of them, for that it must be a purchase and not a gift, as it would not be right to offer a sacrifice at the expence of another. He therefore gave him fifty shekels of silver for the thrashing floor and for the oxen, and immediately offered up sacrifices to God, who, in consequence thereof, was pleased to reinstate him in his favour. This was the place where Abraham brought his son Isaac to sacrifice, but just as he was about to commit the deed, there suddenly appeared a ram which he took, and sacrificed instead of his son.

David was so happy in the thoughts of his prayers being received by the Almighty, and his sacrifices accepted, that, as a memento he called the whole place *The Altar of the People*, and resolved to build a temple on it to the honour of God. This was agreeable to what was afterwards predicted by the Almighty, who sent his prophet to tell David, that a temple should be built in that place by his son, who should succeed him in the government of Israel. In consequence of this prediction he thought no time could not be better employed than in making the necessary preparations for so great a work. He therefore appointed people to take an account of all the strangers in his dominions, the number of whom, upon their return given, amounted to one hundred and eighty thousand. Of these he appointed eighty thousand to be hewers of stone, and the rest to be labourers, except three thousand five hundred, who were to act as superintendants over the rest. He likewise got together great quantities of iron, brass, and cedar wood, the latter of which, by his particular request, was sent him from Tyre and Sidon. When his friends asked him the cause of his gathering together all these materials, he told them, they were to be by till his son should have occasion for them in building the temple, when it would both save time, and be the means of expediting the work; for as yet he was too young and unexperienced to enter upon so important an undertaking.

CHAP. XI.

David gives Solomon orders for the building of a temple [illegible] declares him his successor. His schemes are frustrated. David causes Solomon to be anointed king. Address to the people and his son Solomon, who is declared king a second time.

SOME time after this David summoned together the princes of the respective tribes, accompanied by his son Solomon, to the latter of whom he gave a strict charge that, as soon as he came to the throne, he would immediately enter upon the building of a temple to the honour and worship of God. "I would have done it (says he) my-"self, but being frequently in war and consequently pol-"luted with blood, I was expressly forbidden by the Di-"vine command, and the work reserved for you, my son, "whom God has predicted shall succeed me in the king-"dom. Let me, therefore, beseech you, since the Al-"mighty, even before you was born, designed you to be "king, to endeavour to behave yourself in all things wor-"thy of his Providence, by strictly observing piety, jus-"tice and fortitude. Keep his commandments and laws "as taught us by Moses, and suffer not others to trans-"gress them. As to the temple, which God has ap-"pointed you to build in your reign, I beg you will at-"tend to it with the greatest diligence, and not be in the

(*a*) The [illegible] [illegible] was [illegible] [illegible] [illegible] good [illegible] repentance of [illegible] [illegible] [illegible] that God [illegible] [illegible] upon his [illegible] people [illegible]

"least dispirited at the importance of the undertaking, "for it shall be my care to have all the materials in readiness against you succeed to the government. I have already laid up ten thousand talents of gold, and an hundred thousand of silver; but of brass and iron a quantity not to be summed; and of wood and stone an immense store; besides which I have engaged many thousands of carpenters and masons, whom you can readily supply with all necessaries. Attend therefore, diligently to your business, the performing of which will be so acceptable to God, that he will be your perpetual protector; you will live happy, and die in peace." Having said this, he exhorted the princes of the tribes to assist his son in the undertaking, and to be particularly attentive to their religious duties, in doing which they would be rewarded with the fruits of peace, and a happy administration. He desired, that when the temple was finished, they would place the ark therein, and all the sacred vessels belonging to it, for the reception of which, he said, a temple ought to have been built long ago, if their forefathers had not neglected the commands of God when they first got possession of that country. These last exhortations David gave not only to his son, but also to the princes.

Though David was at this time only seventy years of age, yet he became very infirm, and was afflicted with a disease, resembling the dead palsy, which so chilled his blood that he could not be kept warm, more especially in his bed. In consequence of this a consultation was held among the physicians, who advised that, to supply him with natural heat, a virgin should lie in the same bed with him. Accordingly, one Abishag, a young and beautiful woman of Shunam, belonging to the tribe of Issachar, was brought to him as a mistress or concubinary wife; but David had never any carnal knowledge of her, being, from his infirmities, incapable of possessing connubial enjoyments.

David, being now grown almost inactive from natural infirmities, Adonijah, who (next to Absalom) was his eldest son, taking advantage of his imperfections, entertained thoughts of ascending the throne, on a presumption that his father either could not, or would not obstruct him. He was indeed, a prince of exquisite beauty, greatly admired by the people, and particularly indulged (a) by his father. He was much of the same disposition as his brother, and followed the same measures, having set up a pompous equipage, retained a prodigious number of attendants, and lived in the most sumptuous manner.

Adonijah had got over to his party Joab, the general of the forces, and Abiathar, the high-priest, by whose advice he invited all his brothers (except Solomon) and all the great men of Judah, (except Nathan, the prophet, Benaiah, captain of the guards, and the officers of the army, who, with Zadock, the priest, were not for him) to a sumptuous entertainment, the design of which was, as soon as the company began to be merry, to proclaim him king.

Nathan the prophet, who knew God's designation, and David's concern for the people's interest, having received intelligence of the meeting appointed by Adonijah, gave information of it to Bathsheba, strongly advising her to go to the king and put him in mind, in the most urgent manner, to name his ten years Solomon his successor: things being come to such an extremity, as to threaten them with imminent danger.

Bathsheba, taking Nathan's advice, immediately repaired to the king, and having acquainted him with Adonijah's conspiracy, besought him to name her son Solomon his successor, agreeable to the promise he had formerly made, and ratified with an oath. While she was with the king, Nathan entered the apartment, and confirmed all she had said relative to the conspiracy. In consequence of this David immediately declared Solomon his successor, and commanded Zadock the priest, Nathan the prophet, and Benaiah, the captain of his guards, with the other officers and ministers of state, to mount him on the mule (b) he was accustomed to ride himself, and having in this manner conducted him to Gihon, Zadock and Nathan should anoint him with holy oil, after which, by sound of trumpet, they should proclaim him king. All this was accordingly done, after which Solomon was conducted back to Jerusalem amidst the acclamations of the people.

When Adonijah and his company heard of these proceedings (which was at the time they were at the point of proclaiming him king) they were thrown into the utmost confusion. In dread of the consequences that might ensue, the company instantly dispersed, and the unhappy Adonijah, their leader, fled to the altar for sanctuary, where he continued for protection till having obtained of Solomon a promise of life, on condition that he would never make any future attempt against his government, he was admitted into the king's presence, where he made his obedience to Solomon, in token of thankfulness for his pardon, and acknowledgment of his superiority.

David, thinking the inauguration of Solomon had been too hasty and private, determined to have it repeated in a more public manner, in the city of Jerusalem. On this occasion he summoned all the princes of the tribes, together with the priests and Levites, among whom, on examination, there appeared to be 38,000 from thirty to fifty years of age. Out of these he appointed 24,000 to attend the building of the temple, 6,000 as judges over the people, 4,000 as porters to the house of God, and as many chanters to attend Divine service, and play on the instruments he had made for the purpose. Then he divided into families, and, on separating the priests, from the rest of the tribes, found them to consist of twenty-four, sixteen descended from Eleazar, and eight from Ithamar. He appointed that each ticket should attend for a certain days, that is from Sabbath to Sabbath. The lots of the whole were cast in the presence of David, Zadock and Abiathar, the priests, and the heads of the tribes. That lot that came out first took the precedence, and the rest in their turns as they happened to be drawn. He also divided the tribe of Levi into twenty-four parts, or classes, who, by lot, were to attend the priests in the performance of religious duties. But the greatest honour he conferred on the posterity of Moses, to whom he committed the trust of the holy treasures, and the donations that might arise from royal benefactions.

After this he divided his whole army into twenty-four parts, with their captains, centurions, and tribunes. Each division consisted of 24,000 men, who, in their turns, were to guard king Solomon thirty days together, attended by their centurions and tribunes; and over each division was placed an officer, a man of probity and integrity, as a judge, to administer justice. He likewise appointed [illegible] over the king's treasury, vineyards, [illegible], flocks, herds, &c.

Having made these regulations, David called together an assembly of the magistrates, princes of the tribes, the officers of the army, and those who had the care of the revenue; when, placing himself on an eminence, he addressed them as follows:

"Brothers, and countrymen,

"The reason of my having called you together is to inform you of my ardent desire that a temple should be erect-

(a) [illegible]

(b) In the [illegible] it was a capital offence [illegible] upon [illegible] the king [illegible] the throne [illegible] was [illegible] in the [illegible] chapter of [illegible] of Esther.

ed to the honour of God, for the doing of which I have laid up great quantities both of gold and silver. God by the prophet Nathan has forbid me doing it myself on account of my having embrued my hands in the blood of your enemies, and he has appointed my son and successor to execute it in my stead. Now, since you know our forefather Jacob had twelve sons, and Judah was appointed king over them, and that I, having five brothers, was preferred to them, and received the kingdom at the hands of God, to their satisfaction, I therefore entreat my sons not to be concerned in any rebellion against Solomon, who now receives the government, but to believe God chose him to be king, and on that account, with pleasure, pay obedience to his authority. If God had been pleased that a stranger should have enjoyed the chief command, it would have been the duty of every one of you, to have owned him allegiance to him, but now a brother of yours is raised to that high pinnacle of honour, how great ought to be your joy at so happy an appointment! My prayer is, that the promises God has vouchsafed to make, may have the desired effect, and that the peace [illegible] under the reign of Solomon my son. (Then David, addressing himself to Solomon, said) These [illegible] confirmed to you, if you lead a holy life, continue to enforce the laws of your country; but if you do not, you will become miserable, and die [illegible]."

When David had finished his speech, he gave his son, in the presence of all the people, a plan of the intended temple, the foundation and superstructure of it, the height and breadth, the number of private cells, with [illegible], and how many vessels should be provided of gold and silver, with the precise weight of each, after which he exhorted him to undertake the building with the utmost cheerfulness. He then desired the princes of the tribe of Levi to give them assistance in the undertaking, not only in regard to his son's youth and inexperience, but [illegible]. He told them the work could not be attended with any great [illegible], he having already provided many talents of gold, but still more of silver, great store of wood, emeralds, and all other kinds of precious stones, with a prodigious number of masons, carpenters, and other workmen. "I have likewise, (says he) reserved 3000 talents "of the purest gold out of my own store, for adorning "the holy place, and the chariot of God, that is, the ark, "which is to be ornamented with a cherub at each end, "whose expanded wings will cover the [illegible]."

As soon as David had done speaking, not only the princes and priests, but likewise the whole multitude, showed their zeal for promoting the work, every one contributing something in proportion to their circumstances. They likewise promised to contribute 10,000 talents of gold, as many of silver, and the like number of shekels. In short, so great was the zeal of the people for having the work completed, that if any person had in his possession a precious stone, he brought it to David to be put into the treasury, the care of which was entrusted to one Jalus, a descendant of Moses.

David was so pleased at this great readiness of the people to facilitate the work, that he offered up his prayers to God on the occasion, calling him the Father and Creator of the universe, the Maker of all things both divine and human, the protector of the Hebrew nation, and the fountain of all that happy and peaceable government they had so long enjoyed. He then wished all happiness to the people in future, and commanded them to offer up their praises to God. They immediately obeyed his commands, fell on the ground and worshipped, after which they unanimously returned their thanks to David for the great benefits they had received under his administration.

The next day (after offering up sacrifices in abundance) Solomon was again anointed, and acknowledged by all the people, their lawful king. He was afterwards conducted to the palace, and placed on his father's throne, from which time the people paid him their true allegiance. Zadock, by the general voice of the people, was declared high-priest, in the room of Abiathar, who had publicly espoused the interest of Adonijah.

CHAP. XII.

David's last charge to his son Solomon. His death and burial.

A SHORT time after this, David perceiving his dissolution was near at hand, called for his son Solomon, and gave him this his last exhortation. "I am "now (says he) going a journey common to all, but to a "place from whence no traveller returns. Wherefore, "while I am yet living, let me remind you of those things "I have before said to you, namely, that you exercise "your authority with justice over your subjects, humbly "obey God, who has been pleased to bestow the government on you, and carefully to observe those laws and "commandments which he has transmitted to you from "our great legislator Moses. Be careful that you are not "induced to violate these injunctions, either from the "flatteries of your courtiers, your own corrupt desires, "or any other cause whatever. If you do, be assured "your great and Divine Protector will immediately forsake you; whereas, on the contrary, if you behave "yourself towards him as you ought, and as I most sincerely wish, you will confirm the kingdom to your posterity; no other house but ours will sway the sceptre "of the Hebrews; but it will be continued to you and "yours for ever. Forget not the crimes of Joab, who, "through jealousy put to death two just and faithful generals, namely, Abner, the son of Ner, and Amasa, the "son of Jether; punish him for their deaths, as you shall "think fit; for being more powerful than myself, he has "hitherto escaped the threats of justice. I beseech you "to do all the good offices you can for the sons of Barzillai, the Gileadite, not under the light of an obligation, but as an acknowledgment for the great benefits I "received from their father during my banishment, "which I reckon as a debt incumbent on our whole family to discharge. As for Shimei, the Benjamite, who "reviled me in the days of my persecution, and whom "I afterwards pardoned, you may act with him as you "think proper, but I would not have him escape unpunished." (a)

A short time after David had delivered this exhortation to his son, he gave up the ghost, in the

(a) The substance of the two charges given by David to his son Solomon [illegible] relating to Joab and Shimei [illegible]. Speaking of Joab he says, "Thou knowest what Joab did unto me, with [illegible] against Absalom, how [illegible] and afterward talk [illegible] what he did to [illegible] when I [illegible] to [illegible] the [illegible] forces [illegible] that to Abner who [illegible] of Saul. The injury done to these [illegible] both under my protection [illegible] murdered, basely murdered [illegible] [illegible] murder [illegible] [illegible] [illegible]

"[illegible] against them; let the blood of these two valuable men be charged to his "account, and let him as he has long deserved be put to death."
Speaking of Shimei he says, "Thou hast Shimei with thee [illegible] "perhaps he may have [illegible] not. He is no friend to "kings or kingly power. Remember what he did to me in my distress, how bitterly [illegible] he cursed me to my face, and I make no doubt but this he would do [illegible] to thee in the like circumstances. I forgave him [illegible] because I looked upon him [illegible] instrument in God's hands [illegible] "[illegible] offence. I forgave him [illegible] because he came to me "when my heart was open, and unwilling to damp the joy of my restoration with the effusion of his blood, I promised him his life, and kept that "promise [illegible] my days; but what I did [illegible] obligation to "[illegible], for his offence against me [illegible]

[illegible]1st year of his age, and 40th of his [illegible], [illegible] of which he governed in Hebron, and thirty-[illegible] in Jerusalem (a)

He was a man of most distinguished courage, and possessed all the qualities necessary for the forming of a great king He was temperate, meek, bountiful, [illegible], and never stained the greatness of his [illegible] instance, except in the case of Uriah's wife [illegible] greater treasure behind him than had been done by any of his predecessors, and the purposes to which he [illegible] the greatest part of it rendered his name immortal (b)

He was buried at Jerusalem with great pomp and magnificence, and his son Solomon deposited [illegible] monument an inestimable treasure Some idea may be formed of the great riches Solomon deposited in his father's tomb from the following circumstances

[illegible] Antiochus, [illegible] the Pius, the son of Demetrius [illegible] to Jerusalem Hyrcanus, the high-[illegible] offered him [illegible] if he would raise the siege, and [illegible] The proposal was accepted by Antiochus [illegible] Hyrcanus [illegible] other method of fulfilling the [illegible], but [illegible] David's tomb, from whence he took 3000 talents of gold, with part of which he paid the sum agreed on, and Antiochus [illegible] raised the siege

Many years after [illegible] king Herod opened another part of David's tomb, from whence he took treasure [illegible], of which we shall speak more at large in the [illegible] book of this work

---

[illegible] he should [illegible] to give [illegible] occasion [illegible] to lay hold of it [illegible] in his nature [illegible] good [illegible]

(a) David was buried with great pomp in that part of the city of Jerusalem which [illegible] had taken from the Jebusites and [illegible] after his own name The City of David His sepulchre was [illegible] the Jews [illegible] in being in St Peter's time, for he tells the people [illegible] 29 [illegible] Adrian [illegible] part of it was fallen [illegible] the emperor Adrian's reign Modern travellers [illegible] some [illegible] in a rock not far [illegible] Jerusalem [illegible] are doubtless [illegible] but they do not agree that they are the sepulchres of the kings [illegible] It is however somewhat strange that the place of David's sepulchre (which both the Chaldeans and Romans when they took Jerusalem thought proper to [illegible] should now be so entirely lost that [illegible] not the least traces of it have been to be found But though Providence has so ordered it that the place of David's sepulchre [illegible] not be known yet [illegible] does not [illegible] an eternal monument [illegible] most excellent [illegible] The book of Psalms which for the most part was composed by him doth publish the glory of its author more than the most pompous [illegible] and the son of Sirach has consecrated an epitaph to his memory which will [illegible] when brass and marble shall be no more "As the fat [illegible] (says he) is taken away from the peace offering so was David chosen from the people of Israel He played with lions as with kids, and with bears as [illegible] lambs He slew a giant when he was young and took away reproach from the people, for he called upon the Most High Lord and he gave him strength to his right hand [illegible] warrior and to set [illegible] people So the [illegible] honoured him with [illegible] and praised him in [illegible] the Lord, for he destroyed the enemies [illegible] and brought to nought the Philistines his adversaries In all his works he praised the Holy One Most High and [illegible] the Lord with words of glory [illegible] singers also before the altar [illegible] they might [illegible] sweet melody [illegible] songs [illegible] the beauty [illegible] their solemn [illegible] The Lord took away his sins and exalted his horn for ever He gave him a covenant of kings and a throne of glory in Israel"—Ecclesiasticus chap [illegible] &c

(b) A very learned and celebrated writer [illegible] the character of [illegible] and says that as there was no [illegible] singular translations that to give it in a compass suited to [illegible] readers would not be to do him that justice his great [illegible] He then proceeds to relate the principal incidents that occurred from [illegible] country popular to the period that produced its dissolution, and concludes with the following noble variation "Such (says he) are the outlines of a Jewish [illegible] [illegible] God's [illegible] God himself called to be king over Israel [illegible] the purpose for which God raised him [illegible] he established the throne, with whom he made an everlasting covenant, and who was the great progenitor of the Messiah himself who is to reign over all, and shall [illegible] feet"

END OF THE SEVENTH BOOK

FLAVIUS JOSEPHUS

ON THE

ANTIQUITIES

OF THE

JEWS.

BOOK VIII.

[INCLUDING A PERIOD OF ABOUT ONE HUNDRED AND SEVENTEEN YEARS.]

CHAP. I.

Solomon succeeds his father on the throne of Israel. Adonijah concerts a scheme for dispossessing him. He is assisted by his brother, Joab, and Shimei. Solomon detects the scheme, and avenges himself on the authors.

THE virtues and prowess of king David, with the singular benefits his subjects derived from him, considered both as a statesman and warrior, during an auspicious reign, have been fully treated of in the foregoing book.

On his demise his son Solomon, who had been by him declared king of Israel, assumed the reins of government amidst the joyful acclamations of the people. He received, upon the occasion, the congratulatory addresses of the heads of all the tribes, with their earnest wishes that he might [illegible] and happily.

Solomon, however, was no sooner [illegible] on the throne, than a circumstance occurred, which, though disagreeable, laid him under a necessity of putting into execution the commands of his dying father. Adonijah, his elder brother, who during the life of David made several [illegible] attempts to gain possession of the regal authority, [illegible] to Bathsheba, the king's mother, and [illegible] those [illegible] which [illegible] of effect. When he perceived that she was rendered complacent by his [illegible], he intimated "That though the crown was his right by seniority, as [illegible] the will of the people, yet as it was transferred to Solomon, her son, according to the Divine pleasure, he was contented to act [illegible] him, [illegible] perfectly satisfied with his present station, that he had only to request of her that she would use her interest with her son to obtain the royal consent to his taking Abishag to wife." Bathsheba immediately promised to comply with his request, and encouraged him to hope for a joyful event, persuaded, that her son would hardly refuse the joint petitions of two of his nearest relatives, in a matter of such importance as the present. She accordingly repaired to the king upon the subject of Adonijah's request. Solomon received his mother [illegible], token of duty and affection, conducted her into the palace, and placed her on a throne at his right hand. When she was seated, she entered upon the business, and [illegible] that she had a suit to proffer, which, if he should refuse, would affect her in the most sensible manner. Solomon in the most [illegible] terms, desired her to lay her commands upon him, as it was his duty to grant whatever she should ask. Without farther ceremony she then [illegible] with him for his [illegible] upon that his brother Adonijah might take Abishag to wife.

The king, [illegible] at the subject of her request, dismissed his mother abruptly, observing, "that Adonijah had aspiring views, that he might have been more explicit, and requested of him the resignation of the kingdom to him upon the claim of seniority, and especially as he had [illegible] powerful friends as Joab, the general, and Abiathar the high priest, to back his pretensions." To frustrate at once his [illegible] ambitious designs, he sent for Benaiah, the captain of the guards, and commanded him to put Adonijah to death (7). Summoning Abiathar, the high-priest, he told him, "That although his crime [illegible]

(a) [illegible]

[illegible]

[illegible] behaviour [illegible] he would spare his life in consideration of the [illegible] he had [illegible] his royal father, and [illegible] the assistance he afforded in bringing back the ark; but that as for his punishment, he should be [illegible] and deprived of the dignity of the high-priesthood, [illegible] had rendered himself [illegible] of that sacred function." [illegible] ver- [illegible] man [illegible] been [illegible] [illegible] of [illegible] the [illegible] there, [illegible] the [illegible] him, [illegible] the [illegible]

[illegible] the- [illegible] ap- [illegible] commanded [illegible] there, [illegible] and [illegible] given [illegible] death of [illegible] his com[illegible] [illegible] high-priest.

[illegible] that he should [illegible] to that [illegible] death [illegible] with a [illegible] [illegible] country, [illegible] [illegible] thou [illegible] [illegible] to death [illegible]

CHAP. I[illegible]

[illegible] of Egypt [illegible]

SOLOMON [illegible] throne, [illegible]

himself to his friends took to wife the daughter of the king of Egypt. His next concern was to enclose the walls of Jerusalem upon a more extensive and defensible plan than the former; after which he applied himself to the administration of public justice. Nor [illegible] in the execution of his duty as king, respecting either the awarding of justice, the enforcing of the laws, or the fulfilment, with religious reverence, he commands laid upon him by his venerable father in his dying moments. [illegible] conduct was such in general, as might have become the gravity and judgment of an old and experienced monarch.

In the interval of profound peace both at home and abroad, he resolved to go to Hebron, to sacrifice to God upon the brazen altar that was erected by Moses, [illegible] of the many mercies he had re[illegible] pared [illegible] and offered a thousand [illegible] offering. This [illegible] instance of [illegible] pleasing in the sight of the Almighty, [illegible] in a dream the following night, and [illegible] of him some gifts he was ready to bestow, [illegible] his dutiful and grateful regard. Solomon [illegible] was most excellent in itself, what the bountiful [illegible] bestow with the greatest approbation, and what was most [illegible] table for man to receive. He did not desire [illegible] silver, [illegible] or those gratifications, [illegible] and young persons in [illegible] the [illegible] On the contrary his petition [illegible] "O Lord [illegible] and a good [illegible] "may judge the people according to [illegible]" This [illegible] so acceptable to the Almighty [illegible] [illegible] When Solomon [illegible] [illegible] from his bed, [illegible] [illegible] to Jerusalem [illegible] [illegible] all the [illegible]

[illegible] brought before him to [illegible] think it [illegible] to [illegible] that the reader may [illegible] judgment [illegible] and rectitude, and that [illegible] example, in points which affect the [illegible]

Two harlots applied to him for justice. The [illegible] related her tale in words to this purport: "This woman, O "king, and I dwell together in one house. [illegible] "son at the same hour. On the third day this woman a- "gainst whom I prefer my complaint [illegible] "[illegible] then taking mine to herself [illegible] asleep, [illegible] "[illegible] son in my arms. Being desirous, in the mor- "ning, of giving the infant the breast, I found it [illegible] "[illegible] persuaded that it was this [illegible] dead [illegible] "I demanded my own, but not [illegible] "had recourse to my lord the king for justice. For [illegible] "were alone, and there is no evidence to convict her, she "obstinately perseveres in a denial of the fact."

When this woman had finished her tale, the king commanded the other what she had to say in her defence. Upon her denial of the charge [illegible] against her, and affirming that her child was living, and that of her opponent dead, and none present being able to decide the point in controversy, the king devised the following method of discovering the merits of the cause. He ordered both the dead and living child to be brought in, then commanded one of his guards to [illegible] sword, and cut both the children in halves, that each of the women might have half the living and half the dead child. This was deemed a trifling [illegible] at first, but [illegible] the real mother of the living child [illegible] against it, and consent that the child should be delivered to the other woman as her own, declaring she would be satisfied with the life of the child, and with the sight of it, [illegible] the other. The other woman [illegible] to the judgment, and was ready to see the child divided, [illegible] the [illegible] mother.

tormented. Now the king wisely, inferring that the respective behaviour, upon the occasion, was from the impulse of their passions, adjudged the child to her who cried out to save it, as the real mother, and condemned the other as a wicked woman, who had not only killed her own child, but was endeavouring to destroy that of her friend (a). This determination was applauded by the multitude as an evident token of the king's extraordinary sagacity, and they ever after looked on him as a prince endowed with a Divine understanding.

Solomon's great officers were the following: Uri, the son of Hur, presided over the tribe of Ephraim, including Bethlehem. Aminadab, who married the king's daughter, had the region of Dora and the sea coast under him. The great plain was under Benaiah, the son of [illegible]. He also governed all the country as far as the [illegible] Jordan. Gabaris, the son of Geber, ruled over Gilead and Gaulanitis, as far as mount Libanus, and had under him sixty large and well fortified cities. Ahinadab, who married another of Solomon's daughters, directed the affairs of Galilee [illegible] to Sidon. Baanah had the sea coast about Arce. The mountains Tabor and Carmel, and all the Lower Galilee to the farther side of Jordan, was under the command of Jehoshaphat, as was the whole country of the Benjamites under that of Shimei. And Tabar governed the country beyond Jordan. These governors were all under the superintendance of one [illegible].

The Hebrew nation, and particularly the tribe of Judah, [illegible] now in a flourishing condition, for as they enjoyed [illegible] the blessings of peace and liberty, unmolested by the distractions and tumults of war, they applied themselves to [illegible] and other arts, and by these means advanced both their fame and [illegible].

The king had likewise other rulers, who were over the land of Syria, and other barbarous parts between Egypt and Euphrates, and these collected the receipts from the [illegible]. These people contributed [illegible] the daily supply of the king's table thirty measures of meal, ten fat oxen, twenty [illegible] oxen [illegible], an hundred fat lambs, besides deer, birds, [illegible] and other sporting productions. He had [illegible] a number of chariots, that there were forty thousand stalls provided for the horses that belonged to them, besides twelve thousand horsemen, that were his guards, the half of which were quartered at Jerusalem near his person, and the other half distributed throughout the villages adjacent to the city. The same officer who superintended the supply of the king's table was [illegible] for the [illegible].

The wisdom and knowledge of Solomon were so great, that he exceeded the ancients, in [illegible] the Ethiopians, and was infinitely superior to the Egyptians, who were reputed to be the most accomplished people of their age. He also excelled the most celebrated of his country men and cotemporaries; those were Ethan, Heman, Calcol, and Dodan, the sons of Mahol. He composed fifteen hundred books of poems, and three thousand of parables and [illegible] multitudes. He wrote an history of plants, from the cedar to the hyssop, as also of beasts, and living creatures in general, [illegible] a consummate natural philosopher, and [illegible] perfectly acquainted with their respective properties [illegible] adapted the universal knowledge with which God had favoured him to the good of mankind, according to particular exigencies. He composed incantations [illegible] cure of diseases, and left behind him a prescribed method for the expelling of demons, and this method [illegible] force even at this day. I [illegible] one Eleazar [illegible] the presence of Vespasian, his son, his officers, and a [illegible] of his soldiers, dispossessing people of demoniacal [illegible]. This was his method: he put a ring, that had a root of one of those sorts prescribed by Solomon, to the nostrils of the person possessed, which, by the smell, [illegible] the expulsion of the demon, when Eleazar, reciting the name and incantations of Solomon, adjured it never to [illegible] him more. Eleazar, in order to demonstrate he [illegible] had such a power, placed a cup of water [illegible] from a man who was possessed, and adjured the demon on his leaving the man, to overturn it, and thereby [illegible] it known to the spectators that he had quitted him. [illegible] proved the extraordinary abilities of Solomon, to [illegible] which I have inserted this narrative.

When Hiram, king of Tyre, who had lived in friendship with the king of Israel, heard of Solomon's accession to the throne on the demise of his father, he sent ambassadors to congratulate him on the occasion. Solomon, on their return, sent an epistle to Hiram couched in the following terms:

"Solomon to Hiram greeting,

"Be it known unto thee, O king, that David, my father, would have built a temple to God, but being, during the whole course of his reign, engaged in wars, [illegible] subduing his enemies, he could not [illegible] execute his design, and therefore left it to me to accomplish in a time of peace and tranquillity, according to the Divine prediction. That time I shall now dedicate to that solemn and important purpose. Therefore I make it my earnest request that thou wilt send some of thy subjects with mine to mount Libanus, to assist in cutting down timber, in which the Sidonians are more skilful than our people. Their wages shall be paid [illegible] such a rate as thou shalt determine."

Solomon's epistle was highly approved by Hiram, who returned him this answer:

"Hiram to king Solomon greeting,

"Nothing could have been more grateful to me than to hear that the crown of your excellent father has devolved [illegible] through Divine Providence to so wise and virtuous a successor. Your desire shall be punctually and cheerfully complied with. I will issue my command for the cutting down and exportation of such quantities of the finest cedars and cypress trees as thou mayest require. My subjects shall bring them to the sea side, and ship them away to what port thou pleasest, in order that thy subjects may transport them to Jerusalem. In exchange thou wilt supply us with corn, of which commodity we islanders stand much in need."

Copies of these epistles remain to this day, being preserved not only in our books, but the Tyrian [illegible]

(a) [illegible]

[illegible]

King SOLOMON *building the* TEMPLE *of Jer*

[illegible] so that, [illegible] may apply to the [illegible], which will be full confirmation [illegible] refer the reader to this proof [illegible] of the charge of stating any thing but matter [illegible] history of subjects doubtful and [illegible] at the same [illegible] centers in our endeavouring [illegible], no considera- [illegible] so that we desire nothing that we [illegible], unless we appear able to demonstrate [illegible] the most [illegible] authority.

[illegible] pleased with the urgent [illegible] and thank [illegible] the king of Tyre, in token of which he ordered [illegible] present of two thousand [illegible] of wheat and [illegible] two thousand [illegible] of oil, and [illegible] of wine, [illegible] each seventy-two [illegible]. This was an earnest of [illegible] between these two kings, which was daily more [illegible].

[illegible] on the temple in general, to pro- [illegible] thousand [illegible], [illegible] articles and la- [illegible] employment [illegible] by an impartial and [illegible] of time. He appointed ten thousand to [illegible] upon Mount Lebanon for the space of one month, [illegible] to be relieved by the rest for [illegible], and [illegible], by which means [illegible] were [illegible] and [illegible] in proportion [illegible]. Adoniram was appointed [illegible]. There were also [illegible], [illegible] other [illegible] eighty thousand [illegible] were [illegible] to [illegible] stones for the foundation of the temple, and have [illegible] ready to be conveyed [illegible]. Hiram's people were also employed in [illegible].

Solomon began to build the temple [illegible] year of [illegible] the second month, which the Macedonians call [illegible], the Hebrews [illegible] four hundred and eighty [illegible] out of Egypt. It was also in the reign of [illegible] and [illegible] year [illegible] city. And [illegible] different [illegible] time [illegible] in last time, [illegible] of [illegible] the famous [illegible] temple of Diana in the city of Ephesus.

[illegible] of the temple was laid [illegible], and the [illegible] were such as would resist the [illegible] and other [illegible]. [illegible] and [illegible] to become a base for the superstructure to be [illegible]. [illegible] from the ground to the roof. The height and length were each sixty cubits, and the breadth twenty. [illegible] of the same dimensions, [illegible] entire [illegible] of the temple [illegible] hundred [illegible] cubits, [illegible] to the east. The porch, [illegible] entrance, [illegible] cubits in length, ten in breadth, [illegible] and twenty in height. [illegible] round about the temple [illegible] rooms, [illegible] each of these rooms was [illegible] in length and breadth, and in height twenty [illegible] two other floors, [illegible] altogether to the lower part of the [illegible], [illegible] raised no higher than the top of the [illegible]. The roof, that covered [illegible] of [illegible] every partition had its peculiar roof, [illegible] but they were all fastened together [illegible], so that they appeared [illegible] beams were [illegible] of [illegible] and [illegible] whole [illegible] ornamented, that [illegible] dazzled the eye of the beholder. The whole [illegible] of the temple was of the finest stone, [illegible] [illegible] [illegible] [illegible]

effect of Providence and nature, than the production of art or human invention. The king had an admirable contrivance for an ascent to the upper part, which was by winding stairs, cut through the thickness of the wall, for the second story had not a large door at the east end, as the lower had. The inside of the temple was lined with cedar, and the junction of the beams by iron-work added great strength to the building.

Solomon caused the temple to be divided into two parts, that is, the inner part or *Holy of Holies*, of twenty cubits square, which was inaccessible, and the other of forty cubits, which was assigned to the use of the priests. In the partition-wall betwixt the inner and outer part of the temple, were large cedar doors, superbly gilded and elegantly carved. There were also veils of different colours, beautiful, interwoven with variegated flowers, to be drawn before those doors.

[illegible] consecrated for the most holy place two cherubims of massy gold. They were each five cubits high, and had two wings stretched out to the same extent, so that with one wing they might touch the south side, and with the other the north. With the other two wings they overspread the ark, that was placed between them.

The very floor of the temple was overlaid with gold; in a word, there was no part, internal or external, that was not covered with gold, nor was there any thing wanting that could contribute to its splendour and magnificence.

The king sent for an eminent artificer from Tyre, whose name was Chiram. His mother was of the tribe of Naphtali, and his father, by extraction, an Israelite. This man's chief skill lay in working in gold, silver, and other metals. He was, therefore, employed in the most curious piece of mechanism about the temple, according to the direction of Solomon. He cast two brazen hollow pillars four fingers thick in the metal, eighteen cubits in height and twelve in circumference. Two chapiters of brass on the tops of the two pillars, five cubits each. These were covered with a kind of brass net-work, and below them were flowers, or lily-work, of the same contrivance, with two rows of pomegranates hanging down, an hundred in each row. One of these pillars was placed at the entrance of the porch on the right-hand, and called Jachin, the other on the left, and called Boaz.

Solomon also caused this artificer to make a brazen sea, the figure of which resembled an hemisphere. This vessel was also called a sea, from its largeness, for the laver was ten feet in diameter, and cast of the thickness of a palm. The middle rested on a stout pillar, that had ten spirals round it, and that pillar was a cubit in diameter. Around it were placed the figures of twelve oxen facing, by three and three, the four cardinal points north, east, west and south. This brazen sea contained three thousand baths.

There were also made ten brazen bases for so many quadrangular lavers; the length of each of these bases was five cubits, and the height six cubits. The several pieces were cast apart, and then thus put together. There were four small quadrangular pillars, one of which stood at each corner. These had the sides of the base fitted to them; on each quarter there was a threefold partition; every interval had a border fitted to support the laver, upon which was engraven in one place a lion, and in another place a bull and an eagle. The small pillars had [illegible] engraven on the sides. The whole work was elevated, and stood upon four wheels, which were also cast, and had naves and spokes, and were a foot and an half in diameter. It was admirable to observe with what exactness the spokes of the wheels were turned and united to the sides of the bases, and, indeed, the curious manner in which the whole was wrought. This was their structure. Certain shoulders and hands stretched out held the corners, above which rested a short spiral pillar, that lay under the hollow part of the laver, resting upon the fore-feet of the eagle and the lion, which were adapted to them [illegible] would imagine they were of one piece. Between these were engravings of palm-trees. This was the construction of the ten bases.

To these bases he made ten lavers of the same metal, each containing forty baths, the height four cubits, and the diameter the same. These ten lavers were set upon as many bases, that were called *mechonoth* [illegible], were all placed in the temple; five of them on the left hand, on the north side, and the other five on the south side, on the right, looking towards the east. In the same place also was the brazen sea. They were all filled with water; the sea, for washing the hands and feet of the priests upon entering the sanctuary, and ascending the altar, and the lavers for cleansing the entrails of the beasts, and other parts of the burnt-offering.

He erected also a brazen altar, of twelve cubits in length and breadth, and ten in depth, for the service of the Holy, and [illegible] providing the same with all the necessary vessels, made of the purest brass.

The king likewise dedicated a great number of tables, and one of pure gold to the shew-bread, larger than the rest. There were many others, much inferior to that for the shew-bread, sufficient to hold twenty thousand golden vessels, and forty thousand silver ones.

He also provided twelve thousand candlesticks, according to the appointment of Moses. One of them was peculiarly dedicated to the service of the temple, to be kept burning in the day time, according to the law. The table for the shew-bread was placed on the north side, over against the candlestick, which stood on the south; but the golden altar stood between them. All these vessels were contained in the fore part of the temple, which was forty cubits long, and were before the veil of the *Holy of Holies*, where the ark of the covenant was to be kept.

There were also made pouring cups in number eighty thousand, and ten thousand golden vessels, with twice as many of silver. There were eighty thousand golden chargers, and twice as many of silver, for the sacrifice of offering [illegible] the flour at the altar. Golden measures, such as the Mosaical hin and assaron, twenty thousand, and twice as many of silver. The golden censers, in which they carried the incense to the altar, were in number twenty thousand. The other censers, in which they carried fire from the great altar to the smaller one within the temple, were fifty thousand.

The sacerdotal garments, which belonged to the high priests, with the long robes, and the oracle and the precious stones, were a thousand. [illegible] there was but one crown, upon which Moses inscribed the sacred name, one [illegible], and that hath remained to this day. There were also made ten thousand sacerdotal garments of fine linen, with purple girdles, for priests in ordinary, and two hundred thousand trumpets, according to the institution of Moses, [illegible] two hundred thousand garments for the Levites, who composed the choir. These were furnished with forty thousand musical instruments, as harps, psalteries, and the like, made of a mixed metal, between gold and silver, to accompany the voices.

These expensive and magnificent preparations were made to [illegible] the [illegible] of this mighty work, [illegible] the [illegible] of the Divine Being, nor was there any thing wanting that could express the [illegible] of the [illegible], or [illegible] that of the people in general. When the preparatory part was executed, the [illegible] articles were deposited in the sacred treasury, and [illegible] no longer use.

Round about the temple was a partition, called in the Hebrew *Gison*, [illegible] raised to the height of three cubits, in order to exclude the multitude from the place into which the priests only were to be admitted. Beyond this partition was another building, with large galleries [illegible], and four [illegible] gates, that opened each towards one of the four quarters. The doors were plated and inlaid with gold. Into this place people entered in common, [illegible] were duly outward of the laws.

[illegible] this outward building was an undertaking stupendous beyond description. There were such depths to be filled up as must strike the inclining gazer with horror. [illegible] to a level with the [illegible], [illegible] regular, and the ground level [illegible] with a double row of cloisters, supported by [illegible] the [illegible] of [illegible] were [illegible] required.

When King Solomon had finished his [illegible] [illegible] which [illegible] [illegible] in [illegible] to [illegible] of [illegible] to accomplish, he sent to the elders [illegible] tribes, to summon the people up to Jerusalem, to see the temple, and [illegible] into it [illegible] the covenant [illegible] solemnly [illegible] [illegible] feast of tabernacles [illegible] [illegible] the Hebrews [illegible] their [illegible] [illegible] [illegible], together with the vessels [illegible] lodged them in the temple [illegible] whole congregation, with the Levites, [illegible] their sacrifices and [illegible] [illegible] [illegible] blood, and [illegible] incense, till the very [illegible] most [illegible] throughout the [illegible], who [illegible] circumstance, [illegible] Presence [illegible] but [illegible] [illegible] course of the time in which they [illegible] to the [illegible].

When [illegible] to the most sacred place [illegible] [illegible] [illegible] [illegible] [illegible] [illegible] [illegible] [illegible] contained [illegible] graven upon [illegible] upon mount S[illegible] were [illegible] the [illegible] as [illegible] their [illegible] sacrifices [illegible] by order of Solomon was placed [illegible] the door, [illegible] [illegible] [illegible] the rest of the vessels were collected and deposited in the temple.

When the [illegible] was [illegible], and [illegible] with [illegible], a thick cloud hovered over [illegible] not resembling that which [illegible] [illegible] or more tempestuous [illegible] occasions, indicated the Divine Presence and [illegible], so that the present [illegible] and that [illegible] dwell amongst [illegible] temple [illegible] his service.

While the people were [illegible] upon the [illegible] before them, [illegible] [illegible] in a [illegible] [illegible] the [illegible] on. His prayer was to this effect: "[illegible] thee [illegible] [illegible] "thing [illegible] this universe, the [illegible] "the air, the earth, and the sea, [illegible] "whole, and every thing [illegible] "bounded and incomprehensible, look down [illegible] "upon thy servants, who [illegible] to erect [illegible] "ple to the honour of thy sacred Majesty, [illegible] "then, Lord, to hear our prayers, and accept our [illegible] "ons. Thou that [illegible] "from thy exalted throne [illegible] "supplications of the people [illegible] place [illegible] "ever failest to assist them [illegible] thee, [illegible] "[illegible], and afford us thy gracious [illegible]."

After this solemn address to the Supreme Being Solomon directed his attention to the [illegible] and in a pathetic speech, represented to them the many instances in which the Divine Power and Providence had been exerted in their behalf. He laid before them the important things that had been revealed to his father David (some of which were past, and others were to come) concerning himself, his succession to the throne, his building of the temple, the establishment of the family, and the prosperity of the nation. The use he made of these remarks was, to admonish them to bless God for mercies received, in consequence of his gracious promises, and to rely on the same infallible word for the [illegible] of what had been predicted concerning [illegible] things.

After this brief, but significant discourse, to the multitude, the king again turned towards the temple, and, with his right hand uplifted, thus again, in an humble address, applied himself to the Almighty: "Lord, what are all the returns of which man is capable, compared even with the least of thy mercies? Oh! how can [illegible] requite the smallest of thy bounties? All that we can do is to render [illegible] praise, acknowledgment and thanksgiving. This is, indeed, an honour conferred upon mankind, in distinction from all other creatures, so that it becomes my bounden duty to adore and praise thy holy name for the singular favours bestowed on our house, and thine infinite goodness towards the whole people of Israel. Be pleased, therefore, to accept our most grateful acknowledgments in the only way we are capable of expressing them. First, for thy singular goodness to my deceased father, in raising him from a state of obscurity to the highest pitch of glory, and next for making good to thy servant before thee, all thy gracious promises in his favour. Continue thy bounty to us as [illegible] thy chosen people. Preserve, prosper, and perpetuate the government in our house, according to thy gracious promise to my father, living and dying. Let thy holy spirit descend upon this temple, and though heaven and earth cannot contain thy glorious Majesty, much less a [illegible] wrought by the hands of mortals, deign to afford it thy Divine presence and protection. Preserve it from the power of enemies [illegible], and set apart for thy [illegible]. If this people, by their offences, should at any time provoke thee, [illegible] displeasure, to visit them with famine, pestilence, or any other judgment, be pleased, O Lord, upon their humble supplications to thee in thine own house, to accept of their repentance, and deliver them from their afflictions. This I most humbly implore, not only for the Hebrews, but for all people in general, who shall offer up their prayers to thee in this holy place. Hereby it will appear to the whole world, that this is thy house, and that we are thy people; and further, that such is our good-will to mankind, as to desire that they may all participate of the blessings of thy providence."

After this humble address to the Father of Mercies Solomon cast himself on the ground, and worshipped in the most lowly posture, then rose, and offered sacrifices upon the altar, having the satisfaction of being assured by an evident token that his oblations were accepted of to the Almighty; for a flash of fire from above rushed with violence upon the altar, and instantly consumed the offerings. The whole multitude looked upon this prodigy as a demonstration of the Divine Presence, and therefore fell prostrate in humble adoration of God's goodness, in thus owning both the worship and the temple. Upon this the king proceeded to offer praises and thanksgivings, and exhorted the multitude to do the same, as now having sufficient indications of God's special favour towards them. He enjoined them to pray for the continuance of his mercies, and especially his Divine grace, that they might live in holiness and righteousness, and the strictest observance of those precepts which God had given them by Moses. This he recommended as the only means of securing the happiness of the Hebrew nation, and, indeed, rendering them blessed above all nations upon the face of the earth; observing furthermore, that the best way to secure their felicity, was to persevere in the paths by which it was obtained.

When the king had thus [illegible], he dismissed the assembly, having first completed his oblations, [illegible] and his people: they consisted of [illegible] and one hundred and twenty [illegible] lambs. [illegible] first blood that was spilt in the temple; and the Hebrews, with their wives and children, [illegible] was also celebrated at the [illegible] time, with great solemnity, the feast of tabernacles, which lasted fourteen days, at the king's expence.

After these solemnities were duly performed, and nothing omitted that related to the Divine worship, the people returned to their respective habitations, warmly [illegible] the wisdom, care, and bounty of the king, and adding their prayers to God for the continuance of [illegible], and the prosperity of his reign. They also joined in hymns and psalms of thanksgiving to the fountain of all their mercies, and expressed in every instance, tokens of joy and gratitude.

The [illegible] brought into, and deposited in the temple, [illegible] the beauty and magnificence of that glorious [illegible], [illegible] the congregation dispersed. The king [illegible] that his sacrifices had been accepted, and his prayers heard by the Almighty, that he would [illegible] the temple, and make it the place of his residence, that is, so long as he [illegible], his people and posterity, should continue to walk before him in holiness of life, according to the [illegible] of David his father. Upon that condition [illegible] to the summit of earthly glory, [illegible] should never be wanting of the line of the tribe of Judah, to sway the sceptre [illegible]. But [illegible], on the contrary, [illegible] from the Divine ordinances [illegible] should be [illegible] from the face of the earth, and [illegible] be no more a people; but, [illegible] ravages and calamities of [illegible] world as vagabonds [illegible]. [illegible], that, in case of such apostacy, that temple, [illegible] by the Divine [illegible], should [illegible] hands of barbarians, [illegible] Jerusalem [illegible], such should be the [illegible] as to excite the [illegible] mankind, [illegible] people, [illegible] of nations, [illegible] power, [illegible], should [illegible] to [illegible] state, by the [illegible] exalted them. [illegible] should [illegible] too late, under [illegible] conscience, exclaim, "We have [illegible] God [illegible] our forefathers, [illegible] and [illegible]." This was the purport of what was communicated to Solomon in the vision, as we have translated in the sacred records.

After finishing the temple, as before observed, in the course of seven years, the king laid the foundations of his palace, for the perfecting of which he was thirteen years; for he was not so anxious for the accomplishment of this undertaking as he [illegible] of that of the temple. The building of the temple, a work of vast extent and importance, [illegible] by the Divine blessing and assistance, or it could not have been completed in so short a space of time. But the palace which was building, much inferior in dignity to the temple, [illegible] account that its materials had not been so long before hand prepared, and also as it was a habitation for [illegible], and not for the Omnipotent God, was longer in finishing. It was, however, a very magnificent [illegible], [illegible] honour both to the prince and people. But to form [illegible] adequate idea, and [illegible] the contents of the [illegible], it will be necessary to enter upon description.

This palace was [illegible] extent [illegible] supported by many pillars [illegible] common [illegible], for the purpose of hearing causes [illegible] was an hundred cubits long, fifty broad, and thirty high, [illegible] could it be less spacious to contain the [illegible] through [illegible] from all quarters [illegible] supported by sixteen square columns [illegible] roof was of the Corinthian order [illegible] doors curiously wrought [illegible] ornamental. In this hall was [illegible] cubits square, [illegible] upon massy pillars In one of the apartments was a throne of state, whereon the king himself sat personally in judgment Next to this was the queen's house, and other buildings adapted for the purpose of retirement and recreation These were fitted up with cedar, and raised upon stones of ten cubits square, which were partly plain and partly overlaid with the most precious marble, after the manner of magnificent palaces or temples The rooms were hung with three depths of the richest hangings, and ornamented with images in sculpture, representing trees, plants, branches and leaves, all so curiously wrought, as to appear to the eye as if they were in motion The remainder of the space, up to the ceiling was embellished with delicate party coloured figures, upon a ground of white Besides these there was a great variety of other chambers, long and spacious galleries, superb rooms of state, and others for feasting and entertainment, adorned and furnished with services of plate and massy gold Indeed the variety and extent of the royal palace may be said to surpass description, as they exceeded every thing of the kind in the known world, and exhibited a magnificence almost beyond conception

To complete the dignity of his chair of state, Solomon erected a large ivory throne, with curious carved and engraved work upon it, after the fashion of a tribunal There were six steps upon the ascent, and at each [illegible] of every step was the figure of a lion There were also two lions over [illegible] above, that is, one on either hand of the seat of state As the king rested on his throne, there were arms put forth in order to receive him, and the figure of a bullock placed in a proper posture under him for his support The whole piece was covered with gold

When Solomon had completed these magnificent structures in the course of twenty years, through the assistance of Hiram, king of Tyre who had contributed a great deal of gold, and more of silver, besides a vast store of cedar and cypress wood, he sent him annually, as an acknowledgment, great quantities of corn, wine, and oil, commodities of which, as an islander, he stood much in need He also offered him twenty cities in the land of Galilee, adjoining to his own country, but Hiram, with a respectful excuse, declined acceptance From this refusal, that part of the country was called Chabalm, which in the Phœnician language signifies, *It does not please me*

So great a veneration had Hiram for the sagacity of Solomon, that whenever any difficult case or mysterious question was propounded to him, he applied to him for a solution, for was that wise prince deficient in explaining the most ambiguous matters, or intricate problems Menander, the historian, who translated the Tyrian annals from the Phœnician into the Greek language, makes mention of these two princes as follows "On the death of Abibalus, Hiram, his son, succeeded him in the kingdom "of Tyre He lived three and fifty years, and reigned "four and thirty He raised a bank in a large place called "the Great Field, and dedicated the golden pillar in Jupiter's temple He cut down abundance of timber upon "the Mount Libanus for the roof of temples, and demolishing ancient buildings, he erected new ones to Hercules and Astarte He built a statue for Hercules in the "month of Peritius He made an expedition against the "Lyceans for neglect of the payment of tribute, and having overcome them, returned home In his reign there "was one Abdemonus a young man who undertook to "give Solomon, the king of Jerusalem, a solution of all "mysterious questions that were put to him"

Dius also writes to this effect "Abibalus, being dead "was succeeded by his son Hiram, who raised the east "quarter of the city, enlarged the borders and brought the "temple of Jupiter, that before stood apart, within its "compass, as well as enriched and adorned it with most "valuable presents He ordered cedar wood to be cut down "on Mount Libanus for the building of the temple" He farther writes, "That Solomon, the king of Jerusalem, "sent problems and riddles to Hiram, upon the forfeiture "of a considerable sum if he should not expound them That "[illegible] problems and riddles were not only solved by means "of Abdemonus, a Tyrian [illegible] others [illegible] "[illegible] to Solomon, who was to pay a great "forfeit upon failure of explanation" Thus far goes the testimony of Dius, respecting the intercourse between these princes

The fortifications of Jerusalem being deemed insufficient for the defence of that spacious and opulent city, Solomon applied himself to the erecting of such towers and the completion of such repairs, as he found requisite for the security of the place He also rebuilt and fortified several cities of considerable note as Azor, Megiddo, and Gazara, in the land of the Philistines, the latter of which king Pharaoh had taken by assault, and having [illegible] and slain all the inhabitants gave it as a present to his daughter upon her marriage with Solomon This city the king rebuilt as it was naturally very strong and equally useful to government in peace and in war He also built not far distant Betachora and Baleth, besides other places for the purposes of health and pastime from the temperature of climate, delicacy of fruits, and conveniencies of air and water When he had built this city, and encompassed it with strong walls, he called it Thadamora, which name it bears among the Syrians to this day The Greeks call it Palmyra

If any should enquire wherefore all the kings of Egypt, from Minaeus the founder of Memphis, many years before our forefather Abraham, until the days of Solomon being an interval of thirteen hundred years should be called by the name of Pharoah, it is deemed expedient to give them this information Pharoah in the Egyptian language signifies king I apprehend that they were, other names from their childhood but on coming to the exercise of the regal dignity, they exchanged the distinction of the family for that which denoted their authority Thus it was that the kings of Alexandria, who were called formerly by other names, when they assumed the reins of government, were all called by the name of Ptolemy, from the first of their kings Thus it is with the Roman emperors also, who upon their elevations to that dignity, are styled Cæsars, in consequence of their assumption to the sovereign power Perhaps this was the cause that occasioned Herodotus of Halicarnassus, in his account of the successors of Minaeus the first king of Memphis, to call them in general by the name of Pharoah, though they amounted in number to three hundred and thirty When a woman succeeded to the government she was called by her proper name Nicaulis, the appellation of Pharoah being peculiar to the other sex Nor can I discover from our own history, that after Pharoah, the father-in-law of Solomon, there was ever any other king called by that name I am also well assured that this Nicaulis was the queen of Egypt and Ethiopia that came with [illegible] to Solomon, but of this more hereafter I have rather dwelt upon these particulars to prove the agreement of our history and that of the Egyptians

In process of time Solomon subdued to himself the remnant of the Canaanites between Mount Libanus and the city Amathe, who, for some time, disputed their allegiance to the kings of Israel, till Solomon at last made them tributaries, upon condition of furnishing him yearly with such a certain number of slaves, as was agreed upon to be employed in tilling the land, and other sorts of servility, for none of the Hebrews were subject to servile employments, nor would it have been proper for conquerors to descend to do the business of their captives With respect to the Israelites, their genius lay more towards arms and military exploits The Canaanites, in the mean time, were kept to hard labour and six hundred officers were appointed to superintend them in their respective employments

The king fitted out many ships in Ezon-Geber, an Egyptian bay upon the Red Sea It is now called Berenice, not far from the city of Elat The place formerly belonged to the Hebrews, and became useful for shipping from the donations of Hiram, king of Tyre, who also sent him a number of skilful navigators and expert pilots — These served the king's officers for guides to the land of Ophir, which belongs to India, where they went for four hundred talents of gold and brought them to the king

The fame of Solomon's wisdom having reached

the ears of Nicaulis queen of Egypt and Ethiopia, excited in that princess, who possessed a great share of understanding, much desire to see our celebrated monarch. She wished to be satisfied by her own experience, and not trust to report alone, respecting his magnificence and wonderful qualifications. With this view she set forward towards Jerusalem with a train and equipage suited to her royal dignity, taking with her a number of camels, laden with gold, a variety of rich perfumes, and of precious stones. The king, upon her arrival, received her with all possible honour, courtesy, and respect, solved all the difficult questions she proposed, insomuch that she was struck with wonder at his various excellencies. She could not but admire the magnificence of his palace, the discipline and œconomy of his houshold, and the peculiar grace and propriety with which he conducted his affairs in general. But nothing gave her so much satisfaction as that masterly fabric called the Grove of Lebanon, which displayed such singular beauties. She was likewise infinitely pleased with the daily sacrifices, and the application, care, and veneration with which the priests and Levites performed their parts in the worship. The whole she beheld impressed her mind so sensibly, that in the height of her amazement, she addressed the king in words to this effect:

"Great prince, report is so doubtful and uncertain, that, "without an experimental and demonstrative confirmation of "the truth of what we hear, we are forced to suspend our "judgment, especially when the fame of things relates either "to extreme good or evil. But with respect to your incomparable faculties, that is to the advantages of the mind in a "superlative degree of knowledge and understanding, and the "glory of your outward state, the rumour has been so far "from partial, that it falls short even of common justice. "For tho' report conveyed as much to your honour as words "could express, I have yet the happiness at this present time "to see much more than I heard. Blessed are the Israelites; "blessed are the friends and people of Solomon, that stand "even before him and hear his wisdom; and blessed be God "for his goodness to this land and nation, in placing them "under the government of so excellent a prince."

Nor did this great princess testify her admiration of the wisdom and magnificence of Solomon by words alone as mere professions; but, as a further instance of the high respect she entertained for the king, she presented him with twenty talents of gold, together with a great quantity of aromatic spices, rich perfumes, and precious stones of considerable value. They speak also of a root of balsom that she brought with her, which according to tradition, was the first plant of the kind that ever came into our country, where it has been extensively propagated ever since.

Solomon on his part was not wanting in making a suitable acknowledgment of the favours conferred upon him; for he not only presented the queen with whatever she asked, but added several articles which he thought attracted her fancy. After this reciprocal interchange of presents the queen of Egypt and Ethiopia returned, highly gratified, to her own country.

About the same time the king's fleet returned from Ophir (otherwise called the land of gold) bringing precious stones and pine wood in abundance. The latter was made use of for pillars and supporters to the temple and palace, and partly for the construction of musical instruments, such as psalteries, harps, and cymbals, which the Levites used in their hymns during the course of divine worship. The wood that was brought upon this occasion, was larger and finer than any that had ever been brought before. Let it not, therefore, be imagined, that this pine wood was like that which is so named by the merchants in order to enhance its value in the esteem of the purchaser. It has somewhat of the grain of the fig-tree, but is more white and glossy. It is deemed proper to make this remark that the reader may form a just estimate of so valuable a commodity.

Solomon received by this fleet six hundred and sixty-six talents of gold, exclusive of the merchants adventure, and what the governors and princes of Arabia sent him for presents. Of this gold he caused to be cast two hundred targets, weighing each six hundred shekels of gold, and these were hung up in the great hall of the Grove of Lebanon. He also made cups of gold and of precious stones for the purpose of entertainments, and had them embellished with exquisite art. Indeed his utensils in general were made of this rich metal. No money passed in the carrying on of this traffic, for the king had many ships in the sea of Tarsus which carried out all kinds of merchandize to the remotest parts, so that his subjects exchanged their commodities for gold, silver, ivory, negroes, apes, &c. They finished their voyage usually in the course of three years.

The fame of Solomon's wisdom, power and riches, having by this time extended to the remotest parts, several of the most potent princes were desirous of being witnesses of the same, and embraced every opportunity of testifying their veneration for his character by their submission and munificence. They sent him gold and silver plate, purple robes, spices and perfumes of all sorts, horses, chariots, and mules for burthen, such as they thought for strength and [illegible], would be most acceptable to the king. In short, the richest presents were sent him from every quarter, and it was [illegible] princes of that time [illegible] attend to the instruction of this renowned king of Israel.

By the presents last mentioned, Solomon [illegible] on of four hundred chariots [illegible], that is, he now had [illegible] chariots [illegible] horses, which, in beauty and speed, exceeded [illegible]. Their riders were also [illegible] to them, being men in the flower of their age, completely [illegible] elegantly arrayed, with the advantage of [illegible] of golden threads with their locks, which [illegible] sun, exhibited a most splendid view to the spectators. This was the guard which, with their accoutrements, attended the king mounted in his chariot, and clothed in white on particular occasions, and especially in his morning excursions to a seat he had at Etham, which [illegible] situation, gardens, and fountains, became his favourite [illegible].

The king's dignity and [illegible] appeared in the minutest [illegible]. He [illegible] superintendance of the highways that led to his [illegible] Jerusalem, but ordered them to be paved, as well [illegible] and convenience of passengers, as the support of [illegible] regard [illegible]. He also disposed his chariots in [illegible] order, so that a certain number should be sent [illegible] to [illegible] upon frequent [illegible] those places he called his chariot towns. Silver was as plentiful in Jerusalem in his days as stones, and cedars, which had never been [illegible] Judea before, were now as common as sycamore trees. He gave commission to his [illegible] a chariot, with a pair of horses [illegible] hundred silver drachms each, and these were sent to the kings of Syria and beyond Euphrates.

But though Solomon was become the most [illegible] of kings, the most favoured of heaven, and excelled in wisdom and riches, all his predecessors, and indeed all monarchs upon the face of the earth, he did not persevere in this happy state to the time of his death. The [illegible] actions of his life greatly sullied the glories of the former. It is a melancholy truth, that he departed from the laws of Moses and the religion of his forefathers, and that, prompted by inordinate desires, and not satisfied with women of his own country, he contributed [illegible] those of various nations, such as Sidonians, Tyrians, Ammonites, Idumeans, &c. in violation of the [illegible] forbidding any Hebrew intercourse or [illegible] strangers, it being natural to conclude, that strange women would allure men to the worship of strange gods. This was the true cause of the prohibition against such marriages, for the transgression of one law [illegible] towards the breaking of another, and the taking [illegible] prohibited wife would produce, of course [illegible] of a prohibited religion.

It soon appeared that Solomon's [illegible] were beyond the controul of reason [illegible]— He had no less than seven hundred wives who were princesses, and three hundred concubines, and the passion he had for the personal charms of some, and the captivating demeanour of others, at length led him into compliances with them in the temples, at their practices and opinions, as the most effectual proof he could give them of his affection. As he grew more advanced in years, he experienced a decay, both of his mental and corporeal powers, and as he became more remiss in the exercise of the true worship, he was the more easily prevailed on to join with them in strange worship in a false one (a), though he had been guilty of a flagrant transgression of the law before, in the very figures of the bulls under his brazen sea, and the lions afterwards, that were set as guards upon his throne, which were directly in breach of a positive commandment. He had, at the same time, the most glorious precedent in his pious father, whose steps were recommended to his example in a vision from on high, upon pain of the Divine indignation, and the ruin of the whole family and nation of his people.

This had so highly offended the Almighty, that he was pleased to send a prophet to him with a message to this effect: "That his wickedness could not be hid from God's all-seeing eye, and that he should not long go unpunished." With respect to the promise made to his father, the prophet told him his government should not be taken from him while he was living, but that, after his death, his son should suffer for the iniquities of his father, not that there should be an universal defection, but that ten tribes only should revolt, and the other two continue in their allegiance to the son of Solomon, for the sake of his grandfather David, and for the sake of the temple of Jerusalem, which God had chosen for his peculiar habitation on earth.

This severe denunciation, which foretold the removal of the kingdom from the family of his son, contrary to the consolation, wounded him to the very soul, and to add to it, he could not but acknowledge the justice of the sentence.

Soon after this, pursuant to the prophecy of the prophet, God raised up a bitter enemy against him. His name was Adad, an Idumean by birth, and of the blood royal. His animosity to Solomon arose from the following circumstance: When the Hebrews over-ran the country of Idumea under the command of Joab, who, at that time was David's general, this Joab, having subdued the people, put to the sword all the males he could find of the province that were able to bear arms, and this cruelty was continued for the space of six months. Adad, who was then in his youthful state, happening to make his escape, fled to Pharaoh, king of Egypt, who not only received him with great humanity, but generously gave him houses, lands, and other necessaries for his support, nay, such was his affection for him, that, on his arriving to years of maturity, he gave him his own wife's sister in marriage, who bore him a son, that was brought up with the children of Pharaoh.

In process of time news was brought to Egypt of the death of David and Joab, and Adad, upon these tidings, asked permission of Pharaoh to return to his own country. The king not being pleased with the request, asked him what was the cause of his so earnestly desiring to leave the best friend he had in the world? Adad repeated his solicitations for some time, but could not prevail.

But when Solomon's affairs began to decline, on account of his before-mentioned transgressions, and the Divine displeasure for the same, Adad, with Pharaoh's permission, returned to Idumea, with a design of stirring up the people to a rebellion against Solomon. On his arrival at the place he found the garrison so strong, and the country in such a posture of defence, that nothing could be done effectually by surprize. He therefore adopted another plan, and went from thence into Syria, where he joined interests with one Rezon, a fugitive from his master Adadezer, the king of Zobah, and a famous leader of a body of banditti, who pillaged up and down at pleasure. Adad struck a league with this man, and, with his assistance, subdued that part of Syria, where he was declared king, and made such inroads upon the territories of Solomon, as perplexed him greatly in the declining part of his reign.

But, besides these indignities from a stranger and a fugitive, Solomon found a more dangerous enemy in his own nation. This was Jeroboam, the son of Nebat, a man of turbulent and ambitious spirit, who had an expectation of rising, from a prophecy that had been made to him long before. Jeroboam being left by his father, when very young, to the care of his mother, and Solomon observing that, as he grew up, he became of a bold and enterprizing disposition, made him overseer of his works, being at that time rebuilding the walls of Jerusalem. He executed that office with such care and attention, that Solomon gave him as a reward, the military command over the tribe of Joseph.

As Jeroboam was one day going out of Jerusalem, he was met on the way by the prophet Ahijah, who having saluted and taken him aside, laid hold of his garment, that was new and tore it into twelve pieces, bidding him take ten of them to himself, for it was the Divine pleasure and will it should be so. The prophet added, that the government should be wrested from Solomon, but that, for the sake of the Divine promise, the two contiguous tribes should be given to his son, but the other ten to Jeroboam, as a punishment for giving himself up to strange women, and through them instigated to strange gods. He concluded with admonishing him to take warning from Solomon's miserable case, and observe the statutes and commandments according to the example of pious king David, as the only security for the continuance of the Divine favour and protection.

Jeroboam was much elated at the words of the prophet, and being naturally of an haughty and aspiring temper, whatever conduced to gratify his ambition, rendered him turbulent and restless. The prediction of the prophet was strongly impressed on his mind, and therefore the first step he took, after he came to the army, was to tamper with the people he commanded, and instil into their minds the spirit of disaffection to their sovereign.

The pernicious designs of Jeroboam were soon made known to Solomon, who concerted a plan to surprize and dispatch him, but the plot being discovered, he made his escape, and fled to Shishak, king of Egypt, and there resided till the death of Solomon furnished him with an opportunity of prosecuting his intentions.

CHAP. III.

On the death of Solomon, Rehoboam ascends the throne. Becomes obnoxious to the people. Ten tribes revolt, and Jeroboam, made king, introduces idolatry. He is reproved by a prophet. Jeroboam and Rehoboam equally wicked and idolatrous.

SOLOMON, after a reign of eighty years over Israel, departed this life in the ninety-fourth year of his age, and was interred with great funeral pomp at Jerusalem. He was superior to all his predecessors in wisdom and opulence and might have been deemed so in happiness, had not an inordinate attachment to women, in the decline of life, precipitated him into actions that sullied the glories he had acquired. But of these, with their consequent punishments, we shall treat in the sequel.

On the death of Solomon, the government of course devolved to his son Rehoboam, who was born of an Ammonite, called Naamah. He repaired immediately to Shechem to declare his succession, and obtain the suffrages of the people. Jerobo-

---

(a) ... to imagine that a person of Solomon's ... should have been persuaded ... into the ... in which he had been ... educated, and ... only ... to Moses ... honour ... had brought ... the house of David, and inspired him ... wisdom ... which rendered him famous throughout the earth. It affords however a ... lesson to all mankind to beware of the infatuation of vice, since even Solomon ... his ... weaknesses ... and when once ... happy ... it ... not ... to ... him from it.

The IDOLATRY and APOSTACY of JEROBOAM King of Israel which was followed by the death of his favourite Son & the dreadfull Calamities of his subjects.

am, who was then in Egypt, being urged by some of the ra[illegible] [illegible] hither also on the same [illegible].

On [illegible] he appeared, together with many of the [illegible] of the tribes to Rehoboam, and advised him to adopt a [illegible] form of government, (considering that, in [illegible], his father was oppressive) and, instead of rendering himself an object of terror to his subjects, his interest and happiness required him to regulate his conduct in such a manner, as to [illegible] acquiescence with the measures he pursued from an affection to his person, rather than [illegible] of his power.

[illegible] he [illegible] reason [illegible] to his consideration, and [illegible] desired them to return in three days, when he would give them an answer. The delay raised some jealousy in the minds of the people as to the result, for they considered it so reasonable a request could not be denied, especially [illegible] young prince, [illegible] disposed to promote the [illegible] of his subjects. However, suspending their [illegible] [illegible] denial, they waited the event with hopes of [illegible].

In consequence of this general application, Rehoboam called [illegible] the friends and counsellors of his late father, and [illegible] of them their advice respecting the answer he should [illegible] their request. Being [illegible] affected to the public cause, and [illegible] with the disposition of the people, they recommended to him by all means to treat them with courtesy and condescension, assuring him that he would gain much [illegible] upon them by a compliance, [illegible] [illegible] qualities of majesty and state, nothing giving so commanding [illegible] and [illegible] the loyalty of a people, as the condescension [illegible] prince.

[illegible] counsel could not [illegible] general [illegible] occasion [illegible] [illegible] his present [illegible] young [illegible]. But [illegible] this young prince [illegible] the [illegible] [illegible] of his [illegible], determined [illegible] their opinion [illegible] debated on the point, [illegible] [illegible] of experience and [illegible] passion, advised him [illegible] people an answer to this effect: "That since [illegible] complained of his predecessor, they should feel more [illegible] from his little finger than they had done from the [illegible] of his father: that if they thought they [illegible] oppressed [illegible], they must expect more oppression now: and [illegible] if his father had chastised them [illegible] whips, he was determined to chastise them with scorpions."

The weak king was highly pleased with this pertinacious reply, suggested by counsellors [illegible], thinking it corresponded with his [illegible] of majesty; so that upon the third day, when the people assembled in the utmost anxiety of hope and fear, he appeared and delivered his answer to them precisely in the words which the young men had recommended. It seems as if it had been so decided by Divine Providence, that the prophecy of Ahijah might be fulfilled, [illegible] words uttered with all the pomp of state, so enraged the multitude that they exclaimed [illegible] voice, "What have we to do with the house of David? Let him take to himself the temple that his father built." And this [illegible] [illegible] general revolt.

[illegible] Rehoboam understood this, he sent Adoram, one of his officers in the treasury, to pacify them by laying the blame upon some rash and vehement young men: but the [illegible] from his exculpatory arguments, [illegible] him to death. The king, thinking the violence pointed at [illegible] rather than his officer, thought it high time to consult his own safety, so that he hastened to his chariot, and fled to Jerusalem. The tribes of Judah and Benjamin [illegible] [illegible] proclaimed him king; but the rest of the [illegible] [illegible] of Jeroboam, declaring they [illegible] [illegible] the sovereignty of the house of David. This [illegible] kingdom divided into two [illegible] [illegible] different denominations, [illegible], the kingdom [illegible] [illegible] kingdom of Israel, though the latter [illegible] [illegible] whole people.

[illegible] [illegible] with [illegible] [illegible] [illegible] [illegible] [illegible] [illegible] Benjamin [illegible] allegiance, and drew out 180,000 soldiers professing [illegible] [illegible], with this body of men to march against [illegible] ten tribes, and by force, reduce them to obedience.

While he was preparing for this enterprize, [illegible] [illegible] [illegible] apart, who by the Divine [illegible], exhorted him to desist from prosecuting [illegible] [illegible] the will of God that the division of the [illegible] [illegible] come to pass, that the prediction [illegible] [illegible].

We will now return to some of the actions of Jeroboam, king of the [illegible] tribes, and thence proceed to [illegible] of Rehoboam, and the [illegible].

Jeroboam enlarged and [illegible] Shechem, [illegible] [illegible], and made it a royal city. He then [illegible] Penuel, a fortified place on the other side the river [illegible], where he likewise built a palace, to which he [illegible] [illegible] [illegible] [illegible] the affections of the two [illegible] [illegible] were attached to Jeroboam.

The time was now near for celebrating the feast of tabernacles, when Jeroboam reflected, that [illegible] [illegible] should repair to Jerusalem to celebrate that festival, the ceremonies of religion might furnish opportunities [illegible] induce them to acknowledge allegiance to [illegible], whereby both his life and government would be [illegible] danger. For prevention, [illegible] [illegible] [illegible]. He erected two golden calves, and [illegible] [illegible] for [illegible], the one at Bethel, and the other at Dan, [illegible] town situated at the head of the Lesser Jordan. [illegible] [illegible] were consecrated in both places, [illegible] [illegible] [illegible] ed the ten tribes under his command, [illegible] addressed [illegible]:

"It is unnecessary, my friends [illegible] [illegible] [illegible] "on the omnipresence of the Deity [illegible] [illegible] [illegible] "re, I hope, [illegible] [illegible] [illegible] "fore conceive, that, for the exercise of your [illegible] "totally needless to undertake the [illegible] [illegible] "salem. You will be at no loss for the want of places [illegible] "vine. The builder of [illegible] [illegible] [illegible] "selves. The golden calves, which [illegible] [illegible] "at Bethel and Dan, have been [illegible] [illegible] [illegible] "temple at Jerusalem. Therefore, [illegible] [illegible] "execute the sacerdotal [illegible] [illegible] [illegible] "[illegible] [illegible] [illegible] "ron, the first of the [illegible]"

By these [illegible] the people [illegible] apostasy from the [illegible] worship of the true God, [illegible] [illegible] laws of their country, and [illegible] [illegible] [illegible] [illegible] shall show in due time and order.

The festival of the seventh month, or the feast of tabernacles, was now approaching, and Jeroboam [illegible] [illegible] [illegible] of worshipping the same way at Bethel, that the two tribes did at Jerusalem. To give countenance to this innovation in religion, he erected an altar before the golden calf, assumed to himself the office and office of high priest, and, having gone through the different ceremonies, according to the form of that [illegible] worship, proceeded at length to that of the sacrifices. But as he was preparing to put fire to the victim, in the sight of all the people, [illegible] prophet from Jerusalem, named Jadon, at that very instant, [illegible] rupted him. Having made his way through the multitude, he advanced to the altar, and thus exclaimed, "O altar! altar! there shall arise one out of the house of Judah, Josiah by name, who upon thee shall deal by the false prophets, seducers and impostors of these times, and [illegible] [illegible] their bones. That there may be no doubt of this prediction being fulfilled, [illegible] shall now be [illegible]. Behold the altar shall be rent, and the [illegible] of the [illegible] [illegible] that are upon it shall be poured forth upon the ground."

The king was so incensed at this speech from the prophet, that, stretching out his hand, he commanded the people [illegible] to seize him; but at the very instant his hand became so benumbed, that he could not draw it back again. At the same time the altar was rent [illegible] [illegible] [illegible] [illegible] of the sacrifice [illegible] [illegible] [illegible]. Jeroboam, [illegible], [illegible] that the prophet was [illegible] with a Divine commission, [illegible] [illegible] [illegible], and [illegible] requested him to supp[illegible] the Almighty for the restoration of his withered hand. The prophet readily complied with his request, and Jeroboam, having received the use of his limb, gratefully acknowledged the benefit of the cure, and earnestly pressed his benefactor to stay and take some refreshment with him. But the prophet declined the invitation, in consequence of a Divine injunction, not to taste bread or wine in that city, nor to return the same way he came. His abstinence and refusal induced the king to be more attentive to what he predicted than he otherwise would have been; and his anxiety increased as he continued to reflect upon the event.

There was at this time, in Bethel, a certain false prophet, who by the flattering [illegible] which he pretended would come to pass, had highly ingratiated himself with Jeroboam. He was far advanced in years, and being informed by his sons, of the famous prophet who was come from Jerusalem, and the miracles he had wrought in the sight of the people, notwithstanding he was oppressed with many and great infirmities, he arose from his bed, and being mounted on his ass, went immediately in quest of the stranger. This rapid motion was the result of the false prophet's apprehension of being supplanted in the king's favour. He came up with him as he was resting himself under the shade of a spreading [illegible]. The formality of salutation having passed between them, the false prophet complained of the unkindness of the stranger, in not having called at his habitation, and partaking of the fare which it afforded, strongly urging him at the same time, to return and take some refreshment. The stranger refused his request, alleging the same reason for it as he had done to the king. The old man replied, that the prohibition did not extend to him, for that he himself was a prophet, and sent expressly by the Divine command to eat with him. [illegible] was at length prevailed on by the false prophet to return, and while they were seated at table, and engaged in familiar converse, a voice [illegible] appeared, and not only gave him to understand that he should be punished for his disobedience, but informed him in what manner the punishment should be effected, which was, that he should be torn in pieces on the way by a lion, and that his body should not be laid in the tomb of his ancestors.

Nor was it long before this awful sentence was put in execution. For as Jadon was on his return to Jerusalem, he was suddenly attacked by a lion, and instantly destroyed. But the beast neither tore his body, nor did the least injury to the ass on which he rode. An account of this disaster being brought to the false prophet by some travellers who passed that way, he appointed his sons to fetch the body into the city, which being done, he caused it to be magnificently interred in his own sepulchre, [illegible] charging his sons, whenever he died, to lay his body as near that of this prophet as possible. He declared at the same time, that he was confident that what he had foretold concerning the altar of Bethel, the priests, and the false prophets, would most certainly come to pass.

The funeral obsequies were no sooner performed, and the charge given to his sons than the false prophet, with his usual impiety and perfidy, went to Jeroboam, and, finding him much agitated in his mind, asked him why he should be thus affected by the words of a frantic madman? The king then adverted to the miraculous signs of the altar, and the withering and restoration of his own hand, as the ample cause of his perturbation, adding, that had it not been a prophet [illegible] high he could not have given such proofs of a Divine commission.

The false prophet used every effort to invalidate the [illegible] by which the king was so apparently impressed, and attempted to persuade him that his hand was enfeebled by the labour which it had undergone in supporting the victims, and that upon its resting a short time, it returned to its former state. That the altar was newly erected, and cracked by the weight of the sacrifices laid upon it. He then artfully endeavoured the manner in which the prophet, who had foretold the things that so much alarmed him, was taken off, making use of every means of working the king into a disbelief of the prediction.

Nor were his efforts in vain, for Jeroboam, blinded by his arts and seduced by his insinuations, became totally alienated from God and his true worship, and abandoned to impiety and profligacy in the highest degree. He seemed to have bidden defiance to every thing sacred either in heaven or earth, and to have added presumption to idolatry. But we pass on from the acts of Jeroboam to those of Rehoboam.

The king, who was of the two tribes which maintained their allegiance to him, as the son and successor of David, was as little deserving of his station as his rival. He built and fortified several considerable cities, as Bethlehem, Etam, Tekoa, Bethzur, Shoco, Adullam, Ipa, Maresha, Ziph, Adoram, Lachish, Azekah, Zorah, Ajalon, and Hebron, all in the tribe of Judah, besides several places no less considerable in that of Benjamin. These he provided with garrisons, governors, corn, wine and oil, with all necessaries in abundance, for their maintenance and defence. During his residence at Jerusalem, the priests and Levites that were in all Israel, and such of the people in general as were attached to the true religion left their respective places of abode, that they might enjoy the privilege of worshipping God in the manner of their forefathers. They were disgusted with the tyrannical and idolatrous practices of Jeroboam, in forcing them to the adoration of images, and the dishonour of the one only and true God, and in violation of his positive command. So general, indeed, was the revolt, that in the course of three years, the power and interest of Rehoboam were greatly augmented. The first wife this prince espoused was his kinswoman, by whom he had three children. He afterwards married Maachah the daughter of Thamar, who was the daughter of Absalom, by whom he had Abijah. He had many other children by other wives, but he loved Maachah above them all. He had, in the whole, eighteen wives and thirty concubines, by whom he had twenty eight sons and sixty daughters. But he appointed Abijah his successor in the kingdom, and entrusted him with his treasures, and the command of his fortified cities.

It appeared in the instance of Rehoboam as in many others, that greatness and prosperity has led men into impiety and irreligion. For, elated with his pre-eminence, his son thus [illegible] in the mind, and discovered his inclination towards idolatry, and, as his example was followed by his subjects, they soon forsook the worship of the true God, and carried their idolatrous practices to a most extravagant height. Indeed it is evident from observation that the lower class of mankind become depraved through the pernicious example of their superiors, for the immorality of a prince has a powerful influence on the conduct of the subjects, nay, some foolishly imagine it laudable to imitate even the vices of those who are called the great. Thus it was at this time, when the people became idolatrous in their worship and immoral in their practice, in conformity with the pleasure and example of their king.

CHAP. IV.

Shishak besieges Jerusalem, and plunders the temple. Death of Rehoboam. He is succeeded by his son Abijah. Prediction of a prophet to Jeroboam of the destruction of himself and family.

As a punishment for this defection, the Almighty was pleased, in the fifth year of Rehoboam's reign, to avenge himself on him and his people, by the means of Shishak, king of Egypt, not Sesostris, as related, through error, by Herodotus. This prince invaded his dominions with a most formidable force, amounting to one thousand two hundred chariots, sixty thousand horse, and four hundred thousand foot, the army being chiefly composed of Africans and Ethiopians. With this powerful armament he fell upon the Hebrews, made himself master of their strongest cities without opposition, and having left garrisons in them, proceeded to Jerusalem where Rehoboam and his people were blocked up in the town.

In this dilemma the Hebrews besought the Almighty, by prayer and supplication for victory over, and deliverance from, their enemies: but so flagrant had been their impiety, that they could not obtain the interposition of Divine Providence. When Simeas, the prophet, told them that God would forsake them as they had forsaken his worship, they were in great consternation: and seeing no prospect of deliverance, they most humbly acknowledged their apostacy from his laws, and the just judgement which had ensued. Being thus disposed to confess their sins, and implore the Divine forgiveness, when brought to the very brink of despair, the prophet told the king, that the Almighty was pleased so far to accept of their humiliation and repentance, that they should not be utterly cut off; but that, however, they should become subject to the Egyptians, that they might learn, by experience, their duty to God, in preference to all human authority.

Alarmed at this report of the prophet, Rehoboam delivered up Jerusalem to Shishak, upon certain conditions: but the Egyptians, without regard to faith or honour, violated the treaty, pillaged the temple, and carried away plate and treasure belonging to the temple, as well as the king, to an immense value. He took with him Solomon's golden shields and bucklers, together with the golden quivers that David had taken from the king of Sophene, and dedicated to the purpose of adorning the temple. When he had thus done, he returned to his own country.

Herodotus, of Halicarnassus, makes mention of this expedition, mistaking only the king's name, where he speaks of his march through several other countries, and of his reducing Syria of Palestine without opposition. Now it is manifest that the historian intended to record the subjection of our nation by the Egyptians; for he mentions, "That he left behind him pillars in the land of those who "submitted to him without opposition, and engraved upon them images, emblematical of the pusillanimity of "the men, in giving up their country without one effort to "defend it." It is evident that Rehoboam, our king, surrendered without opposition. He likewise says, "That "the Ethiopians took the custom of circumcising from "the Egyptians." It is also universally agreed that the Phœnicians, and the people of Syria of Palestine had it from the latter, nor are there any other people of that country circumcised but the Hebrews.

Upon the return of Shishak to his own country, after this depredation, Rehoboam was reduced so low as to be under the necessity of repairing the loss of the golden shields and bucklers with the same number of brazen ones, for the use and ornament of his guards. After this transaction there is nothing of importance to be related concerning Rehoboam, his fear being a constant check upon him, with respect to the animosity that subsisted between him and his formidable rival, Jeroboam. He lived fifty-seven years, and died in the eighteenth year of his reign. He was of a temper weak and arrogant, and sacrificed himself, his government, and expectation, to his vanity and obstinacy, in rejecting the wise counsel of sage and upright men. He was buried in the city of David at Jerusalem, amongst the kings of Israel. He was succeeded by his son Abijah, in the eighteenth year of Jeroboam's reign over the ten tribes.

Having brought the reign of Rehoboam to a conclusion, we shall revert to the history of Jeroboam. This prince persisted in his idolatry and immorality. He daily multiplied altars in the high places, and appointed priests to officiate unworthy of the sacred functions. The Almighty, in righteous judgment, soon avenged the indignation offered his sacred name, upon himself and his family. It soon happened that Obimes his son, fell sick, upon which he ordered his wife to dress herself as a private person, and go to the prophet Ahijah, at Shiloh, (who had formerly told that he himself should obtain the royal dignity), and enquire of him the fate of the child. The prophet was now dim-sighted with age, therefore Jeroboam thought it might be easy to impose upon him, and that he would imagine the queen to be no more than a common person. In conformity to the order of her royal husband, his wife, having disguised herself, set out on her journey to Shiloh to make enquiry of the prophet concerning the life of their darling son. Before she arrived at the place, Ahijah was addressed by a voice from heaven, informing him that the woman was coming to apply to him, and upon what occasion, together with the answer he should return to the questions she should propose. Upon her approaching his habitation, he thus addressed her: "Come in, and pretend not "to disguise yourself, for I have received information of "your character and business, together with the speech I "am to deliver to you, from one who is not to be deceived. "Return, therefore, to your husband and deliver him this "message, with which I am charged from on high: As I "deprived the house of David of the regal authority, (saith "the Lord), and, from a mean station in life, exalted thee to "the dignity of a throne, and as thou hast, with the greatest "ingratitude, deserted my worship, and impiously set up "gods of thine own invention, made by the hands of men, "and preferred them to the Creator of the Universe, I will "therefore extirpate thee and thy house from the earth, and "give the carcases of thy people to be consumed by dogs "and the birds of the air. Another king shall be in thy "stead, who shall not suffer one man of thy family to "remain alive. Nor shall the people themselves avoid "punishment, for they shall be driven out of the land "they inhabit, and be scattered beyond the Euphrates, for "imitating thy wickedness, and worshipping thy gods, "in contempt of me and my commandments."

The prophet, having given the queen this message, bid her hasten home, and inform her husband of it as soon as possible; but not till he had assured her that the child should expire the very instant she entered the city.

With this doleful message, and these melancholy tidings, the queen left Ahijah, and no sooner did she arrive home than she found his prediction verified; for the child, a very short time before, had given up the ghost. After her first grief had a little subsided, she delivered the message to the king as she had received it from the prophet, and related every particular that had passed between them.

CHAP. V.

Jeroboam is vanquished by Abijah, son and successor to Rehoboam on the throne of Judah. Death of Abijah. He is succeeded by Asa, a pious and virtuous prince. Death of Jeroboam, and extirpation of his whole race.

NOTWITHSTANDING the late awful and intimidating event, Jeroboam did not appear dismayed, but levied a formidable army, and undertook an expedition against Abijah, son of Rehoboam, who now succeeded to the throne of Judah. Abijah, though young, was a prince of a martial spirit, and so far from being alarmed at this preparation, that, determined to put an end to the dispute which had so long subsisted between the kingdoms of Judah and Israel, he immediately raised an army out of the two tribes, and marched against Jeroboam, whose forces were double the number of those of the king of Judah, though they amounted to four hundred thousand men.

When the two armies were drawn up in order of battle, Abijah advanced to an eminence, and holding up his hand to bespeak silence, spoke to this effect in the hearing of them all:

"You cannot have forgotten that God has promised, "that David and his posterity shall rule this kingdom. I "am therefore surprised to find my father forsaken, and "his subject, Jeroboam, put in his stead, as well as to "see that you have taken up arms against a government "which God hath established, and that you cannot be "contented without driving the legal possessor from what "small portion is still remaining under his jurisdiction. "For Jeroboam has already usurped rather too much of the "greatest part of the kingdom. The Almighty, however, "will not suffer him long to possess what he has so iniqui-"tously obtained, but will severely punish him for his "crimes, and cause those rapacious and oppressive mea-"sures to cease which, instead of endeavouring to termi-"nate, he employs his constant attention to aggravate. "What excuse can be assigned for this falling off? You ne-"ver received any injurious treatment from my father. "One indeed, incited by evil counsel, (of which Jero-"boam was the principal cause), he unhappily made use "of an improper expression, upon which every one of you "departed in a rage, not only relinquishing allegiance to "your sovereign, but your duty to your God. You ought "to have proceeded with deliberation, and to have judged "more favourably of that weakness which is incident to "all mankind. You should also have recollected my fa-"ther's youth, and that he did not affect to be endowed "with the powers of oratory. You should also have con-"sidered him as the son of Solomon, from whom you had "received such signal obligations. I should have suppo-"sed that all these considerations might have induced you "to excuse a hasty expression, and on the father's ac-"count, it would have been [illegible] "tice to have made some [illegible] [illegible] "it is evident you never considered these things, nor is it "probable, if I may form my judgment from the forces "now before us. In what is your [illegible] fixed? "It cannot surely be in your golden figures of calves, your "altars and high places. You confide in your evil deeds, "and not in your religious practices. You act in oppo-"sition to every law, Divine and human, against both, "to meditate in taking up arms against us, who have al-"ways worshipped the true God, not an idol carved "from stone or wood, and imposed upon a [illegible] "credulous multitude, by the [illegible] other prince, "but God the Creator of heaven and earth, who is the "primary and ultimate cause of all things. Repent, "therefore, of the wickedness you have committed, and "follow better courses hereafter; or if you are deter-"mined to contend, let it be for the protection of those "laws from which you derive your preferments and "felicity."

This expostulation from the mouth of Abijah, had not the least effect upon the mind of Jeroboam, who, during the time he was speaking, ordered a detachment to march round, and intercept his retreat. The troops of Abijah were greatly alarmed at this unexpected manœuvre, but their leader encouraged them to place [illegible] exhorting them to depend upon the protection of the Almighty, who would render abortive the most consummate treachery levelled against the righteous cause they were engaged to support. These words from the king revived the courage of his troops, and [illegible] humble supplication to the Almighty for success, till at length the charge being sounded by the priests, they fell on with a mighty clamour, attacked the enemy with such vigour, that they were soon defeated, and a slaughter that is not paralleled in the history of any war either of the Greeks or Barbarians. [illegible] men fell upon the spot, and then [illegible] were taken and [illegible]. After this defeat Jeroboam was never able to make head against his [illegible]. Abijah, however, did not long survive this memorable event; but, after a short reign of hardly three years, paid the debt of nature, and [illegible] at Jerusalem in the sepulchre of his ancestors. He left behind him twenty-two sons and sixteen daughters, which he had by fourteen women. Asa, his son, [illegible] mother's name was Maachah, succeeded him on the throne, and under his government the land [illegible], yet the blessing of peace for [illegible] years.

In the second year of Asa's reign [illegible] of his own, died Jeroboam, the [illegible] of the ten tribes. His reign was [illegible] or the [illegible] of those ten tribes, the [illegible] of idolatry and the victory obtained over him by Abijah, king of the two tribes of Judah.

Jeroboam was succeeded by his son Nadab, who fol-lowed the impious example of his father. His reign was but short; for, at the close of about two years, leading his army against Gibbethon, a city of the Philistines, thinking it might be taken by assault, he was cut off by the treachery of a professed friend, called Baasha, who seized upon the government, and destroyed the whole house of Jeroboam, according to the prophecy denounced by Abijah, "That the dogs should eat of Jeroboam's "flock that died in the city, and that the fowls of the air "should eat him that died in the fields." This was the result of their impious apostacy and most flagitious conduct.

CHAP. VI.

[illegible] and upright prince. Defeats Zerah, king of Ethiopia. Invites the king of Damascus to assist him against Baasha, who is taken off by death, as was his [illegible] and successor, Zimri.

ASA, king of Jerusalem, was a prince of an excellent disposition, and laudably employed the interval of peace, for the first ten years of his reign, in removing the abominable [illegible] which had been introduced among the people. He was in fact, a man of true religion and morals, and [illegible] conformity to the law of God, as handed down by his forefathers. He rectified the errors of government, and purged his dominions from the abominations of idolatry, and the corruption of [illegible].

During this interval of peace he also fortified several [illegible] the frontiers of his kingdom. He likewise trained [illegible] great part of his subjects to the art of war, [illegible] in a short time, he had an army of three hundred thousand men of the tribe of Judah armed with [illegible] and [illegible], and two hundred and [illegible] of the tribe of Benjamin, with shields and [illegible].

[illegible] of the tenth year of his reign, [illegible] king of Ethiopia, invaded Judea with an army [illegible] thousand foot, one hundred thousand horse, [illegible] hundred chariots. When he was advanced as far as [illegible], a city in the dependency of Judah, Asa [illegible] against him, and encamped in a [illegible] called Sephatha, at a small distance from [illegible]. When [illegible] their very formidable [illegible] he [illegible] the Divine aid, declaring that he had taken [illegible] only through the confidence he reposed in the protection of the Almighty, and that his assistance would more than compensate for the inferiority of numbers, and every other apparent disadvantage. Upon this humble application, he was encouraged with tokens and assurances of victory.

Nor was it long before they were made good, for, [illegible], he charged the enemy with such invincible fortitude, that they immediately gave way, and a total rout ensued, attended with prodigious slaughter. He pursued them to the plain of Gerar, and there quitting the pursuit, [illegible] the city itself, and likewise the camp of the enemy, carrying off [illegible] booty in gold and cattle.

Having, through the interposition of Divine Providence, gained this signal victory, the king returned in triumph with his army to Jerusalem. When they had got within a small distance of the city, he was met by Azariah, the prophet, who having commanded him to halt, addressed him in words to this effect:

"It hath pleased the Almighty, on account of your "piety and virtue, to give you this signal victory; and if "you proceed in the like discharge of your duty in future, "you may be assured that success will attend all your un-"dertakings. But if ever you deviate from the religion "and laws of your forefathers, you will suffer the most "dreadful calamities, and the time will come in which "there shall not be a true prophet [illegible] "worthy the dignity of his functions. Your cities shall "be razed, and your people dispersed like vagabonds "throughout the earth. Persevere, therefore, you [illegible] "in the paths of piety, and [illegible] "[illegible] judgment and [illegible] to God for the "[illegible]."

The words of the prophet were extremely grateful to the king in particular, and the people in general, and it became their study and practice, both in public and private life, to maintain inviolate the religion and laws of their country, to promote which laudable purpose the king appointed commissioners throughout his dominions, to superintend both civil and ecclesiastical concerns. Such was the present situation of Asa, king of the two tribes. We now return to Baasha, king of the Israelites, who having taken off Nadab, the son of Jeroboam, usurped the government of the ten tribes.

This usurper reigned four years, during which he resided at his palace in Tarshish. He exceeded Jeroboam and his son in impiety and immorality, was oppressive to his people, and contumacious towards his God, insomuch that a prophet was commissioned to tell him, that "The Almighty would extirpate him and his house from the face of the "earth, as he had done that of Jeroboam before him, for "his ingratitude and disobedience to that power which "had exalted him to the throne, and not paying regard to "righteousness and justice, two qualities most acceptable "to God, and profitable to the people." The prophet added, also, "As he had followed the example of Je"roboam in every instance of iniquity, he should be ren"dered as exemplary in his punishment." Baasha remained inflexible, notwithstanding the judgement denounced against him by the prophet, at the Divine command, continuing daily to add to the measure of his iniquities, regardless of every tie, civil or sacred, and, as it were, setting the Almighty at defiance. Some of his people, having renounced his idolatrous tenets, and gone over to Jerusalem, for the sake of engaging in the true worship, he marched with an army to Ramah, a town belonging to the tribe of Judah, situated about forty furlongs from Jerusalem. This place he fortified, in order to make it the seat of war, and an advantageous situation for making inroads into the territories of Asa, as well as preventing the people from passing to and fro without permission, and thereby cutting off all communication between his tribes and those of Judah.

Asa, apprehensive of his designs, and the danger to which his country would be exposed, from the adjacent situation of so inveterate a foe, dispatched ambassadors to the king of Damascus, with presents, soliciting his alliance upon a principle of friendship that had subsisted between the two houses. The application of Asa had the desired effect, for the king of Damascus instantly broke off with Baasha, suddenly attacked his fortified places, as Achion, Dan and Abelmean, burning some, and razing others. Baasha, by these means, was compelled to abandon his designs of fortifying his frontier towns towards Judah, in order to defend other parts of his territories thus vigorously attacked. Asa availed himself of this opportunity, by demolishing the works raised at Ramah, with the materials of which he erected strong garrisons in the towns called Gaba and Maspha. This was the last of Baasha's military exploits, for he was cut off in his own capital by death, and buried in the city of Arsanes. He was succeeded, on the throne of Israel, by his son Elah, who was as profligate a character as his father. His reign, however, was short, for in the second year, while he was carousing in the house of one of his principal officers of state, he was assassinated by Zimri, one of his grandees, a troop of horse falling upon him, in the absence of his guards, who were then upon a military exploit.

CHAP. VII.

[illegible] king Zimri sets fire to the palace, and perishes in the same. Ahab, a most abandoned prince, succeeds to the throne. Prediction of calamities by the prophet. Jehu ascends the throne of Israel, and Hazael that of Syria. History of Naboth, who is stoned at the instigation of Jezebel, Ahab's queen.

ZIMRI, by treacherous means having advanced himself to the throne, exterminated the whole race of Baasha, as had been the fate of Jeroboam, for his daring impieties, according to prophetic prediction. The news of Elah's death, and the assassin's usurping the crown, reaching Gibbethon, while the army was before the town, they declared for Omri their general, who immediately raised the siege of that place, marched to Tirzah, and took it by storm. This so alarmed Zimri, that seeing all lost, and despairing of any quarter from the enemy, he retired into a private apartment of the palace to which he set fire, and the whole building was consumed, himself perishing in the flames, after a reign of only seven days.

Every thing was now in a most embarrassed state, and the people divided into two factions. The one supported the interest of Omri, and the other that of Thamni, but the former carried it, so the latter being slain, Omri enjoyed the government without interruption. This event happened in the thirtieth year of the reign of Asa. Omri reigned twelve years, six at Tirzah, and six at Mareon, which the Greeks call Samaria. He introduced more abominable practices, if possible, than any of his predecessors. Indeed, it was their general custom to alienate the minds of the people from the love and service of the true God, and lead them to the commission of every enormity. Therefore the Almighty, in his vengeance, rendered them successively instrumental to the destruction of one another, till, in the end, the whole race became extinct. Omri died at Samaria, and was succeeded in the government by his son Ahab.

It is worthy of observation, that, during the reign of Asa over Judah, Israel was subject to seven or eight different princes, as Jeroboam, Nadab, Baasha, Ela, Zimri, Thamni, Omri, and Ahab, yet such was their hardiness in idolatry, that, in all these changes, not one of them ever thought of returning to the house of David, or paying attention to the worship of the true God at Jerusalem. In the course of these occurrences, we are given to understand, how the Divine Providence interposes in human affairs, in showering down blessings on the righteous, and in the extirpation of the wicked.

Asa, king of Jerusalem, and of the two tribes, lived happily in the Divine favour to a great age, in consideration of his piety and virtue, and departed this life in peace, after a reign of forty-one years. His son Jehoshaphat, whom he had by Abida, succeeded him on the throne of Judah. — This prince inherited his father's virtues, and walked according to the example of his illustrious ancestor David, that most eminent king of Israel.

Ahab, king of Israel, took up his residence at Samaria, where he reigned two and twenty years. He was one of the most wicked princes, and abominable idolaters, that ever sat on a throne. He followed the example of the most impious of his predecessors in their most abominable practices, and more particularly those of Jeroboam. He not only continued the worship of the calves which Jeroboam had set up, but having married Jezebel, the daughter of Ethbaal, king of Tyre and Sidon, was by her seduced to the idolatry of worshipping her country gods. To indulge her rash and impetuous disposition, he erected a temple in Samaria, to Baal, the idol of the Tyrians, planted groves for the exercise of superstitious ceremonies, and appointed priests for that impious service. Indeed, Ahab was surrounded with idolaters and profligates, being of a similar disposition, averse to whatever was good, and prone to every kind of evil.

In order to render the abandoned Israelites, in general, and their impious king, in particular, sensible of the enormities they daily committed, there came to Ahab a prophet, who was a Tishbite, and born in the city of Gilead. The purport of his message was to tell the king that, from the time of his departure there should not fall a single drop of rain, nor should there be the least sign of dew in all this province, till the time of his return. This prediction he confirmed with the strongest assurances.

After the prophet had executed the Divine commission, he proceeded to the southward till he came to a brook, where he stopped for the present, in order to refresh himself with water, the ravens, day by day, duly supplying him with food. Through the continuance of the drought the water of the brook began to fail, upon which the prophet moved by Divine [illegible] the [illegible] a town between [illegible] and Sidon, for [illegible] been foretold by a voice from on high that he should there find a widow woman to receive and furnish [illegible] the necessary refreshment.

[illegible] therefore to the Divine command, the prophet set out, and having [illegible], reached the end of his journey, [illegible] observed a woman gathering sticks not far from the [illegible], whom he concluded to be the widow to whom he had been directed. This induced him to call to her, requesting [illegible] she would fetch him a little water to quench his thirst [illegible] also, as she was going for the water, desired she would [illegible] with her a morsel of bread. The woman solemnly [illegible], that [illegible] of meal, and a little oil, were all she had to keep herself and son from starving, and that she was [illegible] into a cake. But the prophet encouraged her to do as he [illegible], as soon as the cake was [illegible], [illegible] that neither her meal [illegible] during the [illegible] of the famine. The woman [illegible] and found his words [illegible] time, for she and her son, together with [illegible], constantly [illegible] to the barrel of meal and [illegible], [illegible] no sooner diminished than an [illegible] took place, nor did it [illegible] brought [illegible].

Menander [illegible] this drought in the history of Ithobal, [illegible] of the [illegible] (says he) there was an [illegible] drought [illegible] continued from the [illegible] of Hyperberetæus till the [illegible] month next year [illegible] and were [illegible] for the [illegible] of the judg[illegible] which were followed [illegible] mighty claps of thunder." [illegible] Botrys, in Phœnicia, and Auzates, in Ab[illegible] drought under Ahab, Menander evidently [illegible], for it was in the reign of Ahab [illegible] king of Tyre and Sidon. But to return.

When the prophet had sojourned with the widow some [illegible] became extremely sick, and the [illegible] the [illegible] of exclamation, [illegible] as if he came to reproach her [illegible] upon her. [illegible] the prophet bid her be of good cheer, and [illegible] to him, with [illegible] he would restore him to [illegible]. He then took him into his [illegible] chamber, where [illegible] the Almighty to restore the child to life. This [illegible] the child revived, and was delivered by him to the mother, who received him with unfeigned gratitude, [illegible] of the Divine mission of the prophet [illegible] (*).

[illegible] the prophet was commanded to return [illegible] of Israel, present himself before Ahab, and [illegible] that, after [illegible] time, rain would descend on the [illegible]. The famine at this time raged with so much violence [illegible] the whole country, of Samaria, that the people [illegible] being starved to death. The king was so [illegible] of provender for his cattle, that [illegible] for Obadiah [illegible] of his flocks, charging him to [illegible] of the prophet [illegible] means bring him to him [illegible] where [illegible], he ordered Obadiah to accompany him, and when they had proceeded [illegible], the king took one way, and the other [illegible]. Obadiah was a man of pure religion, and at [illegible] the cruel queen Jezebel had given [illegible] for [illegible] all the prophets, he concealed and protected an hundred of them in a cave, and there provided them with [illegible] sustenance.

[illegible] and Obadiah were no sooner parted, than the [illegible] Elias [illegible] the way, and [illegible] him with the great [illegible]. The prophet desired him to go to the [illegible], and inform him that he was ready to wait on him. Obadiah, apprehensive that Elias might depart before his return, replied, "In what have I [illegible] that thou would[illegible]

"est [illegible] into the hand of Ahab [illegible]? "As the Lord thy God liveth, there is no nation or king-"dom whither the king hath not sent to seek thee; and "when they [illegible], He is not here, he took an oath of "the [illegible] that they found thee not; and now thou "sayest, Go, tell thy king, Behold, Elias is here. As "soon as I am gone from thee, thou mayest be carried "whither I know not, so when I tell Ahab, and he can-"not find thee, he will slay me. I thy servant feared "the Lord from my youth. Was it not told my lord "what I did, when Jezebel slew the prophets, that I hid "an hundred of them in a cave, and provided them with "sustenance?" Elias bid him fear nothing, but go to the king, solemnly assuring him that he would present himself to Ahab that very day.

Thus assured, Obadiah went in search of the king, whom having found he afterwards introduced Elias [illegible] the first interview the king began to upbraid him with being the cause of the calamity under which the [illegible] had so long laboured. The prophet boldly [illegible] charge, and, after having [illegible] him with the worship of false gods, and suppressing the true religion, desired him to summon the multitude to meet upon Mount Carmel, together with his priests and prophets, and those of his wife. The king summoned them, and they accordingly met. Elias then addressed them in words to the following purport: "How long will you live thus in uncer-"tainty of mind and opinion? If you believe [illegible] God "we worship to be the only living and true God, obey "him, and keep his commandments; if otherwise, per-"sue your own courses." To put the matter to the test [illegible] proposed an experiment. "Since," said he, "there [illegible] "can be no more than one Infinite, Supreme, and Almighty "Being, let us at this time make the experiment [illegible] "Being is. You, who are the worshippers of Baal, have "all the advantage on you [illegible] the favour and protec-"tion of the court, four hundred and fifty priests of [illegible] "[illegible] and four hundred of another, whereas I [illegible] "[illegible], a single prophet, to defend the cause of that power "from whom I receive my commission. Let the priests of "Baal choose the[illegible] ox, and lay it on the altar [illegible] "[illegible] fire thereon. I will then choose my ox, [illegible] "them [illegible] to their gods, and I will call on the name of "Jehovah [illegible] then let the God who, by consuming the "sacrifice with a sudden flash of fire, shall make it appear "that he hath heard the invocations, be declared by this "whole assembly the One, the True, and Supreme Being."

This mode of determination being approved by the multitude, Elias bade [illegible]'s prophets take an ox, and invoke their gods by their names, giving them the precedence, in point of offering sacrifice. When they had invoked their gods a considerable time without effect, Elias ridiculed their superstition, and bade them exalt their voices, as perhaps their might be at a greater distance than they imagined. They then went on with hideous outcries and [illegible] exclamations, scarifying themselves with lances after the [illegible] of their country; but all without the least effect.

When Elias proceeded to sacrifice, [illegible] desired the multitude to draw nearer, and make diligent search in order to discover if [illegible] was secretly conveyed to the spot on which he was about to give proof of the Divine [illegible] of his mission. Upon the approach of the multitude, Elias took twelve stones, to answer the number of the twelve tribes, and erected an altar out of them, making a deep trench around it. The wood being fitted and the sacrifice laid upon the pile, five vessels of spring water were cast upon the altar, so that it ran off and filled the trench. After every thing was duly prepared, Elias approached the altar, and implored the true God [illegible] to manifest his [illegible] by some circumstance that might convince a mis-guided people of their error." Upon this supplication [illegible] descended [illegible] from above, upon the altar, and, in the sigh[illegible]

(*) [illegible]

[illegible]

AHAB King of Israel SLAIN in his Chariot by an ARROW
at the Battle of Ramoth Gilead

[illegible] consumed not only the burnt offering, [illegible] the wood and stones, and even dried up the water in the trench.

This extraordinary display of the divine power so astonished the people, that they fell prostrate, and acknowledged that the God of [illegible] was the only living and true God, declaring, at the same time, that they looked upon [illegible] as the productions of human invention. When the people [illegible] from their surprise, Elias [illegible] all the prophets and priests of Baal to be [illegible] and his command was immediately executed. [illegible] to the king to compose his mind, as he might [illegible] would be refreshed with rain in a very [illegible].

[illegible] having thus taken place of the false prophets [illegible] the top of [illegible], after having prayed for some [illegible] sent his servant to see if he could discover any [illegible]. He went up again and again, but with no [illegible]. At length, after the seventh time, he brought his [illegible] that he saw a small cloud rising out of the sea [illegible] the size of a man's hand. In consequence of this [illegible] he dispatched his servant to Ahab to advise [illegible] to his chariot [illegible] the head of his [illegible] should be [illegible] a very great storm [illegible] the advice of the prophet, who, having [illegible] ran before the chariot till he [illegible] by which time the clouds [illegible] thicker, and discharged abundance of water. [illegible] Jezebel was informed by Ahab of all the wonders [illegible] the prophets had been put [illegible] the command of Elias, she immediately [illegible] revenge [illegible] dispatched messengers to inform [illegible] she would certainly pay for theirs. On that [illegible] prophet [illegible] withdrew to Beersheba, [illegible] in the southern part of Judah and bordering upon [illegible]. In this place he [illegible] and pursued his [illegible] wilderness [illegible] he laid himself down [illegible] of the world, and desirous to leave it. — "[illegible] is no longer desirable." After [illegible] it was not long before he [illegible] before him, [illegible] and by the strength of that [illegible] to Mount Sinai, the place where God [illegible] to Moses. He then betook himself [illegible] cave, intending [illegible] to end the remainder of his days in that of [illegible].

After he had passed some time in this habitation, [illegible] he left the [illegible] desert [illegible] heard the [illegible] where it came [illegible]. His reply, however, was, that the [illegible] for [illegible] pro[illegible] the one only [illegible] commanded him to leave [illegible] and attend to the Divine [illegible] future conduct. He accordingly [illegible], when he heard the noise of an earthquake [illegible] saw in the air the appearance of blazing fire [illegible] followed by a [illegible] time of silence, after which he heard a voice exhorting him not to be [illegible] situation, for his enemies should not prevail [illegible] him. He was commanded to return home by [illegible] of Damascus, and there anoint Hazael king of Syria, and [illegible] the son of Nimshi, king over Israel, and also [illegible] Elisha his successor in the prophetic office, [illegible] intimating that these men would be proper instruments in the hands of Divine vengeance to punish the [illegible] of the [illegible] and extirpate those who encouraged and [illegible] it.

[illegible] did, [illegible] with [illegible] he had seen and heard, [illegible] ing Elisha, the son of Shaphat, ploughing with others, threw his mantle (*c*) over him. [illegible] Elisha immediately upon this began to prophesy, quitted the plough, and declared himself ready to follow Elias, only desiring to take leave of his father and mother before his departure. This being granted him, he returned, and thenceforward became the [illegible] companion of Elias during life.

Ahab, notwithstanding so many repeated tokens of the divine displeasure, [illegible] and, to aggravate his [illegible] former instances of injustice was guilty of an action of the most unjustifiable nature. It happened that one Naboth, a citizen of Jezreel, had a vineyard adjoining to the royal gardens, which the king was desirous of obtaining in order to enlarge his own grounds. To accomplish his desire he offered Naboth an equivalent, either in land or money, but the possessor, as it was his paternal inheritance, refused to part with it on any terms whatever. This so much disgusted Ahab, that he could neither sleep, nor take any convivial or social pleasures.

When Jezebel, after many enquiries, became acquainted with the real cause of her husband's complaint, and that, notwithstanding he had treated Naboth with a degree of courtesy and condescension derogatory to his dignity, he could not obtain his consent to the proposal he had made him, she, at first, upbraided him with pusillanimity, or not knowing how to exert the authority of a king. She afterwards desired him to banish all melancholy, as she had thought of an expedient by which he might be put in possession of the coveted vineyard. The device was this. She caused letters to be written in the king's name, and sealed with his signet, to be directed to the principal men in Jezreel, commanding them to proclaim a fast, call an assembly, and assign Naboth a place amongst the leaders. They were then to suborn two witnesses to give evidence against him for blaspheming God and the king, upon whose testimony he should stand convicted and receive sentence to be stoned to death by the people. Notwithstanding the baseness of the plot, such was the influence of the king over the leading men in Jezreel, that every thing was executed according to the directions of the infamous Jezebel, and the innocent Naboth fell a sacrifice to the covetous disposition of the king, and the infernal machinations of a tyrannical and perfidious woman.

As soon as Jezebel received intelligence that the cruel murder was perpetrated, she repaired to the king, informed him of the circumstance, and desired him to go to Jezreel, and, without any ceremony, take possession of the vineyard. Ahab, pleased with the effect of the plan devised by his queen, immediately followed her directions, and prepared for a visit to his new possessions. But he was suddenly met by the prophet Elias, who, at the Divine command, first upbraided him with having slain the innocent, and then usurping a right to his possessions. When Ahab saw the prophet approaching, he made open confession of the whole transaction, and a tender of any satisfaction he might require. But Elias spurned at the offer, and denounced judgment on him to this effect: "That where the blood of Naboth had been licked by "dogs, they should likewise lick the blood of Ahab and "Jezebel, and that the crime of taking away the life of "an innocent man by perjury, should be punished by the "extirpation of his whole race."

Ahab was so affected at the denunciation of this judgment, that he became deeply penitent, cloathed himself in sackcloth, went barefoot, and gave every proof of the most unfeigned sorrow and humiliation. Hereupon the prophet was commissioned to acquaint him, that in consideration of his contrition, the judgment denounced should be postponed during his life, but that it should certainly take place in that of his son, the truth of which prediction will hereafter appear.

(*c*) [illegible] However the [illegible]

CHAP. VIII.

[illegible] Syria [illegible] Damascus, [illegible] defeat [illegible] mighty [illegible] [illegible] [illegible] to death, [illegible] the great [illegible] [illegible] the [illegible]

DURING the [illegible] between Ahab and [illegible] [illegible], Adad the king of Syria and Damascus, [illegible] [illegible] [illegible] [illegible] parts of his dominions, [illegible] two confederate princes [illegible] [illegible] [illegible] mighty force [illegible] the king of Israel [illegible] [illegible] to hazard the [illegible] of [illegible] plain with [illegible] power to oppose, retreated to fortified places in order to act upon the defensive. He [illegible] in Samaria, [illegible] eligible [illegible], being surrounded [illegible] strong walls [illegible] good [illegible] [illegible] numerous [illegible] [illegible] [illegible] the [illegible] [illegible] [illegible] The king [illegible] [illegible] [illegible] leading [illegible] the [illegible] [illegible] to Ahab [illegible] [illegible] he might dispatch [illegible] [illegible] to [illegible] terms.

[illegible] the [illegible] were [illegible] [illegible] pitched [illegible] to inform Ahab, that [illegible] [illegible] treasures, [illegible] king of Syria, [illegible] [illegible] [illegible] part of [illegible] he pleased, [illegible] [illegible] [illegible] [illegible] Then the [illegible] [illegible] the king the [illegible] [illegible] [illegible] [illegible] [illegible] to defeat [illegible] [illegible] [illegible] [illegible] [illegible] [illegible] [illegible] own [illegible] [illegible] [illegible] [illegible] [illegible] of Ahab.

[illegible] [illegible] to deliver [illegible] [illegible] [illegible] [illegible] [illegible] [illegible] [illegible] [illegible] the [illegible] [illegible] [illegible] [illegible] [illegible] [illegible] [illegible] [illegible] [illegible] [illegible] [illegible] [illegible] [illegible] [illegible] the peace [illegible] the common [illegible] people [illegible] [illegible] [illegible] [illegible] [illegible] [illegible] [illegible] [illegible] [illegible] property [illegible] [illegible] [illegible] [illegible] [illegible] [illegible] [illegible] [illegible] [illegible] [illegible] I am [illegible] [illegible] the matter to [illegible] [illegible] [illegible] [illegible] by [illegible]

The [illegible] [illegible] [illegible] [illegible] [illegible] [illegible] [illegible] [illegible] [illegible] [illegible] to the [illegible] [illegible] [illegible] [illegible] [illegible] [illegible] [illegible] [illegible] [illegible] [illegible] [illegible]

A[illegible] [illegible] [illegible] [illegible] [illegible] [illegible] [illegible] [illegible] [illegible] [illegible] [illegible] [illegible] [illegible] [illegible] [illegible] [illegible] [illegible] [illegible] [illegible] his troops, in order to deter him from opposition [illegible] replied in laconic terms, that, "Men of [illegible] [illegible] "[illegible] with their swords, not with their tongues."

When the ambassadors returned, they found the [illegible] at [illegible] board with his confederate princes, and having informed Adad of Ahab's reply, he gave immediate orders for carrying on the siege with all possible vigour. [illegible] and his people, were greatly intimidated at the [illegible] preparations made by the enemy, in circumvallating the [illegible] and [illegible] strong bulwark, till a prophet came to him and encouraged him with an assurance that he should prevail against this tremendous power. When he expressed [illegible] of being informed by what means the victory was to be obtained, he received for answer, "By the sons of the [illegible] "of the people [illegible] [illegible] conduct [illegible] [illegible] [illegible] Ahab, to avail by this pleasing information, called them together to [illegible] [illegible] [illegible] hundred and [illegible] [illegible] [illegible] the king of Syria [illegible] [illegible] [illegible] the gates were suddenly [illegible] [illegible] the young officers made a [illegible] rapid sally [illegible] [illegible] given by the centinels to Adad, [illegible] he [illegible] orders, that "Whether they come to fight or to treat, [illegible] "[illegible] bring them bound to him." Ahab, [illegible] [illegible] [illegible] within the walls, [illegible] [illegible] [illegible] [illegible] might repair but the [illegible] [illegible] [illegible] [illegible] many of them [illegible] [illegible] the rest to [illegible] [illegible] Ahab found [illegible] succeeded [illegible] [illegible] [illegible] the [illegible] of [illegible] to fally forth, [illegible] the Syrians [illegible] [illegible] [illegible] [illegible] [illegible] [illegible] [illegible] [illegible] [illegible] [illegible] [illegible] [illegible] [illegible] [illegible] were put to the rout, [illegible] [illegible] [illegible] [illegible] [illegible] [illegible] [illegible] [illegible] Ahab following [illegible] [illegible] [illegible] fled [illegible] [illegible] camp [illegible] [illegible] [illegible] [illegible] [illegible] chariots and horses [illegible] [illegible] [illegible] [illegible] the prophet advised him [illegible] [illegible] [illegible] as the king of [illegible] [illegible] [illegible] the next [illegible] [illegible] [illegible] [illegible] [illegible] [illegible] renewal of the contest.

[illegible] friends, [illegible] the remainder [illegible] [illegible] to deliberate on their future conduct. When [illegible] [illegible] [illegible] [illegible] [illegible] another [illegible] [illegible] [illegible] the Hebrews, [illegible] [illegible] [illegible] [illegible] engaging with [illegible] mountains, because [illegible] [illegible] [illegible] [illegible] [illegible] [illegible] [illegible] [illegible] [illegible] [illegible] [illegible] [illegible] [illegible] [illegible] [illegible] [illegible] further personal [illegible] [illegible] [illegible] [illegible] [illegible] [illegible] [illegible] [illegible] experienced [illegible] [illegible] [illegible] [illegible] [illegible] [illegible] [illegible] [illegible] [illegible] [illegible] [illegible] [illegible] places of [illegible] [illegible] [illegible] [illegible] [illegible] [illegible] [illegible] [illegible] [illegible]

In the beginning of the spring the king of Syria [illegible] with his army against the Hebrews, and pitched his camp in a large plain, according to the advice of his [illegible] [illegible] [illegible] [illegible] In the [illegible] Ahab [illegible] [illegible] [illegible] [illegible] [illegible] [illegible] [illegible] [illegible] [illegible] [illegible] [illegible] [illegible] of the Syrians. [illegible] [illegible] [illegible] each other, the prophet came to the Hebrews with the Divine assurance [illegible] [illegible] [illegible] [illegible] their enemies [illegible] [illegible] [illegible] [illegible] [illegible] [illegible] [illegible] [illegible] [illegible] to the [illegible]

The armies [illegible] [illegible] to their respective [illegible] [illegible] [illegible] [illegible] [illegible] [illegible] advanced [illegible] both sides [illegible] [illegible] [illegible] battle. The [illegible] the enemy. [illegible] [illegible] who [illegible] up in flight, and the ... to perish by ... misadventure ... immediately brought on by confusion, the havock was very great; for, indeed they were destroyed by their own hands, and by one another. Those that got to Aphek, their only place of refuge, were but few in number, and it is supposed that about seven and twenty thousand were crushed to death by the walls suddenly falling to the ground, and that an hundred thousand were slain in battle.

Terrified at this dreadful judgment, Adad, with some of his officers and friends, retired for security into a subterraneous ground, where some of them took occasion to applaud the clemency and humanity of the Hebrews, and advise to invite the king to cast himself at Ahab's feet for mercy, in confidence that, upon such application and submission, it would not be rejected.

Adad approved of the advice, and thereupon several of his ... dressed in the habits of suppliants, their ... sackcloth, with ropes about their necks, ... the custom of the country in such cases (a) ... to Ahab, requesting the life of their king upon ... he might be pleased to propose. The king received them courteously, and assured them, that, ... the safety of their king as much as ... Nay, he promised to shew him the same tokens of honour and respect.

... having received assurances, upon oath, that no ... should be offered to his person, he went ... his retirement, and brought him to Ahab, ... his chariot. As soon as the vanquished ... king, he bowed ... Ahab ... him with the utmost courtesy, ... him ... and pledging his ... honour for his perfect security and freedom. ... he acknowledged ... connection, of which he declared he should retain a grateful remembrance ... He ... promised to restore to the Hebrews the cities ... which the former kings had taken from them, and that Ahab should have every ... in the capital city of Damascus. Such mild treatment could not but be acceptable to Ahab, the result ... that the ... immediately took ... between the contracting monarchs, founded on a ... of oaths for the performance of covenants, after which Adad was dismissed with ... to his own country.

... the ... between the kings of Israel and Syria ... prophet, whose name was Michaiah, came ... Ahab's subjects, and bid him smite him on the ... telling him that it was the Divine will ... upon his refusal, the prophet told him he would ... for his disobedience, for he should be destroyed by a lion. When the accident foretold had befallen the man, the prophet applied to another with the same injunction, who immediately smote him, and drew blood. Upon ... bound up his head and went to the king with this ... That he had been one of his soldiers and had ... custody of one of the prisoners delivered to his ... an officer; and that the prisoner having escaped, he was in danger of his own life, by means of that officer, who had threatened him with death if the prisoner was not found, when called for in his custody." When Ahab told him he would suffer justly, he unbound his head and gave him to know his person and office ... him he made use of this artifice as ... the following prediction: "That God would punish him who had suffered Adad, a blasphemer against him, to escape punishment (b), for the time would come when this very Adad whom he now spared, would be the means of his death, and the destruction of his army." Ahab was highly exasperated at the denunciation of the prophet, and commanded him to be imprisoned, though he was much affected, and struck to the very heart, by his prediction. But we shall return to the affairs of Jehoshaphat king of Jerusalem.

CHAP. IX.

Jehoshaphat's ... Jerusalem, ...

JEHOSHAPHAT had not only ... his territories, and put garrisons into all the cities under his jurisdiction, but had ... in those cities which were taken out of the ... of Ephraim ... his grandfather Abijah, when Jeroboam reigned over the ten tribes. This prince was favoured with the Divine blessing, assistance, and protection, in all his undertakings, for ... he ... the ... Almighty ... and employed in acts pleasing to God ... to mankind. His ... integrity and ... gained him the reverence ... of all the neighbouring princes, as appeared from the ... presents ... poured in upon him from different quarters, and ... tended to enhance both his fortune and fame. In the third year of his reign he summoned the elders and priests that were under his jurisdiction, and ordered them to appoint commissioners in their respective cities and towns within his dominions to enforce a regular attendance on divine worship, and ... observance of the laws of Moses. His own concern for the preservation of the pure religion ... the powerful ... on the minds of his subjects, who seemed to vie with each other in the promotion of so excellent a work. Nay, ... seems to have impressed the neighbouring princes with a kind of reverential awe, for they lived in peace and harmony, and studied to render each other mutual services. The Philistines paid their tribute with the most scrupulous regard to justice, and the Arabians their annual tribute of 6?0 lambs, and the like number of kids with the greatest compliance.

Jehoshaphat also fortified ... great cities and towns, and kept in constant pay a well disciplined army, to be in readiness upon any urgent occasion. Of the tribe of Judah there were three hundred thousand chief officers, under the command of Adna; and two hundred thousand under Johanan; and, of the tribe of Benjamin two hundred thousand archers, under the same officers. There was also another officer, called Achobat, who commanded an hundred and eighty thousand men, armed with bucklers, besides the soldiers who were dispersed in different garrisons.

Jehoshaphat at length married his son, Joram, to Athaliah, the daughter of Ahab, ... upon which occasion, when he went to ... sumptuously entertained by Ahab, ... his officers and attendants in general, were presented with the ... productions of the country. At the entreaty of Ahab, upon this visit, he joined him in an expedition against the king of Syria, for the recovery of Ramoth-Gilead, which had been taken, and was detained from him, by that prince. Jehoshaphat promised him powerful assistance, and sent for a numerous army from Jerusalem to Samaria, where both the kings went out of the town, and each of them, seated on ... throne of state, reviewed and gave orders to their forces. Previous to their entering upon hostilities, Jehoshaphat deemed it advisable if there were any prophets at hand, to consult them upon the occasion. For there had been a three years interval of peace between the kings of Israel and Syria.

CHAP. X.

Consultation of the prophets ... Different opinions ... Death ... Ahab.

IN consequence of the advice of Jehoshaphat, Ahab called his prophets together to the number of about four hundred, and commanded them to ... concerning

(a) ... the ... humble suppliants ... The sackcloth ... token of ... for what ... had done, and the ... be ... Ahab should ... proper to ... on their ...

(b) Ahab ... a ... to ... them ... sufficient ...

the event of the war with Adad, and [illegible] the [illegible] the city, on which account it was [illegible]. These prophets [illegible] declare [illegible] their [illegible] of the [illegible] before. But Jehoſhaphat, who [illegible] the [illegible] of both of these prophets and their predictions, asked Ahab if there were no other prophets to whom he [illegible] have recourſe with no certainty. Ahab replied, that "There was, "indeed one Micaiah," but that he [illegible] never foretold [illegible] any ſucceſs, but, on the contrary, had foretold that he ſhould fall by the hands of the king of Syria; for which cauſe he was now in priſon.

Upon Jehoſhaphat's deſire however, that he might be produced, an eunuch was diſpatched to bring him into the royal preſence. The meſſenger informed Micaiah on the way, that the reſt of the prophets had unanimouſly declared that Ahab ſhould be victorious in the [illegible] of the king of Syria. Micaiah declared that he would not [illegible] in ſo ſolemn a matter, but would [illegible] to the king such meſſages as he ſhould receive from the Divine [illegible].

Upon the prophet's arrival, and [illegible] him to ſpeak the truth, he ſaid, "I ſaw [illegible] flying, "and the Syrians purſuing them [illegible] diſperſed when their ſhepherd is ſlain; by which repreſentation I am given to underſtand, that the [illegible] in general, "ſhall return ſafe, but that the king ſhall fall in the action." When Micaiah had uttered this alarming prediction Ahab ſaid to the king of Jeruſalem, "Are you not convinced that "this man is my enemy?" Micaiah declared the contrary, and ſolemnly [illegible] that the words he delivered were [illegible] according to the Divine command [illegible] Ahab, at the inſtigation of [illegible] prophets, had engaged in an expedition, which to him would prove fatal. The [illegible] of this upright prophet threw the king into ſuſpenſe and conſternation.

During his ſtate of anxiety one Zedekiah [illegible] himſelf to Ahab, and in [illegible] of Micaiah, [illegible] his opinion, and [illegible] the falſity of the prediction. In order to this he cited the prediction of [illegible], "That the "dogs ſhould lick his blood in the [illegible] of Jezreel in the field "of Naboth, as they licked the blood of Naboth, who, at [illegible] was ſtoned to death by the multitude." Whence he inferred the falſity of Micaiah, as contradicting a greater prophet than himſelf, by ſaying, that the king within the compaſs of three days ſhould fall in battle. As a further proof of his falſity, Zedekiah ſaid he would ſmite Micaiah, to try if his hand would wither upon ſo doing, as Jadon [illegible] the hand of king Jeroboam to wither upon a former occaſion. Having thus ſpoken, he ſtruck the prophet and Ahab finding no judgment immediately follow, perſevered in his reſolution of entering upon the war, giving more credit to falſe prophets than true, and thereby haſtening the judgment that awaited him. Zedekiah then made horns of iron, and declared to Ahab that thoſe horns were ſignals of his total conqueſt of Syria. Micaiah, on the other hand, [illegible] the falſe prophet, that, in a ſhort time, he ſhould be called to account for his [illegible] pretenſions, and be compelled to ſeek refuge to avoid juſt puniſhment. The king was ſo exaſperated with Micaiah that he remanded him back to priſon, with orders to the governor of the city to allow him only bread and water till his return.

The kings of Iſrael and Jeruſalem now advanced with their forces towards Ramoth, and the king of Syria, no ſooner had the intelligence of it than he marched on to meet them. It had been agreed that Ahab ſhould aſſume the diſguiſe of a private habit, while Jehoſhaphat was arrayed in his royal robes, in order to evade the preſage of the prophet. But this artifice had no effect, for Adad, by his officers, had iſſued ſtrict orders to his army to encounter neither ſmall or great, except Ahab king of Iſrael.

The Syrians, at firſt, ſeeing Jehoſhaphat at the head of the army, conceived that he was Ahab, and advanced towards him to execute the order of their king; but when they found their error, they retreated. They kept the field from morning till night, the one party flying, the other purſuing; but no blood was ſhed during the whole day. Ahab was the object of purſuit, and the Syrians, in general, were in queſt of him; at length one of Adad's attendants [illegible] an arrow at a venture, that entered through his breaſt-plate into his very lungs. Ahab was deſirous of keeping the accident from the knowledge of his men, leſt they ſhould be [illegible], and therefore ordered his charioteer to take him a little way aſide, as he was mortally wounded. He [illegible] in his chariot till about ſun-ſet, when he expired in great agony.

When night came on, the Syrians withdrew to their camp, and as ſoon as the death of Ahab was announced [illegible] they all returned home. The king's body was carried to Samaria and there interred. The chariot in which he was conveyed was ſo ſtained with blood that iſſued from his wound, that they were obliged to [illegible] it in a neighbouring fountain, in doing of which the dogs [illegible] it, thereby fulfilling one part of the prediction of Elias, which he denounced againſt Ahab in [illegible] of Naboth, the citizen of Jezreel. He [illegible] Ramoth, as Micaiah had foretold. [illegible] the [illegible] of the predictions of the true prophets, we [illegible] ſingular inſtances of the interpoſition of Divine providence. This ſhould diſpoſe us to the worſhip of the one only and true God, and diſſuade us from any reliance on falſe prophets and impoſtors, who are actuated by mercenary views, and, inſtead of leading us to our duty to God, divert us from it into the path of infidelity and impiety. The gift of prophecy is of ſingular advantage, as men are thereby ſhewn what they ought to avoid, though they too frequently perſiſt in their obſtinacy till it proves fatal. This was the caſe of Ahab, [illegible] diſbelieved thoſe who foretold his defeat, and was [illegible] for giving credit to what eventually proved falſe. He was ſucceeded in his government by his ſon Ahaziah.

FLAVIUS JOSEPHUS

ON THE

ANTIQUITIES

OF THE

JEWS.

BOOK IX.

[INCLUDING A PERIOD OF ABOUT ONE HUNDRED AND SEVENTY-SIX YEARS.]

CHAP. I.

[illegible] Jehoſhaphat [illegible] Prophecy of [illegible] confirmed by the [illegible] Moabites and their confederates.

WHEN king Jehoſhaphat returned to Jeruſalem, after his going with Ahab againſt the king of Syria, he was met by the prophet Jehu, who ſeverely reprehended him for eſpouſing the cauſe of ſo impious and abandoned a prince as the late king of Iſrael. The prophet, however, aſſured him, that, for the ſake of his own exemplary piety and virtue, the offence for which he had rebuked him, ſhould not only be pardoned, but that God would be pleaſed to deliver him out of the hands of his enemies.

Upon the admonition and encouraging information of the prophet, the king offered up prayers and ſacrifices, as an acknowledgment of the goodneſs of the Father of Mercies. He then appointed a general viſitation throughout his dominions, and iſſued particular orders to thoſe to whom the charge was committed, to inſtruct the people in the laws of Moſes, and the religion of their anceſtors. He alſo erected tribunals, and commiſſioned magiſtrates in all the cities, and conſiderable towns, ſtrictly enjoining them to adminiſter juſtice to all men, without reſpect to perſon, intereſt, or affection, always remembring that they muſt render an account of the diſcharge of their duty, to that Being who ſearches the heart, and cannot be deceived.

Having taken theſe wiſe precautions for the eſtabliſhment of order and good government in the ſeveral cities belonging to the two tribes, he returned to Jeruſalem, where he conſtituted judges out of the moſt conſiderable prieſts and Levites, giving them the [illegible] charge, upon the ſame principle, to adminiſter juſtice with the utmoſt impartiality.

If matters of an intricate or important nature within their reſpective diſtricts, ſhould be brought before them, they were by no means to paſs [illegible] without the greateſt caution and deliberation [illegible] nothing ſhould reflect ſuch foul diſgrace on a king and people, as [illegible] whom the Almighty had been pleaſed [illegible] ple, as a partial adminiſtration of juſtice. He appointed two principal ſuperintendants out of the tribe of Judah, [illegible] were Amariah, the prieſt, for religious, [illegible] dah, a prieſt, for civil concerns.

About this time the Moabites and Ammonites made an expedition against [illegible] who happily with a large army of [illegible] encamped at Engeddi, [illegible] of [illegible] three hundred furlongs diſtant from Jeruſalem, and famous for the production of balſam and palm-trees. When Jehoſhaphat heard that his enemies had paſſed the [illegible] and made an irruption into his dominions, he was [illegible], and [illegible] iſſued orders for calling a general aſſembly of the people in the temple.— When they were convened in a very [illegible] adreſs, he implored the divine [illegible] upon his arms, to enable him to repel [illegible] nation. This was [illegible] agreeable to [illegible] practice of our forefathers upon the firſt [illegible] of that ſacred place, for whenever they had cauſe to apprehend danger of being overcome by [illegible], the people were [illegible] to meet in [illegible], to implore the Divine aſſiſtance towards their [illegible] and the maintenance of [illegible] they enjoyed through the [illegible] [illegible] the [illegible] zeal, [illegible] which were accompanied by the joint ſupplications of the [illegible].

In the midſt of the [illegible] devotions there came into the aſſembly a certain prophet named Jahaziel, exclaiming [illegible] Almighty who would defend them [illegible] and maintain [illegible] He recommended [illegible] proper for [illegible] much [illegible] they ſhould [illegible] encamped between Jeruſalem and Engeddi, at a certain [illegible] the [illegible] of [illegible] which, in our language, ſignifies [illegible]. The prophet added, that there would be no occaſion [illegible] [illegible] in their [illegible] [illegible] ſolicitous [illegible] their favour [illegible] full prospect, worshipped [illegible] accompanied their praise with [illegible] instruments.

[illegible] not [illegible] the city of T[illegible] [illegible] them [illegible] [illegible] the [illegible] [illegible] as would [illegible] and [illegible] and [illegible] upon [illegible] [illegible] Jehoshaphat [illegible] followed.

[illegible] the Ammonites [illegible] ready to begin the attack, [illegible] upon one another [illegible] [illegible] Jehoshaphat [illegible] [illegible] [illegible] he gave his orders [illegible] the [illegible] were three days in collecting [illegible].

On the [illegible] deep [illegible] they joined [illegible] of the Divine [illegible], for the late [illegible] and [illegible] champaign. The [illegible] [illegible] When [illegible] several days were [illegible].

The fame of this [illegible] foreign nations [illegible] of the piety and virtue of Jehoshaphat [illegible] entirely [illegible] the Divine protection, that they held him in awe [illegible] [illegible] of God, and maintained [illegible] during his reign.

[illegible] Ahab's son, [illegible] king of Israel, and [illegible] number [illegible] to Pontus [illegible] then design [illegible] [illegible] [illegible] Indeed, [illegible] [illegible] [illegible] Thus much, [illegible] of Josephus.

Ahaziah, the son of Ahab and king of Israel, took up his residence at Samaria. He [illegible] and [illegible] that fixed [illegible] [illegible] [illegible] Soon after his accession to the throne, the Moabites, [illegible] to the kings of [illegible] took the [illegible] to reduce [illegible] It happened in the second year of his [illegible] received a violent [illegible] from [illegible] the god of Ekron (a) to know [illegible] thus, after the God of the Hebrews [illegible] and not a God of [illegible] [illegible] He was enjoined also to bid them go back, and tell the king [illegible] When the prophet had executed the Divine command, the messengers hastened with the purport of [illegible] the king, who was [illegible] surprised at their speedy return. On his [illegible] concerning the matter for which they had been sent, they informed him that they were met by a man who bade them proceed no farther, but go back and tell their king, in the name of the God of Israel, that the hurt he had received would prove mortal. The king then demanded a description of the man who had presumed to send such a message; upon which they told him that he was an hairy man, and that he wore a leather girdle.

From this description the king immediately concluded the person to be Elias, the prophet, and therefore dispatched an officer, with fifty men to apprehend him, designing to [illegible] his life for his presumption. The officer, [illegible] prophet on the top of a mountain, commanded him to come down, and go with him to the king, for it was [illegible] order, if he refused a ready compliance to bring him by force. Elias told the officer that he would convince him, by a [illegible], that he was a true prophet, and no impostor, he would pray that fire might descend from heaven, and destroy both the soldiers and officer. [illegible] [illegible] (b) instantly descended, and consumed [illegible] The king no sooner received intelligence of the destruction of these men, than, fired with indignation, he sent another officer with fifty more. Upon his [illegible] the same command, enforced with the same menaces, they all shared the same fate. After this the king sent a third officer. This [illegible] very differently from the former, [illegible] to Elias, instead of peremptorily demanding his person, he saluted him with respect, and thus addressed him: "I need not inform you of the purport of my commission, [illegible] in the execution of it; therefore I [illegible] that, in compassion for the lives of [illegible] officers and soldiers, you would come down, and [illegible] to the king." [illegible] was so affected by his discreet and courteous behaviour, that he came down and followed him.

When he came to the royal presence, he without any ceremony thus [illegible] the king: "The Lord saith thus, [illegible] no God, and unable to [illegible] will be the effect of your distemper, [illegible] the God of [illegible] in point of authority, [illegible] that [illegible]." The prediction of the [illegible] soon verified, for the king [illegible] up the ghost, [illegible] dying without [illegible] another [illegible] the pernicious example of his father [illegible] the practice of idolatry [illegible] his [illegible] religion of his ancestors, though he [illegible] his ability [illegible].

At this time the prophet Elias disappeared from among men (c). He [illegible] behind him [illegible] his successor, in the [illegible] of whom we have spoken already.

Upon [illegible] to the throne of his brother, [illegible] of going to war with Mesha, king of the Moabites, [illegible] to pay an annual tribute [illegible] and lambs, which had been paid to his father Ahab [illegible] the [illegible], though denied to his brother Ahaziah. In consequence of this resolution, [illegible] at home, and [illegible] the alliance of [illegible], king of Judah, urging, as a motive, the [illegible] that subsisted between their respective fathers. Jehoshaphat not only complied with his request, but engaged to bring the king of Idumea

(a) [illegible]

(b) [illegible]

(c) [illegible]

THE PROPHET ELIAS CARRIED UP TO HEAVEN
in a fiery Chariot in the presence of his Disciple Elisha

into the league, having, from [illegible] [illegible] influence with that prince.

As Jehoram met with so friendly a reception upon his [illegible], he went to Jerusalem, where he was [illegible] [illegible], and sumptuously entertained, by the king of the [illegible]. The plan of the expedition was debated in council, [illegible] carried unanimous, that the army should march through the desert of Idumea, where the enemy would be [illegible] [illegible] design. According to the [illegible] [illegible] the kings of Judah, Israel, and Idumea, [illegible] towards the desert, [illegible] [illegible] [illegible] [illegible] [illegible] for [illegible] [illegible] to the utmost [illegible], [illegible] distressed, [illegible] [illegible] [illegible] the Moabites without [illegible] [illegible] [illegible] [illegible] [illegible] [illegible] of Jehoram, [illegible] [illegible] prophet [illegible] [illegible] [illegible] concerning the Divine will [illegible] [illegible], by a servant, that he had seen Elisha, the son of [illegible] [illegible] [illegible] [illegible] immediately [illegible] to the prophet, [illegible] would be the consequence [illegible] [illegible] [illegible] [illegible] [illegible] [illegible] [illegible] [illegible] [illegible] [illegible] [illegible] [illegible] [illegible] [illegible] [illegible] [illegible] [illegible] for the people and [illegible] [illegible] [illegible] [illegible] [illegible] [illegible] [illegible] [illegible] [illegible] [illegible] [illegible] [illegible]

The king of Moab, [illegible] had engaged and slain each other, [illegible] [illegible] [illegible] [illegible] [illegible] [illegible] [illegible] [illegible] [illegible] [illegible] [illegible] [illegible] [illegible] [illegible] [illegible] [illegible]. But they found themselves mistaken, [illegible] when they came up to the camp, [illegible] [illegible] [illegible] [illegible] [illegible] [illegible] [illegible] [illegible] [illegible] [illegible] [illegible] obliged to [illegible] [illegible] [illegible] [illegible] [illegible] [illegible] [illegible] [illegible] [illegible] [illegible] [illegible] [illegible] [illegible] [illegible] [illegible] [illegible] [illegible] [illegible] [illegible] Moabites was obliged to [illegible]

[illegible] departments, [illegible]

C [illegible] [illegible] II.

[illegible] of Jehoram [illegible] of Jehoram [illegible] [illegible] [illegible]

THE [illegible] king Jehoshaphat [illegible] [illegible] [illegible] [illegible] [illegible] [illegible] [illegible] [illegible] [illegible] [illegible] [illegible] [illegible] [illegible] brother, [illegible]

[illegible] of Jehoram [illegible] to understand that the prophet Elisha was the man who had discovered and laid open all his counsels, he gave immediate orders to some of his messengers to go in quest of the prophet, and word was soon sent him that he might be found at Dothan. Upon this intelligence he immediately dispatched a number of officers to apprehend him. They beset the town by night, and thereby prevented persons from coming in or going out. When the prophet's servant had notice of this extraordinary incident, and found the design upon his master, he hastened to him, and, with a serious account, related the circumstance. Elisha bid him take courage nor harbour a fear in his breast, as his confidence was firmly rooted in the goodness and power of an over-ruling Providence. Upon this he besought the Almighty to manifest to his servant his presence and protection in such a manner as to inspire him with hope and courage, and lead him to an entire resignation to his Lord's will and pleasure. His prayers were heard, and there appeared in the sight of the servant a multitude of chariots and horses round about Elisha, as a guard to his person. This dissipated the fear, and restored the courage of the servant, as he was convinced of the protection and office of his master.

After this the prophet entreated that the Syrians might have such a mist cast before their eyes, as to affect their sight, so that they should not discern him from another man. In consequence of the grant of his request, he went into the midst of the troops, and asked them whom they sought. They answered, "Elisha the prophet," upon which he told them, if they would follow him, he would lead them to the place where he was to be found. These men, whose understanding ... their sight, followed him with the greatest ... till at length he brought them to Samaria. Upon their entrance into the city, king Jehoram, at the instance of the prophet, commanded the gates to be shut and the Syrians to be surrounded. Elisha then ... ed that their sight might be restored, and his prayer being granted, the mist was withdrawn, and (to their great astonishment) the Syrians found themselves surrounded by their enemies in their own capital Samaria.

While the Syrians were in this state of danger and suspense, apprehending nothing but a retaliation of injuries from ... , the king proposed to the prophet the putting them all to death; but this he positively rejected as means totally inconsistent with honour, justice, and humanity, and never justifiable but in self-defence, or when victory is obtained in battle. He observed that these men had been guilty of no act of hostility ... brought hither by the Divine will ... through the Divine power, without any malicious intention, or without their own knowledge. The prophet, from these considerations, recommended to the king that they should be treated not only with lenity but with civility, and, after affording them every comfortable refreshment, sent them home without any molestation. Jehoram followed his counsel, so that after a splendid and sumptuous regale, they were sent home to their king, without the least injury.

Upon their return they related to the king the particulars of their strange event, which struck him with conviction, that it was certainly brought about by the display of a Divine power, and that what the prophet had delivered were the dictates of Divine inspiration. He therefore determined to make no more secret attempts upon the king of Israel, but resolved, however, upon an open war, relying on the strength and power of superior numbers.

In consequence of this resolution Adad raised a formidable army, and marched with his whole force against Jehoram, who thinking himself incompetent to engage him in the field through great inequality in point of numbers, kept within the walls of Samaria, depending on the strength of its fortifications. Adad however, invested the place, not ... of its surrender, ... through force of arms, by famine, through ... from obtaining provisions. The siege ... carried on before the people were brought to such extremity, that an ass's head was sold for fourscore pieces of silver, and ... given for a pint of pulse. In this extremity Jehoram was apprehensive that the enemy might receive information of the dreadful degree in which the famine prevailed, so that he daily walked round the fortifications, had an eye upon the guards, and was very attentive that no person whatever should enter the city without first undergoing a proper examination.

As the king was one day walking on the walls of the city, upon this business of watchful inspection, a strange woman accosted him, requesting his assistance ... posing she wanted food, he put her off with ... anger, asking her how she could expect relief from him who had neither barns nor any kind of provisions to spare. The woman gave him to understand that she did not come to solicit him for food, but for justice, and earnestly intreated him to determine a dispute between her and another woman. The king asking her meaning, she told him that "Her neighbour and herself, having each a male infant, and being both ready to perish for want of food, came to an agreement to kill their children and eat them, as the only means to prevent starving. She added, that her child was killed and dressed the preceding day, and the other woman partook of it, but that now, when she ought, in turn, to partake of her child, the woman had broke the agreement and concealed it (a)."

Jehoram, deeply affected by this melancholy tale, rent his clothes, and, in a fit of rage and horror, vowed vengeance on Elisha, whom he took to be the cause of this dreadful calamity. While this rage prevailed, he dispatched an officer to take off the prophet's head, and the man immediately set forward to execute his commission. Elisha, by the spirit of prophecy, had notice of this wicked design against his life, and, therefore, having acquainted the people with it who were with him, and particularly informed them, that Jehoram, the son of a murderer, had sent an officer, with a party, who were then on their way to take off his head, he desired them to secure the door and by no means to admit the officer till the arrival of the king, who had sent him to be there, and change his mind, and was hastening after his people to prevent their ... They watched as they were directed, shut the doors upon the men when they came, and kept them out till the appearance of Jehoram, who hastened with the utmost speed to countermand the execution of the order, and save the life of the prophet.

The king, on his arrival, began to reproach the prophet with inhumanity, in beholding himself and his people reduced to such extremity of distress, without interposing and offering up one prayer for their relief. The prophet then encouraged and comforted him with this prophetic assurance, "That by the same hour on the following day Samaria should be so abundantly stored "with all kinds of provisions, that the market price of "a measure of fine flour should be only a shekel, and "that two measures of barley should be sold for the "same sum." This prediction was credited by the king, and those of his attendants, who had seen different proofs of the prophet's veracity. They rejoiced in the presage as if already accomplished, and bore their present distresses with a degree of patient resignation, being revived by the hope of a speedy relief. But one of the king's favourite officers, who commanded a third of his army, could not be brought to place any confidence in it, on the contrary, as the king was that day familiarly leaning on his shoulder, he affirmed it to be "a thing impossible, unless it should rain meal from heaven." The

ND *King of Java* [illegible]
[illegible]

[illegible] him to the prophet's reply to this effect, "That him[self] should see the plenty, but should not be permitted to [partake of it]." And this prediction accordingly came to pass [illegible] in Samaria, that no persons [infected] with the leprosy, and whose bodies were not cleansed from [it], should be suffered to live within the walls of the city. [It] happened, at this time, that there were four leprous persons that had their habitation without the city gates. The famine raged with such violence in the city, that no provisions could be expected from that quarter, and to remain in their habitations would be to give themselves up to the most lamentable of deaths. They, therefore, unanimously, resolved to cast themselves upon the mercy of the enemy, who would either relieve their necessities, or put them to death, so that their miseries one way or other would be soon terminated.

In consequence of this resolution, they proceeded, [illegible] to the camp of the Syrians, which they had no sooner arrived at, than, to their great surprize, they found it [entirely] deserted by the enemy. For, upon the approach [illegible] the Syrians were struck with a panic, by the [prodigious] noise of horses and armed men breaking in upon them, and coaches, [imagining] that the king of Israel had [called in] the assistance of [illegible] and were coming to surprize them. This conjecture threw them into the greatest consternation insomuch that they hastened to [illegible], and told him that the confederate kings were just at hand, with [illegible] of the march of the army. [illegible] did give credit to [illegible], as he himself was influenced by the same false imagination, so that, [illegible] one general consent, the whole camp broke up [illegible] [illegible] [illegible] [illegible] for himself, [illegible] baggage, [illegible] provision, in a word [illegible] possessions [illegible].

The lepers having [illegible] the camp of the Syrians and found all [illegible], regaled themselves with [illegible] and then carried [off] a great quantity of gold, [illegible] [illegible] without seeing so much as one person [illegible]. They [hid] themselves [illegible] and [illegible] holes, which they dug for that [purpose] [illegible]. But while they were thus [illegible] and [illegible] themselves, they reflected that [illegible] a [illegible] town [illegible] by the enemy, and [illegible] to inform [illegible] as soon as possible, [illegible] place. Thus resolved, they made the utmost [illegible] called aloud to the [illegible] walls [illegible] had totally abandoned their camp [illegible] behind them all their tents [illegible] and treasure.

[illegible] of this important event being communicated [to] the king, he immediately summoned a full council, [illegible] he gave it as his own private opinion, [illegible] of the enemy to draw them out of the city, [illegible] they would [illegible] all of them and obtain a complete victory. He [illegible] despair of [illegible] [illegible] recourse to this invention to surprize them [illegible] From [illegible] such [illegible] [illegible] One of the [illegible] stood up, and, with due deference to that venerable board, gave his opinion in consequence [illegible] of saving [illegible], that it [illegible] [illegible] if the [illegible] [illegible] the loss would not be considerable, [illegible] they might [illegible] suppose that all was [illegible] own country.

[illegible] proposal, two [illegible] In [illegible] not [illegible] but that they [illegible] [illegible] they might [illegible]

[illegible] the people [illegible] rushed [out of] the city, in great numbers, in order to plunder the [illegible] camp, where they found an immense booty [illegible] and such [illegible] of grain, that [illegible] amazing [illegible] [illegible], for two measures of [illegible] were sold for one shekel, and [illegible] of flour at the same price, according to the prediction of Elisha. This [illegible] [illegible].

The officer who doubted the veracity of the prophecy, was appointed by the king to guard the gate, [illegible] to the camp, in order to prevent [illegible] and [illegible] to death in the [illegible], but the crowd pressed on with such vehemence that he was trampled to death; so that, though he saw the [illegible] provisions afterwards brought to [illegible], as the prophet had foretold, he did not taste thereof.

When [Adad], upon the miraculous [illegible] of the [illegible], had escaped to Damascus, and was informed [illegible] of chariots and horsemen, [illegible] [illegible] his army [illegible] possession of [illegible] he looked upon [illegible] [illegible] from heaven [illegible] him, and this [illegible] made him as sick in body as in mind.

[illegible], being [informed] that Elisha was at this time in [illegible] he sent Hazael (who was now [illegible] of [illegible]) with magnificent presents to the prophet, and to enquire whether or not he should recover from the sickness under which he then laboured. The messenger took with him forty camels [illegible] the choicest curiosities [illegible] [illegible] Elisha on the [illegible], with the greatest veneration [illegible] of king Adad, telling him, that [illegible] commission to offer him presents, and [illegible] about his defeate, [illegible] might [illegible] The prophet assured Hazael that [illegible], but charged him not to [illegible] [illegible] much [illegible] Elisha poured forth tears [illegible] the [illegible] the people [illegible] of Adad. When Hazael enquired [illegible] of his excessive grief, he replied, "I [illegible] "weeping, when I contemplate [illegible] "you [illegible] are to bring upon the people of [illegible] "You will put their strong men to the [sword], [illegible] "fenced cities, dash their children [illegible] and "destroy their women in a state of pregnancy." When Hazael, struck with surprize, asked, by what power he was to perpetrate all these evils, the prophet [illegible] [illegible] Divine intimation [illegible]

These words of Elisha fixed the ambition of Hazael, who immediately left the prophet, and returning to [the] king his master, gave him great [illegible]. This, however, the treacherous [illegible] took [illegible] [illegible] for the next morning he [illegible] him to death [illegible] him with a cloth dipped in water [illegible] took possession [illegible] [palace] and government [illegible] was an active [illegible] greatly beloved by his people, [illegible], the memory of Adad and Hazael his successor, [illegible] honoured by the Syrians, for their goodness [illegible] and the magnificence of the temples they erected [illegible] together with the ornaments with which they embellished the city [illegible] their images [illegible] [illegible] esteemed [illegible] for several hundred years [illegible] the time of the existence of their original. The [illegible] [illegible] the king of Israel, delivered him from the [illegible] which had long disturbed his quiet, [illegible] [illegible] of peace.

When Jehoram [illegible] the king of Je[rusalem] [illegible] [illegible] the throne he filled the [illegible] [illegible] [illegible]

[illegible] In[illegible]ed, he [illegible] by the [illegible] of his wife, Gotholiah, [illegible] one his [illegible] and [illegible] Now though [illegible] family, for the [illegible] continued his [illegible] as that tended to [illegible] of the real [illegible] of the people.

[illegible] having [illegible] Jeho[illegible] king [illegible] consider [illegible] were [illegible] any farther [illegible] of [illegible] any degree of fear [illegible] example, [illegible] Sec[illegible], [illegible] the people [illegible] and [illegible]

[illegible] desired. Th[illegible] "[illegible] God "[illegible] con- "[illegible] not [illegible] "[illegible] [illegible] "[illegible] and [illegible] "[illegible] the Divine [illegible] [illegible]

CHAP. [illegible]

[illegible]

S[illegible] dreadful [illegible] of the [illegible] [illegible] Ammonites, [illegible] and put to the sword his [illegible] children, except one, who was Ahaziah, [illegible] calami[illegible] [illegible] according to [illegible] prediction of the [illegible] buried in the [illegible] died [illegible] the [illegible] county of [illegible] place in [illegible] Ahaziah.

CHAP. IV.

[illegible]

A[illegible] of [illegible]

[illegible] the [illegible], on the death of Adad, [illegible] Syria, [illegible] hopes of recovering [illegible] he laid [illegible] with a very dangerous wound [illegible] from [illegible] of Samaria, [illegible] to Jezreel, for [illegible] the conveniences of the cure. [illegible] however [illegible] under [illegible] of Jehu, to whom [illegible] during his [illegible] by force. [illegible] his return, to prosecute the war against the S[illegible]. [illegible] the mean time, the prophet [illegible] thinking [illegible] proper [illegible] opportunity for executing the orders [illegible] to [illegible] punishment of the [illegible] of Ahab, ordered [illegible] disciples to go to Ramoth-Gilead, and there [illegible] the [illegible] and by the [illegible] of [illegible] Eliga[illegible]. He [illegible] ordered him to depart [illegible] as possible, and by no means give the [illegible] the purport of his [illegible].

When the young prophet reached the [illegible], [illegible] Jehu engaged with his officers, in consult[illegible] taken [illegible] to the [illegible] offered, he [illegible] chamber, which they had [illegible] young prophet, taking out a [illegible] of oil, poured it on [illegible] telling him, "[illegible] chosen [illegible] of the house of Ahab, [illegible] murder of the [illegible] of Ahab." When he had [illegible] spoken, he hast[illegible] and [illegible] any of the [illegible].

As soon as Jehu returned to the [illegible] of[illegible] [illegible] the [illegible] that [illegible] of [illegible] to them all [illegible] [illegible] of [illegible] Jehu [illegible] [illegible] to the [illegible] received from the [illegible] of [illegible] Ahaziah king of Judah, his [illegible] upon a visit of [illegible] to [illegible] Jehu [illegible] took the opportunity [illegible] where he [illegible] surprise [illegible] his [illegible] upon the allegiance, not to give [illegible] intelligence of their [illegible].

CHAP. V.

[illegible]

J[illegible] before [illegible] had [illegible] the [illegible] to the [illegible] it was Jehu [illegible] and [illegible] with [illegible] who [illegible] to [illegible] a true [illegible]

MAYNARDS

[illegible] the purpose [illegible] intelligence [illegible] much [illegible] convertible [illegible] and the [illegible] on the [illegible] He then [illegible] the messenger [illegible] contractors [illegible] the same [illegible] as the former [illegible] contemptuous [illegible] her to meet Jehu, [illegible] continued his march at a [illegible] slower pace [illegible] it happened that they met [illegible] field of Naboth, the Jezreelite, and very probably [illegible] from the spot where the innocent and injured man was stoned to death. [illegible] meeting Jehu [illegible] concerning the [illegible] his army, and whether it is war or peace? Jehu, in reply, [illegible] the [illegible] and witchcrafts of Jezebel, his mother [illegible] this [illegible] was convinced of the hostile [illegible] of Jehu, [illegible] and [illegible] so [illegible] that he gave [illegible] turned his chariot, and endeavoured [illegible] by flight. But Jehu prevented him from effecting his design, for [illegible] penetrating [illegible] immediately [illegible] As soon as Jehu [illegible] of his principal officers, [illegible] into the field of Naboth [illegible] to his [illegible] of the [illegible] to his father Ahab, "That he would [illegible] on the very spot [illegible] alleged property."

When [illegible] from [illegible] Jezreel, [illegible] Jehu, [illegible] received [illegible] had [illegible] to have [illegible] of Megiddo [illegible] to Jerusalem, [illegible] his ancestors [illegible]

CHAP. VI.

[illegible]

Jehu [illegible] to Jezreel, where Jezebel, the queen, [illegible] to meet [illegible] and [illegible] opposite the window, [illegible] Jehu [illegible] who was, and [illegible] commanded [illegible] that were [illegible] the walls of the [illegible] in falling, were stained with her blood, and [illegible] to the ground, [illegible] trampled on [illegible]

[illegible] had [illegible] arrived [illegible] the [illegible] of [illegible] of the [illegible] of the skull [illegible] of her [illegible] been devoured [illegible] dogs. When Jehu was informed of this circumstance [illegible] conversation [illegible] prophet of Elias, who had [illegible] "Should [illegible] flesh of Jezebel in the [illegible] of Jezreel."

There were at this time seventy [illegible] of king Ahab [illegible] under the [illegible] of the [illegible] [illegible] Jehu [illegible] tion of [illegible] great [illegible] [illegible] pursuers [illegible] of the Israelitish youths [illegible] [illegible] conduct they [illegible] [illegible] disposition [illegible] his interest. Having [illegible] of the letters with great circumspection [illegible] tion that it would [illegible] [illegible] defend the [illegible] sovereignty [illegible] [illegible] "[illegible]" [illegible] "[illegible] earth [illegible]" [illegible] this [illegible] [illegible] place [illegible] that [illegible] of the [illegible] Ahab was [illegible] agreeable to the [illegible] of the prophet [illegible] the race of Ahab [illegible] Samaria [illegible] consisting of forty-two people, and [illegible] and where they were going [illegible] of Ahaziah, king of Judah, [illegible] the court of Samaria, being ignorant of the [illegible] king, Jehoram and [illegible] who they were, [illegible] to death.

[illegible] he [illegible] Jehu [illegible] righteous [illegible] the [illegible] Jehu then [illegible] [illegible] Samaria, [illegible] and [illegible] who [illegible] the [illegible] from the worship of the [illegible] to [illegible] good [illegible] [illegible] and [illegible] to the king's [illegible]

As soon as Jehu [illegible] Samaria [illegible] to be [illegible] round to be put to death, [illegible] race was extirpated [illegible] ing the [illegible] land, [illegible] the [illegible] priests, [illegible] design [illegible] executed [illegible] the people [illegible] them [illegible] was [illegible] worship [illegible] the [illegible] Jehu would [illegible] worship [illegible]

[illegible footnotes]

[illegible] priests of Baal [illegible] to offer to the god of [illegible] [illegible] declaring [illegible] should be punished with death. [illegible]

[illegible]

CHAP. [illegible]

[illegible]

[illegible] called together to consult [illegible] which was of the [illegible] to the people [illegible] in order to carry [illegible] and [illegible] word to [illegible] "Behold your [illegible] the only surviving branch of the "family, which, according to the Divine promise [illegible] "predicted, shall never be wanting to fill the throne of "David. It is my advice that you divide [illegible] "to three parties, one to guard the person of the king [illegible] "the temple, one to secure the avenues leading [illegible] "the other to guard the open gate that leads [illegible] "that none be permitted to enter, except the priests and "Levites, upon pain of death." He also [illegible] [illegible] select number of priests and Levites should [illegible] [illegible] orders as a guard about the king, to put to death whoever should press into the temple [illegible] upon [illegible] and, at all events, to secure the [illegible]

[illegible] approved of the conduct of the high priest, [illegible] next business was to open a [illegible] [illegible] that had been deposited in the temple [illegible] David, and to deliver out lances, bows, and [illegible] to the centurions, priests, and Levites [illegible] as a guard upon the [illegible] as to exclude all those who [illegible] to enter. When these preparations were made, [illegible] placed the [illegible] put the book of the law into his hand, [illegible] and [illegible] king of Judah, the people [illegible] approbation [illegible]

The shouts of the people [illegible] Athaliah, who immediately [illegible] [illegible] to the temple [illegible] the priests, [illegible] the guards, who were [illegible]

[illegible] entered the [illegible] and saw the child upon [illegible] royal crown upon his head, and [illegible] huzzas of the people [illegible] clothes, exclaiming vehemently, [illegible] to exterminate the traitors who had [illegible] Jehoiada, [illegible] officers of the guards to [illegible] out of the temple, as that place [illegible] blood of [illegible] who had the charge of [illegible] conducted Athaliah to the stable-gate [illegible] without any opposition.

As soon as this design upon Athaliah [illegible] the people to the temple, [illegible] an oath of allegiance to [illegible] and defence of his person, and [illegible] of his government. [illegible] king took [illegible] of reign [illegible]

[illegible]

[illegible]

[illegible]

DESTRUCTION of the TEMPLE of BAAL,

[illegible]

MAYNARDS

[illegible] general [illegible], [illegible] the fall of the kingdom of [illegible].

Joash [illegible] crown [illegible] name was [illegible] the [illegible] for the [illegible] death of [illegible] the throne of Judah.

CHAP. VI.

[illegible] of Hazael, king of Syria [illegible] succeeded by his son Jehoash [illegible] Death of [illegible] prophecy of Joash [illegible] by the friends of Zechariah, whom he [illegible] to death.

HAZAEL, king of Syria, [illegible] waged war against [illegible] and then king Jehu, [illegible] land to the [illegible] and [illegible] particularly [illegible] of Reuben, Gad, and [illegible] young men, women, [illegible] to the world, [illegible] Nor [illegible] com [illegible] of the religion [illegible] twenty-seventh [illegible] Samaria, and succeeded in his government by his [illegible]

[illegible]

[illegible] the [illegible] the people [illegible] the [illegible] the priests [illegible] [illegible] the high-priest [illegible] [illegible]

[illegible] the temple [illegible] [illegible] [illegible] [illegible] carpenters [illegible] [illegible] [illegible] [illegible] [illegible] the [illegible] [illegible] [illegible] universally beloved [illegible]

[illegible] the [illegible] [illegible] [illegible] and the [illegible] people [illegible] [illegible] the [illegible] Jehoiada [illegible] pleased to [illegible] both [illegible] and to [illegible] never [illegible] [illegible] reformed [illegible] [illegible] [illegible] as a [illegible] not sufficient [illegible] cautious, as well [illegible] the [illegible] Zechariah [illegible] high-priest, [illegible] he stood [illegible] for the [illegible] strong [illegible] on the general [illegible] [illegible] [illegible] Zechariah [illegible] [illegible] to God [illegible] [illegible] witness [illegible] good [illegible] [illegible]

[illegible] [illegible] Zechariah [illegible] [illegible] [illegible] [illegible] [illegible] of the temple [illegible] [illegible] [illegible] [illegible] [illegible] the siege [illegible]

[illegible] Hazael [illegible] [illegible] revenge [illegible] [illegible] Joash [illegible] [illegible] the [illegible] [illegible] the [illegible]

CHAP. IX.

[illegible] of Hazael, king of Syria [illegible] [illegible] [illegible] Lord [illegible] of Israel [illegible]

JOASH [illegible] the government of Judah [illegible] [illegible] at the time of [illegible] [illegible] Joash [illegible] the government [illegible] [illegible] [illegible] the example of [illegible] [illegible] [illegible] [illegible] his people [illegible] [illegible]

[illegible] to H[illegible], when he [illegible] under [illegible] the possession of towns [illegible].

[illegible] which [illegible] his administration was [illegible] the [illegible] enjoyed.

[illegible] the [illegible] seventh year of the [illegible] He was a pious and [illegible] conduct, [illegible] and govern[illegible] of his father.

[illegible] Lord, [illegible] the [illegible] people, [illegible] to often delivered [illegible] enemies, and [illegible].

[illegible] charged [illegible].

[illegible] the prophet [illegible].

[illegible] of the prophet [illegible].

[illegible] of Hez[illegible].

CHAP. X.

[illegible]

THE second year of the reign of Joash over Israel, Ama[illegible] the throne of Judah, [illegible] Jerusalem [illegible], [illegible] When he found himself fully est[ablished] in the [illegible], he revenged the death of his father upon those who treacherously murdered him under a pretence of friendship. But, though he [illegible] the [illegible] justice, he spared their children, according to the precept of Moses, which expresses, "[illegible] children should not be punished for the iniquity of their fathers."

After this he selected [illegible] out of the tribes of Judah and Benjamin [illegible] of men in their prime, and [illegible] they were incorporated, [illegible] to command them. He also sent to the king of Israel and hired a great number of [illegible] hundred talents of silver, determined upon a war with the Amalekites, the Edomites, and the Gabalites.

When this combined army was ready for marching [illegible] them, he received a visit from a prophet, who, by [illegible] Divine direction, dissuaded him from employing the Israelites, as they were become an abandoned generation, [illegible] certainly be [illegible] together with those who joined them [illegible] that, with his own force and [illegible] he [illegible] overcome the enemy. The king [illegible] with the condition [illegible] the [illegible] he [illegible] the money for payment of th[illegible] the prophet enjoining him to yield [illegible] obedience to the Divine will, he discharged the [illegible] "[illegible] on the [illegible] bounty which they had received [illegible]." On [illegible] the mercenaries, he [illegible] the combined [illegible] ten thousand of them in one [illegible] ten thousand more to the [illegible] they were all destroyed [illegible] down [illegible]. He then returned home [illegible].

But, in the mean time, the hired subjects of the king of Israel [illegible] and contemptuously [illegible] exasperated against Amaziah [illegible] to [illegible] distance, they plundered all the [illegible] to Judah, [illegible] no less than three thousand men, and carried [illegible] considerable booty [illegible] in order to [illegible] they had promised themselves in [illegible] against the Edomites.

Amaziah, elated with this conquest over the Edomites, [illegible] to himself, regardless of the [illegible] hand of Divine Providence, fell from the [illegible] true God, [illegible] on his return to Jerusalem, [illegible] the idols of the Amalekites, to which he paid [illegible] and [illegible]. This was so [illegible] to [illegible] of heaven, that [illegible] prophet was sent to reprove him for [illegible] dependence on those powers which [illegible] to be taken captive by the Hebrews, [illegible] with the rest of the spoil, like abject slaves, [illegible]. The king interrupted the prophet in his [illegible] reproached him with want of deference to his [illegible] and [illegible] him, at his peril, not to interfere with matters that did not concern him. The prophet told him [illegible] but [illegible] that [illegible] would be the certain consequence of his perseverance [illegible].

The king, however, was so transported with pride [illegible] success, that he determined to [illegible] by the [illegible] of the king of Israel, [illegible] he had [illegible] and [illegible] had committed ravages in different parts of his dominions on their return home.

With this view, he wrote an imperious letter, commanding him and his people to pay that allegiance to him which they had formerly rendered to his ancestors David and Solomon, in default of which he might expect a decision of

[illegible]

the sword. Joash treated this haughty behaviour with [illegible] disdain, and returned him an answer couched in a parable to this effect.

"King Joash to king Amaziah, greeting.

"It happened upon a certain time that a thistle, which grew on Mount Libanus, sent to a cedar tree, growing on the same spot, saying, give thy daughter in marriage to my son; whereupon a wild beast passing by trod the thistle to the ground. Learn hence to lower your ambition, nor aspire to things above your reach. Be cautious lest your pride, on having conquered the Amalekites, should lead you to such actions as may terminate in the [illegible] of your life and kingdom."

This sarcastic reply enraged Amaziah to the highest degree, and rendered him more furious and implacable than before, as if Providence had given him up to the influence of his outrageous passion, in order to expose him to the stroke of Divine justice for his impiety. Thus inflamed he took the field, and both armies were drawn up in order of battle, but no sooner were the troops of Amaziah advanced within sight of the enemy, than they were struck with such a panic and consternation that they gave way on the [illegible] onset, and consulting their own safety, fled with the utmost precipitation, leaving the king in the hands of his enemies. Amaziah being now at the mercy of Joash, the latter refused him quarter upon any other terms, than that the citizens of Jerusalem should set open their gates, and receive him and his victorious army into the town. Necessity [illegible] compliance, so that Joash entered Jerusalem with his army [illegible] [illegible] triumphant procession through a breach of three hundred cubits of wall he had caused to be broken down, and [illegible] Amaziah [illegible] before him. He proceeded to the palace, and then to the temple, both of which he plundered of their richest jewels, and then, dismissing Amaziah, returned to Samaria. Thus did misery befall Jerusalem [illegible] the fourteenth year of the reign of Amaziah.

In consequence of this [illegible] of Divine justice, the leading men of Jerusalem entered into a conspiracy against Amaziah. Having received intimation of their design, he endeavoured to escape by flight to Lachish, a town situated on the frontiers of the country of the Philistines; but this attempt proved fruitless, for the conspirators sent [illegible] [illegible] who put him to death. His body was carried to Jerusalem, and buried in royal state. Thus fell Amaziah king of Judah, as a punishment due to *his* neglect of the worship of the true God, and introduction of abominable idolatry. He lived fifty-four years, reigned twenty-nine, and was succeeded on the throne by his son Uzziah.

CHAP. XI.

[illegible] Jonah [illegible] Death of Jeroboam, [illegible] [illegible] [illegible] [illegible] [illegible] conquests of Uzziah. [illegible] [illegible] [illegible] [illegible] with grief, and is succeeded by [illegible] [illegible] Divine [illegible] to the tribes of Israel. Excellent qualities [illegible] king of Judah. [illegible] of the destruction of Nineveh and the Assyrian empire, by the prophet Nahum.

JEROBOAM, the son of Joash, ascended the throne of Israel, and resided in the place of his ancestors, at Samaria. He was a prince most dissolute and licentious, abandoned to the most idolatrous and profligate practices, by which he brought down almost innumerable calamities upon the people of Israel.

It was foretold him by Jonah the prophet, that he should overcome the Syrians, and enlarge his dominions as far as the city Hamath on the north, and the lake Asphaltites on the south, which were formerly the bounds of the land of Canaan, according to the allotment of Joshua, their general. Jeroboam, elated by this prediction, made war [illegible] against the Syrians, took from them all the above mentioned tract of land, and annexed it to his own territories.

As I promised, at my entrance upon this work, to give a faithful and impartial history of our nation, I deem it necessary, in this place, to recount the actions of this prophet, as I find them represented in the Hebrew records.

Jonah had received a Divine commission to go to Nineveh, and denounce the destruction of that great city, because of her many enormous crimes and abominations. But Jonah, afraid of obeying the Divine command, in order to avoid the danger to which such a denunciation might expose him, directed his course another way, and intending to retire to Tarshish, a town in Cilicia, embarked on board a vessel for Joppa. In the course of their passage there arose a violent tempest, which so alarmed the mariners, that, after labouring to no purpose, in opposition to the winds, they found themselves in the most imminent danger of being shipwrecked. It was observed, that amidst the fears of the labour, and devout [illegible] of the mariners, Jonah was the only man that did not exert himself to promote their safety, but lay in the hold totally inactive and useless. The master finding that the violence of the storm increased to such a degree as to frustrate all their endeavours, suspected that to maintain the [illegible] [illegible] [illegible] the [illegible] [illegible] some person on board the vessel [illegible], [illegible] [illegible] agreed among the crew and passengers, that they should cast lots to know who was the [illegible].

The lot accordingly being [illegible], and the lot fell upon Jonah. In consequence of this the mariners enquired of him who he was, and what he had done, to bring on himself and them so great a calamity. Jonah [illegible], acknowledged that he was an Hebrew, and not only an Hebrew, but a prophet to the great God; [illegible] [illegible] [illegible], by disobeying the Divine command, had brought on the present calamity, he wished them to throw him overboard, as the only means of abating the storm, and saving themselves and the vessel.

The mariners being much surprized at the [illegible] [illegible] [illegible] of Jonah, by which he doomed himself to death, hesitated some time, and endeavoured, by rowing hard and exerting their utmost [illegible], to reach the land, in hopes of saving his life; but finding that all their efforts [illegible] [illegible], that the waves still ran higher and higher, and that the vessel was on the very point of sinking, they were at length prevailed on, through the importunity of the prophet, and the imminent danger in which they stood, to throw him overboard.

No sooner was Jonah thrown into the sea than the tempest abated. It is related that Jonah was swallowed up by a large fish (*c*), and, after three days, and as many nights, cast up again, living and sound, upon the shore of the Euxine sea, [illegible] there, [illegible] [illegible] [illegible] and obtained pardon [illegible] disobedience of the Divine command, he proceeded immediately to the city of Nineveh, according to his commission, and standing on [illegible] elevated place, where he might best be heard, foretold them, "That the empire of Assyria was nearly "at an end," and having uttered this prophetical denunciation he took his departure. [illegible] recounted concerning the prophet Jonah in the Hebrew writings, but we return to our main history.

Jeroboam, after a prosperous reign of forty years, departed this life, was buried in Samaria, and succeeded by his son Zachariah, as was Amaziah by his son Uzziah, who began to reign over the two tribes in Jerusalem in the fourteenth year of the reign of Jeroboam. His mother [illegible] [illegible] Achia, and she was a native of Jerusalem.

Uzziah was a pious prince, [illegible], valiant, and [illegible]. He made an expedition against his enemies the Ph[illegible]

[illegible]

(*c*) [illegible]

[illegible] took the cities of Gath and Ja[illegible] [illegible] and demolished their walls. His next expedition was against the Arabians on the borders of [illegible]. He built a town upon the Red Sea, and committed it to the guard of a strong garrison. He afterwards [illegible] the Ammonites, who were so alarmed at the [illegible] and extent of his conquests, that they, as well as [illegible], became his tributaries.

Having thus reduced his enemies to submission, he next turned his attention to Jerusalem, the capital of his dominions. He rebuilt the [illegible], and repaired that breach which had been made by Joash, king of Israel, when he entered the city with his army in triumph, after [illegible] Amaziah his prisoner. He erected also several towers of 150 cubits in height, and built castles and strong forts for the protection of the country. He also constructed aqueducts, cisterns, and [illegible], for the convenience of his cattle, of which he had immense numbers, the lands about him affording pasturage. As he was a great lover of husbandry, he employed prodigious numbers of [illegible] [illegible] on the plains, as also vine-dressers, on the mountains, by which he obtained considerable [illegible].

But the chief [illegible] his country lay in his military force, which consisted of 3[illegible],000 chosen men, under the command of 2000 brave and experienced officers, who had attained the most perfect knowledge of martial discipline. They were all furnished with swords, bucklers, spears, bows, slings, and other implements of war, [illegible] rendered expert by constant practice in their respective exercises. He likewise constructed [illegible] and engines for battering, and casting of stones and darts, with hooks, and other offensive weapons.

But [illegible] the mind of Uzziah was so elated with the [illegible] of his [illegible], and the glory he had acquired, [illegible] the greater, [illegible], and forgetting himself, neglected the [illegible] duties of his worship to God, following the example of his father. [illegible]

[illegible] the king having formed the [illegible], went into the temple [illegible] [illegible] to Azariah, the high-priest, [illegible] a train of eighty priests, [illegible] the temple, and reproached [illegible] [illegible] of the [illegible] privilege of the priests of the [illegible] Aaron. Azariah [illegible] him to desist from such [illegible] [illegible] to the Divine [illegible] conduct [illegible] to the Divine will.

This remonstrance had not [illegible] the king, [illegible] of [illegible] into a violent passion, [illegible] the high-priest [illegible] the greatest indignation [illegible] commanded him and his attendants to depart [illegible] peril of their lives. This menace was followed by a terrible earthquake, and the roof of the temple opening [illegible] shock of it, there passed a beam of the sun through the cleft, that struck upon the face of this sacrilegious and impious prince, who, at that very moment, became a leper.

This awful judgment was accompanied [illegible] a tremendous effect. There was a place, at a small distance to the westward from the town called [illegible], where by the [illegible] earthquake, one half of the [illegible] was torn from the other, and after it had rolled over and over, stopped at the [illegible] of an opposite mountain, having choaked up the highway, and covered the king's garden with rubbish.

When the priests found that the king was infected with leprosy, and that he had been smitten as a divine judgment, they admonished him to depart the city, as an unclean person, and unfit for common society. The disgrace of being [illegible] with so [illegible] a disease humbled his pride so far, that he took the admonition of the priest, and having lived some time in private out of the city (Jotham, his son, taking upon him the administration of government) his [illegible] at length brought him to the grave in the sixty-eighth year of his age, and fifty-second of his reign. As he was a leper, his body was not interred in the royal sepulchre, but in the same field, in a monument by itself.

Zachariah (3), king of Israel, and son of Jeroboam, was murdered in the seventh month of his reign, by Shallum the son of Jabesh, who usurped the throne. [illegible] government was much shorter than that of his predecessor, for he survived his usurpation but thirty days. [illegible] the time of his murdering Zachariah, Menahem [illegible] command of the army at Tirzah, who, upon the news [illegible] had befallen Zachariah, marched with his troops to Samaria, defeated and overthrew Shallum, and put him to the sword, was, not only with the approbation of [illegible], but likewise the heads of the people, raised [illegible] regal dignity.

Menahem, having thus secured possession of the government, returned with his army to Tirzah, in order to [illegible] the [illegible] before [illegible], and reduce the inhabitants to subjection. But the citizens shut the gates against him, and treated him with contempt; at which he was so enraged, that [illegible], [illegible] himself master of the place, he put all to the sword, without distinction either of age or sex, [illegible] [illegible] exercises upon his own countrymen, such as would have been unpardonable even towards the [illegible] [illegible]. In short, his reign was one scene of [illegible], rapine, superstition and [illegible].

[illegible] was invaded by Pul, king of Assyria, but [illegible] to stand the [illegible] of a battle, he [illegible] with him, for the composition of [illegible] talents, which he raised upon the people [illegible] He died soon after, and was [illegible] at Samaria, leaving his son, Pekahiah, to succeed him, who inherited not only the crown, but the ill qualities of his father. The reign of Pekahiah, however, was but short, for after he had been upon the throne about two years, Pekah, the general of his army, conspired against him, and having cut him off, with several of his friends about him, seized upon the government, which he held about twenty years, during which he was as notorious for his impiety towards God, as his tyranny and injustice towards men. In the course of his reign, Tiglath-Pileser, king of Assyria, invaded the [illegible] and, after subduing the land of Gilead, the country beyond Jordan, and that part of Galilee that is adjacent, as also Cydisse and Asora, took the inhabitants prisoners, and carried them away into his own country.

Jotham, the son of Uzziah, reigned in Jerusalem over the tribe of Judah. His mother was a native of the [illegible] and her name Jerusha. He was a pious and virtuous prince, exemplary for the veneration of the Deity, his justice to mankind, and his concern for the [illegible]

(2) [illegible] of any [illegible] town, [illegible] [illegible] [illegible] [illegible] from this time

(3) [illegible] both in [illegible] [illegible] Zechariah [illegible] [illegible] [illegible] of Zachariah [illegible] [illegible] [illegible]

His [illegible] was to [illegible] in all things, and [illegible] [illegible] was found to [illegible]. He repaired the [illegible] porches and galleries of the temple, as well as the walls of the city, [illegible] they were falling to ruin, and built towers, large and [illegible]. He also [illegible] an expedition against the Ammonites, whom he overcame, and laid them under the contribution of an hundred talents annually, thirty thousand measures of wheat, and [illegible] of [illegible]. Indeed, he so [illegible] the kingdom, that his people were happy at home, and a terror to their foreign enemies.

In the reign of this prince [illegible] prophet, whose name was Nahum. He foretold the destruction of Nineveh and the destruction of the Assyrian empire [illegible] to the following purport: "The condition of Nineveh will be like that of a [illegible] agitation of [illegible] great wind. The people [illegible] in [illegible] in trouble and confusion, flying to each other. Take with you your gold and silver, [illegible] [illegible] shall be dearer to them than [illegible]. [illegible] their [illegible] [illegible], and there shall be weeping, wailing, with [illegible] [illegible] Nineveh (faith the Lord), I will [illegible] [illegible] the earth [illegible] end to the [illegible] heads [illegible] forth into the world!"

[illegible] which it is [illegible] to [illegible] the [illegible] to the reader, I shall [illegible] add, that this [illegible] hundred and [illegible] years [illegible] delivered.

CHAP. XI.

[illegible] of Jotham, Ahaz [illegible] [illegible] Pekah [illegible] [illegible] Ahaz.

On [illegible] Jotham, who [illegible] the [illegible] of [illegible] in the forty-first year of his age, and [illegible] of his [illegible] Ahaz by right hereditary, succeeded to the throne. [illegible] a very wicked prince, [illegible] the [illegible] of his father, gave himself up to idolatry, [illegible] the kings of Israel. He built altars [illegible] [illegible] [illegible] upon them, and offered his own son [illegible] offering, after the manner of the Canaanites.

While Ahaz was following these impious practices, Rezin, the king of Damascus, and Pekah, the king of Israel, having joined in a league, marched in conjunction to Jerusalem, and pressing hard, lay before it for some time, but the place was so well fortified and defended, that they made but a slow progress, and afterwards found it expedient to raise the siege.

In the mean time the king of Syria possessed himself of Elath, near the Red Sea, put all the inhabitants to the sword, and introduced in their places a colony of Syrians. His [illegible] took possession of several cities [illegible] Judah, harassed the Hebrews very much, and returned with an immense booty to Damascus.

When the king of Jerusalem had intelligence of the departure of the Syrians, and apprehended [illegible] of the king of Israel, he advanced with his [illegible] against him; but having, by his crimes, incurred the Divine displeasure, the enemy gained the victory, and slew an hundred and twenty thousand of his men. In this action Zechariah, the general of the Israelites, killed Amasiah the son of Ahaz, in a personal encounter. Seven principal officers fell upon the same occasion. Elkanah, the general of the troops of [illegible], was taken prisoner, and the Israelites returned in triumph to Samaria, graced with a long procession of captives of both sexes, and laden with the richest spoils of the enemy.

There was at this time in Samaria a prophet, named Oded, who went out of the town to meet the army on their return, accompanied by a great number of the principal inhabitants. As soon as they approached, the prophet [illegible] [illegible] [illegible] to the conquerors, that they were by no means to impute the late victory to their own valour or [illegible], but considered it as a judgment from heaven upon king Ahaz. He [illegible] them they might rest satisfied [illegible] [illegible] [illegible] spoils, without making slaves of their [illegible] of the two tribes, and ordered them to set them at liberty, and send them home, without offering any indignities to them, upon the peril of falling under the Divine [illegible].

Upon this remonstrance and admonition of the prophet, the Israelites called a council to deliberate on their future proceedings. The point in question being fully debated, one Berachiah, a man of [illegible] and [illegible] [illegible] of the [illegible] [illegible] the [illegible] [illegible] they should themselves thereby incur the [illegible] of the Almighty. He represented that the [illegible] [illegible] had already occasioned the severest denunciations of the prophet, and that therefore it would be [illegible] [illegible] to them [illegible]. The [illegible] of Berachiah [illegible] the assembly, so that the officers of the army, [illegible] of the [illegible], [illegible] the prisoners [illegible]. They were all furnished with necessary provisions, and escorted as far as Jericho, [illegible] [illegible] [illegible] [illegible] was [illegible] to [illegible].

CHAP. XII.

A[illegible] [illegible] [illegible] [illegible] [illegible] [illegible] [illegible] [illegible] [illegible] Pekah.

The [illegible] [illegible] [illegible] a proper force to [illegible] [illegible] Tiglath-Pileser [illegible] [illegible] [illegible] [illegible] Israel, [illegible] Syria [illegible] [illegible] [illegible] [illegible] [illegible] [illegible] [illegible] [illegible] [illegible] [illegible] of Assyria [illegible] [illegible] against them, [illegible] Syria [illegible] [illegible] [illegible] [illegible] the whole [illegible]. He transported the [illegible] of Damascus to the Upper Media, [illegible] [illegible] [illegible] [illegible] to [illegible] [illegible] a great part of the [illegible] of the [illegible], and carried away a great number of prisoners.

After the [illegible] of Syria, [illegible] [illegible] Tiglath-Pileser, king of Assyria, [illegible] to [illegible] [illegible] [illegible], to [illegible] all the gold and silver [illegible] [illegible] [illegible] and the [illegible] [illegible] [illegible] [illegible], and [illegible] [illegible] with him to Damascus, [illegible] [illegible] [illegible] them up to [illegible], with acknowledgments of his great conduct, and then returned to Jerusalem.

Such was the [illegible] and [illegible] of the king of Judah, that, notwithstanding the inveterate enmity [illegible] [illegible] between his subjects and those of Syria, [illegible] [illegible] condescended to worship their gods, and [illegible] their [illegible] ceremonies, [illegible] persuading himself that they would [illegible] to his arms, [illegible] [illegible] [illegible] unhallowed [illegible] for a false religion. When it appeared to him necessary, he would pay homage to the gods of the [illegible]; nay, he seemed to prefer [illegible] kind of idolatry to the adoration of the true God, [illegible] the laws and religion of his ancestors. He [illegible] [illegible] and [illegible] of the Almighty to such a degree, that, having [illegible] the temple of its vessels and ornaments, he [illegible] the [illegible] [illegible] [illegible] [illegible], and, [illegible] [illegible], [illegible] the [illegible] [illegible] their [illegible] his [illegible].

While Ahaz was [illegible] [illegible] his [illegible] the Almighty was [illegible], [illegible] him off in the very [illegible] of his [illegible], being [illegible] years of age, [illegible] [illegible] of his [illegible] [illegible] Hezekiah succeeded him on the throne of Judah.

A[illegible] [illegible] Pekah [illegible] Israel [illegible] [illegible] [illegible] through the [illegible] of [illegible] Hoshea, [illegible] [illegible] [illegible] [illegible] [illegible] [illegible] [illegible] [illegible] [illegible] [illegible]-

doned to the h[illegible] degree, a contemner of God, and an enemy to ju[illegible] [illegible] Salmanezer, king of Assyria, led [illegible] against him, and that Almighty aid which he had rejected and despised, being justly withheld, he [illegible] overcome, and forced to submit to the [illegible] was imposed by the conqueror, who laid him under contribution.

In the fourth year of the reign of Hosea, Hezekiah [illegible] the throne of Judah. He was a prince of distinguished qualities, and revered for his strict adherence to piety and justice. No sooner had he got possession of the kingdom than he began with a laudable zeal to set about [illegible] reformation in matters of religion. To this end [illegible] an assembly of the priests and Levites, whom [illegible] addressed as follows.

"It is unnecessary for me to remind you of the misfortunes [illegible] [illegible] in your refusing [illegible] to God and [illegible] with [illegible] [illegible] [illegible] [illegible] [illegible] [illegible] [illegible] [illegible] taught [illegible] [illegible] [illegible] [illegible] I recommend [illegible] [illegible] [illegible] [illegible] [illegible] selves from former pollutions, and [illegible] purify the temple by sacrifices and consecrations [illegible] [illegible] [illegible] alone you may hope for future prosperity, [illegible] [illegible] or for the sins you have committed."

The priests were so affected [illegible] [illegible] [illegible] [illegible] [illegible] [illegible], that they instantly followed the [illegible] [illegible], by opening the temple, cleaning [illegible] from [illegible] impurities, preparing the vessels and [illegible] [illegible] [illegible] the [illegible] according to the form and [illegible] prescribed by the Mosaic institution.

Hezekiah then sent messengers throughout all his dominion to summon the people up to Jerusalem, to celebrate the feast of unleavened bread, which had been long interrupted through the impious neglect of former kings. He also exhorted and invited the Israelites to relinquish their [illegible] [illegible] institutions, and return to the [illegible] [illegible], and [illegible] worship of the one God, promising them [illegible] those [illegible] [illegible] to pass and [illegible], and celebrate the festival in common with his own people. He observed, that [illegible] was not [illegible] [illegible] [illegible] of [illegible] [illegible] [illegible] [illegible] this [illegible] [illegible] [illegible] [illegible] [illegible] [illegible] real prosperity, [illegible] would [illegible] [illegible] [illegible] [illegible] he would be [illegible] [illegible] [illegible].

[illegible] the Israelites treated [illegible] [illegible] [illegible] [illegible] [illegible] the messengers [illegible] [illegible] [illegible], [illegible] the prophets for their good offices [illegible] [illegible] them to [illegible] [illegible] [illegible] [illegible] [illegible] [illegible] [illegible] [illegible] [illegible] treat them [illegible] [illegible] [illegible] [illegible] [illegible] [illegible] [illegible]. They not only neglected this salutary counsel, but [illegible] [illegible] their bigotry and resentment at the expence of the lives of [illegible] of the prophets. They proceeded [illegible] from one [illegible] to another, till the Almighty in his vindictive wrath [illegible] himself of them for their impieties, [illegible] [illegible] [illegible] up to the oppression and tyranny of [illegible] [illegible], as will appear from the sequel of this history. Many, however, of the tribes of Manasseh, Zebulon and Issachar, were duly impressed with the promotions of the prophets, and cordially [illegible] to Jerusalem, [illegible] the invitation of Hezekiah, to worship the true God according to the form of his own appointment.

As soon as Hezekiah was informed that the necessary preparations were made in the temple for the worshipping of God, he repaired thither early the next morning, attended by the priests, and a great concourse of the people, and sacrificed [illegible] bullocks, seven rams, seven lambs, and as [illegible] goats. [illegible] [illegible] [illegible] on the victims, the priests performed the duties of their function, while the Levites standing round, chanted Divine hymns, and accompanied the vocal with instrumental music, as David had composed and taught them of old.

When this ceremony was over, the king and the people [illegible] themselves prostrate, and paid adoration to the One Supreme. He afterwards sacrificed seventy bullocks, an hundred rams, and two hundred lambs, besides [illegible] hundred [illegible] and [illegible] [illegible] [illegible], which he bestowed as a bounty for the entertainment of the people. When the solemnities were duly observed, and the ceremonies regularly performed according to precise form and order, the king joined in the general festivity, and universal joy prevailed throughout Jerusalem.

The feast of unleavened bread was now approaching, and during the time of the preparation, they offered up a certain [illegible] of other sacrifices for seven days successively. The king again bestowed upon the people, as a bounty, two thousand bulls, [illegible] seven thousand other cattle. The princes likewise following the example of his liberality, offered a thousand bulls, and one thousand four hundred other beasts, insomuch that it might be deemed one of the greatest festivals that had been solemnized from the days of king Solomon.

After the celebration of this festival, the king's next care was to purge the whole country, having first purified [illegible] [illegible] itself from the abominations of idolatry. He [illegible] appointed daily sacrifices according to the law, to be supplied out of his own stores, and enjoined the people to present the priests and Levites with the tenths and first-fruits, that the ordinary concerns of life might not [illegible] them from a due attendance on the offices of their sacred function. He also erected granaries and store-houses to be built, for the common use and service of the [illegible] [illegible] [illegible] children, to be distributed in proportion to their [illegible] [illegible] [illegible], by these means, the ancient discipline was restored.

Hezekiah having thus effected an entire reformation in matters of religion, and established the worship of the [illegible] God throughout his dominions, directed his attention to politics, by endeavouring to recover the places which had been taken by the Philistines during the reign of his father. To this end he made war on them, and [illegible] [illegible] their country from Gath to Gaza, which he [illegible] to his own territories. In the mean time the king of Assyria sent a message to Hezekiah, to demand the tribute which his father Ahaz had agreed to pay annually to the kings of Assyria, with menace, in case of refusal, to lay waste his country. But Hezekiah, relying on the Divine protection, [illegible] of his own integrity, and [illegible] [illegible] on the fulfilment of the prediction of the prophet [illegible] was by no means intimidated by the menaces of the Assyrian. This shall suffice for the present concerning the transactions of king Hezekiah.

CHAP. XIV.

[illegible] [illegible] the Samaritans [illegible] [illegible] the kingdom of [illegible] [illegible] [illegible] [illegible] [illegible] [illegible] [illegible] a colony of [illegible] [illegible] [illegible]

WHEN intelligence was given to Salmanezer, king of Assyria, that the king of Israel had entered into a secret treaty of alliance with So, the king of Egypt, he was greatly exasperated, and advanced with his army against Samaria. This city was besieged by him in the [illegible] year of the reign of Hosea, [illegible] sustained an [illegible] [illegible] the third year, when it was taken by assault, in the [illegible] year of the present king, and seventh of the reign of Hezekiah king of Jerusalem.

The loss of Samaria was attended with the total subversion of the kingdom of Israel, for the people were [illegible] transplanted into Media and Persia, and their king, Hosea, was carried off with them. The king of Assyria brought others from thence in exchange [illegible] [illegible] Chuthæans, [illegible] of Persia, to plant in Samaria, [illegible] up and [illegible] [illegible] country of the Israelites.

This was the miserable end of the Israelites, who impiously, as well as obstinately persisted in their [illegible] [illegible] of the Divine commands, nor would they attend to the voice and admonition of the prophets, though they were told by them that inevitable destruction would be the consequence of their continuance in disobedience to the Divine commands. These calamities took their origin from the seditious revolt of the Israelites from Rehoboam, and advancing to the regal dignity Jeroboam, who in contempt of the laws and religion of their fathers drew the indignation of heaven upon them, by leading them into the practice of [illegible] [illegible] abominations. But this [illegible] of iniquity did not escape unpunished.

"[illegible] king of Assyria extended his [illegible] ages, and carried [illegible] before him, throughout Syria and Phœnicia. His name [illegible] recorded in the history of the Tyrians; for, in the reign [illegible] (as Menander [illegible] his [illegible], that were [illegible] from the [illegible] into the Greek language), he [illegible] (*a*) Menander writes to this purpose. "This king Elulæus reigned thirty-six years, and, [illegible] revolt of the Citteans, [illegible] which [illegible] them to obedience. The king of Assyria also [illegible] against them, and invaded the whole country [illegible] After [illegible] this expedition the [illegible] of (*b*) Sidon, Ace, with many others, revolted [illegible] the Tyrian to the Assyrian [illegible] the Tyrians would not submit, the latter renewed the attack upon them with a fleet of [illegible] sail, and eight hundred [illegible], under the conduct of the Phœni[illegible] This fleet the Tyrians encountered with only twelve vessels, dispersed the enemies ships, and took five hundred prisoners. The naval reputation of the Tyrians was enhanced by this exploit. But the king of Assyria returned, and placed guards at the river and aqueducts to prevent the Tyrians from drawing water. The Tyrians laboured under this inconvenience, and were compelled to dig pits to procure a supply for their relief."

The Chuthites, who [illegible] country of Persia, called Chutha, composed five nations, each of whom brought their respective gods along with them. These idolaters so incensed the Almighty, that they were afflicted with a dreadful plague, insomuch that the greater part of them were [illegible] from the face of the earth, and finding no relief from any human means, they were directed by the oracle to have recourse to the worship of the Omnipotent God, as the only means of averting their calamity. Upon this they sent messengers to the king of Assyria, requesting him to send some of the priests [illegible] captive with the Israelites. This being granted, and the priests [illegible] they had the law of Moses read, [illegible] explanation of the same so far as it related to the theory and practice of religion, [illegible] that, [illegible] attention, the pestilence ceased.

The people of that country still retain the name of Chuthites among the Hebrews, but by the Greeks they are called Samaritans. They are fickle in their [illegible], and in their conduct [illegible] When the Hebrews are in prosperity, they [illegible] kindred, [illegible] adversity, they disclaim all connection. But this will appear hereafter with greater propriety in another place.

[illegible] Tyre [illegible] Sidon [illegible] Zidon [illegible]

[illegible] Lu[illegible] xxx [illegible]

(*b*) Sidon or Zidon [illegible] Canaan [illegible] Joshua [illegible] Great [illegible] Sidon [illegible] Sidon [illegible]

D OF THE NINTH BOOK.

FLAVIUS JOSEPHUS

ON THE

ANTIQUITIES

OF THE

JEWS.

BOOK X.

[INCLUDING A PERIOD OF UPWARDS OF TWO HUNDRED YEARS.]

CHAP. I.

[illegible]'s expedition against Hezekiah. [illegible] and Hezekiah is encouraged by the prophet [illegible].

IN the fourteenth year of the reign of Hezekiah, king of Judah, Sennacherib, the king of Aſſyria, made an [illegible] against him, with a numerous and well diſciplined army, and having taken ſeveral of the fenced cities of Judah by aſſault, [illegible] towards Jeruſalem. Hezekiah, deeming it moſt expedient to compound the matter, ſent an embaſſy to the king of Aſſyria, with [illegible] of ſubmiſſion, and offering him tribute. When Sennacherib heard the propoſals of the ambaſſadors, he determined to decline hoſtilities, ſolemnly engaging, upon condition of receiving three hundred talents of ſilver and [illegible] of gold, to withdraw his army, and give up his deſign of inveſting Jeruſalem. Hezekiah complied with the terms, and, to fulfil the agreement, was under the neceſſity of [illegible] all the treaſure, both of the palace and temple, to raiſe the ſtipulated ſum [illegible] it to Sennacherib. The baſe and perfidious Aſſyrian having received the money, receded from his agreement, for, [illegible] the [illegible] and withdrawing his army, he left Rabſhakeh his lieutenant-general, with [illegible] and [illegible], two other principal officers, to carry on the ſiege of Jeruſalem, while he marched himſelf with a [illegible] againſt the Egyptians and [illegible].

On [illegible] their army, they pitched their camp [illegible] the walls of Jeruſalem, and Rabſhakeh [illegible] with Hezekiah [illegible] king, [illegible] out three of his principal [illegible], Eliakim his deputy-governor, together with [illegible] the [illegible] records. [illegible] the [illegible] Aſſyrian camp, [illegible] the [illegible] to the [illegible] [illegible].

"The mighty potentate, Sennacherib, demands to know upon what principle or preſumption the king of Judah [illegible] of admitting the army into the city, or acknowledging his ſupremacy. Does he rely on the aſſiſtance of [illegible]? Vain and deluſive hope. He [illegible] a broken reed, that will not only deceive, but wound [illegible] ſeverely. Go, tell your maſter [illegible] is undertaken againſt him by the Divine will and [illegible], and that, therefore, the king of Aſſyria will as certainly obtain victory over Hezekiah and his ſubjects, as he hath done over the [illegible]."

Rabſhakeh addreſſed himſelf to Hezekiah's ambaſſadors in Hebrew, a language in which he was verſed. Eliakim, apprehending that what he had ſaid, being generally underſtood, might have an unfavourable effect on the multitude, requeſted him, if he had any thing further to ſay, to ſpeak in Syriac. But Rabſhakeh [illegible] Eliakim's motive for deſiring a change of language, exerted his voice, and continued his harangue in Hebrew, to this effect:

"It is neceſſary that your people ſhould well underſtand the commands of the king, my maſter, [illegible] them to ſubmit before it is too late. I am aware that it is your purpoſe to amuſe the people with [illegible] of [illegible] themſelves by force. But if you have courage to attempt [illegible], or entertain a hope of repelling [illegible], I will ſupply you with [illegible] you will [illegible] put [illegible] the experiment. [illegible] why will you longer delay [illegible]? Your compliance will enſure your ſafety, [illegible] a further oppoſition will involve you in moſt imminent danger, for neceſſity will at length compel the weak to yield to the ſtrong."

When Hezekiah [illegible] acquainted him with the [illegible], he immediately [illegible], put on ſackcloth, [illegible], and [illegible] againſt [illegible],

[illegible] on the ground, fervently [illegible] the Divine [illegible] protection, as the only means whereby he could overcome [illegible] powerful and haughty foe. Having done this he [illegible] some trusty friends, accompanied by a number of priests, to the prophet Isaiah, entreating him to exert his utmost [illegible] sure by prayer, to intercede [illegible] in his behalf, that thereby he might be able to [illegible] the pride and power of his enemies. The prophet complied with the king['s] request, and succeeded so far [illegible] thereafter, that he was authorized to bid the king [illegible] courage, for [illegible] Sennacherib should be overcome and [illegible] in his design with loss and disgrace, [illegible] and the Divine vengeance [illegible] to his [illegible]. He added, that Sennacherib should [illegible] perdition, and returning home [illegible], should fall by the sword in his own land.

At this very time Hezekiah received letters from the king of Assyria, expostulating [illegible] presumption of [illegible] opposition to a prince who had [illegible] so many warlike nations, [illegible] with [illegible] to spare neither age nor [illegible], but put all to the sword, without distinction, unless, without delay, [illegible] the gates of the city, and [illegible] for [illegible]. Hezekiah, relying on the Divine [illegible] and power, was not affected by this imperious epistle [illegible], laid it in the temple, and again had recourse to [illegible] tion for the safety of the city, till [illegible] this encouraging answer, that "His petition was heard, and that he need not apprehend [illegible] undertaking, that [illegible] which they had [illegible] in [illegible] the [illegible] of Jerusalem."

Soon after this the king of [illegible] against the Egyptians [illegible] frustrated, [illegible] upon this occasion. He spent a long [illegible] of [illegible], and at length [illegible] a little of the top of the [illegible] the point of taking the [illegible], he received intelligence that [illegible], king of [illegible] with a powerful reinforcement to the Egyptians, [illegible] took his way through the desert, with a [illegible] by surprise. Sennacherib [illegible] report, that he immediately [illegible].

Herodotus, in the second book of his history, [illegible] of Sennacherib, [illegible] against the [illegible] the Egyptian king was also a priest of [illegible], and assigns this cause for the raising of Pelusium: "The king of "Egypt upon this occasion, called upon [illegible] "[illegible] being granted, was [illegible] to the Arabian [illegible]. Herodotus [illegible], as he should have [illegible] "[illegible] the [illegible] that "there came [illegible] "camp of the Assyrians, that [illegible] "to pieces, and [illegible] several other pieces of [illegible] "arms, even to the [illegible] on "this [illegible], drew off from the [illegible]."

Berosus, [illegible] of this Sennacherib, and writes, that he reigned over the Assyrians, and made war upon all Asia and Egypt. His words are to the [illegible] the following chapter.

CHAP. II.

Judea [illegible] pestilence [illegible] the army of Sennacherib. [illegible] fire.

"WHEN Sennacherib [illegible] Egypt, [illegible] "to Jerusalem, he found the [illegible] "[illegible] the command of Rabshakeh [illegible] "[illegible] by a dreadful [illegible] "[illegible] one hundred [illegible] "[illegible], partly "through [illegible] of Divine [illegible] "[illegible] "[illegible] Nineveh, where [illegible]

"[illegible] "[illegible] "[illegible], "[illegible] "[illegible] "[illegible] [illegible]."

CHAP. III.

[illegible]

H[illegible] took [illegible] for [illegible] in preservation [illegible] the [illegible] the succession of the [illegible] kingdom [illegible] in his [illegible] not [illegible] to which [illegible]

[illegible]

[illegible] prized [illegible] the [illegible] a [illegible] to [illegible] upon his [illegible] the [illegible] temple, [illegible]

[illegible] with [illegible] them [illegible] them [illegible] the [illegible] might [illegible] and [illegible]

[illegible] ... the prophets [illegible] ... in the forty-ninth year of his reign.

CHAP. IV.

[illegible]

[illegible] ... the pious Hezekiah ... succeeded ... the throne [illegible] ...

[illegible]

... the [illegible] commotion, [illegible] his father's time. He [illegible] ... formed [illegible] ... and virtue. He [illegible] ... the temple [illegible] ... Conscious [illegible]

[illegible] ... the people [illegible] ... among them [illegible] example [illegible]. He [illegible] agreeable to the directions of Moses, and offered [illegible] ... oblations.

When he had restored religion to its original state of purity, he [illegible] to the fortifying of Jerusalem, made the necessary reparations in the old walls, and, as a further security, encompassed them with new ones. He erected several strong and lofty towers, and provided the city with stores and ammunition. In a word, his government was so reformed that, from the instance of his return to God and his subjects, he was [illegible] of the happiest of princes. He died after holding the government fifty-five years, and in the sixty-[illegible] year of his age, and was buried in his own garden. [illegible] devolved to his son Amon, whom he had by [illegible] of [illegible]

This prince, following the pernicious example of his father's early life, and indulging himself in the [illegible] ... in the hands of [illegible] ... conspiracy ... formed against him by his own [illegible] ... in the twenty-fourth [illegible] ... of his reign. The people, however, [illegible] to avenge his murder, by putting to death [illegible] who were [illegible] concerned in it. [illegible] ... the monument of his father, and [illegible] ... his son [illegible] ... years [illegible]

CHAP. V.

THE mother of Josiah was a native of Boscath, and her name was Jedidah. He was a prince of an excellent, tender, and most amiable and virtuous disposition, and [illegible] continued to follow the example of David, throughout the whole [illegible] of his conduct, in the promotion of the religion and laws of his country. Before he had completed his twelfth year, he gave an instance of his piety, by [illegible] the worship of idols, and restoring the people to the religion of the true God. Such of the ordinances of his predecessors as he found productive of ill consequences he abolished, such institutions as were expedient he retained, and to those which required alterations he made [illegible], which would have conferred honour on the [illegible] consummate wisdom, and the experience of advanced years.

Having finished his reform in the city of Jerusalem and its environs, he next made a progress through all his dominions, [illegible] resolved to purge religion from all those corruptions which had been introduced in the preceding ages. He [illegible] the groves and altars, together with the carved and molten images which his apostate predecessors had set up, to be destroyed. By these means the people were drawn from the vanity of their superstitions, to a reverence for the [illegible] of the worship of the only true God, and for the [illegible] custom of burnt-offerings and other sacrifices [illegible] ... He also appointed [illegible] ... the regulation of manners, and deciding matters of private concern, in order to [illegible] good government, and the [illegible]

[illegible]

Manasseh King of Judah loaded with Chains [illegible]
confined in the [illegible]

MANASSEH King of Judah RELEASED from CAPTIVITY by order of the King of Babylon.

HILKIAH & SHAPHAN presenting to King JOSIAH the Book of the LAW of MOSES which had been found in the Temple

[illegible] God [illegible] purposes [illegible] communications [illegible] intended [illegible]

[illegible] the earth [illegible]

[illegible] a country [illegible], which [illegible] all [illegible]

[illegible] reasons."

[illegible]

[illegible]

his government in honesty, peace and piety, till he closed his life in the following manner.

CHAP. VI.

Death of Josiah by a wound, in an engagement with Pharaoh-Necho, king of Egypt. Jehoahaz, his son and successor, is carried captive into Egypt, and dies there. The king of that country delivers the government to Jehoiakim.

SOON after the celebration of the passover, Pharaoh-Necho, king of Egypt, advanced with a powerful army towards the Euphrates, against the Medes and Babylonians, who had subverted the Assyrian empire, with a design of making himself master of Asia. When he came to Megiddo, a town within the dominions of Josiah, he refused him passage through his country, in an expedition against the Medes. The Egyptian upon this sent an herald, to give Josiah to understand, that he entertained no thought of hostility towards him, and that his only design was to expedite his march towards the Euphrates, desiring him at the same time not to put him to the necessity of effecting that by force, which he wished to do by courtesy.

Josiah notwithstanding the very mild terms in which the herald's message was couched, persisted in the denial of the passage, as if through the impulse of a fatality that was to bring on his dissolution. For, putting his army in a posture to dispute the passage, and riding up and down from wing to wing, to animate his men, an arrow from the bow of an Egyptian, gave him a mortal wound. He immediately commanded a retreat to be sounded for his army, returned to Jerusalem, and there expired. He was interred with great funeral pomp, in the sepulchre of his ancestors, in the thirty-ninth year of his age, and thirty-first of his reign. Never did a king die more universally regretted by his subjects, the lamentations for his loss were as universal when dead, as had been their affections to his person when living. Jeremiah, the prophet, composed an elegy for the occasion, which is extant at this day. This prophet foretold the approach of the Babylonish captivity, and the calamities of our days, and also, like Isaiah, committed his predictions to writing, for the information of posterity. Nor was Jeremiah the only prophet who foretold these melancholy events, for Ezekiel also left behind him, in writing, two books of the prophecies, concerning the same events. These two prophets were of the sacerdotal line. Jeremiah resided at Jerusalem, from the thirteenth year of the reign of Josiah, to the time of the destruction of the temple and city, of which we shall treat in due order.

On the death of Josiah, his son Jehoahaz succeeded to the government, in the twenty-third year of his age, and kept his court at Jerusalem. His character was the reverse of that of his father, and his mother's name was Hamutal.

The king of Egypt on his return from the expedition against the Babylonians, sent for Jehoahaz to come to him, to a city called Hamath, in the country of Syria, whither he had no sooner arrived, than he caused him to be put in fetters, and delivered up his government to Eliakim, his elder brother by the same father, on condition of his changing his name to Jehoiakim, and paying the Egyptian monarch an annual tribute of an hundred talents of silver and one of gold. (*r*) Jehoahaz was carried captive into Egypt, where he finished his life in disgrace and captivity, having reigned in Jerusalem three months and ten days. The mother of Jehoiakim was a native of Ramah, her name Zabida. He was a prince as destitute of religion as of humanity, having neither reverence for God nor regard for man.

CHAP. VII.

Nebuchadnezzar, king of Babylon, having overcome the king of Egypt, makes the king of Judah his tributary. Jeremiah foretells the calamities and death of Jehoiakim.

IN the fourth year of the reign of Jehoiakim, king of Judah, Nebuchadnezzar, king of Babylon, advanced with a mighty army to Carchemish, a city bordering on the Euphrates, with a resolution of making war upon Pharaoh-Necho, king of Egypt, who, at that time, held all Syria under subjection. The Egyptian, sensible of the power of his adversary, took the field with a formidable body of forces, in order to oppose him, but coming to action, was obliged to retreat, with the loss of many thousands of his men. The victorious Babylonians passed the Euphrates, and subdued the whole country of Syria, as far as Pelusium, Judea only excepted.

In the fourth year of Nebuchadnezzar, and eighth of Jehoiakim, the former made an expedition with a powerful army against Judea, threatening the inhabitants with the greatest extremities, unless they would become tributary, as were those of Syria in general. Jehoiakim, terrified by these menaces, purchased peace for a certain sum of money, which was duly paid for the space of full three years, but the year ensuing, upon the credit of a false report, that the king of Egypt was advancing against Nebuchadnezzar, Jehoiakim refused to pay him tribute any longer. He found himself, however, miserably disappointed in his hopes, for the Egyptians, for fear of the power of the Babylonians, declined the contest.

The prophet Jeremiah had repeatedly foretold these events and pointed out the folly of Jehoiakim, in relying on the assistance of the Egyptians. He likewise presaged the fate of Jerusalem, that it would be suddenly destroyed by the Babylonians, and the king himself fall a captive. But the inhabitants of Jerusalem, instead of being duly impressed with the awful prediction of Jeremiah, treated it with contemptuous ridicule. Nay, a charge was exhibited against the prophet to the king, as a mover of sedition, and being ultimately referred to the decision of the council, the majority were for pronouncing sentence of death. The elders, however, seeing the matter in its true light, would by no means agree to so rigorous a punishment. Their prevalent advice was for discharging Jeremiah the court, observing that he was not the only prophet that had foretold the calamities of Jerusalem, as Micah, and several others, had done the same before him, without being subjected to the censure or punishment of government, but, on the contrary, honoured and caressed as bearing a Divine commission. The council, prevailed on by this cool though forcible mode of reasoning, gave up their former opinion, and revoked the sentence they wished to pass without due deliberation.

Jeremiah committed all his predictions to writing, and upon a day of solemn fasting, when the multitude were assembled in the temple, in the ninth month of the fifth year of Jehoiakim, he read to the congregation those predictions which related to the destruction of the temple, the city, and the people. The rulers, alarmed at the denunciation, took the book from the prophet, and ordered him, and Baruch (*u*) his scribe, to abscond, and conceal themselves from public search. The book was then carried to the king, who ordered his secretary to read it in the presence of his friends. The king was so incensed at the contents, that he tore the book, threw it into the

(*q*) It is very probable that ... [illegible] ... of ... [illegible] ... we may ... [illegible] ... among the prophecies ... how ... [illegible]

(*r*) [illegible]

[illegible] suffered down upon him ... persecutions, and a great ... [illegible]

(*u*) The book called Baruch ... [illegible]

[illegible] and commanded Jeremiah and Baruch to be immediately brought to him and punished, but they had absconded.

CHAP. VIII.

[illegible] Jerusalem. Puts [illegible] to death, and appoints [illegible] his son [illegible] to the succession.

SOON after the king of Babylon made an expedition against Jehoiakim, who, alarmed at the prediction of the prophet, received him with his army into the city, and lived, as it were, into a kind of fatal security, [illegible] But the Babylonian, upon his admittance into the city, violated the covenant previously made, and put the flower of the youth of Jerusalem, together with the king himself, to the sword. He then commanded his body to be thrown before the walls without burial, and constituted Jehoiachin, his son, king, both of the city and country, in his stead. He carried away captive to Babylon three thousand of the principal inhabitants, among whom was the prophet Ezekiel, being at that time a youth. This was the end of king Jehoiakim, who lived thirty-six years, and reigned [illegible]. He was succeeded by his son Jehoiachin. His mother was a native of Jerusalem, whose name was Nehushta. He reigned only three months and ten days.

CHAP. IX.

Nebuchadnezzar violates his faith in imprisoning Jehoiachin and the [illegible] of the people of Jerusalem.

THE king of Babylon soon repented his having placed Jehoiachin on the throne of Jerusalem, apprehending that, in revenge for his perfidious practice, in the life of his father, he would embrace the first opportunity of stirring up [illegible] and tumult. Upon this reflection he dispatched an army to invest Jerusalem. Jehoiachin, being a prince of a [illegible] mind [illegible] and unwilling that the city should be exposed to destruction on his account, entered into a treaty with Nebuchadnezzar's deputies for delivering up the city, upon condition that neither the town itself, nor the inhabitants, should sustain any injury. The treaty was ratified, and his mother and kindred delivered up as hostages to the deputies for the due performance of the articles. But before [illegible] elapsed, the king of Babylon violated his faith, commanded his officers to secure all the youths of the city, and all art[illegible] in general, and bring them bound to him. Their number was ten thousand eight hundred and thirty-two, amongst whom were Jehoiachin himself, his mother and [illegible], who were detained in custody by the king's command.

CHAP. X.

Jehoiachin deposed, and Zedekiah advanced to the throne [illegible] violating his oath, Nebuchadnezzar again invests Jerusalem. Zedekiah opposes the counsels of the prophet Jeremiah.

JEHOIACHIN being still detained in custody (*a*), the king of Babylon appointed Zedekiah, his father's brother, to the government in his place, binding him, by a solemn oath, to attempt no innovation, nor enter into any league with the Egyptians.

Though Zedekiah was no stranger to the fate of his predecessors for their impieties, he followed their pernicious example in the practice of the most detestable abominations. To this he was instigated by a similarity of dispositions and manners in his cotemporaries, and the sycophants who surrounded him. Indeed, an universal depravity seemed at this time to prevail. Such being the declension of true religion, and the prevalence of vice and immorality, Jeremiah, the prophet, frequently warned the king of the evil tendency of his impious courses, and [illegible] He also pointed out to him the danger [illegible] relying on the misrepresentations of the [illegible] predictions of false prophets, [illegible] pro[illegible] as that [illegible] the Egyptians [illegible] the Babylonians. Zedekiah [illegible] the prophet's [illegible] and [illegible] to his best interest, [illegible] the [illegible]ence of the wicked suggestions and corrupt [illegible] of [illegible] whom he [illegible] most intimate, [illegible] good [illegible] might have been wrought on him by the [illegible] counsel of the prophet.

Ezekiel, being at this very time in Babylon, foretold the destruction of the temple, and the [illegible] of the people, and sent his predictions in writing to Jerusalem. The two prophets exactly corresponded as to the taking of the city by force, and Zedekiah's being [illegible], while there was an apparent disagreement between Ezekiel's foretelling that Zedekiah should not see Babylon, and Jeremiah's affirming that the king himself should [illegible] tioner [illegible] [illegible] mercy, [illegible] [illegible] of expression, [illegible] Zedekiah to [illegible] all the particulars in which they agreed, though the [illegible] foretold came to pass exactly according to their prophecies, as we shall render evident [illegible].

After an [illegible] of eight years between the kings of Babylon and Judah, the latter violated the treaty, and went over to the interest of the Egyptians, not doubting but that their [illegible] powers would be able to crush the [illegible] Nebuchadnezzar. But the Babylonian no sooner [illegible] intelligence of this revolt than he advanced with his army against Zedekiah, [illegible] country, destroyed [illegible] fortresses [illegible], and proceeded immediately to the siege of Jerusalem. The Egyptians, hearing of the critical situation of [illegible], posted away to his relief, at the head of a powerful army, with a resolution to attempt the raising the siege. Nebuchadnezzar, upon intelligence of his march and design, [illegible] his army, met the Egyptians, gave them battle, vanquished, put them to flight, and drove them out of [illegible]. In consequence of this temporary [illegible] the siege of Jerusalem, the false prophets again plied Zedekiah with [illegible] delusions, intimating, that the king of Babylon [illegible] longer wage war with him or his people, nor remove them from their own country into Babylon, and that [illegible] them in captivity would return, and all the plate and treasure, which had been carried away, would be restored to the temple.

But Jeremiah contradicted their groundless assertions, peremptorily charged them with imposture and delusion, and affirmed that "The king of Babylon would "renew the war, besiege Jerusalem again, destroy the in-"habitants by famine, carry away those that remained "into captivity, take their private property, and spoil "the temple [illegible], that he would lay it in ashes, [illegible] "[illegible] overthrow their city and, lastly, they should "serve him and his posterity seventy years." The prophet added, that "On the expiration of the term, the "Medes and Persians, should deliver them from bond-"age by the utter extinction of the Babylonish empire; "that then they should be released, return to their na-"tive land, rebuild the temple, and restore Jerusalem." These important declarations of the prophet had great effect on the minds of the people in general: but the leading men, and those who were hardened in impiety, and abandoned to the gratifications of sinful desires, pronounced them the effusions of a distempered brain, and treated them accordingly.

As Jeremiah was on his journey toward Anathoth, the place of his birth, about twenty furlongs distant from Jerusalem, he was met on the way by one of the rulers, who took him into custody on pretence that he was a deserter, and going over to the

(*a*) Jehoiachin continued [illegible] but when [illegible] succeeded [illegible] [illegible] [illegible] continued [illegible] [illegible] his [illegible] [illegible] [illegible] [illegible] [illegible] The [illegible] [illegible] [illegible] [illegible]

[illegible]

CHAP. XI.

[illegible]

which he could not do, as he was brought blind thither [illegible]

[illegible] ignorance [illegible] of the power and wisdom of God [illegible] and the [illegible] to demonstrate [illegible] by the [illegible] prophecies [illegible] Divine [illegible]

Thus [illegible] kings descended from David, [illegible] of [illegible] years, six months and ten days, [illegible] years of the reign of Saul, who was of [illegible] tribe.

And the [illegible] king of Babylon sent Nebuzaradan, his commander [illegible] to Jerusalem [illegible] the ground [illegible] Nebuzar-Adan [illegible] the temple [illegible] golden tables and candlesticks [illegible] Zedekiah, and [illegible]

[illegible] of Jerusalem [illegible] Nebuzaradan [illegible] the high priest, Seraiah [illegible] the king [illegible] Zedekiah [illegible]

Having [illegible] the succession [illegible] from father to son [illegible]

[illegible] high-priest [illegible] of Solomon [illegible] was Zadok. Then [illegible] Ahimaaz [illegible] Azariah [illegible] Jotham [illegible] Sallum [illegible] Jozadak [illegible] to Babylon [illegible] generation.

[illegible] the king's return to Babylon, Zedekiah was [illegible] and [illegible] the holy vessels [illegible] the temple [illegible] gods of [illegible] and Jehozadak [illegible]

Nebuzaradan, the general [illegible] captive [illegible] Gedaliah, the son of Ahikam [illegible] tribute to the king. The prophet Jeremiah [illegible] not to [illegible] Gedaliah [illegible] to Babylon [illegible] Jeremiah [illegible] suffered to remain there, and there in the miseries of [illegible] Nebuzaradan, having the prophet's [illegible]

[illegible] Gedaliah [illegible] Jerusalem [illegible] fled to Egypt [illegible] he [illegible]

Upon the [illegible] Gedaliah, he [illegible] tribute to the king of Babylon.

[illegible] Ishmael [illegible] Gedaliah [illegible]

[illegible] Gedaliah [illegible]

In the [illegible] Gedaliah [illegible] to a famous [illegible]

thought the most favourable opportunity for carrying his execrable design into execution, nor did he fail taking advantage of it. In the midst of the entertainment, when conviviality and intoxication prevailed, Ishmael and his companions, suddenly arose from the table, and falling on the governor, not only put him to death, but all the guards who were present. Being now the dead of the night, and the inhabitants of the city carelessly secure, they sallied into the streets, slaughtering all they could find, whether Jews or Babylonians, without distinction. The day after this horrid transaction took place, it happened that a party of fourscore men came to Mizpah, in order to offer presents to Gedaliah, in acknowledgment of their subjection to his government. Ishmael being apprised of their arrival, went, accompanied by his companions, some way from Mizpah to meet them; which he had no sooner done, than he offered to conduct them to the governor's house. The offer was readily accepted, but they had no sooner arrived there, than Ishmael and his companions shut the doors upon them, fell on and slew them, causing the bodies afterwards to be thrown into a pit, where they might be concealed. Some few of the number were spared in consequence of their promising to make a discovery of some treasure, and other valuable commodities, which were hid under ground in an adjacent field.

Ishmael, after these horrid massacres, took away with him captive the common people of Mizpah, with their wives and children, and, amongst the rest, two persons of distinction, daughters of Zedekiah, whom Nebuzar-Adan had left under the immediate care of Gedaliah. When Johanan, and the rest of the principal men, heard of the horrid barbarities committed by Ishmael, and that he was posting with the news of his exploits to the king of the Ammonites, they collected a considerable body of armed men, went in pursuit, and overtook him at the fountain of Hebron. As soon as the captives who were with him saw Johanan, they rejoiced exceedingly, and immediately [illegible] to his party; while Ishmael, with only eight of his companions, made their escape to the king of the Ammonites.

Johanan, in the mean time, with the people he had rescued out of the hands of Ishmael, consisting of [illegible], women, and children, retired to a certain place called Mandra, where they abode one day, being determined to remove from thence into Egypt, lest the Babylonians should avenge on them the murder of their governor. While this matter was in agitation, they entered into a resolution of applying to the prophet Jeremiah, and consulting him on their present critical situation. The prophet promised them his best advice and assistance, and at the expiration of ten days he received a Divine commission to inform Johanan and the other rulers, "That if they continued where they were, the Almighty would assist and secure them against any injury from the Babylonians, whom they so much dreaded; but that if after this premonition, they were determined to go into Egypt, they might expect the same vindictive judgment for disobedience, as had fallen on their brethren before them."

Though the prophet assured them that this message was delivered to them at the Divine command, they doubted its authenticity, imagining it could not be consistent with the Divine will that they should continue where they were. Supposing it, therefore, an invention of the prophet, to gratify Baruch, his disciple, and expose them to the resentment of the Babylonians, Johanan, and the people under him, in contempt of the Divine commission by the prophet, went away into Egypt, and took with them Jeremiah and Baruch.

Upon [illegible] the prophet received Divine information, that the king of Babylon should bring [illegible] into Egypt, [illegible] commanded to tell the people that Egypt should be taken; that part of them should be [illegible] carried away captive to Babylon; which accordingly [illegible]. For in the fifth year after the destruction of Jerusalem, [illegible] third of Nebuchadnezzar [illegible] into Coelo-Syria, and upon [illegible] forward to the Ammonites and Moabites, [illegible] reduced them to subjection, made a furious incursion into Egypt, [illegible] the then king, set up another in his place, and carried away the Jews that were found there a second time captives to Babylon.

Such was the miserable state of the Hebrew nation, having been twice carried away beyond the Euphrates: for the ten tribes were transported first by the Assyrians, out of Samaria, in the reign of Hosea, and afterwards the other two by Nebuchadnezzar, king of the Babylonians, upon the taking of Jerusalem.

Salmanezer transplanted the Cuthites into the country of the Israelites, out of the land of Media and Persia, and they were called Samaritans, from the name of the place into which they were thus transplanted. But the king of Babylon carried away the other two tribes without introducing any other into their country. From this cause Judea, with Jerusalem and the temple, [illegible] abandoned for the space of seventy years. The interval between the captivity of the ten tribes, and the transmigration of the other two, proved to be one hundred and thirty years, six months and ten days.

Among the number of captives carried away by Nebuchadnezzar, king of Babylon, were many youths of the first distinction, whom the conqueror, in consequence of their great natural abilities, kept in his palace, and employed proper tutors to instruct them in the language and learning of the Chaldeans. The most conspicuous among these were Daniel, Ananias, Mishael, and Azariah. As it was the custom amongst the conquerors to change the names of their captives, especially when they were to [illegible] in any capacity about the court, their names were changed as follow: Daniel was called Belteshazzar, Ananias Shadrach, and Azariah, Abednego. The king held these youths in high esteem for the excellence of their education, their assiduous application to learning, and their extraordinary progress in useful knowledge, insomuch, that orders were given for their daily supply of meat and wine from the royal table. But Daniel, being a devout believer in the religion of his country, and determined to abide by the precepts it enjoined concerning the eating of living creatures, desired Ashpenaz, the chief eunuch who had them in custody, that, instead of the delicacies which the king sent them from his own table, they might have pulse or dates, or any other ordinary food that had no life in it, as a plain diet would be most agreeable to their palates. The eunuch told them he was entirely disposed to gratify their inclination, but if such indifferent diet should cause them to look not so well as those who lived on better food, the king might take offence, and it might endanger his life. Finding the eunuch not entirely averse to the proposal, they urged him to permit them to make the experiment only for ten days, and after that, if he found the least change in their habit or complexion, he might bring them back to their sumptuous fare. The eunuch was prevailed upon to make the trial, and when he found them so far from being worse for the alteration, that they improved both in the habit of their bodies, and their intellectual faculties, he made no further scruple of complying with their desires, but gave them such diet as they requested, and kept the allowance from the royal table for his own use.

This abstemious mode of living agreed so well with Daniel and his companions, that it produced an apparent good effect in preserving them in the strength of mind, and body, fit for study or labour, being neither distended with gross nor effeminated by luxury. In short, through the means of temperance and discipline, their spirits were so perfect and active, as appeared from their astonishing progress in the Hebrew and Chaldee languages. Daniel, in [illegible], exceeded the rest, and soon appeared to possess an extraordinary knowledge in the understanding and interpretation of dreams.

About two years after the destruction of Egypt, Nebuchadnezzar had an extraordinary dream, which so impressed his mind as to make him very uneasy; and what contributed to his perplexity was, that he could not recollect the substance of it. To assist his recollection in this particular, he summoned all his wise men, as Chaldeans, Magi, and the prophets, and told them that he had an extraordinary dream, the substance of which he had forgotten, [illegible] therefore demanded of them the interpretation. They answered, that they could readily give him the interpretation, provided they knew the dream; but without that it would be impossible. This answer further irritated the king, who immediately gave orders that all the wise men of Babylon should be put to death.

As soon as Daniel heard the cause of this dreadful decree, and had reason to apprehend that he and his companions might be included in it, he immediately repaired to Arioch, the captain of the king's guards, requesting to know the crime for which they were to die. The captain informed him, that the king had a dream which he had forgotten, and that they were to die because they could not tell him the substance. Daniel requested him to procure him a reprieve for one night only, and he would not despair of giving him the satisfaction he required, as he had cause to apprehend that by the Divine assistance he should be enabled so to do. The captain related to the king the particulars that had passed between him and Daniel, in consequence of which the execution was respited, to try the effect of the experiment.

Nebuchadnezzar having complied with Daniel's request, he immediately went home, and related the whole matter to his companions, beseeching them to join in prayer with him, that God would be pleased to reveal to him this great and important secret, whereby not only their lives, but also those of all the wise men in Babylon, might be saved. The intercession of Daniel and his companions was heard, and that very night he received in a vision, not only the dream itself but a full interpretation of it, in order that he might communicate the whole matter to the king.

Daniel was so transported with this signal instance of the Divine favour and regard, that he rose early in the morning, encouraged his companions, now brought to the very brink of despair, by assuring them, that they might dissipate their fears, and rest in security. When they had joined in their acknowledgements to the Almighty for his signal interposition in their behalf, Daniel went to Arioch, the captain of the guards, desiring him to introduce him to the king, with assurance that he should have full satisfaction as to the particulars and interpretation of his dream. Arioch, happy in this intelligence, and pleased with the thought of avoiding the execution of the king's decree, readily complied with Daniel's request, and conducted him to the palace.

When he was admitted to the king's presence, he modestly confessed, that he did not arrogate to himself more wisdom than the Chaldeans and Magi, though upon their inability to discover his dream, he had undertaken to give him full information. He acknowledged that it was not through his own prescience, or his possessing an understanding superior to the rest, but purely through the Divine mercy and goodness which interposed in a time of imminent danger, at his intercession, for his own life, and those of his nation, and manifested to him both the dream and the interpretation. He observed, that he had not been so solicitous for the safety of himself and his companions, as for the prevention of the deaths of so many worthy men, who had so severe a sentence pronounced against them, for not being able to do that which could not be accomplished but by a supernatural power. He then proceeded in words to the following purport:

"Your mind, O king, was agitated in your sleep, concerning the succession of the empire of the world on your demise. The dream had a tendency to solve that matter, and point out to you those who will rule when you are no more. You saw a large image, of [illegible], standing before you, the head was gold, the shoulders and arms silver, the belly and thighs brass, and the legs and feet iron. You then saw a stone broken off from a mountain, the fall of which overturned the image, and broke it so small that the dust of the gold, silver, brass, and iron, was as light as chaff, and carried away by a blast of wind to the furthermost parts of the earth, the stone increasing to such a magnitude, that it lay like a mountain upon the face of the earth." (a)

Daniel, having thus related the dream, proceeded thus to give the interpretation:

"The head of gold denotes yourself, and the kings of Babylon, your predecessors. The hands and shoulders portend that two kings shall subvert your empire, and afterwards their empire shall be subverted by another king coming from the west in armour of brass, and he is to be subdued, in process of time, by another power, which, in its nature, is stronger than gold, and not to be resisted."

Daniel also gave an interpretation of the stone, which I shall pass over in this place, as I have undertaken to write of things past, and not of things to come. Those who are desirous of prying into future events, are referred to the book of Daniel, as it stands upon sacred record.

Nebuchadnezzar was so astonished at this wonderful discovery of his dream, and the interpretation of it, that after prostrating himself before Daniel, he appointed Divine honours to be done him: nor would this serve him without giving him the name of his god, Beltheshazzar. He then made him ruler of the whole province, and appointed some of his kindred to offices of dignity. This drew such an envy upon them as to endanger their lives, through a [illegible] the king took on the following occasion.

He caused an image of gold to be made [illegible] cubits in height, and six in breadth, and placed it in the great plain of Babylon. He summoned, upon the dedication of it, the great men and officers, throughout all his dominions, making proclamation that, upon hearing the sound of the trumpet, they should all fall down and worship the image, upon pain of being cast into the fiery furnace.

Accordingly, upon the sound of the trumpet, all the people fell down and worshipped, Daniel and his kindred excepted, who refusing to do it, [illegible] of their country, were informed against, and [illegible] into the fire; but, through a merciful Providence, [illegible] preserved. The flame, as it were suspended [illegible] of its devouring quality in favour of the innocent, so they were not so much as scorched. This miraculous interposition of the Divine power and goodness, in their behalf and justification, recommended them to the king's esteem in such a degree, that they were more honoured and esteemed, if possible, than they had been before.

Soon after this singular circumstance in favour of the worshippers of the true God, who refused to bow down to idols, Nebuchadnezzar had another dream surpassing the former. It was, "That being expelled from the kingdom, he lived seven years among the beasts of the forest, and was afterwards restored to his former state and dignity." Upon this occasion the king again sent for the Magi, and demanded of them the interpretation. But they were at a loss of expounding this dream, which he perfectly remembered, as they were of the former, which he had entirely forgotten. Recourse was therefore, from necessity, had to Daniel, who gave him the interpretation, and his prediction was confirmed by the event; for, after an interval of seven years [illegible] in the desert, during which no attempt was made to seize on his government, the Almighty was pleased to restore him to his regal authority.

Let me not incur censure for representing things in my writings minutely as I find them in ancient history; for I have obviated all cause for this censure, by a public declaration, at the commencement of this work, that it should be my study and endeavour to acquit myself as [illegible] faithful translator of the history from the Hebrew into the Greek, and to adhere precisely to the original, without addition or diminution.

Nebuchadnezzar was a prince of an active disposition, and much more fortunate than any of his predecessors. He departed this life after he had reigned forty-three years.

Berosus, in the third book of the Chaldean [illegible] writes concerning him thus: "Nebuchadnezzar [illegible] [illegible] hearing that a certain great officer, to whom he had committed the government of Egypt, Coele-Syria

(a) [illegible] to Nebuchadnezzar [illegible], name of the Chal[illegible] [illegible] The [illegible] he wished, her [illegible] [illegible]

"[illegible]a, and Phœnicia, was fallen off from his allegiance "and not being in bodily condition himself to suffer the "fatigues of a [illegible] in his own person, sent his son Neb[u]-"chadnezzar, with part of his army, to reduce him to "obedience. He went, found him out, fought, over-"came him, and brought back the revolted provinces to "their duty. His father, in the mean time, was taken "off, by a sickness at Babylon, in the twenty-first year "of his reign. The young prince had no sooner intelli-"gence of [illegible] than he applied himself to the set-"tling of his affairs in Egypt, and the rest of the pro-"vinces, and recommended to some particular friends "the charge of conveying his prisoners, Jews, Syrians, "Phœnicians, and Egyptians, to Babylon with the ar-"my and baggage, while he himself, with a small reti-"nue, took his way [illegible] over the desert. The go-"vernment was reserved for him in the mean time by the "Chaldeans, and secured [illegible] the principal "[illegible] all his return, so that, when he entered upon the "government, he was established in the full possession of "his paternal empire. His first care was to [illegible] "arrange [illegible] of his captives into colonies, [illegible] "after that to adorn the temple of Belus, and other reli-"gious places, with the spoils taken in battle. He re-"paired and enlarged the ancient buildings of the city, "and raised works upon the banks of the river, to prevent "all approaches of an enemy. He erected three walls "of entrenchments within the bounds of the city, and as "many without, and they were all composed of [illegible] "Having thus fortified the city, he ornamented the gates "[illegible], and built another palace "contiguous to that of his father, with all possible [illegible] "and magnificence. The particulars of this structure "are too numerous for insertion in this place, there-"fore I shall only observe, as worthy of notice and ad-"miration, that it was finished in fifteen days. In this build-"ing there were raised stone [illegible], supported upon arches [illegible] "[illegible] mountains [illegible] as the "[illegible] with several sorts of trees, "[illegible] complement to the queen, who being [illegible] "[illegible] the [illegible] of the "[illegible] of her own country."

Megasthenes, in the fourth volume of his History of India, makes mention of these great works, and [illegible] [illegible] [illegible] his perfor-mances [illegible] Hercules himself, having subdued the greatest part of Lybia and Iberia. Diocles writes of [illegible] in the second book of his Persian History [illegible] Philostratus, in his account of the Phœnicians and [illegible], that this prince [illegible] the days of Ithobal, king of Tyre, maintained a siege of thirteen years against that town. These are all the historians, within the compass of my knowledge, who have written concerning this king.

CHAP. XII.

[illegible] by Evil-Merodach [illegible] Babylon. [illegible] Daniel expounds [illegible]

ON the death of Nebuchadnezzar, the government of Babylon devolved to his son, Evil-Merodach, who [illegible] Jehoiachin, king of Jerusalem, [illegible] his confinement [illegible] him with many [illegible] [illegible] and [illegible] government [illegible] Babylon. This [illegible] indisputably [illegible] with Jehoiachin [illegible] his prison [illegible] felt no [illegible] [illegible] country. On the [illegible] Evil-Merodach, after a reign of eighteen years, he was succeeded by his son [illegible], who having [illegible] years, the government [illegible] to his [illegible], Labosordachus, who [illegible] but only nine months [illegible] [illegible] Belshazzar, called, by the Baby-lonians, Naboandel.

Cyrus, king of the Persians, and Darius, king of the Medes, made war upon this prince, and when [illegible] before Babylon, there appeared to Belshazzar an ex-traordinary vision. As he was regaling himself in a spa-cious room with his courtiers and concubines, he [illegible] the vessels of gold and silver, which Nebuchadnezzar had taken out of the temple of Jerusalem, to be brought before him, and converted to the purpose of conviviality, [illegible] had already a most magnificent service of plate [illegible] had never heretofore been put to any kind of use [illegible] this instance of their [illegible], when the [illegible] intoxicated [illegible] to [illegible] the midst of [illegible] the king was [illegible] into the utmost terror and consternation by the appearance of a hand, which wrote on the wall, in three [illegible], the sentence of his condemnation. He immediately [illegible] for the most expert of the [illegible] to tell him the [illegible] of the words that were inscribed on the plaster [illegible] [illegible] the least [illegible] [illegible] under [illegible] of mind that he [illegible] [illegible] that whoever could [illegible] the writing, and give him the signification, [illegible] [illegible] and [illegible] [illegible] [illegible] [illegible] import of the writing, [illegible] had been upon the former occasion.

While the king was labouring [illegible] of [illegible] [illegible] and [illegible] his grandmother [illegible] him, on this emergency, "That there was a cer[tain] captive, who came out of Judea, [illegible] by [illegible] [illegible] by Nebuchadnezzar [illegible] Daniel [illegible] for his [illegible] the most [illegible] [illegible] that could possibly be proposed to him." She added, that he had [illegible] to light such things, and [illegible] on such questions to Nebuchadnezzar [illegible] of the most learned in his kingdom when they were con-sulted. She therefore [illegible] and enquire of him concerning the writing, giving him [illegible] encouragement, at the same time, to speak the truth though it should [illegible] him on the [illegible] of [illegible] his doubts, and exposing the ignorance and [illegible] of pretenders.

Upon this advice Belshazzar caused Daniel to be sent for, pretending, indeed, that he had [illegible] of his [illegible] [illegible] city, and that he apprehended him to be the most capable person in the world to divine the truth of a matter [illegible] [illegible]. When Daniel was brought into the royal presence, the king put the question to him, declaring [illegible] with the [illegible]

[illegible]

The PROPHET DANIEL *in the* LIONS DEN

[illegible] he had caused to [illegible] his lords [illegible], and which would [illegible] throughout the world, when it should be known [illegible] had not tried the [illegible] wisdom.

[illegible] modestly declined receiving the offers proposed, observing that wisdom was a Divine gift, and not to be [illegible] rules, but, on the contrary, bestowing its benefits [illegible] those who seek them; for which cause he would [illegible] to explain the writing.

"The [illegible] (said he) denotes that your death is at hand [illegible] not taken warning from the judgments that [illegible] great ancestor for his contempt of God, and [illegible] of the exercise of piety and virtue. [illegible] know that Nebuchadnezzar was banished [illegible] sentenced to the life and condition of a beast, [illegible] the Almighty on his contrition and [illegible] restored man to his former state [illegible] such signal instance of Divine mercy he [illegible] celebrated during the remainder of his life [illegible] so far from [illegible] you, that you are guilty of the most flagrant [illegible], and glory in the profanation of the vessels [illegible] to the most solemn services. By the [illegible] you have drawn upon your head the Divine sentence [illegible] and the intent of the writing is to demonstrate to [illegible] consequence. MENE, which signifies [illegible] that the days of your life [illegible] or that you have but a short time to live. TEKEL, [illegible] weight [illegible] have been weighed [illegible] balance of Divine justice, and found wanting [illegible] PERES, which [illegible] kingdom shall be divided, and given to the Medes [illegible] Persians."

Belshazzar, [illegible] Daniel, could not but be struck with [illegible] he [illegible] of [illegible] the Divine [illegible].

[illegible] the kingdom of the [illegible] Nebuchadnezzar. [illegible] of the Babylonish empire, [illegible] of Cyrus, his kinsman, which Cyaxares the son of [illegible] Greeks [illegible] took the prophet Daniel to accompany him to Media, [illegible] with honour [illegible] of esteem, [illegible] one of the three chief governors, that had the [illegible] hundred and twenty provinces [illegible] the [illegible] of Darius. Indeed, the king of Media entertained [illegible] high opinion of the [illegible] of Daniel [illegible] consulted him upon [illegible] occasions as an oracle, [illegible] upon any matter of importance without [illegible] advice.

[illegible] with Daniel [illegible] favourites of princes [illegible] the confidence and favour of the king his master [illegible] the envy of the courtiers around him. Daniel, however, was so well aware of their [illegible] his words and [illegible] he was above [illegible] riches, [illegible] and even desire [illegible] to receive [illegible] plot to [illegible] the following manner.

[illegible] that Daniel [illegible] prayers three times a day, [illegible] and [illegible] officers [illegible] to the king [illegible] that whosoever should [illegible] to prefer [illegible] to God [illegible] for the space of thirty days, should be cast into the lions' den [illegible] so [illegible] as not to see [illegible] the malevolence of [illegible], which [illegible] reflection, must have [illegible] of Daniel, consented to the [illegible] ordered the publication of the edict [illegible] counsel. [illegible] to the [illegible] of the edict [illegible] were [illegible] Daniel still continued his [illegible] of paying his devotions to the Almighty three times [illegible] of the world, [illegible] of the terrors of the [illegible] rather [illegible] with the [illegible] of a [illegible] which they immediately [illegible] themselves [illegible] the [illegible] declared, that Daniel was the only [illegible] in contempt of his royal [illegible], and [illegible] to the terrors and [illegible] of the edict, had prayed to his God, and that not [illegible] principle of [illegible] of [illegible]. Such was the [illegible] of the [illegible] apprehension that the [illegible] give so [illegible] was [illegible] with [illegible] that, [illegible] the lions' den.

Darius was compelled to [illegible] the [illegible] and [illegible] Daniel [illegible] that [illegible] world [illegible] into the den [illegible] great [illegible] to his palace. He [illegible] sleeping [illegible] of [illegible] to enjoy the comforts [illegible]. At the earliest [illegible] he went to the [illegible] things [illegible] the preceding day, [illegible] called upon Daniel [illegible] "O king, live for ever." [illegible] out.

But [illegible] enemies would not [illegible] that [illegible] the lions [illegible] given [illegible] the same [illegible] causes on natural principles, would produce the same effects, the [illegible] were [illegible]. The [illegible] as victims of Divine [illegible] well as human justice.

Darius [illegible] the enemies of Daniel, published a decree throughout his empire [illegible] his people to acknowledge the God of Daniel to be the true [illegible] and Almighty God, and [illegible] the prophet [illegible] to his [illegible] and [illegible] his [illegible], [illegible] universal esteem. Daniel erected [illegible] Ecbatana, the capital of Media, [illegible] for the [illegible] the beauty of its structure. [illegible] building still to be seen [illegible] from the [illegible] famous for being [illegible] monument of the kings of the Medes, Persians, and Parthians, [illegible] is [illegible] committed to the custody of a Jewish [illegible] this day.

[illegible] circumstances in the history of Daniel, which [illegible] extraordinary nature, are well worthy [illegible] He was endowed with a [illegible] of prophecy, acquired the highest degree of reputation, [illegible]

[illegible]

[illegible]

honours specified in the proclamation he had caused to be made throughout his dominions, and which would spread his fame throughout the world, when it should be known that he had acquired them by his wisdom.

Daniel modestly declined receiving the offers proposed, observing that wisdom was a Divine gift, and not to be corrupted by bribes, but, on the contrary, bestowing its benefits freely on those who seek them; for which cause he would proceed to explain the writing.

"The writing (said he) denotes that your death is at hand, "as you have not taken warning from the judgments that "befel your great ancestor, for his contempt of God, and neglect of the exercise of piety and virtue. You cannot "but know that Nebuchadnezzar was banished human society, and sentenced to the life and condition of a beast, "though it pleased the Almighty, on his contrition and supplication, to restore him to his former state as a man and a "monarch; which signal instance of Divine mercy he adored "and celebrated during the remainder of his life. But this "example is so far from having a due influence on you, and "those around you, that you are guilty of the most flagrant "blasphemy, and glory in the prophanation of the vessels "dedicated to the most solemn services. By these impious "courses you have drawn upon your head the Divine vengeance: and the intent of the writing is to demonstrate to "you the consequence. MENE, which signifies *number*, intimates that the days both of your life and reign are numbered, or that you have but a short time to live. TEKEL, "which signifies *weight*, intimates that you have been weighed in the balance of Divine justice, and found wanting. "PHARES, which signifies a *fragment*, intimates that your "kingdom shall be divided, and given to the Medes and "Persians."

Belshazzar, having heard this dreadful sentence pronounced by Daniel, could not but be struck with awe and confusion: nevertheless he fulfilled his promise, though he was the harbinger of most disastrous events, justly imputing the cause not to the prophet but his own impious courses, that had so highly excited the Divine indignation.

Soon after this both himself and the city were taken by Cyrus, (*) king of Persia, in the seventeenth year of the reign of Belshazzar, who is said to have been the last king of the family of Nebuchadnezzar. Darius was sixty-two years of age at the subversion of the Babylonish empire, with the assistance of Cyrus, his kinsman, which Cyrus was the son of Astyages, though known among the Greeks by another name. He carried the prophet Daniel to accompany him to Media, where he treated him with singular tokens of esteem, and appointed him one of the three chief governors, that had three hundred and sixty more under them, according to the original institution of Darius. Indeed, the king of Media entertained so high an opinion of the ability and integrity of Daniel, that he consulted him upon all occasions as an oracle, nor would resolve upon any matter of importance without his advice.

But it was with Daniel as with the favourites of princes in general; the confidence and smiles of the king his master excited the envy of the courtiers around him. Daniel, however, was so well aware of their design, that he kept so strict a watch over his words and actions as to elude their secret efforts. As he was above the love of money, he despised bribes, and even disdained to receive a gratuity for services performed. His enemies, however, contrived a plot to ensnare him in the following manner.

Observing that Daniel exercised prayers three times a day, they applied, in the name of his council and state officers, and with their advice and request, to the king intreating him to [illegible] an edict, that whoever should presume to prefer any petition either to God or man for the space of thirty days, should be cast into the lions' den. The king being so short-sighted as not to see through the malevolence of this device, which, on due reflection, must have appeared to strike at the life of Daniel, consented to the request, promised a confirmation of it and ordered the publication of the edict, [illegible] of himself and counsel. The penalty annexed to the transgression of the edict was so severe, that the people, in general, were terrified into compliance with it. But Daniel still continued in his usual course of paying his adorations to the Almighty three times every day in the public view of the world, wholly regardless of the tenour of the edict. This pious resolution furnished his enemies with the opportunity of a pretence for a crimination of which they immediately availed themselves. They waited on the king, and gave him to understand, that Daniel was the only man who, in direct contempt of his royal proclamation, and contrary to the tenour and letter of the edict, had prayed to his God, and that not from a principle of piety, but a spirit of obstinacy, and defiance of his authority. Such was the inveteracy of their hatred, and such their apprehension that the king's personal regard for him would induce him to pass over the offence, that they solicited with an importunity, and urged him with clamour not to be trifled, for justice on the delinquent, and that, according to law, he might be cast into the lions' den.

Darius was compelled to yield to their pressing importunities, but gave Daniel to understand his hope and trust that a divine miracle would be wrought to deliver so good a man from impending destruction. Daniel, [illegible], was cast into the den, and a great stone was laid at the mouth, upon which the king put his own signet and retired, pensive to his palace. He passed that night without eating or sleeping, for the anxiety of his mind for the fate of Daniel would not suffer him to enjoy the comforts and refreshments of life. At the earliest morn he went to the den, where he found everything as left the preceding day, and the royal signet untouched. He called upon Daniel by name, to satisfy himself respecting his fate. Daniel no sooner heard his voice than he exclaimed, "O king, live forever!" At which instant the king ordered him to be taken out.

But his enemies would not admit that his safety was the effect of a providential interposition, and attributed it solely to the lions being glutted with food. The king was so incensed at this instance of their rancour, that he commanded the lions to be fasted with prey and Daniel's accusers cast in among them; pertinently observing, that, as the same causes on natural principles would produce the same effects, the supernatural interference would appear, if they shared the expected, nay, a deserved fate. The lions instantly seized and tore them to pieces, so that they perished as victims to Divine as well as human justice.

Darius having thus executed justice on the enemies of Daniel, published a decree throughout his empire, commanding his people to acknowledge the God of Daniel to be the only true and Almighty God, and, at the same time heaped honours upon the prophet, in preference to all his friends and favourites. Having, by his piety and moderation, procured an universal esteem, Daniel erected a stately tower at Ecbatana, the capital of Media, a work as eminent for the strength as the beauty of its structure. This elegant building is still to be seen, and appears as firm as if it had not sustained the least impair from the shock of time. It is famous for being the royal monument of the kings of the Medes, Persians, and Parthians, to which use it is still applied, and the spot is committed to the custody of a Jewish priest to this day.

There are other circumstances in the history of Daniel which, from their extraordinary nature, are well worthy of observation. He was endowed with a singular gift of prophecy, acquired the highest degree of reputation, both

(*) The manner in which this was effected is related by Xenophon as follows: [illegible] named Cadites and Cobrias [illegible] palace [illegible]

[illegible] of Jeremiah [illegible]

with prince and people, and, at his death, left behind him a character that reflects immortal honour on his memory. We find by his writings that are still extant, and in daily use and reading, that he was highly favoured of God, who was pleased to reveal to him, not only the ſum and ſubſtance of things to come, in common with other prophets, but the preciſe time of their accompliſhment. And whereas other prophets, in general, foreboded calamitous events, and conſequently incurred the odium of princes and people, it was his peculiar honour and happineſs to conciliate their eſteem, by being the harbinger of welcome tidings. The accuracy and veracity of his predictions will be abundantly evident to ſuch as may be diſpoſed to peruſe his writings with candour, in proof of which we cite the following paſſage.

"It happened (ſays he) as I was taking the air with "ſome of my companions at Suſa, the metropolis of Perſia, that we were ſuddenly ſurprized with an earthquake. My friends, in a fit of terror, deſerted me. As "I lay upon the ground, ſtruck with horror and conſternation at ſo awful an event, I perceived the touch, and "heard the voice of a perſon bidding me riſe, and give "due attention, as the revolutions that would befal my "countrymen in future ages, would now be communicated to me. When I aroſe I ſaw a large ram with ſeveral horns, and the laſt was higher than the reſt. Turning my face towards the weſt, I ſaw a goat that paſſed "through the air, encountered the ram, ſtruck him down "twice, and trampled him under his feet. After this "there roſe a large horn out of the forehead of the goat, "and when that came to be broken, there ſprung up four "more, pointing towards the four quarters of the heavens." He alſo writes, "That from one of them came "forth a little horn, which, upon growing up, ſhould "wage war with the nation of the Jews, and deſtroy Jeruſalem itſelf, ſuppreſs the ceremonies of the temple, "and all ſacrifices, for the ſpace of 1296 days."

This was the viſion that Daniel writes he ſaw at Suſa, that was firſt ſhewn by a Divine revelation, and then interpreted after the following manner.

"By the ram was ſignified the kingdoms of the Medes "and Perſians. By the horns the kings who were to ſucceed to the government of thoſe kingdoms. By the laſt "horn the tranſcendency of the laſt king over all his predeceſſors, in riches and power. By the goat was ſignified ſome king of Greece, who ſhould twice overthrow the Perſians, and ſubdue their empire. By the "great horn on the forehead of the goat was meant the "firſt of their kings, and by the budding out of four "horns more, pointing to the four winds, was to be underſtood the ſucceſſors to thoſe kings, and the partition "of their dominions after the death of the firſt, though "ſtrangers to his blood, but that nevertheleſs they ſhould "reign for ſeveral years. And that in proceſs of time "from among them ſhould ariſe a king, who ſhould "make war upon the Jewiſh nation, ſuppreſs their laws, "rifle the temple, and put a ſtop to the exerciſe of Divine worſhip for the ſpace of [illegible]." This prophecy was fulfilled under Antiochus Epiphanes.

In the ſame manner this prophet foretold the deſolation of our people by the victorious arms of the Roman empire. All theſe paſſages he received from the revelation, and tranſmitted them in writing to poſterity as a teſtimony upon record of the exact correſpondence of the prediction and the event.

Theſe particulars may ſerve to eſtabliſh a veneration for the writings of a man whom God was pleaſed to honour in ſo particular a manner. They likewiſe tend to refute the erroneous opinions of the Epicureans, who deny the ſuperintendency of an over-ruling Providence, and eſpouſe the doctrines of chance and neceſſity, and that the whole ſublunary ſyſtem is the effect of contingencies, without any primary cauſe, not ſubjected to the influence of a guide or director (a). Upon this principle the world would reſemble a ſhip toſſed at the mercy of the winds and waves, without a pilot, or a chariot, without a driver, overthrown through the fury of horſes unbridled, or daſhed to pieces. So that from the predictions of Daniel before mentioned, I think the ignorance and ſtupidity of thoſe men will be evident, who diſpute the ſuperintendance of a Divine Providence, and aſſert the abſurd doctrine of chance and fatality. To ſuch opinions I ſhall ſubmit to oppoſe the moſt ancient teſtimonies of the exact correſpondence between preſages and events which could never have taken place without the interpoſition of a ſupernatural power.

(a) St. Paul confuted many of the Epicurean doctrines when he was at Athens.

No providence the ſceptic will allow.
"Then let the ungrateful mortal tell me how
His tender infancy protection found,
"And how his childhood was with health and crown'd
From his youth he came to manly years
Through many dangers which [illegible]

END OF THE TENTH BOOK

FLAVIUS JOSEPHUS

ON THE

ANTIQUITIES

OF THE

JEWS.

BOOK XI

[INCLUDING A PERIOD OF TWO HUNDRED AND TEN YEARS.]

CHAP. I.

Restoration of the Jews from the Babylonish captivity by means of Cyrus, who, by his bountiful influence, promotes the rebuilding of the city and temple of Jerusalem.

IN the first year of the reign of Cyrus, king of the Persians, and the seventieth of the captivity of the Jews in Babylon, the [illegible] was pleased to commiserate their calamity, [illegible] had foretold them, by Jeremiah the prophet, [illegible] the destruction of the city, that, [illegible] for their [illegible] and [illegible] years they should [illegible] to their own country, [illegible] and return their former [illegible] to be vouchsafed [illegible] his providence [illegible]. This was effected through [illegible] of king Cyrus, [illegible] letters throughout all Asia to this purport:

"[illegible] saith Cyrus, the king [illegible] I [illegible] believe that "[illegible] God, of whole [illegible] I [illegible] "[illegible] is the very God whom the children of Israel "[illegible] for I find honour [illegible] made of [illegible] "[illegible] by his prophets of [illegible] "[illegible] to come should [illegible] "[illegible] people."

Cyrus, it seems, had read [illegible] of Isaiah [illegible] wherein the prophet [illegible] the Almighty, "[illegible] the world [illegible] a king of [illegible] and powerful [illegible] with the Hebrews [illegible] [illegible] This [illegible] [illegible] The [illegible] [illegible] [illegible]

Jews to Babylon, and informed them that such of them as were disposed to return to their country, should have passports and permission to rebuild the temple and city of Jerusalem, not doubting but that the Almighty would be propitious to the design. He intended that he would send orders to all his governors and officers bordering upon Judæa, to furnish them with gold and silver for the [illegible], and beasts for sacrifices.

Encouraged by so generous a proposal, the most eminent of the two tribes of Judah and Benjamin, together with the priests and Levites, immediately repaired to Jerusalem. Many of them, however, remained in Babylon, unwilling to quit their possessions. Upon their [illegible] Jerusalem, [illegible] the king's officers contributed largely towards the promotion of the great work, some in gold, others in silver, and others in cattle. Many attended the discharge of their vows, and the solemnity of oblations, as if they had already entered upon the business of rebuilding the city, and the exercise of their ancient discipline. Cyrus also sent back the holy vessels and utensils that Nebuchadnezzar had taken out of the temple. These were committed [illegible] to Mithridates, the king's [illegible], and [illegible] Sabassar, till the temple should be finished, when they were to be restored to the priests and rulers of the people to [illegible] and [illegible] Cyrus then sent [illegible] to the [illegible] of Syria, conceived in terms to the following purport:

"Cyrus, the king, to [illegible] sendeth greeting."

"[illegible] known unto [illegible] "[illegible] [illegible] [illegible]

[illegible]

" for sacrifices, and all this is to be done at my sole charge. " I have also appointed my treasurer, Mithridates, and " Zorobabel my governor of Judea, to cause all the " utensils and vessels that Nebuchadnezzar carried away " from the temple at Jerusalem, to be sent back and re- " stored. Their number is as follows: fifteen golden " censers, and four hundred silver, fifty golden vessels, and " four hundred silver, thirty golden chalices, and three " hundred silver, thirty golden phials, and two thousand " four hundred silver, with a thousand other large vessels, " of divers forms, and for divers uses. It is my farther " pleasure that they receive entirely to themselves all the " profits and revenues that were formerly enjoyed by their " predecessors, and that they have an allowance paid them " of two hundred and five thousand five hundred drachmas, " in consideration of beasts for sacrifice, wine, and oil, " and two thousand five hundred measures of wheat, in " lieu of fine flour, and all this to be raised upon the tri- " bute of Samaria. The priests alone to offer up the sa- " crifices according to the laws and ceremonies of Mo- " ses, and to pray daily for the king and the royal family, " and for the welfare and happiness of the Persian empire. " Let no man presume to do any thing contrary to the te- " nor of this my royal will and proclamation, on pain " of forfeiting both life and possessions."

This was the substance of the king's letter, and the number of those that came out of captivity to Jerusalem, upon this invitation and encouragement, amounted to forty-two thousand four hundred and sixty-two.

CHAP. II.

On the death of Cyrus, his son Cambyses, is solicited to countermand the orders for rebuilding the city and temple of Jerusalem.

WHEN the foundations of the temple were laying, and the Jews were very intent on the advancement of the building, the bordering nations, and especially the Cutheans whom Shalmanezer king of Assyria, had formerly transplanted from Persia and Media into Samaria, when he removed the Israelites into other habitations, applied to the governors to whom the care of the undertaking was committed, importuning them most earnestly not to suffer the Jews to proceed upon the project of rebuilding the city and temple. These commissioners were prevailed on by the force of the bribes and fair promises, to slacken their diligence in the prosecution of their orders; and, during the course of this negligence and delay, Cyrus could not take cognizance of this, being engaged in a war with the Massagetes, in which he lost his life.

Upon the death of Cyrus, Cambyses of course succeeded to the empire. He had an address presented him out of Syria and Phoenicia, and from the Ammonites, Moabites, and Samaritans, signed by Rathymus, historiographer, Semellius, scribe, and the magistrates of Phoenicia and Syria. The tenour of it was to the following purport: "It is fit, O king, you should understand that the " Jews, who were carried away to Babylon, are now re- " turned to their former seats and into our country, where " they are busily employed in rebuilding a city that was " most deservedly destroyed for seditious practices. They " are setting up markets and places of commerce, repair- " ing the walls and raising up the temple. Know, there- " fore, that when these things are finished, they will nei- " ther pay taxes nor yield allegiance; for they are profes- " sed enemies to kings, and will not submit to serve, if " once they have it in their power to command. We con- " sider it as the indispensible duty of faithful subjects, to " apprize you of the true state of the matter, before it is " too late. We beseech you, therefore, to recur to the " history of your predecessors, where you will find the " Jews, from generation to generation, to have been ene- " mies to regal government, and that this very city was " justly laid waste for the daring crime of rebellion. We " beg leave to submit these matters to your royal consi- " deration, and add that, if you suffer them to proceed " with the rebuilding of the city, and the finishing of the " walls, you will find your communication cut off with " Phoenicia and Coelo-Syria."

CHAP. III.

Cambyses sends orders for putting a stop to the rebuilding of the city and temple. On his demise the Magi retain the government of Persia during one year, when Darius is chosen king.

CAMBYSES, who was of himself naturally averse to the Jews, stood in need of very little incentive to excite him to persecution. After reading therefore the remonstrance, and consulting the records of his ancestors, he gave answer to this effect:

> " Cambyses, the king, to Rathymus, historiographer,
> " Semellius, scribe, and the rest of the inhabitants of
> " Samaria and Phoenicia, greeting.

" Upon the reading your letter of address, I have caused " the records of former times to be examined, according to " your request, and have found your observations respecting " the city, consonant with truth and to mere experience. The " Jews there am[illegible] appear ever to have been a vindictive, rebel- " lious people, naturally disposed to rebellion, and their kings " in the highest exercise of violence and tyranny, [illegible] upo- " sition of taxes, in Phoenicia and Coelo-Syria, in particular, " may bear witness against them. On these considerations, it " is my command that you exert your utmost power to pre- " vent the rebuilding of the city and temple, for, in pro- " portion to the increase of power amongst these people, will " their spirit of rebellion revive, and as they have revolted " against former sovereigns, there is the greatest reason to " apprehend they will audaciously contend against the au- " thority of the present government."

Rathymus and Semellius, having received this epistle mandatory, hastened with a considerable body of associates to Jerusalem, and pursuing the king's orders with the utmost rigour, an absolute stop was put to any further proceedings in the work of rebuilding the city and temple, so that it was discontinued for the space of nine years, that is, to the second year of Darius king of Persia. Cambyses, after he had reigned six years, and subdued Egypt, died at Damascus, on his return from that expedition. Upon his death the government remained in the hands of the Magi for the term of a full year, when it was conferred, by the seven Satrapae, or eminent families of the Persians, with common consent, to Darius, the son of Hystaspes.

CHAP. IV.

Darius promotes and accomplishes the work of rebuilding the city and temple, against all opposition.

KING Darius, before his exaltation to the throne of Persia, was well affected towards the Jews, and had made a solemn vow, that, if he ever attained to that dignity, he would send all the holy vessels that were in Babylon back again to the temple of Jerusalem. It happened about that time that Zerubbabel, who had been appointed governor of the captive Jews, came from Jerusalem to Darius. There subsisted between them an ancient friendship, so that he was admitted, with two other great officers, to a post of the most importance and trust, in elevation to that great office his rate of [illegible].

Darius, a short time after he had ascended the throne,

* A certain [illegible] of the captivity [illegible] [illegible] [illegible] [illegible] [illegible] Cyrus gave permission [illegible] [illegible] [illegible] [illegible] [illegible] Babylon.

gave a splendid entertainment, not only to his own courtiers, but the princes and nobility of the Medes and Persians, the general officers of India and Ethiophia, in fine, of an hundred and twenty-seven provinces. When the entertainment was over, the company retired to rest, as did also the king, but [illegible] and [illegible] of [illegible], and having [illegible] indisposed for sleep, entered into conversation on divers subjects with the officers of the [illegible], and told them, [illegible] [illegible] [illegible] [illegible] questions to propose, and that to [illegible] [illegible] give the most [illegible] [illegible] [illegible] [illegible] [illegible] he would [illegible] [illegible] [illegible] [illegible] purple [illegible] [illegible] [illegible] [illegible] [illegible] [illegible] a golden [illegible] [illegible] [illegible] [illegible] place to himself in the council [illegible] [illegible] [illegible] [illegible] [illegible] the questions as follow.

1. Is there any thing stronger than wine?
2. What can exceed the strength of kings?
3. What is superior to the power of women?
4. [illegible] any thing [illegible] truth?

[illegible] [illegible] [illegible] [illegible] questions, the king [illegible] [illegible] the officers to weigh the [illegible] [illegible] [illegible] [illegible] their [illegible] [illegible] [illegible] they thought [illegible] [illegible] wonderful.

The next morning, the king summoned [illegible] [illegible] company [illegible] [illegible] he had [illegible] the [illegible] [illegible] the preceding [illegible], [illegible] [illegible] [illegible] himself [illegible] the place [illegible] he [illegible] [illegible] audience, he called upon the officers, severally [illegible] [illegible], to report their [illegible] on the questions proposed.

The first who [illegible] contended for the [illegible] [illegible] of [illegible], [illegible] declared the following [illegible] [illegible] [illegible] "[illegible] [illegible] [illegible] [illegible], reduces the greatest [illegible] [illegible] [illegible] [illegible] [illegible] [illegible] [illegible], gives money to the slave, [illegible] [illegible] "[illegible] [illegible] equal to an emperor. It [illegible] [illegible] [illegible] [illegible] [illegible] [illegible] the [illegible], the [illegible], [illegible] wine to be most [illegible]."

The second officer [illegible] [illegible] [illegible] [illegible] [illegible] [illegible] [illegible] [illegible], in words to this effect: "[illegible] [illegible] [illegible] [illegible] that the [illegible] "[illegible], [illegible] [illegible] [illegible] to be so far [illegible] over all [illegible] [illegible] [illegible], as to [illegible] them to [illegible] themselves [illegible] the [illegible] of [illegible] [illegible] of the [illegible] [illegible] [illegible] [illegible] [illegible] [illegible] [illegible] [illegible] [illegible] [illegible] [illegible] [illegible] [illegible] [illegible] [illegible] themselves to the [illegible] [illegible] dangers of war, and [illegible] [illegible] [illegible] [illegible] [illegible] [illegible] [illegible] [illegible] command of a prince, who [illegible] to [illegible] the king's store [illegible] whom the public [illegible] such respect [illegible] [illegible]?"

After this [illegible] on the power of kings, Zerubbabel, the principal of the officers to whom the [illegible] [illegible] [illegible] [illegible] [illegible] [illegible] [illegible] [illegible] [illegible] [illegible] [illegible] [illegible] [illegible] [illegible] [illegible] [illegible] [illegible] "[illegible] the force of wine, nor the power of [illegible], [illegible] women [illegible] [illegible] [illegible] the mother [illegible]

"[illegible] [illegible] [illegible] [illegible] [illegible] [illegible] [illegible] [illegible] [illegible] [illegible] we disregard [illegible] [illegible] [illegible] [illegible] [illegible] [illegible] [illegible] [illegible] being the [illegible] [illegible] [illegible] [illegible] [illegible] [illegible] [illegible] [illegible] beloved object. [illegible] [illegible] [illegible] [illegible] [illegible] [illegible] [illegible] [illegible] [illegible] [illegible] [illegible] [illegible] [illegible] [illegible] [illegible] [illegible] and [illegible] [illegible] friends, and [illegible] [illegible] [illegible] [illegible] [illegible] [illegible] "[illegible] [illegible] [illegible] [illegible] [illegible] [illegible] [illegible] [illegible] [illegible] [illegible] valuable [illegible] [illegible] [illegible] [illegible] [illegible] [illegible] [illegible] [illegible] [illegible] [illegible] [illegible] [illegible] the opportunity of [illegible]."

[illegible] [illegible] [illegible] [illegible] [illegible] [illegible] [illegible] [illegible] [illegible] [illegible] [illegible] noble company [illegible] [illegible] [illegible] [illegible] [illegible] the [illegible] [illegible] [illegible] [illegible] [illegible] [illegible] [illegible] [illegible] [illegible] [illegible] [illegible] [illegible] [illegible] [illegible] [illegible] [illegible] [illegible] [illegible] [illegible] the [illegible] [illegible] [illegible] [illegible] [illegible] [illegible] [illegible] [illegible] the earth, the [illegible] the vicissitudes of [illegible], [illegible] [illegible] [illegible] [illegible] [illegible] [illegible] [illegible]."

The [illegible] [illegible] [illegible] [illegible] [illegible] [illegible] [illegible] [illegible] [illegible] [illegible] [illegible] [illegible] [illegible] Zerubbabel, [illegible] and [illegible] temple, and ordered [illegible] [illegible] [illegible] all the sacred vessels [illegible] him [illegible] Jerusalem, [illegible] the burden of [illegible] Samaritans, [illegible] [illegible] [illegible] Coele-Syria, to [illegible] the Levites, [illegible]

When Zerubbabel had met with this gracious reception from the king, he no sooner left his presence, than he returned thanks to the God and giver of all good and perfect gifts, for that degree of understanding by which he had acquired both honour and esteem beyond the rest of his competitors, which he gratefully acknowledged to be the distinguished effects of his Divine bounty. And having concluded his thanksgiving with a prayer for the success of the undertaking, hastened to his countrymen, at Babylon, with the joyful news of their deliverance, and the liberal grants he had obtained from the king. Upon the report of these happy tidings they immediately joined in an universal thanksgiving for the promise of restitution to their native country. After this solemnity they celebrated a festival of seven days continuance, and indicated every token of joy and transport that they could have possibly done if the day of their redemption had been even the first day of a new life.

The heads of the tribes made choice of those that were to go upon the expedition, providing horses and other beasts of burden, as well as carriages for their wives and children, and taking with them those troops which Darius had appointed for a convoy. They passed the time of their journey cheerfully, exulting with vocal and instrumental music, and exhibiting every token of rapturous complacency. There was a select number called out from each of the tribes, but, as a particular account of them would not only be deemed prolix by the reader but break in upon the order of my narrative, I shall only give an account of them in general. There were of the tribes of Judah [illegible] from twelve years old and upwards, four [illegible] hundred and [illegible] thousand. After [illegible] four [illegible] and seventy Levites, and a promiscuous multitude of women and children, to the number of forty thousand seven hundred and forty-two. Of the [illegible] of the Levites there were [illegible] hundred and [illegible] porters, and ten porters, and of [illegible] three hundred and [illegible]-two. There were [illegible] and [illegible] that called themselves Israelites, but could not [illegible] There were [illegible] who had [illegible] [illegible] could not be traced [illegible] [illegible] [illegible] [illegible] hundred and [illegible]-two. The number of [illegible] that attended them was computed at seven thousand three hundred and thirty-seven, [illegible] men and women, two hundred and forty-five camels four hundred, other beasts of [illegible] five hundred and twenty-five. The leaders of this [illegible] was Zerubbabel the son of Salathiel, of the tribe of Judah and the race of David, and with him was Jesus the son of Josedec, and Mardochæus and Serebæus, which two were chosen to the command, by the suffrages of the tribes, and contributed, at their own charge, an hundred pounds of gold and five thousand of silver, towards the expence of this expedition. This was the form and order of the procession of the priests and Levites and that part of the people that went with them on their return from Babylon to Jerusalem, and the rest following [illegible] by degrees [illegible] in the end, they all went back to their own country.

In the seventh month after their departure from Babylon, Zerubbabel, their leader, and Jesus, the high priest, [illegible] expresses throughout all the land, to summon a general assembly at Jerusalem. The people [illegible] [illegible] with the utmost [illegible]. Upon this occasion they erected an altar for sacrifice, according to the [illegible] of Moses, and it was raised up on the same spot [illegible] [illegible] before. This proceeding highly offended the [illegible] nations, who [illegible] [illegible] to the [illegible] their religion, and [illegible] [illegible] celebrated the feast of tabernacles at that time as the legislator had ordained, [illegible] [illegible] [illegible] offerings, and the sacrifices of the sabbaths, and at the new moons of all holy feasts. All those who had made vows now came like [illegible] from the first day of the seventh month

They entered thereupon the rebuilding of the temple and expended vast sums of money upon the artificers in general both for materials and sustenance. The Sidonians generously promoted the undertaking bringing down cedar planks in abundance from Libanus, and afterwards stowing them in boats, which they brought into the port of Joppa, as they had been first directed by Cyrus, and after him by Darius.

It was now the second month of the second year, after the return of the Jews, when the foundation of the temple being already laid, they began, on the first day of the second month, with the superstructure, committing the superintendance of it to the whole family of the Levites of twenty years of age and upwards, and likewise to Jesus the high-priest, with his kindred, and to Zodmiel, the brother of Judah, and son of Aminadab, and to his sons. These excited themselves with such unremitting industry in the discharge of their commissions, that the work went on beyond the most sanguine expectations.

When they were advanced thus far, the priests came and officiated in their vestments, with musical instruments, and the Levites and sons of Asaph, sung some of the hymns of David to the glory of God, according to the first institution. But the priests, and the Levites and the elders of the families, who had seen the splendour and magnificence of the former temple and reflected how inferior the present was in comparison with it, became disconsolate, while those who had never seen the former, and consequently could not be affected by the disproportion, contented themselves with the present state of things, and rejoiced at the [illegible] of so happy an event.

When the Samaritans, who were still enemies to the tribes of Judah and Benjamin, heard the sound of trumpets, with [illegible] clamour, they flocked, in great numbers, to learn the cause of it, and finding [illegible] occasioned by the return of the Jews from their captivity in Babylon, and that they were now at work upon the rebuilding of their temple, they immediately applied to Zerubbabel and Jesus, [illegible] [illegible] [illegible] [illegible] that they might be admitted [illegible] undertaking [illegible] [illegible] common with them [illegible] alleging that "They worshipped the same God, gloried in the same profession and the love and practice of the same religion, from the days of Salmanezer king of Assyria, who transplanted them out of Cuthah and Media into this country." The [illegible] answer to this request was that they could not possibly be admitted into any share of the undertaking, because [illegible] Cyrus, and after him Darius had assigned the work to their particular conduct and care, but that they should have liberty, if they thought fit, to worship there without exception, and that it should be open to all people indiscriminately, who were disposed to worship the true God in the true manner.

The Cuthites (for so we call the Samaritans) were so incensed at this reply, that they incited the Syrians to remonstrate with the leaders [illegible] as they had done first under Cyrus, and then under Cambyses, in such manner as to [illegible] a stop to [illegible] to the undertaking, by slackening the diligence of those who were entrusted with the superintendance of it. In consequence of this proceeding, there went up at this time to Jerusalem, Sisinnes, governor of Syria and Phœnicia, and Sathrabuzanes, with some others and demanded of the principal men by what authority this temple was to be built? And also, as it had rather the appearance of a castle than a temple, to what end the walls of the city were made so strong, and the gates set forth? Zerubbabel and Jesus replied that they were the servants of the great God, to whose honour this temple was to be built, and to his [illegible] [illegible], by the greatest, the happiest, and the [illegible] prince that ever sat on the throne. That it stood [illegible] [illegible] [illegible], in the end, for the wickedness of their [illegible], the city, by Divine permission, was taken by Nebuchadnezzar, king of Babylon and Chaldea, the temple pillaged and [illegible], and the people carried away captive into Babylon. But that when Cyrus came to the [illegible] of Persia and Babylon, he commanded by roy-

[illegible] proclamation, the rebuilding of the temple, and restitution [illegible] the vessels and donations that had been taken away by Nebuchadnezzar, which were delivered to Zerobabel, and his treasurer Mithridates, to be transported to Jerusalem, and [illegible] up again in the temple there: that, by the command of [illegible] king, Abassar was sent to [illegible] to [illegible] expedite the work, and accordingly was present at the [illegible] the foundation, but that ever since that time, by one [illegible] or another, their enemies had found means to obstruct and retard it; and that, for the truth of these allegations they might write to Darius, to the end, that by consulting the public records it might be known whether or not what they had asserted was a [illegible] of facts.

Sisinnes and his associates did not think [illegible] to interrupt the proceeding [illegible] the knowledge of Darius himself, and therefore agreed to [illegible] to him immediately upon the subject. The Jews hereupon were very apprehensive that the king, upon this [illegible], would countermand the orders he had given, [illegible] (Haggai and Zechariah, two prophets among them at that time, [illegible] them [illegible] of good cheer, and [illegible] from the [illegible], for they were certainly informed of [illegible] Divine [illegible] touching [illegible]. The people [illegible] the encouragement given them by the prophets, that they doubled [illegible], and [illegible] without the intermission of a single day.

[illegible] the Samaritans had written a letter [illegible] to Darius, objecting to [illegible] of the city, [illegible] the erecting of a strong place, [illegible] the temple, and produced [illegible] ambitious, which had [illegible] to [illegible] [illegible] orders [illegible] should be [illegible] [illegible] found to the following [illegible]

"[illegible] year of the reign of [illegible] the temple of Jerusalem [illegible] [illegible] [illegible] [illegible] [illegible] [illegible] framed [illegible] one [illegible] of wood, the produce of the country, and the [illegible] out of the [illegible], that the sacred things, taken into Babylon by Nebuchadnezzar, be restored and placed in [illegible] [illegible] the [illegible] work should be committed to [illegible] governor of Syria and Phoenicia, and his officers, [illegible] not [illegible] Jerusalem [illegible], at [illegible] place [illegible] leave the building of the temple to the Jews, and the elders of their tribes: that they supply them out of the taxes upon the province, and furnish them for their sacrifices, with oxen, lambs, kids, [illegible], and whatever else the priests shall desire, [illegible] to put up their prayers to the Almighty [illegible] the welfare and happiness of the king and his people; that whosoever should presume to [illegible] this mandate, be [illegible] and hanged up [illegible] his goods confiscated to the king's use."

On the discovery of this record, Darius ordered a copy of it to be immediately taken, which being done, [illegible] to Sisinnes and his colleagues to this effect:

"King Darius to Sisinnes, governor of [illegible] and [illegible] the other magistrates, greeting.

"[illegible] copy of [illegible] extract from [illegible] Cyrus [illegible] will find com[illegible] [illegible] to the directions contained therein."

Sisinnes and his colleagues, on [illegible] the king's resolution, agreed to obey his commands in every [illegible] point, so that undertaking to assist the Jews, according to the tenor of the mandate, the [illegible] was carried on with such unanimity and alacrity, that the [illegible] [illegible] according to the prophecies of Haggai and [illegible], and the commands of King Cyrus and Darius, in the ninth year of Darius, and [illegible] day of the eleventh month, which is called [illegible], and the Macedonians [illegible]. The priests and Levites [illegible] with the people of Israel, [illegible] and [illegible] hundred [illegible] hundred lambs, [illegible] goats for [illegible] of the twelve tribes [illegible] temple [illegible] ordered [illegible] to them formerly [illegible] new temple. The priests and Levites had their [illegible] [illegible] according to [illegible], the Jews [illegible] erected galleries round about the [illegible].

The feast of unleavened bread was [illegible], and in the first month ([illegible] by us Nisan) the people [illegible] in the city, where they celebrated [illegible] with their wives and children, according to the [illegible] and the practice of their [illegible] [illegible] [illegible] [illegible] [illegible], offering [illegible] to God for [illegible] [illegible] and [illegible] of their [illegible] [illegible] [illegible] [illegible] [illegible] [illegible] [illegible] [illegible] [illegible] [illegible] form of government, [illegible] in the high priest, [illegible] change of affairs, [illegible] captivity for the [illegible] [illegible] [illegible] governed [illegible] [illegible] of their [illegible] [illegible] [illegible] This [illegible] and [illegible]

But the Samaritans who [illegible] [illegible] [illegible] the Jews [illegible] claimed to the Persians and [illegible] people [illegible] [illegible] proved exceedingly vexatious [illegible] endeavours to [illegible] [illegible] which was confirmed [illegible] Darius [illegible] Samaria had [illegible] [illegible] the temple, [illegible] the work being now finished the Samaritans pretended that the [illegible] [illegible] [illegible] expences of the [illegible]

The [illegible] and people of Jerusalem [illegible] Zerobabel, with [illegible] colleagues [illegible] to Darius. The king of Persia [illegible] [illegible] [illegible] to the following effect:

"King Darius to [illegible], governors [illegible] [illegible] Bobelon, and the rest of the [illegible],

"greeting.

"[illegible] Zerobabel [illegible] Ananias and Mardochæus on the part of the Jews, [illegible] [illegible]

[illegible]

"the rebuilding of the temple, and refusing to bear your part "in the charge of the sacrifices, which, by my command, "you ought to have contributed; it is my will, and I require you, "upon sight of this letter, forthwith to supply them out of "my treasury in Samaria with whatever they shall want "for the use of their sacrifices, and wood and [illegible] to the end that "they may offer up daily prayers and oblations both for "myself and for my people."

This letter put an effectual end to all contests between the Jews and Samaritans, the latter paying the tribute demanded for the service of the temple without further opposition. This is the last good office that Darius did the Jews, as he was soon after [illegible] by his subjects.

CHAP. V.

Xerxes, the [illegible] successor of Darius, well disposed toward the Jews. [illegible] Esdras and [illegible] Nehemiah.

ON the death of Darius, Xerxes, his son, succeeded to the government; a prince who inherited his father's piety and virtue, and confirmed all that his predecessors had done in favour of the Jews and their religion, being firmly attached to both.

Joachim, the son of Jesus, was at this time high priest. But the name of the high-priest of the Jews, who resided at Babylon, was Esdras, a man of most exemplary piety and justice, and universally beloved and respected by the people. He was also well versed in the Mosaic law, as to stand high in the king's esteem on that account. Upon a resolution to make a progress to Jerusalem, and take with him several of the Jews [illegible], he desired of him a letter from the king [illegible] to the governors and [illegible] of Syria, which he accordingly obtained. It was couched in terms [illegible]

"[illegible], to Esdras, the priest and reader of the [illegible]

"[illegible] my counsellors, "[illegible] with their "[illegible] company to "[illegible] "[illegible] according to the "[illegible] of their country, [illegible] "[illegible] all the [illegible] that you [illegible] "Babylon [illegible] "[illegible] upon the [illegible] to [illegible] "[illegible] you "[illegible] "[illegible] given you [illegible] "[illegible] should have [illegible] for any thing "[illegible] "[illegible] To this end I have also written "to the [illegible] of Syria and Phoenicia, expressly "commanding them to furnish whatever Esdras the priest, "[illegible] the laws of God, shall demand, without [illegible] "[illegible] to obtain the Divine blessing on my kingdom "[illegible] a hundred measures of wheat "[illegible] according to the [illegible] of "[illegible] I do [illegible] charge [illegible] the [illegible] "[illegible] nothing from the priests, Levites, "holy singers, or others, attendants on the temple, nor lay "any burden upon them. And I do hereby give you, "Esdras, full authority, according to the wisdom you have "[illegible] to constitute judges to execute justice "[illegible] Syria and Phoenicia, who un-"[illegible] in the [illegible] of "[illegible] do you instruct the igno-"rant [illegible] transgressors against the laws of "God [illegible] punished according to their demerit, some "with [illegible], and others with death, according to "[illegible] to the king's command.

Upon the receipt of the king's letter, Esdras acknowledged the Divine goodness, [illegible] to [illegible] of Providence [illegible] conferred on the Jews through the [illegible]

tality of the king. The people were summoned to a general meeting on this occasion at Babylon, where the letter was read, and a copy of it transcribed, and sent away to be communicated to all the Jews in Media, but Esdras reserved the original. When the Jews understood the piety of Xerxes towards God, and his affection for Esdras in particular, and their nation in general, they not only expressed their satisfaction, but hastened in great numbers with their effects to Babylon, with full purpose of returning to Jerusalem. But there was another [illegible] of Israelites, who, being accustomed to the place and settled in their habitations, chose to remain where they were. This is the reason why there are but two tribes to be found in Asia and Europe under the Roman empire. As to the other ten tribes, they are all planted beyond the Euphrates, and so prodigiously increased in number as to be almost beyond computation.

The publication of this [illegible] testimonial brought over [illegible] numbers of people to Esdras, not only priests and Levites, but [illegible] singers and [illegible] attendants appertaining to the [illegible]. He appointed a rendezvous for such as were disposed to return from captivity into their own country at the Euphrates, where they [illegible] three days fast, and offering up their vows [illegible] [illegible] (Esdras having declined [illegible] guard of soldiers offered [illegible] the Divine protection) they began [illegible] on the [illegible] day of the first month, in the seventh year of the reign of Xerxes, and arrived at Jerusalem [illegible] the [illegible] year, when Esdras [illegible] delivered [illegible] the money he brought to the priests [illegible] the [illegible] of the holy [illegible] six hundred [illegible] talents of silver [illegible] hundred talents [illegible] twenty talents of [illegible] gold, and twelve [illegible] brass, that was [illegible] more precious than gold [illegible] These were the presents of the king and his counsellors [illegible] of the [illegible] that continued in Babylon.

When Esdras had [illegible] himself of his trust, he offered up burnt offerings, according to the laws, twelve bulls for the whole people of Israel, seventy-two [illegible] [illegible] and twelve [illegible] for a sin-offering. He communicated also the king's letter to the governors of Coele-Syria [illegible] [illegible] and they [illegible] they could not dispute with the king's authority. These [illegible] were accomplished under the conduct of Esdras, who, doubtless, [illegible] the Divine [illegible] for his exemplary [illegible] and virtue.

Soon after these happy events, a charge was exhibited to Esdras [illegible] some of the priests and Levites had [illegible] from the law, and, of course, from their duty, in marrying into foreign families, and thereby polluting the sacerdotal race. Application was made to him at the same time, to support and assert the laws, lest the Divine vengeance should fall upon the whole body of the people for the [illegible] of a few. Esdras, at this complaint, rent his cloaths, tore the hair from his head, and cast himself on the ground, despairing of effecting a [illegible] as the principal men were concerned in this abomination, and it would be in vain for him to [illegible] them to part with their wives and children.

Those who retained any sense of piety and humanity, both [illegible] his [illegible] In this state of despondency he fervently [illegible] the Almighty, expressing his shame to look towards "heaven, because of the sins that the people had com-"mitted, while they had forgotten [illegible] "and undergone on account of their [illegible] He "[illegible] God, who had saved a [illegible] "calamity and captivity they had been [illegible] "them again to Jerusalem, and to their own [illegible] "had [illegible] "compassion on them [illegible] "the sins they [illegible] "[illegible] "[illegible] the [illegible]"

After Esdras had expressed his grief for the transgression of his countrymen, and implored the Divine mercy and forgiveness, in the hearing of a promiscuous multitude, there came to him one Jechonias, a leading man of Jerusalem, with a public confession of the crime alledged against them, advising him, at the same time, to adjure all those who had married strange women contrary to the law, to cast them out, together with their children, upon pain of the severest punishment, on refusal of submission. Esdras approved the counsel, and exacted an oath from the chief of the priests and Levites, and all the principal men of Israel, that they would put away their strange wives, with their children, according to the counsel of Jechonias. When this was over, he went from the temple to the chamber of Joannan, the son of Eliashib, where he spent the whole day, without taking any sustenance, through an excess of grief and agitation of mind.

He next issued a proclamation, by which all those who were returned from captivity were enjoined to meet at Jerusalem in the course of two or three days, on the penalty of excommunication, and confiscation to the holy treasury, in case of failure, either through neglect or contempt. Within three days the tribes of Judah and Benjamin assembled, on the twentieth day of the ninth month, called by the Hebrews, Thebeth, and, by the Macedonians, Appellæus. When they had placed themselves in the upper part of the temple, the elders being present, Esdras arose, and told them, that, "Whereas they were guilty "of an heinous crime, by marrying with strangers, in "contempt of the express law of their country, there "were no other means of obtaining the Divine forgiveness, and security from the Divine vengeance, than by "putting away the strange women with whom they had "so intermarried." They unanimously signified compliance with the requisition, but observed, that as their number was great, and the season rigorous, a matter of such importance would require mature deliberation. Upon this suggestion it was proposed that a commission of enquiry might be issued out to select a number of leading men, who were innocent of the charge in question. The motion passed without a dissentient voice, and, upon the first day of the tenth month, they entered upon the inquisition, which fully employed them till the first day of the month following. Upon the scrutiny, they found numbers of the kindred of Jesus, the high-priest, as well as of other priests and Levites, and the rest of the Israelites, who, having a greater regard to the observance of the law, than even to natural affection, immediately put away their wives, and the children born of them. After the solemnity of this abdication they offered up rams, according to custom, for peace-offerings; so that it was deemed unnecessary to specify either their characters or names. Esdras, upon the whole, produced a general reformation, and established a precedent as an universal rule of conduct for future generations.

At the celebration of the feast of tabernacles, in the seventh month, when a great multitude of the Israelites were assembled in that part of the temple which looks towards the east, Esdras, at their request, read aloud to them the laws of Moses, repeating the same from morning to noon. This public reading tended much to the edification of the hearers, as they were not only thereby taught a line of conduct for present and future observance, but their reflection was directed to the calamities their forefathers had suffered for the violation of those very laws, to which their obedience would have secured to them permanent peace and happiness. Esdras, perceiving them melt into tears at this affecting consideration, advised them to refrain from inordinate sorrow, as incompatible with the present festive occasion, and that they should indulge themselves in innocent mirth, while they retained in their minds such sense of past transgressions as to prevent a future relapse. The people, embracing the wholesome and friendly advice, celebrated the feast with cheerful conviviality, and then returned to their own habitations; but not till they had [illegible] to Esdras [illegible] the important reformation he had wrought in a point so essential to the laws and religion of their country. Having obtained an universal esteem by this meritorious service, he lived with honour, and died full of years and much regretted, at Jerusalem, where he was interred with a solemnity suitable to his dignified character. Joachim, the high-priest, died also about the same time, and was succeeded by his son Eliashib.

There was amongst the Jewish captives a certain person whose name was Nehemiah. This person, who was cupbearer to Xerxes, walking one day near Susa, the metropolis of Persia, overheard some travellers, that were entering the city after a long journey, conversing in the Hebrew language. This excited him to enquire whence they came. Upon their replying from Judæa, he put several questions to them respecting the state of the people and city of Jerusalem, when they gave for answer, that things, in general, were in a bad state, as their walls had been demolished, and the Jews had suffered the greatest injuries from the neighbouring nations, which annoyed them day and night, overrunning and laying waste their country; insomuch that great numbers were led captive out of Jerusalem itself, and the roads in the day time were found strewed with dead bodies. Nehemiah burst into tears of commiseration for the calamities of his countrymen, and in a suppliant posture, humbly enquired of the Almighty, "How long he would be pleased to disregard the miseries of the Hebrew nation, and suffer them to be made the prey and spoil of all men."

While he was thus deploring the wretched state of his country, word was brought him, that the king was about to sit down to supper, upon which he hastened, in much disorder and confusion, to attend the duties of his office as cup-bearer. The king, being more cheerful than common after supper, cast an eye upon Nehemiah, and observing his countenance dejected, demanded the cause. Having put up an ejaculatory prayer to heaven to give energy to his words, he replied to this effect:

"How is it possible for me, O king, to appear otherwise "than dejected, when the place of my nativity is laid waste, "Jerusalem reduced to an heap of rubbish, the gates burnt, "the tombs and monuments of my ancestors broken up, and "the ashes of the venerable dead sacrilegiously prophaned. "Deign then, O king, to grant the boon I humbly prefer, "that I may have your royal permission to repair to Jerusalem to assist in the rebuilding of the wall, and in the re"maining work of finishing the temple."

The king granted his petition, and having promised him letters recommendatory to the governors of the several provinces through which he was to pass, with orders to treat him with due respect, and supply him with every necessary he might require, dismissed him with an injunction to cast off his melancholy, and proceed in the discharge of the duties of his office with his usual cheerfulness. Nehemiah, upon this gracious reception and assurance, refreshed himself, and acknowledged the blessing of Providence, that had so remarkably interposed in his favour.

On the following day the king sent for him, and gave him letters of credit and recommendation to Sadeus, governor of Syria, Phœnicia, and Samaria, with instructions to receive and assist him according to promise. He went first to Babylon, and from thence, with as many of his countrymen as voluntarily offered to bear him company, proceeded to Jerusalem, in the twenty-fifth year of the reign of Xerxes, and having first exhibited his credentials to the inspection of his private friends, he delivered them to Sadeus and his colleagues, according to the superscription. He then summoned a general assembly up to Jerusalem, and addressed them in the temple to the following purport:

"You must be sensible and know, O men of Judah, that we our"selves are, at this day, under the superintending provi"dence of the same Almighty and merciful Being who "brought about so many wonderful events from a gracious "regard to the piety and virtue of our forefathers Abraham, "Isaac, and Jacob. I am now to declare to you, that it is "through favour [illegible] that I bring to [illegible] the [illegible] permis-

"sion of the king to enter on the rebuilding of your walls, "and the finishing of the work of the temple But taking it for granted, that neighbouring nations are not "only averse to, but determined to counteract you in the "design, I recommend it to you, in the first place, to "rely solely on the power of the Almighty, who will "certainly defeat all the efforts of your enemies, and "next, that you exert yourselves in the prosecution of "the work night and day, without intermission, while "the season affords opportunity"

Having delivered this address, he gave orders to the magistrates to survey the ground, take measure of the walls, and from due computation, make an equal distribution of the work amongst the people, according to the proportions of the inhabitants, in city, town, or village, promising, at the same time, the assistance of himself, and all that belonged to him, in the service, and then discharged the assembly

The authority of Nehemiah had such an effect upon the people, that they applied themselves most assiduously to the undertaking From this time the country was called Judea, and so termed from the tribe of Judah, that formerly possessed that quarter of the world

The report of this undertaking no sooner reached the Ammonites, the Moabites, the Samaritans, and the Cœlo-Syrians, than they determined to leave nothing unattempted, either by force or treachery to counteract it Accordingly they lay in ambush for the Jews up and down in every quarter, and took off many of them by surprize They kept assassins in pay to attempt the life of Nehemiah, and alarmed the multitude with menaces of invasion to such a degree, that through apprehension of impending danger, they were ready to desist from their work But Nehemiah maintained his ground with undaunted resolution, and, under the security of a slender guard, prosecuted the work without sense of weariness, or apprehension of danger Nor was he anxious for his own safety merely in the provision of a guard for his person, but it arose from an assurance that if he should be cut off, the men would never finish the building He therefore ordered that, in future, all the men should work with their swords by their sides, and their bucklers at a convenient distance, to have them in readiness He also appointed trumpeters to be posted within five hundred paces of each other, to give the alarm upon any discovery of an enemy, that the people might have time to stand to their arms, without any danger of a surprize He went round the city almost every night, and became so inured to labour, abstinence, and watching, that he surmounted all those difficulties, taking of food and sleep no more than was requisite to support nature This was the course of his life for two years and three months, at the expiration of which the walls were finished, in the twenty-eighth year and ninth month of the reign of Xerxes

Upon the perfecting of the work, Nehemiah and the people offered up sacrifice, and kept a festival for eight days, an event highly unwelcome and displeasing to the Syrians Nehemiah observing that the city was thin of inhabitants, persuaded all the priests and Levites, who lived contiguous, to take up their residence in town, promising to furnish them with houses at his own expence He likewise ordered people in the country, who followed husbandry, to carry their tenths into the city, for the maintenance of the priests and Levites, that they might not be diverted by any worldly concerns from attending the duties of their office This was readily agreed to, and by these means the city became better peopled

After these, and many other great and glorious actions, worthy of eternal honour, Nehemiah, in an advanced age, departed this life He was a man of unfeigned piety, strict probity, and unsullied virtue, eminent for genuine philanthropy and patriotism, as appears from the whole of his transactions respecting the people and city of Jerusalem This may suffice as a brief narrative of events during the reign of Xerxes

CHAP VI

Xerxes is succeeded by his son Artaxerxes, under whose reign the nation of the Jews was in danger of being extirpated Particulars concerning Esther, Mordecai, &c

ON the death of Xerxes, the government descended to his son Cyrus, whom the Greeks call Artaxerxes in whose reign over the Persians, the whole nation of the Jews, with their wives and children, were in great danger of being destroyed, as we shall shew in due time and place It is necessary that we should previously attend to some particulars that related to the king himself, concerning his marriage with a woman of the blood royal of the Jews, and who is represented in the annals of history as the protectress of our nation

When Artaxerxes had ascended the throne, and settled the government of an hundred and twenty-seven provinces, between India and Ethiopia, he made a most magnificent and sumptuous entertainment at Susa, in the third year of his reign, where he regaled his noble guests in a manner becoming the dignity of so great a monarch, during the term of an hundred and fourscore days After this he prepared another entertainment for several foreigners and their ambassadors, for seven successive days, which was conducted in the following manner There was a tent erected, upon gold and silver pillars, covered with purple and fine linen, and sufficiently capable for the reception of some thousands of people The wine was served in golden cups, ornamented with precious stones in such a manner as at once to excite curiosity, and afford exquisite delight Orders were given to the servants not to ply the guests with wine incessantly, as is the Persian custom, but permit every man to drink at liberty, and proclamation was made throughout the king's dominions, that they should set a certain number of days apart for the celebration of a festival for the safety and prosperity of the kingdom

Queen Vashti also had her apartments in the palace She was so remarkably beautiful, that the king, desirous of shewing her to his guests, sent for her to come into the general chamber, where they were convened But as the laws of Persia do not allow wives to be seen by any besides their domestics, from a regard to that prohibition she refused to go to the king, not only once, but persisted in the denial, notwithstanding several eunuchs brought her by the eunuchs to the same purpose The king was so incensed at this obstinacy, that, after the festival was over he sent for the commissioners that were expressly appointed for the interpretation of the Persian laws, to advise him in what manner he should punish the contumacy and obstinacy of his queen, complaining that she had not only once, but repeatedly disobeyed his commands One of them, whose name was Muchæus, gave it as his opinion, "That it was not only an indignity offered "to royal authority, but a precedent of dangerous conse-"quence to all his subjects, since other women might thereby be encouraged to contemn and disobey their husbands, "and that therefore so heinous an offence should be punish-"ed with a proportionable degree of severity, in fact, with "nothing less than banishment from the king's presence for "ever, by virtue of his royal will and pleasure published by "proclamation" The king was so divided between the love he bore the queen, on the one hand, and the regard he had for his dignity on the other, that he remained some time in a state of most tormenting suspense While he was in this anxiety of thought, his counsellors endeavoured to divert him from the resolution of making himself miserable for the unprofitable love of one woman, while he might make his choice from a collection of the first beauties through the several provinces of his dominions, and select her as a wife to whom, in a general view, he should find the warmest attachment

The king, on second thought, approved the advice, and immediately dispatched commissioners throughout his dominions, to select the most celebrated beauties they could find, and bring them up to him The commissioners were very diligent in the execution of their charge, and amongst others, discovered a virgin in Babylon, whose name was Esther Her parents being dead, she was brought up in the house of her uncle Mordecai, a man of rank amongst the Jews This virgin so far excelled the rest, in the beauties and graces of her person, that she was an object of general attraction and ad-

[illegible]sion. She was committed to the care of one of the eunuchs, treated with all possible delicacy and respect, and presented with essences, perfumes, and all the niceties of art used by the sex as ornamental embellishments. Thus was Esther, together with four hundred virgins, treated, for the space of [illegible] months, in which, being prepared for the king's bed, they were individually and separately introduced by the eunuch to the king, who having received them into his arms, sent them by the same eunuch.

When Esther was presented, he was so transported with the charms of her person, the elegance of her deportment, and the allurements of her conversation, that he immediately resolved to take her to wife, and the nuptials were accordingly celebrated in the seventh year of his reign, and the twelfth month, which is called Adar, with the greatest pomp and magnificence. A most splendid entertainment was given upon the occasion to the great men of the Medes and Persians and other nations, for the space of a whole month. When the queen entered the royal palace, the king placed the crown upon her head, and treated her in every respect worthy of a dignified situation, wholly regardless of her country or extraction. Her uncle Mordecai removed from Babylon to [illegible], and would often enquire, at the gate of the royal palace, concerning the welfare of Esther, who was as dear to him as his own child.

The king at this time, caused a law to be enacted, prohibiting any of his domestics from approaching him while he [illegible] upon his royal throne, unless they were called or sent for, upon pain of losing their heads, and there were officers appointed to be in readiness to exact the penalty. In the mean time he had a golden sceptre in his hand, and when he was disposed to pardon any who had transgressed the law so enacted, he held that sceptre forth, and, upon their touching it, they were exempted from the penalty.

There was formed, some time after this, a conspiracy between Bigathan and Teresh, two attendant eunuchs, against the person of the king. Barnabazus, a servant of one of them, and a Jew by extraction, discovered their treacherous design to Mordecai, the king's uncle, and he, by means of Esther, to the king himself, who put the criminals to the question, and, upon conviction, delivered them both up to justice. The king gave Mordecai no other reward than that of appointing his service to be registered upon the record, and allowing him admittance to the palace, with the privileges of one of his domestics.

Haman, the son of Ammedath, an Amalekite, being now advanced by the king, and coming frequently to court, the Persians, as well as strangers, paid him the greatest reverence, indeed it was the king's will and pleasure that it should be so. Mordecai was the only person that refused to do him the homage, that mode of respect being contrary to the practice of his country. This exasperated the haughty Amalekite to such a degree, that he asked him what countryman he was, and finding him to be a Jew, he broke out into a violent exclamation at the insolence of such a wretch, who, [illegible], and the free-born Persians, made no hesitation at doing him the honour commanded by the king, he should presume to disobey. In this fit of rage he took the desperate resolution not only to be revenged on Mordecai, but to destroy the whole race of Jews in the dominions of Persia. He might indeed, be further induced to carry this design into execution, by recollecting that his ancestors, the Amalekites, had been formerly beaten out of the land, and exterminated by those people. To perpetuate his malicious design, he attended the king according to usual custom, and took the opportunity of representing the Jews to him in the most odious and contemptible light, exclaiming against them [illegible] generation, unsociable in their disposition, barbarous in their manners, devoted to superstitious laws and ceremonies, [illegible] up and down in every quarter of his dominions, and, upon the whole, discovering themselves, [illegible] of word and deed, the common enemies of mankind. [illegible] therefore, to observe that [illegible] being their [illegible] it was not consistent with the rules of policy [illegible] He then [illegible] [illegible] propriety, [illegible], of [illegible] of the Persian empire, and let the [illegible] should be brought [illegible] the king's revenue, he proposed making up the defect out of his own private fortune.

The king was prevailed on by the artful insinuations of this wicked and arrogant favourite, to submit the disposal of the Jews to his entire discretion, and at the same time dispense with his promise of making up the deficiency of the revenue, which was estimated in the treasury accounts, at forty thousand talents of silver. Haman thus authorized, immediately published an edict in the king's name, and dispersed it throughout all his dominions, to this effect:

"The great king Artaxerxes to the hundred and twenty-seven governors of the provinces between India and Ethiopia, greeting.

"Whereas it hath pleased God to give me the command of so many nations, and a dominion over the rest of the world as large as I myself desire, being resolved to do nothing that may be tyrannical or grievous towards my people, and to bear a gentle and easy rule over them, with an eye more especially to the preservation of their peace and liberties, and to settle them in a state of tranquility and happiness not to be shaken: all this I have taken into mature deliberation, and being given to understand, by my trusty and well-beloved friend and counsellor Haman, a man of tried truth, prudence, and justice, and whom I esteem above all others, that there is a mixture of inhuman people among my subjects, who take upon them to govern by their own laws, and to prescribe ways to themselves, in contempt of public and [illegible] government, men, depraved both in their customs and their manners, and enemies not only to monarchy, but to the methods of our royal administration. This is therefore to will and require, that upon notice, given you by Haman, (who is to me a father) of the persons intended by this my proclamation, you put all the said persons, men, women and children, to the sword, without any commiseration or favour, in strict pursuance of my decree. And it is my further command, that you put this in execution on the thirteenth day of the twelfth month of the present year, to make but one day's work of the destruction of all mine and your enemies, in order to the future peace and security of our lives."

This edict was rapidly dispersed throughout the whole empire, and the people prepared themselves accordingly for the abolition of the Jews on the day appointed, but the inhabitants of Susa, the place of the king's residence, were particularly strenuous for carrying it into execution. The king and his favourite in the mean time spent their hours in conviviality, while the few Jews that were amongst the Persians thundered at the rumour of so horrid a massacre as that approaching.

When Mordecai was informed of the tenor and purport of this proclamation, he rent his garments, put on sackcloth, covered his head with ashes, and passed through the streets of the town, exclaiming against the flagrant iniquity of this horrid and barbarous design against the Jews. In this manner he proceeded till he came to the gate of the palace, where he was obliged to stop, no man being permitted to enter in such a garb. Mordecai's example was followed by all the Jews in the several cities within the Persian dominions, who, upon notice of the king's decree, were overwhelmed with despair.

Intelligence of this reaching the queen, (who was a stranger to the decree being passed) she was greatly affected thereby, and sent a messenger to Mordecai, entreating him to lay aside that [illegible] habit, and return the dress that was consistent with his station. But he told the messenger he could not comply with the queen's request, till the cause of his melancholy appearance was removed. In consequence of this answer, the queen sent Hatach, one of the king's eunuchs, who was at that time in her presence, to learn the reason of Mordecai, wherefore he [illegible] from an appearance [illegible] to put it off at her particular request. Mordecai then related the [illegible] and the form of the decree, setting forth that the king, at the instigation of Haman, had affixed his royal proclamation throughout all his dominions, for the extirpation of the Jews, and that Haman had offered a vast sum of money, by way of compensation to induce him to do it. He then gave Hetach a copy of the decree to deliver to the queen, imploring that she would make an humble application to the king, and intercede with him in their behalf, as the lives of the whole nation were now at stake. He represented the necessity of waving delay, as Haman was incessantly calumniating the Jews, and would continue to exasperate the king against them till he had gained his point.

This account was faithfully delivered by the eunuch to the queen, who immediately returned an answer to Mordecai, in which she excused herself from engaging in the affair, setting forth that an ordinance had been passed, prohibiting any person, whether man or woman, on pain of death, from approaching the king when seated on his throne of state, without being called to attend him, unless he would vouchsafe to hold forth his golden sceptre. When Mordecai heard this, he pressed the queen once again, by the same messenger, representing, that it was not her own personal safety that was in question, but the security of the whole race, and admonishing her by no means to neglect the least opportunity of performing an office incumbent on her by every relative tie, and every dictate of humanity. He further intimated his reliance on the Divine interposition in behalf of a people who were unjustly condemned to death by the vile artifices of an arrogant and ambitious man.

This message found Esther, who immediately dispatched the eunuch to Mordecai with this order and promise, that he, and all the Jews in Susa, should fast for three days, as would herself and servants, and offer up their humble supplications to the Almighty, that he would be pleased to prosper her in so hazardous an undertaking, at the expiration of which she would not fail to address the king, though at the hazard of her life. Mordecai duly attended to the queen's instructions, and having circulated the same amongst the Jews, they strictly observed the fast, and humbly besought the Almighty to defeat the malicious designs of their enemies, to extend his mercies according as he was wont to penitent offenders, and finally deliver them from the destruction denounced against them. The whole multitude joined, indeed, in one common address, imploring the Almighty to vouchsafe them his protection, and avert that dreadful judgment from the Israelites that now hung over their heads. Queen Esther also humbled herself before God after the manner of her country, prostrating herself on the earth, assuming a mourning habit, abstaining from every sensual gratification for three days, and imploring the Divine interposition in her behalf, that the king might be disposed to attend to her intercession for a miserable and persecuted people, so that it might prevail, to the confusion of their enemies, and all their malicious designs upon her distressed countrymen.

After three days thus spent in fervent supplication for the Divine mercy and compassion, the queen put on her royal attire, and, with two attendants, bearing up her train, advanced towards the king, her face being covered with a blush expressive both of majesty and grace, though at the same time, not without some indication of doubtful apprehension. The dazzling lustre of the king seated on his throne, and an imagination that his countenance expressed displeasure, so affected the gentle Esther, that she immediately fell into a swoon, and would have sunk to the ground, had she not been supported by her attendants. The king, alarmed at her [illegible], descended from his throne, embraced her in his arms, and, in tenderest phrase, consoled her with an assurance [illegible] no advantage should be taken of the law to her prejudice, though she came uncalled; that decree extending only to subjects, and consequently not to her, whom he esteemed as the partner of his empire. He then laid his golden sceptre gently on her neck, as a token of his affection, as well as confirmation of the [illegible] he had so lately given. These tender proofs of love and [illegible] brought her back to the use of her reason and speech, when she explained to the king the cause of her swoon, which arose from the impression of the awful appearance of his sacred person, and an apprehension that his countenance expressed displeasure. These words were uttered in such a tone of voice and accompanied by such a disposition of feature, as afforded a most lively representation of her sensibility, and thereby acted so compulsively on the king, that, in the most explicit terms, he bade her prefer her request, declaring he would grant it, even if it was one half of his kingdom.

Upon this declaration Esther told him, all she desired, at present, was that he would be pleased to come to a banquet with her that day, and that he would permit Haman to accompany him. Her suit was granted, they came together, and when the entertainment was nearly over, with which the king expressed the highest satisfaction, he again asked Esther what request she had to make, repeating his former promise, that whatever it should be, he would grant it, though it were half his kingdom. The queen, not thinking this a proper time to open the secret to the king, told him, that her desire, at present, was no more than that he would honour her the next day at a like entertainment, accompanied by Haman, when she would take the [illegible] to present her petition. The king was highly pleased with the proposal, but the distinguished honour conferred upon Haman, being invited to accompany the king to the queen's banquet, so increased his pride and ambition, that he expected nothing less than a respect and homage to be paid him as the second person in the kingdom. Nor were his expectations ill-founded, except in the person of Mordecai, who, as he passed him at the palace gate, on his return, neglected to pay him obedience. As soon as he got home, he recounted to his family, and particularly to his wife Zeresh, the many instances of esteem he had received, not only from the king, but likewise the queen, having been at a banquet provided by the latter, and that the next day he was to be present at a like invitation, accompanying the king [illegible].

He could not, however, forbear complaining of the affront and disrespect which Mordecai had put upon him, and advising with Zeresh, his wife and his relations and friends, concerning the manner in which he should [illegible], they proposed to him, as the best expedient, to order a gibbet to be erected fifty cubits high, and the very next morning go to the king, and obtain a grant for the execution of Mordecai upon it. This advice was perfectly agreeable to Haman, who imagining the king would not refuse his request, gave orders for the gibbet to be immediately erected.

But that Omniscient Being who disposes of all events was pleased to direct things in such a manner, as to frustrate the design of the proud and cruel Haman; for, when he went to court the next morning, he found matters turn out very different to what he expected. It happened that the king that morning awoke much sooner than usual, and not being able to compose himself again to sleep, in order to pass the time in some degree profitable, as well as entertaining, he ordered his secretary to bring the [illegible] and state papers, as well ancient as modern, and read their respective contents. The king found, upon the reading them, the name of a person who had great honours and possessions given him as a reward for a glorious and memorable action; also of another, who obtained the [illegible] of his prince for his fidelity. The secretary proceeded till he came to the passage which made mention of Mordecai's discovery of the conspiracy of the two eunuchs, Bigthan and Teresh, against his person; and when the king, upon enquiry, was given to understand, that the man, for so signal a service had not received any [illegible], he seemed exceedingly angry, and commanded the secretary to stop at that record, and enquire of the [illegible] what hour it was. Answer being brought that it was break of day, he demanded to know who waited without, and being told Haman, ordered him to be called in, and, upon his entrance, thus addressed him: "From [illegible] sion of your loyal attachment to my person and government, I would ask of you what token of honour you would advise me to bestow on the man to whom I have the greatest obligation imaginable, and that consistently with the dignity of my royal character?" Haman, not conceiving but his own interest was concerned in the solution of the question, presuming that he [illegible] the person referred to, gave it as his opinion

QUEEN ESTHER fainting before KING ARTAXERXES

King ARTAXERXES presenting to MORDECAI the RING which he had formerly entrusted with his treacherous Haman, as a token of his royal Favour

that the king should clothe the man whom he desired to honour with his own royal apparel, mount him on his own horse, present him with a golden chain and cause [illegible] to make proclamation throughout the city, "Thus shall be done to the man whom the king vouchsafes to honour."

No sooner had Haman delivered his opinion, than the king, quite contrary to his expectation, commanded him to take the horse, apparel and chain, find out Mordecai the Jew, array him in this attire, and when mounted to march before him, making proclamation in quality [illegible] officer, because, as the king's favourite, he was the fittest man to advise with, and to execute his own advice. He concluded that Mordecai merited these honours, since to him he was indebted for his life.

This order cut the imperious Haman to the very heart, was so contrary to his expectation, his thoughts having been wholly employed on his own advancement. But the king's word was a law, and he knew there was no disputing it. Being, therefore, obliged to comply, he went with the horse, habit, and golden chain in quest of Mordecai, and finding him at the palace gate, in his habit of humiliation, bid him divest himself of the sackcloth, and put on the purple. The Jew, ignorant of what had passed, imputed this parade of ceremony to mockery, and reprobated Haman as an hard-hearted, insolent wretch, who delighted to sport with the miseries of mankind. But Haman reasoned with him on the matter, and at length convinced him that the king had commanded this honour to be done him, in recompence of the service he had rendered him, in detecting the conspiracy of the eunuchs, and thereby saving his life. Being thus satisfied, he put on the purple and the golden chain, mounted the king's horse, and paraded through the city, Haman making proclamation before him, "Thus shall it be done to the man whom the king desireth to honour." Mordecai, after this, was ushered into the royal presence, while Haman departed to his own house, stung with vexation, disappointment, and despair, being assured, from the late transactions, that all his efforts to revenge himself on the Jews would prove fruitless, as the king had thus received Mordecai into his immediate favour and protection.

While Haman was relating these doleful tidings to his family, lamenting the disappointment and great mortification he had met with, in being forced to pay so signal an honour to his most hated enemy, the queen's eunuchs came to call him away to supper. One of them, whose name was Sabuchades, observing a gibbet erected in the court, asked one of the servants the meaning of it, and being told it was prepared for Mordecai, for whose execution Haman had obtained permission of the king, he rested apparently satisfied.

When the king and Haman were set down to the banquet, and highly pleased with their entertainment, the king asked Esther again what her request was, at the same time renewing his promise that he would not fail to grant it her, though it should extend to the half of the kingdom. The queen availing herself of this opportunity, with blushing modesty, represented to the king, "That her petition was for the security of her own life, and the lives of her people, as there was a plot laid against them, for their general destruction. Had they (she observed) been made slaves, that calamity might have been tolerable, so that her last was, that he would be graciously pleased to interpose, and avert the imminent extirpation of the whole race."

The king no sooner heard Esther's petition, than he asked, with great emotion, who it was that durst put such a design on foot? The queen, without prevarication, replied, that Haman was the author of that affair, and that it proceeded from the impulse of malice to the people. The king, rising up in a great passion, immediately left the entertainment, and retired into the garden, in order to give vent to his resentment. Haman, in the interim, finding the storm gathering, took the opportunity of the king's absence for supplicating the queen for his life, acknowledging his error, and prostrating himself on the seat (*x*) before her, in the most humiliating manner. At this juncture the king returned, and seeing Haman in such a posture, was more exasperated by this circumstance than all the rest, and reviled him as the basest of men, for so infamous an attempt on the honour of his queen. Then eunuch then informed the king of the gibbet of fifty cubits in height, which, by order of Haman, was erected for the execution of Mordecai, as he was made to understand, by one of his servants when he went to give him an invitation to the queen's banquet. The king immediately fixed a resolution of inflicting the same punishment upon Haman that he had prepared for Mordecai, and ordered him immediately to be executed upon the same gibbet.

I cannot pass over this extraordinary event without a comment on the infinite justice, wisdom, and power of the Almighty, not only in bringing Haman to deserved punishment, but causing him to fall by the very snare he had laid for the life of an innocent man, and thereby justly retaliating so execrable a design on the life of its author.

This was the end of the imperious Haman, who had been so grandly [illegible] with the king's peculiar favour and bounty. His body was delivered up to justice, and his whole estate given to the queen, who appointed Mordecai her steward. The queen had, by this time, made it known to the king, that Mordecai was her near relation, upon which he sent for him, and delivered him the ring with which Haman had been entrusted before. The possessions of Haman, which the king had granted to the queen, she transferred to Mordecai, and then presented a second petition to her royal consort, that he would be pleased to deliver the Jews from that apprehension for their lives which still prevailed, reminding him of the edict which Haman had dispersed, in his name, throughout the empire, and enforcing her request, by declaring that her own life depended upon the safety of her nation. The king gave her his royal word, that nothing should be done to the Jews without her knowledge. He farther granted her the liberty of drawing up any decree or mandate in his name, with assurance that the same should be notified, sealed, and dispersed, by his command, throughout his dominions, which when confirmed by the royal signature, their authority would be unquestionable. Upon this he commanded the attendance of his secretaries, and enjoined them to draw up the following manifesto in behalf of the Jews, to the magistrates of all the provinces that lie between India and Ethiopia, under the command of an hundred and twenty-seven governors.

"Artaxerxes, the great king, to our trusty governors and "magistrates, greeting.

"Whereas it is too general a practice for men, whose "fortune hath been greater than their merit, to insult "both their inferiors and benefactors, and extinguish, as "far as lies in their power, all sense of gratitude and be"nevolence, and likewise to pervert the power vested in "them, and [illegible] under such guises as they vainly ima"gine can elude the penetration of the Great Searcher of "Hearts; nor is it any new matter for favourites, by "misrepresentation of men and things, to gratify their

(*x*) [illegible] the people [illegible] being at that time [illegible] opportunity [illegible] Perhaps [illegible] It can [illegible] that Haman [illegible] attempt to violate the chastity of the [illegible] Artaxerxes was [illegible] order to give a plausible colour to [illegible] In the book of [illegible] Haman [illegible] consistent with the [illegible] "private passions, to the injury of their masters, and thus "endangering the lives of [illegible] by their ill offices with "the prince: this I declare, not only on the credit of "historical report, but on perfect demonstration within "my own knowledge. For the future, therefore, let no "regard be paid to slanderous accusations, but let facts "be carefully enquired into, and ere full proof of the inno- "cence or guilt of the party acquit or condemn.

"You are not unacquainted with Haman; not being a "Persian, but an Amalekite by extraction, nor how [illegible] "[illegible], I have treated, and what honour done this man, "[illegible] and regarded him as my father, and order- "[illegible] to [illegible] him next to myself. Now his "[illegible] induced him to depart from his duty, and "prompted him to think of succeeding to the government, "by the destruction of Mordecai, to whom I owe my life, "and even by the destruction of the queen, the end of his "plotting to usurp my authority, when his plans against "the [illegible] of my friends had succeeded.

"[illegible] whereas the designs of this wicked man to destroy "the Jews [illegible], I hereby certify that far from find- "ing them seditious, I approve of them as a people wor- "shipping that God to whom I and my family owe the pos- "session and support of our dominions.

"These letters are therefore to command that you do not "execute or put in force the severity on the Jews as com- "manded by Haman, whom, as a sacrifice to justice, I have "caused to be executed on a gibbet before the gates of Susa.

"And I further command that copies of these letters be "transmitted throughout my dominions, and that you afford "them help against those who may oppress them.

"And as the thirteenth day of the twelfth month, that is "to say, the month Adar, is fixed for the extirpation of these "people, it is my royal will and pleasure, that you now fix "on that time as the moment of their deliverance, assured "that this proceeding will testify my intents, and afford a "cautionary example to future traitors.

"Be it further known to the parties herein concerned, in "[illegible], towns, and villages, that military execution "shall be the consequence of disobedience to the commands, "of which all our subjects are to take notice, and the Jews "will be ready to avenge themselves on their enemies at the "time appointed." Couriers were immediately sent express with these letters mandatory to all quarters.

[illegible] after the king had put the royal signet to this decree, Mordecai came out of the palace, dressed in the royal robe, gown, and chain, the sight of whom gave the highest satis- faction to the Jews, who thereby imagined themselves safe, and that Haman's decree against them was totally rescinded. The Jews likewise, who resided in the different parts of the kingdom, when they heard the contents of the king's last decree, were elated with joy, and some of the natives, though [illegible], underwent circumcision, supposing that it might be a means of securing them, should the Jews become predominant, as they were greatly animated by the king's [illegible] giving them the same day for their revenge that had been designed for their execution, that is to say, the thir- teenth day of the twelfth month, which the Hebrews call Adar, and the Macedonians Dystrus. Upon the obtaining of this mandate, the princes, governors, and magistrates, all paid a more than ordinary reverence to the Jews, through fear of the power of Mordecai.

When the decree was dispersed, the Jews put five hun- dred of their enemies to the sword at Susa, and the king shewed [illegible] the number of them, but no account was yet taken of those that were slain elsewhere. At the queen's special request, that the Jews might have one day's revenge more upon their enemies, and that the ten sons of Haman might be executed on the gibbet, the king appointed the day following for that purpose. So that [illegible] assembled in great numbers, and slew [illegible] three hundred more of their adver- saries, without so much as touching any of their property. But, throughout the whole empire, the number of the slain, as accounted enemies, was computed at seventy-five thou- sand. This slaughter was on the thirteenth day of the month, and the next was celebrated as a festival by all the Jews throughout the Persian dominions. These days are still ob- served with the same solemnity by the Jews, who make it a point, on their annual return, to regale and present each other with donations of [illegible] kinds. Mordecai, indeed, sent orders throughout the empire to all his countrymen, re- quiring them most strictly to observe these days of festival, and to transmit them to posterity, in order to perpetuate the memory of their signal deliverance from the massacre de- signed by the flagitious Haman, and the advantages which they gained in the result over their most inveterate enemies. For this cause these days are still observed by the Jews who call them Phrurea, or Purim, that is to say, Feasts of Con- servation. Mordecai retained his influence with the king, being the first person in administration, and equally respect- ed by him and the queen. The affairs of the Jews continued to prosper under the auspices of Artaxerxes, whose name therefore stands with honour in our records, and as such will be handed down to future ages.

CHAP. VII.

John, the high-priest, slays his brother Jesus, in the temple. Bagoses offers many injuries to the Jews.

ON the demise of Eliashib, the high-priest, his son Judas, by right hereditary, succeeded to the office, as did his son John, by the same right, at his decease. This said John was the cause of the violation and prophanation of the temple afterwards, by Bagoses, commander in chief of the troops of another Artaxerxes, called Memnon. Bagoses imposed a tribute on the Jews, obliging them to pay, out of the public [illegible], fifty drachmas a day for every lamb they sacrificed before they entered upon their daily oblations (*a*). John, the high-priest, had a brother, whose name was Jesus, and Bagoses, the general, being much attached to him, had pro- mised to exert his influence to advance him to the supreme sacerdotal office. Jesus, relying on the assurance and at the- [illegible] of Bagoses, had the audacity to enter into a contest with his brother John in the temple upon this subject, who was excited by his provocation to such a degree of rage, that, in his fury, he slew him.

The religion of the Jews could not possibly sustain a great- er disgrace, than the commission of so heinous a crime in so sacred a place, by so sacred a character: indeed, as an ag- gravation of its enormity, there never was a similar instance among the Greeks, or even the Barbarians. The Almighty, however, did not suffer it to pass unpunished; for, on that very account, the people were enslaved, and the temple was prophaned by the Persians. When Bagoses heard that the high-priest had spilt the blood of his brother in the very tem- ple, he exclaimed with contempt and indignation against the Jews, as the most daring and abandoned wretches, in perpe- trating the most heinous crime of murder, in a place of all others the most solemn and sacred. Being opposed in his attempt to enter the temple, he cried out, "Am I not purer "in body than he who was slain within?" and with these words forced his way. Bagoses accordingly made use of this pretence for treating the Jews with the utmost severity and rigour, for the space of seven years.

John, the high-priest, was succeeded, at his death, by his son Jaddus. This Jaddus had a brother, whose name was Manasses, to whom Sanballat, who was sent by Darius, the king of Persia, into Samaria, understanding Jerusalem to be a famous city, and that the kings of it had put the Syrians to many difficulties, frankly gave his daughter Nicaso in mar- riage, as a token and earnest of the friendship he wished to cul-

(*a*) The [illegible] on the [illegible] in the government of Syria [illegible] the person who succeed[illegible] in that [illegible] no farther exacted [illegible] tract and maintain with the Jews Sanballat was by birth a Cuthite, from whom the Samaritans derive their origin

CHAP VIII

Alexander the Great overthrows the Persians Makes his entry into the city of Jerusalem, and, instead of destroying it, contrary to expectation confers many benefits on the Jews

ABOUT this time Philip, king of Macedon, was treacherously assaulted and slain, in the city of Egea, by Pausanias, the son of Cerastes, of the family of Orestes He was succeeded on the throne of Macedon by his son Alexander, who crossing the Hellespont, obtained a signal victory over the army of Darius at the river Granicus after which he subdued Lydia and Ionia, and passing his army through Caria, entered into Pamphilia, as is recorded in another place

The elders of Jerusalem were at this time much concerned at the conduct of Manasses, the brother of Jaddus, the high priest, who had taken to wife a strange woman indeed, their indignation arose to such a pitch, as to have been almost productive of an insurrection, for they deemed it a step towards the dissolution of the laws of their country respecting marriages, and concluded if they suffered it to pass unnoticed, it would, by degrees, become an established custom Nor could they be unmindful that this was the very cause of their former captivity, and of all the calamities that ensued thereupon They were too sensible that the transgressions which drew down those heavy judgments upon them, was their intermarrying with strange women, and therefore they peremptorily demanded of Manasses, that he should either dismiss his wife, or never more approach the altar

In consequence of this Manasses repaired to his father-in-law Sanballat, governor of Samaria, told him all that had passed at Jerusalem and declared that though he passionately loved his daughter, yet he was unwilling, for her sake, to be deprived of the priesthood, which was a great honour, and in the highest esteem among the Jews Sanballat, in order to ease the mind of his son-in-law upon this head, told him that if he would but continue his affection to his daughter, and keep her as his wife, he would undertake not only to secure him the exercise of his function, but advance him to the pontificate and establish him as prince of the whole country He further promised to build him a temple upon mount Gerizim, that overlooks Samaria, and the rest of the mountains, not inferior to that at Jerusalem, all which should be performed by the permission and power of Darius Manasses, relying on these promises, remained with his father-in-law the consequence of which was, that many of the priests, as well as laity, of Jerusalem who had engaged in these prohibited marriages, resorted to Samaria, and put themselves under his protection Their removal indeed, was far from being against their worldly interest, for the governor, to encourage his ambitious son-in-law, furnished them with houses, land, stock and money, a circumstance which afterwards occasioned great disorder in the Jewish state

Darius, about this time, receiving intelligence that Alexander had passed the Hellespont and obtained a complete victory over his generals at the river Granicus, to prevent this progress, immediately assembled his forces, with a resolution to give the Macedonians battle, lest they should over-run the whole of his territories which they seemed inclined to do He accordingly marched at the head of his troops beyond the Euphrates, and encamped on the side of mount Taurus, in Cilicia, determined to come to an engagement with the enemy in that quarter

This was agreeable news to Sanballat, who, in full confidence of success, assured his son-in-law Manasses that, on the king's return, he would ratify all he had promised as he, and all the Asiatics, were fully persuaded that Darius would obtain an effectual conquest over the Macedonians, who, with their handful of men, could never sustain the first shock In this, however, he was fatally mistaken, for though the army of Alexander was as represented, very inferior to that of Darius, the Persians were totally routed, a great part of their army was lost, the king's mother, wife, and children were taken prisoners, and he was obliged to save himself by a precipitate flight

Alexander, encouraged by this success, marched directly into Syria, took Damascus and Sidon, and laid siege to Tyre From thence he wrote the high-priest at Jerusalem, giving him to understand, that he expected the same assistance from them which they had formerly given to Darius, and that they should provide a market for the supply of his army, where he might have recruits for his horse, assuring them they should have no reason to repent of such their services The high-priest returned for answer briefly this, that they had bound themselves by oath not to take up arms against Darius and that he was determined to keep that oath inviolable during his life

Alexander was much displeased with this answer and though he determined to prosecute the siege of Tyre with the utmost vigour, he as firmly resolved, upon its surrender, to make an expedition against the Jewish high-priest, and, by his example, teach the world in general, how far oaths were to be preserved or broken At length, after a siege of fatigue and danger, the Macedonians made themselves masters of Tyre by assault, and then proceeded to invest Gaza, a Persian garrison, under the command of a governor named Babemeses

When Sanballat understood that Alexander lay before Tyre, he took that opportunity of going over to him with eight thousand men, whom he had assembled together out of his own province The Macedonian hero received him with great respect, desiring him to open his mind freely without the least reserve as he was ready to grant any reasonable request he might make This gave Sanballat a favourable opportunity of executing the design he had projected He told Alexander he had a son-in-law, named Manasses the brother of Jaddus, the high-priest of the Jews, who is following him with great numbers of people, to assist him in an to erect a temple in that province for divine worship He intimated, at the same time, how much Alexander's interest was concerned in this penetration, as the Jews, who were very numerous, might, if he refused, be as troublesome to him, as they had heretofore been to the Syrians Alexander readily granted Sanballat's request, upon which he immediately gave orders for erecting the temple on mount Gerizim appointed Manasses, his son-in-law, to be high-priest, and ordered that his descendants by his daughter, should succeed to that honour The temple which Sanballat had obtained permission to build was soon completed, and Manasses appointed high-priest, but his father-in-law did not live long to see him enjoy that honour, for in about two months after he paid the debt of nature

As soon as the victorious Alexander had subdued Gaza, he advanced, at the head of his army, towards Jerusalem, fully determined to punish the high-priest for non-compliance with his request Jaddus, being apprized of Alexander's intention, and that he was marching with all haste to Jerusalem, was greatly alarmed, and knowing how incapable he was of making any resistance against so powerful an invader, ordered prayers and sacrifices to be offered up for the general safety and prosperity of the people On the following night it was revealed to the high-priest, in a dream, that he should adorn the city with garlands and flowers, open the gates, and let the people, who should be dressed in white, go out to meet Alexander, himself and the other priests preceding in their proper habits When Jaddus awoke he was highly pleased with what had been revealed to him in his dream, that having in the morning told the others what had passed, he proceeded to make the necessary preparations for meeting the king

As soon as Jaddus heard of the approach of Alexander, he, with the priests and people, left the city, in a solemn procession, and went to a place called Sapha, that is, *the place of prospect*, from its being so elevated as to command an uninterrupted view of the city and temple.

The army of Alexander made no doubt of a speedy conquest, and flattered themselves with reaping great advantages by plundering the city. But in this they soon found themselves mistaken, things taking a different turn from what they expected. As soon as Alexander saw the people marching in procession and clothed in white, the priests in silken robes, and the high-priest in purple, embroidered with gold, wearing his mitre, and having on his forehead a golden plate, with the sacred name of the Deity inscribed on it, the majesty of the spectacle struck him with such reverential awe, that he advanced alone, paid homage to the inscription by falling on his knees, and saluted the high-priest himself. So unexpected a circumstance greatly surprised the Jews, who gathered in crowds about Alexander, and with loud acclamations, proclaimed his praise. The king of Syria, and the great men of Persia, were likewise astonished at his behaviour on this occasion. One of them, named Parmenio, took the liberty to ask him in a familiar way, how it happened that he, who was adored almost by the whole earth, should now descend to bow to a priest of the Jews? The reply that Alexander made was this: "That he did not "pay that adoration to him, but to the God whom he "professed to serve. That while he was at Dion, in "Macedonia, and deliberating with himself in what "manner he should carry on the Asiatic war, and subdue "the Persian empire, that very person, and in that very "habit, appeared to him in a dream, encouraging him "to enter boldly on the expedition, and not to doubt of "success, because the Almighty would be his guide, and "ensure him a conquest: that therefore he made no "doubt of gaining his point in all his undertakings to his "utmost wish, as he made war under the direction of that "Supreme Being, to whom, in the person of the high-"priest, he paid adoration."

After this reply to Parmenio, the king embraced Jaddus, and the other priests escorting him into the city, he went up to the temple, and there offered sacrifice in form, according to order, paying also a singular veneration to the high-priest, who shewed him when the ceremony was over, the book of the prophet Daniel, and, in it, the prediction of the over-throw of the Persian empire by a certain Grecian king whom Alexander interpreted to be himself. Pleased with this reflection, he offered to grant the people any request they should desire of him by their high-priest. Jaddus made answer, that they desired only to enjoy their own country laws, and possess the same privileges as their brethren did in Media and Babylon, with an exemption from the seventh year's tribute, as according to the Mosaic law, they neither ploughed or sowed at the stated returns of that period. Alexander readily complied with their request, and offered moreover, that such of them should be disposed to take up arms in his service, they should be received into his army, and enjoy the free exercise of their religion as before. From this act of generosity and indulgence, many were ready to accompany him in his wars.

Having thus settled matters at Jerusalem, Alexander marched with his army from place to place among the neighbouring cities, at all of which he was received by the people with great testimonies of friendship and submission. The Samaritans, whose capital at that time was Shechem, at the foot of mount Gerizim, and inhabited by Jewish deserters, hearing how king Alexander had treated the people of Jerusalem, resolving to take advantage of it by veering about, and returning to their former professions. It was a common practice with them to assert or deny their origin, as best suited their interest or convenience. When at any time they observed the affairs of the Jews in a prosperous state, they boasted that they were of their nation, and descended from Manasseh and Ephraim. But when they thought it was their interest to affirm the contrary, they would solemnly disclaim all affinity to them. Resolved, however, to profess themselves Jews on the present occasion, in order to answer their intended purposes, they went with great eagerness as far as the territories of Jerusalem to meet Alexander, whom they no sooner saw, than they expressed their satisfaction by the loudest acclamations. The king commending their zeal, these Samaritans (Shechemites) preferred their humble suit, that he would vouchsafe to honour their city and temple with his presence. Alexander told them, that the situation of affairs required his speedy departure, but that, on his return, he would not fail to comply with their desires. Upon their requesting that he would grant them an exemption from the seventh year's tribute, he asked them if they were Jews. They replied they were Hebrews, but that they were called Shechemites by the Sidonians. The question was then put explicitly, whether they were Jews or not? Upon their reply in the negative, they were dismissed with this answer: "The favour you ask I have "granted to the Jews. When I return and have better "information, I shall indulge you in whatever may be "thought reasonable." Alexander, however, took Sanballat's men with him into Egypt, allotting them a distribution of lands to live upon there, which they had afterwards in Thebes, where they were put into garrison.

After the death of Alexander, the empire was parted amongst his successors, but the temple on mount Gerizim remained untouched. If, at any time, the Jews at Jerusalem were found guilty of the violation of their laws, as in eating forbidden meats, breaking the Sabbath, or any other crime of the like nature, they took sanctuary with the Shechemites, upon pretence that they were unjustly accused. About this time Jaddus, the high-priest, died, and was succeeded in the pontifical dignity by his son Onias. Such was the then state of Jerusalem.

END OF THE ELEVENTH BOOK.

FLAVIUS JOSEPHUS

ON THE

ANTIQUITIES

OF THE

JEWS.

BOOK XII

[INCLUDING A PERIOD OF ABOUT ONE HUNDRED AND SEVENTY YEARS.]

CHAP. I.

[illegible] takes Jerusalem by surprize, and transplants many of the Jews to divers colonies in Egypt. Perpetual animosity between the Jews and Samaritans.

WHEN Alexander king of Macedon, had put an end to the dominion of the Persians, and settled the [illegible] of the Jews in the manner already described, he departed this life, and his empire was divided into distinct principalities. On this division, Antiochus took the sovereignty of Asia, Seleucus that of Babylon and the bordering countries, Lysimachus governed the Hellespont, [C]assander reigned over Macedon, and Ptolemy, the son of [La]gus, succeeded his father in the government of Egypt. [T]hese respective princes, not satisfied with their different [al]lotments, continued [at] war with each other for some [y]ears, in the course of which great numbers of lives were [sacr]ificed and many capital cities utterly destroyed. The [wh]ole tract of Syria [illegible] sensible of the [illegible] effects of this discontent, under the government of [P]tolemy, others [illegible] called Soter or [illegible], though [illegible] character more [illegible] to such denomination.

Having a design upon Jerusalem, he took the advantage of storming it upon [illegible] under colour of devotion, as if he would offer [illegible], and then treacherously [pos]sessed himself of [illegible] without any opposition, or [the] least apprehension of danger, for it being a day of rest, [the] Jews would not act on the defensive, which facilitat[ed] his conquest [illegible] and barbarous purposes. [illegible], who record[ed] the acts of the successors of [illegible], reproaches us [w]ith superstition, as if [illegible] we [illegible] lost our liberty [an]d our country. His words [illegible]:

"There are a people [illegible] by the name of Jews, who have their habitation [illegible] populous city, called Jerusalem. This [illegible] fell into the hands of Ptolemy, and [illegible] liberty, upon [illegible] could not [illegible] [illegible] defence upon what they call their sabbath-day." This is what Agatharchides relates of our nation.

Ptolemy carried away a great many captives out of the mountainous parts of Judea, from about Jerusalem, Samaria, and the mount Gerizim, whom he transported into Egypt, and settled there. As he knew that the people of Jerusalem were most faithful in the observation of oaths and covenants, (and this from the answer they made to Alexander, when he sent an embassy to them, after he had vanquished Darius in battle,) he disposed of them in strong holds, garrisons, and places of trust, upon their oath of fidelity to him and his successors, granting them also immunities and privileges in common with the Macedonians; so that, [t]empted by Ptolemy's liberality, on the one hand, and the pleasures and conveniences of a fruitful country, on the other, there came over great numbers of Jews into Egypt from other parts.

But the Jews and Samaritans could never be reconciled upon the subject of their ancient laws and constitutions, the one insisting that the temple at Jerusalem was the only holy place, and the Jews, on that account, not being allowed to send their sacrifices any where else, while the Samaritans as peremptorily and confidentially affirmed the same with respect to their temple at Gerizim. And this was the cause of much bloodshed.

CHAP. II.

Ptolemy Philadelphus, son of Ptolemy Soter, succeeds to the kingdom of Egypt, and causes the Jewish laws to be translated into Greek. Liberates many captives, and presents many gifts [illegible] of the temple.

ON the death of Ptolemy Soter, or the Saviour, Philadelphus his son, succeeded of course to the kingdom of Egypt. He reigned thirty-nine years, and [illegible] for translating the Mosaic laws into the Greek tongue. There were, at that time, captive Jews, in Egypt, to the number of an hundred and twenty thousand, whom this [illegible] commanded to be set at liberty, upon the [illegible] Demetrius Phalerius [illegible] the king's library under his care and custody, from a natural curiosity determined, if possible, to procure a collection of all the books extant, and that upon any terms. This being his peculiar propensity, he bought up all the choice books he could hear of, and which he thought might be worthy a place in the king's study and good opinion. Upon the king's enquiring how many thousand volumes he thought he had collected, he replied, about two hundred thousand; but that he hoped, in a short time, to make them five hundred thousand, as he had certain information, that there was an incredible number of choice manuscripts among the Jews, concerning their laws, customs, and ceremonies, that were deserving not only of perusal, but the honour of a place in the royal library; but being written in their own language and characters, it would be a matter of great difficulty and trouble to translate them into Greek. He observed, that though there might seem to be some resemblance and affinity between the language and writing of the one and the other, yet there were several niceties peculiar to each other; but that he introduced this remark to encourage the translating them out of the Hebrew, and depositing them in the royal library, as long as money could be found to defray the expence.

The king highly commended the purpose of Demetrius concerning such a collection, and wrote to the high-priest of the Jews, to assist him in providing those copies. There was, amongst the attendants on the king, one Aristeus, a man whose modesty and candour recommended him to the confidence of his master. This Aristeus long and heartily desired to obtain the liberty of the Jews, and considering this occasion as the most convenient opportunity of applying to the king on that subject, went first to Sosibius, [illegible] and Andreas, three captains of the guards, to sound their inclinations, and finding them well affected towards his design, he entreated their concurrence [illegible]. Upon this assurance, he modestly [illegible] addressed himself to the king, in words to the following effect:

"It is my desire, with all deference and humility, to "submit my thoughts to your royal pleasure, respecting [illegible] "[illegible] of the Jews. You will permit me to observe, that I "[illegible] done, which so many of that nation "are in bondage under your government, from whom "you expect to derive so much [illegible]. I presume "it is an act worthy of your [illegible] to deliver those "unhappy people from their present state of misery, as I apprehend the same Divine Being [illegible] whom you rule, is "the author of their laws. We and they worship one and "the same God, [illegible] adore the same Almighty Power, "though we differ in name and title. Permit me, therefore, "to intreat that, from a reverence to that Divine Being "whom they love and worship with zeal and affection beyond all other mortals, you will be pleased to restore these "wretched exiles to their own country, that they may end "their days in their own place. I interpose not, Sire, in "their behalf, from a principle of partiality, but from a "consciousness that the same God is the Creator of us all, "and that such an act of clemency must be acceptable to "the Father of all Mercies."

The king, highly pleased with the [illegible] of this address, asked Aristeus how many thousands he thought there were who would derive this indulgence? Answer being made, about one hundred and twenty, [illegible], by observing, that it would be an action worthy of so great a monarch, to [illegible] to miserable captives, as an acknowledgment of the power he had derived from above, the king gave orders, that one hundred and twenty drachmas should be paid to the soldiers for every Jew they had in custody, over and above their [illegible] stipend. He also promised to grant the request of Aristeus in every particular point, and to ratify the whole by a public decree, comprehending not only those who had been [illegible], but those who, [illegible] that time, had been taken into captivity. When this [illegible] to him, that [illegible] would be attended with an expence amounting to [illegible] talents,

he solemnly declared it should be done, as will appear from the following decree, which is preserved as an instance of the magnanimity of this illustrious monarch.

"It is our royal will and pleasure, that all the Jews who "[illegible], who have been made captive by any of our father's "forces upon their incursions into Syria and Phoenicia, [illegible] "those brought away, or sold into any part of my dominions, and all those likewise, that, either before or since "that time, have been sold and enslaved, be all set free upon the payment of one hundred and twenty drachmas for "every slave, the soldiers to receive this redemption-money, "together with their pay, out of the treasury. I cannot "suppose that my father either intended or approved of the "forcing away so many thousands into captivity, or the ravaging of their country by the soldiery, for the mere sake "of plunder, contrary to the great law of equity. Out of "regard, therefore, to justice, and in commiseration of those "who suffer under oppression, I do hereby expressly charge "and command, that all the Jews, who are at this time in "servitude, be immediately dismissed upon the payment of "the sum aforesaid to their respective masters, in obedience "to our own mandate, without fraud or collusion. It is "also our royal will and pleasure, that this our proclamation "be made public for three days successively after the receipt "of it, and, in the mean time, that the aforesaid masters "bring in a list of their slaves to such officers, and in such "manner as shall be prescribed, and all this upon pain of "confiscation, if any man shall be found to act contrary to "the tenor of this our decree."

Upon a review of this decree, it appeared to the king that the provision for the liberty of the Jews, who were taken either before or after the time specified, was not expressed in [illegible] explicit terms, but it might be evaded; so that, from [illegible] of generosity, he [illegible] of indulgence. Nay, such was his liberality, that he gave orders to the collectors of his tribute, and the officers of his treasury, to have the money ready for the ransom of the Jews, by which means, in the course of only seven days, the business was dispatched at the king's charge, amounting to four hundred and sixty talents, the masters insisting on the same rate for the children of [illegible] they had for the adult, though the king's edict extended no further than to those who were brought away prisoners, without comprehending such as were born there.

Having thus far conducted the business, with a munificence that did him the highest honour, the king commanded Demetrius Phalereus to publish his purpose concerning the transcript of the Jewish records in due form and order, so that a copy of the petition of Demetrius was registered, as also of the letters written upon that occasion, together with an account of the donations and donors towards the work, so that from hence might appear both the excellence of the design and the execution. The petition was couched in terms to the following purpose:

"Demetrius to the great King.

"Since it is your royal will and command, that I should "contribute my utmost endeavours to supply what yet may "be wanting towards the perfection of your library, and to "find out what curious and useful books and copies may [illegible] "have [illegible] my search, this is humbly to inform you, "that, after much study and recollection, I do not find any "thing so conducive to that laudable purpose as the books of "the Jewish legislation; but being written in Hebrew character, and in an Hebrew idiom, it will be difficult for "us to understand them. Besides, our present [illegible] "not so correct as it should be, through want of royal patronage. It will, therefore, I presume, be necessary to "have them accurately translated, as a body from their Divine original, of the wisest and most perfect laws that are "extant. For this is the reason, that, according to Hecataeus, "of Abdera, we find none of the poets or historians make "any mention of those laws, or the [illegible] of them: "the origin and institution of them being sacred, and not to "be prophaned by [illegible]

"You will, therefore, Sir, if you judge it meet, be pleased to write to the high-priest of the Jews, to send you out of every tribe six elders, whom he shall choose as men best skilled in the knowledge of their constitution, so that, by their assistance in the interpretation and explication of the writings, we may be able to produce something worthy of your royal approbation."

Upon this motion of Demetrius, the king gave directions for letters to be written to Eleazar, the high-priest of the Jews, agreeable thereunto, informing them the general release of all the captives in Egypt. These letters were accompanied with a present of fifty talents of gold, together with precious stones of immense value, to be submitted to the disposal of [illegible] artists and converted, with the addition of an hundred talents to the use of sacrifices and other sacred services of the temple. I cannot pass over, in silence, the magnificence of the whole proceeding, but shall previously present the reader with a copy of the letter written to Eleazar, premising an account of the manner by which he attained to that dignity.

Upon the demise of Onias, the high-priest, his son, Simon, succeeded to that office. He was a man of singular piety towards God, and exemplary benevolence towards mankind, insomuch that he obtained the honourable appellation of "Simon the Just." This excellent man did not long hold the pontifical dignity, and leaving at his death, an infant son [illegible] in course succeeded by his brother Eleazar, to whom Ptolemy wrote the following letter:

King Ptolemy to Eleazar the high-priest, sendeth greeting.

"Whereas there are great numbers of Jews in my dominions, that were brought hither captive by the Persians, while they were in power, and whereas those were honoured by my father in reposing confidence in them, vesting them with places under his government, and particularly appointing them to garrisons, as a check upon the Egyptians, with extraordinary pensions for their services, be it known unto you that as from the time of my accession to the throne, I have ever retained an affection for your people, I have lately manumitted the same, in setting at liberty above one hundred thousand of them, and paying the charge of their ransom out of my own coffers. Some of them I have employed in a military, and others in a civil capacity, according to their respective character and abilities, deeming it a service acceptable to that Supreme Being to whom I owe both my existence and my crown. From a desire of showing my regard for the Jews throughout the habitable earth, I have proposed to procure a translation of your laws into the Greek, to be deposited in my library. In order to accomplish this design, you will do well to select out of your several tribes six elders from each tribe, well skilled in the laws, and send them to assist in this translation, as I think, if it is well executed, it will redound to my immortal honour. The persons I depute to treat with you in this affair are Andreas, an officer of my body guards, and Aristeus, my most faithful counsellor. I have charged them with a present of an hundred talents of silver, as first fruits dedicated to the sacred services of the temple. Your answer to this letter will be highly acceptable."

Eleazar complied with the king's request, and wrote him in return to the following effect:

Eleazar, the high-priest, to king Ptolemy, greeting.

"If you, your queen Arsinoe, and your illustrious family, are well, it is highly grateful to the Jews. We acknowledge the receipt of your most gracious letter, which was read in full assembly, and afforded infinite joy and satisfaction, not only as an instance of your clemency towards the afflicted people, but your piety and reverence for the worship of the great God. We have received, by the hands of Andreas and Aristeus, (persons highly worthy of esteem and honour), twenty golden cups, thirty of silver, five goblets, and a table, to be dedicated to the service of the altar, together with an hundred talents towards the charge of sacrifices, and other ceremonies of the temple. We have [illegible] in the most affectionate terms of respect and gratitude, and we are all so sensible of the obligations you have been pleased to lay upon us that you may depend on our most implicit obedience to your commands, as a due acknowledgment of your gracious condescension. Pursuant to [illegible], we have recommended to God, in our public prayers, the protection of your royal person, queen and children, together with all that are near and dear to you, with peace and prosperity to yourself and people, and beseeching the Almighty that the work you have in hand of compiling a collection of our laws may be of as much satisfaction and advantage to you as you desire. To promote this desirable end, I have sent you six elders out of every tribe, with the law, to attend your pleasure, relying on your piety and justice for their remittance to us after the translation, and recommending you to the providential care of the Almighty."

Such was the answer of Eleazar the high-priest to king Ptolemy's letter, upon which occasion the names of the seventy-two elders were inserted, but it is deemed unnecessary to enumerate them. But the magnificence and curiosity of the donations for the service of the temple cannot be omitted without doing great injustice to the king's piety and bounty, considering with what liberality he promoted the work, the encouragement and countenance he gave to the prosecution of it, and the great attention he paid to those who were employed in it. In these particulars, therefore, I am bound in duty to be more minute, not as a branch of the history, but a memorial of the king's magnanimity, that it may stand upon record to his eternal honour. To begin with a description of the table.

With respect to the dimensions, the king gave directions to measure the former table at Jerusalem, and see whether the place would not contain a larger. They informed him that he might make it as large as he pleased, upon which he proposed at first to have it made five times as large as the other. But reflecting that so great a bulk would render it unwieldy for use, and have the appearance of ostentation rather than service, he came to a resolution that it should not exceed the former table in size, but in elegance and variety of its materials. The king had a competent knowledge of human nature, and the fashion of things, and a great presence of mind, devising expedients, and forming inventions, so that he commonly planned his own designs, and prescribed to the workmen the rules of proportion. With respect to this table in particular, he gave orders that it should be two cubits and an half in length, and one and an half in height, all of solid gold, and round about it a border of an hand's breadth, set out on three sides with curious carving of [illegible] work, and other agreeable figures, which being triangular, every angle had the same disposition of sculptures, and the same form presented itself when turned about without any variation. This table, in fine, was curiously wrought all over, but especially that part which was most in view, with an intermixture of precious stones, looped together by golden buckles at equal distances from each other. The outside of [illegible] set with other such stones of an oval and embossed work of twigs and branches intermixing. There were also various sorts of fruit wrought together under the figure of a crown, as bunches of grapes, ears of corn, all in their proper and natural positions, and expressed by stones set in gold, bearing the native colour of every [illegible]. Under the crown was another row of ovals, which, for the frame, the order, and ornament, [illegible] so exactly uniform, from top to bottom, that one part could not be distinguished from another. There [illegible] drawn also upon this latter the resemblance of a meander, the course of which was marked with stones of lustre that sparkled like stars, as rubies, emeralds, and whatever else was most precious and excellent in the kind. Along this meander were curious pieces of sculpture in boughs and knots that, in some degree, resembled the figure of a lozenge, and they were so embellished by a regular disposition of crystal and amber for the advantage of the view, that it exhibited all together one of the most finished spectacles that can be imagined. The cornices of the feet resembled the first budding of lilies, the stem upright, with the leaves and tendrils winding under the table. The basis was an hand's breadth over, garnished with rubies, and a border round about it, two hands distant betwixt the feet that rested upon it. The graving work of these feet was incomparable, being the fancy of a foliage of the vine and the ivy, finished so exquisitely to the life that it was difficult to distinguish the artificial from the natural; for upon the least breath of air, the leaves would move and play, as if they had been the produce of nature. This whole consisted of three parts put together with such art, that there were no joints to be discerned, and the thickness of it was half a cubit. This great prince, by the magnificence of his present, the value of the materials, and the exquisite curiosity of the whole work, demonstrated that though it was altered in size and proportion from the first design, it was abundantly supplied by a more rich and excellent expence in ornament and art.

There was also a huge pair of golden cups, wrought half way up the bowls in form of a scollop, and inlaid with all sorts of precious stones, ranged in the resemblance of [illegible] of a cubit over, with elegant figures of twigs, branching out in a kind of net-work up to the brim, and garnished with jewels also. The borders were set out with a miniature of lilies, flowers, vines, grapes and the like round the lips of the vessel. This was the fashion of the goblets, which contained each between three and four [illegible]. The several pieces were so radiant, that they exceeded the brightness of the clear crystal.

Besides these, the king presented thirty golden vessels more, richly decorated with precious stones, and overshadowed, in the parts which were not filled up with vine and ivy leaves in curious sculpture. Nor was the excellence of these curiosities owing to the bounty [illegible], but to the design and execution of the artificers, who took a considerable part in contributing to the perfection of the work, [illegible] his business to superintend the artists themselves [illegible] which rendered them more intent, as they saw the king had the design [illegible] than they otherwise would have been.

Upon the delivery of these donations, and the dedication of them to the use and service of the holy temple at Jerusalem, Eleazar treated the king's commissioners with all due honours, and dismissed them with presents and good wishes to [illegible]. When the king received intelligence of their arrival at Alexandria, and that they had brought the elders with them, he sent to his two ambassadors Andreas and Aristeas, from whom he received Eleazar's letter, and received particular satisfaction as to many important questions. This prince was so intent upon an [illegible] conference with the elders of the tribes, that no person had access to him even on the most urgent affairs, though, contrary to his custom of giving private audience [illegible] days and public once a month.

Having thus secured himself from the importunity of [illegible] interruptions, he only waited the arrival of Eleazar's deputies, who presented themselves soon after with presents from the high-priest, with certain manuscripts of the Jewish laws, written upon parchment in letters of gold. Upon the king's asking for the books they were produced, to his great admiration at their exquisite workmanship, for the leaves were put together with such art that there was no discerning where one skin was joined to another. The king expressed his regard for the persons who brought him the curiosity, [illegible] for the person who sent [illegible] but the greatest of all for the [illegible] those [illegible] brought him. The deputies, and their attendants, [illegible], with one heart and voice, in their joint prayers and acclamations, such striking instances of their zeal for his service, that he could not refrain from tears of joy at the sincerity of their respect.

The writings were then put into the hands of the officers, who were to take them in charge, and the king embracing the deputies told them he would first confer with them on the business they came upon, and then take their persons into his peculiar care. He looked upon the day of their arrival so remarkably auspicious, that he determined to have it observed during his life as an annual festival in commemoration of so great a blessing. It happened, indeed, to be upon the very day of his naval victory over Antigonus.

The care of entertaining and providing for strangers was properly the province of Nicanor, who appointed Dorotheus under him in this, as in other cases, to see that nothing might be wanting. For his own honour and the accommodation of the strangers, the king commanded that they should be served after the manner of their country, and such instructions were given with respect to the officers, that they might not be disgusted with novelty. The conduct of this business was committed to Dorotheus, as a person versed in the customs of the Jews. There were placed two seats, one on the king's right hand, the other on his left, by his own order, for the accommodation of the deputies. When the guests were seated in due form, the king commanded Dorotheus to serve them in the same manner as he had done their countrymen upon a former occasion. So that the Egyptian priests and officers, who attended the king's table, were all dismissed, and one of their own deputies and priests, named Eli[illegible], was called upon by the king to give thanks. After the solemnity of a benediction, and fervent prayer for the prosperity of the king and his people, to the infinite satisfaction of all present, the company cheerfully partook of the entertainment; during which the king took occasion to start several philosophical questions, in order to sound the abilities of the deputies. Their answers were so pertinent, that the king was highly delighted with their conversation, insomuch that the feast was continued for the space of twelve days. Those who may be desirous of knowing the particular points that were discussed, are referred to a book written by Aristeus upon this very occasion.

The conversation of the deputies had a great effect not only upon the king, but Menedemus, the philosopher, who was brought over to acknowledge an over-ruling Providence, and gave up the controversy on that subject to their reason. The king, in testimony of a due sense of the [illegible] he had derived from their learned disquisitions and particularly respecting the art of government, ordered them a gratuity of three talents each, after which they were conducted to their apartments.

At the expiration of three days Demetrius [illegible] over a causeway, of several furlongs, and a bridge of communication betwixt the island and the continent, from whence he proceeded to the northward, and settled them in a mansion by the sea side, quietly and commodiously situated for study and contemplation. Having thus disposed them in a manner most convenient for the prosecution of their undertaking, he requested them [illegible] attention [illegible], wished them success, and took his departure.

They prosecuted their studies with unremitting assiduity, from earliest morn till the ninth hour of the day, which was a time of relaxation, when they were served by Dorotheus, at the king's order, with the choicest dainties from his own table, over and above their ordinary allowance. They came to court every morning, and saluted the king, and then betook themselves to their [illegible], having first washed their hands with sea-water.

The version of the laws was finished within the compass of seventy-two days, when Dorotheus called all the Jews together into the place where it was translated, and, in the presence of the interpreters, read over the laws, the whole assembly unanimously approving the translation, and applauding Demetrius for proposing a work of such essential benefit to the community. He desired also that it might be read by the eminent men of the nation, after which the high-priest, the elders, and magistrates of the people, propounded, that, since the [illegible] was so happily executed, its authority might be ratified, and the text remain unalterable for ever. They were unanimous with respect to the proposal, but came to this resolution, that the work be subject to a further examination [illegible], and that if any superfluity or omission should be discovered, upon mature deliberation, it should be laid before them and corrected, and it was judged expedient that it should stand valid for ever.

The king was charmed with having gained the point and succeeded in an undertaking [illegible] to the public [illegible]. When it was read to him, he was transported with wonder at the wisdom of the [illegible], and expressed his astonishment to Demetrius, that [illegible] poets [illegible] should make no mention of so incomparable a system. Demetrius replied, that their [illegible] immoderately divine, and the subject of them so venerable, none had been bold enough to attempt a defence, [illegible] especially when reflection brought to mind the heavy [illegible] inflicted on several people for their temerity in profaning them. He cited the case of Theopompus, who, as [illegible], having published texts of holy writ, [illegible] to have been the author, was struck with [illegible] the space of thirty days, but that, in the interval of his [illegible], being conscious of his guilt, and imploring the Divine pardon, he was, upon repentance and [illegible] restored [illegible] his right mind, though not without a revelation [illegible] his audacity in confounding [illegible] with [illegible], that brought the [illegible] upon him. That [illegible] Theodectes, the tragic poet, who [illegible] representation, introduced [illegible] of sacred scripture, was struck blind, but, upon confession and repentance of his crime, restored again to his sight.

The king, upon the receipt of the books from Demetrius, [illegible] adoration to the Divine Author, and [illegible] command for preserving them [illegible], ordering the interpreters [illegible] that they could [illegible] it convenient, [illegible] upon all occasions to promote their honour and interest. He observed, that their present [illegible] was [illegible] but that if ever [illegible], they should be disposed to return, they should meet with such reception as was due to the characters of wise and good men, and becoming the dignity of an opulent and powerful prince. He then bestowed on each of them three rich suits of raiment, two talents of gold, the value of one talent in cups, and [illegible] upon. He also sent by them, as presents to Eleazar, the high-priest ten beds with silver feet, and [illegible] of furniture [illegible], [illegible], a chalice of thirty talents, ten [illegible], [illegible] of inestimable value, and an hundred pieces of fine linen, besides cups and goblets of divers sorts, and two golden [illegible] [illegible] dedicated to the service of the temple. [illegible] [illegible] he declined [illegible] the [illegible] be [illegible] to [illegible], he [illegible] them [illegible] [illegible] the conversation of [illegible] [illegible] in returning [illegible] thus, so [illegible] did Ptolemy Philadelphus king of Egypt, towards the Jews.

CHAP. III.

The kings of Asia favourable to the Jews. Antiochus the Great [illegible] them [illegible].

THE Jews were held in great honour and esteem by the princes of Asia, both for their fidelity and skill in military operations, insomuch that Seleucus Nicanor [illegible] them the privileges of freemen in all the cities he built throughout Asia and the Lower Syria, nay, in the metropolis of Antioch itself, declaring it his royal will and pleasure, that they should enjoy the same rights and immunities with the Greeks and Macedonians, of which they are possessed to this very day. For instance, the Jews being interdicted the use of foreign oil, the officers, [illegible] the superintendance of that commodity, were obliged by government, to allow them so much money in [illegible]. In the course of the following [illegible], the people of Antioch insisted on the abolition of this custom, but Mutianus, who was then governor of the province of Syria, would not admit of it.

In the reign of Vespasian, and his son Titus, the people of Alexandria contended for the disfranchisement of the Jews, but [illegible] the honour and justice of the Romans and of [illegible] [illegible] ourageous [illegible], that they could not [illegible]. They certainly did not want pretences for [illegible] a people who had formerly [illegible] them [illegible] ever, but they [illegible] rights and privileges to be [illegible], and [illegible] greatly cut [illegible] them [illegible] to the importunity of two great nations, [illegible] justice [illegible] the [illegible] of their ancient merit [illegible] of their [illegible] indignation. Nor could they be [illegible] by [illegible] to [illegible] [illegible], observing, that those who had taken up arms against the Romans, had suffered sufficiently by the calamities of war, without any other [illegible], and that to [illegible] who had not offended, would be equally contrary to justice and common [illegible].

It is also certain, [illegible] testimony of [illegible], that Marcus Agrippa was [illegible] disposed to [illegible] the Jews [illegible] from [illegible] the [illegible] Agrippa that [illegible] they [illegible] privileges [illegible] which Antiochus, the grandson of Seleucus, [illegible] the [illegible] conferred upon them, and recollected that [illegible] Jews were to be [illegible] with them in their privileges, they ought to be obliged to worship the same gods as the [illegible], the question was brought to trial, [illegible] obtain their suit, [illegible] the Jews, [illegible] cause was ably defended by Nicolaus, of Damascus, [illegible] [illegible] judgment [illegible] that they claimed to the [illegible] [illegible] and [illegible]. Agrippa [illegible] he could not [illegible]. Those who would [illegible] this [illegible] the whole [illegible] in the [illegible] and 124th books of the history [illegible], the [illegible] of Apion does not [illegible] a matter of wonder, [illegible] that time our nation was at war with the Romans, [illegible] and [illegible] of Vespasian and Titus [illegible], nor [illegible] names be mentioned [illegible] notorious [illegible], amidst the outrages of a fierce and bloody war, could not be [illegible] beyond the bounds of humanity and moderation.

Under the reign of Antiochus the Great, [illegible] Judea and Cœlo-Syria, were perpetually harassed [illegible] Antiochus [illegible] that time being [illegible] Ptolemy Philopater, and his son Ptolemy Epiphanes [illegible] conquerors, the Jews [illegible] the [illegible] of Antiochus [illegible] on either side. Antiochus, however, [illegible] and took possession of Judea.

In process of time, after the death of Philopater, [illegible] sent [illegible] army to Cœlo-Syria, [illegible] command of Scopas his general, who [illegible] of their cities and [illegible] Judea, [illegible] in a short time obtained [illegible] victory over Scopas, [illegible] the head of the river Jordan, and recovered [illegible] Cœlo-Syria and [illegible] of which the [illegible] possession. The Jews, upon this [illegible], received the army into the city (Jerusalem) provided plentifully for the [illegible] in the [illegible] of the castle, where Scopas had [illegible] of [illegible]. Antiochus, [illegible] to grant the Jews some honour [illegible] he returned of their good will [illegible] giving testimony of their merit [illegible] the rewards he intended [illegible] copies of the epistles which follow [illegible] concerning the [illegible] of Polybius [illegible] the sixteenth book of his history, [illegible].

Scopas the general [illegible] army [illegible]

"in the winter ſeaſon, into the heart of the country, and ſubdued the nation of the Jews." He writes in the ſame book, that "When Scopas was conquered by Antiochus, the victor took poſſeſſion of Bathanæa, Samaria, Gadara, Gadua, and Abila, after which the Jews of Jeruſalem, and of the glorious temple there, went over to him." He adds, "That he ſhould ſay more on the ſubject, but that he reſerved it for another opportunity." Having thus cited the teſtimony of Polybius, we return to the epiſtle of Antiochus

"King Antiochus to Ptolemy, greeting

"Whereas we have received ſeveral demonſtrations of the good diſpoſition of the Jews towards us and our ſervice, from the time of our firſt coming into their country, in the reſpect of their elders and ruling ſtates in attending us on the way, and the ſplendid reception of our perſon and army into the city, as well as making ſuch ample proviſion both for our horſes and elephants, theſe good offices duly conſidered, we hold ourſelves bound in duty to acknowledge, by beſtowing on them ſome marks of our favour and eſteem, contributing towards the reparation of their demoliſhed city, and recalling their captive countrymen to their former habitations. In order to effect theſe neceſſary purpoſes, we have, in the firſt place, aſſigned twenty thouſand pieces of ſilver towards the charge of their ſacrifices, wine, oil and frankincenſe, and for fine flour, according to the cuſtom of the place, one thouſand four hundred and ſixty meaſures of wheat, and three hundred and ſeventy-five meaſures of ſalt. And it is our will and pleaſure that all this be executed and made good according to order. It is our farther will and pleaſure, that whatever may be wanting towards the repairs of the temple, porch, or galleries, be ſupplied either from Judæa, Libanus, or elſewhere, without any tax or duty. And we do likewiſe grant the ſame immunity for all other materials that ſhall be applied to the uſe of the holy temple, with permiſſion to ſo great an univerſal liberty to live and govern themſelves according to their own cuſtoms and laws. And we do hereby reſpectively diſcharge their elders, prieſts, ſcribes, and ſinging-men, of poll-taxes, royal duties, and all other tributes whatſoever. And as a further encouragement to the ſpeedy repeopling of this city, we do, by our royal authority, grant unto all the preſent inhabitants of the ſame, and to ſuch others as ſhall come over to ſettle up their reſidence there, at any time betwixt this and the month Hyperbereta is next enſuing, an exemption from all public impoſitions for the ſpace of three years to come, and likewiſe from that time forward, an abatement of all taxes, in conſideration of their part of damages and ſufferings. And finally, whereas great numbers of theſe people have been carried away captives, and remain to this day in bondage, we do further command that they be forthwith ſet at liberty, with reſtitution of what hath been taken from them."

This generous declaration in favour of the people was followed by an edict in honour of the temple, which he cauſed to be publiſhed throughout his dominions. It was to this purpoſe. "It ſhall not be lawful for any foreigner to enter the temple but with conſent of the Jews, and without being purified and qualified beforehand for his admittance. No man ſhall preſume to bring into the city either the fleſh of horſes, mules, or aſſes, or of panthers, foxes, hares, or any creatures that the Jews are forbidden to eat. Nor ſhall their ſkins be brought, nor one of theſe animals be bred in the city. Let them only uſe ſuch as their forefathers, according to Divine appointment, applied to the purpoſe of ſacrifices. He that tranſgreſſes any of theſe orders, ſhall be fined for every ſuch offence three thouſand drachmas, to be paid by the offender to the prieſts for their uſe and benefit."

The king took another occaſion of bearing teſtimony to our piety and allegiance. Upon the breaking out of a commotion in Phrygia and Lydia, Zeuxes, the commander in chief of his forces, being at the head of an army in the upland provinces, he commanded him to ſend away from Babylon a number of the Jews into Phrygia, and gave him his inſtructions in a letter to this effect

"The King Antiochus to Zeuxes his friend and general, greeting

"Whereas I am given to underſtand that ſeditious practices prevail in Phrygia and Lydia, and it behoves me therefore to be upon my guard. I am now to acquaint you that I am adviſed by my council to take two thouſand Jewiſh families out of Babylon and Meſopotamia, and to tranſport them into Phrygia, with their goods, and whatever property they may poſſeſs, and there to place them in ſtrong holds and garriſons, being thoroughly ſatisfied of their zeal and allegiance, not only from the principles of their religion, but proofs of their fidelity to my predeceſſors. Wherefore it is my will and pleaſure, notwithſtanding the difficulties with which it may be attended, that they be forthwith tranſplanted, giving them all aſſurances that they ſhall enjoy the liberty of their own laws and cuſtoms. Upon their arrival there, you are to aſſign them lands and poſſeſſions, with all ſorts of conveniences for building, planting and tillage, with an exemption from all taxes and contributions out of the profit for ten years to come. In the mean time, till they may be able to ſupport themſelves out of the fruits of their own induſtry, you are to allow them a competent proviſion of wheat for the maintenance of themſelves and their families, by which kind treatment they will be encouraged to act more cheerfully in our ſervice. You are finally to take care that they be not expoſed to any ſort of moleſtation or trouble. And ſo we bid you farewell."

Theſe teſtimonials are produced to ſhew the eſteem and friendſhip Antiochus the Great bore to the Jews, as well as to commemorate actions noble in their nature and conſequently moſt worthy of imitation.

Soon after this tranſaction, a league of friendſhip and alliance was entered into between this king and Ptolemy Epiphanes, king of Egypt, upon a marriage with his daughter Cleopatra, who he yielded up to him by way of dowry, Cœlo-Syria, Phœnicia, Judæa, and Samaria. The revenue was in partition between the two kings, and farmed out to ſome of the principal men in the reſpective provinces, who ſuperintended the collections, and paid their proportions into the king's treaſury according to contract.

At this juncture the Samaritans were in a flouriſhing ſtate and condition, and greatly harraſſed the Jews, by vexatious incurſions, carrying many of them away captives, and theſe ravages were chiefly committed during the time of the high-prieſt Onias; for after the death of Eleazar, his uncle Manaſſes ſucceeded, and after his death Onias, the ſon of Simon the Juſt, which Simon was the brother of Eleazar, as before obſerved. This Onias was poor in ſoul, weak in intellects, and covetous in diſpoſition, ſo that by refuſing to pay the cuſtomary tribute which his anceſtors had done, he incenſed Ptolemy Euergetes, the father of Philopater, to ſuch a degree, that he ſent ambaſſadors expreſsly to Jeruſalem, with a menace to demand the payment, upon peril of having an army quartered upon their country at diſcretion, and a new plantation of ſoldiers ſettled there, if they did not immediately comply. The Jews were greatly alarmed at the purport of this embaſſy, but Onias was ſo ſordidly avaricious, that with him no menaces could have any effect.

CHAP. IV.

Joſeph the nephew of Onias, the high-prieſt, intercedes for his uncle with king Ptolemy, and advances himſelf and family. His death.

THERE was at this time one Joſeph, a man who had acquired great reputation among the people of Jeruſalem for his prudence and juſtice. He was the ſon of Tobias, by the ſiſter of Onias, the high-prieſt. Being informed by his mother, while he was at Phicola, the place of his birth, of the menacing meſſage delivered by the ambaſſador, he haſtened to Jeruſalem, and reproved Onias for not attending to the ſafety and welfare of his countrymen, as well as expoſing the nation to imminent danger, by refuſing to pay the tribute-money according to the cuſtom of his predeceſſors. He reminded him that, for that very important purpoſe, he had received the authority he held and been appointed high-prieſt. But that if he heart was so clogged by malice, that he would sacrifice his country and friends, rather than refund a part of what was committed to his trust, he advised him to make a dutiful application to the king, and endeavour to persuade him to remit either the whole or a part of the sum demanded Onias replied that he was not so much attached to his office, considered either in a civil or sacerdotal capacity, but that he would resign both, if he might be permitted, rather than apply to the king upon so disagreeable a concern which he therefore desired to waive, as wholly averse to his inclination

Joseph then asked him if he would permit him to go upon the commission, as an ambassador, in behalf of the nation? Having obtained his hearty concurrence, Joseph went up to the temple, and calling the multitude together exhorted them not to be alarmed by terrifying apprehensions from the remissness of his uncle Onias, as he would attend the king in their name, and exert his utmost endeavours to effect a reconciliation of the point in dispute The whole multitude gave him thanks for the proposal, and left the business entirely to his direction Upon this he went to the king's commissioner, and having entertained him splendidly for several days, and made him valuable presents, dismissed him to his master, with an assurance that he would speedily follow him He became more and more anxious for this expedition not only from the invitation and engagement of the king's commissioner but the promise he had given to use his influence with his master, by which he made no doubt that the young adventurer would gain his point Indeed he was so captivated with the grace of Joseph's person, the elegance of his deportment and the gravity of his manners, that upon his return to Egypt he represented the sordid temper of Onias and the agreeable disposition of Joseph, in such terms to his master as greatly prepossessed both him and the queen in favour of the latter before they saw him Joseph sent to his friends for money for his equipage which, in clothes horses, carriages plate, and other necessaries, amounted to twenty thousand drachmas, and, being properly equipped set out for Alexandria He happened in his way to fall in company with a train of the rulers and principal men of the cities of Syria and Phœnicia, who were going to the king to treat with him concerning the farming of the revenue according to annual custom These grandees treated Joseph with a peculiar severity, and made him and his retinue the subjects of their derision nevertheless he prosecuted his journey

Finding, upon his arrival at Alexandria that king Ptolemy was at Memphis he immediately set out for that place, in the way to which, he had the good fortune to meet the king the queen and Athenion, his particular confidant, on their return to Alexandria This Athenion was the person who was deputed with the embassy to Jerusalem, and there so honourably treated by Joseph He therefore no sooner saw him, than he gave the king to understand that he was the young man in whose commendation he had spoken so highly on his return from Jerusalem Ptolemy then saluted him, took him into his carriage and mentioned how ill he had been treated by Onias the high-priest Joseph respectfully answered, "Sir, an old man is a second time a child "impute nothing to Onias but what his age will excuse "As for us who have youth and the power of our faculties, we will give proof of our loyal attachment" The king was so pleased with this candid as well as dutiful reply that, induced thereby to conceive the highest opinion of the ability and discretion of the speaker, he gave orders, on their arrival at Alexandria that he should be lodged in the palace, and entertained every day at his own table This singular token of respect excited the envy of the Syrians, when they observed the honours that were paid to Joseph at Alexandria

The day of auction being now arrived, when the several branches of the revenue were to be put up, the Syrian and Phœnician noblemen, whom Joseph had seen on his way to Alexandria endeavoured to undervalue them, offering no more than eight thousand talents for all the cities of Cœlo-Syria, Phœnicia, Judea, and Samaria Joseph censured the contractors, for offering a composition so inferior to the real value of the revenues, and proposed doubling it himself, over and above the forfeitures which these publicans had reserved for themselves The king was so highly pleased with this proposal for the improvement of his revenue, that he asked Joseph what security he could give Joseph told him his securities were undoubted The king ordered him to name them, and upon his answering that he doubted not but his majesty and the queen would be mutually bound for his justice and honour, the king, from the high opinion he entertained of him, immediately appointed him receiver general of all those provinces, a circumstance which greatly mortified those whose intentions were to have purchased the farming of the revenue at an under value

Joseph, on his appointment to this high office desired a guard of two thousand soldiers to support him in collecting the duty in case of opposition, and thereupon having borrowed five hundred talents of the king's friends in Alexandria, he proceeded towards Syria to execute his office On his arrival at a place called Askalon and demanding the king's tribute, the people not only refused payment, but insulted him in the most outrageous manner, upon which he punished twenty of the ringleaders, by bringing them to exemplary justice, raised a thousand talents out of their forfeited estates, and sent the treasure to the king with an account of his proceedings Ptolemy was so satisfied with the discretion of his conduct, that he left the whole business to him and this recent example of severity upon the people of Askalon had such an effect on the rest of the Syrians, that they set open their gates in all places to Joseph, and paid their taxes without scruple

The inhabitants of Scythopolis followed the precedent of those of Askalon, in an obstinate refusal of their customary imposts and in contempt of the king's officers and authority, so that Joseph was under a necessity of dealing with the ringleaders there as he had done with the former upon the same occasion, confiscated their estates, and applying the forfeiture to the king's use and the support of government He sent valuable presents to the king, queen and their principal adherents, by which means he conciliated many powerful friends

In this situation did Joseph continue for the space of twenty-two years, and became the father of seven sons by one wife, and he had one other son, whose name was Hyrcanus by the daughter of his brother Solymius, whom he took to wife on the following occasion

Travelling to Alexandria with his brother accompanied by his daughter who being marriageable he took thither, in order to give her in wedlock to some Jew of quality As he was at supper with the king, he became passionately enamoured with a beautiful maid that danced there for the entertainment of the royal guests He made his brother the only confidant of the secret, desiring him, as he could not, by a Jewish law marry a stranger, to be subservient to his desire of obtaining a private interview with the object of his affection His brother seemed cordially to accede to the proposal and arraying his daughter in suitable attire, conveyed her to Joseph's bed Joseph, being disordered by the fumes of the regale, passed the first night with his brother's daughter, without discovering the error This abuse was practised on him repeatedly till Joseph, becoming more and more enamoured of his fair, though unknown, partner, complained to his brother of his hard fate, as being prohibited, by the law and religion of his country from marrying the woman he most ardently loved Solymius told him he need not perplex himself with so disagreeable an apprehension, as he might lawfully marry the object of his affection He then discovered to him the whole affair, telling him, that, instead of the admired dancer, he had conveyed his own daughter to his bed, and thinking it less criminal to submit to an indignity in the person of his daughter than suffer his brother to be exposed to contempt and dishonour by an offence against the law ... joining [illegible] to a strange woman, in violation of one of the most sacred laws. The great surprize of this discovery, and the singular instance of the regard Solymius had shewn for the preservation of his religion and honour, had so prevailing an effect on the mind of Joseph, that he immediately married his daughter, and of her was born Hyrcanus, as before observed.

This Hyrcanus, at the age of thirteen years, gave such proofs of superior genius, as well as superior virtue, that he became, as is too natural, the envy of all his brethren, from gaining an ascendancy over the minds of all to whom he had an opportunity of discovering his amiable qualifications. Joseph, in order to make an experiment of the ability and disposition of his several sons, sent them to such masters as had acquired the greatest reputation for instructing of youth; but the seven elder, through dullness or sloth, returned without making the least proficiency in useful or ornamental knowledge. He sent out last his youngest son Hyrcanus upon a seven days journey into the desart, with 300 yoke of oxen, bidding him plow and sow there, having first privately taken away the tyes that should join the yoke and plough together. When Hyrcanus came to the place, and wanted the necessary tackle, he was advised by the husbandmen to send some to his father for it; but being averse to losing his time, he projected a plan worthy of the most experienced age. He caused ten yoke of the oxen to be slain, and dividing the carcases among the husbandmen and servants, cut their hides into thongs, made the necessary tackle of the same, ploughed and sowed the land according to his father's appointment, and then returned home. His father was highly pleased with this instance of his sagacity, and shewed him such peculiar tokens of esteem and favour, as excited the envy and hatred of his [illegible].

About this time Joseph received intelligence that Ptolemy's queen Cleopatra, was delivered of a son, to the joy of the subjects in general. As upon this occasion it might be required of him among other great officers of state, to congratulate the king and queen, he determined, as a journey from Jerusalem to [illegible] too fatiguing to him in his advanced years, to send one of his sons in his stead. To try how they stood affected to this expedition, he called them together, and severally asked them, which would chuse to engage in the business? The eldest positively refused; the next apologized, by saying he was totally unacquainted with the customs and ceremonies of a court; in short, the rest declined the undertaking, on some pretence or other, till at length it was resolved, as well with the approbation of Joseph, as the rest of his sons, that Hyrcanus should be sent, who, though the youngest was, [illegible] distinguished abilities the best qualified for such an occasion.

This matter being adjusted, Joseph asked his son, what he thought would be sufficient to defray the expences of his embassy, and purchase the necessary presents for the king and queen. Hyrcanus told him ten talents, and recommended that instead of sending the presents from Judæa, they should be purchased at Alexandria, for which purpose he might write to his agent there to furnish him with what was requisite. Joseph complied with his son's request, and gave him letters of credit upon Arion, the person in Alexandria to whom he remitted the money collected in Syria to be deposited in the royal treasury, which, at that time, did not amount to less than three thousand talents.

As soon as he arrived at Alexandria, Hyrcanus went to Arion, produced his letters of credit, and demanded instead of ten, a thousand talents. Surprized at so great a demand, Arion refused compliance, saying, "What do you want with such a sum? Your father's fortune was made by industry, and you would do well to follow his example. I will give you ten talents, and those I will see expended in the presents you are to make."

This abrupt reply highly offended Hyrcanus. He for some time expostulated with him, but finding him continue resolute in not complying with his demand, he, by his superiority of power in consequence of his father's authority, had him committed to prison. The wife of Arion, who was on good terms with the queen, informed her of the treatment her husband had received from Hyrcanus, and the queen related the particulars of the whole to the king. In consequence of this the king sent him a message, expressing his astonishment at his conduct, and ordering him immediately to attend, and clear himself of the charge alledged against him. Hyrcanus desired the messenger to inform his master, that by the Jewish law, no man was permitted to eat of the flesh of any thing that was sacrificed that had not been first in the temple, and offered sacrifice himself; in his case, he dare not presume to wait upon the king till he had first presented the oblations, with which his father had entrusted him, in testimony of his gratitude and duty; and that, with regard to punishing a refractory servant, he thought himself justified, as the like impunity in an inferior might at length effect the king himself, where authority was despised, the precedent might be dangerous.

When the king received this answer, instead of being offended with Hyrcanus, he highly applauded him for the dignity of his sentiments; and Arion finding he had no reason to expect favour or protection from the king, compounded for his liberty by paying him the thousand talents he had demanded. Three days after Hyrcanus went to court to pay his respects to the king and queen, where he had the honour, from the singular regard the king entertained for his father, to be admitted to the royal table. As soon as Hyrcanus had received the money of Arion, he contracted privately with certain merchants for an hundred of the most comely boys, and the like number of beautiful girls, at the price of a talent a head. [illegible] after this to a magnificent entertainment [illegible] the king, together with other persons of [illegible] the officers who had the conduct of the ceremony, [illegible] the arrangement of the guests, assigned Hyrcanus, on account of his youth, the lowest place at the table. [illegible] of the company, which sat next him, looking upon him with contempt, endeavoured to shew their disrespect by laying their bones before him and [illegible] on [illegible]. [illegible] the king's jester, to treat him with [illegible] the jester attempted to do; but desiring the king, with an [illegible] to [illegible] the circumstance, saying [illegible] the bones before him, so had the father picked the bones of all Syria. The king could not but smile at the drollery of the conceit, and asked Hyrcanus how he came to have so many bones piled before him. "Sire, (replied he, looking steadfastly on the company) dogs eat bones as well as men, but [illegible] put the bones aside." This facetious answer highly pleased the king, and, instead of a laugh being raised on Hyrcanus, it fell on Tryphon, and the company that affected to treat him with contempt and mockery.

The next day Hyrcanus sounded the servants of the great men, who came on the errand of congratulation on the birth of the prince, as to the sum their masters intended to present. Some said twelve talents, some more, and others less. But Hyrcanus, from design, affected to be uneasy, upon pretence that he could not come up to their proportion, as he could advance no more than five. This [illegible] of poverty was highly pleasing to the servants, who [illegible] not to tell their masters of it, so that the grandees exulted with the thought how contemptible the youth would appear in the king's eye by the meanness of his present. But they were soon mistaken, for, on the day appointed for the ceremony of their oblations, the largest gift was twenty talents, except that made by Hyrcanus, who presented the hundred boys to the king, and the hundred girls to the queen, and with each of them a talent for another present over and above. This was so unexpected and excessive a munificence, that it struck the king and company with astonishment; but Hyrcanus gave many, exclusive of this, to the king's [illegible] and officers, in order to avoid the danger he apprehended from those who were suborned to [illegible] to destroy him.

[illegible] the liberality of Hyrcanus so [illegible] on [illegible] that he became the greatest favourite at court, and the [illegible] granted his request, with assurance of returning [illegible]. Of this generous offer he made no other use than to solicit the king for letters of recommendation to his [illegible] and brethren. The king took [illegible] [illegible] [illegible] of [illegible], bestowed on him [illegible] worthy the [illegible] of a prince, and, with commendatory letters to his father, brethren, and his own governors and officers, dismissed him with every token of respect.

When his brethren heard of the [illegible] reception he had met with from the king and queen, and how much his character was aggrandized [illegible], they entered into a combination to go out of the town, meet him on his return, and take away his life, [illegible] with the privacy of his father, who was greatly disgusted at the enormous expence of his late presents, and therefore, in reality, very [illegible] for his preservation, though he dissembled them [illegible] of [illegible].

It came, however, to the [illegible], [illegible] and assaulted him on his return, [illegible] resistance on [illegible] part [illegible] they [illegible] considerable number of them [illegible] two of [illegible] were slain on the spot, and [illegible] to [illegible] Jerusalem [illegible] that [illegible] into the city; but meeting with a very cold reception [illegible] of danger, he crossed the river Jordan [illegible] his [illegible] and there [illegible] the [illegible] of his life in collecting the king's duties from the Barbarians.

This was in the reign of Seleucus, king of Asia, otherwise called Soter, [illegible] the son of [illegible]. Among his [illegible] of Hyrcanus, [illegible] and magnanimity, [illegible] of his country, [illegible] he [illegible] most important concerns. [illegible] the [illegible] the [illegible] Phœnicia, [illegible] Samaria, [illegible] His [illegible] time, and [illegible], who was succeeded by Onias [illegible] Lacedæmon, [illegible].

CHAP. V.

[illegible] king of Lacedæmon, [illegible] high-priest [illegible].

"Areus, king of the Lacedæmonians, to Onias, high-priest, [illegible].

"WHEREAS there [illegible] manuscript, [illegible] the Jews and the Lacedæmonians [illegible] from the stock of Abraham, [illegible] therefore [illegible] and reasonable for brethren, [illegible] good offices towards one another. [illegible] offer you the command of any thing [illegible] to serve you, [illegible] our own, [illegible] Yours received this [illegible] and [illegible] Demoteles, [illegible] sealed with the [illegible] of an eagle holding [illegible] the [illegible]." This was the purport of the [illegible] which the Lacedæmonians [illegible].

Upon the death of Joseph, [illegible] amongst the people, by means of a [illegible] between Hyrcanus and his surviving brethren about the [illegible] estate. The [illegible] was divided, [illegible] the high-priest [illegible] took the part of the [illegible] [illegible] to return to Jerusalem, [illegible] of the Jordan, where he was [illegible] the Arabians, [illegible] of whom he [illegible] into captivity.

[illegible] his retreat Hyrcanus [illegible] erected a strong castle, the walls of which [illegible], with the figures of animals [illegible] and proportion [illegible]. The castle was [illegible] [illegible] of [illegible] large [illegible] mountain opposite [illegible] of [illegible] [illegible] [illegible]. With [illegible] dining-rooms, and other places of entertainment, with [illegible] courts, gardens and [illegible]. To this [illegible] he gave the name of Tyre. [illegible] between Arabia and Judea, beyond Jordan, [illegible] of the [illegible]. Hyrcanus [illegible] seven years, [illegible] the whole time [illegible] Seleucus [illegible] Syria. Upon his [illegible], he was succeeded by his brother Antiochus, who was called Epiphanes. Ptolemy [illegible] died [illegible] time, and left behind him two sons, [illegible] of the [illegible] Philometor, [illegible] of the younger Physcon. [illegible] Hyrcanus [illegible] of [illegible] [illegible] his [illegible] Antiochus [illegible] treasure [illegible] of his goods [illegible] a tomb.

CHAP. VI.

[illegible] high-priest [illegible] the [illegible] the Romans.

ONIAS the high-priest dying about this time, [illegible] Antiochus Epiphanes [illegible] [illegible] of [illegible] [illegible] [illegible] after [illegible] the king's displeasure [illegible] from the [illegible], and [illegible] to Onias his younger brother. There were three sons of Simon, [illegible] [illegible] had [illegible] the name of Jason, as did Onias that of Menelaus.

[illegible] a party [illegible] the [illegible] of [illegible] [illegible] Menelaus, [illegible] of [illegible] [illegible] to Antiochus, [illegible] the [illegible] [illegible] [illegible] the Grecian [illegible] [illegible] to [illegible] they [illegible] from [illegible] the Greeks. In [illegible], they totally [illegible] religion, laws, customs, and manners of their own country, and [illegible] profession [illegible].

Antiochus, finding [illegible] in [illegible] of Egypt [illegible] contempt of the sons of Ptolemy [illegible] [illegible] Pelusium [illegible] got footing in Egypt. He [illegible] thence to Memphis, and other [illegible], which having reduced, he proceeded to Alexandria, [illegible] of [illegible]. But, upon [illegible] the Romans, who [illegible] if he continued to [illegible] with the force [illegible] his [illegible], [illegible] to [illegible] [illegible] his departure from thence. [illegible] seem [illegible] Antiochus, and they set forth the [illegible] of Jerusalem and the temple, as they are [illegible] record.

CHAP. VII.

[illegible] Jews, [illegible].

ANTIOCHUS [illegible] from the [illegible] of the [illegible] the Romans [illegible].

city in the hundred and forty-third year from the time that the kingdom of Syria fell into the hands of Seleucus He made himself master of the city without striking a blow, the gates being set open to him by a party he had formed in the town, where, having exercised the greatest cruelties and put numbers to the sword, without distinction of friend or foe, he carried away an immense booty to Antioch

This calamity happened in the second year after the taking the city, in the hundred and forty-fifth year from the first Seleucus, the twenty-fifth day of the month, which we call Chasleu, the Macedonians Appellaus and in the hundred and fifty-third olympiad Such was the savage ferocity of the army of Antiochus, that they spared not even those who opened the gates, and thereby paved their admission to the temple, and, through treachery to their country, laid open their dearest possessions to the most rapacious plunderers

The temple, in short, was entirely rifled, all the holy vessels and utensils taken away, with the golden candlesticks, the golden altar, and the table of shewbread The curtains, and the embroidery of silks, fine linen, and the secret places, where they concealed an immense [illegible] of treasure were all laid open and exposed, insomuch, that not a relic remained of this prodigious store of wealth To complete the misery of this [illegible] people the daily sacrifices were forbidden, the city levelled with the ground, its inhabitants partly slain, and partly led away captives, together with their wives and children to the number of ten thousand, their walls demolished and their stately edifices consumed by fire They erected in the city a tower that overlooked the temple into which, when they had fortified it, they put a garrison of Macedonians but not without a mixture of execrable apostate Jews, who were more inimical to the citizens than their most inveterate foreign enemies

They erected an idol altar in the temple and sacrificed swine upon it in palpable violation of the sacred laws and institutions of the Jews Those who refused to renounce the worship of the true God, and pay adoration to idols were subject to the greatest barbarities and throughout all the cities and towns of Judæa, they erected temples and altars for the daily sacrifice of swine They laid a heavy penalty on those Jews who circumcised their children retaining officers and informers, either to prosecute them for disobeying their injunctions, or extort from them obedience, by terror and threatening

Awed by the dreadful apprehensions of the most horrid cruelties, the greater part of the Jews complied with the king's commands Some there were indeed, amongst them, of such inflexible piety and virtue, that they stood firm against the trials of the severest tortures, and even of death itself, rather than depart from the religion and laws of their country, having their bodies lacerated with whips, and then crucified alive with their wives and so many of their children as were circumcised hanging about their necks, according to the king's command The holy scriptures were destroyed wherever they were found, and it was made death for any person even to mention them

When the Samaritans found the Jews reduced to so miserable a state of distress, they disclaimed all kindred with them, extolling the temple of Gerizim as the temple of God, so that they wavered according as their interest led them, as before observed At this crisis they pretended to be the race of the Medes and Persians and that they would entirely detach themselves from so wretched a people as the Jews To this effect they dispatched an address to Antiochus, couched in terms to the following import

"To king Antiochus Epiphanes, the illustrious prince,

"Memorial of the Sidonians, inhabitants of Shechem

"That the ancestors of your memorialists, lying under "the affliction of many grievous plagues in their own "country, were partly wrought on by that calamity and "partly prevailed on by the superstition of ancient custom "to join in the religious observance of a certain festival "which the Jews call the sabbath, and in the erecting of "a temple upon mount Gerizim, where sacrifices were offered to a god without a name Now, since you have "been pleased to order this wicked people to be punished "according to their deserts, and to appoint officers who, "upon a supposition that we are all of the same stock are "thereby induced to involve us with the Jews in the same "crime, and whereas we derive our origin from the Sidonians, as we can make appear by the public records which "are extant to this day, it is our humble request, that, out "of your clemency and goodness, you would issue such order to Apollonius, our governor, and to Nicanor, his deputy, that they may not in future be molested, upon suspicion of any correspondence or confederacy with the Jews, "to whom we are as much strangers in our manners as in "our extraction And we do further pray, that the temple "that hath hitherto stood without any dedication at all, may, "from this time forward, be called the temple of Jupiter of "Greece, to the end that we may live in greater security "and freedom, as to our own private concerns, and the advancement of your service and revenue"

In answer to this memorial of the Samaritans, king Antiochus thus wrote

'King Antiochus to Nicanor

'Having received a memorial from the Sidonians at Shechem, which we have annexed to this letter, this gives 'you to understand, that it appeareth unto us, and to our "council, upon the information of the bearers hereof, that "the Sidonians are in no instance guilty of the crimes charged upon them by the Jews but, on the contrary, entirely 'govern themselves by the customs and manners of the "Greeks It is, therefore, our royal will and pleasure, that "they be no further molested concerning this matter With "respect to the temple, it is our will likewise that it may "from henceforward, be known and distinguished by the name "of the temple of Jupiter of Greece We have written to 'the same effect also to our governor Apollonius Dated in "the forty-sixth year, and the eleventh day of the month of "Hecatombæon'

CHAP VII

The z[illegible] resolution of Matthias and his sons f[illegible] [illegible] the country The goodness of Matthias

THERE dwelt at this time in Modin, a village of Judæa, one Matthias, a priest, of the family of Joarib, a native of Jerusalem This Matthias was the son of John, the son of Simeon, and Simeon the son of Asmoneus Matthias had five sons, Johanan, who was called Gaddis, Simon, who was called Thassi, Judas, who was called Maccabeus, Jonathan, who was called Apphus, and Eleazar, who was called Auran Matthias would frequently condole with his sons on the deplorable state of the Jewish nation, the desolating their city, the pillaging and prophanation of their temple, with numberless other calamities He would often animate each other with this suggestion, that it would be more glorious to fall a sacrifice to the laws and religion of their country, than linger out a wretched life of the most abject servility When the king's officers arrived in the village to enforce the execution of their master's commands, they began with Matthias as a person of authority, and one who might be a leading example to the rest They pointed out to him the danger of disobedience, with the advantages and rewards that would attend compliance, and, upon those terms, warmly enjoined him, in the king's name, to worship as he was commanded These injunctions he not only refused to obey, but moreover assured them, that, if every individual within their master's dominions would obey him in that particular command, he was determined not to submit, and it would be his constant advice to his sons never to abandon the laws and religion of their country

Matthias had no sooner acquainted the officers with his resolution, than one of the Jews proceeding to sacrifice according to the manner prescribed But Matthias and his

JUDAS MACCABEUS defeats the SAMARITAN ARMY and kills Apollonius their General

sons, were so incensed at the indignity of the offence, that, in a rage, they flew not only the apostate Jew, but the king's officer, Apelles, as he was compelling the people to the [illegible] worship. They also overthrew the idol altar, and then cried aloud to the people around them, "As many of you as have any regard to your religion or honour, follow me." Upon this the father and sons withdrew into the wilderness, leaving their goods and effects behind them. Many of the people, inspired by so glorious an example, fled with their wives and children into the same desert, where they lived some time in caves. When the king's officers received intelligence of this desertion, they drew the forces out of the citadel of Jerusalem, and marched after the Jews into the wilderness.

Upon overtaking them, they first expostulated with them mildly, recommending them to act with more moderation and compliance, and not lay them under the disagreeable necessity of proceeding to a military execution. But when they found that neither the harshest menaces, or the mildest persuasions, could prevail, they pitched on the sabbath day for the attack, and accordingly burnt and destroyed them in their caves, without any resistance: for such was the reverence in which the Jews held that sacred day, and the zeal they maintained for the observance of their laws, that they chose rather to perish than profane it. The number of men, women, and children, that were suffocated under ground, amounted to about a thousand; but great numbers made their escape, and enlisted under the banner of Mattathias. This zealous defender of the religion and laws of his country pointed out to them the legality and necessity of opposing an hostile attack on the sabbath, as well as any other day, as such mere scruples would end in their total destruction, for their enemies, availing themselves of that superstition, would certainly fall upon them at a time when they were sure they should meet with no resistance. This argument had a most convincing effect: they were all fully satisfied of the lawfulness of taking up arms in their defence in cases of necessity, and the practice, in such cases, continues to this day.

Mattathias, in process of time, acquired such influence, and raised such numerous and powerful adherents, that he overthrew their idol altars, and slew all apostates, who violated the laws, wherever he could find them. He commanded circumcision, that had been forbidden, to be restored, and put to flight the king's officers who were appointed to suppress that ancient practice; many of them, indeed, had dispersed, through fear of his vindictive power.

Having thus nobly asserted the laws and religion of his country, and removed every obstacle to the observance of the rites and ceremonies, during the course of a full year, Matthias fell into a distemper, which he apprehending to be mortal, called for his sons, and addressed them to the following purport:

"My dear sons, as my life is verging to a period, I am "now to charge you, as your tender [illegible] before I "go hence, that you maintain, with a [illegible] resolution, "the cause your father has asserted before you, with [illegible] "less perseverance. Remember my dying injunction, and "fail not to execute it. Exert your uttermost ability in the "support of the rights and laws of our country, and the "restoration of a nation ready to fall a sacrifice to idolatry. "Shun all connection with those who, either through fear "or interest, have basely betrayed it. Approve yourselves [illegible] "worthy of such a father, and, in contempt of force and "external dangers, expose your lives, and yield them up "with cheerfulness, if occasion should require, in defence "of your country: being assured that such resignation "is acceptable to God, who, as the reward of your pious "resolution, will restore to your country its former glorious "privileges, and uncorrupted religion and laws. Our bodies, indeed, are mortal, but great and noble actions [illegible] "immortalize our memory. [illegible] to this glory I aspire, [illegible] "[illegible] which, by your illustrious atchievements, [illegible] "will accrue [illegible]. Preserve unanimity, among[illegible] "yourselves, and yield to the judgment of each other in

"those points wherein you respectively excel. As, for example, as Simon possesses quick penetration and discernment, I would recommend him as your counsel. Maccabeus, being of a warlike disposition, should be appointed "general, as best qualified for the vindication of his country's cause, and the total overthrow of his enemies. [illegible] "courage and protect men of piety and virtue; and let these "be the sources of your own conduct, and then fear nothing."

CHAP. IX.

Judas Maccabeus succeeds his father Mathias in the command.

WHEN Matthias had given these exhortations to his sons, he addressed his prayers to the Almighty for a blessing on their joint endeavours towards the redemption of their countrymen, and the recovery of their ancient rights and privileges. He departed this life soon after, and was interred with due pomp and solemnity. When the funeral obsequies were over, his son Judas, called Maccabeus, was vested with the public administration of affairs, in the hundred and forty-sixth year after Seleucus the first. He was so well supported by his brothers, that he expelled the enemy from their country, put the [illegible] of its laws to the sword, and purged it from all the abominable pollutions with which it had abounded.

CHAP. X.

Judas overthrows the forces of Apollonius and Seron, and [illegible] the general [illegible]

THE news of this turn of affairs, in consequence of the valiant exertions of Judas, the son and successor of Matthias, in the military command, being made known to the [illegible], Antiochus sent orders to Apollonius, his governor in Samaria, to raise what forces he could, and march immediately against the enemy. Apollonius obeyed the king's orders, but his attempt, happily for the Jews, proved not only fruitless, but destructive. Judas, apprized of his intentions, got his friends together, and prepared them in the best manner he could for battle, encouraging them to persevere in the opposition they were about to make, not only for the security of their own lives, but for the preservation of their descendants, and, above all, for their religion and laws.

Animated by this advice, the forces under Judas marched with great expedition to meet those under Apollonius, the consequence of which was, that a desperate engagement ensued, in which, by the distinguished intrepidity of the Jews, the Samaritan army was then routed, great numbers slain, and the rest put to flight. The brave Judas, finding Apollonius detached from his army, engaged him in single combat, and, by his prowess, soon dispatched him, took away his sword in triumph, and, as a memento of this signal victory, generally made use of it in future encounters.

The news of this defeat soon reached Seron, governor of Cœlo-Syria, who, in consequence thereof, and the farther information he had received, that reinforcements were daily going over to Judas upon his late success, collected his forces, determined to come to an immediate action, holding himself bound in honour to chastise the [illegible], and bring rebels to obedience. To this end, with what men he could muster of his own, and the additional force of a rabble of fugitive Jews, he marched on as far as Bethhoron, a village in Judea, where he pitched his camp. In the mean time Judas made the necessary preparations to engage him, but finding his soldiers rather dismayed, from the superior number of the enemy, he endeavoured to dissipate their fears, by addressing them in words to this effect:

"Be not, soldiers, dependent on yourselves, but on the arm "of Omnipotence for victory. Repose no confidence in "[illegible] but in the almighty God. This is the doctrine by "the history of our ancestors who, with small numbers, have "[illegible] in defence of their religion, laws, and "[illegible] Truth shall prevail, and innocence remain in-"vincible."

Having thus spoken, he led his men into the battle, which they maintained with such courage and resolution, that Seron, general of the Syrians, being slain by Judas, and his army totally routed, the scattered troops betook themselves to flight, as the only means of safety. The number of the enemy that fell in the battle was about eight hundred, and the rest made their escape towards the sea-side.

CHAP. XI.

Judas defeats Lysias [illegible] Gorgias. Proceeds to Jerusalem, [illegible] the temple, and [illegible] the Philistines.

WHEN Antiochus heard of these disasters, he was so enraged, that he vowed revenge on the Jews, [illegible] which, he raised a powerful army from amongst his own people, and, with the addition of some Greek mercenaries, determined to invade Judea early in the next spring. [illegible] however, upon mustering his men, that his revenues fell very short of defraying the expences of so great an army (his coffers being much drained by the frequent re-[illegible] commotions in his own dominions) he thought [illegible] for himself first to go into Persia, and there [illegible] a supply of money to assist him in the [illegible] of his design.

[illegible] he went on this expedition, he constituted [illegible] of approved fidelity, governor of all the [illegible] Egypt and the Euphrates, leaving him [illegible] for Antiochus [illegible] his return. He [illegible] particular orders for the reduction of Judea, and [illegible] of all the inhabitants [illegible] to destroy [illegible] completely [illegible]. Having [illegible] these matters, [illegible] and, [illegible] the upper [illegible] advanced [illegible] higher [illegible].

Lysias, the better to execute his commission, [illegible] chose three eminent commanders, Ptolemy the son of Dorymenes, Gorgias, and Nicanor, whom he put at the head of [illegible] foot, and 7000 horse, with orders to march [illegible] to Judea. These [illegible] as far as Emmaus (-), [illegible] encamped upon the plain, where there came [illegible] great number of auxiliaries from Syria, and other neighbouring countries, with abundance of fugitive Jews [illegible] with [illegible] and fetters [illegible] the [illegible], being [illegible] in their minds, that the Jews should be totally defeated.

[illegible] the [illegible] hastened [illegible] his men [illegible] good courage, place their hope [illegible] Almighty, and [illegible] to [illegible] according to the custom of their country, [illegible] danger, [illegible] prayer, fasting, and [illegible]. His next [illegible] was [illegible] regular [illegible] order of battle, in regiments, [illegible] and [illegible] who were newly married, or [illegible] their [illegible] left, by these considerations, they [illegible] interrupted [illegible] discharge of [illegible]. When he had thus disposed his [illegible], in order to animate them to persevere in the undertaking, he [illegible] the following speech to this purport:

"My [illegible] fellow soldiers and companions, we shall never see [illegible] occasion [illegible] to [illegible] very [illegible] for [illegible] contempt of all dangers, [illegible] upon the [illegible] of [illegible] depends not only our liberty, but [illegible] [illegible] that attend it, and [illegible] above the [illegible] for [illegible] freedom, our [illegible] [illegible] without [illegible] one [illegible], pre-"serving the other. [illegible] well the [illegible] "it is your [illegible] to [illegible]

"less than the sum and substance of the greatest happiness "you ever enjoyed, that is to say, the peaceable possession "of your ancient laws, rights, and [illegible] Now, [illegible] "they you [illegible] to perish with the [illegible] "[illegible] the [illegible] you [illegible] "[illegible] or [illegible] effort [illegible] the [illegible] "[illegible] and your friends, is the [illegible] "[illegible] Death is the same thing to the coward [illegible] to "the man of wisdom, and [illegible] certain to one [illegible] other, but "there is a wide difference between them in point of [illegible] "[illegible] everlasting fame. The gallant man, who [illegible] "[illegible] of his religious laws and country, [illegible] "[illegible] with honour [illegible] the [illegible] "[illegible] is consigned [illegible] Take these [illegible] "[illegible] your thoughts, [illegible] make the [illegible] of the [illegible] "You have nothing to trust to but the providence of God, "and your own concurring resolutions, and, [illegible] "while we contend [illegible], we [illegible]

This [illegible] had the desired effect, the people [illegible] [illegible] declared they would [illegible] with the [illegible] in defence of their religion and country.

Judas, soon after this, [illegible] intelligence that Gorgias was detached from the [illegible] army, with five [illegible] [illegible] and a thousand horse, [illegible] to [illegible] surprize his camp by night, [illegible] to [illegible] and countermine his plot, [illegible] in order to [illegible] surprize, [illegible] in the camp, [illegible] Gorgias, [illegible] deserted, [illegible] had fled [illegible] themselves [illegible] he had nothing to do but [illegible] [illegible] the [illegible] [illegible] his people, [illegible] and protection, [illegible] with these words he ordered the [illegible] [illegible], and his men rushing in upon the enemy [illegible] instant, threw them into such surprize, that, [illegible] to the [illegible] the [illegible] themselves to flight, and the Jews pursued them as far as Gazara, [illegible] of Idumea, [illegible] Azotus, and [illegible] number of the slain [illegible] about three thousand.

But Judas would not suffer his people to take the spoils, as the troops of Gorgias were yet entire, which, when they had routed, he told them they might take possession of the booty [illegible]. While he was uttering those words, the troops of Gorgias, discovering from an eminence, the dead bodies of their fellow soldiers, [illegible] and their camp covered with smoke, [illegible] took it for granted that the Jews were still embodied, and [illegible] condition to [illegible] them. This occasioned so general a consternation, that they immediately fled, and dispersed themselves in different quarters. The victory being thus gained, [illegible] his men to pillage the [illegible] of the field, where they found gold and silver, [illegible] of purple and scarlet, and booty [illegible] great [illegible]. With this they marched off [illegible] [illegible], [illegible] thanks to God, the [illegible] of this victory, which proved both an earnest and a foundation of their future freedom.

The great success of Judas so incensed Lysias, that [illegible] his [illegible], he brought into the field, the [illegible] [illegible] of sixty thousand foot, and five thousand horse, all select men, and with this powerful body he entered into Judea, [illegible] of the mountains, and encamped [illegible] place called Bethsura. Judas, [illegible]

[illegible]

[illegible] number of the enemy, [illegible] [illegible] only ten thousand men, and having offered up [illegible] fervent prayer for success, he attacked the enemy with [illegible] resolution, that, upon the first [illegible], he forced their lines, and killed upwards of five thousand men on the spot. The army of Lysias was so [illegible] at this disaster, that they [illegible] their commander [illegible], were [illegible] to conquer or die; but Lysias, considering [illegible], instead of continuing the battle, [illegible] a retreat, and, with his troops, withdrew to Antioch, where he [illegible], by the [illegible], to be ready for the first opportunity of a revenge upon the Jews.

Animated by these repeated successes, Judas [illegible] ringing his adherents to [illegible] the [illegible] protection of the Almighty, proposed marching to Jerusalem, and [illegible] more to [illegible] of the [illegible], to offer up sacrifices and purify the temple, so that they might again restore the worship of the God of Israel. When they came thither, and found the gates destroyed, the temple abandoned, and the [illegible] [illegible] their [illegible], they could not refrain from weeping at the deplorable situation of the place. The two great works he first [illegible] upon, were the [illegible] of the citadel, and the [illegible] of the temple. [illegible] reserved the care of the [illegible] to himself. [illegible] the [illegible] [illegible] to purge it from those [illegible] [illegible], for [illegible] [illegible]. The [illegible] being [illegible], he [illegible] table, and [illegible] of pure gold. [illegible] versal [illegible] hangings on the walls [illegible] prophaned by the [illegible], [illegible] according to the Mosaic [illegible].

Upon the [illegible] day of the month Casleu, they lighted tapers [illegible], offered [illegible] the altar, [illegible], [illegible] [illegible]. [illegible] happened [illegible] prophanation [illegible] [illegible] three years. [illegible] [illegible] year, [illegible] [illegible] one of the [illegible] Olympiad. It [illegible] [illegible] on the same day, [illegible] of the month Apelleus, on the hundred and forty-eighth year, and the hundred and fifty-fourth Olympiad, as the prophet Daniel had expressly foretold [illegible] hundred and [illegible] years before the [illegible].

Judas continued the [illegible] eight days, with [illegible], rejoicing and feasting, while the [illegible] resounded with thanksgiving, and [illegible] the people, who, during the whole time, were indulged in [illegible] gratifications. The people, in fine, were so [illegible] of finding themselves restored to their religion and [illegible] of their forefathers, that [illegible] [illegible] eight days following [illegible], [illegible] [illegible], which we [illegible] from that time to this, under the title of the feast of Lights, in allusion to that light which Providence was pleased to bestow on the children of Israel.

Judas, in the mean time, [illegible] the walls of the city, and fortified them with strong [illegible] to keep off the enemy, settling a garrison in Bethsura, and putting the place in a state and posture of defence.

The neighbouring nations were so [illegible] at the growing power and confidence of the Jews, that they set their instruments at work by [illegible] and treachery to circumvent them, destroying many of them when off their guard. Judas however used [illegible] means to prevent or disappoint them [illegible]. He fell at this time upon Acrabatene, where he slew [illegible] of the [illegible] the posterity of Esau, making [illegible] great booty. He [illegible] of Baan, [illegible] their [illegible], in the [illegible] were [illegible] and [illegible] and [illegible] [illegible] took the places by assault, killed [illegible], and [illegible] his [illegible] [illegible]. [illegible] Ammonites [illegible]. These [illegible] overcome, [illegible] carried away the wives and children [illegible] captive, and, after [illegible] the city [illegible], he returned to Judea. [illegible] [illegible] heard of his return, that [illegible] [illegible] [illegible] [illegible] together at [illegible] [illegible] [illegible] the [illegible] Jews, who, [illegible] [illegible] [illegible] the [illegible] [illegible] Judas [illegible] [illegible] a design to [illegible] [illegible] expected [illegible]. While Judas was [illegible], [illegible] several messengers came from G[illegible] [illegible] complaint [illegible] Ptolemais, Tyre, and Sidon, and other [illegible] were [illegible] confederacy against [illegible].

CHAP. II.

[illegible] of S[illegible], [illegible] Con[illegible] [illegible] [illegible] the [illegible] [illegible] [illegible] [illegible] [illegible]

To [illegible] the [illegible] of relieving [illegible] [illegible] [illegible] places, [illegible] [illegible] the Jews [illegible] [illegible], to Galaad, [illegible] [illegible] [illegible] command of [illegible] [illegible] [illegible] [illegible], with orders to [illegible] [illegible] [illegible] [illegible] [illegible], [illegible] Galilee, [illegible] [illegible] [illegible] of Ptolemais, [illegible] Sidon, [illegible] [illegible] [illegible] his army [illegible] [illegible] [illegible] captive, [illegible] returned [illegible] [illegible] [illegible].

At the same time Judas and his brother Jonathan, after three days [illegible] Jordan, in the [illegible], were [illegible] [illegible] [illegible] the [illegible] intelligence of the extreme [illegible] their friends and [illegible], who were [illegible] the towns and cities of G[illegible], [illegible] [illegible] to suffer, with all possible [illegible] to their [illegible]. [illegible] [illegible] of Bosor, [illegible] to the [illegible] their [illegible] the city to the ground. [illegible] [illegible], Judas [illegible] [illegible] the Jews were [illegible] [illegible] with them in [illegible] [illegible] [illegible] [illegible], whereupon [illegible] [illegible] [illegible] [illegible] for the [illegible] of their [illegible], [illegible] [illegible] changed [illegible] [illegible] army of Timotheus [illegible] that Judas [illegible] [illegible] of this action [illegible] [illegible] [illegible] [illegible] [illegible] they [illegible] took such [illegible] the very [illegible], that they [illegible] [illegible]. But [illegible] [illegible] them, [illegible] [illegible] them [illegible] the pursuit. [illegible] [illegible] they took [illegible] town of the [illegible], called Ma[illegible], [illegible] the walls to [illegible], [illegible] [illegible] the city by fire. [illegible] [illegible] over [illegible] Casphon, Bosor, and other places in [illegible] country.

Soon [illegible] this [illegible] [illegible] formed [illegible] [illegible] amongst their [illegible], [illegible] of [illegible]. They crossed the river, and [illegible] Raphon, where he exhorted his people to [illegible], [illegible] all events [illegible] the Jews from crossing [illegible] [illegible] [illegible] [illegible] [illegible] [illegible]. When Judas understood that Timotheus was prepared [illegible] [illegible] [illegible], [illegible] [illegible] army, gave the onset, put the enemy to the rout upon the first encounter, killed those that resisted, and forced the rest, who casting away their arms betook themselves to a precipitate flight. Some of them, for sanctuary, fled to the temple of Carnaim, hoping that the place might protect them, but Judas took the town by force, burnt the temple, and destroyed the inhabitants by fire and sword.

Having surmounted these difficulties, he gathered together all the Jews that were in the country of Galaad, with their wives, children, and all the substance that belonged to them, in order to [illegible] them to Judæa. The city of Ephron, lying so exactly in his way, that there was no passing it, without going a considerable space round, he sent a friendly message to the inhabitants for permission to pass with his army through the town. But the gates being shut, and the avenues cut off [illegible], in plain [illegible] a [illegible] passage [illegible] upon this Judas ordered his men, and put them in a posture for an attack upon the town, [illegible] day and night, [illegible] himself master of it, and [illegible] putting all the males that were found in it to the sword. After passing the river Jordan, they advanced to a great plain near Bethsan, called, by the Greeks, Scythopolis, and from thence returned to Judæa, the people rejoicing on their way, [illegible] hymns and triumphal songs, and offering sacrifices of thanksgiving for the safety of the army, as they had not lost [illegible] one Jew in all these encounters.

When Judas, and his brother Jonathan, arrived at Jerusalem, they received a very disagreeable piece of intelligence which arose from the misconduct of Joseph and Azarias, who were left in command in the absence of Simon, that was sent into Galilee against the people of Ptolemais. Hearing of the successes of Judas in Galaad, these commanders, animated thereby, contrary to orders given, in a fit of emulation, formed an ill-projected expedition against Jamnia, but Gorgias, who commanded in that quarter for the king of Syria, and who had under him a very considerable army, attacked them so forcibly, that their troops were thrown into the utmost disorder, two thousand were slain on the spot, and the rest pushed to the very borders of Judæa. This calamity was in consequence of their disobeying the orders of their general, who had privately enjoined them not to engage the enemy upon any terms till his return. The result proved the propriety of the instructions given, from which if they had not erred, Judas from his great [illegible], knew they would [illegible].

The valiant brothers prosecuted the war against the Idumæans with the utmost vigour, annoying them in every part. They took Hebron by force, demolished its fortifications, laid the enemy's country waste, then proceeded to Marissa, and thence to Azotus, both of which they overcame and plundered, and, loaded with the honours and spoils of victory, returned triumphant to Jerusalem.

CHAP. XIII.

Antiochus Epiphanes dies in great torture of body and mind, acknowledging the justice of his punishment.

ANTIOCHUS, in his progress through the upper parts of Persia, hearing there was a very opulent city called Elymais, with a most magnificent temple in it dedicated to Diana, in which were deposited divers valuable donations, and the very shields and breast-plates of Alexander the Great, was tempted thereby to lay siege to it; but the inhabitants, regardless of his power or design, made a noble resistance, and frustrated his towering expectation; nor did they merely keep him from the wall, but pursued him so closely on his retreat, that they cut off great part of the rear, and drove him before them like a fugitive for protection into Babylon. While he was fretting at this disappointment, tidings arrived of the defeat of his other troops, to whom he had committed the conduct of the war with the Jews, and of the daily increase of their number and power. At length one calamity following another, brought on him

such an insupportable anguish of mind, as was attended with a most acute and excruciating bodily distemper, till, finding his dissolution approaching, he called his friends around him, and told them the cause and quality of it. "I am thus justly, though severely, punished (said he) for the miseries I brought on the Jewish nation, for the sacrilegious rifling and prophaning of their temple, and for a heinous contempt of the Almighty God." With these words expired the wicked and cruel Antiochus Epiphanes.

I cannot, upon this occasion, but take notice of a perversion of Polybius, of Megalopolis, (otherwise an historian of credit), in affirming that this judgment befel Antiochus for his design of rifling the temple of Diana, which was a sacrilege only intended, but never came to act. But if Polybius was of opinion that he deserved this punishment only for the design, he might much more reasonably have imputed it to the sacrilege of which he was actually guilty upon the holy temple of Jerusalem. But let facts speak for themselves. Truth and justice need no comment.

CHAP. XIV.

Antiochus Epiphanes succeeded by his son Antiochus Eupator, and proclaimed by Lysias. Judas invests the citadel of Jerusalem. The armies of the Jews and Syrians engage. Bravery and death of Eleazar. Antiochus violates his faith on the surrender of Bethsura.

ANTIOCHUS, a short time before his death, sent for Philip, a confidential friend, and committed the regency into his hand, delivering up to him, at the same time, the crown, the royal robes and signet, with charge to preserve them for his son Antiochus, then in his minority, with the strictest injunction to attend to his education. The death, however, of Antiochus was no sooner made known to the public, than Lysias proclaimed his son Antiochus king, under the name of Eupator, for Lysias, at that time, had the tuition of the young prince.

The Macedonians, who were at that time garrisoned in the citadel of Jerusalem, together with some Jewish runagates, greatly annoyed the Jews as they went up to worship at the temple, which they could do with ease, as the castle was upon an eminence, and of course commanded it. Judas therefore determined to reduce that fort for the common security of the nation, in their attendance upon their religious ceremonies. To this end he caused machines and engines to be formed for battery, and the casting up of works. While this was in agitation, several of the runagates, with others as nefarious as themselves, repaired to Antiochus, and to him represented the wretched condition to which they were reduced by men of their own tribe, for their obedience to the king's command, in opposition to their own law, and that they were now in imminent danger of falling into the hands of Judas, without immediate relief.

The young prince, inflamed by this artifice, immediately gave orders to his officers to levy all the mercenaries they could raise, over and above the choicest forces they could select from his own subjects. His orders were executed with such alacrity, that, in a short time, they mustered a hundred thousand foot, twenty thousand horse, and thirty two elephants. With this formidable army, under the command of Lysias his general, the king marched out of Antioch, advanced to Idumæa, and thence to Bethsura, a well fortified place, both by nature and art. He sat down before the fort, and, to little effect, spent much time, for the besieged, between sallies and stratagems, found means to burn or frustrate all engines of battery that were brought against it.

Judas, upon the intelligence of the approach of Antiochus, raised the siege from before the citadel, and marched the ready way to meet him, pitching his camp upon the very entrance into the straits of Bethzacharias, about seventy furlongs from the enemy. Antiochus, upon this, quitted the siege of Bethsura, and encamped within a distance of engaging Judas, appointing his army, at earliest dawn, to put themselves upon the march in order of battle; but the place being too narrow for the elephants to pass in front, they marched in a defile, with a thousand foot and five hundred horse upon the guard of every elephant. Each had a kind of tower or castle on the back charged with archers. The rest of the troops mounted the hills on both sides, under the command of such officers as the king could best confide in. From this ascent they gave the attack, and that with so horrid a shout and clamour, that the vallies all rang with the echo; so that, with the hideous outcry, and the dazzling flashes of the golden and brazen bucklers, nothing could be more terrific in appearance and sound. But the gallant Judas stood undismayed by empty pomp and noise, and, when they came to action, received them with such dauntless intrepidity, about six hundred fell upon the first onset. While they were thus engaged, Eleazar, otherwise called Auranes, the brother of Judas, taking notice of one elephant that was caparisoned with richer trappings than the rest, with noble ardour made his way to that beast, supposing that the king himself was mounted upon it. Having hewn down his opponents on each hand, and [illegible] the [illegible] to clear his passage, he crept under the belly of the elephant, smote and slew him, perishing himself under the enormous weight of the beast upon his fall. He died, however, in the glorious prospect of victory, and encompassed with the dead bodies of his slaughtered foes.

Judas, finding himself greatly overpowered by numbers, drew off his army to the [illegible] of [illegible] Jerusalem, while Antiochus sent part of his army to sit down before Bethsura, and with the rest under [illegible] proceeded to Jerusalem. The inhabitants of the [illegible] were so [illegible] and [illegible] the appearance of the enemy [illegible] so [illegible] through want of provisions, that they found themselves under a necessity of delivering up the place. This they accordingly did, upon [illegible] most solemnly [illegible], that no violence or molestation whatever should be offered them. But the king [illegible] his faith no farther than the sparing of their lives, for they were all turned naked out of the town, and a garrison of his own was placed in their stead. The [illegible] it must be recorded to their honour, made a most obstinate resistance, as all the efforts of their machines and engines were still eluded by counterworkings and stratagems. Their greatest distress was want of bread, for having already expended their last year's store, and this [illegible] happening to fall upon the seventh year, in which by the Jewish law, they could neither plow or sow, great numbers of the Jews went out of the town purely for want of provisions, insomuch that there was not a competent number to defend the place.

The king, and his general Lysias, receiving intelligence at this time, that Philip was endeavouring to obtain the government, and was marching towards them at the head of an army out of Persia, they came to a private determination to quit the siege, and advance immediately against him. To effect this purpose, without the knowledge even of the first officers in command, the king recommended to Lysias, to sound the opinion and disposition of the soldiers in general, respecting the continuance of the siege, representing the strength of the place, the dearth of provision, and the indispensible necessity of the king's departure, and, from these considerations, inferring the expediency of coming to some terms, and particularly the condition of allowing them the free exercise of their particular religion, laws and customs, which being granted as the grand cause of all their rebellions, the king might return whenever he pleased. This Lysias had in charge to communicate to the army, and the soldiers in general approved of the proposal.

CHAP XV

Antiochus Eupator violates the league he made with the Jews. Onias the high-priest put to death. Philip vanquished by Antiochus.

MATTERS being thus concerted, Antiochus sent an herald to Judas, with an offer of peace, and free exercise of their religion and laws, which being accepted, they left the temple, and the accommodation between them was ratified by oath. But when Antiochus, upon taking possession of it, found the strength of the fortifications belonging to the temple, without any regard to his oath, he ordered the soldiers to demolish the walls, and lay them level with the ground. This being accordingly executed, he returned to Antioch, taking with him Onias, otherwise called Menelaus. [illegible] to the king the absolute necessity of [illegible] if he would wish to conduce to the quiet of the Jews [illegible] his own peace, because it was [illegible] the [illegible] Menelaus that his [illegible] the Jews to the transgressions of the religion and laws of their [illegible] the news of course, the author and promoter of the evils that had befallen him. [illegible] Lysias, the king sent Menelaus to [illegible] he caused him to be put to death, after [illegible] pontificate during the space of ten years. [illegible] Menelaus, was an infamous character, who, to [illegible] office of the high-priest [illegible] to himself, had [illegible] general defection amongst the Jews from the religion and laws of their country. He was succeeded by [illegible], who was also called Jacimus, a man as [illegible] as his predecessor.

When Antiochus found that Philip had usurped the government, he immediately attacked him with [illegible] forces, and, in a short time totally routed his army, [illegible] great numbers of his men, took him prisoner, and ordered him to be put to death. [illegible] Onias being left an infant on the death of [illegible] finding that the king had conferred [illegible] at the instance of Lysias [illegible] no relation to the sacerdotal family, [illegible] application to Ptolemy, king of Egypt, [illegible] he was most graciously received, as well as by his queen Cleopatra, who bestowed on him a place of consideration [illegible] Heliopolis, where he erected a temple after the model of that at Jerusalem.

CHAP XVI

Demetrius gains the crown of Syria, and orders Antiochus Eupator and Lysias to be put to death. On the complaint of Alcimus, sends an army against the Jews. Conduct of Alcimus.

ABOUT this time Demetrius the son of Seleucus having fled from Rome, possessed himself of Tripolis, a city in Syria, took the crown upon him, and, with as many mercenaries as he could gather together, invaded the country, where he was received by the people with open arms. As a further [illegible] of their affection to his interest, they seized on the persons of Antiochus and Lysias, and brought them in custody prisoners to him, upon which Demetrius commanded them both to be put to death. Antiochus having reigned over Syria two years. He had in his party a great number of those Jews, who had been banished for notorious crimes, with Alcimus the high-priest, at the head of them. These all joined in a common accusation against the whole people of the Jews, but more especially against Judas Maccabaeus [illegible] whom they charged not only with the [illegible] of as many of the king's friends as fell into their hands, but the very ejection of themselves out of the country. They therefore made it their request to Demetrius, that he would send certain particular persons, in whom he could confide, to examine into the truth of what they had alledged against Judas and his adherents.

In consequence of this representation, Demetrius, who, from the situation of Alcimus, was readily induced to give credit to all he said, was so exasperated, that he immediately ordered Bacchides, a very powerful man, and governor of Mesopotamia, to march with an army into Judea, and having confirmed Alcimus in the priesthood, joined him in the same commission against the Jews. With this army Bacchides left Antioch, and marched directly into Judea, where he gave Judas and his brethren a solemn invitation to come to a better understanding with him; but the design was under colour of a friendly and peaceable [illegible] to draw them into a [illegible] to surprise them. Judas, however, upon his coming, [illegible] an army, and not [illegible] of an enemy, [illegible], kept upon his guard, without giving any credit to his pretensions. [illegible] to some [illegible] people [illegible] over to him [illegible] the command [illegible] would do them no [illegible], especially, as [illegible] solemn oath [illegible] purpose, [illegible] no sooner [illegible] them [illegible] to death, [illegible] the [illegible] period [illegible]

[illegible], [illegible] Jerusalem, and [illegible] to [illegible] [illegible] was [illegible] to the [illegible], he [illegible] dence, to [illegible] part of his army [illegible] with the [illegible] Demetrius [illegible]

[illegible] of Alcimus [illegible] God [illegible] to [illegible] the people's [illegible] behaviour [illegible] the mind [illegible] [illegible] Jews [illegible] [illegible] to Judas, [illegible]

[illegible] Judas [illegible] his brethren [illegible] the country [illegible] Demetrius [illegible] [illegible] the [illegible] [illegible] [illegible] the country.

CHAP. XVII.

[illegible] Romans.

IN consequence of [illegible] Alcimus, to [illegible] the growing power and influence of Judas, Demetrius became apprehensive of the danger that might result therefrom, if not checked in time. To effect this desirable purpose, he sent [illegible] of the Jews, [illegible] command of Nicanor, one of the principal men of his court, with strict orders to [illegible] the whole nation, and to [illegible] the office of high-priest. Nicanor, [illegible] Antioch, and set out for Jerusalem, [illegible] himself preserve [illegible] under [illegible] intentions. [illegible] to Judas with this message: "Why should we [illegible] the uncertain [illegible] war, when we may adjust [illegible]? [illegible] to [illegible] upon [illegible] [illegible] the [illegible] [illegible] the knowledge [illegible] good [illegible] nation of the Jews."

This [illegible] on Judas and his [illegible] the design [illegible] the Jews, [illegible] Nicanor [illegible] Judas, [illegible] Nicanor, the latter [illegible] to seize Judas; but the plot being discovered in time, he [illegible] his escape to his own people. After this detection of this treachery, no [illegible] [illegible] open hostility, without any [illegible] extremity. The armies [illegible] [illegible] Judas [illegible] was worsted, and obliged to [illegible] retreat to the citadel of Jerusalem.

[illegible] with this success, Nicanor [illegible] with [illegible] Judas. It happened on a certain occasion, as Nicanor was passing by the temple, that [illegible] several of the elders and priests [illegible] sacrifices they had with them, and [illegible] to offer them up for the [illegible] Nicanor, in the [illegible] with blasphemous revilings, [illegible] deliver up Judas to him [illegible] the city. [illegible] and the priests [illegible] that they addressed themselves to the [illegible] priests and [illegible] to protect the [illegible] own immediate presence, and [illegible] who belonged to it, against the outrages of the enemy.

Nicanor, [illegible] no probability of [illegible] Judas [illegible] near a [illegible] called [illegible], where he was joined [illegible] of [illegible], however, [illegible] Judas, who, [illegible] his army [illegible] [illegible] called Adasa, [illegible] the enemy. [illegible] his troops, he told [illegible] the city [illegible] forget [illegible] of God, [illegible] multitudes, [illegible] [illegible] were [illegible] would [illegible] "[illegible] them therefore, [illegible] the [illegible] to deliver."

The Jews, thus encouraged by their leader, attacked [illegible] the utmost intrepidity [illegible] the [illegible] on both sides [illegible] of Judas; for Nicanor [illegible] of his troops, the rest [illegible] that they immediately threw down [illegible] Judas [illegible] of his [illegible] among the fugitives, to whom he [illegible] his victory by sound of trumpet [illegible] all the cities and towns through which he passed, the consequence of which was, that the country people gathered together from all parts, and such of the enemy that fell in their way, [illegible] escape, they put to death, [illegible], by means of [illegible] not a single person of the [illegible] to carry [illegible] [illegible] It was upon the thirteenth day of the [illegible] which the Jews call Adar, and the Macedonians Dystrus, [illegible] commemoration of this [illegible] of Providence in our deliverance, we celebrate [illegible] this very day. The Jews [illegible] had a short respite from [illegible] permanent peace.

At [illegible] in contemplation to pull down the old wall of the sanctuary, and demolish the works of the ancient prophets, but in the very instant of [illegible] execution [illegible] he was smitten with [illegible] [illegible] that he fell [illegible] on the ground, where he lay [illegible] then [illegible] after he had held the pontificate [illegible] Upon the [illegible] the [illegible] people [illegible] Judas to succeed him in his office, when [illegible] the great fame and power of the Romans, in conquering the Gauls, Spaniards, [illegible], and Carthaginians, together with the king Perseus, Philip [illegible] Antiochus, he [illegible] was desirous of forming an alliance with them, in hopes thereby of putting [illegible] to [illegible] the oppression of the Syrians. Judas accordingly dispatched two of his most intimate friends [illegible] [illegible] Jason and Eupolemus, whom he knew were capable of executing such [illegible], to Rome, to request of the senate that the Jews might be admitted as their allies, and that a letter might be written to Demetrius, requiring him to desist from every farther molestation of them. This proposal proved agreeable to the senate, who immediately drew up articles of treaty, the original of which they kept, and sent a copy of them to Jerusalem, which was highly approved by Judas. The purport of the articles was "That no people subject to the Romans, should "make war on the Jews, or supply their enemies with "money, shipping, corn, &c. and that the Jews should "be held to the same, in case the Romans should be at-"tacked. That if the Jews demanded any future altera-"tion of the agreement, the consent of the whole people "should be necessary to ratify it." This was the first alliance that was formed between the Jews and the Romans. This decree of the [illegible] was written by Eupolemus, the son of John, and Jason the son of Eleazar, Judas the high-priest, and his brother Simon, general of the army.

CHAP. XVIII.

The extraordinary valour of Judas and his brethren.

IN the mean time Demetrius having received an account of the defeat and death of Nicanor, sent Bacchides again into Judea, at the head of a very numerous army, to give battle to Judas, and with orders, if possible, to bring him to Antioch [illegible] or alive. The general immediately set out to execute the king's command, and the first place at which he encamped was Arbela, a town in Galilee, where he forced many Jews from the caves to which they had retreated, and cruelly put them to death. From thence he marched towards Jerusalem, and upon intelligence that Judas and his people were at Bethleem, he posted thither immediately with twenty thousand foot, and two thousand horse to encounter him. Judas had no more than three thousand to oppose him, and these were so terrified at the strength and number of the enemy, that the greatest part deserted, so that he had not above eight hundred left.

Notwithstanding Judas was thus distressed for want of men, and had not an opportunity of recruiting his forces, yet he determined to hazard a battle, and therefore used the most powerful arguments he was master of, to prevail on the few he had to stand by him to the utmost extremi-[illegible]. [illegible], however, consulted with him on the impropriety and rashness of attempting to engage so very superior a number, and [illegible] him rather to retreat with caution, and put off his design till he could augment his forces. To this he replied, "It never shall be said of "me that I turned my back upon an enemy. If it be the "will of God that we now [illegible], let his will be done; "but let us not by an ignominious flight, destroy all the "credit of a life of glory." This speech so animated the soldiers that they unanimously resolved to stand the combat, and every necessary preparation was made for opposing the enemy.

CHAP. XIX.

Judas falls in battle, after [illegible] great [illegible] prowess.

THE army of Bacchides was disposed of in the following manner. The front was composed of light armed men, and supported by a large body of Macedonians, while there were two wings of horse, the right being commanded by Bacchides himself. In this order of battle they advanced towards the army of Judas, which they no sooner approached than they sounded a charge, gave a loud shout, and began the attack. The forces of Judas sustained the shock with great intrepidity, and the battle continued desperate for some time, when Judas, seeing Bacchides with his right wing, pressing hard on his men, relieved them with a band of courageous youths, who broke the right wing of Bacchides, and pursued them as far as Aza; but not having sufficient forces to keep the left wing in play, during his absence, he was followed, and closely surrounded by the enemy. The action was very obstinate, and the [illegible] sold their lives at a dear rate. Their general did all that a gallant man could do, till at length, being overpowered with numbers, he was, with the greatest part of his men, slain, and the rest intimidated by the loss of their leader, betook themselves to flight. Thus fell the great Judas Maccabæus, dying as he lived, a zealous asserter of the religion and laws of his country. He was pious, just, and valiant, and equally respectable in the various characters he filled with so much honour and dignity to himself, as well as glory and advantage to the Jewish nation.

His two brothers, Simon and Jonathan, having permission of Bacchides to remove his body, it was conveyed to Modin, and there interred in the sepulchre of his ancestors, with all the funeral honours due to the memory of so brave and excellent a commander. We shall only add, that he acquired immortal fame by the rescue of his friends out of the hands of the Macedonians, and by his three years administration in the office of high-priest.

END OF THE TWELFTH BOOK.

FLAVIUS JOSEPHUS

ON THE

ANTIQUITIES

OF THE

JEWS.

BOOK XIII

[INCLUDING A PERIOD OF ABOUT NINETY-FOUR YEARS.]

CHAP. I.

Implacable hatred of the revolted Jews towards their countrymen. Jonathan succeeds to the government after Judas, and, together with his brother Simon, carries on the war against Bacchides.

THE means by which the Jews were delivered from their slavery under the Macedonians, and the exploits and character of their great patriot and leader, Judas, who, after a life devoted to his country's service nobly fell in a contest for the vindication of its liberties and laws, have been fully set forth in the foregoing book.

This illustrious person was no sooner taken off, than the whole party of profligate apostate Jews, contrary to the dictates of conscience, faith, and honour, abandoned the religion, laws, and customs of their nation, resumed their former animosities, and, at the instance and with the assistance, of Bacchides, treated all the friends and adherents of the Maccabees, wherever they found them, with the greatest barbarity. At this time there happened to be a general famine throughout the land of Judæa which aggravated other calamities, insomuch, that, thro' distress for want of bread, on the one hand, and the difficulty of defending themselves against their enemies, on the other, many of the Jews were, in a manner, compelled to adhere to the faction of the Macedonians. At this juncture Bacchides sends a summons to all the apostate Jews, who were gone over to strange gods, and committed the care of the government principally into their hands, so that they made it their business to seize all the friends and late partizans of Judas, and deliver them up to the Syrian general, to be tortured at his pleasure. In short, the Jews were never so deplorably distressed since the Babylonish captivity, as at this period; insomuch that the late adherents to Judas joined in a request of Jonathan, not only to follow his brother's example, who had so freely sacrificed his life for the liberties of his country, but to take upon himself the command also, as the whole nation was under such desperate circumstances, that, without a leader to assist them in opposing their enemies, they must all be inevitably lost. Jonathan's answer was, he was willing to do or suffer any thing for the public welfare, upon which he was elected general of the Jewish army by the unanimous voice of the people.

Bacchides, hearing of this election, and reflecting that Jonathan was not less likely to give trouble to the king, and to the Macedonians, than his brother Judas, set about concerting measures to take him off by stratagem. But Jonathan, having intelligence of his design, collected what force he could, and, accompanied by his brother Simon, withdrew immediately into a neighbouring desert, and pitched his tent by the pool of Asphar. Bacchides, imagining this retreat into the desert to be no other than a direct flight, immediately advanced towards them with his whole force, and, encamping beyond Jordan, made choice of that place for a rendezvous. When Jonathan heard of this motion, he sent his brother John (otherwise Gaddis) to the Arabian Nabathites, being in friendship with him, for leave to deposit their baggage in their custody, till the battle with Bacchides should be decided. But as John was upon the way, the sons of Amaræus made a sally out of the city of Medaba upon the convoy, took all the carriages, with whatever else they had about them, and killed John upon the spot, with all his people. But his brothers soon had their revenge, as will appear in the sequel.

Bacchides, having intelligence that Jonathan had encamped in the fenny grounds, near the river Jordan, immediately marched after him, and having made himself master of the pass that led to their encampment, fixed on the sabbath-day for the attack, in confidence of their superstitious reverence for the law respecting that day, that he should not meet with the least resistance. In this, however, he found himself mistaken, for Jonathan, after reminding his men of the determination that was made in cases of necessity like the present, encouraged them to dispute the ground, which after a short and fervent prayer [illegible] for the divine aid, they accordingly did, till they slew great numbers of the [illegible] on the spot. During the encounter, Bacchides pressed furiously upon the person of Jonathan, who at the same time aimed a stroke at him; but the other diverting it, Jonathan and his party, took to the river, and the enemy declining to follow them, they got safe to the other side, without the loss of a single man. The Syrian general withdrew to the citadel of Jerusalem, with the loss of near two thousand of his men. He afterwards fortified several strong places in Judæa that had been demolished before, as Jericho, [illegible] [illegible], Bethel, [illegible], Pharathon, [illegible] and [illegible]. These places he strengthened with walls [illegible], and with strong garrisons, to be ready for excursions to fall upon the Jews. But especial care was taken above all the rest to render the citadel of Jerusalem [illegible], in which place the sons of the principal Jews were [illegible] as hostages.

About this time the two brothers received intelligence, that there was a wedding to be celebrated between one of the [illegible] of Amaræus and the daughter of [illegible] Arabian, that the [illegible] of Amaræus were to be [illegible] ceremony, and the bride to be conducted, [illegible] pomp, from the city of Gabatha. Jonathan and Simon, [illegible] this the best opportunity for avenging the death of their brother, [illegible] towards Medaba, and [illegible] among the mountains [illegible] their enemies. Upon the coming up of the bridegroom with the bride, and a long train of their friends, as is usual in such cases, the [illegible] cut them all off without exception, together with their wives [illegible] and friends to the number of four hundred, carried away [illegible] and the [illegible] to the [illegible] of [illegible]. After this [illegible] returned to [illegible] [illegible].

[illegible] Bacchides [illegible] [illegible] [illegible] of two years those Jews [illegible] their [illegible] religion [illegible], but the [illegible] present [illegible] iniquity [illegible] [illegible] by proxies, that Bacchides might be ordered to [illegible] upon Jonathan [illegible] reduce him [illegible] his power, which [illegible] by [illegible] surprizing him [illegible] one night.

The king [illegible] ordered Bacchides [illegible] into Judæa upon this commission, [illegible] letters [illegible] his friends in [illegible] the country, to give their assistance towards the [illegible] of Jonathan. They in consequence, [illegible] [illegible], but, [illegible] [illegible] [illegible] enough the [illegible] of the Jewish general, the Syrian commander [illegible] [illegible] imputed the whole [illegible] to the [illegible] of the [illegible] Jews, which he said had [illegible] [illegible] ordered [illegible] of their [illegible] to be put to death. Jonathan and his brother [illegible] [illegible] had retired [illegible] [illegible] village called Bethalaga, [illegible] to make that [illegible] place of retreat on [illegible] occasions.

Bacchides, having received intelligence of this [illegible], marched [illegible] the forces [illegible] able to [illegible] upon the [illegible] his own troops with an auxiliary [illegible] of the Jews. He opened his [illegible] against the place, and, for some days, carried on his operations. Jonathan, on the other side, making a very stout resistance. While matters were in this posture, he left the defence of the place to his brother Simon, and, with such a body of men as he was able to [illegible] the [illegible] [illegible] Bacchides [illegible] [illegible] killed many of his men, [illegible] [illegible] [illegible] his brother [illegible] [illegible] [illegible] cut off [illegible] [illegible] their [illegible] [illegible] [illegible]

at his assault upon his front and rear, [illegible] [illegible] of an attempt of which he thought [illegible] that it deranged his affairs in the greatest degree. He [illegible], however, the whole of his disappointment to the Jews [illegible] [illegible], who had prevailed with the king to send him upon this expedition. His main business, it [illegible] to deliberate on the best means of raising the siege, and drawing off the army, that he might thereby save his men, and retire without loss of honour to his master or himself.

CHAP. II.

The Syrian and Jewish generals adjust matters [illegible]

WHILE Bacchides was deliberating in what manner [illegible] [illegible] proceed, Jonathan [illegible] [illegible] [illegible] [illegible] of the [illegible] [illegible] and therefore sent [illegible] [illegible] [illegible] [illegible] of friendship, or [illegible] of the respective prisoners. Bacchides found in this proposal so favourable an opportunity of abandoning the siege without disgrace, that he immediately acceded, and [illegible] [illegible] [illegible], [illegible] a mutual exchange of oaths to deliver up and restore all prisoners on both sides, and [illegible] [illegible] from all acts of hostility against each other. This [illegible] been [illegible], Bacchides returned to the king at Antioch, and so strictly did he observe the treaty [illegible] Jonathan, that he never returned [illegible] to Judæa. The war being thus happily [illegible] [illegible] [illegible] [illegible] [illegible] [illegible] [illegible] [illegible] in Machmas, where he [illegible] his [illegible] attention to the concerns of [illegible] and [illegible] administration [illegible] [illegible]. He [illegible] [illegible] [illegible] [illegible] from the [illegible] and [illegible] of the [illegible] [illegible] [illegible] [illegible] [illegible] [illegible] [illegible] [illegible] [illegible] [illegible]

CHAP. III.

[illegible] between Alexander, [illegible] [illegible] [illegible] and Demetrius.

SOON after these transactions Alexander the son of Antiochus [illegible] his [illegible], [illegible] [illegible] to the [illegible] and took possession of Ptolemais, through the connivance of the [illegible] regard [illegible] [illegible] [illegible] [illegible] [illegible] [illegible] [illegible] [illegible] [illegible] However, [illegible] alarmed [illegible] [illegible] of [illegible] [illegible] [illegible] [illegible] his troops with all [illegible] expedition, [illegible] [illegible] [illegible] [illegible]

CHAP. IV.

Demetrius [illegible] [illegible] [illegible] [illegible] [illegible] [illegible] [illegible] [illegible] [illegible]

DEMETRIUS [illegible] [illegible] [illegible] more of [illegible] [illegible], though [illegible] to [illegible] [illegible] [illegible] [illegible] [illegible] [illegible] [illegible] between them. [illegible] purport of the [illegible] [illegible] [illegible] [illegible] [illegible] [illegible] that the hostages [illegible] [illegible] [illegible] the [illegible] prisoners [illegible] castle. Upon the [illegible] of the letter vesting him with this power, Jonathan left Machmas, and repaired to Jerusalem, where he publicly read the contents of the king's letter to the garrison. [illegible] [illegible] [illegible] [illegible] [illegible] [illegible] [illegible] [illegible] [illegible] [illegible] [illegible] [illegible], however, proceeded [illegible] [illegible] [illegible] to the hostages [illegible] [illegible] [illegible] appointed to [illegible] [illegible] [illegible] [illegible] [illegible] [illegible] [illegible] [illegible] [illegible] [illegible] [illegible] [illegible] [illegible] [illegible] [illegible] [illegible] [illegible] [illegible] been [illegible] during the reign of [illegible] Epiphanes. The [illegible] who were [illegible] up and down [illegible] garrisons, quitted their station upon this [illegible] of affairs [illegible], and went to Antioch, but [illegible] in the citadel of Jerusalem, being [illegible] Jewish deserters, remained the [illegible] apprehension of being taken upon removal, and suffering condign punishment.

CHAP. V.

Alexander Balas [illegible] friendship of Jonathan, whom he [illegible] high-priest. [illegible] between Alexander and Demetrius. [illegible] of Demetrius.

In the mean time Alexander, who was no stranger to the character of Jonathan, or to his exertions against the Macedonians, or to the [illegible] that had been offered him by Demetrius [illegible], assembled his friends, and represented to them the advantages that would [illegible] of an alliance with a person of such eminent valour, and a mortal enemy to Demetrius from the highest provocations imaginable. [illegible] resolved [illegible] with him [illegible], a letter was [illegible], dispatched to Jonathan to the following purport.

"Alexander, the king, to Jonathan, his brother, greeting.

"Having been informed of your character, [illegible] honour, [illegible], and courage, and deeming you every way worthy [illegible], we have dispatched ambassadors to offer you our friendship and alliance, and [illegible] By these presents [illegible] we constitute and ordain the high-priest [illegible] of the Jews, and rank thee in the number of the king's friends. We likewise present thee with a crown of gold, and a purple robe, [illegible] for this instance of our respect [illegible]."

Jonathan immediately, on the receipt of this message, put on his sacerdotal robe, it being the day of the feast of tabernacles. This was four years after the death of his brother Judas, the office of high-priest having been so long vacant. He then applied himself to the levying of troops, and making [illegible] of arms. Demetrius was, [illegible] sensible of the error [illegible] in neglecting the opportunity of anticipating his competitor for an alliance with Jonathan. Nevertheless, he exerted his utmost to carry the point, as will appear from the following letter:

"Demetrius, the king, to Jonathan and the Jewish people, greeting.

"As we have already entered into a treaty of alliance with you, we would [illegible] to [illegible] uninterrupted [illegible]. Wherefore it is our pleasure that you [illegible] remitted, and we release all the taxes formerly paid to our predecessors, or ourselves, (exclusive of the salt and crown taxes, with the thirds of [illegible] corn and fruits), and these duties we give up for all future times, as well as the poll-tax on the inhabitants, through Judea, and the three governments of Galilee, Samaria, and Perea. It is our pleasure likewise that Jerusalem and its dependencies be exempted from all tenths and tributes, [illegible], and have their [illegible] of a [illegible]. Let the citadel be delivered to Jonathan the high-priest, with permission to place in it a garrison of such of his friends as he may think proper. We [illegible] command, that, immediately on receipt hereof, [illegible] be given to all Jewish prisoners, in every part of our dominions, without [illegible] imposed even on their cattle: that their sabbaths and solemn festivals, and three days preceding each, shall be deemed days of freedom to the Jews, throughout our dominions, that they [illegible] peace, [illegible] unmolested. Thirty thousand Jews, if so many should be willing,

"may bear arms in our service, and receive the same pay as our own troops; that they be entrusted in garrisons, and near our person, and that our royal family [illegible] the better [illegible] of them as domestics. In Jerusalem and the three dependent provinces, the Jews shall freely [illegible] their own laws, but the high-priest must take care that the temple of Jerusalem be the only one in which the Jews worship. Fifteen thousand drachms of silver [illegible] annually towards the expence of their sacrifices, and we remit the ten thousand drachms formerly paid to the predecessors by the priests and officers attending the service of the temple. We further order that all debtors repairing to the temple of Jerusalem, or the liberties thereof, on account of debt, shall remain unmolested, both in person and property. We also permit and require that the temple be repaired, that fortifications be [illegible], and that such strong places as the Jews think proper to fortify shall have garrisons stationed in them, and all this shall be done at our own expence."

At this critical juncture Alexander levied a mighty army, partly from his own mercenaries, and partly from those that went to him from Demetrius [illegible], and [illegible] them against the enemy. At length they came to action, and the right wing of Alexander's forces were pressed hard by the left of Demetrius, who pushed their advantage [illegible] to the plundering of the camp; but Alexander forced the opposite wing, where Demetrius fought in person, [illegible] was totally routed. Demetrius, however, atchieved wonders, killing and pursuing his enemies, and defending himself for a considerable time, till at length his horse plunging into a bog, and he being oppressed with numbers, he was obliged to yield, though not till his body was covered with darts and arrows. Thus died Demetrius, king of Syria, after having enjoyed the sovereignty of that empire for the space of about eleven years.

CHAP. VI.

[illegible] between Onias and Ptolemy Philometor. The [illegible] permission to build a temple in Egypt, [illegible] that of Jerusalem. [illegible] a dispute between the Samaritans and Jews, which is referred to the king, who [illegible] the latter.

Onias, the son of Onias the high-priest, lived in a kind of exile from his own country, with Ptolemy Philometor at Alexandria. This Onias, finding Judea [illegible] ravaged by the Macedonians, and their kings, [illegible] from an ambition to acquire immortal fame, resolved to try if he could obtain leave from king Ptolemy, and his queen Cleopatra, to build another temple in Egypt, after the plan and model of that in Jerusalem, and to supply it with priests and Levites of his own family. This thought was suggested to him by a prediction of the prophet Isaiah, of at least six hundred years before, presaging that, in time to come, there should be a temple erected in Egypt to the honour of the great God, and that it should be the work of a Jew. Onias was so possessed with the impulse of this revelation that he wrote a letter to Ptolemy and Cleopatra to the following effect:

"At the time when I had the honour to serve you in the field, I passed through several countries, and observed that in the provinces of Cœlo-Syria, Phœnicia, and Leontopolis, in the land of Heliopolis, and several other places, that the Jews had no uniformity in their temples, and therefore could not agree among themselves about it. Such is the case with respect to the Egyptians, by reason of the multitude and variety of their temples, and the diversity of the forms of religion. Having discovered a certain place near the castle of Bubastis, upon the plain, where there is great store of materials for building at hand, and numbers of beasts ready for sacrifice, it is my humble request that you will grant me your royal licence and authority to "demolish a ruinous temple there, that was never consecrated to any deity, and, in its place, to erect another after the model of that of Jerusalem, with a dedication of it To the most High God, upon condition that prayers be constantly offered there for the safety and prosperity of your royal person, and family, to the end that all the Jews in your dominions may by this means, be more united among themselves, and so the more enabled to render you service. This is what the prophet Isaiah has foretold, that God would have an holy place in Egypt, together with several particulars relative to that subject."

The pious disposition of the king and queen will appear sufficiently evident by their answer to this petition of Onias, wherein they exculpate themselves from any concern in the impious violation of the law, and transfer the whole blame to Onias, in the following terms:

"King Ptolemy and queen Cleopatra to Onias, send greeting.

"We have read and duly considered your petition, wherein you request our royal licence and authority to purify an old ruinous temple at Leontopolis, near Bubastes, upon the plain, within the jurisdiction of Heliopolis. We cannot but express our wonder, that you should conceive it pleasing to God to have a temple erected in a place so unclean, and haunted with such a variety of detestable animals. But since you refer yourself for justification to the predictions of the prophet Isaiah, we do hereby grant you full permission, so far as in us lies, to execute your design, provided it be done without violating the Divine law."

Onias had no sooner obtained this permission, than he [illegible] applied himself to the building of the temple, and the altar, according to the model of that at Jerusalem, though much inferior to it in point of size and magnificence. As the dimensions of this edifice, and the holy vessels appertaining to it, are particularly described in my seventh book of the history of the wars of the Jews, I shall pass them over in this place, and only say that Onias, having completed his design, did not want priests and Levites of his own opinion and persuasion, to officiate in the ceremonies of the temple.

In consequence of this transaction of Onias, there arose a violent contest between the Jews and Samaritans who erected the temple at Gerizim, in the days of Alexander the Great, concerning the form of their temple and manner of worshipping. Both parties appealed to the king to take the matter into his own cognizance, and then pass judgment on the merits of the cause. The point in dispute was this: The Jews insisted that the temple at Jerusalem was the only temple extant that was authorized by the laws of Moses. The Samaritans [illegible] contended for the temple at Gerizim. Both parties, as before observed, referred themselves to the arbitration of the king, together with his ministers and friends, desiring that counsel might be heard on both sides, and sentence passed upon the party that should be found guilty. Sabbæus and Theodosius pleaded the cause of the Samaritans, Andronicus, the son of Messalam, that of the Jews, binding themselves on oath on both sides, in the presence of God and the king, to advance nothing in proof of their allegations, but what was strictly conformable with the letter of the law, and desiring that the breach of that oath might be made death to the violator. The king then sat down with his friends and counsellors to try the cause.

The Jews of Alexandria were very apprehensive that their advocate would be incompetent to the business he had undertaken, and took it extremely to heart, to find the sacred authority of the temple at Jerusalem, the most ancient and noble structure and institution in the whole world, brought into question. Upon a debate who should speak first, Sabbæus and Theodosius gave the precedence to Andronicus, who opened the cause, and treated of the sanctity, practice, and venerable antiquity of the temple of Jerusalem, from its very origin, according to the law, setting forth the uninterrupted succession of the priesthood throughout all ages, with the honour and magnificence of the place, as it was celebrated from time to time for the sumptuous and splendid donations of the kings of Asia. He observed in a comparative view, that the temple of Gerizim, then in question, was so obscure in every respect, that little more notice was taken of it than if no such fabric had been erected. By these, and other arguments of the like nature, the king was prevailed upon to give sentence in favour of the temple at Jerusalem, and to adjudge Sabbæus and Theodosius to death, according to the conditions of the proposal. Such was the state of the Jews at Alexandria in the days of Ptolemy Philometor.

CHAP. VII.

Demetrius is succeeded by Alexander, who espouses the daughter of Ptolemy, and confers sudden honours upon Jonathan.

DEMETRIUS being slain in battle, as before related, Alexander took upon him the government of Syria, and wrote to Ptolemy Philometor, desiring his daughter in marriage, and suggesting that it would be neither unreasonable nor dishonourable, after the overthrow of Demetrius, and through Divine favour, the recovery of his kingdom, to receive him into his alliance. Ptolemy received the proposal with the highest complacence, and immediately wrote him back a letter congratulating him on his victories and accession to the throne, promising him his daughter in marriage, and appointing Ptolemais for the place of meeting, where he assured him he would attend with his daughter Cleopatra, and there consummate the nuptials. The king of Egypt, pursuant to this information, repaired with his daughter to the place of appointment, and the marriage was celebrated with the utmost pomp and magnificence, and Alexander received a dowry in gold and silver, worthy the dignity and opulence of the potentate who had given him so convincing a proof of his friendship and esteem, in forming with him an alliance at once so honourable and advantageous.

Jonathan, the high-priest, upon this occasion, came to Ptolemais, where he was received by both kings with the utmost cordiality, and treated with every token of the highest honour and respect. Alexander required him to change his habit, put on a robe of purple, and take his place next to himself upon the throne. He also commanded his principal officers to attend him into the heart of the city, and make proclamation, that no man should presume, on his peril, to complain to accuse him in any respect, or give him molestation. Upon this signal demonstration of the king's esteem and favour, his enemies, who came thither with a view of injuring him by their calumnies, [illegible] thought it prudent to retire, lest they should bring on themselves the mischiefs they designed for him. So great indeed was the respect which Alexander bore to Jonathan, that he was ranked among his most approved friends.

CHAP. VIII.

Extraordinary success of Jonathan. Contest between Demetrius, son of the late king, and Alexander. The former enters into a league of friendship with Jonathan. Death of Alexander and of Ptolemy. Demetrius renders himself independent.

ALEXANDER now thought himself arrived at the summit of happiness, and that he should enjoy a life of uninterrupted tranquillity; but he soon found himself mistaken. A short time after Demetrius, the son of the late king Demetrius, resolving to revenge his father's death, and recover his kingdom, embarked with a body of mercenaries, whom Lasthenes the Cretan had raised for him, and passed with them out of Crete into Cilicia. This expedition alarmed Alexander, who instantly marched from Phœnicia to Antioch, to put his affairs in a posture of security before the arrival of Demetrius. In the mean time Demetrius had gained over to his interest Apollonius, the governor of Cœlo-Syria, who, to oblige Jonathan to quit Alexander's party, and join with Demetris, marched with an army as far as Jamnia [illegible] and thence sent a challenge to Jonathan, desiring him to meet him with his forces [illegible] open field [illegible] and put the issue on their single contest [illegible] boasted also that he was at the head of a number of the bravest men in the empire whose valour had frequently made his enemies yield to their superior power

Irritated at this daring message, Jonathan, accompanied by his brother Simon, left Jerusalem with a select band of ten thousand men, and encamped near Joppa the gates of which were shut by [illegible] garrison belonging to Apollonius. Jonathan [illegible] demanded entrance, which being refused, he immediately [illegible] the necessary preparations for attacking the place, when the garrison, knowing themselves too weak to make opposition against so formidable a body, quietly surrendered

As soon as Apollonius understood that Jonathan was in possession of [illegible] he [illegible] advanced with three thousand horse, and eight thousand foot to Azotus, and thence, by [illegible] marches, to Joppa, where he drew off a little to entice Jonathan into the open plain, depending on the superior numbers of his cavalry. Jonathan, upon this, [illegible] and followed Apollonius towards Azotus, but when the armies approached each other the latter thought proper to make a retreat. Jonathan, however, continued to [illegible] till his antagonist, having got him to a spot of ground which he thought [illegible] advantageous, [illegible] about [illegible] preparation to engage. He [illegible] thousand [illegible] to attack Jonathan [illegible] but the latter, being aware of this [illegible] without any difficulty [illegible] against it, and [illegible] his [illegible] into a [illegible] so that [illegible] might be enabled to engage the enemy on all sides at the same time

[illegible] continued [illegible] evening [illegible] ordered his brother Simon with part of his army, to charge [illegible] the enemy's body, [illegible] his own [illegible] to receive the [illegible] of the [illegible] upon their buckler, [illegible] accordingly [illegible] being [illegible] the enemy [illegible] offensive [illegible] for they stood thick [illegible] than bucklers, and [illegible] though [illegible] The enemy [illegible] this [illegible] was [illegible] fighting [illegible] the enemy [illegible] and was so bravely [illegible] that the troops [illegible] enough [illegible] up [illegible] the [illegible] hopeless condition of the army, for the [illegible] were broken [illegible] and dispersed themselves in the utmost confusion [illegible] pursued them [illegible] Azotus, [illegible] great numbers, and forcing the rest into the temple of Dagon [illegible] But the conqueror entering the [illegible] to it and [illegible] neighbouring villages, which he [illegible] to the ground together with the temple of Dagon [illegible] that had fled to it for protection, without any regard to the [illegible] of idolatry [illegible] the number of those who were [illegible] perished in the flames, was computed [illegible] eight thousand.

Having thus defeated the army of Apollonius, Jonathan [illegible] with his troops to Ascalon, and encamped before the city with a design of investing it. But the inhabitants, [illegible] of attempting to make any opposition brought [illegible] valuable presents as a testimony of their submission, which Jonathan accepted upon the terms, and from the motives on which they were offered, and then [illegible] Jerusalem with the spoils of the enemy in triumph to Jerusalem

As soon as Alexander heard of the success of Jonathan over his general Apollonius, he affected much joy at the event, [illegible] he [illegible] had given [illegible] to [illegible] without his knowledge or consent. In token of the [illegible] in which he held him, he [illegible] a [illegible] of gold [illegible] such as [illegible] but [illegible] at the same time, also gave him the city of Ekron, with all the territories thereunto belonging

About this time Ptolemy Philometer passed into Syria with a considerable body of land and sea forces, to the assistance of his son-in-law Alexander. Agreeable to the king's order he [illegible] received with the greatest honour and respect by the inhabitants of all the cities [illegible] through which he passed except Azotus, where he was [illegible] with complaints of the burning of the temple of Dagon, and exclamations against Jonathan as the [illegible] of the [illegible] as well as the havock made in their country by fire and [illegible] and the destruction of numbers of the people. Ptolemy gave them a patient hearing [illegible] fearful of disobliging Jonathan, did not think proper to say [illegible] in their favour [illegible] about his knowledge [illegible] soon as Jonathan heard of the [illegible] of Ptolemy [illegible] and that he was advanced as far as Joppa, he went [illegible] to [illegible] him his respects, and was received by [illegible] with all honour and magnificence; after which [illegible] attended him to the river Eleutherus [illegible] returned to Jerusalem

As Ptolemy was on his way to the city of Ptolemais, he fortunately discovered a plot, which had been [illegible] ed by Alexander, to be executed by Ammonius, his [illegible] dent, for taking away his life, though no reason could be assigned for such a diabolical intention. In consequence of this discovery, on his arrival at Ptolemais, he demanded that justice might be done to the traitor, but Alexander refusing to give him up, Ptolemy was [illegible] convinced that the king was concerned in the plot, [illegible] therefore entertained an implacable hatred against him, which soon terminated in his ruin. Alexander had [illegible] incurred the ill-will of the people of Antioch [illegible] of [illegible] who had [illegible] [illegible] the cause of [illegible] however [illegible] [illegible] was [illegible] to [illegible] from [illegible] who were employed to bring him to justice

[illegible] Ptolemy [illegible] his daughter Cleopatra from Alexander [illegible] Demetrius [illegible] that he would [illegible] to [illegible] of [illegible] Demetrius was highly pleased with the terms [illegible] by Ptolemy, and as much [illegible] of possessing the beautiful Cleopatra [illegible] had [illegible] an aversion to Demetrius [illegible] account that it was with the utmost difficulty Ptolemy could bring them over to receive [illegible] their king, whom they looked upon as their enemy. Such, however, was their hatred to Alexander, for his [illegible] to the execrable Ammonius, and their hatred to Ammonius himself, for his own sake, that they were easily [illegible] to expel the former from the city. He therefore [illegible] from Antioch into Cilicia.

Ptolemy upon this, made his entrance into the city, [illegible] proclaimed [illegible] king of [illegible] that is, [illegible] of Asia and Egypt. But being a man of honour, reflection and [illegible] considered himself in all public affairs, as [illegible] to [illegible] [illegible] possible, without giving [illegible] of [illegible] to the Romans [illegible] was very [illegible] he [illegible] to [illegible] he modestly declined the compliment, [illegible] having called a council of the heads of the people [illegible] them to receive Demetrius, the true heir to their crown [illegible] sovereign. He told them he hoped [illegible] would be forgotten [illegible] that he would hold [illegible] bound for [illegible] executing the trust reposed in him [illegible] that, with respect to himself, he might be permitted to content himself with the government of his own dominions. This modest address [illegible] the people unanimously received. Demetrius as their king, [illegible] him into the city with great pomp, and placed him on the throne of his ancestors.

When Alexander [illegible] that [illegible] Cleopatra [illegible] had [illegible] Antioch, [illegible] all his [illegible] him, [illegible] he out [illegible] though [illegible] sword. [illegible] and gave him battle, [illegible] he [illegible] and [illegible] fled to [illegible] in the [illegible] He would [illegible] a part of [illegible], but [illegible] that he [illegible] for [illegible] waiting [illegible] that was [illegible] Upon the [illegible] day, [illegible] king, Zabel [illegible] an Arabian [illegible] the order, sent it to [illegible] the report [illegible]. But his satisfaction [illegible] for he soon [illegible] the wound he [illegible] received [illegible]. This Alexander, otherwise called Balas, [illegible] of [illegible] years.

Demetrius, [illegible] known by the name of Nicator, [illegible] ceeded [illegible] he was a man [illegible] without any regard to the obligations [illegible] from them [illegible] of [illegible] The [illegible] to [illegible]

Jonathan, the high-priest, [illegible] having [illegible] of Judea, [illegible] own [illegible] the [illegible] Jerusalem, [illegible] Could not [illegible] Jonathan [illegible] Demetrius [illegible] Demetrius, [illegible] the [illegible] token of [illegible] the [illegible] high-priest [illegible] jot [illegible] Samaria, [illegible] to [illegible] the following [illegible] upon the first word, to [illegible]

"Demetrius, the king, to his [illegible] Jonathan, and the "[illegible] of the [illegible], greeting;

"You [illegible] hereby to understand, [illegible] letter to our [illegible] and well beloved [illegible] copy of which [illegible] herewith [illegible]."

"Demetrius, the king, to Lasthenes, [illegible] greeting.

"[illegible] the friends the Jews have [illegible] to [illegible] "[illegible] their [illegible] "guishing testimony [illegible] "their [illegible] command that the "governments of Aphærema, Lydda, and Ramatha, with "all the lands dependent on these places, be assigned to the "state of Judea; and [illegible] exempt [illegible] from all taxes "heretofore paid to our officers, as well [illegible] crown "taxes [illegible] "command that for the future [illegible] de-"manded. Take care that [illegible] "Jonathan, and [illegible] "[illegible] holy temple [illegible]

Demetrius being [illegible] quiet possession of the crown, and [illegible] he should not be [illegible] rupted by [illegible], dismissed his army without giving them their [illegible], and [illegible] number of mercenary [illegible] which [illegible] This [illegible] old [illegible] without any [illegible] to [illegible] practice [illegible] peace [illegible] kept them [illegible] for [illegible] ther [illegible] general, and the [illegible]

CHAP. XI.

[illegible] Person.

THE [illegible] Demetrius, [illegible] native of Apamia, [illegible] seen, [illegible] the [illegible] Demetrius [illegible] Malchus [illegible] and [illegible] pressing [illegible]

[illegible]

The [illegible] of Antioch [illegible] Demetrius, [illegible] that [illegible] part of [illegible] Demetrius, [illegible] together with [illegible] and charged [illegible] by [illegible] and [illegible] the [illegible] and [illegible] sent [illegible] to the [illegible] and [illegible] that time, [illegible] betook themselves [illegible] the Jews, [illegible] king's orders, [illegible] execution, [illegible] forcing the [illegible] throw down their arms, [illegible]

Thus was this [illegible] Demetrius, [illegible] the Jews [illegible] fidelity, sent them back to Jerusalem, [illegible] most honourable [illegible] of their [illegible] the [illegible]

[illegible] Demetrius [illegible]

threatened him with military execution, unlefs he, in future, made good thofe tributes to himfelf, which the Jews had formerly paid to his predeceffors. This he would accordingly have done, if Tryphon had not diverted him, by forcing him to relinquifh the preparations he had made [illegible] Jonathan for his own fafety, though without effect. [illegible], being now returned out of Arabia into Syria, with young Antiochus, he fet the crown upon his head, and, by the help of the foldiers who were [illegible] to Demetrius for the default of payment, proceeded to open hoftilities, overcame him in battle, took from him his elephants, and the city of Antioch, and forced him back into Cilicia.

Antiochus, foon after his acceffion, fent an embaffy to Jonathan, complimenting him with the title of his friend and ally, confirming him in the office of high-prieft, putting him in poffeffion of the four governments that were affigned to Judæa, and appointing his brother Simon to the command of all his forces from Tyre to the borders of Egypt. He alfo prefented Jonathan with feveral golden cups, purple garments, and [illegible] badges of honour, and adopted him in the number of his chofen friends. [illegible] a fenfe of thefe extraordinary tokens of honour and liberality, [illegible] he had received from Antiochus, that he difpatched meffengers both to the young king and Tryphon, his [illegible], with a [illegible] tender of friendfhip and fervice, efpecially in joining againft Demetrius as a common enemy, whom he reputed [illegible] moft ungrateful of men, in returning evil for the moft fubftantial good.

Having received a commiffion from Antiochus to raife forces, Jonathan proceeded for that purpofe to Syria and Phœnicia, and from thence to all the neighbouring towns and cities, where he was treated with great honour and [illegible], but raifed no foldiers. Upon his arrival at Afkelon, he was received with great [illegible] by the inhabitants, who made him many valuable prefents, and whom he advifed, as he had done thofe in other cities through which he paffed, to [illegible] the caufe of Antiochus [illegible] both they and [illegible] fo to do. He [illegible] upon them, by [illegible] and advice, that they [illegible], he [illegible] to Gaza, upon the defign of [illegible] good [illegible] to Antiochus, but found, to his great furprife, the gates fhut againft him, and the people [illegible] attached to Demetrius.

Jonathan, incenfed at this [illegible], laid fiege to the place, [illegible] of his forces to deftroy the adjoining towns and villages with fire and fword. Seeing, therefore, nothing but [illegible] before them, [illegible] appearance of relief from Demetrius, they came at laft to a compulfive determination of making a [illegible] and fubmiffive application to Jonathan, [illegible] deputies, who were as frankly received on the other hand into his intereft and friendfhip. He readily accepted the conditions they offered, and having received hoftages for the performance of the fame, left Gaza, and proceeded with his forces towards Damafcus.

In the mean time Demetrius had encamped with a powerful army before Cedafa, a place bordering on Tyre and Galilee, with a view of enticing Jonathan out of his way, and [illegible] him. But Jonathan advanced with all fpeed to encounter him, leaving the care of Judæa in the [illegible] to his brother Simon, who, collecting all the forces he was able, [illegible] to Bethfura, and affaulted it, though it was accounted the ftrongeft and moft defenfible place in all Judæa, then in the poffeffion of the partifans of Demetrius. The people of the garrifon, from the neceffity of paying of their [illegible] againft them, [illegible] themfelves in a dangerous fituation, fent a meffenger to Simon, requefting permiffion to march away without violence, or any moleftation, to Demetrius. Indeed, they were at length brought to thefe terms, through fear of being put to the fword. Simon, however, granted the [illegible], and placed another garrifon of his own people in their ftead.

By this time Jonathan had advanced with his forces, which he had greatly augmented on the way, as far as the plain of Azor, where he encamped, unfufpicious of any danger. A party of Demetrius's having intelligence of his fituation, lay in ambufh behind a mountain, while others of them marched to attack him on the plain. As foon as Jonathan found himfelf thus befet, he gave the beft orders to his foldiers, that [illegible] of the time would permit; but the Jews, feeing the party of Demetrius who were placed in ambufh, fearful of being furrounded by the enemy, the greater part of them threw down their arms, and precipitately fled. So general, indeed, was the terror, that only a very fmall party remained with Jonathan, who were encouraged to ftand [illegible] the enemy by means of their leader, together with [illegible] of his guard, Matthias the fon of Abfalom, and Judas, the fon of Chapfæus. Thefe, with a band of gallant followers, charged the front of the enemy in fo defperate a manner, that their lines were foon broken, which being feen by the deferters, fome of them rallied, and fell on with fuch fury, that the army of Demetrius was [illegible] routed, about two thoufand being flain on the fpot, and the reft obliged to fave themfelves by a precipitate flight.

After his glorious victory Jonathan returned to Jerufalem, and, in the height of his fucceffes, fent ambaffadors to Rome to renew former alliances, giving them directions [illegible] Lacedæmon upon bufinefs of a fimilar nature. The Romans received the ambaffadors with the higheft refpect, and difmiffed them with letters, recommending that a fafe [illegible] might be granted them by the potentates of every dominion through which they might have occafion to pafs. On their return they delivered the following letter to the Lacedæmonians:

"By a letter of very ancient date, from your king Areus "to our high-prieft Onias, (a copy of which we fend inclofed), we find that we are nearly allied to you in blood, and "by the teftimony we there gave to Areus, [illegible] "happy we were in the ratification of fuch an alliance. We "would now inform you, that we fhould long [illegible] "[illegible] your friendfhip, but that we left you the honour "of fetting the example. From the firft ratification of our "friendfhip to the prefent time, we have conftantly offered "up our prayers to the Almighty that you might [illegible] "health and profperity, and overcome your enemies. [illegible] "our diftreffes and misfortunes, from the [illegible] of ambitious neighbours, we have been cautious not to [illegible] "you, or other allies. But Divine Providence [illegible] "[illegible] our wars, and our affairs being more [illegible], we "have difpatched Numenius, the fon of Antiochus, and Antipater, the fon of Jafon, (both men of honour and fenators), with letters to the Romans, and to you [illegible] "renewing and ftrengthening the league of friendfhip [illegible] "[illegible]. Return what anfwer you think proper, that we "may know how we may teftify our affection [illegible] by "every means in our power."

At this time there were three fects amongft the Jews, who maintained different opinions concerning human actions. They went under the denominations of Pharifees, Sadducees, and Effenes. The Pharifees held, that fome [illegible] fubjected to a fatality in fome cafes, and left at liberty in others either to do, or not to do, as they pleafed. The Sadducees allowed of no fatality at all in what cafe foever, but affirmed that every man has it in his own power to make his condition better or worfe, according as he purfues meafures right or wrong. The Effenes, on the other hand, afferted the power of an overruling deftiny, working according to the predeterminations of [illegible]. But a more exact account of thefe opinions will hereafter be found in our hiftory of the Jewish wars. We therefore refume our narrative.

In the mean time Jonathan, being informed that the forces of Demetrius, now greatly augmented, were advancing towards him in hopes of recovering the credit they had loft by their late overthrow, he haftened with all expedition to meet them at Amathis, with the full refolution to oppofe their paffage into Judæa. He encamped within fifty furlongs of the enemy, and fending fpies to difcover their defign, found, upon their return with the beft information they could get, and fome prifoners they had taken that night, that the intention of the enemy was to fur-

[illegible] him in his quarters. In consequence of this intelligence, Jonathan made every necessary preparation for counteracting their design, by fixing sentinels in the out-posts, keeping his men under arms all night, acquainting them [illegible] and with the intention of the enemy. When the officer of Dem[illegible] thus understood that their plan had been discovered, they w[illegible] [illegible] how to act, knowing their [illegible] to work for [illegible] on [illegible] his force [illegible] therefore at length [illegible] a resolution of decamping in the night, which they accordingly did, and covered their retreat with [illegible] Accordingly [illegible] Jonathan marched [illegible] [illegible] [illegible] camp abandoned, he pursued [illegible] [illegible] expedition, but his endeavour [illegible] [illegible] having retreated to a secure place, beyond the river [illegible], before he could reach [illegible] [illegible] their [illegible] his course to Arabia, plundered the country of the Nabatheans, made many of the inhabitants prisoners, took great numbers of their cattle, conducted them to Damascus, and there sold them.

Simon in the mean time proceeded with his army through Judea and Palestine, to Ascalon, fortifying [illegible] the places he came to in his way [illegible] [illegible] Joppa, of which he [illegible] made himself master, [illegible] [illegible] [illegible] [illegible] [illegible], and thereby prevent its falling into the hands of Demetrius.

Jonathan and Simon [illegible] [illegible] measures to prevent any injury from the enemy, [illegible] [illegible] to Jerusalem; and [illegible] the people [illegible] to the temple [illegible] the high-priest, he [illegible] [illegible] to repair the walls of the city, [illegible] [illegible] cut off all communication between the [illegible] [illegible] [illegible]; likewise to put the whole country in [illegible] of defence, by [illegible] proper garrisons [illegible] [illegible] thought best for the security of the people. This proposition being unanimously approved, [illegible] [illegible] took the care of the [illegible] upon himself, and committed the country [illegible] to his brother Simon.

Demetrius having passed the river, [illegible] into Mesopotamia, with a design [illegible] [illegible] [illegible] [illegible] [illegible] country, [illegible] [illegible] [illegible], [illegible] [illegible], upon the [illegible] of the [illegible] [illegible] the quarter, the seat of the [illegible]; [illegible] [illegible] [illegible] [illegible] dwelt there, had [illegible] [illegible] [illegible] [illegible] come over to them, with [illegible] [illegible], [illegible] [illegible] the would [illegible] [illegible] [illegible] [illegible] [illegible] [illegible] [illegible] [illegible] king of [illegible] [illegible] this [illegible], Demetrius hasted towards them, [illegible] [illegible] [illegible] the Parthians, of [illegible] Tryphon [illegible] [illegible] [illegible] his arrival he [illegible] [illegible] [illegible] [illegible] considerable army, and marched to [illegible] Arsaces, [illegible] [illegible] utterly routed, his whole army destroyed, [illegible] [illegible] prisoner.

CHAP. [illegible]

[illegible] of the treachery of Tryphon, [illegible] [illegible] [illegible] [illegible] [illegible], who is taken prisoner, [illegible] [illegible] [illegible] of [illegible] people.

DURING these transactions the [illegible] and treacherous Tryphon, who had no other view in getting young Antiochus into his hands, [illegible] to answer his own wicked purposes, and was concerned in the completion of his plan to possessing himself of the crown of Syria, now resolved upon the miscarriage of Demetrius, [illegible] [illegible] [illegible] [illegible] accomplishing his wishes. [illegible] [illegible] [illegible] [illegible] [illegible] than was in the interest of Antiochus [illegible] could not possibly execute his design, and therefore the [illegible] [illegible] [illegible] [illegible] [illegible] him of his power; but [illegible] [illegible] [illegible] [illegible] [illegible] do this by force, he therefore [illegible] [illegible] stratagem. To this end he went from Antioch to [illegible] [illegible] [illegible] Greeks Scythopolis, where [illegible] [illegible] Jonathan [illegible] the [illegible] [illegible] forty thousand chosen men, [illegible] [illegible] [illegible] [illegible] Tryphon, on his arrival, [illegible] [illegible] [illegible] presents [illegible] [illegible] [illegible], affected [illegible] [illegible] [illegible] [illegible] [illegible] respect and obedience to Jonathan [illegible] [illegible] [illegible], by their [illegible] [illegible] [illegible] [illegible] his [illegible] heart, and create in the other such a confidence as would [illegible] [illegible] [illegible] through want of caution, to a fatal [illegible]. At length, after diverse [illegible] [illegible] he told Jonathan that, as the war was over, all things at peace, and Demetrius from his reduced condition was no longer able to [illegible], he thought it [illegible] his army [illegible] [illegible] [illegible] [illegible] [illegible] [illegible] [illegible] [illegible] [illegible] [illegible], [illegible] [illegible] [illegible] [illegible] [illegible] [illegible] [illegible] [illegible] into his possession. [illegible] [illegible] [illegible] [illegible] [illegible] [illegible] and [illegible], [illegible] [illegible] [illegible] [illegible] [illegible] [illegible] [illegible] [illegible] [illegible] [illegible] [illegible] [illegible] [illegible] [illegible] [illegible] [illegible] [illegible] [illegible] [illegible] Tryphon [illegible] [illegible] [illegible] dismissed all his army except [illegible] [illegible] [illegible] two of whom he left in [illegible] [illegible] [illegible] [illegible] Tryphon to Ptolemais [illegible] [illegible] [illegible] [illegible].

[illegible] [illegible] [illegible] the [illegible] [illegible] [illegible] [illegible] [illegible] [illegible] [illegible] [illegible] [illegible] [illegible] [illegible] [illegible] [illegible] [illegible] [illegible] him, [illegible] [illegible] [illegible] [illegible] [illegible] [illegible] all his [illegible] [illegible] [illegible] [illegible] [illegible] [illegible] [illegible] in his design he [illegible] [illegible] [illegible] into [illegible] [illegible], with [illegible] [illegible] [illegible] [illegible] [illegible] [illegible] [illegible] [illegible] [illegible] Jonathan [illegible] [illegible] [illegible] the country, but [illegible], [illegible] [illegible] [illegible] [illegible] of [illegible] [illegible] [illegible] [illegible] their [illegible] [illegible] Ptolemais [illegible] [illegible] to their [illegible] [illegible] [illegible] [illegible] [illegible] to [illegible] [illegible] [illegible] [illegible] [illegible] [illegible] [illegible] [illegible] the [illegible] [illegible] [illegible] [illegible] to [illegible] [illegible], without executing the bloody [illegible] [illegible] [illegible] [illegible].

CHAP. [illegible]

[illegible] [illegible]

WHEN the [illegible] [illegible] [illegible] [illegible] [illegible] [illegible] [illegible] the [illegible] were [illegible] were [illegible] [illegible] [illegible] [illegible] [illegible] [illegible] [illegible] whose power they thought [illegible] [illegible] [illegible] [illegible] [illegible] [illegible] [illegible] [illegible] [illegible] [illegible] [illegible] and remove the gloom [illegible] [illegible] [illegible] on the minds and countenances of the [illegible] [illegible] [illegible] [illegible] [illegible] [illegible] [illegible] [illegible] [illegible] [illegible] [illegible] to this effect:

"It is unnecessary [illegible] [illegible] [illegible] [illegible] [illegible] to say [illegible] my father, brothers [illegible] [illegible] [illegible] [illegible] [illegible] [illegible] ourselves [illegible] [illegible] [illegible] [illegible] [illegible] [illegible] [illegible] [illegible] [illegible] [illegible] [illegible] [illegible] [illegible] of our [illegible] [illegible] [illegible] [illegible] [illegible] [illegible] [illegible] [illegible] example, [illegible] [illegible] [illegible] [illegible] [illegible] [illegible] [illegible] [illegible] [illegible] Such [illegible] [illegible] [illegible] [illegible] [illegible] [illegible] [illegible] I am [illegible] to [illegible] [illegible] [illegible] [illegible] [illegible] [illegible] [illegible] actions [illegible] [illegible] I [illegible] not [illegible] [illegible] [illegible] [illegible] [illegible] [illegible] more than they [illegible] [illegible] [illegible] [illegible] [illegible] [illegible] [illegible] [illegible] [illegible] [illegible] [illegible] [illegible] [illegible] [illegible] [illegible] no doubt but God will [illegible] [illegible] [illegible] [illegible] [illegible] your [illegible] [illegible] [illegible] [illegible] [illegible] and [illegible], from their [illegible] [illegible], and secure the [illegible] temple from destruction."

The people [illegible] [illegible] by this speech [illegible] [illegible] [illegible] [illegible] confidence [illegible] [illegible] [illegible] tears, and [illegible] [illegible] [illegible] [illegible] [illegible] [illegible] [illegible] Simon to succeed to the command [illegible] [illegible] brother [illegible] Jonathan. Therefore [illegible] Simon [illegible] [illegible] [illegible], and [illegible] [illegible] commands [illegible] [illegible] [illegible] [illegible] [illegible] Simon [illegible] thus [illegible] [illegible] [illegible] the [illegible] [illegible] [illegible] [illegible] [illegible] to [illegible] the walls of the city [illegible] [illegible] [illegible] [illegible] [illegible] with [illegible] [illegible] [illegible] [illegible] [illegible] [illegible] which [illegible] dispatched [illegible] [illegible] [illegible] [illegible] [illegible] of Absalom to Joppa, with orders to [illegible] [illegible] [illegible] [illegible] [illegible] [illegible] [illegible] [illegible] [illegible] [illegible]

Tryphon, while himself continued at Jerusalem to look to the city.

Soon after this Tryphon, at the head of a considerable army, marched from Ptolemais to Judæa, having with him Jonathan as his prisoner. Simon, being aware of his approach, headed his forces, and proceeded to meet him, which he did on a mountain that overlooked the plain near the city of Adida. As soon as Tryphon saw the Jewish army, and understood that Simon had been chosen their leader, he thought it most expedient to decline an engagement, and therefore resolved, instead of force, to endeavour to obtain his ends by deceit and stratagem. To effect this, he dispatched one of his principal officers to Simon, with a message to the following effect: "That he had seized Jonathan only because he owed "an hundred talents to the king, but that, in case he "would send the money, and Jonathan's two sons as hos- "tages for their father's fidelity, he would again set him "at liberty, since he was only detained till the king's due "should be paid." Simon, suspecting a deception intended by this message, and yet fearing, if he refused the money as a ransom, or the sons as hostages, it might cost his brother Jonathan his life, and that his death would of course be imputed to him, summoned a council of the principal people, to whom he intimated his suspicion of treachery, but observed at the same time that he thought it would be most proper to send both the young men and the money, as otherwise he might be thought indifferent with respect to the safety of his brother.

This being unanimously agreed to, the money and hostages were accordingly sent to Tryphon, who, instead of fulfilling his agreement, by delivering up Jonathan, retained both him and his sons. He then marched with his army up and down, ravaging the country, till he came at length to Dora, a city of Idumea, with an intention to pass that way to Jerusalem; but Simon watched his motions so closely, as to prevent his carrying his design into execution.

While Tryphon was on the way, he received intelligence from Jerusalem, that the garrison was hard pressed for want of provisions, and that if not speedily supplied he would immediately hasten away to their relief. Upon this he ordered his horse to be in readiness, as he determined to proceed, without delay, to Jerusalem; but a deep snow fell in the night, that the ways were covered, and impassable, especially for the cavalry. Upon this disappointment he decamped, returned to Cœlo-Syria, and passing through the country of Galaad, near the city of Basca, he basely caused Jonathan to be slain, and buried there, and afterwards returned to Antioch.

In the mean time Simon was returned to Jerusalem, where, hearing of his brother Jonathan's death, and that he was buried at Basca, in the land of Galaad, he sent for his remains, which he deposited in the sepulchre of his father, at Modin, and ordered a general mourning to be observed upon the occasion. He afterwards erected a stately monument over the sepulchre, the whole of which was of white marble, polished, and curiously wrought with a variety of figures. He raised also seven pyramids for his father, mother, four brothers, and himself, one for each, a work of such admirable state and beauty, that it is to be seen to this day, and hath the reputation of being an extraordinary piece. This may suffice to shew the care and zeal of Simon, in doing due honour to his family, by so magnificent a monument, and particularly to the memory of Jonathan, who had now governed the people in quality both of prince and high-priest for the space of four years, his brother Simon succeeding him by the universal suffrages of the people.

In the first year of his promotion he freed them from the tribute formerly paid to the Macedonians, and this was in the year 170 from the coming of Seleucus Nicanor to the kingdom of Syria. Simon had obtained such esteem and authority among the people, that they dated their writings, public and private, in such a year of Simon, the governor of the Jews, adding, "and most deserving person of the "nation." For under his administration all things succeeded well, both in war and peace, through the advantages procured his friends, and the victories he obtained over common enemies, destroying the cities of Gaza, Joppa, and Jamnia, and laying the citadel of Jerusalem level with the ground. He also took care to prevent inconveniencies in future, by putting it out of condition, either to annoy the town, or serve as a place of refuge to fugitives or [illegible]. To this end he gave his advice to the digging up and levelling of the mountain itself that the castle stood upon, as to leave the temple the advantage of the higher ground. Upon this consideration, he summoned an assembly of the people, and laid before them the damages they had suffered from this castle, and the inconveniencies they might reasonably expect from it in future, if it should ever fall into the hands of an enemy. This plain, but just, mode of reasoning, wrought so effectually on the multitude, that they unanimously approved the purpose of demolishing the castle. They then immediately fell to work, and plied it incessantly, night and day, for three years, till, in the end, by means of indefatigable labour, they brought it under the command of the temple.

CHAP. XII.

Tryphon proceeds in his iniquitous practice. Simon forms an alliance with Antiochus Soter. They expel Tryphon from Syria. He at length falls a victim to [illegible] and is put to death.

SOON after the taking of Demetrius Nicanor prisoner, Tryphon caused his pupil, Antiochus, the son of Alexander, to be secretly murdered, and a report to be spread that he lost his life by an unlucky accident that happened in his exercises. This report being credited, Tryphon, by his artifices and deceit, so wrought on the [illegible] of the people, that they unanimously chose him for their king, and placed him on the throne of Syria, alledging, that Demetrius was a prisoner to the Parthians, and that Antiochus would never forget the deserters of his brother.

The treacherous and perfidious Tryphon, having thus possessed himself of the throne of Syria, began to display that turpitude of heart which had been distinguished while in a private character. His point was no sooner gained than he threw off the mask, and proved that the name of Tryphon (which signifies a dissolute wretch) was an epithet he justly merited. His disposition and conduct proved so disagreeable to the soldiers in particular, that they deserted in great numbers, and went over to Cleopatra, the wife of Demetrius, who was at this time in retirement with her children at Seleucia, while Antiochus (otherwise called Soter, and the brother of Demetrius) was in an obscure situation in Crete, [illegible], that scarce any person dared to receive him, through fear of Tryphon.

Cleopatra, encouraged by the advice of her friends, and the appearance of the soldiers, who had deserted from Tryphon, as well as urged by the fears she had lest the people of Seleucia should deliver up the place to the usurper, dispatched a messenger to Antiochus Soter, offering him the crown of Syria, and, at the same time, making a proposal of marriage. Antiochus immediately embraced the offer both of her kingdom and person, so that, upon coming to Cleopatra, the people flocked to him in such numbers, that he soon found himself at the head of a very considerable army. With these forces he marched against Tryphon, overcame him in battle, drove him out of Syria, into Phœnicia, and at length pent him up in the strong fortress of Dora. Antiochus then sent ambassadors to Simon, the high-priest of the Jews, with a treaty of amity and alliance. The terms were thankfully accepted by Simon, who soon after sent him a supply of money and provisions for carrying on the siege, which was at that time so acceptable to Antiochus, that he ranked him amongst the number of his best friends. The siege of Dora was carried on for some time, till, at length, Tryphon made his escape, and, after flying from [illegible] to place, endeavoured to shelter himself in Arabia, his place of nativity, but an universal disgust prevailing against him among the [illegible], they seized him, and put him to death, in the fourth year of his government.

CHAP. XIII.

[illegible] of Antiochus [illegible] Simon, who [illegible] him, [illegible] renews a league with the Romans.

ANTIOCHUS being of a covetous, and consequently [illegible] disposition, was no sooner settled on the throne of Syria, than, forgetful of the good offices Simon had done him, and the promises he had made him in return, he sent an army, under the command of his general Cendebeus, to lay waste Judæa, and seize upon his person. The thought of this base perfidy, on the part of Antiochus, [illegible] Simon, that heedless of the infirmities of age, with a juvenile resolution, he made the necessary preparations for giving him a warm reception. Having assembled his forces, he dispatched two divisions of them, under the command of his two sons, while himself took charge with the main body of the army, planning ambuscades in different parts of the country. Nor did he fail of success in his attempts, for he forced his enemies [illegible], and justly retaliated the injuries he had sustained, after which he renewed his alliance with the Romans, and [illegible] the rest of his life in peace.

CHAP. XIV.

[illegible] treacherously murdered by Ptolemy, [illegible] [illegible] his son [illegible] [illegible] [illegible] the [illegible] of [illegible].

WHEN Simon had been eight years governor of Judæa, he was barbarously murdered by the treachery of his son-in-law Ptolemy, whom he had made governor of the [illegible] of Jericho. This [illegible], who was [illegible], had laid a design of usurping the government of Judæa to himself, but this could not well be done without the destruction of Simon and his family. To perpetrate the horrid design, he invited his father-in-law to a [illegible], where, as he was [illegible] in a [illegible] of [illegible], he caused him to be assassinated. He then made his wife, and two of his sons, prisoners, and sent his ruffians in quest of his third son, John, (otherwise called Hyrcanus) [illegible] to take him off, as they had done his father; but Hyrcanus being apprized of the design, went to a [illegible] at Jerusalem, where he was received with open arms by the multitude, though the veneration they had for the memory of his father, and their aversion to Ptolemy for his perfidy, when they bravely repulsed upon an attempt to enter it [illegible], because they had then [illegible] received Hyrcanus in another.

CHAP. XV.

Hyrcanus is declared high-priest [illegible] besieges Ptolemy in the castle of Dagon. The fortitude of the mother and two brothers of Hyrcanus, who are put to death by Ptolemy.

WHEN the fall of Simon was known at Jerusalem, Hyrcanus was declared high-priest and prince of the Jews, in the place of his father, whose death was universally lamented, and a general mourning throughout the whole country was observed on the melancholy occasion (*a*).

The first thing Hyrcanus did, after he entered upon his office, was to offer up prayers and sacrifice in due form, which being done, he marched an army against Ptolemy, who had retired to the castle of Dagon. [illegible] grand difficulty he met with, in the prosecution of this design, was to surmount a natural affection towards his mother and brethren, whom Ptolemy caused to be [illegible] whipped and otherwise publicly tormented on the battlements, threatening to cast them down headlong, unless he [illegible] raised the siege. This terrible menace abated the resolution of Hyrcanus, who thought, if he persisted in his attempt, the consequence would be an aggravation of cruelty to his relations. His mother, observing his embarrassment, called aloud, urging him not to consider the sufferings of herself and sons, but to avenge the injury his father had received; and expressed a willingness to expire under the most excruciating torments [illegible] condition that the barbarous and unnatural tyrant Ptolemy, should meet with a punishment proportioned to the enormity of his crime. This instance of fortitude and generosity animated Hyrcanus to make a vigorous effort; but observing that in proportion to the force he exerted for reducing the fort additional cruelty was exercised upon his mother, and his desire of revenge yielding to filial tenderness, the siege was protracted till the coming on of the sabbatical year, wherein the Jews were obliged to rest, so that Ptolemy, by this means being delivered from the war and the siege, [illegible] putting to death the mother and brothers of Hyrcanus, withdrew to the [illegible] [illegible] surnamed Cotylas, who at this time had usurped to himself the city of Philadelphia.

CHAP. XVI.

Antiochus makes war upon Hyrcanus, [illegible] [illegible] enters into a [illegible] [illegible] Antiochus is defeated and slain, and [illegible] to the throne of Syria by [illegible] Demetrius.

ANTIOCHUS stimulated by the disappointments and disgrace so lately brought on him by Simon, the father of Hyrcanus, made an inroad into Judæa, in the fourth year of his reign, the first of the government of Hyrcanus, and the [illegible] hundred and sixty-second olympiad. Having first ravaged the country, he [illegible] Hyrcanus into the city itself, dividing his army into seven bodies round about it. The siege was carried on with great resolution, and the defence of the place [illegible], supported for some time. The camp was for some time distressed for want of water, but that defect was at length plentifully supplied by a great fall of rain. Upon a general survey, they found the town most accessible upon the north side, and therefore directed their force principally to that quarter, raising an hundred turrets, of three stories high, which were lined with soldiers to cover [illegible]. They had likewise drawn a double circumvallation of great length and depth, to cut off the means of communication and relief. But this did not intimidate the defendants from making frequent sallies and doing execution, when they found the assailants off their guard. [illegible], they found them in a posture to receive them they could make good their retreat at pleasure. Hyrcanus [illegible] foreseeing the inconvenience of retaining in the town many useless people, turned such out, having taken care to separate those that were fit to bear arms; so that between Antiochus, on the one hand, who stopped them from going farther, and Hyrcanus, on the other, who would not suffer them to go back, the poor wretches wandered about the walls, till many of them perished for want.

(*a*) The [illegible] of [illegible] book [illegible] [illegible] Simon [illegible] [illegible] [illegible] [illegible] kingdoms [illegible] Jews lived [illegible] [illegible] [illegible] [illegible] [illegible] [illegible] [illegible] [illegible]

[illegible] [illegible] [illegible] Romans [illegible] [illegible] Simon [illegible] [illegible] [illegible] [illegible] [illegible] it so fell out that it was now the feast of tabernacles, so that those who were within the town commiserated their condition, and received them again. Upon this occasion the inhabitants addressed themselves to Antiochus only to grant a truce for seven days in honour of the solemnity, with which, from a conscientious motive, he [illegible] complied. Nor did he only gratify them in their request, but sent them sumptuous presents for sacrifices, such as bulls with gilded horns, cups of gold and silver replenished with costly perfumes, and in fine treated them in a manner wholly the reverse to that of Antiochus Epiphanes, who, when he had taken the city, sacrificed swine upon the altar, and committed other abominable prophanations in contempt of the religion, laws and ceremonies of the Jews: which was the cause of [illegible] irreconcilable animosity between that prince and our nation; whereas the present Antiochus obtained the firname of "the Pious," in token of the reverence he had for the [illegible] of religion.

Hyrcanus was [illegible] by this instance of the king's [illegible] and moderation, to sollicit him by an embassy [illegible] of the Jews, for the liberty of living once [illegible] according to the laws and customs of their own country. The major class of his subjects were for the [illegible] of the Jews, as a people who affected to be more holy than their neighbours, and prized themselves of a singularity of manners from the rest of mankind. But the king, conceiving this peculiarity in the [illegible], could not be [illegible] to rigorous measures, but, on the contrary, sent word back to Hyrcanus, that, upon condition the [illegible] would deliver up their arms, undertake to pay tribute for Joppa, and the rest of the cities about Judea, and [illegible] a garrison into the town of his appointment, he was ready to put an end to the war. The Jews agreed to all the terms but that of receiving the garrison, from [illegible] of intermixing with strangers, and therefore proposed, as a composition for that article, to give the king hostages for the performance of covenants, and five hundred talents, over and above. The king accepted the proposal, the [illegible] talents were deposited in part, and the brother of Hyrcanus sent as one of the hostages. Upon the fulfilling of the treaty, Antiochus raised the siege and departed.

Hyrcanus after this caused the sepulchre of David to be opened, who excelled all other princes in opulence, and took [illegible] three thousand talents for his own use. [illegible] he raised mercenary troops, being the first of the nation that ever entertained an army of strangers. He then ratified the league of friendship with Antiochus, invited him to [illegible] entertainment in the city, and accompanied him with his army to the Parthian war, as we have it from the history of Nicolaus of Damascus, who writes to the following purpose:

"Antiochus, upon the routing of Indates, the Parthian "general, erected a trophy, [illegible] upon the bank of the "river Lycus, where he rested two days, at the request of "Hyrcanus, a Jew, being at the time of one of their "festivals, upon which [illegible] a confluence of travel-"ling." The account of the historian is certainly authentic in this particular, for the feast of Pentecost fell out, at that time, to begin the next day after the sabbath, and it is unlawful for us to travel upon either of these two [illegible].

Antiochus at length came to an engagement with Arsaces, king of Parthia, in which he lost both his army and his life. His brother, Demetrius, succeeded to the kingdom of Syria, through favour of Arsaces, who freed him from captivity at the same time that Antiochus invaded the dominions of Parthia.

CHAP. XVII.

Hyrcanus [illegible] Forms a new alliance with the Romans. The death of Demetrius. [illegible]

UPON the death of Antiochus, Hyrcanus marched immediately with his army into Syria, [illegible] that he should find the country [illegible]. In [illegible] effect [illegible], with some difficulty, he took Medaba, and after that Samega and other adjacent places. He then made himself master of Sichem and Garizim, with the land of the Cuthæans, where stood the temple which by permission of Alexander was built, after the model of that at Jerusalem, by Sanballat, one of his governors, to gratify his son-in-law Manasses, brother of Jaddus the high-priest, as we have already related. This temple was deferted two hundred years after it was built.

Hyrcanus also took several strong places in Idumea, Adora and Marissa, and, at length, when he had subdued the whole province, issued a proclamation to all the inhabitants to depart the land who would not submit to circumcision; so that, rather than abandon their native country, the inhabitants not only complied in the point of circumcision, but in conformity to all other rites and ceremonies of the Jews: insomuch, that they were reckoned [illegible] common with the nation.

Hyrcanus being now about to renew a league with the Romans, sent an embassy to the senate with letters upon that subject. The letters being read and debated, a [illegible] was concluded upon according to the following form.

"Fannius, the son of Marcus Prætor, called a senate "in the field of Mars, on the eighth of the ides of Feb-"ruary. Present Lucius Manlius, the son of Lucius Me-"[illegible] and Caius Sempronius, the son of Caius F[illegible], "upon the business of the embassy of Simon, the son of "Dositheus, Apollonius the son of Alexander, and Dio-"dorus, the son of Jason, persons of rank and probity, "and deputed by the nation of the Jews to treat about "[illegible], and other public matters, with the senate of "Rome. [illegible] it then [illegible] agreed upon, that Joppa and "the ports, Gazara, with the fountains, and other places "that had been taken away by Antiochus, contrary to "a decree of the senate, be all restored, and the king's sol-"diers not to pass through that or any other part of the "Roman territories without permission. That [illegible] "had been done by Antiochus [illegible] be "declared void, and commission be appointed to [illegible] "an estimate of what the people had suffered in their "lands and goods by his depredations, and to see repa-"ration made for all losses."

Upon these conditions the senate was pleased to accept of the proposals that were presented them by these honourable persons, in the name of their good friends and allies the people of the Jews. With respect to the returning answer in form, they said it should be done at their leisure, and care taken that no injury should be offered them in future. Pains had orders likewise to furnish the ambassadors with money, out of the public treasury, to defray the expences of their return home, which he accordingly did, with recommendatory letters to all governors and officers in their way, for the security and accommodation of their passage.

While the affairs of the Jews under the conduct of Hyrcanus, were in this flourishing condition, he was no want of disposition in Demetrius to urge him [illegible] hostilities, provided he could have relied on being able in his design. But he behaved in so tyrannical a manner, and pursued such wicked courses, that he became universally detested by his people, who, uniting in a conspiracy against him, sent messengers to Ptolemy Physcon, king of Egypt, requesting that he would send them a descendant of the house of Seleucus, whom they would immediately invest with the sovereignty. Ptolemy, who was no friend to Demetrius, readily complied with the request of the Syrians, to whom he sent Alexander, surnamed Zebina, attended by a very considerable army. In consequence of this a desperate battle took place, in which Demetrius being totally defeated, he fled to Ptolemais, where his wife Cleopatra then resided, not doubting but to find protection [illegible], however [illegible] found himself mistaken, for on his arrival he was refused entrance into the city, [illegible] he took himself to refuge to Tyre, where [illegible] to the [illegible], they first made him a prisoner, and then put him to death.

Alexander Zebina being now possessed of the kingdom of Syria, entered into a league with Hyrcanus, the high-priest, who was engaged some time after in a war with Antiochus Grypus, the son of Demetrius, and in a battle ensuing, Alexander was slain. Antiochus by this means obtained the kingdom of Syria, but was intimidated from making war upon the Jews, upon hearing that Antiochus Cyzicenus his brother, was at that time, raising an army against him in the town of Cyzicus: indeed, he was fully employed in making preparations to sustain the repeated attacks from this brother, who took his surname from the name of the place where he had his education. Antiochus Cyzicenus was the son of Antiochus Soter, who was detained prisoner by the Parthians. Cleopatra, as before observed, had been wife to the two brothers, Demetrius and Antiochus. Upon the coming of Antiochus Cyzicenus into Syria, a perpetual animosity prevailed between the brothers, so that Hyrcanus enjoyed an uninterrupted tranquillity: for, after the death of Antiochus, he detached himself entirely from the Macedonians, nor had he the least concern with them either as an ally or a subject. In the days of Alexander Zebina, his affairs were in a prosperous state, but more so in the reign of the two brothers, for, while they were employed in harassing each other with perpetual hostilities, Hyrcanus had full possession of Judæa, and an opportunity of [illegible] [illegible] treasure. His attention, in a word, was devoted to the promotion of the interest of his country, regardless of and defying the [illegible] [illegible], of the rival brothers.

CHAP. XVII.

During the contest between the rival brothers, Antiochus Cyzicus and Antiochus Cyzicenus, Hyrcanus [illegible] [illegible] [illegible] [illegible]. Hyrcanus [illegible] [illegible] [illegible] of the Sadducees, [illegible] [illegible] of the Pharisees. His death.

IN consequence of these disturbances in Syria, Hyrcanus marched at the head of an army to the strong city of Samaria, now called Sebaste, since it was rebuilt by Herod, of which we shall speak in due time and place. He was so incensed against the Samaritans for the indignities they had offered to the people of Marissa (a colony of the Jews, and confederate with them) that he determined to attack the place with the utmost vigour. Upon sitting down before it, he [illegible] the town with a large ditch, and a double wall of eight furlongs compass, and gave the conduct of the siege to his two sons, Antigonus and Aristobulus; [illegible] they were both young they prosecuted the undertaking with the judgment of experienced warriors, and displayed the greatest courage and magnanimity, insomuch that the besieged were so pressed for want of provisions as to be reduced to the necessity of eating carrion. In this distressed situation they applied for relief to Antiochus Cyzicenus, who came with the utmost haste at their request; but being routed by Aristobulus, and pursued by the brothers as far as Scythopolis, he with great difficulty escaped being taken.

The brothers then returned to Samaria, and forcing the people into town again, renewed the siege, which caused them to repeat their application to Antiochus, who prevailed with Ptolemy [illegible] for a supply of six thousand men, [illegible] against the consent of his mother, as to endanger the loss of his kingdom. With these Egyptian auxiliaries Antiochus over-ran and ravaged the whole country of Hyrcanus, he not having at that time, a body of forces sufficient to cope with him. His grand point in view was to divert Hyrcanus from the prosecution of the siege. However, through surprizes, defections, and other casualties, he found his party, in a short time, so diminished that he committed the conduct of the Jewish war to his generals Callimander and Epicrates, and retired himself to Tripoli. Callimander, with more courage than conduct, ventured on a rash encounter, was immediately routed, and lost his life. Epicrates, from a principle of avarice, betrayed Scythopolis, and several adjacent towns [illegible], to the Jews, so that all hopes of relieving Samaria were cut off. At length, after a siege of a year's continuance, which subjected the inhabitants to the greatest distresses, it was surrendered to Hyrcanus, who gave orders for its total demolition, after which he caused trenches to be dug in various parts across the ground where it stood, that it might not be afterwards rebuilt. [illegible] strange, if not incredible, report, that, upon the day of the battle which the sons of Hyrcanus had with Antiochus Cyzicenus, it was revealed to him, as he [illegible] in the temple, in a supernatural manner, that his sons [illegible] out in the victory. This he not only declared [illegible] to the multitude on his coming out of the temple, but it was soon literally fulfilled.

The affairs of the Jewish nation were now in a flourishing state, not only in Jerusalem and throughout Judæa, but in Alexandria, Egypt, and Cyprus: for queen Cleopatra being at variance with her son Ptolemy, delegated the command of her troops to Chelcias and Ananias, the sons of that Onias who erected a temple in the territory of Heliopolis, according to the model of that at Jerusalem, as before observed. These two persons were the queen's chief counsellors, according to the relation of Strabo, the Cappadocian, who writes that "Great numbers of those that either came to Cyprus with us to "Cyprus, or were sent thither afterwards by Cleopatra, "immediately quitted the service of the queen, and went "over to Ptolemy, only the Jews, that were of the party "of Onias stood firm to the queen [illegible] the "queen on account of the respect [illegible] to Chelcias "and Ananias, their friends and countrymen."

The prosperous state of affairs, however, drew upon Hyrcanus, in a great measure, the envy of the Jews, and particularly the Pharisees, a prevailing sect among them. The authority of that people was so great, from their pretence to extraordinary [illegible] in religion, that they obtained the most distinguished reputation and interest among the multitude, whose conduct they could direct even in opposition to the sentiments of the high-priest, and the heads of the nation. Hyrcanus, having been educated among this sect, and being sensible that their popularity might, in time, produce some disagreeable consequences, tried various means to gain their esteem. Among other [illegible] to effect this, he one day invited several of their leading men to a splendid entertainment, when his [illegible] had caused a circulation of good humour, he rose from his seat and thus addressed them: "Since, my good friends, I "profess your principles, it is entirely necessary to observe, "that my most [illegible] wish is to render myself acceptable to the Almighty by observing the duties to my neighbour. If I have violated my duty, it is your business to "admonish me, and it shall be mine to effect a reformation in my conduct."

As soon as Hyrcanus had finished this address, the generality of the company gave him the applause, as a brave man and a worthy governor. But one of the guests, named Eleazar, a man of a rough [illegible] disposition, who had been hitherto silent, now arose, and [illegible] addressed Hyrcanus as follows: "Having declared yourself [illegible] "for truth and plain dealing, you cannot be offended if I "recommend a resignation of the high priesthood, and that "you apply yourself only to the discharge of your authority." Surprized at this, Hyrcanus asked Eleazar what reason he had for giving him such advice. "Because," replied the other, "we are assured, from authentic testimony, "that, in the days of Antiochus Epiphanes, your mother "was a captive taken in the wars, and being the [illegible] "[illegible] of a [illegible] woman, you are incapable of the office "and dignity of high-priest."

As this allegation was known to be totally void of truth, the company resented it with just indignation, and Hyrcanus himself was so exasperated, that he vowed revenge [illegible] the [illegible] had attended for this [illegible]. With [illegible] disposition one Jonathan, a [illegible] of his, (that is, one of the Sadducees) took the opportunity of [illegible] to incense Hyrcanus against the whole sect of the Pharisees. To this end he suggested to him that it was not the single act of Eleazar, but a thing concerted by the whole party, that Eleazar, in pointing the [illegible], delivered the sentiments of the sect: and that the truth of this observation would be confirmed on demanding what punishment was due to the man who had dared to so scandalous a defamation of the character of the prince and high-priest of his nation.

Hyrcanus took the advice of his friend Jonathan, and [illegible] of the Pharisees what punishment [illegible] the calumniator, they returned for answer, [illegible] that, being a people inclined to lenity, they did "not [illegible] it to be an offence deserving of death, "[illegible] of opinion, that imprisonment and scourg-"ing would be sufficient penalty." This answer [illegible] Hyrcanus that what Jonathan had suggested was true, and, [illegible] that very moment, he became [illegible] to the whole sect of the Pharisees, abrogated their [illegible] constitutions, and enjoined [illegible] should observe them [illegible] and going over to the other sect, the Sadducees, this was the source of that disturbance [illegible] allowed them more latitude [illegible] of time and place.

It is here proper to observe, that the Pharisees had many traditions handed down from their fathers, which were not to be found amongst the laws of Moses, and [illegible] rejected by the Sadducees, from a persuasion [illegible] and [illegible]. This, then, is the grand subject of controversy [illegible] Sadducees [illegible], the great [illegible] the [illegible].

[illegible], Hyrcanus [illegible] and [illegible] both civil and ecclesiastical [illegible] the debt of nature, [illegible] had lived thirty-one years. He was [illegible] of [illegible] honours, the [illegible] of the Jews, the high priesthood, and the [illegible] which had [illegible] from the [illegible] two of [illegible] should not long enjoy the government [illegible] the death of their father, and his prediction was verified in the event.

Hyrcanus was a most excellent governor, and [illegible] prudent conduct, obtained [illegible] privileges [illegible] had ever enjoyed since the Babylonish captivity. He was a man of the strictest probity, and [illegible] administered justice with such impartiality, as to acquire the general esteem of the people, so that he lived respected, and died lamented.

CHAP. XIX.

A[illegible], the eldest son and successor of Hyrcanus, after exer-[illegible] and [illegible] barbarity, and [illegible] [illegible], ex-[illegible] conscience, [illegible].

ON the death of Hyrcanus, his eldest son, Aristobulus, succeeded him, and determining to change the form of government into [illegible], assumed the title and dignity of king. This happened [illegible] years and three months after the return of the Jews from the captivity of Babylon. Aristobulus, though a man of [illegible], [illegible] protested, on this occasion, so particular a regard for his next brother, Antigonus, that he admitted him as a kind of partner in the government, [illegible] his mother, whom he committed [illegible] in the sovereignty, (Hyrcanus having left her all [illegible] could possibly confer,) he ordered to close confinement and consigned his [illegible] younger brothers to the [illegible]. His cruelty [illegible] was so horrid and [illegible], that he caused his mother to be starved to death in [illegible] ment, and afterwards [illegible] the life of his favourite brother, upon [illegible] grounds of suspicion. It was, indeed, [illegible] he would credit the [illegible] reports [illegible] affection he bore for Antigonus, [illegible] entertained, that they [illegible] envy and malevolence. Antigonus, returning from [illegible] expedition, on which he had been sent by his brother, just upon the solemnity of the feast of tabernacles, and hearing that Aristobulus was dangerously ill, [illegible] up to the temple attended by his guards [illegible] in order to offer up prayers for the restoration of his brother's health.

This being made known by the enemies of Antigonus, they immediately repaired to the king, telling him it was high time to look to himself, that his brother [illegible] to the temple, in [illegible], and with armed men [illegible] his coming in private [illegible], and that, in all probability it would not be long before he would come with a troop of armed soldiers, and, by dint of force, divest him of his crown. Aristobulus did not give credit to all these reports concerning his brother, but yet supposing there might be some foundation for a part, he devised such methods for providing for his safety as he thought might end his [illegible] of being apprehensive of danger [illegible] therefore, he sent [illegible] to his brother, [illegible] that he [illegible], [illegible] concluding that if [illegible] his condition, there was no [illegible], but if he did otherwise there might be something in what had been said. Before he dispatched the message to Antigonus, he ordered his guards [illegible] a [illegible] passage that led from the [illegible] to the temple, [illegible] his brother in his passage, and [illegible] come [illegible] for him to pass unmolested, but otherwise [illegible] to put him to death. But the queen, [illegible] of the conspirators, to [illegible] the messenger [illegible] to tell Antigonus [illegible] on his [illegible] long since [illegible] an elegant suit of [illegible] was desirous of [illegible] [illegible] that he would come to him [illegible] attire. Antigonus, [illegible] upon the good faith of his brother, and [illegible] left the temple completely armed [illegible] the messenger, [illegible] obedience (as he thought) to the king's commands. Upon his coming to a place called the Tower of Straton, the guards, which [illegible] posted there to watch him in his passage, fell on him and put him to death. This disaster may induce to [illegible] the power of [illegible] on the human mind, and [illegible] that good [illegible] may be corrupted by its [illegible] suggestions. But the most extraordinary circumstance that attended it was the prediction of one Judas, a [illegible] prophet of those times, [illegible] This Judas, [illegible] Antigonus coming to [illegible] exclaimed among his disciples, that he [illegible] of his life, for Antigonus, whose death he had foretold upon that very day at Straton's Tower, was yet alive, [illegible] place [illegible] then [illegible] off, [illegible] the day more than half spent, so that he had lost his reputation as a prophet for ever. While he was in this state of [illegible], the news arrived of Antigonus being slain in a subterraneous passage [illegible] the tower. This was [illegible] Straton's Tower, [illegible] that upon the coast, which was [illegible] known by the name of Cæsarea, and this event fully reconciled the [illegible] of the prophet.

When Aristobulus [illegible] his commands were executed in the death of his brother, he was seized with a conscientious remorse [illegible] of his [illegible] the distemper of his body, [illegible] great [illegible] that he could find no cure for the one, nor any ease to the other.

(DEATH of ARISTOBULUS King of the JEWS.)

At length, his agonies increasing, he fell into a violent vomiting of blood. As one of the servants was conveying some of the blood away in a vessel, he spilt a part of it on the very spot where Antigonus had been slain, and where the stains of his blood were still to be perceived. The spectators imagining this to be the effect of design, so loudly expressed their surprise as to be overheard by the king, who instantly enquired the cause. But as he became anxious to be informed, the people about him were the more desirous of concealing it. However, by the force of threats and entreaties he at length prevailed on them to tell him: but his desire was no sooner complied with, than he shed an abundance of tears, and fetching a deep sigh he broke into the following exclamation:

"The all-seeing power hath detected my iniquity, and my brother's murder hath called down the vengeance of heaven upon me. How long shall I hold this life, which is forfeited to the blood of a mother and a brother? Rather, why do I not expire at once, than thus yield my life drop by drop, as if [illegible] were a punishment inadequate to my guilt?"

With these words he gave up the ghost, having governed only one year, under the surname of Phihellen, that is to say, Lover of the Greeks. He did his country some services, in making war upon Iturea, and annexed a considerable part of it to the territory of Judea, compelling the people of that part of the country to live in conformity to the religious rights and forms of the Jews. His character is thus drawn, described by Strabo in the name of Timagenes: "He was a man of candour and, [illegible] serviceable to the Jews, for he enlarged their dominion by adding to it Iturea, bringing the people into union by the common bond of circumcision."

CHAP. XX.

Alexander, on his coming to the throne, [illegible] Ptolemais [illegible] Ptolemy Lathyrus [illegible]

ARISTOBULUS was succeeded on the throne by his brother Alexander Jannaeus, who had been kept in prison during the whole of the late reign; but, on the decease of Aristobulus, his wife, Salome, (by the Greeks called Alexandra) released him and his two brothers from confinement, and advanced Alexander, being the elder, to the regal dignity. It was the misfortune of Alexander to incur his father's aversion almost as soon as he was born, which was imputed to the following circumstance. Hyrcanus had a vision one night, from which he obtained information upon enquiry, that Alexander should succeed him in his government, and the information was conveyed by a lively representation of the figure of his [illegible]. Aristobulus and Antigonus, being his favourites, and Hyrcanus finding that neither of them was designed by this figure, he applied it to Alexander, under the double mortification both of his crown and his throne falling to a younger son. Alexander, upon this account, was sent for education into Galilee; but the event, however, verified the prediction, for Alexander, upon the death of Aristobulus, entered upon the administration, and taking off one of his brothers that would have supplanted him, treated the other with great honour through the continuance of a private life.

As soon as Alexander had settled the affairs of state, he marched with an army to Ptolemais, and meeting with the enemy, a defeat [illegible] ensued, in which Alexander proved victorious, [illegible] into the town, and then shut them up in it. [illegible] was only Ptolemais and Gaza of all the sea-coast towns that stood out, beside Dora and the Tower of Strato, which was in the hands of Zoilus. Antiochus Philometor, and his brother, Antiochus Cyzicenus, were so wasted with the war, in which they were engaged with each other, that the people of Ptolemais could [illegible], [illegible] than Zoilus [illegible] to [illegible] advantage of the [illegible] that the [illegible] of Zoilus [illegible].

The besieged, [illegible], had no hopes of relief but from Egypt, and therefore applied to Cleopatra, and to Ptolemy Lathyrus, who, being driven out of Egypt, reigned over his kingdom of Cyprus. The Ptolemaites [illegible] Ptolemy, requesting his immediate [illegible], and assuring him that as soon as he should [illegible] them, the inhabitants of [illegible] would [illegible] to his [illegible] on his entering [illegible], [illegible] would be supported by Zoilus, the Sidonians, and other neighbouring people. The king was so elated with these assurances, that he [illegible] the [illegible] immediately [illegible] and [illegible] [illegible] in the [illegible].

While this business was carrying on, [illegible] a man of [illegible] [illegible] the [illegible] make [illegible] the inconsiderate [illegible] consequences [illegible] the people, whom [illegible] effect.

"It is [illegible] (said he) is [illegible] [illegible] not eligible to [illegible] to accept of the relief we had requested, for it were [illegible] ourselves under the protection of Ptolemy, [illegible] slavery must be the consequence. [illegible] provoke [illegible] [illegible] to be [illegible] Cleopatra [illegible] while Ptolemy is preparing for [illegible] powerful army [illegible] [illegible]. Besides, the queen [illegible] determined to drive him out of Cyprus; and when [illegible] he [illegible] engaged [illegible] strengthening his interest with the neighbouring provinces, she will [illegible] the opportunity [illegible] to give the [illegible] [illegible] that Ptolemy [illegible] driven back to Cyprus [illegible] shall then be left without succour, [illegible] to encounter [illegible]."

This audacious [illegible] the people [illegible] had been contracted by the people of [illegible] of which Ptolemy was informed on [illegible] but notwithstanding this, he resolved to proceed on his voyage [illegible] the [illegible] to which he had been invited. He continued his course to Sycaminum, where he landed his forces to the amount of thirty thousand [illegible] and [illegible] advanced [illegible] he [illegible] Ptolemais. [illegible] the [illegible] place had [illegible] to [illegible] his [illegible], but, to his great surprize, they refused to receive the message, or hold any intercourse either with him or his agents.

This [illegible] embarrassed Ptolemy, who, while he was considering what measures to take, received a message from Zoilus, and the people of Gaza, requesting that he would immediately come to their assistance against Alexander, who was committing great depredations in their territories, and whose forces were too powerful for them to subdue.

This solicitation was very agreeable to Ptolemy, who immediately marched his army to their relief; but Alexander not thinking it advisable to hazard an engagement with them, withdrew his army, and placed them in winter quarters. But though he had raised the siege, and withdrawn all his troops, he [illegible] was unable to cope with Ptolemy, and therefore thought of effecting that by policy which he could not by force. To this purpose he entered into a treaty with Ptolemy, covenanting to pay him four hundred talents of silver, on condition that he would deliver Zoilus and his territories into his hands.

This Ptolemy Lathyrus agreed to do, and accordingly soon after got Zoilus into his custody, but being informed that, at this very time, Alexander was clandestinely treating with Cleopatra, to bring her upon him with [illegible] forces he looked upon the covenant as void, and instantly laid siege to Ptolemais, where the gates were shut [illegible]. Upon this he divided his army, leaving one part before the city to carry on the siege, and marched off himself with the remainder to lay waste the country of Judea. Alexander, on the other hand, to counteract the design of Ptolemy, levied many of his own people, (some say fifty, and others say eighty thousand men,) and with it advanced against the enemy, while Ptolemy, in the mean time, taking the [illegible] Sabbath-day, fell upon Asochis, a city of Galilee, and took it by assault, with ten thousand prisoners, and an immense booty.

CHAP. XXI.

Ptolemy Lathyrus defeats Alexander, who is afterwards joined by Cleopatra. Ptolemy expelled out of Egypt. Ptolemais taken [illegible] at Gaza. Instances of the [illegible]

HAVING subdued Asochis, Ptolemy, elated with success, made a [illegible] upon Sepphoris, a place not far distant from that which was destroyed, but, in this attempt, he was defeated, and [illegible]. He then led his army against Alexander, whom he found in the neighbourhood of Asophon, near the river Jordan, and encamped near [illegible] the enemy. Alexander had in his van eight thousand of those they called Hecatontomachi. These were all armed with brazen bucklers, as were also some of Ptolemy's [illegible] in the front, but the generality of the [illegible] adventures, were rather [illegible] engagement. Philostephanus, however, a man of great military skill and experience, and the chief officer [illegible], gave them all possible encouragement, [illegible] there was no doubt of their success against the enemy. The [illegible] pass the river that parted the two armies, [illegible] confident of victory, if he could but engage them with the river behind, to cut off their retreat. When the two armies met, a [illegible] battle ensued, which, for some time, [illegible] with great [illegible], both armies, and with [illegible] success. At length, on the [illegible] Ptolemy's troops giving way, victory seemed to incline to Alexander, but Philostephanus coming to their relief with a seasonable reinforcement, the Jews were entirely routed, with great slaughter. Some relate that thirty thousand men were slain in that battle: but, according to Timagenes, in his history, the number amounted to fifty thousand. The rest were either taken prisoners, or compelled to save themselves by a precipitate flight.

After this carnage Ptolemy went to some villages belonging to the Jews, and commanded his soldiers to murder the women and children, and then put their bodies into vessels of water, which were to be placed over fires. He is said to have had recourse to this bloody device in order to strike terror into those that had escaped by flight, by making them think that his army was accustomed to feed on the flesh of the enemy. This horrid transaction is confirmed by the joint testimony of Strabo, and Nicolaus of Damascus. The same forces also took Ptolemais by force.

Cleopatra now became sensible of the overgrown power of her son, [illegible] of Gaza, and the laying waste of Judea, that she thought it necessary to curb his ambition, which might prompt him to attempt the invasion of Egypt. Upon this precaution she mustered, with the utmost expedition, all the force she could possibly raise, both naval and military, constituting Chelcias and Ananias, two Jews, her commanders in chief of the different departments. She sent the greatest part of her [illegible], [illegible] her last will and testament, and her grand-children, to the isle of Cos, and ordered a powerful fleet into [illegible] to keep that province in awe, while she herself proceeded to Phoenicia, and being received [illegible], laid siege to the city.

Ptolemy, receiving intelligence of this, quitted Syria, and hastened into Egypt, imagining that, arriving so unexpectedly, and in the absence of the queen, he should find the country unprovided to receive him; but he was much disappointed in his expectation. At this time Cleopatra [illegible] Chelcias, one of her generals, [illegible] pursuit of Ptolemy in Cœlo-Syria.

When Cleopatra heard of Ptolemy's miscarriage in his attempt upon Egypt, she sent a strong detachment after him, which drove him out of the country, and forced him to return, and take up his winter quarters at Gaza, while she, in the mean time, took the city and garrison of Ptolemais by assault. Upon this Alexander repaired to her with many valuable presents, and was kindly received by the queen, who considered him as an unhappy prince, who, [illegible] persecution and oppression of a common enemy, [illegible] her for protection. Some of her [illegible] embrace this opportunity of [illegible] both [illegible] his dominions, but this motion was [illegible] Ananias, who represented to her the [illegible] of such a proceeding, which would be a violation of the laws of hospitality, and [illegible] as well as raise the ill-will of every Jew upon the face of the earth that had the interest of his country [illegible]. The queen was so pleased with the plain dealing of Ananias [illegible], that she not only forbore every injury to Alexander, but entered into a league of friendship with him at Scythopolis, a city of Cœlo-Syria.

Alexander, thus delivered from the power, and consequently the fear, of Ptolemy, made an expedition into Cœlo-Syria, where, after a ten months siege, he took Gadara, and after that Amathus, a very strong fortress on the [illegible] side Jordan, the place where Theodorus, the son of Zeno, in the first [illegible] of revenge fell upon the Jews [illegible], and slew ten thousand of them, and took Alexander's baggage. But this misfortune did not deter him from laying siege upon Raphia, a seaport town, and Anthedon, which was afterwards, by Herod, called Agrippias, both which he took by force.

Ptolemy by this time had left Gaza, and returned to Cyprus. Cleopatra had also returned to Egypt, so that Alexander took the occasion of revenging himself upon the people of Gaza, for calling in Ptolemy to their succour, and therefore laid siege to the town, and, at the same time, laid waste their country. While Alexander was before the place, Apollodotus, the commander, made a desperate sally by night, with two thousand mercenaries, and ten thousand of the citizens, well armed, upon the camp of the Jews. During the night the besieged prevailed, upon an apprehension of the enemy, that they were attacked by Ptolemy. But when day-light appeared, and freed them from that error, the Jews rallied, and so furiously charged [illegible], that they destroyed [illegible] thousand of them. [illegible] withstanding this defeat the people of Gaza were determined to encounter all difficulties of hunger, force, and [illegible] itself, rather than submit to the enemy. They were encouraged to persist in this resolution by Aretas, an Arabian prince, who had promised to come at the head of a large body of forces, to their assistance; but before his arrival with the supply, the place was reduced through the base treachery of Lysimachus, brother to Apollodotus, who, envying the credit and esteem he had [illegible] for his gallant defence of the place, first murdered him, and then delivered up the city to Alexander. This prince, on his first entrance, affected a degree of moderation and lenity, but the very appearance soon vanished, for he turned his soldiers loose among the people, with a commission at large, to kill, burn, and destroy at pleasure. So that more dreadful scenes of barbarity took place than [illegible] conceived. The inhabitants, finding they [illegible] no quarter, fought hand to hand, and [illegible] so dear [illegible], that, in the general carnage, [illegible] nearly as many of his own men as he killed of the [illegible]. Some of the inhabitants set fire to their own houses, that they might not be plundered by the enemy, [illegible] ever so far as to lay violent hands upon their wives and children, choosing rather that they should die in freedom than live in bondage. The magistracy of the [illegible] happened to be in council when these barbarous [illegible] entered, and the senators, to the number of five hundred, retired to the temple of Apollo for sanctuary; but they were all slaughtered to a man; the town was [illegible] and levelled; and Alexander, after a year spent before it, returned to Jerusalem.

During these transactions some material revolutions took place in the court of Syria. The first was the death of Antiochus, otherwise called Grypus, who was assassinated by the treachery of Heracleon, in the forty-fifth year of his life, and nine and twentieth of his reign. His son Seleucus, who succeeded him, soon after his accession, waged war with his uncle Antiochus, called Cyzicenus, whom he defeated in battle, and afterwards put to death. After his decease his son Antiochus, surnamed Eusebes, being greatly beloved by the people, was crowned in Aradus, immediately made war upon Seleucus, defeated and drove him out of Syria. Seleucus fled for safety to Cilicia, where, in requital for the inhospitable reception he met with, he treated the inhabitants with the greatest tyranny, and subjected them to enormous taxes, so that, incensed [illegible] to the highest degree, they set fire to the palace, and he, [illegible] [illegible], perished in the flames.

While Antiochus Cyzicenus was in possession of the government of Syria, there was another Antiochus, the brother of Seleucus, who waged war with him, in which he lost his life and his army. After this his brother [illegible] the crown, and governed part of Syria. Ptolemy Lathurus, upon this, sent for a [illegible] brother from Cnidus, called Demetrius Eucaerus, and [illegible] him king of Damascus. Antiochus maintained [illegible] [illegible] to these brothers for the time he lived; but, being called to the assistance of Laodice, queen of the Galadenians, he was slain in the field of battle, with his sword in his hand, and fell like [illegible] of [illegible]. After his death the government of Syria descended to his own brother, Philip and Demetrius.

Alexander, on his return to Jerusalem, found things in a very different situation to what he had expected, for the people, being incensed at his conduct, were ripe for a[illegible] rebellion, on which, however, so [illegible] [illegible] demonstration. It happened, soon after his return, [illegible] [illegible] for celebrating the feast of tabernacles, during which it was a custom among the Jews to carry in their hands branches of citron or palm-trees. As Alexander was preparing to assist at the solemnity as high-priest, the multitude had the insolence to throw citrons at him, and [illegible] [illegible] opprobrious language, telling him he was [illegible] [illegible] [illegible] to go up to the holy altar to offer solemn sacrifices. This treatment enraged him to such a degree, that ordering his soldiers to fall upon them, no less than six thousand were instantly put to death. After this he ordered the court of the priests to be surrounded with a wooden partition to prevent the people from coming near him while he was officiating as high-priest, and, to secure his person against all future attempts, he hired mercenaries from Pisidia and Cilicia, not daring to trust his own countrymen.

Having by these means, in some measure, put a stop to the tumults at home, Alexander marched with his forces in pursuit of new conquests, subdued and laid the Moabites and Galaadites under contribution, and destroyed Amathus, without the least opposition from Theodorus. He made war upon Obed, the king of Arabia, but falling into an ambush near Gadara, in Galilee, he was forced, by a [illegible] of camels, into the mouth of a narrow [illegible] passage, from whence, with infinite difficulty, he made shift to clear himself, and get back to Jerusalem. This disaster was followed by a six years rebellion, during which were slain no less than fifty thousand Jews. The king, wearied with intestine broils, sought for a reconciliation with his people, and, to that end, asked them upon a public occasion, what conditions they could wish him to pursue to give them satisfaction. They replied, with one voice, "That he should cut his own throat;" and thereupon entered into a [illegible] [illegible] alliance with Demetrius Eucaerus, king of Damascus.

CHAP. [illegible]

Demetrius Eucaerus [illegible] [illegible] [illegible] [illegible] [illegible] from the [illegible] [illegible] [illegible] [illegible] [illegible] Demetrius is carried [illegible] to Parthia, [illegible] [illegible]

DEMETRIUS, in consequence of the [illegible], marched with a considerable army [illegible] [illegible], [illegible] reinforced by the [illegible] Jews [illegible] [illegible] [illegible] the [illegible] number of his forces amounting to [illegible] [illegible], and 4[illegible]000 foot. Alexander [illegible] [illegible] [illegible] [illegible] [illegible] [illegible] [illegible] [illegible] [illegible] [illegible] [illegible] [illegible] twenty thousand Jews, who [illegible] [illegible] [illegible] [illegible].

When the [illegible] [illegible] [illegible] [illegible] [illegible] [illegible] [illegible] [illegible] [illegible] [illegible] [illegible] [illegible] stratagem, to [illegible] [illegible] [illegible] [illegible] [illegible] [illegible] Demetrius [illegible] [illegible] [illegible] [illegible] [illegible] to desert and join [illegible] [illegible] [illegible] [illegible] [illegible] [illegible] [illegible] the Jews [illegible] [illegible], but neither party was [illegible] [illegible] [illegible] [illegible] the battle took place, which [illegible] [illegible] [illegible] [illegible] for some time, [illegible] [illegible] in favour of Demetrius. [illegible] [illegible] [illegible] [illegible] [illegible] [illegible] [illegible] [illegible] [illegible] Demetrius [illegible] [illegible] [illegible] [illegible] [illegible] [illegible] Alexander's forces were so [illegible] [illegible] [illegible] obliged to [illegible] [illegible] [illegible] shelter [illegible] [illegible] [illegible], where, by [illegible] [illegible] [illegible] [illegible] [illegible] [illegible], [illegible] six thousand Jews [illegible] to him, [illegible] [illegible] him. This circumstance proved [illegible] [illegible] [illegible] [illegible] [illegible] who [illegible] [illegible] that the rest of [illegible] [illegible] [illegible] [illegible] might follow the example of [illegible] [illegible] [illegible] [illegible] [illegible] [illegible] [illegible] [illegible] [illegible] [illegible] [illegible] of his forces, retired into Syria.

But the Jews, [illegible] [illegible] the departure of Demetrius, continued to [illegible] the war against Alexander, though they were [illegible] [illegible] [illegible] [illegible] [illegible] [illegible] [illegible] [illegible]. At length, however, he [illegible] to a [illegible] [illegible] with them, cut off the greater part, and obliged the rest to fly for protection to a place called Bethome, which was fortified by nature and art. Alexander [illegible] [illegible] to the [illegible], and [illegible] the town, [illegible] [illegible] [illegible] prisoners to Jerusalem, where he exercised [illegible] [illegible] [illegible] [illegible] [illegible] that could be imagined. As he was [illegible] [illegible] his concubines [illegible] of his [illegible] [illegible] [illegible] [illegible] [illegible] [illegible] [illegible] eight hundred Jews [illegible] [illegible] [illegible] [illegible] [illegible] [illegible] [illegible] [illegible], [illegible], to [illegible] [illegible] [illegible] [illegible] [illegible] [illegible], he ordered the throats of [illegible] [illegible] [illegible] [illegible] [illegible].

[illegible] [illegible] [illegible] [illegible] [illegible] [illegible] [illegible] [illegible], and greatly [illegible] [illegible] by their [illegible] [illegible] [illegible] against their lawful prince, which was [illegible] [illegible] with respect to the subjects of Alexander [illegible] [illegible] [illegible] reduced to the necessity of surrendering to the king of Arabia what he had taken from the Moabites and Galaadites, as a compensation not to assist his revolted subjects against him, but yet all these considerations [illegible] [illegible] [illegible] to justify the exercise of such [illegible] [illegible]. His [illegible], in short, was so detestable, that the Jews gave him the appellation of Thracida. About eight thousand of [illegible] [illegible], who made their escape by night, [illegible] [illegible] [illegible] [illegible] [illegible] of exile during the life of Alexander, who, after this [illegible], enjoyed a peaceable reign, without any interruption from his subjects.

[illegible]

Demetrius went from Judæa to Berea, where his brother Philip was, and, with an army of 10,000 foot, and 1000 horse, laid siege to the town. Strator, the prince of the place, and a friend to Philip, called into his assistance Zizus, an Arabian prince, and Mithridates Sinaces, the Parthian general, who with a powerful army, attacked Demetrius, and pressed him hard both with darts and arrows, which, together with drought for want of water, forced him and the people to surrender. Demetrius was taken prisoner, and sent as a present to Mithridates, a Parthian prince, who treated him with great honour and respect, but he was soon taken off by a malignant distemper. Philip afterwards repaired to Antioch, and entered upon the government of the whole kingdom of Syria.

CHAP. XXIII.

Antiochus Dionysius, otherwise called Antiochus, makes expeditions into Judæa. Alexander makes several conquests, deposes Demetrius, returns to Jerusalem, and there dies, having given his last advice to his queen Alexandra.

DURING these transactions Antiochus, otherwise called Dionysius, having an eye upon Damascus, got possession of the place, and caused himself to be proclaimed king there. The tidings of this adventure brought his brother Philip in all haste to Damascus, where, by corresponding with Milesius, the governor of the fort, he was quietly received into the town. But to disguise the matter, he gave the officer no reward, lest he should be thought to come in rather by treachery, than the influence of terror. Milesius, however, retaliated upon him, for Philip being one day taking exercise at the circus, he shut the gates upon him, and secured the city for Antiochus, who, upon the first intelligence, posted from Arabia, and, with an army of 8000 foot, and 800 horse, marched directly into Judea.

Alexander upon this occasion, drew a large and deep ditch from Capharsaba, now called Antipatris, up to the very sea of Joppa, which was the only accessible way to the town. He erected a wall also, with several wooden towers at intervals, which he carried on for an hundred and fifty furlongs in length, and there waited for Antiochus, upon whose arrival a most desperate battle ensued. Antiochus at first had so much the advantage, that he thought himself secure of victory; but observing one of the wings of his troops in danger of being overpowered, he only hastened to its relief, and fell in the attempt, at which his troops were so dispirited, that they threw down their arms and flew to Cana, where the greater part of them perished by famine.

Aretas came next to the government of Cœlo-Syria upon the choice of the people of Damascus, from a spirit of opposition to Ptolemy, the son of Menneus. He entered Judea with an army, overthrew Alexander near Addida, and then, upon terms of accommodation being settled between them, returned to Damascus. Alexander then went in pursuit of new conquests, took Dion by assault, and thence marched to Essa, where Zeno's treasure lay, which was of inestimable value. He first raised three walls about it, and then took it by storm, as he did afterwards Gaulon and Seleucia, the vale of Antiochus, and the fortress of Gamala. Many misdemeanours being alledged to the charge of Demetrius, who had formerly the government of these places, he divested him of his authority, and, after a successful expedition of three years continuance, returned to Jerusalem.

By virtue of such numerous conquests, the territories of the Jews were greatly extended at this time. They were in possession of Syria, Idumæa, and Phœnicia; the tower of Strato upon the sea, Appollonia, Joppa, Jamnia, Azotus, Gaza, Anthedon, Raphia, Rhinocura, and in the midland of Adora and Marissa, all Samaria, and the mountains of Carmel and Itabyrium, also Scythopolis, Gadara, Gaulanitis, Seleucia, and Gabala. In the land of the Moabites they held Esebon, Medaba, Lemba, Oran, Telithon, Zara, Cilicia, Aulon and Pella. This last they demolished for refusing to conform to their laws and customs.

After this Alexander became violently addicted to intemperance and drinking, on a certain occasion drank to great excess, he fell sick, and was afterwards seized with a quartan ague, which was so powerful as to baffle the skill of the ablest physicians. He was afflicted with this distemper for three years, during which time he not only continued his attention to the affairs of government but likewise prosecuted several military undertakings, till at length, being quite exhausted, he was forced to submit, and expired upon the frontiers of the country of the Gerasens at the siege of the castle of Ragaba, on the further side of the river Jordan.

When his queen Alexandra, who attended him to this place on account of his indisposition, found he was near his end, she was greatly perplexed in her mind, from the precarious state in which she and her children must inevitably be left on his decease. In the height of her melancholy reflections she broke out into the following exclamation: "My beloved partner, what will be the fate of your wife and children, if deprived of your protection and exposed to the mercy of your inveterate foes!" In answer to this, he gave her the following advice, which were the last words he was heard to utter.

"I particularly request (said he) that you strictly follow the directions I am now about to give you, as the only effectual means to secure a peaceable succession to yourself and children. Keep my death a profound secret from the army till the castle shall be surrendered: then repair in triumph to Jerusalem with the marks of victory, and endeavour principally to be to ingratiate yourself into the favour of the Pharisees, for you must remember that they can reap the interest you form with that sect to whom others, as those of the multitude are entirely subservient. The former clamour against me hath been carried on in opposition to them. On your arrival at Jerusalem, send for the principal men among the Pharisees, expose my dead body before them, and say, that, from a veneration for their piety and justice, you leave the body either to be honoured the ceremony of interment, or to be treated with contempt and indignity, as their discretion shall dictate; and, at the same time assure them that, in this and all other matters of a public nature, you will offer an implicit obedience to their authority. Follow this counsel, and there is no doubt but my remains will be favourably interred, and yourself and offspring established in the dignities of the royal station."

Thus closed his counsel and life in the 49th year of his age, and 27th of his reign.

CHAP. XXIV.

Alexandra, queen regent, obtains the favour and interest of the Pharisees, holds the government nine years, and dies, after having suffered through many perplexing scenes in a reign advanced state.

AS soon as the fortress of Ragaba had surrendered, Alexandra, pursuant to the dying counsel of her husband applied herself to the Pharisees, and submitted the disposal both of the body and the government to their absolute pleasure and direction. This alluring method of proceeding conciliated the esteem of those who had been her most inveterate enemies; insomuch, that the most eminent amongst them harangued the multitude on the glorious exploits of their deceased sovereign Alexander, and their irreparable loss of so excellent a prince; and by such eulogiums raised their passions to such a degree, that they deemed him more worthy of the rights of funeral solemnity than any of his predecessors.

Alexander, at his death, left [illegible] two sons, Hyrcanus and Aristobulus, but committed the regency to his queen Alexandra. Hyrcanus the elder [illegible] was of an indolent disposition and consequently disqualified for the cares and intrigues of the [illegible]. Aristobulus, the younger, on the contrary, was active and resolute, [illegible] the mother had acquired great popularity by [illegible] approbation she now discovered [illegible] the exceptionable parts of her husband's administration during his life. Through her prevailing [illegible] Hyrcanus was promoted to the dignified office of high-priest, not [illegible] abilities, but rather through a persuasion that his disposition would never prompt him to aspire to the [illegible].

But notwithstanding these instances of [illegible], she was little more than a tool in the hands of the [illegible]; for although she had the name of sovereign [illegible] submitted the conduct of all public affairs to their direction, [illegible] gave it in charge to the common people to pay them obedience. She also [illegible] the [illegible] Pharisees [illegible] ordinances and traditions which her father-in-law Hyrcanus had abrogated, and gave the sanction of her [illegible] and authority to the acts and [illegible] of the leaders of her favourite sect. Hence they recalled exiles, set prisoners at liberty, and in divers instances, assumed even [illegible] prerogative. In some cases indeed [illegible] authority, and particularly in augmenting her forces to such a degree, and retaining in pay [illegible] of mercenaries [illegible] keep the adjacent countries in awe, [illegible] security they gave [illegible] hostages [illegible] favour. Her reign [illegible] the [illegible] Pharisees [illegible] suggesting to her [illegible].

They [illegible] whole instigation [illegible] put to death in Jerusalem [illegible] as well as many [illegible] among them, [illegible] adherents, [illegible] Aristobulus, her younger son, at the [illegible] of such proceedings. Having [illegible] had [illegible] manner, [illegible] countenance, the [illegible] measures. They [illegible] that in the most extremity [illegible] they [illegible] an unshaken loyalty to their late sovereign, who had generously rewarded their services [illegible] since they had escaped the [illegible] of war, they ought not [illegible] domestic enemies. They told her that if [illegible] directors would proceed no farther in their [illegible] purpose, they would [illegible] complaints on [illegible]. They observed that to countenance the destruction of her deceased [illegible] friends, would be [illegible] Aretas, the Arabian king, and other hostile princes, would enjoy [illegible] pleasure [illegible] that she had drawn from her court those who had once been so powerful that their very names had struck terror into their enemies. [illegible] that if she was determined to [illegible] every consideration to the ambition of the Pharisees, [illegible] regard was to be paid to their [illegible], they had only one request to make, and [illegible] that they might be permitted to retire into the different [illegible] of the kingdom, where they would [illegible] existence, honourably, sharing the common calamities which [illegible] to await the friends of the deceased king.

These expostulations greatly [illegible] the queen, who for some time knew not how to act, being fearful [illegible] should give countenance to the petitioners, she might [illegible] the displeasure of the Pharisees, of whom they [illegible] [illegible] good in general. At length she resolved on complying with their last request, and therefore consented to their returning to the several garrisons and places of strength throughout the kingdom; but with this restriction, that they should not enter Hyrcania, [illegible] or Machaerus, because in those places she had deposited her jewels, and other valuable treasures. Soon after this she sent her son Aristobulus, with an army, towards Damascus, to [illegible] Ptolemy, surnamed Menneus, who had greatly annoyed the adjacent provinces; but he shortly returned [illegible] without doing any thing of [illegible].

While affairs were in this situation, intelligence was received that Tigranes king of Armenia had [illegible] army of 50,000 men into Syria, with a design to [illegible]. Alexandra was so alarmed [illegible] she dispatched ambassadors to Tigranes, with [illegible], hoping thereby to procure his friendship [illegible] impending danger [illegible] dominions. Tigranes was at that time [illegible] the ambassadors acquitted themselves [illegible] on behalf of Alexandra, and [illegible] of the Jews, but, with every instance of [illegible] for the honour of the embassy, he [illegible] in return. Upon [illegible] Lucullus [illegible] from [illegible] into [illegible] could not overtake [illegible] necessity of immediately [illegible] to the defence of his own dominions.

[illegible] Aristobulus [illegible] Hyrcanus, both in the priesthood and sovereignty. He [illegible] design to [illegible] privately left the city, [illegible] all the castles and forts in which his [illegible] garrison. Alexandra had long been [illegible] at [illegible] the danger, [illegible] her family [illegible] exposed, [illegible] power of the Pharisees [illegible] wholly [illegible] for any public [illegible] Agaba, where he was [illegible] Galaestes, a [illegible] eminence in the [illegible].

The day [illegible] Aristobulus left Jerusalem, his absence was known to Alexandra, who, however, did not entertain a suspicion of his intentions, till [illegible] informed, by messengers, that several forts [illegible] to him, [illegible] one place [illegible] followed by the rest.

Intelligence of these proceedings threw the queen and her adherents into the greatest consternation; for they knew Aristobulus, from his great abilities, [illegible] disposition, to be well qualified to [illegible] the enterprize he had undertaken. They were further [illegible] the [illegible] the outrageous barbarities she had exercised upon several of his particular friends. In this state of perplexity they thought the best expedient would be to confine the wife and children of Aristobulus under a strong guard, in the [illegible] the temple. While this was in agitation, Aristobulus became exceedingly powerful, and the people [illegible] him in such numbers, that [illegible] assembled [illegible] space of only fifteen days [illegible]. Having [illegible] theſe reſpective fortifications, he ſoon raiſed troops from Mount Libanus, Trachonites, and places adjacent, which were readily inclined to ſupport his party, from the expectation of the advantages they ſhould derive, by aſſiſting in the eſtabliſhment of a new king, who, they had reaſon to expect, would remove that tyranny and cruelty which had been exerciſed in the late reign

At this critical juncture Hyrcanus, and his principal adherents, repaired to the queen, requeſting that ſhe would give them directions what further meaſures ſhe would wiſh them to purſue They informed her of the great power of Ariſtobulus, by virtue of the places that had already ſubmitted, and were daily ſubmitting to him, and aſſured her, that, though their ſituation was deſperate, and ruin likely to enſue, yet they would not by any means act without her concurrence The queen replied, " That the ſtate of her " mind and body rendered her wholly incapable of the " cares of government, which ſhe therefore wholly reſigned " to their conduct and management, adding, that there " was no defiance either of men or money, in which con- " ſiſted the ſtrength of the nation " Having ſaid this, Alexandra gave up the ghoſt, in the ſeventy-third year of her age, and ninth of her reign

This princeſs may be ſaid to have aſpired beyond the generality of her ſex, in an ambition to attain to ſovereign power, which, in ſome inſtances, ſhe exerciſed to the reproach of the male monarchs of the earth She ever adverted to the preſent ſtate of things, without wandering into the perplexing uncertainty of future events She obſerved ſome degree of moderation, even in the ſtretch of her power Her grand foible was an attachment to a peculiar ſect, and a conſequent connivance at actions unjuſtifiable in principles, either of religion, or even common humanity By theſe ſhe entailed the ſubſequent calamities that befel her family, though, it muſt be acknowledged, that her adminiſtration was ſuch, during her life, as to preſerve the internal peace of the nation

END OF THE THIRTEENTH BOOK

FLAVIUS JOSEPHUS

ON THE

ANTIQUITIES

OF THE

JEWS.

BOOK XIV

[INCLUDING A PERIOD OF ABOUT THIRTY-ONE YEARS.]

CHAP. I.

An engagement between Hyrcanus and Ariſtobulus, wherein the former being defeated, they came to an agreement, that Ariſtobulus ſhould govern, and Hyrcanus enjoy the honours ſuitable to his dignity in peaceable retirement.

IN the third year of the hundred and ſeventy-ſeventh olympiad, when Quintus Hortenſius and Quintus Metellus Creticus were conſuls at Rome, Hyrcanus entered upon the office of high-prieſt, and Ariſtobulus immediately made war upon him. The neceſſary preparations were made on both ſides; but when they came to action, on the plain of Jericho, the greater part of Hyrcanus's ſoldiers deſerted, and went over to his brother. Hyrcanus himſelf fled for refuge into the citadel in which the wife and children of Ariſtobulus were impriſoned, by order and direction of his mother, the late queen; while the reſt of the party took ſanctuary for a time, within the verge of the temple; though they ſoon after ſurrendered themſelves.

Matters being come to this paſs, the two brothers entered into a treaty of accommodation, and, in concluſion, came to this agreement, that Ariſtobulus ſhould be eſtabliſhed in the poſſeſſion of the government, and Hyrcanus allowed to live at eaſe and liberty upon his own fortune, with the privileges and dignities due to his rank, without moleſtation. This contract was ſigned and ratified with the due formalities of joining hands, and interchanging promiſes, reciprocally for performance of covenants, in the preſence of the people; after which Ariſtobulus retired to the palace, and Hyrcanus, to the private apartments, which had been before occupied by his brother.

CHAP. II.

Antipater ſtirs up a faction againſt Ariſtobulus in favour of Hyrcanus, and prevails with Aretas to join in attempting his reſtoration.

AMONGST the adherents of Hyrcanus was a certain Idumæan, a man opulent, powerful and reſolute, and a profeſſed enemy to Ariſtobulus, whoſe name was Antipater. Nicolaus, of Damaſcus, affirms, that he was of the firſt ſtock of the Jews that came out of Babylon into Judæa, probably to gratify his ſon Herod, who, by divers revolutions of fortune, were afterwards advanced to the throne. This Antipater was firſt called by his father's name, Antipas, who, as it is related, was preferred, through favour of king Alexander and his wife, to the government of Idumæa, where, by means of fair words and ſumptuous preſents, he formed a conſiderable intereſt with the Arabians, Gazæans, and the people of Aſkalon. Antipater, no doubt, ſtood in awe of Ariſtobulus, from a conſciouſneſs of his power to do him injury, and the animoſity that ſubſiſted between them. As the moſt plauſible means of leſſening the reputation and popularity of Ariſtobulus, he had recourſe to the inſidious arts of calumny and detraction, in order to excite the fears and jealouſies of the people. He inſinuated to them, that it was unreaſonable for the younger brother to ſupplant the elder, deprive him of his birthright, and uſurp the government himſelf; pointing out, at the ſame time that it was unworthy of them tamely to bear ſuch invaſion of the hereditary right. He alſo told Hyrcanus, that ſo long as he continued in Judæa, his life would be in danger, as Ariſtobulus could never deem himſelf ſecure in the poſſeſſion of the crown while he was in exiſtence. Hyrcanus, being of an open, undiſpicious temper, the suggestion of Antipater had not the effect upon him which he desired, though, as he never ... seemed inclined to listen to his counsel, the other took care to ply him with importunities to use caution with respect to the designs of his brother. At length, however, he prevailed with him to apply for protection to Aretas, king of Arabia, with offers of his own best services by way of mediation with that prince, in his behalf. Hyrcanus acceding to the proposal, Antipater immediately repaired to Aretas to prepare him for his reception; and having exacted from him a promise upon oath, that he would not deliver him up into the hands of his enemies, Antipater returned, and informed Hyrcanus of the result of the interview.

Having prepared Hyrcanus to petition, and Aretas to comply with his request, Antipater conducted the former out of the city by night, and accompanied him to Petra, where the royal palace of Arabia is situated. Upon their arrival he used the most plausible arguments with the king in favour of Hyrcanus, to induce him to assist him in the recovery of his paternal right. In ... he urged him so ... both with solicitations and presents, that Aretas promised to comply with his request, on condition, that if ever Hyrcanus should be restored to his kingdom through his means, he should cede to him the country and the twelve cities, which his father Alexander had taken from the Arabians, viz. Medaba, Naballo, Livias, Thabana, ... Athone, Zoara, Orone, Marissa, Rydua, Lusa, and Oryba.

CHAP. III.

Aretas ... Aristobulus, ... and besieges him in the temple. ... The Divine vengeance ... the people.

ARETAS, in consequence of these promises, advanced against Aristobulus with an army of fifty thousand ... to fight and overcame him, insomuch that finding himself abandoned by his soldiers going over to Hyrcanus, he was forced to fly to refuge to Jerusalem, where Aretas, with his whole army, ... him in the very temple. The people ... Aretas, with the united forces of the Arabians and Jews, prosecuted the siege with the ... vigour.

The feast of unleavened bread, which we call the passover, coming on at this time, the chief men among the Jews ... the country and went into Egypt. At the same time one Onias, a man of ... integrity ... the ... had privately withdrawn to a place of concealment. The Jews reflecting on the great reputation he had acquired through the sanctity of his life, and that by his prayers, he had been ... to obtain rain from heaven in a ... of drought, and ... that his curses might be as prevalent as his prayers, brought him out into the camp, and there made it their request that he would denounce a malediction upon Aristobulus and his whole party. He opposed their request as long as he could; but at length finding no rest from their importunities, and that they were resolved to maltreat him ... he lifted up his hands to heaven, and offered a prayer to this purport: "Almighty Ruler of the universe, since both we that stand here ... thy people, and they that are besieged in the temple are thy priests, I humbly beseech thee not to hear the prayer of either of them against the other." Upon these words, those who had brought him to the place were so enraged, that they immediately fell upon him, and stoned him to death. But the Divine vengeance pursued the perpetrators of this horrid barbarity.

While Aristobulus and the priests were thus beset in the temple, the paschal festival came on, at which season, according to custom, the Jews offered up a great number of sacrifices. But the besieged not having so many as they had occasion for, requested that their countrymen would furnish them at their own price ... them demanding one thousand drachmas for each head; and the money to be deposited, the demand was agreed to, and the money accordingly let down to them by means concealed over the walls.

When the besiegers received the money, they refused to deliver the victims; and such was their flagitious impiety, that they not only violated their faith ... but prevented their brethren from performing a service dedicated to the honour of their God. The priests therefore, finding themselves perfidiously imposed upon, under pretence of contract, imprecated vengeance on their abandoned countrymen. Nor was the judgment delayed, for there fell immediately a violent tempest, that destroyed all the fruits of the earth throughout the whole province, so that one measure of wheat sold for fifteen drachmas.

CHAP. IV.

Scaurus is sent by Pompey into Syria. ... into Judea, and causes the siege of Jerusalem to be raised.

AT this time a war subsisted between Pompey the Great, and Tigranes, king of Armenia: so that the former commanded Scaurus, one of his generals, to lead the army under his command into Syria. Scaurus accordingly ... but, on his arrival at Damascus, finding the city had been reduced by Metellus and Lollius, he drew off his forces, and led them into Judea. On his arrival ... ambassadors ... from Hyrcanus and the other from Aristobulus. They both ... upon the same ... to ... an alliance offensive and defensive with the Romans.

Aristobulus offered four hundred talents, and Hyrcanus no less. Though they were equal in ... the Roman general gave the preference to Aristobulus, as he was opulent and magnanimous, and would require nothing more than what was reasonable; whereas the other was penurious and pusillanimous, and might ... more than was adequate to the conditions; ... that it was a much more arduous undertaking to carry ... by assault, than to ... and ... Nabatheans, ... the country. ... therefore, with Aristobulus, Scaurus dispatched messengers to Aretas, commanding him, in the name of Pompey the Great, and the Roman senate, immediately to draw off his troops, and raise the siege, upon pain of a declaration of war. Scaurus then returned to Damascus, and Aristobulus advanced with a powerful army against Hyrcanus and Aretas, and engaging them at a place named Papyron, gave them a total overthrow, and put about seven thousand to the sword, among whom was Cephalo, the brother of Antipater.

CHAP. V.

The cause of the contest between Hyrcanus and Aristobulus, is brought before Pompey. The trial is adjourned, and Aristobulus, ... withdraws to Judea.

A SHORT time after this, Pompey himself went into Syria, and took up his residence at Damascus where he received embassies from the princes of several nations ... his friendship and protection. Aristobulus ... the rest, sent him a most valuable present, which was a golden vine of the value of five hundred talents. Strabo of Cappadocia, thus describes it: "There was a present made to Pompey out of Egypt, a crown that was valued four hundred pieces of gold, and another out of Judea, of a golden vine, or garden, to which they gave a name, which, in the Greek language, signifies *delight*. These presents were brought by ambassadors, and I myself saw the vine at Rome, in the temple of Jupiter Capitolinus, with this inscription, *Alexander king of the Jews*. It was valued at five hundred talents, and ... for the present of Aristobulus, the prince of the Jews."

There came to Pompey, soon after this, other ambassadors, Antipater, on the part of Hyrcanus, and Nicodemus, on the part of Aristobulus, who charged Gabinius and Scaurus with taking sums of money (the former three hundred talents, and the other four) as bribes.

Pompey took the cognizance of the cause into his own hand, and appointed the parties concerned to attend him. As the spring advanced, he drew out of his winter quarters, and marched to Damascus, destroying the fort of Apamia (a fortification of Antiochus Cyzicenus) by the way, and making, at the same time, a descent upon the territories of Ptolemy Mennæus, a man of vicious character, imposing a fine on him, to what his relative Dionysius Tripolitanus, who fell a victim to the offended laws of his country. He also razed the fort of Lysias, of which Silas, the Jew, had got possession, and passing from thence towards Heliopolis and Chalcis, went into Cœlo-Syria, and then to Damascus, to decide the point in dispute between Hyrcanus and Aristobulus. Being determined first to hear the voice of the people, it was argued in their favour, "That it had been formerly the usage of their nation to be governed, not by kings, but the high-priest of the God whom they worshipped, who, without assuming any other title, administered justice according to the laws handed down to them from their forefathers. They did not deny but that the two contending brothers were of the sacerdotal race, but charged them with a design of enslaving the people, and subverting the fundamentals of the constitution."

Hyrcanus pleaded, "That though he was the elder brother, Aristobulus had usurped his birthright, and, contrary to justice, robbed him of his birthright, and reduced him to a dependence on his own bounty. That, as a man fraught with mischief, he had played piracy at sea, and rapine and depredation on land, towards his neighbours, and that it was the violence of his disposition which had engaged the people against him." Having said this, he called upon a number of the principal Jews, whom Antipater had engaged in his interest, to [illegible].

Hyrcanus, and his party, having thus done, [illegible] contended, "That Hyrcanus was not displaced from the government through any ambition of his own, but through his own incapacity to govern, and [illegible] sloth and inactivity had brought him into the contempt of the people. He declared, that, with respect to himself, he had no other choice than either to assume the government, or suffer it to be transferred into another family, and that as to the title of king, he held it only as he received it from his father Alexander." As a testimony of the truth of what he had said, he called several young men of eminence among the Jews, who, by the gaudiness of their appearance, and the [illegible] of their carriage, did no great credit to the cause which they endeavoured to espouse.

After Pompey had heard both parties, he seemed to be of opinion that Aristobulus had been too hasty in his proceedings, but dismissed them, for the present, with fair words, and referred the full determination of the matter until he came to Jerusalem, which he declared he would not fail to do, as soon as he had finished the war with the Nabatheans. He enjoined them, in the mean time, to behave themselves peaceably; but Aristobulus perceiving that his inclinations were in favour of his brother Hyrcanus, abruptly left Pompey, and returned to Judea, where he took every means he could devise to prepare himself against those consequences which, from his proceedings, he might rationally expect would afterwards take place.

CHAP. VI.

Pompey prosecutes revenge on Aristobulus.

THE abrupt and disrespectful departure of Aristobulus so highly offended Pompey, that he resolved to take the part of Hyrcanus, without paying any further attention to their respective complaints. He accordingly marched in pursuit of him, with the Roman troops which he had under his command, and a considerable body of Syrian auxiliaries. Having passed Pella and Scythopolis, he came at length to Coreæ, where he was informed that Aristobulus had shut himself up in the castle of Alexandrium, a strong fortress built by his father, on an high mountain, near the entrance of the country of Judea, towards the side of Samaria. Pompey immediately marched his army to the place, and having encamped before it, he sent a message to Aristobulus to come down to him. Aristobulus, considering this message as an insult, at first refused to comply, but the people expressing their disapprobation at his conduct, and his friends representing the impossibility of withstanding so formidable an enemy as the Romans, he was at length prevailed on to leave the place, and accordingly went to Pompey, accompanied by the chief of his particular friends.

Pompey had been previously informed, that Aristobulus had commanded his governors of [illegible] to give up the [illegible] as were given under his own hand, and therefore, as soon as Aristobulus appeared, he insisted on his writing to the respective officers of those forts, ordering them immediately to surrender the place. Aristobulus thought it necessary to comply with this injunction, but was so exasperated at the imperious conduct of Pompey, that he immediately departed to Jerusalem, with a full resolution of opposing him with all his strength.

CHAP. VII.

Pompey and Aristobulus come to [illegible].

ENDEAVOURING to prepare Aristobulus, [illegible] making preparations for war, as soon as Pompey knew of his departure he immediately marched after him, intending to [illegible] him, and therefore, when he [illegible], he proceeded towards Jerusalem. Aristobulus was alarmed at his expedition, and alarmed at the approach of Pompey. He now repented of his conduct, and to prevent further consequences, he had no sooner come to [illegible] than he offered him a considerable sum of money, with the command of the city, and whatever else he should require, provided he would stop hostilities. These terms were accepted by Pompey, who immediately dispatched Gabinius, one of his officers, with some troops to the city to receive the offered money. But when they came there, the people who commanded in the city, by the means of Aristobulus's partisans, refused them admittance, telling them that they would not stand to any such agreement.

This was a kind of treatment the Roman general could not digest, and therefore, after ordering a strict guard to be kept on Aristobulus, he marched with his army to Jerusalem, and immediately proceeded to reconnoitre, in order to form a judgment which was the most likely part to make a successful assault.

CHAP. VIII.

Faction at Jerusalem in the different interests of Pompey and Aristobulus. [illegible] and the temple taken by assault [illegible] Aristobulus [illegible] sent to Rome.

NO sooner did Pompey appear before Jerusalem, than an insurrection took place between the two parties respectively attached to Aristobulus and Hyrcanus. The adherents of the former were for attempting to rescue their king by force of arms, while the other party were equally strenuous for admitting Pompey into the city; and the majority of the people conscious of the superior power of the Romans, were friends to the latter. The partisans of Aristobulus took possession of the temple, and cut away the bridge of communication between that and the city, being firmly resolved to defend themselves to the last extremity. The other party not only gave entrance to the army, but delivered up both city and palace into the hands of Pompey, who dispatched [illegible], his lieutenant, with part of his army, to take charge of [illegible]. When things were come to this pass, [illegible], in the first place made a proposal of peace, but finding the other party averse to any compromise, he made the necessary preparations for an assault, in which he received every possible assistance from Hyrcanus and his [illegible].

The north side of the temple being the weakest quarter, Pompey [illegible] there. It was encompassed with high towers, and surrounded by a very deep [illegible] [illegible] on the other side towards Pompey's [illegible] now the bridge [illegible] down, for [illegible] the Romans, [illegible] labour [illegible] to fill up the [illegible], [illegible] they had collected, and so to [illegible] platforms [illegible] to such a prodigious height, that, [illegible] [illegible] brought from Tyre [illegible] in the temple [illegible], had it not been [illegible] of our seventh day's sabbath, they would [illegible] the engine that point: for though [illegible], the law permits us to defend ourselves upon that day, and to repel force by force, we are not [illegible] upon it, even to [illegible] the [illegible] [illegible] the Romans observing, therefore, that we [illegible] opposition to the advancing of their batteries, and fixing their machines upon that day, [illegible] the next day, [illegible] [illegible].

[illegible] the great deference we pay [illegible], [illegible] even [illegible] from the [illegible] [illegible] devotion, [illegible] [illegible] with all the prescribed [illegible] [illegible] the [illegible], even [illegible] [illegible].

[illegible] the [illegible] month, [illegible] Caius [illegible], [illegible] Cicero [illegible] [illegible] [illegible] [illegible] [illegible] [illegible] [illegible] [illegible] [illegible] [illegible] the time, paid no [illegible], even [illegible] the [illegible] of [illegible] [illegible] exercising their [illegible]. The Jews [illegible] to Pompey, [illegible] no [illegible] [illegible] [illegible] of Aristobulus [illegible] [illegible] [illegible] place [illegible] [illegible] [illegible] of [illegible], [illegible] of Pompey, amongst [illegible] Strabo, Nicolaus of Damascus, and Titus Livius, the famous Roman historian. [illegible] [illegible] engines [illegible] [illegible], [illegible] they [illegible] it to pieces, and brought it down to the ground, carrying [illegible] part of the next wall [illegible] [illegible]. The breach was no sooner made, than the enemy [illegible] crowds to enter it. The first that [illegible] was Cornelius [illegible], the son of Sylla, with his company, [illegible] the centurion [illegible] both [illegible] the same part. So great was the slaughter, that the place was covered with dead bodies, some killed by the Romans, others by [illegible], dispatching one another, some casting themselves down headlong from the walls, and others setting fire to the houses over their heads, rather than be spectators of the [illegible] that were [illegible] [illegible] thousand [illegible] Jews were slain, but of the Romans comparatively [illegible] [illegible] the uncle, and father-in-law, of Aristobulus, was made prisoner.

The [illegible] were accompanied with several indignities to the very mysteries of our religion, by the admittance of profane persons into the holy of holies, where none [illegible] but the high-priest [illegible] [illegible] of [illegible], [illegible] candlesticks, lamps, [illegible] the performance of Divine service. He likewise visited the treasuries, where he found two thousand talents of silver, besides [illegible] of gold, and other things of great value. He would not, however, suffer a single article to be touched, but left them entirely for the sacred uses to which they were appropriated. He likewise ordered the temple to be purified, and that the oblations, and other ceremonies of religion should be performed according to our ancient customs and ordinances. He restored Hyrcanus to the office of high-priest, partly for the services he had received from him [illegible], and partly for his influence in preventing the Jews from espousing the interest of Aristobulus. All those among the Jews, whom he discovered to have been the promoters of the late [illegible], he condemned to the loss of their heads; but such as had signalized themselves in the prosecution of the siege, he liberally rewarded. He made Jerusalem [illegible] tributary to the Romans, deprived the Jews of the [illegible] in Cœlo-Syria, and, by annexing them [illegible] the [illegible] of the Romans, reduced the possessions of the Jews to their former limits. He caused Gadara (demolished a little before, to gratify Demetrius, his freed man) to be rebuilt, and restored, Hippon, Scythopolis, [illegible], [illegible], Azotus, Jamnia, and Arethusa, being [illegible], to their former inhabitants; [illegible] maritime towns of [illegible], Joppa, Dora, and Strato's Tower, [illegible] [illegible], [illegible] annexed to the province of [illegible]. [illegible] Tower of Strato, which [illegible] afterwards rebuilt by Herod and [illegible] with stately ports and temples, was called Cæsarea.

[illegible] Hyrcanus and Aristobulus, we may [illegible] the ruin of Jerusalem, [illegible] subjection of the Jewish nation to the Roman yoke, [illegible] compelled to [illegible] to the Syrians [illegible], [illegible] the [illegible] of a long war, as well as [illegible] to the imposition of above ten thousand talents, and the translation of the sovereign authority, which had [illegible] till then descended in the priesthood, to private and obscure individuals. He appointed [illegible], one of his generals, to the government of [illegible] Cœlo-Syria, and [illegible] the country of Egypt to the [illegible] Euphrates, giving him likewise the command [illegible] that he might be the better enabled [illegible] repose in him. He then left Jerusalem, and set forward on his journey to Rome, taking with him Aristobulus, his two sons, Alexander and Antigonus, and two of his daughters, as captives, whom he [illegible] be led before him, when he made his triumphant entry into his capital.

CHAP IX

Scaurus enters into a league with Aretas, the Arabian prince

SCAURUS made an expedition against Petra, the capital of Arabia, and [illegible] all the places round about it [illegible] difficulty of access to it. As his army was pinched for want of provisions, Antipater, by order of Hyrcanus, furnished him with corn, and other necessaries, out of Judæa. Being well known to Aretas, Scaurus sent him upon an embassy to him, in which he acquitted himself with such address that he prevailed upon him, for a composition of three hundred talents to free his country from ruin. Scaurus, upon this, renounced hostilities, and the parties formed a league of amity and [illegible] to their mutual satisfaction.

CHAP X

Alexander, the son of Aristobulus, makes an expedition into Judæa, but is overcome by Gabinius, the Roman general

AT the expiration of about three years after Pompey's return to Rome, Alexander, one of the sons of Aristobulus, who had found means to effect his escape, [illegible] into Judæa, and having assembled a considerable number of forces, possessed himself of several places in different parts of the country. In consequence of this Gabinius was sent from Rome to take the command of general, and upon an expedition against Alexander, [illegible] he performed [illegible] memorable exploits. [illegible] [illegible] not own to [illegible] [illegible] contemplation to rebuild the walls of Jerusalem that Pompey [illegible], but the [illegible] [illegible] to put [illegible] into execution. [illegible] and collected [illegible] of Jews, [illegible] [illegible] [illegible] [illegible] force, and [illegible] the borders of Arabia. [illegible] Gabinius [illegible] principal officers, [illegible] [illegible] of Jews [illegible] the command of Pitholaus and [illegible] [illegible]

[illegible] Alexander [illegible] Gabinius [illegible] [illegible] Jerusalem, [illegible] [illegible] [illegible] [illegible] [illegible] [illegible] Alexandrium, [illegible] [illegible] [illegible] Alexander [illegible] [illegible] [illegible] [illegible] [illegible] [illegible] [illegible] [illegible] [illegible] Gabinius [illegible] [illegible] [illegible] [illegible] [illegible] [illegible] [illegible] [illegible] [illegible] [illegible] [illegible] Alexander [illegible] [illegible] [illegible] [illegible] Alexandrium, Hyrcania, and [illegible] [illegible] [illegible] [illegible] [illegible]

Gabinius [illegible] [illegible] country [illegible] [illegible] [illegible] [illegible] the cities of [illegible] [illegible] [illegible] [illegible] [illegible] [illegible] [illegible] [illegible] [illegible] Alexander [illegible] [illegible] [illegible] Pompey [illegible] [illegible] [illegible] [illegible] Rome [illegible] [illegible] [illegible] [illegible] insomuch that Hyrcanus was [illegible] Jerusalem [illegible] [illegible] [illegible] [illegible] [illegible] were constituted, at this time, [illegible] [illegible] [illegible] [illegible] [illegible] equal [illegible] viz. Jerusalem, [illegible] [illegible] Jericho, [illegible] Sephoris, which is a city of Galilee. [illegible] came, [illegible] means, to be delivered from the tyranny [illegible] [illegible] of and were again under an aristocratical form of government.

CHAP. XI.

Aristobulus makes his escape from Rome. [illegible] [illegible] [illegible] [illegible] [illegible] [illegible] [illegible] to Persia, [illegible] [illegible] [illegible] by Crassus.

A SHORT time after this, Aristobulus (with his son Antigonus) escaped from Rome, and going into Judea was joined [illegible] [illegible] [illegible] Jews, some of whom were influenced to countenance him merely from a desire of changing the [illegible], and others from [illegible] [illegible] fidelity and affection. [illegible] [illegible] [illegible] [illegible] the fortress of [illegible], but, on receiving [illegible] [illegible] Gabinius had dispatched an army [illegible] [illegible] [illegible], he retreated to Machaerus, where he [illegible] [illegible] the useless part of his followers, retaining only [illegible] men, whom he thought capable of bearing [illegible] [illegible] resolution enough to [illegible] the contest. [illegible] Roman army [illegible] [illegible] [illegible] [illegible] [illegible] great bravery, but were [illegible] [illegible] superior [illegible] [illegible] [illegible] two [illegible] [illegible] [illegible] [illegible] [illegible] [illegible] [illegible] [illegible] [illegible] [illegible] Machaerus [illegible] [illegible] [illegible] [illegible] that Crassus [illegible] [illegible] [illegible] [illegible] [illegible] [illegible] [illegible] [illegible] [illegible] [illegible] for two days, [illegible] the Parthians, and [illegible] [illegible] [illegible] [illegible] [illegible] [illegible] Jews [illegible] [illegible] [illegible] [illegible] [illegible] [illegible] [illegible] [illegible] [illegible] [illegible] [illegible] [illegible] [illegible] [illegible] [illegible] [illegible] [illegible] [illegible] of the Jews [illegible] [illegible] the Parthians [illegible] [illegible] [illegible] [illegible] Gabinius [illegible] [illegible] [illegible]

Gabinius, [illegible] Jews, [illegible] [illegible] [illegible] [illegible] [illegible] [illegible] [illegible] [illegible] [illegible] [illegible] the Jews [illegible] [illegible] [illegible] [illegible]

[illegible] being thus settled in Jerusalem, [illegible] [illegible] the advice of Antipater marched against the Nabateans, [illegible] [illegible] [illegible] [illegible] [illegible] [illegible] noble Parthians, Mithridates and Orsanes, who [illegible] [illegible] [illegible] [illegible] [illegible] [illegible] [illegible] [illegible] [illegible] [illegible] [illegible] [illegible] returned to Rome, and Crassus succeeded him in the command. [illegible] [illegible] exploits of Pompey and Gabinius, against the Jews, may be seen in the histories of Nicolaus, of [illegible] [illegible] Strabo, of Cappadocia, and they concur in their testimony.

CHAP. XII.

Crassus, the successor of [illegible], [illegible] [illegible] [illegible] [illegible] [illegible] the Parthians. [illegible] [illegible] [illegible] progress of the Parthians, and [illegible] [illegible] Jews.

CRASSUS, having undertaken the prosecution of a war against the Parthians, came to [illegible] and seized not only the [illegible] that [illegible] [illegible] [illegible] Pompey left untouched from a motive of conscience, [illegible] [illegible] the temple of all the treasure he could find, to the amount of eight thousand talents more. He [illegible] [illegible] [illegible] [illegible] wedge of gold, of the weight of three hundred mina, reckoning every mina, according to the Jewish computation, at two pounds and an half. Eleazar the priest, who had the custody of the holy treasure, delivered it up to Crassus, not from a censurable motive; for he was a man of probity; but as a composition for all the rest. This ingot of gold was lodged in a wooden beam, that was made hollow for its reception, nor had any man knowledge of it but Eleazar himself, who finding Crassus very desirous of obtaining it, resigned it up to him, upon his most solemn oath that he was abundantly satisfied, and that the hangings, of inestimable value, and other rich ornaments, belonging to the temple, in the possession of the high-priest, should remain untouched. But he perfidiously violated his oath, rifled the temple from the top to the bottom, and [illegible].

It will not be matter of wonder that so prodigious a mass of wealth was lodged in this temple, when it is considered how long the Jews were in collecting it, [illegible] [illegible] [illegible] of the [illegible] God was known. Besides [illegible] and [illegible], [illegible] and, [illegible] the [illegible], Strabo, the Cappadocian, [illegible] writes, that "Mithridates [illegible] to the isle of Cos [illegible] "[illegible] of Cleopatra, that she had deposited there, and "[illegible] talents belonging to the Jews [illegible] [illegible] [illegible] and dedicated to the service of God, and [illegible] [illegible] that the [illegible] Jews [illegible] from [illegible] to Cos, upon the apprehension [illegible] Mithridates. Nor can it be [illegible] that the [illegible] of Judea, who had [illegible] [illegible], [illegible] the temple [illegible] [illegible] would [illegible] [illegible] [illegible] [illegible] to Cos [illegible] the Alexandrian Jews, for they were too [illegible] to [illegible] upon [illegible] of [illegible].

Strabo [illegible] [illegible] [illegible] [illegible] ancient place, [illegible] he writes, [illegible] "Greece, to [illegible] Mithridates, [illegible] "Lucullus to Cyrene, the [illegible] "and factions among the [illegible] "themselves over the [illegible] "ther relates, "That the Cyrenians [illegible] to "four classes, viz. Burghers, [illegible] "and Jews [illegible] [illegible] "posed, that there is scarce [illegible] "earth where they have not [illegible] "[illegible] Egypt, Cyrene, and [illegible] "they were [illegible] [illegible] of the [illegible], "embraced, in many places, their [illegible] laws, [illegible], "[illegible] customs, and [illegible] "[illegible] to the Jewish discipline; [illegible] in Egypt, they "had whole colonies of [illegible], they had [illegible] "of property, by [illegible] a [illegible] considerable "part of the city of Alexandria, where they had magistrates, courts of [illegible], and [illegible] of deciding "claims to property, [illegible] to themselves, [illegible] "as regular in [illegible] [illegible] established [illegible] of "government." Let this suffice [illegible] the testimony of Strabo.

When Crassus had disposed of the affairs of Judea according to his pleasure, he marched [illegible] [illegible] [illegible] he and his whole army were cut off. But Cassius made his retreat into Syria, where he checked the progress of the Parthians, who were now grown [illegible] upon their success. He went afterwards to Tyre, and so to Judea, where he took Tarichea by assault, and made thirty thousand prisoners. Among the rest was Pitholaus, a partizan of Aristobulus, whom he caused to be put to death, at the instance of Antipater, a man of [illegible] with the Idumeans, through a marriage with an Arabian wife of illustrious descent. Her name was Cypron, and by her he had four sons, Phasael, Herod (who was afterwards king), Joseph, and Pheroras, and one daughter called Salome. This Antipater, through [illegible] generosity and affability of disposition, [illegible] conciliated the esteem of all the princes and characters of rank about him, but more especially the king of Arabia, to whom he committed the protection of his children, during the war with Aristobulus. Cassius, having by this time reinforced [illegible] [illegible] advanced to the river Euphrates, to meet the Parthians, who were preparing to oppose him.

CHAP. XIII.

Aristobulus, and his son Alexander, are taken off by Pompey's party.

WHEN Cæsar had prevailed in a contest between him and Pompey, who together with the whole senate, had abandoned the city of Rome, and fled beyond the Ionian sea, he formed a design of setting Aristobulus at liberty, and dispatching him to S[illegible] [illegible] the command of two legions, to [illegible] that province [illegible] [illegible]. But the situation Aristobulus proposed [illegible] [illegible] from the friendship and favour of Cæsar, was [illegible] [illegible], for before he could get out of Rome, [illegible] Pompey's factions found means of dispatching him by poison. His body lay embalmed for a considerable time, till it was [illegible] by Antony, who caused it to be carried into Judea, and there honourably [illegible] [illegible] [illegible].

The [illegible] of Alexander, the son of Aristobulus, was no less deplorable than that of his father; for Pompey having sentenced him to death, on [illegible] [illegible] against the Romans, [illegible] [illegible] to have his head struck off, which was accordingly executed in the city of Antioch. Ptolemy Menneus, governor of Chalcis, near Libanus, [illegible] [illegible] [illegible] to the [illegible] of Aristobulus, [illegible], to request that [illegible] [illegible] [illegible] [illegible] [illegible] and his sisters [illegible] [illegible] be [illegible] with one of them, [illegible] Alexandra, [illegible] [illegible], but he was afterwards [illegible] by Ptolemy, his father, who married Alexandra, and took the family under his protection.

CHAP. XIV.

Gallant exploits of Antipater.

AFTER the death of Pompey, and the victory which Cæsar had gained over him, Antipater [illegible] [illegible] [illegible] [illegible], through the many considerable [illegible] he rendered [illegible] at the instance of [illegible] [illegible] [illegible] Egypt. When Mithridates, of Pergamus, was [illegible] [illegible] [illegible] [illegible], and not able to continue his [illegible] [illegible], [illegible] [illegible] to [illegible] [illegible] [illegible] Ascalon. Antipater joined him with an armed body of 3000 Jews, and brought [illegible] [illegible] leading men of Arabia, and [illegible] Syria, to his assistance. Among these were Jamblicus, a prince of the country, and his son [illegible] [illegible] [illegible], of Lebanus, the [illegible] [illegible] [illegible], with the governors of the cities in general, among whom there [illegible] an emulation of signalizing themselves in his [illegible].

Mithridates, thus reinforced, advanced out of Syria into Pelusium, where the inhabitants refusing him [illegible], he [illegible] [illegible] [illegible] to the place, and [illegible] [illegible] Antipater [illegible] [illegible] [illegible] [illegible] [illegible], and was so well [illegible] in the [illegible], that, by this means, the town was taken. [illegible] [illegible], together with Mithridates, [illegible] [illegible] to Cæsar, the Egyptian Jews, in the country of Onias, opposed their passage, till, through the power and interest of Antipater, their countryman, and especially on the sight of a letter from Hyrcanus, the high-priest, they were brought over to his terms with Cæsar, and, upon that consideration, supplied them with whatever they had occasion for upon their march. This important service was effected through the mediation of Antipater and the letter of the high-priest, which also induced the inhabitants of Memphis to espouse the same cause and interest.

CHAP. XV.

Antipater [illegible] highly honoured by Cæsar, [illegible] depending between Hyrcanus on the one side, and Antigonus on the other, [illegible]

SOON after this, Mithridates and Antipater came to a pitched battle with the enemy, at a place called Delta, and upon a particular spot of ground [illegible] by the name of the Jewish Camp, the former commanding the right wing, and the latter the left. It happened that Mithridates, being hardly pressed [illegible], and the [illegible] order was very near being [illegible] with a total [illegible], but Antipater, at the very [illegible], [illegible] along the [illegible] of the river with a detachment to his relief, [illegible] and in one word, vanquished the enemy [illegible] victory. Having [illegible] [illegible] [illegible] [illegible] his part of the [illegible]. In this [illegible] [illegible] of the party of Mithridates fell, but [illegible] Antipater, not more than fifty.

[illegible] Mithridates, [illegible] to Cæsar, [illegible] the honour of victory, both [illegible], and [illegible] at the [illegible] Cæsar, [illegible] [illegible] and [illegible] him in the most honourable [illegible] [illegible] testimony [illegible] he received [illegible] [illegible].

[illegible] Cæsar [illegible], [illegible] [illegible] tokens of respect [illegible] the [illegible], and the [illegible] with all the privileges [illegible] [illegible] that Hyrcanus was [illegible] [illegible] come into Egypt [illegible] Cappadocia, [illegible] to this, when he affirms, [illegible] the [illegible] [illegible] upon the coming of [illegible] [illegible] [illegible] [illegible] in [illegible] other place [illegible] [illegible] Mithridates came [illegible] "for Antipater, the governor of Judea [illegible] "[illegible] brought him [illegible] "[illegible] "[illegible] of the [illegible], [illegible], and "[illegible] the [illegible], Hyrcanus, [illegible]."

About this time, Antigonus, [illegible], came to Cæsar, [illegible] [illegible] relative to the [illegible] the said were [illegible] of the partizans of the late Pompey [illegible] [illegible] against [illegible] Antipater [illegible] represented as the cause of [illegible] being [illegible] driven from their native [illegible] [illegible] charged them [illegible] [illegible], for the sake of indulging their own [illegible]. He further said, that the assistance they had rendered [illegible], proceeded rather from fear than [illegible], [illegible] to make some compensation for their former [illegible] to Pompey.

Antipater, one of the parties [illegible] by Antigonus, was at this time with Cæsar, and, in order to destroy the intended effect of these reproaches, [illegible] his wounds, as the best testimony he could [illegible] of his loyalty to Cæsar, which having done, he spoke [illegible] follows: "It is a matter "of astonishment (said he) that this man, the son of a [illegible] "ared enemy to the [illegible] of Rome, [illegible] the "rebellious principles of his father, [illegible] "tery, this is to receive the [illegible] of [illegible] "and to arrogate a merit to himself, which his conduct [illegible] "rendered him deserving of [illegible]."

Cæsar, having heard both parties, instead of giving the least countenance to Antigonus, immediately conferred the pontificate upon Hyrcanus, gave [illegible] [illegible] command he might prefer, and conferred upon him the dignified post of lieutenant-governor of Judea.

CHAP. XVI.

Hyrcanus obtains permission, from Cæsar, [illegible] the walls of Jerusalem. [illegible] of the Romans [illegible], respecting [illegible] [illegible] the [illegible] [illegible] the people of Jerusalem.

THE walls of Jerusalem having been demolished by Pompey, [illegible] [illegible] request to Cæsar, for permission [illegible] them, which [illegible] immediately granted, [illegible] letters being [illegible] [illegible] [illegible] the [illegible] [illegible] of the [illegible]. The [illegible] the decree ran as follows,

Decree of the Senate [illegible] in the Temple of Concord, upon [illegible] [illegible] Lucius Coponius, the son of [illegible], and Caius [illegible] Quintus.

"Whereas [illegible] [illegible] upon the report "of [illegible] [illegible] [illegible] "[illegible] [illegible] [illegible] Numenius, the son of [illegible], [illegible] the son of "Dorotheus, [illegible] [illegible] "[illegible] [illegible] [illegible] friendship "[illegible] [illegible] [illegible] [illegible] of a golden cup "[illegible] [illegible], [illegible] [illegible] "[illegible] [illegible] [illegible] "[illegible] [illegible] [illegible] [illegible] "[illegible] [illegible] [illegible] [illegible] "[illegible] [illegible] [illegible] and "[illegible] [illegible] agreed to and "[illegible]."

[illegible] in the [illegible] year of the pontificate of [illegible].

[illegible] by the [illegible] of Athens, [illegible] of [illegible], as [illegible] the following decree:

Decree of the [illegible] [illegible] [illegible] [illegible], Dionysius Asclepiades [illegible] [illegible] [illegible], Agathocles, Aminon, [illegible], the son of [illegible], [illegible], on the [illegible] [illegible] at the [illegible] [illegible] [illegible] [illegible] in the theatre, and [illegible] [illegible] to the people, by the [illegible] [illegible], and [illegible], [illegible], the [illegible] [illegible] as follows.

"[illegible] Hyrcanus, the son of Alexander, high-"priest [illegible] the Jews, has, upon all occasions, "[illegible], [illegible], as well in the generous recep-"tion [illegible] [illegible], [illegible], given proof of a "[illegible] [illegible] and [illegible], both [illegible] "[illegible], and [illegible] Athenians in particular, whatever "[illegible] [illegible], and for [illegible] "we [illegible] [illegible] for Theodo-"[illegible] [illegible], of Sunium, of the virtue "of the [illegible] excellent prince, and his [illegible] [illegible] "[illegible] [illegible] power, we have resolved "to present him with the [illegible] of "[illegible] gold to erect a [illegible] to him in the "temple of the people, and the [illegible] of his [illegible] "to [illegible] in the [illegible] theatres "and places of public exercises, and [illegible] in honour "of Bacchus, Minerva, Ceres, &c. that we have pro-

"[illegible] with this crown [illegible] of a [illegible] [illegible] the [illegible] far [illegible] will and [illegible] [illegible] Herod [illegible] our [illegible] name, [illegible] [illegible] fers."

When [illegible] had [illegible] the affairs of [illegible], he took [illegible] departure, [illegible] his return to [illegible] [illegible] [illegible] [illegible] [illegible] would himself prove [illegible] governor, [illegible] [illegible] of Hyrcanus, [illegible] [illegible] and [illegible] [illegible] concluded with [illegible] [illegible] rate of Rome [illegible] [illegible] over them."

CHAP. [illegible]

[illegible]

[illegible]

held [illegible] his [illegible], created him many [illegible] the [illegible] men of the Jews, more [illegible] [illegible] favour of the emperor, [illegible] [illegible] [illegible] [illegible] [illegible]

"[illegible]

[illegible]

"[illegible]

[illegible] Herod took the advice [illegible]

[illegible] and immediately [illegible] to his friend Sextus Cæsar, [illegible] at Damascus, [illegible] he declared a full [illegible] that [illegible] the [illegible] to the court, he [illegible] their jurisdiction. This contempt of court [illegible] of the judges, [illegible] to incense Hyrcanus [illegible], but though [illegible] was sufficiently evident, he was so pusillanimous, [illegible] had not courage to take the necessary means to pre-[illegible].

[illegible] was greatly embarrassed at this representation, [illegible] receiving information that Sextus had appointed [illegible] the command of his troops in Syria, he [illegible] to such a degree, that he [illegible] that he had meant to [illegible] him. Nor was his apprehension without foundation; for Herod, exasperated [illegible], [illegible] with [illegible] was so resolute, and would certainly have [illegible] into execution, had it not been for the [illegible] of his father and brother, who, by their arguments, [illegible] him to [illegible] imprudent a proceeding. [illegible] to think of offering violence to his [illegible], whose favour and countenance he [illegible] the [illegible] he enjoyed. They told [illegible], [illegible] indignation, at being insulted, [illegible] by the friendly [illegible] of [illegible] on his power, he [illegible] to [illegible], was not [illegible] could [illegible] received [illegible] that the [illegible] he [illegible] to oppose, [illegible] [illegible] who [illegible] him, except [illegible] suggestions of his enemies." Herod [illegible] by these arguments, [illegible] his design of proceeding to [illegible] returned with his [illegible] to Galilee.

[illegible] on his return to Rome, made preparations for [illegible] against Scipio and Cato, [illegible] from Hyrcanus, [illegible] This suggests the propriety of [illegible] formal [illegible] the honours that [illegible] paid to [illegible], and leagues [illegible] have formed with [illegible] it may be [illegible] that [illegible] esteem [illegible] have been [illegible] by the [illegible] Europe, is taken [illegible]. [illegible] will not [illegible] histories of the [illegible] and Macedonians, [illegible] not [illegible] [illegible] the Romans, [illegible] the capitol, [illegible] upon [illegible]. [illegible] Julius Cæsar [illegible] the Jews of A[illegible] the decrees made [illegible] by Julius Cæsar, in honour of Hyrcanus in particular, and of [illegible] in general.

"Caius Julius Cæsar, emperor, Pontifex Maximus, and "the second time dictator, to the magistracy, senate, "and the people of Sidon, greeting.

"I send you a copy of [illegible] to Hyrcanus, the "son of Alexander, the prince and high-priest of the Jews, to be engraved upon a brass table, [illegible] "in Latin and Greek, and to remain among your archives [illegible]-times. The letter [illegible] in substance as follows."

"Caius Julius Cæsar, emperor, Pontifex Maximus, and "the second time dictator, [illegible] the advice and "consent of the senate, appointed the publication of "this decree.

"[illegible] Hyrcanus, the son of Alexander, a Jew, hath at all times, as well in war as in peace, approved himself to be our [illegible] good friend and ally, as [illegible] by [illegible]

"and particularly by the supply of [illegible] hundred choice "men, [illegible] the late Alexandria [illegible] and [illegible] "[illegible] Hyrcanus and his [illegible], the perpetual government of the "[illegible] "[illegible] time forward, [illegible] well "beloved friends, and [illegible] "affection. And [illegible], that the "[illegible] "[illegible] "[illegible] concerning the [illegible] "[illegible] "[illegible] "[illegible]

"It is [illegible] that the "government of the Jews [illegible], "to his [illegible] "[illegible] "[illegible] "[illegible] And [illegible] "[illegible] to Hyrcanus the son of Alexander, "the high-priest of the Jews [illegible] "about [illegible] "[illegible] "[illegible] and Greek, to [illegible] in [illegible] capitol [illegible] "[illegible] "this [illegible] may be [illegible] "[illegible] "[illegible] "[illegible] "[illegible]

"Caius Cæsar, emperor, did [illegible] "[illegible] and "[illegible] "[illegible] of Rome, "[illegible] into Hyrcanus, [illegible] "[illegible] "[illegible] "[illegible] "be by them [illegible] "the [illegible] "[illegible]

"Caius Cæsar [illegible] the fifth time consul [illegible] "and appointed that the city of Jerusalem [illegible] "[illegible] and [illegible] Hyrcanus [illegible] prince "and high-priest of the Jews, [illegible] of Alexander [illegible] the administration of the [illegible], "with [illegible] upon the [illegible], "[illegible] part of their taxes, an exemption from [illegible], "and other tributes.

"Caius Cæsar, emperor, hath likewise [illegible] that "the inhabitants of Jerusalem [illegible] "[illegible] its dependencies, [illegible] "[illegible] of Joppa, [illegible] "the seventh year, which they call [illegible] the "Year of Rest, [illegible] "[illegible], either [illegible] or grain. And [illegible] "[illegible], that the Jews, in Sidon, pay a tribute, or the "tenth part of their fruits, every [illegible] "duty, beside the tenths to Hyrcanus [illegible] his sons, as "they have paid formerly to their predecessors. And "[illegible], that no governors, [illegible] officers, or [illegible] "[illegible], presume to raise any [illegible], or [illegible] "any charges, upon the lands of the Jews, whether [illegible] "winter-quarters, or upon any other pretext whatsoever, but that they may hold all [illegible] "[illegible] peaceably and quietly to themselves [illegible] "out any let or molestation [illegible] "[illegible] and [illegible] the city of Joppa, "which the Jews [illegible] possessed [illegible] "[illegible] alliance with the Romans, [illegible] under the "government of Hyrcanus, the son of Alexander, and "his family, with all the revenues and advantages arising from [illegible] whether upon husbandry, port-duties, taxes, [illegible], anchorage, impositions upon goods and exportations of corn for Sidon, except in the [illegible] (as [illegible] before) they [illegible] plough, plant, [illegible] to gather. As to the villages that Hyrcanus and his [illegible] formerly enjoyed in the Great Plain, it is the will of the senate, that they continue to Hyrcanus and the Jews [illegible] as before, and that [illegible] laws and customs be [illegible] and [illegible] and the priests, and all [illegible] had been formerly granted to them by the [illegible] people of Rome, [illegible] privileges [illegible] to Lydda itself. And [illegible] the Roman [illegible] formerly bestowed upon the kings of Syria and Cilicia, certain lands and estates, [illegible] still continue [illegible] of the Jews [illegible] that [illegible] him [illegible] and his [illegible], shall have place [illegible] among the [illegible] and other public [illegible] and [illegible] upon [illegible] giving them [illegible] the [illegible] drive them to their [illegible] [illegible] them."

Caius Julius, the fourth time emperor, the fifth time consul, and perpetual dictator, [illegible] following [illegible] of Laodicea [illegible] to the Jews.

"Whereas my [illegible] as [illegible] formerly [illegible] to my honourable [illegible] on the [illegible] of the high priest [illegible] of the Jews, [illegible] the senate and people of Rome, [illegible] the [illegible] good [illegible] in [illegible] respects [illegible] obliged [illegible] people of Rome [illegible] of the [illegible] have [illegible]."

"Caius Julius [illegible] consul to [illegible] greeting.

"Whereas [illegible] been made to us, at Delos, by [illegible] of the Jews [illegible] cities, [illegible] against [illegible] presume [illegible] your own [illegible] to [illegible] the [illegible] country [illegible] and sacrifices, they have [illegible] the [illegible] instruments [illegible] to let you understand that we will not [illegible] [illegible] to [illegible] to [illegible] and [illegible] that our [illegible] on the contrary, that [illegible] the [illegible] when [illegible] they enjoy in Rome [illegible] Caius Cæsar, [illegible] congregations [illegible] the Jews [illegible] permitted to [illegible] the Jews [illegible] out of that restraint, [illegible] to their own [illegible] and [illegible]. Wherefore [illegible] it be, that you [illegible] in order to the [illegible] that, in the privileges that we have [illegible] to allow them, it is but just and reasonable [illegible] to revoke and [illegible] such decree out of respect to us, [illegible] to them [illegible] our [illegible] they [illegible] ourselves."

After the death of Cæsar, Marcus Antonius, and Publius Dolabella [illegible] consuls [illegible] [illegible] to the ambassadors of Hyrcanus, upon the subject matter of their instructions, formed [illegible] with [illegible], and came to [illegible] on [illegible] [illegible] demands. Dolabella having [illegible] letters from [illegible], took occasion from the [illegible] to dispatch [illegible] Asia, and [illegible] to [illegible] the [illegible] of [illegible] province, [illegible] should [illegible].

"The emperor Dolabella to the magistrates, senate, and people of Ephesus, greeting.

"Whereas [illegible] given to understand [illegible] Alexander the son of [illegible], ambassador of Hyrcanus, the high priest [illegible] prince of the Jews, [illegible] that the Jews, being tied [illegible] [illegible] and constitutions of their country not to bear arms, travel [illegible] so much as [illegible] [illegible] sabbath day [illegible] rendered incapable of [illegible] the duties [illegible] of the [illegible] do [illegible] order [illegible] according to [illegible] [illegible] the same [illegible], that the Jews be, [illegible], exempted [illegible] [illegible] permitted the use of [illegible] according to [illegible] [illegible] to come [illegible] be given through all the cities of [illegible]."

[illegible] of the [illegible] and [illegible] the [illegible] in favour of Hyrcanus [illegible] the [illegible] Pretence [illegible] the [illegible] we have [illegible] the [illegible] We have produced [illegible] to the [illegible] with the Romans, [illegible] the capitol [illegible] monuments of [illegible] ought to [illegible] evidence, and [illegible].

CHAP. VIII.

[illegible]

About this time [illegible] Julius Cæsar [illegible] [illegible] Cæsar [illegible] the [illegible] of the [illegible] The [illegible] borders of [illegible] attacked by Julius Cæsar [illegible] and [illegible] Julius Cæsar in the senate-house, that [illegible] had [illegible] the [illegible] for the space of three years [illegible] months.

The death of Julius Cæsar occasioned [illegible] contentions and disorders among the subjects of the Roman empire. [illegible] of the people were [illegible] into factions, and, regardless of the public [illegible] according to their respective [illegible] and passions, and an universal [illegible]. [illegible] obtained the command of the army in Syria which was then before Apamea, [illegible] soon brought over to [illegible] Marcus and Delius, [illegible] fled the [illegible]. He then proceeded from place to place collecting men, money, and arms, wherever he went, but the place he most oppressed was Judea, on which he levied an enormous tax of between seven and eight hundred talents of [illegible].

During this confusion, Antipater committed the care of gathering part of the money levied on Judea, to his two sons, [illegible] Malichus (who was next to him in power, and [illegible] his enemy) was concerned [illegible] others in collecting there [illegible]. Herod, who was desirous of obliging the Romans, though at the [illegible] of his countrymen, [illegible] the [illegible] Cassius, of [illegible] of Gadara, as the [illegible] Coponius, [illegible] for [illegible]. He [illegible] negligence, formed [illegible] Hyrcanus, by the [illegible] Cassius had [illegible] collected, [illegible] Malichus [illegible] of his [illegible], which he considered as the [illegible] view. Antipater, entertaining suspicion of his design, [illegible], and placed himself at the head of [illegible] body of Jews [illegible] Malichus, who was bold and artful [illegible] went to Antipater and his sons, and, by [illegible], attempted to prove his innocence. [illegible] that Herod had the [illegible] of Antipater, he [illegible] to [illegible].

CHAP. [illegible]

Herod [illegible] Syria [illegible] Malichus.

At this time a war commenced between Antony and the younger Cæsar, (afterwards called Augustus, [illegible]) Cassius, sensible of the great talents of Herod, [illegible] him to the government of Cœlosyria, and [illegible] him a strong guard both of horse and foot, [illegible] the same time, that, after the war was over, he would promote him to the sovereignty of Judea. The advancement of Herod proved of fatal consequence to [illegible], for Malichus, thinking that Antipater would, [illegible] become still more powerful, resolved to dispatch him, and, to that end, taking the opportunity of Antipater's [illegible] with Hyrcanus, he bribed the butler to put poison into his wine, with which [illegible] Malichus, who [illegible] armed force, took possession of the city [illegible] of Antipater, a man of [illegible], a friend to the distressed, and a true lover of his country.

When Herod and his brother heard of this barbarous murder upon the person of their father, they were greatly incensed against Malichus, who, in their own minds, they were convinced was the author of it. But Malichus had the [illegible] to disown all, and [illegible] upon his justification. Herod was desirous of wreaking instant vengeance on the head of the traitor, but his brother Phasael dissuading him from this measure, through an unwillingness to disturb the public peace, they permitted him to make a defence, and [illegible] the appearance of being [illegible] his innocence.

[illegible] which they proceeded to the interment of their father, the ceremonies of which they caused to be performed with the most distinguished magnificence.

Herod [illegible] went to Samaria, [illegible] great disorder, [illegible] matters, and [illegible] law and justice. Soon after [illegible] came on a feast [illegible] upon he advanced with [illegible] Malichus, being [illegible], persuaded Hyrcanus not to [illegible] preparation of the [illegible] of the [illegible] to [illegible]. [illegible] Malichus, who, perceiving [illegible] to be [illegible] Herod and his [illegible] to [illegible] or Herod to [illegible], and the next [illegible].

CHAP. XII.

The [illegible] of [illegible].

Cassius, [illegible] in [illegible] orders [illegible] Tyre, in consequence of [illegible] Cassius, [illegible] to [illegible] of the [illegible], contrary [illegible] Tyre, where [illegible] the Jews might [illegible]. [illegible] Malichus [illegible] But [illegible] was frustrated through the [illegible] of Herod, who sent out [illegible] to meet Malichus [illegible] certain [illegible] of Herod, [illegible] to [illegible] general.

Cassius had no sooner left Syria, than great disturbances arose in Judea, for Felix, [illegible] his command in Jerusalem, [illegible] Phasael, and the people betook themselves [illegible] in his defence. Herod applied himself [illegible] governor of Damascus, desirous of [illegible] of his brother, but was prevented, [illegible] by a prevailing indisposition [illegible] thered the storm, and, with his own [illegible] This tumultuous [illegible] for [illegible].

proper to impose. Phasael reproached Hyrcanus with the highest ingratitude, in [illegible] after the [illegible] he had derived from him, [illegible] the possession of [illegible] the strongest fortress in the country. But Herod, [illegible] took all the places that had been [illegible] by [illegible], and brought him quietly to submit [illegible].

CHAP. XXI.

Antigonus, the son of Aristobulus, [illegible], and is defeated by Herod, who [illegible] Mariamne, the [illegible] daughter of Hyrcanus.

HEROD had [illegible] powerful enemy to [illegible] Fen[illegible] Antigonus [illegible] into [illegible] of [illegible] him, for the purpose [illegible] and, in consideration of [illegible], governor of Damascus, [illegible] also assisted by Marion, [illegible] of the [illegible] of [illegible], having [illegible] there, [illegible] Cassius [illegible] Herod, however, [illegible] to [illegible] brought [illegible] the [illegible] [illegible], [illegible] of them, a token of [illegible] He then [illegible] and being met by Antigonus, at the head of [illegible], in which Herod [illegible] victorious, the [illegible] opposite [illegible] rest, with the [illegible] flight. After this [illegible], Herod returned in triumph to Jerusalem, where he was received with [illegible] tions of joy [illegible] the family of Hyrcanus [illegible] with Mariamne, (c) [illegible] Aristobulus and Alexander [illegible] [illegible] had, by his wife, [illegible] [illegible] Doris, [illegible] [illegible].

CHAP. XXII.

Complaints brought by the Jews against Phasael and Herod [illegible] [illegible] of the [illegible] [illegible].

DURING these transactions, a decisive [illegible] in Macedonia, [illegible] Anthony and Augustus Cæsar [illegible] to Cassius [illegible] Anthony [illegible] Asia [illegible] ed at [illegible], he was [illegible] ambassadors from several parts and [illegible] to congratulate him on his late success [illegible] against Phasael and Herod [illegible] they [illegible] having [illegible] Herod [illegible] pleaded his cause so powerfully [illegible] by the [illegible] his adversaries could not obtain a hearing [illegible] Lysias, Tyrannus, and a body of the principal Jews [illegible] to [illegible] and [illegible] at the same time [illegible] their countrymen who were carried [illegible] by Cassius contrary to the rules of war, [illegible] restored to [illegible] when they [illegible] depart [illegible] Anthony, to the respective provinces in [illegible]

Anthony, pleased with the compliment, and that the request made by the Jews [illegible] general compliance, in consequence thereof [illegible] Tyrians and the Jews, [illegible] dispatched [illegible] the Tyrians, to the following effect:

"[illegible] Antonius, Emperor, to Hyrcanus the high [illegible], and [illegible] of the Jews, greeting.

"Whereas [illegible] we received from Lysimachus, the son of Pausanias, Joseph the son of Mennæus, and Alexander [illegible] of Theodorus, your ambassadors [illegible] at Ephesus, [illegible] of the continuance of [illegible] and [illegible] according to [illegible] [illegible] to us at Rome, [illegible] faithfully and worthily [illegible] and whereas we are [illegible] of your [illegible] [illegible] of your [illegible] the force of [illegible], we [illegible] agree to your [illegible] Now [illegible] and the [illegible] of Rome, [illegible] ravaged the whole country [illegible] without any regard to laws [illegible] [illegible] against the [illegible] of [illegible] [illegible] own [illegible] as in the [illegible] of Cassius [illegible] Philippi [illegible] up to the [illegible] almost [illegible] [illegible] at [illegible] [illegible] gave us [illegible] friends, [illegible] [illegible] [illegible] [illegible] [illegible] shall be our care [illegible] to provide [illegible] people may [illegible] for [illegible] country of [illegible] blessing. To [illegible] [illegible] [illegible] immediate discharge of all [illegible] [illegible] [illegible] been exposed [illegible] by Cassius, [illegible] you shall quietly [illegible] to yourselves [illegible] your [illegible], all the grants and privileges [illegible] [illegible] Lentulus and Dolabella, [illegible] [illegible] the Tyrians, [illegible] [illegible] full restitution of the goods [illegible] taken away from the Jews, [illegible] [illegible] [illegible] [illegible]."

"Marcus Antonius, Emperor, to the ruling [illegible] and people of Tyre, greeting.

"[illegible] we have been [illegible] [illegible] of Hyrcanus the high-priest [illegible] the Jews, that, in [illegible] possession of this [illegible] [illegible] [illegible] [illegible] of [illegible] against [illegible] of [illegible] [illegible] [illegible], with [illegible] you, not only

(c) [illegible]

[illegible]

"[illegible] in peace, [illegible] our allies, but also to "restore to the former [illegible] whatever you have [illegible] that [illegible] taken from them [illegible] the hands of our "enemies, who, as they had no [illegible] of right there-[illegible] themselves, by any [illegible] from [illegible], so neither could they [illegible] ought to [illegible] upon what any pretence [illegible], being [illegible] [illegible] And now [illegible] our adversaries [illegible] [illegible] [illegible] the [illegible] of their [illegible] [illegible] [illegible] the Jews, which [illegible] to be [illegible] [illegible] countenance, or [illegible] [illegible] [illegible] [illegible] portion [illegible] [illegible] [illegible] parts, [illegible] both sides, and to do impartial "justice."

"Mark Antony [illegible] to the magistrates, senate "and people of Tyre, greeting.

"I have sent you my [illegible], which you are to see "[illegible] [illegible] Lentulus, [illegible], and expect "[illegible] among your [illegible], where all people may take notice of [illegible]."

"[illegible] Antonius, emperor and triumvir, &c. as follows:

"Whereas Caius Cassius, [illegible] [illegible] [illegible] [illegible] [illegible] [illegible] the Jews, [illegible] [illegible] [illegible] [illegible] [illegible] upon [illegible] "our [illegible]."

[illegible] the people of Sidon [illegible] we think proper [illegible] in this place, that posterity may [illegible] honour and respect our nation has received, from [illegible] to time, from the state of Rome.

CHAP. XXIII.

[illegible] Herod and Phasael. [illegible] Herod [illegible].

WHEN Anthony, after this, came into Syria, he [illegible] [illegible], by Cleopatra, where he became [illegible] of her person and accomplishments.

Notwithstanding the repulse which the enemies of Phasael and Herod had met with, not [illegible] one hundred of the most eminent persons among the Jews repaired in a body to Anthony, with complaints and accusations against them, and the most eloquent speakers were appointed to urge their complaints. Anthony now thought proper to give them a hearing. The defence of the two brothers was undertaken by Messala and Hyrcanus, who, at this [illegible], became [illegible] to Herod. The cause was tried at Daphne, [illegible] full hearing of both parties [illegible] [illegible] whom he considered as [illegible] public administration? He replied [illegible] [illegible] capable of [illegible] [illegible] [illegible] was highly [illegible] Anthony [illegible] [illegible] [illegible] [illegible] [illegible]

[illegible] [illegible] [illegible] sent his [illegible] to the [illegible] place to [illegible] Herod [illegible] [illegible] [illegible] [illegible] [illegible] [illegible] [illegible] [illegible] [illegible] [illegible] [illegible] [illegible] [illegible] of [illegible] Jews [illegible] [illegible] commanded [illegible] [illegible] to death.

CHAP. XXIV.

[illegible] Herod [illegible] [illegible] [illegible] [illegible].

IN the year following, Pacorus, son of the [illegible] Parthian, and Barzapharnes, a [illegible] commander of that country, possessed themselves of Syria. [illegible] Ptolemy Mennæus dying at the same time, his son Lysanias succeeded him, having contracted a particular friendship [illegible] Antigonus, the son of Aristobulus, by means of Barzapharnes, who held him in great esteem.

Antigonus, who had long looked upon Herod with an eye of jealousy, had established an interest among the most leading persons of the Parthian nation, and contracted with them, for a thousand talents, and five hundred women, on their deposing Hyrcanus, putting him and Herod's party to death, and receiving him for governor in his stead.

Though the sum promised was not deposited, the Parthians embarked in the undertaking, and [illegible] with

---

[illegible] The word [illegible] [illegible] [illegible] [illegible] [illegible] [illegible] [illegible] [illegible] [illegible] kingdom, which [illegible] [illegible] [illegible] [illegible] [illegible] [illegible] [illegible] [illegible]

[illegible] [illegible] Ptolemais at the end of one book by [illegible] the sea-coast, and [illegible], the generals [illegible] the [illegible] through the inland parts. The [illegible] [illegible] the entrance of Pacorus into the city, but the people [illegible] and Sidonians opened their gates. Upon this he [illegible] a troop of horse upon the [illegible], to [illegible] a view of the state of the country, [illegible] Antigonus, at [illegible] request. The Jews of Mount Carmel espoused his interest, by whose assistance he was induced to think he should be in [illegible] of that part of the country which they call Drymi. At the [illegible] of others who came over to him [illegible] considerably augmented his force, he [illegible] even to [illegible], with a resolution to attack the [illegible] Phasael and Herod, at the royal palace [illegible] considerable part of them [illegible] fell upon them in the market-place, and driving them from their post, they [illegible] to the temple. Herod placed a guard [illegible] the adjacent [illegible] [illegible] the [illegible] of the sacred edifice, [illegible] impetuosity [illegible] [illegible] to the [illegible], [illegible] both them and the guard [illegible] [illegible] however, soon revenged [illegible] on his [illegible] [illegible], [illegible] defeat he gave them, with very great [illegible].

They [illegible] on [illegible] thing from day to day [illegible] [illegible] of Pentecost, [illegible] of Antigonus [illegible] great [illegible], on account of the [illegible] people [illegible] thither on that solemnity. When the time came, [illegible] gathered together [illegible] the temple [illegible], and others [illegible] Indeed they had seized on both city and temple. Herod [illegible] with a small party, the charge of the wall and the [illegible] being committed to Phasael. The enemy having [illegible] themselves in the suburbs, Herod [illegible] desperate[illegible] upon them, in which he did great execution, [illegible] before him, some into the temple, and some into the city, and forcing others to take [illegible], behind a rampart that was near at hand, while Phasael acquitted himself as became a man of valour.

[illegible] in the mean time entered the city, at the instance of Antigonus, with a small party, under pretence of quelling the [illegible], but, in reality, to effect the purposes [illegible] the Parthians had concerted with him. [illegible] received him and his party courteously, [illegible] other [illegible] [illegible] upon his life, for he prevailed [illegible] to go on an embassy to Barzapharnes, [illegible] to [illegible] him. But Herod was so averse to [illegible] of [illegible], that he [illegible] his brother to [illegible] and his whole party, to prevent [illegible], being [illegible] of the perfidy of the barbarians with whom they were engaged in a contest.

However, through some fatality, Hyrcanus and Phasael [illegible] [illegible], under the conduct of Pacorus, leaving a guard of two hundred horse with Herod, and ten of the people they call *Eleuteri*. Upon their arrival at Galilee, the commanders of the [illegible] garrisons met them [illegible] arms, but received them courteously, [illegible] than Barzapharnes, though he was designed as one of the principal instruments of the plot. Phasael and his train were conducted to a quarter upon the sea-side, where, being given to understand that the Parthians were to receive [illegible] talents, and five hundred women, of Antigonus, to assist him against them, they became apprehensive of the design, in which they were presently after confirmed by notice given to Phasael of their intention that very night, and there being a guard in readiness to seize on his person.

The plot would certainly have been carried into execution, had they not waited for the intelligence of Herod's being secured at Jerusalem by the Parthians, as had been previously concerted; for they inferred, that, if the other [illegible] had been secured first, it would of course afford Herod opportunity to escape.

[illegible] of the information was soon evident, from the coming up of the guards who were to execute the design. Upon the discovery, Phasael was [illegible] to [illegible] horse, and betake himself to immediate flight. [illegible] a man of the first rank and fortune in Syria, had [illegible] the plot, and having given the [illegible], offered him the convenience of shipping for his departure. But Phasael was [illegible] generous to abandon his friends in their distress, and [illegible] rather to go to Barzapharnes, and reproach him with the indignity of so foul a practice, by representing to him, that as money had been his object, so he was better able to gratify him than Antigonus, that he might have [illegible] entering on the conclusion of so horrid a deed on the [illegible] of ambassadors, in violation of the laws of good faith, hospitality, and nations. The barbarian had the [illegible] to deny the foundation of his suspicion, affirming that it [illegible] mere conjecture, and then went to Pacorus, his confederate in the design.

CHAP. XXV.

Hyrcanus and Phasael [illegible] taken up by the Parthians. Herod's flight. Jerusalem besieged. Antigonus obtains the government. Phasael destroys himself. [illegible] [illegible] [illegible] of Herod.

BARZAPHARNES had no sooner departed, than a party of armed men took Phasael and Hyrcanus into [illegible], [illegible] the [illegible] against the perfidy of the Parthians. An eunuch was also dispatched to apprehend Herod, if they could decoy him out of his palace. But Herod, having intelligence of the perfidious conduct of the Parthians, eluded their designs, and immediately went and [illegible] with Pacorus, and his principal officers, on their [illegible] proceedings, who also had the hardiness to disown all concern in the plot, though they had been privy to every [illegible]. They told him, that [illegible] ought to go out with them before the walls, and [illegible] the [illegible] who were bringing him his letters, for they were not taken by his enemies, but were coming to give "him an account of the [illegible] of Phasael." But having [illegible] of his brother's ill usage, and being confirmed in his [illegible] of the Parthians, from the opinion of Alexandra, a woman of singular prudence, and whose daughter he was to marry, Herod governed himself by her counsel and advice in preference to all others. Upon this [illegible] the Parthians deliberated on the measures that were [illegible] to be taken, not deeming it expedient to make an open [illegible] a person of such rank and eminence. But Herod, reflecting on the present distracted state of things, as well as the perfidy of the Parthians towards his brother, resolved to take advantage of the dusk of the evening to attempt an escape. He took with him all the troops he had about him, his mother, sister, and Mariamne, his contracted spouse, the daughter of Alexandra, and niece of Aristobulus, with his wife's mother, the daughter of Hyrcanus the youngest brother, and the rest of the family. This was a spectacle that must have affected the most obdurate heart: for who, without commiseration, could have beheld the women, with their infant children, lamenting their [illegible] abandoning their country, and being subjected to the most poignant calamities that could befal human nature.

But Herod sustained this reverse of fortune with invincible magnanimity, and, by his advice and example, endeavoured to animate his friends and companions. He told them there was no hope, either of one of safety, life, but in flight, and observed, that grief and despair were not only fruitless, but would be obstacles to their pursuing the means of their deliverance. Upon these words they formed a resolution necessary for the present occasion. They had not proceeded far, when an unfortunate accident happened in the overthrow of one of the carriages, that endangered the life of his mother. This disaster affected him to so great a degree, from the tender regard he had for his parent, and the apprehensions of being overtaken by the enemy through the

only occasion in which he certainly cast himself upon the point of his own [illegible], had he not been prevented by his friends, who [illegible] represented to him, that such an action would expose them to the fury of their enemies, and that it was not becoming a brave man to give way to despair. He then prosecuted his journey to the castle of Masada, with the utmost speed possible, though pressed on his march by the Parthians, with whom he had many skirmishes, but still got the better. He was also harassed by the very Jews themselves, who came up with him, when he had proceeded about threescore furlongs in his way from Jerusalem, but they were repulsed and put to the rout.

When he afterwards came to the [illegible] of Judah, he erected a famous palace upon the spot of ground where he obtained this victory, and built a city which he called by the name of Herodium. Coming afterwards to Resa, in Idumea, he was met by his brother Joseph, with whom he consulted on the most expedient means of getting rid of the multitude of useless and superfluous people they had in their train, as the castle of Masada, which they had fixed upon as their retreat, could not contain the whole body. He therefore dismissed about 9000 to provide, in the best manner they could, for themselves up and down in Idumea, and gave them money to purchase provisions, till they could find some place of defence. He took those who were fit for action, together with his near relations, into the castle where he disposed of the women and their families, to the number of about 800 persons, and leaving them a competence of provision, hastened to Petra, the capital of Arabia.

As soon as the Parthians understood that Herod had fled from the city, they seized on all that he left behind him, and plundered the houses of the principal people, who had left them for the safety of their persons. They made booty of all the property they could find, and even seized the treasure of the royal palace, but the spoil was not so considerable as they expected; for Herod, being sensible of their rapacious disposition, had the precaution to remove his most valuable treasures, and his example was followed by all those who attended him to Masada.

Having plundered Jerusalem and the adjacent country the Parthians put Antigonus in possession of the government, and then delivered to him Hyrcanus and Phasael in bonds. But the escape of the women was a mortifying disappointment to him, as the Parthians were by contract, to receive the women with money. As for Hyrcanus Antigonus ordered that both his ears should be cut off, in order that he might be incapacitated for ever after from becoming high-priest, blemished or maimed persons being deemed ineligible to the pontifical dignity. Phasael knowing that his death was determined, put a voluntary end to his life and sufferings; and not having the use of his hands to dispatch himself, such was his resolution, that he beat out his brains against the walls of the prison. Some affirm that the contusion was not mortal, and that the surgeons appointed by Antigonus, under pretence of assisting him, were in truth to dispatch him, and that they applied poison to the wound instead of remedies. He lived long enough, however, to understand that his brother Herod was at that time safe, and out of the hands of his adversaries, which made his death more welcome to him in the satisfaction of leaving one behind him that would avenge his blood upon the heads of his adversaries.

In the mean time Herod, so far from sinking under his misfortunes seemed the better disposed to encounter them. His first application was to Malchus king of Arabia, to borrow a sum of money of him, in his present state of distress, either upon credit and consideration, or upon the score of bounty and humanity, not doubting of a full and friendly return from a prince who was already indebted to him for many signal obligations. At this time Herod was unacquainted with the death of his brother, and his principal view in going to the king of Arabia, was to obtain a sum of money from him to [illegible] ransom, leaving a son of Phasael's along with him as security for the return of the money. But all his expectations proved abortive, for, before he reached Petra, he received an order from Malchus desiring him immediately to quit his dominions, as the Parthians were absolutely against receiving him. His answer was that he did not come with a view to put the prince to trouble or expence, but to treat upon some important affairs of his own. Upon reflection however, he thought it most prudent to depart, and therefore proceeded on his way to Egypt. In the evening of the first day he met with a [illegible], where he [illegible] then shelter in a castle, and were friends to his interest, and the day following he arrived at Rhinocorura, where he received the first information of the [illegible] of Hyrcanus, and of the death of his brother Phasael.

In the mean time Malchus, being [illegible] remorse at his ingratitude towards Herod, dispatched messengers after him to solicit his return, but as he had reached Pelusium, he found that it was too late to repair the injury he had done him. The inhabitants of Pelusium refused him the liberty of embarking from that place, upon which he applied to the magistrates of the town, who granted him permission to take what course he pleased. He set sail for Alexandria. Cleopatra, who was at this time [illegible] preparing for an important enterprize, gave him an honourable and magnificent reception, in order to induce him to take up his residence there for some time, but he was so desirous of proceeding to Rome, that neither the entreaties of the queen, the extremities of the season, and the danger of the seas could not divert him from his purpose.

He accordingly left Alexandria, and after a very tremendous voyage, at length reached Rhodes, where he found public affairs in a very embarrassed state. He was here received in a very generous and hospitable manner by two friends named Sappinius and Ptolemy, and though he was greatly distressed for want of money, yet he procured a vessel to convey him to Brundusium, from whence he proceeded with all possible expedition to Rome. Upon his arrival he repaired to Anthony, to whom he related an account of all his adventures in Judæa, the seizure and murder of his brother Phasael, the imprisonment of Hyrcanus, and the contract of paying the Parthians a thousand talents, and presenting them with five hundred women upon the advancement of Antigonus to the government through their assistance. He represented to him with much difficulty he had effected the escape of the women by night, into a place where they were since besieged, and in hourly expectation of falling into the hands of the enemy, and, having related these particulars, earnestly intreated some assistance, that he might recover the right which Anthony had [illegible] bestowed on him, and of which he had been unjustly and cruelly deprived by his enemies.

CHAP. XXVI.

Herod [illegible] Antigonus [illegible]

THE melancholy story of Herod's adventures excited the tenderest compassion in Anthony, who recollecting the former friendship that had subsisted first with his father, Antipater, and afterwards with him, and at the same time, being exasperated against Antigonus when he looked upon as a man of a busy, turbulent spirit, and a professed enemy to Rome, determined to espouse the interest of Herod with all his powers. Augustus concurred likewise with Anthony in promoting his defence, partly on the score of acknowledgment for former services, and partly for the sake of the friendship that had subsisted between the two families; for his father and Antipater had served together in a military capacity in Egypt. He wished also to gratify Anthony, by serving the person of his recommendation.

[illegible]

CHAP. [illegible]

[illegible]

HEROD [illegible] affairs thus prosperous [illegible] people and [illegible] accordingly [illegible] of Galilee, towards Antigonus [illegible] and [illegible] from Antony [illegible] kingdom [illegible] of Moses [illegible] who [illegible] advantage [illegible]

[illegible]

[illegible] on [illegible] of Silo [illegible] of the [illegible] to [illegible] royal [illegible] the Romans [illegible] and that, therefore, [illegible] to deprive [illegible]

[illegible] at length to acts of [illegible] Antigonus commanded the [illegible] from the walls, which they [illegible] by plying them with darts and arrows, that they were compelled in general to retire. It was now no longer a doubt but that Silo was corrupted, for he had [illegible] officers, that they encouraged [illegible] on pretence of the want of forage [illegible] quarters, and [illegible] great uneasiness to Herod, who [illegible] to apply, not only to Silo's officers, but [illegible] the common soldiers, being fearful lest a general [illegible] should take place and he, who, instead of [illegible] bribed [illegible], proved [illegible] to him [illegible] different. He accordingly repaired to them, [illegible] had received his commission from Cassius, Anthony, and [illegible], and encouraged them to [illegible] maintain their station, assuring them that [illegible] they should want nothing that could conduce to their satisfaction. He then appointed [illegible] to procure a supply of provisions, which were immediately distributed [illegible] and in order to [illegible] [illegible] with [illegible] under his protection.

But notwithstanding all this, he found some inconveniences from the treachery of Silo, who gave notice to Antigonus of all that passed; he [illegible] to Jericho, and the [illegible] frequently intercepted and cut off the convoys that were [illegible]. Herod, on the other side, was as watchful on his part, and, with ten companies, one half [illegible], the other Jews, together with [illegible] and a few troops of horse, proceeded towards Jericho. Upon his arrival he found the town [illegible] that [illegible] of the inhabitants, with their families, had fought refuge amongst the mountains.

The Romans rifled the city, and [illegible], in money, jewels, and other articles, [illegible]. After [illegible] he returned with his forces [illegible] his army [illegible] quarters in the new conquests, as Idumea, Galilee, and Samaria. Antigonus, through the prevailing influence [illegible], brought upon Silo so that part of the Roman army [illegible] means, might be quartered in Lydda, [illegible] to court the favour of Anthony.

But Herod, who could not remain inactive, dispatched his brother into Idumea, with 2000 foot and 400 horse, and went himself to Samaria, where he provided for his mother and the rest of his kindred, who he brought from Massada, and then proceeded to Galilee, to take the [illegible] garrisons which were then in possession of Antigonus. Coming up to Sepphoris in a deep snow, he found the place [illegible] abandoned, but abounding with provisions of every kind. The adjacent country being infested with robbers, who from the fastnesses of the caverns [illegible] the neighbourhood, Herod [illegible] horse and three companies of foot to drive them from their lurking places. About forty [illegible] after which he marched against them with his whole army, upon which they drew out, and made so vigorous a charge, that Herod's left wing gave way, till, upon a vigorous reinforcement, with Herod himself at the head of it, he brought his own men on again, put the adversaries to a total rout, and pursued them as far as the river Jordan. This overthrow brought all Galilee over to Herod, those only excepted who had sheltered themselves in the recesses of the mountains. The intended operations being now over, Herod ordered the common soldiers an hundred and fifty drachmas a man, and the officers a sum in proportion to their rank, and they were dismissed to their winter quarters. Silo, and the officers, who had been hitherto billetted upon Antigonus, now gave Herod to understand, that he not only refused to allow them more than one month's entertainment, but sent orders to all the country around to convey what they had to the mountains, and carry off, in fine, all the necessaries [illegible] so that the Romans might be starved out of their quarters. But Herod prevented this mischief, by committing the charge of providing for the army to his younger brother, Pheroras, with orders also to repair the fort of Alexandrion, which then lay in ruins; in both which commissions he acquitted himself much to his reputation.

Anthony was now at Athens, and Ventidius in Syria where he ordered Silo to join him, with the auxiliary troops of the Parthians, [illegible] to assist Herod if occasion should require. Herod, however, [illegible] people to Ventidius, [illegible] who lay lurking in the [illegible] hills. These recesses [illegible] caves and holes [illegible] to come at them, [illegible] of the mountains [illegible] impossible [illegible] from below, or from above to [illegible] [illegible] [illegible]

These [illegible] were even [illegible] that they [illegible] his permission to [illegible] themselves to [illegible] the [illegible] who [illegible] [illegible] but [illegible]

Herod [illegible] [illegible] foot, [illegible] [illegible] the Romans [illegible] had [illegible] [illegible] [illegible] [illegible]

[illegible] the loss of [illegible] Ventidius, according to [illegible] Machæras to Herod, [illegible] legions and a [illegible] horse. But Machæras, at the instigation of Antigonus [illegible] the [illegible] of Herod, was [illegible] to [illegible] of giving intelligence and [illegible] doing, however, at his approach the Antigonians [illegible] so far from [illegible] admitting him, that he ordered his people to keep [illegible] he [illegible] convinced of the propriety of Herod's [illegible] ing him, and [illegible] in [illegible] with [illegible] Hereupon he returned to the city of Emmaus, and in the fury of his rage put all the Jews to the sword he found in his way, without distinction of friend or foe. [illegible] was [illegible] this wanton barbarity, that [illegible] withdrew to Samaria, [illegible] resolution to [illegible] Anthony on the [illegible] [illegible] he was [illegible] of himself to cope with Antigonus, without the assistance of such as were [illegible] to their own [illegible] Machæras [illegible] [illegible] him on the way, to [illegible] him [illegible] to desist from his journey, or, if he was determined to prosecute it, to leave his brother Joseph behind, in order to carry on the [illegible] continued on with him [illegible] and Antigonus [illegible], upon this importunity, granted him his request [illegible] was [illegible], leaving the army under the command of Joseph, with express orders not to run any unnecessary hazard, or enter into any [illegible] with [illegible].

[illegible] being thus settled, [illegible] with [illegible] to [illegible] Anthony, who [illegible] at [illegible] Samosata, [illegible] Euphrates. Upon his coming to Antioch, he found a great number of people who were desirous to go over to Anthony, but [illegible] for fear of being set upon by a troop of [illegible], who had [illegible] upon and [illegible]. Herod, however, put himself at the head of them, and [illegible] both [illegible] protection, they proceeded [illegible], and when they were [illegible] within [illegible] days [illegible] of Samosata, they [illegible] behind [illegible] the enemy's [illegible] close behind the [illegible], upon the [illegible], to [illegible] Anthony. [illegible] Herod [illegible] coming up with the [illegible], fell [illegible] upon him [illegible]. But the king [illegible] violence [illegible] his [illegible], he [illegible] the ground [illegible] his own scattered troops, and [illegible] himself master of the [illegible] they had taken, [illegible], horses [illegible] and the baggage, [illegible] very considerable [illegible] Herod [illegible] journey, [illegible] with troops of barbarians, [illegible] progress [illegible], he [illegible] and cut them to pieces [illegible], the [illegible], the people [illegible] protector.

Anthony [illegible] of the [illegible] upon [illegible] troops to receive [illegible] possible honour and respect, [illegible] at [illegible] from [illegible] him with [illegible] under he had [illegible] him. [illegible] Anthony [illegible] put an end to the [illegible] the government of the [illegible], and the command [illegible], to Sosius, with orders to [illegible], and [illegible] to Egypt [illegible] the king [illegible], or the [illegible] himself with the [illegible] of [illegible].

During [illegible] transactions, Joseph, [illegible] was [illegible] in Judea, [illegible] went [illegible] to [illegible], when he went to Anthony. He [illegible] towards Jericho with [illegible] companies which he had from Machaeras, and encamped upon the mountain. The Romans [illegible] and undisciplined troops, [illegible] part [illegible], on the [illegible] of the place where he was posted, and [illegible] under his command, and [illegible] them, surprized and routed them, entirely destroying [illegible] companies, and cutting Joseph to pieces, fighting [illegible] at the head of them. Antigonus being master of the [illegible], and finding Joseph among the dead bodies, [illegible] though his brother [illegible] at the price of [illegible] talents. [illegible] the [illegible] of Galilee, and the [illegible] of Herod's [illegible] could [illegible] hold [illegible] in Judea [illegible] the [illegible] called [illegible].

The news of these disasters were brought to Herod at a place called Daphne, in the suburbs of Antioch, and [illegible] less [illegible] to him, from some foreboding dreams [illegible] had a little before, which manifestly pointed at the death of his brother. From this place he went to Mount Libanus, and taking eight hundred of the people along with him and a Roman legion, advanced to Ptolemais. In passing by [illegible] country of Galilee, he was set upon by [illegible], but repulsed the enemy, forced them back into the castle out of which they came the day before, [illegible] and disposed the troops early [illegible] attack. A violent tempest, however, arising, [illegible] obliged to draw off into some of the [illegible] shelter. Just as this happened [illegible] from Anthony, which reinforcement [illegible] they evacuated the place, and retired through favour of the night.

Herod, impatient to revenge the death of his brother, [illegible] with all [illegible] towards Jericho, where he [illegible] with great magnificence, all the grandees of the [illegible] upon his arrival. When the entertainment was over, he dismissed his guests, and retired to his own chamber. He had no sooner departed than the roof fell in; but no damage [illegible] in point of life, it was deemed a singular [illegible] of Providence in his deliverance from [illegible] danger.

The next day [illegible] of the enemy came [illegible] the mountains, and resolutely falling upon Herod's forces, the Romans were thrown into [illegible] confusion, that they immediately retreated. The [illegible] them, and [illegible] great [illegible] advantage was obtained on either side, only that Herod received a wound in the side from a [illegible].

Antigonus, at [illegible], sent Pappus, his general, [illegible], with [illegible] troops under his command, being [illegible] the enemy his strength, and that he [illegible]. [illegible] Herod got possession of five towns, [illegible] that were there [illegible] went [illegible] in quest of Pappus, who was then encamped at a place called Isana, [illegible] numbers, who came over to [illegible] Jericho. Herod [illegible] the enemy [illegible] for a battle, [illegible] immediately upon [illegible], [illegible] out, doing execution upon the [illegible] of his brother's death in the [illegible] they [illegible]. The houses were presently crowded with soldiers from top to bottom, some in [illegible], and [illegible] of the roofs, by means of some [illegible] instruments those within were all laid open to a universal slaughter. The most dismal part of the spectacle was the piles of dead bodies that lay in heaps [illegible] above and below, which could not fail of filling the spectators with horror.

[illegible] the remainder of their broken troops fled in such disorder, and in such numbers, that, had it not been for a furious tempest at that very time, the victors had [illegible] directly up to Jerusalem, and put an end to the war, for Antigonus was [illegible] upon the point of [illegible], to abandon the city. It was now too late in the evening, and Herod [illegible] ordered his soldiers to [illegible] he retired to a chamber to take the bath, as he was much fatigued after the engagement. As he was naked in the bath with only one attendant, out started three soldiers with swords in their hands, and [illegible] the room [illegible], rushed out at the door. Such was their consternation, however, that they hurried away, [illegible] to [illegible] themselves, without dreaming of doing any violence to the king, whom they might have most easily destroyed. The body of Pappus being found among the slain, Herod the next day ordered his head to be struck off, and sent to Pheroras, as a kind of consolation revenge for his brother Joſeph, whom Pappus put to death with his own hand.

When the rigour of the ſeaſon was over, Herod removed his army, and encamped near Jeruſalem, taking up his quarters on the temple ſide of the town, as Pompey had done long before him, and as the ſpot that lay faireſt for an attack. When he had collected his pioneers, with all neceſſary materials, and given orders for the caſting up the trenches and bulwarks, and made every proper diſpoſition for the ſiege, he went to Samaria, to conſummate his marriage with Mariamne, to whom he had been ſome time contracted, as already obſerved.

CHAP. XXVIII.

[illegible] and Herod [illegible] with a [illegible] army [illegible] againſt Jeruſalem, and lay ſiege to the city. The inhabitants, [illegible] from being [illegible] great [illegible]. Herod takes meaſures to ſubdue the ſiege of the [illegible]. The [illegible] take [illegible] ſet fire to the [illegible] works. Their [illegible] reſolution, and [illegible] progreſs. The Romans ſcale the walls of the city [illegible]. The Romans [illegible] the Jews [illegible] Antigonus [illegible] put to death. The end of the Aſmonæan family.

AFTER the celebration of the nuptials, Soſius ſent away his troops before him, being a conſiderable body of horſe and foot, ſoon after following them himſelf by way of Phœnicia. The king alſo returned from Samaria, with a reinforcement of about 30,000 men, which being joined, the whole army drew up together towards the walls upon the north quarter of the town, to the number of 11 legions of foot, and 6,000 horſe, with other auxiliaries out of Syria. The two generals were Soſius and Herod, the former ſent by Antony as an aſſiſtant, the other acting on his own account with a view of ſetting himſelf in the poſſeſſion of a kingdom, which the ſenate had conferred upon him on the overthrow of Antigonus, the profeſſed enemy of Rome.

The Jews within the city were numerous and reſolute, and made a very obſtinate defence; for the whole nation may be ſaid to have been gathered together at this important criſis. They animated each other by exclaiming inceſſantly, "*The temple of the Lord! The temple of the Lord!*" and ſome [illegible] ſuch preſages of victory, as ſeemed prophetically to foretell their deliverance. Nor were they wanting in their endeavours, by frequent excurſions and [illegible] into the country, to diſtreſs the aſſailants; for they ſwept it ſo bare, that there ſcarcely remained any ſuſtenance either for man or horſe. But Herod ſoon remedied this inconvenience, partly by the ambuſhes that he laid to enſnare the pillagers, and partly by commiſſaries and convoys he employed far and near for the ſupply of the camp. The ſeaſon being remarkably favourable, and an extraordinary number of hands employed, the pioneers ſoon finiſhed the approaches, and the aſſailants advanced to the battery, leaving nothing unattempted to carry their point. The beſieged, on the other hand, made a ſtout reſiſtance, oppoſing ſtratagem to ſtratagem, and by one invention fruſtrating another. They made many deſperate ſallies, and ſet fire to divers of the enemy's works, as well thoſe that were finiſhed, as thoſe that were only begun. Their courage and reſolution were in no reſpect inferior to the Romans; but, in point of military ſkill and experience, they were greatly ſurpaſſed by them. As faſt as one wall was thrown down, the defendants ſupplied it with a retrenchment that ſerved for another. They counter-wrought mine againſt mine, and in ſhort, with undaunted reſolution, oppoſed fatigue, danger, and difficulty, making a moſt gallant and deſperate reſiſtance. This bravery they exerted in defiance of a formidable enemy before the city, and a dearth of proviſions and other neceſſaries within the walls; for they were now in the ſabbatical year, when it was unlawful for them to till the ground.

Upon the fortieth day after breaking ground, twenty choſen men mounted the firſt wall, and were ſeconded by ſome of the centurions under the command of Soſius. The ſecond wall was ſcaled fifteen days after, and ſeveral galleries about the temple ſet on fire, which Herod imputed to Antigonus, in order to expoſe him to the hatred of the Jews. When the out-quarter of the temple, and the lower town, were taken, the Jews betook themſelves into the inner-court of the temple, and the upper part of the town; and, leſt the Romans ſhould interrupt them in their daily oblations, they deſired permiſſion of Herod, by their ambaſſadors, only to bring in ſo many beaſts as ſhould be neceſſary for the ſervice. Herod readily granted their requeſt, hoping it might prevail with them in his favour; but finding his miſtake, and that they were more and more ſtrenuous in their attachment to Antigonus, he fell on immediately with his whole ſtrength, and took the city by aſſault.

The Romans were ſo exaſperated by the oppoſition and the delay, and the Jews, in the intereſt of Herod, ſo averſe to thoſe of the other party, that they put all to the ſword without mercy, as well in the ſtreets, as in the houſes, without regard to age or ſex. Nor was the very temple itſelf any more a ſanctuary to thoſe who fled to it. Never was exhibited ſo ſhocking a ſpectacle of blood and ſlaughter, for the ſoldiers were ſo tranſported, betwixt fury and revenge, to ſuch a degree of implacable inhumanity, that notwithſtanding the injunction of Herod on their allegiance to withhold their rage, they continued the maſſacre, and death triumphed in all its horrid forms.

The conduct of Antigonus was unworthy the dignity of his ſtation; for, as ſoon as he found all was loſt, he came down from the tower, and, in the humbleſt manner, caſt himſelf at the feet of Soſius, who, inſtead of pitying, inſulted him in the higheſt degree, calling him by the name of *Antigona*, in token of contempt of his puſillanimity and cowardly behaviour. But, though he gave him a feminine appellation, he did not treat him like a woman, for he was put in chains, and kept in cloſe cuſtody.

Though Herod had gained a compleat victory over his enemies, he had ſtill more difficulties to encounter. The foreign auxiliaries were ſo preſſing and importunate to be prying into the temple, and the very ſanctuary itſelf, that neither authority, intreaties, threatenings or even force itſelf, could hardly reſtrain them. Indeed, he would have deemed his ſucceſs worſe than a defeat, if conqueſt had proved the cauſe of expoſing the ſacred and incommunicable myſteries of religion to the curioſity of the profane multitude.

Being deſirous that the city ſhould not be plundered, Herod informed Soſius, that if the treaſure was ſeized, and the town depopulated, he ſhould be ſovereign of a deſart, and that he would not purchaſe the government of the univerſe at the price of ſo much blood. Soſius replied, that it was according to juſtice and common practice, upon taking of places by aſſault, to allow the ſoldiers the advantage of the booty. Herod, admitting the force of Soſius's plea, as to what concerned the ſoldiers, undertook to compound himſelf for the plunder, and declared that every man ſhould be duly recompenſed out of his own private coffers. According to his promiſe he rewarded both private men and officers in proportion to their reſpective ſtations and merits, and preſented Soſius with gifts worthy his rank and character. In ſhort, the liberality and munificence he diſplayed on this occaſion, alſo gave univerſal ſatisfaction.

This memorable event happened in the conſulate of Marcus Agrippa and Caninius Gallus, on the 185th olympiad, in the third month, and upon the day of a ſolemn faſt, being the very anniverſary of their deſtruction by Pompey, for the city was taken upon that very day 27 years before.

Soſius after making a handſome preſent for the ſervice of the temple, departed from Jeruſalem, taking the puſillanimous Antigonus with him in bonds to Anthony, and leaving the courageous Herod in full poſſeſſion of the ſovereignty of Judæa. Herod entertained doubts that Anthony would not take away his life, and of courſe, apprehenſive, that, on his appearing at Rome, and preferring his claim to the government of the ſenate, as he was of the blood royal, and himſelf only a plebeian, it might ſtill tend to his degradation. He was conſcious that he might ſuggeſt, that though for his own part, he could not pretend to deſerve the dignity, having been in arms againſt the Romans, yet he might hope they would not puniſh his innocent ſons for the guilt of their father, but admit them to the ſucceſſion. Impreſſed with theſe ſuſpicions he prevailed with Anthony, for a conſiderable ſum of money, privately adminiſtered, to have Antigonus diſpatched, which being done, reſtored his tranquility.

With this prince ended the reign of the famous and illuſtrious houſe of the Aſmonæans, after being in poſſeſſion of the government an hundred and twenty-ſix years.

This family was illuſtrious in itſelf, for the long continuance of the regal and ſacerdotal ſucceſſion in it, and for the ſignal ſervices which they and their anceſtors, from time to time, had rendered our nation. But, through inteſtine broils, the adminiſtration was transferred from them to Herod, the ſon of Antipater, a perſon who had no claim from lineal deſcent, or dignity of extraction.

END OF THE FOURTEENTH BOOK.

ANTIGONUS King of the Jews BEHEADED at ANTIOCH, by order of Anthony.

FLAVIUS JOSEPHUS

ON THE

ANTIQUITIES

OF THE

JEWS.

BOOK XV.

[INCLUDING A PERIOD OF ABOUT TWENTY-SIX YEARS.]

CHAP. I.

Herod, having obtained possession of Jerusalem, and the sovereignty of Judæa, gratifies his friends, and revenges himself on his enemies.

AS soon as Herod obtained the sovereign rule of Judæa, he made it his business to promote and provide for those who had espoused his interest while he was in the rank and condition of a private man. He also took care to revenge himself on those whom he knew to have been his enemies, insomuch that hardly a day passed without a capital execution upon some one or other of them.

Pollio, the Pharisee, and his disciple, Sameas, were highly in his favour for the good offices they did him, in advising the citizens, when he lay before Jerusalem, to open the gates and receive him. This Sameas was the person who formerly foretold to Hyrcanus, and the rest of the judges, upon the questioning of Herod for his life, that, if they acquitted him, the time would come when he should as certainly take away their lives, as they might then take away his; and the prediction was verified in the event.

No sooner was Herod in possession of the city, than he got together all the royal ornaments, with the rich booty, in goods, gold, and silver, that had been taken away by the wealthy citizens, and commanded the whole to be conveyed to the royal palace, out of which he made a magnificent present to Anthony, and divided the rest amongst his friends and favourites.

He ordered 45 leading men, in the interest of Antigonus, to be put to death, and set guards at the gates of the city, that nothing might be carried out but the dead bodies. They also searched the dead, and whatever was found, either of gold or silver, or other treasure, was carried to the king. There was, indeed, no end of the miseries brought upon them by a covetous prince, for their whole possessions were not sufficient to satisfy his avarice. They were also in their sabbatical year, and had consequently no harvest to supply their wants.

Anthony, having, at this time, Antigonus in bonds, thought to expose him publicly in honour of his triumph; but when he heard that the Jewish nation grew seditious, and that, from their aversion to Herod, they continued to bear good will for Antigonus, he caused him to be beheaded at Antioch, as we have before observed towards the close of the last book. This is attested by Strabo, of Cappadocia, who thus writes: "Anthony ordered Antigonus, the Jew, to be brought prisoner to Antioch, and there to have his head struck off. He was the first king that ever the Romans put to death in this manner; but he had this to offer in his own behalf, that the Jews would not acknowledge Herod for their king while Antigonus was living. Nay, so great a reverence had they for their former prince, that they were not to be wrought upon, even by torments, to allow Herod so much as the name of king. But Anthony proposed to himself, by this dishonourable proceeding, to blast the memory and reputation of the one, and soften the popular aversion to the other."

CHAP. II.

Hyrcanus is set at liberty by [illegible] ... [illegible] ... by Aristobulus.

HYRCANUS, being at this time in the hands of the Parthians, news was brought him of Herod's promotion to the government. He had before made his court to the new king, from whom he obtained his liberty in the following manner.

Phraates, king of Parthia, being informed of the

irth and character of his prisoner Hyrcanus, held him in such high esteem, that he ordered his chains to be taken off, and allowed him the freedom of the city of Babylon, where there were many of his own sect, and where he had the same reverence paid him, not only by the Jews of that city, but those likewise on the other side of the Euphrates, as if he had actually been their sovereign and high priest; circumstances which could not but afford him considerable satisfaction.

When he came to understand that Herod was advanced to the government, judging [illegible] in his favour, and flattering himself with mighty expectations from Herod in his grateful return for an ancient engagement to the preserver of his life and honour, he determined to pay him a visit, but not without first advising with his particular friends. Having informed them of his design, after long deliberation they unanimously opposed it, alledging "that as long as he was amongst them, he might assure "himself, from them, and all their people, of a reverence "and obedience suitable to the dignity of his character, "which he could never expect in his own country, by reason of the maim he had received from Antigonus, which "rendered him unfit for such a charge." They also observed that, in point of good offices or acknowledgment of services, it was not with princes as with private persons, since their elevation in general altered their attention from past transactions. But these remarks, though pertinently suggested by his friends, had no weight with Hyrcanus, who nevertheless persisted in his resolution.

Herod, indeed, gave him an invitation, by letter, to come over to him, and take his part in the government, persuading him to desire Phraates, and his brethren, the Jews, not to envy him so great a happiness, as he had now an opportunity of shewing his gratitude to the person to whom he stood indebted for his advancement. To enforce the matter, Herod sent Saramallas upon an embassy to Phraates, with pressing arguments, and frequent presents to obtain his favour towards his worthy and endeared friend. But this zeal in Herod did not flow from principle, but from a caution, as being [illegible], to secure himself from every change of fate, and for that consideration, either to get Hyrcanus in his power, or put him out of the world, as the event afterwards proved.

Hyrcanus, having at length obtained his discharge from Phraates, and being amply supplied with money and necessaries by the Jews in Babylon for his journey, proceeded to Jerusalem, where he was received with every token of regard, honour and respect. Herod appointed him the first place at all public meetings and entertainments, treated him in the style of a father, and maintained such an appearance of amity, as could not fail to elude all doubt and suspicion of the integrity of his disposition. In fine, he omitted nothing that could give a favourable opinion of his regard for Hyrcanus, till at length he sullied all he had done before, by an act that caused the greatest disturbance in his own family. Being conscious of having any man of honour [illegible] advanced to the pontificate, he sent to Babylon for one Ananel, a person of obscure condition, and constituted him high-priest. The promotion of this mean person greatly disgusted Alexandra, the daughter of Hyrcanus, and mother of Aristobulus, (brother to Mariamne, the wife of Herod,) to whom by right of birth, the office of high-priest belonged. In order therefore to resent the affront offered to her family in taking it from her son, and of putting a foreigner into the pontificate, she wrote to Cleopatra, queen of Egypt, who had an absolute authority over Anthony, to request her influence for Aristobulus.

Anthony at first, did not attend to the matter. It happened, however, that one Gellius, a particular friend of his, being in Judæa about some affairs of his own, by chance saw Aristobulus and Mariamne, the uncommon beauty of which persons so affected his eye, that he could not refrain from complimenting Alexandra, as the mother of two such accomplished productions of nature, and recommending her to send their pictures to Anthony, as the most effectual means of securing his best services. Alexandra accordingly sent the pictures, and Gellius being disposed to inveigle Anthony into a passion for Mariamne, exaggerated the representation in the drawings, and in words described them as of angelic form.

Anthony deemed it imprudent to send for the wife of a prince who was his friend, and fearful of giving Cleopatra any ground for jealousy, wrote to Herod, informing him of his desire to see Aristobulus, if a convenient opportunity should offer. Herod did not think proper to send a youth of so attractive a person to Anthony, with whose excessive passion he was well acquainted, so that he put him off with a pretence that the Jews were so seditious and bent upon the experiment of another king, that if Aristobulus should leave the kingdom, it would excite dangerous commotions.

Herod having thus excused himself to Anthony, kept up appearances with Aristobulus and Alexandra, his wife Mariamne pressing him, upon every occasion, to do her mother justice in the instance of the pontificate, urging withal, that it was his interest so to do, and that the [illegible] incumbent on the office would excuse him [illegible] exception from taking the [illegible]. Herod, incensed at this spirited exertion, called his friends about him, and, in the severest terms, inveighed against Alexandra, telling them she had entered into a conspiracy against him, and influenced Cleopatra to prevail with Anthony to dispossess him of the government, and transfer it to her son, in which, he said, she was the more to blame, as she could not, in that instance, assert the cause of Aristobulus without degrading her daughter, and provoking the nation, by intestine feuds, for dethroning her son-in-law, and removing him from a dignity he had acquired by so much toil and hazard. Upon the whole, he declared himself ready to forget and forgive all injuries, and in a proof of the reverential regard he had for his mother, and all her relations, he would immediately vest her son with the exercise of the office, which he would have conferred on Aristobulus, had he been of proper age to have executed.

This declaration he tendered merely to amuse the women and friends about him, very much embarrassed Alexandra, who was so greatly affected by the joy of having accomplished her wishes on the one hand, and a concern of angering him lest he suspected on the other, that, in a transport of passion, she thus vindicated her conduct, declaring, that, with respect to the pontificate, she was hurt by the affront put upon her son, that she was determined to leave no lawful means unattempted to do him right, but as to any design she had of raising him to the throne, it was so far from her, that if offered she would have refused it. Her ambition, she said, went no farther than to see justice done to her son in that station, in which the honour of her family was concerned; and as that point was to be settled, she was so sensible of the king's gracious regard to her in the person of Aristobulus, that she would ever retain a most dutiful sense of the favour, and if she had in any instance, exceeded the bounds of respect and moderation, through a mistaken punctilio of honour she implored the pardon of the royal personage who might be offended. This pertinent address soothed the king, and the parties re-assumed at least the appearance of friendship.

CHAP. III.

Herod's first suspicions of the designs of Alexandra. Causes Aristobulus to be taken off. Exhibits a proof of [illegible] hypocrisy.

THE king deposed Ananel from the office of high-priest, alledging, as the cause, that he was a foreigner, and of the race of the Jews that were formerly carried away by the Syrians beyond the Euphrates, many thousands of whom took up their habitations in Babylon. He was, indeed, of sacerdotal extraction, and a friend of Herod's, who, upon Herod's coming to the crown, had created him high-priest and afterwards deposed him, though contrary to law, for the high priesthood is an office for life, and not to be taken away, when it is conferred. The first who broke in upon this rule was Antiochus Epiphanes, who removed Jesus to make way for his brother Onias. Aristobulus was the second, who took that dignity from his brother Hyrcanus; and Herod the third, who deposed Ananel, and conferred the pontificate on Aristobulus.

By this expedient Herod thought to have healed the divisions in his family; but it appeared from consequences, that the reconciliation was not so permanent as might have been expected, for he entertained suspicions that Alexandra would be no longer quiet, than till she had an opportunity of compassing her ends by reviving dissention. For this cause he confined her to her palace, and absolutely forbid her interfering in public concerns. He set guards over her, that the least transaction might not pass without his knowledge. This method of proceeding highly disgusted her; for, being a woman of spirit, nothing touched her so near as this officious scrutiny into her conduct, insomuch that rather than endure to subject it thus, and being deprived of the liberty of speech, she was determined to run any hazard to deliver herself from it. Thus resolved, she fully stated her case in a letter to Cleopatra, and requesting at the same time her advice and assistance, received, from that princess, an invitation to come away privately, with her son, to her in Egypt. Alexandra approved the counsel, and bethought herself of an expedient to put it into execution. She ordered two coffins to be provided, contrived for herself and son to be put in them, and appointed the servants, who were privy to the contrivance, to see them carried out by night, and put on board a ship that lay ready at hand to transport them into Egypt.

But this stratagem miscarried through the treachery of one of the servants, who communicated the whole scheme to a man named Sabbion. This person had been suspected of assisting in the death of Antipater, the father of Herod, and therefore, in order to obviate the consequences that might follow, he divulged the whole secret. The king suffered them to go some way from the city, and then surprized and brought them back. But fearing the power and influence of Cleopatra, he suspended his design, and making a virtue of necessity, pretended, with great clemency, to pardon in both what he dared not punish. It was not long, however, before he embraced an opportunity of taking a full revenge on young Aristobulus.

The feast of the tabernacles (which is one of our principal festivals) now approaching, Herod seemed disposed to celebrate it with the utmost mirth and good humour: but a circumstance occurred, that induced him to execute his design upon the youth sooner than he intended. Aristobulus who was to officiate as high-priest upon the occasion, possessed a most engaging person and demeanour, and was in the eighteenth year of his age. Having advanced towards the altar, he discharged his duty with so becoming a reverence, and the splendour of the pontifical robes added such a lustre to the graceful-ness of his person, that, by both these, he captivated the affections of the people, insomuch, that they could not forbear expressing the love, honour and esteem, they bore, in the warmest prayers and acclamations, and accompanying those tokens of regard and affection, with the most grateful acknowledgments of the various obligations they had to his noble family. This stimulated Herod's jealousy to such a degree, that he in his mind meditated a scheme for taking away the life of Aristobulus, which he effected as follows.

As soon as the feast of tabernacles was over, Herod went to partake of an entertainment with Alexandra at Jericho, where he took Aristobulus, in point of complacency, to bear him company in the diversion of the day. The weather being too warm for exercise, the company withdrew into the cool of the shade, near certain fish-ponds, in which several of them proposed to bathe. Aristobulus was prevailed on to be one of the party; and no sooner had he plunged into the water [illegible] who were there before [illegible] and dipped him, according to the direction of Herod, [illegible] held him under the water so long [illegible] he was at length actually drowned. Thus was this accomplished youth taken off, through the wicked device of a wicked king, in the eighteenth year of his age, and the first of his pontifical office, which was immediately restored to Ananel. When this lamentable catastrophe [illegible] to the women, distraction [illegible] countenance [illegible] despair and horror reigned around. It [illegible] loss, as to be mourned throughout Jerusalem [illegible] family seemed to [illegible] But Alexandra was more deeply affected than all, and it was [illegible] of her calamity, that, though she was convinced of the treachery [illegible] necessity, for her own security, to pass [illegible] Such was her despair at [illegible] violent hands on herself, but on cooler [illegible] checked her passion, hoping [illegible] slight [illegible] With [illegible] and seemed to have no knowledge of [illegible]

Herod to wipe off all suspicion [illegible] affected more than ordinary tokens of sorrow, [illegible] tears and exhibited an [illegible] might probably have been [illegible] remorse for forfeiting the blood of the [illegible] of youth; but as he held [illegible] for the security of the other, [illegible] to keep [illegible] clear of suspicion [illegible] were performed with the utmost pomp and magnificence, which he attended himself as chief [illegible] he [illegible] in some degree [illegible] for the loss they had sustained in the death of [illegible]

CHAP. IX.

[illegible]

NOTWITHSTANDING external appearances, Alexandra could not suppress her great [illegible] desire of obtaining revenge, [illegible] had recourse to Cleopatra, whom she [illegible] the untimely death of her son and the [illegible] was effected. She represented the villainy of Herod in such a light, and pictured her own [illegible] in such affecting terms, as moved the compassion of the queen, who resolved to do the utmost in her power to procure her redress. She accordingly made immediate application to Antony, pressing him, with the utmost importunity, to see justice done on the perpetrators of so barbarous a murder. She represented to him the disgrace [illegible] king, whom he had raised to the throne, and who was the usurper of the right of another, to commit so horrid an outrage upon the lawful heir [illegible] Anthony, [illegible] by the incessant solicitations of Cleopatra, was at length prevailed upon to cite Herod to account, and accordingly repaired to Laodicea, whence he cited him to appear before him, in order to clear himself [illegible] imputation laid to his charge for the death of Aristobulus.

Herod [illegible] of his guilt to [illegible] of his [illegible] and dreading the influence of Cleopatra, who had incensed Antony against him, he was greatly perplexed in what manner to proceed [illegible] He well knew, however, that it [illegible] will of the all-powerful Anthony, and [illegible] hazards to appear. He committed [illegible] of the government, in his absence, to [illegible] giving him privately [illegible] put him to death [illegible] for such was his attachment to her, that he could not bear the thoughts of her being in the possession of another even after his death; besides, he had received an intimation that the fame of her beauty had captivated Anthony. Having given these orders, he took his departure with a mind fraught with the most dismal apprehensions.

Joseph, being now vested with the administration of affairs, attended to his trust, and made frequent visits to Mariamne, partly on business, and partly from the respect due to her character as a queen. At these interviews he would frequently take occasion to insinuate the very affectionate regard Herod had for her, representing him as the tenderest and most loving of husbands. The women, and particularly Alexandra, treated his declarations with raillery, which rendered Joseph so zealous in the cause, that, to confirm the character he had given him, he insisted, as an incontestible argument of his affection, "That as he found he could not live without her, so he was resolved that death itself should never part them." But the women, as was natural, [illegible] this as an evidence of love, they rather construed it to be an intimation of a tyrannical purpose he had [illegible], in case of his own death, not to suffer them to survive him. A rumour was spread at this time, by some persons who bore the king ill-will, that Anthony had caused Herod to be put to the question, and after that to death.

The whole court was alarmed at [illegible] and particularly the women, insomuch, that Alexandra [illegible] to Joseph [illegible] for protection to the Roman legion, under Julius, that was then quartered without the city, and to take them along with him. She observed, that if there [illegible] the Romans would [illegible], or if ever Mariamne should come to the sight of Anthony, he would deny her nothing that she should ask him, though it were the kingdom itself, or all the royal privileges she could pretend to.

[illegible] his affair was under deliberation, letters arrived [illegible] Herod [illegible] the true report, for it appeared that Anthony, by force of presents and fair words, was so far brought over to his interest, that Cleopatra could no longer [illegible] the prejudice of Herod, for he not only exculpated him from every imputation of having been accessary to the murder of Aristobulus, but gave him [illegible] tokens of favour, [illegible] declared that kings were not to be accountable to their subjects for their actions. Herod [illegible] in his letters, that the generous Anthony had [illegible] him, setting forth that he had called him to his councils, and to his own feasts, in despite of all the calumnies of Cleopatra, who had a design upon the government herself, and did all she could to effect his destruction. Anthony, he added, was a prince of honour and justice, and told them they might expect him back again in a short time, better established in the possession of his kingdom, and in the assurance of Anthony's friendship, than ever. Cleopatra being entirely detached from him, [illegible] her acceptance of Cœlo Syria as a present, upon condition never to trouble him more in Judæa.

[illegible] Anthony's advancing on his expedition against the Parthians, Herod returned to Jerusalem, and his mother and sister, Salome, informed him of what had passed. The latter accused Mariamne of having had too great a familiarity with Joseph, her husband, whom she was willing to [illegible] rather than not obtain her revenge of the innocent Mariamne. This [illegible] some disagreeable words between Salome and the queen, who reproached her with the meanness of her original, in comparison of the royal stock of the Asmoneans, from whom she was descended.

This accusation, however, threw Herod into the utmost transport of rage and jealousy, so that it was with the greatest difficulty he could restrain his passion within the bounds of discretion. However, on cool reflection, he took Mariamne aside, and clearly examined her respecting her intimacy with Joseph. She said every thing in vindication of herself that it might be supposed innocence could dictate, insisting, that, as for any thing that might look criminal or dishonourable in her conduct, she was not only innocent with regard to Joseph, but (except himself) to all mankind. The king, enamoured with the charms of his wife, and overcome by the extremity of his passion for her, relaxed, by degrees, from the violent rage into which he had been thrown, and not only absolved her from all suspicion of the crime that had been imputed to her, but confessed himself perfectly convinced that she had not given the least cause of offence. He likewise repeatedly entreated her pardon for that inconsiderate haste, which induced him to give credit to a report, by which she had been so vilely traduced, and, with tears and embraces, besought her pardon for his indiscreet conduct.

Notwithstanding all this appearance, Mariamne had some doubts of the reality of Herod's regard for her; but the more she seemed, by her expression and manner, to entertain this notion, the more anxious was he to give her every testimony he could of his sincerity. At length, however, she exclaimed, "Truly, you give abundant proofs of the tenderness of your regard, as a husband, by ordering an innocent wife to be put to death, in case you should happen to die first." She had no sooner uttered these words, than Herod broke from her arms in the utmost rage, and cried out, with all the fury of a mad-man, "It is now evident, beyond a doubt, that the purity of my wife has been corrupted by Joseph, for nothing less than the confidence arising from such an intimacy, could have prompted him to give up [illegible] secret which had been committed to his care with such solemn injunctions not to reveal it."

In the impetuosity of his passion Herod had almost determined to put Mariamne to death on the spot, but after several violent struggles on his part the warmth of his affection prevailed for her preservation. With regard to Joseph, however, he gave strict orders for his being put to death, even without suffering him to speak a word in his own defence; and directed Alexandra, whom he considered as the cause of all the mischief, to be committed to close confinement.

At this same time great tumults prevailed in Syria, through the means of Cleopatra, who having absolute power over Anthony, was incessantly persuading him to take the dominions from the several princes and bestow them on herself. Her avarice and ambition, in fine, were so insatiable, that she attempted to gratify them at all hazards. She dispatched, by poison, her brother, a youth of about fifteen, to prevent his being king of Egypt. She prevailed on Anthony to have her sister Arsinoe taken off at Ephesus, at her very devotion in the temple of Diana, so that neither temples, sepulchres, or sanctuaries, escaped her, when there was money or spoil to be got by a sacrilegious violation of them. In fine, the world would have been too small to gratify the ambition and avarice of this licentious woman, for which cause it is no matter of wonder that she instigated Anthony to take from others that which she coveted herself, and that she no sooner set her foot in Syria with him, than she formed projects to gain possession of it. [illegible], suggesting that Lysanias, the son of Ptolemy, was a friend to the Parthians, she caused him to be put to death. She obtained also from Anthony, Judæa and Arabia, from the princes who had them in possession. Anthony, indeed, was so entirely at the command of this woman, that he may be said to have been enslaved by her, and subjected to many instances of conduct that sullied and debased his character. To avoid more trouble and importunity, he gave her some cities [illegible] parts of both provinces, and all the cities from the river Eleutherus to Egypt, excepting Tyre and Sidon, which have ever been free; but this did not prevent her from [illegible] Anthony with solicitations to procure them.

HEROD *reproached by* MARIAMNE *for his* CRUELTY
whom he throws from his Arms with scorn and indignation
falsely accuses her with inconstancy & orders her to be put to death

CHAP V

Cleopatra comes into Judea, and is honourably received by Herod, who afterwards is dissuaded from putting her to death, and [illegible] protected by his friends. He then conducts her on her way to Egypt. She is loaded with presents by Anthony.

WHEN Cleopatra had obtained these acquisitions, and accompanied Anthony, in his expedition to Armenia, as far as the Euphrates, she returned, and took Apamia and Damascus in her way to Judea, where she was honourably received by Herod, who treated with her for the revenue of that part of Arabia and Jericho which had been granted her, the latter being famous for balsam, which is the most precious of all gums, and likewise for the finest palm trees in the world. Upon her arrival, she attempted to form an intrigue with the king, nor did she affect secrecy, but exhibited evident and open tokens of affection for him, though most probably with a treacherous design. Herod, who well knew her abandoned and dissolute character, was, in some degree, fortified against her, but when she made such advances as exceeded the bounds of decency, he determined to repulse her, and called a consultation of his friends upon it. The question he put to them was, "Whether it was not most prudent to make sure of this lascivious woman, now he had her in his power, as it would be both a satisfaction to those she had abused heretofore, and a certain security from her abuse hereafter." He observed, that Anthony himself would derive an advantage from it, as she was the common enemy of mankind, and would no [illegible] [illegible] to him if ever he should oppose her will.

Herod was absolutely for taking her off, but those about him were no less positive against it, as a thing beneath the dignity of a prince. They therefore besought him not to think of acting so rashly, as Anthony would resent it, however conducive it might be to his advantage. They observed, that the love of his mistress, by force of secret practice, would but tend to enhance the value he had for her before, and irritate him to revenge. That with respect to [illegible] a violence upon the person of a princess of her illustrious quality, it would be no means be [illegible] [illegible] they represented to him the tumult and confusion which would inevitably follow, both in the kingdom and the royal family, if he carried his purpose into execution, and that he was justifiable in rejecting the importunities of the woman, upon every principle of reason and sound policy. Through dint of argument, and the confidence reposed in their judgment, Herod was brought over to an acknowledgment of his error, and was diverted from his desperate resolve, so that, as an instance of conduct totally reverse, he bestowed rich presents on Cleopatra, and conducted her some part of the way to Egypt.

Anthony, having subdued Armenia, sent Artabazes, the son of Tigranes, prisoner into Egypt with the princes his sons, and presented them to Cleopatra, together with the immense booty he had taken there. Artaxias, the eldest son of the Artabazes, who fled out of the country at the breaking out of the war, succeeded his father, but was afterwards driven out by Archelaus and the emperor Nero, who put Tigranes, the youngest brother of the family, into his place.

With respect to the revenues of the country, which Anthony had given to Cleopatra, Herod made a point of paying it most punctually, being well assured that it was his interest to keep upon [illegible] terms with her. The Arabians considering that Herod had the [illegible] of the tax, made due payment, from time to time, of the proportion of two hundred talents a year, [illegible] [illegible] continue, so it gradually fell off, till at length it was reduced to less than one half.

CHAP VI

Herod makes war upon, and conquers the king of Arabia. But [illegible] of [illegible] the Jews [illegible] overcome.

IN consequence of this deficiency of payment on the part of the king of Arabia, Herod had himself in readiness to take revenge for the [illegible], but was prevented by the civil broils of the Romans. The battle of Actium was now depending, which, it was apprehended, would put an end to the competition between Augustus and Anthony for the empire. This fell out in the 187th olympiad.

Herod having been now a long time, through the favour of Anthony, master of a rich and populous country, raised a very powerful army, with which he intended to have marched to the assistance of his patron. But Anthony, instead of accepting his services against Augustus, prevailed on him to proceed against the Arabians, whom he knew to be a [illegible] [illegible] [illegible] people, [illegible] [illegible] [illegible] [illegible] [illegible] [illegible] past [illegible] [illegible]. This [illegible] [illegible] [illegible] to the counsel of Cleopatra, [illegible] [illegible] [illegible] [illegible], [illegible] [illegible] the Jews and [illegible] [illegible] [illegible] [illegible].

In obedience to the direction of Anthony, Herod marched back with his army, and [illegible] [illegible] [illegible] to Arabia, having under his command a very considerable body of horse and foot. The Arabians having received intelligence of Herod's motions, [illegible] [illegible] [illegible] battle near a place called Diospolis. As soon as the armies met, an engagement took place, which was, for some time, maintained with great obstinacy on both sides, till at length victory declared in favour of the Jews, great numbers of the Arabians being slain, and the rest put to flight.

Soon after this the Arabians raised another considerable army at a place called Cana, in Coelosyria; Herod having received authentic information, and [illegible] [illegible] that they were upon their march, advanced with the main body of his troops to that part of the country, intending there to encamp, and fortify himself, till he should have a favourable opportunity of attacking the enemy with a [illegible] [illegible] of success. But the soldiers were so [illegible] with the consideration of their former victory, and so well assured of the resolution, fate, and [illegible] to [illegible] [illegible], that they besought Herod not to suffer them to be held, but give the command to fall on immediately. Nay, [illegible] was then [illegible] [illegible], that they were ready to break through all the bounds of discipline to obtain their desire.

This uncommon ardour and alacrity of the troops, gave Herod so much satisfaction, that he was determined to encourage their humour, and not to check the eagerness of disposition which he thought might [illegible] [illegible] [illegible] to victory. He therefore immediately put himself at their head, grasped his sword, gave the word of command, and begun the attack, telling them to follow me [illegible] [illegible]. [illegible] upon they marched forward to the [illegible] [illegible] such [illegible] resolution, that the Arabians were [illegible] [illegible] [illegible] courage before the encounter began. [illegible] [illegible] [illegible], indeed, they made [illegible] [illegible] show of resistance, but, [illegible] [illegible] the first onset, they gave way, and [illegible] [illegible] pursued in the utmost confusion.

This rout would in all probability, have occasioned the total destruction of the Arabian army, had it not been for Athenion, Cleopatra's general in that quarter. This Athenion, who had long been an inveterate enemy to Herod, had been in a kind of neutrality, but with his men drawn up in order, attending the issue of the battle. Finding the Arabians worsted, and the Jews [illegible] [illegible] [illegible] [illegible] [illegible] cut with [illegible] but [illegible] [illegible] [illegible] [illegible] in the confidence of victory, Athenion, with a considerable body of the natives, took the Jews off their guard, and [illegible] them by surprise, dispersed them with an [illegible] [illegible] sued them through the woods, and other places of rugged passage, and put great numbers to the sword. Upon this defeat, the Arabians took courage, rallied, and renewed the action, and made such terrible slaughter in the pursuit, that a very small party of this great body escaped with life.

After this melancholy issue, Herod posted away with all possible speed for relief; but before he could bring it, the Jewish camp was taken and pillaged. This fatal catastrophe was owing to a sudden and unexpected surprize, through confidence and carelessness on the part of the Jews. Herod, in consequence of this disaster, was compelled to have recourse to the making depredations and incursions upon the Arabians, as opportunity would admit, and, by small advantages, gain some compensation for the capital defeat his army had sustained. But the time thus spent was not absolutely thrown away, for the troops were thereby kept in a perpetual exercise, instructed in the duties of military discipline, inured to hardships and fatigues, and in some degree qualified to redeem their lost honours at a future period.

CHAP. VII.

[illegible] earthquake in Judæa. The Jewish ambassadors are put to death by the Arabians.

THE hope of Herod's being able to conquer his enemies, was greatly checked by a dreadful earthquake, that happened in Judæa, in the seventh year of the reign of Herod, and the year of the famous battle of Actium. It destroyed prodigious numbers of cattle, and by the falling of the buildings in the several towns and villages, it was computed that not less than 10,000 people lost their lives. But the soldiers, who were in the open fields, escaped with much less injury; for though most of their tents were thrown down, yet little other damage took place, than some being maimed, and the whole greatly frightened.

Though this providential calamity was sufficiently terrible in itself, yet it was greatly magnified by report; and the Arabians, imagining the Jews to be utterly ruined, cherished the flattering idea, that no difficulty would attend their possessing themselves of a province, which now had not a sufficient number of inhabitants to sustain a defence. The Jews, in the height of their distress, dispatched ambassadors to the Arabians humbly soliciting terms of accommodation, and that a peace might be established between them. But the Arabians not only put the ambassadors to death, but, in a short time after, marched, with a powerful army, into Judæa, in full confidence of making themselves masters of that country.

As soon as the Jews understood that the Arabians had entered Judæa, they were thrown into the utmost consternation. Their spirits were greatly depressed, by the reflection of their late calamities; and they despaired of being able to make any resistance against their enemies. The king seeing this, did all in his power to raise their spirits, begged of them to dismiss their unreasonable anxiety, and intreated an exertion of as much courage as might be necessary to prepare themselves for their own defence. Some of the more timorous sort of his people felt their misfortunes so severely, that, while the sense of them was recent in their minds, they could not be easily prevailed on to attend to the arguments of prudence and wisdom: but Herod, having brought them at length to a more tractable temper, in order to encourage and support, addressed them to the following effect.

CHAP. VIII.

Herod's [illegible] inspires the Jews with courage [illegible] vanquish the Arabians. In their distress for want of [illegible], [illegible] surrender.

"YOU are not unacquainted, my fellow soldiers, that we have had, not long since, many accidents, that have put a stop to what we intended to accomplish, and it is probable that even those that are most distinguished for their courage, can hardly keep up their spirits in such circumstances. But since we cannot avoid fighting, and nothing, that hath happened, is of such a nature, but may, by yourselves, be recovered into a good state, and this by one brave action, I have proposed to myself, both to give you some encouragement, and, at the same time, some information. Both which parts of my design will tend to this point, that you may still retain your own proper fortitude. I will, then, in the first place demonstrate to you, that this war is a just one on our side, and that on this account, it is a war of necessity, and occasioned by the injustice of our adversaries; for if you are once satisfied of this, it will be a real cause of alacrity to you. After this, I will farther demonstrate, that the misfortunes we are under, are of no great consequence, and that we have the greatest reason to hope for victory. I shall begin with the first, and appeal to yourselves as witnesses to what I say. You are not ignorant, certainly, of the wickedness of the Arabians, which is to that degree as to appear incredible to all other men, and to include somewhat that shews the grossest barbarity and ignorance of God. The chief things wherein they have affronted us, have arisen from covetousness and envy; and they have attacked us in an insidious manner. What occasion is there for me to mention many instances of such their procedure? When they were in danger of losing their own government of themselves, and of being slaves to Cleopatra, what others were they that freed them from that fear? It was the friendship I had with Anthony, and his kind disposition towards us, that hath been the occasion that even these Arabians have not been utterly undone, Anthony being unwilling to undertake any thing which might be suspected by us of unkindness. But when he had a mind to bestow some parts of each of our dominions on Cleopatra, I also managed the matter so, that, by giving him presents of my own, I might obtain a security to both nations, while I undertook myself to answer for the money, and gave him two hundred talents, and became surety for those two hundred more, which were imposed upon the land that was subject to this tribute. This they have defrauded us of, although it was not reasonable that Jews should pay tribute to any man living, or allow part of their land to be taxable. But although that was to be, yet we ought not to pay tribute for these Arabians, whom we have ourselves preserved. Nor is it fit that they, who have professed, and that with great integrity and sense of our kindness, that it is by our means that they keep their principality, should injure us, and deprive us of what is our due; and this while we have been still not their enemies, but their friends. Whereas observation of covenants takes place among the bitterest enemies, but among friends is absolutely necessary. This is not observed among these men, who think gain to be the best of all things, let it be by any way whatsoever, and that injustice is no harm, if they may but get money by it. Is it, therefore, a question, with you, whether the unjust are to be punished or not? when God himself hath declared his mind that so it ought to be, and hath commanded that we should ever hate injuries and injustice, which is not only just, but necessary, in wars between several nations. For these Arabians have done what both the Greeks and the barbarians own to be an instance of the grossest wickedness, with regard to our ambassadors, whom they have beheaded, while the Greeks declare that such ambassadors are sacred and inviolable. As for ourselves, we have learned, from God, the most excellent of our doctrines, and the most holy part of our law, by messengers, or ambassadors. For this name brings God to mankind the knowledge of God, and is sufficient to reconcile enemies one to another. What wickedness, then, can be greater than the slaughter of ambassadors, who come to treat about doing what is right? and when such have been their actions, how is it possible they can either live securely in common life, or be successful in war? In my opinion this is impossible. But, perhaps, some will say, that what is holy, and what is righteous is, indeed, on our side, but that the Arabians are either more courageous, or more numerous, than we are. Now as to this, in the first place, it is not fit for us to say so, for with whom is what is righteous, with them is God himself. Now where God is, there is both multitude and courage. But to examine our circumstances a little: we were conquerors in the first battle, and when we fought again, they were not able to oppose us, but ran away, and could not endure our attacks, or our courage. But when we had conquered them, then came Athenion, and made war against us without declaring it. And is this an instance of their manhood, or is it not a second instance of their wickedness and treachery? Why are we, therefore, of less courage on account of that which ought to inspire us with much stronger hopes? And why are we terrified at those who when they fight upon the level, are continually beaten? and when they seem to be conquerors, they gain it by wickedness? If we suppose that any one should deem them to be men of real courage, will not he be excited by that very consideration to do his utmost against them? For true valour is not shewn by fighting against weak persons, but in being able to overcome the most hardy. But then if the distresses we are ourselves under, and the miseries that have come by the earthquake, have affrighted any one, let him consider, in the first place, that this very thing will deceive the Arabians, by their supposal that what hath befallen us is greater than it really is. Moreover, it is not right that the same thing that emboldens them should discourage us, for these men do not derive their alacrity from any innate virtue of their own, but from their hope as to us, that we are quite cast down by our misfortunes. When we boldly march against them, we shall soon pull down that insolent conceit of themselves, and shall gain this by attacking them, that they will not be so insolent when we come to the battle. For our distresses are not so great, nor is what hath happened an indication of the anger of God against us, as some imagine, because such things are accidental, and adversities that come in the usual course of things. If we allow that this was done by the will of God, we must allow that it is now over by his will also, and that he is satisfied with what hath already happened; for had he been willing to afflict us still more thereby, he had not so soon put a stop to our calamities. As for the war we are engaged in, he hath himself demonstrated, that he is willing it should go on, and that he knows it to be a just war; for while some of the people, in the country, have perished, all you who were in arms have suffered nothing, but are all preserved alive, whereby God makes it plain to us, that if you had universally, with your children and wives, been in the army, it had come to pass, that you had not undergone any thing that would have much hurt you. Consider these things, and what is more than all the rest, that you have God at all times for your protector, and prosecute these men with just bravery, who, in point of friendship are unjust, in their battles perfidious, towards ambassadors impious, and always inferior to you in valour."

This speech had the desired effect, the soldiers shaking off all despondency, and resuming their natural courage and alacrity. Herod, having sacrificed in form, marched away immediately towards the Arabians beyond the river Jordan. Between the two armies was a castle, of which the contending parties were equally desirous to get possession. A party of Arabians attempted to gain the castle, but the Jews, without much difficulty, repulsed them, and soon after took possession of the hill. Herod duly arranged his men in order of battle, and took every possible method to provoke the enemy to an engagement. In point of numbers, the Arabians had the superiority, but the Jews were by far the most courageous and intrepid. A general consternation appeared in the Arabian army, which so animated the Jews, that they pushed them to their very trenches, where, for a time they made a faint shew of resistance, while despair was evident from their looks and actions. They maintained, however, a kind of fight, partly as encouraged by their numbers, and partly as compelled by inevitable necessity, till at length, after a long contest, and much bloodshed, they were put to a total rout, and with so terrible a slaughter, that, between those who fell by the enemy's sword, and their own, and those that were trodden to death in the crowd, there were missing 5000 of their number. The rest made their way to their camp, but with a miserable prospect before them, being destitute of all the necessaries of life, and, to add to their desperate condition, they were so blocked up by the Jews, that there was no possibility either of relief or escape.

In this extremity they sent deputies to Herod, requesting that he would either grant them peace, or free them from their present distress for want of water; but he would admit neither of proposal or request, till at length their thirst became so intolerable, that, in the space of five days, no less than four or five thousand came out, and surrendered themselves prisoners, to avoid the insupportable calamity of a raging drought. On the 6th day all the rest made a sally, by consent, and attacked the besiegers, chusing rather a present certainty of death, than to perish gradually and ingloriously. Having taken this resolution, they issued out of their camp, but without either strength or spirit to sustain so desperate an action, so that, on the first attack, there fell above 7000, by which the rest were taught that Herod was a skilful commander, and being thus effectually humbled, they surrendered themselves to the protection of the conqueror.

CHAP. IX.

The battle of Actium. Hyrcanus put to death by Herod, who repairs to Cæsar, and commits his government to his brother Pheroras.

THE reduction of the Arabians highly gratified the ambitious Herod, who went back to Jerusalem in full possession of his utmost wishes. *But this tide of prosperity* was greatly eclipsed, by his receiving intelligence of the defeat of Anthony, at Actium, by Augustus, for both friends and foes were agitated at his situation, as it was by no means probable that he, who had shewed so much friendship for Anthony, should remain without punishment. The former did not affect to disguise their apprehension of his ruin, while the latter, under a pretence of condoling with him, inwardly rejoiced at the pleasing prospect they had of a change in affairs. It occurred to Herod, that Hyrcanus, being the only surviving branch of the royal family, it would be much for his interest to have him taken off, whatever might be his own fate, with respect to Cæsar, since, whether he escaped his resentment or fell under it, he thought it necessary to remove his own fears, by cutting him off from the succession. While Herod was ruminating on this horrid design, the very family of Hyrcanus furnished him with an opportunity of executing his purposes. Hyrcanus he knew to be of an easy and indolent disposition, averse to business, and content in an easy station of life. But his daughter Alexandra, on the contrary, was of an aspiring turbulent spirit, and exceedingly anxious for a change in the government. Seeing her father so [illegible] and unconcerned at the [illegible] state of their family, she represented to him the disgrace of [illegible] the indignities which Herod daily put upon [illegible] and advised him to apply to Malchus, at this time governor of Arabia, requesting [illegible] occasion, to receive him into his protection [illegible] that if Herod should fall under the displeasure of Cæsar, which might reasonably be expected [illegible] could not fail of being restored to his dignity, and

ing an indisputable right and title, and the good-will of the people manifestly on his side.

Hyrcanus at first turned a deaf ear to the solicitations of his daughter; but her importunities at length prevailing, he wrote to the Arabian, and committed the charge of the letter to one Dositheus, whom he considered as a confidential friend to himself, as well as an inveterate foe to Herod. The purport of the letter was, to desire that Malchus would send him a party of horsemen to the lake Asphaltites, about three hundred furlongs from Jerusalem. But he was greatly mistaken with respect to the confidence he reposed in Dositheus, who choosing rather to form an interest with the present king, no sooner received the letter, than he carried it to him. When Herod had read the contents, he made his acknowledgment to Dositheus for his good office, and requested that he would seal the letter up again, and carry it forward to Malchus, and receive his answer, as it would afford him the highest satisfaction to know how he would act in so interesting a business.

Dositheus executed his commission with the utmost punctuality, and brought back the Arabian's answer, which was to this effect: "That he was willing to give entertainment to Hyrcanus and his family, that if he chose to bring with him all those Jews who remained true to his interest, they should likewise be received in the most hospitable manner; that he was ready to send a proper force to conduct them with safety, and, in fine, heartily disposed to afford Hyrcanus all possible assistance in any way he might require."

Herod, upon the receipt of this letter, sent for Hyrcanus, and demanded of him whether he held any correspondence with Malchus. Hyrcanus answered in the negative; upon which Herod produced the letter, read it publicly, and ordered Hyrcanus to be put to death. This is according to the account contained in the commentaries of king Herod. Other historians record, that he was put to death for a conspiracy, and not for the crime that is here related. They write, that Herod and Hyrcanus, being once at an entertainment, the former, without any apparent suspicion, asked the latter whether he had received any letters from Malchus? and when he answered in the affirmative, but that the contents were merely complimentary, he was again asked if ever he had received any presents from him: to which he also replied in the affirmative, but they were only four horses for his recreation. It is said that Herod charged those upon him as crimes of corruption and treason, and gave orders for his immediate execution. To demonstrate that he had been guilty of no offence, when he was brought to this end, they alledged the peculiar complacency of his temper, which he ever maintained from his earliest youth, and that even when he came to be king, he committed the management of the greatest part of the public affairs to Antipater the father of Herod; that he was upwards of fourscore years old, and knew that Herod's government was in a secure state, and himself on the wrong side of the Euphrates, having left his friends behind him, and all these in submission to Herod's dominion. From these considerations they infer the incredibility of his attempting any enterprize, by way of innovation; and thence conclude that it was a plot of Herod's contrivance.

Thus ended the life of Hyrcanus, a life long and troublesome, and chequered with a vast variety of fortune. He was advanced to the pontificate during the reign of his mother Alexandra, and continued to discharge the duties of it nine years, at the expiration of which his mother died, and he assumed the reigns of government. He did not, however, be in possession of the sovereignty above three months, when he was expelled by his brother Aristobulus. After this he was restored to his former station by Pompey, who put him in possession of all his dignities, and, for the space of forty years, he continued in the enjoyment of them, but was at length dethroned by Antigonus, suffering the pains and disgrace of having his ears cut off, and being carried away prisoner among the Parthians. After remaining some time in this situation, he obtained his liberty, and returned home, flattering himself with great advantages from his friendship of Herod. But in this hope he was so disappointed, that the latter caused him to suffer an ignominious death at a most advanced age, after having experienced so many of the malicious turns of fortune. He was distinguished by the candour and moderation of his disposition, as well as by his regard to the laws of equity. He was remarkable for his love of ease, and generally entrusted the administration of public affairs to the care of others, from a conviction, that he was himself ill-calculated for the management of them. This easiness of disposition laid the principal foundation of the fortunes of Antipater and Herod; yet, in the end he fell a sacrifice to that very goodness of temper which ought to have been his protection.

Herod, having obviated all grounds of fear by the death of Hyrcanus, prepared to wait on Cæsar, though he had no reason to expect any favour from him, as he was a man who had so heartily espoused the interest of Anthony. He had strong suspicion of Alexandra, and not knowing what advantage she might take of his absence to occasion some tumult, committed the care of the government to his brother Pheroras, placed his mother Cyprus with his sister, and other relations, in the castle of Massada, laying a strong injunction on his brother, if any misfortunes should befal him, to maintain his authority, and continue the administration in his own name. His wife Mariamne, and her mother Alexandra, he secured in the castle of Alexandrion, as such animosity prevailed betwixt his wife, his mother, and sister, that they could not possibly live together in peace. He put the government of the fort into the hands of two friends of approved truth, Joseph and Sohemus, under pretext of doing honour to those princesses, but with private orders, if any violence was offered to his person by Cæsar, immediately to put them to death, and use their endeavours to fix his brother and sons securely in the government.

CHAP. X.

Herod addresses Cæsar, by whom he is confirmed in his government of Judea. Magnificently entertains Cæsar in Ptolemais.

HEROD, having given these directions respecting what he would have done in his absence, left Jerusalem, and proceeded with all expedition to wait on Cæsar, who was at this time at Rhodes. Upon his arrival he immediately made application for being admitted to an audience of the emperor, which being granted, before he entered into his presence he laid aside his diadem, and remitted nothing else of his usual dignity. As soon as he came into the presence of the emperor, without needless apologies, as is common in such cases, he frankly addressed him in words to this purport:

"Illustrious Cæsar, (said he,) I wait not upon you to disavow the sincerity of a friendship I have always entertained for Anthony; and I must be free enough to declare, that, if it had been in my power to have made him master of the world, he had not wanted that distinguished station. I acknowledge, great prince, that I am indebted to Anthony for the regal state I at present enjoy, and had not my duty called me against the Arabians, I would have manifested my gratitude by being personally with him in the last battle. I did, however, my utmost to serve him by supplying him with soldiers, provisions, and money. Notwithstanding the unfortunate event at Actium, I still entertain for Anthony the greatest warmth of friendship, and venerate him as a generous patron. Though I could not attend him in person, yet I gave him such advice, that, had he pursued it, would have been of the most material advantage. I urged him to abandon Cleo-

"patron, telling him that while his connection with "her subsisted, he would be in continual danger; but "he chose to proceed in another mode, and has promoted your interest rather than his own, for want of an "exertion of that prudence which his situation demanded. Now, though you may have conceived the less "favourably of me, because I attached myself to the interest of Anthony, at a time when you was his professed enemy, yet I shall not, on that account hesitate "to make known and defend the services I have done "him, and the perfect esteem I have ever had for him. "If you will, for a moment advert to his rank, and the "friendship I bore him, without retrospect to the peculiarities of his situation, I conceive that you will see so "much gratitude and good faith in my conduct, that "you may think the acceptance of my friendship worthy "your notice: for the dignity of my character will suffer no alteration, whether I vow this friendship to Cæsar or to Anthony."

Herod delivered this speech with such an air of magnanimity, and such grace of demeanour that Augustus who possessed a natural benignity of mind, was not able to resist its power. He treated Herod with singular instances of regard and esteem, directed him to re-assume his crown, and be the same friend in future to himself, that he had formerly been to Anthony, giving him also to understand, that Cappidius had made him sensible of the good offices Herod had done him in the affairs of the gladiators. When Herod had obtained so kind a reception, and had beyond all his hopes, been reinstated in his kingdom, more securely than ever, by a decree of the Roman senate, upon Cæsar's immediate application, he could not but be affected with a degree of transport, and take every opportunity of testifying the sense he entertained of such liberal favour. Upon this consideration he attended Augustus into Egypt, treating himself and his friends upon the way, with a magnificence suitable to his dignity of character, and due acknowledgment of obligation. He interceded with the emperor on the behalf of Alexander, a friend of Anthony, in order to obtain his pardon; but Augustus, having bound himself by solemn vow not to spare him, his request could not be granted.

The Jews who, on Herod's departure, had given him up for lost, were now so astonished at his return with a greater degree of reputation and splendour than that with which he had left them, that they looked upon him as a person under the peculiar care of Providence, which turned to his advantage all those circumstances that appeared to lead him only into disgrace and danger.

When Cæsar was upon his return from Egypt, Herod went out to meet him at Ptolemais, where he treated him with most superb magnificence, and amply supplied his whole army with necessaries. Upon this occasion Cæsar gave him every token of friendship and familiarity, insomuch, that they ordinarily rode out together while their troops were reviewing. Having a train of 150 attendants, richly habited, and perfectly instructed in the duties of their office, Herod appointed them to wait on Cæsar and his friends in their passage, and take care that neither himself, or his army, should want either wine or water, over the dry and barren desert, which gained him great reputation amongst the soldiers. Besides, he presented Cæsar with five hundred talents, and gave so universal a satisfaction that they held him in the highest veneration. Having thus improved a signal opportunity of demonstrating his generosity to divers Romans of the first rank, in their passage out of Egypt, he acquired the character of one of the most illustrious princes upon earth.

CHAP. XI.

Distracted state of Herod's family. Deaths of Anthony and Cleopatra. Herod causes Sohemus to be put to death. Pusillanimity and perfidy of Alexandra. Death and character of Mariamne. Herod is inconsolable for the loss of her. A great pestilence in Jerusalem. Alexandra endeavours to possess herself of several strong fortresses in the neighbourhood of the capital. Is put to death by order of Herod. Cruelty of Herod to his friends. Herod rules with despotism.

THE satisfaction which Herod felt in consequence of his very great success in his late expedition, was greatly eclipsed by the disturbances he found among his own family on his arrival at Jerusalem. Mariamne, his wife, as well as his mother-in-law, had been very unhappy on account of the situation in which he left them at his departure, considering themselves rather as prisoners, in the castle of Alexandrion, than as being lodged there for the security of their persons. His wife was strongly possessed with an opinion, that, in the whole of his professions of regard to her, he had no farther view than the consulting of his own convenience. But the circumstance she held most heinous, was her husband's resolution not to suffer her to survive him in case of his death. Being apprehensive that he might have left orders for the execution of his sanguinary purpose both with Joseph and Sohemus, she tried various means to discover if her suspicions were justly founded. For some time Sohemus remained true to his trust; but on Mariamne's treating him with great complaisance, and presenting him with several very valuable articles, he began to recede by degrees, and at length discovered the whole secret with which Herod had entrusted him. Mariamne was so incensed with these conditional orders which Herod had repeatedly given respecting her, that she conceived the greatest antipathy against him, and such was the horror and dread of her mind, at the thought of living with a man who could harbour such a design, that she made it the subject of her daily prayer that he might never return to her alive; and, at a future period, when she had not the power to conceal her sentiments any longer, she acknowledged this circumstance in the most open and explicit manner.

As soon as Herod returned from Cæsar, he immediately repaired to Mariamne, and delivered to her the happy tidings of his success, at the same time embracing her with an apparent tenderness of affection. But while he was relating the circumstances of events which he thought would afford her the highest satisfaction, she looked upon her with an air of the greatest indifference, without paying the least attention to what he said. She was, in fact, entirely unreserved in her neglect, and being a woman who prided herself in acting without disguise, took no pains to assume a look foreign from her heart, but gave Herod the opportunity of reading in her countenance that his good news and endearments gave her more pain than pleasure.

This apparent aversion in Mariamne tortured the mind of Herod, who, partly through the indignation he felt at finding his love rejected, and partly through his confusion from the transports of his rage, was for a time almost distracted. He saw no means of gratifying his love without offering violence to his resentment, and at the same time dreaded giving scope to his vengeance more than the opposite extreme; for he felt a principle of self-love in his breast which told him, that, should he take vengeance on his wife, the most unhappy consequences would arise to himself, when future experience should convince him, that life was not to be supported without the endearments of her conversation.

The restless anxiety of Herod's mind leaving him in doubt how he should conduct himself with regard to Mariamne, his mother and sister thought this a fit opportunity of increasing the difference between them, by doing all kinds of ill-offices, and propagating every species of calumny that might tend to promote that hatred which had already taken possession of the breast of Herod. In consequence of this, Herod became daily more and more discontented in his mind, and behaved with a greater degree of severity to [illegible] wife. On the contrary Mariamne took [illegible] pains to disguise the discontent which rankled in her heart; so that the excessive regard that Herod entertained for her, was, by degrees, converted to the utmost rancour and hatred; and it is probable she might have fallen an immediate sacrifice to his resentment, had he not, just at this juncture, received intelligence of the deaths of Anthony and Cleopatra, and that Egypt was then in the possession of Cæsar. Upon this information Herod hastened away to [illegible] his [illegible] with the greatest dispatch, and once more committing Mariamne to the care of Sohemus, with acknowledgments for his care [illegible], [illegible] the grant of a command in Judea, as [illegible].

When Herod arrived in Egypt, he was received by Cæsar, with the greatest kindness and respect, and having [illegible] him to Antioch [illegible] so [illegible] with the emperor that he put him in possession of that [illegible] which Anthony had bestowed on Cleopatra, with the addition of Gadara, Hippos, and Samaria, towns, and the [illegible] of Gaza, Anthedon, Joppa, and the Tower of Strato, which [illegible] no [illegible] to his royal state.

But [illegible] Herod [illegible] himself [illegible], on his return, he found nothing but trouble and vexation at home. Mariamne still [illegible] her resentment for the [illegible] given to Sohemus; so that when he [illegible] offered [illegible] she not only rejected them [illegible] the utmost [illegible] but reproached him, in the bitterest terms, [illegible] of her relations; which enraged Herod to such a degree, that he could hardly [illegible] laying violent hands on her. [illegible] his [illegible] Salome, the sister of Herod, and [illegible] the [illegible] time, took the [illegible] of [illegible] cup-bearer, whom she had [illegible] that purpose, to accuse the queen of having tempted him to [illegible] poison, under pretence of [illegible] the [illegible]. Herod [illegible] had [illegible] with which he [illegible] to [illegible] of [illegible] ordered [illegible] particular conduct of Mariamne to the [illegible] it [illegible] would [illegible] that was [illegible] this [illegible] to this order [illegible] could [illegible] until, [illegible] hearing [illegible] some words, [illegible] that the [illegible] of Mariamne [illegible] from some [illegible] that had been communicated to her by Sohemus. The sufferer [illegible] when Herod burst out into the most [illegible] passion [illegible] that "Sohemus, who had [illegible] to be a loyal subject, [illegible] "received himself [illegible] "never could have betrayed [illegible] "tions that with which he had been entrusted, but in the "confidence of [illegible] Mariamne." He therefore gave immediate orders that Sohemus should be put to death; [illegible] he directed that his wife should be [illegible] before a court of justice, and [illegible] ready [illegible] to do his will.

When [illegible] the charge exhibited against her was, having conspired to poison the king Herod [illegible] against her, both by his words and [illegible] with the conduct of any man in a court of justice, and the judges [illegible] the disposition of the king, followed his example, and Mariamne was pronounced guilty of the charge exhibited against her. Herod, however, [illegible] of his conduct, observed, that [illegible] would be more [illegible] to [illegible] her life, and detain her in prison [illegible] put her to death; which proposition was approved of, not only by the judges, but the greatest part of the [illegible] by Salome and her adherents, who [illegible] violent in their [illegible] [illegible] for immediate [illegible] consequence of what they urged, that a [illegible] would [illegible] among the people

if the queen's life was spared, Herod was prevailed on to agree to her execution, and a day accordingly appointed for the tragical scene.

As soon as Alexandra found to what extremity the proceedings against her daughter had been carried, [illegible] every reason to apprehend that her own life was in danger. In order, therefore, to avoid the dreadful consequence, she descended to a conduct that was altogether derogatory to the dignity of her [illegible]. Her fears [illegible] induced her to go such lengths [illegible] she was [illegible] of not being thought to have combined with her daughter, [illegible] she sought every opportunity of [illegible] her, [illegible] as the most [illegible] of women, and extolling the justice of the [illegible] which had doomed her to death for continuing [illegible] to [illegible] husband, to whose tenderness [illegible].

Alexandra carried [illegible] to such a degree, that she became [illegible] despised, [illegible] who could [illegible] to [illegible] commiserating the extremity of her misfortunes. But Mariamne, even while she was conducting to the place of execution, [illegible] mother's unnatural behaviour, though her countenance [illegible] the sense she [illegible] of the [illegible] such her [illegible], she maintained her spirits with the greatest degree of firmness and constancy, [illegible] exhibiting, [illegible] the change of her countenance, [illegible] the least [illegible] of apprehending death. In a word, [illegible] she [illegible] the [illegible] ing [illegible] the world [illegible].

[illegible] would have been [illegible] [illegible] to [illegible] a [illegible] her [illegible] Her beauty was so great, [illegible] of [illegible] [illegible] the charms of [illegible] to render [illegible] to such [illegible] of any degree [illegible] these superiour [illegible] in a great degree to the [illegible] of [illegible] in the [illegible] Herod. He was [illegible] that [illegible] the [illegible] opposed [illegible] permitted her to do what she [illegible], and indulged her in every gratification she chose [illegible] the [illegible] gave [illegible] to those frequent and intemperate reproaches which she cast upon Herod, without reflecting that she was thereby destroying her own happiness; for, by this kind of conduct she rendered herself obnoxious to the mother and sister of her husband, and finally to himself, [illegible] he conceived to [illegible] excessive [illegible] could not, by any circumstance whatever, be alienated more especially to such a degree as to affect her life.

After the death of Mariamne, the passion which Herod had entertained for her in her life-time, displayed itself with redoubled violence. When he came to reflect upon the sentence which had [illegible] ordered to be carried into execution, he broke out into the strangest and most unmanly exclamations, frequently repeating the name of Mariamne, and saying, that her blood cried loud for vengeance. The agonies of his mind [illegible] to such a degree, that he sought to divert his melancholy by feasting, company, [illegible] a variety of entertainments. But all these endeavours proved fruitless, and, instead of finding any relief, he grew [illegible] [illegible], talked in a [illegible] manner, and, while the [illegible] were on him would frequently call for Mariamne, and direct that she should be brought before him.

While Herod was in this distracted state, a most dreadful plague broke out in Jerusalem, which raged with such prodigious violence, that people of all ranks and degrees fell [illegible] to its [illegible], and many thousands were taken off in a very short space of time. This dreadful calamity was universally considered, by the people, [illegible] consequent on the murder of the unfortunate and innocent Mariamne.

Herod's disorder [illegible] daily increasing [illegible] he withdrew [illegible] [illegible] and [illegible] take the exercise of hunting. L— however, he had been long in this retreat, he was attacked with a disorder in a more violent than the former, and attended with such a racking pain and inflammation in the head, that he was not master of his own conduct. The prescriptions applied for his relief were found to do him more injury than service, so that his case was considered as no other than hopeless. The difficulties that arose in the attempt to conquer this disease, the peculiar situation of the patient, and the impossibility of relieving him in the regal — way, being considered, the physicians reflected that it would be in vain to interpose their advice any longer, and therefore left him entirely to his own management, on the — to prosecute every — he might — — in every thing he desired. This was at Samaria, now called Sebaste.

The wretched situation of Herod being made known to Alexandra, who was then at Jerusalem, — reflecting on the circumstance, she began to consider whether or not it might be possible for her to obtain possession of the strong fortresses in the — of the capital. She was particularly desirous of becoming mistress of two above the rest, one of which was situated in the city, and the other close adjoining to the temple, being assured that the people must be altogether at the mercy of the party who should be in possession of these two towers. Both the Jews were so attached to their religion that they would on no consideration dispense with their daily sacrifices, and it must have been at the option of whoever commanded these — whether they should have any sacrifices or not. Alexandra, therefore pursuing her design, thus applied to the governors of these respective towers in words to this effect: "I need not inform you of the very deplorable state of the king's health, which strongly convinces you that the two towers may be given up to the possession of the master of the king's wife, or the children of Herod and Mariamne, lest, in case of his death, a different family should succeed to the throne; and even if the king should recover, the persons of his nearest relations are those to whom the government may with most safety be trusted."

The governors (one of whom was named Achiab, and nephew to Herod) partly from a sense of their duty, but chiefly from attachment to Alexandra, refused to acknowledge the force of her arguments for delivering up the towers, telling her, it would ill become them to make a kind of prejudice upon the king's life, to whom, during many years, they had entertained the most perfect friendship and loyalty. No sooner was their conversation ended than Achiab repaired to his uncle, and gave him a particular account of the proposal made by Alexandra. Herod, who was by this time much recovered from his illness, was enraged to the highest degree, and without suffering Alexandra to his presence, or allowing her to say any thing in her own defence, he issued immediate orders that she should be put to death.

This fit of sickness, of which Herod recovered with the greatest difficulty, produced a very strong and singular effect both in his body and mind, particularly the latter. His disposition was totally altered, and he became so extravagantly cruel and suspicious, that the least trifle ruffled his temper, incited him to acts of the greatest barbarity, and — friends or foes — the objects of his vengeance. — instance, Costobarus, Lysimachus, Antipater, — called Gadias, and Dositheus, were taken off upon various pretexts.

Costobarus was an Idumean by birth, a man of the first rank, and descended from — whose ancestors had formerly officiated as priests of Coze, — held in great veneration, till, in the days of Hyrcanus, they embraced the religion of the Jews. Herod no sooner obtained the government than he gave this Costobarus the command of Idumea and Gaza, with his daughter Salome to wife, who — Joseph, he — —

— to him — This — so much — hope and — of Costobarus, — him to — sufficient — the — of — deeming it — Idumeans, to own themselves the subjects of the Jews, in consequence of embracing their — He therefore sent — to Cleopatra, reminding her that — had been — the dominion of her forefathers, and that — to make application to Antony — command, promising — the — at her entire devotion. — not — from any preference he gave to the government of Cleopatra, but because he thought that upon the — of Herod's power, it would not be difficult — to obtain for himself the government of the Idumeans, — for the execution of — the — both, and — brought the — of — Cleopatra tried her influence with Antony, but without — and this — to — Herod would have put — to Costobarus, — the intercession of his — he obtained his pardon, though he was — under — suspicion.

Some time — a disagreement prevailed between Costobarus and Salome, who, in consequence, sent — a bill of divorce, though directly repugnant to the custom of the country, — the privilege of the husband, who — — and — — — Salome, — — her — alleging that she — her motive — and — — — from — Lysimachus, Antipater, and Dositheus, was forming a confederacy against — As — of what she — — were — — of Babas, whom he had — — — When Herod, upon an enquiry, discovered the truth of this allegation — the — — — the — known enemies to his interest — — from the — —

When Herod was before Jerusalem in the — of Antigonus, the besieged were so distressed by the — of famine, and the — of the siege, that the greater part were for opening the gates, and — Herod into the town. The sons of Babas, — — — of birth, and — great — — as friends to Antigonus, — — — to — the — — and — the government in the — line. Upon the taking the city, Herod — charge to Costobarus to keep strict watch upon the avenues of the city, — — of the party — to his interest to escape. Costobarus, sensible of the esteem in which they were held by the multitude, and supposing that their preservation might conduce to his interest in case of a change in the administration of affairs, — them to — — — in a place of — Herod suspected them — — — that — knew not what was become of them. A proclamation was then published, and other means followed, to detect the offence the king had received in the disobedience of his orders, but without any effect, — after the — there was no — — but at the most imminent — —

At length the whole plan was — open by Salome, and the king having ordered the — — to be made for the — — — they were found and all cut to pieces. — — Hyrcanus was extinct.

Herod had no sooner established an absolute power, than he gradually departed from the antient constitution and laws of his country, by the introduction of foreign inventions and innovations. He appointed games to be celebrated, every fifth year, in honour of Augustus, and, for that purpose, erected a theatre in Jerusalem. He also built a stately amphitheatre without the walls of the city; and these were wonderfully magnificent, and attended with an enormous expence. But these edifices were opposite to the Jewish laws and customs, which gave no sanction to the exhibition of games and public spectacles. To add to the magnificence and extent of these entertainments, Herod caused them to be proclaimed far and near, with large promises of reward to such as should excel in the different performances. By these means he brought in competitors, in the various kinds of exercise, from all quarters, and the greatest adepts in the several professions, not only wrestlers, but musicians, vocal and instrumental, horse-racers, charioteers, &c. In fine, it was his peculiar care that nothing might be wanting to contribute to the pleasure, ornament, and curiosity of the main design. He imitated whatever was superb and sumptuous in other nations, for the intent of giving public demonstration of his grandeur. Inscriptions of the great actions of Cæsar, and trophies of the nations he had conquered, made of the purest gold and silver, encompassed the theatre itself. To diversify the entertainment, he provided lions, tigers, and [illegible] wild beasts as were extraordinary either for ferocity, [illegible], or any quality of a singular nature. Some of these beasts of prey were set loose upon each other, while others were selected to encounter condemned criminals.

Foreigners were greatly surprised and delighted with these spectacles; but to real Jews they appeared no other than [illegible], introduced to the dissolution of those ancient customs they held in the highest veneration. For [illegible] be more horrid than to take pleasure in the beastly practice of sacrificing men to beasts, and spilling human blood in sport and derision? Besides, they deemed it the most egregious folly, as well as impiety, to change good old customs for frivolous new ones. But, above all, the Jews were most disgusted with the trophies, which they imagined to be images of men covered with armour, and consequently to be repugnant to the institutions of their country. They discovered their aversion to these trophies in such animated terms, that Herod chose rather to overcome their prejudices by mild than rigorous means; but all the arguments he could throw out had no effect, for they unanimously exclaimed against the impiety of his proceedings, declaring they could submit to any thing except the introduction of images, (meaning the trophies) into the city, which was absolutely contradictory to the laws of their country.

Herod, finding their disgust more and more increase, and that they were not to be pacified, either by the force of arguments or persuasion, took some of eminent rank to the theatre, shewed them the trophies, asked their opinion of them, and what they took them to be. Upon their declaring they were the images of men, Herod gave orders that they should be stripped of their external ornaments, and exposed as naked frames of wood, which rendered their assertion ridiculous, because they had ever before held the ornaments of images in contempt and derision.

Though Herod, by these means, satisfied the multitude, and allayed the vehemence of their indignation, there were many who persisted in their abhorrence of the introduction of foreign customs, esteeming it a violation of the laws of their country, as likely to be the origin of very great mischief. For this cause they held it their duty, at the hazard of their lives, to assert these laws against the infringements of Herod, who, under the function of royal authority, would act the part of an enemy, in thus imposing on their consciences and liberties.

The people were at length so inflamed with this innovation, that ten citizens entered into a conspiracy against the person of the king, in defiance of all danger that might attend the enterprize. Having preconcerted the matter, they concealed daggers under their garments, ready for the execution of their resolve. They then went, by common consent, to the theatre, with full resolution to stab the king, and, in case of disappointment, with respect to himself, of making such havock among his attendants, that their example would render him [illegible], and that this instance of their bravery, in the vindication of their religion and discipline, would be an incitement to others to follow their steps.

As Herod was just entering the theatre, one of his spies, who had found out the whole affair, discovered it to him; whereupon, being conscious to himself of the odium he lay under, he retired to his palace, and sent for the conspirators every man by name. Being now, as it were, surprized in the fact, and bereft of any probable means of escaping, they sustained the shock with undaunted resolution, avowing and justifying the charge exhibited against them, at the same time that they produced the daggers with which they were to have acted, alleging, "that they were not engaged in a criminal combination to gratify any passion or interest, but in a solemn league, for the common good, and the defence of their laws, which the Jews in general were bound to maintain with their lives." After this open and spirited declaration, they were led away to execution by the king's guards, and underwent, with [illegible], all the exquisite torments that were inflicted on them, till death came to their relief. Nor was it long before the spy who had discovered them was seized by some of the people, from the detestation in which they held him, by whom he was not only slain, but cut to pieces limb from limb, and thrown to the dogs, and this in the presence of numerous spectators. Yet not one man concerned in this matter was detected for a considerable time, till, upon Herod's making strict search for the [illegible] and threatening the severest tortures, certain women confessed what they had seen done, upon which the [illegible], and their whole families, were destroyed for this rash attempt. The multitude, however, [illegible] in the vindication of their laws and customs, [illegible] Herod, apprehensive of the danger of this [illegible], determined to take effectual [illegible] for the prevention of a revolt.

He [illegible] two forts in the city, the one at [illegible] the other (Antonia) which served for [illegible] temple. He fortified Samaria (otherwise called Sebaste) [illegible] which served to keep the whole country in obedience. It was about a day's journey from Jerusalem, and commodiously situated to quelling broils in the city. There was also another strong hold that lay [illegible] for this purpose, formerly known by the name of Strato's Tower, but by Herod, called Cæsarea. He built a castle also in the great plain, round which he placed a select body of horse. These fortifications were so [illegible] stationed up and down the country, that it was impossible for the people to enter into any plot or practice against the state, as they were ready, upon any occasion, either to observe sedition or crush it. He made it his first business to settle affairs in Samaria, as a place naturally strong and fit for his purpose. To this end he drew a great body of troops into the city, both foreign and domestic, partly for the security of the temple which he proposed to build there, and partly for the reputation of the work, but principally for his own interest, which, under the pretext of magnificence, was abundantly provided for. He changed the name of the town of Samaria to that of Sebaste, and divided it among the inhabitants of the country about it, by which means the lands, being fruitful about it, they soon became rich and easy. He surrounded the city with a strong wall, and enlarged it in such proportion, as to render it not inferior to the most famous cities. It was [illegible] and twenty furlongs in circumference, and a furlong and an half in the middle, which he reserved for a temple, [illegible] accordingly erected one, that, for size and magnificence, was not inferior to

whatever. In a word, he man [illegible] improvements [illegible] as not only conducive to [illegible] but intended to perpetuate monuments of the glory of his reign.

CHAP. XII.

Dreadful famine in Judea. Prudence of Herod in procuring provisions for the inhabitants. He builds a castle, etc. [illegible]

IN the thirteenth year of the reign of Herod, very great calamities fell upon Judea, whether from the effects of divine vengeance, or, according to natural causes, we shall not undertake to determine. The first instance of distress was a long-continued drought, which rendered the soil so barren, as totally to obstruct vegetation. The want of food, as well as the sudden change of diet, [illegible] a dearth of corn, brought on some terrible diseases, which terminated in pestilence, and, to aggravate their calamities, the sick were almost abandoned, and left without remedy, or any means of consolation. So universal was the [illegible], that each individual was in hourly expectation of dissolution. The last year's stores being expended, and no hopes of supply remaining, the case was desperate, and pining want stared them in the face, and [illegible] to threaten a total extermination of their race. The miseries of the first year followed them in the second, as what seed they had sown perished from the [illegible] as the former, and extremity almost produced a state of despair.

Nor was the king, or any means of [illegible] himself, his revenue, [illegible] have been, was not at this time able [illegible], his treasure being sunk, and his [illegible] kept [illegible] on building and fortifications. As an aggravation of his private distress, amidst the [illegible] of the people, he was subject to calumny, as [illegible] and [illegible] supposed to have caused the infliction of such severe judgments.

In this deplorable situation Herod deliberated within himself on the means of procuring some relief, which, [illegible], appeared a matter of insurmountable difficulty. His neighbours [illegible] same condition with himself, so that no supply could be expected from them, [illegible] could they even [illegible] his [illegible] were so reduced, that he had it not in his power to defray the expence.

Determining, however, to persevere in his endeavours to assist his people in the day of their despair, as the last and only resource, he melted down all his plate, both silver and gold, ornaments, and reduced the whole mass into one aggregate [illegible], and sent it away into Egypt, which was, at that time, governed under a commission from Cæsar. Petronius had been [illegible] by people from different quarters, urged by the most pressing necessity, had most [illegible] solicited his [illegible] but from a particular regard to Herod, [illegible] anxiety for the preservation of his people, he gave him the preference to all others, a grant for the exportation of corn, and gave him all possible assistance, both in the purchase and conveyance. By procuring this very [illegible] relief, he not only obviated the ill opinion the people entertained of him, but enhanced him still in their esteem, as a prince of consummate wisdom, generosity, and humanity.

His first care on the receipt of it was to contrive so as to make an equal and impartial distribution of it, in proportion to the number and condition of those who were to reap the benefit of it. Those who, by reason of age, or any infirmity, could neither fetch their corn, or prepare it for food, were supplied with such as was ready for immediate use. He also took care that they should be provided amply, not only with food, but also raiment, to secure them from the [illegible] of the season, as they had been as destitute of wool for clothing, as of corn for food.

When he had thus provided for his own [illegible], he took care to [illegible] the necessities of his neighbours, and furnished the Syrians with a quantity of grain [illegible] for the ensuing season. [illegible] benevolence turned greatly to his own advantage, for the [illegible] arriving [illegible] the crops [illegible] prodigious an increase of the following crop, [illegible] sent [illegible], he preserved [illegible] to help [illegible]. By these [illegible] he [illegible] of his own country and of [illegible] his neighbours, who [illegible] under the same [illegible] to [illegible] the [illegible] it appears [illegible] of wheat, [illegible] were [illegible] 10,000, and [illegible] distributed in his own kingdom, to be [illegible].

The [illegible] of the king [illegible] among the Jews as [illegible] character, [illegible] favour [illegible] from [illegible] his [illegible] that [illegible] to [illegible] was the [illegible].

[illegible] out of his own guards [illegible] to serve [illegible] with Cæsar [illegible] [illegible] of Judea, [illegible] command [illegible] Herod [illegible] of [illegible] of Jerusalem [illegible] for the [illegible] and [illegible] to [illegible] Jewish [illegible] Cæsar, [illegible]

While he was [illegible] this undertaking, he became disposed to [illegible] for [illegible] Herod, [illegible] a prince of great [illegible] to [illegible] Herod [illegible] became enamoured of, determined to make no tyrannical use of his authority, made proposal of an honourable marriage. It is [illegible] beneath his dignity, though in his opinion, too [illegible] to be rejected. To [illegible] therefore, the [illegible] in some degree, augmenting the honour of the family, and thereby [illegible] him for the proposed alliance, he deposed Jesus the son of Phabet from the pontificate, [illegible] him, [illegible] married his daughter.

When the [illegible] were solemnized, Herod erected a fortress upon the spot where he formerly defeated the Jews when he had with Antigonus. This castle is about sixty furlongs distant from Jerusalem, and so strong by nature, as to be capable of being rendered impregnable. The [illegible] effect, as it is [illegible] the figure of it is round, and the castle encompassed with several towers, and 200 stone steps to it. The apartments are stately and magnificent, and the whole structure [illegible]. At the bottom of [illegible] several buildings worthy of [illegible] particularly [illegible] aqueducts which with [illegible] brought [illegible] and [illegible] were brought the [illegible] distance. The plain [illegible] the city is covered with edifices to the proportion of a considerable city, having the [illegible] above [illegible] in the form of a castle.

Herod [illegible] now succeeded in his designs in general, supposed himself totally free from future commotions and tumults. He kept his people in due subjection, partly by awe and fear, and partly through attachment and interest, for he was a prince of most inflexible severity in the punishment of delinquents, as he was of most unbounded liberality in promoting the public good. He maintained such a guard upon himself, and kept every thing in such a posture of defence, as to render it apparent that the prince and people must stand or fall together. He deported himself with affability to all around him, and, upon all occasions, exhibited instances of munificence worthy of an emperor. By these means he acquired a general esteem, that greatly facilitated the accomplishment of his designs.

But the ambitious affectation of conciliating the favour of Augustus, and the most powerful men of Rome, induced him to swerve, by degrees, from the customs, and discipline of our forefathers, in the erecting of cities and temples to the honour of his patrons. This was not done in Judæa itself, for the Jews would not have suffered it, as we are forbidden to pay any honour to images after the manner of the Greeks: so that he built these cities only upon the borders of the province, and not within the jurisdiction of it, offering as an apology, that he was not incited to these acts by his own inclination, but purely from a motive of obedience to the higher powers, and particularly Cæsar and the Roman state. Whatever desire he might have of securing the favour and protection of those potentates of the earth, his main view seems to have been directed to the promotion of his own interest, and the gratification of his ambition, in perpetuating his name by the memorials of his magnificence and liberality.

CHAP. XIII.

Herod erects divers spacious and elegant edifices. Sends his sons Aristobulus and Alexander to Rome, where they are honoured by Augustus Cæsar, who, in divers instances, displays his bounty to Herod.

HEROD, observing a certain place near the sea-side, formerly called Straton's Tower, which he considered as a very commodious spot to erect a city upon, drew its model, employed artificers, and completed his design. The buildings were, in general, of marble, but the master-piece was the harbour, equal in size to the Pyræum at Athens, replete with all conveniencies, and a secure station for shipping against all winds and weathers. The work was the more remarkable, because all the materials were conveyed from a great distance at an enormous expence.

This city is situate in Phœnicia, in the passage by sea, into Egypt, between Joppa and Dora, two miserable seaports, where vessels cannot ride at anchor when the wind is south-west, as it beats so furiously upon the shore, that merchant-men are frequently obliged to keep out at sea, lest they should be run aground. To rectify this inconvenience, Herod ordered a mole to be made in the form of an half moon, and large enough for ships of war to ride in. He directed also vast stones to be let down there in twenty fathom of water. These stones were fifty feet in length, not less than eighteen in breadth, and nine in depth; some greater, and some less, than those dimensions.

This mole was two hundred feet in extent, the half of which was opposed to the current of the waves, the other half served for the foundation of a stone wall, fortified with turrets, the largest of which was called Drusus from Drusus, the son-in-law of Augustus Cæsar, who died in infancy. There was several arched vaults in which the mariners dwelt occasionally. There was likewise a quay or landing place, with a large walk upon it round the harbour, accommodated to the purpose of healthful exercise and recreation. The port opens to the northward, which is the clearest quarter of the wind: on the left side of the entrance there was a turret erected upon a large platform, with a sloping bank to shoot off the washing of the sea, and on the right hand were two stone pillars opposite to the tower, both of an height. The edifices about the harbour were erected upon an uniform plan, and composed of the most excellent kind of marble. Upon an elevation in the middle stood a temple dedicated to Cæsar, which was of great use to mariners as a land-mark. There were in the temple two statues or images, one of which was that of Cæsar, and hence the city took the name of Cæsarea, which was no less celebrated for the materials than the workmanship. Nay, the subterraneous vaults and cellars were finished specimens of architecture, as well as the buildings above ground. They were laid at equal distances one from the other, and so discharged themselves into the sea. Herod built also a stone theatre, and, upon the south side of the harbour, an amphitheatre, with a commanding prospect of the sea. This work was brought to perfection, at immense labour and expence, in the space of twelve years.

When Herod had finished his design with respect to the cities of Sebaste and Cæsarea, he dispatched his two sons Alexander and Aristobulus, to Rome, to pay their respects to Cæsar. Pollio, who was Herod's particular friend, accommodated them with accommodations, though Augustus had given positive orders for their being entertained in his own palace. He received them with the greatest cordiality, and after the additional bounty of conferring upon Herod the three provinces of Trachon, Batanea, and Auranitis, gave him his choice which of his sons he would appoint to succeed him in the kingdom of Judæa. This particular favour arose from the following cause.

One Zenodorus had taken upon him to farm the lands of Lysanias, and not contenting himself with the lawful advantage of the agreement, became partner with the free-booters in Trachon, a set of men who lived upon the spoil they take from the people of Damascus. Those of the country who were great sufferers, applied themselves to Varro, who was at that time governor of the province, for a letter to Cæsar, complaining against Zenodorus. Cæsar was so averse to their mal-practices, that in his answer, he recommended them to destroy those nests of robbers, and commit the command of the province to Herod, to keep the Trachonites in order for the future. It was very difficult to restrain them, as they had been long accustomed to this mode of pillaging, nor had they towns, houses, or possessions, but lived, like brutes, in dens and caves. The entrance into their hiding places was so narrow, that no more than one person could pass at a time, but the receptacle was large beyond imagination, and the roof plain and flat. They are, in fine, a people of so rapacious a disposition, that, when they have not an opportunity of preying upon their neighbours, they prey upon one another; insomuch, that they are guided by no principle of justice, or common humanity. When Herod had received this grant from Cæsar, and was come into the country, he procured skilful guides, put a stop to their lawless depredations, and set the neighbours at rest. Zenodorus was so irritated at this proceeding, from the loss of his commission, on the one hand, and the envy he bore Herod on the other for having supplanted him, that he hastened to Rome to prefer an accusation against him, but returned without effecting his design.

During these transactions Augustus sent Agrippa into Asia, to take upon him the command of the provinces beyond the Ionian Sea. Agrippa being a particular friend of Herod, he met him on his way at Mitylene, and then returned to Judæa. However, some of the Gadarenes came to Agrippa to accuse Herod, when they were not only dismissed without a hearing, but sent back to the king in chains.

Notwithstanding the prevailing interest of Herod, the Arabians from an ancient grudge, attempted to raise a sedition in his dominions, and upon an occasion specious enough, just thus. Zenodorus, finding his affairs grown desperate, agreed to consign over to the Arabians a certain proportion of his principality, on consideration of an annual payment of fifty talents. But as this was a [illegible]ed in Cæsar's grant to Herod, the Arabians contested the point, sometimes by law, and sometimes by force, and, to render the latter means more coercive, they engaged a party of soldiers, of desperate fortunes, who were willing to exert themselves in any cause that might retrieve them. Herod was well apprized of the design, but deemed it expedient to counteract it rather by mild than rigorous measures, in order to prevent fresh commotions.

In the seventeenth year of Herod's reign Cæsar came into Syria, where he was immediately applied to by the greater part of the inhabitants of Gadara, with clamorous accusations, against Herod, as a most insupportable tyrant and oppressor. They were instigated to prefer these complaints by Zenodorus, who had bound himself by oath never to quit the prosecution of Herod, till he was dispossessed of his dominions, and they reverted to Cæsar. Thus instigated by Zenodorus, they became more and more vehement in their exclamations, and especially because those prisoners that were delivered up to Herod by Agrippa, continued unpunished. Indeed, lenity, towards the injuries of strangers was a striking trait in Herod's character, however inexorable he might have been towards the delinquents of his own subjects. The misdemeanours with which he was charged were, rapine, oppression, the violation and demolition of temples, with others of a similar nature.

Herod boldly presented himself in justification, and was treated with every token of respect and honour by Cæsar, notwithstanding the clamours of the multitude, insomuch that the Gadarenes, finding his powerful interest with the emperor, and thence expecting that they would fall into his hands, had recourse to [illegible], by various means, to prevent the infliction of severer torments, and Cæsar thence inferring they had condemned themselves, acquitted Herod of every part of the accusation.

A combination of events at this time, seemed to favour Herod, and particularly the death of his implacable enemy Zenodorus, by a violent dysentery, at Antioch, in consequence of which he obtained, from Cæsar, a considerable part of his dominions between Galilee and Trachon, comprising Ulatha, Paneam, and the adjacent country. He was also vested with a sovereign command over the governors of Syria, who were accordingly under his sole rule and direction.

Herod was now advanced to such a pitch of good fortune, that whereas there were but two men that governed the vast Roman empire, first Cæsar, and then Agrippa, who was his principle confident, Cæsar preferred no man to Herod besides Agrippa, nor did Agrippa any one to Herod besides Cæsar. By virtue of this interest, Herod obtained a tetrarch's commission, in Judæa, from Augustus, for his brother Pheroras, upon whom he bestowed an annual income of an hundred talents out of his own proper revenue, to obviate the consequences of any contingencies that might reduce him to a dependence on his children. After this, Herod waited upon Cæsar, till he saw him embarked, and, on his return erected to his honour a most beautiful temple, of white marble, upon the domains of Zenodorus, near the cave they call Panius, which is at the bottom of a mountain famous for being the source of the river Jordan. The cavern is very steep, and the springs of water in it perpetually bubbling. The mountain is famous for a delightful prospect, but more especially so for the magnificent temple of Augustus Cæsar.

The king took an opportunity, at this time, of ingratiating himself with his people, by remitting a third part of their taxes, under pretence of commiserating the distresses they had undergone during the time of the late famine, but, in reality, to conciliate their good will. The innovations he had introduced, in violation of their laws and religion, gave universal disgust, and were loudly complained of, so that, to preserve order and decorum, he enjoined every man diligently to attend to his own concerns, prohibiting [illegible] assemblies, and fixing spies in all places of resort, to take into custody all who should disobey the order, and [illegible] them to be punished with the utmost rigour. The [illegible] very roads, streets, and avenues, were beset [illegible], [illegible] was he for the detection of any [illegible] [illegible] in this particular, that, [illegible] he would mix himself, in disguise, with the rabble [illegible] how they stood affected. Those who could by no [illegible] be brought to acquiesce with his scheme of government, were persecuted with the greatest [illegible], while [illegible] more moderate were put to an oath of allegiance, and [illegible]. By these means he brought the [illegible] or [illegible], to a compliance with him, [illegible] resolution to contend the point and [illegible] were taken off by some device or other. He endeavoured to impose his oath upon Pollio the Pharisee, [illegible], together with their [illegible], [illegible] refused it, he excused [illegible] [illegible] the regard he bore to Pollio. The Essenes were [illegible] exempted from this oath. These Essenes were [illegible] respects resembling the Pythagoreans among the Greeks, and though we have already detailed the [illegible] they hold, it will be [illegible] [illegible] but the causes for which they were [illegible] regard by Herod.

There was one among the Essenes whose name was Manahem, a man of singular piety and virtue, who was endowed with the gift of prophecy. This person seeing Herod in his juvenile days, going to school, greeted him with the salutation of "King of the Jews." Herod, either not knowing him, or thinking [illegible] he was not descended from a family to [illegible], [illegible] Manahem, smiling, and laying his hand gently on his shoulder, replied, "You are to be king, and [illegible] happily, for it is the Divine will that it should [illegible] [illegible] these words of Manahem in your [illegible] [illegible] give you to understand the change of [illegible]. It will be your duty to govern with justice [illegible], but, by a secret impulse, I know that you cannot [illegible] be regulated by those excellent maxims, [illegible] stances, you will swerve from them, though, in other respects, you will be fortunate, [illegible] commendation. Remember your crimes cannot be concealed from the penetrating eye of the Almighty, who will most severely punish you for them."

Herod, at that time, was totally regardless of what Manahem predicted, having no reasonable view of [illegible] advancement. But when he afterwards came to the [illegible], and attained to the summit of his glory, he sent for Manahem, and asked him how long he thought he should reign. [illegible] Manahem returning an indefinite answer, Herod [illegible] the question whether he thought he should reign ten years? He replied, yes, and twenty and thirty, but did not assign the determinate limits of his reign. Herod, [illegible] with what he had heard, dismissed him in a friendly manner, and, from that time forwards paid great honour to the sect of Essenes. We have related this circumstance, strange as it may appear, as another proof of the many instances in which the secret purposes and counsels of the Divine Being have been revealed to men of singular piety and virtue.

CHAP XIV

Herod rebuilds the temple, [illegible]

AFTER so many signal transactions and the finishing of so many sumptuous edifices, Herod in the eighteenth year of his reign, turned his attention towards the rebuilding of a temple in honour of the true God, in every respect larger and more stately than the former. This work he was persuaded would perpetuate his memory beyond all he had accomplished heretofore. But as he knew many of the people might be reluctant to assist him in so vast a design, he thought proper to call them together, and address them, upon the occasion, to the following purport:

"It would be time lost, my friends and countrymen, "to give you the history of my transactions since I came "to the crown; therefore let it suffice, that I have more "attended to your benefit and security, than to my own "particular interest. You know what care I have taken for "you in your greatest extremities, and without any regard "to my own profit. You know, likewise, that you your"selves have had the greatest [illegible] in the advantage of "the mighty works which, by God's blessing and assis"tance, I have brought to perfection, insomuch, that "Judæa is in a better state at this day than ever; wherefore "there will be no need of citing the particulars of the ci"ties, castles, palaces, &c. that I have either built, forti"fied, or repaired, in Judæa, and the tributary provinces. "But the aim of my present business is religion, and "what concerns the reputation of your country. You "will do well to observe that this temple, that was "erected by your forefathers at their return from Baby"lon, wants sixty cubits of the height of Solomon's; "though this was no fault of our ancestors, for it was "not owing to them that it came not up to the proportion "of the first, being raised according to the express model "of Cyrus, and Darius, the son of Hystaspes, under "whose dominion they then lived, [illegible] under the "Macedonians, so that they had it not in their power to "advance that monument of their piety and [illegible] up to the "measures of the original. But since God [illegible] now pleas"ed, in his gracious providence, to put the government "into my hands, and, at the same time, to furnish me "with all necessary means to that end, [illegible] "as peace, [illegible], a large competency of [illegible] "which [illegible] all the rest, we are [illegible] "whole world (that is to say, the Romans,) [illegible] "[illegible] and [illegible] to [illegible] "[illegible] peace [illegible] "to [illegible] and to do [illegible] to the glory of "God, [illegible] "[illegible] to his holy name, [illegible] "the mercies we have received."

This speech raised much anxiety, and many doubts, in the minds of the people, particularly, with respect to the demolition of the old temple, till they were assured of another being erected in its place, which, in fact, the [illegible] ed [illegible] almost [illegible]. In this [illegible] the king encouraged them with the assurance, [illegible] not [illegible] the old one, till all the "[illegible] were [illegible] prepared for building the intended "new one."

[illegible] to his word, he ordered a thousand carriages to be [illegible] to bring stones, chose ten thousand of the most skilful artificers, purchased a thousand sacerdotal garments for that number of priests, and caused them to be instructed in the different branches of workmanship, in order to [illegible] the general concern.

Having made all necessary preparations, both as to artificers and materials, Herod caused the old foundations to be removed, and others to be laid, upon which basis they raised the superstructure of a temple an hundred cubits in length, and an hundred and twenty in height; but the twenty cubits sinking afterwards, it fell so much short of the original design, which our ancestors had in contemplation to raise again in the days of Nero. The whole fabric was composed of stones, white and durable, in length twenty-five cubits, in height eight, and in breadth twelve.

The front of this magnificent structure bore the resemblance of a palace, the middle being much higher than the sides, and commanding such a view over the fields, as was very agreeable to those who either resided directly opposite to it, or were travelling towards it. This view extended several furlongs into the country. The porch, in elegance, was proportionate to the rest of the building, the [illegible] part being adorned with a variety of rich tapestry and delicate purple flowers, with pillars interwoven, and a golden vine creeping and winding about them, the branches of [illegible] [illegible] with clusters of grapes pendent from the cornice.

Round about the temple were large cloisters, not inferior to the rest of the building in magnificence, but rather exceeding all that went before them for symmetry and elegance. Two of these cloisters were supported by strong walls, a work as singularly curious as had ever been executed.

The hill was a rocky ascent, that declined by degrees towards the eastern parts of the city, till it came to an elevated level. This was the hill which Solomon [illegible] before, by Divine direction, encompassed with a wall, and was of excellent workmanship, upwards and round the top of it. He also built a wall below, beginning at the bottom, which was encompassed by a deep valley. This wall was composed of large stones, clamped together with iron, including the whole and reaching down to the bottom of the hill. The form of the work was [illegible], and, considering the magnitude and depth, it was an [illegible] performance. The [illegible] of the stones in the [illegible] was plainly visible on the outside, yet so that the inner parts were preserved by joints immovable.

When the foundation was finished in the manner described, Herod caused [illegible] the outer [illegible], filled up the hollow places which were about the wall, and made them level. He [illegible] within the [illegible] another stone wall [illegible] the top of the hill, [illegible] double porch to the east, and facing the [illegible] stones in the middle. This portal was magnificently [illegible] ed by the munificence of many princes in former times, and [illegible] about the [illegible], [illegible] and [illegible] taken [illegible] [illegible] Herod [illegible] others of [illegible] [illegible] from the Arabians.

[illegible] the work of [illegible] [illegible] Herod, [illegible] They called [illegible], or the Tower [illegible] sited the vestments of the high-priest [illegible] taken out but at the time he was to offer sacrifice [illegible] applied it to the same use, but after his death, it [illegible] be lodged in the hands of the Romans, till the time of Tiberius Cæsar, in whose reign Vitellius being [illegible] governor of Syria, and going to take upon him the command, was so magnificently received at Jerusalem, that, in acknowledgment of the honour done him by the Jews, he prevailed with Cæsar, at their earnest request, that they might have those sacred vestments under their own immediate deposit. They continued in the custody of the Jews till the death of king Agrippa, when Cassius Longinus, governor of Syria and Cuspius Fadus, procurator of Judæa, enjoined to deposit those vestments in the town of Antonia, insisting that they ought still to be in the power of the Romans as they were formerly. Hereupon the Jews sent deputies to Claudius Cæsar, to intercede for their continuance with them. The young king Agrippa, happening to be at Rome upon the arrival of the deputies, obtained the grant of the request from the emperor, who accordingly sent orders to Vitellius to deliver them up. Before that time they were kept under the seal of the high-priest, and treasurer of the temple, who, upon the eve of a solemn festival, applied to the commanding officer of the Romans, shewed him their seal, and took out the vestments, which, when the festival was over, they brought to the same place, and there deposited in the presence of the officer. I have been thus minute in this particular point, because its various changes have essentially affected the concerns of our nation. As to the Tower itself, when Herod had fortified it more firmly, in order to secure the temple, he gave it

…name of the Tower of Antonia, in honour of his great …d Anthony, who once presided over the Romans
…the western quarter of the enclosure of the temple were … gates The first led to the king's palace, two more …he suburbs of the city, and the last to the city itself …a descent of many steps down to the valley, and an …on the other side, of as many steps, up to the top …city stood over against the temple, in the manner of a …tre, encompassed, towards the south with a deep valley …the middle of the square was another gate, equi-distant …n the two angles, with stately royal cloisters, with three …s, that reached, in length, from the east valley to the …l, for they could not possibly reach any further This …ded a most extraordinary spectacle, for the valley was …ry deep, and the height of the building over it so stu…dous, that it caused a giddiness in the brain to look down …n the top of the battlements This cloister had pillars …stood in four rows equi-distant, with a stone wall …ight up betwixt those of the fourth rank The pillars …e as much as three men could fathom, being seven and …ty feet in length, and upon a double base The num… of them was one hundred and sixty-two The chapi… were exquisite beyond description, and the sculpture of …inthian workmanship These four rows of pillars in…led three intervals for walking in the middle of this …ster, two of which walks were made parallel to each …r, and were contrived after the same manner, the …dth of each being thirty feet, the height fifty feet, and …length a furlong The roof was adorned with curious …pture representing a variety of figures

This was the first enclosure, in the midst of which, and …far from it, was the second, upon an ascent of a few …s, with a partition of stone, and an inscription upon it, …hibiting any strangers from entrance, upon pain of death It had on its southern and northern quarters, three gates, equi-distant; and on the eastern quarter one large gate, where men, who were purified, had admittance with their wives but the women were not permitted to pass any farther

There was a third enclosure, into which it was lawful only for the priests to enter This was the temple itself, before which stood the altar, where the sacrifices were offered up Into neither of these three did king Herod presume to enter because, not being a priest, he was prohibited by the law, so that he committed the holy work to the priests themselves which they finished in eighteen months, when he himself was eight years in finishing the rest

The people were transported with joy at the completion of so glorious a work, returning thanks to the Almighty for his blessing upon the undertaking, and extolling the king for the alacrity he had shewn in the execution of it The event was celebrated with festivity The king sacrificed three hundred oxen, and the people according to their respective abilities, so that the number of oblations could hardly be computed This memorable dedication of the temple fell upon the day of the king's inauguration, which added greatly to the solemnity

There was an occult passage built for the king, leading from fort Antonia to the eastern gate of the inner temple, over which he erected a tower, this passage being designed as a private and safe retreat, either for himself or his successors, in case of any sedition against the government It is reported, that, during the building of the temple, it never rained but in the night, so that the work was not hindered. This tradition has been handed down to posterity, and is, by many, deemed a peculiar interposition of Providence in favour of the work

END OF [illegible] BOOK.

name of the Tower of Antonia, in honour of his great end Anthony, who once prevailed over the Romans In the western quarter of the enclosure of the temple were r gates The first led to the king's palace, two to the suburbs of the city, and the last to the city itself h a defcent of many fteps down to the valley, and an ent on the other fide, of as many fteps, up to the top e city ftood over againft the temple, in the manner of a re, encompaffed, towards the fouth with a deep valley the middle of the quarter was another gate, equi-diftant m the two angles, with ftately royal cloifters, with three lls, that reached, in length, from the eaft valley to the ft, for they could not poffibly reach any further This oned a moft extraordinary fpectacle, for the valley was very deep and the height of the building over it fo ftu- ous that it caufed a giddinefs in the brain to look down m the top of the battlements This cloifter had pillars t ftood in four rows equi-diftant, with a ftone wall ought up betwixt thofe of the fourth rank The pillars re as much as three men could fathom, being feven and enty feet in length, and upon a double bafe The num- of them was one hundred and fixty-two The chapi- s were exquifite beyond defcription, and the fculpture of rn than workmanfhip Thefe four rows of pillars in- ded three intervals for walking in the middle of this fter, two of which walks were made parallel to each e, and were contrived after the fame manner, the dth of each being thirty feet the height fifty feet, and length a furlong The roof was adorned with curious lpture reprefenting a variety of figures

This was the firft enclofure, in the midft of which, and t far from it, was the fecond, upon an afcent of a few ps, with a partition of ftone and an infcription upon it, hibiting any ftrangers from entrance, upon pain of death It had, on its fouthern and northern quarters, three gates, equi-diftant, and on the eaftern quarter one large gate, where men, who were purified, had admittance with their wives, but the women were not permitted to pafs any far- ther.

There was a third enclofure, into which it was lawful only for the priefts to enter This was the temple itfelf, before which ftood the altar, where the facrifices were offered up Into neither of thefe three did king Herod prefume to enter because, not being a prieft, he was prohibited by the law fo that he committed the holy work to the priefts themfelves which they finifhed in eighteen months, when he himfelf was eight years in finifhing the reft

The people were tranfported with joy at the completion of fo glorious a work, returning thanks to the Almighty for his bleffing upon the undertaking, and extolling the king for the alacrity he had fhewn in the execution of it The event was celebrated with feftivity The king facrificed three hundred oxen, and the people according to their re- fpective abilities, fo that the number of oblations could hardly be computed This memorable dedication of the temple fell upon the day of the king's inauguration, which added greatly to the folemnity

There was an occult paffage built for the king, leading from fort Antonia to the eaftern gate of the inner temple, over which he erected a tower, this paffage being defigned as a private and fafe retreat, either for himfelf or his fucceffors, in cafe of any fedition againft the government It is reported, that, during the building of the temple, it never rained but in the night, fo that the work was not hindered. This tradition has been handed down to pofterity, and is, by many, deemed a peculiar interpofition of Providence in favour of the work

END OF [illegible] BOOK.

FLAVIUS JOSEPHUS

ON THE

ANTIQUITIES

OF THE

JEWS.

BOOK XVI.

[INCLUDING A PERIOD OF ABOUT SIX YEARS.]

CHAP. I.

Herod enacts a law against theft, goes to Rome, and is graciously received by Cæsar, who restores him his two sons. They are calumniated on their return to Jerusalem, but without effect.

AS Herod was very zealous in the administration of government, to promote the impartial execution of justice, throughout, both in town and country, in public and in private, he made a new law for the punishing of house-breakers, to this effect: "That all offenders of that kind should be sold for slaves to any that would purchase them, without exception even to strangers." This law was by no means approved by the people in general, who did not animadvert upon it as it immediately respected the malefactor, but as it manifestly encroached on the laws and customs of the nation, by subjecting the Jews to the impositions of those who lived according to different rules and measures, which they therefore considered as a violation of the institutions of their forefathers, rather than a punishment to those who were found to have offended. Such punishment was avoided in our original laws, which ordains that the felon should make a fourfold restitution; or, if insolvent, shall be sold, but not to strangers, nor into perpetual slavery, and at the end of seven years discharged. This new law was construed as a deliberate contempt, in Herod, against an established practice and discipline not becoming a king, but an unjust and oppressive tyrant, a character to which he again exposed himself by carrying the penalty into execution.

Herod about this time made a voyage to Italy, to pay his court to the emperor, and inquire into the circumstances and situation of his sons, who had been sent to Rome to finish their education, where he had the happiness to find them accomplished in the different branches of polite literature. He was received with singular honour by Cæsar, who delivered to him the young princes in a much more improved state than he received them. They were tall and graceful in figure, affable and winning in conversation and deportment; so that it might be said, the endowments of their minds were not inferior to their personal accomplishments.

Having paid his respects to the emperor, and had leave to depart, Herod returned to Jerusalem with his sons, where they no sooner arrived, than they attracted the admiration of the multitude, as youths possessed of every quality that could adorn their elevated rank and station. But they were objects of envy to Salome, the king's sister, and the whole party, who had raised calumniating reports to effect the destruction of Mariamne. Indeed, they beheld them with awful dread, as instruments whom Providence had raised up to revenge the death of their mother, and made this apprehension a motive to scandalous reports against them. They gave it out that they would never endure the conversation of their father, after imbruing his hands in the murder of their innocent mother. They supposed that slanderous insinuation was the most effectual means of prejudicing the father against the sons, and accordingly practised it with all the art and subtlety that envy and malice could possibly suggest, hoping, in the result, so to work upon the mind of Herod, as to destroy that natural affection which is the basis of all the ties of consanguinity, as well as of reciprocal duty and regard.

CHAP. II.

Herod marries his sons. Pays a visit to Agrippa.

THE artful design of Salome, and her party, had not yet prevailed on Herod, so as to withdraw his paternal affection and confidence from his sons, to whom he continued to behave with his usual openness and cordiality, without any reserve or suspicion. His first concern was to form princely alliances for them, by marrying Aristobulus to Berenice, the daughter of Salome, and Alexander to Glaphyra, the daughter of Archelaus, king of Cappadocia.

When Herod had dispatched these affairs, he received intelligence that Marcus Agrippa had left Italy, and was gone to Asia, where he therefore immediately repaired, with a generous tender of all respect and service, and earnestly entreated of him the honour of a visit. Agrippa complying with his request, Herod, on his part, omitted nothing that could contribute to the entertainment of his noble guest. He shewed him all the stately edifices that he had lately erected or repaired, carrying him to Sebaste, the port of Cæsarea, and the forts of Alexandrion, Herodion, Hyrcania, &c. where he treated him and his retinue with the utmost splendor and magnificence. After this tour he conducted him to the city of Jerusalem, where he was received, by the whole multitude, with all the acclamations and pomp of a solemn festival. Agrippa, upon this occasion, made an oblation of an hecatomb, and feasted the people in the most sumptuous manner. His journey and entertainment afforded him so much pleasure and satisfaction, that he was desirous of protracting the visit; but the winter approaching, and those seas being dangerous, he was under a necessity of returning to Ionia, for which he took his departure, laden with presents and honours.

CHAP. III.

Herod revisits Agrippa, and many offices of friendship pass between them.

HAVING passed the winter at Jerusalem, Herod made another voyage, on the opening of the spring, to visit Agrippa, who, according to intelligence received, was gone upon a campaign towards Bosphorus. He embarked for Lesbos, with expectation of meeting him there; but, after he passed Rhodes and Coos, he was driven, by contrary winds, upon the isle of Chios, where he was detained for some days. During the course of this voyage, he had many visits made him, which he returned in a suitable manner; and observing, on his short stay upon this island, that several public buildings lay yet in ruins ever since the Mithridatic war, for want of money to repair them, he gave them credit for a sum sufficient to accomplish the work, with an express charge to put it in hand, and finish it as soon as possible.

Upon the change of wind, Herod sailed to Mitylene, and then to Byzantium; and hearing that Agrippa had already passed the Cyanean rocks, he followed him with the utmost speed, and joined him at Sinope, a city of Pontus, at a juncture that Agrippa had no expectation of such assistance. This interview was equally agreeable to both parties, and reciprocal tokens of friendship passed between them. In fine, they seemed to be actuated by the same views, with respect to enterprize and pastime. When Agrippa had dispatched his affairs in Pontus, he took his way upon the return over land; so that they passed through Paphlagonia, Cappadocia, and the Greater Phrygia to Ephesus, and thence, by sea, to Samos. Herod displayed many instances of generosity during the passage, as well as of the great power and influence he had with Agrippa, whose favour he had conciliated in the highest degree. All became intercession with him in behalf of the people of Ilium, against whom he had been highly incensed, and paid arrears, which were due from the people of Chios, to the emperor, provided them many privileges, and rendered them, in divers particulars, the most essential services.

CHAP. IV.

Agrippa, at the instance of Herod, and through the prevailing arguments of Nicolaus against the natives of Ionia, in favour of the Jews, confirms their laws, and assures them of his protection.

WHEN Agrippa and Herod arrived in Ionia, a great multitude of Jews, of that province, embraced the opportunity of laying before them the injuries they had sustained from the natives, in the infringement of their laws and worship, their depriving them of the money they used to send to Jerusalem, forcing them to bear arms, and pay public duties out of their subsistence money, and all this contrary to common faith, and the liberties and exemptions granted them by the Romans. Herod, desirous of using his influence in behalf of the Jews upon this interesting occasion, prevailed with Agrippa to grant them a hearing, and procured them one Nicolaus, an advocate of most distinguished abilities, and his most intimate friend, for their counsel. At a court called upon the occasion, Agrippa, himself being present, together with a bench of Romans of great rank, Nicolaus thus opened and enlarged upon the cause of the Jews.

"Whither, most illustrious Agrippa, should the miserable and oppressed fly for sanctuary and relief, but to those princes that are able to protect and relieve them? This is the case with your humble supplicants, and we must presume to appeal from your authority to your justice, in a full confidence of your royal goodness: for we have nothing more to desire at present, than the possession and enjoyment of what you yourselves have granted us already, and which our fellow-subjects are now endeavouring to take from us. If the favours we enjoy be great, we doubt not but you will now think it worthy to retain them. If the benefit be small, it reflects upon your honour to imagine that you are not able to make it good. Neither is this a greater injury to us, than it is an indignity to yourselves, in the contempt of your judgment, and in the disappointment of your pious intentions. If it were put to these very people, whether they would rather part with their lives, or with their laws, customs, discipline, sacrifices, festivals, &c. in honour of their God, I think, with submission, that we may safely answer for them, they would choose the former. It is a common thing to take up arms for religion; and what is the great blessing of the peace and freedom the world enjoys under the Roman empire, but that every man may live and worship after his own way? What pretence is there for people to impose that upon others, which they will not submit to themselves? As if it were not all one whether we hinder another man from doing his duty, or neglect our own. It is a thing farther to be considered, that there is no city, people, or nation, extant, that does not depend on the administration, and the power of Rome, for all the happiness they can pretend to? Will any thinking man deem it his interest to frustrate your bounties, when every man living, some way or other, will be a loser by it? Our enemies are not aware, that while they labour to invalidate our rights, they destroy their own; for why should the same concessions be good to them, and void to us, and that inestimable privilege among the rest of living at ease and liberty, under the protection of the Roman emperors, while several other nations lie groaning in a state of servitude, at the mercy of rigorous kings? Neither is ours, at the best, a condition to be envied for, as to other matters, we desire nothing more than a common share of advantage with the rest of our fellow subjects, provided we may but be allowed to worship God after the manner of our forefathers, which, as it is innocent in itself, on the one hand, so it is for the service of those that permit it on the other; for God not only loves those that worship him themselves, but those also that encourage the worship of him in others. What is there in our way of holy offices that any moderate man can take offence at? or, in truth, that is not in all respects, agreeable to piety and justice? We make no difficulty of owning the rules of our lives and profession. The Seventh Day is a day of rest from all our labours, and a day that we set apart for the study of the law, as a discipline that much conduces to the rectifying of our manners. Now these customs ...

"no only blameleſs in themſelves, even upon the ſtricteſt
"examination of them, but venerable even for their anti-
"quity, (all cavils to the contrary notwithſtanding), ſo
"that there can be no cauſe for controverting the authority
"of laws that have ſtood the teſt of ſo many ages. The
"injuries we complain of are theſe: they ſacrilegiouſly
"make ſeizures of monies dedicated to holy uſes. They
"impoſe taxes upon people that ought, in right, pay none.
"They hurry them up and down to courts of juſtice, and
"other common attendancies, upon our days of ſolemnity
"and religious worſhip, and for no other end but to turn
"our piety and devotion to ſcorn, and theſe practices they
"know to be unwarrantable and cauſeleſs. Your wiſdom
"conſults and ſteadily the common welfare of all your peo-
"ple, in the promoting of peace, and the preventing of
"feuds. It is againſt theſe injuries, moſt excellent Agrip-
"pa, that we crave to be relieved, and that we may be al-
"lowed the ſame liberty hereafter, that we have enjoyed
"heretofore, and that our adverſaries may have no more
"advantage over us, than we pretend to, over them. We
"take this to be juſtice not only in the nature of the thing,
"but in the right which your goodneſs has given us to it,
"by declaring it our favour, to which purpoſe there are,
"at this day, to be ſeen in the capitol, ſeveral decrees of
"the ſenate, in tables of braſs, for a perpetual memory.
"Monuments and records were undoubtedly grounded upon
"the experiment of our truth and loyalty to the ſtate. Be-
"ſide, that the obligation would be yet ſacred and inviola-
"ble, even without any antecedent merit on our part, for
"your generoſity hath been ever ſo far from leſſening or re-
"voking the bounties you have once beſtowed (and that not
"only to us, but to any) that it hath been your practice ra-
"ther to amplify and enlarge them, even beyond every
"thought and expectation, as I could give inſtances abund-
"antly, if time would permit. But not to value ourſelves
"too much upon our own ſervices, let our royal maſter's
"friendly offices ſpeak for us. When did he ever fail, to
"the uttermoſt of his power to oblige your nation? Has not
"his faith and zeal for your intereſt been tried over and over?
"Has he not made the advancing of your honour his buſineſs and
"his ſtudy? Were your affairs ever in any difficulty and he not
"eſpouſe them as his own? So that if it were but for our
"king's ſake, we might pretend to ſome ſort of conſidera-
"tion. We muſt not forget the ſervices of his father Anti-
"pater, nor the reinforcement of two thouſand auxiliaries,
"that he brought to Cæſar in Egypt, where his behaviour
"was ſo ſignally brave, and ſo much to the advantage of
"the empire, that he had the reputation of being not inferi-
"or to any commander, either at ſea or land, for conduct
"and courage. We might appeal to the glorious preſents
"that Cæſar made him, or rather to the letters recommen-
"datory that he wrote to the ſenate, in his favour, upon
"this occaſion, by which he obtained for him the privilege
"of a citizen of Rome, with other additional honours.
"This ſingle argument, great prince, might be ſufficient,
"even of itſelf, to evince that thoſe favours were at firſt
"well beſtowed, which we are now imploring may be con-
"firmed. Beſide that, conſidering the preſent league of
"friendſhip betwixt yourſelf and our royal ſovereign, we
"rather hope for an augmentation of your bounty than fear
"any abatement of it. I might enlarge upon your holy
"vows and ſacrifices at Jeruſalem, the ſplendour of your
"entertainments, and the ſatisfaction you were pleaſed to
"own in the reciprocal exchange of offices of hoſpitality and
"reſpect, which were all evident proofs of an affectionate
"regard, and an amicable underſtanding betwixt the Jews
"and the Romans, confirmed and ratified under the very
"roof of the king himſelf. Now our final requeſt to the
"majeſty of Agrippa, and the preſence of the king of the
"Jews, is only this, that we may reap the fruits of your
"own bounty, without being made a prey to other."

When Nicholaus had finiſhed his ſpeech, in vindication of the rights of the Jews, there was no reply on the part of the Greeks, for it was not a matter of enquiry, as in a court of juſtice, but a petitionary complaint, to prevent violence from being offered to the Jews. They did not attempt to deny the fact. Their pretence was that the Jews were ſtrangers, and would be a burden to them, while the Jews, on the contrary averred, that they were no ſtrangers, but a people who lived according to their own laws and cuſtoms without giving offence to any man. Agrippa thus convinced that they were oppreſſed, declared in their favour, as well from the juſtice of their cauſe, as from the reſpect he bore to Herod. He ſaid he thought their requeſt ſo reaſonable, that if it had been more extenſive, he would have granted it, ſo far, at leaſt, as was conſiſtent with his duty to the ſenate, and ſtate of Rome. He then made this formal declaration: "I do hereby pronounce a confirmation of the claim the "Jews make of their privileges, as ſpecified in the repre-"ſentation of their counſel, and pledge myſelf, that ſo "long as they keep themſelves within the bounds of their "profeſſion and diſcipline, they ſhould not be moleſted "for the future." With theſe words Agrippa diſmiſſed the aſſembly, when Herod ſtood up and made acknowledgment of the favour, in the name of the whole Jewiſh nation, which done, he and Agrippa, after mutual ſalutations, took their departure from Leſbos.

CHAP. V.

Herod, upon his arrival at Jeruſalem, calls an aſſembly of the people, and gives them a relation of his late tranſactions in Aſia.

HEROD, having taken his leave of Agrippa, embarked for Cæſarea, where, through means of favourable winds, he landed in a few days, and from thence immediately proceeded to Jeruſalem. As ſoon as convenient after his arrival, he ſummoned a general aſſembly, ſtrangers as well as citizens, and laid before them a particular account of his voyage, and the very important grant he had obtained for the Jews in Aſia, by which they were exempted from the impoſitions of the Ionians, and fully confirmed in their ancient national privileges. He repreſented to them the ſeveral and great advantages they had derived from his government, and pointed out that the welfare of his ſubjects was the grand ſpring of his actions. As a peculiar gratification, he remitted them a fourth part of their taxes for the laſt year, a circumſtance which, added to his moſt agreeable repreſentation of affairs in general, conciliated the univerſal eſteem of the people, who, with loudeſt acclamations teſtified their loyalty, and moſt fervently prayed for the proſperity of their king.

CHAP. VI.

Great diſturbances prevail in Herod's family, through the contrivance of Salome and Pheroras, who inſinuate againſt his ſons Ariſtobulus and Alexander, and induce Antipater to endeavour to ſupplant them in the government. Herod treats the two princes with great ſeverity, and expreſſes a partiality for Antipater, who attends Agrippa to Rome.

DURING theſe tranſactions abroad, great domeſtic animoſities prevailed at home, through the artful practices of Salome, againſt the two young princes, Ariſtobulus and Alexander, to whom ſhe had a mortal averſion. As ſhe had ſucceeded to her utmoſt wiſhes in her calumnies upon the mother, ſhe proceeded with greater confidence in her deſign upon the ſons, determined that none of her poſterity ſhould be left alive, who might have it in their power to revenge her death. The deſign was carried on with ſome proſpect of ſucceſs, for the young princes gave inſtances of a refractory behaviour towards their father, and let fall raſh words, expreſſive of their resentment at the [illegible] treatment, with threats of revenge upon those who had been the [illegible] of it. Two factions now prevailed, [illegible] the two princes, and that of Salome and Pheroras, the [illegible] of Herod. They cast the bitterest reproaches on each other, and had recourse to all means of calumny and [illegible]. But though their hatred was equal on both sides, their manner of gratifying it was different. The young princes were explicit in the profession of aversion, and the real cause of it, while the others had recourse to the arts of insinuation, and oblique suggestion. The princes, in the heat of blood and simplicity of their hearts, did not hesitate to [illegible] the [illegible] of their mother's death; but Salome and Pheroras gratified [illegible] provoking them to calumniate [illegible], in order to [illegible] they [illegible] the highest honour to be the sons of [illegible] mother, insisting on it that she was basely murdered. This expression was a sufficient ground for calumny [illegible] construction [illegible] revenge [illegible] hands. These [illegible] became the topic of conversation throughout the city, and, [illegible] upon such [illegible], the inexperience of the youths was esteemed [illegible] lation of the [illegible] exaltations, which Salome artfully improved to her own purposes [illegible] deeply affected with the death of [illegible] mother [illegible] would frequently exclaim, "That, [illegible] the [illegible] of that unhappy princess, they looked upon their own circumstances to be [illegible] able of all others, in the [illegible] of [illegible] letters, and, [illegible] becoming partakers of the crime, by [illegible] with the company."

These disorders increased greatly, and the [illegible] had afforded no opportunities for terminating the animosities that prevailed between the parties. When the king [illegible] ed, and addressed the [illegible] the occasion, Pheroras and Salome dropped words intimating [illegible] danger as the young princes [illegible] on the authors and abettors of the death of their mother. They added another circumstance, which was, that their hopes were fixed on Archelaus, king of Cappadocia, by whose means they might be [illegible] Caesar, and to prefer their [illegible] against their father. This information alarmed Herod, [illegible] it was confirmed by the [illegible] of many others. Upon this occasion, he could not [illegible] on the calamities that had heretofore been [illegible] faction [illegible] family, and deprived him of his dearest friends, [illegible] These considerations [illegible] reduced him to a state of despair. He had been fortunate abroad beyond expectation, but he had been no less miserable at home, so that, upon a ballance of the [illegible], it became a [illegible] whether or not he might have been happier [illegible] tion, which could not have [illegible]

In this state of anxious perplexity it appeared to him expedient to introduce a son, [illegible], into the gay circle of [illegible] court, in order to [illegible] haughty and insolent brothers. His name was [illegible]. He had no intention, at that time, of [illegible] him to the first dignity, but had recourse to [illegible] as a check upon the conduct of the sons of Mariamne, and to bring them to sober reason, as they would thereby be convinced, that, at all events, the government would not want a successor. With this view Herod gave Antipater the ceremonies of trust and authority, and paid him such honours as if he had been [illegible] appointed to the succession, not doubting but, by these means, to bring his sons to an acknowledgement of their duty. The event, however, proved otherwise, for they resented it in the highest indignity, and, instead of a check, it became a provocation. Antipater was both shrewd and ambitious, so that when he had once attained to this degree of elevation, and began to form towering prospects, he was determined to pursue the path into which his father had conducted him. He exerted every effort of calumny to supplant his brothers in the affection of their father, who was [illegible] credulous and open to his arts, [illegible] that he gained his point to his utmost wish, and [illegible] in him an aversion, [illegible] grew more and more implacable. His whole aim was to keep up the [illegible] of his father, and, at the same time, [illegible] [illegible] to himself, so that he employed [illegible] as he knew would work upon the [illegible] a discovery of the chief agent.

[illegible] an ascendancy, [illegible] to [illegible] court to him, as the road to preferment [illegible] design was [illegible] to the service of Herod. [illegible] or commands, they soon [illegible] the young princes could not support, [illegible] reported [illegible] and [illegible] [illegible] [illegible] [illegible] [illegible] [illegible] to [illegible] [illegible] [illegible] [illegible] [illegible] [illegible] [illegible] [illegible] to court, [illegible] recommendatory letters to Caesar, [illegible] Upon Agrippa's return to Rome [illegible] Antipater [illegible] when he [illegible], he obtained [illegible] permission for his son to attend him to Rome, [illegible] promising of introducing him to Caesar. This [illegible] to Antipater, [illegible] brothers their father's resolution of cutting them off from the succession.

CHAP. VII

Herod exhibits an accusation against his sons, [illegible] before Caesar.

ANTIPATER's voyage to Rome, with the [illegible] of recommendatory letters from the king [illegible] [illegible] His only [illegible] of [illegible] being [illegible] the opportunity [illegible] perpetually [illegible] to the [illegible] of [illegible] His [illegible] upon to engage his [illegible] thereby [illegible] to act [illegible] occasion [illegible] Mariamne. To prevent [illegible] maintained an epistolary correspondence with his father, and thereby took opportunities of [illegible] the [illegible] under which he laboured for his father, though his real motive was to preserve [illegible] his mind, the antipathy he [illegible] excited him to conceive against his brothers. But notwithstanding he [illegible] incensed in the highest degree [illegible] Alexander and Aristobulus, by the artful practices of their brother Antipater, Herod thought it most prudent, before he proceeded too [illegible], to go to Rome, and there openly exhibit an accusation against his sons before Caesar. [illegible] he happened to meet with the emperor [illegible] the city of Aquileia, and having obtained audience in form, preferred [illegible] the following effect, stating to Caesar, "That he had "not only made him master of his sons' destiny, but that "the very laws of the Jews declared, that, [illegible] "accused by his parents, and they put their hands upon "his head, all who were present should stone him [illegible] "put him to death, and therefore though he might "treat his sons in this manner, after the crimes of which "they stood convicted, yet he [illegible] to have their "opinion upon the matter, not doubting but that he would "[illegible] with him in giving an example to future ages, of "that just severity which ought to be ever used upon unnatural children."

This was the main point of accusation brought by Herod against his sons, who, during the time of his speaking, were so affected, as to burst involuntarily into tears. Though they were conscious of their innocence, yet being accused by their father, they were sensible of the necessity of exculpating themselves from the crime alledged against them, or remaining under the censure that had been brought upon them by means equally fallacious and wicked. Cæsar, observing their confusion, and that the reluctance with which they proceeded on their defence did not arise from conscious guilt, but the prevalence of modest diffidence, was disposed to judge with candour of their cause, as was, indeed, the whole assembly present.

CHAP. VIII.

Alexander's defence. The princes are acquitted by Cæsar. Herod returns to Jerusalem, and declares his succession.

IT being by this time evident that they had excited the commiseration both of Cæsar and the audience, and that all present expressed concern for the unfortunate situation of the young princes, they were emboldened to hope for the prosperous issue of an event, which, at first, appeared to them replete with the greatest danger. Alexander the elder, therefore, thus addressed his father upon the subject of the charge.

"We cannot, Sir, but take it for a clear evidence of "your good intentions towards us, that you have brought "us to this place, before so great and just a judge, and "so gracious a prince for the decision of our cause, "without employing either your regal, or your paternal, "power over your own children and people. But, in "referring us to Rome, by an appeal to Cæsar, it "is given us manifestly to understand, that you have a "desire and purpose to preserve us, for men do not use "to carry those to temples and altars that they intend to "destroy. Yet, after all this, as an aggravation of "our misfortunes, we are conscious to ourselves, that "we are not worthy to live, if we had but done any "thing that looks like disloyalty or ingratitude towards so "good a father, and we had much rather die innocent, "than survive the scandal of such a suspicion. If Providence should enable us to defend the truth, the proof "of our innocence will be a much greater comfort to us, "than the deliverance of our persons; but if calumny "should prevail, a life, under those infamous circumstances, would be worse than a thousand deaths. The "pretext of an ambitious design upon the government, "is well accommodated to the inordinate passions of "young men, and the instance of our unfortunate mother furnishes more colour for it. But whose case, I "beseech you, Sire, may not this be as well as ours, "and why may not the children of all other princes, under our circumstances, be charged with the same design, "if suspicion shall pass for a proof? For here is only an "invidious accusation, without the least shadow of evidence, or so much as a probability to support it. "Why is not the poison itself, or the accomplices and "instruments of the practices, produced? Where are the "conspirators, the conspiracy, the bribery, or the defamatory letters? But the whole story, in fine, is "founded on invention and slander, without any countenance to give it credit. A divided court, it is true, "is a great misfortune, but the hope of preferment, "which you are pleased to call the reward of virtue, "proves often an incentive to all sorts of wickedness. "Nay, we insist so far upon our integrity, that we defy "the whole earth to disprove it. As for scandals, there "is no resisting them, where the ear is open to the calumny, and deaf to the defence. If we have talked at "large it was not meant against yourself, but against "your tale-bearers. If we have passionately lamented the "loss of our dear mother, it was not purely for the death "itself, but out of a zeal to the honour of her memory, "which we found blasted where she least deserved it. "And to what end again should we aspire to the government in the life-time of our father? For if we "already enjoy the honours belonging to the royal family, (as effectually we do,) what have we further to "struggle for? Or, if we are at present barred of our "right, may we not presume to wish and hope for it? "Can it be imagined that the murderers, in such an instance, should ever set up for successors, when sea and "land, after so flagitious a villainy, would conspire "against them? How would it consist with the piety of "the subject, or with the religion of the country, to set "up parricides for kings, and to see the holy temple, "that you yourself erected to the great God, profaned "by the basest of assassins? Or, all other consideration "apart, how can any man think to destroy Herod, the "emperor yet living, and not fall under the power and "justice of Cæsar? Now, if there appears nothing "against us, upon any colourable pretence, where is the "ground for the accusation that exposes us for such impious wretches? As to the death of our mother, it is a "consideration to make us rather cautious than outrageous. We might multiply words, but there is no need "of excusing a thing that never was done, wherefore "we have only to beg of the mighty Cæsar, and to "refer our sovereign judge, that, if you can in your conscience, discharge us of any further suspicion for the "future, we may be allowed to live however miserable "ever; for what can be more grievous than to lie under "the imputation, even, though falsely, of the most horrid of crimes? but if you go on suspecting us, the torments of our own thoughts will put a period to our "existence without your help; for we are not so fond of "life, as to think of preserving it to the torture of him "from whom we received it."

Cæsar who before could scarcely give credit to so gross a calumny, was greatly moved by this spirited address of the young prince, which, added to the visible effect it had upon the countenance of Herod, during the time of delivery, confirmed him in the opinion of an iniquitous design. The whole court, indeed, commiserated the case of the princes, and could not avoid censuring the conduct of the king, in commencing so rigorous a prosecution against them. In fine, from the improbability of the charge, and their concern for the lives of two most promising youths, they determined to interpose most strenuously in their behalf. The princes continued in a state of dejection, anxiously waiting the decision of the case, while the king discovered the utmost confusion both in visage and gesture, till, at length Cæsar, having duly attended to what had passed, delivered it as his opinion, "That, although the sons were entirely innocent of the charge alledged against them, yet they were censurable in having given their father any suspicion of the probability of the calumniating reports that had been spread concerning them." Upon the whole, he acquitted them, and exhorted the father to banish all groundless suspicion, and admit them to former favour and confidence, as the only means of establishing his and their present and future prosperity. After this declaration and admonition, a signal was given to the brothers to approach the imperial seat, near which stood Herod. They advanced with such becoming grace and modesty, and were about to cast themselves at their father's feet, with most dutiful submission, when, with all paternal affection, he embraced them alternately, and gave every proof of the most perfect reconciliation. The surprize of this unexpected encounter, drew tears of joy from the whole assembly, when, after mutual salutation, and the most grateful acknowledgment to Augustus, Herod and the princes took their departure, together with Antipater, who hypocritically pretended to rejoice at this reconciliation.

During the four last days they abode at Rome, Herod presented Cæsar with three hundred talents, as he was then exhibiting public spectacles; and Cæsar, in requital, bestowed upon him half the revenue of the copper-mines in Cyprus, and the charge of the other half, together with other honourable bounties and commissions. With respect to his government, he left it in his own power to appoint which of his sons he pleased for his successor, or so to distribute, that each of them might partake of the dignity: but declared that he would by no means permit him to deprive himself, during life, of the power over his kingdom, or over his sons.

Having adjusted these affairs, Herod returned, accompanied by his three sons, to Judea. During his absence, great part of his dominions about Trachon had revolted, but were reduced to submission, by the vigilance and activity of his several governors and officers, civil and military. Herod, and his sons, touching, upon their return, at Eleusa, a city in the district of Cilicia, they met with Archelaus, king of Cappadocia, who received them kindly, and discovered the utmost pleasure in finding a reconciliation was happily effected, and that Alexander, who had married his daughter, was acquitted of the accusation brought against him. After a reciprocal exchange of salutations and presents, the two kings parted, and Herod set out for Judea, where, upon his arrival, he called an assembly of the people in the temple, when he related the transactions which had passed during his journey, enumerated the particular honours conferred upon him by Cæsar, and, at length, directed his speech to the admonition of his sons, exhorting them, and the people in general, from the highest to the lowest degree, to live in concord. He then informed the multitude, that he appointed his sons to be his successors, Antipater first, and then Alexander and Aristobulus, the sons of Mariamne, in their order. During his life, he claimed all duty and esteem, as sovereign, from his own family, his officers, civil and military, and all ranks and degrees of subjects. These he enforced and recommended as the only effectual means to promote good government on the part of the prince, and consequently the general happiness and prosperity of the prince and people. Having spoken to this purpose, he dismissed the assembly. The sentiments he communicated coincided with the opinion of some, but differed much with that of others, who looked upon the late commotion amongst his sons, and the subsequent transactions, as introductory of mischievous innovations.

CHAP. IX.

Upon the finishing of the building of Cæsarea, Herod celebrates games in honour of Augustus. Builds and adorns many places, and performs divers actions to perpetuate his memory.

THE city of Cæsarea was now finished in the tenth year from laying the foundation of it, the twenty-eighth of Herod's reign, and the 192d Olympiad. The most sumptuous preparations were made for its dedication, the most expert masters in the different entertainments were engaged from all parts, such as musicians, swordsmen, wrestlers, racers, and the like, who were to exhibit, with the utmost dexterity, in their several professions. In short he collected entertainments in all their variety, whether exhibited at Rome, or in other places.

This festival was instituted in the honour of Augustus Cæsar, and because it was to be repeated every fifth year, it was called in the Roman language, *certamen quinquennale*. It was attended with immense expence to the king, in contributing magnificent curiosities to its pomp, collected, at any price, from all quarters: to add to which, Julia, the wife of Cæsar, sent great part of her most valuable furniture from Rome, with the choicest rarities of Italy, estimated at the value of five hundred talents; so that nothing was wanted to complete its splendor. This grand spectacle was attended by an innumerable concourse of people from all quarters, and ambassadors from divers potentates, resorted to it out of compliment to Herod, who were all entertained at the king's charge, with curious spectacles by day, and sumptuous feasts at night, so that he acquired the reputation of a most magnanimous and generous friend. In every instance of this extraordinary exhibition, his ambition was to eclipse the glory of all those that had gone before: and it is related that Cæsar and Agrippa had been heard to say, "The "dominions of Herod were too little for the greatness of his "soul."

After the ceremony of this festival, Herod applied himself to the building of another city, upon a plain called Capharsaba, a spot of ground agreeably situated for the convenience of wood and water, and a plantation of most curious trees. This town he called Antipatris, from his father Antipater. He built upon another spot of ground beyond Jericho, a delightful seat, which he called Cypros from the name of his mother. He also dedicated several monumental structures to the honour of his beloved brother Phasael; he erected a tower in the city itself, not inferior in strength and height to the tower of Pharos in Alexandria, to which he gave the name of Phasael. After this he erected a town upon the north side of the valley of Jericho, which he called by the same name, and by this means rendered the country more fertile, through the cultivation of the inhabitants he introduced, who were called Phasaelites. It would be endless to enumerate the benefits he conferred on cities both in Syria and Greece, and all the places through which he passed in the course of his tour. He amply supplied whatever could contribute to the relief of their necessities and the advancement of their public works, nor did they want money to support them on the failure of their revenues.

But it was the most magnificent and illustrious of all his undertakings, he rebuilt, at his own particular charge, the temple of Apollo, at Rhodes, and bestowed upon the inhabitants a great number of talents of silver for the repairs of their fleet. He expended a vast sum for the repair and finishing of several public edifices for the inhabitants of Nicopolis, near Actium. He also built two cloisters at Antioch, (the largest city of Syria,) that ran across the town, with a wall between them. They were magnificently adorned, and the streets were paved with polished stone, which was of very great advantage to the inhabitants. He recovered the reputation of the Olympic games, which were in a low state, through want of money to support them, appointed revenues for their maintenance, and rendered them more venerable as to sacrifices and other pompous expences; so that, on account of his great liberality, he was declared, in their inscriptions, to be a perpetual director of the games.

From what has been already related concerning the transactions of Herod, his character must appear extremely diversified. If we have respect to his magnificence and liberality, it will be impossible to deny that he was of a beneficent disposition. But if, on the other hand, we advert to the punishment he inflicted, and the injuries he offered, not only to his subjects, but his nearest relations, we must confess he was lost to the feelings of humanity. Upon this view of things, his very nature may seem to many, a contradiction in itself; but I must differ from that opinion, and conclude, that the actions above-mentioned spring from one and the same principle. Being a man ambitious of honour, he was induced to be magnificent, wherever there appeared any hopes of present reputation or future memorial. As his profusion exceeded his income, he became burthensome to his subjects; for his enormous expences could not be supported by justifiable measures. He was conscious of the hatred he had incurred through his oppression, as well as of the difficulty of appeasing those seditious tumults that must ensue thereupon, without either retrenching his disbursements, or shortening his revenue. This circumstanced, he endeavoured to render the ill-will of his fubjects conducive to his emolument. It, therefore, any of his court was not obfequious to him in behaviour, or dropped the moft diftant hint of any innovation in his government, they became the objects of his vengeance, and his very kindred and friends were perfecuted with relentlefs cruelty. This arofe from a [illegible] ambition of being honoured, as did the monuments he erected to Cæfar, Agrippa, and other illuftrious friends, intimating thereby his defire of being honoured in like manner, fo that the one might be exemplary to the other. Thefe dedications and materials are repugnant to the Jewifh laws, which prefer reverence to [illegible] for [illegible] the difpofition of [illegible] was no [illegible] the king, whofe ambition it was to be [illegible] with ftatues, temples, and other monuments, [illegible] in a word, whofe ambition was the fource and fpring of his liberality to ftrangers, and his oppreffion of his fubjects.

CHAP. X.

The Jews petition Cæfar againft the Greeks. Copies of the decrees of Cæfar and Agrippa in their favour.

THE Jews who dwelt in Afia, and in Cyrene, in Africa, fuftained, at this time, the greateft injuries from the Greeks, who committed depredations on them, under pretence that they carried their money out of the country, and, in many inftances, deprived them of thofe privileges and immunities they held, by grant of former kings, in common with the reft of the natives. And upon remonftrance, they found no redrefs of grievances, they fent deputies to Cæfar, with an appeal againft the Greeks, which fo effectually prevailed with the emperor, that he fent letters to the governors of the provinces, enjoining them to confirm to the Jews the full enjoyment of all their privileges and immunities as heretofore. Copies of thefe letters are hereunto fubjoined, as teftimonials of the favourable difpofition of the Roman emperors towards our nation.

1 "Cæfar Augustus, high-prieft, and tribune of the "people, ordains this: Since the nation of the Jews "hath been found grateful to the Roman people, not on-"ly at this time, but in time paft alfo, and chiefly Hyr-"canus, the high prieft, under my father Cæfar, the "emperor, it feemed good to me and my counfellors, "according to the fentence and oath of the people of "Rome, that the Jews have liberty to make ufe of their "own cuftoms, according to the law of their fathers, as "they made ufe of them under Hyrcanus, the high-prieft "of Almighty God; and that their facred money be not "touched, but be fent to Jerufalem, and that it be com-"mitted to the care of the receivers at Jerufalem; and "that they be not obliged to go before any judge on the "fabbath-day, nor on the day of preparation to it, after "the ninth hour. But if any one be caught ftealing their "holy books, or their facred money, whether it be out "of the fynagogue or public fchool, he fhall be deemed a "facrilegious perfon, and his goods fhall be brought into "the public treafury of the Romans. And I give order, that "the teftimonial which they have given me, on account "of my regard to that piety which I exercife towards all "mankind, and out of regard to Caius Marcus Cenfori-"nus, together with the prefent decree, be propofed in "that moft eminent place, which hath been confecrated "to me by the community of Afia, at Ancyra. And if "any one tranfgrefs any part of what is above decreed, he "fhall be feverely punifhed." This was infcribed upon a pillar in the temple of Cæfar.

2 "Cæfar to Norbanus Flaccus, fendeth greeting: "Let thofe Jews, how many foever they be, who have "been ufed, according to their ancient cuftom, to fend "their facred money to Jerufalem, do the fame freely." Thefe were the decrees of Cæfar.

3 Agrippa alfo himfelf, wrote after the manner following, on behalf of the Jews: "Agrippa, to the ma-"giftrates, fenate and people of the Ephefians, fendeth "greeting: I will that the care and cuftody of the facred "money, that is carried to the temple at Jerufalem, be left "to the Jews, of Afia, to do with it according to their an-"cient cuftom; and that fuch as fteal that facred money of "the Jews, and fly to a fanctuary, fhall be taken thence "and delivered to the Jews, by the fame law that facrile-"gious perfons are taken thence. I have alfo written to "Sylvanus, the prætor, that no one compel the Jews to "come before a judge on the fabbath-day."

4 "Marcus Agrippa to the magiftrates, fenate, and peo-"ple of Cyrene, fendeth greeting: The Jews of Cyrene "have interceded with me for the performance of what Au-"guftus fent orders about to Flavius, the then prætor of "Libya, and to the other procurators of that province that "the facred money may be fent to Jerufalem freely, as hath "been their cuftom from their forefathers, they complain-"ing that they are abufed by certain informers, and, under "pretence of taxes, which are not due, are hindered from "fending them, which I command to be reftored, without "any diminution, or difturbance given to them. And if "any of that facred money in the cities, be taken from their "proper receivers, I farther enjoin that the fame be exact-"ly returned to the Jews in that place."

5 "Caius Norbanus Flaccus, proconful to the magiftrates "of the Sardinians, fendeth greeting: Cæfar hath written "to me, and commanded me not to forbid the Jews, how "many foever they be, from affembling together, according "to the cuftom of their forefathers, nor from fending their "money to Jerufalem. I have therefore written to you, "that you may know that both Cæfar and I would have "you act accordingly."

6 Nor did Julius Antonius, the proconful, write otherwife: "To the magiftrates, fenate, and people of the "Ephefians, fendeth greeting: As I was difpenfing juftice "at Ephefus, on the Ides of February, the Jews, that "dwell in Afia, remonftrated to me, that Auguftus and "Agrippa had permitted them to ufe their own laws and "cuftoms, and to offer thofe their firft fruits, which every "one of them freely offers to the deity, on account of pie-"ty, and to carry them in a company together to Jerufa-"lem, without difturbance. They alfo petitioned me, that "I alfo would confirm what had been granted by Auguftus "and Agrippa by my own fanction. I would therefore "have you take notice, that according to the will of "Auguftus and Agrippa, I permit them to ufe, and do ac-"cording to the cuftoms of their forefathers, without dif-"turbance."

We have cited thefe inftances and precedents, that the Greeks may find, on perufal, the honours which have been done us by antiquity, and the privileges, in point of cuftom, doctrine and worfhip, that have been, from time to time, granted us by fovereign powers, even to the toleration of our religion, and the fervice of the true God. Thefe decrees are alfo recorded to foften the prejudices which men, deftitute of liberality and candour, entertain againft us. Nations in general, and places in particular, may change their manners and cuftoms, but the grand law of nature is immutably the fame, and extends indifferently to Jews, Greeks, and Barbarians. Upon this principle our laws are formed, and fo long as we maintain them facred, we muft conciliate the efteem of all mankind. This affords me an opportunity of recommending candour and benevolence to men of all perfuafions, which, when they prevail, will reconcile thofe animofities that arife from difference of opinions, and recommend to all mankind virtue, which is the grand and folid bafis of human fociety.

HEROD the Great in search of TREASURE breaking open the ROYAL SEPULCHRE of KING DAVID when two of his attendants were KILLED by LIGHTENING during the Sacrilegious Attempt—

CHAP. XII.

Great family dissensions ensue upon Herod's rifling the sepulchre of David. [illegible] on the [illegible]. The hypocrisy of Antipater, and general policy of the king's relations. Herod [illegible] for the greatest suspicions and [illegible] [illegible] to a state of [illegible] horror.

HEROD having lavished vast sums in ostentatious munificence, both within and without his kingdom, and heard that Hyrcanus, his predecessor, had opened David's sepulchre, and taken out of it three thousand talents of silver, and that there was a much greater sum [illegible] behind, he determined on making the like attempts. Taking therefore, with him, some of his confidents, he conveyed himself by night into the sepulchre, but with all possible caution, to keep it from the knowledge of the people. He found a great store of rich plate and vessels, both gold and silver, which he carried off; but was disappointed in his expectation of money, as it had been all taken away by Hyrcanus. Being desirous, however, of making further search, he advanced [illegible] to the very coffins in which the bodies of David and Solomon were deposited. It is said, that two of his guards were killed by a flash of fire which burst out of the recess, which was interpreted as a judgment on the rashness of the undertaking. Herod was so alarmed at this prodigy, that he not only quitted his design of prosecuting the search, but, to expiate the sacrilege in [illegible] measure, he erected a most sumptuous monument of marble at the mouth of the sepulchre, to [illegible] the [illegible] [illegible].

Nicolaus, the historian of these times, makes mention of this monument, but is silent as to the king's going down into the sepulchre; [illegible] he [illegible] so inglorious and dishonourable, that he thought it expedient to suppress it. [illegible] [illegible] [illegible] with the king in writing his history under his immediate inspection, he was under an obligation of inserting such circumstances only as would tend to his honour, without [illegible] [illegible] those that would be productive of a contrary effect. The plan he adopted, was either to palliate or disguise his most notorious cruelties, and, in some instances, pass them over unnoticed. His partiality, in [illegible] [illegible], is evident in his plausible colouring of the murder of Mariamne, and the base indignities offered her two sons, under pretext of incontinency in the one, and a design upon the life of the father in the other. Such actions as would be admitted praise-worthy, he extolled by the most lavish encomiums, while those that were highly reprehensible were either extenuated, or passed over unnoticed. It might be said, in favour of Nicolaus, that he wrote a panegyric rather than history, not so much for the information of posterity, as the gratification of his patron. With respect to myself, being nearly allied to the Asmonean kings, and, on that account, attained to the dignity of the priesthood, it is my incumbent duty to relate matters as I find them, with all reverence to the [illegible] of that prince, but yet with an undeviating regard to truth, to which I am determined inflexibly to adhere throughout the whole of my history.

The troubles in Herod's family [illegible] to be much augmented after this sacrilegious attempt upon the sepulchre of David, whether from a judicial vengeance, to increase former calamities so as to render them incurable, or whether fortune assailed him at a particular season, as a punishment for his enormous crimes, cannot be determined. The feuds in his family resembled the tumults of a civil war, and were maintained by [illegible] [illegible] of outrage and calumny; but the grand [illegible] were the artifice and hypocrisy of Antipater, who, while, on the one hand, he suborned his creatures to bring accusations against his brothers, acted himself, on the other hand, as an advocate in their defence, thinking, under this [illegible], to accomplish their destruction. He wrought so far upon the king, by these practices, that he looked upon him as the guardian of his life only, [illegible] [illegible] [illegible] and [illegible], that he recommended his [illegible] [illegible] Ptolemy, to advise with Antipater on the most important concerns of the state; so that these two, in [illegible] [illegible] with the mother, might be said to mould the king either into love or hatred, as best served their particular interests.

Alexander and Aristobulus, on the other side, who [illegible] men [illegible] of a due sense of honour, could not tamely submit to so [illegible] a [illegible], as to be trampled on by them; and their wives were affected in the same manner. Glaphyra, the daughter of Archelaus, and wife of Alexander, [illegible] Salome, both from the love she bore her husband, and [illegible] jealousy, on seeing the daughter of Salome, who was married to Aristobulus, put upon the [illegible] [illegible].

There [illegible] [illegible], at the same time another unfortunate circumstance, [illegible] [illegible] Pheroras, the king's brother, in the dispute, which [illegible], at length, to a high degree of jealousy and hatred. Herod made an offer to Pheroras of his daughter in marriage with [illegible] [illegible], [illegible] [illegible] [illegible], [illegible] was [illegible] [illegible] with [illegible], who, [illegible] of [illegible] [illegible], he was determined to [illegible] [illegible] could [illegible] by this [illegible] to [illegible], [illegible] [illegible] a [illegible] to [illegible] he had given [illegible] [illegible] [illegible] [illegible] [illegible] [illegible] [illegible] [illegible] [illegible] [illegible] [illegible]. But [illegible] [illegible] [illegible] [illegible] [illegible] he offered him rejected, his [illegible] [illegible], and that he could [illegible] [illegible] [illegible], he [illegible] his daughter [illegible] of Pheroras [illegible] [illegible]. Some time [illegible] [illegible] he thought his brother's [illegible] [illegible] [illegible], he sent to him, reprimanded him for [illegible] [illegible] [illegible], and, as [illegible] [illegible] of his [illegible], made him a second offer of his own daughter [illegible] Cypros.

[illegible] [illegible] of this proposal, Pheroras applied to Ptolemy, [illegible] him, by all means, to close with his brother's [illegible], as well as [illegible], in the [illegible] of the king's favour, which would subject him to the most [illegible] danger, and all through means of [illegible] [illegible] [illegible] amour. Pheroras approved the [illegible] [illegible], [illegible] the king's pardon, and [illegible] [illegible] [illegible] although he had one child by her, promised the king [illegible] [illegible] oath [illegible], his second [illegible] [illegible] himself by oath to hold no further [illegible] with [illegible] whom he had renounced.

But when thirty days had elapsed, Pheroras became [illegible] [illegible] to his [illegible], that regardless of his promise given to the king, he took the former woman home, and cohabited with her again. This provoked Herod to such a degree, that he could not restrain his wrath, nor keep from the bitterest invectives on his brother, for a conduct at once [illegible] dishonourable and perfidious. As there was not wanting incendiaries to blow up the [illegible] of domestic discord, Herod was deprived of all the peaceful enjoyments of life, circumstances furnishing incessant occasions for quarrel amongst his nearest and dearest relations. So deadly was the hatred of Salome to the sons of Mariamne, that she would not suffer her daughter to enjoy so much as the conjugal conversation of her own husband Aristobulus, but tampered with her to disclose what had passed between them in private; and if, at any time an occurrence had made a disagreement between them, she was particularly careful to widen the breach, and add her utmost endeavour to bring it to a mutual hatred. By these means she became acquainted with all their concerns, and induced her daughter to divulge what she had heard from the brothers, which they [illegible] by their [illegible], respecting Mariamne and their father, whom they declared [illegible], [illegible] [illegible] continually threatening, that when they got possession of the kingdom, they would make Herod's sons, by his other wives, country schoolmasters, as [illegible] [illegible] [illegible] [illegible], and their diligence in learning fully qualified them for that employment. She added, that [illegible] [illegible], if ever they [illegible] [illegible] of Herod's women [illegible] [illegible] them to [illegible] [illegible] they would cause them to be clothed in [illegible] [illegible] and confined to cloſely, that they ſhould not ſee the light of the ſun. Theſe tales were carried by Salome to the king, who, though they could not but give him much concern, endeavoured to make matters up by fair means rather than foul, ſo that having rebuked his ſons, and heard the defence they made he contented himſelf, for the preſent, but ſoon after he was beſet with ſevere trials.

Pheroras informed Alexander, the huſband of Glaphyra, who was daughter of Archelaus, king of Cappadocia, that he had heard from Salome, that Herod was enamoured of Glaphyra, and that his paſſion for her was unconquerable. Alexander, upon hearing this, from his youth and jealouſy, was all on fire, and concluded it was true, from obſervations he had made of Herod's obliging behaviour to her. This ſtrong ſuſpicion made ſuch an impreſſion upon him, that he went immediately to his father, and, with tears in his eyes, told him what had paſſed between him and Pheroras. This calumniating ſuggeſtion incenſed Herod more than ever, as it proceeded from one of his own family, to whom he had ever rendered all the good offices within his power; ſo that he ſent for Pheroras, and upbraided him, in the ſevereſt terms, with ingratitude, and the vileſt deceit.

Pheroras, in order to exculpate himſelf declared that Salome was the framer of the plot, and that he had the ſtory from her mouth; but happening to be at hand, ſo as to hear this declaration, ſhe vehemently exclaimed, that it was a malicious falſhood, contrived to take away her life in revenge for the zeal and affection ſhe had ſhewn for the ſaving of the king's, who, at this inſtant ſhe averred was in greater danger than ever. She added, it was no wonder that Pheroras ſhould hate her, as ſhe was the only perſon who perſuaded her brother to put away the wife he now had, and to take the king's daughter. As ſhe ſaid this, ſhe tore her hair, and beat her breaſt, and gave proof of the greateſt acts of diſſimulation. Pheroras was now in the greateſt anxiety of mind, between two inextricable difficulties; for he could neither deny what he told to Alexander, or diſprove what Salome had ſaid to him. They, however, maintained the diſpute a conſiderable time, till Herod, being diſguſted with the ſubject, diſmiſſed them both, highly commending the moderation of his ſon, as well as his candour, in coming ſo frankly to him with the ſtory. Salome incurred the diſgrace of being the ſuppoſed author of this calumny, and the king's wives were ready to avail themſelves of it, ſo that he was inceſſantly diſturbed with complaints from one or the other, and his uneaſineſs was not a little increaſed by the following incident.

Obodas was at that time king of Arabia, a prince totally addicted to indolence. His affairs were under the ſole management of Syllæus, a man of graceful perſon and addreſs, and in the prime of life. This Syllæus, coming upon ſome occaſion to Herod, and ſeeing Salome, became enamoured of her, and made her an overture of marriage. Salome loſing her brother's eſteem daily, diſcovered no averſion to the propoſed match, ſo that, upon farther converſation, it was obſerved, by their countenances and geſtures, that the amour advanced on both ſides. The women acquainted the king with the affair, and repreſented it in a moſt ridiculous light. But Herod did not give credit to it, till having ſet Pheroras as a ſpy over them, he brought him word, that, by what he had gathered from the information of looks and ſigns, there was an amour between them. Syllæus, ſoon after this, took his departure; but within the ſpace of two or three months returned, and treated with Herod himſelf concerning the match, pointing out the advantages that would accrue therefrom to him, not only in point of commerce, but with reſpect to his own right to a conſiderable part of the country already. The king, upon this, aſked his ſiſter if ſhe was diſpoſed to the match, and ſhe, without heſitation, replied in the affirmative. But when Syllæus was informed of the neceſſity of conforming to the Jewiſh religion, if he eſpouſed the king's ſiſter, he could not aſſent to theſe terms, aſſigning, as a reaſon, that the Arabians would ſtone him to death, and ſo the treaty ended. Pheroras from thence took occaſion to hint to the king, that Salome had in ſome degree, ſullied her reputation, while his wives peremptorily charged her with incontinence.

Herod now determined, at the importunity of Salome, to marry his own daughter, whom Pheroras had refuſed, to a ſon Salome had by Coſtobarus. But Pheroras diſſuaded him from it, alledged that a ſenſe of the death of his father would cool his affection, and adviſed him rather to give her to his own ſon, who was to ſucceed him in the government. The king took his counſel, gave her an hundred talents for her portion, and all former miſunderſtandings were forgotten.

Notwithſtanding this compromiſe between Herod and his brother Pheroras, feuds and animoſities ſtill prevailed in his family. It ſeems he had three attendant eunuchs, for whom he had a great partiality, and that ſome officious tale-bearer had told him, that Alexander had been tampering with them, for a ſum of money, to betray him. Upon this information, the eunuchs were put to the torture to diſcover what had paſſed between them and Alexander. They confeſſed that they had ſome conference with Alexander, but denied any knowledge of his having a treaſonable deſign upon the life of his father. The tormentors, at the inſtance of Antipater, preſſed them ſtill harder and harder, till, at length, in the extremity of anguiſh, they declared "That Alexander bore a mortal hatred to his father, and endeavoured to ſeduce them from their allegiance to him, "as a prince infirm and impotent, though he uſed artifices "to conceal the decay of nature; that, if they would come "over to him, they ſhould ſoon be preferred to the firſt "offices of ſtate, as the government muſt not only deſcend "to him of courſe, but matters were ſo concerted, as to "put it out of his father's power to diſappoint it, as he had "formed a powerful party among the officers and the king's "friends, who were determined to ſtand by him at the hazard of their lives and fortunes."

Herod was greatly agitated by this confeſſion, which carried in it both reproach and menace, and for ſome time, at a loſs how to proceed, in order to prevent ſurprize, and avoid impending danger. Upon deliberation, it appeared moſt expedient not to go openly to work, but carry on his deſign of detection by ſpies and informers. He was now fraught with ſuſpicion and hatred againſt all about him; and, by indulging thoſe ſuſpicions for the ſake of his preſervation, he continued to ſuſpect thoſe who were guiltleſs. Nor did he ſet any bounds to his ſuſpicions, for the nearer the relation, the greater was his apprehenſion, as ſuppoſing they had better opportunity of effecting his deſtruction. With reſpect to ſuch as were totally diſregarded from him, the ſlighteſt information was their certain deſtruction. The ſituation of his attendants and domeſtics was ſingularly embarraſſing; for their only ſecurity was to calumniate each other, by which practice, even when they ſucceeded, they drew upon themſelves ſuch envy and deteſtation, that ſeldom failed of meeting with its deſert. So it was alſo with reſpect to private piques; for informers were generally entrapped in the ſnare they laid for others. The king had occaſionally ſome qualms of conſcience, for taking away the lives of ſuch numbers without trial or conviction, though he perſiſted in the ſame iniquitous and cruel proceedings. At length however, in the concluſion and after the deſtruction of ſo many innocents, he was ſo far commendable, as to execute juſtice upon the falſe witneſſes, who had ſo vilely ſold the blood of their fellow-creatures.

The palace was now in a ſtate of diſtraction, many of the king's friends were baniſhed thence, and thoſe in particular to whom he had been moſt attached, as Andromachus and Gemellus, two of his principal favourites. Theſe miniſters had ſerved him both abroad and at home, in embaſſies and councils, in the careful education of his sons, and, in fine, in offices of the greatest trust and importance He renounced Andromachus for the kindness Alexander had shewn to his son Demetrius, and Gemellus, for the respect he bore to Alexander, having been his tutor and companion in his travels to Rome It is probable he would have treated them with more severity, had he not been awed by their great popularity, so that he contented himself with depriving them of their offices, and banished them the court, that he might carry on his cruel purposes without controul

These distractions, so disgraceful to Herod, as a prince and a man, sprang from the pernicious counsels of Antipater, who, finding him fearful and suspicious, insinuated himself into his confidence, gratified his humours, and caused him to imbibe, as a political maxim, "that it is necessary to make sure of all those who have power to do mischief" Herod followed this maxim, for when he had expelled Andromachus, and the rest of his friends, who had the honesty and courage to tell him plain truths, and gave him wholesome advice, he put all the confidants of Alexander to the question, concerning treasonable plots and commotions, when they all died upon the torture, having nothing to confess This generous constancy being taken for obstinacy, induced this suspicious and cruel prince to increase the torments, though with no extremity they could not extort the shadow of a disloyal thought expressed at any time by his son Alexander Antipater, with his wonted artifice insinuated that it was a point of honour in them, rather to deny the truth in question, than violate the trust reposed in them, by which means he incited Herod to attempt to discover, by the torture of great numbers, what attempts might be concealed

At length, one under torture declared, that when Alexander was commended, as a graceful person, and a skilful marksman, he observed that these qualifications, given by nature, though desirable in themselves, were not advantages to him, as they excited the envy and jealousy of his father He added, that when he walked along with his father, he endeavoured to depress and shorten himself, that he might not appear too tall, and that when he was hunting, if his father was near, he missed his mark from design, as he knew his father was ambitious of excelling in those exercises Upon this pretended discovery they released the man's torture, and he proceeded with his declaration that Alexander and Aristobulus had entered into a conspiracy once to take away their father's life as he was hunting, and if they succeeded, Alexander was to fly to Rome, to demand the succession There were certain letters also produced from him to his brother complaining of his father, for giving away two hundred talents a year in land to Antipater Herod looked upon all this as sufficient evidence to confirm the suspicion he had of his children, and, in consequence, had his son apprehended and made prisoner, not that he gave much credit to what he heard, as they could have no interest in his destruction, nor was it probable they should go to Rome to solicit his kingdom, after a most notorious parricide In the mean time however, Alexander being imprisoned without any plausible pretext to justify such a measure in the opinion of the multitude, Herod could not think himself secure, without giving them some satisfactory reason, and to that end, put divers of Alexander's confidants and friends to the torture, and afterwards to death, in order to colour the pretence of his guilt, but they could not bring them to confess

While the palace was in this confusion, and nothing to be seen or heard of but tumult, terror, and torment a young man in the utmost agony of torture, confessed that Alexander had written to some friends of his at Rome to move Cæsar, that there was a conspiracy against him, and that if he was sent for thither he would discover it, for that his father had abandoned the interest of Rome, to treat with Mithridates, king of the Parthians, adding withal, that there was a poison already prepared at Askalon This accusation had such credit with Herod, that he immediately ordered the strictest enquiry to be made after the poison, but could obtain no information

Alexander was so far from sinking under this oppression, that he neither attempted denial or defence, but rather to exasperate his father by shewing contempt of his outrageous behaviour, and partly to put him to shame, for his absurd credulity and suspicion He sent him four letters, in which he gave him to understand that he need not to torture any more people upon questions to learn the truth of things, as he could inform him there was a conspiracy against his life, and that Pheroras, and several others, whom he least suspected, were concerned in it He told him of the indecent behaviour of Salome and, in a word assured him, that there was a general resolution formed for taking him off, as neither freedom or happiness could be expected while he was living and amongst the list of conspirators were two named Ptolemy and Sapinnius, in whom he most confided

The court at this time, resembled a den of ferocious animals, rather than a society of the most polished of mankind, as nothing prevailed therein, but calumny, treachery and murder The palace, which was the seat of mirth and festive sport, was now become the [illegible] of gloomy despair, and Herod was as weary of his own life, as he had made others of theirs, for, as he could not repose confidence in any man living, his present state was truly miserable and he had no prospect before him, but that of confusion and horror He could not be [illegible] to enjoy a moment's rest, sleeping or waking, for hideous representations, and horrid imaginations At one time fancy would point out to him his son with a dagger at his breast, and at another time suggest some tremendous [illegible], so that, in a word, he was as miserable as conscious guilt, and the dread of justice, could possibly make him

CHAP XII

Archelaus, king of Cappadocia, [illegible] to effect a reconciliation between Alexander and [illegible] [illegible] obtains pardon of Herod, who goes to Rome, and [illegible] Titius governor of Syria, to [illegible]

WHEN Archelaus heard of the distracted state of Herod's mind, through the suspicions and dissentions which prevailed in his family, he deemed it the part both of a father and friend, to exert his best endeavours to compose the differences betwixt the king and his daughter and son-in-law, for whom he had a very great affection When he found, upon his arrival, that Herod was almost transported beyond the bounds of reason, he thought it imprudent to reprove him, or charge him with the rashness of his conduct, as it would most probably bring on a dispute that would defeat the design on which he came He therefore transferred the blame to Alexander, declaring the king had done nothing but what was just and honourable and that, for his part he would totally reject Glaphyra his daughter, if he should find she had been privy to a plot, and not discovered it This affected zeal of Archelaus in vindication of Herod, brought him upon reflection, to a sense of his late conduct, so that he greatly abated of his rigour towards his son From this sudden change of disposition the king who lately accounted every man his enemy that spoke in favour of Alexander, now burst into tears on hearing Archelaus censure him severely, and request that he would not transport himself to that degree of passion, to the folly and rashness of an inexperienced youth

When Archelaus had thus brought Herod into a more tractable temper, he palliated the matter, by transferring the blame to the advice of evil counsellors, observing, it must be owing to them, that a young man who had no [illegible] in his nature, was corrupted; and that he apprehended there was more reason to suspect the brother than the son This excited Herod's displeasure with Pheroras who, reflecting that Archelaus had the greatest influence with his brother, most importunately requested his intercession with him in his behalf. Archelaus did not reject his suit, but gave him to understand that he could not undertake to change the king's disposition towards him immediately, recommendigg to him, as his best advice, to cast himself at his brother's feet, confess himself the cause of the calamities of the family, and humbly implore his pardon and forgiveness. By following the advice of Archelaus, Pheroras gained his point in both respects; for the calumnies raised against Alexander, were, beyond all expectation, wiped off, and Herod at the instance of Archelaus was reconciled to his brother. Herod was so sensible of the obligations he lay under to the king of Cappadocia, that, on his return to his own country, he dismissed him with the most valuable presents. It was agreed upon between the two kings, that Herod should go to Rome, to inform Cæsar of the present state of his family, as he had written to him upon that subject. They went together as far as Antioch, where Herod effected a reconciliation between Archelaus and Titus, the governor of Syria, and then returned to Judæa.

CHAP. XIII.

Revolt of the people of Trachon. They are overcome by Herod's troops, and received and protected by Syllæus. Herod applies to the Roman governors to deliver up the rebels, who are refused, and makes war on them.

ON Herod's return from Rome, a war broke out between him and the Arabians, on the following occasion. The inhabitants of Trachon, a province that Cæsar had taken away from Zenodorus, and given to Herod, when they could no longer live by pillaging, were reduced to the necessity of following agriculture, an employment that yielded them neither satisfaction or profit. Herod for some time, maintained a degree of order amongst them, and restrained them from making depredations on their neighbours, by which he acquired a deserved reputation. But, upon his going to Rome, to accuse his son Alexander, and commit Antipater to Cæsar's protection, the Trachonites spread a rumour of his death, revolted from his dominion, and betook themselves again to their accustomed way of pillaging their neighbours. But they were quickly suppressed by the king's troops. Only forty of the leaders of them made their escape, and retired into Arabia, where Syllæus (still disgusted at the refusal of Salome) afforded them an hospitable entertainment within a well fortified place. From thence they not only over-ran Judæa, but Cœlo-Syria, and carried off their prey, while Syllæus afforded them protection during their iniquitous practices.

When Herod returned from Rome, and found his dominions had sustained great injury by them, and that he could not come within reach of the free-booters themselves, so long as they were under the protection of the Arabians, he was so incensed that he made an incursion into Trachon, where he put whole families to the sword. This transported them to such a degree of rage, being obliged by the law of their country to avenge themselves on the murderers of their kindred, that Herod's dominions were never free from their incursions. Under these circumstances he applied himself to Saturninus and Volumnius, Cæsar's governors of those provinces, to deliver those plunderers into his hands. This requisition enraged them the more; and collecting in a body, to the number of a thousand, they ranged up and down, committing depredations in town and country, and laying all waste before them, so that their proceeding had, in every respect, the appearance of a war. Herod, therefore, insisted on the free-booters being delivered up, and the repayment of the sixty talents which he, by the hands of Syllæus, had lent to Obodas.

Syllæus, who had now usurped the government of Obodas, denied that the plunderers were in Arabia, and put off the payment of the money, till the Roman governors Saturninus and Volumnius ordered the debt to be fully discharged within the compass of thirty days, and that they should reciprocally deliver up the subjects on each side. This mandate discovered the fallacy of Syllæus, for not one Arabian had taken sanctuary with Herod, while great numbers of robbers were found under the protection of the Arabians.

CHAP. XIV.

Syllæus violates his word. Herod obtains permission to recover his right by force. Takes Repta by assault. Defeats the Arabians. Marches with three thousand Idumæans into Trachon.

WHEN the time appointed for the payment of the money according to the order of the Roman governors, was past, without Syllæus having fulfilled his agreement, Herod, hearing he was gone to Rome, peremptorily demanded satisfaction, both as to the debt, and the delivering up of the plunderers. But finding the Arabians obstinately persist in withholding justice, he obtained permission of Saturninus and Volumnius, to attempt the recovery of his right by force; and, in three days, made a considerable progress with an army into Arabia. Arriving at length at the castle called Repta, whither the free-booters had retired for shelter, he took it by assault, and then demolished the fortifications, without doing the least injury to the inhabitants. In the mean time Nacebus, the Arabian general, advanced with a reinforcement to the succour of his party, and there ensued an engagement, in which the army of Herod sustained very little loss, but many of the Arabians together with their general, were slain, and the remainder scattered and put to flight.

The king having now chastised these free-booters, marched with 3000 Idumæans into the country of Trachon, in order to keep the plunderers in that quarter under. After this Herod sent a particular account of these proceedings to the Roman governors in Phœnicia, giving them to understand that he had not exceeded the bounds of his commission in bringing to condign punishment the refractory Arabians, which, upon an investigation of the matter, they found to be consistent with the authority he had received from the Roman state.

CHAP. XV.

Syllæus gives false intelligence at Rome, and prejudices Cæsar as to the particulars. Cæsar in a letter of reproof, censures the conduct of Herod. The insolence of the Arabians. Herod's embassadors are denied audience of Cæsar. Death of Obodas, and succession of Aretas, whose embassadors and presents are refused by Cæsar. Nicolaus, of Damascus, is sent on an embassy by Herod.

IN consequence of Herod's conduct towards the Arabian free-booters, Syllæus hastened to Rome, where he totally misrepresented every circumstance concerning it. He had already insinuated himself so far as to be personally known to Cæsar, to whom, as he was walking before his palace, he addressed a complaint of Herod's having entered Arabia with an army, overturned the government, ravaged the country, slain 2,500 noble Arabians upon the spot, with his friend and kinsman Nacebus, their general, amongst the rest, pillaged Repta of vast treasure that had been deposited there, and all this through the advantage he took of the infirmities of Obodas, who had neither troops in readiness to oppose him, or a general in his absence fit for command. Syllæus added invidiously, that he would not have undertaken this journey to Rome, but in full confidence that Cæsar would provide for the public peace of all his people, and that, had he been there, he would have exerted himself in such a manner as would not have redounded either to the honour or advantage of Herod.

This representation of the matter enraged Cæsar, who enquired of Herod's friends, as well as his own, who lately came out of Syria, whether or not Herod had led his army to any place out of his own jurisdiction. When this could not be denied, he admitted the truth of all that had been laid before him by Syllæus, and immediately sent a letter of reproof to Herod, giving him to understand, that "whereas formerly he had used him as his friend, he "should now treat him as his subject." Syllæus also wrote an account of this to the Arabians, who, finding that Herod was in disgrace with Cæsar, neither delivered up the robbers, who had fled to them, or paid the money that was due, according to the contract subsisting between them. The people of Trachon, availing themselves of this opportunity, rose against the garrisons in Idumæa, joined the Arabian ravagers, laid waste the country, and took ample vengeance of Herod for his late rigorous proceedings against them.

Herod, having lost the favour of Cæsar, was under a necessity of bearing these insults, for both his courage and credit had failed him. He endeavoured to exculpate himself by his ambassadors, who were, at first, denied audience, and afterwards peremptorily dismissed, without any attention being paid to the business of their embassy. Herod could not but entertain apprehensions of the subtle insinuations of Syllæus, who improved the displeasure of the emperor to his own advantage, and finding him extremely credulous, and pliant to his will, made the best of his opportunity to work upon him in his own behalf to the prejudice of Herod.

Obodas being dead and succeeded by Æneas, whose name, on his accession to the government, was changed to Aretas, Syllæus endeavoured, by calumnies and presents to Augustus, to bring about his expulsion from his principality, and engross the power to himself. He was induced to this attempt from the disgust that Cæsar took to Aretas for entering upon the administration without his knowledge and consent. The new king sent ambassadors to Cæsar, with complimentary letters, and magnificent presents, and, amongst the rest, a golden crown of immense value. These letters contained a positive charge against Syllæus for poisoning his sovereign Obodas, usurping his government, debauching the wives of the Arabians, and taking up vast sums of money to accomplish his purposes. But Cæsar rejected his embassy, as he had done that of Herod, without paying the least regard to his accusation of Syllæus.

In the mean time affairs in Judæa and Arabia became more and more perplexed, partly through the anarchy and confusion which prevailed, and partly because there was no rule maintained, one of the kings being not yet established in his government, and the other carrying no sway over his people: for Herod was so circumstanced, that he could not assert his regal authority without offending Augustus, and therefore was under a necessity of submitting to all indignities. At length, being brought to the last extremity, he took up a final resolution of attempting to appease the anger of Cæsar, through the mediation of his friends, and trying the effect of a third embassy to Rome, on which important business he deputed Nicolaus, of Damascus, an expert logician, and an accomplished orator.

CHAP. XVI.

Great dissentions in Herod's family. Eurycles ingratiates himself with Herod. Obtains the confidence of Alexander. His perfidy and fraud [illegible]. He is banished out of Lacedæmon. Herod's [illegible] jealousy. Jucundus and Tyrannus brought [illegible] and forced by torture to accuse Alexander. The [illegible] of Alexander put to the question. Counterfeit letters produced against Alexander. [illegible] Salome's information. Examination of Glaphyra and Alexander, who deny the charge. Cæsar is reconciled to Herod. Nicolaus exhibits an accusation against Syllæus, and defends the cause of Herod. Syllæus [illegible] his death. Cæsar [illegible] Herod a letter of condolence.

HEROD's family was now in a state of the utmost distraction, through the prevalence of intestine jealousies, which threatened the direst calamities, and chiefly arose upon the following occasion. There was one Eurycles, a Lacedæmonian, a man of noble extraction, but perverse disposition, and an adept in all the arts of the profoundest dissimulation. This Eurycles cultivated the friendship of Herod, through a mutual exchange of presents, and other good offices, with him in the house of Antipater, by which means he became [illegible], acquainted with Alexander, as pretending to him that he was in great favour with Archelaus, king of Cappadocia, and also that he entertained the highest respect for Glaphyra. Under this semblance he minutely observed whatever passed in the family, in order to [illegible] as opportunity might offer. In fine, he was so arch an hypocrite, as to conceal his designs from the keenest penetration, and, though a monster of perfidy, pass upon mankind as the most ingenious and disinterested man in the world. By his arts he obtained the confidence of Alexander, who disclosed to him all his secrets, and reposed in him an unlimited trust. He gave him a detail of his misfortunes, such as the unkindness of his father, the death of his mother, and the increasing power and influence of Antipater. He represented his oppression as intolerable, as the king's aversion was now come so inveterate, that he would not admit his children to his table or conversation. These complaints Alexander credulously imagined would remain undisclosed in the breast of Eurycles, but they were all by him conveyed to Antipater, whom he told, that he did not bring him the information from any interested view, but from a motive of friendship, and a sense of the very great importance of the concern, warning him, at the same time, to beware of Alexander.

Antipater looked upon this as a singular instance of the respect and friendship of Eurycles, made acknowledgement of it by very considerable presents, and at length related the purport of the information to Herod. The king was so prepossessed with a disposition to believe every evil report against Alexander, that, through the force of such prejudice, and divers ambiguous hints in the course of conversation, he contracted a hatred for him more implacable than ever.

Having obtained from him a present of fifty talents for his supposed generous service, the perfidious Eurycles went to Archelaus, with lavish encomiums on his son Alexander, insinuating to him, at the same time, the great pleasure and happiness he had received in being accessary, upon several occasions, towards composing the differences between him and his father. His arts prevailed likewise with Archelaus, who gratified him with a pecuniary present, and this imposture he carried on without detection by any one of the several parties. He then returned to his own country, where he followed the practice of his base arts, till he was at length discovered, brought to justice, and, as the vilest of malefactors, banished Lacedæmon.

Herod was not now disposed, as before, towards Alexander and Aristobulus, when he was content with hearing the calumnies which others raised against them, but entertained so implacable an hatred, as to urge many to determination contrary to their will. He observed all that passed, put questions, and attended to all informations that he thought might tend to criminate them, till, at length, he heard, that one Evaratus of Coos, was confederate with Alexander, a circumstance that [illegible] great satisfaction.

Calumnies against the brothers daily increased, and it [illegible] of general concern, to exhibit some deadly charge, under pretence of the regard for the preservation of the king. There were two persons, called Jucundus and Tyrannus, formerly of Herod's guards, men much admired for their stature, strength, and agility, but having incurred the displeasure of Herod, they were banished the court. Alexander knowing the valour and activity of these men, entertained them as guards of his person, and treated them with every instance of liberality. The king, therefore, being suspicious of them, had them put to the question upon the rack, concerning the conspiracy. Having sustained the anguish for some time, with incredible resolution, they at length confessed that Alexander had solicited them to take an opportunity of killing the king, while he was upon the hunt, as the fact might be concealed under colour of a fall from his horse upon his own spear, especially as he had [illegible] escaped that accident once before. They made a further discovery of money, hid in the stable, and some of the king's lances and darts, delivered out by the master of the [illegible] to the servants of Alexander, by his own order.

The [illegible] the governor of Alexandrion was put to the torture, upon the questions of promising to receive the brothers into his fortress, and of putting into their hands the king's [illegible] there deposited. The governor denied the charge, but his son avowed it, and produced letters under Alexander's hand, as he pretended, to this effect: "When we have finished all that we have projected to do, "we will attend you, but do you [illegible] "to promise, to receive us into your fortress." After this [illegible] produced, Herod was confirmed in his suspicion of the treacherous design of his sons, but Alexander peremptorily insisted that it was the malicious contrivance of Antipater, and forgery by his secretary Diophantus, who was a man skilled in such illicit practices, and afterwards convicted and punished for the same.

[illegible] Jericho, for putting the witnesses to the torture, had them brought thither to accuse his sons before the people, who [illegible] stoned them to death; as, in [illegible], they would have done Alexander and Aristobulus, had not Herod prevented them by means of Ptolemy and Pheroras. They were, however, committed to close custody, and spies set upon them to observe every thing they did or said, and, in fact they were treated as condemned criminals.

In this extremity Aristobulus endeavoured to excite Salome, his aunt, and mother-in-law, to compassion for his distress, and to a just indignation for the author of it, representing to her the danger she was in, from lying under an accusation of holding private correspondence with Syllæus, about the king's affairs, [illegible] him. Salome carried their words to her brother, who, in the heat of his passion, commanded both his sons to be bound, kept separate from each other, and enjoined to communicate severally, in writing the particulars of their treasonable design. They wrote according to the king's command, and both agreed in the same declaration, that they had never conceived a treacherous design. They acknowledged indeed, an intention of making their escape, and the life they led under perpetual jealousy was worse than death.

About this time there came an embassy to Herod, from Archelaus, king of Cappadocia, one Mela, a person of distinguished rank in that country. Herod, desirous of shewing the ill will he supposed Archelaus bore him, sent for Alexander out of prison, and examined him in the presence of the ambassador concerning his escape, whither he intended to go, and in what manner to dispose of himself. He frankly replied, that he proposed to go to Archelaus, his father-in-law, who had promised to send him to Rome, declaring most solemnly, that neither he or his brother had entertained the shadow of a treacherous thought, against their father, whatever sycophants and liars might have insinuated to the contrary. He had declared, he said that Jucundus and Tyrannus might be examined more [illegible]ly, but it was agreeable to the design of Antipater to have them dispatched, so that, at his instigation, they fell by the hands of the [illegible].

After this declaration, in the hearing of the ambassador, Herod commanded him and Alexander to be taken to Glaphyra, and that she should be strictly interrogated as to her knowledge of the conspiracy against his life. They were no sooner come within view of the princess, than, upon sight of her husband in chains, she exhibited tokens of the utmost phrenzy, tearing her hair and uttering the most piercing groans, which were answered by deep fetched sighs from Alexander, insomuch that the surrounding multitude was struck with astonishment. Ptolemy at length put the question to the prince, whether his wife was privy to his actions? He replied, "[illegible] that the woman I "love dearer than life, and by whom I have had even pledges of that love, should be unconscious of my actions?" The princess then exclaimed, that "she never knew he entertained a wicked design, but that, if her accusing herself falsely would tend to his preservation, she would confess it all." Alexander declared, that "they were innocent of the charge alledged against them, by those from whom they had deserved better things, but if an intention of making their way to Archelaus, and then to Rome, was to be imputed to them as treason, they were certainly answerable for it." Glaphyra also made the same confession.

Herod, construing this declaration as a proof of the ill-will of Archelaus towards him, dispatched Olympus and Volumnius with letters to him, with orders to touch at Eleusa, [illegible] in Phenicia, and there deliver them. They had instructions also to expostulate with him, upon a strong presumption of his being engaged with his son in the conspiracy. Their orders were from thence to sail for Rome, in case they should find that Nicolaus of Damascus, that Cæsar was become more tractable than formerly, they were to present another express to him, with the proceedings against Alexander and Aristobulus, and copies of the evidence upon which they were convicted. Archelaus acknowledged his readiness to receive the princes, and that he undertook to afford them such sanction, as the best service he could render both the father and the sons, being fearful lest Herod in the heat of rage and jealousy, might drive them to extremities. He affirmed upon the whole, that he had no design of sending them to Cæsar, or supporting them against their father.

When Herod's deputies arrived at Rome, and found Cæsar reconciled to their master, they delivered their letters according to order. They were previously laid before Nicolaus for his inspection, who managed his commission after this manner. As soon as he came to the emperor's palace, at Rome, exceed[illegible] above the instructions that he had in charge, he brought a formal accusation against Syllæus having procured proofs upon him from the Arabians (who were greatly divided among themselves), of the most flagitious practices that could be imagined, particularly the murder of Obodas, which was rendered undeniably manifest, by intercepted letters under his own hand. Nicolaus, whose main concern was to effect a permanent reconciliation of Herod, with Cæsar, greatly improved this discovery to the advantage of his principal, being assured that he would not be allowed to make a direct defence of Herod, but if he desired to accuse Syllæus, an opportunity would present itself for speaking in Herod's behalf.

The day being appointed for a hearing, Nicolaus in the presence of the ambassadors of Aretas, delivered an accusation against Syllæus, as the murderer of his lord and master the king, and great numbers of the Arabians, as having taken up immense sums of money towards disturbing the public peace, as an abandoned debauchee, both in Rome and in Arabia, and as guilty of the most daring effrontery in imposing falsehood and calumnies upon Cæsar himself, and particularly with respect to the account he gave of the conduct of Herod, which was fallicious throughout the whole. When Nicolaus came to the last article, Cæsar interrupted with a command to speak to this single point, and shew that he had not led an army into Arabia, nor slain two thousand five hundred men there, nor taken prisoners, nor pillaged the country. Nicolaus made answer, that he should take the liberty to demonstrate that either none at all, or but very few of the imputations, were true, of which the emperor had been informed. This assertion drew the attention of Cæsar, and Nicolaus thus proceeded in his plea for Herod:

"There was a debt due to Herod of five hundred talents upon a bond, wherein it was specified, that, when "the time appointed for payment was expired, it should "be lawful to make a seizure of any part of his country. "With respect to a body of men that Cæsar calls an army, it was merely a party sent out for putting a legal "claim into execution. This party was not sent immediately according to the tenor of the bond, because Syllæus had come before Saturninus and Volumnius, and "at last had sworn at Berytus, by the fortune of Cæsar, "that he would pay the money in the course of thirty "days, and deliver up the fugitives that were under his "protection. The time arrived: but neither the money "was paid, nor the fugitives delivered up, so that Herod "was obliged to address the governors again, who gave "it as their opinion, that he might do himself right by "distress. This was the occasion of his going into Arabia, and of the war which this adventurer so tragically "describes. How can this be deemed a war, when it "had the approbation and permission of the governors, "in prosecution of a lawful compact, and after a violation of a solemn oath, both in the name of the gods "and Cæsar?

"With respect to the captives, they were robbers that "came from the country of Trachon, where the number at first amounted to no more than forty, but increased afterwards. They escaped the punishment "Herod would have inflicted upon them, by taking refuge "in Arabia. Though the common enemies of mankind, "they were entertained by Syllæus, who gave them lands, "and went shares with them in their booty. These "were the men that Syllæus bound himself by oath to "restore, together with the borrowed sum within the "time limited. I can now with confidence defy any "man to say that Herod took any other prisoners in Arabia, than these free-booters, of whom several escaped. "Thus does the calumny of the captives, which has "been represented in so odious a light, appear to be no "better than a fiction to provoke the indignation of the "emperor: for I can take upon me to affirm, that, when "the forces of the Arabians came upon us, and one or two "of Herod's party fell, he then only defended himself, "and there fell Naccbus, their general, and, in all, "about twenty five others, and no more. This number "Syllæus hath enlarged, by multiplying every single soldier to an hundred, so that he reckons the slain to have "been two thousand five hundred."

Cæsar was so incensed at this relation, that, turning towards Syllæus, he sternly asked him, how many Arabians were slain in that action? After some hesitation, he confessed himself mistaken in the number, upon which they read the conditions of the bond, the arbitration of the governors, and the remonstrances of the several cities and towns, complaining of the injuries sustained from the robbers. Augustus, being now fully informed of the matter, passed sentence of death on Syllæus, took Herod into favour again, acknowledged a concern for his mistake in listening to the calumnies that transported him to such severities against him, and reproached Syllæus as the compulsive cause of his ingratitude towards his best friends. In fine, Syllæus was sent back to Arabia, there to discharge the debt, and afterwards to be punished with death.

Cæsar was still offended with Aretas, for presuming to usurp royal authority, without having obtained his consent, insomuch that he determined to transfer the government of Arabia to Herod, but changed his mind, on reading the letter which Olympus and Volumnius brought him, containing invectives against his own sons. The deputies were instructed, if they found Cæsar propitious, disposed, to deliver him those letters, which they accordingly did; and Cæsar, upon reading them, reflecting on the advanced age and turbulent temper of Herod, retracted his resolution, called for the ambassadors of Aretas, and, after having spoken a word of reproof on the temerity of their master in not waiting till he had received the authority from him, accepted their presents, and confirmed Aretas in his government.

Cæsar, upon this reconciliation, wrote a letter of condolence to Herod, on account of his sons, giving him full power, if he found them engaged in so unnatural and impious a conspiracy, to proceed against them as parricides: but if, at length, it should happen that their misdemeanours amounted to no more than an intention to escape, he should content himself with an admonition, and not proceed to extremity. The sum of his advice was to call a council at Berytus, a city under the Roman jurisdiction, and there, with the assistance of the governors of the adjacent provinces, together with Archelaus, king of Cappadocia, hear and determine upon the whole matter, and bring the point to a final decision.

CHAP. XVII.

Herod upon his reconciliation with Cæsar, calls a council at Berytus, and prefers his [illegible] against [illegible]. They [illegible] that Herod [illegible] a stage of [illegible] to [illegible]. S[illegible] for [illegible] the [illegible] [illegible] dead, [illegible]. Herod goes for Tyre, [illegible] to Cæsarea. Tyro's generous [illegible], [illegible] Herod, in behalf of the [illegible]. Tyro's [illegible] against Tyro. [illegible].

THIS letter from Cæsar afforded Herod the highest satisfaction, not only as a token of his reconciliation with the emperor, but as vesting him with full authority over his sons. It is remarkable, that, though in former times of prosperity, he had treated his sons with great rigour, when life was in question, he abated his severity, and affected a degree of moderation. But, upon the change of affairs, and his reinstatement in the favour of the Roman emperor, he became outrageous in his resentment, and proceeded against them with ungovernable rancour.

Pursuant to Cæsar's direction, he summoned a council to meet at Berytus, but excepted Archelaus, perhaps from personal pique, or apprehension that he would endeavour to frustrate his design. When the council was met according to summons, he did not produce his sons, but kept them in a village belonging to Sidon, that they might appear when called for. He then entered the council-chamber alone, and there preferred an accusation against his sons, in the presence of one hundred and fifty persons; but without premising his own misfortunes, or pointing out the necessity of the present proceeding. It was a charge fraught with language unbecoming a father, and accompanied with boisterous exclamations and violent gestures, that indicated symptoms of his labouring under phrenzy. His arguments were confused and inconsistent: no proofs were tendered to govern the opinion of the court. His assertions were founded on his own authority alone, and the letters he produced composed rather of the parties, than judges to determine upon evidence, and according to the grand principles of right and wrong.

There were some letters of the young princes read; but not one of them contained the remotest hint of any plot or contrivance against the prosecutor. All that could be inferred was, a consultation as to the method of escaping, together with some expressions of dissatisfaction and offence. When Herod came to that part of the letters, he endeavoured to pervert their obvious meaning, by adducing them as demonstrative evidence of a conspiracy, and most solemnly declared, it was worse than death to peruse their contents. He affirmed, he might insist on the power he had received over his own children, both from nature and the grant of Cæsar; and added an allegation of a law of his own country, which enjoins, that, "If parents laid their hands on the head of him "that was accused, the by-standers were obliged to stone "him to death;" which, though he was ready to do in his country and kingdom, yet, at present, he would rather decline his privileges, and submit the matter to the further consideration of the counsel, not as judges to determine whether the case be as is represented, or not, since it is so indubitably manifest, but to take their opinion with respect to the justification of the sentence, as an instructive lesson to posterity, against such impious practices on the life of a parent.

The assembly plainly perceiving, from the evasive finesse displayed throughout the whole proceeding, as well as the withholding of the princes from the presence of the court, that equity was totally suppressed, and a reconciliation impracticable, confirmed the authority of Herod with respect to the disposal of his sons. Upon this occasion Saturninus, a person of consular dignity, who had executed many honourable commissions, arose and observed, that "he was for "punishing the princes, but not with death; as having "children of his own, he was duly impressed with the case, "and therefore would be very loth, after the calamities that "the king of Judæa had endured already, to oppress him "with the heaviest of all at the last." He was followed by his three sons, who spoke with feeling and spirit, and enforced the opinion delivered by their father. Volumnius, on the contrary, exerted himself with great vehemence against the princes, exclaiming that nothing but death could expiate the horrid crime of parricide; and the majority concurring with his opinion, carried the question.

The sentence was no sooner passed than Herod hastening to Tyre, taking his sons with him, and meeting with Nicolaus, on his return from Rome, he related to him the circumstances that had passed at Berytus, and enquired of him the opinion that prevailed concerning the matter at Rome. Nicolaus informed him that the princes were generally blamed for their foul practices, and deserved to be laid in chains; nay, that death was their legal due, if the conspiracy could be clearly proved; though the world imputed the prosecution rather to malice than justice. But if Herod found himself otherwise disposed, he might acquit them, without involving himself in an irretrievable difficulty. Thus Nicolaus gave as the opinion and judgment of his friends at Rome; upon which Herod, after a long pause, without making a single comment, bid Nicolaus put to sea with him, and they proceeded together to Cæsarea.

Upon their arrival at Cæsarea, they found that the point in dispute between Herod and his sons, was the general topic of conversation, and that the people waited the issue with the utmost anxiety. An apprehension prevailed, that the feuds and animosities of the family would come to a fatal conclusion. The case of the brothers was sincerely compassionated, though opinion was suspended, and popular resentment smothered.

As an exception to the general conduct upon the occasion, Tyro, a veteran in the military service, of distinguished valour, gave his opinion on the point with the utmost freedom. To this he might have been induced from having a son of the same age, and who had the strictest intimacy with Alexander. This honest veteran publicly exclaimed, that justice and truth were banished the earth, that nothing prevailed but malice and deceit; and that mankind were so blinded by their inordinate passions, that they could no longer discern right from wrong, or good from evil. This, though a dangerous freedom, was so noble an instance of virtue and resolution, that it could not fail of meeting with universal approbation; so that those who durst not follow the example, could not but revere the man who generously stood forth in vindication of oppressed innocence, and to stem the torrent of corruption.

Nor did his efforts stop here; for he boldly presented himself before the king, and being granted a private audience, thus addressed him: "Since, Sire, I labour under "insupportable grief, I am determined to give it vent, "though at the hazard of my life; and probably the liberty "I take, if you are so disposed as to hear me with patience, "may tend to your advantage. May I be permitted to enquire "whither are fled that understanding and magnanimity, "that, in time past have carried you through so many dif"ficulties? Whence comes this solitude and desertion of "your friends and relations? For those I cannot deem "such, that can behold the horrid transactions in your "court and family, and stand still unconcerned spectators. "Do you not perceive the tendency of these things? Can "you resolve to take away the lives of these two princes, "accomplished with every virtue, and subject yourself to an "ambitious son, and those of your relations you have so of"ten doomed to punishment? Do you not find yourself ta"citly condemned, and the case of your sons universally "lamented; and is not your whole army, both officers and "private soldiers, particularly afflicted for the princes, and "enraged with the authors of their miseries?"

Some part of this expostulation the king heard with calm composure; but when Tyro touched upon the perfidy of his confidants, and launched out into an unbounded freedom, he deemed it rather a reproach than a caution, and sternly asked who these officers and soldiers were, to whom his declaration referred? Upon Tyro's naming them, Herod ordered them all together, with the veteran himself, to be taken up, and committed to prison.

Upon this occasion one Tryphon, who was the king's barber, laid an information against Tyro, importing that he repeatedly tampered with him, by promises of pecuniary reward, as well as the favour of Alexander, to cut the king's throat, while he was under the operation of the razor. Orders were immediately given, that Tyro, his son, and the informer, should be put to the torture. The son seeing his father so cruelly tormented, and so resolute in sustaining the anguish, without hope of mitigation, declared, "that, "if the king would free him and his father from those excru"ciating pains, he would relate the truth." When the king had passed his word so to do, he said, "that an agree"ment was made, that his father, having private access "to the king, should lay violent hands on him, if he suffered "death, as he was almost certain it would be an act of "generosity in favour of Alexander." Upon this declaration his father was delivered from present torture; but whether the confession was founded on truth, or whether it was a mere pretence to obtain deliverance, has not yet appeared.

Herod was now finally resolved to proceed to the execution of his purpose, without any further doubt or deliberation; so that calling the people together, he ordered 300 officers, together with Tyro, his son, and the informer, to be brought forth, who, upon his accusation of them to the multitude, were all stoned to death upon the spot. Alexander and Aristobulus, by their father's command, were sent away to Sebaste, and there strangled. Their bodies were deposited in a sepulchre at Alexandrion, with divers of their ancestors.

TYRO vindicating the Innocence of HEROD's two SONS.

... afterwards put to Death ...

It may perhaps seem unnatural to suppose, that such an inveterate hatred would prevail between a father and sons, as to overcome all natural affection, and be productive of such dire effects. But [illegible] may justly deserve censure, whether the cause arose from a continued course of provocation in the young princes, or from the imperious jealousy and unnatural disposition of the king. [illegible] to the sons, they might, perhaps, in the heat of youthful passion, become haughty and [illegible], ready to [illegible] evil reports of their father [illegible] his conduct. They might be [illegible] in their words and actions, as to [illegible] informers, who sought [illegible] against them. On the other hand, what could argue greater weakness in Herod, or be more [illegible] than, without any proof or conviction of a treasonable design, or even so much as the presumption of a contrivance, to indulge a lawless, nay, more than brutal, passion, by putting to death his own sons, who possessed such rare accomplishments, both mental and personal, and in particular Alexander, the elder.

If he was determined on a condemnation, might not imprisonment or banishment have sufficed? Under such circumstances, there would have been no fear of treachery, and as little of open force, because of the patronage of the Roman power. But to deprive them of life, to gratify an ungovernable passion, can never be justified by any law, human or divine. He lived, indeed, afterwards to give additional proofs of his towering ambition, rancorous envy, and relentless cruelty, which he exercised, as occasion offered, upon the rest of his relations, though, as will be seen in the sequel, some of them deserved the punishment. However, upon the whole, the barbarity of Herod must be an eternal stigma on his character.

END OF THE SIXTEENTH BOOK

FLAVIUS JOSEPHUS

ON THE

ANTIQUITIES

OF THE

JEWS.

BOOK XVII

[INCLUDING A PERIOD OF ABOUT TWELVE YEARS.]

CHAP. I.

Antipater is universally detested by the Jewish nation, for being accessary to the murder of the princes Alexander and Aristobulus. Maintains great sway in Judæa. Endeavours in vain to delude Salome. Herod compels her to marry Alexas. Sends Glaphyra, the widow of Alexander, back to her father, Archelaus, king of Cappadocia. Antipater much disgusted at the respect in which the people held the memory of the princes. Herod is prevailed on to dissolve certain contracts.

ANTIPATER having, by his insidious arts, effected the destruction of his brothers, paved the way for compassing his design upon the life of his father, and indulged the most sanguine hopes of attaining to the very summit of his ambition. But he was soon disappointed in his towering expectations; for, although he was delivered from the fear of his brethren being rivals, as to the government, he found the general odium he had incurred throughout the nation on their account, to be an obstacle almost insuperable. The alienation of the soldiery was a more disagreeable circumstance, as the security of these kings depended upon them, whenever they found the people desirous of innovations. These mischiefs he drew upon his head by fraud and perfidy; yet, if the exercise of his power was his delight, it might be said that he actually governed at this time, his father being king only in name, while the affairs of the state were under his guidance and direction. Nay, the very crime for which he deserved to die, passed for an instance of his affection and respect, as if he had consulted the preservation and safety of the king in the death of the princes; whereas, in reality, he grafted his aversion to the father in what he did; and such was the inveteracy of his malice, that he detested the brethren for the father's sake.

All Antipater's arts and contrivances now tended to make way for the taking off Herod, that he might have none to accuse him of the vile practices he was devising, and that Herod might have no refuge, nor any to afford him assistance, since such must have Antipater for their avowed enemy. He looked upon the government as his own after the death of Herod, but thought that delays would be dangerous, so far as they might lead to a discovery of his insidious arts to his father, and thereby frustrate his ambitious design. To this end he spared neither cost or pains to gain the good will of his father's friends, by a winning courtesy, and most unbounded munificence. The objects of his regard were his friends at Rome in general; but he was particularly desirous of conciliating the esteem of Saturnius, governor of Syria, as also of his brother.

Nor did he despair of bringing over to his interest Salome, the wife of a particular friend, and confident of Herod. Antipater possessed all the art of address and insinuation, and could assume the mask of complacency to conceal the basest intentions. But he could not impose upon his aunt Salome, who saw through all his disguise, opposed artifice to artifice, and defeated his designs, though he had so ordered it, that her daughter, the widow of Aristobulus, was married to his uncle, by the mother's side, and the other daughter to Calleas. Salome was passionately fond of Syllæus; but Herod, by means of the assistance of the empress Julia, who represented to her the train of ill consequences that would result from her disobliging her brother, prevailed with her to marry Alexas.

Herod, at the same time, sent Glaphyra, the widow of his son Alexander, back to her father Archelaus, king of Cappadocia, returning the portion which he had with her, in order to obviate all ground of controversy; and took moreover great care of the education of his grandchildren. Alexander had two sons by Glaphyra, and Aristobulus by Bernice, the daughter of Salome, had three sons and two daughters. Herod would occasionally present these children to his friends, deploring the hopeless fate of his sons, and praying that they might avoid the fame, improve in virtue, and live to acknowledge the care of their education He designed the daughter of his brother, Pheroras, for wife to the eldest son of Alexander, and the daughter of Antipater to the eldest son of Aristobulus, and to the son of Antipater, one of the daughters of Aristobulus, the other daughter to his son Herod, whom he had by the daughter of the high-priest, for polygamy according to our law, is allowable

The principal motive of the king, in these alliances, was the commiseration of their orphan state, and to render Antipater, by these inter-marriages, more affectionate towards them But Antipater returned the same disposition for the children as he had before done for their fathers, and Herod's tenderness was so far from softening him, that, on the contrary, he became fierce and jealous, and the more the king favoured them on the one hand the more Antipater hated them on the other, lest they should rival him, and especially with the assistance of Archelaus and Pheroras, the tetrarch, whose son at that time stood fair to marry one of the daughters It was the greatest mortification to Antipater to observe the compassion the people returned for the care and memory of the unfortunate princes, and with what detestation they beheld the contrivers of their ruin, while they waited for an opportunity of exposing Antipater for his malicious practices against his brethren It occurred to him upon reflection, that the most effectual method of securing the government to himself, was to prevail with Herod to dissolve the contracts above-mentioned, which, with much importunity, he brought to pass, and obtained the promise of the daughter of Aristobulus for himself, and for his son the daughter of Pheroras, whereupon the former marriage agreements were annulled

King Herod, at this time, had nine wives The first was the mother of Antipater The second was the daughter of Simon, the high-priest, by whom he had a son, called by his own name The third was the daughter of his brother He fourth his cousin german, by whom he had no issue The fifth a Samaritan, by whom he had two sons Antipater and Archelaus, and one daughter, called Olympias, who was married to Joseph, the king's kinsman Archelaus and Antipater were brought up at Rome, by a particular friend His sixth wife was Cleopatra, of Jerusalem by whom he had Herod and Philip who was also bred up at Rome The name of his seventh wife was Pallas, by whom he had Phasael His eighth was Phœdera The ninth was Elpis, by whom he had two daughters, Roxana and Salome As to his elder daughter by Mariamne, the mother of Alexander and Aristobulus, and whom Pheroras refused to marry, he gave the one to Antipater's sister's son, and the other to Phasael, the son of his brother This was the posterity of Herod

CHAP II

Zamaris, a Babylonian Jew, settles a colony in Syria It is invited by Herod to Batanea Herod protects theborders of the Jews Philip levies taxes Death of Zamaris and Jacimus, the latter of whom leaves his son Philip general of the army

HEROD, being now desirous of securing himself on the side of the Trachonites, resolved to build a spacious village in the middle of the country, and to put a strong garrison in it, to serve as a check upon the inroads from that quarter, and, upon occasion, to sally out upon the enemy While he was ruminating upon this project, he was given to understand that a certain Jew had come from Babylon with 500 horsemen, with bows and arrows, and near a fifth part of them his own relations, and that, with these troops, he had passed the Euphrates, and now sat down near Daphne, in Syria where Saturninus the governor, gave him a little called Valatha, not far from Antioch, for an habitation Herod, upon this intelligence sent an invitation to the Jew to come over to him with all his people, promising them lands, and other conveniences, in the territory of Batanea, upon the borders of Trachon, with privileges of exemption from all duties and tributes to the land as well as for the men, and a commission only to defend that quarter against the incursions of vagrant plunderers

The Babylonian, induced by these offers, came hither with his people, took possession of the land and built in it fortresses and a town, which he named Bathyra By these means he not only protected the inhabitants from the inroads of the Trachonites but secured the Jews also in their processions from Babylon to Jerusalem, according to the duty and practice of their profession From this consideration he was joined by vast numbers of such Jews as conscientiously adhered to the religion and laws of their forefathers, and the country was well peopled on account of their universal freedom from taxes This continued during the life of Herod but the person who succeeded him charged them with some small impositions, they were continued, however, for only a short time Agrippa the Great, and his son, of the same name imposed very heavy taxes upon them, as did the Romans after them, but never deprived them of personal liberty, as we shall take occasion to shew hereafter

At length Zamaris, the Babylonian, to whom Herod had given this country for a possession, departed this life, having maintained an upright character and left behind him children that inherited the virtues of their father, and amongst others Jacimus, a gallant commander, who had served the kings of Babylon in their guard This Jacimus died in an advanced age, and left behind him a son, called Philip, who, for his exemplary probity and valour, was in such esteem with king Agrippa, that he made him general of his army

CHAP III

Antipater intrusted with the administration of public affairs A female combination Salome informs Herod of it They take part with the Pharisees, who refuse the oath of allegiance to Herod A penalty put upon them for their refusal is paid by the wife of Pheroras Bagoas, a number of the Pharisees put to death Pheroras refuses to divorce his wife He is banished Antipater and his uncle in communication with Pheroras

WHILE the affairs of Herod were in this confused state, he placed such confidence in the faith, zeal, and affection of his son Antipater, that he vested him with the entire administration of government, so that all public affairs absolutely depended on his will But he flagrantly abused the trust reposed in him, by gross gloss over falsehoods and injustice, with specious pretences of duty and loyalty to his father, so that, in effect, his authority was as dangerous as his power But none in appearance cultivated so strict a friendship with him as Pheroras, while Antipater at the same time encompassed him with a female clan, that watched his words and actions, for Pheroras was in absolute subjection to his wife and her mother, notwithstanding the hatred he bore them for the indignities they had offered his virgin daughters But these were matters too trivial to cause a breach between parties so necessary to each other in carrying on the main business, and who were all privy to so many important secrets, besides, Antipater was attached to them both on account of himself and his mother

Salome, the king's sister, frequently thwarted their intentions, and being particularly informed of the whole plan of this female combination, had determined to make discovery of it to Herod, so that the accomplices having their motions watched, and fearful of coming under the jealousy and displeasure of the king, contrived that their meetings in future should be more private than they had been, as the most effectual means of avoiding suspicion As time and opportunity served, they would take occasion to revile each other, especially in the presence of Herod, or any of his friends, who would report [illegible] to him, and the plot was carried under the guise [illegible]

But they could conceal from Salome neither the first continuance, or the means through which they had made [illegible] progress [illegible] She traced their projects step by step, and communicated every particular to her brother, and not without aggravation She represented to Herod, that "if "their private assemblies, and clandestine counsels, were "not founded upon a design on his life, they might as well "be open and public, that their affectation of variance and "feuds, when in public, while they preserved an intimacy in "private, were evident tokens of fraud and collusion, and "that, in fact, they acted in perfect concert to accomplish "one common purpose and design"

Thus did Salome state the matter to Herod, who, though he had [illegible] previous hints of it, to which he gave credit, did not [illegible] depend on his sister's veracity, conscious that calumny was one of her darling vices

This female clan were much attached to a certain sect amongst the Jews, who valued themselves highly upon the [illegible] they had in the [illegible] of their fathers, and would impose upon [illegible] a belief that they were the peculiar favourites [illegible] These were the Pharisees, a sect [illegible] and crafty, who, through [illegible] pride and [illegible] made no conscience of insulting majesty, and [illegible] authority [illegible] when the whole [illegible] of the Jews were called upon to swear allegiance to [illegible] Cæsar, there refused of this sect [illegible] Being condemned by the king [illegible] a fine for this refusal, the wife of Pheroras deposited it for them In order to requite this kindness, as they pretended to a fore-knowledge of events from Divine inspiration, [illegible] foretold that it was the Divine decree, that the kingdom [illegible] transferred from Herod and his sons, to the [illegible], Pheroras, and their issue

Salome gave the king notice of this, and of the bribery and corruption that had been practised at court in favour of [illegible] Upon strict search and inquiry, several Pharisees were apprehended and put to death, as the authors of this [illegible] Amongst those who suffered upon this occasion was Bagoas, and Herod's minion Carus, besides [illegible] of his family, that were convicted of the conspiracy upon the testimony of the Pharisees themselves Bagoas was persuaded to maintain the notion, that he was to be celebrated as the benefactor of the prince that was [illegible] the throne, and every thing was to succeed with the new king, and the government to be established in his family

When Herod had punished the criminal Pharisees, he called a council of his friends, and exhibited an accusation [illegible] the wife of Pheroras, alledging, "that it was "through her counsel and advice, that his brother so contemptuously rejected the tender of the royal virgins to "him in marriage, and that she had most unnaturally, and "[illegible] all [illegible] fomented feuds between brethren, both "by deeds and words, that she had abetted the sedition "[illegible] Pharisees in easing them of the fine, which he himself "had imposed, and, in short, that she was the principal "agent in the conspiracy" From these premises he took occasion to recommend to Pheroras the propriety of putting away a woman of so infamous a character, without any [illegible] him, especially as matters were come to such a pass, that he must either disown her as a wife, or never expect to be owned by the king as a brother

Pheroras was much affected by this passionate declaration of Herod, and peremptorily declared, that no consideration should move him to renounce his wife, since he would rather die than live without her company Herod then moderated his anger, only forbidding Antipater and his mother any communication with Pheroras, and the female clan their usual [illegible] He promised obedience to the king's orders, but kept up their former intercourse, and especially that between Antipater and Pheroras

CHAP IV

The jealousy of Herod [illegible] Antipater, who [illegible] to Rome with [illegible] and Herod's last will and [illegible] Syllæus [illegible] with the [illegible], and [illegible] Rome

ANTIPATER having now strong suspicion of his father's jealousy and displeasure, and being apprehensive of experiencing their effects, wrote to his friends at Rome, to have him sent for with all expedition to wait upon Augustus His request being immediately complied with, Herod dispatched him with rich presents, and his last will and testament, wherein he declared Antipater his successor, or in case of his decease, his son Herod, whom he had by the daughter of the high-priest

At the same time Syllæus, the Arabian, went to Rome, though he had neglected to obey the injunctions of Cæsar Antipater there accused him of the same crimes of which he had formerly been accused by Nicolaus of Damascus, as advocate for Herod Syllæus was also accused by Aretas, of having put to death, at Petra, several men of rank and character, without his knowledge or consent, and amongst others, Soheimus, a person worthy of universal esteem, and likewise Fabatus, one of the emperor's servants The circumstance relative to Fabatus was this

There was one Corinthus in Herod's guards, a man in whom he particularly confided Syllæus tampered with this man for a considerable sum of money, to take off the king, and the offer had such an effect, that he had promised to execute his proposal Fabatus, having been made acquainted with this circumstance, immediately related it to the king Corinthus, being put to the torture, confessed the whole plot He also caused to be apprehended two Arabians, the one the head of a tribe, and the other a friend of Syllæus, who being both put to the torture, confessed that they came thither to press Corinthus to the execution of what he had undertaken, and to assist him in it, if there should be occasion The information was sent by Herod to Saturninus, and by him to Rome, where the cause was to be heard and decided

CHAP V

Pheroras, at Herod's command, retires to his government, and swears not to return during the king's life Herod falls sick, and sends for Pheroras, who excuses himself upon the plea of his oath Death of Pheroras

WHEN Herod found Pheroras inflexibly attached to his wife, he commanded him to retire to his government, and he most willingly obeyed, taking a solemn oath not to return during the life of Herod Nor did he swerve from his vow, for the king soon after falling sick, he was requested to pay him a visit, and receive some secret orders from him before he died Pheroras pleaded in excuse, that he was under oath, and durst not break it Herod, however, so far relaxed in his hatred to his brother, that when Pheroras himself fell sick soon after, without following his example, he of his own accord, paid him a visit The distemper carried him off, and the king gave orders for the conveyance of his body to Jerusalem, where it was honourably interred The death of Pheroras became the origin of Antipater's misfortunes, though he was now at Rome for justice at length arrested and brought him to an account for the blood of his brothers I shall give a minute detail of this circumstance, that it may be a warning to mankind to conduct their lives by the rules of virtue [illegible] of [illegible], who [illegible] [illegible] [illegible] the [illegible] was carried [illegible] [illegible] [illegible].

[illegible] Salome [illegible] the first con- [illegible] [illegible] [illegible] she [illegible] [illegible] [illegible] [illegible] to her brother, and [illegible] [illegible] She represented to Herod, that "[illegible] "[illegible] private [illegible], and [illegible] [illegible], were "[illegible] [illegible], they [illegible] "be open and public, [illegible] affectation of variance and "[illegible] with the [illegible] [illegible] in "[illegible] [illegible] and collusion, [illegible] "[illegible], they acted in perfect concert to accomplish "[illegible] [illegible]."

[illegible] Herod was [illegible] [illegible] [illegible] he gave credit, [illegible] depend on [illegible], con- [illegible] of her daring [illegible].

[illegible] much [illegible] a certain sect [illegible] the Jews, [illegible] valued themselves highly upon the [illegible] of their fathers, and would [illegible] [illegible] [illegible] These were the Pharisees, a sect [illegible] who, though [illegible] [illegible] and [illegible] [illegible] [illegible] [illegible] when the [illegible] of the [illegible] [illegible] a [illegible] [illegible] [illegible] and to [illegible], there [illegible] [illegible] [illegible] [illegible] [illegible] [illegible] [illegible] [illegible] [illegible] [illegible], that the [illegible] [illegible] transferred [illegible] and his sons, to [illegible] [illegible] Pheroras, and their [illegible].

[illegible] the king [illegible] of this, and of the [illegible] [illegible] had been [illegible] [illegible] [illegible] [illegible] [illegible] [illegible] and put to death, as the authors of [illegible] [illegible] [illegible] [illegible] Herod's minion Carus, be- [illegible] [illegible] of his family, that were convicted of the [illegible] [illegible] the testimony of the Pharisees themselves [illegible] [illegible] [illegible] [illegible] [illegible] [illegible] [illegible] [illegible] to succeed him in [illegible] king, and the government to be established in his [illegible].

When Herod had punished the criminal Pharisees, he [illegible] a council of his friends, and exhibited [illegible] [illegible] [illegible] [illegible] alledging, "that it was [illegible] [illegible], that his brother so con- "[illegible] [illegible] [illegible] [illegible] royal [illegible] to "[illegible], and that she had most unnaturally, and "[illegible] [illegible] between brethren, both "[illegible] [illegible] [illegible] the seditious "Pharisees [illegible] the [illegible] of the fine, which he himself "had [illegible], and, in [illegible], that she was the principal "[illegible] the conspiracy." From these premises he took occasion to recommend to Pheroras the propriety of putting [illegible] [illegible] [illegible] character, without any [illegible] [illegible] [illegible] were come to [illegible] [illegible], that he [illegible] [illegible] a wife, or never [illegible] by the king [illegible] brother.

[illegible] so much affected by this passionate declaration of Herod, [illegible] declared, that no consideration should move him to [illegible] his wife, since he would [illegible] than live without her company. Herod then [illegible] [illegible] Antipater and his mo- ther [illegible] [illegible] [illegible] [illegible] [illegible] [illegible] [illegible] obedience to the king's orders, but kept up their former intercourse, and especially that between Antipater and Pheroras.

CHAP. IV.

[illegible] of Herod [illegible] Antipater [illegible] [illegible] Rome [illegible] Herod's last [illegible] [illegible] Syllaeus [illegible] [illegible] [illegible] Rome.

ANTIPATER having now strong suspicion [illegible] [illegible] the [illegible] displeasure, and being [illegible] [illegible] five of experiencing, the [illegible] wrote to his friends at Rome, to have him sent for with all expedition to [illegible] upon Augustus. His request being immediately complied with, Herod dispatched him with rich presents, and his last will and testament, wherein he declared Antipater his successor, or in case of his decease, his son Herod, whom he had by the daughter of the high priest.

At the same time Syllaeus, the Arabian, went to Rome, though he had neglected to obey the injunctions of [illegible]. Antipater then accused him of the same crimes of which he had [illegible] been accused [illegible] Nicolaus of Damascus, advocate for Herod. Syllaeus was also accused by Aretas, for having put to death, at Petra, several men of rank and character, without his knowledge or consent, and amongst others, Schemus, a person worthy of universal esteem, and likewise [illegible], one of the emperor's servants. The circumstances relative to [illegible] was this.

There was one Corinthus in Herod's guard, a man in whom he particularly confided. Syllaeus [illegible] with [illegible] a considerable sum of money, to [illegible] of the king, and the offer had such an effect, that he had [illegible] to execute the proposal. [illegible], having been [illegible] [illegible] with this circumstance, immediately revealed it to the king. Corinthus being put to the torture, confessed [illegible]. He also caused to be apprehended two Arabians, the one the head of a tribe, and the other a friend of Syllaeus, who, being both put to the torture, confessed that they came thither to press Corinthus to the execution of what he had undertaken, and to assist him in it, if there should be occasion. This information was sent by Herod to Saturninus, and by him to Rome, where the crime was to be heard and decided.

CHAP. V.

Pheroras, at Herod's command, retires to his government, and swears not to return during the king's life. Herod falls sick, and sends for Pheroras, who [illegible] himself upon the plea of his oath. Death of Pheroras.

WHEN Herod found Pheroras inflexibly attached to his wife, he commanded him to retire to his government, and he most willingly obeyed, taking a solemn oath not to return during the life of Herod. Nor did he swerve from his vow, for the king soon after falling sick, he was requested to pay him a visit, and receive some secret orders from him before he died. Pheroras pleaded in excuse, that he was under oath, and durst not break it. Herod, however, so far relaxed in his hatred to his brother, that, when Pheroras himself fell sick soon after, without following his example, he, of his own accord, paid him a visit. The distemper carried him off, and the king gave orders for the conveyance of his body to Jerusalem, where it was honourably interred. The death of Pheroras became the origin of Antipater's misfortunes, though he was now at Rome; for justice at length arrested and brought him to an account for the blood of his brothers. I shall give a minute detail of this circumstance, that it may be a warning to mankind to conduct their lives by the rules of virtue.

CHAP. VI.

Enquiry into the death of Pheroras. Poison is administered to ... of Sylleus. Several women put to the ... exhibited and proved against the mother of Antipater. Doris stripped of her jewels and banished. Antipater joins in a plot to poison the king. The ... of Pheroras makes discovery of the plot. Last words of Pheroras ... discharge of his conscience. More witnesses examined. Herod puts away his wives. Bathyllus brings poison from Rome for Antipater's mother and Pheroras.

AFTER the performance of the funeral obsequies, two of Pheroras's freed-men, who had been much esteemed by him, applied to Herod, and intreated him not to suffer the murder of his brother to pass unrevenged, but to make the minutest search in order to bring the perpetrator of it to condign punishment. They informed the king, who gave credit to their words, that their master supped with his wife the night he was taken ill, and that a certain potion was brought him with a sort of food that he had not been accustomed to eat; that when he had eaten, he died of it; that this was brought out of Arabia under pretence of its being a love potion, ... to take him off, as the Arabian women are skilled in compounding such poisons. The woman, against whom they alledged this charge, was confessedly an intimate friend of one of Sylleus's mistresses. It was also deposed, that both the mother and sister of Pheroras's wife had been at her place of abode, persuaded her to sell this potion, and brought it with them the day before it was administered to him at supper.

The king was so enraged at hearing the story, that he ordered several of the women to be put to the torture, free as well as slaves. They continued some time without confessing, till at length, one of them in the agony of torment exclaimed, "Would to heaven the mother of "Antipater were now under the same anguish, for that "... woman has been the cause of all our miseries." This discovery put Herod upon a resolution to extort from them every particular of the plot, and to run through the whole process from circumstance to circumstance; as, at their private meetings and consultations, the occasional discourses that passed betwixt Herod and Antipater had been minutely divulged, as well as the means that were to be used to keep matters from the knowledge of Pheroras.

The female witnesses further enlarged upon the hatred Antipater bore his father, and that he had complained to his mother how very long he lived, insomuch, that, as he was himself advanced in years, if the kingdom should devolve to him it would not afford him any great pleasure; that as there were many brothers, who had children bringing up, his hopes were but uncertain; that, in case of his death, Herod had ordained that the kingdom should be conferred not on his son, but rather on a brother. It was added, that he had accused the king of great barbarity, and of the slaughter of his sons; and that it was from the fear he was under, lest he should do the like to him, that he contrived his journey to Rome, as well as sent Pheroras back to his government.

These particulars were consonant with what his sister had told him, and therefore tended to corroborate her testimony, and free her from the suspicion of unfaithfulness. Being perfectly satisfied of the treasonable designs of Doris, the mother of Antipater, Herod immediately stripped her of all her jewels to the value of many talents, and expelled her the palace, while he treated the women of Pheroras's family with more lenity on account of their information.

There was abundant proof against Antipater, but the most unpardonable article of his accusation was drawn from the confession of one Antipater, a Samaritan, an officer of great trust under Antipater, the son of Herod. This man, among other things, averred, that his master had put a mortal poison into the hands of Pheroras, for the king to take in his absence, as the work might then be effected with less suspicion. The poison (he said) was brought out of Egypt, by Antiphilus, a friend of Antipater, and sent to Pheroras by Theudion, the brother of the mother of Antipater, and by that means came to the wife of Pheroras, her husband having given it to her to keep. When the king interrogated her concerning it, she confessed; and, as she was running to fetch it, she cast herself down from one of the palace galleries into the court, but the bruise she received was not mortal. As soon as she came to herself, the king promised her and her domestics pardon, upon condition of their declaring the whole truth; but threatened them with the severest torments, if they concealed any part of the design.

Upon this Pheroras's widow bound herself, by a solemn oath, to lay open the whole matter, without the least reserve, and declared what was generally supposed to be true; that "the potion was brought out of Egypt "by Antiphilus, and that his brother, who was a phy"sician had procured it; that when Theudion brought "it, she kept it, upon Pheroras's committing it to her, "being prepared, at the instance of Antipater, for the "king; that, when Pheroras fell sick, and the king "treated him with such brotherly kindness, he was great"ly affected thereby, and calling to her, after his depar"ture, exclaimed, that Antipater had inveigled him into "a most unnatural plot for poisoning his brother, and "the traitor's father; that Pheroras recoiling at so horrid "an act, had determined not to incur such heinous guilt "in leaving this mortal life, requested her immediately "to bring the poison, and throw it into the fire before "his face; that, upon these words, she fetched it, and "threw the greater part into the fire, reserving a small "remainder for herself, in case it should be her lot, "after the decease of her husband, to be put to ex"tremities."

With these words she produced the box containing the poison before them all; when the mother of Antiphilus and another brother of his, being both put to the question, they confirmed the matter, by giving evidence as to the identity of the box itself.

There was an accusation exhibited also against one of the king's wives, the daughter of the high-priest; and as they could not bring her to confession, Herod cast her off, and struck her son, of his own name, out of his will, though he had appointed him his successor, if Antipater had died before him. He deposed Simon, his father-in-law, from the pontificate, and raised Matthias, of Jerusalem, the son of Theophilus, to that dignity.

In the mean time Bathyllus, one of Antipater's freedmen, came from Rome, and being put to the torture, confessed that he had brought poison for Antipater's mother, and for Pheroras; that if the former potion did not operate, they might try the other. There came also, at the same time, letters from Herod's friends at Rome, by the approbation, and at the suggestion of Antipater, to accuse Archelaus and Philip, as if they calumniated their father on account of the murder of Alexander and Aristobulus, and they commiserated their unhappy fate, suggesting also, that they were recalled to be treated in the same manner with those that went before them. These letters had been procured for great rewards, by Antipater's friends, while he himself wrote to Herod in his usual prevaricating manner, both accusing and excusing the brothers, to gloss over the matter, by means of specious pretence, and ambiguous hints. The controversy was still maintained between Sylleus and Antipater, the latter of whom had procured a number of friends and advocates, by means of presents, amounting to an expence of two hundred talents. It seems a matter of wonder, that there should be so many accusations exhibited against him in Judæa, during the space of seven months, without his having knowledge of them; though this may be reconciled to probability, when it is observed, that the roads were strictly guarded, and that Antipater was generally detested, so that none would risque the hazard of information.

CHAP. VII.

Artful correspondence between Antipater and Herod. News of the death of Pheroras. Antipater goes to Sebaste, where he is universally execrated. Quintilius Varus, governor of Syria, holds council with Herod at Rome. Antipater comes in state to the palace. Is admitted, but his train excluded. A charge of treason and fratricide exhibited against him. Trial appointed for the next day. Quintilius Varus to preside on the bench. Salome and all the evidences produced. Herod prefers his accusation. Antipater makes his own defence. Nicolaus of Damascus, counsel for Herod, urges the prosecution, and applies to Varus for justice. Divers charges alledged to Antipater. His character painted in the most odious colours. He is committed to prison. Letters intercepted, [illegible] made. Herod sends a state of the whole case to Rome.

ANTIPATER, having written to the king, that he was settling his affairs at Rome, and preparing for his return, Herod concealed his resentment, and wrote back to him, desiring him not to defer his journey, lest any misadventure should befal him in his absence. The king avoided any hints of displeasure in his letter, except some trifling complaints against his mother, which, on his return, he declared should subside. Indeed, he made professions of confidence and friendship, fearing that, through suspicion, he might defer his journey, and that, during his continuance at Rome, he might concert plans for supplanting him in the government.

This letter came to Antipater's hands as he was upon the way in Cilicia: but he had received the news of the death of Pheroras before, at Tarentum, and with much concern, not from any affection to Pheroras, but from disappointment in his not taking the life of his father, according to promise. Upon his arrival at Celenderis, a city of Cilicia, he deliberated with himself, whether he should proceed or return, being much chagrined at the disgrace his mother had sustained in her ejection. Some of his friends advised him to wait, the necessity of farther intelligence, others to hasten home without delay, not doubting but, upon his arrival, he would invalidate all charges brought against him, as his accusers derived all their weight and importance from his absence, he being thereby prevented from refuting their tales and calumnies.

These arguments prevailed with him to proceed so that he continued his course, and soon landed at Sebaste, a port erected by Herod, at an incredible expence, in honour of Augustus Cæsar, and called after his name Cæsarea. Here he found himself in a most mortifying situation, as now, on his return, he received not one token of respect: nay, on the contrary, was insulted with execrations, whereas before, at his departure, he was followed with warm benedictions, and joyful acclamations. Nor could the people out [illegible] an aversion for him, while they supposed he was going to receive punishment, for the horrid crime of fratricide.

Quintilius Varus, successor of Saturninus in the government of Syria, was at this time at Jerusalem, coming thither at the request of Herod, to assist him with his advice in the present state of affairs. As they were sitting together in council, Antipater came into the palace, arrayed in his robes of state, the gates having been set open to him, though his train were excluded. This circumstance threw him into some agitation of mind, which was greatly increased, upon his presenting himself to his father's embrace, when he was spurned from him with reproaches of fratricide and treason, and given to understand, that he would be publicly in court charged with those crimes the following day, and that Varus would preside as judge upon his trial. Receiving with the utmost consternation, he was met by his mother and wife, the daughter of Antigonus, Herod's predecessor, from whom having learned all circumstances concerning him, he then prepared himself for defence upon his trial.

On the day following the court assembled, Varus and the king sitting in judgment, with their friends about them. Salome, the king's sister, was cited thither also, with others of their relations. There were brought thither likewise all those who had made any voluntary discoveries, or on confession upon torture, and besides, some of the domestics of Antipater's mother, who had been taken up a little before his return, and brought with them letters, importing, by way of caution, "that he should by no means come back, "since the whole matter was come to his father's knowledge, and Cæsar was the only refuge he had left." Antipater then threw himself at the king's feet, requesting only to be admitted to his defence, and not condemned unheard. Herod ordered him to rise and stand forth to take his trial. The king then addressed himself to the court, in words to the following purport:

"I confess myself an unfortunate man, to have been the "father of such children, and to fall at length, in my advanced age, into the hands of such a wretch as Antipater. "I have been assiduously attentive to his education, nor "have I denied him any request he ever made. And what "is my return? A conspiracy against my life, and an attempt to seize on the crown by impious violence, which "by the double right of title and free gift must devolve "upon him. What advantage could he propose to himself, "the [illegible] of so extravagant an ambition, after I had made "him my successor by will, and effectually a partner with me, "in dignity, glory, and power, even during my own life, "settled on him an annual income of fifty talents, and "made him an allowance of three hundred more for the expence of his journey to Rome? With respect to the "charge brought by him against his brothers, if they were "guilty, he has imitated their example; if not, he has "alledged groundless charges against his near relations, and by "that means abused them, and incurred himself the guilt "of parricide."

The king could not proceed through an involuntary effusion of tears, and therefore desired Nicolaus of Damascus, his old and particular friend, who was thoroughly instructed in every circumstance relative to the case, to proceed to the examination of the witnesses, and an explanation of their respective evidences. Antipater, by way of prevention, applied himself to his defence, and turning to his father, thus spoke:

"Can there be a probability (said he) that, after having "rescued my father from the treacherous designs of so many "others, I should at length turn traitor to him myself, or "sully the reputation of a tried allegiance with so foul a "blot? Could I do it to be greater or more happy than I "was? Or could I be actuated to such egregious folly, "under the most splendid circumstances, to expose myself "to infamy and misery? The succession was settled upon "me according to every form of law, and I was so far admitted by the king's bounty into a share with him in the "exercise of his royal power, that I was in the possession of "the government, in effect indeed the respectable title, "without any one to controul me, or envy my claim. Why "should I risk that with danger, for which I required the "quiet enjoyment by the rectitude of my conduct; or expose myself to certain infamy, for the vain flattery of an "uncertain hope? especially considering the consequences of "this ambition, with respect to my brothers, whom I myself "[illegible], convicted, and punished. This I did, and of this "I shall never repent, but, on the contrary, value myself on

HEROD rejecting the treacherous Emb[illegible] ANTIPATER
[illegible] Conspiring against his Life [illegible]

"the merit of that fervice, as the higheſt inſtance I could "give my honoured father of filial duty, and inviolable alle-"giance. With respect to my general conduct in the city "of Rome, I dare appeal to Cæſar himſelf, who can no "more be impoſed upon than an oracle, and could produce "ſeveral letters, under his own hand, in my favour. Would "it not be unjuſt, would it not be impious, to oppoſe the "calumnies of abandoned men to the authority of ſuch un-"queſtionable evidence? or a ſet of miſcreants, whoſe chief "[illegible] is to [illegible] the royal family, and who have "taken the advantage, in my abſence, of poſſeſſing the "people with defamatory rumours againſt me, which they "would never con[illegible] ſo long as I was within diſtance of "[illegible]king for myſelf. With reſpect to the evidence ex-"torted by the rack, it is commonly falſe, becauſe the an-"guiſh of [illegible] pain naturally impels the ſufferer to ma-"ny things to gratify thoſe at whoſe inſtance they are put "to the queſtion." This ſaid, he offered himſelf to be put to the queſtion, and abide the iſſue of it.

Antipater delivered his defence with ſuch energy as to excite the compaſſion of the whole court, and draw tears even from his enemies; nay, Herod himſelf was diſpoſed to relent, although he did his utmoſt to conceal it.

When Antipater had gone thus far, Nicolaus took up the cauſe where the king left it, ſummed every article, cited and ſummed up the proofs, the names of the witneſſes, and the particular [illegible] of thoſe that had been put to the queſtion. He [illegible] then to the ſubject of the king's boun-ty, care, and tenderneſs, in the education of his children, and how ill it was requited. "As for Alexander and Ari-"ſtobulus, while they were under the dominion of ambi-"tion, rather than avarice, and hurried on by the intem-"perate notions of youth and blood, it was not ſo much "a wonder to them (ſaid he) to be deprived [illegible] "[illegible], [illegible] negligence or contempt of their [illegible], but as to "the caſe of Antipater, it was worſe than brutal; for "in the very [illegible] beaſts there is a kind of natural "gratitude for their keepers, whereas this man was ſo "far from being [illegible] by the goodneſs and boun-"ty of an indulgent father, that [illegible] he was not to be de-"terred by the calamitous example of his brothers, ſo, "on the contrary, he valued [illegible] upon an imitation "of their wickedneſs and cruelty. Was it not you your-"ſelf, Antipater, (ſays he) that firſt diſcovered their "deſign? Were not you then the proſecutor? and [illegible] "you ſelf again, the director of the [illegible], and con-"ſequently of the puniſhment. This is not to reflect up-"on your zeal and indignation in ſo juſt a cauſe; but it "[illegible] me to find you ſo bitter againſt your brothers "for the very ſame thing that you do yourſelf, which "manifeſtly ſhews that your bitterneſs was not ſo much "the preſervation of the father, as the ruin of the chil-"dren, and under a colour of a ſevere brother to get the "reputation of a tender and dutiful ſon, and ſo with the "more ſecurity to make [illegible], to the king himſelf. This "was the expedient you went about. How came it to paſs "elſe, that the brothers were put to death, and not their "accomplices? What could be the meaning, or the end "of this, but firſt, that you and they were agreed upon "the matter, and ſecondly, that, as ſoon as the firſt "[illegible] ſhould be over, they might be at hand to help "you out with the next? So that you had a double ſatiſ-"faction in the contemplation of your wickedneſs: the "one was by impoſing publicly upon the world a moſt "[illegible] impiety for meritorious virtue, the other was "in carrying on, and the hopes of executing that horrid "barbarity yourſelf, which you took upon you to revenge "in others. If you had really deteſted that malice, "you would as well have abhorred the imitation of it. "But you have had the precaution, however, to take the "beſt [illegible] [illegible] to ſet yourſelf clear of "[illegible] [illegible] [illegible] "witneſſes, [illegible] [illegible], to crown [illegible] "of the brothers with that of the father; and by ſo do-"ing, not only to eſcape the puniſhment you have de-"ſerved, but to bring your parent to bear the burden of "your crimes, in ſuch a parricide as was never heard of "before; for the treaſon was not formed againſt a perſon of "the common rate of fathers, but againſt a parent ten-"der and indulgent to the higheſt degree, the conſpira-"tor marked out for the ſucceſſion already, a half-ſhare "in the crown by advance ſettled before, and in the pre-"ſent enjoyment of his greatneſs, and ſecure in the re-"verſion of it by his father's will. But your inſatiable "deſires were not to be bounded by his goodneſs, but "by ſuch meaſures only as your own [illegible] per-"verſeneſs ſhould preſcribe. Your own [illegible] of his right "would not ſerve your end, unleſs you [illegible] have him "[illegible] too. Your pretence was the ſaving of him, when, "at the ſame time, the plot was to deſtroy him; and the "crime was not all your own, but your [illegible] was made "a party in it, and the whole family was by it embroil-"ed. After all this, what can you think of the [illegible] "of calling your father beaſt? But neither [illegible] "of your benefactors [illegible] [illegible] [illegible] "[illegible] [illegible] as if the venom of your own heart had "not been ſufficient to [illegible] and [illegible] revenge, you "have called to your help your guards, counſellors, and "ſuborners of both ſexes in a confederacy [illegible] "[illegible]; and now, after the torturing of [illegible] "men and women, free and ſlaves, one [illegible] "upon your account [illegible] "evidences you have, of the con[illegible] "truth [illegible] to [illegible] enterprize upon [illegible] "[illegible] [illegible] "[illegible] ſuch [illegible] and [illegible] "in contradiction to the quality of [illegible] and to the [illegible]-"[illegible] meaſures of [illegible] juſtice. [illegible] "think [illegible] extorted teſtimonies, but [illegible] "you would [illegible] from the circuit of theſe [illegible] "[illegible] open to your wickedneſs, and conducive to the [illegible]-"ſervation of your father."

"Sir, (ſays Nicolaus to Varus) by the majeſty of the "Roman empire, and by your own honour, I [illegible] "that you vindicate the king from the indignities of his "own family, and deliver up this monſter of hypocriſy "to death, [illegible] reverence to his father, "hunted after the blood of his brothers, and [illegible] "not been [illegible] detected, his father's turn would "have been next, to make his own way to the crown. "You know well that parricide is no private crime, but "a public affront to the laws of ſociety, and of reaſona-"ble beings, and ſo abominable a [illegible] in the very "thought as well as in the act, that whoever ſuffers it "to paſs unpuniſhed, offers an indignity to [illegible] na-"ture itſelf."

Nicolaus adverted farther to ſome [illegible] expreſſions which fell from the mother of Antipater concerning predictions, [illegible] relating to the king and the ſucceſſion of the crown (ſtories Antipater had related in an hour of [illegible] with Pheroras' family) examinations upon other [illegible] matters which concerned the teſtimony of witneſſes, [illegible] time, every thing was advanced by this able advocate for Herod that could tend to criminate Antipater. To add to his mortification and perplexity, thoſe men who were acquainted with his practices, but had concealed them through fear, when they ſaw he had been expoſed to the accuſations of former witneſſes, and that his extraordinary fortune, which had ſupported him hitherto, [illegible] evidently betrayed him into the hands of his enemies, who were inſatiable in their revenge, diſcovered whatever they knew.

His ruin was, indeed, effected; but not by the enmity of thoſe who were his accuſers ſo much as by his own abominable devices againſt his father and [illegible] the [illegible] diſorders in the family, [illegible] [illegible] the blood of each other, and expressing his detestation and regard, not from principle, but merely to subserve his present purpose

The evidence in proof of what had been alledged against him could not be set aside, because the witnesses neither spoke out of favour to Herod, nor were they obliged to conceal what they knew by any apprehension of danger, so that they frankly inveighed against his enormous crimes, which they declared deserving of the highest punishment, not so much for the king's safety, as to deter mankind from following so infamous an example So many accusations were voluntarily exhibited against him, that Antipater, notwithstanding his shrewdness and effrontery, had nothing to advance by way of refutation

When Nicolaus, and the rest of the accusers, had left off speaking, Varus, addressed himself to Antipater, telling him if he had any thing to offer in his own defence, the court was ready to hear him, as his father and himself were equally desirous of finding him entirely innocent Antipater then cast himself upon the ground, and appealed to the Great Searcher of Hearts, beseeching him to vindicate his innocence, as to any injurious design upon his father, by some evident token from heaven, that would convince the world of his integrity This is the usual method with men destitute of virtue, when they undertake actions, it is in conformity to their own inclinations, as if they believed the Supreme Being had no concern with human affairs but when once they are found out, and are in danger of undergoing the punishment due to their crimes they endeavour to overthrow all the evidence against them by an hypocritical appeal to the great fountain of truth and justice This was the very case of Antipater who, when he acted, in every instance, as if there had been no Supreme and Super-intending Being, and was in consequence arrested by justice, but had nothing to invalidate the evidence adduced against him, presumptuously insulted the Majesty of Heaven, ascribed it to his power that he had been preserved hitherto, and produced to all who were present the difficulties he had undergone in exerting himself for the preservation of his father.

Varus finding he could give no direct answer to any of the questions, except appeals to heaven, ordered the potion to be brought before the court in order to make trial of the force of it It was accordingly brought and being administered to a criminal under sentence of condemnation, he immediately expired Upon this experiment the court rose, and Varus went away the next day, to Antioch, the place of his usual abode, as the kings of Syria commonly make that the place of their general residence

The particulars that passed between Varus and Herod were not known to the generality of the people, though it was supposed upon the whole, that his proceedings towards his son were according to his entire approbation When Herod had committed him to prison, he sent letters to Cæsar at Rome by messengers, who were directed to inform him of the heinous crime of which Antipater had been found guilty At this very time a letter was found written to Antipater, by Antiphilus, out of Egypt which, when opened, appeared to contain the following contents "I have sent you Acme's letter at the hazard "of my life You well know I am in danger from two "families, if I am discovered I wish you success in "your present undertaking"

The king made a strict enquiry for the other letter of Antiphilus's servant, who brought that which had been read; but he denied having received it, till at length it was discovered enclosed within a seam of his upper garment the contents were these "I have written to "your father according to the purport of your desire "I have taken a copy, and sent it as if it came from Sa- "lome to my mistress (Julia) You will find, when "you read it, that Herod will punish Salome as plotting "against him" This pretended letter of Salome to Julia was composed by Antipater, as to its real meaning, but in the words of Acme it ran thus "I have done my "endeavour that nothing which passes should be conceal- "ed from you therefore, upon finding a letter written "from Salome to my mistress against you, I have taken a "copy and sent it you, at the hazard of my life but for "your advantage The reason she wrote it was her great "desire of being married to Syllæus Do you therefore "destroy this letter, that I may not come into danger of "my life" Acme had written to Antipater himself, and informed him that, in obedience to his command, she had herself written to Herod, as if Salome had laid a plot against him, and had also sent a copy of a letter, as coming from Salome to her mistress This Acme was a Jewess, and servant to Julia, Cæsar's wife She carried on this device from an attachment to Antipater, by whom she had been bribed with large presents to assist him in his infamous practices against his father and his aunt

Herod was so enraged at this late instance of the baseness of Antipater, that he was ready to order him to immediate execution, not only for having plotted against his life and his sister's, but even corrupted Cæsar's domestics Salome did all in her power to instigate him to it, calling upon him to slay her, if he could produce any credible testimony that she had acted in this manner Herod sent for his son, interrogated him on the matter and called upon him to offer what he could in his own vindication Being detected in his villainy, he stood mute, upon which Herod commanded him, without delay, to make discovery of his associates, in these abominable practices, when he laid the whole upon Antiphilus, mentioning none else Herod hereupon had resolved to send this miscreant to Cæsar to answer for his crimes, but fearing, lest, through the assistance of his friends there, he might escape condign punishment he kept him close prisoner, and sent ambassadors to Rome with a state of the case, instructions and copies of the letters given in evidence, and in particular, with an account of Acme's being concerned in the plot

CHAP VIII

Herod is seized with a distemper and makes his will An insurrection among the Jews abetted by two eminent men, Judas and Matthias Herod's life despaired of The golden eagle thrown down from the temple at the instance of Judas and Matthias They are taken into custody Justify the action Sent bound to Jericho Matthias is deposed from the priesthood, and Joazar advanced to that dignity The Insurgents are burnt alive Herod's distemper increases He sends for Salome and Alexas His fixed cruelty

WHILE Herod's ambassadors were making the best of their way with their letters and instructions for Rome, he fell into a distemper, made his will, and having conceived an unfavourable opinion of Archelaus and Philip, through the calumnies of Antipater, he declared Antipas, his youngest son his successor He bequeathed a thousand talents to Cæsar and to his wife Julia, his children, friends, and freedmen, five hundred talents The rest of his money, with his lands and revenues, he distributed amongst his children and grand children, and left his sister Salome a very considerable fortune, in acknowledgement of her unshaken fidelity Being now in the seventieth year of his age, and despairing of recovery, he became so petulent and choleric, as to be the plague and detestation of all around him and he seemed to have indulged this disposition and temper, through a prevailing conceit that he was fallen into contempt and odium with the people, who were therefore pleased with his misfortunes Indeed, he was confirmed in this opinion by a commotion that soon happened upon the following occasion

There were two men, Judas and Matthias, who had acquired [illegible] amongst the Jews, for their learning, eloquence, and skill in the laws, and were particularly beloved by the people, for the care they took in training the rising generation to the knowledge and practice of the duties of their profession. When these men, [illegible] to the religion and customs of their country, as [illegible] from their ancestors, found that his [illegible] [illegible] of the [illegible] part of the people to [illegible] the [illegible] which the king had erected, [illegible] the law of their fathers, giving them full assurance of [illegible] was due to their exertions in so noble a cause. They [illegible] that all the broils and [illegible] the king's family, and the miserable temper with [illegible] were judgments upon him for [illegible] amongst other instances of superstitious [illegible] mentioned the huge golden eagle or [illegible] weight [illegible] over the portal of the temple, observing, that as that was a direct violation of the [illegible] law, which positively forbids the use of images in [illegible], it would be a [illegible] action to pull down the [illegible].

To enforce [illegible], they laid before them, "that [illegible] be [illegible] of danger, a glorious [illegible] that a life of conformity to [illegible] the blood could not be [illegible] the [illegible] of the laws and [illegible] of [illegible] immortalize their names, when [illegible] that they should be [illegible] after this [illegible], to [illegible] all men, of [illegible] and [illegible], to [illegible] the decree of [illegible] of these most glorious occasions, [illegible] [illegible] they would [illegible] the [illegible]."

[illegible] was no sooner [illegible], than a rumour was [illegible] death, which encouraged the [illegible], [illegible] pulled down the portal [illegible] the temple, [illegible] to pieces with axes, [illegible] persons, who were in [illegible]. The [illegible] of the king's [illegible], [illegible] with a band of soldiers [illegible] hatchets, [illegible] [illegible] to the spot, [illegible] forty [illegible], [illegible] [illegible] the [illegible] charge, except [illegible] Judas and Matthias [illegible] upon [illegible] of [illegible].

[illegible] carried [illegible] to the king, who [illegible] of them, [illegible] they had been [illegible] [illegible] upon the sacred [illegible]? They replied, [illegible] the [illegible] a long time, and at length [illegible], they resolved [illegible] and courage, in putting it in execution, that what they [illegible] were, [illegible] the honour of the supreme [illegible] and the precepts of their great [illegible], whose disciples they [illegible] themselves to be [illegible] humbly [illegible] the king would not make it a [illegible] of [illegible] if they [illegible] the laws which they received from Moses, and, indeed, from their Creator, [illegible] whatever, that they did not [illegible] for [illegible], but for the [illegible] of conscience, and that they were ready to [illegible] their bodies in this cause, either [illegible] punishment or death." [illegible], from this [illegible] of their conduct, that their profession and [illegible] were, and that they were ready to suffer with the same [illegible] as they had acted with before.

The king ordered them to be sent in chains to Jericho, where he summoned a great council of the leading men [illegible] the Jews, and being [illegible], [illegible] was carried in a [illegible] to the assembly. He [illegible] before them, "that he had [illegible] and indefatigable [illegible] for the service of the [illegible] at an immense [illegible], a work that [illegible]. Asmonean race had not

"been able to compass [illegible] in [illegible] hundred and twenty-five "years, but he had not only rebuilt the temple, but [illegible] "[illegible], enlarged and enriched it with ornaments and pre-"sents [illegible] this magnificent undertaking." He concluded [illegible] "that [illegible] he [illegible] he had "[illegible] the [illegible] in the [illegible] he "had performed in his public character, he was treated with "ingratitude and indignity, and [illegible] the face of his peo-"ple, his gifts and oblations to [illegible] the very temple, and "an act of [illegible] from pious motives, construed into "sacrilege."

The leading men of the council, to prevent the dangerous consequences of that degree of rage to which Herod might probably be [illegible] on the occasion, exculpated themselves, [illegible] the innocence of the fact, [illegible] the [illegible] to be [illegible]. [illegible] Herod [illegible], [illegible]. As [illegible] of his [illegible] resentment, he deprived Matthias of the high priesthood, [illegible] better on the [illegible], and conferred the dignity on [illegible]. After Herod [illegible] Matthias [illegible] he gave orders for the burning of [illegible] Matthias, whom [illegible] the [illegible] of the sedition, and all his companions [illegible]. As it fell out, there was that night an eclipse of the moon.

Herod's distemper now greatly [illegible], [illegible] [illegible] [illegible] [illegible]. He laboured under a most malignant [illegible] [illegible] fistula, cramps, and [illegible] of the [illegible], together [illegible] other [illegible] symptoms. Notwithstanding his [illegible] deplorable [illegible], he [illegible] hope of recovery, [illegible] the [illegible] of his [illegible], [illegible] and passed over the river Jordan [illegible] the [illegible] Callirrhoe, that empty themselves into the lake Asphaltites, [illegible] virtues, [illegible] [illegible]. On coming to the place, the physicians ordered him to bathe in a vessel of oil, which had such effect upon him, that [illegible] the point of death [illegible], he survived [illegible] on [illegible]. [illegible] at length [illegible] of recovery [illegible] he [illegible] amongst the soldiers, [illegible] amongst his friends and officers, and to return to Jericho, where he became so choleric, that he formed [illegible] resolution, [illegible] the extreme.

He sent out [illegible] to all the principal men of the Jewish nation to [illegible] to him at Jericho, and not fail upon pain of death. Upon their appearance, according to the proclamation, he ordered them all to be shut up in the circus (a place for horse-races), one [illegible] [illegible], and [illegible] his sister, [illegible] and Alexas, he [illegible] them in words to the following effect: "The time of my departure approaches. I am "oppressed with pains, and death is the common lot of "mankind. I can [illegible] myself against the "thought of being deprived of those funeral honours "which are due to royalty. I [illegible] of the [illegible] "[illegible] the [illegible] of the Jews, that they [illegible] "[illegible] me when living, and will of course rejoice when "I am no more. [illegible] is in the power of [illegible] to "afford me some [illegible] of my grief [illegible], "and [illegible] more than [illegible]. Follow "my directions, and I [illegible] you promise [illegible] most "magnificent funeral solemnity that ever prince had [illegible] "my [illegible] restriction, and [illegible] [illegible] "or hypocritical affectation. The moment I expire, let "the circus be surrounded with soldiers, and the word of "command given to destroy every man within the enclo-"sure. [illegible] my death be kept a profound secret till the "work be accomplished. In the due execution of this, "you will lay a double obligation upon [illegible], in "the performance of my will, and [illegible] the ce-

"lebration of my death, with the honour of a public "mourning."

He accompanied these words with tears and sighs, adjuring his relations, by all that was sacred, and by every tie of consanguinity and friendship, to be punctual in the discharge of the trust reposed in them, which they accordingly promised to execute in the minutest particular.

From this circumstance it will be easy to form a judgment of the temper and disposition of this most execrable of mankind, who not only took a pleasure in exercising cruelties upon his nearest relations, from a principle of love for life, but, on his departure, left a commission, that, by its execution, should put the whole nation into mourning, as one of every family was to be slain, and this without any injury, provocation, or exception; whereas, amongst people who are not dead to the feelings of humanity, it is usual to bury all animosity in the grave of our departed fellow mortals.

CHAP. IX.

Acme put to death by order of Augustus Cæsar. Antipater left to Herod's discretion. Herod attempts to kill himself. Is prevented by his nephew Achiab. Antipater, upon a presumption of the death of the king, treats with the keeper of the prison about his escape. The keeper gives information to Herod, who orders him for immediate execution.

AS Herod was giving these commands to his relations, his ambassadors arrived from Rome, with an answer to the letter they were commissioned to deliver to Cæsar. The substance was briefly this: "That Augustus had caused Acme to be put to death for a correspondence with "Antipater, and had left Antipater himself to the king his "father, either to be put to death, or banished, according to his direction." It afforded Herod the greatest satisfaction to find himself both revenged on Acme, and at liberty to dispose of his son as he pleased. But though this information gave him some temporary relief, he soon relapsed into his former extremity of pain, and, in an outrageous fit, called for an apple and a knife, it being usual with him to pare his own apples. He was observed to look suspiciously about him, as if he had some intent of stabbing himself: but his nephew, Achiab, kept an eye upon him, and, at the very instant of the attempt, caught hold of his right hand, with an outcry, and prevented it.

The exclamation alarmed the court a second time, and it was generally supposed that the king was at that moment expiring. Antipater therefore taking it for granted, and making no doubt of the death of his father, entertained an assurance of procuring his liberty, and by that means of paving his way to the throne. In this confidence he treated with the keeper of the prison about his discharge, holding forth to him large offers and promises, both of present reward, and future preferment, when he should come to the crown. The keeper, so far from complying with his proposal, discovered the whole matter to the king, who detested him before, but, was so enraged by this representation, that, though in the very agonies of death, he commanded one of his guards to slay Antipater without further delay, and ordered his body to be interred, without any funeral honours, in the castle of Hyrcania.

CHAP. X.

Herod alters his will, and declares Archelaus his successor. Death of Herod is kept secret. The leading men are discharged the circus. The king's death published. Archelaus acknowledged as king. Pomp and order of Herod's funeral. Archelaus waits the ratification of Herod's will by Cæsar.

HEROD, upon changing his mind, changed his will also, and appointed Antipas (to whom, in his former testament, he had bequeathed the government) to be tetrarchy of Galilee and Peræa, but gave the crown to Archelaus. The provinces of Trachon and Gaulan, Batanæa and Paneas, he assigned to his son Philip, brother-in-law of Archelaus, under the title of a tetrarchy. Jamnia, Azotus, and Phasaelis, he gave to his sister Salome, with five hundred thousand drachmæ of coined silver. He also made provision for the rest of his kindred, by leaving them sums of money, and annual revenues to a very considerable amount. He bequeathed also to Cæsar, ten millions of drachmæ in ready coin; and to the empress Julia, five millions more, besides vessels of gold and silver, with sumptuous apparel.

Affairs being thus settled, Herod departed this life five days after he had caused Antipater to be slain, thirty-four years after the expulsion of Antigonus, and in the thirty-seventh year from his being declared king of the Jews by the Romans. He was a man inexorably cruel, a slave to his passions, whose will was his law; and yet upon the whole, he may be said to have been fortunate. He ascended the throne of Judæa from the condition of a private man, was involved in many difficulties, but surmounted them all, and lived, at last, to a great age. With respect to his domestic broils, however unfortunate he may have been in the opinion of others, he seems to have been very fortunate in his own, as he ever found himself able to overcome his enemies.

The death of Herod was kept a profound secret by Salome and Alexas, who immediately dismissed the leading men that were confined in the circus, telling them, in the king's name, they might repair to their respective estates, and attend to their own affairs, as there was no farther occasion for them. It being now deemed a proper time for publishing the king's death, Salome and Alexas gathered the soldiery together in the amphitheatre at Jericho, where Herod's letters to the army were read, containing gracious acknowledgments of their past faith and services, and desiring them to continue the same dutiful affection to his son Archelaus in future, whom he had declared his successor. Ptolemy, the keeper of the king's seal, read after this the testament itself, with this express clause in it, that the act itself was not to be deemed valid, without the consent of Cæsar. This was followed with acclamations, saluting Archelaus as king, and wishing him a happy reign, both from the officers and soldiers, with promises of the same loyal attachment to the new king, as they had shewn to his predecessor.

The next object of attention was, to prepare for the funeral solemnity; and it seemed to be the peculiar care of Archelaus, that nothing should be wanting to complete its pomp and splendour, resolving himself to bear a part in the ceremony. The body was carried upon a golden bier, adorned with precious stones, covered with purple, a diadem upon his head, and over that a golden crown, with a sceptre in his hand; his son and relations marching by the side. Next to these were the soldiers, in their proper distinctions and divisions. First the body guards, then the Thracians, after them the Germans, and next the Galatians, all of them armed, and arranged as for battle. Behind these marched the rest of the army, under their respective officers, with five hundred of the court attendants in the rear, bearing perfumes of different kinds. They proceeded in this order as far as Herodium, eight furlongs from Jericho, where the body was interred according to appointment; and this was the end of Herod.

When seven days had been spent in attending upon the funeral obsequies of the deceased king, according to the custom of the country, and the appointed time for mourning was at an end, Archelaus entertained the multitude, and afterwards went up to the temple, where he placed himself upon a golden throne to receive the congratulatory acclamations of the people, which were answered on his part, with every token of respect, intimating the sense he had of their kindness, after the hard usage they had met from his father assuring them that their good-will should never be forgotten. "He did not pretend (he said) as "yet to assume the name of king, having no right so to "do without the authority of Cæsar in the ratification of "his father's testament, for which cause he declined the "dignity offered him by the army at Jericho, but whenever he should be settled in the government, it should "be the constant object of his care to do all things for "the benefit and satisfaction of his people, to make his "reign much easier to them, than what they had found "during the reign of his father."

The people were charmed with the apparent candour and modesty of behaviour of their new prince, and depended, as is usual in such cases, upon the good faith of every particular for which he pledged himself. In order to put this complacency to the test, they preferred several petitions. Some importuned a desire to be eased of their taxes, others to have their friends released who had been imprisoned by Herod. Some exclaimed against duties and impositions that were laid upon provisions, and divers pleas were offered upon divers pretences. In fine, Archelaus found it was his interest to deny them no one favour they asked, esteeming the good-will of the people the most effectual means of securing to himself the continuance of the government.

CHAP. XI.

A plot to remove the government. Satisfaction demanded of Archelaus for Herod's misdemeanors. A dangerous tumult. A party of seditious Jews croud into the temple. Archelaus sends a party to controul them, and they are mostly destroyed. Archelaus going to Rome, and appoints Philip to the administration of affairs in his absence. Salome's perfidy to Archelaus. He meets Sabinus at Cæsarea in his way to Judæa. Varus stops his journey, being engaged in the same business. Archelaus goes to Rome, and Varus for Antioch. Sabinus goes to Jerusalem, and demands Herod's books and keys, but the officers keep them for Cæsar. Antipas goes to Rome, and sets up for himself with a strong party. Sabinus lodges an information against Archelaus. Cæsar calls a council, where Caius, the son of Agrippa, sits as president. Antipater against Archelaus. Antipater's speech, and Nicolaus manages the cause. Archelaus submits himself before Cæsar.

AT the commencement of the government of Archelaus, there arose a party of malecontent Jews, who seemed determined to bring about an innovation. The subject of their complaint was the case of Matthias and his associates, whom Herod had ordered to be put to death, for their assembling in a tumultuous manner, and pulling down the golden eagle which had been erected upon the top of the temple. During the life of the king, not one was to be found who durst make any attempt in vindication of these reformers; but, on his demise, a popular clamour was raised against him, and a great concourse assembled and demanded of Archelaus, justice upon the friends of Herod, who had advised the execution of those who so nobly asserted the cause of the religion of their country. They peremptorily insisted upon the removal of the high-priest whom Herod had promoted in lieu of Matthias, and the appointment of another more worthy of that sacred function. This was granted by Archelaus, though he was much offended at their importunity, having proposed himself to go to Rome, and submit the case to the determination of Cæsar. However, he sent one of his principle officers to try what might be done upon terms of reason and moderation. The officer represented to them, "that the punishment inflicted upon those men was according to law; that their petitions were carried to too great a height; that they would do well to consider that Archelaus was going immediately for Rome, and that, upon his coming back with his commission ratified, every thing would be settled to their utmost content; and that therefore, it was both their duty and interest to preserve the public peace, without incurring the danger of a sedition."

This candid representation, so far from having the desired effect, rendered the populace so clamorous, that, regardless of all law, they repeated their demand of revenge, now Herod was dead, for their friends whom he had destroyed whilst he was living. In the impetuosity of their zeal, they paid no respect to persons or the rules of right and wrong, and were so intent on the ruin of those whom they considered as the objects of their vengeance, that they neglected the most necessary means of their own safety. In the mean time there was no want of seasonable applications to them, as well from Archelaus himself, as those whom he deputed; but these moderate proceedings rendered them more outrageous, insomuch that they wanted nothing but numbers to turn the tumult into a direct rebellion.

The Feast of Unleavened Bread, or the Passover, that celebrated memorial of the delivery of the Israelites out of Egypt, being now at hand, a more than ordinary concourse of people, as well from abroad as at home, came up to Jerusalem, to worship and offer sacrifices upon the solemn occasion. A party of seditious Jews, availing themselves of this opportunity, crouded into the temple, and there made a stand, with a resolution not to quit the place, though they were threatened with the most fatal consequences. They alledged, that they came thither to condole with the people for the loss of their two great teachers of the law, Judas and Matthias, and to stir them up to avenge their deaths. Archelaus, to prevent the mischiefs that might arise from the tumult of a multitude actuated by a zeal bordering on phrenzy, sent an officer, with a party of soldiers, to suppress the riot in due time, giving orders to seize the ringleaders, and bring them before him, if they should persevere in their resistance. The guards no sooner appeared, than the mutineers attacked them with the utmost fury and clamour, and the whole multitude falling upon them, with stones and other implements of destruction, slew the greatest number of them; so that the officer, with some few of the wounded men, were under the necessity of making their escape in the best manner they could. After this action they proceeded with their sacrifices.

The contest was now brought to such a pass, that Archelaus concluded he must either suppress this tumultuous faction, or fall himself, sent out a powerful body of forces to encounter them, with orders to his horse to put all to the sword who should endeavour to make their escape, and to keep all succours from them. The body of horse, pursuant to command, cut off three thousand in the action, and the rest fled to the neighbouring mountains for shelter; so that Archelaus, having carried this necessary point, ordered proclamation for every man to retire to his own habitation, with which they readily complied, lest greater mischief should ensue.

Archelaus now prosecuted his journey to Rome, taking his mother, Nicolaus, Ptolemy, and several other friends along with him, leaving the care of his government and family to his brother Philip. He was accompanied also by Salome, and many of her kindred, under pretence of joining interests to assist Archelaus in obtaining the confirmation of his succession, but, in reality, to obstruct it, by exhibiting a complaint against him for his late conduct in the affair of the temple. Archelaus, being on his way with his attendants, was met by Sabinus, governor of Syria, at Cæsarea, who was posting to Judæa to secure the effects of Herod. But Varus arriving very opportunely, restrained him from interfering in the matter, being there upon an invitation from Archelaus by Ptolemy on the same business; so that, out of respect to Varus, Sabinus ne-the [illegible] in Ju[illegible] not settled up their [illegible] power [illegible] Archelaus, [illegible] declare [illegible] upon [illegible] made he an[illegible] Cæsar.

But when Archelaus [illegible] embarked for Rome, and Varus had departed for Antioch, Sabinus proceeded to Jerusalem, seized on the palace, sent for the officers of the garrison, and those who had the charge of Herod's effects, [illegible] demanded their keys [illegible] books. They informed him, however, that they could not be [illegible], as they had particular orders from Archelaus to keep the things till his return, in the [illegible] they received them, for the use and service of Cæsar.

At the same time Antipas, one of the sons of Herod, went to Rome, in hopes of obtaining the kingdom for himself. He was instigated to this [illegible] by Salome, under colour of a prior right to be successor by an antecedent will, which (as he maintained) ought to be deemed more valid than the later. Antipas took with him his mother, and Ptolemy, the brother of Nicolaus, [illegible] was [illegible] of Herod, [illegible] part. [illegible] But [illegible] fed his ambition, and [illegible] his [illegible] attempt, was Irenæus, an accomplished orator, and [illegible] of great sagacity, [illegible] concerns of Herod. When he was advised by others to consider the [illegible] of Archelaus [illegible] held [illegible] succession [illegible] his deceased father, the [illegible] of Irenæus, [illegible] with his own ambition, [illegible] to [illegible] Upon his [illegible] Rome [illegible] over to him, not from any [illegible] than aversion to Archelaus, [illegible] being [illegible] a Roman governor, or, if they must have a king, preferring Antipas to Archelaus.

Sabinus had lodged an information [illegible] Archelaus, and [illegible] by the [illegible] presented the papers [illegible] memorial of what [illegible] containing [illegible] of his claim, a recital of his [illegible] an account of [illegible] together with [illegible] submitted [illegible] whole [illegible] determination of Cæsar. When Cæsar had perused these writings with the letters also of Varus and Sabinus [illegible] an account of the monies Herod had left [illegible] the [illegible] of the government [illegible] that Antipas himself had [illegible] his own right, he called a council [illegible] to advise upon the whole matter, with [illegible] to [illegible] Caius, the son of Agrippa by his daughter Julia, whom he had adopted, being [illegible] president. Antipater, the son of [illegible] in the advocacy [illegible] to [illegible] spoke to this purpose, [illegible] "curious to Archelaus to [illegible] the [illegible] given him, since he had [illegible] taken [illegible] power over it to himself, before Cæsar had granted it to him, and appealed to those [illegible] of his destroying so many of the Jewish [illegible] punished [illegible] might have been reserved [illegible] country, [illegible] had the power to punish them, and not been executed [illegible] that [illegible] pretended to [illegible] king [illegible] to Cæsar [illegible] before [illegible] determined to him by Cæsar [illegible] as much worse [illegible] he, who was putting in for the kingdom, could by no means expect to have that power granted him, of which he had already deprived Cæsar by taking it to himself. He also [illegible] changing the [illegible] in the army, and his [illegible] on the [illegible] and his determination of [illegible] as if he were no other than a king [illegible] to his concessions to those that petitioned him on a public account [illegible] doing such

"things, than which he could devise no greater, if he had been already settled in the kingdom by Cæsar. He [illegible] to him the releasing of the prisoners that were [illegible] Hippodrome, and many other things that either had been [illegible] done by him, or were believed to be done, and [illegible] might be believed to have been done, the [illegible] of such a nature, as to be usually done by young men, and by such as out of a desire of ruling, seize upon the government too soon. He also charged him with his neglect of the funeral mourning for his father, and with having merry meetings the very night on which he died [illegible] that the [illegible] took the handle of raising a tumult. And if Archelaus could thus requite his dead father, who had bestowed such benefits upon him, and bequeathed [illegible] great things to him, by pretending [illegible] the day [illegible] good [illegible] for having [illegible] to be the same Archelaus with regard to Cæsar, if he granted him [illegible] which he had been to his father, since he [illegible] though an enemy [illegible] fallen, and not [illegible] were carried to his funeral [illegible] related, and had been so great [illegible] But he said, that [illegible] of all was this, that he came now before Cæsar to obtain the kingdom by his grant, which he had before [illegible] all things, as he could have [illegible] Cæsar himself [illegible] had fixed him in the government. And what he most aggravated [illegible] of those about the temple [illegible] at the festival [illegible] were [illegible] themselves, (some of whom were foreigners, and others of their own country) [illegible] dead bodies, and all [illegible] one who pretended to the kingdom [illegible] complete the [illegible] opposed him to, and which [illegible] Cæsar [illegible] his [illegible] power to [illegible] giving him his [illegible] the kingdom, [illegible] to [illegible] because he knew his disposition and in his former [illegible] more authentic testament appointed [illegible] Antipas, to succeed, but that Archelaus [illegible] called by his father to that dignity, when he was in [illegible] condition, both of body and mind, while Antipas [illegible] he was ripest in his judgment, [illegible] of body as made him capable of managing [illegible] And if his father had the like notion of him formerly, that he hath now [illegible] hath he given a [illegible] specimen what a king he is like-ly to be, when he has (in effect) deprived Cæsar of that power [illegible] the kingdom, which he justly [illegible] and has not [illegible] from making a terrible slaughter of his fellow-citizens in the temple, while he was but a private person."

When Antipater had made this speech, and had confirmed [illegible] producing many witnesses from among [illegible] own relations, he ended his pleading. Upon which Nicolaus [illegible] to plead for Archelaus, and said, "That [illegible] had been done at the temple [illegible] to be [illegible] of those that [illegible] authority of Archelaus [illegible] those who were the authors of such things, are not only wicked [illegible] injuries [illegible] in forcing sober persons [illegible] Now it is evident that what [illegible] in the way of opposition was done [illegible] pretence, indeed [illegible] Archelaus, but in reality against Cæsar himself [illegible] they, after an injurious manner, attacked and slew [illegible] by Archelaus, and [illegible] only to [illegible] their doings. They had no regard [illegible] to God or to the festival, whom Antipater yet is not ashamed to patronize, either out of his [illegible] of [illegible] to Archelaus, or out of his hatred of virtue [illegible] as to those who began such "results [illegible] but [illegible] righteous actions, "they [illegible] for [illegible] them to "betake themselves to arms, even against [illegible] "so that Augustus, in effect, assists the [illegible] "[illegible] those who were of council to the [illegible] "[illegible] of [illegible] has been done, but what was derived from [illegible] "[illegible] Nor are those things evil in themselves, "but [illegible] only, in order to do harm to Archelaus. Such are these men's inclination to do any injury "to a man that is of their kindred, their father's benefactor, [illegible] with them, and that hath "[illegible] in friendship with them. For that, as to "this [illegible], it was made by the king when he was "of a [illegible], and so ought to be of more authority "than his former [illegible], and that for this reason, "because Cæsar is therein left to be the judge and disposer of all therein contained. And for Cæsar, he will "[illegible] the [illegible] proceedings of "those men, who, during Herod's whole life, had, on "all occasions, been [illegible] partners of power with him, "[illegible] injure his [illegible] "while they have not themselves had the same regard to "their kinsmen, (which Archelaus had;) Cæsar will not "therefore [illegible] the settlement of [illegible] man whom he and "[illegible], of his friend and confederate, and "[illegible] committed to him in trust [illegible]. Nor "will Cæsar's [illegible] and upright disposition, which are "known and uncontested through all the habitable world, "[illegible] concerning a king "[illegible] his reason, while he "[illegible] bequeathed the succession to a good son of his, and "to one who fled to Cæsar's upright determination for refuge. Nor can Herod at any time have been mistaken "in his judgment about [illegible], while he shewed so "much prudence as to submit all to Cæsar's determination."

When Nicolaus had finished this speech, Archelaus cast himself at Cæsar's feet, upon which the emperor, raising him with the utmost courtesy [illegible] judgment upon him that he was worthy of the crown, and this was confirmed as a [illegible] of his authority. Cæsar then finding the young prince so highly gratified, dismissed the assembly [illegible] determination, in order to deliberate whether he would settle the government on Archelaus alone, or in partition on the whole family, as they depended in general upon his will and pleasure.

CHAP. XI.

As [illegible] Sabinus, [illegible] brought [illegible] by [illegible] Sabinus, [illegible] the [illegible], is threatened by the Jews. Sends to Varus for relief. The Jews mount the [illegible] galleries, and [illegible] the Romans, who [illegible] to the galleries [illegible] on the Jews. The temple [illegible]. The palace [illegible] by the Jews. Rufus and Gratus [illegible] to the Romans. Divers insurrections in Judea. Simon, formerly a [illegible] to Herod, sets up for king. His [illegible], and [illegible] his head. Athronges, a man of the [illegible] extraction, aspires to the crown with [illegible] of his [illegible]. [illegible] and suppressed. Varus marches to the relief of Judea. [illegible] Sepphoris [illegible]. The [illegible] occasions the burning of divers places. The Jews flee [illegible] Varus [illegible] thousand of them to death [illegible] two thousand of them prisoners. [illegible] Varus leaves a garrison [illegible], and returns to Antioch. The Jews send an [illegible] to Cæsar, [illegible] temple of Apollo [illegible] invective against Archelaus. Nicolaus pleads in defence of Archelaus and Herod.

BEFORE these matters could be finally adjusted, Malthace, the mother of Archelaus, paid the debt of nature, and news arrived from Varus, one of the governors of Syria, that the Jews had [illegible], [illegible] been a very [illegible] time ever since the departure of Archelaus; [illegible] Varus, [illegible] upon the [illegible] the whole [illegible] examples of the [illegible], and [illegible] returned to Antioch, leaving one legion in Jerusalem to prevent further [illegible], [illegible] out [illegible] measures [illegible] Varus was no sooner departed than Sabinus [illegible] the forces that were left to [illegible] his [illegible] against the Jews, [illegible] several of their forts and castles [illegible] under pretence of searching for concealed [illegible] [illegible].

The [illegible] of [illegible] people [illegible] from all quarters, for [illegible] Pentecost [illegible] to [illegible] table [illegible] from Judæa, [illegible] from Galilee, Idumea, Jericho, and [illegible] Jordan. [illegible] to [illegible] Sabinus to [illegible]. They divided [illegible] one of them took possession of the [illegible] posted upon the [illegible] of the temple [illegible] west, where [illegible] palace [illegible].

When they had [illegible] the Romans [illegible] ready for the [illegible] Sabinus [illegible] the [illegible] day, and [illegible] they [illegible] conquered [illegible] for [illegible] relief, assuring [illegible] certainly be cut to pieces. He [illegible] ascended [illegible] called Phasael, which was erected [illegible] Herod [illegible] who was [illegible] the Romans [illegible] to the Romans [illegible] the Jews, expecting others should [illegible] to gratify his avarice, [illegible] appear among [illegible] his friends. The Romans pushed to the hazard [illegible] encounter ensued, both parties exerting [illegible]. The Jews [illegible] possessed themselves of [illegible] the [illegible] galleries of the temple, whence they galled the Romans [illegible], with stones and arrows, from their slings [illegible], [illegible] the Romans below were [illegible] to [illegible] enemies. The [illegible] to the [illegible] of the Romans, [illegible] they set fire to the timber work of the galleries, [illegible] it to [illegible], that the flames rapidly [illegible] up the roof, [illegible] took hold of the pitch, wax, [illegible], [illegible] the ornamental part, [illegible] blaze, [illegible] was certain [illegible] of those that were crushed to death by the fall of the building, and those that were put to the sword upon the ground, there was not [illegible] of the [illegible] possessed the galleries. Several of them, in [illegible] and despair, [illegible] others cast themselves upon the points of their swords. Those who thought to conceal themselves [illegible] the same [illegible] could not avail them in such a situation.

As the fire [illegible] the Romans pressed through the flames up to the very treasury of the sacred treasure, a considerable part of which was plundered by the soldiers, and not above four hundred talents (as Sabinus pretended) were brought to him. The Jews were not a little [illegible] distressed, though the loss of so many of their friends on the one hand, and the [illegible] of the temple on the other. However, in this state of desperation, they collected a body of the most resolute men, and [illegible] the palace, threatening immediately to set fire to [illegible] put every man to the sword that should [illegible] if they did not instantly quit the [illegible] and [illegible] promises of impunity to Sabinus and all his people upon [illegible] condition. Rufus and Gratus, with [illegible] of Herod's [illegible] men, went over to the Romans [illegible] with [illegible]

[illegible]

horſe that were under the command of Rufus which was a very conſiderable as well as ſeaſonable reinforcement. Nevertheleſs, the Jews plied their work, mining the walls, threatening and adviſing the enemy to depart, without reducing them to the extremity of deſperation, as they were reſolved, at all hazards, to maintain their liberties, with the laws and cuſtoms of their forefathers. Sabinus was willing to comply, but being conſcious of what he had deſerved from the Jews, durſt not truſt to their promiſe. Beſides, he thought the conditions too advantageous to be made good, and ſo determined to venture the holding it out, in hope and expectation of ſuccour from Varus.

While matters were in this deſperate ſituation in Jeruſalem, there were ſeveral inſurrections in divers parts of Judæa at the inſtigation either of profit or vindictive malice. About 2000 of Herod's diſbanded men gathered together upon the occaſion, with a reſolution to encounter a party of the king's under the command of Achiab, Herod's nephew. But Achiab, ſenſible that he was oppoſed by experienced veterans, avoided coming to action as much as poſſible, by ſhifting into defiles and faſtneſſes.

Judas, the ſon of Ezechias, the notorious robber, who had long annoyed Herod with a band of deſperadoes that he had collected, at Sepphoris, a city of Galilee, made an inroad into the king's country, ſeized his magazines and military ſtores, armed the inhabitants, pillaged wherever he came, and aſpired, in fine, to government himſelf from a moſt rapacious diſpoſition, and lawleſs ambition.

During this ſtate of confuſion, one Simon, formerly a ſervant of Herod, but a man of extraordinary ſtrength, agility, and gracefulneſs of perſon, having the vanity to aſpire to the crown, got together a body of guards, and was ſaluted by the frantick crowd as king. As the firſt inſtance of his dignity and power, he burnt and rifled the palace at Jericho, ſet fire to many of the king's buildings, and allowed his followers the advantage of the booty. Nor would he have ſtopped there, had he not been repreſſed by Gratus, who, having eſpouſed the cauſe of the Romans, advanced with his troops againſt him, when an obſtinate engagement taking place, Simon's party, though reſolute, being wanting in military ſkill, were totally routed and cut to pieces, and he himſelf being made priſoner, Gratus ordered his head to be ſtruck off.

This tumultuous diſpoſition ſeemed univerſally to prevail; for the royal palace at Amatha, by the river Jordan, was burnt to the ground, by a ſet of lawleſs banditti, reſembling thoſe under the direction of Simon. Indeed, a ſpirit of outrage, or rather epidemical madneſs, poſſeſſed the multitude; and that through want of good order under a confirmed king of their own, for the introduction of foreigners, through their intolerable pride and avarice, rather inflamed than reclaimed them.

After the example of Simon, one Athronges, a man who had no pretence either to birth, virtue, ability, or fortune, but a mere clown, of enormous bulk, and vaſt ſtrength, put in a claim to government, and pretended to have formed a reſolution of venturing his life for the obtaining a prerogative to plunder at will. This Athronges had four brothers of the ſame gigantic form with himſelf. They had each of them a band of men under command, which they deemed a ſufficient means for gaining their point. Great multitudes came over to theſe five brothers, ſo that Athronges appointed his four brethren to act as his lieutenants, while he himſelf ſat in council with a diadem upon his head, forming reſolutions, and giving orders in affairs of ſtate. This pageantry continued ſome time, during which the royal ſtile and title ſeemed to be maintained, for they acted according to their own will and pleaſure, none diſputing their authority, or diſobeying their commands. They were cruel to the extreme, whenever either the Romans or the king's forces fell into their power, for they held them in equal averſion, the latter for their licentious conduct under the government of Herod, and the former on account of injuries of a later date. The animoſity grew daily more implacable inſomuch, that they might be ſaid to diffuſe devaſtation and maſſacre, from motives of rapine on the one hand, and cruelty on the other. They fell upon a Roman convoy, out of an ambuſh, with corn and arms for the camp, ſlew Arius, the commander, with forty choice men upon the ſpot, and the reſt would have ſhared the ſame fate, if Gratus had not advanced with a party at the critical juncture, and compelled them to retire. They maintained theſe ſkirmiſhes a conſiderable time, to the great annoyance of the Romans, but at length to their own ſuppreſſion, for they were all taken, particularly in an encounter with Gratus, and another with Ptolemy. Archelaus took the eldeſt of them priſoner, and the laſt finding their caſe deſperate, the men ſpent with toil and ſickneſs, and no proſpect of recruit, ſurrendered himſelf to Archelaus, upon oath for the performance of conditions.

During this general ſcene of tumult, or, as it may be called, terms of licence for outrage and robbery, every new band of mutineers was for ſetting up new kings, which cauſed univerſal diſtractions in the ſtate. The Jews were torn by feuds and factions amongſt themſelves, while the Romans ſuſtained ſome injuries, but not of equal detriment with thoſe of the former.

As ſoon as Varus received intelligence of the ſtate of Judæa, by a letter from Sabinus, he was in great apprehenſion for the third legion, and therefore took the other two legions, and four troops of horſe, with the ſeveral auxiliary forces, which either the king, or the tetrarchs afforded him, and haſtened away to Judæa to the relief of the beſieged. He gave orders that all that were ſent out upon this expedition, ſhould make Ptolemais their place of rendezvous, and took with him 1500 auxiliaries, with which he was ſupplied by the citizens of Berytus. Aretas alſo, king of Arabia Petræa, from his averſion to Herod, and in order to ſecure the favour of the Romans, ſupplied them with a very conſiderable reinforcement both of horſe and foot. When Varus had collected all his forces, and drawn them up in a body at Ptolemais, he gave the command of part of it to his ſon, and one of his particular friends, with orders to march into Galilee, which lies in the neighbourhood of Ptolemais.

Upon this inroad into the country, he carried all before him in ſpite of oppoſition, took Sepphoris, laid the city in aſhes, and made its inhabitants ſlaves. Varus himſelf advanced with his army towards Samaria, but ſuffered no damage to be done to the city, becauſe he knew the inhabitants to be well affected and peaceable in their diſpoſitions. He pitched his camp in a certain village, called Arus, which the Arabians burnt in revenge to the very friends of Herod for Herod's ſake. The army advanced afterwards to Sampho, which the ſame Arabians rifled, though a ſtrong place, and then ſet it on fire. In fine, they filled all places wherever they went with devaſtation and ſlaughter. Emmaus was burnt after the inhabitants had deſerted it, by order of Varus, in revenge for his ſoldiers that were ſlain there.

When Varus approached Jeruſalem, the Jews who had beſieged the Roman legion in that quarter, abandoned their poſt, and fled into lurking places with precipitation. But as to the Jews of Jeruſalem, when Varus reproached them ſeverely for what they had done, they cleared themſelves of the accuſations, alledging that the conflux of the people was occaſioned by the feſtival, that the war was not made with their approbation, but through the raſhneſs of ſtrangers, while they were on the ſide of the Romans, and beſieged together with them, rather than having any inclination to beſiege them. There came alſo before-hand to meet Varus, Joſeph, couſin-german of king Herod, as alſo Gratus and Rufus, who brought their ſoldiers along with them, together with thoſe Romans who had been beſieged. But Sabinus, from conſcious guilt, avoided the ſence of Varus, ſtole out of the city, and went to their [illegible]

Varus, upon this, ſent a detachment from his army into the country, in queſt of the ringleaders of the revolt, and upon diſcovery, and clear proofs being adduced againſt them, puniſhed thoſe that were moſt guilty, and diſmiſſed the reſt. The number of thoſe who were crucified upon this occaſion, amounted to about 2000. After this he diſbanded his army, as they had committed many outrages againſt his will, in the heat and rage of a military licence. But hearing ſoon after, that 10,000 of the Jews were collected into a body, he ordered a ſtrong detachment to fall upon them in their quarters; ſo that, by the advice of Achiab, they ſurrendered themſelves without making any reſiſtance. Hereupon Varus ſet the common people at liberty, ſent the ringleaders to Cæſar, and pardoned all the reſt, except ſome relations of Herod, who, without any regard to affinity or juſtice, had engaged in ſo unnatural and ruinous a war. Matters being thus compoſed, Varus left the ſame legion in garriſon at Jeruſalem, and returned to Antioch.

The commotions in Judea were no ſooner quelled than Archelaus had many embarraſſments to encounter at Rome, which aroſe upon the following occaſion. The Jews, by permiſſion of Varus, ſent an embaſſy to Auguſtus Cæſar, petitioning for liberty of living according to their own laws. There were fifty Jews joined in the commiſſion, and upwards of 8000 in the city of Rome, that preferred themſelves to countenance the embaſſy. Cæſar hereupon appointed a ſelect number of his friends and others of the firſt rank, to attend him in the temple of Apollo, a moſt magnificent ſtructure of his own erecting. The Jewiſh ambaſſadors attended by a long train of Jews, and Archelaus with his friends likewiſe. But his kindred were at a loſs how to act upon the occaſion, for, on the one hand, they abhorred and therefore could not join him, and on the other, if he had cloſed with the ambaſſadors, they would have appeared to the king as enemies to a prince of their own blood. Philip his brother, came thither alſo out of Syria, by the perſuaſion of Varus, with an intent of eſpouſing the cauſe of Archelaus, for whom he had a particular regard, though he was not without hope, that if the ambaſſadors ſhould gain the point, and the government be divided among the children of Herod, a part of the ſame might be allotted to himſelf.

When the Jewiſh ambaſſadors were admitted to the audience of the emperor, the following was the purport of their commiſſion.

"They declared that Herod was, indeed, in name, a "king, but that he had taken to himſelf that uncontroulable "authority which tyrants exerciſe over their ſubjects, "and had made uſe of that authority for the deſtruction of "the Jews, and did not abſtain from making many innova-"tions among them according to his own inclinations. "That whereas there were many who periſhed by that "deſtruction he brought upon them, (ſo many, indeed, as "no other hiſtory relates,) they that ſurvived were far more "miſerable than thoſe that ſuffered under him, not only "by the anxiety they were under, from his looks and diſ-"poſition towards them, but from the danger their eſtates "were in of being taken away by him. That he did, in-"deed, never leave off adorning thoſe cities that lay in their "neighbourhood, but were inhabited by foreigners, ſo that "the cities belonging to his own government were ruined, "and utterly deſtroyed. That whereas, when he took the "kingdom, it was in an extraordinary flouriſhing condi-"tion, he had filled the nation with the utmoſt degree of "poverty. That, when, upon unjuſt pretences, he had "ſlain any of the nobility, he took away their eſtates; that, "when he permitted any of them to live, he condemned "them to the forfeiture of what they poſſeſſed. That, be-"ſides the annual impoſitions which he laid upon every one "of them, they were to make liberal preſents to himſelf, "to his domeſtics and friends, and to ſuch of his ſlaves as "were vouchſafed the favour of being his tax-gatherers, "becauſe there was no way of obtaining a freedom from un-"juſt violence, without giving either gold or ſilver for it. "That they would ſay nothing of the corruption of the "chaſtity of their virgins, and the reproach laid on their "wives for incontinency, and thoſe things acted after an "inſolent and inhuman manner, becauſe it was not a "ſmaller pleaſure to the ſufferers to have ſuch things con-"cealed, than it would have been not to have ſuffered them. "That Herod had put ſuch abuſes upon them, as a ſavage "would not have put on them, if he had power given him "to rule over them. That although their nation had "paſſed through many ſubverſions, and alterations of go-"vernment, their hiſtory gave no account of any calamity "they had ever been under, that could be compared with "this, which Herod had brought upon their nation. That "it was for this reaſon, that they thought they might juſtly "and gladly admit Archelaus as king upon this ſuppoſition, "that whoſoever ſhould be ſet over their kingdom, he would "appear more mild to them than Herod had been; and that "they joined with him in the mourning for his father, in "order to gratify him, and were ready to oblige him in "other points alſo, if they could meet with any degree of "moderation from him. But that he ſeemed to be afraid "leſt he ſhould not be deemed Herod's own ſon, and ſo, "without any delay, he let the nation underſtand his "meaning, and this before his dominion was well eſtabliſh-"ed, ſince the power of diſpoſing of it belonged to Cæſar, "who could either give it to him, or not, as he pleaſed. "That he had given a ſpecimen of his future virtue to his "ſubjects, and with what kind of moderation and good ad-"miniſtration he would govern them, by that his firſt action, "which concerned them, his own citizens, and God him-"ſelf, when he made the ſlaughter of 3000 of his own "countrymen at the temple. How then could they avoid "the juſt hatred of him, who, to the reſt of his barbarity, "hath added this, as one of our crimes, that we have op-"poſed and contradicted him in the exerciſe of his au-"thority?" The main thing they deſired was, that "They "might be delivered from kingly and the like forms of go-"vernment, and might be added to Syria, and put under "the authority of ſuch preſidents as ſhould be ſent them. "For that it would thereby be made evident, whether they "be really ſeditious people, and generally fond of innova-"tions, or whether they would live in an orderly manner, "if they might have governors of any ſort of moderation "ſet over them."

Nicolaus vindicated the kings from theſe accuſations, by obſerving, that, "As for Herod, ſince he had never been "thus accuſed all the time of his life, it was not fit for thoſe "that might have accuſed him of leſſer crimes than thoſe "now mentioned, and might have procured him to be pun-"iſhed, during his life, to bring an accuſation againſt him "now he was dead. He alſo attributed the actions of Ar-"chelaus to the Jews, injuries to him, who, affecting to "govern contrary to the laws, and going about to kill thoſe "that would have hindered them from acting unjuſtly, "when they were by him puniſhed for what they had done, "made loud complaints againſt him. He accuſed them of "their attempts for innovation, and of the pleaſure they "took in ſedition, by reaſon of their not having learned to "ſubmit to juſtice and to the laws, but ſtill deſiring to be "ſuperior in all things." This was the ſubſtance of the plea of Nicolaus.

CHAP. XIII.

Cæſar's generous proceedings in this point [illegible] Partition of the kingdom [illegible]

WHEN Cæſar had heard the allegations and petitions of the ambaſſadors on the one part, and the pleading of the council on the other, he diſmiſſed the aſſembly, and, after a few days, declared Archelaus ſucceſſor to one moiety of Herod's [illegible] jurisdiction, [illegible] the title and name of king, though [illegible] promise [illegible] he should approve, from [illegible] to obtain [illegible], to be [illegible] of the honour.

The [illegible] was divided betwixt the two sons of Herod, Philip and that Antipas who had the dispute with Archelaus concerning [illegible] the succession. Antipas had, for his portion, Galilee, with the country beyond Jordan, and two hundred talents yearly revenue. That of Philip was [illegible], and Auranites, and a part of what was called the [illegible] of Zenodorus, with an [illegible] talents in yearly revenue.

Archelaus had Idumæa, Judæa and the [illegible] Samaria, which was discharged by Cæsar of a fourth part of the duty, for [illegible] loyalty when other places were in rebellion. There fell also to his lot the Tower of Straton, [illegible], [illegible] for [illegible], Gadara, and Hippon, living [illegible] to the Greek customs and manners, were no longer dependent upon the kingdom, but annexed to Syria. The revenue of Archelaus was [illegible] six hundred talents.

Thus stood the partition of the sons of Herod. With regard to Salome, besides the cities of Jamnia, Azotus, [illegible] Phasaelis, with five hundred talents [illegible] coined silver bequeathed her by [illegible] Cæsar presented her [illegible] palace in Ascalon, [illegible] the dominions of Archelaus [illegible] was claimed at sixty hundred talents [illegible] of the king's relations, being [illegible] to the will of Herod [illegible] Herod's two virgin daughters [illegible] father had left them [illegible] which [illegible] them to the [illegible]. [illegible] to complete his generosity and magnificence, he divided his own legacies among the sons of Herod, [illegible] pieces of plate excepted, which he reserved [illegible], not for their [illegible] value, but as memorials of the donor.

CHAP. XIV.

A spurious Alexander [illegible] Cæsar [illegible]. The Jews [illegible] at Rome. [illegible] by Cæsar [illegible] the [illegible] petition.

THESE affairs being settled by Cæsar, a certain young man, by birth a Jew, but brought up at Sidon by a certain man of Rome, insinuated himself into the [illegible] There [illegible] resemblance [illegible] figure [illegible] to that of Alexander [illegible] Herod [illegible] supposed to be [illegible] the [illegible] some [illegible] might [illegible] to the government. To assist him in the execution of his plot, he had recourse to one of his own [illegible], who was versed in the [illegible] of courts, together with the arts necessary for carrying on [illegible] imposture [illegible] deception. [illegible] the matter, they came to a determination, that the Jew, who bore the resemblance, should declare himself to be the very Alexander who was said to be dead; and the report was to be propagated to this effect, "That the persons entrusted with the execution of the two brothers, Alexander and Aristobulus, had [illegible] other bodies in their place, and preserved them both."

The impostor was not only pleased with the conceit of the [illegible] to play, but [illegible] other people [illegible] coming to Crete [illegible] the Jews to [illegible] the [illegible] several [illegible] them upon the credit of [illegible] blood royal. [illegible] so far [illegible] of [illegible]

powers, what favourites he would make, and to what [illegible] [illegible].

With these [illegible] fancies he went for Rome with [illegible]. Upon his arrival at Puteoli, the Jews [illegible] regard for Herod [illegible] about him, and received him as their [illegible] being [illegible] credulous where they have resemblances to work upon their imaginations. This person [illegible] was so very like the prince, that several of his [illegible] friends not only [illegible], but [illegible] that it was Alexander himself, and could not [illegible] otherwise. The rumour of this discovery [illegible] throughout Rome, brought all the Jews from the [illegible] to meet him [illegible] things [illegible] for so surprizing a deliverance.

Upon his arrival at Rome he was carried [illegible] litter, with [illegible] magnificence [illegible] officers and followed by multitudes of people with the loudest acclamations. All these [illegible] him for the sake of his supposed mother, the [illegible] much-injured Mariamne.

But Cæsar, [illegible] Herod [illegible] to be imposed upon in a matter of such importance, [illegible] credit the report. However, for the sake of curiosity and satisfaction, he sent a freedman of his, one Celadus, a [illegible] and confidant of the two brothers, to bring the new Alexander into his presence, which he accordingly did, being [illegible] imposed on as any of the rest. He could not, however, deceive Cæsar; for, although there was a resemblance between him and Alexander, yet it was not so exact as to elude a nice discernment. Besides, the hands, or the [illegible] were rough and callous, through the hard labour to which he had been accustomed, instead of the softness and delicacy of the prince; his body, in general, was found to be coarse and rugged. Cæsar, observing how exactly the parties agreed in their tale, demanded [illegible] become of Aristobulus, and [illegible] delivered [illegible] together, and urge their claim to the [illegible].

The impostor made answer that Aristobulus [illegible] through fear of the designs of the [illegible], for [illegible] should both have returned together, the whole race of the [illegible] would have been extinct, so that regard was had to the preservation of Aristobulus. [illegible] this [illegible] the contrivers of the story coming exactly [illegible] concert, Cæsar took him aside, and thus [illegible] him: "Be ingenuous with me, and [illegible] shall be spared as a reward. Tell me who you are, and who it is that has been so base and arrogant as to contrive and propagate so flagrant an imposture, for it is too intelligent a scheme to be laid by one of your age."

When he found there was no means of [illegible], he [illegible] to Augustus the author, the contrivance, and the [illegible] proceeding. Cæsar fulfilled his promise to the impostor, condemning him [illegible] to the galleys, being of a robust habit of body, and proper for that service. His adviser he [illegible] to death; and as for the people of Melos, he [illegible] sufficiently punished, in having lavished so much money on their counterfeit Alexander. Such was the ignominious conclusion of this scene of imposture.

CHAP. XV.

Archelaus, [illegible] a second accusation, is banished to Vienne [illegible] his [illegible] confiscated. Simon, an Essene, [illegible] interprets [illegible] dream.

ARCHELAUS, on returning to Judæa, and entering upon his ethnarchy, deprived Joazar, the son of Boethus, of the pontificate, upon pretence of having abetted the seditious faction, and conferred the dignity upon [illegible], his brother. He rebuilt the palace at Jericho at a great expence, and brought down one half of the water that watered the village of Neara, to a grove of palm-trees, which he had planted in the [illegible]. He built, also a village, which he called after his own name, Archelais, and, without any regard to the laws of his forefather, took to wife Glaphyra, the daughter of king Archelaus, and widow of his brother Alexander, by whom he had several children, though such marriages were expressly forbidden by the Jewish law. Nor did Eleazar long continue in the enjoyment of his dignity, for Jesus the son of Sie, was put into his office, while he was yet living.

In the tenth year of the government of Archelaus, the principle men of Judæa and Samaria were so disgusted at his tyrannical administration, that they jointly exhibited an accusation against him before Cæsar. They proceeded in it with more confidence, because they knew that severity in the extreme was directly contrary to the commands of Cæsar, who had expressly enjoined him to govern with moderation and justice. Upon hearing this complaint, he sent for Archelaus, who was his agent at Rome, to come to him immediately, and ordered him to go and bring Archelaus, the ethnarch, before him, without vouchsafing him a letter. The messenger, pursuant to command, posted away to Judæa, where he found Archelaus feasting with his friends, and having communicated the emperor's order, called upon him to hasten away. Upon his arrival at Rome, Cæsar heard both charge and defence, and passed sentence of banishment upon Archelaus, with confiscation of all his goods, and sent him away to Vienna, a city of Gaul.

Archelaus, the ethnarch, a little before his summons to Rome, had an extraordinary dream, which he related to his friends, and was to the following purport. He fancied that he saw ten ears of wheat, all ripe and full, and oxen devouring them. This vision dwelling upon his mind when he awoke, he consulted several sages, skilled in divination, about the meaning of it. But the wise men being divided in their judgment, one Simon, an Essene, with the permission of the rest, gave his opinion of the signification of that dream, which was that it foreboded some misfortune to Archelaus, for the dreaming of oxen, being animals designed for labour, seemed to import affliction, and a change of affairs, because upon their turning up the ground every thing changed its place and form. He added, that, by the ten ears of corn, was marked the same definite number of years, which take their revolutions in course, and that the government of Archelaus seemed now to be at an end. This was Simon's interpretation of the dream, and, upon the fifth day after the vision, Cæsar's agent came to Judæa, by his order, to cite Archelaus before him.

His wife Glaphyra, whose first husband was Alexander, the son of Herod, and brother of Archelaus, but, on his being put to death by his father, was married to Juba, king of Mauritania, and afterwards to Archelaus, on the divorce of his former wife Mariamne, this Glaphyra, it is to be observed, during the time of her cohabiting with Archelaus, had the following dream. "She fancied that she saw Alexander her first husband, standing by her, at which she rejoiced, and embraced him with great affection, but that he expostulated with her on her conduct, observing, that she had verified the adage, that women are not to be trusted, since, after pledging her faith to him, who was the husband of her virginity, she had not only engaged in a second marriage, but a third, and violated the express injunction of law and decency, in taking for her husband his brother Archelaus." He added, however, "that ancient kindness should never be forgotten, and therefore it should be his care to deliver her from reproach." She related this dream to several of her female companions, and within a few days afterwards departed this life.

I have introduced these circumstances relative to the princes which are the subjects of the present part of my history, as the examples held forth thereby is worthy of consideration, and as they seem to afford an instructive lesson with respect to our immortal state, and the wisdom of Divine Providence.

Cæsar annexed the lands of Archelaus to the province of Syria, and sent Cyrenius, a man of consular dignity, to tax the province, and dispose of the palace of Archelaus.

END OF THE SEVENTEENTH BOOK.

FLAVIUS JOSEPHUS

ON THE

ANTIQUITIES

OF THE

JEWS.

BOOK XVIII

[INCLUDING A PERIOD OF ABOUT THIRTY YEARS.]

CHAP. I.

Cyrenius appointed governor of Syria, and Coponius, governor of Judæa, sent with him. Cyrenius levies taxes in Syria and Judæa. The Jews therefore become seditious, but are brought to submission by the persuasion of Joazar the high-priest. Judas and Sadducus stir up the people to rebellion, and the commission of outrages. The temple burnt to the ground. Dangerous effects of innovation. The ringleaders start a fourth sect.

CYRENIUS was at this time appointed by Cæsar to the government of Syria. He was a man of eminent character, a senator of Rome, and one who had passed through all dignified offices. Coponius, a man of the equestrian order, was sent together with him, as governor of Judæa, but that province being already annexed to Syria, it came within the department of Cyrenius to take and affess the people, and dispose of the effects of Archelaus. The Jews at first murmured at this mode of assessment, but, through the authority and persuasion of the high-priest, Joazar, they were brought to submissive compliance, without further trouble.

There started up, soon after this, one Judas, a Gaulanite, of the city of Gamala, who, together with one Sadducus, a Pharisee, excited the people to a revolt, by his maintaining that taxes were the badges of slavery, that it was the incumbent duty of the nation to contend for liberty unrestrained, and that one fortunate turn might make them free and easy for ever, advance their reputation, and secure them in their possessions. The multitude, fired by the suggestions of these incendiaries, proceeded to the most outrageous violence, murders, robberies, and depredations, without distinction of friend or foe, universally prevailed, under pretence of advancing the common cause of liberty and property, but, in reality, to subvert all government and good order, gratify the vilest of passions, and promote the private interest of the most abandoned members of society. While intestine broils prevailed to such a degree of ferocious madness that the citizens were sheathing their swords in the bowels of each other, they had to encounter the destruction of a war abroad, and the desolations of a famine at home. Yet to such excess of outrage were they transported by their frantic rage, that the scene of blood and devastation continued, till the sacred temple itself was laid in ashes.

These were the fatal consequences of aiming at innovations in our laws and customs, and desiring to reject fundamental rules and maxims. To that absurd disposition the multitude were excited by Judas and Sadducus, who, from conceit and caprice, introduced a fourth sect, and gaining over many disciples, laid the foundation of our future miseries, by a system of philosophy, with which we were before unacquainted. As these principles proved so fatal in their tendency, it will not be improper to present the reader with their definition.

CHAP. II.

The opinions and practice of the Pharisees, a sect in great repute with the people. Opinions of the Sadducees. Doctrine and manners of the Essenes. Principles of a fourth and new sect.

THERE were, amongst the Jews of old, three peculiar sects of religion. They were distinguished by the denominations of Essenes, Sadducees, and Pharisees. Though I have taken frequent occasion to treat of them, I cannot, on account of the new sect introduced, pass them over unnoticed with propriety in this place.

The manner of life preferred by the Pharisees is rigid and simple, disdaining luxurious delicacies. They scrupulously adhere to the dictates of their reason, and pay such veneration to the judgment and opinion of their seniors, as to follow them implicitly. They ascribe all contingencies to fate, but not as to exclude men's freedom of actions, laying it down as a maxim, that, though all are done by Divine appointment and permission, this by no means excludes the concurrence of the will in points which respect either good or evil. They affert the doctrines of the immortality of the soul, and a future state of rewards and punishments, that the wicked are to be consigned to perpetual chains and darkness, and the good to rise again to a state of bliss. By these doctrines they have acquired great esteem with the people, insomuch, that all forms of worship, prayer, and sacrifices, are presented by them, and an universal opinion entertained of their wisdom, temperance, and integrity.

The Sadducees, on the one hand, deny the immortality of the soul, and affirm, that we have no other obligation upon us but to observe the law, insomuch, that they value themselves upon a right they have to dispute the most important points with their teachers. This sect is not numerous, but mostly composed of men of rank, who when properly qualified for offices of state, are compelled to conform, at least in profession, to the principles of the Pharisees, otherwise they would incur the resentment of the multitude.

The Essenes ascribe the government of the world to Divine Providence, without any exception, hold the immortality of the soul, and revere justice, both in theory and practice, as the cardinal virtue. They send their gifts to the temple, without going thither themselves, for they offer sacrifices apart in a peculiar mode, and with more ceremonies. They are men of excellent morals, and their chief employment is agriculture. They are eminent for their rectitude of conduct, beyond either Greeks or Barbarians, which seems to be the chief object of their study and application. They have all things in common, without any distinction of rich and poor. They have neither wives or servants, as they look upon the one as an encroachment upon the natural liberty of mankind, and the other as a state of life attended with trouble and anxiety, so that they chuse rather, by a mutual exchange of good offices, to assist each other. This is the sum of their principles and manners, and the sect is supposed to amount, in number, to upwards of four thousand. Their treasurers and commissaries are men of integrity, chosen from among their priests, and it is their care to make provision out of the fruits of the earth, for the maintenance of the whole body. Their manner of living, upon the whole, much resembles that of the Plisti, among the Dacians.

The founder of the fourth and new sect was Judas Galilæus, and this was much the same with that of the Pharisees, except in the maxims of an uncontroulable liberty: they will rather expose themselves, and their dearest relations, to the most exquisite torments, than call any man by the name of master. But this is a truth so well confirmed by every day's observation and experience, that it needs no comment, besides, the invincible constancy of this people in the endurance of pains, is beyond expression. The sect, which maintained these principles, were farther enflamed by the intolerable cruelties of Gessius Florus, which ended at length in a general revolt from the Romans. Thus much for the distinct sects among the Jews.

CHAP. II.

The end of the taxation of Cyrenius. Joazar is deposed from the priesthood, and Ananus promoted to that dignity. Herod and Philip being settled in their tetrarchy, build several cities in honour of Cæsar. The Samaritans profane the holy temple. Coponius returns to Rome, and is succeeded in the government of Judæa by Marcus Ambivius. Death of Salome. Death of Augustus Cæsar, emperor of Rome, and succession of Tiberius. Ambivius is succeeded by Annius Rufus, as is the latter by Valerius Gratus. Ananus removed from the high-priesthood, and replaced successively by Ismael, Eleazar, Simon and Joseph. Gratus returns from the government of Judæa, and is succeeded by Pontius Pilate. Herod builds a city, and calls it Tiberias, in honour of the emperor. Phraates, king of Parthia, murdered by his son Phraataces, who is destroyed by a tumult. Orodes taken off by a conspiracy. An embassy to Rome, recommending one of the Parthian hostages for king. Vonones elects Artabanus into Media. Is himself afterwards routed and pursued by Artabanus, and seeks the protection of Tiberius, but in vain. A dispute about the form of government. Germanicus sent to adjust the matter, is poisoned by Piso.

WHEN Cyrenius had disposed of the effects of Archelaus, and settled the taxation according to order, which fell out in the thirty-seventh year after the battle of Actium, Joazar, the high-priest, becoming unpopular, he deprived him of the dignity, and appointed Ananus, the son of Seth, to succeed him. Herod and Philip being settled in their tetrarchies, adjusted affairs in the best manner possible. The former built a wall about Sepphoris, which he made the bulwark and capital of all Galilee. After this he fortified another town, which, at that time, was called Betharamphtha, but he afterwards changed the name to Julias, in honour of the empress. Philip, on his part, beautified and enlarged Paneas, at the head of the river Jordan, and called it Cæsarea. He also advanced the village Bethsaida, upon the bank of the lake of Genezareth, to the rank of a city, both as to bulk, magnificence, and number of inhabitants, calling it also Julias, in honour of Julius Cæsar's daughter.

During the government of Coponius, who was sent, as before observed, with Cyrenius into Judæa, a circumstance happened upon the following occasion. It is customary for the priests, upon the feast of unleavened bread, which we call the passover, to open the gates of the temple soon after midnight. A band of Samaritans, who stole into Jerusalem, watching the opening of the gates, immediately entered, and threw the carcases of dead men into the cloisters. Upon this account the Jews excluded them from the temple, which they were not accustomed to do at such festivals, and watched the sacred spot more carefully than they had formerly done.

A short time after this, Coponius, returning to Rome, Ambivius succeeded him in the government of Judæa, under whose administration died Salome, sister of Herod, and left to Julia, Cæsar's wife, Jamnia, Phasaelis, and the plain of Archelais, with its palm-trees, that bear most excellent fruit.

Annius Rufus succeeded Ambivius, and in his time Augustus Cæsar departed this life. He was the second emperor of Rome, and reigned fifty-seven years, six months, and two days, having been fourteen years of that time colleague with Antony in the government. The term of his life was seventy-seven years. He was succeeded by Tiberius, the son of his wife Julia, being the third emperor of the Romans, who appointed Valerius Gratus to the government of Judæa. He also deposed Ananus from the priesthood, and put Ismael, the son of Fabus, in his place, who was soon after deposed, and the dignity transferred to Eleazar, the son of Ananus, the late high-priest. The office, however, was taken from him, after he had held it a year, and given to Simon, the son of Camith, who, after another year, was compelled to relinquish it to Joseph, who was named Caiaphas. Gratus having now held the government eleven years, returned to Rome, and was succeeded by Pontius Pilate.

Herod, the tetrarch, was now in great favour with Tiberius, and built a city to his honour, called Tiberias. It was built upon the best spot of ground in all Galilee, on the bank of the lake of Genezareth, not far from the hot baths of Emmaus. The city was peopled partly by strangers, the greater part of Galileans, who were compelled to become inhabitants, who took up their residence there by choice, [illegible] the [illegible] of their [illegible] contributions, re collected from all quarters, and of all conditions, high, low, rich and poor, free men and slaves. For the encouragement of these people to settle there, he gave them very considerable privileges and immunities, to some houses, to others land; for he was sensible that, to render this place habitable, was to transgress the ancient Jewish law, because many sepulchres were ordered to be taken away, in order to make room for the building of the city of Tiberias, and our law pronounces, that such inhabitants are unclean for seven days.

About this time died Phraates, king of Parthia, through the treachery of his son, upon the following occasion. The king among other presents that were formerly sent him by Julius Cæsar, had an Italian woman whose name was Thermusa. He made her first his concubine, but being enraptured with her charms, and having a son by her whose name was Phraates, he made her his lawful wife, though he had several legitimate children. This Thermusa perceiving the great affection he had for her, determined to attempt the means to procure for her son the succession to the throne of Parthia. Finding that her efforts could not succeed without removing the legitimate sons out of the kingdom, she prevailed with their father to send those sons as hostages to Rome: such was her ascendency over the mind and will of her husband.

Phraates, being trained up at home to the expectation of the kingdom, thought it tedious to wait for a crown in reversion, and therefore formed a treacherous design, by the assistance of his mother, with whom he was supposed to have been criminally concerned, of [illegible] for taking away his father's life. This being accordingly done, Phraates rendered himself so odious to the people, both for parricide and incest, that, before he could enter upon the government, he was expelled, and perished in a tumult raised against him. Now the Parthians not having agreed, that government and good order could not be maintained without a king, and resolving at the same time not to let any prince up on the throne that was not of a lineal descent from Arsaces, (the blood of Phraates being tainted by a marriage with an Italian concubine,) sent ambassadors and invited Orodes to take the crown. But Orodes being odious to the multitude, on account of his cruel and unaccountable temper, a band of conspirators set upon and slew him. Some say the execution was done at a feast or a banquet, but the more general report is, that they slew him when they had drawn him out to a hunt.

Upon this the Parthians sent an embassy to Rome, desiring one of the hostages for their king, and made choice of Vonones in preference to the rest. He was a prince worthy of the honor conferred on him, by two of the greatest empires upon the face of the earth, the Roman and the Parthian. But his own countrymen being naturally fickle and haughty, quickly repented of their choice, and spurning the idea of a slave, (for so they construed the word hostage,) as well as rejecting the imposition of a king, not by any law of arms, as it was a time of profound peace, in the heat of their resentment, they sent for Artabanus, who was then king of the Medes, and of the blood of Arsaces. Artabanus immediately accepted the offer, and, upon his arrival at the head of a considerable army, was encountered by Vonones, who repulsed him, the generality of the Parthians as yet maintained their allegiance; but Artabanus, being in a short time reinforced, gave Vonones a total overthrow in a second battle, so that, with great difficulty, he escaped, with some few horse in Seleucia. Artabanus taking advantage of the consternation of his opponents, pressed on the pursuit with terrible slaughter, and retired to Ctesiphon with his victorious army. This action put him in possession of the kingdom of Parthia. Vonones, in the mean time, fled into Armenia, expecting to obtain the government there, soliciting Cæsar also to assist him in his design. But whether the emperor suspected his courage, or himself was afraid of incurring the resentment of the Parthians, Tiberius stood off, and Vonones despairing of the attempt delivered himself up to Syllanus, governor of Syria, who, out of regard to his education at Rome, gave him an honourable reception. Artabanus, being now settled in the government of Parthia, made his son Orodes king of Armenia.

At this time died Antiochus, king of Comagene, which occasioned the multitude to contend with the nobility, the latter being desirous of reducing the kingdom into the state of a province, while the former were for being under a kingly government, as they were before. Upon this dispute Germanicus was ordered away into the east, to compose the difference, but it proved the occasion of his ruin; for, after he had settled all his affairs, he was poisoned through the treachery of Piso, as will be shewn hereafter.

CHAP. IV.

Standards set up in Jerusalem with Cæsar's image [illegible]. A tumult raised upon the occasion. Pilate orders the images to be removed. Demands money out of the sacred treasury. A great destruction of the Jews. Josephus bears illustrious testimony. Decius Mundus [illegible] Paulina, a woman of [illegible] virtue, forms [illegible] tions. [illegible] the priests of Isis, bring them [illegible]. A criminal intercourse ensues. The priests and [illegible] are [illegible], and the temple of Isis destroyed.

PILATE, governor of Judea, upon the removal of the army from Cæsarea to Jerusalem, to take up their winter quarters there, brought several standards into the city, with the image of Cæsar, to the violation of the Jewish laws, which expressly prohibit the use of such figures; for which reasons no former governors brought ensigns with such ornaments upon them before. The present governor was the first that ever transgressed this rule, and to do it, he brought them in by stealth, and fixed them up in the dead of the night, when none were present. When the citizens observed them next morning, they assembled in great multitudes, and attended Pilate at Cæsarea, with a petition for the removal of those images to some other place. After several days waiting, and Pilate still refusing upon pretence that it was a request not to be granted without offering an indignity to Cæsar, they still persisted in their importunities. But the governor, upon the seventh day of the Jews attendance, commanded a party of soldiers to be ready in arms, where he appointed them, and thereupon mounted a tribune which he had caused to be erected in the circus, as a place most commodious for a surprize. When the Jews renewed their petition, he gave a signal to the soldiers to encompass them round, and threatened that their punishment should be immediate death, unless they would quietly depart to their respective habitations. The Jews, notwithstanding this alarming menace, cast themselves upon the ground, and laid their necks bare, thereby intimating that their lives was not so dear to them as the laws of their country. Pilate was so deeply impressed with this instance of their fortitude in preserving their laws inviolate, that he commanded the images to be carried back to Cæsarea.

The next thing Pilate undertook was to bring an aqueduct to Jerusalem about two hundred furlongs from the city, for which purpose he demanded money out of the sacred treasury. The Jews, enraged at this proceeding, assembled in great numbers, to try the effect of popular clamour in diverting him from his purpose. Some, as is usual upon such occasions, used reproaches, and poured forth the most provoking invectives, insomuch that he ordered a certain number of soldiers to assume the habit of the vulgar class, carry daggers under their garments, and be ready to obey a private signal. He then commanded the Jews to depart, but as they persisted not only in denial, but reproach, the signal was given to the soldiers, who fell upon them, dealing destruction indiscriminately, and the Jews being unarmed, and consequently unprepared for resistance, an end was put to the tumult.

At the same time there appeared in Judæa an extraordinary person called JESUS, if it be lawful to call him a man. He was a famous worker of miracles, a teacher of those who were desirous of receiving the truth in simplicity, and brought over to him many disciples, both Jews and Gentiles. This was the CHRIST, whom Pilate, at the accusation of the princes and great men of the nation, delivered up to the ignominious punishment of the cross, notwithstanding which, those who first loved him did not forsake him. He appeared to them alive again the third day after his crucifixion, which the divine prophets had foretold, together with numberless other wonders concerning him. And thence, to this day, there is a set of people, who bear the name of CHRISTIANS, as owning him for their Head, Lord and Master.

About this time another calamity caused great disorder among the Jews, which arose from certain shameful practices about the temple of Isis that was then at Rome. The particulars are as follow. There was at Rome, one Paulina, a woman no less eminent for her virtue than her birth, possessed of an ample fortune, most exquisite beauty, and had withal consummate modesty. She was married to Saturninus, a husband worthy of such a wife; but it so fell out, that one Decius Mundus, a Roman knight, in the prime of life, fell desperately in love with her. As she was a person above the temptation of presents, he was the more inflamed with a desire of gaining her, and proceeded so far, however, as to offer two hundred thousand drachmæ to ingratiate himself with the object of his adoration. When these means proved ineffectual, and he became more and more enamoured, he began to meditate his own destruction. There was a female domestic belonging to the father of Mundus, called Ide, a woman of intrigue and cunning, who observing his passion had transported him beyond all reason, encouraged him to hope for the possession of Paulina, by suggesting to him, that, for a consideration of fifty thousand drachmæ, his desire might be accomplished. Mundus, charmed with the proposal, produced the money; but Ide, persuaded that one had no attraction with Paulina, and reflecting that she held the goddess Isis in the highest veneration, she had recourse to this invention. Having convened several of the priests of Isis, sworn them to secrecy, and secured them by a deposit of twenty-five thousand drachmæ, and a promise of as much more when the business was effected, she communicated to them the circumstances towards facilitating an interview between the parties.

The priests, lured by the temptation, promised fair, and one of them went immediately to Paulina, and, in a private conference, told her, that the god Anubis was passionately enamoured of her, and that she must favour him with a visit. Paulina welcomed the messenger, and was so elated with the ideal honour, that she could not forbear disclosing to her female companions the kind regard which the god Anubis entertained for her. She even made her husband acquainted with it, and told him that an assignation was made between them, to which, from a reliance on her insuperable virtue, he chearfully acceded.

Paulina, in pursuance of this pleasing fancy, went into the temple of Isis, where, in the evening, she was shut up by one of the priests; and meeting with Mundus in the dark, had intercourse with him during the night, supposing she was honoured with the caresses of Anubis. In the morning they separated, and Paulina returned to her husband charmed with the late adventure, which she failed not to relate to her female companions in exaggerated terms.

Upon the third day after the interview Mundus happened to meet Paulina, and, in terms pregnantly satirical, lampooned her credulity, that had induced her to take him into her arms, as a substitute for her adorable Anubis, intimating at the same time, that it had saved him two hundred thousand drachmæ.

When the woman reflected on the deception, she rent her clothes, burst into vehement exclamations, related the whole circumstance to her husband, and requested, if he had any regard for her, that he would not suffer so flagrant an indignity to pass unpunished. The husband represented the matter to Tiberius, who, upon full enquiry and information, caused these sanctified, or rather sacrilegious, impostors, together with Ide, the inventress of the plot, to be crucified. He commanded the temple of Isis to be pulled down, and her statue to be thrown into the Tiber, but mitigated the sentence of Mundus to banishment, as a young man overcome by the irresistible force of his passion.

CHAP. V.

Profligate Jews impose themselves on the credulous as teachers of the law. Extort money upon fraudulent pretences. Cause the expulsion of their brethren from Rome. A Samaritan impostor. Siege of Tirathaba. The assailants cut to pieces. The Samaritans exhibit a complaint against Pilate. Marcellus made governor of Judæa. Pilate ordered before Tiberius Cæsar.

A Certain Jew, a notorious profligate, who, to avoid the stroke of public justice, was compelled to fly his country, passed at Rome, in these days, as a kind of rabbi, together with three more of the same abandoned character and destruction. Holding themselves forth as professors and expounders of the laws of Moses, they gained several proselytes, and, among others, one Fulvia, a woman of rank and integrity, and a Jewess by profession. This person, having delivered herself up to their authority and guidance, was prevailed upon by them to send oblations of gold and purple to the holy temple at Jerusalem, which, from time to time, they converted to their own use. Saturninus, induced by his wife, who had detected the fraud, exhibited a complaint against the impostors to Tiberius, who commanded all the Jews forthwith to depart the city. There were 4000 soldiers entered the consul's roll, and sent away for Sardinia, besides great numbers who made conscience of bearing arms for the sake of their religion; and these were put to grievous torments, so that, for the infamy of four flagitious impostors, the Jews were all banished to a man.

Nor was Samaria free from tumults, which were excited by a certain impostor, who gave out, that, if the multitude would assemble at mount Gerizim, a spot held sacred in that country, he would undertake to shew the holy vessels which Moses had caused to be there deposited. A credulous rabble lured by this plausible tale, betook themselves to arms, waiting for others to join them, in order to march up to the mountain in a large body. But Pilate anticipated their design by pre-possessing the mountain with a strong band of horse and foot, whence they charged the Samaritans, who had surrounded the village, routed and slew great numbers of them, and took and carried away a multitude of prisoners, the principal of whom were put to death by order of the governor of Judæa.

When this tumult was appeased the leading men of the Samaritans applied to Vitellius, a person of consular dignity, and at that time governor of Syria, and brought a charge of murder against Pilate. Vitellius, upon this sent his friend Marcellus to take charge of the government of Judæa and ordered Pilate to Rome, to answer before the emperor, the accusations exhibited against him. Pilate had held the government of Judæa ten years, when he prepared for his journey to Rome. But Tiberius departed this life before his arrival.

collected from all quarters, and of all conditions, high, low, [illegible] poor, free men and slaves. For the encouragement [illegible] gent to settle there, he gave them very considerable [illegible] privileges and immunities, to some houses, to others land; for he was sensible that, to render this place [illegible], [illegible] great [illegible] Jewish law, because [illegible] sepulchres [illegible] to be taken [illegible], in order to [illegible] the building of the city of Tiberias, and our [illegible] pronounce, that [illegible] inhabitants are unclean for seven days.

About this time died Phraates, king of Parthia, through the treachery of his son, [illegible] the following occasion. The king [illegible] other presents that were formerly sent him by Julius [illegible] for [illegible] Italian woman whose name was Thermusa. He made her first his concubine, but being captivated with her [illegible], and having a son by her whose name was [illegible], he made her his lawful wife, though he had before [illegible] legitimate children. The [illegible] perceiving the great [illegible] he had for [illegible], determined to attempt [illegible] to procure for her son the succession to the throne of Parthia. Knowing that her son could not succeed [illegible] the legitimate sons out of the kingdom, [illegible] with her [illegible] to send those sons [illegible] hostages [illegible] Rome [illegible] over the mind and [illegible] of [illegible] husband.

[illegible], being trained up at home to the expectation of [illegible], thought it tedious to wait for a crown in reversion, and therefore formed a treacherous design, by the [illegible] of [illegible], with whom he was suspected to [illegible] criminal [illegible], for taking [illegible]. This being accordingly done, [illegible] to the people, both for [illegible], that after he could [illegible] the government, [illegible] expelled [illegible] tumult raised against him. Now the Parthians held it agreed, that government [illegible] good order [illegible] not be [illegible] king, and [illegible] at the same time, not to let any prince [illegible] royal descent [illegible] the blood [illegible] being [illegible] Orodes to [illegible]. But Orodes being [illegible] to the [illegible], [illegible] cruel and [illegible] temper, [illegible] set upon and slew him. Some say the execution [illegible] done at a [illegible], or a banquet, but the more general report is, that they slew him when they had drawn him [illegible].

Upon this the Parthians sent an embassy to Rome, desiring one of the hostages for their king, and made choice of Vonones in preference to the rest. He was a prince worthy of the honour conferred on him, by two of the greatest empires upon the face of the earth, the Roman and the Parthian. But his own countrymen being naturally fickle and [illegible], quickly repented of their choice, and [illegible] the [illegible] of a slave, (for so they construed the word hostage) as well as rejecting the imposition of a king, not by any law of arms, [illegible] time of profound peace, [illegible] the heat of [illegible], they sent for Artabanus, who was then king of the Medes, and of the blood of Arsaces. Artabanus [illegible] accepted the offer, and, upon his arrival [illegible] head of a considerable army, was encountered by Vonones, who repulsed him, the generality of the Parthians [illegible] their allegiance. But Artabanus, being in a short time reinforced, gave Vonones total overthrow in a second battle, so that, with great difficulty, he escaped, with some few horse, to Seleucia. Artabanus taking advantage of the consternation of his opponents, pressed on the pursuit with terrible slaughter, and retired to Ctesiphon with his victorious army. This action put him in possession of the kingdom of Parthia. Vonones, in the mean time, fled into Armenia, expecting to obtain the government there, soliciting Cæsar [illegible] his design. But whether the emperor suspected his courage, or [illegible] was afraid of incurring the resentment of the Parthians, Tiberius [illegible] [illegible], and [illegible] despairing of the attempt, [illegible] himself up to Silanus, governor of Syria, who, out of regard to his education at Rome, gave him an honourable reception. Artabanus being now settled in the government of Parthia, made his son Orodes king of Armenia.

At this time died Antiochus, king of Comagena, which occasioned the multitude to contend with the nobility; the latter being desirous of reducing the kingdom into the state of a province, while the former were for being under a kingly government, as they [illegible] before. Upon this dispute Germanicus was ordered [illegible] into the east, to compose the difference, but it proved the occasion of his ruin; for, after he had settled all his affairs, he was poisoned through the treachery of Piso, as will be seen hereafter.

CHAP. II.

[illegible] Jerusalem [illegible] Cæsar [illegible]. A tumult [illegible] Pilate [illegible] images to be removed. [illegible] money out of the sacred treasury. A great destruction of the Jews. [illegible] illustrious testimony. [illegible] Paulina, a woman of [illegible] virtue, [illegible]. [illegible] the priests of Isis, [illegible] of this [illegible].

PILATE, governor of Judæa, upon the removal of the army from Cæsarea to Jerusalem, to take up their winter quarters there, brought several standards into the city, with the image of Cæsar, to the [illegible] of the Jewish laws, which expressly prohibit the use of [illegible] figures, for which reasons no former governors [illegible] with such ornaments upon them before. The present governor was [illegible] the [illegible] rule, and [illegible] brought them in by night, and fixed them up in the dead of the night, when no [illegible] present. When the Jews observed them [illegible], they [illegible] in great multitudes, and [illegible] Pilate [illegible], with a petition for the removal of those images to some other place. After [illegible] days waiting and Pilate still refusing, upon a pretence that it was a request not to be granted without offering an indignity to Cæsar, they still persisted in their importunities. But the governor, upon the seventh day of the Jews attendance, commanded a party of soldiers to be ready in arms, [illegible] appointed them, and thereupon mounted a tribunal which he had caused to be erected in the circus, as a place most commodious for [illegible] surprize. When the Jews renewed their [illegible] petition, he gave a signal to the soldiers to encompass them round, and threatened that their punishment should be immediate death, unless they would quietly depart to their respective habitations. The Jews notwithstanding this alarming menace, cast themselves upon the ground and laid their necks bare, thereby intimating that their lives was not so dear to them as the laws of their country. Pilate was so deeply impressed with this instance of their fortitude in preserving their laws inviolate, that he commanded the images to be carried back to Cæsarea.

The next thing Pilate undertook was to bring an aqueduct to Jerusalem about two hundred furlongs from the city, for which purpose he demanded money out of the sacred treasury. The Jews, enraged at this proceeding, assembled in great numbers, to try the effect of popular clamour in diverting him from his purpose. Some, as is usual upon such occasions, used reproaches, and poured forth the most provoking invectives, insomuch that he ordered a certain number of soldiers to assume the habit of the vulgar [illegible], carry daggers under their garments, and be ready to obey a private signal. He then commanded the Jews to depart, but as they persisted not only in denial but reproach, the signal was given to the soldiers, who fell upon them, dealing destruction

CHAP. VI.

Vitellius magnificently received at Jerusalem. Hyrcanus builds a castle, afterwards called Antonia. Caiaphas deposed. Vitellius forms a league with Artabanus. The Parthians seize Armenia. Artabanus banished, but reinforced, and recovers his kingdom. Treaty between Tiberius and Artabanus. Darius sent as hostage. Vitellius returns to Antioch. Death and character of Philip.

AT this time Vitellius went into Judæa, and visited Jerusalem, (it being the feast of the passover,) where he was most honourably received, and remitted the inhabitants all the taxes upon fruits bought and sold. He restored to the priests also the keeping of the pontifical vestments in the temple, as they had been of old, but were of late deposited in the castle of Antonia, upon the following occasion.

Hyrcanus, the high-priest, and first of that name, having built a tower near the temple, passed the greater part of his time there, keeping in his own custody the pontifical vestments and ornaments, in order to reserve them for his own use, as did his successors for a considerable time after him. But Herod, upon his succession to the throne was so well pleased with the situation, beauty and strength of this fort, that he caused it to be improved at a very great expence, and called it by the name of Antonia in honour of Anthony, his particular friend. In this castle he found the sacred vestments, and there he ordered them to be kept from an opinion, that having them in his possession, would keep the Jews in proper decorum. Archelaus, his son and successor, followed his example, and from the time above, as did the Romans also after the reduction of the kingdom into a province, and these pontifical robes were deposited in a cabinet appropriated to that service, under the seal of the priests and keepers of the holy treasury, the governor of the castle being obliged to have a lamp burning before the place. Upon the seventh day preceding the three solemn festivals he delivered out the vestments to the high-priest, who having caused them to be purified, performed the sacred functions in them, and the day following deposited them in the usual place. This was the practice at the three annual festivals, and upon the solemn fast.

But Vitellius was now pleased, in favour of the Jews, to give up all the pontifical robes into the possession of the priests again, and to discharge the governor from any further care of them. This he did to conciliate the esteem of the Jewish nation. He then deposed Joseph, who was also called Caiaphas, from the office of high-priest, and conferred it upon Jonathan the son of the high-priest Ananus, after which he returned to Antioch.

Upon his arrival, he received letters of instruction from Tiberius Cæsar, to form a league of friendship with Artabanus, king of Parthia, the emperor being apprehensive, if he should get possession of Armenia, that he might become a dangerous enemy; but Vitellius was enjoined to form the league upon no other condition than that of having one of the king's sons as an hostage. This induced Vitellius to tamper with the kings of Iberia and Alania, by the offer of a great sum of money, to engage them in a war with Artabanus. His utmost efforts could only prevail with the Iberians to open a free passage for the Alanians through their city, and so, by the Caspian mountains, to enable them to pave the way for an incursion into the kingdom of Armenia. By means of this irruption, Armenia was again taken from the Parthians, and that stroke was followed with so desperate a ravage of their own country, that the principal men were almost entirely cut off, together with the king's son, and such vast numbers of the common people, that the nation may be said to have laid all waste before it.

Artabanus now fatally perceived that he had been betrayed under his very roof, and that his friends and relations were bribed into a plot with Vitellius for his destruction, so that not knowing in whom to repose confidence, and suspecting treachery under the guise of friendship, he made his escape into the upper provinces, where he was not only protected but reinforced with so considerable an army of the Dahæ and Sacæ, that he not only overthrew his enemies, but recovered his kingdom.

Upon this turn of affairs, Tiberius proposed an alliance with Artabanus, and upon this invitation, Artabanus and Vitellius went to the Euphrates, and a bridge being laid over the river, they each of them came attended by their guards, and met upon the middle of the bridge. At the conclusion of the treaty, Herod, the tetrarch, gave them both a very splendid and magnificent entertainment in a tent he had erected at a great expence, upon the same river. Artabanus soon after sent his son, Darius as an hostage to Tiberius, with a variety of presents, and one amongst the rest was a man seven cubits in height, by profession a Jew, whom they called Eleazar the Giant. Vitellius after this returned to Antioch, and Artabanus to Babylon.

Herod, desirous of giving Cæsar the first information of their having obtained hostages, dispatched a messenger with every particular of the treaty, to Rome, and every circumstance being so accurately described, the intelligence of Vitellius became needless. He was, however, much disgusted at his officious anticipation, but smothered his resentment till Caius came to the government.

At this time died Philip, the brother of Herod, in the twentieth year of the reign of Tiberius, and the thirty-seventh of his tetrarchy, of Trachon, Gaulanitis and Batanea. He was a man of a quiet, easy disposition, and spent his whole life in the compass of his own jurisdiction. He scarcely ever went abroad but in company with some few of his select friends, and had a chair carried after him, which upon several occasions, he used as a seat of justice. If it happened he was met on by any for his decision of any matter in controversy, he immediately proceeded to the examination of the cause, and gave sentence according to validity of evidence. He died at Julias, and was buried with great funeral pomp in a monument he had prepared for himself; but leaving no issue behind him, Tiberius annexed his dominions to Syria, upon condition that the tributes in that tetrarchy should not go out of the country.

CHAP. VII.

A war between Herod, the tetrarch, and Aretas the king of Parthia. Particulars of the occasion of it. John the Baptist imprisoned by order of Herod. Vitellius marches on the army of Judea towards Petra. The Jews are offended at the images in the Roman ensigns. Vitellius, Herod and attendants go to a public festival held at Jerusalem. The priesthood transferred from Jonathan to Theophilus. Intelligence of the death of Tiberius. Progeny of Herod the Great.

A WAR broke out at this time between Herod and Aretas king of Parthia, upon the following occasion. Herod, the tetrarch, married the daughter of Aretas, with whom he cohabited a considerable time, but being called afterwards to Rome he paid a visit to Herod his brother-in-law, (the son of the daughter of Simon, the high-priest,) in his way, where he became so passionately enamoured of Herodias, wife of his brother and daughter of Aristobulus, their brother, that he had the confidence to make a proposal of marriage to her, upon his return from Rome, and of putting away his wife, the daughter of Aretas, which was agreed on both sides, as the condition of their marriage. He then prosecuted his voyage for Rome, where, having done his business, he returned home. His wife having by this time received intelligence of his intrigue with Herodias, artfully intimated a desire of obtaining his permission to go to Machærus, a castle upon the borders of the dominions of Aretas. Herod not suspecting the cause of her request, readily complied; and, as Machærus was placed under the command of her father, every necessary preparation was then made, for her journey. The governor, immediately upon her arrival, furnished her with Arabian guards, who conducted her from stage to stage, with all possible speed, to her father's palace. When she related the circumstance of Herod's amour, Aretas became naturally incensed; and there being, at that time, a dispute concerning the boundaries of some land in Gamala, and the two armies in the field ready to decide the point in question, they laid hold of this pretence, and brought it to a battle, in which Herod was totally routed, through the treachery of a band of refugees that came over from Philip, and were at that time in the pay of Herod. The tetrarch no sooner gave Tiberius intelligence of this disaster, than he dispatched orders to Vitellius to make war upon Aretas, to retaliate the supposed indignity, and either bring him prisoner, or send his head to Rome.

There prevailed amongst the Jews a general opinion that this disaster was the effect of Divine vengeance upon Herod and his army, for the blood of John, surnamed the Baptist, who was [illegible] by order of this tetrarch. He was a man [illegible] character, whose grand concern was to exhort the Jews to the practice of piety and virtue, to [illegible] the necessity of repentance, and hold forth, by baptism, the [illegible] and meaning of regeneration and a new life, not as consisting in abstaining from a particular sin, but [illegible] in habitual purity both of mind and body. Such was the influence and authority of this great and good man, as appeared from the multitude of his disciples, and the veneration they had for his doctrine, that Herod was apprehensive he might instigate them to a revolt. Acting therefore by [illegible] sordid principle, he sent him away bound to Machærus, (the castle before mentioned,) where, by the malice and contrivance of Herodias, his brother's wife (with whom he was greatly enamoured,) the Baptist was afterwards put to death; and that impious barbarity was followed by a Divine vengeance on the execrable cause of it, as the Jews, from the best foundation, were firmly persuaded.

Vitellius was now preparing for the Arabian war, and upon his march towards Petra, with two legions, and all the auxiliaries, horse and foot, of the Roman allies. When he was advanced as far as Ptolemais, thinking to take his passage across Judea, the leading men of the country met him on his way, entreating him to steer some other course, as the images which the Romans usually bear on their ensigns are repugnant to the religion and laws of the Jews. The general complied with the request, and sent his army about, through the compass of an extensive plain; while he himself, with Herod the tetrarch, and his friends, went up to Jerusalem, to the celebration of a public festival which then approached. He was received with the utmost respect and honour, and took his abode there three days, during which time he transferred the office of high-priest from Jonathan to his brother Theophilus. Upon the fourth day he received intelligence of the death of Tiberius, and, in consequence thereof, made the people swear allegiance to Caius Caligula, the successor, called back his troops, and ordered them into winter quarters, putting a stop to the war upon a change of government.

There prevailed a report that upon the intelligence of the expedition of Vitellius, Aretas consulted the diviners and soothsayers respecting the event of the undertaking, and that they foretold, " That the army then upon the march should never reach Petra, as either one of the princes would die, or the general appointed to the command, or the person against whom the war was made; so that Vitellius returned to Antioch." As I am now relating these vicissitudes of human events, I deem it not foreign to the purpose to make some remarks on the fate of Herod and his family, which certainly display [illegible] instances of the wisdom and power of Divine Providence. It tends to shew, that dignity of birth, the most splendid fortune, or numerous progeny, are objects of no consideration with piety and virtue. We find this maxim confirmed in the case of Herod; who, within the course of an hundred years, had not any remains left of so numerous a family. This should serve as a check to the vain pretensions of arrogant mortals, and lead them to admire the wonders of Providence, and, amongst the rest, the advancement of Agrippa from a private fortune, to so eminent a degree of dignity and power. We have given an account of the progeny of Herod in the abstract, but shall now give it in detail.

Herod the Great, by Mariamne, the daughter of Hyrcanus, [illegible] two daughters, Salampso, who married Phasael the son of Phasael, the king's eldest brother, with the father's consent, and Cypros, who married Antipater, the nephew of Herod, by his sister Salome.

Phasael had, by Salampso, five children, Antipater, Herod, Alexander, and two daughters, Alexandra and Cypros, who married Agrippa, the son of Aristobulus; but Alexandra was married to one Timius, a nobleman of the isle of Cypros, who died without issue. Agrippa had, by Cypros, two sons and three daughters. The latter were Bernice, Mariamne, Drusilla; the former Agrippa, and Drusus, who died in his minority. Agrippa the father, was brought up under his grandfather Herod the Great, together with his brothers, Herod and Aristobulus; as was also Bernice, the daughter of Salome and Costobarus.

The children of Aristobulus were at that time infants, when their father, and his brother Alexander, were put to death by Herod. When they arrived to years of maturity, this Herod, the brother of Agrippa, married Mariamne, the daughter of Olympias (who was king Herod's daughter), and of Joseph, Herod's brother, by whom he had Aristobulus. Aristobulus, the third brother of Agrippa, married Jotape, the daughter of Sampsigeramus, king of the Emesenes, by whom he had a daughter called after her mother, and that was born deaf. These were the children of the three brothers. But Herodias, their sister, married Herod, the son of Herod the Great, whom he had by Mariamne, the daughter of Simon, the high-priest; and from hence came Salome, after whose birth Herodias made no scruple in defiance of the law of our country, of taking Herod the tetrarch of Galilee, for her second husband, though her husband's brother, by the father's side, having also abandoned a former husband who was yet living. Salome, the daughter, married Philip the son of Herod the tetrarch of the Trachonites, who died without issue; after which she married Aristobulus, the son of Herod, and brother of Agrippa, by whom he had three sons, Herod, Agrippa, and Aristobulus. Thus much for the family of Phasael and Salampso.

Cypros had by Antipater, a daughter, called after the mother, who was married to Alexas Selcias, the son of Alexas, who, by her, had one daughter, Cypros. But Herod and Alexander, the brothers of Antipater, died without issue. Alexander the son of king Herod, that was put to death by his father, had by Glaphyra, the daughter of Archelaus, king of Cappadocia, Alexander and Tigranes.

This Tigranes was that king of Armenia, who had an accusation brought against him by the Romans, and died without children. Alexander had a son called Tigranes also, after the name of his uncle, whom Nero advanced to be king of Armenia, and had a son named Alexander, who married Jotape, the daughter of Antiochus, king of Comagena, and was made king of Lesis, in Cilicia, by Vespasian. The race of Alexander's sons declined from the Jewish law and discipline to the religion of the Greeks; and the other daughters of Herod the Great left no children behind them. Having thus gone through the posterity of this prince as far as the reign of Agrippa, we shall now advert to the history of Agrippa himself, and the various zing ſucceſſion of events that at length advanced him to ſo great a degree of dignity and power

CHAP VIII

Extravagance and profuſion of Agrippa He conciliates the favour of the great Diſguſts in hatred of his brother Ariſtobulus Is graciouſly received by Cæſar at Capreæ Charged with a fraud by Herennius Diſmiſſed the court Succeſs of his wiſhes Dilatory temper of Tiberius Agrippa committed to priſon upon an accuſation of Eutychus Prediction of a German upon an owl's perching over Agrippa's head Tiberius favourable towards him Popularity of Caius Tiberius, upon conſulting the oracle, as to the ſucceſſion, is directed to Caius Transfers the government to him Death of Tiberius, and ſucceſſion of Caius Character of the late emperor Agrippa diſcharged from confinement, and treated with ſingular honour Marcellus appointed to the government of Judea

AGRIPPA, being at Rome, a ſhort time before the death of Herod the Great, and frequently admitted to the emperor's palace, had inſinuated himſelf into the graces of his ſon Druſus, as alſo of Antonia, the wife of Druſus the elder, by means of his mother Bernice, for whom Antonia had great eſteem Agrippa was naturally of an open generous temper, but kept within the bounds of moderation, in his expences during the life of his mother, but, upon her demiſe, gave into every exceſs of extravagance, and eſpecially amongſt the creatures of the court, inſomuch that he had incurred ſuch loads of debts that he was under a neceſſity of abandoning Rome Tiberius, at the ſame time, ſo loſing his ſon could not bear the ſight of any of the companions of Druſus, as they would remind him of his loſs

Having ſquandered his property, and injured his character, through his profuſion, and being preſſed by creditors without the means of making ſatisfaction Agrippa returned to Judea, and partly through ſhame for his indiſcretion, retired to Malatha, a caſtle in Idumea reſolving there to put an end to a miſerable life Cypros apprehending the moſt fatal effects from the anxiety and terror of his melancholy, wrote to her ſiſter Herodias an account of his very calamitous condition, intreating her, by all the ties of honour and affinity, to afford him ſome aſſiſtance This application ſo far wrought upon Herodias that ſhe prevailed with her huſband to ſend for Agrippa allow him a penſion, and the government of Tiberias, for his preſent maintenance But Herod did not long continue his protection nor did Agrippa diſcover much ſatiſfaction with his ſituation inſomuch that, at a convivial board, Herod reflected upon his poverty, and reproached him with having, by his profuſion, rendered himſelf a dependant on his bounty

Agrippa diſguſted at ſo palpable an affront, betook himſelf to Flaccus a particular friend at Rome, and that time governor of Syria Flaccus gave him a kind reception, having, as a gueſt, Ariſtobulus, who, though his brother was inimical to Agrippa but this circumſtance did not prevent Flaccus from dividing his good offices indiſcriminately betwixt them Ariſtobulus however indulged his ſpleen, and an incident occurred, that furniſhed him with the means of working Flaccus into an unfavourable opinion of Agrippa There was a diſpute betwixt the people of Sidon concerning the limits of their territory The cauſe was to be tried before Flaccus, and the people of Damaſcus being informed of the weight of influence Agrippa had with the governor determined, by a valuable conſideration, to engage him in their intereſt The bargain was ſtruck, and promiſes exchanged, ſo that Agrippa ſtrenuouſly contended for the claim of Damaſcus in oppoſition to that of Sidon Ariſtobulus, finding that his brother was actuated by a pecuniary motive communicated of him to the governor, who, upon examination, and proof of the charge, rejected Agrippa, ſo that being again abandoned to the wide world, he went to Ptolemais with a reſolution of going back again into Italy In this extremity he employed Marſyas, one of his freedmen to procure a ſum of money upon any terms to ſupply his preſent exigencies Marſyas accordingly applied to Protus, a freedman of Bernice, the mother of Agrippa, and his late patroneſs, the, under her will and teſtament had recommended him to the ſervice of Antonia, for the loan of a ſum of money to him on his bond Protus accuſed Agrippa with non-payment of what was already due, and by that means compelled Marſyas, when he made the bond of twenty thouſand attic drachmæ to accept of two thouſand and five hundred leſs than what he deſired

Upon the receipt of this ſupply, Agrippa went to Anthedon, took ſhipping, and prepared himſelf to put to ſea But intelligence of this being given to Herennius Capito, procurator of Jamnia, he ſent a band of ſoldiers to demand of him payment of a debt of three hundred thouſand drachmæ of ſilver, which he borrowed from Cæſar's treaſury when he was at Rome This accident, for a few hours ſuſpended his purpoſe He made fair promiſes, but when night came on, cut his cables, ſtood off to ſea, and ſteered his courſe for Alexandria Upon his arrival, he deſired Alexander, the principal officer of the revenue, to lend him two hundred thouſand drachmæ upon his own ſecurity The officer rejected his requeſt, but complimented his wife upon her known integrity, and offered the loan of the money upon her bond In fine, upon the ſecurity of Cypros, Alexander ſupplied Agrippa with five talents at Alexandria, and letters of credit for the reſt at Puteoli, for he was not willing to venture the whole ſum in his hands together, from a knowledge of his profuſion and extravagance Cypros, finding, by this time, that her huſband was reſolutely bent upon his journey, went back with her children to Judea by land

Agrippa, upon his coming to Puteoli, informed Tiberius Cæſar (who then reſided at Capreæ) by letter, that he was come ſo far to pay him his duty, and requeſted permiſſion to wait upon him Tiberius, without delay returned him the kindeſt anſwer, with aſſurance of his gracious reception at Capreæ, and accordingly upon his arrival, ſaluted him with the greateſt tenderneſs, introduced him into his palace, and entertained him in the moſt ſumptuous and magnificent manner But the day following Cæſar received letters of complaint againſt Agrippa from Herennius Capito, ſetting forth that "being three hundred thouſand drachmæ in the emperor's debt and the money long ſince due, he had only demanded ſatisfaction in the bond, but that Agrippa having ſtolen away to evade juſtice, the emperor was in danger of loſing his money" Tiberius reſented this in ſo heinous a light, that he ordered the officers of his court not to admit Agrippa till he had paid his debt Agrippa took no notice of the emperor's diſpleaſure, but went immediately to Antonia the mother both of Germanicus and of Claudius, (who came afterwards to the empire), and ſetting forth the danger he was in of loſing the favour of Cæſar, for the want of three hundred thouſand drachmæ, obtained the loan of that ſum from her, as a teſtimony of her reſpect to the memory of Bernice, and the friendſhip that had ever ſubſiſted between them With this money he diſcharged the debt and not only re-inſtated himſelf in the emperor's favour, but gained on it upon him, that he committed his grandſon Tiberius, the ſon of Druſus, to his care and government Agrippa was ſo ſenſible of the obligations he had to Antonia, that he paid his court to her grandſon Caius, who was held in general eſteem, both for his own ſake, and the reverence he had for the memory of Germanicus, his father Agrippa found means of borrowing a million of drachmæ from one Thallus, a freedman of Cæſar, part of which he appropriated to the payment of Antonia, and the overplus to the defraying of the expences in his attendance upon Caius, who had now taken him into his greateſt confidence [illegible] [illegible] Caius [illegible] [illegible] [illegible] [illegible] [illegible] on [illegible] Tiberius, as they were riding together [illegible], to [illegible] [illegible], that "[illegible] [illegible] [illegible] and [illegible] [illegible]." [illegible] [illegible] [illegible], who was [illegible] [illegible] [illegible] [illegible] [illegible] [illegible] [illegible] [illegible] [illegible] [illegible] [illegible] upon [illegible] [illegible] of [illegible] [illegible] some wrong [illegible], [illegible] [illegible] [illegible] [illegible] [illegible], and brought before Piso, [illegible] [illegible] [illegible] the cause of it, [illegible] [illegible] [illegible] [illegible] to [illegible] [illegible] [illegible] to his [illegible] [illegible] [illegible] [illegible] [illegible], was sent [illegible] Caius, [illegible] kept in chains by Tiberius, [illegible] [illegible] [illegible] [illegible] [illegible] [illegible] [illegible] [illegible] and [illegible] [illegible] [illegible] [illegible] [illegible] with [illegible], [illegible] [illegible] [illegible] provinces, till he re- [illegible] [illegible] of former deputies, [illegible] [illegible] [illegible] negligent also in hearing the [illegible] [illegible] [illegible] [illegible], by his [illegible] the [illegible] [illegible] [illegible] [illegible], "If [illegible] [illegible] [illegible] [illegible] [illegible], they, of course, [illegible] [illegible] [illegible] [illegible] places, to [illegible] [illegible] [illegible] [illegible] [illegible] no [illegible] ambition. With respect to officers, whose places are once filled, [illegible] [illegible] the [illegible] to keep [illegible] to change them, so [illegible] [illegible] [illegible] [illegible] covetous, and more so when they suppose their offices will not be of long duration.

[illegible] [illegible] the true character of Tiberius needs no other proof than that, during the course of a reign of [illegible] [illegible] years, he sent only two governors into Judea, which were Gratus, and his successor, Pilate, and that he [illegible] the [illegible] in all other parts of the empire. The reason he gave for the [illegible] in bringing prisoners to their trial, [illegible] [illegible] them the longer in [illegible] and to punish them for their just crimes, by a lingering torment worse than death itself.

This was the true cause of Eutychus being kept so long in chains before Caius could [illegible] to [illegible] [illegible]. [illegible], after some time coming from Capreæ to Tusculanum, about [illegible] [illegible] from Rome, Agrippa desired Antonia to move [illegible] [illegible] [illegible] that he might have a hearing, that it might be known what he had to object against his person. Tiberius [illegible] [illegible] [illegible] to Antonia, [illegible] [illegible] though consanguinity, as [illegible] [illegible] [illegible], and [illegible] widow of Drusus, and [illegible] [illegible] [illegible] [illegible] or [illegible] virtue in the denial of a second marriage, though [illegible] [illegible] importuned by Augustus himself. Besides these [illegible], Tiberius had [illegible] [illegible] obligations to Antonia, [illegible] [illegible] [illegible] been [illegible] her [illegible], faith, and industry, that [illegible] [illegible] [illegible] of [illegible] [illegible] Sejanus, had certainly cost him his life. As he was [illegible] of power and credit, the captain of his guards had engaged several men of senatorial dignity, divers of Cæsar's freedmen, court favourites and military officers [illegible] the conspiracy. Sejanus had certainly gained his point had not the vigilance and resolution of Antonia defeated his schemes: for when [illegible] [illegible] [illegible] his designs against Tiberius, she wrote him an exact account of the whole, gave the letter to Pallas, the most trusty of her servants, and sent it to the emperor at Capreæ. By virtue of this discovery, both the conspiracy itself, and the agents concerned in it, were brought to light, and justice done upon Sejanus and his [illegible]. This added to Cæsar's former obligations to her, who, with propriety, could deny her no request. So that, upon the importunity of Agrippa, she pressed Tiberius to give Eutychus a hearing. The emperor consented, observing, that, if Eutychus had traduced Agrippa, he must abide by the consequence, and, on the other hand, if the accusation upon enquiry, appeared to be true, the punishment would certainly fall upon the criminal. Antonia gave Agrippa [illegible] [illegible], [illegible] the more [illegible] [illegible] [illegible] [illegible] [illegible] [illegible] [illegible] [illegible] to bring it to a [illegible] scrutiny; insomuch, that Antonia, when she found he would [illegible]

[illegible] [illegible] death, [illegible] [illegible] [illegible] [illegible] [illegible] [illegible] [illegible] preferring a request, that Eutychus might be [illegible] and heard. He [illegible] [illegible] [illegible] appealed to [illegible], but [illegible] he was about to [illegible] [illegible] [illegible] [illegible] [illegible] [illegible] [illegible] with [illegible] [illegible].

[illegible] [illegible] commanded Macro, [illegible] [illegible] to [illegible] [illegible] [illegible] [illegible] [illegible] [illegible] [illegible] [illegible] [illegible] [illegible] [illegible] [illegible] [illegible], and [illegible] [illegible] [illegible] [illegible], [illegible] him [illegible] the [illegible] [illegible] [illegible] [illegible], who [illegible] [illegible] [illegible] [illegible] He [illegible], with [illegible] [illegible], "[illegible] [illegible] one day driving Caius and Agrippa, [illegible] [illegible] [illegible] the [illegible] [illegible] [illegible] [illegible] that [illegible] between them, and [illegible] [illegible] [illegible] [illegible], [illegible] [illegible] from Agrippa, [illegible] [illegible] [illegible] [illegible] [illegible] [illegible] might be taken off [illegible] [illegible] [illegible] [illegible] to the [illegible]," [illegible] [illegible] [illegible] [illegible] [illegible] [illegible] [illegible] [illegible]. Tiberius was disposed to believe [illegible] [illegible] [illegible] [illegible] [illegible] [illegible] incensed at Agrippa, because that, after his having committed the care of his grandson to him, he [illegible] [illegible] [illegible] wholly to the service of Caius. [illegible] [illegible], [illegible] [illegible], turning to Macro, exclaimed, "[illegible] [illegible] [illegible]" [illegible], [illegible] [illegible] [illegible] to whom Tiberius [illegible], [illegible] [illegible] [illegible] that man? The emperor [illegible] [illegible], [illegible] [illegible] [illegible] [illegible] [illegible] [illegible] [illegible] [illegible] [illegible] [illegible] [illegible] [illegible], [illegible] [illegible] [illegible], by the [illegible] [illegible] [illegible] [illegible] the memory of [illegible], [illegible] [illegible] [illegible] [illegible] [illegible] [illegible] be [illegible] accused, and for the [illegible] [illegible] [illegible] [illegible] [illegible] [illegible] to [illegible] [illegible] [illegible] [illegible] [illegible] [illegible] [illegible] [illegible] [illegible] were in vain, so that [illegible] was dragged [illegible] to prison in his purple robes [illegible] [illegible] [illegible] him. The [illegible] being extremely hot, and [illegible], [illegible] [illegible] [illegible] for the service [illegible] [illegible] [illegible] [illegible] [illegible] [illegible] [illegible] [illegible] to [illegible] [illegible] Caius to [illegible] him his freedom. Nor [illegible] [illegible] [illegible] [illegible] [illegible], [illegible] [illegible] he [illegible] [illegible] came to the crown, he procured [illegible] [illegible] [illegible] [illegible] [illegible] him [illegible] [illegible] [illegible] [illegible] [illegible], [illegible] his death recommended him to his son Agrippa [illegible] Bernice his daughter, to continue him in [illegible] [illegible], wherein he acquitted himself with great honour [illegible] the remainder of his life.

As Agrippa [illegible] [illegible] [illegible] chains before the palace, with others of his fellow-prisoners, and leaning in a melancholy posture against a tree, there came an owl and perched upon it. A German, that was there in bonds, observing it, enquired of one of the soldiers, who that man in purple was? Being informed that he was a Jew of the first rank in point of extraction, he desired [illegible] [illegible] to [illegible] him to approach in order to speak to him, as he wished to enquire concerning [illegible] things relating to his country. This being granted, the German, by an interpreter, thus addressed him: "[illegible] [illegible], young man, "this sudden and surprizing change [illegible] [illegible] [illegible] you "down, nor will you [illegible] [illegible] [illegible] how near your "deliverance approaches under the [illegible] and protection "of a Divine Providence that watches over you. I call "the gods to witness, both [illegible] and ours, by whose "permission we are here in bonds, that I speak not this to "amuse and flatter you with vain [illegible], for well I know "that prognosticks of this kind, if the event does not accord with the prediction, aggravate [illegible] [illegible] [illegible] "the ills of life. But I deem it my incumbent duty [illegible] "[illegible], to assure you, that you will experience such "a change of times and things, as [illegible] [illegible] you, "from this state of misery and dejection to the highest "pinnacle of honour and power [illegible] [illegible] [illegible] the envy "of those who either despised or pitied you before. Th[illegible] "[illegible] [illegible] of [illegible] [illegible] shall [illegible] [illegible], [illegible] [illegible] [illegible] "[illegible] children behind you to [illegible] [illegible] [illegible] [illegible] [illegible] [illegible] "[illegible] [illegible] [illegible] [illegible], [illegible] [illegible] [illegible] see this bird "[illegible] the fifth day after it will be your last. This is the "[illegible] what you are given to understand by the good "[illegible] My revelation is certain, and I deliver you the truth "to support you in your present trouble, with the hope of "better things to come. I am not to deceive you further, "[illegible] you find these things come to pass, you will "[illegible] get your fellow-sufferers, [illegible] consult the deliverance "of those you leave behind you."

The prophecy of this German appeared as [illegible] and improbable to Agrippa, in the relation, as it was afterwards wonderful and surprising in the accomplishment. Antonia, in the mean time, was deeply [illegible] by the hard usage of her friend; but taking it for granted, that Tiberius was not to be wrought upon, and that all applications and intercessions would therefore be in vain, all that she could do was to prevail with Macro, to render [illegible] somewhat more tolerable, by setting affable tractable men as guards over him, allowing him to sit at table with the officers who had him in custody, and giving access to his friends that were disposed to visit him. All this was accordingly granted, insomuch that Silas, his friend, and Marsyas and Stechus, two of his freedmen, brought him the most acceptable diet, and afforded him many other indulgencies under the connivance of the soldiers, from the hints they had received from Macro.

When Agrippa had remained in confinement six months, Tiberius, upon his return to Capreæ, was taken with an indisposition, which increased upon him to such a degree, that he had no hopes of recovery. Perceiving his case desperate, he sent Evodus, a freeman, in whom he confided, to bring his children to him early the next morning, to take their leaves of their dying father. I would here be understood as speaking of adopted children, for he had none of his own, Drusus, his only son, being deceased: but Tiberius, surnamed Gemellus, the son of Drusus, was living, as was Caius, the son of his brother Germanicus, who had now attained to man's estate, and possessed most excellent accomplishments. He was the darling of the people, from the reverence they had for the memory of his father's virtues, who was a prince of the greatest moderation, affability, and condescension. This illustrious example not only gained the favour of the senate and people of Rome, but of the provinces in general that were subject to the empire, which he conciliated by every good office, and token of justice and humanity. His death, at [illegible], was not so much celebrated with external pomp and show, as with tears flowing from real affection and compunction of heart: for the whole body of the people lamented the death of this prince as if each individual subject had lost a father. The reputation of Germanicus tended greatly to the interest of his son Caius, [illegible] particularly recommended him to the soldiers, who were ready to lay down their lives for his service.

Tiberius, having given orders to Evodus to bring his sons to him the next morning, he prayed to the gods of his country to direct him, by some manifest signal, as to the appointment to the succession. He gave himself the preference to Tiberius, but durst not venture to pre-judge or determine in a point of such importance, without consulting the oracle. He then proposed to govern himself by this token, that he of the two that came first to him in the morning should be his successor. Having thus resolved, he gave it in charge to the tutor of Tiberius, his grandson, to bring his pupil to him by break of day, taking it for granted that the sign he requested would be in his favour. But it fell out otherwise; for upon his sending Evodus, by peep of day, to bring in him whom he should first see, he found only Caius, and accordingly informed him that the emperor required his presence. Tiberius, it seems, not suspecting the importance of the business upon which he was to attend, had rather loitered than hastened upon the occasion.

The emperor was not a little startled at the sight of Caius, considering in what manner Providence had defeated him in his design of disposing of the government, by setting [illegible] contrary to [illegible] [illegible]. [illegible] he was more [illegible] that [illegible] [illegible], by apprehension for the [illegible] [illegible] his grandson, than for [illegible] the empire [illegible] [illegible] [illegible] power must [illegible] [illegible] kindred [illegible] amongst [illegible] [illegible] [illegible] [illegible] took [illegible] [illegible] [illegible] [illegible] other.

Tiberius had been very much given to astrology, and the calculation of nativities, and had governed his actions, in a great measure, by the direction of wizards and fortune-tellers. Accordingly, happening once to cast his eye upon Galba, he turned to some particular friends about him, and exclaimed, "That man will be emperor of Rome." Upon the whole, none of the emperors were so much addicted to divination as Tiberius. But nothing touched him so sensibly as this foreboding encounter of the two [illegible]; [illegible] which wrought upon him in such a manner, that he gave his grandson for lost, abandoned himself to a kind of despair, and involved himself in perplexed researches into the decrees of Providence, that are wisely concealed from mortals, though he might have lived happily in a patient resignation to the will of heaven. Though he was much dissatisfied [illegible] unexpected resolution of the government for those to whom he did not intend it, yet deeming it a point of expediency to speak upon the occasion, he delivered himself to the following effect:

"I need not tell you, Caius, that Tiberius is nearer to "me in blood; yet, upon consulting the will of the immortal gods, and my own reason, I do hereby transfer the "government of the Roman empire to your hands. I do "likewise adjure you, that, in the exercise of this power, "you never forget the obligation you have to him from "whom you received it, and that you shew your gratitude "to your patron by every demonstration of love and friendship to your brother Tiberius. [illegible] nothing [illegible] "[illegible] for the dignity I have now conferred upon you (for "next to the gods you owe it all to me) than that you be "[illegible] [illegible] [illegible] thing to him, whom nature [illegible] "made [illegible] [illegible]. I am farther to remind "you, that [illegible] as much your interest as your duty to follow "my injunction, for the security and splendor of your own "fortune depends, in a great measure, upon the [illegible] "[illegible] of your brother, and the day of his death will be "the [illegible] of your misery. Sovereignty is a giddy slippery "height, and a dangerous ascent for a man to stand upon "alone, because crimes against the ties of consanguinity and "nature, never fail of being followed by Divine vengeance." These were the last words of Tiberius to Caius, who promised punctual obedience in every point, though it was evident, from the result, he never intended it, for he no sooner possessed the command, than he put his brother to death, and he himself, according to the presage of Tiberius, was assassinated some years after.

Tiberius, having declared Caius his successor, within a few days after departed this life, having reigned twenty-two years, five months, and thirteen days. Caius was now the fourth in the roll of the emperors. The rumour of the death of Tiberius was grateful to the Romans, though they durst not venture upon the truth of it, being fearful lest, through their credulity, they might discover a satisfaction that would subject them to the information of spies, and be attended with certain death. Tiberius was in disposition [illegible] and inexorable to the highest degree; his passion was easily inflamed, and his resentment was implacable. He conceived aversion without cause, and executed vengeance without decency, pronouncing the rigorous sentence of death to the slightest offences. It therefore concerned the people to be cautious, as to the discovery of their joy for the report, considering the [illegible] danger of being found in a mistake.

Marsyas, Agrippa's freeman, no sooner heard of the death of Tiberius, than he posted with the glad tidings to his patron, whom he found going into a bath, and ad-

[illegible] in the Hebrew tongue, "The lion is dead!" Agrippa [illegible] understood his meaning, and bursting forth into a kind of [illegible] "How can I requite thee for this, and [illegible] other good offices that thou hast rendered me, if it be [illegible]?" The officer who had Agrippa in custody, observing the haste with which Marsyas delivered the message, and the rapture with which Agrippa received it, and concluding that the words implied some great import, [illegible] Agrippa to give him an explanation. He at first declined it, but upon being pressed, told him in confidence the whole story. The officer congratulated him on the good news, and treated him with a sumptuous regale; but, as they were in the [illegible] of their conviviality, [illegible] longer arrived with advice that the emperor was past danger, and would [illegible] come to town. These words threw the officer into the greatest confusion, from a consciousness that he had forfeited his head, by regaling with a state prisoner upon the news of Cæsar's death. He therefore pushed Agrippa, in a rage, from his seat, and exclaimed, "Dost thou think to impose upon me with a lie, concerning the death of the emperor, without punishment? Be assured, that thy head shall be the price of this [illegible]." He then ordered him into chains again, and a stronger guard to be kept over him than before.

When Agrippa had passed the night in this aggravated state of misery, [illegible] of the death of Tiberius reached the next day, [illegible] that it was publicly spoken of, and [illegible] offerings of gratitude. [illegible] Caius, one to the senate, to inform them, that [illegible] had declared him his successor, and the other to Piso, governor of the city, to the same purpose, giving orders also, that Agrippa should be discharged the prison, and allowed the liberty of the house he had before his confinement, so that he was now out of all danger, and, though in custody, in [illegible] of freedom.

Upon the return of Caius to Rome with the body of Tiberius, the funeral obsequies were performed with the utmost pomp and solemnity. The emperor would have discharged Agrippa the same day. But Antonia objected to it, not from any ill will, but because it would be deemed an instance of disrespect to the memory of Tiberius, to set free his prisoner so hastily. However in the course of a few days, Caius sent for him home, caused him to be shaved, and to put on royal habiliments, put a diadem upon his head, and made him successor to Philip's tetrarchy. He also gave him the tetrarchy of Lysanias, and changed his iron chain for a golden one of the same weight. Marcellus at the same time was sent governor into Judæa.

In the second year of the reign of Caius Cæsar, Agrippa requested permission to go home, in order to settle the affairs of his government, with a promise of returning at a stated time. The people, on his arrival, were astonished to see him [illegible] upon his head; though it demonstrated to them the vicissitude of human events, in the sudden change from the extreme of one condition to that of another. Some looked upon him as the happiest of men, whilst others were so amazed at the circumstances of the revolution, that they could scarcely believe even what they saw.

CHAP. IX.

The envy of Herodias. She presses her husband to apply to Cæsar. [illegible] Herod with much reluctance, consents. Fortunatus sent by Agrippa as [illegible] of accusation exhibited against Herod. Conspiracy of Sejanus and Artabanus against Caius. Herod confesses, and [illegible] to perpetual exile. Caius [illegible] at first, but afterwards presumptuously arrogates to himself Divine honours.

HERODIAS, the sister of Agrippa, and wife of Herod, the tetrarch of Galilee and Peræa (the country beyond Jordan) became envious at the present condition of her brother, who, from a state of penury and dejection, was now advanced to splendor, dignity, and power, above her husband. Her haughty spirit was particularly [illegible] at seeing him appear in all the pomp and magnificence of royalty, and exhibited himself as a public spectacle to the multitude. In the violence of her passion, she urged her husband to go immediately to Rome, and intreat Cæsar to confer on him the same honours. In order to incite him to compliance, she represented, "that it would be death to her to see her husband, who was the son of a king, and stood in the high affections of the people, as well as in his pretensions to the succession, stand [illegible], and behold the son of Aristobulus, a bankrupt, and [illegible] that had [illegible] under the hands of justice, [illegible] to a throne." She also observed, "that if Herod had hitherto patiently [illegible] with the dignity of his father's [illegible], it was now time to exert himself in vindication of the honour of his family, without suffering himself to own the superiority of a wretch who had been a dependant on his bounty." She therefore insisted on their going immediately to Rome at any expence, as money could not possibly be applied to a better use than that of obtaining a kingdom.

Herod, from a natural love of ease, and an unfavourable opinion of the court of Rome, used every means to divert his wife from her design; but the more he refused the more she pressed him, having formed an unconquerable resolution to pursue her point at all events. In fine she was so urgent, that he seemed under a necessity, in his own defence, of complying with her importunities, so that they set off for Rome together with an equipage suitable to the dignity and importance of [illegible].

Agrippa, having intelligence of every [illegible], resolved on the means of counteracting [illegible] sent his [illegible] certain Fortunatus, [illegible] presents for the emperor, and [illegible] should sail for Rome, he was to put [illegible] particular instructions as to his mode of proceeding on his arrival. Fortunatus [illegible] and arrived at Puteoli at the same time with Herod. But Caius happened at that time to be at the Baiæ, a small town in Campania, about five furlongs from Puteoli [illegible] famous for grand apartments in the royal palaces, the emperors, that frequented the hot baths there, striving to outdo each other in the magnificence and convenience of their buildings.

Herod, on coming to this place, paid his dutiful obedience to the emperor, and Fortunatus immediately after presented his letters. The emperor on perusal, found them to contain a direct charge against Herod, first, for being a party in the confederacy of Sejanus against Tiberius, and now for joining with Artabanus, king of Parthia, against the government of Caius, as a demonstration of which he alledged, that he had then a magazine of arms sufficient for seventy thousand men. Caius, moved at this information, demanded of Herod, whether he had such a store of arms or not? The fact was so clear that he could not deny it: so that the emperor, deeming this sufficient ground of evidence for treason, took away his government, and gave it to Agrippa, with his money also, as a reward for his discovery. He sentenced Herod to exile during life, and fixed Lyons, a city of Gaul, for the place of his residence. As for Herodias, whom he knew to be the sister of Agrippa, he gave her the full command of what [illegible] to her; and, without making her a partner in the husband's calamity, promised to treat her with [illegible] for the sake of her brother. But Herodias spurned his offered favours, declared she was not in a condition to enjoy the benefit of his bounty, nor could she, after having shared in her husband's better fortunes, now abandon him in adversity. This greatness of mind, laudable as it was, gave such offence to Caius that, though in respect of its being an [illegible] of [illegible], he banished and confined the one to the other. [illegible] this seems to have been [illegible] ment inflicted on her for the malignity of her envy to the success of her brother, as also a punishment on Herod for being over-ruled by a vain, ambitious, and impetuous woman.

The reign of Caius, during the two first years of his government, was prudent and moderate, and his conduct gained exceedingly on the people both at Rome itself, and in the provinces. But such was the pride and vanity of his heart, in the contemplation of his greatness and dignity, that, after a time, he assumed to himself to be more than mortal, blasphemed the higher powers, and had the audacity to usurp to himself divine honours.

CHAP. X.

Tumult at Alexandria between the Jews and the Greeks. Three persons are sent as an embassy to Caius. Apion's accusation against the Jews on the part of the Greeks. Philo's reply to [illegible].

A TUMULT having arisen at Alexandria, betwixt the Jews and the Greeks, three ambassadors were chosen from each party at that place, and sent to Caius to decide the matter. Apion was the chief on the part of the Greeks, as was Philo on the part of the Jews. The principal allegation of Apion against the Jews was, "that whereas temples and altars were erected by all the subjects of the Roman empire elsewhere in honour of Caius, and the same adoration paid to the emperor as to the rest of the gods, the Jews alone refused [illegible] to dedicate images to Caius, or to swear by his name." Apion began with this invective, and used his utmost efforts to inflame Caius against the Jews. But Philo, the brother of Alexander, chief officer of the revenue, and a man of [illegible] literary abilities, standing up in defence of the Jews against the allegations of Apion, Caius, in a violent rage, commanded him to depart. Philo, on his choler re[illegible], turned to the Jews, who were about him, and bade them be of good courage, adding [illegible], "Now Caius is against us, God will be for us."

CHAP. XI.

[illegible] Petronius [illegible] The Jews expostulate with Petronius, and collect [illegible] Aristobulus, [illegible] who desire Petronius to lay the case before Caius. Petronius [illegible] and summons the Jews to Tiberias. [illegible] to Cæsar, [illegible] that Agrippa gives a splendid entertainment to Cæsar, who promises [illegible] Agrippa requests him to revoke the [illegible] to Petronius. Caius grants his request. A [illegible] among the Jews. Caius sends a [illegible] letter to Petronius. His death.

CAIUS was so highly offended at the imagined insult of the Jews in standing in defiance of his orders, that he sent Petronius to take upon him the government of Syria instead of Vitellius, directing him to enter Judea with a powerful army, and set up his statue in the temple. He was further instructed, if they refused compliance with his commands, to enforce compulsion by dint of arms. Petronius accordingly took upon himself the government, and hastened with all possible expedition, to execute the commands of Cæsar. To this end he collected a body of auxiliaries, which, with two Roman legions, he put into winter quarters in Ptolemais, to be ready to march early in the ensuing spring. He wrote an account of his proceedings, from time to time, to Caius, who commended his zeal and attention, and encouraged him to his conduct, being resolved, as he declared, to punish the contumacy of those stubborn people.

There came at this time multitudes of Jews to Petronius at Ptolemais, to [illegible] not to compel them to transgress, and violate the laws of their forefathers, [illegible] that if he was determined to erect statues in their temple he must first take their lives, for that as long as they had breath they could not suffer such things to be done as were directly prohibited by their great and much revered legislator. Petronius sternly replied, "that if he were at his own liberty, their petitions might have an effect, but that being under Cæsar's command he must [illegible] obey Cæsar's order." The Jews, in answer said, "that he could not depart from his master's order, neither could they from theirs; and that through Divine assistance, they were resolved to tread in the steps of their forefathers [illegible], that they preferred the consideration of eternity to that of time, and the preservation of their religion and laws, to that of their lives and fortunes; that their trust was in the providence and protection of the Almighty; and that, in fine, they [illegible] it to his determination, whether they should obey the voice of heaven, or the voice of Caius."

Petronius gathering from this discourse that they were inflexible in their resolution, and that without a profusion of blood, he could not be subservient to Caius in the dedication of his statue, took some friends and attendants with him, and hastened to Tiberias, to the [illegible] instance of being more particularly informed of the manners, customs and affairs of the people [illegible] to call. The Jews were alarmed at the approach of the Romans, not so much from the apprehension of [illegible] as an invasion upon their religion and laws, so that many thousands went in a body to Petronius, most passionately requesting him, not to drive the multitude to the last desperation, by offering to prophane the temple with forbidden images. Petronius then exclaimed, "Will you go to war with Cæsar without considering his mighty preparations, and your own weakness?" They replied, "We would not, by any means, wage war with him, but we are still determined to die rather than live to see the violation of our laws." Upon this they cast themselves upon the ground, laid bare their necks, intimating thereby that they were resigned to death. In this manner they passed forty days, without attending to the business of husbandry, though the season of the year required it. Indeed, the common offices of life were wholly neglected, as they were unanimously resolved rather to die than be spectators of the dedication of the statue.

While matters were in this state, Aristobulus, the brother of king Agrippa, and Helcias, surnamed the Great, with several of the first rank among the Jews, applied themselves to Petronius, desiring him, "as he saw the resolution of the multitude, not to proceed to such measures as would drive them to despair, but rather to inform Caius of the difficulty of the undertaking, and the inflexible resolution of the party, who had neglected all the offices of life not from the least principle of disloyalty, but a determination rather to die than suffer the violation of their religion and laws." They suggested also, "that in consideration that this neglect of their husbandry must of necessity expose the country to rapine, and cut the inhabitants from paying their taxes, might induce Cæsar to relent, and consequently remove all cause for a rebellion, or that, if nothing could divert him from entering on a war, he must use his pleasure." This was the purport of their address, as delivered by Aristobulus.

Petronius was no stranger to the revengeful temper of Caius, especially upon any delay in the execution of his commands; but such were the horrors of his conscience, when he thought of sacrificing so many lives to [illegible] frantic fury, that from this consideration, together with the rank and credit of the intercessors, the importance of the affair, and the danger of driving an obstinate people into desperation, he came to a resolution, at all hazards, of laying the state of the case plainly before Caius, reflecting, that, though he might incur his hatred [illegible]

[illegible] the [illegible] were [illegible] moved to [illegible], to [illegible] which, from [illegible], [illegible] the [illegible] on him.

[illegible] turn'd [illegible], summoning [illegible] people [illegible], where he attended in great num[illegible] upon the occasion. "[illegible] my own will [illegible] done, [illegible] I have under[illegible] [illegible] commands of Caius. I need [illegible] the danger [illegible] deferring the execution of my [illegible] orders, [illegible] (which I never [illegible] will not be [illegible] with) to [illegible] to [illegible] instrument [illegible] me to fulfil the [illegible] whom [illegible] my [illegible]. But [illegible] the [illegible] stand, I [illegible] not to much [illegible] my [illegible] "[illegible] the [illegible] shall [illegible] experience of [illegible] on [illegible] I [illegible] secret [illegible] to Caius, and [illegible] "[illegible] the [illegible], nor [illegible] any thing [illegible] "[illegible], that can move him to comply with every [illegible] can [illegible] the Divine Prov[idence] [illegible] powers [illegible] [illegible] of the [illegible] may be due to my pre[illegible] sent [illegible]. [illegible] to [illegible] to fall under [illegible] to the loss of fortune, [illegible] that I may [illegible] the destruction of [illegible] good men for [illegible]-doing. Let [illegible] to his own home [illegible] Rome [illegible] and [illegible] the [illegible] with the [illegible], and [illegible] "[illegible] to give [illegible] all "[illegible] satisfaction." [illegible] the [illegible].

Petronius [illegible] to the Jews [illegible] contrary to [illegible] expectation [illegible]. This hap[illegible] [illegible] of [illegible] it [illegible] with [illegible] law, as [illegible] the prayers of Petronius [illegible] behalf. [illegible] Petronius [illegible], as [illegible] appeared [illegible] in favour of the Jews, that [illegible] would not bear the least [illegible] of con[illegible]. He [illegible] in his report to the empe[illegible]ror, and [illegible] necessary points before him, representing the consequences of [illegible] of resolute [illegible] to extremities, [illegible] no [illegible] desperate, as nothing but absolute force would ever compel them to desist. But [illegible] the violent prosecution of them, he would [illegible] his own revenue, and [illegible] punishment [illegible] to his reproach, and [illegible] that the Jews were a people accept[illegible]able to God, who had given them many wonderful tokens of his peculiar f[avour].

King Agrippa [illegible] Rome [illegible] time, and was insinuating himself [illegible] into the graces of the emperor, to [illegible] whose esteem was his whole study and application. To this end he prepared an enter[illegible]tainment for Caius, which, for variety, [illegible], delicacy, order, and expence, exceeded every thing of the kind that went before, not excepting the most sumptuous regales of Caius himself. Caius was so charmed with the magnificence of the treat, and the hearty welcome of the donor, that he determined to enter into a kind of competition, and vie with him in good offices. When [illegible] were [illegible] with generous wine, he [illegible] disclosed his mind [illegible] to this import: "[illegible] the first proof, Agrippa, I have had of your friendship and affection. In the days of Tiberius, I had [illegible] evidences of [illegible], [illegible] you have now obliged me to your [illegible] excessive [illegible] that you have conferred my honour [illegible] the [illegible] of [illegible] your [illegible] it would be [illegible] of my character to suffer myself to be overcome [illegible] benefits. I am therefore resolved to make compensation by the ad[illegible]vancement of your station and [illegible], as well as your fortune." Upon this frank and unlimited promise, Caius imagined that Agrippa would have mentioned commissions, provinces, or ample revenues. But Agrippa, having [illegible] determined [illegible] of his boon, suspended the declaration of it till he could introduce it with a better grace, and contented [illegible] with this answer: "As I had no private views, [illegible] in the little services I did you in the time of Tibe[illegible]rius, so I propose nothing more to myself at present, than [illegible] the [illegible] and happiness of your favour and protection. [illegible] You have done more for me already than I could [illegible] "[illegible] expect; and though I am persuaded you have greater "[illegible] in your power, [illegible] to make this profession "with grateful acknowledgments for what I have received, "that I neither deserve nor seek for any thing farther."

Caius was so amazed at the [illegible] of Agrippa, that he urged him to prefer his request, assuring him that no[illegible]thing should be denied him. Agrippa then thus addressed [illegible]: "Since, Sir, you are so generous as to lay this kind command upon me, I [illegible] presume to offer you [illegible] request. It will be neither riches, nor honours, "[illegible], though your bounty, I enjoy a plenitude of them. "The grant of my request will recommend you to the "[illegible] both of God and man, and it will redound to "[illegible] honour [illegible], if I can obtain this concession, [illegible] to many others to crown all the [illegible], [illegible] "that you will be pleased to revoke your orders to Petro[illegible]nius for setting up your [illegible] in the temple of the "Jews." Agrippa was conscious that he preferred this request at the [illegible]. Caius, however, though [illegible] in the entertainment, and the [illegible] of refusing a request he had himself exhorted, to[illegible]gether with the [illegible] paid to the modesty and [illegible] of the petitioner, immediately complied, and wrote to Petronius, approving his general conduct, and [illegible], if the statue was erected to let it remain, [illegible] not, to trouble himself no further about it, but disband his army, and return to Syria; assuring him, at the same time, that he remitted the punishment due to [illegible] contempt of his orders [illegible] the instance of Agrippa, for whom he entertained so great a respect, that he could deny him nothing.

This was the substance of the emperor's letter to Petro[illegible]nius, which was written before he had the least intima[illegible]tion of an insurrection intended amongst the Jews: but, upon receiving intelligence that they were ready to revolt, [illegible] fell into such a burst of passion, to find his authority [illegible] by that obstinate people, that he immediate[illegible]ly changed his style, and wrote a second letter to Petro[illegible]nius to this effect: "Since you appear to prefer the Jews' "[illegible] to my commands, [illegible] your neglecting the "one to obtain the other, judge [illegible] "to expect from my [illegible] and justice. I am resolved "to make an example of you, both to the present age and "to posterity, that all the world may know that sovereign "power is not to be defied." This letter was sent to Petronius by Caius; but he did not receive it while Caius was living, for the letter [illegible] having a lingering passage, he received letters in the mean time with intelligence of the death of the emperor. It seems to have been a kind [illegible] of Providence in favour of Petronius for the zeal he had shewn, and the dangers he had undergone [illegible] of his own honour, and the religion of the Jews. [illegible] Caius being cut off in the eve of his blasphe[illegible]mous vanity in arrogating to himself Divine honours, Petronius had the thanks of the Romans, as well as of the Jews, for his [illegible] services to the public upon that occasion, and [illegible] especially the [illegible] of [illegible] instances, [illegible] contempt [illegible] he had written the letter to Petronius, denouncing his death. But the ground of the conspiracy and the manner of executing it, we shall treat of upon a future occasion. The news of the emperor's death to Petronius, was followed by the letter that contained the menace of his own: and as he could not, under those circumstances, but rejoice at the former, so neither could he but admire the Divine Providence, that in the same instant, rewarded the veneration he had paid to the holy temple, and his deliverance of the Jews out of their distress. Thus was the life of Petronius wonderfully preserved.

CHAP. XII.

Origin of the calamities of the Jews in Babylon and Mesopotamia. The ancient treasure of Neerda and Nisibis, two strong places upon the Euphrates. Asinæus and Anilæus, [illegible] form [illegible] build an impregnable fort. [illegible] king of Parthia [illegible]. [illegible] of the approach of the enemy. The law of necessity a justification for the [illegible]. Asinæus totally routs the enemy. Artabanus courts the alliance of the two brothers. The Parthian general [illegible] the king's [illegible] to put Asinæus to death, but [illegible]. Artabanus advises Asinæus to [illegible] and [illegible] the command of Babylon. The brothers [illegible] [illegible] by falling from the religion and [illegible] of their country. Anilæus becomes enamoured of a Parthian woman, slays her husband and takes her to [illegible]. [illegible] to idolatry, and a general [illegible] against Asinæus, who is at length poisoned [illegible]. Anilæus breaks in upon Mithridates and [illegible] booty. Mithridates [illegible] his army [illegible] fighting [illegible] the sabbath. Anilæus [illegible] Mithridates [illegible], and routs his army. [illegible] [illegible] total defeat. The Jews and Babylonians [illegible], but cannot come to an [illegible]. The Greeks and Syrians [illegible] the Jews, of whom upwards of fifty thousand are slain.

THE Jews of Mesopotamia and Babylon were now in a more calamitous state than had ever been known heretofore. It is therefore necessary to trace the origin of the various evils that befel them.

There is, in the province of Babylon, a city, called Neerda, very populous, and fruitful in soil, as well as fortified and encompassed by the river Euphrates. Near it is another strong city, called Nisibis, upon the same river. The Jews depending on the strength of these two places, deposited the common stock of their sacred treasure, as it was brought in and dedicated, from time to time, according to custom. From hence it was transmitted to Jerusalem, in the proper season, under strong convoys, for fear of the ravages of the Parthians, to whom the Babylonians were then subject. There were among the Jews of Neerda two brothers, Asinæus and Anilæus. Their father being dead, they were put out by their mother, to learn the art of weaving and making [illegible]-cloth, which amongst the inhabitants of that place, was accounted no disparagement. Having been remiss in their attention to business, they were punished by their superintendant, which they resented very highly, armed themselves with the weapons that were kept in the factory, and went to a certain place upon the partition of the river, where was great plenty of corn, grass, fruit, and all manner of provision for a winter store. While they continued in this retreat, a successive band of youthful, daring adventurers enlisted themselves under their command, so that they acted without controul. By the assistance of this party, they built an impregnable fort, and then sent their emissaries to raise contributions throughout the adjacent country, with [illegible] of friendship and protection to [illegible] who [illegible] [illegible] menaces against those who refused [illegible]

were, compelled to a compliance with their requisition, they became, in a short time, so numerous and powerful, as to defy opposition, insomuch that the king of Parthia was alarmed at their conduct.

The governor of Babylon receiving intelligence of these proceedings, determined to suppress them in their rise, and, to that end collected his troops, both out of Parthia and Babylon, and marched with all expedition, in order to surprize them. When he had advanced through by-ways to the skirts of a lake, he made a halt, and depending that (the next day being the sabbath) they would not dare to fight, proceeded gradually, thinking to fall upon them suddenly, and make them prisoners without resistance.

But Asinæus, who was at that time sitting upon a bank, with his companions and arms about him, imagining he heard the neighing of horses, and the champing of the bits, in order to obviate the circumvention of an enemy, proposed that scouts should be dispatched to make discovery. They were accordingly sent out, and, in a short time, hastily returned, with assurance, that the apprehension of Asinæus was well founded, as the enemy was at hand, and upon the very point of executing their revenge. The scouts added, that they had cavalry enough to over-run and trample them under-foot, while many urged, that they were restrained by their religion from making resistance on the sabbath-day. But Asinæus was of a different opinion, and represented the folly and pusillanimity of suffering themselves to be tamely butchered to gratify a barbarous enemy. He then propounded to them the law of necessity and self-preservation, as the most powerful of all motives, encouraged them to follow his example, that, at all events, they might not fall unrevenged, and so commit the rest to Providence. Animated by the exhortation of their leaders, the party of Asinæus boldly advanced to the combat, and finding the enemy in a careless supine posture, as if ready to take possession of victory, rather than dispute it, they fell upon them, slew great numbers, and put the rest to flight.

The intrepidity of the two brothers, upon the news of this defeat, alarmed the king of Parthia to that degree, that he became desirous of an interview with them, and, to that end dispatched one of his guards, in whom he most confided, with a message purporting, "that he had a commission from Artabanus, king of Parthia, to inform "Asinæus and Anilæus, that, although he had been unjustly treated by them, in making inroads upon his territories, he was ready to bury past injuries in oblivion, "from the character he had heard of their personal bravery "that, in the name of his master, and without any fraud or "indirect meaning, he desired to enter into a league of "friendship with them: that he had to offer them, upon "his faith and honour, all assurances they could possibly "desire of security in their journies, backwards and forwards, and lastly that they would find the king a magnificent and generous prince, ready, upon all occasions, to give them farther proofs of his gracious intentions."

Notwithstanding the frankness of the invitation, Asinæus from cause of suspicion, declined the visit, himself, but sent his brother Anilæus with such presents as he could procure. Upon his arrival, he was admitted to the presence of the king, who, finding that he came alone, enquired wherefore his brother did not accompany him: and Anilæus giving the king to understand, that he remained in his station near the lake from apprehension of danger, he swore by the gods of his country, that neither of them should suffer the least injury, in person or property, and as a ratification of his oath, gave Asinæus his right-hand, which with these barbarians, is the most sacred tie of good faith that can be given. After that ceremony is past, they are free from all suspicion of false dealing. Artabanus, upon this, [illegible]

[illegible]ance, sent Asinæus back again, to persuade his brother to pay him a visit, in contemplation of the services they might render him conjunctively, by keeping those provinces in awe, that seemed inclined to revolt in his absence. Nor could he be certain, that while he himself was employed in the suppression of a rebellion on the one hand, Asinæus was not fortifying himself, and doing mischief about Babylon, on the other.

Asinæus understanding, by the report of his brother, how well disposed Artabanus was towards them both, and with what oaths and protestations he had confirmed the sincerity of his professions, was prevailed upon to visit him, which he accordingly did, accompanied by Anilæus. The king received them courteously, and could not but admire the greatness of Asinæus's mind, especially when placed in comparison with the diminutive figure of his person, which then appeared so disproportionate, that he passed this remark to his friends, "That the soul of that "man was not made for his body." Taking occasion one day at table, to mention the martial character, and feats of arms, achieved by Asinæus to Abdagases, his general, in terms of the highest commendation, the general made no other reply than that of requesting permission to put him to the sword for the indignity he had offered the Parthians. The king returned, "that he "would never consent to the massacre of a man, who "had committed himself to his honour, and whom he "was bound by solemn oath to protect; but that if the "general was inclined to signalize his valour, he might "find means, of taking revenge for the indignity offered "to the Parthians, without involving him in the guilt "of perjury, and this by attacking him on his return, "without making him privy to his purpose."

The king next morning sent for Asinæus, and thus addressed him: "Return home, gallant youth, lest, "through the animosities and resentment of my officers, "you should meet with what I cannot prevent. Let me "commend Babylon to your care: exert your utmost ef-"forts to maintain the peace, and preserve the province "from harm. You have committed your life into my "hands, and your safety shall be as dear to me as my "own." With these words, and a profusion of presents, the king dismissed Asinæus to take charge of his command. He no sooner arrived there than he applied himself most assiduously to the duties of his commission, building forts, repairing and fortifying as he saw occasion, and acquitting himself to such universal satisfaction, that none of his predecessors ever acquired so much power and fame, from so slender a beginning; and this not only among the people of Babylon, but the Parthian governors and commanders, who, holding him in the highest esteem, his authority increased to that degree, that Mesopotamia might be said to be under his direction.

The brothers went on in a most flourishing state to the space of fifteen years, to their own honour, and the approbation of all around them. But when once they deviated from those principles and manners, by which they had obtained both their power and fame, and abandoned the precepts and discipline of their forefathers, to the addicting themselves to sensual pleasures, and foreign innovations, they fell in their credit, and experienced the [illegible] of their declension, as will appear from examples in the sequel.

There came into those provinces a Parthian governor, accompanied by his wife, a woman of exquisite beauty, and most engaging qualities. Anilæus became passionately enamoured with her, and having no other means of consummating his inordinate desire, provoked her husband to single combat, killed him in the first encounter, and took the woman to his bed.

This adventure was the source of all the terrible calamities that befel them afterwards. The woman, when she came from abroad, had constantly with her images of her country gods. She was now a widow, and in custody; but having privately concealed some of these idols, she took an opportunity of worshipping them for a while, by stealth; but upon Anilæus taking her to himself, and owning her publicly for his wife, she worshipped them in her accustomed manner, and with the same appointed ceremonies as she had done in the days of her former husband. The most esteemed friends of the two brothers were highly offended at this licentious practice, in open violation of the religion, rites, and laws of the Jews. But neither the good counsel, or reproof of friends, had any effect in reclaiming him: on the contrary, he was so infatuated in his attachment to the idolatress, and so incensed at the liberty his advisers had taken, that he stabbed one of them upon the spot, for discharging his conscience, in telling him plain truths; and in his expiring moments, he imprecated vengeance upon this murderer Anilæus, Asinæus, and their companions also, upon the two first, as the examples and abetters of this violation of religion and friendship, and upon the rest, as the [illegible] accessary to the neglect of the protection of their laws and liberties, which they ought to have defended.

Though these companions were greatly affected by the death of their friend, the most inordinate affection of the brothers, and the sense they retained of their obligations to them for their advancement, induced them to avoid any interference in the matter. But at length the flagrant and barefaced profession of idolatry, became intolerable, insomuch, that the people thronged, in tumultuous crowds, to Asinæus, with complaints against his brother, representing to him the absolute necessity of adopting proper measures, in due time, to prevent further mischief, as the corruption would become universal. They added, that the marriage with this woman was a violation of their ancient laws, and her idolatrous practices a reproach to the worship of the true God. Asinæus acknowledged that he was fully convinced of the dangerous tendency both to himself and people, of his brother's iniquities conduct; yet, from the impulse of affection for him, as so near a relation, and an allowance for human frailty in so irresistible an attachment, he palliated the matter without proceeding to an examplary severity. But being persecuted with daily clamour, more and more, he took upon him to reproach his brother for his past conduct, and to caution him as to his future state, charging him withal to put away the woman, and send her home to her relations. But this had no effect with him, and the woman finding the mutinous disposition of the people increase, and fearing that some mischief might befal Anilæus for her sake, poisoned Asinæus, not doubting of the security of her life, as her husband was to be her judge.

Anilæus now took the government upon himself alone and made an incursion with his arms into the territories of Mithridates, a man of the first rank in Parthia, and husband to the daughter of king Artabanus. He found money, slaves, and cattle there in great abundance, besides other rich booty, that he carried away, to an immense value. Mithridates was not far off at that time, and hearing of this incursion and rapine without any kind of provocation, collected a body of his choicest troops, and marched at the head to give Anilæus battle. The next day being the Jews sabbath, which they observe most religiously as a day of rest, he halted at a village that night, with an intent of falling upon them by surprize the ensuing morning. A Syrian, who lived in the neighbourhood, gave Anilæus intelligence of the design, and particularly where Mithridates was to be that night at an entertainment.

Anilæus upon this advice ordered his men refreshment, and they marched, by night, to anticipate the design, and take them by surprize. He succeeded to his utmost wish, for about the fourth watch he fell into their quarters, and took some asleep, whilst others, in consternation, were put to flight in the dark. Mithridates was taken prisoner, and mounted naked upon an ass, which, amongst the Parthians, is deemed the highest indignity. When they had cut [illegible] Anilæus [illegible] would [illegible] as [illegible] and [illegible] it [illegible] would [illegible] of the world might [illegible] on the other hand, [illegible] to extremities with Mithridates, they [illegible] would never rest till he [illegible] in Babylon [illegible] is the [illegible] would be punished, in case of any [illegible] of [illegible]."

[illegible] Mithridates, was set at liberty, by common consent. But his wife, upon his return, finding out the terms of his release, reproached him, for neglecting, as [illegible] the king, to revenge himself on those that injured him, and suffering himself to hold a life owing to their mercy. She then enjoined him to go back, and redeem his honour, vowing, upon failure, to dissolve the marriage. Terrified by the taunts of this woman, and dreading a repetition of them, he put himself, though reluctantly, at the head of an army, but with this conviction, that the Parthian did not deserve to live who would submit to a Jew. As soon as Anilæus had intelligence that Mithridates was marching towards him, he made it a point of honour not to take advantage of the fastnesses he was possessed of, but to put the dispute to the issue of a battle in the open plain, so that he advanced to meet him with a body of men flushed with former conquests, and, over and above the veteran troops, they were joined by several reinforcements, that fell in with them for the booty. In the utmost confidence of victory, therefore, they marched fourscore furlongs into a dry sandy country, and when they were spent with the drought of the place, the fatigue of the march, and the heat of the day, Mithridates fell upon them with fresh men, put them to a total rout, and cut off several thousands in the pursuit. Anilæus, with those that escaped, made to a forest in the greatest consternation, leaving Mithridates in the happy possession of an absolute victory.

There came over to Anilæus, after this defeat, such multitudes of loose desperadoes, that his army was not long recruiting to its former number, but they were raw, undisciplined men, and by no means comparable to those that fell in the late action. With these recruits, however, he marched into the territories of the Babylonians, and laid all waste. Upon this the Babylonians sent to the Jews at Nearda, to deliver up Anilæus to justice, but this could not be obtained, for it was not in their power so to do. Their proposal then was to invite him to a treaty, in order to accommodate matters upon terms to which they agreed, and sent commissioners on both sides, Jews as well as Babylonians, to conduct the treaty. But the Babylonians, instead of keeping the spot where Anilæus and his men lay, surprised them in the dead of the night, and finding them unprovided and drowsy, slew all before them without opposition, and Anilæus himself was slain amongst the rest.

The Babylonians and Jews were perpetually at variance, by reason of their contrariety of laws and customs, and waged war with each other with different success. But the Babylonians, who were kept in awe during the life of Anilæus, took opportunity, on his death, to renew their depredations on the Jews, insomuch that they compelled them to quit their habitations and withdraw themselves to Seleucia, the capital of that province, and so called from Seleucus Nicanor, the founder of it, being a place of liberty, where Macedonians, Greeks, and Syrians lived promiscuously together. The Jews lived quietly here during the space of five years, but the plague breaking out in Babylon in the sixth, the inhabitants were forced to withdraw more and more to Seleucia, which proved the occasion of the greatest calamities.

The Greeks and Syrians in this city were at perpetual discord, but in their contentions, the Greeks ever had the advantage, till, upon the coming in of the Jews, being a bold and warlike people, with their assistance the Syrians prevailed. The Greeks finding their power decline, and their situation desperate, unless they could disunite the Syrians and the Jews, engaged such of their particular friends amongst the former as [illegible] in bringing about an accommodation. The proposal was well received, and the consideration of it referred to some leading men on both sides, to advise upon the expedient. They interposed and put an end to the contention upon this condition, that the Greeks and Syrians should join in a league offensive and defensive against the Jews. Pursuant to this agreement, they fell upon the Jews by surprize, and slew upwards of fifty thousand, not an individual escaping, unless protected by some neighbour or friend. The miserable remainder retired to Ctesiphon, near Seleucia, where the king of Parthia generally resides in the winter. In this place they took up their abode, not doubting of their security in the verge of the place, but they soon had cause to entertain such apprehensions from both Babylonians and Seleucians, that the greater part betook themselves to Nearda and Nisibis, depending on the strength of those cities, and the martial disposition of the inhabitants. This was the then state of the Jews in Babylon.

END OF THE EIGHTEENTH BOOK

FLAVIUS JOSEPHUS

ON THE

ANTIQUITIES

OF THE

JEWS.

BOOK XIX

[INCLUDING A PERIOD OF ABOUT SIX YEARS.]

CHAP. I.

Caius Caligula commits outrages upon the Jews. Styles himself the brother of Jupiter, and challenges adoration. Plunders the Grecian temples. Orders Regulus to send the statue of Jupiter Olympius to Rome. Arrogates equality with [illegible]. Three conspiracies formed against his life. He [illegible] Chaereas, [illegible], who meditates revenge [illegible] to [illegible]. Caius orders Chaereas to put [illegible] to the torture, [illegible] with great [illegible]. Noble speech of Chaereas. Minucianus and Chaereas conspire about taking off Caius. Liberty, the [illegible]. Chaereas encouraged by a voice from among [illegible] to prosecute his design. The execution put off from day to day. Chaereas, impatient of delay, animates his companions, and they come to a final resolution. Caius sacrifices, and goes to the theatre. Description of the theatre. The [illegible] execute their design. The glory ascribed to Chaereas. Chaereas with his associates, retire to the [illegible]. The German guards of Caius [illegible]. Proclamation of the death of Caesar. [illegible] to restore the aristocratical form of government.

These violent outrages and barbarous cruelties of Caius, called, by the Romans, Caligula, were not confined to [illegible] alone, and the neighbouring provinces, but extended over sea and land throughout the whole Roman empire, and that to a degree unheard of before. Nor did any [illegible] the effects of his [illegible] barbarities more sensibly than [illegible] Rome [illegible], where senators, patricians and nobles in general, were treated with all manner of [illegible], banishment, confiscation, and [illegible]. He had the vanity and presumption to arrogate to [illegible] and honours of a god [illegible] with respect to its dedication, by the name of brother, together with other actions equally frantic. Having a design to pass from Puteoli, a city of Campania, to Misenum, a sea port on the other side of the water, and deeming it a derogation to his dignity to cross it in a galley, he laid a bridge over it, from one promontory to the other, and so passed and re-passed in his chariot, triumphing that he had subjected the sea as well as the land, as became the power and dignity of a god.

There was not so much as one temple throughout Greece, which he did not rifle of all the curious paintings, sculptures, ornaments, and donations in general, giving orders for the transportation of the spoil to his palaces, gardens, and retirements of pleasure, and observing that the most glorious city in the universe was the most proper cabinet for the deposit of the choicest rarities which the universe afforded. He had the confidence to send to Memmius Regulus for the statue of Jupiter Olympius, that admirable piece of Phidias, the famous Athenian statuary, and so called from the place in Greece where it is so highly honoured, in order to have it brought to Rome. But in this instance he did not compass his end, for the architects told Regulus, to whom the care of it was committed, that the workmanship would be defaced by the removal. It is reported, that while Memmius had it under consideration, he was alarmed by a prodigy, which caused him to delay it, as he gave Caius to understand in a letter, by way of excuse; but that apology would have cost him his life, if the death of the emperor had not prevented it. His frantic pride came to such a pitch, that, upon the birth of a daughter, he had the child carried into the capitol, and placed upon the knee of the statue of Jupiter, as if there had been an alliance between Caius and the supreme of the gods.

As he prophaned the religion, so he violated the laws of his country, not only in permitting, but encouraging slaves to accuse their masters, and signifying his pleasure in [illegible]. As an instance, Claudius was charged [illegible], Pollux, and Caius had the [illegible], or the bench to commence [illegible] execution against the life of [illegible], with a resolution of taking him off.

By the licence which he gave to calumniators, sycophants, and informers, in the advancement of their own [illegible] their patrons, he provoked the same practices against himself that he had countenanced against others. [illegible] was [illegible] for him on all hands, some in revenge of [illegible] received, and some by way of prevention to [illegible] mischiefs apprehended. Justice and law were corrupted [illegible] and power bore universal sway, and so critical was the situation of affairs, that either Caius must have sunk, or the commonwealth been annihilated. The Jews, in particular, by the seasonable exit of this tyrant, were rescued from impending destruction. It [illegible] equally to instruction and entertainment, to be [illegible] minute and particular in this part of our history, as the concurrence of so many providences in the disposal of events, must serve as a lesson to good men, not to despair in the greatest extremities, of the infinite and mercy power of the Almighty, and also as a caution to the great men of the earth, how they build their hopes on trusts to addictions, or [illegible] their [illegible] on transitory enjoyment, which in the end lead to disappointment and misery.

There were three several conspiracies laid against Caius, and each of them conducted by a person of eminence. [illegible] Regulus, a Spaniard of Corduba, conducted one party, and had a troop of resolutes to assist in the enterprize. Cassius Chaereas, the tribune, had another detachment; and Annius Minucianus a third. These were all determined on the destruction of this tyrant, as they deemed him a monster of [illegible]. Minucianus was animated to it partly in revenge for the death of Lepidus, his singular friend, a citizen of unsullied honour, whom Caius most barbarously put to death, partly through apprehension of the tyrant's design upon his own life. [illegible] directed him from a natural [illegible] to [illegible], being himself a man of [illegible] probity. Chaereas was [illegible] at the reproaches he had received from Caius with effeminacy and cowardice; and alarmed at the imminent danger under which he lived in the service of so outrageous a master.

Different as the causes might be, they all agreed in this one common end of delivering their country and the world, from the outrages of so inhuman a tyrant; esteeming the success of their design the salvation of the public, and persuaded that it was the duty of a patriot to lay down his life for his country. But Chaereas was more zealous than the rest, partly through ambition of acquiring a name, and partly, through the advantage he had above others, (being tribune) of executing his design from freedom of access to the person of his master.

It was the season of the Circensian Games, an entertainment of which the people of Rome were highly delighted. It had formerly been the custom of the multitude to crowd into the palace, and petition the emperor for what they required, and as they rarely met with a denial, their request on the present occasion was, an abatement of their tributes and taxes. Caius was so enraged at their petition and their clamour, that he ordered his guards immediately to seize those that made the outcry and put them to death; in consequence of which numbers were slain on the spot. The people then ceased their importunities, taking warning by the fate of those who had suffered.

These horrid barbarities excited Chaereas to hasten the attempt, who had it in contemplation to dispatch the tyrant as he sat at table. He deferred it, however, from time to time, not from any change of mind, but to wait an opportunity of giving a decisive stroke. He had commanded the guards a long time, and being now in commission for collecting the revenues, he incurred the displeasure of Caesar for not proceeding with rigour against those that were in arrears, (poor and insolvent as they might be,) insomuch that he upbraided him with cowardice in not enforcing the payment, [illegible] a number of reflections on him, which no man of spirit and honour could possibly bear without resentment. [illegible] more, [illegible] brought the word from Caius to the rest of the officers, but he suggested some [illegible] either the [illegible] or contempt. Indeed he was [illegible] the very butt of their derision.

This was so impudent a provocation, and so powerful an incitement to revenge, that to forward the design he communicated it to some confidential friends, and among the rest to Pompedius, a man of senatorial dignity, but in principle an epicurean. Pompedius had been accused by Timidius, a professed enemy of [illegible], [illegible] reproachful expressions against Caius, and the charge was founded on the pretended testimony of Quintilia, a very beautiful woman, who belonged to the theatre. Quintilia being generally beloved, had the good fortune to stand in the favour of Pompedius among the rest. The accusation being groundless, and Quintilia refusing to take away the life of an innocent [illegible] false evidence, Timidius called for her being put to the torture, and Caius commanded Chaereas to see it executed, while he reserved those offices of cruelty for him whom he had frequently upbraided with effeminacy. As they were conducting Quintilia to the rack, she trod upon the foot of the associate, giving him thereby to understand that he was safe, for she would not confess any thing. It was much against the inclinations of Chaereas to execute this decree, but he was compelled to torment her with the greatest severity. Not being able, however, to extort confession, he conducted her into the presence of Caius, miserably torn and disfigured, even to such a degree that the emperor himself took compassion on her, and discharged Pompedius, presenting the woman with a considerable sum of money, as a compensation for the excruciating pains she had [illegible] with manly fortitude.

The tenderness of the emperor aggravated the concern of Chaereas, who [illegible] reflected on the disgrace brought upon him, in being the appointed instrument of so merciless a cruelty as even Caius himself relented at. Thus enraged he disclosed his design to Clemens and Papinius, one of whom was an officer in the army, and [illegible] as well as himself. He represented to Clemens "that neither of them had been wanting in dedication to the emperor, that it had been their care and business to discover and defeat several conspirators against him, some of whom they had put to death, and others to torture, all [illegible] even excited his pity, which proved they were commanders fit for savages, not for soldiers and men of honour."

Clemens made no reply, but indicated by his countenance, the aversion he had to be employed in so infamous a [illegible], though he durst not utter a word against the majesty of Caesar. Chaereas, however, having disclosed the matter, thus continued his discourse: "I need not recount the calamities either of the city or empire: they are too notorious to be concealed, and Caius is the reputed [illegible] of them. But if I speak truth I must confess [illegible] the effectual cause, nay, I must include both you, Papinius, and Clemens: we are the men who have brought this ruin upon Rome, and upon mankind, in executing the orders of others. When we might put an end to the outrages daily committed on the citizens and subjects in general, we prostitute ourselves to the vilest offices. We [illegible] the cause not of the Roman empire, nor of glorious freedom, but of those who enslave both our bodies and minds. In fine, what do we but execute the commission of an inhuman tyrant in perpetrating horrid murders, and inflicting execrable tortures upon others, till the time comes [illegible] shall be executed upon us. The tyrant is so accustomed to the effusion of human blood, that he never consults the reason of things, but acts according to his humour and caprice. We seem all destined to destruction, one after another, and our turn will probably be the next, if we do not, in time, provide for the security both of our own lives and the common liberty."

Clemens, though he could not but approve the opinion and resolution of Chæreas, charged him not to be too hasty, as [illegible] the execution of the design, he said, [illegible] came to execution, would prove fatal to every one concerned. He observed, that "time would bring forth opportunity, that his age would not permit him to make any attempt, though, perhaps, he might suggest safer means than those proposed by Chæreas." Clemens having spoken thus briefly, departed, revolving in his mind both what he had heard and said.

The caution of Clemens raised in the mind of Chæreas a suspicion of the sincerity of his attachment to the cause: he therefore immediately repaired to Sabinus, another of the tribunes, whom he knew to be a man of honour, an asserter of the liberty of his country, and totally averse to the present [illegible] government. He never doubted his integrity or judgment, and determined to consult him upon the whole affair. When he found that Sabinus concurred in opinion with him as to the [illegible] point, [illegible] kept the secret to himself, he observed that there was no need of deliberating with a man who had already formed his resolution, insomuch that Sabinus promised him both his good [illegible] and assistance, which confirmed Chæreas the more in the purpose.

As they were both for bringing the matter to a speedy issue, they applied to Minucianus, a man of a similar disposition, and equally zealous in the cause of liberty. Caius had a jealousy of Minucianus, on account of Lepidus, his most [illegible] [illegible], besides the aversion he had to him as a man of [illegible] a character that ever incurred his hatred. [illegible] privately [illegible] each other's mind from [illegible] respecting the mode of government, [illegible] they were, they [illegible] common [illegible] in the same [illegible].

[illegible] that Chæreas and Sabinus had for the virtue and dignity of Minucianus, and as they formerly [illegible] upon the [illegible] [illegible], they desired to have his opinion on the present business. Minucianus [illegible] of Chæreas, what was the word the emperor had given [illegible] for the insults which Caius had offered him [illegible] were notorious throughout the city. Chæreas took the hint, and [illegible] on the motion of Minucianus, [illegible], "Whatever the emperor's word was, let "yours be [illegible], and I return you a thousand thanks "for encouraging me to attempt what I had long resolved. "I rejoice to find that we concur in opinion. My single "[illegible] will [illegible] us both; do you lead the way, and "be assured, that whatever you command shall be obeyed. "[illegible] and resolved, to a brave [illegible] arms are [illegible] "[illegible] not the weapon, but the will, that does the "execution. [illegible] lost all [illegible] action, and as to "the event, whether I stand or fall, I am [illegible]. "[illegible] or fortune are no objects, when "the [illegible] country, and the laws and liberties of so "[illegible] in danger of being swallowed up "by this merciless tyrant. I hope you will not envy "Chæreas the honour of a part at least, if not of striking "the blow, in the plot that must meet the general approbation." Upon this generous declaration, Minucianus embraced him, wishing him success in the undertaking, and, after an interchange of mutual assurances, they parted. It was rumoured that, to confirm the conspirators in their design, there was a voice heard among the people, calling out to Chæreas as he entered the palace, to go on and prosper in his undertaking. He, at first, suspected that he was betrayed; but afterwards found it to be either an intimation from some of the accomplices, or a declaration from heaven in favour of his design.

There was at this time assembled a number of persons, of all ranks and degrees, that were well affected towards the purpose; as senators, knights, soldiers, and commonalty; for it was universally agreed that either Caius or the commonwealth must fall. [illegible] a competition prevailed which [illegible] either by word or deed, towards the saving of his country, or, which was one and the same thing, towards the destruction of Caius. Nay, Callistus himself, the emperor's freedman and favourite, made one of the party. This man had vast influence with Caius, which he perverted to such a degree, that he was equally hated and dreaded; indeed he conceived himself more like a partner in the government than a subject. He had amassed great wealth by corruption; notwithstanding which, he could not think himself safe under a prince of so fickle and implacable a disposition. He was in danger from many causes, but more especially for his wealth, which, in those days, was a temptation hardly to be resisted. Callistus finding the situation of Caius very precarious, thought he could not do better than secure the friendship of the next successor; and, with that view, to ingratiate himself with Claudius, he went over privately to that prince, telling him in confidence, that Caius had frequently put him on to poison him, but that he had ever found out some device to evade it. This rather appears to me an invention of Callistus to obtain the favour of his new patron, than a matter of fact; for if Caius had been disposed to murder his uncle, it could not have been in the power of Callistus to evade it; [illegible] would he have excused himself, if he had been remiss in the execution of the emperor's commands. Claudius however looked upon him as the instrument of Providence for his deliverance, so that the insinuation subserved his purpose.

In the mean time, through the deliberation of the confederacy, the main design was put off from day to day, though much against the will of Chæreas, who was ever of opinion that no opportunity should be lost for the execution of so necessary a purpose. Nay, he did not [illegible] to declare, that he could not have wished for a better time or place, than the capitol itself, when Caius went up to sacrifice for his daughter; or when he stood on the battlements of his palace scattering his donations amongst the people, or upon any solemnity at his own private ceremonies; for Caius seemed careless, and free from suspicion of danger, though most of his attendants were traitors in their hearts. Chæreas was at length so impatient of these delays, that he reproached the confederates with want of activity and resolution, and declared that, if they persisted in making obstacles, he would undertake to dispatch the tyrant himself, and be answerable for doing it, even without a weapon. His associates commended his zeal for the common cause, but they were for deferring the design till the celebration of the games instituted in honour of Augustus, who first took the sovereign power out of the people into his own hands.

There was a theatre erected before the palace for the Roman nobility, with their families, in the presence of the emperor himself. As, upon this occasion, thousands of spectators crowded into so narrow a compass, it was concluded, that the design might be executed with the greater ease, because the guards could not come up in time to rescue; whereas, upon an attempt elsewhere, there would be danger of miscarriage, and a tumult in the city, which, through searches and soldiers, might expose the party to detection, and frustrate the whole contrivance.

Chæreas having given his consent, a resolution was formed to do the deed on the first day of the exhibition of the public shews; but fate seems to have over-ruled in the case, and put it off to the third and last day. Indeed it would have been further delayed, if Chæreas had not called his associates together, and animated them with a speech to this effect: "We are here assembled "in a righteous cause, and upon a just and honourable "design; but, to our shame be it spoken, through "sloth and cowardice, without advancing one step in "the business. Not only has much time been lost, but "our lives, liberties, and fortunes, are in imminent "danger while Caius rides triumphant. What is the "consequence of this pusillanimity but loss of liberty, and increase of tyranny? Whereas we should "attend to our own security in the first place, the welfare "of the public in the next, and, in fine, acquire for ourselves immortal glory."

Having thus spoken, he gave them some time to deliberate, but finding they stood mute, he rejoined, "My brave "comrades, wherefore these delays? Do you not know that "the games are upon the point of breaking up, and that "Caius is going for Alexandria, to take the tour of Egypt? Would it redound to our honour to part with this scandal "to humanity out of our hands, as if we had sent him to "proclaim to the world the servility of the Romans, and to "afford occasion for some free-spirited Egyptian to do that "justice to mankind, upon this blood-thirsty tyrant, which "we were afraid to do ourselves? Away then, my friends, "with deliberation. I will assist the man, and put the "point to immediate issue, nor will I suffer mortal to contend with me for the glory of so noble an action."

This zealous address fired the conspirators with resolution, and Chæreas put on his equestrian sword, and went to the palace as the tribunes usually did, it being his turn that day in course, as commanding officer of the guard, to go to the emperor for the word. The people were pressing in great multitudes towards the palace, crowding to get places, and Caius himself seemed not a little pleased with this scene of confusion, for there were no seats set apart for senators, knights, or other degrees of people, according to their quality, but men, women, masters, and slaves, were all promiscuously huddled together.

This solemnity being dedicated to the honour of Augustus, Caius advanced, and offered up sacrifice to the imperial patron. It so happened that, upon the fate of the victim, some of the blood flowing out, fell upon the robe of Asprenas, one of the senators. Caius sported at the omen, but it proved fatal to the senator, for he was slain at the same time with Caius. It was much noticed that Caius was in better humour this day than usual. When the sacrifice was over, he went with his friends to the theatre, which was only a frame of wood-work, so constructed as to be taken to pieces and put together again, as it was annually upon this occasion. It had two gates, one towards the open court, and the other over against the passage, for the actors to enter without incommoding the audience, and near at hand was an orchestre for the musicians.

When the multitude had taken their places, and Chæreas with the other tribunes, were seated near Cæsar, upon the right wing of the theatre, Bathybius, a senator and military man, in a whisper, asked Cluvitus, a person of consular dignity, who sat next to him, if he had heard any news? Upon the reply of Cluvitus in the negative, the other informed him that the tragedy of the death of the tyrant was to be performed that day. Cluvitus, in a quotation of a verse out of Homer's Iliad, cautioned him to beware that none of the Grecians overheard him. The vulgar then proceeded to their usual clamour and outrage, with which Cæsar seemed highly delighted. Two circumstances then followed that had an ominous appearance. One was the representation of a corrupt judge brought to public justice; the other was the tragedy of Cinyra, wherein she and her daughter were slain with great fictitious effusion of blood. It is said that this was the anniversary of the day upon which Philip, the son of Amyntas, king of Macedonia, was killed by his friend Pausanius, upon entering the theatre.

This being the last day of exhibition, Caius was undetermined whether he should sit it out, or whether he should go first to the bath, then to dinner, and return. Minucianus taking his place near the emperor, and observing him disposed to move, rose from his seat to encourage him in his resolution, lest the present opportunity should be lost; but Caius, taking him gently by the skirt, asked him, with a friendly smile, whither he was going? Upon this Minucianus, with affected reverence to Cæsar, sat down, but, in a short time, from the former apprehension, he rose again, and Caius did not oppose his exit, imagining, some necessary business might call him hence. Asprenas, one of the confederates, then persuaded him to go out, to the bath, and dine as he was used to do, and so return.

Chæreas having by this time placed his associates in their proper stations, and giving them their necessary instructions, was impatient of longer delay. He at first resolved to assault him on his seat, though he knew this could not be done without much bloodshed both of the senatorial and equestrian orders, preferring the deliverance of his country, to the loss of the lives of a few dignified individuals. As Chæreas was going towards the theatre, word was given the croud that Cæsar was up and returning to his palace. The conspirators called to the multitude to make way for the emperor, as if by his order and direction, but in reality to afford them scope for the execution of their design. Claudius the uncle, went first, then Marcus Minucianus, the husband of his sister, and Valerius Asiaticus, persons whose rank entitled them to precedence. Caius himself, with Paulus Aruntius, followed them. When he entered the palace, he left the ordinary way which Claudius and the rest had taken before him, and turned off to a bye path, leading to the baths, to see some boys that were sent him out of Asia for their skill in singing hymns, and in the Pyrric way of dancing. In this passage Chæreas met him, and asked for the word, which being given according to former ridicule and insult, the tribune returned the indignity with a stroke of his sword, but the wound was not mortal. Some were of opinion it was contrived by Chæreas to render his death more painful by a repetition of strokes; but this to me seems improbable, as it was not a business to be protracted. The wound, in short, was betwixt the neck and shoulder, where it struck upon a bone that prevented its going further. He cried not out, or called to any around him for help, conscious, perhaps, he did not deserve protection. He uttered a groan, however, and made an attempt to escape, but Cornelius Sabinus prevented it by a stroke that brought him on his knees, which being followed by an unanimous outcry of "Down with him, dispatch him," they fell upon him together and executed their purpose. It is said that Aquila gave him the finishing stroke, but the generality of the people, ascribed the glory of the action to Chæreas. Though many concurred in it, he was the original proposer, and most essentially conducive to the execution of it. He formed and united the confederacy, animated and supported his associates, and, when it came to the decisive point, struck the first blow, and, by his personal bravery, laid this haughty tyrant in the dust. So that this laudable exploit must be attributed to the virtue and resolution of Chæreas. Thus fell the emperor Caius, by many hands, and by many wounds.

Chæreas and his associates were not a little embarrassed as to the manner of getting off after the accomplishment of their design. They had to contend with the outrage of a wild and seditious multitude, and the fury and revenge of the soldiery for the death of their prince. The avenues were narrow where the fact was committed, and filled with guards then upon duty. Finding it impossible to return the way they came, they struck off to the palace of Germanicus, the father of Caius, whom they had lately slaughtered. These apartments bordered on the palace royal, and the whole pile is as uniform as the efforts of the several emperors, from time to time, could make it. Being now freed from the rabble they were secure, so long at least as the death of Cæsar could be concealed.

The German body guards, known by the name of the Celtic Legion, were the first that got intelligence of it. These were men naturally fierce and choleric, in common with other barbarians, without any degree of reason or reflection. They were enraged at the news of the emperor's death, not so much from personal regard to him, as [illegible] own interest, for he had been bountiful to them [illegible] conciliated their attachment by force of frequent donations. This corps, under the command of Sabinus, (originally a gladiator, and preferred merely on account of his bodily strength,) marched, with drawn swords, from house to house, in quest of the murderers of Caius. The first man they met was Asprenas, whose robe was stained with the blood of the emperor, a most unfortunate token for him, as they immediately cut him to pieces. The next they seized was Norbanus, a man of the first rank, and descended from some of the most eminent commanders. Finding the dignity of his extraction availed nothing with those barbarians, he disarmed the first man that assaulted him, and being a person of extraordinary strength and courage, would not have fallen unrevenged, had he not been oppressed by numbers. The third that fell into the hands of these Germans was Anteius, who was drawn out from curiosity to see the dead body of Caius, as he had banished his father of the same name with himself, and afterwards put him to death. Anteius came to gratify himself with this spectacle; but as he was endeavouring to avoid the tumult, the Germans found him out, and involved him in the common [illegible]. This was the fate of these unhappy men.

When the news of Caius's death was brought to the theatre, the multitude were astonished, though they could not believe it; for, though it would have given them pleasure, they were fearful of disappointment, and therefore would not entertain a hope precariously founded. There were others who greatly distrusted it, because they were unwilling that so fatal an accident should befal Caius. These, for the most part, were women, children, slaves, and some of the soldiers, [illegible] the double advantage of their services [illegible] as the ministers of pride and tyranny [illegible] good men, and became [illegible]. The women, children, and common people were engaged with spectacles, drolls, prizes, and other amusements, under pretext of making them easy, but, in reality, to gratify the vanity of the oppressor.

Bondmen, who were indulged in the licence of insulting their patrons, under the protection of Caius, also lamented his death, as they found no difficulty during his reign, of making good any accusation against them, and were assured of advantage in discovering where their masters' money was deposited, since the law entitled the informer to one eighth part of the value of the confiscation.

With respect to persons of condition, to whom the report might appear credible, as either privy to the design, or well-wishers to it, they were so far from appearing to rejoice at it, that they affected to be ignorant of it. Those, indeed, who were deepest in the conspiracy, disclaimed all knowledge of it [illegible] that death, without mercy, would be the result of the slightest suspicion.

The story of the death was represented in various lights; some had it that Caius was wounded and under the care of the surgery. It was by no means prudent for people, under these circumstances, to declare themselves one way or the other, for either the authors of the report were partizans of Caius, and consequently under a suspicion of partiality on that hand, or if they were enemies it was dangerous to publish ill-news. There started, at the same time, another report, that alarmed the higher class more than all the rest. This was that Caius, upon receiving of his wounds, ran into the [illegible], and, without staying to be dressed, all bloody as he was, made his appeal, by way of declamation, to the people. This variety and uncertainty of reports put people in general upon their guard; but they durst not stir for fear of calumny and misconstruction; for the point was not so much what they intended, as the face the judges and informers would put upon it.

In this unsettled state of affairs the Germans, sword in hand, beset the theatre, every man giving himself up for lost upon the sight of them, expecting nothing but immediate death. While they stood trembling, with anxious suspence, whether to go or stay, as there was danger both ways, the soldiers breaking in upon them, put the whole theatre into an alarm; and the people, with supplications, deprecations, and protestations accompanied with tears, groans, and invocations upon all the gods attested their innocence. This dismal spectacle drew compassion from the obdurate hearts even of the Germans themselves, and put a stop to the further progress of their fury, and caused them, in some measure, to repent of their inhumanity in the massacre of Asprenas, and his companions, and carrying their heads up and down by way of ostentation, till, in the end, they were deposited upon the altar. What could be more afflicting to their friends, considering the dignity of their characters, and the insolent barbarity of their triumph, than this horrid action? Indeed, the greatest enemies that Caius left behind him could not now rejoice at his death, from the danger they were in of sharing his fate.

While things were in this confusion, one Arruntius, a public cryer, a man of property, and of great credit and influence with the people, came to the theatre, dressed in deep mourning like a senator of Rome, and, with all the formalities of sorrow and lamentation, that were customary upon the loss of the nearest relations, made proclamation of the death of Caius. Upon this the Germans relented, and the officer commanded the soldiers to put up their swords, so that the uproar entirely ceased. To this the people that were pent up in the theatre solely owed their lives, as did all those in general that might have fallen into the hands of the Germans; for so long as they could have flattered themselves with any hope of the emperor's being alive, they would have proceeded in their outrage. They had so great an affection for Caius, that they would have redeemed his life even with the loss of their own, and without any regard to the distracted state of the commonwealth. But now, upon the certainty of the event, the desire of revenge ceased of itself, as there could be no longer any occasion for conferring obligations on one side, or returning acknowledgments on the other. Besides, they had apprehension from the power of the senate, if the democratical form of government should be revived. Thus was the rage of the Germans appeased.

Chaereas, in the mean time, being very anxious lest Minucianus should fall into the hands of the Germans, enquired of as many of the soldiers as he could trust, one by one, if they could give any account of him, recommending him, with earnest entreaties, to their especial care and protection. By this means he had an interview with Clemens and Minucianus, the latter of whom told him, that he could not but infinitely honour him for so noble a resolution, and that he would take upon himself to return him thanks in the name of the commonwealth, for so public a service, as well for his conduct in the undertaking, as his courage in the execution of it. This, he observed, might serve to shew the fate of tyrants, which seldom fail, after the short-lived pleasure of usurpation, to terminate in an untimely death, or such a conclusion as exposes the oppressor to an universal odium. This was the case of Caius, who laid the foundation of this conspiracy by a violation of the laws of his country, and acts of intolerable insolence and injustice towards the very best of his subjects, who upon these provocations, became his enemies, and then the instruments of his destruction: but it must be allowed, on all hands, that he was the author and first moving cause of his own ruin. The guards being now withdrawn, the people in the theatre were all rising to shift for themselves. The occasion of it was this: Arcyon, a physician, was called away to attend some wounded men, and dispatched several about him, under pretence of going for remedies, but, in truth, to secure them from danger.

The senate, in the mean time, met in the palace, where the multitude pressed in upon them in throngs, to demand justice for the murder of the emperor; but the senate, from prudential motives, shewed [illegible] an appearance

While the rabble were in quest of the assassins, Valerius Asiaticus, a man of consular dignity, in the midst of these clamorous outcries, to know what was become of the murderers of Caius, exclaimed, "Would I had been the man," and so departed.

The senate then proceeded to a decree in condemnation of Caius, and passed an order for both people and soldiers to depart quietly to their own habitations and quarters, with promises of certain exemptions and privileges to the one, and of rewards and gratuities to the other, if they deemed themselves peaceable as they ought to do. By this means there was a seasonable stop put to the uproar, which otherwise might have broken out into fresh tumults, sacrilegious violences, rapine, and all manner of confusion. The whole bench of senators being now met, and those especially that were of the plot, began to deliberate on assuming the power themselves, and re-establishing the democratic form of government.

CHAP. II.

The senate and soldiers divided about the form of government. The latter are for monarchy, and declare Claudius emperor. Oration of Saturninus against tyranny. Chereas goes to the soldiers for the word. They give him LIBERTY. *The wife and daughter of Caius put to death by Julius Lupus. Character of Caius. Character of Claudius. Gratus puts Claudius in possession of the empire. His interest espoused by the soldiers. Disputes still pending between the senate and common people.*

WHILE the senate were debating on one hand, the soldiers were deliberating in a council of war on the other, upon the grand point in dispute, whether a popular or imperial government should now take place. The latter came at length to these resolutions, that a democracy was incapable of conducting the weighty affairs of state; that, if it should be set up, it would not redound to their interest; that if any of those, already in administration, should obtain the supreme power, it would tend to their disadvantage, unless they afforded him their countenance and protection; and that, therefore, in the present unsettled condition of things, it would be most expedient to chuse Claudius emperor, being the uncle of the deceased, and much superior, as to birth, qualities, and education, to any of those who were assembled in senate, not doubting but he would reward those according to their deserts, who had promoted his advancement. This being the sense of the whole council, Claudius was immediately brought from his house by the soldiers, and declared emperor. The news of this event being carried to the senate house, Annius Sentius Saturninus, finding matters come to this pass, rose, and delivered his sentiments upon this important occasion in terms worthy of an orator and patriot. This was the tenor of his speech:

"Who would have thought, my noble countrymen and fellow-citizens, after so long an interruption of our natural freedom, that we should have ever lived to draw one breath of liberty after it! and yet, through the goodness of Divine Providence, in whose power it is to give, or to take, we are at this very day and hour, freemen, in some degree, once again. How long it will last we know not.

"But let the event be what it will,
"A comfort short is yet a comfort still.

Shall we account it as nothing for a freeman to live free in a free country, and to have some relish of the sweets of our ancient liberties in the flourishing condition of our once free commonwealth, even though we were to enjoy the satisfaction of it but for one single hour? I can say little, it is true, to the liberty of former times, before I came into the world, but I have a great desire, I must confess, for the preserving and improving of that liberty which we enjoy at present. I cannot but esteem those men to have been exceedingly happy, whose lot it was to fall in an age that affected the common liberty of mankind, and the study of virtue. But the blessing of all others, that, in my opinion, deserves most to be honoured, next to the immortal gods themselves, are those heroic spirits that have had the courage to give us yet some taste of it, how late soever, even in this abandoned state of the world, a blessing which I fervently wish may be perpetuated. As to what concerns ourselves, our own experience is abundantly sufficient for our comfort and instruction, both young and old. Those that are in years will leave the world with less regret, when they shall better understand the advantages that attend liberty; and so those that are growing up, the very example will inflame them with a virtuous emulation of treading in the steps of their famous ancestors. Virtue, in short, is the main business of human life, and so it ought to be; for, in truth, virtue is liberty itself; that is to say, the liberty of the mind, whatever becomes of the body. Now I do not take upon me all this while to speak of things before my time, any farther than upon the grounds of tradition; but when I come to the subject of tyranny, and the calamitous consequences that attend it, I shall say no more upon that topic than I can make good from what I have seen and felt, and upon the infallible certainty of woeful and miserable experience. It confounds the order of government, and of all civil communities. Great minds, generous dispositions, and glorious actions are discountenanced and suppressed. It makes mens souls as servile as their bodies, quenches all honourable emulations, and accommodates all rules of law and equity, by fear and flattery, to the arbitrary caprice of ambitious and fantastical princes. If we look back to the usurpation of Julius Cæsar upon the power of the people, and the trampling of their laws, liberties, and government under foot, in the erecting of a tyrannical monarchy upon the ruins of the commonwealth, and all this only to gratify ambition, what a train of miseries has that insatiable affectation of dominion drawn after it, both upon the government and the nation? What has the succession been, but a kind of violent competition, betwixt the predecessor and the successor, who should do most mischief, either in the subverting of the laws, or depopulating of the city, by the suppressing of all men of honour and virtue in it, and by all sorts of persecution, even to the degree of death itself? for they could not be safe but in the hands of wicked instruments that had abandoned themselves to all sorts of iniquity, without either shame or conscience. There was not one individual in the number of these imperious masters, that had not acted the part of a most barbarous oppressor. But the tyrant Caius, who hath this day received his fate, perhaps has outdone all the rest in the licentious rage of a brutal and ungovernable fury, sparing neither citizens, friends, or relations, in a defiance at the same time, both of humanity and justice, and of all the laws both of God and man. It is not enough for tyrants to give themselves up to their vanity, and their pleasures, rapines, adulteries, and extravagant appetites, (for these are only human frailties,) but their satisfaction lies in the diabolical practices of rooting out whole families, and involving children and infants in their fathers quarrel. Being conscious, to themselves, of the indignities they multiply upon their subjects, they find no security at last, but in the deaths of those they have wronged, and in the seasonable removal of them out of the way. But since so it is, that we have now shaken off the yoke, and recovered the possession of our primitive freedom, all that we have to do for the preserving of unity among ourselves, and providing for our future safety, is to join in repairing the ruins of our ancient glory, and restoring the commonwealth to its original state of union and integrity. We are now at liberty to propose and to debate, and to like and dislike at pleasure, without any superior power over our

CÆSONIA wife of CAIUS CÆSAR the Roman Emperor while lamenting over the mangled Body of her murdered Husband discovers LUPUS who by order of CHEREAS one of the Tribunes immediately puts her & her Children to Death.

"heads to confound, and call us to an account. For "what was it that gave birth and growth to the unbound- "ed progress of the late tyranny, but the dull patience "of a deluded people, that had no spirit to make head "against it? Those that were flatterers to their plunderers, and "men that on all occasions acted and lived like slaves, were "the people that chusing rather to lead a mean inglo- "rious life, than venture an honourable death, cast the "city into those insupportable miseries, of which we "ourselves have been both ear and eye-witnesses. But "let me recommend it to you, in the first place, to do "right to Chaereas, in conferring upon him the honours "he deserves for freeing the world, and the common- "wealth, of this abominable monster. For it was his "counsel, and his hand, by the impulse of a Divine as- "sistance, that brought our liberty; and it is but rea- "sonable that he that procured us our freedom with the "hazard of his life, should receive acknowledgments "and rewards from the persons he rescued, answer- "able to the nature of the obligation. It is the part "and duty of an honest man to be thankful to his "benefactor, especially to such a benefactor as this, "who has involved us in common hope. The action of "Brutus and Cassius upon Julius Caesar was great and "glorious, but Chaereas, over and above the emulation "of their bravery, hath, in this respect, gone much be- "yond them. That exploit was followed with a civil war, "that ran through and ravaged the whole Roman empire; "but Chaereas cut off the tyranny together with the "tyrant, and delivered the whole world at one blow."

This speech of Sentius obtained the approbation of the whole body of the senate; but he was so intent upon the point in immediate consideration, that he forgot himself at that very time, a ring upon his finger, with a head of Caius engraved upon it. Trebellius Maximus observing it, rose up hastily, and took it off his finger, and it was ordered to be broken.

As it was now far advanced, Chaereas went to the consuls for the watch-word, and they gave him *Liberty*. The face of things were so strangely changed on a sudden as appeared almost incredible; this being the first act of authority in which the senate had appeared since the time they were deprived, for the soldiers had their orders from the consuls till the Caesars took it out of their hands. Chaereas, upon receiving the word, delivered it of course, to the troops which espoused the cause of the senate, that is, to four companies which had been affected to lawful government, and declared themselves against the usurpation. These men went away with their officers, and soon after them the people, rejoicing at the thought of the present change, and hoping that the ancient glory of the commonwealth was about to be restored, with loud shouts and acclamations, they hailed Chaereas as their deliverer.

Chaereas, apprehending it might be dangerous, after the death of Caius, to suffer his wife and daughters to survive him, sent Julius Lupus, one of the tribunes, with a command to kill them, chusing him the rather for that commission, both as the kinsman of Clemens, and as it seemed proper for a man who was so deep in the conspiracy to have his part in the execution. But several of the confederates were of opinion, that it was an unmanly action to commit so barbarous an outrage upon the person of a woman, as she had no concern in the execrable cruelties perpetrated on the flower of the nobility, which was the sole effect of her husband's malignity. Others imputed horrid deeds to her suggestion, and the administration of a potion that turned his brain, and from thence considered her as the principal cause of the ruin of the state. The latter opinion prevailing, Julius Lupus hastened to the execution of his commission, in order to demonstrate his zealous attachment to the interest of his country.

When he came into the palace he found Caesonia stretched upon the ground with her daughter by the body of her husband, besmeared with the blood of his wounds, and, in bitterest accents, exclaiming against Caius for not attending to the advice of so affectionate a wife, who had repeatedly told him what would be the consequences of his wild proceedings. These words were taken in a different sense, esteemed equally ambiguous by those that heard them, and artfully interpreted according to the various inclination of various people. Those who took them in a more favourable sense, intimated that she advised him to restrain his outrageous fury, and keep himself within the bounds of moderation, assuring him that, if he persisted in these acts of cruelty and oppression, he would incur the hatred of his people, and draw the blood of his subjects on his own head. Those who put another construction upon them, insinuated, that she pressed him to consult his own security in due time, and [illegible] himself on all suspected persons, since, where the life of a prince was at stake, a just ground of suspicion would have been sufficient to proceed upon. Thus was the matter differently interpreted.

Lupus approaching Caesonia, who was bewailing her forlorn condition in all the bitterness of anguish and distress, she intreated him, with tears and lamentations, to draw near, and behold the horrid spectacle of her mangled husband. But reading his design in his countenance, and assured of it from his words, after a short ejaculation, she presented her bare throat to the executioner, pressing him to dispatch what he had undertaken, and finish the tragedy his companions had begun. She encountered the stroke with wonderful constancy of mind, and her daughter died by the same hand with her, and the tidings were sent to Chaereas as soon as the business was accomplished.

This was the end of Caius, after he had reigned four years within four months. He was a man of a savage, malicious disposition, even in a private state, insatiate in his appetite, a patron of calumniators and informers, timid in cases of danger, and consequently bloody in his revenge. He enjoined exorbitant power to oppress the innocent, and make way to confiscations and forfeitures by rapine and murder. He was charmed with the servile adulations of the common people, nor would any thing short of temples and altars satisfy his frantic ambition. He was neither restrained by law or virtue, nor would spare the best friend upon the least pique, or a pretended cause for revenge. He was an enemy to all good men, impatient of contradiction, nor would bear reproof even in the case of incest with his own sister. This, indeed, was a vice so abominable in those days that it was scarcely credible, and such a scandal as had not so much as been heard of among them for many ages. It does not appear that he ever did, or so much as attempted, one action truly magnificent and royal for the honour of the empire, or the common good of mankind, excepting the harbours and store-houses he built about Rhegium, near Sicily, for the convenience of the ships that brought corn out of Egypt. This design was laudable, though it was not brought to perfection, partly through the infirmity and neglect of his agents, and partly through the instability of his own temper; for his mind was diverted by unprofitable pursuits, and he thought his money better employed upon his own private pleasures, than upon those undertakings that might conduce to the honour or interest of the state. He was an excellent orator, and a great proficient in the Latin and Greek languages, had a wonderful presence of mind, and an admirable faculty in speaking extempore; to which was added a peculiar talent for gaining upon the judgment, as well as affections, of mankind in affairs of the greatest moment. Being trained up in the emulation both of his father Germanicus, and his uncle Tiberius, his predecessor, two persons so illustrious for their literary accomplishments, he seems to have made it a point of honour not to degenerate from the dignity of his birth or education. But what avails a virtuous education, unless its influence is diffused through our life? What a train of ill consequences ensue when it is perverted to ignoble purposes? How hard a task it is to men possessed of power, and, in ſome degree, above law, to act virtuouſly for virtue's ſake. At his firſt entrance on the government he made an excellent choice of men of integrity and abilities for his friends and miniſters, by which he gained a deſerved reputation with the people. But in a ſhort time he took another bias, turned them off with inſolence and ſcorn, and, by intolerable provocations, forced his ſubjects to thoſe outrageous extremities of deſpair and revenge that afterwards brought on his own deſtruction.

Claudius, as before obſerved, hearing of the death of Caius, and the tumult occaſioned by it, betook himſelf to an obſcure retreat, though he had no reaſon to apprehend danger, unleſs it might ariſe from the dignity of his birth. In private life he conducted himſelf with moderation, and ſeemed content with his fortune, applying himſelf to literature, eſpecially the cultivation of the Greek language, and avoiding, as much as poſſible, ſcenes of hurry and confuſion.

The multitude was now in a ſtate of diſtraction: the palace thronged with ſoldiers, hurrying from one part to another in furious conſternation, and the common people running from place to place at a venture, without any regard to order or authority or government, ſo that the guards, being men of the greateſt credit among the ſoldiers, in this tumultuous confuſion, began to deliberate on the moſt expedient meaſures of proceeding. They were not ſo much troubled at the death of the emperor, who they thought ſuffered according to his deſert, as at the difficulty of ſettling their own affairs. Indeed, the rage of the Germans againſt the aſſaſſins, rather proceeded from a regard to private intereſt than good will to the public. Theſe circumſtances weighed together, increaſed the apprehenſion of Claudius, eſpecially when he beheld the heads of Aſprenas and his companions, that were carried up and down in triumph. Having concealed himſelf in a dark retreat, Gratus, one of the emperor's guards, eſpied him in a corner, but not being able to identify his perſon, advanced towards him (though the other requeſted him to retire,) and upon drawing near, finding he knew him, he called aloud to thoſe that followed him, "This is Germanicus, and no man fitter to fill up the vacancy of the empire." Upon theſe words the ſoldiers were ready to lay hold on him, and Claudius, for fear they ſhould put him to death for the ſake of Caius, earneſtly entreated them to ſpare him, ſolemnly proteſting his innocence of the whole matter. Gratus, upon this, took him by the right hand, aſſumed a pleaſing countenance, deſired him not to entertain the leaſt apprehenſion for his ſafety, but rather diſpoſe his mind for receiving the empire, which the gods he ſaid, had taken from Caius, and now offered to Claudius by the hands of Gratus, for the relief and preſervation of mankind, who had been long groaning under the weight of numerous oppreſſions. He added, "Riſe therefore, and take poſſeſſion of the throne of your anceſtors." They then took him up and carried him, as, through the effect of the ſurpriſe, between joy and apprehenſion, he was hardly able to ſtand.

During theſe tranſactions between Gratus and Claudius, the guards gathered about the former in great numbers, lamenting the fate of the innocent Claudius, whom they imagined to be carrying to execution, while others were for appealing to the conſuls. As the ſoldiers crowded in more and more, the people that had no arms, conſulted their ſafety, and departed different ways. This put a ſtop to the progreſs of Claudius, for he was not in a condition to walk, and his bearers had withdrawn themſelves for fear of ſharing his expected fate. The military corps being now poſſeſſed of the palace, their numbers increaſing, and having none to oppoſe them, took into conſideration, at this juncture, in what manner they ſhould proceed in order to ſettle the commonwealth. They rejoiced in the preſence of Claudius, and were unanimous for advancing him to the empire, partly in honour to his brother Germanicus, whoſe memory was held in univerſal eſteem, and partly to exclude ambitious pretenders from among the ſenators who, having heretofore embroiled the ſtate, would probably do as much miſchief if they had it in their power. They looked upon the republican form of government as loſt beyond recovery, and therefore, ſince an emperor was of neceſſity to be choſen, they inferred the expediency of taking the utmoſt care that no perſon ſhould be advanced to the dignity without owing his preferment to them. From this conſideration they concluded that they could not do better than make choice of Claudius, and by that mean engroſs the merit of the obligation entirely to themſelves. The whole body of the ſoldiery were ſo well ſatisfied with this mode of reaſoning, that, upon conferring with one another, they all joined in the ſame reſolution; ſo that taking up Claudius, they carried him away to the camp, there to finiſh what they had begun, and he was attended by the whole army as his guards.

In the mean time there fell out a miſunderſtanding between the ſenate and the populace. The former were for re-eſtabliſhing the commonwealth in all its ancient glory, and vindicating their authority from tyrannical uſurpations. The latter, envious of the power of the ſenate, deſired nothing more than an imperial check upon their pride and avarice, and a ſecure appeal for themſelves to an higher court from republican oppreſſions. So that the people were overjoyed at the elevation of Claudius, hoping that, under his protection, they might be preſerved from civil wars, and the renewal of thoſe horrid ſcenes that took place during the conteſt between Pompey and Cæſar.

The ſenate were no ſooner informed of the ſoldiers conducting Claudius to the army, than they diſpatched a certain number of choſen men of their own order, with inſtructions to admoniſh him "not to attempt to aſſume the government to himſelf by violence, but rather content himſelf in the ſtation of one of the ſenators, and leave the care of the public to that body who are qualified by the laws, to manage by themſelves, and by their direction all the officers of adminiſtration." They then reminded him how tyrannically the people had been ruled by former emperors, and particularly by Caius, and alſo of the danger in which himſelf ſtood from the wanton cruelty of that tyrant. They then aſſured him, that, if he would ſubmit to the ſenate, and re-adopt his former principles, he ſhould be crowned with honour by a free and powerful people, and gain the reputation of a wiſe and good man, by contenting himſelf to take his lot in the courſe of things in this world, whether it be higher or lower, as Providence ſhould appoint: but that, if he was determined to follow the example of the late emperor, they muſt certainly oppoſe him in his deſign, as they wanted neither ſoldiers or arms, nor any other neceſſaries for ſuch an undertaking, and that, after all, their dependence was upon the juſtice and power of the gods in favour of ſo righteous a cauſe as the defence of their country.

When the deputies, Veranius and Brocchus, who were both tribunes of the people, had acquitted themſelves of their commiſſion to Claudius in words to this effect, they caſt themſelves at his feet, with the moſt earneſt ſupplications to avoid any proceeding that had a tendency to bring the people into a civil war. But finding him beſet with the ſoldiers, and that the power of the conſuls was far inferior to that of the army, they briefly added this requeſt, that if he was reſolved upon the ſovereignty, he would rather accept it from the ſenate, and take it upon him without violence, as it would be much more auſpicious to receive with the good-will of the people, than to take it from them by force. They concluded with obſerving, that, if he received the ſovereignty from the hands of the ſenate, it would indicate a diſpoſition to govern with that mildneſs and ſerenity that ſhould be the characteriſtic of royalty: but that, if he refuſed to accept it from them, it would indicate a deſign of his wiſhing to tyrannize over the people, inſtead of governing them in a manner conſiſtent with the principles of a prudent man, and good ſovereign.

CHAP. [illegible]

[illegible] of Agrippa, [illegible] Claudius [illegible] to accept [illegible] the [illegible] of Agrippa [illegible] the [illegible] The [illegible] Claudius [illegible] Claudius [illegible] the [illegible]

CLAUDIUS, being well acquainted with the haughty [illegible] of the senate, gave their deputies a courteous answer for the present, as he could [illegible], without [illegible] at their mercy. But, through the advice [illegible] of the soldiers, the instigation of Agrippa, and the [illegible] to stand by him in asserting his pretensions, he was prevailed upon not to decline his claim to the dignity which they had conferred upon him.

When Agrippa had decently disposed of the [illegible] of the late emperor Caius, to whom he owed his crown, and [illegible] every thing in as good order as circumstances would admit, he went to the guards, and gave it out that Caius was not dead, but [illegible] wounded, and that therefore he [illegible] to him. Being informed soon after that Claudius [illegible] by the soldiers [illegible] sent for him [illegible] found him [illegible] involved [illegible] delivering [illegible] to the senate [illegible] Agrippa [illegible] him to [illegible] on [illegible]

[illegible] this [illegible] to the senate [illegible] the same, [illegible] in the [illegible] to him [illegible] opinion of the [illegible] Agrippa replied, "that there [illegible] to [illegible] the [illegible] that he was [illegible] to the [illegible] could [illegible] would rather [illegible] the [illegible] good [illegible] commonwealth, than the speaking of [illegible] of [illegible] it was [illegible] provision of arms, [illegible] and money, for a foundation [illegible] would be fruitless [illegible] for ambition and power." He replied, "[illegible] had abundance of the articles he mentioned, and [illegible] numbers they had [illegible] ought to [illegible] them [illegible] of [illegible] freedom [illegible] the partizans of Claudius were [illegible] experience [illegible] on the other hand, [illegible] was composed of [illegible] and untractable [illegible] and [illegible] propose, with their concurrence, [illegible] deputies to Claudius to endeavour to prevail with him to [illegible] his crown, and that, with their approbation, he would be one to go upon the business."

The senate, [illegible] the proposal was reasonable, [illegible] and [illegible] others, upon the [illegible] But Agrippa, [illegible] means of [illegible] Claudius [illegible] prevailed in the [illegible] to [illegible] answer to the deputies becoming [illegible] of [illegible] prince, Claudius [illegible] the [illegible] person, [illegible] considering [illegible] the [illegible] of [illegible] to [illegible] their [illegible] and [illegible] and [illegible] the

"[illegible] the [illegible] the [illegible] for the [illegible] to the [illegible] he [illegible] the [illegible] made [illegible] even in [illegible]" With [illegible] the [illegible] of the [illegible] and [illegible] and [illegible] to the [illegible] that were [illegible]

Upon this the [illegible] the [illegible] of [illegible] Caius [illegible] the [illegible] to [illegible] who [illegible] in [illegible]

[illegible] of the [illegible] to [illegible] for [illegible] they found [illegible] them [illegible] the [illegible] three [illegible] men [illegible] not [illegible] to [illegible] Caius [illegible] the [illegible] Claudius [illegible] of [illegible] and [illegible] and [illegible] Claudius [illegible] spirit [illegible] and [illegible] to [illegible] then [illegible] that the [illegible] themselves.

After [illegible] of [illegible] Caius [illegible] the [illegible] and [illegible] that they [illegible] their [illegible] the government [illegible] the dignity of the [illegible] of [illegible] of the [illegible] "[illegible] once [illegible] of Caius [illegible] to [illegible] that he could [illegible] to the [illegible] Claudius [illegible] of the [illegible]

Thus [illegible] and [illegible] Agrippa [illegible] the [illegible]

[illegible] to [illegible] and [illegible] his [illegible] Sabinus, one of the conspirators, [illegible] that he would [illegible] his [illegible] in the [illegible] of every man, rather than [illegible] to acknowledge the imperial authority of Claudius [illegible] He reproached Cherea, for having [illegible] the principal [illegible] of the common liberty, [illegible] Caius, in [illegible] to [illegible] for ordinal, [illegible] could [illegible] Cherea declared his [illegible] resolution [illegible] but that he [illegible] to know in the [illegible] how Claudius [illegible]

During [illegible] in the [illegible] to [illegible] from all quarters, to pay their court to Claudius [illegible] the rest, one of the [illegible] Quintus Pomponius, who had [illegible] the [illegible] of [illegible] the [illegible] to [illegible] and [illegible] with the [illegible] and [illegible] Claudius [illegible] were not [illegible] by blows as they [illegible] wounded and [illegible] of [illegible] danger [illegible] king Agrippa, who [illegible] and the [illegible] extirpation of the [illegible] to treat the [illegible] general, with courtesy [illegible] for [illegible] game or [illegible]

[illegible] Cherea and Sabinus [illegible] the [illegible] of the [illegible] Claudius [illegible] to [illegible] into [illegible] of [illegible] Cherea [illegible] to the place of [illegible] and several [illegible] of [illegible] According to [illegible] Cherea [illegible] degree of [illegible] the dignity of an exalted mind [illegible] the contrary [illegible] token of [illegible] Cherea [illegible] contempt [illegible] upon [illegible] for [illegible] stripping [illegible] of [illegible] the import of his [illegible] Roman language [illegible] he asked him, whether [illegible] and desired [illegible] weapon with which he slew Caius [illegible] dispatched him at one stroke. But [illegible] the position of his [illegible] by [illegible] before the office [illegible] business. Some few days after, on the festival [illegible] the people's [illegible] ghosts of their deceased [illegible] by casting their offerings into the fire [illegible] to the usual ceremony, they paid the same honour to Cherea as to the dead, begging [illegible] for their late ingratitude, to so [illegible] a patriot [illegible] Cherea [illegible] the glorious cause of [illegible] He was a man who possessed [illegible] of [illegible] rarely to be found among elevated characters. His being the instrument [illegible] of that abominable tyrant [illegible] justly applauded by the people in general, who lamented the death of so distinguished a patriot for the cause of liberty and his country.

Claudius not only pardoned Sabinus, but continued him in his command. The noble Roman, however, made no [illegible] of his [illegible] to rid himself of a [illegible] by falling upon his own sword.

CHAP. IV.

[illegible] to Agrippa [illegible] the [illegible] of Claudius [illegible]

THE [illegible] of Claudius, [illegible] from the [illegible] the [illegible] of [illegible] confirming [illegible] the [illegible] conferred upon [illegible] Caius, [illegible] services [illegible] Samaria, over which [illegible] death Herod had [illegible] them to the right of his [illegible] Abila, and [illegible] Lysanias, [illegible] his [illegible] out of his own territories. [illegible] between [illegible] Agrippa, and the people of Rome, were set up in the middle of the forum, as [illegible] He also [illegible] of which he was possessed, [illegible] Chalcis and [illegible] Alexander Lysimachus [illegible] his old friend, and superintendant of the [illegible] his [illegible] Alexander, who had been imprisoned [illegible] Herod Berenice, [illegible] to his son Marcus [illegible] the [illegible] by [illegible] Claudius, the king [illegible]

[illegible] there was a tumult [illegible] the Jews and the Greeks, in the city of Alexandria [illegible] of Caius, during whose reign the Jews of Alexandria had been greatly oppressed, they took up arms [illegible] Claudius [illegible] the [illegible] of Egypt to [illegible] endeavours to suppress [illegible] at the request of the kings Agrippa and Herod, sent an edict to Alexandria and Syria, according to the following contents:

"Tiberius Claudius Cæsar Augustus Germanicus, [illegible] "[illegible] of the [illegible] greeting.

"Whereas we [illegible] to understand [illegible] from time to time enjoyed "[illegible] privileges, from former kings of Egypt, "in common with the rest of the inhabitants, as appears by "several royal decrees, and [illegible] of record, at this day "extant in confirmation thereof, and likewise that the "rights and benefits have been continued to them ever "since the annexing of that city by Augustus to our empire, "[illegible] by the governors of Alexandria successively, "[illegible] also in the same Augustus [illegible] "to substitute another in his stead [illegible] the free exercise of their religion and discipline, without any molestation or control.

"Now, forasmuch as Caius Cæsar, in a blasphemous "excess of madness, hath [illegible] upon the Jews "to worship him as a god, contrary to the good faith and "honour of the imperial [illegible] [illegible] violence "upon the [illegible] and breaking into [illegible] the [illegible] [illegible] "[illegible] against the Jews, their fellow-citizens, [illegible] to declare all those proceedings of Caius null and void, [illegible] the "said privileges of the Jews [illegible] "virtue, requiring and commanding, both the one and the "other, by this our [illegible] authority, to live [illegible] "[illegible] together, without "troubling the public peace." These are the contents "of the [illegible] and after this, in particular for Alexandria, there was another sent abroad by the same prince, in favour of the Jews all over the empire, in the following terms:

"Tiberius [illegible] Augustus Germanicus, "high-priest, tribune of the people, [illegible] consul [illegible], given to [illegible] that

"Upon [illegible] of the kings Agrippa and Herod [illegible] great [illegible], to [illegible] same liberty to the "Jews [illegible] empire [illegible] and [illegible], "that we [illegible] granted them in Alexandria, [illegible] "[illegible] comply [illegible] their desire, not "only [illegible] of the [illegible], but out of a respect "[illegible] of the people, [illegible] acknowledgement "[illegible] friendship and good offices that have ever [illegible]-"ded to the [illegible] Rome. Wherefore we judge it "reasonable to [illegible] committed to [illegible] the com-"[illegible] cities, as well Greek "[illegible] of them [illegible] maner as "they [illegible] Augustus [illegible] "And [illegible] there [illegible] that, where-"ever [illegible] within the com-"[illegible] be allowed to govern "them [illegible] without any let or in-"terruption [illegible] that they [illegible] modest [illegible] or "[illegible] other people "[illegible] they them-"[illegible] to [illegible] the [illegible] "[illegible] we have thought fit to decree. And it "is [illegible] command that [illegible] proclamation "[illegible] all [illegible], nations, towns "[illegible] of our do-"minions [illegible], and comes "[illegible] governors "[illegible] and com-"pose [illegible] point."

CHAP. [illegible]

Claudius [illegible] deposes Theophilus [illegible] dig-nity [illegible] of Simon [illegible] of a [illegible] the Jews.

CLAUDIUS CÆSAR [illegible], having made [illegible] hold [illegible] he conceived [illegible] of his government [illegible] to a greater dig-nity [illegible] of special recom-[illegible] provinces [illegible] to [illegible] dispatched all [illegible] with expedition [illegible], he has-tened [illegible] acquitted [illegible] holy [illegible] greatest [illegible] of the [illegible] for the sufferings inflicted upon [illegible], Tiberius, who had formerly commanded [illegible] chain, [illegible] a golden chain of equal weight [illegible] Agrippa caused to be suspended [illegible] the temple, over the receptacle of the [illegible] severity of his pun-ishment [illegible] on his behalf, as well as [illegible] that the same Divine Power [illegible] dejects. The chain re-[illegible] a prince more the most [illegible], with his deliver-ance [illegible] to greater dignity [illegible], circum-stances [illegible] vicissitudes of hu-man nature.

When Agrippa had attended to the duties of Divine worship, he deposed Theophilus from the high-priest-hood [illegible] Simon, the son of [illegible] was [illegible], and whose daughter [illegible] had [illegible] Simon, therefore, held the [illegible] and with his [illegible] Simon the son of Onias, [illegible] held it under the Macedonian [illegible]

[illegible] high-priest-hood, he [illegible] acknowledge the [illegible] and [illegible] received from the [illegible] of Jerusalem, by [illegible] to [illegible] Heasson [illegible], a man who had [illegible] him in [illegible]

Soon [illegible] of Doris [illegible] had the [illegible] into the syna-gogue of the Jews [illegible] Agrippa, [illegible] and laws of his country. He [illegible] to [illegible] governor of Syria, [illegible] of the most [illegible] Agrippa, [illegible] laws [illegible] the [illegible] of Doris, [illegible]

CHAP. VI.

Petronius [illegible] of Doris [illegible] good [illegible] Petronius [illegible]

"Publius Petronius, governor of S[illegible] "ment of Claudius Cæsar, [illegible] "the magistrates of Doris, greeting.

"WHEREAS I have rec[illegible], "that, notwithstanding [illegible] full liberty [illegible] "the Jews [illegible] Claudius Cæsar Augustus "Germanicus, to live according to [illegible] "[illegible] of their own [illegible], some of you [illegible] "been so audacious, in contempt of [illegible] "edict, to prophane their synagogue, [illegible] "Cæsar's statue there to [illegible] "religion, being [illegible] the [illegible] "dom Cæsar hath [illegible] "their consciences, but [illegible] "of Cæsar himself, [illegible] should [illegible] "set up in his own temple [illegible] especially "in the synagogue [illegible] the emperor himself [illegible] "it meet [illegible] to leave every man [illegible] him-"self. I shall [illegible] of my own [illegible] this [illegible] "tain, [illegible] upon the [illegible] "[illegible], who has not only indulged the Jews in the "matter of their religion, but granted [illegible] the pri-"vileges of free men [illegible] "they inhabit, in common with the Greeks. [illegible] "[illegible] that this [illegible] "been committed, and the majesty of Cæsar [illegible] "despised, [illegible] on yourselves [illegible] "in the thing, [illegible] to turn it off to the [illegible] "[illegible], this is [illegible] require, [illegible] "you [illegible] Vitellius Proculus [illegible] "the guilty persons to [illegible] "have done [illegible] him who [illegible] "not your lives will be [illegible] "tors [illegible]. In the mean time, [illegible] "the public peace, [illegible] "would put all [illegible]. But as [illegible] "ter and myself [illegible] "hands, as to keep [illegible] the Jews [illegible] "tion or pretext [illegible] troublesome [illegible] "defence. And now for your [illegible] "opinion the emperor [illegible] "lest you [illegible] "[illegible] "shewed me (though every body knew it already) as I "was sitting upon the tribunal positively requiring that "the Cæsar's concessions to the Jews should be made "good. Wherefore I do now charge and require it of "you, for the future, to forbear all manner of seditious "controversies, and leave them to worship their God quietly "in their own way."

Petronius, by these means, removed the grievance complained of by the Jews, and rendered the Greeks cautious of attempting the like infringement for the future.

Soon after this king Agrippa removed Simon from the high-priesthood, with an intent to transfer it to Jonathan, the son of Ananus, as a person more deserving of that dignity. But he declined it, with due acknowledgement of the favour designed him, observing "that, since God had been pleased to judge him unworthy of holding it, he should content himself with the honour of having once worn the [illegible] belonging to it, as he could better justify his entrance upon the holy function at first, than he could [illegible] it, begging permission to recommend [illegible] in his [illegible], inoffensive before God [illegible] consequently better qualified for the [illegible] office." The king was so pleased with the [illegible] modesty of [illegible] that, with his advice, he transferred the pontificate to his brother Matthias. Much about the same time Petronius was dismissed from the government of Syria, and Marcus appointed to succeed him.

CHAP. VII.

The [illegible] by the king, who, at the [illegible] of [illegible], [illegible] the [illegible] of Jerusalem [illegible] of the [illegible] and [illegible] of Agrippa. The [illegible] are transferred to [illegible] Games [illegible] at [illegible] of Agrippa, [illegible] of [illegible] his folly [illegible] He [illegible] [illegible] of Cæsarea [illegible] [illegible] his friends, [illegible] to Cæsarea [illegible]

SILAS the king's generalissimo, presuming on his fidelity to his master, and the very singular personal services he had rendered him, as well as the great [illegible] that had subsisted between them, began to aspire at [illegible] with him, and dictate to him on the most important occasions, as if he absolutely thought himself entitled to a share in the government. He took upon him to [illegible] not only with [illegible] freedom, but frequently [illegible] insolence, [illegible] of his own merit, reminding the king of his former [illegible] estate, and ostentatiously representing the good offices he had done him.

[illegible] repetition of these circumstances could not fail to [illegible] the king, as it is disagreeable to human nature to be reminded of unpleasing events, nor can any thing be more dangerous than a perpetual intimation of obligations. Silas persisted in this arrogant behaviour so long as to incense the king [illegible] to such a degree, that he not only deprived him of his commission but sent him in bonds to his own country. When his resentment, however, began to subside, and he reflected on his [illegible] to a man who had undergone so many dangers and difficulties in his service, the anniversary of his [illegible] appointed [illegible] for Silas to be present at the [illegible] But [illegible] being a man of a frank disposition, and one that could not disguise his sentiments, especially when he thought he had reason on his side, [illegible] to the messengers that brought the invitation, "that, notwithstanding the apparent honour the king did him [illegible] of complacency, as he had often experienced, were [illegible] that, after he had taken away not only his commission, but, as far as he could, his reputation, he could not imagine that, aggrieved as [illegible] as, he could conceal such flagrant injustice, that the world should know the distress from which he had delivered him, the difficulties and dangers he had encountered [illegible] as [illegible] the reward he had received [illegible] a dungeon and a chain." He then [illegible] the messengers with advice, or rather orders, that they would carry back this answer to the king. This being done, and Agrippa finding his petulance incurable, commanded him to continue in prison.

Agrippa now turned his thoughts towards the concerns of the city, and repaired the walls of that part which was called the New Town at the public charge, making them [illegible] stronger and higher than they were before. Such was his zeal and assiduity, that, in the end, he would have rendered Jerusalem impregnable had not Marcus, the governor of Syria, given Claudius Cæsar cautionary notice of it, and the emperor, from suspicion of attempts at innovation, [illegible] command on Agrippa, by letter, to desist from the work.

The king of the Jews was of so affable and generous a disposition, that his greatest delight was to display his munificence, and acquire fame by the exercise of [illegible] He was a character in contrast with that of Herod who reigned before him, the one being inflexibly rigid, implacably cruel, and notoriously partial to the Greeks in preference to the Jews, as appears from his profusion of treasure upon foreign works both in structure and ornament, as baths, theatres, temples, galleries, promenades and the like, whereas he was never known to have put himself to any extraordinary expence to [illegible] the nation of the Jews. Agrippa, on the contrary, was gently benevolent, the common [illegible] of mankind, but particularly attached to the common interest and welfare of his country. He made Jerusalem his constant residence, strictly conformed to all the rites and ceremonies of the religion, without the corruption of any [illegible] superstitious mixture, nor did he suffer a day to pass without its appointed sacrifice.

Notwithstanding the very respectable character Agrippa had justly acquired, one Simon, a professor of the law, endeavoured to vilify him. The king being absent at Cæsarea, this man took occasion, in a public assembly, to reflect on him, as not living according to the [illegible] precepts of the Jewish religion, and therefore deserving of exclusion from the temple. One of Agrippa's principal officers sent him information of the charge alleged against him by Simon, who was immediately cited to appear before the king. At the time of his arrival, Agrippa happening to be in the theatre, called to him, and asked him, in a gentle tone, "if he knew of any thing he had done contrary to the laws of his country?" Simon having no reply to make in justification of his charge, with confusion of face implored his pardon, which the king granted beyond all expectations, and, to confirm his character, added to this singular proof of his clemency as remarkable an instance of his bounty, valuing himself more upon the exercise of mercy than power, and esteeming it more worthy a king to be humane than rigorous.

All the different places through which he passed had some taste of his bounty and magnificence, but Berytus [illegible] above the rest, for there he erected at an immense charge a stately theatre, an amphitheatre, with several baths and porticoes, sparing no cost to render the respective edifices the models of perfection. The pomp of the dedication of these eminent buildings was equal to the stateliness of them, as the entertainments of the theatre were composed of most pleasing variety. In the amphitheatre were exposed the combats of gladiators, and man to man, and after that a whole army of condemned malefactors, to the number of seven hundred on each side. This might be deemed an execution of justice [illegible] the form of a battle, as they were all destroyed, to the very last man.

Agripp... rately ... ttes, ... to ... s city of ... coverted ... kings ... king of Comagena, ... Sampsigeram ... of ..., Cotis, king of the lesser Armenia, Polemon, a ... prince, and Heron, brother of Agrippa, and king of Chalcis. ... were treated with a magnificence and hospitality becoming the dignity of the host and his guests, ... redounded to the honour of Agrippa ... royal visits. During the ... of these kings with him, Marcus, the governor of Syria, came over to him, and Agrippa, to preserve ... due to the sovereignty of the empire, went seven furlongs out of the city to meet him. But this proved ... an occasion of a misunderstanding between him and the governor; for as the kings accompanied ... Marcus ... such apparent friendship among them, ... to ... that ... might be ... to ... potentates; and therefore he ... to each of them enjoining them to depart without delay, which gave Agrippa such offence, that ... reconcile ... to him. The pontificate was ... from Matthias, ... conferred upon ... the son of Cantheras.

Agrippa, in the third year of his reign over ... Judæa came to the city of Cæsarea, formerly called the Tower of Straton, where he exhibited games and shews in honour of Cæsar. ... this festival drew together great numbers of persons of ... rank, from ... parts of the province. On the second day the king went to the theatre in most ... and ... apparel, his vest ... being of ... costly ..., and ... interwoven with ... as well as ornamented with jewels of ..., that ... the eyes of the ... to ... with veneration. Some ... flatterers, ... addressed him as a god, ... their ignorance ... hitherto ... whereas they were now ... excellency in his ... The king ... rebuked them not ... their ... ; but while he was gratifying his vanity to this excess, he espied an owl perched on a rope over his head, which he soon found to be a presage of ill to him now, as it had been of good heretofore. He fell into an extremity of internal pains, and turning to many about him, thus addressed them: "Behold your god ... condemned to die, and thereby prove "the fallacy of your flatterers, and convince the world "that he is ... I have had no reason to envy the "happiness of any prince upon the face of the earth, but "yet ... beyond the ... of human nature. The "will of ... be done."

At these words, ... he was removed to the palace, and it was rumoured throughout the city, that the king was at the point of death. The multitude was so affected the ... that men, women, and children, put on sackcloth, according to custom, and joined in fervent supplications to ... for the recovery of the king; who, looking down from his apartment in the palace, could not forbear weeping at the sight of the ... prostrate upon the pavement below. After struggling with the acutest pains, without an interval of ease, for five successive days, he departed this life in the fifty-fourth year of his age, and seventh of his ... He ... of ... Caius ... of them ... the tetrarchy of Philip, ... that of Herod, ... that of Claudius ... to the government of Judæa, added those of Samaria and Cæsarea. His ... revenue was computed at twelve millions of drachmæ, ... he was so profuse ... that ... not being adequate to his expences, he frequently borrowed great sums. Before his death ... Chelcias, ... and Herod, prince of Chalcis, both of them ... to ... as ... had been done by the king ...

This was the end of king Agrippa, who left behind him a son of his own name, a youth in the seventeenth year of his age, and three daughters. Bernice, the eldest, at the age of sixteen, was married to Herod, his father's brother. Mariamne was contracted to Julius Archelaus, the son of Chelcias; and Drusilla to Epiphanes, the son of Antiochus, king of Comagena.

When the ... of king Agrippa was ... the people of Cæsarea and Sebaste, forgetting the obligations he had laid upon them by so many instances of his ... treated his memory with the utmost disrespect. A body of soldiers ... statues of his daughters ... the palace ... and ... their characters in a manner too indecent to be related. They also celebrated festivals, with garlands on their heads, ointments and libations to Charon, ... the death of the king. Nay, they were not only ungrateful to Agrippa, who had abundantly extended his liberality to them, but to his grandfather Herod also, who had himself ... their cities, and raised their temples and harbours at a vast expence.

Agrippa, the son of the deceased, was at this time at Rome, and trained up in the court of Claudius, who no sooner had intelligence of the death of his father, and the indignities offered to his memory, by the inhabitants of Cæsarea and Sebaste, than he expressed great sorrow for the loss of Agrippa, and resentment of the ingratitude. He then determined to send away the son to succeed his father in the kingdom, pursuant to the oath he had taken, and agreeable to the laws of equity and reason. But his friends representing to him the danger of reposing a trust in the hands of an inexperienced youth, that was equal to the best ... in the empire, he was diverted from his purpose, and, through their insinuations, gave the whole government to Cuspius Fadus, with this deference to the memory of the deceased, that he should by no means introduce Marcus, who had been at variance with him, into any office within his jurisdiction. He also gave Fadus express charge to chastise the inhabitants of Cæsarea and Sebaste most severely for the indignities they had offered to the memory of the deceased, and the diligence they had ... upon the characters of his daughters. He gave orders that he should send away the troops which were in those two cities of Pontus, and detach a body of chosen men out of the Roman legions in Syria to supply their places. But this last order was not obeyed; for Claudius was prevailed upon, with humble supplication, to continue those troops still in Judæa. These very men became the source of the great calamities that afterwards befel the Jews, and sowed those seeds of contention, from which sprung the war under the government of Florus, insomuch that Vespasian though conqueror, was obliged to transport them out of that country.

END OF THE NINETEENTH BOOK.

FLAVIUS JOSEPHUS

ON THE

ANTIQUITIES

OF THE

JEWS.

BOOK XX

[INCLUDING A PERIOD OF ABOUT TWENTY-ONE YEARS.]

CHAP. I.

Claudius appoints Caſſius Longinus to the government of Syria. Diſſentions between the Jews and Philadelphians. Tholomæus, leader of a band of robbers, put to death. Agrippa, ſon of the late king, moves Claudius in favour of the Jews. Joſeph appointed high-prieſt.

UPON the death of king Agrippa, Claudius Cæſar appointed Caſſius Longinus ſucceſſor to Marcus in the government of Syria, out of reſpect to the memory of his deceaſed friend, who, in his life time, had often requeſted, by letters, that he would remove Marcus from his office.

When Cuſpius Fadus entered upon his command in Judæa, he found great contentions prevailed between the Jews beyond Jordan, and the Philadelphians, about the bounds of a ſmall village, called Mais, the inhabitants of which were a brave and warlike people. The Jews of Perea had taken up arms, without any colour of authority from their ſuperiors, and killed ſeveral of the Philadelphians. Fadus was ſo incenſed at this ſeditious inſolence, that he cauſed three of the ringleaders to be put in chains, Annibas, Amaram, and Eleazar. The firſt was afterwards put to death, and the other two were baniſhed.

Soon after this Tholomæus, the notorious leader of a band of robbers, who had committed ravages in Idumæa and Arabia, was brought to him in chains, and ſentenced to death; nor was any thing wanting on the part of Fadus to clear the country of theſe plunderers. He ſent after this to the prieſts and rulers of Jeruſalem, and ſhewed them Cæſar's mandate, requiring that the veſtments peculiarly belonging to the high-prieſt ſhould be depoſited in the caſtle of Antonia, and there remain in the cuſtody of the Romans, as they had done in former times. The Jews durſt not diſpute the commands of the emperor, and therefore choſe to make reſpectful application to Fadus and Longinus (who had his troops about him by way of ſecurity) for permiſſion to move Claudius upon that point, and reſpite the proceeding till they might receive the emperor's anſwer. This requeſt was granted, upon condition of delivering up their ſons for hoſtages in the mean time, to which they readily agreed, and the deputies proceeded on their embaſſy.

Agrippa, being then in Rome at the court of Cæſar, and having timely notice of their arrival and buſineſs, petitioned Cæſar in behalf of the Jews, that the ſacred veſtments might remain in their own poſſeſſion, and that he would vouchſafe to ſignify his pleaſure to Fadus by an order to that purpoſe. Claudius, upon this, ſent for the deputies into his preſence, and having told them that he had granted their requeſt, and called upon them to thank Agrippa for his interpoſition in their behalf, gave them the following letter.

"Claudius Cæſar Germanicus, tribune of the people, the "fifth time conſul elect, the fourth time emperor, and "the father of his country the tenth time, to the ſenate, "the people of Jeruſalem, and the whole nation of the "Jews, greeting.

"Whereas we are given to underſtand by our dearly beloved Agrippa, whom we have trained up as tender as our "own child, that you have ſent us your deputies (which deputies he hath alſo preſented to us) with acknowledgment "of our conſtant cares for the good of your people, and "likewiſe with your earneſt deſire of having the pontifical "robes and ornaments in your own cuſtody, we do freely "grant ye your requeſt, in ſuch manner as was formerly "allowed you in the days of that excellent perſon Vitellius, "our very dear friend. And be it further known unto you, "that we have deſcended to theſe conceſſions, partly out of a "motive of piety, it ſeeming unto us a reaſonable thing for "all men to enjoy the religion of their country, and partly "to gratify king Herod and the young Aristobulus, whose "friendship we have a great value for, upon the certain "knowledge of the friendship they both have for us."

"We have written to our lieutenant Caspius Fadus about "this matter, by Cornelius the son of Ceron, Tryphon, "the son of Theudion, Dorotheus, the son of Nathanael, "and John, the son of John. Dated the fourth of the ca-"lends of July. Rufus and Pompeius Sylvanus consuls."

Herod, brother of the deceased Agrippa, and prince of Chalcis, petitioned Claudius Cæsar for the charge of the temple and holy treasure, with the privilege of appointing the high-priest. All this was granted him: and the power continued in the family till the end of the Jewish war. This prince removed Canthara from the pontificate, and appointed Joseph the son of Canæus to succeed him.

CHAP. II.

Helen, queen of Adiabena, and her son Izates, embrace the Jewish religion. Zeal of Izates for their rites and ceremonies. Eleazar, a professor of the Mosaic law, enforces the necessity of circumcision. The king Izates is convinced, and complies with it. A dreadful famine in Jerusalem. Liberal contributions of the queen and Izates for the relief of the inhabitants. Conspiracy against Artabanus, king of Parthia. Izates interposes in his behalf. Gratitude of Artabanus. His death. Vardanes, his son and successor, presses Izates to a war with the Romans. Makes war upon Izates, is cut off by his own people, and the government transferred to his brother. Izates detects a conspiracy and punishes the traitors. Izates involved in various disputes. His fortitude, modesty, piety, and humility. Death of Izates, and succession of Monobazus. Death of Helen, who, with her son, is interred in Jerusalem. Punishment of Theudas, a false prophet.

ABOUT this time Helen, queen of Adiabena, and Izates her son embraced the Jewish religion upon the following occasion. Monobasus, king of Adiabena, became enamoured of his sister, and took her to wife. As he was reposing one night in the term of her pregnancy, he fancied he heard a voice admonishing him to be cautious, lest, by any pressure, he might hurt the infant, which was designed by Providence as a blessing to mankind. The voice startled him, and when he awoke, he related the circumstance to his queen. The child at the birth proved to be a male; and the father gave him the name of Izates. He had another son by the same princess, whom he called after his own name, as well as several children by other wives; but his affection concentered in Izates.

This partial preference in the king, excited the jealousy and envy of the rest of the brothers. The king at first took no notice of it, hoping that, through his own prudent conduct, these passions by degrees would subside: but finding them on the contrary, rather increase, he thought it expedient, by way of security, to remove Izates from the palace, and the kingdom. He therefore dispatched him, with a particular recommendation, and sumptuous presents, to Abennerigus, at the fort of Spasinus, who esteemed him so highly, that he gave him his daughter Samacnas in marriage, with a very extensive portion of land as her dowry.

Monobasus being advanced in years, and apprehending the approach of his dissolution, had a great desire to see his darling son, and therefore sent for him to that purpose. Upon his arrival he embraced him with the tenderest affection, and bestowed upon him the province of Cæron, a spot famous for aromatic plants, and particularly for the remains of Noah's ark that escaped the deluge, and were there exposed to view. Izates took up his residence in this place during the life of his father. But upon the very day of the king's decease, queen Helen called her great officers of state and commanders together, and thus addressed them:

"I need not inform you that the late king, my husband, "designed Izates for his successor, as esteeming him of all his "sons most worthy of that honour. However, I wait your "determination, as the happiness of a prince depends not "on the approbation of an individual, but the suffrages of the "people in general." This courteous address was delivered to sound their opinion. It had a very good effect; for the council had no sooner heard of it, than, with the profoundest reverence, according to the custom of their country, they declared themselves unanimously disposed to advance Izates to the throne, being fully satisfied that it was agreeable to his father that it should be so, as the person of his family he accounted best qualified for that dignity. They assured her that the people were in his interest, and that themselves were not only ready to acknowledge him for their sovereign, but, in case of any danger from the pretensions of brothers, to obviate such obstacles, and pave him a safe and easy passage to the throne.

The queen most gratefully acknowledged this zeal and affection; but could by no means consent to the effusion of any blood, till Izates should be consulted upon that point. When the council found the queen thus disposed, they urged, however, that for the better security of the new king, they might be kept in safe custody, and some other person that the queen should best approve of, entrusted with the administration in his absence. The queen approved the proposal, and made choice of Monobasus, the elder brother, for the viceroy, set the crown upon his head, gave him his father's signet, and committed the care of the government into his hands, till his brother should come to take it himself. Izates did not long delay after he heard of his father's death, and immediately on his arrival Monobasus resigned his charge.

While Izates resided at the fort of Spasinus, a certain Jewish merchant, by name Ananias, having introduced himself to some of the female attendants belonging to the court, instructed them in the knowledge of the true God, and the rites and customs of the Jewish religion. By these means he became acquainted with Izates, whom he converted to the same religion, and attended him in his journey to Adiabena, whither his father sent to see him a short time before his death. Queen Helen was also converted to our profession by another Jew. Izates, upon his return to Adiabena, was much concerned to find his brothers, and others of his kindred, prisoners there. His conscience recoiled at the idea of either putting them to death, or keeping them in chains. On the other hand he thought it might be dangerous to set them at liberty under provocation to revenge; so that he prudently steered a middle course, and sent them away for hostages; part, with their children, to Rome, to Claudius Cæsar, others to Artabanus, king of Parthia.

When Izates began to find how highly his mother approved of the Jewish mode of worship, he thought it an incumbent duty to make public profession of his religion; and supposing he could not be in reality a Jew, without undergoing the form of circumcision, determined to perfect the work, by initiating himself with that ceremony. His mother endeavoured to divert him from it, apprehending that it would be attended with dangerous consequences. To this end she suggested to him, "that his subjects "would renounce their allegiance, if they heard their "own king had embraced another religion, and that they "would never endure a Jew upon the throne." This dissuasive suspended the execution of his purpose, and, in the mean time, he advised upon the point with Ananias, who assured him he entirely coincided in opinion with his mother, and threatened to leave him if he persisted in his resolution. Ananias very pertinently observed "that if the matter should become public, he "himself would be the greatest sufferer, as the author "of this change, and under the stigma of a seducer "and public enemy: besides, that religion being an act of "the heart, God might be worshipped in sincerity and truth, "without the external ceremony of circumcision, upon "principles of obedience to the precepts of Moses, and that "God would dispense with the omission of the operation, "when the peace and safety of his dominions would be en-"dangered by the observance of it." This persuasive of one of argument prevailed with the king according to the desire of his mother.

But the king soon wavered again in his opinion, it happened in short time that there came a Jew out of Galilee, whose name was Eleazar, and was versed in the Mosaic laws. This Eleazar being introduced to Izates as he was reading in the pentateuch, thus addressed him: "You do not consider, O "king, how great an injury you do the law, and how "heinous an offence you offer to God, in knowing his "will without obeying it. How long will you continue in "a state of uncircumcision? If you have not met with the law "that recommends it, read it, that you may be convinced of the "enormity of your crime in the omission of it." This address of Eleazar wrought so powerfully upon the king, that he immediately retired to a drawing-room and underwent the operation. He then sent for and gave information of the transaction to his mother and Ananias, who discovered the greatest astonishment and apprehension lest the discovery should hazard the loss of his kingdom, as his subjects would not endure a prince of another religion, and also lest themselves should be subject to danger, as the supposed abettors of the innovation. But Providence mercifully interposed in this behalf, by delivering Izates out of great perplexities and [illegible] desperate extremities, in order to demonstrate that piety and virtue shall never go unrewarded, and that the great disposer of all events will never forsake those who put themselves under his care and protection.

When queen Helen had the happiness of seeing her son settled in the peaceable possession of his crown, and finding he had acquired the reputation, both at home and abroad, of a prince highly favoured of God and man, she was much inclined to visit the city of Jerusalem, in order to worship and sacrifice in that temple, which was so famous all over the world. Her son not only readily gave his consent, furnished her amply with money and every other necessary for her voyage, and conducted her [illegible] upon her way.

She arrived at Jerusalem in a happy hour for the citizens, as so dreadful a famine prevailed at that time, that multitudes were perishing for want of bread. Their distress was no sooner made known to this benevolent princess, than she sent several of her train, some to one place, and some to another, to search for relief, insomuch that, in a short time, great quantities of wheat were brought from Alexandria, and dried figs from Cyprus, which she immediately caused to be distributed among the poor, and thereby acquired immortal honour throughout our nation. Her son Izates likewise on receiving intelligence of the famine, sent great benefactions in money to the rulers of Jerusalem, for the use of their poor; but a detail of these royal bounties will be more properly introduced in another place.

Artabanus, king of Parthia, perceiving that a combined party of powerful and factious noblemen had formed a plot against him, determined to apply to Izates for his advice, assistance, and protection, in his then embarrassed situation. Accordingly, having collected about a thousand of his kindred and servants, he proceeded, and met Izates by the way. He had no personal knowledge of him, but imagined him to be the prince to whom he was repairing, by the magnificence of his retinue. On approaching near, he saluted him with reverential awe, according to the custom of the country, and then made known his circumstances in words to this effect: "Behold, great prince, "your humble suppliant, and despise the object of your "generous compassion. It has been my fortune to be "cast down from the throne of majesty to a private and "obscure state, which has compelled me to have recourse "to your benevolence for succour. Of this I cannot de-[illegible] "from [illegible] so well acquainted [illegible] the vicissi-"tudes of human affairs, and considering that we cannot [illegible] "be our own, [illegible] degree of elevation is [illegible] "more formerly was [illegible] I might observe that it tends to "the common interest of princes to [illegible] each other, as the "success of one rebellion becomes a precedent for another, "by emboldening disaffected subjects." [illegible] words were accompanied with tears, and a dejected countenance.

Izates, by this time, perceived his petitioner was no less than Artabanus, king of Parthia. In that distressed condition he requested him to collect his scattered spirits and console himself with this assurance, that the injury was not past relief and that Providence would [illegible] speedy end to his distress. He added, that he should find in him a more effectual friend than he could possibly [illegible] and it was his determined resolution to see him restored to his crown, or give up his own. After [illegible] Izates set Artabanus on his own horse, and walked on foot by his side, in honour of a king he owned to be greater than himself. But Artabanus [illegible] at the compliment, and swore by all his hopes he had of recovering his dignity and fortune, that he would alight, unless the other would take his horse and go before him. Izates, in compliance with this resolution, ordered another horse and conducted him to his palace with all the deference and honour one prince could pay to another. He gave him the precedence in all places private and public, respecting his former glory and dignity, without the least degradation from his change of fortune; wisely considering it as the common lot of mortals to be exalted one day, and dejected another.

His mind being intent on rendering the promised services to Artabanus, Izates wrote a pressing letter to the Parthians to receive their king again, engaging his honour for their indemnity, and assuring them, that all past injuries should be forgiven and forgotten. The Parthians did not absolutely refuse, but pleaded by way of excuse, that they had transferred the crown to Cinnamus, and thereby precluded themselves from receiving Artabanus again, adding, that however, it might offer [illegible] could lay the foundation of an intestine commotion. Cinnamus, being of a generous and grateful disposition and having been educated under the immediate care and inspection of Artabanus, informed him in a letter, that if he would return, he would himself be answerable for his reception and security. Artabanus, upon this assurance returned. Cinnamus met him on the way, paid him reverence in form, saluted him with the title of king, took the crown from off his own head, and placed it upon the head of Artabanus. This was the manner in which he was restored to the kingdom, through the means of Izates, after he had been expelled from it by a faction of his own people. Artabanus expressed his gratitude to his benefactor, by a return of all honourable duty and respect. He gave him the privilege of wearing the Tiara upright, and to sleep upon a golden bed, which are marks of honour peculiar to the kings of Parthia. He bestowed upon him the country of Nisibis, formerly belonging to the king of Armenia, a large and fruitful territory, and famous for the ancient city of Antioch, afterwards called Mygdonia, that the Macedonians had erected there. These were the acknowledgments which Izates received from Artabanus, in consideration of the good offices he had rendered him.

Artabanus dying soon after appointed his son Vardanes to succeed him in his kingdom, who immediately tampered with Izates to draw him into a war with the Romans. But Izates was too well acquainted with the strength and conduct of those people to be drawn into a league against so powerful an enemy. Besides having five sons trained up among them, to learn their language and discipline, he had some marks of honour upon him as well as discretion, to render it prosperous. As he was himself convinced of the impropriety of such an undertaking he endeavoured to divert Vardanes from it, by representing the extraordinary strength and prowess of the Romans. But so far was the Parthian from being discouraged by the pomp of words, that he made war immediately upon Izates. Providence, however, so ordered matters for the humbling his vanity, that he was convinced of the advantages he would hence derive from giving up the enterprize. When the Parthians found Vardanes bent upon a war with the Romans, they took their opportunity to cut him off, and committed the government to his brother Gotarza, who was after taken off by treachery too, and his brother Vologeses succeeded him. He divided the government between his two brothers by the father's side. Pacorus, the elder, had Media, and Tiridates, the younger had Armenia.

Monobazus, the brother of the king, observing his exemplary piety and virtue, the blessings that attended his general conduct, and the universal esteem he acquired thereby, became desirous of renouncing the religion of their country and embracing that of the Jews. When this was made known to the grandees of the kingdom, they were not a little displeased, but stifled their resentment till a proper opportunity for shewing it. To this end they wrote to Abias, king of Arabia, and tempted him, with large promises of money, to make war upon their prince, with a solemn assurance that, upon the very first encounter, they would desert him, because they were determined to punish him for having abandoned the religion of his country. They entered into a league with the Arabian king, and pressed him to prosecute the design without delay. Abias complied with their desire, and forthwith marched with a considerable army against Izates. At the first onset, before they came to a close engagement, the army of Izates, according to former assurance, deserted their posts in a panic of consternation, without striking an effective blow. Izates, by this time, found himself evidently betrayed, but retreated without disorder to his camp, where, upon strict enquiry into the cause of this defection, he discovered it to be a manifest treason betwixt his people and the enemy, detected some of the conspirators, and punished them according to their deserts. The day following he went in pursuit of Abias, routed him, made a great slaughter of part of his army, put the rest to flight, and drove their king into a castle of Arsamus, which he took by storm, rifled, and carried off rich booty, and returned in triumph to Adiabena. Abias, finding himself encompassed on every side, fell by his own sword.

The grandees of Adiabena, however, though they failed in their first attempt, and were now at the mercy of the king, would not desist, but in a supplicatory letter to Vologeses, then king of Parthia, requested him to take them under his protection, rid them of Izates, and appoint some potentate of his own nation to rule over them, observing, that their king had incurred an universal odium, by apostatizing from the religion of his country.

The Parthian king, upon this application, commenced hostilities against Izates, without any colourable pretence. His first step was a revocation of all the honours and privileges which his father had conferred upon him, together with a menace of immediate war, if he dared to dispute his pleasure. This at first alarmed Izates, who deemed it reproachful to be thus forced into a resignation of those privileges he so honourably possessed and deserved. Persuaded that submission to the Parthian would avail him nothing he came to a determinate resolution of committing his cause to Providence, and, in full dependence on the Divine aid, of setting life, honour, and fortune, upon the issue of a battle. Thus resolved he secured his wives and children in a strong castle, laid up stores of corn in his magazine, burnt and destroyed all the forage about him, and put himself in a posture to receive the enemy. The king of Parthia had raised a formidable army of horse and foot, with great expedition, and pitched his camp upon the bank of a river that parts Adiabena from Media. Izates encamping also not far from thence with a body of six thousand horse, Vologeses gave him to understand by a messenger, that he was now advancing against him with the whole force of the empire, from Bactria to Euphrates, to chastise him for his ingratitude to his master, impiously observing, that the God whom he adored could not deliver him out of his hands. Izates replied to the messenger, that he was sensible of the superiority of the king of Parthia in point of numbers, and as sensible that he was under the protection of an omnipotent God, who was infinitely above all the controul of human power.

With this declaration he dismissed the messenger, and prostrating himself, with his wives and children, in a suppliant posture thus offered up his prayer to the Father of mercies to this effect

"Great God, and Governor of the universe, whom none of thy creatures ever served in vain, vouchsafe in mercy to look down upon thy servant, who hath now wholly cast himself upon thy Almighty power and infinite goodness. Deliver him out of the hands of his enemies, repress the presumptuous boldness, for the vindication of thine own honour, and avenge thyself upon them, for their blasphemous defiance of thine omnipotence."

The prayer and humiliation of this pious prince appeared so effectual, that, upon intelligence, the very same night, of the Dahæ and Sacæ (people of Scythia) falling into Parthia with a strong army, Vologeses drew off his forces without carrying his menaces into execution, which was an indication of the interposition of Divine Providence in favour of Izates.

This pious prince died soon after, in the fifty-fifth year of his age, and twenty-fourth of his reign. He left four sons behind him, but appointed his brother Monobazus for his successor, as a due acknowledgment of the integrity of his conduct, in delivering up the crown which he held in trust, in the absence of Izates, upon the death of their father. Queen Helen, the mother, could not but be greatly afflicted for the loss of so dear and dutiful a son, but it was some alleviation to her grief, to find that the elder brother succeeded to the government. She therefore immediately repaired to Adiabena, but did not long survive her favourite son Izates. Monobazus sent the bones of his brother and mother away to Jerusalem, to be deposited in the pyramids which she had built there. They were three in number, and about three furlongs distant from the city. The history of Monobazus will be given in another place.

While Fadus was governor of Judæa there was a certain magician, called Theudas, who, by his arts, brought the common people into a belief, that if they would follow him to the river Jordan, and take their effects along with them, he would but give the word, and the waters should divide, and afford them an easy passage over it on foot. This impostor drew after him a numerous train of followers, but they suffered for their presumption and folly, for Fadus, sending a troop of horse among them, before they were aware, many of them were slain, and many taken alive, and among the rest their deluded Theudas, whose head was carried as a spectacle to Jerusalem.

CHAP. III.

Tiberius Alexander succeeds Cuspius Fadus in the government of Judæa. A great famine in that province. Crucifixion of James and Simon. Cumanus taxes Galilee. Cumanus succeeds Tiberius Alexander. Death of Herod, brother of Agrippa. Claudius transfers the government to the younger, Agrippa.

FADUS was succeeded in the government of Judæa by Tiberius Alexander, son of Alexander, of Alexandria, a much more respectable character than his son, who renounced the religion of his country. Under these procurators, the great famine happened in Judæa before mentioned, when the benevolent and humane queen Helena procured relief for the distressed out of Egypt at immense charge. It was at the same time also, that Alexander caused to be crucified James and Simon, the sons of Judas of Galilee, who, while Cyrenius was taxing Galilee, was inciting the Jews to revolt from the Romans. Herod king of Chalcis removed Joseph, the son of Camydus, from the office of high-priest, and appointed Ananias the son of Nebodeus, to the succession. Cumanus succeeded Tiberius. At the same time Herod brother of Agrippa the Great, departed this life, in the eighth year of the reign of Claudius Cæsar, leaving behind him three sons, Aristobulus, whom he had by a former wife, and Berenicianus and Hyrcanus whom he had by Berenice, his brother's daughter, but Claudius conferred the government upon Agrippa the younger.

CHAP. IV.

A tumult between the soldiery and populace, upon the feast of the passover, is productive of the most fatal consequences. The books of Moses found among the spoils, and exposed [illegible]. The multitude apply to Cumanus for justice [illegible] condign punishment on the offender.

WHILE Cumanus ruled in Judæa a tumult happened at Jerusalem upon the following occasion, which proved fatal to many thousands of the inhabitants. The festival of the passover, or unleavened bread, now approaching, vast multitudes of people repaired to Jerusalem to be present at the solemnity. Cumanus, the governor, thought it expedient, for fear of any disturbance, to set a band of soldiers as a guard upon the temple sufficient to suppress a tumult, if occasion should require it, as had frequently been done by his predecessors. Upon the fourth day of the festival, a soldier exposed himself naked to the people, an act at once so indecent and insolent, that they exclaimed most outrageously against it, not so much as an affront put upon them, as an indignity offered to God himself, to whose honour this feast was dedicated. Some of them reproached Cumanus as if the soldier would not have had the hardiness to behave in this manner without his encouragement. Cumanus though [illegible] fo [illegible] an imputation, suppressed his resentment, and desired them, in fair terms, to avoid any instance of behaviour that might look like sedition. But he soon found that gentle means would have no effect, as they tended to increase rather than suppress the outrage. He therefore commanded the whole army, completely accoutred, into the castle of Antonia, which, as [illegible] observed, overlooked the temple. The common people were so alarmed at the approach of the soldiers, that they betook themselves to flight with the utmost precipitation, and pressing one upon another, through several narrow avenues, many of them were thrown down and trodden under foot, insomuch that twenty thousand persons perished upon the occasion, a circumstance that turned that day of festival into a day of mourning, in which outcries and lamentations universally prevailed.

This calamity was attended by another equally fatal, for some of those, who had escaped the pressure of the crowd, and advanced a hundred furlongs from the town, meeting with a domestic of the emperor's on the highway, whose name was Stephanus, they insulted and robbed him of all he had. Cumanus receiving intelligence of this outrage, dispatched a band of soldiers to the spot where it was committed with orders to take all the adjacent villages, and bring away some of the principal inhabitants prisoners. In the midst of this pillage, one of the soldiers seized upon the books of Moses among the other plunder, and presenting them to the populace, [illegible] both against them and the whole nation of the Jews in the most opprobrious terms, and then tore them to pieces. This flagrant contempt of what they held most sacred was no sooner made known to the Jews than they assembled in great numbers, and preferred their complaint to Cumanus, who was then at Cæsarea, and called upon him to do them right on the offender, not as guilty of a private injury, but [illegible] heinous offence to the majesty of [illegible]. The governor durst not deny them justice, lest a popular revolt should ensue, so that after consulting his friends, he ordered the criminal's head to be struck off for the violation of the law, and by that means put a stop to the progress of the tumult.

CHAP. V.

A dissention between the Jews and the Samaritans. The Jews [illegible] the [illegible] Cumanus [illegible] to the [illegible] the multitude. The Samaritans call upon the governor for justice on the Jews, who had [illegible] several [illegible] Ananias and [illegible] sent to Rome. Claudius [illegible] the cause between the Samaritans and Jews [illegible] former [illegible] condemned to die. Cumanus banished, and Celer, the tribune, dragged to death in the streets. Claudius [illegible] governor in Judæa [illegible] great favour to Agrippa, [illegible] Drusilla [illegible] Death of Claudius Cæsar, [illegible] to have been [illegible] poison. Nero [illegible] emperor of Rome. [illegible] Aristobulus [illegible] government of the lesser Armenia [illegible] Aristobulus, and [illegible] part of Galilee [illegible] Agrippa.

AFTER this tumult a dissention arose between the Samaritans and Jews upon the following occasion. It being usual for the Galileans to travel by the way of Samaria to Jerusalem, upon the celebration of their festivals, they happened to pass by a village called Nais [illegible] the jurisdiction of Samaria, and situated on the great plain, where a dispute arose between the passengers and the villagers, and several of the Galileans were slain. Some of the chiefs resented this matter so highly, that they animated the Jews to take up arms, and assert their [illegible] at the point of the sword. Slavery, they observed, was, at best, base and disgraceful, but when accompanied with injury and insult, intolerable. The magistrates did all in their power to appease them, and undertook for Cumanus, that he should do them satisfaction upon the authors of the tumult. But the multitude were deaf to all terms of pacification, were resolutely bent upon having recourse to arms, and made choice of Eleazar, the son of Dinæus, to head them. This Eleazar was a mountaineer, and one that made it his profession to live upon the spoil of ravaging up and down in Samaria with fire and sword. Cumanus, having intelligence of the present situation of affairs, drew out some squadrons of horse from Sebaste, and four companies of foot, with a body of the Samaritans in arms, advanced upon the Jews, slew many of them, and took more prisoners. The most eminent persons in Jerusalem, finding things in this hopeless and forlorn situation, betook themselves to prayer and humiliation in sackcloth and ashes, for the averting of those dreadful judgments they feared were impending, not omitting, at the same time, such powerful hints and arguments, as appeared most conducive to bring the multitude to sober reason. They set before them the desolation of their country, the demolition of their temple, the casting of their wives and children to prophane nations, and intreated them, upon the whole, as they loved their country, their lives, liberties, fortunes, laws, and religion, to adopt more moderate counsels in future, return to their own habitations, and peaceably lay down their arms. This representation so far prevailed, that the common people dispersed, and the tumult subsided, but the freebooters betook themselves to their lurking places, so that Judæa was exposed to continual ravages.

The heads [illegible] to Numidius Quadratus, governor of Syria, who [illegible] with charges [illegible] panding [illegible] their violences, [illegible] they were not so [illegible] on the [illegible] on the sovereign [illegible] which had singly and solely the cognizance [illegible] nature. They observed, that they [illegible] depredations, and usurped a right of judging, thereby [illegible] the Roman legislature [illegible] own [illegible].

The Jews, on the other hand, affirmed that the Samaritans were the authors of this tumult, and consequence of [illegible] which ensued. [illegible] the [illegible] of the charge upon Cumanus, who, they said, had been bribed into a connivance at a most notorious [illegible]. Quadratus, having [illegible] to the allegations on both sides, adjourned the hearings, [illegible] the parties that he would go himself into Judea [illegible] more [illegible], [illegible] so that they were admitted [illegible] the [illegible]. [illegible] into Samaria, where [illegible] the cause he concluded that the Samaritans [illegible] was likewise informed [illegible] to commotions, and [illegible] Cumanus had [illegible] into [illegible], to [illegible] death. From thence he went to Lydda, [illegible] place of considerable extent, where he heard the Samaritans [illegible] second time, and understanding that one Dortus, [illegible] more of his own tribe, had excited [illegible] to an insurrection, he passed sentence of death [illegible] all. But Ananias the high priest, and Ananus, [illegible] officer, were sent bound to Rome, [illegible] to [illegible] before Cæsar. He likewise ordered into Italy [illegible] both of the Samaritans and the Jews, [illegible] Cumanus, the governor, and Celer [illegible] to [illegible] and determine [illegible], but returned himself to Jerusalem [illegible] might [illegible] the sedition of his [illegible]. [illegible] a peaceable state, [illegible] upon the celebration of [illegible], he would not interrupt them [illegible] their [illegible], and so went on to Antioch.

When Cumanus and the Samaritans arrived at Rome, they were ordered to appear at the time and place appointed for the [illegible] and having made very powerful interest [illegible] him, would not probably have carried the cause, had it not been for the interposition of Agrippa the younger, who finding the Jews in danger of being overpowered by numbers, [illegible] Agrippina, the wife of Claudius, to press her husband for a candid and impartial hearing, and an [illegible] execution of justice upon the authors of this [illegible] on the sovereignty of the Roman empire. Claudius was so prevailed upon by this intercession, that [illegible] both sides at [illegible] hearing, and finding, upon the whole, that the Samaritans had been the authors of this tumult, passed sentence of death upon those who came up to him, [illegible] upon Cumanus, and commanded Celer, the tribune, to be carried to [illegible], and dragged to execution through the streets in the face of all the people. He then appointed Felix, the brother of Pallas, to the government of Judea.

Claudius Cæsar, in the twelfth year of his reign, conferred upon Agrippa the tetrarchy of Philip, with Batanea, [illegible] added to it Trachon and Abila, which had been the tetrarchy of Lysanias; but he took Chalcis from him, after it had been under his government four years. Agrippa having received these bounties from Cæsar, gave his sister Drusilla in marriage to Azizus, king of Emesa, who was now become a Jew. She had before been promised to Epiphanes, the son of Antiochus, on condition of his embracing the Jewish religion, but, upon refusal, the match broke off. He married Mariamne, another of his sisters, to Archelaus, the son of Chelcias, to whom she had been contracted some time before by her father Agrippa, from which marriage was derived a daughter, whose name was Berenice.

Soon after this, Drusilla and Azizus were parted on the following occasion. Drusilla's [illegible] Felix, the governor of Judea, became passionately enamoured of her. To obtain his end, he sent for Simon, his particular friend, (a Jew of Cyprus, who pretended to divination,) and [illegible] him to use all his art with Drusilla to detach her from her husband, and persuade her to marry him, with full assurance that nothing should be wanting to complete her happiness. Drusilla, to avoid the envy of her sister Berenice, on account of her beauty, imprudently [illegible] to [illegible] of [illegible] her husband, and married the Roman governor, by whom she had a son, called Agrippa, who, in the days of Titus Cæsar, and in the [illegible], perished with [illegible], at a conflagration of the mount Vesuvius.

Berenice [illegible] of widowhood a considerable time after the death of Herod, who was both her uncle and her husband, [illegible] under the disgraceful imputation of incestuous [illegible] her brother, in order to wipe off that stigma, [illegible] Polemon, king of Cilicia, to embrace the Jewish religion, and take her to wife, as it might pass for a confirmation of the [illegible], [illegible] by her fortune [illegible] to the proposal; but Berenice being a woman of a licentious disposition, soon parted with her husband [illegible] with his new religion. Mariamne also [illegible] Archelaus, and was married to Demetrius, the most eminent Jew of Alexandria, as well for birth as fortune, and [illegible] of this [illegible] by whom she had a son called Agrippinus.

Claudius Cæsar, having reigned thirteen years, eight months and [illegible] days, departed this life, not without a strong suspicion of his having been poisoned by his wife Agrippina. She was the daughter of Germanicus, the emperor's brother. Her first husband was Domitius Ænobarbus, a man of eminence in the city of Rome, who [illegible] her a widow she remained in that state till Claudius took her to wife. She had a son by Domitius, who was called by his father's name, which, upon his being adopted by Claudius, was changed into that of Nero. This emperor had a former wife, whose name was Messalina, by whom he had issue, Britannicus, and Octavia. He caused Messalina to be put to death, upon a suspicion of [illegible] and [illegible]. And [illegible] his [illegible] child, whom he had by Petronia, a former wife, to Nero his adopted son.

Agrippina being bent upon the advancement of her own son to the empire, it is reported that she consulted the death of Claudius, [illegible] securing the succession to Nero, at the same time, lest Germanicus should interpose and supplant him. She had suborned Burrhus, commanding officer of the guards, with some tribunes [illegible] friends, and [illegible] to be in immediate readiness, upon the demise of Claudius, to carry Nero into the camp, and proclaim him emperor. This they no sooner did but his first exploit, after his elevation, was the poisoning of Britannicus, which was followed by the atrocious murder of his own mother, in requital for the life she had given him, and the empire she had procured him. He put his wife Octavia to death, and divers persons of the first eminence for integrity and honour. But the history of Nero is so well known, that it is needless to enlarge upon the subject. Some writers [illegible] extravagant in their panegyrics, as others have been in their accusations, so that truth, the chief excellence of [illegible] history [illegible]. Nor do I much wonder at the palpable contradictions evident in the recital of the acts of Nero by different authors of his [illegible], when I consider the partiality and prejudice that [illegible] is evident in the histories of [illegible] predecessors. With respect to myself, truth shall ever [illegible] my [illegible]. Matters foreign and contingent shall be passed over with brevity, [illegible] particular attention shall be paid to the concerns of our own nation, which shall be related without the [illegible] of exaggeration, [illegible] or [illegible] of [illegible]. [illegible] thing [illegible]

Azizus, king of Emesa, died in the first year of the reign of Nero, and was succeeded by his brother Sohemus. Nero gave Armenia the Lesser to Aristobulus, the son of Herod, king of Chalcis. He also gave to Agrippa a part of Galilee, subjecting Tiberias and Tarichæ to his government, with the addition of Julias beyond Jordan, and fourteen villages under that jurisdiction.

CHAP. VI.

Judæa infested with robbers and impostors. Felix seizes Eleazar, a ring-leader, and sends him bound to Rome. Jonathan, the high-priest, is assassinated, through the contrivance of Dora, at the instance of Felix. The people seduced by the wiles of magicians and false prophets. Disputes between the Jews of Cæsarea and Syria, concerning the privileges. Felix turns the soldiers upon the contending parties, and gives them the booty. The high-priests tithe from, and oppress the priests in ordinary.

THE affairs of the Jews grew daily worse and worse, as the country was infested with robbers and impostors, who deluded the credulous multitude. A day scarcely passed in which Felix did not cause some of them to be apprehended, and brought to condign punishment. Theudas, the son of Dinæus, a ring-leader of the party, was taken by stratagem. Felix gave him a solemn invitation to come over to him with assurance of perfect security, which inducing Eleazar to compliance, he no sooner arrived, than the governor sent him in chains to Rome.

Felix conceived a mortal aversion to Jonathan, the high-priest, because he frequently gave him wholesome advice, concerning the regulation of the affairs of Judæa, to prevent the murmurs of the people, and insure the approbation of those friends who had recommended him to the government. Felix considered his counsel as reproach, and therefore concerted means for ridding himself of the ungrateful importunities of the high-priest, as men of depraved minds cannot bear to be chastised for their faults. To this end he tampered, by presents, with Dora, a citizen of Jerusalem, one of Jonathan's particular friends, to suborn a set of bravoes to fall upon and assassinate him. Dora undertook and executed the commission. Matters were so concerted, that these ruffians went to Jerusalem on pretence of devotion, with daggers concealed under their garments, and intermixing with the promiscuous multitude, took an opportunity of stabbing the high-priest. As these miscreants came off with impunity, others were encouraged to perpetrate the same massacres, under the same disguise, upon such festive occasions, so that murders were frequently committed, from motives of revenge or other execrable causes, not only in divers parts of the city, but in the very temple itself, as if that sacred spot could sanctify the foulest of crimes. Can it then be matter of wonder, that, for the practice and connivance of such abominable profanations, the Almighty, in his wrath and indignation, should deliver up his city, nay, his own house, into the hands of the Romans, and that the whole nation of the Jews, with their wives and children, should be condemned to misery and bondage, to bring them to a due and penitential sense of their enormous offences?

While plunderers and murderers were injuring the public in one quarter, magicians and impostors were preying upon them in another, and alluring the multitude by thousands, to see the signs and miracles they pretended to work. But they suffered severely for their credulity and curiosity, being apprehended and many of them put to death, by order of Felix. There arrived, at that time, out of Egypt, a certain reported prophet, who invited the populace, and misled the common people to follow him to the top of Mount Olivet, about five furlongs from the city, assuring them, that when he came thither, he would but give command, and the walls of Jerusalem should be levelled with the ground, and open to them an entrance into the city through the ruins.

When Felix received intelligence of this adventure, he commanded his soldiers to take their arms, and breaking in upon them with horse and foot, they soon routed them, slew four hundred on the spot, and took two hundred alive; but the Egyptian impostor made his escape. Those who fled endeavoured to incite the people to a rebellion against the Romans, notwithstanding their late defeat, by insinuating that their yoke was intolerable, and should therefore be shaken off, and committed ravages upon all those who would not join them.

There happened, at this time, another dispute between the Jews of Cæsarea and Syria on a claim to some certain privileges. Those of Cæsarea claimed a precedence in right of their king Herod, the founder of that city. When the report of this contest came to the knowledge of the neighbouring governors, they caused the incendiaries on both sides to be apprehended, and punished with stripes, in consequence of which the tumult for some time subsided. But the Jewish citizens, depending on their wealth, reproached the Syrians in the most vehement terms. The Syrians, though inferior in wealth, relying on the assistance of the soldiers, returned the opprobrious language of the Jews, so that they proceeded from words to stoning one another, and many were wounded and fell on each side; but the Jews came off conquerors. When Felix found this contest was brought to a kind of war, he urged the Jews to decline it; but when words proved ineffectual, he sent armed troops among them, who killed many, took more prisoners, and permitted the soldiers to plunder the houses of the opulent for their booty. The more respectable and moderate part of the Jews dreading worse consequences, applied to Felix, and intreated him to call off the soldiers, and afford them time to repent of their rashness. Felix complied with their request.

King Agrippa, at the same time, gave the high-priesthood to Ismael, the son of Phabeus; and the high-priests began to divide themselves from the other priests and the governors of Jerusalem, each of them taking a guard of the boldest and most seditious partisans, insomuch that all authority seemed to be set at defiance, as if there had been a total vacancy of administration. Such was the insolence of the high-priests, that they sent their emissaries up and down into Barns to seize upon the tithes of the priests, so that the poorer sort of that holy order perished for want of bread. These were the dire effects of faction.

CHAP. VII.

Portius Festus being appointed to succeed Felix, the Jews of Cæsarea accuse him before Nero. His brother Pallas obtains his pardon. Beryllus procures a mandate for disfranchising the Jews. They are annoyed by robbers. An impostor decoys the multitude into the wilderness. Festus destroys both the seducer and the followers. Agrippa builds a magnificent palace that overlooks the temple, which occasions a murmuring amongst the Jews. They appeal by commissioners to Cæsar. Joseph appointed to the office of high-priest.

FELIX being removed from his government, and Portius Festus appointed, by the emperor, to succeed him, some of the principal Jewish inhabitants of Cæsarea, went up to Rome, to accuse Felix, and would certainly have brought him to condign punishment, had not Nero yielded to the solicitations of his brother Pallas, who at that time stood highly in his favour.

There were two eminent Syrians of Cæsarea, who, by a vast sum of money, formed so powerful an interest with Beryllus, tutor and Greek secretary to Nero, that he obtained the emperor's letters mandatory to Cæsarea, for the disfranchising of the Jews, and abrogating all the privileges they enjoyed within that city, which had been hitherto common to Jews and Syrians. This grant was the source of all the calamities that afterwards befel our nation; for the Jews of Cæsarea, after this mandate, would never rest till they waged war with their enemies.

When Felix came into Judæa, he found the country desolate, the people forced from their habitations, their houses exposed to fire and pillage, and all at the mercy of a brutal clan of free-booters, who ravaged up and down, in great numbers, at pleasure. These robbers were denominated Sicarii, from Sica, alluding to the short sword they wore, a weapon, bending towards the point, and formed in a manner betwixt a Persian scimetar and a Roman faulchion. With these weapons they did great execution, by intermixing with the multitude at festivals, under colour of religion, and dispatching whom they pleased in that confusion, without difficulty, or danger of discovery.

There were in those days a notorious impostor, who had deluded a credulous rabble into an opinion, that, if they followed him into such a wilderness, they would be protected from harm. But Festus, with a detachment of horse and foot, destroyed the seducer and his besotted followers together.

About the same time king Agrippa caused to be erected, near the porch of the royal palace, at Jerusalem, belonging to the Asmonean family, a stately, magnificent apartment, for the entertainment of guests. It stood upon an eminence, commanded a noble prospect of the city, and was so contrived, that the king could see every thing that was done in the temple, which afforded him very great satisfaction. This gave much offence to the principal men amongst the Jews, as it is contrary to our laws, that our rites and ceremonies, and especially our sacrifices in the temple, should be exposed to the view of others. They therefore erected a wall, by way of prevention, before the seats, that enclosed the inner part of the temple, towards the west, which not only intercepted the prospect from the king's apartment, but also the view of the galleries to the westward on the other side of the temple, where the Roman guards were placed upon days of festival. This proceeding highly displeased Agrippa, and more so Festus, who ordered the wall to be pulled down. The citizens, upon this, assured him that they prized the temple above themselves, and therefore desired permission to send deputies to Cæsar, before they proceeded to the execution of his orders. Their request being granted, they sent to the emperor ten eminent citizens, with Ismael, the high-priest, and Chelcias, the treasurer of the temple, as their commissioners. When Nero had heard their petition, he not only passed over what they had done, but gave them his grant for the continuance of the wall they had built. This indulgence they obtained on the intercession of the empress Poppea, a religious woman, who was greatly disposed to favour the Jews. The ten deputies were permitted to return, but Poppea detained Ismael and Chelcias, as hostages. When Agrippa heard of these transactions, he transferred the pontificate to Joseph, otherwise called Cabus, the son of Simon, formerly high-priest.

CHAP. VIII.

Death of Festus, and succession of Albinus. Ananus the high-priest [illegible] Agrippa deposes Ananus, and transfers the pontificate to Jesus, the son of Damneus. Agrippa [illegible] Cæsarea Philippi [illegible] Nero. Builds a magnificent theatre at Berytus. Deprives Jesus of the high-priesthood, [illegible] the son of Gamaliel [illegible] Albinus in the government of [illegible] particular privileges. The temple finished. High-priesthood frequently transferred. Enumeration of the high-priests.

CÆSAR, upon hearing of the death of Festus, sent Albinus to take upon him the government of Judæa, and Agrippa, at the same time, deposed Joseph and conferred the dignity of high-priest upon Ananus, the son of Ananus. Ananus the father, was esteemed singularly honoured, as he had five sons that came successively into the pontificate after him, a circumstance of which no other of an high-priest could boast. The younger Ananus, of whom we are now speaking, was naturally fierce and impetuous, and of the sect of the Sadducees, a very censorious and uncharitable people. Actuated by these principles, he took an opportunity in the interval between the death of Festus and the arrival of his successor Albinus, to call a council, with the assistance of judges, and then to cite James, the brother of Jesus, together with some other persons, to appear before him, and answer a charge brought against them, upon which they were all condemned, and delivered up to be stoned. The considerate part of the city were so displeased at this proceeding, that they privately represented it to the king as highly unjust, requesting that Ananus might be so reproved for it, as to caution him not to act in the same manner for the future. Others were sent with an account of it to Albinus, who was then upon his journey to Alexandria, setting it forth as an usurpation upon his authority. Albinus was so offended, that he wrote a menacing letter to the high-priest upon it, and king Agrippa, at the expiration of three months, removed him from his office, and conferred it on Jesus, the son of Damneus.

Albinus no sooner arrived at Jerusalem, than he applied himself, with all possible diligence, to the maintaining of the public peace; and to that end brought many of the robbers, called Sicarii, to deserved punishment. Ananias, the high-priest, by his bounty and affability, greatly contributed to the esteem of the people, and also cultivated the friendship of Albinus, and the high-priest Jesus, by means of largesses and presents. But he had a number of abandoned servants, who, joining with others as profligate as themselves, went from barn to barn, and took away the tithes that belonged to the priests by violence, beating and maiming those that resisted to deliver them. Many other high-priests acted in the same unjust manner, as they were subject to no controul; insomuch that the priests in ordinary were perishing for want of food, being deprived of the only means of support.

A band of these Sicarii entered the city by night, on the eve of a festival, and surprized the secretary of Eleazar, an officer of the first rank in the army, and son of Ananias, the high-priest whom they bound, and carried away with them. They then sent information to Ananias, that they had the secretary in custody, and were ready to deliver him up, on condition of his prevailing with Albinus to release ten of their party, whom he held in prison. The deportment of the secretary was of such importance, that Albinus was under a kind of necessity of complying with the request of Ananias, though it was productive of disastrous events; for when the robbers had found out this mode of compounding their villainies, they were incessantly contriving means for surprizing some of the domestics of Ananias, in order to obtain their [illegible] and thereby procure the release of any of their party who might be in custody; so that they were more and more emboldened, and infested the whole country with their ravages and depredations.

King Agrippa had now enlarged Cæsarea Philippi, and gave it the name of Neronias, in honour of the emperor Nero. He also erected at Berytus a magnificent and sumptuous theatre, which he largely endowed, for the exhibition of annual shews, and distribution of corn and oil among the people in due proportions. He caused the city to be beautified, and adorned with curious statues and pictures, and a collection of antique originals, from the hands of the greateſt maſters in the ſeveral branches so that this town might be deemed a repoſitory for all that was rare or precious in the kingdom But this munificence to ſtrangers, to the impoveriſhing of his own people, of courſe incurred their ill will

Agrippa ſoon took away the pontificate from Jeſus, and gave it to another of the ſame name, who was the ſon of Gamaliel This created ſuch feuds between them, that they formed parties of abandoned followers, and reviled each other in the public ſtreets in the moſt opprobrious terms From words they ſometimes proceeded to ſtones, but Ananias, by dint of money, had the ſtrongeſt party

Coſtobarus and Saul being of the blood royal and nearly related to Agrippa, had great intereſt, and drew together a band of reſolutes ready to execute their commands They were inſolent and rapacious towards the lower claſs of people who had no patronage or protection, ſo that from this juncture we may date the declenſion of the Jewiſh nation

When Albinus heard that Geſſius Florus was appointed to ſucceed him, he thought the moſt effectual means of ingratiating himſelf with the Jews, was to do juſtice upon thoſe whom he had in cuſtody He therefore cauſed all the priſoners to be brought before him, and, upon due examination, proceeded againſt them according to their demerits, putting to death thoſe who were manifeſtly guilty of capital crimes, and diſcharging thoſe who were only convicted of miſdemeanors upon a fine and ranſom These means might tend to clear the priſoners, but they let looſe robbers upon the country

Thoſe of the tribe of Levi, that officiated as choriſters in the temple, prevailed on the king to call a council, and grant them the uſe of the linen veſtments which had been peculiar to the prieſts, ſuggeſting that ſuch a conceſſion would ſtand upon record as an act of grace to the king's eternal honour This requeſt was heard and granted in form and manner according to deſire, and the choriſters were permitted to wear the linen veſtments There was another claſs of Levites who officiated in the ſervices of the temple, and were likewiſe allowed to ſerve promiſcuouſly as choriſters But theſe licences were repugnant to our national laws and cuſtoms, which were never abandoned without a judgment upon the violation

The repairing of the temple being finiſhed and near eight thouſand artificers and labourers deſtitute of employment, and conſequently of the means of ſubſiſtence, the people, unwilling to ſtock their money as an eaſy prey to the Romans, and deſirous of making ſome proviſion for them, propoſed the repairing of a building on the eaſt ſide of the temple, which overlooking a deep narrow valley, was ſupported by a wall four hundred cubits in height, and ſix in depth, being the work of Solomon, the firſt founder of the temple But Agrippa, who was entruſted by the emperor with the repairing of this glorious ſtructure, revolving in his mind how much eaſier it would be to deſtroy ſuch a work than to rebuild it, did not think it expedient to comply with the deſire of the people, and therefore gave them to underſtand, that if they would reſt content with beautifying the city by paving the ſtreets with white ſtone, he would not oppoſe it Agrippa alſo deprived Jeſus the ſon of Gamaliel, of the pontificate, and conferred it on Matthias, the ſon of Theophilus, in whoſe time commenced the war between the Jews and the Romans

It appears to be neceſſary, as introductory to a work under contemplation, to give an account in this place of the origin of high-prieſts the qualifications requiſite for that ſacred function, and the number of thoſe who were admitted to ſuch dignity, as far as to the end of the war

The firſt of this order was Aaron the brother of Moſes, and after his death his children ſucceeded him and ſo the honour deſcended in courſe to his family This right of hereditary ſucceſſion prevailed ſo far with our forefathers, that none but thoſe of the blood of Aaron were accounted worthy of that holy office, kings themſelves not excepted From Aaron to Phanatus, who was declared high-prieſt by a faction in a time of war, there were eighty-three in number, thirteen of whom officiating in the ſtation from the time that Moſes erected a tabernacle to God in the deſert, to their entrance into Judæa, where king Solomon built and dedicated the holy temple At firſt there was no ſucceeding to the pontificate but by a vacancy upon death, though it became a practice afterwards, to appoint ſucceſſion during the lives of predeceſſors Theſe thirteen perſons deſcending from two of the ſons of Aaron, ſucceeded in their turns to that dignity The form of government was at firſt ariſtocratical, then monarchical, and laſtly regal The number of years from the time in which Moſes carried our forefathers out of Egypt, to the building of the temple of Solomon, was ſix hundred and twelve

After thoſe thirteen high-prieſts abovementioned there followed eighteen more in the courſe of four hundred ſixty-ſix years, ſix months and ten days, in ſucceſſion one to another under the government of kings These are computed from king Solomon to the days of Nebuchadnezzar, king of Babylon, when he marched up to Jeruſalem, and took it, burnt the temple, and carried away the whole nation, together with Jozedeck, their high-prieſt, captives

After a captivity of ſeventy years in Babylon, Cyrus, king of Perſia, diſmiſſed the Jews to their own country, with permiſſion to rebuild their temple, Jeſus, the ſon of Jozedeck, exerciſing, at that time, the function of high-prieſt Fifteen of his poſterity ſucceeded him in the ſame dignity, but under a democratical form of government, till the time of king Antiochus Eupator, a term of four hundred and fourteen years, when this ſame Antiochus, with his general Lyſias, took away both the dignity and life of Onias, otherwiſe called Menelaus, at Beryttus, excluded his ſon from the ſucceſſion, and, in his place, appointed Jeſinus, one of the race of Aaron, but not of the pontifical family

Upon this Onias, ſon of Onias deceaſed, went away into Egypt and inſinuating himſelf into the good opinion of Ptolemy Philometer, and Cleopatra his wife, prevailed upon them to build and dedicate a temple to God at Heliopolis, in imitation of that in Jeruſalem, and to conſtitute him high-prieſt there Jacimus died at the expiration of three years, in the execution of the pontifical office, without a ſucceſſor, ſo that there was a vacancy for ſeven years

When the Jews revolted from the Macedonians, the dignity was transferred to the family of the Aſmoneans, and Jonathan advanced to the pontificate, which he enjoyed for the ſpace of ſeven years, and then being taken off by the treachery of Tryphon, his brother Simon was promoted to his place Upon his being afterwards aſſaſſinated by his ſon-in-law at a public entertainment, his ſon Hyrcanus ſucceeded him, and held it for the ſpace of one and thirty years Upon his death it devolved on his ſon Judas, otherwiſe called Ariſtobulus, who was the firſt that took upon him the name and quality of king After a reign of one year he left his brother Alexander heir and ſucceſſor both to the kingdom and pontificate, in both which capacities he adminiſtered for twenty-ſeven years, and then departing this life, tranſmitted the regency to his wife Alexandra, with authority to diſpoſe of the pontificate, in conſequence of which ſhe conferred it upon her brother Hyrcanus, who enjoyed it during the nine years of her reign At her death Ariſtobulus, the younger brother, made war upon him, overcame him, and reduced him to the condition of a private man, aſſuming both the kingdom and the pontificate to himſelf, which he held for three years, and as many months When Pompey, upon the taking of Jeruſalem, carried away him and his children priſoners to Rome, Hyrcanus, being reſtored to the pontificate, accepted alſo of the principality, but not under the title of king enjoying the high-prieſthood twenty-three years more beſides the nine above-mentioned. At the expiration of this time, Barzaphernes and Pacorus, Parthian generals, paſſed the Euphrates, made war upon Hyrcanus, and carried him away priſoner, advancing Antigonus, the ſon of Ariſtobulus, to the crown, who, in three years and three months after, was taken in Jeruſalem by Herod and Soſius, and then, by command of Anthony, put to death at Antioch.

Herod having now received the kingdom from the Romans, made no ſcruple of chuſing the high-prieſts out of the Aſmonean race, but conferred the dignity indiſcriminately upon perſons of obſcure birth, provided they were in holy orders, except in the inſtance of Ariſtobulus, of whom he made choice, being the grandſon of Hyrcanus, that was taken by the Parthians, and brother of his wife Mariamne, to ingratiate himſelf with the people, who held the memory of Hyrcanus in great veneration. He was, in fine, ſo generally beloved, that Herod grew jealous of him, and cauſed him to be drowned in a fiſh pond at Jericho, as before related. After this time he would never veſt any of the Aſmonean family with that dignity. His ſon Archelaus took the ſame meaſures, and ſo did all the Romans after him who were ſucceſſively appointed governors of the province.

From the days of Herod to the burning of Jeruſalem, and the temple by Titus, there were, in all, twenty-eight high-prieſts, in the courſe of an hundred and ſeven years. Some of theſe were political governors under the reign of Herod, and his ſon Archelaus, but after their deaths, the government was changed to an ariſtocracy, and the high-prieſts held dominion over the nation.

CHAP. IX.

Geſſius Florus ſucceeds Albinus, and cauſes the Jews to take up arms againſt the Romans. Concluſion of the Jewiſh Antiquities.

GESSIUS Florus, appointed by Nero to ſucceed Albinus in the government of Judæa, entailed upon our nation the direſt calamities. He was a native of the city of Clazomena, and the huſband of Cleopatra, a character as infamous as himſelf. Through her intereſt with the empreſs Poppea, he obtained the dignity, which he abuſed to ſuch a degree, that the Jews wiſhed for the reſtoration of Albinus, as the latter endeavoured to conceal his vices, whereas the former openly gloried in his ſhame. He was rapacious to a degree, inexorably cruel, and ſo inſatiably covetous, that he ſeemed diſpoſed to univerſal depredation. He ſhared in the plunder of robbers, and thereby gave a ſanction to rapine. Such, in fine was the oppreſſion under his government, that the wretched Jews were forced to abandon their habitations, their country, and their altars, and fly for ſanctuary even to the moſt barbarous of foreign nations. Florus laid us under a neceſſity of taking up arms againſt the Romans, reſolving rather to fall together, than periſh ingloriouſly one by one. This was commenced in the ſecond year of the government of Florus, and twelfth of the reign of Nero. The particulars of it may be accurately known, by peruſing the books we have written upon that ſubject.

The Jewiſh Antiquities I have deduced from the creation of the world to the twelfth year of the reign of Nero, recounting in hiſtorical progreſſion, the ſeveral events which related to the Jewiſh nation throughout ſo many ages, as in Egypt, Syria, under the Aſſyrians, Babylonians, Perſians, Macedonians, and laſtly the Romans. I have enumerated the high-prieſts in regular order and ſucceſſion for the ſpace of two thouſand years. I have faithfully extracted, according to promiſe, at the firſt entrance upon this work, from holy writ, the deſcent of our kings, and the courſe of other forms of government, as they ſucceeded one another, with their power, and adminiſtration of affairs.

I will be bold to affirm, that no man living could have written the Jewiſh Antiquities in a ſtyle and manner ſo accurate, or ſo acceptable to the Greeks, as myſelf, for thoſe of my own nation acknowledge me to be perfectly verſed in the learning of the Jews, and my proficiency in the language of the Greeks has been cultivated with unremitting aſſiduity. The knowledge of different languages, and the embelliſhment of diſcourſe, by pointed accents, and turned periods, are not ſo highly eſtimated by our nation, as the knowledge of our laws and the holy ſcripture. This is an excellency to which two or three, of all that ever aſpired to it, have attained, to their immortal honour, and to the eſſential benefit of ſucceeding ages.

It will not I preſume be deemed amiſs, to relate ſome memoirs of my own life, as there are living witneſſes to expoſe falſhood, and confirm truths. Thus I cloſe my Antiquities, which are here compriſed in twenty books, intending, with the Divine permiſſion, to draw up a conciſe narrative of the whole war, from the period of its commencement, to the preſent ſtate, being the thirteenth year of Domitianus Cæſar, and the fifty-ſixth of my own life. I alſo intend to write a treatiſe on the peculiar tenets and opinions, as held by the different Jewiſh ſects concerning the nature and eſſence of the Divine Being, and the particular licences and reſtrictions of our laws.

END OF THE JEWISH ANTIQUITIES OF FLAVIUS JOSEPHUS.

PREFACE OF JOSEPHUS

TO THE

HISTORY

OF THE

WARS OF THE JEWS.

AS the wars between the Jews and the Romans were, in point of events, the moſt memorable of all others, whether national or civil, many have been induced to preſent the public with a pretended hiſtory of them. But it has appeared, upon impartial examination, that their ſeveral productions have been deficient in the ſtatement of facts, or that they have tended to veil truth by partial repreſentation, either from a deſire of conciliating the favour of the Romans, or manifeſting their hatred to the Jews.

Actuated by theſe conſiderations, I, Joſephus, the ſon of Matthias, an Hebrew by birth, and a prieſt of Jeruſalem, have undertaken to tranſlate thoſe books, which I formerly compoſed in the language of our country, into the Greek tongue, for the common benefit of the ſubjects of the Roman empire, and having firſt borne arms, for the Jews againſt the Romans, I find an irreſiſtible impulſe to proſecute my deſign.

Theſe dreadful wars commenced at a very critical juncture, when the Roman ſtate was embroiled by faction, and the affairs of the Jewiſh nation flouriſhed in an eminent degree. Power and opulence incited ſedition, which was inflamed into tumults that alarmed the whole eaſtern world, for the Jews, as well thoſe beyond the Euphrates as the reſt, ſeemed all in a confederacy to riſe as one man. Commotions prevailed among the Gauls upon the borders of Italy, as alſo among the Germans. In a word all was in diſorder upon the death of Nero, ſome arrogating ſovereignty to themſelves, and ſome attempting innovations from motives of perſonal advantage.

In this ſituation of affairs I hold myſelf bound, in honour and conſcience, to vindicate ſo many important truths from impoſture and miſtake, and after having inſtructed the Parthians, the Babylonians, the moſt remote of the Arabians, the Jews on the farther ſide of the Euphrates, with the Adiabeni, in the particulars of the riſe, progreſs, and event of the wars, not to ſuffer the Greeks, and ſo many of the Romans, to be impoſed upon by fictions, and remain ignorant of the moſt eſſential tranſactions.

Theſe writers, indeed, have the confidence to call their accounts hiſtories, though they are deſtitute of ſenſe, connection, and even truth itſelf. An evident partiality runs through the whole; and to vilify the Jews without cauſe, in order to aggrandize the Romans, ſeems to be their main and principal deſign. Where is the glory of triumphing over an enfeebled adverſary? Why was not the conqueſt more ſpeedily atchieved, conſidering the mighty power of the Romans, and the valour of their commanders? All their honours are ſullied, if they deny or miſrepreſent the bravery and reſolution of the vanquiſhed.

Far be it from me to exaggerate the exploits of the Jews, as others have done thoſe of the Romans. I profeſs to do right indiſcriminately to both parties, without addition to, or diminution from, plain matter of fact, to content myſelf with an affectionate concern for the ruin of my country, while I juſtly impute our unhappy diviſions, and the very burning of the holy temple itſelf, to the tyranny of our own governors, who compelled the Romans to proceed to that extremity. As an inſtance of this I ſhall cite Titus Cæſar, who compaſſionated our miſeries, when we were rent by inteſtine factions, to that humane degree, as to ſuſpend the final deſtruction of the city, (which he afterwards laid in aſhes,) to give the authors of the war time for reflection and repentance. If it ſhould be urged that, in the warmth of paſſion for the oppreſſion of my country, I have tranſgreſſed the bounds of an hiſtorian, I have only to offer, by way of excuſe, that I was impelled by an irreſiſtible concern for the fate of my country. It is beyond a doubt, that of all the places that ever fell under the dominion of the Roman empire, none arrived at ſo great a degree of eminence, or was reduced to ſo abject a ſtate, as the city of Jeruſalem. As the calamities of our nation were brought on by our own countrymen, I could not but be particularly affected by *them*; nor can any candid reader cenſure me for the tragical ſtile in which I have related them.

The Greek hiſtorians have diſcovered a very reprehenſible partiality, not only in the omiſſion of the tranſaction of as memorable a war as ever occurred in the revolution of time, but in derogating from the merits of thoſe who have undertaken ſo laudable a taſk. They have compiled the hiſtories of the Medes and Aſſyrians from the productions of ancient writers, to whom they are greatly inferior both in ſtile and manner.

It is the part of a judicious and faithful historian, to furnish himself, if possible, with such materials as have not been previously transmitted to the world Pursuant to this maxim I have, at great expence and labour (being a stranger,) furnished both Greeks and Romans with a memorial of transactions worthy of being known In points of controversy the Greeks have sufficiently displayed their abilities but they seem to have neglected the province of history, or assigned it to men inadequate to the task But the inattention of the Greeks does by no means depreciate the merit of the History

I might here relate the origin of the Jews, the cause of their leaving Egypt, the countries through which they passed, and the vicissitudes of fortune they underwent But all this would be superfluous, as these subjects have been amply treated by several of our own people, and faithfully translated by some of the Greeks into their own tongue I shall begin my history where their writers and our prophets left off With respect to the transactions of the wars, of which I was eye-witness, I shall be as copious and particular as possible, and, on the other hand, as concise and general, with respect to such events as preceded my own time

The method I propose shall be to set forth the cause of the expulsion of Antiochus, surnamed Epiphanes, after taking Jerusalem by force, and keeping possession of it three years and a half, by the sons of Asmonæus I shall then relate the contest betwixt the successors about the government, and the advantage the Romans under the government of Pompey, took of that division, together with the manner in which Herod, the son of Antipater, with the assistance of Sosius, the general, put an end to the power of the Asmonean line

The popular revolt under the government of Quintilius Varus, the war that commenced in the twelfth year of the reign of Nero, together with the exploits of the Jews upon their taking up arms under the command of Cestius, will comprize a part of my plan In this narrative I shall endeavour to observe the strictest impartiality, and do justice to the merits of the Romans as well as our own countrymen Nor will I suppress any part of the calamities that befell the Jews as I have cotemporaries ready to controvert whatever may be advanced contrary to the truth

It will also be necessary to state the events which took place on the death of Nero, and succession of Vespasian, who was called back to assume the Imperial government as he was going back to attack Jerusalem with the presages he had of his future greatness, the changes that happened at Rome under his government and his being declared emperor against his will To this will be added the sedition that arose amongst the Jews upon his going into Egypt to give necessary orders, the slavery they endured under the tyrannical oppression, and the animosities that prevailed amongst them

The acts of Titus will also be attended to, such as the inroads he made into Judæa, the number of his approaches the strength of his works, the fortifications of the city and of the temple, and the model and dimensions of the altar Nor shall I omit an account of our solemn festivals the ceremonies that attended them, the several sorts of purification, the offices of the sacerdotal function, the vestments of the priests, or whatever is sacred belonging to the holy temple

I shall represent, with impartiality, the cruelty of our governors towards those of their own tribe and profession, the humanity of the Romans even towards strangers, and the candour and liberality of Titus, in inviting the Jews to come to an agreement amongst themselves, from an honourable design of saving both the temple and city I shall enlarge upon the sufferings and calamities of the people that arose from war, sedition, and famine, till, in the end, they were made prisoners, nor shall I pass over the destruction of the fugitives or the torments inflicted upon those that were taken I shall also advert to the conflagration of the temple against the will of Cæsar the consumption of the sacred treasure, the sacking of the city, the prodigies that preceded the [illegible] of our tyrannical masters, and the slavery of the people that were carried away Lastly I shall describe the progress of Titus through the city and country, together with his return into Italy and his triumph

These are the heads of the seven following books, which I have written in confi[illegible] to [illegible] to excuse myself from the censure of those who are well acquainted with the subject.

4 I

FLAVIUS JOSEPHUS

ON THE

WARS OF THE JEWS.

BOOK I.

CHAP. I.

Contention between Antiochus and Ptolemy. Antiochus cruelly [illegible] and takes Jerusalem. Profanes the temple, as do [illegible]. Matthias avenges their cause. Judas restores the worship of the true God. Death of Antiochus and Judas.

THE great men of the Jews being divided into factions among themselves, at a period at which there was a competition between Antiochus Epiphanes and Ptolemy the Sixth, Onias, the high-priest, got the ascendancy, and drove the sons of Tobias out of the city, who applied themselves to Antiochus, with intreaties that he would make an inroad into Judæa, and use them for his guides. The king being easily persuaded to an exploit he had in contemplation before, marched into Judæa with a powerful army, took Jerusalem by assault, and put great numbers to the sword that were suspected to be the friends of Ptolemy. The pillage in general, he gave to the soldiers, rifled the temple himself, and for three years and an half, discontinued the prayers that were there daily offered up to the Almighty God. Onias the high-priest fled to Ptolemy, who gave him permission to build a temple and city near Heliopolis, after the model of that at Jerusalem, of which we shall have occasion to speak hereafter.

Antiochus was not satisfied with his unexpected taking of the city, or with its pillage, or with the great slaughter he had made there; but, being overcome with the violence of his passion, and remembering what he had suffered during the siege, compelled the Jews to renounce the laws of their country, keep their infants uncircumcised, and sacrifice swine's flesh upon the altar. These were violations dreadful to all good men, but none dared to oppose them without hazard of their lives.

Bacchides had, at this time, the command of Judæa under Antiochus, who could not have found out a fitter instrument for his purpose, being a man naturally fierce and merciless, and as ready to execute cruelties as the other to enjoin them. It was his common practice to treat men of quality with the greatest indignity, and Jerusalem was little more than a city in name, without privileges, and without commerce. Thus proceeded this insolent tyrant, till the suffering of the people spurred them on to immediate revenge. Matthias, the son of Asmonæus, one of the priests, that lived at a village called Modin, drew up a band of his own domestics, who arming themselves with daggers, slew Bacchides, and withdrew immediately to the mountains out of the reach of the garrisons for their safety. The people came flocking unto Matthias, till he found himself strong enough to venture coming into the plain, where he gave the enemy battle, and forced them out of the borders. This success gave him such reputation, that the people, in acknowledgment for their deliverance, chose him for their general, in which command he died, leaving the government to his eldest son Judas.

Judas, upon a presumption that Antiochus would renew his hostilities, levied a considerable army of his own countrymen, and entered into an alliance with the Romans. Antiochus, upon this, made another incursion into Judæa, where he met with a total repulse. Judas availed himself of this advantage, and assaulted the garrison, in which action the soldiers were beaten out of the upper city (commonly called the holy place) into the lower. He then got possession of the temple, purified it, threw it out, ran up a wall about it, and furnished it with all forms of vessels for Divine worship, the old ones having been polluted and prophaned. He caused a new altar also to be erected, and sacrifices to be offered upon it, as soon as the true religion was restored. [illegible] [illegible]

This Antiochus was succeeded by a son of the same name, who bore as much enmity to the Jews as his father had done before him. He put himself at the head of an army of fifty thousand foot, five hundred horse, and eighty elephants, and fell upon Judæa by the way of

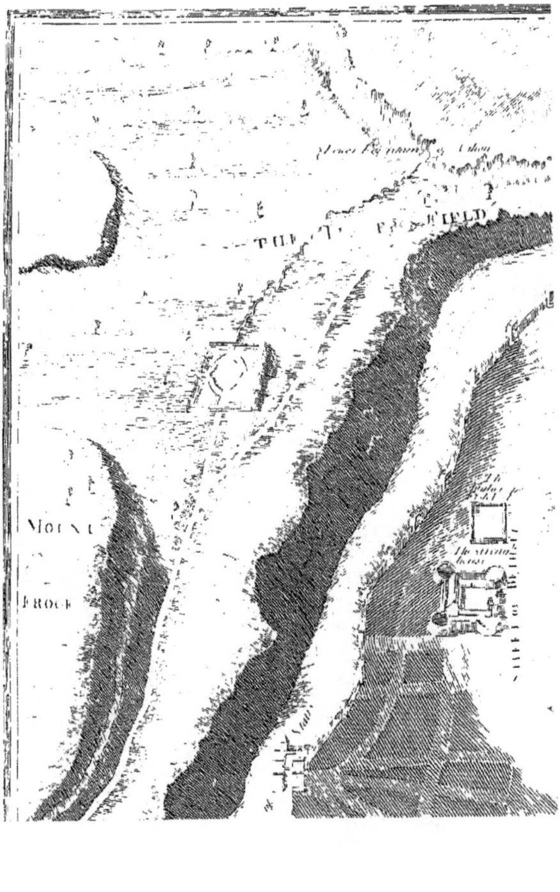

Engraved for the AMERICAN Edition of Maynards Josephus

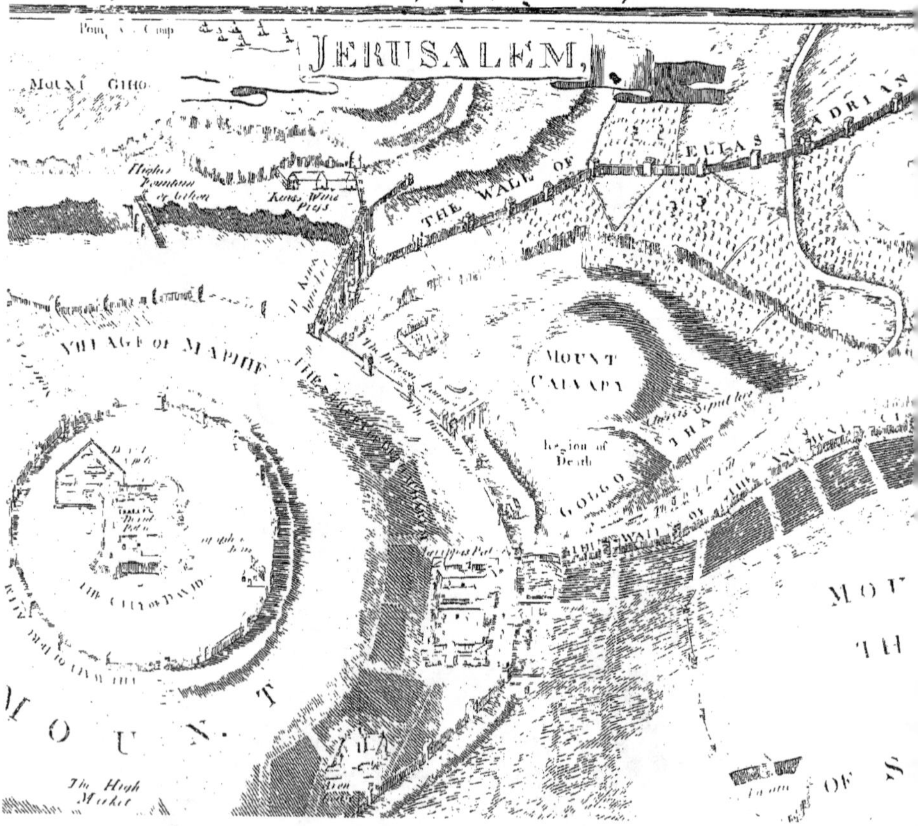

Titus's Camp
Old Gate
N T A C R A
E CITY
A L E M OF

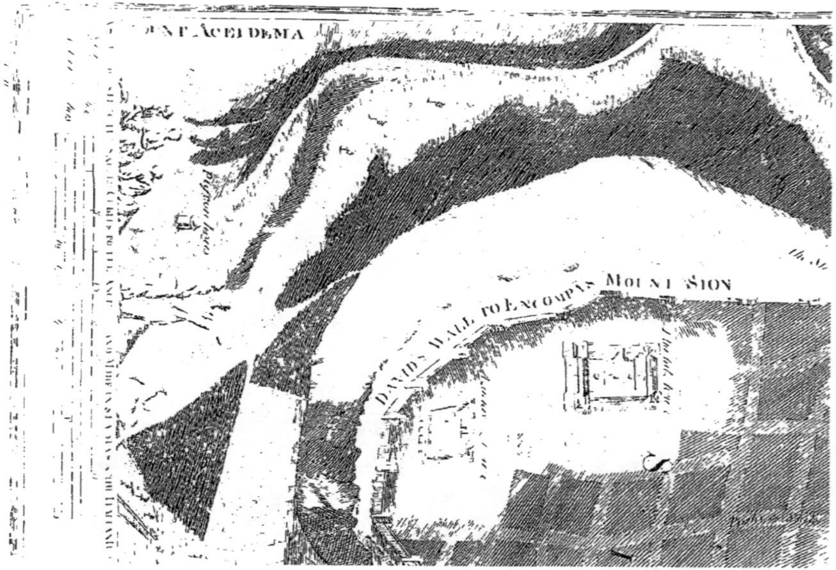
ACELDEMA
DAVIDS WALL TO ENCOMPASS MOUNT SION

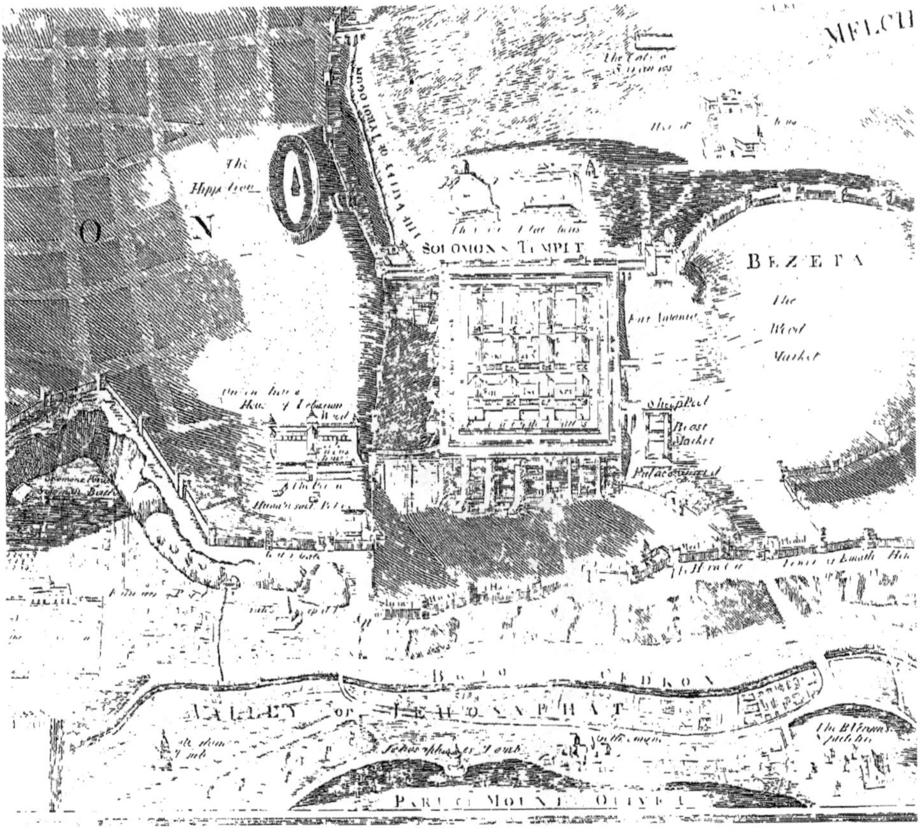
SOLOMONS TEMPLE
BEZETA
Beast Market

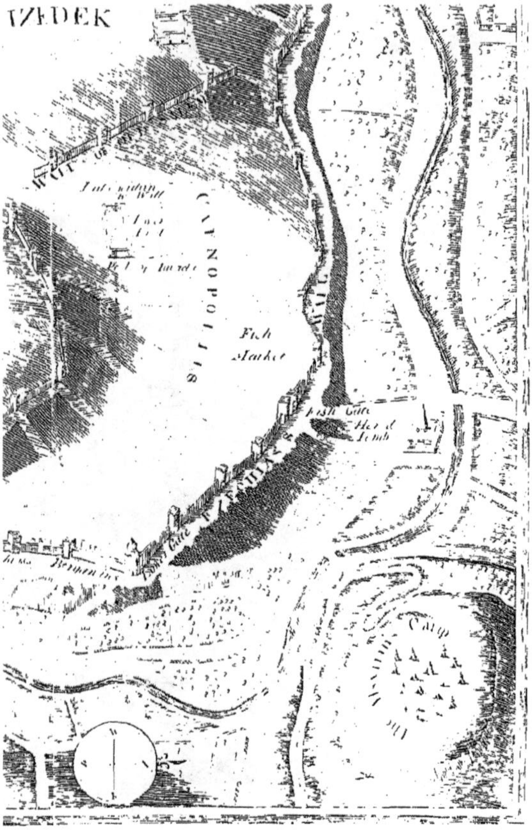
ZEDEK
Fish Market
Fish Gate
Camp

Je mo[illegible] [illegible] going through a narrow defile, in a place called Beth-zacharias. Jews engaged him in the pass, and, before the [illegible] enemies could [illegible] his brother Eleazar, [illegible] one of the elephant, [illegible] a castle upon his back, and arrayed [illegible] trappings, he took it for granted, that the [illegible] Antiochus. In this confidence he advanced upon the enemy, and made his way up to the elephant but finding the [illegible] upon him, whom he took for the king, out of his reach, he stabbed the beast with a weapon [illegible] was crushed to death under the weight of him upon his fall, giving [illegible] to understand, how much he [illegible] his honour above his life. But it seems [illegible] the rider of the elephant was only a private man, [illegible] Antiochus himself [illegible] Eleazar could have got [illegible] the reputation of sacrificing his life to [illegible] This disappointment was looked upon by his brother as presage to the fate of the battle, for, though the Jews maintained a long and obstinate engagement, they were, in the end, [illegible] number, and after a great loss of men, Judas with the [illegible] retired into the toparchy of Gophna, [illegible] Antiochus repaired to Jerusalem. After a few days [illegible] he was [illegible] to withdraw, though [illegible] of necessaries, leaving [illegible] competent garrison, and sending the rest to take up their winter quarters in [illegible]

Judas, [illegible] of the king's [illegible] being obliged [illegible] to recruit his [illegible] men [illegible] escaped out of the last battle once more [illegible] of Antiochus, [illegible] where he [illegible] his valour that he was [illegible] His brother John [illegible] friends of Antiochus, [illegible] him his life.

CHAP. [illegible]

[illegible]

JONATHAN succeeded, as prince of the Jews, to his brother [illegible] who conducted the [illegible] strengthening [illegible] and [illegible] of Antiochus [illegible] for [illegible] treachery, [illegible] the means of depriving Jonathan of the [illegible] Jonathan's [illegible] at Ptolemais, [illegible] him by [illegible] and having [illegible] Judea [illegible] his brother [illegible] Upon this he [illegible] against Jonathan, [illegible]

Simon pursued his success, took Gazara, Joppa, and Jamnia, [illegible] of Accaron, [illegible] demolished [illegible] who, before his [illegible] laid siege to Dora. But such was the [illegible] of the king, that, though Simon had contributed to the [illegible] Antiochus [illegible] with an army to [illegible] Judea, and to [illegible] Simon himself. This prince of the Jews, though [illegible] in the [illegible] the [illegible] His [illegible] with a chosen band of [illegible] and took [illegible] among the mountains, he [illegible] victory, and [illegible] the [illegible] of the Macedonians, [illegible]

[illegible] Ptolemy, [illegible] who had, [illegible] time, [illegible] He [illegible] to despatch John, who [illegible] Having notice of the design, John [illegible] to the city, where he had many friends, [illegible] veneration for the memory of [illegible] Ptolemy, for [illegible] Ptolemy, endeavoured to get into the city by another gate, but the people, having admitted [illegible] repulsed him. Upon [illegible] Dagon, [illegible] Jericho [illegible] being [illegible] possessed of the [illegible] in succession [illegible] his father, [illegible] the [illegible] Ptolemy in the castle, [illegible] his mother and brothers [illegible] Hyrcanus [illegible] the [illegible] had even a [illegible] Ptolemy [illegible] When Ptolemy [illegible] himself [illegible] to be [illegible] them [illegible] [illegible] [illegible] his [illegible] the [illegible] of his [illegible] [illegible] the [illegible] upon [illegible] Ptolemy, [illegible] the [illegible] the [illegible] the siege to [illegible] the Jews [illegible] the [illegible] the siege, [illegible] Ptolemy [illegible]

Antiochus, [illegible] Simon, [illegible] before Jerusalem, [illegible] Hyrcanus, who [illegible] opened the [illegible] of David [illegible] took [illegible] a [illegible] with Antiochus [illegible]

Antiochus [illegible] Jerusalem, [illegible] wards Syria, [illegible] he [illegible] took Medaba and [illegible] the Cutheans, a people [illegible] upon a famous temple, erected [illegible] of the [illegible] at Jerusalem. [illegible] Dora and Marissa, [illegible] Samaria, [illegible] called Sebaste. He [illegible] and [illegible] the care of the siege to [illegible] Antigonus, who [illegible] [illegible] their own [illegible] two brothers, [illegible] Samaria, [illegible] [illegible]

[illegible] of [illegible] circumstances, and then made [illegible] which he subdued the Gileadites, and the Moabites, made them his tributaries, and returned to [illegible]. [illegible] therefore, [illegible] the success [illegible] quitted the peace and the other, [illegible] [illegible], razed it to the ground.

His next [illegible] was against Obodas, king of Arabia, who [illegible] for him near Golan. Alexander [illegible] driven into a deep valley, [illegible] was crushed by the multitude of camels, [illegible] with great difficulty, to Jerusalem, [illegible] his [illegible] foes more implacable than ever [illegible] his [illegible]. They encountered him much [illegible], in every encounter, he overcame them, insomuch that, within the course of six years, he destroyed at least 50,000 of them. But he could derive no satisfaction from [illegible] with the [illegible] of his kingdom, so that, in the end, [illegible] from arms to reason, [illegible] to [illegible] himself with his people by [illegible] measures. But the instability of his conduct, instead of gaining them over, rendered him so odious and contemptible, that on his asking them what he should do [illegible] that he must die, adding, [illegible] could hardly [illegible] his grave for the injuries [illegible] in the time of his life.

The Jews [illegible] to their assistance king Demetrius [illegible], who, finding it his interest to come over to them, [illegible] and advancing with his army, [illegible] the Jews [illegible]. They were computed to [illegible], to 3000 horse, and 40,000 foot. [illegible], however, with only 10,000 well affected Jews, [illegible] them [illegible] the two kings, before they engaged, used their endeavours to gain deserters from [illegible], [illegible] to the mercenaries of [illegible], and the [illegible] to the Jews [illegible]. [illegible] Demetrius [illegible] found that neither the [illegible] nor [illegible] could be wrought upon to prove unfaithful [illegible] to the decision of a battle, in which Demetrius [illegible] conqueror, though Alexander [illegible] [illegible]. Demetrius, indeed, was [illegible] of the [illegible] that invited him to come over to them [illegible] compassion of several of the Jews [illegible] king, and [illegible] 6000 of those who [illegible] join him, [illegible] the mountains, where he had taken refuge. This [illegible] Demetrius to that degree [illegible] the rest of the army would follow [illegible], he gave up his design and withdrew.

But the defections of the auxiliaries had no effect on [illegible] against Alexander [illegible] the greatest part of them, and [illegible] the remainder into the city of Bemeselis, where [illegible] were [illegible] prisoners and carried to Jerusalem. [illegible] a shocking picture of the ungovernable [illegible] of an imperious [illegible]. Alexander, revelling with his concubines, as one part of the entertainment, ordered to be exhibited the horrid spectacle of 800 prisoners on crosses in the midst of the city, having first commanded the throats of their wives and children to be cut before their faces. This dreadful scene had such a terrible effect on the opposing multitude, that 8000 of them fled the country the next night, nor did they return till after the death of this prince. By these inhuman means he at length suppressed the tumults that disturbed the peace of his kingdom.

CHAP. IV.

[illegible] expedition against the Jews [illegible] defeated by Aretas, king of Arabia. [illegible] Alexander. The kingdom left to his queen [illegible] Hyrcanus and [illegible] [illegible] Aristobulus [illegible] the kingdom [illegible] [illegible] Hyrcanus [illegible]

THOUGH Alexander [illegible] the Jews had subdued Antiochus Dionysius, the brother of Demetrius, and the last of the race of Seleucus, [illegible] in fresh troubles. This prince, having overcome the Arabians, put Alexander into some apprehension for himself, so that he raised a [illegible] and [illegible] high wall, between [illegible] with wooden towers, in order to prevent his sudden approaches. This [illegible] retrenchment was carried [illegible] Antipatris, to the borders of Joppa. But it was no obstruction to the progress of Antiochus, for he set fire to the towers, filled the ditches, and [illegible] his army, [illegible] against the Arabians, regardless of his revenge upon Alexander.

Aretas, king of Arabia, upon the approach of Antiochus, drew his army into strong holds, and then [illegible] sudden, when the latter thought himself secure, fell upon him with ten thousand horse. The action was obstinate and bloody; for while Antiochus survived, his army stood bravely by him, though the Arabians made very great slaughter. When he fell in the heat of the battle, they turned their backs and fled, so that upon the whole, between those that were cut off in the engagement and the pursuit, the army was nearly destroyed. Some escaped into the village of Cana, where the greatest part of them perished with famine. The people of Damascus had such an hatred for Ptolemy, the son of Mennæus, that they entered into a league with Aretas, and made him king of Cœlo-Syria. He carried the war into Judæa, defeated Alexander, and then retired upon mutual agreement.

The king of the Jews having taken Pella, [illegible] Gerasa, and [illegible] it, though [illegible] with a triple circumvallation, making himself master not only of the place, but of all the treasures of Theodore deposited therein. After this he demolished Gaulan, Seleucia, and a place called the Valley of Antiochus, together with the strong castle of Gamala. In this place he took prisoner Demetrius, the governor (a man of infamous character) [illegible] returned to Jerusalem, where he was received with joyful acclamations, after a success of three years. At the expiration of the war he fell into a quartan ague, and being of an opinion that action would do him good, entered [illegible] a fresh and unseasonable war, and struggling beyond his strength, wore himself out with fatigue, and thus closed the scene of life in the twenty-seventh year of his reign.

Alexander left the kingdom to Alexandra, his queen, as one that had acquired popularity by her moderation and virtue, he therefore made no doubt of the people's ready submission and resignation to her authority. Nor was he deceived in his opinion, for the reputation of her goodness atoned for the disadvantages of her sex, being a woman versed in the Jewish [illegible] and customs, and one that had given constant proof of her zeal for the observance of those holy laws. As she had two sons by Alexander, she made Hyrcanus, the elder, high-priest, not only on account of his seniority, but the inactivity of his disposition, which would prevent him from disturbing the public peace. Aristobulus, the younger, being of an enterprizing spirit, she thought it more expedient to keep him in a private station.

There was amongst the Jews a certain sect called Pharisees, who valued themselves upon being thought more holy than their neighbours, and better skilled in the law. Alexandra, who was bigotted in her religion to a degree of superstition, held these men in the most profound reverence upon account of their mighty pretensions; and they availed themselves so far of her favourable opinion, as to engross the honours and privileges of government, [illegible] commended to places under administration, and in [illegible] or discharge [illegible] they [illegible]. [illegible] both the honourable and profitable commissions of government to the Jews, but the chief expences and dignities, were left to Alexandra. She having great ingenuity in the conduct of affairs, made a point of augmenting the militia, kept two armies on foot, and a great number of foreign auxiliaries, which rendered her formidable at home, and formidable abroad. But though she had the full command of others, she was herself under the subjection of the Pharisees.

The leaders of this sect caused Diogenes, a man of the first rank, and a particular friend of the late king, to be put to death, upon an allegation that he had a concern in crucifying the eight hundred prisoners at the command of Alexander. Nay, further, they prevailed with the queen not to suffer one man to escape that was privy to that horrible proceeding. The queen was so captivated that she could deny them nothing, so that under the colour of fashion and religion, they destroyed whom they pleased, and carried their violence to such lengths, that no good man was safe; insomuch, that several persons of condition were forced to take sanctuary with Aristobulus, who persuaded his mother to spare those persons out of respect to their dignity, and for the future to expel those from the city upon the slight subject of having been guilty. This being granted, they were banished, instead of being put to death.

Alexandra, about this time, sent an army to Damascus, upon a pretext that Ptolemy grievously oppressed that city, and got possession of it without any considerable resistance. Cleopatra was now besieged in Ptolemais, by Tigranes, king of Armenia, while Alexandra plied him with presents and proposals; but Lucullus having already entered Armenia with a Roman army, he marched away to prevent further mischief at home.

Soon after this Alexandra fell dangerously ill; whereupon the younger brother, Aristobulus, with a train of adherents, in the prime of youth, faithful and brave, got possession of the castles, seized what money he could find, engaged a body of mercenary troops, and declared himself king. Hyrcanus complaining of this usurpation to his mother, she, [illegible] compassionated his case, caused the wife and sons of Aristobulus to be confined in the castle on the north side of the temple formerly called Baris, and afterwards Antonia, under the government of [illegible], as Sebaste and Agrippias derived their names from Augustus and Agrippa. Alexandra, after a reign of nine years, departed this life, before she could revenge herself upon Aristobulus for endeavouring to depose his brother.

She left Hyrcanus all she possessed, and transmitted the government to him while she was living; but Aristobulus was much his superior in power and magnanimity. The dispute between the two brothers came to a battle near Jericho, where the greater part of Hyrcanus's men went over to Aristobulus, while he, with his wretched partizans, escaped, with much difficulty, into Antonia, where they had their security, the wife and sons of Aristobulus being there in custody. The brothers, however, before matters proceeded to extremities, came to this agreement, that Hyrcanus should yield up the kingdom to Aristobulus, and content himself with such honours and privileges as belonged to the dignity of the king's brother. The reconciliation being interchangeably declared in the temple, they embraced each other, and Aristobulus repaired to the royal palace, while Hyrcanus went to the former residence of his brother.

CHAP. V.

Hyrcanus, at the instance of Antipater, applies for assistance in the recovery of his kingdom, to Aretas, king of Arabia, who enters Judea with a formidable army, forces Aristobulus into Jerusalem, and besieges him there. Scaurus, on Pompey's [illegible] [illegible], raises the siege. [illegible] [illegible] [illegible] Pompey, [illegible] [illegible] [illegible] Pompey [illegible] [illegible] Hyrcanus to Pompey [illegible] [illegible] [illegible] [illegible] [illegible] by [illegible] [illegible] Pompey [illegible] [illegible] [illegible] [illegible] [illegible] [illegible] [illegible] [illegible] [illegible] [illegible] [illegible].

THE sudden elevation of Aristobulus to the royal dignity was a great mortification to his enemies, and especially to Antipater, with whom he had been long at variance. Antipater was by extraction an Idumean, and for birth and estate, a man of the first rank in the country. Hyrcanus being now deposed, and arrogantly deprived of his dominions, Antipater advised him to apply to Aretas, king of Arabia, for assistance towards the recovery of his kingdom, employing his own interest, at the same time with Aretas, to gain the point, by censuring the usurpation of Aristobulus, and applauding the pacific disposition of Hyrcanus. He advanced arguments supported by the honour of contributing to the restoration of a much injured king, and enforced them by representing it as becoming the character of a great prince to vindicate the prerogative of royalty.

Having thus pre-disposed Aretas in favour of Hyrcanus, Antipater conveyed him out of the city by night, and brought him, with the utmost expedition, to Petra, the royal palace of Arabia, where he consigned him, with plausible words, and sumptuous presents, to the care and protection of the king, who promised to exert his utmost endeavours to restore him to his crown.

To this end he entered Judea with an army of 50,000 men, horse and foot, so that Aristobulus, through a fear of inferiority in point of numbers, [illegible] the [illegible] of [illegible] resistance, was routed at the first charge, and forced to take sanctuary in Jerusalem. He was there besieged, and had certainly been taken, if Scaurus, the Roman general, had not seasonably interposed, and raised the siege. Pompey the Great, who was then at war with Tigranes, sent Scaurus, with an army, out of Armenia into Syria, but, upon his arrival at Damascus, he found the place taken by Metellus and Lollius, and their troops drawn off. Receiving intelligence of the state of affairs in Judea, he thought it most expedient to bend his course that way, and had no sooner reached the borders, than he was encountered by two deputies from the brothers, who had each of them instructions to implore the assistance of the Romans for their respective masters. But the three hundred talents presented by the deputy of Aristobulus, had much more weight than the pretensions of his brother Hyrcanus, as appears from an herald being sent by Scaurus to Hyrcanus and the Arabians, threatening them with the resentment of Pompey and the Roman senate, unless they immediately raised the siege. Aretas, terrified into compliance, withdrew with precipitation out of Judea into Philadelphia; and Scaurus returned to Damascus. Aristobulus, not satisfied with this escape, assembled all his forces, and pushed the enemy to a place called Papyron, where he engaged them, and cut off above six thousand of their men, and amongst the rest Cephalon, the brother of Antipater.

Hyrcanus and Antipater, thus deprived of their hopes from the Arabians, transferred the same to their very adversaries; and upon Pompey's entering Syria, and coming to Damascus, cast themselves upon his honour for protection. They used the same means of presents and arguments which they had done with Aretas, entreating Pompey to consider the violent usurpation of Aristobulus, and the right of Hyrcanus, as well with respect to seniority as character. Aristobulus, relying upon his interest with Scaurus, arrayed himself in royal attire, and presented his person to Pompey with the train and equipage of a king. But finding that his assuming of royal dignity had no weight with Pompey, and disdaining a servile application, he abruptly took his departure, and retired to Diospolis.

The [illegible] Pompey great [illegible] countenance to Hyrcanus and his adherents. He immediately drew out his Roman troops, and some Syrian auxiliaries, and marched after him. When he had passed Pella and Scythopolis, and came to Corea, upon the borders of Judea in the Mediterranean parts, he heard that Aristobulus was fled to Alexandrion, a strong hold, situated on an high mountain, which he sent, and commanded him to come down to him. Aristobulus naturally proud and ambitious, could not brook the imperious mandate, and therefore determined to run all hazards rather than comply with it; but, through the [illegible] of the people, and the [illegible], to consider the power of the Romans and the urgency of the case, he was at length prevailed upon to come down, and after speaking in defence of his pretensions, went up again. He afterwards, at the [illegible] of his brother, came down a second time, and [illegible], and each of them preserved their [illegible] Pompey, he returned without the least molestation. He was now divided between hope and fear, and [illegible] till, upon [illegible], he was resolved to go up to the castle [illegible], lest he should be tempted to do any thing derogatory to his royal state.

Pompey was now strongly inclined to the possession of the castle; but being told that Aristobulus had given a positive command to all the governors to attend to no orders but those under his own hand and seal, he commanded him to [illegible] them, to deliver them up [illegible] upon the sight of his letter. Aristobulus obeyed [illegible], but [illegible] were [illegible], indignant and [illegible] Jerusalem, intending a war with [illegible].

The Romans [illegible] time to make preparations [illegible] him and he was [illegible] in his progress, by the [illegible] death of Mithridates. The [illegible] the most fruitful [illegible] of Judea, bearing a vast number of palm-trees, besides the balsam-tree [illegible] upon the incision of the bark, with a sharp stone, drops down like tears. He staid there that night, and posted away the next morning for Jerusalem. Aristobulus, [illegible] this expedition, cast himself at Pompey's feet, with supplications and tears, and made him promises of money, and proposals of giving up both the city, and his own person, into Pompey's hands. This pacified him for the present, but Aristobulus did not perform the conditions; for, when Gabinius was sent to receive the money, his partizans would not admit him into the city.

This procrastinating behaviour irritated Pompey to so great a degree, that he kept Aristobulus his prisoner, and advanced to the city, took a view of the fortifications, and considered upon what quarter to attack it. He observed that the walls were strong and impregnable, and the temple so invincibly sure, that if the city itself was taken, the work would be but half accomplished.

While Pompey was deliberating on the most expedient means to pursue, a violent sedition arose in the town between the parties of Aristobulus and Hyrcanus. The former were for putting the matter to the decision of an engagement, and rescuing their king by dint of arms, the other for opening the gates and admitting Pompey into the town without any opposition. This was the sense of the majority, from the awe in which they held the Romans. The friends of Aristobulus, upon this, retired into the temple, and cut down the bridge of communication betwixt that and the city, determining to maintain it to the last. But as the other had received the Romans into the city, and put them into the palace, Pompey sent Piso, one of his general officers, with a strong detachment [illegible]. When he perceived the obstinacy of [illegible] the temple, and that there was no longer any prospect of accommodation, he posted his [illegible] and [illegible] attack, Hyrcanus and his party contributing [illegible] to his assistance.

The first business was to fill up the ditch and valley upon the north side of the temple, and the soldiers were obliged to carry materials for that purpose. It was a work of infinite difficulty, both with respect to the prodigious depth and the advantage the Jews had of annoying them from their superior station. Nor could the Romans have succeeded in their efforts, had not Pompey [illegible] them of the Jews [illegible] observance of the [illegible] day or sabbath. This great leader, knowing that the Jews made a conscience of doing any work upon that day, but what was of absolute necessity, either for the support of life, or the defence of it in case of immediate danger, commanded his soldiers only to ply their entrenchments on that day, without any other act of hostility. When the ground was now levelled, the bulwarks advanced, with strong and large turrets planted upon them, and manned, the Romans, with the engines they had brought from Tyre, began the battery, the soldiers, at the same time, beating the defendants out of the towers above, with stones from the walls, till, in the end, they were tired out with the labour.

Pompey could not but admire the fortitude of these people, and more especially in this particular, that in the midst of extremity and danger, they never [illegible] the ceremonies of their religion, but offered up their daily prayers and sacrifices as [illegible] as if it had been a time of profound peace. Nor, indeed, did they relax in their attention to Divine worship, even after the temple was actually taken, and [illegible] were slain before the altar. [illegible] short after [illegible] this siege, and the loss of one tower, the temple was taken by assault.

The first that entered the breach was Faustus Cornelius, the son of Sylla, and after him Furius and Fabius, two centurions, with their cohorts, who beset the temple, and put to the sword all that fell in their way. There were several priests at that time in the very exercise of their holy function, who, with the point of the sword at their breasts, went on with their oblations and incense without any regard to the safety of their lives, out of the veneration they had for the duties of their profession. The greater part of them were slain by their own countrymen of the adverse faction, and an innumerable multitude threw themselves down precipices; others, in a rage of desperation, set fire to what they could reach about the walls, and then cast themselves into the flames. There perished in this outrage 12,000 of the Jews. Few of the Romans were slain, but great numbers wounded.

But nothing affected the Jewish nation so much in their present calamities, as that their holy place, which had hitherto been seen by none, should be exposed to the view of strangers. Pompey, with a train of attendants, went into the temple itself, where it was not lawful for any but the high-priest to enter, and saw what was deposited therein, the candlesticks, lamps, and tables for incense, with other vessels, all of gold, a mass of spices, and 2000 talents of sacred treasure. Yet such was his liberality, that he would not suffer any thing to be touched that was dedicated to Divine worship, but commanded the ministers about the temple, the very next day after he had taken it, to superintend the purification of it, and go on with their ceremonies as before.

He also declared Hyrcanus high-priest, in consideration of the good offices he had rendered him, both in the siege and otherwise, by drawing off great numbers of the faction from Aristobulus. By these means, like a wise and good man, he secured himself the affections of the people. Amongst the captives was the father-in-law of Aristobulus, who was also his uncle. Pompey caused the principal authors of the revolt to be beheaded; and conferred upon Faustus, and those of his party, [illegible] signalized their bravery, the most honourable rewards. He imposed a tribute upon Judea, [illegible] the Jews [illegible] had possessed themselves of in Cœlosyria [illegible] restoring them to the jurisdiction of the [illegible] governors, [illegible] them to their own friends. [illegible] rebuilt Gadara, which the [illegible] destroyed, to gratify Demetrius, one of his [illegible] and a native of the place. With respect to the [illegible] of Hippos, Scythopolis, Pella, Samaria, Marissa, Azotus, Jamnia, and Arethusa, and the sea-coast towns of Gaza, Joppa, Dora, and that which was formerly called Strato's Tower, and afterwards Cæsarea by Herod, who beautified it with magnificent buildings, he took them all from the Jews, to restore them to their [illegible] and so joined them to the province of Syria. After the passing of these orders, and settling Scaurus in the government of Judea, and of all the countries [illegible] Egypt to the borders of the Euphrates, with the command of two legions, Pompey [illegible] to Rome by way of Cilicia, carrying Aristobulus, and his family, [illegible] with him, that is, two daughters, and two sons, Alexander, and Antigonus, the former of whom made his escape on the [illegible], but the latter, with his sisters, were carried to Rome.

CHAP. VI.

[illegible] upon Aretas, king of Arabia, [illegible] Antipater [illegible] Alexander [illegible] by Gabinius, and [illegible] to Alexandrion. Mark [illegible] several cities from [illegible] Gabinius [illegible] the government of Judea, and [illegible] Aristobulus [illegible] by the Romans [illegible] Gabinius [illegible] Alexander [illegible] Gabinius [illegible] Rufus [illegible]

IN the mean time Scaurus made an expedition into Arabia [illegible] Petra, but [illegible] the country so rugged [illegible] he could not advance without the greatest difficulty. He had [illegible] and his cannons, though he met [illegible] hardships to encounter, through want of provisions [illegible] his army. Hyrcanus, however, [illegible] found [illegible], by the assistance of Antipater, to furnish him with [illegible] Scaurus well knowing that there was a good understanding subsisting between Antipater and Aretas prevailed with the former to go to him upon terms of amity, and endeavour to bring him to consent to [illegible] composition of the war for a stipulated sum of money. [illegible] undertook the commission, and brought the king of Arabia into compliance with the proposal, who, entering into an agreement to pay three hundred talents [illegible] the purchase of a peace, Scaurus drew his army out of Arabia. Alexander, the son of Aristobulus, who escaped from Pompey, and by this time, raised a considerable body of [illegible], was ravaging Judea, and putting [illegible] Hyrcanus that Jerusalem was [illegible] to be in danger, upon a pretence that the walls which Pompey had broken down were not as yet repaired. But Gabinius, the successor of Scaurus, an officer eminent for his conduct and valour, being sent into Syria, [illegible] against him, Alexander found the necessity of putting himself in the best posture of defence against so formidable an enemy. He had raised an army, consisting of 10,000 foot, and 1500 horse; and had fortified several defensible places, as Alexandrion, Hyrcanus, and Machærus, near the mountains of Arabia.

Gabinius sent Mark Anthony before him, with a detachment of some of Antipater's choice troops, and a great number of Jews, under Malichus and Pitholaus to join him. Gabinius himself followed with the main body, and advanced towards Alexander, who finding himself so greatly overpowered in number, was forced to retire. But Gabinius [illegible] upon him in his retreat, came up with him and engaged him not far from Jerusalem, where he lost 6000 men, of whom 3000 fell in the action, and the remainder were taken alive, while he [illegible] with those that [illegible] Gabinius [illegible] the [illegible] offered [illegible] all [illegible] that would come over to him, and join him before [illegible] but as they were so [illegible] to listen to [illegible] recommendation, he fell upon them [illegible] and [illegible] Mark Anthony [illegible] fell in the action, and though [illegible] displayed his valour and conduct, he seems upon the [illegible] to have outdone himself.

Gabinius, leaving a sufficient force before the castle [illegible] all the cities and towns in the province, with an intention of repairing those that had sustained damage, and [illegible] those that had been destroyed. He [illegible] peremptory orders for the re-peopling of Scythopolis, [illegible] Anthedon, Apollonia, Jamnia, Raphia, Marissa, [illegible], Gadara, Azotus and several other places, where the inhabitants came flocking in with the utmost joy, to resume their former habitations.

When Gabinius had thus disposed of these places, he returned to the siege of Alexandrion, and [illegible] vigour. Alexander was so alarmed at the desperate situation of his affairs, that he sent ambassadors with an absolute resignation of himself to his pleasure, and acknowledgement of his errors and [illegible] pardon. They were commissioned to tender to him not only Machærus and Hyrcanion, but Alexandrion itself [illegible] being made and accepted, Gabinius demolished them at the instance of Alexander's mother, lest they might prove the occasion of another war. Such was her tenderness for her husband and children that [illegible] prisoners to Rome, that she omitted no application or access that might ingratiate herself with the general.

After this Gabinius brought Hyrcanus to Jerusalem committed the temple to his charge, appointed [illegible] for the civil constitution and divided the whole province of Judea into five jurisdictions. The first was Jerusalem, the second Gadara, the third Amathus, the fourth Jericho and the fifth Sepphoris, a city of Galilee [illegible] gave great satisfaction to the people to find themselves delivered from a monarchy to [illegible].

It was not long before Aristobulus afforded [illegible] for new disturbances. He made his escape from Rome, and collected a great body of Jews [illegible] love of innovation, [illegible] through the regard they bore him. His first attempt [illegible] the repairing of Alexandrion, but upon information, that Sisenna, Anthony, and Servilius were marching towards him with an army from Gabinius, he withdrew to Machærus, where he dismissed the unprofitable multitude, and took with him only a body of eight thousand men well armed [illegible] among a thousand fugitive Jews, that Pitholaus had brought out of Jerusalem. The Romans followed their [illegible], and brought them to action. Alexander and his men behaved gallantly upon the occasion; but in the end [illegible] overpowered [illegible] the Romans obtained a decisive victory, [illegible] upon the [illegible], two thousand withdrew to an hill and [illegible] and the other [illegible] with Aristobulus [illegible] way through the Roman army, [illegible] marched to Machærus. [illegible] upon them [illegible] they [illegible] ruins, Aristobulus did not despair of [illegible] repair the castle, and [illegible].

The Romans in the mean time plied the attack and at the end of two days, after a very [illegible] on the part of the besieged, took the place with Aristobulus and his son Antigonus, that fled from Rome with him. They were both bound and sent to Gabinius, and thence to Rome again. The [illegible] under confinement, but sent the sons back to Judea at the instance of Gabinius who had [illegible] to the wife of Aristobulus upon the delivery of the castles.

Gabinius was now preparing for a war upon the Parthians, but Ptolemy having quitted the Euphrates, and been [illegible] from Egypt, [illegible] Hyrcanus [illegible] assistance, supplying [illegible] with [illegible] money, arms, [illegible] with all [illegible] necessary for carrying on a war. They [illegible] the Jews, [illegible] the avenues to [illegible] Gabinius pass over at his return. His [illegible] the other places of Syria, and caused such [illegible] the Jews, that Alexander, the son of Aristobulus, [illegible] of people, took [illegible] Roman to death that was to be found [illegible] the general was not [illegible] the [illegible], he made use of his interest with Antipater [illegible] to an [illegible] and having an army of thirty thousand men, as eager to come to [illegible] engagement, [illegible] the mountain [illegible] thousand of Alexander's army [illegible] slain upon the [illegible] the rest [illegible] dispersed. Gabinius then returned to Jerusalem, to settle the government, according to [illegible] of Antipater. [illegible] he marched after the Nabatheans, [illegible] Parthian deserters that came over to him, Mithridates and Orsanes, pretending to [illegible] had made their escape.

Crassus, who succeeded Gabinius in the government of Syria, [illegible] the temple not only of the two thousand talents that Pompey left untouched, but all the gold that was deposited there [illegible] the purpose of carrying on the Parthian war [illegible] where he himself was [illegible].

Crassus [illegible] succeeded by Cassius, who put a stop to the Parthians, [illegible] they were just ready to break into Syria. He was [illegible] his government, [illegible] he marched [illegible] took Tarichea, and carried off near three [illegible] into bondage. He also caused to be put to death [illegible] who had supported the [illegible] followers of [illegible] though [illegible] of Antipater. Cypros, the wife of Antipater, was a noble Arabian, by whom he had four sons, Phasael, Herod, afterwards king, Joseph and Pheroras, and one daughter whose name was Salome. He was [illegible] universally beloved for his many excellent qualities, but his most particular friend was the king of the Arabians, to whom he recommended the care of his children when he undertook the war against Aristobulus. When Cassius had forced Alexander to come to terms, [illegible] his post at the Euphrates, to take possession of the pass, and prevent the inroad of the Parthians.

CHAP. VII.

Aristobulus [illegible] Julius Cæsar, emperor of Rome, [illegible] Pompey's faction, [illegible] son Alexander by Scipio. Antipater [illegible] friendship of Cæsar, [illegible]

UPON the sudden flight of Pompey, and the Roman senate, [illegible] and the Ionian sea, Julius Cæsar was left in the sole possession of the empire, and immediately released Aristobulus from his bonds. He then dispatched him with two legions into Syria [illegible] granted, that the country would [illegible] on the appearance of the Roman soldiers upon their borders. But the expectation of the emperor, and the confidence of Aristobulus, were both disappointed, the latter being soon poisoned by some of Pompey's faction. The body was embalmed, and lay some time uninterred, till Anthony caused it to be transported to Judea, and there deposited in the royal sepulchre. Nor did Alexander, his son, long survive his father, for he was beheaded by Scipio, at Antioch, according to the direction of Pompey, upon an accusation exhibited against him before his tribunal, [illegible] the Romans. But Ptolemy the son of [illegible], and prince of Chalcis, upon [illegible]

Libanus, sent his son Philippion to Ascalon, to the widow of Aristobulus, in order to bring with him his son Antigonus, and his daughters. Philippion became enamoured of the younger, whose name was Alexandra, and took her to wife, for which his father caused him to be slain, and afterwards married her himself. This alliance greatly attached him to her brother Antigonus, [illegible]

On the demise of Pompey, Antipater changed his system of politics, and made court to Cæsar and Mithridates, of Pergamus, finding a stop put to his expedition into Egypt, by prohibiting his troops a passage through the avenues about Pelusium, [illegible] with his army at Ascalon, and not only prevailed with the Arabians for assistance, though [illegible] but raised upon his own account, three thousand [illegible] Jews. He brought also over [illegible] of Syria into the party, as Ptolemy of Libanus, Jamblicus, and another Ptolemy, so that men of their reputation and interest induced the whole country to engage in this war. Mithridates finding himself, through the help of Antipater, in a condition to enter upon action, marched forwards to Pelusium, and, upon the inhabitants opposing his passage, laid siege to the city. Antipater added to the honour he had acquired by his intrepid behaviour in this encounter, for he was the first man that mounted the breach, and entered the town with his people after him.

Thus was Pelusium taken: but the Egyptian Jews of the province of Onias, stopped their further progress. Antipater, however, prevailed with them not only to offer no hostilities, but to furnish provisions for the army. This example wrought so far upon the people of Memphis, that, of their own accord, they delivered themselves up to Mithridates. Upon this he went to Delta, and engaged the rest of the Egyptians at a place called "The camp of the Jews;" where Mithridates and the whole right wing, were in extreme danger of being totally cut off, but Antipater having already broken the enemy's other wing, wheeled about, passed the bank of the river, and came up so seasonably to the rescue of Mithridates, that he turned upon his pursuers, slew many of them, and followed the remainder to their camp, which he plundered, and all this with the loss of only four score men on his side. Mithridates lost in the pursuit about eight hundred men. He escaped with his life beyond all expectations, and became an irreproachable witness to the Roman emperor of the gallant exploits of Antipater. Cæsar was so frank and generous in his professions and acknowledgments to this great man, that he became more and more zealous and ambitious, upon every occasion, to lay down his life for so illustrious a master. He needed no other proofs of his fidelity and courage than the honourable marks he wore on his body. When Cæsar had settled the affairs of Egypt, and returned to Syria, he gave Antipater the privilege of a citizen of Rome, and rendered him [illegible] object of admiration and envy, by the singular tokens of respect and esteem he conferred upon him. On his account he confirmed Hyrcanus in the dignified office of high-priest.

CHAP. VIII.

Antigonus addresses himself to Cæsar, and contrary to design, promotes the interest of Antipater. Cæsar appoints Hyrcanus to the pontificate, and Antipater to the government of Judea. Antipater prefers his sons Phasael and Herod. Herod [illegible] to appear before the council, and acquitted of the charge exhibited against him. He is declared general in Syria and Samaria. Sextus Cæsar [illegible] off by the treachery of Bassus, and succeeded by Murcus.

ABOUT this time Antigonus, the son of Aristobulus, addressed himself to Cæsar, and became very contrary to his design, the means of the advancement of Antipater. He seems to have been actuated by a desire of pouring forth the most extravagant invectives against Hyrcanus and

4 L

Antipater [illegible] his own [illegible] upon them [illegible] that he had [illegible] respected the [illegible] in gratitude [illegible] [illegible] price he also [illegible], that the [illegible] [illegible] to Cæsar [illegible] was [illegible] often [illegible] hoping to merit, in some measure, [illegible] they had formerly rendered to Pompey. Now [illegible] he would have imputed the death of his father to the instrument [illegible] of [illegible] faction, and [illegible] of [illegible], to-[illegible]

[illegible] to [illegible] all these reproaches, the [illegible] [illegible] of his garment [illegible] exposed his wounds [illegible] testimony of his fidelity [illegible], enforced by declaring, "that he could not but wonder at the confidence of Antigonus, [illegible] to the Romans, after he, "[illegible], like his father [illegible] in exhibiting "[illegible] to Cæsar [illegible] the most faithful and [illegible] "of his subjects, and insisting upon pretensions to merit "of which he was wholly devoid, [illegible] in "obtaining power, was to employ [illegible] posing the will "of his benefactor."

Cæsar was so wrought upon by this manly conduct, that he declared Hyrcanus [illegible] for the office of high-priest, and gave Antipater the liberty of nominating his commission. As he referred the matter to the good pleasure of his master, the emperor constituted him governor of Judea, with the additional favour of permission to repair the walls of his country. These honorary grants, Cæsar ordered to be engraven on brass, and the table hung up in the capitol, as a memorial of the deserts of Antipater, and his [illegible].

When Antipater had conducted the emperor to the borders of Syria, he returned to Judea, where the first thing he did was to rebuild the walls of Jerusalem, that Pompey had caused to be overthrown. He then [illegible] through the [illegible] to prevent disorders, and keep the peace, [illegible] the people [illegible], that, if they behaved with [illegible] to Hyrcanus, they should live in plenty [illegible], but if they should prove refractory, and [illegible] avenging themselves by the ruin of their country, [illegible] instead of a gentle governor, a rigid master, and Hyrcanus a cruel tyrant, instead of a gracious prince.

Notwithstanding this apparent deference paid to Hyrcanus, Antipater took upon him to settle the state of the province, [illegible] the defect and incapacity of the other for [illegible]. He [illegible] his eldest son, the government of Jerusalem, and the provinces adjacent, to Herod, his second son, that of Galilee, with the same [illegible]. Herod, being naturally bold and active, soon found honourable occasion for the display of his genius. Syria was greatly infested with bands of robbers, till he took Hezekias, the leader of them, and caused him to be put to death, with several of his followers. This exploit was so acceptable a service to the Syrians, that the towns and villages resounded with acclamations to the honour of Herod [illegible] the restorer of their liberties and possessions. It also made him known to Sextus Cæsar, the kinsman of Cæsar the Great, who [illegible] then governor of Syria. The fame of this [illegible] inspired Phasael with a generous emulation to excel his brother, and to gain more and more upon the hearts of the people of Jerusalem, where he exercised his power with such moderation and justice, as to produce universal satisfaction. The wise conduct of this administration inspired the people with as great a reverence of Antipater, as if he had been their absolute sovereign, and he behaved himself at the same time, with the profoundest respect towards Hyrcanus.

But as the human mind is too susceptible of envy, we find, upon this occasion, a notorious instance of it in Hyrcanus. The renown these young governors had acquired in their respective provinces, and the daily informations he received of the exploits of Herod in particular, raised this ignoble passion in the heart of Hyrcanus. There were not wanting [illegible] about the palace [illegible] sycophants, to [illegible] the [illegible] jealousy of the fame they had obtained [illegible]. They suggested to this end, that it was derogatory to the dignity of Hyrcanus, that the administration of government should be divided betwixt Antipater and his sons, while he held but an empty name, that it was [illegible] keep kings in opposition to him, and that they [illegible] his authority in their general conduct, but more especially in the instance of Herod's causing so many to be put to death in direct violation to the Jewish law, and without any mandate from him. In short, they demanded if Herod was a private man or a king, reflecting, that if he was only the former, he was amenable to the king himself, and [illegible] contrary, for the murder of so many innocent persons.

Hyrcanus was gradually incensed by these insinuations to so violent a pitch, that he commanded the proper officers to summon Herod to make his appearance for trial. Herod, conscious of his innocence, with the advice of his father, secured his garrison in Galilee and repaired to Jerusalem, taking with him only a competent guard for the security of his person, without any design of offering [illegible] to Hyrcanus. Sextus Cæsar however, anxious for his safety, sent a [illegible] to him to acquit Herod of the charge alleged against him. Hyrcanus seemed [illegible] to compliance, but Herod, too cautious to depend upon fair words, went to Sextus at Damascus, with a resolution not to attend to a second summons. The court sycophants renewed their [illegible] to Hyrcanus, and represented the abrupt departure of Herod as [illegible] a design of some desperate attempt. [illegible] Hyrcanus credulously admitted of their intimation [illegible] remained undetermined as to the steps he should pursue, [illegible] the enemy too powerful for him, till Sextus declaring Herod general of all his troops in Syria and [illegible], it struck such a terror into Hyrcanus, [illegible] of his own strength, and the affections of the people, that he conceived him marching at the head of an army against him.

Nor was he mistaken in his conjecture, for Herod, in a transport of indignation at finding himself treated as a criminal, collected a body of forces, and marched towards Jerusalem, with a full determination to depose Hyrcanus from the government, which he had certainly done, if his father and brother had not stopped the violence of his passion. They advised him to carry his revenge no farther than threatening, and to spare the prince under whose patronage he had been advanced to his present dignity. They reminded him, that, though he might have been [illegible], yet, as he was acquitted, it was but letting the conversation of his life [illegible] the hazard of it, and that if the Almighty was the author of success in war, an unjust cause would meet with a deserved fate, and that therefore he should not be too presuming nor confident [illegible] attempt upon a prince who had been his supporter and benefactor, and would never have treated him with rigour had he not been misled by calumny and evil counsel. Herod was prevailed on by these arguments, and contented himself with giving the nation [illegible] proof of his great power and interest.

In the [illegible] time the Romans fell into a civil [illegible] Apamia [illegible] occasioned by the treacherous [illegible] of Sextus Cæsar by Cecilius Bassus, which he [illegible] out of his good will to Pompey, and then assumed his command. The officers of Julius Cæsar, in revenge for the death of Sextus, fell with their utmost force upon Bassus. Antipater also sent his sons to join them with succours, from a regard to the character of the living, and the memory of the deceased Cæsar. The war was protracted to a considerable space of time, and Murcus was ordered out of Italy to succeed Sextus Cæsar in the government of Syria.

CHAP. IX.

[illegible] Cassius [illegible] the [illegible] purpose [illegible] Malichus [illegible] Antipater. Augustus Cæsar and Anthony [illegible] Cassius. Herod made governor of Syria. [illegible] of the treachery of Malichus [illegible] death [illegible] influence of Herod.

THERE fell out, at this time, a most desperate war among the Romans [illegible] the murder of Julius Cæsar, in the third year and seventh month of his reign, by the treachery of Brutus and Cassius, was followed by tumultuous factions in divers parts of the empire. The great men were divided into parties, each individual acting as his humour or interest led him, without any regard to the public good. Cassius proceeded to Syria, to possess himself of the forces that were there before Apamia, where he effected a reconciliation between Marcus and Bassus, and the raising of the siege of Apamia at the same time. He laid the cities under excessive contributions, and imposed a tax of seven hundred talents upon the Jews, which Antipater provided for in time, by an equal distribution of the charge, appointing his sons, friends, and Malichus, though his professed enemy, to take a seasonable care of the levy. The first that wrought himself into the good graces of Cassius was Herod, who presented him with an hundred talents for the quota of Galilee, and for that very important cause was ranked amongst his friends. But Cassius resented the delay of others [illegible] in their proportions to such a degree, that he razed Gophna, Thamna, and two other places of less note, to the ground; and when this was done, formed a resolution of cutting off Malichus for being so [illegible] in acting his tribute. But Antipater prevented his death and the destruction of several cities, as well as [illegible] the effects of Cassius, by bringing in an hundred talents [illegible].

Cassius, however, had no sooner taken his departure, than Malichus, dead to every sense of gratitude and moral obligation, entered into a plot upon the life of the very [illegible] he had so often acknowledged as his friend, [illegible] he termed [illegible] to remove as an obstacle to his [illegible] practices. Antipater perceived of his power and [illegible] him with a curious eye, and therefore passed [illegible] in order to raise forces to guard himself against [illegible] treacherous designs. Malichus finding himself [illegible], had recourse to delusive arts with the sons [illegible], and plied both Phasael and Herod so effectually [illegible] excuses, oaths, and protestations of his [illegible] and integrity, that he engaged them in a mediation [illegible] the father for a reconciliation, and by the same [illegible] peace with Marcus, governor of Syria, who had determined to put him to death as a mutineer.

[illegible] Cæsar and Anthony being now at war with Brutus and Cassius, the latter having had convincing proof of the bravery of Herod, appointed him governor of the whole province of Syria, with a considerable guard of horse and foot. Nay, Cassius went so far as to promise him the kingdom of the Jews at the end of the war. But it so happened, that the hope and bravery of the son was the cause of the destruction of the father; for Malichus had him in such dread, that he bribed one of the cup-bearers of Hyrcanus to put a poison with his drink, by which means he lost his life at a banquet. Thus was this great man requited for the favours he conferred on the most ungrateful of wretches. He was a man of singular prudence and prowess, to which Hyrcanus might be said to be indebted for his kingdom. The people were so enraged at Malichus, from a suspicion of this execrable practice, that they were ready to sacrifice him to their resentment. But, upon his renouncing and abjuring any knowledge of the [illegible], [illegible] purpose, and Marcus, [illegible] the mean time, by way of prevention put himself into a posture of defence, as it could not be expected that Herod would suffer so atrocious a murder to pass unrevenged. He knew that Herod was absolutely for taking his revenge at the head of an army; but his brother Phasael dissuaded him by all means from that resolution, for fear of a tumult [illegible]. The [illegible], upon this, gave him a hearing, with a semblance of allowing his defence, and [illegible] countenance as if they thought him innocent, and then proceeded to the funeral obsequies of their father, which were very sumptuous and magnificent.

Sextus being at this time taken up with factions, Herod went thither to appease them, but returned upon all [illegible] to [illegible] Jerusalem being [illegible] his going and coming by his guard. Hyrcanus, upon this, at the request of Malichus, who feared [illegible], forbad the introduction of foreigners to mix themselves with the people of the country while they were exercising the rules of their holy profession. But Herod [illegible] both of the cause itself and of the authority that issued the command, entered the city by night. Upon this Malichus came to him, and with tears, bewailing the loss of Antipater. Herod, on the [illegible], dissembled his rage and indignation. But, at the same time, he wrote to Cassius for justice upon Malichus for the murder of his father. This was easily obtained, as the man was odious to Cassius: so that he left Herod to the due course of law, and sent private orders to his officers to give him assistance as occasion might require.

Laodicea being lately taken, persons of rank resorted from all parts to Herod with congratulations and presents. This, therefore, he looked upon as the fairest opportunity for the execution of his [illegible]; but Malichus, suspecting his design, laid a plan to evade it, by getting [illegible] his son from Tyre, who was an hostage there, and conveying him privately to Judæa. Fearing this plan might fail, he conceived a greater exploit. This was to stir the whole nation of the Jews against the Romans, while Cassius was fully engaged in the war with Anthony. By this means he flattered himself he could effect the deposition of Hyrcanus, and the acquisition of the government to himself. But the fates had otherwise determined it; for Herod, suspecting what his design, invited Malichus and Hyrcanus to an entertainment, and sending a servant to [illegible], under pretence of making preparations, gave him private instructions for the tribunes to [illegible] and execute the plan concerted between him and Cassius. The tribunes accordingly marched out with their drawn swords towards the sea side, where they met Malichus, surrounded him and cut him into pieces. Hyrcanus was so alarmed at this incident, that he fell down in a swoon, from which as soon as he recovered, he enquired of Herod who it was that killed Malichus? One of the tribunes replied, that it was done by order of Cassius. Hyrcanus then rejoined, that Cassius had saved both him and his country at once, in the destruction of a tyrant so dangerous to both. Whether Hyrcanus spoke the sentiments of his mind cannot be determined. But thus was the revenge of Herod, and the end of Malichus.

CHAP. X.

A [illegible] in Jerusalem. [illegible] Herod [illegible] of Tyre, [illegible] Cassius [illegible] Anthony [illegible] Herod [illegible] Phasael [illegible] of Judæa.

WHEN Cassius departed from Syria, a [illegible] [illegible] arose in Jerusalem, where Felix made [illegible] upon Phasael and Herod, to revenge the death of Malichus. It so happened that Herod being then at Damascus, with Fabius, the governor, was prevented, by indisposition, from marching to the relief of his brother. But Phasael stood in no need of his assistance in the defence. Felix with his own troops ... took an opportunity of reproaching Hyrcanus for his ... in affording aid to Felix, and putting several fortresses into the hands of the brother of Malichus, and amongst the rest Massada, one of the best fortified places in the country. But this availed them little against the ... of Herod, who no sooner recovered from his indisposition, than he re-took all he had lost, and brought Hyrcanus to submission, even in Massada itself. He drove Marion, king of Tyre, out of Galilee, and recovered three castles of which he had possessed him ... He not only treated however, the lives of those Tyrians whom he took, but gratified many of them with donations, thereby attaching them to himself, and rendering them inimical to Marion. This Marion was a fit instrument for Cassius ... to many tyrants over Syria ... to Herod, that he assisted Antigonus, the son of Aristobulus, and Fabius also, who ... the hiring of Antigonus ... Ptolemy, the kinsman of Antigonus supplied them all with necessaries.

Herod made every necessary preparation for the encounter, which soon took place on the borders of Judea, and was decided in his favour, so that having totally defeated Antigonus, he returned to Jerusalem, and was received with every token of honour and respect, even ... had despised him before; but this was from ... to his family alliance with Hyrcanus. Herod had formerly married a woman of his own country, who was of noble extraction, called Doris, by whom he had a son Antipater. He afterwards took to wife Mariamne, the daughter of Alexander the son of Aristobulus, and of Alexandra, the daughter of Hyrcanus.

Upon Cæsar's coming into Italy, and Anthony into Asia, after the death of Cassius, at the battle of Philippi ambassadors were dispatched from several places to Anthony in Bithynia, whither the chiefs of the Jews were repaired also with complaints against Phasael and Herod for usurping the ... power to themselves, and allowing Hyrcanus merely the name of sovereign. Herod appeared ready to answer this accusation, but had so effectually ingratiated himself with Anthony, by dint of presents, that the plaintiffs were dismissed without any hearing.

Anthony being some time after this at Daphne in the suburbs of Antioch (about the beginning of his intrigue with Cleopatra) there came an hundred of the principal men among the Jews to prefer their complaints to him against the brothers. They selected their best orators for the purpose of advancing their plea. Messala undertook the cause of the brothers, and was seconded by Hyrcanus, upon the score of alliance. When Anthony had heard the allegations of both parties, he demanded of Hyrcanus whom he esteemed the fittest man for the administration of government? Hyrcanus replied that he knew of none so capable as the two brothers. Anthony was highly gratified at this declaration, having been greatly obliged to Antipater of old for a generous reception and entertainment upon his coming into Judæa with Gabinius. So he promoted them both tetrarchs of Judæa, and committed the whole administration to their conduct. The deputies were so disgusted at this proceeding, that, for their behaviour, he committed fifteen of the hundred to prison, and the rest escaped narrowly with their lives ... he first reprimanded, and then dismissed them. This served to inflame the mutineers at Jerusalem to a greater degree; so that instead of a hundred, they sent a thousand deputies to Anthony at Tyre, who was preparing at that time to fall upon Jerusalem. They were so clamorous, that the magistrates of Tyre were ordered to disperse them, and, in case of resistance, to put all to death whom they took. Anthony giving them further charge to maintain the authority of the tetrarchs whom he had set up. Herod and Hyrcanus being apprized of this order, went up towards the shore ... and advised the ambassadors to ... the ... that they ... bringing ruin upon themselves ... their country ... by their ... But as they grew outrageous, Anthony was under a necessity of ordering ... many of them, who ... and wounded great numbers of them. Hyrcanus, however, took care of the wounded, and provided for the burial of the dead. This had no effect upon those that escaped, for they continued their tumults till they provoked Anthony to such a degree, that he ordered all his prisoners to be put to death.

CHAP. XI.

Lysanias, by ... of Ptolemy, ... to depose Hyrcanus, ... Antigonus. The ... Jerusalem. Hyrcanus and Phasael ... Antigonus ... the Arabians ... Herod ... to ... Antigonus ... king ... Herod ... by ... king ... Herod ... the Jews.

ABOUT two years after this time, when Barzapharnes, a noble Parthian, held the government of Syria with Pacorus the king's son, Lysanias, the successor of Ptolemy the son of Mennæus, entered into an agreement, and ... to deliver up to them a thousand talents, and five hundred women, upon ... dethroning of Hyrcanus, and setting up Antigonus in his place. The ... immediately proceeded to the execution of the project. Pacorus took his way ... the sea-coast and Barzapharnes marched over the midland. Ptolemais and Sidon opened the gates to Pacorus, but the Tyrians ... He sent before him a party of horse to Judea, under the command of Pacorus, one of the king's cup-bearers, (an officer of his own name,) with instructions to attend to the enemy's motions, and to ... Antigonus ... occasion might require.

The Jews of Mount Carmel spontaneously offered their services to Antigonus, who directed them to ... and possess themselves of that quarter of the country they call Drymi. An action ensued, in which the party of Antigonus prevailed, and when the enemy was routed and dispersed, their numbers increasing, they marched at once to Jerusalem, where Hyrcanus and Phasael made a very brave resistance, and, after a smart contest in the market-place, forced them to retire to the temple. Herod upon this placed a guard of sixty men over the adjoining houses, but the people set fire to them from the aversion they had to the two brothers. These practices transported Herod to such a degree of indignation, that he fell upon the enemy, and cut off great numbers of them, ... daily ... slaughter.

The feast of Pentecost being now at hand, the city upon that occasion being crowded up to the very temple, and many of the multitude coming under arms, Phasael took charge of the walls, and Herod, with a small party, of the palace. The latter made so unexpected a sally into the suburbs that he killed several, and dispersed the whole multitude. Some fled into the city, others into the temple, while others sheltered themselves behind the ramparts.

When things were brought to this pass, Antigonus proposed a treaty of peace, and nominated Pacorus as the arbitrator. Phasael acquiesced, admitted the Parthians with 500 horse into the city. His pretence was to compose the mutiny; but his real intention was to assist Antigonus. This perfidious ... prevailed ... with Phasael to send an embassy to Barzapharnes upon the same subject. This was very contrary to the opinion of Herod, who advised Phasael to use the utmost caution in trusting him, as perfidy was the characteristic of a barbarian. Pacorus, however, went on, and took Hyrcanus with him, that he might be less suspected. He also left with Herod some of the horsemen which they called freemen, and conducted Phasael with the rest.

When they came to Galilee, they found the people of that country had revolted, and were in arms, but the governor, however, came out to meet them. Barzapharnes had the art to conceal his intention with the external civilities of compliments and presents, but as soon as they were departed had an ambush in readiness to surprize them on the road. They were conducted to a place near the sea, called Ecdippon, where they were informed of the particulars of the plot, that a thousand talents, and five hundred women, were to be delivered to the Parthians, upon their betraying Hyrcanus and Phasael. They were further informed that the plot would not have been deferred so long, but that they waited for Herod's coming up to Jerusalem, lest it should take air, and be frustrated.

Ophellius was the man to whom Saramalla (a Syrian of great opulence) had communicated the particulars of the whole design. Ophellius importuned Phasael to provide for his safety, but he determined at all events not to abandon Hyrcanus, and therefore went up to the Parthian general, and reproached him to his face, for entering into this treacherous design against him, from mercenary, the meanest of all motives, telling him, that if money was his object, he could give him more for his life than Antigonus had promised him for the kingdom. The subtle Parthian endeavoured to remove the suspicion by protestations and oaths, and then went immediately to Pacorus. But no sooner had he departed than Phasael and Hyrcanus were taken into custody by the Parthians who were left behind, according to their orders, and they [illegible] the liberty of exclaiming against so [illegible] perjury.

The Parthian, in the mean time, was instructed to attempt to get Herod out of the town, and seize upon him. He made the effort, but Herod was so well acquainted with the treacherous practices of those barbarians, that he would not venture out of the city. He did not doubt but that Phasael had sent him information of the plot, though the Parthians might have intercepted the letters. Pacorus, however, could not draw him out by the most plausible pretences he could use, and the strongest assurances of his personal security, for he still kept upon his guard, having heard that his brother Phasael was apprehended. Besides, Mariamne, a woman of great sagacity, conjured him by no means to go forth, nor expose himself to the manifest designs of those barbarians.

Pacorus finding it impossible to circumvent a man of Herod's prudence and penetration by open attack, began to deliberate how they might bring their plot to bear privately. But Herod, while this was in agitation, made his escape, with some of his nearest relations, by night, towards Idumea. The Parthians no sooner received intelligence of his departure, than they pursued him, upon which he sent his mother, brother, Mariamne, (to whom he was contracted,) and her younger brother, before him, whilst he himself, with his party, made a stand against the barbarians and overcoming them in several encounters, retired, at last, to the castle of Masada. The Jews pressed him more in his flight than the Parthians, attacking him sixty furlongs from Jerusalem, so that at length a regular engagement ensued. Herod obtained the victory, slew great numbers, and, to perpetuate the honour of the action, erected a magnificent palace, upon the spot, with a strong castle, which he called Herodium, from his own name.

As great numbers repaired to his standard in his retreat, his brother Joseph, when he came to Thresa in Idumea, advised him by all means, to lessen his train, which amounting, according to computation, to upwards of three thousand men, the castle of Masada could not contain them. Herod attended to his counsel, and commissioned the most cumbersome part of his retinue, disposing of his kindred and the best disciplined of his followers, in the respective departments of the castle, with an extra body of 800 men for the protection of the women, and provisions sufficient to hold out a siege if occasion should require. Having thus arranged matters, he went forward to Petra, in Arabia.

The Parthians at Jerusalem were wholly intent upon plunder, breaking into the houses of those who were absent, and rifling the royal palace itself, sparing nothing but the treasure of Hyrcanus which did not amount to more than three hundred talents, though they possessed themselves of the riches of others, but not equal to expectation, for Herod having a suspicion of the perfidy of the barbarians, had taken care to convey what was most precious to Idumea, and his companions had followed his example. But the Parthians, not content with the spoil of the city, infested the adjacent country with a bloody and implacable war. They laid waste the city of Marissa, and not only constituted Antigonus king, but delivered up Phasael and Hyrcanus bound into his hands. Such was the cruelty of Antigonus, that he tore off the ears of Hyrcanus with his teeth, to render him incapable of the priesthood, as no maimed person was eligible to that sacred function. Phasael, however, frustrated his inhuman designs, for having neither the command of his sword or his hands, he prevented all further abuses by dashing out his brains against a stone, demonstrating thereby his alliance to Herod, while Hyrcanus had given proof of degeneracy. He died like a man of honour, and his end was suitable to the glory of his life. It is reported that he survived that violence upon himself, and that a physician was sent him from Antigonus who poisoned the wound, and so dispatched him. There prevails another report, that being told by a woman a little before his death, that Herod had made his escape, he exclaimed, "I shall now die in peace, as I shall leave behind me a friend to avenge my wrongs." But we do not contend for the authenticity of either of these reports.

Thus was the end of Phasael, and the Parthians, though they were disappointed in the promise of the women, put the government of Jerusalem into the hands of Antigonus, and sent Hyrcanus bound into Parthia. Herod was not yet made acquainted with the death of Phasael, so that concluding, from his knowledge of the avaricious disposition of the barbarians, that a sum of money would be the only means of his redemption, he determined upon a journey into Arabia, in hopes of supplying himself from the king upon that occasion, either as a bounty upon the score of the old friendship betwixt him and Antipater, or a loan upon the security of the pledge of his nephew, the son of Phasael, a youth of seven years of age, whom he proposed to take with him for that purpose. The sum he intended to give was three hundred talents, and the Tyrians were to intercede to procure his request.

But fate unhappily prevented the execution of his generous design in the death of Phasael. Nor could he trust himself among the Arabians, for Malchus, their king, ordered him to depart immediately out of his territories, pretending that the Parthians had demanded, by their ambassadors, that Herod might be driven out of Arabia, though the real motive was to withhold what was due to Antipater, and to avoid the obligation of making a requital to the son for the bounty of the father. He was instigated to act thus illiberally by those about him, who were destitute of both faith and honour.

When Herod found that the Arabians were his enemies and for the very cause which he imagined would have conciliated their friendship, he dispatched the messengers with such an answer as was suggested by the resentment of his passion, and then proceeded to Egypt. He came in the evening to a certain temple where he had left several of his companions in his passage. He next day arrived at Rhinocolura, where he received the first news of the death of his brother [illegible]
[illegible]

[illegible] him, but when he had given vent to the feelings of natural affection, and discharged his last duty to his brother, he proceeded on his journey.

The king of Arabia soon repented of what he had done, and dispatched messengers to prevail on him to return. But it was now too late, as he had advanced as far as Pelusium, where the officers stopped his progress, till, upon application to the magistrates, he was permitted to pass on, from the respect they had for his character. He embarked for Alexandria, whither, upon his arrival, he was received by Cleopatra with all pomp and splendor, hoping that he might be prevailed upon to accept the command of an army which she was then raising for some important design. But Herod was so intent upon his voyage to Rome, that neither the entreaty of the queen, the rigour of the season, nor [illegible] of the seas, could divert him from the prosecution of it. Putting therefore to sea, and taking his course by way of Pamphylia, there arose so violent a tempest, that the mariners were under a necessity of casting the goods overboard to save the vessel. At length, with great difficulty, they got safe to Rhodes, where he found *things in* great disorder, on account of the war with Cassius. He was there received by two friends, Ptolemy and Sapphinias, and, notwithstanding his then want of money, found means to provide himself a stout vessel, which conveyed him and his friends to Brundusium, and thence to Rome. Upon his arrival he paid his court to Anthony, between whom and his father Antipater an ancient friendship had subsisted, and revealed to him the adventures and misfortunes of his family, particularly that of his relations, being then shut up in the castle of Massada, which induced him to hazard a voyage, in the most rigorous part of the season, to wait upon him, and implore his protection.

Anthony was so affected by compassion for his distress, and tender regard for the memory of his father, together with the due sense he entertained of his own personal merit, that he determined to have him declared king of the Jews, as he had made him tetrarch before. To this he was moved, not only from respect to Herod, but aversion to Antigonus, whom he looked upon as of a turbulent, seditious spirit, and inimical to the Romans. Augustus was, if possible more attached to Herod than Anthony, nor was any thing more pleasing to him than to enter into a detail of Antipater's services in Egypt, the hardships they had there encountered together, and the mutual friendship they had long enjoyed.

Upon this an assembly of the senate was called, where Messala, and after him Atratinus, (Herod being present,) enlarged upon the merits of Antipater, and his fidelity to the people of Rome, holding forth Antigonus, at the same time, as a public enemy, not only from his defection, but receiving a crown from the hands of the Parthians, in contempt of the sovereignty of the empire. The senate were so wrought upon by these representations, that they gave their voices unanimously for Herod to be king of the Jews, which was enforced by Anthony, who pointed out the advantages that would accrue from it in the conduct of the Parthian war. When the senate rose, Cæsar and Anthony went out, preceded by the consuls and other magistrates, to give orders for sacrifice, and the depositing the decree of the senate in the capitol. Anthony also made a splendid entertainment for Herod on the first day of his reign.

CHAP. XI.

Massada besieged by Antigonus. Defended by Joseph, the brother of Herod. [illegible] *and Silo* [illegible] *Herod against Antigonus. Herod takes Joppa. Relieves Massada, and advances to* [illegible] *which* [illegible] *offers* [illegible] *The* [illegible] *of Silo. A* [illegible] *supported* [illegible] *Herod,* [illegible] *takes Jericho, and* [illegible] *His encounters with the robbers. Herod returns to Samaria,* [illegible] *Ptolemy assumes the command in his place.* [illegible] *Anthony,* [illegible] *Antigonus* [illegible]

DURING this time Antigonus besieged the castle of Massada, where the family and friends of Herod suffered much through an extreme drought, insomuch that Joseph, his brother, understanding that Malchus, king of Arabia, had repented of the injuries he had done to Herod, took a resolution to leave the castle by night, with two hundred chosen friends, and apply to the Arabians for succour. But at the very precise time that they were about to make the sally, there fell so copious a shower of rain, that their pits, cisterns, and other vessels were all replenished, which obviated the necessity of carrying their design into execution. After this seasonable relief, the garrison made several resolute sallies; and, between surprize and open force, did considerable execution upon the enemy, though they frequently met with severe repulses.

In the mean time Ventidius, one of the Roman generals, being sent to restrain the incursions of the Parthians into Syria, entered *Judæa, under colour of a design to relieve* Massada, but in reality to seize upon the treasure of Antigonus. When he had accomplished his purpose at Jerusalem, he withdrew, with the greatest part of the army, but left Silo, with a small body, behind him, in order to countenance his pretence; for if he had taken with him all the forces, his motive to enrich himself would have been too evident. Antigonus, however, maintained a good understanding with Silo, hoping that the Parthians would come again to his assistance.

Herod having now sailed out of Italy to Ptolemais, raised a considerable army, both of his own nation and strangers, and then marched through Galilee towards Antigonus, with the assistance of Ventidius and Silo, who were prevailed upon, by the solicitation of Dellius, at the instance of Anthony, to aid Herod in obtaining the possession of his kingdom. Ventidius was then intent on quieting the commotions which the Parthians had raised in divers cities, while Silo was corrupted by the bribes of Antigonus in Judæa. Herod, however, was not destitute of forces, as numbers repaired to his standard every day during his march, and the greatest part of Galilee came over to his interest. The principal object of his attention was the raising the siege of Massada, to set his kindred and friends at liberty; and Joppa was the first obstacle to be removed, as they could make no attempt upon Jerusalem with that enemy so near at hand. Silo took the opportunity to withdraw, and the Jews of the party of Antigonus pursuing him, Herod, with an handful of men, engaged, defeated them, and brought off Silo, after a very faint resistance.

After this Herod took Joppa, and then hastened, with all expedition, to set free his kindred and friends, that had been shut up a considerable time in the castle of Massada. *The inhabitants of the country seemed in general disposed to* join him; some for the sake of his father, others for his own sake, and others for their obligations to both; but the greater part were actuated by the hopes of honour and reward. Herod was by this time at the head of a considerable army; but Antigonus used his utmost endeavours to obstruct his passage, by planting ambushes in his way, though with little or no damage to the adverse party. He found, upon the whole, a great difficulty in raising the siege, and removing his friends and effects out of the castle. From hence he advanced to Jerusalem, where many of Silo's men, and of the inhabitants, came over to him, awed by his increasing power.

He pitched his camp upon the west side of the town, where the enemy galled him with showers of darts and arrows, and the defendants made divers vigorous sallies. As a prelude to his design, he caused a proclamation to be issued in form by an herald, round the walls of the city, setting forth that he had only in view, by his expedition, to promote the common good of the people and the safety of the place; with an offer of burying in oblivion the efforts of all his enemies, of every rank and degree without exception. Antigonus, on the other hand, did all he could, with noise and harangue, to keep his people from hearing the conditions of the declaration, or being moved by the force of it, and at length commanded them to fall on, upon which the assailants were repulsed from the tower, and forced to a retreat. The corruption of Silo was now evident beyond a doubt, from the clamours of the soldiers that he had suborned to put all in a flame. They exclaimed that they were lost for want of necessaries, as well as convenient winter quarters, through means of the army of Antigonus, that had carried every thing off. By these means the people were stirred up to a revolt, and Silo would have accompanied them in their retreat. His attempt threatened so much danger, that Herod was under the necessity of applying not only to Silo's officers, but to the common soldiers, representing to them the mischiefs that must inevitably ensue if they deserted him, and requesting that, as he had the commission of Cæsar, Anthony and the senate, for what he did, they would stand by him one day longer, and all their wants should be supplied. Upon this assurance Herod went himself to give orders for the provisions, and forthwith sent them so abundant a supply, that all Silo's pretences were obviated, and to secure them a future competence he wrote to Samaria, which was then under his protection, to send him all sorts of provisions to Jericho, such as corn, wine, oil, cattle, and every other necessary article. When Antigonus had intelligence of this, he dispersed his troops abroad, and laid ambushes to intercept the convoys. They obeyed their orders, so that a considerable army was posted near Jericho, and parties placed up and down the mountains to obstruct any kind of relief.

Herod, in the mean time, with his usual activity, advanced with ten companies, half Romans, half Jews, and a small body of horse, to Jericho, where he found the city totally abandoned, but five hundred men, with their wives and children, had taken possession of the summits of the mountains. These he took, and then dismissed them. The town contained abundance of valuable plunder, which the Romans carried away, and Herod leaving a garrison in the place, returned, and assigned the Roman troops their winter quarters in the cities that came over to him, as Idumæa, Galilee, and Samaria. Antigonus also, by bribing Silo, had part of his army quartered in Lydda, to stand fair in the opinion of Anthony.

The Romans now lived in the full enjoyment of peace and plenty, but Herod, whose active spirit could not rest, sent his brother Joseph, with 400 horse, and 2000 foot, to fortify Idumæa, lest Antigonus should enter upon any new device, while he went with his kindred, whom he had rescued at Massad, to Samaria. When he had settled them securely, he advanced into Galilee, to reduce certain garrisons possessed in that province by Antigonus. He came up to Sepphoris in a deep snow, and took the place without any difficulty, for the garrison quitted it without making any resistance. When he had given his men time to refresh themselves after the fatigue of the winter, there being in that city abundance of necessaries, he turned his arms against the free-booters that sheltered themselves in caves, and, by sallies and incursions, annoyed the inhabitants more than an open and professed enemy in the course of war. He sent three companies of foot, and a troop of horse, before him to Arbela, and followed them himself forty days after, with the rest of his army. The free-booters were not in the least alarmed at this incursion, but, on the contrary, advanced against them in a body, confident of the conduct and courage of their leader. When it came to a pitched battle they put to flight Herod's left wing, but Herod wheeling upon them immediately with his right, not only stopt the flight of his own men, but brought them on again with such fury, that the robbers, not being able to stand before them, were pursued as far as the Jordan, many of them cut off, and the rest got over the river. Thus was Galilee delivered from these ravagers, except some stragglers, that kept still in their fastnesses, which occasioned Herod to prolong his stay in the country.

After this exploit, as the first fruits of his soldiers services, he gave to every man an hundred and fifty drachmæ, and to the officers so much more in proportion, and then dismissed them to their winter quarters. He gave it in charge to his younger brother, Pheroras, to superintend the supply of provisions, and the raising of a wall about the castle of Alexandrion, which was accordingly performed with the utmost punctuality.

In the mean time Anthony took up his residence at Athens, while Ventidius sent to Silo and Herod to join him in the war against the Parthians, but instructed them first to settle the affairs of Judæa. Herod willingly dismissed Silo to go to Ventidius, but went himself in quest of the robbers that lurked in the caves. These dens or caverns were in the crags of the rocks, hardly accessible on any side, but by narrow turnings and windings, with a direct precipice from top to bottom. As it appeared, from the situation of the place, that the attempt would be attended with the utmost difficulty, the king hesitated for some time, but at length hit upon a bold and desperate expedient. There were strong chests, with soldiers in them, let down with ropes from the top of the mountains to the mouth of the entrance into the caves. These soldiers destroyed the robbers in their holes, some with their arms, and others, that resisted, with fire. As Herod was desirous of saving some of them, he made proclamation that they should surrender themselves, but not one of them came spontaneously, and many, that were compelled, preferred death to captivity.

There was a very remarkable instance of the resolution of an old man, the father of seven sons. His wife and children entreating him to suffer them to go out and surrender themselves, according to the tenor of the proclamation, he commanded them to come forth one after another, and as they respectively appeared, put them to death. This spectacle struck Herod with compassion, so that he entreated him, by signs, to spare his children. But neither words nor actions could prevail with him, for he maintained his resolution, killed the children first, and then the mother, casting their dead bodies down a precipice, and himself at last, and reproached Herod with the meanness of his spirit.

When Herod had exterminated these robbers, he left only such a force behind him as he judged necessary to preserve the public tranquility. He left the command to Ptolemy, and returned to Samaria, in order to march against Antigonus, with three thousand foot, and six hundred horse. The malecontents of Galilee took advantage of Herod's absence, fell upon Ptolemy by surprize, and slew him. They also laid the country waste, and then retired to bogs and places almost inaccessible. Herod no sooner received intelligence of this disorder than he returned, cut off great numbers of the seditious, raised the siege of the fortresses they had attacked, and fined the cities an hundred talents for their crimes.

The Parthians being now defeated, and Pacorus slain, Ventidius, by order of Anthony, dispatched Machæras to Herod, with a thousand horse, and two legions, as auxiliaries to him against Antigonus. Antigonus had sent Machæras a letter complaining of the indignities he had received from Herod, with a very considerable offer to enter into his interest. Though Machæras did not comply, as he had greater expectations of advantage from espousing the cause of Herod, he kept fair with the other party, and seemed disposed to treat with him on the business, but this was to sound him as to the present state of his affairs, though directly repugnant to the opinion and advice of Herod.

Antigonus, by this time, discovering his intention, not only refused him entrance, upon his approach to the city, but kept him off with darts and arrows as a professed enemy. Machæras was so mortified at this disappointment, that he went to Herod at Emmaus, and, in the fury of his rage, put all the Jews to death he could meet with, whether friends or foes, or attached to the interest of Antigonus or Herod.

Herod was so enraged at this merciless outrage, that at first he determined to avenge himself on Machæras as an open enemy; but he cooled upon reflection, and chose rather to accuse him before Anthony. Machæras, conscious of the atrocious nature of his conduct, instantly followed Herod, and by submissions, protestations, and importunities, sued for pardon. But this did not divert him from going to Anthony; and hearing that he was at that time besieging Samosata, a strong place upon the Euphrates, he made the greater expedition to come up to him, in order to ingratiate himself by some special proofs of his fidelity and courage. His arrival put a speedy end to the siege; he slew great numbers of the barbarians, and obtained immense booty. Anthony, who always maintained a favourable opinion of Herod, held him, upon this occasion, in higher esteem than ever, which redounded much to his honour, and encouraged his hopes of obtaining the kingdom. Antigonus, in fine, was compelled to deliver up Samosata.

CHAP. XIII.

Joseph, the brother of Herod, is slain in a battle with Antigonus, who treats his remains with indignity. Sosius made general of Syria. Prediction of Joseph's death. Herod besieges Jerusalem, and takes it by assault. Commands the head of Pappus to be cut off, in revenge for the death of Joseph. Pusillanimity of Antigonus. He is sent in chains to Anthony, and beheaded. Avarice and cruelty of Cleopatra.

DURING these transactions, the affairs of Herod were in a precarious situation in Judæa, which he left, in his absence, under the command of his brother Joseph, upon this express condition, that he should make no attempt against Antigonus during his absence. This advice proceeded from a suspicion he entertained of the perfidy of Machæras, founded upon former circumstances. But Joseph, when his brother was at a distance, became unmindful of his injunction, and marched towards Jericho, with five companies that Machæras had provided him, to carry off the corn that was now fit for the sickle. The enemy fell upon him from the mountains, and, from the advantages of the place, and the occasion, gave him a total defeat, cutting all the Romans to pieces, and the general himself, who left behind him the character of a great and valiant man. There were only new raised troops, levied in Syria, and had no veterans amongst them to supply the want of skill and experience in their fellow-soldiers.

But such was the brutality of Antigonus, that, not content with the victory, he committed the most unmanly insolences upon the remains of the dead, insulting over the body of Joseph himself, and then striking off his head, though Pheroras offered a composition of fifty talents to avoid that indignity. Affairs were so changed in Galilee upon the success of Antigonus, that they took the partizans of Herod, of the first quality, and plunged them into the lake. The affairs of Idumæa underwent several alterations where Machæras repaired the walls of the castle of Gitth. Herod was ignorant of these transactions; for, upon the taking Samosata, Anthony made Sosius governor of Syria, with a charge to assist him against Antigonus, and so he departed into Egypt. Sosius upon this sent away two companies into Judæa, to join Herod, and he himself followed soon after with the rest of the army.

When Herod was at Daphne, near Antioch, he had a presage of the death of his brother in a dream. As he leaped out of his bed in a confused manner, messengers arrived at that very instant to acquaint him with the calamity. The surprize struck him at first, but when his grief had a little subsided, he hastened with all expedition, in quest of the enemy. Upon his arrival he took eight hundred of the mountaineers, and one Roman cohort of his strength. With this body he entered Galilee before day, charged the enemy, and beat them back to the castle which they had left. He sat down before it and assaulted it day after day; but, before he could make himself master of it, the weather became so tempestuous, that he was under a necessity of drawing off his army into the next village. Anthony some few days after, sent him a reinforcement of another company, which put the garrison into such apprehensions, that they escaped from the castle through favour of the night.

After this Herod proceeded to Jericho to avenge himself of the death of his brother, where he seems to have been preserved by a miraculous interposition of Providence. That evening he gave a grand entertainment to several persons of the first distinction; and when the company had retired, and the hall was cleared, the roof fell to the ground. He took this remarkable escape as so auspicious a presage with respect to the war in which he was engaged, that he decamped early the next morning. The enemy, in a body of about 6000 men, came down the mountains, and had a skirmish with his van guard; but they did not press on to close action with the Romans, assaulting them only with darts and stones at a distance, by which means Herod, as he passed, received a wound in his side.

Antigonus, who piqued himself in being supposed superior to Herod, not only in the number but the courage of his men, sent Pappus his familiar friend, with an army into Samaria, to try an encounter with Machæras. Herod in the mean time took five towns, ravaged the enemy's country, destroyed 2000 of the inhabitants, laid their houses in ashes, and so returned to the main army, not far from a village called Cana.

Now a great multitude of Jews resorted to him daily, both from Jericho and other parts of the country. Some were moved from their hatred to Antigonus, others from their respect to Herod, and others from their love of innovation. Herod was most sanguinely desirous of bringing on an engagement, nor were Pappus and his army less anxious for the encounter; so that without dismay, they boldly advanced to the charge. When they came to close action, they made a stout resistance for some time; but wherever Herod came, he was so transported with the spirit of revenge for the death of his brother, that his enemies fled before him. In a word, a most terrible slaughter ensued; some were forced back into the place whence they came, Herod still pressing and pursuing them, till he fell in with the thickest of them in the town. The houses were soon crouded with fugitives, and the very roofs covered with them. But these were easily destroyed; and, upon beating down the buildings, several perished under the ruins, and others by the sword, and those who escaped the one perished by the other. The streets were so blocked up with carcasses, that they found some difficulty to march over them; and the spectacle was so hideous, that it could not be seen without the most thrilling horror. Upon confidence from this victory, Herod would have certainly marched immediately to Jerusalem, if the extreme rigour of the season had not rendered the ways impassable. This was the only point wanting to crown his victory, and effect the irreparable ruin of Antigonus, who was now making the previous dispositions for abandoning the city.

Herod, in the evening, having dismissed his friends, to refresh himself after the fatigue of the day, went to bathe, as is usual in such cases, with only one servant to attend him, and was met on his way by one of the soldiers of Antigonus with a drawn sword, then by a second, then by a third, and afterwards by several more. These were men who had fled thither with their arms out of the battle for refuge. Upon sight of the king they were seized with such dread and tremour, that they passed by in all precipitately, and none being at hand to apprehend them, got off, while Herod fortunately escaped untouched. The day following he ordered the head of Pappus, the general of Antigonus, to be struck off, and sent to his brother Pheroras in revenge for the blood of Joseph, who was slain by that very Pappus.

When the spring season came on, Herod advanced to Jerusalem, drew his men to the walls, and for the advantage of the attack, encamped before the temple, being the quarter from which Pompey had taken it before. This was the third year since Herod had been declared king at Rome. He assigned all his troops their proper stations, and every man his post in the suburbs. He ordered the casting up of three ramparts, and the building of turrets over them, and when he had given these commissions in charge to such of his officers as he could best confide in, he went himself to Samaria, to consummate a marriage with Mariamne, (the daughter of Aristobulus, son of Alexander,) to whom he had been contracted some time before, so that the siege and the match went on together in spite of his foes.

Upon this marriage he returned to Jerusalem with a number of additional troops, besides a strong body of horse and foot, under Sosius, the Roman general, who was sent to join him. The greater part of them took their march through the midland, and he himself through Phœnicia. The whole army upon the muster, amounted to eleven regiments of foot, and six thousand horse, besides a strong reinforcement of Syrian auxiliaries. The assault was made on the north side, Herod founding his right upon the decree of the Roman senate, that had constituted him king, and Sosius pressing the commission of Anthony for the assistance of Herod with the troops under his command.

The Jews within the city were now in the utmost confusion and distress, the common people crowding about the temple, and passing their judgment about the times, in a kind of enthusiastical foreboding of future calamities. The more bold and hardy part of the rabble went up and down, pillaging whatever they could reach, especially within the purlieus of the city, where they left no necessaries for man or horse. The soldiers omitted nothing to the defence of the place, kept the assailants from the walls and opposed one instrument and stratagem to another. But their chief manœuvre was in mining, and breaking in upon the enemy before they were aware.

The king, on the other hand, took care to provide against the depredations of the plunderers and for a supply of provisions by convoys from abroad. The Jews must be allowed to have displayed the greatest resolution and courage, but were constantly excelled by the Romans in military skill and experience. They maintained the contest, however, with the utmost bravery, and, in case of any surprize of the enemy from their trenches, by sally or attack, found some means or other to frustrate their attempts. In fine, they spared neither art or labour in the resolution they had taken to defend the city to the last. But, after five months resistance against so vast an army, a chosen band of Herod's men were so hardy as to mount the wall, with some of the Roman centurions to second them, and thereupon fell into the city.

Immediately upon their entrance, they posted themselves round the temple, and as nearly as possible, while the army dispersed, and carried death and desolation, in the most hideous forms wherever they went. The Romans were exasperated to revenge, by the hardships they had endured in the course of the siege, and the Jews of Herod's party were implacably cruel, in preventing the escape of any of their adversaries. The avenues of the city were covered with piles of mangled carcases, for the conquerors spared neither age or sex, nor was the temple itself any longer a sanctuary, nay, though the king himself commanded them, upon their allegiance, to hold their hands, and desist from the massacre, they went on with the carnage to a degree of inhuman phrenzy.

Antigonus, with the most dastardly pusillanimity, without any regard to his rank, or past or present fortune came down from the citadel, and prostrated himself before Sosius, who, without discovering the least pity for his calamitous condition, taunted him with a declaration that his name should be no longer Antigonus, but *Antigona*. But though he named him, he did not treat him like a woman, for he was loaded with chains, and kept a prisoner. Herod's present concern, after subduing his enemies, was to restrain the impetuosity of his foreign auxiliaries, as the multitude pressed so violently into the temple, prompted by curiosity to see the building, and its valuable contents, that it was with the utmost difficulty he could keep them in order, either by menace, entreaties, and sometimes blows, accounting that his victory would be worse than a defeat, if it tended to expose those sacred things, which, by the Jewish laws, were to be veiled from the sight of the profane.

He then proceeded to the regulation of the soldiery in the matter of pillage, pertinently observing to Sosius, "that, by leaving neither men or money, the Romans would render him king of a desert, rather than of a citizen people, and that he judged the dominion of the whole habitable earth too small a compensation for the slaughter of so many citizens." Sosius replied, "that it was but just to allow the soldiers this plunder, as a reward for what they had suffered during the siege." Herod rejoined, "that he would see justice done every individual out of his own private fortune." By this generous manner of proceeding he preserved the remainder of his country, and afterwards fulfilled his promise to the army, by making liberal presents to each private soldier, and in proportion to the officers, with a royal bounty to Sosius himself, so that, upon the whole, he gave universal satisfaction. Sosius after this dedicated a golden crown to sacred services, and then left Jerusalem, carrying Antigonus bound to Anthony, flattering himself with the hope of mercy, till the axe put a period to an existence not worthy of being prolonged.

The multitude in the city were divided, and Herod distinguished party from party, conferring honours on his friends to attach them to his interest, and putting the adherents of Antigonus to death. When his finances ran low, he divided the most valuable of his effects betwixt Anthony and those immediately about his person, but this did not prove an effectual security, for Anthony was so infatuated with a predilection for Cleopatra, that he could deny her nothing. This execrable woman having sated her cruelty with the blood of all her own kindred, turned her implacable fury against strangers, by calumniating men of rank and fortune to Anthony, and prevailing with him to cause them to be put to death, to obtain possession of their estates. Her avarice transported her so far against the Jews and Arabians, that she entered into a secret practice on the lives of their kings, Herod and Malchus. Anthony amused her with fair words, and seeming countenances, but, though he could not indulge her so far as to take away the lives of two kings who had treated him with such singular respect, he violated the terms of friendship that subsisted between them, and put her in possession of great part of their territories, for instance, the lands in Jericho, so famous for palm-trees and the balsam plant, and all the cities upon the river Eleutherus, except Tyre and Sidon. When he had gratified her with these presents, she accompanied him as far as the Euphrates in his expedition against the Parthians, and so took her way into Judæa, by Apamia and Damascus.

Herod had already attempted, by large presents, to conciliate the favour of Cleopatra, but her cruelty was so implacable, and her avarice so insatiable, that former largesses had no effect, so that he found himself under a necessity of allowing her two hundred talents out of the revenues of Judæa, and then with the utmost obsequiousness conducted her to Pelusium. Anthony soon returned from the Parthian war, with Artabazes, the son of Tigranes, his prisoner, whom he presented to Cleopatra with the whole booty.

CHAP. XIV.

[illegible] Cleopatra [illegible] Herod [illegible] earthquake [illegible] The [illegible] of Jewish ambassadors [illegible] Herod's soldiers [illegible] Herod [illegible] They [illegible]

ON the breaking out of the war at Actium Herod being at liberty, resolved to accompany Anthony in that expedition, to he had gained possession of Hyrcania from the sister of Antigonus, and all things were now compleated and quiet at home. But Cleopatra, left Herod should be continued in the favour of Anthony, [illegible] diverted him from his design. This princess, having [illegible] to the kings both of Judæa and [illegible] persuaded Anthony to commit the conduct of the [illegible] to Herod, foreseeing as the consequence, that, if he succeeded in the enterprize, she should be queen of Arabia; if otherwise, queen of Judæa.

This [illegible] to the advantage of Herod, who having levied a great body of horse, sent them against the Syrians about Diospolis, who met, attacked them, and, after some resistance, drove them out of the field. Upon this defeat the Arabians drew together a formidable army, and posted themselves at Canatha, in Cœlo-Syria, there to wait the arrival of the Jews. Herod was now advancing towards them; but, upon sight of their number and disposition, he found it expedient to be more than ordinarily watchful, and therefore ordered the raising of a wall about the camp. But the people were so elated with one victory, that, regardless of Herod's precaution, they fell on without ceremony, and routed the Arabians at the very first onset. But Herod himself escaped very narrowly upon the pursuit by a body of troops of Canatha, which were sent in by Athenion to the relief of the Arabians. This Athenion was one of Cleopatra's generals, and a deadly enemy to Herod. Animated by this reinforcement, the Arabians rallied, scattered Herod's army, and pursuing them through crags and woods, slew many of them in the chace. Those who escaped fled to an adjacent village, called Ormiza, where they were pent up and surrounded, and the Arabians made themselves masters of the camp, and of all that was in it. Soon after this severe check, Herod [illegible] his forces, but could not repair the losses sustained by the late disaster, which was owing to the contempt and disobedience of his officers; for if they had not been so [illegible] and precipitate, Athenion could never have had an opportunity of putting his plot in execution. But he avenged himself afterwards upon the Arabians by many incursions, and, by several victories, compensated for one defeat.

There befel Herod in the course of his successes one providential calamity. This was in the seventh year of his reign, in the beginning of the spring, and in the midst of [illegible] of Actium. It was a tremendous earthquake, that destroyed an immense number of cattle, and near thirty thousand people: but the army that lay in the field sustained no injury. It was [illegible], but gaining as [illegible], the Arabians took it for granted that Judæa was totally overthrown, and flattered themselves into an opinion, that they should get a land destitute of inhabitants into their power. In this confidence they put certain Jewish ambassadors, who were then with them, to death, and advanced into the country to take possession of it. This formidable inroad of the Arabians struck the Jews with such a terror, especially as they had undergone so many calamities upon one another, that Herod was under a necessity of attempting to reduce them to reason and resolution by the following speech:

"You are here [illegible] (said he,) under most un-reasonable apprehension. I will allow you to indulge your sorrows under the hand of an offended God; but to subject yourselves to the same despondencies and passions, for fear of the power of men, is a meanness of soul below your courage. Nay, so far am I from any dread of an enemy, after this earthquake, that it looks to me rather as if Providence had ordered the ensnaring of your adversaries, by this temptation, into a vengeance for the injuries they have done you: nor do they lay so much stress upon the force of their own arms or valour, as upon the opinion they have of our abject and miserable state. But those are false hopes, when men support themselves upon the infirmities of others, rather than upon their own virtue. Nor is there any certainty either in prosperous or adverse fortune, as they are both unsteady, and take their turns. For a confirmation of this doctrine, you need go no farther than to the late battle, where we were masters one hour, and at mercy the next. This is the very case of our enemies at present, or I am much deceived: they think they take, and they are taken. People that are over-confident are unwary; but a considerate fear makes men provident, so that the very ground of your apprehension is the foundation of my assurance. You would needs be charging the enemy contrary to order, and forwarder than you should have been, and Athenion, you see, made advantage of your [illegible]; but you yourselves are now upon the reserve, and your deliberations are sober and not fantastical, which is a disposition that I look upon as an earnest of a certain victory. This is the right temper of a brave man before he comes into action, but let him reserve his spirit till he [illegible] occasion for it in the field. So let it be your business now to convince your enemies, by force of arms, that the Jews will sooner part with their lives than their reputation, and stand firm at last under all misfortunes; nor ever own the Arabians for their masters, who have so often been their slaves.

"But why this fear at last for things inanimate? How comes an earthquake to be a portend, or a presage of things to come? Is there any thing more natural than the agitations and disorders of the elements? They do not foretell calamities, but they actually bring and create them. It is possible that there may be some forerunning signs of plagues, famine, and earthquakes, to come; but when they are once come, the greater they are, the sooner will they be over. Or put the case we should be conquered now, which is worse, the war or the earthquake? But there's a destination of these people to ruin, even by their own hands, without the help of enemies, that could be so impious and inhuman, as, contrary to the laws of nature and nations, to dip their hands in the blood of our ambassadors, and devote them as a sacrifice to God for the success of the war. Can they ever think to escape the all-seeing eye and almighty power of a vindictive God, whenever we shall but rouze in us the courage and zeal of our forefathers, and call these perfidious violators of leagues and public faith to a severe and just account? Wherefore stand up my fellow-soldiers, not for your wives, children, or country, but to revenge the murder of your ambassadors, whose very blood will consecrate the cause: and those heroes dead as they are will do you more good in the head of your army than the living commanders of it. Do you but follow where I will lead you, and I will ask no more. Only one word of caution. Remember this, that when it comes to the trial, they will not dare to look you in the face."

This animated address inspired such ardour into the soldiers, that Herod availing himself of the opportunity, sacrificed, and, without delay, passed his army over the river Jordan. He pitched his camp at Philadelphia, not far from the enemy, with a castle between them, which looked as if the castle was to be the subject of dispute.

Herod, at that distance, provoked them to a battle,

desiring nothing more than to bring it to a speedy issue, for the enemy had sent a corps before to take possession of this castle, but Herod's party, without much difficulty, repelled them and gained the ascent. Herod drew out every day in order of battle to dare the Arabians to a combat; and when he perceived they would not answer the challenge, (for they were all in consternation, and Altemus, their general, above the rest,) he attacked them in their trenches, and so forced them to a battle, upon which they entered in such disorder, that their horse and foot were mixed together. They were, indeed, superior to the Jews in number, but inferior in valour, although they were obliged to expose themselves to danger from their desperate situation.

While they resisted, the slaughter was not great, but when once they turned their backs, between those that fell in the pursuit, and those that were trampled to death by their own people, there were 5000 missing, and the rest were driven into their camp, where Herod soon encompassed and besieged them. They were also much distressed for want of water. In this embarrassed situation they sent ambassadors to Herod, with an offer of fifty thousand talents for a composition, but he would not so much as deign them an hearing. They came out after this in troops in the torment of raging thirst, and delivered themselves up to the Jews at discretion, so that, in the course of five days, Herod had four thousand of them in bonds. Upon the sixth day the remainder of them, in a transport of despair, provoked the Jews to battle, where about 7000 men were slain on the spot. This stroke finished Herod's revenge upon the Arabians, for it humbled them to that degree, that they chose him afterwards as their protector.

CHAP. XV.

Herod's [illegible] Cæsar at Rhodes, upon the defeat of Anthony at Actium. [illegible] for the emperor. He is [illegible] his [illegible] with large [illegible].

THE affairs of Herod now took a prosperous turn, but the news of the defeat of Anthony at Actium affected him most sensibly, as he entertained the highest regard for him. His apprehension, however, was not justly founded, for Cæsar could never think Anthony absolutely suppressed, as long as Herod continued to assist him. Herod, in consequence of this unfortunate event, repaired to Rhodes, where Augustus was at that time, and presenting himself without any ensigns of royalty, in the habit of a private man, but with the majesty of king, thus candidly and frankly addressed him:

"I must confess, mighty Cæsar, that as Anthony made "me a king, I have exerted my legal authority in the ser"vice of the benefactor from whom I received it. And "you yourself, if I may be permitted to speak freely, "would have found the effects of my services, had I not "been diverted by the Arabian war. It did not how"ever prevent me from sending supplies both of troops "and provisions, nor has this last fatal blow at Actium "in the least abated my zeal for the interest of my patron. "I could not, indeed, furnish him with men and arms, "nor attend him in person upon the occasion, but I gave "him this salutary counsel to detach himself from Cleo"patra, which done, I promised him money, fortresses, "troops, nay, my very self, as an assistant in the war "against you. But, through his infatuation to a woman "on the one hand, and your success in arms on the "other, all our efforts are frustrated, so that the fate of "Anthony and Herod are involved, we fell upon the "same day, and with his fortune I now laid down my "crown. All my pretences to gain clemency, is founded "upon a consciousness of having acted consistently "with the character of an honest man and a sincere "friend."

Cæsar, struck with this address, thus rejoined:

"Herod, be secure, be happy, be still a king, and that "more firmly than ever, as I am confident so generous a "friend must make a good governor. Bear [illegible] "your attachment to the conqueror [illegible] you have been to "the vanquished, and I shall cherish the hope of [illegible]"ing mighty benefits from so exalted a mind. [illegible] "has been [illegible], the counsel of Cleopatra to our "mutual advantage. Rest, therefore, content [illegible] "confirmation of the kingdom [illegible], and I shall take "care that in future you shall find no detriment from "the loss of Anthony."

Augustus Cæsar after this [illegible] with [illegible] admitted Herod not to doubt of his friendship, and then putting the crown upon his head, confirmed his title to it by an act of state, with honourable commemorations of his character. When Herod [illegible] acknowledgments, by [illegible] words and [illegible] presents, [illegible] with the emperor in behalf of Alexander, one of Anthony's friends, to obtain his pardon, but Cæsar would not hearken to his solicitation, declaring that his offences were unpardonable.

As Augustus was afterwards passing through Syria to Egypt, Herod entertained him with royal magnificence, and Cæsar, in return, did him the honour of causing him to ride by his side while he was reviewing his troops about Ptolemais. Herod also made a plentiful provision of water for them, during their march to Pelusium through a dry country, nor were there any necessaries wanting, insomuch that Cæsar, impressed by these extraordinary instances of his magnificence, declared to his train, that the kingdom of Judæa was too little for the mind of so great a prince.

Cleopatra and Anthony being now deceased, upon Cæsar's arrival in Egypt, he not only conferred new honours upon Herod, but annexed to his kingdom those parts which Cleopatra had taken from him, with Gadara, Hippon, Samaria, and the maritime cities, Gaza, Anthedon, Joppa, and the Tower of Strato. He also presented him with four hundred Gauls, who had been Cleopatra's body guards. He also gave him the province of Trachon, with Batanea and Auranitis, upon the following occasion.

It had been a common practice with Zenodorus, who possessed in a much [illegible] the land of Lysanias, to [illegible] out of Trachon to Damascus. The inhabitants applied themselves to Varus, at that time governor of Syria, for relief, entreating him to represent their calamitous situation to Cæsar. Varus accordingly complied with the request, and the emperor sent him orders immediately to suppress these robbers, in consequence of which parties being dispatched to all suspected places, they freed the country from these pests of society. The governor also having been enjoined to deprive Zenodorus of a part of his estate, Cæsar bestowed it upon Herod, to secure it from being [illegible] a receptacle for those caterpillars, appointing him at the same time, governor of all Syria. He also enjoined the subordinate rulers to consult Herod in all matters of importance, and, upon the demise of Zenodorus, gave him all the land between Trachon and Galilee. But Herod was more eminently gratified by the consideration that he was beloved by Cæsar above all men living, next to Agrippa, and by Agrippa next to Cæsar. [illegible] circumstances he was advanced to [illegible] felicity, and evinced a [illegible] equal to his exaltation, by [illegible] his [illegible] purposes.

CHAP XVI

Herod erects several magnificent buildings both at home and abroad. Repairs the temple. Calls the castle on the north side Antonia, in respect to Anthony, and two other sumptuous edifices Cæsareon and Agrippion, in honour of Cæsar and Agrippa. Immortalizes their names by special dedications, particularly that of Sebaste in Samaria. Cæsar's additional favours to Herod. Herod builds Antipatris, to the memory of Antipater, Cypros to that of Cypros, and Herodion to that of Herod. Repairs Straton's Tower, and adds to it a stately palace. A spacious port between Dora and Joppa. Detail of the various instances of Herod's extensive munificence, and extraordinary achievements of mind and body, which acquired him an universal fame.

HEROD in the fifteenth year of his reign, applied himself to the repairing and rebuilding of the temple, which he accomplished with splendid magnificence, and at immense charge, as appeared from the stately galleries round about it, that were raised from the very foundation, and the castle on the north side adjoining to it, which, for grandeur and elegance, was not inferior to the royal palace itself, giving it the name of Antonia, alluding to his favorite Anthony. He greatly enlarged the enclosure round about the temple, and raised upon an eminence, that overlooked the city, two superb spacious structures, comparable to any temple, which he called Cæsarion and Agrippion, in honour of his two illustrious friends Cæsar and Agrippa.

Nor did he restrain his zeal for perpetuating the memories of these celebrated characters to palaces and particular fabrics, but dedicated whole cities to the immortalizing of their fame to posterity, for instance, Sebaste, in Samaria, a city twenty furlongs in compass, with a stately wall about it, a colony of 6000 inhabitants planted in it, and an endowment of fruitful lands belonging to it, with particular immunities to the people. Amongst other eminent works he erected a majestic temple, with an area of three furlongs and an half about it, and this temple he dedicated to Augustus Cæsar.

After this Cæsar gratified Herod, with an additional donation of lands, and Herod, in acknowledgment, erected another temple, of white polished marble, near the head of the river Jordan, at a place called Panium, which he also dedicated to his illustrious patron. Not far from hence stands a mountain of stupendous height, that overhangs the crags and rocks, and looks down into a deep valley. At the bottom is a dark and hideous cavern, worn and hollowed to such a depth by the constant fall of waters upon it, that it cannot be founded. From the foot of this cavern there bubbles forth an issue of several springs, which according to tradition, passes for the source of the river Jordan.

The king gave equal proofs of his magnificence at Jericho, where he caused to be erected, betwixt the castle of Cypros and the old palace, other stately and commodious buildings, and called them by the names of the same august personages. In fine, he did not leave one considerable place in the whole kingdom without some monumental memorial to the fame of Cæsar. When he had ornamented the borders of the temples throughout Judæa, he did the like in the provinces, distinguishing several of them by the name of Cæsarea.

As Herod was on his progress along the coast, he observed one maritime city amongst the rest, with all the decays of antiquity about it. It was known by the name of Straton's Tower, and appeared, from its situation, worthy of the king's royal care and bounty. He not only repaired the castle with beautiful white stone, but erected a palace there equal in grandeur to his other works. It lies betwixt Dora and Joppa, where there is no good haven, and the passage is so dangerous, that mariners who shape their course that way towards Egypt from Phœnecia, run great risque from a south-west wind, which sets in with such violence upon the rocks, that it rebounds in eddies, and makes a turbulent sea.

But the king's liberality and resolutions surmounted all the difficulties and obstructions that could arise, either from situation or expence, for he built an haven there larger than the Pyreneum at Athens, with stations, for the largest ships to ride in with the utmost security from wind and weather. It was so fortified against the violent surges of the sea, and ornamented so agreeably to the view, as to admit of no addition, either of strength or beauty of contrivance.

Upon taking measure for the dimensions of the port, he ordered huge stones to be cast into the sea at twenty fathoms water. The greatest part were fifty feet in length, and nine in depth, and ten broad, and some still larger. When they had filled up the space to the surface of the water, they carried on a wall two hundred feet wide, the one half to break the force of the waves in the nature of a mole, from whence it was called Procymæa, and the other for the support of the turrets that were fixed upon it, to one of which he gave the name of Drusion, in compliment to Drusus, Cæsar's kinsman.

There were also a great number of vaults for stores, and before and above these vaults a pavement of flat stones, that served both as a landing place and walk for recreation. It fronted the north, which, upon that quarter, is the most gentle of all winds. On each side of the entrance stood three colossi, mounted on pillars. Those on the left hand were supported by a strong tower of one entire stone, and those on the right by two large stones, in the form of columns joined together. The buildings next the port were all of white stone, and the streets that led from the city to the quay exactly uniform. Upon an hill, opposite to the mouth of the haven, stood Cæsar's Temple, a building, in magnitude and curiosity, not inferior to that of Jupiter Olympus, from the model of which it was taken, as also of another at Rome, that did not fall short of the temple of Juno at Argos. Herod's design in erecting this stately tower and port, was the advantage of the province, and the security of voyagers, and, to the honour of Cæsar he called it Cæsarea.

There was other famous works of Herod worthy of record, as a spacious market-place, a theatre, an amphitheatre, and the institution of the *Ludi Quinquennales*, so called from their being games appointed to be celebrated every fifth year, which he dedicated to the honour of Augustus. He was the first who, in the 192d olympiad, propounded honorary rewards, not only to the victors themselves, but to the second and third competitor, in course one after another. He repaired Anthedon, which had been nearly demolished in the war, and called it Agrippion and, as a testimony of respect for his friend, inscribed the name of Agrippa on the gate of the temple he had built there.

Herod was a dutiful son, as well as a generous friend and patriot, for he founded a city to the honour of his father, in the most pleasant and fruitful part of his dominions, abounding with plants and rivulets, which he called Antipatris. There was a castle also near Jericho, which was strong and delightfully situated. This place he walled in, and gave it the name of Cypros, after his mother. Nor was he unmindful of his brother Phasael on several occasions, as in a tower he built at Jerusalem, which he called Phasaelis, and likewise a city to the north of Jericho, which he also called by the same name.

As he transmitted to posterity the memories of his family and friends, he did not omit a memorial for himself, for he built and fortified a castle on a mountain of Arabia, which he called Herodion, after his own name. He gave the same appellation also to an hill, which he caused to be thrown up in form of a woman's breast, about sixty furlongs distant from Jerusalem. This mount was encompassed at the summit with round turrets, the circuit of it filled with royal apartments, as splendid and brilliant, within and without, as art and cost could render them. The stairs were of pure white marble, comprising two hundred steps from the bottom to the top. It was of stupendous height. At the feet of it he built other magnificent apartments for the accommodation of his friends: insomuch, that considering it was adapted to every use and convenience, it seemed to be a city rather than a castle, though it was nothing more than a structure erected for the temporary residence of the king.

Having given so many proofs of munificence to display his liberality to his own subjects, Herod seemed disposed to render foreigners partakers of his generosity. To this end he caused public baths to be set up at Tripolis, Damascus, and Ptolemais, built strong walls at Byblos, galleries, council-chambers, public magazines, market-places, and temples, at Berytus and Tyre, theatres at Sidon and Damascus, an aqueduct at Laodicea, water-works at Ascalon, with piazzas of exquisite workmanship. To some he gave groves and harbours, to others lands. He appointed annual revenues for the support of baths, distributed [illegible] the necessitous, and frequently furnished the inhabitants of Rhodes with money for the equipping a navy, when occasion required it. He repaired the temple of Apollo (called Pythium,) and rendered it more magnificent and commodious than it was in its pristine state. I might add, to these instances, his liberality to the Lycians and Samians, his largesses throughout Ionia, Athens, Lacedæmon, Nicopolis, and particularly his bounty to Antioch, one of the principal cities of Syria, that [illegible] a bog for the space of many furlongs, till he caused the passage to it to be paved with white marble, and shelters to be put up against foul weather.

Men of narrow minds may suggest that these favours were confined to a few particular places, to such we need only oppose the obligations he laid upon the Eleans, wherein not only the people of Greece, but the whole world were concerned, at least all those who have heard the fame of the Olympic games; for when he found, upon his arrival at Rome, that these games were all that remained of ancient Greece, and that they were upon the decline for want of money to support them, he not only took upon him the charge of that year, but settled an annual allowance for the perpetual continuance of them. It would be endless to recount the debts and tributes which he remitted, and particularly those of the inhabitants of Phaselis, Batanea, and the small towns in Cilicia, where he discharged them from the payment of their pensions. He would have extended his liberality still further, but was prevented by an apprehension of incurring envy from other monarchs.

Herod possessed great strength and agility of body, was an excellent horseman, and discovered perfect skill in the lance, for he darted forty beasts upon the chace in one day. He was a consummate soldier, and finished swordsman. In a word, he was as fortunate as accomplished: and if he failed in any warlike exploit, it was attributed to treachery, or the rashness of his soldiers, and not to their gallant commander.

CHAP. XVII.

Herod exhibits a reverse of character. Great disorders prevail in his family. He puts away his wife Doris, and marries Mariamne. Expells his son Antipater. Puts Hyrcanus to death. Causes Aristobulus to be drowned. Becomes jealous of the designs of his wife and sister. Joseph and Mariamne put to death. Marries his sons. Calls Antipater [illegible]. The craft of Antipater. Herod accuses Alexander before Cæsar. [illegible] Reconciliation between Herod and his son. Herod [illegible] by [illegible]. Character of [illegible]. Machinations of [illegible] mother and Salome, the sister of Herod. Herod's advice to [illegible]. Pheroras and Salome their mutual calumnies. A plot [illegible] upon Herod's life. His cruelty and injustice. Alexander apprehended and his friends put to the torture. Archelaus debates the point with Herod. Pheroras confesses and obtains his pardon. Herod an advocate for Alexander. Archelaus brings Alexander to his father. Eurycles the confidant of Herod. An accusation brought against Alexander and Aristobulus. Several put to the torture. Herod listens to calumnies. Salome incites the father against the youths, and causes him to lay the brothers in chains. The king open[s] the case before council at Berytus. Sentence of death passed upon the brothers. The bravery of Tyro, and offences of Tryphon. The brothers strangled at Sebaste.

HEROD, in the midst of his external successes, was greatly perplexed by domestic broils, which took their rise from his putting away one wife, and taking to himself another; for he no sooner became possessed of the kingdom, than he dismissed Doris, and married Mariamne, the daughter of Alexander the son of Aristobulus. He banished out of the city Antipater, whom he had by Doris, for the sake of the sons he had by Mariamne, and permitted him to come into it at no other time than the festivals. He then put to death Hyrcanus, his wife's grandfather, upon his return from Parthia, under pretence of having plotted against his life: for Barzapharnes having carried him away prisoner to the king of Parthia, after the taking of Syria, the Jews, on the other side of the Euphrates, from pure compassion, set him at liberty, and paid his ransom. If he had followed their counsel, and not passed over the river to Herod, he might have lived safe and happy; but through a passionate desire to revisit his own country, he was inveigled to his ruin, as Herod was conscious of his right and title to the government, though he had no reason to entertain a thought of his design to lay claim to it.

Mariamne had five children by Herod, two daughters and three sons. The youngest of the latter died in the course of his studies at Rome. The two elder were educated according to the royal descent, both with respect to the dignity of their mother's extraction, and their being born when their father was in possession of the crown. But nothing moved Herod so powerfully in their favour, as the wonderful ascendancy Mariamne had over him, which grew to such an height, as to render him insensible of all indignities and affronts. Mariamne requited this warmth of affection with an equal degree of aversion. She did not want matter of pretence for disgust, and presuming upon the extravagant passion he had for her, she peremptorily charged him with the murder of Hyrcanus, and her brother Aristobulus, and highly aggravated her reproaches. The latter, an innocent youth, she observed, but seventeen years of age when he was created high-priest, was cut off as soon as he obtained that sacred function, amidst the approbation of the people, who wept with joy at his appearance in the pontific vestments to officiate at the altar; but the very same night he was sent away to Jericho, and there drowned in a lake, by the Gauls, at the instance of Herod.

Mariamne did not content herself with these outrages against Herod, but uttered the foulest invectives upon his sister and mother: which he heard with patience, through the excess of his affection. This incensed them to that degree, that they concerted means to raise the indignation of Herod, and to that end dropped some oblique hints to him touching the honour and virtue of his wife. Amongst other plausible matters they related the circumstance of Mariamne's sending her picture to Anthony, and the pains she took to ingratiate herself with him from a principle of concupiscence; adding, that Anthony was so great a libertine as to gratify his inordinate desires at the expence of his very life. Through the rage of jealousy, the consideration of Cleopatra's insatiable avarice and cruelty, and the power [illegible]

[illegible], [illegible] and Malichus, [illegible] of Sabin, [illegible] put to death the [illegible]. Herod was [illegible] ſtruck at this [illegible] of his [illegible] apprehending danger of loſing not only [illegible] but his [illegible].

In this perplexity of mind he determined to go to Anthony, and recommend the care of his wife during his abſence, to Joſeph the huſband of his ſiſter Salome, whom he had [illegible] to him, but with this ſecret inſtruction, [illegible] Anthony [illegible] away his life, he ſhould cauſe the death of Mariamne. [illegible] this to the queen, as a proof of the king's [illegible] affection for her, [illegible] could not endure the thought of ſeparation even in [illegible]. Herod, upon his return, in an hour of [illegible], was proteſting the [illegible] of his affection for Mariamne, and [illegible] had a paſſion for any other of the [illegible], upon which the queen ſarcaſtically replied, "[illegible] he had given an [illegible] in the order he had left [illegible] to [illegible] her." The diſcovery of this very important [illegible] the mind of Herod with indignation, as he was perſuaded Joſeph would never have divulged it but in the confidence of an [illegible]. In this ſtate of diſtraction he ſuddenly aroſe from his couch, went into the court-yard [illegible] Salome, who [illegible] herſelf of ſo fair [illegible] for calumniating the queen, ſo effectually confirmed Herod in his ſuſpicion, that, in the rage of jealouſy he ordered both Joſeph and Mariamne to be put to death. The command was no ſooner iſſued than he repented of it, but the execution was done before it could be recalled. [illegible] extreme commiſeration, [illegible], [illegible] the extraordinary pomp of the funeral ſolemnities, and the grief [illegible] upon the occaſion, [illegible] that he bore the ſame eſteem for the memory of his deceaſed wife, as he had [illegible] for her perſon [illegible] living.

The ſons of Mariamne were ſo [illegible] by the [illegible] of this proceeding [illegible] their mother, that they looked upon their father [illegible]. They had entertained [illegible] unfavourable opinion of him, even when they were at Rome together, [illegible] upon their return [illegible] Judea, [illegible] knowledge [illegible] by experience and obſervation. [illegible] years of maturity, one of them married the daughter of his aunt Salome, [illegible] averſe to their mother. The other took [illegible] daughter of Archelaus king of Cappadocia. In proceſs of time they indulged themſelves in a greater liberty of ſpeech [illegible], and that confidence [illegible] them to [illegible] informers, inſomuch that their enemies [illegible] the king, that they had entered into a conſpiracy againſt his life, and [illegible] of Archelaus deſigned to go privately to Rome, with a complaint againſt Herod himſelf to Cæſar. When Herod had information of theſe tranſactions he recalled Antipater to court whom he had by his former wife, Doris, propoſing to uſe him as [illegible] againſt the brothers, and to this end treated him with ſingular tokens of reſpect.

The brothers reſenting this preference given to the ſon of an old [illegible] woman, as the higheſt indignity offered to [illegible] defcent on the mother's ſide, took every occaſion of ſignifying their diſguſt, and even indignation. But theſe [illegible], inſtead of furthering their deſign, tended to the advantage of Antipater, for he managed matters ſo artfully with his father, that, through the prevailing efficacy of flattery on the one hand, and calumny on the other, he brought it to this iſſue at laſt, that the brothers were totally excluded from the ſucceſſion, which was to devolve to him by virtue of his father's will and teſtament. He was ſent after this to Cæſar in a kind of royal ſtate, having the robes and train of a king, and only wanting the crown. [illegible] with this [illegible], [illegible] the means of [illegible] and ſlander he [illegible] his mother [illegible] bed, and at length [illegible] his father, by degrees, [illegible] deſign upon the lives of his brothers.

When [illegible] Herod to [illegible] to Rome with [illegible], and there [illegible], before Cæſar, [illegible] king [illegible]. When Alexander [illegible] to his defence, and before a judge that [illegible] impoſed on [illegible] by Herod [illegible] Antipater, he [illegible] avoided laying [illegible] on his father, but, with great force of argument, refuted the calumnies brought againſt himſelf, demonſtrated the innocence of his brother, who was involved in the ſame [illegible], and from thence proceeded to lay open the impoſtures, fraud, and [illegible] of Antipater, and this with ſuch power of elocution and grace of action, as carried the ſtrongeſt conviction to the minds of the auditors, and impreſſed them with a [illegible] ſenſe of his integrity, as well as his accompliſhments as an orator. This ſpeech had ſo powerful an effect upon Cæſar, that rejecting the accuſations, he made them all friends, provided that the ſons, in future, ſhould be obedient to their father, and the father at liberty to appoint whom he pleaſed to ſucceed him in the kingdom.

Herod, at his return from Rome, could not but acquit his ſons of the accuſations brought againſt them, yet he could not caſt away his ſuſpicions, for Antipater [illegible] with him ſo effectually, that he kept jealouſies alive, though he durſt not openly avow his ſentiments, leſt he ſhould ſeem to diſpute the authority of the [illegible]. He took his paſſage by Cilicia, and ſo to [illegible], where he was received by Archelaus with great pomp and reſpect, who congratulated him on the reconciliation effected between him and his ſons. Archelaus had not in the mean time been wanting by letters, and other inſtances, to his friends at Rome, to make intereſt for Alexander. He conducted him [illegible] where he preſented him with thirty talents, and took his leave.

The king, upon his arrival at Jeruſalem, called an aſſembly of the people, and in the hearing of his three ſons, thus addreſſed them on the ſubject of the late reconciliation.

"[illegible] is a bleſſing which I ſhall ever value incomparably
"above the glories of a crown, and which I ſhall endeavour
"to preſerve and improve accordingly. It is to Cæſar that
"I ſtand indebted for my dignity and eſtate, and to Cæſar
"again that I owe the liberty and privilege of appointing
"my own ſucceſſor. It is to him [illegible] that I am to pay my
"acknowledgments, with this declaration, that I deſign
"them all three both for the ſovereignty and the ſucceſſion,
"if it may be agreeable to the will of God and your good
"pleaſure. The eldeſt of them has the title of [illegible],
"the other two [illegible] pretend to the dignity by their ex-
"traction, and the command, at laſt, is extenſive enough
"for all three.

"As for thoſe that Cæſar hath united, and the father [illegible]
"[illegible], you muſt be ſure to pay them all due reſpect, that is
"to ſay, it muſt be impartial, equal, and juſt, [illegible]
"to a precedency of birth-right, for the advancing of [illegible]
"man before his time, will not be ſo great an [illegible]
"upon him that is preferred, as a diſguſt to the [illegible]
"that is poſtponed. But now, for fear of evil [illegible]
"or example, it ſhall be my care to place wiſe and [illegible]
"people about them, ſuch as I can depend upon, and
"ſuch as ſhall be anſwerable for their good order and
"decorum.

"I do further expect from theſe miniſters, as well as [illegible]
"the officers of my army, that, for the preſent they ſhall
"own no other maſter than myſelf, for it is not the government
"but the honorary part of it, that I have communicated
"to my ſons, ſo that they may have the pleaſure of a kind
"of regency, but the burden of adminiſtration to reſt upon
"my ſhoulders, and the laſt reſult of matters in the judg-
"ment [illegible] of things, muſt be my province.

"if you consider [illegible], the [illegible] of my age, or my manners, I am not so far advanced upon the point, but, by "the course of nature, I may live to see many days. "Neither have I done any thing to shorten my life by "intemperate pleasures. As to my duty to God, I have "been so true to his holy worship, that I will not despair "of the blessing of a longer time yet in this world, even "in consideration of that zeal and devotion. But if any "of you shall take upon him to advance the sons while I "am yet living, in contempt of the father, let him expect "to be severely punished for it. It would give me pleasure to have my children honourably treated in the "world, but young men are hot and pragmatical, and "'tis but throwing a temptation in their way to inflame "their desires. People would do well to consider before "they make their applications, for it is my part, as "men do well or ill, to see them rewarded or punished. "Nor will I be wanting in the [illegible] of my duty. The "best way will be for the sons and father to be all of a "mind, for it is their interest to have me govern, and it "is mine for them to agree among themselves.

"And now, my dear children, (says he) consider, in "the first place, that natural affection which Providence "hath made common even to beasts with men, and acquit "yourselves like dutiful children to your father. Bless "Cæsar in the next place, for the good office of his "mediation, and receive it kindly from me, in the third "place, that I only desire what I have a right to command, that is to say, let me intreat you to live amicably as brethren. I shall now take care to provide "you such attendants and equipages as may be suitable to "your quality. Be sure you live peaceably one with another, and I beseech God to keep me steady in the "same mind."

When the king had thus spoken, he embraced his sons, and dismissed the multitude. Some [illegible] contents went away, muttering that he was not in earnest in his [illegible], [illegible] [illegible] on particular [illegible] of it, and others doubting the sincerity of his declarations.

The brothers were still divided among themselves, and their dissentions grew [illegible] to [illegible] separation. Aristobulus and Alexander [illegible] that Antipater should have the preference. Antipater, on the other hand, that his brethren should be allowed any share in the government. Antipater being of a malicious and reserved disposition, disguised the mortal aversion he had to his brothers, whereas the other two, being frank and open, [illegible] the [illegible] of [illegible]. Their enemies had their instruments planted up and down to watch their words and actions, provoke them to indulge their natural frankness of disposition, and gain upon them by insinuation, under the mask of confidence and friendship, insomuch that not a word passed from Alexander, but it was brought to Herod with considerable additions. The most simple remark had a criminal interpretation, and every thing was misrepresented that could tend to calumniate.

The agents of Antipater, on the other hand, were like [illegible], ever on the reserve, either from disposition or the force of bribery, so that their whole proceedings were enveloped in mystery and ambiguity. Antipater, in fine, conducted matters with such art and address, that the friends and servants of Alexander were all corrupted, either by flattery or rewards, into the betraying of him in whatsoever he said or did. Instead of appearing himself an open enemy to his brothers, he had his confidents at hand ready to accuse them, while he stood forth speciously himself in their vindication, but introduced such oblique hints, and [illegible] insinuations, as greatly alarmed Herod, and fully persuaded him that the report of Alexander's plot upon his life was well founded; indeed, Antipater's artful manner of misrepresentation gave the semblance of truth to every [illegible].

Herod was greatly incensed against the two brothers by these practices of Antipater, insomuch that [illegible] stood upon [illegible] the king in [illegible] [illegible] [illegible] [illegible] that means [illegible] the [illegible] of the [illegible], particularly [illegible] of Ptolemy, his [illegible], [illegible] his brethren and domestics. The [illegible] of Antipater was prevailing, [illegible] of his mother [illegible] every circumstance to mortify [illegible] Alexander, [illegible] bore in the whole [illegible], [illegible] her mortal hatred to the children of the queen. [illegible] respect was paid to Antipater, from a consideration of his influence with the king, who absolutely prohibited [illegible], [illegible] from holding any intercourse with Alexander or his brothers, [illegible] [illegible] his [illegible] displeasure. [illegible] [illegible] [illegible] on [illegible] [illegible] [illegible] [illegible], but their friends abroad: for Herod [illegible] privileges conferred upon him by Augustus which [illegible] [illegible] other, as the liberty of bringing [illegible] [illegible] [illegible] [illegible] [illegible] [illegible] princes, where [illegible] [illegible] [illegible] [illegible] [illegible] authority.

The brothers were not as yet conscious of [illegible] [illegible], offence, as Herod had not exhibited any public [illegible] against them, which made the danger so much the greater, through want of precaution for a necessary defence. They inferred, however, [illegible] [illegible] of their [illegible] from the king's coolness towards them, which consequently increased their anxiety.

Antipater had also prejudiced their uncle Pheroras, and their aunt Salome, against the brothers, and [illegible] them to use their influence with Herod to their disadvantage. The feud already ran very high, but was greatly inflamed by Glaphyra, the wife of Alexander, who, upon all occasions, would be [illegible] upon the [illegible] of her birth, and claiming a superiority [illegible] [illegible]. She came from [illegible] on the father's side, and from Darius [illegible] on the mother's, reflecting at the same time, on the [illegible] of Herod as upstarts, and treating [illegible] with [illegible] contempt, observing that Herod did not marry for rank, but for beauty. We have already observed that he had several wives, and much approved of polygamy, it being allowed by the Jewish law, and they were all [illegible] at Alexander [illegible] the haughty and [illegible] behaviour of Glaphyra. Aristobulus married Salome, his [illegible]-in-law, to his [illegible]. She was [illegible] piqued at the pride of Glaphyra, who was continually upbraiding her of the meanness of her origin. He would [illegible] reproach his wife in like manner, and complain that he had married a woman of low descent, whereas his brother had taken to wife one of royal descent. The daughter of Salome carried these taunts to her mother, adding, that Alexander threatened the mother of his other brethren with the vilest indignities if he should come to the crown, and declared he would put their children, male and female, to the most servile and menial offices, as best becoming their mode of education. These intimations [illegible] the resentment of Salome to that degree, that [illegible] [illegible] the whole to Herod, nor could her testimony be suspected, since it was against her son-in-law.

There was another calumny propagated, that inflamed Herod more than all the rest. It was given out that Alexander and Aristobulus were continually bemoaning the face of their mother, and execrating their father for his cruelty, and farther suggested that upon Herod's dividing Mariamne's wardrobe among the rest of his wives, the brothers foreboded that their gaudy apparel would soon be turned into mourning.

Herod on these intimations, conscious of the [illegible], [illegible] of the princes was not without apprehension of [illegible] from them, yet did not despair of reducing them [illegible] [illegible] duty and obedience. Being on the point of [illegible] to Rome, he ordered his sons to [illegible] with the authority of a king and tenderness of a father, [illegible] them to agree among them [illegible] [illegible] [illegible] [illegible] [illegible] promise of [illegible] [illegible] [illegible] [illegible] had long armiſs upon condition of their repentance and amendment. By way of reply, they refuted the calumnies that had been raiſed againſt them, and alledged, that their actions were ſufficient for their vindication; adding, that the king ſhould not credulouſly admit of ſuch tales, as there never would be wanting thoſe who would poiſon the royal ear with them.

Though they had thus pacified him, and freed themſelves from any further apprehenſion and danger, they ſoon fell into new anxieties. They knew that Salome, and their uncle Pheroras, were their deadly enemies, who were both of them highly ſevere. The latter alſo had great power and influence, as he ſhared with Herod in all the dignities of royalty, the crown only accepted. His own proper revenue was fixed at an hundred talents, beſides the amount of all the land beyond Jordan, which he enjoyed through the bounty of Herod, at whoſe requeſt Cæſar was prevailed upon to make him a tetrarch. Herod honoured him alſo with a royal match, beſtowing upon him his wife's ſiſter in marriage; and upon her demiſe, offered him his eldeſt daughter, with a portion of three hundred talents. But Pheroras was ſo captivated with a paſſion for a private perſon, that he declined the propoſal of the royal marriage, which Herod reſenting, gave her to the ſon of his brother, who was afterwards ſlain by the Parthians. But though Herod was incenſed for the preſent, upon reflection, he imputed the refuſal to the violence of his paſſion, and ſo pardoned his folly.

It ſeemed that a rumour had long prevailed of Pheroras having entertained a deſign, even in the life-time of Mariamne, of poiſoning his brother. This was a ſeaſon ſo favourable to ſpies and informers, that Herod, though poſſeſſed of great fraternal affection, was alarmed at the report, though he did not abſolutely credit it. Many were apprehended upon ſuſpicion, and ſeveral put to the queſtion, paſſing from one to another, till they came at laſt to the friends of Pheroras. They confeſſed nothing of the poiſonous intention, but acknowledged that Pheroras had made preparations to ſteal away with his miſtreſs to Parthia, and that Coſtobarus, Salome's ſecond huſband, was privy to the deſign. Herod had delivered her up to this Coſtobarus, after her former huſband had been put to death for adultery. Nor was Salome free from accuſations, for her brother Pheroras exhibited a charge againſt her, of having entered into a marriage treaty with Silæus, governor of Arabia, under king Obodas, one of Herod's moſt implacable enemies. Salome was found guilty of the charge alledged againſt her by Pheroras. Herod, however, pardoned them both.

The ſtorm of faction now reſted upon the head of Alexander, and from the following cauſe. There were three eunuchs who were in high eſteem with the king, and employed in offices immediately about his perſon. Alexander, by flatteries and rewards, had rendered them his creatures, ſubſervient to his purpoſes. Herod, ſuſpecting ſome colluſion, put them to the torture, and extorted from them a confeſſion that Alexander had expreſſed to them "the vanity and folly of the king in colouring his hair, from an affectation of youthful gaiety; whereas he was entitled to their attention, as being ſucceſſor to the crown, and having, on the attainment of it, power of avenging himſelf on his enemies, and rewarding his friends, amongſt whom he ranked them in particular." The informers added, that the great officers of ſtate were in their hearts all attached to the intereſt of Alexander, and concerted their ſchemes in private meetings and cabals.

Theſe confeſſions alarmed Herod, though he would not venture to publiſh them immediately; but he had his ſpies at work, night and day, to make diſcoveries in all places, and amongſt all families; and death was the certain conſequence of ſuſpicion. This part of Herod's hiſtory was one ſcene of cruelty and injuſtice. Every diſguſt made way for calumny, and that calumny was conſtrued a mortal crime; for Herod executed the malicious deſigns that were ſuggeſted to him by others. No witneſs ſo infamous, no impoſture ſo groſs and ridiculous but it gained credit, and the puniſhment immediately followed even the ſuppoſed evidences; ſo that the accuſed and the accuſer frequently went off together. As Herod contemned the formalities of law where the life of a prince was in danger. Nay, he was tranſported, by ſuſpicion and apprehenſion to that degree, that he could not behold an innocent perſon with complacency; and his nominal and quondam friends became as it were, the objects of his averſion.

Antipater was the ſource of Herod's diſquiet and turbulent proceedings. He firſt ſuggeſted, and then exaggerated charges. Nay, he ſo terrified the king with groundleſs inſinuations, that he fancied Alexander ſtood before him with a drawn ſword ready to aſſaſſinate him. Under theſe frantic apprehenſions, he cauſed him to be taken and bound, and then proceeded to put his adherents to the torture. Many of them died mute, and ſacrificed their lives to a good conſcience; others, who wanted reſolution to bear the torment, framed a falſhood, charged the brothers with plotting againſt the life of the king as he was upon the chace, and a deſign afterwards of flying to Rome. Improbable as this ſtory was, it had ſuch an effect upon the credulity and ſuſpicion of the king, that he urged it in his own juſtification for committing his ſons to priſon.

The jealouſy of Herod raging to an incurable degree, Alexander diſmiſſed all thoughts of vindicating himſelf by way of argument, and had recourſe to another expedient, which was to concur with his enemies, in their declarations, and, by confeſſing his own guilt, involve them in the ſame condemnation. To this end he drew up four narratives, acknowledging himſelf a confederate againſt the life of his father, with the names of divers of the conſpirators, but particularly thoſe of Pheroras and Salome, charging her with forcing him to a criminal intercourſe with her.

Thoſe narratives which contained the ſevereſt allegations againſt ſeveral perſons of the firſt rank, being put into the hands of Herod, it ſo happened that Archelaus came into Judæa at that very juncture of time, anxious for the deliverance of his daughter and ſon-in-law from their preſent very alarming ſituation. Archelaus managed matters with ſuch art and addreſs, that he reſtored Herod to the uſe of his reaſon, and accompliſhed a much deſired purpoſe. When he came into his preſence, he began to exclaim moſt bitterly againſt his ſon-in-law as a traiterous parricide; to wiſh for an opportunity of ridding his daughter from ſuch an huſband with his own hands, and to lament the taint ſhe had received from intercourſe with ſo flagitious and abandoned a character. He profeſſed the patience of Herod to be miraculous in ſparing the life of a conſpirator at the hazard of his own; and his wonder at finding Alexander alive. He then ſoothed him, by obſerving that his feelings would be too tender to inflict condign puniſhment upon ſo rebellious a ſon, and therefore requeſted that he would leave to him to do him right, as he would recommend to his generoſity the diſpoſal of his daughter. Theſe ſpecious means, as they cauſed Herod to abate of his rigour towards Alexander, inflamed him the more againſt Pheroras, as he was the principal ſubject of the four narratives which Herod gave Archelaus to peruſe. Every thing appearing opportune for his purpoſe, Archelaus inſinuated himſelf by little and little, into the merits of the cauſe, laying the blame upon the ringleaders, and chiefly upon Pheroras, and finding the effect of one artifice, had recourſe to another.

He repreſented to the king, "that, in his opinion his ſon was in more danger of being undone by a faction, than he was of being deſtroyed by his ſon: that Alexander muſt be frantic to entertain ſuch a deſign, as he had already a fair pretence to the ſucceſſion: that young men were raſh, inconſiderate, and eaſily impoſed upon by evil company and corrupt counsels, through want of knowledge and experience; and that he had made provision of arms, etc. [illegible], and calumnies of incendiaries, that they [illegible], in general, as irresistible as destructive."

Herod began now to coincide with Archelaus in opinion, and think more favourably of Alexander, and worse of Pheroras than he had done, from the substance of the four narratives. Pheroras perceiving the king in a more tractable temper, through the influence of Archelaus, he left Alexander, and had recourse to him, by whom he was told plainly, that he could not possibly escape himself from the charge [illegible] proved against him, as there was not clearer than the evidence of his being in a conspiracy against the life of his brother, and [illegible] contrivance of the detraction of Alexander. To enforce his former remarks, he submitted, that it would be much more to his advantage to give up his evasive manner of behaviour, and frankly confess that part of his charge of which he was conscious of being guilty; [illegible] his brother had a natural tenderness for him, by which he might be prevailed upon to pardon him; and that, if he would make the experiment, he would do his utmost to render it effectual.

Pheroras took the hint, and having assumed the appearance of contrition, [illegible] countenance [illegible] himself at Herod's feet, with confusion, implored forgiveness, [illegible] as a plea for his behaviour, the foolish passion he had [illegible], which transported him beyond the bounds of reason and duty. Pheroras having thus made his confession, and pleaded for his pardon, Archelaus availed himself of the circumstance to work Herod into a more complacent humour.

[illegible] having [illegible] Herod towards Pheroras, to carry on his design, treated Alexander with reproaches [illegible], and, in the conclusion, threatened to take away his daughter. This seeming concern of Archelaus wrought so sensibly upon Herod, that he became an advocate for his son, and made his suit to Archelaus not to annul the marriage. [illegible], out of the reverence he had for the rights of marriage, he was content to let his daughter [illegible] Herod's disposal, provided only that he should not give her to Alexander. [illegible] this was counterfeit [illegible] Herod was [illegible] confusion, and confessed, that, as they had children, and the affection was so evidently mutual, it would be death to part them; besides [illegible] perpetual barrier to the [illegible] of the family.

This conversation was no sooner at an end, than Archelaus entered, and, in a very short time returned, bringing with him Alexander, whom he reconciled to his father. He approved of Herod's resolution to go to Rome, with an account to Cæsar of the late transactions, as he had written at large to him on that subject. Thus did Archelaus accomplish his purpose, and deliver his son-in-law from impending danger. The reconciliation was celebrated with festivity and most agreeable entertainments. Herod presented Archelaus on his departure, with seventy talents, a throne set with precious stones, a train of eunuchs, and a concubine called Pannychis. All his great officers and friends were treated, by Herod's express order, with rich presents according to their rank; the king himself, and his nobility, conducting him on his way as far as Antioch.

There came a person into Judæa not long after this, a man of superior policy to Archelaus, one who not only overthrew the project of Alexander's reconciliation to his father, but so ordered matters, that he brought Alexander himself to his end. His name was Eurycles, a Lacedemonian by birth, a man so exorbitantly luxurious and profuse, that the revenue of a prince could not answer his demands. He made Herod several valuable presents, which being deemed allurements to conciliate his friendship, were returned by gifts of much greater value. He used divers means to conciliate the favour of Herod, and, through [illegible] speeches, and the grossest flattery, wrought so effectually upon his temper and disposition, that whatever he said or did met with his approbation. By this practical behaviour he acquired great interest at court: besides being a Spartan, they had a respect for his country as well as his person.

When Eurycles discovered the factions and divisions that prevailed in Herod's family, and noticed how the king stood affected towards the different parties, he took up his residence with Antipater, and pretending a [illegible] regard for Alexander, related to him the good offices that [illegible] had between him and Archelaus. This served as a passport to Alexander, who not only gave credit to the whole matter, but got [illegible] his brother Aristobulus with [illegible]. [illegible] Eurycles had sounded the different parties, he [illegible] several [illegible] of proceeding, as [illegible], his grand business being to obtain money from [illegible], and [illegible] Alexander. To [illegible] former, "that it was surprizing to him, that, as the eldest son, and next heir to the crown, he could suffer himself to be imposed upon by pretences [illegible]." [illegible] he exercised his [illegible], "that the son and husband of a great princess could endure to see the son of a private woman [illegible] betwixt him and the crown, especially having [illegible] such [illegible] importance as king Archelaus." This [illegible] upon the credit of procuring a friendship for Archelaus, Alexander was so [illegible], that he took Eurycles into close confidence, and disclosed every particular to him relative to the [illegible] with Antipater, observing that it was no matter of surprize that Herod, who [illegible] their mother, should deprive the son of the king [illegible] both in countenance and [illegible], [illegible] the inhumanity of such a practice, [illegible].

When this [illegible] had derived the [illegible] from them both, he went to Antipater, [illegible] him the story, with some [illegible] of his own, intimating, that the conspiracy was upon the point of execution, and the king [illegible] moment [illegible] in danger. [illegible] with a considerable sum of money, [illegible] and recommendation, [illegible] above, [illegible] of which he offered [illegible] himself as an evidence against [illegible]. He then went to Herod, and thus addressed him:

"I am here come in gratitude to acknowledge [illegible] your favours, and to give you [illegible]. It is now a long time that your death has been resolved upon [illegible] that Alexander [illegible] and once, with full determination to have done the deed [illegible] and let me tell you [illegible], this horrid wickedness had been compleated, if I had not put a stop to the dispatch, by seeming to approve of the thing, and offering myself to join in the exploit. What! says Alexander, cannot Herod content himself with the usurpation of a kingdom, the death of my mother, and the dividing the government to pieces, without declaring that [illegible] his successor, to a [illegible] of [illegible]? But it belongs to me to do justice to the names of Hyrcanus and Mariamne [illegible] would [illegible] the government should descend from such [illegible] without blood. Not a day passes over [illegible] fresh [illegible] and provocations. [illegible] a syllable upon the [illegible] of [illegible] the families and connections, Herod [illegible] me with [illegible] that strikes [illegible]. When I am a hunting with him, if I say nothing, Why do you not [illegible]? [illegible] hold your tongue? Nay, I cannot so [illegible] him but he suspects my truth. I can do nothing, in fine, to his liking, and it is only Antipater that has the good fortune to please him. So that (says Alexander) if this plot should miscarry, I had rather [illegible] my grave than outlive the conflict. If I [illegible] get off [illegible] my father-in-law, [illegible] who knows but little [illegible] of this history, [illegible] the temper of Herod. I shall not now [illegible] when I come to Rome, [illegible] "father, who was then present, nor shall I much insist upon private injuries done to myself, but rather turn my discourse to public grievances, as how the corruptions and oppressions, and the squandering away of exorbitant impositions in luxury and pleasure. I shall shew what ways they were turned into what him is, the miserable slavery of the Jews, and the true reasons of it. And, to conclude, I shall deliver the true history of the death of my grandfather Hyrcanus, and my mother Mariamne, and make such a discovery of the wicked effect the palace that no man living, after these necessary truths, shall ever esteem me the murderer of my father."

When Eurycles had finished this invective against Alexander, he turned the remainder of his discourse into a panegyric upon Antipater, declaring him to be the only son that truly loved his father, and put a reasonable stop to the progress of the design. The king still labouring under his former prejudices, took fire at this hint, so that it was now the business of Antipater to inflame his passion by producing new witnesses against the brothers. The evidence was thus: "That Alexander and Aristobulus held a private correspondence with Jucundus and Tyrannus, two officers of horse, who for some misdemeanor, had been dismissed from their command."

This information so enraged Herod, that he commanded them immediately to be put to the torture. They denied any former knowledge of the matter, but a certain letter was sent from Alexander to the governor of Alexandrion, desiring him to receive himself and his brother Aristobulus into the castle, in case of their father's death, and to furnish them both with arms and other necessaries, if that event should happen. Alexander charged this letter as a forgery of Diophantus, an enterprizing man, and very expert at counterfeiting hands, besides which, he was the king's secretary, and it is to be observed, that he suffered death for forgery. The governor of the castle was also tortured, but made no confession. The brothers were honourably acquitted; yet Eurycles, the author of forgery, and projector of this vile accusation, was applauded by Herod as his friend and preserver, and rewarded with fifty talents for his service.

This abandoned wretch, before Archelaus could have any certain information of the imprisonment of the brothers, went to him by stealth, and had the effrontery to assure him, that he himself had effected a reconciliation between Herod and his son Alexander. From thence he went into Achaia with his treasure, and spent it in riot and luxury, till, in the end, he was arraigned by Cæsar for seditious and corrective practices, and condemned to banishment. This was the punishment he suffered for his abominable practices.

It will be very pertinent in this place, to adduce the character of Evaratus, of Coos, in opposition to that of Eurycles, of Sparta. He was one of Alexander's most intimate friends, and was at Herod's court at the same time with Eurycles. The king demanded of him, upon his honour, what credit he gave to the report of the conspiracy, and to the accusation given out upon it. Evaratus declared upon oath, that he had never heard the most distant hint of any such design from either of the brothers. This testimony, however, was of no avail to them, for Herod was so open to calumny, as to be entirely prepossessed by it, nor was there any other method of obtaining his favour, than by saying, doing, and believing as he did.

In the mean time Salome exasperated Herod against his sons, in order to secure herself. Aristobulus cautioned her, as a relation, to take care of her words and actions, intimating, that she was still in danger from Herod, as she lay under a second charge for the same crime of which she had been accused before, which was, that she entered into a contract of marriage with Syllæus, the Arabian, though she knew him to be the king's enemy, and that she gave him, from time to time, secret information of the king's council. This caution proved eventually the very means of the ruin of the brothers, for Salome acquainting the king with it, he was transported to such an impetuous passion, that he commanded them to be separated, and laid in chains.

In his fury he dispatched Volumnius, a general of his army, and Olympus, one of his chief friends, to Cæsar with copies of the proceedings. The emperor upon reading them, was much affected by the situation of the princes, but, at the same time very fearful of exerting his civil power to the prejudice of the natural feelings of a father over his children, so that he returned Herod for answer, "That he was master over himself and those that belonged to him, but that he thought it adviseable to call an assembly of respectable persons, to enquire into the conspiracy, and proceed to justice according to substantiated evidence."

The emperor having pointed out Berytus as the place of meeting, Herod, in conformity to his direction, called a council there. It was composed of Saturnius and Pedanius ambassadors, Volumnius the governor of the province, the friends and relations of Herod, not omitting Salome and Pheroras, the principal men of Syria, Archelaus only excepted, Herod having suspicion of him as father-in-law of Alexander. The council did not approve of bringing the sons into court, and from prudential causes, for their very presence would have tended to excite compassion, and if they had been heard in their own vindication, Alexander, with the greatest ease, would have baffled all their objections, so that they were rather kept under custody at Platane, a village of Sidonia.

When the king stood up, he began to inveigh against his sons with great acrimony, and exhibit tokens of passion as if they had been present. Touching on the subject of the conspiracy his voice faultered, and he seemed rather disposed to pass it over, because he was destitute of evidence; but when he came to speak of expressions, indignities, injuries, and instances of disobedience respecting himself, he was abundantly vociferous, giving the assembly to understand that those reproaches were worse to him than death, and finding every allegation pass without contradiction, he only lamented his own unhappiness in giving a cause so ruinous to himself, and then called upon the court to proceed to pass sentence.

Saturnius gave it as his opinion, that the brothers deserved to be punished, but not with death, as it was by no means just in him, who had three sons present in the assembly, to pass sentence upon those who were absent. The two ambassadors were of the same mind, as were others who spoke after them. The first who voted for sentence of death was Volumnius, and others followed him, as they were influenced by their passions or interest, but none from a principle of ill-will to the prisoners.

Judæa and Syria were in dread and suspence for the issue of this affair, though it could hardly be supposed that Herod could be so inexorably cruel as to be the murderer of his own offspring; but so destitute was he of the feeling of nature, that he sent his sons in chains to Tyre, and thence by sea to Cæsarea, deliberating, at the same time, on the means of their execution.

There was a certain old officer of the king's much attached to the princes, and whose son was upon terms of friendship with Alexander. His name was Tyro, and being greatly incensed at the proceedings of Herod, he went up and down exclaiming, in a fit of phrenzy, "that justice was trampled on, and truth lost, that nothing but iniquity prevailed in the world, and that there was neither humanity nor natural affection to be found among mankind." He had even the resolution to go to the king himself, and remonstrate with him to this effect. "Of all men living, Sire, you are certainly the most inexorable, in believing the allegations of the most abandoned characters to the prejudice of your best friends. Permit me to point out Pheroras and Salome as persons you have pronounced deserving of death, yet upon their testimony you are about to take away the lives of your sons. You do not consider that, when the "ghbours are removed, they will have in the succes-" sion of Antipater a king framed to their purpose. " But let him beware of the soldiery, they will not tame-" ly suffer the mischief to pass unavenged, as they com-" passionate the case of the unfortunate Princes, and there " is not a man of honour but murmurs at such foul proceed-" ings." Tyro upon this named several of the malecon-tents, who were instantly removed, by order of the king, and the old officer and his son were put into custody.

There was one Tryphon at that time the king's tonsor, who offered to the court himself suddenly as a witness, and depose, "that Tyro offered him a considerable reward, in the name of Alexander, to dispatch the king during the operation of shaving." Upon this allegation Tyro, his son, and the tonsor, were ordered to be put to the question. Tyro and his son denied the charge, and Tryphon was wholly silent, whereupon Herod commanded Tyro's torments to be increased with his son, from filial piety to his father, promised the king a discovery of the whole transaction, on condition of his granting him a pardon. The old man being taken from the torture, the son declared that his father had been instigated by Alexander to take away the life of the king. This was in general, supposed to be an evasion of the son, yet there were those that gave credit to it. Herod, in an harangue to the public, soon after this, took occasion to inveigh against some officers of rank, together with Tyro, by which the rabble were so exasperated, that they fell upon those officers, Tyro and Tryphon, and stoned them to death. Herod caused his sons to be strangled at Sebaste, and then dead bodies carried to Alexandrion, and there deposited by the remains of Alexander, their mother's uncle. This was the end of Alexander and Aristobulus.

CHAP. XVII.

Antipater conspires against the life of his father. Dissimulation and duplicity of Herod. The issue and children of Aristobulus. The issue of Salome in Syllaeus. The issue of Antipater. Conduct of women. Foul practices on a plea upon Salome. Herod sends Antipater to Rome with his last will declaring him his successor. A design upon the life of Herod proved against Syllaeus.

ANTIPATER had so far wrought upon the credulity and suspicion of his father, that he entertained not a doubt of succeeding to the throne of Judaea; but, through one continued scene of falsehood and perfidy, he had rendered himself obnoxious to the people. Nor was he free from apprehension that the children of the murdered brothers would revenge the deaths of their parents. Alexander had by Glaphyra two sons, Tigranes and Alexander. Aristobulus had by Berenice the daughter of Salome, Herod, Agrippa, and Aristobulus, and two daughters, Herodias and Mariamne. Glaphyra was sent away with her portion, into Cappadocia, after the death of Alexander, and Berenice, the widow of Aristobulus, was married to the uncle of Antipater, who promoted this marriage to effect a reconciliation with Salome, and put an end to all dissention. Antipater plied Pheroras with compliments and presents, and cultivated the esteem of Caesar's friends, by sending vast sums of money to Rome to engage them in his interest. Nor was he less bountiful to Saturnius, and the rest of his friends in Syria. But this munificence, instead of conciliating their esteem, incurred their contempt, as they considered it as arising from a notion of fear. Indeed he was generally obnoxious to the people, notwithstanding his liberalities, as they were convinced of the malevolence of his disposition, and the fallacy of his conduct.

Herod, having summoned his friends and kindred, sent for the young princes, and, with tears of compassion, addressed them in words to the following effect:

"You have here before you the children of an unfortu-" nate family. Their fathers have been taken from me " by a sad fate, and I find myself bound in humanity to " do the best I can for the orphans, in discharging the " part of a grandfather more to my satisfaction than I did " that of a father. In pursuance of this purpose, I shall " make it my care, in the first place, to put these chil-" dren in good hands, and under the charge of the best " friends I shall leave behind me when I am gone. To " begin with you, Pheroras, I would have you marry " your daughter to Alexander's eldest son, and supply the " place of a father and guardian. As to your part, An-" tipater, I would have your son to take one of the daugh-" ters of Aristobulus, under which relation you will be " as good as a parent to the orphan. As for my son He-" rod, the grandchild of Simon, the high-priest, by the " mother's side, let him marry the other sister. This is " my will and desire, and no relative that has any regard " or kindness for me will dispute it. Thus I would " have it, and I beseech God to prosper these alliances " to the comfort of my kingdom and family, and grant " mercy that the children may be looked upon with " more favourable eyes than their fathers."

With this benediction Herod concluded, and joined the hands of the princes, and weeping over them, affectionately embraced, and then dismissed them. This instance of Herod's behaviour greatly alarmed Antipater, nor could he conceal his surprize, as he considered the respect paid to the fathers, through the children, as a degradation to himself. This he likewise imagined would be the means of supplanting him, especially if Pheroras, the tetrarch should join interest with Archelaus in favour of the sons of Alexander. He also considered the universal hatred he had incurred, the compassion of the people for the fatherless children, and, in fine, the concern the whole nation had for the living children and reverence for the memory of the dead, of whom he was deemed little better than the murderer. These circumstances duly weighed, Antipater had no other remedy but to dissolve the contracts, a point of the greatest difficulty, as Herod, being rather rigid and suspicious, was not to be wrought upon by craft and circumvention. He therefore adopted a more frank and open manner of proceeding, and desired him, with all modesty and deference, that he would deign him the honour of which he thought him worthy, as without it all other grants were but the mere shadow of a kingdom without the substance, as would certainly be the case, if Alexander's son should not only have Archelaus for his grandfather, but Pheroras also for his father-in-law. Antipater pressed Herod, with vehement importunity, to change the disposition of the marriages, which might easily be done, as he had so numerous a family.

Herod had nine wives, and children by seven of them. Antipater by Doris. Herod by Mariamne the daughter of the high-priest, Antipas and Archelaus by Malthace, a Samaritan, and a daughter Olympias, whom his brother Joseph married. Herod and Philip by Cleopatra, of Jerusalem, and Phasael by Pallas. He had also two other daughters Roxana and Salome, the one by Phaedra, the other by Elpis, and two wives that had no children, the one was the daughter of his brother, the other his cousin-german. Besides these he had by Mariamne, the two sisters of Alexander and Aristobulus. Since therefore the royal family was so numerous, Antipater requested him to change the intended marriages.

The king perceived by this time the disposition of Antipater towards his children, and was very much disturbed at it, lest he should follow his own example, and dispatch the survivors as he had done their predecessors. In this humour he commenced him to quit his presence, but was soon after prevailed upon, by soothing flattery, to lay his jealousy, so that he gave to Antipater himself the daughter of Aristobulus, and obtained the son of the daughter of Pheroras. This circumstance evinces the prowess and energy of Antipater over the mind of Herod, in effecting that in which his own sister failed by the means of the empress Julia, but failed before. For when Salome was disposed to marry Syllæus, the Arabian, and engaged Julia to intercede in her behalf, Herod not only opposed the match, and rejected the intercession, but commanded her, on pain of being treated as his greatest enemy, if she did not give up the project. He caused her, against her consent, to be married to Alexas, a friend of his, and to give one of her daughters to his son, and the other to the uncle of Antipater by the mother's side. He likewise gave one of the daughters of Mariamne to Antipater, his sister's son, and the other to his brother's son, Phasael.

When matters were thus changed, and every thing settled to the mind of Antipater, and confident by the manifest violation of the orphans' [illegible], became intolerable. As he was conscious that he had incurred the hatred of the people, he founded his security on rendering [illegible] terrible to them. Besides, Pheroras [illegible] him [illegible] established his sovereignty.

[illegible] the court by a [illegible] [illegible], for the wife, mother, and sister of Pheroras, together with the mother of Antipater, behaved with insolence even towards the king's daughters. [illegible] Antipater was well pleased, [illegible] declaration. The rest of the women, who [illegible] of the court, except Salome, who informed the king of their [illegible] consultations, and pointed out to him that they did not tend to the promotion of his interest. When the women came to understand that the king had notice of their [illegible], and took great offence at it, they desisted from their [illegible], and pretended, in his hearing, to be at [illegible] with one another. Antipater [illegible] himself of [illegible] in public, opposed the [illegible] of Pheroras, but they had still private [illegible] and consultations in the night, though not [illegible] the [illegible] of Salome, who acquainted Herod with every particular.

This put him in a rage, especially against the wife of Pheroras, upon whom Salome laid the greatest [illegible]. Herod, upon this, called a council of his friends, and, among other foul practices, complained against her for insulting his daughters, encouraging the Pharisees in opposition to him, and giving his brother a potion to render him his enemy. At length he turned to Pheroras, and asked him which of the two he would part with, his brother or his wife? Pheroras replied he would part with life itself rather than with his beloved wife. Herod, struck with this resolute answer, directed his [illegible] to Antipater, and charged him to hold no intercourse either with Pheroras or his wife, or any person belonging to him. Antipater pretended compliance with the king's injunctions in public, though he continued to attend their nocturnal meetings. However, for fear of discovery, he so ordered matters with some friends he had in Italy, that letters were written to Herod by all means to send Antipater to Rome, to pay his court to Cæsar. Upon this intimation Herod immediately provided him a splendid equipage, furnished him with money, and dispatched him for Rome, with his last will and testament, wherein he declared Antipater his successor, and after Antipater, Herod whom he had by Mariamne, the daughter of the high-priest.

Syllæus, the Arabian, went also at this time to Rome, without any regard to Cæsar's injunctions, to dispute the same cause again with Antipater, that he had formerly defended against Nicolaus. It was a controversy of great moment that he had with Aretas, his own king, having put several of his friends to death, and, amongst the rest, Soëmus, a most eminent person for wealth and power in the whole city of Petra. He likewise corrupted Fabatus, one of Cæsar's governors, with a sum of money, to assist him against Herod; but Herod, by out-bidding, induced him to leave Syllæus, and made him receiver of his duties. Syllæus, finding that he came to no account, gave Augustus to understand, by way of complaint, that Fabatus was not Cæsar's governor, but Herod's. This provocation transported Fabatus to such a degree, that, being yet in great credit with Herod, he went and betrayed Syllæus to him, telling the king that he had engaged Corinthus, one of his guards, for a sum of money, to join with him in a conspiracy, advising withal, that he might be forthwith taken into custody. The king complied, for this Corinthus, though he had his education in the court, was by birth an Arabian, so that Herod ordered not only him to be apprehended, but two Arabians, who were found with him. One of them was a friend of Syllæus, the other the head of a tribe. This last being put to the question, confessed that they had prevailed with Corinthus, for a large sum of money, to undertake the killing of the king. Saturninus, the governor of Syria, took the examinations, and sent the parties to Rome.

CHAP. XI.

Pheroras is banished the court, and refuses to be present at the [illegible] Herod's sickness, and [illegible] for Pheroras, who [illegible] to [illegible]. Herod recovers, [illegible] becomes sick, [illegible] Herod's [illegible]. Death of Pheroras. [illegible] of his being poisoned at the instance of Syllæus. [illegible] of Antipater [illegible] his [illegible]. Herod's inexorable [illegible] of the [illegible] of Pheroras. His own confession at [illegible] death. Proof adduced of Mariamne's being [illegible].

HEROD continued his importunities with Pheroras to put away his wife. He found abundant cause to hate her, but could not devise any means of bringing her to punishment; and, in the height of rage, he banished both herself and her husband the court. Pheroras submitted to the disgrace very patiently, and retired to his tetrarchy, binding himself, by an oath, never to return during the life of Herod, so that nothing but his death should put an end to his banishment. Herod soon after fell into a dangerous fit of sickness, and sent several times for Pheroras, having something of moment to communicate to him before he died. But Pheroras could not be prevailed upon to go, and Herod, on the other hand, beyond all expectation, recovered. Pheroras, a little after this, became indisposed himself, and the king, his brother, upon that occasion, displayed some degree of humanity, for he not only made him a visit, but gave him singular proofs of fraternal affection. The disease, however, carried him off in a short time. Though Herod had evinced this kindness for his brother in his expiring moments, a rumour went forth that he had caused him to be destroyed by poison. The body, however, was conveyed to Jerusalem, where public mourning and a most pompous funeral were appointed. This was the end of one of the murderers of Alexander and Aristobulus.

But the punishment was soon transferred to the author, Antipater, and took its rise from the death of Pheroras, for certain of his freemen, in the agony of their passion for so irreparable a loss, went boldly to the king, and told him, "that his brother had been destroyed by poison, that his wife had brought him something prepared after an unusual manner, that, upon eating it, he fell into his distemper; that the mother and sister of Antipater, two days before, brought a woman out of Arabia, that was skilled in drugs, in order to prepare a love potion for Pheroras, that, instead thereof, she had given him deadly poison; and that this was done at the instance of Syllæus, who was well acquainted with this woman."

So many suspicions started, and the presumptions were so strong, that the king ordered the putting of several persons, bond and free, to the question. A female servant exclaimed in the agony of her torture, "May "the Almighty ruler of heaven and earth, avenge himself and us upon the mother of Antipater, for all the "miseries we suffer for her sake!" The king availed himself of this confession, and proceeded to further enquiry into the truth of the matter. Another woman laid open the whole circumstance of the familiarity betwixt the mother of Antipater and Pheroras and his women, the clandestine meetings, that Pheroras and Antipater, when they came from court, regaled together all night, nor would admit a servant into the chamber. It was one of the free-women that gave this evidence.

When the witnesses came to be examined apart, there was such an agreement in their information, that the truth of the charge was no longer to be doubted. It was occurred to Herod, that Antipater's withdrawing to Rome, and Pheroras's procuring his own banishment, were only contrivances to get out of the way; for they had often been heard to say, "that, after the taking off Alexander and Aristobulus, they must prepare for their turns, since, from the execrable murder of his own wife and children, they had no ground to expect to fare better; and the only fence against such a monster of barbarity was to be out of his reach."

The women deposed further, that Antipater would often complain to his mother, "that he had already grey hairs on "his head, that his father grew younger every day, that "perhaps he might die before he came to govern; that, in "case of the death of Herod, the enjoyment of the succession would be but transitory, as those heads of Hydra, the "sons of Alexander and Aristobulus were shooting up; "that he was deprived, by his father, of the hope of being "succeeded by his children, as Herod the son of Mariamne, was appointed to succeed him; that, in this point, "Herod was plainly distracted, to think that his testament "should take place in that, as he would take care that none "of his posterity should remain, being, of all parents most "averse to his children, and more so, if possible, to his brother, as appeared from his giving him an hundred talents "to hold no intercourse with Pheroras; that, however, "though they could expect nothing but inhumanity and "barbarity from such a monster, that if they had but the "hearts and hands of men, they might assert their rights and "submit to no the [illegible]."

To this confession it was added, that Pheroras had some thoughts of flying with them to Petra. The discovery was credited upon the whole, but the most corroborating circumstance to Herod was that of the hundred talents, for he had only mentioned that particular to Antipater. He first vented his rage against Doris, his mother, took from her all her jewels and trinkets, which he had purchased for her at an immense charge, and then ejected her from the palace. After this he caused the women of Pheroras to be tortured to death, though he trembled all the while, and was distracted between fears and jealousies; nay, he was so rigid in inflicting punishments, that he put the innocent to the torture without distinction, lest any of the guilty should escape.

The next that passed examination was Antipater, the Samaritan, and steward to Antipater, the king's son. It appeared, upon putting him to the torture, that Antipater sent for poison into Egypt, by Antiphilus, his friend, with a design upon the king's life, which he received from Theudion, the uncle of Antipater, and, upon his order, delivered it to Pheroras, who had taken upon him to execute the design while he was at Rome, and, from distance of situation, freed from suspicion; and that he committed the care of the poison to his wife.

Herod sent for the widow of Pheroras, and commanded her, without delay, to shew him the secret she had received. She went out on a pretence to fetch it, but cast herself headlong from the top of the house, to prevent both the torture and the discovery. But Divine Providence would not suffer Antipater to escape thus, for her fall was not mortal. She was taken up and carried to the king, who, as soon as she recovered herself, demanded of her to tell him the cause of so desperate an act, assuring her, upon his oath, that if she spoke the truth, she should have no further punishment; but if she deviated from that, she should die upon the rack, without being allowed the rites of a funeral.

By this time she recovered her senses, and thus rationally expressed herself:

"Am I to keep secrets now Pheroras is dead and gone, "in favour of Antipater, that has been the ruin of us all? "Give patience! Give ear to [illegible], and I call that God, "who cannot be deceived, to bear witness to the truth of "what I say. When you came upon a visit to Pheroras in "his sickness, and weeping over him, my husband called "me to him. See, my dear wife, says he, how much I "have been mistaken in my opinion of my brother's kindness to me; for, in plain terms, I hated him, and meditated the death of this man, that shewed so generous a pity for me in my distress, (though yet among the living,) "but I have the just reward of my impiety. Fetch me "immediately the remainder of the poison that Antipater "gave you to keep, and burn it before my face, else I shall "carry the vengeance of a troubled conscience into the other "world. I brought it as I was bid, and threw the greater "part of the poison into the fire before his eyes, and the rest I "reserved for a time of need."

With these words she produced a box, containing a little of the poison. The brother and mother of Antiphilus were then put to the question, and they informed the king, that Antiphilus brought the box out of Egypt, and that he received the poison from a brother of his at Alexandria, that practised physic. It was now evident that Mariamne, the daughter of the high-priest, was concerned in the plot, as appeared from her brothers upon the question. But Herod punished the mother in the son, for he struck her son Herod out of his will, in which he had formerly declared him his successor.

CHAP. XX.

Antipater [illegible] Pheroras [illegible] Antipater [illegible] The [illegible] conduct of Herod [illegible] upon [illegible] Antipater's [illegible] The evidence of the [illegible] Antipater [illegible] Antipater to [illegible] Herod [illegible] Antipater to the [illegible]

THE last and convictive evidence was Bathyllus, one of Antipater's freemen, who was just returned from Rome, and brought with him the poison of an asp, and other serpents, for Pheroras and his wife to compleat the work, if other attempt should fail. He brought also, as an addition to Antipater's devices against his father, several letters, which he had written to the prejudice of his brothers Archelaus and Philip, though they were princes of most generous disposition.

Archelaus and Philip were at that time at Rome, pursuing their studies. They were youths of promising genius, and consequently such objects of envy to Antipater, that he entertained no hopes of gaining his point unless he could get them removed. To this end he forged letters against them, in the names of several of his friends at Rome. Some of them insinuated the [illegible] which they had treated their father, openly [illegible]

Alexander and Ariſtobulus, and diſcovering much reluctance at their being recalled, a circumſtance that gave Antipater more diſquiet than all the reſt Antipater, indeed, was in a practice of forgery and ſecret intelligence even before he left Judæa, and procured letters from Rome to Herod upon the ſame ſubject, while he himſelf, to evade ſuſpicion, joined himſelf to his father as a kind of advocate for his brothers, alledging that ſome of the charges contained in the letters were falſe, and others only the effects of youthful folly The intelligence he obtained to circumvent his brothers was attended with great expence, to compenſate which, he purchaſed a variety of rich apparel, furniture, gold and ſilver plate, and ſeveral other curioſities of great value, to the amount of two hundred talents, which he placed to the account of the ſuit they had with Syllæus, to diſguiſe the ſubornations

But, notwithſtanding theſe artful practices, the whole country rang with the parricide, and all witneſſes and letters concurred to prove repeated deſigns upon the lives of the brothers, yet not one that came to Rome took any notice of the preſent ſtate of Herod's family, though ſeven months had intervened between his conviction and his return Indeed, he was an object of univerſal deteſtation, ſo that their ſilence might ariſe from a deſire of ſeeing juſtice executed upon ſo many horrid murders He then wrote from Rome, informing Herod that he was upon the return, after having been moſt honourably diſmiſſed by Cæſar

The king, being deſirous of ſecuring this plotter, in order to divert him from any precaution, diſſembled his anger in his epiſtle to him, and, in a familiar ſtyle, deſired him to be with him as ſoon as poſſible, upon which condition he would lay aſide the complaints he had againſt his mother, for Antipater knew ſhe had been ejected from the palace The firſt news he had of the death of Pheroras was by a letter he received at Tarentum, which very much affected him Some looked upon his lamentation as the reſult of the feelings of nature, but others, with much greater reaſon, imputed it not to his tenderneſs for Pheroras, but his concern for the loſs of ſo neceſſary an inſtrument for the execution of his plot He was alſo under ſome apprehenſion of being detected However, upon his receiving the king's letter when he came into Cilicia, he purſued his journey with all expedition At his coming to Celenderis, he had a kind of foreboding of his mother's ſtate and condition The moſt cautious of his friends adviſed him not to go raſhly to his father, till he had learned the cauſe of his mother's ejectment, leſt he ſhould be involved in the ſame calumnies that had been caſt upon her But thoſe who were leſs conſiderate and preferred the ſight of their native country to his intereſt, perſuaded him to haſten his return, leſt delay ſhould raiſe ſuſpicion, and ſuggeſt matter for his enemies to work upon For if any thing ſhould be moved againſt him, he could not clear himſelf in his abſence, but if preſent, they would be more circumſpect in their proceedings They added, it would be abſurd to deprive himſelf of a kingdom from uncertain ſuſpicion So that, from theſe ſpecious repreſentations Antipater ſeems to have been actuated by the fatality of an impulſe to proſecute his voyage to Sebaſte, a port of Cæſarea

Upon his arrival, to his great ſurprize, he found himſelf univerſally ſhunned He was, indeed, as much deteſted there as upon his former viſit, but the people were not ſo much at liberty to ſhew their averſion Some were fearful of incurring the diſpleaſure of the king, for the country was filled with rumours concerning Antipater, and himſelf was the only perſon that was ignorant of them Never was man diſmiſſed more magnificently when he ſet out upon his voyage to Rome, or treated with more ignominy and contempt upon his return, than was Antipater He ſuſpected the broils that prevailed in Herod's family, but concealed his apprehenſions as much as poſſible, and aſſumed a cheerful countenance to veil a perplexed mind There was no poſſibility of eſcaping, nor had he any view of extricating himſelf from the difficulties with which he was encompaſſed Nor could he obtain any certain intelligence of the affairs of the royal family from the menaces the king had iſſued, ſo that he had ſome intervals of hope, either that things were not diſcovered, or that, in caſe of extremity, he might bring himſelf off by confidence and impoſture, the only means upon which he relied

Encouraged by theſe hopes, he advanced to the palace without his train, for they had been contemptuouſly repulſed at the firſt gate It ſo happened that Varus, the governor of Syria, was then preſent Antipater, at his entrance, with his uſual effrontery, approached his father with a dutiful ſalutation, but Herod rejected his embraces, exclaiming againſt his preſumption as a parricide, and denouncing a curſe upon him, till he cleared himſelf of the crimes alledged to his charge He alſo aſſured him he ſhould be judged by Varus, who would paſs ſentence according to his demerit, and then ordered him to depart, and prepare for his defence the next day, that being all the time allowed him Antipater was ſo confounded, that, without reply, he took his departure He was afterwards viſited by his wife and mother, who informed him of the evidence they had procured to ſubſtantiate the charge, which induced him to reflect on the moſt effectual means of defence

Upon the following day Herod ſummoned a court compoſed of his kindred and friends, ordered the friends of Antipater to attend alſo, and, together with Varus, aſcended the bench He cauſed all the witneſſes to be brought in, among whom were certain domeſtic ſervants of Doris, who had brought letters from the mother to the ſon, purporting, "that, ſince every thing had been diſcovered by Herod, he ſhould be cautious of coming near him, unleſs he could prevail upon Cæſar to afford him his protection" When the witneſſes were introduced, Antipater entered the court, and throwing himſelf at his father's feet, ſupplicated the grant of an impartial hearing, without prejudging his cauſe, as, in that caſe he entertained not a doubt of demonſtrating his innocence

Herod vehemently enjoined him to hold his peace, and then thus addreſſed himſelf to Varus

"I do certainly know that you, Varus, or any other unbiaſſed judge, will be fully ſatisfied that Antipater deſerves "to die but I am afraid, in the mean time, of the opinion you may conceive of my invidious fortune, as if this "calamity had juſtly befallen me for being the father of "ſuch children I have ſome right, however, to your humanity and compaſſion, for having been ſo indulgent a "father to ſuch profligate wretches As for the young "princes that are gone, I deſigned them for the government, "and trained them up at Rome, in the court and favour of "Cæſar, the better to prepare them for the exerciſe of royal "dignity and none, at laſt, were ſo great enemies to my "peace and ſafety, as thoſe that I had raiſed even to be the "envy of princes Antipater made his profit of their ruin, for "he found his account in it, as a ſecurity to himſelf in the "ſucceſſion What is now the requital this monſter deſigns me "for all theſe tokens of favour, but the entering into a practice againſt my life? I was likely to live too long, he "thought, nay, I had lived too long already, that was his "grievance The crown alone would not content him, it "ſeems, unleſs he made his way to it through the blood of "his father And in this truly he ſeemed to have ſome "colour of reaſon, for my bringing him back to court out of "a private condition, to the excluſion of the ſons I had by "the queen, in declaring him my ſucceſſor

"To confeſs myſelf to you, Varus, I am convinced "of my error I did not do well to provoke my ſons, "by cutting off the ſucceſſion, to their injury, in favour "of Antipater for what did I ever do for them comparable to what I did for him? He had a very great part "of the adminiſtration ſettled upon him during the con-

"tinuance of my life, and the ſucceſſion after my death; and, beſide other gratifications, a ſeparate revenue of fifty talents, and his expences every where upon my charge; three hundred talents upon his voyage to Rome; and himſelf the only perſon of my whole family that I recommended to Cæſar as my preſerver. Take them altogether, they had not half the wickedneſs in them of Antipater; the proofs againſt them were infinitely ſhort of what I have againſt him; and yet this daring wretch has the face to plead innocent, and does not deſpair, I perceive, of baffling truth by impoſture. Varus, look to yourſelf, for he will tell his tale well; but I know the monſter well through all his diſguiſes.

"This is the man that was ſo earneſt with me, in time paſt, to have a care of Alexander, and how I expoſed my perſon. How often would he come into my bed-chamber, and ſearch about, for fear of treachery! This man was my guardian, and my ſecurity, while I ſlept; my comforter in my mourning for the dead brothers, and one that would undertake for the duty of thoſe that were living; my champion, in fine, and my guard. When I call to mind, and conſider the addreſs and hypocriſy of this man, how artfully he laid his ſnares, and covered his deſigns, I can hardly think myſelf alive at this day, or how it was poſſible for me to eſcape the danger. But ſince my fate would it ſo, and that my greateſt enemies are to be thoſe of my own family, and thoſe I have been the kindeſt to, I ſhall only deplore the hardſhips of my inevitable deſtiny, and keep my ſorrows to myſelf; but with this reſolution, that not one man comes off that ſhall be found guilty of thirſting after my blood, though the whole houſe ſhould fall in the condemnation."

Herod being then interrupted by the confuſion of his mind, directed Nicolaus, one of his counſel, to produce the evidence againſt Antipater, who being proſtrate before the king, raiſed his head, and, in an exclamatory tone, thus proceeded:

"You have had the goodneſs, Sire, to plead my cauſe; for how can I be a parricide, and yet recorded by yourſelf for your preſerver? If my piety be only impoſture and pretence, as you are pleaſed to ſay it is, how came I to be ſo crafty in one caſe, and ſo ignorant in another, as not to underſtand, that, though men may be impoſed upon, yet the all-ſearching and all-ſeeing eye of God, that knows our hearts, will not ſuffer ſo great a wickedneſs to paſs unpuniſhed! God's vengeance overtook my brothers becauſe of their undutifulneſs to you. But what temptation had I now to practiſe upon your life! The hope of a kingdom? Why, I did reign in fact already. Was it that I thought you hated me? That was impoſſible, after ſo many demonſtrations to the contrary. Was I afraid of you? When, quite on the other hand, others ſtood in awe of me, in conſideration of the zeal I had for your ſafety. Or was it that I wanted any thing? So far from it, that all my profuſions were ſupplied out of your treaſure. So that certainly I muſt be the worſt even of men and of brutes, to be wanting in good offices towards ſo kind a father, being a perſon that you yourſelf, as you ſay, received into your favour, preferred before ſo many of your other ſons, and whom you declared king, while yourſelf were yet living, beſide other benefits in proportion, to make me the envy of other men.

"Wretch that I am! that this fatal journey ſhould afford ſo much time and matter for envy and treachery to work upon. But it was, Sire, for the ſervice of yourſelf, and of your affairs, that I undertook this voyage, and to keep Syllæus from putting affronts upon your old age. Rome is witneſs to my loyalty, and ſo is the prince of Rome, and of the world, Cæſar himſelf, that has ſo often celebrated me for my reverence to my father. Be pleaſed, I beſeech you, to receive theſe letters, that have more truth in them than all the forgeries that have been trumped up againſt me; theſe letters are my juſtification, and the infallible argument of a ſincere affection for you. You may remember, Sire, how unwillingly I took that journey, to lay myſelf at the mercy of all the enemies I left behind me. It was your command, Sire, that ruined me, how unwillingly ſoever, in forcing me to give my adverſaries time for concerting their malice againſt me.

"If I had been a parricide, divine juſtice either by ſea or land would have found me out. But I ſhall not lay the ſtreſs of my innocence upon that argument, for I know very well that you have condemned me in your heart already. All that I beg, even in this ſtate, is only that I may not ſuffer upon the credit of proofs extorted by torment; but let me rather be put to the teſt either of fire, ſcrews, or what other inſtruments of cruelty you ſhall think fit, without any mercy to a miſerable carcaſe. For if I am a parricide, no pain can be too much for me."

Theſe words were attended with ſuch energy and pathos as to excite the commiſeration of the whole court, and of Varus in particular. Herod alone remained unaffected, from a conſciouſneſs of the clearneſs of the evidence, and the conſummate hypocriſy and fallacy of Antipater.

Nicolaus then, at the king's command, having premiſed many inſtances of the craft of the culprit, and thereby obviated the effects of the commiſeration he had excited in the minds of the auditors, exhibited a long catalogue of charges againſt him, aſcribing to him all the miſchiefs of the kingdom, and eſpecially the murders of his brethren, whom he demonſtrated to have periſhed by the calumnies he raiſed againſt them. He obſerved, that he had laid plots againſt the ſurvivors as ſtanding in the way of his preferment, and commented on the folly of ſuppoſing that he, who prepared poiſon for his father, would ſpare the lives of his brethren. He then proceeded to convict him of the attempt to poiſon Herod; recapitulated the ſeveral diſcoveries that had been made, produced the evidences, and repreſented Antipater as principally acceſſary to the crime of Pheroras, the corruption of the court, and, indeed, all the calamities that had lately befallen the kingdom; nor did he conclude without expatiating largely on the ſeveral accuſations.

Varus then called upon Antipater to produce what he had to offer to clear himſelf from the accuſations laid againſt him. After ſome pauſe he briefly ſaid, "God is my witneſs that I am entirely innocent." Varus then called for the poiſon, and cauſed it to be adminiſtered to a condemned malefactor, who, having drank it, inſtantly expired. He then, after ſome private diſcourſe with Herod, tranſmitted the proceedings of the court to Cæſar, and the next day took his departure. The king commanded Antipater to be bound, and ſent the emperor an account of his proceedings.

He was charged after this with a treacherous deſign upon Salome; for a ſervant of Antiphilus brought letters from Rome, from a female attendant of the empreſs Julia, whoſe name was Acme. By her a meſſage was ſent to the king, that ſhe had found a letter, written by Salome, amongſt Julia's papers, and ſent it him privately from a motive of good-will. This letter contained the bittereſt invectives againſt the king. They were forged by Antipater, who had bribed Acme, and employed her as an inſtrument to convey them to Herod. This was rendered evident from Acme's letter to Antipater, which ran thus: "I have written to your father according to your direction, and diſpatched the letter. I am perſuaded the king will not ſpare his ſiſter after reading it. I have executed the buſineſs; do you look to the performance of your promiſe."

Upon the detection of this plot against the life of Salome, Herod was greatly alarmed, to [illegible] how [illegible] only his sister had [illegible] the [illegible] snare, nor could he avoid suspecting that [illegible] was taken off by [illegible] similar [illegible] He therefore renewed a peremptory [illegible] of bringing him to justice for all his crimes, domestic and [illegible] but was diverted from the execution of it by a severe distemper. He transmitted, however, a detail to Cæsar of Acme's part in the intrigue, and the treacherous practices against Salome. He then also for his testament, altered it, appointed Antipas to the succession in lieu of Antipater, but omitted Archelaus and Philip, through former suggestions of their excessive [illegible] He bequeathed to Cæsar, besides other presents, a thousand talents, and to the empress, her children, friends, and freemen, about five hundred more, with [illegible] considerable bounties to others. [illegible] his regard for his sister Salome by many valuable bequests. This was the purport of his last will and testament.

CHAP. XXI.

Herod's [illegible] [illegible] the golden eagle, [illegible] the [illegible] [illegible] the rabble. [illegible] Herod [illegible] [illegible] Death of Herod. [illegible] Archelaus [illegible] [illegible]

HEROD's distemper became more and more severe, [illegible] through the bodily decay [illegible] years, and the [illegible] of his mind. His calamities were not a little aggravated by the consideration of Antipater being still alive, whom he determined to bring to condign punishment in the most public manner, as soon as the state of his health would permit.

These calamities were followed by a popular sedition, which was headed by Judas the son of Sepphoris, and Matthias, the son of Margalus, two sophists, famous for their skill in the laws, and consequently highly revered by the people. They had many disciples, and were attended at their lectures by numerous audiences. When these sophists were informed of the king's languishing condition, they intimated to their friends that the present would be a convenient opportunity for [illegible] the [illegible] of God, [illegible] of all works erected in contradiction to the laws, and observed further, that the setting up of [illegible] in the temple, or the [illegible] of any living creature, was absolutely forbidden. It was [illegible] alluded to the golden eagle, which Herod had caused to be fixed over the great gate of the temple. The multitude therefore came to a resolution to pull it down, as the most glorious hazard they could run in support of the laws of their country, even if they should die in the attempt. It was represented to them, that, should they do this, it would be followed with everlasting happiness and immortal honour; while the mean spirited, and those who were regardless of virtue, [illegible] would prefer death in their beds by a disease, to an [illegible] adherence to religion and virtue.

While this populace [illegible] in [illegible] a report prevailed that the king was at the point of death, which emboldening the multitude, they mounted the temple at noon-day, and letting themselves down with ropes and axes, demolished the golden eagle in the presence of a numerous congregation of spectators. The commanding officer of the garrison no sooner had notice of this outrage, than he fell in among them with a party, seized about forty of the most active, and brought them before the king, who demanded of them if they had been so [illegible] as to demolish the golden eagle? When they replied in the affirmative, and he interrogated them whose command they had done it? they rejoined, at the command of the laws of their country; and when he further asked them how they could be so cheerful, as they must shortly die? they returned for answer, because they were assured of a [illegible] life after death.

This incensed the king to such a degree, that, seemingly unmindful of his disease, he reproached them in the most opprobrious terms, for having attempted innovations in government under colour of law, and declared, as they had behaved themselves like abandoned wretches, that they should undergo an exemplary punishment. The people, upon this, apprehending that the severity might be too far extended, preferred their request to the king that he would content himself with justice upon the ring-leaders and the prisoners, and shew mercy to the rest. Herod was at length prevailed upon, and ordered that those that came down by the ropes, and the two heads of the faction, to be burnt alive, and those that were taken together, to be delivered up to the proper officers, in order to be put to death.

By this time the king's distemper seized upon his whole frame, and produced various symptoms, such as an intermitting fever, an intolerable itching, dropsical tumours about his feet, an inflammation in the abdomen, putrefaction that caused worms, contraction of the nerves, and convulsions in general. It was the opinion of those who pretended to divination, that these calamities were inflicted upon him as a judgment for his rigorous proceedings towards the rabbies. But notwithstanding the complication of his diseases and the torments under which he laboured, he was still so desirous of life, that, in this very extremity, he forgot [illegible] [illegible] [illegible] hopes of his recovery. He crossed the Jordan, and [illegible] the warm baths of Callirrhoe, which [illegible] the [illegible] [illegible] a water not only medicinal, but [illegible] the [illegible]. Here the physicians advised him to [illegible] the whole body in warm oil; but upon his being let down into the vessel, his eyes and senses failed him together, and his fit was so alarming, that his attendants exclaimed with horror, and [illegible] a little [illegible] But at length, when he found there was no hope, he ordered the soldiers fifty drachmæ a man, and left money [illegible] great amount, to be divided amongst his governors and friends.

When he came back to Jericho, and found himself in despair, he seemed to set death at defiance, but resolved upon the most dreadful that ever entered into the heart of man. He sent an order throughout Judæa for seizing all the nobility, and shutting them up in the circus, called also the hippodrome, or horse-course. He then called to him Salome, his sister, and Alexas, her husband, and gave them this charge: "I know that the Jews will celebrate my death by a festival; but I shall take care not to want mourners, or the splendid pomp of funeral solemnities, provided you will but follow my directions. Be it your care then, the moment I expire, to send soldiers to encompass the circus, and slay all those who are in their custody. This will be an infallible means of making "the whole province of Judæa, and every particular family in it true mourners for my death."

Herod had no sooner given these orders, than his deputies brought him letters of information from Rome, that Acme was put to death at Cæsar's command, and that Antipater was under sentence of condemnation; but it was added, that, if Herod chose to mitigate the punishment, and banish him, he had the emperor's permission. This complaisant message procured him some little relief; but soon relapsing, as he was at that time afflicted with a violent cough, he had some thoughts of laying violent hands on himself, and, to that end, called for an apple and a knife, as if he had been about to cut and pare it. Hiing looked round him with an eye of caution, he raised his hand with the point towards his breast, which being perceived by his nephew Achiab, he wrested the knife out of his hand, and prevented the seemingly intended mischief

Upon this a rumour was spread that the king was dead, of which Antipater availing himself, tampered with his keepers, for a sum of money, to release him but the principal officer not only rejected his request, but gave instant notice of it to the king, who, upon hearing it, burst out into a vehement exclamation, and ordered his guards immediately to dispatch him, and see his body deposited in the castle of Hyrcanion He then altered his testament once more, declared Archelaus, his eldest son, successor, and constituted Antipas a tetrarch

Herod died five days after his son, having reigned thirty-four years from the death of Antigonus, and thirty-seven since he was declared king by the Romans He was fortunate in every other respect but that of his family, being advanced to the throne from a private station, which he maintained a series of years, and was at length succeeded by one of his sons

Before the soldiers knew of the king's death, Salome and her husband went to the circus, and dismissed those who were confined there, in order to be slain by the king's command They did this upon a pretence that Herod had changed his mind, but as soon as they were released, proclamation was made of the king's death The soldiery and populace being assembled at the amphitheatre of Jericho, Ptolemy the keeper of the royal signet, made a speech in honour of the deceased, whom he mentioned as a fortunate prince, condoling with them, at the same time, for so sensible a loss He then read the epistle which had been left for the soldiers, and contained an earnest recommendation of his successor to their loyalty and allegiance After this he read the will by which Philip was to inherit Trachon and the adjacent country, Antipas was made tetrarch, and Archelaus appointed to succeed to the throne He left orders for the delivery of his ring to Cæsar, who was to be informed of every transaction; as the whole was to be confirmed by the emperor's sole authority and direction

This was followed with joyful congratulations to Archelaus upon his accession to the throne, both from the soldiers and populace Preparations were then made for the funeral of Herod, for which neither care or cost was wanting to render it as pompous as possible The bier was covered with an embroidery of gold and jewels, and an intermixture of purple The corpse was placed on a purple bed of various contexture, a diadem was put on the head, with a golden crown about it, and a scepre fixed in the right hand Next the bier were the deceased king's son and kindred The guards, Thracian troops, Germans and Gauls, marched at the head of the solemnity, as in form and order of battle To close the procession, five hundred officers, domestics and freemen, brought up the train The body was carried two hundred furlongs to Herodion, where it was interred according to mandate

END OF THE FIRST BOOK

FLAVIUS JOSEPHUS

ON THE

WARS OF THE JEWS.

BOOK II

CHAP I

Archelaus appoints the ceremony of mourning and feaſting. His gracious declaration in favour of the people. They are clamorous on the ſubject of grievances. Raiſe a tumult on account of thoſe who had been put to death for the demolition of the golden eagle. The multitude overcome the guards, but are afterwards routed by the whole army. Three thouſand Jews are ſlain. Archelaus goes to Rome, leaving the adminiſtration to Philip in his abſence. Sabinus advances to Cæſarea in his way to Judæa. Varus puts a ſtop to his journey. Sabinus goes to Jeruſalem, and demands poſſeſſion of ſome caſtles and treaſure. Meets with a formal refuſal from the officers. Antipas goes to Rome, and prefers his claim to the ſucceſſion. Sabinus and Salome exhibit a charge againſt Archelaus. His defence. Cæſar attends to the reſpective allegations of the parties, and proceeds to trial. Antipater, the ſon of Salome, opens the cauſe againſt Archelaus. Nicolaus pleads for the defendant. Archelaus graciouſly received by Cæſar. The court adjourned.

THE neceſſity Archelaus was under of going to Rome proved the occaſion of new diſturbances. After a public mourning for his father ſeven days, and he had given a very expenſive feaſt to the multitude, (a cuſtom ruinous to many of the Jews, who cannot diſpenſe with it,) he arrayed himſelf in white, and went up to the temple, where the people accoſted him with the loudeſt congratulatory acclamations. He returned the compliment, from a throne of ſtate, in a manner becoming the dignity of his character. Having returned them thanks for the zeal they had ſhewn in the funeral of his father, and the royal honours they had paid to himſelf as to an anointed king, he obſerved withal, "that he would not at preſent take upon him either the authority or name of a king, until Cæſar, the declared lord "and maſter of all by the teſtament of his father, ſhould confirm the ſucceſſion: that, for this cauſe, when the army "would have ſet the crown upon his head at Jericho, he "would not accept it, but that he would make abundant requitals, not to the ſoldiers only, but the people, for their "good will towards him, when the ſuperior power ſhould "have given him a competent title to the kingdom, as it "ſhould be his ſtudy, upon all occaſions, to be more complacent than his father."

The people were highly gratified by this declaration, and preſently put him to the teſt by preferring ſeveral petitions. The purport of ſome was to have their taxes abated, of others to have them wholly remitted, and of others for a general releaſe of priſoners. Archelaus readily complied with the whole, in order to ſecure their attachment, which being done, he ſacrificed and feaſted with his friends.

Soon after this, however, a great multitude, deſirous of innovations, aſſembled together, and declining the ſubject of the common mourning for the death of the king, began to murmur at the public grievances, and particularly to lament the caſe of thoſe who were put to death by order of Herod for demoliſhing the golden eagle which he had placed over the gate of the temple. This lamentation was expreſſed by beating their breaſts, tearing their hair, and outrageous exclamations for the loſs of ſo many pious virtuous men, who had died martyrs to the religion and laws of their country. They demanded juſtice upon Herod's mercenaries, thoſe accurſed inſtruments of his cruelty, the expulſion of Herod's high-prieſt, and the appointment of a man of more piety and integrity to that ſacred and dignified office.

Archelaus was highly incenſed at theſe mutinous proceedings, but reſtrained himſelf from taking vengeance on the ringleaders, as his journey to Rome required expedition, and immediate ſeverity might be productive of diſaſtrous conſequences. Thinking it more adviſeable to have recourſe to ſoothing admonitions, he ſent a principal officer of his army to quiet the ſeditious by perſuaſion, rather than by force. But the ringleaders of the tumult drove him away by ſtones from the temple, without ſuffering him to ſpeak a word. Archelaus ſent other officers on the ſame errand but they were treated in the same manner, insomuch, that it plainly appeared, they wanted only numbers to commence an open rebellion

The feast of unleavened bread, or the passover, being near at hand, and annually celebrated by abundance of sacrifices, crowds of people resorted from all parts of the metropolis, on account of being present at that solemnity Amongst the rest were divers of the faction of the two rabbies, Judas and Matthias, who came thither to lament the death of those two venerable martyrs, and wait an opportunity of inflaming the multitude to sedition

Archelaus had the prudent caution to send a tribune, with a band of soldiers, with orders to seize the ringleaders if they should continue refractory, as the most effectual means of obviating the danger of a general riot The multitude made head against this party some they slew with stones, dangerously wounded the tribune, and afterwards betook themselves to their sacrifices as if nothing had happened Archelaus, finding that the riot could not be suppressed without bloodshed, turned the whole army loose upon them, the foot by way of the city, and the horse before the walls The former fell suddenly upon them as they were sacrificing, and killed near three thousand at the very altar The remainder dispersed and fled to the mountains, and Archelaus causing proclamation to be made, commanding all people to depart to their own habitations, to put an end to the festival

This sedition being quelled, Archelaus, with his mother, and his three particular friends Poplas, Ptolemy, and Nicolaus, embarked for Rome, leaving Philip behind him, both as viceroy and trustee of his private affairs Salome, with her sons accompanied him, as did several of his kindred under pretence of assisting him in the confirmation of his succession, but [illegible] to prefer an accusation against him for his breach of the laws in the violation of the holy temple

Upon their arrival at Cæsarea, they were met by Sabinus governor of Syria who was then going up to Judæa, to secure the effects that Herod had left behind him But Varus at the instance of Archelaus, and mediation of Ptolemy, restrained Sabinus from proceeding any farther So that to gratify Varus, he neither demanded the castles or the treasure to the prejudice of Archelaus, and passed his word that he would do nothing in the business without the approbation of Cæsar, and remained where he was

But as soon as Varus, was gone for Antioch, and Archelaus for Rome, Sabinus, upon the removal of these obstacles, went to Jerusalem, seized on the palace, and sent from thence to the governors of the castles, and the officers of the treasury, the former to deliver up to him possession of the castles, and the latter the accounts of the treasure But the officers faithful to the trust reposed in them by Archelaus, evaded compliance with this answer, "That what they had in charge was rather the property of Cæsar than Archelaus"

In the mean time Antipas went to Rome also, in order to prefer his claim to the kingdom, insisting upon the validity of the former testament, in which the succession was settled upon him Besides he was promised the interest of Salome, and others of their kindred that sailed with Archelaus in the support of his claim He was accompanied by his mother and Ptolemy the brother of Nicolaus an approved friend of Herod, a circumstance of weight but his chief dependance was upon Irenæus, a shrewd and subtle logician Antipas relying on the ability of these advocates, totally disregarded those who advised him to pay some deference to the seniority of Archelaus, and the authority of his father in his second testament, and seemed perfectly secure of the kingdom when they came to Rome, he was joined by all the pretended friends of Archelaus, those especially who were desirous of shaking off the yoke of monarchy and being immediately under the Roman government, who, in case they could not obtain their wishes, preferred Antipas for their king

Antipas had great dependance on the interest of Sabinus, who had already exhibited an accusation against Archelaus, by letters to Cæsar, and on the other hand, highly commended his character Salome and her adherents stated their charge against Archelaus, and presented it to the emperor Archelaus then drew up the grounds of his claim, and the several heads of his justification, which with his father's signet, and an account of the bequests he made him were transmitted to Cæsar by the hands of Ptolemy

When the emperor had duly weighed the respective allegations, the greatness of the kingdom, the variety of large revenues, the numerous family of Herod, together with the contents of the letters of Varus and Sabinus he called a council of the Roman nobility, where Caius Cæsar, the son of Agrippa, and his daughter Julia, was, for the first time, called to take his place at the board and then proceeded to the trial The cause was opened by Antipater the son of Salome, an advocate of great abilities, who urged his plea against Archelaus by stating, "That Archelaus had long since exercised sovereign authority in effect, and that it was now but matter of form to contend about the name A hearing before Cæsar was nothing to him that has already refused him for judge That Herod was no sooner dead, but people were immediately engaged, and suborned, to set the crown upon his head, while he himself, did not only sit like a king in royal state, and upon a golden throne, but acted like one too, as in changing the order of the militia disposing of charges, receiving and granting petitions, exercising the power of life and death in public crimes, setting his father's prisoners at liberty &c which are all regal privileges That this person, that has already engrossed to himself the powers and ensigns of royalty, coming to Cæsar only for the title of it, makes Augustus but a shadow of a prince, or a king in name, not in effect Farther, (says Antipater,) what avails all the solemnity of his mourning weeds for his dead father? He looks sorrowfully all day, and then sits up feasting and making merry all night What was it, at last, but the detestation the people had for this hypocrisy that raised the late sedition? But the main stress of the charge was yet to come, which was a horrible slaughter about the temple It was a festival day, the people gathered together to worship, and pay their devotions, and they themselves were made the sacrifice Their throats, in short, were cut, and such heaps of dead bodies piled up in the temple, as, in the most implacable and merciless of foreign wars, was hardly ever heard of Herod was so well acquainted with the cruelty of this man's nature, that it was almost impossible for him ever to give him the least hope of a crown, so long as he was in his right mind And that, alas! was the king's case in the latter testament his mind was more out of order than his body, and he did not know what he did Beside this, after all this, there was no inability or defect charged upon Antipas, the successor, by the former will, but the people give him the character of a prince very well qualified for the royal function Or if it should be supposed that Herod was in truth, sound, and in his right senses, Archelaus has as good as abdicated the royal dignity, by acting against the laws of the constitution What havock would he make now, if he had Cæsar's authority to cover him in his cruelties, that does all this upon his own account, without any power at all"

When Antipater had thus powerfully argued the point, and produced a great number of the kindred of Archelaus to prove the several parts of his accusation he sat down, and Nicolaus rose in behalf of the defendant, alledging, "That the slaughter committed in the temple was not only of absolute necessity, but the people that were killed were Cæ-

"ſar's enemies. He ſhewed likewiſe that for the other pre-"tended crimes, the preſent oppoſers of Archelaus were "themſelves the adviſers of them. As to the validity "of the ſecond teſtament, he argued, that it ought to "ſtand, in regard that Herod, had at that time, the con-"ſideration and reſpect to refer the confirmation of it to Cæ-"ſar. Now he that had the judgment to know the right "lord and maſter, had certainly ſenſe enough to appoint the "right heir."

Nicolaus having thus ſpoken conciſely, but pointedly, in vindication of Archelaus, the latter ſuddenly caſt himſelf at Cæſar's feet, who raiſed him with ſuch ſingular grace and benignity, as indicated that he thought him worthy of the ſucceſſion, but no poſitive reſolution was entered into at that time. This being done, Cæſar diſmiſſed the council for that day, and entered into a conſultation with his friends reſpecting the deciſion of the caſe, whether it were fitting to conſtitute any of thoſe named in Herod's teſtaments as his ſucceſſor, or make an equal participation of the principality amongſt the whole family, as they were numerous, and would require a great revenue to ſupport them with honour.

CHAP. II.

Death of Malthace, the mother of Archelaus. Great uproar amongſt the Jews. Sabinus inflames it. The feaſt of Pentecoſt. The Jews draw up in form. Sabinus preſſes Varus for relief, and takes ſanctuary in the Tower of Phaſael. A bloody conflict between the Jews and the Romans. The Romans ſet fire to the galleries of the temple, which makes great ſlaughter amongſt the Jews. The ſoldiers plunder the ſacred treaſure. The Jews ſummon the palace to ſurrender, and ſit down before it. They offer Sabinus conditions, which he refuſes. Factions and broils throughout Judæa. Exploits of Judas, a notorious robber. Ambition and courage of Simon. Athronges and his four brothers enterpriſing men.

BEFORE Cæſar came to any poſitive determination as to the ſucceſſion, Malthace the mother of Archelaus, fell into a diſtemper, and departed this life. Letters alſo at the ſame time were received from Varus out of Syria, containing information of a revolt amongſt the Jews, and of his going up to Jeruſalem upon Archelaus's journey to Rome, to reſtrain the incendiaries, and reſtore peace and good order. When he found advice and remonſtrance ineffectual, and that the multitude were ſtill refractory, he quartered one of the legions he brought out of Syria in the city, and ſo returned to Antioch.

But when Sabinus came afterwards to Jeruſalem, he furniſhed them with new occaſion for tumults; for depending on the reinforcement of troops of Varus, and a band of his own domeſtics well armed, and at hand, to ſubſerve the purpoſe of his avarice and rapine, his deſign was to get poſſeſſion of the caſtles and Herod's treaſures by force, and menace upon the governors and officers who had them in charge. It was now the feaſt of Pentecoſt, or fiftieth day, ſo called from the term of the revolutions, after ſeven times ſeven days after the paſſover, ſo that the people aſſembled in great numbers, not from a religious motive, but diſcontent with the preſent ſituation of affairs. They repaired to Jeruſalem from Galilee, Idumæa, Jericho, and the country beyond Jordan, with the inhabitants of Judæa, who for number and courage, ſurpaſſed all the reſt. They divided themſelves into three bodies, and pitched their tents in three quarters; one upon the north ſide of the temple, another upon the ſouth towards the circus, and the third to the weſtward of the palace, ſo that the Romans, by theſe means, were beſet on all ſides.

Sabinus, alarmed at the number and reſolution of the enemies, preſſed Varus, by divers meſſengers, to come to his ſuccour immediately, or his legion would be cut to pieces. He reached, however, the higheſt tower of the fortreſs, that commands all the reſt, and, from the name of Herod's brother, that was ſlain by the Parthians, is called Phaſaelus, and then gave a ſignal to the ſoldiers of that legion to break in upon the enemy; for ſuch was his puſillanimity, that he durſt not lead on the very men he was appointed to command.

The Romans, according to order, made a vigorous attempt upon the temple, and a deſperate engagement took place between them and the Jews, in which the latter, while they had no help from above, either with darts or arrows, were worſted; but when once the Jews got poſſeſſion of the galleries, and galled the Romans from thence, many of them were cut off, and the reſt were too far diſtant to take their revenge; though, if they had been hand to hand, they would have been much too hard for them.

After this the Romans ſet fire to the galleries, which, for workmanſhip, proportion, and ornament, were incomparable. Many of the Jews periſhed in the flames; ſome were cut off by the enemy upon their fall, others puſhed from the battlements; ſome again in deſpair, chooſing rather to die by the ſword than by fire, laid violent hands on themſelves. Thoſe that made an attempt on the Romans from the walls, were deſtroyed without any difficulty, till, at length, they were either ſlain or ſcattered. The ſoldiers plundered the ſacred treaſure, carrying off four hundred talents, and leaving to Sabinus the remainder.

This loſs of men and treaſure brought a more powerful reinforcement of the Jews upon the Romans than the other, both for valour and number. They ſummoned the palace to ſurrender, and ſet down before it, with a menace of giving no quarter unleſs they immediately quitted it, and offering Sabinus liberty if he would depart with his legion. There were many of the king's party who deſerted the Romans, and aſſiſted the Jews. But the moſt warlike body, amounting to three thouſand men of Sebaſte, went over to the Romans, under the command of Rufus and Gratus. The Jews ſtill preſſed the ſiege, and attempted the walls of the fortreſs, calling upon Sabinus to retire, without oppoſing himſelf to the reſolution they had taken of recovering their liberty. Sabinus was inclined to provide for his ſafety, but diſtruſted the aſſurances the Jews gave him, and ſuſpected their preferred lenity as a bait laid to enſnare him. This conſideration, together with the hope of relief from Varus, induced him to ſtand the ſiege.

Judæa was at this time involved in tumults and factions, an opportunity now offering for pretenders to ſtart their claim to government. A band of two thouſand veterans in Idumæa, who had ſerved under Herod, had ſeveral encounters with the king's troops, and in particular with Achiab, Herod's kinſman, who often ſallied upon them out of ſtrong holds, but could not cope with them in the open plain.

In Sepphoris, a city of Galilee, one Judas, the ſon of Hezekias, leader of the band that was taken by Herod, aſſembled a conſiderable party, forced the king's magazines, and arming himſelf and companions out of thoſe ſtores, ſet oppoſition at defiance, and ravaged the country.

In Peræa alſo, on the other ſide of the river, Simon, one of the late king's domeſtics, relying on the ſymmetry, agility, and ſtrength of his perſon, placed a crown upon his head, and, aſſiſted by a band of robbers he had collected, burnt down the palace at Jericho, laid ſeveral ſtately buildings in aſhes round about it, and procured immenſe booty by rapine. Nay, he would have laid waſte the whole country, if Gratus, who commanded the king's foot, had not brought the Trachonite archers, and a warlike body from Sebaſte, to their relief. In fine, they came to action, when the robber was overcome, and great part of his foot cut off. As he himſelf was upon the flight acroſs a ſteep bottom, Gratus felled him by an oblique ſtroke on the neck, and thereby put an end to his life and depredations The royal palaces, about Amathus and the borders of Jordan, were also burnt down by another fearl ous gang that came out of Perea

There was also at the same time a certain shepherd, named Athronges, who had the confidence to set up for king He had strength of body, and resolution of mind, equal to any enterprize and was aided and abetted by four brothers of the same qualifications, who served him in his incursions both as officers and counsellors Upon affairs of moment, he ascended a throne, with a crown upon his head, pronounced judgment without appeal, and in every instance assumed regal authority Under this usurped sanction he continued to over-run the country for some time destroying whatever he met with, and exercising hostilities towards the Romans, the king's troops, and even the Jews themselves, if there was a probability of gaining any booty These free-booters once met, near Emmaus, a convoy with corn and arms, which the Romans were carrying to one of their legions, and encountering them, killed Arius, their centurion, with forty of his best men, and would have destroyed the whole, if Gratus, with his troops from Sebaste, had not come speedily to their relief Having thus plundered both foreigners and their own countrymen for some time, three of the brothers at length were taken, the eldest by Archelaus, the two next by Gratus and Ptolemy, and the fourth surrendered himself to Archelaus, upon conditions Thus ended the enterprizes of these desperadoes while Judæa might be said to be over-run with depredations and rapine

CHAP III

Varus joins the Romans against the Jews Sepphoris burnt to the ground Sappho taken and plundered Emmaus laid in ashes Upon the approach of Varus to Jerusalem, the Jews quit the siege into fermation The citizens clear themselves of all seditious practices and welcome Varus into the town Near 2000 of the ringleaders are punished with crucifixion Varus discharges the Arabian auxiliaries for their non-conformity to military discipline His generosity towards the Jews of Idumæa

VARUS having received intelligence from Sabinus, and the chief officers at Jerusalem, that the Roman legion there was in danger of being cut off, he hastened with all expedition to their relief, and marched with the two other legions he had under his command and four troops of horse, to Ptolemais, ordering the auxiliaries, that were sent by the kings and governors of cities, to join him there at the rendezvous The people of Berytus, as he passed through their city, furnished him with a reinforcement of fifteen hundred men, well armed Upon his coming to Ptolemais, Aretas king of Arabia, (a bitter enemy to Herod,) joined him with a considerable number of horse and foot When he had mustered his forces, he sent a detachment into Galilee, under command of his friend Gallus, who soon after encountered a party, totally routed them, entered the city of Sepphoris, burnt it to the ground, and made all the inhabitants slaves

Varus himself marched with the main army into Samaria, but spared the city, because he found the inhabitants had not joined in the late commotions He encamped at Arus, a village belonging to Ptolemy, which the Arabians plundered, merely because he was a friend to Herod The army advanced next to Sappho, a fortified place, which they took, rifled, and pillaged The Arabians carried all before them with fire and sword Emmaus was abandoned by its inhabitants, and then burnt by command of Varus, in revenge for the deaths of Arius and his companions

Thence he marched to Jerusalem, where the Jews, upon the very tidings of approach, quitted the siege, dispersed, and took shelter in the fields and woods, but the citizens, on the contrary, maintained their ground, and received the conqueror with due honours They cleared themselves from all suspicion of joining in the late revolt, alledging that they had raised no commotions, but had been forced to admit the multitude on account of its being the day of a grand festival, so that they were rather besieged themselves, together with the Romans, than accessary to the least mutiny or sedition

Varus had been met on his entrance by Joseph, the nephew of Archelaus, with Rufus and Gratus, the king's generals, at the head of the Roman soldiers and the troops of Sebaste, all in their military habits Sabinus, from consciousguilt, to avoid the presence of Varus, had stolen away out of the city, and landed about the sea-side Varus, in the mean time, dispersed his troops up and down the country, in quest of the ringleaders of this tumult They apprehended great numbers, of whom those who appeared to have the least concern were put into custody, but such as were most criminal he ordered to be crucified, to the amount of about two thousand

Varus was informed that there remained in Idumæa ten thousand Jews still in arms Finding, however, the Arabians did not act like soldiers and men of honour, but gave themselves wholly up to spoil and rapine, laying the country waste wherever they came, in opposition to his will, he dismissed them, and, at the head of his own legion, marched against the revolters but, before it proceeded to blows, at the instance of Achiab, they surrendered and laid down their arms The Roman governor treated the commonalty with lenity, but sent the officers to answer for their conduct to Cæsar Finding some of Herod's kinsmen in the number of revolters, he proceeded against them as traitors, for taking up arms against their king, and having thus restored tranquility to Jerusalem, he left the former legion as a guard, and then returned to Antioch

CHAP IV

The Jews accuse Archelaus before Cæsar, and petition for the free exercise of their religion The emperor calls a council upon the occasion Hears the allegations of both parties, by their deputies, on the one hand, and those of Archelaus, and his adherents, on the other Nicolaus pleads the cause of Archelaus Cæsar, having duly weighed the whole matter, settles the government, and makes the disposition according to the will of Herod

AFTER matters had been thus accommodated in Judæa, the pretensions of Archelaus were delayed by an accusation which the Jews had preferred against him at Rome, by fifty deputies, who had been sent from Jerusalem before the tumults broke forth, and that with the permission of Varus The purport of their embassy was to address the emperor for the liberty of their country, and the exercise of their religion, and their petition was signed by 8000 Jews, principal inhabitants of Rome

This being a point of importance, Cæsar called a council of the Roman nobility, and his own particular friends, to meet in the temple of Apollo, upon mount Palatine, a stately and superb structure of his own erecting The council being assembled the Jews and their ambassadors were ranged on the one hand, and Archelaus and his adherents on the other His kindred maintained a neutrality, as, from their envy and hatred, they would not espouse his cause, nor would they be seen to take part with his accusers, so that they acted from a two-fold motive Amongst others was Philip, the brother of Archelaus, whom Varus sent before for two reasons the one that he might be enabled to assist his brother upon the occasion, the other, that, in case Augustus Cæsar should think fit to make a distribution of the possessions of Herod amongst his children he might come in for his share

The deputies of the Jews being called upon to ſet forth their complaints, and then prefer their petition, addreſſed the court to the following effect

"That Herod never demeaned himſelf like a king; but, "on the contrary, as the moſt intolerable tyrant upon the "face of the earth That his cruelty did not ſtop at the pro-"fuſion of innocent blood, and the violation of juſtice but "that he made the very living wiſh themſelves dead That "he had not only tear the bodies of his ſubjects to pieces with "torments, but ſtript his towns and cities of all that was "choice and precious, and gave it away in oſtentation to "foreigners, facrificing the very lives too of the Jews to "ſtrangers Inſtead of the bleſſings of their ancient laws "and liberties, he left his people nothing but beggary and "iniquity in exchange, inſomuch that they ſuffered more "plagues ſince his coming to the crown, than their forefa-"thers had ever felt ſince their deliverance from Xerxes out "of the captivity of Babylon

"The Jews (they ſaid) had been now ſo uſed to ſlavery, "that they were grown modeſt and patient under the yoke, "even to the degree of entailing a voluntary ſervitude upon "their poſterity in the perſon of Archelaus, the ſon of the "late tyrant whom they ſaluted as king immediately upon "the death of his father They mourned for Herod toge-"ther, and offered up their joint vows for the long and "proſperous reign of his ſucceſſor, and, then to put it out "of doubt that he was the true ſon of the inhuman father, "he made his auſpicious entrance upon the government "with the ſlaughter of three thouſand citizens and, the "better to entitle himſelf to the ſucceſſion this maſſacre "was his oblation to Court three thouſand victims, and "all this upon an holy day, and the carcaſſes piled up in the "holy temple

"What wonder is it for men that have outlived ſo many "miſeries, and eſcaped ſo dangerous a reel to own their "averſion to this man, and to fall (if periſh they muſt) like "men of honour with their faces to the enemy? All the "Jews deſire at the hands of the Romans, is only that Cæ-"ſar will judge the wretched remainder of them ſo far wor-"thy of pity, as not to expoſe them to the rigour of their "merciless oppreſſors, but rather to annex Judæa to Syria "and range them under the laws and rules of the Roman "government It will then be ſeen whether the Jews are, "in truth, ſo turbulent and ſeditious a ſort of people as they "are given out to be, when they fall once into the hands of "humane and temperate governors" With this petition the deputies cloſed their charge

Nicolaus roſe in behalf of Archelaus and, in his reply, cleared both him and Herod from the accuſations brought againſt them, and then proceeded, in very pointed language, to characterize the nation of the Jews as averſe to any government, and more particularly to that of monarchy, concluding his ſpeech with ſome ſevere remarks upon the relations of Archelaus, who had deſerted his cauſe and joined his accuſers

When the emperor had heard the arguments on both ſides, he diſmiſſed the court and, after ſome few days deliberation, beſtowed upon Archelaus one half of Herod's kingdom, under the title of ethnarch, with a promiſe of making him king, if he ſhould appear worthy of that dignity The other half he divided into two tetrarchies, which he gave to two other ſons of Herod, one to Philip, the other to Antipas, who had conteſted the ſovereignty with Archelaus There fell to his lot the country beyond the river, and Galilee, producing a revenue of two hundred talents But Batanæa, Trachon, Auranites, and ſome part of the land of Zenon, about Jamnia, were aſſigned to Philip, and yielded a revenue of an hundred talents In Archelaus's ethnarchy were comprized Idumæa, all Judæa, and Samaria, which laſt was remitted a fourth part of its tribute, as a reward for not joining in the rebellion with their neighbours Straton's Tower, Sebaſte, Joppa, and Jeruſalem, were all caſt into the ſhare of Archelaus but Gaza, Gadara, and Hippon, Grecian cities, were detached from the kingdom, and annexed to Syria The revenue of Archelaus amounted, upon the whole, to four hundred talents

Cæſar beſtowed upon Salome, beſides what was bequeathed by will of Herod, Jamnia, Azotus, and Phaſaelis He gave her alſo a palace at Aſkalon, which was valued at ſixty talents; but was ſubjected to the juriſdiction of the ethnarchy. When Cæſar had thus diſcharged all Herod's bequeſts, he granted to his two virgin daughters 500 000 drachmæ, and gave them in marriage to the ſons of Pheroras But after this family diſtribution he made a liberal diviſion of a thouſand talents more, which were bequeathed to himſelf, reſerving only ſome particular preſents in memory of the deceaſed

CHAP V.

Exploits of a ſpurious Alexander His impoſtures detected, and he is ſent to the gallies The firſt projector put to death

AT this time there was a man, by birth a Jew, but brought up at Sidon with the freeman of a Roman citizen, who falſely pretended on account of the reſemblance of their countenance, to be that very Alexander who was ſlain by Herod This man came to Rome to practiſe his impoſture, and had with him, for countenance and counſel, another Jew who was perfectly acquainted with the attendants and intrigues of the court of Herod His companion inſtructed him to give out, that the people who were employed by his father to put him and Ariſtobulus to death, had ſo great a compaſſion for them, that they ſubſtituted other bodies in their places, and conveyed the brothers out of the way This paſſed current with many Jews in Crete, who furniſhed the pretender with plentiful ſupplies for travelling in ſplendour From thence he proceeded to Melos, where he experienced more reſpect and bounty, nay, he ſo far impoſed upon the public credulity, that he took ſeveral of his friends along with him to Rome Upon his arrival at Puteoli, the Jews of that place made him ſumptuous preſents, and the friends of his father treated him as a ſovereign prince The ſtriking reſemblance, in fine, procured him ſuch credit, that as many as had ſeen Alexander would not heſitate to ſwear this was the man The report was ſo prevalent, that the whole body of the Jews who were at Rome came in crowds to ſee him, and innumerable multitudes ſtood in the avenues, through which he was carried in a ſedan by the inhabitants of Melos, who kept him a degree train at their own proper charges

But Cæſar, who knew perfectly well the lineaments of Alexander's face, becauſe he had been accuſed by Herod before him, ſuſpecting the fraud, ſent to one Celadus, and ordered him to bring the young man to him When Cæſar ſaw him, he immediately diſcerned the fallacy in his countenance, and when he diſcovered that his whole body was of a coarſer texture, and more robuſt form, like that of a ſlave, he was convinced that the whole was an impoſture But he was moſt aſtoniſhed at the effrontery of his reply, on being aſked concerning Ariſtobulus, which was, "That he was living, but left on purpoſe at Cyprus, for fear of treachery, as it would be more difficult for plotters to get them into their power while they were ſeparate"

Cæſar then took him by himſelf privately, aſſured him he had diſcovered the fallacy and that he would ſpare his life, if he would own to him who had perſuaded him to adopt that mode of impoſition Having promiſed compliance, he went with Cæſar, and pointed to the Jew that had adviſed him to it in order to get money for, in fact, the ſum he raiſed upon this piece of chicanery, was more than Alexander himſelf could have procured had he been alive Cæſar laughed at the contrivance and condemned the ſpurious Alexander to the gallies on account of his ſtrength, and the projector of the impoſture to death but the people of

Melos had been sufficiently punished for their folly, by the expences they had been at on his account

CHAP VI

Archelaus is accused of oppression to Cæsar, and banished to Vienna, a city of Gaul A foreboding dream The exposition Another very extraordinary dream of the princess Glaphyra, who has a vision of her first husband Her death

WHEN Archelaus took possession of his ethnarchy, he treated not only the Jews but the Samaritans with great rigour, from a resentment of former disputes between them In consequence of this they sent embassies to complain to Cæsar, who in the ninth year of his government, banished him to Vienna, a city of Gaul, and sequestered his effects

A report prevailed that Archelaus before his summons to attend the emperor, dreamt he saw nine ears of corn large and full, devoured by oxen, and that when he sent for several who were supposed to be skilled in divination, some said one thing, and some another, till at length Simon, one of the sect of Essenes, gave it this interpretation "That the ears of corn denoted years, and the oxen the vicissitude of things, as the earth is overturned by the plough, that the ethnarch should reign as many years as there was ears of corn, and, after many revolutions, depart this life" It so fell out that, five days after this interpretation, Archelaus was called upon his trial

There was another memorable dream of the princess Glaphyra, daughter of Archelaus, king of Cappadocia, and wife of Archelaus, the present subject of our history Her first husband was Alexander, the son of Herod, by whom he was put to death This princess, after his death, married Juba, king of Lybia, and, upon his decease, returned home, and lived with her father in a state of widowhood Archelaus, the ethnarch, became so enamoured of her at first sight, that he put away Mariamne, and married her Soon after this she came back into Judæa, and had there a vision of her first husband Alexander, who thus seemed to reproach her "Could not your marriage with one husband after me suffice but you must take a third, and this under my own roof? and, to add to thy criminality, my own brother? These are injuries not to be borne But you shall soon return to me again" Glaphyra survived this dream but two days

CHAP VII

The ethnarchy of Archelaus reduced into a Roman province The sedition of Judas of Galilee Three sorts of Jews Pharisees, Sadducees, and Essenes Of the Essenes Their sentiments and opinion of marriage, their effects in common, their apparel, frugality, and manner of living, their principles of conscience, peaceable disposition, and fidelity The method of admission into the society, and of punishing offenders Their piety, virtue, and contempt of death Their opinion of the soul Veneration for the ancients A different sort of Essenes Brief description of the sects of the Pharisees and Sadducees

THE ethnarchy of Archelaus being now reduced into a Roman province, Coponius a man of equestrian rank, was vested by Cæsar with a full commission to govern it Under his administration a certain Galilean, named Judas, stirred up the people to revolt, on a suggestion that, in submitting to the Romans, and paying them tribute, they acknowledged a supremacy due to God alone This Judas was the leader of a peculiar sect, and entertained tenets peculiar to himself

There are among the Jews three philosophical sects distinguished by the different denominations of Pharisees, Sadducees, and Essenes, which last maintain a more rigid discipline than the rest

The Essenes are Jews by birth, and seem to have a greater affection for one another than the rest of the sects They reject pleasure as an evil, but esteem continence, and a conquest over the passions as a cardinal virtue They neglect wedlock, but select the children of others, while they are young and docile, and adopt and train them up as their own They do not absolutely deny the moral fitness of marriage, and the succession of mankind continued thereby, but guard against the frailty of women, and can hardly admit an inviolable attachment to one man

They hold wealth, and what are called the good things of this world, in contempt, so that they are equally strangers to riches and poverty, as they have all things in common or, in other words, the whole society live like brethren, being all equal sharers in one common patrimony upon such a principle no man can be contemptible for being poor, nor honourable for being rich

They think oil a defilement and value themselves upon the simplicity of their appearance, provided the garments are white and clean

They appoint stewards for the management of their common stock, and leave it to their discretion to make distribution out of it to every man in proportion according to his need

They have no certain place of abode, but disperse themselves through different cities, towns, and villages, where they are ever ready and open to receive and entertain any of their own sect and treat them, though strangers, with the same familiarity as if intimately acquainted

They carry nothing with them, when they travel but arms for the security of their persons They appoint, in every place, some one to take care of their strange brethren, and provide them with lodging, food apparel, and necessaries in general Their dress the wear resembles that of children when they are under the charge of masters and governors Nor do they change their garments or shoes, but when one is torn, and the other worn out

They neither buy or sell among themselves but supply each other's wants, not by way of exchange, but an obligation on the one party to give, and the other to receive

Their piety towards God is extraordinary, as they never speak a word of the common affairs of life before sun-rise, but upon certain traditional forms of prayer, imploring the Divine protection for the day After this act of devotion they betake themselves to their several occupations and employments, in which they labour with great diligence till an hour before noon, when they assemble in white veils, and bathe in cold water Upon this purification they retire to their apartments, into which it is not permitted to any one of another sect to enter From thence they enter into a refectory or dining-hall, as into an holy temple, and sit down without uttering a word The attendants place their loaves in order, and bring each one a single plate of one kind of food, which is not touched before the priest pronounces a blessing, as in like manner he returns thanks to the divine donor after meat. This duty performed, they lay aside their white garments, as in some degree sacred, and resume their ordinary avocations till evening, when they return to supper in the same manner, and if there be any strangers they sit down with them Their houses are free from clamour and disturbance They speak by turns, and observe a gravity and silence which excite the veneration of strangers, and arise from a constant course of moderation and sobriety

They are not allowed to do any thing without the advice of their superiors, except in offices of compassion and assistance, in which they are at liberty; for every man is free to help the virtuous, though they are restrained from their superiors. They curb their passions and are eminent for their fidelity, and preserving peace and good order. Their word is as sacred as an oath, which they avoid as worse than perjury, accounting a man, who cannot be believed without bringing God for a witness, as a liar, and unworthy of confidence.

They hold the works and writings of the ancients in great veneration, and select from them what is conducive to the benefit of their minds and bodies, as in the cases of ethics, or morals, or remedies for diseases, the virtues of plants, metals, minerals, and the like.

When any person is disposed to become a member of the society, he is not immediately admitted, but prescribed the mode of living for one whole year, and presented with an axe, a girdle, and a white garment. If, in that course of time, he has given evidence of his continence, they, in some respect, change his diet, and allow him the benefit of the water of purification. But he is not permitted to enter the refectory till he has passed two years probation of his integrity, upon which trial he is taken into the society upon the following conditions.

He is first to bind himself, by solemn oaths, to love and worship God, and observe justice towards man, to injure no one of his own accord nor at the command or persuasion of others, to declare himself an enemy to the wicked, and a friend to the righteous, to shew fidelity to all men, and especially to those in authority, as they are the ministers of God by his own appointment. He is likewise to declare, that if ever he should attain to an elevated station, he will never abuse that power to the injury of those who are subordinate to him, nor distinguish himself, by any peculiar ornament of dress, that he will love and embrace the truth, and reprove those who speak falsehood. He binds himself also to keep his hands clean from theft and fraudulent dealing, and his mind from the desire of unlawful gains. He swears that he will not conceal from those of his own sect any of the mysteries of his religion, nor communicate any of their doctrines to others, though it should be to save his life, and finally, that he will communicate their doctrines in no other manner than as he received them himself, and will preserve the books belonging to their sect, and the names of those by whom they are written.

Those who are detected in heinous offences are excluded the society, and generally come to a miserable end, as they are bound by oath not to receive even a morsel of bread from the hand of a stranger, and thus compelled to graze like beasts till they perish. In this distress the society sometimes compassionate a case, and receives the delinquent again, deeming the punishment, in some degree, an atonement for the offence.

In the administration of justice they are singularly strict, determining nothing without the concurrence of at least an hundred voices, and from their sentence once passed there is no appeal.

Next to the supreme authority of God himself they hold in reverence that of their legislator, (Moses,) whom if any one blasphemes, he is punished with death. They ascribe great honour to their elders, and to the majority of the people, deeming it highly reasonable to obey the one and hearken to the other. When there are ten members in council, no particular one is to speak if the other nine are against it. They hold it indecent, and even immoral, to spit towards the middle of the assembly, or upon the right hand of it.

They observe the sabbath with greater strictness than any other sect of the Jews, as they not only prepare their food the preceding day, to avoid kindling a fire upon that day, but will not move an utensil from one place to another.

Those who profess these tenets and practices, are divided into four sorts, according to their respective obligations. The younger are required to [illegible] such inferior to their elders, that if the senior is touched by the junior, he must purify as it were upon the contact of a stranger.

They live to a great age, many of them an hundred years and upwards, which must be ascribed to the simplicity of their diet, and their temperance in general. They are also firm and hardy, contemning the miseries of life, and accounting an honourable death more desirable than an inglorious existence. Indeed our war with the Romans abundantly proves this part of their character, as, upon divers occasions, neither burning, or the most exquisite torture, could force from them an irreverent word of their legislator, or the breach of one of their rites or ceremonies. Tortures they also endured not only without supplication and tears, but with cheerfulness of countenance, deriding the tormentors, and yielding up their breath with serenity and composure, in the assurance of exchanging the present life for a better in future.

They firmly believe the mortality of the body, and that the soul, being of the same nature with the subtilized air, is incorruptible and immortal, and by a kind of attraction enclosed in the body as in a prison, but that when it shall be freed from these corporeal bonds, or from a long slavery, it shall ascend to the regions of bliss. This tenet seems to correspond with a certain opinion of the Greeks, who conceit that there is a region beyond the ocean, where there are neither rain, snow, or raging heats, but only gentle refreshing breezes: this they make the residence of the blest in a future state. As for the wicked, on the other hand, they stand, in their opinion, condemned to impetuous tempests, destroying frosts, and everlasting agonies and groans.

This is analogous to what Grecian fabulists relate of the fortunate islands, describing them as places set apart for the beatific enjoyment of those glorious spirits they call heroes and demi-gods. They have also their places, or hell, which their fabulists inform us is an infernal prison, when Sisyphus, Tantalus, Ixion, Tityus, and the like, are consigned to different, but eternal plagues and torments. This is built on the first supposition that souls are immortal, and from thence are derived exhortations to virtue, and dissuasive from vice, for good men are rendered better, even in this world, by the hopes of reward in another, and the vehement inclinations of bad men are restrained by the fear and expectation they have, though their wickedness may be, in some measure, concealed in this life, of suffering eternal punishment after death. These are the doctrines of the Essenes concerning the subject of the soul, and we find very few when once they have imbibed the same, that ever depart from it.

There are amongst the Essenes, those who pretend to the spirit of prophecy, founding their presumptions upon holy writ, and using preparatory purifications to fit them for the work, and it is observable that they seldom fail in their predictions.

There is another order of Essenes, agreeing with the former as to meats, manners, and laws, but differing from it in the point of marriage, as thinking that, by not marrying, they cut off succession, and thereby tend to extinguish the human race. The woman, however, must be subject to a three years probation, and if she should be found in a condition for child bearing, she is to be esteemed, after that trial, qualified for wedlock. Thus much for the Essenes.

The Pharisees are professors of the law, and learned in the Jewish rites and ceremonies. The first article of their creed is, in effect, that fate and Providence do all, and yet that, whether we do well or ill, it is much in our own power, only that destiny interposes sometimes in this or that particular. They believe the soul to be immortal. They likewise believe a transmigration of the souls of good men into other bodies, but, at the same time, [illegible] ſouls of the wicked are tranſmitted to a ſtate of everlaſting woe.

The Sadducees, on the other hand, abſolutely deny fate, affirming that God can do no ill, and that he leaves men at liberty to do what they liſt. They have good and evil before them, and they take their choice. The former ſect are ſociable, and live upon good terms with one another; while the latter are harſh and ill-natured among themſelves, and abſolutely inhuman and intolerable to ſtrangers. But to return to the main ſubject.

CHAP. VIII.

Death of Auguſtus Cæſar. Succeſſion of Tiberius. Pilate made governor of Judæa. A tumult upon conveying Cæſar's enſigns into Jeruſalem. Pilate ſummons the Jews under colour of hearing. Is induced, by the generous behaviour of the Jews, to remove the enſigns. Another tumult occaſioned by a tax upon the holy treaſure. Agrippa complains of Herod to Tiberius, and in conſequence of an expreſſion to Caius, is kept priſoner till the death of that emperor. Caius Cæſar ſucceeds Tiberius, and advances Agrippa. Herod, at the inſtance of Herodias, ſeeks the favour of Caius. Deaths of Herod and Herodias in exile in Spain.

THE ethnarchy of Archelaus being now reduced into a province, the two brothers Herod and Philip, (called Antipas, continued in the adminiſtration of their tetrarchies. Salome, upon her demiſe, bequeathed her toparchy to Livia, the wife of Auguſtus, together with Jamnia, and a plantation of Palm-trees at Phaſaelis.

Auguſtus dying after a reign of fifty-ſeven years, ſix months, and two days, Tiberius, the ſon of Livia, ſucceeded to the Roman empire. Philip, the tetrarch, built a city in Paneas, which he called Cæſarea; and another in Gaulanitis, which he called Julias. Tiberias in Galilee was built by Herod, as was Julias in Peræa.

Pilate being appointed governor of Judæa by Tiberius, ſecretly conveyed, by night into the city certain enſigns, with the image of Cæſar inſcribed upon them. This excited a tumult amongſt the Jews, who were alarmed at ſo flagrant a prophanation of their religion, and violation of their liberties, as the introduction of images to the city was a thing totally forbidden. This tumult in town was ſpeedily inflamed by a vaſt concourſe of people from all parts of the province, in conſequence of which the Jews went in a great body to Cæſarea, to move Pilate for relief, and there earneſtly beſought him to be tender of their laws, and order the removal of the images out of the city. Upon Pilate's inattention to their requeſt, they fell proſtrate, and in that poſture continued immoveable five days and as many nights.

On the ſixth day Pilate mounted the tribunal, which was in the great court, and called to him the multitude, as if deſirous of giving them an anſwer, when ſuddenly upon a ſignal given, the Jews were ſurrounded with armed troops, and Pilate, in the inſtant of their conſternation, declared that every man ſhould die, unleſs they admitted the images into the city, and gave intimation to the ſoldiers to draw their ſwords. The Jews, in this ſtate of terror, caſt themſelves proſtrate one and all before him, ſtretched out their necks, and offered themſelves to the execution, crying out with one voice, that they would rather die than ſee the prophanation of their laws. Pilate was ſo aſtoniſhed at the daring zeal of theſe people in defence of their religion, that he gave immediate orders to have the ſtatues removed.

This tumult was followed by another. The Jews have a a ſacred treaſure, which they call corban, and Pilate laid a tax upon it towards the charge of aqueducts for the bringing in of water at the diſtance of three hundred furlongs. The common people were ſo irritated at this impoſition, that they came with complaints to Pilate about it as he ſat upon the tribunal. But he had caution to provide againſt a tumult, by intermixing ſoldiers in diſguiſe with the multitude, to be in readineſs to fall on whenever a ſignal ſhould be given; but, in caſe of riot, to uſe ſtaves only, and not their ſwords. The people growing clamorous, Pilate gave the ſoldiers the ſignal, who did execution according to their orders. Many of the Jews were deſtroyed, ſome dying by blows, ſome crouded and trampled to death, and others periſhing in the purſuit. The multitude alarmed at this chaſtiſement, ceaſed from murmuring; ſo that this ſeverity put an end to the tumult.

In the mean time Agrippa, the ſon of that Ariſtobulus who was put to death by his father Herod, went to Tiberius with a complaint againſt Herod the tetrarch. Tiberius did not attend to the accuſation; ſo that Agrippa continued at Rome in the condition of a private man, and made his court to perſons of the firſt quality, and in particular to Caius, the ſon of Germanicus. Regaling him upon a certain occaſion with a collation, Agrippa took an opportunity, in the hour of conviviality, of exclaiming, "how joyful he ſhould be in ſeeing Caius emperor of the world inſtead of Tiberius." This being told to the latter by one of the company, he ordered him to be put in chains, and hardly treated in priſon for the courſe of ſix months; at the expiration of which he departed this life himſelf, after a reign of twenty-two years, ſix months, and three days.

Caius Cæſar, upon his ſucceeding to the empire, diſcharged Agrippa, and gave him the tetrarchy of Philip, who was now dead, with the title of king annexed. The advancement of Agrippa excited the envy and ambition of Herod the tetrarch, which were not a little inflamed by his wife Herodias, who reproached him for his ſloth, and told him it was only becauſe he would not attend Cæſar, that he was deprived of greater dignity; for ſince the emperor had made Agrippa king from a private perſon, it was much more probable that he would promote him from a tetrarch to that rank. Theſe arguments ſo far prevailed with Herod, that he repaired to Caius; but was followed by Agrippa, in order to prefer accuſations againſt him. The emperor was ſo far from gratifying his ambition, that he reproved him ſeverely, and gave his tetrarchy to Agrippa; in conſequence of which he retired to Spain with his wife, and there died in exile.

CHAP. IX.

Caius Cæſar arrogates divine honours. His horrid cruelties. He ſends Petronius, one of his generals, to ſet up his ſtatue in the temple, and put all malecontents to the ſword. Petronius advances with an army from Antioch towards Judæa. Deſcription of Ptolemais. The Jews repair thither, and petition Petronius, who ſummons them to Tiberias, and there reaſons the caſe with them. He relents, and diſmiſſes the court without coming to any reſolution. Promiſes his mediation with Cæſar. Writes to the emperor to that purport. He orders him to be put to death, but his own premature fate prevents the execution.

SO elated was Caius Cæſar with his fortune, that he had the vanity to aſſume the name of a god, and aſpire to divine honours. His cruelty alſo kept pace with his blaſphemy, for he cut off great numbers of the Roman nobility, and extended his barbarity to Judæa, whither he ſent his general Petronius, charged with a commiſſion to ſet up his ſtatue in the temple, and put every individual to the ſword who ſhould dare to make the leaſt oppoſition, and make ſlaves of all the reſt of the Jews. But the Divine Providence interpoſed and defeated his deſigns.

Petronius marched with all expedition from Antioch towards Judæa with three legions, and a conſiderable number of auxiliaries out of Syria. The report of this expedition gained no credit with the greater part of the Jews, nor were those who believed him in a condition to put themſelves in a poſture of defence but when the army advanced as far as Ptolemais, they were ſtruck with an univerſal conſternation

Ptolemais is a city on the coaſt of Galilee, ſituated on an extenſive plain, and encompaſſed with mountains That on the eaſt ſide, at the diſtance of ſixty furlongs belongs to Galilee that on the ſouth to Carmel, which is diſtant an hundred and twenty furlongs that on the north is the higheſt of them all, called, by the people of the country, "The ladder of the Tyrians," and diſtant alſo an hundred and twenty furlongs The ſmaller river Belus runs by it at the diſtance of two furlongs Not far from it ſtands Memnon's ſepulchre, bordering upon a proſpect of near an hundred cubits over, which has ſomething in it well worthy of obſervation There is the appearance of a round valley, that yields a kind of glaſſy ſand It is carried off by ſhipping, and as faſt as they fetch it away, the winds from the ſummit of the mountains fill the place again It is the nature of the ſoil to turn every thing to glaſs that comes into it, and, what is more extraordinary, that glaſſy ſand, which is ſuperfluous, once removed out of the place, becomes common ſand again

In this ſtate of conſternation the Jews, with their wives and children, went to Petronius at Ptolemais and there beſought him for their country's ſake, and their own, not to enforce the violation of their laws, to the utter deſtruction of ſo many wretched people Petronius was prevailed upon by the number of the ſuppliants, and their deplorable condition, to leave his army, and the ſtatues of Cæſar, at Ptolemais advance towards Galilee, and ſummon the Jews, of all ranks and degrees, to attend him at Tiberias Being there aſſembled, he entered upon a detail of the ſtrength and power of the empire, and the menaces of Cæſar, adding, that this requeſt was an affront, as they could claim no right to diſpute theſe orders, to which all the ſubjects of the Roman empire beſides themſelves, had ſubmitted, which was the placing of the emperor's ſtatue in the temples amongſt thoſe of their other gods He added, that their oppoſition was little ſhort of a revolt, and would be conſidered by Cæſar as the moſt palpable indignity

They had only to alledge, that the laws and cuſtoms of their country would not allow them to ſet up any images whatever, either of God or man or in any place whatſoever either ſacred or prophane Petronius replied, that he was under as indiſpenſable a neceſſity of obeying the injunctions of the emperor his maſter, as they were of thoſe of their legiſlator, ſo that, in conſequence of tranſgreſſing in their favour, he muſt be liable to puniſhment, being as much under command as they were Hereupon the whole multitude exclaimed, that they were ready to lay down their lives in vindication of their laws

When the outcry ſubſided, Petronius demanded if they were reſolved to take up arms againſt Cæſar? They not only replied in the negative, but declared that not a day paſſed but they offered up ſacrifices for the proſperity of Cæſar, and the whole Roman people, but that, if he was determined to place images in the temple, he would make the nation of the Jews one common ſacrifice, as they were ready to expoſe themſelves, with their wives and children, to the ſevereſt torments Petronius was ſo affected by this demonſtration of invincible ardour, for the preſervation of their religion, in the unanimous reſolutions of ſo vaſt a multitude, that he diſmiſſed them without coming to any final deciſion

Petronius then aſſembled the higher claſs in private, and the multitude in public, and ſometimes had recourſe to perſuaſion and advice, but chiefly to threatenings, inſiſting upon the power of the Romans, the high diſpleaſure of Cæſar, and the neceſſity he was under of enforcing his injunctions But when he found that no conſideration would prevail with them, and that the ſeed time was almoſt elapſed, having employed fifteen days in urging their ſuit, he told them that for their ſakes, he was determined to expoſe himſelf to a deſperate hazard, in attempting to ſatisfy Cæſar, in failure of which his life would be at ſtake He then diſmiſſed the multitude, who offered up a thouſand prayers for his proſperity, and drew off his army from Ptolemais, to Antioch From thence he immediately tranſmitted to Cæſar an account of the manner in which he entered Judæa, of the petition in which the whole nation joined, and the danger to which the whole province would be expoſed in caſe of denial They deſired nothing more, he obſerved, than the maintenance of their laws againſt all innovations

Caius very conciſely anſwered the epiſtle of Petronius, by an order for putting him to death for not executing his command, but it ſo fell out that the bearers of this order were detained three months by contrary winds, and, in the mean time Petronius received intelligence of the death of the emperor by a quicker paſſage, twenty-ſeven days before the arrival of the other

CHAP X.

Claudius declared emperor by the army He is oppoſed by the ſenate Agrippa courted both by Claudius and the ſenate Eſpouſes the intereſt of Claudius Harangues in juſtification of Claudius and the army Anſwer of the ſenate to Agrippa Of Claudius to the ſenate A ſoldier ſtands up for the honour of Claudius Deſertion of the ſoldiers followed by that of the ſenate Agrippa prevents the deſtruction of the partizans of Claudius Claudius acquires popularity Sacrifices in form Bountifully rewards Agrippa and Herod The immenſe wealth and power of the former Jeruſalem is walled in Death of Agrippa at Cæſarea Deſcendants of Alexander and Ariſtobulus

CAIUS Cæſar being taken off by treachery, after he had maintained the imperial ſway three years and ſix months, Claudius was advanced to the government by the army, which was then at Rome. The conſuls Sentius Saturnius and Pomponius Secundus appointed, according to the reſolution of the ſenate, three regiments of ſoldiers for the guard of the city, whilſt they met in the capitol, determined to oppoſe the elevation of Claudius, on account of the barbarous treatment they had met with from Caius, as well as from a deſign of reſtoring the ariſtocratical form of government, when men of rank and integrity were taken into adminiſtration At this time Agrippa happening to be at Rome, he was invited into the council by the ſenate, and into the camp by Claudius, as a conſiderable addition to what party ſoever he eſpouſed Agrippa finding Claudius emperor in effect, eſpouſed his intereſt, and was immediately employed upon an embaſſy to the ſenate He repreſented to them, upon the occaſion, "That the army's ſetting him up as emperor was an act of abſolute force, in which his will was totally unconcerned, that it being paſſed, he could not recede with honour or ſafety, as it would provoke them to revenge if he ſhould ſeem inſenſible of the obligation, inſiſting again and again, on the danger he muſt inevitably incur by a puſillanimous reſignation of the power veſted in him by the grand bulwark of the empire He added that ſince the main point was gained, and he was in poſſeſſion of the government, Claudius had determined with himſelf to attend and execute the office, not as a tyrant to domineer at will and pleaſure, but as a prince to expreſs the tendereſt regard for the welfare and proſperity of his people That he ſhould content himſelf with the honour of the name of emperor, and in caſes of importance, be ever ready to hearken to the advice of the ſenate, as the exemplary fate of Caius was a warning to him to exerciſe moderation

When Agrippa had proceeded thus far in his addreſs, the ſenate, relying upon their credit with the army, and the prudence of their own councils, gave him this conciſe reply; "That they were not a body to be made voluntary ſlaves" Agrippa retorted the anſwer to Claudius, who ſent him back to assure them, "That Claudius was not a man to betray his friends that had raised him to the empire; that he was much concerned at the thought of entering into a dispute with the senate; but if it must come to a decision by dint of arms, he desired they would appoint some spot of ground without the city for the place of action, as it would be dreadful, beyond conception, to have Rome laid in blood and ashes to gratify the humour of a few rash and turbulent people." With this message Agrippa was charged by Claudius to the senate, and he accordingly delivered it.

At this very critical juncture of affairs, one of the soldiers then present, belonging to the senate, stood forth, and drawing his sword, thus exclaimed: "My brave companions, why are we thus at daggers with our best friends, and upon the brink of a civil war only for adhering to Claudius, an emperor of so good a character, and a prince whom we should rather treat with duty and respect as our protector, than threaten with arms as an enemy?" Having thus spoken he marched through the whole senate, followed by the rest of the soldiers. This defection alarmed the nobility, that, to avoid more serious consequences, they gave over opposition, and following the example of the soldiers, went their way, and declared for Claudius. In the mean time divers of the malecontents ran up to the walls, with their swords drawn, under the walls, to fight them as they were coming out, and they would have been all cut off, before Cæsar could have had any knowledge of the matter, had not Agrippa given him notice to prevent it, telling Cæsar plainly, that if he did not restrain the insolence of the army, especially towards the nobility, a universal massacre would shortly ensue, and instead of being master of a glorious empire, it would leave him only prince of a depopulated nation. Claudius, prevailed on by the advice of Agrippa, restrained the violence of the soldiery, received the senate into the camp with due honours, and then went out with them, according to custom, to offer vows and sacrifices for the prosperity of the empire. He bestowed upon Agrippa not only his father's kingdom entire, but over and above, those places that Augustus had conferred upon Herod, as Trachon and Auranitis, with what was called the kingdom of Lysanias, appointing the particulars of this grant to be notified by proclamation to the people, and giving it likewise in charge to the senate to have it cut in brass, and set up in the capitol. He gave the kingdom of Chalcis to Herod, the brother of Agrippa, who was become his son-in-law, by his marriage with Bernice, his daughter.

The reign and power of Agrippa now exceeded the bounds of imagination, and he soon made the most of what he had acquired, in vain and trifling objects. His first undertaking was the walling in of Jerusalem, which had it been brought to perfection, would have rendered it impracticable for the Romans to take it by siege. But after three years reign as king he died at Cæsarea, and left the work unfinished, having governed three years before in quality of tetrarch. He left three daughters by Cypris, Bernice, Mariamne, and Drusilla, and one son, whose name was Agrippa. Being very young when his father died, Claudius reduced the kingdom into a province, and made Cuspius Fadus governor, and after him Tiberius Alexander, who making no innovations in the laws and customs of the country, preserved the public peace. A little after this died Herod governor of Chalcis, and left, by Bernice the daughter of his brother two sons, Bernicianus and Hyrcanus, and by Mariamne, his former wife, Aristobulus. There was another brother named Aristobulus, who died in a private station, and left a daughter, whose name was Jotapa. These, as before observed, were the children of Aristobulus, the son of Herod; but Alexander and Aristobulus were the sons of Herod by Mariamne, who were slain at the instance of their father. The posterity of Alexander ruled afterwards in the Greater Armenia.

CHAP. XI.

Herod of Chalcis dying, is succeeded by Agrippa, as is Tiberius Alexander by Cumanus. An insult offered by a Roman soldier to the Jews occasions a tumult. Ten thousand Jews are taken off. A Roman soldier tears the book of the law. The offender put to death by order of Cumanus. A dispute between the Jews of Galilee and those of Samaria. A universal tumult in Jerusalem. Eleazar and Alexander ravage and murder in the villages. Jerusalem infested with robbers. Complaint made to Quadratus, who goes to Jerusalem to be further informed. Cæsar gives Cumanus and the Samaritans a hearing at Rome. He passes judgment against the Samaritans, and orders the execution of them. Death of Claudius, and succession of Nero, a most prodigious and abandoned prince.

ON the death of Herod, who reigned in Chalcis, Claudius introduced Agrippa, the son of Agrippa, into the kingdom of his uncle, and Cumanus succeeded Tiberius Alexander in the government of Judæa. During the time of his administration the Jews fell into new grievances and disturbances. The people being assembled together in vast numbers at Jerusalem, to celebrate the feast of unleavened bread, and a band of soldiers being stationed at the gate of the temple, as was customary upon those occasions, to prevent tumults, one of the soldiers turned his back, and stood in an indecent posture towards the Jews. This put the whole multitude in such a rage, that they pressed in throngs to Cumanus for justice upon the soldier for that affront, and those who were most tumultuous amongst them began to reproach the soldiers. Cumanus, apprehending further mischief from a popular outrage, sent a reinforcement of men to support the former band. This so alarmed the Jews, that they pressed to get out of the temple with all haste, insomuch that the passages were so crowded, that ten thousand of them were trodden and squeezed to death. This accident rendered it a melancholy solemnity to the whole nation. Tears and wringing of hands were seen in every house, nor was there a family but had a share in the mourning.

There soon followed another calamity, which arose from a tumult occasioned by robbers. One Stephen, a domestic of Cæsar's, carrying some furniture from Bethoron, was set upon and robbed by a band of thieves. Upon this Cumanus sent a party to apprehend the people in the neighbouring villages, and bring them bound to him, making them responsible for not pursuing and taking the robbers. While they were upon this enquiry, a soldier happening in the search, to lay his hands upon the books of Moses, rent them in pieces, and threw them into the fire. The Jews assembled in an instant as if the whole country had been in a flame, and, actuated by the most fiery zeal for their religion, hastened to Cumanus at Cæsarea, and there pressed him most importunately not to suffer the wretch to escape unpunished, who had offered so daring an insult to God and his sacred laws. Cumanus, finding there was no appeasing the enraged multitude without some sort of satisfaction, commanded the soldier to be brought out, and put to death in the sight of the whole field; which putting an end to the tumult, the Jews departed.

There happened, at the same time, an unfortunate difference between the Jews of Galilee and those of Samaria. There was a certain Jew of Galilee passing through a village called Geman, in the great plain of Samaria, that was there killed as he was going up to Jerusalem to worship at a solemn festival. The people of Galilee, upon this, drew out a body to revenge themselves upon the Samaritans; but the better sort applied to Cumanus, and advised him by all means, before the dispute went too far, to go over to Galilee and, upon strict enquiry into the matter, see justice done on the murders. Cumanus having other concerns in hand, dismissed the petitioners, without entering into the cause. The report of this outrage afterwards reaching Jerusalem, so enraged the whole multitude, that, leaving the business of the day, they determined, without either officer or order, to fall upon Samaria, in spite of the efforts of superiors to restrain them. The ringleaders of this robbery and murder were Eleazar, the son of Dineus, and Alexander, who breaking into the borders of Acrabatena, laid waste all before them, and put men, women, and children to the sword.

Cumanus, upon receiving intelligence of this ravage, came with a party of horse to the relief of the country, took many of Eleazar's band, and cut off many more. The remainder of this rabble committed such depredations in Samaria, that the great officers and leading men of Jerusalem went out with mournful appearance, and used every art and argument to prevail with them to desist from their outrages. They entreated them not to destroy Jerusalem to be revenged of Samaria, to have pity upon their country, their temple, their city, their wives, which were all at stake, and not to sacrifice all that was dear to them in this world in revenge for the loss of one poor Galilean. The Jews at length became cool, and the tumults subsided.

It might now be said to be the period of universal rapine, in which the main business of the people was to prey upon each other, and the most powerful plundered the lower class of their countrymen. Numidius Quadratus being then governor of Syria, several of the heads of the Samaritans applied to him at Tyre with a heavy complaint against the robbers that infested that country. There were divers of the leading men of the Jews then present, and amongst the rest Jonathan, the son of Ananus, the high-priest, who turned the blame upon the Samaritans as the first authors of the tumult in the death of the Galilean. He charged the consequences also upon Cumanus, for not bringing the offender to justice in due time.

Quadratus, having heard the cause, deferred the further consideration of it till he came into Judæa, where he might receive more particular information. He then went to Cæsarea, and there caused all those that Cumanus had taken alive to be put to death. From thence he proceeded to Lydda, where he heard the Samaritan cause over again, and ordered eighteen leading men of the Jews to be beheaded, as they were found to have been abettors of the tumults. He sent the two high-priests, Jonathan and Ananias, with Ananus, the son of Ananias, and some other Jews of the first rank, to Cæsar, together with some noble Samaritans. He also ordered Cumanus, and Celos, the tribune, away to Rome, to give an account of what had been done to Claudius. Having thus finished these matters, he went up to Jerusalem from Lydda, and finding the multitude celebrating their feast of unleavened bread without any tumult, he returned to Antioch.

When the parties returned to Rome, where Agrippa appeared a zealous advocate for the Jews, and Cumanus was supported by some weighty friends, Cæsar hearing the respective cases, gave sentence against the Samaritans, condemning three of the most powerful of them to be beheaded, Cumanus to be banished, Celos, the tribune, to be sent bound to Jerusalem, delivered over to the Jews to be tormented, his body drawn round the city, and then beheaded.

He constituted Felix, the brother of Pallas, governor of Judæa, Samaria, Galilee, and Peræa, and preferred Agrippa from Chalcis to a greater dominion, giving him the tetrarchy that had belonged to Philip, which contained Batanea, Trachon, and Gaulanitis, superadding the kingdom of Lysanias, and the province which Varus had governed.

When Claudius Cæsar had reigned thirteen years, eight months, and twenty days, he departed this life, and left the succession to Nero, whom his wife Agrippina had artfully introduced to the empire, notwithstanding he had at that time a legitimate son, Britannicus, by his first wife Messalina, and a daughter, Octavia, whom he married to Nero. He had also another daughter, by Petina, called Antonia.

No man, perhaps, perverted power and wealth more than Nero to the injury of others, as appears from the imbruing his hands in the blood of his brother, his wife, and his mother. He merited the complicated character of tyrant and buffoon, incompatible as they may seem; for he not only exercised the most horrid barbarities towards his nearest relations, but introduced subjects of dignity and importance in a most ridiculous point of view upon the public stage. But as the history of this emperor is so generally known, I shall pass over trivial matters, and confine myself to those particulars in which the Jews were chiefly concerned.

CHAP. XII.

Nero's liberality to Aristobulus and Agrippa. Felix chastises the robbers. A new set of free-booters, called Sicarii. Jonathan, the high-priest, the first that fell by their hands. Anarchy and confusion prevailing throughout Jerusalem. Dangerous effects of enthusiasm, seduction, and imposture. A magician pretends to the spirit of prophecy, and marches with thirty thousand followers towards Jerusalem. Felix meets and totally routs him. Ambitious bandits persuade the Jews to revolt. An outrageous tumult between the Jews and Syrians. The matter in dispute finally referred to Cæsar. Felix succeeded by Festus.

NERO, soon after his accession to the imperial dignity, conferred upon Aristobulus, the son of Herod, king of Chalcis, the government of Armenia the Lesser, and annexed four more cities to the territory of Agrippa; that is to say, Abila and Julias in Peræa, and in Galilee, Tarichee and Tiberias, with their dependencies. The remainder of Judæa he gave to Felix, who was no sooner vested with his commission, than he went in quest of the robbers, took Eleazar, their leader, with several others, and sent them all bound to Rome, after they had ravaged the country for the space of twenty years; so that the number of robbers whom he caused to be put to death, and the country people that joined them, was almost incredible.

These ruffians were no sooner suppressed, than there sprang up another set of robbers, under the name of Sicarii, from *sica*, the weapon they used. They made no scruple of executing their destructive practices in the open day, and in the very streets of Jerusalem. Their custom was to carry short daggers under their garments, and mixing with the multitude at festivals in particular, deal death around them without being detected. They continued this horrid practice some time, not only without discovery, but without being so much as suspected. The first man slain by these assassins was Jonathan, the high-priest, after which not a day passed without several executions of the same kind. This occasioned a general alarm, insomuch, that the apprehension was almost as dreadful as the mischief itself; and it was as dangerous to walk the streets as to be in a field of battle. Every man at a distance was suspected for an enemy, nor could even reputed friends be trusted upon their approach to each other. Nor was the utmost watchfulness, and minutest caution, a sufficient security, so dextrous were these bravos in the exercise of their profession.

There started up at this time another sort of miscreants, who did more mischief with their tongues than the others did with their weapons. They shed no blood, indeed, but caused more destruction by their pernicious doctrines than the others did with their daggers, raising disorder and confusion throughout the city. These were impostors and seducers, who, under pretence of divine inspiration, inculcated vague opinions and absurd innovations. They drew the multitude into woods and solitudes, pretending that God would there set them at perfect liberty, and re-

[illegible] himself to them by such tokens from heaven, as would give them [illegible] the assurance of it. Felix foresaw the design of this proceeding, and was convinced of the necessity of nipping the attempt of a revolt in the bud; so that he sent [illegible] body of horse and foot in pursuit of these enthusiasts, who destroyed great numbers of their disciples and followers.

These mischiefs were followed by those of an Egyptian pretender, that proved more fatal to the Jews than the former. He was a magician, but passed for a prophet, and [illegible] of followers, to the number of about 30,000, whom he inveigled into his trammels. These deluded people he led, by the way of the wilderness, to mount Olivet, proposing to march thence to Jerusalem, expel the Roman garrison, and make himself master of the city and country, [illegible] his followers and guards about him to assist in the enterprize. Felix, finding it to be a growing evil, advanced up to the Egyptian with his Roman legions, and a considerable body of Jews that joined him. He then gave him battle, and totally defeated him; the Egyptian himself, and some few of his followers, saving themselves by flight. Great numbers of them were slain, others taken and put into chains, and the rest dispersed to their own habitations.

[illegible] of a nation resembles the state of the body, in [illegible] disease is generally followed by another; for these [illegible] and free-booters were now concerting a scheme for [illegible] liberty, and engaging the multitude in a resolution to shake off the Roman yoke. This they attempted both by argument and menace, threatening death, [illegible] to any man who acknowledged the Roman jurisdiction; and proposing to reduce those by terror, that would not otherwise subject themselves to a voluntary slavery. They formed themselves into different bodies, and dispersed throughout the country, diffusing slaughter and devastation; so that Judea was brought to the very extremity of desperation, and the destructive flame raged more and more every day.

At the same time a disturbance happened at Cæsarea, upon a commotion [illegible] the contest between the Jews and Syrians living promiscuously together. The Jews claimed it as their city, arguing, that a Jew was the founder of it, referring to King Herod. The Syrians could not deny that a Jew had been the founder of it, but insisted, on the other hand, that it belonged to the Gentiles, since, if it had been a Jewish city, they would never have suffered statues to be erected in it. The contest between the parties became so warm, that they had recourse to arms, [illegible], but there was mischief done by the most resolute of each party. The elders exerted their authority and counsel to quiet the Jews on the one hand, and the Greeks had too exalted an idea of their own importance to submit to the Jews. The latter were esteemed to possess more wealth and courage than their competitors, who had, however, greater interest with the soldiery; for a considerable part of the Roman army being drawn out of Syria, they were the readier to assist them, both as their countrymen and kindred. The magistrates and officers did their utmost, by severity of discipline, to suppress the tumult, taking the incorrigible into custody, and inflicting punishment with rigour. But the exemplary sufferings of part had no effect upon the whole; on the contrary, that which was designed to intimidate, served but to harden them in the daring pursuit.

When Felix found that no means would bring them to [illegible], he commanded the factious out of the city, by proclamation, at their utmost peril; but divers remaining there in contempt of authority, the governor sent a party of soldiers amongst them, who slew many, and seized on their effects. But the sedition still prevailing, he dispatched some of the principal men of both parties to Nero, as commissioners to plead their cause before him. Festus succeeded Felix, and was very active in suppressing these disturbances, and bringing the authors to condign punishment.

CHAP. XIII.

Festus is succeeded by Albinus, who proves a corrupt and tyrannical governor. His successor, Gessius Florus, is more flagitious. Their characters compared. Florus is subject to Cestius Gallus, governor of Syria. He endeavours to excite the Jews to rebellion. The rise of the Jewish war.

ALBINUS, who succeeded Festus, did not tread in the steps of his predecessor. He was a man universally depraved, addicted to corruption, avarice, extortion, and oppression; so that the nation groaned under most intolerable burthens during the time of his government. He adopted the most destructive systems of policy, was influenced in every measure by venality, would pass or revoke sentences as bribed; in fine, as money was his god, so it [illegible] his conduct in general, to the utter perversion of justice, and abolition of every principle of virtue.

There prevailed, at this time, a faction [illegible], which had determined to introduce an innovation, and compounded with Albinus to connive at their practices. The ringleaders of this faction had each of them a band of desolates at command, while the governor himself, as an arch robber, with his guards about him, perverted his authority in the plunder of those who were not in a condition for resistance or defence. These iniquitous proceedings came at length to that pass, that those who sustained the loss of their property durst not complain; and those who escaped, were under a necessity of giving up a part of what they had to secure the rest. In fine, all good faith was lost, tyranny and oppression universally prevailed, and paved eventually the [illegible].

Such was the character of Albinus, but Gessius Florus, his successor, exceeded him [illegible]; for the former had recourse to privacy and [illegible] practices, while the latter gloried in his [illegible] upon the enormity of his crimes, and [illegible] professing himself an enemy to the whole [illegible] province [illegible] the part of an executioner rather than of a governor, taking the whole body of the people [illegible] common [illegible], without [illegible] his tyranny. He was [illegible] or honour, merciless to the [illegible] to the [illegible] blush at the foulest actions. He [illegible] truth with [illegible] under the sanction of [illegible] would not [illegible] his rapacious desires [illegible] be laid desolate to gratify his more [illegible]. He gave as much liberty and encouragement to rapine as if it had been publickly tolerated; nor was any one prohibited from plundering, if he might be admitted to share in the booty. Such, in effect, was his avarice that the whole province was drained, and consequently deserted by its inhabitants as a dreary waste.

Cestius Gallus was [illegible] governor of Syria, and so much attached to [illegible], that not a Jew, even of the first rank, durst prefer a complaint against him; but, upon his coming up to Jerusalem at the feast of the leaven [illegible], the multitude, to the number of three hundred thousand, [illegible] their application to take pity of [illegible] people, [illegible] the province out of the hands of Florus [illegible] of society, and tyrant of a governor. Florus was [illegible] of this complaint, but so far from being moved at it, that he turned it into ridicule. Cestius used his utmost [illegible] pacify the people, [illegible] Florus should [illegible] with more lenity in future, and [illegible]. Florus attended him in his way [illegible] Cæsarea, [illegible] him with many vague reports [illegible], in order to induce him to [illegible] the only means of [illegible].

of [illegible] In case of a peace the Jews, he thought, would embrace that opportunity for bringing the cause before Cæsar, which would subject him to danger; whereas, if he could but once work them up to a revolt, the greater mischief would divert their attention from the lesser; and therefore his only means were to force them, by degrees, into a rebellion in his own defence.

The Cæsarean Greeks had, at this time, carried their cause against the Jews before Cæsar, and obtained a decree in their favour, which sentence gave rise to the Jewish war. It bore date the twelfth year of Nero, and the seventeenth of Agrippa, in the month Artemisius.

CHAP. XIV.

[illegible] of Cæsarea, and the Greeks [illegible] sacrifice of fowls [illegible] The Jews [illegible] for [illegible] He [illegible] of the Jews [illegible] Florus [illegible]

THE tyranny of Florus [illegible] dangerous temptation to a rebellion, but the Jews stood firm against that temptation, till, at length, it was brought about by an incident that fell out in Cæsarea.

A certain Greek had a house in Cæsarea near the spot upon which stood the Jewish synagogue. The Jews were desirous of making a purchase of this house, and treated with the proprietor several times about it, offering much more for it than the intrinsic value. But the proprietor was so far from complying with their proposal, that from a spirit of aggravation, he raised other buildings, and so blocked up the avenues, that there was scarcely room for a single person to pass to the synagogue. Upon this, some of the Jewish youths applied to the inspector of the buildings, and wanted them, at their peril, to order the workmen to desist. Florus countenanced the prohibition, so that the Jews had only to tamper with the governor by the offer of a sum of money. Several of their principal men met about it, and, amongst the rest, John, a publican, or collector of revenues, who contracted with Florus, for eight talents, to forbid the prosecution of the work. They paid him the sum according to a stipulated agreement, and he promised to fulfil the conditions; but immediately after, upon the receipt of it, he went from Cæsarea to Sebaste, and left the parties at liberty to contend the point, as if he had taken the money to furnish an opportunity for them to massacre one another.

The next day being the Jews sabbath, when the people were assembled in the synagogue, a seditious Cæsarean placed an earthen vessel just at the entrance, with a sacrifice of birds upon it. This contemptuous mockery incensed the Jews to a degree of madness, as it was an open derision of their laws, and a profanation of their most sacred rites. The more moderate and substantial men of their party were for appealing to government for redress; but the younger, and more hot-brained, determined on revenge; and the Cæsareans being as ready for an encounter, which was the design of the insult, the contest accordingly took place.

Jucundus, an officer of horse, who was left to keep the peace, coming up at this juncture, ordered the earthen vessel to be taken away, and endeavoured to put a stop to the tumult. But the Jews finding Jucundus overborne by the Cæsareans, took up the books of their law, and carried them off to Narbata, a place about sixty furlongs distant from Cæsarea. John, above mentioned, and twelve of their principal men, went to Florus at Sebaste, with a complaint of what had passed, and a petition for redress, reminding him, though with the utmost delicacy, of the eight talents he had received. But Florus, notwithstanding, ordered them to be apprehended, and put in prison, for presuming to remove the books of the law from Cæsarea.

This action of Florus struck the Jews of Jerusalem with horror and detestation; but they found it expedient, [illegible] present to restrain their passions. Florus still [illegible] aggravate matters, and to add to the [illegible] sent, in Cæsar's name, for seventeen talents out of the sacred treasury, pretending they were for the service of the emperor. This threw the Jews into the utmost confusion, [illegible] much that they ran up and down the temple, [illegible] calling upon Cæsar to free them from the tyranny of Florus, whom they upbraided with the severest reproaches, [illegible] ecrated if possible, beyond the power of malediction [illegible] of the malecontents carried an alms-basket, [illegible] entreating charitable donations for the [illegible] way of derision. But these taunts had no other effect than that of increasing his avarice, and inflaming his resentment, so that instead of checking the tumult, [illegible] his duty, in consequence of the contract, he marched [illegible] an army of horse and foot, to Jerusalem, [illegible] the power of the Roman empire subservient to [illegible] vate passions, either of pride, profit, or revenge, [illegible] minds of the people, wherever he came, with confusion or terror.

The multitude, however, not [illegible] [illegible] ies offered them, assumed the appearance of [illegible] spect in going out to receive him upon the way, and preparing to entertain him with all the [illegible] esteem usual upon such occasions. But, as an [illegible] of their [illegible] submissive design, Florus sent Capito, a centurion, before him, with a band of fifty horses, to stop their progress, and deliver them a message to the following purport, "I am to command you in the name of Florus, to "return home, and to let you understand, that the man with "whom you have so freely sported, is not to be cajoled into "a better opinion of you by pretended appearances. If you "are as you would be thought to be, men of courage and "resolution, ave your reproaches to his face, and assert your "liberty by dint of arms, you have no [illegible] "do by tumult and clamour." This message alarmed the multitude, so that, upon the approach of the centurion with his band of horse, they dispersed without waiting for the ceremony of saluting Florus, and manifesting their submissive disposition. They retired to their own habitations and passed the night in disquieting apprehensions.

Florus took up his abode at the palace, and the next day ascended the tribunal, the high-priest and great officers of the city being there present. He animadverted, with great severity, upon [illegible] reproachful and sarcastic speeches that had been thrown out against him, peremptorily insisting that the authors should be produced, and threatening to take vengeance upon those [illegible] were upon the spot, if they did not find out the guilty.

The heads of the [illegible] assured Florus, that the people in general were peaceably disposed, and implored pardon for those who had [illegible] reproachful expressions, observing that in [illegible] a matter of time must be some rash and headstrong men, nor was it possible to distinguish the guilty, for even those who repented of what they had done, would not make confession. They submitted it to his consideration, whether any thing could tend more to the honour and interest of the Roman empire, than to consult the safety of the people and city by preserving them firm in their allegiance to Cæsar, and whether it might not be more adviseable to spare some few of the guilty for the sake of a great number of innocent people, than to destroy so many innocent for the sake of a few guilty.

Florus was so incensed by this remonstrance, that he immediately ordered the soldiers to plunder what was called the upper market-place, and slay those who oppos [illegible] them. The soldiery therefore, finding themselves supported [illegible] claims to pillage by the concurring authority of their commander, not only executed their orders on the places and people they were sent to, but forcing themselves into every house, rifled at pleasure, and put the [illegible] to death without distinction, as well those they took upon their flight in bye-ways and secret passages as those they found in their houses. In fact, no booty came amiss to them. Several men of rank, whom they seized and brought to Florus, were, by his order, whipped and crucified. The whole number of the slain upon that day, including women and children, (for they spared not infants at the breast,) amounted to six hundred and thirty. The calamity was aggravated by a new species of Roman severity; for before the time of Florus, it was never known that any of the equestrian order were whipped, or ignominiously nailed to the cross; for though the persons, thus disgraced, were, by extraction Jews, they were notwithstanding, of Roman dignity.

CHAP. XV.

[illegible], the sister of Agrippa, goes to Jerusalem to pay a [illegible]. The [illegible] of [illegible] the city. She [illegible] Florus in behalf of the Jews. The [illegible] Florus. [illegible] brought to [illegible]. Florus re-kindles the flames of discord. The [illegible] The [illegible] of Florus [illegible] He [illegible] Return to the palace. The [illegible] Antonia and the temple [illegible] to Cæsarea.

AGRIPPA was at this time gone to Alexandria, to congratulate Alexander upon his having obtained the government of Egypt from Nero. His sister Berenice was then at Jerusalem, and in extreme concern for the barbarous outrages practised there, insomuch that she sent several officers of her guards to Florus, earnestly to entreat him to desist from effusion of human blood. But Florus was equally insensible of the atrocious nature of the sin, and dignified rank of the mediatrix. His heart was so set upon lucre and pillage, that he looked upon all other considerations (the intercessions of Berenice not excepted) with neglect and contempt. Nay, to such a degree did the violence of the soldiery proceed, that they not only perpetrated their murders before her face, but would have wreaked their cruelty on her person, if she had not made her escape into the palace, and remained there during the night, with her guards under the strictest watch for fear of a surprize.

The occasion of her coming to Jerusalem was to offer up a vow to the Almighty, as is customary in providential deliverance from sickness or any great danger. It is usual, with persons under these circumstances, to continue in prayer for thirty days before they sacrifice, abstaining from wine and shaving the head. Berenice was now in the regular performance of this duty, and took an opportunity of standing barefoot before the tribunal, to intercede with Florus in behalf of the people of the Jews. But as on the former, so on the present occasion, she met neither with success or respect, but incurr[illegible] imminent hazard of life for her pious offices.

This happened on the sixteenth day of the month Artemisius, and upon the following day the people gathered together in the market-place in the upper-town, outrageously exclaiming against the murderers of their friends who had been slain there the preceding day. The whole stress of their rage and invectives fell upon Florus. The leading men, and the high-priests, were so sensible of the danger of adding provocation to provocation, that they rent their garments, and, in the humblest tone, besought the multitude to desist from exclaiming, as the exasperating of Florus would be attended with inevitable ruin to them all. This mode of interposition appeased them, and they ceased their outrages, partly through respect to the intercessions, and partly through hope that the governor would relent.

Florus, who seemed to delight in broils, bethought himself of a device to rekindle the flame. He sent for the high-priests, and some of the chief men of the Jews, to come to him, and told them, that as there were two companies of soldiers coming from Cæsarea, it would be a convincing evidence of the peoples good affection to government, if they would go forth and meet them on the way. This being agreed upon, Florus [illegible], and gave it in charge to the centurions, that [illegible] the Jews greeted them with any [illegible] of compliment or respect upon the meeting, they should not [illegible] the least token of a return; and that, upon the smallest appearance of disgust, they should betake themselves to their arms. The high-priest assembled the people in the temple, and there [illegible] them, by all means, to go out and compliment the Romans upon the way, giving [illegible] friendly salutation to prevent future mischief. [illegible] rash and resolute opposed this counsel, [illegible] them revolving in their minds the [illegible] of their [illegible] and friends, [illegible] to comply [illegible].

While this was in agitation, the priests and Levites entered, expos[illegible] the [illegible] vessels, and other ornaments of the temple, and [illegible] the [illegible] musical instruments, and [illegible] to the people with the earnest entreaties to preserve the honour of the temple [illegible], without provoking the Romans [illegible] contumelious affronts to [illegible]. There also [illegible] of the high-priests, who, covered with sack-cloth [illegible], and with garments rent, applied themselves to all the men of rank both individually and collectively, [illegible] them not to betray their country [illegible] trivial a consideration to [illegible] people who [illegible] contributing to the [illegible] its destruction. They justly observed, "That the Roman soldiers would derive no benefit from a [illegible] from the Jews, nor the Jews, on the other hand, any advantage from neglecting the [illegible]. That, on the contrary, if they treated them with honour and according to the [illegible], Florus could have no pretence for [illegible] hostilities, so that, at [illegible], it would tend to the [illegible] of their country from the calamities they had [illegible] further, that they [illegible] the peaceable majority of the multitude [illegible] few [illegible] gling mutineers [illegible] of the greater part over-ruling the less."

These arguments [illegible] authority and merit [illegible] the most resolute were brought to attend to the dictates of reason, [illegible] were brought to this [illegible], the people marched out to meet the [illegible] multitude followed them in good order.

When the Jews were [illegible] within distance of [illegible] ceremonious [illegible] them with every expression of respect, but [illegible] the mere choice [illegible] Florus [illegible] contrive of mischief. The soldiers [illegible], and began to fall upon the Jews, [illegible] sion and [illegible] upon the [illegible], trampled [illegible] under the horses feet, so that between those that [illegible] of blows and wounds, those that were [illegible] in the crowd, or smothered in the [illegible] great [illegible] horrid carnage ensued, [illegible] dreadful a spectacle, that from [illegible] suffocation, the bodies were so [illegible], relation did not know [illegible] to provide a decent funeral. [illegible] all they came up with in the [illegible] mercy. But [illegible] the Jews and the gates [illegible] that led to the [illegible]

Florus, at the same time, made a sally out of the palace, with what troops he had, upon the back of the Jews, with a view of forcing the castle, but the people immediately rallying, and making head against him, he failed in his attempt. Having got possession of the houses, they annoyed the Romans to such a degree with their darts from the roofs, that, finding no defence against the mode of attack, nor any possibility of breaking through the throng which stopped up the narrow passages, Florus was obliged to retire with the remainder of his army to the palace.

The Jews being now under some apprehension that Florus would return to the assault, and make an attempt upon the temple by the way of Fort Antonia, they cut down a certain gallery of communication betwixt the fort and the temple, which so mortified Florus, that, finding his project hopeless, and his avarice disappointed, (the sacred treasure being all his aim,) he gave up the enterprize.

Upon this he conferred with the high-priest and Sanhedrim, assuring them that he was now leaving the city, and [illegible] to them as large a garrison as they should desire. They promised, in consequence of this liberal proposal, that they would make no innovations, provided he would leave them one company, but not that which had maintained the contest against them, on account of the prejudices the people had imbibed from the injuries they had sustained from them. Florus changed the company according to their desire, and, with the rest of his forces, returned to Cæsarea.

CHAP. XVI.

Florus accuses the Jews to Cestius, governor of Syria, as [illegible] Cestius [illegible] the matter, and charges Politianus to make strict enquiry concerning it. The people of Jerusalem represent to him the destructive measures pursued by Florus. Give proof of their obedience to other governors. Address themselves to Agrippa for his concurrence in sending deputies to Nero to prefer a complaint against Florus. Agrippa calls an assembly, and, in an elaborate speech, dissuades the Jews from prosecuting a war with the Romans. His speech produces a momentary effect, but the Jews lapsing into their former outrages, he leaves them, and retires to his own kingdom.

FLORUS, upon his arrival at Cæsarea, pursued other means for inflaming a war, which was by sending a letter to Cestius, and charging the Jews falsely with a design of revolting from the Roman government, and imputing to them the very misdemeanor of which he had been guilty himself. But the queen Berenice, and the principal men of Jerusalem, were so equitable and candid in this matter, as to state the particulars in the clearest light, and represent to Cestius, without exaggeration or palliation, the government of Florus.

Upon receipt of this intelligence, Cestius consulted with his principal officers respecting the most expedient method of proceeding. Some were for his advancing with an army immediately into Judæa, in order to bring the offenders to justice, if the report should appear true, or otherwise to encourage them in their loyalty, if they were falsely accused. Cestius was of opinion that it would be more adviseable to send some person of honour and address beforehand, to investigate matters, and transmit to him a faithful account of their present state. He accordingly made choice of one of his tribunes, named Politianus, who meeting king Agrippa near Jamnia, on his return from Alexandria, told him by whom he was sent, and what was the purport of his mission.

There was then present several high-priests, as well as members of the Sanhedrim, and others of the first rank amongst the Jews, who came to congratulate the king upon his safe return. These had no sooner paid their obedience in due form, than they proceeded to lay before him a lamentable detail of the piteous condition to which they were reduced by the barbarities of Florus. Agrippa felt for their distress, but, from secret designs, apparently turned his invectives against the Jews rather than the governor, in order to restrain the impetuosity of their passion, as the less they might seem to suffer, the less [illegible] cation they could pretend to revenge. Those who had most property at stake, and consequently most reason to [illegible] a peace, looked upon this gentle reproof as intended by the king for their good.

The people of Jerusalem met Agrippa and Politianus upon their way sixty furlongs from the city, to escort him with all respect and honour, while the women [illegible] the loss of their murdered husbands, and the whole multitude joined in one general lamentation; [illegible] Agrippa generously to compassionate the [illegible] nation, and others entreating Politianus but to go into the city, in order to be an eye witness of the desolations [illegible] Florus. Upon this they took him into [illegible] and pointed out to him its abandoned and forlorn [illegible]. They then prevailed with him, though [illegible] Agrippa, to make the tour of the city [illegible] only one servant, that he might thereby have demonstrative proofs how obedient the Jews were to all other Romans in authority, though the horrid cruelties of Florus were utterly intolerable. When he had taken a view of the city, and informed himself sufficiently of the [illegible] disposition of the Jews, he called the people together, and went up to the temple, where he entered into a declaration of commendations of their approved fidelity to the Romans, earnestly exhorted them to keep the peace, and having performed such parts of Divine worship as he was allowed to do, returned to Cestius.

Immediately upon the departure of Politianus, the multitude addressed themselves to the king and high-priests, importunately soliciting permission to send deputies to Nero with a complaint against Florus, lest [illegible] their silence would afford suspicion that they [illegible] occasion of the havock which had been made, [illegible] were disposed to revolt, and were the [illegible] and thence inferred [illegible] to the emperor. It was evident, on the one [illegible] nothing could satisfy them but the grant of [illegible] and it appeared an invidious profession on the other to suffer the multitude to prefer such an invective against their governor under the sanction of [illegible]. So that Agrippa, in this dilemma, called the multitude together in a large gallery, and having placed his sister Berenice in a chair of state in the Asmonean palace, which overlooks that gallery from the upper part of the town, [illegible] them in words to the following manner:

"If I found you under any sort of disposition to make "war upon the Romans, as I am at this time clearly con"vinced of the contrary, and that the greater part of you "profession [illegible] peace [illegible] I should [illegible] "[illegible] both you and [illegible]. For what "would [illegible] to [illegible] "[illegible] But "[illegible] experimental "knowledge of the [illegible] of you, [illegible] "and inconsiderate [illegible] "for the advantage of the body and making profit to "themselves out of a general confusion, I have now "thought fit to call you together, and tell you what I "think convenient to be done under your circumstances, "in order to the rectifying of your errors, and to prevent "the ruin of a loyal majority by the intemperate heat of a "few desperate libertines. All I desire is your patience "and silence, and to be heard without murmuring and "noise, whether you approve what I say or not. As to "those that are abandoned to the spirit of disorder and "confusion, and irrecoverably lost, they are still at liberty, to go their own way, let my opinion be what it will But it is to no purpoſe for me to ſpeak at all, unleſs I may be heard by thoſe that deſire to hear me

"I well know that the faults of governors, and the bleſſings of liberty, are two common topics for men of art and paſſion to work upon Before I enter upon the diſquiſition of what you yourſelves are, and the force you are pretending to encounter, I muſt, in the firſt place, divide two points that you confound, by taking them into one If revenge upon your oppreſſors (or let it be called juſtice) be the thing that you contend for, what is the meaning of your crying up liberty at ſuch an extravagant rate? Or, if ſubjection be in itſelf ſo intolerable why quarrel with your governors? Subjection is but ſubjection ſtill

"Conſider upon what ground it is that you pretend to calumniate and cavil, and in what manner you are to behave yourſelves, even if your governors ſhould be to blame It is your intereſt, as well as duty, to moderate things with offices of tenderneſs and reſpect, and not to treat your ſuperiors with unbecoming language when you make things greater than they are, you provoke thoſe that are over you to make things worſe than they would otherwiſe be, and to turn that mal-adminiſtration, that they were half-aſhamed of before, into a bare-faced tyranny Nothing takes off the edge of oppreſſion like patience, reſignation is enough to put perſecution out of countenance, even let it be ever ſo violent and unjuſt

"Suppoſe it the caſe now that you are, in truth, extremely injured by the Roman government, will you have [illegible] the Romans, nay, and of Cæſar himſelf too? There's your quarrel You cannot imagine that thoſe governors are [illegible] their commiſſion to oppreſs you, or that Cæſar himſelf can look eaſt and weſt, and ſo through the four quarters of the world, all at a time, when it is no eaſy matter for him to get a faithful account, at Rome, even of what is done here How great a madneſs is it, then, to run the riſque of ſo dangerous a war for trifles? and, in fact, for we know not what! Beſides, matters may mend in time, for governors are neither immortal, or perpetual, but take their turns, and it is reaſonable to hope and promiſe ourſelves that the ſucceſſion will be better When a war is once commenced, it is neither to be given up, or to be continued, without inconveniences As for thoſe that ſet up for liberty, let them beware, in the firſt place, not to run themſelves out of it, for the laſt ſlavery is always the moſt burthenſome, and to avoid that yoke muſt be acknowledged a juſt cauſe of war He that is once a ſubject, and then falls off, is rather a ſtubborn ſlave, than a generous advocate of freedom

"If any thing could have been done againſt the power of the Romans, why was it not done when Pompey broke in upon us? But if your forefathers, and the princes of thoſe times, (though much your ſuperiors in men, money, and conduct,) were not able to ſtand before ſo inconſiderable a detachment of their power, with what face or ſenſe can you pretend, at this time, to bid defiance to the whole body of the empire? To ſay nothing of the obligation of an hereditary allegiance of ſo long a continuance, that hath deſcended from your predeceſſors to their poſterity

"What do you think of thoſe brave and generous Athenians that contended for the liberty of Greece to the very extremity of laying their country in aſhes? thoſe people that brought down the proud heart of the vain and inſolent Xerxes, put him to flight at Salamis, and, having broken the whole power of Aſia, forced him to ſhift for himſelf in a boat, that haughty prince, that turned the ſea into land, and the land into ſea, to make room for his fleets and armies, that looked as if they would have ſwallowed Europe? and yet the nation that did all this, are now ſubjects to the Romans; and Greece receives laws from Italy

"The caſe is the ſame with the Lacedæmonians, after all their famous exploits at Thermopylæ and Platea, and Ageſilaus's carrying their victorious arms into the heart of Aſia, and yet, at preſent theſe heroes own the ſame maſters ſtill

"To come now to the Macedonians, with their Philips and their Alexanders, a people that, to this very day, propoſe little leſs to themſelves than the empire of the univerſe, has not fortune reduced theſe people alſo to the ſame fate and of conquerors made them ſubjects, and ſubjects alſo to the ſame governors? I might reckon up a great many other nations now, much more conſiderable than yourſelves that in the [illegible] of an ambitious contention for liberty, have been forced to ſubmit and obey and are you the only men in the world that are too good to ſerve the ſovereign lords of all other people? Where is your militia, or the arms that you depend upon? your fleets to ſcour the Roman ſeas? Where is your treaſure to anſwer the expence of this undertaking? You fancy an Egyptian or an Arabian war, perhaps, but you proceed altogether upon falſe meaſures, without computing the diſproportion betwixt your ability and your undertaking, and the inequality betwixt a weak and a diſordered people, and the ſtability of a formidable empire It is a common thing for you to be over-run and ſurprized by your next neighbours, when, at the ſame time, the Romans carried the whole world before them

"Nay, and the known world would not content them neither, for though they were poſſeſſed of the courſe of the Euphrates to the eaſt, the Danube to the north, the Lybian deſert to the ſouth, and as far as Cadiz to the weſt, nothing would ſerve them but another world beyond the ocean, and the carrying their arms into Britany, which, at the ſame time was looked upon as inacceſſible What is it that you pretend to? Would you be thought richer than the Gauls hardier than the Germans, or wiſer than the Greeks? Or do you take yourſelves to be hard enough for all mankind beſide? Upon what ground is it that you are ſo bold and confident againſt the Romans? It will be ſaid, perhaps, that it is an uneaſy and irkſome thing to ſerve, but if it be ſo to you, what muſt it be to the Greeks, who over and above a large extent of territory, are looked upon as men of the nobleſt extraction [illegible] under the ſun? And yet theſe [illegible] as they are, live in obedience to the Romans, as do the Macedonians alſo, who have undoubtedly more right to a claim of liberty than you can pretend to [illegible] ye to the five hundred cities of Aſia that peaceably ſubmit themſelves to a conſul, without any guard or garriſon to over-awe them? To ſay nothing of the Heniochians, the Colchians, the [illegible] about the Boſphorus, and the inhabitants of the coaſts of Pontus and the lake of Mæotis, people ſo free in former times, that they never had ſo much as a maſter among themſelves and yet three thouſand Romans were enough to keep them in perfect ſubjection and forty gallies ſufficient to preſerve all theſe ſeas in peace and obedience which no power durſt venture upon before

"Had the Bithynians, Cappadocians, [illegible] Lydians, and Cicilians, nothing to ſay for themſelves upon the point of liberty? and yet they are [illegible] tributaries, and pay their duties without [illegible] to compel them How is it with the [illegible] large country of ſeven days journey [illegible] over, and much more [illegible] yours, being almoſt impoſſible for [illegible] deep ſnows there, and [illegible] ſaid Romans keep them all [illegible] for the Illyrians, from beyond the Danube, as far as Dalmatia, and ſo likewiſe the Dacians, they are all under the guard only of two legions. Nay, the Dalmatians themſelves, after ſo many conteſts for liberty, ſo many battles in the attempt, and ſo many rallies and reinforcements afterwards, in proſecution of the ſame deſign, how quiet and eaſy are they under the command of one ſingle legion!

" But, after all this, if any pretence whatſoever might juſtify a revolt, the Gauls, of all men living, have the greateſt encouragement and temptation to do it, from the very ſituation of their country. They are naturally fortified, on the eaſt with the Alps, the Rhine on the north, the Pyrenæan mountains on the ſouth, and on the weſt with the ocean. But, notwithſtanding all theſe advantages, three hundred and fifteen nations in the ſame intereſt, and an inexhauſtible fountain of all good things within themſelves, both for uſe and commerce, not only for their own, but likewiſe for the common benefit of mankind, we find theſe people under the Roman allegiance, and propounding no other happineſs to themſelves than in that of their maſters. This reſignation does not ariſe from the want of courage, either natural or acquired, or from the want of brave examples in their anceſtors, who had ſtood a diſpute of eighty years for the maintenance of their liberty; but finding ſo admirable a concurrence of fortune and virtue in the actions of the Romans, the Gauls were ſo awed betwixt the veneration they had for the one, and the dread of the other, that the Romans gained as much upon them by their goodneſs as by their arms, inſomuch that, at this day, with only twelve hundred men, they ſecure almoſt as many cities in their allegiance.

" What was Spain the better for their golden mines, when they came to contend with the Romans for their freedom? Or I might inſtance nations more remote from Rome, both by ſea and land, as the Luſitanians and Cantabrians, where neither valour, diſtance, or poſition could warrant them againſt the power of Rome, though bordering upon a ſea ſo impetuous that it cannot be ſo much as named, or thought of, without dread and horror. What ſignified Hercules's pillars, or the Pyrenæan mountains, ſo many warlike nations in the way, diſtance, or any other difficulty, to the obſtructing the progreſs of their victorious arms? But they were reduced as well as the reſt, and one ſingle legion ſerved for a guard upon them all.

" I need not tell you that the Germans are a populous nation, and that their country is of vaſt extent, the people ſtrong, their courage anſwerable to their ſize and ſtature, and firm to the very contempt of death itſelf. But part of this you are eye-witneſſes of, for the Romans have ſlaves of that nation all over the earth. In their anger they are more outrageous than brutes, and the Rhine is at this day their frontier. They have a guard of eight Roman legions upon them, that make ſlaves of as many of them as they take, and the reſt ſave themſelves by flight.

" As for thoſe that place ſo much confidence in the walls of Jeruſalem, they would do well to conſider the walls of Britain, where the inhabitants are ſurrounded by the ſea, in a kind of a new world, not much inferior to the other. They have made themſelves maſters of this vaſt iſland too, and aſſigned only four legions for a guard upon it. What ſhall we ſay of the Parthians, a powerful and warlike people, that have heretofore given laws to ſo many great nations themſelves? Why do they ſend the flower of their nobility for hoſtages to Rome, but as a tacit acknowledgment of ſubjection under the colour of peace? Are we the only men in the world to make war upon the empire, when all other nations tremble under the apprehenſions of their arms?

" Call to mind the fate of Carthage, a people that valued themſelves as branches of the noble race of Phœnicians, that had the honour of the famous Hannibal for their commander. What was the end of that brave people, but to fall under the conquering arms of Scipio?

" But neither the Cyrenæans of the Lacedæmonian race, or the Marmaridans, that ſtretched their dominions as far as the parched deſarts, or the Syrtes, ſo frightful to our apprehenſions, or the Naſamonians, or the Moors, or the numberleſs multitude of the Numidians, were able to check the Roman courage. They had reduced, I ſay, the third part of the world to their ſubjection, ſo large that the very nations are hardly to be numbered, beginning from the Atlantic ſea, and the pillars of Hercules, to the red ſea, and comprizing all Æthiopia. All this they took by arms, receiving, over and above, to themſelves, a yearly tribute of corn, ſufficient to maintain the people of Rome for eight months, beſides other duties that they pay chearfully and readily, though there be but one legion in garriſon to raiſe the contribution.

" But there is no need of recourſe to remote examples for proof of the uncontrolable power of Rome, when we may have inſtances ſo much nearer at hand, as in Egypt, a kingdom that ſtretches out as far as Æthiopia and Arabia Felix, contiguous to the Indies, and an infinite multitude of people in it, beſides thoſe of Alexandria, and yet this mighty populous kingdom ſubmits to be rated by the poll towards the ſervice of the ſtate, and as a tributary to the Romans, and ſuffers impoſition, though not without our plauſible ground to murmur at it.

" How comes it about that Alexandria does not revolt too? a ſtrong, large, and opulent city, thirty furlongs in length, and ten in breadth, peopled, and fortified round about, either with deſerts, ſeas without ports, deep rivers, or boggy quagmires. But the fortune of Rome ſurmounted all theſe difficulties, for two legions in the city, were enough to ſecure the peace of Egypt, and to bridle the Macedonian nobility. This city paid more tribute in a month than you do in a year, and four months proviſion in corn for the people of Rome, beſides money.

" If this be the caſe, what deſerts do you propound to repair to for companions in your undertaking? For all the habitable part of the world is clearly againſt you, and, in effect, Romans, unleſs you flatter yourſelves with hopes of aſſiſtance from your countrymen, the Adiabenians, on the other ſide of the Euphrates. Suppoſing that they could be guilty of ſo groſs an overſight as to engage in a war ſo deſperate, upon ſo unreaſonable a ground, the Parthians themſelves would never endure ſuch diſreſpect towards the Romans, as muſt inevitably end in a rupture, by countenancing a war againſt them. So that you have no retreat left, but a recourſe to God's power againſt his providence, which is moſt evidently ſeen in the advancement, eſtabliſhment, and protection of the Roman empire.

" Conſider war in a religious view, even if you yourſelves were the ſtronger of the two. How can you pretend to diſpenſe with the violation both of God's and of your own laws, or to expect a bleſſing from heaven in the very act of your diſobedience? If you keep the ſabbath-day as ſtrictly and religiouſly as you profeſs, and as your laws bind you to do, you will moſt certainly be caught in the ſame ſnare over again, that your predeceſſors were hampered in by Pompey heretofore, that is to ſay, by taking advantage of your ſcruples, and falling upon you on thoſe days when you dare not ſo much as move an hand to defend yourſelves. If you make no conſcience of breaking the laws, in fighting one day as well as "another how do you fight for the maintaining of them, "and how can you look for any favour from God in the "deliberate breach of his own commandments? Whoever "made war but in hope of assistance either from God or "man? and when both fail, what can be the consequence "but a voluntary wilful slavery? If this be your resolution, "what have you more to do than to lay violent hands upon "your wives and children, and to lay your glorious country "in ashes? The extravagant madness of the action will be "some sort of excuse for it, besides, that it will save you the "dishonour of falling by the hands of an enemy.

"It is a high point of wisdom, my good friends, and a "very necessary point, to foresee and to provide for a "storm while the ship is yet in the harbour, and it is as "dangerous, on the other hand, to put off the consideration "of it till the tempest is upon you, and then to stand trem-"bling, and at a loss which way to turn yourselves. As "for those calamities that threaten us unawares, and by "surprize, people that fall into them are to be pitied, for "there is no preventing of evils not to be foreseen, but for "men that run headlong into visible hazards, they fall not "only unlamented, but with infamy also and scandal.

"Your way of proceeding, in this affair, would almost "persuade one that you have already agreed upon terms "with the Romans how they are to behave themselves in "case of gaining their point, that is to say, with tenderness "and moderation, and not according to the practice of other "nations, with fire and sword, burning your sacred cities, "extirpating your whole race and destroying every man "upon the pursuit that outlives the battle; for which way "can you fly, but into the very mouths of your enemies, who "are either the subjects of Rome already, or such as are in "fear of being quickly made so?

"Nor are you to flatter yourselves that this calamity will "stop here: all the Jews upon the face of the earth are to "expect your fate, and the whole universe will join as one "man to the punishing of this rebellion. You will remem-"ber what I tell you now, when you shall see the streets run "with blood to gratify the impetuous violence of a few hot-"brained councils. The Romans are not to be blamed in "that, for doing that which you yourselves have forced "them to, and you are to consider, on the other side, in "case they should spare you, what an impiety you have "to answer for, in the abuse of so much humanity and "goodness.

"If you have no longer any sense of natural tenderness "for your wives and children, have at least some compas-"sion for your capital city, and the sacred walls of it, have "mercy even upon the temple, your laws, as the holy sanc-"tuary, which you yourselves are now about to destroy "with your own hands, for you are never to hope for "mercy again from the Romans, after so ungrateful an "abuse of the indulgencies you have formerly received from "them.

"But, to conclude, I hereby call God and our whole "country to witness, that I have done the utmost in my "power towards your preservation. If you will follow my "counsel, you may yet live in peace, but if you are deter-"mined to perish in tumult and outrage, I have only to con-"sult my own safety."

This address, which was enforced by tears from his sister Berenice, in some degree abated the rage of the multitude, who acknowledged that they were not inimical to the Romans, but to Florus, for the indignities he had so repeatedly offered them. Agrippa replied, "that what they had already done was, in effect, professing enmity to the Romans, as they had broken down the galleries of the castle of Antonia, and refused paying tribute to Cæsar." He added, "that if they would obviate all suspicion of revolt, they had only, without further delay, to discharge the one, and rebuild the other, since neither the citadel or the tribute belonged to Florus."

The people hearkened to this advice, and went with the king and Berenice into the temple, where they applied themselves to the rebuilding of the galleries, and, at the same time, sent the proper officers up and down the province, to collect the duties which were deficient, and then paid in the whole arrears, amounting to forty talents. Having brought them thus far to reason, Agrippa counselled them to submit to the government of Florus till Cæsar should appoint a successor. But this incensed them to such a degree that they not only reviled him in the most opprobrious language, but stoned and drove him out of the city. The king, sensible of this contemptuous behaviour in the highest degree, and finding the rabble irreclaimable and desperate, sent several men of rank to Florus at Cæsarea, in order that he might make choice of collectors of the revenue for the whole province, and then retired to his own kingdom.

CHAP. XVII.

The Jews surprize Massada, and put the Roman garrison to [illegible] kept the Roman [illegible] at the instance of Eleazar, [illegible] The first beginning of the war. The leading men [illegible] Representation of the [illegible] Of [illegible] Pharisees [illegible] [illegible] Jews [illegible] [illegible] Agrippa [illegible] The [illegible] the upper town [illegible] The [illegible] [illegible] depart.

SOON after this a strong party of the whole seditious people to revolt [illegible] Massada, [illegible] the Roman garrison, took it by surprize, put all the Romans to the sword, [illegible] people. There happened at the same time another disorder in the temple at Jerusalem. One Eleazar, the son of Ananias the high-priest, an intrepid young man, and [illegible] officer then in command, prevailed upon some of the priests to receive neither offering or sacrifice [illegible] the nation of the Jews. This was the very foundation of the war with the Romans, for, at the instance of Eleazar, the sacrifices of Cæsar which were offered [illegible] for the welfare of the Roman people, were rejected. The high-priests and men of the first rank, declared [illegible] tion of the novelty of such [illegible] desired the continuance of so pious a custom as the offering up of prayers for princes and governors. But the factious party were resolute and inexorable, [illegible] upon their numbers, and all those who were desirous of innovation espoused their cause, which was the more countenanced, was [illegible] supported by Eleazar, an officer both in [illegible] and [illegible] command.

This occurrence brought together the rulers, the high-priests, and the Pharisees of the first quality, to deliberate on the most expedient measures to be taken at this juncture, for they plainly foresaw the calamities [illegible] continuance of the tumult must entail [illegible] debated the point, and came to the [illegible] tempt, by representation and counsel [illegible] of the people. In order to this, they called [illegible] assembly before the brazen gate [illegible] temple to the eastward, and the [illegible] rashness of the enterprize, and, indeed madness of involving their country in so destructive a war. From thence they proceeded to shew the unreasonable ground of the dispute, and the injustice of the cause; observing that their predecessors were so far from prohibiting any oblations from strangers (which was the highest instance of impiety,) that, in some sort, they made it a part of their worship, as appears from their donations being preserved in the temple as ornaments, and in honour of the memories of the donors. It was represented, that, to provoke the Romans to a dangerous war, to the scandal, if not ruin of Jerusalem itself, by setting up new modes of religion, to the exclusion of all sorts of people, but Jews, from offering up prayers and oblations to God in his holy temple, was so extravagant a measure as could not admit of excuse, even in the instance of a private person; but further, to make it general, to the absolute excommunication of Cæsar himself, the insult would justly be deemed unpardonable. It was inferred from these premises, that the contempt would revert to themselves; and that, in consequence of their refusal to offer up prayers and oblations to others, they would not be allowed the liberty of worshipping themselves, when the city would be left without discipline and good order. It was concluded they must expect, unless they gave up so idle a project, and relinquished so impious a design before it came to the knowledge of Cæsar.

After these representations, several of the sophists versed in the Jewish rites and ceremonies, produced precedents and reports of the practices of former times upon the point in question; and the conclusion drawn upon was, that their ancestors never refused oblations from strangers. But those who were bent on innovation, and therefore for stirring up contention, would not hearken to their opinion, nor would the Levites attend Divine service, being wholly intent upon the war.

The men of rank finding the multitude too strong for government, and that the resentment of the Romans would first fall upon them, deliberated upon the matter, and agreed upon sending deputies, some to Florus, of whom Simon, the son of Ananias, was to be chief; others to Agrippa, the principal of whom were to be Saul, Antipas, and Costobarus; which last was the kinsman of Agrippa. Their commission was to solicit them to come with some troops to Jerusalem, and crush the sedition in time.

This message was grateful to Florus, who was disposed to inflame the war at all events, as appeared by the delay of his answer to the deputies, in order to give the seditious an opportunity to collect their force. But Agrippa who was for the common interest, was desirous of saving both parties as much as lay in his power, the guilty as well as the innocent, and by that means securing the Jews to the Romans, and Jerusalem to the Jews. Finding also his own interest at stake, he sent two thousand auxiliary horse, collected from Auranites, Batanea, and Trachon, with Darius at the head of them; and Philip, the son of Joacim, their general.

The rulers of the people, with the high-priests, and all that were disposed for peace received these deputies into the upper town, the lower part of the temple being in the hands of the faction. They began a skirmish with slings and darts, bows and arrows, and maintained it without intermission. Sometimes they made sallies and excursions, and sometimes fought hand to hand. The seditious were the more resolute and daring, but the king's soldiers were superior in military skill. Their principal aim was to force the sacrilegious faction out of the temple, while Eleazar, and his accomplices, laboured as hard on the other side, to make themselves masters of the upper town. The contest lasted seven days, without any material advantage on either side, but with great slaughter on both.

The festival of Xylophoria now drawing on, which took its name from the custom of carrying wood to the temple, to keep fire all the year round, they excluded the seditious from their worship. But while a party of the Jews were abroad upon this office, a band of assassins, called Sicarii, fell in amongst them, and improving the advantage of the king's troops being overborne, both with hardiness and numbers, they forced them out of the upper town, and the faction immediately took possession of it. They then set fire to the house of Ananias, the high-priest, and to the palaces of Agrippa and Berenice, proposing, in the next place, to burn the offices of record, and the contracts belonging to the creditors, and thereby dissolve their obligation for paying their debts. This was done to gain to their interest multitudes of debtors, who might then join in an insurrection with safety against the more wealthy. The keepers of the records, in fine, abandoned their trust, and consulted their own personal safety, and both writings and offices were all burnt. After this stab to the strength and credit of the city, they applied themselves more particularly to the prosecution of the war.

In this scene of confusion many of the rioters, and high priests, were forced to fly for safety to subterraneous caverns, while others got amongst the king's troops into the upper palace, and immediately shut the gates. In this number were Ananias the high-priest, Hezekias, his brother, and the deputies of Agrippa.

The seditious contented themselves, for the present, with the advantage they had obtained, and the mischief they had done, and proceeded no farther. But the day following, being the fifteenth of the month Lous, they attacked the castle of Antonia, and after two days carried it by assault, cut off the whole garrison, and set fire to the place. Passing from thence to the palace where the troops of Agrippa had taken sanctuary, they divided themselves into four bodies, and attempted the undermining of the walls; but the defendants were obliged to keep close, not being strong enough to venture a sally. The assailants plied their works, and several of the faction, as well as the Sicarii perished under the walls. *In fine, they fought day and night, without* respite, the faction, in hopes of rendering the besieged miserable by starving them; and the besieged thinking to tire out the faction with the fatigue of unremitting duty.

There was amongst the seditious one Manahem, the son of Judas of Galilee, a subtle and specious orator, who had formerly upbraided the Jews, under Cyrenius, for professing to worship one God, and at the same time acknowledging the supremacy of the Romans. This Manahem, having a design upon Herod's arsenal at Massada, inveigled several men of rank into his party, took them with him, and forced the place, armed a band of vagrants, and marched with the state of a king to Jerusalem, where he set up as head of the mutineers, and gave orders in form for carrying on the siege of the palace.

But they wanted proper instruments, for it was impracticable to undermine the wall, as the enemy showered darts upon them from above; so that they began to break ground at a distance, and carried on a covered way to the foot of one of the towers, which they undermined at the foundation, and then propped it with timber to support the weight. When they had finished the work, they set fire to those timbers, and so withdrew; and the pillars being consumed, the turret fell to the ground. But the king's troops, it seems, were aware of this stratagem and ran up another wall immediately behind the turret to make the place good. This discovery, upon the fall of one of the towers, and when they deemed their work accomplished, threw the besiegers into the utmost consternation. The king's people in the palace, however, sent to Manahem, and the other heads of the faction, for permission to depart, and those of his religion, who forthwith took their departure.

The Romans, in consequence of this, were greatly dejected, as they were incapable of coping with so vast a number, nor could they, in honour, descend to treat with rebels. In this extremity they quitted the camp as indefensible, and betook themselves to the king's forts, Hippon, Phasaelus, and Mariamne. Manahem's party brake in [illegible] the fold [illegible] quitted, slaying all that came near them, plundering whatever was left behind, and, in conclusion, burning the camp. This action bare date the sixth of the month Gorpiæus.

CHAP. XVIII.

Death of Ananias and Hezekias. Eleazar and his party [illegible] Manahem [illegible] [illegible] the Romans [illegible] upon terms [illegible] Eleazar [illegible] oaths and articles. The [illegible] of Eleazar. [illegible] of the [illegible] of the Jews. [illegible] upon a sabbath-day.

ON the day following, Ananias, the high-priest, and his brother, Hezekias, were taken out of one of the [illegible], wherein they had concealed themselves, and both put to death by one of the guards. The faction [illegible] the guard about the forts, insomuch that none of the [illegible] could make their escape. Manahem was so elated with the [illegible] of so many fortified places, and the death of Ananias, the high-priest, that he became a most inhuman and insupportable tyrant, and behaved as if he had engrossed to himself the government of the [illegible]. These overbearing tyrannies gave occasion to Eleazar, and some of his confidents, to reason amongst themselves upon the subject. It was observed, that it was by no means [illegible] that those who had revolted from the Romans from a desire of asserting their liberty, should betray that liberty to any of their own people, and submit to [illegible] governor, who, though he should be guilty of no violence, was inferior to themselves, concluding from thence, that if there was an absolute necessity of setting up one man above the rest, it should by no means be Manahem. In the heat of this resolution they went up to the temple, where they found Manahem at his devotion, [illegible] robes in all the state of a prince, both as to dress and train, with all his guards about him.

While he was [illegible] in all his glory, some of Eleazar's party made a violent assault upon his person. The multitude then began to stone him, [illegible] that the death of the sophist would bring about the [illegible] of their liberty. His guards made a slight [illegible], till they found he was opposed by the people, when they respectively shifted for themselves. They slew all they took, and made diligent search for the rest. Some few got privately into Massada, and amongst the rest Eleazar, the son of Jairus, and Manahem's near kinsman, who [illegible] exercised a tyrannical government in that place. Manahem himself was taken lurking in a place called Ophlas, dragged out, exposed, tortured, and then put to death. His deputies and assistants were treated in the same manner, and amongst the rest Absalom, who was the chief abettor of the tyranny.

The people espoused the cause of the opposers of Manahem, imagining, as before observed, that it would be a ready means of effecting an accommodation, whereas the party, in truth, was only in [illegible] to Manahem, that were setting up for themselves, not so much with the design of suppressing one tyranny, as promoting another. The multitude [illegible] pressed the prevailing faction [illegible] to bear so hard upon the Romans, but rather to raise the siege, and suffer them to depart. But the more they pressed it on the one side, the more it was opposed on the other. When Metilius, the Roman general, and his people, had exerted their utmost power for the defence of the place, and were now reduced to the last extremity, they offered to capitulate with Eleazar, to deliver it with all that was in it, upon condition only of sparing their lives. The terms were readily accepted, and Gorion, the son of Nicodemus, Ananias, the son of Saddaca, and Judas, the son of Jonathan, were appointed to ratify the treaty, and sign and seal the articles. As soon as the agreement was confirmed, and the [illegible] formalities had passed, Metilius drew off his soldiers, without interruption, or the least suspicion of danger, as long as the Romans were under arms. But when, according to compact, they came to deliver up their swords and shields, Eleazar's guards broke in upon them, [illegible] and [illegible] assassinated them, without resistance or [illegible] on the part of the Romans, or so much as one word of reproach, except those of "oaths and articles." Metilius [illegible] the only [illegible] that begged it, which, however, was granted him upon promise of turning Jew.

The Romans sustained no real [illegible] by this [illegible], [illegible] upon the occasion, [illegible] into comparison with their vast armies. [illegible], the leading cause of destruction to the Jews, [illegible] became inevitable, and [illegible] just grounds [illegible] very city which took [illegible] so polluted with [illegible] and rebellion, that, [illegible] escape the vengeance of the Romans, it would [illegible] a victim to Divine justice. Never did the [illegible] wear so melancholy an aspect, [illegible] and the [illegible] were [illegible] in [illegible] face, as they were to be answerable [illegible] the guilt [illegible] slaughter being perpetrated on the sabbath-day, [illegible] the most horrid and heinous, as upon that day [illegible] not allowed to perform any work, though ever so [illegible] praise-worthy.

CHAP. XIX.

Slaughters and calamities by [illegible] Jews. [illegible] of them to [illegible] Seditions [illegible] Ferment [illegible] bring [illegible] the [illegible] of 13,000 Jews [illegible] Exploits of Simon, a man of [illegible] strength [illegible] His confession and [illegible] his wife and children [illegible] his own hand, [illegible] himself, to avoid the [illegible]

UPON the very same day, [illegible] tion of Providence, there [illegible] at Cæsarea to the number of above twenty thousand [illegible] was there a Jew left in the place, [illegible] carried [illegible] fled to be apprehended, and [illegible] to [illegible] This horrid carnage [illegible] the [illegible] that the Jews divided [illegible] and began their inroads upon some of the villages of Syria, and then laid waste several of the [illegible] delphia, Gebonitis, Gerasa, Pella, [illegible] they broke in upon [illegible], destroying some places, and setting fire to others. Thence they advanced to Cedasa, belonging to the Tyrians, to Ptolemais, Gaba, and Cæsarea. They [illegible] Sebaste and Ascalon without opposition [illegible] reduced those places to ashes, they [illegible] Gaza. They [illegible] also, and laid waste, several villages upon the frontiers, and put to death as many of the inhabitants as they could find.

The Syrians, on the other hand, [illegible] the Jews not [illegible] put to the sword, but the persecution [illegible] inhabitants of [illegible] time most deplorable, as every [illegible] times in it; and there were no means of preserving [illegible] but by destroying the other. [illegible] shed, and [illegible] The pretence of the Syrians [illegible], but they were so divided concerning others, [illegible] suspected to be Judaizers, or favourers of their [illegible], they thought it [illegible] they were so fearful of suffering them to [illegible] should afterwards prove to be Jews.

Those who before had discovered some degree of humanity and moderation, were now become inexorably cruel, from malevolence, and the hope of lucre, for they plundered all they killed, and had the booty for a reward, reputing him the bravest man who obtained the greatest share, as having overcome the greatest number of his enemies. It was an horrid spectacle to behold the streets filled with dead bodies of men, women and children, that lay there not only unburied, but uncovered. The provinces laboured under the same calamities, besides the dreadful prospect of [illegible] and much greater miseries in future.

The conflict had hitherto been maintained betwixt Jews and strangers, but drawing towards the borders of Scythopolis they found the very Jews of that quarter inimical to them, so much did they prefer their interest and convenience to every other consideration, for the Jews of Scythopolis joined the inhabitants against the other Jews. Nay, such was their alacrity, that the citizens of Scythopolis suspected them, lest they should join against them with the other Jews, surprize the town in the [illegible] and impute it, at last, either to a desire of revenge for their sufferings, or the necessity of their condition. The citizens, upon this account, told the confederate Jews, that if they would confirm their agreement and demonstrate their fidelity to them, they should withdraw, for the present, with their families, into a certain grove adjacent. This they accordingly did, and for the two following days all was quiet at Scythopolis; but, upon the third night, their scouts bringing them intelligence that they lay in a careless, easy, and supine posture, the inhabitants fell upon and cut them all off, to the number of 13,000, seized the plunder, and so departed.

Having given this general account, I cannot pass over [illegible] relating to one Simon, who perished in this [illegible]. He was the son of Saul, a man of [illegible] among the Jews, and distinguished from the rest of his companions for the firmness of his mind, and the strength of his body, both which faculties he had employed [illegible] of the Scythopolitans, to the injury of his country. [illegible] did daily execution upon several of the Jews living near the place, and would frequently put whole troops [illegible] that his single person was [illegible]. But in the end, a vengeance overtook him adequate to his crime, for when he saw the Jews surrounded by the Scythopolitans, and [illegible] all over the grove, he drew his [illegible], (which he found of no avail against such a multitude,) thus passionately addressed himself to the men of Scythopolis "How [illegible] am I [illegible] the wrongs I have done, and "purchasing [illegible] with the lives of so many "of my fellow-citizens. As I am now to die, and it "will not become a man of honour to fall by the hand of "an enemy, but rather to do justice upon myself, I will "not therefore put it in the power of an enemy to glory in "my ruin, and triumph over me in my calamity."

Having thus spoken, he surveyed his wife, his children, his aged parents, and whole family, with a mixture of rage and commiseration, and while gazing, as in suspence, he took his father by his grey hairs, and ran him through the body, and after him his mother, who willingly submitted to the stroke. After the father and mother, he did execution upon his wife and sons, who appeared rather to meet the weapon than avoid it, as by that means they prevented the enemy. When he thus put all his kindred to death, he piled them up, and ordering their bodies to be seen by all, he stretched out his right hand, and sheathed the sword in his own bosom. This man, from the strength of his body, and firmness of his mind, deserves to be remembered with compassion; but whoever considers his attachment to strangers, must confess that, in the end, he met with a deserved fate.

CHAP. XX.

Massacre of the Jews at other places. Agrippa goes to Antioch, and leaves Varus his viceroy. Batanea sends [illegible] deputies to solicit for a garrison. Varus sends a band of armed men to cut them off upon the way. Agrippa deprives him of his commission. The seditious take possession of the castle of Cypros. The Romans surrender up Machærus to the Jews.

AFTER the massacre at Scythopolis, other cities rose up against the Jews that were amongst them. The people of Askalon slew two thousand five hundred, those of Ptolemais two thousand, those of Tyre a considerable number, but kept more of them in bonds. In Hippon and Gadara they cut off all that were young and active, imprisoning the rest, and proceeded in like manner elsewhere, as they were actuated by hatred or fear. But in Antioch, Sidon, and Apamia they were safe and quiet in the enjoyment of their lives and liberties. Whether it was that they were not powerful enough to be dangerous, or from compassion to a people who did not seem to have any design upon the state, cannot be determined; but the latter seems the more probable cause. As for the Gerasenes, those who were dispersed were permitted to abide with them in peace, and they gave the rest safe conduct to their borders.

There fell out, at the same time, an unfortunate incident for the Jews in the kingdom of Agrippa, who, having occasion to visit Cestius Gallus at Antioch, committed the administration of his government to Varus, a kinsman of king Sohemus. The province of Batanea, during the king's absence, sent seventy deputies of the first rank to solicit the indulgence of a garrison, to the end that, in case of a commotion or tumult, they might be able to suppress it. Varus immediately sent out a party of the king's troops to cut them off upon the way. This he had the confidence to do, not only without the knowledge of Agrippa, but entirely against his approbation. He was induced to this horrid outrage by his avarice, so that, after so flagitious a beginning, he stopped at no manner of tyranny or iniquity, but continued his havock throughout the kingdom. When Agrippa had intelligence of his destructive proceedings, for the sake of Sohemus he spared his life, but removed him immediately from his government.

The seditious, in the mean time, got possession of the citadel of Cypros, upon the frontier of Jericho, put the garrison to the sword, and demolished the fortifications. At the same instant another considerable body of the Jews treated with the Romans in Machærus to deliver up the garrison, who, choosing rather to part with it by agreement than compulsion, surrendered it upon conditions.

CHAP. XXI.

[illegible] of the Jews for [illegible] from [illegible] the Alexander the Great, and afterwards [illegible] to the Cæsars. A violent tumult at Alexandria between the Jews and the Greeks. [illegible] composed by Tiberius, who turned [illegible] loose upon them [illegible] commission [illegible]. [illegible] Fifty thousand Jews slain upon the spot, and the rest beg their lives. The implacable rage of the Alexandrians.

THE natives of Alexandria conceived a mortal antipathy to the Jews, from the days of Alexander the Great, who, in acknowledgment of the services they had done him against the Egyptians, made them free of this city, with the grant of all privileges in common with the Greeks. These privileges were continued to them by the successors of Alexander; a peculiar quarter was assigned apart to themselves, where they lived in a manner seques-

[illegible] from the converse of other people, being also entitled to the privilege of calling themselves Macedonians. When Egypt came afterwards to fall into the hands of the Romans, the Jews had their ancient privileges still confirmed by Cæsar and his successors; but they were perpetually at variance with the Greeks; and though they suffered [illegible] on both sides for their misdemeanors, it had [illegible] other effect than to inflame the contention.

Things were extremely out of order at this time every where, but particularly so at Alexandria. The inhabitants [illegible] in assembly about an embassy to Nero upon an extraordinary occasion, there came rushing into the amphitheatre a mixed crowd of Jews and Greeks. The latter immediately exclaimed that the Jews were enemies and spies, and at the same instant fell furiously upon them. They took three of them, and the rest made their escape; but these three they dragged away in order to burn them alive. This commotion brought in the whole body of the Jews to their rescue. They began with casting stones at them, and after that ran with lights in their hands up to the amphitheatre, threatening the whole multitude to burn them to ashes, which they had certainly done if Tiberius Alexander, the governor of the city, had not restrained their fury. He did not [illegible] violent measures, but employed some of the most popular men among themselves to attempt, by mild persuasion, to bring them to reason, advising them to moderation, and [illegible] how they incensed the Roman soldiers. The seditious Jews, however, made a jest of the [illegible] of Tiberius, and reproached him for the [illegible] he had [illegible].

When the governor found the tumult was not to be suppressed without having recourse to arms, he sent out upon them two Roman legions that were then in the city, and five thousand Libyan troops, to harass the mutineers. Their orders were not only to slay all that opposed them, but to seize their effects, and the [illegible] their houses. The word of command was no sooner given, than they marched to a quarter of the town called Delta, where the Jews chiefly resided, and there executed their orders to the utmost extremity. The Jews placed their best armed men in the front, who for some time, made an obstinate resistance; but, upon the first disorder, they were scattered and cut to pieces, though it proved to the conquerors a bloody victory. Death and destruction never appeared in more hideous forms. Some were caught in the open field, others forced into their houses, which were first plundered, and then set on fire by the Romans. No mercy was shewn to age or sex, till the place ran with torrents of blood, and fifty thousand of them lay dead in heaps, nor had the remainder been preserved, had they not betaken themselves to supplication for their lives, so that the governor, commiserating their case, gave orders for the Romans to retire, which they did at the first word, out of the deference they paid to order and discipline. But the populace of Alexandria bore so implacable an hatred to the Jews, that it was with difficulty they were prevented from insulting the very carcases. Such was the consequence of the tumult at Alexandria.

CHAP. XVII.

Cestius marches with a powerful army against the Jews. The inhabitants of the country [illegible] upon his [illegible] to Ptolemais. He is [illegible] Zabulon, the strongest city of Galilee, plundered and burnt. Cestius returns to Ptolemais. The Jews cut off two thousand Syrians. Cestius removes to Cæsarea. [illegible] of Joppa by the Romans.

CESTIUS finding the Jews, from their seditious disposition, become so totally obnoxious, determined on a vigorous prosecution of the war. To that end he drew out his troops, and marched for Ptolemais. He took with him the twelfth legion entire, which he had at Antioch, two thousand chosen men out of the other legions, four troops of horse, besides the kings auxiliaries, that is to say, two thousand horse, and three thousand foot, belonging to Antiochus, armed with bows and arrows, a thousand horse, and three thousand foot, belonging to Agrippa, a body of four thousand men from king Sohemus, a third part horse, and the remainder of them foot, chiefly archers. The people came flocking in to Cestius out of the cities through which he passed in his way to Ptolemais, who though they might be deficient in military skill, were zealous in the cause, from their implacable hatred to the Jews.

Agrippa assisted Cestius not only with his troops, but his counsel, so that at this instance the general [illegible] with part of his army to Zebulon (otherwise called [illegible] or [illegible]) which divides Judæa from Ptolemais. When he came up to the place, he found it totally deserted by the inhabitants, who had all fled up to the mountains, abounding in all sorts of provision, so that he gave the soldiers the plunder of the town. Though he could not but admire the beauty of the buildings, which [illegible] those of Tyre, Sidon, and Berytus, he caused the whole [illegible] to the ground, [illegible] the [illegible] country [illegible] fell in his way. [illegible] had [illegible] a blaze, he [illegible] turned to [illegible]. The Syrians were [illegible] upon the booty, [illegible] of Berytus, [illegible] behind for the [illegible], so that the Jews, taking courage upon the [illegible] of Cestius, and [illegible] upon them by surprize, cut them off to the number of near two thousand.

From Ptolemais Cestius removed to Cæsarea, and from thence sent a detachment of his army to Joppa, with orders to preserve the place, if they could quietly get possession of it; but, in case the inhabitants should put themselves in a posture of defence, they should wait for the bringing up the rest of the army. The Romans, in fine, assaulted the place both by sea and land, and mastered it without much difficulty, for the inhabitants were so far from attempting to dispute it by force, that they had no opportunity [illegible] [illegible]. They were all put to the [illegible] men, women and children, without distinction. The city was plundered and burnt, and the number of the slain is [illegible] to amount to eight thousand four hundred persons. Cestius also sent a body of horse into the [illegible] of Narbatene, near Cæsarea, where they laid the country waste, put great numbers of the inhabitants to the sword, seized upon their effects, and burned their [illegible].

CHAP. XVIII.

Cestius sends Cæsennius Gallus into Galilee. Sepphoris, and [illegible] with the Romans. The [illegible] Cestius [illegible] from Cæsarea to [illegible] with his army to [illegible]. [illegible] The Jews [illegible] on the [illegible] day, and [illegible] Cestius [illegible]. The [illegible] the Romans [illegible] Jerusalem [illegible].

CESTIUS now sent Cæsennius Gallus, the commander of the twelfth legion, into Galilee, with such additional forces as he judged sufficient for the reduction of that province. The inhabitants of Sepphoris, the strongest city, opened their gates to him, [illegible] of the towns had the prudence to follow their [illegible]. But the mutineers and free-booters [illegible] the mountain of Asamon, that crosses Galilee, [illegible] to Sepphoris. Gallus advanced upon them [illegible] their own post; but so long as they maintained [illegible] ground they were too hard for the Romans, and slew [illegible] two hundred of them in the encounter. But when the Romans came to take a compass, and, by degrees, had gained the top of the mountain, and were [illegible] to cope with them upon even terms, the fugitives were presently routed, their light-armed men not being able to stand the shock, nor those that fled to escape the pursuit of the horse. Some few, indeed, concealed themselves in lurking places among the mountains, but upwards of two thousand of them were cut to pieces.

Gallus, apprehending no cause for innovation in Galilee, drew off his troops to Cæsarea, and Cestius with his whole army, went to Antipatris. He was there given to understand, that a considerable body of the Jews were got together into the tower of Aphec, and sent a party thither to dislodge them. The Jews, not being in a condition to stand the attack, left it to the Romans, who razed it, and then setting fire to all the adjoining villages, took their departure. From Antipatris Cestius removed to Lydda, where he found only fifty men, the rest being gone up to Jerusalem to the feast of tabernacles. He put those fifty to the sword, burnt the town, and then advanced, by the way of Bethoron, to a certain place called Gabaoth, fifty furlongs from Jerusalem, and there pitched his camp.

The Jews, finding the enemy approach their metropolis, left the festival, and betook themselves to their arms. They thought their number of the enemy, ... and in that confidence sallied out upon the Romans, with ... clamour, and ... confusion, regardless of ... it being ... the sabbath, which ... is by them most scrupulously observed. But ... rage which caused them to ... with the ... of the sabbath, proved an advantage to them in the execution of their design upon their enemies; ... the Romans into disorder upon the first charge, ... and made so furious an attack ... main body, that if they had not been supported by a party of foot which was then ... that came up to their relief in ... and his whole army, had been ... There fell five hundred and fifteen of the Romans in this skirmish, four hundred of them foot, the rest horse; two and twenty only of the Jews were slain upon the spot. Those who signalized themselves upon this occasion were Monobazus and Cenedæus, two kinsmen of Monobazus, king of the Adiabenians. The next in reputation to these two heroes were Niger of Perea, and Silas the Babylonian, who went over from king Agrippa, whom he had formerly served, into the interest of the Jews.

The Jews, at length, being forced to retreat, returned into the city, while the Romans, drawing off likewise to Bethoron, were pressed upon the rear by Simon, the son of Gioras, who cut off several of them, seized their carriages and baggage, which they found upon the road, and so went off to Jerusalem. Cestius continued three days after this in the field, as the Jews had possessed themselves of the elevated parts of the city, set watches at the entrances, and appeared resolved to fall upon the Romans as they had quitted their stand.

CHAP. XXIV.

Agrippa proposes to the Jews an alliance with the Romans. The people ... upon it, and treat the ambassadors ... Cestius falls upon them, and pursues them to the wall of Jerusalem, bringing his whole army up to the city. He encamps near the palace. The Jews repair to the defence of the walls. The Romans are repulsed upon several assaults. An invention to secure the pioneers. Cestius raises the siege, and the revolters fall upon his rear. A great slaughter of the Romans by the Jews. Cestius ... great perplexity. The miserable condition of the Romans. Cestius saves himself by a stratagem.

AGRIPPA, observing that the affairs of the Romans were in a dangerous situation, while such an immense number of their enemies had seized upon the mountains round about, determined to try if the Jews were to be influenced by words, flattering himself that the parties might be reasoned to a better understanding one of another; or thinking, however, if he could not reconcile them, he might possibly be able to divide them, and abate something of the rancour of the quarrel. Pursuant to this design, he sent two of his officers, Borceus and Phebus, men of approved integrity, to offer them a treaty of alliance with the people of Rome, with an assurance of pardon and indemnity for all that was past, upon condition of laying down their arms, and coming over to Rome. The factious, upon hearing of this proposal, were so apprehensive of the people going over to Agrippa, in hopes of this amnesty, that they determined to assassinate the ambassadors. Accordingly they slew Phebus before he could open his commission, and Borceus was wounded, but prevented his fall by flight. But the multitude was so enraged at the baseness of this action, that they drove the seditious before them into the city.

This intestine division gave Cestius the first opportunity to break in upon the factious, so that he advanced upon them with his whole army, charged, routed and pursued them to the walls of Jerusalem. He then marched off to a place called Scopus, seven furlongs from the city, and there pitched his camp. He remained three whole days in a state of inactivity, without so much as making an attempt upon the place, hoping, perhaps, that the people might become disposed to peace; but in the mean time, sent out a party of soldiers into the neighbouring villages, to procure corn and other necessaries.

On the fourth day, which was the thirtieth of the month Hyperberetæus, he advanced with his whole army, in good order, up to the city, while the people ... through fear of the factious party. But the ... were so intimidated by the apparent order and ... of the Romans in their march, that they retired ... the suburbs, many into the inner parts of the city, and ... into the temple. Cestius took his way by Bezetha, ... he advanced, burnt Cenopolis and a place called ... market. Thence advancing to the upper ... he ... his camp near the palace. If he had then ... assault, he might easily have carried the place ... to the war. But Tyrannius and Priscus, ... other great officers, had been corrupted ... divert him from his purpose. Thus ... the absolute ruin of the Jews, and the source of ... future calamities.

... these circumstances divers of the principal men ... the Jews, at the instance of Ananus, the son of ... invited Cestius into the city, proposing to open the gates to him, but he delayed his resolution so long, ... through indignation or diffidence, that the ... was discovered, and Ananus, with his party, forced, by stones from the walls, to fly for sanctuary to their own ...

The Jews dispersed themselves upon this into the turrets, for the defence of the walls, and they made good for five days against the utmost efforts of the Romans, though pressed with the most impetuous violence. On the sixth day Cestius, with the choicest of his troops and bowmen, assaulted the temple on the northern quarter, but the Romans were so galled with ... and arrows from the porches and galleries, that they were not only obliged to give way, but ... repulsed. After these disappointments the Romans had recourse to the invention of the first rank ... their ... the wall, and guarded themselves with what they called testudo, from its resemblance to the back of a ... which ... being proof against all the enemies darts and arrows, they were at liberty to undermine the wall without further danger. They then made preparation for setting fire to the gate of the temple. This so ... the factious, that they gave up all for lost, and many of them quitted the town. But it was matter of joy to the more ... and peaceable part, insomuch, that they called out to open the gates to Cestius, whom they deemed their friend and preserver.

Ten Thousand JEWS *Massacred in one Day by the Inhabitants of* DAMASCUS.

To such a plight were they reduced, that if Cestius had [illegible] the siege [illegible] little longer, the Romans would certainly have had possession of the city; but it seems not to have been agreeable to the Divine will, that this dreadful war should thus terminate; for Cestius [illegible] unconscious of the good disposition of the people in general, or the desperation of the seditious [illegible], by [illegible] of judicial infatuation, drew off his men on a sudden, even when their hopes were [illegible] the [illegible], and contrary to all reason, quitted the [illegible]. This unexpected [illegible] so emboldened the [illegible] that they [illegible] the [illegible] of the Romans, and cut off a considerable [illegible] both of their horse and foot. Cestius lodged that night at the camp he had fortified at a place called Scopus [illegible] the next day he continued his march, [illegible] the enemy [illegible], who putting [illegible] cut off many of the hind [illegible]. They also fell upon the flanks on each side of the army, and galled them with darts; nor [illegible] they so much as [illegible] to look the enemy in the face, [illegible] of those that pursued them [illegible] not even attempt to repel those that pressed them on [illegible], [illegible] of breaking their ranks, whereas [illegible] the Jews on the other hand [illegible], [illegible] and [illegible] upon any [illegible]. Upon this [illegible] Romans suffered greatly, [illegible] themselves upon their defence [illegible], in fine, were covered with dead and wounded [illegible], [illegible] the [illegible], [illegible], [illegible], [illegible] of horse, so [illegible], [illegible] got to [illegible] their baggage [illegible].

Cestius [illegible], doubtful [illegible] to proceed [illegible]. Upon [illegible] found the number of Jews [illegible] the country [illegible]. From this [illegible] this delay [illegible] not only [illegible] but end-[illegible] the more [illegible] he [illegible].

Upon [illegible] order [illegible] army to be disengaged of all incumbrances [illegible] and expedition of the [illegible]. The mules, [illegible] burthen, [illegible] to be kill[illegible] reserving [illegible] of those which [illegible] that he might have [illegible] occasion for [illegible] which [illegible] left the [illegible] with [illegible] the [illegible].

[illegible] was the fate [illegible] on their march to Bethoron. [illegible] were not [illegible] the Jews so long as [illegible] in open country, but when they came into narrow passages, they charged [illegible], to separate the [illegible], and forced them [illegible] valley, while the multitude, from [illegible] rocks and crags, galled them with their darts. While the foot [illegible] these distressed [illegible], not knowing how to defend [illegible] enemies, the condition of the horse was much more [illegible], [illegible] they could neither advance up to the Jews to attack them upon the mountains, nor secure themselves against [illegible] could they keep their own troops [illegible] the shower of arrows that poured down among them. They were at length in such a situation [illegible] they could neither fight nor fly, and in this desponding [illegible] they had recourse to all the [illegible] of tears, groans and outcries, that are usual in such cases, whilst the rocks and the vallies rung, on the other side, with transports of joy, triumph, and [illegible].

Such was their advantage, that if the Jews had been favoured with day-light the army of Cestius had been totally destroyed; but night coming on, the Romans escaped to Bethoron, and the Jews secured all the passes round about, to cut off the retreat of the Romans.

When Cestius found in what manner he was beset, he bethought of a stratagem to assist him in his escape. He selected about four hundred of his bravest men, and placed them at the strongest of the fortifications, giving orders that, when they went up to the morning guard, they should erect their ensigns, that the Jews might be induced to believe the army had not yet decamped. In the mean time Cestius slunk away with the rest of his forces without any noise, about thirty furlongs during the night.

When the Jews perceived in the morning that the place was abandoned, and the main army withdrawn, they immediately fell upon the four hundred Romans who had deluded them, slew them to a man, and then went in pursuit of Cestius. But having [illegible] himself of the night to promote his escape, they could not overtake him. The soldiers fled in such confusion, that [illegible] behind them all their [illegible], which the Jews took up, and afterwards [illegible] the [illegible]. They followed the pursuit as far as Antipatris, but finding it vain to continue it longer, secured their engines, [illegible] the dead, collected the booty, and so returned [illegible] and triumph to Jerusalem, [illegible] victory [illegible] had [illegible] [illegible] the twelfth year of the [illegible] Nero.

CHAP. XXI.

The most eminent Jews [illegible]
to Nero, [illegible]
[illegible]
[illegible] in the [illegible]
[illegible] Cestius [illegible]
[illegible]
[illegible]
[illegible]
[illegible]

AFTER [illegible] Cestius, the most considerable [illegible] Jews [illegible] the city [illegible]. Costobarus [illegible] brother [illegible] of Jerusalem, [illegible] general, [illegible] to Cestius. But Antipas [illegible], [illegible] to [illegible]. Now Cestius [illegible] to Nero in Achaia, with [illegible], and to transfer the [illegible] upon Florus. Cestius [illegible] culpability himself, and [illegible] of the [illegible] against the other.

When the people of Damascus [illegible] of the destruction of the Romans, they entered into [illegible] of cutting off all the Jews in that place. [illegible] could effect, if they could [illegible] the baths, or any other places of [illegible]. Their principal ground of apprehension [illegible] coming to the knowledge of their wives, who were mostly attached to the Jewish religion. [illegible], the opportunity when the Jews [illegible] these public meetings, in an [illegible] upon them [illegible] ten thousand [illegible] day without any difficulty.

The Jews who gave Cestius [illegible], being by this time returned to Jerusalem, [illegible] by every means, fair and foul, to [illegible] Romans as they could in their [illegible] had a meeting in the temple, for the [illegible] for the government of the [illegible] sastical departments. The [illegible] Gorion, and Ananus, the high priest, [illegible] in the city, [illegible] more especial manner, the rebellion [illegible] for Eleazar, the son of Simon, [illegible] session a mighty booty taken from the Romans, a considerable sum of money from Cestius, and a mass of public treasure to an immense value over and above, they did not think him worthy of having any commission conferred upon him, looking upon him as a man of an imperious, tyrannical disposition, and upon his special friends and confidents rather as guards than companions. But this did not prevent Eleazar from insinuating himself, by degrees, into the affections and esteem of the people, for he so prevailed upon them by the popular means of money and address that, in their professed opinions, no man was so well qualified for governor as himself.

The commanders they sent into Idumea were Jesus, the son of Sapphas, one of the high-priests, and Eleazar, the son of the new high-priest, at the same time enjoining Niger, the present governor of that province, to obey their orders. This Niger, coming from Peræa, beyond Jordan, was called Peraites. Nor did they neglect the care of other parts of the country. They sent Joseph, the son of Simon, to Jericho; Manasses to Peræa; John, the Essene, to Thamna; while Lydda, Joppa, and Emmaus, were to be governed in the room of the same John. John, the son of Ananias, was made governor of Gophnitis and Acrabatene; and Josephus, the son of Matthias, governor of both the Galilees, adding to his command Gamala, the strongest place in the whole country.

These governors discharged their duty with alacrity and prudence, according to the extent of their respective commissions. ... Josephus, when he came into Galilee, was to obtain the good-will of the people, ... knew to be more conducive to the preservation of order and good government. He was also convinced that the certain way to make sure of the great men, his friends, was to admit them to a share in the government, and that the most effectual means to secure the affections of the multitude, was to employ natives, and particular inhabitants in popular offices. His plan was therefore this: he selected a council of seventy out of the elders and ablest men of the nation. To this council of seventy he committed the whole government of Galilee, under some few restrictions, appointing seven to every city, to hear and determine all common causes in such manner and form as he had prescribed, reserving to himself the judgment of capital causes, and matters of great importance.

Having thus regulated affairs at home, so far as related to domestic policy, he took it into consideration the necessary means of securing his people from foreign injuries and insults. Taking it for granted that the Romans would break into Galilee, he took care, in the first place, to wall in all the defensible cities, as Jotapata, Bersabee, Selamis, Pereecho, Jappha, Sigoh, ..., and Tiberias, with the mountain Tabor. He fortified also the caves about the lake of Genezareth, in the Lower Galilee, and in the Upper, Petra of the Achabarians, Seph, Jamnith and Meroth, and Seleucia, Sogane, and Gamala, in Gaulanitis. The people of Sepphoris being wealthy and warlike, had liberty to build their own walls. John, the son of Levi, by order of Josephus, walled in Gischala. As to the rest of the castles, they were fortified by the direction and assistance of Josephus himself. He collected an army out of Galilee of more than an hundred thousand young men, and armed them with old weapons, which he had collected together, and prepared for them.

The next thing that occurred to him was the mighty power of Rome, and the means by which it became invincible, which evidently appeared to be their strict attention to military discipline. Observing, therefore, that their readiness in obeying orders was owing to the multitude of their officers, he made partitions in his army after the Roman manner, dividing and subdividing officers of command into several subordinations. He had his officers over tens, hundreds, and thousands, and all these subjected to other superiors. He taught them the discipline of signals, the points of war in the sound of the trumpet, to distinguish an alarm, a charge and a retreat, the disposition of an army and form of battle, the order of bringing off or on, seconding the weak, or relieving the weary. He explained to them the nature and effects of fortitude, mental and corporeal, and whenever he treated on military subjects, held forth the Roman discipline as the grand instance of authority and example. He told his soldiers, that, if they would lay a foundation for success in their military undertaking, they must renounce beforehand, all violence, robbery, fraud, pilfering, and the like, that they must do justice to all people without exception, nor seek to raise themselves upon the downfall of others, observing, upon the whole, that a good conscience is the only real foundation of genuine courage.

Josephus had now raised his complement of forces; they consisted of sixty thousand foot and two hundred and fifty horse, and besides these four thousand five hundred mercenaries, with six hundred select men for the guard of his person. These men were no very heavy charge to the country, for all but the mercenaries were maintained by the different cities, which, as they sent one half of them to the war, employed the other half in providing necessaries, so that one part wrought for the other, and those that were in arms protected their purveyors.

CHAP. XXVI.

Character of John of Gischala. He obtains the confidence of Josephus, and then abuses it. Raises a jealousy against him ... is deserted by all his friends but four. ... to the Jews. He gains upon the multitude, ... puts John upon other treacherous practices. ... gives notice of it to Josephus, who hastens to Tiberias. John counterfeits sickness. Josephus ... escapes. John is execrated for his perfidy. All ... reconciled to Josephus. Terms of accommodation ... accepted. Secret plots against Josephus. ... go over to the enemy.

WHILE Josephus was engaged in his administration in Galilee, there started up an extraordinary kind of impostor. He was a native of Gischala, the son of one Levi, and his name was John. He possessed cunning and fraud in an extraordinary degree, and was capable of the most flagitious practices. His poverty for a long time prevented the execution of his wicked designs. Though he was a notorious liar himself, he was as credulous as those he imposed on. Fraud by him was estimated a virtue, and his best friends were the objects of his delusion. He made great pretence to humanity, but was barbarously cruel where he had hopes of gain. His ambition had no bounds, and the foundation of his hopes was laid in his crimes. He was so naturally addicted to theft, that he acquired its various tricks, and particularly of alluring others, insomuch, that he collected accomplices, by degrees, till they amounted to a train of four hundred, in which number there was not one irresolute man, or inexpert in the use of arms, so scrupulously careful was he in his choice for mental and corporeal qualifications. The greatest part of this band was raised from the villages and borders of Tyre. With this banditti, however, he made great ravages, and put many of those to the sword who had withdrawn upon the apprehension of a war. But he aspired to far greater things, and wanted only money to put himself at the head of a well formed party.

When he found that Josephus was greatly pleased with the activity of his disposition, he employed his influence with him to obtain the superintendence of the re-building the walls of Gischala, upon which pretence he drew huge sums of money in contributions from all the citizens of property. He had then recourse to another invention, concerted with wondrous shrewdness. He procured ...

order from Joſephus to all the Jews in Syria, forbidding them expreſsly to ſend any oil into the bordering parts, but of the produce of their own nation Upon this prohibition John engroſſed the oil, and ſold it again at eight times the price it coſt him

This being a plentiful year, and Galilee a country abounding with oil, the monopoly which he practiſed in ſending ſo much abroad, where there was a great ſcarcity, brought an incredible ſum of money into his coffers, which credit he converted afterwards to the miſchief of his benefactor Perſuaded at this time, if he could once overthrow Joſephus, he ſhould himſelf obtain the government of Galilee, he gave it in charge to the ruffians under his command to harraſs the inhabitants more and more, which would either exaſperate the people into practiſes upon his perſon, if he controlled them, or elſe expoſe him to accuſations and complaints, if he let them alone As an introduction to his deſign, he cauſed a report to be circulated far and near, that Joſephus was in a plot to betray the province to the Romans, and many other ſtratagems did he continue to effect his ruin

There was at that time a party of young men of the village of Dabaritta, who kept guard on the great plain, and as Ptolemy, king Agrippa's and queen Berenice's ſteward was travelling that way, ſet upon him, and took away all his horſes and baggage, to a great value, in rich robes, ſilver plate, and ſix hundred pieces of gold This was a prize not to be concealed, ſo that they carried it whole as it was to Joſephus at Tarichee, who checked them for the violence they had offered to the king and queen, and ordered the booty to be depoſited in the charge of one Eneas an eminent man of that city, and to be forth coming upon demand This act of juſtice had well nigh coſt Joſephus his life, for when the villagers came to underſtand that they were excluded from all ſhare in the prey, and that the governor reſerved it entirely for the king's uſe they ran through all the neighbouring cities and villages, exclaiming that Joſephus had betrayed them

This outcry raiſed ſuch an uproar, that, by day-light next morning, there was a body of an hundred thouſand people aſſembled who ran to the Circus at Tarichee, exclaiming againſt Joſephus, ſome being, for depoſing, ſome for ſtoning, and others for burning him as a traitor The tumult at the firſt time was encouraged by John, and Jeſus, the ſon of Sapphias who were magiſtrates of Tiberias This violent outrage of the people threw the attendants and guards of Joſephus into ſuch a conſternation that all but four perſons deſerted him He was at that time in a ſound ſleep, and as they were juſt ſetting fire to the houſe his four friends waked him. Joſephus maintained an extraordinary degree of compoſure, nor diſcovered the leaſt emotion, either at the number of his enemies, or the deſertion of his friends, but frankly preſented himſelf to the view of the people in rags and aſhes, with his hands behind him, and his ſword about his neck This generous conſtancy moved his friends, and eſpecially thoſe of Tarichee, to the higheſt degree of commiſeration But the ſavage mob, both of the town and country, to whom his government ſeemed burthenſome, reviled him for his treachery and oppreſſion, calling upon him again and again, to reſtore the money, and confeſs the fact They concluded in fine, from his habit and behaviour, that he was now diſpoſed to declare the truth, and that with a view of obtaining both pardon and pity Under theſe circumſtances he thought it moſt expedient to divide his enemies, and ſet them at variance, and to this end promiſed them a frank confeſſion of the whole matter, ſo that having obtained an hearing, he ſpoke to this effect

"I neither did intend to ſend this money back again to "Agrippa, or to convert it to my own uſe, as it never "was my deſign to court the friendſhip of any prince "that was inimical to you, or propoſe to myſelf any be"nefit to your prejudice But (addreſſing himſelf to the "people of Tarichee) conſidering the defenceleſs ſtate of "your city without walls, your own inability to rebuild "them, and the avidity with which the people of Tiberias, and ſeveral other cities, have beheld this prize, I "thought I could not do better than increaſe it for the "accompliſhment of ſo laudable a purpoſe If you agree "with me in opinion, you are bound in honour to ſupport "me in what I have done, if otherwiſe, I am ready to "lay all that I have taken at your feet, to be diſpoſed of "at your pleaſure"

The people of Tarichee loudly applauded this ſpeech, but thoſe of Tiberias loaded him with calumnies, menaces, and reproaches, and their rage and animoſity became fiercer than ever In the heat of their diviſion, however, they declined their quarrel with Joſephus, and entered into a war to conteſt one with another

When Joſephus found he had ſecured the people of Tarichee in his intereſt (who amounted to near forty thouſand) he addreſſed them with more freedom, pointed out to them their error, and aſſured them that, for his part, he was reſolutely for employing the money they had in the fortification of the town He recommended to them to leave to him the care of the other cities alſo, aſſuring them, if they would follow his direction, nothing ſhould be wanting towards the charge of the work

This carried ſo fair a face, that part of the mutineers, though ſtill diſſatisfied, withdrew but, at the ſame time, another party of two thouſand armed men advanced furiouſly towards Joſephus, who eſcaped into the houſe, while the rioters ſtood preſſing and menacing without Joſephus was now under a neceſſity of having recourſe to another invention he went up to the top of the houſe, and waving his right hand as a ſignal for ſilence, when the uproar ſubſided a little, thus addreſſed them "I cannot underſtand the drift "of your debate, for it is impoſſible for us to underſtand each "other in this confuſion of noiſe I ſtand here ready to "fulfil your commands, if you will depute any perſons to "come to me, that we may treat on the matter with com"poſure and temper"

Upon this propoſal, ſome of the leaders repaired to Joſephus, were admitted into the houſe, taken into the inner quarter, and there ſcourged with the utmoſt ſeverity The rabble thought they had waited long enough at the door for the iſſue of the conference, imputing the delay to ſome difficulties in the caſe, when, on a ſudden, the doors were thrown open, and the commiſſioners diſmiſſed in the bloody hue after the flagellation, which ſtruck the people with ſuch terror, that thoſe who were higheſt in their menaces before, were the firſt to caſt down their arms, and betake themſelves to flight

This diſappointment ſo mortified and exaſperated John againſt Joſephus, that he concerted other practices to gratify his revenge He counterfeited ſickneſs and deſired permiſſion of Joſephus to go to the hot baths at Tiberias for the recovery of his health Joſephus, upon this, gave him recommendatory letters to the governor of the city to afford him aſſiſtance in what might be requiſite for his accommodation, without the leaſt ſuſpicion of treachery But John was no ſooner poſſeſſed of the advantages he deſired, than he tampered with ſome, and corrupted others with money [illegible] fair words, to abandon Joſephus When Silas, who [illegible] time, had charge of the city, received information of this practice, he forwarded advice of it to Joſephus, who, [illegible] the very inſtant of receiving the letter, (though [illegible] it) haſtened away for Tiberias, and arrived there [illegible] next morning The people in general received him [illegible] utmoſt deference, John only excepted, who [illegible] matter, and the fiction which he had [illegible] He ſent him, however, a complimentary excuſe for not doing himſelf the honour of waiting upon him [illegible] ing to be confined through ſickneſs [illegible] Tiberias were now aſſembled by order of Joſephus [illegible] intent to acquaint them [illegible]

[illegible] John, [illegible] notice of it, sent a band of bravoes to destroy him [illegible], at the instant of their drawing their swords, the people gave a shriek, and Josephus [illegible] the [illegible], when the weapons were just at his throat, leaped down from a standing of six cubits high which he had mounted for his harangue, and made his escape to a little boat upon the lake, with only two of his guards to protect him.

The soldiers immediately [illegible] to their [illegible], to avenge their general [illegible] the [illegible]. But Josephus, fearful lest [illegible] should be [illegible] by the envy of a few men, and [illegible] the city [illegible], sent a messenger to his people, [illegible] to proceed to further [illegible] for their own preservation, and [illegible] followed his orders with the strictest [illegible].

When the rumour of the [illegible], and the [illegible] of it, was spread [illegible] the country, the people [illegible] in great multitudes and [illegible] John, but he [illegible] them [illegible] by flying to Gischala, his native place. The cities of Galilee [illegible] to [illegible] on the occasion, and with [illegible] thousand [illegible] men, who offered their best services against John, whom they reviled as a traitor, and the common enemy of mankind, and declared him deserving of being condemned to the [illegible], with the city that [illegible] him. [illegible] that he [illegible] thanked them for [illegible] goodwill, but [illegible] to moderate proceedings [illegible] the [illegible] would [illegible] his enemy, by [illegible] and prudence, than destroy them by [illegible]. He declared, however, at the same time, that he would wish to find every man out of their respective cities [illegible] John, [illegible] should not [illegible] five days [illegible] decree, abandon the interest of John, and return to their allegiance.

The heads of [illegible] cities were unanimous in the promotion of these conditions [illegible] was made [illegible], and all things [illegible] duly executed. This declaration brought over [illegible] of John's party, who cast themselves and their [illegible] at the feet of Josephus. [illegible] with the remainder, which consisted of about a thousand Syrian fugitives, betook himself to [illegible], where he found he could not carry [illegible] open attempt. He sent private emissaries to Jerusalem [illegible] his [illegible] extravagant [illegible], and [illegible] that he would soon become tyrant, unless restrained by a superior power. The people in general discredited this intimation, but some of the [illegible] to [illegible] John with money towards maintaining the contest with Josephus. Nay, they even passed a decree for recalling him from his government, nor did they think this [illegible], but sent a detachment of two thousand five hundred armed men, and four persons eminent as lawyers and orators, to order to supplant Josephus [illegible] and with the people. They were [illegible] to offer him no violence, if he would come away [illegible], but, in case of refusal, to treat him as an enemy. The commissioners were Jonzar the son of Nomicus, Ananias the son of Sadduc, and Simon and Judas, the sons of Jonathas.

The friends of Josephus gave him intelligence that an army was coming against him, but the design of the enemy was kept so close, they could not form the least judgment of it. For this cause four cities immediately revolted from him, these were Sephoris, Gamala, Gischala and Tiberias, but he soon recovered them without bloodshed. Four of the principal men he had taken, both for arms and counsel, he sent back to Jerusalem, which enraged the people to so violent a degree against them, that, if they had not escaped in time, they would have been all cut to pieces, both those who were sent, and those that sent them.

CHAP. XXVII

Tiberias again revolts, and is recovered by a notable stratagem. The inhabitants surrender, and send hostages for the performance of articles. Clytus [illegible] himself, and cuts off one hand with the other, according to [illegible].

DURING this time John was in such dread of Josephus, that he kept himself close within the walls of Gischala. Within a few days Tiberias revolted again, [illegible] Agrippa to take possession of the town and acknowledge him for their king. But, as he did not come at the time appointed, some Roman cavaliers appeared and expelled Josephus out of the city. When the news of this [illegible] reached Tarichee, Josephus was in a very embarrassed situation, as he durst not venture himself alone among the whole body of the deserters, nor could he stay [illegible] for fear of being surprized by the king's soldiers. [illegible] the next day was the sabbath, no plan could be [illegible] execution. Thus circumstanced, he found himself under the necessity of circumventing the revolters by [illegible] the gates of Tarichee to be all [illegible] present any intelligence being conveyed to Tiberias [illegible] design. Upon this he caused all the vessels [illegible] together, to the number of two hundred and thirty, [illegible] men to be put in each of them [illegible] sailed early in the morning for Tiberias. [illegible] at a distance of [illegible] the [illegible] the number of the fleet, [illegible] what men they had on board, he ordered all [illegible] to come to anchor, and stay [illegible], with [illegible] seven of his guards, and those unarmed, rowed up so near the town as to be within view of the place. [illegible] from the walls, but, upon sight of [illegible] that taking it for granted that the vessels were full of men, they threw down their arms in consternation, [illegible], by tokens of the most submissive intercession, [illegible] to [illegible] the city.

Josephus uttered terrible menaces against them, and reproached them, that, when they took up arms against the Romans, they should spend their force before-hand in civil dissensions, and do that which their enemies desired above all things, that besides, they should endeavour to [illegible] him who took care of their safety, and [illegible] to shut the gates of their city [illegible] their walls. He, however, told them, that he [illegible] of such intercession from them as he could [illegible] with for the security of the city.

Upon this they dispatched [illegible] of the principal men as deputies, whom Josephus ordered to [illegible] a boat [illegible], and conveyed to [illegible]. He afterwards [illegible] fifty of the principal [illegible] for the performance of the conditions, [illegible] proceeded, upon one pretence or other, [illegible] the whole senate in his hands, to the number of [illegible] persons, besides two thousand of the [illegible], as fast as the vessels could be filled, were all conveyed to Tarichee, and there kept in custody.

The people now exclaimed against Clytus as the author and ringleader of this tumult, desiring Josephus to make him an example, and to accept of his punishment for satisfaction. Josephus had no design of [illegible] any man to death, but, however, on the supplication of the people, he ordered Levi, one of his guards, to cut off [illegible] the hand of Clytus. The soldier durst not venture upon the execution in such a crowd of enemies, [illegible] which Josephus was inclined to go on shore and do it himself. Clytus, perceiving this, entreated Josephus to content himself with one of his hands. The request was granted, upon condition that he himself should cut it off. Clytus drew out his sword

ncd, and with the right hand cut off his left Such was the awe in which Josephus was held and thus was Tiberias recovered by Josephus, seven soldiers, and a number of empty vessels

Not many days after this, upon the revolt of Sepphoris, and some other cities, Josephus gave his soldiers the plunder of that place and Gischala, but, upon application of the inhabitants, he caused restitution to be made of all they could discover, and the like at Tiberias, proposing at the same time, to chastise and oblige them

CHAP. XXVIII

The inhabitants of Jerusalem prepare for war. Ravages and cruelties of Simon, the son of Gioras

THUS were the disturbances of Galilee quieted, and the Jews no sooner ceased the prosecution of civil dissentions, than they applied themselves to making preparations for a war with the Romans, Ananus, the high-priest, and the men of power in Jerusalem, that stood in opposition to the Romans, both repaired the walls and procured numbers of warlike implements, such as darts, arrows, and the like All hands were employed upon warlike preparations, and the youth in general, were trained to the exercise of arms. In this confused state of affairs the more moderate and candid part of the people could not restrain from lamentation at the prospect of calamities to come Those of a pacific turn beheld with horror the discord that prevailed, but public incendiaries were pleased with the expectation of mischief The city, in fine, wore the aspect of destruction, before the Romans came against it Ananus contended for laying aside these preparations for a war, and endeavoured to bring them to reason, but he miscarried in the attempt, as will appear from the sequel of this narrative.

Simon, the son of Gioras, was, at this time, at the head of a band of free-booters, who lived upon the spoil in the toparchy of Acrabatena, where they not only plundred great mens houses, but injured their persons also, and treated the masters themselves with the greatest ignominy, exercising indeed, the most barefaced tyranny, He went on in this lawless manner till he was forced, by the troops sent against him by Ananus, and other rulers, to retire with the small party he had remaining to Massada, where he continued till Ananus, and his other adversaries, were cut off He made such ravages in Idumæa and its environs, and committed such horrid outrages, that, for the security of the country, government was under a necessity of putting garrisons into the very villages This was the state of affairs in Judæa at this juncture

END OF THE SECOND BOOK OF THE WARS

FLAVIUS JOSEPHUS

ON THE

WARS OF THE JEWS.

BOOK III.

CHAP. I.

Instances of the vanity and ostentation of the emperor Nero. Distracted state of the Roman affairs. Nero appoints Vespasian to the government of Syria. His qualifications for such a trust. Vespasian, and his son Titus, draw together a powerful army. The defeat of Cestius renders the Jews rash and insolent. They advance towards Askalon. The armies engage, and the Jews are totally routed, as incompetent to cope with the Romans. Great slaughter of the Jews upon another occasion. Niger, their general, preserved in a wonderful manner. The inhabitants of Sepphoris friendly to the Romans.

WHEN Nero was informed of the ill success of the Roman arms in Judæa, a consternation and terror, as is usual upon such occasions, fell upon him; though he openly affected unconcern, intimating, that what had happened was rather owing to the negligence of the commander than to any valour of the enemy. It seems he thought it becoming him, who bore the burthen of the whole empire, to contemn such misfortunes, which he pretended to do, as possessing a soul superior to all the casualties of fortune. But after all this ostentation of invincible courage his solicitude for the want of a general equal to the necessities of the empire was plain and evident; for the east was now wavering and falling off, the Jews were in deep rebellion already, other nations prepared to revolt, and the state of affairs universally perplexed. The great points necessary to be attended to, were to keep the one quiet, reduce the other, and prevent the seditious spirit of the third from tainting the whole body. Vespasian was the instrument pitched upon as the only person Nero deemed competent to the discharge of so important a trust. He was now advanced in years, and had been exercised during the whole course of his life in military exploits. This was the man that settled the peace of the empire in the west, upon the revolt of the Germans. This was the man who completed the conquest of Britany, which before was neither perfectly subdued or known; and he presented his father Claudius with the honour of a triumph for it, without any danger or fatigue of his own. Considering Vespasian under all these circumstances, his years, resolution, faith, and conduct, the children he had, (hostages for his fidelity,) together with other incidental matters in favour of the empire, Nero was induced to constitute him general of his forces in Syria. For his further encouragement, his commission was accompanied with many fair words and alluring promises, according to the custom of the world in an hour of necessity.

Vespasian had no sooner received his commission from Nero, in Achaia, than he dispatched his son Titus for Alexandria, to draw off the fifth and tenth legions there, while he himself crossed the Hellespont, and so made his way by land into Syria, where he came to a rendezvous with all the Roman troops, and the auxiliaries sent in by the princes bordering upon that province.

The Jews, in the mean time, were so transported with the unexpected advantage they had gained over the Romans under Cestius, that they behaved in the most extravagant manner, carrying on the war beyond all the bounds of moderation and prudence. They collected with expedition a multitude of their most hardy troops, and marched towards Askalon, an ancient city, distant near 520 furlongs from Jerusalem. They ever had an aversion to the inhabitants of this place, and therefore made choice of it for their first attack. They had for their leaders three celebrated commanders, Niger, of Perea, Silas, a Babylonian, and John, an Essene, men eminent for sagacity and resolution.

Askalon had a wall of prodigious strength; but there had been but men to defend it, the whole garrison consisting only of one company of foot, and a troop of horse, under the command of Anthony. The Jews were impatient till they came to blows with the Romans, and therefore marched with more than ordinary expedition to fall upon them by surprize. But Anthony, being apprized of it, had drawn his horse out of the town before hand, to be in readiness for the encounter, without being intimidated either by their numbers or their courage Upon their advance, he received their charge with great bravery, and so put a stop to their progress towards the walls of the town The Romans, through the advantage of veteran horse to foot order to confusion, troops well appointed to people without arms, counsel and conduct against rage and passion, and men, in fine, of obedience and resignation, against a loose headstrong multitude, made no difficulty of putting the Jews to the rout, for their first ranks were no sooner broken by the Roman horse, than they fled several ways, some towards the town, where they were crushed to death by crowds of their own people while others were scattered all over the plain, with the Roman cavalry at their back, and spacious room for the horse to play in These circumstances greatly favoured the Romans, and occasioned the slaughter of great numbers of the Jews as which way soever they fled, the Romans were upon them, overtaking some, crossing others, while they surrounded many, and dispatched them with their darts In this calamitous state of desperation their vast multitudes were no more than so many single men, and the Romans, greatly flushed with victory, cut off their small number had enough to spare The Jews, on the other hand, as they were ashamed of having turned their backs, so they did all that was possible towards the recovery of their honour but the Romans in the course of their success, without weariness or intermission, pursued their victory the greatest part of the day, killed ten thousand Jews upon the spot, two of their generals, John and Silas, being of the number The rest were mostly hurt, and made their escape, with Niger their only surviving general, to Salis, a town in Idumæa, and during the whole contest there were but few wounded on the Roman side

But the Jews were so far from desponding under so great a calamity, that the losses they had sustained seemed rather to have quickened their resolution for other attempts This confidence entailed on them a second overthrow When they had paused a little, scarcely long enough to dress their wounds, they got together in the most outrageous indignation, all the power they were able to make, and in a much greater body attempted Ascalon once again, under the same disadvantages of want of skill and discipline, and with the same fortune as before, for they fell unawares into an ambush laid by Anthony in the way they were to pass, where they were beset, charged, and routed by the Roman troops, before they could put themselves in order of battle Eight thousand were slain upon the spot The rest got off with their general Niger, who acquitted himself several times on that occasion like a gallant officer but the enemy pressing them closely, they were driven, for sanctuary, into a strong castle, belonging to a village called Bezedel This castle was deemed impregnable, so that Anthony, to bring matters to a speedy conclusion, set fire to the fort, as the only means of destroying the castle and the general at once Upon this exploit the Romans went their way triumphing and rejoicing, making no doubt but Niger was destroyed in the flames But it seems, to avoid the fire, he leapt down from the top of the castle into a deep vault, and as some of his friends were searching for his body, in order to give him a decent funeral, he presented himself before them yet living, which transported the Jews out of an affliction almost inconsolable into an excess of joy, to find their commander delivered by so signal a providence

Vespasian being now come with his army to Antioch, the capital of Syria, and, without dispute, for beauty and situation, the third city of the Roman empire, he found king Agrippa with all his forces waiting his arrival He passed from thence to Ptolemais, in which city the inhabitants of Sepphoris a town of Galilee, were ready to attend him These people had prudently provided for their own safety, and being sensible of the formidable power of the Romans, without staying for the arrival of Vespasian, to shew their good affection to the government they had, by anticipation, promised as much to Cestius Gallus, receiving a garrison from him, acknowledging him for their governor, and binding themselves to serve him even against their own countrymen Vespasian, granted them, at their request, such a body of horse and foot for a garrison, as might be a sufficient security against incursions, if the Jews should make any such attempt Sepphoris, indeed, being the largest and strongest city of all Galilee, Vespasian judged it a matter of high importance to have it in good hands

CHAP. II

Description of Galilee, Samaria and Judea Division or distribution of Judæa

THERE are two Galilees, known by the names of the Upper and the Lower Galilee, which are encompassed by Phœnicia and Syria They are bounded on the west by the city of Ptolemais and mount Carmel formerly belonging to the Galileans, at present to the Tyrians To this mountain adjoins Gaba, or the *city of horsemen*, so called from the plantation of Herod's horsemen that settled there upon their dismission They are bounded, on the south by Samaria and Scythopolis, as far as the river Jordan, on the east by Hippene, Gadaris, and Gaulanitis, together with the borders of the kingdom of Agrippa, and on the north by Tyre, and the frontiers of the Tyrians

The Lower Galilee extends in length from Tiberias to Zebulon, near Ptolemais on the sea-coast In breadth, from Xaloth, on the great plain, as far as Bersabe, and there begins the breadth of the Upper Galilee, which extends as far as the village of Baca, that divides it from the territory of the Syrians Its length is computed from the Thella, a village near Jordan, to Meroth

These two provinces are of large extent, and surrounded by several distinct nations, but yet have ever been able to make powerful resistance upon all occasions of controversy, for the Galileans are inured to war from their infancy, and have been always very numerous The men neither wanted courage, or the country provisions The soil is universally rich and fruitful, and full of plantations of trees of every kind, insomuch that it invites the hand of cultivation, and courts the cherishing art of the husbandman The grounds are every where dressed, and not a foot of it lies unmanured There are cities, towns, and villages in abundance which in so plentiful a country, must be populous, for the inhabitants of the least of them are computed to amount in number to fifteen thousand Though Galilee falls short of Perea beyond Jordan, in point of magnitude, it is much superior to it in strength and value, for, besides the fertility of the soil, every spot is so improved, that no ground is lost, whereas that vast track of land beyond Jordan is in general, dry and barren, and not so proper for corn, as the milder kind of fruits In some places indeed, as Perea in particular, the soil is more fruitful, and produces excellent fruits, which appears from the vines palm-trees, and other plants scattered up and down the fields in great abundance and perfection They are all watered and refreshed with torrents from the mountains, and with quick springs in the season of excessive heat

The length of Perea is from Machærus to Pella the breadth from Philadelphia to Jordan, with Pella on the north, the river Jordan on the west, the land of the Moabites on the south, and Arabia, Silbonitis, Philadelphia, and Gerasa, on the east

Samaria is situated betwixt Judæa and Galilee, beginning at a village called Ginea, upon the plain, and extending to the toparchy of Acrabatena The country is much of the same nature with that of Judæa, which is well tilled and manured, abounding in trees and autumn fruits both those which grow wild, and those which are the effect of cultivation

vation It is naturally dry, but amply supplied with showers. The waters of those few rivers they have are exceedingly sweet, and, as they have excellent grass, their cattle yield abundance of milk. But the superior advantage of these provinces is the incredible number of inhabitants The boundary of Samaria and Judæa is Annath, otherwise called the village of Borceos

The same village likewise bounds Judæa on the north The length of it runs from the south side to a village, upon the borders of Arabia, called Jordan The breadth is from the river Jordan to Joppa In the midst of it stands the city of Jerusalem, which has been aptly denominated by some the "Navel," or center of the province Judæa wants nothing to render it as delightful as it is fruitful, and that by sea as well as land, as far as Ptolemais

It is divided into eleven parts Jerusalem, the first, as the sovereign head of all the rest, is called emphatically the royal city The other ten are distributed into as many toparchies, Gophna is the second, and the Acrabatena, Thamna, Lydda, Emmaus, Pella, Idumæa, Engedi, Herodion, and Jericho The neighbouring countries are under the jurisdiction of Jamnia, and Joppa, as Gamala, Gaulonitis, Batanea, and Trachon, are comprized in the kingdom of Agrippa This country, which is inhabited by the Syrians and Jews promiscuously, extends in breadth from mount Libanus, and the sources of Jordan, to the lake of Tiberias, and in length from the village of Arpha as far as Julias Thus have we, with all possible brevity, described the country of Judæa, with its boundaries and confines

CHAP III

Vespasian sends succours to the people of Sepphoris under the command of Placidus Josephus attacks Sepphoris, but is frustrated in his attempt Galilee is miserably harassed Titus comes with a great army to Ptolemais The order of the Roman discipline The Roman method of encamping and decamping The order they observe in marches Extent of the Roman empire

THE auxiliaries sent by Vespasian to the relief of the people of Sepphoris, being a thousand horse and six thousand foot, were distributed, after drawing them up on the great plain, into two divisions The horse continued in the camp, but the foot were quartered within the walls, for the security of the city They made daily excursions up and down the adjacent parts, which, though they committed no act of hostility, either by assault or surprize, was very disgusting to Josephus and his men Besides, they pillaged all the places which were out of the liberty of the city, and intercepted all the inhabitants that durst venture out of the gates

Upon this account Josephus made a bold attempt upon the city, but finding to his cost, that he himself, before his going off from the Galileans, had made the place almost impregnable against himself, and that it was not to be gained from the Sepphorites by any means, he dropt his enterprize This practice, however, as the Romans deemed it highly treacherous, rendered the war much fiercer, and the enemy more outrageous than before, depopulating the country, night and day, with fire and sword pillaging whatever they could lay their hands on, putting all to death, without mercy, where they found resistance, and making slaves of the rest Galilee, in fine, was one tremendous scene of fire and blood not exempt from any kind of calamity, with no refuge left but the places which Josephus himself had fortified

Titus was by this time come up to Vespasian at Ptolemais, with the troops he brought from Alexandria, and his arrival was much sooner than could have been expected from a winter's march He then joined the fifteenth, fifth, and tenth legions, which were reputed the choicest troops of the empire These legions were followed by eighteen cohorts There came also five from Cæsarea, with one troop of horse, and five troops of horse from Syria Ten of these cohorts had a thousand men each, and the rest six hundred and thirteen, with an hundred and twenty horsemen There was also a considerable number of auxiliaries from neighbouring princes, as Antiochus, Agrippa, and Sohemus, each of whom contributed two thousand foot and a thousand horse Malichus, king of Arabia, sent five thousand foot, mostly armed with bows and arrows, and a thousand horse so that the whole army, including the auxiliaries sent by the respective princes, amounted to sixty thousand horse and foot, besides the train of baggage and servants that followed the camp, who had been so trained to military exercises, that they could scarcely be distinguished from the professed soldiers

The policy of the Romans, in thus training their servants, cannot be too much admired, or too closely imitated, as it renders them, at the same time, not only useful to private families, but also to the commonwealth in the important particulars of war and government Whoever attends to the excellency of the Roman discipline in military matters, will find that fortune had the least hand in the success of their arms and that they raised themselves to the command of the world upon the foundation of their own honour and virtue They were not to learn the art of war when they were under a necessity of exercising it, but they made it their practice in times of peace, and handled their arms with as much ease as if they were then constant engagements Peace and war were in every respect the same to them, and they were ever in readiness for all occurrences, times, and seasons Their very trials of skill resembled real conflicts not a day passed but every man went through all his exercises, which kept them in disposition and in breath By these means they were always in order, without feeling the inconveniences either of fear or fatigue. Their exercises are effectually combats without drawing blood, as their fiercest encounters are but bloody exercises

To secure themselves from surprize, when entering into an enemy's country, the first thing they do is to pitch and fortify their camp, not slightly or disorderly, but with regard to the situation and condition of the place, levelling the ground where it is uneven, and making it into a form resembling a quadrangle To improve the execution of this business, they have with them smiths, carpenters, pioneers, and other workmen for operations, to attend the army The inner part of the camp is distributed into quarters of lodgments, for the officers and soldiers The outside bears the resemblance of a wall, where they raise turrets at an equal distance one from another In the intervals they have all sorts of weapons to be used at a distance, as darts, arrows, stones, &c as well as instruments and machines for casting them The camp has four large gates, for horse and foot to pass and repass at pleasure On the inside there are several streets, orderly disposed, with lodgments in the middle for the principal officers, and within them a tent erected for the general, after the form of a little temple, a market-place, with shops and standings for artificers and tradesmen, courts of justice and tribunals, for the hearing of causes, civil and military, so that, upon a general view, it looks like a city rebuilt on a sudden, so wonderful is the dispatch where there are great masters to direct and many hands to execute If occasion requires, a trench is drawn round the whole, whose depth is four cubits, and its breadth equal

When they have thus secured themselves, they live together in a kind of military brotherhood, orderly and peaceably one with another Upon any occasion of foraging, they go out in parties, and as for their times of repast, they do not eat singly, but jointly, and all together, and the trumpet directs them when to sleep, when to rise, and when to set the watch, so that they do nothing but by rule and command In the morning the soldiers wait upon their officers, from whom they receive the word or signal, and such other orders to be communicated to them subordinates as the occasion requires, to the end that every man may be instructed in his duty, and how to behave himself in action, how and when to sally out, or to retreat, and to do all things in order The trumpet informs them when they are to decamp, and then they take up their tents, pack up their baggage, and prepare to be gone Upon the second sounding they load their carriages, and stand ready for motion They then set fire to the camp, which may be easily repaired by throwing up another, while it prevents the enemy from taking an advantage Upon the third sounding the army marches, and all possible care is taken to prevent stragglers, and to move every man in his rank

On the right hand of the general stands the herald, who, with an audible voice, puts the question thrice over to the army, whether they are ready for battle The soldiers, in martial tone and motion, return for answer thrice in the affirmative Nay they often prevent the very demand, by first lifting forth their right hands, and giving other tokens of joy and satisfaction, in hopes of coming to that close After this the army advances with order and composure, as if in the face of the enemy

The footmen are armed with breast-plates and head-pieces, and have swords on each side, but the sword on the left side is much longer than the other Those that are chosen from the rest to be about the general have a lance and a buckler, a saw, a basket, a pick-axe, a hatchet, a [illegible], a scythe, a chain, and bread for three days, so that the men carry little less burthen than the beasts

The horsemen wear long swords girt to their right sides They carry [illegible] in their hands a buckler in a [illegible] hanging across the horse's side, a quiver with three or more darts upon it, broad pointed, and about the length of a short javelin Their helmets are like those of the foot The arms of the cavaliers that attend the person of the general, are the same with the rest only being chosen by lot, the [illegible] troop has the precedence

This is the Roman mode of marching and encamping, with the various manners of their arming They do nothing, in their military enterprizes and combats, that is rash and inconsiderate, but their actions are the result of deliberate councils, by which means either their failings are few, or those that happen are easily redressed for, provided that matters are well digested, it is more eligible to suffer disappointment from the ill success of a well-grounded enterprize, than become indebted to fortune for an advantage gained from an ill-concerted plan These blind events give persons an ill habit of abandoning all to chance, without any precaution or foresight, whereas men become wiser and better for instructive examples, even in cases of miscarriage, and have the consolation of having acted with propriety, though a calamity may have befallen them, which human prudence could not prevent

The constant exercise of arms not only tends to strengthen the bodies of men, but to fortify their souls for daring enterprizes It is death, by the Roman martial law, for a soldier not only to desert his station, or betray his trust, but for being in the least degree remiss in any point of duty Their officers if possible, are more severe than their laws, and make amends for the punishment they inflict upon criminals, by the honours and rewards they confer upon men of merit Such is the reverence in which they hold the authority of military discipline, that a Roman army exhibits a most glorious spectacle in time of peace, but when under preparation for action, it appears awful and tremendous Every individual moves as a member of the same body, and there is such harmony of motion as if they were all governed by the same mind. Their ears are ever open to the word of command, their eyes watching for the signal, and their hands ready to execute the orders of their superiors, in contempt of all difficulty and danger

When they come to the encounter, and a battle is once resolved upon, they are not at all solicitous as to the number of the enemy, or danger of the passes but break through all obstacles, and think themselves sure of the victory before the first onset In their councils are thus guided by political maxims, and executed with a proportionable degree of vigour, what wonder is it to behold the Roman empire giving laws to the universe, and extending itself as far as the Euphrates on the east, the ocean on the west, the fertile climes of Africa on the south, and the Rhine and Danube on the north? And yet, after all, the dominion seems too narrow for the great souls of the possessors

I have not recounted these particulars from a [illegible] of writing a panegyric in honour of the Romans, but by way of consolation to those who have been obliged to submit to their all conquering arms and to [illegible] innovators and male-contents from absurd and [illegible] attempts This summary of the Roman military [illegible] will also afford a very instructive lesson to such as may be disposed to enter into a martial life

CHAP IV

Placidus breaks into Galilee Attempts to take Jotapata, but is repulsed

WHILE Vespasian remained with his son Titus at Ptolemais, he gave all necessary orders for the supply, and government of the army, and in the interval Placidus made an inroad into Galilee, over-ran the whole country, took a great number of prisoners, and put many to the sword There were [illegible] pusillanimous people, but the more daring Galileans took sanctuary in the cities and other strong holds, that Josephus had fortified Placidus, observing this, resolved to set upon them by assault, and to begin with Jotapata the strongest place they had, making no doubt of carrying it upon the first attack, [illegible] acquiring a reputation among the rest of the generals, and opening a way to the taking of other places as the very [illegible] of Jotapata would then intimidate the rest to make a [illegible] But Placidus was much mistaken in his conjecture, for the inhabitants, being apprized of his design, and [illegible] upon his march, went out of the city to encounter him, and falling upon the Romans [illegible] with a considerable body, and in high spirits [illegible] their country, wives, children, and all [illegible] they put them to the rout, but killed only seven of them, they being well armed, and making an orderly retreat Of the Jews there were only three slain and [illegible] few wounded, for being light armed, they were obliged to [illegible] their weapons from a great distance, without venturing a conflict at close quarters, and upon this repulse Placidus took his departure

CHAP V

Vespasian comes from Ptolemais into Galilee [illegible] the order of [illegible] Shews [illegible] to the G[illegible] Josephus is deserted by his soldiers [illegible] [illegible] to Tiberias

VESPASIAN, being resolved upon an incursion into Galilee, left Ptolemais, and [illegible] the army [illegible] marching orders, according to the form of the Roman discipline The auxiliaries, being light armed, [illegible] bow-men, advanced before the rest, to keep [illegible] at a distance, and, by scouting out into the woods and other suspected passages, for the discovery of ambushes, to prevent surprize These were followed by [illegible] of Roman horse and foot, and after them [illegible] ten men out of every company, with their [illegible] necessary provisions for the forming of a camp [illegible]

[illegible] the pioneers, to level and mend the ways, and cut down the trees and bushes that incommoded them in [illegible]. After these came the general's baggage, with [illegible] officers, and a strong party of horse for [illegible] convoy. Next marched Vespasian himself, with a [illegible] horse and foot, some troops of lances, and [illegible] his own men, drawn out of so many squadrons. The engineers, with their machines and instruments for assault and battery, took their place next; then followed the [illegible] and other officers, with a choice body of troops about them. These were followed by the [illegible] at the head of all the rest of the Roman ensigns, as the prince of [illegible] for authority and power, [illegible] good omen of success in [illegible]. After the [illegible] ensigns came the trumpets, and after the trumpets the [illegible] of the army, six in front, with the proper officers to keep them in rank and file, according to order and [illegible]. The servants of every legion marched [illegible], and took care of the carriages and baggage. In the last place were the [illegible], and other [illegible] to the service of the army, under a convoy of horse and foot.

In this order Vespasian advanced to the confines of Galilee, and then encamped with his soldiers [illegible], earnestly [illegible] for action, but partly in confidence that the enemy's courage would fail upon the very approach of the army, or otherwise that they might change their minds before it came to a battle, he gave them time for [illegible], and made the necessary preparations for a siege.

Such was the fame of this great general, that the Jews were struck with consternation at the very report of his approach, insomuch, that the soldiers of Josephus, who were then encamped near Sepphoris, abandoned their commander, not only without striking a blow, but without so much as a sight of the enemy. Finding himself thus deserted, and out of condition to encounter the Romans, the [illegible] of the Jews totally sunk, the greater part gone over to the enemy, and the remainder in all appearance ready to follow them, he declined all further warlike pursuits, and, consulting his own safety, withdrew to Tiberias.

CHAP. VI.

[illegible] Gadara, [illegible] Tiberias [illegible] Josephus [illegible] to the council of [illegible] the propriety of [illegible] treating [illegible] Romans.

VESPASIAN marched to the city of Gadara, attacked [illegible] and carried it without any difficulty, there not being men to make necessary defence. The Romans, upon the forcing the town, put all to death without distinction, through hatred to the Jews, and revenge for the overthrow of Cestius. They set fire not only to the city itself, but to the small towns and villages about it, laying them utterly waste, and making the inhabitants slaves.

The retreat of Josephus to Tiberias for sanctuary, greatly alarmed the inhabitants, as they concluded that nothing but desperation would have driven him to flight. Nor were they mistaken in their judgment; for he foresaw the tendency of the war, and that nothing but submission and repentance could save the Jews from inevitable destruction. With respect to himself, he made no doubt of obtaining lenity from the Romans, if he should request it; but rather than betray his country and his trust, he was determined to suffer a thousand deaths, without soliciting the friendship of a public enemy.

He wrote upon this to the principal and leading men of Jerusalem a plain state of the case, without extolling or depreciating the merit of the Romans, lest, by aggrandizing the power of the enemy, he might intimidate them; or, by representing it in an inferior light, he might encourage them to make resistance without ability. He, in fine, referred the whole matter to the council, requesting them, after due deliberation, to send him word if they were disposed to treat, or if, on the contrary, they were determined to prosecute the war, to send him an army, without delay, to encounter the Romans. This was the purport of the letter which Josephus sent express to Jerusalem.

CHAP. VII.

[illegible] to besiege Jotapata, [illegible] Josephus [illegible]. A desperate conflict between the Jews and the Romans [illegible] five successive days. The situation of Jotapata [illegible] of the siege [illegible] and defence. [illegible] of [illegible] stones and [illegible]. The Romans [illegible].

JOTAPATA was deemed the strongest place [illegible] which Vespasian [illegible] that the Jews [illegible] difficulties, [illegible] and [illegible] horse, foot, and [illegible] mountains [illegible] rugged, and [illegible] to the foot but utterly impracticable [illegible] four days [illegible] the whole [illegible] any trouble.

C[illegible] day, being the twenty-first [illegible] went privately out of [illegible] to Jotapata, which in force [illegible] of the Jews [illegible] of Josephus being arrived [illegible], by all means, to [illegible] within his power, [illegible] Vespasian was so transported [illegible] a particular providence [illegible] enemy they had, and the [illegible] kind of voluntary bondage [illegible] commander [illegible] council [illegible] army along with him [illegible] orders, without delay, to march [illegible], and take particular care that Josephus did not make his escape.

Vespasian followed the [illegible] marching up to Jotapata in the evening, when he drew up his army on the north side of the city, seven furlongs distant, encamping upon an hill within the view of the enemy, in order to strike them with so tremendous a sight. This was accordingly effected, for the people were in such consternation, that not an individual durst so much as [illegible] the walls. The Romans were so fatigued by the march of the day, that they [illegible] at [illegible]. Vespasian, however, ordered [illegible] the town with two great bodies, and a third troop of horse [illegible] at a distance, to cut off all communication with the place. When the Jews found that they were [illegible] and [illegible] the [illegible] desperation inflamed their courage, as daring enterprizes take their rise from necessity.

The next morning the Romans began to play upon the walls, and the Jews at first, [illegible] stood firm, but when Vespasian [illegible] to force them from the walls, and [illegible] at the same time, with a body of foot, assaulted [illegible] upon an hill over against the other [illegible] to the danger of a battery, Josephus was so [illegible] of the town, that he fell most outrageously upon the Romans, at the head of the whole body of the Jews, beat them from the walls, and followed the advantage with a [illegible] resolution. The havock they suffered was not [illegible] to what they did, both parties being equally provoked and inflamed, the Jews by desperation, and the Romans by shame and indignation, to find themselves opposed by [illegible] so powerfully. There were skill and valour on the one [illegible] opposed to fury and rage on the other. Of the Romans there were several wounded, and thirteen slain, of the Jews six hundred wounded, and seventeen killed upon the spot. The fight was maintained all the day, until night parted them.

The assailants renewed the conflict the ensuing morn, and in this encounter both parties performed wonders. The Jews took courage from the repulse they had given the enemy already beyond all expectations, and the Romans from the shame of being so long in play, for the very delay of a victory was little less to them than an overthrow. The combat continued five successive days, the assailants pressing still harder and harder upon them, the Jews, on the other hand, not only supporting the defence, but at the same time, making occasional sallies, without being daunted by the prodigious number they had to encounter. Nor did the Romans abate any thing of the vigour of their attack from the difficulty and hazard of the enterprize.

With respect to the situation of Jotapata, it stands upon a rock utterly inaccessible, saving only upon one quarter. It is encompassed, on three sides, with such precipices of steep and profound vallies, that, to look down from the top to the bottom, is enough to cause a vertigo of the brain. It cannot be approached but towards the north, where part of the city is built upon the brow of the mountain, and that way, as one of the accessible. But Josephus had ordered this place to be fortified, and taken into the town, to secure a mountain that overlooks and commands it, which with other mountains adjacent, kept the place so close, that it was not discernable till they came close upon it. This was the situation and strength of Jotapata.

Vespasian, finding that he had the natural difficulties of the place, and the rugged bravery of the people, to contend with, took up a resolution of proceeding the siege with more vigour and called a council of his officers to deliberate on the manner in which they should carry on the attack. The debate came to this issue, that a large terrace should be erected on the weakest part of the town, pursuant to which, Vespasian set the whole army to work, to provide necessary materials for raising such a mount, fetching vast quantities of stone and timber from the neighbouring mountains, with provisions for hurdles to shelter the besiegers against the darts and shot from the town. Under the cover of these defences they advanced their design, though the weapons from above fell down in showers upon them. They procured the earth they used from the neighbourhood, and so handed it from one to another, so that, with the multiplicity of hands they had to assist them, and the undertaking going on without intermission, the work advanced with great expedition. The Jews in the mean time, did their utmost, by darts and stones from the walls, to divert them from their design, but all they were able to do could only retard the proceeding, without defeating or disappointing it.

Vespasian had by this time sixty engines at work, casting lances at the defendants, besides larger machines, to throw stones and javelins, arrows and artificial fires, which were all managed by the Arabians, and rendered not only the wall itself, but the whole space betwixt that and the terrace, too hot for the defendants.

This, however, did not hinder the Jews from sallying out upon the Romans, stripping them of all their defences, setting fire to every thing about them that was combustible, and by these means counteracting all their efforts. Vespasian, finding the mischievous contrivances of the Jews prevail more and more, and that there was no means of preventing their effects, but by filling up the intervals, so as to exclude their passage, joined his troops in a close body, and put a final end to their excursions.

The mount being now brought up almost to the height of the town wall, Josephus did not think it expedient to have more done on the one side to destroy the town, than on the other to defend it. He therefore called the workmen together, and gave orders for the raising of the wall, and keeping it up still above the height of the terrace. But, upon their representing the impossibility of advancing the work under such showers of weapons, he bethought himself of an invention to keep off both stones and fire. It was by driving several large stakes fast into the ground, and stretching up a number of raw hides against them, these were to be interspersed betwixt the enemy and the bodies of the besieged, as the moisture of the skins could resist and damp the flame, and then yielding to pressure throw off the stones and lances with little or no impression.

Under the protection of this cover, the workmen plied it hard day and night ... in a short time, they raised a wall of twenty cubits, and fortified it with turrets and strong battlements. This greatly discouraged the Romans, who before looked upon themselves as masters of the place, while they were ... astonished at the contrivance of Josephus, and the resolution of the defendants.

CHAP. VII.

Vespasian's attempt to effect by famine what he could not by force. No provisions wanting at Jotapata but water. The Stratagem of Josephus to conceal this ... frustrate the hopes of the enemy. Vespasian ... recourse to arms ... by the ... Josephus ... proposes an escape. The Jews force him to stand ... He refuses ... with them ... importunities. Josephus deliberates and ... Vespasian declines the assault. ... courage and resolution of the Jews.

THE citizens of Jotapata were so ... by the ... of this stratagem, that ... daily ... sallies, ... plunder, and violences, by fire, sword and pillage. Vespasian was greatly ... at this ... and disappointment, ... upon mature reflection, deferred the assault, and determined on starving the place instead of storming it, concluding that either want would bring them to submission, or, if they held it out, ... by weakening or ... them, put them out of a condition of defence. ... resolution ... ... there was no ... ... in order ...

The besieged had plenty of ... ... and, indeed, of all other necessaries, except water ... not so much ... ... for their common ... ... in summer, and ... ... The very thought of a drought was a great ... ... indeed, they had ... ... The place being plentifully ... ... provisions, and ... ... the garrison upon an allowance ... ... hold out ... ... the longer, ... tion disgusted them ... ... or an approaching drought ... ... refractory, and desisted from ... work.

This froward disposition of the Jews could not ... kept from the knowledge of the Romans ... ... in distance of observing, from ... ... whatever passed among them, ... the measuring of their portions, and ... ... therewith, so that many of them ... ... spot by showers of darts from the enemy.

The pit-water being by this time ... ... Vespasian in hourly expectance of ... ... hands, Josephus, to frustrate his hopes ... ... stratagem. He caused a great number of clothes ... made very wet and then ... exposed ... ...

[illegible] of the Romans, by which means he induced them to believe that there could not be such a scarcity of water in the place where they were so lavish of it. Upon that [illegible], they despaired of ever taking the place for [illegible] of water. Nay, Vespasian himself gave over all hopes of carrying it by a siege, and therefore [illegible] in his [illegible] recourse to arms. This was exactly the desire of the Jews, [illegible] themselves, as well as the city, were reduced to the last extremity, and wished nothing more earnestly than to [illegible] [illegible] state of [illegible] of water, [illegible] an honourable [illegible] than the field of battle.

While Josephus was [illegible] his invention for some expedient, it occurred to him that, on the west side of the town, there was an hollow gutter, that stood so much out of the way as to be in general unobserved. He proposed through the convenience of this passage to get relief into the town, such as water and whatever else was [illegible]. To [illegible] the [illegible] of the [illegible] no [illegible] out that quarter, to [illegible], from time to time, [illegible] supplies as [illegible] be [illegible], together with [illegible] to cover [illegible] with hair [illegible] and [illegible] them to creep along, to [illegible] if they should be observed by the watch, they [illegible] dogs, or some other four-footed animals. This [illegible] the correspondence was discovered, and the communication cut off.

Josephus, perceiving [illegible], the utter impossibility of defending the city, and [illegible] [illegible] his [illegible], called a council of the leading men in order to deliberate on the means of escape. When this came to the knowledge of the multitude, they [illegible] [illegible] treating him not to overlook their [illegible] their sole reliance was upon him. They observed that there was still hope of the city's deliverance if he would remain with them, as they were in general ready to undergo [illegible] hardships on his account; that, if they should be [illegible] upon, it would be recorded to his eternal honour, that he was too brave either to fly from his enemies or to [illegible] his friends; as, in that case, it would [illegible] a man leaving a vessel in a storm, of which he had taken charge in a calm, upon a comparative view of the case of the vessel with that of their city, for [illegible] they [illegible] who shall [illegible] defence of our country, when we have lost the very man whom we looked upon as the only means of our safety?

Josephus, [illegible] to have it thought he consulted his own particular safety, gave them to understand, in a plausible discourse, that his motive for withdrawing was more for their sakes than his own, observing, that if he [illegible] with them, he should be able to do them little good while they were in such a condition, and that, if they were once taken, he should only perish with them to no purpose; but that if, on the other hand, he was at liberty, [illegible] he might bring an army into the field out of Galilee time enough to raise the siege, while, as long as he continued pent up in the town, the Romans would be more eager for the prosecution of the siege, as their great object was to have him in their possession.

This plea was so far from moving the people to accord with his desire, that they urged him with greater importunity, men, women, and children, mothers with their infants at their breasts, bathed in tears, embracing his knees, and casting themselves at his feet, entreating him, with outcries and supplications, not to forsake them in their distress. This, it is presumed, they did, not from envying his deliverance, but from a certain impulse of persuasion, that the presence of Josephus would be a kind of protection to his friends.

It occurred to him, upon reflection, that, if he determined to stay, it would be ascribed to their entreaties; if to go he should be taken into custody. His commiseration of their state, deplorable as it was, had also much weight with him; so that at length he resolved to stand it out with them, and bear his part in the common desperation of the city. Having fixed this determination, he thus addressed them: "This is the time, my friends and "countrymen, to display our valour, when we have no "hope of safety but in our arms, when we are sure to receive immortal honour in exchange for [illegible] life, "and, by acting as firm patriots, to have our names "celebrated by posterity as devotees to the good of our "country."

From these words Josephus advanced to action, and putting himself at the head of the bravest men he had, charged the enemy's guards, beat them from their trenches, and drove them to the very camp, tearing the coverings of their tents to pieces, and setting fire to their works. [illegible] they did from time to time for three [illegible] [illegible] and nights, with insuperable boldness, and [illegible] labour.

When Vespasian found the Romans distressed by these sallies, and though they were worsted, disinclined to turn their backs, when he also observed that [illegible] [illegible], [illegible] the letter, they were too heavy armed to [illegible] the advantage, so that the Jews never [illegible], [illegible] [illegible] their [illegible], he commanded his troops to [illegible] the attack, and not throw away their lives [illegible] who desired to die under the provocation of [illegible] [illegible]. [illegible] rage, he observed, [illegible] [illegible] would go out of itself, if it wanted [illegible] matter [illegible] [illegible] the case of the Romans was [illegible] from that of the Jews, as the former fought [illegible], the latter for life and liberty, [illegible] much more in need of victory than the other. [illegible] the Arabian and Syrian slingers, archers, and engineers, were all busily employed, as the [illegible] found to their cost. But this was so far from staggering their resolution, that, on the contrary, they pressed through all difficulties to single out the Romans man to man, and they fought it out without quarter, the [illegible] on both sides stepping up to supply the place of the dead.

CHAP. IX.

Description of the battering ram. The manner of working [illegible]. A contrivance to repel the force of [illegible]. The Jews [illegible] [illegible] to fire. [illegible] signalizes his [illegible]. Two brothers distinguished heroes. Vespasian is [illegible]. The extraordinary effect of battering engines. A [illegible] slaughter of all [illegible] men. The Jews [illegible] [illegible] [illegible] to the last.

THROUGH the length of the siege, [illegible] the perpetual excursions of the besieged, Vespasian looked upon himself as in a manner besieged; but having now carried up his works near the height of the walls, he resolved to bring matters to an issue by dint of battery, and ordered an engine called a ram, to be brought up to the place of action.

This ram is a machine of prodigious bulk and size, like the mast of a ship, fortified with a strong piece of iron at the top of it, wrought into the form of the head of a ram; from which, and the manner of playing it in the use of it, like the butting of that animal, it derived its name. This machine is hung up by the middle, with great cables, or ropes, fastened to cross timbers, well cramped together, and strongly supported. There it lies upon a poise, like the beam of a pair of scales, and, as it hangs thus balancing in the air, it is moved backward and forward by the force of many hands, and falls with such violence upon the place where it is to batter, with the iron part that is pre-eminent, that no wall is able to withstand its repeated attacks.

Delay was now death to Vespasian, as the length of the [illegible] the exertions of the Romans, while the Jews were incessantly annoying them by some [illegible] or other, so that he was now determined on dispatch. The first thing he did was to bring his slingers, [illegible], and ordinary machines, closer up to the town to [illegible] the defenders from the walls, and to make way [illegible] battering ram, which was then brought on, that [illegible] soon as the bowmen and their companions had [illegible] too hot for the Jews to shew their heads [illegible] with hurdles, and wrapt in hair-skin, for [illegible] both of the directors and the machine. The [illegible] the very first stroke of this engine, [illegible] amongst the people in the city, as if all were lost, and Josephus finding that [illegible] battering would bring down the [illegible] in a short time, ordered several sacks [illegible] to be provided, and let down by ropes from the [illegible] the place where the engine played, and [illegible] charged their battery, the Jews en[illegible] them with their sacks, by which means they [illegible] the stroke, or failed of the effect.

[illegible] impeded the efforts of the Ro[mans] [illegible] direction they pointed the [illegible] the Jews [illegible] before to meet them with their [illegible] the wall sustained very little damage [illegible] the Romans [illegible] another means [illegible] that contrivance. They procured some long poles [illegible] hooks fastened to the ends of them [illegible] they cut the strings of the bags, [illegible] the [illegible] its office again, [illegible] could [illegible] any longer.

Josephus and [illegible] companions had no other resource than [illegible] so that collecting all the combustible matter they could [illegible] sulphur and [illegible], they divided it several [illegible] and set fire to the Roman machines, huts, and [illegible] that would [illegible] in three several places at the same time. The rage of [illegible] the Jews were so terrible that there was [illegible] place for relief, and the danger of perishing both ways [illegible] equal. The conflagration, in fine, was so dreadful [illegible] in a moment it destroyed that which had cost the Romans long [illegible] labour and hazard.

There was one Samaes, of Saab, in Galilee, and the son of Eleazar, who signalized himself, on this occasion, [illegible] most memorable action. He took up a stone of [illegible] bulk, and cast it down from the wall upon the machine with such prodigious force, that he broke off the [illegible] head of it, and then leaping down into the middle of his enemies, carried it off, without any apprehension of danger, to the top of the wall, where he stood awhile [illegible] as he was, a common mark for the enemy, till he had five arrows stuck in his body. In this condition he remounted the wall, where he stood, for a short time, [illegible] spectacle, without any change either of countenance or behaviour, till at length he expired with the anguish of his wounds, and the head of the machine in his arms, which he would never quit till the last.

There were also two brothers, of Ruma, in Galilee, Netiras and Philip, who exhibited singular instances of resolution. These men fell upon the soldiers of the tenth legion with such impetuous fury, that they broke into the Roman army, and drove all opposition before them, while Josephus, at the head of a troop of men with fire-brands, burnt the machines, huts, and works of the fifth and tenth legions, and those that followed made the same havoc with what was left.

By the evening of the same day, the Romans were at work with the same engine upon that part of the wall that had been shattered and broken before. Vespasian, at the same time, received a shot upon the ancle, by an arrow out of the town, but it proved a slight wound, as the force of the arrow, through the great distance, was spent. Those who were near enough to see their general's blood, so alarmed the whole army with the report, that the principal officers quitted their posts, and came to the head quarters to learn the particulars of the incident; Titus himself being at the head of them, from an [illegible] regard for the welfare of his father; but this generous concern [illegible] into a [illegible].

Vespasian, however, quickly put them all out of their pain, both his son and the army, by shewing himself [illegible] the utmost frankness, and pointing out to them that the accident was attended with no injurious effect; so that the [illegible] which they had before, or fear of a mortal stroke, were now turned into the thoughts of an honourable revenge. Vespasian encouraged the soldiers, and the soldiers one another, to renew the [illegible] in defiance of all opposition. [illegible] stones and [illegible] destroyed great numbers of the Jews; but Josephus and his people did not desert the wall, but, with fire, sword, and [illegible] galled those who had the direction of the battering engine. The Jews, however, [illegible] could advance but very slowly, as they were forced to engage in sight of the enemy, and the very [illegible] of [illegible] the Romans, also dead the enemy light against themselves, so that they stood so fair a mark, that there was no minding it on the one side, nor [illegible] on the other, for they could not so much as see the [illegible] whence the [illegible] came. By the force of stones from the [illegible] the battlements and the corners of the tower were broken down, and where they fell [illegible], they carried away whole files before them. But those who would be [illegible] the [illegible] effect of these [illegible], need only look into the history of the tremendous events of that memorable night.

One of the guards of Josephus, as he was upon the walls of Jotapata, had his head struck off with a stone from one of these engines, which was carried three furlongs from the place, as if it had been thrown out of a sling; and [illegible] coming across a pregnant woman, [illegible] the child [illegible] her half a furlong from the body. [illegible] of the machines, and the [illegible] of the wounded falling from the walls, the [illegible] women within the town, the [illegible] miserable [illegible] without, the town-ditch running with blood, the [illegible] piles of carcasses sufficient to mount an enemy to the [illegible], and the echo from the mountains reverberating the [illegible] sounds during that tremendous night served to fill [illegible] and ear with inexpressible horror. [illegible] slaughter of gallant men in this action, who fell in defence of the liberty of their country, which they maintained [illegible], against the utmost efforts of the enemy's machines, till [illegible] of day, and then the walls fell to pieces. Yet the Jews, even in this extremity, made the breach good with their bodies and their arms, before the Romans could [illegible] over the ditch to the attack.

CHAP. [illegible]

[illegible] makes ready to [illegible] the city. Josephus takes the necessary preparations [illegible]. Harangue [illegible] the approach of the Romans [illegible] fight between the Jews and the Romans. The Romans [illegible] the walls [illegible] of the [illegible]. Josephus orders [illegible] to be poured on [illegible] them off. The [illegible] of the Romans. Vespasian [illegible] the rising of his [illegible], Jews are [illegible].

WHEN the army had a little refreshed themselves after the fatigue of the [illegible] exertion, Veſpaſian made every neceſſary preparation for an aſſault, taking care, in the firſt place, to keep the Jews from daring to ſhew themſelves in the breach. To this end he diſmounted a party of the beſt horſe he had, armed them at all points, and ſo ranged them in three diviſions with pikes in their hands, to make good the breach, and upon the advance of the bridges, to be the firſt to enter the town. The horſe were ſeconded by a body of choice foot. The remainder of the horſe were to be diſtributed round the mountainous parts of the city, to prevent any of the enemy from eſcaping upon its ſurrender. The next in order were the archers, with their bows and arrows fixed at hand, and then the ſlingers and engineers. Others were employed with ladders to attempt the ſcaling of ſome parts of the wall that were entire, which was intended only for an amuſement, and draw off the aſſiſtance from other places that more needed it, and to force them, by this diverſion, to abandon the attack.

Joſephus was ſo well informed of the purpoſes and deſigns of the Romans, that he employed only men that were ſuperannuated for the guard of thoſe parts of the wall that were ſound. But wherever there was the leaſt flaw, he appointed none to that duty, but thoſe of tried integrity and courage. He put himſelf, with five more, at the head of them, to receive the firſt ſhock of the enemy, giving them in charge, not to heed the outcries or inſulting clamours, but rather to ſhut the ears againſt them as they were but empty ſounds. He directed them to cover their heads with their ſhields, as the beſt defence againſt the arrows of the enemy, or to withdraw a little till they had emptied their quivers; but added, that, if they once came to lay over their bridges, the only reſource then was fighting, not as in defence of a country that is to be preſerved, but for the honour of a country that is already loſt, and that therefore they ſhould make the authors of their deſtruction pay dear for their acquiſition, for they muſt expect, upon the ſubduing of their city, that their adverſaries would gratify their cruelty with the blood of their fathers, wives, and children.

When the common people, the women, and the children, ſaw the town ſurrounded by a three-fold army, and no force ſent out to encounter them, the enemy marching up with their drawn ſwords towards the weak ſide of the wall, the mountains round about glittering with arms, and the Arabians ready with their arrows, they made a lamentable outcry, as if deſtruction not only threatened, but was actually come upon them. Theſe clamours were ſo moving, that Joſephus ordered the women to their houſes, leſt they ſhould intimidate the ſoldiers, enjoining them, at the ſame time, ſilence at their peril; while he himſelf went to that part of the town which fell to his lot, paſſing by the ſcaling ladders without the leaſt fear, his thoughts being wholly taken up with the enemy's way of attack by their darts and their arrows.

Upon the ſeveral Roman legions ſounding their trumpets together, and the warlike ſhout of the army, the very ſky was darkened with a cloud of arrows. The ſoldiers of Joſephus, however, were not unmindful of the charge he had given them, but ſtopped their ears againſt the clamours, and covered themſelves with their ſhields againſt the darts. Upon the leaſt advance of the bridges, they ſet upon the Romans with amazing intrepidity to put a ſtop to their deſign, either keeping them off, or beating them off, and diſputing every inch of the poſſeſſion. As faſt as the Romans endeavoured to mount the bridge, the Jews violently puſhed them down again, with ſignal inſtances both of their ſkill and courage in the conduct and execution, ſhewing themſelves bold and fearleſs in the extremity of danger, as were the Romans where there was any at all; nay, the greater their hazard, the firmer was their reſolution, ſo that when they were once engaged, there was no parting them, till one or the other fell upon the ſpot.

But the Jews being kept upon perpetual duty, and no reinforcements to relieve them, while the Romans had continually a freſh ſupply of men to ſubſtitute in the place of thoſe that were wearied or worſted, numbers muſt of neceſſity prevail in the proceſs. The Romans were ſenſible of the advantage they had in thus preſſing as cloſe together as poſſible, they threw long bucklers over their backs, and making an impenetrable figure, drove the Jews before them as if the ſtrength of the whole army had been united in one body, and thus they advanced up to the very wall.

In this ſtate of diſtreſs, or rather deſperation, Joſephus reſolved upon the trial of an experiment. The Jews having a great deal of oil by them, he ordered a conſiderable quantity to be boiled, and caſt down ſcalding hot upon the ſoldiers under their wall, together with the very pots and veſſels in which it was boiled. This was accordingly done, and paſſing between the bucklers, and over the bodies of the Romans, it utterly broke their order, and deſtroyed the men, by forcing them down from the wall in their extreme miſery; for the oil flowing under their arms from head to foot, and ſo all over the body, conſumed the fleſh like fire itſelf, being naturally apt to take heat, and long in cooling. Their armour alſo being braced and buckled to their bodies, there was no getting clear of the torment; ſome of them leaping and ſprawling in their pains, others drawn double, and all falling from the bridge down to the ground. Thoſe that attempted to get off to their own people were eaſily maſſacred by the Jews at their backs.

In the whole courſe of this calamitous circumſtance, there was no failure either of courage in the Romans, or prudence in the Jews; for the former, notwithſtanding the miſery they endured by the ſcalding oil, had the reſolution to preſs upon thoſe that poured it among them, and not without a competition who ſhould be foremoſt. The Jews, after this, put another check to the progreſs of the Romans by caſting boiled fenugreek, a ſeed of a glutinous nature, upon the boards of the bridge, which rendered them ſo ſlippery that the Romans could not keep their feet, ſo that they could neither fight or fly. Some fell at their length upon the planks, where they were trampled upon by their own people; others fell lower, and were ſlain by the Jews. Veſpaſian found his people ſo harraſſed out by this way of fighting, that, toward evening, he called them off, having loſt ſeveral men, and had many wounded. Of Jotapata there were only ſix men ſlain, although three hundred were carried off wounded. This action happened upon the twentieth day of the month Deſius.

Veſpaſian was ſo ſenſible of this miſcarriage of his, that he took an opportunity of conſoling the army upon the occaſion; but finding the ſoldiers ſo far from being dejected, that they were rather inflamed, and deſirous of being continued in action, he ordered the raiſing of his platforms, and the erecting of three wooden turrets upon them, each fifty feet high, covered with plates of iron, to keep them ſteady with the weight, and not ſo liable to be ſet on fire. In theſe turrets were the choiceſt of his markſmen and engineers, with their machines, inſtruments, and arms. The people in them had this advantage of the beſieged, that they were out of ſight and reach of the others, whereas thoſe upon the walls were eaſily ſeen, and wounded from the turrets. The Jews, therefore, being neither able to avoid the arrows from above, or ſo much as to ſee thoſe that annoyed them, quitted the breach, but ſtill, upon all attacks, made a vigorous and brave reſiſtance. Thus did the people of Jotapata defend themſelves againſt the Romans, though with daily loſs of men, without being able to retort the miſchief upon their enemies.

CHAP XI

Vespasian sends Trajan to besiege Japha The people meet him on the way to give him battle The Jews put to flight, and driven into the first enclosure A great slaughter Trajan desires Vespasian to send Titus to his assistance Titus, in consequence, brings his troops to Japha The Romans mount the walls, and enter the town A warm conflict in the street for six hours, attended with an horrid massacre

VESPASIAN being given to understand that Japha, a neighbouring city to Jotapata, after the example of others, was inclining to a revolt, and especially as being encouraged by the defence of that place, which held out beyond expectation, sent Trajan, the commander of the tenth leg on, with two thousand foot, and a thousand horse, to reduce it But he found the town impregnably fortified, as, besides the natural strength of situation, it was encompassed with a wall He was likewise encountered on the way by the inhabitants of the place, in a posture to give him battle The parties accordingly joined, and, after a slight resistance, Trajan put them to flight, and pursued them so close to the out-wall, that they fell in together with them But, upon their pressing to get up to the second wall, the inhabitants shut the gates, lest they should admit friend and foe one with another

This extraordinary mode of the Galileans being delivered into the hands of the Romans, seems to have been in consequence of a judicial providence, as they were shut out of their own gates by their own people, and given up for a sacrifice to an enemy that thirsted for their blood They crowded in throngs up to the gates, called to the officers by their names, and begged admittance, yet they were massacred in the midst of their supplications The Romans kept one gate, and the citizens the other Some of those who were pent up in this enclosure, laid violent hands on themselves, others fell by the swords of their companions, besides an immense number that were slain by the Romans Nor had one of these the spirit to lift up an hand, or so much as offer to revenge, for, besides the dread of an enemy, they were daunted by a sense of treachery amongst themselves There died, in fine, to the number of twelve thousand persons, cursing not the Romans, but their own citizens

Trajan now taking it for granted that their martial men were in a manner all cut off, and that these few who remained would take warning from the fate of their companions, sent to Vespasian requesting that his son Titus might have the honour of completing the victory Vespasian, apprehending that something was still requisite to be done, dispatched Titus accordingly, with a reinforcement of five hundred horse and a thousand foot, which immediately, on his arrival, he formed into two divisions, that on the left he gave to Trajan, that on the right he commanded himself

The first thing the Romans did was to plant scaling ladders, and then mount the wall upon all quarters at the same time The Galileans made a faint resistance, but soon quitting the wall, Titus and his party leaped down after them and entered the town There was now a desperate conflict in the street, which, through ambushes and sallies from narrow passes, where a number of resolutes were posted, together with annoyances of every kind they received from the very women at the tops of the houses, lasted near six hours But the bravest being by this time cut off the remainder of the multitude, whether in their houses or not, young men or old, were all destroyed indiscriminately, and not a male left alive, but infants, who were carried away captive with the women The number of the slain in the city, and in the first encounter, was fifteen thousand, and the prisoners were two thousand one hundred and thirty This calamity befel the Galileans on the twentieth day of the month Desius

CHAP XII

The Samaritans assemble upon mount Gerizim, and seem to threaten a revolt Vespasian sends Cerealis against them The Samaritans raise a formidable body A [illegible] Cerealis offers them an indemnity, which they reject, [illegible] all put to the sword

NOR did the Samaritans escape the calamity [illegible] times They assembled themselves together [illegible] mount Gerizim, which is by them deemed an holy mountain, and there seemed to wait the event of things [illegible] in the mean time, the complexion of the [illegible] the manner of their behaviour, seemed menacing [illegible] bulent, and indicated a disposition to revolt They [illegible] not become wise by the example of others, but [illegible] considering either their own weakness or the might [illegible] of the Romans were precipitating their [illegible] lion which Vespasian took early care to prevent [illegible] the province of Samaria was well garrisoned, he [illegible] without some apprehension of what such a tumult [illegible] such an union of ill affection, might produce, [illegible] fore, by way of prevention, dispatched Cerealis, [illegible] of the fifth legion, with six hundred horse a[nd] [illegible] thousand foot to maintain the public tranquility

When Cerealis came up with his troops to the [illegible] tain, he found the Samaritans gathered together [illegible] a body, that he did not think it expedient to attack [illegible] upon that post, but rather intrenched himself round [illegible] them at the foot of the mountain and there [illegible] watched their motions It so fell out that [illegible] in the height of summer and a very hot season, the Samaritans were in great want of water, (the people [illegible] made no provision to supply it) insomuch that some [illegible] ed [illegible] by a parching drought whilst others went over to the Romans, preferring slavery to so miserable a death

Cerealis being informed, by deserters that those [illegible] stayed behind were as much [illegible] as their fellows advanced up the mountain, and surrounding them [illegible] his army, not only offered them life and liberty, [illegible] condition of laying down their arms but courteously [illegible] treated them to accept of the [illegible] an assurance that it should be made good But [illegible] Roman commander found they could not be prevailed on he caused them all to be put to the sword, to [illegible] of eleven thousand six hundred persons This [illegible] on the twenty-seventh day of the month Desius

CHAP XIII

The Romans [illegible] Jotapata [illegible] forms Vespasian of the [illegible] to assault it about break of [illegible] He takes [illegible] The Romans [illegible] the city [illegible] Forty thousand [illegible] the city razed, [illegible] castles burnt

THE people of Jotapata held out manfully, and stood firm against all extremities with admirable constancy, but, upon the forty-seventh day of the siege, when the Romans had carried their works to over-top the walls, Vespasian had an account brought him, by a deserter of the miserable state of the town, which was, that with loss of men, watching, and hard duty, the garrison was so weakened, that with one hard [illegible] the Romans might certainly carry the place, or, as the other way, they might take an opportunity of surprising them The deserter advised Vespasian to make his time about break of day, when he would be sure to find them secure and careless, and the guard so drowsy and [illegible] that he could not fail of carrying his point

Vespasian was so well acquainted with the natural fidelity of the Jews, and how much they contemned force or torments, that he gave little or no credit to this fugitive, and particularly from an instance he had of a wonderful constancy of mind in one of that city already. He was a prisoner of Jotapata, and being put to the question about the condition of the town, he stood all manner of tortures, even to fire, and the cross itself, to the contempt of death in all forms, rather than make the least discovery. But as there was some probability in the account, he thought he should run no [illegible] in seeming to believe it, upon which consideration he ordered the informer to be taken into custody, and every thing made ready for the [illegible].

Pursuant to this resolution, at the hour assigned, the army made a silent march up to the walls, Titus at the head, with Domitius Sabinus, and some chosen men from the fifteenth legion. They killed the guards, entered the city, and were followed by Sextus Cerealis, the tribune, and Placidus, with the troops under their command. The Romans were now in possession of the fort, masters of the town, broad daylight, and yet the garrison was so spent with fatigue and over-watching, that they did not so much as know the town was taken. [illegible], those that were awake were almost as ignorant as the rest, for there [illegible] very instant that the they saw nothing, [illegible] knew not what they saw. This fog continued till the whole army entered the place, the people [illegible] till they felt the danger, and [illegible] were convinced, by the fatal consequences, that they were undone.

The Romans had suffered too much in the siege to have [illegible] in the storm. Some [illegible] from the top of the fort to the bottom, others, that wanted neither good-will nor resolution [illegible] were either pressed to death in crowds, forced down precipices, or dashed to pieces by the [illegible] over their heads. This was the case of several of the [illegible] of Josephus, who chose rather to die by their own hands, [illegible] of an enemy, and to lay themselves in [illegible] when they could not have the satisfaction of [illegible] Romans along with them. This induced [illegible] of them to [illegible] together into a remote part of the city, and [illegible] the last office for one another.

[illegible] who first perceived that the town was lost, got into a certain turret towards the north, and, for a while, defended themselves, but being overborne by numbers, they offered to treat, and finding no terms would be [illegible] them, they were cut to pieces upon the place, and [illegible] like men of honour. This action closed the siege, [illegible] the day had passed without the shedding of one drop of Roman blood, had it not been for the death of Anthony, a centurion, who was basely slain at the taking of the city.

There were several of the Jews that fled into caves, and one of them called out to Anthony for quarter, desiring that he would give him his right hand upon it, as an obligation of honour for the performance of the condition. Anthony unwarily stretching out his right hand for the satisfaction of the Jew, the other stabbed him under the loin with a dagger, and killed him on the spot.

The Romans slew all they met that day without distinction, and for some days following they searched all hiding places, vaults, and cellars, for fugitives, putting all to death they could find, women and children only excepted. There were twelve hundred taken prisoners, and forty thousand slain during the whole course of the siege. Vespasian ordered the city to be razed, and the castles to be burnt. Jotapata was taken the first day of the month Panemus, in the thirteenth year of the reign of Nero.

CHAP. XVI.

The strictest search is made after Josephus, who is betrayed by a woman. Vespasian offers him quarter. Nicanor endeavours to prevail with him to comply. The soldiers [illegible] at his hesitation. He calls to mind former revelations [illegible] delivering himself up to the Romans. The Jews [illegible] against him. Expostulation of Josephus with the Jews [illegible] continue their declamation. [illegible] lots for their lives [illegible] and one more left to live. He is set at liberty [illegible] conducted by Nicanor to Vespasian, who confers with him [illegible] private. Titus conceives esteem for him. Josephus [illegible] tells the succession of Vespasian and Titus to the empire [illegible] prophecy [illegible] predictions [illegible] afterwards come [illegible]. Vespasian receives [illegible] Ptolemais, and thence to Caesarea.

THE Romans made the strictest search for Josephus, partly through personal animosity to him, [illegible] through an officious desire of obtaining the favour of Vespasian, who looked upon him as the main [illegible] war. It was his good fortune, upon the taking of the city, to make his escape through the midst of the enemy, [illegible] conceal himself in a deep pit, with a passage that led [illegible] into a large cavern, which could not be discerned from above. In this recess he found forty persons of [illegible] under his own circumstances, with provisions [illegible] for several days. The enemy being in possession of the whole country [illegible] under the necessity of keeping [illegible] the day-time, but went abroad in the night [illegible] the posture of the guards, and look for [illegible] his escape. But the watch were so strict [illegible] particularly on his account, that it being impossible to elude their vigilance, he went back to his retreat, and there [illegible] for some time.

On the third day he was betrayed by a woman that [illegible] taken up, and Vespasian sent two tribunes to him, [illegible] and Gallicanus, to invite him from his recess, and [illegible] him, upon the word of the general, of the most liberal treatment. Josephus could not think it prudent to trust so far to the Roman generosity as to venture himself upon the general's parole, [illegible] being conscious, from the mischiefs he had done them, he had more reason to expect revenge than favour. He excused himself from complying with the proposal. Vespasian then sent a third time to him, Nicanor, his familiar friend. Nicanor represented to him the humane disposition of the victorious Romans towards those whom he had subdued, and assured him, moreover, that, so far from resenting his conduct, considered in the light of an enemy, he highly approved his bravery, and esteemed his virtues. He farther proceeded to reason with him, when he had only to enjoin subserviency to his will, that his behaviour was a proof of his respect for a worthy man, and his disposition to treat Josephus in a manner becoming his character; that, if duplicity had been his design, he would not have employed a friend in the office of a [illegible], nor would he himself have submitted to be the instrument of treachery.

Josephus still continuing to hesitate, notwithstanding the pertinent reasoning of his friend Nicanor, the soldiers became so incensed, that they would have set fire to the cave, if the tribune had not prevented it, by assuring them that he was desirous of taking him alive. As Nicanor became more pressing in his [illegible] to bring him to compliance, the rage and menaces of the soldiers increased. This recalled to his mind certain dreams he had, in which had been revealed to him the calamities that were to befall the Jews, and the grandeur and prosperity of the Romans. He was endowed with a gift of expounding dreams, and revealing many things which had been veiled under the guise of mystery. As he was a priest himself, and of the [illegible] race, he was [illegible] versed in the writings of the inspired prophets; and at the very instant, as if impressed by a divine emotion, and under the immediate impulse of the tremendous images represented in his former visions, he thus addressed the Almighty

"Great God! since it is thy blessed will to depress the Jews, and to exalt the Romans, and to make me the instrument to foretel thy purpose, I submit myself to thy providence, and to the acceptance of my life upon condition of surrendering myself to the Romans: but in the presence of thy sacred Majesty, I do likewise declare, that I do it as a minister of thy good pleasure, and not as a betrayer of my country."

He had no sooner complied with Nicanor's invitation, than his companions, in the recess, reproached him with invectives to the following purport:

"What is become of the laws of our country, or of the honour of our profession? the spirit of our ancestors, and that primitive vigour of the Jews, that, with the first breath of life, grew up in a contempt of death? Can Josephus be so fond of that life now, as to think of looking the sun in the face, and seeing himself a slave? Why does he not according to his doctrine, and practise what he teaches? He recommends liberty to others, and renounces it himself. You were certainly very much mistaken (they exclaimed) in the measures you took of true wisdom and courage, either if you could hope for quarter where you have so little deserved it, or if you can sink so low as to accept of life upon dishonourable terms. But however the fortune of Rome may fright you into a forgetfulness of yourself, it shall never make us depart from the duty we owe to the good of our nation; and we have yet hearts and swords ready to stand by you in that quarrel. If you are otherways resolved, you have it now at your choice, whether you will die a general of the Jews, or the death of a coward and traitor. Fall upon your sword, and you do the former, or leave it to us, and it will be the latter; for the work must be done."

Having uttered this invective, they unsheathed their swords, and threatened him with immediate death, if he entertained a farther thought of submitting to the Romans. Josephus, apprehensive that he might be taken off before he had delivered to the Jews what he had been enjoined by Divine revelation to communicate, thus expostulated with his companions:

"What can be the meaning, my good friends and companions, of this desperate fancy you have taken up of laying violent hands upon yourselves, and setting the two dearest friends in nature at variance, the soul and the body? Am I changed? Ask the Romans. Is it a glorious fate to die in war? It is so undoubtedly, if it be in a war according to the law of arms; that is to say, where a man falls by the hand of the conqueror. Neither should I make any more conscience of killing myself than of desiring a Roman to do it; but if the Romans have a mind to spare an enemy, shall that enemy, on the other hand, be so cruel as not to spare himself, or so foolish as to be more rigorous in his own case than he would have an enemy to be? No man dies so great, it is true, as he that sacrifices his life to his liberty; but then it must be in arms, and in the act of contending for it, and that life must be taken away in the contest by the competitor, that would take away that liberty. But we have to do with an enemy at present, that neither kills us, or fights with us, for the quarrel is over. Now he is as pusillanimous a wretch that presses to die when he should not, as he that is afraid to die when his honour calls him to it. What is it, at last, but the fear of death, that keeps us from going up to the Romans? Shall we cast ourselves into a certain death one way, for fear of an uncertain death another? But it is, you will say, perhaps, to avoid slavery; and do you think yourselves now at liberty? But it is looked upon as the part of a brave man to take away his own life with his own hand. What would you think of the master of a vessel, that for fear of a storm approaching, would sink the boat before it comes? Would you account that man a brave commander? To say nothing of the affront that is offered to the common wisdom of Providence, in the nature of things (for the desire of self-preservation is a principle implanted in all living creatures), for any thing to destroy itself, it is contrary to nature, and consequently a sacrilegious wickedness against God himself. There is no creature that seeks or covets its own death, in opposition to the universal impulse of a desire to live; and therefore we pronounce those people our enemies that would take away our lives, and punish those that lie in wait to destroy us. It is from God that we have received life, and it is to him again, at his good time, that we are to render it. What can be more provoking and ungrateful than the despising his gifts? Our bodies are all mortal, and so are the materials of which they are compounded; but the soul is a divine particle, infused into the body by God himself, and it can never die. If any men shall embezzle or abuse a deposit betwixt man and man, we can say nothing bad enough of him. Now the soul is strictly but God's deposit, and shall we presume to rob the Divine Majesty, and think to come off at last without either discovery or punishment? We find it reasonable enough to punish servants who desert, though it be from the worst of masters; and shall we at the same time, that forsake a generous and a righteous God, pretend to justify ourselves? As for those that govern themselves according to the instinct of nature, and pay the debt of life back again to him that gave it, whenever he comes to call for it, do not you know that everlasting honours attend the memory of those blessed souls from generation to generation, which, after a certain number of ages in the heavenly mansions provided for them, shall return, and animate bodies, pure like themselves? Whereas the deepest pit of hell is reserved for self-murderers, and God will revenge the iniquities of the fathers upon the children in after ages. They are hateful to God; and the wisdom of our great law-giver hath been so severe upon them, that he that kills himself is not allowed burial till after sun-set, though a privilege never denied to an enemy. In other places the right hand is cut off from the body of the dead, as armed against himself; for it is reasonable that the hand that parts the soul and the body should be cut off from the body itself. It is a great blessing, my good friends, to make a right judgment of things, and not to render our condition worse than it is, by blaspheming or renouncing our Maker. If we are disposed to live, what hinders us? for life can be no dishonour to us when we have given so many signal proofs of our virtue. But if nothing will serve us but dying, let us fall by the hands of those that have mastered us. I am not for going over to the enemy in such a manner as to deprive myself of life by doing the same thing to my destruction that a deserter does to save himself. If the Romans should be treacherous, and break faith with us, it would be no more in some respects than what one might honestly wish for, as it yields matter for a steady and generous mind to work upon not only in the the sufferance, but in the contempt of death; for the very baseness of the perfidy will be some sort of comfort to us, when we consider that the authors of our ruin have made themselves infamous and odious to posterity."

These, and many arguments of a similar nature did Josephus use to dissuade his companions from their impious resolution of suicide. But desperation had rendered them deaf to all prudent advice, as having long ago devoted themselves to destruction. In the most frantic rage they pressed upon him with their drawn swords one after another, reviling him as an infamous coward, and declaring him deserving of death at their hands. Josephus, in this extremity, conducted himself with all possible calmness and [illegible] proposing one while the authority of his command, which carried a kind of reverence with it, at another [illegible] commending, at another the force of argument, [illegible] or a [illegible] application to their respective [illegible] dispositions, he diverted the blow. When [illegible] the point of execution, however, the venerable [illegible] of the general struck them with remorse, and compelled them to drop the weapons they had uplifted to deprive him of life.

[illegible] with his usual ingenuity, and [illegible] to the providence of the Almighty determined [illegible] to the hazard, observing to his companions, "That, since they were resolved upon death, [illegible] nothing [illegible] do [illegible] commit [illegible] death to [illegible] by lot, so that he [illegible] upon the lot fell first, might [illegible] and so [illegible] through them all [illegible] might be [illegible] own hand, [illegible] when the rest were gone, that [illegible] crime."

[illegible] just and equitable [illegible] drawn, and the persons upon [illegible] but to death [illegible] next [illegible] general would [illegible] con- [illegible] At length [illegible] through [illegible] there was only Josephus and one [illegible] upon which Josephus [illegible] companion "I [illegible] or I must kill [illegible] in the blood of [illegible] country- [illegible] common [illegible] engagement for his security.

[illegible] in which [illegible] not only with the Romans but his own [illegible] committed himself to Nicanor, who conducted him to Vespasian. The multitude [illegible] to [illegible] him, and were variously affected by the incident. Some rejoiced [illegible] threatened him, [illegible] to get near him, and others, at a distance [illegible] enemy. Those [illegible] near enough to observe his person, [illegible] on his extraordinary emergencies in a comparative [illegible] were struck with the [illegible] in the change. Nor was there any of the Roman [illegible] however prepossessed against him before, [illegible] Titus, [illegible] his character [illegible] of his mind in [illegible] remembered [illegible] with [illegible] of him now in [illegible] making pertinent re- [illegible] of war, and the [illegible] Such were the sentiments [illegible] and he brought all that [illegible] to concur with him, but rather not excepted, [illegible] very instrumental towards effecting [illegible] Vespasian gave strict orders, that he [illegible] kept with great caution, as he intended to send him to the emperor.

When Josephus heard him give those orders, he informed the general that he had something to communicate to him in private. Vespasian, upon this intimation, ordered all to withdraw, except Titus and two friends, and then giving him audience, Josephus addressed him to this effect:

"You have now, general, in your hands, Josephus, a "prisoner of war, and your present thoughts, perhaps, "extend no farther. But I come as a messenger of greater "tidings, in a matter of much more importance. Had "it not been for this commission, I could not have been "here at present, contrary to the duty of a Jewish gene- "ral, living, and in the hand of an enemy. But why am "I to be sent to Nero, when Vespasian himself is so near "the empire, that I can hardly distinguish between Ves- "pasian and the emperor, or Cæsar? Besides, his son "Titus is to succeed him. Keep me at pleasure, but "let me be the prisoner of Vespasian, who is not only "my master, but in effect, sovereign of the universe. This "is what I have in charge to deliver, and whenever I "am found so sacrilegious an impostor as to call God "witness to a fallacy, deal with me as I deserve."

This address carrying with it the resemblance of [illegible] was not attended to at first by Vespasian; but comparing the particulars with other predictions of the [illegible] tendency, which appeared exactly to correspond, he was at length induced to give credit to the presage. A [illegible] and confident of Vespasian, expostulating with Josephus on the credibility of his declaration, observed to him, "that, as he was so skilful in divination, it was extraordinary he should know nothing of the ruin of Jotapata, and his own imprisonment." Reply was made by Josephus, "that he foretold the inhabitants very particularly what was to befal the town and himself; that the town was to be destroyed on the forty-seventh day, and that he himself was to be taken prisoner by the Romans." Vespasian caused strict enquiry to be made in private of the truth of this relation, which he found verified by the prisoners. Though Josephus was not admitted [illegible] ty, he was, in every instance of accommodation, treated with great courtesy and respect, but by Titus in a more peculiar manner.

On the fourth day of the month Panemus, Vespasian returned to Ptolemais, and thence proceeded to Cæsarea on the sea-coast, which is one of the first cities of Judea. The greater part of the inhabitants were Greeks, so that they received the Roman army with great acclamations, not only from the respect they bore the empire, but the aversion they had for the Jews, on which account they pressed Vespasian with clamorous importunity to [illegible] Josephus to death. But the general, considering this tumultuous way of proceeding only as the act of a [illegible] multitude, dismissed the petitioners without an answer. Deeming Cæsarea commodious [illegible] to winter quarters, he placed two legions in it, and sent the fifth and tenth legions to Scythopolis, that he might not distress Cæsarea with the entire army. This town is situated upon a plain near the sea, and is extremely hot in the summer, but temperate in the winter season.

CHAP. XV.

Joppa a refuge for revolters and robbers. Vespasian sends an army thither. Description of Joppa. The inhabitants [illegible] shipwreck. It is taken [illegible] by the Romans. [illegible] pieces [illegible] Josephus [illegible] to [illegible] been [illegible] thereupon [illegible] the Jews, [illegible] they found that he was [illegible] with the Romans [illegible] the [illegible]

THERE was at this time, a great multitude gathered together, partly revolters from the Romans, and partly fugitives from some ruined cities of the Jews. They applied themselves to the repairing of Joppa, which Cestius had demolished, and, for want of subsistence in the country which he had laid waste, resolved to try their fortune at sea. To this end they put out with a fleet of piratical ships, hovering Syria, Phœnicia, and the coasts of Egypt, pillaging all trading vessels in those seas, and thereby wholly obstructing commerce. Vespasian, receiving intelligence of these proceedings, sent a body of horse and foot to Joppa, which being loosely guarded, they entered the town in the night with much ease. The inhabitants were so alarmed at this surprize, that, without attempting to oppose the Romans, they fled to their ships, and lay off at sea all night, out of the reach of their darts.

JOSEPHUS in a CAVE after the Siege and Destruction of JO[illegible] agreeing with his Companions which should first destroy each other in order to avoid [illegible] the hands of the Romans when only Josephus with one of his Companions escaping [illegible] they surrendered themselves to the Romans by whom they were [illegible] —

Joppa may be said to be a [illegible] town, without any manner of port, the shore is steep and craggy, with two pointed rocks on each side, stretching a considerable way into the sea, and bending in the form of an half moon, which renders it very tempestuous there in foul weather. Here are said to be seen the marks of Andromeda's chains, which attest that fable of antiquity. A cross wind upon the quarter [illegible] the waves against the rocks in so dreadful a manner, that nothing can be more hideous or dangerous.

While the people of Joppa were standing in this station, there arose a furious storm at break of day, which is called by the name of the Black-north. This wind dashed their vessels to pieces, some against one another, and others against the rocks. Great numbers, that laboured against the tide, to get out to sea, were [illegible], and swallowed up, for the [illegible] was so rocky, and had so many of the enemy upon it, that they were afraid to come to land. Their situation, indeed, was desperate, betwixt the wind at sea, and the Romans on shore. Their lamentations and outcries were horrible; some were drowned, others died on board of the wrecks, some fell upon their swords, to prevent other consequences, several were washed away by the billows, and dashed to pieces against the rocks, till the water was discoloured with blood, and the whole coast covered with dead bodies, the soldiers waiting all the time upon the land to dispatch those that were driven on shore. The [illegible] supposed to be four thousand two hundred [illegible] cast up with the [illegible].

The Romans being now masters of Joppa without a stroke (this being the second time of their taking it,) [illegible] it to the ground, but Vespasian, lest it should become an harbour for pirates, once again fortified the castle and placed in it a competent garrison, leaving a considerable body of horse in the place, to [illegible], and lay waste the circumjacent towns and villages, which orders were accordingly executed.

The report of the surrender of Jotapata was so extraordinary, and therefore so difficult to [illegible] that it gained little or no credit. Indeed, there [illegible] of the place to carry the tidings, though a rumour was spread at random, that the city was taken, as adverse [illegible] began to transpire. By degrees, however, it passed for current, and in the course of [illegible], was generally [illegible]ted, with many additional and [illegible] circumstances. It was confidently reported that, upon the taking of the city, Josephus was slain, to the extreme affliction of the inhabitants of Jerusalem in general. Some [illegible] were lamented by particular families, others by particular friends, but the general, being a public loss, was the subject of universal mourning, insomuch, that for thirty days there was no intermission of the solemnity, nor any cost spared for the celebration of the funeral pomp. But when time brought truth to light, and represented the transactions at Jotapata in their true colours, when it came to be known that Josephus was not dead, as reported, but still living, and in such credit with the Romans, that their generals, instead of treating him as a captive, conferred the highest honours upon him, the veneration they had for him, while they supposed him dead, was turned into the most rancorous envy and hatred. They reproached him with cowardice and treachery, in abandoning the cause, and the whole city joined in calumny and detraction against him. Wise men avail themselves of one misfortune as a precaution against another, but those devoted people, when they had once deviated pursued their error, and made the end of one mischief the beginning of another. The Jews, by a kind of fatality, were now thrown into a greater rage against the Romans than ever, as if the wreaking of their vengeance on them was the most effectual means of revenging themselves upon Josephus. These were the tumults in Jerusalem at this time.

CHAP XVI

Vespasian goes to Cæsarea Philippi, where he is entertained [illegible] Agrippa twenty days. Tiberias and Tarichea revolt from the Romans. Vespasian [illegible] to [illegible], and encamps at Sennabris, within sight of the rebels. The [illegible] fall upon Valerian, who is sent by the general to [illegible] matters. Vespasian, at the [illegible] of Agrippa, pardons [illegible] offence. Titus takes possession of the city. Vespasian [illegible] the city, [illegible].

KING Agrippa having invited Vespasian to pass [illegible] some time with him in his country, and to bring his army with him, partly from a motive of generosity, and partly from the hope of bringing some [illegible] to better order, the general embraced the offer with civility, and marched from Cæsarea upon the sea-coast to Cæsarea Philippi, where he stayed twenty days, refreshing himself and his troops, and returning public thanks to the greater disposer of all events for the success which he had been pleased to crown his undertakings. He was then given to understand that Tiberias [illegible] at that time wavering, and that Tarichea had already revolted, (both of which cities were parts of the kingdom of Agrippa,) and therefore thought he could not have a fairer opportunity of acknowledging his obligations to Agrippa, than by reducing those people to allegiance, especially [illegible] resolved with his [illegible] to press hard upon the Jews. With this view he sent his son Titus for the troops that were quartered at Cæsarea, to bring them to Scythopolis, a place not far from Tiberias, and [illegible] largest town in the district of Decapolis. [illegible] and waited the arrival of his son, when he advanced with three legions [illegible] the [illegible] of [illegible] and encamped at a place called Sennabris, within sight of the rebels. From thence he sent Valerian [illegible] fifty horse, to [illegible], [illegible] to [illegible] to their duty. He was inclined to [illegible], that the generality [illegible] the people to be [illegible] inclined, but they were not moved to [illegible] a [illegible] contents. When Valerian approached the [illegible] alighted from his horse, and ordered his companions to do the same, to obviate any suspicion of a hostile [illegible].

The faction under the command of Jesus the son of Tobias, leader of a band of rovers, [illegible] Valerian and his people without giving [illegible] vious notice. Valerian, though [illegible] durst not [illegible] contrary to [illegible] though he had every probable [illegible], [illegible] and five of his men [illegible] forced to leave their horses behind [illegible] when Jesus [illegible] his crew carried off in triumph into the [illegible] of victory, rather than the booty of an [illegible].

This [illegible] and [illegible] conduct [illegible] the leading men of the place [illegible] vengeance, that they immediately retired to the Roman camp, under the countenance and protection of Agrippa, and cast themselves [illegible] Vespasian's feet, to [illegible] and pardon, imploring him not to [illegible] particular persons to the whole body [illegible] retained veneration for the Romans, and likewise to [illegible] the innocent, and punish the authors of the [illegible]. Vespasian could hardly forgive the seizure of the [illegible], however, upon the mediation of Agrippa, he granted [illegible] request. As soon as this act of grace [illegible] his party, not thinking it safe for them to [illegible] ber, [illegible] made the best of their way to [illegible].

Vespasian sent Titus, [illegible] following [illegible] of horse, to take possession of the [illegible] common people, if they were of the same [illegible] with their deputies. Upon [illegible] mind, Vespasian marched up to the city [illegible] my, the citizens opening the gates, [illegible] in the way with the honours [illegible].

their benefactor and protector. But the gates being too narrow for the troops to march at liberty, the Roman general commanded part of the south wall to be beaten down to widen the passage, but with a command of the utmost penalty, not to offer any violence to the people. This he declared was for the sake of Agrippa, as it was that he spared the remainder of the wall, upon the king's undertaking for the good behaviour of the people for the time to come. Thus did he restore this city to a quiet state after it had been grievously afflicted by sedition.

CHAP. XVII

Vespasian leads his army against Taricheæ. Its situation and proportions. The Jews break in upon the Roman pioneers. The Romans pursue the Jews up to their shipping. Great numbers of Jews assembled in a plain. Titus sent to [illegible] [illegible] his father. Total destruction of the Jews [illegible] about the city. The [illegible] [illegible] [illegible] account of the [illegible] [illegible] of the fugitives.

VESPASIAN, having departed from Tiberias, encamped betwixt that city and Taricheæ, but fortified his camp with a wall, upon the [illegible] that the taking of the place would be a work of time. It was remarkably strong, both by art and nature, and being fortified by the lake of Gennesareth, it was looked upon [illegible] the reception of all the disaffected [illegible] people of the faction [illegible] [illegible], [illegible] [illegible] [illegible] [illegible] not-side that [illegible] washed by the sea, Josephus had [illegible] [illegible] strong wall, but in some degree [illegible] to [illegible] of Tiberias [illegible] the commencement of the [illegible], there wanted neither men, money, or provisions to render the place impregnable [illegible] there was a surplus to spare for Tiberias. The [illegible] had likewise a fleet of [illegible] [illegible] upon the lake for a retreat, in case of an adverse stroke by land, and to serve for a naval fight, if there should be an occasion.

While the Romans were fortifying and entrenching, Jesus and his party made a furious attack upon them, scattered the pioneers and overthrew a good part of their works, without any dread either of the Roman discipline or of their numbers. The Romans pursued them to the lake, when they embarked on board their vessels, and when they had got out of the reach of the enemy's darts and arrows they came to anchor, and there lay arranged, as if drawn up in order of battle.

During these transactions Vespasian received intelligence that a considerable body of the Jews were gathered together on the next plain, and thereupon sent out his son, with a detachment of six hundred chosen horse, to disperse them. Titus accordingly proceeded, and finding himself greatly overpowered by numbers, sent to his father for a reinforcement. Finding however the greater part of his troops eager for action, notwithstanding a disparity in point of numbers, he took up his stand where he might best be heard, and thus addressed them.

"Romans (for I cannot begin my discourse more appositely than by putting you in mind of your race, telling you whence and what you are, and whom you have to do withal. As to the Romans, the whole world allows them to be invincible upon undeniable proof and experience. I have this to say for the Jews too, that, though they have been often conquered, they would never own themselves to be overcome so that we have no more to do, than to stand as firm at least in our prosperity, as they do in their adversity,) I read cheerfulness and courage in every face, and it joys me to see it but yet I am uneasy sometimes for fear the vast numbers of your enemies should strike a secret damp upon that resolution. Wherefore let every man duly consider his own force, and that of his adversary. The Jews, it is true, are generally bold, and fearless of death, but utterly deficient in military conduct and discipline, and may be more properly called a croud of people than an army, whereas nothing can be more regular than our order and experience. What are we the better for the practice of arms in time of peace, if it does not help us to supply the want of numbers by skill and address? Or, what is the benefit of a perpetual exercise of war, if it gives us no advantage over men that are raw and inexperienced? Do but consider what it is to encounter naked bodies with men in arms, foot with horse, men that understand nothing of government, with eminent commanders [illegible] that we are as good as double the number we appear to be at that rate of advantage, and the enemy [illegible] [illegible] so strong as they may appear. It is not [illegible] [illegible] [illegible] does the business in war, let the [illegible] [illegible] be ever so stout, but true courage, as we see every day, does wonders with a few, for moderate numbers are manageable to the best advantage of the party, but great bodies are liable to disorder and confusion, and [illegible] [illegible] dangerous to themselves than an enemy. The daring, desperate and brutal fierceness of the Jews, does a great deal, I must confess, in a prosperous course of fortune; but, upon the least check of a disaster or disappointment, [illegible] impetuous ardour abates, and comes to nothing; whereas virtue, resignation, obedience, and true valour, will support us in all our fortune, good or bad, without [illegible] puffing us up, or deceiving us. Besides, we have a greater interest at stake than the Jews, for theirs is only a personal quarrel for liberty, and their country, but we contend for glory, and for the fame of immortal memory, and not without some indignation neither, after the conquest of the world beside, to find ourselves [illegible] in competition with the Jews. You may observe again, even in case of the worst, that we shall run no great risque neither in the contest, being sure to be well seconded with so many of our allies, so strong, and so near us. But what have we more to do now than to anticipate the victory, and engross the honour of it to ourselves, without waiting for the reinforcement we expect from my father? The glory will be the greater when it comes home to us alone, without sharing. The point at present in question, is no less than the characters of my father, myself, and my fellow soldiers, that is to say, whether or no my father deserves the honour the world has done him. And am not I his son then, and are not you my soldiers? My father has been so accustomed to victory, that I should never dare to look him in the face again after one defeat, and would not you be as much ashamed of tardiness on the other hand, where the general leads the way? The first post of danger shall be mine; do you but stand by me, and commit the rest to Providence; only remember what I tell you, that a close fight will be to our advantage."

This address of Titus greatly animated the Roman army, throughout which the spirit of heroism seemed now to be diffused insomuch, that the arrival of Trajan with four hundred horse, before the engagement [illegible], disgusted them so much, as they could not bear the thought of having more partners to share in the glory of the day. Vespasian had also sent Antonius and Silo, with two thousand archers, and given them in charge to take possession of the mountain that was over against the city, and [illegible] [illegible] that were upon the wall, which was accordingly done. Titus, in order to render his army more formidable in appearance than it was in reality, drew up in a line, to answer the front of the enemy, and was the first man himself that charged in upon their body, the men following him with the loudest exultations. The Jews, though surprized at the resolution of their attack, made some resistance till they were beaten down and trampled upon by the horse, when they dispersed, and precipitately fled for refuge towards the city, and many had been slain upon the spot. Titus pressed upon the hindmost, crossed others, and maimed them, and forced others back that made for the walls, insomuch that very few escaped, but those who got into the town.

There fell out at this time a terrible sedition in the city betwixt the old inhabitants and the strangers. The former were concerned for their possessions, and ever [illegible] to a win, and more so now than their defeat. But their foreigners, who were violent and numerous, were the more eager on that account for action. The dispute [illegible] loud clamours and outrages, that Titus, being near the wall, and overhearing the whole, improved the occasion, and [illegible] addressed his soldiers to this effect:

"The time is now come, my fellow soldiers, [illegible] have but hearts to make use of it, for God hath delivered [illegible] the Jews into our hands, and we may have a victory, for the taking it up. Do you not hear the outrageous contentions of the very men that have escaped our hands, and [illegible] to cut one another's throats? The city is our own, if we do not slip the opportunity. [illegible] as well as [illegible] to be done [illegible] And why, do we not [illegible] coming to [illegible] of [illegible] but of the [illegible] of the [illegible] [illegible] shall have both the [illegible]"

[illegible] the town followed by his troops. The [illegible] such confusion [illegible] bold [illegible] [illegible] The [illegible] Jews, [illegible] [illegible] Other [illegible] were [illegible] others by [illegible] There was great slaughter in the city, [illegible] to [illegible] having [illegible] the town [illegible] slaughter out of [illegible] The town being now taken, those that [illegible] to the lake [illegible] reduction of the city [illegible] [illegible] to be [illegible] and [illegible]

CHAP. XVII.

Description of the lake of Genezareth. [illegible] of the river Jordan. Description of the country [illegible] of Genezareth. [illegible]

THE lake of Genezareth derives its name from the country adjoining to it. Its breadth is forty furlongs and in length an hundred. Its waters are sweet and agreeable to the palate, as they are purer than those of other fens. It lies upon a gravel, is more convenient for drawing, and milder than any river or fountain water, yet so cool, that the natives cannot warm it by setting it in the sun in the hottest season of the year. It abounds with a variety of fish, which for form or flavour, are not to be found any where else, and the river Jordan runs through the middle of it. The head of this river has been thought to be Panion, but, in reality, it is carried thither after an occult manner, from a place called Phiala, an hundred and twenty furlongs distant from C[illegible], a little on the right hand, and not much out of the way to [illegible] It is called Phiala from its round figure, and the water always continues up to its edge, without ever shrinking or [illegible] flowing. The first discovery of this was by Philip the tetrarch of Trachonitis, who caused chaff to be thrown into Phiala, which came out again at Panion, till [illegible] taken for the head of the Jordan. Panion [illegible] delightful from situation, but most [illegible] and enriched by the royal bounty of Agrippa. [illegible] stream of Jordan [illegible] from this [illegible] and fens of the lake [illegible] hundred and twenty furlongs [illegible] of Julias, and so over [illegible] into the desert [illegible] the lake Asphaltites.

[illegible] that [illegible] proved [illegible] a peculiar [illegible] is cultivated [illegible] [illegible] One, indeed, might term [illegible] that had claim to the [illegible] [illegible] Capernaum [illegible] Coracin, [illegible] found but at Alexandria. [illegible] the lake is thirty furlongs [illegible] this suffice for a description of the [illegible]

CHAP. XX.

[illegible]

WHEN the vessels were [illegible] Vespasian embarked as many [illegible] deemed sufficient to cope with [illegible] [illegible] of them. Those who [illegible] to the land, where they [illegible] into the hands of the enemy, or to [illegible] at [illegible] as their vessels, being [illegible] were too small to encounter with the [illegible] they were to [illegible] upon [illegible] to approach the Romans, who [illegible] good order. The only manner in which [illegible] them was [illegible] stones [illegible] greatest [illegible] but the Romans [illegible] stones [illegible] they lay open and exposed [illegible] [illegible] they could execute their designs, [illegible] men drowned. The enemy [illegible] distance with the [illegible] with their swords, and [illegible] [illegible] Those who were tumbled overboard, [illegible] life, no sooner [illegible] were taken off by [illegible] [illegible] of them [illegible] their adversaries, they were sure to have their hands or their heads chopped off

Nothing was to be seen but death and destruction in all the variety of horror, till they were totally broken and routed, pressing through the midst of the enemy to get on shore In this confusion, many were killed upon the water, and more upon the land, nor was any thing to be seen upon the lake, or the borders of it, but blood and carcases The putrid bodies, in a few days, tainted the air to such a degree of malignancy, that the case was not only dreadful to the sufferers of the calamity, but the very conquerors were shocked at the scene, and many expressed abhorrence at the barbarity of it This was the issue of the naval battle, and the whole number of the slain, in both actions, were 6500 persons

When the fight was over Vespasian took his place upon the tribunal, and separating the strangers that were the cause of the war, from the natives and old inhabitants, who were merely passive in it, he called a council of his officers about him, to consider what was to be done with these people, and whether they were to be treated all alike The council opposed the sparing of the strangers, as they would ever be restless, having no habitation, and consequently dangerous and troublesome to any prince that would receive them Vespasian acknowledged that they deserved to die, and that he made no doubt of their rebelling against their preservers, but the difficulty was, the manner of disposing of them, as the inhabitants would lay it to heart to see so many people put to death after a promise of quarters upon their mediation, besides the general's scruple upon a point of honour and justice of breaking faith with his prisoners His friends, however, insisted on it, that he was not tied up to punctilios with the Jews, and that where strict honour and policy are inconsistent, the common good ought to have the preference

Vespasian was over-ruled by his council, and gave the strangers leave to depart, upon condition they kept the way that led to Tiberias As mankind are ready to believe what they wish to be true, in this confidence they set out for Tiberias, without the least apprehension of any violence in their passage, either upon their persons or property The Romans had beset the road that led to the city, so that it was impossible for any one to escape When they got them into the town, they made them all prisoners, Vespasian causing them to be shut up in the amphitheatre, where he ordered both old and young, to the number of 1200, that were not able to bear arms, to be put to death, 6000 of the strongest of them to be sent to Nero, and 30,400 were sold for slaves, besides those given to king Agrippa, whom he left at liberty to dispose of as he thought fit The rest were inhabitants of divers places, most of them incendiaries and fugitives, and promoters of the war, because they could not live in peace These prisoners were taken upon the eighth day of the month Gorpiaus

END OF THE THIRD BOOK OF THE WARS

FLAVIUS JOSEPHUS

ON THE

WARS OF THE JEWS.

BOOK IV

CHAP I

Siege of Gamala. Formidable ſituation of that city. Veſpaſian advances up to it. The Romans make an aſſault. Are afterwards repulſed with great loſs. Veſpaſian's bravery and preſence of mind. Noble action of Gallus, a Roman centurion. Noble ſpeech of Veſpaſian to his ſoldiers. Second attempt upon Gamala.

THE cities and towns of Galilee, which, after the taking of Jotapata, had revolted from the Romans, upon the conqueſt of Tarichæa, returned to their allegiance, ſo that they were now in poſſeſſion of all the fortreſſes except Giſchala, and the mountains of Itabyr. Gamala alſo, a city over againſt Tarichæa, ſituated upon the lake, and under the government of Agrippa, joined in the rebellion. Sogane revolted alſo, and ſo did Seleucia, after their example. They were both cities belonging to the province of Gaulanitis, Sogane in the upper part of it, which is called Gaulana, and Gamala in the lower. Seleucia ſtands upon the lake Semechonitis, which is ſixty furlongs in length, and thirty in breadth; and its marſhes reach as far as Daphne. This is a delightful country in many reſpects, but more eſpecially for the curious ſprings in it, that feed the Leſſer Jordan, as it is called, and then take their courſe to the Great Jordan, at the foot of Jupiter's golden temple.

King Agrippa, at the beginning of this defection, entered into an alliance with the people of Sogane and Seleucia; but Gamala, depending on its own ſtrength, as being much ſtronger than Jotapata, refuſed to be of the party. Gamala, which ſtands upon the cliſt of a rock, that ariſes out of the middle of a mountain, and, in the poſture of elevation, with crags before and behind it, has ſome reſemblance of the figure of a camel, from whence it originally took its name, but time and cuſtom have corrupted the manner of writing it. Upon the front and the two ſides are inacceſſible vallies. The part that joins the mountain is not of itſelf ſo hard of acceſs, but as the inhabitants have fortified it with trenches and defences, it is next to impregnable. The houſes ſtand as thick upon the ſteep of the hill to the ſouthward, as if they were dropping into the precipice. There is alſo an hill of ſo prodigious an height, that it may ſerve for a citadel to the valley in the bottom. There was alſo a fountain within the circuit of the city, which terminates the town.

Notwithſtanding all that nature had done towards making this place impregnable, Joſephus had cauſed a wall to be run about it, and caſt up artificial works, trenches, and fortifications, for a further ſecurity. The inhabitants were much more confident in the defenſible condition of the place, than thoſe of Jotapata, though neither ſo many, or ſo martial. But the difficulties of [illegible] had made amends for the want of numbers. The city, indeed, was well manned, as it was the ſanctuary of all the refugees; inſomuch that king Agrippa ſpent ſeven months before it without any manner of advantage.

Veſpaſian at this time decamped from Emmaus, near Tiberias (the former of which was ſo called from a warm bath of ſovereign virtue againſt ſeveral diſeaſes) and ſo proceeded to Gamala, where he found it impoſſible to draw a regular line of circumvallation about it, but ſet guards, however, upon all the paſſes he could come at, and poſſeſſed himſelf of the mountain above. The Romans, according to their cuſtom, fortified their camp, carried up a wall about it, and ſo entrenched. The fifteenth legion was poſted againſt a tower, eaſtward, upon the higheſt part of the town, the fifth toward the middle of the town, and the tenth was appointed to level the ditches, and other hollow places.

While things were in this ſituation, king Agrippa drew up cloſe to the wall, to try if he could bring the people to ſurrender the place, and reaſon them into a ſenſe of their duty. But at this inſtant he received a terrible ſtroke with a ſtone from a ſling upon his right elbow. His [illegible]

[illegible] m[illegible] about him to bring him off, and the [illegible] tented, by reflecting how barbarously they [illegible] strangers and enemies, [illegible] prince, then countrymen and [illegible] that [illegible] them to their good [illegible] pressed the siege with all possible vigour.

[illegible] many [illegible] and diligent application, the walls [illegible] and the next thing to be done [illegible] of their [illegible] Chares and Joseph, [illegible] the principal men in the town, had the ordering of the defence and to hold up the soldiers to the [illegible] exhortations and encouragements to behave themselves [illegible] or honour [illegible] and [illegible], they [illegible] not much disposed to the [illegible] they could not hold out long. Upon [illegible] Romans [illegible] made some [illegible] them [illegible] with their [illegible] nothing could [illegible] without and within the [illegible] trumpets, and the noise of the [illegible]

The defenders [illegible] the [illegible] great [illegible] the Romans [illegible] of [illegible] parts of the city, [illegible] Romans [illegible] their backs.

[illegible] turned short [illegible] parties, [illegible] precipices before them, [illegible] passages, where the [illegible] upon them [illegible] the Romans, finding [illegible] enemies over their heads, betook themselves [illegible] to [illegible] the [illegible] they sunk under the weight [illegible] brought down another, [illegible] that [illegible] the Romans perished under [illegible] they chose rather to commit [illegible] to the [illegible] of those tottering houses, than be openly exposed [illegible] public [illegible]. Some were crushed to pieces with the [illegible], others maimed in attempting [illegible], and some again were suffocated with the dust.

The Jews were so far from being troubled at the loss of their habitations, that they esteemed themselves gainers by the fall of so many of their enemies in the charge, and [illegible] one [illegible] another, in order to bring down that [illegible] lost their hold, were forced to [illegible] from [illegible] with which the [illegible] bodies [illegible] their [illegible] [illegible] the common [illegible] Some [illegible] from the tops of the houses, [illegible] to death in the fall of them, and [illegible] the good fortune to escape out of the town, [illegible] general destruction.

Vespasian was deeply affected to find his army thus broken by the [illegible] city, so that, fearless of personal danger, according to his common practice, he [illegible] to a post in the upper part of the town, where he was left with some resolute men about him, [illegible] the greatest [illegible], his son Titus being abroad at this time in Syria, upon a commission of Mutianus. Such was his condition that he could not retreat with safety or honour; so that calling to mind former gallant exploits and resolving to persevere in the path to fame, a very extraordinary expedient occurred to his mind. This was to plant himself, with the few valiant men he had, as close to each other as possible, and covering themselves with their arms stand firm against all attempts of violence from above. The Jews were so startled at this astonishing instance of resolution, that, deeming it a kind of providential impulse, and dreading the vengeance of opposing the higher powers, they abated somewhat of the vigour and fury of the action. Vespasian, observing this, drew off by degrees, and [illegible] turned his back till he had got from the walls. The [illegible] many Romans, both officers and private soldiers, in the encounter, and among others, Ebutius, a decurion, who, as he lived, so he died, exhibiting proofs of invincible magnanimity.

One Gallus, a centurion, being in a certain house with [illegible] Syrian soldiers, and overhearing some [illegible] to be taken with the Romans, which [illegible] being [illegible] Syrians, they perfectly understood, fell upon them in the night, slew them all, and got off safe to the Romans.

Vespasian finding, at length, his soldiers cast down [illegible] series of disasters, and not [illegible] general alone to encounter the greatest difficulties and dangers, bethought himself of a method of affording them [illegible] degree of comfort, without [illegible] To this end he thus addressed them:

"Since, my fellow-soldiers, misfortunes [illegible] borne [illegible] "let them be generously [illegible] It [illegible] for [illegible] men to expect an exemption [illegible] common [illegible] of mankind. Whoever considers the nature of war, will find that victory is not to be [illegible] without blood [illegible] this [illegible] but [illegible] the thousands of Jews that we [illegible] before [illegible] vanity and weakness to be [illegible] upon prosperity, so it is the mark of a mean soul to be cast down by adversity. Consider again, how variable the change [illegible] from one extreme to the other, and that no man is truly great, but he that stands his ground and keeps up the same [illegible] of mind in all conditions, correcting the malignity of [illegible] one by the prudence of the other. We are not now to impute our present miscarriage either to the want of resolution on our parts, or to the valour of the Jews; for, if they fought bravely [illegible] the [illegible] was the odds of the ground [illegible] If you were to blame for any thing in this encounter, it was truth for your rashness, in pursuing the enemy when they had up the town for you. You should have held your hands, and contented yourselves with the possession of the lower town, till necessity should have forced them to engage you upon a fair [illegible] and [illegible] equal terms. But you were so impatient to have the [illegible] never attended to the right way of doing it. The Romans are a people famous for order and discipline, and not for this impetuous and [illegible] the Jews and Barbarians. Wherefore let us have recourse to our own methods of reformation and discipline, and let [illegible] like men that are [illegible] with indignation for what they have done [illegible] under the burden of a [illegible] [illegible] his own [illegible] hand to the work, and give himself the comfort of revenging [illegible] of his friend upon the heads of those that destroyed them. In this respect and confidence you shall find [illegible], as you have [illegible] already, [illegible] the [illegible] in [illegible] dangers."

The army of Vespasian was greatly animated by this spirited address, and resumed their former courage and resolution.

The people of Gamala could not but be elated by a [illegible] of such unexpected success for a short time, but afterwards reflecting that they had no hopes of any terms of accommodation, no possibility of escaping, or prospect of supply of provisions, their spirits were depressed, and they were seized with the horrors of despair. They persisted, however, in the exertion of their utmost efforts for the defence of the place, setting their best men to guard the breaches, and disposing of the rest to the greatest advantage.

The Romans, by this time, having repaired their platforms and made ready for another attack, divers of the citizens stole away through occult and intricate passages, where no guards were posted Others concealed themselves in subterraneous caverns, where they perished for want of food as the provisions were wholly reserved for such as bore arms Such were the distresses with which the people of Gamala had to encounter

CHAP. II

Vespasian sends Placidus against a factious party that had taken possession of mount Tabor He draws them some distance from the mountain into the plain, and there subdues them

WHILE Vespasian was so harrassed by this vexatious siege, he was under a necessity in the midst of his confusions of sending out Placidus, with a party of six hundred horse, to mount Tabor, to disperse a seditious multitude that were assembled there This mountain lies betwixt the great plain and Scythopolis The ascent is supposed to be thirty furlongs It is inaccessible on the northern part The top is a plain of twenty furlongs, and encompassed with a wall which though extensive, had been erected by Josephus in the space of forty days He furnished it with water and other necessaries from below, for the inhabitants had only rain water for their use

When Placidus, upon his arrival at the place, according to orders, found it impossible to ascend the mountain, he amused the enemy with the flattering hopes of peace and pardon, and brought numbers of them down to him upon a pretence that they were wrought upon by the reason of his address, though in reality the design was to draw him into a snare, and surprise him Placidus had also a design upon them His plan was to get them into the plain, and take them unawares They feigned compliance with what he proposed, but the scheme of Placidus succeeded in the result When the Jews began the fray, Placidus and his men, as if they were afraid, betook themselves to flight The Jews pursued them till in the pursuit they were dispersed throughout the field Placidus watched his opportunity, and turning quickly upon them with his horsemen, slew several, and put the rest to flight or and one of them return to the mountain Those of the faction who were left at Tabor, now quitted it and hastened to Jerusalem, but the natives surrendered themselves and the place to Placidus, upon security for their good behaviour

CHAP III

Destruction of Gamala Three Roman soldiers are thrown into a consternation by the fall of a tower Titus enters the town without opposition and terrible slaughter of the inhabitants

THE bravest of the people of Gamala had now recourse to flight or concealment, while the rest pusillanimous and inferior perished by famine But the resolute in arms sustained the siege till the twenty-second day of the month Hyperberetæus when three soldiers, of the fifteenth legion, stole out before break of day, to the foot of the highest tower upon their quarter, and undermined it so privately as to elude the vigilance of the guards They made not the least noise, but having rolled away five of its principal stones, retired that very instant The tower immediately fell to the ground with a most dreadful noise, dashing the guards, and all that were in it, under the ruins The horror of this accident frightened the other guards from their posts and some of them fell into the very teeth of the Romans Amongst these was one Joseph, who was slain by a dart as he was running away over that part of the wall that was broken down Such was the terror that prevailed in the city, that it excited as universal a panic as if the whole Roman army had entered the town. Chares was at that time much indisposed, and it was believed that this stroke hastened his end But the Romans were so impressed with a remembrance of their former ill success, that they postponed any farther attempt till the following day

Titus was by this time returned, and, from indignation at the disasters which had befallen the Romans in his absence, drew out a body of foot, and two hundred chosen horse, and entered the city without opposition The watch were the first that took and gave the alarm, and the news was spread throughout in an instant It was no sooner confirmed, than the citizens, in the utmost confusion took their wives and children and fled to the citadel, amidst horrid outcries and lamentations Some were cut off by the Roman soldiers, others, that could not get into the citadel, and straggled about fell into the hands of the guards. Death, in fine, prevailed in all its forms of wounds and groans, and horror had diffused itself throughout every quarter

Vespasian then drew up his whole army to attack the castle It stood upon the point of a rock, high and steep, and almost inaccessible, with many crags and precipices round about it Upon this disadvantage it was impossible for the Romans to avoid the stones and darts of the Jews that were cast down from above, or to reach the Jews from below Through a wonderful providence, however, in favour of the Romans, and for the destruction of the Jews, there arose a violent storm, which drove the Roman arrows directly in the faces of the defendants and kept theirs from the Romans, or diverted them away from them The blast, at the same time, was so strong, that the besieged could not maintain the ground on which they were to make their defence, nor see the people with whom they had to engage The Romans, with these advantages, made themselves masters of the mountain which they surrounded immediately, and in a rage of revenge for their former miscarriage upon that attack, put all to the sword indifferently, whether they resisted or not In this state of desperation many cast themselves, with their wives and children, down the precipice from the castle They were supposed to amount to the number of five thousand, of whom four thousand were thus slain: so much more merciful were the Romans to the Jews, than the Jews were to themselves The very infants were thrown down the rocks, without sparing so much as a single creature, two women only escaped who were the daughters of Philip a man of rank, and formerly a general in the army of Agrippa The two sisters were not, indeed so much beholden to the clemency of the Romans for their preservation, as to the good fortune of lying undiscovered till the rage, in some degree, subsided The rebellion at Gamala began on the twenty-fourth day of the month Gorpiæus, and the place was destroyed on the twenty-third of the month Hyperberetæus

CHAP IV

The people of Gischala are suddenly a sanguinary disposition [illegible] volt from the Romans [illegible] Titus [illegible] intending [illegible] to attack [illegible] The [illegible] Titus treats the people [illegible] John of Gischala [illegible] in the night The [illegible] entered into Gischala [illegible] Galilee

THE province of Galilee was now wholly reduced except the small city of Gischala where the people in general, were disposed to pacific obedience, being mostly employed in the pursuit of agriculture and commerce [illegible] on the produce of their lands. They [illegible], however, with a band of libertines, [illegible] and there was some citizens of [illegible] with [illegible] principles. The chief [illegible] the faction, and perverter of the people, was one [illegible] of dissolute morals, a vile impostor, [illegible] with [illegible] and chicanery, destitute of honour and [illegible], and a promoter of sedition from sinister views [illegible] the son of one Levi, and the head of the rabble in Gischala. Had he not interfered, the people would [illegible] have sent their deputies to the Romans, with [illegible] of submission; but, at his instigation, they [illegible] upon to put it off, till a war should be [illegible].

[illegible] upon this juncture, sent away Titus to [illegible] with a thousand horse, and the tenth legion to [illegible], with the other two legions, to Cæsarea [illegible], in order to prepare their [illegible] for the [illegible] they had yet to encounter. [illegible] that [illegible] of the inhabitants of Jerusalem would [illegible] arduous [illegible], not only as it was populous and [illegible], and the capital city, but as it was an [illegible] fugitives of faction from other quarters, [illegible] men, naturally strong, as well [illegible], though not impregnable in point of [illegible]. The Roman general revolving these circumstances in his mind, trained his soldiers like champions [illegible] exercise of their arms, to render them more expert [illegible] into action.

[illegible] he rode up to Gischala, finding from the [illegible], that it was not a place to stand an assault, and [illegible] at the same time that the soldiers would undoubtedly [illegible] the inhabitants of the city as they had [illegible] Gamala, confounding the innocent with the guilty, if once they should take it by storm, [illegible] of compassion for the people, and the detestation in which he held those inhuman cruelties, bethought himself how he might gain upon them by treaty. The walls being now covered with soldiers, and the majority within the town of the corrupted party, he thus addressed them in an humble tone of voice:

"It is wonderful to me, that, when all the rest of your [illegible] are gone, and places much better manned and "fortified than yours, taken without any difficulty, (many "of them at the very first attack,) you should be now so "[illegible] as to think of standing out, especially "when you may yet be safe, easy, free and happy, upon "a return to your duty. This, I dare undertake, shall "be made good to you, and all your insults pardoned "[illegible] and imputed only to an inordinate desire of "liberty. But if you do not know when you are well "offered, and refuse to cast yourselves upon the faith and "honour of the Romans, if you resolve, at last, to run "headlong to your certain destruction, and to contend "with impossibilities, you must expect to feel the weight "of the Roman power and displeasure, and you will "find, before you are aware, that your paper walls will "fall like dust before their engines. Is this the way "to shew yourselves to be the most arrogant fools of all "the Galileans?"

Not one of the populace durst make a reply, or even come up to the wall, for the faction over-ruled, and had posted guards at all the gates, that none of the rest should pass in or out, to propose any terms of submission. John, at length, took upon him to return for answer, in the name of the people, "That he accepted the conditions "and that the town should agree to them likewise, or he "would force them to it: only he made him this request, "with regard to the inviolable strictness of the Jewish "law for the observance of their sabbath, which would "no more suffer them to treat of peace than to fight a "battle, that he would indulge them that day; it being a "case wherein either their complying on the one hand, "or, as the Romans knew very well, the enforcing them "on the other, would be equally unwarrantable. Besides, "there could be no danger in putting off the treaty to "another day, for, if they imagined that any man would "attempt to escape that night, it would be an easy matter, "by placing guards at all the avenues, to prevent it. Besides, the reputation he would get by shewing himself "a [illegible] of their laws [illegible] they were of them [illegible] "of their consciences as well as of their persons, [illegible] "was a favour beyond the expectation."

John had recourse to this manœuvre with Titus, not so much from a regard to the seventh day, as to his own preservation, for he was apprehensive of being deserted if the city should be taken, and all his hopes centered in [illegible] his escape that night. But [illegible] providence, it eventually tended to the destruction of Jerusalem [illegible] was the occasion not only of the [illegible] of the encampment of Titus, farther off the city [illegible], one of the strongest and most populous places in [illegible] and mortally averse to the Galileans.

The night being now come, and the town unguarded, John seized the opportunity, and made his escape to Jerusalem, taking with him not only his military people, but several substantial inhabitants of the town. [illegible] women, and children, that had left the place at his instigation, with difficulty kept up with their leaders for the first twenty furlongs; but finding themselves spent, and not able to continue the march, they betook themselves to lamentation, for those that had outstript them, and gone before, as the farther their friends were advanced from them one way, the nearer they accounted themselves to their enemies the other. Nay they fancied the very noise of their own feet to be the tread of their adversaries, and still looking behind them, took their own people for their pursuers. In this imaginary fright they fell one over another, and the way was covered with the bodies of women and children, that were crushed to death by the crowd pressing who should get foremost. There was little more to be heard than the cries of miserable wretches to their husbands and friends to stay for them. But John [illegible] who [illegible] to save themselves by flight [illegible]. He observed, that if the Romans found these upon those whom they left behind, they would be revenged on them for it. The multitude upon this dispersed themselves, and every one made the best of his way.

When Titus came to the walls of the town to execute the treaty, he found the gates open, and the inhabitants ready, with acclamations, to receive and acknowledge him as their benefactor and preserver. They informed him of John's escape, entreated clemency for the innocent, and justice upon those left in the town, that should be found to have been abettors of the revolt. Titus sent out a party of horse in pursuit of John, but they could not overtake him before he got into Jerusalem. They slew, however, [illegible] thousand of his party, and brought back near three thousand women and children, whom they found wandering up and down.

Titus was highly displeased at the escape of the impostor, which prevented his being brought to exemplary punishment; but then [illegible] the advantages of the prisoners, [illegible], and the taking of the town, against the disappointment of missing the single person of such a miscreant, he balanced the one with the other, and entered the place with a friendly disposition towards the people. He took possession of it in form, by the ceremony of his soldiers breaking off a piece of the wall, [illegible] the authors of the sedition rather by menaces than actual punishment. Titus wisely and humanely thought that, in a case where so many family feuds, personal piques, and inordinate passions were concerned, it might be dangerous to inflict punishments, as a common rule of distinction between the good and bad, for fear of injuring the innocent, while doing justice to the guilty.

Upon this deliberation, he thought it more honourable and humane, rather to spare the lives of some criminals, than run the risk of destroying some innocents, there being no place left for remedy and atonement in the latter, whereas, in the other case, there might be hope of amendment, whether from fear of punishment, sense of shame, or the impulse of virtue. Upon condition, however, he placed a garrison in the town, partly to restrain turbulent spirits, and partly for the security of those who were disposed for peace. This action finished the conquest of Galilee, at the expence of much labour and blood.

CHAP. V.

[illegible] of Gischala [illegible] Jerusalem [illegible] Senate [illegible] Cestius [illegible] Simon, [illegible] Ananus [illegible] of John of Gischala.

UPON John's coming into Jerusalem with his party, the whole body of the people came in an uproar [illegible] thronging about them to enquire concerning the [illegible] abroad. John and his companions had been so expeditious in their flight as to read [illegible] apparent tokens of want of breath; nevertheless, they endeavoured to support their pretences, by insinuating, that they had not fled from the Romans but were come [illegible] to find out some spot for the encounter, where they might engage upon equal terms, alledging that it would be unreasonable to expose themselves to desperate hazards for the defence of Gischala, and other places of little importance, when the metropolis itself was in safety, and every way more obliged in duty and honour, to exert its utmost efforts to defend it.

But, notwithstanding the plausible manner in which they related the capture of Gischala, and their own departure from that place, many of the people saw through the disguise, and considered that honourable retreat, as it was termed, as little less than an absolute flight.

The [illegible] and story of the prisoners the Romans had taken struck the people with so much terror, as if the [illegible] of Gischala had been the prelude to the destruction of Jerusalem. But John, regardless of the miserable condition of those he had left behind him, went amongst the multitude, animating them to the prosecution of the war, [illegible] affirming that the power of the Romans was much declined, and that of the party resolved to oppose it much enlarged, so that by these means of the [illegible] [illegible] [illegible] [illegible]. He further insinuated the impossibility of the Romans taking Jerusalem, even if they had wings, from their finding so much difficulty after so many of their projects were [illegible] in subduing some inconsiderable places in Galilee. These pompous harangues, had the desired effect upon the rash and inexperienced, but men of sober reflection foresaw impending ruin.

Such was the confused state of things in Jerusalem at that time, but the country led the way to the sedition that followed afterwards in the city. For Titus being gone from Gischala to Cæsarea, Vespasian went also from Cæsarea to Jamnia and Azotus, and subdued them both, settled garrisons in them and so returned, bringing up a vast number of people along with him, that were now entered into a league with the Romans. The cities were infested with tumults and intestine broils, and no sooner [illegible] with the Romans, than contention prevailed amongst themselves, and particularly between those of a warlike and those of pacific turns. The quarrel began in private families, which had [illegible] long adversaries upon the score of hereditary feuds. It thence passed into divided multitudes, and those who had been friends became enemies. It terminated in matter of fact and opinion, when men of the same mind formed in opposition of party to party, and so incorporated in a rebellion. Sedition and faction, in fine, universally prevailed, the young men, and active being bent upon arms and innovations, and the more grave and prudent disposed to moderation and candour; but the former overpowered the latter.

A general licentiousness now broke through all restraint and a right to pillage was now assumed, without any regard to law or conscience. Besides, the parties were found who committed such [illegible] outrages and depredations in the [illegible] of which the fears of the sufferers were [illegible] as they could [illegible] the calamity would have been much more tolerable from an enemy than from their own countrymen.

The garrisons placed to guard the cities, consulting their own ease on the one hand, and being generally averse to the people on the other, would not exert themselves in their protection or defence, till, [illegible] the [illegible] of the [illegible] [illegible] [illegible] parts [illegible] [illegible] government the [illegible] with no opposition. Besides, [illegible] [illegible] were open to them, without exception, and at this time more especially, when they took [illegible] people [illegible] [illegible] [illegible] [illegible] the [illegible] of the city, [illegible] [illegible] provisions [illegible] [illegible] the [illegible] [illegible] who had [illegible] the place. [illegible] [illegible] were added to the [illegible].

There came [illegible] the [illegible] a band of robbers [illegible] of the country, who [illegible] with those they found in the town [illegible] [illegible] and [illegible]. To [illegible] the [illegible] crime of murder, [illegible] [illegible] [illegible] persons, but [illegible] and upon the most considerable [illegible] in the city. They began with the [illegible] of Antipas, a [illegible] of the royal [illegible] and [illegible] authority that he [illegible] in the [illegible] treasury. They seized Levias and [illegible], the son of [illegible], with divers other persons of rank with the same [illegible].

Nor did these profligate wretches stop here, but finding their prisoners to be [illegible] of [illegible], [illegible] and apprehending [illegible] keeping [illegible] [illegible] of a rescue or revenge [illegible], [illegible] [illegible] [illegible] [illegible] sentence of death [illegible] bloody [illegible] (son of Dorcas) [illegible] to [illegible] the sentence. [illegible] [illegible] [illegible] up the city to the Romans, [illegible] service, in [illegible] [illegible] [illegible] [illegible] traitors of the liberty of the country.

The [illegible] [illegible] [illegible] [illegible] [illegible] selves the right of [illegible] [illegible] [illegible] [illegible] sedition, and [illegible] [illegible] [illegible] [illegible] [illegible] [illegible] [illegible] [illegible] [illegible]

Artificial calumnies, and feigned stories, were propagated to create mistrust and dissension amongst those who had it in their power to frustrate their designs, and take advantage of their disagreements; till, in the end, having glutted themselves with their injustice and cruelties towards men, they carried their impieties against God himself, against his laws and holy sanctuary. But upon this daring attempt, the people, at the instigation of Ananus, the high-priest, made head against them. Ananus was a person no less venerable for his years, piety, and wisdom than his general character, and might probably have protected the city, if he could have escaped the hands of those who conspired against them.

The faction took sanctuary in the temple as a place of defence against the resentment of the multitude, as well as the seat of their tyranny and usurpation. But the most sensible part of the contempt was the contemptuous mockery that attended it, in the wanton experiment of their own power over the credulous dependence of the people. For instance, they took upon themselves the pontificate by lot, contrary to precedent, as they pretended, whereas the succession of the chiefs was originally a family privilege, and descended in the line of election. This practice was no better than the abrogation of a positive law, to get the power into their own hands, for they were themselves the owners of it; so, upon summoning one of the sacerdotal tribes, called ... to make choice, the lot fell upon a person that showed the iniquity and corruption of the proceeding. His name was Phanias, the son of Samuel, of the village Aphthas, a man unworthy ... and not only unworthy of the high-priesthood, but wholly ignorant of the nature and duties of that sacred function. They compelled him however, to relinquish his rustic occupations and dressing him up in his pontifical robes gave him ... of ... what he was to do ... and exhibited him as a buffoon on the ... stage. This horrid prophanation greatly affected the other priests, insomuch that they could not refrain from tears, to see the holy laws trampled upon, and their profession and worship so impiously mocked. The people were at length so enraged with the sense of this oppression, that they had no longer patience to endure it, but zealously joined as one man to depose the tyrant, and cast off the yoke. Those who principally encouraged them in this necessary opposition, were Gorion, the son of Joseph and Simeon, the son of Gamaliel, who inculcated the doctrine of liberty, and exhorted them, one and all, to stand up for the vindication of their religion and laws, against their profane and ... enemies.

There were also Jesus, the son of Gamala, and Ananus, the son of Ananus, two priests eminent for their piety and ... who ... frequent discourses to ... to excite their detestation of the ... and practices of the zealots. They had assumed the denomination of zealots, from an hypocritical ostentation of holiness; though, in their lives and practices, they were the most abandoned and dissolute of men. The people being now assembled were inflamed to a degree of indignation bordering on phrenzy, to see the havock they made ... in their holy places and the murders and rapine they had committed without controul.

But notwithstanding this passionate zeal, they did not attempt to oppose them in their impious proceedings, not thinking themselves able to encounter the zealots by force of arms, as indeed they were not, till at length, Ananus standing in the midst of them, and casting his eyes, deluged with tears towards the temple, thus addressed them:

"Why did I not rather die, than live to see the house of "God thus polluted and prophaned, and the wickedest of "men admitted promiscuously into those sacred places of "privilege that were only reserved for the high-priests? "Why do I live and see all this in my sacerdotal robes "too and with the venerable name of the great God written on my forehead? Why do I live any longer, after "so glorious an opportunity now in my age, of ending my "days with honour? What have I more to do, in fine, "under my circumstances, but to fall alone, and give up my "life to my God and my duty? Why should any man desire to live in an insensible generation, and among people "that have neither the prudence to foresee calamities, or the "courage to resist them? You stand still to see yourselves "robbed, beaten, and abused, and your friends and companions murdered before your faces, without so much as one "look, word, or action of tenderness or compassion that you "dare own. A shameful and an insupportable tyranny! But "why do I talk of the actors of the tyranny, and not rather "of those that suffer it, and that trained up the tyrants themselves to the power of exercising what they now practise? "Why did you not crush them when you might have done "it? when they were but few, weak, and inconsiderable? "It was your patience, and nothing else, that made these "people your masters. When you should have turned your "arms against your enemies, you must be cutting throats among yourselves. You should have called them to account betimes, for the outrages they put upon one another. You should have considered that the suffering of "one affront naturally draws on and encourages another, as "so ... in what followed. For when they found that "they might commit all manner of insolence without controul, they advanced a step further, and put several of the "best men of the city in chains (who were effectually betrayed by your tameness,) and dragged them to prison, not "only unheard, and without a sentence, but without so much "as an accusation, and all this was done without one creature appearing in their favour. After the loss of their "estates and liberties, there remained nothing more to be "taken away but their lives, and that was done too, and "their throats cut, like so many beasts drawn out of the herd "for sacrifices, before our very faces, and not a mouth "opened, or an hand lifted up, in their defence. After all "these sufferings, one after another, can you have the patience now to see your holy altars profaned, and our religion exposed to scorn, without showing some resentment worthy of your profession? What, ... that you are "afraid at last but monsters of your own creating, and "the ... enemies of all that is good and holy? If they "don't here, it is not for want of good-will to be yet more "and more wicked, but for want of fresh matter to work "upon, for it is impossible for men to ... the ... things "they have done already. They are possessed, you see, of "the strongest place of the city, and that which you call "the temple serves them only for an impregnable castle, "maintained against you. Considering ... the strength of "the place, and your enemies the masters of it, (as that you "see is the case,) what is there ... propose to yourselves? "Or what do you imagine ... the end of these things? "unless you fancy that the Romans will espouse the cause "of your religion and ceremonies, and, in truth, such is "the misery of our present condition, that our very enemies cannot but pity us. If so many beasts were in your "place, hunted, affected, and wounded, as you yourselves "are, they would have the spirit to turn again upon their "pursuers, and to revenge themselves upon their enemies, "while you, at the same time, suffer all this, without so "much as the sense or apprehension of the brutes. Let it will "you bear this always? and sink in ... under the affronts, public and private, that have been put upon you, "without avenging yourselves? This abject patience looks "as if you had no longer any sense of the most natural and "powerful of human affections, the desire of liberty, but, "as if you had taken up on the contrary, the love of slavery, instead of it, a temper which ... you never "inherited from your ancestors, witness the many dangerous wars they underwent against the Medes and Egyptians, to assert their freedom. But what need of looking "back for precedents, when the very war we are now engaged in against the Romans (whether it succeed well or "ill) is advanced evidently upon the same foot? And shall

" ... now, that dispute our liberties with the masters of " the whole world, crouch like slaves, to our own coun-" trymen? To be overcome by strangers is the chance of " war, and may be imputed without loss of honour, to " the iniquity of fortune; but for people to give them-" selves up in subjection to their own brethren and coun-" trymen, and to the very worst of them too, betrays a " sordid servility of spirit, and a soul prepared for bon-" dage.

" With respect to the Romans, make it the case that " we were all actually now their prisoners (which hea-" ven forbid!) whether would our condition in probabi-" lity, be better or worse than it is now? For what mise-" ry could the enemy inflict upon us that we have not " suffered already? Can any man stand a spectator to " look upon the Jews, and see them robbing the temple " of the oblations and donations that the Romans have " bestowed upon it? Defacing the most glorious city un-" der the sun, and [illegible] their hands in the blood of " those heroes, which the Romans themselves, in the " very triumph of their victories, would have had a ve-" neration for? Can ... see all this, without tears " in his eyes, and a bleeding heart? whereas the Romans, " on the other side, made a conscience of passing the " bounds of sacred and prophane, and of breaking in up-" on the solemnities of holy customs, so that so much as " casting a look, unless with reverence, and at a distance, " toward the sacred residence. We have a sort of people " among ourselves, and ... of our way, too, and cal-" ling themselves Jews, that make no more scruple of " walking in the temple than in a common place, and that " while their hands are reeking with the blood of their " fellow-citizens. Shall we ... after this, stand in dread " of a foreign war, compared with such a domestic one? " The enemy is, in truth (to call things by their right " names) the greater friend of the two; for while the " Romans shew themselves the preservers of our laws, " our pretended friends betray them. Certain it is that " these tyrants have betrayed your liberties, and that no " punishment can be equal to their crimes. I tell you no " more in this, than what you all knew before I opened " my mouth; and you need no other instigation against " these men, than the sense of your own sufferings. But " you are afraid of their numbers, perhaps, the daring " boldness of these men, and the advantageous post they " are possessed of. What was it I beseech you but your " want of resolution, that raised them up to this, and " made them so considerable? You have no way left " you now but a steady, a generous, and a joint resolu-" tion among yourselves to bring them down again; for " delay gives time for the[m], opportunity to increase, and " heart to gather courage. The whole faction will flow " to one party, which will make them numerous. They " have nothing to lose where they meet with no opposi-" tion, and that makes them bold; and so for deferring " the attempt, the longer it is put off, the more time they " have to fortify and strengthen. It is but one bold push, " to shew that you are in earnest to bring down their in-" solence, and you will find that, betwixt the terrors of " a guilty conscience, and the infamy of their actions, " they will have little joy of their station. Who knows " but these impious wretches may be cut off by the just " judgment of a righteous God, as a vengeance upon them " for their contempt of his Divine Majesty? and that the " very weapons they launch at us may, by a providential " miracle, be turned against their own breasts, so that they " shall not be able to stand the very sight of us, but with " confusion. Or, to put matters at the worst, if we " should fall every man of us in the contest, could any " thing be more glorious than to lay down our lives at " the gates of the temple, for the honour of God, and in " the defence of his holy house and cause? As to the con-" duct of the enterprize, you shall have my heart, hand, " example, and advice along with you."

This spirited address of Ananus encouraged the multitude to persevere in their resolution against the zealots; but being fully informed of their numbers, their conduct or men, and their courage, together with the circumstances of the place, and the posture they were in, and finally their despair of pardon, in case they should be overcome, he was not too sanguine in his expectation of immediate advantage from the measures that were taken. He was determined, however, to run all hazards, rather than abandon his country in this distress, while the people pressed the most importunate desire that he would lead them on against these miscreants, in defiance of every danger they could possibly encounter.

Ananus, finding the multitude thus bravely resolute, selected the best men he could find, and ranged them in the best order the time would permit. The zealots receiving intelligence from their spies of this motion and design, advanced immediately to withstand it, in small parties, and in large bodies, sparing all before them. Ananus collected his men with great expedition, and in point of numbers exceeded the others, but the zealots had the advantage of being better armed. The ... of ... each party formed ... all other defects. The rage and indignation of the citizens ... supplied the ... in opposing the progress of the zealots, and the ... on the other hand, were ... the ... of the multitude. The ... concluded they could not be safe, unless they ... the city of the faction; and it was certain death to the faction if they came not off victorious.

This disposed, both parties engaged, and a skirmish began, not far from the temple, with casting stones, and throwing javelins, at each other. Those that fled were cut off by the swords of their enemies, so that many fell on both sides. When any of the multitude happened to be wounded, they were carried off by their friends to their own houses; but the zealots were carried ... to the temple, where their place they polluted with their blood. The faction, however, in all these ... encounters, obtained the advantage.

The populace ... been ... , and lost all patience ... , insomuch, that ... the way before them in their flight, they turned them back again upon the enemy ... that they were forced to cut out their way for ... their own defence. By ... they were brought every man to the combat ... and ... the shock of the whole body ... the ... gates of the temple, where Ananus and his party ... at the same time together ... ven the faction ... of the first court, ... got into the second ... the ... . Ananus had too great a reverence for the holy place, to ... any sort of violence ... the force ... this passage, though the ... be done by ... forces ... . But such was the ... of polluting the holy temple with the ... of unpurified multitude, that ... might ... cause by ... , he would ... it. All that he did ... was to order ... guard, of six ... chosen men ... of the temple ... a succession of the ... be relieved. The first men of the ... not exempt from their part in this ... permitted ... to their lot to ... watch in their stead.

The populace ... now carried all before them, ... John of Gischala, the fugitive, ... measures and counteracted their designs. He was ... , ambitious to a degree, ... perfidious traitor to the public. ... purposes, he ... the mask of a patriot ... the councils of Ananus ... .

round the guards at night. But the traitor divulged their secrets to the zealots, and every thing deliberated upon was, by his means, known to their enemies even before it had been well agreed upon amongst themselves. In order to evade suspicion, he cultivated, with assiduity, the greatest friendship with Ananus and the people, was most officiously complaisant in his behaviour to the high-priest, and, in short, to every man of rank and power.

But his flattery was so gross, and his officiousness and assiduities were so [illegible] deceptive, that they naturally raised suspicions and jealousies, which were not a little augmented by his constant attendance on councils, without summons or [illegible]. It was evident, from divers circumstances, that the [illegible] were apprized of all resolutions taken against them at their consultations, nor was there any one whom they had so much reason to suspect of the discovery as this John. But he had played his part so artfully, and insinuated himself [illegible] into the good opinion of several great men, that it was deemed impossible to remove him from his [illegible] condition. [illegible] no better expedient [illegible] than administering to him an oath [illegible] to keep their counsels, and [illegible] to the utmost of his power.

He most readily took the oath, and Ananus and his party seemed [illegible] as they not only admitted him into their consultations, but sent him on a commission to the zealots, with proposals of accommodation. They were [illegible] to adopt such measures, by an earnest desire of avoiding the pollution of the temple with the blood of the Jews, and the blame they should consequently incur. This [illegible] availed himself of the trust reposed in him to perpetrate his base designs, and accordingly [illegible] to the zealots, and [illegible] misrepresented the whole matter by intimating to them, most artfully and maliciously, in the following address, that the oath he had taken was a confirmation of his good will towards them.

"I have run (said he) all hazards for your sakes, in order "to give you authentic information of the designs and prac-"tices of Ananus and his party against you. I am now to "assure you that neither you nor I were ever in such great "danger as at present, if some providential interposition does "not avert it, as Ananus has prevailed with the people to "send deputies to Vespasian, to desire him to come imme-"diately and take possession of the city, having ordered the "people to purify themselves the next day, to the end "that, under the pretext of religion, they might, either "by fair means or foul, get into the town. I do not "find, under these circumstances, how they should be "able to hold out against such a number of armed men, "but, as it hath pleased the Divine will, I am deputed "to bring you proposals of peace, which, in fact, is no "other than a stratagem of Ananus to amuse you with a "treaty, and fall upon you by surprise when you think "yourselves most secure. You have now no other "choice than to throw yourselves at the feet of the be-"siegers, or call in a foreign power to your rescue. If "you are taken, the consciousness of what you have done "must exclude you from all hope of mercy. Besides, "criminals prove frequently worse for repentance. Con-"sider again, what you are to expect from the friends "and relations of those whom you have slain, and from "a furious multitude, in the height of their rage, for the "abrogation of their laws and customs. A single indi-"vidual may have some sense of humanity and tenderness, "but what will that avail against the violence of an irri-"tated million?"

This artful speech alarmed the factious party; but John durst not name what foreign assistance he hinted at, though there was every reason to think it was that of the Idumæans. After this he took some of the leaders apart, and loaded Ananus with calumnies and reproaches, in order to inflame their resentment against him.

CHAP. VI.

The Idumæans, being sent for to the assistance of the zealots, repair to Jerusalem with a formidable army. Jesus, the high-priest, reasons the matter with them. Simon makes a reply to the particulars of his speech. The Idumæans resolve to make good the siege.

ELEAZAR the son of Simon, and Zacharias, the son of Phalek, were deemed two of the ablest men the zealots had in their counsel, and the best qualified for business, either in point of advice or execution, and they were both of the sacerdotal race. These persons taking for granted, that, besides the general menaces, their lives in particular were threatened, and that Ananus and his party had called in the Romans to their assistance, as John had represented, imagining also, that they should fall a sacrifice to the fury of the multitude, and that no foreign succours could arrive in time to prevent the execution of the plot, they came at length to a resolution of applying to the Idumæans, and wrote them a letter upon the occasion, to this effect:

"Finding that Ananus, having first seduced the people, "hath designed the betraying Jerusalem to the Romans, "we have retired into the temple in defence of the com-"mon liberty, where we are now besieged, and upon "the very point of falling into the hands of Ananus, and "the rest of our enemies, and the city itself into the hands "of the Romans, without immediate relief." The bearers had charge to relate many other circumstances verbally to the principal of the Idumæans. The persons chosen for this commission were both called Ananias: they were active, good speakers, endowed with the faculty of persuasion, and (which was equal to all the rest upon this occasion) men of resolution and dispatch. They made no doubt of the ready compliance of the Idumæans, being a people fond of broils and changes, brutal and churlish, that needed no great pains to be wrought upon, as they go to war with as much alacrity and delight as other people do to a banquet. Expedition was therefore the main business, and the messengers did their duty.

When they arrived at Idumæa, and delivered their letters and instructions to the governors, the people were no sooner informed of the particulars than they caught the flame, and encouraged and provoked one another to take up arms; insomuch that they soon assembled in a body of 20,000 men, which was speedily raised, and dispatched to Jerusalem, under the command of John and James, the sons of Sosas, Simon, the son of Cathlas, and Phineas, the son of Clusoth.

Though Ananus knew nothing of the deputation to the zealots, he had intelligence of the Idumæan expedition, and ordered the gates to be shut, and the walls guarded, but no act of hostility to be committed, till he had tried the effect of reason and fair words towards composing the broil; so that Jesus, the first priest, next Ananus, mounted a tower over against the Idumæans, and thus addressed them:

"Of all the calamities that ever befel this famous city, "nothing amazes me more than to see fortune in a conspi-"racy with the most abandoned people in nature to destroy "it. Who could ever have thought to have seen you join-"ing with a band of miscreants against us, even more hear-"tily than would have become you toward barbarians "themselves, if Jerusalem had desired your aid? But if you "are of the same mind with your superiors, this you have "to say for yourselves, that a similitude of manners natu-"rally begets an agreement of affections. This, however, "cannot be the case betwixt you and them. For if you "consider their lives and actions, you will not find one "man of them that does not deserve a thousand deaths. As to their quality, they are the very scum of mankind: then "for their manners, after their squandering away their for-"tunes in luxury and debauch, they proceeded to rapine "and pillage, and stealing afterwards into the city like "thieves, they advanced to sacrilege and bloodshed, even in the holy temple itself, wallowing in drink at the very altar, without either fear or shame, devouring the spoils of those they have murdered, and prophaning the sacred place with all manner of pollutions. In the middle of this confusion, I find your people here in as regular a formality of order and equipage, as if your army had been brought in at the request of a whole body of the city against a foreign enemy. What shall I call this, but the iniquity of fortune, to see your whole nation united in so infamous a confederacy against your own brethren? I cannot but admire. I must confess the suddenness of your resolution, as well as the thing itself. It must be some great matter, sure, that could move you to take up arms for thieves and vagabonds against your allies. But you have a report among you, I perceive, of our calling in the Romans, and betraying [illegible] to them, and upon the pretence you take upon you to set up for asserters of the liberties of Jerusalem against a foreign power. Though it was a gross and malicious calumny, it was yet pertinent enough to the purpose of the inventors of it. For our enemies could never have gained their ends upon men that valued liberty at the rate that you do, and would venture so far for the preserving of it, but by possessing you with a rage against us, as the base and unmanly betrayers of a blessing and privilege that you have so great a veneration for. But you will do well to consider who they are that thus belie and traduce us, and then form a judgment upon the whole, not upon the credit of plausible tales, but upon the force of clear truths and convincing reason.

"How will it be consistent that we should dispute our liberties thus long with the Romans, and just now own them for our masters? How came it that we fell off from them at first? Or how came it that we did not go over to them again, before our lands, towns and villages were totally laid waste and destroyed? Neither is this a time for a treaty if we had ever so great a mind to it, for the conquest of Galilee hath made them too proud to hearken to any conditions. And then to go out suing to them for a peace as soon as they show themselves before our walls, would be an infamy more unsupportable than death itself. For my own part, I am rather for peace than war, but, on the other side, when the war is once begun and inevitable, I am rather for a glorious death than the life of a slave.

"But how stands the case, I beseech you, of our sending to the Romans? Is it that the ring-leaders have privately sent some particular persons out of their own number or families? Or will you have it to be a deputation at the command of the people? If this was done by a particular commission, why are we not told the names of the commissioners? Are there any letters to be produced in proof of this suggestion? Or hath any man been taken up going or coming upon this errand? How comes it, that, among so many thousands of people as we daily converse with in the city, not so much as one man ever heard of it? And how comes it again that this secret, that has been managed with so much caution out of the city, should be only known to a few persons that are locked up in the temple, and not at liberty so much as to stir out of the walls? Is it not a strange thing too, that this treason should never be heard of, till the reporters of it were in danger themselves, and in dread of being called to an account for their own crimes? Neither could it be called the people's act, without passing the vote of a general assembly, which would have made it impossible to be kept so long a secret. Or to what end should there be a deputation, when the thing was resolved before hand, and no room left for a treaty? Then, as before observed, they would have done well to have named the commissioners. But drowning men will catch hold of any thing, and all this prevarication is only to save themselves. If it must be the city's fate, at last, to fall by treachery, none are so likely to bring it to that end as our accusers themselves, for it is but adding treason to blood, sacrilege, and the rest of the impieties they are guilty of already, to fill up the measure of their iniquities.

"But since you are here upon the place with us, and in arms, what can you do better than to join with us in the relief of the city, and in the rooting out of these tyrannical monsters? Wretches that have trod all our laws under foot, to make way for tumult and violence, treated our governors worse than bond-slaves or common criminals, in prisons, chains, nay, with death itself, though ever so innocent, and, which is worse, without so much as any pretence to the contrary, and without any place at last, for prayers or intercessions in favour of the miserable. [illegible] what you may be eye-witnesses of yourselves, if you will but enter the city as friends, and believe your eyes. There you will see the ransacking of houses, and the whole town in mourning for their murthered kindred and friends, your ears will be shocked with cries and lamentations, and not one creature to be found, in the whole, but [illegible] in this oppression. They have [illegible] to so extravagant a pitch, that, after the innumerable robberies and outrages committed in the country towns and villages, they have brought the scene of blood into the [illegible] though the head and glory of the nation, carrying their outrage from thence also into the very temple, which they have made the seat of the war. From thence it is that they make their sallies, and that [illegible] their retreats there they keep their guards, their stores, and their magazines. At this rate it is, [illegible] disgrace and dishonour, and trample upon God's holy habitation, and the place that is venerable all over the world, [illegible] only among our own people. They are never so desperate, but in the depth of their despair, they will take delight in forcing all things to extremities, and in setting cities and nations against each other, and all in a confusion of civil broils. The most generous and reasonable things that you can do (and that which would best become you) would be, to go hand in hand with us, in delivering the nation from these [illegible], and in taking your revenge upon them for the [illegible] they have put upon you, and for presuming to [illegible] their party for assistance, whereas they should rather have dreaded the vengeance and justice from you, that belongs to a common enemy. If you think it more [illegible] decency and respect, to pay some sort of deference to their requests, let it be pleaded to pass into the city as friends; leave your arms at the gates [illegible] the cause [illegible] hearing and be yourselves the judges of the controversy. [illegible] for those people that have so many notorious crimes to answer for [illegible], and particularly the barring [illegible] to death, without so much as [illegible] defence, to these people, [illegible] partial and easy a way of trial, will be a [illegible] extraordinary, and it will become them to acknowledge [illegible] obligation they have to you for the favour. But if you will neither join with us in the course of the case, [illegible] pear in the capacity of judges betwixt us, [illegible] both parties, without either insulting over [illegible] them [illegible] your mother city. [illegible] of our innocence, [illegible] any secret correspondence [illegible] Romans, send your [illegible] and agents to [illegible] and [illegible] whensoever you [illegible] guilty of such a practice, spare neither [illegible] party. That will be the only proper [illegible] upon your metropolis, and [illegible] time, for, as you are posted, [illegible] is not [illegible] to interpose to your prejudice. If this [illegible] it is well, but if otherwise, [illegible] for us to open our gates till you lay down your arms.

[illegible] this [illegible] and reasonable address of [illegible], the [illegible] continued much enraged because they [illegible] into the city, and the gen[illegible] very [illegible] of [illegible] on their arms [illegible] that could be offered them. Simon, [illegible] one of their principal officers, [illegible] they had [illegible] standing upon an [illegible] might near him, spoke to [illegible]:

"[illegible] wonder [illegible] of our country's "[illegible] very besiegers of "[illegible] the city itself, which "[illegible] to the whole nation: but at the "[illegible] enough, perhaps, to entertain the Romans "[illegible] enough for us, you "think, [illegible] advise us to lay "[illegible] (though [illegible] in the common cause,) "[illegible] nearest friends with the [illegible] of the "[illegible]. But, instead of [illegible] our country, we [illegible] "in [illegible] of the [illegible], "[illegible], and, in the [illegible] you [illegible] "[illegible] upon [illegible] "without any [illegible], you yourselves pronounce "[illegible] upon the whole nation, and "[illegible] your own [illegible] gates "[illegible], upon the account of [illegible] to all "[illegible]. But [illegible], the [illegible] acknowledg[illegible] "[illegible] Do [illegible] "[illegible] "[illegible] At the [illegible] are those in the temple "your enemies, and [illegible] have just as much [illegible] "[illegible] against [illegible]. You have, at present, the very supporters "of the common [illegible] and we are "[illegible] with a pretence, that the [illegible] of your keep"ing all the world out of the city, is to [illegible] tyranny, "when, [illegible], the very tyranny you complain of, you"selves [illegible]. This is too gross to pass on any man who "hath eyes to see. Keeping us out of the city is not all "[illegible], for we are barred, by that exclusion, from the "[illegible] and enjoyment of the religious rites and cere"monies of our profession. And it is the same case again with "those who are charged in the temple, for punishing cer"tain [illegible], whom you are pleased to honour with the "[illegible] of honest men and persons of quality, for the [illegible] of "the [illegible]. The only thing they were to blame for "[illegible], that they did not begin with you: that is to say, at "the root of the conspiracy. But if they were over tender, "[illegible] with more vigour, for the main"[illegible] of the house of God, and of the rights of our "country, as well within the city as without, in against all "enemies. So that this siege we are resolved to make "[illegible], till either the Romans deliver you, or the con"[illegible] of what you have done [illegible], bring you back "to your duty."

CHAP. VII.

The Idumæans [illegible] the city walls. A dreadful [illegible]. The [illegible] of the zealots for the [illegible] of their friends. The Idumæans [illegible] the city by night, and join the [illegible]. [illegible]. The [illegible] Ananus and Jesus put to death.

THE Idumæans testified, by their acclamations, the approbation of the speech of their general; while Jesus, on the other hand, went away pensive and sorrowful, on finding the Idumæans opposed all moderate counsels, and that the city was besieged on both sides. Nor were the minds of the Idumæans at rest, being enraged at the affront offered them by their exclusion from the city, as well as at their disappointment with respect to the supposed strength of the zealots, together with the difficulties they had met with in their expedition. But the shame that would attend them, in case they returned without making any attempt, outweighed all other scruples, so that they lay all night before the wall, though in a very bad encampment. The following night there arose an horrible storm of wind and rain, accompanied with such peals of thunder, flashes of lightning, and [illegible] earthquakes, as produced an universal consternation. [illegible] prodigies were deemed a manifest indication of some approaching destruction, as the system of the world appeared to be in general disorder.

The inhabitants and Idumæans were both under the [illegible] apprehension. Their opinion was, that the Almighty was displeased with them for taking arms, and that [illegible] judgment [illegible] them both, if they persisted in a war against the mother city.

But Ananus and his party looked upon it as a declaration from heaven in their favour, [illegible] the Providence would interpose in their behalf, and give them victory without a battle. But the event proved [illegible] of their conjecture, for that which they applied to their enemies, befel themselves in the conclusion. In this storm the Idumæans fenced one another by edging together as close as they could press, thereby keeping themselves warm, and connecting their shields over their heads, were not so much hurt by the rain. [illegible] zealots [illegible] more pain for the Idumæans than for themselves [illegible] entered into consultation to devise means for [illegible] their friends. The most daring [illegible] were [illegible] the guards with their arms, and, then [illegible], bursting open the gates, and [illegible] the Idumæans, as supposing the guards would [illegible], and give way [illegible], [illegible] the greatest part of them were [illegible] and unskilful [illegible]. Besides the multitude would not be [illegible] assembled, as they were dispersed to their several habitations by the [illegible]. They were determined, however, at all events, and in spite of every danger, to support and protect their friends and [illegible], who came so generously to their assistance.

But the more prudent part disapproved of this method, persuaded that the guards, at this critical time, were doubled, and that a stricter watch than ordinary was set upon the [illegible] on account of the Idumæans. They also supposed that Ananus would be every where up and down at all hours, to keep the soldiers to their duty. This, indeed, was the case every other night but that, when Ananus went to retire [illegible] himself, not through slothfulness or inattention, but [illegible] kind of fatality, to the ruin of himself and the people, [illegible] the night being far spent, and the tempest raging, Ananus permitted the guards at the temple gates to go to rest.

At this fatal instant it occurred to the zealots, that, if they could but destroy the bars of the gates, their design would be accomplished. Upon this they took certain [illegible] belonging to the temple, and [illegible] asunder, and it fell out fortunately for them, that, [illegible] the raging of the wind, and roaring of the thunder, the noise was not heard by the besieged. They then went privately to the gates next to the Idumæans, which they opened as they had done the former. The Idumæans at first apprehended that Ananus and his party were [illegible] false, so that every man made towards the passage sword in hand, but, on finding them in safety, they entered the city, and with such rage, that, if they had discharged it upon the people, they might have put the whole body to the sword. But, as their first concern was to deliver the zealots out of custody in the temple, according to their earnest request, and it was pointed out to them how much easier they would find the enterprize, if they began with the guards, whereas, if the inhabitants took the alarm, they would gather in multitudes, and dispute every inch of the ground upon such advantages, that they would never carry their point. The Idumæans were [illegible] to co[illegible] with them in opinion, and therefore [illegible] their main business to pass directly through the [illegible] to the relief of their friends, who were prisoners in the temple, and waited their coming with great impatience.

[illegible] had no sooner entered, than the zealots came boldly out of the inner temple, and joined with them in an attack upon the guards. Some they killed in their sleep, but the multitude, alarmed by the outcry, noise, and in great amazement and confusion, seized upon their arms, and stood in their own defence. Imagining at first, that they were only a party of the zealots, they had no doubt of overpowering them by numbers, and therefore pressed on boldly; but when they found others advancing, and that the Idumaeans had joined the zealots, the greater part dropped their arms with their courage, and lamented the horror of their situation. Some few, more brave and resolute than the rest, covered themselves with their armour, and valiantly encountered the Idumaeans, but the major part ran up and down bewailing, [illegible] yells, the ruin of the city. Not a blow [illegible] struck, [illegible] generally known that the Idumaeans were mas[illegible] [illegible], the [illegible] of the [illegible] were rendered more [illegible] by the shouts of the Idumaeans and zealots, and the [illegible] violence of the winds and thunder. [illegible] the [illegible] and fierceness of the Idumaeans, ig[illegible] the thought of being shut out of the city, and exposed to the [illegible] of weather, that they spared neither age or sex. Some of the distressed mortals pleaded religion, others kindred, but deaf stopped all mouths. There was neither place for flight, or hope of preservation; but as they were driven one upon another in heaps, so were they slain. Nay, the very fear of death contributed as much to the execution of it as the rage of the enemy. In this extremity of distraction, some of them to avoid one death, leaped headlong down a precipice into another. Rivers of blood flowed round the temple, and by day-light, the place was strewed, upon computation, with 8,500 dead bodies.

The rage of the Idumaeans was not satiated by this horrid massacre, but afterwards turned upon the city, where they pillaged all the houses indiscriminately, and slew every one they met. The rabble they looked upon as below further notice, and chiefly wreaked their vengeance upon those of the sacerdotal order, which they did by taking off their heads without the least distinction, and then trampling on their bodies, deridingly upbraided Ananus with his popularity, and Jesus with his elaborate harangue upon the wall. They proceeded to that degree of impiety, as to forbid the rites of burial, though the Jewish laws, from a [illegible] reverence to the dead, have provided for the taking down even of executed criminals from the very cross, and burying them before sun-set.

I presume I shall not be found guilty of an error, if I date the destruction of this city from the death of Ananus, and affirm that Ananus and Jerusalem fell both on one and the same day; for, in the loss of this man, they lost the [illegible] of their government, and all [illegible] of safety, and Jerusalem was [illegible], as much extinct as Ananus. Besides the dignity of his extraction and character, he was highly esteemed for his personal virtue and justice, and his humility was an ornament to all his good qualities. He was a zealous [illegible] of the cause of liberty, and ever preferred the public to private interest. His study and concern were to promote peace, well convinced of the insuperable power of the Romans, and that the only security of the Jews was to maintain a good understanding with them. To sum up the whole, if Ananus had survived, the Romans and Jews would have come to an agreement. He was a powerful orator, and endowed with the faculty of persuading his hearers in an eminent degree. He had already humbled those incendiaries called zealots, and the Jews, under such a leader, would have made a vigorous opposition to the power of the Romans.

He was so happy as to be aided in his councils by Jesus, a person of very great abilities, though inferior to Ananus. But it seems to have been the Divine will to doom this city to destruction, and purge the [illegible], as it were, by fire, for all the pollutions and abominations that had been committed in it. This was done by removing these two illustrious persons, who were the only means of preserving it. These, who, a little before, were venerable for their sacred garments, the protectors of our holy religion, and the delight not only of their own people, but of all foreigners who had the honour to know them, were now wantonly exposed as a prey to dogs and wild beasts, to the astonishment and grief of all good men, who lamented to see virtue dejected, and vice triumphant.

END OF THE FOURTH BOOK OF THE WARS

FLAVIUS JOSEPHUS

ON THE

WARS OF THE JEWS.

BOOK V.

CHAP. I.

Cruelty of the zealots and Idumæans. Zachariah falsely accused of treason. Makes an honourable defence, and is acquitted. Is afterwards murdered in the temple. The Idumæans discover the iniquitous practices of the zealots, discharge their prisoners, and leave the city. Gorion, and Niger of Peræa, put to death. Divine vengeance overtakes the tyrants.

AFTER the murders of Ananus and Jesus, the people in general, were treated with the most horrid barbarities by the Idumæans and zealots, who carried devastations and slaughter every where before them. As to persons of rank, and those who were in the prime of life, they only kept them in custody, in hopes that, for the sparing of their lives, they might be brought over to their party; but they chose rather to die than join in a conspiracy with traitors against their native country. Death, however, might be accounted the least part of their miseries, as it was brought on by the most exquisite tortures: their bodies were torn and lacerated with scourges till they were covered with ulcers; and, when they could no longer sustain the torments, they had recourse to the sword for finishing the work. Those whom they caught in the day were crouded into prisons, and slain in the night; and then their dead bodies were carried out in order to make room for others. These horrid massacres excited such terror in the minds of the people, that they durst not affect sorrow, or perform funeral rites for their nearest relations: nay, they were even afraid to shed a tear in their own houses without the utmost caution, lest any should be privy to it; for humanity was become so dangerous a crime, that it was death even to shew a tender regard for the memories of those who were departed. All they could do, was, now and then, in the night, to cast a little earth upon the body, though some few were so daring as to venture upon it in the day. There perished, in this manner, 12,000 persons of the first rank.

These inhuman monsters being almost surfeited with their barefaced cruelties, had the effrontery to set up fictitious tribunals, and constitute judicatures, under a pretended form of law and equity. The first who became amenable to this mock court was Zachariah, the son of Baruch, a man of the first rank, and a character eminent for piety and virtue. He was looked upon by the zealots as a man so dangerously popular, that, to ensure their own safety, it was necessary to remove him. Resolving, therefore, to take away his life, they put him upon his trial, and to that purpose convened seventy of the principal men amongst them, under the name of judges, but without even the semblance of juridical authority. This self-constituted court being met, the zealots exhibited a formal charge against Zachariah, of a design to betray Jerusalem to the Romans, and treating with Vespasian about it. There appeared not the least colour of a proof; nevertheless, they attempted to establish their affirmations as sufficient evidence. Zachariah perceiving manifestly that his life was at stake, and that the whole design was fraudulent, in this state of despair, prepared for his defence with that serenity and freedom of mind which are the inseparable concomitants of conscious integrity.

He began with pointed reflections on the scandalous practices and frivolous pretences of his accusers, and proceeded to shew the evident calumnies and inconsistencies of their allegations, exposed the futility of their objections, and turned all their arguments against themselves, setting forth the whole course of their iniquities, and the dreadful consequences which had attended them. The noble and spirited conduct of Zachariah enraged the zealots to such a degree of malice, that they had certainly murdered him on the spot, if they had not been restrained by a remaining deference to their pretended court of judicature, and a design of making the experiment whether their new judges would venture their lives on so dangerous a point.

When it came to the issue, the whole court pronounced the prisoner innocent, nor was there one out of the seventy judges, but chose rather to run the hazard of his own life, than take away that of so good a man by a sentence repugnant to conscience and equity. This judgment of acquittal highly incensed the zealots, who censured the judges as idiots, in not comprehending the design of their appointment. Two of the most splenetic and daring fell outrageously upon Zachariah, and murdered him in the middle of the temple, and having insolently exclaimed, "Thou hast also our verdict, which will prove a more sure acquittal than the other," cast the body down a precipice into the valley. The lives of the judges were spared; their punishment was a sentence of infamy, to be beat out of the temple with the backs of their swords. By this means they were dispersed up and down as so many eye-witnesses of the slavery of the capital city at that time.

By this time the Idumæans repented of their coming, and were disgusted at the horrid proceedings of the zealots. While they were consulting on the subject they had secret intelligence sent them by one of the party, of the transactions and principles of the people that invited them, to the following effect:

"That they took up arms upon the credit of a report, that "the high priests were treating with the Romans for be-"traying of the city; however, upon strict enquiry, they "found nothing at all in it, but, on the contrary, the pre-"tended assertors of our liberties, were actually the subverters "of them, and they themselves the tyrants that ought to have "been timely suppressed. But (said the writer) since it hath "been your unhappy lot to join with them thus far in their "iniquities, it will be time for you to break off so criminal "an alliance with the professed enemies of your laws and "country. You took it ill to be kept out of the city, "and are you not [illegible] revenged upon those that "excluded you in the death of Ananus, and so many "thousands of the citizens in one night? an action which "many of your people will live to repent. [illegible] "only to [illegible] the [illegible] of [illegible] that "[illegible] to commit the [illegible] merciless cruelties "even before the face of their preservers, and by doing "the basest things that ever were heard of in the sight of "their allies, to transfer the infamy from the zealots to "the Idumæans, who, in truth, should either have de-"livered them, or left them. Now, since it is so clear to "the [illegible], that the whole story of the conspiracy is no-"thing but a calumny, and that there is no such thing in "prospect as the dread of a Roman army, beside the im-"pregnable strength of this city, if it were true to a tittle; "since this it is, what [illegible] you more to do than to return "whence you came, and, by [illegible] the monsters "[illegible], in some degree [illegible] the ill things you did in their "company? Wherein you are thus far excusable, that "you were rather passive under a well meaning mistake "than voluntary actors at your own liberty and choice."

These persuasions wrought so effectually on the Idumæans, that they immediately set the prisoners at liberty, being about two thousand, left the city, and returned home. Their unexpected departure greatly surprised both the inhabitants and the zealots on several accounts: the people, who knew the cause, took courage, from the consideration of being delivered from so many of their enemies. The zealots, on the other hand, became insolent upon it, in confidence of their own strength; and, from reflecting that the check was removed which kept them in some degree of awe of the Idumæans, they were now at liberty to pursue their own measures without the least restraint or delay, they went on without deliberation or council, perpetrating whatever could be iniquitous or cruel.

But their deadly rancour was levelled at men of honour and valour, whom they persecuted to the utmost extremity; those of rank from a principle of envy, those of resolution and virtue, from a principle of fear; for they could never think [illegible] selves safe [illegible] of that character was living. This was their motive for taking off Gorion, a man of birth and virtue, and a generous asserter of the cause of liberty. Niger of Perea fell under the same calamitous fate. He [illegible] who had displayed his courage against the Romans, and gloried in the wounds he had received in the [illegible] of his country, as they dragged him along the [illegible]. When they brought him out of the gates, [illegible] of life, he made them this request, that [illegible] might be buried; but it was denied him, [illegible] death with this prophetical imprecation [illegible] "that the Romans might come to [illegible] and Divine Justice overtake them with famine [illegible] lence, and mortal [illegible], [illegible] in proportion to the enormity of their crimes."

Nor was it long before the Almighty, in righteous judgment poured down all those plagues upon them according to the good man's imprecation, [illegible] brOils. The removal of Niger [illegible] [illegible], that there was no part of the people [illegible] found out some pretence to destroy. Some they put to death for pretended [illegible]. In [illegible] cases where matter of fact could not be produced, [illegible] or poverty was sufficient. If they [illegible] court to [illegible], they were foes; if they [illegible], it was construed into enmity and contempt. [illegible] crime was great or small, the penalty was [illegible] and none escaped that possessed either dignity or property.

CHAP. II.

[illegible]

THE [illegible] of the Roman officers pressing them to the capture of Jerusalem, [illegible] a fairer opportunity for [illegible] than that afforded by the present [illegible]. To this end they urged Vespasian [illegible] chief to improve the [illegible] proper time to concert [illegible]. They represented to him, that the interposition of [illegible] [illegible]. The general replied to them [illegible] following effect, observing,

"That their bravery was [illegible] "that they consider [illegible] glory [illegible], in the "ostentation of their courage [illegible] "more than the prudence [illegible] advantage [illegible] "attack the city [illegible] "to make them all friends again [illegible] "upon us, which [illegible] "against the common enemy, whereas, if we could "wait with a little patience [illegible] "our hands, in spending their [illegible] "one upon another. [illegible] "do for ourselves, [illegible] "mans without [illegible] "[illegible] "solved in [illegible] "judgments [illegible] "[illegible] with madmen, [illegible] "being [illegible] "bullet [illegible] "people are [illegible] "strayed [illegible] "[illegible] a cheap [illegible] "well to set the advantages of a temporary accommoda-"tion, without blood, against the uncertain chance of "war. This is not to derogate from the honour of mi-"litary virtue, no; provided the same things be done it "matters not whether it be by arms or council. Un-"doubtedly that must be the best way of doing it which "at the same time that it weakens the enemy, keeps our "own men by [illegible] exercise, in discipline and in "breath. Neither is that a time for us to propose to "ourselves the fame of a glorious exploit, when the "Jews are playing our game for us, and [illegible] neither "their arms, their works, or their walls, or the making "of [illegible] and friends, but [illegible] destroying one another, "and laying the part of the world of enemies on to ano-"ther, till they have brought themselves into such a con-"dition, that the best they can hope or wait for is to be "ourselves [illegible] to the [illegible] or the matter "[illegible], if they [illegible] to [illegible] one ano-"ther, [illegible] then? Nor is there [illegible] "[illegible] reputation to be got by a victory that was [illegible] "[illegible] upon us by the faction of the one side, than "[illegible] the [illegible] or the other. And this is the "[illegible] of the case."

This [illegible] Vespasian [illegible] his opinion, with which, [illegible] liquid, the others [illegible] for [illegible] came over to him [illegible] the zealots, in great numbers, [illegible] though the passages were to [illegible] to escape. They [illegible] to the sword that fell in the [illegible], upon pretence that he was going over to the Romans, unless he released himself for a sum of money, which he [illegible] to procure his deliverance. [illegible] no change [illegible] there was no want of money, so that the rich [illegible], and the poor were obliged to submit [illegible] to oppression, but even murder itself. The [illegible] was so outrageous, that the dead bodies lay piled in heaps upon the high ways, and many, who had mounted [illegible] changed their minds, and chose [illegible] from the mere hope of a little earth to cover them. But such was the inhumanity of those monsters, [illegible] allow the burial either to those [illegible] or without the city, but, like professed enemies to the instinct of nature as well as the laws of their country, they offended God and man, and exposed the bodies to rot above ground in the face of the sun. Nay, it was deemed as unpardonable a crime to attempt the burial of a friend, as to go over to the enemy, and he that had buried another, wanted, perhaps the [illegible], a friend to do the same office for himself. [illegible] the most humane of affections, seemed to [illegible] wholly extinguished in the hearts of these miscreants, and [illegible] was [illegible] provocation to rage than [illegible] to pity.

The spectacle [illegible] so hideous, that it caused the living to envy the dead [illegible] the want of [illegible] as [illegible] prison. Nor [illegible] they [illegible] with the Deity, and paid as little regard to the predictions of the prophets, as they did to the fabulous reports of [illegible]. But, notwithstanding this contempt of the laws and precepts of their forefathers concerning [illegible] of good and evil, they found the predictions verified, in the conclusion, concerning themselves and their country. There was a traditional prophecy handed down to them from antiquity, that, in future time, there should break out a violent sedition in Jerusalem, and that the Jews themselves, with their own hands, should prophane the holy temple, that the city should be afterwards taken, and all that was sacred in it laid in ashes. The zealots made no doubt of the authority of this prophecy, and contributed the utmost in their power towards the fulfilment of it.

CHAP. III.

John usurps sovereign power. The faction [illegible] parties, zealots and anti-zealots. [illegible] Heavy judgments fall upon the Jews. An excursion of Sicarii from the citadel of Massada. [illegible] Jordan becomes the seat of war. The Jews [illegible] secret correspondence with Vespasian, and [illegible] Gadara [illegible] The [illegible] themselves to flight. Placidus follows [illegible] The [illegible] make their way to [illegible] [illegible] the place [illegible] with a [illegible] are [illegible]

SUCH was the ambition of John of Gischala, that nothing would content him less than sovereign power, so that withdrawing himself from the [illegible] of his companions, [illegible] to his [illegible] doned miscreants, he [illegible] way. He took upon him to [illegible] opinions [illegible] the [illegible] and [illegible] affection [illegible] Some [illegible] him out of fear, and [illegible] good [illegible], so he was a great [illegible] knew how to work upon the [illegible] loved him for [illegible] security [illegible] members would be [illegible] they should be called to an account [illegible] But [illegible], fell off from him, some from envy, and others [illegible] dain of subjection to one that had been their equal; but the grand objection was [illegible] the despair of dispossessing him of that power if he once [illegible] it. Besides, they [illegible] would [illegible] that opposed him in his [illegible] beginning.

The people, upon these [illegible], [illegible] to a resolution, rather to stand the [illegible], than [illegible] under the infamy of making themselves [illegible]. The faction, upon this, divided into two parties, John putting himself at the head of the [illegible] upon their guard one against the other, and not without some slight skirmishes, but rather with the people in general, [illegible] betwixt themselves, for the main point, which of the two parties should get the greatest booty.

Jerusalem [illegible] at this time [illegible] ments, war, tyranny, and sedition, the people taking the former to be the most tolerable of the three, quitted their habitations, fled from their own country [illegible] to strangers, and found afterwards that safety and protection from the Romans they could not obtain [illegible] from [illegible].

The three fore-mentioned judgments were followed by a fourth, which contributed as much to the destruction of the Jews as any of the rest. There is [illegible] not far from Jerusalem, called Massada, a place of great [illegible], strength, and importance. It was [illegible] use of by the kings, in former times, [illegible] magazine of all kinds of [illegible] for an impregnable [illegible] in times of danger. It was now in possession of a band of [illegible], called Sicarii, who over-ran, plundered, and [illegible] the country [illegible] happening, at this juncture, that the Romans lay quiet, while the Jews were divided between sedition and tyranny, [illegible] these assassins took the opportunity of making still bolder attempts than they had ventured on before. It was now the feast of unleavened bread, a festival celebrated by the Jews with great solemnity, in commemoration of their deliverance from Egyptian bondage, and translation into the land of [illegible]. On that night the ruffians broke into Engaddi by surprise, scattered the people, and made themselves masters of the place, before the inhabitants could take to their arms. They drove them out of the town, and having put to death upwards of seven hundred persons, mostly women and children, rifled their houses, and seized upon all the fruits that were in season which they carried to Massada Indeed, they laid waste all the villages in the neighbourhood of the fortress, for their numbers increased daily by the accession of an abandoned rabble, that came flocking in to join them

The region of Judæa now became one scene of violence, and, as it is with the human body, when any of the nobler parts are indisposed, all the rest sympathize so it is with respect to a seditious and disorderly city When the capital is rent by faction, the subordinate parts suffer, of course, in proportion as they are tainted by the example Having plundered all within their reach, those robbers marched off with the booty into deserts, joined in conspiracies, and gathered together in multitudes little inferior to armies, sufficient to destroy cities, and lay temples desolate

The sufferers, as was very natural, availed themselves of every opportunity to revenge themselves upon their oppressors but that was rare, for the robbers were too dexterous and active, and generally got off with their prey before the pursuers could reach them so that there was not a spot in Judæa but what partook of the calamity of the metropolis

The faction had guarded all the avenues with the utmost caution so that there was no stirring without imminent danger of life But, notwithstanding all this vigilance, deserters stole away with intelligence of the state of the city to Vespasian, and to implore his relief, in the name of the miserable remainder of [illegible], as great numbers had lost their lives through their attachment to the Romans, and many more were at present in danger of perishing by the same fate Vespasian, a generous compassion for the [illegible] condition of [illegible] people, advanced with his army nearer the town, not, as some imagined, to lay close siege to it, but with a view of drawing them from any siege at all, by reducing all the strong holds about it, so as to leave no obstacle to impede him in the prosecution of his design

When he came to Gadara, the chief and strongest city beyond Jordan, and the metropolis of that province, he entered the place on the fourth day of the month Dystrus, upon an invitation of some of the leading men by their deputies, to take them under his protection This they did to save both their lives and estates, being a very wealthy people The opposite party knew nothing of this embassy, but suspecting it, when they found the Roman general drawing near the walls, they became greatly embarrassed They were assured it was utterly impossible for the town to hold out against so many enemies, both within and without, the majority of the citizens being against them, and the Roman army at hand They had nothing to trust to but flight, which was a point that in honour could not be resolved upon, without first taking revenge upon some of the authors of their ruin. Upon this consideration they apprehended Dolesus, the first man of the city, both for rank and merit, caused him to be put to death, and ordered the dead body to be scourged, which being done, they went privately out of the town

Upon the nearer approach of the Romans towards the city, the inhabitants met Vespasian on the way, and congratulated him with congratulatory acclamations, and, besides the ceremony of oaths of allegiance, and assurances of that kind to [illegible], they [illegible] it their own act and deed to [illegible] their own walls, as a further security of their good faith and peaceable intention Vespasian, after this gave them a garrison for their safe guard, and sent away Placidus with 500 horse and 3000 foot, after the fugitives, while he himself, with the rest of his troops, went back to Cæsarea

When the fugitives found themselves pursued, and a party of horse behind them, they turned off into a village, called Bethennabris, before the Romans could come up to them, There they engaged a number of young men to join them, and with this party sallied out, and made a desperate charge upon Placidus, who gave way at the outset, but it was only to draw his adversaries a little farther from the town. The scheme succeeded, for Placidus got them into a place of advantage, and there attacked and put them to the rout Those that fled for their safety were intercepted by the Romans, and those that fought were cut off by their rear In fine, they were totally defeated When they attacked the Romans, it was to no effect, for they stood so firm and close, that there was no breaking the body, and there lay upon such a guard under their arms that no lance or dart could touch them Whereas the Jews, on the other hand, lay exposed to all sorts of weapons, and to all manner of assaults, till, in the end, in a fit of despair and brutal rage, they cast themselves, with the utmost fury, upon the points of their enemies swords, and so perished Some were dispersed by the horse, and trampled under foot Placidus made it his particular care as far as possible, that none of the fugitives should get back into the town [illegible] of them attempted it, he intercepted them [illegible] and forced them off again [illegible] lances Some, however, [illegible] made their way to the very wall, [illegible] puzzled whom to admit, and whom to exclude, [illegible] it hard to open the gates to their townsmen, and [illegible] entrance to those of Gadara On the other hand, they were fearful lest, by opening to all indiscriminately, they [illegible] endanger the loss of the place, as had like to have been the case soon after, for the Romans, [illegible] the fugitives up to the wall, had [illegible] into the town, but, with much difficulty, they shut the gates, and thereby prevented them

Placidus, upon this, vigorously assaulted the place, insomuch that he made himself master both of the wall and the village in a few hours The [illegible] people, who had no means of defence, were [illegible] sword, but the rest [illegible] to save the [illegible], [illegible] carrying terror along with them [illegible] To finish the calamity, they first pillaged the houses, and then laid the village in ashes The [illegible] of the [illegible] was great in fact, but much greater in appearance, for it was given out that the whole Roman army was coming [illegible] This terror so terrified the people, that [illegible] habitations, and repaired in great numbers to [illegible] [illegible] garrison [illegible], the [illegible] to which they could betake themselves Placidus, in [illegible] of his success, pursued them to the river Jordan, putting to the sword all that were taken on the way

When the fugitives came to the river side a great fall of rain had caused an overflow of the waters, so that there was no passing, nor, as the case stood, any possibility of getting away In this extremity [illegible] absolute necessity of coming to [illegible] the Jews [illegible] themselves along the bank of the river, [illegible] for some time, but [illegible] those who were [illegible] could hardly be computed It is estimated [illegible] fare killed on the spot, and about two hundred taken, besides a mighty booty of sheep, camels, and oxen This was one of the greatest [illegible] the Jews [illegible] [illegible] ways where they marched, [illegible] covered with dead bodies, the river Jordan so choaked [illegible] that there was no [illegible] [illegible] channels that lead to the lake Asphaltites

Placidus being now in the [illegible] good fortune, proceeded [illegible], Julias, [illegible] and other [illegible] the lake, where he settled [illegible] [illegible] from [illegible] those that [illegible] to the Romans His next [illegible] the [illegible] all the fugitives that [illegible] much, that, by this time, the Romans were [illegible] Peræa as far as Machærus.

CHAP IV.

Gaul revolts Vespasian fortifies all the places he had taken in Judæa Description of the country about Jericho Of the lake of Asphaltitis and Tiberias. Elisha's fountain

DURING these transactions in Judæa, advice was received that Gaul had revolted from Nero, and that Vindex, and several principle men of the country, abetted the male-contents Vespasian, on this intelligence, prosecuted the present war with more vigour, as it was probable that one revolt might be productive of another, and the whole empire at length be in danger from a civil war, whereas, if the troubles in the east were first composed, Italy would have the less to fear But it being the winter season, all that could be done to it at present, was to place garrisons in all the towns and cities he had subdued, and order such reparations as might be found needful

In the beginning of the spring he marched, with the greatest part of his army, from Cæsarea to Antipatris, where he stayed two days to put things in order, and on the third day proceeded, laying all the neighbourhood waste with fire and sword, from the borders of the toparchy of Thamna, and thence to Lydda and Jamnia.

When he had peopled them with inhabitants from other towns, such as he thought he might best confide in, he advanced to Emmaus, and possessing himself there of the passage that leads to the capital city, pitched his camp, and ran a wall about it Having left the fifth legion there, he moved with the rest of his troops into the toparchy of Bethlepton, which he burnt and destroyed, together with the neighbouring country, and the borders of Idumæa, saving only some strong castles, which he manned and fortified Having taken two towns in the very midst of Idumæa, called Bethabris and Caphartoba, he slew upwards of ten thousand of the people, reserving near a thousand for slaves, drove out the rest, and left a considerable part of his troops to sally out and commit outrages upon the mountainous part of the country

He returned, after this, with the remainder of his army, to Emmaus, and passing from thence to Samaria and Neapolis, (called, by the natives, Mabartha,) arrived, the second day of the month Desius, at Corea, where he encamped, and shewed himself next day before Jericho At this place he was joined by Trajan, one of his principal officers, with the troops under his command, after the entire reduction of all the country beyond Jordan But most of the inhabitants were withdrawn to the mountains over against Jerusalem before the arrival of the Romans A great part, however, of those that stayed behind were put to the sword

Vespasian found Jericho a desolate city It is situate in a plain, that is overlooked by a naked and barren mountain, and of such extent, that it reaches upon the north side to the region of Scythopolis, on the south as far as Sodom, and the borders of the lake Asphaltitis, a country uninhabited by reason of its barrenness Opposite to this, and on the farther side of the river Jordan, lies another mountain, which rises at Julias towards the north, and stretches southward up to Gomorrha, and so borders upon Petra, a city of Arabia There is also another mountain, which they call the Iron mountain, and runs out as far as the land of Moab Betwixt these mountains lies a place call'd the great Plain It begins at Genabara, and stretches out to the lake Asphaltitis The length of it is two hundred and thirty furlongs, its breadth an hundred and twenty, and the river Jordan crosses the middle of it

There are two remarkable lakes, the one called Asphaltitis, the other Tiberias, but of very different, if not contrary, qualities, the former being salt and crude, without fish, the other sweet, kindly and fruitful The summer heats there are excessive, the country being burnt up with them, and the air hot and sickly, without any refreshment, but from the river Jordan, as appears from the palm trees, which thrive much better upon the banks than at a distance

Near Jericho there is a large and plentiful fountain, which overflows all the grounds thereabouts, and takes its rise not far from an ancient city the first place that Joshua, the son of Nun, and famous general of the Hebrews, gained from the Canaanites by the sword There goes a tradition that this fountain in time past was so dangerous, that it not only corrupted the fruits of the earth, as well grain as plants, but likewise caused abortions in women and tainted with a blasting infection whatever it touched that was capable of such an impression It is further reported, that from the days of the prophet Elisha, the illustrious successor of Elijah the waters of this fountain became not only innocent but wholesome and nourishing, and upon this occasion Elisha having been treated with great hospitality and respect by the people of Jericho, he thought himself of such an acknowledgment as they themselves, their country and posterity, might be the better for to time immemorial The prophet upon this, went out to the fountain, and casting an earthen vessel, full of salt to be let down into the bottom of it advanced his right hand towards heaven and presenting his oblations at the side of it besought the Almighty, in his goodness, to correct the water and to sweeten the veins that passed from them, to soften the air and render it temperate and fructifying to bestow children as well as fruit upon the inhabitants in abundance and never to withdraw this blessing so long as they continued in their duty Upon the offering up of this prayer, with all due form and ceremony the quality of the fountain was changed, and instead of sterility and famine the waters were become ever since means of plenty and increase insomuch that the bare touching of the ground with them gives extraordinary increase ... I find there is not another water in the country that runs through such a track of land

The country is seven furlongs in length, and twenty in breadth, abounding with curious gardens and thick groves with palm-trees along the banks, of different sorts, names and tastes They press out of some of them great quantities of a sort of honey, not much inferior to other honey, which they have there also in plenty There is great store of balsam, cypress and myrobalanus and it is undoubtedly a remarkable blessing from heaven for a country to produce not only the choicest of all the fruits of the earth, but the largest and best of the several sorts Nor are they less happy than other countries in the production of other fruits, and in the improving of them as well in growth as in virtue This, I presume, may be referred to some peculiar property of the water, and to a certain kindly warmth in the air the latter to draw out and diffuse the virtue of the subject matter it has to work upon, as in the disclosing of leaves, flowers, and the like The other serves to bind and confirm the roots, and to fortify them, by increasing the sap, against the parching heats, which are so excessive, that nothing would sprout or bud without it In the extremity of these heats, they have likewise every morning such refreshing breezes, that the very breath of them renders the water, that is drawn before sun-rise cool and comfortable In the winter it is warm and salutary to bathe in Such is the temperature of this climate that even when the rest of Judæa is covered with snow, the natives of this place are cloathed in linen It lies an hundred and fifty furlongs from Jerusalem, and sixty from the river Jordan, and the whole country, betwixt it and Jerusalem, is rock and desart Thus much for the happy situation and natural advantages of Jericho

CHAP. V.

Extraordinary qualities of the lake of Asphaltitus. Sodom produces a fair fruit to the eye, that falls to ashes upon the touch.

THE nature of the lake of Aſphaltitus is alſo worthy of deſcription. It is bitter and unfruitful, and ſo light, that it bears up the heavieſt things that are thrown into it. Veſpaſian, having heard of the ſtrange qualities of this water, took a journey out of curioſity to ſee it, and ordered ſeveral perſons, that could not ſwim, to be thrown into it, with their hands tied behind them. They all roſe as if by means of a puff of wind, and floated on the ſurface of the water. This lake changes colour thrice a day, according to the various refractions of the light of the ſunbeams upon it. There are alſo to be ſeen, in ſeveral parts of it, large lumps of a dark bituminous matter, not much unlike the bodies of bulls without heads. The natives draw them up in their boats, but the ſubſtance of them is ſo viſcous, and one part ſo glued to another, that there is no getting the veſſel off again, but by diſſolving the lumps, and ſeparating that part without the boat, from the other within, which is effected by moſt extraordinary means. This bituminous matter is not only uſed for caulking of ſhips, but as a medicine for the cure of many diſorders. The length of the lake is five hundred and eighty furlongs, the breadth an hundred and fifty, and it reaches to Zoaradin in Arabia.

The lake Aſphaltitus borders on the land of Sodom, once famous for the wealth of its inhabitants, and the fruitfulneſs of its ſoil, but it is ſince become totally deſolate, having been deſtroyed by a judgment of fire from heaven, for the abominations of the people. There are yet to be ſeen ſome remains of five cities that periſhed in that conflagration, and there are mock fruits to be ſeen to this day, ſpringing out of the aſhes, fair and lovely to the eye, but diſſolving into ſmoke and aſhes upon the touch, ſo that we have not only tradition, but occular teſtimory of this hiſtory.

CHAP. VI.

Veſpaſian inveſts Jeruſalem. Gerara taken by ſtorm. Veſpaſian receives intelligence of the death of Nero, and, in conſequence thereof, ſuſpends his deſign upon Jeruſalem.

VESPASIAN, being determined to inveſt Jeruſalem on every ſide, raiſed two forts at Jericho and Adida, putting into each of them garriſons both of Roman and auxiliary troops. He then ſent Lucius and Annius, with a body of horſe and foot, to Gerara, which he took by ſtorm upon the firſt attack. He cauſed a thouſand young men to be ſlain, whom he intercepted in their flight, carried away whole families priſoners, and gave the ſoldiers the pillage, which done, he ſet fire to the place, and ſo went forwards. The men of power fled, the weaker part were deſtroyed, and whatever they took they burnt. Nothing, in ſhort, eſcaped them, neither mountains or vallies places or people, but all ſuffered in the outrages of the war. Thoſe who were ſhut up in Jeruſalem could not ſtir, the zealots keeping ſo ſtrict a watch upon thoſe that were friends to the Romans, and the town being ſo beſet by the enemy, that the zealots durſt not venture forth, through fear of falling into their hands.

When Veſpaſian was returned to Caſarea, and preparing to advance with the whole army againſt Jeruſalem, he received intelligence of the death of Nero, who had now reigned thirteen years and eight days. I deem it needleſs for me to relate minutely and circumſtantially the particulars of his hiſtory, reſpecting the diſhonour he reflected on his character, in ſuffering himſelf to be impoſed on by Nimphidius and Tigillinus, two infamous miſcreants, that attended on his perſon, his being betrayed by them, abandoned by his ſenators and guards, and being forced to fly into the ſuburbs only with four of his freemen, the death he inflicted upon himſelf, the iſſue of the war with the Gauls, the ſucceſſion of Galba to the empire, who, upon his coming out of Spain to Rome, was calumniated by the ſoldiers as a puſillanimous being, and afterwards ſlain in the middle of the great market-place, the ſucceſſion of Otho, who marched with his army againſt Vitellius; the troubles of Vitellius, the combat before the capitol, the defeat of the German troops by Antonius Primus and Mucianus, who, having ſlain Vitellius, put an end to the civil war: theſe particulars I omit, as they have been accurately deſcribed by ſeveral eminent hiſtorians, both Greek and Latin, and contenting myſelf with this ſketch, return to my own narrative.

Veſpaſian, upon this intelligence, put a ſtop, at firſt, to his expedition againſt Jeruſalem, till he could learn how the government was diſpoſed of after the death of Nero, and finding Galba appointed to the ſucceſſion he deemed it imprudent to proceed without orders. Hereupon he ſent his ſon Titus to Galba, to congratulate his acceſſion to the empire, and to receive inſtructions and commands as to his future conduct. King Agrippa accompanied Titus on the commiſſion but, as they were upon their paſſage near Achaia, they were informed of the death of Galba, who was ſlain after a government of ſeven months and ſeven days, as alſo of the ſucceſſion of Otho, who reigned three months. This revolution did not hinder Agrippa from proceeding to Rome, but Titus, through an extraordinary impulſe, ſailed from Achaia into Syria, and from thence very ſeaſonably got back to his father at Caſarea. They were now both in ſuſpenſe concerning the public affairs, the Roman empire being in ſo fluctuating a condition. They ſuſpended their expedition againſt the Jews, nor was it a time to think of extending the empire, when inteſtine broils prevailed amongſt thoſe of their own country.

CHAP. VII.

Another war in Jeruſalem. Simon commits ravages and depredations. Attempts the conqueſt of Idumæa. Encounters the zealots. Eleazar, one of his party, ſummons Idumæa, and the garriſon receives him. He is deſerted at the gate of Simon, and puts an end to his life. Perfidy of James of Idumæa. Idumæa is taken without a ſtroke, and after various likewiſe. The zealots ſeize upon Simon's wife, but, upon his dreadful menaces, they ſend her [illegible]

ON this revolution there broke out another war in Jeruſalem. There was one Simon, the ſon of Gioras, by birth of Gerara, in the prime of life, and though not ſo dextrous and artful as John of Giſchala, who had already ſeized upon the city, ſuperior in bodily ſtrength and reſolution of mind. As he was found to be a perſon dangerous to the community, Ananus the high-prieſt, drove him out of his government in the toparchy of Acrabatene, and made him fly to the free-booters in Maſada for refuge. At firſt they ſuſpected him, and only permitted him to come, with the women he brought with him into the lower part of the fortreſs, while they dwelt in the upper part of it themſelves. Finding at length his diſpoſition and manner correſpond with theirs, they repoſed confidence in him, and appointed him leader of a party upon an adventure, in pillaging and depopulating the country about Maſada. He endeavoured to inflame them with an ardour to attempt greater things, and aimed to affect ſovereignty, but all his efforts proved abortive, till the death of Ananus.

Immediately upon the removal of this obſtacle, he took his courſe into the mountainous parts of the country, and ſent out proclamations of liberty to all ſlaves, and rewards to all freemen who would enliſt under his banner. This brought over to him a number of licentious rabble from all quarters, and as his power thereby augmented daily, he firſt ravaged the villages that were ſituated upon the hills, and then proceeded to the plains, rendering himſelf formidable to all the places through which he paſſed. His party, in proceſs of time, was not compoſed merely of ſlaves and robbers, for many men of power came over to his intereſt, and the populace ſeemed to treat him with the reſpect and reverence due from a ſubject to a prince. He then made ſeveral incurſions into the toparchy of Acrabatena, and the Greater Idumæa, where he made choice of Nain, a town he had himſelf walled in and fortified, for his retreat. In the valley called Pharan, he found many caverns ready for his purpoſe, and others he enlarged, for granaries, ſtores, magazines, [illegible], and, [illegible], repoſitories for the fruits of his rapine. From theſe preparations it was generally taken for granted that his main deſign was upon Jeruſalem. The zealots being of the ſame opinion, and finding it dangerous to ſuffer him to augment his ſtrength, only determined by one vigorous effort, to ſtop the career of his ambition, before it was too late. Purſuant to this reſolution they advanced in a full body to charge him at the head of his troops. Simon met and encountered them with great vigour, made a conſiderable ſlaughter amongſt them, and put the reſt to the rout.

But not thinking his forces yet adequate to an attempt upon Jeruſalem, he choſe rather to begin with the conqueſt of Idumæa, and therefore marched, at the head of twenty thouſand armed men, towards the borders of that country. Upon their appearance the leading men, with great expedition, raiſed a body of twenty-five thouſand choice troops, leaving a competent number to ſecure the country from the ravages of the freebooters in Maſſada. They then waited for Simon upon the borders, where, upon his advance, the two armies engaged, and the action continued from morning till night, upon terms ſo equal that the ſuperiority could not be decided. It appeared, however, that both parties had ſuſtained great loſs, for Simon retired to Nain, and the Idumæans returned home.

Not long after this Simon took the field again, with a very conſiderable reinforcement, and encamping near the village of Thecue, ſent Eleazar, one of his aſſociates, with a commiſſion to the governor of Herodion, requiring him to deliver the caſtle into his hands. The officers received him, at firſt, with all tokens of reſpect and honour, but, upon coming to underſtand his commiſſion, they all drew upon him in an inſtant, and Eleazar, finding it impoſſible to make his eſcape, leaped down the precipice from a wall, and was daſhed to pieces.

The Idumæans were poſſeſſed with ſuch apprehenſions of the power and ambition of Simon, that they were not diſpoſed to contend with him again, till they were perfectly well informed of the force and ſtrength of his army. James, one of the commanders, very readily (but with a treacherous deſign) took upon him the office of a ſpy. Upon this commiſſion he went away from Olurus, where the Idumæan army lay encamped, and thence proceeded to Simon. After ſome diſcourſe upon the buſineſs, he entered into a ſolemn contract with him, to deliver up his country to him, upon condition of being treated, after the performance of it, as his firſt miniſter and favourite, and undertaking, in the next place, to aſſiſt him in ſubjecting all Idumæa. When Simon had gratified this treacherous inſtrument with a ſplendid entertainment, fair words, and large promiſes, he returned to his own people, and magnified every particular, as to ſtrength, conduct, number, and order, which made ſuch an impreſſion not only upon the ignorant multitude, but the very officers themſelves, that they came to a reſolution not to diſpute the point any longer by arms, but rather ſurrender themſelves to Simon, for fear of worſe conſequences.

James, at that inſtant, diſpatched meſſengers to Simon, to come off immediately, and by no means neglect ſo fair an opportunity, aſſuring him that Idumæa would be his own without ſhedding a drop of blood. His aſſurance proved valid, for, upon the approach of the army, James was the firſt man that took horſe, and fled, together with thoſe whom he had corrupted, and this ſtruck the whole multitude with ſuch a terror, that they diſperſed ſeveral ways, and the whole army was diſſolved without coming to any action.

Simon being now almoſt miraculouſly poſſeſſed of Idumæa without bloodſhed, ſurprized the town of Hebron with the corn in it, and other booty of immenſe value. This city is of great antiquity, not only as it reſpects that province, but, if we may credit the natives, of more ancient date than Memphis in Egypt, being computed to be of 2300 years ſtanding. They have a tradition that Abraham, the grand father of the Jews took up his habitation there upon his leaving Meſopotamia, and that his poſterity removed from thence into Egypt, where there are monuments of the moſt excellent marble, with inſcriptions confirming the ſame. There is alſo to be ſeen, at the diſtance of ſix furlongs from the place, a very large turpentine tree, that, according to report, has remained there from the creation of the world.

From this place Simon made his inroads throughout Idumæa, not only ravaging the cities and villages, but laying waſte the whole country, for, beſides thoſe that were completely armed, he had a train of 40,000 followers. The progreſs of this multitudinous throng was as deſtructive to the people as locuſts are to the vegetable creation. They left every place deſolate behind them, nor was there to be ſeen the trace of any thing that contributed to human [illegible]. It was utterly impoſſible to find proviſions for such a [illegible], which, added to the natural temper of Simon, and the reſentment of his rage againſt the Idumæans, aggravated the [illegible] want. In fine, from their burning, demoliſhing, and devouring the fruits of the earth, or trampling them to duſt, Simon's troops did not leave so much even in a fruitful well cultivated country, as the leaſt ſign or memorial of what it had been formerly.

Theſe rapacious proceedings of Simon could not fail to incenſe the zealots, though they durſt not bring it to an open war, but contented themſelves with what they occaſionally got by ſurprize. At length a valuable acquiſition fell into their hands, for they took Simon's wife priſoner, with ſeveral of her attendants, and carried her away to Jeruſalem with as much joy and triumph as if it had been the huſband himſelf, making no doubt but he would lay down his arms, and enter into a compoſition. But [illegible] upon the woman wrought, [illegible], a contrary effect upon the huſband, and, inſtead of moving him to tenderneſs and compaſſion enraged him into the moſt furious extravagance.

He haſtened immediately to the gates of Jeruſalem, and there vented his ſpleen upon all that fell in his way, including men, women, and children, that came out of the city upon any neceſſary occaſion, to be [illegible] and ſcourged to death, young and old, without diſtinction. He cut off the hands of many, and ſent them [illegible] to affright his enemies, and in order to make the people [illegible] ſedition, and deteſt thoſe who had been the authors of his wife's ſeizure. He alſo commanded them to declare, "that Simon ſwore, by the Great God of the Univerſe, that unleſs they immediately reſtored him his wife, he would force the walls, and inflict the like puniſhment upon every creature, whether young or old, guilty or innocent." Theſe menaces ſo terrified not only the multitude, but the zealots themſelves, that they ſent back his wife, and thereby ſo far appeaſed him, that he ſuſpended the continuance of his dreadful maſſacre.

CHAP VIII

The Roman empire rent by [illegible] and intestine broils. Transactions and fate of Galba, Otho, and Vitellius. Vespasian completes the absolute conquest of Judæa. Cerealis takes Capharis, and lays Hebron in ashes.

SEDITION and [illegible] now not only throughout Judæa, but in Italy also. Galba was slain in the midst of the market-place at Rome, and Otho was declared his successor. Then [illegible] up Vitellius, who, being elected emperor by the German legions, disputed his title with him. They had two battles near Bedriacum, in Gaul. Otho gained the advantage [illegible] the first day, and Vitellius the next, under the command of his two generals, Valens and Cecina. After much slaughter, Otho, when he heard of his defeat at Brixellum, slew himself, after a nominal reign of three months and two days. Upon this event Otho's soldiers went over to the party of Vitellius, who presently marched away with his army to Rome.

Vespasian, in the mean time, removed from Cæsarea, on the fifth day of the month Desius, with a design of making an absolute conquest of Judæa, [illegible] those places that yet stood out. He went [illegible] the mountainous country, and made himself master of [illegible] of Gophna and Acrabatena, [illegible] of the cities of Bethel and Ephraim, and, when he had [illegible] garrisons in them, proceeded [illegible] Jerusalem, in his way to which he took captive and slew great numbers of Jews.

Cerealis, one of his commanders in chief, in the mean time, with a body of horse and foot, over-ran the upper Idumæa, took and burnt the celebrated Caphethra, on the way, and laid siege to Capharis, a strong walled town, and supposed capable of making a good defence; but the inhabitants opened their gates, and surrendered themselves to the assailants. Having thus carried every thing before him, he went to Hebron, the ancient town upon the mountains before mentioned, not far from Jerusalem, which he attacked and carried on the first assault. He put the people to the sword, and sacked and burnt the city. There were yet three castles in the possession of the free-booters, Herod on Massada, and Machærus; though nothing might be said to be wanting to put a final period to this destructive war, but the conquest of Jerusalem.

CHAP IX

Simon, [illegible] the seizure of his wife, [illegible] the Idumæans. [illegible] principles and practices of the zealots. The Idumæans [illegible] the zealots, [illegible] them to the palace, and thence to the temple. [illegible] Simon into the city, [illegible] the [illegible] of the people [illegible] upon [illegible]

AS soon as Simon had recovered his wife from the zealots, he turned his rage upon the remainder of the Idumæans, and driving them before him from all quarters, divers of them, in a fit of despair, fled to Jerusalem for sanctuary. He pursued them to the very foot of the wall, putting to death all that came within his reach; so that Simon without the wall, was a greater terror to the people, than the Romans themselves; and the zealots within were more furious to them than both. They seem to have imbibed these principles from the Galileans, who improved them in the arts of wickedness, by instruction, encouragement, and example. John of Gischala, having been advanced by them, made them [illegible] requital [illegible] the authority he had obtained, [illegible] them to live in the most licentious manner [illegible] the least degree of control. In matters of rapine and pillage, their avarice was insatiable. They sported with the lives of men and the honour of women, and when they had fated themselves with blood and confusion, they wallowed in the very sink of [illegible], [illegible] in the commission of horrid and unnatural crimes, and polluted the whole city with impurities that decency forbids us to mention. At the same time [illegible] they proceeded in these infamous practices, they continued their bloody [illegible], and had their weapons constantly ready to slay all that opposed them. He that escaped John fell into the hands of Simon, the most inhuman monster of the two; and those who got clear of the tyrant within the walls, were certainly the other before the town, so that the passages were blocked up, and there was no possibility of [illegible] the Romans.

At length the Idumæans, through [illegible] of John [illegible] and detestation of his [illegible], [illegible] tyrant, and made head against him. An engagement [illegible] and many of the zealots were [illegible], [illegible] the rest [illegible] fled into the royal palace, which was [illegible] Grapte, a relation of Izates king of the Adiabeni. [illegible] Idumæans pressed in with them, and [illegible] the zealots into the temple, made themselves masters of the [illegible] treasure, which was there deposited [illegible] the [illegible] inhabitants. Upon this, the zealots that were [illegible] throughout the town, [illegible] those of them that were got into the temple [illegible] prepared to [illegible] the [illegible]. The Idumæans were [illegible] numbers of the opposite party, [illegible] the [illegible] out of the temple, [illegible] Upon this occasion the [illegible] the high priest, [illegible] providence [illegible] posed themselves would [illegible] themselves, to [illegible] John [illegible] Simon [illegible] tyrant, into the city. [illegible] Matthias, the high-priest, was [illegible] for the governor [illegible] Jerusalem by the zealots, [illegible] of [illegible] told them their petition [illegible] and [illegible] the city [illegible] the [illegible] protection and deliverer. He [illegible] his troops, than he [illegible] as he looked upon those that [illegible] him [illegible] enemies [illegible] those against whom [illegible]

Simon got possession of Jerusalem [illegible] called Xanthicus, upon [illegible], John [illegible] hindered from coming out of the temple, and [illegible] their power in the [illegible] mon, with the assistance of the [illegible] the temple, but the [illegible] darts, and arrows, [illegible] head, that they were repulsed [illegible] others carried off wounded, [illegible] were fatally [illegible] of situation, [illegible] not reach them. [illegible] their own [illegible] to the eastward, [illegible] at the corner [illegible] the top of [illegible] one of the priests [illegible] trumpet, when [illegible] people [illegible] return to it again [illegible] appointed to [illegible] there. Simon, however, [illegible] pending on his [illegible] just [illegible] parts.

CHAP X.

[illegible] the [illegible] chan[illegible] of Rome [illegible] Vespasian [illegible] to the empire. The [illegible] The [illegible] Vespasian [illegible] He accepts the [illegible]

IN the midst of these intestine broils in Jerusalem, Rome [illegible] civil dissensions. [illegible] of Germany with a prodigious multitude of foreign troops, and, as the departments allotted for the [illegible] could not contain them, was under the necessity of quartering many of them in private houses. The [illegible] of the [illegible] and [illegible] such an [illegible] to [illegible] that they [illegible] as to [illegible] the [illegible] of [illegible] taking it by force. Such was the state of [illegible]

[illegible] Caesarea after [illegible] the intelligence of all [illegible] had been [illegible] was a man of [illegible] and [illegible] to a [illegible] the empire, without one requisite qualification [illegible] foreign [illegible] at home. But as [illegible] on the one hand, so [illegible] of so long [illegible] the execution [illegible] especially in the [illegible] might happen before he could [illegible]

While [illegible] the officers and soldiers formed [illegible] and [illegible] consulted about a change in public affairs. The [illegible] as follows:

"That the [illegible] soldiers at Rome [illegible] and
"delicate, that the [illegible] of war would [illegible]
"them [illegible] were well qualified to
"dispose of empires, or rather to sell them to the best bid-
"der. That [illegible] and labour of a [illegible]
"[illegible] ever [illegible] to an emperor of their
"[illegible] while they [illegible] among themselves one much
"[illegible] of government. That if they let the present
"[illegible] the [illegible] for the favours so
"generously conferred upon them by Vespasian, it was pro-
"bable [illegible] never [illegible] That Vespasian was in
"[illegible] to Vitellius, with respect to qua-
"[illegible] they were themselves, in point
"[illegible] That they had a
"[illegible] greater part in the war, as
"the [illegible] legion, that [illegible] the usurper into the ne-
"[illegible] well skilled in military discipline as
"[illegible] that, as to Vespasian, there could be no possi-
"ble competition. [illegible] the people and senate of Rome would
"never [illegible] so licentious an emperor as Vitellius, when
"compared [illegible] eminent for moderation and
"temperance [illegible] Vespasian. That it could not be expected,
"[illegible] Titus, though a prince of extraordinary virtues,
"should be chosen in preference to his father, but that,
"however, [illegible] of experience, or vigour of
"youth, might be allowed a title to choice, they had the
"one in Vespasian, the other in Titus, with all the advan-
"tages that [illegible] wisdom and resolution. That it was far-
"[illegible] to be considered, that, in electing the admirable father
"of so [illegible] the three imperial legions and
"[illegible] would be strengthened by the whole power of
"the east. [illegible] out of the reach of
"Vitellius, [illegible] the friends of Vespasian,
"[illegible] (Domitian,) [illegible]
"(the one being præfect of Rome, a charge of great influ-
"ence, and the other as popular,) and the flower of the no-
"bility, would espouse him in the [illegible] cause and that,
"finally, if they delayed in this point, the senate might chuse
"an emperor who might be obnoxious to the soldiers."

This was the topic of discourse amongst the soldiery in their several companies, and their confidence increasing with their numbers, they came unanimously to the point, and declared Vespasian emperor, requesting him, at the same time, to take the tottering state under his protection. Notwithstanding he might [illegible] be said to have been the [illegible] the [illegible] a long time, he wished to decline the [illegible] absolutely resisted it, pretending that he had much rather spend the remainder of his days in the freedom of a private life, than amongst the snares and difficulties of a more illustrious station. The more he refused, the more pressing were the officers for his acceptance, till at length, [illegible] perseverance [illegible] they [illegible] to him with [illegible] threatened to kill him [illegible] he would [illegible] to accept of the honour [illegible] so that, [illegible] reluctance, when he found [illegible] he yielded to their importunity.

CHAP. XI.

[illegible] to [illegible] against [illegible] to begin [illegible] Alexandria [illegible] Egypt, and [illegible] port of Alexandria [illegible] Tiberius Alexander joins [illegible]

VESPASIAN was no sooner advanced to the empire, than Mucianus and the rest of the officers who [illegible] him to the government were unanimous for his [illegible] against Vitellius. But Vespasian thought it more [illegible] to begin with Alexandria, Egypt being one of the [illegible] considerable spots with respect to the [illegible] could but reduce that country, he was in hopes that [illegible] itself would rather dethrone Vitellius [illegible] famine, which must inevitably be the [illegible] Egypt. He also desired a reinforcement of two legions [illegible] at Alexandria. He likewise considered with himself, that he should then have that country as a defence against the uncertainty of fortune.

Egypt is hard to be entered by land, and has no good [illegible] towards the sea. It is bounded on the west by the [illegible] corners of Libya, on the south, Syene divides it from Ethiopia, and the unpassable cataracts of the river Nile, on the east, the Red Sea serves it for a rampart as [illegible] Coptos and on the north, it stretches [illegible] Syria, and that which they call the Egyptian sea. The [illegible] it has no havens for ships, so that nature seems to have provided for the [illegible] of Egypt in the very [illegible] of it. Its length, from Pelusium to Syene is computed at two thousand furlongs, and the passage by sea, from [illegible] to Pelusium, is three thousand six hundred furlongs. The Nile is navigable as far as Elephantine beyond which there is no passing for the cataracts.

Alexandria, in the fairest weather, is a dangerous [illegible] the entrance being very narrow, and the rocks so [illegible] up and down in shallow water that it requires the utmost skill in the pilot to steer without accident. On the left hand it is encompassed with a dyke, and on the right lies the isle of Pharos, which has been so celebrated for a famous land-mark. The light of it is seen three hundred furlongs out at sea, and serves as an [illegible] signal to mariners. About this island there are great piers, against which, when the sea dashes, and its waves are broken, the passage is rendered very dangerous. But the haven, when once entered, is very safe. The length [illegible] thirty furlongs, and it is furnished with con-

JOSEPHUS brought before the EMPEROR VESPASIAN who orders him to be restored to LIBERTY his Chains to be broken and afterwards confers on him great HONOURS and REWARD

...e-horses both for the importation and exportation of ... commodities.

With ... Vespasian desire ... to settle the empire, ... Tiberius Alexander, ... the importunity ... the burden of government ... his ... Alexander ... to Vespasian ... His distinguished ... for the reception ...

CHAP. VII

...

FAME spread the report over ... that Vespasian was emperor ... could have been imagined, so that every city kept festivals, and celebrated sacrifices ... upon the auspicious event. The legions that ... in Mysia and Pannonia, and had lately taken up arms against Vitellius for his tyrannical conduct, ... took the oath of allegiance to Vespasian on his accession to the empire.

Upon his removal from Cæsarea to Berytus, ambassadors from Syria, and other provinces presented him with congratulations, ... in particular, ... with what joy people received the news of his advancement, ... had pretended an inviolable attachment ...

Vespasian succeeding in his undertakings to his utmost wish, began to consider that he had not arrived to the summit of human grandeur without the interposition of Divine Providence. He ... called to mind several prophetical hints and tokens he had observed in the course of his life, all tending to one and the same point. But he was most sensibly impressed with the prediction of Josephus, who ventured to foretell his advancement to the empire in the very life time of Nero. This produced such a concern for his imprisonment, that, calling for Mucianus, and several of his friends and officers, he took occasion to mention the bravery of Josephus, in the instance of the siege of Jotapata, and then related the prediction he at that time suspected to be fictitious, and suggested by apprehension and personal danger; but had now been demonstrated to be of Divine origin. From these circumstances he concluded, that it was shameful in him to suffer the man that had foretold his coming to the empire, and been the means of conveying to him a Divine message, to be retained in the ... of a prisoner, and therefore caused Josephus to be sent for, and ... This instance of generosity in Vespasian ... stranger, afforded his officers a most pleasing prospect of his future administration, as conducive to the interest and honour of the empire. Titus, however, being then present, represented to his father, that the scandal should be taken from Josephus, together with his iron chain, as barely to loose his bonds, without cutting them to pieces, would not be a sufficient reparation for the injury he had sustained. Vespasian approved the observation, and ordered the chain to be destroyed. Josephus not only obtained his freedom, but every token of honour and respect, as a testimony of his integrity.

CHAP. VIII

Vespasian ... and ... Vitellius ...

WHEN Vespasian had ... government ... and proceeded ... Cappadocia and ...

Antonius Primus, governor ... legion, that lay in ... and ... Cæcina ... join him ... upon the borders of Italy, ... he had ... the ... took this opportunity to ... Vespasian and ... of Vitellius over to Vespasian. He ... that the former had but the name ... other the right and authority ... in imperial ... therefore better for them to ... would ... over ... was able of himself to ... able to ...

Cæcina, by these means ... the soldiers ... but ... repentance ... punishment, if Vitellius ... Cæcina ... which they would ... not ... his ... life, they kept him in chains, ... to Vitellius as a traitor.

When Antonius heard of this, he commanded out a party to fall upon them ... stand, but, after the first shock ... took their flight towards Cremona. Antonius with his horse, cut off their entrance into the city, ... slew great numbers on the spot, ... pillage. There perished promiscuously, ... foreign merchants ... together with the whole army of Vitellius to ... of thirty thousand two hundred men ... whom Antonius brought out of Mysia ... thousand five hundred. He then ... Cæcina ... and sent him to Vespasian ... where he ... to ... the ... teachers to him ...

Upon the news that Anthony was approaching Rome, Sabinus, the brother of Vespasian, took courage, and drawing together the city guards, seized upon the capitol in the night. Great numbers of persons of rank came into him in the day, and amongst the rest his nephew Domitian, who had a great hand in the glory of that action. Vitellius was not so much incensed against Anthony as against Sabinus, and those who joined with him in the revolt, and, being naturally ferocious and cruel, especially to such of them as were of noble extraction, he sent a body of his own troops against the capitol, who, as well as those in the temple, gave signal proofs of valour. At length the Germans, being too numerous for their adversaries, got the hill in their possession. Domitian, and several of the principal Romans, escaped by a miracle, but Sabinus was brought to Vitellius, who ordered him immediately to be slain. The soldiers then plundered the temple of its ornaments and treasures, and then set it on fire.

The next day Anthony came up with his army, and being met by Vitellius, they engaged in three several places, till the army of Vitellius was totally destroyed. Vitellius then came out of his palace, wallowing in gluttony and drunkenness, where he was taken up, and dragged through the streets, and [illegible] with every kind of scurrility and insult, and then put to death in the midst of the city. He had now reigned eight months and five days, and such was his profusion, that it was supposed, if he had lived longer, the revenue of the empire would not have been adequate to the charge of his luxury. This action happened on the third day of the month Appellæus, in which it is computed that fifty thousand men were slain, over and above those already mentioned.

Mucianus, the following day, entered Rome with his army, and, having restrained the fury of Anthony's soldiers, who were slaying all before them, whether guilty or innocent, pointed out to the people the expediency of choosing Domitian for their governor, till his father should arrive. But the people being freed from every disagreeable apprehension, would hear of no other governor than Vespasian, whom they extolled to the skies, celebrating a double festival, one for the blessing of the accession of Vespasian to the empire, and the other from the deliverance from the tyranny of Vitellius.

CHAP. XIV.

Vespasian is congratulated from all quarters at Alexandria. Sends Titus towards Jerusalem. His several stations in the course of his progress.

WHEN Vespasian arrived at Alexandria, he not only received the agreeable news of what had passed at Rome, congratulatory addresses from all quarters, upon his advancement to the imperial dignity. Though Alexandria was deemed the largest city in the world, Rome excepted, it proved too small to contain the multitude that resorted thither upon that occasion. The state of affairs at Rome being now settled and secured, the people quiet and easy beyond all expectation, and the winter season passed, Vespasian turned his thoughts towards subduing the remainder of Judæa, and preparing for his journey to the seat of his empire. When he had put every thing in order at Alexandria, he dispatched his son Titus, with a select part of his army, upon an expedition against Jerusalem. Titus went as far as Nicopolis by land, which is twenty furlongs distance from Alexandria, and there embarked his troops, passed down the Nile, along the banks of the Mendesian Canton, to the city of Thmuis, and went on shore at a small town, called [illegible]. From thence he proceeded to Heracleopolis, and so to Pelusium, where he stayed two days to refresh his troops, and then marched away across the desert, and encamped near the temple of Jupiter Casius.

The next day he came to Ostracine, a place so extremely dry, that the inhabitants have no water, but what they fetch from other places. His next station was at Rhinocolura, where he stayed awhile, and then went on to Raphia, the first city upon the borders of Syria, thence to Gaza, thence to Ascalon, so to Jamnia and Joppa, and lastly to Cæsarea, in order to strengthen himself by reinforcements.

END OF THE FIFTH BOOK OF THE WARS.

FLAVIUS JOSEPHUS

ON THE

WARS OF THE JEWS.

BOOK VI

CHAP I.

A threefold sedition in Jerusalem. Eleazar begins the breach by setting up the zealots against the people. John of Gyscala and Eleazar contend for power. Ar[illegible] afterwards John and Simon. A terrible slaughter in the temple. The deplorable state of Jerusalem. March and order of the army of Titus.

WHEN Titus had marched over the desert, which lies between Egypt and Syria, in the manner before mentioned, he at last came to Cæsarea, with a resolution to draw his troops together and form his army. But while he was assisting his father Vespasian, at Alexandria, in settling the administration of the empire which Providence had put into their hands, the sedition at Jerusalem was revived, and the factious split into three parties, each faction contending with the other. With respect to the faction of the zealots, which may be deemed the leading cause of the destruction of the city, we have described its rise and progress. It was, in fact, one sedition originating from another, and resembled the fury of a wild beast, that, for want of prey, [illegible] its ravenous appetite by devouring, as it were, its very self.

Eleazar, the son of Simon, was the first who began the separation in the temple, by setting the zealots against the people, upon a pretence of indignation at the insolent attempts of John of Gischala, while himself was guilty of the same enormities. But the fact was, that the former tyrant could not submit to the tyrant that came after him; and being desirous of gaining the entire power and dominion to himself, revolted from John, and took to his assistance Judas, the son of Chalcis, Simon the son of Ezron, and Hezekiah, the son of Chobar, all men of rank and eminence, and each of them followed by a great party of the zealots. This party took possession of the inner temple, and placed guards on the there [illegible] gates and doors, in confidence that the provisions of the place, from the multitude of daily oblations, would supply them with all necessaries, and making no difference betwixt things sacred and profane.

Being thus posted, the only thing they feared was want of men for the execution of any considerable design. John was much the stronger of the two, but what Eleazar wanted in number, was abundantly made good by the advantage of the place, for he had his enemy under him. John could not attempt any thing without loss, so that through fear of a rash action on the one side, and impatience of inactivity on the other, he was greatly embarrassed. Ambition, however, at length prevailed over discretion: he made several attacks, with darts and other weapons, till the temple was polluted with the gore of dead bodies.

On the other side, the tyrant Simon, the son of Gorias, whom the people, in their distress, had invited and entertained as their governor and protector, having in his possession the upper town, and a great part of the lower, made a vigorous assault upon John and his party, seeing how he was pressed from above by Eleazar. John had the same advantage over Simon that Eleazar had over him, so that, in fact, he had [illegible] to maintain, and his efforts proved as powerful [illegible] ineffectual with the other: for, in proportion as Eleazar was too hard for John, whom he had under him, so was John too hard for Simon, who was below him [illegible] little or no difficulty in repelling the [illegible] from [illegible] but was obliged to repel those from above by [illegible] war, while the [illegible] on those who [illegible] people in arms, but on those who [illegible] worship. It must be acknowledged [illegible] even in the outrages of their [illegible] all who offered themselves on religious [illegible] the Jews were more liable to examination [illegible] ing, strangers, that were so happy as to [illegible] of a military [illegible], frequently fell [illegible] machines being [illegible] by stones and [illegible] the very altar [illegible], the priests themselves, [illegible] cise of their holy function, fell victims, [illegible]

[illegible]

a multitude of persons assembled for the [illegible]. The altar, by these means, was [illegible] not only by the Greeks, but even the wildest barbarians, who had the greatest veneration for the [illegible] of our holy religion. The dead bodies of strangers and of natives, persons holy and prophane, were promiscuously confounded, and their gore streamed in one common flow.

"O wretched city! The [illegible] of the Romans, which entered by force and purged it from the pollutions of faction and apostacy, with all the desolation that ensued thereupon, could not be compared with its present deplorable state. It was now no longer [illegible] of the Most High, being converted [illegible] into a common charnel-house, a just punishment for its most impious provocations. But yet it is not impossible but that unfeigned repentance might appease the incensed [illegible] of a righteous God, that inflicted [illegible] but deserved judgment." But here let me stop [illegible] passions which [illegible] to relate the consequences of [illegible].

As before observed, [illegible] Eleazar and his party [illegible] upon John. John [illegible] Simon [illegible] that assisted him with provisions [illegible] Eleazar. When John happened to be [illegible] at the same time, by Eleazar and Simon, he divided his forces, and held those in play that assaulted him on the city side with stones and arrows from his engines. If at any time he had a little respite from those above him, he was at liberty to make stronger sallies upon Simon and his accomplices; and as he drove him farther into the town, he burnt all before him, whether magazines or granaries, and, in fact, whatever came in his way. Upon his retreat Simon followed him, and acted the same destructive part as John had done before. Such, in a word, were the [illegible] malevolent efforts that they seemed to have been actuated by a most diabolical spirit, as if they had entered into a conspiracy for betraying Jerusalem to the Romans, by putting [illegible] for defence in the destroying [illegible] necessary to preserve it. Accordingly all places about the temple were burnt down, the city was turned into a desert by the [illegible] intermediate [illegible] were open to them for shedding the blood of each other. The provision of corn and other necessaries, sufficient to have maintained a siege for several years, was [illegible] consumed, which led inevitably to a famine, and the [illegible] which they brought upon themselves.

The [illegible] the faction within the town, and [illegible] without it, was like a great body rent asunder. The [illegible] were so distressed by their [illegible] calamities, that they prayed for the success of their very enemies the Romans, and for a foreign war in exchange for a civil one. The citizers were under terrible [illegible] no opportunity of taking council, or changing their measures. All passages were [illegible] and the heads of the factions, [illegible] to each other as they [illegible] in other points, were agreed in this, that whoever [illegible] to [illegible]. They suffered not an individual to escape, who was but suspected to be amicably disposed towards the Romans, but treated them all as common enemies. The clamour of shouts, and the clangour of arms, was heard day and night. The fear of [illegible] to come was a greater misery, though present consternation prevented outward lamentation. No regard was paid to those that were lying by their relations, nor was any care taken of burial for those that were dead. The [illegible] of all this [illegible] desperation; as he who had nothing to hope for, had nothing to fear. Every man that was not of the faction gave himself up for lost, and carried his life in his hand, as if he were to resign it the next moment. The faction at the same time, maintained their conflict, with heaps of carcases under their feet, with a triumphant ostentation, as if the horror of the spectacle had rendered the living as insensible as the dead. They meditated mischief against themselves, and when they had resolved upon any thing, they executed it without mercy, nor omitted any instance of torment or barbarity. John even perverted to prophane uses the sacred materials that were set apart for the service of the holy temple.

The people and the priests had formerly determined to raise the temple twenty cubits higher, and [illegible] to support the work. To this end king Agrippa, at incredible charge and labour, brought from mount Libanus certain curious pieces of timber [illegible] and size; but the war breaking out [illegible] John having occasion for the [illegible] into lengths for his own purposes [illegible] into turrets for his security and defence [illegible]. There were [illegible] against the inner wall [illegible] as there [illegible] John [illegible] his impious contrivance would [illegible] his feet, but [illegible] by bringing the Romans upon [illegible] the work.

When Titus had collected a part of his forces, [illegible] to meet him at Jerusalem, he went to Cæsarea, where he had with him [illegible] which had formerly made [illegible] Judea [illegible] the twelfth legion also [illegible] desire of revenge [illegible] had under Cestius. He ordered the [illegible] legion [illegible] way of Emmaus, and the tenth by Jericho, while he himself marched with the rest, and [illegible] body of royal auxiliaries [illegible] great number of Syrians. The detachments that were sent by Vespasian, under Mucianus, into Italy, out of the four legions, he made good out of 2000 chosen men of the Alexandrian army that he brought along with him, and 3000 men that followed him from the Euphrates. His best friend and counsellor was Tiberius Alexander, formerly governor of Egypt, but now appointed to command the army, being the first man that espoused the interest of Vespasian in the infancy of his government, entered into a league with him, and stood firm to it, in defiance of all the hazards of an uncertain fortune. He possessed [illegible] every qualification, natural and acquired, for [illegible] undertaking.

CHAP. II.

[illegible] Jerusalem [illegible] narrowly [illegible] preserved. His [illegible]

THE following was the order in which Titus marched with his army into the country of the enemy. [illegible] auxiliaries led the way. After them came the pioneers, to prepare the roads, and [illegible] out the camp. These were followed by the officers' baggage, [illegible] guard [illegible] came Titus himself, with a select body of men, and his ensign bearers about him in a body, or [illegible] them [illegible] the head of the engineers of war. After them the Roman eagle, with the ensigns of the legions [illegible], and [illegible] before them, the body of the [illegible] marching rank and file six in front, and the common servants, every one following the legion he belonged to, with the baggage before them. The mercenaries and their guards brought up the rear.

In this order Titus advanced, according to the [illegible] of the Roman discipline, by the way of Samaria up to Gophna, a place that his father had formerly taken, in which there being a garrison, he passed that night, and prosecuted his march next morning to a place the Jews call "The Valley of Thorns," near the village of Gabath Saul, or "The Valley of Saul," where he encamped, about thirty furlongs distant from Jerusalem.

After this Titus put himself at the head of six hundred chosen horse, and led them toward Jerusalem, to take a view of the city, and learn what he could of the state and disposition of the Jews. Being well assured that the people were desirous of peace, weary of their oppressors, and the event wanted nothing but strength and opportunity for a revolt, he apprehended that, upon sight of him and his army, they might be inclined to bring matters to an accommodation, rather than proceed to extremities.

With this idea he marched towards the city; and, while he went forward in the direct road to the walls, nobody appeared upon the battlements. But upon crossing over towards the turret called Psephinos, there sallied out a vast number of Jews from the gate over against the sepulchre of Helena, in the quarter they call the Womens' Tower, that broke through the main body of the Romans, and cutting off the communication between the two divided parties, they could not relieve one another. Thus confused, the Jews singled out Titus, with a very small number of his people about him, in a place where there was no going forward for the enclosures, gardens, and ditches betwixt him and the wall, and his retreat was intercepted, on the other hand, by a strong body of the enemy, who had got between him and his own people. The guards, not knowing the danger their general was in, supposing him to be very safe, and in the crowd thought they had nothing to do but to follow on. Titus, therefore, finding, in this extremity, that he had nothing but his sword and his courage to trust to, called out to his fellow-soldiers to follow him, and, at the same time, rushed into the midst of the enemy, to force his way through to the rest of his men.

We may hence learn how far Divine Providence interferes in the events of war, and in the personal preservation of princes. For Titus, who came not to fight, but to make discoveries, had not provided himself with armour either for his head or body; and yet not one dart or arrow, out of the showers that were launched at him, touched him, but were carried off from the mark, as if they had been designed to miss it.

Titus, in the mean time, cleared his passage on both sides with sword in hand, overbearing all before him, and trampling his enemies under his horse's feet. This dauntless resolution of the Roman general, drew the rage of the whole party upon him with fury and clamour, insomuch, that they cried out one to another, to fall upon him, as the only check to their success. But which way soever Titus turned, the Jews fled before him, yet at the same time others pressed him flank and rear, whilst his guards bravely supported him. They found at last, there was no means of coming off, but by one honourable, resolute charge quite through the enemy. This gallant effort was made. One of the companions of Titus was slain, another overthrown from his horse and carried off, while Titus, with the remainder of his noble few, got back to his camp without so much as one wound. The Jews were elated by this temporary advantage, and looked upon it as an earnest of future success, but they were totally deceived in their expectation.

CHAP. III.

Titus [illegible] Jewish factions [illegible] together. The Jews [illegible] out [illegible] the Romans, [illegible] The Romans [illegible] Titus [illegible]

ON the coming up a legion that night from Emmaus, to join Titus he marched away early next morning to Scopos, a place seven furlongs to the northward from the city. It stands low, and a fair prospect both of the town and temple, and is therefore very properly called Scopos, or The Prospect. He ordered two legions to encamp upon that spot, and the fifth legion to [illegible] where they might entrench [illegible] enemy, being [illegible]. These legions had no sooner [illegible] their orders, than the tenth legion [illegible] place lately taken and garrisoned by [illegible] was appointed to encamp [illegible] of Jerusalem, and the Mount of Olives [illegible] city, and the valley of Cedron [illegible].

The factions continued [illegible] upon [illegible] interest [illegible] war, and [illegible] on the very sight of the Romans [illegible] began to think of [illegible] equity and [illegible] their present [illegible] what [illegible] safer ourselves to [illegible] remain pent up within [illegible] the advance of [illegible]. We [illegible] of each other, to [illegible] with the blood."

Upon this the [illegible] lengthened [illegible] the valley, upon [illegible] outcries, as they [illegible].

[illegible] was given [illegible] turned, being [illegible] divisions [illegible]. The soldiers being [illegible] upon them [illegible]. Some ran away, [illegible] before they could make [illegible] ces, the Jews [illegible] though they were not [illegible] torture made [illegible] selves.

Though the Romans, [illegible] cern, and [illegible] called a [illegible] ardness [illegible] surprize, that [illegible] lowed them [illegible] increased though [illegible] confusion of the [illegible] they were [illegible] to abandon [illegible] gion had been [illegible] precipitate [illegible] their cover [illegible] the other put a stop to them [illegible] opportunity of joining the [illegible] of the [illegible] veral of them [illegible] whole body [illegible]. Upon their passing the valley [illegible] tained a [illegible] reinforced the [illegible] cover it, and [illegible] this [illegible] the more [illegible].

The Jews, that were [illegible] motion from the walls, [illegible] the centinel gave the [illegible] against them, as a signal [illegible] they rushed out upon [illegible] that they [illegible] than a number of men. The [illegible] not so much as one man of the [illegible] in the [illegible], and [illegible] by a blow [illegible] ing up the [illegible].

In the midst of this activity, Titus made a stand with a few of his generous resolute friends, who, from the veneration in which they held the dignified character of their general, besought him not to expose his own life any longer against the lives of a desperate rabble of Jews, whose condition was such, that death was the best thing that could befall them, but rather consult his own quality and safety. They reminded him, that he was not then in the circumstances of a soldier only, but in the character of the sovereign of the universe, on whose preservation the state of things upon this habitable earth absolutely depended.

Titus paid not the least attention to their exhortations, but stood upon his guard against all opposition, and encountered all assaults, wounding some, [illegible] others that pressed upon him, and forcing some [illegible] down the mountain into the valley. The vigour and resolution of the prince kept them in some degree [illegible] though not sufficient to frighten them into the city [illegible] to the opening to the [illegible], and left they [illegible], [illegible] Titus, [illegible] the flank, gave some obstruction to the pursuit.

[illegible] the Romans, who were [illegible] their camp upon the [illegible], observed the havock that was made of their companions below, it struck them with [illegible] amazement, that the whole legion [illegible], taking it for granted that the Romans [illegible] the Jews, and that Titus himself being [illegible] they thought his soldiers would never [illegible] him. In the midst of this distraction, an alarm was given to the whole legion, by some who had seen Titus [illegible] for his life in the midst of his enemies, calling upon them to hasten away to the rescue of their general. The reproach of having abandoned their commander enraged them to such a degree, that, without regard to consequences, they fell with all their might upon the Jews, and drove them [illegible] down [illegible] the Jews however [illegible], disputed every inch of ground they [illegible] till the Romans, through the advantage of the higher station, forced them all down into the valley. Titus [illegible] effectually [illegible] the Jews as they [illegible], and sent the legion back [illegible] to fortify their camp, staying with those who were with him [illegible], to keep the enemy at a distance. It may be affirmed, with that truth which becomes an impartial historian, that this was the second time that Titus saved his legion [illegible], which afforded the soldiers [illegible] to fortify and settle their camp.

CHAP IV

The [illegible] of [illegible] full of [illegible] John [illegible] Eleazar. The [illegible] Jews are reduced to two [illegible] Jerusalem.

FOREIGN hostilities ceasing for a time, internal sedition was revived. The Paschal feast, or the feast of unleavened bread, being now at hand, Eleazar, and his party, caused the temple gate to be set open for a free entrance to all the people that came up to worship. John made use of this religious pretext as a cloak for his treacherous designs, and armed the most inconsiderable of his own party (of whom the greater part were not purified) with weapons concealed under their garments, with instructions how they were to proceed. A tumult immediately arose both within and without, and the uproar was looked upon as a general design upon the whole multitude, by all those who were not in the plot. But Eleazar and the zealots were persuaded that the malice of this exploit was principally levelled at them. The guards drew off from the gates, others leaped down from the battlements without striking a blow, and crept into the temple vaults to hide themselves. The common people, that betook themselves to the altar, were miserably destroyed, some of them crushed and trampled to death in the crowd, others lay weltering in their blood, up and down, as spectacles of horror and despair. Many were slain from private enmity, and to call a man a zealot was a sufficient pretence for taking away his life. But, amidst these barbarities towards the innocent, they granted a truce to the guilty, and connived at their escape out of the caverns, where they had absconded. John's party now seized upon the inner temple, and, by resolutely opposing Simon, reduced the factions to two.

Titus, forming a design of decamping from Scopos, and advancing nearer Jerusalem, in order to his removal, posted a competent number of his best troops, to prevent [illegible] inroads, and gave it in charge to [illegible] to see all the ways levelled between that and Jerusalem. Upon this they demolished all the hedges and walls that the inhabitants had made about their gardens and groves, cut down all the fruit-trees that lay between them and the wall of the city, filled up all the chasms, and [illegible] rocky precipices with iron instruments. The whole space was by this means levelled from Scopos, [illegible], to Herods [illegible], which [illegible] to the pool, called The Serpent's Pool.

CHAP V

The Romans are deluded by the Jews. The [illegible] Titus [illegible] The [illegible] their [illegible]

THE Jews at this time concerted a plot to delude the Romans. [illegible] the most resolute of the factions went out of the town [illegible] the place called The Womens Tower, on a pretence that they were ejected by those who were for peace, [illegible] venture an [illegible] for fear of the Romans. [illegible] there they kept themselves close, and as much out of sight as possible. There was at the same time, another party upon the walls, that [illegible] to peace and an alliance with the Romans, imploring them, at the same time, to come over to them, and assuring [illegible] that they would open the gates. To grace the imposture, they counterfeited a squabble among themselves, some pretending to press out to the Romans, and others calling stones at them to hinder them, and [illegible], [illegible] either by fair means or foul, to make their way. After several feigned attempts and repulses, they went their way, affecting the utmost chagrin at their disappointment.

The stratagem lured the common soldiers, who looked upon the tower as in their possession [illegible], and [illegible] most eagerly to be in [illegible], as if there had been nothing wanting but the ceremony of opening the gates to make them masters of it. But Titus had too much penetration and discernment to place confidence in the present invitation, having made them an offer by [illegible], but the day before, of what they now affected to desire, which they peremptorily rejected the proposal. He therefore commanded the soldiers in general to stand to their arms, and [illegible] posts. But in the meantime, [illegible] employed in the trenches, betook themselves to their weapons, and [illegible] the gates. Those who pretended to have been ejected let them pass without any interruption, but as soon as they had reached the towers on each side of the gate, the Jews followed them close upon the rear, hemmed them in within reach of stones, darts, and other missile weapons, from their engines, plied them with vigour, and killed and wounded great numbers, being so pent up by them that [illegible] that there was no getting out of the wall. Besides, though shame and confusion on the one hand, and the fear of punishment on the other, they were hardened into a resolution of prosecuting what they had begun. At length, after a long dispute, and [illegible] on both sides, the Romans forced their way through the body of the Jews, who yet pursued them, in their retreat with lances, and such like weapons, as far as the sepulchre of Helena, and not without conspicuous reproaches for their foolish credulity. For as they did by waving their bucklers over their heads, and exulting all the way with shouts of joy and triumph.

The Roman soldiers, in consequence of this delusion, were upbraided by their officers, and reproved by Titus himself, who, with a degree of resentment and indignation, thus addressed them:

"How comes it (says he) that the Jews, who have nothing but their despair for their directors, should yet manage their affairs with so much consideration, stratagem, and success? The question is answered in one word. They live in obedience to their superiors, and keep good will and union one with another. Whereas the Romans, that have been hitherto so famous for their excellent order and discipline, and consequently for their good fortune, are now fallen off and disobey[illegible] [illegible] the head-strong intemperances of their own folly, [illegible] making war without officers [illegible], which is worst of all, Cæsar himself to be a spectator of this. What a scandal will this be to the very rules and orders of [illegible]! Or what will my father say, when he shall come [illegible] hear of it? A general that, in the whole course of a long and military life, never met with any thing like [illegible]. Now, such is the severity of martial law, that it makes it capital for any man to depart from the [illegible] a rule of this nature, even in a small matter, but in this case the whole army are deserters. And be it known to you all that, according to the strictness of the Roman discipline, victory itself is a scandal when it is gained without order for fighting."

From the manner in which Titus delivered these words, it was evident to the officers that he determined to put the martial law into execution, so that the whole body of offenders gave themselves up for lost, being conscious they deserved the justice they feared. The other legions, however, applied to the general with petitions in behalf of their unfortunate fellow-soldiers, imploring his pardon for the failings of a rash few, for the sake of a great number that stood firm, upon assurance that they would atone, by their future services, for their past faults. Titus, upon reflection, calling to mind, that however requisite severity might be towards individuals who are delinquents, the same reason did not hold good with respect to numbers, complied with the petition of the intercessors, and forgave what was past, upon condition of their behaving in a more prudent, as well as obedient, manner in future, and therefore turned the future means of revenging himself upon the Jews for their treachery.

When the space between the Romans and the walls had been levelled, which was done in four days, he ordered the choice part of his army to advance towards the [illegible] parts betwixt north and west, the foot drawn up in seven battalions, and the horse in three squadrons, with archers betwixt them. This being a force sufficient to prevent or repel all sallies, was of course, a security for the baggage and train thereunto belonging. Titus himself encamped at the distance of two furlongs from the city, over against the tower called Psephinos, upon that angle of the wall where it winds off from the north to the westward. He entrenched another part of his army towards the tower of Hippicos about two furlongs from the city, while the tenth legion continued in its former station upon the mount of Olives.

CHAP. VI.

Description of Jerusalem. Three famous towers. A dismal conflagration. Structure of the temple. Its utensils and appurtenances. The fort of Antonia particularly described.

THE city of Jerusalem was fortified with three walls on those parts which were not encompassed with impassable vallies, where there was but one. It was built upon two hills opposite to each other, and a deep valley betwixt them covered with houses. Of [illegible] [illegible] which contains the upper city is much higher [illegible] length more direct. [illegible], from the [illegible] of its situation, king David formerly called it "The Citadel;" but it is now called by us "The Upper Market-Place."

The lower town is seated upon another hill, that bears the name of Acra, with a steep declivity round about it. There was formerly another hill over-against this, [illegible] lower than Acra, and formerly parted from it [illegible] by a broad valley, but the princes of the Asmonean race caused it to be filled up, being desirous of joining the city to the temple, which by [illegible] [illegible] [illegible] commanded all the rest. The [illegible] [illegible] valley, that divides the upper town from the lower [illegible] [illegible] it stretches as far as the fountain of Siloam, [illegible] affords an excellent water, and in great abundance.

The oldest of the three walls was almost impregnable, by reason of the depth of the valleys [illegible] and the overhanging of the rock from above, upon which it was erected. Besides the natural [illegible] [illegible] David, Solomon, and [illegible] [illegible] [illegible] to the farther strengthening it [illegible] [illegible] industry, and expence. This wall began on the north, at the tower of Hippicos, and [illegible] called the Xystus, [illegible] at the west [illegible] temple. It passes on the other [illegible] place by Bethso to the [illegible] [illegible] southward by the fountain of Siloam [illegible] to the eastward, towards [illegible] [illegible] by Ophlas to the east [illegible] [illegible].

The second wall began at [illegible] [illegible] belonging to the former wall, and so [illegible] the [illegible] of the city to the fort of Antonia.

The third wall began at the tower of Hippicos [illegible] ran northward to that of Psephinos [illegible] sepulchre of Helena, queen of Adiabene, [illegible] king Izates, passing along by the royal [illegible] [illegible] tower at the corner towards the [illegible] [illegible] Monument of the Fuller [illegible] [illegible] wall in the vale of Cedron. This wall was [illegible] Agrippa, for the security of [illegible] [illegible] he had built, which before was [illegible] [illegible]. The city, by this time being [illegible] [illegible] was too circumscribed for the [illegible] [illegible] degrees they crept out [illegible] [illegible] the north side of the temple, [illegible] [illegible] ing increased extremely.

There was another hill [illegible] [illegible] ditches cut out of a prodigious depth [illegible] that there was no coming at the [illegible] to undermine it, besides that the [illegible] added so much to the [illegible] of the [illegible] the fourth hill the name of Bezetha [illegible] an enlargement only of the [illegible]. When [illegible] came to be inhabited, the people [illegible] have it fortified, and Agrippa [illegible] the same name mentioned his design [illegible] wall about it that we [illegible] described [illegible] to him that Claudius Cæsar [illegible] [illegible] and jealousy at the pomp and ostentation of [illegible] magnificent a work, Agrippa went no [illegible] foundation, and so dropped the project [illegible] had pursued it, Jerusalem might never have been [illegible]

The stones of this wall were twenty cubits [illegible] and ten in breadth, and so [illegible] [illegible] proof against either mining or [illegible] also ten cubits thick, and would have been [illegible] portion, if they had persisted in the work [illegible] indeed, carried it up afterwards to [illegible] battlements of two cubits [illegible] [illegible] three which, in all, make twenty-five [illegible] wall was fortified with [illegible] as substantial as itself, and not inferior, for strength and beauty, to the stones and workmanship of the temple.

These towers were raised twenty cubits above the wall, with winding staircases leading up to them, convenient apartments at the top, and cisterns for rain water. Upon the third wall there were ninety towers of the same form, and at the equal distance of two hundred cubits one from the other. The middle wall had only fourteen towers, and the old wall sixty. The compass of the whole city was thirty-three furlongs.

The third wall was an exquisite piece of workmanship from one end to the other, but yet not comparable to the tower called Psephinos. It stood upon the angle of the wall, north-west of the city, upon that quarter where Titus had encamped. Being seventy cubits high, it afforded, on a clear day, a prospect of Arabia, the sea, and uttermost confines of the Hebrews. It was, in figure, an octagon, and over against it was the tower of Hippicos, and hard by it were two other towers, erected by Herod on the old wall, which, for magnitude, beauty, and strength, were looked upon as master-pieces. For, besides other instances of the magnanimity and magnificence of this king towards the city of Jerusalem, he caused these to be erected in so extraordinary a manner to gratify a particular inclination, dedicating them to the memory of three persons, for whom he professed the greatest esteem, his brother, his friend, and his wife, the two former having signalized themselves by dying gloriously in the field of battle, and the other being slain at his own instance in a fit of jealousy.

The tower of Hippicos, so named from one of his friends, had four angles, five and twenty cubits in breadth, and thirty in height, and the whole body of it solid. Above this was a platform of stone accurately joined, and a receptacle for rain water of twenty cubits depth. On this terrace were two stories of five and twenty cubits each, divided into several apartments; and over that building were two battlements of two cubits in height, and parapets of three cubits all round, amounting, in the whole, to the height of eighty-five cubits.

Herod called the second tower Phasael, from the name of his brother. Its breadth and height were forty cubits. It was solid within from top to bottom. Above this was a porch ten cubits high, supported with arches, and embellished with divers curiosities. Over the middle of this porch was another, with elegant baths and apartments belonging to it, suitable to the magnificence of the royal founder. On the top of it were battlements and fortifications, the whole height of the tower falling little short of ninety cubits. It had, at a distance, some resemblance of the watch-tower of Pharos, the famous land-mark to those that sailed towards Alexandria, but much larger, and at this time the residence of Simon, that oppressive tyrant.

The third tower was Mariamne, so called from the name of his queen. It was twenty cubits square, and fifty-five cubits high. It must be allowed, that the structure, apartments, and furniture of the other two towers were pompous and elegant, but they were as much beneath the curiosity, beauty, and ornament of this, as this fell short of the strength of the other two, being properly adapted to the delicacy of the fair sex.

Though these towers were very high, they appeared more so from the place on which they were raised. For the old wall they stood upon was itself erected upon a very high piece of ground, and those turrets were advanced upon the top of a hill that was yet thirty cubits higher than the ancient wall. Nor were they less admirable for the materials they were composed of than the structure. The stones were neither common, nor of a weight to be removed with hands: they were of white marble, cut out into planks, twenty cubits in length, ten in breadth, and five in depth, and put together with such art, that there were no joints to be found, so that every distinct tower looked like one entire piece.

As these towers were on the south side of the wall, the king had thereunto adjoined a palace, magnificent beyond description. It was enclosed with a wall thirty cubits high, and adorned with turrets, of the best workmanship, planted around it, at an equal distance one from the other, with elegant apartments and spacious halls for public entertainments. There was an incredible collection of the choicest marble, for variety of colours, that could possibly be purchased. The roofs were wonderful, both for the length of the beams and the splendour of their ornaments. The number of apartments was very great, and they were amply furnished with whatever could tend to elegance or convenience. There were porches and galleries in abundance, lying in a kind of circle from one to another, and in each of them a row of pillars. The courts that lay to the open air had the agreeable prospect of divers groves, [illegible] many nurseries of plants, long and pleasant walks, [illegible] with cisterns, fountains, pipes, and brazen figures [illegible] forth water, with flights of tame pigeons [illegible] about it for refreshment. But, indeed, it is impossible to give a complete description of this sumptuous [illegible]; besides, it sinks one to call to remembrance the devastation that was made of it by an impious crew of incendiaries and traitors. This conflagration was not the work of the Romans, but a band of miscreants, as we have already observed, upon the breaking out of these troubles, who burnt all from the fort of Antonia, and [illegible] ing the fire into the palace, set the roofs of the three towers into a blaze.

The temple, as before observed, was built upon a very hard rock, which was so steep, that, at first, there was scarce ground on the top sufficient for the [illegible] and the enclosure that was to be about it. When king Solomon erected this edifice, he commanded [illegible] up a wall to the eastward of it to keep up the [illegible]; and having thus far secured it, he built a porch upon the rampart. There was not as yet any other fort here [illegible], but the people carrying up mould from time to time, the banks became greatly enlarged. They broke [illegible] some time after this, the north wall, and took in as much ground thereto as served, at length, for the foundation of the whole temple.

The design succeeded so much beyond expectation that they encompassed the hill with three walls, at a prodigious expence of time and treasure; for it was not only the work of ages, but the whole mass of religious oblations from all parts of the world to the honour and service of the Most High, was expended upon this undertaking, computing the charge as well of the upper as of the lower temple, which latter was erected upon a foundation of three hundred cubits deep; but the depth did not appear, as the valley was not filled up to the very level of the streets in the city. The stones provided for this immense work, were forty cubits in length; which proves, upon the whole, that liberality, constancy and perseverance can effect astonishing things.

As the foundations were wonderful, so the magnificence of the superstructure was not inferior to that of the ground-work. The galleries were all double, upheld by pillars of white marble, all of a piece, and five and twenty cubits in height, wainscotted with cedar, [illegible] curiously carved, so that they exhibited a most elegant view to the spectator. They were all thirty cubits over, and six furlongs the whole compass of them, including the tower of Antonia. These entire courts that were exposed to the air, were laid with stones of all sorts; but the second court was lined on each side with stone ballustrades of three cubits high, defensively wrought, and highly polished. In this passage were several pillars disposed in regular form and order, with moral precepts inscribed upon them in Latin and Greek, positively forbidding strangers to enter into that holy place; for the second court was called the sanctuary, and was ascended by fourteen steps above the first. The figure of it was four square, with a wall peculiar to itself, which, though forty cubits without, was but twenty-five within, the place being covered with steps that led to ascend it. This wall being built upon an advanced ground, with steps to it, part of the inside was so obscured by the hill, that it could not be discerned. At the top of these fourteen steps there was a plain level of three hundred cubits up to the wall, and from thence five steps more to the gates of the temple. There were also four from the north, as many from the south, and two from the east.

The women had an oratory, or place of worship by themselves, with a partition wall to it, and two gates, one to the south, and the other to the north, which were the two only passages of entrance for the women, nor were they permitted to pass the other. This place was free indifferently to women, inhabitants as well as strangers, that came thither on purposes of devotion. The west side was a dead wall, without any door at all. Betwixt the aforesaid gates, and over against the wall, near the treasury, there were galleries with stately pillars to support them, single, and excepting their magnitude, not inferior to those of the lower court.

Some of the gates were plated over with gold and silver, posts, fronts, and all; but there was one without the temple of Corinthian brass, which was much the richer metal of the three. There were double doors to every gate, each thirty cubits high, and fifteen broad. They were wider within, and had crowning rooms on each hand, of thirty cubits square, after the manner of turrets, upwards of twenty cubits high, each of them borne up with pillars of twelve cubits in thickness; the other gates being of the same dimensions in proportion. As to the Corinthian portal, on the east side of the temple, where the women entered, it was certainly the highest and most magnificent of them all, being fifty cubits high, and the gold and silver plates upon it more substantial than those that Alexander, the father of Tiberius, had put on the other nine. There were fifteen steps which led from the wall of the court of the women to the greater gate, whereas those that led thither from the other gates were five steps shorter.

The holy temple itself, called emphatically the sanctuary, was placed in the middle, with twelve steps to ascend it. The height of it was an hundred cubits, and the breadth as many in the front, but behind it wanted forty of that number. The height of the first gate was seventy cubits, and twenty-five over, but it had no doors, being an emblem visible and open to the whole world. The front and outsides were gilt, nor was there any thing in the middle of the temple that had not a brilliant lustre.

The inner part was divided into two partitions. The first of them in sight was open to the top, which was ninety cubits in height, forty in length, and twenty in breadth. There were five golden branches of vines over head, and huge clusters of grapes that hung pendant, between five and six feet deep, all of gold. The other partition of the temple, being called above, appeared the lower of the two. The doors also of it were of gold, fifty-five cubits in height, and sixteen in breadth, with a piece of Babylonian tapestry hanging before them of the same dimensions, interwoven with blue, purple, and scarlet, in a most curious manner. Nor was this mixture of colours without a mystical interpretation, as it alluded to the four elements, either by the colours themselves, or the matter of which they were compounded, the scarlet representing the fire, the silk the earth that produced it, the azure the air, and the purple the sea from whence it comes. So that this veil, or hanging, was, in miniature, an emblem of the universe.

The entrance led to the lower part of the temple, the height and length of it was sixty cubits, and the breadth twenty. The length of sixty cubits was then sub-divided into two unequal parts, one of forty cubits, and the other of twenty. The former part, of forty cubits, had in it the three wonders that had been celebrated over the whole world, the candlestick, the table of shew-bread, and the altar of incense. The candlestick had seven branches [illegible] out of the same stem, with seven lights, representing the seven planets. The twelve loaves of shew-bread, upon the table, pointed at the twelve signs of the zodiac, and the course of the year. By the thirteen sorts of perfumes in the censer, upon the altar of incense, with which the [illegible] replenished it, we are given to understand, that the [illegible] Creator is sovereign of the universe, and that all things are formed for his honour and service.

The inner part of the temple being only twenty cubits in height, was also divided by a veil from the other [illegible] any man permitted to enter, or so much as look into it [illegible] was called the Sanctuary, or Holy of Holies [illegible] the sides of this lower temple there were several [illegible] leading from one to another, with three [illegible] and passages into them out of the great portal. The [illegible] part, being narrower than the other, could not [illegible] venience of the same order of chambers, [illegible] cubits higher, though the less splendid [illegible] we collect that the whole [illegible] from the floor, amounted to an hundred cubits.

The curiosity and beauty of the outside of the temple was charming to a degree, being [illegible] substantial golden plates, that [illegible] the beams of the sun, and dazzled the eye of the beholder. [illegible] no gilding, the parts were so delicately white [illegible] peared, at a distance, to [illegible] like a [illegible] or pillar of snow. The roof was [illegible] ed spikes, to prevent any pollution by birds sitting upon [illegible] Some of the stones of this building were forty-five cubits in length, five in height, and [illegible] in breadth.

The altar before the temple was fifteen cubits high, and forty square, with four angles [illegible] The passage to the altar was by an [illegible] It was formed without any iron tool. The [illegible] tition raised of stone-work, curiously wrought, of one cubit in height, enclosing the temple [illegible] and the altar, and separating the people from the [illegible] No unclean persons, either male or female, were [illegible] in the temple, or even in the [illegible] not [illegible] ed to enter the inner temple without being first purified, and even then also they were not to mix with the [illegible]

Those of the sacerdotal race, that were [illegible] any defect from the exercise of their [illegible] places with those that had none [illegible] in common with the rest [illegible] lay habit; for no man is allowed to [illegible] of a priest, but he that [illegible]

The priests that ministered in the temple [illegible] altar, were to be men [illegible] versation, and without [illegible] clothing was to be fine linen [illegible] abstemious and temperate in their [illegible] out of reverence to their holy [illegible] went up, with the other priests [illegible] seventh day, upon the first day of every month, and [illegible] all public anniversary festivals [illegible] veil girt about him, and [illegible] thighs with a linen veil [illegible] the ground. On both [illegible] loured garment, fringed at the bottom, [illegible] and pomegranates [illegible] representing the thunder [illegible] the other [illegible] His pectoral, or girdle, that tied the [illegible] was embroidered with five rows of [illegible] gold, purple, scarlet, linen, and violet, [illegible] colours also of the temple.

The like embroidery was upon the [illegible] more gold in it, its form [illegible] It was bound together with two golden [illegible] the largest and richest sardonyx stones, [illegible] graved, with the names of the twelve tribes [illegible] upon them. There were also four rows [illegible] down in the order of three and three [illegible] fix a fardonyx, a topaz, and an emerald, a carbuncle, a jasper, and a fapphire, an agate, amethyft, and a lynx, an onyx, a beryl, and a chryfolite, with the fame names upon them refpectively as before. He had upon his head a filken tiara, with a crown over it of a violet colour, and another crown over that of gold, with the facred name of the Deity engraved upon it.

The high-prieft's ordinary habit was not fo rich and magnificent, the grand veftments were only put on for the annual folemnity, and when he entered into the holy of holies, which day was ftrictly obferved as a religious faft.

The fort of Antonia was built in an angle between the two galleries of the firft temple looking weft and north. It was raifed upon a rock of fifty cubits in height, inacceffible from on all hands, and, in fine, the greateft of Herod's works, both for magnificence and convenience. The rock was faced with thin fcales of marble from the bottom to the top, both for ornament and fecurity, and it was fo flippery there was no poffibility of afcending or defcending it. This tower was enclofed with a wall only of three cubits high, and within that compafs ftood the fort of Antonia, of fifty cubits, with the ftate, fplendor, and conveniences of a court, containing apartments and offices for all purpofes, with fpacious halls and places of parade for the ufe and fervice of a camp, fo that, in point of accommodation, it might be deemed a city rather than a fort, and, in point of magnificence, it vied even with a palace. It bore upon the whole, the refemblance of a tower, and was encompaffed with four other towers at equal diftances from each other, and one from each corner. Three of them were fifty cubits in height, but the fourth, that looked to the fouthward and eaftward, was feventy, and from thence had a view of the whole temple. In the place where the galleries joined them were, upon the right and left paffages for the foldiers to go down to the temple. For when the Romans were mafters of Jerufalem, there were guards pofted ftill at that quarter to prevent feditions upon their public feftivals and meetings. The temple commanded the city, as fort Antonia commanded the temple. This place had a guard upon it and Herod's palace was a good fort to the upper town. The hill Bezetha was cut off from Antonia, and joined to part of the new town, and was the only place that hindered the fight of the temple on the north fide. Let this then fuffice for a defcription of the city of Jerufalem and its appurtenances.

CHAP. VII.

Simon's party great [illegible] of the [illegible] poffeffed of the temple. [illegible] [illegible] the Romans [illegible] [illegible] of the city. [illegible] [illegible] [illegible] Orders [illegible] The fuccefs [illegible] to the Romans [illegible] The Romans [illegible] back to their camp. A [illegible] the honour of the day. [illegible] the Jews into the city.

THE party of the feditious Jews, under Simon, amounted to ten thoufand men, befides Idumaeans, which were five thoufand more, comprizing in the whole fifteen thoufand. The ten thoufand Jews had fifty commanders, of whom Simon was chief. The other five thoufand, under twenty officers, were the moft daring of the whole faction. The principals were James, the fon of Sofias, and Simon the fon of Cathlas.

John was now in poffeffion of the temple, with fix thoufand men, under the command of twenty principal officers. There came into him alfo two thoufand four hundred of the zealots, who enlifted themfelves under Eleazar, whom they had formerly ferved, and Simon, the fon of Arinus.

In this oppofition of the two parties, the people were common robbers, and thofe who were peaceably difpofed, were plundered by both factions. Simon was now mafter of the upper town, and the great wall as far as Cedron, and as much of the old wall as bent from Siloam to the eaft, and reached down to the palace of Monobazus, who was king of the Adiabenians, a people beyond the Euphrates. He was poffeffed alfo of the hill of Acra, the feat of the lower town, as far as the palace of queen Helena the mother of Monobazus. But John, in the mean time, held the temple, and the places thereunto adjoining. As for Ophlas, the vale of Cedron, and that lay between both and Simon, it was all confumed to afhes, and could only ferve as a field for action.

Though the Romans were at this time drawn up at the very gates of Jerufalem, internal fedition did not ceafe. The enemy preffing upon them brought them fometimes to a degree of reflection and moderation, but, upon the leaft fufpenfion or refpite, they relapfed into factions among themfelves, and contended together upon fome new pretence. They turned to the advantage of the Romans, as they treated each other with more malignity than they were treated by the common enemy, and were at length reduced to a ftate that they had no new calamities to fear. They were reduced to harder extremities, indeed, before the city was totally deftroyed, but the Romans atchieved a much greater exploit than the taking of the city, for, as the fedition deftroyed the city, the Romans deftroyed that fedition, which was a far greater work than the demolition of the walls. So that, for the Jews they brought this ruin on their own heads, and the Romans were only the executioners of Divine juftice upon them for their wickednefs.

While affairs were in this pofture in the city, Titus, with a felect party of horfe, took the whole circuit of the walls, to find out upon what quarter he might make an attack. It was totally inacceffible on the one fide by the way of the vallies, and on the other fide, the firft wall was fo firm as to repel the force of battery. After fome paufe, he pitched upon that part of the wall over towards the fepulchre of John, the high-prieft, as the moft convenient place for an affault, the firft wall being lower there, and the fecond cut off from the fecond wall, for they had neglected the fortifying it, the new city being but thinly inhabited. Here alfo was an eafy paffage to the third wall, and fo to the upper town, and, with the help of fort Antonia, they might take the very temple itfelf.

While Titus was weighing thefe matters in his mind, one of his particular friends, by name Nicanor, was wounded in his left fhoulder by an arrow from the walls, as he was endeavouring, together with Jofephus, to perfuade the Jews to pacific meafures. Titus was fo incenfed at this inftance of ingratitude towards thofe who endeavoured to perfuade them to what tended to their own prefervation, that he immediately determined on a moft vigorous profecution of the fiege. He alfo, at the fame time, gave his foldiers leave to pillage and fet the fuburbs on fire, ordering them to make ufe of the rubbifh and ruins for works and platforms. He divided his army into three bodies, affigning to each diftinct employment and ftations. He difpofed of his archers and flingers in the midft of the banks, then were the engines with engines to caft javelins, darts, and ftones before them. This ferved for two purpofes, either to repel the enemy's fallies or to hold them in play upon the walls. The trees were all cut down, the fuburbs laid naked in an inftant, and the timber employed in raifing the banks. The whole army, in fine, were bufily engaged in their works, nor were the Jews idle at fo important a crifis.

Thofe of the citizens of Jerufalem, who had been formerly expofed to robberies and murders, finding the faction fo wholly taken up in their own defence began to flatter themfelves with fome profpect of eafe, in the very hope that the Romans themfelves, if they obtained the

victors, would be avenged on those who had been the authors of their miseries.

John's party made a resolute defence against the assailants; but he himself durst not stir out of the temple, for fear of Simon. Simon, being posted next the enemy, was never out of action. He planted all along the wall the engines he had formerly taken from Cestius, and out of the fort of Antonia. But they were of little advantage to the people, through a want of understanding the right use and management of them, as all the skill they had was derived from the information of a deserter. They plied them, however, so as to gall the enemy from the ramparts with arrows and stones, sallying out also in small parties, and entering into skirmishes with the Romans, who, on the other side, covered their workmen with hurdles.

The Roman legions had engines of wonderful contrivance to repel the efforts of the enemy, and especially the tenth, not only for the casting of large stones, but throwing them more forcibly, and to a greater distance. Every stone cast by these engines was of a talent weight, and did execution not only at hand, but at the top of the walls and ramparts, though at the distance of a furlong, and where it fell it carried a whole file before it. The Jews were several ways apprized of these stones: first, as they were white, and easily discerned in their passage; secondly, by the noise they made in the air; and, thirdly, from the notice given them by the watchmen placed upon the walls, who had instructions to observe the playing of these engines, and when any of them was discharged, to exclaim, in the mother tongue, "The stone comes." This gave every man time to secure himself. The Romans, after this, discoloured the stones, that they might not be discovered in their course, and, by means of that invention, sometimes slew several Jews at one blow. But all was not sufficient to divert them from opposing the progress of the enemy in raising their banks; for they persisted, night and day, in doing all that was possible to be done, by policy, and courage, to obstruct their proceedings.

As soon as the Romans had compleated their works, they measured the distance from the bank to the wall by the lead and line, for it could not be done otherwise, as there was no approaching it on account of the arrows and darts that were showered down from above. When they found the engines could reach the walls, Titus ordered them to be brought up, and placed at proper distances, but nearer the objects, that they might have more liberty to play. Hereupon they set three batteries to work at a time upon three several parts of the wall. The terrible noise of the engines was heard throughout the city; the citizens exclaimed with horror at it, and the factions trembled with apprehensions. The divided members of this sedition, finding themselves exposed to one common danger, deemed it expedient to join in one common defence. They were now sensible that, as they went on, they were furthering the design of the enemy; and that, if they could not come to a final accommodation, it was indispensably necessary, at present, to join unanimously against the Romans.

Simon, upon this, dispatched a messenger to those who had shut themselves up in the temple, with a commission to tell them, that so many of them as were disposed to come out, and advance to the wall, had free liberty so to do. John, however, placed no confidence in the good faith of the message, but left his party to their own freedom.

The factions coalesced immediately upon this overture, and laying aside particular quarrels, marched up to the walls in a full body. When they had posted themselves for their purpose, they plied their fires and torches upon the Roman engines, pressing furiously upon those who had the direction of them, with darts and other weapons without intermission. Nay, in the heat of their rage and resolution, the Jews leaped down desperately from the walls in troops upon the very engines, tore off their covers, and broke in upon the guards that were to defend them.

Titus, in this confusion, dispatched, with all expedition, a party of horse and archers upon the guard of the engines, to keep off the fire, and, by holding the Jews in play upon the walls, leave the engineers at liberty to do execution. But all this battering made little or no impression. One ram, of the fifth legion, indeed, shook the corner of the tower, but without any damage to the wall itself; for the tower being much higher than the wall, it fell without drawing any part of the wall after it.

The Jews having, for a short time, intermitted their sallies, the Romans imputed it either to fear or weakness, and so became indolent and inattentive, as in a state of security. But when the Jews observed this from the town, and that they were scattered and out of order, they made a furious sally from the tower of Hippicos, set fire to their works, and in the heat of this success, forced the assailants back to their very camp. The alarm spread immediately through the whole army, and the Romans, far and near, drew presently together for the relief of their companions. The grand conflict was about the engines; how to burn them on the one side, and save them on the other. The air was rent with outcries from both parties, and many brave men fell in the encounter; but the Jews were much the bolder and more adventurous. The fire at length seized the engines, and they had certainly been destroyed, with all that belonged to them, had they not been supported by a choice party of Alexandrian troops, who performed wonders upon the occasion, and had a great share in the honour of the action.

This was the state of things, till the general himself, with a select body of horse, attacked the enemy, slew twelve men with his own hand, and drove the rest before him into the city. This exploit was the saving of the engines. It happening in this encounter that a Jew was taken alive, Titus ordered him to be crucified before the wall, to try how far such an exemplary terror might work upon the rest. But after the Jews were retired, John, a principal officer of the Idumæans, as he was talking with a soldier before the walls, was shot with an arrow through the heart by an Arabian, to the great grief of all that knew him, being a man eminent for his valour and wisdom.

CHAP. VIII.

The Romans are alarmed by the fall of a tower in the night. The Jews are greatly annoyed from the towers. They behave with great intrepidity, and make several bold sallies; but the Roman discipline prevails against their temerity. Attachment of Simon's men to their leader. Extraordinary fortitude of Longinus.

THERE happened the next night a dreadful tumult in the Roman camp. Titus had given orders for the raising three towers, of fifty cubits, upon three several ramparts, so as to have the command of the town wall. In the dead of the night one of these towers fell down to the ground with so dreadful a noise, that the surprise alarmed the whole army. Supposing that the enemy was coming to attack them, they all ran to their arms, which occasioned a great tumult and disturbance amongst the legions. Some fancied the Jews might have a hand in it. Various, indeed, were their conjectures, till, in the end, they became jealous of each other, and every one demanded of his neighbour the "Watchword" with great earnestness, and with the same formality and strictness, as if the Jews had invaded their camp. They lay under the consternation of this panic till Titus was informed of the whole matter, and made the truth of it public by proclamation. This, with some difficulty, put an end to the commotion.

The Jews stood firm against all difficulties but those of the towers, which could not be disputed nor avoided from thence they were galled by all kinds of engines, arrows, &c. while they had no remedy againſt them; for it was impoſſible for them to carry up the platform to the height of their turrets: they were alſo too ſtrong and heavy to be overturned, nor could they be burned, as they were plated with iron. The Jews had, therefore, only to retire out of reach of the darts, arrows, and ſtones, without endeavouring to oppoſe the force of the battering-rams, which, through the ſhock of repeated ſtrokes, at length prevailed.

The Romans had one formidable engine, which the Jews called Nicon, or the conqueror, and it was this that made the firſt breach. The beſieged were by this time, ſo ſpent with watching and fighting, (having been upon duty all night) that, betwixt diſpoſition and ill advice, they came to an agreement among themſelves to quit the firſt wall, having two others yet to truſt to.

Upon this they retired, and the Romans mounted the breach that the Nicon had made, and after that opened the gates to the whole army, the Jews being all withdrawn to the ſecond wall. Thus did the Romans get poſſeſſion of the firſt wall on the fifteenth day of the ſiege, which was the ſeventh day of the month Artemiſius, when they demoliſhed great part of it, as they did of the northen parts of the city, which Ceſtius had ruined before.

Titus, being now removed to a place they call the Camp of the Aſſyrians, poſſeſſed himſelf of all betwixt this and the valley of Cedron, ſomething more than a bowſhot from the ſecond wall, reſolving from thence to begin his attack, and accordingly immediately entered upon it. The Jews poſted themſelves upon the wall, and made a gallant reſiſtance. John and his party, engaged in the fortreſs of Antonia, and at the north ſide of the temple, from the ſepulchre of Alexander. Simon, and his party maintained the paſſage from the monument of John, the high-prieſt, to the gate, by which water is conveyed to the tower of Hippicos. The Jews made ſeveral deſperate ſallies, and fought cloſely with the Romans a conſiderable time, but the diſcipline of the latter overcame the inexperience and temerity of the former, who were therefore repulſed with great loſs; only upon the walls they had the better of them. The Romans had both fortune and conduct on their ſide, but the Jews ſupported themſelves by a kind of deſpairing ferocity, and a hardneſs againſt fatigue and danger.

It is farther to be conſidered, that the Jews fought for life and ſafety, and the Romans for victory and honour, and they were neither of them to be tired out, for approaches, aſſaults, ſallies and combats of every kind, were their daily exerciſes. They began with the dawn of the day, and ſo continued till night parted them, when both ſides were kept walking, the one from fear of their walls, and the other from fear of their camp, all night in arms, and the next morning, by day-light, ready for a battle.

The Jews valued themſelves ſo much upon contempt of death and danger that they made it a point of emulation, who ſhould dare moſt, as the only way to ingratiate themſelves with their ſuperiors. Such were the fear and reverence they had for Simon, that all and every man of his party would have died at his feet, if he had but ſaid the word, nay, would have been their own executioners. As to the Romans, they were ſo accuſtomed to victory, that they ſcarcely knew what it was to be overcome, ſo that they needed no other incentive to behave gallantly than experience and ſucceſs. Beſides, war was familiar and habitual to them, by the continual exerciſe of arms in the ſervice of a glorious empire, which, with the preſence and aſſiſtance of a martial prince, over and above the reſt, could not but inſpire them with more than ordinary courage. What could be more infamous than cowardice under ſo gallant a leader? Or what more glorious, on the other hand, than the bounty and eſteem of a leader famed for great and noble exploits? Such ardour and ambition have tranſported heroic ſpirits to ſoar to daring attempts almoſt beyond human power.

There was, at this time, a ſtrong body of Jews drawn up before the walls, and they were come within diſtance of exchanging weapons with the Romans. While they were engaging, Longinus, one of the equeſtrian order, rode into the midſt of the enemy, and ſlew two of their braveſt officers. One of them he ſtruck through the jaw with his lance, and ran the other through the body with the ſame weapon, coming off to his party without a wound. He gained renown by this action, and inſpired others with a generous emulation of following his example.

The Jews, at this time, were ſo intent, through deſpair, of doing miſchief, that they were heedleſs of what they ſuffered, and ſet death itſelf at defiance, if they had but one life in exchange for another. But Titus, on the other hand, had regard to the lives of his men as well as the obtaining the victory, and juſtly looked upon an inconſiderate temerity as another kind of deſperation. Nor would he deem any exploit truly valiant that was not directed by caution or prudence.

CHAP. IX.

Caſtor, a bold, crafty, and treacherous Jew, impoſes on the humanity of Titus. Makes his eſcape through the enemy's ſtratagem. Mercy miſapplied, bad policy.

TITUS having ordered one of his engines to be pointed againſt the middle of the tower, on the north ſide of the city, it poured in ſuch ſhowers of arrows upon the beſieged that they all quitted their poſt but a certain crafty Jew, whoſe name was Caſtor, and ten others like himſelf, lay in ambuſh behind the battlements. Being alarmed by a violent ſhock, that cauſed the tower to totter under them, they aroſe, and Caſtor, in behalf of himſelf and the reſt, addreſſed Titus, in the poſture and language of an imploring ſupplicant, for mercy and pardon. The Roman general, from a principle of moderation and candour, thinking that the Jews repented of their raſhneſs, and obſtinacy, ordered a ſtop both to the engine and the archers, and gave Caſtor to underſtand that he was diſpoſed to hear what he had to offer. The ſubtle Jew ſubmiſſively aſſured him that he deſired nothing ſo earneſtly as a treaty. Titus cordially aſſented, and told him, that, if his companions were of the ſame mind, he was ready to grant them his pardon. Five of the ten diſſembled with their principal; the other five exclaimed, that while they could die free they would never live ſlaves. This occaſioning a ſuſpenſion of the attack, Caſtor, in the interval, ſent privately to Simon, and informed him that he had now time to deliberate on future meaſures, as he would delude the Roman general, under the pretext of adviſing thoſe of his aſſociates, who remained inflexible, to come into terms of peace.

The artful Jew performed his part with admirable adroitneſs; ſwords were drawn by the contending parties, blows given, and men apparently ſlain. Titus, and thoſe about him, were amazed at the obſtinacy and hardneſs of the Jews, nor could they refrain from compaſſionating their miſerable ſtate, but being upon the lower ground, they could not ſee ſo diſtinctly what was done above. While this paſſed, Caſtor, being wounded with an arrow upon the noſe, drew it out, and held it up to Titus, as an appeal to him for juſtice. The noble Roman reſented the ſeeming injury to ſuch a degree, that he ordered Joſephus, who ſtood by him, to go to Caſtor, with aſſurance, in his name, of amity and fair quarter. Joſephus begged to decline the commiſſion, and diſſuaded his friends from going upon it, telling them, that the pretended ſubmiſſion was founded on a fraudulent deſign. Eneas, however, one of the deserters to the Romans, undertook to go upon the invitation of Castor, who promised him a gratuity for the execution of his commission. Allured by these terms, Eneas hasted, and had no sooner put himself in a posture to receive the present than Castor dropt a huge stone down from the wall, which Eneas with difficulty avoided; but it wounded a soldier who stood near him. When Titus, by this means, detected the delusion, he was convinced of the danger of humanity misapplied, and, persuaded that rigour was the best defence against fair words and plausible pretences to avenge himself upon Castor and his companions, he ordered the engines to be plied with greater violence than before. The treacherous accomplices finding the tower totter, and ready to sink under them, set it on fire, and made their escape into a vault through the very flames. From this last exploit the Romans were as much astonished at their resolution, as they had been incensed at their treachery.

Titus made himself master of this part of the wall within five days after taking the first, and now finding the way open to the second wall, he drove out the Jews before him, and, with a thousand choice men, entered the town, and passed through the cloth-market, and other avenues, up to the wall. If Titus had immediately demolished the greater part of this wall, as by the martial law he might have done, he would have obtained the victory at an easy rate; but considering the miserable state of the Jews, on the one hand, if they stood it out, and the security of their retreat, on the other, if they were disposed to fly, he once again relented, in confidence that they would be duly sensible of his clemency, nor treat again with treachery and ingratitude, the man to whom they owed the preservation of their lives.

CHAP. X.

Extraordinary humanity of Titus. Malice and calumny of the faction. The Jews overcome the Romans in an encounter. Fight renewed every day. The Romans gain the second wall, but are quickly repulsed. Famine a greater calamity to the Jews than the war. Titus carries the second wall on the fourth day of the assault.

THE Roman general, having entered the town, would not permit his soldiers so much as to put to death one prisoner, or set fire to one house; nay, he was so candid to the very faction, that he left them at liberty to contend the point in dispute, provided they did not force or oppress the people. He promised the inhabitants also, at the same time, to maintain them in their lawful possessions, and to restore to them what had been taken from them.

These proposals were generally acceptable, some desiring the city might be spared for their own sakes, others that the temple might be spared for the sake of the city. But this humanity and tenderness was imputed, by the obdurate and relentless faction, to pusillanimity in the general, whom they represented as having offered these conditions, because he was apprehensive he could not perfect his design of reducing the city. They also threatened those with death who should even throw out a hint of a surrender.

The Romans were no sooner got into the town, than the Jews annoyed them by divers means, such as blocking up the narrow passes, galling them from the tops of the houses, and forcing the guards, by sallies from the walls, to quit their towers, and retire to the camp. Never was greater confusion and outcry than betwixt the soldiers within the town in the midst of their enemies, and those without the town for fear of their companions within. The Jews, being more numerous, and better acquainted with the by-ways and secret passes, than the Romans, had the advantage of them in their encounter; and the breaches not being wide enough to march out many abreast, they were so hampered in the crowd, that they would have been cut to pieces, if Titus had not come to their relief. By posting a body of archers at the end of every street, and taking place himself where there was most danger, with Domitius Sabinus for his second, (a man eminent for his valour,) they held the Jews in play with their darts and lances, till they brought off their men under cover of that diversion. Thus were the Romans, after gaining the second wall, again repulsed.

The resolute part of the citizens flattered themselves into an opinion, upon their success, that the Romans would never venture into the city again, and that if they kept within themselves, they should not be any more conquered. But these devoted objects seem to have been judicially infatuated, or they would have considered, that the Romans, whom they had lately worsted, bore no comparison, in point of numbers to those with whom they had to encounter; nor did they foresee the dreadful famine that approached. They had hitherto rioted on the public, and drank, as it were, the very blood of the city. Many excellent members of society fell into extreme necessity, and not a few died of want and famine itself. But the loss of men of candour and moderation afforded joy to the factious, who only wished such to survive as were for carrying on the ruinous war with the Romans. The rest they looked upon as an useless burden, so averse were they to their own real interest.

The Romans made another attempt to recover the wall which they had failed in before, and for three days without intermission, plied the assault, attack upon attack, and were as valiantly repulsed; but on the fourth day Titus gave so furious a charge, that they could resist no longer, and by that means got possession of the wall, demolished the northern part of it, and immediately placed garrisons in all the towers to the southward.

CHAP. XI.

Titus prepares for the prosecution of the war. Titus the subject of [illegible] and argument with the Jews. Josephus's [illegible] to the Jews [illegible] blessings of peace and miseries of war [illegible] history of their own nation. [illegible] the good of his country. The Jews [illegible] their own destruction.

A RESOLUTION was taken by Titus to suspend the siege for a short time, and afford the faction an interval for consideration, in order to try whether the demolition of their second wall would not render them more compliant, or whether they were not fearful of a famine, as the spoil they had obtained by rapine would not last long for their support. Upon a day of general muster, he commanded his troops to be drawn up, and paid in sight of the enemy, the foot advancing with their swords drawn, and the cavalry with their horses elegantly caparisoned. No sight could be more grateful to the Romans, or so tremendous to the Jews, who were assembled in multitudes upon the old wall on the north side of the town. The houses were crowded, and the whole city covered with people, gazing at this pompous display of the power and greatness of the Romans. A consternation seized the boldest of the Jews, and would probably have brought them over to the Romans had not a consciousness of their provocation and affronts worked them up to a despair of pardon. Assured, therefore, that immediate death would follow surrender, they rather chose to fall in the contest; but it seems to have been so ordered by the overruling power, that the innocent should fall with the guilty, and the city itself with the faction.

When Titus had passed four days in muster[illegible] and paying his army, without any act of hostility, but found no disposition in the Jews towards peace, he divided his legions, and began to raise banks at the fortress of Antonia, near John's monument, in order to [illegible] the upper town from that quarter, and make himself master of the temple from Antonia, for he knew that [illegible] taking the fort, the city was not to be maintained At each of theſe parts he raiſed banks, each legion raiſing one Thoſe that worked at John's monument were annoyed, and, in ſome degree, obſtructed by the Idumæan, and Simon's party, who made occaſional ſallies upon them, while John's faction, and the multitude of zealots with them, did the ſame to them that were before the tower of Antonia These Jews had the advantage of the Romans, not only as they ſtood upon higher ground, but, through conſtant practice, had attained a perfect knowledge of the uſe of the engines They had three hundred engines for darts, and forty for ſtones by which means they greatly annoyed the Romans, and impeded their deſign of raiſing the banks

Titus, however, aſſured that the city, whether ſaved or deſtroyed, would eventually fall into his hands, not only proſecuted the ſiege with vigour but tried again the effect of advice and perſuaſion to bring the Jews over to reaſon and reflection Being ſenſible that exhortation is ſometimes more prevalent than force, he counſelled them to ſurrender the city, in a manner already taken, and thereby ſave themſelves, and ſent Joſephus to addreſs them in their own language, imagining that they might yield to the arguments and remonſtrances of their countrymen.

Joſephus, purſuant to commiſſion from the noble and generous Roman, went round about the wall and finding a place ſecure from weapons, and convenient for hearing, delivered himſelf in words to the following purport

" I am now to beſeech you, my dear friends, as you love
" your lives and liberties, your city, your temple and your
" country, let your tenderneſs appear upon this occaſion,
" and learn to be merciful to yourſelves from your very ene-
" mies The Romans, you ſee, have ſo great a veneration
" for holy things that they make conſcience of laying vio-
" lent hands upon any thing that is ſacred, and without
" pretending to any part or intereſt in the communion,
" whereas, inſtead of defending the religion you were
" brought up in you are engaged here in a direct conſpi-
" racy to ſuppreſs it Do you not ſee that your ſtrength is
" all beaten down already, your weakneſs expoſed, your
" walls defenceleſs, and that, in this condition, it is morally
" impoſſible for you to hold out any longer againſt ſo for-
" midable a power? Neither is it a new thing (in caſe of the
" worſt) for the Jews to be ſubject to the Romans It is
" truly a glorious cauſe when liberty is the queſtion, provi-
" ded it be early enough, and before that liberty is either for-
" feited or loſt, but for people to talk of ſhaking off the
" yoke, after they have once ſubmitted to it, and continued
" in that obedience till they become ſlaves by preſcription,
" is not the way to live free, but rather to die with infamy
" It would be a ſcandalous bondage, indeed, to ſerve a maſ-
" ter that a man of honour would be aſhamed to own, but
" *it is another caſe to be ſubject to a people that have the*
" whole world at their feet As where is that ſpot in the
" univerſe that has eſcaped the dominion of the Romans,
" ſaving only where extreme heats or colds have rendered
" the places intolerable and uſeleſs Fortune is effectually
" gone over to them, and the Great Diſpoſer of Empires
" himſelf hath, in his providence, at preſent made Italy the
" ſeat of the univerſal monarch Beſide that, it is according
" to the ſovereign law of nature, that governs in beaſts, as
" well as in men, to give way to the ſtronger, and ſubmit
" quietly to the ſword It was this that made your anceſ-
" tors, though in power and politics much your ſuperiors,
" pay allegiance to the Romans, which they would never
" have done, if they had not been thoroughly convinced
" that it was God's will to have it ſo But to what end is
" it for you now to diſpute a point any longer that is the
" ſame as loſt already? For if the walls were yet entire, and
" the ſiege raiſed, famine alone would do the work. It has
" begun with the multitude, and the ſoldiers turn will be
" next, and every day ſtill worſe than the other for the
" calamity is inſuperable, and there is no fence againſt hun-
" ger Wherefore you would do well to bethink yourſelves
" in time, and to take wholſome advice before it be too
" late The Romans are naturally a generous enemy, ready
" to forgive and forget all that is paſt, provided you do not
" carry on the affront to an unpardonable extremity They
" are not a people to ſacrifice their intereſt to their revenge,
" and to charge themſelves with the incumbrance of a de-
" populated city, and a deſolated province, but rather for
" receiving you with open arms into their friendſhip But
" if ever you come to be taken by ſtorm, you muſt expect
" to be put to the ſword every man, thoſe eſpecially that,
" in defiance of the emperor's grace and mercy, ſhall con-
" tinue obſtinate to the laſt As for your third wall, what
" have you to look for from it, but the fate of the other
" two that are gone before? Or what if your works were
" abſolutely impregnable? the very want of bread, as I
" have before obſerved, would do the office of the ſword"

This exhortation had ſo little effect upon the obſtinate contumacious Jews, that they not only derided and reproached the ſpeaker, but diſcharged weapons at him from the walls Deſirous, however, from a principle of genuine patriotiſm, if poſſible, to avert their impending deſtruction he proceeded thus to expatiate on many hiſtorical facts, that he might terrify, if he could not perſuade

" Ah miſerable and ungrateful wretches, to forget your
" beſt friends, and encounter the Romans with common
" weapons, as if the victories you have formerly obtained
" had been the effect of your own wiſdom and virtue?
" Can you ſay that the great Creator of heaven and earth
" ever failed of protecting the Jews when they were op-
" preſſed? Will you never be wiſer? Do but conſider
" whence you come, where you are, what you are doing,
" and how glorious a Protector it is that you provoke by
" theſe outrages Do you not call to mind the divine ex-
" ploits of your illuſtrious anceſtors, and the wonderful
" deliverances that God hath wrought for them by the
" ſacredneſs of this holy place? It gives me horror to think
" of expoſing the hiſtory of God's miraculous diſpenſations
" to a people ſo unworthy of the bleſſing, but yet, upon
" this occaſion, I ſhall diſpenſe with that ſcruple, to ſhew
" you that the war you are now engaged in, is not ſo much
" againſt the Romans as againſt God himſelf

" Pharaoh Necho, king of Egypt, carried away, with a
" mighty army, Sarah, the queen and mother of us all
" You would have thought, perhaps, that Abraham, the
" huſband of Sarah, and our common father, having, at that
" time, the command of three hundred and eighteen
" lieutenants, and troops innumerable under them, ſhould
" have attempted the righting of himſelf by arms but he
" choſe rather to lie quiet, and offered up his prayers to-
" *wards this holy place, which you have poluted, to im-*
" plore God's aſſiſtance What came of it, but the king's
" ſending the queen back again untouched to her huſband,
" the ſecond night after ſhe was taken away, the Egyp-
" tian, in the mean while, contracting a veneration for the
" place which you have defiled with the blood of your
" countrymen till in the end having himſelf haunted
" with frightful dreams and viſions, he poſted back again
" to his own country, but firſt ſcattered large donations of
" gold and ſilver among the people, in token of the reve-
" rence he had for a nation ſo much in God's favour

" What ſhall I ſay of our predeceſſors tranſporting them-
" ſelves into Egypt, their four hundred years bondage un-
" der a foreign tyranny, and their ſubmitting with patience
" and reſignation to God's good pleaſure, even at a time
" when they were ſtrong enough to have redeemed them-
" ſelves by force? If I ſhould tell you now how the
" Egyptians were infeſted with ſerpents and tainted with
" all manner of diſeaſes, how the fruits of the earth
" were blaſted, the Nile corrupted, and ten plagues

"succeeded one another, it would be no more than what "every body knows but those of our ancestors that "God had designed to the priesthood, were conducted "out safe and sound, without either blood or danger un- "der the guard of a special Providence.

"So when the Assyrians forced away from us the holy "ark, how did Palestine, Dagon, and the whole nation "fare that was concerned in the seizure of it? Their "bowels became putrid, and their pain intolerable, in- "somuch that their bowels and blood came away to- "gether. What was the end of it, but the bringing of "the ark back again to us with the sound of musical "instruments, and with the same sacrilegious hands that "took it away to expiate, in some degree, for the "wickedness? This was the work of God himself in "favour of our ancestors, for casting themselves entirely "upon his Providence and mercy, without having any "recourse to common means.

"What became of Sennacherib, king of Assyria, and "that prodigious army of his, when he sat down before "this place with the whole strength of Asia at his com- "mand? Was he cut off by the arm of flesh, or any hu- "man power? No. But when the Hebrews were quietly "at their prayers, the angel of God confounded in one "night that mighty army, and the Assyrian found "185 000 of his men dead upon the place next morning, "and the rest flying in consternation from the unarmed "Hebrews that had no thoughts of pursuing them.

"You know likewise that our people were seventy "years captive in Babylon, without making any attempt "towards the recovery of their liberty, till God put it in "the heart of Cyrus to discharge them, and dismiss them "to their own country where they began to offer sacri- "fices again to God, as their only deliverer and preserver. "To be brief what great thing did our forefathers ever "bring to pass, either with arms or without, but by God's "particular direction and assistance in the execution of "his orders? If they stayed at home, they were victori- "ous without fighting, it being God's pleasure that it "should be so and when they fought in confidence of "their own strength, they never succeeded. For instance, "when the king of Babylon laid siege to this city, our "king Zedekiah gave him battle, contrary to the advice "of the prophet Jeremiah, what was the event, but the "routing of his army, the taking of Zedekiah prisoner, "and the destruction both of the city and temple before "his face? Do but observe the difference now betwixt the "moderation of that prince and people, and yours. The "prophet told them plainly, that they were fallen under "God's displeasure for their wickedness, and that, if "they did not deliver up the city, it should be forced from "them by assault yet for all this forboding, neither "prince, or people, offered him any violence. To say "nothing of what passes within your walls, (an iniquity, "in truth, not to be expressed,) I shall only take notice "how barbarously I myself have been treated by you "both in words and actions and what is my crime, I "beseech you, but the honest liberty of telling you your "faults, and advising you for the best?

"It was much the same case too, when Antiochus, "called Epiphanes, laid siege to this city. Our fore- "fathers having by many ways incurred God's high "displeasure, pressed the enemy to a battle, without "waiting for his Divine direction and assistance the "Jews were totally defeated, the town taken and pillaged, "and the sanctuary, for three years and six months, "wholly abandoned. In few words, what was it but "the contumacy of our own people that first irritated the "Romans against the Jews? Whence are we to date our "slavery but from our own seditious countrymen, when "the two factions of Aristobulus and Hyrcanus, in an "ambitious heat of competition, brought Pompey into "the city, and made the Jews, that were unworthy of "liberty, slaves to the Romans? When they had held it "out three months, they surrendered the place, though in "a much better condition to defend it than you are and "infinitely short of what you are to account for to the "laws and religion of our country. We all know what "was the end of Antigonus, the son of Aristobulus, in "whose reign the Jews were punished with another ju- "dicial captivity for the sins of the people. Did not "Herod likewise besiege Jerusalem with the assistance of "Sosius, a Roman general, and at the head of a Roman "army? After six months the town was reduced, and "rifled by the enemy, as a just judgment upon the party "for their iniquities.

"Enough has been said to shew that this way of arms "and sieges hath ever been fatal to our brethren, and "that the end of such a war would be certain ruin. "Therefore it seems reasonable to me, that those, who "are in possession of this holy place, should entirely "submit themselves to the conduct of God's providence "who will never be wanting to them that serve him, and "keep his commandments. But you lead lives in direct "opposition to his holy will, leaving undone what you "are commanded to do, and doing what you are forbid- "den. How much have you more to answer for, than "those that you have seen taken off by a vindictive ju- "stice in the career of their wickedness? As for the secret "sins of theft, fraud, treachery, and adultery, you look "upon them as trifles. But you value yourselves upon "oppression, murder, and other sins of the first magni- "tude, that were hardly ever heard of. Nay, you have "made the holy temple itself the scene of your wicked- "ness, a place so sacred, that the Romans themselves "have a veneration for it, notwithstanding the inconsis- "tencies of their religion yet this place, that the very "Romans have so great a reverence for, is polluted and "blasphemed by those who have been trained up to the "temple worship. With what face now can you pretend "to expect assistance from a power that you have so "daringly provoked? But taking it for granted that you "are just, humble, and righteous, and your hands as "clean as our king's were when he stretched them out "to implore succour from heaven against the Assyrian, "and when the return of his prayer was the next night, "the utter ruin of the enemies army, if you will have it "that the Romans behave themselves as the Assyrians "did, you may expect that God will deal with them "after the like manner. But this is quite the reverse, "for the Assyrian compounded for a sum of money to "save the city, and then broke his oath and set fire to "the temple whereas the Romans only demand a yearly "tribute, and no more either than what had been paid "them formerly time out of mind. Let this be made "good to them and the temple and city have nothing to "fear you shall enjoy your families, your liberties, and "your estates, with the free exercise of your religion, "and under the regulation of your own laws. You must "be frantic to imagine that God will treat tyrants and "murderers, and men of moderation and justice, alike, "especially when punishment and vengeance are but the "work of a moment to the Almighty.

"The Assyrians, you see, were destroyed the first night "they came before the town, and if it had been the will "of God to set the one free and to chastise the other, he "would have poured down his wrath upon the Romans "as he did upon the Assyrians either when Pompey "first forced Jerusalem, or Sosius after him or when "Vespasian harrassed Galilee or now, at the ... upon ... "attack of Titus. But neither Pompey or Sosius met "with any signal opposition from heaven ... they both "succeeded in their enterprizes upon the ... As to "Vespasian, he advanced himself to the ... upon the "credit of the war he made upon us. And what do ye "you think of (also [illegible]) a miracle, wrought ... of "Titus? Siloam, you know, ... to ...

"[illegible], were dried up so low before Titus came hither, that water was hardly to be got for money; but since his arrival here, the springs are grown so quick again, that there is sufficient for the Romans, for all manner of purposes, and not only for themselves and their cattle, but for their gardens too. The same thing happened at the [illegible] when the king of Babylon, before-mentioned, marched up to Jerusalem with his army, took the town and city, and laid them both in ashes. This prodigy was the forerunner of that ruin and conflagration. Not that I take the wickedness of those days to have been comparable to that of the present age, but it looks as if God had abandoned his own house and people in favour of the enemy. Make it the case now of the master of the house, with a [illegible] and debauched family. If he be a virtuous man he will shift his quarters, and never endure to be under the roof with that sort of people. How can you imagine then that God will countenance your abominations? An all-seeing God that searches your inmost souls, and reads your thoughts in their very conception? but, alas! you have no [illegible] but make your very enemies confidents of all you do. You live in a kind of competition who shall be most abominable, and value yourselves upon an ostentation of wickedness."

"God is not inexorable to those that confess their misdoings and truly repent, which is the course that you must take, if ever you hope for mercy. Wherefore cast away your arms, let your hearts bleed for the judgments you have brought upon your country. Do but look well about you, and consider the beauty of the place, the glory of the city, and the majesty of the temple, that you are now about to betray, with the inestimable mass of treasure that is there deposited, in donations and oblations from all quarters. Can any man have the heart to think of exposing those magnificent curiosities to fire and pillage? or of seeing those excellencies destroyed, which, of all things under the sun, are best worth preserving? If you were not harder, and more insensible, than stones, this reflection would move you; or if nothing else will work upon you, bethink yourselves of your parents, your wives, your children, and your families, that are at this instant upon the brink of perishing, either by famine or the sword. It will be said perhaps, because I have a wife of my own, a mother and a family, (of some credit formerly) concerned in the common hazard, that it is for their sakes, and my own interest, that I give this counsel; but if either the sacrificing of their lives, or mine, or both, may conduce to your safety, I am ready to deliver up all, upon condition that you will be wiser and honester after my death."

This recapitulation of historical events was heard by the factions with the same unfeeling disregard as the preceding exhortation; but the multitude were disposed to desert to the Romans. Accordingly, some of them sold what they had, and even their most valuable effects, which they had treasured up, for a trifling consideration, and swallowed down pieces of gold, for fear of being robbed in their way, by which they supplied themselves with necessaries when they got over to the Romans. Titus gave many of them free liberty to go whithersoever they would, which was a great inducement to them to desert, as they were thereby not only freed from the miseries they endured in the city, but also from slavery to the Romans. John and Simon, with their factions, however, as carefully watched their exit as they did the entrance of the Romans, and death was the immediate consequence of the least shadow of a suspicion.

The rage of faction, and the pinch of famine, increased daily. No man appeared publicly; the plunderers searched private houses, and, if they found any corn, abused the tenants for denying them what they had; if they found none, they abused them the more, from a supposition that they had concealed it. The indication, whether they had any or not, was taken from the bodily state of these miserable wretches. If they were in good case, they supposed they were in no want of food; if wasted, they went off without further search. Nor did they think it necessary to put such to death, as they would soon destroy themselves with famine. Many, indeed, sold what they had for one measure, that is, of wheat, if the richer; or but of barley, if the poorer. When they had so done, they shut themselves up in the most retired part of their houses, and eat what they purchased, some without grinding, through extremity of want, and others making bread of it, as necessity or fear dictated to them. A table was no where spread for a regular meal, but they snatched the bread out of the fire half baked, and devoured it most greedily.

A more shocking spectacle never presented itself to human view, where the stronger had more than sufficient, and the weaker were bemoaning absolute want; starving being certainly of all deaths the most deplorable, as it takes away all sense of shame, tenderness, and respect. Wives tore the meat from the mouths of their husbands, children did the like by their parents, and, what was yet more barbarous, mothers by their infants, taking from them, as they lay languishing in their arms, the very last support of life. Nor could this be done so privately but some one was still at hand to take away that from them which they had taken from others. Wherever they saw a house shut up, they concluded there was food within, and therefore broke open the door, ran in, and took the meat from them by force, as they were rapaciously devouring it. They had mercy for neither age or sex, but beat the old men who offered to defend what provision they had got, and dragged the women by the hair for endeavouring to conceal the last trifle. Nor did sucking infants escape their fury, but were torn from the breast, and dashed against the ground; so that children and grey hairs had the same quarter. But, if possible, they were more barbarously cruel to those that prevented their coming in, and had actually swallowed down what they were going to seize upon, as if they had been unjustly defrauded of their right. They also invented dreadful torments to discover where any food was, and a man was forced to bear what is too horrid to relate, in order to make him confess that he had but one loaf of bread, or that he might discover an handful of barley, that was concealed. All these cruelties were perpetrated not from the compulsion of hunger, which had been some degree of palliation, but merely to keep their savage practices in exercise, as rapine and murder were the very soul of their existence.

This was the treatment the common people suffered from these tyrannical guards; but persons of dignity and opulence were carried before the usurpers themselves. Some of them were put to death for treason, and under pretence of betraying the city to the Romans, upon the testimony of false witnesses, and this was sure to be one of the articles, that they had an intention of going over to the enemy. Those whom Simon had pillaged were carried to John, as John's prisoners were to Simon, as if they had been drinking together, and sharing the prey between them. Their contention was, who should be uppermost, though they were perfectly well agreed in the methods of their tyranny and usurpation. They divided the spoil they took, and it was deemed an unpardonable crime in every one to deprive his companion of his moiety, as it was his just claim according to contract.

It would be needless to recount the iniquities of these miscreants, or the miseries of our nation at this time. To be brief, therefore, I am persuaded there never was so wretched a city and people upon the face of the earth. In order to palliate their inhumanity to strangers, they reviled the very name of the Hebrews, and confessed themselves, as in truth they were, slaves and vagabonds. At length they laid the city in ashes, nay, the very burning was, in effect, their own act, as they forced Titus, against his inclination, upon these extremities. As the upper town was in flames, the Romans indicated a generous compassion, but not a sigh was heard, or a tear seen, amongst the hardened Jews.

CHAP. XII.

The Jews are crucified before the walls of the city. Instances of their malice and resolution. The Romans raise four mighty works in seventeen days. The Jews set fire to the [illegible]. The Romans are driven from their works, and [illegible]. A sharp encounter upon mounting [illegible]. Titus begins to despair of carrying his point.

THE banks were now far advanced, notwithstanding the Roman soldiers had been much annoyed from the walls. Titus then sent out a party of horse, and ordered them to lay in ambush for those Jews who went abroad for provisions. The greater part of these were poor people, who were deterred from deserting by the concern they were in for their relations, nor durst they take their families with them for fear of a discovery. Hunger had rendered them desperate, so that they went out and fell into the ambush of the enemy. When they found themselves hampered, they were compelled by necessity to fight, through fear of some punishment worse than death itself; besides, it was now too late to think of suing for mercy. In fine, they were overpowered, and, after being exposed to all manner of torture, they were crucified in sight of the besieged. Titus was not gratified by these rigorous proceedings, but he did not think it safe either to discharge so many obstinate prisoners, whom he had now at mercy, or spare men enough to look after them, from the service of the army. He likewise entertained hopes that the terror of such examples might move them to bethink themselves, lest it should come to be their own case. They were all crucified, but in several ways and postures; some to express rage, others hatred, and others contempt and mockery. The number of unhappy persons thus put to death was so great that room was wanting for the crosses.

So far was the horror of this dreadful scene from softening the faction, that it produced a contrary effect. The friends and relations of the fugitives, and those who had but the least inclination to peace, were dragged out to the walls, in order to shew them what they had to trust to that went over to the Romans, while they endeavoured to persuade them that the men they saw in chains were not prisoners of war, but deserters that fled for mercy. This device kept many from going off till the truth came to be known, though some immediately escaped to the enemy to avoid starving, which, on a comparative view, appeared much the more miserable death of the two.

Titus, upon this, caused several of his prisoners hands to be cut off, and sent away to John and Simon in such a plight, advising them at the same time, to put an end to the war, without forcing him upon the destruction of the city, as it was not yet too late, upon a seasonable submission, to preserve their lives, their country, and the temple. Titus, however, at the same time advanced his works, quickening and encouraging the men, being resolved very suddenly to follow those works with effect, and gain his point by force, if he could not compass it by reason and persuasion.

The factious Jews, notwithstanding their desperate situation, cast out curses from the walls against both Vespasian and Titus, declared, one and all, their contempt of death, and how much dearer their liberties were to them than their lives. They had the hardiness to add, that, provided they could plague the Romans, they cared not what became either of themselves or their country, which Titus assured them were in danger of perishing. As to their temple, they looked upon the world to be a much more magnificent structure, but made no doubt of its being preserved by him that inhabited therein, in despite of all the threatenings of the enemy.

Antiochus Epiphanes, in the mean time, came up with a train of armed troops, one company of which was composed of men in the prime of life, accoutered after the Macedonian manner, from whence they took the name of Macedonians.

Of all the princes that were ever subject to the Roman empire, the king of Comagena was undoubtedly the most prosperous and successful for the former part of his life; but, in his latter days, his fortune forsook him, and verified the old adage, "That no man can be pronounced happy before death." He had a son of a martial enterprizing spirit, robust, firm, and daring to the utmost degree of rashness. This son observed, upon a certain occasion, that he wondered the Romans stood trifling before the walls, and did not push the attack with vigour. Titus replied, that the way was open, and had no sooner uttered these words, than Antiochus led up his Macedonians to the assault, and gave proof both of his valour and conduct in the action. But his select company were almost all killed or wounded. Having boasted before of the feats they would perform, they could not in honour recede. From this it was evident that Macedonian courage would never conquer without Alexander's fortune: so that they were forced to give up the attempt, and bring off the remainder of the men as they could.

The Romans began to raise their banks on the twelfth day of the month Artemesius, and finished them on the twenty-ninth, after they had laboured hard for seventeen days; for there were now raised four great banks. There was one at the fortress of Antonia, raised by the fifth legion, over against the middle of the Struthian pool. There was another cast up by the twelfth legion, within twenty cubits of the former. The tenth legion, which was more considerable than the other two, threw up another work to the north, opposite the pool called Amygdalon; and at thirty cubits from the last was another, raised by the fifteenth legion, not far from the monument of John, the high-priest.

These works were no sooner finished than John caused a mine to be wrought under that which looked towards Antonia, and several wooden props to be set up along the trench to keep the weight of the earth above from falling, plastering the wood-work with a bituminous matter that would take flames immediately. John had now no more to do than to set fire to the pillars, which, when the props where gone, brought down the whole bulwark with a most hideous noise. There was no fire to be seen at first, but only a smothering dust and smoke, till the flame burst through all opposition, and shewed itself. This was such a surprise to the Romans that they were much embarrassed as to their future proceedings, especially as it would answer no purpose to quench the fire when the ramparts were gone.

Two days after this Simon and his party made an attempt to destroy the other banks, where the Romans had planted their engines, and began to play. There was one Jepthæus, of Galilee, Megassarus, a domestic of queen Mariamne, and one of Adiabena the son of Nabatæus, who from an accident was called Agiras, which signifies, lame. These three with torches in their hands, flew directly to the machines, and breaking through the enemies troops with no more concern than as if they had been among their friends, set fire to them, and, in despite of all opposition with darts and arrows, pursued their design till the engines were all in a flame. These were reputed three of the bravest men that appeared in that war.

Upon the mounting of the fire, the Romans dispatched a detachment from the camp to the relief of their companions, but the Jews in the mean time, poured their shot upon them from the walls, and, without any regard to their own lives or persons, fought it out hand to hand with those that were endeavouring to put a stop to the fire The Romans did all they could to save their engines, the covers of them being consumed already The Jews ventured into the very flames to hinder them, and would not let go their hold, though the iron-work was burning hot The fire passed from thence to the ramparts, nor could it be prevented The Romans at length, finding themselves encompassed with flames and no hopes left of saving the works, withdrew into their camp The Jews had so many reinforcements out of the city, that the increase of their numbers rendered them more and more pressing and inconsiderate, insomuch, that, in the heat of their success, they advanced to the very camp itself, and attacked the guards

The office of these guards according to the rule of the Roman discipline, was to do duty by turns, and relieve one another, and not a man upon pain of death, without mercy, to quit his post under any pretence whatsoever These people, having this charge before-hand, either to fall like men of honour, or suffer an infamous death as deserters, made a gallant resistance, and brought several of those back again, who, betwixt shame and necessity, had abandoned their stations, and, with their engines, put a stop to the excursions of the Jews from the city They made their sallies without any guard or defence for their own security, encountering all they met at a venture, and casting themselves as frantic upon the enemies pikes It must be confessed that the Jews gained more upon the Romans by a rashness and fool-hardiness than by real courage, and that the Romans, on the other hand, gave way rather to the outrageous boldness of the Jews, than any apprehension of mischief they could do them

Titus, at his return from Antonia, where he had been to find out a commodious spot for advancing his attacks, severely reprimanded the soldiers for suffering themselves after gaining the enemies works, to be distressed in their own, and, in a manner, besieged by those that were no better than prisoners themselves Upon this, with some of his choice troops, he surrounded the Jews, and charged them in the flank, while they, on the other side maintained their ground with amazing intrepidity This encounter raised such a dust and clamour, that there was nothing to be seen or heard distinctly, nor friend or foe to be known asunder Neither were the Jews thus obstinate out of any confidence in their own strength, but out of despair of safety, while the Romans were so enraged on the other side, betwixt the punctilio of military honour, and the regard they had for the person of their general, which was then in danger, that, if the Jews had not retired into the town just as they did, they had undoubtedly been all cut to pieces But the Romans were greatly chagrined at the loss of their bulwarks, and to find it the work of but one hour to destroy what had cost so much labour and time in raising This disappointment together with the dismounting of their engines, caused them to despair of gaining the place

CHAP XIII

Titus calls a council of war The result of their deliberations A wall is built round Jerusalem in three days by the Roman army

IN this situation of affairs Titus called a council of his great officers, to give their opinion and advice respecting future operations The most resolute and active were for a general assault, and falling on with the whole army, observing, that hitherto nothing had been done but in skirmishes and parties, and that if once it came to a main action, the Jews would never be able to stand the shock of the very darts and arrows The cooler, and more considerate part were for renewing and repairing the ramparts Others were for having no works at all, and recommended a strict guard to prevent the Jews from bringing provisions into the city, as a famine would do the business of the sword without striking a blow.

Titus, indeed, did not think it honourable to continue inactive at the head of a formidable army, nor was he for fighting with a people so bent upon their own destruction He pointed out to the council the impracticability of casting up any more banks for want of materials, and the difficulty of encompassing the whole city with his army, on account of its magnitude, situation, and the sallies they had reason to expect from the enemy For though they might guard the known passages out of the place yet the Jews, when they found them under the greatest embarrassment, would find out private conveyances, as being well acquainted with all the different avenues, so that carrying provisions by stealth, the siege would be considerably protracted He confessed his fear, that delay would diminish the honour of the conquest, and therefore gave it as his opinion that if they aimed at expedition, joined with security, they must run up a wall round the whole city, by which means all excursions would be prevented, and the Jews compelled either to deliver up the place in the extremity of their despair, or, weakened by pinching want, into an incapacity of defending themselves He added, that this should not hinder him from giving orders for repairing the works, more especially when the situation of things should render it necessary, but that, at the same time, the difficulty of the project respecting the wall should not deter them from undertaking it, as great things were to be brought about by exertion, and the assistance of an Almighty Power

These arguments prevailing with the council, Titus gave orders to his officers to attend immediately to the erecting this wall and to enter upon it with a regular distribution of the whole army into their proper stations The word was no sooner given, than the soldiery seemed transported into a generous emulation of out-doing one another, for, after measuring the ground, and dividing the legions, the same spirit of competition ran through the whole body, insomuch that each soldier was ambitious to please his decurion, each decurion his centurion, each tribune his superior officer, and all this in subordination to their noble general, who was so intent on the design, that he surveyed the whole works, by taking his rounds several times every day

The wall was begun at a place called the camp of the Assyrians, where Titus took up his quarters, and carried forward to the lower Cenopolis, and so by the way of Cedron to the mount of Olives, which was enclosed, on the south, as far as the rock Peristereon, together with a neighbouring hill that overlooks the vale of Siloah From thence it turned a little to the westward, and so on to the valley of the fountain It then went on to the sepulchre of Ananus, the high-priest, and so enclosing the mountain where Pompey had formerly encamped, turned again to the northward, and went to a village called Erebinthonicus, took in Herod's monument towards the east, and there joined one end to the other where it was begun

The compass of this wall was nine and thirty furlongs Thirteen forts were built on the outside of it, the circumference of each amounting to ten furlongs That which might have required some months, was compleated in three days, so that it might be deemed a work of incredible dispatch When Titus had encompassed the city with this wall, he posted guards upon it every night under arms He went the first round himself, Tiberius Alexander went the second, and the commanders of the legions the third The soldiers and the watch slept by turns, so some or other were still upon the guard in the forts all night

CHAP. XIV.

A famine amongst the Jews, attended with a great mortality. The Romans make ostentation of their plenty, to reproach the Jews in their extreme necessity. Four ramparts raised at the tower of Antonia larger than the former.

THE Jews, by the raising of this wall, were not only cut off from all hopes of escape, but driven to the utmost degree of despair by a most outrageous famine, that swept away whole families. The houses were strewed with carcases of women and children, and the narrow lanes with the bodies of old men that lay dead there, while the younger part of the inhabitants wandered about like shadows, being wholly emaciated through hunger. There was no burying the dead. Some wanted strength to perform the office, others wanted will, as being discouraged partly by the great number of them, and partly by an apprehension that their own turn might be next. Some expired in the very act of burying others, and some hastened away to the grave before their time, to ensure a resting place while they were yet living. Yet, in the extremity of all this misery there was not heard so much as a groan or an outcry, as all other passions were stifled in the pain of a tormenting hunger. Those that were ready to expire stood gazing with dry eyes and ghastly looks, upon such as were gone to rest before them. The city was wrapt in profound silence, and enveloped in a kind of deadly gloom. But the most deplorable part of the calamity was the insolence and brutality of robbers, who broke into houses, put to death all they met with, stripped them, and made wanton sport with their naked bodies. If any one called for an hand or a sword to dispatch him, the kind office was refused, and the sufferer left to perish by famine. As they came to the point of death, they directed their eyes towards the temple, grieving to the heart that they should leave those miscreants among the living, who had so abominably prophaned that sacred place.

When the seditious were no longer able to endure the stench of the carcases, they gave orders for their interment at the public charge; but, for want of room to dispose of them, these monsters in inhumanity caused them to be cast down headlong from the walls into the valleys, which was so horrid a spectacle, that Titus, upon taking the round of the place, finding the ditches so infected with pestilential vapours, stretched out his hand in an appeal to heaven, that it was against his will to have it so. Such was the miserable state of the city at that time.

While the faction was thus pent up within the walls, and laboured under the complicated calamities of famine and despair, the Romans passed their days in ease and jollity, and were abundantly supplied with provisions from Syria and the neighbouring provinces. Some of them, from an invidious ostentation of their stores, came up to the very walls, to augment the wants on the one side, by exposing the plenty on the other. But all this had no effect upon the insensible hearts of the seditious, insomuch that Titus, in pure compassion to the remainder of a miserable people, resolved to expedite the casting up new works as much as possible. The only difficulty was the providing materials, for the wood near the city was cut down already, so that they were now forced to fetch timber, for a second supply, at ninety furlongs distance from the place, and there were four ramparts erected at the fortress of Antonia, larger than the former. Titus lost no time, and rendered his dispatch apparent to the faction; but they went on without remorse, as regardless of themselves as others, and delighting in whatever was derogatory and shocking to human nature.

CHAP. XV.

Simon causes Matthias to be put to the torture, and afterwards to be massacred, by Ananus, upon the bodies of his three sons. Ananias is put to death, and the father of Josephus made a prisoner. Judas lays a plot to destroy Simon. Simon surprises the town. Josephus wounded, and reported to be slain. Is rescued by Titus, and recovers. The Jews swallow their gold. Two thousand ripped up in one night. Titus is alarmed at so horrid an outrage. Force of the love of money.

THE tyrant Simon, having first put Matthias to the torture, afterwards put him to death, notwithstanding he got possession of the city through his means. This Matthias was the son of Boethus, a priest in high esteem, and universally beloved by the people. The multitude were distressed by the zealots; and upon John's joining them, Matthias moved the calling in Simon to their assistance, but without the necessary caution of previous conditions. Simon was no sooner in possession of the town, than he treated Matthias as one of his greatest enemies, and imputed the advice he gave to gross simplicity and oversight. Upon this pretence Matthias was arraigned, and accused of holding correspondence with the Romans; and sentence of death was passed upon the father and his three sons, (the fourth having escaped to the Romans,) without so much as hearing what he had to offer in his own vindication.

The only favour this venerable old man had to desire of Simon, in return for the obligation of letting him into the town, was, that he might die first himself; but the inhuman monster refused that grace, and commanded the father to be executed last, to keep him so much the longer in pain. Matthias, in the conclusion, was put to death upon the bodies of his three sons, and in the sight of the Romans, according to Simon's order to Ananus, the son of Bamadas, the most barbarous of all his party. Nor did he content himself barely with the execution of this detestable sentence, but, in a frolic of insolence and derision, when he was just upon the point of striking the stroke, reviled the old man, by telling him he might now see whether the Romans, to whom he intended to go over, would lend him any succour to bring him off. In fine, to consummate the inhumanity, the bodies were all refused burial, by the special command of Simon himself.

Ananias, a priest, the son of Masbalus, nobly descended, and Aristeus, a native of Emmaus, and secretary to the sanhedrim, with fifteen men of rank, were all put to death. The father of Josephus was made prisoner, and proclamation issued that no man should presume to associate with him upon pain of death.

It fell out after this, that Judas, the son of Judas, an officer of Simon, and commander of one of the towers, feeling for the oppression of a miserable people, and anxious at the same time for his own security, took occasion to address a select party of his most trusty friends upon that subject, to the following purport: "How long shall we crouch under the burden of this tyranny? or what hope of safety can we have from such [illegible] merciless a monster? We have sword and [illegible] to encounter, and the Romans in a manner [illegible] of the city. Simon, of all men living, the vilest and most ungrateful; the Romans, on the other hand, are men of faith and honour, so that we have only to deliver up the walls, and preserve ourselves and our country. Nor has Simon any cause of complaint, [illegible] less [illegible] that he will be brought to justice a little sooner than he expected."

The friends of Judas being prevailed on by these arguments, he sent the rest of those that were under him several ways, to prevent the discovery of his design; and, about the third hour of the day, called out to the Romans from the turret, and gave them to understand the resolution they had taken. Some gave no credit to it, others [illegible] delaying the matter, from an assurance they should get possession of the city in a short time without hazard. [illegible] Titus had just drawn some troops up to the wall, [illegible] that [illegible] surprized the town, killing the guard [illegible] throwing the bodies down the wall.

[illegible] Josephus was going round the city, and doing the [illegible] by encouragement and advice, it was [illegible] wounded by a stone from the battlements, upon which the Jews made a desperate sally, and would have carried him off prisoner, if Titus, at that instant, had not sent a party to his rescue. During this skirmish they [illegible] Josephus before he was well recovered from the shock of the blow, so that the faction exulted in the hope of his being slain. The rumour [illegible] current through the city, and gave the inhabitants infinite concern for the loss [illegible], and [illegible] among the Romans. The [illegible] of Josephus being brought to his mother [illegible] she had heard the same, and mourned [illegible] him more. Upon this occasion the women condoled with her, and she deplored her own misfortune, [illegible] in having a son, whom she hoped would have buried [illegible], she was now deprived of the power of performing the funeral rites for her son. The report, however, did [illegible] his [illegible] pleasure, for the danger of the [illegible] was quickly over, and, upon returning to his post, he gave the seditious to understand, that they should pay dearly for what they had done, while he exhorted the people to continue their allegiance to the Romans. The sight of Josephus animated his friends as much as [illegible] dispirited the faction.

In this extremity several deserters went over to the Romans. Some leapt the wall, and made their escape that way, others got off under colour of pursuing the enemy with stones. But, instead of avoiding one calamity within the town, they fell into a worse without, and the [illegible] they contracted by gorging in the Roman camp, were much more mortal than the famine they left at home; for being empty, and puffed up with a dropsical distemper, without a prudent restraint on their appetites, they were in danger of bursting. But the most miserable circumstance remains yet to be related.

There was a fugitive surprized, among the Syrians, in the very act of searching for gold that had been swallowed and [illegible] through him. Now the faction put all to the search, [illegible] was such plenty of gold in the city, that as much [illegible] sold (in the Roman camp) for twelve attic drachms, [illegible] had been [illegible] for twenty-five. But when this [illegible] was discovered, the Arabians and Syrians ript up [illegible] their bellies, in one night, for their treasure, which was one of the greatest barbarities the Jews ever suffered.

Titus was so enraged at the brutality of this action, that he [illegible] ordered every man that was concerned in it to be put to death, if the number of the guilty had not been [illegible] greater than that of the slain. Hereupon he called his officers together, both Roman and auxiliaries, and [illegible] into an expostulatory reproof with them on the subject. He asked if it were possible that any Roman soldier could be guilty of so inhumanly a cruelty for an uncertain advantage, and not blush at the thought of so infamous a pursuit. Turning to the auxiliaries, he demanded, if they thought it reasonable, that the murder and inhumanity of the Syrians and Arabians, in a foreign war, should be imputed to the Romans?

But as some of his own soldiers were supposed to have been guilty of this infamous practice, he threatened death, without mercy, to any man that should presume, in future, to commit such outrages, appointing the legions also, at the same time, to make strict search after all suspected persons, and bring them before him to stand their trial. Avarice, however, overcame all fear of punishment, and a vehement desire of gain appeared to be unconquerable. Other passions have certain bounds, while that alone is unlimited. When a people are given up to a spirit of reprobation, the ordinary means of security turn to their destruction; so that what Titus so severely prohibited in public, was nevertheless executed upon the Jewish deserters in secret. Their custom was, upon any fugitives coming over, first to make sure that none of the Romans should be within sight, and then dissect them for the execrable booty. This horrid practice at length terrified the Jews from deserting, and kept them from going over any longer to the Romans.

CHAP. XVI.

Instances of John's sacrilege. The [illegible] the Jews [illegible] [illegible]. Six hundred thousand dead bodies carried out of the city.

WHEN John could no longer plunder the people, he had recourse to sacrilege, appropriating to his own use and service several donations and oblations consecrated for the worship of God in his holy temple, such as cups, dishes, tables, together with the vessels which were presented by Augustus and his empress, who held that sacred place in the highest veneration. But this miscreant, on the contrary, prophaned it, and stripped it, of the very bounties of strangers, encouraging his associates to take all manner of liberty with holy things, and alledging, that it was reasonable those who fought for the temple should live by it. He made no scruple of distributing, among the people, the sacred wine and oil that was reserved in the inner part of the temple for sacrifices; and as John made the distribution, the multitude took their parts of it, drinking and anointing without any difficulty. I cannot relate these circumstances without horror; and I am persuaded that if the Romans had deferred calling these abandoned wretches to account any longer, this city would either have been deluged by water, or swallowed up by an earthquake, or destroyed like Sodom, by thunder and lightning; the Jews, if possible, being more abandoned, insomuch, that for their notorious prodigacy the whole race was extirpated. It would, indeed, be endless to relate the several instances of their misery.

Manneus, the son of Lazarus, who had the command of one of the city gates, gave them the following account: that, from the time of the Roman army's encampment before the town (that is from the tenth day of the month Xanthicus, to the first of the month Panemus) there passed through that gate 115,080 dead bodies, and this was no more than what fell to his share to notice by virtue of a commission for that purpose; besides those that were buried by their relations, or, in other words, thrown out of the city, for there was no other mode of burial.

After this, upon the computation of divers men of rank who came over to Titus, there were no less than 600,000 poor people carried out of the gates, besides others innumerable, that, for want of friends to remove them, [illegible] out of the city, were piled in heaps, and [illegible] up in large houses. Wheat, at this time, was estimated at a talent, or medimnus, the bushel; and, since walling up the city so close, they were cut off from all provisions, and brought to that pitch of extremity, that they were [illegible] to search the common sewers for sustenance, and to feed upon the most nauseous articles. The very relation of these calamities drew pity from the Romans; but the faction in the city, who saw and felt their sufferings, were wholly insensible that their own rebellious obstinacy had been the cause. They persisted under the fatality of a blind infatuation, that led them into the irreparable ruin of themselves, their city, and their country.

FLAVIUS JOSEPHUS

ON THE

WARS OF THE JEWS.

BOOK VII.

CHAP. I.

The Jews reduced to extremity in Jerusalem and its environs [illegible]. The Romans are attacked by the Jews, who attempt firing their engines, but fail. The Romans attack the tower of Antonia, which is gallantly defended by the Jews. The Romans fail to [illegible]. Titus harangues his army. Sabinus signalizes himself by his bravery.

THE miseries of Jerusalem daily increased, and the faction became more and more fierce and turbulent, as they became more and more wretched, the famine now preying upon great and small, without distinction. The multitude of carcases that lay in heaps one upon another, afforded an horrid spectacle and produced a pestilential stench, which hindered them from making sallies out of the city upon the enemy; but all this excited in them neither terror or pity; so that after destroying one another, they proceeded in their endeavours, to oppose the Romans, as Providence had doomed them to destruction; for they did not contend so much from any hope they had of victory, as from a degree of rage and despair.

The Romans were greatly distressed for materials to finish their works; however by means of cutting down all the woods within ninety furlongs of the city, they raised their platforms in the space of one and twenty days. Never was a more dismal reverse of appearance than the present. That spot, which was once deemed a paradise, was now become a desert; and, instead of the most beautiful country upon the face of the earth, for curious gardens and fruitful plantations, not a tree was left standing, or any thing to be seen, but the marks of desolation and ruin, insomuch that strangers could not forbear weeping to see the difference between the former Jerusalem and the present, for war had so defaced its beauty and glory, that it was hardly to be known; and the place that was once so peculiarly distinguished for its grandeur, was now nothing more than a scene of desolation.

Upon finishing the works, the Jews and Romans were equally solicitous for the event. The Jews were either for destroying them by one decisive effort, or losing the city; and one disappointment on the other hand, would put them out of condition to repair them; for no more wood could possibly be procured, and the soldiers were harrassed out with fatigue of the service. The Romans, however were more afflicted for the obstinacy of the city than the Jews themselves who maintained their resolution in spite of every thing. When the Romans found themselves over-reached by stratagem, their invention eluded, the wall proof against their engines, and themselves foiled at every manœuvre, their courage failed, especially as they found they had an enemy, that, instead of sinking under the pressure of faction, famine, and war, rather gathered spirit from the opposition. They inferred, from their bravery, in defiance of every disadvantage, that they would atchieve wonders if they had fortune on their side. From these considerations the Romans doubled their guards.

John and his party, in the castle of Antonia, did all that could be done before the engines were mounted, to prevent the danger of a breach. But it was only labour lost, for the design they had of setting fire to the engines was frustrated. In fact, they wanted union and vigour, and so were forced to a retreat. As the Jews fell short of themselves on the one hand, so the Romans exceeded themselves on the other, in planting so strict a guard on the bulwarks, that there was no possibility of doing any execution by fire; besides they were resolved every man to die upon the spot, rather than submit to so irreparable a mischief, as the losing of that post. Nothing indeed could put soldiers more on the mettle, than to see brave men deluded, their courage baffled and injured by an audacious temerity, military discipline and experience confounded by popular outrage, and the Romans, in fine, worsted by the Jews

While the Jews advanced the Romans were ready with their darts to encounter them, and the foremost that fell, not only hindered his next man, but the exemplary danger of the one served as a warning for the other. Some of those that pressed upon the enemies weapons, were surprized at the dignity of the Roman order, others at their numbers, and some again marched off with their wounds. At length they reproached one another for their cowardice, and retired without doing any thing.

The attack was made upon the first day of the month Panamus, and the Jews having now retreated, the Romans advanced with their engines towards Antonia, in defiance of all they were able to do by fire, sword, stones, and all other implements of hostility. Though the Jews depended much upon the strength of their walls against the battery of the engines, they exerted their utmost efforts to keep the Romans at a distance from fixing them. The inference they drew from this exertion of the Jews was, that they were conscious to themselves, Antonia was in danger, and this apprehension was the cause of it. They continued the battery, and the wall stood hitherto firm, but the Romans fortifying themselves, under the defence of their bucklers, against the weapons from above, they applied themselves to digging and mining; and when, with indefatigable labour, they had loosened four stones under the foundation of the work, they betook themselves, when night drew on, to rest. In this interval that part of the wall which John had undermined for the destruction of the former works, fell down on a sudden. This unexpected accident alarmed both parties. The Jews, who had reason to be troubled at it, especially when they might have foreseen and prevented it, were yet in as high spirits as if Antonia had been still standing, and the joy of the Romans on the other hand, for an accident that appeared so seasonable, was as quickly dashed upon the sight of another wall, that John had carried up within the former, only the latter seemed to be the least defensible of the two, both as the ruin of the one facilitated the passage to the other, and as the work of the new wall could not yet be so firm and settled as that of Antonia. But no one durst scale it, from a conviction that whoever attempted to scale it must certainly be killed.

Titus now considering that the alacrity of soldiers in military exploits was to be excited by hopes and fair words, and that exhortations and promises frequently cause men to forget the hazards they run, and sometimes to despise death itself, summoned the flower of his army, and thus addressed them.

"My brave fellow-soldiers, there can be no room for "encouragement where there is no danger. Exhortations "are more properly for doubtful cases, wherein all brave "men will advise themselves. It will be a hard work, "I must confess, to master the wall we have here before "us, but great souls are given us for great and glorious "exploits, and death is desirable, when it is followed "with immortal fame for a reward. Besides, it shall be "my care to reward those that deserve it. In the first "place, I would have you think on that for your en-"couragement that works a contrary effect upon others; "I mean the insuperable patience and constancy of the "Jews in the worst of fortunes. What can be more ig-"nominious than for the military Romans, that study "war in peace, and are so wont to conquer, that it is "almost natural to them to be victorious, for these, I say, "to be beaten out of their strength and courage by the "Jews, and at the end of the day too, with God's provi-"dence most evidently on their side, and the enemy nothing "to support them, but the fury of their own extravagant "despair? besides, that they suffer daily under the judicial "vengeance of God's high displeasure in our favour: wit-"ness their factions, famine, siege, and the ruin of their "walls, even without battery, which are but so many de-"clarations from heaven against them, to our advantage. "It will not become us therefore, to crouch to our "inferiors, and to cast off the Divine protection. Shall "the Jews, that have been trained up to slavery, "and consequently have little or no credit to lose upon "that account, shall these people, I say, have the brave-"ry to charge into the middle of the Roman troops, and "look death in the face, rather than run a risque of the "same condition over again, and all this in a frolic of "ostentation and vanity, without the least hope or pros-"pect of success? And shall we, on the other hand, that "are effectually the lords and masters of the universe, "and in a manner entitled to a right of conquest, shall "we, I say, lye still and inactive, without so much as "one bold attempt upon our adversaries, waiting only in "our arms, till hunger and fortune shall give up the ene-"my, without any difficulty, into our hands? It is but "taking Antonia, and the town is our own. Or, in "case we should meet with any resistence from within, "(which I do not expect,) it would not be worth men-"tioning, for the advantage of the higher ground lays "the enemy at our feet, without all hope of recovery. "I do not take upon me here to celebrate the history of "those heroes, that, having ended their days in the field "of battle, yet live in the memory of future ages to "perpetuity. As for those worthless wretches that think "of going down body and soul into the grave together, "I wish them a death suitable, to so abject a mind. "Since death is inevitable, and that the sword compar-"ed with any disease, is the easier death of the two, "how mean and degenerate a cowardice would it be to "withdraw the use of a life from the service of the "public, which is an indispensible debt of nature, and a "man's country?"

"This may look, perhaps, as if I took the storming "of this wall to be certain death, but resolution is a-"bove danger, and he that fears nothing, despairs of "nothing. The fall of the first wall has opened a way "to the rest, and the second will be easily over-borne, "if you do but encourage and support one another, only "stand firm, and your very numbers will do the work; "and who knows at last, but you may carry your point "without blood too? You are to prepare, however, for "a vigorous opposition, and to assure yourselves, that, "upon any advantage, either by stratagem, or by force, "they will never be able to withstand us. As for him "that first mounts the breach, it shall be my care, whe-"ther he lives or dies, to crown him with honours and "rewards."

This address of the general cast such a damp upon the soldiers, that only one person was animated by it. His name was Sabinus, a Syrian by birth, one of [illegible], and a man eminent both for courage and [illegible]. He had not a military appearance, being short in stature, and of a wan complexion, but possessed a soul capable of valiant enterprizes. This man, bowing to Titus, thus addressed him. "I do here tender myself to the ge-"neral as the first man to give the assault. May the "result answer my good will. If I should miscarry in "the attempt, I shall have the honour of laying down "my life for my master, which renders it indifferent to "me whether I live or die."

Upon these words, with his sword drawn in his right hand, and his shield over his head in his left, he advanced towards the wall about the sixth hour of the day, with a train of eleven men, that followed him purely in emulation of his magnanimity. Sabinus, in this action, encountered the enemy's weapons with a resolution more than human, and several of his followers were wounded in the attack; nevertheless, he pressed forward, amidst darts and arrows, till he had well nigh mounted the wall, and forced the Jews to abandon their station for fear of a reinforcement of greater numbers to overpower them. But alas! an accident frustrated this heroic attempt, for, when this valiant soldier had nearly gained his point, he was unfortunately overborne by the fall of a stone. The noise alarming the Jews, they looked behind, and finding Sabinus lying alone, they all fell upon him with their darts. He defended himself upon his knees, with his buckler over his head, as long as he could, and revenged himself upon his enemies with his sword, killing some, and wounding others, till, in the end, being able to strike no longer, he breathed his last, covered with wounds.

The valour of this man deserved a more propitious fate, though he died as great as he lived. Three of his companions were dashed to pieces with stones from the top of the wall, and the remaining eight were carried off wounded to the camp. This action happened upon the third day of the month Panemus.

CHAP. II.

The Romans march up to Antonia, find the guards sleeping and possess [illegible]. A desperate [illegible] with great slaughter [illegible] sides.

SHORTLY after this, twenty of the Roman vanguard upon the works, the ensign of the fifth legion, two horsemen, and a trumpeter, made a silent march over the ruins up to Antonia, in the dead of the night, without any opposition, and finding the enemy's advance guard fast asleep, slew them, got possession of the wall, and ordered the trumpet to sound. Upon this alarm the rest awoke and fled without waiting to see what numbers had entered the place; but, between fear and fancy they took it for granted they were very strong.

Titus, upon intelligence of this exploit, put himself at the head of a chosen band, and advanced up to the ruins. The Jews were so startled at this surprize, that some of them made for the inner temple, and others towards the mine that John had wrought to supplant the Roman works; but the two factions of John and Simon giving up all for lost, as the Romans should once get into the temple, there followed a most desperate contest before the very doors of the place, the one fighting for life, the other for victory. Lances and darts being of no use on either side, the matter in the upshot was decided by the sword.

In this confusion they fought at random, the men being intermixed one with another, without order or distinction, by reason of the narrowness of the place, and a medley of outcries prevented their hearing any word of command. The slaughter was great on both sides, and the ground covered with arms and carcases. There was no room either to fly or pursue, but, as they had the better or the worse, they advanced or retired, exulting on the one hand, and lamenting on the other. There was a necessity for the front of both armies either to kill or be killed, for there was no distance left betwixt them for a retreat.

The battle lasted ten hours, that is, from the ninth hour of the night to the seventh the next morning. The furious obstinacy of the Jews carried it from the resolution and conduct of the Romans, and happily for them it was so, as their all [illegible] was at stake. But the Romans were content, for the present, with getting possession of the tower of Antonia, with only one part of their army, for the legions upon whom they chiefly depended were not as yet come up.

CHAP. III.

A gallant exploit of one Julian, a centurion. The Romans are shut up in the tower of Antonia. The names of the Jews that signalized themselves in this action.

THERE was in the Roman army one Julian, a native of Bithynia, and a centurion. He was a man of eminent fortitude, resolution and martial skill, as any that had signalized themselves in the course of the war. Standing by Titus at the tower of Antonia, and observing the Romans give way to the Jews, he took an opportunity of leaping on a sudden into the thickest of the enemy, and gave them chace in his single person up to the innermost court of the temple. The multitude fled from him in crowds, being, as it were, thunderstruck at such amazing exertions of strength and resolution, which seemed to them to be more than human.

Julian pursued his course; some he overturned, others he overtook, and put to death; nor, indeed, was there any sight that appeared more wonderful in the eyes of Titus, or more terrible to his enemies. But this gallant man was at length himself pursued by fate, which, as mortal, he could not escape; for having his shoes shod with iron nails, according to the fashion of other soldiers, as he was running on the pavement near the temple, he slipt, and the Romans, upon the clash of his armour, broke into an outcry, fearing he might have done himself a mischief. The Jews fell upon him at the same time with swords and darts, while he fenced himself with his buckler; but, as he attempted to rise, he was borne down by multitudes. Such were his vigour and agility, that, even at his length upon the ground, they had some difficulty to dispatch him, till at last, through loss of blood, and none to succour him, he gave up the ghost.

Titus was deeply affected to see so brave a man made so public and deplorable a spectacle, and especially to find himself under an utter impossibility of saving so valuable a life. There were others, indeed, who might have relieved him, if they had had the courage to attempt it. Julian, in fine, after a long struggle with human frailty, and leaving several of his murderers wounded behind him, closed his life to his immortal honour both with friends and foes. The Jews at last carried off the dead body, and after giving another check to the Romans, shut them up in the tower of Antonia.

The Jews that signalized themselves in this action, were Alexas and Gyptheus, of John's party; and of Simon's faction, Malachias and Judas, the son of Merton, James, the son of Sozas, commander of the Idumæans, and of the zealots, two brothers, Simon and Judas, the sons of Jair.

CHAP. IV.

Titus gives orders for the demolition of the tower of Antonia. [illegible] John to an engagement. John [illegible] the Jews according to commission from Titus. [illegible] instance of the piety and prudence of Josephus. [illegible] of Jesus [illegible] The Jews [illegible] of the Romans. The general [illegible] Romans [illegible] the temple [illegible].

TITUS now resolving to give orders to his soldiers to dig up the foundations of the tower of Antonia, to make a ready passage for his army, called for Josephus, and (being informed that on that day, which was the seventeenth of the month Panemus, the solemnity of their daily sacrifice could not be performed for want of a congregation, and that the people were much troubled at it) sent him a second time upon the same errand. The purport of it was, "that if John was inclined to fight, he might bring what number he pleased, and put matters to the decision of battle, provided only that the city and temple might not be exposed to the common ruin, and that he would cease to prophane the name and worship of the Almighty God, or, if he was desirous of reviving the religious services that had been for some time discontinued, he might appoint which of the Jews he pleased to officiate."

Josephus, not thinking it sufficient to acquit himself of this commission to John alone, mounted an eminence, and then communicated to the multitude the pleasure of Titus, in the Hebrew language, and in the tenderest terms of which he was capable, begging the Jews to have compassion on their country, and prevent the burning of the temple before it was too late, by solemnizing their prayers and sacrifices as formerly. The people sent a melancholy [illegible] upon this occasion; but the tyrant John, after [illegible] Joseph [illegible]

[illegible] responded this irony, "That [illegible] is [illegible] of Jerusalem, [illegible] was the city of [illegible]" Josephus interrupting him, thus replied

"[illegible] have made conscience of keeping every [illegible] and of paying your duty to that [illegible] you pretend to look for help. What [illegible] of that man, but in the worst of enemies, that should rob you of your daily bread? Yet, [illegible] time, you make no difficulty of robbing [illegible] his daily sacrifices and oblations. [illegible] with the Romans, but for standing up in defence of your own laws and worship, [illegible] you yourself suppress? Nor [illegible] there so much [illegible] change in religion and state! Strangers and [illegible] friends [illegible] and the [illegible] barbarians one to [illegible] As [illegible] of Jechonias, king of the [illegible] the Babylonians made war upon Jerusalem, [illegible] the town upon choice before it was [illegible] relations, [illegible] and temple from [illegible] honour of his [illegible] in an anniversary for [illegible] of that illustrious action. I [illegible] more pertinent or seasonable [illegible] Let your distress or offence be what it [illegible] the Romans will pardon it. [illegible] yourselves who [illegible] they are to whom I [illegible] this [illegible] and in whose [illegible] I [illegible] that I should ever [illegible] to forget what I owe to the place of [illegible] and to the laws of my country. After all this, what do I get for my good-will, but fresh [illegible] and injuries? Yet all this is [illegible] for endeavouring to preserve a [illegible] of people that fate and Providence are resolved to destroy. [illegible] than the frequent predictions we meet with in history, pointing at the destruction of this miserable city? and that the time of it is near at hand, when the Jews are tearing out the [illegible] one another? This is so far come to pass that not only the houses, but the temple are polluted with the blood of your own tribes. What is all this but the divine judgment of God, putting the Jews in the hands of the Romans, which will probably end in [illegible] the city by fire."

Josephus was interrupted by an overflow of tears, which [illegible] the Romans to compassionate his affliction, and admire his humanity; but the more he lamented the deplorable [illegible] the more implacable were John [illegible] against the Romans, as well as [illegible] of getting Josephus into their power. But his [illegible] great influence with the better sort. Many of the faction also, finding the case desperate, and giving [illegible] have gone over to the Romans, [illegible] of their own guards. Others there were who took [illegible] of eluding the vigilance of their companions, among whom were the high-priests, Joseph and Jesus, the three sons of Ishmael, who was beheaded at Cyrene, four sons of Matthias, and one son of another Matthias, who made his escape to the Romans, after Simon the son of Gioras, had put the father and three of his sons to death, as before-mentioned. There were many persons of condition that deserted with the priests, who were graciously received by Titus Cæsar, but sent away to Gophna for the present, with a promise of large possessions to be distributed amongst them at the end of the war. Titus gave them this assignment apart, to avoid the uneasiness of mixing with people of different manners, laws, and customs, and they were highly pleased with their allotment.

When they were all withdrawn to their colony, and none of them seen any longer in the city, the faction spread a report, that these deserters were slain by the Romans, to deter the rest from making their escape. This device succeeded once again as before; but Titus, [illegible] aware of the design, recalled them from Gophna, [illegible] ordered them to take the tour of the walls with Josephus, and shew themselves to the town, which brought over more proselytes to the Romans than ever. As they were assembled upon this occasion, they stood before the Romans, and pressing the faction with importunities and lamentation, intreated them either to receive the Romans into the city, and deliver their country, or otherwise quit the temple, to prevent the firing it, which the Romans would never agree to but upon the last extremity. This rendered the faction more outrageous against the fugitives, with their stones, darts, arrows, slings, and engines, [illegible] being planted at the very gates, the temple [illegible] repository of arms more than a place of religious [illegible] ship, and the dead bodies lay as thick every [illegible] about it as if it had been a common burial ground.

Those sacrilegious wretches rushed into the [illegible] sanctuary with their arms still warm and reeking with the blood of their countrymen; nay, they went to the extremest degree of impiety and profaneness, [illegible] the Romans, to the [illegible] for the Jews, had a greater reverence for that [illegible] than the [illegible] themselves. There was not a man in the [illegible] Titus who had not a veneration for [illegible] the Supreme Being that was there [illegible] and did not heartily wish for [illegible] while mercy was yet to be obtained.

Titus was so deeply affected with the [illegible] of these wretched people, that he once more endeavoured, by an appeal as follows, to bring the faction to reason:

"Tell me, inhuman miscreants! what were all these [illegible] and partitions for about this holy place, with the [illegible] and Greek inscriptions upon these pillars, forbidding all people, upon a penalty, not to pass this enclosure? Nor have we ourselves been less tender of your privileges, in making it death for any man to pass these bounds, not excepting the Romans themselves. [illegible] comes the sanctuary, after this, to be prophaned with assassinations and murders, and the temple [illegible] with blood, foreign and domestic? I appeal to all the [illegible] of my country, and to the late patron of this holy temple, (who hath now forsaken it,) to my [illegible] the Jews that have joined with me, and [illegible] to yourselves, that I am innocent of all these abominations; and I do farther promise, that if you will [illegible] in quitting this holy place, no [illegible] offer [illegible] indignity; for I will preserve and protect your temple."

CHAP. V.

The [illegible] full [illegible] Titus [illegible] He forms [illegible] Antonia. [illegible] and confusion. The R[illegible] Jewish officers [illegible] The Jews fire the temple [illegible] of one Jonathan [illegible]

THUS, upon this occasion, had Josephus [illegible] his interpreter; but the faction erroneously construed his generous application to them unto timidity, and thereupon grew more insolent and outrageous. The noble Roman therefore, finding they had no regard either for the preservation of the temple or themselves, took a resolution, though against his inclination, to prosecute the war. As there was space sufficient to [illegible], he detached thirty out of every [illegible] the tribune of every thousand, and [illegible] commander in chief. With this detachment [illegible] upon the enemy's guards [illegible] hour of the night, and Titus himself was to [illegible] the attack. But, upon a council of war, the [illegible] opinion, that it would be more advisable [illegible] himself upon Fort Antonia, where he might [illegible] acquitted themselves, without [illegible] of danger in his own person, besides, that [illegible] his people to improve their bravery in the [illegible].

[illegible] the opinion of his officers and friends, [illegible] tower on Fort Antonia, where he [illegible] judge of the whole action, charging his officers [illegible] time, to observe minutely who did well or [illegible], might be rewarded or punished accordingly. [illegible] no longer suspended but orders were given, [illegible] the attack. The Romans did [illegible] asleep, as was expected, so that the [illegible] readily to action, [illegible] their commanders [illegible] multitudes to accord them [illegible] the numbers that [illegible] their own people, without [illegible] betwixt the noise of [illegible] the night, the knew neither [illegible] following the impulse of blind [illegible] their way to venture [illegible] themselves in order under the cover of their [illegible] one another by the word [illegible] the enemy whereas the [illegible] confusion, and, by taking foes [illegible], and friends for foes, destroyed more of their own men than the Romans [illegible] break of day, when [illegible] evaded their order, they proceeded more regularly, [illegible] their darts and arrows on both sides with as much [illegible] not been engaged in the night. The Romans, who had Titus for their judge, the witness and spectator of their behaviour, looked upon the valour of [illegible] as the foundation of their future fortunes, [illegible] fought, one and all with a noble emulation, [illegible] at the same time, had their lives and their [illegible], with the [illegible] John at the head of them, exciting some with fair words and threatening others with menaces or blows. The fight was mostly hand to hand, but with various changes backwards and forwards, for there was scarcely room for flight or pursuit. Antonia was, in effect, a kind of theatre of war, and Titus and his friends the spectators, calling out to the actors to follow their advantage, at other times to stand their ground, as they saw occasion, and nothing passed that escaped their observation.

The contest lasted from the ninth hour of the night to the fifth the next day, both sides maintaining their ground till it came, in the conclusion, to a drawn battle. Several noble Romans behaved like heroes, and those who signalized themselves amongst the Jews were the following, Judas the son of Merton, Simon, the son of Josias, Jason, the son of Sosa, and Simon, the son of Cathlas, who were Idumæans. Of John's party were Gyphæus and Alexas, and of the zealots was Simon, the son of Jai[illegible].

In the course of seven days the foundations of Antonia were all turned up, and a broad way cut for the legions to march up to the wall, where they immediately fell to work upon four banks. The first was against the corner of the inner temple, that looks north and east, the second against the gallery, to the northward, betwixt the two gates, the third toward the west porch of the outward temple, and the fourth towards the north porch. But the bringing of the materials an hundred furlongs from the place, was attended with infinite charge and labour, besides the many surprizes they met with in the way, for the Romans were too confident and careless, and the Jews rash enough to attempt any thing.

It was the practice of several of the Romans when they went out to forage, to turn their horses loose to graze, and it was as common for the Jews to sally out upon [illegible] opportunity, and carry them off. This happened so often, that Titus imputed it, at last, rather to the negligence of the Romans, than the daring efforts of the Jews. Nor did he judge erroneously, for, upon punishing some of the [illegible] for the loss of their horses, it secured all the rest, as they were all more wary in future.

When the Romans had raised their banks and [illegible] themselves in a posture to begin their attacks upon the temple, many of the faction were so pressed by famine, or the fear [illegible] of their ravages, that they assembled in a body, about the eleventh hour of the day, and made an assault upon the Roman guard towards the mount of Olives, in hopes of [illegible] taking them unawares, or [illegible] them without [illegible]. [illegible] Romans, apprized of their [illegible] with all the strength they were able to make, and [illegible] most desperate attempt [illegible] projected upon the [illegible]. It came, [illegible] to a bloody [illegible] both [illegible] [illegible] the Romans [illegible] the foolish [illegible] for [illegible] the other [illegible] graceful in the Romans to suffer [illegible] were now [illegible], and the Jews had [illegible] themselves, but by [illegible] the Romans.

An instance of the fortitude of one Roman [illegible] upon this occasion, is worthy of [illegible]. The Jews being routed and pursued by the [illegible] into the valley, this Pedanius pressing full speed [illegible] took a common man, [illegible] on foot. Such was his strength, [illegible] that he took the fugitive Jew off his horse, [illegible] and carried him as his prisoner to Titus, who [illegible] of the young Roman, but ordered the prisoner to [illegible] punished with death [illegible] the Roman [illegible], after which he prosecuted his design of [illegible] the temple, and [illegible] the banks.

The Jews finding themselves every day become more weak, as the war grew more hot, [illegible] temple itself, followed the example of [illegible] distempers, by cutting off the infected part to [illegible]. According to their [illegible], they began with setting fire to that part of the gallery that [illegible] from the north to the east, faced Antonia, where they made [illegible] twenty cubits, and thereby made a beginning of [illegible] their sanctuary with their own hands.

On the twenty fourth day [illegible] the month [illegible] the Romans put the [illegible] gallery [illegible] fifteen cubits [illegible] the Jews [illegible] and so went on, [illegible] Antonia. They might [illegible] flames, but they not [illegible] spreading to [illegible] their own advantage. However [illegible] daily skirmishes and [illegible] every [illegible] temple.

There was at this time a man amongst the Jews [illegible] stature, [illegible] appearance, of neither birth [illegible] to claim respect, whose name was Jonathan. This [illegible] went out to the monument of [illegible] high-priest, and there in a vain-glorious [illegible] any man of the whole Roman army to [illegible] in hand. No man dared appeared [illegible] used, and others [illegible] disposed to encounter with [illegible] of death, who feared neither God [illegible] [illegible] could not be tempted [illegible] When this [illegible] Jews [illegible] contempt, defending [illegible] one Pudens, of the equeſtrian order, incenſed at his taunts, ſtood forth, and accepted the challenge. The contempt in which he held the inſignificant Jew rendered him raſh and careleſs, ſo that unfortunately ſtumbling, Jonathan took the advantage, and ſlew him when he was down, [illegible] then ſtanding on the dead body, brandiſhed his ſword, [illegible] and ſhook his ſhield with his left hand, [illegible] over his antagoniſt at his feet, and deriding [illegible] in the Roman army. While the Jew was [illegible] height of his exultation, Priſcus, a centurion, ſhot [illegible] through the heart with [illegible] which laid him dead upon the body of his enemy, and was deemed a [illegible] judgment upon him for [illegible] an action [illegible] courage, but intemperate zeal.

CHAP VI

[illegible] the temple and the [illegible]. The Jews [illegible] the Romans [illegible] a ſtratagem. [illegible] the [illegible] of Longus, and the [illegible] of Artorius.

THE faction in the temple now openly endeavoured [illegible] to beat off the Roman ſoldiers that were upon the [illegible], and, on the [illegible] of the month afore-[illegible] contrived the following ſtratagem. They [illegible] of the weſtern porch, betwixt the top and [illegible], with a quantity of dry wood, ſulphur, and [illegible], and then pretending to give way upon [illegible] themſelves to be beaten out, as if they [illegible]. Many of the raſh and [illegible] among the Romans followed them cloſe [illegible], and [illegible] ladders to make good what [illegible] had quitted, but the cool and diſpaſſionate [illegible] conceived it to be a ſtratagem, and remain-[illegible] ſituation. Upon the Romans crowd-[illegible] the porch, the Jews ſet fire to it, and all was [illegible] in a blaze, to the aſtoniſhment of thoſe that [illegible] and moſt deſperate horror [illegible] confuſion of the reſt. Some plunged themſelves into [illegible], others leaped headlong down the horſes, [illegible] were ſmothered in the flames, and others run upon their [illegible] to prevent one death by another.

[illegible] could not but commiſerate thoſe who thus miſe-[illegible], though they raſhly ventured upon the at-[illegible] orders, and thereby ſubjected themſelves to [illegible] death by their own law, if they eſcaped [illegible] ſtratagem of the enemy. They had this com-[illegible] diſtreſs that, to balance the loſs of their [illegible] the love and pity of their prince for whom [illegible], as they could ſee him calling and labouring [illegible] to do all that was poſſible for their relief, [illegible] inſtance of his affection was looked upon as a [illegible] to his immortal honour. Thoſe who ſurvived [illegible] cataſtrophe were beſet by the Jews, and after a [illegible], every man of them put to the ſword.

[illegible] brave men fell in this deſperate adventure, but [illegible] more valiant than one Longus, who, in juſtice and honour, cannot be paſſed over in ſilence upon ſo memo-[illegible] occaſion. This Longus was a Roman, and in the vigour of his youth. The Jews found him a daring and dangerous man, and had no way of cutting him off, unleſs they could get him down to them, upon honour that he ſhould return ſafe again without any violence to his perſon. His brother Cornelius taking notice of this, called out to him on the other hand, adjuring him not to do any thing that either his country or himſelf ſhould have reaſon to be aſhamed of. Longus upon this drew his ſword, and ſlew himſelf in the ſight of both parties.

There was one Artorius that delivered himſelf from [illegible] by his ſubtlety. Being reduced to an extremity, he called out to Lucius, one of his fellow ſoldiers, [illegible] declaring, "that if he would catch him in his arms, and break his fall, he would make him his heir." Artorius accordingly took his leap, and the other, diſpoſing himſelf to receive him, the weight of the [illegible] daſhed the other with ſuch violence on the ſtone pavement, that he immediately expired.

This melancholy accident greatly affected the Romans, but it kept them afterwards more upon their guard againſt the frauds and ſtratagems of the Jews, by which they had been moſt eſſentially injured, in divers inſtances.

The porch was burnt as far as the tower that John erected in his war with Simon, and the Jews, after burning of the Romans, brake down the reſt. The following day the Romans ſet fire to the north porch, and carried it before them to that on the eaſt, that overlooks the valley of Cedron from a ſtupendous precipice. Such was the ſtate of the temple at that time.

CHAP VII

A dreadful famine in Jeruſalem, with the [illegible] it.

TO add to the diſtreſs which befel a devoted nation, a dreadful famine now raged in Jeruſalem, and the miſeries that attended it were inconceivable. The city was well nigh depopulated. The bare mention of food was ſufficient to create family diſcord, and diſſolve friendſhip cemented by the deareſt ties. Thoſe that were evidently expiring with hunger, could [illegible] at the laſt gaſp, and they would ſearch the very bowels of the dead for bread. If they were diſappointed [illegible] expectation, deſpair hurried them up and down, [illegible] like mad dogs, and ſtaggering like drunken men, [illegible] ſacking the ſame houſes over and over again. Their hunger was ſo intolerable, that they gathered and [illegible] things as the moſt filthy animals would not touch, nor did they abſtain from their girdles, ſhoes, nor the very leather which belonged to their ſhields. An handful of old hay was ſold for four attics. But why ſhould I [illegible] out their dreadful judgment by referring to things [illegible], when I have a perſonal inſtance to cite, that cannot be equalled in hiſtory, either among the Greeks or Barbarians? As the fact cannot be related or heard [illegible] horror, I was inclined to ſuppreſs it, but, upon reflection [illegible] there were ſo many living witneſſes to confirm it, I hold it my duty to hand it down upon record to poſterity.

CHAP VIII

Mary, a woman of rank and quality, is ſo tormented [illegible] hunger, that ſhe eats the fleſh of her own infant. [illegible] proteſtation of Titus upon the occaſion.

THERE was a certain woman that dwelt beyond Jordan, whoſe name was Mary. Her father was Eleazar, of the village of Bethezob, which ſignifies the houſe of hyſſop. She was opulent, as well as noble, celebrated, and had fled to Jeruſalem with the reſt of the multitude, where, at this time, ſhe was with them beſieged. The tyrant ſtripped her of her moſt precious treaſure which ſhe had brought out of Perea, and her houſe was [illegible] broke open and rifled by the ſoldiers, for either goods or proviſions, which ſhe had concealed. In conſequence of ſuch outrages, ſhe reviled the faction in the moſt opprobrious terms, but could not work them up to [illegible] of indignation as to put her to death. When ſhe found herſelf brought to the laſt extremity, totally deprived of the means of ſupporting exiſtence, the pains of a tormenting famine having already ſeized her, ſhe [illegible] to have given herſelf up to all the fury of the direſt want, and formed the moſt horrid and unnatural reſolution that can either be conceived or expreſſed.

She had an infant ſucking at her breaſt, which [illegible]-ing up, and looking tenderly upon, ſhe burſt out into this rhapſody. "What ſhall I ſay to thee, unfortunate child,

DAUGHTER of ELEAZAR ... SIEGE and FAMINE at JERUSALEM.

[illegible] brought into the world under a complication [illegible] such dreadful judgments as war, famine, and [illegible]? To which of the three shall I reserve thee? [illegible] Romans will give thee thy life, perhaps, but not [illegible] liberty. Famine will also prevent slavery; but [illegible] shalt find our present tyrants incomparably worse [illegible] the other two. Be thou then my food, and finally [illegible] complete the history of the Jews with the only ex[illegible] abomination that is yet wanting to perfect their [illegible]." With these words she slew her child, dressed [illegible] and having eaten one part herself, set by the re[illegible] and kept it covered. Some of the faction en[illegible] and smelling the unusual scent, threaten[illegible] death if she did not bring out her [illegible] this [illegible] the remainder of [illegible] and the robbers being struck with [illegible] "This is [illegible] child, and [illegible] I have myself pre[illegible] the other [illegible] tender [illegible] however, [illegible] as I have one [illegible] for me." They [illegible] horror and amazement, as the [illegible] they [illegible] shown.

[illegible] of this horrid deed soon spread throughout [illegible] not equal terror and de[illegible] part in the crime [illegible] aversion to life, and [illegible] dead that were taken away before [illegible] extremity of woe. The dread[illegible] the Romans, some of whom pitied [illegible] detested them, and others [illegible].

[illegible] of having been accessory to [illegible] solemnly protested, as in the presence of [illegible] had proposed to the Jews peace and [illegible] as well as an oblivion of all their former insolent [illegible] instead of concord had chosen [illegible] war, and instead of plenty [illegible] famine. That they had begun with [illegible] hands to burn that temple which the Ro[illegible] had [illegible] preserved, and that therefore their [illegible] were [illegible]. That he was de[illegible] in their ruin, and not [illegible] upon the face of the earth, where [illegible] devoured their own children, and the fathers, [illegible] perished in a war after so [illegible] of the Divine vengeance." Titus [illegible] obstinacy of these people, [illegible] they had any sensibility the [illegible] they had [illegible] reclaimed them.

CHAP. [illegible]

[illegible] The Romans [illegible] The ten[illegible] con[illegible] opinions [illegible] make [illegible] Romans. Titus [illegible] and forces [illegible] temple [illegible] of the [illegible]

WHEN two of the legions had finished their works on the eighth day of the month [illegible] Titus ordered the battering rams to be placed against the [illegible] gate of the outward temple, having played the [illegible] of battery he had for six whole days without [illegible], but to no purpose, for the edifice was proof against the engines [illegible] others, [illegible] sapping the foundation [illegible] found that with incredible labour, they could [illegible] some of the outward stones, without moving [illegible] rest, (for the porch yet stood firm,) [illegible] nothing effectual could be done [illegible] so that the Romans [illegible] ladders.

Though the Jews could not [illegible] their ladders, they made a brave [illegible] would admit of, [illegible] hand before they [illegible] casting others [illegible] cutting off [illegible] The loss of the Romans [illegible] siderable, especially [illegible] or recovering their [illegible] Jews kept the ensigns [illegible] bearers, which terrified the rest, and forced [illegible] [illegible] justice to the [illegible] tell [illegible] died like [illegible] one of the [illegible] former encounters did so [illegible] Simon, [illegible] that [illegible] his own men, [illegible] his people [illegible] fire to the gates.

In the mean time [illegible] deserted to him [illegible] the most [illegible] guards, [illegible] Magadatus [illegible] forgiveness from [illegible] was so well [illegible] barbarous practices of these pretended [illegible] was [illegible] inclined [illegible] standing this pretence [illegible] convinced [illegible] necessity [illegible] design, not [illegible] brought them over [illegible] the who had [illegible] [illegible] overcome the [illegible] resolution [illegible].

The gates of the [illegible] the silver [illegible] and the [illegible] a flame, [illegible] The Jews [illegible] wrapped [illegible] in flames [illegible] other in [illegible] without [illegible] thing toward the [illegible] for what [illegible] one, in [illegible] their [illegible] [illegible] prevailed all that day [illegible] till, by degrees, it burnt down the [illegible].

Titus gave orders next [illegible] for the [illegible] fire, and levelling the ways for the [illegible] After this he called a council of his general [illegible] consisted of Tiberius Alexander his lieutenant [illegible] Sextus Cerealis commander of the fifth legion, [illegible] Lepidus, of the tenth, Titus Frigius, of the [illegible] [illegible] Fronto, Julius [illegible] officers of the first rank. This [illegible] council [illegible] to deliberate on what measures were necessary [illegible] in the business of the temple, some were for [illegible] the rigour of the law of [illegible] so long as [illegible] stood, and the [illegible] Jews [illegible] [illegible] but [illegible] [illegible] [illegible] [illegible]

[illegible]

[illegible] the stubbornness of a [illegible] and by [illegible] the [illegible] He added [illegible] Rome itself, to [illegible] of so illustrious an orna-[illegible]

[illegible] Cerealis, and Fronto, found how [illegible] they came over to his opinion, and [illegible] with orders to the army to rest [illegible] several [illegible] ordered out, in the mean time, to [illegible] was over the ruins The [illegible] fatigued and harrassed, remained in-[illegible] following, when they had [illegible] spirits, they made a [illegible] second hour, through the eastern gate, upon the [illegible] of the outward temple The Ro-[illegible] their backs, [illegible] could not long have op-[illegible] resolutely bent, if Titus, [illegible] had not seasonably [illegible] of horse, to their relief, be-[illegible] think upon this [illegible] upon their front, [illegible] to flight, but when the Ro-[illegible] rallied, and came [illegible] turns interchang-[illegible] till about the fifth hour of the day, when the Jews were forced into the temple, and [illegible] retired to the tower of Antonia, with [illegible] to storm the temple, with his whole [illegible] the next morning, as it seems to have been [illegible] by Providence to fire, and, in course of time, [illegible] was now at hand, according to the revolu-[illegible] It was upon the tenth day of the month, [illegible] same day whereupon it was formerly burnt [illegible] Nebuchadnezzar, king of Babylon But this was [illegible] conflagration which the Jews brought upon themselves, [illegible] had no sooner left them quiet, than the rebels [illegible] upon his guards, as they were [illegible] to extinguish the fire But the Romans put the Jews to flight, and pursued them to the temple itself

CHAP [illegible]

[illegible] of [illegible] fire to the [illegible] quenched [illegible] of the Jews

AT this [illegible] one of the Roman soldiers, without [illegible] any orders, or without any concern or [illegible] upon him for so impious an act, and being hurried on, as he afterwards pretended, by a certain Divine im-pulse, mounted the shoulders of one of his comrades, and cast a flaming brand into the golden window, that looks towards the apartments on the north side of the temple The place took fire immediately, which raised such a [illegible] among the Jews, that they hastened with all possible expedition to prevent its progress, for this was not a time to consult their personal security, when all that was dear and precious to them was at stake

The news of this conflagration being brought to Titus, as he was reposing himself in his tent, after the fatigue of the combat he arose in great haste, and immediately [illegible] his chariot, passed to the temple, in order to have a stop put to the fire His great officers followed him, and the legions after them, in such confusion as is natural to a [illegible] multitude without discipline Titus did all that could be done, by words and signs, towards quenching the fire, but it was ineffectual, for the greater noise [illegible] and they were as blind to the signals he gave with his hand, as they were deaf to the words he uttered from his mouth Nor were the soldiers to be swayed by menaces or commands, but followed the im-pulse of rage and passion Some were trampled to death in crowds, others choaked in the sultry ruins of the gal-leries over the porches, and it was the same, in effect, whether they overcame, or were overcome The com-mon soldiers in the temple pretended, in excuse of their disobedience, that they could not hear the word of com-mand from their general, and those who followed, gave the word forward to throw fire

The faction were in too great distress to afford any assistance, for wherever they turned themselves [illegible] nothing but blood and destruction The [illegible] and unarmed, were put to death in every quarter [illegible] tains of dead bodies were piled upon the altar, and [illegible] of blood flowed down the steps leading to it [illegible] of miserable wretches weltering in their gore

When Titus found there was no restraining the [illegible] fury of his soldiers, and that the fire continued to gain more and more, he took some of his chief officers with him into the inward temple, where upon [illegible] of matters, he found the glory and [illegible] of the place even beyond the very fame of it, [illegible] equal to the report of the Jews themselves [illegible] flames had not reached it, and there was there [illegible] to hope it might not yet be too late to [illegible] Titus, in person, endeavoured to [illegible] earnestly besought, his soldiers to do their utmost [illegible] the progress of the fire giving [illegible] centurion of his guards, to [illegible] inflicted corporal punishment upon [illegible] But, through ungovernable rage [illegible] zy, [illegible] respect were [illegible] within the bounds of duty [illegible] hearts were set upon booty, not doubting but, [illegible] doors were plated with gold, they should find [illegible] filled with hidden treasure

While Titus was so very intent upon [illegible] one of the soldiers at the same time [illegible] door-posts, whereupon the general and his officers, were forced to withdraw out of distance of preventing [illegible] chief, so that the temple was destroyed at last, in despite of whatever Titus could do to hinder it

This desolation was a calamity [illegible] great [illegible] most obdurate heart if we duly consider the ruins of [illegible] most stupenduous fabric that ever was seen [illegible] both for structure, bulk, state, magnificence, [illegible] of religion, and of holy things But it is [illegible] bered, to our comfort and instruction, that [illegible] fatality attends all terrestrial works, [illegible] inanimate, and that all things must have [illegible] most remarkable revolution also, that [illegible] gration should so exactly answer the very [illegible] of the former under Nebuchadnezzar, [illegible] We reckon from the beginning of the first [illegible] lomon, to the destruction of this, in the [illegible] Vespasian, one thousand, one hundred, [illegible] seven months, and fifteen days, and from [illegible] building of it by Haggai, [illegible] six-hundred and [illegible]

CHAP XI

The distress [illegible] the Jews [illegible] of the temple [illegible] with the Romans [illegible] by the advice of a false prophet

WHILE the temple was in flames, the soldiers mur-dered all that came to hand and [illegible] all they met, without respect to age or sex, both young and old, sacred and prophane, priests, and [illegible] all went toge-ther, and men of all sorts and conditions were involved in the common calamities of the war, and, whether they resisted or submitted, whether they stood it out, or begged for quarter, they all fared alike, falling victims in the common destruction. As the fire advanced, the crackling of the flames was heard in unison with the dying groans of people at their last gasp; and betwixt the depth of the hill, and the extent of the conflagration, the whole city seemed to be but one continued blaze. The tumult and uproar was so dreadful, that nothing more terrible can possibly be conceived. The raging outcries of the Roman legions, the howlings of the rebels under the devastation of fire and sword, and the dismal lamentation of distressed wretches in the temple, betwixt the enemy and [illegible] could not but pierce the [illegible] [illegible] wound the heart of the most obdurate [illegible]. The adjacent mountains and places beyond Jordan [illegible] the same complaints and grievances over and over [illegible] and the clamours exceeded the noise. The flames were so impetuous and violent, that the very mountains, upon which the temple stood, appeared as one body of fire from the bottom, and the blood in proportion was answerable to the flames, for the number of the men were [illegible] to that of those that did the execution. The [illegible] was covered over with the dead [illegible], and the soldiers [illegible] over the bodies of the dead. But, in the end, a band of [illegible] beat the Romans, and having forced their way into the outer court of the temple, made their escape into the city, and the rest of the multitude got into the outward court.

There were several priests engaged in the quarrel with the Romans, [illegible] the [illegible] spikes [illegible] and discharged them at the enemy; but when they found [illegible] nothing, and [illegible] upon them, they covered themselves [illegible] under [illegible] wall, [illegible] eight cubits in breadth [illegible] of this number, who were [illegible] the [illegible] of Belgas and Joseph the son of Daleus, that might have saved themselves by going over to the Romans, [illegible] to [illegible] with their companions, and [illegible] themselves into the flames, share in the common fate.

When the Romans found [illegible] ten [illegible] itself reduced to ashes, they looked upon the rest of the buildings as [illegible], and so fired [illegible] of one of the galleries on the east side, and another on the south, but they soon after followed the [illegible] of [illegible]. They burnt also the treasury of the wardrobe, [illegible] vessels, money and [illegible] habits, to an inestimable value. The place [illegible], as the repository [illegible] the Jews had, that was precious.

There was now [illegible] in one gallery, vast numbers, women, children, and a mixed multitude, that fled from the rabble, to the number of near six thousand persons. But before Titus had determined any thing concerning these people, or given the officers any orders relating to them, the soldiers in a rage of brutal fury, set the place on fire, and plied it so closely, that betwixt those that were burnt to death, and others that had cast themselves headlong down the ruins to save themselves, there was not one that escaped death.

A false prophet was accessary to all this mischief, by making proclamation in the city, that it was the will of the Almighty they should go immediately up to the temple with an assurance that there they should have an infallible proof of his Divine favour and protection. It was, indeed, a common practice [illegible] fiction, to pretend to revelations, in order to keep the credulous multitude firm against all dangers, and so secure them from deserting. But men in adversity are apt to hope the best, especially where they are promised relief, though it be only upon the credit of a false prophet.

CHAP. XI.

The portentous signs which [illegible] the destruction of Jerusalem. A comet resembling a sword. [illegible] about the altar. An [illegible] gate of the temple opens of itself. [illegible] the signification. Chariots and [illegible] crying in the temple "Let us be gone." [illegible] clamation of one Jesus, a [illegible] death. The prophecy of [illegible] emperor [illegible] fulfilled in the person of Vespasian.

THUS were these miserable people deluded [illegible] while they did not attend nor give credit to [illegible] were most evident, and plainly foretold them [illegible] tion. Indeed, like infatuated men [illegible] pable of seeing, nor [illegible] pable of reflecting [illegible] not perceive the denunciations of the Almighty [illegible], amongst which were the following. There was a [illegible] resembling a sword, which stood over the city, [illegible] that continued a whole year.

Thus [illegible] motions which preceded the war, when [illegible] in multitudes to the feast of unleavened bread, on the [illegible] day of the month Xanthicus, [illegible] day, so great a light [illegible] that it appeared [illegible] upon by the ignorant [illegible] by the more discerning [illegible] mystery unfolded before it came to pass.

At the same feast [illegible] high-priest to be sacrificed, [illegible] of the temple.

Moreover the eastern gate of the inner temple, which was of brass, and very ponderous, and [illegible] shut by twenty men, [illegible] upon a [illegible], and had bolts fastened very deep into the [illegible] was there [illegible] one [illegible] about the sixth hour of the night [illegible] to the proper officer [illegible], and with much ado [illegible] near [illegible] to the vulgar to be an happy presage [illegible] formed a contrary judgment, and apprehended [illegible] ing of the gate was an [illegible] the desolation of the [illegible]

A few days after the [illegible] of the month Artemisius [illegible] vince, that [illegible] produce several witnesses [illegible] it, and if the calamities that [illegible] pass. There were seen [illegible] set, chariots and armed men [illegible] rounding several cities.

At the feast of Pentecost [illegible] night, to officiate in the [illegible] they heard, at first a kind of [illegible] that, a voice, crying [illegible] "[illegible] us be gone."

But what is still [illegible] Ananus [illegible] and an husbandman [illegible] before the commencement of the [illegible] the city enjoyed peace and plenty [illegible] tabernacles [illegible] the east, a voice from the west, a voice from [illegible] a voice to Jerusalem, and [illegible] the bridegrooms and the brides, [illegible] tion." This was his cry [illegible] through every street [illegible] nence were so offended [illegible] him to be apprehended, and [illegible] submitted without a murmur [illegible] defence, but still [illegible] tioned [illegible] that he was [illegible]

[illegible] at that time our procu-[illegible] he scourged with the utmost ri-[illegible] same manner as before, without [illegible] at every stroke, in [illegible] woe, woe to Jerusalem! When [illegible] of him who he was, whence he came, [illegible] these words. He made no manner of [illegible] till the procurator [illegible] him [illegible]

[illegible] the beginning of the war, he was never [illegible] of the citizens, but every [illegible] "Woe, woe to Jerusa-[illegible] to those that scourged [illegible] that fed him; but this was his [illegible] no other than a melancholy [illegible] to come. He [illegible] to be much [illegible] than upon other days, and in [illegible] to proceed, nor did his voice or [illegible] Jerusalem verified his pre-[illegible] the top of the wall once [illegible] to the city, the [illegible] con-[illegible] his [illegible]

[illegible] destruction of [illegible] Creator, [illegible] at the [illegible] of future events, and [illegible] own [illegible] after the taking of Antonia, make the temple [illegible] they were conscious to themselves of a pre-[illegible] that both temple and city should be taken, when [illegible] but they were chiefly in-[illegible] war by the misconstruction of a [illegible] days, there should one come [illegible] that should have the command of the whole [illegible] applied to their own nation, and [illegible] error. But this prophecy [illegible] Vespasian, who was created emperor in Ju-[illegible] suggests divers interpretations, and thus [illegible] the Jews, till in the end, they suffered for their [illegible] the destruction of themselves and their country.

CHAP. XIII.

[illegible] The force [illegible] the leaders of [illegible] The emperor agrees [illegible] upon the occasion. The [illegible] of Jere-[illegible] den [illegible]

[illegible] on the burning of [illegible] the buildings about it, the Romans [illegible] the eastern gate, where they [illegible] acclamations, pro-[illegible] Titus [illegible] such name [illegible] reduced to one half of [illegible]

[illegible] upon the wall, that [illegible] Roman guards to defend, and get [illegible] the parching thirst under which he [illegible] considering his tender years and [illegible] their right hands as a security [illegible] The boy accordingly descended, drank, filled [illegible] with him, and returned to his friends with [illegible] expedition, that the guards could not overtake him.

The Romans, upon this, charged him with perfidy; but he ingeniously pleaded that he covenanted only for liberty to fetch the water, not to continue with them when he had it, and consequently had not violated any agreement. The plea was admitted, and the delusion looked over on account of his tender years.

On the fifth day after this, the priests, urged by outrageous hunger, came down from the walls, and being conducted by the guards to Titus, cast themselves at his feet, and implored his mercy. But he told them the time of pardon was over; for the temple being destroyed, it was but reasonable they should follow, since the priests and their temple should be inseparable; and upon this he ordered them to be put to death.

The heads of the faction, finding themselves [illegible] passed that there was no possibility of escaping, desired a conference with Titus, who, with his natural goodness, was inclined to grant it, partly from a desire to save the town, and partly at the instance of his friends, in hopes that the rebels might be brought to better terms for the future.

Titus then made a stand on the west side of the inner temple, near the gate that led to the gallery, where there was a bridge of communication betwixt the temple and the upper town, which at this time parted the Romans and the Jews. The multitude on both sides gathered about their generals, the Jews about Simon and John, to learn what hopes there were of pardon, and the Romans about Titus, desirous of seeing the manner in which he would receive the suppliants. Having commanded silence, and an intermission of all hostilities, he delivered his mind to them, by an interpreter, to the following effect:

"Is not your country wretched enough? Will you [illegible] be brought to a sense either of your own weakness, or of "the Roman power, but like so many madmen, ruin [illegible] "people, city and temple at once, and yourselves too, [illegible] "deservedly in the conclusion? When were you ever out of "broils and tumults, since Pompey [illegible] "Nothing will serve you now but open war against the "Romans. Is it your numbers you depend upon? [illegible] "have seen the time that one half our army have been [illegible] "to cope with you. Do you value yourselves upon the [illegible] "of your auxiliaries and allies? Where is that people under "the sun, that is not more or less in our allegiance, or that "would not rather have the Romans as friends, than the "Jews? If you reckon upon the strength of your [illegible] "take notice that the Germans are our subjects. And is "the firmness of your walls, are they stronger than the "Britons' wall, the ocean? and yet these people, with [illegible] "fence have not been able to withstand us. If you rely upon "the address and resolution of your leaders, we have been "too hard, you know, for the Carthaginians themselves. "But it is the humanity of the Romans that hath raised "enemies to themselves; first, in giving you land [illegible] "first, and then setting up kings of your own [illegible] "to govern them. We have [illegible] "and exercise of your country's laws, and permitted you to "live both at home and abroad, according to your own "[illegible] And, what is more than [illegible] we have al-"lowed [illegible] the privilege of collecting, receiving and em-"ploying [illegible] and tributes, for the maintenance of "your [illegible] and God's holy worship with all freedom to "yourselves [illegible] your friends. What is the use you have made "of all these benefits, but to enrich yourselves into a capacity "of doing us the more mischief, in the employing of our "own money against ourselves? You do, in truth, behave "yourselves like the worst of serpents, that practise upon the "lives of those that take them into their bosoms.

"It is agreed that the contempt you had for the spiritless "disposition of Nero, made you forget the quiet that at the "same time you enjoyed, and put you upon ambitious and "extravagant designs.

"My father, you must know, did not come into Judæa "to call you to an account for your defection from Cestius, "but rather to reform you by admonition and good advice. "If the depopulating of this nation had been his business, "he would have struck at the root, and begun with Jerusalem, [illegible] than Galilee, and those parts, which he did "on purpose to give you room and leisure to repent. But "his humanity passed for weakness, and our lenity hath given "you a boldness that you take for courage.

"At the death of Nero, according to the custom of "[illegible] wicked men, you took advantage of our divisions, "[illegible] my father and myself were no sooner gone to Egypt, "[illegible] of our being absent, to la[illegible] "[illegible] notwithstanding "[illegible] have given of our tenderness and hu"manity in the government of those provinces, you had yet "[illegible] to practices against us, even when "[illegible] declared emperor, and myself "[illegible] further yet, for, after the very "[illegible] by the common consent, in the "quiet and peaceable [illegible] of the empire, and congra"[illegible] that were paid us by foreign [illegible] "[illegible] to the government, who but the "Jews were still our enemies, as appeared by [illegible] dispatches of embassies and denunciations beyond Euphrates, "to [illegible] their [illegible]. To [illegible] of your new "fortifications, factions, and competitions, till it came, in the "end, to a civil war, an ingratitude that none but the "wickedest of men could have been guilty of.

"When my father [illegible] brought with great difficulty and "reluctance) [illegible] this stubborn and rebellious city to a[illegible] "count, how pleased I was to hear that the people were "disposed towards a peace! [illegible] I beg of you to pre"vent [illegible] before [illegible] How [illegible] Can you say that "I did not [illegible] to you afterwards [illegible]? "Did I ever refuse any [illegible] of you that offered himself? "Did I ever [illegible] with any man that came over to "me? How [illegible] was I of your prisoners! [illegible] was I ever "hard upon any man that did not inflame the quarrel? "With what reluctance did I come to the battering of your "[illegible] I avoided all bloody executions as much as possible. "When did I ever get the better of you, and not sue for "peace, as if you yourselves had been the conquerors? "Whenever I came near your temple, I took no advantage "of the right I had, by the law of arms, to destroy it, but "only made it my request to you, to spare yourselves, and "all that was now that belonged to you. Did I not offer "you free leave to depart and upon terms of secu"rity too? Or, if nothing but fighting would serve your "turn, I gave you the choice of your own time and place. "What is the fruit now of all this tenderness, but the "burning of the temple with your own hands that I would "so willingly have preserved? Have you the hardiness "now at last to invite me to a parley, as if you had any "thing left to atone for what you have destroyed? How "can you expect a pardon for yourselves, that would not "so much as pardon your own temple? Your present your"selves in arms too, without so much as pretending to be "supplicants. But to come to the ground of this miserable "confidence, your people are wholly disheartened, your "temple is gone, the city mine, and yourselves all at my "mercy: and yet you would be thought to insist upon "terms of honour [illegible]. Not to stand expostulating any "longer with you on your follies, lay down your arms, "and surrender yourselves, and I am content to give you "your lives. When I have once done necessary justice "upon the principal rebels, you shall find me a gentle "master to the rest." The faction returned him this answer, "That they could not deliver themselves up upon "any promise or assurance he could give them, because they "were under an oath to the contrary, but that they were "ready to be gone, if he pleased, with their wives and "children, into the desart, and leave the town to the Ro"mans." Titus was so incensed at prisoners giving laws, "and imposing conditions upon the conquerors, that "he caused proclamation to be made, that no Jew should "presume, for the future, to make any further application "to Titus, or expect either protection or quarter, but that "they might now defend themselves by arms as well as "they could, for Cæsar was resolved to govern himself "by the rules of war."

Titus then gave orders to the soldiers to plunder and burn the city, so that on the day following they set fire to the repository of the archives, to the council chamber, and a place called Ophilas, at which time the fire proceeded as far as the palace of queen Helena, which was in the middle of Acra. The lanes were also consumed, as were the houses that were full of the dead bodies of those who perished by famine.

On the same day the sons and brethren of king Izates, with several other persons of rank, [illegible] petition to Titus for their lives, which, according to his [illegible] benevolence, he granted, though the [illegible] had [illegible] dignation [illegible] and the sons and relatives of Izates [illegible] tages to Rome.

CHAP. [illegible]

The faction move to the [illegible] where the [illegible] 8400 persons, and [illegible] of honour amongst the [illegible] for the crown. [illegible] Miserable [illegible] of the faction.

THE faction now [illegible] into the royal [illegible], where many had deposited their effects on account of its strength drove the Romans out of it, slew about 8400 persons, and plundered them of all their substance. They took upon this occasion, two Romans [illegible] alive, the one belonging to the infantry, the other to the cavalry. The former they slew, and [illegible] dragged [illegible] about the city, as revenging themselves upon the whole body of the Romans by this one instance. [illegible], on pretence of having something to communicate relative to the interest of the faction, was brought before Simon, but the pretence appearing frivolous, he was delivered over to Ardalas, one of Simon's officers, to be punished. He was brought out with his hands bound behind him, and a band over his eyes, in order to be beheaded within sight of the Romans; but as the executioner was [illegible] for his office, the prisoner started away, and made his escape to the Romans.

Though Titus could not think of putting him to death for this escaping from the enemy, yet he deemed it unworthy of a Roman soldier to be taken alive, he was condemned cashiered, an indignity to a man of honour more piercing than the loss of life.

The next day the Romans drove the rebels out of the lower city, and set all on fire as far as Siloam. Their soldiers, indeed, had the pleasure of seeing the city destroyed, but they missed the plunder, for the Jews had carried off all their effects, and were retreated into the upper city. Such was their obstinacy, that, so far from repenting of the mischiefs they had done, they became insolent [illegible] beheld the conflagration of the city with joyful countenances, in expectation of death, as they declared, to end their miseries. The people were now wasted, the temple burnt down, and the city in a blaze, so that there was nothing further left for the enemy to do.

In this utmost extremity however, Josephus did [illegible] could be done to save the [illegible]

He remonstrated with them on their barbarity and impiety, and gave them advice as to their future proceedings But they derided his counsel, as they were bound on oath not to surrender themselves, as well as so accustomed to slaughter, they could not restrain from the commission of it

In this distracted state of things, they dispersed themselves throughout the city, and laid in ambush amongst its ruins, to surprise those that might attempt to desert to the Romans Accordingly, many of them were taken, for they were too much reduced by famine to escape by flight Their dead bodies were thrown to the dogs but of all deaths [illegible] was the most frightful and ghastly, insomuch that many went over to the Romans, despairing of mercy, and merely to exchange one death for another The streets were strewed with dead bodies from one end of the city to the other that had been either murdered or starved

The [illegible] heads of the faction were in their recesses in subterraneous caverns, from a vain fancy that there they might lie concealed till the Romans were gone, and that [illegible] might make their escape, not considering that no recess could hide them from the all-seeing eye [illegible] They depended, however, on these subterraneous [illegible], and did more mischief than the Romans by fire, killing and robbing all they could meet, that came for sanctuary [illegible] those caverns Nay, they now fought one with another [illegible] about their plunder, and I cannot but think, if their destruction had not prevented it, their barbarity would have induced the living to eat the flesh of the dead

CHAP XV

The Romans begin to raise banks against the upper town The Idumæans offer their service to Titus who accepts [illegible], and grants them pardon Simon puts the deputies of the Idumæans to death Men, women, and children [illegible] of being sold in a market Titus sets 40,000 [illegible] at liberty Phineas, treasurer of the temple, [illegible]

THUS observing that the upper town was seated on such crags and precipices, that it could not possibly be taken without raising banks against it, entered upon that arduous undertaking the twentieth day of the month The conveyance of the materials was attended with much difficulty, as all the trees within the distance of an hundred furlongs from the town, were cut down for the former works The four legions threw up a bank on the west side of the city, over against the palace royal The auxiliaries, and the rest, cast up another towards the gallery with the bridge, and a fort that Simon built in his war with John, known by the name of Simon's Tower

At the same time the Idumæan officers concerted a plan of desertion to the Romans, and sent five deputies with a tender of their services to Titus, and a petition for mercy in the name of the rest Though the application was rather late, Titus, from an opinion that the rebel tyrants, John and Simon, would never stand it out after such a defection, sent the deputies back with a promise of their lives, for he looked upon the Idumæans as the most considerable part of their army The plan, it seems, had transpired, for the deputies were apprehended, immediately put to death, and their leaders imprisoned, of whom James, the son of Sosas, was the chief Though much could not be expected from the common soldiers, now deprived of their officers, they were kept under a stricter guard, but even that precaution could not prevent their deserting Many were cut off, but more escaped, for Titus had too much generosity to press his former prohibition to the utmost rigour, and the very soldiers themselves, betwixt the hopes of booty, and a glut of blood, became more humane and moderate. The common people were sold, with their wives and children, like beasts in a market, and at easy rates, there being but few purchasers

Titus reflecting upon this, and upon his own proclamation, forbidding any more Jews to come over to him singly, was now pleased to dispence with his order, and to receive as many of them, one by one, as presented themselves, but with superiors over them to distinguish the good from the bad, and to deal with them according to their merits Vast numbers of them were sold, and upwards of forty thousand set at liberty by Titus, to go whithersoever they pleased

There was, at the same time, one Jesus, a priest, and the son of Thebuth, who compounded with Titus for his life, upon condition of delivering up to him some of the vessels, donations, and other ornaments belonging to the temple He came out, and delivered to him, from the wall, two candlesticks, some tables, cups, and goblets, all like those in the temple, of gold He gave him also several veils, sacerdotal habits, and a great number of sacrificing vessels

Phineas, the treasurer of the temple, produced many priests' habits and girdles, purple and scarlet stuffs, that were folded up for use There was also a proportion of cinnamon, cassia, gums, and perfumes, for daily incense, besides several sorts of holy ornaments, and private goods This man, in consideration of those services, obtained from Titus the same pardon that he allowed to such as voluntarily deserted

CHAP XVI

The banks are finished and the Romans advance with their engines against the upper wall Some of the faction [illegible] while others stand their ground Simon and John are terrified by false alarms They [illegible] resign the strongest places they had to the Romans, [illegible] all before them Titus imputes his success to [illegible] Providence, and causes a monument to be erected [illegible] of it Gives orders concerning the disposal of the prisoners

THE works being finished on the seventh day of the month Gorpieus, the Romans advanced their engines and that part of the faction that despaired of holding out, quitted the walls, and withdrew to the castle, and others into subterraneous vaults, while the more resolute maintained their ground, and opposed those who had the direction of the battery The Romans overcame them by their numbers and strength, though chiefly by the alacrity with which they executed their orders, while the Jews were dejected, and become weak As soon as they observed any flaw in the wall, or that any of the turrets gave way to the engines, the defendants shifted away as fast as they could Simon and John themselves were seized with a panic, and fled, even before the Romans were come within distance of doing them any hurt These men, whose insolent and arrogant practices had been so notorious, now trembled with the direst apprehensions, and exhibited every proof of dread and pusillanimity They made an attempt, indeed, upon the wall of circumvallation that the Romans had raised about the city, attacked and made a breach in it, with a resolution of falling upon the guards, and making their escape, but perceiving, when they expected to be seconded, that their friends had all forsaken them, they hurried away in confusion, as their fears and necessities moved them

In this fantastical variety of frightful imaginations, ore brought news that the whole wall to the westward was overthrown, others that the Romans were just at the foot of it, that some were entered, and some of them seen in possession of the tower Whatever they feared they saw, falling prostrate upon their faces, and bemoaning their follies, as if they had been thunder-struck, and knew not which way to turn themselves

The interpoſition of Divine Providence was very remarkable upon this occaſion, for the tyrants wholly deprived themſelves of the ſecurity they had in their own power, by quitting thoſe holds of their own accord, that could never have been taken but by famine, and this after they had ſpent ſo much time to no purpoſe, upon other places of much leſs importance. By this means the Romans became maſters of three impregnable forts by fortune, that could never have been taken any other way, for the three famous towers formerly mentioned were proof againſt all battery.

Upon their quitting theſe towers, through the impulſe of a Judicial infatuation, they haſtened away to the vale of Siloam, and, after ſome recollection and refreſhment, made an aſſault upon the new wall there, but it was ſo faint and weak, that the guards beat them off, for, betwixt fatigue, deſpondency, dread, and miſery, their ſtrength failed them, and they again retired into ſubterraneous caverns.

The Romans being now maſters of the walls, planted their enſigns upon the towers, with acclamations of triumph for the victory they had gained, as having found the end of the war much lighter than the beginning, it, at laſt, the war was now at an end, which they could not well doubt without diſtruſting their own eyes.

The ſoldiers were now broke looſe all over the town, with their ſwords drawn, ſlaying all that fell in their way without diſtinction, and burning entire houſes, and whatever was in them, in one common flame. In many places, which they entered to ſearch for plunder, they found the carcaſes of ſuch as had periſhed by famine, ſo that, ſtruck with horror, at ſo hideous a ſpectacle, they came out without touching any thing, but this commiſeration for the dead did not render them in the leaſt degree more humane to the living, for they ſtabbed every one they met, inſomuch that the channels of the city ran down with blood, as if it had been to quench the fire. In the evening they deſiſted from ſlaying, and proceeded to burning.

The eighth day of the month Corpius put an end to the conflagration of Jeruſalem, and if all the bleſſings it ever enjoyed from its foundation had been in proportion to the calamities it ſuſtained during this ſiege, it would certainly have been the envy of the world. The ſource of all its miſeries aroſe from its producing ſo iniquitous and abandoned a generation, as brought on its total overthrow, and ſheathed their ſwords in the very bowels of their country.

As Titus was taking a ſurvey of the upper town, the works, the fortifications, and particularly the towers, which the tyrants in their infatuation had abandoned, when he contemplated on their altitude, dimenſions, and ſituation, together with the curious deſign and execution of the whole fabric, he broke forth into this pious rhapſody. "If an Almighty arm had not ſtretched forth to "our aſſiſtance, we could never have ejected the Jews "out of theſe fortifications, as it was certainly an under-"taking not to be accompliſhed by human power alone." Having made this remark to his friends about him, his next care was to ſet all the priſoners at liberty whom the tyrants had left in the towers and afterwards, upon demoliſhing the city, to preſerve thoſe turrets, as a monument of his ſucceſs through Divine aid, without which their reduction would have been impracticable.

The Roman ſoldiers being quite ſpent with doing execution, and numbers ſtill remaining alive, Titus gave orders that only ſuch ſhould be put to death as were found to make reſiſtance, appointing Fronto, one of his own council, to determine the fate of every one according to his merits. The robbers and ſeditious impeached one another and were all put to death. Thoſe of comely and graceful perſons, and in the prime of youth, were reſerved to adorn his triumph. As for the reſt of the multitude, all thoſe above ſeventeen years old were ſent in bonds to Egyptian mines. Others were diſtributed up and down the provinces for the uſe of the theatres, as gladiators, and thoſe under ſeventeen were ſold for ſlaves.

While the priſoners were under the charge of Fronto eleven thouſand of them were ſtarved to death through the churliſhneſs of the keepers on the one hand who neglected to bring them food, and their own diſguſt on the other, that reſtrained them from eating. But their numbers in fact were ſo great, that there was not proviſion adequate to their ſuſtenance.

CHAP. XVII.

The number of thoſe that periſhed in the ſiege, and of thoſe taken captive. John and Simon taken. The one kept for triumph, the other a priſoner for life. The city [illegible] aſhes, and the walls thrown down.

THE number of thoſe taken captive during the whole war was computed to amount to ninety-ſeven thouſand, and the number of thoſe that periſhed during the ſiege, was eſtimated at eleven hundred thouſand. The greateſt part of them were Jews by nation, though not citizens of Jeruſalem, for it was a general [illegible] in that metropolis, from all quarters, to celebrate the feaſt of the paſſover that they were ſurpriſed into a war. The multitude was ſo prodigious, that, for want of decent accommodation they firſt brought the plague into the city, which, through want of competent proviſion, was followed by a famine. That the city was capacious enough to contain ſo many people is manifeſt, if credit may be given to the calculation of Ceſtius.

Nero held the Jews in ſuch contempt that Ceſtius made ſuit to the high-prieſt, to deviſe ſome method of numbering the people, and this he did from a deſire of convincing the emperor that the Jewiſh nation was not ſo deſpicable as he imagined. They took their time to enter upon the computation at the celebration of their paſchal feaſt. When offering up their ſacrifices, according to cuſtom, from the ninth hour of the day, to the eleventh, which ſacrifices were afterwards to be eaten in their families, by ten at leaſt, and ſometimes twenty, to a lamb, the number of ſacrifices was 25,650, which, at the rate of no more than ten to a lamb, amounts to two million five hundred and ſixty-five thouſand perſons, all pure and ſound, or ſuch as labour under epidemic or infectious diſorders, are not admitted to any part of this ſolemnity, nor any ſtrangers, but ſuch as repair thither from religious motives.

This prodigious concourſe of people, which might be ſaid to comprize the Jewiſh nation, was afterwards by a kind of fatality, ſhut up in the city as in a priſon, for the Roman army encompaſſed it when crowded with inhabitants. Accordingly, the number of the ſlain in the ſiege was the heavieſt judgment that ever was inflicted upon mankind. Some were put to death openly, others kept in cuſtody by the Romans, who ſearched the very ſepulchres and vaults for them and put all they found alive to the ſword. There were upwards of two thouſand that had either laid violent hands on themſelves, or killed one another by conſent, beſides thoſe that periſhed by famine. The putrid exhalation of the dead bodies poiſoned as many as came within the reach of it. Some went out of the way to avoid it, others had their [illegible] ſo ſet upon booty, that they [illegible] the very [illegible] and trampled upon the dead bodies in a putrified ſtate. They brought out ſeveral priſoners the two [illegible] had [illegible] chains there, for they perſevered in their [illegible] to the laſt, but Divine vengeance [illegible] them [illegible] for John and his brethren, in the [illegible], [illegible] inſupportable hunger, to beg that mercy they [illegible] deſpiſed, and Simon, after a long ſtruggle [illegible] inſuperable neceſſity, delivered up himſelf. The [illegible] reſerved for triumph and John made a priſoner for life. The Romans now ſet fire to the [illegible] and threw down the walls.

CHAP XVIII.

Jerusalem taken and destroyed. Brief account of its history

THUS was Jerusalem taken, and utterly destroyed, in the second year of the reign of Vespasian, on the eighth day of the month Gorpieus It had been taken five times before, that is to say, by Azochæus, king of Egypt, Antiochus Epiphanes king of Syria, Pompey, Herod, and Sosius who still preserved it But Nebuchadnezzar, king of Babylon laid it waste, one thousand, four hundred, sixty-eight years, and six months after it was built.

The first founder was a man of power amongst the Canaanites, called Melchisedeck, which in the Hebrew language, signifies a righteous king, for such he was in an eminent degree He first dedicated the city to the Almighty, erected a temple in it, and officiated in quality of a priest, gave it the name of Jerusalem, which before was called Solyma

When David, the king of the Jews, came afterwards to drive out the Canaanites, he planted his own people there, and, in four hundred seventy-seven years, and three months, after this, it was laid waste by the Babylonians From the reign of David to the destruction of the city, under Titus, were one thousand, one hundred, and seventy-nine years, and two thousand one hundred, and seventy-seven, from the foundation of it Yet neither its antiquity, nor its vast riches, nor the diffusion of its glory over all the habitable earth, nor the great veneration paid it on a religious account have been sufficient to preserve it from destruction This was, in fine, the issue of the siege

When the soldiers had neither rapine nor bloodshed to satisfy their spleen, Titus gave orders for laying the city and temple level with the ground, and leaving nothing standing but the three famous towers, Phasaelus, Hippicos, and Mariamne, and so much of the wall as enclosed the city on the left side, where he designed to keep a garrison The towers were to remain as so many monuments to posterity of the power and conduct of the Romans in taking them This order was punctually executed, but all the rest was laid so level, that the place seemed as if it never had been inhabited This was the miserable end to which Jerusalem was reduced, from the inordinate propensity of the inhabitants to innovations

CHAP XIX

Titus distributes honours and rewards amongst his soldiers, accompanied with an elegant and generous address Offers a thanksgiving sacrifice for his victory

TITUS having formed a resolution to leave the tenth legion in garrison in Jerusalem, with some squadrons and battalions of horse and foot, and having discharged every duty incumbent on a vigilant and careful general, was desirous of bestowing proper rewards upon those who had signalized themselves in the service of their country To this end, he mounted a tribunal, with his principal officers about him, and from an eminence, where he might best be heard, delivering himself to the army in terms to the following effect

"It is impossible, my brave fellow soldiers, to express "the sense I entertain of the respect and obedience you "have shewn me during the whole course of this war "Your invincible firmness, upon all occasions, and in "the most imminent danger, the reputation you have "acquired in advancing the honour, and enlarging the "territory, of your country, and, finally, the proof you "have given, that neither superiority of numbers, advan- "tages of forts, strength of places, nor the outrageous fu- "ry of brutal adversaries, can ever discompose the Roman "conduct and courage, claim every mark of gratitude "and respect It was but reasonable for you to put an "end to a war that had lasted so long, which was your "chief desire when you entered upon it, It must afford "you singular pleasure and satisfaction, to see your choice "of the Roman emperor and generals not only admitted "but universally approved I cannot but esteem and ad- "mire you for all what you have done, but those who "have rendered themselves exemplary in their enter- "prizes, and thereby done honour to their characters and "professions, may depend on my care to make an equi- "valent return Every emulation to excel shall have "proportionate acknowledgment, as I am more diligent "in rewarding the meritorious, than in punishing the "delinquent"

Titus hereupon ordered the proper officers to produce the list of those who signalized themselves by their gallant exploits in the course of the war They were mentioned by name, and highly applauded, both by the general, and all the respectable persons present on the occasion From words he proceeded to substantial instances of liberality and bounty They were crowned with coronets of gold, had golden ornaments put about their necks, lances, pointed with gold, put into their hands, presented with silver medals, and advanced every man according to his station He gave them money in gold and silver, out of the booty, with rich robes, and other things of value

Having made this distribution according to the merit of each individual, Titus, accompanied by the vows, prayers, and acclamations of the whole army, descended from his tribunal, to offer sacrifices, and give thanks for his victory A great number of oxen were sacrificed, and distributed among the army, Titus having treated his officers for three days, the troops were dismissed to their respective quarters, and Jerusalem committed to the guard of the tenth legion, without sending it back to Euphrates whence it came

Bearing in memory that the twelfth legion had given way to the Jews under Cestius, then commander, he expelled them out of all Syria, (for they had laid formerly at Raphanea,) and sent them away to a place called Meletine, that lies along the Euphrates, upon the borders of Cappadocia and Armenia, keeping two legions to himself, as a competent guard to convoy him into Egypt From hence he took his passage to Cæsarea upon the coast, but it being winter, he durst not venture into Italy, so that he deposited his treasure for the present and took every precaution for the security of the prisoners

CHAP XX

While Titus lay before Jerusalem, Vespasian visits several ports Simon taken prisoner by Terentius Rufus, and put in chains Promotes farther discoveries The birth-days of Domitian and Vespasian celebrated with great pomp

DURING the siege of Jerusalem by Titus, Vespasian embarked on board a trading vessel for Rhodes, where he took a galley, and so passed out of Ionia into Greece, visiting all the towns in his way, where he was most magnificently received He then proceeded to Corcyra, and so to Iapygia, whence he took his journey by land

Titus was now come back from Cæsarea upon the sea-coast, to that called Cæsarea Philippi, where he made a considerable stay, entertaining himself with a diversity of spectacles, as combats betwixt men and beasts man and man, troop and troop, which cost him the lives of many of his captives

At this juncture Simon, the son of Gioras, happened to be taken in the following manner Simon, upon the siege of Jerusalem, was forced into the upper town, and the Romans breaking into the city, he was much puzzled to devise means of effecting his escape, till at length he hit upon this contrivance. He got together a number of miners, stone-cutters, smiths, and men well skilled in iron works, and having laid in a stock of provisions for several weeks, they let themselves all down into a subterraneous cavern. When they had made their way as far as they could, and found the passage too narrow to proceed, they betook themselves to digging and mining, hoping to work a thoroughfare, and so to make their escape. But, before they could make any considerable advance, their provision fell short, and the plan of course failed, though they managed their stores with the utmost œconomy,

Simon had now recourse to another device, which was to alarm and terrify the Romans. To this end he put on a white garment, over which he threw a purple cloak, and in this garb presented himself out of the ground from under the ruins of the late temple, to the amazement of the soldiers and others, that first saw the supposed apparition. But, on his approach, they took courage, asked him his name, and who he was; upon his refusing to satisfy them, and calling to speak with the officer of the guard, Terentius Rufus, who had the command, was immediately sent for, and learning the truth from Simon, ordered him to be put in chains, and transmitted an account of the whole affair to Cæsar.

Thus was this inhuman tyrant, who had taken away so many of his countrymen's lives by subornation and false evidence, upon pretence of their going over to the Romans, brought to justice himself, and delivered into the hands of his enemies, without any force upon him but his own act. But the stroke of Divine vengeance cannot be avoided: nor is the power of innocence and justice to be contended with, while the punishment is frequently aggravated by being deferred, and when notorious offenders hug themselves in security. This was the case of Simon in the hands of the Romans, and his fantastical scheme of rising out of the ground proved an occasion of discovering divers of his companions in their lurking-places.

Simon being presented to Titus in chains, on his return to Cæsarea by the sea-side, was ordered to be kept for his triumph at Rome. While Titus was at Cæsarea, he set a day apart for the celebration of the nativity of his brother Domitian, and a great number of his condemned prisoners were dedicated to the honour of the solemnity. The number of those that were destroyed by beasts, fire, and in combat one with another, were supposed to amount at least to two thousand five hundred, and all this too little in the opinion of the Romans, who bore them a mortal aversion. Titus went afterwards to Berytus, a city of Phœnicia, and a Roman colony, where he continued for some time, and celebrated his father's birth-day with more splendour and magnificence than the former, both for spectacles, and other sumptuous entertainments.

CHAP. XXI.

The Jews dispersed throughout the habitable earth, especially in Syria and Antioch. Antiochus, the son of a Jew, occasions many disasters, by setting up the Pagan worship, and suppressing the observation of the sabbath. The city takes fire, and Antiochus imputes it falsely to the Jews.

THE Jews in Antioch were now accused for divers misdemeanors against them, of a public rather than a private nature. But it is necessary to enlarge upon this subject, for the better understanding the sequel of this history.

The Jews are a people dispersed over the face of the whole earth, particularly amongst the Syrians, as they are their near neighbours, and more especially in Antioch, where there are great numbers of them, not only on account of its being a large and populous city, but also by reason of the privileges and immunities they have enjoyed through the favour of government ever since the days of Antiochus Epiphanes, who laid waste the city of Jerusalem, and rifled the temple. The successors of Antiochus caused restitution to be made to the Jews of all the brazen vessels that had been taken away, in order to be dedicated to the service of their synagogue at Antioch, allowing them the same freedom of the city with the Greeks, and they were likewise treated by the succeeding kings in the same manner, their numbers increasing, and their temple rich and flourishing, insomuch that several Pagan proselytes came over to them, and incorporated with their nation.

But, upon the breaking up of the war, and Vespasian's passing by sea into Syria, the Jews rendered themselves extremely odious from one particular incident. There was one Antiochus, son of one of the most eminent Jews in Antioch, both for rank and power. This Antiochus coming into the theatre upon a public assembly, directly charged his father, and certain other foreign Jews, by name, with a design to fire the city in one night. This enraged the multitude to such a degree, that they called immediately for fire, and burnt the pretended conspirators in the midst of the theatre. Their rage went on to doing the same execution on all the rest, and rescuing the country before it was too late. Antiochus aggravated their rage as much as possible, and, as an argument of the affection he had for the Pagan worship, and his aversion to that of the Jews, he not only sacrificed after the Pagan manner himself, but forced others to do so too, upon pain of death in case of refusal. Some of the inhabitants of Antioch complied with this injunction, but most of the Jews stood out, and were put to death.

Antiochus being by this time in a better condition to wreak his vengeance upon the Jews, having a command given him by the governor, exercised more rigour towards the citizens, not permitting them to rest on the sabbath day, forcing them to work and treating them upon that day as upon others, and carried matters to such an extremity, that the observation of the sabbath was not only abolished at Antioch, but in danger of being abrogated every where else.

The persecution of the Jews at Antioch was followed by another calamity. The square market, with several offices where public records were deposited, and other stately buildings, happening to take fire, the flame was so fierce, that the whole city was in danger of being burnt to the ground. Antiochus imputed the guilt of it to the Jews, and the natives were apt enough to believe it, for the very sake of the late story, even if they had not been prepossessed against them beforehand. Taking the matter, however, for granted, they fell upon the persons accused with so outrageous a fury, that Callegas, the deputy-governor to Cerennius Petus, had the utmost difficulty to keep the people quiet, till the emperor might be duly informed of the affair. Cerennius had his commission as the governor, but was not as yet come to his command. Callegas, upon a strict examination of the matter, evidently discovered that not one of the Jews accused by Antiochus had any hand in it. It appeared, on the contrary, to be the scheme of a few abandoned profligates of desperate fortunes, whose only means of securing themselves from being apprehended by their creditors, was to destroy their evidence. But the Jews were yet under great terror from uncertain expectations of the issue of these false accusations.

CHAP. XXII.

Titus expresses the greatest joy for his father's [illegible] Vespasian is received at Rome [illegible] acclamations.

TITUS, on receiving the news of his father's happy arrival in Italy, and of the honourable reception he had met with in the course of his progress, and particu-

CHAP. XVIII.

Jeruſalem taken and deſtroyed. Brief account of its hiſtory

THUS was Jeruſalem taken, and utterly deſtroyed, in the ſecond year of the reign of Veſpaſian, on the eighth day of the month Gorpieus. It had been taken five times before, that is to ſay, by Azochæus, king of Egypt, Antiochus Epiphanes king of Syria, Pompey, Herod, and Soſius, who ſtill preſerved it. But Nebuchadnezzar, king of Babylon, laid it waſte, one thouſand, ſix hundred, ſixty-eight years, and ſix months after it was firſt built.

The firſt founder was a man of power amongſt the Canaanites, called Melchiſedeck, which in the Hebrew language, ſignifies a righteous king, for ſuch he was in an eminent degree. He firſt dedicated the city to the Almighty, erected a temple to it, and officiated in quality of a prieſt, giving it the name of Jeruſalem, which before was called Solyma.

When David, the king of the Jews, came afterwards to drive out the Canaanites, he planted his own people there, and, in four hundred ſeventy-ſeven years, and three months, after this, it was laid waſte by the Babylonians. From the reign of David to the deſtruction of the city under Titus, were one thouſand, one hundred, and ſeventy-nine years; and two thouſand, one hundred, and ſeventy-ſeven, from the foundation of it. Yet neither its antiquity, nor its vaſt riches, nor the diffuſion of its glory over all the habitable earth, nor the great veneration paid it on a religious account, have been ſufficient to preſerve it from deſtruction. This was, in fine, the iſſue of the ſiege.

When the ſoldiers had neither rapine nor bloodſhed to gratify their ſpleen, Titus gave orders for laying the city and temple level with the ground, and leaving nothing ſtanding but the three famous towers, Phaſaelus, Hippicos, and Mariamne, and ſo much of the wall as encloſed the city on the left ſide, where he deſigned to keep a garriſon. The towers were to remain as ſo many monuments to poſterity of the power and conduct of the Romans in taking them. This order was punctually executed, but all the reſt was laid ſo level, that the place ſeemed as if it never had been inhabited. This was the miſerable end to which Jeruſalem was reduced, from the inordinate propenſity of the inhabitants to innovations.

CHAP. XIX.

Titus diſtributes honour and rewards amongſt his ſoldiers, accompanied with an elegant and generous addreſs. Offers a thankſgiving ſacrifice for his victory.

TITUS having formed a reſolution to leave the tenth legion in garriſon in Jeruſalem, with ſome ſquadrons and battalions of horſe and foot, and having diſcharged every duty incumbent on a vigilant and careful general, was deſirous of beſtowing proper rewards upon thoſe who had ſignalized themſelves in the ſervice of their country. To this end, he mounted a tribunal, with his principal officers about him, and from an eminence, where he might beſt be heard, delivering himſelf to the army in terms to the following effect:

"It is impoſſible, my brave fellow ſoldiers, to expreſs "the ſenſe I entertain of the reſpect and obedience you "have ſhewn me during the whole courſe of this war. "Your invincible firmneſs, upon all occaſions, and in "the moſt imminent danger, the reputation you have "acquired in advancing the honour, and enlarging the "territory, of your country, and, finally, the proof you "have given, that neither ſuperiority of numbers, advantages of forts, ſtrength of places, nor the outrageous fury of brutal adverſaries, can ever diſcompoſe the Roman "conduct and courage, claim every mark of gratitude "and reſpect. It was but reaſonable for you to put an "end to a war that had laſted ſo long, which was your "chief deſire when you entered upon it. It muſt afford "you ſingular pleaſure and ſatisfaction, to ſee your choice "of the Roman emperor and generals not only admitted "but univerſally approved. I cannot but eſteem and admire you for all what you have done, but thoſe who "have rendered themſelves exemplary in their enterprizes, and thereby done honour to their characters and "profeſſions, may depend on my care to make an equivalent return. Every emulation to excel ſhall have "proportionate acknowledgment, as I take more delight "in rewarding the meritorious, than in puniſhing the "delinquent."

Titus hereupon ordered the proper officers to produce the liſt of thoſe who ſignalized themſelves by their gallant exploits in the courſe of the war. They were ſpecified by name, and highly applauded, both by the general, and all the reſpectable perſons preſent on the occaſion. From words he proceeded to ſubſtantial inſtances of liberality and bounty. They were crowned with coronets of gold, had golden ornaments put about their necks, lances, pointed with gold, put into their hands, preſented with ſilver medals, and advanced every man according to his ſtation. He gave them money, in gold and ſilver, out of the booty, with rich robes, and other things of value.

Having made this diſtribution according to the merit of each individual, Titus, accompanied by the vows, prayers and acclamations of the whole army, deſcended from his tribunal, to offer ſacrifices, and give thanks for his victory. A great number of oxen were ſacrificed, and diſtributed among the army. Titus having feaſted his officers for three days, the troops were diſmiſſed to their reſpective quarters, and Jeruſalem committed to the guard of the tenth legion, without ſending it back to Euphrates, whence it came.

Bearing in memory that the twelfth legion had given way to the Jews under Ceſtius, their commander, he expelled them out of all Syria, (for they had laid formerly at Raphanea,) and ſent them away to a place called Meletine, that lies along the Euphrates, upon the borders of Cappadocia and Armenia, keeping two legions to himſelf, as a competent guard to convoy him into Egypt. From hence he took his paſſage to Cæſarea upon the coaſt, but it being winter, he durſt not venture into Italy, ſo that he depoſited his treaſure for the preſent, and took every precaution for the ſecurity of the priſoners.

CHAP. XX.

While Titus lay before Jeruſalem, Veſpaſian viſits ſeveral ſea-ports. Simon taken priſoner by Terentius Rufus, ... in chains. Promotes further diſcoveries. The birth's of Domitian and Veſpaſian celebrated with great pomp.

DURING the ſiege of Jeruſalem by Titus, Veſpaſian embarked on board a trading veſſel for Rhodes, where he took a galley, and ſo paſſed out of Ionia into Greece, viſiting all the towns in his way, where he was moſt magnificently received. He then proceeded to Corcyra, and ſo to Japygia, whence he took his journey by land.

Titus was now come back from Cæſarea upon the ſea-coaſt, to that called Cæſarea Philippi, where he made a conſiderable ſtay, entertaining himſelf with a diverſity of ſpectacles, as combats betwixt men and beaſts, man and man, troop and troop, which coſt him the lives of many of his captives.

At this juncture Simon, the ſon of Gioras, happened to be taken in the following manner. Simon, upon the ſiege of Jeruſalem, was forced into the upper town, and the Romans breaking into the city, he was much puzzled to deviſe means of effecting his eſcape, till at length he hit upon this contrivance. He got together a number of miners, stone-cutters, smiths, and men well skilled in iron works, and having laid in a stock of provisions for several weeks, they let themselves all down into a subterraneous cavern. When they had made their way as far as they could, and found the passage too narrow to proceed, they betook themselves to digging and mining, hoping to work a thoroughfare, and so to make their escape. But, before they could make any considerable advance, their provision fell short, and the plan of course failed, though they managed their stores with the utmost œconomy.

Simon had now recourse to another device, which was to alarm and terrify the Romans. To this end he put on a white garment, over which he threw a purple cloak, and in this manner presented himself out of the ground from under the ruins of the late temple, to the amazement of the soldiers and others, that first saw the supposed apparition. But, on his approach, they took courage, asked him his name and who he was, and, upon his refusing to satisfy them, and calling to speak with the officer of the guard, Terentius Rufus, who had the command, was immediately sent for, and learning the truth from Simon, ordered him to be put in chains, and transmitted an account of the whole affair to Cæsar.

Thus was this inhuman tyrant, who had taken away so many of his countrymens lives by subornation and false evidence, upon pretence of their going over to the Romans, brought to justice himself, and delivered into the hands of his enemies, without any force upon him, by his own act. But the stroke of Divine vengeance cannot be avoided, nor is the power of innocence and justice to be contended with, while the punishment is frequently aggravated by being deferred, and when notorious offenders hug themselves in security. This was the case of Simon in the hands of the Romans, and his fantastical scheme of rising out of the ground, proved an occasion of discovering divers of his companions in their lurking-places.

Simon being presented to Titus in chains, on his return to Cæsarea by the sea-side, was ordered to be kept for his triumph at Rome. While Titus was at Cæsarea, he set a day apart for the celebration of the nativity of his brother Domitian, and a great number of his condemned prisoners were dedicated to the honour of the solemnity. The number of those that were destroyed by beasts, fire, and in combat one with another, were supposed to amount at least to two thousand five hundred, and all this too little in the opinion of the Romans, who bore them a mortal aversion. Titus went afterwards to Berytus, a city of Phœnicia, and a Roman colony, where he continued for some time, and celebrated his father's birth-day with more splendour and magnificence than the former, both for spectacles, and other sumptuous entertainments.

CHAP. XXI.

The Jews dispersed throughout the habitable earth, especially in Syria and Antioch. Antiochus, the son of a Jew, occasions many disasters, by setting up the Pagan worship, and suppressing the observation of the sabbath. The city takes fire, and Antiochus imputes it falsely to the Jews.

THE Jews in Antioch were now accused for divers misdemeanors against them, of a public rather than a private nature. But it is necessary to enlarge upon this subject, for the better understanding the sequel of this history.

The Jews are a people dispersed over the face of the whole earth, particularly amongst the Syrians, as they are their near neighbours, and more especially in Antioch, where there are great numbers of them, not only on account of its being a large and populous city, but also by reason of the [illegible] through the favour of government ever since the days of Antiochus Epiphanes, who laid waste the city of Jerusalem, and rifled the temple. The successors of Antiochus caused restitution to be made to the Jews of all the brazen vessels that had been taken away, in order to be dedicated to the service of their synagogue at Antioch, allowing them the same freedom of the city with the Greeks, and they were likewise treated by the succeeding kings in the same manner, their numbers increasing, and their temple rich and flourishing, insomuch, that several Pagan proselytes came over to them, and incorporated with their nation.

But, upon the breaking up of the war, and Vespasian's passing by sea into Syria, the Jews rendered themselves extremely odious from one particular instance. There was one Antiochus, son of one of the most eminent Jews in Antioch, both for rank and power. This Antiochus coming into the theatre upon a public assembly, openly charged his father, and certain other foreign Jews by name, with a design to fire the city in the night. This enraged the multitude to such a degree, that they called immediately for fire, and burnt the pretended conspirators in the midst of the theatre. The rabble were for doing the same execution on all the rest, and [illegible] together country before it was too late. Antiochus [illegible] their rage as much as possible, and, as an argument of the affection he had for the Pagan worship, and his aversion to that of the Jews, he not only sacrificed after the Pagan manner himself but forced others to do so upon pain of death in case of refusal. Some of the inhabitants of Antioch complied with this injunction, but most of the Jews stood out, and were put to death.

Antiochus being by this time in a better condition to wreak his vengeance upon the Jews, having a command given him by the governor, exercised more rigour towards the citizens, not permitting them to rest on the seventh day, forcing them to work, and [illegible] upon that [illegible] upon others, and carried matters to such an extremity, that the observation of the sabbath was not only abolished at Antioch, but in danger of being abrogated every where else.

The persecution of the Jews at Antioch was followed by another calamity. The square market, with several offices where public records were deposited, and other stately buildings, happening to take fire, the flame was so fierce, that the whole city was in danger of being burnt to the ground. Antiochus imputed the cause of it to the Jews, and the natives were apt enough to believe it, for the very sake of the late story, even if they had not been prepossessed against them before-hand. Taking the matter, however, for granted, they fell upon the persons accused with so outrageous a fury, that Collegas, the deputy-governor to Cerennius Petus, had the utmost difficulty to keep the people quiet, till the emperor might be duly informed of the affair. Cerennius had his commission as the governor, but was not as yet come to his command. Collegas, upon a strict examination of the matter, evidently discovered that not one of the Jews accused by Antiochus had any hand in it. It appeared, on the contrary, to be the scheme of a few abandoned profligates of desperate fortunes, whose only means of securing themselves from being apprehended by their creditors, was to burn their evidence. But the Jews were yet under great terror from uncertain expectations of the issue of these false accusations.

CHAP. XXII.

Titus expresses the greatest respect [illegible] arrival in Italy. Vespasian is received at Rome [illegible] acclamations.

TITUS, on receiving the news of his father's happy arrival in Italy, and of the honourable reception he had met with in the course of his progress [illegible]

[illegible] on his entering the city of Rome, could not but give every demonstration of [illegible] and satisfaction. Vespasian was held in the same [illegible] at all instances, as if he had been present, and the [illegible] expectation the people had of seeing him, [illegible] compensated for his absence. The [illegible] who [illegible] the miserable revolutions they [illegible] during the sovereign rule from one [illegible] themselves happy in the bless[illegible] reputation, con[illegible] the administration. The com[illegible] the change, [illegible] civil wars, [illegible] hope of being restored, by his means, to [illegible] had given [illegible] and genu[illegible] in the [illegible] them [illegible].

[illegible] so universally beloved, that [illegible] of dignity under the govern[illegible] distance [illegible] out to meet him a considerable way [illegible] with such a train of the populace after [illegible] came out than stayed behind. As he [illegible] word was brought him how the [illegible] of the people by his affability [illegible] being thronged with women and children, [illegible] longing to see him, breaking [illegible] of admiration at the elegance of his person, [illegible] of his manners, calling him their be[illegible] and protector, and extolling him as the only prince under the [illegible] deserved an imperial crown. The whole city was so set out with garlands and perfumes, that it resembled a temple, and the streets so crowded, that there was hardly any passing to the palace. [illegible] the same time, offered up to his household [illegible] for his safe return, while [illegible] themselves up to feasting, with their tribes [illegible] neighbours, wishing a long and happy reign to Vespasian, and a continuance of the imperial sovereignty to his son, and those of the line that should come after him. This was the manner in which the citizens of Rome received Vespasian, and the empire immediately experienced the happiness of his auspicious reign.

CHAP. XXIII.

The Germans revolt, [illegible] the cause of it. Cassius and Civilis [illegible] of [illegible] rebellion. [illegible] some [illegible] of Sarmatians [illegible] the Roman garrisons. Rubrius Gallus [illegible] to the [illegible].

BEFORE the arrival of Vespasian at Alexandria, and during the time that Titus was before Jerusalem, there happened a revolt among the Germans, to which they were animated and encouraged by their neighbours the Gauls, in hopes of shaking off the Roman yoke. The Germans being naturally ferocious and inconsiderate, readily engaged in any rash undertaking; besides, they were incited to it by a mortal aversion to the Romans, as the only power they feared: to which may be added, a favourable conjecture of the times, with respect to the [illegible] factions and divisions of the empire upon so many changes of government.

Cassius and Civilis, two men of rank among the Germans, took advantage of these distractions to promote a sedition, to which they had been disposed long before. Upon sounding the multitude, they found them eager for the attempt, and in all probability they would in general have embarked in it, had they not been prevented by a fortuitous circumstance: for the Romans, Petilius Cerealis, formerly governor of Germany, received letters from Vespasian, appointing him consul, and commanding him to repair immediately to Italy, and take upon him the command. Having intelligence, on his way, of this insurrection, he marched against them as they were in a[illegible], charged and put them to the rout with very great slaughter, and brought the rest back again to their duty. Had not Cerealis fallen thus suddenly upon them, it had not been long before they would have been brought to [illegible] punishment. For the news of this rebellion had no sooner reached Rome, than Domitian, the son of Vespasian, [illegible] inherited the heroic spirit of his [illegible] father, [illegible] himself at the head of an army against the [illegible] upon the very rumour of his approach [illegible] themselves, deeming it a happiness to return to [illegible] allegiance, without suffering. [illegible] the [illegible] Domitian had appeased the commotions in Gaul, [illegible] any suspicion of [illegible], he returned [illegible] with the acclamations of the people, [illegible] performed [illegible] above his own age, and [illegible] the son of so great a father.

The [illegible] of the Germans was [illegible] incursion of the Scythians, or Sarmatians, [illegible] ing themselves over the Danube, [illegible] into Mysia, without being perceived, surprized [illegible] Roman garrisons, and with relentless cruelty, put them to the sword. They also slew Fonteius Agrippa, a [illegible] of consular authority, at the head of his troops, and proceeded to lay waste the whole province. When Vespasian received intelligence of the havock they made in Mysia, he sent Rubrius Gallus to call them to account. This officer did great execution upon them, so that the insurrection was quickly at an end, and the general took care to secure the passages leading to the province from [illegible] such incursions in future.

CHAP. XXIV.

Titus marches in triumph with his prisoners. The S[illegible] [illegible], and whence it derived that appellation. The people of Antioch rejoice at the arrival of Titus. [illegible] petition against the Jews, which is rejected. Titus [illegible] Egypt, and is much affected at the [illegible] Jerusalem. Vast treasures buried [illegible] John, with seven hundred chosen men, [illegible] the triumph. The order and magnificence of the [illegible] concluded in the temple of Jupiter [illegible] Death of Simon Giora. Ves[illegible] Jews.

TITUS, on his return from Berytus, exhibited magnificent spectacles in all the cities through which he passed, carrying his captives with him for the honour of his arms, and the ornament of his triumph. In his progress he observed on his way, between Arca and Raphanea, cities in the kingdom of Agrippa, a river of so peculiar a nature as deserves to be recorded in history. While this river flows, it has a full stream of a strong current, after which its springs fail for six days together, and leaves the channel dry to the very bottom. On the seventh day it fills again, as though it had undergone no change, and keeps exactly the same course as before. Hence it is called the Sabbatical river, alluding to the seventh day's festival among the Jews.

When the people of Antioch were informed that Titus was approaching, they were so rejoiced at the tidings, that the populace posted away thirty furlongs out of the town, to meet and welcome him on his way. As he drew near, they made a lane to receive him, and with all possible demonstration of affection and respect, conducted him to the city, intermixing with their acclamations earnest importunities to banish all the Jews out of the city. Titus did not yield to their intreaty, but gave them the bare hearing quietly. The Jews, however, were in fearful apprehensions of the result.

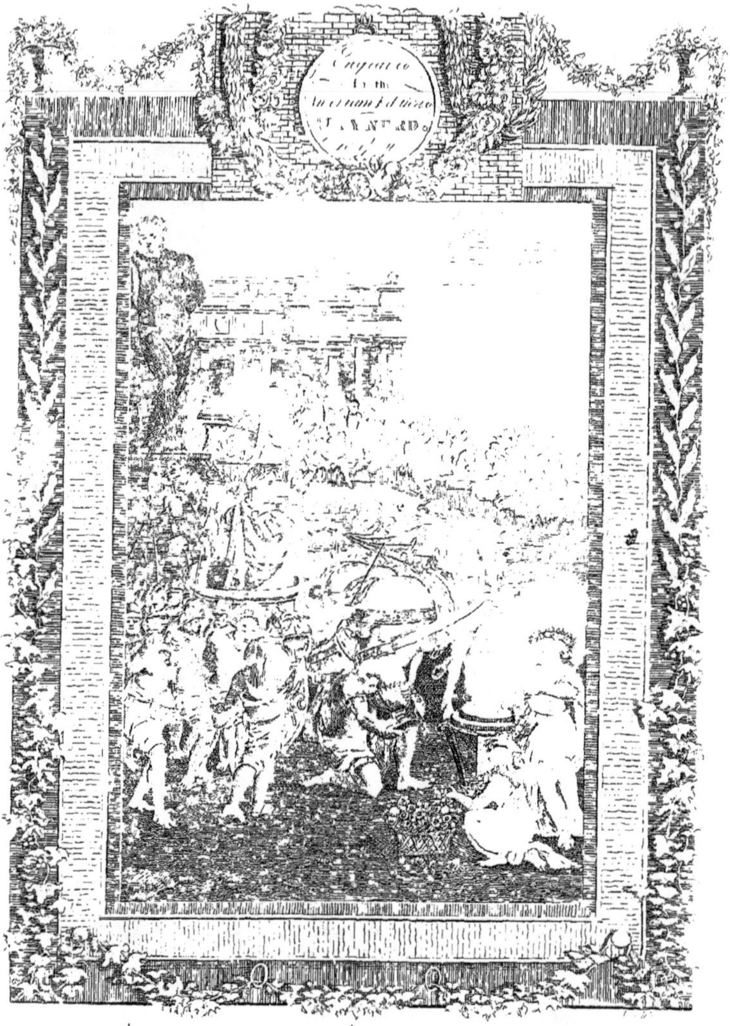

Magnificent TRIUMPH of TITUS after the Reduction of Jerusalem

Titus made no stay at Antioch, but continued his progress [illegible] Zeugma, which lies upon the Euphrates, where [illegible] with an embassy from Vologesus, king of [illegible] the compliment of a golden crown in congratulation [illegible] his victory over the Jews. This accepted of the [illegible] the [illegible], and went back again [illegible] no sooner arrived, than the magistrates [illegible] with great earnestness, to the theatre, with [illegible] and there found a mighty con[illegible] his entrance. They immediately [illegible] for the expulsion of [illegible] presence of mind, [illegible] reply, "[illegible] own country was destroyed [illegible] world [illegible]." When they failed in [illegible] they [illegible] another request, which was, that [illegible] upon them of the [illegible] might either be removed or defaced [illegible] [illegible] himself in either, but left the Jews at [illegible] the [illegible] as he found them [illegible]

[illegible] journey, and saw the [illegible] the country [illegible] comparison between the [illegible] and [illegible] the one resembling a paradise, the other a desert. [illegible] to deplore the [illegible] authors of [illegible] the cause of it. [illegible] he [illegible] upon a public [illegible] instructions that forced him upon the [illegible] treasures buried in the ruins of [illegible] gold, silver, and other precious commodities, to [illegible] the [illegible] had concealed [illegible] of the enemy [illegible] the Romans found [illegible] to Egypt, passed over [illegible] and formed [illegible] the [illegible] having [illegible] back [illegible] quarters the [illegible] the tenth into [illegible]. But Simon and [illegible] prisoners, selected from the rest for [illegible] of their persons, were transported to Italy, in order to [illegible] the triumph.

[illegible] prosperous voyage, Titus arrived at Rome, where [illegible] the same honours and respects as his [illegible] Vespasian [illegible] out with the rest to meet his son, [illegible] which the people looked upon as an earnest of [illegible] the father and his two sons [illegible] so propitious a Providence.

[illegible] this, the senate having resolved upon two triumphs, one for the father, the other for the [illegible] honour of their [illegible] achievements, Vespasian [illegible] notwithstanding this decree, declared themselves [illegible] triumphs into one. Previous notice having been given of the day appointed for this pompous solemnity, not one of the immense multitude was left in the city, but every one went out to secure a station, insomuch that [illegible] there was hardly any passage [illegible] the procession. The soldiers, with their officers at the head, marched in good order before day, up to the gates near the temple of Isis, where the princes rested the foregoing night, in order to wait their coming up. At break of day, Vespasian and Titus advanced, with crowns of laurel upon their heads, and purple robes, after the manner of their country, as far as the Octavian Walks, where the senate, nobility, and Roman knights waited for them. A tribunal was erected before the portico, and two seats upon it, which they mounted, and sitting down, were saluted with the acclamations of the whole field. As they were going on with their eulogies on the princes, Vespasian made a signal for silence, and when all was hush and quiet, he stood up, and covering part of his head with his garment offered up certain vows and prayers according to custom, and, after him, Titus did the like. Vespasian then, in a short speech, addressed the spectators in general, and sent away the soldiers to an entertainment prepared for them at the charge of the emperor. He then went to the triumphal gate so called [illegible] the procession in triumph passing that way [illegible] there, taking a repast, putting on their triumphal habits, they offered [illegible] and so led on the triumph, and marched through the theatre for the better view of the people, and the greater glory of the solemnity.

The magnificence and variety of these spectacles [illegible] not be conceived, much less expressed; whether they are considered in point of exquisite workmanship [illegible] value, or attracting novelty: for they comprehended [illegible] of curiosities many years collecting, and now combined to complete the triumph of this auspicious day, to the honour of the [illegible] Roman [illegible]. There was a vast quantity of gold, silver, and ivory, [illegible] a multiplicity of [illegible] and so disposed as to [illegible] [illegible] some [illegible] with the [illegible] purple hangings, others [illegible] to the life, figures [illegible] by the art [illegible] There were also jewels and precious stones [illegible] [illegible] to [illegible] images of their gods [illegible] [illegible] and publicly attended [illegible] by a vast number of people [illegible] with gold, and [illegible] the [illegible] of the solemnity, had their [illegible] of state and splendour. The very captives [illegible] out something graceful in their habits, to [illegible] of their condition, and [illegible] the [illegible]

For nothing was more worthy of [illegible] the [illegible] of the pageants, which were of such [illegible] that it was almost incredible that the bearers could support them. The cost was [illegible] [illegible] wrought with gold, silver and ivory. There were [illegible] the most lively [illegible] with all the circumstances that attend it. In one place was the delineation of a beautiful country [illegible] whole armies cut to pieces, [illegible] prisoners, strong walls battered to the ground, fortresses demolished [illegible] taken by assault, fires devouring [illegible] [illegible] implored mercy [illegible] upon the heads of their [illegible] streams, [illegible] from refreshing the fields, [illegible] their course through a general [illegible] in a word, pourtrayed a lively image of the miseries of the Jews, and was so [illegible] that it might furnish a picture [illegible] of the ruin of our once famous city, for those who were not eye-witnesses of it.

Upon each of the pageants [illegible] ners of the place that was [illegible] ing it. [illegible] spoils, that were dispersed up and down [illegible] The most considerable pieces were the golden [illegible] and the golden candlestick, that were taken out of the temple of Jerusalem; the former weighing several [illegible] and the other not applicable to the use to which it was intended. There was [illegible] root of it, and out of that [illegible] as from the [illegible] of a tree, seven branches, every branch having [illegible] resemblance of a lamp, the number of seven importing the veneration the Jews have for the seventh day. After this came the Jewish law, which was the last trophy of their conquests that the Romans exposed. Vespasian himself, with Titus, brought up the rear [illegible] upon horseback, mounted [illegible] his station. They marched together [illegible] the temple of Jupiter Capitolinus, and there [illegible]

[illegible] remained some little time in this place, it being according to ancient custom so to do upon the like occasion, till news was brought them that the general of the enemy was [illegible]. This general was Simon Gioras, one of the captives that walked in triumph through the market-place, with a rope about his neck, and put to death by those that drew him, according to the Roman law and practice in the [illegible] of malefactors. Word being brought that Gioras was [illegible], the whole field rang with shouts and acclamations, and the people betook themselves to their vows and [illegible], and when the solemnity was over, the princes returned to the palace, where they gave an elegant entertainment [illegible] others, [illegible] throughout the day, but [illegible] and giving thanks for the final victory they had obtained over their enemies, to the glory of their generals, and the [illegible] of public tranquillity.

When the triumph was over, and the empire settled [illegible] Vespasian erected a temple dedicated to Peace [illegible] so short a time, and so [illegible] human expectation. He [illegible] over and above a collection of the choicest [illegible] painting and sculpture, to adorn it, insomuch, [illegible] people flocked from all quarters to see the glory and order of this admirable structure. In this temple he deposited the golden table and the candlestick, as the most valuable trophies of his victory; giving orders that the Jewish laws, and purple veils of the sanctuary, should be lodged with great care and reverence in the place.

CHAP. XXV.

The situation of Machærus. Name of the plants, rue and [illegible] [illegible] Machærus. The natural fend [illegible] [illegible] the [illegible] town. [illegible] A valiant exploit of Eleazar. Bassus discharges [illegible] Eleazar [illegible].

When Lucilius Bassus was sent, by Cæsar, as legate into Judæa, he took upon him the command of the army from Cerealis Petilianus, and made himself master of the castle of Herodion, with the garrison that was in it. After this he drew his troops together, that lay scattered up and down, proposing, with the help of the tenth legion, to attack Machærus, a design of the utmost importance, as the strength of that place would ever be an inducement to a rebellion, and as the situation of it gave confidence to the town, so it struck an awe, on the other hand, upon any that should attempt it.

The mountain, upon which Machærus stands, is prodigiously high and rocky, to the degree of rendering it almost impregnable. Nature has made it well nigh inaccessible too, by enclosing it with valleys that are neither to be passed, nor to be filled up, and so deep likewise, that the eye could not reach their bottoms. It reaches to the westward sixty furlongs in length, and borders on the lake Asphaltitis, the [illegible] an unbounded prospect over all that quarter. On the north and south it is encompassed with vallies of the same dimensions, and as secure from any attempt as on the other parts. The depth on the east, is, in length, an hundred cubits, and reaches to the mountains over against Machærus.

Alexander, king of the Jews, was the first that fortified this place, and built a castle upon it, which Gabinius afterwards demolished in his war with Aristobulus. Then Herod the Great, deeming it an object worthy of his regard, as a piece of defence against the Arabians, [illegible] a substantial wall about it, with strong turrets at the corners, of sixty cubits in height; and in the middle built a magnificent palace, which was abundantly supplied with water from cisterns, wherever there was occasion for it, as if nature and art had been at strife which should exceed the other, the one by situation, the other by improvement. He likewise furnished this castle with a plentiful magazine of arms, arrows, engines, and provisions of every kind, both for war and sustenance, that the garrison never need to fear either force or famine.

Within this palace there grew a sort of rue, that excited admiration on account of its size, being as tall and well spread as any fig-tree. According to report, it has been there ever since the days of Herod, and might have continued longer, if the Jews had not rooted it up upon taking the place. In the valley on the north side of Machærus, called Baaras, there grows a plant of the same name. [illegible] colour resembles that of a flame, and towards the evening, sends forth a ray like lightning. It is not easily taken, [illegible] recedes from the touch; nay, it is certain death to touch it without a piece of the root [illegible] the hand. It [illegible] without danger in the following manner. [illegible] trench quite round it, till the hidden part of the root becomes very small, and then tie a dog to it, and when the dog struggles hard to follow him that tied him, the root is pulled up, but the animal expires immediately, as if it were to redeem the man. After this it may be touched with as much safety as any other plant, but it [illegible] that compensates for the trouble in obtaining it, being, on the touch, a certain remedy for the expulsion of demons.

In the same place there is a wonderful diversity of springs and fountains, of very different qualities and tastes, some being hot, others sweet, and others bitter. There are also cold springs, intermingled one with another, in the low ground. But that which is more surprizing, is a hollow cave, with a rocky stone over it, and two figures of [illegible] breasts, like two fountains, prominent from it, the one discharging hot water, and the other cold, and they compose a most agreeable bath, which is salutary in many maladies, and especially those of the nerves. There are also mines of sulphur and allum.

When Bassus had taken a full view of the place, he resolved to besiege it, proposing to fill up the valley to the east of the town, and make his approaches that way. He first, with great pains and expedition, raised a battery against the castle, as the most probable means of facilitating the attempt. The Jews resident divided themselves from those who were strangers, and turned them off as an insignificant herd to sustain the first shock, while they seized on the upper citadel, and held it, not only as the most defensible of the two, but as a place where they might make better terms with the Romans in case of the worst. They determined, however, to use every effort to divert the siege; and there passed not a day without resolute sallies and skirmishes, and a considerable loss of men on both sides, one party sometimes having the advantage and sometimes the other. The Jews, when they fell upon the Romans by surprize, and the Romans, when they were aware of the Jews coming, provided to receive them. But the conclusion of the siege did not depend on these skirmishes, for an incident happened that reduced the Jews to an absolute necessity of giving up the castle.

There was amongst the besieged, one Eleazar, a young man, of a bold and enterprizing spirit, who made several vigorous sallies, and did all that was possible, both by council and example, to obstruct the progress of the Romans, and put a check to their undertakings, insomuch that he became at once a terror to his enemies, and a support to his friends. He was the first that presented himself in all encounters, and the last in case of a retreat that came off. It happened, on a certain time, when a skirmish was over, and both parties were withdrawn, that Eleazar, in a vain glorious contempt of the enemy, made a stop without the gate, and began to talk to some of the defendants upon the walls. This being within view of the Roman camp, one Rufus, an Egyptian, availing himself of the opportunity, seized him unawares, and carried him off, armed as he was, into the enemy's quarter. The Roman general ordered him to be stripped and scourged upon the ground in the sight of the city. The Jews were so confounded at the calamitous accident that befel this gallant youth, that became a subject of [illegible] had [illegible], which Bassus perceiving, he naturally concluded that, if he could but excite their compassion, he might gain his point, and bring them to a composition [illegible] giving up the place to save Eleazar's life. This [illegible] succeeded to his wish; for, upon the setting up of a cross [illegible] Eleazar was to be forthwith crucified, the garrison [illegible] cry with one voice, "that their affliction was intolerable." Eleazar, upon this, begged of them to consider both his case, who was now to die a wretched death, and [illegible] not contend longer with the valour and fortune of the Romans, since the world had already submitted [illegible] to their empire.

The submission and supplication of Eleazar, together with the powerful intercessions of his friends, who were men of [illegible] and influence, softened the defendant [illegible] that they sent deputies immediately to the Romans, [illegible] proposal to deliver up the castle, upon condition of [illegible] Eleazar and leaving the garrison at liberty to go [illegible] would. Bassus accepted the terms, [illegible] the agreement that was made by the Jews for themselves [illegible] to [illegible] in the night. Upon opening the gates, [illegible] it from those who [illegible] with him, but the most courageous [illegible] the enemy from entering the town, and got off, while the rest, to the number of 1700 men, were put to the sword, and the women and children made slaves. But as Bassus deemed it expedient to fulfil his articles, he dismissed the garrison, and set Eleazar at liberty.

CHAP. XXVI.

[illegible]

WHEN Bassus had [illegible] the affairs, he [illegible] marched [illegible] the army to the forest of Judes, upon intelligence that great numbers of Jews, who had escaped from Jerusalem and Machærus, were there assembled. [illegible] upon his arrival, that the information was authentic, he [illegible] the whole place with his horse, where he ordered so strict guard to be kept, that not a Jew could possibly pass [illegible]. He employed his foot at the same time, to [illegible] the trees and bushes of the thickets where the Jews [illegible] and [illegible], so that there [illegible] no way of escaping [illegible] through the troops of the enemy. This being [illegible], they drew [illegible] body, and, with an [illegible] upon those [illegible] them, [illegible] were as bravely received. The [illegible], in fine, through the [illegible] of the one [illegible] on the other, was hot and obstinate, [illegible] for the Romans, with the loss of twelve killed, and not many wounded, whereas of the three thousand Jews that were in this action, not so much as one man came off. Among the rest was Judas, the son of Jair, that leader, who had formerly a command at the siege of Jerusalem, and made his escape at last out of a vault.

The emperor, at the same time, wrote to his officer Liberius Maximus, to make sale of all the Jews lands, as he would not trouble himself with rebuilding any other cities but take them all to his own use, leaving only eight hundred soldiers in Emmaus, about sixty furlongs distant from Jerusalem, and imposing a poll-tax upon every Jew of two drachmæ, or half a shekel a year, to be paid into the capitol [illegible] had been formerly done into the temple. Such was the miserable state of the Jews at this time.

CHAP. XXVII.

The calamities that befel Antiochus, king of Comagene. He is represented as an enemy to Cæsar, by Cesennius, who makes an incursion into his dominions. Antiochus [illegible] to withdraw, and not return any act of hostility. Epiphanes and Callinicus his two sons [illegible] to the [illegible]. Antiochus flies into Cilicia. The brothers [illegible] to the king of Parthia, who [illegible] Vespasian kindly treats Antiochus, his captive. The [illegible] and sons are conducted to Rome, [illegible]. The Scythians [illegible]. Narrow escape of Tiridates, king of Armenia.

IN the fourth year of the reign of Vespasian, it happened that Antiochus, king of Comagene, with his whole family, fell into very great calamities, and this was the occasion. Cesennius Pætus, who was governor of Syria at this time, wrote Cæsar word that Antiochus, with his son Epiphanes, were resolved to revolt from the Romans, and had treated with the king of Parthia [illegible] at the same time, the necessity of preventing [illegible], by striking the first blow. Whatever might be the motive on the part of Cesennius, Cæsar could not, in prudence, neglect the advice, as the vicinity of the kingdoms rendered the consideration of importance, and as Samosata, the capital of Comagene, lying upon Euphrates, might afford the Parthians [illegible] passage, or a secure retreat.

Vespasian, however, was so possessed [illegible] the event of the story, that he left Cesennius at his own discretion, [illegible] a commission to act as might seem to him most expedient. The Roman governor [illegible] his departure and fell immediately into Comagene with the [illegible] legion, and some [illegible] of horse and foot. He also called in to his assistance Aristobulus, king of Chalcis, and Sohemus, king of Emesa. Antiochus [illegible] suspecting his design. His entrance met with no opposition, for the natives were not in a condition to encounter him, nor had Antiochus, when he heard of the [illegible] least thought of a misunderstanding with the Romans. [illegible] this embarrassment he determined to leave his kingdom in its present state, and retire, with his wife and children, to Rome, in order to demonstrate his good [illegible] to the empire. Hereupon he withdrew about [illegible] furlongs from the city, and encamped upon a plain, Cesennius, in the mean time, sent soldiers to take possession of Samosata, and keep garrison there, [illegible] other troops, marched away [illegible] Antiochus. [illegible] this violence and injustice did not provoke the king to any unfriendly act against the Romans. He [illegible] his hard fate, and endured, with patience, what he was not able to prevent.

But his sons, Epiphanes and Callinicus, who were youthful, brave, and martial, could not, however, [illegible] themselves to arms, so that drawing [illegible] were able to raise, they gave the Romans battle, [illegible] the whole day, and, in the end, carried a conflict equal to their valour, for they came off with very little loss.

The fortune of this day, though favourable to Antiochus did not stop the retreat upon which he had resolved, for he took his wife and daughters away with him into Cilicia, and by that means greatly discouraged his soldiers, who having nothing to hope when their king [illegible] ed, and went over to the Romans. It [illegible] necessary for his sons to provide [illegible] their own [illegible] before it was too late, so that, with ten horsemen, they passed the Euphrates (where they were now safe) [illegible] to Vologeses, king of Parthia. [illegible] upon [illegible] not treat them as fugitives, [illegible] [illegible] the [illegible]

[illegible] having reached [illegible], in [illegible], Cesennius [illegible] to take him into custody, and carry him [illegible] to Rome. But Vespasian was too generous to treat [illegible] with indignity, and chose rather to shew [illegible] friendship than to revenge himself for [illegible]. He therefore ordered his chains to be [illegible] off upon the way, and his journey to Rome [illegible], that he might make some stay at Lacedæmon, where he furnished him with a provision of money suitable to the [illegible] of his character.

This frank and [illegible] proceeding towards Antiochus, not only delivered the brothers from the anxiety they [illegible] for their father, but encouraged them to hope [illegible] reconciliation with Cæsar himself, especially at the [illegible] of Vologeses, that they might be permitted to go to Rome, being ever desirous of living within the pale of the empire. They [illegible], in fine, to Rome, whither [illegible] was soon after conducted; and they were all [illegible] treated with every token of affection and esteem.

[illegible] people now known by the name of Alanes, formerly called Scythians, inhabiting the country near the river Tanais, and the lake Mæotis, formed in confederacy with the king of Hyrcania, to break into Media, and commit depredations, for he was master of that passage which Alexander shut up with iron gates. This pass being [illegible] they possessed themselves of the place, without [illegible] suspicion or resistance, and carried off a booty, in goods and cattle, to a considerable value. This [illegible] so alarmed Pacorus, then king of the place, that he left his [illegible] and fled, for his own safety, into obscure [illegible], till he found means at length, with some difficulty, to redeem his wife and concubines for an hundred talents. Tiridates, who afterwards became king of that country, met and fought them, but was nearly taken [illegible] in the battle, by the noose of an halter that was thrown over his head, but, in the very moment as they were [illegible] him off he cut the rope with his sword, and made his escape. The success of this combat rendered those barbarians more bloody and insolent than before, insomuch that they ravaged the country, and carried off with them an immense booty.

CHAP XXVIII

[illegible] those robbers called Sicarii, [illegible] The abominable [illegible] Roman general, besieges Massada. [illegible] Inspiration, [illegible] by Eleazar [illegible] Reflections on the opinions of the [illegible] philosophers and Brachmans. The effects of [illegible] Jews. The Romans [illegible]

ON the death of Bassus, Flavius Silva was appointed governor of Judæa, and finding the whole country reduced to the obedience of the empire, excepting one rebellious castle, he drew out his utmost strength, with a resolution to attack it. The name of the castle was Massada, and it was under the command of one Eleazar, ringleader of the Sicarii, who had seized upon it. This Eleazar was a descendant from that Judas who persuaded a great number of Jews not to submit to the taxation, when Cyrenius executed the office of censor in Judæa. The faction of the Sicarii, it is to be observed, were professed enemies to all that shewed any manner of respect to the Romans, and treated them in that light, even to the degree of pillaging their goods, driving away their cattle, and burning their houses, alledging, "that those men were no better than strangers who betrayed their country in a dastardly manner, and had rather live slaves than freemen, notwithstanding freedom is a blessing that can never be too dearly purchased."

But this specious declaration was only a cover for their inhumanity and avarice, as most evidently appeared in the conclusion, for, when these very men, whom they branded with perfidy and cowardice, came to join the revolt, and in the common cause against the Romans, they were more injuriously treated than before, especially those that laid open the hypocrisy of their pretensions, and the iniquity of their practices.

There never was an age since the creation, in which [illegible] manner of impiety prevailed amongst the Jews [illegible] at this juncture. Invention seemed too [illegible] species of wickedness, men seemed to agree in every [illegible] of corruption, and there was an emulation to excel in [illegible] doing. Those in power oppressed the common people [illegible] the common people opposed the authority of those in [illegible] the one contending for dominion, the other for [illegible]

The Sicarii were the first that led the way to this [illegible] course of massacre and rapine [illegible] opportunity, either by word or deed, of [illegible] But the cruelties of John were of all the rest the most extravagant. This inhuman monster not only [illegible] men to death as common enemies, and [illegible] for presuming to advise measures profitable for the [illegible] but multiplied all manner of outrages upon his [illegible] What better, indeed, could be expected from a [illegible] seemed to set the majesty of heaven at defiance, [illegible] particular instances of the use of forbidden meats, [illegible] the purity of his profession, and de[illegible] laws and customs of our forefathers? [illegible] ly prove humane to his fellow-creature, that [illegible] wards his Creator.

Simon, the son of Gioras, seems to have [illegible] John of Gischala in his nefarious practices. What barbarities did he not inflict upon the very [illegible] He enslaved those that were born free, violated the [illegible] and friendship, inflamed his myrmidons to [illegible] the most horrid butcheries, who [illegible] strangers a kind of disgraceful exploit, compared with the heroic bravery of trampling upon their own flesh and blood.

The Idumæans bore their part in the [illegible] of the times. These execrable miscreants, after [illegible] the high-priests, and thereby cutting off, as much as in them lay, the whole frame and order of religion at one stroke, endeavoured to destroy the remains of [illegible] government, and introduced every species of [illegible] practicable. This was the province of those that were called zealots, to whom that appellation was justly [illegible], as they were the warmest [illegible], the most [illegible] advocates for vice and irreligion, under the colour of [illegible] and virtue seducing those they [illegible] giving evil the semblance of good, and good that of evil. At length however, Divine vengeance overtook and stopped them in their career, for they suffered all the calamities and torments that is possible for human nature to undergo, and that throughout the whole [illegible] their lives. It might be justly said, that they suffered [illegible] they deserved, because they could not be punished according to their deserts. Indeed, their crimes were of [illegible] hue, as to exclude them almost from pity, [illegible] But to return to our main point.

Silva, the Roman general, was now upon his march to besiege Massada, where there was a garrison of the Sicarii, under the command of Eleazar, who was the head of that party. He had gained possession of the [illegible] country about it, without much difficulty, [illegible] in the most convenient places, and [illegible] the castle, to prevent excursions or escapes, and [illegible] the guards. He made choice of a quarter [illegible] ou[illegible] com[illegible] for his purpose, this was upon [illegible] of the castle rock to the next mountain. Pro[illegible], indeed, were extremely scarce, for they were [illegible] great length of way, and with much trouble to [illegible] Jews, whose business it was to supply them, besides [illegible] water another way, as there was no foun[illegible] in the place.

[illegible] taken these previous steps, Silva made the neces[illegible] for the siege, which was like to be a [illegible] of time and labour, as will appear from a description [illegible] of the castle.

[illegible] upon a large high rock, with deep and craggy precipices round about it. There is no discerning the [illegible] other rocks, that interpose and cover it. The access is so difficult, that even beasts cannot climb it, except by two passages, one to the eastward from the [illegible] Asphaltites, which is very dangerous, the other from [illegible] which is more practicable of the two. One of [illegible] is called by the name of the Serpent, from [illegible] windings and turnings in the ascent, for the [illegible] many places double upon themselves. The pas[illegible] likewise so narrow, that there is a necessity for [illegible] upon one foot while the other is advanced, be[illegible] false step is certain death, as, on each side there [illegible] precipice tremendous to behold. This passage is esti[illegible] at thirty furlongs from the bottom to the top of the [illegible] upon which is a plain, where Jonathan, the [illegible], built a fortress, and called it Massada.

[illegible] the Great afterwards adorned and fortified it at [illegible] charge and labour. He built a wall round it [illegible] furlongs in compass, composed of [illegible] white stone, twelve cubits in height, and eight in breadth. He erected also upon that wall twenty-seven turrets, each fif[illegible] cubits in height, and these turrets had a communi[illegible] with all the buildings on the inside of the wall. The [illegible] above was of so fruitful a soil, that Herod ordered [illegible] to be set apart for tillage, that those who should take [illegible] the citadel, might never want provision. He built a magnificent palace for himself within the com[illegible] of the castle, the entrance from the west and [illegible] a little to the north. The walls of it were high and strong, with towers in the four corners, each sixty cu[illegible] in height. The apartments, galleries, and baths, for construction and ornament, equalled any of his works, [illegible] supported by pillars each of one entire stone and wrought with exquisite skill. In each quarter of the pa[illegible] were many large cisterns, hewed out of the rock, for the preserving of water, so that [illegible] reservoirs abundant[illegible] supplied the want of fountains. There was also a way [illegible] ground from the palace up to the castle, which was not to be discovered from without, and that on the east side, as before observed, was impassable. On the way to the westward, and in the narrowest place, was built a large tower, a thousand cubits distant from the castle, and thus was their citadel fortified by art and na[illegible] to frustrate the attempts of assailants.

Nor was this fortress provided only against force and stratagem, but also against the [illegible] of famine, being stocked with corn, wine, oil, pulse, and dates for many years, all which Eleazer found there when he, with the Sicarii, took it by surprize. Moreover, the provisions [illegible] as fresh and sound as if they had been recently depo[illegible], though they had remained there little less than an hundred years, which probably might be owing to the purity of the air at that height abstracted from gross vapours.

There was also found here a magazine of arms sufficient for ten thousand men, stored there by order of Herod, to[illegible]gether with a great quantity of unwrought iron, brass, [illegible] and tin, from which it may be presumed, he had [illegible] important design in contemplation. According to [illegible], Herod prepared this fortress as a refuge against two [illegible] of danger: the one, lest the people should depose [illegible], and restore the Asmonean family to the throne, the other, and much greater danger, lest Cleopatra should prevail with Anthony to seek his life, in order to raise her to the government of Judæa, as she acknowledged to have tampered with him to accomplish such a purpose. What[illegible]ever was the motive, Herod put Massada in such a condi[illegible]tion, that it was long deemed impregnable, and [illegible], in[illegible]deed, the finishing stroke for the Romans in the Jewish war.

Silva, the Roman general, having by the wall he built on the outside, precluded the Jews from escape, advanced with his engines, there being but one place that could [illegible] up to raise a bank, for behind the tower which [illegible] the road that led to the palace, and to the top of the hill from the west, there was a large long rock, called Leuce, but not so high by three hundred cubits as Massada. [illegible] general had no sooner gained this rock, than [illegible] fell to work with such alacrity, that [illegible] ed two hundred cubits high, but not being [illegible] to support the engines, they raised [illegible] on it, wrought [illegible] stones, fifty [illegible] breadth and height. [illegible] besides these [illegible] they had others, of [illegible] afterwards by Titus. They [illegible] platform, a tower of sixty cubits, plated with iron.

The Romans, from [illegible] with darts and stones from the engines to such a degree, that they were forced to retire. At the same time Silva ordered the great battering ram to be brought forward, and plyed against the wall, and, in course of time [illegible] some impression. The Sicarii, however, quickly sup[illegible]ed the defect, by building another wall within [illegible] which [illegible] cluded the force of the engines, [illegible] the matter being pliant, it deadened the strokes.

When Silva found his engines ineffectual, he resolved to attempt that by fire which he could not com[illegible] by [illegible]tery, and therefore ordered his soldiers to try what might be done by fire-brands towards destroying the defences. The new works, being chiefly composed of timber, took fire immediately, and burst out into a mighty flame, which began with the wind at the north, and beat terribly upon the Romans, that they almost despaired of saving their engines, but the wind fortunately, [illegible] ing about to the southward, drove so [illegible] upon the wall that it set all in a flame from top to bottom. The Romans were so sensible of this providential [illegible] in their favour, that they returned [illegible] to their camp with full resolution to attack the enemy next morning at day-break, and to keep careful [illegible] that they might not escape in the night.

But Eleazar never entertained a thought of [illegible] or suffering any of his people to do so. [illegible] however, being confined to the [illegible], and no [illegible] possibility left of safety or relief, he [illegible] to consider how they might deliver [illegible] from the ignominious treatment they had reason to expect at the hands of the Romans, whenever they came to be masters of the place. Eleazar upon weighing the mat[illegible]ter, concluding that a glorious death was infinitely pre[illegible]ferable to a life of infamy, and that the noblest [illegible] they could take was not to outlive their liberties, [illegible] together the most courageous of his friends, and, [illegible] following address, endeavoured to prevail with them to a compliance with it.

"It is no new thing, my generous friends, [illegible] people to disclaim all [illegible] and [illegible] the true and sovereign Lord and Master [illegible] God himself, [illegible] mans, or to any other [illegible] is now at hand to make [illegible] us [illegible] run [illegible] perpetuated [illegible] years [illegible] that fell [illegible]

[illegible] The matter duly considered, we are to look upon it as a [illegible] grace and favour from above, [illegible] at liberty to chuse our death, a blessing [illegible] gone before us. We are certain [illegible] to-morrow if we do not prevent it [illegible] ourselves free this very night, and [illegible] of our enemies to hinder it, neither [illegible] thing they desire more than to take us [illegible] too late to think of contending [illegible] Something might have been done at first, [illegible] our liberties had but duty [illegible] For they would have found that [illegible] merely his choosen [illegible] have exposed us to what we [illegible] divisions [illegible] of our [illegible] which laid waste with fire [illegible] are [illegible] up [illegible] of [illegible] [illegible] ? Yea [illegible] extravagant hopes, and the [illegible] What are [illegible] the [illegible] castle with ample provision [illegible] necessaries on our support when God [illegible] destruction. What do you [illegible] that left the Romans [illegible] ? Or, was it not [illegible] upon us for [illegible] we had been [illegible] our punishment [illegible] will it not be much [illegible] do justice upon ourselves, [illegible] the [illegible] Romans, as the executors of Divine vengeance? By this means we secure [illegible] of our wives and the freedom of our children. [illegible] to them, let us honourably take our own [illegible] that memorial behind us as [illegible] of monuments. But first, let the castle be set [illegible] gold and silver melted down, [illegible] of their purchase, without [illegible] of our treasure, or of our persons [illegible] be left behind as a [illegible] not starved into this condition, [illegible] resolution of chusing death rather [illegible]."

[illegible] speech was differently received by the people [illegible] was addressed. Those of a tender turn [illegible] of using violent hands upon themselves, [illegible] betrayed the softness of their hearts. [illegible] with the proposal, and desirous of putting it into execution. To work the former, however, into compliance, he proceeded in his exhortation, and [illegible] the doctrine of the immortality of the soul, [illegible] to the following effect.

"I [illegible] wonderfully mistaken I perceive, in my opinion, that brave men, in a contest for liberty, had rather lose their lives than their [illegible] For it is [illegible] to die, though to [illegible] worse than death [illegible] that neither needs counsel, [illegible] We have it from antiquity, the [illegible] the laws and customs of our country, [illegible] practice of our forefathers, that it is [illegible] but death that makes a man happy. What [illegible] and transmits [illegible] into those [illegible] blessed regions where it shall never know corruption? But so long as it communicates with the mortal [illegible] with the evils of that [illegible] for what affinity is [illegible] divine and mortal? Soul and body in conjunction, it is true, may do much, for the body is but the soul's instrument [illegible] secret offices and operations [illegible] But when the soul comes once to be discharged of its clog and weight that keeps it [illegible] and to recover its proper station, it enjoys a vigorous and perfect liberty, not visible to human eyes, but invisible as God himself is, and it is invisible also in our bodies. It comes into us unseen, and so it goes out again, incorruptible in itself, but causing variety of changes in the body, for whatsoever the soul influences it puts life and vigour into it, and wherever it withdraws itself, the separation is certain death. The [illegible] not hinder the soul yet from being immortal. As [illegible] for instance, how quietly does the soul repose [illegible] that respite from the distractions of the body [illegible] shews the happiness of the soul is wrapt up [illegible] self, and likewise that it holds some sort of [illegible] tion with the Almighty, in foretelling things to come. But how can any man pretend to fear death that loves [illegible] or who, but a madman, for the sake of [illegible] would grudge himself a life eternal? Besides, [illegible] ned up, by the laws and institutions of [illegible] fession, not only to the contempt of death [illegible] but [illegible] to recommend and practise it [illegible] to others.

"If there needed any recourse to strangers [illegible] or authority upon this subject, what [illegible] Indian philosophers and Brachmans [illegible] of this sort of people. They look upon life [illegible] sary function of nature, an office which [illegible] unwillingly enough, and not without some [illegible] to be quit of the trouble. They are not [illegible] neither, upon the account of pain or inconvenience, but, for the love of immortality, [illegible] sition that shall never have an end. Nay, they [illegible] lemn leave of their friends too, as if it were but [illegible] journey, and tell them when they are going [illegible] does any body offer to hinder them, but, on [illegible] wish them happy, and send [illegible] to their friends, in full and certain [illegible] they understand one another. So when they [illegible] ceived all their orders and instructions [illegible] their bodies to the fire, as a preparation [illegible] go off with acclamations, and [illegible] spectators. Among them, friends [illegible] more chearfully to death than [illegible] long journey, congratulating those [illegible] ing into a state of immortality, and only [illegible] rest that stay behind. What a shame will it [illegible] to now to fall short of the Indians, in a matter of [illegible] portance, and to bring a scandal upon the [illegible] and religion of our forefathers by [illegible] I might! Or put the case that we had been [illegible] instructed, and brought up in the contrary [illegible] from our infancy, as if life were the [illegible] mankind, and death the most [illegible] very occasion should make us [illegible] necessity and the will of God will [illegible] now to be punished with the loss of life [illegible] abuses of it, by the ordering of Divine Providence. Neither have we to ascribe it to our [illegible] generosity of the Romans, that we were [illegible] cut off in this war. Nor was it simply [illegible] the effect of a more powerful [illegible] like one. What had the Romans to do in the [illegible] massacre of the Jews at Cesarea, [illegible] place, where man, woman, and child [illegible] their seventh day's festival, without one word [illegible] spiracy or the least resistance? Where is the [illegible] ver looked upon the Jews as their enemies, but [illegible] they revolted. It will be said, perhaps, that [illegible] an old grudge betwixt the Jews of Cesarea [illegible] tizens, and that the latter took this opportunity for revenge. What shall we say, then, of the Scythians [illegible] that joined with the Greeks against us, and not [illegible] friends against the Romans? What did they [illegible] for their good-will, but the utter [illegible] selves and their families? This was the [illegible] that we had for our assistance, they [illegible] the same extremity, out of which we [illegible]

The MEN *of* MASSADA *(previous to destroying themselves)* MURDERING *their* WIVES *and* CHILDREN *to prevent their falling into the hands of the Romans*

"It would be too tedious to cite particular instances, "for you well know that there is not so much as one "city in Syria that has treated us better, and that has "not been incomparably worse to us than the Romans "What think you of Damascus, that, without any co- "lour, or pretence of disgust butchered ten thousand "Jews, with their wives and children, in that single "city? Then they reckon at least sixty thousand killed "in Egypt That is no wonder, you may say, in a "strange land, where they had no seconds to stand by "them But to come to our own case, we, who had "the courage to assert our liberties against the Romans in "our country and wanted neither men or arms, fearless "spirits, impregnable cities, strong holds, or any other "manner of provisions that might encourage or strengthen "a revolt, and entitle us to a reasonable hope of a vic- "torious issue How long did this last, and to what end "did this pompous preparation serve, save only to ag- "gravate confusion? For all is lost, and only to the ho- "nour of the enemy without any advantage to our- "selves, for, and by whom these stores were provided

"How happy are they that fell with their swords in "their hands, contending for their liberty, and in the same "act preserving it, compared with the surviving remain- "der of us, that are reserved in chains! some for torture, "some for the fire, others for spectacles, some for combat, "and others to be torn with scourges, some half eaten by "beasts Who would not suffer a thousand deaths rather "than lead such a life? But the most deplorable of all the "rest are those that are living, calling upon deaths and yet "having not the resolution to dispatch themselves

"Summon up your thoughts and consider what is be- "come of your glorious metropolis, your strong walls and "fortifications, your impregnable towers and castles your "vast treasuries and magazines, stores of ... for "your stores of ... prodigious ... , your "holy place too, known by the ... house, "Is it not all torn up by the roots, and nothing to be "seen of it, but the ruins, the ... , for a camp "to the conqueror, a few unfortunate old men, mourn- "ing over the ashes of the temple, and a number of un- "happy women set part for the most ignoble purposes?

"Can any thing, that hath the soul of a man, submit "to look another sun in the face after this? Though he "might live without ... or danger, can any man "be so unnatural to his country, so mean and narrow- "spirited as not to be grieved that he ever lived to see "this day? It would have been well if we had been all "in our graves before ever we beheld these sacrilegious "ruins, and this glorious pile of Jerusalem lain in rub- "bish But so long as we had lenes and courage we "flattered ourselves with the possibility of a redemption "This conceit, however, being now over, and nothing "left us to trust to but the consideration of an insuperable "necessity, we have nothing more to do than to take pity "on ourselves, our wives, and our children, and to make "all the haste we can, while we have the means in our "hands We are all born to die, the brave and the cow- "ard alike, and all subjected to the same fate As to these "points of indignity and slavery, the seeing of our wives "dishonoured, and our children led in triumph, these are "not evils arising from the necessity of our nature, but the "results of cowardice, when a man might have died, and "would not As to us, that had the heart to abandon the "Romans, fly in the face of our masters, and afterwards "refuse quarter and pardon, when it was offered us, and "not so much as accept of an indemnity, though they "themselves begged it of us, can it be thought that, if "ever they take us alive, this will be forgotten?

"It is shocking to think of the miserable condition "both of young and old betwixt the strength of body, "on the one hand, to lie languishing under a lingering "torment, and the weakness of age, on the other, that is "not able to support it The husband must expect to "see his wife dishonoured before his face, and the fa- "ther to hear his children begging in chains for relief "But while we are free, and masters of our swords, let us "make a glorious use of them, and preserve our liberties "Let us die freemen, with the comfort and company of "our wives and children about us It is but what they "themselves desire, what our laws require at our hands, "and what Providence itself hath made necessary for us "Only the Romans are against it, for fear we should do "their work for them Let us dispatch them ... it will "be to our immortal honour to take the prize ... "for out of their hands, in leaving them only the poor "satisfaction of dead bodies for their triumph"

As Eleazar was proceeding in his exhortation they cut him off short, and expressed the greatest eagerness of ac- complishing the design recommended, contending with a kind of demoniacal fury, who should be foremost as a mark of superior bravery, so ardent was the passion of the people for the destruction of themselves and ... Nor did their courage fail them when they came to the execution, they retained their natural affection to the last, from a confirmed opinion that they could not do their friends a better office The husbands tenderly embraced their wives, took their children into their arms, and with gushing tears compleated their last resolve The ... of the action was at once a source of comfort and a plea of excuse from a consideration of deliverance from those mi- series they had to expect from the hands of their enemies Not a man at length refused to act his part in the ... scene, but dealt destruction, with a relentless hand, amongst the nearest and dearest friends and relations Miserable men indeed! whose poignant woes compelled them to slay their wives and offspring, as the lightest of evils that were before them

When they were no longer able to sustain the grief they were under for what they had done, deeming it an injury to those they had slain to survive them even the shortest space, they piled up all their goods in an heap and burnt them, then chusing ten men by lot, out of their number, to do execution upon all the rest, they ranged themselves as close as possible to the dead bodies of their friends, gave them a parting embrace, and cheerfully submitted to the decisive stroke When these ten had discharged their of- fice with unshaken resolution, they cast lots among them- selves which of them should dispatch the other nine, on condition that the surviving tenth man should ... upon the bodies of the rest These nine died with the same constancy as the former, and the last man, having sur- veyed the bodies of those he had slain, to assure himself of their being effectually dispatched, set fire to the palace, cast himself upon his sword, and fell among his friends

Thus concluded the fatal tragedy, upon a presumption that not a soul remained to become subject to the Romans Yet it appeared afterwards, that there was one ancient woman, and a female relative of Eleazar (a person of ad- mirable qualities,) with five small children, who had con- cealed themselves in caverns, and escaped ... The number of the slain was nine hundred ... in- cluding women and children in the computation ... dreadful calamity happened on the fifteenth day of the month Xanthicus

Next morning, at break of day, the Romans made ready preparation for an assault but as no enemy ... or any noise was to be heard but the crackling of ... they stood in amazement and suspence ... a general shout, to try if they could be answered ... clamour alarming the women they came out of the ca- verns, and related the melancholy story of what had been done to the Romans, which appeared to them incredible, till, attempting to quench the fire and following their [illegible] up to the palace, a dreadful spectacle of piles of suicides convinced them of the truth of it. They were struck with admiration at the courage and resolution of the Jews, who had thus magnanimously braved death, and maintained their freedom to the last gasp.

CHAP. XXIX.

Many of the Sicarii retire to Alexandria, and raise commotions [illegible] impute to them all their misfortunes. Refuse to acknowledge the supremacy of Cæsar.

MASSADA being thus reduced, the Roman general left a garrison in the fortress, and marched with his army to Cesarea, leaving the country in perfect peace behind him, for the Jews of Judæa were so broken and subdued by the length and continuance of the war, that not an enemy was to be heard of in that quarter. Yet [illegible] nces soon after prevailed in Alexandria, where several Jews were put to death.

Many of the faction of the Sicarii had fled thither for [illegible], and not content with living in safety and [illegible] endeavoured to raise fresh commotions, by persuading many of the citizens to assert their liberty, esteem the Romans no better than themselves, and acknowledge no other lord than the Almighty Sovereign of the universe. They proceeded to avow their principles, which, if any of their own countrymen presumed to contradict, they were immediately put to death. Some they terrified, others they seduced from their allegiance to the Romans, till in fine, their practices became so bold and dangerous, that the leading men took the alarm, and summoned a general meeting of the Jews, to arraign the temerity and folly of the Sicarii, and demonstrate that they had been the authors of all the evils that had fallen upon them. They observed, that as soon as their design should be known to the Romans they would certainly avenge themselves upon all promiscuously, so that the innocent and guilty would be involved in one common calamity. From these considerations they cautioned the multitude to beware of bringing destruction on themselves through their means, and admonished them to provide for their own safety, by delivering these miscreants up to the Romans.

The multitude, thus apprized of their danger, complied with what had been proposed, fell violently upon the Sicarii, and seized six hundred of them immediately. The rest fled to Egypt, Thebes, and places adjacent, where they were soon taken, and brought back again; but so insuperable was their resolution, that they endured the most exquisite torments, rather than acknowledge Cæsar for their master. And what is more astonishing, the very children sustained the same tortures with the same resolution as the adults: in fine, not one soul of them would acknowledge Cæsar to save life: so far did their contempt of pain prevail over the fear of it.

CHAP. XXX.

Onias moves Ptolemy to grant the Jews permission to build a temple, and enjoy the exercise of their religion. Ptolemy grants the request. The temple is erected, and afterwards rifled and shut up.

LUPUS being at this time governor of Alexandria, gave Cæsar early intelligence of this commotion; and the emperor, well knowing the turbulent and seditious temper of the Jews, thought it adviseable to be cautious of their meetings and cabals, to prevent faction and parties being raised, and therefore sent orders to the governor, to demolish their temple in the city of Onias, in Egypt. This temple was built, and had its appellation from the following occasion.

Onias, the son of Simon, one of the high-priests being driven out of Jerusalem, in the time of the war between Antiochus, king of Syria, and the Jews, withdrew to Alexandria, where he was kindly received by Ptolemy, king of Egypt, partly as an enemy to Antiochus, and partly upon a condition agreed upon betwixt them. Onias undertook to bring the Jews over to the interest of Ptolemy, if he would grant him one request. The king signifying compliance, Onias preferred his petition for permission to the Jews to erect a temple in some spot in Egypt, where they might meet for Divine service according to the laws and religion of their country. By these means he intimated Antiochus would be rendered more obnoxious to the Jews, and the Jews more attached to his interest; besides, vast multitudes would (he added) put themselves under his protection for the free exercise of their religion.

Ptolemy acceded to the proposal, and assigned the Jews a spot of ground, distant about one hundred and eighty furlongs from Memphis, in the tract of Heliopolis. Onias built a castle there, and after that a temple, not comparable, indeed, to that at Jerusalem, though the tower bore a resemblance, being composed of huge stones and sixty cubits in height. There was an altar, after the model of that at Jerusalem, and adorned in the same manner, with a diversity of donations, excepting that there was no candlestick, but a golden lamp of great brilliancy, which hung upon a golden chain before the altar. This temple was encompassed with a brick wall, and had gates of stone. It was endowed with a considerable revenue both in land and monies, that there might be nothing wanting to the solemnity and celebration of the service. Onias was not influenced to this undertaking by an unfeigned regard for the cause of religion, but the aversion he had to the Jews at Jerusalem who [illegible] him away, and he proposed to himself, by the erecting of this temple, to draw a great number of them over again to himself. There had been also an antient prediction of the prophet Isaiah, about six hundred years before, that a temple should be built in Egypt by one of the Hebrew race.

Lupus, pursuant to the emperor's orders, went to the temple, took out of it several donations presented to it, and then shut it up. But Paulinus, who succeeded to the government on the demise of Lupus, not only rifled the temple of all that it contained, but threatened the priests severely if they concealed the least article. Nor would he permit any one to enter it on the account of religion, but rendered it wholly inaccessible, insomuch that there was not even the semblance of Divine worship there. The duration of time, from the building of that temple to the shutting it up, was three hundred and [illegible] years.

CHAP. XXXI.

Jonathan, one of the Sicarii, sets up a [illegible] Cyrene. He is taken and brought before Catullus governor of [illegible] Proves an adept in the [illegible] of [illegible] and corruption. Josephus, the historian, [illegible] but acquitted by Vespasian, who [illegible] on the calumniators. Catullus [illegible] and mind.

THE baneful influence of the principles of the Sicarii spread like a contagion, and extended as far as Cyrene. One Jonathan, an enthusiastic weaver, having [illegible] his escape thither, drew a credulous multitude [illegible] into woods and deserts, under pretext of [illegible] signs and apparitions; and this imposture [illegible] with the lower class of people. But [illegible] ears of some of the leading men of Cyrene [illegible] immediate notice of it to Catullus, governor of Libia Pentapolis, respecting their design [illegible] they took They were immediately purſued by a military band, and being unarmed eaſily overcome. Many were ſlain, and the reſt taken and carried priſoners to Catullus.

Jonathan, the ringleader of this miſerable clan, at firſt made his eſcape, but, after a long and ſtrict ſearch, was taken, and likewiſe carried to Catullus But he found means to divert the ſtory from himſelf, and to furniſh the governor with an acceptable occaſion of turning it another way. This he effected, by bringing the wealthieſt Jews of the place into the plot as the promoters of the conſpiracy Theſe accuſations, falſe as they might be, were welcome to Catullus, who aggravated matters to ſuch a degree, that a war with the Jews ſeemed inevitable He not only lent a ready ear to thoſe calumnies himſelf, but encouraged the Sicarii to alledge falſe accuſations, and ſuborned witneſſes to impeach one Alexander, a Jew, (to whom he had long profeſſed enmity,) and his wife Berenice, who were condemned upon the ſame evidence Theſe were the firſt that ſuffered, and after them a train of three thouſand more were put to death at once, whoſe only crime was, that they were men of property and character This he thought he might do with ſafety, ſo long as their eſtates were confiſcated to the empire Nay, through fear of being detected in his villainy by Jews of credit elſewhere, he prevailed with Jonathan, and certain others, to exhibit matter of accuſation againſt the moſt eminent, both in Rome and Alexandria, and among the reſt Joſephus the hiſtorian Catullus *now coming to Rome*, and bringing Jonathan and his companions with him in bonds, made no doubt but the ſtory would paſs as he had conceited and repreſented it But the event of this contrivance did not anſwer his expectation; for Veſpaſian, ſuſpecting the matter, determined upon inveſtigation, and finding out the iniquity of it, he pronounced, at the inſtance of Titus, Joſephus, and the reſt of the Jews, innocent, who were thereupon diſcharged, while, at the ſame time, he ſentenced Jonathan to be firſt ſcourged, and then burnt alive which was accordingly executed

As for Catullus, ſuch was the bondage of the two princes, that they proceeded no farther againſt him at preſent, but, in a ſhort time, he fell into a complication of diſeaſes, both mental and corporeal, though the former were moſt poignant and diſtreſſing; for he was tormented with all the horrors of conſcious guilt, and ſaw, in imagination, the ghaſtly apparitions of thoſe whom he had murdered, inſomuch that he ſtarted from his bed as if he would endeavour to avoid approaching flames His bodily diſtemper, in fine, increaſed upon him, till his inteſtines were corroded, and came from him; and thus was brought to his end, by the Divine vengeance, a man *who acted in defiance of all the laws of humanity and juſtice.*

Thus concludes our hiſtory, in which we have ſtrictly adhered to truth and candour, according to promiſe, for the information of thoſe who may be deſirous of becoming acquainted with the particulars of the wars between the Romans and the Jews The ſtyle muſt be ſubmitted to the judgment of the reader, but *as to the facts recorded, I muſt be bold to* aver, that the truth has been my invariable aim throughout the whole compoſition

END OF THE JEWISH WARS

FLAVIUS JOSEPHUS

TO

Epaphroditus,

ON THE

ANTIQUITIES OF THE JEWS,

IN ANSWER TO

Apion.

BOOK I.

IT is preſumed, moſt excellent Epaphroditus, that I have already incontrovertibly proved the antiquity of the Jewiſh nation, which originated with themſelves, and maintains a claim of priority to this very day. The antiquities contain the hiſtory of five thouſand years, are founded on the ſacred writings, but tranſlated by me into the Greek tongue. Since, however, this arduous, and I may add, unprejudiced undertaking, has not been ſufficient to exempt the author from illiberal cenſure, or his productions from fabulous imputation, (and that upon the mere preſumption of the Greek hiſtorians having neglected to record the antiquity of the Jewiſh nation) I am bound, in duty to myſelf, and my country, firſt, to refute the invidious aſſertions of opponents; ſecondly, to inform the ignorant; and, thirdly, to ſtate plain facts, in terms obvious to the underſtanding of thoſe who deſire to inveſtigate truth.

The authorities I ſhall cite will be derived from men of unleniable reputation among the Greeks; and I ſhall ſet aſide the aſſeverations of thoſe who have malevolently or ignorantly traduced me or my nation, by recurring to their own writings. I ſhall alſo aſſign the cauſes for which many of the Greek hiſtorians have paſſed over our nation without mention of their records, and then endeavour to obviate vulgar prejudices in general.

There are many people ſo ſuperſtitiouſly attached to the Greeks, that they conſider them abſtractedly from all others, as the very oracles of hiſtory, to the contempt and diſparagement of the reſt of the rational creation. In point of antiquity I am convinced the reverſe will appear, if mankind will not be led by vain opinions, but ſearch for facts upon the baſis of ſubſtantial evidence. They will then find little or nothing amongſt them that is not novel; I mean with reſpect to the building of their cities, the invention of their arts, and the deſcription of their laws. The writing of hiſtory is of very late date among them; whereas, by their own confeſſion, the Egyptians, Chaldeans, and Phœnicians, (to ſay nothing of ourſelves,) have, from time to time, recorded and tranſmitted to poſterity, memorials of paſt ages in monumental pillars and inſcriptions, with the advice and direction of the wiſeſt men, to perpetuate tranſactions of moment. Beſides, theſe people living in a clear air, the very climate contributed to the preſervation of theſe antiquities from corruption and decay: which was quite otherwiſe with the Greeks, reſpecting duration, order, and appointment.

Their bare pretence to the knowledge of letters is of late date, and their ſkill in that particular is at this very hour defective. The antiquity of which they boaſt goes no farther back than to the Phœnicians, and they value themſelves upon the reputation of having had Cadmus for their firſt maſter. But ſo far are they from being able to produce, either in their temples or public regiſtries, any one authentic memorial of their times, that, when it came to be propounded as a queſtion, whether the uſe of letters was found or known at the end of the Trojan war, it was carried in the negative. It is univerſally acknowledged that there is no Greek manuſcript in date antecedent to the poems of Homer; and it is certain that the Trojan war was over before that poem (the Iliad) was written. Nor has it been admitted that Homer ever committed this production to writing. The prevailing opinion runs, that it paſſed like a kind of ballad, which the people committed to memory, till the end copies were taken from oral dictation, which is aſſigned as the cauſe of many contradictions and miſtakes found in the tranſcripts.

With reſpect to Cadmus, the Mileſian, Acuſilaus, and other Greek hiſtorians, they lived but a ſhort time before the inroad of the Perſians into Greece. Pherecydes, Pythagoras, and Thales, who firſt introduced philoſophy, and the inveſtigation of ſubjects Divine and celeſtial, unanimouſly acknowledge that they derived their information from the Egyptians and Chaldeans. Nay, it remains a doubt to this day, whether theſe men were the authors of the works attributed to them.

From these premises it appears extremely absurd for the Greeks to claim to themselves not only the sole knowledge of antiquity, but a preference in point of historical accuracy, candour, and credit. Nay, is it not evident, from their own writings, that their histories are the result of fancy and conjecture, rather than records of substantial fact? As their authors clash one with another, and report one and the same thing in a manner totally different.

It would be tedious to point out the disagreement between Hellanicus and Acusilaus respecting their genealogies, the differences between Hesiod and Acusilaus, the proofs repeatedly brought by Ephorus to demonstrate the representations of Hellanicus, those of Timeus to the same purport against Ephorus, those of succeeding writers against Timeus, and in fine, those of all the latter authors against Herodotus. Nor could Timeus agree with Philistus or Callias, about the Sicilian history. The historians of Athens and Argos differ essentially. So that doubts must arise in the minds of the readers, when they discover such palpable contradictions amongst writers. Nay, Thucydides himself is called in question upon several occasions, though the most cautious, candid, and impartial historian of his age.

Upon due consideration, many reasons might be assigned for the great differences which prevail amongst Greek authors; but I apprehend the principal parts are these. First, the neglect of the Greeks in not laying a timely foundation for history, in records and memorials to preserve the remembrance of great atchievements; for, without these monumental traditions, posterity are apt to err, having no clue to guide them into the path of truth. This mode of recording antient traditions was not only neglected in other parts of Greece, but even in Athens itself, which has been deemed the very seat of the polite arts. Draco's penal laws, now extant in manuscript, are the most antient of their public records, though bearing date but a short space before the tyrant Pisistratus. As to the Arcadians, whatever their pretensions to antiquity, they came later to the use of letters than any of the rest.

Now there being no authorities extant, there must naturally arise great differences among the writers, because such vouchers might be introduced to confirm truth, and refute error, and thereby distinguish between the authentic and groundless historian. Another cause of contradictions is the motives which induce writers to take up the pen. Some write for the applause of their cotemporaries, and prefer the reputation of being esteemed florid in style, rather than candid in narrative. Some write to gratify fancy or humour, without any regard to bulk and justice; others deal in panegyric, to court the patronage of the great; and there are some that lavish their time and talents in calumniating the writings and characters of their predecessors, which are all contrary to the duty and office of a genuine historian.

The characteristic of true history is the concordance of several writers, as to the subject, time, and place; but the Greeks seem to adduce their diversity as an argument of their authenticity. If the matters in dispute betwixt them and us, were mere arguments of words, and precisions of periods, we would yield them the palm; but we cannot but contend for superiority in point of fact and antiquity.

That the Egyptians and Babylonians of old were precise in the care of their annals, which was committed to the care of their priests, who were punctual in the discharge of that office; that the Chaldeans followed the example of the Babylonians, and that the Phœnicians, who were intermixed with the Greeks, instructed them in the use of letters, is universally acknowledged. It therefore only remains for me to shew, that our forefathers provided, at least, as well for the security of this order and regulation, if not better, than any that went before them, in charging the high-priests and prophets with this commission; and these records have been handed down to our times with the utmost accuracy; and I dare pronounce that our future annals will bear the same stamp of authority. Care was taken, from the beginning, to make choice of men of exemplary piety and virtue for this function, and further was made for preserving the sacerdotal race pure and untainted, as no man is qualified for the office of a priest, whose mother was not of priestly extraction, and therefore, without any regard to wealth and honour, whoever pretends to the priest-hood, must prove his descent in a right line by a multitude of witnesses. This is the practice not only in Judæa, but wherever our people are dispersed over the face of the whole earth; for our priests make it a kind of conscience only to intermarry with their own tribes. In this case, they send from the father to Jerusalem the name of the woman they intend to marry, with her pedigree well and duly attested.

But in time of war, as for instance, in the days of Antiochus Epiphanes, Pompey the Great, and Quintilius Varus, and principally within our own memory, the surviving priests compose new tables of genealogy out of the records, and examine the circumstances of the women that remain. The priests marry no captive, through a suspicion they might have had intercourse with foreigners; and, as an incontrovertible proof of their purity, the names of all our priests, in an uninterrupted succession, from father to son, have stood upon record throughout a space of two thousand years. If any of them prevaricate, they are forbidden the altar, and deposed from the exercise of the sacred function. And this is justly or rather necessarily done, because every one is not permitted to write, nor is there any disagreement in what is written. The writings of the prophets we hold of Divine original; and as to those who have written the history of their own times, their number is not great, nor are they very repugnant one to another.

We have not a multitude of books amongst us, disagreeing and contradicting one another, as the Greeks have, but are confined to twenty-two, that we are bound to believe; and those twenty-two books comprise the history of the world from the beginning to this day. [illegible] them treat of the creation of the world, and the generation of mankind, and so to the death of Moses, in a space of little less than 3000 years.

From the death of Moses to the reign of Artaxerxes, the son of Xerxes, the king of Persia, every one of our prophets wrote the history of the times in which he lived, comprehending the whole in thirteen books; the other four books containing Divine poems and moral precepts. There has indeed, been a continuation of our history from Artaxerxes to this instant; but it is not esteemed, in point of authenticity, comparable to that of our ancestors, as there has not been an exact succession of prophets since that time. The former writings are the objects of our implicit belief; for, during many ages of the world, no attempt has been made, either to add to, or diminish from them, or even so much as to transform or [illegible] them. As we hold these writings Divine, we call them so, and are trained, from earliest infancy, to meditate upon, observe, and maintain them as such: nay, we are disposed rather to suffer death than give them up.

How many are there of our captive countrymen at this day, struggling under exquisite torments, because they will not renounce the laws of their country, nor blaspheme the God of their forefathers? When did any of the Greeks undergo such trial? They would not venture [illegible] to preserve all they hold most d[illegible] writings in no other esteem than as [illegible] same opinion of antient as of modern productions [illegible] have taken upon them to write [illegible] were wholly ignorant, and that without [illegible] to mention to those who were acquainted with [illegible] We have an example of this in the histories of [illegible] published by persons who were never on the [illegible] but who nevertheless, have the confidence to [illegible] the world a jargon of [illegible]

But this I can aver, with respect to my history of our wars, that it is genuine and authentic, as I had occasion [illegible], fit in knowledge, and the means of informing myself particularly of every occurrence. I have been as faithful in my report, as I was minute in my investigation. I had a command in Galilee as long as our nation was able to oppose the Romans, and it was my fortune in the end to be made prisoner, and carried to Vespasian and Titus, who, at first, ordered me to be kept bound, but I was afterwards generously released, and sent to accompany Titus, when he came from Alexandria to the siege of Jerusalem. During the whole time there was nothing done that escaped my knowledge. Whatever [illegible] in the Roman camp was open to me, nor was any care wanting, on my part, most faithfully to represent every circumstance. With respect to the state of the city, I had accounts of it from deserters, with an express from the emperor to take minutes of each occurrence.

Being furnished with these materials, and finding leisure at Rome, I applied to some friends to assist me in acquiring a competent knowledge of the Greek tongue, and then proceeded to the compilation of my history, in which I am so conscious of having observed the utmost candour and justice, that I dare appeal to the generals Vespasian and Titus as my vouchers. To these illustrious personages I first presented my work, and next to them to certain noble Romans, who commanded in the same war. Others I disposed of to several of our own nation, who were skilled in the Greek tongue, as Julius, Archelaus, Herod, and the most excellent king Agrippa. These bear honourable testimony, that I acquitted myself as a faithful historian, and surely I could never have obtained such sanction and patronage, if, through ignorance or favour, I had in any instance deviated from facts. I have been exposed to the censures of the illiberal, who have censured my productions in a vein of irony and sarcasm, but they would do well to consider, that whoever pretends to [illegible] in the relation of transactions, should first render himself intimately acquainted with them, either from his own personal observation, or the information of others of both these advantages I have fully availed myself.

With respect to our Antiquities, I have, in character of priest, translated them from our sacred writings, and digested them in methodical order. But in the history of the war, I was an actor in some cases, a spectator in others, and, upon the whole, a stranger to nothing that was either done or said. What insolence therefore, it is in those, who would endeavour to deprive me of my title to authenticity! They pretend to have inspected the journals of the commanders, but can that invalidate my history, in points absolutely unknown to those commanders?

I have been under a necessity of making this digression, in order to expose the vanity of many who pretend to write histories, and I apprehend, that what I have observed, is sufficient to satisfy any man, that the very barbarians have better preserved this custom of transmitting down the histories of antient times than the Greeks themselves. I would now offer some matters for the consideration of those who endeavour to prove, that our constitution is but of modern date, because the Greek writers have made no mention of us. I shall then produce testimonies of our antiquity from the writings of foreigners, and demonstrate the injustice of those who cast reproaches on our nation.

We neither inhabit a maritime country, nor do we delight in merchandise, nor in that intercourse with other nations which naturally arises from it. Our cities lie remote from the sea, our soil is fruitful, and cultivated with care. Our grand concern is the education of our children, to train them in pious exercise, and strict obedience to the laws of our country: this indeed, we esteem the main business of our lives. Besides, we have a peculiar way of living to ourselves, which gives us to understand, that in times past, we had no communication with the Greeks, as the Egyptians and Phœnicians had, as also other nations, by a common tie of navigation, trade, and commerce, for the advancement of their fortunes. Nor did our predecessors make inroads upon their neighbours, as others have done, for the enlarging their estates, though they wanted neither numbers or courage, to be dangerous and troublesome, had they been so disposed.

Thus it was that the Phœnicians became known to the Greeks, and through them the Egyptians, and other traders into Greece. After these the Medes and Persians, having become lords of Asia, carried the war into Europe. The Thracians were also known by being contiguous, the Scythians by holding a correspondence with those that sailed to Pontus, and so all along the eastern and western sea, there was a sufficiency of subject matter for history.

But those whose habitations were remote from the sea, were for the most part unknown: [illegible] Europe also, where the Roman empire, [illegible] long had possessed such mighty power and greatness, performed such gallant exploits in war, are not even mentioned by Herodotus, Thucydides, nor any of the cotemporaries; and it was very late, and with great difficulty, that the Romans became known to the Greeks. What shall we say of writers in ordinary, when Ephorus himself, the most celebrated of their historians, was so ignorant of the Gauls and Iberians that he supposes the kingdom of Spain, with the vast continent it stands upon, to be no more than one city, and so ascribes to them things that were never done, said, nor heard there? Whence comes this ignorance of the truth, but from the writer's having no knowledge of the parts alluded to? Nor can it be any wonder that our nation was no more known to many of the Greeks, nor had given them occasion to mention them in their writings while they were so remote from the sea, and had a conduct of life so peculiar to themselves.

But if I should turn the Greeks' mode of reasoning upon themselves, and alledge, by way of disproving their antiquity, that no mention is made of it in our records, would not such an inference be exploded as ridiculous? Would they not appeal to neighbouring nations to confirm their claim? If this manner of proceeding may be admitted on the one side, why not on the other? The Egyptians and Phœnicians are the chief witnesses that I shall [illegible] in this case, nor can there be any ground of exception to their evidence, as the former are known to be our [illegible] enemies, and the latter no better disposed towards us, particularly the people of Tyre. But the Chaldeans are of another opinion, as having been formerly under their command, likewise on account of consanguinity and country, as appears from the honourable mention they make of us in their chronicles. When I have cleared our nation from the aspersions of the Greeks, and wiped away the slanders they have cast upon us, I will then revert to their own historians, and so obviate all farther cavil. I shall begin with the writings of the Egyptians, and cite [illegible] from the works of Manetho, an Egyptian by birth, but well skilled in the Greek language, as appears from his history he took from holy writ about the Jewish [illegible]. He finds much fault with Herodotus, [illegible] misrepresentation of the Egyptian manners and [illegible]; and, in the second book of his history, delivers himself in these very words, which I quote without the least alteration, that they may suffice to confirm his testimony.

"We had a king whose name was Timaus, [illegible] "reign we fell, beyond all imagination, under God's heavy "displeasure. There came flowing in upon us, a rugged, "robust people out of the east, that made an [illegible] "the province, and there encamping, took it by force, "and carried all before them without so much as [illegible] "putting our princes in chains, and [illegible] "ashes, demolishing our temples, and miserably [illegible] "strong our inhabitants, some being cut to pieces and others "with their wives and children, kept [illegible] in bondage

"After this, they set up a king from among themselves, whose name was Salatis.

"The new king advanced to Memphis, and having subjected both the upper and the lower provinces, and put garrisons into all tenable places, he fortified to the eastward in a more especial manner, for fear of an invasion from the Assyrians, whom he looked upon as the stronger of the two. He found in the country of Saites, a city, formerly called Avaris, which was situated very conveniently for his purpose, to the east of the river Bubastis. This city he improved and repaired, and fortified it with strong works and walls, and a body of two hundred and forty thousand men to cover it. He made choice of harvest time for the execution of his design, with a regard both to the plenty of the season for provisions, to the means of paying his soldiers, and to the securing himself likewise against all assaults, or [illegible], by his excellent discipline and conduct.

"Salatis died in the nineteenth year of his reign, and one Beon succeeded him, who governed forty-four years. After him came Apachnas, and reigned six and thirty years and seven months. Apochis came next, and ruled sixty years and one month. Janias, fifty years and one month: and last of all came Assis, who ruled forty-nine years and two months. These six were the first kings, and perpetually in war, to exterminate the Egyptians. The people we called *Hycsos*, that is to say, *king shepherds*: for *hyc*, in the holy tongue, is as much as *king*; and *sos*, according to the vulgar, is a *shepherd*: so that *hycsos* is taken as a compound. Some will have it that these people were Arabians. According to some other copies, *hyc* does not signify *king*, *shepherd*; but *shepherd captive*, for *hyc* and *hac*, with an aspiration, found, in Egyptian, as much as *captive*; and it seems to me the more rationable interpretation of the two, as it [illegible] better with the ancient history."

"We have it upon credit of the same author, that when these (by whatever name they may be called) kings or shepherds, and their train, had kept the government of Egypt in their own hands for the space of 511 years, the king of Thebes and the remainder of Egypt, that was not as yet subjected, made a violent and obstinate war upon the shepherds, and routed them, under the command of king Alisfragmuthosis; and when the greatest part of them were driven out of Egypt, the rest withdrew into a place called Avaris, of ten thousand acres in extent; and this the shepherds (according to Manethon) enclosed with a strong substantial wall, that secured to them all necessaries within themselves." He says further, "that Themosis, the son of Alisfragmuthosis, laid siege to it with four hundred and eighty thousand men; but when he found the place was not to be carried by assault, they came to conditions, upon articles to depart Egypt, and a free convoy to go whither they would. Upon these terms they marched out with their goods and families to the number of two hundred and forty thousand souls, by the way of the wilderness, into Syria, and for fear of the Assyrians, who were then masters of Asia, [illegible] into a country that is now known by the name of Judea, where they erected a city large enough to receive this vast multitude, and called it Jerusalem."

The same Manethon tells us, in another book of his Egyptian history, "that he finds these people in books of great authority, distinguished by the name of Captive Shepherds," our ancestors having been brought up to grazing, and from that pastoral employment taking the name of shepherds. They imagine that they had some ground for calling them captives; it was by that name that our father Joseph made himself known to the king of Egypt, when he obtained permission to send for his brethren. But of this more particularly elsewhere. So that it will be sufficient, at present, to consult the testimonies of the Egyptians upon this subject, and to hear Manethon, in his own words, about the time when this happened.

"King Themosis reigned five and twenty years and four months, from the departure of the shepherds out of Egypt, to the building of Jerusalem. His son Chebron took the kingdom after him, and governed thirteen years; and after him Amenophis, twenty years and seven months; his sister Amesses, one and twenty years and nine months; her son Mephres, twelve years and nine months; his son Mephramuthosis, five and twenty years and ten months; his son Themosis, nine years and eight months; his son Amenophis, thirty years and ten months; his son Orus, thirty-six years and five months; his daughter Acencheres, twelve years and one month; Rathotis, her brother, nine years; his son Acencheres, twelve years and five months; another Acencheres, his son, twelve years and three months; his son Armais, four years and one month; his son Armesis, one year and four months; his son Armesses Miamun, sixty-six years and two months; Amenophis, nineteen years and six months. Sethosis, having raised a great force both at sea and land, constituted his brother Armais deputy-regencial of Egypt, and vested him with all sovereign powers and privileges, the wearing of the crown excepted, and, with a caution not to oppress the queen or her family, nor to intermeddle with the king's concubines."

"Sethosis upon this, marched up to Cyprus and Phœnicia, and so forward to the Medes and Assyrians, conquering still as he went, some by the [illegible], others by the very terror and reputation of his arms. He was so [illegible] by his successes, that he stopt at nothing; but [illegible] all waste to the east, [illegible] the whole country before him. While this was doing, his brother Armais, without any [illegible] [illegible] with his brother [illegible] [illegible]. He [illegible] the queen, [illegible] the king's concubines [illegible] [illegible] arms against his brother [illegible] the [illegible] from [illegible], upon which [illegible] the king [illegible] again by the way of Pelusium, and [illegible] government. From this prince the [illegible] of Egypt, for Sethosis [illegible], and his brother Armais named [illegible] Danaus."

This is the account of Manethon, [illegible] evident, upon a clear computation, that our [illegible], otherwise known by the name of shepherds, left Egypt three hundred and ninety three years before Danaus went to Argos, though the Greeks [illegible] themselves [illegible] the antiquity of that prince. Manethon therefore advances two great points for us out of the Egyptian records; the first, that our forefathers came out of another country into Egypt; the second, that their deliverance [illegible] was of so ancient a date, as to precede the siege of Troy almost a thousand years. With respect to some other particulars which Manethon adds, not out of the Egyptian records, but, as he himself confesses, from stories of an uncertain original, I shall demonstrate hereafter, that they are no better than groundless fictions.

I shall now pass from these records to those of the Phœnicians, concerning our nation, and from them [illegible] testations of what I have advanced. The [illegible] Tyrians [illegible] public records of great antiquity, [illegible] carefully preserved, as to contain all [illegible] worthy of memorial. Amongst other [illegible] our nation, they make mention of [illegible] a temple at Jerusalem, an hundred [illegible] years and eight months before their predecessors [illegible], [illegible] also, in their annals, the very [illegible] the temple. Hiram, king of Tyre, had so great a friendship for David, and his son Solomon for his sake, that he presented [illegible] hundred and twenty talents of gold towards the ornament of the fabric, and furnished him with the most excellent timber from mount Libanus for the roof and wainscot. Nor was Solomon wanting, on the other hand, in a magnificent return, as, among other acknowledgments, he made him a present of Zebulon in Naphtali. But the love of wisdom, or a kind of philosophic passion, cemented the friendship betwixt them. They sent problems and intricate cases to be solved by each other, and Solomon evinced a superiority to Hiram. There are extant among the Tyrians, to this day, divers copies of the letters that passed betwixt them; and for confirmation of the same, I shall refer to Dius, an historian among the Phœnicians of unquestionable credit. These are his words:

"Hiram, the son of Abibal, succeeded his father in the "government. He acquired and improved divers cities in "the eastern parts of his dominion, enlarged Tyre, and, by "raising a causeway between them, joined it to the temple "of Jupiter Olympus, standing in an island, and beautified it with many rich donations. After this he went up "to mount Libanus to cut down wood for temples. They "say farther, that Solomon, king of Jerusalem, and Hiram, "interchanged certain problems to be solved, upon condition that he who failed in the solution, should incur a "forfeiture; and that Hiram, finding the question too difficult for him, paid the penalty, and proposed new ones "for Solomon to interpret, upon the penalty of paying forfeit to Hiram." This is what Dius records upon this subject.

I now proceed to Menander, the Ephesian, an author who made an historical collection of the transactions of the Greeks and barbarians under every one of the Tyrian kings, which, for the better authority of the work, he has extracted from their own records. Having passed through the succession of the Tyrian kings as far as Hiram, he thus writes:

"Upon the death of Abibal, his son Hiram came to the "crown, and lived to enjoy it thirty-four years. This "prince threw up a large bank, that joined Eurychorus to "the city of Tyre, and dedicated a golden pillar to Jupiter, which was there deposited in his temple. He went "after this into a forest, to a mountain called Libanus, "where he cut down all the cedar for roofs for temples, "razing the old buildings, and advancing others. One he "dedicated to Hercules, another to Astarte: the former in "the month Peritius, and the other when he marched against "the Tyrians, for not paying their taxes; but, upon their "reduction, he presently returned.

"Hiram had, at this time, a young man, a servant in "his house, whose office it was to expound Solomon's riddles, his name was Abdemonus. From this king's time "to the building of Carthage, the computation runs thus.

"Beleazar, the son of Hiram, succeeded his father, and "died in the forty-third year of his age, and the seventh of "his reign. The next was Abdastartus, the son of Beleazar, who died in the twentieth year of his life, and the "ninth of his reign. This prince was murdered by his "nurse's four sons, and the eldest of them governed twelve "years in his place; and after him came Astartus, the son "of Delæastartus, who lived sixty years, and reigned twelve. "After him came his brother Aserymus, who lived fifty-"four years, and reigned nine, and was murdered by his "brother Phelles, who took the government upon him in "the fiftieth year of his age, and, after a reign of eight "months, was slain by one Ithobalus, a priest of the "goddess Astarte, who lived to the age of sixty eight years, "and ruled thirty-two. His son Badezor succeeded him, "who lived forty-five years, and reigned six: and then his "son Margenus lived two and thirty years, and reigned "nine. The next was Pygmalion, who lived fifty-six "years, and governed forty. It was the seventh year of "his reign, that his sister Dido built Carthage, in Africa. "So that from the time of Hiram to the erecting of Carthage, we account an hundred and fifty-five years and "eight months. Taking for granted that the temple of "Jerusalem was built in the twelfth year of king Hiram, "it makes an hundred and forty-three years and eight "months, from the raising of the temple to the building "of Carthage."

Nothing can tend more to confirmation than this testimony of the Phœnicians; for our ancestors certainly came to Judæa long before the building of the temple, nor did they build that temple till they had obtained possession of the country by dint of arms, as I have clearly proved from the sacred writings in my Antiquities.

We will now proceed to shew how far the Chaldean records agree with others concerning our history, and begin with Berosus, by birth a Chaldean, well known by the learned from his publication of the Chaldean treatises on astronomy and philosophy among the Greeks. Berosus, following the most antient records, gives us an history of the deluge, and the destruction of mankind thereby, exactly consonant with the description of Moses, as also of the ark, and the preservation of Noah in it, when it was brought to the highest part of the Armenian mountains. He gives us a catalogue of the posterity of Noah, and adds the years of their chronology, from Noah himself to Nabulassar, king of the Babylonians and Chaldeans, with an account of this king's exploits. He tells us that he sent his son Nabuchodonosor with a mighty army into Egypt and Judæa, where, upon his being informed of a revolt, he reduced the people to subjection, set fire to our temple at Jerusalem, and carried off our whole nation in captivity to Babylon. After this our city lay desolate during an interval of seventy years, till the days of Cyrus king of Persia. He then says, that this Babylonian king conquered Egypt, Syria, Phœnicia, and Arabia, and exceeded in his exploits all his predecessors. But to quote his own words:

"Nabulassar, the father, understanding that his [illegible] "in Ægypt, Cœlo-Syria, and Phœnicia, [illegible] "being old himself, and past the fatigues of war, [illegible] "his son Nabuchodonosor (in the vigour of his [illegible] "the head of a strong army, to bring [illegible] to [illegible] "prince encountered the rebel, defeated [illegible] "all the provinces that were engaged in the revolt.

"It happened, at the same time, that Nabulassar [illegible] "at Babylon, and died, after [illegible] "years. It was not long before the son heard of his "father's death, whereupon he [illegible] "fairs in Egypt, and the rest of the provinces, and com-"mitting the captive Jews, Phœnicians, and Syrians, [illegible] "had been in Egypt, to the care of some [illegible] "confidents, to see them brought up to Babylon, [illegible] "with the army and the baggage, he himself, [illegible] "[illegible], took his journey for Babylon [illegible] "desert. Upon his arrival, he found all the [illegible] "his [illegible], the Chaldeans, and all the great men, [illegible] "themselves in his interest, and for his establishment [illegible] "the throne of his father.

"In this interim, while the prisoners were [illegible] "he ordered them the most commodious [illegible] "city for their quarters, and all accommodations [illegible] "vided for them. The spoils of the war [illegible] "wonderful munificence, to the enriching [illegible] "the temples, as that of Bel, [illegible] "he erected a new town [illegible] "and to prevent the turning of the [illegible] "upon, from the place, in case of [illegible] "triple wall, part of it brick [illegible] "tumen, about the whole. [illegible] "made such gates as might have [illegible] "temple. He built likewise a glorious palace, near that of "his father, but incomparably beyond it, both for extent "and expence. The description of it would be too tedious, "but it must be observed, that this admirable piece was the "work of only fifteen days.

"There were in it also several artificial rocks, that had "the resemblance of mountains, with nurseries of all sorts "of plants, and a kind of hanging garden, suspended in the "air by a most admirable contrivance. This was to gratify "his wife, who being brought up in Media, among the hills, "and in the fresh air, found relief from such a prospect."

Thus [illegible] Berosus respecting the king, and there are other [illegible] worthy of remark in his Chaldean antiquities, [illegible] where he censures the Greek [illegible] that Babylon was founded by Semiramis queen of Assyria. Moreover, we meet with a confirmation of what Berosus relates, in the records of the Phoenicians, concerning the king of Babylon, and his conquest of Syria and Phoenicia. Philostratus agrees with him in his history of the siege of Tyre, as does Megasthenes, in the fourth book of his Indian history, wherein he pretends to prove that this king of Babylon was superior to Hercules in strength and prowess, adding, that he had the greatest part of Lybia and Iberia at his devotion. With respect to the temple of Jerusalem, we have the authority of Berosus, [illegible] laid in ashes by the Babylonians, and [illegible] Cyrus, when he had reduced Asia, began to rebuild [illegible] thus writes in his third book.

"When Nabuchodonosor was just entered upon the third [illegible], in the forty-third year of his reign, he fell "sick, and died. Evil-Merodach, his son, succeeded him, "but having rendered himself odious to the highest degree, "by his [illegible] oppressions, he was cut off by the treacherous practice of Niriglisoror, his sister's husband, in "the second year of his reign. After his death, the traitor "advanced himself to the crown, and kept it four years. "His son Laborosardochus came very young to the government, and continued in it only nine months, being destroyed by the treachery even of his very friends, who "looked upon him as a youth of vicious and dangerous "inclination, and therefore removed him. He was no "sooner dispatched than the conspirators met, and consulting together, chose one Nabonidus for their king, being "both a Babylonian, and of the same family. The walls "about the river of Babylon were finished by this prince.

"In the seventeenth year of this king's reign Cyrus, "with a mighty army out of Persia, over-ran all Asia, "and marched directly for Babylon. Nabonidus fairly "met him in the field, fought him, and lost the battle. [illegible] himself, and some few of his people, got into "the town of Borsippe. Cyrus was now before Babylon, making no doubt but, upon forcing the first wall, "he might carry the place. But, upon second thoughts, "he quitted the siege, and went back to Borsippe, with a "design to attack the place. Nabonidus chose rather to "cast himself upon Cyrus's mercy, than to stand the "shock; so that, upon his humiliation, Cyrus banished "him out of Babylon, and gave him quiet possession "of Carmania, where he ended his life in a private "station."

These accounts of Berosus exactly correspond with our sacred books, in which it is related that Nabuchodonosor, in the eighteenth year of his reign, destroyed our temple, and that it lay desolate for fifty years. But that, in the second year of the reign of Cyrus, its foundation was laid, and it was finished again in the second year of *Darius*. I shall now add the records of the Phoenicians, as too many proofs cannot be adduced, provided they agree in point of chronology. The computation stands thus.

Nabuchodonosor besieged Tyre for thirteen years, in the reign of king Ithobal. After him reigned Baal ten years. After him judges were appointed of whom Ecnibalus, the son of Baslec, judged the people two months. Chelbes, the son of Abdæus, ten months. Abbar, the high-priest, *three months. Mytgonus and Gerastus Betus the sons of* Abdelimus, six years. After them Balatorus, one year. Upon his death they sent for Merbalus from Babylon, who governed four years, and was succeeded by his brother Hirom, who ruled twenty years, during which Cyrus obtained the empire of Persia. The whole interval amounts to fifty-four years and three months; for, in the seventh year of the reign of Nabuchodonosor, he began to besiege Tyre, and Cyrus entered upon his reign over the kingdom of Persia in the fourteenth year of Hirom. So that the records of the Chaldeans and Tyrians agree with our writings concerning this temple, and the testimonies here produced are an indisputable attestation to the antiquity of our nation.

But it is now expedient to satisfy those who disbelieve the records of barbarians, and think those of the Greeks only worthy of credit, by producing many of those very Greeks who were acquainted with our nation, and setting before them such as, upon occasion, have made mention of us in their own writings.

Pythagoras, of Samos, lived in very antient times, and was esteemed superior to all philosophers in piety and wisdom. It is evident that this great man was not only versed in our laws, but, in many instances, an admirer and observer of them. This is not inferred from any thing that he ever wrote, but from what others have said and reported concerning him. Hermippus, an historian of credit, in his first book concerning Pythagoras, informs us, "that upon "the death of Calliphon, of Croton, one of his associates, "the philosopher affirmed, that the soul of this man conversed with him night and day, and enjoined him not to "pass over a place where his ass had stumbled, to drink "only of clear fountain water, and to speak evil of no man. "This he did in imitation of the Jews and Thracians, "with an application to himself." And it was truly said, for Pythagoras incorporated divers customs of the Jews into his own philosophy.

Nor was our nation unknown of old to several of the Grecian cities, or, indeed, thought unworthy of imitation by some of them, as appears from Theophrastus in his book of laws, where he speaks of the Tyrian law against swearing by any strange god, naming the Corban, amongst other oaths, prohibited, that is to say, in Hebrew, the gift of God; and this oath was only to be found amongst the Jews.

Herodotus, of Halicarnassus, was no stranger to our nation; for he makes some mention of us in his second book, where speaking of the people of Colchis he has these words: "With respect to circumcision, I find only the Colchians, the Egyptians, and the Ethiopians, to have used it "of old. But the Phoenicians and the Syrians in Palestine, "confess that they derived it from the Egyptians. The "Syrians that border upon the rivers Thermodon and Parthenius, and their neighbours the Macronians, are reputed to have taken it up of late from the Colchians. These "are no others that are circumcised, and they practised it "after the manner of the Egyptians. As for the Egyptians "and Ethiopians, I cannot determine which of them received it from the other." This author says, that the Syrians of Palestine are circumcised. [illegible] there are no people circumcised in Palestine but the Jews, it must therefore be his knowledge of them that induced him to speak concerning them.

Cherilus also, a more antient writer, and a poet, makes mention of our nation, and informs us [illegible] the alliance of king Xerxes, in his expedition against the Greeks. [illegible], in his enumeration of other nations, he last of all inserts ours, when he says,

" The people, with an admirable grace,
" Brought up the rear: their language Tyrian was;
" The natives unknown; the mountains their abode
" By Solymus, that near a vast lake stood
" Their heads cut round, and their heads cover'd o'er
" With head-pieces of tann'd horse-hides they wore."

From hence, I think, it is evident, that, speaking of the mountains of Solyma, or Jerusalem, and of a large lake at hand there, it can be understood of no other than the Jews that dwelt amongst those mountains, and of the lake Asphaltites, which is by much the largest in all Syria.

Nor were the Jews only known to the common sort of the Greeks, but likewise to their philosophers of the first rank, by whom they were honoured with singular marks of [illegible] Clearchus, who was the disciple of Aristotle, and [illegible] to none of the Peripatetics, in his [illegible] the subject of sleep, says, from Aristotle, [illegible] " It would be tedious to run through the whole [illegible] the people of the Jews and therefore I shall [illegible] give you a specimen of a particular person's admira[illegible] [illegible] Hyperochides made answer, that it would be [illegible] to them. Aristotle then proceeded [illegible] " This was a Jew of the Lower Syria, of the [illegible] of those philosophers whom the Indians call Calani, and the Syrians Jews, from the country of Judæa, " which they inhabit. The capital city has a hard name, " and they call it Jerusalem. He was a person of great " hospitality to strangers, and no less considerable for his " learning [illegible] It was my fortune to be in Asia with [illegible] this man paid us several visits there, " to the [illegible] and improvement of those who [illegible]"

This is the character, according to Clearchus, that Aristotle gave the Jews, to which he added his extraordinary temperance and moderation in the government of his passions.

Hecatæus the Abderite, a man learned and active, who was educated with Alexander the Great, and lived afterwards with Ptolemy, the son of Lagus, and king of Egypt, wrote an entire treatise upon the subject of the Jews, from which I shall extract some passages that tend to elucidate the matter under present consideration. He relates an account of a battle fought between Ptolemy and Demetrius, at Gaza, eleven years after the death of Alexander, and in the hundred and seventeenth olympiad, according to [illegible] history. " It was in this olympiad (he writes) " that Ptolemy, the son of Lagus, defeated Demetrius, the son of Antigonus, otherwise called Poliorcetes, in a battle, not far from Gaza." Now it is agreed, on all hands, that Alexander died in the hundred and fourteenth olympiad, and it is therefore evident that the Jews were a flourishing people in the days of that great prince. Hecatæus says farther, that after the battle of Gaza, Ptolemy made himself master of Syria, and the country round, and that the people were so charmed with his humanity and moderation, that many followed him into Egypt, and were willing to share him in his concerns. Among the rest, was one Hezekiah, an high-priest of the Jews, and a person of the first rank. He was a man fifty years of age, possessed of the powers of eloquence, and great knowledge of the world. The same author says likewise, that the number of priests who received tenths and lived in common, had amounted to about fifteen hundred. Speaking afterwards of Hezekiah, he thus proceeds:

" We have had several conferences with this great man, " and others about him, concerning our different customs, " practices, and opinions, insomuch that he carried us to " his habitation, and instructed us in the polity of his " country, which he had down in writing."

Hecatæus proceeds to shew the zeal and veneration we have for our laws, and that we are ready to submit to the most excruciating torment, rather than be guilty of the least violation of them. He then expatiates on the subject of our patience under calumny and reproach in the following manner:

" What indignities have these people endured from their " neighbours? How have they been persecuted by the Persian kings and their officers, and [illegible] " [illegible] against [illegible] For [illegible] the temple " of Belus was fallen down at Babylon, [illegible] " being at that time in the place, had [illegible] " it, and accordingly ordered all the soldiers to [illegible] " rying timber and materials to [illegible] the advancement of the " work. The Jews were the only people that [illegible] " and were severely punished for their disobedience [illegible] " when the king saw nothing would work upon them [illegible] " of generous tenderness for such constancy, he [illegible] " them to be discharged. Upon their return to their " own country they demolished all the temples [illegible] " that they found erected to strange gods, [illegible] " of them were fined and punished [illegible]"

The historian enlarges [illegible] upon our [illegible] ness and resolutions, the vast multitudes of our people, the prodigious numbers that were carried away captive, [illegible] Persians, into Babylon, and others [illegible] after the death of Alexander, transported into Egypt and [illegible] occasion of a sedition in Syria. He [illegible] likewise [illegible] extent, the beauty, and the fruitfulness of our country, (that is to say, of Judæa) which he computes at [illegible] three millions of acres and affirms it to be a most [illegible] soil. Of the city of Jerusalem, its spaciousness, [illegible] ple, and the temple, he speaks to this effect:

" The Jews have in their possession a great many towns, " villages, and strong holds, but one city [illegible] " all the rest for its greatness and strength. It is [illegible] " fifty furlongs in compass, to contain an hundred and " fifty thousand inhabitants, and the name of it is Jerusalem. In the middle of this city stands an enclosure of " stone, an hundred cubits [illegible] " [illegible] Within this enclosure is a quadrangular altar [illegible] " of unwrought stones, that never tool touched, the superficies of it twenty cubits over, and the [illegible] " Next about it there stands a spacious building [illegible] " [illegible] " and lamps burning continually night and day [illegible] " images, plants, groves, [illegible] in other temples [illegible] " they were wholly wanting. [illegible] " pass their time there [illegible] " they drink no wine." The [illegible] relates a story of [illegible] under one of Alexander's successors.

" As I was travelling towards the Red Sea [illegible] " one Mosollam [illegible] " [illegible] " [illegible] " they were advancing on their way [illegible] " took upon him to interpret the [illegible] " bade them all stand, and then did [illegible] " them what they stood on? [illegible] " them a bird, replied, if that bird stand [illegible] " stand; if it rises, and goes on [illegible] " too, but if the bird turns its course [illegible] " you must all go back again. The Jew [illegible] " more words, let fly an arrow, and killed the bird [illegible] " diviner, and his companions, fell [illegible] " Jew, in most outrageous terms. [illegible] " Mosollam,) you are all mad, to be [illegible] " a foolish bird. How shall that poor wretch pretend to " tell us our fortune that knew nothing of its own? If " this bird could have foreseen [illegible] " would have kept itself out of the way [illegible]" Thus much of Hecatæus.

I shall add one word out of Agatharchides, not as any friend of ours, though I take him, in charity, to be no enemy. "He relates a story, how Stratonice cast off her "husband Demetrius, and passed out of Macedonia into "Syria, with a design to marry the king Seleucus. But "Seleucus not answering her expectation, she stirred up "a commotion in Antioch, while he was with his army "in Babylon. At his return he took Antioch, and Stra-"tonice making for Seleucia, she was taken, and it cost "her her life." Her only course had been to have taken her passage by sea, but she was diverted from it by a dream. Agatharchides, reflecting upon Stratonice's superstition on this occasion, to treat more at large upon the [illegible], and so enters upon an invective against the Jews.

"The people (says he) they call Jews, are possessed of "a city by the name of Jerusalem, a place of impregnable "strength. They have a custom there of resting the se-"venth day, without either bearing of arms, tilling the "ground, or attending any common business whatsoever, "but they employ it wholly in their temples, and upon "[illegible] devotion, from the morning to the evening.

"[illegible]cus, the son of Lagus, took advantage of this "custom, and entered the city with an army upon that day "[illegible] it was the consequence. When the Jews should "have been defending their lives and liberties, their at-"tention was altogether taken up with the superstitious "[illegible] of not violating their Sabbath, and so they de-"livered themselves up to an insupportable tyranny, "[illegible] taught them, by experience, the [illegible] "[illegible] of so pernicious a [illegible]. From hence it is, "that men fly to dreams and opinions, never considering "that things necessary are not to be controuled by human "reason." Thus Agatharchides reflects upon our con-duct; but whosoever passes a sober judgment upon the whole matter, will find the proceedings grounded upon the most glorious foundation of honour and virtue: for what can be more heroical than to give up life and coun-try to the duty we owe to God's holy laws and religion?

That some writers have omitted to mention our nation, not because they know nothing of us, but because they en-vied us, or from some other unjustifiable cause, I think I can demonstrate from particular instances. Jerome, who wrote the history of Alexander's successors, lived at the same time with Hecataeus, who was a friend of king An-tigonus, and had the government of Syria. Now Heca-taeus wrote a complete volume of our affairs, while Jerome never mentions us in his history, though from the vici-nity of the place of his nativity, he might be said to have been bred up amongst us. But men act according to their different inclinations. The one thought our actions worthy of being transmitted to posterity, while the other was unduly disposed to suppress the truth.

But surely [illegible] evidence to demonstrate our claim to antiquity, as the Egyptians, Chaldeans, Phoeni-cians, together with many of the Greek writers, for, besides those already mentioned, there are Theophilus, Theodotus, Mnaseas, Aristophanes, Hermogenes, Euemerus, Conon, Zopyrion, and many others, who have made particular mention of us. The greater part of these writers must undoubtedly be in the dark, for want of the holy scriptures for their guide, yet they all afford their testi-mony to our antiquity, which is sufficient for my present purpose. The errors of Demetrius Phalereus, the elder Philon, and Eupolemus, may be passed over with can-dour, as they had not the means of better information.

There remains behind one material circumstance, to which I hold myself bound in duty to attend. This is to demonstrate the calumnies and reproaches laid upon our nation, and turn the asseverations of the authors against themselves. To all men who are conversant in history, the prejudice and partiality of writers must have been obvious. Some exercise their malignity and prejudice upon whole nations, some cast the shaft of detraction at one object, some at another. Thus Theopompus in-veighed against the Athenians, Polycrates against the La-cedemonians, and Tripoliticus (not Theopompus as some imagine) against the Thebans. Some of these writers are actuated by malevolence and envy, some from the hope of acquiring fame, and others by reporting things ex-travagant and extraordinary. [illegible] effect such illiberal efforts may have with the weak and superficial, men of sober judgment will treat them with the contempt they deserve.

The Egyptians being our professed enemies, the most effectual means of [illegible] to pervert truth, and misrepresent the [illegible] for [illegible] coming into Egypt, and their departure [illegible]. Indeed they envied and hated us for many [illegible]. First, for [illegible] power and [illegible] amongst them [illegible] the [illegible] prosperous [illegible] to our country. The difference of our religion from theirs [illegible] cause of enmity, [illegible] conception, for they paid adoration to brute [illegible]. This practice they [illegible] their [illegible], and rendered them incapable of sublimer ideas, excited their aversion to their proselytes who came over to us, [illegible] of them have proceeded to that degree of [illegible] in their conduct, as not to scruple to contradict their own antient records. This assertion I [illegible] prove by quoting the words of one of their principal writers, who I have already cited in confirmation of our antiquity.

Manetho, having [illegible] Egyptian history, solemnly pro[illegible] upon sacred writ-ings, and premises, "that our ancestors carried an army "into Egypt, and subdued the country, but that, being "expelled [illegible] settled themselves in a pro-"vince that is now called Judea, built a city [illegible] "[illegible] Jerusalem, and erected a temple." Thus far he fo-llowed the [illegible] records. But he afterwards becomes eccentric, [illegible] and [illegible] and in-troduces incredible [illegible] representing us as intermixed with a rabble of Egyptian lepers, [illegible] driven out of the country. He [illegible] the fictitious name of [illegible], but [illegible] of his im-posture, does not [illegible] the year of his reign, which he has accurately [illegible]. He [illegible] even fabulous stories [illegible] the king [illegible] forgotten what he [illegible] that is, that it is now five hundred and eighteen years since the [illegible] went out of Egypt [illegible] Jerusalem, [illegible] the reign of Tethmosis [illegible]. Now, from his days, the reign of the [illegible] kings, according to Manetho, amounted to three hundred and ninety-three years, till the two brothers, Sethos and Hermeus, of whom the one [illegible] called Egyptus and Hermeus Danaus. He also says, that Sethos cast the other out of Egypt, and reigned fifty-nine years, as did his eldest son Rhampses, [illegible] six years.

Having acknowledged that our forefathers were gone out of Egypt so many years ago, he introduces his ficti-tious king Amenophis [illegible] like Orus, and Isis, [illegible] desirous to become a spectator of the gods. He [illegible] communicated [illegible] to one of the same name with his own, who was the son of Papius, and [illegible] of prior [illegible] this sad pass, Amenophis, told him that his [illegible] seeing the gods should be granted, upon [illegible] clearing the kingdom of all lepers and other [illegible] sons, and that the king, [illegible] gathered together out of Egypt, [illegible] rejects, to the number of fourscore thousand, whom he sent to work in the quarries to the eastward of the Nile, with a mixture of other Egyptians, to whom that service was allotted He says further, that there were some of the learned priests polluted with the leprosy

In prosecution of his purpose, he goes on to observe, that the wise and heavenly priest Amenophis, in a horror of conscience for what he had done, and in dread of a judicial vengeance from heaven upon himself for giving that counsel, and upon the king for taking it, durst not mention it to him, but left a writing behind him, and put an end to his own existence The author then goes on in these very words

"The king being plied with petitions on the behalf of these miserable people and particularly for some place of retreat, where they might live safe and easy, they pitched upon Avaris, formerly known by the name of Typhon, and the seat of the shepherds The prince granted them this boon, and they were no sooner settled in it than, finding it a commodious post for a rebellion, they listed themselves under Osarsiph, a priest of Heliopolis, and took an oath of fidelity to him, to obey whatever he should command them, upon these preliminaries, that they should neither worship any of the Egyptian gods, nor abstain from any of the meats that they count holy, nor intermarry but with people of their own opinion When they had gone thus far, in opposition to the Egyptian interest and customs the commander presently ordered the fortifying and walling of the city, and the levying war against Amenophis, holding other priests along with him, sent in embassy to the shepherds at Jerusalem, whom king Thetmosis had forced away out of Egypt, with instructions to the deputies to consult upon the common cause, and to invite them into a league against Egypt, with a promise to conduct the confederates, and receive them into Avaris, the seat of their ancestors, where they were sure they could want nothing, but they might fight when they found it convenient, and, with the utmost ease, make themselves masters of the province They were transported with joy at this proposal, and immediately drew out to the number of two hundred thousand men, and so marched away to Avaris

"Amenophis, upon the news of this invasion, was in great confusion of mind, as to the prophetical paper the priest left behind him, immediately called a great council of his princes and people together, and sent away all the beasts that passed for sacred among the Egyptians, with a strict order to the priests to keep all their idols as close as possible He committed his son Sethos, otherwise called Ramesses, after his father's name, Rhampses a child of five years of age, to the care of a particular friend, and so marched away himself, at the head of three hundred thousand fighting men, to encounter the enemy But, upon second thought, and a check of conscience, he turned short without fighting, and went his way to Memphis, where he and his people took shipping, and, with Apis, and the rest of their gods, fled into Egypt The king of the country gave him and his people so generous a reception, that they wanted for nothing the place afforded, neither provisions or habitations, for their entertainment and convenience, to serve them the whole course of that fatal thirteen years banishment Thus it fared with the Egyptians in Ethiopia, besides that they had a guard allowed them upon the frontier, for the safety of their king's person

"But, in the mean time, the Jerusalem auxiliaries made infinitely more ravage in Egypt, than they that called them in For there was nothing they stuck at that was either inhuman or wicked, and the very spectacle of their impiety was a calamity not to be expressed The razing, burning, and rifling of towns and villages, was nothing to them without sacrilege, and breaking the images of their gods to pieces; most barbarously tearing the consecrated creatures, that the Egyptians adored, limb from limb, forcing the priests and prophets to be the executioners of them themselves, and then turning them off naked"

The author says yet further, "That the founder of that polity was one Osarsiph, a priest of Heliopolis, so called from Osiris, a god that was worshipped there" and he says that this priest, changing his religion, changed his name too, and called his name Moses This is an Egyptian story of the Jews, but contradicted for brevity-sake

Manethon says yet again, that "Amenophis and his son Rhamses marched afterwards to Ethiopia with two great armies, encountered the shepherds and the lepers, routed and chased them with great slaughter to the borders of Syria" This is the account we have from Manethon, which is most ridiculously trivial, as will evidently appear

Now this fabulist takes it for granted, in the first place, that our forefathers were not originally of Egypt, but came thither from another country, and having subdued it went up and out of it But that these Egyptians, who were thus diseased, did not afterwards intermix with us, and that Moses, who brought us out of the land of Egypt was not one of that number, I shall endeavour to demonstrate from Manethon's own account, and prove that it is not only a fiction, but that the foundation of it is as ridiculous as false

Manethon supposes that "King Amenophis desired to see the gods" I ask what gods? If he meant the gods their laws ordained to be worshipped, as the ox, the goat, the crocodile, and the baboon, he had already seen them But if he meant celestial gods, they are altogether invisible What could excite this desire? Another king, it seems, had seen them before He might have been informed what they were, and after what manner they had been seen, without any new artifice for obtaining his desire However the prophet, it is said, by whose means the king thought to compass his design, was a good and wise man If so, he must have known that the king's desire was unattainable But he failed of his end To come more closely to the point, what pretence could there be to suppose that the gods would not be seen by reason of any defect in the human body? The gods are not offended at the defects of the body, but at those of the mind How can it be conceived that so many thousand diseased persons should be gathered together in one day? Why did not the king follow the direction of the prophet, and rather expel them out of Egypt, than condemn them to the quarries, as if he rather wanted labourers than to purge his country? He says further, that the prophet slew himself in dread of a Divine vengeance, and left this prediction for the king in writing How came the prophet not to foresee his own destruction as well as that of the rest? Why did not the king follow the advice of the prophet, and rather expel them out of Egypt, than condemn them to the quarries, as if he rather wanted labourers than to purge his country? He says further that the prophet slew himself in dread of a Divine vengeance, and left this prediction for the king in writing How came the prophet not to foresee his own destruction as well as that of the rest? Why did he not oppose the king from the indulgence of so fantastical a desire? Was that dread upon him of judgments that were not to happen during his life? Or was the matter, here rehearsed, any worse than death itself? but the most ridiculous part of the story remains for comment

The king, although he had been informed of these things, and was terrified at the apprehension of them, did not eject these diseased people out of his country, but as Manethon relates, gave them that city to inhabit, which had belonged to the forefathers, and was called Avaris, where they made choice of the high-priest of Heliopolis for their governor. This priest first ordained that they should never worship the gods, nor abstain from those animals that were adored by the Egyptians, but kill and eat them [illegible] they should associate with none but their confederates, and he bound the multitude by oath to the observance of these laws. In fine, they fortified Avaris, and took up arms against the king, sending to Jerusalem for assistance, with a promise of putting Avaris into their hands, not doubting but from thence, upon a conjunction, they might [illegible] of Egypt.

He farther says, [illegible] they advanced with two hundred thousand men, but that Amenophis, king of Egypt, because he would not fight against the gods, took his flight into Ethiopia, and took Apis, and other sacred animals, along with him [illegible] Jews, afterwards breaking into Egypt, [illegible] wise, [illegible] temples, put the nobility to [illegible], and committed other things without mercy or [illegible] [illegible] that the priest who settled their polity was an [illegible] [illegible] Osarsiph [illegible] from their [illegible] [illegible] named the name of [illegible] out of Ethiopia [illegible] in the thirteenth year after his [illegible] [illegible] elephantine, and the [illegible] [illegible] many of them, and [illegible]

[illegible] note that [illegible] his stories [illegible] [illegible] though the defeated people [illegible] them, might despair, [illegible] such rigour by [illegible] the prophet, yet, when they [illegible] liberty [illegible], and allowed a [illegible] they must certainly have entertained [illegible] him. Or, admitting their aversion to [illegible] immutable, they would rather have continued [illegible] upon his person, than involve not only [illegible] relations, in the calamities [illegible] men, not with the gods [illegible] contrary to the laws in which [illegible] acknowledgements to [illegible] that the ringleaders of this [illegible] out of Jerusalem, [illegible] Egyptians themselves, and especially their priests [illegible] bound [illegible] oath to these practices. How [illegible] is to suppose, that, when they found none of their [illegible] could be revenged upon [illegible], they should [illegible] to [illegible] the force of such [illegible] for on the contrary they were [illegible] enemies, from a total repugnance [illegible]

[illegible] complied upon [illegible] Egypt, as if they [illegible] condition of that country out of which [illegible] by force. Had they been [illegible] [illegible] taken so hazardous [illegible] people, living [illegible] and [illegible] fruitful and agreeable country [illegible] danger for their [illegible] [illegible] so [illegible] determined, argues a degree [illegible] frenzy. They could not [illegible] the flight of the king at the head of three thousand men, [illegible] according to the fabulist, he brought [illegible] him to encounter the revolters.

He charges also upon the army from Jerusalem, the [illegible] of [illegible] Egyptians [illegible] provisions, the embezzlement of [illegible], and the commission of the most horrid acts. What less could be expected from an open and declared enemy, especially when the Egyptians had done the same things before, and bound themselves by oath to continue the same practices?

In what light shall we view the story of the rout Amenophis gave his enemies, together with the slaughter and pursuit of them to the borders of Syria? Does Egypt lie so open on all hands? and would not those who had the conduct of the war, when they were informed he was upon the march, have secured the avenues out of Ethiopia, and drawn an army together to oppose him? But, says the fabulist, he followed them over the sandy desert, and pursued the slaughter as far as Syria. A very probable supposition! to pursue an enemy over a desert hardly passable, and that without any interruption. It is evident, even from Manethon's own account, that we neither derived our origin from the Egyptians, or ever intermixed with them. As to the [illegible] part of them, it is not doubted but that many died in the quarries, more in the war, and great numbers in this last [illegible] and flight. But we now proceed to examine into the validity of what Manethon advances concerning Moses.

The Egyptians universally acknowledged Moses to have been a man of singular wisdom and integrity, and for this reason it seems, they were desirous of having it thought that he was of their country, and therefore represent him as one of the priests of Heliopolis, who was [illegible], [illegible] [illegible] It has been [illegible] from the [illegible] records, [illegible] [illegible] hundred and eight [illegible] earlier [illegible] [illegible] [illegible] Egypt [illegible] [illegible] to [illegible]

[illegible] from [illegible] [illegible] any [illegible] villages, [illegible] them [illegible], [illegible] [illegible] the same [illegible] with them, [illegible] [illegible] [illegible] of the [illegible], and restored [illegible] [illegible] certain purifications, [illegible] [illegible] the [illegible], and [illegible] [illegible] [illegible] Moses had been [illegible] himself, he would [illegible] upon others.

Nor [illegible] ordained for persons afflicted with the leprosy only, but they disqualified any man for the sacerdotal office, who had [illegible], or corporeal defect. Now [illegible] should have such a [illegible] nature, he [illegible] deprived of his function. Can it then be supposed, that if Moses had been a leper, he would have ordained laws to his own reproach?

Nor is there any probability of his changing his name from Osarsiph to that of Moses, as there appears not the least [illegible] between the one and the other [illegible] in the Egyptian language, [illegible] [illegible] person who is preserved out of the water. [illegible] the whole, [illegible] presumed, [illegible] while Manethon followed the ancient records, he [illegible] of the truth, but when [illegible] guided by fiction and [illegible], there is no longer any [illegible] truth [illegible]

I shall now enquire into the [illegible] of Cheremon, another Egyptian historian, who [illegible] the same [illegible] [illegible] Amenophis, [illegible] Manethon. He relates that the goddess [illegible] [illegible] Amenophis in his sleep, and reprehended him [illegible] for suffering her temple to be [illegible] in the war. But that Phritiphantes, a sacred [illegible], suggested to the king, [illegible] [illegible] all persons labouring under [illegible] [illegible] he should never more be troubled with those frightful apparitions. That Amenophis accordingly [illegible] two hundred and fifty thousand of those that were thus [illegible] [illegible] of the country under the command of Moses and [illegible] two of the number, and holy men [illegible] were originally Egyptians, Moses being [illegible] and Joseph, Peteseph [illegible] hundred and eighty thousand, that [illegible] [illegible] them [illegible] struck [illegible] joined [illegible] Egyptians [illegible] [illegible] behind him [illegible] there brought forth [illegible]

M[illegible]ses, who, when he was grown to man's estate, drove about two hundred thousand of the Jews into Syria, and brought back his father Amenophis out of Ethiopia. Thus much for the account of Cheremon.

To invalidate the credit of these writers, it will be only necessary to [illegible] them [illegible] truth and error can never be [illegible], nor can truth be divided against itself. When [illegible] to fable and fiction, what they write [illegible] disagree [illegible] rather than [illegible]. Manetho im-[illegible] the expulsion of the lepers to the desire of Amenophis to see the gods; Cheremon to the vision of Isis. The [illegible] makes [illegible] Amenophis [illegible] of the ex-[illegible] of the contaminated people out of the king's domi-[illegible], [illegible] that it was Phritiphantes. They [illegible] respect to their numbers as their [illegible], [illegible] them at eighty thousand [illegible] and fifty thousand. Mane-[illegible] the lepers [illegible] to the quarries, and after [illegible] to Avaris, whence they apply to the [illegible] that the [illegible] of the war [illegible], that being driven out [illegible] of the three hundred and [illegible] Amenophis had left at Pelusium, [illegible] Amenophis to fly into Ethiopia [illegible] he gives us no information who [illegible] they came, whether they [illegible], or why Amenophis would not [illegible] the dream as the supposed [illegible] of the expulsion of the lepers, he writes that Moses [illegible] together, whereas the latter was [illegible] generations before the time of Moses, which space [illegible] of one [illegible] and seventy years. According [illegible] Ramesses, the son of Amenophis, was a young [illegible] his father in the war, left the country with [illegible] and fled into Ethiopia. By Cheremon's account, he [illegible] after the death of his father, in process [illegible] Jews in [illegible], and drove about two [illegible] of them into Syria. What incoherence! [illegible] inconsistency! [illegible] the three hundred and eighty thousand [illegible] as [illegible] to learn, as we are the man-[illegible] perished, whether [illegible] to Ramesses. But what is [illegible], we cannot gather from Cheremon who they [illegible] he calls Jews, or to which of the two [illegible] denomination, whether to the two hundred [illegible] fifty thousand lepers, or to the three hundred [illegible] that were about Pelusium. It would, however, be [illegible] of time to dwell upon the confutation of [illegible] writers, who [illegible] confute themselves.

[illegible] former [illegible], I shall add those of Lysimachus, whose [illegible] far exceed those before-[illegible], [illegible] rancourous hatred of our [illegible]. His words are these:

"[illegible] reign of Bocchoris, king of Egypt, the Jews [illegible] leprosy [illegible], and over-run with foul distem-[illegible] into the temples to beg for chari-[illegible] number of them of contagious "[illegible] there followed a famine in Egypt. "Bocchoris, [illegible], sent to consult the oracle of "Jupiter Ammon about the dearth. The answer was, "[illegible] should purify the temples, by sending away all "unclean [illegible] persons out of them into the desert, "[illegible] those that were ulcerated and leprous, for "[illegible] so abominable a sight, "[illegible] being gone, the earth should bring forth fruit again, "[illegible] return to her course. Bocchoris, upon this, "calls his priests and diviners about him, and with their "advice, orders the [illegible] people to be gathered together, and "delivered up to the soldiers; the lepers to be wrapped up "[illegible], and cast into the sea, and the others to be car-"ried into the wilderness, and there exposed to destruction.

"The night coming on, these poor people began to think "what to do with themselves: they made fires, set watches "and guards, and the next night kept a fast, to reconcile "themselves to the gods whom they had offended. The "day following there was one Moses that advised them to "decamp, and march on together till they met with better "accommodation, with a charge to do no good offices upon "the way, nor so much as to give any man good counsel "that should desire it, and likewise to break down all the "temples and altars they found in their march. These pro-"posals were no sooner approved and the resolution taken, "than the multitude presently put themselves upon the "march over the wilderness, and, after many hardships, "came at last into a country that was both cultivated and "peopled. They treated the inhabitants cruelly in the "highest degree, burnt and pillaged their temples, came in "the end to a place that they now call Judea, and built a "city there by the name of Hierosyla, (according to the "occasion) being as much as to say, *The [illegible]*; "but coming afterwards into power and reputation, they "were ashamed of their own name, changed Hierosyla into "Hierosolyma, and called themselves after their city."

It is here observable, that this last fabulist does not discover or mention the [illegible] with the others, but feigns a more modern [illegible], and passing over the dream and the Egyptian prophet, brings him to Jupiter Ammon, to ask counsel concerning the lepers and other unclean persons. He says, that the Jews gathered together in multitudes about the temples. Now it is uncertain whether he ascribes this appellation to the lepers, or to those that were subject to such diseases among the Jews only, for he seems so to restrict it in calling them the people of the Jews. But why not be explicit, and point out whether he means natives or strangers? If Egyptians, wherefore call them Jews? If strangers, why not inform us whence they came? If, by command of the king, so many were drowned, and the rest cast out to desert, it is extraordinary that there should be so great a multitude remaining, which should pass the wilderness, possess the country, build a city, and erect a temple celebrated throughout the world.

Again, how comes it to pass that he mentions [illegible] the name of our legislator, without a word concerning his country, his person, or his descent? Or without [illegible] the reasons for his making such extravagant [illegible] in his passage, to the dishonour both of gods and men? Whether these exiles were Egyptians or not: if they were, they would not so suddenly have changed the customs of their country. If they were not, they had certainly [illegible] of their own, which they attained from long [illegible]. It is likewise to be considered, that, if they had bound themselves by oath never to bear good will towards those who ejected them, they had a plausible reason for so doing; but for men, in their wretched plight, to [illegible] an implacable war against all mankind, nothing could argue greater folly, or even phrenzy: but the attempt to impose so monstrous a fiction upon rational and intelli-gent beings. He has the effrontery to affirm, that a [illegible] implying "robbers of the temple" was given to the city, and that this name was afterwards changed. But how was it that the very name, which at that time, according to his report, was so great a scandal to the city, should afterwards be accounted the highest honour to its inhabi-tants? It seems that this malevolent detractor in fact only imagined, ignorantly imagined, that the word Hierosolyma implied the same thing in Hebrew as it did in Greek. But wherefore multiply words to detect an imposture so glaringly manifest, especially since it is pictured, that the very face of the narrative bears a stamp of the [illegible] of its author? I shall proceed therefore, in the following book, to accomplish my design.

END OF THE FIRST BOOK IN ANSWER TO APION

FLAVIUS JOSEPHUS

TO

Epaphroditus,

ON THE

ANTIQUITIES OF THE JEWS,

IN ANSWER TO

Apion.

BOOK II

HAVING, in the former book, moſt excellent Epaphroditus, demonſtrated the antiquity of our nation, and confirmed the truth of what I advanced, from the writings of the Phœnicians, Chaldeans and Egyptians, together with thoſe of ſeveral Greek authors, in my remarks upon Manethon, Chæremon, and others of our enemies, I ſhall now direct my attention to perſonal opponents, and, in the firſt place, to Apion, the grammarian, if he may be deemed worthy of notice

His writings contain much the ſame accuſations as thoſe with which we have been charged by others They are contemptible, dull and ſcurrilous Palpable ignorance, and malevolent [illegible], pervade the whole, inſomuch that they beſpeak at once, the author's want of judgment, of learning, and of [illegible]

But, as the frivolous and ſuperficial part of mankind far exceed the conſiderate and diſcerning, and the illiberal delight rather in detraction than encomium of character, I [illegible] felt under ſome kind of neceſſity to detect and expoſe the errors of this man, who has the arrogance to [illegible] himſelf judge in the cauſe, and I am particularly [illegible] to the undertaking, from conſidering that perſons in general, are gratified in finding reproach and ſcandal [illegible] upon their authors

His manner of writing is ſo dark and intricate, that his meaning frequently cannot eaſily be conceived, and his [illegible] abound with contradictions and inconſiſtencies At one time he miſrepreſents the circumſtance of the departure of our forefathers out of Egypt, in the ſame manner with thoſe whom I have already confuted At another he inveighs againſt the Jews of Alexandria, and then [illegible] forth into moſt outrageous clamours againſt the [illegible] and ceremonies of our temple and worſhip

Now, although I cannot but think I have already abundantly demonſtrated, that our forefathers were not originally from Egypt, nor thence expelled on account of bodily diſeaſes, or any ſimilar calamities, yet I hold it expedient to animadvert particularly to what Apion advances in the third book of his Egyptian hiſtory, where he thus writes "I have heard from ſome antient men "of Egypt, that Moſes was a native of Heliopolis that "the people formerly had their religious meetings in the "open air, till Moſes who was well ſkilled in the wor-"ſhip of his country, brought their congregation out of "the fields into private houſes in the city enjoining the "people to addreſs their prayers [illegible] towards the ſun" He adds, "that, with reſpect to the ſituation of the place, there were, [illegible] of obeliſks, certain pillars advanced "upon the [illegible], with engravings upon "them, and the ſhadow falling upon the [illegible], (for "all was open [illegible]) [illegible] the ſun moved, the ſha-"dow moved along [illegible]"

This was the profeſſed opinion of our grammarian, to confute which I ſhall [illegible] any [illegible] from myſelf, but only advert to the writings of Moſes It is [illegible], from his works, that when [illegible] erected a [illegible] for the purpoſe of divine worſhip, he [illegible] gave orders [illegible] for any ſuch repreſentation to be made [illegible] ordained that thoſe who came after him ſhould make [illegible] one When, in a future age, Solomon built his temple in Jeruſalem, he avoided all ſuch fantaſtical decorations as Apion hath here deviſed

With reſpect [illegible] of the [illegible] who informed him that Moſes was a native of Heliopolis, it ſeems he was too young to know [illegible] therefore conſulted ſome of his cotemporaries [illegible] ſays, were well acquainted with him [illegible] pregnant with abſurdity This grammarian [illegible] the country either of Homer [illegible] the latter was [illegible] then to poſitive [illegible] many ages before them [illegible] of his antient men [illegible] Romans less divided as to chronological [illegible] of the time when Moses led the lepers, the [illegible] out of Egypt According to Manetho [illegible] Tethmosis, three hundred and [illegible] years before Danaus fled into Argos [illegible] Lysimachus, it was in the reign of King [illegible] one thousand seven hundred years ago [illegible] others determined it as they pleased [illegible] claims more authenticity than all the [illegible] it to have been precisely upon the first [illegible] Olympiad, the very year, he says of the building of Carthage He makes mention of Carthage [illegible] that would infallibly confirm the truth [illegible] computation But he was not aware that, by this [illegible] arguments and evidence against himself [illegible] credit may be given, in this case, to [illegible] records For we find in them that Hiram [illegible] years before the building [illegible] Carthage, [illegible] that he had a particular friendship [illegible] for Solomon, the founder of the [illegible] contributed materials in abundance towards the perfecting of that work But Solomon [illegible] foundations of the temple [illegible] years after the Jews came out of Egypt

As to the number of the Jews that were expelled out of Egypt, Apion agrees with Lysimachus that they were [illegible] hundred and ten thousand But the origin he gives of [illegible] is involved and nugatory beyond comprehension [illegible] says, that, "when the Jews had travelled [illegible] days, they had inflammations about the [illegible], for this cause, they rested the seventh day [illegible] safely arrived in the country now called [illegible] gave that day the name of the Sabbath, from the Egyptian word [illegible], which signifies the *[illegible]*" Could any thing more absurd or ridiculous [illegible] imposed on the credulity of mankind under the [illegible] history? An hundred and ten thousand men [illegible] under the same disease! If they were blind [illegible] distinguishing, as Apion elsewhere reports them, how could such a multitude hold out so much as one day's journey in the desert? Besides, they [illegible] through all opposition The improbability [illegible] hundred and ten thousand men falling [illegible] at the same time, must be universally [illegible] and is such an incident could never be accounted [illegible] ordinary course of nature, it would be the [illegible] to chance Our author had before told [illegible] they came to Judæa in six days," and [illegible] "Moses ascended a mountain, betwixt Arabia and [illegible], called Sinai, was concealed there for [illegible] days, [illegible] when he came down, he delivered [illegible] to the Jews" [illegible] would ask him if it is possible [illegible] to march over so vast a desert in [illegible] forty days in a place that afforded [illegible]

[illegible] of the origin of the word Sabbath is [illegible] the [illegible] degree of ignorance and insolence, [illegible] Sabbath are widely different [illegible] the word Sabbath, in the Hebrew [illegible] denotes *[illegible] sorts of work* but the word [illegible], denotes the name of the *Egyptian [illegible]* This is the novel account which the Egyptian Apion has given us concerning the Jews departure out of Egypt, and is nothing more than a contrivance of his [illegible] But why should we wonder at his misrepresenting the origin of our fathers, when he affirms them to have been Egyptians when he [illegible] concerning his own? He was born at Oasis, in Egypt, but renounces [illegible] of his nativity, to be thought an Alexandrian, which shews what an opinion he had of the Egyptians, [illegible] name he gives to [illegible] whom he would represent in an odious light, and this is the cause for which he takes [illegible] to disguise his extraction

Those that glory in the dignity of their country, deem it a point of honour to make good their title, and maintain the rights and privileges belonging to it This is the case of the Egyptians with respect to us Either they claim country and kindred with us to aggrandize themselves, or to involve us in their own infamy But Apion seems to vent his splenetic passion against us merely to gratify the Alexandrians for the privilege they allowed him of being a fellow citizen with them, apprized of the ill-will the Alexandrians bear those that are [illegible] their fellow citizens, and yet though he pretended to expose only one sort of Jews, the poison of his detraction extended to the whole race

Let us now attend to the abominable crimes which Apion charges with so much rancour upon the Alexandrian Jews, "They came (he says) out of Syria, and inhabited the spot along the sea coast at a place within the wash of the tide [illegible]" [illegible] Apion [illegible] (being a [illegible] so much [illegible] and falsely however,) as the place of his nativity [illegible] dependency upon Alexandria [illegible] most commodious habitation [illegible] Jews took it by force, and so maintained it [illegible] opposition the more it redounds to their honour

But, to be candid and ingenuous [illegible] Alexander the Great that put the Jews in possession of the place, and granted them the [illegible] with the Macedonians [illegible] Apion would have said, had the [illegible] them at Necropolis instead of that royal city, and their [illegible] been called Macedonians to this day [illegible] read the epistles of King Alexander, of Ptolemy the son of Lagus, and the succeeding kings of Egypt [illegible] which he [illegible] to be [illegible] upon the pillar of Alexandria, [illegible] of the privileges by him granted to the Jews [illegible] record, he must have been lost to all sense of [illegible], to have perverted truth, and opposed the conviction of his own mind

What [illegible] the Jews being called Alexandrians [illegible] ignorance or prejudice Is it not notorious that all colonies take their [illegible] first founders? Need we seek for foreign instances [illegible] we have so many near home? The Jews of Antioch [illegible] Antiochians, because Seleucus the founder of that [illegible] them with the privileges belonging thereto [illegible] like manner the Jews of Ephesus [illegible] Ephesians [illegible] Ionia [illegible], to which right they [illegible] by the successive privileges of foreign [illegible] is a favour which the Roman state hath [illegible] only to particular persons, but to whole provinces [illegible] now called [illegible] If Apion [illegible] the privilege of a citizen of Alexandria [illegible] the title of an Alexandrian [illegible] any man, according to his [illegible] the inland part of Egypt, to call himself an Alexandrian [illegible] and especially an Egyptian [illegible] whom [illegible] this privilege? But [illegible] proof of title to this [illegible] who are in the [illegible]

In the erecting of this city, Alexander [illegible] assistance and service of the Jews [illegible] in testimony and approbation of their [illegible] with a design to shew them [illegible] as Hecatæus says, "Alexander [illegible] "a degree, that, for the equity and [illegible] "gave proof of, he permitted them to hold the [illegible] "of Samaria free from tribute" Ptolemy [illegible] Lagus, acted [illegible] the same manner, with respect to the Jews who dwelt at Alexandria [illegible] entrusted the [illegible] fortresses of Egypt in their hands, [illegible] confidence [illegible] loyalty and allegiance, and for the better securing [illegible] Cyrene, and other cities of Libya with [illegible]

Ptolemy Philadelphus succeeded Ptolemy the son of Lagus, who not only set those of our nation free, but remitted them several duties, and, what is more extraordinary, had so great a desire of being instructed in our laws and customs, and in the sacred scriptures, that he requested interpreters might be sent him for his better information For the more speedy advancement of the work, the care of it was committed to Demetrius Phalerus Andreas, and Aristeus Demetrius was one of the most learned men of the age, the other two were officers of rank, and belonged to his body guards Can it now be reasonably supposed, that this prince could have had such a veneration for the Jewish laws and customs, and for the piety and wisdom of our forefathers, without a degree of affection and regard for the professors of those laws and customs? Apion must be little versed in that history, if he did not know that most of the kings of these Macedonians, whom he pretends to have been his progenitors, were well affected towards the Jewish nation

The third Ptolemy, called Evergetes, when he got possession of all Syria by force, did not offer thanksgiving for his victory to the gods of the Egyptians, but sacrificed, and returned thanks, to the Almighty God of the universe, in the temple of Jerusalem, after the manner of the Jews

Ptolemy Philometer, and his queen Cleopatra committed the charge of the whole government to Onias and Dositheus, who were both Jews Apion treats them with ridicule, but he ought rather to admire their actions, and [illegible] for the preserving the [illegible] [illegible] to be a citizen [illegible] [illegible] upon the [illegible] these two Jews interposed, and [illegible] to former obedience Apion says, that Onias, [illegible] this, entered the place with a small army, in the presence of Thermus, the Roman ambassador In this trite manner he recounts an exploit worthy of being celebrated by a much more candid and able historian

Upon the death of Ptolemy Philometer, Ptolemy Physcon, his brother, marched out of Cyrene, and would have ejected Cleopatra, and her sons out of the kingdom, that he might obtain it unjustly for himself For this cause, Onias undertook the defence of Cleopatra, nor would he desert the trust the royal family had reposed in him now they were in distress Never was there a more remarkable demonstration of the Divine power and justice than upon this occasion When Ptolemy Physcon had prepared for action with Onias he caused all the Jews in Alexandria, men, women, and children, to be exposed naked, and in bonds, to the elephants, to be trampled to death, nay, the beasts were made drunk to inflame their fury But the event proved contrary to his expectation, for the elephants left the Jews, who were exposed to them, turned their rage another way, fell violently on the friends of Physcon, and destroyed a great number of them [illegible] at the [illegible] a horrid spectre appeared to Ptolemy, warning him to leave off persecuting the Jews His favourite concubine (by name called Ithaca, by others Hirene) joining her office of mediation, he not only complied with her request, but repented of what he had already done or intended to do This is a circumstance so notorious, that the Jews of Alexandria keep, to this day, an anniversary festival, in commemoration of their deliverance Yet such is the inveteracy of Apion, that common detractor, that he reproaches the Jews for joining in this war against Physcon, whereas he should have extolled it as a most laudable action

But the partial and perverse principles of Apion most flagrantly appear in the instance of Cleopatra, the last queen of Alexandria, for he applauds that most infamous woman for her ingratitude towards the Jews, whereas he ought to have reprobated her for every species of injustice and wickedness, with respect to her nearest relations, the tenderest of husbands, the Romans in general, and her Imperial benefactors in particular Did she not cause her sister Arsinoe to be put to death in the temple without a crime? Her brother to be taken off by treachery? Did she not rifle the temples of the gods of her country, and the sepulchres of her progenitors? Did she not receive her kingdom as a bounty from the hand of the first Cæsar, and afterwards rebel against his adopted son and successor? Did not her seducing wiles render Anthony a traitor to his country and his friends?

Besides these instances of her ingratitude, inhumanity, and avarice, I might enlarge on the infamous disposition she evinced at the naval battle of Actium where she abandoned even her beloved Anthony himself, who had been father of many children by her, and compelled him to resign his army and his honor to follow her to Egypt In fine I might add to all this, that upon Cæsar's taking Alexandria, she was fired to such a degree of rage, that she valued herself upon the score of merciless [illegible] and declared she would have esteemed it some compensation for the loss of the town, if she could have put all the Jews that were in it to death with her own hand If Cleopatra, according to Apion's reproof, refused corn to the Jews in a time of famine, why does he charge that upon us as a disgrace, which in effect redounds to our honour? However, she at length met with the punishment she deserved

But we can appeal for our own justification to Cæsar himself, to the public decrees of the Roman senate and to the testimonials of Augustus Cæsar in his epistles These, in general, bear witness of the true allegiance we [illegible] and the empire, and [illegible] against the Egyptians

Apion, if he would have done us right, should have [illegible] these authorities, and particularly the opinion [illegible] the Ptolemies, and [illegible] of the Roman [illegible] of the Jews [illegible] the inhabitants of Alexandria [illegible] Jews The [illegible] of the emperors to [illegible] Alexandrian Jews was never called in question [illegible] they demand [illegible] more than their neighbours, but, on the contrary, found credit upon all occasions, as in the command of the river, and other considerable trusts [illegible] they were trusted, [illegible] in all places and matters of moment, beyond all others

Apion brings another objection, and demands, if the Jews be citizens of Alexandria [illegible] the same gods with the rest of their fellow citizens? I reply by putting another question [illegible] wrangle and maintain [illegible] implacable [illegible] concerning a [illegible] of opinion, [illegible] Shall we on that account pronounce that [illegible] Egyptians? [illegible] whether you are, in truth, [illegible] worship [illegible] selves, why should you wonder that the Jews [illegible] Alexandria, who came from another country, and have original laws of their own, should persevere in the observance of them?

Moreover Apion charges us with being the authors of sedition If the point [illegible] Alexandrian Jews, why [illegible] Jews [illegible] wherever dispersed, [illegible] Whoever looks minutely [illegible] revolutions, will find that they were [illegible] of similar principles with Apion himself [illegible] the Greeks and Macedonians were [illegible] city the Jews had the free exercise of their [illegible] the people lived in [illegible] of the Egyptians [illegible] grew more and more [illegible] continued the same throughout all [illegible] others, having neither [illegible]

[illegible] the [illegible] of the Greeks, stirred up these commotions [illegible] in their evil practices, and retained their former [illegible] to our people. The Egyptians, therefore, [illegible] all the differences that prevailed, though we are charged with those very errors and misdemeanors of which our very accusers appear to have been so palpably guilty.

[illegible] likewise disposed to vilify us as strangers, though [illegible] to all purposes of the rights of citizens, yet our [illegible] that privilege without the least colour or pretence. We do not read, in antient history, any more [illegible], or any prince, or any emperor, ever granted such [illegible] to the Egyptians. The first that introduced us [illegible] to that claim was Alexander the Great, and the [illegible] has been enlarged by other kings, and since that, [illegible] have been continued, and confirmed to us by the Romans.

[illegible] further takes occasion to pass a heavy censure upon [illegible] not setting up images and statues in honour of the [illegible], as if he could not have judged of this matter, [illegible] defence. Instead of arraigning our [illegible] have celebrated the magnanimity and [illegible], in allowing their subjects the freedom of their religion, without extorting from them such [illegible] could not conscientiously pay them, and [illegible] tokens of respect as they could with pro[illegible]. It is the good-will that stamps the obligation, [illegible] upon the benefit, without the intervention [illegible] or violence. It may be urged, perhaps, [illegible] a common practice both with the Greeks and [illegible] to hold the images of their relatives, friends, [illegible] their very servants, in high esteem, it argues [illegible] pride in those who withhold that deference [illegible] lords and masters. To this I reply, with respect to [illegible], that we pay implicit deference to our venerable legislator, who has positively forbidden us the use of [illegible] images, and of any creature whatever, whether animate or inanimate. He did not lay this injunction with any view of derogating from the dignity of the Roman empire, but he would by no means suffer any corporeal image, or representation, to be made of an invisible and incomprehensible Deity. We are not, however, forbidden from paying reverence to great and good men in due subordination to the one Supreme Being, as in the case of the emperor and people of Rome, for whose welfare and prosperity we offer daily sacrifices at the public charge, and this we [illegible] no other person whatever. Let this suffice for [illegible] in general to Apion as to what he urges with re[illegible] to the Jews of Alexandria.

I cannot but admire the confidence of Posidonius and [illegible], who furnished Apion with his materials, [illegible] us with not worshipping the same gods as others [illegible] themselves guilty of impiety, in spreading [illegible] reports even to the ridiculing and propounding our [illegible] of all vices one of the most unmanly, [illegible] especially so where the scandal falls upon a temple, [illegible] throughout the world for the exemplary solemnity of its devotion.

Apion [illegible] that, in this holy place, the Jews had the golden head of an ass, of immense value, and that they worshipped this head as a deity; that the image was deposited in the treasury, there found, and carried away, by Antiochus Epiphanes, upon the rifling of that sacred place. To [illegible] I say, that, supposing the story to have been true, it became not an Egyptian to reproach us with it, for an ass is not a more contemptible animal than a goat, or other beast which they adore. It is strange that Apion could not perceive this to be a palpable lie, and the very extreme of contradiction and absurdity. Have we not, from time to time, retained the same laws and customs, without variation? Though Jerusalem has shared the fate of other cities, and repeatedly fallen into the hands of enemies, as Theos, Pompey the Great, Licinius Crassus, and at last Titus Cæsar, and our temple has been thus taken, yet nothing bearing such resemblance was ever found, nor any thing contrary to rules of the strictest piety.

Antiochus Epiphanes is chargeable with the highest degree of perfidy and sacrilege in pillaging the temple. He did not obtain possession of it as an avowed enemy, but as a pretended friend, and a traitor to his allies. His principle was avarice, which he gratified as a common plunderer. We have, however, the testimonials of many respectable writers, that there was nothing found, upon the rifling, to render the party or the cause, ludicrous, as was fallaciously represented. Amongst others I may enumerate Polybius, of Magalopolis, Strabo, of Cappadocia, Nicolaus, of Damascus, Timagenes, Castor, the chronologer, and Apollodorus, who all agree that Antiochus, through necessity, violated his league with the Jews, and spoiled their temple of a vast mass of gold and silver. If Apion was not as obdurate and senseless as the animals which the Egyptians worship, he would have taken those circumstances into consideration, and not contended for such palpable fictions. We have not that veneration for our asses which the Egyptians have for their asps and crocodiles, when they esteem such as are stung by the former, or bitten by the latter, happy persons in being translated to the gods. Asses are to us the same as they are to other considerate men, creatures to bear our burdens, but if they spoil our corn, or become refractory, we chastise them with stripes. But this Apion was so frivolous in his inventions, and so defective in his descriptions, that he could never obtain sufficient credit with the world to do us essential injury.

There is another malicious tale which he borrows from the Greeks in order to reproach us. Of this we need only observe, that they are little acquainted with divine subjects, who are not sensible that it is less impious to pass through temples, than to cast aspersion upon those that minister in sacred things. But it was evidently their design to palliate the sacrilege and perfidy of a prince, by imputing his actions to necessity, rather than do justice to truth, to our nation, and our temple.

Apion writes that "Antiochus found, upon entering the "temple, a man lying upon a bed, with a table before him, "set out with all the delicacies that either sea or land could "afford. This man was so surprized at the encounter, that "looking upon Antiochus as his good angel, and one that "came to rescue him, he threw himself at his feet, and, "in a posture of adoration, implored his assistance. The "king bade him speak freely, tell him who he was, what "he did there, and finally what was the meaning of the "table's being thus set out. The man, upon this, burst "into tears, and proceeded to answer: I am a Greek, and, "wandering up and down in quest of the means of subsistence, was taken up by some foreigners, brought to "this place, and shut up, with positive orders not to suffer "mortal to approach me. I was pleased, at first, with "entertainment so unexpected, but [illegible] in "process of time, I enquired of my keepers into the cause "of this extraordinary treatment. They gave me to understand, that the Jews had a custom among them, once "a year, upon a certain day prefixed, to seize upon a "Grecian stranger, and when they had kept him [illegible] "one whole year, to take him into a wood, and offer him "up for a sacrifice according to their own form, tasting "a taste of his blood, with an horrid oath [illegible] and the "sworn enemies to the Greeks, after which they cast the "remainder of the miserable carcase into a ditch. The "man added, that his time was nearly expired, and adjured him, by the veneration he had for the Grecian "gods, to deliver him from the fate he apprehended at the "hands of the Jews."

This tragical invention was carried to the highest pitch of extravagance, but not so far as to exempt Antiochus from the imputation of perfidy and sacrilege, as those who endeavour to vindicate him would insinuate. For it was not on account of the Greek that he entered the temple, but he found him there without any foreknowledge of the matter, so that the iniquity of his design is manifest, nor can it be justified upon any principle of equity or reason. Now the difference is much greater betwixt our laws and those of the Egyptians, and several other nations, than betwixt us and the Greeks. Where is the country through which, in the course of time, people of all religions do not pass? And how comes it to pass that this fantastical barbarity should be exercised only upon the Greeks? How is it possible that all the Jews should join in these sacrifices, and that the entrails of one man should suffice for so many thousands to taste? How comes it that we have not the name of this perfected Greek, and that Antiochus did not send him back in state to his own country, which would have given him the reputation of a patriotic prince, and formed a powerful party against the Jews?

But as the vulgar and superficial part of mankind are not to be wrought upon by argument, I shall have recourse to the demonstrative evidence of fact. No man ever saw our temple, but can witness that it was so constructed as to preserve every thing in purity and perfection. It had four partitions encompassed with cloisters. The first division was open to all, even foreigners, without reserve; Jews and their wives (if clean and purified) were admitted into the second, and the Jews purified in like manner, into the third. The fourth was only for the priests in their sacerdotal habits, and none but the high-priest, in the robes peculiar to his dignity, was to enter the holy sanctuary. Nay, so strict and punctual are they in their adherence to form and decorum, that the very priests themselves could not have admittance but at certain hours.

Upon opening the temple in the morning, the priests, who were to officiate, attended, and so at noon, upon shutting it up. There were in the temple an altar, a table, a censer, and a candlestick, according to the direction of the law, nor was it legal to carry any other vessel into it. There was no feasting, nor any mysteries carried on, but in the face of the whole congregation, and such method was observed, that, though there were four tribes of priests, and in every tribe upwards of five [illegible] they took their turns of attendance upon [illegible] and that in due regular succession. Meeting [illegible] together in the temple, they delivered [illegible] one to another, some distinguishing [illegible], others of the vessels, without [illegible] being carried into that [illegible] to offer any thing [illegible] for sacrifice. But [illegible] allegations, without considering whether [illegible] founded on truth or not? What can reflect greater disgrace upon any man that sets up for an historian, or a lover of letters? Besides, it is farther observable, that, while Apion puts forth his invectives against us without any foundation, on the one hand, he suppresses [illegible] facts on the other. The fancy of his Greek prisoner, his luxurious entertainment, and the people passing through the temple in a thoroughfare, are evidently the contrivance of malice or spleen, to seduce those who will not be at the pains of investigating truth.

Apion, led by a vein of fiction, enumerates fable upon fable, to render us, if possible, more and more odious, and his inventive faculty suggested the following story.

"While the Jews and Idumæans were engaged in a long and obstinate war, there came a man over to the Jews, "out of some city of Idumæa, where they worshipped "Apollo. This man, whose name was Zabidus, promised to put Apollo, the god of Dora, into their hands, "if they could but get the Jews to gather all together in- "to the temple in a body. Zabidus upon this, contrived "a certain machine of boards, and conveying himself into "it, set three rows of lights upon it, which appeared at a "distance, like a comet on the ground. This appearance "so surprized the Jews, that they gazed at it afar off, with- "out speaking a word. Zabidus, in the mean time, slipped "into the temple, and, without any difficulty, seized the "ass's golden head, and carried it away to Dora." This ridiculous fiction proves the author more stupid than the animal, for he writes of places that exist only in his imagination, nor does he know where Idumæa lies, or that there is any such city in it as Dora. There is, indeed, a place of that name in Phœnicia, not far from mount Carmel, but this is four days journey from Judæa.

How is he to be justified in condemning us for not worshipping the gods of other nations, if, as he says, our forefathers were so credulous as to believe that Apollo would come to them in the form of a comet. It was rather extraordinary that the Jews should not know a lamp, or a torch, when they saw it, from a star, when they had so many at their festivals. And it was little less miraculous that Zabidus should get clear off, with the ass's head, through so many thousands of people, and that there should be no guards to stop his progress, even in a time of war.

The very circumstances of the tale prove its fallacy. How the temple gates, sixty cubits in height, and twenty in breadth, plated over, and no fewer than two hundred men required to shut them every day, could be managed by one single man, is submitted to the determination of common sense. It remains, upon the whole, a question whether Zabidus brought the head back again, or gave it to Apion to be laid in the temple, that Antiochus, finding it, might give rise to another story.

Apion is equally false respecting the oath, when he declares that the Jews do solemnly swear by the maker of heaven, earth, and the sea, to bear no good-will to any foreigners, and more especially, to the Greeks. If this falsifier had said to none of the Egyptians, he would have been more consistent with himself, at least if our predecessors were driven out of Egypt not for their ill conduct, but the calamities under which they laboured. The Greeks and Jews were so remote in point of situation, that there was not the least colour for envy or jealousy betwixt them. On the contrary, many of them came over to our religion [illegible] persevered in it [illegible] receded from it, but, for this pretended oath, no man ever heard it, nor was it any thing more or less than a project of Apion.

[illegible] argument [illegible] the [illegible] of our laws, [illegible] the truth of our holy religion, that we are under the burden of servitude and oppression, and that our city, [illegible] powerful as it might once have been, is no better than tributary to the Romans. But where are the people now [illegible] able to contend with them? Who but Apion would reason in this absurd manner? Governments are subject to [illegible] by turns. The [illegible] are the only [illegible] in immunity from all services to [illegible] of Asia and Europe, which [illegible] on [illegible] having [illegible] into their country, and [illegible] being changed into the [illegible] hands. Whereas these Egyptians are the very people that appear to have never in all past ages enjoyed one day of [illegible], either at home or abroad. But I will not reproach them by relating the manner in which the [illegible] insulted them, not once, but many times, when they laid their [illegible] demolished their temples [illegible] their idols [illegible] vilified their worship [illegible] to imitate the example of Apion, who turned into contempt the misfortunes of the Athenians and Lacedemonians, though there never was a braver people than the latter, or a people of more exemplary piety than the former. Yet neither the piety of the one, or the courage of the other, was sufficient to secure them against the chances of war [illegible] common fate of states and kingdoms.

When we reflect on the miserable [illegible] the best of kings, and particularly Crœsus, [illegible] of the tower of Athens, the [illegible] and several other magnificent [illegible] in such instances [illegible] their tragical devastations But our accuser Apion has discovered a new mode of crimination, forgetful of the [illegible] of his own people the Egyptians He seems to have been blinded by Sesostris, once a celebrated king of Egypt

We will not boast of our kings David and Solomon, though many nations were conquered by their victorious arms, but rather confine ourselves to the case in point Were not the Egyptians at first slaves to the Persians, with other princes of Asia, and so to the Macedonians, when they were lords of Asia, while we lived in a state of freedom, with the command of all the neighbouring cities, for the space of an hundred and twenty years, that is to [illegible] to the time of Pompey the Great? At length, when the Romans had conquered all the other kings with whom they had to do, our ancestors were the only people they [illegible] as friends and allies on account of their fidelity and [illegible] Apion, however, affects ignorance of these facts, though they [illegible] to all the world besides

We are [illegible] reduced, by this malevolent writer, for [illegible], ignorant people The Jews, he affirms, have among them no eminent men for their knowledge of the arts and sciences, or of politics, or the government of states, such as Socrates, Zeno, Cleanthes, and the like He does not forget [illegible] himself in the list of celebrated persons, [illegible] happy in the honour of having [illegible] He was the properest man to be his [illegible], as other people maintained a despicable opinion of him, from the general depravity of his manners, so that [illegible] to be pitied than envied, for valuing himself upon such a support As to the point in competition between the two nations, which should have the preference [illegible] learning and abilities, the reader is referred to our ant[illegible] for his satisfaction As to the other part of the scandal that remains unanswered, we cannot do better than refer him to his own contradictions, wherein he accuses himself and other Egyptians

He seems to take great offence at our sacrificing ordinary beasts, [illegible] we make of eating swine's flesh, and turns the ceremony of circumcision into absolute mockery As for the slaughter of tame animals for sacrifice, we do it in common with all other men, and as to our sacrifices, he [illegible] himself, before he is aware, to be an Egyptian in speaking against them, for a Greek, or a Macedonian, that makes profession of offering whole hecatombs to their gods without any [illegible], would never have discovered aversion to this practice They also make use of the sacrifices [illegible] without any danger of destroying the species [illegible], as Apion seems to apprehend But if [illegible] the Egyptians, the world [illegible] with the wildest of the brute [illegible], which are the objects of their adoration

If the question was put to Apion, what class of the [illegible] as the most wise and pious men, his [illegible] be the priests, for they have [illegible] handed down to them from their first [illegible] worship the gods, and to apply themselves to the [illegible] wisdom This they profess to do, they are all circumcised, abstain from swine's flesh, and join with no other class of Egyptians in their sacrifices Apion therefore [illegible] from his purpose when, instead of gratifying the Egyptians with invectives against us, he advances a direct [illegible] against those he pretended to favour, in charging them with the same ceremonies for which he blames others, and [illegible] advising and encouraging circumcision in others, as we have it upon the credit of Herodotus It seems, that Apion was justly punished for casting such reproaches on the laws of his country, for it so fell out, that, through the prevalence of a disease, he was under a necessity of being circumcised The wound putrifying, a cancer ensued, which carried him off in great torment This should serve [illegible] warning to those, who, regardless of the duties both of religious and social life, prostitute their time and talents, to the base purposes of envy and detraction This was the case of Apion, he apostatized from the laws of his own country, and misrepresented those of ours, and thus concludes our discourse concerning him

But since Apollonius Molon, Lysimachus, and several others, have cast dishonourable reflections on Moses, our excellent legislator, aspersing and vilifying his character as an impostor and magician, and representing his laws as injurious to society, partly through ignorance, but chiefly through enmity to our nation, I shall endeavour, with all possible brevity and precision, to treat on the constitution of our government, and its several particular branches I apprehend it will thence be rendered evident, that there never was such a code of laws framed, for the common good of mankind, as those of Moses, for the advancement of piety, justice, charity, industry, the [illegible] of [illegible], patience, and perseverance in well doing to the very contempt of death itself I have therefore only to request the candour and impartiality of the reader, as I solemnly declare my design is not to write an encomium upon our nation, but to assert the cause of truth and justice, against the efforts of calumny and detraction

Apollonius does not vent his spleen like Apion, in a continued succession of accusations, but varies as to time and mode of aspersing us At one time he reproaches us as Atheists and Misanthropes, at another he upbraids us as cowards, at another he charges us with temerity and fool-hardiness, and represents us as ignorant and savage as the widest barbarians, declaring that the Jews never invented any thing for the benefit or improvement of mankind To confute these malevolent suggestions, it will be necessary to examine the constitution of our laws, and the conformity of our lives to those precepts If, in the course of this undertaking, I should be compelled to make mention of the [illegible] and policy of other nations, it is to be imputed to those who have provoked us to an opprobrious comparison, and rendered the reproach we cast upon them necessary to our own defence

There are in the case under present consideration two essential points First, the tendency of our laws, and secondly, the degree in which we observe them [illegible] such as deny the former, we are ready to produce an abstract of those laws, those who call in question the latter, will be referred to demonstrative evidence

It is an incontrovertible maxim, that the first founders of laws for the establishment of discipline and good order in society, are to be preferred to those who live without any form or method at all, for they appeal to antiquity, and deem it a greater honour to teach others what they ought to do, than barely to imitate what they see done before them This position being admitted, the excellency of a legislator is apparent from his providing such laws as may tend to promote the interest of the community, from a conviction that they are [illegible] beneficial, so that the people firmly adhere to the observance of them, both in a prosperous and adverse state

The antiquity of our legislator gives him an un[illegible] right to precedence, for Lycurgus, Solon, and Zaleucus of Locris, with the rest of [illegible] held in such esteem amongst the Greeks [illegible] when compared with Moses The [illegible] name of [illegible] was not yet so much as heard of, and Homer [illegible] to the truth of this observation [illegible] found throughout his poems The people [illegible] were not governed by written precepts, but by the [illegible] will and pleasure of kings, and so it continued for [illegible] long time by authoritative orders and provisions, occasionally made and issued Our legislator, having this claim of priority admitted by his very enemies, [illegible] himself to general admiration, in all the offices of administration and council first, in composing such a body of laws as might affect all the [illegible] of human life, and afterwards in obtaining a most cordial reception of them by the people, and their solemn declaration of [illegible] and maintaining them. But let his works speak for him.

When our forefathers, to the number of many thousands, marched out of the land of Egypt, into the country appointed for them by Divine Providence, through a [illegible] sandy desert, without water, and had several encounters with the enemy, by the way, in defence of themselves, their wives, and children, they were guided through these almost insuperable difficulties by our vigilant legislator, who maintained the character of a valiant general, a prudent counsellor, [illegible] common protector. He was a man of such [illegible] moderation, that, though he held the people in [illegible] obedience to his injunctions, he never availed himself of his authority to promote his private advantage, [illegible] tyrannized, and [illegible] the greatest licentiousness, he observed the rules of [illegible] and, by his example, encouraged the [illegible] conduct as proved their best [illegible] of [illegible].

[illegible] Being as [illegible] and [illegible], and being persuaded that he could not err, so [illegible] to the care of Divine Providence [illegible] to imprint that belief on the minds of [illegible], for nothing so effectually [illegible] the [illegible] of the Divine [illegible]. [illegible] character of our legislator, [illegible] that he was not a sorcerer or a magician, as he [illegible] Minos, and other [illegible] among the Greeks, some ascribing their [illegible] laws to Jupiter, others to Apollo, or the [illegible] Delphian [illegible] whether [illegible] they [illegible] or were desirous of imposing such a [illegible] people, I pretend not to determine. But the [illegible] excellence of these laws will best appear by [illegible] comparative point of view which is the [illegible] to which we shall attend.

[illegible] nations have their several forms of government, and [illegible] of laws. Some governments are committed to a single person, others to the people. Our legislator had no regard to any of these forms, but ordained a government, [illegible], by a strained expression, may be termed The [illegible], or Holy Commonwealth, in ascribing the [illegible] and power to God, and persuading the people to regard him as the author of all the good things that were [illegible] either in common by all mankind, or by each [illegible] in particular. To him he directs us to fly for [illegible] in our distresses, as he hears our prayers, and [illegible] the very secrets of our hearts. He inculcates the doctrine of one God, the uncreated, immutable, and eternal Being infinitely glorious, and incomprehensible one, further than what we know of him by his works.

This is what [illegible] be derived in some measure, from the wisest of the Greek philosophers, who, from the light of nature, unanimously agree on the congruity of these principles to the majesty and excellence of God, as for instance, Pythagoras, Anaxagoras, and Plato and the stoics, that succeeded them, were of the same sentiments, and had the same notions of the nature of the Divine Being. But the multitude being actuated by a violent and superstitious prejudice against these opinions, the philosopher durst not venture too far in promoting them.

But our legislator was the only man that lived as he taught, both to the satisfaction of the present age, and to the establishing and confirming posterity in the truths which he delivered, governing himself by this constant rule, to make the public good the grand end of all his laws. He pointed out, that the worship of the Divine Being was but the one part of a good man's duty, annexing to it the other parts, such as resignation, temperance, justice and a constant interchange of good offices towards mankind, insomuch that all his precepts and ordinances tended to the advancement of piety, and of course to the honour and glory of God, this being the main object he had in view.

There are two ways of attaining to a degree of excellence in religion and morality, the one is by instruction in words, the other by practical exercises. Now law-givers, in general, commonly attended to one part, and neglected the other. [illegible] for example, the people of Lacedæmon and Crete taught by practical exercises, without rule and precept, while the Athenians and most of the Greeks, [illegible] prescribed laws for every thing, though they fell short in the practice.

But our legislator wisely connected these two methods of instruction, for he neither left these practical exercises to go on without verbal instruction, nor did he permit the hearing of the law to proceed without the [illegible] practice. [illegible] begins with the [illegible] meats [illegible] diet, which we [illegible] to eat and what not [illegible] whom, [illegible] people in general to [illegible] of [illegible] and [illegible]. He [illegible] the [illegible] in respect to [illegible] in matters of [illegible], to [illegible] end that no [illegible] may be ignorant of [illegible] or what the law enjoins us [illegible] and command of our maker, and [illegible] offences. To leave [illegible] without [illegible] of [illegible] necessaries, [illegible] once, twice, thrice, or [illegible] (as [illegible]) [illegible] commanded [illegible] work or [illegible] apart) to meet [illegible] full congregation, expressly to attend the reading of the law, and learning it exactly. [illegible] was never [illegible] by any other law-giver. Indeed the greatest part of mankind are so far from living in conformity to their own laws, [illegible] yet, [illegible] they enquire of others [illegible] the [illegible] knowledge [illegible] to confess their ignorance [illegible] and assistance. But our people [illegible] well [illegible] they [illegible] are [illegible] and [illegible] there are but few, and those who do offend cannot [illegible] escape punishment.

This is the foundation of that admirable [illegible] of [illegible] We [illegible] same sentiments concerning the Divine Being [illegible] of [illegible] and [illegible] life, and the same rule of manners. It is not with [illegible] others, who entertain [illegible] opinions concerning [illegible] the Divine God, and this is the [illegible] people, but the [illegible] men have denied [illegible], others [illegible] intending providence, [illegible] men are equal, [illegible]. We affirm, on the contrary, that God [illegible]. Nay, [illegible] children, [illegible], that our actions, in general, [illegible] and service of God.

This has given rise to a [illegible], [illegible] being [illegible] no [illegible] we continually [illegible] there is men of genius and speculation [illegible] improvement and innovation. While others think [illegible] to deviate from every thing [illegible] forefathers, we, on the contrary, [illegible] of wisdom and virtue, to admit of no actions or [illegible] that are repugnant to our original laws [illegible] is the infallible mark of a good and well [illegible] which neither [illegible] ment will ever [illegible] destroy. Besides, as we truly believe [illegible] Divine institution, we have only to preserve [illegible] and inviolate. Who shall dare to [illegible] those foundations which have been laid by the [illegible] Almighty? Who can amend [illegible] securing the most beneficial provisions [illegible]

[illegible] ents, to the code of his commonwealth? Can any inſtitution be more firm or juſt than that of which the King of kings is king?

As for the prieſts, they are qualified, in common, for their ſpecial ſervices, and the high-prieſt is veſted with power and ſuperiority above all the reſt. They are not promoted, by the legiſlator, to this dignity for ambition, wealth, or any corrupt influence, but for the ſignal teſtimony they have given of their piety, temperance, and wiſdom; and to them is committed the care of religion, and the particular functions of divine worſhip. They ſerve alſo as judges in controverſies between man and man, and have a power to puniſh thoſe who are guilty of miſdemeanors.

What form of government can be more ſacred and venerable than this? Or what greater honour can we do to the Almighty, than to ſpend our lives in a duly attendance on his ſervice, and under the inſpection of prieſts who ſee that all things are performed with due order and reverence? We ſeem to celebrate a perpetual feſtival, and whereas foreigners diſcover a laſſitude, in a few days after their attendance on their myſteries, we are as firm, chearful, and vigorous in the diſcharge of our religious duties at this time as we were many ages ſince, upon their firſt inſtitution.

Among other known precepts of our religion we are taught, in the firſt place, that God is all in all, perfect, ſelf-ſufficient, and ſupplying all other beings, the beginning, middle, and end of all things. He is glorious in all his works, and tremendous in his power and greatneſs, but, at the ſame time, ſo incomprehenſible, that it is not for the tongue of man to expreſs, nor the heart to conceive, any reſemblance of the Divine Majeſty. He is, in fine, incomparable in all his excellencies and attributes, infinitely beyond our art and invention, ſo that it is impoſſible to ſee or imagine any thing like him, for, being a Spirit, he is inviſible.

But we are allowed to read the great Inviſible Being in his works, as in the light, the heavens, the earth, the ſun and moon, the ſtars, the rivers, the ſea, ſeveral ſorts of animals, and various kinds of plants. Theſe things hath the Creator formed, not with hands, nor by labour, nor as wanting the aſſiſtance of any to co-operate with him. But as it was his Divine will they ſhould be made, and be made good alſo, they were made and became good immediately. This is the Almighty Sovereign whom we are all bound to love and adore in the ſtudy and exerciſe of virtue, which is the only way to pleaſe him.

As there is but one God, and one world in common to all mankind, it holds the analogy, that there ſhould be but one temple, for likeneſs is the conſtant foundation of agreement. This temple ought to be common to all men, becauſe he is the common God of all men.

His prieſts are to be continually about his worſhip, over whom the firſt in order is to be perpetual ruler. His buſineſs is to offer ſacrifices to God, aſſiſted by thoſe who are joined with him, to ſee that the laws are obſerved, to determine controverſies, and to puniſh thoſe who are convicted of injuſtice. Such as do not ſubmit to him, ſhall be ſubject to the ſame puniſhment as if he had been guilty of the greateſt impiety.

In eating what has been offered in ſacrifice, we muſt avoid extending the liberty to a degree of gluttony and exceſs, for that Being, who delights in ſobriety and temperance, can never be pleaſed with luxury and profuſion.

The prieſt begins his office with prayers for the general good of mankind, and after that to every man for himſelf, as a part of the whole, being well aſſured, that nothing is more acceptable in the ſight of God, than mutual charity, tenderneſs, and forbearance among mankind.

When we offer up our prayers to Almighty God we are not to petition for wealth, honour, and the good things of this world, for theſe are bleſſings which he is pleaſed to beſtow in common upon mankind, but our prayers muſt be for grace to make a right uſe of what we have.

The law hath preſcribed us certain formal purifications, under kinds of imitations and reſtrictions, too many and too tedious to be enumerated and ſpecified. This is the doctrine concerning God and his worſhip, and what the law enjoins for our attention and practice.

In point of marriage, the law approves no other junction of the ſexes than that upon ſuch principles which nature hath appointed, not from regard to intereſt, or the gratification of inordinate paſſions, but for the procreation of children, and that with the conſent of parents. The very attempt of an unnatural crime is puniſhed with death.

The law farther ordains, that the woman ſhall be ſubject in all things, to her huſband, which muſt not be taken for a diſpenſation to abuſe her, but a proviſion for the maintenance of decency and good order; for God hath given the authority to the huſband. The woman is to have no carnal knowledge of any other man, upon pain of death without mercy; and he that abuſes a betrothed virgin incurs the ſame penalty. It is the ſame alſo in caſe of corrupting a married woman, or a mother of children. Our law is no leſs ſevere upon thoſe women who either conceal their children when they are brought into the world, or otherwiſe deſtroy them. Purification is to be uſed after intercourſe of the ſexes, for which purpoſe water is to be provided for the preſervation of a becoming decency and cleanlineſs.

The law does not permit us to make ſumptuous feaſts at the births of our children, and thereby afford opportunity of drinking to exceſs, but ordains that the earlieſt period of our education ſhould be directed to the purpoſes of ſobriety. We are alſo enjoined to bring up our children to a general knowledge of things, but more eſpecially of law and hiſtory, the one to furniſh them with a perfect acquaintance with their duty to God and man, and the other with great examples, to incite them to the imitation of noble actions.

Care has alſo been taken of the decent burial of the dead, but without extravagant pomp in funeral ſolemnities, or ſumptuous monuments. The law ordains that the neareſt relatives ſhould perform the obſequies, and that thoſe who paſs by when any one is conveying to the place of interment, ſhould attend the funeral, and join the lamentation. It alſo ordains that the houſe, and its inhabitants, ſhould be purified after the funeral is over. Every one is directed not to deceive themſelves with the imagination of being excuſed by purification, if he hath been once guilty of murder.

We are enjoined reverence to parents next to God himſelf, and the law appoints ungrateful and diſobedient children to be ſtoned to death. The younger are commanded to pay reſpect to their elders, as God was before all things. Secrecy among friends is prohibited, as friendſhip imports an entire confidence without any reſerve. Nay, where friendſhip is diſſolved, we muſt not be falſe to a former truſt.

The judge who takes a bribe is to be puniſhed with death, for countenancing the guilty and oppreſſing the innocent. He that diſregards the petition of an indigent perſon, when he is able to relieve him is held guilty. No one is to touch the property of another. He that lends money muſt not demand uſury. Theſe and many others of the like kind, are the rules by which we are united in the bonds of ſociety one with another.

It may be worthy of our pains to enquire into the equity our legiſlator would have us exerciſe in our intercourſe with ſtrangers, whence it will appear, that he hath not been wanting in any thing that can tend to the public good, either by keeping us firm to our laws or communicating the benefit of them to others, who may be diſpoſed to cultivate a knowledge of them. He receives with open arms, all who come over to us, of every nation indifferently, provided they agree in the same common principles of life and manners. Those who come by accident, and without intent to join us, are not suffered to intermix with us in our solemnities, but we are obliged to render them our best offices in many instances: as for example, if they should want water, fire, wood, or the like, we are commanded to supply them; to set any of them right who [illegible] in their way, and to give the dead a decent burial. These are duties of humanity, and [illegible] from the [illegible] laws of our religion.

He prescribes also rules of moderation to be observed towards enemies, to prevent the dreadful extremities of [illegible]. This [illegible] extends to the taking of prisoners, and [illegible], nor would he suffer [illegible] to be stripped.

[illegible] the cultivation of tender principles [illegible] recommended them even to be [illegible] no other power over them than for [illegible]. Domestic creatures, brought [illegible] to be spared, nor, in other [illegible] together [illegible] common use, are likewise to be forborne, though [illegible] mischievous.

[illegible] lawgiver contrived, by every means, to [illegible] conduct [illegible] such sentiments [illegible] excellent purpose, while, at the [illegible] transgressors shall be punished [illegible]. In capital offences the punishment [illegible] death; for instance, in murder, [illegible], and unnatural practices: nor are any [illegible] free, exempt from the penalty.

We [illegible] laws concerning weights and measures, and all sorts of fraud in buying and selling, taking away another man's goods, or appropriating to ourselves what is not our own. Offenders of this kind are punished with much more severity under our laws than those of other nations.

[illegible] want of dignity towards the Majesty of heaven, together with contumacious behaviour towards parents, incur the penalty of immediate death upon the very spot where committed. But the reward of conforming to their laws is not gold, silver, imperial crowns, or precious stones, but the testimony of a good conscience, with the assurance of future bliss, founded not only on the prediction of the legislator, but the promise of [illegible]. In this confidence, therefore, they look upon death only as the blessed means of transporting them from this life to a better. This is evident from many occurrences in the history of our ancestors, particularly the resolution with which they have undergone the most excruciating tortures, rather than let fall one word to the dishonour of their profession. Supposing now the Jews were a people never heard of upon the face of the earth, and there were no witnesses to the veneration we have constantly paid to our laws, what opinion would the Jews form, if an account was [illegible] to them of a people in some imaginary [illegible], who had stood firm so many ages to the religion, laws, and customs of their predecessors? Would they not deem it matter of admiration, especially those that are fickle and changeable themselves?

Modern writers, on the subject of political government, are much censured for having advanced many absurd and improbable stories. Plato himself, the very oracle of the Greeks, and a man in singular esteem for his piety, wisdom, and virtue, as well as the excellency of his philosophy, is exposed to contempt and ridicule by arrogant pretenders, for his wild notions of government, as they term them; while those who peruse his writings with attention and candour, will find them conformant both with reason and nature. Plato himself ingenuously confesses, that "it is not safe for a wise man to publish his notions "concerning the Deity amongst the ignorant multitude." Yet some affirm that Plato writes like a man of vanity and licence.

Lycurgus was a man eminent as a finished legislator; and the Spartans were commended for having continued in the firm observance of his laws for a long space of time. From thence it is inferred, that it is confessedly a mark of virtue to submit to laws. But then let those who admire and applaud this constancy in the Spartans remember, that their continuance in point of duration bears no comparison to that of ours. Let them also remember, that, though the Spartans maintained exact obedience to their laws while they enjoyed their liberty, yet, when fortune abandoned them, they fell off, and abandoned their laws.

But it cannot be said of us, that under all the vicissitudes of fortune which happened to us in Asia, when we were driven to the last extremity, we ever departed from the laws and customs of our forefathers. Nor can it be objected to us, that we ever consulted either our ease or our pleasure when called upon to maintain them. Whoever compares the conditions of both parties, will find the labour and difficulties of the Jews to exceed those of the Spartans; for they were exposed to no service [illegible], but lived in their city at ease, in the enjoyment of repose and plenty. Notwithstanding these advantages, they went over to their enemies in frequent defections, and, contrary to law, duty, and the common obligations of citizens and soldiers, tamely delivered themselves up with their arms. I cannot recollect more than one or two of our people that ever betrayed their cause through fear of death; I mean not the death of a soldier, sword in hand, and in the field of battle, but a death of exquisite cruelty and torment: a calamity to which [illegible] our nation have been exposed, not, I apprehend, through hatred, but to try the experiment of [illegible] constancy, and to try if there were such men in the world, as could endure the acutest pains rather than be guilty of any one word or action derogatory to the dignity of their laws.

Nor is this resolution in the Jews above all other nations matter of surprize; for our ordinary mode of living would be a kind of severity to any other sort of people, [illegible] with respect to the fatigue of labour, hard fare, days of abstinence, coarse clothing, hard lodging, and the like. These people, in the [illegible] military life, would not brook the forbearance of meats [illegible], and many others of the [illegible]. Whereas it is our glory, to engage ourselves, with unchangeable constancy, to the obedience of the laws of our country. Let the partizans of [illegible] and Molon, and other [illegible] censors and perverters of youth [illegible] their reproach and detraction [illegible] in discharging our duty to God, our country, and ourselves.

It is our custom to keep firm in the observance of our own laws, but not to traduce those of others. Nay our legislator had expressly forbidden us to offer the least indignity or contempt to the reputed gods of other nations; and this he did from a reverence to the very name of Deity. But we cannot remain altogether silent, where it is both so easy and necessary to confute the assertions of our opponents, and where, [illegible] other authorities, ready to our hands. The most [illegible] among the Greeks for wisdom have heartily exclaimed against the most celebrated of their poets, and especially their law-givers, for poisoning the minds of the common people with the impious [illegible] advancing the account to [illegible], and deriving their origin from what [illegible] they please. Nay, they allot them their proper [illegible] places like other creatures, for they [illegible] neous gods and [illegible] gods, and [illegible] race, or [illegible], they keep up in [illegible] religions. With respect to their celestial gods, [illegible] give Jupiter the name of Father, but represent him [illegible],

[illegible] tyrant [illegible] his wife, his brother, and the daughter of his own brain entered into a conspiracy, according to the fiction, to destroy him, as he himself had [illegible].

This was the light in which all wise men held those [illegible] deities, the idea being so ludicrous, that they could not [illegible] without scorn and derision. Some of their gods they represented as stripplings, others in the prime of their youth and strength, and others as seniors, [illegible] beards. They have their gods, or patrons of [illegible] arts or trades, as smiths, weavers, harpers, archers, and so on. They have their feuds and factions among themselves, and take part with mortals against one another. They receive wounds in the contest, grieve and [illegible] of them. Nay, these pre[illegible] gods and goddesses go farther still, even to the [illegible] of [illegible] and embraces, and fiercely wi[illegible] [illegible]. What was the case of their Jupiter [illegible] the [illegible] of the whole train of gods [illegible] many goddesses, he suffers them to be kept [illegible] in the sea. He is himself so bound [illegible] that he cannot [illegible] his own offspring, nor can he [illegible] this without shedding tears.

[illegible] of [illegible] practices, and worse consequen[illegible] [illegible] yet remained. Open violation of the [illegible], not only committed, but applauded by [illegible]. If the sovereign, Jupiter himself, could not [illegible] harlot, what are we to expect from [illegible] weaknesses of inferior deities? What shall [illegible] of gods adoring the forms of shepherds [illegible] made close prisoners in the infer[illegible] [illegible] crowned with corn on [illegible] the inventors, the encouragers, and [illegible] [illegible] stories? In some cases they [illegible] passions, as fear, madness, and the like, [illegible] them in the worst of forms so that there can [illegible] amongst men, but it may be [illegible] the character of one of their gods, nor is [illegible] people from sacrificing to the be[illegible] [illegible] monsters. They look upon the gods as the authors of good and evil, and consequently as their friends or their enemies, in proportion to the one or the other. Upon this consideration they deal with their deities as with the vilest of men, they worship and make them presents, for fear they should do them injury.

[illegible] deserves our enquiry how mankind came to lay [illegible] so many desperate and dangerous mistakes concern[illegible] the Deity. I suppose it to have been derived from the imperfect knowledge the heathen legislators had, from the beginning, of the Divine nature, or else from [illegible] of communicating to the world the notions they [illegible] things, as matters of little moment, perhaps, in their opinion, and [illegible] the poets and orators to in[illegible] their own gods, and by this means confounded [illegible] system of politics with idle tales of uncouth deities, and strange [illegible].

The [illegible] and painters of Greece contributed in a great measure to this abuse, in the liberty they took of representing their gods in what shape and figure the artist thought [illegible]. They had their variety in point of matter as well as form, some working in plaster, others in gold and ivory, some in sculpture, and others in colours, and the last piece, for the sake of novelty, was reputed the best. [illegible] the old gods fell off, and went out of fashion, they were [illegible] succeeded by new, and, upon the failure of one religion another started up. It was so with temples as one was laid in rubbish, another was raised out of the ruins of it, according to the fancy of the age, whereas the true worship of the Almighty ought to be as unchangeable as his own nature.

Appollonius Molon was puerile, weak, and superficial in his understanding, but those among the Greeks, who deserve the name of philosophers, are no strangers to the truth of what I have delivered, and entertain the same exalted ideas of the Deity that we do, and with as hearty a contempt of the absurd fables of their countrymen. Whence it was that Plato would suffer no poets in his commonwealth, nay, he dismissed even Homer himself, though with all the honours of a poet laureat, lest fables should destroy right notions of the Deity.

This great man of all others comes nearest to the example of Moses in the model of his commonwealth, where he charged all his subjects to study their laws, get them by heart, and never intermix with strangers, but preserve their government in its original purity, and pay strict obedience to their ordinances and decrees. Appollonius Molon did not consider this, when he preferred his accusation against the Jews, for not joining and communicating with men of different persuasions, as if, in that instance, we were singular, whereas all people [illegible] generally speaking [illegible] do the same thing, the Greeks themselves, and the most discreet men amongst them too.

The Lacedæmonians would admit no strangers among them, nor so much as suffer their citizens to travel abroad, lest they should contract such habits as might tend to a dissolution of their laws. Perhaps there may be cause to censure this rigid severity, in debarring strangers the common privileges of society and commerce. But so far are we from this uncharitable restriction, that, tho' we do not interfere with the concerns of others, we are ready to entertain proselytes, and receive those who are disposed to join with us, which must be acknowledged a certain [illegible] dication of humanity.

The Athenians, on the other hand, contrary to the custom of the Lacedæmonians, make it their glory to give admittance to all strangers, but of this I suppose Apollonius was ignorant. They are so zealous for the honour of their gods, that it was made capital to [illegible] as one irreverent word upon the subject. On what account was Socrates put to death? Not for betraying the commonwealth, or burning their temples, not for [illegible] or sacrilege, but for framing new oaths [illegible] the [illegible], as he suggested, of a certain demon. Whether he [illegible] jest or earnest is not known to this day, but for this he was tried, condemned, and put to death by poison. [illegible] was also charged with propagating false doctrines, and endeavouring to supplant the religion and laws of his country. This was the case of Socrates, [illegible] citizen of Athens.

As another instance of their rigour, Anaxagoras the Clazomenian was put to death for [illegible] which the Athenians thought to be a god, was a [illegible] fire. A [illegible] was offered by proclamation to any man that would bring in the head of Diagoras of Melos for ridiculing the mysteries of their religion. They would have proceeded in like manner with Protagoras, if he had not made his escape in due time. His offence [illegible] was the writing of a tract wherein he delivered himself [illegible] ambiguously of the gods of the Athenians. But why should we wonder at their treating men with this severity, when the women themselves were not spared? For instance, they put a priestess to death, upon an accusation of worshipping strange gods. It was made death also for any man to introduce a foreign religion. What therefore can be more evident, than that so far as these laws were in force, the people could have no faith in other gods. Besides, if they had, they would never have deprived themselves of the comfort and benefit of their favour.

The Scythians themselves, though the most barbarous and brutal people upon the face of the earth, were so scrupulous of preserving the mysteries of their profession, that they slew Anacharsis, a man of eminent parts, only for speaking too reverently of the gods of the Greeks. We read likewise, that many amongst the Persians suffered death upon the same account. Appollonius Molon was [illegible] attached to the laws and customs of the Persians, and [illegible] that held them in admiration, as well as the Greeks, for their firmness and agreement in the matter of worship, as exemplified in the burning of their temples. Molon had not only a good opinion of their customs, but, in some degree, imitated them in the extravagant liberties he took with other mens wives, and the cruelties he exercised towards their children, barbarities that are declared death by our laws, though committed upon any of the brute creation.

Such is the veneration we have for the observance of these laws, that neither power, profit, fear, or any other consideration, can divert, or deter us from the conscientious discharge of our duty. Nor have we exerted ourselves in military exploits from motives of ambition or avarice, but for the support and maintenance of our lawful rights. We have submitted to every kind of outrage with patience and resignation, but we feel most sensibly for every violation of our laws, and are thereby rendered daring and obstinate to the last degree. What reason can we have for desiring to imitate the customs of other nations, which we see abhorred by their very founders? Why do not the Spartans abandon their inhospitality, as well as their contempt of matrimony? And the people of Elis and Thebes their abominable propensities. The most shameful practices generally prevailed among the Greeks through connivance, and they ascribe to the very gods the gratification of the most criminal passions.

What shall be said of those legislators who have been more industrious in devising means for the escape of malefactors, than for bringing them to condign punishment, compounding for a fine in cases of adultery, and atoning for debauchery by marriage? It would be endless to recount the temptations to swerve from the rules of piety and virtue, that are thrown out to the unwary by these compositions, even to the total subversion of their laws.

But nothing of this kind is permitted amongst us; for, though we be deprived of our wealth, our cities, and every thing we hold most dear, our laws continue inviolate, and immutably the same. Now if this be our disposition towards our laws, and that from their intrinsic value, let our enemies make this confession, that they are most excellent. If they deny us this requisition, we demand of them wherefore they neglect the observance of their own laws, which they esteem so far superior to ours?

Time is the surest touchstone in all human cases; nor is there a more convincing proof of the goodness of a law than the antiquity of it. We therefore cast our case upon this issue for the honour of our legislator, and of the laws themselves with regard to God's holy worship. It will be granted us that Moses was the first legislator for many ages, and that as our laws had their origin thence, so they were followed and imitated, more or less, by all other nations. That the generality of the antient Greeks had, in appearance, their own peculiar laws, I admit, but their philosophers held the same notions of the Deity with us, and inculcated the same doctrines of life and manners.

Such is the reputation we have held in the world for our religion and polities, that there is hardly any nation, either Greek or barbarian, that does not act in some conformity to our example, either in the observance of our seventh day's Sabbath, the use of lamps, the celebration of fasts, or abstinence from certain meats; as also in matters of humanity, charitable agreement in society, indefatigable labour and industry, and an invincible constancy in suffering for the truth. In some of these particular instances they generally imitate us.

But the matter of greatest admiration, is that our laws have no baits of pleasure to allure men, but prevail through their own force, and seem to pervade the human mind as the Almighty pervades the universe. Those who look into their own country, or their own families, will bear testimony to my assertion. Can there be any propriety then in the idea of changing our old laws for new ones? If not, let the reproach cease. We are not actuated by a malevolent and envious principle, but a veneration we have for the memory of our prophet, and in full persuasion of his divine authority. If we were not fully convinced of the intrinsic excellence of our laws, the great number of their admirers and professors would be sufficient to give us an high esteem for them. I have treated on this subject more copiously in my Antiquities, and therefore only hint now what is necessary for my present purpose, without any design of depreciating the laws of other nations, or making a panegyric upon those of our own, but merely for the vindication of truth against calumny and injustice.

To draw towards a conclusion. I presume I have sufficiently completed what I proposed in writing these books; for whereas our accusers have pretended that our nation is of late date, I have demonstrated the antiquity of their origin. I have likewise produced several eminent authorities, that make honourable mention of us in their annals. I have incontestably refuted the assertion, that our ancestors came originally out of Egypt, and, with respect to the fable of our being expelled for epidemic maladies, I have rendered it evident, on the contrary, that they cut their way through troops of their enemies into their own country. There are those who asperse the character of Moses, in opposition to the concurrent testimony of several ages to his immortal honour.

In vindication of our laws, more words are superfluous. Those who read and understand them, must be convinced of the piety and wisdom of their institution. They are declared enemies to iniquity, luxury, and faction; promoters of peace, charity, industry, and justice. They allow of no war founded on ambition or avarice, nor do they approve of returning evil for evil. They inspire valour and resolution in the defence of the dearest right of mankind. They are vigorous in the punishment of malefactors, and point out that actions, not words, are the standard of merit.

From these premises I may justly conclude, that we have the most perfect laws extant. For what can be more excellent than unfeigned piety towards God? What more reasonable than submission to laws? What more beneficial than union in prosperity, and a well cemented friendship in adversity? a dauntless resolution in arduous exploits? a sedulous application to arts and husbandry in times of peace? and, finally, a perpetual consciousness of an omnipresent, omniscient, and superintending Providence?

If these precepts had been written at first, or more exactly retained by any others before us, we should owe them thanks, as disciples owe their tutors. But as it is evident that we derived them from no foreign origin, and that the institution of them is our own, that, from time to time, we have handed them down, as the precise and invariable rules of our profession and practice, let Apion, Molon, and the whole tribe of calumniators and detractors, stand confuted. I have completed my design, in dedicating to thee, and others, most excellent Epaphroditus, an authentic history of our nation.

END OF THE SECOND BOOK IN ANSWER TO APION.

FLAVIUS JOSEPHUS

ON THE

MARTYRDOM

OF THE

MACCABEES.

1 MACCABEES.

CHAP I

AS my design, in this discourse, is to shew that reason is the perfection of wisdom, and ruler of the passions, when duly improved by study and religion, I cannot but exhort my readers to apply themselves, with the utmost assiduity, to the attainment of knowledge, the most important of all acquisitions. Reason is a necessary preliminary to knowledge, in which, if we excel, we may be said to excel in the noblest and most comprehensive of all virtues, which is prudence. It is reason alone that can effectually restrain the inordinate affections of the mind, correct the depravity of nature, and those corrupt inclinations which are opposed to the love and practice of virtue. That branch or degree of it which subdues the passions of anger, fear, and grief, and whatever else enervates the mind, may properly be denominated fortitude.

To this it may perhaps be objected, if reason has this dominion over the passions, or perturbations of the mind, why has it not the same controuling power over ignorance and forgetfulness? This is a frivolous objection, and foreign to the case in point, for when we affirm that reason has a controuling power over the passions, we mean those defects of nature only as are opposite to justice, temperance, and fortitude, all which are of a distinct kind, and belong to the sensitive soul, but not such as are defects peculiar to itself, and appertain to the rational system. Again, in this objection the nature of this sovereignty is misrepresented, for we do not mean that reason entirely removes those affections but does not so far submit as to suffer itself to be vanquished by them.

That it is in the power of reason to command and subdue the passions, I could demonstrate by a variety of arguments, but shall, at present, confine myself to the most approved and undeniable one, matter of fact. I mean the example of persons who have signalized themselves irresolutely asserting and dying in defence of truth and virtue, among whom I apprehend none are more conspicuous, or more deservedly admired, than those of our country, Eleazar and the seven brethren martyred with their mother. These, despising the most exquisite tortures, and persevering even unto death, have incontestibly proved the command of reason over the passions. I mean those of the sensitive kind, as before alluded to. I shall endeavour to give just commendations to these brave men, and their incomparable mother, for their immoveable constancy, and to transmit their names with honour to posterity, for their stedfast adherence to virtue and their duty. These men excited the admiration not only of those who were indifferent spectators, or readers, of their sufferings, but even of their very enemies, and most prejudiced tormentors, who stood amazed at the courage and patience which their own unplacable malice exercised after so inhuman and barbarous a manner. Thus they became the means of releasing their nation from oppression, conquering the rage of a tyrant by their sufferings, and becoming a sacrifice of expiation for their country.

The method in which I propose to proceed, will be, first, to make some general remarks on the point in debate, and then attend to this particular instance, giving glory to God, the fountain of wisdom, who hath been pleased to leave such undeniable evidence of this truth in the persons whose virtues I am now about to celebrate.

The question to be resolved is plainly this. Whether reason can controul and govern the passions? In order thereto it will be necessary to explain what is to be understood by reason, what by passion, how many species there are of passions, and whether reason bears sway over them all.

By reason then I understand the intellectual faculty improved and rightly guided by reflection, preferring a life conducted by wisdom and truth. By wisdom I understand the knowledge of divine and human affairs, and the true causes and grounds of each [illegible] by the discipline and instruction of the laws, which teaches us to embrace those truths which relate to God with reverence, and those respecting men as things directed to, and designed for the benefit of mankind. Wisdom may be divided into four particular branches, Prudence, Justice, Fortitude, and Temperance. The noblest and most comprehensive of these is prudence, because reason through its assistance and influence, attains dominion over the passions.

These passions that are most general are two, pleasure and pain, each of which acts upon the body and soul. In these two passions of pleasure and pain are comprehended many others. Thus, in the instance of pleasure, it is preceded by desire and followed by joy. In that of pain it is preceded by fear, and followed by sorrow.

Anger is a mixed passion between pleasure and pain of which those must be sensible who minutely observe how they are affected by it. In pleasure is comprehended a base and wicked affection, which of all the passions is the most diffusive. In the mind are avarice, envy and contention; in the body greediness and voraciousness. Pleasure and pain, like certain branches growing out of the body, have several scions, which reason, like the common husbandman, by lopping, tying up, watering, transposing, and ordering, corrects in their nature, and tames their wildness. Reason is the guide of the virtues, and governess of the passions. That this is not affirmed without ground, is evident from the mighty effect it has in matters where the virtue of temperance is obstructed. Temperance restrains the desires, some of which belong to the soul, others to the body, both of which are under the government of reason. When our appetites incline to such fish, fowl, or other delicious foods as are forbidden by our laws, and we abstain from them upon that very account, this is a demonstrative proof of the dominion of reason over the passions. For the impulse of the appetite by the assistance of reason is restrained, and all the motions of the body are bridled by its coercive power.

CHAP. II.

BUT this is a matter of small weight when compared with the more stimulating desires of the mind, especially those that are excited by beauty. Joseph acquired immortal renown for conquering his passion by the strength of reason and sound reflection, though in the bloom of years, and urged by the united impulse of beauty and importunity. It is not the mere allaying the fury of vehement pursuits after pleasure, and abstaining from the impure act, that reason can or ought to do, since it is plain that all inclinations are under its jurisdiction, otherwise the law would have been most absurd in laying upon us [illegible] practical laws that, "Thou shalt not covet thy neighbour's wife, nor any thing that is thy neighbour's." For it is evident that when the law forbids us to covet at all, it more strongly implies that reason is able to curb and conquer our desires. And thus it is not only in those things which are opposite to the virtues of temperance, but justice also. Otherwise what remedy could there be for reforming the luxurious, avaricious, or sinful man? When a man of a covetous disposition, is prevailed upon to conform to the precepts of our law, he refrains his desires, lends to the poor without taking usury, and remits the debt at the year of jubilee, and though he be ever so frugal, yet he is obliged by this law neither to gather in the fruits of his field or his vineyard in the sabbatic year.

Many other instances might be produced to shew that reason governs our passions: for the law, in some cases, exercises dominion over natural affections to parents, forbidding us, for their sakes, to betray the cause of truth and virtue; so it does over tenderness to our wives, commanding us to punish them for the transgressions of their duty; so again over love to our children, enjoining us to make them examples when they do amiss; and lastly, over-kindness to our friends, in directing us to reprove their vices. In confirmation of this truth, it is further to be observed, that reason, when influenced by the law, overcomes hatred to enemies, for it prohibits the cutting down their fruit trees; it orders us to restore to our enemies things which they have lost, and to help their cattle when fallen and in distress.

Further, it is evident that reason bears sway over the more violent passions, such as ambition, vain-glory, and envy; for all these unseemly dispositions are removed and subdued by a mind instructed by sound reason; as is anger also, though the most ungovernable of all passions. If this were not the case, how could our wise ancestor Jacob so severely condemn that fact of his sons, Simeon and Levi, when they, contrary to reason, utterly destroyed the whole race of the Shechemites? saying, in abhorrence of their intemperate rage, "Cursed be their anger, for it was fierce, and their wrath, for it was cruel." He had certainly no view in speaking thus, unless persuaded that reason was able to conquer wrath.

CHAP. III.

WHEN God created man, and endued him with reason and a freedom of will, he at the same time, implanted in his nature variety of passions and dispositions, and set his intellectual mind upon the throne, to exercise government over all the sensual appetites within. He then imposed a law as a rule, whereby he might direct himself, and lead a life of temperance, justice and goodness. What ground can there be then for that objection which makes a doubt whether reason can master the passions, because it does not appear that it [illegible] absolute dominion over forgetfulness and ignorance? We are not to expect that reason should totally exempt us from all evil dispositions, but [illegible] con-flicts with such dispositions, it being the proper office of reason not to [illegible], but assist [illegible], not to be a destroyer but an auxiliary.

This matter may receive some illustration from the example of David. We read that, after having engaged a whole day with an army of Philistines, and made great slaughter among them, the king retired in the evening into the royal tent, fatigued and [illegible] where [illegible] the forces of our forefathers were encamped [illegible]. The rest of the company refreshed [illegible], but the king being exceeding thirsty, could not [illegible] his appetite with any water drawn out of [illegible] which they had plenty. An inconsiderate desire [illegible] him to drink of the water fetched from the enemy's quarter. Hereupon some of his officers, desirous of [illegible] ing him, armed themselves, took a vessel, [illegible] the enemies trenches, passed their guards, [illegible] well of Bethlehem, and thence brought to the king [illegible] water he so ardently desired. But David, [illegible] with thirst, recollecting how inhuman [illegible] thing it would be to gratify his appetite [illegible] men's lives, and that drinking the water would [illegible] fect to drink blood, opposed reason to inclination, and made a libation of it to the Deity.

Thus a mind, strictly temperate and wise [illegible] come the impulse or the passions [illegible] the most furious desires, [illegible] bodily pains, and, in one [illegible] quell all the perturbations [illegible] discompose the human frame, by a [illegible] vir-tue. But it now becomes necessary to confirm the argument by demonstrative proofs of this power of reason exemplified by practice, of which our forefathers have given undeniable instances. When, through the observance of their laws, they had ingratiated [illegible] foreign princes, and prevailed upon Seleucus Nicanor, king of Asia, so far, that he set apart a portion of his private revenues to defray the expence of the [illegible] approving their institutions, it happened [illegible] found [illegible], some of them were brought under various and severe trials, by the ill offices of wicked men, who disturbed the public peace in the manner hereafter related.

CHAP. IV.

A CERTAIN man, named Simon, creating a quarrel with Onias, who was high-priest for life, and a man of the greatest integrity, after having endeavoured to vilify his character by the foulest aspersions, and finding his attempts [illegible] him in the esteem of the people, fled [illegible] foreign country, with wicked intent to betray his country [illegible] to Appollonius, who was then governor of [illegible] Phœnicia, and told him, that, from [illegible] for the king his master, he was come to [illegible] vast sum of money deposited in the temple [illegible] appropriated to the temple, or [illegible], but wealth hoarded up by [illegible] of course the right of Seleucus [illegible] received this account, commended [illegible] for the king's service, waited upon Seleucus, [illegible] to him the secret. Upon this information, [illegible] from the king, and marched [illegible] with him the traitor Simon, and [illegible].

[illegible], he gave out, that he came, by order [illegible], to remove the private money that was in the [illegible], and complaining of it as an horrible injustice to deprive those of [illegible] deposited it in the sacred treasury, [illegible] they were able. But Appollonius [illegible], marched up to the temple [illegible] and children, prostrating [illegible] before the sacred place, implored the [illegible] his own temple from prophanation [illegible].

Appollonius [illegible], and entering the place with [illegible] he was about to seize upon the [illegible], behold angels from heaven suddenly appeared, mounted on horses, clad in shining armour, and struck Appollonius and his soldiers with fear and trembling. The governor fell to the ground in the court of the Gentiles, stretching out his hands to heaven, and supplicating [illegible], with many tears, to offer their prayers for [illegible], that he might not be destroyed by that tremendous [illegible] the high-priest Onias, moved with compassion, [illegible] fearing lest Seleucus should impute the death of Appollonius to human treachery, granted his request, so that [illegible] miraculously saved, he returned back to the king, [illegible] related to him the particulars that had befallen him.

The king Seleucus dying soon after, he was succeeded [illegible] by his son Antiochus, a man of an imperious [illegible] disposition, who deprived Onias of the [illegible], and put into that office his brother Jason, upon a compact of [illegible] an annual tribute of three thousand six [illegible] and sixty talents, which he had covenanted to pay [illegible]. The king having constituted this Jason superintendant, not only over ecclesiastical matters, as high-priest, but also over civil affairs, he put our nation under [illegible], and by introducing new customs, contrary to the law, hurried them into all manner of impurity. [illegible] only instituted Grecian games in our metropolis, but abolished the use of the temple, insomuch that the Divine vengeance being provoked, Antiochus was stirred up to [illegible] against the Jews. Being engaged in an [illegible] against Ptolemy, king of Egypt, and informed, at the same time, that some of the inhabitants of Jerusalem had expressed joy at the report of his being dead, he turned his forces that way, and made great havock among them, publishing withal an edict, forbidding any of them to observe the customs of their country, upon pain of death. Finding this edict had not its intended effect, but that all his severest threatenings and punishments were so far despised, that even the women (who continued the practice of circumcising their children) were cast down headlong from the walls of the city, (though they knew what they were to suffer,) he was so amazed at the little regard shewn to his authority, that he came in person, and by torments compelled those that were brought before him, to eat of meats unclean and forbidden by the law, and thus abjure the religion of their country.

CHAP. V.

WHEN Antiochus, that cursed tyrant, had seated himself upon a tribunal, surrounded by his counsellors and a strong body of armed men, he commanded many of the Hebrews to be brought by force before him, and compelled them to eat of swine's flesh and meats offered to idols, upon pain of the torture in case of [illegible]. After many had been thus barbarously treated, a certain man, named Eleazar, of the family of the priests, by profession a lawyer, far advanced in years, and known to several who stood round the tyrant, was brought before him. Antiochus observing the venerable sage, thus addressed him:

"Before I proceed to use any severity, let me advise
"thee, reverend old man, to save thy own life by submitting to eat of swine's flesh, for I pay great respect
"to thy age and grey hairs, and am surprized that the
"experience of so many years should not have made thee
"wiser than still to persevere in the Jewish superstition.
"It seems to me a most unreasonable thing for men to
"abridge themselves of any innocent pleasures, and an
"injustice to themselves, and ingratitude to nature to
"refuse any of those enjoyments which her bounty has
"provided for us. Why shouldest thou then entertain
"such abhorrence of that most delicious of all meats,
"which seems, in the flesh of swine, to have been designed as our best entertainment, in a singular manner?
"This may in others seem somewhat [illegible]
"but in you, who are a person of better judgment, it
"would be a most unaccountable folly, to be [illegible]
"by a false and empty notion of religion, [illegible]
"idle fancy to contemn my authority, and draw [illegible]
"this punishment upon your own head. [illegible] not thou
"then suffer thine eyes to be opened, [illegible]
"out of this dream of thy peculiar [illegible]
"thyself free from the bondage of so mean and [illegible]
"a notion? Will this friendly expostulation prevail for
"no deference to be paid my kindness? and the compassion I have for thy age move thee to comply
"upon this? Methinks it should [illegible] enough what I
"have said does not convince thee of the vanity of thy
"opinion [illegible] this point, yet you must allow, that if there
"be a power above which [illegible] [illegible]
"the observance of this religion, that power [illegible] so
"much goodness as to pardon the transgression of his
"laws, when it is not the offender's own [illegible]
"but the effect of force and [illegible]."

Eleazar having duly attended to these words, [illegible] of the king permission to speak for himself, which being granted, he stood forth, and, in the midst of the [illegible] assembly, spoke to the following effect:

"Know, Sire, that we who are [illegible] that
"it is our duty, in all things, to behave ourselves according to the law given us by God, are perfectly persuaded, that no necessity can [illegible] oblige us, [illegible]
"be stronger upon us, than that by which we are
"bound to obey his law, and for this reason [illegible]
"our acting contrary to it cannot be [illegible]
"any terms whatsoever. Nay, [illegible]
"as you are, pleased to suggest [illegible]

ELEAZER by command of ANTIOCHUS [illegible] to the TORTURE [illegible]

[illegible]

"muſt crave leave to ſay, that ſo long as we continue to "believe it divine, that very perſuaſion ought to be an "effectual reſtraint upon us from violating, or thinking "meanly of, any religious ordinances eſtabliſhed by it "Do not therefore imagine, if we ſhould ſubmit to de- "file ourſelves by unclean meats, that this would be "deemed a ſmall and pardonable fault For the pre- "ſumption of the offender is the ſame, and the authority "of the law equally inſulted, be the inſtance in which a "man tranſgreſſes greater or leſs The fact itſelf makes "no difference in point of guilt You were pleaſed, Sire, "to ſpeak contemptuouſly of our religion, as an inſtitu- "tion unbecoming men of reaſon and philoſophy But "I muſt be bold to ſay, it is the beſt and moſt conſum- "mate philoſophy, for it teaches us temperance, the "conqueſt of our paſſions and deſires, and ſets us above "all our pleaſures It trains us up in the exerciſe of "fortitude, and commands us to undergo all manner of "pain willingly and chearfully It teaches us the moſt "exact juſtice, and orders us to confine our worſhip "and abſolute reverence to the one true God, where alone they are of right due Upon this account we dare not "eat things prohibited and unclean, for we are fully "perſuaded that God, who created our nature had due "regard to it, that the very inſtitution of this law was "ſo far from a hardſhip, as in itſelf to be an act of "goodneſs and mercy, and that the things forbidden are "hurtful to our [illegible], whereas thoſe allowed for food "are uſeful and convenient It is therefore the very ex- "tremity of tyranny to force us not only to ſin againſt "our law, but to eat that which is therefore not allowed "us becauſe of its quality not fit to be eaten But this is "a ſort of triumph which I ſhall never give you over me "Never will I [illegible] the ſolemn oaths, and only engage- "ments whereby our anceſtors have bound themſelves, "and their poſterity, to the faithful obſervance of this "[illegible], no though you ſhould command my eyes to be "put out, and my bowels to be burnt Old [illegible] I [illegible] "not ſo impaired my mind, or enfeebled my body but "that, when religion and duty call me to it, my reaſon "can yet approve itſelf youthful and vigorous If this "will increaſe you, prepare your inſtruments of torture, "and heat your furnace hotter ſtill all that ſhall not "prevail to ſhame my old age, ſo as, for the ſaving my "perſon, to violate the law of my country and my God "The holy law, to which I owe my inſtruction, I will "never deſert Thou deareſt of all virtues, temperance, "by which we preſerve our native ſovereignty over our "appetites, I will never forſake thee, thou beſt of all "philoſophy, I will never diſgrace thee Thou holy "order of prieſthood, and ſtudy of the law, I will nei- "ther forego, or be a blemiſh to you My anceſtors "ſhall find me come to you pure and conſtant, a ſoul "[illegible] from ſuch a ſtain, and undaunted under all manner "of torments, even unto death"

CHAP VI

ELEAZAR, having made this noble and ſpirited reply to the tyrant's exhortation, was dragged by the guards that ſtood round to the crueleſt torments They pulled off the old man's garment, the venerable habit of his religion, and having bound both his hands behind him unmercifully ſcourged him, an officer calling out at every ſtroke, "Obey the kings commands" The brave Eleazar ſuſtained his torment as if he had been in a dream, without deviating a tittle from his profeſſion

The good old man ſtood with his eyes uplifted to hea- ven, while the blood ſtreamed down from his body to the ground, till, no longer able to ſuſtain the torments, he fell upon the pavement but this was owing to bodily infirmity, for his mind was as conſtant and reſolute as ever Upon this one of the guards ſtamped upon him in order to raiſe him Still he bore their barbarous inſo- lence, and, with ſurprizing conſtancy ſuffered their ſtripes, till his very tormentors ſtood in admiration of his extra- ordinary magnanimity, and wondered to find ſo noble a ſoul in a body ſo aged and infirm At length ſome of them, touched with compaſſion at his decrepid age, and moved by remembrance of antient friendſhip, thus ad- dreſſed him

"Why doſt thou thus for no manner of reaſon, expoſe "thyſelf to all theſe ſufferings? Permit us, Eleazar, to "ſet before thee ſome lawful and clean meats, and do "thou make as though thou didſt eat ſwine's fleſh, ac- "cording to the king's command, ſo ſhalt thou ſave thy "life and yet commit no wickedneſs" But Eleazar re- ſolutely anſwered, "Far be it from us, who are children "of Abraham, to be guilty of ſuch cowardice and wicked "ſubtilty, by ſo much as ſeeming to do an act that does "not become us How abſurd would it be for me, who "have lived a life of ſincerity and truth hitherto, and "preſerved my reputation free from blemiſh by a ſtrict "obſervation of the law, to change my conduct now in "extreme old age, and ſet an ill example to others to "purchaſe a little remainder of life at the expence of ſoul "diſſimulation, and live that little with the ſcorn and de- "riſion of all the world for my fear and baſe compli- "ance?" When they perceived him thus reſolute and inflexible, and that their pity could have no influence upon him they changed their diſpoſition and brought him to the fire There they applied new inſtruments of torture, threw him upon the fire and, as he burnt, poured ſtinking and nauſeous liquors up his noſtrils But being to the very bone and ready to expire, he lifted up his eyes to heaven, and ſaid, "Thou ſeeſt, my God, the miſeries I "endure, and that I chuſe to die by fire and torment for "the ſake of thy law, when it was in my power to pre- "ſerve my life for tranſgreſſing it Be thou, therefore, "gracious, O Lord, to thy own people, and let the ven- "geance executed on me ſuffice for what they have de- "ſerved Make thou my blood a purification for them "and accept my life inſtead of their lives" With theſe words this pious man gave up the ghoſt

Hence it is evident, that reaſon improved by religion is conqueror over the paſſions, if it were otherwiſe, it is to them that the praiſe of this nobleſt triumph [illegible] and conſtant virtue ought to be aſcribed But ſince from this inſtance, it appears plain, that the former was victo- rious, we cannot with truth deny that reaſon is the go- verning principle [illegible], indeed, it is no leſs [illegible] to con- feſs the ſame, not only of all demonſtrations [illegible], of bodily pains, but likewiſe of pleaſures too [illegible] vanquiſhed for the [illegible] of our paſſions is to indulge pleaſure and to decline pain

CHAP VII

OUR reverend father Eleazar may be deemed a ſkilful pilot, holding the rudder of the ſhip of piety in the ſea of the paſſions toſſed to and fro with the threatenings of the tyrant, and overwhelmed with the waves of [illegible] Nevertheleſs, he changes not the rudder till he reaches the haven of victory by a direct and proſperous courſe A city beſieged with various engines, never made ſuch reſiſ- tance againſt the furious aſſaults of an enemy, as the di- vine mind of this pious [illegible] againſt the attacks of ſtripes, tortures and death till, at length he vanquiſhed through the aid of reaſon engaged in the cauſe of religion

"O prieſt moſt worthy of the [illegible] who didſt not pollute thy ſacred body with [illegible] O guardian of the law, and profeſſor of a philoſophy all divine! O noble aſſertor of the religion of thy country [illegible] ſpite of paſſion, of torture, and of death! Thou haſt glo- riouſly confirmed the equity of our law, thy ſufferings and perſeverance, rendered our rites [illegible], but [illegible] them, and by [illegible] deeds [illegible] liſhed the precepts and doctrines of [illegible] O, venerable age, ſuperior to torments, [illegible] o[illegible] [illegible]ng f[illegible]r[illegible]ces, most glorious of conquerors, who hast [illegible] thy passions in triumph! As heretofore our father Aaro[n], armed with a censer, ran into the midst of the temple, and vanquished the destroying angel, in like manner did Eleaz[ar], descended from the same Aaron, steadily adhere to his profession, and conquer in the midst of devouring f[lames]. And, what is most astonishing, when [illegible] had [illegible] his body, he exerted an [i]mmoveable resolution of mind. O happy age! integrity [illegible] [illegible] inquest [illegible], that gave testimony of so il[lustrious a] death!"

W[hat] [more] [sa]tisfactory evidence can be required of the [illegible] of reason over the passions, than that of an aged [illegible] [illegible] much for the cause of piety and virtue, [illegible] [illegible] undaunted intrepidity. But as it may be alleged [illegible] [illegible] objection, that this age is less to be [illegible], because, [a]s strength and courage decrease, [illegible] [illegible] and love of life may then be supposed to [be] [consi]derably abated, I shall proceed to shew, that even young men, [illegible] [illegible] has been fixed upon true prin[ciples] [illegible] [illegible], and overcome, torments heavier [illegible] [illegible] terms.

W[he]n the tyrant found himself foiled in the first att[empt], [a]nd that he could not compel the venerable Eleaz[ar] [to] viol[ate] the laws of his country, he became so in[censed] that he commanded others of the Hebrew captives [to] [be] brought before him, promising them immediate [illegible], upon condition of their eating forbidden meats, [and] [threa]tening them with greater torture than had been [illegible] in case of refusal.

CHAP. VIII.

PURSUANT to the order aforesaid there were brought [illegible] [illegible] [illegible] seven [illegible], with their antient mo[ther]. The [illegible] in the symmetry of their form, and [illegible] of their deportment, attracted his notice, and [illegible], after beholding them with a kind of appro[bation], he commanded them to approach, and thus ac[costed] [them]:

"Young [me]n, from an approbation of your person[al] [illegible], I have kind intentions towards you: nor "can I but pay a more than ordinary respect to your fa"mily, which hath the unusual blessing of so many such "[chi]ldren. To advise, therefore, that you would not be "[illegible] [illegible] [illegible] and most [illegible] zeal, with that "poor old bigot, whom you saw perish in the midst of "[illegible] and tortures, is a kindness far below what I "design for you. I invite you to comply with me, with "an [a]ssurance of my particular friendship: for I have it "in my power to oblige and advance them that obey me, "[illegible] manner as I have to punish those that "[stan]d out against my commands. Be assured then you "[illegible] [illegible] of preferments, but have places of honour "[illegible] and great trust under me, provided you will re"[nounce] [illegible] [co]untry's customs, and be content to live "[after] the Greek manner, laying aside the foolish dif"[illegible] [illegible], and indulging those appetites and "[pleasures] [illegible], in which youth, ever fond of restraint, "[illegible] [illegible] delight now denied you by the tyrant of "your own superstition. Consider too, that if such ad"vantageous offers be rejected, you must expect that "your obstinacy will be the more provoking, and I "shall be obliged to make every one of you examples, "by deaths as full of pain and horror as the anger of an "[i]ncensed king can inflict. Be persuaded to pity your"selves, when a stranger and an enemy has set you an "example of pity. Throw not lavishly away so much "youth and beauty, which I am very loth should perish: "but perish it must, unless you will save it by that one "way; therefore consider well. Methinks you should "consider, and not resolve too rashly, when I assure you, "that, in case of disobedience, you have nothing to ex"pect but racks, fire and death."

The tyrant had no sooner thus spoken, than he commanded the instruments of torture to be produced, in order to work more strongly upon their fears, than words and menaces he imagined could do. When the guards had set before them the wheels, racks, manacles, combustible matter, and other implements of horror and execution, Antiochus, taking the advantage of the impression he supposed this spectacle would make, once more applied to them in terms to this effect: "Young men, consider the "consequences; your compliance is no longer a wilful "offence: you may rest assured that the Deity you wor"ship will consider your case in being compelled to vio"late your law." But they were so far from being terrified at the consequence of a denial, that their resolutions became stronger, and through the power of reason aided by religion they triumphed [over] his barbarity. What is it reasonable to suppose would have been the measures pursued, had there been but an individual [am]ong them [illegible]rous, or more [illegible] fond of life? Would not such a one have addressed himself to the rest, in terms similar to the following?

"What stupid and fool-hardy wretches are we [illegible] to "continue deaf to the invitations and kind advice of a "king, who calls us to gain and promotion, upon our "obedience! Why should we amuse ourselves with vain "imaginations, and persist in a fatal obstinacy, which can "end in nothing but death? Shall we be so [illegible] "to have no regard to these dreadful engines of cruelty? "None to the menaces of an unrelenting tyrant, inexo"rable enough to put in execution all that he hath threa"tened? Shall we not rather abandon this empty point of "honour, and that false pride of constancy that is certain "to prove our destruction? It can be no crime to have "some respect to our youth, which promises many happy "years, some pity to our poor aged mothers, whose grey "hairs must be brought down with unspeakable [illegible] "to the grave, to see so many sons cut off at once, and "herself made childless in an instant by our disobedience. "What the king says is very rational, that God [illegible] "and good not to make allowance for the hard circum"stances we lie under. Why should we [illegible] [our]"selves out of life at a time when we are best [able] to "taste the sweets of living? Why hurry ourselves [head]"long out of a world where every thing conspires to de"light and entertain us [illegible] [agree]ably? [illegible] "any longer with our fate, nor [illegible] [illegible] "at the expence of racks and death. [illegible] "not so severe as to condemn [illegible] [illegible] "and the more just our fears are, the less [illegible] "in the compliance. What pretence can we [illegible] "for this obstinacy? Or why should we [illegible] "mistaken courage, which is indeed no better than [des]"pair and obstinacy, when nothing [illegible] "[illegible] we stand out, and life and [illegible] "pleasure, are surely ours, if we do but submi[t]?"

CHAP. IX.

BUT no language similar to this was uttered from the mouth of one of these brave youths: for [the] apprehension of the racking pains they were about [to] [illegible] little affected their mind. They triumphed over their [im]pending misfortunes; and when the tyrant commanded them to eat of the forbidden viands, they, with one voice, and, as it were with one spirit, made him this reply;

"To what purpose, O king, [illegible] ? [If] with de"sign to know our final resolution, [illegible] [illegible] we are "ready to encounter death in its most [illegible] forms, ra"ther than transgress the laws of our fathers. [illegible], be"sides the reverence due to the example of [illegible] "upon other accounts, this is what our obedience to the "law, and the precepts of Moses require [illegible]. Do "not then attempt any more to [illegible] [illegible]

do not [illegible] counterfeit pity for those who know you
" hate them, even death itself is more supportable than
" such an insulting, dissembling compassion, as would save
" our lives with the loss of our innocence Thou thinkest
" to terrify us by threatenings of death and torture, not-
" withstanding the same experiment made upon the old
" man hath so lately taught thee how ineffectual all such
" methods are upon the servants of the true God, and if
" the old men of our nation endure so courageously such
" exquisite pains for their religion, is it reasonable to sup-
" pose that the young ones will suffer the reproach of being
" behind them in constancy and patience? As we have
" been educated under his particular care and instructions,
" so we shall conquer after this example Try us, there-
" fore, and see if it be in thy power to destroy our souls,
" when we suffer in the cause of God and religion? This
" is impossible [illegible] cruelty cannot hurt us, for all the
" effect of [illegible] pains [illegible] will be to secure us the glorious
" reward due to [illegible] patience and injured virtue
" Upon you the consequence will be very different and
" dreadful, for [illegible] of so many innocent men,
" you [illegible] the Divine vengeance against yourself, and, for
" the [illegible] punishments which you inflict, will become
" so obnoxious, as to suffer the punishment of everlasting
" torments "

The tyrant enraged at their contumacy, gave the word of command, and the guards immediately brought forth the eldest of the seven brethren, and having torn off his garment and tied his hands behind him cruelly scourged him, and continued their lashes till they were tired, but could avail nothing They then put him on the wheel, [illegible] his body being extended, he underwent the severest [illegible] of the rack, thus reproaching his tormentor " [illegible] enemy to the Divine Justice! you [illegible] me in this manner not for homicide or impiety, " [illegible] defender of the sacred law" The guards [illegible] him to comply, eat of the king's meat, [illegible] obtain a respite But he answered, " Think " [illegible] men, that your wheel can destroy my reason " Break my limbs in pieces, burn my flesh, distort my [illegible] " [illegible] all the torments you can inflict on me shall " serve but to convince you that it is the peculiar glory of " an Hebrew to be invariably firm in suffering for the " cause of virtue" They then put fire under him, and exposed his body, as much extended as possible, to the devouring flames, insomuch that he exhibited a spectacle horrible [illegible] destruction, and thus continued till nothing was left of human form, but a skeleton of broken bones

During the shocking scene, this brave youth, and worthy descendant of [illegible] Abraham, was not heard to utter a groan, but bore his torments with such invincible fortitude, [illegible] he had been transflated to immutability in the midst of the flames, exclaiming " My brethren follow my example [illegible] desert me not in this noble conflict nor disclaim " [illegible] generous constancy by which we are all " [illegible] in soul more nearly than in blood Engage, resolutely engage, in the [illegible] war [illegible], nor doubt but that " the Almighty, Creator of the universe will be propitious " [illegible] nation and avenge himself on the cruel tyrant" With these words the brave youth expired

While the spectators stood fixed in astonishment and [illegible], the guards advanced with the second brother [illegible] fixed his hands in manacles of iron but, before they put him to the rack they demanded if he would accept the conditions Finding by his reply, he had adopted the same noble resolution with his brother, they tore off his flesh with pincers and flayed off the skin of his beard, face, and head He bore this torture with singular magnanimity crying, " How welcome is death in any form, when " we suffer for our religion and laws! Art thou insensible, " inhuman tyrant, that thou art rather thine own tormen-" tor than mine, in finding thy tyrannic aims defeated by " our constancy? The comforts of conscious virtue allevi-" ate my pains, while the dreadful load of your impiety " shall fall on your own head, and the Divine vengeance " make an example of such a monster to the whole world"

CHAP X

THE second brother having made this glorious exit, the third was produced, and pressed with arguments and entreaties to taste and preserve his life But he replied, with vehemence, " Are you ignorant that I am the son of " the same father and the same mother with those that went " before me? Shall I then, in this last scene of life, renounce " the honour of the alliance? The same institutions were " taught us all and I will abide by them until death" The freedom of this speech enraged the executioners, who, to express their malice and resentment, stretched his hands and feet on the engine, and broke them to pieces But when they found this method did not deprive him of life, they drew off his skin at the ends of his fingers and flayed him from the very crown of his head Not content with mangling his body in this merciless manner they dragged him to the wheel where, being yet more distended, he saw his own flesh torn from him, and streams of blood gushing from his body When at the point of death, he exclaimed, " Merciless tyrant we suffer thus for the religion and law " of that God who is able to reward us but remember, " thou shalt suffer pains much more insupportable for thy " impiety and cruelty"

Having died thus equally glorious with his preceding brothers, the fourth was produced by the guards, and persuaded to bethink himself, and be wiser than those who had gone before him His answer was, " Your fire has not " heat enough in it to make me despond or renounce my " opinion I solemnly swear by the happy exit of my brothers, " by the eternal destruction of the tyrant, and the glorious " life of the pious I will not renounce their magnanimity Invent and bring thy torments, tyrant, and " make the experiment whether I am not a branch of the " same stock and animated with the same soul, as those " whose blood thy impious hands have spilt" Antiochus on hearing these words, was so excessively enraged, that all the force of passion was visible in his countenance He gave immediate orders to cut out his tongue, whereupon he thus proceeded " You may, deprive me of the " instrument of utterance, but that God who seeth the " heart, knows the inward sensations of the silent Here " is the member, you cannot by this act, deprive me of " reason O that I could lose my life by inches, to support the cause of religion Though you take away the " tongue, which chants the praises of God remember " that his high hand will very soon let his vengeance fall " down upon your head"

CHAP XI

NO sooner had this brother exhausted with pain and miserably mangled, finished his course, than the fifth sprang forward of his own accord, exclaiming " Prepare your torments I am here ready to suffer the " worst you inflict I come voluntarily to die in the " cause of virtue, and, by a cruel death, to bring down " an endless punishment on you for the barbarities you " have committed on the bodies of my brothers [illegible] " enemy to virtue, religion and mankind, what have I " done, wherein have I transgressed, to deserve these merciless treatments? Do we not worship the [illegible] " Parent of Nature according to his own decrees? Do " we not act in conformity to the institutions of his " holy laws? These are things that ought to meet with " reward instead of punishment"

While these words were in his mouth, the tormentors bound and dragged him to the wheel, [illegible] his knees with iron rings, they fastened him round the engine, and then broke his joints [illegible] tortured in this manner, he thus ſpoke in unſpeakable anguiſh "Tyrant, thou doſt us the greateſt honour againſt thy inclination, for the glorious torments you inflict upon us, only ſerve to teſtify our extraordinary zeal for our laws and religion."

When he had borne teſtimony to the truth of his religion, after the example of his heroic brothers, the ſixth youth was brought before Antiochus, and being demanded, by the tyrant, whether he would accept deliverance on the terms aforementioned, reſolutely anſwered, "It is true, indeed, I "am younger than my brothers, but my mind is the ſame "with theirs. We had all of us the ſame parents, and the "ſame inſtructions, and it is but neceſſary that we ſhould "all die alike for them; therefore if you are determined "to put me to the torment on my refuſal to eat, torment "me." Hereupon they faſtened him to the wheel, and having broken his bones, put fire under him. Then the [illegible] their ſpears, and thruſt them into his back [illegible], till his very entrails were burnt up. In the midſt of theſe torments he exclaimed, "O glorious conflict, in "which ſo many brethren have engaged for the ſake of "their religion, and all came off victorious; for a mind "[illegible] of the truth, and armed with ſteady "principles of virtue, muſt for ever be impregnable. I "will accompany my brothers, and relying on my own "[illegible] my defence, now ſubmit to death. But thou, "tyrant, muſt not think to avoid a puniſhment which your "[illegible] deſerve; for a death, attended with the moſt "dreadful of torments, hangs over your head. Six of us "[illegible] fled thy rage and malice. As for your fire, it "[illegible] to us, your tormenting engines are far from "giving us pain, and all the violence you can uſe is fruit"leſs and of no conſequence. For ſo long as our law is "[illegible], we retain a reaſon that all the world and "its [illegible] cannot ſubdue."

CHAP XII

THE ſixth brother being diſpatched at laſt, by being thrown into a boiling cauldron, the ſeventh, and youngeſt, appeared, whom, when the tyrant ſaw fettered and [illegible], and though ſo implacably outrageous againſt the reſt of his brethren, his heart began to relent. Calling upon him, therefore to approach the tribunal, he endeavoured to ſoothe him with theſe words.

"You ſee what kind of deaths your brothers have un"dergone, but their diſobedience and contumacy have "been the ſole means of all their torments, and the cruelties "they have ſuſtained. Yet you, if you obey not my com"mands, ſhall be expoſed to the ſame, nay, worſe torments, "and to ſuffer an immature death; but if you comply "with my deſires, I will take you into the number of my "friends; you ſhall have a conſiderable poſt in my king"dom, and be a governor in the ſtate." Not content with theſe perſuaſions to the ſon, he addreſſed himſelf to the mother with ſeeming compaſſion for her loſs, entreating her to prevail upon her child, in pity to her at leaſt, to ſave the ſmall remains of the family, and not to bring on her the affliction of having all her offſpring ſo ſadly torn away at once. But his mother, addreſſing him in the Hebrew tongue, exhorted him to ſuffer, as we ſhall ſhew in the ſequel. Upon this he ſuddenly exclaimed, "Take off my fetters, for I have ſomething to communicate to the king, and all his friends." The king and his nobles hearing the promiſe the young man made, ſeemed greatly rejoiced, and his chains were immediately knocked off. Taking the advantage of this circumſtance, he thus exclaimed.

"Impious and curſed tyrant, have you no fears nor "apprehenſions in your mind, after having received at "the hands of the Almighty the kingdom and riches you "enjoy, than to put to death his ſervants, and torment his "worſhippers? Theſe cruelties ſhall be returned with an "eternal puniſhment from the hands of the Divine ven"geance. Is your conſcience touched with no ſcruples, "inhuman monſter, thus to deprive of their tongues thoſe "who ſhare alike the ſame nature and paſſions with you, "and who are born of the ſame elements, and thus put "innocent perſons to cruel torments, and take away their "lives in the moſt unmerciful and barbarous manner? They "have undergone a glorious death, and ſhewn how much "their piety and obſervance was for the maintenance of the "true religion; whereas thou, impious man, ſhall be ex"poſed to [illegible] you little dream of, for taking away unjuſtly "the lives of thoſe who were worſhippers of the Supreme "Being. For this reaſon I will ſuffer death, and, in my "laſt pangs, diſcover how much my deſire was to follow "the brave example of my brothers. I beg and entreat "the God of my fathers that he would be propitious and "merciful to our nation, but that he may chaſtiſe you "while you live, and after death, that your puniſhment "may be augmented." Having finiſhed this addreſs, he threw himſelf into the boiling cauldron, and ſo gave up the ghoſt.

CHAP XIII

FROM theſe particulars we have enumerated, it muſt be confeſſed that reaſon, guided and ſupported by religion, has power over the paſſions, when we ſee ſeven brothers in perfect agreement, and upon the ſame principle, deſpiſing and vanquiſhing the moſt exquiſite pains, and even death itſelf. Is it not manifeſt, that had theſe men been governed by their paſſions, they had ſubmitted to pollute themſelves with unlawful meats, refuſed no condition to procure eaſe and ſafety, and been totally ſubdued? But ſince they combated theſe paſſions by a judicious uſe of reaſon, we are bound to acknowledge, with abundant praiſe to the holy martyrs who ſuffered, that, as they deſpiſed the moſt dreadful torments, ſo reaſon never more diſcovered its dominion over the ſubject paſſions than in thoſe inſtances. For as the moles and forts upon the ſhore break all the force of the waves and weather, and render the harbour commodious and ſafe to ride in, ſo did the ſevenfold fortification of reaſon protect the harbour of piety from all the ſtorms and boiſterous inundations of paſſion.

How moving, how affecting a ſight was ſuch a company, encouraging and aſſiſting each other in the exerciſe of their piety, like the voices which contribute, every one by its diſtinct part, to make up a perfect melody? With ſuch an harmony of hearts did they exclaim, "Let us die like "brethren in the defence of our laws; let us imitate the "brave example of the three Aſſyrian youths, who deſpiſed "the furnace of the king of Babylon, in fighting for the "cauſe of virtue; let us never deſpair, nor once be caſt "down. When religion and a good conſcience are at ſtake, "let us abandon all ignoble fears, and act with becoming "reſolution." Another ſaid, "Aſſume courage, my bro"ther, and ſuffer all with an inſurmountable bravery of "mind." Others of them recognized their anceſtors. "Re"member whence you derive your origin, and what father "Iſaac could ſuffer in the cauſe of piety." Then in general looking on each other with countenances ſerene, and highly pleaſed, they exclaimed, "Let us cheerfully conſe"crate our bodies to God. Let us pay him back the lives "he lent us for his ſervice, and devote theſe bodies to the "defence of his moſt holy law. Why ſhould we ſtand in "fear of one who only ſeems to kill the body? The only "danger worthy of our dread is that of ſouls abandoned "to torments everlaſting, which can never be the fate of "ſuch as keep and honour the truth. Let us then arm "ourſelves with an holy fortitude, ſo ſhall Abraham, Iſaac, "and Jacob receive us when we die, and all our progenitors "congratulate and applaud our conſtancy."

As they were dragged one by one to the place of execution, thoſe whoſe turn was not yet come, encouraged those that went before them, with words to this purport "Brethren, do not dishonour us, nor elude the expectation "of your brethren who have already suffered death"

These must have been very engaging exhortations, for none can be insensible what charms, what powerful influence so near a relation carries with it, what tender affections the All-wise Providence hath infused into their hearts, who have derived their being from the same father and mother, been maintained at one common table, conversed perpetually together under the same roof, instructed by the same teachers, and initiated in the same religion Such was the affection, such the endearment, and, of course, such were the weight and efficacy the admonitions and mutual encouragements of these seven brothers to one another, for they were brought up in the same faith, trained up in the exercise of the same virtues, and the better men they were, the better they must love each other Natural affections is never so happily improved [illegible] by perfect [illegible] in goodness, and [illegible] zeal in the love and service of God And as each of these would love the [illegible] more tenderly in proportion as he himself was more religious, so would he necessarily, in the same proportion and upon the same account, become more worthy to be beloved by all the rest And yet we may observe in this very [illegible] mighty conquest of reason over passion, for though the [illegible] had all the tender concern th[illegible] the same blood, birth and education, acquaintance and personal worth, could inspire them with, yet these [illegible] endearments were [illegible] and borne down when religion [illegible] at stake, that, in a cause so noble, the very tortures [illegible] deaths of their dearest relations gave a sensible satisfaction to those of the number who yet survived, and were the undaunted, nay, even pleased, spectators of them

CHAP XIV

THE pious and virtuous youths not only excited one another to suffer these terrible conflicts so as to make them surmount all the pains they might be put to, but [illegible] [illegible] that their [illegible], during their torments bore every thing with astonishing resignation [illegible] minds more absolute than the most sovereign princes, and more free than liberty itself! Not one of them was observed to betray any fears, nor have any scruples on the approach of death but all, [illegible] running the race of immortality, embraced death amidst their torments As the hands and feet [illegible] motions of the mind and so direct their [illegible], even so did these [illegible], from [illegible] of piety, consent to [illegible] in its cause As the number of days in which the world was created gave us the idea of God, and shews the perfection of his majesty and goodness, so do these more [illegible] by [illegible] the whole circle of pains and torments, compose one unmixed piece of [illegible], and teach us [illegible] perfection of fortitude [illegible] the slavish fear of death But this [illegible] pattern do we stop [illegible], who cannot [illegible] or read without trembling and amazement, what they not only heard, not only saw, but felt and bore without the least disorder of mind

Nor ought we to wonder that reason in man should have this dominion over his passions, when the mind of a woman contemned more cruelties than these, and of a different [illegible] For the mother of these seven youths had such presence of mind as to be a spectator of the tortures her children endured Reflect on the force of natural affection, how diffusive to one's offspring [illegible], this we observe in the brute creation, who have a tincture of the same kind of affection and love for their young as mankind But there is no necessity for producing examples of brute animals to confirm this love for their young, when the very bees, at the time they are employed about making their honey, revenge themselves on those that approach them, and make their stings to do the office of swords, and other [illegible] weapons, upon those that would attack their little ones

CHAP XV

BUT so true a daughter of Abraham was the mother of these gallant youths, that even compassion to her own children could not break [illegible] upon her duty Such was her noble zeal, that, when two things were offered to her choice, religion and the present safety, and great preferment of seven sons, she wisely gave the preference to the former which leads to eternal life and happiness By what language shall I describe those tender passions of parents, that union of nature between them and their children, which, in a wonderful manner, draws upon the offspring the same lines and features of body, and impresses the same dispositions of soul? How can I [illegible] the [illegible], feel for these [illegible] and parts of themselves, when [illegible] manner of distress? How especially that of mothers [illegible] weaker minds, and [illegible] excess of [illegible] still more [illegible] [illegible] dren, than fathers are wont or expected to be? [illegible] was more under the influence [illegible] mothers in common [illegible] man, additions to this love, and [illegible] was repeated it was a fresh [illegible] endearment towards all for whom she had endured the [illegible] pangs

But, notwithstanding all this, the fear and love of God overcame her concern for the present [illegible] or her children [illegible] ever did she love them [illegible] when their steady virtue, and constancy in the truth [illegible] ed her affections, and endeared them [illegible], to the [illegible] and wise, temperate and [illegible] each other, and dutiful to their [illegible] [illegible] in the cause of [illegible] [illegible] [illegible] her sons, yet [illegible] the eloquent [illegible] were [illegible] to [illegible] once divert the opinion [illegible] she [illegible] turned with her breast, for the exhort [illegible] them [illegible], and all of them together, not [illegible] suffering [illegible] death, for the sake of religion Though she was an eye-witness to the torments [illegible] each of her sons, yet [illegible] of [illegible] [illegible] maintained the [illegible] of her intentions Her [illegible] [illegible] that it [illegible] the thrilling spectacle of her children [illegible] to [illegible] [illegible] torture [illegible] pangs [illegible] [illegible] into the [illegible] [illegible] second [illegible] draw a tear from those eyes [illegible] terrible [illegible] torments

The songs of Syrens, and the [illegible] all their [illegible] persuasive to your ears [illegible] their expiring moans [illegible] ed [illegible] with thee, and [illegible] ferings of thy children [illegible] then wouldst not [illegible] gavest them up to [illegible] Thou didst [illegible] him, as heirs of [illegible]

Mother of our nation [illegible] of piety [illegible] more patient [illegible] fortitude to undergo [illegible] [illegible] [illegible] upon [illegible] of the [illegible] [illegible] violent [illegible] a dreadful [illegible]

CHAP. XVI.

TO return to the point at which I have been aiming, [illegible] woman, aged, and the mother of seven sons, [illegible] only [illegible] in the sight of those children expiring [illegible], in consideration of the cause for which they suffered and died, it is evident, beyond dispute, that [illegible] protected by religion hath a power superior to [illegible]. It has been abundantly proved, that not [illegible] overcome vast difficulties, but that a woman [illegible] the most exquisite pains. The lions among [illegible] were not so fierce, nor was [illegible] though heated with the most [illegible] as those violent passions which naturally [illegible] kindled in her breast, when [illegible] expire in agonies inexpressible [illegible] religion quenched those so [illegible] affections.

[illegible] to suppose that had this woman the [illegible] composition, she would [illegible] to the following [illegible]:

"[illegible] who having brought seven [illegible] world am now parent of none! To what [illegible] have I borne the many sorrows I [illegible], and the many solicitudes in [illegible] beloved children, whose faces I shall [illegible] no rejoice in their marriage and posterity [illegible] blessing in being [illegible] happy in any descendants of the second and third generation. I once was happy, happy above my [illegible], when surrounded with seven comely children; but now I am deprived of them and left desolate [illegible] have I a son to pay me the last duty of interment."

[illegible] piety of this eminent woman disdained such complaints. She was so far from desiring any of her children to live that it would have been matter of grief to her had they not died as they did. She therefore besought them to fulfil her joy, and encouraged them in dying for the cause of religion. Noble matron! the tyrant was [illegible] by thy perseverance, and, both in thy words and actions, thou hast approved thyself mighty; for when thou wert apprehended with thy sons, and saw [illegible] put to the torture, thou stoodst immoveable, and thus [illegible] them in the Hebrew language:

"My sons, you have a glorious conflict before you, [illegible] being called that you may leave your nation [illegible] of your faith and religion, contend cheerfully [illegible] the laws of your country. It would [illegible] from our characters, to suffer an aged man to be exposed to the pains of the rack, while you [illegible] in the prime and vigour of youth, under the [illegible]. Remember what life is, from whom you received it, to whom you owe it, and that it is your [illegible] duty to undergo every difficulty and danger [illegible] the cause of the religion of its grand author [illegible] did our father Abraham hasten to sacrifice his son, the future parent of our nation. Nor did that son [illegible] or once recede, when he saw a father's hand, [illegible] weapon of death, uplifted to give the first stroke. For how was pious Daniel cast a prey to [illegible] lions, and the three children into the fiery furnace. You, who are partakers of the same faith, should [illegible] be disheartened if you are made partakers of the [illegible] sufferings; for it is most dastardly, in those who [illegible] true sense of religion, to betray a pusillanimity, when called upon to sustain difficulties."

Thus did this matron exhort her seven sons, whom she enjoined rather to suffer death than violate the divine law, especially when assuredly persuaded that those who die in the cause of God, shall live with God, with Abraham, Isaac, and Jacob, and all the succeeding patriarchs, [illegible] of immortal bliss.

CHAP. XVII.

IT is said of this dauntless woman, that, after being scourged, and otherwise severely tortured, by order of Antiochus, she finished her punishment by voluntarily throwing herself into the flames.

Courageous matron! thus defeating the tyrant's rage, disappointing his infernal schemes, and exerting a most noble faith, proof against all shocks that laboured to overturn it! Take comfort, therefore, thy patience is supported by a firm reliance on the divine goodness, [illegible] well grounded hope of future reward. The moon encircled with her attendant stars, shines not so bright in the firmament of heaven as dost thou, reflecting light upon, and receiving it back again from thy seven [illegible] sons, fixed in the celestial mansions, and honourable in the Divine presence. [illegible] from the [illegible] of Abraham. Were we able to depict this [illegible] of piety in true and lively colours, our pathos [illegible] the mere representation. Were a monument to be erected as a memorial by the nation to which they are so great an honour [illegible] the following might become it:

"Here lies a venerable priest, [illegible] mother, and seven gallant sons [illegible] tyrant [illegible] attempting, but in vain, to overthrow [illegible] constitution. The brave champions stood [illegible] fended the religion and rites of their country, committed themselves and their cause to God, and persevered in dispite of torments and death."

The encounter was truly divine: virtue was the judge of the combat and disposer of the prize, and [illegible] was the proof and exercise of it [illegible] the victory was one adjudged, and immortal bliss was to be the reward of the conquerors.

Eleazar was the first champion, the mother of the seven sons made a glorious defence, the brothers [illegible] fought, the tyrant was their adversary, and the world were the witnesses. Religion obtained the victory, and yielded the crown to her champions [illegible] admire their noble [illegible] on gazing on them, [illegible] himself, and the whole court [illegible] tion at their fortitude. But now [illegible] of heaven, and enjoy [illegible] writes, "All his saints are in thy hand." [illegible] being devoted to God, are celebrated with immortal renown. Nor was the benefit of [illegible] confined to their own persons; but the blood shed upon this occasion was accepted by divine justice as a propitiatory sacrifice, and delivered Israel from the oppression under which they groaned.

Antiochus, considering the extraordinary virtue and resolutions of these [illegible], gave testimony to their [illegible], and, by a public officer, pronounced it as a pattern worthy the imitation of his own soldiers. He enlisted many of the Hebrews into his service, and by their valour, having subdued his enemies, became an absolute conqueror, learning, by experience, that religion inspires men with the truest courage, and that none are capable of serving their prince [illegible] comparably to those undaunted contemners of life, who dare to encounter tortures and death for the sake of God, and a good conscience.

O sons of Israel! race of faithful Abraham! pay obedience to this law [illegible] that reason, aided by religion, has dominion over the passions, not only of those which are called internal, but also external pains and troubles.

CHAP. XVIII.

THUS did these heroes nobly fight and conquer: nor did they overcome death and torments only, but the enemies alſo that inflicted both, reſtoring peace to their nation, and the obſervance of that long neglected law, the contempt whereof provoked the Almighty to ſcourge the people with that word of calamities, the tyrant Antiochus. But while he became an inſtrument of vengeance to others, he treaſured more againſt himſelf; for, when he found he could by no means force the Jews to embrace foreign cuſtoms and rites, and abdicate their own, he departed from Jeruſalem, and undertook an expedition againſt the Perſians; nor was it long before the divine juſtice overtook him, and cut him off the face of the earth by a moſt miſerable death.

For duty to the memory of the pious mother, I add another exhortation ſhe gave to her ſeven brave and virtuous ſons.

"I was long a chaſte virgin, nor did I wander from my "father's houſe. No ſeducer or youth corrupted me in the "fields, nor did I fall a prey to the ſubtle craftineſs of a "deceiver. The prime of my life I paſt in the ſtricteſt "conjugal fidelity to my huſband. When you, my chil-"dren, were grown up, your father died, happy in the "eſteem of all that knew him. He had the ſatisfaction of "being the parent of dutiful ſons, nor did he ſurvive the "loſs of one of them. While he continued with you, he "uſually inſtructed you in the knowledge of the law and "the prophets, and ſet before you the renowned examples "of patience and ſuffering virtue. Abel murdered by his "own brother Cain, Iſaac deſigned for a burnt offering, "Joſeph impriſoned for his chaſtity, and Phineas zealous "for the divine law. He diſplayed the virtues of Ananias, "Azarias, and Miſhael, and of Daniel caſt into the den of "lions. He would frequently remind you of God's pre-"ſerving providence, by repeating from Iſaiah, 'When "thou paſſeſt through the waters I will be with thee, and "when through the rivers they [illegible] not [illegible] thee. "When thou walkeſt through the fire thou ſhalt not be "burned, neither ſhall the flame kindle upon thee.' He "taught your infant tongues that ſong of David, 'Many "are the afflictions of the righteous, but the Lord deliver-"eth him out of them all,' and [illegible] to [illegible] "that maxim of Solomon [illegible], '[illegible] "is a tree of life to all [illegible].' Nor did "he forget to teach that [illegible] of Moſes, 'I kill "and I make alive;' and again, what he [illegible] of the "law, and the diligent obſerver of it [illegible], and "through this thing ye ſhall prolong your days.'"

O melancholy, or rather glorious day! when the merciless Grecian tyrant kindled his impious [illegible] the cauldrons, and, with infernal fury [illegible] to the engines of torture, and exerciſed, with the moſt excruciating pains, the [illegible] fold offspring of the daughter of Abraham! when he [illegible] cut [illegible] tongues, and put them to death with all the cruelties that [illegible] could invent! Those horrid barbarities were [illegible] of their perpetrators, while these ſons of Abraham, with their victorious mother, are tranſlated to bliſs unſpeakable, admitted to the triumphant ſociety of their pious anceſtors, and enjoy with them a glorious immortality in the viſion of that beatific Being whom they had ſo faithfully ſerved, and to whom be aſcribed all glory and praiſe, both now and for evermore. Amen.

END OF THE MARTYRDOM OF THE MACCABEES.

PHILO's ACCOUNT

OF HIS

EMBASSY FROM THE JEWS OF ALEXANDRIA

TO THE

EMPEROR CAIUS CALIGULA.

PREFACE OF THE AUTHOR

HOW long will men, though advanced in years, entertain notions, and exhibit a conduct in life, incompatible almoſt with the inexperienced youth? This can only be imputed to a reliance on fortune, and a deviation from the dictates of reaſon and nature, the former being ever fickle and wavering, the latter unchangeable and permanent. In this manner we invert the order of things, eſtimate uncertainties as certainties, and ſo on the contrary. The beſt reaſon which can be aſſigned for ſuch errors is, that weak and ſhort-ſighted men are incapable of forming a judgment of what is to come, led away by things preſent, and influenced by a fallacious ſenſe rather than the conviction of deliberate inveſtigation. The eye, indeed, is a fit inſtrument to receive ſuch objects as are near and conſpicuous, but it is reaſon that penetrates future and inviſible things. This eye of the mind is clearer than that of the body, which is too frequently rendered dim by luxurious exceſſes, or by ignorance, as the reſult of indolence, and greater miſchief of the two.

Theſe our times, however, and the many remarkable events that have fallen out in them, are ſufficient to perſuade us to a belief of a Divine Providence, a providence that takes particular care of the virtuous, and thoſe eſpecially who devote themſelves to the worſhip and ſervice of the Almighty. Theſe are the people called, in Chaldee, Iſrael, which ſignifies "Seeing God," a bleſſing, in my opinion, more eſtimable than the treaſure of ten thouſand worlds. For if the aſpect of ſeniors, of magiſtrates, of parents, if precepts can excite in us an awe and reverence, and correct our manners and demeanour, how much more muſt we ſuppoſe it contributes towards the perfection of virtue, to ſoar above vulgar minds, beyond all created beings, to the contemplation of the great ſource of all things, even that Supreme Being, who is the chiefeſt good, and the chiefeſt happineſs?

The human mind cannot comprehend, nor human language deſcribe his excellencies. They cannot [illegible] the perfections of the Diety, who is ſuperior to every thing. If the whole creation were but one tongue it would fall ſhort in declaring his attributes, and diſplaying his omnipotence in the creation of the world, his ſovereignty in the diſpoſition of it, his wiſdom in the order and government of it, and his juſtice, both towards good and bad, in the retribution of rewards and puniſhments.

Vengeance itſelf muſt be ranked amongſt the Divine benefits, not only becauſe it is a part of the Divine law and naturally reſults from a principle of rectitude in the diſtinction of the good from the bad, but as it frequently brings offenders to a due ſenſe of themſelves, and checks their progreſs in their enormities; for it is an obvious maxim, that the puniſhment of ſome is often the reformation of many.

CHAP. I.

The happy ſtate of the firſt ſeven months' reign of the emperor Caius Caligula, after the death of Tiberius.

THE commencement of the reign of the emperor Caius Caligula affords an ample example of the maxims advanced in the preface. Never did there prevail ſuch profound peace and tranquility throughout the whole empire. North, ſouth, eaſt and weſt, concurred in perfect harmony. Greeks and Barbarians, ſoldiers and burghers, living together like brethren in the mutual exchange of all neighbourly offices of friendſhip and commerce. It was a degree of felicity almoſt incredible, for a young prince to aſcend the throne, not only with the univerſal acclamations of the people, but the immediate poſſeſſion of whatever his heart could deſire, ſuch a treaſure, both in money and plate, wrought and unwrought, as well for ornament as convenience, a mighty armament, military and naval, and a revenue flo[illegible] it were, from a perpetual source, for he had the whole habitable earth under contribution. His empire was bounded by two rivers, the Euphrates and the Rhine, the latter separating Germany, and other barbarous nations, the former Parthia, and the people inhabiting Sarmatia and Scythia, no more civilized than the Germans.

From the east to the west, as well upon the continent as in the islands, prevailed an universal complacency and joy. The people of Rome performed a general festivity, and all Italy, with the provinces, both in Europe and Asia, partook of the d[illegible] o'ering; for if compleat happiness was enjoyed under the reign of any emperor, it was certainly under the present at this time, when mankind did not fluctuate between hope and despair, but had sure possession both of their public and private rights, and were blessed with a plenary indulgence of propitious fortune. Through[out] the cities and towns, nothing was to be seen but altars, victims, sacrifices, garlands, blithe and jocund aspects, musical performances, crouded theatres, banquets, and every species of entertainment and pastime that could gratify the sense. There was no distinction between the rich and the poor, the lofty and humble, the creditor and debtor, the master and slave, but all promiscuously mixed together. Such, in fine, was the felicity of the times for plenty and pleasure, and the universal satisfaction of persons and families, that what we find described in the fabulous accounts of poets, concerning the Saturnian days of old, now appeared to be verified. This was the happy state of things during the first seven months of the reign of Caius.

CHAP. II.

The emperor falls into a desperate disease in the eighth month of his reign, which [illegible] general [illegible] of the provinces, [illegible] [illegible] which [illegible] his recovery.

CAIUS, in the eighth month of his reign, and in the [illegible] of his prosperity, fell into a very severe distemper, for having quitted the temperate, and consequently healthful, course of life, he led under Tiberius, he addicted himself to every species of luxury and dissipation, and pursued more [illegible] gratifications to a degree of bestiality. He followed, in a word, every corrupt and sensual practice that could tend to enervate both the mind and body; and as health and strength were the attendants on temperance, so were weakness and disease the concomitants of debauchery and riot.

It was now about the beginning of autumn, at which serene season the returning ships from all quarters are upon their voyage homeward bound, that is to say, such as do not winter in foreign parts. By this opportunity the news of the emperor's indisposition was immediately dispersed, so that a sudden sorrow and dejection succeeded the late universal content and joy, for all the cities, towns, and houses, were filled with mourning and sadness, and a gloomy aspect appeared in every place. The provinces were seized with an indisposition worse than that of the emperor, which was confined to the body alone, but the other reached the mind. They were anxiously apprehensive of losing not only the peace they enjoyed, but their lives, liberties, and estates. They reasonably recollected all the calamities that generally rose up in the empire when deprived of its prince, such as wars, depredations, devastations, banishments, plunder, imprisonments, fears, dangers, and even death itself. The only remedy against this train of calamities, they imagined, was placed in the preservation of the emperor.

Upon hearing, therefore, that his distemper was somewhat abated, (for nothing moves with such velocity as fame,) they seemed to enjoy an interval of happiness, which was soon diffused to the farther frontiers of the empire. All the cities were pleased with the tidings, though they retained their anxiety, till they received the welcome news of Caesar's perfect recovery, which gave them as much joy as if the case had been their own. The inhabitants, both on the continent and islands, immediately returned to their mirth and festivity. It never was known, in the memory of man, that any nation or country so nonfrazed [illegible] a general and public rejoicing, for the recovery of their prince, as was seen, upon this occasion, throughout the world, for the safety of Caius, when he was restored to his former health. It appeared like a momentary [illegible] from savage to social life, from deserts to [illegible] communities, from confusion to order, and all this was owing, as they thought, to the government and protection of a generous and rightful prince. But [illegible] [illegible] not penetrate into the hearts of [illegible], and [illegible] pleased and rejoice without sufficient ground.

CHAP. III.

Caius gives proof of a [illegible] [illegible] [illegible] [illegible] of young [illegible].

IN a very short time the traits of the [illegible] [illegible] appeared in the insolence of Caius, who [illegible] [illegible] been celebrated for the profusion [illegible] all over Europe and Asia, as the most illustrious [illegible] to all glorious purposes, public and private, [illegible] [illegible] of [illegible], and discovered that he had been [illegible] [illegible] a [illegible] [illegible] simulation.

The late emperor [illegible] [illegible] [illegible] Drusus, a grandson, called Tiberius, and [illegible] [illegible] Germanicus, called Caius, [illegible] [illegible] to the imperial throne. He was recommended by [illegible] to the succession, provided [illegible] [illegible] the obligation [illegible] [illegible] [illegible] [illegible] [illegible] had been the [illegible] [illegible]. But [illegible] Caius [illegible] joy [illegible] by adoption, [illegible] [illegible] by [illegible] [illegible] [illegible] [illegible] [illegible] and next succession to [illegible], to [illegible] [illegible] that he was [illegible] [illegible] which, from his [illegible] [illegible] for suspicion. Indeed, [illegible] [illegible] if the youth [illegible] [illegible] would have [illegible] [illegible] very [illegible] [illegible] died [illegible] had recourse to [illegible] his common right, [illegible] [illegible] [illegible] births, and then calling [illegible] [illegible] these words to [illegible].

"My intentions [illegible] [illegible] tion, in making [illegible] [illegible] youth, [illegible] without experience, [illegible] government itself, more [illegible] If [illegible] [illegible] calling [illegible] of one part of the [illegible] my office over so many nations, [illegible] for fear of [illegible] [illegible] mean time let him depend [illegible] [illegible] to [illegible] denomination."

This [illegible] effectually [illegible] er, and the young prince [illegible] plot [illegible] [illegible] [illegible] [illegible] which he [illegible] him already, so that Caius [illegible] his [illegible]

[illegible]

Roman [illegible] parents an absolute authority over their [illegible] supreme magistrate an uncontroulable power [illegible] Caius therefore, in order to gain his point, [illegible] Tiberius an enemy, and proceed against [illegible] penalties. This, without scruple of con- [illegible] to his years, or consanguinity, or to [illegible] having been [illegible] up by the emperor with [illegible] to the succession.

[illegible] commanded him to put an end to [illegible] prohibiting many tribunes and centu- [illegible] to add to so detestable an act, as [illegible] of not spilling royal blood [illegible] He was desirous of appearing tena- [illegible] his hypocrisy with the mask [illegible] upon this, who had never [illegible] had been trained up to the [illegible] sons of kings generally are [illegible] office, he took [illegible] should strike, to put [illegible] Thus died, at the in- [illegible] the [illegible] innocent [illegible]

CHAP. IV.

[illegible]

WHEN Caius had thus removed the first and prin- [illegible] of his journey, and there remained no [illegible] disaffected party to [illegible] up against him, [illegible] Macro the second sacrifice, in which [illegible] ungrateful disposition. Macro [illegible] services, not only after he [illegible] (for it is the province of flatterers [illegible] but also previous to his advance- [illegible] the chief instrument that indu- [illegible] him to the succession.

[illegible] through years and experience, was [illegible] mankind, and had sagacity to discern [illegible] motives of human actions, nor was he [illegible] prudent. He was sensibly touched with [illegible] of Caius, and had too much reason to [illegible] to the whole family of Claudius, or [illegible] relations, it was for those [illegible] He had therefore many appre- hensions for his grandson, lest being left in his minority, [illegible] should prove but of short date. Nor did he look [illegible] as competent to sustain the weight of empire, [illegible] and inconsistent, without genius for [illegible] rule or a mind [illegible] to sublime pursuits.

[illegible] however, exerted his utmost efforts to dispossess [illegible] prejudices, lest their prevalence should [illegible] He would frequently [illegible] deference and veneration he had [illegible] dignity, and that he retained so gene- [illegible] respect for his kinsman, that he would [illegible] yield the [illegible] to him alone, adding, that his modesty and reserve were unfortunately taken for want of [illegible]

When he found that the specious arguments he offered were of no effect he made no scruple of covenanting for him, and being his security, as he had sufficiently proved his loyalty to the Cæsars, and particularly to Tiberius, to whom he had been of singular service, in discovering and suppressing the conspiracy of Sejanus. In short, he extol- led Caius to the skies, [illegible] defending him against causes of [illegible] and uncertain and dubious charges, may be deemed [illegible] commendation. Not to multiply words, he could not have done more for his nearest relative than he did for Caius. Many pretend to say that this extraordinary respect was founded on the several good offices which Caius re- dered Macro, as he was at that time highly in credit [illegible] the emperor. Others alledge that the wife of Macro, [illegible] a certain attachment to Caius, was constantly importuning her husband to espouse his cause, and it is well known that female solicitation is very powerful, and [illegible] fails [illegible] success.

Macro, who had no suspicion of dishonour, [illegible] these blandishments of his wife to conjugal affection, [illegible] was thereby so far imposed on, that he took his most [illegible] enemies for his sincerest friends. In consequence of this, as he was conscious to himself that he had been the [illegible] of preserving Caius at several times, he took [illegible] liberty of counselling him openly, without harbouring [illegible] least suspicion, for his design [illegible] a great master, [illegible] make his work perfect and lasting, that it might not perish through his own negligence, or be destroyed [illegible] For instance, if at any time he saw him sleep [illegible] entertainment, he would take the freedom to [illegible] secretly hinting that [illegible] exposed him to danger. So [illegible] he [illegible] gazed at dancers, or [illegible] the ribaldry of buffoons, or [illegible] instruments, he would [illegible] to check him, by [illegible] suggestions to the following purport.

"It is not for you, Sire, to [illegible] senses like other men, but [illegible] your "[illegible] is [illegible] above the rest of [illegible] in the dignity 'of your mind, as [illegible] of your person. For "what can be more incongruous than for the [illegible] "world to entertain himself with the amusements of sing- 'ing, dancing, [illegible] and other trifles of that [illegible] 'Whereas it is his part, in all cases, times, and places, to "uphold the majesty of an [illegible] as a shepherd [illegible] over the whole flock, and aggrandize his character [illegible]

"When you are at the circus, the theatre, [illegible] 'public spectacle, you are not so much to attend [illegible] "[illegible] as the pains taken to form the entertainment, "and to reason the matter thus: if people take such care "and pains to please spectators, [illegible] "mankind, purely for popular applause, [illegible] "it as ample reward to [illegible] "shall we expect from the protection of [illegible] "cellent art? That is the art of government, [illegible] "vides for tillage, planting, navigation, and [illegible] "commerce, in the establishment [illegible] "of commodities all over the [illegible] "of mutual [illegible] Some persons [illegible] 'tainted with a venomous envy for this [illegible] "and agreement, but the malignity [illegible] "however, is to poison the [illegible] for the greater "part of it, here and there a man, or a family, or [illegible] "a city or two, might be concerned, but for whole coun- "tries, or nations, there has been nothing of it, especially 'since your illustrious family has had the administration of 'the government. The monsters that formerly had the "confidence to domineer in the very heart of [illegible] "are now glad to shift for themselves, like wild beasts [illegible] 'caves, and hiding places, and have left us in exchange "beneficial intercourse of correspondence with all quarters "of the earth, which is [illegible] subjected [illegible] "good pleasure and conduct. [illegible] empire [illegible] looks "like a mighty ship, and yourself, [illegible] "the helm, where you are [illegible] "of the vessel, as you tender the [illegible] "Wherefore be sure to have [illegible] "business and pleasure of your [illegible] "piness of your people. [illegible] "good offices among themselves [illegible] and "some another, both public and private, [illegible] "bounty and wisdom of the prince [illegible] people "can ever pretend to [illegible] 'open hand, and an expanded [illegible] to [illegible] "liberality but what shall be found necessary for a reserve, "to answer all the ends and chances of government."

Thus did this unfortunate counsellor endeavour to work upon the mind of Caius, but all in vain, for his admonitions were not only scornfully rejected, but he was frequently reproached with taunts to the following effect:

"Here comes my preceptor, but, I thank my stars for "it, I am out of my wardship. He sets up for my master, but I am past my childhood, so likewise am a "monitor that understands the world better than himself. "The pedant takes upon him to instruct an emperor "how to behave himself towards his subjects, and an "emperor who understands all the arts of court politics "much better than he can pretend to. This man has "the vanity to act the part of my master, but I would "willingly know where he learnt that skill himself that "I want? And I have been trained up, from my cradle, "to the mysteries of state under a variety of tutors, as "fathers, brothers, uncles, cousins, grand-fathers, and "great-grandfathers, besides a continued succession of so "many great princes in a right line, both by father and "mother, [illegible] nothing of the seeds of royal virtues, "that [illegible] commonly in the forming of a "governor. For as children often resemble their parents, "not in face and manners only, but in their very motions, humours, habits, and gestures, so does nature "[illegible] into the very veins of a governor. "And shall an idiot take upon him now to instruct me "in the mysteries of an art that I brought into the world "with me? Yet an obscure mean wretch tutors me "upon a subject of which he knows nothing himself."

In this manner did Caius alienate himself from Macro, devising [illegible] to lay to his charge, and cloaking them over with the semblance of the truth. While he was ruminating on this matter, he availed himself of certain expressions that Macro had uttered as the ground of an accusation. They were these:

"Caius is a man of my preferring, and more obliged "to me for what he is, than to his very father. It was "my interest that not only once, but thrice, rescued him "from the rage of Tiberius, when he would have put "him to death. After the death of Tiberius, when the "prætorian bands were under my command, I gave up "my guards into his hands, with this admonitory precaution, that the empire could never be safe and entire, "but in the hands of a *single person*."

This was not only true beyond contradiction, but believed by many who heard it, as they were not acquainted with the mutable and inconstant temper of Caius, and of that dissimulation and hypocrisy of which he was master. However, not many days after this, the unfortunate Macro and his wife were removed out of the way to gratify the ambition and barbarity of Caius, and recompence for loyalty and affection in the extreme! It is beyond dispute that Macro, who, with sedulous endeavours strove first to serve Caius, and then caused the empire to be vested in him alone, received this reward for his pains. It was reported that the unhappy man and his wife were forced to lay violent hands on themselves, notwithstanding the former attachment of Cæsar to the latter; but the sallies of unlawful passions are irregular and unaccountable.

CHAP. V.

The cruelty of Caius towards Syllanus, his father-in-law, and [illegible].

WHEN this treacherous prince had rid himself of the danger of a competitor, and taken off Macro and all his domestics, he turned his mind to a third exploit, in the conduct of which he had recourse to deeper stratagem than that of the two former. He had a father-in-law, named Marcus Syllanus, a person brave in arms, and of illustrious descent, who, though his daughter was snatched away by an untimely death, paid Caius the same respect as before, not doubting of a reciprocal return; but he cherished hopes that proved vain and fallacious in the end.

Syllanus, being a man frank and open in his temper, would frequently introduce the topics of morals and politics, as the offices and functions of a prince, and the measures of government and good order. He often admonished him upon these points, with a freedom becoming his quality and station, besides the death of his daughter being fresh in his memory, the sense of the affinity he thought could not be so soon forgotten. But the emperor interpreted this friendly counsel as reproach, and looked upon it as a dishonour [illegible], for any man to arrogate a degree of prudence, temperance, fortitude, or justice, superior to himself, so that he conceived an aversion to Syllanus, as he had done to other [illegible] tors, and considered him as his professed enemy. He supposed him a main obstacle to the pursuit of his inordinate desires, and therefore, [illegible] of outrage, bid a final adieu to the memory of his deceased [illegible], and followed the [illegible] upon the life of her father, though one of the most respectable [illegible] his time. The fame of this [illegible], and others [illegible] less considerable that followed upon it, struck the whole world with horror and indignation; but fear restrained open reprobation, while every one maintained their own private opinion.

The common people, however, who [illegible] are given to change both in point of words and actions, could scarcely be brought to believe it possible that a prince who was [illegible] candid and generous one day, could prove so [illegible], [illegible] and bloody the next, and therefore, took upon them the justification of his conduct, and urged in his defence, the equity of the cause. They said, that as to Tiberius his co-heir, the law of nature would not admit of a partner in sovereignty; that it was only an act of prevention to take away the life of a man who would have slain him, had it been in his power; that it could not have been so justly termed homicide as a favour of Divine Providence, in removing Tiberius for the common good of mankind, to prevent them from being divided into parties, and to escape as well foreign as civil wars, that might follow thereupon: for nothing is more [illegible] than tranquility and peace, that peace was the [illegible] of good government, that is a government where no competitions are encouraged by any divisions of the princes.

Their opinion respecting Macro was, that he had become immoderately ambitious, having [illegible] from his mind the Delphic oracle, which enjoins every one to know himself; and would have been the [illegible] of his [illegible], had he not defeated it by [illegible] [illegible] since that it was unbecoming a man to [illegible] part of the prince, or [illegible] the emperor Caius to a level with himself; and that it was the sovereign's province to command, the subject's to obey. In this manner did some [illegible] people reflect upon wholesome counsels and admonitions, either owing to their resentment or want of knowledge to distinguish things and true effects from their true cause.

Syllanus, in the mean time, was not free from the censure of the envious, who insinuated, that it was [illegible] in him to suppose or pretend that a father-in-law was vested with so much authority over his son-in-law, [illegible] father; that private citizens, on their [illegible] to dignified stations, mind no scruple of giving their [illegible] precedence; that Syllanus discovered [illegible] and ignorance in his meddling with affairs that by no [illegible] concerned him, nor was he silent to know that his [illegible] to the emperor expired with his daughter [illegible] marriage connects families [illegible] dissolved by death.

[illegible] observations were handed about to save the emperor's credit as much as possible, for the public having [illegible] opinion of his humanity and probity, could not be [illegible] that [illegible] total reverse of character could [illegible] produced.

CHAP. VI.

[illegible] ambition of Caius [illegible] arrogating Divine honours.

HAVING thus gained his point, in the disputes above [illegible] mentioned, against three principal parties, and ob[illegible] citizens of equestrian and senatorial [illegible] another over one of his own family, Caius [illegible] supposed that the most powerful being removed out of the way, [illegible] formidable to all around him [illegible] ambition and arrogance, he could [illegible] within any bounds, or even the [illegible] but aspired to Divine honours, [illegible] a demi-god. The [illegible] pretence was, "that, as the mis[illegible] herdsmen, and the [illegible] more excellent nature than the [illegible] so the [illegible] of men in society ought to be esteemed [illegible] of human nature, and ad[illegible] the gods."

[illegible] this opinion, like a man infatuated [illegible] a romantic tale instead of a true one. At [illegible] to publish his consecration, he [illegible] further and attended by certain gradations. At [illegible] the demi-gods, as Bacchus, Hercules, Castor, [illegible], Amphiaraus, Amphilochus, and the [illegible] was continually changing character [illegible] like the mimic in the dramatic scene. At one [illegible] would personate Hercules, with his club and lion's [illegible] he would assume a martial bonnet, and [illegible] Castor. Sometimes he would appear in a fawn's [illegible] wrapt in ivy, in imitation of Bacchus. [illegible] If this peculiar privilege, [illegible] demi-gods were content with the [illegible] ceremonies respectively appropriated to them [illegible] considered, Caius engrossed them all to himself, [illegible] he might soar above those whom he envied.

[illegible] excited the admiration of his followers was his [illegible] dinary aukwardness in metamorphosis, not that [illegible] bodies, like Gerion, but his transforming [illegible] into so many shapes, like Proteus, whom Homer [illegible] turning himself into a variety of ap[illegible] elements, animals, and rivers.

[illegible] O Caius, do you assume the figures and [illegible] of those images, without imitating the virtues [illegible] respectively ascribed to them? The labours and [illegible] of Hercules were all employed for the good of [illegible] delivering the world, both at sea and land, from the monsters that infested it. Bacchus cultivated the [illegible] and extracted a cordial drink, in the juice of the grape, that cheers both the body and mind. It subdues our cares, and soothes our misfortunes. Wine recreates the health and makes us more active and valiant. It is of signal advantage to private persons, families, and cities; and a cheerful cup is but a transition from labour to rest. The Greeks and barbarians introduced it to crown their festivals, which without it would have been languid, dull and spiritless.

Of the twins of Jupiter, Castor and Pollux, it is reported that the one gave immortality to the other. For as the one was born subject to mortality, and the other immortal, he whose condition was the happier, chose rather to dispense with his privilege than not discover his love to his brother. Accordingly he devised an expedient to compound the difficulty, which was by dividing the immortality and mortality of the two brothers equally betwixt them, and fixing two different natures upon the same basis of equity and reason. And this is the very fountain and spring of all justice.

These worthies having distinguished themselves by their good offices, as the friends of mankind, were [illegible] that score held in profound admiration, and declared [illegible] of divine honours. But with respect to Caius, it may be asked, what great or good act he ever performed [illegible] entitle him to the honours of a demi-god? To begin with Castor. Instead of emulating the heroic bravery of [illegible] generous friend and brother, he put to death his brother and co-heir in the flower of his age, and condemned his sister to banishment to secure his usurpation. What [illegible] he done after the example of Bacchus? Has he [illegible] any invention beneficial to the community? Has he diffused with Bacchus joy and gladness? Did [illegible] partake of his munificence? Inventions he [illegible] deed, discovered, but such as, like an epidemic [illegible] turning joy into mourning, and render mankind [illegible] of their lives. He [illegible] the east and west, [illegible] other regions extending north and south, for their choicest commodities, to satisfy his [illegible] which he returned by taxes and imposts, to make [illegible] burden of the oppression intolerable. So much [illegible] imitation of Bacchus.

In like manner did he exhibit a noble portrait of Hercules, by the valiant and indefatigable atchievements [illegible] by his wholesome laws, [illegible] by a plentiful increase of the fruits of the earth, [illegible] he blessed the islands and the continent? Might [illegible] rather exclaim, indolent, pusillanimous mortal! who expelled peace and tranquility from his cities, and [illegible] the inhabitants mutinous and seditious!

Was Caius desirous of being stiled a god for the [illegible] nations and destructions which he brought upon [illegible] subjects in general, and that they might be [illegible] must differ in opinion, perhaps that if he had been [illegible] mitted to rank with the gods, his sinister and [illegible] views would have soon degraded him to a level [illegible] tality. If divinity is the consequence of [illegible] tue, it follows that mortality results from [illegible] vice. He could not therefore pretend to the [illegible] that subsisted between the sons of Jove, who [illegible] homicide and fratricide. Nor could he [illegible] cellent nature either of Hercules or Bacchus [illegible] guished themselves by their good offices, [illegible] acted in contradiction to every principle of [illegible] virtue.

CHAP. VII.

The vanity and arrogance of Caius [illegible] he aspires to a more exalted [illegible] the gods [illegible]

CAIUS at length was actuated by such a degree of infatuation, that, not content with entering into competition with demi-gods, he proceeded to [illegible] the [illegible] of an higher class, as Apollo, Mars, and Mercury [illegible] imitated the latter, by assuming an [illegible] caduceus in his hand, and binding winged [illegible] feet. Having laid aside these ornaments he [illegible] Apollo, encircling his temples with a [illegible] ing a bow and quiver in his left hand [illegible] in his right, intimating that we should [illegible] doing good offices.

Next to this he instituted dances to the [illegible] Pæans to him who just before was represented [illegible] for whenever he assumed the habit of this god, they called him Evius, Lyæus, and Lycæus. Several [illegible] peared with a breast-plate, a helmet, a shield, [illegible] ced in a pompous manner, with sabre drawn, in imitation of Mars. On each side he had a band of homicides [illegible] bravoes, called Sali, ready to execute any cruelty he enjoined them, and gratify his savage disposition, that delighted in blood. By these horrid spectacles he struck terror into the people, who were surprized that he should assume the honours of those whose virtues he despised, and content himself only with their ensigns, though those outward habiliments are annexed to the images as intimations of the bounty and goodness of the gods to those that truly love and fear them. For example, to what purpose is Mercury represented with winged buskins? because, being the messenger or ambassador of the gods (whence he has a Greek appellation that denotes the same) he is prodigiously swift, and borne along with expanded wings, and surprizing rapidity. He is also depicted with a caduceus, which is the badge of a conciliator or peace-maker, for it is the herald that determines war, either by striking peace, or making truces; if these means were not admitted, there would be no end put to the hostilities of jarring princes, and injuries and insults would be continued to be committed without controul.

What could be the design of Caius in putting on the winged buskins? Was it to publish the depravity of his principles and conduct throughout all the provinces of the empire? a scandal that, on the contrary, should have been buried in silence. Nor was there a necessity for this rapid course, because had he not remained upon one spot, he would have poured mischiefs upon mankind, as it were, in a deluge. Why assume the caduceus, that emblem of peace, when he was constantly raising feuds and animosities, and filled every city, Grecian and barbarian, with intestine sedition, and civil discord? Away then with every claim to the character of Mercury. Let us now consider in what instance he resembles Apollo.

He wore, it is true, a radiant crown, the rays of which representing those of the sun are beautifully imitated by the artist, as if either the sun, or a general light, pleased him much better than the night and the thick darkness, to perpetuate his horrid designs. Honest and virtuous actions stand in need of the noon-day to render them conspicuous, but base and sinister practices, that will not stand the test, require the thickest darkness to cover them. Let them, therefore, be condemned to the regions of Tartarus, and never see the light. He cast great contempt upon Apollo with the greatest propriety, putting the bow and quiver into his right hand, that he might strike with jave[illegible] men, women, children, cities, and armies, according to custom, and the Graces into his left, unless he had rather slain them entirely, for it is plainly evident he does but imitate them, in coveting the possessions of other people, and, after having stripped the owners, putting them to death, bringing this calamity upon them because they were rich. As to Apollo's medicinal quality, he invariably inverts it, for that god was the inventor of salutary remedies, and so well disposed, that he was always ready to heal those disorders of which others had been the cause.

Caius, on the contrary, brought diseases on those that were well, maimed ones on those that were found, and inflicted death, with his own hand, on the living, before nature had determined their time. He made diligent search after several sorts of poisons, whereby, had not the divine justice prevented him, all the best and noblest citizens in every city, under his dominion had certainly been destroyed. This criminal preparation was designed for the noble and wealthier sort, chiefly the Italians, and those within the metropolis, as there was more gold and silver hoarded up within that compass of ground, than in the whole world beside. Therefore he made his own country the point to aim at, and shewed himself the scourge, the plague, and the destruction of his subjects.

Apollo was likewise as famous for his prophetic mind as his medicinal knowledge, but all his endowments were applied to the benefit of mankind. By his oracles he directed the doubtful, who were in danger of taking good for evil, and kept them from wavering, or deviating into the paths of error. Nay, his foreknowledge of future events was so certain, that men placed an implicit reliance on the result of their consultations.

If we oppose to these the [illegible] oracles of Caius, which prognosticated infamy, confiscations, exile, and death, to all men of rank and merit, what affinity will they appear to bear to those of the true Apollo? Away then with these false Pæans made to imitate those that are genuine, for if the adulteration of coin be deemed criminal, it is much more so to prostitute divine honours.

But nothing could be more ludicrous or contemptible, than for a body and mind, so enervate and effeminate, to rival the strength and fortitude of Mars, and endeavour to impose on the spectators by various and singular appearances, as the mimic does upon the stage. We are no strangers to the courage of Mars. I speak not of the fabulous deity, but of that by which we understand natural fortitude, exerted in behalf of the innocent and oppressed, as is evinced from the original Greek word, which signifies [illegible]. Mars has two names; one of them imports a lover of peace, for it conduces to the good of the public, and the other a friend to war, to [illegible] fatal [illegible] attended with bloodshed and confusion.

CHAP. VIII.

[illegible] of Caius towards the Jews for refusing to pay him divine honours.

IT has been rendered sufficiently apparent that Caius had no pretence to rank amongst the gods, either junior or inferior, as there was no kind of affinity between them, either in nature or essence, in inclination or manners. Our desires are often directed by a blind fatality, especially when ambition and an unbounded liberty are granted to them, and this was formerly the ruin of our nation. The Jews were the only people that raised suspicions in the mind of Caius, and not [illegible] in obstructing his design, because they had been taught from their infancy, by their parents, their preceptors, and chiefly by their [illegible] laws, that there was but one God, the Father and Creator of the Universe. The rest of the world, through the terrible apprehensions for the consequence of his proceedings, were obliged to join the general voice, in extolling that [illegible] to the skies.

Some introduced the manners and customs of the barbarians into Italy, by which the Roman worship and rites were much corrupted. The nation of the Jews, in fact, was the only one that by tradition opposed, or opposing the deity of this [illegible] [illegible]. They were known to have resigned themselves voluntarily to death, as if it were but entering upon a better and more lasting life, rather than suffer an infringement upon the least article of the rites of their country. Because, as we observe in buildings, if one part be wanting, though the rest [illegible] to stand firm, yet time will moulder it by degrees, and it falls to pieces.

The [illegible] was [illegible], but [illegible] the highest [illegible] for men, [illegible] meta-morphosed [illegible] God, [illegible] majesty [illegible] nothing can be more [illegible] [illegible] [illegible] and ingratitude to the [illegible] benefactor, [illegible] attributes his bounties to the [illegible] of mankind. This [illegible] left [illegible] [illegible] [illegible]

[illegible]

[illegible]

arbitrary ſway of a monſter of tyranny, inſtead of the father of his people

CHAP IX

The horrid outrages of the Alexandrians againſt the Jews, upon the occaſion of the perſecution of Caius

WHEN the tumultuous and ſeditious people of Alexandria had notice of the rigorous proceedings of Caius towards the Jews, they immediately took advantage of the opportunity of executing a long meditated revenge Had the Emperor permitted, or given expreſs orders for their violent proceedings, we could not have been more expoſed to their rage and fury, or, by the right of war, become more reduced to their power They maſſacred us with relentleſs cruelty, broke into houſes, turned men, women, and children out of doors, and plundered and carried off all effects of value This they did not after the manner of thieves in the night, who act under the apprehenſion of being detected and brought to juſtice, but committed their depredations in the very face of the ſun, boaſting of what they had done, and expoſing their plunder with as much confidence as if it had been their legal property Nay, they formed themſelves in bands and companies, who ſhared in the booty, and divided the ſpoil in the market-place, while the proprietors looked on, and were groſsly reviled and inſulted

It was certainly a hardſhip in the extreme for men of rank and property, who lived in affluence, to be turned out of their habitations, and expoſed to want, and that without a moment's warning, or the leaſt default on their ſide But no conſideration had weight with thoſe miſcreants, who perſiſted in their outrages, and were more cruel and rapacious than the moſt ſavage of the brute creation.

Theſe calamities, however, are more tolerable than thoſe which will appear in the ſequel; for they forced, out of every corner of the city, thouſands of men, women, and children, like ſo many ſheep, into a narrow place, reſembling a cave, making no doubt of finding them, within a few days, a pile of carcaſes, for want of food or breath, the place being cloſe and ſmothering, and the air tainted with the frequent reſpirations of ſo great a concourſe of people Theſe miſerable wretches, when they could no longer ſuſtain the hardſhips to which they were expoſed from hunger and ſuffocation, betook themſelves, ſome towards the ſea-ſide, others to remote burying-places, all deſirous of a little pure and wholeſome air Thoſe who were found remaining behind in other parts of the city, or ignorant of the calamities that threatened them, appeared abroad, and were unmercifully treated, either wounded with ſtones, or beaten to death with clubs. A few out of the number, who were pent up in a narrow corner of the city, were beſet with ſpies, who watched narrowly that none of them privately made their eſcape, which was naturally to be expected, not ſo much for their own ſakes, as to ſave their families from periſhing by hunger The Alexandrians kept a ſtrict guard upon that quarter, to prevent their getting away, and as many as they intercepted, they firſt put to the torture, and then to death, with all the rage and cruelty imaginable

There was another party of them that lay in ambuſh about the ports of the river for the Jewiſh merchants, whoſe effects they took away in the ſight of the owners, and then making piles of the planks of their veſſels, burnt many to death Others were burnt in the midſt of the city after a moſt miſerable manner There being no dry wood to be found, they brought branches that were green and in ſap, and having ſet theſe on flame, the poor wretches were thrown in, and endured greater torments from the ſmoke than the fire, becauſe, from the greenneſs of the matter, a thick ſmoaky fire aroſe that burnt but weakly, and was ſoon extinguiſhed, leaving few or no aſhes at all Several were dragged with cords through the middle of the market-place, amidſt the inſults of the mob, who ſpared not even the bodies of the dead, which with more barbarity than ſavage beaſts, they cut into pieces, inſomuch that no remains could be found for burial

The governor of the province, who, by the interpoſition of his authority, could, in a very ſhort time, have put a ſtop to the outrages of theſe miſcreants, affected ignorance of the very things he ſaw and heard, ſo that having liberty to purſue their meaſures, they proceeded to acts of greater violence Having collected themſelves into numerous parties, they went to the oratories, or places of prayer, which were in ſeveral parts of the city, and either plundered them, cut down the trees about them, or entirely levelled them with the ground: ſome they burnt, by throwing fire into them, with ſo much rage and fury, that the houſes adjoining could not eſcape their deſtructive hands, as it is difficult to ſtop a conflagration where there is combuſtible matter to work upon

I decline relating an account of the monumental and illuſtrious memorials of the Roman princes that were made a ſacrifice in this conflagration by this frantic mob ſhields, crowns, and golden ſtatues, which they ought to have held in veneration But their fury was beyond all reſtraint To fix themſelves in the good graces of the emperor as far as was poſſible, and promote the execution of his deſtructive deſign on the Jews, to whom they knew he was mortally averſe, they had recourſe to new arts of flattery [illegible] and thus proceeded.

As there were many of our oratories which they had not been able to ſet fire to, becauſe of the great number of Jews that dwelt in them, they deviſed other means of deſtroying them, together with their rites and manner of worſhip They ſet up the ſtatue of Caius in all of them, but in the greateſt and moſt famous, his ſtatue was erected aloft, but with ſo much haſte, and over-officiouſneſs, that, having no new horſes caſt, they took out of the gymnaſium or place of exerciſe, four ruſty ones, with their ears, tails, and feet very much worn, which, according to report had been dedicated to Cleopatra, the laſt queen of that name Now the inſult committed in this action was palpable Was it according to the rules of decorum to dedicate to a Roman emperor who endeavoured to emulate a god, what had been erected to the honour of a woman, things that were foreign to the purpoſe and had been the enſigns of another? Were not they fearful of incurring the diſpleaſure of Caius by honouring him with ſuch a gift, an emperor paſſionate, and one who had arrogated to himſelf all honours, and thoſe the moſt ſplendid and magnificent? However [illegible] they were in hopes of obtaining [illegible] than they had hitherto done They changed however their oratories into new temples, and increaſed the number of temples that were dedicated to Caius, not ſo much to honour him in the action, as to gratify their own [illegible] ing their vengeance by any means upon the Jews [illegible] be rendered evident It is obſervable that during the reign of ten kings, whom they count in ſucceſſion for three hundred years, not one of them had a ſtatue dedicated to him in the oratories, though they gave theſe very princes the title of gods in their ſuperſcriptions and for what reaſon? becauſe they certainly knew that they were men ſince, among their deities, they have abundance of creatures belonging to land and water, as well as birds of the air with whoſe altars, temples, and groves, all Egypt is well ſtocked

But as theſe people are the groſſeſt of flatterers, and court princes for their fortunes rather than their perſons they might ſay, perhaps, that, as emperors are greater and more conſiderable than the Ptolemies, ſo it is but reaſonable they ſhould have more honours done them A moſt ridiculous pretence! Why did they not decree the ſame honours to Auguſtus before Caius, who ſtood indebted to him for the empire? a prince who for the whole ſpace that he held the government never occaſioned one war, either in Greece or Barbary, but every place, to his death, enjoyed the ſweets of peace and the ſecurity of a quiet government [illegible] noble deſcent at obstacle to his preferment? Evidently otherwise, for he was much superior to Caius, both by father and mother. Was he inferior in point of erudition? It is denied, for none of his cotemporaries could pretend to more learning or prudence. Could any valid objection be founded on his advanced age? Far from it, for he not only gave signal proofs of his understanding in early life, but was eminent for the continuance of his abilities in its decline. Yet such a character must be passed over in silence, while one, in every instance of merit deficient, arrogates a claim to being deified. Augustus was a virtuous man, and virtue, according to the maxim of the greatest philosophers in every age, is the only nobility. He obtained the venerable name of Augustus, not as an hereditary honour transmitted from his ancestors, but as due to his personal merit, and thence descending to his posterity.

The whole world seemed to [illegible] for some eighty when he came to the empire. The [illegible] Mediterranean provinces, under the conduct of each Roman general, distinguished [illegible] his dignity, and [illegible] prizes in the [illegible] struggle. The vast countries [illegible] regions of the world followed one another, [illegible] engaged in the grand decisive battle that was to award [illegible] globe to the conqueror. The [illegible] nations were roused to partake of the two interests, one side or the other, and the land and sea joined their forces. So that during this great revolution almost all mankind had been swallowed up in the destruction and mutual defeats that were given on either side, had not one man, a prince of an August family, come in time, and given his assistance when affairs were at the last gasp. This prince was Cæsar, who, after he had driven back the storm that raged on every side, restored a perfect calm to the afflicted race of mankind, who remedied the public calamities that visited both the Greeks and barbarians, that beginning at east and south diffused their baleful influence to the west and north, while the countries that lay betwixt them were exposed to all manner of evils. This was he that restored liberty to all the provinces, and freed them from their chains. This was he who removed not only the terror of wars, but also all manner of depredation and plunder. This was he who scoured the sea of pirates, and caused it to be navigated by vessels of merchandize, who brought order out of confusion, and reduced the most barbarous and inhospitable of nations to a social and benevolent disposition. He gave large [illegible] to the Grecian cities, and annexed to Greece the richest and best situated countries of the barbarians. He maintained peace, administered justice, and scattered his bounties amongst the people in so generous a profusion, that they wanted for nothing, and this was his course and practice to the end of his days. Yet, after all these obligations to so great and glorious a benefactor during his auspicious reign, there was never heard of any such things as statues or images to his honour in any of their oratories, though, if any mortal had a right to such extraordinary tokens of respect, it was certainly this prince, not only as the founder of the august imperial family, and the best deserving of all mankind, but as taking the power out of many hands into one, and assuming the conduct of it himself; for it is a very just maxim, "that many rulers are the cause of many mischiefs." Besides, the whole world had decreed him divine honours, such as temples, groves, porticos, more beautiful than which, none, either antient or modern, were ever seen in any cities; particularly that temple dedicated to Cæsar in Alexandria, under the name of Sebaste, a piece incomparably transcending all others. It stands situate opposite a most commodious harbour, very high, and large in proportion. It is an eminent land-mark, full of choice paintings and statues, with donations in abundance. It is ornamented with gold and silver. The model is curious and regular in the disposition of the parts, as galleries, libraries, porches, courts, walks, and consecrated groves, magnificent and elegant as expence and art could render them. Can it then reasonably be supposed, that, amidst so universal a consent of nations, any thing was wanting that was justly due to the honour of Cæsar, without setting up statues in the Jewish oratories? Why therefore were they omitted? Without prevarication for this reason.

They were so well convinced of the generosity and justice of Cæsar, that they were persuaded he would be as tender of the rights and privileges of the several provinces as of the Roman ceremonies. He received these honours from blind flatterers, not from any principle of approbation, but because the dignity of the empire seemed to require it, as these acts procure a veneration for government. That he was never elated by these obsequious duties, is evident from his never suffering himself to be addressed in the style of the gods, so great was his aversion to so servile a way of adulation. Nay, he declared his satisfaction when the Jews refused to comply with that abominable practice. He would never else have suffered so considerable a part of the city beyond the Tiber to be inhabited [illegible] Jews, and the greater part of them freemen too, that is [illegible] men who having been prisoners of war, were set at liberty by their masters, and permitted to live according to the laws and religion of their country. He was no stranger to the nature of their oratories, and their worship on the sabbath days, conformably to the practice of their forefathers. He knew likewise that they collected their first fruits, and sent them to Jerusalem, together with certain [illegible] who obtained sacrifices for them, yet he never expelled them the city, or punished them otherwise, as he might have done. In Palestine itself they were allowed the free exercise of their religion, without check or restraint. Nor did he prohibit them from holding the assemblies where they taught their laws, nor, by any edict or proclamation, annul their solemn custom of sending and offering their first fruits. On the contrary, he held our worship in such veneration that many of his domestics presented gifts which are extant in our temple, where [illegible] victims to be offered every day, at his own charge, to the Most High God. These solemnities are still performed, and will so continue as a lasting monument to the virtues of this excellent emperor. Upon all occasions of distributing money and corn amongst the people [illegible] pleased to order the Jews their proportion, and if the day for dispensing it happened on the sabbath, when we are not allowed to give nor receive, the officers were commanded to reserve their share till the next [illegible]. This generous care so enhanced the reputation of the Jews, that it kept their enemies in awe, and deterred them from violating their customs and rites.

The Jews were likewise favoured with the protection of Tiberius, though Sejanus endeavoured to irritate him against them, and to involve Italy in new commotions. [illegible] rius on the death of the traitor discovered that [illegible] he had laid to the charge of the Jews were [illegible] ties, and that his principal design was to remove them out of the way, as the men most likely of all others to oppose his wicked measures and the scheme he had concerted to take away the life of the emperor. In consequence of this, orders were dispatched to all the governors of provinces to treat such of the Jews, as appeared to retain their allegiance, with lenity, so that upon the whole, no innovation was made within the tribes; but, on the other hand, they were commended as lovers of peace, while laws of morality tended to establish the public tranquility.

CHAP. X.

C[illegible] suspected against the Jews. A[illegible] fal[illegible] of an Egyptian [illegible]

CAIUS was at length so puffed up with [illegible] vanity, that he believed himself [illegible] pretended; and amongst all his [illegible] barians, none were so inclined to co[illegible] as the people of Alexandria [illegible] in the highest degree to dissimulation, flattery, and hypocrisy. They possess the arts of prevarication and insinuation, and are highly qualified for raising public commotions and overturning a system of good government. Those who wish to form an idea of the veneration they have for the name of God, need only reflect that their asps, and [illegible] other creatures, are honoured with it: there[illegible] [illegible] the [illegible] of this sacred name, they im[illegible] on the [illegible], and such as are not acquainted with [illegible] piety, but to such as are duly informed, [illegible] things, it is as open as the day.

[illegible] this, was so infatuated as to believe that the Alexandrians held him to be a god; for such was their [illegible], that there was no apparent difference between the [illegible] worship and the true, the acclamations and external [illegible] being the very same. Thus mis[illegible] imagined the innovations they brought into their [illegible] of their minds, and a strong [illegible]. He had frequent accounts sent him from Alexandria of these transactions, nor could any [illegible] celebration of him, afford him such pleasure, [illegible] to his satisfaction, the intelligence was [illegible] to him by one of his domestics, who well knew how to gratify the honour of his master. The greater part of the creatures about him were Egyptians, vile abject [illegible], [illegible] up in the worship of serpents and crocodiles, and totally corrupted in mind and body. Of this Egyptian band one Helico was the principal, a sordid [illegible], who, by [illegible], had crept into the palace. He had received his education under a former master, who presented him to Tiberius Cæsar. But the turn of that prince being rather grave and serious, and Helico's talent confined to ribaldry, instead of affording him entertainment, he excited his disgust; for that emperor, even in [illegible] had an aversion to things light and trivial. But, [illegible] the demise of Tiberius, and the succession of Caius to the imperial throne, Helico consoled himself, from the character of his new master, with a promising view of working him up to a subserviency of his utmost wishes.

The [illegible] miscreant now ruminated in his mind that there was [illegible] hand in which he should exert himself. He was conscious that he possessed talents adapted to the [illegible] of his present master, and that his peculiar turn [illegible] joke, banter, [illegible], and repartee, would gain upon him. He knew that his ears were open both to adulation and calumny; that the laws and ceremonies of the Jews was a forcible subject to work upon, and therefore determined to avail himself of those objections to them, which he had begun to acquire from his earliest infancy.

Such was the design this sycophant and impostor intended to prosecute to alienate the mind of Caius from the Jews, in the prosecution of which he used every artifice that was practicable. He did not deem it expedient to behave openly in this affair, but acted under covert, and through the disguise of hint and allusion, did the Jews more injury than he could have done in quality of a professed enemy.

This was no sooner known to the ambassadors from Alexandria than they made it their business to bring Helico over to their interest, by present gifts and large promises of treasure and honour, as soon as Caius should come to Alexandria. Helico was extremely pleased with the reflection of the respect he was to receive in the presence not only of his master, but of so many eminent persons as would be sure to appear from all quarters upon so solemn an occasion, and in veneration of so great a prince, so that he promised himself the accomplishment of his utmost wishes.

The attention of the Jews had been hitherto so taken up by known and open enemies, that they never suspected the danger of a secret one in the person of Helico. But when they came to be convinced of their mistake, they endeavoured to sooth him by fair words, as the man whom of all others they had most reason to dread. He was the emperor's constant companion at all his exercises and entertainments, indeed, in every scene of sensual pleasure. Being principal of all his attendants, he had the entire command of his ear, and as he was free *from other avocations, he had constant opportunity of* poisoning his mind with fables, interspersed with detraction and ribaldry, calculated at once to amuse and prejudice him against our nation. His apparently principal aim was the pleasure of the prince, but this in reality was transient; for the main scope of this pernicious slave's intention was to throw oblique accusations, in order to ruin us in his opinion. At length he seemed to have laid [illegible] the *mask, employed the whole force of his battery against* us, and plied his artillery with such addresses, as could not fail to work a most powerful impression on the mind of the emperor.

CHAP. VI.

The Jews of Alexandria send deputies to the emperor [illegible] Caius to complain of their grievances. Philo is [illegible] chief of the embassy.

THE Jews exerted their utmost endeavours to sooth Helico, and dispose him in their favour; but finding him remain intolerably proud and inaccessible, they let that project fall, and bethought themselves of another expedient, which seemed no less necessary, and yet to promise a better effect, not knowing at this time, but that the malicious designs of Helico might arise from some personal and particular pique. They came to a determination of presenting Caius with a petition and remonstrance on their grievances, with a prayer for relief annexed. This petition was no more than an abstract of a longer address, that was delivered a little before to king Agrippa, who fortunately, put into Alexandria in his way to Syria, to take possession of the kingdom conferred upon him by the emperor. We were thus far advanced in our way towards Rome under a great mistake as it happened; for whereas we made no doubt of finding Caius a prince of honour and justice, he proved, on the contrary, our most implacable enemy, though, in words and countenance, he assumed the mask of a generous friend. On our first reception [illegible] in the Campus Martius, where he complimented us with his right hand to indicate that he was propitious. [illegible] sent a person to us, whose office was to receive all ambassadors, to inform us he would take cognizance of our cause at leisure, from which the people in general, both Jews and strangers, concluded that the purport of our embassy was as good as accomplished. But [illegible] experience taught me better than to judge from appearances, so that I was inclined to suspect that with which others seemed so highly pleased. These reflections sprang up in my mind: "What can the emperor mean, when he [illegible] almost every nation under the sun here, by saying he will give audience to us [illegible]? He [illegible] that we are Jews, and would be satisfied with being [illegible] upon an equality with the rest. [illegible] height of phrenzy in us to hope for such a privilege from a youth who is a stranger to us, and a prince of absolute authority. He must be more favourably disposed to [illegible] the people of Alexandria, and for their sakes he prefers [illegible] matter to our [illegible]. I sincerely wish that the parties may find an impartial judge in him, and [illegible] a patron to them, and an enemy [illegible]."

CHAP. VII.

Caius orders Petronius, governor of Syria, to [illegible] in the temple of [illegible] [illegible] Philo and his colleagues.

WHILE I [illegible] [illegible] in my breast, I was surprised with a [illegible] accident that boded destruction not only to the Jews, but all [illegible] w[illegible] g[illegible] ons to a[d]drefs the emperor, we followed him out of town to Puteoli, whither he went to take the air at the fea-fide, and divert himfelf from place to place, vifiting [illegible] towns and villas, which are there very numerous [illegible]. During our abode there, in daily expectation of an audience, a perfon came to us trembling, out of breath, with his eyes fwoln, and having beckoned us [afide], as it were out of hearing, demanded in flow accent, if we had heard any news? With this he endeavoured to d[illegible] fomething, but a flood of tears put a flop to his fpeech. He attempted it again and again, and was ftill prevented, till at length, alarmed at fo horrid a fpectacle, we entreated him to acquaint us with the reafon of his coming, as we could not fuppofe it was merely for the fake of weeping, adding a requeft, that, if there was caufe for mourning, we might bear our part in an exercife [to which] we had been fo long accuftomed. At length [illegible] fetched fighs, he faid "Our temple is [illegible] to deftruction. Caius has commanded his image [to be fet] up in the fanctuary, with the infcription of the [illegible] Jupiter." This affecting information ftruck us [with] amazement; we ftood like perfons mute and fenfe[lefs]. The truth of it was quickly confirmed by other mef[fengers]. At length we withdrew into our apartment, [fhut] ourfelves up, and condoled our misfortunes, public [and] private, with uncommon dejection of mind.

After [a] long fatigue, we repented of having expofed ourfelves to the hazards of raging feas, to petition for a [redrefs] of injuries to which we were every day liable, [not] knowing but a greater and more terrible tempeft [than] what we had fuffered at fea hung over our heads [on] land. The laft ftorm was no more than the confequence of a natural caufe, which diftinguifhes the fea[fons], for the works of nature are but, in other words, the [illegible] of Providence to promote the common good of mankind. But the author of this tempeft had [neither] good or humane in him, he was a turbulent and [illegible] youth, and fo much the more dangerous in having the power of the whole empire to fupport him. Who could have courage enough to approach him with a petition or open his mouth in behalf of the temple to the moft facrilegious of all men living? It would be repugnant to common fenfe to expect mercy out of cruelty [or] to place the hope of protection in the breafts of perfecutors. It was further very apparent that he would condemn every one who had refrained from doing honours to his infamous temple, which the laft had well worfhipped as religioufly as if it had been the fun. Befides, if [illegible] had been granted, what could be expected but certain death? In this dilemma I thus addreffed my [colleagues]:

"Why fhould not one die then, efpecially when he hath [no] other life for the laws and religion of his country, [illegible] more glorious in exchange? But [illegible] that cafts away [his] life at this [rate], which no body is the better for. So that fuch an inftance as this would but be the addition of one more to the roll of our former calamities, efpecially, as we are under the characters of ambaffadors, and in a point [where] the principals are more concerned than the deputies. Nor fhall we want envious and malignant fpirits, and of our own people, to make the worft of things, and to impute any glorious refolution to a wrong caufe. The ambaffadors they will fay, found themfelves [in] a crifis and fo quitted the ftation, deferting the commonwealth when they found it in danger in order to the promoting of their own private intereft. But the lefs muft give way to the greater, private matters to public, and wherever this order is broken or confounded, the whole government is at ftake, and out of frame. In one word, when the polity of the Jews come once to be fubjected to the queftion, 'tis a ftep towards abolifhing the very name of a nation, where there is an agreement of power and good will in the doing it. We cannot, in fine, abandon the Alexandrian Jews, for the whole nation of the Jews is here at ftake, and it is to be feared, that this cruel oppreffion will extirpate us all from off the face of the earth. It will be faid perhaps, that if we can make nothing of [illegible] we are at liberty to come off at laft, in cafe of the worft. To this I anfwer, he that makes fuch a propofition has neither courage or foundation in fcripture in him. Generous natures will hope the beft, and holy writ [illegible] foundation of that hope to all thofe that heartily embrace the doctrine. Who knows [illegible], but this may be for a trial of our conftancy and virtue in the world of fortunes? Admitting that all human comforts and fupports, they are falfe and feeble, and leave us when we have moft need of them. Adieu [illegible], and let us caft ourfelves in a firm and invariable faith upon the goodnefs of God, who hath fo often delivered us therein, and will [not] forfake us." After this manner we comforted ourfelves and one another, in all cafes of furprize and in the [illegible].

Having [illegible] this addrefs, we applied ourfelves to the [bearer] of this difmal news: "[illegible] to confider [illegible] tidings you have had as [illegible] thrown into our ears as you have uttered [illegible] words, for you have only told us the matter of fact, which tends nothing to our fatisfaction [illegible] reafon of it, and without knowing what was the [caufe] [of] the emperor's horrid [illegible]."

The bearer [illegible] replied "[illegible], Caius has [illegible] in looking upon the Jews as the only people likely to oppofe [illegible] his blafphemous [illegible] it poffible to [illegible] the way, towards [illegible] the world. This could not be better done, he thought, than by [illegible], with contempt and indignity upon [illegible], [illegible] ed, [illegible] hands, to [illegible] [illegible] univerfe, [illegible] prefents and [illegible] been [illegible] in collecting [illegible] Caius, in the conclufion [illegible] confidence [illegible]. Befides, [illegible] further [illegible] Capito was [illegible] the [illegible] tributes in Judea, [illegible], by [illegible] and oppreffors, and [illegible] made himfelf odious [illegible]. He came [illegible] poor, and [illegible] corruption [illegible] of being called to an account, he [illegible] provement of [illegible] opportunity [illegible] Jamnia is [illegible] of Judea [illegible] the [illegible] all Jews, [illegible] that [illegible] countries [illegible] without fome plot [illegible] the Jews [illegible] foon as thefe people [illegible] extravagant [illegible] of Caius [illegible], and his [illegible] the whole [illegible] out of pure [illegible] the [illegible] to [illegible] for the Jews [illegible] together [illegible] the party [illegible] with the [illegible] and [illegible] to [illegible] Caius [illegible] look worfe than it was. This [illegible] prince [illegible] received the [illegible] gave [illegible] glorious Co[illegible] of Jerufalem, [illegible] laid down [illegible] and [illegible] counfel of his two [illegible]; Helico, [illegible]

"Apelles the tragedian, who, from a libertine in his "youth, went over afterwards to be an actor upon the "stage, [illegible] sort of people that are looked upon, in their "theatrical liberties, to be the lowest and the most shame-"less of all professions. These were the men that Caius "pitched upon to instruct him in the arts of singing and "talking, without so much as ever thinking of the duties "[illegible] and the care of maintaining the public peace. "Thus did Helico, like a scorpion, attack the Jews with "Egyptian venom, and Apelles, at the same time, as an "[illegible], that is to say, as a member of a nation "[illegible] to be reconciled to the bordering Jews."

Every word of this wounded us to the very soul. However, these learned counsellors lived to receive the reward due to their iniquitous actions. Apelles was commanded by Caius, on several crimes being exhibited against him, to be laid in irons, and put to exquisite torture at particular intervals, and so consequently a lingering death. Helico was afterwards put to death by Claudius, successor to Caius, for crimes of the like nature.

CHAP. XIII.

Petronius [illegible] difficulty in executing the [illegible] of Caius [illegible] his statue in the temple of Jerusalem.

AT this time arrived the order of Caius, for erecting and consecrating his statue, drawn up not rashly, but with all the care and accuracy possible. Petronius, governor of Syria, was expressly commanded to draw out one half of the army that lay upon the river Euphrates, as a guard of defence against any inroads and incursions of the eastern kings and nations, and with these troops to attend the statue, not for the solemnity of the dedication, but for a terror to any that should dare to oppose him. "Cruel prince! who well knew that these people would rather die a thousand deaths than submit to such an imposition. Wherefore then bring out an army, but to consecrate the impious act with the blood of many thousand innocents?"

Petronius having perused the order, was divided within himself as to the execution of the commission. There was danger in refusing, and danger in delaying, besides [illegible] on the other hand, in case of compliance, for he made no doubt of the Jews standing out, [illegible], and encountering all hazards. Nations in general are tender and jealous of their privileges and customs, but the Jews are particularly so, as they believe their laws to be of a divine stamp, and are trained up to the love and study of them from their infancy. They are so deeply impressed on their minds, and the more they think of them, the greater reverence they have for them. [illegible] their proselytes with the privileges of free citizens, and the veneration they have for the dignity of the profession is so sacred, that they would rather part with any thing than the minutest point of their duty. But there is nothing which they hold in so much esteem as the temple, which appears from the law, that makes it death, without mercy, for any man to set foot within the sanctuary, while the exterior part is open to all of their own nation from whatever quarter they come.

This was a matter of such great importance, that Petronius bethought himself over and over upon it, without coming to any resolution. He called a kind of council in his own mind, and, upon summoning up divers arguments and opinions, this was the result. That there must be no innovation in matters of religion, first, because nature and equity are both against it, secondly for fear of unhappy consequences, not only from God himself, but the passions of violent, revengeful men. He also adverted to the prodigious extent of this populous nation, that was not comprehended within the space of one country, but diffused almost throughout the world. All the provinces of the continent, and the islands, were peopled with them, so that their numbers were not much inferior to that of the natives. To provoke, therefore, so many myriads of men, must appear hazardous, for a general insurrection might probably arise in all countries at once, to repel this injury, and thereby give birth to an insuperable war, without taking notice of the vast numbers of inhabitants in Judæa, remarkable for their extraordinary strength and mighty valour, being ready, at all times, to die gloriously rather than [illegible] the rites of their country, though in the opinion of [illegible] they are called barbarous, when, in fact, they are free born, and brave men.

The governor entertained jealousy also of the [illegible] on the other side of the Euphrates, as Babylon, [illegible] other provinces he knew to be in the interest of the Jews. He was well assured that large sums of money were annually remitted to the temple in the name of [illegible] through [illegible] difficult and dangerous, which their piety and resolution rendered easy. He had therefore reason to apprehend, that, as soon as they heard of this [illegible] attempt, they would immediately rise up in arms, [illegible] surround, and cut them to pieces.

When Petronius had [illegible] all these particulars in his mind, he reflected a little on the humour and character of his master. He considered that the person [illegible] command he was under was a young [illegible] being his law, it was dangerous to oppose [illegible] or wrong that should be [illegible] the command of the emperor, fierce war would be the consequence, and the event precarious. On the other hand should he disregard the royal mandate, his destruction must [illegible] from the hands of Caius.

CHAP. XIV.

Petronius, governor of Syria, gives orders for making the statue of the emperor [illegible] the [illegible] of the [illegible] Petronius [illegible] to [illegible] of Caius [illegible]

MANY of the Roman officers, who served under Petronius in the government of Syria, [illegible] to undertake the work, taking it for granted, that there [illegible] the prince would [illegible] upon them [illegible] sedition. What gave them opportunity for this [illegible] having time to deliberate matters whilst the statue was preparing, for it was not yet sent over from Italy. This seems to have been a special act of Providence in favour of the Jews, to protect them from [illegible]. Had this [illegible], the consequences would have been dreadful. [illegible] would have [illegible] broke out [illegible] violation of the [illegible] they could have consulted on due methods of [illegible] for future events [illegible].

Petronius, at length, gave orders [illegible] hence [illegible] not far from his residence, [illegible] the greatest masters of [illegible] [illegible] on their coming, supplied them with the [illegible] materials, appointing Sidon [illegible] for [illegible]. He sent notice likewise of the emperor's pleasure to the high-priests and magistrates of the Jews [illegible] patiently, to submit to the mandate of his master, and guard against the ills that threatened them in [illegible]. He acquainted them that he had a great army of Romans at hand, who were [illegible] the whole country with fire and sword. Petronius was of opinion, that, if he could but soften the minds of the [illegible] the multitude of course would follow [illegible]. But he was grossly mistaken [illegible], for [illegible] bare mention of the [illegible] indignation, that they burst into a profusion of tears, [illegible] expressing every token of lamentation [illegible]

"[illegible] all our former felicity, to [illegible], at an advanced period of life, to be eye-witnesses of that which none of our ancestors beheld before? But we will sooner deprive ourselves of the eyes than survey so great an abomination."

The report of this strange innovation no sooner reached Jerusalem, and the region of Judæa, than the people, all as one man, proceeded towards Phœnicia, where Petronius then [illegible]. The officers of the Roman governor, upon first sight of their prodigious multitude, advised him to take care of his own security. As the Jews advanced still nearer and nearer, they appeared as a cloud overspreading the country, but without either arms or guards. The air was filled with outcries and lamentations, and when the noise was gone, the echo still continued. At length, when the clamour ceased, they entertained themselves with discourses and ejaculations suitable to the melancholy occasion. They marched in six divisions; old men, young men, and boys, old women, young women, and virgins, three on the one hand, and three on the other.

When they came within sight of Petronius, who was seated in a chair of state, they fell prostrate before him, all in the rank of suppliants, observing such decorum in their [illegible] as if they had been actuated by one spirit. Petronius commanded them to rise and draw near, which they [illegible] with much reluctance. At length, covered with [illegible] and ashes, they advanced towards the governor with their hands behind them, like condemned prisoners, [illegible] of their chiefs thus addressed him:

"We are without arms, to shew that we bring no hostile intention with us; but those hands, that nature gave us for the use of arms, are put out of condition to serve us in that capacity. We bring our very bodies at mercy too, our wives, children, and families, in quality of petitioners, first to Petronius, and then, by his means, to Caius. We have not left one soul at home, and our prayer is either that we may be all preserved or all destroyed. We are naturally lovers of peace, and it is our interest, as well as our inclination, so to be, in regard to benefits we receive from it. When Caius came to the empire, and the notice of it to Vitellius, your predecessor in the government, at that time living among us, we were the first of all Syria to congratulate his accession to the sovereignty, and to spread the joyful news of his elevation throughout other cities and places. Was it not our temple also that first offered up vows and sacrifices for the happiness of his life and reign? and is our's to be the first, if not the only temple, that is to be deprived of the exercise and enjoyment of our religious worship? If the quitting of our houses, privileges, and possessions, public and private, may be worth your acceptance, we are ready to lay them all at your feet. Also our plate, household goods, or what is more precious, [illegible] for asking, and with so good [illegible], that we shall reckon ourselves upon the receiving [illegible], even in what we give upon this single condition, that the temple may stand as it did, and continue inviolate, as we received it from our forefathers. Grant us this single request, and we ask no more. But if nothing less than our religion will content you take away our lives too, without forcing us upon a life of torment, worse than a thousand deaths. We are threatened here with armed troops and military executions, if any of us shall presume to obstruct the intended dedication. No man is so mad as to set himself up in contradiction to his master; but let them strike, cut and hack, us to pieces, and do all that a victorious enemy can pretend to, so long as they may do it, [illegible], without any danger of their own blood. What needs an army to be drawn out for such an execution, where there is only a massacre on the one side, and not so much as a defence on the other? As for sacrifices, we may do the work of our own priests ourselves, upon the victims of our own wives, brothers, sisters, sons, and daughters, and content ourselves with the denominations of men, women, and children slayers, for [illegible] must have hard names. What have we to do, after spilling so much innocent blood of other people, but to lay violent hands upon ourselves, and mingle our own with it in one common mass? ending our [illegible] last with this prayer in our mouths, that God [illegible] be offended with us for an action that carries along with it so great a deference to the authority of the emperor and at the same time to the [illegible] of our profession. This will be the [illegible] to condemn a life that [illegible] would [illegible] to lead. There is an old [illegible] the Greek [illegible] of Gorgon's head, that [illegible] to stone that did but look upon [illegible]. The [illegible] but a fiction, and yet [illegible] and striking resemblance of [illegible] accidents of [illegible] fare of [illegible] Now, Petronius, [illegible] our people should [illegible] temple, as you have [illegible] forbid,) they would [illegible] be [illegible] and out of [illegible] But to come to a conclusion [illegible] absolute discharge of our [illegible] other [illegible] partial [illegible] [illegible] worship, [illegible] the world [illegible] nations enjoy [illegible] those rites and traditions [illegible] lation from our [illegible] [illegible] the [illegible] condemned [illegible] if we should find [illegible] but where it was, [illegible] affirmed that he [illegible] Caius's request, Petronius, [illegible] is, that you would [illegible] embassy [illegible] upon it, [illegible] tent for profit (but for [illegible]) [illegible] as goodness [illegible]"

CHAP. [illegible]

P[illegible]

THIS [illegible] with such [illegible] the compassion of all [illegible] and gestures [illegible] the rest, for the [illegible] disposition, and [illegible] upon [illegible] actions. The Jews [illegible] was [illegible] titude was [illegible] affection [illegible] with his friends, he [illegible] friendly against the [illegible] to favour them, [illegible] [illegible] the [illegible] time, or the [illegible] [illegible] or [illegible] by a regard for [illegible]

We cannot determine [illegible] sue [illegible] of the Jews, [illegible] time instructed in their [illegible] ters from their books, [illegible] of Asia and Syria, in the several towns of which the Jews .... in abundance, or whether he acted as a man whose ... him to the study and knowledge of things in general, or whether God suggests good counsel to good men ... benefit of themselves and the public, as it ... on this occasion. The statuaries had been orders ... perfect a figure as art and hands could make, ... as works expedited are seldom of any ..., whereas perfect models endure time and age.

The Jews, however, could not obtain leave to send deputies, ... was it safe for them to commit an affair of this importance to the will of a prince, at once powerful, ... and ..., so that Petronius found it dangerous either to grant or refuse. At length he determined on sending a letter to Caius, without any accusation of the ..., ... the cause of the delay of the dedication to the statue, who ... required a certain space of time to complete the statue. It occurred likewise to the governor, that such delays would inevitably occasion a longer ..., Caius, in the mean time, might suffer himself to be ... over. Besides, the grain was now ripe, ... reason to fear that the Jews, abandoning ... in despair for the sake of their religion, would ... in contempt of their lives, destroy ..., and lay the whole country waste.

... apprehension? so that early care was ... by ..., for reaping the grain, and gathering the ..., partly for ... of need. It was at that time reported, that the emperor ... a design of a visit to Alexandria, though it did not seem very probable that so great a ... should expose himself to the dangers of a voyage ..., ... when ... of Syria and Syria would have been ... and ... Had he taken this method, he might have embarked ... at pleasure, having at command, two hundred vessels for the use and service of the coasts, besides others of considerable burthen, for navigating the ocean.

In consequence of this report, all the cities of Syria ... necessity of procuring a sufficient store of provision, especially those on the sea-coast. A prodigious multitude was expected to come, not only from Rome, but other parts of Italy, besides numbers from the provinces that lay between, and those of all conditions, as men of rank, civil and ..., together with soldiers, ..., and servants .... there was not only required necessary accommodation ... supply of every thing suitable to the dignity of ... prince.

... the general opinion of those whom Petronius consulted ... that the emperor, on perusing the ... letter, would commend the prudence or deferring the dedication not so much for the sake of gratifying the Jews, ... the advantage of securing the harvest ..., ... approved, transferred, and dispatched ... all possible expedition. Caius no sooner inspected ... he betrayed a visible indignation, and at length broke out into this exclamation:

"... Petronius! you are yet to learn obedience to an emperor. Your continuance in office swells your ambition. You know not that I am persuaded of your partiality in the laws of the Jews, a nation to me most obnoxious. You neglect the command of your prince. You shew yourself a coward to a base multitude, when you have a power under your command sufficient to encounter the kings of Parthia, and the whole force of the .... You urge compassion for neglect of duty, and plead ... as an excuse, but it shall not be long before your head shall pay the forfeit. You likewise adduce, by way of palliating your disobedience, the gathering in of the fruits, as though if Judæa were barren, the border ... provinces were not able to supply provisions, or make up the deficiency of a country, which is but one government, with all their increase. But why do I deign to reason upon this business? or why suspend the execution of my menaces on a miscreant that deserves my highest displeasure?"

After some pause, Caius determined to dissemble his anger for a time, and therefore dictated, to one of his secretaries, an answer to Petronius, apparently in commendation of the governor's foresight and precaution. He was fearful of some of his governors, lest they should introduce innovations, especially in large provinces, such as that ... comprehending Syria to the Euphrates; so that having cajoled Petronius in this letter, with formalities of respect and fair words, he only concealed his resentment, which was implacable, till a fit opportunity should offer for ... it, though he enjoined him, at all events, to attend to the dedication of the statue, in preference to all other pursuits.

CHAP. XVI.

... Agrippa ... to Rome, ... of the ... upon the ...

SOON after this king Agrippa came to Rome, to pay his duty to the emperor, after his ... without any knowledge of what had passed between Petronius and Caius. However, from the emperor's disordered state he conjectured that some resentment lurked ... brooding in his breast. He considered with himself if he had ... the ... word or action, offended him, but, being unconscious of any misdemeanor, he concluded, as was the case, that his resentment was against others. Yet perceiving again that his stern aspect was directed at him, he fell into his former apprehensions. He was several times ... of enquiring the cause, but as often ... upon himself, lest his ... curiosity should bring ... own head those menaces which were designed for others.

Caius, who was very expert in reading the mind ..., observing Agrippa fearful, thus addressed him: "Agrippa, I perceive you are in doubt, and will ... remove your scruples. You cannot ... the long time you have conversed with me, ... discourse with my eyes as well as with my .... good people of your nation ... from the rest of mankind, refuse Caius the ... styled a god, and, in their contumacious ..., plunge themselves into ... destruction ... tive commanded to have the statue of ... their temple, and ... multitudes ... quarters, under the pretext of supplicants, ... to trample my orders under their feet."

As the emperor was proceeding, Agrippa ... changed ... legs ... him to that degree, that ... must have fallen to the ground .... conveyed to his apartment speechless, and ....

Caius, by this accident was more exasperated against the Jews, and ... "... friend, who is ... offices, has so great a veneration for the ... country, that he cannot hear a word ... being affected almost to death, ... others, who have no consideration ... with them to my favour?"

Agrippa all that day was in a kind of stupor, till towards the evening he began to raise his head a little ..., much difficulty, opened his eyes, though his ... so much impaired, that he could not ... who stood around him. ... gentle repose, and seemed to rest better than he had done, from the drawing of his breath, and the beating of his pulse. When he awoke he ... "...

emperor? Is he present?" His attendants, in answer, [illegible] be of good courage, for he was in his own [illegible] and the emperor was not there." They desired him, as he had slept long enough, to raise himself a little and look on those round him, who were his friends, domestics, and faithful servants. The tenderness they expressed for him in this distress, brought him to some measure to himself again. Upon the physicians [illegible] to withdraw, that the patient might be quiet, and at liberty for remedies and refreshments, he said, "Trouble not yourselves about delicacies for my palate, a coarse diet, and good appetite, are all I ask, and more yet than I should make use of, if it were not for the hopes I have left me of living to be serviceable, even at this last extremity, to my miserable country."

[illegible] accompanied with a flood of tears. [illegible] contented himself with what was barely necessary to [illegible], drinking water without the least mix[illegible] having [illegible] his [illegible], made this [illegible] paid [illegible] to nature, and has nothing [illegible] left [illegible] to do, but dutifully to solicit Caius on the [illegible] melancholy state of the Jews." Having thus spoke, he called for a tablet, and wrote to the emperor [illegible]

"SIRE,

"BETWIXT the fear and reverence I have for your Imperial Majesty and the dread of your high displeasure on the one hand, and in the veneration I have for the dignity of your sacred character on the other, I have [illegible] rather presume to lay my humble duty at your majesty's feet in writing, than to venture upon it in a verbal address.

"It may be laid down for a maxim, that all men living have a natural affection for the place where they were born, and as [illegible] reverence for the laws they were brought up in; which is a truth that hath been abundantly attested in the piety [illegible] great prince of your profession [illegible] and it is as natural for every man to approve of his own way, because we are governed, in particular cases, more by passion than by reason.

"As to myself, I need not inform you, Sire, that I am by nation a Jew, by birth of Jerusalem, the seat of the holy temple, that stands there dedicated, in a most peculiar manner, to the honour of the Most High God. As to my predecessors, some of them have been kings, others high-priests, upon which dignity they valued themselves more than upon the authority royal, [illegible] that as God is above man, so the sacerdotal [illegible] above the civil, the one exercising itself in Divine matters, and the other only in human.

"Such is the nature of my relation and manifold obligations to this nation, country, and temple, that I cannot but implore your royal grace and favour on their behalf [illegible] for the nation, that they may not be [illegible] over from the profession of their own religion [illegible] especially considering how [illegible] and [illegible] they have ever been to your illustrious family, [illegible] to [illegible] marks of their vows and prayers for the welfare and prosperity of your empire, [illegible] of their sacrifices and oblations, not only [illegible] festivals, but daily, and this not only in [illegible] words and [illegible] but with a piety of reverence, and affection that came from their very hearts and without any exceptions, saving only in cases of [illegible] with their laws and religion.

"I have this to say further now for the holy city and [illegible] of my birth, which is not to be looked upon as the metropolis only of Judæa, but of many other colonies that have been planted from thence, as Egypt, Phœnicia, Upper and Lower Syria, Pamphilia, Cilicia, and several parts of Asia, as far as Bithynia and Pontus; and so in Europe there is Thessaly, Bœotia, Macedonia, Ætolia, Athens, Argos, Corinth, and the better part of Peloponnesus; and not only the continent, but the islands also of most eminent note, are filled with Jewish plantations, as Eubœa, Cyprus, and Crete, to say nothing of those beyond the Euphrates: for, in short, a [illegible] part of Babylon, and some other governments excepted, there is hardly a city of eminence, but is in the possession of the Jews. That if this be the case, I am not a suitor for my own country alone, but for the common good of Asia, Europe, and Africa, [illegible] land, islands, and continent all under one; for the interest of the whole depends upon the [illegible] of clemency; and I hope my confidence will be the more pardonable for the [illegible] I have to be [illegible] so much to the honour of Caius: for what can be more agreeable to the [illegible] genius of so glorious a prince, than the [illegible] an occasion of obliging the whole world at once, and consequently the perpetuating of your name and memory to all ages, as the guardian angel of mankind.

"You have been [illegible] at the request of some particular friends [illegible] whole towns free citizens of Rome, and masters of those that were but slaves before, and [illegible] your kindness was [illegible] to the [illegible] of this bounty, [illegible] the [illegible] being [illegible] the condition of [illegible]; and yet give me leave to [illegible] myself upon the title of a [illegible], a friend [illegible] but above all [illegible] good [illegible] for it [illegible] continue [illegible] I [illegible] the confidence to intercede for my [illegible] and privileges [illegible] for the common freedom of [illegible] the [illegible] that I have to beg, would be of [illegible] advantage to them [illegible] and of no sort of inconvenience to Caius [illegible] what greater [illegible] the favour of his prince? Was it not Jerusalem that first congratulated Caius on his accession to the empire? Was it not Jerusalem again that sent the joyful tidings of it to all the neighbouring [illegible] transported [illegible] the Jews [illegible] such [illegible] as the eldest son of the family is [illegible] honourable, because it was he that [illegible] to the reverend [illegible] of father and mother, so this city [illegible] would think [illegible] Caius by the name of emperor should [illegible] at least, if not better, than any other [illegible]

"I have been [illegible] country, [illegible] Holy Temple, Caius, is the holiest [illegible] any image made with hands [illegible] works of [illegible] sensible gods [illegible] representation of the invisible God [illegible] Agrippa [illegible] grandfather [illegible] mighty reverence for this temple [illegible] expressly [illegible] apply [illegible] certain [illegible] of [illegible] great grandfather [illegible]

"Neither Greek [illegible] condition [illegible] tive of our ceremonies [illegible] receive the idol of [illegible] that had no enemies, but [illegible] for being devoted to [illegible] it struck people into [illegible] frequently [illegible] not [illegible]

[illegible]

"of reaping the fruits of it themselves. We need not to look abroad for instances, having so many nearer home.

"In the reign of Herod, my grandfather, your grandfather Marcus Agrippa, passed the compliment upon him of a visit into Judæa, where he coasted along the sea-side up to Jerusalem. Upon a view of the temple, he was so transported with the glories of the fabric, the solemnities of the sacerdotal rites and ceremonies, the simplicity of the people's manners, and, in fine, with the delight of so curious and wonderful a spectacle, that he was continually enhancing the honour of that illustrious structure, insomuch that for the time he staid there, he never missed so much as one day's attendance, but still paid his constant visits, entertaining himself all the while with the contemplation of the holy vests, the order of the sacrifices, and the awful majesty of the high-priest, in his rich pontifical robes, as he sat exalted above the rest. In fine, when he had presented his donations to the holy temple and shewed himself as indulgent to the citizens as was possible, saving only an exemption from taxes, Herod accompanied Agrippa to the sea-side, upon his return where they exchanged mutual acknowledgments of the high obligations they had the one to the other, the people strewing the passage all the way he went with boughs and flowers, in token of the veneration they had for his piety and bounty.

"So, Sire, your great uncle Tiberius, was not he mindful of the same principle and judgment? Did not our religion and temple stand firm and safe through the whole three and twenty years of his reign, without any sort of innovation? Nay, there is something that I both can and must say to Tiberius's honour, though I myself had very hard treatment from him. But truth is truth, and I am sure you will have the patience to hear it.

"When Pilate was governor of Judæa, he dedicated to Tiberius certain gilt bucklers, not so much out of respect to the emperor, as in pure spite to the Jews, and they were erected in the palace of Herod in Jerusalem. They had no sort of figure upon them, nor any thing that was prohibited, but barely the two names of the dedication, and the person to whom they were dedicated. When this story came to be noised among the people they made application presently to the king's four sons with some other branches of the royal family, and several other persons of eminence to employ their interest with Pilate to have these bucklers removed as a violation of the laws and religion of their country, which former kings and emperors had ever regarded them. Pilate, who was harsh in his disposition made the *mediators so rude and churlish a* reply to the [illegible], that it put the multitude into wild and disorderly exclamations.

"Let people be quiet, they cried, that would be quiet, as those [illegible] men to war and sedition, and to the embroiling of the publick peace, as if the honour of the emperor depended upon the violation of the law, never think of covering an injustice with so weak a pretext. If you have any thing to shew in your justification, from Tiberius whether edict, letter, or any thing like it, shew us the warrant, and we have no more to do than to address ourselves, with humble petitions and remonstrances, to our lord and master, for redress without taking any further notice of Pilate, for Tiberius, we are sure, will never approve of this oppression.

"This mode of applying themselves to Cæsar, by remonstrance or deputation, startled Pilate more than any thing else, for fear of laying him open to the world with the history of his other iniquities, as corruption, justice exposed to sale, rapine, violence, ruin, torments, innocent blood, and the most barbarous of cruelties. This cholerick man was yet so divided within himself, that, as he had no mind to gratify the subject, so he had not the confidence to withdraw any thing that was made sacred by a dedication, being well acquainted with the humour of Tiberius in such cases. When the great men found matters in this state, and that Pilate repented himself of what he had done, however he dissembled it, they represented the case to Tiberius by way of letter, in the most tender and dutiful manner that could be devised. Tiberius had no sooner notice of Pilate's language and behaviour than he brake out into a violent passion, though [illegible] not easily moved.

"The first thing he did was without any delay, to write to Pilate about it, with a severe rebuke for his insolence, and a positive command immediately to remove the bucklers, and to have them transported into the temple that was built at Cæsarea (a sea port) in honour of Augustus. This expedient [illegible] a salvo to the honour of the emperor, and the [illegible] customs of the city. These bucklers [illegible] had no gravers work upon them, and the point now in question is the graven image. It was then only in the governor's palace but it is now to be erected as I am informed in the [illegible] a place so venerable and sacred that only the high-priest is allowed once, and that but upon one day in the year too, and after a solemn fast, to burn incense to the glory of God, and to offer up prayers to the Almighty, according to custom, for a happy year, and the common peace of mankind.

"If any other of our own people, either priest or layman, shall presume to enter this holy place, contrary to the law, it is made death without mercy. As for example, if the high-priest shall dare to enter above one day in a year, or thrice or four times over for the purpose, upon that day of his entrance it will most certainly cost him his life, so tender was our lawgiver of preserving the reverence of that holy place [illegible] and inviolate. Now if the rigour was so strict and capital in these nice cases, you may easily imagine, Sire, what an uproar it would create to have an image set up there, where the high-priest himself was not to be admitted but upon certain limitations. How many of our priests would sacrifice themselves, their wives, and children, in one common pile of carcasses, rather than outlive the sight and [illegible] of such [illegible].

"This was the case in the days of Tiberius. [illegible] Augustus the best and the greatest prince that ever sat upon the imperial throne, [illegible] give him out of a [illegible] to his conduct [illegible] prince to whom the whole world was indebted [illegible] blessing of an universal peace this illustrious prince [illegible], upon some discourse he had concerning our temple, was given to understand that there [illegible] suffered to be brought into [illegible] that the invisible God was not to be represented [illegible] visible figure [illegible] which he [illegible] with the reason and the [illegible] of the thing [illegible] a prince moreover of profound literature [illegible], he passed several reflections [illegible] partly recollecting what he had heard [illegible] the learned men he had constantly about him, and [illegible] the matter in his own thoughts. He was [illegible] great a lover of letters, that his [illegible] table discourses were as good as philosophical lectures, and his [illegible] entertainments were [illegible] to [illegible] satisfaction both of body and mind. Not to multiply instances in proof of this prince's generosity and good-will towards our people, I shall [illegible].

"First, upon notice that there was not such care taken for the return of our first fruits as the matter required, the emperor wrote to the governors "of the provinces in Asia, not to give any sort of interrup-"tion to the Jews meeting in their synagogues, (but this "tribute, was not to be extended to any other.) For the Jews "meetings are not like the feasts of Bacchus to encourage "[illegible] and sedition, but schools rather to piety and "common justice. And as for their yearly first fruits, they "were only [illegible] for sacrifices to be offered up to God "in the temple. This was followed with an express com-"mand, not to put the Jews to any trouble about their "meetings or collections after the manner of their country. I may mistake the word but the substance I well know of, as your majesty will find in a letter from Norbanus, where-"of this is a true copy.

"Norbanus Flaccus, proconsul, to the magistrates of Ephe-sus, greeting.

"Cæsar has signified unto me by letter, that whereas the "[illegible] used [illegible] custom of religious meetings, "and of gathering money to send to Jerusalem, under the "[illegible] of first fruits, it is his imperial majesty's will and "pleasure that they be allowed liberty so to do. Of this "[illegible] to take notice, and to pay your obedience accor-"dingly."

"What clearer evidence, Sir, can there be in the world "of Cæsar's opinion of our temple, than the indulging of the "Jews in the public exercise of their worship, the freedom "of their collections for holy uses, and the countenancing of "them in other offices of piety?

"There is yet another argument of the good will that "Augustus bare us, that is to say, he ordered the daily sa-"crifice of a bull and two lambs, out of his own revenue to "be offered up to the honour of our God, and the practice "of it hath been kept up ever since to this very day, [illegible] "any intermission. This oblation Cæsar designed for the "altar, and yet he very well understood that there was no "image in the case, either within or without. But this "wise and learned prince was nevertheless convinced of the "necessity of having some glorious temple upon earth dedi-"cated in a peculiar manner to the invisible God, where "men might offer up their devotions in hopes of having "their prayers heard and granted, and without any visible "figure.

"With your majesty's leave once again. What did your "great grandmother the empress Julia, but copy her great "master and husband, Augustus, *in the profusion of her* "royal bounties upon this temple in vessels of gold and sil-"ver, with other ornaments and presents to an inestimable "value? [illegible] without image work? "For women's minds are commonly weak and hard to be "wrought upon, but only by sensible objects. This prin-"cess, however, that was as much beyond other women in "perspicacity and judgment as in all other excellencies, sup-"plied the failings of the sex by study and meditation, and "gave herself up so entirely to thought and speculation, that "she looked upon the practical part to be only a shadow of "the other.

"Now, great Sir, after so many glorious instances of ten-"derness and clemency out of your own family, and those "of your ancestors in particular, from whom you have re-"ceived both your life and government, be but so gracious "towards our people as your predecessors have been every one "of them before you. Here are emperors interceding for our "[illegible] to an emperor, several august princes to one, grand-"fathers and great grandfathers to a grandchild, many to "a single person. And what is the request at last, but this? "They do humbly beg of you not to make void those laws "and customs, that, from their first establishment, have been "[illegible] to this very day. These acts, it is true, may "be vacated, and these innovations wrought perhaps, with-"out any judicial vengeance upon the transgression; but "whoever considers future uncertainty, and that Divine "Justice is nevertheless sure for being so active [illegible], will "tremble to think of the consequences, if at the same time "he believes there is a God.

"If I should take upon myself to enumerate the infinite "obligations I have to your majesty, [illegible] would not "serve me to recount them, neither would it become me "to handle so sacred a subject, but the thing speaks itself. "It is no secret, Sir, that I [illegible] irons and that I [illegible] "indebted to yourself for my liberty, but I hope [illegible] "not take me of those chains [illegible] "that case my sufferings [illegible] only in one part of my body, "but in this my very soul [illegible] the [illegible]. You "did first deliver me from the dread of death, and you re-"ceived me afterwards out of [illegible] Agrippa "desires no more now, than [illegible] "life he has received, for [illegible] "less calamity to perish by [illegible]

"It is to your royal bounty that I am [illegible] the "gift and dignity of a crown, and [illegible] "[illegible] of another, and a greater [illegible] "and Galilee. But after the multiplying [illegible] ex-"traordinary favours upon me, do not [illegible] "you, or things the most necessary of all [illegible] "solicitous for fear of either losing my [illegible] "being [illegible] to my former station, [illegible] "once for all, that the laws of my country [illegible] "tected and maintained. For what will [illegible] "me [illegible] Jews [illegible] One [illegible] "must necessarily follow, [illegible] I shall [illegible] "a betrayer of my [illegible] "the honour of your friendship [illegible] "[illegible] For [illegible] "self to be still in the number of [illegible] "[illegible] "I must certainly [illegible] "employing my [illegible] "emperors and princes [illegible] "vours. Or, [illegible] "your gracious [illegible] "as Tiberius did, [illegible] "life [illegible] "[illegible] "is the only hope and [illegible]

CHAP. XVII.

Caius, [illegible]

AGRIPPA, having [illegible] Caius, kept close in his apartment, [illegible] with the greatest [illegible] he [illegible] to the liberty [illegible] Jews [illegible] the face of the [illegible]

While the emperor [illegible] his design [illegible] the justice of so good a cause [illegible] tus [illegible] in part accused him [illegible] love and affection [illegible] had been the only people [illegible] obedience, had refused [illegible] ever he commanded the [illegible]

[illegible] differed [illegible] great soul, and generous disposition [illegible] appearance he seemed perfectly reconciled, [illegible] to Agrippa's letter, couched in very [illegible] terms. He gave the king a kind of promise, that there should be no more mention of the dedication, and at the same time ordered a letter to be written to [illegible] to suffer no innovation to be made in the temple [illegible]. However, to render it apparent that his disposition and resolutions were not entirely changed, it was [illegible] in the letter, that though he ex[illegible] purpose, if any of the bordering cities were [illegible] were desirous to erect temples [illegible] to him, such as gave the impediment were [illegible] put [illegible] to death, or be sent to him.

[illegible] seditions, and the cause [illegible] thrown and then abro[illegible] seemed to have consented with so [illegible] peace. Those who were enemies to [illegible] against them than [illegible], who punished such very severely [illegible] disturbance. He gave orders [illegible] to be set up in the temple; but [illegible] the people were quiet beyond [illegible] the least pretence for so doing, [illegible] was attended with the [illegible] continued busy and troublesome [illegible] he had granted rendered him uneasy, [illegible] kindled within his breast. He gave [illegible] to be made at Rome, of brass covered over with gold, throwing aside that cast for him [illegible] arise among the people. Care [illegible] this statue privately on ship-board that it [illegible] into Judæa, and set up in the temple [illegible] were aware. He also took shipping for [illegible] thereby to accomplish his design the [illegible].

[illegible] desire to see Alexandria, [illegible] accommodation upon his passage, being [illegible] was the properest place in the world [illegible] his [illegible] designs, both with respect to the authority and example of a leading city, and its convenient [illegible] for universal commerce. Indeed, it is generally found, that not only the lower class of men, but cities too, [illegible] the example of their superiors.

[illegible] so variable and inconstant in his temper, that [illegible] good, he would immediately re[illegible] into one prejudicial [illegible]. [illegible] he once set some prisoners at liberty, [illegible] nothing criminal could be alledged against them, [illegible] into chains again, merely to render [illegible] more miserable and helpless than it had been before. Others, [illegible] expected to die, were only banished, [illegible] circumstance, not that [illegible] because the rigour [illegible] judges made them despair of [illegible]. These people, in fine, went into banishment [illegible] others commonly return from it, [illegible] as cheerfully in their exile, as if they had been at liberty in their own habitations. But it was not long before Caius cut them all off by a [illegible] execution, without assigning any cause of offence, so that all the noble families in Rome were put into mourning for the loss of their [illegible] relatives by this execrable assassination.

If he presented any with sums of money, he would neither [illegible] gift, or as a loan upon consideration of interest, but find some means or other to recover it as a fraud or theft, to the great detriment of those who received it. Nor did he deem it sufficient to force back what he had given, [illegible] the whole estate he had [illegible] and acquired, went along [illegible] those who imagined they stood highest in his favour and esteem, were dealt with in another manner, a pretence of [illegible] being the constant snare by which they were inveigled and fleeced to an intolerable degree. This was by putting them to prodigious [illegible] to support frequent journeys, as [illegible] him luxurious entertainment. Whole fortunes were sometimes squandered in the preparation [illegible], insomuch that they were reduced to the necessity of [illegible] up sums of money at interest, to give [illegible] splendour and magnificence upon these occasions. This [illegible], however caused some to [illegible] and [illegible] as not only unprofitable, but dangerous [illegible] they found that all his plausible appearances were only snares to entrap the unwary.

Thus variable and violent [illegible] the Jews, to whom he had [illegible] aversion, [illegible] sensibly experienced their effects. He began [illegible] Alexandria, by seizing on their [illegible] with statues representing his own image, and [illegible] [illegible] to dispute [illegible]. The [illegible] holy city was now [illegible] the Jews had left [illegible] attempt to appropriate to his own [illegible] the title of "The temple of the new Jupiter, [illegible] Caius." [illegible] arrogating the [illegible] of the [illegible] who [illegible] the world at his disposal [illegible] aspiring to the heavens? [illegible] [illegible] of his own [illegible] of eternal God? What [illegible] Caius [illegible] himself and his empire [illegible] without dread [illegible].

CHAP. XVIII.

[illegible]

We shall now enter [illegible] subject of the embassy, to which [illegible] address, when we first opened our commission. We [illegible] no sooner entered into the presence than we plainly perceived, from the behaviour of the emperor, that instead of a judge, we should find him an accuser and enemy. A fair and impartial judge would have [illegible] council, investigated it from point to point, [illegible] sides [illegible] commissioners, passed sentence in open [illegible] more, would have been [illegible] of this consequence, [illegible] should the Alexandrian Jews [illegible] had [illegible] was [illegible] rule [illegible]

[illegible] and [illegible] and the town, which [illegible] retreat of Caius, [illegible] the spectato[illegible] opened, his profane [illegible] It was not long [illegible] reverence before him [illegible] a man [illegible] who [illegible] called a god [illegible] At the [illegible] blasphemous [illegible] These outrages were looked upon [illegible] as the prognostics of a certain victory, and there was not one attribute peculiar to God himself, but [illegible] to Caius.

Upon this occasion one Isidore, a crafty sycophant, took occasion to insinuate to Caius, that, "if he did but know the mortal hatred the whole body of the Jews had for his imperial majesty, he would abhor them much more than he did; for while the whole world were offering their prayers and vows for the safety of his person, and the prosperity of his government, the Jews were the only people that refused to do him honour." Upon hearing this calumny, we unanimously exclaimed, that "we were slandered [illegible] having had our sacrifices in form for the prosperity of Caius and the empire, and that we did not feast upon the victims as some did, but committed the sacrifice [illegible] to the sacred fire, and that upon three remarkable occasions. First, [illegible] to the imperial throne; secondly, upon his recovery from a dangerous illness, which so [illegible]; and thirdly, for the success of his [illegible] in Germany."

Caius, in a [illegible] tone, replied, "I grant you did sacrifice, but not to me, [illegible] to another. Where then is the [illegible]?" This unexpected answer threw us into the greatest consternation; we stood amazed, and knew not what to say. The emperor, in the mean time, went into the villas, surveying all the apartments, commending some, disapproving others, and giving orders for alterations to be made where he thought proper. We followed him up and down wherever he went, being all the time exposed to the reproaches of our enemies as objects of general ridicule. Indeed, the whole affair had the appearance of a farce, where the judge personated the accuser, and the accuser represented an unjust judge. It was one scene of faction and malice, without any semblance of justice and truth. But such accusers, and such a judge, ought much rather to be buried in silence, than have their proceedings exposed in writing. We could make no answer that could please him, and the laws of our country imposed silence in several cases.

When Caius had given some necessary orders about the buildings, he asked us, with a grave, serious countenance, what was the reason of our abstaining from swine's flesh? Our adversaries were highly gratified by this enquiry, as it indicated the disposition of the emperor, and was poignantly satiric upon us. Some of his attendants, however, reprimanded others for the licentious freedom of their smiles in the presence of the emperor, who might justly deem it the greatest indignity that could be offered him.

With respect to the question concerning the swine's flesh, our answer was, that several people and places had their several fashions and customs, and our adversaries were prohibited the use of some things, as we were the use of others. After some arguments had passed, we came to the point in question; but the emperor perceiving that we were about to produce such vouchers that were incontestable, broke off the discourse, and hastily withdrew into a spacious apartment, where having walked and ruminated with himself some time, he came out, and demanded of us, "what we had to say?" We represented our case as concisely as possible; but he left us again, and withdrew into another apartment, where he [illegible] a collection of ancient paintings carefully deposited.

The prosecution of our cause being thus delayed, we grew impatient, and, indeed, had nothing to apprehend but certain death. In this anxiety of mind we betook ourselves to the true God, with prayer and supplication to protect us from the rage and menaces of the false one. In compassion to his servants, he mitigated the fury of the emperor, who only [illegible] this short reflection, "those men who would not believe him to be a god, were, in his opinion, more miserable than wicked;" and having thus spoken, he retired, and commanded us also to withdraw.

Thus were we delivered from a scene of torment, hatred, and ridicule, being grossly reviled by the surrounding spectators, as well as shocked with the blasphemies to which we were under a necessity of being ear-witnesses. What was the ground of his implacable rage against us, but that we were the only people in the world who refused to own him for a god? We speak not this as men fearful of death for the sake of the love of life; on the contrary, we should have deemed it the highest blessing, had it advanced the common cause of our profession. But in this case death would rather have been an ignominious, for the miscarriage of deputies are generally imputed to the ill conduct of their principals. This reflection pointed out to us the propriety of seeking a deliverance, while we were in anxious uncertainty as to the sentence the emperor might pronounce upon the [illegible]; for how could he enter into the merits of the cause who would not hear the particulars? Was it not a matter of extraordinary weight and importance for all the Jews upon the face of the earth to rest their dependence upon us five deputies? If Caius had gratified the Alexandrians, what would have been the consequence? We should have had neither friends, towns, or oratories left. Our laws, rites, and privileges, would have been involved in one general destruction, and we must have sunk under the burthen of an insupportable oppression. Thus have we briefly shewn the cause that excited the aversion of Caius to the Jews, and induced him to persecute the whole race with unrelenting cruelty.

THE END OF PHILO'S EMBASSY.

THE

LIFE

OF

FLAVIUS JOSEPHUS.

AS every nation has its peculiar marks of distinction, so amongst the Jews nothing tends more to aggrandize a family than a lineal succession to the sacerdotal dignity. In that respect I may put in my claim, not only as I derive my origin from a race of priests, but also from those of the first rank in the twenty-four courses which indicates the highest degree of advancement. By my mother's side I am allied to blood-royal, for the Asmonæan family, from which she is descended, enjoyed, during a series of time, both the kingdom and the priesthood together: but to give a detail of the succession.

Simon, otherwise called Psellus, was my great great grandfather, who lived when Hyrcanus, the son of Simon, the high-priest, and the first of that name had the pontificate. This Psellus had nine sons, one of whom was Matthias, surnamed Aphlias, who, in the first year of King Hyrcanus, married the daughter of Jonathan, the high-priest. This Jonathan was the first of the sons of Asmonæus. Matthias had a son called Matthias Curtus, in the first year of the reign of Hyrcanus. His son's name was Joseph, born in the ninth year of the reign of Alexandra; and from him descended Matthias, in the tenth year of Archelaus, to which Matthias I was born, in the first year of the reign of Caius Cæsar. I have three sons: Hyrcanus, the eldest, was born in the fourth year of Vespasian, Justus, the second, in the seventh, and Agrippa, the youngest, in the ninth. This is a short account of my extraction as it stands upon record, as an indefagable testimony, in opposition to the authors of invidious and calumniating reports.

My father Matthias was greatly esteemed in Jerusalem, not only from his honourable descent, but his strict probity and justice. I had a brother, called after my father, with whom I was trained up in the different branches of literature. Being blessed with a sound judgment and retentive memory, I made so early a progress in my studies, that, at fourteen years of age, the high-priests and elders did me the honour of advising with me on some intricate points of law. At sixteen I began to inform myself of the different opinions of our three sects, the Pharisees, the Sadducees, and the Essenes, proposing to myself to investigate their respective tenets, and fix my choice where I most approved. I passed through them all with much labour and mortification, but supposing the experience I had attained from them insufficient to the end proposed, and hearing of one Banus, who led the life of an hermit in caves and solitudes, no covering but the bark of trees, fed upon nothing but the spontaneous productions of the earth, and bathed himself night and day in cold water to allay inordinate desires, I followed his example, and having passed three years with him in these austerities and gratified my curiosity in the experiment, I returned to the city in my nineteenth year, and conformed myself to the sect of the Pharisees, whose principles much resemble those of the stoics among the Greeks.

In the six and twentieth year of my age I happened to go to Rome, on the following very particular occasion. Felix, being at that time governor of Judæa, had sent several priests, worthy men of my acquaintance, as prisoners to Rome, upon a very frivolous pretence, to clear themselves of what might be objected to them before Cæsar. They shewed the utmost constancy, chusing rather to suffer any thing than depart from their duty, which consideration induced me to determine at all events, to attempt to procure their deliverance. Accordingly I embarked for Rome, and falling into a desperate storm, with about six hundred in company, we were cast away, and the vessel was lost in the Adriatic gulph. Only eighty of the whole number, by a wonderful Providence, were preserved, being taken up early the next morning by a vessel of Cyrene, when we had kept ourselves a whole night above water by swimming.

Having thus escaped and got to Dicearchia, (the Italians called Puteoli,) I became acquainted with Aliturus, a comedian, by birth a Jew, and in great favour with the emperor Nero. This man brought me to the knowledge of the empress Poppea, who immediately, [illegible] th[illegible] [illegible] difcharge [illegible] and loaded me with prefents, [illegible] which I returned to my own country.

[illegible] my arrival I found affairs in a very precarious [illegible], and the people appeared difpofed to a revolt, [illegible] that I endeavoured to keep the [illegible] within the bounds of duty, by reprefenting to them the circumftances [illegible] with whom they had to do, who were po[illegible] martial, and well difciplined, that I could not but [illegible] them from expofing their country, wives, and [illegible], and all that could be dear to them, upon terms fo very unequal. I plied them with argument, counfel, and importunity, to divert them from an outrage that could not but be attended with many fatal confequences. But whatever [illegible] before them had no effect, fo great was the [illegible] caufed by their defperate condition. But [illegible] that too often inculcating the leffons I gave them would draw upon me their hatred and fufpicion, as if I fided with the enemy, which might in the end en[illegible] my life, I took fanctuary in the inner temple, and [illegible], and the principal robbers were put to death [illegible] to the priefts and chief men of the Pharifees. We were prefently in a panic at the people [illegible] up [illegible], and [illegible] we were not able to reftrain their fury, we pretended to approve the fteps they had taken, but [illegible] them to decline any hoftilities, as we were in hopes that Geffius Florus would come to our [illegible] with a fufficient body of forces to quell the [illegible].

But upon [illegible] coming, and giving battle to the rebels, he [illegible] the ill fortune to be defeated, and feveral of his [illegible] were flain, which overthrow became the fource of [illegible] calamities to our nation, for thofe that were difpofed for war entertained hopes of finally conquering the Romans. Befides, another caufe occured for rekindling this war, which was as follows.

The Syrians and Jews living promifcuoufly together in feveral great towns bordering upon Judæa, the former took their opportunity of feizing upon all the Jews, with their wives and children who dwelt among them, and inhumanly put them to death, without any fort of provocation or offence; for there was nothing of a confpiracy, or fo much as difaffection to the Romans charged upon them. But the barbarity of the Scythopolitans exceeded all the reft; for they not only forced the Jews of that place, that were their fellow citizens, to bear arms againft thofe of their own tribe that came before it, (a thing expressly forbidden by our laws,) but when they had worfted the enemy by their affiftance, without any regard to juftice, gratitude, or common faith, put them all to the fword, without mercy or diftinction, to the number of feveral thoufands. The Jews of Damafcus were treated [illegible] in the fame manner, as is related at large in our hiftory of the Jewifh wars. We mention this circumftance in particular in order to make it generally known that we did not undertake this war upon choice, but were forced upon it by extreme neceffity.

After the overthrow of Ceftius, the leading men of the Jews finding themfelves weak and unarmed, and in danger of a turbulent and powerful faction, thought it time to provide for their own fecurity, fo that confidering how Galilee was divided, they fent me, and two other priefts, [illegible] and Judas, as commiffioners, to try if we could prevail with the feditious people to lay down their arms, not to [illegible] with them [illegible], but only to depofit them, for the prefent, in the hands of their governors till they fhould have occafion to ufe them, and wait till they were better informed what the Romans intended to do.

When I had received thefe inftructions, I proceeded to Galilee, and found the people of Sepphoris very much agitated by a concern for their country, into which the Galileans had made inroads on pretence of their ftanding up [illegible] the Romans and their adherence to Ceftius Gallus, then governor of Syria. But I effectually removed all their apprehenfions, by obtaining for them a licence to fend as often as they pleafed to Dora, a city of Phœnicia, to their hoftages they had given to Geffius. The citizens of Tiberias had taken arms on the following occafion.

There were three factions in [illegible] city. The firft confifted of men of honour and integrity, and Julius Capellus was then chief, who was joined by Herod, the fon of Miarus, Herod the fon of Gamalus, and Compfus the fon of Compfus; but as for his brother Crifpus, whom Agrippa had made governor of the town, he now lived upon his eftate beyond Jordan. All thefe [illegible] urgent for the citizens continuing their allegiance to the king and the people of Rome, Piftus being the only man of [illegible] who, in compliance with his fon Juftus, [illegible] the other way. The fecond faction was compofed of rabble, and feemed determined for [illegible]. The third was the abovementioned Juftus, who pretended to have fcruples with refpect to [illegible], but [illegible] defirous of innovation, from a view of [illegible] himfelf by means of the confufion.

To this end he endeavoured to perfuade the people, "That this city [illegible] Galilee [illegible] in the days of Herod the tetrarch, its founder, [illegible] of the province [illegible] never [illegible] from [illegible] the father and the governor [illegible] it away to the [illegible] Sepphoris, [illegible] neighbours, till they [illegible] themfelves to the Roman yoke, and [illegible] revolution."

When Juftus, by thefe means, [illegible] to a revolt, [illegible] the Scythopolites [illegible] of the Romans, [illegible] no other means [illegible] their rights [illegible] arms, and join with the Galileans [illegible] Sepphorites." This popular [illegible] greatly upon the people. For as he was [illegible] in the Greek tongue, [illegible] actions, [illegible] conducive to his purpofe. But I [illegible] define to the character of this Juftus, [illegible] the progrefs of the [illegible] well nigh [illegible] the deftruction of [illegible] he [illegible] fome of the citizens by [illegible] others by force, to take up arms [illegible] in a body, and fet fire to the [illegible] and Hippenians, [illegible] Tiberias and Scythopolis.

To pafs over from the [illegible] of Tiberias [illegible] Gifchala. John the fon of [illegible] his fellow-citizens highly [illegible] the Romans [illegible] endeavour to keep them [illegible] and obedience. But [illegible] the Gadarens, Tyrians, [illegible] forces, attacked and took Gifchala [illegible] afhes, and then returned home. John [illegible] at this [illegible] fought and [illegible] them [illegible] place, and, for better fecurity, [illegible] ftrong wall.

But the people of Gamala [illegible] to the Romans from [illegible]. Philip the fon of [illegible], king Agrippa's lieutenant, having [illegible] Jerufalem, while the city was [illegible], [illegible] danger of being [illegible] of robbers, but was [illegible] relations who were then at [illegible] day after his [illegible] him and [illegible] his own [illegible] to fome of his [illegible] he was feized with a fudden fever, [illegible] prevented the [illegible] of fixing his [illegible] into this diftemper, [illegible] a certain freeman of trust and credit, with orders to deliver his letter to Varus, to whom had been committed the care of the palace in their absence, on a journey to Berytus, with an intention of meeting Gessius.

When Varus found, by these letters, that Philip had made his escape, he was greatly concerned, lest the king and queen should discharge him from their service upon his return, so that he exposed the messenger to the people as an impostor, alledging that Philip was at that time at Jerusalem with the Jews, making war against the Romans, and upon this calumny he caused him to be put to death. When Philip had waited a considerable time and received no news either of the messenger or the letters, he dispatched a second with another packet, to inquire what was become of the former, and he was taken off upon the same pretence. Now the Syrians of Cæsarea had persuaded Varus that the Romans would certainly revenge themselves upon Agrippa for this rebellion of the Jews, and that, upon his death the crown would devolve to him as a branch of the royal line descending from Soemus the tetrarch of Libanus. Varus became so puffed up with this conceit, that he intercepted the king's letters, and guarded all the passes, in order to deprive him of intelligence of what was done. He put great numbers of the Jews to death, to make an interest with the Syrians of Cæsarea, and likewise proposed engaging the Trachonites of Batanea with him in a war with the Jews at Ecbatana, which they called Babylonians.

In order to the prosecution of this design, he sent for twelve of the principal Jews in Cæsarea, and dispatched them away in his name, with a message to their friends at Ecbatana, purporting that Varus had heard of their entering into a conspiracy against their king, but that though he did not believe the report, he required them to lay down their arms, as the most demonstrative proof of their innocence. He also enjoined them to bring seventy of their principal men, to answer all objections in behalf of the rest. The twelve deputies accordingly went, and acquitted themselves of their commission, but, upon strict enquiry at Ecbatana among people of their own tribe, not finding the least colour for any such rumour, they took, according to their instructions, seventy of the principal men along with them, and proceeded towards Cæsarea. Varus, in the mean time, having planted himself in the passage with a guard of the king's troops about him, fell upon them, and cut all to pieces except one man, after which he advanced upon his design against the Jews at Ecbatana.

But, by a wonderful Providence, the only one of the seventy who escaped got thither before him, with the news of this abominable treachery, upon which the inhabitants put themselves in arms, and, with their wives and children, retired to the castle of Gamala, leaving their goods and cattle behind them to a mighty value. As soon as Philip heard of this adventure, he repaired thither, and was welcomed with universal acclamations of the people, who tendered him their lives and fortunes in a contest with Varus and his Cæsarean abettors, if he would but do them the honour to command them; for it was now reported that the king was slain. Philip, however, endeavoured to restrain their zeal, by reminding them of the benefits the king had conferred upon them, the formidable power of the Romans, and the desperate hazard of a rebellion, insomuch that they were brought in the conclusion to better reason. When the king had intelligence of the resolution of Varus, with respect to the massacre of all the Jews in Cæsarea, he removed him from his government and appointed Equus Modius to succeed him; Philip keeping possession of the citadel of Gamala, and the country bordering upon it, that continued their allegiance to the Romans.

When I came into Galilee, and received the news of these transactions, I wrote to the Sanhedrim at Jerusalem respecting every circumstance, and requesting their commands as to my future proceedings. Their instructions were for me to remain where I was, and provide the best I could for the defence and security of the place, and to retain my colleagues if they approved it. But having acquired great riches from the tythes which were due to them as priests they resolved to return, but at my request staid a little longer, till matters were better accommodated. We went together from Sephoris to Bethmaus, about four furlongs distant from Tiberias, where, sending a messenger, I summoned the elders of the people to appear before me. Upon their arrival, (and Justus among the rest,) I told them I was sent to them by the people of Jerusalem, together with my colleagues, to consult with them about the demolition of the palace which Herod, the tetrarch, had erected there, and adorned with the images of divers animals, in direct violation of our laws, and requested them to put the work into immediate execution. Capellus, and the rest of his faction opposed it a long time, but at length, after a hard contest, we carried the point.

While this controversy was on the tapis, Jesus, the son of Sapphias, instigated an abandoned banditti to set fire to the palace royal, in expectation of considerable booty, for every thing he saw was magnificent and sumptuous; so that they pillaged many things, notwithstanding our utmost precaution. Having transacted our business, we withdrew from Bethmaus to the Upper Galilee. But the faction of Jesus put all the Greeks in Tiberias to the sword, and all whom they deemed enemies before their hostilities.

When I had intelligence of these proceedings, I was much enraged, went down to Tiberias, and used my best care and diligence possible to save the rest of the furniture of the palace from the hands of the pillagers. Among these were candlesticks of Corinthian brass, royal tables, and a great quantity of silver in the rough. Resolving to preserve whatever I saved for the king's use, I sent for ten of the principal men in the senate, and Capellus the son of Antyllus, and delivered to them the aforesaid articles, with an express charge not to part with them to any one without my particular order.

From thence I proceeded with my colleagues to Gischala, to watch the motions of John, whom I found manifestly engaged in forming a party, and setting himself ... He importuned me to give him authority to export the corn that belonged to the emperor, which lay in several magazines in the Upper Galilee. I easily saw the drift of his intention in this request. I answered that I could not possibly permit him, as being obliged, by virtue of my commission from Jerusalem, to take care of things within that jurisdiction. I could not dispose of such stores any other way than for the service of ... good of the province. Finding he could not prevail with me, he applied himself to my colleagues, who, through want of foresight, and the prevalence of ... were induced by bribes and fair words to comply with this request, so that having a majority of voices on his side, it was carried against me. John, having no sooner gained this point, than he brought himself ... ... vention.

The inhabitants of Cæsarea Philippi were complaining to him (he said) for want of pure virgin oil, and desired him to supply them, the Grecian oil being forbidden them, and the king's proclamation barring them from going ... town to fetch it. John was evidently actuated by self-interest, not religion, for he knew that the oil bore at times the price of ... he sent away the ... from ... under colour of authority from me, which ... not grant him ... but from ... fused, of being stoned by the multitude ... gained a vast sum of money by this stratagem.

Having sent my colleagues from Gischala ... ... him, I ...

[illegible] ſtate, provide the beſt I could for the defence of my province. The free-booters I found were not to be reduced by force, and therefore tried the effect of compoſition, ſo that a treaty was entered into with ſeveral leading men among them to take them into pay, being all convinced that the charge of the penſion would not be comparable to the ſpoil they would make by rapine and pillage. We came in fine to an agreement, and I took their oaths for the performance of articles, and ſo diſmiſſed them. The conditions were theſe, that they ſhould not offer any violence either to Romans or natives, nor ever ſet foot into our country, but when they were called, or behind hand in their pay. For it was my principle concern to keep Galilee in peace, in order to which I made choice of ſeventy of their beſt men to go along with me, and made uſe of them as companions, counſellors, and aſſiſtants, and, with their approbation, pronounced my ſentences, but with an inviolate regard to [illegible] juſtice, ſo that under the appearance of friendſhip they [illegible] me in quality of hoſtages.

I was now in the thirtieth year of my life, an age wherein the utmoſt virtue and moderation cannot ſecure a man from the laſh of envy and detraction, eſpecially in an exalted ſituation. [illegible] I can undertake to aver that I never was charged with any capital miſdemeanour. I wanted nothing, I coveted nothing, nay I refuſed my very tenths, though due to me as a prieſt, even when offered. I confeſs I took part of the ſpoil upon the defeat I gave the Syrians, and ſent them to my kindred at Jeruſalem. But when I twice ſtormed Sepphoris, four times Tiberias, once Gadara, and ſeveral times brought John, who treacherouſly acted againſt me, into my power, I paſſed all over without taking revenge either of the one or the other, and the Omniſcient Being, to whom the ſecrets of the heart are open, was ſo gracious as to deliver me from the ſnares of powerful enemies, and not upon that occaſion only, but divers times afterwards, as will be ſeen in the ſequel.

Such was the regard and benevolence of the people of Galilee towards me, that, when their cities were taken by aſſault, and their wives and children carried into ſlavery, [illegible] a much greater concern for my ſufferings than their own. [illegible] the envy of John, who, in a letter, requeſted me, when he came to Tiberias, to grant him permiſſion to uſe the [illegible] baths there for the recovery of his health. I immediately complied, having no ſuſpicion of any wicked deſign, and gave him recommendatory letters to thoſe to whom I had committed the adminiſtration of the affairs of Tiberias, to provide neceſſary accommodations for him and his whole train. At this time I took up my abode at a certain village of Galilee, called Jana.

John was no ſooner come to Tiberias, than he tampered with the inhabitants to revolt from their fidelity to me, and come over to his intereſt. Several were won over by his intreaties, being fond of innovation, and glad of any opportunity that offered to promote their ſeditious views. Amongſt his principal adherents were Juſtus, and his father Piſtus, who immediately cloſed with the propoſition, and joined intereſts with John againſt me. But, by good foreſight, I prevented their deſign; for Silas, whom I had made governor of Tiberias, ſent me a meſſenger to inform me of the diſpoſition of the inhabitants, and adviſed me to haſten thither, as the only means of preventing the city's coming under the juriſdiction of another. Upon the receipt of this intelligence, I took two hundred men with me, and travelled all night, having ſent a meſſenger before me to inform the inhabitants of my approach. In the morning a great multitude came out to meet me, and amongſt them John, whoſe countenance betrayed his guilt. Being conſcious that his life was at ſtake, if he was diſcovered, he haſtily withdrew to his apartment. When I had reached the place for public exerciſes, I diſmiſſed the guards I had about me, excepting one, and ten armed men that were with him, and then addreſſed the people of Tiberias from an eminence, upon the ſubject of good faith and allegiance, the honour of a generous conſtancy, and the dangerous conſequences, as well as actual baſeneſs of betraying a truſt, for one treachery would moſt certainly be avenged upon the head of the traitor by another, and after one act of perfidy their credit would be loſt for ever.

I had ſcarcely uttered theſe words, when I heard a voice earneſtly calling to me to come down and provide for my own ſecurity, as my enemies were juſt upon me, and this was no time for ſpeeches. The truth was that John, having me at advantage in a place where I was little better than alone, drew a ſelect number of men out of the thouſand that he commanded, with orders to fall upon me by ſurprize. They were already advanced within a little of executing their deſign, which they had certainly done, if I had not leaped down that very moment by the help of one of my own guards, who led me off to the lake, where I found a veſſel that conveyed me to Tarichea, beyond all expectation, and out of the power of my enemies.

The inhabitants of this city, when they came to hear of the perfidious conduct of the Tiberians, were greatly exaſperated, betook themſelves to their arms, and requeſted me to head them, that they might avenge the cauſe of their commander. The report of this outrage was quickly ſpread all over Galilee, in order to irritate the Galileans, who preſently aſſembled in prodigious numbers, and with great earneſtneſs entreated me to aſſault Tiberias, and upon the taking of it, utterly demoliſh it, and expoſe all the inhabitants, with their whole families, to [illegible] my friends, who had eſcaped out of Tiberias, gave me the ſame advice. But I did not comply with it, dreading the thoughts of being the cauſe of a civil war, and being deſirous of putting a ſtop to the diſpute before they proceeded to blows. I alſo pointed out to them, that it was not their intereſt to purſue ſuch meaſures, as a ſpectacle for the Romans that were to ſtand looking on. By theſe means, though with much difficulty, I aſſuaged the impetuous rage of the Galileans.

But John, when he found his ſtratagem diſconcerted, began to have apprehenſions for himſelf; ſo that taking the forces he had about him, he quitted Tiberias, and went to Giſchala, whence he wrote a letter in excuſe for what he had done, as if he had acted againſt his inclination, and begged of me to entertain no ſuſpicion of him, affirming the ſame with dreadful execrations, in order to obtain credit to what he had aſſerted.

This however, did not ſatisfy the Galileans, who were too well acquainted with his perfidy in divers inſtances, ſo that they preſſed me [illegible] (being a mighty body of men) to lead them on to the aſſault, that they might deſtroy him and Giſchala, the place of his nativity, at once. I gratefully acknowledged my obligation to them for the reſpect and good will they had ſhewn me, and aſſured them of the beſt ſervices I could render them in requital; but, at the ſame time, importuned them to reſtrain the impetuoſity of their rage, and permit me to endeavour to put an end to the tumult without bloodſhed. When I had pacified the multitude I withdrew to Sepphoris.

The inhabitants of this city (determined to continue in their allegiance to the Romans) were not without apprehenſions upon my approach, and ſo contrived for their own ſecurity how they might divert me from other ways. With this view they ſent a meſſenger to Jeſus, the head of the robbers, upon the borders of Ptolemais, with promiſe of a large reward, if he would bring his company, conſiſting of 800 men, to make war upon [illegible] prevailed, and it was reſolved to fall upon me by ſurprize. In conſequence of this, Jeſus [illegible] that he was deſirous of making me a viſit. When I granted his requeſt, having no ſuſpicion of his treacherous deſign, he took a band of his robbers, and [illegible] to his journey with all expedition. [illegible] for, upon his approach within a little of the town, I had intelligence brought me [illegible] contrivance.

[illegible] on I went into the market-place, as [illegible] of the plot against me, and I was there attended by [illegible] of Galileans [illegible], and several Tiberians amongst them. I then gave orders for the guard [illegible] the gates, to let in only [illegible], with some few of his followers, and exclude [illegible], or, if they should attempt to break in by violence, [illegible] by force. They did as they were ordered, [illegible] admitted Jesus with some few of his train, and then shut [illegible] against the rest. Upon his entrance, I commanded [illegible] down his arms upon pain of death in case of [illegible], with which he complied, [illegible] himself surrounded with a guard of soldiers. Those of his followers, who [illegible] the city, when they heard [illegible] was [illegible] to a precipitate flight.

[illegible], I took Jesus aside and told him I was not ignorant of the plot [illegible] against me, nor by whom he [illegible] I would grant him pardon [illegible] all these [illegible], if he would promise, in future, to behave as [illegible]. He accordingly pledged himself, in the [illegible] to do, upon which I set him at [illegible], and [illegible] him to collect the men he had brought [illegible] with respect to the Sepphorites, I charged them to [illegible] in future at their peril.

[illegible] to me, about this time, out of the country [illegible] two grandees, who had been vested with [illegible], bringing with them horses, arms, and money. The [illegible] absolutely against receiving them, unless [illegible] to the rite of circumcision; but I would [illegible] violence of that kind to be offered them, [illegible] every man ought to be at liberty to worship [illegible] according to his own conscience, and that these [illegible] to us for protection, ought not to be so [illegible] coming hither. When I had [illegible] the matter, I furnished the men, that came over to [illegible] in abundance.

During these transactions, king Agrippa sent Equus Mo[illegible], with a body of forces, to lay siege to the castle of [illegible]. The detachment being too few to invest the place, [illegible] could only post guards at the avenues, in order to block [illegible]. But when [illegible], the centurion, who had command of the great plain, understood that I was come to [illegible], upon the confines of Galilee, distant [illegible] he drew up an hundred horse, that he [illegible], two hundred foot, and some militia [illegible] from Gaba, and making [illegible] night's march [illegible] the village. Having drawn up my forces in order of [illegible], [illegible] to bring me into the plain, as his [illegible]. But as my army consisted [illegible] of foot, I found it would not be safe to venture [illegible] that [illegible] of ground, and so kept my [illegible] did what he could to force me from my [illegible], [illegible] he found he could not effect by means [illegible], [illegible] his design, and withdrew to Gaba, [illegible] three men in the action. I followed him [illegible] with a body of two thousand men, and when [illegible], a town upon the confines of Ptolemais, about [illegible] furlongs distant from Gaba, where Ebutius [illegible] me, I took possession of all the passes about it [illegible] quarters, and, in the mean time, carried off the [illegible] other grain to a prodigious quantity, that had been taken from the neighbouring villages, and belonged to [illegible] Berenice, sister to king Agrippa. This provision I [illegible] to be transported to Galilee, upon a number of camels I had brought thither on purpose. When this business was [illegible] I offered Ebutius battle, which, when he declined, I bent my course towards Neopolitanus, who was then in garrison with a body of horse at Scythopolis, and committed ravages in the country about Tiberias, so that having [illegible] from further annoyance, I determined to attend to the affairs of Galilee.

During these transactions John, the son of Levi, who was, as before observed, at Gischala, being galled to the very [illegible] every thing succeeded to my wish, and that I was actually established in the good opinion of my people, and at the same time a terror to my enemies, tampered with the inhabitants of Tiberias and Sepphoris, as well as those of Gaba, to revolt from their obedience to me, and join his party, insinuating to them how much easier their condition would be under his government than they found it under mine. The Sepphorites were, in truth, neither for one or the other of us, being wholly attached to the Romans. The Tiberians, though they would not be persuaded to revolt, promised to hold an amicable correspondence with him. But the Gabarenes espoused his interest at the [illegible] of Simon, a citizen of eminence, one of John's particular friends and companions. These people did not at first openly discover their defection, having [illegible] of the Galileans, whose kindness and loyalty to me they had several times experienced; but when they [illegible] opportunity, they threw off the mask, and plainly shewed their treachery, in consequence of which I was exposed to imminent danger on the following account.

A company of adventurous young men, of the village of Dabaritta, observing the wife of Ptolemy, the [illegible] procurator, travelling with a pompous retinue over the great plain, out of the king's jurisdiction into [illegible] province of the Romans, suddenly sallied out upon them, forced the woman to fly, and plundered all the carriages. This passed while I was at Tarichea, whither they brought four mules laden with rich clothes, costly furniture, a great number of silver vessels, and five hundred pieces of gold. Being desirous of preserving the property of Ptolemy, who was of my own tribe, (and our law prohibiting us from robbing even an enemy,) I told the people, who brought them to me, that they were by all means to be kept till they could be sold to the best advantage, and the money to be laid out upon repairing the walls of Jerusalem. These adventurers regretting the loss of so considerable a booty, of which they had made themselves sure, spread a report throughout the country adjoining to Tiberias, that I had a design to betray the province to the Romans. I pretended, indeed, they said, to employ the profit of the purchase upon rebuilding the walls of Jerusalem, but that my real design was to restore it to the proprietor. Nor were they much mistaken, for, after their departure, I sent for Dassion and Janneus, two citizens of the first rank, and both in great esteem with the king, and ordered them to take the effects that had been stolen, and see them conveyed to the king, threatening them with death if they communicated the affair to any one else.

A rumour now spreading throughout Galilee that the country was to be betrayed by me into the hands of the Romans, put every thing into confusion, and so exasperated the populace, that they vowed revenge. The people of Tarichea, among others, gave so much credit to the story, that they tampered with my guards, and other soldiers, to abandon me when asleep, and [illegible] immediately into the circus, there to consult with the rest what measures were to be taken against their general. When they came thither, they found a great concourse of people assembled beforehand, calling out, with one voice, for vengeance upon the traitor. But the ringleader of the tumult was Jesus, the son of Sapphias, at this time chief magistrate of Tiberias, a man seditious, turbulent, and naturally disposed to innovation. Presenting himself to the multitude, with the two tables of Moses in his hand, he thus addressed them: "If, citizens, you have no regard for your own "interest and safety, let me recommend to you, how-"ever, to preserve a reverence for these holy laws, which "Josephus, your governor, has made no scruple to be-"tray, and consequently rendered himself so odious to "all good men, that no punishment can be too exemplary "and severe."

The multitude applauded this address with the loudest acclamations, upon which he took [illegible] armed men, and hastened to the place where I [illegible] with full determination to take away my life [illegible] reposing myself without the least apprehension of danger. But

Simon, my body guard, and the only man who now attended me, upon sight of the crowd pressing roused me, told me the danger I was in and advised me rather to fall by my own hand, than be insulted at the will and pleasure of an insolent enemy. I therefore committed myself to Providence, disguised myself in black, girded on my sword, and went through a bye-way, where I supposed none of my adversaries would meet me, into the circus. I there threw myself prostrate on the earth, and exhibited so mournful a spectacle as excited general compassion. When I found the people in some measure softened, I endeavoured to influence their opinion in my favour before the return of the soldiers from the place of my residence. I admitted the truth of what had been objected to me, but requested them to permit me to inform them in what manner I had disposed of the money which arose from the plunder, when I assured them, I would chearfully submit to death if it was their pleasure.

The people were [illegible] hearing me, but the soldiers, who were just returned [illegible] for putting me to instant death. Through the [illegible] ever, that prevailed, they respited the e[illegible] granted that, after the confession of [illegible] ould have just ground for taking [illegible] this, silence being proclaimed, I thus [illegible] ded them.

"I [illegible] e, my countrymen, if I shall be [illegible] it, provided I may lay before you a [illegible] cause for which I suffer before I go. I [illegible] upon this city as a sanctuary to strangers [illegible] much, that numbers of people have been "prevailed upon to quit their native soil, and transplanted "themselves hither to share with you their fortunes. What "is my crime, but the dedicating a sum of money, from [illegible] for the public service, towards the repairing of "your walls? This, in short, is the ground of your displeasure."

The Taricheans, and other strangers, exhorted me to be of good courage, but the Galileans and Tiberians, on the other hand, were untractable and outrageous, so that it came to a direct feud between them, the one side plying me with menaces and hard words, the other undertaking for my security and protection. When I had promised to build walls in Tiberias, and other cities they dropped the contest, took my word for the performance, and dispersed, after which unexpected deliverance I returned home, attended by my friends, and a guard of twenty soldiers.

But the heads of the sedition, apprehensive of being called to account for what they had done, collected about 600 soldiers, and came to my abode in order to set it on fire. When I heard of their approach, I thought it dishonourable to turn my back, and resolved to expose myself [illegible] to the danger that threatened me. In order to this, I gave orders for the doors to be shut, went into an upper apartment [illegible] required them to send a party to receive the money [illegible] the most effectual means of appeasing the tumult. Upon their sending one of the boldest of them all, I ordered him to be seized, severely scourged, one of his hands to be cut off, suspended about his neck, and thus turned out to tell his tale to those that sent him. At this procedure they were in no small consternation, from apprehension that I had a strong guard in my house, insomuch that they moved off for fear of being treated in the same manner, and thus, through this stratagem, I escaped a conspiracy formed against me.

Notwithstanding this there was still some that irritated the multitude against me, and remonstrated, that the grandees, who fled to me for refuge, were unworthy to live, [illegible] they refused to conform themselves to the rites and customs of those with whom they lived for the sake of their own security. They traduced them with being sorcerers, and advising the Romans to come against them, so that the multitude were deluded by such plausible pretences as were agreeable to their own inclinations. Upon information of this, I represented to them, that it was neither generous or discreet to persecute those that sought refuge amongst them, and ridiculed the charge they had brought against them of sorcery, alledging, that the Romans would never be at the expence of maintaining so many thousand soldiers, if they could overcome their enemies by dint of spells and witchcraft.

This, for the present, pacified them, but they were soon stirred up again through the insinuations of some contentious persons, against the grandees, and a party of them, armed, went to their residence at Tarichea, in order to put them to death. When I heard this, I collected what men I could, and posted away to prevent the mischief, for the sufferance of so barbarous an inhumanity would have rendered me odious to mankind. Upon my arrival, I locked the doors of the house, and had a trench drawn round it leading to the lake, sent for a vessel, embarked with them, and sailed to the confines of Hippos, where I gave them money to provide themselves with horses, and then d[illegible] them with earnest advice to [illegible] in their misfortunes with courage and resolution. I was extremely concerned that I was compelled to expose those that had fled to me to go again into an enemy's country, yet I thought it more eligible th[illegible] they should perish by the hands of the Romans, th[illegible] lose their lives by treachery w[illegible]. However, they escaped at length, and king Agrippa frankly pardoned them, and thus ended their commotions.

The people of Tiberias having offered, by letter, their service to king Agrippa, provided he would furnish them with troops sufficient to protect them, I went among them, and, upon my arrival, they reminded me of my promise of rebuilding their walls, as I had [illegible] of Tarichea. I immediately consented, and gave orders for providing materials and workmen to put it in hand without delay. After three day's stay there, as I was travelling [illegible], some thirty furlongs distant, it happened that certain Roman troops, being on their march within sight of Tiberias, the inhabitants took them to be of Agrippa's party, and suddenly burst into acclamations of the king, and most contemptuous reflections upon me. I soon received information from a messenger, in great haste, that the people were upon the very point of revolt, an event that embarrassed me much, for the Sabbath being now at hand, I had dismissed the soldiers from Tarichea, for the more quiet celebration of the festival. Beside, I seldom kept a guard about me in that place, as I had received [illegible] proofs of the [illegible] of the people, so that having only [illegible] and a few friends about me, I found myself in great perplexity what course to take. It would have been to no purpose to recall my troops now, the day was far spent, [illegible] make no use of them [illegible] I [illegible] liberty to the people of [illegible] their number was not sufficient for the [illegible]. Nor was there time for [illegible] forces were hourly expected from the king, who would [illegible], and excited me [illegible] concurring [illegible] me to try the [illegible]. I set over the gates of the town some persons in whom I could confide, with orders to be [illegible] diligent in observing those who wanted to go out, and summoned the heads of the chief families to come to me, every one of whom I enjoined to go on board some vessel which I had provided for that purpose, having also [illegible] them to follow me [illegible] with my friends, and [illegible] [illegible]

When th[illegible] no forces came [illegible] the lake covered with vessels, [illegible] for the safety of their city, [illegible] former [illegible]. They then [illegible] to meet me with their [illegible] submission congratulated me on my arrival, wished me success in my undertakings, and invited me into their city, imagining I was wholly ignorant of their former design. Upon drawing near the shore, I ordered the pilots to cast anchor at a distance from the land, that the people might not discover the vessels were empty. When I approached them, (being conveyed in a certain vessel) I upbraided them with [illegible], in relinquishing their allegiance without any [illegible] cause. However, I assured them of forgiveness of what was past, provided they would send me ten of their ringleaders, with which they complied, and I immediately ordered them away for Tarichea, there to be [illegible] custody.

By this stratagem I gradually got the whole senate of Tiberias, and many of their principal citizens, into my power, whom I sent to the beforementioned city. The [illegible], reflecting upon the condition they were in, imputed [illegible] cause to one Clitus [illegible], resolute [illegible] desperate [illegible], and requested that I would bring him to condign punishment. As I could not [illegible] of my own to be to death, and yet was [illegible] of making him an example by some means or other, I ordered Levi belonging to my [illegible] guard, to cut off one of his hands. But the soldier fearing to execute this order among so numerous a multitude, and I, being desirous of veiling his timidity, thus exclaimed "Since you deserve to lose both hands "be your own executioner, lest, on refusal, you expose "yourself to a severer punishment." Upon his earnest petition to [illegible] one of his arms, I granted him that boon, when he immediately took a sword and cut off his own left hand, and this put an end to the tumult.

When the people of Tiberias, after I was gone to Tarichea, perceived the stratagem I had put in execution, they were astonished to think I had terminated the sedition without effusion of blood. Matters being thus quiet, I having ordered some of the prisoners to be released, amongst whom was Justus, and his father Pistus, I invited them to [illegible] and took that opportunity of observing, that I was not ignorant of the superiority of the Roman power, though I confessed to have dissembled in that [illegible] with which I had to contend. I endeavoured to bring them to the same opinion, and advised them in the mean time to live quietly under my administration, as they would never find a governor of more lenity than myself. I reminded Justus of the Galileans cutting off the hands of his brother before I [illegible], upon a pretence of forging some letters, and of the Gamalites upon a dispute they had with the Babylonians after Philip's departure, putting his kinsman Chares to death; whereas I had not [illegible] his brother-in-law Jesus [illegible] matter. Having communicated these particulars at table, I gave orders for Justus, and all his followers, to be set at liberty early the next morning.

A little before this, Philip the son of Jacimus, went out of the citadel of Gamala upon the following occasion. When Philip was informed that Varus was put out of his government by king Agrippa, and Modius Equus, his [illegible] friend and companion, succeeded him, he wrote him letters acquainting him with every circumstance that had befallen him, and requesting him to take care that the enclosed were forwarded to the king and queen, who were then at Berytus. Modius was overjoyed to hear of the welfare of his friend, and dispatched the letters according to address.

As soon as the king perceived these letters, and found that the report of Philip's putting himself at the head of the Jews against the Romans was false, he sent for him to court by a party of horse, and receiving him, on his arrival, with great cordiality, told his commanders about him that that was the person they heard had revolted from the Romans. He sent him soon after this with some troops of horse to the fort of Gamala, with instructions to bring away all his family, resettle the Babylonians in Batanea, and take all possible care to keep the people quiet. Philip had no sooner received his orders, than he hastened to execute his commission.

About this time one Joseph, the son of a mountebank, having, by his insinuations, induced several adventurous young men, to espouse his interest, made an insurrection upon the inhabitants of Gamala, and then [illegible] them to renounce their allegiance to the king and take up arms as the only means of recovering their liberty. Some were compelled to enter into their measures, and those who would not acquiesce were slain. Chares fell a sacrifice to their fury, as did his kinsman Jesus, with the brother of Justus of Tiberias whom we have already mentioned. The inhabitants wrote to me desiring I would send them troops for a garrison, and workmen to build their walls, with both which requests I immediately complied.

This procedure was followed by a revolt of the country of the Gaulanites, as far as the town of [illegible] the king. I built a wall about Sogannis and Seleucia, two very strong places by situation, and fortified several towns in the Upper Galilee, as Jamnia, Amerith, and Charabe, among the rocky mountains, and in the Lower Galilee the towns of Tarichea, Tiberias, [illegible], together with the villages of the cave of Arbela, [illegible], Selame, Jotapata, and the mount Itabyrium, in which places I had my magazines of corn and arms.

This prosperous course of my affairs excited such envy in the breast of John the son of Levi, that he [illegible] resolution of accomplishing my destruction. [illegible] end, having walled in Gischala, the place of his nativity, he sent to his brother Simon, the son of Gamaliel, [illegible] Jerusalem, to request him to use his interest with the sanhedrim to remove me from my government, and [illegible] John as my successor. This Simon was [illegible] of the first rank, by sect a Pharisee, who were supposed to excel others in an accurate knowledge of the laws of their country. He was also a man of eminent political [illegible] admirably adapted to regulate affairs of state. [illegible] this, he was warmly attached to the interest of John, and as singularly averse to me.

In consequence, therefore, of this application from John, he advised Ananus, the high-priest, and Jesus, the son of Gamala, with others of the party, to stop my progress now I was raising myself to dignity, nor suffer me to arrive at the highest pitch of grandeur, it being their common interest to remove me from the government of Galilee. He pointed out the necessity of being expeditious in effecting such a design, lest I should gain intelligence of it, [illegible] the city with a numerous army. This was the counsel of Simon. But Ananus [illegible] to them, that this was not to be effected so easily as had been suggested, because many of the high-priests, and heads of the people could bear witness to the [illegible] of my administration, [illegible] that it would not appear reasonable to proceed to judgment [illegible] without assigning his crime.

Simon [illegible] hearing this from Ananus, [illegible] the matter might rest [illegible] [illegible] might not reach the knowledge of the people [illegible] make it his business to [illegible]. Upon this he applied [illegible] to the brother of John, and proposed the distribution of money and presents among the friends of Ananus, as the most likely [illegible] to take for gaining his point [illegible] Simon [illegible] gained his end, for Ananus and [illegible] receiving these bribes, concerted the means for deposing me from my government, without suffering one citizen to be privy to the matter.

With this view they concluded [illegible] to send into Galilee some persons who were [illegible] birth, and versed equally with me in the [illegible]. Two of these happened to be [illegible], who were [illegible] mias, and of the sect of the Pharisees [illegible] descended from the [illegible] line [illegible] the fourth, who was Simon, was the chief of the [illegible]. These four had instructions, when they came before the assembly of the Galileans, to enquire into the [illegible] of their partiality to me. If it was said, because [illegible] born in Jerusalem, it might be answered, so were [illegible]; if because I was versed in the laws, it might be [illegible], they were not ignorant of the constitution of [illegible] country. But if they proceeded to say, that they re[illegible] me for the dignity of the priesthood, they should [illegible] that two of their members were priests.

[illegible] and his companions had received these [illegible] they were presented with 40,000 drachmæ [illegible] the public money, to defray their expences; but [illegible] that a certain Galilean named Jesus, was [illegible] to Jerusalem with a band of six hundred men, they [illegible] him, presenting him with three months pay [illegible] ordered him to follow Jonathan and his col[illegible], and pay obedience to their commands. They [illegible] gave money to the three hundred citizens to de[illegible] their charges in general. These necessary prepara[illegible] being made, Jonathan and his associates set for[illegible], taking in their retinue the brother of John, and [illegible] soldiers, who were ordered by those that sent [illegible] on condition I voluntarily laid down my arms to [illegible] me prisoner, and send me to Jerusalem, but upon [illegible] opposition they were to put me to death, without [illegible] relying entirely on the command that had been [illegible]. There were letters also dispatched away to [illegible] in readiness to make war upon me, and the [illegible] Gabarenes, and the Tiberians were com[illegible] to aid them with supplies.

Now Jesus the son of Gamala, who was attached to [illegible] and privy to the whole contrivance, sent my father [illegible] from time to time, of every thing that passed, and [illegible] I received a particular account of the whole [illegible]. I was [illegible] to think of the ingratitude [illegible] not a faction in the city against [illegible], nor was I less [illegible] to find the trouble my father [illegible] for my sake, and with what [illegible] he pressed [illegible] to come over to him, that [illegible] yet once [illegible] before he departed this life. Hereupon I made these [illegible] known [illegible], and informed them, that, [illegible] three days, I should leave the country, and visit the place [illegible]. They were much concerned at hearing the [illegible] entreated me, with tears in their eyes, not to [illegible] them, as they should certainly fall to ruin if they [illegible] my government. But not [illegible] all their entreaties [illegible] the Galileans, apprehending my departure [illegible] contemptible to the robbers, [illegible] messengers through the whole province to notify [illegible] bringing great numbers [illegible] together with their wives and children to the [illegible] as I [illegible], to prevail with me [illegible] out of affection to me perhaps, as [illegible] apprehensions on their, thought them[illegible] I remained with them.

[illegible] a surprising dream: for having [illegible] sorrow and confusion from the [illegible] which I received, it seemed that a [illegible] and addressed me to this purpose: [illegible] banish thy sorrow, and dis[illegible], for all these calamities shall only [illegible] thy greatness and distinction, not only for the [illegible] but likewise for the time to come, wherefore [illegible], remember you were told, that you must [illegible] war with the Romans."

Upon waking out of this dream, I arose with a design [illegible] into the plain. When the whole multitude of [illegible] Galileans, men, women, and children, saw me, they [illegible] themselves prostrate, and with tears and supplica[illegible] besought me not to leave them in this extremity, at [illegible] mercy of their enemies. When they found prayers [illegible] they pressed me with adjurations not to forsake them, and threw out many a heavy curse upon the people of Jerusalem, that it would never let them be quiet.

When I heard these words, and saw the sorrow of the multitude, I was melted down to pity and compassion, and brought, in the end, to a resolution of running any hazard whatever for their service. I now commanded them to draw me 5000 men out of their whole number, and furnish them with arms and provisions for a march, and sent away the rest to their respective habitations. As soon as these five thousand were ready, I joined them with three thousand more, and advanced with them to the town of Chabolo, on the frontiers of Ptolemais, where I took up my station, as if my design had been to fall upon Placidus, whom Cestius Gallus had sent into those parts, with a troop of horse and two companies, to burn all the villages in that quarter. Both armies were several times drawn out with a design of coming to action, but proceeded no further than to slight skirmishes, for the more I pressed the bringing of it to a combat, the more the other declined it; yet did he not draw off from the neighbourhood of Ptolemais.

While matters were in this posture, Jonathan, with his colleagues, appeared, who had been sent from Jerusalem by the faction of Simon and Ananus, the priest. At first they endeavoured to take me by stratagem, not having the resolution to attack me openly. To this end they consulted together, and sent me the following letter.

Jonathan, and his colleagues, from the Sanhedrim at Jerusalem, to Josephus, greeting.

"Whereas the elders are given to understand, that "John of Gischala hath been engaged in several perfidious "practices against your person, they have sent me, in "their names, to give him a severe reproof for so doing, "and to require him, for the future, to pay all respect "and obedience to your commands. And to the end "that we may agree upon some better provision for the "regulation of things hereafter, we make it our request "that you will come hither to us with all speed: as "the village is but small, we desire you will not bring "any considerable retinue, as there is not convenience to "accommodate a numerous train."

This letter put me to the pause, for it occurred to me, that if I went unguarded, they might seize my person, and treat me as they pleased; and, on the other hand, if I went attended with military force, it might serve as a pretext for condemning me as an enemy. The letter was brought me by an officer of horse, an intrepid youth, who had been formerly in the king's service. The evening was advanced, and being regaling with some friends, and several Galileans of rank, about me, word was brought me at table, that a Jew horseman desired to speak with me. Having ordered him to be introduced, he entered, and, without any deference to the company, delivered me a letter, which he brought, he said from the Jerusalem deputies, and required an immediate answer, as he was to return without delay. The company were amazed at the confidence of the soldier, whom I desired to sit down, and partake of the conviviality, keeping the letter in my hand without opening it. Though he excused himself from accepting the invitation, I took care to protract the time, by introducing various subjects of discourse, and passing now and then out at the door, in complimentary attendance on some of my guests that were going to repose, availed myself of that opportunity, for breaking open the letter, and glancing at the contents, then instantly folding it up, I held it still in my hand as before, without discovering that I had read it. All the company at length retired, but four particular friends, when I presented the soldier with twenty drachmæ as a gratuity. From the warmth of his acknowledgment, I found that money was his object, and resolving to attack him on his weak side, I promised, if he would sit down and be cheerful, for every cup he took he should be gratified with a drachma. He caught the bait, and becoming speedily [illegible], unravelled the whole mystery of the plot laid in the way in [illegible]. Upon this discovery I gave him the following answer to his letter.

Josephus to Jonathan, and his colleagues in embassy, greeting.

"I rejoice to hear of your health and arrival in Galilee, as I can now return to my native country, this being a [illegible] opportunity for my delivering up the care of the public administration into your hand. I should esteem myself happy in attending you at Xilo, or farther, without invitation, but am under a necessity of remaining where I am to watch the motions of Placidus, who has a design of breaking into Galilee. I therefore think it more advisable, upon receipt of this letter, for you to come hither." Farewell.

This letter I delivered to the bearer, and sent with him thirty trusty Galileans, with orders to compliment the deputies on my part, but to proceed no farther. I joined to each of them a soldier in whom I could confide, to watch their motions, and observe that they did not combine, or enter into any schemes, against me with Jonathan and his colleagues. After their departure the deputies, [illegible] the [illegible] effort abortive, sent a letter to the following effect:

Jonathan and colleagues to Josephus greeting.

"This is to require you to appear within three days before us at the village of Gabara, without any fail, to make good the charges you have exhibited against John of Gischala."

When they had written this letter, and [illegible] the Galileans whom I sent, they went to Japha, one of the strongest and most populous villages of Galilee. Upon their approach the inhabitants, with their wives and children, went out to meet them, and with [illegible] voices, [illegible] upon them [illegible], nor interrupt their [illegible], for they would own no other governor than Josephus. The deputies, after this [illegible] went hence, [illegible] to Sepphoris, the largest city of all Galilee. The inhabitants of this place being in the Roman interest, went out to meet them, [illegible] [illegible] [illegible] [illegible] [illegible]. From thence they proceeded to Asochis, where they [illegible] [illegible] [illegible] [illegible]. This contempt [illegible] [illegible] them to [illegible], [illegible] [illegible] [illegible] [illegible] [illegible] the clamour [illegible] the [illegible] [illegible] [illegible] [illegible] [illegible] [illegible] to Gabara. John [illegible] [illegible] [illegible] [illegible] [illegible], [illegible] [illegible] [illegible] [illegible] [illegible] resolution [illegible] to [illegible] [illegible] battle, I left Gabaroth with [illegible] men, and having [illegible] one of my [illegible] friends to guard my camp, without [illegible] to Jotapata, being [illegible] [illegible] about forty furlongs from them, [illegible] I wrote the deputies the following letter.

"If you find it absolutely necessary for me to come to you, there are four hundred and forty cities and villages in Galilee, and I will come to any one of them you please, Gabara and Gischala excepted, one of them being the place of John's nativity, and the other [illegible] [illegible] [illegible]."

The deputies having received this letter, returned no answer, but convening a council of their friends, among whom was John, advised in what manner they should attack me. John was for sending circular letters to all the cities, towns, and villages of Galilee, [illegible] a presumption that there was one or more in every place [illegible] to me, who might be suborned to [illegible] an information [illegible] me as a public enemy. He observed further, that nothing more need be done towards gaining [illegible] [illegible] of [illegible] over to the opinion of his being an [illegible] to the Galileans, than to send them the [illegible] [illegible] [illegible] [illegible] would certainly [illegible] [illegible] [illegible] [illegible] people. The council of John met with general approbation.

Notwithstanding this [illegible] proceeding, I [illegible] [illegible] [illegible] [illegible] [illegible] [illegible] [illegible] of one Sachaeus, who brought me an account [illegible] [illegible] [illegible] [illegible] [illegible] I found now I had no time to lose, [illegible] I immediately called one Jacob, (a brave man [illegible] [illegible] me) and sent him away with 200 men [illegible] [illegible] [illegible] and Gabara, with instructions to [illegible] [illegible] passengers he thought fit, and send them to me [illegible] [illegible] if they had any letters about them. At the same time I dispatched Jeremiah, one of my friends, with 600 foot another way, to watch the [illegible] from [illegible] to Galilee, expressly charging them to seize all whom they [illegible] about them, commit the parties to prison, and send me their papers. I sent [illegible] [illegible] [illegible] the whole province of Galilee, requiring them [illegible] to meet me at Gabara [illegible] [illegible] [illegible] [illegible] three days provision. Having divided the soldiers [illegible] with me into four parts, I [illegible] [illegible] and commanded them to be [illegible] my [illegible], and set centinels over them to watch that no unknown soldier got among their number. Coming to Gabara [illegible], I found the whole plain before the town covered with [illegible] troops that came out of Galilee to [illegible], [illegible] [illegible] multitude of country people. Upon my [illegible] [illegible] [illegible] I was interrupted with [illegible] [illegible] [illegible] [illegible] [illegible] me the benefactor [illegible] [illegible] [illegible] the country. I made them due acknowledgments for their [illegible] affection, advised them to [illegible] [illegible] [illegible] [illegible] [illegible] individually or collectively, [illegible] [illegible] [illegible] [illegible] [illegible] satisfied with [illegible] [illegible] [illegible] [illegible] [illegible] put a period to the commotion [illegible] [illegible] [illegible] [illegible] day, the messenger [illegible] [illegible] [illegible] [illegible] happened to fall into the hands of [illegible] [illegible] [illegible] in the roads, whom [illegible] [illegible] [illegible] [illegible] fined and sent me the letters which I found [illegible] [illegible] to abound with invectives [illegible] [illegible]. I determined therefore, without taking [illegible] [illegible] of the [illegible] to be as expeditious as possible [illegible] [illegible].

When Jonathan and his colleagues heard of my arrival they collected all their forces, and withdrew with John to the house of Jesus, which was a large tower, built in the manner of a citadel. As soon as they [illegible] [illegible] [illegible] [illegible] they fastened all the doors except one, where they [illegible] [illegible] for me, waiting for my coming to pay them my compliments, now I was upon my journey. Besides, they gave orders to their soldiers to let me enter [illegible] [illegible] as [illegible] [illegible] appeared, but refuse admittance to the rest of my attendants. This [illegible] imagined they [illegible] [illegible] [illegible] [illegible] power, but I effectually disappointed their [illegible] [illegible], [illegible], to having had some apprehensions beforehand of their design against me, as soon as I arrived [illegible] [illegible] place, I retired to a lodging over against them [illegible] [illegible] [illegible] to betake myself to rest. The deputies [illegible] [illegible] me much fatigued [illegible] [illegible] to the [illegible] [illegible] and the multitude dispersed [illegible] [illegible] [illegible] [illegible] [illegible] [illegible] me and my [illegible] [illegible] [illegible] [illegible]. But matters proceeded otherwise, for no sooner had the Galileans [illegible] them, than they fell upon them [illegible] [illegible] [illegible] [illegible] [illegible], calling out that I had acted the part of a [illegible] faithful governor and thereby [illegible] [illegible] them to my [illegible] by the firmest and most indissoluble ties. At the same time they upbraided the deputies with coming, without [illegible] having offered them the least injury, to [illegible] [illegible] [illegible] [illegible] to the affairs of the country, [illegible] [illegible] [illegible] [illegible] [illegible], as all their efforts would prove abortive.

Upon this encouragement I appeared, and presented myself to hear what Jonathan and his colleagues had alledged against me. When I came publicly among them, the whole multitude received me with loud acclamations, [illegible] applauded my upright and generous conduct. The deputies hearing this, were extremely apprehensive [illegible] they should be exposed to the designs of the Galileans, [illegible] the consequences of which might [illegible] [illegible] [illegible] [illegible] to them; they therefore thought themselves [illegible] [illegible] [illegible] [illegible]. But finding themselves [illegible] [illegible] [illegible]

[illegible] them to [illegible], they [illegible] [illegible] [illegible] dejected [illegible], could [illegible] their eyes from the earth. [illegible] [illegible] their [illegible] [illegible] engaged the [illegible] to be [illegible] careful in guarding the [illegible], to prevent John from [illegible] expected [illegible] [illegible], and [illegible] the Galileans at the same time to [illegible] their arms for fear of an irruption of the [illegible], which might [illegible] into disorder, and [illegible] them. I [illegible] the deputies of a letter [illegible] [illegible] sent me [illegible] a command from Jerusalem to [illegible] and [illegible] on certain matters in controversy between John and myself, producing the letter at the same time in proof of [illegible]. I observed that, "[illegible] [illegible] John and [illegible] colleagues [illegible] presence for calling [illegible] account [illegible] as governor of [illegible], [illegible] pronounce [illegible] upon the evidence of [illegible] unquestionable [illegible]." I further appealed not only [illegible] two or three [illegible], but to every one present [illegible], both [illegible] and [illegible], as [illegible] a man of [illegible] and [illegible] [illegible] of [illegible], [illegible] to [illegible] the truth, and the [illegible] truth, [illegible] were [illegible] in the cause, [illegible] men [illegible] called themselves [illegible] [illegible].

[illegible] [illegible] [illegible] pronounced me [illegible] [illegible] [illegible] [illegible] [illegible] [illegible] [illegible] wives had been [illegible] [illegible] [illegible] [illegible] [illegible] [illegible] [illegible] [illegible] letters [illegible] [illegible] I had acted [illegible] [illegible] people, [illegible] not [illegible] [illegible] know that I had [illegible] [illegible] [illegible] [illegible] [illegible] enter their [illegible] [illegible] time, to [illegible] ended [illegible] [illegible] to me [illegible] by the messengers [illegible]. [illegible] hearing these things, [illegible] exasperated [illegible] and his colleagues, that [illegible] have [illegible] [illegible], had I not [illegible] [illegible] [illegible] them. I gave them, however, [illegible], [illegible] their [illegible], and returned [illegible] [illegible] [illegible] acquainting them [illegible] [illegible] [illegible]. I then [illegible] [illegible] [illegible] would never [illegible] [illegible] [illegible] [illegible] continued [illegible] [illegible], [illegible] to permit them to punish them [illegible]. I still desired them to refrain, [illegible] the least [illegible] be prejudicial [illegible]. All I could do could not [illegible] [illegible], [illegible] length they [illegible] house where Jonathan and his colleagues [illegible].

When I found my [illegible] efforts [illegible] not [illegible] them, I took [illegible] and ordered them to follow me to [illegible] a village [illegible] about forty furlongs [illegible] [illegible], and [illegible] this [illegible] I [illegible] [illegible] [illegible] of a civil war. Being [illegible] [illegible] the place, [illegible] troops [illegible] [illegible] [illegible] [illegible] [illegible] [illegible] [illegible] [illegible] [illegible] [illegible] [illegible] [illegible] [illegible], [illegible] complaint [illegible] [illegible] [illegible] [illegible] [illegible] [illegible] I gave them, moreover, [illegible] [illegible] [illegible] disposed to my [illegible] [illegible] [illegible] [illegible] [illegible] [illegible] [illegible] John [illegible] [illegible] [illegible] I [illegible] [illegible] [illegible] [illegible] [illegible] men [illegible] [illegible] [illegible] [illegible] [illegible]

[illegible] passing through their country, [illegible] [illegible] that [illegible] the Roman [illegible], and it was necessary for those who were desirous of making [illegible] speed, [illegible] [illegible] them to [illegible] [illegible] that they arrived in three days. I [illegible] them myself to the frontiers of Galilee, [illegible] on the road to prevent a report being spread of their departure. After this I [illegible] [illegible] [illegible].

Jonathan and his colleagues finding themselves wholly disappointed in [illegible] they had formed against me, [illegible] John [illegible] [illegible] [illegible] themselves to the [illegible], of [illegible] [illegible] of reducing [illegible] to obedience, as [illegible] the chief [illegible], had, in a letter, promised [illegible] bring the people over to their interest. But [illegible], my [illegible] word, from [illegible] of every [illegible] [illegible] me with the most expedition, [illegible] I complied with [illegible] solicitation, [illegible] [illegible] nearly lost my life, from the following [illegible].

[illegible] [illegible] [illegible] formed a scheme of [illegible] against me [illegible] [illegible] [illegible] [illegible] coming [illegible] [illegible] [illegible] [illegible] [illegible] [illegible] [illegible] report [illegible] acquired [illegible] [illegible] [illegible] [illegible] in the administration of Galilee, [illegible] [illegible] [illegible] [illegible] there [illegible] [illegible] [illegible] and [illegible]. [illegible] promised a much greater [illegible] for me than John, [illegible] [illegible] [illegible] [illegible] [illegible] [illegible] [illegible] [illegible] every degree of [illegible] [illegible] [illegible] countenance. They then [illegible] [illegible] [illegible] other place, suggesting [illegible] the matter that the Sabbath approached, [illegible] [illegible] occasion the [illegible] [illegible] that day.

Upon this [illegible] I repaired to Tiberias, not [illegible] [illegible], [illegible] for the [illegible] of [illegible] I [illegible] [illegible] [illegible] to [illegible] observe and report to me [illegible] [illegible] concerning me. On [illegible] [illegible] [illegible] [illegible] [illegible] [illegible] [illegible] [illegible] [illegible] Jonathan [illegible] [illegible] open declaration [illegible] in need of [illegible] [illegible] [illegible] [illegible] finding [illegible] [illegible] [illegible] clared, that [illegible] [illegible] "four [illegible] [illegible] [illegible] [illegible] "honourable [illegible] [illegible] [illegible] [illegible] stood [illegible] [illegible] [illegible] [illegible] brought [illegible] [illegible] [illegible] of the people [illegible] [illegible] [illegible] [illegible] [illegible] [illegible] [illegible] [illegible] to keep the assembly, for [illegible] [illegible] [illegible] our nation [illegible] [illegible] [illegible]. The deputies [illegible] [illegible] [illegible] [illegible] [illegible] [illegible] [illegible].

Having intelligence of every thing that was transacted, I resolved to go [illegible] in the morning, and upon my [illegible] the people assembled [illegible] the oratory [illegible] [illegible] [illegible] [illegible] meeting. The [illegible] [illegible] [illegible] [illegible] [illegible] they [illegible] [illegible] contain. At length they meditated the [illegible] [illegible] of a report [illegible] [illegible] Roman horse [illegible] [illegible] the confines at one distance, about thirty furlongs from the [illegible] at a place called [illegible]. They then [illegible] b I marched out of the city But finding at the place not the least foot-step of an enemy, I hastened back to the city, where the senate and people were assembled together, and the deputies were laying before them a long accusation against me, as inattentive to the duties of my station, and addicted to wanton pleasures They then produced four letters, pretended to have been written them from those who dwelt on the frontiers of Galilee, entreating them, through a pretence that a body of Roman troops would be with them in three days to ravage their country, to hasten their arrival amongst them as much as possible, and not defer the time. The credulous Tiberians admitted the whole story as correct, and unanimously exclaimed, that it was now high time to send a seasonable relief to their allies As I knew the drift of the colleagues, I answered, I would readily obey their orders, and promised, without hesitation, to go and carry on the war in their defence But as it appeared, from the letters, that the Romans had made their irruptions into four several places I persuaded them that there was a necessity to make a division of the army into so many parts and put the four deputies at the head of them as it was the duty of good patriots and valiant men to serve their country in their persons, as well as with their conduct and counsel, at the same time I pointed out to them the impossibility of my being at the head of any more than one party This advice was approved by the multitude, who obliged the deputies to take a share in the expedition, though they were [illegible] chagrined when they found their designs frustrated by the stratagem I used to disconcert their measures

But one of them named Ananias, a seditious turbulent man, persuaded the multitude to have a fast kept the next day by all the people, and ordered them to come without arms, which, he observed, would avail nothing unless favoured by the assistance of the Almighty This proceeded from no religious motive, and was, in reality, designed to [illegible] I was, however, under a necessity of complying with the proposal, as I would not seem averse to so pious an admonition, in consequence of which every one [illegible] to his own habitation

The colleagues wrote in all haste to John to come early the next morning with all the force he could make, for if they could but get me into their hands, the [illegible] done John receiving the letter resolved to obey the summons The following day I ordered two of the most resolute and faithful of my guards to conceal their daggers under their garments and attend me in order to resist any violence that might be offered me I put on a breast-plate, and girt on my sword, as secretly as I could, and in that manner went to the proseucha

Jesus, however, refused to admit all my attendants, and only suffered me to enter with some particular friends As we were just on the point of entering upon our devotions, Jesus began to discourse on the rich furniture, and the ingots of silver, that were taken upon the firing of the royal palace, and asked where it was to be found, and who had it in possession? This was done to spin out the time, till John might come up with his army I answered in brief, that it was all deposited in the hands of Capellus, and ten other principal citizens of Tiberias, to whom I referred them for the truth of my declarations They then enquired what I had done with the twenty pieces of gold I told them I had given them to the envoys I had sent to Jerusalem to defray the expenses of their journey The colleagues replied, I was highly culpable in paying my particular agents out of the public treasure

These proceedings exasperated the multitude, who plainly observed their malice against me, and I, desirous of irritating them more, if possible, against the colleagues, added that, "if I was culpable in gratifying my messengers out of the public stock, I would willingly [illegible] them" The fewer matters appeared on my side, the more outrageous were the multitude, when they perceived [illegible] whole story founded upon envy and calumny This fell out so contrary to expectation, that Jesus ordered all but the senators to depart, pretending that the business could not be transacted amidst the tumult of a multitude The people exclaimed, on the other side, that they were determined not to suffer me to remain without them Upon this a messenger whispered Jonathan, that John would be with him immediately, with his party, so that, upon this encouragement, he broke out into these words "Imagine not, citizens of Tiberias, that I would have Josephus punished for "the undue appropriation of the gold, but for imposing upon "a credulous multitude, in the tyrannical affectation of "exercise of an arbitrary power" At that word certain bravoes, that were in the plot, set upon me, and had undoubtedly destroyed me, if my particular friends had not immediately drawn, and kept them off the common people at the same time threatening to stone John, so that betwixt them both, I was rescued out of the hands of my enemies Upon my withdrawing to make my escape, I met John upon the way with his troops, upon their march to the assistance of Jonathan This put me upon some apprehension of danger, but I found means to evade them, and reach the lake, where having the good fortune to find a vessel, I embarked and passed over to Tarichææ, a deliverance beyond all expectation

The first thing, after my arrival, was to summon the chief men of the province, and relate to them the barbarous treatment I had received from Jonathan and the Tiberians, contrary to common faith, humanity, and justice This so incensed the Galileans, that they insisted on an immediate declaration of war against John and his colleagues, in order to extirpate such monsters of iniquity. I endeavoured by fair means, to restrain their impetuosity, advising them for the present, to wait till we had an answer from the deputies we sent to Jerusalem; for there was no resolution to be taken without their approbation With these words they were pacified, and John, when he found his design ineffectual, went back to Gischala

Not many days after this the deputies brought word from Jerusalem, that the government there was much offended with Ananus, and Simon, the son of Gamaliel, for presuming without any public authority, to send their agents to remove me from the government of Galilee, and that the people were so incensed at this proceeding, that they were ready to set fire to their houses They brought letters also, in which the head men of Jerusalem, with the consent of the people, confirmed me in my government, and commanded John, and his associates, instantly to depart the place

Upon the receipt of these letters I went to Arbela, where the Galileans being assembled, the deputies made report of what passed at Jerusalem, how heinously they took the base actions of Jonathan and his colleagues, and how they confirmed me by their decree, in the government of the country, with a command to the pretended deputies to quit their pretences I took care to send them the letters by messengers, to whom I gave orders to be very strict in observing their design Upon the receipt of the letters, they were put into the utmost confusion, and sent for John, and the leading men of Tiberias and Gabara, to consult about the present state of affairs, and advise what measures it was expedient to pursue The Tiberians were for their keeping the power still in their own hands, and not abandoning a people that had delivered themselves up to their protection, especially against an enemy that had threatened them with an invasion, as they falsely and maliciously represented I had done

John not only gave into this opinion, but advised the sending two of their body to Jerusalem, with a charge of maladministration against me, which he said, betwixt the credit of the accusers and the variable humour of the common people, could not fail of making an impression The counsel of John being approved, they sent Jonathan and Ananias to Jerusalem upon the commission, with a [illegible] an hundred soldiers to attend their persons, the other two staying behind at Tiberias. The inhabitants of that place immediately set about repairing their walls, betook themselves to their arms, and sent for John's troops, that were then at Gischala in a considerable body, to be within distance of joining them against me, if there should be any occasion.

Jonathan and his people being now upon their march, and advanced as far as Dabaritta, a village upon the borders of Galilee, fell about midnight into a party of my out-guards, who took away their arms, and kept them prisoners according to order. Levi, who commanded the party, gave me notice of the encounter, and two days after, as if I had been ignorant of what had happened, I sent a messenger to the Tiberians, to advise them to lay down their arms. But they returned a very scurrilous answer, supposing that Jonathan and his party were by this time arrived at Jerusalem. I was resolved notwithstanding to requite them by means of one stratagem or another, though I could not be persuaded to make war against my own fellow-citizens. In order to decoy them out of the town, I took 10 000 of my choicest troops, and divided them into three bodies. Part of them I placed privately in Dora, and a thousand of them in another village, upon the mountains, four furlongs from Tiberias, with orders to be ready upon the first signal to make a sally. I came out of the village myself, and encamped on an open plain within sight of the Tiberians, who marched towards me, and treated me with reproachful language; nay, they proceeded so far in their folly and insolence as to provide a mock funeral for me, and, with fantastical pomp, exposed my image in the bier, surrounded by mourners. But I only made this farce the subject of my mirth and diversion.

Being desirous to intercept Simon and Joazar by a stratagem, I sent a messenger to them, desiring them to come a little way out of the city, conducted by their friends, as I was desirous upon meeting them, to enter into an alliance, and divide the government of Galilee with them. Joazar, who was crafty and suspicious, kept himself at a distance, but Simon, lured by the prospect of advantage, came over to me, attended by his guards and friends. I received him with becoming respect for the honours he had done me, but presently taking him aside, through a pretence of speaking with him apart, and thinking I had conveyed him far enough, I gave him up to my friends to carry him to the next village, and then giving the signal for my men to come forth, marched with them instantly to besiege Tiberias. A sharp encounter followed, and the Tiberians were almost in possession of the victory, till observing my men inclined to retreat, I roused their courage; when they rallied, and with extreme difficulty and hazard pursued the enemy to their very gates. Other forces passing the lake at this juncture to my relief, I ordered them to set fire to the first houses they could seize upon. The Tiberians seeing this, and imagining their city stormed, threw down their arms, and, with their wives and children, cast themselves at my feet imploring me to spare the place of their nativity. Prevailed upon by their entreaties, I restrained the fury of my soldiers, and as night was drawing on, returned with my men from the siege, and refreshed myself. I sent for Simon to regale with me, and gave him comfortable assurance of sending him safe back to Jerusalem, with all necessaries and conveniences for his journey.

The next day I marched into Tiberias with an army of 10 000 men, and summoning the principal citizens into the circus, enjoined them to tell me who were the ringleaders of the revolt. Upon their information, I sent them all prisoners to Jotapata, except Jonathan and his colleagues, whom I set at liberty, with a guard of 500 soldiers to conduct them to Jerusalem, and an allowance for the expence of their journey. The Tiberians came again before me, and entreated pardon for what they had done, promising to make ample amends by their future fidelity, and requesting that the pillage, which the soldiers had taken, might be restored to the right owners. Hereupon I ordered the whole booty to be produced before me, but being not uniformly obeyed, and observing one of my men with a garment more splendid than ordinary, I enquired whence he had it, and being told out of the plunder of Tiberias, I commanded him to be severely scourged, with a menace of a greater rigour upon any man that should presume to withhold any part of what he had taken. By this means abundance of things were brought to me, which were restored to the Tiberians, every part to the respective claims.

I cannot dismiss this subject without taking notice of some palpable calumnies imposed upon the world, and transmitted to posterity by Justus, and certain other writers, who have treated of these matters, and, through partiality [illegible] prejudice on the other, misrepresented facts, and thereby perverted the grand end of history. This kind of men may justly be compared to those who, by the forgery of instruments or writings concerning conveyances of property, [illegible] to the [illegible] spirit of these sticklers [illegible] detract [illegible] truth. Justus, upon this ground, took upon him to write of [illegible] of Tiberias, and has feigned [illegible] lies of me and [illegible] many particulars of his own account, which are not founded on the basis of truth. [illegible] I am bound to defend myself against his calumnies, and shall take the freedom to [illegible] because I hold it as a maxim [illegible] that [illegible] history should not [illegible] any subject without conviction of its authenticity, though at the same time he is bound to observe the laws of candour and moderation. Thus, then, I expostulate with Justus, as if he were present.

"Sir, Justus, you that art the greatest pretender of "all men living to the good faith of a candid historian, "how was it possible for me and the Galileans to be the "cause of the revolt of thy countrymen from their prince, "and from the Roman empire, when you yourself, and "your Tiberians had already made war upon the Deca-"politans in Syria, and burnt their villages, by the "token that one of your servants [illegible] the action, and all "this before ever I received my commission from Jeru-"salem for the government of Galilee? I do not deliver "this barely upon my own credit, but refer the reader, "for his better satisfaction, to the memorials and records "of the emperor Vespasian, wherein it will appear, "that, while he was at Ptolemais, the people of Deca-"polis were still pressing him with restless importunities "to do them justice upon you, as the principal promoter "of all their troubles, which he had undoubtedly done, "if king Agrippa, to whom the care of the execution "was committed, had not given you your life, at the in-"termediation of his sister Berenice. Even this pardon did "not yet hinder you from being still kept in a prison "for a long time after. Besides, the whole course of "your life was uniform, as may be seen from your "following practices, for I shall make it as clear as the "sun, that it was upon your tampering and instigation, "that your people broke out into a rebellion against the "Romans. I must now give the reader to understand "that neither you yourself, nor the rest of the Tiberians "were ever faithful either to our king, or to the emperor.

"The fairest cities of Galilee are Sepphoris and Tibe-"rias, the latter the place of your birth, Justus, the "former seated in the middle of the province, with se-"veral villages depending upon it, and the people so "true to their masters, that they did not only refuse "me entrance into the place, but, by a public edict, pro-"hibited all their citizens from bearing arms for the "Jews. And for their better security, they hired me to "[illegible] small town, which I had no sooner "[illegible], then they turned me off with contempt, submitting also, at the same time, without any difficulty, to a Roman garrison, under Cestius Gallus, who was then governor of Syria, and this at a season too, when I held the whole neighbourhood in awe. Nay, so tender were they of giving the least colour for a suspicion of their breaking faith with the Romans, that, when the temple of Jerusalem was besieged, and the common cause and interest of our nation at stake upon that action, they would not so much as contribute in any sort to the relief. But Justus considering the situation of your country, as it stands upon the border of the lake of Gennesareth, some thirty furlongs from Hippos, [illegible] from Gadara, and an hundred and twenty from Scythopolis, (places under the king's allegiance, and none of the Jews garrisons [illegible] besides this [illegible] wanted neither [illegible] nor [illegible],) what should hinder [illegible] now, with all these advantages on your side, from discharging your duty to the Romans, if you had a mind? Or supposing the matter to be as you say, and that in truth, I was at that time in some measure the cause of the war [illegible] Yet [illegible] know very well that the Romans had got [illegible] power before the siege was laid to Jerusalem, Jotapata and divers other castles taken [illegible], and great numbers of the Galileans cut off from several encounters. Now [illegible] be that as you suggest, that the war was altogether against your will, and that you were [illegible] by force, how [illegible] to pass that you [illegible] your arms [illegible] It at the feet of your prince, and of the Romans, when that [illegible] was over? For [illegible] not [illegible] I could do you. But you were [illegible] disposed to stand it out, till Vespasian was [illegible] his army [illegible] then [illegible] when [illegible] without [illegible] neither without the intercession of the king to Vespasian in your behalf, for [illegible] had been razed to the very ground, if [illegible] the emperor's pardon for your [illegible] so that your city [illegible] rely [illegible] own heart [illegible] How many times have I protected you and had you at mercy without spilling [illegible] one drop of your blood. Whereas it is notorious [illegible] in the rage of your intestine broils, not [illegible] the king's cause, nor [illegible] the Romans, but out of [illegible] and rancour one against [illegible] you put to death no less than an hundred and [illegible]-five citizens at a time, when I was blocked up in Jotapata. And were there not two thousand Tiberians killed and taken at Jerusalem? Were you no enemy [illegible] cause you [illegible] at that time with the king? No, [illegible] duty, but because I [illegible] you thither [illegible] Justus [illegible] that Vespasian pronounced sentence of [illegible] though the execution of it was afterwards [illegible] King Agrippa [illegible] upon the [illegible] sister, and finally, [illegible] of a secretary, which [illegible] the honour to have conferred upon him, [illegible] his preference for [illegible] Justus, [illegible] your misdemeanours, I cannot sufficiently [illegible] the arrogance of your setting up for the most perfect and exact historian of this war, to the disparagement of all others, when [illegible] but a mere stranger to the whole [illegible], even to what passed in Galilee itself, for in the time of the [illegible] you were with the king at Berytus. And as to the siege of Jotapata how was it possible for you to make [illegible] report of my behaviour [illegible] when there was not one man left

[illegible] but [illegible] to tell [illegible] You will perhaps [illegible] you have given of what passed at Jerusalem may be more correct. But it is a thing hardly to be [illegible] that you who [illegible] so much as read Vespasian's commentaries [illegible] should be so well [illegible] I have [illegible] you nor [illegible] Vespasian [illegible] contradict [illegible] you have [illegible] Agrippa [illegible] in the Greek tongue? Why was this history of yours kept [illegible] it has been now [illegible] twenty years) when you might have had [illegible] of the [illegible] good [illegible] work? Why was it [illegible] published at last [illegible] of the world [illegible] people were [illegible] that were [illegible] to [illegible] you. I [illegible] another way to [illegible] to the hands of [illegible] the government of [illegible] while [illegible] of it was [illegible] fresh in every one's memory, my conscience [illegible] that I [illegible] which [illegible] my writings [illegible] received [illegible] could [illegible] I recommend [illegible] very [illegible] then, [illegible] in the war, as king Agrippa, and some [illegible] of his [illegible] has [illegible] such [illegible] approbation of this history, [illegible] the world [illegible] record [illegible] his own hand, [illegible] King Agrippa was so pleased with the [illegible] and candour of [illegible] me sixty-two letters [illegible] firmation of the credit of [illegible] subjoined to the end, that the [illegible] speak for [illegible]."

King Agrippa to [illegible] dearest friend, Josephus, greeting.

"I HAVE read [illegible] with great delight, and look upon it to be the most pertinent and exact account of any I have yet seen. Send me the remainder [illegible] so I bid you farewell, my dear friend."

King Agrippa, to Josephus, his dearest friend, health.

"UPON the perusal of your writings, I perceive you have little need of any thing farther that I can tell you: only when we meet next, I may, perhaps, suggest some certain passages to your consideration that have [illegible] your knowledge."

Thus [illegible] with regard to Justus, with whom I [illegible] myself in justice [illegible] obliged to make this comparison.

When I [illegible] the [illegible] of Tiberias [illegible] a council of my friends, I advised what measures were to be put in execution concerning John. All the Galileans were of opinion, that [illegible] upon John as the [illegible] author of the late troubles. But I could not concur with them in opinion, as [illegible] desirous to terminate the difference without bloodshed: wherefore I desired them to be very diligent in [illegible] a list of the whole faction. [illegible] the names of the most considerable of John's party, I [illegible] liberty [illegible] to all that would come in [illegible] twenty days, [illegible] their [illegible] duty, but [illegible] those who [illegible] beyond that [illegible] the sword, and pillage

This being an invitation as well as a menace, wrought [illegible] effectually on the associates of John, that four thousand of them threw down their arms, and came over to me. [illegible] his fellow-citizens of Gischala staid behind, [illegible] one thousand five hundred Tyrian mercenaries. [illegible] effort so effectually affected the measures of John, [illegible] through fear, he confined himself within the limits of his own country.

About this time the people of Sepphoris, confiding in the strength of the place, and seeing me engaged in other [illegible] grew insolent, and took up arms. They sent to [illegible] who was then governor of Syria, desiring he would come in person and receive the obedience of their city, [illegible] send thither a garrison of soldiers. [illegible] to come, but gave no intimation of the time [illegible] of what had passed between them, I marched [illegible] the place attacked and carried it [illegible]. The Galileans [illegible] us of improving this advantage, [illegible] their revenge on the Sepphorites, [illegible] the town, with a resolution of destroying [illegible] city. The people had quitted their habitations, and retired into the castle for protection, while the soldiers [illegible] houses, and committed depredations without bounds. I was much concerned at these violences, and commanded the soldiers to desist from such unnatural proceedings against [illegible] their own tribe and profession. When I found that neither entreaties or commands had any effect upon them, I ordered some of my trusty friends to divulge a report, that the Romans, with a great body of forces, had attacked the other part of the city. This I did with no other design than that the report spreading abroad, the fury of the Galileans might be restrained, and Sepphoris preserved from ruin. At length the stratagem had its effect; for, upon hearing this report, they were apprehensive for themselves, ceased from plundering, and betook themselves to flight, especially when they saw [illegible] general do the same; for, in order to gain more credit to the report, I pretended to be terrified in like manner, with the danger that threatened. Thus the Sepphorites, by this artifice preserved their lives and effects.

Tiberias was upon the point of being plundered by the Galileans on the following occasion. The principal men of their senate wrote to the king, desiring he would come to them, and take possession of their city. The king promised to come, and wrote a letter in answer to theirs, which he gave to one of his attendants named Crispus, by birth a Jew, to carry it to Tiberias. Some of the Galileans happening to meet with Crispus as he was bringing the letter, apprehended and brought him to me. When this came to the ears of the people they were enraged, and immediately betook themselves to arms. Many of them assembling the next day, came to the city of Asochis, where I then resided, and, with loud exclamations, called the Tiberians traitors, and of the king's faction, and desired leave of me to go down and utterly destroy their city; for they were as averse to the Tiberians as the Sepphorites.

When I heard of this proceeding, I was doubtful in what manner to preserve the city from the enraged Galileans; for there was no denying or palliating the charge brought against the inhabitants of surrendering up their city, the letter the king had written back being too convincing a proof of it. Weighing the affair, therefore, some time in my mind, I reasoned the case with them in the following manner, by way of answer: "That the Tiberians were highly culpable, nor would I be any obstacle to the sacking of their city; 'nevertheless nothing of that kind should be put in execution without previous advice, and mature consideration; for that upon further scrutiny, a faction might be found among the noble Galileans as deep in this plot upon their liberties as the Tiberians themselves. That, therefore, I recommended patience, till better information could be procured of the authors of the defection and treachery, and then that every one should be surrendered up and brought to condign punishment." By these means I pacified [illegible] [illegible] they quietly dispersed.

Having ordered the man sent by the king to be put in [illegible] I pretended I was obliged to leave the [illegible] for a few days to attend [illegible] [illegible] privately to Crispus, I engaged to him to [illegible] [illegible] and then make his escape to the king. [illegible] [illegible] he left [illegible] [illegible] from the danger which threatened [illegible]

While affairs were in this situation, Justus the son of [illegible] without [illegible] over to the king, and [illegible] [illegible] the Romans, [illegible] perseverance in their obedience to the king, and in [illegible] [illegible] the Romans. [illegible] notwithstanding [illegible] [illegible] to suffer them to [illegible] [illegible] [illegible] for a change, [illegible] [illegible] [illegible] king [illegible] [illegible] country.

[illegible] for the Galileans, who [illegible] the Tiberians, from [illegible] [illegible] could not [illegible] [illegible] I myself also, [illegible] of Galilee from the hands [illegible] [illegible] situated by [illegible] [illegible] have been ready to put him to death [illegible] [illegible] [illegible] to the king, [illegible]

The Sepphorites [illegible] escaped [illegible] from their [illegible] sent to Cestius Gallus, [illegible] immediately [illegible] possession of their city [illegible] them [illegible] a force [illegible] At length they prevailed [illegible] supply of cavalry and infantry, which they received into [illegible] The bordering country being exposed to [illegible] of the [illegible] soldiers, after I had [illegible] I went to Garisme, where I encamped about twenty furlongs from Sepphoris, and in the night [illegible] with my arms to [illegible] [illegible] the [illegible], and then ordering a [illegible] men to ascend the walls with their scaling ladders, I made myself master of the greatest part of the city; [illegible] being unacquainted with [illegible] [illegible] to retire, having lain twelve foot soldiers and two horsemen belonging to the Romans, [illegible] after [illegible] Roman horse, [illegible] which having [illegible] long time [illegible] victory [illegible] [illegible] surrounded by the enemy, [illegible] [illegible] [illegible] upon me, [illegible] enough [illegible] this action lost Justus, one of [illegible] [illegible] in the service of the king.

About this time a great body of horse and foot forces sent by the king under the command of Sylla, captain of the royal guards, who encamped about five furlongs from Julias, and planted his scouts along the roads which led to Cana and the castle of Gamala, to cut off [illegible] other.

As soon as I came to learn this, I sent two thousand [illegible] men under the command of Jeremias. Both armies [illegible] about a furlong from Julias, [illegible] [illegible] but slight skirmishes till I had an opportunity to come up with three thousand more of [illegible] [illegible] The day following, after placing a strong ambush in a bottom, [illegible] distance from the enemy, I ordered the king's troops to battle, with orders to [illegible] [illegible] on the first charge, [illegible] [illegible] the enemy, [illegible] they had drawn them within the reach of the ambuscade.

This stratagem was crowned with the desired success, [illegible] to have been a [illegible]

[illegible] ed them. [illegible] when I had [illegible], [illegible] fell upon them, [illegible] When I saw this, I [illegible] my [illegible] and the royal army, and [illegible] to fight [illegible] certainly become [illegible] me that [illegible] I not [illegible] accident prevented it [illegible] place, the fall [illegible] of my joint, so [illegible] I was obliged to be carried off to Cepharnome, [illegible] my [illegible] that [illegible] had [illegible] me [illegible] the [illegible] ha [illegible] to [illegible] there but [illegible] con- [illegible] that night.

[illegible] and [illegible] the news of [illegible] this [illegible] accepted, the challenge [illegible] with [illegible] through [illegible] ed.

[illegible] Vespasian [illegible] Titus [illegible] him [illegible] the Tyrians [illegible] Tyrians [illegible] and the Roman [illegible] Vespasian [illegible] to the [illegible] to Rome to [illegible] ed [illegible] this [illegible] and [illegible]

[illegible] Jews [illegible] Vespasian, [illegible] government, [illegible] came into Galilee [illegible] and the [illegible] of his [illegible] I had [illegible] the Jewish war, [illegible] I had been [illegible] the [illegible] remains [illegible] that [illegible] the [illegible] Vespasian to [illegible] with the [illegible] of [illegible] frequently exposed to danger, for the Jews were [illegible] from [illegible] he [illegible] and [illegible] to [illegible] with the [illegible] and return- [illegible] soldiers

When [illegible] on the point of being [illegible] peace, [illegible] out [illegible] and [illegible] brother, [illegible] of my [illegible] which I [illegible] to go [illegible] concerned to [illegible] and, without [illegible] for [illegible] and [illegible] them [illegible]

[illegible] the [illegible] and [illegible] of the place [illegible] there [illegible] and at any other [illegible] of long [illegible] I went to [illegible] because [illegible] them taken down, [illegible] Two of them died [illegible] the third [illegible]

When [illegible] to the [illegible] made me a [illegible] my [illegible] troops, that were [illegible] to the metropolis for the [illegible]

[illegible] me the honour, upon [illegible] Rome, [illegible] the palace [illegible] He favoured [illegible] gave me an [illegible] hatred of my [illegible] a [illegible] of the [illegible] by the governor [illegible] province, he was sent to [illegible] emperor, before whom he aver- [illegible] that I had [illegible] Vespasian not [illegible] brought [illegible] but through Divine Providence, I got [illegible] and had a [illegible] through the bounty of Vespasian.

About this time [illegible] wife, [illegible] of her conduct, having had [illegible] by her [illegible] the [illegible] living. After [illegible] took another [illegible] by birth a [illegible] of noble [illegible] the eldest, Simonides, the younger, who was [illegible] Agrippa. [illegible] circumstances of my family.

I [illegible] as to [illegible] the [illegible] of Vespasian, Titus treated me [illegible] honourable respect as his father had [illegible] Domitian [illegible] who succeeded Titus, [illegible] the highest [illegible] of [illegible] to be [illegible] punish- ed [illegible] testimony [illegible] been [illegible] less [illegible] Titus [illegible] of my life, [illegible]

THE

TESTIMONIES

OF

FLAVIUS JOSEPHUS,

CONCERNING

Our Blessed Saviour JESUS CHRIST, JOHN the BAPTIST, &c.

CLEARLY VINDICATED,

FROM THE

Concurrent Authorities of Ecclesiastical and other writers of Authenticity, such as Historians, Biographers, the Ancient Fathers of the Church &c

AS we meet with many important testimonies in Josephus, the Jewish historian, concerning John the Baptist, the harbinger or forerunner of Jesus of Nazareth, concerning Jesus of Nazareth himself, and also James the Just, the brother of Jesus of Nazareth, and since the principal testimony has been questioned by many, and rejected by some as spurious, I hold it my duty, having ever declared my firm belief that these testimonies are genuine, to produce original evidences, in order to confirm them, and then make proper observations for the more compleat satisfaction of the reader Before I enter upon my main design, it may not be impertinent, by way of preparatory, to quote the opinion of perhaps, the most learned person, and competent judge, that ever was, as to the authority of Josephus, I mean Joseph Scaliger, from whose works, in Latin, the following is a translation.

" Josephus is the most diligent, and the greatest lover of " truth, of all writers. We can confidently affirm of him, " that it is more safe to believe him, not only as to the affairs " of the Jews, but also as to those that are foreign to them, ' than all the Greek and Latin writers, and this because " his fidelity, and his compass of learning, are every where " most conspicuous

TACITUS

TACITUS writes, in his annals, that ' Nero, in order ' to stifle the rumour, (though he himself set Rome on " fire,) ascribed it to those people who were hated for their " strange practices, and called, by the vulgar, Christians " These he punished exquisitely The author of this name " was Christ, who, in the reign of Tiberius, was put to death " by Pontius Pilate the procurator "

Since Josephus gives us his testimony, and since almost all the rest that is true of the Jews in Tacitus, was directly taken by him out of Josephus, there can remain no reason to doubt but this passage was taken from him also. He could not have this account from that other Jewish historian, Justus, of Tiberias, for Photius, who perused his history, assures us, that Justus made no mention at all of Jesus Christ The true writing of these names, Christ and Christians, as in Josephus, is another argument that Tacitus had this account from him, which names he would otherwise most probably, with Suetonius, and other old Romans, have written Chrest and Chrestians. The words of Tacitus are all so very like those of Josephus, that it is most reasonable to conclude they were taken from him, and no other author.

JUSTIN MARTYR

YOU (Jews) knew that Jesus was risen from the dead, and ascended into heaven, as the prophecies did foretel was to happen

ORIGEN

THIS James was so shining a character among the people, on account of his righteousness, that [illegible] Josephus, when, in his twenty books of the Jewish Antiquities, he describes the cause why the people suffered such miseries till the sacred temple was demolished, says, that these things befel them through the Divine anger, for what they had dared to do with James, the brother of Jesus, who was called Christ He says further, that the people thought they suffered these things for the sake of James

Josephus testifies, in the 18th book of his Jewish Antiquities, that John was the Baptist, and that he promised purification to those that were baptized The same Josephus also, when enquiring into the cause of the destruction of Jerusalem, and [illegible] of the temple ought to

6 C

[illegible]

[illegible] When I [illegible] [illegible] Lord. [illegible]

[illegible] a [illegible] accident [illegible]

[illegible]

[illegible] [illegible] said me the [illegible] [illegible]

[illegible] He [illegible]

[illegible] in Cyrene, [illegible] the [illegible] of the [illegible] of the [illegible] by the governor [illegible] he was [illegible] before whom [illegible] that I had [illegible] him to [illegible] accusations brought against me [illegible] that [illegible] me [illegible] Vespasian.

About this time [illegible] my wife, [illegible] of her conduct, having [illegible] three children, [illegible] Hyrcanus [illegible] by birth a Jewess, [illegible] Simonides, [illegible] who was [illegible] named Agrippa. These [illegible] of my family.

[illegible] to be [illegible] favour [illegible] of Vespasian, [illegible] respect [illegible] Domitian, [illegible] Titus, [illegible] of my Jewish [illegible] accusers, [illegible] favour of mine, to be [illegible] punished [illegible] has been [illegible] [illegible]

[illegible]

AMBROSE, OR HEG[illegible]

[illegible]

[illegible] Jews [illegible] to Christ, [illegible] from Josephus, [illegible] "That [illegible] lawful to call him a man, [illegible] appeared to [illegible] the earth, alive again, according [illegible] prophets, who foretold these and [illegible] concerning him. [illegible] the denomination of Christians [illegible]. Nor does [illegible] in the Roman [illegible]. If the Jews [illegible] believe [illegible] Josephus, whom they esteem a very [illegible] man, [illegible] he hath [illegible] such [illegible] that is historical [illegible] though he [illegible] which neither confirms [illegible] invalidates his [illegible]

RUFINUS

NOW there was at that time Jesus a wise man, if [illegible] be lawful to call him a man, for he was a doer of wonderful works, a teacher of such things to [illegible] were willing to hear the truth. He [illegible] many of the Jews, and many of the Gentiles. He was Christ. And when Pilate, [illegible] principal men of [illegible] those that had loved him from the beginning did not forsake him, [illegible] he appeared to them [illegible] third day, according [illegible] prophets had foretold [illegible] miracles [illegible] than the name [illegible] of Christians [illegible] continues [illegible]

HIERONYMUS

JOSEPHUS [illegible] Antiquities, [illegible] Christ was slain by the Pharisees on account of [illegible] and John [illegible] was truly a prophet [illegible] Hebrew [illegible] "At the same time there was Jesus a wise man, if yet it be lawful to call him a man. He was a doer of wonderful works, a teacher of those who [illegible] the truth. He had many followers, [illegible] the Jews and Gentiles. He was believed to be Christ, [illegible] though the envy of our principal men [illegible] he had condemned him to the cross, notwithstanding [illegible] those who had loved him at first persevered [illegible] appeared to them alive [illegible] the prophets had [illegible] concerning him. And the sect of Christians [illegible] from him, [illegible]

ISIDORUS PELUSIOTA

SCHOLAR OF CHRYSOSTOM.

THERE was one Josephus, a Jew of the greatest [illegible] for the Jews, [illegible] would not suppose [illegible] necessary to set down his words. What then does he say? [illegible] at that time Jesus, a wise man, if it be lawful to call him a man, for he was a doer of wonderful works, a teacher of [illegible] the truth [illegible] many of the Jews, and many of the Gentiles. He was the Christ. And [illegible] of the principal men [illegible] him to the cross, [illegible]

[illegible] that [illegible] not forsake [illegible] alive [illegible] prophets [illegible] concerning [illegible] of Christians, [illegible] from him, [illegible] [illegible] which he [illegible] a testimony [illegible] ceived [illegible] same."

SOZOMENUS

N[illegible] the son of Matthias, a priest [illegible] [illegible] Jews [illegible] Romans [illegible] of Christ's [illegible] [illegible]

CASSIODORUS

NOW [illegible] the son of Matthias, a priest [illegible] Christ [illegible] was condemned to the cross [illegible] alive, [illegible] things [illegible] ever, [illegible] them [illegible] Greeks and [illegible] they continued to love him, [illegible] named from him was [illegible]

EPIPHANIUS SCHOLASTICUS

OF JOHN THE BAPTIST.

IT was the opinion of some of [illegible] Jews [illegible] John [illegible] good man, and [illegible] Jews to [illegible] [illegible] by [illegible] [illegible] and [illegible] Herod [illegible] to obey [illegible] precepts [illegible] [illegible] John [illegible] Jews [illegible] of opinion that God [illegible]

EPIPHANIUS

OF OUR LORD JESUS CHRIST

NOW there was at this time Jesus, a wise man, if at least it be lawful to call him a man, for he was a doer of wonderful works, a teacher of such men as willingly heard the truth. He also drew over to him many of the Jews, and many of the Gentiles. He was Christ. And when Pilate, at the accusation of the principal men of our nation, had decreed that he should be crucified, those that loved him from the beginning did not forsake him; for he appeared to them the third day alive again, according to what the divinely inspired prophets had foretold, that those and innumerable other miracles should come to pass about him. Moreover, both the name and sect of Christians, who were denominated from him, continue in being to this day.

EPIPHANIUS

OF JAMES, THE BROTHER OF OUR LORD

ANANUS, the high-priest, believing that he had found out a proper time to exercise his authority, Festus, the procurator, being dead, and Albinus only upon the road, appointed a council of judges, and bringing several before him, among whom was the brother of Jesus, who is called Christ, whose name was James, he accused them of acting against the law, and delivered them up to be stoned. But those of the citizens that seemed the most moderate, and were concerned to have the law exactly observed, were greatly offended, and sent to the king (Agrippa) entreating him that he would write to Ananus, that he would desist from such actions as were not well done, &c.

ANASTASIAS ABBAS.

NOW Josephus, a Jewish author, says of Christ, that he was a just and good man shewn and declared so to be by Divine Grace, who gave aid to many by signs and miracles.

FRECULPHUS.

JOSEPHUS, in the 18th book of his Antiquities, most expressly acknowledges that Christ was slain by the Pharisees, on account of the greatness of his miracles; that John the Baptist was truly a prophet; and that Jerusalem was demolished on account of the slaughter of James the Apostle. Nay, he wrote concerning our Lord after this manner: "At that time there was Jesus, a wise man, if it be reasonable to call him a man, for he was a doer of wonderful works, and a teacher of those who willingly receive the truth. He had many followers, both of the Jews and Gentiles. He was also believed to be Christ. And when, through the envy of our principal men, Pilate, had condemned him to the cross, those who loved him at first persevered. Now he appeared to them on the third day alive, as the oracles of the prophets had foretold many of these and other wonderful things concerning him. And the sect of the Christians, so named from him, are not extinct at this day."

JOHANNES MALELA

FROM that time began the destruction of the Jews, as Josephus, the philosopher of the Hebrews, hath written, who also said this, "that, from the time the Jews crucified Christ who was a good and righteous man, (that is, if it be fit to call such a one a man, and not a God,) the land of Judæa was never free from trouble." These things the same Josephus, the Jew, hath related in his writings.

PHOTICUS

I HAVE read the treatise of Josephus about the universe, the title of which I have elsewhere read to be, of the substance of the universe. It is contained in two very small treatises. He treats of the origin of the world in a brief manner. He speaks, however, of the divinity of Christ in a way much resembling ours, declaring that the same name of Christs belongs to him, and writes concerning him, in general, in a manner that cannot be justly censured. The phraseology of this treatise does not at all differ from his other works. Besides others have written on the same subject.

Herod, the Tetrarch of Galilee, and of Peræa, the son of Herod the Great, fell in love, as Josephus says, with the wife of his brother Herod, whose name was Herodias, the grand-daughter of Herod the Great, by his son Aristobulus, whom he had slain. Agrippa was also her brother. Now Herod took her away from her husband, and married her. This is he that slew John the Baptist, that great man, the forerunner of Christ, being afraid (as Josephus says,) lest he should raise a sedition among his people; for they all followed the directions of John, on account of the excellency of his virtue.

MACARIUS

JOSEPHUS, a priest of Jerusalem, and one that wrote with truth the history of the Jewish affairs, bears witness that Christ was incarnate and crucified, and the third day arose again, whose writings are deposited in the public library. Since, therefore, the writer of the Hebrews hath given this testimony concerning Our Lord and Saviour in his own books, what defence can there remain to unbelievers.

SUIDAS

WE have found Josephus, who hath written about the taking of Jerusalem, (of whom Eusebius makes frequent mention in his Ecclesiastical History) saying openly, in his memoirs of the captivity, that Jesus officiated in the temple with the priests. This we have found Josephus saying, a man of ancient times, and not very long after the apostles, &c.

SOPHRONIUS

JOSEPHUS, the Jew, that lover of truth, speaks of the forerunner of Christ, and of our Lord and Saviour Jesus Christ. In the 18th book of his Antiquities, he openly acknowledges, that Christ was slain by the Jews on account of the greatness of his miracles, and that John the Baptist was truly a prophet, and that Jerusalem was demolished on account of the slaughter of James the apostle.

CEDRENUS

JOSEPHUS does, indeed, write concerning John the Baptist as follows: "Some of the Jews thought that the destruction of Herod's army came from God, and that he was punished very justly for the punishment he had inflicted on John, that was called the Baptist; for Herod slew him that was a good man, and exhorted the Jews to exercise virtue both by righteousness towards one another, and piety towards God, and so to come to baptism." But as concerning Christ the same Josephus says, "That about that time, there was Jesus, a wise man, if it be lawful to call him a man, for he was a doer of wonderful works, and a teacher of such men as receive the truth with pleasure; for that Christ drew over many even from the Gentiles, whom when Pilate had crucified, those who at first loved him, did not leave off to preach concerning him. For he appeared to them the third day al-

again, as the Divine prophets had foretold and spoken these and other wonderful things concerning him.

We will produce Josephus himself for a witness, who was one of the sect of the Jews. Consider the love of truth that was in this man, who although he were a Jew, yet he did not permit himself to follow the Jewish evasions and falsehoods.

THEOPHYLACIUS

THE city of the Jews was taken, and the wrath of God was kindled against them, as also Josephus witnesses that this came upon them on account of the death of James.

ALEXANDRIAN CHRONICLE.

JOSEPHUS relates, in the 18th book of his Antiquities, that John the Baptist, that holy man, was beheaded at the instigation of Herodias, the wife of Philip. For Herod had divorced his former wife, who was still alive, and had been his lawful wife. She was the daughter of Aretas, king of Arabia Petrea. When, therefore, Herod had taken Herodias away from her husband, while he was yet alive, (on whose account he slew John,) Aretas made war against him because his daughter had been dishonourably treated. In this war, he says, that all Herod's army was destroyed, and that he suffered that calamity because of the wickedness he had been guilty of against John. The same Josephus relates, that Herod lost his kingdom on account of Herodias, and that with her he was banished, &c.

Now that Our Saviour taught and preached three years is demonstrated both by other authentic writings, as also out of the Holy Gospels and out of the writings of Josephus, who was a wise man among the Hebrews, &c.

Josephus, in the 18th book of the Jewish Antiquities, writes that, when Annas, there were three high-priests, Ismael the son of Baphi, and Eleazar, the son of Ananus, and Simon, the son of Camithus, &c.

Josephus also relates, in the 7th book of the Jewish War, that Jerusalem was taken in the second year of Vespasian, and many years after they had dared to put Jesus to death; in which time he says, that James, the brother of Our Lord, and bishop of Jerusalem, was thrown down from the temple, and slain by stoning.

ZONARAS

THERE also you have an abridgment of what Josephus wrote concerning Our Saviour Jesus Christ and John the Baptist.

Josephus wrote thus concerning this John, that Herod slew him that was a good man, and exhorted the Jews to exercise virtue, both as to righteousness towards one another, and piety towards God, and so to come to baptism, for by that means the washing with water would be acceptable to him. Now Herod, who feared lest the great influence John had over the people might put it in his power to raise a rebellion (for they seemed ready to do any thing he should advise,) thought it best, by putting him to death, to prevent any mischief he might cause, and not to bring himself into difficulties by sparing a man who might make him repent of it when it should be too late. Accordingly, he was sent a prisoner, out of Herod's suspicion, to Macherus, and there put to death. Now the Jews had an opinion that the destruction of the army was sent as a punishment upon Herod, and a mark of God's displeasure to him.

About this time also did Our Lord Jesus Christ appear in Judæa, concerning whom Josephus, in the 18th book of his Antiquities, says thus: "Now there was about this time a wise man, if it be lawful to call him a man, for he was a doer of wonderful works, a teacher of such men as receive the truth with pleasure. He drew over to him many of the Jews and many of the Gentiles. He was the Christ. And when Pilate, at the suggestion of the principal men among us, had condemned him to the cross, those that loved him at first did not forsake him, for he appeared to them the third day alive again, as the Divine prophets had said these and many other wonderful things concerning him. And the tribe of Christians so named from him, are not extinct at this day." These things Josephus wrote in his Antiquities concerning Christ.

Johannes Sarisburiensis, Petrus Comestor, Gertrudus Viterbiensis, and Vincentius Bellovacensis, all add their testimonies concerning Josephus in words to the same effect.

GLYCAS

THEN did Philo and Josephus flourish. The last was stiled the lover of truth, because he commended John, who baptized our Lord, and because he bore witness that Christ, in like manner, was a wise man, and the doer of great miracles, and that after he was crucified he appeared the third day.

NICEPHORUS CALLISTUS

NOW this (concerning Herod the Tetrarch) is attested to, not only by the book of the Holy Gospels, but by Josephus that lover of truth, who also makes mention of Herodias his brother's wife, whom Herod had taken from him, while he was alive, and married, having divorced his former lawful wife, who was the daughter of Aretas, king of Arabia Petrea. On whose account, also when he had slain John the Baptist, Aretas made war upon him, because his daughter had been dishonourably used. In which war he relates, that all Herod's army was destroyed, and that he suffered this on account of the most unjust slaughter of John. He also adds, that John was a most righteous man. Moreover, he makes mention of his baptism, agreeing in all points thereto relating to the gospel. He also informs us, that Herod lost his kingdom on account of Herodias, with whom also he was condemned to be banished to Vienna, which was then place of exile, a city bordering upon Gaul, and lying near the utmost bounds of the west. However, in the 18th book of his Antiquities, he says this farther concerning John. "Some of the Jews thought the destruction of Herod's army came from God, and that very justly, as a punishment for what he did against John, that was called the Baptist. For Herod slew him who was a good man, and one that exhorted the Jews to exercise virtue, and piety towards God, and so to come to baptism, as by that means the washing with water would appear acceptable to him, when they used it not for the putting away of some sins only, but for the purification of the body, supposing still that the soul be thoroughly purified before-hand by righteousness. Now when many others came in crowds about him (for they were greatly moved by hearing his words,) Herod was afraid that his great power of persuasion might tend to sedition, for they seemed disposed to do every thing he should advise them to. He supposed it better to prevent any attempt at innovation from him by cutting him off, than that such change should be brought about, and the public suffered to repent of that negligence. Accordingly he was sent a prisoner, out of Herod's suspicious temper, to the castle of Macherus, and there slain." This is also the account of Josephus.

This writer concurs with the foregoing in his testimony of Josephus concerning Our Saviour Jesus Christ.

HARDMANNUS SCHEDELIUS

JOSEPHUS, the Jew, who was called Flavius, a priest, and the son of Matthias a priest of that nation, a most celebrated historian, and very skilful in many things, was certainly a good man of excellent character, and one who had the highest opinion of Christ.

PLATINA

I SHALL avoid mentioning what Christ did, till the thirtieth year of his age, when he was baptized by John, the son of Zacharias, because not only the Gospels and Epistles are full of those acts which he performed in the most excellent manner, but such books as are quite remote from his way of living and acting. Thus Josephus himself, who wrote twenty books of Jewish Antiquities in the Greek language, when he had proceeded as far as the emperor Tiberius, says, "There was in those days, Jesus, a certain wise man, if at least it be lawful to call him a man, for he was a doer of wonderful works and a teacher of men, especially of such as willingly hear the truth. On this account he drew over to him many, both of the Jews and Gentiles. He was Christ. But when Pilate, instigated by the principal men of our nation, had decreed that he should be crucified, yet did not those that loved him from the beginning forsake him. Besides, he appeared to them, the third day after his death, alive, as the divinely inspired prophets had foretold, that these and many other miracles should come to pass about him. And the famous name of Christians taken from him, as well as their sect, do still continue in being."

The same Josephus also affirms, that John the Baptist was a true prophet, and on that account esteemed by men in general, that he was slain by Herod, the son of Herod the Great, a little before the death of Christ, in the castle of Machærus, and that this cruel order was given by Herod at the instigation of Herodias, the sister of Agrippa, and the wife of his brother Philip, whom he had incestuously married.

TRITHEMIUS, THE ABBOT

JOSEPHUS, the Jew, although he continued to be a Jew, did frequently commend the Christians, and, in the 18th book of his Antiquities, wrote down an eminent testimony concerning our Lord Jesus Christ.

Whether Trithemius found more passages concerning the Christians in his copies of the genuine works of Josephus now or formerly extant, or ascribed the book concerning the universe to him, and therein met with other commendations of the Christians that were in his genuine works, cannot now be determined. So far, however, is plain, that this very learned Abbot who affirms that Josephus frequently commended the Christians, had more testimonies, in the works he believed to be Josephus's, to this purpose, than we are at present acquainted with. Which seems to have been the case with Origen, Eusebius, the author of the Alexandrian Chronicle, Suidas, and Theophylactus, as appears in our quotations out of them.

More quotations from the most respectable writers might be adduced, such as the Latin Version from Hanno, Anonymus Bambergensis, Conradus Urspergensis, Albertus Stadensis, &c. &c. mentioned by Fabricius, all which authors cite the same testimony concerning Christ; but as we presume those already quoted are sufficient to satisfy the candid and impartial reader, we pass them over to obviate a tedious prolixity.

OBSERVATIONS

FROM THE

FOREGOING EVIDENCES

AND

CITATIONS.

I.

THE style of all these original testimonies belonging to Josephus is exactly the style of the same Josephus, and especially his style about those parts of his Antiquities wherein we find these testimonies. His testimonies concerning John the Baptist and James the Just, have been rendered equally undeniable as that concerning Christ.

II.

THE clauses in *Josephus concerning John the Baptist and James the Just*, especially those in all our present copies as well as those cited from their copies by the ancients, are plainly and undeniably genuine. One writer seems desirous of setting aside that concerning John the Baptist, though expressly quoted by Origen himself out of Josephus; but since he hardly produces any thing like an argument to support his pretence, I shall take no farther notice of it.

III.

THESE testimonies therefore, being confessedly and undeniably written by Josephus himself, it is next to impossible that he should wholly omit some testimony concerning Jesus Christ. Nay, while his testimonies of John the Baptist, and of James the Just, are so honourable, and give them such respectable characters, his testimony of Christ can be no other than very honourable, or such as is afforded him a still greater character. Could the very same author, who gave so full and advantageous a character of John the Baptist the forerunner of Jesus of Nazareth, (all whose disciples were by him directed to that Jesus of Nazareth as to the true Messiah, and all whose disciples became afterwards his disciples,) omit to speak honourably of that Jesus of Nazareth himself? and this in the history of those very times in which he was born, lived, and died? This is almost incredible.

Further, could the very same author, who gave so advantageous a character of James the Just, and this under the very appellation of James, the brother of Jesus, who was called Christ, which James was one of the principal disciples, or apostles, of this Jesus Christ, and had been many years the only Christian bishop of the believing Jews of Judæa and Jerusalem, in the very days, and in the very country of this writer, could he, I say, wholly omit, nay could he withhold, a very honourable account of Jesus Christ himself, whose disciple and bishop this James most undoubtedly was? This is almost incredible.

IV.

THE famous clause in this testimony of Josephus concerning Christ, "This was Christ, or the Christ," clearly points out that this Jesus was distinguished from all others of that name, of which there were not a few, as mentioned by Josephus himself, by the addition of the other name of Christ, or that this person was no other than he whom all the world knew by the name of Jesus Christ, and his followers by the name of Christians.

V.

THOUGH Josephus did not design here to declare himself openly a Christian, yet he could not possibly believe all that he asserts concerning Jesus Christ, unless he were so far a Christian as the Jewish Nazarenes, or Ebionites, then were, who believed Jesus of Nazareth to be the true Messiah, without believing that he was more than a man; who also believed the necessity of the observation of the ceremonial law of Moses, in order to salvation for all mankind, which were the two main points of those Jewish Christians faith, though in opposition to all the apostles of Jesus Christ in the first century, and in opposition to the whole Catholic Church of Christ in the following centuries. It seems then to appear that Josephus was, in his own mind and conscience, only a Nazarene, or Ebionite Jewish Christian, and it is observable, that his entire testimony, as well that he gives of John the Baptist and of James, as well as this his absolute [illegible] above all the rest of the apostles, exactly agrees with him under this character, and no other. We all know that the many thousands of Jews who believed in Christ (Acts xxi. 20) [illegible], were all zealous of the ceremonial law, and by consequence, if there were any reason to think our Josephus to be [illegible] this sense, a believer or Christian, [illegible] testimonies there are very great ones, [illegible] [illegible], could not but conspire to [illegible] he was no other than a Nazarene, or Ebionite Christian.

VI.

[illegible] Josephus appears to have been, [illegible] no other than a Nazarene, or Ebionite Christian, and in consequence with them rejected [illegible] Greek gospels, the Greek books of the New Testament, and received only the Hebrew gospel of the Nazarenes, or Ebionites, we ought also to have that Nazarene or Ebionite gospel, [illegible] Nazarene or Ebionite fragments [illegible], when we consider [illegible] passages of Josephus [illegible] Christ or to Christians. Thus, since that gospel [illegible] in the beginning of our St Matthew's and St Luke's gospels, and began with the ministry of John the Baptist, in which first parts of the gospel history are the accounts of the [illegible] of the infant, and of the [illegible] under Augustus Cæsar and Herod, it is no [illegible] wonder that Josephus has not taken one particular [illegible] to [illegible] those stories.

[illegible] Josephus calls James the brother of [illegible] James the Just, and [illegible] a righteous man in [illegible], that such is his name and character in the gospel according to the Hebrews, and the other Ebionite [illegible] of Hegesippus, but no where else.

[illegible] prophecy [illegible] referred to [illegible] [illegible] which was [illegible], [illegible] (Thuc [illegible]) before he converted Christianity, professed himself to have been [illegible]. Thus when Josephus [illegible] Jews [illegible] the [illegible] that nation [illegible], with the destruction of Jerusalem, to the barbarous murder of James the Just, we must [illegible] from the Ebionite fragments of Hegesippus, [illegible] those Ebionites [illegible] a prophecy of [illegible] this very murder, and the consequent [illegible] [illegible] the just one, for he is unprofitable to us, therefore shall they eat the fruit of their own ways."

[illegible] as we have seen, but the most [illegible] of Jerusalem, and those that were not [illegible] condemnation [illegible] of his [illegible], Caiaphas, [illegible] high-priest, [illegible] Sanhedrim, and declares that he himself [illegible] Jews who thought the following calamities of that nation effects of the Divine vengeance for the [illegible] of this [illegible], we may [illegible] these opinions [illegible] converted Jews or Ebionites. The high-priest and Sanhedrim, who [illegible] the Christians and the body of those unbelieving Jews who are supposed to [illegible] for murdering this James, could not [illegible] that opinion. This lastly, when Josephus is [illegible], [illegible] that [illegible] with the [illegible], this account [illegible] means disagreeable to the [illegible] of the Ebionites, Hegesippus, the Ebionite, affirming the very same thing of James the Just.

I have already made some observations on the famous testimony concerning our Saviour in Josephus from [illegible]. The next [illegible] I have alledged [illegible] Justin Martyr, one [illegible] with Josephus, that he might be born about the time [illegible] his Antiquities. Justin [illegible] to the same Antiquities by that very name, and though he does not here directly quote them, yet does he seem to me to allude to [illegible] mon, [illegible] concerning our Saviour, when he [illegible] this place to Trypho, the Jew, that "his [illegible] [illegible] that Jesus was risen from the dead, and ascended [illegible] heaven, as the prophecies did foretel [illegible]." [illegible] indeed, does he seem to me to [illegible] any thing else [illegible] in his view, but those clauses of this very testimony, where Josephus says, that "Jesus appeared to his followers alive the third day after his crucifixion, as the Divine prophets had foretold these and other wonderful things concerning him." I must leave this [illegible] to the impartial reader's own consideration.

The next author I have quoted for Josephus's testimonies of John the Baptist, of Jesus of Nazareth, and of [illegible] Just, is Origen, who [illegible] allowed, on all hands, [illegible] have quoted him for his excellent character of John the Baptist, and of James the Just, but [illegible] about this testimony concerning Christ, [illegible] alledged as the principal argument against its being genuine, and particularly as to the clause "This was the Christ," and [illegible] as we have seen, because he twice assures us that [illegible], Josephus did not himself acknowledge Jesus for Christ. As to this latter clause I have to observe, that Josephus [illegible] not here, in writing to Greeks and Romans, mean any [illegible] thing by these words as Jews and Christians naturally understand by them. I have also to observe, that all the ancients allow still with Origen, that Josephus did not, in the Jewish and Christian sense, acknowledge Jesus for the true Messiah, or the true Christ of God, notwithstanding the [illegible] quotation of that clause in Josephus as genuine [illegible], unless we suppose Origen to have had a different [illegible] of these words from all the other ancients, we can [illegible] from this assertion, that he had not those words in his copy. However, it seems to me, that Origen affords us four several indications that the main parts, at least, of this testimony itself were in his copy.

1st. When Origen [illegible] the testimony of Josephus concerning James the Just, that he thought the miseries of the Jews were an instance of the Divine vengeance on the nation for putting James to death instead of Jesus, he [illegible] an expression no way necessary to his purpose, nor occasioned by any words of Josephus there, I mean that they had slain "That Christ which was foretold in the prophecies." Whence could that expression come into Origen's mind, when he was quoting a testimony from Josephus concerning the brother of Christ, from his remembrance of a clause in the testimony of the same Josephus concerning Christ himself, that "the prophets had foretold his death and resurrection, and many other wonderful things concerning him?"

2dly. Why was Origen so surprized at Josephus's ascribing the destruction of Jerusalem to the Jews murdering of James the Just, and not to their murdering of Jesus, as we have seen he was, if he had not known that Josephus had spoken of Jesus and his death before, and that he had a very good opinion of Jesus, which yet he could learn in no [illegible] so authentic as from this testimony? Nor do the words he uses, that Josephus was "remote from the truth," perhaps allude to any thing else but this very testimony before us.

3dly. How came Origen, upon a slight occasion, when he had just set down that testimony of Josephus concerning James the Just, the brother of Jesus, who was called Christ, to say that, "It may be questioned whether the Jews thought Jesus to be a man, or whether they did not suppose him to be a being of a diviner kind?" This appears to me, like those clauses of this testimony in Josephus that "Jesus was a wise man, if it be lawful to call him a man," that it is highly probable Origen thereby alluded to them. And this is the more to be depended on, because all the unbelieving Jews, and all the rest of the Nazarene Jews, esteemed Jesus, with one consent, as a [illegible] the son of Joseph and Mary; and it is not, I think, possible to [illegible] one Jew but Josephus, who [illegible] than human, or according to the [illegible] of [illegible] " [illegible] person." I take [illegible] very [illegible]-ble one, but submit it to the consideration of the judicious.

4. Why does Origen affirm [illegible], that "Josephus did not himself own in the Jewish and Christian sense that Jesus was Christ," notwithstanding his quotations out of him are eminent testimonies for John the Baptist, his forerunner, and for James the Just, his brother, and one of his principal disciples? There is no passage [illegible] likely to persuade Origen of this, as in the famous testimony before us; wherein as he and all the [illegible] understood it, he was called Christ, the common name whence the sect of Christians was derived, and where he all along speaks of those Christians, as a sect [illegible] author was a wonderful person, and his followers [illegible] lovers of him and of truth, yet as such a sect [illegible] joined himself to. Nor can I devise any other reason for this, and parallel language of Josephus elsewhere, when he speaks of James, as the brother not of Jesus who was Christ, but of Jesus who was *called* Christ, that could so [illegible] induce Origen and others to be of that opinion.

IX

As to that great critic Photius, in the ninth century, [illegible] is supposed not to have had this testimony in his copy of Josephus, or else to have esteemed it [illegible], because [illegible] extracts from the Antiquities of Josephus it is [illegible] mentioned, I cannot withhold surprize that a [illegible] had been cited out of the copies of Josephus all along [illegible] the days of Photius, as well as it has been all along [illegible] of them since his days, should be supposed not to be in his copy, because he [illegible] not [illegible] short and imperfect extracts, no way particular [illegible] to such matters. Those who [illegible] of Photius seem to have a [illegible] brevity of those extracts. They contain little or nothing, as he in effect professes at their entrance, but what concerns Antipater, Herod the Great, his [illegible] and [illegible], with their exploits, till the days of Agrippa the younger [illegible] Cumanus, governor of Judea, sixteen years after the [illegible] of our Saviour, [illegible] one word of Pilate, or what happened under his government, which yet was the only proper place in which this testimony could come to be mentioned. However, since Photius [illegible] therefore [illegible] taken, to suspect the treatise of the universe [illegible] to Josephus, because it speaks highly of the [illegible] of Christ [illegible] of [illegible] the time Josephus [illegible] could [illegible] than this testimony [illegible]. And [illegible] we have also seen, when he speaks of the [illegible] of Tiberius, [illegible] the [illegible] in taking no manner of notice of [illegible] the miracles of Jesus Christ, [illegible] of Josephus himself, [illegible] also that there was not the like occasion here [illegible], but Josephus has not wholly omitted [illegible] miracles, which yet he has [illegible] learned Photius [illegible] Sonatius is most [illegible] Photius [illegible] this testimony in his copy, but also [illegible] it [illegible] be genuine.

X

As to the [illegible] of Clement of Alexandria, who cites [illegible] but never [illegible] any of [illegible] testimonies now before us, it cannot be deemed [illegible] in him, since he [illegible] of Josephus [illegible] but [illegible] a report of [illegible] that the [illegible] Moses to the days of Josephus, so that his silence [illegible] be [illegible] against an hundred other remarkable passages in Josephus as against those before us.

XI

NOR does the [illegible] prove that [illegible] these testimonies, or [illegible] of his [illegible]. [illegible]

[illegible] prophecies [illegible]

[illegible]

[illegible] of ancient testimonies, [illegible] concerning Our Saviour Christ [illegible] of [illegible] the middle of the second century [illegible] probable [illegible] of O[illegible] about the middle of the third, [illegible] of [illegible] Eusebius in the former part of the fourth, [illegible] [illegible] made [illegible] of the Ecclesiastical history, [illegible] copy [illegible] of the [illegible] century.

[illegible]

[illegible] Christ [illegible] Jesus [illegible]

[illegible] Festus [illegible]

[illegible] learned [illegible] produced [illegible] Caesarius [illegible]

[illegible], and Albertus Stadensis, in the thirteenth century, which though not transcribed, are to be esteemed real confirmations of all the former allegations. This, as we have already proved, has been the case of this testimony, in all the past ages of Christianity, and in all the several countries of Europe, during the first [illegible] centuries of the [illegible].

There is also another argument in favour of the authenticity of this testimony, belonging to all the passages, which [illegible] Christians, that [illegible] I think [illegible] that [illegible] contempt all the unbelieving Jews [illegible] Josephus, the best historian, [illegible] nation ever produced [illegible] reason of this [illegible] genuine Greek Josephus [illegible] that the Hebrew Josephus [illegible] Josephus unless it were the [illegible] concerning Jesus [illegible] the unbelieving Jewish nation, as [illegible] by them? This must appear to the impartial world the principal cause of their rejecting this excellent author, nor can I devise any other probable cause for this rejection, which if [illegible] as the true reason, the authenticity of these testimonies, and especially of that concerning Jesus Christ, which of course also be [illegible] to be wholly genuine.

Nor are [illegible] destitute of evidence, that, when this testimony had been inserted in a manuscript of Josephus in Hebrew, [illegible] were in an Hebrew version of his Antiquities, [illegible] Hebrew edition, some Jews [illegible] Prolegomena, and Dr Cave's Historia Literaria, Vol II [illegible] of Josephus. This [illegible] concerning the first [illegible] began.

[illegible] printing began, [illegible] and in every [illegible] of Josephus, [illegible] Greek [illegible] century, and [illegible] century, [illegible] &c. &c. have been [illegible] every one of them [illegible] found [illegible] testimony, and almost every one to contain [illegible] place, under the government of Pilate, and [illegible] considerable [illegible]. Nor do we discover that any author from the days of Josephus to that of [illegible] that he knew of any copies in any language without it, nor give us the least reason to suppose they suspected it or else [illegible] it as any otherwise than an [illegible] truly certain and [illegible]. To this [illegible] added the high probability there is, from the [illegible] testimonies about John the Baptist and James the Just, that Josephus must have [illegible] some such testimony [illegible] Christ, and the very great probability there is [illegible] own private opinion was that of the Nazarene, or Ebionite Jewish Christian, with which character [illegible] agrees [illegible]. Since, therefore, this is no other than the true state of the case, I think every upright judge, who considers it, must declare, that this testimony is [illegible] evidently and undeniably genuine but, upon the whole, as fully so as any other clauses or sections in the works of Josephus now extant.

It will also here be [illegible] to vindicate Josephus in a point wherein some [illegible] have dealt very [illegible] with him, I mean when they accuse him as flattering Vespasian with [illegible] the Jews. We shall take the two passages upon which [illegible] is built in Josephus's own words. The former is in the 6th book of his History of the Jewish War, and runs thus "If these things are duly considered, it will be found that God [illegible] provide [illegible] many means did [illegible] to them before [illegible] their preservation, but that they [illegible] and their misfortunes [illegible] voluntary [illegible] Jews made the temple four-square, by the [illegible] of the tower of Antonia, while they had it written in their own oracles, that their city, and the sacred house, should be taken, when the temple should become four-square [illegible] what chiefly excited them to the war, was an ambiguous oracle, that a certain person would arise about that time out of their country, who should have dominion over the world. This they took to refer to themselves, and many of the wise men were deceived by that determination, while the oracle designed the dominion of Vespasian, who was proclaimed emperor when he was in Judæa."

The other passage is in Josephus's own speech to Vespasian, in the third book of the same history [illegible] "have now in hand Josephus [illegible] prisoner, [illegible] you [illegible] perhaps [illegible] no farther but I come to you as a messenger of greater things. Had it not [illegible] for his commission, I could not have been [illegible] contrary to the [illegible] of a Jewish general [illegible] the hands of an enemy. Wherefore [illegible] to be sent to Nero, when [illegible] so near the emperor that I can hardly distinguish [illegible] Vespasian [illegible] emperor, or Cæsar? Besides this [illegible] is to come [illegible] Keep me close [illegible] you please, provided [illegible] may be Vespasian's [illegible] who is not only my master, but in effect Lord of the Universe. This is what I have in charge to deliver, and whenever I shall be found to use the Divine authority to countenance a fraud, make an example of me."

Now in all this we have not one word of those predictions relating to the Messiah, which Josephus in his famous testimony concerning Christ, declares to be very numerous, but of one only concerning the taking of Jerusalem, and the holy house, when the temple should become four-square, and one only which foretold that about that time a very great potentate should arise out of Judæa. This last prediction the other wise men then interpreted [illegible] of Jewish extraction, but Josephus of Vespasian, who was first proclaimed emperor when he was in Judæa, without the least intimation that he thought him to be the Messiah of the Jews. All the Jews, with one consent, ever expected that their Messiah was not only to arise in Judæa, and that of Jewish parents in general, but to be of the seed of David, and of the town of Bethlehem where David was [illegible] to be a great prophet like Moses, and to come peculiarly for the salvation, and not the destruction of Israel, with many other characters entirely inconsistent with Vespasian. To what particular oracles or predictions Josephus referred is hard to determine, since he does not name them. I suppose, with Reland, that the first of them might be Dan. ix. 26, 27, as then read and interpreted by the Jews, as also that the second was no other than the famous prophecy of Balaam, that "a star should arise out of Jacob, and a sceptre out of Israel, &c. Num. xxiv. 17, 18, 19." Josephus every [illegible] looking on Balaam as a true prophet.

It will also be necessary here to vindicate the [illegible] Josephus from another imputation, which hath been laid upon him, viz. that when in his second book against Apion, he makes a comparison between Moses, the Jewish legislator and Minos, with other old Heathen legislators, he insinuates "that though Moses artfully pretended to a Divine revelation for the laws he gave the Israelites, as did the others as to their own laws, yet that this was only in the way of a pious fraud, and that he did [illegible] himself believe that any such Divine revelation was made to him."

This is I suppose a new hypothesis, that our Josephus, after all his zeal for Moses, and for the Mosaic laws should still believe him to be no better than a direct cheat and impostor. And as I suppose this hypothesis to be entirely new, so do I venture to affirm, and that upon no small acquaintance with the writings of Josephus, that the hypothesis is entirely false, and entirely contrary to the whole drift and tenor of Josephus in all his works.

Josephus begins his Antiquities with this most true and [illegible] observation, that Moses did not act as did the [illegible] sages; he did not found a government on human [illegible], nor [illegible] by political maxims, but laid [illegible] foundation on the belief of the being, attributes, and providence of the one true God the Creator and governor of the whole world, and in the fear of that God being [illegible] impressed on the minds of the Israelites, through a persuasion that he gave them the laws by which they were to be governed, and that in consequence, those, and only those would be miserable who broke them, and were under his displeasure.

[illegible] he appears to give firm credit to the most difficult parts of the sacred books, and assures you every Jew [illegible] is brought up in this profound veneration for them, and that they were always ready to yield up themselves rather than contradict them. He still gives his assent to the [illegible] Adam, to the translations of Enoch and Elijah, to the deluge of Noah, to the long lives of the patriarchs, to the burning of Sodom, [illegible] this of accounts [illegible] in the sacred writings, as also to the scripture prophecies, [illegible] observation of their constant completion [illegible] even down to his own time. He places the [illegible] of the prophet Daniel's predictions [illegible] their completions, and [illegible] such evidence for [illegible]. He [illegible] Moses [illegible] inspired [illegible] in Deuteronomy of his death [illegible] place [illegible] not to have been added by [illegible] expositors since have done, but written by himself [illegible] behind. He frequently [illegible] his belief in good and bad angels, [illegible] demons, and their concern with mankind, [illegible] in divine and prophetic dreams, sometimes afforded eminent persons, [illegible] professes to have had such dreams or divine communications himself, of which we have produced a remarkable example about Vespasian's succession to the Roman empire before any [illegible] knew the death of Nero himself, much less of the successions and deaths of Galba, Otho, and Vitellius, who came between them, the truth of which is also fully attested by Suetonius and Dio, the heathen historians. He has given us a large and valuable collection of the most ancient and authentic heathen testimonies, strongly confirming the truth and divinity of the sacred books of the Old Testament, which he was enabled to do by the vast number of ancient Pagan writers which he perused and quoted. He had indeed, contrary to the body of his own nation, most liberal notions as to freedom of enquiry among all sects whatsoever, was utterly averse to all tyranny, persecution, and oppression of mankind, and was for giving all sober men of every party, liberty to think freely, and speak freely, for themselves as they thought proper, without taking offence at one another; yet do his sentiments always go along with the sacred books and the sacred history. Nay, what is most of all remarkable, this was all said and done by Josephus under the most unpromising circumstances of himself and his nation possible, or, when Jerusalem, with its temple, and temple worship, were utterly destroyed, and when he himself was become a captive at Rome, under Idolators. At this very time he firmly retained his faith in God, in Moses, and in the prophets, and even then said plainly, that Daniel, the Jewish prophet, had long ago foretold the destruction of Jerusalem, by the Romans, which [illegible], as did Jesus of Nazareth interpret that prophet also, Matt. xxiv. 15. Mark xiii. 14. Nay, he farther intimated to observing readers, that the Messiah of the Jews, (or Jesus of Nazareth,) the stone cut out of the mountain in the same prophet, would in time break that Roman monarchy to pieces, and set up a better kingdom, which should endure for ever.

If any are still offended with Josephus's frequent permission of his heathen readers to determine as they should think proper concerning [illegible] of those miracles which he relates from the Jewish Scriptures, as if he himself [illegible] doubted of their truth and reality, which has been, and may be, a common objection against him, I must beg liberty to adduce in his vindication the very [illegible] words of the [illegible] accurate and judicious Reland, who has the following note upon one of Josephus's remarkable expressions of this nature, I mean that concerning the miraculous passage of the Israelites over the Red Sea. [illegible] expression is, "Let every one judge and determine as he pleases," and this is the note.

"Josephus (says Reland) does not by this way of speaking, signify that he doubted whether what was said of the passage of the Israelites through the Red Sea were true or not, but he only uses these words in writing to Gentiles, that if this appeared incredible to them, they might enjoy their own liberty of belief, and not be thereby deterred from reading farther what he was to deliver; for that he himself did not doubt of this is sufficiently apparent from the manner of his narration, and from his own testimony, that he took it out of the sacred volumes. He uses the same expression after he had said that it was falsely believed that Moses and the Israelites were expelled Egypt for leprosy. Is it therefore to be inferred, that he intended to suggest this also was uncertain? This is no other than the very calumny which Josephus himself confutes and exposes in his first book against Apion. He thus speaks, when he relates the ascent of Moses to Mount Sinai, and with the same conclusion ends his third book of Antiquities, where he treats of the divinity of the laws of Moses. He also uses the same words where he relates the age of Noah, which he did in the first book, and produces examples from prophane history, that the thing may appear more probable to the Gentiles. In fine, he uses this expression on divers other occasions.

"But while he is so frequently wont to introduce this phrase, or mode of speaking, in his books of Antiquities, I do not remember that I have once met with them in his books of the Jewish Wars. I apprehend the cause of his so frequently introducing the expressions alluded to in the books of Antiquities, to be, that he wrote those books for the use of the Gentiles, while the others were for certain written for the use of those of his own nation that dwelt beyond Euphrates. I might confirm this interpretation from other writers, but I think I have already rendered the matter plain beyond a doubt." Thus far the learned and candid Reland.

The observations of this professor, where he intimates that Josephus never used the expression, "Let every one judge and determine as he pleases," concerning the miracles of the Old Testament, in his seven books of the Wars of the Jews, is certainly true, for having read those books over several times with care and attention, the same observation has occurred to me.

As to any pretence of forgery, which it has been supposed some Catholic Christian might here have been guilty of with regard to the testimony of Josephus concerning Christ, and that as early as the days of Eusebius, if not Eusebius himself, I must aver that it is the effect of the grossest ignorance and partiality.

REMARKS

ON THE

ACCOUNTS

OF

TACITUS AND SUETONIUS,

CONCERNING

Divers Particulars relative to the JEWISH NATION.

WHOEVER has read, or may be disposed to read the annals of Tacitus, the best writer of his age, must observe the great regard he had to the history of Josephus, while, though he never names him, as he very rarely does any of those Romans authors whence he derives one part of his history, yet does appear that he refers to the different books of the Jewish wars, very frequently in the course of a few pages, and almost always depends on his accounts of the affairs of the Romans and Parthians, as well as of the Jews, during the space of upwards of 200 years, to which those books extend.

Speaking of the origin of the Jews, (Liber 5 Cap 2) he writes, "There are those who report that they were "Assyrians, who, wanting land, got together and obtained part of Egypt, and soon after found themselves "in cities of their own in the lands of the Hebrews, and the parts of Syria that lay nearest to them." This account comes nearest the truth of all his others, and is most probably derived from Josephus, though he [illegible] his name.

Again, (Cap [illegible])

"Many authors agree, that [illegible] once in [illegible] this "distemper was [illegible] in Egypt [illegible] bodies "[illegible], Bocchoris their king went to the oracle of "Jupiter, (Ammon) and [illegible] would grant him "some [illegible] against this evil and that he was enjoined to "purge [illegible] of them and to banish this kind of men "into other countries as [illegible] the gods."

This [illegible] have [illegible] of Josephus, [illegible] the [illegible] Lysimachus and Manetho, [illegible] very particularly [illegible] not angry [illegible] bodily imperfections, but at wicked [illegible]

Again, (Cap 5)

"Accordingly they [illegible] "[illegible] temples [illegible] this piece of flattery [illegible] this kind of honour [illegible]"

These concessions were to be learned from Josephus and almost only from him. Out of whom, therefore, I conclude, Tacitus took the finest part of his character of the Jews.

Again, (Cap 6)

"The limits of Judea eastward are bounded by Arabia "Egypt lies on the south. On the west are Phœnicia "and the great sea. They have a prospect of Syria on "their north quarter, [illegible] at some distance from them." See the chorography of Josephus in the 3d book of the Wars, whence most [illegible] Tacitus [illegible] this [illegible] ment [illegible] it comes [illegible] both authors naturally before [illegible] [illegible]'s first [illegible]

Again, (Cap 7)

"Not far from this [illegible] are those plains, which are "related to have been of old, fertile, and [illegible] "many cities full of people." This is exactly according to Josephus, and must have been taken from him in the place [illegible] particularly because it is [illegible] to [illegible] as I know [illegible] thought the [illegible] the lake is, [illegible] Josephus and Tacitus [illegible] is [illegible]

([illegible] 8)

"[illegible] a temple of im"mense wealth [illegible] the [illegible] "the city itself [illegible] royal palace [illegible] "[illegible] "[illegible] the gates, [illegible] "excluded from [illegible]" [illegible] See his [illegible] of the temple of Jerusalem [illegible]

(Cap 10)

Upon his [illegible] Gallus) [illegible] [illegible]

Josephus says noth[illegible] death of Caius [illegible] Tacitus seems to have known [illegible] about [illegible]

"[illegible] Vespasian was [illegible] [illegible] "[illegible] triumph and consulships, and the glory [illegible] over the Jews. After he had once [illegible] "believed it was portended that he should come to the "empire." Josephus takes notice, in general, [illegible] of Vespasian's advancement to the empire, [illegible] adds his own remarkable prediction of it also [illegible] of the Wars, 3d and 4th.

(Book 5. Chap. [illegible])

"At the beginning of the same year [illegible] "pitched upon by his father to finish the conquest of "Judæa: and while he and his [illegible] were private persons, "Titus was celebrated for his [illegible] actions, and after [illegible] "now with greater vigour [illegible] reputation, [illegible] "kind invitations [illegible] the [illegible] "striving one with another [illegible] encourage "him." The character of Titus [illegible] agree exactly with the history of [illegible] as do a variety of passages in the [illegible]

Since Suetonius has [illegible] Josephus and Tacitus [illegible] them, was about twelve or thirteen years younger than Tacitus, and, by consequence, more than thirty years younger than Josephus, it may be worth our while to examine whether he gives us any indication that he had read the works of Josephus or Tacitus. Now we may take notice that Suetonius never mentions Tacitus at all, but he mentions Josephus once, as having foretold Vespasian's coming to the empire, and touches both upon the Jews and Christians. He informs us that "The Jews raised a tumult at Rome, "under Chrestus, in the days of Claudius, and were thence "banished by him." He says farther, that "Nero inflicted "punishments on the Christians, as a superstitious and per-"nicious sect of men then lately arisen." He says moreover, that "Josephus, one of the captive nobility amongst "the Jews, did affirm most constantly, when he was put "into bonds, that he should be loosed by Vespasian, but "not till he was emperor." He also fully attests to the antiquity and uninterrupted duration of that opinion, that "some one who should arise out of Judæa at this time "should obtain the empire over the world," and supposes, with both Josephus and Tacitus, that "such prediction was "fulfilled in a Roman emperor," (Vespasian.) From all these passages it is natural to suppose that Suetonius had seen Tacitus at least, if not Josephus himself, when he wrote his twelve Cæsars. Yet, because he supposes Chrestus to be alive, and at the head of a Jewish tumult at Rome in the days of Claudius, which, one would think, was impossible in any one that had read either Josephus or Tacitus, who both attest that he was put to death in Judæa under Tiberius, and because he says not one word of that remarkable history concerning the statue of Caius, which Petronius was commanded to set up in the temple at Jerusalem, [illegible] [illegible] Tacitus, and [illegible] [illegible] of which we have an [illegible] the [illegible] [illegible] to [illegible] did not [illegible]

Nor does he [illegible] to [illegible] Suetonius [illegible] in one place, [illegible] the [illegible] [illegible] followers, which [illegible] the other Jews, [illegible] the [illegible] Christians.

As [illegible] Dio Cassius [illegible] [illegible] Josephus, [illegible] [illegible] the reign of [illegible] Severus, and [illegible] had [illegible] that [illegible] no addition to the [illegible] [illegible]

With respect to Strabo, that excellent geographer and [illegible], he lived about [illegible] a considerable [illegible] [illegible] and is [illegible] [illegible] not himself see the [illegible] of Josephus. It may be worth [illegible] notice here, how [illegible] geography, which has errors concerning Judæa, and [illegible] [illegible] [illegible], [illegible] [illegible] [illegible], [illegible] and so cannot be [illegible]

[illegible] Trogus Pompeius, [illegible] by Justin, lived is not exactly known, but most probably, a considerable time before Josephus, so that he could not cite him. However it appears manifestly, that [illegible] Josephus [illegible] his antiquities, his own life, and his books against Apion, he understood the geography and history of his own country much better [illegible] either Strabo, Tacitus, Suetonius, Dio Cassius, or any other foreign writers whatever.

Some of our later and lesser critics, who have preferred the Greek and Roman profane historians and writers to the Jewish, and particularly to Josephus, should have learned more candour and modesty from their great father Joseph Scaliger, who, after all his enquiries, he solemnly pronounced that "Josephus was the most diligent and greatest "lover of truth of all writers," and is not afraid to affirm, that "it is more safe to believe him, not only as to the affairs "of the Jews, but also as to those that are foreign to them, "than all the Greek and Latin writers, and that because his "fidelity and compass of learning are every where conspi-"cuous." To this assertion of Scaliger we are obliged to assent as the proper result of our observations.

To conclude, let the guilty Jews, since the days of Josephus, and the guilty heretics that followed Simon Magus, bear their own burthen of forgery, corruption, and interpolation, of ancient histories and ancient records, for they too plainly and undeniably deserve it. But let not Josephus, or the innocent Christians, before antichristianism and popery, bear any such burthen; for so far as we can judge, and we speak it upon full examination, they have the least relation to be it of any part of mankind whatever, from the beginning of the world to this day.

TABLES

OF

JEWISH MEASURES, &c.

I. *Measure of Length*

		Cub.	Feet	Inches	Dec. pts
A Cubit			1	9	888
A Span	a ½ Cubit		0	[illegible]	944
A hand's breadth	a 6th		0	[illegible]	148
A Finger's breadth	a [illegible]		0	0	9 2
A Fathom		4	7	3	[illegible]
Ezekiel's Reed		6	10	1	328
The Measuring Line		8[illegible]	145	1	0[illegible]0

	Cub.	Miles	Paces	Feet	Dec. pts
A Sabbath-day's Journey	[illegible]	0	729	3	
The Eastern Mile	4000	1	403		
A Furlong, or Stadium	[illegible]	0	14[illegible]	[illegible]	[illegible]
A Day's Journey	96000	33	[illegible]		

Note, [illegible] Feet make 1 Pace and [illegible] Paces make [illegible] Mile.

II. *Measures of Capacity*

Liquid Measures	[illegible]	[illegible]	[illegible]	[illegible]	[illegible]
The Homer, or Cor			[illegible]	[illegible]	6
The Bath		7	4		
The Hin		1	[illegible]		
The Log		0		[illegible]	
The [illegible] of [illegible]		0	7	[illegible]	[illegible]

Note, [illegible] equal to [illegible]

Dry Measures	[illegible]	[illegible]	[illegible]	[illegible]	[illegible] pts
The Homer		[illegible]	0	[illegible]	6
The Lethech	[illegible]	4	0	0	3
The Ephah	[illegible]		3	3	[illegible]
The Seah	3[illegible]	0		1	1
The Cab	[illegible]0	0	0	[illegible]	
The Gomer	[illegible]01	0	0	[illegible]	9

III. *Jewish Money*

	Shekel	[illegible]	[illegible]	[illegible]	d.
A Shekel [illegible]				3	
The [illegible]	[illegible]	[illegible]	1	[illegible]	[illegible]
The Zuz	4	[illegible]	0	[illegible]	8
The Gerah	[illegible]0		0		
The Shekel of the [illegible]			3	0	
A Maneh	3[illegible]	[illegible]	12		5
A Shekel [illegible]		1	1		
A Talent of [illegible]			[illegible]	8	[illegible]
Golden Daric, [illegible]				12	5

			s.	d.
A Piece of Silver [illegible]				5
The [illegible]	[illegible] Den.			
A Piece of Silver [illegible] the State[illegible]	[illegible]			2
A Pound [illegible] the M[illegible]	100	[illegible]		0
A Denarius [illegible] the Den[illegible]		0		3
A Farthing, [illegible]	[illegible] Den			1
A [illegible]	10 [illegible]	[illegible]	0	[illegible]	0
A [illegible]	[illegible]	[illegible]	0	0	1

Note, The [illegible] Ounce [illegible] per Ounce.

IV. *Jewish Weights*

	Shekel	lb.	Oz.	Dwts	Grains	[illegible]
A Shekel		0	0	9	2	[illegible]
The Maneh	60		3	9	10	[illegible]
A Talent	300[illegible]	3	10	1	10	[illegible]

V. *The Jewish Months compared with ours*

1 Nisan or Abib	[illegible]	[illegible]	7 [illegible]	[illegible]	September / October
2 Ijar or Zif		[illegible]	8 [illegible] chesvan		October / November
3 Sivan		[illegible]	9 Chisleu		November / December
4 Thammuz		[illegible]	10 Thebet		December / January
5 Ab		[illegible]	11 Shebath		January / February
6 Elul		[illegible]	[illegible]		[illegible] / [illegible]

The Jews [illegible] Two Sorts [illegible] which began in September and [illegible]
Before the [illegible] of Babylon [illegible] accounted [illegible] Months [illegible] 2 3 [illegible] the [illegible]
the Chaldees [illegible]

VI. [illegible] *Days of the Week*, [illegible] *of the Day*, [illegible]

[illegible] Day [illegible]	Sunday
[illegible]	[illegible]
3d [illegible]	Tuesday
4th Day	[illegible]
[illegible]	[illegible]
[illegible]	F[illegible]
[illegible]	S[illegible]

[illegible]

The [illegible]
[illegible]

[illegible]

[illegible]

[illegible]

The [illegible]
The [illegible]
The 3d [illegible] to [illegible]
The 4th [illegible] to [illegible]

AN

ACCOUNT

OF THE

JUDGES, KINGS, GOVERNORS, &c.

OF THE

JEWISH NATION

[illegible] Nation in their beginning was governed by the following Judges

Moses	Jair
[illegible]	Jephtha
Othniel	Abfan
Ahud	Abdon
Barach and Debora	Elon
Gideon	Samfon
Abimelech	Eli
Thola	Samuel

After them [illegible] these Kings

Saul	Amasias
David	Ozias
Solomon	Jonathan
Roboam	Ahaz
Abiam	Hezekiah
Asa	[illegible]
Jehoshaphat	[illegible]
Jehoram	Josias
[illegible]	Joachaz
Ochozias	Joachim
Athalia	Zedechias
Joas	

The [illegible] of Babylon continued 70 years [illegible] the Governors after the Captivity were

[illegible]bel	Nagge
[illegible]	[illegible]
[illegible] Ben R[illegible]	[illegible]
Judas [illegible]nus	[illegible]os
[illegible]	Mattathias
[illegible]	Joseph Artes
[illegible]	[illegible] Hyrcanus
[illegible]	Mattathias

The Maccabees [illegible] were [illegible] Priests

[illegible]	Simon
[illegible]an	John Hyrcanus

The following [illegible] Kings and [illegible]

Aristobulus 1	Hyrcanus
John Alexander	Aristob[illegible] son of Aristob[illegible]
Alexander	Aristobulus 3
Aristobulus 2	[illegible]

The [illegible] of Herod

Antipater	Archelaus [illegible]
Herod the Great	Agrippa, son of Agrippa

The [illegible] Priests, [illegible] Temple of Solomon

Aaron	Achitob
[illegible]	Achimelech
[illegible]	Abiathar
Abishua	Sadoc
[illegible]	Achimaas
[illegible]	[illegible]
Heli	

[illegible] Babylon

Joram	[illegible]
[illegible]	[illegible]
Azarias	[illegible]
[illegible]	[illegible]
Jo[illegible]	[illegible]

[illegible] Babylon [illegible]

Sarah	[illegible]
Jofeded	Jonathan
[illegible]	[illegible]
[illegible]	Onias
[illegible]	Simon
Eleazar	[illegible]
Manasse	[illegible]
Onias	Lysimachus
Simon	Alcimus
Onias	

High Priests from the Maccabees *time till the final destruction of* Jerusalem

Simon Boethus	Joseph 3
Joseph 1	Ananus
Joseph 2	Ismael
Joazar	Joseph
Eleazar	Annas
Jesus *the son of* Sias	Eleazar
Joazar	Simon
Ananus	Joseph Caiaphas
Ismael	Jonathan
Theophilus	Joshua *son of* Danneus
Simon	Joshua *son of* Gamaliel
Mattathias	Mattathias
Elion	Phineas *or* Panaas

Kings of Israel, *otherwise called Kings of the ten Tribes, or of* Samaria

Jeroboam 1	Jehoahaz
Nadab	Joash
Baasha	Jeroboam 2
Elah	Zachariah
Zimri	Menahem
Omri	Pekahiah *son of* Menahem
Ahab	Pekah *son of* Remaliah
Jehoram	Hoshea.
Jehu	

Kings of Assyria *and* Babylon

Phulbelocus	Nabuchodonosor 1
Phulasser	Nabuchodonosor *the Great*
Salmanasser	Evilmerodach
Sennacherib	Neriglissorar
Esarhaddon	Labosordach
Merodach Benmerodach	Baltassar

Kings of Persia

Cyrus	Xerxes
Cambyses	Sogdianus
Smerdus Magus	Darius *the Bastard*
Darius *son of* Histaspis	Artaxerxes Mnemon
Xerxes *son of* Darius	Artaxerxes Ochus
Artabanus *the Tyrant*	Arsames
Artaxerxes *with a long hand*	Darius *son of* Arsam

Kings of Syria, *after the Death of* Alexander the

Seleucus Nicanor	Alexander Epiphanes
Antiochus Soter	Demetrius Nicanor
Antiochus	Antiochus Sedetes
Seleucus Callinicus	Demetrius Nicanor
Seleucus Ceraunius	Alexander Zebina
Antiochus *the Great*	Antiochus Gryphus
Seleucus Philopater	Antiochus Cyzicenus
Antiochus Epiphanes	Seleucus Gryphus
Antiochus Eupater	Antiochus Pius

Sovereigns of Egypt *after the death of* Alexander the

Ptolemy Soter	Euergetes Phiscon
Philadelphus	Lathyrus
Euergetes	Alexander
Philopater	Auletes
Epiphanes	Cleopatra
Philometor	

Kings of the Tyrians

Abibalus	Phelletes
Hiram	Ithobalus
Bellastartus	Badezor
Abdastartus	Metinus
Astartus	Pigmalion.
Astarimus	

NAMES OF AUTHORS MENTIONED BY JOSEPHUS

A

Acusilaus Argivus
Agatharchides
Alexander Polyhist
Anaxagoras Glazom
Antiochus
Apion Grammat
Apollodorus
Apollonius Molonis F
Ariphanes
Aristoteles

B

Berosus Chaldæus

C

Cadmus Milesius
Callias
Castor Chronologus
Chæremon
Chœrilus
Clearchus
Cleodemus, or Malchus
Conon

D

Diagoras Melius
Diocles
Diodorus, or Tryphon
Dius
Demetrius

E

Ephorus
Euemerus
Eupolomus

H

Hecatæus
Hellanicus
Hermippus
Hermogenes
Herodotus
Hesiodus
Hestiæus
Hieronymus Egyptius
Homer

I

Justus
Isidorus

L

Lysimachus
Livius

M

Malchus
Manethon Ægyptius
Megasthenes
Menander Ephesius
Menedemus
Messala
Mnaseas
Mochus

N

Nicholaus of Damascus

P

Pherecydes Syrius
Philistus
Philo Histor
Philostratus Histor
Plato
Polybius
Polycrates
Posidonius
Protagoras
Pythagoras

S

Sibylla
Strabo

T

Thales
Theodectes
Theodotus
Theophilus
Theophrastus
Theopompus
Thucidides
Timæus
Timagenes
Tryphon

Z

Zopyrion.

CONTINUATION

OF THE

HISTORY OF THE JEWS,

FROM THE TIME OF

FLAVIUS JOSEPHUS.

INCLUDING A

PERIOD OF UPWARDS OF ONE THOUSAND SEVEN HUNDRED YEARS

CONTAINING AN

[illegible] OF THEIR *DISPERSION INTO THE VARIOUS PARTS OF EUROPE, ASIA, AFRICA, AND AMERICA.*

WITH

THEIR DIFFERENT PERSECUTIONS, TRANSACTIONS, AND PRESENT STATE,

THROUGHOUT THE KNOWN WORLD

BOOK I

CHAP I.

INTRODUCTION

THERE is not a circumſtance, amongſt the various events of revolving time, more worthy of admiration then the preſervation of the people of the Jews, in the midſt of all the calamities they have un[illegible]e for the ſpace of upwards of 1700 years It has be[illegible]rked with propriety, that religions of every k[illegible]on temporal proſperity, that they triumph [illegible]tec-[illegible]on of a conquering prince, and lan[illegible]ying monarchies The Chriſtian church it[illegible]lf, ſo renowned for its martyrs, has yet been conſiderably injured by perſecutions, and the [illegible] that have [illegible]n made by v[illegible]o-lence could [illegible]t eaſily be repaired. However, we have now before us a people, and a religion, which, though perſecuted for 1700 years, ſtill ſubſiſt, and are very numerous [illegible] Kings have frequently applied the ſeverity of [illegible]dicts and corporal puniſhments to deſtroy them Seditious mu[illegible] have exceeded the rigour and cruelties of princes [illegible]oth princes and people, however divided in opinions, either political or religious, have concurred in [illegible] this people, but have not been able to effect it

The Jews have been driven from moſt parts of the world, which has only ſerved to produce a general diſperſion They have, from age, to age, undergone miſery and perſecution, but ſtill live, notwithſtanding the diſgrace and hatred that attend them in all places, whilſt nothing remains of many of the greateſt monarchies but the name

Their diſtreſſes are peculiarly aggravated, from this circumſtance, that, though in former captivities, the Almighty was pleaſed to point out a time in which he would be reconciled, break the yoke impoſed by tyrants, and reſtore his people to their liberty, no term is now fixed to the duration of their miſeries, and we have more certain aſſurance from the New Teſtament of their being recalled, than they have in the writings of the prophets, whoſe race is extinct nor is one of them to be ſeen who promiſes the end of a calamity which has already continued ſuch a number of ages.

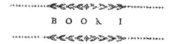

The Romans when they made themſelves maſters of Judea left the inhabitants a public worſhip, and the exerciſe of their laws The ſynagogues, as thoſe of Damaſcus, without appeal, determined the affairs of religion even where the Chriſtians were concerned The high-prieſt had an eminent power They had their judges even in Chaldee, but at preſent they have no ſhadow of [illegible] ther; still [illegible] upon [illegible] Add [illegible] the [illegible] other world [illegible] another [illegible]

[illegible] ders [illegible] age of [illegible] in- [illegible] to partition as [illegible] Hoveman, revolutions have happened [illegible] long [illegible] succession of ages. And yet the Jews [illegible] God [illegible] is [illegible] ground, [illegible] only [illegible] could [illegible] against [illegible] Jerusalem [illegible]

[illegible] the West Indies [illegible] disseminated [illegible]

[illegible] the death of [illegible]

[illegible] the innu [illegible]

[illegible] is to [illegible] There [illegible]

[illegible] marriage [illegible]

[illegible] They [illegible] the same [illegible] to eat no [illegible] own [illegible] and the [illegible] of their conversion.

If we consider what prov[illegible] be [illegible] of [illegible] particular [illegible] numbers dispersed [illegible] little [illegible] arguments for [illegible] Christian [illegible] as [illegible] very particulars [illegible] themselves are the depositaries of [illegible] other prophecies [illegible] Their [illegible] Their dis[illegible] all parts of [illegible] their religion [illegible] their [illegible] tion [illegible] Hitherto [illegible] if the [illegible] converted [illegible] we should certainly have [illegible] all the prophecies [illegible] the [illegible] history of our Saviour [illegible] have looked [illegible] the Gospels.

[illegible] the religion of the modern Jews [illegible] authors [illegible] the same manner. The first comprehends the written law, which is [illegible] contained in the five books of Moses. The second comprehends [illegible] law, or [illegible] delivered [illegible] contains the comments and expositions of the Rabbins [illegible] the Pentateuch; that is, commonly [illegible] collected into a large [illegible] called the Talmud. The third order comprehends the [illegible] which [illegible] authorized [illegible] Of these three orders [illegible] Karaites [illegible] Jews [illegible] and customs of [illegible]

[illegible] French [illegible] for the [illegible] Jews, since the preaching of Christianity [illegible] It [illegible] God [illegible] Gospel [illegible] the Jews [illegible] longer.

The Jews came into England in the reign of William [illegible] in divers parts, [illegible] London, where they [illegible] the [illegible] the king [illegible] the Jews [illegible] protect [illegible] between them and the Christians [illegible] the keys of [illegible] As to their [illegible] that they were [illegible] the crown [illegible] in England [illegible] However [illegible] the English [illegible] money [illegible] obliged [illegible] the [illegible]

[illegible] frequently [illegible] revenge upon them at discretion. However [illegible] to turn Christians [illegible] pardon for all former crimes [illegible] Henry [illegible] convert Jews [illegible] a pension for their maintenance. In 1290 [illegible] proclamation of King Edward I [illegible] the kingdom [illegible] pretence that they [illegible] Christians [illegible] They departed [illegible] number of 15,000, and it was commonly reported [illegible] over the sea, the seamen plundered them, cut their throats [illegible], and threw them overboard. This [illegible] perpetual. However, in process of time, [illegible] England, [illegible] are tolerated [illegible] exercise of their religion. But [illegible] proceed to our [illegible].

CHAP. I.

[illegible] from the taking of Jerusalem [illegible] [illegible].

IT is needless to repeat what has been heretofore related [illegible] Josephus concerning the desolate condition to which [illegible] and metropolis of Judæa [illegible] reduced, or [illegible] the greatest part of the surviving Jews were condemned by the conqueror. Those [illegible] this sad catastrophe, and [illegible] the fury of the Romans, retired some into Galilee, and [illegible] Egypt and Cyrene, where [illegible] new rebellions, committing horrid [illegible], and [illegible] the [illegible] Romans against them.

To pretend that the Sanhedrim was removed to Jamnia, [illegible] to Tiberias, where it subsisted till after the death of Judas the Saint, that academies were established [illegible] cities, and that the nation continued to be governed by a patriarch, is to [illegible] merely [illegible].

There remained no shadow of power [illegible] to [illegible] wretched people in the country that God had given [illegible] Domitian, [illegible] even to excess, helped to sink [illegible] his taxes [illegible] been [illegible] oppression [illegible] only the Jews of Rome, who [illegible] expelled out of the [illegible] not [illegible], but it is a mistake [illegible] demanded by Domitian related to all the Jews, [illegible] not a new one.

[illegible] Judæa to the Romans, made it [illegible] according to [illegible] Julius Cæsar [illegible] Hyrcanus, [illegible] the Jewish people, [illegible] Nevertheless, Josephus adds, that they were obliged to carry [illegible] every two years to Sidon. The privilege then [illegible] to [illegible] collection, [illegible] in those [illegible] nations. They were also exempted from winter quarters, [illegible] entertainment of soldiers. They paid [illegible] the sabbatic year, because the [illegible] allow [illegible] Cæsar had granted the same privilege before Herod [illegible] made king, and a friend to the Roman people, [illegible] he was [illegible] the [illegible] kings, and [illegible] of their [illegible] forcing [illegible] to pay [illegible] would have [illegible] thanks to the immortal gods that [illegible] had [illegible] Cuthage [illegible] king of the kings [illegible] Mark Anthony and made tributaries, [illegible] Herod, with those of Pontus and [illegible], and [illegible] from this general law the princes of the Upper Armenia. That [illegible] might have maintained the [illegible] not seeing any intendants, or receivers, [illegible] Herod and Archelaus's [illegible] a sort of [illegible] this people, to suffer them to collect their taxes by their own receivers, as Josephus has observed, but it cannot be [illegible] concluded that they were not tributary, and [illegible] this kingdom was the only exception to the general [illegible] It cannot be doubted but this tribute was regularly [illegible] our Saviour's lifetime, since the Pharisees [illegible] Jesus Christ [illegible] Cæsar's [illegible] the [illegible] for the rich, [illegible] They should render to Cæsar the things that [illegible]

Cæsar's

The [illegible] then paid two sorts of taxes: one was a subsidy laid upon the lands, of [illegible] paid the [illegible] penny. But, besides this, Appion observes, that there was a capitation, more intolerable to the Jews than all the other tributes, and therefore Judæa petitioned [illegible] to be exempted from this impost, with which [illegible] was [illegible], as well as Syria.

This capitation [illegible] to be great, since they only paid one denarion, that is, [illegible] pence halfpenny per head. But it was equal for [illegible] as the rich. As the didrachm was [illegible] to God, so the tribute [illegible] Cæsar [illegible] one and the same to all the inhabitants without any distinction. There were two reasons [illegible] this [illegible], one, that the people [illegible] themselves [illegible] God, and thinking [illegible] not [illegible] especially [illegible] and the capitation made them feel their slavery. Therefore Judas of Galilee rebelled [illegible] Augustus [illegible] enrolled. [illegible] reason that rendered this yoke [illegible], [illegible] was to be brought to the [illegible] treasure was stamped [illegible] prince's image, and [illegible] to them, [illegible] only [illegible] the worship of images [illegible] emperor's [illegible] upon [illegible] and [illegible] to pay [illegible] without a [illegible].

[illegible] Judæa paid [illegible] lands, and the capitation, which brought [illegible] hundred and [illegible] thousand [illegible] hundred and [illegible] three pounds, [illegible] shillings and [illegible] pence, into the emperor's exchequer. [illegible] Jerusalem, Titus [illegible] Cicero observes, that [illegible] sent it from Rome and the other cities of Italy, to Jerusalem, because they looked [illegible] as a tribute which they paid to God as his subjects. But the emperor usurped the place of God, whom they had forsaken, and appropriated this tribute to himself. [illegible] didrachm was worth fifteen-pence, [illegible] demanded of them was very [illegible] this [illegible] tax was the more disgraceful because they were obliged [illegible] the liberty of their [illegible] by it, and [illegible] most [illegible].

Xiphilin [illegible] that Titus, after the conquest of Judæa, ordered all the Jews, that would profess their religion, to pay the didrachm annually to Jupiter Capitolinus. The Romans [illegible] liberty of conscience [illegible] Tertullian [illegible] that [illegible] had ranked the Christians among [illegible] be suffered at Rome. The Jewish religion therefore being grown [illegible] were obliged to pay [illegible] for [illegible] Suetonius speaks of Domitian's [illegible] the payment. [illegible] of his [illegible] quality or persons, [illegible] rather to pretend [illegible] demanded, were respected. A man of ninety [illegible] was forced [illegible] which were committed [illegible].

Domitian [illegible] the Jews were comprised [illegible] Christians. We cannot doubt [illegible] the opinion of the Romans [illegible] they [illegible] ped only one God, and rejected idols, which was reckoned an [illegible], and added [illegible] persecution. [illegible] the Jewish religion, were condemned [illegible] the crime of impiety [illegible] had some were punished with death, [illegible] sequestration.

Nerva, Domitian's successor, [illegible] the advantage of this nation [illegible] were accused of impiety, and [illegible] Domitian [illegible] design, he was [illegible] to execute [illegible] being prevented by his assassins. He forbid, for the future, the foundations of the emperor to be tormented for the sake of religion, ... And he discharged the Jews of the imposts which even Domitian had oppressed them ...

... placed the first of all the patriarchs of Judæa in this reign, because he was more favourable to the Jews, ... because there is no probability that they could so ... have re-settled themselves after an almost general dispersion. According to this account Gamaliel II. was then the head of the fathers, which the Greeks call patriarch. ... was elected father of the senate, Eleazar was connected with Gamaliel, and they enjoyed their dignity together. Historians ... that Eleazar presided two sabbaths and Gamaliel one, which shews that this office especially related to religion, and the divine service.

The Jews endeavoured to raise the glory of their desolate nation, by making many learned men flourish after the ruin of the temple, and live in the beginning of the second century.

Eleazar the Great lived at that time. They make him the son of a person of quality, called Hyrcanus, who had so neglected his education, that at twenty-eight years of age he was ignorant of the law. He bewailed his ignorance for many days, but at last ... to ... a master. He made a journey to ... son of Zachai, who taught at Jerusalem, by whom he was instructed in his prayers, and some points of the law. Eleazar wept ... till he had learnt them, and eight days passed over ... His father came to ... to disinherit him, ... with the learning and ... he ... he would not ... and, ... his brothers ... The Jewish rabbies ... their ... almost divine, but they are ... with absurdity, and ... to give credit with a ... religious reader.

At that time lived the poet Ezekiel, who composed the departure from Egypt ... Greek verse. He was a Jew, and probably ... the ... to confer ... Romans, in giving ... after Josephus, who ... and before Clemens Alexandrinus, who had quoted him. We must therefore place him at the end of the first or rather at the beginning of the second century.

We must also place at the same time the author of the ... of the twelve patriarchs. This man has disguised his religion, and speaks so often like a Jew, that a learned man who was the first publisher of this work in Greek, maintains that the original was in Hebrew, composed by a doctor of that nation some time before the manifestation of our Lord, ... the author has followed the common prejudices of the doctors of that time, who expected a general of an army, famous for his battles, rather than a spiritual teacher.

The ... of the twelve patriarchs was, however, composed at ... time, for the author speaks of the destruction of ... the actions of the Messiah, and even ... the evangelists, like a prophet who had read their writings.

The miserable are more mutinous and restless than other people. ... is a spirit of sedition imputed to some religions, and to the tempers and inclinations of certain nations. But this is imaginary, ... men naturally love peace and quiet, leave them liberty of conscience, and the free enjoyment, or ... of their estates, and few rebellions will arise in nations. The hatred of parties, persecution, and the harshness of government, are the common springs of tumults and seditions ... do not swerve from their natural state, except when they are forced by despair or violence. We must not ... the Jews notwithstanding their ... have so frequently an inclination to rebel. Misery puts men into agitation, and makes them turn on all sides to be easy, and commonly instead ... accomplishing their desires, they add fresh weight to their burthen. The Jews ... their attempts in Trajan's reign. What could make them so venturous as to brave the power of so great a prince? ... provoked by their precedent misfortunes, they carried, in their turn, cruelty and barbarity to a detestable excess, beginning at Cyrene, a city of Lybia, where they had been settled, and ... for many ages. They had at first some advantages over the Greeks (for so they called the Egyptians), but the fugitives escaping to Alexandria, and carrying consternation, and a thirst of revenge, into this great city, they murdered all the Jews that were there. Those of Cyrene, enraged with a reprizal they had justly deserved, fell into the greatest fury, and being headed by one Andrea, ravaged the plain country under his conduct, and massacred two hundred and twenty thousand inhabitants in Lybia. The Romans returned into the field, under Martius Turbo, then general, whom Trajan had commissioned to quell these disorders. He effected it, but could not defeat the rebels, without long and violent battles, and the loss of many men. Lybia remained so depopulated by the massacre the Jews made in the beginning of the war, that the emperor Adrian was obliged to send a colony to inhabit it.

Eusebius has run into a manifest contradiction as to this rebellion of the Jews, for he affirms, in his history, that it happened in the beginning of the eighteenth year of Trajan's reign, and he places it a year sooner in his chronicle. The history being exacter than the chronicle, we ought to give it the preference, and place this event in the beginning of the second century, and in the hundred and fifteenth year of Jesus Christ. The Jewish historians say, that the war was caused by the ambition of the refugees who had retired to Alexandria after the destruction of Jerusalem, and had built a temple there. Some would fain ... the ... and the weaker party called in Trajan to their assistance, who killed two hundred thousand of them. But the temple of Alexandria was imaginary, that of Onias being the only one they built.

The Talmudists vary more grossly. Some say it was Adrian that killed twice as many Jews in Egypt as Moses had conducted out of it. Others place this event in Trajan's reign, and others affirm matters with as little foundation.

Nor did the disorder stop there, for the news came of new insurrections in Mesopotamia. The ... of ... the inhabitants of this government into ... who saw themselves menaced with the same misfortune. But Trajan sent a Moor thither, called Lucius Quietus, the greatest general the empire then had, or ... his commission ... withstood the seditious, ... a vast number of Jews, ... the rest. Nevertheless, as his presence was thought necessary to retain them in their duty, and there was reason to fear they would take up arms again the very moment the conqueror withdrew, the emperor made him governor of Palestine, to keep a strict eye upon their motions.

A new storm arose in the island of Cyprus. The Jews in this island began with the massacre of two hundred and forty thousand inhabitants. Their own historians do not dissemble this action, but swell the number of the dead instead of abating it, for they tell you, that the noise of the insurrections elsewhere arrived at Goplin, that is to say Cyprus, the Jews, who were very numerous in this country, fell upon all the heathens, and made such a general massacre, that not one of them remained, "Which obliged Trajan to send Adrian, the general of "his forces, against them, who reduced them, and af-"terwards the Romans published an edict, absolutely "prohibiting the Jews access to this island."

CHAP. IV.

[illegible] of the Jews [illegible] A[illegible] of Barchocheba and [illegible] that distinguished [illegible] of the Christian [illegible].

THESE m[illegible] the f[illegible] to be only the beginning of the [illegible] of the Jews, which w[illegible] length compel[illegible] [illegible] Adrian, who [illegible] to [illegible] in [illegible] object state of [illegible] the [illegible] means of [illegible] they were [illegible] of [illegible] recourse to [illegible] of dreams.

We [illegible] Adrian himself, [illegible] Jews in Egypt [illegible] to [illegible] enthusiasm [illegible].

The cause [illegible] They [illegible] to plant a [illegible] was born, and to [illegible] slaughter. These trees grew [illegible] then they were cut down [illegible] couple. The princess, [illegible] to Judah [illegible] to [illegible] one of [illegible] whereupon [illegible] relation, and [illegible] obliged th[illegible] to [illegible].

Chrysostom [illegible] who [illegible] three times [illegible] at their first [illegible] Adrian, that [illegible] on the con[illegible] it was [illegible] princes [illegible] placed [illegible] Jerusalem [illegible] ever ordered [illegible] which was still [illegible] Chrysostom [illegible] of precious [illegible] seemed to restore them [illegible] they made [illegible] the first of the attempts [illegible] The same [illegible] to re-establish them [illegible] attempted to rebuild [illegible] had been built [illegible] go by the name of [illegible] council of Nice [illegible] in this city, and [illegible] there, it retained its [illegible] bius, who [illegible] it Jerusalem [illegible] of the [illegible] that [illegible].

There [illegible] great rebellion [illegible] Adrian. First, This [illegible] forbidden them like Domitian and Nerva to be circumcised. Spartian says so, and I know not how [illegible] any other author can be contested who lived under [illegible]. Modestinus observes also that the Jews [illegible] addressing themselves to Antoninus, he permitted them to circumcise only their own children, and forbid doing it to any person of another religion under heavy penalties. Secondly, There is a law forbidding all the Roman citizens to be circumcised like the Jews, or to cause their slaves to be circumcised, upon pain of banishment, and awarding death to the physicians that should do it. It also banishes and condemns, sometimes to death, the Jews that cut[illegible] children of another religion. But the Jews attempted to circumcise strangers, in order to increase their numbers, whereby to go on afterwards more effectually in the restoration of their commonwealth, as St Chrysostom [illegible] it. Some great men have said it after him. But it is not probable they believed that the converted Roman citizens, or their slaves, could make up a considerable army to restore their state. The Roman proselytes were never so numerous to possess them with this conceit. These edicts were given only to prevent any changes of religion, which now and then happened at Rome, and [illegible] the heathens. Besides, Antoninus [illegible] them to circumcise themselves after his war with them [illegible] this prince, being [illegible] of their rebellion, and seeing [illegible] this custom experienced them [illegible] they were not [illegible] condition to proselyte sufficient numbers to form armies, and restore the [illegible] Adrian, who had forbid [illegible] circumcision [illegible] Jews [illegible] one of the principal [illegible] of their religion [illegible] of the zeal o[illegible] the covenant, the mark that distinguished them from heathens, and the [illegible] annexed this custom [illegible] that they [illegible] deprived of this ceremony.

This prince [illegible] also [illegible] Jerusalem, and built a city upon its ruins, to [illegible] he gave his own name, and consecrated it to Jupiter C[illegible]. The second cause of the war [illegible] first since Eusebius says that the colony [illegible] after the taking of Bither. But Dion [illegible] the colony was the cause of [illegible] not bear to have strangers [illegible] their [illegible] and worship strange gods [illegible] doubt of the truth of the fact. To reconcile Eusebius and Dion, it appears that the emperor's first design was crossed by the Jews revolting before it was full executed, because the Jews had expected the new inhabitants, though the emperor accomplished it when he had subdued them. So that he had sent the colony before the war, as Dion affirms, and he completed his project, when the rebellion was quelled, as Eusebius relates.

Barchochebas's ambition, who knew how to make his advantage of the disturbance which these two circumstances created in the minds of the people, fully determined the nation to prosecute the war. But to speak of the false Messiahs that have deceived the nation.

The time was come in which impostors appeared with [illegible]. Gamaliel had seen two of them perish and was so moved with the ill success of their enterprize, that he would not have the progress of Christianity opposed, being persuaded that Providence would bring the design to nought if it was not from heaven. "Theudas (said he) before these days rose up, who was slain, and [illegible] as many as obeyed him, were brought to nought. After this man rose up Judas of Galilee in the days of the taxing, and he also perished; and now I say unto you, if this counsel be of men it will come to nought." The Christians [illegible] of his great moderation [illegible] afterwards canonized him.

[illegible] the [illegible] chapter of the acts of the Apostles, particularly speak of the impostors. There is said Judas of Galilee [illegible] the people [illegible] living [illegible] here of [illegible] deceive [illegible] which (though [illegible] to invalidate the [illegible]) it is evident [illegible] had been [illegible].

The Romans [illegible] forces against Judas and he miserably perished [illegible] persecuted his children [illegible] His followers [illegible] with an unshaken constancy [illegible] tortures. They [illegible] that was ordered [illegible] when they were [illegible] carried

(T)

being prevented by his aſſaſſins He forbid, for the future, the ſubjects of the empire to be tormented for the ſake of religion, impiety, or Judaiſm And he diſcharged the Jews of the impoſts whe with Domitian had oppreſſed them.

We have placed the firſt of all the patriarchs of Judæa in this prince's reign, becauſe he was more favourable to the Jews, and becauſe there is no probability that they could ſo ſuddenly have re-ſettled themſelves after an almoſt general diſperſion According to this account Gamaliel II was then the head of the fathers, which the Greeks call patriarch Joſhua was elected father of the ſenate; Eleazar was reconciled with Gamaliel, and they enjoyed their dignity together Hiſtorians ſay, that Eleazar preſided two ſabbaths, and Gamaliel one, which ſhews that this office eſpecially related to religion, and the Divine ſervice

The Jews endeavour to raiſe the glory of their deſolate nation, by making many learned men ſurvive the ruin of the temple, and live in the beginning of the ſecond century

Eleazar the Great lived at that time They make him the ſon of a perſon of quality, called Hyrcanus, who had ſo neglected his education, that at twenty-eight years of age he was ignorant of the law He bewailed his ignorance for many days, but at laſt a certain perſon told him of a maſter He made a journey to John, the ſon of Zachai, who taught at Jeruſalem, by whom he was inſtructed in his prayers, and ſome points of the law Eleazar wept and ſighed till he had learnt them, and eight days paſſed over before he eat His father came to Jeruſalem to diſinherit him, but was ſo ſtruck with the learning and modeſty he found in him, that he would not ſit down before him, and, inſtead of diſinheriting him, he gave him his brothers portions, who had put him upon this deſign The Jewiſh rabbies enumerate theſe patriarchs, and aſcribe to them properties almoſt divine, but they are two big with abſurdity, and it may be deemed prophanation, to gain credit with a rational or religious reader

At that time lived the poet Ezekiel who compoſed the departure from Egypt in Greek verſe He was a Jew, and probably meant to ſing a miraculous deliverance to comfort his nation, dejected by the Romans, in giving it an idea of a redeemer like Moſes He lived after Joſephus, who did not know him, and before Clemens Alexandrinus, who had quoted him We muſt therefore place him at the end of the firſt, or rather at the beginning of the ſecond century

We muſt alſo place at the ſame time the author of the will of the twelve patriarchs This man has diſguiſed his religion, and ſpeaks ſo often like a Jew, that a learned man, who was the firſt publiſher of this work in Greek, maintains that the original was in Hebrew, compoſed by a doctor of that nation ſome time before the manifeſtation of our Lord, ſince the author has followed the common prejudices of the doctors of that time, who expected a general of an army, famous for his battles, rather than a ſpiritual teacher

The will of the twelve patriarchs was, however, compoſed at this time, for the author ſpeaks of the deſtruction of Jeruſalem and ſeveral actions of the Meſſiah, and even of the writings of the evangeliſts, like a prophet who had ſeen theſe things.

The miſerable are more mutinous and reſtleſs than other people There is a ſpirit of ſedition imputed to ſome religions and to the tempers and inclinations of certain nations But this is imaginary, for all men naturally love peace and quiet, leave them liberty of conſcience, and the free enjoyment, or increaſe of their eſtates, and few rebellions will ariſe in nation. The hatred of parties, perſecution, and the harſhneſs of government are the common ſprings of tumults and ſeditions men do not ſwerve from their natural ſtate, except when they are forced by deſpair or violence We muſt not wonder then if the Jews notwithſtanding their miſeries, have ſo frequently an inclination to rebel Miſery puts men into agitation, and makes them turn on all ſides to be eaſy, and commonly inſtead of compaſſing their deſires, they add freſh weight to their burthen The Jews miſ-timed their attempts in Trajan's reign What could make them ſo venturous as to brave the power of ſo great a prince? Being provoked by their preceding misfortunes, they carried, in their turn, cruelty and barbarity to a deteſtable exceſs beginning at Cyrene, a city of Lybia, where they had been ſettled, and potent, for many ages They had at firſt ſome advantages over the Greeks, for ſo they called the Egyptians, but the fugitives eſcaping to Alexandria, and carrying conſternation, and a thirſt of revenge, into this great city, they murdered all the Jews that were there Thoſe of Cyrene, enraged with a repriſal they had juſtly deſerved, fell into the greateſt fury and being headed by one Andrea, ravaged the plain country under his conduct, and maſſacred two hundred and twenty thouſand inhabitants in Lybia The Romans returned into the field, under Marcius Turbo, their general, whom Trajan had commiſſioned to quell theſe diſorders He effected it, but could not defeat the rebels, without long and violent battles, and the loſs of many men Lybia remained ſo depopulated by the maſſacre the Jews made in the beginning of the war, that the emperor Adrian was obliged to ſend a colony to inhabit it

Euſebius has run into a manifeſt contradiction as to the rebellion of the Jews, for he affirms, in his hiſtory, that it happened in the beginning of the eighteenth year of Trajan's reign, and he places it a year ſooner in his chronicle The hiſtory being exacter than the chronicle, we ought to give it the preference, and place this event in the beginning of the ſecond century, and in the hundred and fifteenth year of Jeſus Chriſt The Jewiſh hiſtorians ſay, that the war was cauſed by the ambition of the refugees who had retired to Alexandria after the deſtruction of Jeruſalem, and had built a temple there Some would fain lord it over the reſt, and the weaker party called in Trajan to their aſſiſtance, who killed five hundred thouſand of them but their temple at Alexandria was imaginary, that of Onias being the only one they built

The Talmudiſts vary more groſsly Some ſay it was Adrian that killed twice as many Jews in Egypt as Moſes had conducted out of it Others place this event in Trajan's reign, and others affirm matters with as little foundation

Nor did the diſorder ſtop there, for the news came of new inſurrections in Meſopotamia The fate of Egypt threw the inhabitants of this government into a conſternation, who ſaw themſelves menaced with the ſame misfortune but Trajan ſent a Moor thither, called Lucius Quietus, the greateſt general the empire then had, or has had ever ſince, who, in execution of his commiſſion, withſtood the ſeditious, and by killing a vaſt number of Jews, intimidated the reſt Nevertheleſs, as his preſence was thought neceſſary to retain them in their duty, and there was reaſon to fear they would take up arms again the very moment the conqueror withdrew, the emperor made him governor of Paleſtine, to keep a ſtrict eye upon their motions

A new ſtorm aroſe in the iſland of Cyprus The Jews in this iſland began with the maſſacre of two hundred and forty thouſand inhabitants Their own hiſtorians do not diſſemble this action, but ſwell the number of the dead inſtead of abating it, for they tell you, that the noiſe of the inſurrections elſewhere arrived at Gophri, that is to ſay Cyprus, the Jews, who were very numerous in this country, fell upon all the heathens, and made ſuch a general maſſacre, that not one of them remained, "Which obliged Trajan to ſend Adrian, the general of "his forces, againſt them, who ſubdued them, and af-"terwards the Romans publiſhed an edict, abſolutely "prohibiting the Jews acceſs to this iſland"

CHAP. III.

Rebellion of the Jews under Adrian, of Barcochebas and [illegible], till the hundred and thirty-eight year of the Christian aera.

THESE might be said to be only the beginning of the sorrows of the Jews which were at length completed by Adrian, who reduced them to such an abject state of wretchedness, [illegible] the ordinary means of subsistence they were [illegible] to the study of magic [illegible] of dreams.

We need to [illegible] of the emperor Adrian himself, who says [illegible] one Jew in Egypt but what was [illegible] present so [illegible] apply to this study, was [illegible] mathematicians were [illegible].

The cause of this [illegible]. They say that it was the custom [illegible] to plant a cedar at the door of the [illegible] was born, and to set a pine-tree [illegible] daughter. These trees grew till the [illegible] and then they were cut down to make [illegible] married couple. The princess [illegible] passing in Judea, her chariot broke, and her [illegible] the insolence to cut down one of these [illegible] before a house, wherewith they mended [illegible]. But the relations and [illegible] murdered, and massacred [illegible], who being enraged, obliged the emperor [illegible] so fierce a nation.

Chrysostom [illegible] Jews, who always, from their prejudices [illegible] own maxims, have three times attempted to rebel [illegible] their first effort to restore their [illegible] under Adrian, that they rebelled against him, without [illegible] on the consequences [illegible] impossible [illegible] this prince having [illegible] them, placed [illegible] Jerusalem [illegible] knowing that [illegible] would not [illegible] for ever ordered [illegible] his [illegible], which was still [illegible] called [illegible]. Chrysostom [illegible] of precision, [illegible] restore their temple [illegible] is deceived, since they made no [illegible] the attempts after [illegible]. The same must be said of the second [illegible] the Jews went to re-establish their republic. [illegible] attempted to rebuild Jerusalem [illegible], Ælia had been built before the rebellion [illegible] still go by the name of Ælia [illegible] council of Nice, but Constantine [illegible] temples in this city, and Christianity [illegible] triumphant there, it resumed its [illegible] Eusebius, who had called [illegible] Jerusalem [illegible] of the edifices that [illegible].

There were two causes of the great rebellion under Adrian. First, this prince [illegible] forbidden them like Domitian and Nerva, to be circumcised. Spartian says so, and I know not how [illegible] of an author can be contested who lived under [illegible]. Modestinus observes also, that the Jews [illegible] themselves to [illegible] he permitted them to circumcise only their own children, and forbid doing it to any person of another religion under heavy penalties. Secondly, There is a law forbidding all the Roman citizens to be circumcised like the Jews, or to cause their slaves to be circumcised, upon pain of banishment, and awarding death to the physicians that should do it. It also banishes and condemns, sometimes to death, the Jews that cut the children of another religion. Did the Jews attempt to circumcise strangers, in order to increase their numbers whereby to go on afterwards more effectually in the restoration of their commonwealth, as St Chrysostom [illegible] said? Some great men have said it after him. But it is not probable they believed that the converted Roman citizens, or their slaves, could make up a considerable army to restore their state. The Roman proselytes were never so numerous to possess them with this conceit. These edicts [illegible] given only to prevent any changes of religion, which now and then happened at Rome, and scandalized the heathens. Besides, Antoninus licensed them to circumcise themselves after his [illegible] with them. This prince, being weary of their rebellion, and seeing that denying them this custom exasperated them, yielded [illegible] but they were not then in a condition [illegible] proselyte sufficient numbers to form armies, and restore their commonwealth. Adrian who had forbidden them circumcision affected the Jews in one of the principal points of their religion [illegible] the seal of the covenant, the mark that distinguished them from heathens, and the grace of God [illegible] annexed this custom [illegible] no surprising thing that they should [illegible] deprived of this ceremony.

This prince had also sent [illegible] colony to Jerusalem, and built a city upon its ruins, to [illegible] his own name, and consecrated it to Jupiter Capitolinus. The second cause of the war is [illegible] disputed [illegible] the first, since Eusebius says [illegible] the colony [illegible] to Jerusalem till after the taking of Bither. But Dion says this colony was the cause of their rebellion, because they could not bear to have strangers [illegible] in their city, and worship strange gods [illegible]. To reconcile Eusebius and Dion, it appears that the emperor's first design was crossed by the Jews rebelling before it was fully executed, because the Jews had expelled the new inhabitants, though the emperor accomplished it when he had subdued them. So that he had sent the colony before the war, as Dion affirms, and he completed his project, when the rebellion was quelled, as Eusebius relates.

Barchochebas's ambition, who knew how to make his advantage of the disturbance which these two circumstances created in the minds of the people, fully determined the nation to prosecute the war. But to speak of the false Messiahs that have deceived their nation.

The time was come in which impostors appeared with full assurance. Gamaliel had seen two of them perish, and was so moved with the ill success of their enterprize, that he would not have the progress of Christianity opposed, being persuaded that Providence would bring the design to nought if it was not from heaven. "Theudas" (said he) before these days rose up, who was slain, and "all, as many as obeyed him, were brought to nought. "After this man rose up Judas of Galilee, in the days of "the taxing, and he also perished: and now I say unto "you, if this counsel be of men it will come to nought." The Christians, from a high sense of his great moderation [illegible] afterwards canonized him.

St Luke in the 5th chapter of the Acts of the Apostles, particularly speaks of the impostors, Theudas and Judas of Galilee, whom Gamaliel mentions to the people, as having [illegible] heretofore to deceive, from which (though his design was to invalidate the [illegible] doctrine) it is evident such delusions had been practised.

The Romans sent [illegible] forces against Judas, and he miserably perished [illegible] Alexander, Judas's successor persecuted his children, and caused them to be murdered. His followers maintained their master's doctrine with an unshaken confidence, in the midst of the most cruel tortures. They subsisted, notwithstanding the violence that was offered them, after the taking of Jerusalem, in a very ancient castle, where they were [illegible] carried.

this doctrine into Egypt, where it occasioned new massacres.

Other impostors started up, and, with the same fallacious pretensions, endeavoured to delude the credulous multitude; but the most impious, daring and injurious was *Coziba* or *Barchochebas*. He was a robber, like the rest, who hoped to enrich himself with plunder, and acquire some authority in his nation by his outrages against the Romans. It is pretended that there were two impostors of this name, the grandfather and grandson, and their history is thus related by the Jews. Coziba I. was elected king by the Jews two years after the ruin of the first temple, [illegible] at Bither, a city in the neighbourhood of Jerusalem, which was the capital of his empire. His son the Red succeeded him, and afterwards reigned his grandson Romulus, who was called Coziba. The Jews assembled about him, and acknowledged him for the Messiah. The emperor Adrian, having notice of it, came with a numerous army, took Bither, and destroyed a multitude of the Jews in the seventy-third year after the ruin of the temple. Hence it is concluded that the reign of the three Cozibas lasted one and twenty years. Some extend it much farther, and make the first Coziba's reign under Domitian. The antient chronicle of the Jews, on the contrary, assigns but two years and a half to Coziba's reign.

It is absurdly supposed there have been two Cozibas, or Barchochebases. Most of the Jews acknowledge but one, and they are right. For he that induced the Jews to rebellion, towards the end of Trajan's reign, was not called Barchochebas, but Andrea. Neither did he call himself the Messiah, and this rebellion was in Egypt, whereas that of Barchochebas happened in Judæa. They were unacquainted with Trajan's genealogy, since they say that he sent Adrian, his sister's son, against the Jews in Egypt, for Ulpia, Adrian's grandmother, was Trajan's aunt, and these two princes were only cousins. They err in making the war with Coziba last so long, and give him, and his heirs and successors, a reign of one and twenty years, for his race ended with him, and the war [illegible] in a little time, as we shall see in the sequel. They make him perish in the seventy-third year of the ruin of the temple. Adrian was already dead, in the year 14[illegible], and the city of Bither, by which the war was concluded, had been taken in the eighteenth of Adrian. This chronological error suffices to shew the misrepresentations of the rest. The author of the chronicle of the Jews is more exact than his commentators, for he makes Coziba to reign but two years and a half, and speaks but of one impostor. We must therefore acknowledge but one Coziba, who took the title of Barchochebas, lived in Adrian's reign, and was the source of infinite mischiefs to his nation.

This impostor, to facilitate the success of his enterprize, changed his name, and took that of the Son of the Star, or Barchochebas, in order to have it believed that he was the Star that "Balaam had seen afar off." He maintained that he was one of the stars of heaven sent to succour the people, and relieve them from the oppression under which they groaned. He also made choice of a forerunner of the same character with himself, who was very assistant to him in his designs.

This was Akiba, whom, they say, descended from Sisera, general of the army of Jabin, king of Tyre, and from a Jewish mother. He had spent forty years upon the plains, in looking to the flocks of a rich citizen at Jerusalem, called Calba Chuva. His master's daughter being in love with him, and unwilling to marry a shepherd, advised him to apply himself to study. They made a clandestine marriage, after which Akiba went and spent twelve years in the academies, and brought back with him twelve thousand scholars. His wife advised him to return again. He continued full twelve years more, and brought with him twenty thousand disciples. His wife came to meet him with her clothes rent, because her father provoked with her marriage, had disinherited her; but no sooner had he seen Akiba than he fell at his feet, revoked his oath, and gave him a great part of his estate. He continued teaching and writing books, one where[illegible] is cabalistical, and is called Jezirah, but it must be distinguished from that which is ascribed to the Patriarch Abraham, and bears the same name. He was so learned as to give an account of the least letter of the law. We find in the Mishnah and Thalmud [illegible] of [illegible] sentences ascribed to him, and which are looked upon as [illegible] judicious decisions. These are the commendations they give this doctor, who caused the desolation of [illegible] nity, and supported the fraud of an impostor. No great weight therefore can be laid upon what the Jews relate concerning the birth and death of Akiba, since they are perfectly ignorant of that time.

Barchochebas appearing at the time that Akiba's [illegible] was at the height when he was head of the Sanhedrim, he exclaimed, "Behold the Star that was to come out of Jacob!" and made himself his forerunner. These two impostors availed themselves of the prejudices of the people, who were for a conquering Messiah, that should deliver them from the Roman yoke, which the last war and Adrian's persecution, had made more insupportable. Barchochebas, who found the people disposed to follow him, mustered up an army of 200,000 men, and Bither was chosen for his residence, and the capital of his kingdom. The Jews called it Bither, or the *House of Spies*, because, after the ruin of Jerusalem, centinels were placed there to [illegible] those that went to Jerusalem, who were accused of courting the Roman favour, and defaming others, or of selling their estates, of which they stripped them by virtue of these calumnies. They even sometimes impeached them to the [illegible] [illegible] Eusebius places this city in the neighbourhood of Jerusalem, but there were two cities of this name, one twelve, and the other fifty-two, miles distant from the holy city.

Jerome called these two cities Bethoron, and maintains they were built by Solomon, and [illegible], the war Bethoron was given by Pharaoh for a portion to his daughter, when she married Solomon, who restored it to the Levites in whose partition it lay. But if we believe the Jews, this is not the true Bither, since one signifies a *House of Spies*, and the other a *House of Liberty*. Barchochebas chose this place to receive the royal unction, and afterwards caused money to be coined, declaring himself at the same time the Messiah and the Jewish prince of the nation. He waited to declare war when the emperor Adrian had left Egypt, but it broke out in the year 134 in the seventeenth of Adrian's reign.

Dion asserts, that Adrian, having sent a colony to Jerusalem, and placed a statue of Jupiter where the temple of God stood, this foreign worship violently affected the Jews. "However Adrian's presence, who was then in "Egypt, and who went from thence to Syria, stopped "them for some Time. They contented themselves, "during his time, with making imperfect arms, and "selling them to the Romans, that they might not employ them against themselves; but they revolted when "the emperor was gone."

Phlegon, Adrian's secretary, has preserved a letter of his master addressed to Servian, the consul. He gives him an account of what he had seen in Egypt, and of the turbulent inclination of its inhabitants, and makes him a present of some vessels, which he had designed for him and his sister. It is easier to know the time of the Jewish war from this letter, than from the medals of the cities of Syria, for it must have been written when the emperor left Egypt or Syria. Servian, to whom this letter was written, was his brother-in-law, since he made him a present in common with his sister and himself. This Servian was called consul, which dignity he had not till after Adrian's [illegible] 134. We must therefore conclude from that the emperor left [illegible]

Egypt and Syria till the beginning of that year, and that his absence the same year instigated the Jews to rebellion. Another Heathen historian, quoted by Eusebius, asserts, that the war was in its whole vigour; and that Bither, which the rebels had fortified, was taken the tenth of August, in the eighteenth year of Adrian. The war therefore began the preceding year, since it was in its vigour, and near its conclusion. The emperor gave his name to the city he had built about the ruins of Jerusalem in the year 130, in which he celebrated his Vicennalia. So that the war began in the year 134, and ended two years after. Buonarotti produces a medal struck by this prince in the eighteenth year of his reign, for having obtained a great victory over the rebels, and driven the Jews from Jerusalem. To this nothing can be objected, but the authority of the Jews quoted by Jerom, who say the war lasted three years and a half.

The Romans at first seem to have neglected this revolt; as the Jews had been so effectually humbled by Trajan's wars, they could hardly imagine they would so soon be in a condition to oppose them. But when they saw the numbers of the [illegible] increase, and that they fought with a valour that seemed [illegible] upon despair, that all the robbers of the neighbouring provinces joined them in hopes of plunder, and that not only Judæa, but all the world was in motion, they were obliged to change their measures. Some think that the emperor marched in person against the rebels, because they observe, that this prince, writing to the senate, had not ventured to preface his letters with the ordinary form [illegible] of the great losses he had sustained in this war; but, on due enquiry, it appears that he carried it on by his generals.

Barchochebas, who was superior in troops, at first committed great [illegible]. Justin Martyr complained that he openly attacked and massacred the Christians, because they would not abjure their religion. His hatred against these professors of religion, and despair of making the Christians embark in his violent measures, who had the same interest as himself to declare against the Romans, might redouble his cruelty. But can it be imagined that the Heathens, against whom he declared war, and the colony which Adrian had begun to send to Jerusalem, were more humanely treated by this usurper than the Christians? This impostor only favoured his own nation, and treated with the utmost barbarity all others that fell into his hands.

We find, by Eusebius and Syncellus, that the general, who commanded the army in Judæa against Barchochebas, was called Tinnius Rufus. Adrian, who was not acquainted with the importance of the war, sent him at first a great reinforcement; but this commander being often defeated, he sent for Julius Severus, one of the greatest generals of his age, from Britain. This able commander deeming it imprudent to engage so powerful an army, attacked them in parties, straitened them in their camp, cut off their provisions, and by that means growing superior, laid siege to Bither, which they made their retreat.

The rabbins say, that there were in that city four hundred colleges, in each college four hundred professors, and that each professor of these colleges had four hundred scholars, who being mustered up made a great army. They sustained the first efforts of the siege, though they were very badly armed, and unacquainted with discipline. Barchochebas encouraged all his subjects, and executed Tryphon, a famous rabbin, who talked of surrendering. Nevertheless the city was taken, and Barchochebas was killed. Adrian, to whom they brought his head, was desirous to see his body; but when they attempted to carry it, they found a serpent about his neck, which frightened the soldiers, and the prince acknowledged that God alone could kill that man. However, they have since owned the imposture of this man, whom they afterward called Barcozibo, or, *The Son of* [illegible]. The scholars who had so well defended the place, were bound with their books, and thrown into the [illegible]. They add, that the slaughter was so great, that more people died in this war than came out of Egypt. Upon one single stone were found the skulls of 300 children. The inhabitants of that place did not dung their ground for seven years together, being sufficiently fattened by the carcasses; therefore they have inserted in their liturgy a [illegible] appointed for the fast which is fixed the eighteenth of the month of Ab, [illegible] to the months of July and August, in which they call Adrian a second Nebuchadnezzar, and pray God to remember this [illegible] prince, who destroyed [illegible]. As for Akiba, after a very severe imprisonment, he was condemned to a cruel death, and with him [illegible] the glory of the Jewish laws.

Indeed, Dion represents this war as one of the cruellest that ever was. The Romans were frequently beaten, and lost abundance of good troops. The Jews, who had, at that time, a profound veneration for Solomon's tomb, saw it fall, and at once the wild beasts entered [illegible], which [illegible] was an omen of the following slaughter. The presage was not insignificant, for five hundred and eighty thousand persons were killed in the battles, and the numbers that perished by famine, misery, or fire, cannot be reckoned. After the taking of Bither, the Jews had still [illegible] fortified castles and troops to defend them. It seems [illegible] from a medal that the emperor [illegible] the year following [illegible] he had obtained [illegible] over them [illegible], the resistance was not long, and the leaders being taken off, the rest more easily submitted.

Adrian finished the building of Ælia, (Jerusalem) [illegible] the Jews of [illegible] [illegible] this work to Thus Titus, [illegible] in his [illegible], that he gave Aquila, his brother-in-law, the care of these buildings; but this proselyte, who turned Jew after he had embraced Christianity, had no court [illegible] with this prince, nor do we find that he was entrusted with the inspection of these buildings. The circumference of the new city was somewhat different from the old, several places being included in it that were formerly without its gates; but, in the main, they made use of the foundations of the first city. [illegible] denies it, and, [illegible] for a reason, alledges, that Adrian could be far from rebuilding a city [illegible] to the Romans and favouring the Jews, who had brought upon him such a wretched war. But this prince did not do it in favour of the Jews, for he gave it to other inhabitants. And therefore historians observe, that they began to receive a bishop there, who came of heathen race. The design was to mortify the old inhabitants, by excluding them for ever from their primitive habitation.

The truth is, Adrian prohibited their return for ever; and to make the city odious, if it were possible, he changed the use of the remaining monuments of old Jerusalem, for he employed the stones that had been used in the building of the temple to make a theatre, and he erected statues of false gods in the place where the temple formerly stood. And, lastly, St Jerome says, that he caused the image of a hog to be placed over the gate that led to Bethlehem, to shew that the Jews were subject to the power of the Romans; but he is mistaken, the swine was not placed there to indicate the Jews slavery, but to make them abhor entering into Jerusalem, because they hated this animal, the use of which was forbidden by their law, and they thought the gate was defiled and profaned by this figure.

Adrian the more effectually to excl[illegible] the [illegible] inhabitants, caused a great [illegible] to be [illegible] or Terebinth. Hegesippus says, that [illegible] a tree that had continued from the creation of the world, under which they [illegible] to [illegible] where Abraham had pitched his tent, [illegible] the angels, which made it venerable [illegible] there at the [illegible] could not be found, were carried to [illegible] was [illegible] at [illegible] words, "A cry was heard in Ramath, Rachael weeping for her children" because their misery and affliction were excessive. This Father also applied to the miseries that happened under Adrian this prophecy of Zechariah, "I will feed the flock of slaughter," because that he had learnt, from the tradition and ancient history of the Jews, that this prince had put a great number to death, punished others with the most rigorous severity, and sold them at Terebinth, or carried them into Egypt. This Father acquaints us with three things. 1. That he had read the traditions and history of the Jews concerning their calamities, and therefore there must have been such at that time. 2. That Terebinth fair still continued, but that the Jews were ashamed to be present at it, because they remembered the usage of their fathers. 3. That the Jews assembled and came, in his time, to buy, of the soldiers, the liberty of seeing Jerusalem. They could not weep without paying for it. The old men and women came there with tears in their eyes, to go to the mount of Olives, and bewail the destruction of the temple. The soldiers made great advantage of the Jews veneration for the remains of the holy city, and of Adrian's severity of forbidding their entrance for ever, for they sold them, at a dear rate, the sight of this place and the liberty of strewing perfumes upon a stone there. He once assures us, that Adrian conveyed part of these prisoners to Egypt, where their number was considerably augmented.

Adrian having successfully concluded the war in Judæa, struck medals, on which was seen a woman holding two naked children, and sacrificing upon an altar, with these words.

ADVENTUS AUG. JUDÆÆ.

The arrival of the Emperor in Judæa.

Tristan thought that the woman who sacrifices represents a subdued province, which consents to become heathen, and to sacrifice to the false god, and that she brings to the altar two naked children, to shew that she renounced circumcision. The emperor meant rather to signify, by the altar and sacrifice, that the old religion was abolished in this province, which he had colonized with new inhabitants. We see another medal of this same prince, where JUDÆA is represented as a woman on her knees, giving her hand to the emperor, and three children imploring mercy. One of these children is naked. Will it be said that the design of it was to shew his not being circumcised? The medalist's intention was to impress a monument, representing the submission and desperate misery of Judæa, after Barchocnebas's defeat.

Those that dealt in the east were much more fortunate. Trajan had carried the war against them as far as Mesopotamia. But Adrian, upon his accession to the throne, having preferred an inglorious peace to a doubtful war, consented that the Euphrates should be made the boundary of the Roman empire. So that the Jews of this country had no share in this prince's war against their nation.

It is true a confederacy had been formed of three sorts of Jews. Some inhabitants of the neighbouring provinces, animated with the hopes of plunder, and the first advantageous success, joined their antient enemies to fight the Romans. Many Jews of other provinces of the empire, who still breathed after their liberty, and sought an opportunity of recovering it, laid hold on this. Perhaps too some came from the remotest parts, and from beyond Euphrates, to the succour of their brethren, and therefore the number of the dead amounted to above six hundred thousand, which number could not have been found in Judæa alone, after what it had suffered under Trajan. Nevertheless it cannot be said that Adrian himself carried the war into the east, and passed the Euphrates, for he went in to his retreat at Tivoly, where he diverted himself completely and only by the exercise of his various exercises.

We find that this prince had added a new degree of misery to the Jews, by imposing on them a tribute for liberty of reading the Bible in Hebrew, and that this tribute was still paid in Tertullian's time, for he says, in his Apology, that the Jews, every sabbath, purchased the liberty of reading publicly by a tax they paid. They say that the Jews that had highly esteemed the Septuagint version, became to abhor it, when they perceived it was more favourable to the Christians than the Hebrews. But Adrian commanded them only to use this version, so that they were forced to pay money to read the Hebrew in the synagogues on the sabbath.

CHAP. IV.

Of the disciples of Akiba, and of the other learned men that lived at that time.

WE are told that Akiba left many disciples who distinguished themselves by their learning. But the most celebrated amongst them was Judah Hakkadosh, who compiled the Mishnah, or Commentary on Leviticus. He was the son of Simeon the Just, born at Sepphoris and flourished during the reigns of the three emperors, who were great enemies to the Christians, but very favourable to the Jews, viz. Antoninus Pius, M. Aurelius, and Commodus. He became very considerable on account of his sanctity and much more for his great learning, and presided over the great academy of Tiberias with uncontrouled authority. But he was esteemed above all for his famous book called the Mishnah, or repetition of the law, of which the following is an abstract.

The Mishnah is divided into six parts. The first, intitled "Seder Zeraim," and treats on seeds in the ground, trees, fruits, plants, &c.

The second, "Seder Moadim," treats of the Jewish feasts.

The third, "Seder Nashim," treats of women, and all matrimonial causes.

The fourth, "Seder Nezikim," treats of losses, damages, trade, and law-suits arising from them, and the manner of proceeding in them.

The fifth, "Seder Kodoshim," treats of sacrifices, oblations, and all other holy or sacrificed things.

The sixth treats of all kinds of expiations, and all things relating to purification. Each of these books contained several tracts, amounting in the whole to sixty-three.

This code, or body, of oral traditions, is founded upon a five-fold authority.

1st. Upon the writings of Moses, whose exposition are contained in the Pentateuch, and are either decisive of themselves, or by consequences fairly drawn from them.

2d. Upon the ordinances of that legislator delivered to him on the mount, or, as they are commonly stiled, the oral law, which is looked upon to be of the same authority with the written.

3d. Upon the different decisions of the antient doctors concerning which a man is at liberty to take which side he pleases, whether, for instance, those of Hillel or Shammai.

4th. On the maxims and sayings of the prophets and wise men, which are on that account stiled the hedges or fences of the law, but from which the Rabbins do on occasion swerve, though in the main, they hold them in great esteem.

5th. Of the ancient [illegible] and customs, which have once gained the sanction of [illegible] Jews, and are made by it equally obligatory.

This is the sum of that so much boasted treatise, which is therefore the whole body of civil and ecclesiastical rights of the Jews, and is a collection of their oral laws, rules &c. However, it is probable this book was not published, or, at least, received immediately, since we find mention made, in Hegesippus, of such oral traditions being still appealed to, and compiled towards the latter end of the second century. Those who want a fuller account of [illegible] may consult the Latin version of Surenhusius, with the [illegible] and learned commentators.

Jeremiah [illegible], who lived also in Adrian's reign, [illegible] "that every age [illegible] that was made in the name of God remained, and that others were dispersed," because virtue is the soul of societies, and that not [illegible] them close, but vice [illegible] destroys them. We should not speak of Eleazar, the son of Simeon Jochaides, who was pursued by the Romans, and concealed among [illegible] with his father, were not some prayers ascribed to him which the [illegible] and German Jews make use of.

One of the most famous of all Akiba's pupils was the illustrious Meir. [illegible] gave him this name because he was the light of the learned, and opened the eyes of his disciples. He married a learned woman, whose decisions the Thalmudists receive with [illegible] reverence than those of her husband, notwithstanding all their veneration for him.

Dositheus was one of Meir's disciples, but we must not confound him with one Dositheus a priest [illegible] Esdras' [illegible] to the Cuthaeans to teach them the law, that they might not be devoured by lions. There was also another Dositheus, who was [illegible] [illegible] who could not have lived under Meir, [illegible] lived not till the end of the second century. This man determined that it was no crime to forget [illegible] except when it was done voluntarily, [illegible] forgetfulness became innocent, [illegible] was the cause of it. This decision is not very curious, [illegible] yet it has advanced Dositheus into the rank of [illegible] whose sentences are religiously preserved.

Somechus the son of Joses, was another of Meir's [illegible] and a most excellent casuist.

Chipeta, a citizen of Sipporis, had two sons that flourished under Meir. Joses [illegible] famous. The emperor Adrian banished him from Tiberias, and sent him to live in his native country, where the learned were [illegible] as in an academy. [illegible] he took to the trade of a currier. The Jews who find most part of the [illegible] to be only mechanics, [illegible] the [illegible] such a custom by making a law, commanding all Rabbins to learn a trade. Some Christians [illegible] this was done in imitation of the apostles and disciples, who laboured with their own hands; but this reasoning is unjust, for [illegible] of the apostles was a subject of jealousy, the [illegible] ought not to have destroyed this [illegible] changed it into a reproach, by forbidding the [illegible] of a man that had not a benefice [illegible] Besides [illegible] like St. Paul, [illegible] authorise such an [illegible] indolence as that of the Monks.

His younger brother, Simeon, who lived under Antoninus, and the following generation [illegible] is a man eminent for his skill in the learned and more [illegible] sciences.

The same age produced another Simeon, the son of Eleazar, a man of learning, but of excessive [illegible] which, however, according to the account of [illegible] [illegible] the graces of modesty or candour.

[illegible] Judah, the author of the Mishna [illegible] large, and presume these sketches will suffice to shew the genius of the doctors of that age.

CHAP. V.

Antoninus Pius becomes a [illegible] to the Jewish religion. Is offended with the Jews, and makes war against them. Defeats them, and grants them privileges [illegible] restrictions. Justin Martyr holds a conference with Trypho. Principles of the [illegible] Marcus Aurelius [illegible] [illegible] and punishes them for [illegible] [illegible] Conspiracy [illegible] [illegible] [illegible] by Justin Martyr [illegible] Samaritans.

ANTONINUS Pius, who [illegible] Adrian, and [illegible] to the highest [illegible] represented as a great friend and patron of [illegible] been a [illegible] of [illegible] circumcision. He always, however, [illegible] and though he professed Judaism, which [illegible] perfectly acquainted with [illegible] devoted to the service of idols. He could not [illegible] the Jews, and so strenuously applied himself to the study of the law and tradition, that he joined with his master Judah in the composition of the Mishnah.

Antoninus, however, instead of countenancing the Jews, was soon under a necessity of making war against them, because they had rebelled. Adrian's [illegible] of circumcision was still in force [illegible] emperor who had forced them to it [illegible] of his [illegible] and power of [illegible] could not long brook their being deprived of this accustomed sign of their religion. They rose the first opportunity, and were resolved sword in hand to compel Antoninus to give them this liberty. [illegible] [illegible] compared [illegible] [illegible] of five or six [illegible] occasioned Baronius to believe that the [illegible] of the Jews happened in the first year of his reign [illegible] the Jews [illegible] perfect and extremely debilitated [illegible] years to collect a body [illegible] [illegible] account is [illegible] [illegible] [illegible] different [illegible] The Jews were [illegible] ed, Antoninus [illegible] when he had conquered them, he restored them the privilege of circumcision under these restrictions.

1. It only related to the Jews, but the Samaritans, who professed the same religion, had not the benefit of it. 2. Proselytes were also excluded, and none of them were suffered to be made Jews by this rite.

Justin Martyr had at that time a conference with Trypho. The Jews speak of a famous Rabbin, who was [illegible] or colleague with Akiba, called [illegible] and Dr. Lightfoot thinks [illegible] he that Justin [illegible] ed with. He was [illegible] for we are told that Akiba, being employed [illegible] of the poor, [illegible] him [illegible] [illegible] Though he was [illegible] of Samai's school, yet he has been esteemed, and many [illegible] his are preserved and inserted [illegible] of the Talmud. [illegible] them [illegible] because of the [illegible] God commands, and the recompence will be considerable. Nevertheless he teaches, "That man is not obliged to the performance of the whole, [illegible] provided he does his endeavour to know [illegible] part of it, yet he shall receive a great [illegible]"

We [illegible] from him, that the name of twelve letters [illegible] to be pronounced in that [illegible] The name of Jehovah [illegible] because it expresses the essence of

God without ambiguity, whereas the others only make him known by his attributes. There was moreover a dispute among the doctors about the manner of pronouncing it. The prophane, who increased their numbers after the death of Simeon the Just, abused it, and therefore they left off pronouncing it. Instead of this ineffable name was substituted one of twelve letters, which the priest uttered in giving the blessing to the people. But Tarphon affirms, that one day coming near the priest to hear him pronounce his benediction, he perceived that he did not articulate the twelve letters, but that he only muttered whilst the brethren sung, and the reason of this change proceeded from the number of the prophane, which was increased. They highly commend the wisdom of this Tarphon and his knowledge in the law.

Though Marcus Aurelius was naturally of a mild temper, yet this exempted not the Jews from great miseries during his reign. This prince had such an opinion of them, that, as he once passed through Judea in his way to Egypt, he cried out, that he had found people as wicked as the Marcomans and Sarmatians, those barbarous nations that made continual war, and ravaged a great part of his empire in his reign.

Besides, there were two circumstances very prejudicial to them. Vologesus, king of Parthia, was making war-like preparations at the time that Antoninus died, and he commenced the war a little after his death by violent incursions. Severian, the governor of Cappadocia, attempting to oppose him, perished with his whole army. Marching afterwards into Syria the Parthians made terrible destruction. The eastern Jews, who were subject to the Parthians, and enemies to the Romans joined them, and increased the number of their troops. Marcus Aurelius sent Lucius Verus, his colleague, with the best officers of the empire, but he stopped at Antioch to relax, and left the war to the management of his generals. Cassius who commanded, beat Vologesus, and pursued him to his capital Ctesiphon, which he took, and demolished the palace of the kings. Babylon, which still made some figure, Mesopotamia, and the lands of the Medes where there were a great number of Jews, were laid waste. Seleucia, upon the banks of the Tigris, voluntarily surrendered; but the Romans violating the capitulation, killed four or five hundred thousand persons. By a treaty of peace concluded four years after the beginning of the war, Mesopotamia and Osrœne, however remained subject to the Romans. Thus the Jews of this country were reduced once more under their obedience.

Cassius who left the east to vanquish the Sarmatians, flushed with so many exploits and victories, which raised him to the rank of heroes, encouraged as is said, by Faustina, Marcus Aurelius's wife, who was for making him an emperor, that she might marry him after her husband's death, assumed the title of emperor in Syria, where he was governor, having first spread a report that the throne was vacant by Marcus Aurelius's death. His reign was but a dream, for it lasted but three months and six days. However, the Jews, who only waited for an opportunity to rise, seeing the fire kindled in the neighbourhood, added fuel to the flames, by joining with the rebels. Marcus Aurelius pardoned the children of Cassius, whose head had been brought to him, and spared the blood of the senators who had engaged in the conspiracy. He even caused his letters to be burnt, that they might not be known. But he could not bear the insult which the Jews had offered him, and to punish them he renewed Adrian's laws against them. Whether these laws were all executed, particularly in Asia where the Jews were numerous, and very remote from the capital, or that they purchased the liberty of annoying the Christians, they signalized themselves in this country by their hatred. Justin Martyr had before charged them with the consequences of his [illegible], which frequently broke out. But they manifested it at Smyrna, in Polycarp's martyrdom, for they not only joined their voices with the heathens, [illegible] the theatre, "He is an Atheist," but were [illegible] vehement [illegible]. They [illegible] after his death, by soliciting the judge to deny his body to the Christians, [illegible] at last, the captain of the [illegible] seeing the bitter rage of the Jews against the [illegible] caused it to be reduced to ashes.

[illegible] might be [illegible] ble, and tolerated by reason of the [illegible] to the Christians, yet it is certain that the Jews enjoyed great [illegible] of conscience in Smyrna, since they [illegible] [illegible] ablished themselves [illegible]. Moreover we find some footsteps of their [illegible] in Phrygia, [illegible] that [illegible] the Montanists, who [illegible] the prophets. "Is there one [illegible] from the "origin of the sect has been persecuted [illegible] Jews, "or killed by the impious? Is there [illegible] "has been whipped in the synagogues or stoned?" This author attributes to the Jews the persecutions of the Christians, and the branches that divided [illegible]. He adds the power of scourging. The [illegible] tumultuous rabble in Asia, in Marcus Aurelius's time, pursued the Christians in the streets with stones, and sometimes crucified them. It is even very probable that Thraseas, bishop of Eumenia, or [illegible], in Phrygia Pacatiana, was martyred in this manner. The circumcised must have been numerous in this part of the world, since Montanus endeavoured to allure them, by giving the name of Jerusalem to two little cities of Phrygia, which he looked upon as the principal seats of his sect.

This time produced the conversion and [illegible] baptism of a Jew. A man of this nation travelling, in the reign of Marcus Aurelius, with Christians in a desert, [illegible] with so violent thirst, that it was thought he was going to expire. He demanded baptism with great importance, which [illegible] the Christians uneasy, as [illegible] destitute of water. One of them supplied [illegible], by taking sand, which he threw upon the [illegible] body, pronouncing the baptismal form. The Jew recovered by this new baptism, and marched on to the city of Alexandria. Dionysius who was then bishop there, being informed of the fact, ordered the Jew to be rebaptized with water. Nicephorus adds, that another instance happened under Athanasius, and he [illegible] a third example, that fell out in his time at Constantinople.

The conversion of Hegesippus who lived at that time, seems also dubious to many. It is agreed that he was a Jew, and that he embraced Christianity, but some Socinists represent him as a kind of half Christian, not being brought to give up certain tenets he had imbibed from his infancy.

Though the truth would not be weakened by the [illegible] of its defenders, and by [illegible] imagine we form [illegible] his [illegible] of his doctrine, yet we cannot forbear saying, that the arguments produced against him are very weak. For Eusebius only says, that he had published several things drawn from the Hebrew and Syriac gospel, and the unwritten traditions of the Jews. It should therefore be concluded, that he continued a Jew [illegible] received the unwritten traditions of the synagogue, as it is concluded he was [illegible], because he has sometimes quoted the Hebrew gospel. Nevertheless, nobody denies that he embraced Christianity. Hegesippus says, that he went to Corinth, where the church continued constant in the [illegible] ity of the faith, and that Primus, who was then bishop of it, gave him great comfort by the discourses they [illegible] concerning the truth. From thence he went to Rome and maintained constant communion with the bishop [illegible] the see. The church of Corinth was neither Arian nor [illegible] [illegible]. Hegesippus attributes to it the profession of [illegible] faith. He united with this bishop, and consented [illegible]

[illegible] about this pure faith. It is therefore indisputable [illegible] Hegesippus was of the same religion with the bishop and the church, whose purity of faith he commends, and [illegible] he held the doctrine received at Corinth and Rome.

Hegesippus informs us, that there were traditions among the Jews, and that they were not written in his time. We have reason therefore to think, that Judah the Saint, did not compose the Mishnah till Commodus's reign, towards the end of the second century, since they were not yet published in Hegesippus's time, who lived under Marcus Antoninus. [illegible] had first placed him under Adrian, but it seems [illegible] he discovered his error and corrected it.

Hegesippus speaks of four famous sects among the Jews, [illegible] the Pharisees, the Sadducees and the Essenes, [illegible] which he adds the Galileans. These were the followers of that famous Judas, who rose in the days of the taxing made by Augustus, and who would not have the emperors acknowledged for their lords, nor tribute paid to them. This spirit of sedition was still in being, and these sectaries were those who had caused the terrible rebellions which completed the ruin of the nation. The Hemero-baptists are charged by Epiphanius with having incorporated all the errors of the Pharisees and Sadducees. But I do not see what reason there is for this accusation, for their name only denotes their care to wash themselves every day, or many times in a day. It was a branch of the Pharisees that [illegible] first taxed with fondness for washings, and who afterwards separated from the body of the sect to make a particular [illegible], and perhaps a more rigid one in point of washings.

Hegesippus reckons the Masbotheans amongst the Jewish sects. This sect arose after our Saviour, for they are not known from the gospel, nor by any more antient author. We discover their true opinion in the apostolical constitutions: they denied a Providence, and believed that every thing happened by chance: they also rejected the doctrine of the immortality of the soul. So that the Masbotheans were a branch of the Sadducees, as the Hemero-baptists proceeded from the Pharisees. I know not wherefore it has been thought that their name was borrowed from the sabbath, which they observed more religiously than others, for there is no analogy between the terms Masbotheans and Sabbatarians. It was the character of the heretics of that time to confound languages, and to coin uncommon words from them. There [illegible] other Masbotheans, disciples to Simon Magus, which Theodoret has distinguished from the Jewish sectaries, and with reason, for they derived their pedigree from one Masbothæus, their founder, and may be ranked among Christian heretics.

Justin Martyr gave Trypho a very different account of the sects that divided the Jews of this age, though he was cotemporary with Hegesippus. He passes over the Essenes in silence, as if they were vanished, and I could easily believe that Hegesippus only mentioned them because they had formerly made a considerable schism in the nation. Justin Martyr maintains three sects, the Genists, the Merists, and the Helenists. It is said the Genists derived their glory from being the descendants of Abraham the father of the faithful. The Merists divided the scripture, and would not receive all the prophets, because they were animated by different spirits. These Merists might be those mentioned by Benjamin of Tudela. He found a schism at Cairo, because the Jews at Babylon, and of the Irack divided the scripture differently from those of Syria. The former so portioned it, as to read it all in one year, the others multiplying the sections, read it but in three years. Scaliger imagined that the schism was between the Greeks and Babylonians, because he had read in Benjamin the word [illegible], which he translated the Greeks. But Constantine the emperor, who published and translated his travels, read [illegible]. The Jews of the Irack were perhaps Hegesippus's Merists, who began to separate about the manner of reading and dividing the scripture.

The Helenists began also to set up a new sect, of which it will not be amiss to trace the original. After the conquests of Alexander the Great, a distinction was made of the Helenist Jews, which is often [illegible] great characters in the gospel. This name was given them because they were mingled with the Greeks, [illegible] language, and read the Holy Scriptures in it, after they were translated. We observe this only difference between them and the other Jews, with whom otherwise they partook in the same religion, sacrifices, and ceremonies.

Scaliger [illegible] of very long [illegible] and that [illegible]. They reproach [illegible] the Scripture [illegible] and this was a kind of an affront. [illegible] came to blows, and whilst the second temple stood [illegible] Jerusalem said [illegible] Scaliger found traces of this [illegible] as low as the [illegible] century.

If Scaliger [illegible], the sect of the Hellenists would be much more antient [illegible]. But though there were some [illegible] between the Hellenists and the Jews of Palestine, yet it proceeded not to a separation or schism. The Hellenists [illegible] many synagogues at Jerusalem [illegible], where they performed their devotions, whilst [illegible] no disputes in this matter, [illegible] that his countrymen were ill used.

The [illegible] are divided, and [illegible] as to the [illegible], cause, and [illegible] of the division. Some, as Salmasius, think [illegible], that the Bible was never read in Greek, because it was not read in Arabic, which was more common, and better known by the Jews than the Greek could be. [illegible] both Hellenists and Jews into one synagogue at Jerusalem, and fancies that he finds a proof of it in the history of the Acts, where the Jews and Greeks were divided about the creation of the deacons, which could not have happened had they not been both in the same synagogue, [illegible] the question there was not about the converted Greeks and Jews, [illegible] but one body in the church, where they could not continue long without dividing.

Others [illegible] prepossessed in favour of the Septuagint version [illegible] above the original. [illegible] required that the Hellenists, who [illegible] Hebrew, should read them in Greek in their [illegible]. [illegible] true that Philo and some other of the learned understood the [illegible], there would still [illegible] Greek version for the great number of [illegible] that were in Egypt [illegible] the Roman jurisdiction [illegible] could not [illegible] in this [illegible] they [illegible] such another [illegible] the Chaldee [illegible] when [illegible] were [illegible], they [illegible] this defect by an explication or [illegible], which [illegible] being [illegible] that of the C[illegible] versions [illegible] the places where the Chaldee was not the language of the country [illegible] who lived at the time of [illegible] might be read and written in [illegible] hereafter why the Gemara has limited this [illegible] the five books of Moses. We [illegible] coming to Cæsarea, where there were [illegible] Greeks [illegible] surprized to hear the Hebrew [illegible] pronounced in Greek. But R. Jose [illegible] those that had stood [illegible] the Hebrew [illegible] the law, and [illegible] without [illegible],

"That whoever reads in a language he knows or understands, does his duty."

Lightfoot, who could not deny but that there were Greek copies in the synagogues, imagined that they were placed there by way of precaution, that when the heathens came in to explode their religion, they might be convinced by their own eyes it was not bad.

To own that there were Greek copies in the synagogues, is to confess that the law was read in this Language, and the Hebrews hindered not a custom that was universally received in the regions of the Roman empire. Nevertheless, they both of them considered the original as sacred, and preferable, as well to the versions as to Chaldee paraphrases, because it was God that had made choice of this tongue.

Christianity disturbed the harmony of the Jews. The Christians disputing with them, always used the version of the LXX which not only was better known, but [illegible] advantageous to them. Justin Martyr produce[illegible] proof [illegible] it, for he taxes the Hebrews with [illegible] having struck [illegible] these words of Jeremy, "I am like a [illegible] that is led to the slaughter," which were found in the seventieth [illegible] He carried his proofs farther, in quoting a passage [illegible] which is no where to be found, and [illegible] accused [illegible] having put into Greek, though [illegible] that this fraud was [illegible] it. These reproaches, [illegible] the Jews with the Greek version, [illegible] for those who were [illegible] were raised up above the version, [illegible] four [illegible] they flew into [illegible] produced four [illegible] The [illegible] and those that bore [illegible] with bitter reproaches, set up the feast [illegible] Justin Martyr. Here then you have the origin of [illegible] attempt [illegible] new versions, of which we shall give [illegible] The Gamarists, not being able to [illegible] the reading of the Greek book, confined it to the Pentateuch, because these five books contained less disputed prophecies than those of the other prophets. [illegible] the hatred of the Hellenists continually increased, those [illegible] brought [illegible] were invented, said to be wrought at the time that the Septuagint version was composed, and they talked of a fast that was celebrated on the account of this version, of which no mention is made in the Talmud. Thus [illegible] we discover [illegible] the history of the Hellenists, and not only [illegible] with probability but our opinions are founded upon many incontestable testimonies. These new sectaries appeared therefore a little before Justin Martyr, or rather the name of Hellenists, which was hitherto [illegible] great [illegible] and became the title of a sect.

The different parties fell to work upon several translations of the Scripture, and this sort of business became much in [illegible] among the Jews, which the Hellenists we have been speaking of desired, or else they became more necessary to dispute against the Christians [illegible] over all the Roman empire. Aquila was the first that engaged [illegible] whose version was received with a general applause of the Hellenists. Origen affirms, That all the Jews, who did not understand Hebrew, were accustomed to this version, which they looked upon to be the best of all. [illegible] not only says [illegible] but adds, that some heretics followed it. In the mean time the Thalmudists, full of that jealousy that had for some time prevailed against the Hellenists, made their efforts to disgust the people with it, and reduce them to the Hebrew Bible. We find, in their [illegible] several strokes of censure against the Greek one. The Christians complained of it, because it came from a suspected hand, and which had robbed them of many passages of Scripture, but, however, they sometimes [illegible] of it and St Jerome, who had condemned it [illegible] the exactness of the author. Theodotion [illegible] another of them. The Jews carried off this conquest from the church, for Theodotion, who was born an heathen, had embraced Christianity, but being brought over to Judaism, was circumcised. He was a native of Pontus, where he had known Marcion, his countryman, and had entered into his sect. From thence he went to Ephesus, where the Jews were numerous and considerable, and he listened to the synagogue. It seems that this was an [illegible] Antoninus's law who forbad the Jews the making of proselytes, and circumcising them. But we have [illegible] observed, that these laws were ill executed in Asia, and perhaps [illegible] had [illegible] made no [illegible] of [illegible] circumcision, and the Christians knew [illegible] enough. He learnt of his new masters Hebrew enough to translate the Scripture or rather to correct the Septuagint, for he followed them so [illegible] that Origen made use of his version to fill up the chasms and [illegible] that were found in the Septuagint. [illegible] the fifth year of Commodus's reign, according to the custom of the time, for the learned [illegible] to publish their works on the Decennalia [illegible] Vicennalia, and at the birth of princes, or when they came to the throne. Not to dispute [illegible] this custom did [illegible] make a sufficient figure in the [illegible] to honour Commodus's coronation by a version of the Holy scriptures? As odious as his person [illegible] the Christians reaped some advantage by his work, and read publicly his translation of the prophet Daniel, because that of the Septuagint was full of faults, either [illegible] because this version was by a hand that was much inferior to those that had worked upon the Pentateuch. Also the Ebionites and Nazarenes preferred it before all others. Symmachus composed a third translation in Severus's reign [illegible] appeared much clearer, and more useful than the preceding ones, because this author had more respect to the [illegible] than to the signification of words. The Christians made use of all these translations, though they were only made to their prejudice, and by [illegible] Howe[illegible] the [illegible] of the Septuagint still raised its head above all [illegible] new mangled pieces. [illegible] mean time [illegible] ordered, that [illegible] indictment to [illegible] its authors, no longer to be [illegible] in the synagogues, as it hitherto had been [illegible] to prevent the Christians, who disputed with the Jews from drawing objections [illegible] the [illegible] interpreters had echoed to or [illegible]'s oracle, "A virgin shall bring forth."

CHAP. VI.

The Jews [illegible] to Severus, who [illegible] the Parthians [illegible] is very [illegible] to the Jews [illegible] Jews [illegible] The Jews [illegible] Caracalla [illegible] Heliogabalus [illegible] the Jews [illegible] the Talmud [illegible] Alexander Severus [illegible] Jews.

PESCENNIUS Niger being proclaimed emperor [illegible] endeavoured to make [illegible] which was ad[illegible] for him, and finding this people [illegible] for Severus, he [illegible] the [illegible] could permit him [illegible] at first [illegible] ought to have [illegible] attachment to him. Besides he was [illegible] important affairs, being obliged to carry the [illegible] against Vologesus, king of Parthia. The Jews, who were numerous betwixt the Tigris and the Euphrates [illegible] much from this war. Adiabene whose kings [illegible] Judaism at the end of the last century [illegible] of this, was ravaged, Babylon and Seleucia were taken. The siege of Ctesiphon lasted long, [illegible] reduced to the necessity [illegible] city being carried by storm, [illegible] hearts were put to the sword, and 100,000 [illegible] carried prisoners out of it.

[illegible] Severus, being apprehensive that the Jews [illegible] Vologesus, [illegible] But it does not appear that they were distinguished from the rest of the subjects of the [illegible] empire, and the favourable edicts were not promulgated till after the war.

On the contrary, Severus [illegible] his return marched into Judea, and Eusebius says positively that he made war with the [illegible] and Jews. [illegible] the senate, confounding what the [illegible] Syria and the [illegible] decreed a [illegible] emperor [illegible] time, one of [illegible] left [illegible] by his custom. They [illegible] Jews [illegible] the [illegible]

[illegible] to them, which [illegible] Accordingly we [illegible] grievous [illegible]

[illegible] the same prince's reign [illegible] of the Jews [illegible] might prejudice their religion, [illegible] of the heathens like [illegible] some [illegible] ages. Nevertheless [illegible] from [illegible] at Rome, and [illegible] without being a denizen of [illegible] great city. Nevertheless, this prince persecuted [illegible] promoting them to dignities.

[illegible] that the Jews were looked upon as Roman citizens, [illegible] were charged with the [illegible] of the [illegible] that they were [illegible] and this [illegible] for [illegible] years, but [illegible] Leo [illegible] clause in the law [illegible] the Jews the [illegible] of all the privileges of Roman citizens, [illegible] of [illegible] offices of [illegible] if there was any [illegible] were too burthensome [illegible] for, and those [illegible] forced to an acceptance. The [illegible] exempted from [illegible] Constantius made a trade of [illegible] they sold. His successor Julian has been [illegible] extended [illegible] their exemptions, [illegible] that he scarcely [illegible] endeavoured to discharge themselves [illegible] pretences. Severus therefore shewed great [illegible] to the Jews in allowing them these exemptions, and his [illegible] with pride and insolence, especially against the persecuted Christians.

St Jerome says, that, in the twelfth year of Severus, a jubilee was celebrated. This term is peculiar to the Jews, [illegible] Scaliger has remarked, that whatsoever way we reckon the years, the Jewish jubilee could not happen in this. The Christians had borrowed this word from the synagogue. [illegible] it was not a jubilee of the church, and those that should refer the origin of that celebrated at Rome to this would be grossly mistaken, but Severus causing the secular games to be celebrated in the empire, the Christians, who partook in the feast, called it a jubilee.

Caracalla followed his father's steps, nor can it be doubted but that he loved the Jews from his childhood, since one of them at court, who was his playfellow, being whipped by the emperor's order, he was so afflicted that he would not [illegible] father for [illegible] days. So that, as we do not find [illegible] the Jews, we have reason to believe that they took the advantage of a quiet interval to make their [illegible]

There were two sorts of traditions, some that were peculiar to the [illegible] and others received by the Hebrews of the Holy Land, descended from the Pharisees [illegible] by the [illegible] and rejected by the [illegible] contempt and hatred of the Greeks increased [illegible]

Traditions, both Jewish and Hellenist, were by this [illegible] grown very numerous, and the teachers and writers [illegible] In this century flourished the famed [illegible] of the Amoraim, or commentator [illegible] and compiler of the Jerusalem Talmud. The [illegible] is, that he was born about the [illegible] of the second century [illegible] Anno Dom. 184 or 185. Some [illegible] that he was the chief of [illegible] the fifteenth year of his [illegible] the province of the [illegible] still alive, [illegible] is said to have enjoyed [illegible] years [illegible] the [illegible] cannot be supposed [illegible] 225 [illegible] he [illegible] his masters, in order to [illegible] which he was assisted by two other [illegible] Samuel, and Rab, or Rav, [illegible] disciples of his two masters, Judah the Saint and [illegible]

The following is a brief account of [illegible] production, commonly known by the [illegible] Talmud.

The word Talmud signifies "Doctrine," [illegible] this work [illegible] religion and [illegible] they have two of [illegible] and import, viz. this of Jerusalem, which is the [illegible] two, [illegible] and that of Babylon, of which we shall speak [illegible] It is properly a comment upon the Mishnah of Judah Hakkadosh.

Judah had scarcely finished his own work before he had the [illegible] to see a collection of different [illegible] published, and afterwards inserted in the Mishnah. To remedy, therefore, this evil, [illegible] three [illegible] wrote this comment upon it, which [illegible] in Judæa and in the Hebrew [illegible] Gemarah, or *Perfection*, and this [illegible] Mishnah [illegible] made that which is called the Thalmud of Jerusalem.

This Thalmud distinguished [illegible] Hierosolymitan," [illegible] is too obscure, [illegible] Babylonian Thalmud, compiled by Rab Asi, [illegible] the great [illegible] which [illegible] were [illegible] near Babylon [illegible] he compiled his Gemarah [illegible] Judah, [illegible] wrote it [illegible] Ase did not live to finish [illegible] sons, [illegible] body of oral traditions [illegible] of the Jews, [illegible] law, wherein the Mishnah is the text, and the Gemarrah the comment upon it.

The Jews in general prefer this Babylonian Thalmud, on account of its clearness and fullness, above that of Jerusalem, and though it abounds with ridiculous fables, and stories, they will not suffer any one to call it in question without the censure of heresy. We shall dispense with giving a further account of that voluminous work, and only observe that the learned Maimonides hath given us an excellent abridgment of it, in which he has thrown out all that was trifling and ridiculous, and confined himself to a collection of the most material cases and decisions that are contained in it. This epitome, which he calls "Yad Khazekah," or, "*Strong Hand*," is [illegible] preferable to the Thalmud itself, as being one of the most complete bodies of the Jewish laws [illegible]

Hitherto the Jews had lived in peace and happiness [illegible] fal persecution in the reign of [illegible] [illegible] He [illegible] from the [illegible] in whose neighbourhood he had been brought [illegible] even [illegible]

[illegible] relates that this prince having built a fine temple [illegible] ordered the Palladium [illegible] the number of the gods and whatever was [illegible] sacred by the Romans, to be conveyed [illegible] being resolved that Heliogabalus should be the only [illegible] To render this union of worship more complete, he formed the design of introducing the Samaritans [illegible] Jews religion, [illegible] were well known [illegible] the lives and fortunes of the Jews depended upon the execution of this design, for they never would have contented to have worshiped the [illegible] in the emperor's temple, with that heap of ceremonies their religion consisted of, and they could expect nothing but death and the most [illegible] tortures, from a prince whom the historians compare to the Neros and other monsters that have governed the empire. The unexpected [illegible] of this [illegible] was assassinated by his soldiers, secured them from this impending danger. Indeed, he only [illegible] design of the emperor's and that he [illegible] [illegible] though [illegible] his god [illegible] ordered it to be placed in the [illegible] even before his entrance into Rome [illegible] he [illegible] required time to build the temple [illegible] religions were to be combined [illegible] till the year of his death, [illegible] God [illegible] them, as well as the Christians, from [illegible] that was likely to destroy them.

The clemency of [illegible] Severus contributed doubtless [illegible] of the Jews; for indeed this prince openly [illegible] The wits of that time called him [illegible] of Syria, because he favoured the Jews [illegible] them, and was instructed [illegible] he had received some [illegible] Mammea. Indeed, this prince had [illegible] in his head. He never abandoned the [illegible] heathen idolatry, which still prevailed. But [illegible] gods Abraham, the Father of the faithful, and the great patriarch of the Jews. It seems as if he only did it to destroy the design Heliogabalus had formed of making the Samaritans, Jews, and Christians, with the heathens in the same temple, but he did it with wisdom and charity.

Alexander Severus was for having the names of the officers he sent into the provinces proclaimed, and the people licensed to accuse them, because, as the Jews and Christians proclaimed their priests [illegible] might be known, it was fit the same [illegible] of governors who were [illegible] times of the people. [illegible] he often repeated the maxim which he had learnt from the Jews and Christians [illegible] not to others what ye would not have them do [illegible]

The following emperors continued the [illegible] which this nation enjoyed. Philip [illegible] born in Arabia, where the Jews [illegible] them countenance [illegible] church [illegible] to the protection [illegible] might have confounded them [illegible] the difference of these two religions [illegible] does not appear that they had any [illegible] violent persecutions [illegible] Nor must they be [illegible] not considered as the [illegible] Alexandria says, this prince was compelled [illegible] chief-synagogue of Egypt.

We [illegible] observe [illegible] at the end of the third century. [illegible] less [illegible] He had [illegible] the Christians [illegible] [illegible] the [illegible] upon the Scripture.

CHAP. VI.

State of [illegible] the [illegible] the Persian Jews [illegible] word [illegible] Zenobia [illegible]

IT is now time to pass over the Euphrates [illegible] some account of the [illegible] Jews [illegible] of their captivity [illegible] doctors, [illegible] deemed worthy of not [illegible] not begin before the third century [illegible] and to [illegible] most celebrated [illegible] fore think that this [illegible] to Babylon till the time of [illegible] of N[illegible] who was cotemporary with Judah the Saint, [illegible] about the year 220 [illegible] about the beginning of the third century [illegible] authority could be but [illegible] which the Jews [illegible] and other [illegible] them to [illegible]

Artaxerxes [illegible] died about anno 244 [illegible] from whence [illegible] Romans [illegible] and shewed [illegible] They [illegible] the following reigns [illegible] state was governed [illegible] time that their [illegible] grew famous [illegible] shed, the following [illegible]

Samuel the astronomer [illegible] east. He [illegible] famous by his [illegible] method of [illegible] solstices. He [illegible] tury. He [illegible] [illegible] His [illegible] born at Babylon, [illegible]

course of the sun than his predecessor. There were, indeed, at that time very considerable men of their nation at Babylon, as well as learned men in their academies.

The honour of this academy was supported by two great men who lived in the same century, one of whom was Jehudah, the son of Ezekiel. He raised himself by his learning much above the professor of Sora, who could not stand against him, but by his alliance with the princes of the captivity. We find in the Babylonian Talmud abundance of his decisions. His hatred of the heathens, whom he compares to asses, [illegible] appears there. But this aversion to strangers has generally raised the glory of doctors instead of diminishing it. Nachman also possessed this chair, and kept up the succession of eminent doctors. This was the [illegible] of [illegible] in the third century. Let us pass to that of Sora, which is no less noted.

Abba Arecha, who is called Rab, by way of excellence, [illegible] known only by that name, and [illegible] to study under Judah the Saint with Samuel the [illegible] but, after his master's death, he [illegible] to Babylon, to [illegible] there [illegible] to Nahardea, to avoid competition, but erected his academy at Sora, where he remained till his death. One of the princes of Babylon, called [illegible], was so fond of him, that he went to hear his lectures, and was circumcised. They make him the author of a commentary upon Ruth, and some other books. But as the number of [illegible] was very great at that time, their works [illegible] hard to be distinguished. Rab determined that the synagogues ought to be [illegible] the houses of a city. The city where it is not so shall perish, said he, for God hath [illegible] to [illegible] his house. He never went to sea with an infidel, lest God should execute his judgment at that time. He [illegible] the Romans were to become masters of all the world.

[illegible], a relation to the prince of the captivity, and of the same name, succeeded him [illegible] and [illegible] [illegible] of [illegible], was the [illegible] that took [illegible] He [illegible] hundred [illegible] of the law, [illegible] was found [illegible] The [illegible] of the [illegible] or these princes of the [illegible] they [illegible] for [illegible].

Let us add [illegible] called [illegible]. He [illegible] Julian [illegible] was not thought to [illegible] he remained to Babylon, where he [illegible]

[illegible] learned, [illegible] the Persian emperor [illegible] demonstrate that An-[illegible] with [illegible].

But the [illegible] an accomplished scholar [illegible] the [illegible] of Sora [illegible] had done [illegible] compared [illegible] the Rabbins, [illegible] with them. As it was not the custom of the Persians to bury their dead, he wondered that the Jews should do it. He sent to [illegible], one of the learned of that time, who was afterwards president of the academy of Sora, and had under him twelve thousand scholars. He asked the reason of this custom, and required him to prove it by an express passage of the law. The doctor was reduced to silence: but another that was more subtle, evaded the objection, and, instead of a precept produced examples. [illegible] he quoted the example of Moses, who was not buried. The doctors still evaded the difficulty, by saying, that the people wept for him.

This prince from controversy came to persecution; as appears from a Jewish historian, who [illegible] read, in the [illegible]

[illegible] of Persia, which had been [illegible] to the king of Spain, that the people of his nation [illegible] happy under the dominion of the [illegible] had learning and [illegible] the doctors who lived before the [illegible] the people [illegible] by the esteem they [illegible] the king [illegible] to persecute them. He resisted the [illegible], but fearing the people [illegible] the [illegible] against his will, [illegible] nions, and endeavoured [illegible] to renounce their religion, [illegible] Being mortified [illegible] the princes of [illegible] utmost extremity. [illegible] Persians were no longer [illegible] The [illegible] Persian [illegible] of [illegible] [illegible] The [illegible] exercised [illegible] the [illegible] of [illegible]

[illegible] Persians [illegible]

[illegible]

[illegible] but the Jews made great use of her protection, and [illegible] very potent in the [illegible] Odenatus, her husband, who carried every thing before him. When she came to the throne, she added Egypt to her conquests, extended her arms into Asia Minor, [illegible], and [illegible] passed into Bithynia, where she took Chalcedon.

In [illegible], however, Aurelian began to restore the [illegible] empire, which Zenobia had ruined. He entered into [illegible], which acknowledged its former master [illegible] thence he went on to Cappadocia [illegible] Zenobia was at [illegible] the battle was fought [illegible] Orontes. Aurelian's troops [illegible] Zenobia [illegible] empire [illegible].

[illegible] Aurelian's cavalry [illegible] cut in pieces. Zenobia [illegible] to shut herself up in Palmyra, [illegible]. The Persians, Saracens, and [illegible] nations, still devoted to this princess, notwithstanding [illegible] to succour her [illegible] were beaten, and the Saracens obliged to lift [illegible]. Zenobia secretly departed out of the city to seek for succour among the Persians. But, as she [illegible], Aurelian's courtiers, who pursued her, took her prisoner. Palmyra surrendered. Zenobia [illegible] She was adorned [illegible] upon a stately chariot, on which [illegible] a triumphant entry into Rome, [illegible] The chariot of her husband [illegible] ornaments of Aurelian's triumph [illegible] to view whatever was most rich and precious in the [illegible] his splendid victories he had re-united to the empire. Zenobia went to Rome, or [illegible] where she had a small villa, and lived in [illegible].

[illegible] of prosperity and authority of [illegible] that Vaballat [illegible] some sovereignty in [illegible] favoured the Jews [illegible], which is very uncertain.

[illegible] of the Jews [illegible] cities of Persia, where [illegible] some respite. They boasted [illegible] the son of [illegible], who not being [illegible] competence, threw himself into [illegible].

[illegible] at this time a famous disputant, who not only [illegible] doctors, but, to shame them the more, [illegible] with them. He was called Jeremy, [illegible] sophistry. Other doctors had flocked to Sora, [illegible] the academy of Nahardea was fallen [illegible], which was taken and plundered. Zira, [illegible], was [illegible] there. He at first left his country to go and study at Tiberias, where he had also received the imposition of hands; but the authority and friendship of [illegible] recalled him to his academy, where he lived till the year 330, when desiring to lay his bones in Judæa, he [illegible] to carry his living body thither himself, than [illegible] conveyed after his death. So that though the Jews of Babylon had a great esteem for their own country, yet that hindred not their going to study in Judæa, whence they commonly returned before they died.

But the most famed among them was Manes. He could by no means be reconciled to the religion of the Jews, nor to what was recorded of their nation destroying and exterminating such numbers of people and kingdoms. He preferred the doctrine of the Christians, which recommended nothing so much as love and benignity. Nevertheless, he held great conference with the Jews of Persia, where he had much correspondence, whether he designed to be fully instructed in the law, or rather desired to recover them from what he called their infatuation. The modern Jews are not agreed about their ancestors conference with Manes, and in their kalendar they fix the origin of his sect towards the end of Constantine's reign.

The persecution which was raised against the Christians under Dioclesian did not much affect the Jewish nation, either in the east or west, though those of the former pretend that he designed to have made them feel the severest marks of his [illegible], for some [illegible] reflections which the disciples of Judah the Saint had cast upon him; but that they found means to appease his wrath.

CHAP. VIII.

[illegible] of the Jews under the Christian emperors [illegible] Providence [illegible] The Jews [illegible] Constantine [illegible] The [illegible] Christian [illegible] to suppress the [illegible] of the Jews [illegible] Jews [illegible] the Jews raise [illegible] Persia [illegible] Constantius [illegible] of Constantius [illegible] Jews [illegible] Julian [illegible] great protection to the Jews [illegible] by the [illegible] of [illegible] The Jews [illegible] by [illegible] Jerusalem [illegible] Julian [illegible] Julian's [illegible]

THE Jews were not much happier under the Christian emperors than they had been under the reign of idolaters. Their fate varied according to the genius of princes. The Christians [illegible] the persecutions they had suffered, that they could not [illegible] a change of maxims. Constantine contented himself with making some laws that confined the Jews' liberties to narrower bounds, [illegible] of his hatred, but, by degrees, way was [illegible] which tend to the [illegible] and persecution [illegible] us in point of religion [illegible] to have [illegible] equitable, [illegible] came necessary [illegible] of a miserable nation. We often boast of humanity and fancy that [illegible] us [illegible] passionate to other men, but we do not well consider the matter. Pride is another principle [illegible] the ascendant over humanity, and [illegible] considerable parts of mankind, who [illegible] us, and [illegible] the privilege of [illegible] the truths we believe or riches possessed of. Humanity suggests motions of lenity, but [illegible] heart, and [illegible] equity. And as all men are obnoxious to this [illegible] is no wonder to find persecutions in all religions [illegible] more immediately appertain to [illegible] the wickedest, because they are not only puffed up by opinion, which raises them above the level of men of equal birth, but fancy the opposition made against the mysteries of which they are the defenders and ministers, to be a personal affront upon themselves. So that councils commonly authorize and begin persecutions, which kings afterwards carry to the utmost excess.

The first event we find in the life of Constantine concerning the Jews is related by *Zonaras*. This historian says, they had a conference at Rome with Helena, this emperor's mother, who was yet unconverted. They represented to this princess, that though her son had reason to forsake heathenism and its idols, yet he had made no great progress towards his own salvation, since instead of the heroes of antient heathenism, he worshipped a man who had been crucified but a few ages before. Helena, who was devout, and anxious for her son's salvation, called the doctors to conference with pope Sylvester, who quickly triumphed over the enemies of the Christian religion.

It is said, likewise, that Constantine persecuted the circumcised, for St Chrysostom affirms, that, upon their assembling once to re-build Jerusalem, this prince, disgusted with their rash attempt, surprising them, caused their ears to be cut off, and afterwards dispersed them into all the territories of his empire, as so many fugitive slaves. Eutychius adds, that Constantine obliged them all to be baptized, and to eat swine's flesh on a passover day. Persecution cannot be carried farther; but I question the truth of these particulars. Though Chrysostom has great authority in the church, he is liable to error; for the Jews say themselves, that it was the emperor Adrian who caused their ears to be cut off, like the slaves which he sold at the fairs of the emperor. Besides, Jerusalem had been rebuilt under Constantine's empire, its bishop had assisted at the council of Nice, and the emperor had raised such stately edifices in it, that Eusebius told him it was the new Jerusalem. We may add, that though the Theodosian code contains many laws against the Jews under Constantine's name, yet there is not one condemning them "to the loss of their ears, to be baptized, or to eat swine's flesh."

But this prince published several edicts, which acquaint us with the condition and restless humour of the Jews under his reign. The first is one of the most important; it was issued upon occasion of Joseph, who had abandoned the synagogue to embrace Christianity. The Jews, incensed by his conversion, went to insult him in his house, and finding that he read the gospel, forced his book from him, loaded him with abuses and blows, and dragged him to the synagogue, where they unmercifully scourged him. But not content with this first outrage, they pushed him into the river Cydnus, whose current carried him far enough to give them the joyful hopes that he was drowned. But God preserved him. He received baptism, made himself known at court, and obtained the emperor's leave to build temples in several places where none had been erected before. The Jews were settled at Diocaesarea, Tiberias, Nazareth, and Capernaum, and had so appropriated these cities to themselves, as not to admit any strangers, not excepting the Samaritans, who professed the same religion. Joseph undertook to introduce the Christian religion into all these cities, and to that effect built churches in them.

The Jews, however, were still powerful in Judaea, under Constantine's empire, since they alone possessed four cities, one of which was Nazareth. Their numbers rendered them insolent, and they abused those that had turned Christians, and publicly opposed the execution of the prince's orders for the building of temples.

This doubtless obliged Constantine to publish the edict before mentioned. "He taxed them with stoning or burning whoever had a mind to renounce their religion," and he condemned them to the same punishment, with all their accomplices. Herein we still see the footsteps of that furious zeal which they thought authorized them to kill those who were taken in a notorious crime. They imagined these were the precepts of the oral law, and said, that Phineas had executed the verbal order of Moses. They produced another example under the Maccabees, when Mattathias killed a Jew, who was practising heathen ceremonies. The doctors authorized this practice; for Philo doubted not but God had established it. The Essenes, those austere votaries, ordered that if any man had blasphemed against Moses, he should be killed. Josephus says, that they "punished him with death." The interpreter has improperly translated it, they "condemned him to death." For as this sect had no power of life and death, it punished blasphemers by a motion of zeal. Notwithstanding the terrible disorders, and the torrents of blood that the zealots had caused to flow at Jerusalem, yet this dangerous maxim was still preserved; and the Mishnah teaches that if any one "renounces the foundation," (that is the articles of faith,) he ought to be killed; and, pursuant to this principle, they stoned, burnt and drowned those that deserted them in Constantine's reign. This obliged him to repress that violence, and as they did not obey the first law, he was forced to make a second.

He also forbid the Christians to turn Jews, upon pain of an arbitrary punishment. There was more danger in point of slaves, who might be brought over by their masters, and therefore this prince published a law, six months before his death, prohibiting the Jews to circumcise those in their service, and giving liberty to all who accused their master of having circumcised them, or that embraced Christianity.

Constantine farther ordered, that the Jews might be made decurions, because it was fit that they should have their share in the public burthens; but he exempted the patriarchs and priests, and those that had considerable employments in the synagogues, because, being taken up in their functions, they could not attend to the duties of those offices. For, indeed, the post of decurion was not an honour, but a servitude. Every one endeavoured to be discharged from it, by taking other employments in the army and government. They endeavoured to exempt themselves by some privilege which they begged of the emperor. Constantine granted so many of them, that there was nobody left to fill up their posts in Julian's time, which obliged him to revoke them all without exception; and this raised much against him even after his death, whilst others commended him for it. No wonder, then, that Constantine, who did not love the Jews, made decurions of them. Such was the condition of the Jews under the first Christian prince.

Under his reign is placed the council of Elvira, which made two decrees against the Jews of Spain, in which country they had great correspondence with the Christians. They eat and lived sociably together; but the council forbid this table society, upon pain of excommunication to those that eat with a Jew. The penalty was grievous, and absurdly inflicted, for eating together is an action purely civil, and excommunication ought not to be issued except for ecclesiastical crimes. The learned commentator of the council of Elvira pretends, that the council of Nice ordered the same thing in one of its decrees, which had been dictated by Osius, who was president of it, and who was for having the discipline established in the Spanish churches extended to all. But Mendoza is mistaken, for the canon he quotes was never made by the council of Nice. He took it from the Arabians, who have falsely imputed to this council many canons it never made. Nor do we know what the Arabians meant by quoting the apostles in this decree; for St Paul was so far from condemning the commerce of civil society, that he made himself all things to all men, a Jew to the Jews, and a Greek to the Greeks.

If we have recourse to the canons that bear the name of those holy men, we shall only find, that they condemned usury, without forbidding eating and society with the Jews. Recardoe, who renewed the decree of the Elvira council, and supported it with his authority, grounded [illegible] upon the authority of St Paul, who says that "All things are impure to the defiled and unbelieving." From whence he concluded, that the Jews being impure, their meats must be so too: but this is a weak and inconclusive argument.

The same council, by another decree, forbade "the possessors of lands to suffer their fruits to be blessed by the Jews, because their benediction frustrated that of the Christians, and it threatened absolutely to cast out of the church such as should not obey it." This custom of blessing the fruits of the earth, at certain seasons, was common to Pagans and Jews, as well as Christians. But who would have imagined that the latter should have made use of either of the former, if this decree had not informed us of it? However, this and the other decree plainly [illegible] that the Jews had lived very peaceably in Spain, and in good harmony with the Christians, till that time, whatever they m[ay] have done since.

The Jews enjoyed no less benign sunshine in the east, and [illegible] academies went on in a flourishing manner, if [illegible] the persecution raised against one of their greatest doctors. This was the famous Ravena, or Rabba [illegible] head of the academy of Sora. They mention two [illegible] of that name, one ancient and the [illegible]. The latter lived in the year 474; but the [illegible] died before the council of Nice, in 322. He was so [illegible], that they reckon twelve thousand disciples in [illegible]. He was commonly called the Remover of [illegible]; not that he had power to work miracles [illegible] mountains into the midst of the sea, but to [illegible] knowledge as to solve the greatest difficulties [illegible]. He wrote a book that was in great esteem whilst he lived, and [illegible]. It was a commentary upon the first book of Moses, containing the history of the Holy Land, with the literal and mystical sense. The [illegible] of it was Bereshith Rabba. It must not be confounded with another work of the same name, which is a commentary upon [illegible] Judah the Saint, composed by one of his disciples.

Raven, having long taught in the academies of Babylon, was accused of divers crimes by the king of Persia. [illegible] fear of being taken, and condemned to death, obliged him to fly and conceal himself, and he died in his retreat. It is said he was committed prisoner, and that Sapor was [illegible] to [illegible] him but that the empress his mother, [illegible] to tell him, that "he should have nothing to do with the Jews, because she had suffered much on their account." However this persecution was not general, for the academies flourished at Babylon, and the neighbouring parts.

Ravena left a nephew, whom he stiled *Aca*, for two reasons; one was, that he meant to signify that he had been an orphan, and that he had entertained him out of charity; the other was, that he would not [illegible] go by the name of his grandfather Nachman, lest afterwards the nephew should be confounded with the uncle, and the disciple with the master. He made such progress by Ravena's lectures, as to become head of the academy of Pundebita in the year 325, which he governed till 339. At the latter end of his life he married a widow, by whom he had a son, who is known by the name of Rau Bibi.

There was also a professor in the academy of Sora, called Joseph of Great Light, or Sight [illegible]. He was blind, nevertheless he was a man of great knowledge. He was [illegible] named Sinai, because he knew to perfection all the traditions that had been given Moses upon Sinai. He is supposed to be the author of the Chaldee paraphrases upon some of the holy pen[me]n, the Psalms, the Proverbs, Ecclesiastes, Ruth, and Esther. This paraphrase is highly esteemed, [illegible] by the number of its particular editions.

At the close of Constantine's reign the Jews, who were potent in the court of Persia, revenged themselves for what they suffered in the Roman empire, by raising a cruel persecution against the Christians there.

The gospel had some time before reached Armenia. We are told that one of its kings, called Tiridates, had embraced the Christianity. From thence it passed into the Persians, who had great correspondence with the Armenians. They began to build churches, and to consecrate priests. There was [illegible] bishop [illegible] two cities of Seleucia, and Ctesiphon, which were the most considerable of the country. The Jews were [illegible] because, as Jerome observes, they [illegible] and [illegible] were persecuted by one of the Persian kings, being jealous of the progress of Christianity, they [illegible] but when they saw [illegible] principal eunuchs, [illegible], they [illegible] bounds, and made a league with [illegible] bishop of Ctesiphon, was accused [illegible] correspondence with Constantine, which was [illegible] destroy him. [illegible] to [illegible] and the king, when he was brought [illegible] throne "I [illegible] my knee formerly [illegible] it voluntarily [illegible] homage, but I cannot do it when you make it [illegible] religion, and would make me renounce my God." The king, being enraged, caused him to be chained [illegible] geon. The Jews and the Magi, taking [illegible] this opportunity, pulled down all the Christian churches. The persecution was long and bloody. [illegible] old eunuch of Sapor, and eminent for his [illegible] also one of the first martyrs.

The sons of Constantine were much severer than their father had been. Constantius [illegible] obliged to make war against them. This [illegible] [illegible] by the disorders the Jews had committed at Alexandria when Gregory the Cappadocian, sent to succeed at St Athanasius. Joining with the heathens, who were then numerous in this great city, they burnt the sacred books and [illegible] to [illegible] manner, [illegible] The violence went so far as to [illegible] they had stripped [illegible] indignities they were [illegible] by the [illegible] bishop, who was [illegible], so that they went on with the utmost boldness [illegible].

The inhabitants of Diocaesarea [illegible] the same [illegible] Marcellus [illegible] Cardinal Baronius [illegible] have the Laborum, [illegible] supposes him to have [illegible] [illegible] in his heart like Julian, [illegible] could push the hatred [illegible] master of [illegible] The Jews could expect nothing from him, especially since it was in the [illegible] the greatest [illegible] But as he was [illegible], and his troops had often been [illegible] obliged to go personally [illegible] the Persians, [illegible] [illegible] and attack [illegible] siege. The Jews, [illegible] of the empire, could not forbear [illegible] favourable conjuncture.

Diocaesarea [illegible] little known [illegible] the second Palestine [illegible] this name, one in [illegible] a third in [illegible] in Isauria, [illegible] the geographers, [illegible] [illegible] of Judea [illegible] city of P[illegible]

[illegible] G[illegible]. This learned man's error, which has been [illegible] copied, proceeded from his not understanding [illegible] me. [illegible] father says, that G[illegible] was but a mile [illegible] an half from Sepphoris, called at present Diocæsarea [illegible] Jerome speaks [illegible] neighbours, and he was thought to [illegible] Sepphoris had been famous, and the Ro[illegible] be [illegible] metropolis, when Agrippa II was put in [illegible] of Tiberias, which occasioned great jealousies and [illegible] between those two cities. It retained its name till [illegible] empire of Trajan. As, after the taking of Jerusalem, [illegible] great number of Jews were retired to Sepphoris and Ti[illegible], the heathens and Christians, who continued with [illegible] these two cities, suffered much in their revolt against [illegible], in which the rebels put all to the sword that came [illegible] hands. When, therefore, the emperor had delivered [illegible] from their insults, they testified their acknowledgements with [illegible]. Those of Tiberias built a temple [illegible], which they called Adrianeon, and Sep[illegible] [illegible] ancient name to be called Diocæsarea [illegible] Tiberias.

[illegible] great [illegible] had been made of the Jews in the country, [illegible] got together there, under the [illegible], in such numbers, that, in Constantine's [illegible], they were [illegible] and suffered no [illegible] to settle there. It is no wonder [illegible] was the rendezvous of the malecontents [illegible], and that the inhabitants of [illegible] the [illegible] understood [illegible] was able [illegible], and that the Romans made a great [illegible] he [illegible].

[illegible] Constantine [illegible] against the [illegible] the rebels [illegible], which had [illegible] of the [illegible]. Nevertheless [illegible] again, and the Jews [illegible].

Constantine being incensed against the Jews, and being withal zealous for the Christian religion, made some [illegible] against them. There is [illegible] St [illegible], who lived at that time, an edict of the emperor, which hinders them at present from entering into Jerusalem. He [illegible] the [illegible] [illegible] the walls of this great city without [illegible]. They continued [illegible], [illegible] of this hard usage, in being excluded the gates of a city which had been the residence of their ancestors for many ages. All this is an argument that Christians had [illegible] Adrian's edicts, or [illegible] upon the same subject. This prince also made it death for a Jew to [illegible] Christian, or to circumcise [illegible]. He also prohibited their having Christians [illegible] their service, [illegible] forbid, under [illegible] punishments, the [illegible] their religion. [illegible] liberty of conscience for [illegible] they [illegible] permitted to receive proselytes [illegible]. He loaded them likewise with [illegible] had procured new [illegible] against them [illegible].

[illegible] that Epiphanius was converted from [illegible] Christianity, not (as [illegible]) without [illegible] extraordinary [illegible] trouble [illegible] elders, and they were not powerful enough to keep him from running into the wild [illegible] of the sect of Gnostics, whom he [illegible] Egypt [illegible] much more troublesome than Constantine. This prince had no reason to love the Jews, who worshipped but one God, and [illegible] the heathen idolatry. But he [illegible] to augment the number of the enemies of Christianity, which he thought most formidable, and to [illegible] religions at war, that paganism might triumph [illegible] the [illegible] [illegible]. He [illegible] changed the circumstances [illegible] the [illegible] where [illegible] Constantius had lowered them. He wrote to them, and in his letter honoured their patriarch with the [illegible] brother, [illegible] proof that they were then considerable [illegible]. He gave them liberty to [illegible], [illegible] rebuild the temple at Jerusalem, because they represented to him that they could not offer sacrifice out of [illegible] Holy Land. They availed themselves of the emperor's [illegible] to insult the Christians, for they [illegible] cities of Judea and Syria, pulled down their [illegible] Gaza, [illegible] and [illegible], and [illegible] Damascus. Those of Egypt did the same thing, [illegible] magnificent of all the temples [illegible] fell [illegible] of Jerusalem [illegible] but this event, which [illegible] circumstance, deserves to [illegible].

The emperor not only [illegible] of the temple of Jerusalem [illegible] and money. [illegible] they [illegible] years after their [illegible] were [illegible] of the Romans, [illegible] Jerusalem, and [illegible] [illegible] fine [illegible] [illegible] pro[illegible] the Christians, whether [illegible] to [illegible] lent [illegible] the [illegible] [illegible] from [illegible] and [illegible] of the [illegible] Christ[illegible] [illegible] when digging for the foundation of the [illegible] with a variety of [illegible] large in the [illegible]

[illegible] who had permitted [illegible] He [illegible] there a [illegible] between the [illegible] [illegible] would [illegible]

[illegible]

"flatters themselves that they are exempted from the offices "of court, as loaded by their presents; for even the clergy "are not allowed to consecrate themselves to the service of "God, without having first paid what is due to their coun-"try, and he that will truly give himself to God, ought to "furnish a man to fill up his place in public offices."

Though Theodosius had not revoked this law of Valens, which was executed in the reign of Arcadius, yet the Jews continued happy enough at that time. Maximus rebelling in the west, and obliging Valentinian to implore the protection of Theodosius, who was then in Illyricum, thought it most expedient to gain the Jews, and bring them over to his interests. He not only favoured them, but understanding that the people had burnt one of their synagogues at Rome, he ordered it to be rebuilt. Indeed, Maximus's reign was short. Theodosius having often beat his troops, had his head to be cut off at Aquileia, and came after to Milan, where Valentinian and he revoked all they had enacted [illegible] the rebuilding of the synagogue at Rome [illegible] particular ordinance, and Theodosius was persuaded the Jews ought not to be deprived of their religious [illegible], it is doubted whether he annulled that relating to the Jews.

St Ambrose was, indeed, very inveterate against the Jews, strenuously opposed the rebuilding another synagogue in lieu of that which the Christians had set on fire at Callinicum, and which Theodosius had ordered to be rebuilt, at their charge; but what Zonoras, a Greek monk, and some other writers of later date, say of his preaching before him, taking him to task, and reproaching him for suffering the Jews to enjoy the privilege of their synagogues in his capital, is entirely false and absurd. He did not preach, but wrote, to him, and his letter is still preserved, importing that they were so far from thinking themselves obliged to observe the Roman laws, that they thought it a crime to submit to them.

The contrary, however, appears, by all that we have hitherto said of the edicts made for and against them; and much more by the new law which that prince published, in the last year of his life, against the untimely zeal of some Christians, who, under pretence of religion, plundered and demolished their synagogues, contrary to the laws which allowed them liberty of conscience, and for punishing such offenders for the future. He even granted them a particular jurisdiction, on account of the frequent law-suits which they had either among themselves, or with the Christians, by which they were not only free from the trouble and charge of seeking for justice from strange tribunals, but were likewise more easily to obtain it from judges that were nominated by themselves; all which privileges would hardly have been granted them, if, as is pretended to have been alledged by St Ambrose, they had looked upon it as a crime to submit to the laws of the empire.

St Jerome had not the same prejudice against the doctors of this nation as St Ambrose; for, on the contrary, he paid them a pension, and made use of their instruction for understanding the Hebrew tongue, and the Holy Scriptures. This father, who thought that he had taken too much pleasure in reading Cicero and Virgil, (you are not a Christian, but a Ciceronian, said a judge to him,) changed his opinion for the Hebrews, learned their language with difficulty, consulted their doctors, studied under them, and made use of them to compose a Latin version of the scripture.

He acquaints us, that, to restrain the sallies of his youth, he put himself under the discipline of a young Hebrew, that had turned Christian, and underwent very uncommon labour to learn a strange language.

He was not contented with the instruction of this converted Jew, but took another, who so passionately loved him, that he fetched the books from the synagogue, under pretence of reading them, and brought them to his disciple. This master was an ingenious man, and St Jerom has quoted some of his explications. He sent for a third from Tiberias, whom he employed to revise, by the Hebrew, his version of the Chronicles, which he had made from the Septuagint. He says that this new master was admired by the synagogue. He sent for a fourth from Lydda, whom he paid very dear, because he was a learned man, and interpreted the traditions in the synagogue. It was this Rabbin that helped him to translate the book of Job. He had occasion for new assistance to translate Daniel and Tobias, because of the Chaldee expressions that are scattered in these books. But as he laboured with great application, he employed but one day in the translation of Tobias, which a Rabbin equally skilled in the Chaldee and Hebrew, dictated to him.

St Jerome grew so much the haughtier from these [illegible] which he had drawn from the synagogue, because this erudition, which was new, and almost unknown in the Christian church, distinguished him from the rest of the priests, and even from the bishops, who hardly [illegible] more than their mother tongue. In doing some justice to his masters, he boasted of his own skill and understanding of the Scripture. St Austin, who did not love him, admired him as a prodigy, because he understood three languages. An author, who has taken his name, adds, that St Jerome understood the language of the Greeks, the Hebrews, the Chaldeans, the Persians, the Medes, the Arabians, and of all nations. The moderns have gone farther than the ancients; and because this Father understood the holy tongue, they have espoused his observations as those of an almost infallible commentator.

CHAP. IX.

Equitable conduct of Theodosius the Younger. His pious and liberal disposition. The synagogues destroyed in Macedonia. A remarkable impostor in the island of Candia. Many Jews embrace Christianity. The Jews raise a tumult in Alexandria. Riot and murder, the effects of party zeal. Bishop Cyril censured for his violent proceedings. The patriarchal dignity suppressed.

MOST of the edicts which the Christian emperors had published in the fourth century, were enforced in the succeeding. Some of them were renewed, and others added, that were thought necessary to check the Jews' insolence against the Christian religion. Theodosius the Younger was obliged to renew this misery, but he always did it in an equitable manner, for he only punished those who had deserved it by their crimes. In the beginning of this century new troubles sprung up in Macedonia and Dacia. On the one hand the Jews of those countries continued to insult the Christian religion, and, on the other, the Christians burnt their houses and synagogues, and even sometimes condemned the Jews to death for no other crime than their religion. Theodosius, who was always equitable, condemned this oppression of the Jews, forbad the magistrates to punish them for religion, and not suffer the edifices belonging to them to be burnt, on condition that, on their part, they would not violate the respect that was due to the prevailing church. But yet the inhabitants of Inmester, three years after, fell into an excess. Debauchery prevailed over the respect that was due to the prince's laws; for they fastened a young Christian to a gibbet, and scourged him so cruelly that he died. The Christians of that country, enraged at such a barbarous outrage, ran to arms. The battle was violent, because the Jews were numerous. The governor of the province giving Theodosius information of it, he sent orders to chastise the guilty, and the tumult was appeased by their punishment.

Theodosius, who spent the winter at Constantinople (in the year 425,) made many edicts there, one of which forbad the celebrating games and spectacles on Easter Sunday, and during the principal feasts of the year. The Jews and heathens might have alledged, that this decree did not relate to them; but the emperor declared, that they were subject to the law, and told them, there was a time for devotion, and another for pleasure. They thought to excite the prince's jealousy, by complaining, that this mistaken devotion hindered the people from crowning and saluting the emperor's statues: but Theodosius put himself above this, and declared, it was honouring of him to do service to God. However, we see that this remains of heathenism was still retained in this prince's reign, of saluting the emperor's statues, and inserting the stile of Numen in the laws.

Those that profess the predominant religion are apt to imagine that every thing is lawful to them. They think [illegible] signalize their zeal in proportion to the outrages they commit; and under this notion, prescribe no bounds to their passion. It is the highest prudence, in kings, to restrain these excesses, and to ensure the public peace, by punishing an inordinate zeal. But this is not commonly [illegible] from being convinced of its necessity, [illegible] succeed. They often render their religion [illegible], expose themselves to the [illegible] of the people, and [illegible].

The Christians in Theodosius's empire, pulled down the synagogues, without any other reason than their hatred to this religion. If a private person thought himself affronted by a Jew, immediately he engaged the populace in his quarrel, and the next thing was to run in shoals to the synagogue, and set it on fire. This was often done in Macedon [illegible] the emperor was obliged to represent to his subjects, that it was not lawful for private persons to do themselves justice; that there were tribunals appointed to hear their grievances, and to judge of their complaints; and that he had commanded the judges of that country to take cognizance of them. The ecclesiastics, accustomed to religious broils, joined with the people of those of Antioch, where the Jews were numerous [illegible], plundered the synagogue, and thought to sanctify the theft by consecrating the booty to the church. Complaints were made of so scandalous a conduct, which were so notorious, that they were backed by the prefect of the prætorium, who gave informations of the disorder, and the occasions that had produced it. Theodosius condemned the clergy to restore what they had taken, or the value, and ordered a place to be assigned the Jews to build a temple. The decree was equitable, since the Jews lived in the empire upon the public faith of the edicts. But it did not seem so to Simeon Stilites, who was then alive, and violently espoused the interests of the clergy, and the mutineers at Antioch. He wrote so pressingly in their favour to Theodosius, that he not only revoked the orders he had given, but cashiered the prefect who had advised him to punish the robbers. This favour which Theodosius granted upon his request, not only encouraged the Christians of Antioch, but those of the cities and neighbouring provinces to make new assaults upon the synagogues. They were obliged to have recourse to Theodosius, to obtain some security against these frequent insults. This prince, who was an enemy to violence, forbad them doing it. The Christians were disgusted at it: they retorted the charge against the Jews, and complained that the emperor's protection had rendered them insolent. In explication of the preceding decrees, it was said, that, in answering the sad and doleful complaints of the Jews, it was designed to screen them from the persecution that some turbulent spirits exercised on them, under pretence of religion, and to prohibit the burning of their churches; but, at the same time, it was declared that, if they had nothing to fear for the temples they were in possession of, it was not lawful for them to build new ones, and that death should be inflicted on all those that undertook the circumcising of a Christian. There were still Christians, at that time, that embraced Judaism [illegible] for [illegible] were only made against reigning abuses; and it was difficult for the Jews to enforce circumcision on a Christian, if he was not disposed to submit to it.

The losses of the church were repaid by an accident that happened, in the year 4[illegible]4, in the island of Crete, where there were a great many rich Jews, the greatest part whereof were converted, after they had been grossly deceived by an impostor. His name was Moses, and he pretended to be the antient lawgiver of the people, who descended from heaven to procure [illegible] deliverance, by leading them through the sea to return to the Land of Promise, as they had done when they left Egypt. We cannot conceive how [illegible] could be so frantic as to attempt such a deceit, or to persuade himself that he was able to effect it. But yet Socrates affirms that [illegible] not only had this imagination, but [illegible] that he had in one year, run over [illegible] the villages of the island and persuaded the inhabitants into a belief of [illegible]. The infatuation was so great [illegible] expectation of the [illegible] prepared to throw themselves into the sea, [illegible] neglected [illegible] their fields and the [illegible] of their lands and [illegible] [illegible] with taking [illegible] Moses having [illegible] top of a rock, the fish [illegible] into the water, without any wavering of faith [illegible] children plunged themselves in with [illegible]. But it was quickly perceived [illegible] was an impostor, for some were drowned, [illegible] the Christian fishermen [illegible] their barks, and went to [illegible] their credulity had [illegible] to seek the impostor [illegible]. In consequence of this, many Jews embraced [illegible] [illegible] putting so much confidence [illegible] impostor.

There were other adventures that happened in the reign of Theodosius. A Jew of Constantinople, who had been [illegible] for many years, [illegible] [illegible] thought he might recover [illegible] were baptized [illegible] the [illegible] attended the patriarch, entreated [illegible] instructed, he received [illegible], and coming out of the baptism [illegible] found himself cured. This [illegible] extraordinary, [illegible] great an impression upon the Jews [illegible] great numbers became converts, though the [illegible] part of the former [illegible].

As we [illegible] writing the [illegible] of the church [illegible] very strange conversions [illegible] ed and [illegible] observe [illegible] the Christians [illegible] contented themselves [illegible] converts, induced many [illegible] not only to become Christians with that view [illegible] to run [illegible] from one sect to another [illegible] all for the [illegible] of obtaining their [illegible].

Socrates [illegible] Theodosius [illegible] is a remarkable instance of a Jew, who [illegible] then at Constantinople [illegible] discovered [illegible] singular [illegible] by the Novatians [illegible] that he had been baptized [illegible] but [illegible] cheats could not [illegible] the Jews [illegible] Christians [illegible] made them more [illegible] the several [illegible] such as the Novatians [illegible] &c. [illegible] Jews.

The [illegible] Mo[illegible] upwards of [illegible] the [illegible] tended to [illegible]

"[illegible] flattered themselves that they were exempted from the offices "of [illegible], [illegible] by these presents, for even the clergy "[illegible] to consecrate themselves to the service of "God, without having first paid what is due to their coun- "try, [illegible] ought to "[illegible] to fill up his place in public offices"

Though Theodosius had not revoked this law of Valens, [illegible] which was executed in the reign of Arcadius, [illegible] the [illegible] that the [illegible] the [illegible], and obliging a [illegible] man to [illegible] the [illegible] who was then in Illyricum, [illegible] the Jews, and [illegible] them [illegible] to [illegible] He [illegible] them, but [illegible] [illegible] Indeed, [illegible] [illegible] his troops [illegible] to [illegible] Aquileia, [illegible] and he revoked all they [illegible] the synagogue [illegible] and Theodosius [illegible] to be deprived of their religious [illegible] relating to the [illegible]

[illegible] indeed [illegible] inveterate against the Jews, [illegible] opposed the rebuilding another synagogue [illegible] Christians [illegible] on [illegible] Callinicum, [illegible] Zenorus, a Greek monk, and some [illegible] by his preaching before him, [illegible] him for suffering the Jews to [illegible] the privilege of their synagogues in his capital [illegible] He did not preach, but [illegible] him, and his letter is still preserved, importing that [illegible] thinking themselves obliged to observe the Roman laws, that they thought it a crime to [illegible]

The contrary, however, appears, by all that we have [illegible] of the edicts made for and against them [illegible] much [illegible] by the new law which that prince published, [illegible] the untimely zeal of some Christians, who, under pretence of religion, plundered and demolished their synagogues, contrary to the laws which allowed them [illegible] commerce, and for punishing such [illegible] He even granted them a particular [illegible], on account of the frequent [illegible] which [illegible] themselves, or with the Christians, [illegible] only free from the trouble and [illegible] from strange tribunals, but [illegible] to obtain it from judges that were [illegible] themselves, all which privileges would hardly [illegible] them, if, as pretended to have been [illegible] Ambrose, they had looked upon it as a crime [illegible] to the laws of the empire

St Jerom had not the same prejudice against the doctors of this nation as St Ambrose, for, on the contrary, he paid [illegible] made use of their instruction to understand the Hebrew tongue, and the Holy Scriptures [illegible] had taken too much pleasure in reading Cicero and Virgil, (you are not a Christian, but a Ciceronian, [illegible] to him,) changed his opinion for the Hebrews, learned their language with difficulty, consulted their doctors, studied under them, and made use of them to compose a Latin version of the scripture

He acquaints us, that, to restrain the sallies of his youth, he put himself under the discipline of a young Hebrew, that had turned Christian, and underwent a very uncommon labour to learn a strange language

He was not contented with the instruction of this converted Jew, but took another, who so passionately loved [illegible], that he fetched the books from the synagogue, under pretence of reading them, and brought them to his disciple This master was an ingenious man, and St Jerom has quoted some of his explications He sent for a third from Tiberias, whom he employed to revise, by the Hebrew, his version of the Chronicles, which he had made from the Septuagint He says that this new master [illegible] admired by the synagogue He sent for a fourth from Lydda, whom he paid very dear, because he [illegible] interpreted the traditions in the synagogue [illegible] was this Rabbin that helped him to translate the book of Job He had occasion for new assistance to translate Daniel and Tobias, because of the Chaldee expressions [illegible] scattered in these books [illegible] he employed but one day in [illegible] Tobias, which a Rabbin, equally skilled in the Chaldee and Hebrew, dictated to him

St Jerom [illegible] the [illegible] synagogue [illegible] Christian [illegible] the [illegible] of the scripture [illegible] Austin [illegible] [illegible] Greek, the [illegible] Christians, the Fathers [illegible] and been [illegible] Luther [illegible] they have espoused his [illegible] infallible commentator.

CHAP IX

Equitable conduct of Theodosius the Younger [illegible] liberal disposition The synagogue [illegible] in [illegible] A [illegible] the feast of [illegible] Christianity The Jews [illegible] Patriarchs [illegible] Cyril [illegible] for his violent proceedings The patriarchal dignity [illegible]

MOST of the edicts which the Christian emperors had published in the fourth century, were [illegible] in the succeeding Some of them were [illegible] others added, that were thought necessary to check the Jews' insolence against the Christian religion [illegible] sius the Younger [illegible] obliged to [illegible] but he always [illegible] equitable [illegible] punished those who had deserved [illegible] the beginning of this century [illegible] Macedonia and Dacia On [illegible] the [illegible] countries consented to [illegible] the Christian religion, [illegible] on the other, the Christians [illegible] gogues, and even sometimes condemned the [illegible] for no other crime than their religion [illegible] was always equitable, condemned [illegible] the Jews, forbid the magistrates to punish them for religion and not suffer the [illegible] belonging to them to [illegible] on condition that, on their part, they [illegible] the respect that was due to the [illegible] yet the inhabitants of Inmestar, three years after, fell into an excess [illegible] over the respect that was due to the prince's laws [illegible] a Christian to a gibbet, and [illegible] him to crucified [illegible] The Christians of that country, [illegible] barbarous [illegible] The [illegible] because the Jews were [illegible] province giving Theodosius information of it, he [illegible] ders [illegible] and the [illegible] by their punishment

Theodosius, [illegible] at Constantinople (in the year 42?) made many edicts [illegible]

[illegible] spectacles on Easter Sun[illegible] and during the principal [illegible] of the year [illegible] that this [illegible] but the [illegible] declared, that [illegible] subject [illegible] and told them there was [illegible] another for pleasure. They [illegible] by comprising [illegible] the people from [illegible] statues [illegible] it was ho[illegible]. However, [illegible] still remained in this [illegible] statues, and in [illegible] of Simon [illegible].

[illegible] predominant religion [illegible] The [illegible] the changes [illegible] bounds [illegible] the public peace [illegible] ornament [illegible]

[illegible] Theodosius's edicts, pub[illegible] with many others [illegible] In private [illegible] the next thing [illegible] to run [illegible] This [illegible] is often done [illegible] were obliged to [illegible] lawful for private persons [illegible] do themselves justice, [illegible] grievances, [illegible] complaints, and [illegible] commanded the judges of the county to take cognizance of [illegible]. The [illegible] religious [illegible] took of Ant[illegible] the Jews were numerous [illegible] plundered [illegible] to the church. Complaints were [illegible] conduct, [illegible] by the prefect [illegible] who gave [illegible] of the disorder [illegible] proceedings. The [illegible] had taken, or the [illegible] the Jews [illegible] equitable [illegible] the Jews [illegible] the public [illegible] of the edicts. But [illegible] Simon Stylites, who was then alive, [illegible] espoused the interests of the clergy [illegible] so pressingly, in the [illegible] he not only [illegible] he had [illegible] the robbers. This [illegible] which Theodosius granted upon his request, not only encouraged the Christians of Antioch, but those of the cities in the neighbourhood, to make new assaults upon the synagogues. They were obliged to have recourse to Theodosius [illegible] against these [illegible] to violence, forbid [illegible] The Christians were disgusted [illegible] the Jews, and complained [illegible] rendered [illegible] insolent. In [illegible] of the preceding decrees, it was said, [illegible] complaints of the Jews, it was decreed [illegible] them from the [illegible] exercised on them under pretence of religion, and to prohibit the burning of their churches. But [illegible] it was declared that if they had [illegible] temples they were in possession of [illegible] lawful for them to build [illegible] should be [illegible] all those that undertook the [illegible] Christian. [illegible] Christians,

[illegible] that [illegible] Jerusalem [illegible] Jew [illegible] a Christian, [illegible] exposed to former [illegible]

[illegible] in the [illegible] there were a great many rich Jews [illegible] to be the [illegible] from heaven [illegible] the hand of [illegible] We cannot [illegible]

[illegible]

[illegible] ſuch commotions frequently happened in this great city, and ſeldom ended without bloodſhed Sabbaths were noted as so many days of battle because the Jews, who devoted that day to idleneſs and debauchery, inſtead of going to the ſynagogues ſought occaſion to ſignalize themſelves, and the Chriſtians and heathens commonly inſulted them when they went to the ſynagogue There were alſo [illegible] on that day, and the Jews choſe rather to [illegible] their devotion, whereupon the people that [illegible] often engaged in quarrels with them [illegible] proceeded to come to blows, and the governors had ſeldom [illegible] authority to reſtrain theſe riots One day Oreſtes, the governor of Alexandria, was in the theatre, [illegible] to make ſome political regulations in the entertainments He deſigned, perhaps, by good laws, to prevent the diſorders which had been attended with ſuch [illegible] conſequences to the public peace and good of the city [illegible] for, as he was attempting [illegible] that he was ſurrounded by the party of Cyril [illegible] It was ſuſpected that they [illegible] only there to [illegible] the governor, and dictate to him [illegible] Jews. The preſence of Hierax [illegible] only in ſome of the lower claſſes, but one of Cyril's [illegible], who uſed to applaud this biſhop [illegible], ſerved to provoke them, inſomuch, [illegible] that that man, whom they looked upon as their enemy, was come only to inſult them, and [illegible] He muſt have given occaſion for theſe [illegible] ſince the governor cauſed him to be ſeized by his officers, and ſcourged upon the ſtage, without any form of trial Cyril was not a man that would bear ſuch an inſult from the [illegible], whom he mortally hated Inſtead of complaining to him of his injuſtice, (if it was true that he had been guilty of any,) he ſent for ſome [illegible] his palace and threatened them They deſpiſed the threatenings of an eccleſiaſtic whom the governor openly oppoſed, and even reſolved to maſſacre the Chriſtians In order to this deſign, a body of the conſpirators [illegible] the ſtreets in the night, crying that the principal church of the Chriſtians at Alexandria was on fire. The crowd [illegible] without arms to extinguiſh it the Jews who had a mark to diſtinguiſh themſelves, killed them as faſt as they came Cyril, having notice of it came out with a multitude of people, entered into the ſynagogues, appropriated them to the church, gave up the houſes to be plundered, and drove the Jews quite naked out of the city The governor was highly enraged, becauſe the biſhop encroached upon the juriſdiction of the officers of the empire and becauſe he ſaw this great city almoſt unpeopled by ſuch a general expulſion of the Jews He informed the court of it, whilſt Cyril alſo ſent his complaints againſt the Jews The people ſided with the governor againſt their patriarch and obliged him to go and [illegible] for peace to Oreſtes, who refuſed to be reconciled

Cyril brought religion into the affair and went to the [illegible] with the goſpel in his hand, to oblige him upon ſight of that book, to a reconciliation but Oreſtus being inflexible in his reſentment, Cyril, who had a troop of ſoldiers in the habit of monks ordered them all down from the mountains of Nitria These anchorets were never ſeen to deſcend, but they put the people into a conſternation They marched down that day to the number of fifteen hundred, and obſerving the governor as he went into his chariot, began to load him with abuſe, and accuſed him of being an heathen, that they might have a pretence to get rid of him, under a ſhew of juſtice It was in vain for him to cry out, that he had been baptized at Conſtantinople Inſtead of hearing him, they fell upon him with ſhowers of ſtones, wounded him on the head, and covered him with blood His guards deſerted him, being oppreſſed by numbers, and the governor would have been left to periſh, if the people had not run to his aſſiſtance Ammonius, one of the monks, was arreſted, and condemned to puniſhment Oreſtus wrote to the court Cyril, on his part juſtified the proceedings of the Monks by declaring Ammonius a martyr, and making his panegyric in the pulpit on the man who died in ſo glorious an action The tumult began again ſome time after, and Cyril was loaded with all the odium of the event, in which the celebrated Hypatia, an heathen virgin of great [illegible], learning, and virtue, loſt her life, whom this biſhop, jealous of his reputation had cauſed to be aſſaſſinated

It is in vain to extol Cyril of Alexandria, and to make him one of the principal ſaints of the pureſt church People ſuffer themſelves to be eaſily dazzled in favour of ſome men, and canonize thoſe who have been actuated by violent and criminal paſſions inſtead of [illegible] devotion It is owned, that Cyril incurred Oreſtus's hatred by his ambition, and encroachment upon the authority of the imperial officers How did he take his revenge on him? He cauſed him to be aſſaſſinated by the monks Is this conduct conſiſtent with the character of a biſhop? But he ſtops not here [illegible] his [illegible] ſo many aſſaſſins, againſt a virtuous [illegible], who unmercifully killed her at [illegible] church door [illegible] had reaſon to ſay, that this act [illegible] involved Cyril and his eccleſiaſtics in ſhame and confuſion This ſame prelate had drawn upon him the people's hatred, ſince they always engaged againſt him, notwithſtanding their reverence for religion and ſacred perſons How could one eſteem an ambitious prelate who [illegible] people to applaud his ſermons in public as Cyril did [illegible] who [illegible] acted the votary and [illegible] a ſeditious monk who had been puniſhed for his crimes with martyrdom? We cannot juſtify his conduct againſt the Jews, ſince they were not of his juriſdiction, it belonged to the governor to expel them the city if he thought it expedient, and the biſhop was no judge of their privileges and ſettlements It was a perfect rapine to head a rabble, to plunder their ſynagogues, and appropriate them to themſelves with their houſes and effects It was uncharitable to the laſt degree, to expel people quite naked, who had lived there ever ſince the time of Alexander the Great, under the protection of [illegible]

The Jewiſh nation received a ſevere blow in this century in the total ſuppreſſion of their patriarchs, for their way of living raiſed murmurs and complaints againſt them, and the taxes they levied upon the nation occaſioned their fall We have already ſpoken of their privileges and have only to add that Theodoſius and Valentinian deprived them of that income, and appropriated an impoſt made upon their ſubjects to the imperial treaſury By this means the patriarchal dignity was more effectually ſuppreſſed than if it had been annulled by an edict for that, for want of competent ſupport it [illegible] led away Photius pretends that the [illegible] who ſucceeded the patriarchs, were charged with this collection anſwerable for it and obliged to ſee it conveyed into the treaſury

Thus was the patriarchal dignity abſolved in the year 429

CHAP X

State of the Jews, in the weſtern empire, under Honorius [illegible] of Honorius reſpecting the Jews [illegible] privileges [illegible] Determination of [illegible] the Jews State of the Jews under [illegible] in Africa Their privileges confirmed [illegible] The Jews protected by Theodoric king of the Goths.

HONORIUS who poſſeſſed the weſtern part of the empire, was harraſſed with many revolts Never did prince maſter ſo many tyrants, and therefore we ſee him, in moſt of his medals, holding a labarum in one hand, a victory in the other, and trampling a rebel under his feet St Chryſoſtom who derived this prince's glory from hence, did not aſcertain the [illegible] for it is most commonly the weakness or cruelty of the governor [illegible] rebellions, and it is no great honour to a prince to see his subjects vanquished, and in chains at his feet. [illegible] zealots persuade [illegible], that his victories were the recompence of his vehemence against the [illegible]. It is true he sometimes persecuted them, but he shewed great equity to the Jews who lived in his dominions. There is even a law preserved, made upon their account, which is an honour [illegible], for [illegible], "That the glory of [illegible] prince consists in permitting every society quietly to enjoy the privileges they have acquired, and that, though a religion is not approved by a sovereign, yet he ought to preserve its privileges." Pursuant to these [illegible] he decreed that none could [illegible] or appropriate the synagogues with impunity. He ever forbad them to [illegible], under pretence of the public good, and [illegible], because the rest of the week was sufficient [illegible] the [illegible] of the [illegible].

Nevertheless, [illegible] the abuse of their liberty, he forbid the [illegible] of synagogues, and deprived the protectors of it of [illegible], and of that of agents. The [illegible] were distinguished [illegible] militia, having three sorts of employments, to [illegible] in the provinces, to convey [illegible] to the [illegible] the subsistence of the troops, and to be [illegible] couriers to the princes. Augustus had appointed these inspectors in every province and region: they brought an account of all that was done to the prince, and to this purpose had the disposal of the public [illegible]. Honorius deprived the Jews of this employ, who were, [illegible], commissioned to furnish the magazines [illegible] at this day in some states.

This prince severely restrained the sect of the Cœlicolæ, who had no image of the deity in their temples; they prayed to God in open places, and on flat roofs, [illegible] the temples, (says Tertullian,) and make their prayers upon the banks in the air. They swore by the heaven, it is said, that this more particularly agrees with the Samaritans, who had formerly an oratory near Neapolis, built in the form of a theatre, where they went to pay their devotions. Besides, they had a baptism like the sectaries we speak of. They were called Cœlicolæ, because they read the Bible in Hebrew. Scaliger thought it was a sect of the Essenes that bore the name of Cœlicolæ, or angels, by reason of the angelical life they led. And thus, in the latter ages, the monks have been intitled Cœlicolæ, as if they had led the life of heavenly citizens whilst they were upon earth.

There was another sect in this nation called Schamain, or the Heavens. Benjamin of Tudela found [illegible] in Egypt, [illegible] so much resemblance to that of the Cœlicolæ, that [illegible] very probable it was a remainder of those who were condemned in the Theodosian code. It has been further [illegible], that they were apostates, who forsook Christianity, and turned Jews.

Honorius looks upon these heretics as people that were [illegible] and whose doctrines he was yet unacquainted with. This character cannot be applied to the Jews, or Samaritans, or Essenes, nor to the apostates that returned to Judaism, whose doctrine, worship, and ceremonies, could not be unknown to the emperor. Besides, the Schamaim, which Benjamin of Tudela found in Egypt, were not Cœlicolæ, nor so much as sectaries. This is easy to be observed by any one that reads this traveller with attention, for he distinguishes two different synagogues he saw at Grand Cairo, one whereof belonged to the Jews of the Irack, and the other to the Jews of Schamain. As the first name is that of a province from which these Jews came, viz. the Babylonian Irack, from whence they went into Egypt, the second name must also signify a province from whence the Jews who possessed that synagogue proceeded; and Syria is actually called Scham, and the Syrian, Schamain: or rather, there needed no more than to forsake Arias Montanus's version, and to follow that of the emperor Constantine, [illegible] all the difficulty. Indeed, Benjamin makes no difference between these two synagogues, except in their manner of dividing [illegible] reading and the sections of the law, which [illegible] situation in the worship.

An ingenious commentator has differed from [illegible] by observing, that the Cœlicolæ are accused, by Honorius, of disturbing the rules of the church, whence he suspected they were baptized in the name of heaven, instead of the common form, and by heaven they [illegible] God that reigns there. This was the Jews' [illegible] they say still, that the name of [illegible] the term of heaven is necessary, and that [illegible] by heaven shall remain.

These Cœlicolæ, or worshippers of heaven, were in Africa, for it was to the governors of this province that the emperor directed his orders against them. [illegible] Honorius was for reducing them [illegible] the church. These [illegible] the [illegible] Catholick faith, and the worship [illegible] which is an argument, that they [illegible] for these latter [illegible] re-baptizing those who [illegible] the Catholics, and by the addition of some ceremonies [illegible] that Major, one of the Cœlicolæ, [illegible], who had invented a new baptism among them, [illegible] many people. Here you have the Cœlicolæ in Africa, and their principal was Major, of the sect of the Donatists, with whom St. Austin would [illegible] conference had he not been call[illegible] tion of the bishop. The baptism Major had invented [illegible] new, and little known: he had set up [illegible] congregation and [illegible] many people by this [illegible]. St. Austin's passage so perfectly agrees with Honorius's [illegible], that the one seems to be a comment of the other.

They departed also from the worship of God [illegible] know that the Donatists ever [illegible] the [illegible] religion, says Optatus [illegible] for them, by [illegible] oracles. This is enough to make them pass for Cœlicolæ, since the saints are regarded as the inhabitants of [illegible] by them, which was not done in the [illegible] church.

This [illegible] is little known because it continued but a short time. And as the Donatists soon [illegible], the Cœlicolæ, who made [illegible], quickly disappeared, and [illegible] their name in St Austin and the [illegible]. We find no track of them among the [illegible] the catalogue of [illegible] have forgot them, as well as the [illegible].

They must not be confounded with the Jews [illegible] we find them in the Theodosian code [illegible] and included in the same [illegible]. [illegible] observed that the law ought to be [illegible] two articles, one [illegible] of [illegible] obliged to return to the church [illegible] de pain of being confounded [illegible] the other to [illegible] Jews [illegible] bring [illegible] proselytes.

It is true [illegible] the Cœlicolæ had a worship [illegible] worshipped the [illegible] ship of the [illegible] Jews and the Donatists had a baptism [illegible] worship to [illegible] ing two different religions. And therefore [illegible] the synagogues from this new [illegible] hitherto been thought convicted [illegible].

Between Africa and Spain is the [illegible] which were two considerable [illegible]

tion [illegible] that commotions frequently happened in this great [illegible] seldom ended without bloodshed. Sabbaths were [illegible] days of battle, because the Jews, who [illegible] day to themselves and delicacy, instead of go[illegible] [illegible] to signalize themselves [illegible] the Christians [illegible] commonly insulted [illegible] went to the synagogue. There were also [illegible] the Jews chose rather to [illegible] devotion, whereupon the people that [illegible] engaged in quarrels with them [illegible] to come to blows, and the governors had sel[illegible] authority to restrain these riots. One day [illegible] the governor of Alexandria, was in the theatre [illegible] political regulations in the enter[illegible]. He designed, perhaps, by good laws, to pre[illegible] which had been attended with such [illegible] to the public peace and good of the [illegible], for as he was attempting [illegible] he was surrounded by the party [illegible] of the [illegible]. It was suspected that they [illegible] the governor and dictate to him [illegible] the Jews. The presence of Hie[illegible] of the lower classes, but one [illegible] who used to applaud this bishop [illegible] to provoke them, insomuch [illegible] man, whom they looked [illegible] only to insult them, and [illegible] [illegible] given occasion for these [illegible] him to be seized [illegible] upon the stage, without any [illegible]. Cyril was not a man that would bear [illegible] insult from the [illegible] whom he mortally hated [illegible] to him of his injustice, (if it was [illegible] that he had been guilty of any,) he sent for some [illegible] threatened them. They despised [illegible] whom the governor [illegible] and even resolved to massacre the Chris[illegible]. [illegible] a body of the conspirators [illegible] the night, crying that the princi[illegible] of the Christians at Alexandria was on fire [illegible] without arms to extinguish [illegible] mark to distinguish themselves, [illegible] they came. Cyril, having not [illegible] with a multitude of people, entered into [illegible] synagogues, appropriated them to the church, gave [illegible] to be plundered, and drove the Jews quite [illegible] out of the [illegible]. The governor was highly enraged [illegible] bishop encroached upon the jurisdiction of the [illegible] of the emperor, [illegible] saw this great city [illegible] such a general expulsion of the Jews. [illegible] the court [illegible], while Cyril also sent his [illegible] against the Jews. The people sided with the [illegible] and obliged him to go [illegible] to Orestes, who [illegible] [illegible] into the [illegible], and went to the [illegible] with the gospel in his hand, to oblige him upon [illegible] of that book, to a reconciliation. But Orestus being [illegible] in his resentment, Cyril, who had a troop of [illegible] in the habit of monks, ordered them all down from the mountains of Nitria. These anchorets were never seen to [illegible], but they put the people into a con[illegible]sternation. [illegible] marched down that day to the number of fifteen hundred, and observing the governor, as he went into his chariot, began to load him with abuse, and accused him of being a heathen, that they might have a pretence to get rid of him, under a shew of justice. It was in vain for him to cry out, that he had been baptized at Constantinople. Instead of hearing him, they fell upon him with showers of stones, wounded him on the head, and covered him with blood. His guards deserted him, being oppressed by numbers, and the governor would have been left to perish, if the people had not run to his assistance. Ammonius, one of the rioters, was arrested, and condemned to punishment. Orestus wrote to the court.

Cyril, on his part, justified the proceedings of the Monks by declaring Ammonius a martyr, and making his panegyric in the pulpit on the man who died in so glorious an action. The tumult began again some time after, and Cyril was loaded with all the odium of the event, in which the celebrated Hypatia, an heathen virgin of great fame, learning and virtue, lost her life, whom the bishop, jealous of his reputation, had caused to be assassinated.

It is in vain to extol Cyril of Alexandria, [illegible] him one of the principal [illegible] of the [illegible] church [illegible] themselves to be [illegible] [illegible] those who have been [illegible] by violent and criminal passions, [illegible] on. It is owned that Cyril mounted [illegible] his ambition [illegible] encroachment upon the [illegible] imperial officers. [illegible] his revenge [illegible]. He caused him to be [illegible] by the monks. Is this conduct consistent with the character of a bishop? [illegible] he [illegible] not [illegible] his [illegible] so many [illegible] who [illegible] had [illegible] to [illegible] ecclesiastics in [illegible] upon him the people's hatred, since [illegible] ways engaged against him [illegible] once for [illegible] persons. How could [illegible] esteem an [illegible] his [illegible] in public [illegible] the [illegible] been punished for his crimes [illegible] martyr [illegible]. We cannot justify his conduct against the Jews, [illegible] not of his jurisdiction. It belonged to the governor [illegible] pel them the city, if he thought it expedient, and the bishop was no judge of their privileges and settlements. It was a perfect [illegible] to head a rabble to plunder their synagogues, and appropriate them to themselves with their houses and [illegible]. It was uncharitable to [illegible] degree, to expel people quite naked, who had lived there ever since the time of Alexander the Great, under the protection of [illegible].

The Jewish nation received [illegible] severe blow in this century, in the total suppression of their patriarchs, for their way of living raised murmurs and complaints against them, [illegible] the taxes they levied upon the nation occa[illegible]sioned their fall. We have already spoken of their privileges, [illegible] have only to add that [illegible] deprived them of that income, and appropriated an impost made upon them [illegible] to the imperial treasury. By this means the patriarchate was more effectually suppressed [illegible] for want of [illegible] support [illegible] away. [illegible] the [illegible] succeeded [illegible] the patriarchs, were charged with this collection, and [illegible] for it, and obliged to see it conveyed into the treasury.

[illegible] was the patriarchal dignity abolished in the year [illegible]9.

CHAP. [illegible]

[illegible] Honorius [illegible] of Honorius [illegible] the Jews [illegible] Jews. State of the [illegible] Then [illegible] The Jews [illegible] by Theodoric king of the [illegible]

HONORIUS, who possessed the western part of the empire, was harrassed [illegible] Neve[illegible] did prince master [illegible] and therefore [illegible] him, [illegible] his [illegible] victory in the [illegible] his feet. St Chrysostom, who [illegible] ry from hence did not [illegible] for [illegible] most commonly th[illegible] weakness or cruelty of the gove[illegible] rebellion [illegible] so great [illegible] to a prince to see his subjects [illegible], a [illegible] the zealots persuade [illegible], that his victories were the [illegible] power of his [illegible] the [illegible] them, b[illegible] shewed [illegible] Jews who lived in his dominions. There [illegible] even a law [illegible] upon them [illegible] "Thus the [illegible] every society [illegible] to enjoy the privileges they have acquired, and [illegible] by a sovereign, [illegible] privileges." [illegible] to these [illegible] to appropriate the [illegible] ever forbad them to [illegible] the public good, and [illegible] the [illegible] of the week was su[illegible] [illegible]

[illegible] liberty, he [illegible] the [illegible] the profes[illegible] agents. Th[illegible] has [illegible] three sorts [illegible] employments, [illegible] to conce[illegible] to the [illegible] subsistence of the [illegible], [illegible] to the princes. Augu[illegible] [illegible] province and [illegible] gone to [illegible] the [illegible] the emplox, [illegible] commissioned to furnish the maga[illegible] [illegible]

The prince severely chastised the sect of the Calicolæ, [illegible] in their worship [illegible] to [illegible] in open places, and on [illegible] the temples, (says Leunclavius,) [illegible] upon [illegible] in the air. They [illegible] that th[illegible] more particularly agrees with the Samaritans, who [illegible] formerly [illegible] Neapolis, [illegible] where they went to pay their [illegible] they had [illegible] like the sectaries [illegible] called Cœlicolæ, because they [illegible] Scaliger thought it was a sect of the Essenes [illegible] the name of Cœlicolæ, or angel[illegible] [illegible] they led. And thus, in the [illegible] have been entitled Cœlicolæ, as if [illegible] citizens whilst they were [illegible]

There was another sect in this nation called Schamain, [illegible] Benjamin of Tudela found it in Egypt, [illegible] that of the Cœlicolæ, [illegible] the remainder of those who [illegible] the Theodosian code. It has been [illegible] were apostates, who forsook Christ[illegible] [illegible] Jews.

Hono[illegible] upon these heretics as people that we[illegible] [illegible] in Africa, and whose doctrines he was [illegible] This character cannot be applied [illegible] Jews [illegible] nor to the proselytes that [illegible] to Judaism, whose doctrine, worship, and [illegible] could not be unknown to the emperor. Be[illegible] the Schamain, which Benjamin of Tudela found in Egypt, were not Cœlicolæ, nor so much as sectaries. [illegible] easily to be observed by any one that reads this traveller with attention, for he distinguishes two different synagogues he found at Grand Cairo, one whereof belonged to the Jews of the Irack, and the other to the Jews of Schamain. As the first name is that of a province from which these Jews came, viz. the Babylonian Irack, from whence they went into Egypt, the second name must also signify a province from whence the Jews who possessed that synagogue proceeded, and Syria is actually called Scham, and the Syrians, Schamain [illegible] rather, they needed no more than to [illegible] Arias Montanus's version, and to follow that

of the emperor Constantine, [illegible] Benjamin [illegible] these two synagogues, except in their manner of [illegible] reading, and the [illegible] nation in the worship.

Ant[illegible] different [illegible] observing, and the Cœlicolæ [illegible] of admitting the rules of the church [illegible] were baptized in the [illegible] the common form, [illegible] God that reigns [illegible] necessary, that the name of [illegible] the son of heaven is necessary, [illegible] tized by heaven shall [illegible]

These Cœlicolæ, or worshippers of [illegible] Africa, [illegible] to [illegible] [illegible] the [illegible] church [illegible] Catholic [illegible] all which [illegible] for these [illegible] rebaptizing those who [illegible] and by the admission of some [illegible] the Majors, one of the Council [illegible] had [illegible] among [illegible] deceived many people [illegible] Africa [illegible] Donatists, with whom [illegible] [illegible] had he not been [illegible] new, and little known [illegible] and [illegible] Honorius [illegible] [illegible] seems to be a [illegible]

[illegible] demanded [illegible] the name of God [illegible] that the [illegible] religion [illegible] reason for them, [illegible] articles. [illegible] the Jews are [illegible] church.

This sect is little known [illegible] And [illegible] Donatists, [illegible] the Cœlicolæ, [illegible] [illegible] St. Austin [illegible] forgot them, [illegible]

They [illegible] and included in the [illegible] [illegible] articles [illegible] [illegible] Jews [illegible]

It is true, [illegible] Cœlicolæ had [illegible] [illegible] two [illegible] [illegible] from [illegible] Jews [illegible]

Between Africa and Spain [illegible] which were two [illegible]

[illegible] resided, was inaccessible to the Jews: there were neither wolves or wild beasts there, and the serpents, which were very numerous, lost their venom. On the contrary, in the other city, called, at present, Port-Mahon, the Jews were so considerable that, though it was subject to the emperor Honorius, yet they arrived to titles, and exercised all civil dignities: for Theodosius, who was doctor of the law, and head of the synagogue, bore the first rank among the Christians, because he had passed through all the offices.

Severus, being appointed bishop of this island, was easily persuaded by Orosius, who had lately returned from Jerusalem, loaded with singular relics, to undertake the conversion of the Jews. They began with private conferences, and proceeded to public disputes, the last of which was held in their synagogue, where finding some Jewish women had armed themselves with stones to throw at them, they provided for their own defence. The consequence was, that the synagogue was pulled down, and nothing saved out of it but the books and plate: but the bishop, through the power of oratory, brought their greatest men to reason, and, in about eight days, the greater part of them were converted, and the synagogue turned into a church. Many, however, that remained obdurate, went and hid themselves in caverns, till hunger forced them out; and others leaving all they had behind them, went and sought an asylum in foreign countries; all which circumstances shew that there was some violence used against them by the bishop and his clergy. Baronius seems to own as much, and adds, that his example would have been followed in many other places, had not the crowned head put a stop to this method of conversion.

The irruption of the Vandals, a barbarous people, who had no notion of toleration in point of religion, was very likely to create them new troubles. But yet it is probable they brought upon this nation only such confusions as are inevitable in great revolutions; for we find in St. Austin's works several tracts composed against the Jews, which shew that their condition was not grown more hard or unhappy here, than in the other parts of the empire.

In the "Plea of the synagogue against the Christian church," written by a lawyer of that time, the synagogue alledges, "that she is neither a slave or a servant of the "Christians, since they are not committed prisoners, and "instead of wearing irons, and other marks of slavery, "they were left the liberty of sailing and merchandizing." The Vandals, therefore, promised them the liberty of professing their religion and trading. But, on the other hand, the church answers, "That she is obliged to pay tribute to "the Christians: that a Jew cannot pretend to the empire, "nor become a leading man or governor of a province; "that he cannot enter into the senate or the camp; and "that if he is left the liberty of getting his livelihood, it "is only to prevent his dying with hunger."

Valentinian confirmed all their privileges at Rome, and in the rest of the empire under his obedience. He left the synagogues remaining, that had been built in the preceding reigns, but at the same time opposed innovators, and understanding they were building a temple, he caused it to be pulled down, and fined the undertaker. When the empire changed its master, and the Goths seized on Italy, the Jews still found protection from these barbarous kings.

Theodoric defended them against the insults of the people. He attended to, and followed, the maxims infused into him by the secretary Cassiodorus, of forcing no one; because all violence in point of religion is criminal. This prince often represented to them, their excessive love of riches, and a temporal rest, whilst they lost immortality. But he would not have them driven into this road by violence, since they obstructed their salvation, when they did not enter it with their whole desire. He was much affected when he heard that, to revenge a private quarrel, the synagogue of Rome was burnt. He censured the senate for permitting it, and represented the consequences such tumult might have had, since the flames of that building, carried by the wind, might have consumed a great part of their city. He also severely reprimanded the ecclesiastics of Milan, who went to seize upon a synagogue and its appurtenances. The Christian religion does not authorize robbery. The citizens of Genoa were going to vacate all the privileges which the Jews possessed, who had been settled there for a long time. The Jews, therefore, [illegible] their leaders, murmured, and went to plunder the synagogue, of which they carried away the roof. The oppressed had recourse to Theodoric, whose equity was known to them. They were not mistaken, for this prince maintained their privileges, and permitted them to rebuild the synagogue on condition that they would add no ornaments, nor make it larger than it was before. And thus the Jews concluded the fifth century in the Roman empire. They frequently submitted to the hatred and tumults of the people: but they preserved the best part of their privileges by the authority of the sovereigns.

CHAP. XI.

State of the Jews in Persia, and Rise of a Method of [illegible] [illegible] in Tiberias [illegible] Age [illegible] [illegible] and [illegible] of the [illegible] Composition of the Thalmud obstructed in [illegible] the [illegible] of the Sebureans or Sceptics. A new Sect called Gueonim, or Excellents.

LET us now take a view of the Jews in Persia during that interval when we find their academies in a flourishing condition, under their famed chief, [illegible], the compiler of the Babylonish Thalmud, lately mentioned. [illegible] was the place of his birth, and the most celebrated academy of all the east, of which he was chosen president at a very early age.

He invented a new method of instruction, for, instead of fixing his disciples constantly to the college, and reading them lectures all the year, he only [illegible] them in the months of February and August. In February he [illegible] [illegible] a treatise, and sent them to study it some [illegible] months. They returned in August, and gave an account of their proficiency. The subjects were examined [illegible] in his presence, and afterwards he removed the difficulties by the decisions of preceding doctors.

Ten persons were [illegible] [illegible] against him, [illegible] of were called Princes of the Captivity, [illegible] to paraphrase upon the [illegible] of [illegible] [illegible], and to [illegible] repetitions to the scholars, who [illegible] [illegible] 2400. Those that distinguished themselves [illegible] [illegible] gence were praised and rewarded. [illegible] [illegible] collection of all the subjects that had been [illegible], [illegible] from this [illegible] Thalmud was composed [illegible] gave them a [illegible] [illegible] [illegible] [illegible] owing, and to the school broke.

Asce, having taught in this manner [illegible] years, published a collection of his decisions, which [illegible] into different parts. The first contained the [illegible] of the Mishnah, with the commentaries [illegible], and their solutions. In the second [illegible] questions, and related the opinion of the [illegible] and Casuists about them. The third [illegible] [illegible] maxims that had been published [illegible] the [illegible] and in the last [illegible] all the [illegible] [illegible] for the determination of [illegible] [illegible] [illegible] of the principal doctrines [illegible] [illegible] of the Babylonish Thalmud. [illegible] could not finish his undertaking, [illegible] [illegible] him.

[illegible] the method, and made additions, which have rendered it much more confused.

This great doctor died in the year 427. Some make Mar [illegible] his successor, but others say, that the sect of R. [illegible] was [illegible] deferred, that is that this master was made president of the academy of Sora, in Asce's place. His son Thobiomi (according to the pompous Jewish stile) ascended the throne of his father in the year 455, and reigned thirteen years, which the nation enjoyed such profound [illegible], that they called this doctor their daily Prosperity. He must needs have contributed to their felicity, since they gave him the name of it. We must not be surprized to hear them use the phrases of succession to the throne, and thirteen years reign, though the questions are only about the office of a doctor, or the pedagogue of a school. It is the rabbinical stile to give great ideas of their masters, and to caress them with flattering titles. [illegible] that are unaccustomed to this stile are easily dazzled by it, not imagining that a pedant is placed upon the throne, and that they should expressly say, he reigned thirteen years, when his empire extended no further than [illegible] to whom he taught tradition. They also called plain students princes of crowns, because they [illegible] of [illegible].

Seeing such a glorious title is given to the scholars, we need not wonder that the princes of the captivity wore it likewise. They entertain lofty notions of these princes, whereas their power was not so considerable as is commonly supposed. The whole nation did not depend on them, as is said, since as far as the year 429, the patriarchs of Judæa extended their jurisdiction over many provinces, and since that time, the Jews, dispersed in the Roman empire, could not acknowledge a prince residing in the territories of the Persian or Arabian kings, with whom there were continual wars. Would the Grecian emperors, so extremely jealous of their authority, have suffered a foreign Jew to raise taxes upon his subjects, and correspond with them in time of war? This prince's revenues were but small. The doctors say, he obtained of the Persians the privilege of setting up but one judge for the determination of differences between man and man, [illegible]hout being obliged to repair the damage, when the sentence was given wrong, whereas, by the common laws, they were to be judged by three persons. This observation is futile, for it was the Thalmudists that [illegible] the number of these judges to three, and it was impertinent to desire of the king of Persia dispensation from a law which they had voluntarily imposed on themselves. However, the prince established three judges at Naresa, a town half a day's journey from Babylon, and here they paid the Dirachim when they came to be twenty years old. He also punished the violators of the law by fines, which were reserved for the prince. There was [illegible] another tribunal at Chalonn, five days journey from Babylon. There was a third at Kesar, and the last at Babylon, where the prince resided; and in all these courts they collected but seven hundred gold crowns, which composed the prince's revenue; and supposing his dignity proportioned to his income, it could not be considerable. By this we discover the reason of the silence of all the historians concerning these heads of the captivity. They say that all these princes were of the house of David. They assign them a great empire, by which they say the scepter was preserved in the tribe of Judah. However, these historians, who preserve the succession, these names, and some actions of the doctors, who taught in the schools of Sora, Pundebita, and elsewhere, hardly ever mention the heads of the captivity, and if we discover some names of them, it is not without great uncertainty. R. Asce is highly celebrated, they enumerate his successors in the academy; but in all the fifth century we are examining, we find but one name of a prince of the captivity. It is impossible they should have been so entirely forgotten, if they had performed any important actions in the fifth century, or had been princes, as they are stiled. But to return to the Babylonian Thalmud, which the head of the academy composed.

This work was interrupted by the death of Asce, though he left able disciples, that might have finished it. But this interruption was caused by a persecution that lasted seventy-three years. It was violent, for the observation of the sabbath was suppressed, the synagogues were shut up, and the holy houses given to the Magi. The principal doctors of the nation were made prisoners. Aminar, Mor, Asce's disciples, and Huna his son, who was prince of the captivity, were condemned to death, and suffered it courageously; but the Jewish youth, more addicted to the pleasures of life, deserted their religion, so that the Jews were severely afflicted towards the end of the fifth century. However, they resumed courage some time after, and the *Thalmud* was accomplished in the year 500.

Towards the end of the same century, arose a new sect, called Seburcans, or Sceptics, at the head of which was R. Jose. These doctors pretended to [illegible] of [illegible] and seem to have started up to oppose the [illegible] which the Thalmudists attributed to the [illegible], but whether by openly [illegible] its [illegible] of its decisions, we cannot tell [illegible]. However [illegible] usurped pre-eminence became so odious to the [illegible] Jews, that it did not last long. It began to appear about the close of the fifth century, and was driven out of the world before the middle of the next, by the Geonim, or Gaons, a new sect of doctors, who took that pompous title upon them, which signifies [illegible], or [illegible] and who, in the [illegible] century, became the idols of the academies, and of the people.

CHAP. XII.

Persecution of the Jews in Persia, under Cavades. [illegible] [illegible] [illegible] [illegible] [illegible] Persecuted [illegible] [illegible] Persecuted [illegible] [illegible] [illegible] number slaughtered at [illegible] [illegible] [illegible] of [illegible] [illegible] [illegible] end of the Persian monarchy.

THE sixth century commenced with the persecution [illegible] the ten tribes suffered in the east. Cavades, a violent and haughty prince, who could not bear a difference of religion in his kingdom, caused many Christians to be severely tortured. He designed also to force the Iberians to forsake Christianity for the Persian religion, but having first demanded of their king, that their bodies should be left unburied a prey to birds and wild beasts, and the Iberians not being willing to consent to an action so manifestly repugnant to humanity, they put themselves under the protection of the Romans. We must not therefore wonder that this king tormented the Jews of his empire, and it is probable [illegible] the frequent alterations that happened in the [illegible] of the heads of the captivity, for in [illegible] ten years we find four of these princes succeeding one another.

There were Huna, to whom they give but two years reign, Acni, who reigned three, Ieter, who reigned four, and Zeutra, who reigned [illegible] years.

In his time arose the famous Meir, a learned Rabbi and great doctor of law, who having declared war against the Persian king with [illegible], was very successful against him during seven years, [illegible] his men having polluted themselves with [illegible] and female [illegible], he was defeated, [illegible] death by the Persians. He went [illegible] to the city where Zeutra resided, [illegible] that prince, and the president [illegible] hanged them upon a bridge. His [illegible] was forced to betake themselves to flight, [illegible] Zeutra II retired into Judæa, where he became president of the ſenate, or Sanhedrim This the Jewiſh hiſtorians tell us was the ſource of that ſeries of misfortunes which attended them in Perſia, inſomuch that their great maſter Hahonai never dared to ſhew his face during the ſpace of thirty years, that is, during the whole time of the reign of Cavades

Choſroes the Great was not more favourable to them than his father They had endeavoured to purchaſe his favour by betraying the emperor Juſtinian This prince had ſent ambaſſadors to the eaſt to negociate a peace, and had loaded them with preſents, which were received with ſuch acknowledgments, that there was reaſon to hope for a ſpeedy iſſue of the treaty, when the Jews, who had their ſpies and deputies at this court, inſinuated to Choſroes, that if he was willing to continue the war, they would furniſh him with fifty thouſand men in Judæa, by which means he might take Jeruſalem, one of the richeſt cities in the world Choſroes accepted the propoſal, broke off the negociation with the emperor, and was preparing to ſecond the endeavours of the traitors when news was brought that the deputies who were departed to execute the deſign, had been ſeized upon their return, and ſentenced to death, having firſt confeſſed their crime

This deſire to oblige the foreign prince did not engage him in their intereſts, and they not only had their ſhare in the general miſeries of the empire, when Choſroes, who often took arms againſt the Romans, pillaged Syria, and advanced to Judæa, to make himſelf maſter of Jeruſalem, but this prince alſo ſhut up the academies of the eaſt, which obſtructed the progreſs of the ſciences We do not ſo much as find that there was then a prince of the captivity, ſince Zertra II had been obliged to retire to Judæa, where he long exerciſed an office infinitely beneath that he would have poſſeſſed at Babylon, if he had been ſuffered there

Hormiſdas III reſtored them their liberty, for the academy of Pundebita was opened R Chanon Mehiſchka began to teach but this unhappy prince reigned not long his rebellious ſubjects took him priſoner, and his own ſon, Choſroes II deprived him of his life

This young prince did not peaceably enjoy the fruits of his parricide, for Varance, who had been his father's enemy, declaring himſelf alſo his, and pretended to aſcend the throne expelled him Perſia, having firſt beat his army He was obliged to engage in many battles, before he could get the maſtery of Varanes, who had made a conſiderable party in the ſtate, and defended himſelf with great bravery The Jews were in his intereſt "This faithleſs, reſtleſs, imperious, jealous, envious, implacable nation (ſays the Greek hiſtorian) was then ſo powerful in Perſia, as to raiſe the people againſt their prince, and to fortify the rebels, becauſe it was extremely multiplied, and had amaſſed prodigious wealth" Choſroes, getting the maſtery, expiated this treachery with their blood Thoſe of Antioch fell firſt into the hands of Mebodus, the Roman general This was not the Syrian city, but another, which Choſroes I had built in Perſia and had given it that name, becauſe he had formed it by the other's model, and had tranſplanted its inhabitants It is ſaid they were amazed, when they entered it, to find their country again, a ſecond Antioch the ſame ſtreets and houſes they had left Mebodus, having taken this place, put numbers of Jews to the ſword, deſtroyed others by different puniſhments, and reduced the reſt to a miſerable ſlavery

However, Choſroes being reſettled, was reconciled to them, and uſefully employed them in his deſigns indeed, this prince, who delighted in war, gave out, that he armed to revenge the death of Mauritius, his benefactor, upon Phocas, who had killed him, and made himſelf maſter of the empire Choſroes broke into Syria and Judæa, where he did terrible execution. He returned again in Heraclius's time, took Jeruſalem, and carried with him a croſs which a Jew had found It is moſt probable this nation had correſpondence with Choſroes, ſince, upon his being maſter of Jeruſalem, he returned them all the Chriſtian priſoners, which they only bought to ſatiate their implacable malice, for ninety thouſand perſons were unmercifully butchered

Elmacinus, and other Arabian hiſtorians, add, that Choſroes going to beſiege Conſtantinople, there was a neceſſity of evacuating all the places of Syria and drawing out all the garriſons, to come to the aſſiſtance of the capital, and the Jews, ſeizing this opportunity conſpired with all their nation in Judæa, to murder, on Eaſter-day, all the inhabitants of the city of Tyre and make themſelves maſters of that important poſt All the conſpirators came ſecretly to the walls but finding greater reſiſtance than they expected, they ſpread themſelves in the country, where they burnt the Chriſtian churches The Tyrians, who beheld this ſpectacle from the ramparts and towers ſtruck off a Jew's head upon every church that fell, or was burning and as they killed two thouſand Jews, they muſt have burnt two thouſand churches The citizens going out found this company diſperſed like a flock of ſheep in the field, and made great ſlaughter of them It is no wonder that Choſroes then favoured the eaſtern Jews, ſince they made ſuch advantageous diverſions on his account

Hiſtorians relate, that Choſroes continued always devoted to judicial aſtrology, that entering, one day, the church of Dora whilſt the ſervice was performing the Chriſtians were diſturbed as if their myſteries had been profaned, and their religion diſhonoured, by the preſence of this heathen prince Domitian, biſhop of Melitene, not being able to bear the affront he offered the church, went out, and threatened to bring his troops Choſroes ſent his apology to the prelate, who received it returned, cenſured the prince, and drove him out of the church

This prince was impriſoned by his ſubjects and his ſon, and they gave him gold and ſilver inſtead of bread, ſaying "Enjoy at thy pleaſure all the things thou haſt deſired with an inſatiable thirſt" He died of famine in the midſt of his treaſure in the year 628, and three years after concluded the Perſian monarchy which went to the Saracens, Iſdigerdes, the laſt of their kings, having been conquered near Cadeſia

CHAP XIII

Conqueſt of Omar, ſucceſſor to Mahomet Taking of Jeruſalem Fall of the Perſian monarchy Omar ... caliph His conqueſts Is ſucceeded by Aly Moa... at Damaſcus Iſdigerdes perſecutes the Jews ... ty and ... of the Arabians Almanzor ... of Perſia to the head of the empire ...

THE Arabians made great conqueſts and the Jews of the eaſt univerſally changed maſters Omar, the ſecond caliph, after the death of Mahomet, his predeceſſor, reigned but ten years and a half, during which he took thirty-ſix thouſand cities or caſtles pulled down four thouſand temples belonging to the Chriſtians or Magi built fourteen hundred moſques, and made himſelf maſter of all the eaſt

Notwithſtanding all that Heraclius could do to relieve Damaſcus which this caliph beſieged by his generals he entered in at the ſame time by aſſault and capitulation, for they had forced the intrenchments on one ſide, whilſt they capitulated on the other

Syria being conquered, by the taking of this place they proſecuted the ſiege of Jeruſalem, which was already begun, and in a ſhort time totally reduced the place Omar walking the ſtreets with an air of devotion, deſired them to ſhew him Solomon's temple, intending to raiſe a moſque in the place

The Arabians aſſert, that their caliph granted the biſhop of Jeruſalem a very honourable capitulation for the city, that he entered it without ſuffering any diſorders of his troops, and not allowing any church to be taken from the Chriſtians very modeſtly deſired of Sophronius a place where he might build a moſque The biſhop ſhewed him Jacob's ſtone, and the place where Solomon's temple ſtood, followed by the principal officers of his army, where, in time, he built a moſque

This caliph at the ſame time attacked the Perſians by his generals, and, after many battles, Iſdigerdes, the laſt of the Perſian kings, loſt Cadeſia His capital, children, and treaſures, fell into the enemy's hands For his own part he fled to Chorazan, where he lay concealed for ſixteen years, ſhifting from place to place, till one of his ſubjects, the governor of Merou, betrayed him, and invited Tarcan, king of the Turks, to take upon him the government Iſdigerdes gave him battle, loſt it, and attempting to paſs a river in his flight, the boatman diſputed with him about the price of his paſſage, and whilſt they were wrangling, the Turkiſh horſe, who purſued him cloſe, arrived, and took away his life Thus ended the Perſian monarchy, and the Jews, who had been long under its dominion, came under that of the Saracens and Omar, who puſhed on his conqueſts, on the one hand, to the river Oxus, and on the other to Egypt, where he made himſelf maſter of Alexandria Mahomet had educated him, ſo that two parties appealing from his judgment to that of Omar, when he had heard them, he fetched his ſabre, and ſtruck off the head of him that had refuſed to ſtand by Mahomet's deciſion He took the title of Commander of the Faithful, and obſerved ſuch great humility in the midſt of all his glory, that the governor of Suſiana going to wait upon him in a temple, he found him aſleep upon the ſteps among the poor and it was only to do an honour to his nation before this ſtranger, that he went and ſat in the pulpit of the moſque, which ſerved him for a throne Renouncing the ties of nature, and the endearments of blood, he declared the caliphſhip ſhould be elective, and that his ſon ſhould not have a place in the council, unleſs he was found worthy to reign He was killed by a ſlave as he was at prayer

After his death the ſix electors met to nominate a caliph One of them renounced the election of himſelf, upon condition he might chuſe the caliph alone The thing was agreed to, and he made choice of Othman, in preference to Aly, the ſon-in-law of Mahomet, and who was the moſt eminent for that dignity. He entirely ſubdued Chorazan, and many provinces of the eaſt, and puſhed his conqueſts as far as Andalou, that is, Andaluſia, in Spain In the mean time Aly, who always looked upon him with a jealous eye, raiſed ſome Arabians againſt him They beſieged him in his caſtle of Medina, where water failing after a three months ſiege, he came out to the rebels with the Alcoran in his hand, and proteſted he would have no other judge than that book, which was to be the rule of their conduct This did not ſtop the mutineers they ſtabbed him in many places, and put an end to his exiſtence

Aly was elected in his room, and though his paſſion for the caliphſhip was violent enough to make him kill his brother-in-law, yet he wanted to be entreated to accept this dignity

Aiſchah, Mahomet's widow, rebelled againſt her ſon-in-law, and as ſhe had great intereſt with the Muſſelmen, already provoked by the conſpiracy againſt Othman, ſhe was at no trouble to form a numerous army The battle was fought near Baſſora Aly got the victory, and took Aiſchah, after a great deal of blood was ſhed about the camel ſhe rode upon, becauſe brave men had ſurrounded this woman, and loſt their lives in her defence, and for that reaſon it was called the Battle of Camel He reſpectfully ſent back his mother-in-law to Mecca, and ſeeing Arabia and the Babylonian Irach fully ſubjected to his command, he marched to ſtifle another rebellion, which was raiſed againſt him in Syria.

Moavia headed this revolt, reſolving to revenge the death of Othman, his benefactor and relation. This prince prided himſelf in his humanity and clemency "The one is brave, and the other courageous, (ſaid he, ſpeaking of his enemies,) but for my own part I am content to be conſidered among the Muſſelmen as a merciful and gentle prince" It was he that firſt made a gallery or a ſeparate place, in the moſque, for the caliph, who was at once the pontiff and ſovereign It was from thence he repeated the office of the Muſſelmen, and made them a ſort of homily, as the biſhop and curate do in the church of Rome This prince was maſter of Syria, and made Damaſcus his capital he puſhed his conqueſts as far as Conſtantinople, and beſieged it ſo long, as to ſow and reap in the neighbouring fields

Moavia was a formidable enemy for Aly, who, notwithſtanding, marched againſt him, and arrived in a little time upon the frontiers of Syria Water failing him, he aſked for ſome of a Chriſtian hermit, who had his cell near the camp The hermit had only three hogſheads of water in his ciſtern, but told Aly, there was a well in the neighbourhood, ſhut up with a huge ſtone, where he might plentifully ſupply himſelf Aly diſcovered the well, and cauſed it eaſily to be uncovered, and having procured [illegible] refreſhment, returned thanks to God, and continued his march againſt Moavia

The armies were quickly in ſight, but not venturing to give a deciſive battle, fought in little parties they reckoned ninety of theſe ſkirmiſhes in an hundred days Moavia loſt forty-five thouſand men, but Aly infinitely leſs The former perceiving himſelf too much weakened, faſtened many copies of the Alcoran at the end of lances, and cauſing them to be carried at the head of the army, cried, this was the book that was to decide all differences, and that it was not lawful, without reaſon, to ſhed Muſſelmens blood. Aly was ſenſible of the artifice, but his troops being ſtruck with an inſtinct of devotion for that book, demanded that arbiters ſhould be choſen to terminate the differences betwixt Moavia and Aly

Aly's umpire was nominated by his generals, who choſe a man of great devotion and integrity Moavia's arbitrator was a man of art They agreed to depoſe the two pretenders, and to elect a caliph who ſhould rule over all the countries which the Muſſelmen had conquered Aly's arbitrator ſpoke firſt, and uſed, he depoſed Aly and Moavia, as he took the ring from his finger Moavia's arbitrator approved Aly's depoſition, and confirmed Moavia in the caliphſhip with which he inveſted him in the ſame manner, by putting his ring upon his finger It was in vain to appeal to upright dealing and the agreement, which the laſt umpire openly violated They curſed and excommunicated one another In the mean time Aly, who faithfully obſerved the ſuſpenſion of arms, had the mortification to ſee a great part of his army rebel againſt him, becauſe he had acknowledged another judge betwixt him and Moavia He beat the mutineers, and marched a ſecond time againſt Moavia, with different ſucceſs There he loſt Abdallah one of his beſt generals [illegible] the misfortune to hear that his own brother had deſerted him [illegible] with his enemies At laſt three reſolute men [illegible] to ſee ſo much bloodſhed, reſolved to ſlay the heads of a faction who cauſed ſo great a diviſion between the Muſſelmen Aly was killed in the moſque by one of [illegible] aſſaſſins, and Moavia was only wounded Haſſan, Aly's ſon, was forced to yield the caliphſhip to Moavia who remained maſter of Syria and Egypt [illegible] the chief founder of the race of the Ommiades, which was always an enemy to that of Aly

Jeſid, his ſon and ſucceſſor, was cruel and impious; and therefore the Perſians never ſpeak of him without execration

However, he was acknowledged caliph in Persia, and in all the lands of the Mussulmen, except Mecca, Med[illegible], and some cities of Chaldea.

Moavi[illegible] succeeded his father, but he was of so weak a constitution, that he voluntarily resigned the caliphship three months after he had excepted it, and went and shut himself up in a chamber, which he seldom or never came out of. Being wiser, or more resigned, than Charles [illegible] he never repented his abdication, and lived happily in [illegible] retreat; but the people regretted the loss of him, and caused the man to be buried alive who advised him to quit [illegible] dignity. He was so scrupulous as not to charge his co[illegible] science with the choice of a successor, because he did not know any one sufficiently accomplished to sustain so [illegible] a burden. His motto upon his seal was, "The Wo[illegible] nothing but a Cheat."

Mervan was elected, upon condition, that his children should not succeed him, and that the caliphship should return to the house of Moavi[illegible]. Marvan at first designed to execute his promise, but having humbled all his enemies, he declared Khaled, who was to succeed him, and called him bastard. This young prince's mother, whom Marvan had married, could not bear this insult, but revenged her son, by strangling her husband.

We have related the great revolution by which the Persian monarchy fell, and the dispersed tribes came under the empire of the Mussulmen, who became masters of the ea[illegible]. Let us now see what share they had in these events.

The historians assert, that Isdigerdes, king of Persia, persecuted them some time before the war of the Arabians against him. Their synagogues were given to the Magi, their academies shut up, and the persecution caused the fall of many persons. No wonder then that they rejoiced upon the change of their master. It is an inclination rooted in the heart of the oppressed, to desire, and rejoice at, the humbling of their persecutor. They imagine that God, a just protector of the innocent, punishes the oppressor, and makes him sensible of the iniquity. The Jews passed this judgment upon Isdigerdes and the Persians, who had given them such hard treatment.

They are accused not only of rejoicing at the conquests of the Mussulmen, who destroyed abundance of churches, and did great mischief to the Christians, but of associating with them, of taking their mark, and encouraging them to carry their arms into the empire. But their joy must have often been interrupted by their own misfortunes. For the havock which the conquerors made in Persia, and Syria, must have given them disturbance. Besides, it was not necessary that they should provoke the Saracens to war, who were insolently inclined to it; and from the moment they had tasted the pleasure of wealth, by plundering some province, they forgot their antient poverty, and thought of nothing but enriching themselves with the spoils of their neighbours. We ought therefore to found the motives of the war and the invasion of so many kingdoms, on the avarice of the Arabians, and the ambition of their leaders, which was never satiated.

The Jews highly extol the humanity of the Arabians, who condemned the violence offered to conscience, and restored them to the free possession of their religion. They lived peaceably under the first caliphs and their academies were open. Chanin taught at Pumbedita, under Omar. Mar Rabba succeeded him, whilst Chenina Surhæus, the son of Cahpta, reigned at Sora.

Omar sometimes favoured the Jews: for a Mussulman having gained his cause by Mahomet's decision, and the process being brought before him to be revised, he took his sabre, and cut off the obstinate Mussulman's head, to avenge the Jew of his adversary's cavils. After he was caliph, a Jew complaining to him of a governor of a province, to whom he had delivered some goods which he did not pay for, Omar called for ink, and there being none in the place, he took a brick from the wall of Medina, which he was building, and drew upon it these words: "Put an end to the complaints that are brought against you, or leave your government." The Jew carrying the brick, was presently paid the money. This shews what access this nation had to the caliph, and this prince's love of justice. But [illegible] equity for private persons, he was very [illegible] to [illegible] for that part which continued in Arabia after [illegible] conquests he totally expelled.

[illegible] Jewish nation, instead of suffering under Jesid, and [illegible] successors, enjoyed a full and absolute peace. [illegible] of the captivity reigned with almost as great [illegible] as if he had been king. The academies had been [illegible] abandoned during the revolution. So great was the desertion of scholars and masters, that they were forced [illegible] Sora to make a weaver professor, because he had studied the law. But then they began to relish the sciences again. The profession of physic, which is always profitable, resumed its former lustre. A [illegible] of Alexandria, named Aaron, was at once a physician and teacher. He had published a book, intitled, "The Pandects, or, the [illegible] of Remedies." The Jew, Messe[illegible], who was [illegible] caliph's court, then translated it into Arabic.

CHAP. XIV.

Justinian's [illegible] against the Jews. [illegible] Africa changed [illegible] council [illegible] Jews. Their [illegible] Cesarea. [illegible] of Beyrut [illegible] Jews [illegible] the Goths. [illegible] and [illegible] of the Jews at Antioch. [illegible] Great [illegible] moderation and equity [illegible] of religion. [illegible] the Jewish [illegible] under [illegible] Jewish [illegible]. Their [illegible] in Spain [illegible] Decrees of the council of Toledo. A [illegible] decrees against the Jews. Their [illegible] gave them [illegible] of the [illegible] Their [illegible] in France [illegible] Severity of prelates towards them [illegible] of the Jews. They are [illegible] France.

We shall now turn our attention to the Jews in the West, under the Roman emperors at Constantinople, Africa, Italy, Spain and France, during the [illegible] centuries, which we shall [illegible], to avoid breaking the chain of their history.

The first mark of complaint which the emperor Justinian gave them, was his edict, which forbad them [illegible] their passover according to their [illegible] and enjoined them to [illegible] at the [illegible]. This was no more than what we [illegible] letter, who [illegible] obliged to follow [illegible] which [illegible] less confusion [illegible] very tenacious of their old [illegible] right.

They were soon after exposed to a more [illegible] edict, by which that emperor deprived them of several privileges, particularly, of making wills, and becoming [illegible].

He [illegible] deprived the [illegible] of Africa of [illegible] of their religion, [illegible] Carthage, and sent orders to the [illegible] turn all their synagogues [illegible] churches, and [illegible] them from performing [illegible].

This law [illegible] Borium, [illegible] of Africa, situate at the [illegible] the [illegible] bounded Pentapolis on the [illegible], was strong, because [illegible] trance, and left but [illegible]. The Jews had [illegible]. Here [illegible], lived the more peaceably because the emperor de[illegible] no taxes of them, and no imperial collector was [illegible] seen there. They had a stately temple, the founda[illegible] whereof they referred to Solomon's time. We are to conclude from this, that they had been a long time settled in this place, and that they were rich notwithstanding the neighbourhood of the Moors. Justinian undertook the conversion of the inhabitants of this city, as well as of that of Augila, where heathenism still remained, and where they [illegible] sacrificed to idols, in temples consecrated to Alexander the Great, and Jupiter Ammon. He succeeded in his design, for the Jews as well as heathens embraced Christianity. The synagogue, or temple of Solomon [illegible] a church; and Justinian caused the city to be walled in to make it more safe.

[illegible] which were, by the Jews, looked upon [illegible] persecution failed not, as usual, to produce [illegible] ordinary discontent, which, by degrees, ripened into a revolt as soon as a proper opportunity offered. [illegible] was caused by an impostor, named Julian, [illegible] appeared in Palestine, and deluded the people of their [illegible]. As he took the title of Conqueror, the [illegible] to [illegible] his nation, he [illegible] all his credulous followers to [illegible] themselves. The [illegible] falling [illegible] upon the Christians, who fancied they had nothing to [illegible] from a nation so often [illegible] made great slaughter of them; but Justinian's troops ran to the relief of the [illegible] found they were led by a misguided [illegible], and punished with death [illegible] revolt.

There was [illegible] disturbance, twenty-five years after [illegible] Cesarea [illegible] and Jews though mortal enemies [illegible] united against the Christians of this city. They demolished the churches, murdered many people, and assassinated the governor in his palace. His wife [illegible] the danger [illegible] her complaints to [illegible], who [illegible] speedy orders to Adamantius to [illegible] the [illegible] Informations being laid, and the Jews charged with all the odium and cruelty of this violence, Adamantius confiscated the estates of the rich, put to flight great numbers of the mutineers who had a share in the action, and took off the heads of others. The execution was performed with such severity, that it made all the Jews of that country tremble, and prevented, for a time, their taking up arms against the Christians.

In Italy the Jews declared loudly against Justinian and Belisarius, who besieged Naples. This famous general had recovered Africa to the emperor's obedience, vanquished the Vandals, and, in the triumph decreed him for it at Constantinople, brought out the sacred vessels of the temple of Jerusalem, which Titus had brought to Rome, and Genseric had carried away, when he plundered that great city. This spectacle which revived the remembrance of the taking of Jerusalem, and the ruin of its temple, must have disturbed the Jews of Constantinople. Upon this sight, one of them exclaimed, "that these precious vessels ought not to be brought to Constantinople, nor placed in the emperor's palace. They can not (said he) be preserved in any other place than that where Solomon consecrated them; and this is the reason that Genseric has taken Rome, and the Romans have conquered Genseric."

Belisarius, having conquered the Vandals in Africa, passed over into Italy to fight the Goths, who were masters of the principal places, and first attacked Naples.

There were two factions in this great city, one for the emperor, and the other for the Goths, whom the Jews, who were numerous and considerable there, favoured. The imperialists, to free themselves from the inconvenience of a siege, had represented to Belisarius, that it was more advantageous to lay siege to Rome, because if he took that capital, Naples, which continued in subjection to the barbarians but by force, would naturally return to its obedience; but he rejected this proposition, and only made them great promises if they would capitulate. Articles of capitulation were already drawn up, and excepted by Belisarius, who granted all their demands, when the friends of the Goths pathetically addressed the inhabitants, and supported their arguments by the presence of the Jewish merchants, who were there, to assure the people that they would neither want provision or ammunition during the siege. The citizens, encouraged by this assurance, took heart, and defended the place for twenty days with an [illegible] vigour. Belisarius lost many good officers and soldiers in the different assaults in which he was repulsed. The Jews defended that part [illegible] the sea, and [illegible] were persuaded they should have no quarter, since they were the principal [illegible] of the resistance that was made, they fought like desperate men. The city was [illegible] taken on another [illegible] whilst they still held out [illegible] the enemy's [illegible] forced from the [illegible]. Belisarius exhorted his [illegible] to clemency, but whether he spoke [illegible] the soldiers bent on [illegible] and plunder, [illegible] general's advice [illegible] religion, and without distinction of persons [illegible] slaughter. This cruelty [illegible] quelled the [illegible] for a time, and we hear of [illegible] the subsequent reigns.

Though the reign of [illegible] the [illegible] of the A[illegible] came from the Danube [illegible] frequent incursions into Thrace, yet the Jews remained quiet [illegible]. This prince's [illegible] to it, for [illegible] to procure their [illegible] on him. But as he [illegible] so remote from Judea and Syria, [illegible] they could not flatter themselves with drawing any hope [illegible] from thence; and perhaps their motions were but little known. But Phocas [illegible] the throne by [illegible] his master and his children, it was apprehended this revolution might cause many alterations.

Those of Syria finding themselves [illegible] Antioch laid hold on the opportunity [illegible] the Christians. The sedition [illegible] and [illegible] resolutely on both sides, but the Jews being [illegible] rest [illegible] the, had set on fire [illegible] in a barbarous manner; for they [illegible] streets, and after exposing him [illegible] manner, threw him into the [illegible] were at length, with great difficulty [illegible] Count Bonosus, who [illegible] sent with [illegible] force against them. [illegible] were banished [illegible].

The Jews were [illegible] isle of Cyprus, where they had [illegible] establish themselves, notwithstanding [illegible] been taken in [illegible] travellers of [illegible] years after the [illegible] an bishop Leontius, [illegible] them, resolved, if possible, to convert [illegible] and succeeded so [illegible] his [illegible] were baptized.

Gregory the [illegible] performed [illegible] the Jews ought to be [illegible] hated, because they were [illegible] general [illegible] vehement [illegible] fires [illegible] the [illegible] of the [illegible]

"Th[illegible]
"by [illegible]
"as [illegible]
"[illegible]
"of [illegible]

"method to convert them is not to make them fear us, by carrying severity to excess, but to oblige people to come and hear the word of God."

He imagined it lawful to employ money, without believing these presents could infuse faith; for, said he, if we convert not the fathers, we may win the children. The Jews have praised this pontiff, in their annals, for his lenity and indulgence to them; and they had reason; for the abbess of St. Stephen de Gergenti, in Sicily, desiring to signalize her zeal to the pope, gave him notice, that a great number of Sicilian Jews desired to be converted. But he would not be dazzled with a notion of increasing the church. He ordered the abbess not to be too hasty, but to wait till these catechumens were well instructed, before she suffered them to receive baptism.

He had the equity to condemn the extravagant zeal of a new convert of Cagliari. A Jew, who had received baptism the day before, thinking to distinguish himself in his new religion, put himself at the head of a company of young people and went to the synagogue on Easter-day, and set up a cross there. The chief officers, military and civil, instead of approving this violence, certified against the Jews. The bishop himself, whom he had consulted, denied his consent, and condemned the action. Gregory the Great, declining to coincide with this prelate in his equitable notions, praised him for not communicating the evil with the good, and advised him to pass censure upon the new convert, without hearkening to the excuses he might make by laying the fault upon his zeal, and love for religion. He required that the cross should be removed, and the synagogue left to the Jews; since, though the law forbids them to build new ones, it appoints that they should be left the enjoyment of those they had already. With the same spirit he condemned the bishop of Terracina, who had taken away a synagogue in his diocese, which the laws had established, and had driven the Jews from another place where they had retired for their devotion.

This pontiff not only revived the old edicts issued against their having Christian slaves, which had been long since shamefully neglected; but declared that all the Jewish slaves who should take refuge in the churches, and be baptized, should become free.

The condition of the Jews altered much for the worse as soon as the emperor Heraclius had concluded a peace with Persia, by which some relics formerly taken by them had been restored to him, and sent to Jerusalem. It plainly appears, from his own words, that he hated the Jewish nation because they were enemies to the Christian religion: but what gave him the first handle against them was his meeting with one at Tiberias named Benjamin, a man so wealthy as to have alone furnished his army, and court with provisions, and so elated on this account, that he harrassed the Christians with troublesome lawsuits, and malicious prosecutions. Benjamin, fearing his resentment, found no better expedient to avoid it than turning Christian. But this circumstance did not lessen the emperor's aversion to the nation, whom he ordered soon after to be banished out of Jerusalem, with a severe prohibition against those who should, from that time, approach within three miles of the city.

The prediction of some soothsayers, whom he had consulted, gave him greater provocation against the Jews. This restless prince questioned them about the fate of the empire, which was in violent convulsions; and they answered him, "It should be ruined by a circumcised nation." As he saw the Jews numerous, he gave credit to the soothsayers, and persecuted the Jews by obliging them to abjure their religion.

Not content with this, the emperor carried his zeal against them into the neighbouring kingdoms, and particularly to Sisibut, king of Spain, who made great numbers prisoners; and, to avoid the most cruel torments, many abandoned their religion.

Isidorus, bishop of Sevil, who was one of Sisibut's admirers in other respects, has yet condemned [illegible] zeal, which was without knowledge; and, instead of impressing faith in the hearts of the people, [illegible]. Being afterwards at the head of the fourth council of Toledo, he caused a very solemn decree to be made concerning it. This council was [illegible] by order of Sisinand, who had dethroned Suintilla, the former [illegible]; but, he perceiving the people's minds [illegible], because his competitor was still alive [illegible] to unite them. He convened the prelates of the kingdom to Toledo, [illegible] himself before the [illegible], in profound humiliation, [illegible] reform [illegible]. The council furthered the designs of the [illegible], by giving instructions to the Goths to [illegible] prince for the defence of the nation, and pronouncing anathemas on those who should violate the oath of fidelity they had taken to the [illegible] that neither Suintila, who had [illegible], his wife, nor children, [illegible] his brother [illegible] had [illegible] him, [illegible]. They [illegible] on the [illegible] made regulations about the state of the Jews. [illegible] condemned the violence that had been done them by Sisibut's order, declaring that they ought to be [illegible] that [illegible] the first man [illegible] promises, [illegible] version of his mind, and that he ought to be [illegible], and not driven to the faith.

Chintila, who succeeded Sisinand, and was perhaps his brother, thought also he ought to [illegible] in his interest. To this effect he [illegible] the sixth council of Toledo, which made many decrees [illegible]. But to render the laws more authentic, it [illegible] be confirmed by another council [illegible] in the same place. This council [illegible] against the Jews. It recommended this king, who was [illegible] with persecuting zeal, [illegible] the law that this prince had made to banish all the Jews out of his kingdom. Lastly, it decreed, that no king, for the future, should ascend the throne till he had taken an oath never to violate this law, [illegible] if he broke it. It is probable this [illegible] two councils was caused by the [illegible]. This prudent and moderate man, who [illegible], presided in the fourth council of Toledo, but he died before the [illegible] of the prelates who, having lost their only [illegible], [illegible] into violence.

Recesuinth afterwards assembled several councils at Toledo, where he ordered [illegible] to be the subject of their deliberations. He proposed that they should debate about the election of [illegible], in which the clergy [illegible] Jews were [illegible] their conversion [illegible]. The [illegible] was [illegible], it would have [illegible]. However, it seems [illegible] this motion of the king and the [illegible] of the [illegible] met and wrote to the king [illegible] of Toledo and of all Spain, [illegible] circumstances [illegible] to him, [illegible] being [illegible] Christians [illegible] Jews they were [illegible] and [illegible] embraced the Christian [illegible]. They [illegible] any [illegible] would [illegible] their goods should be confiscated.

[illegible] appeared totally opposite to their [illegible] they not only espoused the cause of Judaism, but [illegible] Christianity, insomuch that [illegible] was obliged to order Julian, then archbishop of Toledo, to write [illegible], which he accordingly did, with [illegible], in a learned treatise which he published a little before the close of the seventh century.

[illegible] complained of a conspiracy the Jews, and their [illegible], had made against his government. [illegible] this prince represented to the council assembled at [illegible], that the mischief was [illegible] to all the provinces [illegible] that it had not passed the Alps, nor [illegible], but [illegible] that it could not be [illegible] or tolerated, [illegible] the council's advice [illegible] it was resolved, that all the [illegible] should be degraded of their privileges, [illegible] that [illegible] should be considered, and their children [illegible] Christians.

[illegible] the Romans being expelled, [illegible] the Jews had [illegible] to make their way into several places they had not [illegible] before. At least we find, after Clovis, the kings [illegible] of this kingdom made many regulations relating to their conduct and [illegible]. They must [illegible] been [illegible] in Paris, and the adjacent parts, since Childebert, to whom this kingdom fell by lot, published an ordinance, forbidding them to appear in the streets from [illegible] and Easter Sunday, because he feared that the [illegible] devotion might cause some insurrection against them, or that they might take advantage of that conjuncture, when the churches were full and the streets empty, to execute some villainous design. The council of Orleans, held in the year 540, made such another ordinance, which shews that they were dispersed throughout the kingdom.

They were still more numerous and potent in the diocese of Uzes. Since, Ferreol, the bishop of it, fell under the king's displeasure, and was banished on their account. He thought that he might convert them by living familiarly with them. This familiarity rendered him suspected: it was imagined he engaged in their interests, and probably in their opinions. He was obliged to quit his bishopric, and go to Paris, to justify himself to Childebert, where he continued many years in exile. But the king being convinced of his innocence, and having restored him to his bishopric, he fell into another extreme, and expelled all the Jews from his diocese.

[illegible], bishop of Clermont, went also to convert the Jews of Auvergne, but the means he employed [illegible] on the other hand, the [illegible] criminal violence. [illegible] a new convert entering the city [illegible] his white habit, upon his receiving baptism, [illegible] nation, enraged to see him in that dress, threw upon him a pot of [illegible] oil. The people [illegible] violence, were going to tear him to pieces [illegible] had not opposed it; but their revenge was only [illegible] Ascension day, Christians of the Clermont [illegible] the procession to pull down the synagogue. [illegible] to write to the Jews, that he [illegible] violence, but that, as a shepherd, [illegible] his flock, and [illegible] straggling sheep, he exhorted them to believe as he did, or leave the city. The [illegible] of the bishop, and the fury of the people, [illegible] of a cruel death [illegible] Jews, and on the third day a part of the people sent their [illegible] to the bishop, desiring to be baptized, which [illegible] on Whitsunday. Those who [illegible] were banished the city, and obliged to return to Marseilles, from whence they came.

St Germain, bishop of Paris, was [illegible] conversion, and the historians of those times [illegible] instances of his zeal, [illegible] circumstances.

King Chilperic, who found them [illegible] in his kingdom of Soissons and [illegible] conversion. Being an abandoned [illegible] point to force the Jews, and present them to the font [illegible] this custom was [illegible] no great advantage was derived from the [illegible] of Chilperic, indeed, he was actuated by [illegible] succeed.

[illegible] became afterwards one of the most famous academies of the Jews in the west. The youth came [illegible] from the remotest countries, and found [illegible] doctors that instructed them, [illegible] Benjamin of Tudela affirms, that the doctors maintained the scholars, and supplied them with clothing, all the [illegible] their stay in the academy.

After the persecution of the Jews in France great numbers fled for protection to other countries, where, [illegible] the instigation of the Catholic priests, they were [illegible] persecuted. Some were put to death, and others confined in prisons, while great numbers [illegible] heads and [illegible] shaved, and were treated with other marks of [illegible] obnoxious to the Jews, than degrading to their [illegible].

THE END OF BOOK I.

CONTINUATION

OF THE

HISTORY OF THE JEWS,

FROM THE TIME OF

FLAVIUS JOSEPHUS.

INCLUDING A

PERIOD OF UPWARDS OF ONE THOUSAND SEVEN HUNDRED YEARS.

CONTAINING AN

ACCOUNT OF THEIR DISPERSION INTO THE VARIOUS PARTS OF EUROPE, ASIA, AFRICA, AND AMERICA.

WITH

THEIR DIFFERENT PERSECUTIONS, TRANSACTIONS, AND PRESENT STATE,

THROUGHOUT THE KNOWN WORLD.

BOOK II.

CHAP. I.

The King of Cozar's converſion to Judaiſm. The occaſion and manner of it. Chaſdai's pains to find out the kingdom of Cozar. His letter to king Joſeph. Import of the anſwer.

THE eighth century is chiefly celebrated for the converſion of Cozar, king of an heathen nation, and is one of the moſt conſiderable events of the Jewiſh hiſtory. Cozar was a ſerious, thoughtful prince, who, after examining all religions, and holding conferences with philoſophers, Chriſtians, Mahometans, and Jews, determined in favour of that of Moſes.

His converſion was effected by the obſervations and reaſonings of a famous Rabbi, named Sangari, who explained ſeveral learned matters to him much to his ſatisfaction. The king, however, fearful of alarming his idolatrous ſubjects, and thereby inſtigating them to a revolt, communicated the ſecret only to the general of his army, and departing privately with him, they arrived at a certain mountainous deſert near the ſea, where the night ſurprizing, and obliging them to enter a cave, they found there the Jews keeping their ſabbath. The prince and general, overjoyed at this adventure, made their abjurations to these Jews, and being circumciſed, reſumed their way back to the capital. In the mean time, the noiſe of the king's converſion being ſpread abroad, thoſe who had hitherto diſſembled their Judaiſm, openly profeſſed it, and converted the Cozars. Rabbins and doctors were ſent for from ſeveral places to inſtruct the new converts, and convert the reſt, ſo that [illegible] hundred thouſand embraced this religion. A tabernacle was built after the model of that which Moſes ſet up in the wilderneſs. The original Jews were exceedingly honoured, and the king himſelf reſolved to give [illegible] that nation, to remove his remaining doubts, and to open to him all the precepts of the law. He had no [illegible] for the Caraites, who were ſcrupulouſly addicted to the law, and more zealous than the traditionaries, but he yielded to the reaſons of Sangari, who was a Thalmudiſt. The king grew happy and potent; he [illegible] his enemies, and made new conqueſts, which rendered him ſtrong and formidable to his neighbours.

Judaiſm muſt have continued long in this kingdom, since, more than two hundred [illegible] years after, king Joſeph gave an account of it [illegible] Rabbi, who deſired to be informed [illegible] method of governing his people. The [illegible] Chaſdai, who, according to the moſt authentic [illegible] that can be produced, lived in the tenth century.

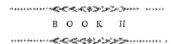

Chifdai was treasurer-general to Abderamus, and had so great an authority at this prince's court, that nothing was done without his advice. He confesses he had often heard mention of the kingdom of Cozar, without being able to discover it, till the ambassadors from Constantinople informed him, that merchants frequently came from this country, whose commodities were skins, and who told him that the reigning king's name was Joseph. He resolved to write to this prince, and be at the charge of sending an express with his letter. He took the opportunity of the ambassadors return to Constantinople to conduct him so far. The envoy resided there for six months, after which he was obliged to return the same way he came, upon information that the roads to Cozar were impassible. Chifdai, much chagrined at this disappointment, designed to send this letter to Jerusalem, that it might be [illegible] to Nisibe, thence to Armenia, and from Armenia to the country of Bardas, and the kingdom of Cozar. But two ambassadors of the king of Giblim arriving at Cordua, [illegible] to make a more certain and speedy expedition. He was also informed, that there was a [illegible] blind man in Spain who had been a favorite of the king of Cozar, but upon search after him, he was not to be found, which obliged him to commit this letter to the Giblim ambassadors, who caused it to be delivered to king Joseph.

He was desired to give a description of this kingdom, the number of its provinces and cities, what people he made war upon, whether there were any adjacent isles, whether any of these inhabitants turned Jews, and the names of the kings his predecessors. He was asked too, whether war expelled the sabbath [illegible]. Whether it was allowed to defend themselves, and attack the enemy on the sabbath-day.

That prince, at his request, gave him an account of his kingdom, government, and religion, which, if genuine, would prove, no doubt, that the Jewish religion was not only established in that kingdom under one of his predecessors, whom he named Bula, but likewise prove that it still continued to flourish in his dominions, though there is very little in the description of them, of their situation, limits, climate, cities, rivers and products that can direct a reader where to find them, so that we deem it ridiculous to dwell longer on that legend.

CHAP II

Jews [illegible] Christians persecuted in Egypt, [illegible] to the house of Abbassides. They are [illegible] Gehan the Jew [illegible] of Mobed [illegible] Charlemagne [illegible] Rabbi [illegible] successor Motawakkel [illegible] Removal of the house of the [illegible]

ABDALMELIC held the caliphship in the beginning of the eighth century. His avarice was so exorbitant [illegible] content [illegible], and he was so violent [illegible] to the house of Aly, as not to bear even to be commanded by a poet of that sect. He pushed his conquests as far as Spain, and triumphed wherever he carried [illegible]. In the height of his victories he preserved a great moderation: he neither persecuted the Jews or Christians of his dominions, but allowed the former their residences and privileges, and would not take from the latter, by force, one of their churches at Damascus, which they had refused him, but left them in the peaceable enjoyment of it.

Valid, the eldest of sixteen sons, succeeded his father, and though he reigned but nine years, yet he conquered many provinces in Spain and Sardinia. The islands Majorca and Minorca were reduced to his obedience, and his troops penetrated even into the Narbonnese Gaul. He was a bigot to this law, and so had no kindness for the Christians. He erected a mosque at Damascus upon the ruins of a church, and built another at Jerusalem. Soliman, that is Salomon, his brother, succeeded him, but continued not long in his sovereignty. He was obliged to fortify Rama, in Palestine, to stop the incursions the Arabians made into the Holy Land. Omar II Abdalasis's son, was his successor, at whose death the caliphship returned into the family of Abdalmelic, and was possessed by his third son called Jesid II. He made himself famous by his conquests, it being in his reign that the Saracens besieged Toulouse and Narbonne. The Christians of Egypt suffered so much in his reign, that the king of Nubia, which lies betwixt Thebais and Æthiopia, came to their succour with an hundred thousand men, and would not return till Hatchem sent the patriarch of Alexandria to assure him he would not disturb the church. It is probable the Jews had an hand in these violent proceedings, since they were caused by the avarice of the Egyptian governors.

The house of the Ommiades ended a little after under Marvan. The Abbassides had already for some time, meditated a rebellion in Chorazan, the governor whereof wrote a letter to his master in these words: "I see through the ashes the light of some coals which will break out to your confusion: fire is kindled with wood, and war by discourse. I would know whether Ommia wakes or sleeps?" He answered but this, "The present is more than the absent: cut off the mischief, for it spreads farther." But as he studied [illegible] how to remedy the disease, the Abbassides as being descendants of Haschem, broke out into a rebellion in the reign of Marvan. This prince was brave and unfortunate. Abul Abbas Saffa, whom Elmacin calls Abulgebbes, revolting against him, and being proclaimed caliph, the war proved cruel and fatal to Marvan by a particular accident. This prince, having drawn his army in battle array, went aside on a particular occasion. His horse, that he had left, took the bit in his teeth and running to the army threw them into a panic, as believing the caliph was killed, so that, without any further information, they took to flight. Marvan made fruitless attempts to rally his frightened troops, and was forced to fly with them to Damascus, from whence, not thinking himself secure, he passed into Egypt, where giving battle again, he lost his life, and his head was carried to his enemy, who remained master of the caliphship. He used his advantages so outrageously, that he was styled Saffa the Bloodshedder, because besides those who were killed in the battle, he put all the house of Ommiades to the sword, except one man who fortunately escaped, passed into Spain, and reigned there. Abdallah, the new caliph's uncle and general, having gathered together fourscore princes of the family of the Ommiades, caused them all to be knocked on the head with massy wooden clubs, and having their bodies laid on a table covered with tapestry, gave to his soldiers a [illegible] of a new invention, and the entertainment was carried on among the sighs and groans of expiring men. Afterwards he caused the sepulchres of this family to be opened, and taking out the dead bodies, hung them upon gibbets. Thus perished that house which had produced fourteen caliphs. That of the Abbassides succeeded, and reigned above five hundred years. As the former caliphs had their seat at Damascus, these chose [illegible] Coufa for their capital, situate upon the banks of the Euphrates, four days journey from Bagdad. This city [illegible] ceased long since, and considerable for nothing but the sepulchre of Aly, which is in its neighbourhood, and visited by his followers with great devotion. The Abbassides, when they changed the seat of the empire, brought their capital nearer the habitation of the Jews, who had still their academies on the banks of the Euphrates. Almansor, who succeeded his brother, built also Bagdad for greater security. He called it the city of Peace, but it retains the name of the hermit Bagdad, who had his cell [illegible] where the city was built. And it was in the neighbourhood of the Tigris and Euphrates that the [illegible] at that time.

[illegible] favourably. In fact this [illegible] was unavoidable, and common [illegible] in the revolutions of an empire, resumed [illegible] under Almansor, who was a man of letters, and drew to his court [illegible] of his time, [illegible] about the difference of religions. His first physician was a Christian. Almansor, who loved him, [illegible] to make him a Turk, but he answered, that he would either be burnt, or saved with his ancestors. [illegible] the answer, and dismissed him to die in peace at home. Almansor, who delighted in astronomy, [illegible] also some men from Persia well versed in that science. He had especially Jews in his attendance, who took advantage of that circumstance to bring their academies into new repute. R. Joseph and Samuel presided in the university of Pumbeditha. Dormis, Ananias, and Mal[illegible] succeeded them. There were likewise two famous [illegible] of Sora, who went both [illegible] of Judah, one was the son of Nachman, and [illegible]. His book called the Great Lessons was received with so general an applause, that Judah, [illegible] soon after made an abstract of it. [illegible] However, he had the title given [illegible] Great Light, because the Jews, thinking it an [illegible] to their learned men to call them blind, concealed [illegible] under an honourable title. There was [illegible] doctor in the [illegible] century, called R. Mari, whom they also stiled Light of the Eyes, from his great knowledge and penetration. Acha was another doctor profoundly skilled in the precepts of the law, upon which he composed a large volume, [illegible], but as he clashed with the head of the captivity, he could not arrive to the quality of sublime doctor or excellent, which mortification was attended by another. Samuel, the head of the captivity, when he died, named another person to succeed him; but so far from having any regard to the reputation and learning of this doctor, he chose his servant to preside over the [illegible]. Acha could not digest this last affront, so that leaving the academy, he went into Judæa, whilst his servant Nathronai possessed the principality, which he enjoyed for thirteen years. Ananias had the same misfortune as Acha. This Rabbin was a man of parts, but could not be admitted to the number of doctors, because his doctrine was suspected of some [illegible]. This suspicion was well-grounded, for he put himself at the head of the Sadducees, which sect was believed to be almost buried in the ruins of Jerusalem. They recovered strength, and, under the conduct of this famous leader, became formidable to their enemies. Some consider this Ananus as the father of the Caraites rather than the restorer of Sadduceism. But we [illegible] the Caraites could not claim him for their founder, because they were of a more antient standing.

Giafar, surnamed the Just, [illegible], who lived at that time, heavily afflicted the Jews of Arabia, and also of Persia. He was the sixth of the Imams, so the Musselmen stile their supreme pontiff, who presides over the mosque. He has a temporal as well as spiritual authority. Such as cast off their subjection to him are looked upon as atheists. The Persians have a particular reverence for twelve of these Imams, the immediate successors of Aly, among whom Giafar is one of the most considerable. This Iman made an order that the Jews and Christians who turned Musselmen should be sole heirs of their family; and as this law was precisely executed, it caused many to apostatize, who by this means succeeded to the estates which they could not obtain in a lawful way.

Almansor, having reigned two and twenty years, departed this life. Abdullah, his uncle, had disputed the caliphship with him, which he pretended to be due to his valour, and the services he had done to Saffa. But being overcome, he was shut up in a house supported by stones of rock salt, and Almansor, by conveying a water-stream under the palace, dissolved these stones, threw down the building, and buried Abdullah in the ruin. The rest of his reign would have been very happy had he not disgraced it by his avarice. Finding his death approaching, he sent for Mohadi, his son and heir, whom he commanded to honour his relations, because the honour he did them reflected upon himself, and to treat his freedmen kindly because they were persons who would serve him in time of need. He forbid him to build the city of Bagdad on the east side, and to admit women into affairs of state, after which he recommended him to Providence and expired. Historians give quite a different character of this prince. He was as liberal as his father was covetous. He spent six millions of gold crowns in one pilgrimage to Mecca, having conveyed thither a [illegible] of snow and ice, which [illegible] surprized the inhabitants, who had never seen any before. He held his court of justice attended by the most able Musselmen, and [illegible] the unjust judges [illegible]ly, he obliged the empress Irene to pay him a tribute of seventy thousand gold crowns, [illegible] from the incursions of the Arabians, who [illegible] Constantinople. He was an enemy to the Jews, and would either have them embrace his religion, or wear a badge to distinguish them from the Musselmen, [illegible] sent Theshas, one of his generals, to [illegible] the commission, which he executed with great [illegible].

Aaron, surnamed the Just, [illegible] after the death of his brother in the year [illegible] one of the greatest of the Arabian [illegible]. He [illegible] men of letters, but, instead of [illegible] belief, exactly weighed whether their [illegible] consisted with the good of the state. "You [illegible] than I," (said he once to one [illegible] who would have put him upon a false step, upon pretence of observing the Musselmen law) "but I have more prudence and understanding than you."

Charlemagne thought it expedient to make an alliance with this prince [illegible] to make a diversion [illegible] the empire [illegible] east, [illegible] might [illegible] him the conquest [illegible] in the west. He had [illegible] which the caliph's [illegible].

In order [illegible] chose Isaac, a Jew, [illegible] counts Lanfrede and Sigismund [illegible] proper [illegible] to negociate [illegible] peace with [illegible] who hated the Christians. He best knew [illegible] manner of the councils, [illegible] who were [illegible] Aaron's [illegible] upon the whole, [illegible] reign, and made their synagogues [illegible].

Aaron was succeeded by his son Amin, about the beginning of the ninth century, but he proved [illegible] prince, and so addicted to his pleasures, that his brother Mamoun found an opportunity to dethrone him.

He was a prince eminent for his noble [illegible] of learning, and endeavoured to bring it into the esteem of the Arabians, who had neglected it till that time, and, in order to succeed in it, caused all the good books of the Jews to be translated into that language.

This step was not at all relished by his subjects, who were ready to revolt, but that consideration did not prevent him from daily gathering [illegible] men of letters, among whom [illegible] celebrated Jewish astronomer who had been in high repute ever since the reign of Almansor, but was now esteemed at this court as the phœnix of his age. He was therefore highly esteemed by Mamoun, during whose reign the Jewish academies of Sora and Pumbeditha abounded with men of letters.

Mamoun, at his death, preferred his brother Motassem before his own son Abbas, who, at the [illegible] of some lords, had at first a design to assume the caliphship, but afterward yielding to his uncle's remonstrances, not only took an oath of fidelity, but obliged all his party to do the same. As Christian princes call themselves kings, by the Grace of God, he would be called Motavakel Billah, that is, a prince, preserved by the Grace of God. Disgusted with Bagdad, by the frequent seditions of its inhabitants, he drew nearer to Syria, where he built Samarrah, or Samarra, which became the capital of these caliphs. He governed [illegible] with great justice, and won a battle against the emperor [illegible], which cost the Christians above [illegible]

[illegible] been a bitter enemy to the Jews, upon [illegible] that they had been guilty of great [illegible] of the finances, which had been committed [illegible] the reign of his predecessor [illegible] the Alcoran, for which [illegible] forced to pay [illegible]

[illegible] particularly [illegible] concerning the question [illegible] in his capital, nor in the rest of his dominions, during [illegible]

[illegible] met with opposition upon [illegible] of the caliphship [illegible] the death of his father [illegible] the disease [illegible] to the death of [illegible] to fly [illegible] he [illegible] made to his throne.

[illegible] against [illegible] for [illegible] admitted [illegible] in the government [illegible] that they were admitted [illegible] that [illegible] their having iron stirrups [illegible] this prince not only degraded them [illegible] but stigmatized them [illegible] infamy [illegible] Motavakel [illegible] his empire, but into the neighbouring [illegible] it is [illegible] stated [illegible] in many places where the [illegible]

[illegible] Jews had another misfortune in this caliph's reign [illegible] kindled in one of their academies. [illegible] the son of [illegible], was the president at Pumbedita [illegible] the people were about to give him a partner, called [illegible]. He could not bear this competitor [illegible] the [illegible] were violent, but at last [illegible] He died two years after, and left the place and authority to Mattathias, who enjoyed it a much longer time.

Motavakel was slain by his son. This cruel prince had an iron stove, pointed within, which he caused to be heated in proportion to the punishment he designed for the offender, and when the sufferer cried, "Have pity on me," he answered, "Pity is a weakness of soul." He never died in this stove after forty days torture. He spared not his own son Mountasser, who, tired with these hardships, caused him to be slain. He was no longer a gainer by his parricide. Being tormented with cutting remorse, he thought [illegible] his father reproaching him with his crime. His brother Mosthain was as unfortunate as he, for the Turks and [illegible] which he had in pay, revolting against him, entered into his palace, dragged him from his throne by the [illegible], exposed him to the sun, and beat him with their batt[illegible] he had signed his deposition. They contrived [illegible] soon after, either by debarring him of drink, or by giving him poison with water and ice. Mothadi, who succeeded him, was quickly deposed by Mothamed, a man, addicted to his pleasures, who was absolutely governed by his brother and nephew. It was in his reign [illegible] Egypt was dismembered from the caliphship [illegible] refusing to depend upon him, was declared a rebel, and ordered to be execrated in all the mosques of the empire [illegible] hindered not a new dynasty being set up in Egypt, and the beginning of a succession of new caliphs.

CHAP. III.

Violent effects of a dispute concerning images. Jews [illegible] in Syria. Favoured under Nicephorus. [illegible] Judah [illegible] Leo [illegible] Basil [illegible] Distressed [illegible] They are [illegible] Occasions its particular [illegible]

THE question about images [illegible] the empire [illegible] contrary decisions [illegible] evolved [illegible] after it torments [illegible]

The [illegible]

[illegible] and the [illegible] by [illegible] Christians [illegible] only the [illegible] suffered them [illegible] the Jews took [illegible] lives. But as the [illegible] images [illegible] finding the [illegible] and his followers, they obliged the Jews, on [illegible] they had not [illegible] to [illegible] acknowledging themselves worshippers of images, [illegible] Divine vengeance [illegible] not [illegible] in their possession.

The Jews found themselves avenged [illegible] of Jerusalem and Syria. Abdalla, the [illegible], commanded the Christians [illegible] and [illegible] Arriving at Jerusalem, [illegible] as well as Christians, [illegible] to distinguish them [illegible] the Christians to [illegible] or [illegible] more violent [illegible] But the Jews, who were as much [illegible] of the caliphs [illegible] obedience. It is certain that [illegible] Abdalla [illegible] the Christians. Indeed, this [illegible] a considerable number of them [illegible] sold the [illegible]

They [illegible] under Nicephorus, who succeeded Leo [illegible] beginning of [illegible] century, and [illegible] images, for which [illegible] it [illegible] themselves, as [illegible] direction of the [illegible] to whom they [illegible] power and influence with respect to the [illegible] of the kingdoms. Nicephorus, however, protected the Jewish nation, and suffered them to [illegible] molested during his reign.

Michael, surnamed the Stammerer, was still more favourable to them than Nicephorus. It is certain, that he was [illegible] a Jew. This prince came from Amonum, a city of Phrygia, in which a great variety of ſectaries had taken ſanctuary. It is pretended that Michael borrowed ſomething from all theſe ſects, which he had known and ſtudied in his youth; that he had taken baptiſm from the Chriſtians, which he ſubſtituted in the room of circumciſion; [illegible] otherwiſe he generally obſerved all the Jewiſh ceremonies.

The ſtate of the Jews in Italy, at this time, cannot be [illegible], and Spain furniſhes out a very ſlender account. The Saracens had entered and reduced it to their obedience. Moſes, or Muſe, the governor of Africa, upon the invitation of the Chriſtians, ſent one of his generals, named Tarif, into Spain, who making his deſcent at the foot of the mountain Calpe, gave it its name, whence it is called Gibel Tarif at this day, or, the mountain of Tarik. Roderick loſt his life, and crown that was given him in the [illegible]. Muſe, [illegible] age, puſhed his army into Spain, and [illegible] his conqueſts not only to Toledo, [illegible] Saragoſſa. But as he depended upon Olic, the [illegible] was called ſome time after.

A Jew was [illegible] to take advantage of this revolution, and of the war the new governors made with the French [illegible]. He was called Serenus, and pretended to a [illegible]. He found in Spain abundance of people [illegible] to believe and follow him into the Holy Land, where he was to eſtabliſh his empire. Ambiſa, who was [illegible], took advantage of this deſertion, and ſeized [illegible] they had vacated by their credulity. It is not [illegible] Serenus carried theſe credulous people; but it is moſt probable that ſome died by the way, and that the reſt returned into their country, to bewail the loſs of their [illegible], which they had ſo imprudently quitted.

The houſe of the Ommiades, which enjoyed the caliphſhip in the eaſt, ſent governors and troops hither to confirm their antient conqueſts, and to make new ones. This family was ruined by that of the Abbaſſides, which made a general maſſacre of all that belonged to it. Abdalrahman, whom we call Abderame, muſt not be confounded with a general of the ſame name, who was defeated by Charles Martel, and had the good fortune to eſcape into Spain with his father. Moors [illegible] acknowledged him caliph in all the weſt. He reigned there a long time, and began to build the famous moſque of Cordua, which his ſon finiſhed by the help of the Chriſtians, whom he ordered from Narbonneſe Gaul, to work upon the ſumptuous temple of his prophet. In the reign of this caliph appeared R. Judah, who diſtinguiſhed himſelf in his nation by his learning. As he had ſtudied philoſophy, he inveſtigated the cauſes that hindered the ſea from overflowing the land, and publiſhed a treatiſe on it, which got him great reputation. He publiſhed alſo an Arabic dictionary, and tranſlated many books of that language into Hebrew, which ſhews not only that this man was learned, and that the ſciences flouriſhed then in the Spaniſh ſynagogues, but alſo that theſe firſt caliphs were more favourable to them than to the Chriſtians, who were forced to labour upon the building of a moſque, after having taken the materials from them.

As Languedoc was added to Spain ever ſince the Viſigoths were maſters of it, that province was the firſt expoſed to the incurſions of the Arabians, who had defeated the Viſigoths. In the firſt years of their conqueſts they made themſelves maſters of Narbonne, and came and beſieged Toloufe. It is aſſerted that the Jews, who had made a particular treaty with them, aſſiſted them, upon condition that all the Chriſtians ſhould be murdered that were in the town after it was taken. It is alſo ſaid that the Jews of Toloufe, weary of the tyranny of the preſent biſhop, called in the Saracens from Spain, and promiſed to deliver up the city, upon condition that, having maſſacred all the Chriſtians upon their entrance, the traitors ſhould be permitted to enjoy ſeveral privileges, and an entire liberty. The Saracens took Narbonne in their march, and advanced as far as Lyons, deſtroying all that fell into their hands. Vaiſier, duke of Aquitaine, vainly endeavoured to oppoſe their paſſage, he was defeated, and loſt his life. After his death, the victor beſieged Toloufe, took it, and put all the inhabitants to the ſword, except the Jews, to whom he religiouſly performed the promiſe he had made them. But Charlemagne having won three battles over Abderame, and retaken the city of Toloufe, was reſolved to puniſh the traitors for their baſeneſs, and all the blood they had cauſed to be ſpilt. They were condemned to death, and the inſtruments of their puniſhment were already prepared, when the cries and groans of ſo many poor wretches moved Charlemagne, and obliged him to mitigate the puniſhment. Inſtead of a general execution, he was contented with the heads of the principals in the treaſon, and ordained, for the future, that all the Jews living at Toloufe ſhould receive a box on the ear thrice a year at the gate of a church, that ſhould be appointed by the biſhop, and pay a perpetual fine of thirteen pounds of wax.

They were ſtill more favoured under Lewis, ſurnamed the Debonnair, whoſe chief phyſician was a Jew, whom ſome hiſtorians have repreſented as one of the greateſt magicians in the world. He was in ſuch high credit with that prince, that all the courtiers were glad to gain him and his countrymen's friendſhip with the moſt ſumptuous preſents. The emperor gave them liberty to build new ſynagogues, and granted them very advantageous edicts. So powerful a protection bred jealouſy and great diſorders in the dioceſe of Lyons.

Agobard, who was biſhop of it, had forbidden his flock to ſell Chriſtian ſlaves to the Jews to be carried into Spain, and to keep the ſabbath. It cannot be doubted but this prelate had a power to make ſuch laws as theſe for the government of the people committed to his care, and he did what is uſual with the men when inveſted with authority. He forbid the Chriſtians to buy wine of the Jews, and to eat with them during Lent. The Jews complained of theſe laws to Lewis, who being provoked againſt Agobard, and the citizens of Lyons, ſent three commiſſaries to take information. The biſhop was much ſurprized to ſee them arrive at his houſe. Some inhabitants, who probably were guilty of more capital oppreſſions, betook themſelves to flight. The biſhop, having more authority, waited the conſequences of the inqueſt, which was not to his advantage, ſince the Jews were reſtored to the poſſeſſion of their privileges, and the market on Saturday was changed to another day of the week, that the neceſſity of trading [illegible] might not oblige them to violate their ſabbath. The emperor had in his turn the power of making [illegible] relating to the police. In the mean time Agobard was [illegible] diſguſted: he queſtioned whether theſe were the true orders of the emperor, though he could not [illegible], ſince his ſeal was put to them. He accuſed his miniſters of corruption: he charged the Jews with ſtealing frequently Christian children, in order to ſell them, and of doing the baſeſt actions, and related this upon the declaration of a fugitive of Cordua, who ſaid, that they had told him in his youth.

Theſe accuſations were not believed at court, and his remonſtrances had no effect. Evrard, the emperor's commiſſary, continued to protect the Jews, [illegible] archbiſhop of Lyons, who omitted nothing [illegible] what he had done. He wrote a [illegible] to the emperor, and ſent him a treatiſe on the Jewiſh ſuperſtitions ſigned by two biſhops he had joined with him, to give [illegible] weight and authority to his book. He endeavoured to prove in this piece, that we ought to have no commerce with heretics, and particularly with the Jews, because there is no ſect [illegible] but what has ſome [illegible] the church.

All theſe efforts failing, Agobard made [illegible] to ſolicit more effectually againſt the Jews, who were looked upon as perſonal enemies. He had [illegible] of the emperor, but it was only [illegible] having permitted to return to his diocese without giving him any satisfaction. The disappointment of this journey [illegible] [illegible]. He was afraid of provoking the court, by [illegible] [illegible] who were in the service of the Jews, [illegible] took refuge in the churches to turn Christians. [illegible] Therefore, as he durst not venture upon the [illegible] [illegible] without the emperor's leave, he sent to beg his permission. What answer he had we cannot learn, but we [illegible] conclude, from a most uncharitable and [illegible] [illegible] the work of this great and learned [illegible], [illegible] [illegible], that it was not acceptable.

The protection the Jews found at Lewis's court, [illegible] [illegible] most learned bishops of this age, [illegible] [illegible] in France. It was [illegible] openly at court that the [illegible] [illegible] ought to be [illegible] [illegible] began to [illegible] to the Jews [illegible] [illegible] reproach to the [illegible] [illegible].

[illegible] Jews was not [illegible] entirely agree[illegible] [illegible] [illegible] [illegible] [illegible] [illegible] [illegible] [illegible] [illegible] [illegible] to [illegible] [illegible] [illegible] [illegible] [illegible] [illegible] the other children [illegible] [illegible] their consent [illegible] [illegible] [illegible] [illegible] to Vienne in Dauphiné, [illegible] [illegible] [illegible] other places, where they were [illegible] [illegible] [illegible] [illegible] to [illegible], and beg [illegible] [illegible] orders to the [illegible] of [illegible], [illegible] to [illegible] [illegible], representing that the conversion of these children was a [illegible] [illegible] [illegible] from living [illegible] [illegible] [illegible] [illegible] probably Charles consented to this request, [illegible] number of Jewish children [illegible] baptized [illegible] [illegible] [illegible] [illegible] [illegible] [illegible] [illegible] [illegible] by [illegible], [illegible] [illegible] [illegible], [illegible] [illegible] [illegible] [illegible] [illegible] [illegible] by those of his own nation.

[illegible] [illegible] [illegible] [illegible] in the troubles that happened under this reign by the incursion of the Normans into several provinces, particularly that of [illegible], where they were very numerous. They were [illegible] to the ignominious [illegible] against them by Charlemagne, of being [illegible] [illegible] a year at [illegible] [illegible], which was not, indeed, executed on all [illegible] [illegible], but was [illegible] confined [illegible] [illegible] [illegible], [illegible] [illegible], who received that punishment in [illegible] [illegible]. We may [illegible], that, though their [illegible] [illegible] [illegible] during the life of the treacherous [illegible], [illegible] they [illegible] [illegible] from [illegible] [illegible] [illegible] from it. This, for instance, [illegible] Beziers, [illegible] [illegible], [illegible] yearly [illegible] [illegible] [illegible] of [illegible], [illegible] the [illegible] [illegible] [illegible] [illegible] [illegible] [illegible] [illegible] [illegible] they paid to the [illegible] [illegible] indeed, [illegible] wonder that the Jews, [illegible] [illegible], should be obnoxious to the [illegible] of [illegible].

CHAP. IX.

State of the Jews in the tenth century. Learning begins to [illegible]. [illegible] [illegible]. His [illegible] [illegible] [illegible] [illegible] [illegible] [illegible] [illegible] [illegible] of David [illegible] [illegible] [illegible] [illegible] [illegible] [illegible] [illegible] [illegible] [illegible] [illegible] [illegible].

THE tenth century, which is in such discredit with the Christians, was not so unreputable to the Jews. Instead of deploring the gross ignorance that overspread Christ[illegible] [illegible] this time, they boast that they never had such excellent [illegible] [illegible]. They erected a new academy in the east, because those which had subsisted for many ages were not sufficient to contain the numbers of professors and scholars. The Arabians applied themselves to study, [illegible] the oppression that destroyed the authority of the [illegible]. There appeared among them able physicians and logicians, and [illegible] [illegible] had [illegible] the [illegible] of [illegible] [illegible], yet they studiously cultivated the science that was useful at court. The Jews [illegible] [illegible] and inclination and genius for learning [illegible] [illegible] [illegible] revived among them. However, their progress was interrupted by the [illegible] that [illegible] between the professors and heads of the captivity. [illegible] [illegible] these academies fall, and the whole nation [illegible] [illegible] the east, were forced to seek a new [illegible] [illegible] and France. [illegible] [illegible] [illegible] [illegible] [illegible] the zeal of the crusaders, who made it a piece of [illegible] [illegible] all the Jews before they proceeded to the conquest of Judea.

[illegible] of the captivity, a haughty man, [illegible] [illegible] [illegible] the authority of [illegible]. [illegible] Jews [illegible] complained, that his predecessors [illegible] [illegible] [illegible] [illegible] [illegible] but that David re[illegible] privileges, and enforced [illegible] [illegible] [illegible] [illegible] [illegible] [illegible] [illegible] [illegible] of David, [illegible] [illegible] [illegible] [illegible] [illegible] [illegible], and the [illegible] [illegible] [illegible] [illegible] [illegible] He was [illegible] young, but [illegible] prudent [illegible] [illegible] devoted [illegible], and [illegible] [illegible] [illegible] of his [illegible] [illegible] that [illegible] could not find any [illegible] in the [illegible] of the [illegible] to [illegible] [illegible] [illegible] [illegible] [illegible] government gave [illegible] an opportunity to [illegible] [illegible], and [illegible] [illegible] [illegible] [illegible] [illegible] [illegible] [illegible] [illegible] of [illegible], by [illegible] his authority [illegible] [illegible] [illegible] [illegible] elected [illegible] [illegible] [illegible] [illegible] [illegible], and the jealousy [illegible] [illegible] two professors, who had [illegible] privileges, [illegible] the former. The division was [illegible] for [illegible] years, [illegible] there was no way to appease it, but [illegible] [illegible] two [illegible] schools in the same place.

That of Sora was so [illegible] from [illegible] [illegible] [illegible] nobody could be found, either willing or able, to teach it. David sent for one named Joseph [illegible], but [illegible] [illegible] [illegible] instead of raising [illegible] [illegible] [illegible] [illegible] as he found it. They were then forced to [illegible] Rabbi Saadias to fill up the [illegible], and [illegible] scholars to the place [illegible], and [illegible] [illegible] [illegible] [illegible] [illegible] [illegible] [illegible] [illegible] [illegible] [illegible] the [illegible] of souls, [illegible] [illegible] [illegible] the [illegible] for many ages, [illegible] [illegible] [illegible] [illegible] [illegible] frequent revolutions [illegible] [illegible] there, [illegible] [illegible] [illegible] [illegible] progress [illegible], but the [illegible] [illegible] [illegible] to sign [illegible] [illegible] [illegible] [illegible] [illegible] [illegible] [illegible] refused [illegible] [illegible] [illegible] David did not [illegible], [illegible] [illegible] [illegible] [illegible] [illegible] [illegible] [illegible] [illegible] him with [illegible] [illegible] [illegible] [illegible] [illegible] ders, but the Rabbi [illegible] [illegible] [illegible] [illegible], they [illegible] [illegible] David, and [illegible] [illegible] [illegible], obliged him to retire. [illegible] [illegible] [illegible] [illegible] [illegible] [illegible] [illegible] Saadias's faction [illegible] [illegible] [illegible] [illegible] David deposed, and Joseph [illegible] [illegible] [illegible] [illegible] captivity, but his authority [illegible] [illegible]. David [illegible] [illegible] by his party, [illegible] [illegible] [illegible] [illegible] [illegible] constrained to fly, and seek a place of retirement, [illegible] he continued seven years, and it was in this [illegible] that he composed most of the works which have perpetuated his name after his death. He came out [illegible] [illegible] to be reconciled with his prince, but he [illegible] [illegible] [illegible] [illegible] him, and have the peaceable [illegible] [illegible] academy.

We may learn from this event, [illegible] [illegible] [illegible] the heads of the academy was [illegible] [illegible] [illegible] the prince, f[illegible] could not enact any laws but what was signed [illegible] there hath been frequent in[illegible] Saadias, though a stranger [illegible], the brightest and most potent [illegible] had [illegible] for many ages.

[illegible] academy might at the same time be [illegible], though this did not always hap[illegible], one of the fabulous, was at the same [illegible] of the nation. Be[illegible] to the others. They [illegible] reigned alone in the academy, and [illegible] of Rab Nehemiah, head of Pundebita, in [illegible] century, lifted eight years, the [illegible] empire only relating to their institu[illegible], in the Jewish chronicles, the [illegible] of the academy, whilst we see no [illegible].

[illegible] and the heads of the acade[illegible] majority of voices. The example of [illegible] proves, that the power [illegible] absolute or independent of the [illegible], the government was not hereditary in [illegible] sometimes succeeded the father, [illegible] the same thing must be said of [illegible] prince continued to them [illegible] the doctors [illegible] also of the peo[illegible] not always. We find an instance [illegible] century, when there was a professor want[illegible] offered himself as [illegible] people were to Ne[illegible] named Aaron, [illegible] preceded him seven[illegible].

[illegible] at that time, [illegible] Jews lived in the city of Pu[illegible] signifies the rapture of Sapor [illegible] Sapor should be acknow[illegible] of this city, and, amongst many [illegible], it might be attributed to Sa[illegible] prisoner, and treated him so [illegible] not only enlarged his kingdom by [illegible], but also built many cities in them, and [illegible] this honour to a Rab[illegible] Sapor, who founded the academy [illegible] the academy, but the city [illegible] this name. It was situated five miles [illegible] nine hundred thousand Jews [illegible] been peopled by that nation, and also of [illegible] cities in the world [illegible] so many inhabitants. Sche[illegible] of this school, kept it flourish[illegible] years together. He was a mortal enemy of [illegible] of the monks, whom he [illegible]. This rendered him [illegible] to his disciples, who commonly look upon [illegible] zeal. Scherira, finding [illegible] years, resigned his place to his son Hai, the most excellent of all the doctors.

[illegible], that this doctor descended, in a direct line, from David the prophet, the king of Judah. As a proof of it they affirm, that he had a lion in his escutcheon, which was also in the arms of the antient kings of Judah. But his principal glory did not arise from so illustrious a birth. He distinguished himself in his nation by many different works, which he published upon purchases, sales, and [illegible]. He has one upon the interpretation of dreams. Another contains his questions upon the book of Jetsira, or the formation, in which he [illegible] the manner they formerly wrote the name of Jehovah at Jerusalem. Hay was a poet, and some of his verses are still remaining, in which he in[illegible] mankind also in the duties of piety. He had so great a reputation, that they came from the east and west to consult him. He became head of the academy of Pundebita, as well as of Phrutz Schibbur, in which he had been professor from nine and twenty years of age. It seems too that he was elected prince of the captivity, but happening to draw upon him the jealousy of his own nation, he [illegible] and his father fell into disgrace.

The caliph, who then reigned, was called Caler, though he was of the house of the Abbassides. He [illegible] with a neighbouring prince, who reigned in the [illegible] that are formed by the waters of the [illegible]. But the sultan having deposed Ther, [illegible] throne. He quickly showed himself [illegible] of the empire he was raised to. He restored the [illegible] the state, and extended his conquests as far as Egypt, where he proved to the Fathers [illegible] there, that he, [illegible] not Aly's family, as the [illegible] Cader, who had [illegible] eighty-one years, [illegible] resolved also [illegible] to the Jews, who had taken the advan[illegible] of the [illegible] troubles, [illegible] authority. Sche[illegible] wealth and power, [illegible] governed the nation, [illegible] put in prison. The caliph [illegible] wealth, and [illegible] Scherira [illegible] above an hundred years [illegible] fortune to [illegible] in the [illegible] taught [illegible].

After Hay's death, [illegible] captivity [illegible] but his reign [illegible] at [illegible] years, the caliph [illegible] and put them to death except [illegible]. The academies were shut up, and the [illegible] seek sanctuary in the west, [illegible] followed them.

It was in the reign of Ezechias that the [illegible] between the children of [illegible] to be the first Masorethes, at least [illegible] masters who applied themselves [illegible] Scripture. Father Simon, well versed in [illegible] for Aaron's manuscript and [illegible] believing them to be [illegible] tors, and pretty modern. [illegible] by the rules [illegible] these two masters [illegible] for people often [illegible] grammar. But if [illegible] of the Hebrew text [illegible] a proof [illegible] the original text had [illegible] and entirety and [illegible].

The persecution which continued [illegible] and the affairs of this nation. The house [illegible] fides, which had always favoured the Jews, [illegible] sion [illegible] by the name of Hakem, resolved to [illegible] that [illegible] open [illegible]. He burned [illegible] to banish themselves, [illegible] the west. He destroyed the prince of the captivity [illegible] his family. The people also suffered extremely [illegible] secution, which was so bloody, [illegible] inconsiderable body, [illegible] bia, and [illegible].

The Jewish historians say, [illegible] of the [illegible] which [illegible] began to [illegible] of David [illegible] and [illegible]. They [illegible] for masters to be obliged to obey [illegible] to kill him, which [illegible] with the princes of the [illegible] madness [illegible] of [illegible] murderers [illegible] but they [illegible] too late. [illegible] the nation took advantage of [illegible] to [illegible].

[illegible] uses of potentates, and to wait till Providence [illegible] to send them one who might give them [illegible]

[illegible] authors [illegible] to the hours of [illegible] Benjamin of [illegible] the following century into the [illegible] found a prince [illegible] from [illegible] the same century, found [illegible] Bagdad, in Persia. His [illegible] the tribe of [illegible] The [illegible] Spain [illegible] a figure [illegible]

[illegible] persecution [illegible] the [illegible] young [illegible] interests [illegible] to the Duke [illegible] to the Jews [illegible] to return [illegible] his opinion, and permitted them to [illegible] old religion. This prince died in [illegible] where he had reigned.

CHAP. V.

[illegible]

[illegible] the Christians, who [illegible] conversion [illegible] of Christians, and [illegible] were not [illegible] to either party [illegible] This prince, who reigned above fifty years [illegible] the number of his enemies, that they could find no soldiers. They [illegible] to retire before his army, which amounted to eighty thousand [illegible] But the [illegible] having prevailed, the Christians, who were [illegible] them with that resolution, that the Arabians betook themselves to flight, leaving [illegible] the spoils. His son Hakem [illegible] the city of Leon, but the [illegible] so vigorously that he was [illegible] Hescham had the famous Almansor for his general, who [illegible] account of the great victories he had [illegible] the Spaniards and Arabians. The latter [illegible] subjects, often revolted against him. [illegible] officers had the insolence to give out [illegible] causing a body to be buried [illegible] in order to delude the people. [illegible] reigned, till a faction, being [illegible] brought him out of his prison [illegible] the throne. But he fell [illegible] happened at [illegible] to live [illegible] thirty-three years. [illegible] in Spain, who were [illegible] Christians, and who, besides [illegible] against the [illegible]

[illegible] the Christians in [illegible] Ordogno, king of Leon, had [illegible] after his death, [illegible] divided the government [illegible] of the [illegible] the command of [illegible] the hatred of the [illegible] Christians [illegible] the army [illegible] gave up part of Castile to his [illegible] capital [illegible] causing [illegible] to reduce [illegible]

[illegible] left [illegible] of Spain [illegible] the Jews of Cordova [illegible] who [illegible] than a [illegible] to resolve [illegible] the questions [illegible] have [illegible] to [illegible] the [illegible] of state [illegible] Hescham, who [illegible] to [illegible] his country [illegible] in order to stop [illegible] give him [illegible] Moses [illegible]

This [illegible] the history of [illegible] the [illegible] fugitives, and was [illegible]

Hescham II. king of Cordova [illegible] Jews [illegible] caused to be translated into [illegible] Arabic [illegible] them [illegible] make it more common [illegible] the [illegible] and Jews.

[illegible] undertook this great work [illegible] fully accomplished it [illegible] to [illegible] than divine [illegible] but [illegible] was excommunicated. He appealed to the king, but Hescan would not meddle with this affair, either out of policy, or because living in dependence upon his hated ... Joseph, being deprived of the protection ... from court, left Spain, and took the road to ... where he thought to find a retreat near the ... but he gave him to understand, that he could not receive him, because he was excommunicated by the ... synagogue. He remained therefore at Damascus, where he died, without being able to procure a revocation of the sentence which had been pronounced against him.

The divisions of the Saracens increased more and more ... during the eleventh century. They had been ... the Ommiades, who ... though after they had changed their ... the people ... by ... Ommiades, who survived the ... of his house, offered himself to them. They re... to him, that to ... attempting to ascend the throne ... certain death. But ambition overcame love ... "Kill me to-morrow, (said he,) provided you ... me this day a king."

These revolutions in Spain were advantageous to the Jews; for R. Samuel Levi became secretary and minister ... to the king of Granada, who afterwards made him prince of his nation, and he employed his credit at court in protecting it. He even scattered his bounties among foreigners, for the African, Egyptian, and Babylonian doctors were his pensioners. The Jews had the satisfaction to see his son succeed him in his posts, and the only thing which moderated their joy was the haughtiness of this young man, whose riches had rendered him proud, whereas his father had preserved his humility in his great exaltation.

But an unexpected turn of affairs disturbed the repose and tranquillity they enjoyed. Joseph Hallevy, one of the learned men of that age, set up for a converter of the Mussulmen. The translation of the Talmud into Arabic, which was made some years before, facilitated this design, though it miscarried. The king of Granada could not bear this insult offered to the established religion, so that the Rabbi was put into prison, and afterwards ... The persecution began by the king's ... in which fifteen hundred families in this one kingdom ... This calamity was the more ... their prosperity had made them rich and ... They were apprehensive lest the neighbouring kings should imitate so dreadful an example; but the violence was soon stopped, and went no farther than the kingdom of Granada.

They would have undergone a more severe and destructive oppression under king Ferdinand, who, at the instigation of his bigoted wife, was going to sanctify his war against the Saracens by the extirpation of the Jews, had not the bishops, and even the pope, (Alexander II.) put a stop to his furious zeal, by publicly opposing and condemning it. But what most probably extricated them out of all danger from that monarch and his successor was, the revolution which the Moors occasioned in Africa, in consequence of which Alphonso, distressed on every side, found himself obliged to befriend and caress, instead of oppressing them, in order to procure their money and assistance. Accordingly they were promoted by him to considerable posts, and obtained such other privileges, that Pope Gregory quite disapproved of them.

Peter I. his grandson, had not more regard to the exhortations of Nicolas of Valencia. The crusade being published in Spain, as in other Christian kingdoms, Peter resolved to engage in this war against the infidels. Nicolas represented to this king, that it was in vain to go in quest of foreign enemies so far, when he had so many at home, and added that the Jews had such an inveterate hatred to the Christians, that they never met them without denouncing curses on their heads, with many other articles as absurd and ridiculous, to which the king, who was averse to persecution, only lent a deaf ear. However, the moderation of this prince did not ... the Jews from being massacred by the crusaders in several other parts of Spain.

Notwithstanding these persecutions, this country had abundance of Jewish doctors in the eleventh century. Samuel Cophni, born at Cordova, published a commentary upon the Pentateuch, the manuscript whereof is in the Vatican library. Those ... read it esteem it a fine piece ... a great many allegories. He had a dispute with a ... of his nation, and died in the year 1034.

At that time appeared the five Isaacs. One of them was called Isaac Alphesi ... out of Africa, from the kingdom of Fez, into Spain. He ... one of the most learned men of his ... and became prince of the exile in Spain. His epitaph written in Spondaic verse ... which shews that at that time they ... quantity, after the manner of the Greeks and Latins, ... one. The second of the Isaacs was the son of Baruch. He derived his genealogy from ... Baruch, Jeremy's secretary; and pretended that his ... which came to Spain in Titus's time ... then. He understood Latin, Greek, and Arabic. He had studied the mathematics, and was so eminent in this science, that the king of ... called ... for his ... sent for him to court ... instructed by him. He was received there with ... and ... with such satisfaction ... the ... Saracens, that he became ... of his country, ... continued here to his death, which happened in the year 1094. He had a violent quarrel with the first of the Isaacs ... could not be reconciled whilst they lived; but at the hour of death, one of them gave an example of repentance, and the other of charity. Isaac, the son of Baruch died first, and finding himself ill, sent his son to beg his enemy's pardon, and to throw himself into his arms as ... a father and a faithful friend. The ... Alphesi received him into his house, treated him as ... and continued teaching him, to his death ...

Another more general ... The learned Rabbins multiplying in Spain in the eleventh century, gave birth to many controversies respecting the study of the sciences, ... the Talmudists designed to ... their scholars, to oblige them to a simple ... principles. They ... study of ... and the human sciences was ... from the ... Titus's time, lest the people ... dispersed among the nations, should be drawn into idolatry by ... of the ... The ... to the text of the Mishnah contains ... him who keeps swine, or teaches his son Greek, as it was equally impure to feed an unclean beast, and to give ... good education.

These laws were not always religiously observed. It was impossible for the Jews who dwelt in Egypt not to ... Greek, or those of Rome not to ... the Spaniards, mingled with the Saracens, not to ... continual use of Arabic. R. Solomon, who ... at Barcelona, in the eleventh century ... to ... those rigorous decrees of the ... but he durst not ... He pronounced an anathema, and sentence of excommunication ... began to study Greek before twenty years ... The bounds being once removed, R. ... the anathema, which Solomon had decreed ... young students, and ...

applied themselves therefore to the languages, mathematics, and other sciences, which produced a considerable number of great men.

France was not so fruitful in famous Rabbins as Spain, ... during all the century which we have ... there being not above five ... to be found ... of any note. The ... who ... have to be born in ... he was a Frenchman, ... of Constitutions there. It ... than ... for they ... a long time about the ... of his collection of laws, which began not to be ... in the middle of the thirteenth century. He was ... called the Light of the ... Captivity.

One of his chief disciples was Jacob, the son of ... who ... the succeeding doctors ... laws that cannot ... without ... he ... the same ... his master Solomon, ... made to ... Chronologers are ... however, upon this article, for some make him ... in the ... of the twelfth century, ... the thirty-five years before.

... another famous disciple, ... Barcelona ... doctor, who ... upon the privileges of women. He published another upon the ... historically ... the different ways the Jews have reckoned the times ... epocha was that of the departure from Egypt ... the creation of ... because ... of ... government was then changed. There was ... entering into Jerusalem ... was followed to the ... of the Christian ... obliged ... to ... the years from the creation of the world ... distinguished ...

... the Prophet, was also ... that time to make ... which had been much neglected ... perhaps ... this custom, since ... became famous by the ... Moses, ... from Narbonne, was doubtless ... eloquent, ... the title of preacher given ... excellence. ... in the middle of the eleventh century, and died in the year 1070, with the glory of leaving the famous Solomon the lunatic ... disciple.

CHAP. VI.

The Pseudo-Josephus, a ... of ... this century. ... Jews ... Germany ... Bohemia ... produced ... the same consequences ...

AS we are treating of the French Rabbies of this century, we must not omit the author of the pretended history of Joseph Ben Gorion, whom the Jews have substituted for the Greek historian Josephus. This Jewish impostor, to give the greater credit ... begins with giving himself out for a royal prince and priest of the Jewish nation, in whose person Providence had united those two ... to war against their enemies. He calls himself the Josephus full of the spirit of wisdom and understanding, of counsel, fortitude, knowledge, and of fear of the Lord, who ... for the ... and for his nation. ... grossly ... that one of his soldiers one day ... to him, "Thou art the man of God ... by the God of Israel, who hath created the soul "that animates thee, and hath endowed thee with such "extraordinary wisdom." And when taken by the Romans, their army asked each other with tears, "Is that the person "so admired among the Jews, and so dreaded by the Ro-"mans? How is he caught, who was alone once able to "fill our army with terror, and hath spread throughout "the universe the fame of his valiant deeds?" Titus himself was no less taken with his person and courage, and raised him above all the priests and Levites of his nation.

His imposture succeeded so well, by his putting, from the Greek and original Josephus, such facts as were to his purpose, ... and adding others, and ... his history in the Hebrew tongue, that the Greek copy became not only neglected, but suspicious, and at length rejected as a forgery by those of his nation. So that we need not wonder if many of them have been deceived ... and extolled it to the skies. But as this author and his history have been fully confuted by several able ... matters, ... shall therefore proceed with ... of the ... they were ... to ...

We begin to find them flourishing in ... the latter end of the eleventh century ... then reigned, ... as the old words ... a Christian ... the ... of them ... for Common ... the Jews ... dom.

The Jews ... synagogues in ... places, particularly in ... had ... even to ... his people ... Bohemia, ... the ... century, ... such considerable ... to the ... the irruptions of the barbarians, that they ... the privilege of a synagogue. They ... It is said they were terrified ... prodigies, which happened at the beginning of the ... century, and fearing the end of the world ... they turned Christians. These prodigies, however, ... to such numbers of them, but that ... posed to acts of violence and outrage.

A priest, named Gotescal, ... fifteen thousand ... he had got together in Germany, and declared war against the Jews ... procured him the veneration of the people, ... protection of kings. He overran ... from whence he passed into Hungary, ... an entire liberty to exercise his ... perceived, that, under the pretence of ... plundered and ravished the wives of the ... the Jews, they ... Gotescal was slain, with the best part of his troops ... tragical an end, however, hindered not the ... of Germany by declaring ... persecutor of the ... but attempting to ... into Hungary, ... stopped ... being resolved to force it, he ... that ... elated with ... divided the kingdom ... his companions ... Hungarians, ... them ... as they were deliberating, put them to the rout. The ... Henry, who was then at ... declared ... the Jews restored them to the ... had been expelled, and made them ... This ... encouragement ...

as they were charged with having magnified their losses, in order to enrich themselves by a more plentiful restitution

The crusades rekindled a fresh zeal against the Jews They complain that these votaries, passing through Cologne, Mentz, Wormes, and Spiers, committed a massacre, from the month of April till July, in which were stabbed and drowned five thousand persons and that the number of those who were forced to abjure the religion of their fathers cannot be ascertained They do not exaggerate the matter, on the contrary, historians amplify the number, with the addition of hideous circumstances. They assert that fourteen hundred of them were burnt at Mentz, and that, from the resistence and disorder which happened on that occasion, half the city was reduced to ashes Those of Wormes at first retired to the bishop, but he would not receive them, unless they turned Christians The people suffered them not to deliberate long some embraced Christianity, which they abjured as soon as the storm was over, and others destroyed themselves Something like this happened at Triers The women, seeing the crusaders coming, murdered their own children saying, "It were better to send them thus into Abraham's bosom, than to abandon them to the Christians" Others, laden with stones, threw themselves into the river, and were drowned, and some fled to the bishop's castle Egilbert, who resided in it, preached them a sermon, by which they were apparently converted, but the year following all of them, except one, relapsed into Judaism The bishop of Spire had more humanity for he not only protected the fugitives but caused some of their persecutors to be hanged This mischief went so far, that the Bavarian annalists reckon twelve thousand that died in that country, and others affirm, that the number of those who perished in Germany was almost incredible.

Another crusade was published fifty years after Rodolphus, who was commissioned to preach it up on the banks of the Rhine, did it with great success As it was one of the articles of his religion and his doctrine, that the enemies of Christianity were first to be taken off, and those that lived among them at hand, before they went to seek them in foreign lands, the people were inflamed by his exhortations but the massacre was not so great as designed, because part of them took their flight betimes, and retired to Nurenberg, and other cities depending upon the emperor, under whose protection they found more security We must do justice to St Bernard, and acknowledge that Rodolphus's doctrine did not please him He wrote to the archbishop of Mentz, whom this hermit had inflamed by his preaching, to prove to him, that he ought to look upon the persecution of the Jews as inhuman, and therefore he advised that he might be sent back to his desart

Nevertheless, the flame was spread far and near by his trumpeters, not only in Germany, but in most other parts of Europe, and great numbers of Jews were massacred, if we may credit their chronologers, while others, being driven to despair by the cruelties they were likely to undergo, put an end to their own existence With these persecutions ended the eleventh century

CHAP. VII

Benjamin of Tudela's character and travels Jews in the east from Benjamin's account Decay of the academy of Pumbeditha Power of the caliph's in ecclesiastical affairs Jews favoured under the caliph Mostanged Heads of the captivity dependent on the caliphs Jews in other eastern parts Ezekiel's tomb Jews in Egypt At Tyre Peculiar superstitions Jews in Jerusalem In upper Galilee Account of Aben-Ezra, another Jewish traveller Jews in Greece At Constantinople At Rome, &c The prince of the nation at Capua In Germany, Bohemia, &c In France The holy assembly of Lunel General remarks upon the whole R Petachia's account of the Jews in Tartary and Nineveh In Bagdad Of their chiefs Persecution in Persia

WITH respect to the state of the Jews in the east during the twelfth century, we shall be obliged to refer, as the best guide we can procure, to Benjamin, surnamed of Tudela, a city of Navarre, the place of his nativity, who tells us that he had visited most of these parts His accounts, indeed, sometimes appear fabulous, nor has he scrupled to interlard them with absurd and incredible stories to raise the credit of his nation

Our author informs us, that he found several considerable synagogues, and a number of Jews, who lived there at ease, and enjoyed the liberty of their religion unmolested That the city of Pethora, upon the banks of the Euphrates, contained 4000 Jews

He found another 7000 also at Almosal, which answers to the antient Nineveh, the one having been built from the ruins of the other, upon the opposite bank of the Tigris and being only separated by a bridge There was Zaccheus, a descendant of the house of David There was also a famous astronomer, called Beren Alpuecce, who served as a chaplain to king Zin-Aldin It may seem strange that a Jew should officiate as chaplain to a Mussulman, for Zin-Aldin was of that religion and brother to Noraldin, king of Syria, whom the Mussulmen reverence not only as one of their most illustrious conquerors, but as one of their greatest saints But perhaps this Jewish astronomer did not scrupulously weigh the difference of religions, but conformed his own to that of the prince he served, as that nation are so apt to temporize

Benjamin, before he arrived at Bagdad, passed through Rohobot, where he found 2000 persons of his nation Carchemis, famous for the defeat of Pharaoh Nachor, and situate upon the banks of the Euphrates, contained five hunored Pundebita was but two days journey from hence But this city, so well known, had changed its name, being then called Alnobari, or Alnebar He discovered here some footsteps of the grandeur of his nation, for there was the tomb of Bostenai, the prince of the captivity, who had married a daughter of the king of Persia [illegible] also those of two illustrious doctors, [illegible] they had built before their death, but it [illegible] flourishing academy of scholars [illegible] famous in former ages there was only 2000 Jews some of whom applied themselves to the study of [illegible]

The same fate had befallen that of Sora, of which the author is content to revive the remembrance, and to add, that many heads of the captivity, descended from the house of David, had taken up their residence there He only celebrates the city and academy of Nahardea He observes also of Nahardea, that its schools were demolished, and the doctors had retired into the west

The authors of the Talmud, and the excellent doctors, were no longer found at Sora and Pundebita, in Benjamin's time, nor even in other places, where there were still many Jews

The Persians ascribe great antiquity to this capital It was built by Almansor, and afterwards became the residence of the succeeding caliphs Benjamin gives a magnificent description of their palace and city The reigning caliph was invested with a supreme, and even despotic, authority He kept his brothers chained in their respective palaces because they had conspired against him His subjects hardly ever saw him, though he was very affable to others The pilgrims that passed that way earnestly desired a sight of him, but instead of shewing himself, he caused a skirt of his robe to be hung upon the window, that every one might see it, and a herald cried out, "Go in peace, for our Lord, the light of the Ismaelites, is favourable to you."

He was supreme in ecclesiastical as well as civil authority. The people believed him almost equal to Mahomet, and he held the same rank among the Mussulmen, as the pope has among the Christians. At the fast of Ramadan he came out of his palace, clad in sumptuous attire, having among other articles, a piece of black cloth upon his head, to signify that all his glory was only vanity, and that joy was quickly changed into sorrow. He was attended by all the great officers of his court, and a vast multitude of people, who came that day from far to have the satisfaction of seeing him. When he arrived at the oratory near the gate of the city, and had received the acclamations of the people, he lifted his robe to give a blessing, and ascending into a lobby of the chapel, expounded the Mahometan law to them. He then killed a camel, pieces of which he distributed to his principal officers, who looked upon it as an extraordinary favour. The ceremony being over, the caliph returned alone to his palace, by the banks of the Tigris, which were covered with thousands of barks, and the ground he had trod was held so sacred, that no one durst walk in the place where he had set the sole of his foot.

It was under the protection of the caliph Mostanged, who reigned ten years, that the Jews then lived peaceably at Bagdad. He esteemed them and had many in his service. He perfectly understood their language, and wrote it, and had also some knowledge of their law. There were but a thousand Jewish inhabitants in this city; and the error of Isaac, the son of Arma, who says there were many thousand Jews, would be deemed a gross one, were we not accustomed to find these Jewish writers magnify whatever contributes to the glory of the synagogue. If there were few inhabitants, there were yet twenty-eight synagogues, and ten tribunals, or councils, at the head [illegible] were ten eminent persons, employed only upon the affairs of the nation, and called the ten Otiosi, or Idlers. Above these was the head of the captivity. He that had then that post was a descendant of David, and his [illegible] Daniel. The Jews gave him the title of Lord; [illegible] Mahometans that of Lord, the Son of David. His authority extended over all the Jews which were in the dominions of the caliph, from [illegible] to the Iron Gates and the Indies. Our author represents this prince of the captivity as a kind of sovereign, for the Mahometans were obliged to respect him as well as the Jews, and he that, meeting him on the road, refused to rise and salute him, received an hundred stripes. The nation was obliged to have their teachers and doctors from him, who gave the imposition of hands. That he might support his dignity, the merchants of his nation raised an impost in the fairs, and paid him a kind of tribute. Some provisions were also sent him from the remote provinces. Daniel, besides this had his patrimony and lands that were given him. He kept a table, and had hospitals, where he maintained the poor. But he was forced to purchase this grandeur and liberty, by a tribute paid to the caliph, and by rich presents to the principal officers of his court.

This observation is of great moment, not only because it shews that there was still a prince of the captivity in the twelfth century, though they had been abolished an hundred years before; but farther, we learn, that this head of the captivity had only a power borrowed from the caliph, which he did not exercise till he had received imposition of hands from the infidel prince.

The Jewish Rabbies, who pretended that those eastern chiefs were independent of any other monarchs, and still retained the power of life and death, have left no stone unturned to prove that favourite point, insomuch that Origin himself believed that those Assyrian monarchs, under whom they lived, being content with their subjection and dependence, allowed them to govern their people according to their own laws, and to inflict even death on the guilty; and proved it not only from the apocryphal book of Susanna against Africanus, but from more recent instances under the Roman emperors, after the destruction of the temple by Titus. He has been followed by others both ancient and modern, who pretend they had a power to raise a tribute on the nation, and to punish recusants, as well as other criminals with death.

Leaving the province of Bagdad, Benjamin passed through Resen, where he found near five thousand Jews, who performed their devotions in a great synagogue. He proceeded towards the antient Babylon, where was Nebuchadonosor's palace, grown the habitation of owls and reptiles. But some leagues from thence were a thousand Jews, who said their prayers in the palace which Daniel built for his [illegible]. H[illegible] but five miles from it, where there are four synagogues and ten thousand Jews. A little farther were discovered the foundations of the antient tower of Babel, built [illegible], after the flood. At length he came to the tomb of Ezekiel, upon the banks of the river Chebar, where there were sixty towers, with a synagogue in each of them. Near this place [illegible] another edifice built by Jeconias, when Evil-merodach gave him his liberty. This palace fronts the [illegible] on one side, and has the Chobar on the other. Thirty-five thousand Jews were employed in this great work for the service of their prince. His picture was still seen in the room, and those of all the officers who accompanied him, and [illegible] up the [illegible] this prophet's tomb, which [illegible] preserved, drew people from all parts. The heads of the captivity visited it every year with a numerous train. [illegible] a place of devotion, not only for the Jews, but for the Persians, the Medes and [illegible] of [illegible], who came to bring their presents, and pay their vows at the synagogue. They reverence [illegible] sacred thing, [illegible] persons, which vanquished [illegible] ever touch it. A lamp burns night and day upon the tomb, and the head of the captivity, and [illegible] council of Bagdad [illegible]. There is [illegible] library, and all that die without [illegible] augment it by sending their books. Here was also [illegible] the original of Ezekiel's prophecies written [illegible] pretended, his own hand.

Coufa had for some time been the capital city of the caliphs, but they had changed their residence. However, Benjamin coming there, found near [illegible] thousand Jews, who had but one synagogue.

Egypt is one of those places where the Jews have resided longest; they were numerous [illegible] when Benjamin paid them a visit. [illegible] thousand of them in one single [illegible] of Ethiopia, which he calls Chous [illegible] Jews, and [illegible] Cairo. There was [illegible] hibited at [illegible]. The occasion [illegible] came from Judea, [illegible] nished the reading [illegible] but one [illegible] the other antient inhabitants of E[illegible], as was done in Spain, and other places [illegible] head of all the synagogues of [illegible] the doctors, and supported [illegible] the caliph.

Our traveller was far from forgetting the land of Goshen, where the Israelites dwelt so long. [illegible] he could observe some traces of their [illegible]. Many Jews were settled [illegible], two [illegible] in one place, five hundred in another, and near three thousand in the city of Goshen, as many at Alexandria, and very few at Damietta.

The rest he represents as dispersed [illegible] the other provinces and towns of Egypt in great numbers, [illegible] vastly short of what they once were, when the single city of Alexandria was reckoned to contain [illegible] thousand of those people.

We now pass into Judah. Our author [illegible] to Tyre, where he found four hundred of [illegible] were glass-makers. [illegible] the Tyrian glass was then in great esteem, and transported [illegible] by the sea-faring Jews However, there [illegible] that were learned, particularly in the Talmud, [illegible] an Egyptian, called R Ephraim, was the [illegible]

[illegible] Samaritans had abandoned their capital city but [illegible] two hundred at Cesarea, and an hundred at [illegible], which they made the seat of their religion [illegible] priests descended from Aaron, who never [illegible] other families, that they might more certainly preserve the succession of the priesthood They [illegible] upon Mount Gerizim in all their former [illegible] that their altar was built with the [illegible] the tribes placed in the Jordan, when they passed [illegible] under Joshua's conduct They are very superstitious about washings, and the choice of their cloaths [illegible] religiously preserve those which they wear in the synagogue, and never put them on on other days

[illegible] Jerusalem, where God had once [illegible], which the Jews ought to consider [illegible] his habitation, was almost entirely abandoned by [illegible] Our author found not above two hundred [illegible] who were, for the most part, dyers of wool, and [illegible] the privilege of the monopoly of [illegible] They lived all together under David's tower, [illegible] there a very mean figure

[illegible] had so few Jews in it the rest of the Holy [illegible] still more depopulated Benjamin found two [illegible] one city, and twenty in another, most of [illegible] dyers He says, that Schunem was one of [illegible] that had the greatest number, wherein he reckoned [illegible] hundred

[illegible], but some leagues from that, and of which [illegible] often speaks as belonging to the Philistines [illegible] fifty-three persons the [illegible] made of Samaritans, the least of the [illegible] traditions, and the rest were Talmudists

[illegible] Upper Galilee that the nation was in greatest [illegible] of Jerusalem, for the Jews retired [illegible] destruction of the holy city The academy [illegible] grew famous from its doctors, and there [illegible] was composed Many changes [illegible] to the twelfth century, for [illegible] Jews in Galilee of the Gentiles [illegible] but fifty persons of his nation, [illegible] some ancient tombs In fine, he only [illegible] its excellent waters and hot baths

[illegible] gives a sufficient account of Tiberias from that of Benjamin [illegible] for, having travelled thither [illegible] years after him, he says, that he consulted the doctors that were in it So considerable a [illegible] have happened to this city in so short [illegible] to restore an academy and produce doctors [illegible] credible that Benjamin, who, on all occasions, [illegible] so much honour to his nation, designed to detract from [illegible] lustre of Tiberias

These two travellers, however may be reconciled in a degree, by observing, that there was a synagogue, and, of consequence, some Rabbins, who managed it, and these, perhaps, were the doctors Aben-Ezra consulted in his travels This city, having lost its walls, continued a long time exposed to the perpetual incursions of the Arabians, who often pillaged it till Solyman walled it in This advantage made it more populous The author of a letter, entitled, 'The Genealogies of the Righteous of the Land of Israel," says that there were in his time two kinds of academies, situate without the gates of Tiberias, one small, and the other very mean In effect, Rabbi Juda Zeno, who, from a Jew turned Christian, and died at Rome in the middle of the last century, pursued his studies in one of the academies of Tiberias There was another much more esteemed academy at Sepheta, but as Benjamin does not mention it it is reasonable to suppose it was not yet erected.

Benjamin passed through Greece, and found mount Parnassus (which had been so long the mansion of Apollo and the Muses) inhabited by two hundred Jews, who cultivated it, and sowed pulse upon it They had some Rabbins, but, whatever be the reasons, they have been since forbidden to settle within some leagues of it

There were three hundred Jews at Corinth Thebes, so well known in antiquity, but infinitely decayed in the twelfth century supported two thousand Jews, silk-workers and dyers The Rabbins there were so learned, that none but those of Constantinople could equal them though we [illegible] nothing of their productions in that kind Two of the most ingenious were S[illegible] but it is a question, whether they had not renounced their schism and opinion, to engage in the study of traditions since they taught the Rabbinists There were some at Patres, at L[illegible], and in most of the cities of the empire, but their number was inconsiderable, the chief being reckoned but fifty in one and twenty in [illegible]

Benjamin [illegible] Greece, [illegible] Egripho, a great city, situate on the sea-coast, where merchants [illegible] resorted from all parts of the world, and where there were two hundred Jews It is supposed this was the ancient Chalcis, in the neighbourhood of Negropont From thence he went to Jabaste [illegible] another sea-port city, containing an hundred Jews There were as many [illegible] which is but [illegible] journey removed from [illegible] about an half from the River of Dogs, (Genocteria[illegible]) through which he entered into Walachia in his way to Constantinople whither he at length arrived He observes, that there were there about two thousand Jews, silk weavers and merchants Besides this there were five hundred Caraites who lived peaceably with the other Jews, but were, however, separated from them by a wall, to prevent their communication They were all placed in the suburbs of Galata, or Pera upon the coasts of the Straights, which habitation had been long ago assigned them by Theodosius, for which reason the suburbs were called by French[illegible], "The Jews." They had hitherto preserved the privilege of depending only upon the governor of the [illegible], but Manuel deprived them of this privilege, and submitted them to the common judges It is probable that this prince had already done it when Benjamin came there, [illegible] represents his nation as very odious in his reign, though his physician who was a Jew, did all he could to [illegible] them It was not only unlawful for them to go on horseback into the city, but the Greeks would [illegible] crowds, revile and maltreat them They broke open their doors, defiled their waters, and pelted them [illegible] and yet they have continued there ever since that time

Benjamin passed into Italy He observed that at that time the Genoese enriched themselves by the pirates [illegible] sent to [illegible] the burghers being divided one [illegible] another had almost all of them towers on their houses, from whence they might war they reckoned [illegible] of these towers in Pisa, designed to the same use These two cities had but very few Jews in them He came to Rome, which he represents as the capital of the [illegible] nites, and the pope is the head of that religion whom he describes a great prince, and affirms, there were many learned Rabbies there, that did honour to their nation

There were Jews also at Capua, where [illegible] the prince of the nation There were doctors famous throughout the universe, and yet there were but [illegible] hundred inhabitants of this nation From thence he proceeded to Naples, where he found five hundred inhabitants of his nation There were [illegible] hundred more of them at Salerno, an ought from the priest [illegible] of the Greek Latins, and [illegible] R Abraham of [illegible] the greatest [illegible] There were Jews also at [illegible] Benevento, Amalphi, and [illegible], in the kingdom of Naples, which [illegible] the pilgrimage of the Holy Land [illegible] at Corfu [illegible] reckoned two hundred at Messina, five hundred at Palermo, and in all these places they paid no tribute

He travelled from thence into Germany, where he found the Jews not only more numerous, quiet, and peaceable, but likewise more zealous, devout, and hospitable to strangers They bewailed the desolation of their city and temple, and expressed a longing expectation of hearing the voice of the turtle dove, as they termed it, by which they meant their glorious recall into that once happy land He penetrated as far as Bohemia, which, he tells us, was then called the New Canaan, because the inhabitants sold their children to all the neighbouring nations

This traveller also visited the synagogues of France, which he entered The number of the Jews was inconsiderable here, as well as at Gironne, but there were three hundred at Narbonne, at the head of which was the Rabbi Calonimus, descended in a right line from David, rich and potent, especially in lands, which had been given him by the lords of the country, in recompense to the services he and his ancestors had done This city was looked upon as the centre of the Jewish nation and their law

Montpelier was then full of Mahometans, Greeks, Christians, and Jews, which shews that this city had, at that time, great commerce with the remotest countries In the neighbourhood was Lunel, where the learned assembly studied the law day and night Meschullum, the president of it, had five sons, all of eminent abilities, one of them profoundly versed in the study of the Talmud The strangers who came to study there were maintained Beaucaire had also its professors, one of which, called Abraham, disbursed, out of his own finances, all that was necessary to maintain six poor scholars, lest poverty should obstruct their application There were in the twelfth century synagogues at Arles, Marseilles, and not only in cities, but even in boroughs Our author concludes with Paris where Lewis reigned, and there was also an assembly much addicted to the law, and abounding in charity, for it received all the Jews that came there as so many brethren

We shall only observe that the Jews were very low in the East in the twelfth century, that they had not been able to restore themselves since the misery that had befel them above an hundred years before, for they were found only in small numbers upon the banks of the Euphrates, and in the ancient cities, where sometimes they had been reckoned at nine hundred thousand The crusaders did not suffer them to settle again in Judaea Thus they were miserable in all the places where they had appeared with greater lustre, and there was a general decline in point both of fame and learning

Before we conclude the twelfth century, it will be necessary to give our readers a short account of some other Jews dispersed in other parts, according to the relation of Rabbi Petachia This Rabbi was born at Ratisbon, and travelled not only through most parts where Benjamin of Tudela had been, but agrees with him as exactly as if they had copied each other, so that we shall forbear repeating from this what has been said by the other, and take notice only of such facts, or curious particulars, as are not mentioned by him

The account R Petachia gives of those Jews he saw in Tartary, is, that they were heretics, that is, they did not observe the traditions of the fathers, and, upon his asking them the reason why they did not, they answered, they had never heard of any They were, however, such strict observers of the sabbath, that they cut the bread on the preceding which they were to eat on that day, when they hardly stirred from their seats, eat their victuals in the dark, and knew of no other prayers, but those contained in the book of psalms

When he arrived at the New Nineveh, he found about 6000 Jews there, whose chiefs were called David and Samuel, two near relations, descended from David All the Jews of that country were obliged to pay them a certain capitation, one half of which was to be conveyed to the lieutenant of the king of Babylon, and the other belonged to them. They had lands of their own, fields, gardens and vineyards, well cultivated It was, it seems, here, as well as in Persia, Damascus, &c the custom among them, not to maintain any singers, but the chiefs, who kept at their table a number of doctors, obliged them, sometimes one, sometimes another, to perform that office The authority was so great that they could punish strangers, as well as those of their own nation, when, upon their pleading before them, they were found in the wrong, and there was a prison kept for all such delinquents

Upon his coming to Bagdad, he found about one thousand Jews settled there, but speaks of two thousand disciples, under the chief of the synagogues, and other learned men These sit on the ground, whilst he taught them from an high desk, covered with a gold tissue, and every one had a copy containing the books of sacred writ The Jewish women went forth veiled, and avoided speaking to strangers, either in the streets, or even at their homes We shall only add with respect to the chiefs here, to what we mentioned out of Benjamin, that, upon the death of Daniel, who left no male successor, the Jews, who had preserved the right of chusing their chief, divided their votes, one party nominating David, and their other Samuel, to that dignity, both lineally descended from David, which division still subsisted when our author left Bagdad, where, he adds, the Jews were treated with great lenity, exempt from any tribute to the king, and only paid a piece of gold to the chief of the synagogue But they were used with severity in Persia, where, nevertheless, they were computed to amount to 600,000, for which reason he only went through one of the Persian cities

He went thence into Judaea, of which he gives much the same account as his brother Benjamin So that having now gone through the most material account of these two Jewish travellers, we shall supply the rest from other authors, with respect to some other countries and facts by them omitted

CHAP VIII

The Jews favoured by St Bernard Protected by Pope Innocent II By Alexander III Persecuted in Spain In France, by Philip the Augustus [illegible] Afterwards recalled Jews in England [illegible] by grant of Henry II [illegible] through the kingdom [illegible] in the twelfth century [illegible]

St BERNARD who, as already [illegible] was a great enemy to the Albigenses, espoused the part of the Jews, and not only would not have them persecuted, but reprehended the violent zeal of some persons bent upon their destruction, and justified the excesses of [illegible] manded of the Christians He held, [illegible] conversion rendered their present [illegible] that, in reality, if their [illegible] were compared [illegible] were many Christians who were guilty of [illegible] extortion St Bernard also gained Pope [illegible] their favour, for, as he was very serviceable to [illegible] who was obliged to fly into France, it is thought [illegible] inspired him with these sentiments of [illegible] which were so much the more necessary [illegible] himself in a foreign kingdom, where he [illegible] ration and assistance They brought him [illegible] interests when he made his entry at Paris [illegible] ed in the [illegible] in procession [illegible] the law to be carried before them, which they presented to him with great respect, and this is one of the ceremonies of the installation of the popes, which has long continued. The Jews of Rome are obliged to wait for him in the way to St. John de Lateran, and to present him with a copy of the law, when he returns this answer: "I reverence the "law which you have received of God by Moses, but I "condemn your exposition of it, because you still expect "the Messiah, which the apostolical church believes to be "Jesus Christ our Lord."

Some time after they had occasion for pope Alexander the third's protection, who granted it them so much the easier, because the Rabbi Jahiel was superintendent of his household affairs. The people of Italy insulted them in several places, and hindered them from celebrating their [illegible]. They made their complaints to the pope, who granted them his protection, prohibiting any from taking away their synagogues, and disturbing them as they celebrated their sabbaths, or exercised their religion. But, at the same time, he ordered that they should not have the privilege to cite churchmen before a civil tribunal, nor take possession of the churches by virtue of pledge or sale.

Under so powerful a protection the Jews flourished in Italy at the end of this, and even in the following century. [illegible], the metropolis of the Milanese, grew famous for the [illegible] Rabbies it produced. Monza, the city where the kings took the iron crown, produced many others. [illegible], in the marche of Ancona, had the same honour.

The [illegible] of Alphonso the eighth's reign in Spain was favourable to them. He was yet a child, when his father Sanchez the Desired was killed by the Saracens. He ascended the throne young. Moreover, as he was well [illegible], he was easily over-reached. Joseph the Jew was [illegible], and grew so potent, as to have his [illegible] and guards to attend him. Gonzales, an officer under him, having committed some fault that deserved disgrace, resolved to destroy his benefactor and his [illegible]. He declared to the king, he could devise the means of procuring him vast sums; in order to which he demanded [illegible], the eight heads of the Jews at his own choice, which [illegible] granted him. Thus he found an expedient at [illegible] two passions, [illegible] and hatred of that nation. [illegible] chose eight considerable persons, whom he caused to be beheaded, and confiscated their estates, part of which he gave to the king, and converted the rest to his own use. The [illegible] offered a much larger sum for the [illegible] of twenty more. But this offer was not accepted, [illegible] the king [illegible] to retain the profit without the [illegible] by ordering the richest of the synagogue to [illegible] their lives. [illegible] did not stop there, for it was [illegible] whether they would not be expelled the kingdom, and their effects seized on, in order to defray the charges of the war, without burthening the people with new impositions. The opinions were divided in council, [illegible] the Jews time to deliberate among themselves, and to offer [illegible] of money. They were, however, highly rejoiced, when they saw Gonzales fall into disgrace, [illegible] who caused him to be arrested, notwithstanding his great services. So that his fall established their tranquility. But what further ingratiated them with him, was his falling deeply in love with a beautiful [illegible], to whom he facrificed his honour and interest, and, for her sake, to her nation; for the Jews taking that advantage, grew so powerful and insolent, that the court and clergy became quite scandalized at it, and at length dissolved the charm, by the death of the beloved object. The Jews took advantage of this happy juncture, and grew so potent, that R. [illegible], who then lived, and wrote at this time a ritual of the ceremonies observed in all the synagogues, and which is called the Custom of the Universe, reckoned [illegible] thousand persons of his religion in the city of Toledo.

They were also very numerous in Andalusia, where they applied themselves closely to learning. But study served only to disturb the union of the doctors, who were divided into three different sects, which Maimonides, who then lived, has distinguished, and which he looked upon as an unhappy consequence of the abolition of the Sanhedrim. Indeed, whilst that tribunal remained, the oral law was not written, by which they avoided diversity of opinions, and the difficulties and errors that arise from the text or a [illegible], or from the different readings of the copiers.

It was during this quiet interval, or, perhaps, a little before this time, that, according to the Jewish chronologers, copies came to be dispersed of the sacred Hebrew, according to the manuscript of the celebrated Hillel, which had appeared some time before, (yet what year cannot be determined, nor what became of it) in which two [illegible] were found wanting in the twenty-first chapter of the book of Joshua. These were the 36th and 37th verses, which mention the four cities of refuge appointed to the Levites out of the tribe of Reuben; [illegible], being [illegible] in the book, made Grotius imagine they had been since transplanted from thence into the text of Joshua above mentioned, though without foundation, being they are not only found in the Septuagint, or Greek version, which is allowed to be more ancient than Hillel's manuscript, [illegible] the [illegible] explain that text, by telling us that these towns were on this side Jordan, and on one side of Jericho.

Their fortune in France was much diversified. They were accused at Paris of murdering St. [illegible], and, for their punishment, sentenced to the flames. Indeed, they deserved death if they were guilty of that crime, and if no innocent person was involved in the fate of the guilty, they had nothing to complain of, but themselves, and their own cruelty.

They were very hardly dealt with at Beziers. On Palm Sunday, every year, commenced a certain pastime, which amused the people, who were therefore careful to renew it. The rabble flocked out at night, scoured the streets, broke the Jews windows, and stoned all those that fell in their way. The bishop, having often noticed this inhuman proceeding, which was then preparation for the holier ceremonies, treated with the Jews, and prevailed with them to buy off this insult by paying him a tribute. The treaty is very singular, for the bishop engaged himself, and his successors, to protect the Jews from insults, from war, and a lapidation, by day and by night, all the time between Palm-Sunday and Easter, declaring that he would shut the doors of the church against all that should break open those of the Jews, and, on their part, he obliged them to pay annually, to the bishop, two hundred [illegible], which might amount, at that time, to four marks in silver. They paid, moreover, above four silver marks to the church of St. Nazarius, to purchase ornaments. This treaty was concluded at Beziers, and rendered them pretty easy, till they were expelled under Philip, surnamed Augustus.

This prince, at the beginning of his reign, under pretence of devotion, banished the Jews out of his kingdom, confiscated their estates, and only permitted them to sell their moveables, and carry away their money, which was reducing them to the last extremity. [illegible] people, taking advantage of this circumstance, refused to purchase or pay [illegible].

Rigord, who wrote the life of Philip, says, that, by this [illegible] he revenged the death of a young man, named R[illegible], whom the Jews had crucified at Paris, and that [illegible] was convinced, by this example, of what he had [illegible] heard the young princes say that were educated [illegible], that the Jews every year committed such a murder [illegible] [illegible], and that [illegible] charge this [illegible] upon the Jews, whilst [illegible] this [illegible]. However, [illegible] a martyr, and was buried [illegible] the church [illegible] Field, which still preserves his name. [illegible]

[illegible] to Innocents church, from whence, we are told, the [illegible] hath carried away his body, in Charles V reign, [illegible] only his head in the church. This was the ground [illegible] pretence to fall upon the Jews. They were seized [illegible] all their synagogues, plundered of every thing that was most valuable, and at length expelled the kingdom.

But Philip did not [illegible] remain an enemy to this nation. Whether he had only made the decree of banishment at the [illegible] of the cardinal de Champagne, brother to [illegible] or was willing [illegible] pope Innocent III for a flagrant [illegible], or whether he was sensible that the state [illegible] such a multitude of rich merchants [illegible] recalled them from their banishment. [illegible] blamed the recall of the enemies of [illegible] the people murmured. However, the [illegible] for no long continuance.

[illegible] England, which had been [illegible] out of it ever [illegible] found means to settle again [illegible] become so numerous [illegible] but one burying ground [illegible] they petitioned that monarch to grant them to have [illegible] new ones, which [illegible] granted.

But [illegible] suffered much under Richard I because the [illegible] were prepossessed with a notion that the Jews were all magicians, and might practice some witchcraft upon the king, if they were present at his coronation. [illegible] orders were given to all the Jews not to appear [illegible]. Some, who came from far and near, at great expence to see the ceremony, were resolved not to lose their labour or money. They flattered themselves they should not be known, because they were strangers in the [illegible], but they were mistaken. The officers, having discovered some of them at Westminster, fell upon them [illegible]. They dragged them out of the church half dead [illegible] the noise of this execution being spread in the [illegible] the people in an uproar, who broke open the houses of the Jews, and killed those they met with. [illegible] were [illegible] found [illegible] friends to shelter them [illegible] spread from [illegible] to the counties, where [illegible] were slain [illegible] after the coronation, [illegible] to stop the [illegible] proceeding [illegible] which [illegible] were ill executed or that it was impossible to put such [illegible] check to the fury of the people, the [illegible] which was that of the jubilee.

[illegible] calamity [illegible] when Richard [illegible] the Jews [illegible] this prince's favour [illegible] brought into his treasury to support his expences [illegible] resolved to [illegible] where [illegible] more [illegible] at York, where 1500 [illegible] to defend themselves, but being [illegible] they offered to capitulate and to ransom their lives [illegible]. The other [illegible] refused, one of them cried out: "That it was better [illegible] own hands than in the hands of barbarous [illegible]." This [illegible] they became the executioners of their own wives and children, and retiring [illegible] to the king's palace, set it on fire, and expired themselves amidst surrounding flames.

Before we close this century, we think to give some account of the most celebrated Rabbies who flourished in that period. We begin with the learned Rabbi Nathan Ben Jechiel, chief of the Jewish academy at Rome, and author of the book called HARUCK, where he explains all the terms of the Talmud in so copious a manner, that he has in some measure, exhausted that subject; insomuch that those who have come after him, have rather plundered than improved him, particularly the great Buxtorf, who made frequent use of his remarks, without quoting him.

The next in time, though superior in learning and merit, was the great Aben-Ezra, surnamed, by way of excellence, the Wise, as he really was one of the most learned men of his age and nation. He had been a great traveller, and a diligent searcher after learning; was a good astronomer, philosopher, physician, poet, and critic, in which last science he hath excelled all that went before him, and is chiefly admired by the Christians for his judicious explications of the sacred book.

We have in this century three famous Rabbies of the name of Levi. One born at Cologne, who, after [illegible] conferences with the Christians, was baptized, and [illegible] under the name of Herman. 2. Judah Levi, a good poet, and author of the [illegible] entitled, "Cozar." 3. Abraham Levi, a learned Rabbi, said to be related to Aben-Ezra, and who was a most zealous antagonist against the Caraites, though [illegible] inferior to them in point of reasoning and judgment, [illegible] being [illegible] cope with them, he had recourse to king Alphonso VIII [illegible] to whom he had rendered signal services, and obtained an order from him to have all his adversaries [illegible].

CHAP. IX.

D[illegible] of the Jewish [illegible] [illegible] [illegible] of the Month [illegible] [illegible]

WE shall here again be obliged to join [illegible] [illegible] centuries together, to [illegible] being frequently forced to speak of [illegible] begin with the [illegible] east, [illegible] [illegible] respect either to [illegible], or [illegible] [illegible].

Petachia [illegible] to [illegible] the [illegible] of his nation, [illegible] Benjamin his [illegible] that he still found a [illegible] of the [illegible] east, when he arrived there. [illegible] it is probable [illegible] persecution raised at the end of the twelfth or thirteenth century, completed the ruin of the nation in this country. Nasser Ledin [illegible] one of the Abbassides, was then caliph [illegible] forty-seven years, all which time he [illegible] the Jews. He was succeeded by two [illegible] [illegible] that he was very zealous for his religion, [illegible] a great number of mosques and [illegible] service, to be built [illegible] his dominions [illegible] was an excessive [illegible] which he wished to [illegible] gold and silver, but which still wanted two [illegible] "Shall I not live long enough to fill it?" On the contrary, his grandson Mostanger [illegible] "How happy should I be [illegible] empty it!" Both of them [illegible] accomplished. Nasser, who delighted to [illegible] of the law of [illegible] before unknown [illegible] the succession of all foreign merchants who [illegible] dominions. The riches of the Jews [illegible] extortions from a [illegible] persecution, for Nasser [illegible] his provinces, or [illegible] exile, and the rest [illegible].

Joseph, the son of [illegible] physician [illegible] had assembled for some time. He went [illegible] He had studied the mathematics [illegible] that science with wonderful [illegible]. He [illegible] weight of

Naſſer's perſecution, and having ſold his eſtate, through means of diſſimulation, retired into Egypt with all he had. He there found Maimonides, and, with his aſſiſtance, corrected a treatiſe on aſtronomy which he had written. After Maimonides's death, he quitted Egypt, to retire to Aleppo, where he purchaſed an eſtate, married, and practiſed phyſic, under the protection of Malik Aidaher.

Judæa was much depopulated by the wars which the Saracens and Chriſtians waged there, as well as in Syria. Moſt of the cities frequently changed maſters. Nevertheleſs, there were ſtill doctors and ſynagogues in it. For here it was that the famous Moſes Nachmanides retired, and built a ſynagogue. He was born at Gironne, and applied himſelf to phyſic, but afterwards made great progreſs in the ſtudy of the law, which has given him the name of the Father of Wiſdom, the Luminary and the Flower of the Crown. A ſermon, he preached before the king of Caſtile, obtained him the character of the Father of Eloquence. Ramban (which is the name he commonly goes by) at firſt deſpiſed the cabaliſtical law, but when he had once reliſhed it, he attained to the greateſt perfection in it.

We cannot conjecture why Ramban who enjoyed ſo great a reputation in his own country, left it to go to Jeruſalem, but it is certain he retired thither, built a ſynagogue, and died there. Authors do not agree about the preciſe time of his death. He compoſed a prayer upon the ruin of the houſe or Temple, Letters to induce men to Piety, and particularly to recommend the holy ſtate of marriage. He entered deeply into the reigning diſputes of that time, concerning Maimonides's ſentiments, and made an apology for R. Alphes, which he entitled the Book of Wars. It would be uſeleſs to affix a catalogue of his works, which may be ſeen elſewhere. Baruch Germerſheim alſo quitted his country to effect the reformation of the Spaniſh ſynagogues. From thence he went to Candia, and at length ſought a retreat in Judæa, where he died.

The tranquillity of Egypt was no leſs diſturbed than that of the Holy Land. St Lewis endeavoured to make a conqueſt of this country, he took Damietta, and defeated Malek Almohadam, who ſucceeded his father, and then reigned in Egypt, but this caliph won a ſecond battle, in which the king was made priſoner. Almohadam's mother cauſed him to be killed by Ibek, the leader of the Mamalukes, whom ſhe was diſpoſed to marry. Thus the love or ambition of an unnatural mother threw Egypt into foreign hands. There was no deliberation about the election of St Lewis, for Ibek, the ſultaneſs's gallant was proclaimed king, and the Mamalukes became maſters of this great kingdom.

These Mamalukes ſo famous at that time, were of different nations: the firſt were ſlaves of Great Armenia, or Turcomans, which ſome Tartars had ſold to the Egyptians. The king of Egypt took a thouſand of them into his ſervice, and employed them in building a fortreſs upon the ſea-coaſt, from whence they took the name of Mamalukes Baharia, that is, maritime ſlaves. Theſe people, accuſtomed to labour, arrived to the greateſt employments, till at length Ibek became king of Egypt. The ſultaneſs having cauſed him to be ſlain, Coutus was elected by the Mamalukes. He vanquiſhed the Tartars, who had hitherto been thought invincible, but, on chaſing a hare, he was killed by Bibars, one of his principal officers, and the greateſt man the Turcoman Mamalukes ever had. He reigned but ſeventeen years, but ſpent them all at the head of his armies, which were generally victorious. Helaun, one of his ſucceſſors, committed the ſame fault as the Egyptian ſultans, for he brought a number of ſlaves from Circaſſia, to whom he entruſted the guard of the towers of Cairo, from whence they took the name of Jorghite Mamalukes, and growing potent and numerous, dethroned the marine Mamalukes, and made themſelves maſters of Egypt.

It is ſaid that theſe Mamalukes received none but Chriſtians among them, whom they cauſed to abjure their religion, and that all deſcended from Mahometan or Jewiſh parents were excluded. If this conjecture were ſolid, we could not doubt but the Jews were ſuſpected by the governors of Egypt for near three centuries, for they were as much miſtruſted as the natural Mahometans. Theſe latter were miſtruſted becauſe they were thought to be ſtill attached to the houſe of the caliphs, the deſcendants of their prophet, who ſubſiſted ſtill in Egypt, but had no authority, and only concerned themſelves with the affairs of religion. The Jews had no reaſon to raiſe againſt this decayed houſe, why then ſhould they be miſtruſted, and hindered from entering into the body of the Mamalukes, when they renounced their religion? It is, however, true, that the Jews made no great figure in Egypt under their empire, and that they were great gainers by changing their maſter, as we ſhall ſee in the ſequel. They preſerved their ſynagogues, but had no ſhare in public tranſactions. It looks as if they had renounced ſtudy, ſince no learned men appeared among them.

We only find, in the fourteenth century, one Simeon Duran in ſome city of Africa, but he was not originally of this country. He had paſſed thither from Spain, from whence he had carried the commentary of Alphes, which he had tranſlated. He compoſed a chronology of the ancient Rabbins, the Buckler of the Fathers, Diligent Judgment, and the Judgment of Juſtice, which Buxtorf has confounded, as if they were but one book, becauſe they are always joined together.

The Tartars, or Moguls formed a new monarchy in Aſia, and immediately ſeized upon Chorazan. This great revolution was occaſioned by one of the moſt frivolous ſubjects that could embroil ſovereigns. Mohammed ſurnamed Chovarezm Shah, reigned in Chorazen, and had obliged all the neighbouring princes to ſubmit to his laws. He had even forced the great Tartars to raiſe the ſiege of Samarcand. A numerous caravan of Tartarian merchants arrived at Otrar, a city of the Tranſoxane, under the guard of a conſiderable officer of Ginghizkhan's ſpies. That which exaſperated him was, that, being a Turcoman by birth, he had been brought up in the ſeraglio with the ſlaves, and had changed his name to conceal his origin. He wrote to his maſter, that he muſt puniſh all theſe ſpies with death, and as the Perſians have a ſaying, 'The wiſeſt are blind, when the decrees of Providence are come.' Mohammed, who had ſo great an intereſt to live peaceably with the cham of Tartary, ordered the priſoners to be put to death without examination, and would give no ſatisfaction to Ginghizkhan, who demanded it before he engaged in the war which broke out betwixt theſe princes. Mohammed loſt his courage as ſoon as he ſaw the vigorous reſiſtance that was made by a handful of Tartars, who ſtopped his army in paſſing the Oxus. He deliberated whether he ſhould paſs that moment to the Indies, where he had made great conqueſts, but changed his deſign. The Tartars puſhed him to ſuch extremities that he was forced to make his eſcape to the iſles of the Caſpian ſea, where he died, and was buried. His mother, whom he had put into an impregnable caſtle, was obliged to ſurrender for want of water, but no ſooner had ſhe got out, than there fell ſuch a torrent of rain, that the ciſterns overflowed. Ginghizkhan ſent her home dreſſed in mourning, but the crowd of thoſe, who deſired to ſee her before ſhe went, was ſo great, that ſhe was ſtifled for want of guards to diſperſe them.

The Tartars puſhed their conqueſts much farther, and took Bagdad. Moſthadem, the laſt caliph of the houſe of the Abbaſſides, who then reigned, was a prince of very indifferent intellects, and ſo devoted to his pleaſures, that he could not refrain from them, even when Helagou, the ſultan of the Moguls, inveſted the city, and preſſed him hard by a ſiege of two months. This prince being taken, was led through the ſtreets of the city wrapped up and ſmothered in a felt, in which he ſoon expired. One of his ſons was taken off as he courageouſly defended [illegible] the city, whilst his [illegible] was revelling, and the [illegible] was slain by the conqueror. Thus ended the illustrious house of the Abbassides, that had produced thirty-five caliphs, and the east was subjected to the plunders of the Tartars and Moguls.

As these barbarous nations depopulated all the places they passed through, the settlements which the ten tribes had in this country were destroyed, and the nation again dispersed. However, they devoted themselves to these new masters of Asia, and sometimes found favour at their court. Ahmed Khan, surnamed Nicouder Ogian, after he had usurped his nephew's monarchy, turned Mussulman, and [illegible] upon him his subjects' hatred, who had [illegible] inclination for Christianity, [illegible] Argoun Khan, who impatiently bore his uncle's usurpation, issued out of Chorasan, where he had retired, was defeated and taken prisoner. This disgrace [illegible] him to the throne, for [illegible] Bega, who was ordered to kill him, joined with him, and surprising his uncle's general, and the sultan who was diverting himself at Bagdad, he caused him to be taken off, and ascended his father's throne. Argoun [illegible] gave the government [illegible] to [illegible], who had done him so important a service, but this [illegible] with his [illegible], and unable to bear his [illegible], rebelled, was [illegible] ages [illegible] become [illegible] of the [illegible]. [illegible], that he deprived the Christians [illegible] Argoun's [illegible]. But he [illegible] and to [illegible] it [illegible] the Jews of the east began to revive, [illegible] the advantages they had been so long deprived of.

The Mussulmen [illegible] held the [illegible] of the dispersed tribes [illegible] kept out of all employments [illegible] of the prince's camp, but they were [illegible] while the Jews prospered [illegible] provinces [illegible].

Saadeddoulet, who foresaw the consequences of the [illegible] to himself and brethren, [illegible] to redress the grievances which were complained of during his ministry, and to appease the people by a speedy satisfaction, but [illegible] Argoun died, and, even before [illegible] the minister of state was accused of having poisoned [illegible] his accusation, invented by the Arabian historians, [illegible] improbable. Nevertheless, Saadeddoulet was taken [illegible] after the prince's death, which the Mussulmen [illegible] every fortunate event, they fell upon the Jews, [illegible] of them, to revenge the [illegible] they had [illegible] them.

We read likewise, in Abou'lfeda[illegible], who was [illegible] at the beginning of the fourteenth [illegible] appeared at his court with a [illegible] inferred that notwithstanding [illegible] after Argoun's death, the Jews [illegible] at the court of the Moguls, [illegible] monarchy was [illegible] Abousaid's death, which [illegible] to [illegible] years, [illegible] neighbouring [illegible] same [illegible].

It is probable that the Jews enjoyed tranquillity in the Grecian empire [illegible] we meet with nothing [illegible] to the contrary. We [illegible] enjoyed full liberty of conscience since the Greek [illegible] of those times condemned the [illegible] which [illegible] exercised against them, in forcing them to be baptized, though none were more ready than themselves to [illegible] these reproaches were but [illegible] the cruel usage the Jews met with [illegible] till the [illegible] they set out, and [illegible] the east where they arrived.

CHAP. X.

State of the Jews in the east [illegible]

[illegible]

This [illegible] who [illegible] having [illegible] what [illegible]

[illegible]

Portuguese synagogues, and Spaniards, differing upon this matter, raised commotions in the beginning of the thirteenth century, for R Baruch made a journey from Germany to Spain, to reproach them with the novelties which they introduced into their synagogues

In Spain they were guilty of a more palpable misdemeanor, for they no longer scrupled to marry strange women As marriages with Christians had been severely forbidden, it is probable they contracted oftener with the Saracens' daughters Moses de Cozzi reprobated these marriages He was of an Italian family, and therefore retained the name of the town of Cozzi, in the [illegible], whence he came but he was born in Spain and [illegible] the most learned Rabbi in his time He was averse to these heterogeneous marriages He preached often upon this subject, and, at last, had the good fortune to be heard, for many sent away the strange wives they had married [illegible] were near 12,000 Jews in the city of Toledo

Raymond de Pennaforte, prior of the Dominicans, [illegible] already condemned the violence that had been [illegible] [illegible] to destroy rather than convert the Jews, [illegible] recommended gentle instruction As he had great credit [illegible] James I King of Arragon, whose confessor he was, a[illegible] often [illegible] to the pope, he persuaded this prince, that he ought to repress the insolence of the people, to [illegible] many to the study of Arabic and Hebrew, to qualify them to dispute with Jews and Saracens, and to lead them [illegible] Christianity, by convincing them of their errors [illegible] boast much of the success he had with the Saracens and [illegible] that he converted above ten thousand ea them, and that the Moors of Africa had a sincere desire to do the same thing, but they do not so confidently speak of the conversion of the Jews It is only observed that they entertained great respect for his person, as an acknowledgment of his gentle and equitable way of dealing with them King James of Arragon, at his request [illegible] edicts, and though they were not so rigid as others had been yet they infringed upon their ancient [illegible]

The exertion of this Dominican produced the [illegible], or [illegible] of Faith This book [illegible] to him, as if he was the author, but he was only the [illegible] of it, nor did it appear till [illegible] composed by Raymond Martin a monk of the same [illegible] it has been supposed that he was born a Jew, [illegible] that he became monk after his conversion, [illegible] does not upbraid him with being an apostate from [illegible] [illegible] this violent and passion [illegible] gross abuses He had been [illegible] to be employed in the [illegible] of the Jews, [illegible] at the conference held at Barcelona [illegible] [illegible] and, in his presence, [illegible] [illegible] the famous [illegible] Raymond [illegible] his adversary [illegible] to quit Spain, and retire to Jerusalem [illegible] shame and reproach [illegible] he would have [illegible]

About the same time Alphonso X [illegible] Castile [illegible] employed the Rabbi, Isaac, the son of [illegible] astronomical tables, which have since been called the Alphonsine, and held in great esteem by all [illegible] who have applied themselves to that study [illegible] Tibbon, who then lived in the kingdom of [illegible] translated all Euclid's elements, whose manuscripts [illegible] It is said he taught at Montpelier when he [illegible] this work

Alphonso likewise made use of them [illegible] proving so generous a patron, it excited the [illegible] zealots, and put them upon devising new [illegible] accusations against them, and it was [illegible] three villains, of the city of Orense [illegible] [illegible] dead body into the house of a Jew, and [illegible] murder This calumny being spread [illegible] the people massacred all the Jews that [illegible]

Some of them escaped into [illegible] being [illegible] of [illegible] of it to [illegible] with, [illegible] dying with hunger, [illegible] break [illegible] The inhabitants of [illegible] the Orense [illegible] slaughtering the Jews, who [illegible] their brethren to lend a [illegible] to the court, to put a stop to [illegible] [illegible]

[illegible]

CHAP [illegible]

[illegible]

[illegible] Arragon, [illegible]

communications and anathemas. The count de Toulouse executed the laws and justice upon them. He seized [illegible] of them, and made them prisoners, but the people opened the prisons and the monks broke their chains. The count was willing to save some Jews, but the [illegible] to whom he had entrusted their custody delivered them to their enemies, and he had the mortification to see them come into his city to force the remainder of that nation to turn Christians. They submitted to it to avoid death. The massacre continued at Bourdeaux, Agen, Castel-Sarasin, and other cities. Those who were retired to Narbonne, imagining the storm was over, came out of their retreat, but they found in their way a troop of ruffians, who supported by the peasants put them to the sword. The king of France, tired with so many cruelties, ordered them to be prosecuted without quarter. The nobility armed by the king's order, and obliged them to retire to Navarre and Arragon. They carried the same disposition thither, and caused the same disorders. The king of Arragon armed against them, put prince Alphonso at the head of his army, who caused the leader of the ruffians to be killed by his master of the horse, and dispersed the rest. Part of them perished by the sword, and more by pestilence.

The plague was a fresh subject of misfortune to the Jews, who were supposed to be the cause of it. They were accused of conspiring with the [illegible] of Messina to poison the waters of the river, and of furnishing them with [illegible]. They were cast into prisons, and informations were lodged against them. Their innocence was proved; but the king, who was unwilling to acknowledge the injustice he had committed in retaining such vast numbers of prisoners so long upon a false pretence, declared that he had shut them up only to convert them, and upon their refusal to embrace Christianity, fifteen thousand of them were sentenced to the [illegible].

Alphonso the Eleventh, their friend and protector, though wholly guided by one Joseph of Astigi, the intendant of his finances, was prevailed upon, nevertheless, by his mutinous subjects, to issue out an edict against them on account of an insult pretending to have been offered by a Jewish boy to the [illegible] of a sacred ordinance as it was carried through the streets. A council was called that very night, to deliberate whether they should be massacred or banished, when the advice for banishment prevailed. He [illegible] for them the [illegible] [illegible] of the process by which it was found that it was a young Christian whose curiosity had brought him to the window to see the procession, and had by chance overset a vessel of water upon the child. The king, upon this, revoked his edict, to the mortification of the zealots, who gave out that the Christians had been suborned to make a deposition in favour of their enemies. This, however, did not hinder the populace from falling upon the Jews in another city, where they massacred them upon the same pretence, and might have gone a much greater length, had not the king caused ten of the mutineers ringleaders to be hanged.

No sooner had they escaped this danger, than they fell into another much more dreadful. There was a mutiny against them at Toledo. R. Ascher, having fled some time before from his native place Northembourg, retired to Toledo with his eight sons. One of his children seeing the [illegible] breaking open his house in order to murder him, fell into such an excess of rage, as to kill all his relations that were shut up with him. He stabbed his own wife, and that of his brother Jacob, a man remarkable not only for his disinterestedness, while he lived, as teaching always gratis though he was poor, but for leaving behind a famous book intitled Turim, which is a body of civil and ecclesiastical law. This Jew having killed all his relations, dispatched himself, for fear of falling into the hands of the Nazarenes. Some place this persecution in the year 1340, but others date it nine years later, and with reason, not only because in the year 1340 R. Jacob composed the book before mentioned, but Alphonso XI. who had countenanced the nation from the beginning of his reign, was living in 1349. At his death he tolerated a sedition which he could not suppress. Peter the Cruel, his son, who came to the throne in the year 1350, saw several factions formed in his kingdom, either by the insolence of the people or of the great, who usurped part of his authority, and caused most of it [illegible] commotions. Henry de Tristemare, his natural brother, supported by Bertrand du Guesclin, took Toledo, [illegible] him, and came before Burgos, which still [illegible]. The Jews fortified themselves in their quarter, and refused to surrender to the conqueror. Peter, they alledged, was their lawful king, and that they would rather lose their lives than receive another master [illegible] his [illegible]. Henry could not forbear esteeming their fidelity for a deceased king, and [illegible] their honourable conduct when they [illegible] his side.

Tristemare, at his accession to the crown, made Don Meir his physician, but dying soon after, not without a suspicion of having been poisoned. Meir [illegible] the [illegible], and [illegible] the king. Other [illegible] however, [illegible] and Meir [illegible] [illegible], [illegible] the king [illegible] had sent them for that purpose. But as his death was occasioned by a weakness in his nerves, there is no great probability that he was poisoned, especially by his physician, to whom he had been so good a friend.

The Jews were not treated more favourably at the end of this century than they had been at the beginning. They complained that the [illegible] who were willing to make themselves [illegible] [illegible] with a [illegible] [illegible] principle of zeal [illegible] [illegible] their [illegible] [illegible]. One of [illegible] [illegible] [illegible] [illegible] means to banish the [illegible] from Spain. [illegible], being advised [illegible] [illegible] [illegible] [illegible] [illegible] [illegible]. [illegible] of Henry III. [illegible] Castile [illegible] [illegible] [illegible] [illegible] of Mi[illegible] [illegible] the [illegible] [illegible] the minds of [illegible] to [illegible] [illegible] [illegible]. [illegible] Valencia and Barcelona [illegible] [illegible], and others resolved, whilst [illegible] [illegible] their religion, to escape the fury [illegible] [illegible] synagogues of Sevil and Cordova [illegible] [illegible] [illegible] [illegible] [illegible] [illegible]. Those that [illegible] [illegible] were murdered by the inhabitants.

His son John was as [illegible] [illegible] [illegible] [illegible]. They who concealed themselves in the [illegible] [illegible] [illegible] in the towns, because they were [illegible] [illegible] [illegible] and were easily [illegible] [illegible] by the badge which they were forced to wear.

Nor were they more happy in [illegible] [illegible] being [illegible] to prevent [illegible] [illegible] [illegible] upon the [illegible] Jews [illegible] [illegible] [illegible] [illegible] [illegible] [illegible] [illegible] [illegible] [illegible] [illegible] reduced [illegible] to the lowest [illegible].

However, this century [illegible] [illegible] [illegible] among whom [illegible] Solomon [illegible] [illegible] [illegible] Constantinople to [illegible] [illegible] the Prophecies of the [illegible]. His [illegible] of a book in which he expounded the [illegible] of the Pentateuch, [illegible] the [illegible] [illegible] were [illegible] [illegible] [illegible].

His son Sche[illegible] [illegible] [illegible] St. Matthew's gospel into [illegible] [illegible] his Paradise, in which he maintains, that most of the Talmudic stories ought to be interpreted allegorically.

[illegible]rechias the younger also lived at that time, who must not be mistaken for another of the same name, who lived in the twelfth century, and passes for a Spaniard, though he was born at Lunel, in Languedoc, because this province then depended upon Spain.

The king of Castile had two Jewish physicians in his [illegible] later called Meir Algudes, was at the same [illegible] for head of all the Spanish synagogues. He [illegible] Aristotle's ethics. This philosopher's works were so esteemed by the Rabbies, that Schem Tou, another learned man, inserted them in his Excellency of the [illegible] This mark of esteem is the more extraordinary, because the doctors hardly ever read the works of foreign[illegible], which they generally despised.

CHAP. XI.

The Jews [illegible] popes. [illegible] of the conduct of the [illegible] Gregory IX. [illegible] of the Jews in France. A persecution [illegible] Jews protected [illegible] by Clement V. [illegible] by Clement VI. [illegible]

Of all those [illegible] one is to be found whose authority has been more indulgent to the Jews than that of the popes, who, whilst they persecuted Christians [illegible] subject to their laws, countenanced this nation, one [illegible] the [illegible] of their princes. They [illegible] them privileges, and left them full liberty of conscience. Some popes, indeed, have been their enemies; [illegible] impossible that in so long a succession of [illegible] they should all have been of the same [illegible], and followed the same principles. They still live more quietly under the dominion of the [illegible] of the [illegible] than any where else, and it is [illegible] to [illegible] the [illegible] of the popes conduct towards the Jews, whilst the [illegible] quite opposite one towards the Christians.

[illegible] Jews [illegible] not so much [illegible] against the Jews, [illegible] had not sufficient power to give them [illegible] opposed the pontifical authority, [illegible] to restore the privileges that belonged to [illegible] therefore the popes have made constant efforts [illegible] weaken and destroy them. Besides, the Jews have no [illegible] grudge to the popes [illegible] all Christians to them. [illegible] The desire of revenge, and the glory of destroying [illegible] have no place here; instead of [illegible] the respect to their revenues interests [illegible] their preservation.

Gregory I[illegible] nephew to Innocent III. was one of the [illegible] pontiffs. He was for having all princes leave [illegible] to make the conquest of the Holy Land [illegible] He had the pleasure to see the isles of Minorca and Majorca, that were full of Mussulmen, [illegible] into Christian hands, after Ferdinand had destroyed the [illegible] of the Moors. It is said too, that all the inhabitants of these two isles turned Christians. Though he had a [illegible] with Frederick the emperor, yet he [illegible] to write to him, to let him know that he might deliver the incredulous Jews to the secular arm [illegible] punished, in which he departed from his uncle's [illegible], who preserved them in their ancient privileges. But he himself altered his opinion; for being informed that the Jews were massacred in several places, when the expedition was on foot for the Holy Land, he prevented these barbarous executions.

He also delivered them from another persecution they fell into, under pretence that they used human blood in their medicines. The inhabitants of Haguenau accused the Jews, their fellow-citizens, of stealing some children from the Christians, and murdering them in a mill in order to use their blood in some of their remedies. The imposture was gross, and the emperor, who [illegible] investigated the matter, was convinced of their innocence. The like fury prevailed in Spain. The English Jews would have been treated with the same inhumanity, had they not warded off the [illegible], by buying the minister's and the king's favour. They were killed and persecuted in several places; but the greatest massacre was in Paris. It had lasted longer, if pope Gregory IX. who had then the see, had not written [illegible] to Lewis to stop the course of these cruelties, and not to force the consciences of the Jews [illegible] they were indebted [illegible] their lives to the pope's [illegible], not only in his [illegible], but also in France.

They were severely treated in Trani, where a pontifex [illegible] was [illegible] upon [illegible] pretences. They were [illegible] potent in these two [illegible] in the whole kingdom of Naples, where they had numerous synagogues and learned Rabbies. [illegible] the poets of this country with those of Provence, who were then in so great reputation. The [illegible] protected them, because they had done him [illegible] in his wars. He gave them a [illegible] when he died, but it was thought [illegible] greater service done them, [illegible] to Christianity. [illegible] to change their religion, upon condition they [illegible] wives from good houses, and the [illegible] of Naples. Every body was deceived in this [illegible] except the [illegible]. The Jews were [illegible]. In the mean time there was [illegible], and they [illegible] Christians. It [illegible] to others, to see several marriages made [illegible] of so recent and suspected a conversion [illegible] returned to their old [illegible] of Trani in order to be revenged on the Jews, [illegible] of them [illegible] indignity to the rites of the Christian religion. This incensed the common people [illegible] and [illegible] all they met with. The [illegible] proceeded from Trani to Naples, where the Jews would have been all murdered, if some men of power had not concealed them [illegible] the popular fury. All the Jews would have been to [illegible] if they had [illegible] the pope of [illegible] as he had no [illegible] Gervais to Naples, to [illegible] the Guelfs, and to [illegible] his authority. But Gervais could not succeed [illegible] pope died soon after the ill success of his [illegible]. So that he could neither cure nor remedy the mischiefs the Jews suffered.

They were more at rest in Ancona. That [illegible] was not in the ecclesiastical [illegible] pope Clement VI. had not seized [illegible] with his troops [illegible] the year 13[illegible], upon pretence of defending it against the Turks.

Clement V. who removed his see to Avignon, because of the troubles [illegible], was [illegible] the beginning of the fourteenth century, [illegible] them there against the fury of their enemies.

This pontiff who endeavoured to secure them from violence [illegible] care of their instruction; for he appointed professors in all universities, to teach Hebrew, and train up scholars to [illegible] the [illegible] them after they had learned their language [illegible], and then [illegible] arguments to convince them.

Clement VI. succoured them in a signal manner [illegible] persecution they suffered [illegible] commonly [illegible] that the [illegible] ing out at one end of [illegible] not only in [illegible] adjacent provinces, but the neighbouring states. [illegible] pretence for this, which was [illegible] universal, was [illegible] poisoning fountains [illegible] to destroy all those that drink of them. Such [illegible] examine the matter acknowledge, that [illegible] this [illegible] poison [illegible]. Many people, however, [illegible] and the Jews were thought guilty of the [illegible]. They were [illegible] in Spain and Germany [illegible] the mischief [illegible]

Twelve [illegible] of [illegible] in [illegible]. The imperial [illegible] of the houses of the Jews [illegible] must have [illegible] despair, suffered themselves [illegible] their houses, and [illegible] falling into the hands of their persecutors. [illegible] most of all their disasters, [illegible] whilst they were [illegible] in other places, and did all that was in his power to stop the torrent of this excessive [illegible].

The Jews were then potent in Bologna, for, besides the synagogue they [illegible], they built another, larger and [illegible] set up in [illegible] there. It was one of the [illegible], who removed from Rome to Bologna, that made this new settlement [illegible] which bears the name of children, is still [illegible] to be so at that time, [illegible] Moses, [illegible] his genealogy as high as those Jews whom [illegible] to Rome. They lived in this great city till the end of the fourteenth century, and then made choice of Bologna, where they made great improvements, and built [illegible] synagogue in [illegible].

CHAP. XI.

[illegible] of Philip [illegible] Augustus [illegible]. The Jews expelled [illegible] Britany. [illegible] of [illegible] under St. Lewis [illegible] by Philip the [illegible] [illegible] privileges [illegible]

PHILIP the August [illegible] at the beginning of the thirteenth century, and many [illegible] to him against the usury of the Jews, who, not content with their excessive interests, and the mortgages of the church-plate, made their debtors slaves. The princes connived at their extortions [illegible] bought their protection, and because, upon [illegible], they were condemned to great fines, and the confiscation of their estates to the royal treasury.

The king, however, was forced [illegible] by the remonstrances of the people [illegible] several decrees, forbidding the lending of money to [illegible], unless he could produce the letters-patent of his [illegible], the taking in pledge the ornaments of the church, [illegible] of [illegible] men. The soldier [illegible] his horse, [illegible] the husbandman and carpenter, [illegible] were prohibited borrowing of a Jew, [illegible] the debt. The edict [illegible] Normandy, where there were Jews as in other places, [illegible] creditors were obliged to cite the [illegible] before the bailiff, and the debts were invalid that were [illegible] in his presence.

These remedies did not [illegible] the [illegible] upon [illegible]. It was declared in the assembly of Melun, convened by St. Lewis at the beginning of his reign, which it was forbidden to borrow of the Jews, or take up money [illegible] from them, to deprive them of all pretences [illegible] violence and injustice. But among all the laws, the statute of the duke of Britany, in the year 1239, is the most [illegible].

The Jews dispersed in this province were very numerous, and, being for the most part [illegible], impoverished the people. The merchants [illegible] complained [illegible] John [illegible] was then duke of Britany, [illegible] having laid down the government [illegible] assembled the [illegible], by which it was enacted, [illegible] abbots, barons, and vassals of Britany, that the Jews should be banished out of the province for ever.

The debtors of the Jews were discharged from the debts [illegible] contracted with them, and those that had received [illegible] from them [illegible] allowed to keep them.

All that killed a Jew were declared innocent, and the Judges were to [illegible] against them, or to bring them to trial.

It was resolved to [illegible] the king of France to cause this statute to be [illegible] dominions, that is to expel the Jews, to [illegible] their fortunes, and gave licence to kill them.

The duke of Britany engaged for himself and his posterity, for [illegible] future, "to maintain the said ordinance, and [illegible] of its violation, the bishops had not "only power to [illegible] him, but to confiscate his "lands in their diocese, without any respect to the privileges "he had obtained [illegible]."

[illegible] that not one of his [illegible] Britany should [illegible], till he had taken [illegible] two bishops, [illegible] his law, [illegible] any Jew [illegible] territories."

The general [illegible] was [illegible] excommunicated, [illegible] who [illegible] Jewish [illegible] to [illegible] the crusades [illegible] upon [illegible] excommunication [illegible] the second [illegible] Jews [illegible] demanding their debts of [illegible] received [illegible]. The council of Vienna also, [illegible] in the same century, was obliged to [illegible] the Christians against [illegible] by the usury of the Jews.

Notwithstanding all these decrees and precautions, the Jews still found means to maintain their influence [illegible], in some provinces of France, particularly in Languedoc, they had the privilege of [illegible], and in most places of the kingdom, to have Christian slaves, [illegible] which was [illegible] great inconvenience, and of [illegible] enormous abuses.

Saint Lewis, zealous for his own religion, [illegible] others. The inquisition, [illegible] the [illegible] upon [illegible] the [illegible] who engaged in the holy league to commit [illegible] outrages. [illegible] the people to [illegible] the Jews, [illegible] on Good Friday, [illegible] Christian blood that day. Many of them [illegible] suffered. The same fury raged in the provinces of [illegible], Touraine, Anjou, Poitou, and Maine, where about 2500 persons suffered violent deaths, who refused to abjure their religion. Things at length proceeded so far, that the pope was obliged [illegible] to the king, [illegible] to moderate his rage, [illegible] that the Jews ought to be allowed [illegible] of their own conscience.

During this prince's unfortunate [illegible] in the Holy Land, a [illegible] body of [illegible] together to go and [illegible]. They [illegible] James of [illegible], [illegible] the Cistercian order, [illegible] to Orleans, [illegible] priests and monks he met with. [illegible], [illegible] his road to Bourges, where he [illegible] the Jews [illegible] to be seized, in order to be burnt, and plundered them wherever he could. But at length [illegible] their plunderers, [illegible] in which they lost their [illegible].

We are told of a [illegible] Jews, [illegible] Judaism, [illegible] The Christians and Jews [illegible] success of it, but that St Lewis was no friend to the Jews plainly appears from the edict which he sent, whilst under his confinement, to have them banished out of France, which was punctually executed. The Jews, however, pretend that it was the king himself that banished them after his return.

[illegible] the Bold recalled them, urged, as it is said, by the [illegible] of [illegible] affairs, for the imprisonment and schemes of [illegible] had [illegible] the finances of the kingdom, and the wars which Philip was obliged to sustain accomplished [illegible]. It was thought therefore, they could not better [illegible] the revenues, than by recalling a people that [illegible] along with them, together with the art of [illegible] plate. Philip's natural lenity contributed [illegible]; however, they were expelled under Philip the Fair.

The [illegible] claimed Leon, the son of Gerson, grandson of [illegible] by his daughter, as one of those doctors that [illegible], though he was born in P[illegible] the ancient Frenchman, if we consider the [illegible] compose that monarchy, and have [illegible] of Gaul. This Rabbi maintained pecu[illegible], and was totally averse to every [illegible] to countenance the imposition of ap[illegible] till the fourteenth century, in which [illegible] upon Samuel, and many other [illegible] of the miseries that [illegible].

C[illegible] a great number of Jews, who [illegible] an alienation [illegible], that complaint was made to [illegible] of it, by an English knight who, having mortgaged some lands to one of them and [illegible] before a judge, refused to appear or render the mortgage. The king gave the Jew to understand that he must comply, and that, though he had suffered them to enjoy all the privileges which his father had granted to them, [illegible] pledge, and that he did not design to give them the preference over the Christians, upon which the Jew submitted to the law. But the king having soon after [illegible] by a clap of thunder, which passed over [illegible] and killed two of his officers [illegible] chamber, he [illegible] banished them out of Guienne and [illegible] his other dominions in France. There had, by this time, crept [illegible] abuses, both amongst the Jews and Christians, in [illegible] parts, that pope Nicholas IV [illegible] to all his inquisitors there to be more watchful [illegible] conduct, and they executed his commands with great punctuality.

His example was not long after followed by Philip the [illegible], who banished them out of his dominions. It [illegible] that he did a good deed from an evil principle, the desire of plundering and becoming rich. The king was covetous, and so violently oppressed his people, that the P[illegible] and [illegible] in the temple, where he remained a whole day without food, the besiegers having [illegible] whatever was valuable in the synagogues. He banished all the Jews, upon pain of death or conviction, and confiscated the estates of the exiles to his own use, permitting them only to carry their clothes and a sum of money out of the kingdom. Part of them died by the way with fatigue and hunger; the rest retired into Germany, from whence the Jews of that country look upon themselves as originally of France, descended from those persecuted people.

Some turned Christians, to prevent the misery they thought unavoidable in foreign countries, and amongst the rest, Nicholas de Lyra, who wrote more learnedly and strongly against the Jews than any either before or after him.

But most of the rest relapsed into the Judaism they had abjured, and four years after one of these proselytes was burnt in Paris the same day with Margaret of Hainault.

The avarice and interest which had expelled the Jews out of France, caused them to be recalled again eight years after [illegible] Hutin, or the Mutineer, (for these two words signify the same thing,) succeeding [illegible], and finding great disorder in his finances, the kingdom exhausted of money, the people ready to mutiny, remembering the oppressions they had suffered in the preceding reign, was not contented with sacrificing Enguerrand de Margini, his father's favourite, to their resentment, but as this execution did not remedy the mischief, he demanded a large sum of money of the fugitive Jews, and upon that condition recalled them to his dominions, where they lived [illegible] in his reign, which, to their misfortune, was very short, and they were again exposed to new troubles.

In the year 1320 they underwent a [illegible]. This misfortune was no sooner over than [illegible] another. Historians relate, that the [illegible] of Granada, mortified to find himself to [illegible] Christians, sought an expedient to [illegible] than by arms. He [illegible] and asked them, whether there was [illegible] Christians? They undertook the [illegible] they could not execute it themselves, as [illegible] suspected, they corrupted some [illegible] their design to them, which was [illegible] wells and fountains. [illegible] to enrich themselves with the spoils of the dead [illegible] in so [illegible], and [illegible] their project [illegible]. The waters were found poisoned in France and Germany. A leading man of Perigny [illegible] to the king the deposition of a [illegible], whom he had seized [illegible], and who confessed he had been [illegible] Jew, that gave him a receipt, which [illegible] and thrown into a well, immediately rendered all [illegible] baneful. The lepers were tried, some [illegible] prisons, and others in their pest-houses, [illegible] to go out. The people of Languedoc, without [illegible] the necessary formalities of law, murdered them in [illegible] barbarous manner as cannot be read without horror [illegible] the pretended criminals in [illegible] to the flames, and other cruel executions, with as much joy as if they had been [illegible] a festival. At P[illegible] were put to death. Some [illegible] prisoners till they had discovered [illegible] Philip the Long [illegible] tain. Some historians, however, affirm, that they were [illegible] expelled out of the kingdom.

The exigencies of the state obliged Charles, dauphin of Vienne, and duke of Normandy, to recall them during the disorders caused by the imprisonment of his father in England, by the oppression of the great men and the mutinies of the people, who were weary of their tedious tyranny. When he came to the king, he confirmed what he had done as dauphin, obliging only the Jews of his kingdom to wear a badge of distinction.

Their last calamity happened in the reign of Charles VI. This prince, being disordered in his senses, or as some affirm, bewitched, the Jews were accused of committing some murders and other outrages, for which some of them were hanged, others scourged, and the synagogues [illegible], severities which obliged many of them to turn Christians. At length appeared the edict which for ever banished their whole nation from the French dominions, and it is from that sad epocha that they begin the date of their years.

They have been tolerated in France, though they have not an entire liberty. Profanus, the celebrated [illegible], taught at Montpelier in the middle of the [illegible] century. Mary de Medicis not only [illegible] Montalto to Paris, to be her physician, but obtained of Henry IV [illegible] liberty of conscience for him and all his family. [illegible] Jews afterwards in Gascony, and from thence came [illegible] Castro de [illegible], who being taken at B[illegible] by the Portuguese, was put into the inquisition, and burnt alive. Ba[illegible] if the Jews [illegible] in France, it was only by way of toleration [illegible] public [illegible]. Most dissembled, and [illegible] profession of a religion they abhorred. [illegible] in that kingdom some of these disguised Jews [illegible] offices in the church, to [illegible] the royal authority, which prosecutes them with the greatest severity even into their retreats.

We must, however, except the city of Metz in Lorrain, in which they preserved their antient privileges and a synagogue. This was afterwards confirmed to them by Lewis XIII. and an edict passed in their favour, by which all criminal causes relating to them were to be referred to the council, and their ancient privileges confirmed, which edict, given at St. Germain's bears date 1670.

CHAP. XIV.

Oppressions of the Jews [illegible] Henry III. Crusaders [illegible] Jews [illegible] taken [illegible] Henry decrees the crusaders [illegible] sold to Richard, [illegible] of [illegible] against them [illegible] Lincoln [illegible] the king's [illegible] Their expulsion [illegible].

WE [illegible] of nothing worth mentioning concerning the Jews in England till the time of king John, except that [illegible] into this kingdom by William the Conqueror. [illegible] early as the reign of king Stephen, anno 1135, they were accused of crucifying a young Christian in contempt of that religion, and were accordingly punished for it. They were again prosecuted for the same atrocious act in Gloucester, in the reign of Henry II. anno 1181; but some have supposed, and not without probability, that these accusations were forged, in order to oppress and fleece the individuals of that nation.

King John [illegible] with severity, used his subjects ill, and incurred the displeasure of the court of Rome by his oppressing the [illegible] of Canterbury, which obliged the pope to [illegible] his kingdom. The Jews [illegible] with heavy taxes [illegible], began to refuse him money, [illegible] by violent punishments, [illegible]. Not satisfied with [illegible] extortions, he confiscated the estates of all the Jews in his kingdom, and banished them by proclamation.

The English [illegible] king John, and invited a foreigner to reign in his stead, but his death put a stop to the calamities that threatened the kingdom. The barons joined with young Henry III. raised an army, and gave battle to Lewis of France, who with difficulty, had much ado to [illegible], after he had given up all that he had taken. Henry reigned fifty six years, during which long term the Jews had several turns of fortune.

Henry III. proposed to convert the Jews of his kingdom, which he thought he could not more effectually promote than by founding a seminary for the maintenance of converts. He committed the conduct of it to an ingenious man, who carried on the design with great assiduity. All that were willing to be converted had here a safe retreat, where they lived in peace, without being subject to servile labour or usury. There were many induced by idleness, and the temptation of being maintained without pain or labour, to come into it, so that the number of the converts multiplied, and the house continued a long time.

The Jews of Norwich were accused some time after, of taking away a Christian child, of having kept it for a year, and after they had circumcised him, designed to crucify him at the feast of the passover. But the design being discovered, the crime passed not unpunished.

The same accusation was brought against those of London four years after, with some remarkable circumstances. The child having been sold to them by his parents and crucified, and the facts discovered by some travellers, circumstances not worth mentioning, he was canonized for a martyr, and his relics carefully preserved. However, the murderers could not [illegible] found out, only [illegible] Jews having left London about that time, were [illegible] suspected.

All the Jews were alarmed the year following, from the persecutions of the crusaders in South France and Germany, fearing there [illegible] that this storm would [illegible] over the [illegible] them, they prevented [illegible] procured an edict of the king, prohibiting [illegible] be done them throughout his dominions.

[illegible] the king having frequent occasions for money, [illegible] his prime minister, there [illegible] could not be easier found than among the Jews. Upon their refusal, therefore, to pay the great sums [illegible] demanded, they were accused of [illegible] a murder at London, [illegible] numbers [illegible] vexatious sufferings, obliged to pay [illegible].

Nor [illegible] this suffice for their entire security [illegible] four years [illegible] this insatiable prince [illegible] from his subjects [illegible] rejected those who [illegible] and [illegible] brought when they were not [illegible] enough, and demanded [illegible]. The Jews [illegible] suffered in his demands. He received [illegible] that was preferred, and [illegible] his officers [illegible]. One particular Jew, called Aaron, [illegible] him four [illegible] and two [illegible] of silver. [illegible] seven years after, [illegible] marks [illegible] the queen [illegible] obtain his release [illegible]. [illegible] were not more [illegible] accused of [illegible] the [illegible] and [illegible] they [illegible] and particular [illegible] knowledge [illegible] that [illegible] obliged [illegible] himself [illegible] this [illegible]. He [illegible] receiving great sums from [illegible] Jews [illegible] at the bar, and [illegible] been still greater [illegible] procured his pardon. [illegible] afterwards [illegible] the same [illegible] he was in [illegible] the Jews, [illegible] oversee [illegible] having forged [illegible] king's seal, [illegible] Complaint was brought to the king [illegible] the Jews who [illegible] him. [illegible] rescue himself from the hands of [illegible] of his post, and [illegible].

The [illegible] furnished Henry with a new pretence for oppressing his subjects. The pope had [illegible] cogent letter to him, to oblige him [illegible] court the king of France [illegible]. He [illegible] it, but at the same time pillaged the Jews [illegible] remaining, and [illegible] of their jewels and every thing that was valuable.

Henry afterwards spread [illegible] report [illegible] Spain designed to declare war against him [illegible] advanced as a new motive [illegible] subsidies from his people. The peers of the realm, assembled at London, remonstrated, that [illegible] former taxes they could contribute [illegible] the king of Castile had effectually [illegible] they would not refuse their assistance; but his [illegible] concealed, they could not raise subsidies upon uncertain ru-

[illegible] they had the better reason for what they did, because the king's desire was only to satisfy the avarice of [illegible] his court. The weight of this refusal fell upon the J[ews], who had less authority, but more wealth [illegible] of them, which they could [illegible] London [illegible] for them all, and [illegible] that, since they had resolved to sink [illegible] the kingdom [illegible] perhaps, they might [illegible] a prince who had some sentiments of [illegible] but the king knew well that [illegible] However the [illegible] of departing, but the tax was [illegible] by [illegible] they drew from them [illegible]

[illegible] these extortions the year following [illegible] represented that, notwithstanding all the taxes he had [illegible] involved in debt. He [illegible] declared his debt amounted to two or three hundred thousand [illegible] He observed that [illegible] must defray the expences of his houshold, and therefore he demanded [illegible] of the Jews. They represented [illegible] to the king that they were ready to quit the kingdom [illegible] had compleated their ruin. The king enraged with this refusal, sold them to his brother Richard. It was not doubted but that Richard [illegible] his brother, [illegible] the payment of his debt, but he [illegible] because he was convinced of their [illegible]

[illegible] which overwhelmed them, the Jews of Lincoln were accused of murdering a child [illegible] circumstances in this accusation [illegible] the Jews of Lincoln had invited [illegible] in England to assist at this [illegible] that the murderer confessed, when [illegible] that this sacrifice was renewed every year, though it was not always discovered. The third was, that the king refusing to ratify the [illegible] the Jews, they not only put him to death, but arrested [illegible] prisoners at London, and punished [illegible] others of that [illegible]

The king, who reigned [illegible] such extortion, and [illegible] his subjects by his avarice must of necessity create himself cruel enemies, therefore they combined [illegible] The earls of Leicester and [illegible] the [illegible] Richard [illegible] king of Germany [illegible] had been elected emperor by the [illegible] princes and king Henry, with his son [illegible] prisoners of war. Edward made [illegible] the liberty of exercising his [illegible] He defeated the earl [illegible] who was [illegible] slain upon the spot, and [illegible] the throne [illegible] of those who had [illegible] But none of these revolutions [illegible] the Jews [illegible] fortune turned, this [illegible]

It is recorded that Henry III banished them out of [illegible] The [illegible] A Jewish historian says they were accused to the king of [illegible] The king easily perceived the innocence of the accused, and that the deponents were guilty of the crime they had charged on others. But, notwithstanding, they went on with their accusation and produced witnesses. The king seeing them so cruelly bent, was afraid that the people would exterminate that nation, and therefore ordered them to depart his territories.

Most Christian authors [illegible] concerning this edict of banishment [illegible] the end of the thirteenth century [illegible] reign, and many records are found of it [illegible] England [illegible] that Edward I banished the Jews out of his kingdom, gave them money for their passage into France [illegible] Polydore Virgil [illegible] council held at London in the year 129[illegible], which [illegible] to separate the sheep from the goats [illegible] all the Jews to [illegible] giving them liberty to carry [illegible] They [illegible] the decree; and thus this nation [illegible] still wandering from one [illegible] is entirely lost [illegible] if they leave us their books, without which it would be [illegible] Such is the [illegible]

[illegible] the [illegible] year [illegible] out of France. The motive [illegible] Jews entering into two [illegible] corrupted them. However [illegible] they never appeared in [illegible] till they were recalled to it in the time of Oliver Cromwell, as will be seen in its proper place.

CHAP XV

Frequent accusations against the Jews in Germany. They [illegible] Persians [illegible] Tartars [illegible] Decrees of the council of [illegible] Protection [illegible] Richard [illegible] Bishop of Spires [illegible] Flagellants [illegible] Germany [illegible] Bohemian Jews [illegible]

WHETHER the Jews were really more wicked in Germany than in other countries, or the people more [illegible] against them, there is no kingdom where they have been accused of more enormous crimes, and of a greater variety and number of them, during these two centuries.

One of the principal crimes charged upon the Jews in Germany, was favouring the conquests of the Persians and Tartars, a multitude of whom quitted the east to ravage in the west. Their incursions did not last long, for they returned into Persia, [illegible] astonished at the obstacles they found [illegible] conquests, gave up a design which [illegible] of the same nation at Cologne had [illegible] It is said that the Jews of this country [illegible] inclined them to listen to every [illegible] the Persians would become their deliverers. [illegible] and [illegible] the Christians, because they [illegible] that he would [illegible]

[illegible] hopes [illegible] in this particular [illegible] multitude of Tartars [illegible] the neighbouring countries [illegible] are forced to see [illegible] enemies of the Christians [illegible] because Frederic's enemy [illegible] the emperor's son [illegible] The emperor [illegible] his son, giving them battle, obliged them to retire. [illegible] Jews [illegible] perity they had enjoyed, imagined that the Tartars were of their nation, and that they came to their assistance. They pretended that their ancestors, who were taken to the banks of the Caspian Sea, had brought forth this people, that carried desolation and terror wherever they went, and therefore resolved to join and succour them with supplies of provisions and arms. To do this the more effectually, they promised the princes to poison the wine they carried, and thus to destroy these barbarians. But their fraud being discovered, they were made prisoners, delivered to the executioners, and died by their own swords. The most favourable thing for the Jews in this event was, that the emperor Frederic was also suspected of calling in these barbarians. However, the accusation was false, for the clergy and the pope had invented it to render him odious; and so far was he from joining and corresponding with this nation, which came only with designs to ravage the empire, that he expelled them, and restored the king of Hungary to his throne.

They were accused, the same year, of obstructing the conversion of a young man of their nation, who was inclined to be baptized at Frankfort. This accusation seems better grounded than many others, because, as it was common for this people, and particularly amongst their fathers, in order to prevent the desertion of their children, frequently to go beyond the bounds prescribed by reason and the laws, the councils and emperors were often obliged to restrain the violence of the Jews in opposing these conversions. This opposition cost the city of Frankfort and the Jews very dear, for the people being incensed that a conquest of this kind should be taken out of their hands, mutinied, and betook themselves to arms. Some Christians were killed in the fray, and 180 Jews were destroyed by the sword, or the fire that had been kindled; but the flames continuing, and raging from house to house, half the city was consumed, which subjected the rest of the Jews to fresh danger. The more prudent, to the number of twenty-four, were baptized, to avoid death, and among them the chief of their synagogue.

The accusation of killing children at the passover was current in Germany, and in all other places of the west. This crime was imputed to them at Haguenau, in the Lower Alsatia. They were accused of taking three children, of seven years old, which were found dead in one of their houses. Complaints of it were brought to the emperor, who dismissed the plaintiffs with an evasive answer, which still more exasperated the people.

A more alarming accusation was preferred in Bavaria, where an old woman confessed that she had delivered a child to the Jews, who had drained his blood for some sacrifice. The people of Munich rose, and, without staying for the sentence of the judge, massacred all the Jews they could meet with. The officers in vain opposing this fury, advised the rest of the nation to take sanctuary in a synagogue, which was a building of stone; but this rendered their misery the more general, for the people pursued them thither, set fire to the place, and burnt all those who thought themselves safe, whilst neither the duke or his officers could stop their rage.

Much such another accusation was brought against the Jews of Wertzburg and Bern, where they were massacred in the same manner, and the two children killed by them canonized for martyrs.

Notwithstanding all these accusations, the nation of the Jews continued to multiply in Germany. Learning flourished in the synagogues, which were governed by learned and illustrious Rabbins. The city of Germeshein alone produced two, one of which was Baruch de Germesheim: for then they began to take surnames, and as noblemen took theirs from the fiefs and lands they possessed, men of letters commonly derived theirs from the cities where they were born. We have spoken sufficiently of Baruch. Eliezer de Germeesman was of the same city, and one of the greatest casuists, who produced a work of great worth and learning.

Isaac of Vienna, author of "The Light sown," took the pains to transcribe books for the synagogues of his country, to render them more correct and exact. He had Meir de Rottembourg for his disciple, who excelled his master, and became the judge and doctor of his nation, which drew upon him a long train of misfortunes; for, as he was thought to be very rich, or to have the management of his disciples purses, the emperor, who loved money, laid a great tax upon him, and imprisoned him for default of payment. One of his disciples bailed him, but he died before he obtained his liberty. A work is ascribed to him, intitled, Hattusbats, but he is but indirectly the author of it, as it was his disciples, after his death, who made a collection of his decisions, and gave them this title.

The German Jews likewise extol their R. Amnon for his learning, riches, and beauty, as well as his miraculous recovery of all his fingers and toes, which the bishop of Mentz had caused to be cut off for declining to confer with him, which he had promised three days before. But this last circumstance has every semblance of a Jewish legend.

Besides the advantage they enjoyed in the thirteenth century, of having a considerable number of great men, they met with another; for Boleslaus, surnamed the Chaste, gave them liberty of conscience in Lithuania, with the addition of many considerable privileges, which they made use of for many ages. He only imitated other princes, who generally took this nation into their protection. This appears from the council of Vienna held at that time.

The council observed, that the number and power of the Jews were so great, that the revenues of parish priests were considerably lessened by them, and therefore they were obliged to make them amends proportionably to the profits they would have received from Christian families living in their parishes; that they hindered their wives and children from embracing Christianity, and yet circumcised Christians, which was a prejudice to religion; and, lastly, that they multiplied their synagogues, making them larger, higher, and more sumptuous. The council restrained these abuses by new decrees, and, [illegible] allowed the ancient synagogues, ordered the new ones to be pulled down.

But these decrees were insignificant, whilst princes and great men protected those who refused to obey them, and ordered their officers to defend those who implored their succours. The [illegible] proceeded to [illegible] insomuch that it was declared to the princes and their officers, that they were excommunicated and banished the church, if they continued to protect the Jews, and refused to execute what the ecclesiastical [illegible] against them.

They were obliged soon after to make fresh regulations at Augsburg, on account of the [illegible] oaths which were till then administered to them, and which they made no scruple to break, and to oblige them to swear by the laws of Moses, holding their hand on the Pentateuch. The misfortune is, that even this kind of oath is held by them to be annulled on the grand expiation day, so [illegible] at the most they can be of force but one whole year. We [illegible] add, that they have their casuists likewise, who allow them to equivocate according to that decision of the Talmud, that it is lawful to dissemble for the sake of peace.

[illegible] disputes with the Caraites [illegible] were headed by a learned [illegible] content to expose the extravagancies of the [illegible] composed a treatise on them, under the title of [illegible], explained all the articles of [illegible] Tree of Life, because he [illegible] without believing the articles [illegible] of the dead, but confined it only to the houſe of Iſrael. As zealous as he was for his ſect, it began then to degenerate from its firſt preciſion, for being fond of traditions, Niſi, the ſon of Noah, who lived at that time, was obliged to explain the Miſnah, becauſe it was earneſtly deſired of him. Aaron was alſo forced to pay ſome deference to his diſciples, and that he might not diſguſt them, gave an allegorical explication of ſeveral ſcripture paſſages. The Talmudiſts were glad to ſee their enemies make an advance in their favour, but they were not reconciled, for their controverſies continued as violent as ever.

They ſoon laboured under a greater misfortune than that of diſputes and diviſion. A peaſant, named Raind Flaiſch, roſe up during the wars that diſturbed Germany, through the competition of Adolphus of Naſſau, and Albertus of Auſtria, who were elected emperors, and taking advantage of this confuſion, gave out in the upper Palatinate, that he had a divine commiſſion to exterminate the Jews. He ran over Franconia, and the neighbouring provinces, proclaiming every where the ſame thing. To give his pretence the more weight, aſſerted, that they had ſtole a conſecrated wafer. The people roſe upon this occaſion, without examining it further. The inhabitants of Nuremberg, Niewmark, Rottenbourg, Amberg, and other cities of Bavaria and Franconia, excited by Raind Flaiſch, ſeized all the Jews in that country, and committed them to the flames. Some choſe rather to burn themſelves with their furniture, wives and children, than be thrown into the fire by the Chriſtians. Ratiſbonne more humanely ſaved its citizens. Duke Albertus of Auſtria was willing to reſtrain this violence, but he durſt not make a bold experiment at a time that his power tottered, and the leaſt diſcontent of the people, who looked upon Raind Flaiſch as a meſſenger from heaven, would have made them declare for the Count de Naſſau. He was forced, therefore, to wait for a more favourable opportunity, which at length occurring, the Jews were reſtored to their privileges, and Nuremberg amerced in a great fine, which was ſo much the more burthenſome, becauſe part of the city had been reduced to aſhes by the fire the oppreſſed had put to their houſes.

The hatred of its inhabitants was not extinguiſhed, for it burſt out again ten or twelve years after, and the famous R. Mordecai of Auſtria loſt his life by it. He had compoſed a commentary upon ſome books of the Talmud, and ſome works of Iſaac Alphez, which are in great eſteem. He collected all he thought worthy of notice from the books of ten Rabbies to which he added his own obſervations. He left Auſtria to come and teach at Triers, where Iſaac, whoſe family came from Dijon, was his colleague, but returning to Nuremberg, he was condemned to be hanged there.

The confuſion, inſtead of leſſening, increaſed. One Armleder, in the neighbourhood of Naſſau, heading ſome peaſants, and encouraging them with the hopes of plunder, cauſed them to take up arms againſt the Jews. They overran ſeveral places, killing all they met with, to enrich themſelves with the ſpoils. The emperor Lewis of Bavaria, fore-ſeeing the conſequences of this commotion, put a ſtop to it, by taking off Armleder's head, who had occaſioned ſo deſtructive a ſedition.

Pope Clement V. having called a council at Vienna againſt the templers, made a decree againſt uſury, and thoſe that exacted it. He alſo condemned the approvers of it as heretics. This decree being publiſhed, the Jews were expoſed to many oppreſſions, which their exorbitant uſuries upon the Chriſtians drew upon them. They were brought before the tribunals, and diſputed their principal for having violated the law of the Chriſtians. They eſpecially felt the effects of this law in Germany. But Menicho, biſhop of Spires, took upon him their defence; he urged, that the law did not reſpect them, becauſe the church does not judge thoſe that are without. He was perſuaded that it was lawful for them to demand uſury, ſince they had been dealt with without any deſign of fraud, and therefore he ſeverely prohibited their being diſturbed about uſuries for the future.

The zeal of the Flagellants was a freſh ſource of their calamities. This ſect, which had been almoſt extinct, reſumed vigour in the year 1349, and cauſed new maſſacres. A company of people, muſtered under certain leaders, aſſembled twice a-day, and ſtripping before the people, ſcourged themſelves with cords. They drew into this fraternity the people of Spires, Straſbourg, and ſome other places. Theſe people, exaſperated by the Flagellants againſt the Jews, ſeized them, and burnt them in great numbers at Thuringia. But their greateſt calamity happened at Frankfort, where the Flagellants, having committed ſome diſorders, had conſented to an accommodation, when a Jew, named Cicogne, whoſe family was numerous in the place, deſiring to revenge his brethren, threw a piece of fire-work into the town-houſe. The flame reached the church, which was preſently reduced to aſhes, and burnt as far as Saxenhauſen. Such a crime as this could not be ſuffered to go unpuniſhed: not only the guilty periſhed, but all the Jews in the city, except a few that eſcaped into Bohemia.

The Jews were accuſed, the ſame year, of poiſoning the wells, fountains, and rivers, though upon no other foundation than that they eſcaped the common mortality, which, through the prevalence of the plague, happened in moſt parts of Europe. A ſuſpicion was ſufficient to condemn them, and people employed all the remains of ſtrength and life they had to murder their enemies. They ... the Jews in ſome places, and maſſacred them in others. Thoſe of Mentz defended themſelves, and ſurpriſing two hundred diſarmed Chriſtians, were cruel in their turn, and took an unmerciful revenge of them. The populace, provoked at this barbarity, ran to arms, and fell upon their enemies with ſuch fury, that twelve thouſand of them periſhed on that ſingle occaſion. "They ſet fire to their "houſes, and the flames ſpread to that degree, as to melt "down the great bell and glaſs of the church of St. Quintin. This torrent over-ran all Germany; the imperial "cities pulled down their houſes, and made uſe of the materials to build caſtles and towers. They were the more "violently bent upon the ruin of the houſes of the Jews, "becauſe they found great riches in the ruins." All the inhabitants of Ulm were burnt, with their families and effects. The princes durſt not engage in ſo critical an affair, and the Jews found no where any place of retreat. There was no place but Lithuania where they enjoyed any quiet, becauſe Caſimer the Great, who was in love with a beautiful Jeweſs, named Eſther, had granted them great privileges.

Thoſe that fled to Bohemia could not find long quiet there. The people of Prague, diſguſted at ſeeing them celebrate the feaſt of the paſſover, choſe that day above all others, to burn their ſynagogue, and thoſe that performed their devotions in it. The project was eaſily executed: none made oppoſition, or eſcaped the death that was prepared for them. This was ſo doleful an event, that the ſynagogue of Prague preſerves the memory of it in a prayer made ſome time after, to deplore its calamity.

Two years after Wenceſlaus, king of Bohemia, and emperor, with deſign to pleaſe his ſubjects, to whom his vices had rendered him extremely odious, diſcharged the nobility from all their debts to the Jews. This decree induced people to believe they might attempt any thing againſt a nation which the emperor refuſed to protect. The maſſacre began at Gotha, and grew terrible when the peaſants joined the inſurgents. Thoſe of Spires put all to the ſword, without regard to age or ſex, except ſome children whom they carried to the church to be baptized. However, as ſuch ſort of executions are odious, and depopulate countries, a ſtop was put to them, by puniſhing ſome of the murderers.

The Jews were again accused of poisoning the wells, and this accusation, which drew death after it, and the most cruel tortures, spread itself into Germany, Italy, and Provence, at least the Jewish historians give us this account but in the same time they add, that the emperor acknowledged their innocence and represented to his council, that it was impossible to poison a running fountain that constantly supplied fresh waters But the people maintaining, that they had seen the Jews throw poison to them and pronouncing some words in a low voice at the same time, the emperor, upon their importunities, resolved to banish them The notice of this caused great rejoicing among the seditious, as if there is no punishment too cruel for those that had been the destruction of so many Christians and thus the emperor was obliged to order them, by proclamation, either to fly, or change their religion

CHAP XVI

Co[illegible] between the Christians and Jews Tenor [illegible] The constitution of pope [illegible] XIII [illegible] the Talmud Different [illegible] His [illegible] at Toledo Co[illegible] Alphonso [illegible] Jews [illegible] out of Spain [illegible] effects of [illegible] Illustrious refugees Miseries of the [illegible]'s [illegible] Jews [illegible] to [illegible] The [illegible] of king Emmanuel [illegible] them [illegible] of [illegible] Jews, and [illegible] for [illegible] and learning

THE Jews had lived for a long time, and multiplied in Spain, where they had their synagogues, famous doctors, and considerable settlement. When Ferdinand, pretending a zeal for religion, resolved to banish them the synagogues were pulled down, the people exiled, and the families who were terrified with this banishment, reduced to dissemble from one generation to another But as this revolution did not happen till the end of the fifteenth century and was preceded with many considerable events, we shall give an account of them before we pass on to their final expulsion

The anti-pope Benedict XIII was in Arragon, the only place he had remaining, and which was his whole jurisdiction, He was inclined to signalize his zeal by attacking the Jews He began with conferences Jerome de Sancta Fide, who had deserted the synagogue, and was his physician, put him upon this design, by assuring him, that he could convince all his adversaries, from passages out of the Talmud, of the rectitude of their tenets The principal Rabbies of the kingdom were summoned, and Don Vidal was chosen for the defendant on the part of the Jews in this controversy

As Benedict defrayed all the charges, the Jews treated him with singular complaisance and respect, though they expressed themselves with some acrimony against his physician, who, as appears, was the chief promoter, as well as conductor, of this conference. The tenor and success of it are variously related by the Jewish and Christian historians, who have transmitted it to us, though they both were present, and bore a share in it

The Jews own that they gave many bishops who were present, money to prevail with the pope to put a speedy end to it, but that the pope remained steady, and would have Jerome de Sancta Fide stand to his promise They add, that their doctors came off with honour, that they were only ordered to restore part of the excessive usuries they had taken from the Christians, but that, upon application to Mark, pope of Florence, they were discharged, and set at liberty

The Christians assert, that Jerome, having presented a writing the same year to the anti-pope, containing the dangerous errands of the Talmud against the law and the Christians, one of the Rabbies present gave the cardinal of St Angelo a writing, in which he declared, that the passages drawn from this book appeared to him offensive and erroneous that it was true, another sense might be given them, but that he did not know it, and therefore he confesses, that he does not pretend to defend them, nor justify them, and disowns all the answers he might have made to elude them And all the Rabbies present except Joseph Albo and Ferrer, subscribed the same declaration.

The Christians add, that three or four thousand persons were converted by Jerome's piece, which rendered it infinitely valuable and that Joseph Albo, who was afraid all the synagogues would be deserted, composed the Articles of Faith in which he endeavoured to [illegible] the wavering faith of the people

It is most certain that Benedict XIII the year following published a constitution against the Talmud and the Jewish usuries But as this anti-pope was deposed for a time after, his constitution was [illegible] with his other ordinances, so that the Jews felt not the effect of it It is known too that Joseph Albo endeavoured to [illegible] the faith of the Jews that was [illegible] by this conference. He published his Articles of Faith, which are reduced to the existence of God, the law of Moses, and future punishments and rewards His work is in such esteem, that Gedalia, a Polander, has commented upon it, under the title of the Planted Tree his notes are the [illegible] of [illegible], the references to scripture passages are the branches, and the allegorical explications the leaves This the commentary is a perfect or planted tree

Vincent Ferrer, another famous converter, appeared at this time They call him, "The Splendor of Spain, "the Light of Valencia, the Prodigy of the Universe, "and the Model of the Dominicans He was chosen to maintain to the people the validity of Ferdinand's election, who by that means became king of Spain and [illegible] afterwards made him a noble recompence He was [illegible] of the prince, and confessor to the anti-pope Benedict XIII [illegible], they have not failed to canonize him, and there is [illegible] a church in Spain but receives his office

The Jews call him Mumar, that is apostate, as if he had deserted the [illegible] to [illegible] Christianity But yet it is [illegible], that he was born a Christian of [illegible] illustrious family, and known at Valencia [illegible], for a long time, had gone by the name of [illegible]

Notwithstanding all this eclat, the conversions [illegible] must be still much suspected, because they were [illegible] short duration There is a writing [illegible] in the Vatican library, of one Duran a Rabbi, who [illegible] embraced Christianity wrote to [illegible] his father The whole letter is equivocal It was believed, at first reading, that it was an exhortation to stand fast in the religion he had [illegible] but the mystery was easily discovered, and it appeared from an attentive consideration, that this father [illegible] to oblige his son to return to Judaism, which he had left at Vincent Ferrer's instigation, and embraced [illegible] Indeed, most of the new converts, having dissembled for some time, took off the disguise and made it known, that they had only yielded to force and necessity

Such were the conversions of Vincent Ferrer in Spain The Jews, whom he had drawn by [illegible] to the church, were no sooner at home, than they fell into the practice of their ancient ceremonies They [illegible] their children in [illegible] [illegible] and all other Jewish festivals [illegible]

As the Jews were [illegible] the [illegible] that befel [illegible] which they [illegible] had a good part in the [illegible] To [illegible] which complained [illegible] privileges had [illegible]

by the imposition of a tax, though a light one, and necessary to the war. The mutineers plundered the houses of the richest citizens, and slew those that resisted. The Jews were not spared, but the violence was carried even to the posterity of the converts, when laws were enacted, excluding all, both Jewish and heathen new converts, from [illegible] offices. The clergy protected them, for the dean of the cathedral church of Toledo reprobated this order of the inhabitants, and caused public theses to be held, in which he opposed it. The better to [illegible] the consequence and injustice of it, or rather to engage a greater number of people in his interest, he mentioned many illustrious families by name, who were allied to those of the converted Jews, and therefore deprived of employments. Pope Nicholas V then published a bull against this decree, excommunicating all those who offered to exclude the converted Jews and heathens from political and ecclesiastic offices, from the priesthood and government.

All this while the Jews were esteemed and protected by king Alphonso the Great, and his grandees, [illegible] it is under his reign that one of their writers places a conference which happened between that monarch and one Thomas, surnamed the Subtle Philosopher, who came opportunely thither, as one of the bishops had preached a severe sermon against them, in which he [illegible] that they could not celebrate their passover without mixing some Christian blood. The king was happy in having so learned a man to confute that absurd notion, which he accordingly did, and with that strength and energy that might be expected from a person of his character.

However, the synagogue was then in possession of great advantages, for, besides the learned of Arragon before mentioned, many others appeared. Chamai was famous at that time for his casuistry.

Joel, the son of Sciocu, published sermons. This preacher was prolix and diffuse, the too common error of those who harangue the people; yet he was much esteemed as a learned man, and competent judges have thought his explication of some chapters of the Pentateuch very instructive.

Lastly, the family of Alcadeb produced two famous astronomers, the uncle and nephew, who both compiled astronomical tables. But we shall not insist longer upon this head, as we shall find hereafter many learned men included in the sentence of condemnation and banishment, and involved in the last calamity that swallowed up this nation, and expelled it out of Spain.

Ferdinand and Isabella accomplished this work. After they had put an happy end to the war against the Moors, they thought of nothing more than demolishing the synagogues, and getting rid of the Jews. To this end they issued an edict, commanding that nation to depart the kingdom of Spain within the space of four months, or embrace Christianity. [illegible], who was the instigator of this persecution, advised shortening the term, and forbid the supplying them with provisions, under great penalties, or lending any assistance to those who should not be gone in April. Some historians are of opinion, that the liberty granted them of carrying off their gold and jewels was revoked, and that they were only permitted to change them for cloth, wine, and other merchandize. But this prohibition was not rigorously executed, since the Jews found means to carry off [illegible] millions of ducats. Such as had the courage to leave their country, were obliged to pay some ducats per head to the king for their freight, and those that would not, or could not go for the want of money, became slaves, and their goods were confiscated. This last clause was so rigorously executed, that two vessels which were laden not able to sail at the fixed time, they unmercifully sold all those that were on board to the Spaniards.

Marianus affirms, that seventy thousand families, or eight hundred thousand persons, left Spain pursuant to this edict. The Jews reckon an hundred and twenty thousand families, and six hundred thousand individuals. The favour Abravanel so long had with the king and queen could not preserve him from the same fate. He was obliged to embark, and depart with the rest, to Italy. He must have been accustomed to exiles, for however glorious his life was, he was often obliged to fly. In the bloom of his youth he appeared at the court of Alphonso in Portugal, and had a great share in his favour, but John II his son, having sufficient motives, Abravanel stole secretly into the kingdom of Castile. Ferdinand and Isabella appointed him to the superintendance of their finances. They say he amassed great treasure in a short time, and was expelled with the rest of his nation. He retired to Naples, and quickly procured the king's favour, to whom he did great services. [illegible] this prince being dead, and Charles VIII having possessed himself of the kingdom of Naples without any opposition, Abravanel was obliged to fly to Sicily, with Alphonso, [illegible] who succeeded his father. He preserved his fidelity to his prince in the midst of distresses which dispossessed him of his riches and crown. Alphonso died in Sicily, and Abravanel was obliged again to change his place of [illegible]. This Rabbi is famous, not only [illegible] [illegible] vicissitudes, but especially for his works. He is [illegible] useful of all the Rabbies for the understanding of [illegible]. He wrote in a pure and intelligible style, though [illegible] too [illegible], and hath more of the [illegible] than a commentator. He [illegible] the literal sense of scripture, and handles the most important questions that are found in the books he [illegible] comments on. He was a good-natured man, and [illegible] [illegible] with the Christians.

There was also at that time famous refugees of [illegible] time, Isaac, the son of Arama, a great philosopher and great casuist. The Jews highly esteem his Exposition of the Law, though some critics think it too [illegible] [illegible], and full of morals altogether [illegible]. He brought with him R. Meir, his son, one of the principal Rabbies of his time, and author of a commentary upon Job, which [illegible] attributed to his father. Another was Joseph Gigatilla who, during his exile, applied himself to the exposition of the divine attributes [illegible] [illegible]. [illegible] was one of these exiles. He retired first into Portugal and went thence to Jerusalem, but he lost his children and his books by the way. He lived a [illegible] life, and composed the Generations of the Children of Israel, to comfort those that had lost them. Abraham Zacuth, lived [illegible] at that time. Bartolocci confounds him with Abraham the Jew, who has translated a Treatise about the Virtue of Medicines out of Arabic. These two authors published a perpetual almanack, and both [illegible] [illegible] studiers of astronomy. The latter was of [illegible], and taught at Saragossa, but he was obliged to quit his country by Ferdinand's edict. He [illegible] Portugal, where king Emanuel gave him the title of his [illegible]ographer. Here it was he composed the Juchasin, the famous book of Generations from the creation of the world to the year 1500.

The misery of the exiles was extreme. The fire seized some of their vessels, and consumed all the passengers. Many were shipwrecked, and perished in the sea, either through default or design of the pilots. The pestilence having infected the rest, the pilots set them on shore. Part of them that landed being cured, died of hunger. Others arrived at Fez, where the inhabitants, frightened [illegible] [illegible] of fugitives, shut up the gates. They were forced to set up tents in the fields, and to live upon herbs, which the drought and barrenness rendered very scarce. Besides the injuries of the air they were compelled to submit to the insolence of some inhabitants, who thought all things were permitted them against the miserable. One of them took a virgin by force from [illegible] [illegible] and afterwards murdered her, for fear she had conceived, and would bring forth a Jew. A [illegible] surprized a company of children, who came to look for shell and other fish when the sea retired. He brought them on board his bark, where he gave them [illegible] which attracted a great number of them. One [illegible] he weighed anchor, and carried off all the young children, which he sold to some persons of quality, and made slaves of the rest. Many other and more atrocious cruelties were perpetrated by these barbarians.

People murmured greatly against the politics of the king of Spain, who depopulated his kingdom by so mistaken a persecution. Besides, he ran the risk of a rebellion, since 800,000 people, driven to despair, were capable of making a dangerous insurrection; and Abravanel had reason to extol the exemplary fidelity of his nation, when it [illegible] taken arms against its persecutors, and [illegible] for so severe a decree. Ferdinand [illegible] had taken precautions against an event he had [illegible] to fear. Religion seemed only a veil to cover the conduct of Ferdinand, who was infinitely ambitious. We [illegible] answer for the motions of the human mind, whose [illegible] are not only hidden, but different, according to the circumstances of times. But it seems that the king and queen sacrificed the prosperity of the kingdom to [illegible] their predominant passion.

[illegible] II. king of Portugal, lying at the very gates of [illegible] to enrich himself with his neighbours [illegible]. The interest of his kingdom demanded, that he should afford a retreat to the Jews, from whom he had [illegible] services. He had sent some of them to the coast of Ormus, and the Red Sea, who brought him a faithful account, and served him in the discovery of the [illegible] Indies; but yet he did not love them. Nevertheless, from motives of policy, he received them, but imposed on them most rigorous conditions. Each was obliged to pay him eight gold crowns for the privilege of [illegible]. He moreover fixed a time, beyond which it was not lawful for them to continue in his territories without [illegible] to slavery. These two conditions were discharged [illegible] that retired into this kingdom; and [illegible] rather to live in slavery, than expose themselves [illegible] misfortunes. They complained that he [illegible] Isles of Thieves, newly discovered [illegible] they miserably perished. But at the [illegible] comfort themselves with a notion, that [illegible] vengeance on him, for he died young, and [illegible], by marrying Isabella, became heir to many kingdoms, fell from his horse into the Tagus, from [illegible] to a peasant's cottage where he died: so that the crown devolved to another branch.

Emanuel, John's successor, at first seemed to compassionate these oppressed wretches, and restored them to their liberty. But the alliance he made with Isabella [illegible] Ferdinand altered his first notion. Isabella [illegible] declared, that she would not have a man to her [illegible] that suffered the enemies of their religion in his kingdom. Emanuel, therefore, sacrificed the Jews and Moors to an alliance he thought more advantageous. He allowed both of them to depart out of his dominions. He kept his word with the latter, as fearing reprisals would be made in Africa upon the Christians. But he doubly violated his faith with the Jews, by depriving them of the liberty to carry away their children above fourteen years of age, which reduced them to that despair, that some of them killed themselves, and others, sacrificing nature to their religion, became their own executioners. Besides, after they had assigned them three ports whither they were to embark, they reduced them to one, so that they were obliged to alter their measures, make a double journey, and exhaust their treasures. In fine, the delays that were given to the embarkation made great numbers miserable.

Amongst those that turned Christians, to avoid such a train of disasters as they saw before them, many were harshly used, from a too just mistrust of their sincerity; and a great number were massacred upon the first slight occasion: all which outrages seem to have been but too much encouraged by the cruelty and treachery with which king Emanuel had used that unfortunate people.

Some historians charge this disaster upon the Jews, affirming, they drew it upon themselves, because some of them, after publicly professing Christianity, and being baptized, were found celebrating the feast of the passover in secret: but Mariana ought to be preferred before all foreign and German authors. Nevertheless it is [illegible] of those that remained in Spain and Portugal [illegible] instead of being converted, which is the natural effect of persecution in matters of religion. The most surprizing thing is, that this religion [illegible] from generation to generation, and still subsists in the persons of [illegible] to a remote posterity. In vain the great men of Spain [illegible] change their names, and take ancient [illegible], they are still known to be of a Jewish race, and Jews themselves. The convents of monks and nuns are full of them. Most of the canons, inquisitors, and bishops, proceed from this [illegible]. Moreover, [illegible] proof of his assertion, [illegible] that there are in [illegible] synagogue of [illegible] brothers and sisters, and their relations [illegible] families of Spain and Portugal, and even Franciscan monks, Dominicans, and Jesuits, who come to do penance, and [illegible] for the crime they have committed [illegible].

Among those who [illegible] with such [illegible] there [illegible] men of great [illegible] been [illegible] Joshua, who [illegible] chronology [illegible] 1554, was a Spaniard, and the best [illegible] has had since Josephus. Ben Virga [illegible] who has collected several [illegible] standing the Gemara, which are [illegible] they were forgotten by other interpreters. Isaac Cardoso, a descendant also from the Portuguese [illegible], being one of the principal physicians of Castile, [illegible] wrote his Spanish tract concerning the [illegible] of water and snow, and cold or hot drink. But at length, being tired with his disguise, he quitted Spain and the Catholic religion with his name Ferdinand, which he had received at his baptism, and retired to Verona about the middle of the last century. He printed his [illegible], in which he expatiates on the particular prerogatives of the Jewish people, which ought to be [illegible], notwithstanding their miseries and dispersions, which God only sends for the punishment of their sins. He [illegible], that this nation was chosen by God; that it [illegible] separated from all other nations [illegible] the [illegible] the Divinity instructed [illegible] men. For [illegible] the inquisition is [illegible] over these new Christians, and they are still suspected by the cruel ministers of this tribunal, who enrich themselves with their spoils. The least suspicion suffices to make them guilty. For, indeed, whenever any accident happens in the kingdom, the people accuse them of judaizing in secret, and bringing down the Divine vengeance. An instance of it was seen at the beginning of the last century, when a Dominican put himself at the head of these mutineers, and they plundered, ravaged, and killed, four or five thousand of their converts.

The Jewish authors bitterly complain that these [illegible] are still continued in full vigour against them in Cordova, Lisbon, [illegible] and even in the East and West Indies.

CHAP XVII

Jews under Tamerlane Establishment of the empire of the Great Mogul Arguments proving that there were Jews at Cachemire Conquests of Ismael Sophi Succession of Sophi Contract between the Jews and Mussulmen Amurath IV favours the Jews Execution of the treaty Horrid massacre of the Jews Jews disgraced and distinguished by dress in Persia Jews at Schiras At Goa In Armenia and Media

THE Jews suffered much by the rapid conquests of Tamerlane, for this conqueror, having fixed his capital at Samarcand passed on to Chorazan, where they were numerous He seized upon Bagdad and all the Irak, and passed into Syria, where he plundered Damascus He overcame Bajazet, who reigned in Anatolia, where his nation had considerable settlements, and, as he laid waste all places where his armies marched it is no wonder that the Jews were ruined and dispersed by his invasions Tamerlane followed Gengizkan's religion, which consisted in seven or eight precepts dictated by the law of nature Though he has been represented as a barbarian and illiterate, because he had followed no other precepts than these, yet he was a lover of men of letters, and maintained a great number of them, with whom he often conversed Physicians and astronomers were very well received [illegible] his court Hence we have reason to believe that many Jews were in it, since they excelled in these two sciences

The conquests of Tamerlane were divided between his sons and grandsons, who could not agree about sharing the succession, and weakening themselves by their confusion Nevertheless they supported themselves an hundred years till a commander of the Usbecs entered Chorazan and, by conquest, took it from them Arbek, a descendant of Tamerlane was obliged to fly to the Indies, where he set up the empire of the Great Mogul We are told there was a province of Cachemire full of Jews, that [illegible] in Solomon or Salmanasar's time, who have [illegible] of their establishment, by which they are [illegible] at this day Mr Thevenot desired one or his [illegible] to examine whether the inhabitants of this country had the Holy Scripture, and whether their Old Testament was [illegible] but he answered, that though there were formerly Jews [illegible], there were none at present "All "are (said he) either Heathens or Mahometans P[illegible] "[illegible] some of them might be found in China, [illegible] "[illegible] in the [illegible] R P Jesuit of "Delhi, [illegible] of a German Jesuit, written from Pekin "signifying that he had seen such as had preserved Judaism "[illegible] and the Old Testament, and that they would ever "have [illegible] [illegible] provided he would "abstain from swines flesh However, we may still "find here some traces of Judaism The first is, that "as you enter this kingdom after the passage of the "Pire-Penjale mountain, all the inhabitants I saw in the "first villages seemed to me to be Jews, by their [illegible] "and looks, and, in fine, by something particular which "ever distinguishes this nation This notion is no peculiar to me, for our Father Jesuit, and many of our "Europeans had it before me The second is, that I "observed the name of Mousa, which signifies Moses "to be much used among the people of this city, though "Mahometans The third, that they say commonly "that Solomon came into their country, and that it was "he who cut the mountain Baramoule, to give current "to the waters The fourth, that Moses died at Cachemire, and that his tomb is a league from this city [illegible] "the fifth, that they pretend this little and very ancient "edifice, which appears here upon an high mountain "was built by Solomon, for which reason it is still called "Solomon's throne Thus I should not be willing to "deny that some of them have penetrated as far as this "place But in the course of time, these people might "have lost the purity of their law, turned idolaters, and "at last Mahometans "

The writer, who gives this account, is in the right, for it is not to be doubted but that there were some Jews in the dominions of the Great Mogul The miseries they were reduced to in the east, by frequent wars, obliged some of them to follow Arbek, with his other fugitive subjects, and as they go into all places where they can make their fortunes, the prosperity of these princes might, in their turn draw over merchants, [illegible], and physicians

The body of the nation remained in Persia and Media but as their academies had been destroyed, and the sciences could not flourish amidst the confusions of war, their learned men and heads of the captivity, have for a long time disappeared, and even the private persons, dispersed in the provinces and cities [illegible] because they had been ruined It is said they raised their heads under Ishmael Sophi, founder of the family that reigned in Persia This prince, who reckoned himself a descendant from Ali, gathered all those who were devoted to this sect, and all the unfortunate that would follow him, He found but seven or eight thousand men in Caramania, which is the antient Cilicia, [illegible] he threw himself into one of the provinces of Media [illegible] slew Feiokhead, the king of it This first victory obtained at fourteen years of age, put him in a capacity to take Tauris, which some geographers confound with Ecbatana, and make himself master not only of the rest of Media, but also of Persia

Ishmael Sophi died in the year 1520 being thirty-eight years old, and left the empire to his son [illegible], who, being engaged in a long war with Soliman was at last obliged to ruin his own country, that he might not be pursued, nor taken in his retreat The [illegible] forced him, to set a son [illegible] but as this son was [illegible] his father [illegible], his [illegible] caused him to be slain by the [illegible] to execute her design She [illegible] her other brother, out of prison, to place him upon the throne but he ungratefully slew her a little [illegible] His subjects unable to [illegible] him after a reign of two years and established [illegible] son of Thahamasb, who was blind and called Ishmael From this blind prince proceeded the famous Shah Abbas, who undertook to [illegible] which gave occasion to a general massacre a long time after his death The [illegible] is thus related

Shah Abbas's council representing to him that Persia was very thinly peopled, he resolved to grant great privileges to all that would come and settle there Multitudes of people [illegible] from all the neighbouring parts and particularly a great number of Jews, who [illegible], amassed great riches They soon excited the jealousy of the other inhabitants, who brought their complaints against them to the Sophi There was no expedient to part with them without giving umbrage to other strangers, whom the violation of privileges, granted for some years would oblige to retire But it was found in the Alcoran, that this nation was to embrace the Mahometan religion six hundred years after its [illegible] Abbas, who was naturally cruel, would have executed Mahomet's orders and [illegible] all the Jews if the mufti had not stopped him It was resolved, [illegible] to cite the [illegible], or [illegible] of the nation before the Sophi's tribunal, to answer [illegible]

Shah Abbas questioned them particularly about the abolition of the sacrifices, and the other [illegible] the use of which had ceased for some time [illegible] or [illegible] and interrogatories, Abbas [illegible] should [illegible] time for the appearance of their [illegible] [illegible] that till then they should be tolerated, [illegible] he came accordingly, he and his successors would embrace their religion, but if, on the contrary, he did not [illegible], the Jews should either turn Mussulmen, or suffer the [illegible] of their lives, children, and effects. After mature [illegible], they fixed the period at seventy years. Abbas [illegible] for their toleration, caused the agreement to [illegible] signed on both sides, and fixed the [illegible] at [illegible] of gold.

An hundred and [illegible] years elapsed after Abbas's reign, and [illegible] thought of the contract he had made with the Jews. Indeed, the empire of the Persians was disturbed with almost continual wars with the [illegible], who seized upon [illegible], while the [illegible] against the Great [illegible]. [illegible] IV found [illegible] Jews there, who had [illegible] his [illegible] person [illegible] though this prince [illegible] put the Persians [illegible] than [illegible] his enemy by this [illegible] he thought it [illegible].

[illegible] in the Persian court, [illegible] treaty Shah Abbas [illegible] with the Jews was [illegible]. But [illegible] Abbas II who began his reign [illegible], and [illegible] over [illegible] his father's [illegible] the contract [illegible] the Jews and Shah Abbas [illegible] Zabeth [illegible] Jews made [illegible] of the Jews looked upon [illegible] person [illegible] to disengage them from [illegible]. He [illegible] great council to deliberate [illegible], and it was [illegible] unanimously [illegible] delay, [illegible] only to [illegible]. Orders [illegible] given to all the [illegible] of the Sophi's dominions, to [illegible] upon [illegible] and to spare neither age or sex, except [illegible] Mussulmen. This massacre [illegible] his kingdom. It was executed [illegible] in the provinces of Seyra, [illegible], where the Jews [illegible] from the Persians, [illegible] Jews in all [illegible] where they had [illegible] the barbarity, by going into the [illegible] the fathers, and abjuring Judaism.

[illegible] Abbas observed that most of these converts [illegible] and forced, it is not improbable that they [illegible] him from proceeding farther, and induce him [illegible] the free liberty of their religion, [illegible] of the Persians to indulge all strangers. [illegible] accordingly, but they enjoyed it a long time, [illegible] engaged his malice to oblige them to turn Mahometans. He employed his utmost efforts [illegible] neither violence [illegible] to succeed in his design. There was also an [illegible] of the prince, forbidding the exercise of the Jewish religion in his dominions; but, notwithstanding all this, he could not effect it, for, upon a [illegible] observation, it was found, that whatever pretences they made to Mahometism, they practised Judaism still, so that there was a necessity of permitting them to turn back Jews again, since they could not be made good Mussulmen. In the mean time all those that are at Ispahan are poor and miserable, and in small number. They pay annually [illegible] per head to the king, and are obliged to wear a little square piece of stuff, of two or three fingers breadth, sewed to their cap or robe, in the middle of their breast, about two inches above their girdle. It signifies nothing of what this patch is made, provided the colour be different from that of the habit it is sewed to.

It is plain, moreover, from Thevenot, who travelled in this country from the year 1663 to 1665, that is some years before the time of the Jewish massacre, that, upon his going thither, they enjoyed full liberty of conscience, since he adds, that the Persians thought it strange that [illegible] Doulet should have undertaken, some time before, to constrain the Jews to turn Mahometans.

The tribe of Levi [illegible] to have maintained themselves at Sel[illegible], where the Persians have a fine academy, a great number of scholars, and professors to teach philosophy, physic, and divinity. It is certain that there [illegible] more Jews there than at Ispahan, but [illegible] without foundation, they pretend to be of the tribe of Levi, [illegible] Cashan [illegible] and [illegible], [illegible] to trade [illegible] They [illegible] a province, [illegible] at the foot of the [illegible] They [illegible] of Ormus and Bander [illegible] little part [illegible] Indies, where [illegible] they were distinguished [illegible] were born [illegible] Jews, [illegible] descended from the race of [illegible] of Portugal, though [illegible] tolerated them all at [illegible] public worship.

Bagdad, which was [illegible] of the captivity, has [illegible] They do not reckon above [illegible] since its being taken by [illegible] IV [illegible] the Jews maintain [illegible] synagogue, [illegible] but there [illegible] every year [illegible] the Jews [illegible] the Persians, [illegible] remain there [illegible] and the Kurds, [illegible] make a [illegible] among the Mussulmen, and are very powerful [illegible] correspondence with them.

They are said to live more peaceably in Armenia, though their own writers tell us, that [illegible] of Media [illegible] he was [illegible] confidence [illegible] a celebrated physician, [illegible] the [illegible] to them, [illegible] Complaint being made of it to [illegible] the [illegible] This story, [illegible] field. The fathers [illegible] if they live quietly [illegible] owing to the protection of [illegible] between them.

We also find some [illegible] great city of Media [illegible] spent the winter [illegible] has [illegible] trade of [illegible] Samarcand [illegible] but enjoyed [illegible]

[illegible] that if he came accordingly, he and his successors would embrace their religion; but if, on the contrary, he did not appear, the Jews should either turn Mussulmen, or suffer the loss of their lives, children, and effects. After mature deliberation, they fixed the period at seventy years. Abbas [illegible] for their toleration, caused the agreement to be registered and signed on both sides, and taxed [illegible] two millions of gold.

An hundred and fifteen years elapsed after Abbas's reign, [illegible] thought of the contract he had made with [illegible]. Indeed, the empire of the Persians was disturbed with the [illegible] which the [illegible], who seized upon [illegible], while the [illegible] against the Great [illegible] IV. found [illegible] Jews there, who had [illegible] the country [illegible] [illegible], at the same time, [illegible] put the P[illegible] [illegible] his enemy by this [illegible], because he thought it [illegible]

[illegible] Persia [illegible] Shah Abbas [illegible] the Jews was [illegible] who began his [illegible] peace, turning over [illegible], in his father's [illegible] contract between the Jews and Shah Abbas [illegible] [illegible] of the Jews looked upon [illegible] disengage them from [illegible] a great council, to deliberate [illegible] and it was [illegible] without [illegible] only to [illegible] Orders were given to all the [illegible] dominions, to [illegible] or [illegible] This [illegible] was executed [illegible] in the provinces of Se[illegible], [illegible] the Jews were [illegible] years, without [illegible] from the Persians [illegible] not one [illegible] in all [illegible] where they had heaped up [illegible] by going into [illegible] and abjuring Judaism.

[illegible] that most of these converfions were feigned and forced, it is not improbable that they [illegible] from needing farther, and hence [illegible] of their religion [illegible] of the Persians to indulge all strangers [illegible] they enjoyed it a long time, [illegible] [illegible] to oblige [illegible] He employed his utmost efforts [illegible] to succeed in his [illegible] There was also an edict of the prince, forbidding the exercise of the Jewish religion in his dominions but, notwithstanding all this, he could not effect it; for, upon [illegible] observation, it was found, that whatever pretences they made to Mahometism, they practised Judaism still, so that there was a necessity of permitting them to turn Jews again, since they could not be made good Mussulmen. In the mean time all those that are at Ispahan are poor and miserable, and in small number. They pay annually [illegible] to the king, and are obliged to wear [illegible] the square piece of stuff, or two or three fingers breadth, [illegible] to their cap or robe in the middle of their breast, about two inches above their girdle. It signifies nothing of what this patch is made, provided the colour be different from that of the habit it is sewed to.

It appears, moreover, from Thevenot, who travelled in this country from the year 1663 to 1665, that is some years before the time of the Jewish massacre, that, upon his going thither, they enjoyed full liberty of conscience, since he adds, that the Persians thought it strange that [illegible] Father [illegible] Potier should have undertaken, some time before, to constrain the Jews to turn Mahometans.

The tribe of Levi pretend to have maintained themselves at Schiras, where the Persians have a fine academy, a great number of scholars, and professors to teach philosophy, physic, and divinity. It is certain there are more Jews there than at Ispahan, but [illegible] conjecture upon what foundation they pretend to be of the tribe of Levi, [illegible] tribe, [illegible] Chaldea [illegible] and Nehemiah [illegible] to trade [illegible] [illegible] They [illegible] provinces, [illegible] at the foot of the [illegible] They [illegible] of Ormus and Bender [illegible] little part of the [illegible] Indies, [illegible] they were [illegible] were born [illegible] descended from the [illegible] [illegible] though he had [illegible] them [illegible]

Bagdad, which was so long the [illegible] captivity, has [illegible] city. They do not reckon [illegible] [illegible] its being taken by [illegible] IV. [illegible] Jews [illegible] [illegible] prerogative [illegible]

[illegible] [illegible] with the [illegible] make a particular [illegible] the Mussulmen, and [illegible] is powerful [illegible] [illegible] them.

They [illegible] in Armenia, [illegible] Moses, [illegible] Christians [illegible] [illegible] Jews [illegible] [illegible] that [illegible] conf[illegible] [illegible] the [illegible] [illegible] the Christians [illegible] the [illegible] was found [illegible] to them, and [illegible] [illegible] magistrates [illegible] [illegible] [illegible] if they [illegible] [illegible] between them.

[illegible] there [illegible] Christian [illegible] [illegible] [illegible] the [illegible] trade [illegible] [illegible] provinces of [illegible] [illegible] entrusted [illegible]

They are not suffered at Samachia, seated upon the Caspian Sea, a place of great trade, but the Tartars, who bring thither girls and boys, and horses to be sold, tolerate them out of necessity and mingle with them for the sake of commerce. We find some of them as far as at the foot of mount Caucasus, which the Arabians thought encompassed the whole earth, that the sun rose upon one of its points, and set behind the other. It is related, that the prince of Mingrelia pretends to be descended from David. The king of Imaretti asserts the same thing. The ancient kings of Georgia believed it likewise, and the cham of Georgia puts it among his titles, that he issues from this great king by Solomon his son. But these pretensions indeed are supported by no solid proofs. It is true that there is a synagogue at Alcalzike, a little city situated at the foot of mount Caucasus, which the Georgians had built to defend themselves against the irruptions of the enemy, and which the Turks have taken from them.

This is the state of the Jews in all the parts of the east, by which it appears, that the tribes, which were dispersed there, still remain in Persia, Armenia, and Media, where they have their synagogues, and are still numerous, since ... all the trading cities from Balsora and the Indies to Mongolia. But the tribes are too much confounded to be any longer distinguished. They are ignorant, poor, miserable, and reduced to the vilest offices to get their bread. They have so little correspondence with their western brethren, as hardly to know any thing of them. About this time those the famous impostor, named Sabatai Tzevi, who, after deluding a variety of the most distinguished ... in order to delude the public, was at length detected in his iniquitous designs, and received that punishment he justly merited.

CHAP. XVIII.

Sapheta peopled with Jews. An academy there. ... Moses Cordovero. Dominic of Jerusalem. ... of Trani, and Joseph de Karo. Moses Alsech. Samuel Ozeda. A printing press set up at Sapheta. The Jews ... Jerusalem.

It might naturally be expected that Judah should have a greater number of Jews than either Syria or Egypt, but as all its noble streams of milk and honey have been long since dried up, their love for it hath cooled in proportion. Indeed, it is frequently visited by their devotees, who go thither in pilgrimages, as well as the Christians, but few of either sort come to settle in it, since they find it so difficult even to get a tolerable subsistence in that quarter.

Sapheta, or, as the Jews commonly call it Saphet, or rather Tzephath, in Galilee, is the most populous and ... city that the Jews have in this province. They enjoy many privileges there. This city, situated nine miles from Bethsaida, upon a mountain with three tops, is of most difficult access, and therefore it is sheltered from the incursions of the Arabians, who plunder and lay waste the country where they can enter. It is also certain there are ... no where ... kindly treated as at Sapheta, than in all the ... of the Ottoman empire. It has an academy in it, which is grown very famous, and though for many years the oriental Jews have much neglected study and sciences, yet they still keep up professors and doctors here, that are men of repute. Hither they send their children to study, as believing the Hebrew tongue is here taught in its purity, as if this language was annexed to the Holy Land, and that the doctors who teach it, who are often strangers, spoke it better than other Rabbies. But it is the common prejudice, and the academy of Sapheta has been, for some ages, what that of Tiberias was before, to which it has succeeded.

In this academy taught the most famous cabalist that has appeared since Simon Jochaides. He was born at Corduba, which gave him the name of Moses Cordoverus, but quitting Spain, towards the end of the thirteenth century, he was one of the pillars, and perhaps one of the first founders, of this academy.

Dominic of Jerusalem taught in the same academy for some time. He became doctor after he had finished his course of studies, and read lectures upon the Talmud. His profession of physic, he practised at the same time, made him better known than the titles of Rau and judge that were given him. The sultan invited him hither to Constantinople, to be his physician. He lived to the beginning of the last century, and turned Christian; translated the New Testament into Hebrew, and, at the same time, answered some objections of the Rabbies against St Stephen's martyrdom.

Few have done more honour to this academy than Moses of Trani, and Joseph de Karo, who had the conduct of it about the middle of the sixteenth century. The ... was born in a city of Apulia, and taught with so much ... at Sapheta, that the Jews called him the "... the Sinaite of ... the ... that plucks up mountains," because he resolves the difficulties that are raised upon the law. The title of his book maintains, that it is an abstract of the Jewish civil law, in which he goes to the ... head of the laws, and distinguishes between those that proceeded from Moses, and others that had been handed down by oral tradition, and a third sort, which are founded only upon the decisions of the Rabbies.

Joseph de Karo was a Spaniard, and went into Galilee, where he died in 1575. He ... explained the law of the ... tradition with so much ... applause, that he was called the Prince of the Universe.

This academy has not always been governed by foreigners, but had doctors of its own growth. Moses Alsech was born in this city, and distinguished himself in the seventeenth century, not only by the eloquence of his sermons, but the commentaries he composed upon a part of the law. All the titles of his works are metaphorical, one is called the Eye of Moses, another the Rose of Sharon, the third, the Lily of the Valleys. He is much ... for attempting, in his explication of scripture, to produce something new, and, being more devoted to the old interpreters than the modern, has exactly related their sentiments, even when they favoured the Christians.

Samuel Ozeda was another teacher at Sapheta, the place of his birth. He explained Jeremy's Lamentations, and intitled his commentary, the Bread of Tears.

Moses de Nagara was also a Galilean, though some make him a Portuguese, because of the family of Noghera, which was, and still is, in this country. He taught at Sapheta, and has left a commentary upon the Pentateuch, which the Jews greatly esteem. The Jews had a press there ... when they printed the ... which Moses Galant, head of ... academy, composed in 1560.

Julius ... who, after his conversion, became the ... Bartolocci's master, and put him upon the design of his rabbinical library, was born at Sapheta, ... to the degree of doctor or Rabbi, in this academy. He was descended of a ... family, which, after Ferdinand's expulsion, retired into Italy. Pius V having expelled them from thence, it passed into the east, where Julius ... was born. Having gone through his course of studies, he came into the west, and determined at Amsterdam the validity of a will, on which depended some points of importance. The sentence which he gave was approved by ... Rabbies of Germany and ... The Jews of Hamburgh ... him afterwards their judge and ... him a salary, but he went from thence to Poland, where he turned Christian. He afterwards retired to Rome and taught Bartolocci Hebrew, who ... him from the errors imputed to him. He had so strong a memory, that if the Talmud had been lost, he could have restored it.

Of all the cities of Judea there is none where the Jews [illegible] longer and still continue with greater lustre [illegible] than at Saphet. They are more numerous here than in Jerusalem, where they reckon but about [illegible] hundred families, who [illegible] their chief habitations [illegible] mount Sion. Some of them [illegible] employs in the custom-house and others are secretaries to the governor, [illegible] great part is made up of mendicants, who live [illegible]. They [illegible] in quest of them even to the west, [illegible] learning [illegible]. It was upon this [illegible] that Jacob [illegible] journey to Frankfort [illegible] in the year 16[illegible]. His father had retired [illegible] Holy Land [illegible] return, [illegible] to the Sam[illegible] [illegible] Jews of Jerusalem [illegible]

[illegible] sixteen [illegible] Rabbi [illegible] compiled [illegible] contained in the [illegible] had compiled before [illegible] corrected [illegible] but Rabbi [illegible] collected the places of the law that were [illegible] [illegible] could not finish his design, [illegible] as the [illegible] the last [illegible]

[illegible] occasioned the commotion of the [illegible] contemned the doctors [illegible] their doctrines. They found in [illegible] Levi doctors at Jerusalem, things [illegible] violent, and the [illegible] but the jealousy of [illegible] him. His memory was honoured, and his work, which fixed the reading of [illegible] large volumes, was received with wonderful [illegible] [illegible] in the last century, [illegible] adding [illegible] many doctors that were [illegible] of the passages that they might be the easier found. He [illegible] his additions, [illegible] index, the House of [illegible] Juda.

CHAP. XIX.

[illegible] "The Book of [illegible]" [illegible] Egypt [illegible] synagogues [illegible]

ETHIOPIA is one of the places where the Jews have [illegible] least [illegible]. They agree more easily with the Christians of this country, because these latter conform to many of their rites. They eat no swines flesh, and religiously observe the [illegible]. Even the kings [illegible] themselves descendants from the ancient Jews, and have [illegible] holding a cross, with these words, "The Lion of Judah hath prevailed." In the letters King David wrote to Clement VII. he took these titles "I David, beloved of God, the Pillar of Faith, sprung from the tribe of Judah, the Son of David, the Son of Solomon, the Son of the Pillar of Sion, and of the Seed of Jacob." A modern traveller, who was well acquainted with the genius and [illegible] of these remote nations, says that these were not the common titles of the kings of Ethiopia, but that they [illegible] them upon that occasion, to give [illegible] to their embassy to the pope. The conjecture is probable; nevertheless, it is certain, that the kings of [illegible] believe themselves the posterity of the Jews, which [illegible] render them more favourable to this nation.

On the other hand, the Jews in this country have not received the Talmud, nor all that heap of traditions which cloud their religion in other places.

When the Saracens made themselves masters of Ethiopia, the Jews, fearing their persecution, retired and took sanctuary in Abyssinia. They were treated with more humanity than the natives of the country, since an Arabian author affirms, that a general massacre of the inhabitants being resolved upon, they begged, [illegible] of the king, that they might be treated like the People of the Scripture. These scripture people, [illegible] the Arabians still [illegible] Jews. This name is given [illegible] for Mahomet speaking of them, calls them the People of the Book, because of the books of the law and the prophets. The Ethiopians therefore desired the same fate as the Jews, and the king [illegible] their request, on condition that they should give themselves a mark on the face by which they might be known [illegible]

It is not easy to ascertain how early the Jews were settled in Ethiopia, but [illegible] traveller, who [illegible] be found [illegible] Here [illegible] they were [illegible] plain, of [illegible] [illegible] the [illegible] Gideon, king of [illegible] [illegible] and [illegible] during his whole reign.

Oviedo, whom [illegible] had made patriarch of Ethiopia, [illegible] this kingdom [illegible] says, that the Jews [illegible] which they were masters of, [illegible] the kings of Ethiopia could [illegible] it was very difficult to [illegible] of their rocks.

They [illegible] beginning of the [illegible] for[illegible] midable to the kings of the Abyssinians. For indeed, they possessed [illegible] [illegible], having [illegible] called Gi[illegible] whom [illegible] even into the rocks of the Jews [illegible] them out. They were obliged [illegible] they had possessed, [illegible] kingdom. Some retired [illegible] the Kings of the [illegible] the Caffres, where [illegible] in the province of Dem[illegible] the woollen and [illegible] to the Abyssinians [illegible] take to furnish them [illegible] have [illegible] [illegible] Hebrew [illegible] follow the court of the [illegible] Arabia, [illegible] the last century, [illegible] them were at court, [illegible] and live very friendly with them [illegible]

Egypt [illegible] sanctuary. They [illegible] in the [illegible] Ponde[illegible] [illegible] had [illegible] him, and resolved, at the same time to make himself master of his new subjects' estates. The soldiers had already begun to plunder the Jews houses, as being persuaded they might do all things safely at the beginning of the rebellion. Achmed, resolving to enrich himself, taxed this nation two hundred talents. They represented their inability, and only brought fifteen talents to the [illegible]. Achmed, enraged at this refusal, ordered all to be [illegible] prisoners that had not paid the tax. The very moment that Sadis, one of his officers, was executing his orders, news came of a conspiracy against Achmed, who [illegible] been surprized in the bath by a plot, was obliged to fly with [illegible] men with him, that he was pursued [illegible] in [illegible] of Circassians, and that it was impossible [illegible] him to escape his enemies. He was actually [illegible] peace and tranquillity were restored to the city of Cairo. The Jews being delivered made a great [illegible] [illegible] [illegible] the [illegible] [illegible] [illegible] which Achmed had [illegible].

Moses [illegible] [illegible] [illegible] [illegible] [illegible] Egypt [illegible] [illegible] had [illegible] [illegible] [illegible] confiscated [illegible] [illegible] had [illegible] [illegible].

The liberty which they have enjoyed in Egypt [illegible] them [illegible] [illegible] were dispersed [illegible] [illegible] country [illegible] in all the cities [illegible] the [illegible] Grand Cairo. In [illegible] they [illegible] so numerous in this country than when Moses [illegible] [illegible] but their numbers [illegible] [illegible] [illegible] affirm, that they have no settlement except [illegible] Cairo, and the [illegible] of Egypt, and that they [illegible] from being [illegible] places, [illegible] [illegible] [illegible] to go [illegible], they are forced to [illegible] themselves, because the country people [illegible] [illegible] [illegible] them.

There are [illegible] other parts of Africa. It [illegible] [illegible] country that [illegible] Muley Archy, king of Tafilet [illegible] [illegible] to whom he [illegible]. For [illegible] to the castle of D[illegible] Mach[illegible], upon pretence of visiting the governor, he seized the castle, [illegible] to manifest his revolt; but he [illegible] [illegible], had [illegible] not found a Jew [illegible] [illegible] [illegible] by means whereof he [illegible] [illegible] [illegible] the province, was elected [illegible] [illegible] his brother then king of Fez and Morocco. He acknowledged the service the Jew had done him, he granted them the same liberty [illegible] enjoyed [illegible] Ben Amosleeh prince of [illegible] M[illegible] [illegible] brother to the king of Tafilet and [illegible] [illegible] [illegible] to them, for [illegible] [illegible] for Don [illegible] [illegible] Toledo's services during his [illegible] [illegible] [illegible] [illegible] of [illegible] [illegible], but sent him to the courts of [illegible] princes [illegible] with them [illegible] [illegible] [illegible] [illegible] United Provinces [illegible] the year 16[illegible]. [illegible] [illegible] [illegible] [illegible] his father.

The [illegible] likewise been a long time settled at Oran, and [illegible] with some of the most important offices in that city; yet such is their fidelity to the Spaniards, notwithstanding the treatment they had received, that they were the very people that betrayed it to them, if it was not rather their avarice, and the great sums with which Cardinal Ximenes bought their perfidy. However [illegible], they have continued very faithful to them ever since. When the town was in great danger from the neighbours, of being retaken, the Jews exposed [illegible] [illegible] in its defence; and when the garrison threatened to [illegible] another time, for want of pay and provisions, they [illegible] by a timely supply of both. All these services, however, did not prevent their being banished from the place in the year 1669, but on what account it is not easy to determine.

They had likewise been very numerous and flourishing in the province of Suz, which formerly depended on the kingdom of Morocco, but has since been dismembered from it. They had, in the capital of that principality, a very rich and sumptuous synagogue, served by several priests and officers. They had then judges and interpreters of the law, that were maintained at the charge of the people, who lived by traffic and labour. There are great numbers of them in the mountains of Morocco, who are employed in [illegible] [illegible], building, and other laborious employments, to which the inhabitants are averse; but this [illegible] [illegible] [illegible] hinder others from trying their fortunes at court, and raising themselves to eminent posts. [illegible] [illegible] named Pal[illegible], was sent [illegible] [illegible] to [illegible] [illegible] Provinces at the beginning of the [illegible] century, [illegible] [illegible] after their [illegible] having been [illegible] [illegible] [illegible] [illegible] [illegible] [illegible] [illegible] [illegible] [illegible] [illegible] [illegible] [illegible] [illegible] [illegible] his [illegible] [illegible] [illegible].

CHAP. XX.

State of the Jews in Italy [illegible] [illegible] [illegible] [illegible] [illegible] [illegible] [illegible] [illegible] [illegible] [illegible] [illegible] [illegible] [illegible] [illegible] [illegible] [illegible] [illegible] [illegible] [illegible] Rome [illegible] [illegible].

THE Jews have for many ages, preserved their liberty and great privileges in the territories of the grand seignior, not excepting Constantinople itself. Two [illegible] [illegible] [illegible] [illegible], which was called Jewry [illegible] the [illegible] [illegible] [illegible] they had been settled there a long time. The ambassadors of foreign princes reside amongst them. They [illegible] [illegible] thirty synagogues, and [illegible] [illegible] [illegible] [illegible] [illegible] in the [illegible] the neighbouring villages. They are allowed the privilege of selling wine, which is the more considerable, as others [illegible] the preference to [illegible] of the Christians, because the law of Moses containing mixtures it is imagined that the Jews [illegible] [illegible] [illegible] it, and that they [illegible] their wine in its purity.

They are [illegible] [illegible] where the much [illegible] [illegible] [illegible] [illegible]. [illegible] it often happens that poverty makes them turn Mussulman. It has [illegible] that they are required to espouse Christianity first, as a preliminary to [illegible] [illegible] [illegible] is without [illegible] tion. [illegible] [illegible] circumcised, because they [illegible] [illegible] [illegible] the covenant [illegible] [illegible] [illegible] to make them [illegible]. Having enquired into the motives of [illegible] [illegible] they [illegible] [illegible] [illegible] [illegible] words, [illegible] is not lawful, upon [illegible] [illegible] [illegible] without becoming Mussulman [illegible] "Illah Illalla Mehemet Resoul Allah. *There is but one God, and Mahomet [illegible] [illegible].*"

The [illegible] charge the Jews with the murder of [illegible] [illegible] II. [illegible] [illegible] [illegible], his son [illegible] [illegible] of [illegible] excluded [illegible] [illegible] by his father's [illegible] [illegible] Achmed, [illegible] [illegible] [illegible]. He [illegible] [illegible] [illegible] [illegible] not [illegible] [illegible] [illegible] the justness [illegible] [illegible] [illegible], [illegible] [illegible] was obliged to quit Constantinople, [illegible] [illegible] [illegible] [illegible] the place of his birth [illegible] [illegible] [illegible] [illegible] [illegible] Jewish physician [illegible] [illegible] [illegible] [illegible] in the bath, and [illegible].

A [illegible] of this nation called Michi[illegible] [illegible] [illegible] [illegible] [illegible] the conquest of the [illegible] Cyprus, and [illegible] [illegible] [illegible] of this fine kingdom. It [illegible] that this man, being enraged at the refusal of the Venetians to receive a great number of refugees [illegible] who were desirous to leave Portugal and Spain, or else at the punishment he had received for some crimes, retired to Constantinople. [illegible] obtained an admittance to [illegible], and being resolved to take vengeance of his old masters, he extolled to Selim II. the beauty of the island, called, The Country of the Blessed. He also cried up the excellency of the wines, of which Selim II. was a great lover, notwithstanding the law forbade their use. He represented, that the Venetians, who were masters of it, [illegible] in Syria, and obstructed the passage of the caravan to Mecca. At length the unfortunate blowing up of the magazines of powder at Venice contributed to Selim's determination. One day in his cups, he promised [illegible] the crown of Cyprus, as a reward for [illegible] his [illegible] Nicosia, one of [illegible], was taken, Famagusta submitted the next [illegible], and [illegible] was hereby reduced. Michles was [illegible], as was promised; but this nation had [illegible] (which they did [illegible]) [illegible] did none, for [illegible] Venice, [illegible] to negotiate [illegible].

[illegible], a short time after, the [illegible] Constantinople. It was a new [illegible] to [illegible] printed, and they were the [illegible] Alcoran [illegible], which would hereby [illegible] from the Jews to the [illegible]. This [illegible] to the [illegible] nation [illegible] copies of [illegible], which were grown very scarce [illegible] were [illegible], and people [illegible] the [illegible] of the law, [illegible] more easily, and [illegible] had greater assistance to [illegible].

This produced [illegible], and [illegible] heads of synagogues. [illegible], who had [illegible] native [illegible], came thither soon after. He explained the Talmud of Jerusalem, and rendered it more complete, by adding to [illegible]. He published two other works, which he called [illegible], and [illegible] the [illegible], alluding to his name, [illegible] contained [illegible], and the other the explication of [illegible] Rabba upon the Pentateuch.

[illegible], who pretended to be of the race of David, came also to leave his father, and his birth-place, Lisbon, [illegible] at Constantinople. But as most of the Jewish physicians are also doctors, [illegible] the [illegible]. He was made head of the synagogue, and [illegible] to reconcile the Caraites and the [illegible]. He says that the Caraites desired [illegible], and [illegible] them over to the synagogue; but [illegible] the Rabbanists were too [illegible], that they thought the [illegible], [illegible] the reconciliation was not effected, and the [illegible] the advantage enjoyed at Constantinople, of printing books, [illegible] published some of their works, which nevertheless are very scarce.

The [illegible] we shall mention is Mardochai. He was son of Eliezer, and took the title of Constantinopolitan, though he [illegible] commonly resided at Adrianople. He explained the grammar which Aben Ezra published, with the title of Jesod Mora, the Foundation of Fear.

There are some cities of Greece where the Jews have not the privilege to settle themselves, such is the city of [illegible]. The inhabitants, who are at present Turks and Greeks, hate the Jews so much, that they will not suffer them in their territories. They [illegible] the same usage at Athens, where they settled in St. Paul's time. Perhaps, as the number of Christians is there greater than that of Turks, who are more inclined to toleration, the Christians have obtained an order that excludes the Jews from this city.

But if they are denied access in some places, there are many others where they have still considerable establishments. They have four synagogues at Patras, and their own judges here, which they chuse from among themselves. They have also their particular burying place upon a neighbouring mountain, which looks like a great city, because it consists of several little stone houses, in which each family is buried, and a marble stone, on which the name of the family the tomb belongs to is engraved, serves as a door. [illegible] there are but few [illegible] in this city, the Jews, which are not above a fourth [illegible], amount only to about a thousand persons. [illegible] Lepanto, Livadia, Corinth, and other cities where they live by commerce. But Greece is so depopulated by the revolutions it has undergone, by the [illegible] it pass, and still more by the oppressions of the [illegible], that their condition is become very miserable.

[illegible], where we find [illegible] they [illegible] as well [illegible] Rabbies, [illegible] their children from Constantinople to be taught in Hebrew [illegible].

[illegible] have continued and [illegible] Cairo [illegible] Thin at Christ's [illegible] the [illegible] confounded [illegible] [illegible] the [illegible] thousand [illegible] considerable at Prodi [illegible] Cyprus [illegible] of the Ottoman [illegible] before the taking of Constantinople, [illegible] but by the [illegible] thousand [illegible], they are not permitted to [illegible], [illegible] and [illegible] honour of [illegible] of [illegible] this city.

The Jews have [illegible] Rhodes. They had formerly [illegible] near the [illegible] "The [illegible] Quarter of the Jews," and [illegible] Mahomet II. besieged [illegible] St. Stephen's [illegible] a [illegible] of his [illegible] violent assault, and the [illegible] were already [illegible] to [illegible], but he [illegible] the [illegible], though he [illegible] and the [illegible], the grand master, d'Aubusson, [illegible] resolved to expel all the [illegible] but [illegible].

[illegible] come, [illegible] was [illegible] all [illegible] canonists, [illegible] Jews [illegible] parents, [illegible] power of their [illegible] be baptized [illegible] allowed to [illegible] were prohibited [illegible] this preference [illegible] be baptized, [illegible].

Rhodes, [illegible] Jews settled [illegible]

[illegible]

They are more numerous at Smyrna, where they reckon six thousand of their nation, and they have many synagogues. In fine, there are few cities or great towns in the Ottoman empire but have some Jews. They suffer much by the avarice of the sultan's officers, but this in short is common to them with most of the subjects of this great and extensive empire.

CHAP. XXI.

[illegible] pope John XXIII. [illegible] Decree of the [illegible] [illegible] Paul [illegible] [illegible] Gedaliah [illegible] [illegible] Jews [illegible] Rome [illegible] XI [illegible] to the Jews [illegible] promote [illegible] Synagogues [illegible]

THE Jewish writers complain that they had a terrible [illegible] in John XXIII. and affirm, that this pope, [illegible] general, and to head an army, [illegible] was their violent persecutor. He tried every course to force them to turn Christians, [illegible] not content [illegible] them in his own dominions, [illegible] wrote to the [illegible] Spain, who was eager in the [illegible] [illegible] acting in conjunction with him [illegible] made the greatest number of proselytes, and this [illegible] forced fifteen thousand [illegible] abandon their religion. Part of the rest that [illegible] perished by the fire, and part by other punishments to which they were sentenced, while others, that fled, fell [illegible] murdered them. A very few [illegible] of them [illegible] their liberty, and lives by [illegible] they [illegible] the pleasure of hearing that the [illegible] reduced to a more desperate state than their [illegible]

[illegible] He [illegible] the Jews of his territories [illegible] their religion, and granted them his protection. He [illegible] the inquisitors, who continued to [illegible] He wrote likewise in his turn [illegible] the forcing of [illegible] and [illegible] the voluntary converts [illegible] into offices, which the inhabitants [illegible] from them by a solemn oath.

They had not enjoyed the fruits of that pontiff's patronage [illegible] before a new [illegible] [illegible] had been prevailed upon to [illegible] [illegible] been murdered by the [illegible] the city of Trent in a most cruel manner. [illegible] full view in that city [illegible] a pair of pincers, [illegible] needles, with which they [illegible] out his blood, and two silver [illegible] which they had drank [illegible] The whole tragical story [illegible] full length [illegible] one of the [illegible] to the [illegible]

[illegible] drew great calamities upon the Jews, [illegible] in the bishoprick of Trent where they pretend [illegible] the crime was committed, but also in all the territories of the republic of Venice. The preachers inflamed the people, who, wrought on by the notion of a false miracle, plundered and murdered all the Jews they met with. So great was the disorder, that the doge and senate were obliged to suppress it, and order the magistrates of Padua to treat the Jews like their other subjects, and prevent their being abused, because the report spread at [illegible] to them appeared a falsehood, contrived by art, [illegible] the senate would not examine into. They were [illegible] out of the city of Trent, where the [illegible] less [illegible] But some time after they obtained the liberty of tarrying three days, because they carried on a considerable commerce. We are told that, some time after, the three days liberty were reduced to three hours, as a punishment for their obstinate defence of [illegible] against the Christians, [illegible] the last war with the Turk.

[illegible] received [illegible] [illegible] Spain by [illegible] Catholic, and becoming [illegible] those [illegible] Rome were ill-treated by their other brethren, who would have suffered them to die with hunger, if he had not succoured them.

In effect that pontiff, though a Spaniard by birth, and head of the church, [illegible] the Jews, who had been long settled in Rome, left the exiles in misery, without attempting to [illegible] them, threatened to expel them, unless they altered their conduct, and gave their [illegible] brethren [illegible] of settling in the ecclesiastical [illegible] He thought it expedient to profit by Ferdinand's edict, and to enlarge his revenues at the cost of others. There have been many who would not persecute the Jews, nor yet suffer their numbers to multiply in their [illegible] by the conjunction of strangers. But the pope [illegible] to the reasons dictated by [illegible] but would have the [illegible] comers have the same privileges at Rome with the old inhabitants.

Amongst those whom that pontiff's kindness had invited to Rome, was the [illegible] R. Jochanan, a [illegible] who came from Constantinople, and was taken into the [illegible] of [illegible] count of Mirandola, as his preceptor. This prince, for many years, had been fond of the [illegible] of the Rabbies, and even of their [illegible] He is [illegible] to have [illegible] that those who read the Hebrew books [illegible] the [illegible] in their hand [illegible] to the Greeks, [illegible] that [illegible] were found among the [illegible] He [illegible] had [illegible] certain cabalistical books [illegible] which he had purchased at a great price, and that Sixtus IV. had ordered them to be translated into [illegible]

[illegible] part of the [illegible] and Portugal [illegible] to [illegible] [illegible] that the [illegible] He [illegible] the truth of the old [illegible] [illegible] there was no [illegible] [illegible] his wounds, and led them [illegible] [illegible] His conduct was authorized [illegible] who would not suffer the Jews [illegible] [illegible] The truth is, this [illegible] the [illegible] he had discovered [illegible] it.

This severity, however, did not discourage one Ricci, a converted Jew, from dedicating to that monarch his [illegible] at he stiled [illegible] He was [illegible] in Germany, and produced [illegible] and explications of some points in theology; but it will be apparent to those who read them, that they [illegible] not [illegible] [illegible] which some learned men have [illegible] on the contrary, that they are far beneath [illegible] found in [illegible] divines.

The Jews were become so powerful under the pontificate of Paul III as to provoke the rage of cardinal Sadolet. He was bishop of Carpentras, in the diocese of Avignon, where the Jews had ever been tolerated, since Joan, queen of Sicily, made a present of this city to the pope. They had then synagogues there, as they have at this day, though the city is in the midst of France, from whence they were banished. The prelate, not able to bear it, wrote to cardinal Farnese representing, that the pope had never been such a benefactor to the Christians as he was to the Jews [illegible] he had granted them titles, new [illegible]ges [illegible], which [illegible] them haughty and [illegible] [illegible] the Christians were but like sheep [illegible] they were driven from their [illegible] from the cities, where they [illegible] that it was unaccountable, how a [illegible] the [illegible] and grant, [illegible] protection, and such singular [illegible], who seemed more worthy of his in[illegible]. He [illegible], that the true method for a man [illegible] his [illegible], and to rise to ecclesiastical dignities, was to countenance [illegible]. He laid open the real source of this protection, and pointed out that this favour proceeded from the pope's treasurers and the intendants of his finances, to whom the Jews were necessary men. However, some regard was paid to the cardinal's remonstrances, and, in this case, they did what is commonly done at Rome, when any abuse is discovered that tends to pecuniary purposes, they palliate it, and [illegible] its too manifest and glaring enormity.

Some time after Julius III being persuaded the allegorical interpretations of the Gemara were dangerous, caused the Talmud to be burnt, so that all the books of the Gemara, which were in Italy, according to the Jewish writers, were destroyed.

It was in this pontificate that Joseph Tzarphati, a famous Rabbi, who had taught a long time at Rome, embraced Christianity. He [illegible] in France, but retired into Italy, where he [illegible] the Talmud in the synagogue and the [illegible] of [illegible], and, to do more honour to pope Julius, took the name of Monte.

[illegible] at this time, other famous Jews [illegible] Rome. Elias, the Levite, was born at Padua, but [illegible] all, when this city was taken, he was received [illegible], whom he taught Hebrew. Being an [illegible], when the constable [illegible] Rome. He retired to Venice, and [illegible], but being unaccustomed to the [illegible] of that country, he returned to Italy, where he died [illegible] of [illegible]. He was suspected to have great [illegible] for Christianity, and this suspicion was a ground [illegible] for his nation to hate him, but he did not abjure the faith of his ancestors, though some have believed and [illegible].

[illegible] woman at Rome, called Deborah, who then began to distinguish herself by her poems and other works. She died in the beginning of the seventeenth century.

Paul IV declared himself an enemy to this nation, and the first year of his pontificate issued two bulls, of which the Jewish writers vehemently complain. By the first he ordered each synagogue in his territories to pay ten ducats annually for the instruction of the catechumens, who should abjure Judaism, and by the second, which was more rigorous, obliged the men to wear a yellow hat, and the women a veil of the same colour. He compelled them all to live in the same quarter of the city, the gates whereof were to be shut at night. They were deprived of all societies, offices, or professions among the Christians, without excepting physic and merchandize, for their commerce was confined to small wares, and they were forbid having more than one synagogue in each city. They were commanded to sell all their lands within six months, a circumstance which [illegible] lowered the price of them, that they could not get the [illegible]th part of their value.

The cardinal Charles de Boromes, bishop of Milan, not only enacted several canons against them in the first council he held in that metropolis, much of the same kind with those of Paul IV before mentioned, but desired all the Christian princes to do the same, and all this to promote, as much as possible, their conversion. But that edict shews, at the same time, they were become so numerous and powerful, that there was some reason to fear them, not only at Milan, but in other places of Italy, unless they were confined to their own separate quarters and [illegible], as much as possible from all kind of conversation with the Christians.

[illegible] V was still severer towards the Jews [illegible] the Constitution he published against them [illegible] sufficient to render them odious to all the world, for he [illegible] them of [illegible] the Christians, of ruining the ecclesiastical state by the exorbitant usuries they drew from it, of sheltering robbers and thereby promoting theft, together with a train of various other vices. They were also charged with dealing in magic, and foretelling things to come, and for these reasons were expelled all the cities of the ecclesiastical state, except Rome and Ancona.

Sextus V [illegible] more [illegible] towards them, and [illegible] owned that the advantage he [illegible] from them was the chief motive of his [illegible], called Meir Magin, of French origin, who resided at Venice, came to Rome, and being a man of [illegible], was very agreeable to the pope. He dedicated a book to him and wrote verses in his commendation, which [illegible]. He at length [illegible] of a silk manufacture, [illegible] secret for [illegible]. The pope granted him several privileges [illegible] and bulls of his predecessors, [illegible] been made with an [illegible] of [illegible] himself, by [illegible] period of [illegible], was [illegible] Jew [illegible] which raised the rest.

Clement VIII shewed them but little [illegible] the [illegible] of Pius V who banished them [illegible] the ecclesiastical state. Two things are observable [illegible], one, that he added the city of Avignon to those of Ancona and Rome, where they still preserve their liberty of conscience, the other, that this pope founded the privilege of tolerating them at Rome upon this reason, that the Jews ought not to be removed far from Rome, that they might be always at hand to be converted, as if conversions were more frequent at Rome than other places. According to this principle he should have given liberty of conscience to all heretics at Rome, and have filled the city with them, that they might always be at hand to be converted.

This nation had then other considerable settlements in the cities of Italy, but one of the most noted was that of Venice. That republic received them into all its territories, and gave them very hospitable encouragement [illegible] is found to have in part deserved this [illegible] by their fidelity, and the great services they had rendered [illegible] with the Turks, and particularly at the [illegible] of C[illegible]. Here it was that Daniel Bomberg printed their Hebrew Bible the [illegible] time. This printer came from Antwerp to Venice, and chiefly dealt in Hebrew books [illegible] them the more correct, he employed [illegible] Jews, whom he kept in pay, to the number of [illegible] Felix Pratensis had the care of the edition of the [illegible] the Chaldee paraphrases and the commentaries [illegible] Rabbies, which he dedicated to pope Leo [illegible] but [illegible] post of the [illegible].

Bomberg [illegible] Hebrew grammar [illegible] compiled [illegible] accordingly, [illegible] finished [illegible] a learned Jew [illegible] at Venice [illegible], he printed a great number of other works of the Jewish Rabbies, for which his memory is still dear to the learned world, especially to the Jews.

It was to Venice that David (the son of Isaac) de Pomis retired, who, by a way of acknowledgment, wrote a treatise to prove, that the laws of that republic are of divine original. This learned Rabbi asserted, that his family descended from one of the heads of the captives whom Titus carried from Jerusalem to Rome. He was a prodigy of learning at his tenderest years. His father lived at Spoleto, but the Germans having pillaged Rome, he who feared of being ruined by the like fate, and therefore carried off all his effects, and went to seek a retreat some where else. He fell into the misfortune he sought to avoid, for [illegible] troops meeting the mules that carried his treasure, seized it, and reduced him to extreme poverty. He [illegible] [illegible], where his son, who was born in the year [illegible], intending, applied himself to study. The [illegible] [illegible] of [illegible], who lived in the beginning of the [illegible] century, and who had then composed an Hebrew Dictionary, [illegible] fell into his hands. He [illegible] [illegible] it, but resolved to make another larger, in which [illegible] the terms that the Rabbies often make use of, though they are not Hebrew. He inserted into his work all that was valuable from those of Rabbi Nathan, Elias the Levite, and Kimchi's roots. In it we find the Hebrew words, and the foreign terms, with the Latin and Italian.

The republic maintained its rights in the war with the Uscoques. These robbers often pillaged the merchants of this nation, and the house of Austria pretended to dispute with the Venetians their privilege to protect those [illegible] they were not Christians. But no regard was had to a pretension that deprived sovereigns of the right of defending their subjects, and the Jew, Henriquez, was chosen by the senate to go into Dalmatia, to endeavour to accommodate this affair, which caused an unhappy war.

R. Sichma, since named Simon Luzati, at the same time published here his Socrates, in which he shews that the greatest genius's are weak and wandering when they are guided by prejudice. He composed another treatise concerning the state of the nation. It was at Venice also that Samuel Nachmias lived, though he was of a Thessalonian family. Here he abjured Judaism, with David, his son, and part of his family, which took the name of Morosini. To shew that this conversion was sincere, he published an Italian treatise intitled Via della Fide, or the Way to the Faith, in which he explains the ceremonies of his nation, and shews the usefulness of them, proves that the six hundred and thirteen precepts, which they distinguish in the law, are observed by nobody, and confutes all the Jewish superstitions and sects. He died in the year 16[illegible], at Rome, whither he retired. Mardochai Korkos who taught in the year 1672, performed a task that was [illegible] [illegible] and odious to the doctors of his nation, for he composed a treatise against the cabala, and their prejudices for that science are so great, that all seem to strike the foundation of their religion who attack it, and therefore the doctors have had the precaution not to print it.

At the same time that Bomberg had his press at Venice, some Jews, from Spire, in Germany, were employed in the same [illegible] at Soncino, a small town [illegible] [illegible] of Milan, near the river Oglio, where they began to print Hebrew books about the end of the fifteenth century. [illegible] quitted the name of their family to take that of the city of Soncino. Their principal business was to print Hebrew books, and as they were almost the first that did this service to the nation, they grew famous and considerable. By this means they rescued from oblivion a great number of rabbinical writings, which would have been buried in the dust, and were now easily read. The doctors, that hereby found it much easier to read the works of their predecessors, gave great encomiums to the Soncinati,

which a long time continued in this post, and from thence dispersed themselves into other cities of Italy. There have been also very famous doctors of this name, and R. Asher was of this family.

There was also a synagogue at Imola, where the famous Gedaliah was born, who was of Portuguese descent. [illegible] boasted to be of the family of the Jechia, and maintained that his family, proceeding in a right line from Jesse, father of David, had maintained itself in Portugal, where Athanaric, son to the great Athanaric, first of the name, had given three cities in fief to one of his grandfathers, and made him intendant of his household, and his [illegible] kingdom.

This Rabbi had composed [illegible] volumes, but the principal, and almost the only one, which was printed, is the Chain of the Cabala, or [illegible] [illegible]. He wrote it at Imola, in the year 1549. And though the author [illegible] a great many things from a work like his own, and is very frequently mistaken in chronology, yet he has been serviceable to [illegible], in his rabbinical bibliotheque, [illegible] [illegible], and it is one of the most necessary books to those that are fond of the [illegible] of tradition, and the [illegible] [illegible] of the doctors.

At Modena was another synagogue, with R. Samuel [illegible] the head of it, who, in the year 1550, published the judgments of Solomon. We have already observed what pompous titles these writers give their books. This is a course of canon law. Solomon is renowned for the wisdom and equity of his judgments, and the author fears not to give the same idea of himself and his decisions, which are [illegible] [illegible] much esteemed.

There was an academy at Padua, which also brought up a considerable number of doctors. R. Meir was its president. Joseph of Padua, who took the name of his native place, likewise taught there. Isaac Phen published there, at the same time, his Way of Faith, which acquired him great reputation. They had their great preacher Menachem Rabna, whose sermons upon the four seasons of the year have been since printed by his son. He was living in the beginning of the last century. The Jews were here admitted doctors of physic, and they might afterwards practise in the territories of the republic. They have moreover three synagogues, eight hundred persons of their nation, and a considerable ghetto. This is the name in Italy they give the streets and quarters of the Jews, in which they are shut up at night.

The synagogue and academy of Mantua, have been famous for a long time. Two Rabbies, Messer Leone di Mantua and Kolon, who governed it at the end of the fifteenth century, were divided. Jealousy perhaps was the true cause of their enmity, but they concealed this shameful passion under the cloak of religion, and [illegible] [illegible] [illegible] about faith. Not only the Jews of Mantua, [illegible] [illegible] the Christians engaged so far in this dispute, as to come to blows. Lewis Gonzaga, who was then Marquis of Mantua, tried in vain all ways to reconcile them; but at length he took the resolution which is always most effectual, that is, [illegible] the leaders of the faction, and by their exile, restore tranquillity to synagogue and academy.

[illegible] doctors succeeded the expelled, and Moses [illegible], [illegible] Moses the Old, made a great figure in the following century. Alphes whom we have already mentioned [illegible] a course of law so conformable to the Talmud, that sometimes one is mistaken for the other [illegible] commentaries instead of censuring several things he had inserted in his book, approved them, or endeavoured to soften them by a favourable interpretation. But Moses the Old setting himself above Alphes and his commentators, published at Mantua his corrections upon their works, which did him great honour.

The Jews were settled at Pesaro, a very antient little city mentioned by Catullus. It belongs at present to the church, and is situate in the dutchy of Urbino, upon the Adriatic sea. Here was born R. Jechiel, who, having some time heard the sermons of an inquisitor at Florence, went to Rome to desire leave to abjure Judaism. Gregory XIII was present at the speech he made to a numerous assembly, and received him, as he descended from the chair, with the highest marks of satisfaction. The pope baptized him some days after. He became a preacher, and some of his Italian sermons have been printed, which he preached at Florence.

They have, generally speaking, upheld themselves in most cities of Italy, and have had many learned Rabbies during the foregoing century, the most celebrated among whom were the following.

R. Juda Arie, commonly known by the name of Leo de Modena, the place of his nativity, is that of Leo (Arie) answered to his Hebrew name of Arie. He was a very learned man, and hath given the world a treatise on the ceremonies of the Jews, which is highly esteemed in the world of all nations. His book, entitled, "The Mouth of the Lion," is another useful work, wherein he hath judiciously collected and explained all the words used by the Rabbins, which are neither quite Hebrew nor altogether Chaldee, and hath endeavoured to fix the pronunciation of them so as to be understood by Jews of all nations. He was for a considerable time chief of the synagogue, and reckoned a good poet both in Hebrew and Italian. He wrote several other treatises, and formed the design of translating the Old Testament into Italian, but was forbidden to proceed by the inquisitors, instead of which, therefore, he wrote his Lexicon. He died at Venice in the year 16[illegible], at the age of almost 80 years.

Here flourished, in the year 1574, Mordochai Korkos, who had a much better judgment than most doctors of his nation; instead of going into the tenets of the cabala, he endeavoured to make the Jews dislike it. He even had the courage to write against the famous Sephirots, which [illegible] his good taste for theology.

Jacob Zaphalon taught at Ferrara. He was born at Rome in 1630, and had also taken his degree of doctor of physic in the university of this city, but bent his studies to the law, and became one of the principal doctors of the last century. Being rendered uneasy in his native country, he forsook it and retired to Ferrara, where he governed the synagogue of that place. This situation was the more convenient to him, because he came near Venice, where he printed several books. He published a collection of devout thoughts, to which he prefixed several prayers. He wrote other books. The title of one is taken from the prophet Micah, "Thou wilt perform the Truth to Jacob." The second is, "The Light of the Fathers." A third, which turns upon physic, is called "The Tree of Life," in which he treats of fevers, poisons, remedies, and diseases peculiar to each part of the human body.

Judas Ariel was eminent also for his preaching in the last century. His reputation was so great, that the Christians went out of curiosity to hear him. He published a book, called, "The Thrones of the House of David." He died at Ferrara in the year 1677.

Jehoshuah Menahem was president of the academy at Rome at the end of the last century, and there was another doctor at the same time called Jacob Danilo [illegible] Pont[illegible]. He came of a distinguished family of his nation at Rome, and was considered as one of the best qualified masters to instruct youth. The R. Tribotti appeared also in the middle of the same century. In a tract which he published, he maintained some propositions that occasioned the doctors of Italy to oppose him. The synagogue and academy of Rome, to prevent the multiplication of books, and the course of the division pronounced upon all these questions, declared for Tribotti, and the other doctors submitting to its decision, peace was restored.

They reckon twelve or fifteen thousand Jews in Rome, who are governed by triumvirs, whom they call Memmonim. These three determine all the differences that arise betwixt man and man, and takes care to preserve the privileges the popes have granted them. They are changed every year, in order to prevent the abuse of their authority. The Jews lived so familiarly with the Christians, that the latter made no scruple to go frequently to their synagogues, and they did it in such numbers, that Innocent XI was obliged to threaten them with excommunication and a fine of twenty-five crowns upon all who entered them. They have an academy here, and their professors also, among whom was the famous Joseph Kimki. They have nine synagogues, and it seems they preserve a kind of superiority over [illegible] of those in Italy, since they are consulted in doubtful cases, and their determinations regularly regarded.

Innocent XI gave them, some years [illegible], a [illegible] token of his protection. This pontiff, who censured the king of France for persecuting his Protestant subjects, to oblige them to change their religion, [illegible] the Venetians to give liberty to some Jews whom they [illegible]. Morosini, general of this republic, returning [illegible] from the Morea, brought with him from thence several Christians and Jews he had found under the [illegible] of the grand seignior. The first were set at liberty, but the latter kept in slavery. The pope resented the injustice that was done them, since they offered to dwell in the territories of the republic, where they are more at full liberty of conscience. They have their cemetery at Venice, which has produced some epitaphs. They have also their synagogues, and reckon near two thousand persons of their nation in this city. But yet they could not obtain their desire, and their fate would have been miserable if the pope, whose protection they implored, had not interposed in their behalf. Not satisfied with writing to Venice, he appointed a congregation at Rome to take cognizance of this affair, and to regulate it; whereupon the republic granted what was demanded, and the Jews were set at liberty.

This pontiff also strove much to promote their conversion. Gregory XIII had ordered a sermon to be preached weekly to instruct them. An ingenious man was to be chosen for the purpose, who was to prove that the [illegible] of the gospel had abolished the Jewish [illegible], and to enlarge upon the long misery this nation had suffered for a prodigious course of years. He obliged one-third of the Jews of Rome to be present at this [illegible] sermon, and the children who had reached [illegible] were registered among the auditors. He built [illegible] for the maintenance of the new converts, and hospitals for the sick. But, after all, the greater part [illegible] in unbelief, and [illegible] But [illegible] expence to forward the work, acknowledged [illegible] his death, that such conversions were only [illegible] insignificant.

We have now brought the history of the Jews in Italy to the end of the seventeenth century. Those who desire a more exact knowledge of the number and present state of their synagogues, may consult the tax of these in the ecclesiastical state. They are [illegible] at Rome and nineteen in Campania, [illegible] in the marquisate of Ancona, [illegible] in the patrimony of St. Peter, [illegible] Bologna, and thirteen in Romandiola. Their [illegible] somewhat above seven hundred crowns, which they [illegible] every year.

We may further observe the will of Zachary a [illegible], who died at Florence towards the end of the [illegible]. This merchant had composed a kind of concordance [illegible] the commentators of the Talmud. When he died [illegible] trusted his work with the doctors at [illegible], and bequeathed his library to the school [illegible] twenty-four thousand piasters to his [illegible] part to be divided among the [illegible] Venice, and the [illegible] piasters to be distributed in portions for [illegible] or the synagogues of Rome [illegible] (which was his birth-place,) Peſaro, Ceſino, Venice, Padua, Verona, Rovigo, Florence, Sienna, Piſa, Leghorn, Mantua, Modena, and Reggio This enumeration ſhews there is ſtill a conſiderable number of ſynagogues in that part of the world, where the church of Rome reigns with the greateſt authority

CHAP XXII

History of the Jews in Germany, *from the fifteenth to the ſixteenth century*

Jews in Germany oppreſſed Hebrew concordances Creation of doctors, and origin of the title Ordinance of the council of Baſil against the Jews Baniſhed Bavaria [illegible] Mecklenburgh Baniſhed Nuremberg and Cologne [illegible] Capnio's book againſt them Simeon a [illegible] Pfefferkorn's advice against the Jews [illegible] Continuation of the diſpute Pfefferkorn [illegible] State of the Jews under [illegible] Martin Luther [illegible] The [illegible] more many and learned R [illegible]'s [illegible] Other Jewiſh tracts [illegible] a canon of [illegible] Jewiſh ſ[illegible] Baniſhed from Mer[illegible] Protected by Ferdinand and a Solomon L[illegible] Simeon de Gunzbourg a good geometrician Other learned Rabbies Condition of the Jews in Bohemia Expelled [illegible] [illegible] Bohemia Jews in Hungary and Moravia Settled in the territories of Brunſwick

THE fifteenth century began unhappily in Germany for the jewiſh nation A great many were ſettled in Thuringia and Miſnia But the landgraves made them pay dear for their quiet and liberty Whether it was that neceſſity required it, or they were driven to it by avarice, which prevails in the minds of princes as well as private perſons but they often demanded conſiderable ſums, and it had not been long perhaps, that they had paid one [illegible], when a new one was demanded of them and, upon their refuſing to pay it, they were all committed to [illegible] and [illegible] ſet at liberty till they paid a conſiderable ranſom

[illegible] Moulin, at that time made himſelf famous by the great number of his diſciples as well as by his judicious anſwers to the queſtions that were propoſed to him A Hebrew concordance was compoſed by Nathan, at the beginning of the fifteenth century Reuchlin printed it, becauſe he found it very uſeful There have been [illegible] [illegible] it ſince, but the beſt of all is the Roman [illegible] the work of a monk, called Marius Calaſio, for he not only added the concordance of Eſther and Daniel, which were wanting, but we find illuſtrations upon the Chaldee notes, and upon all that relates to the deſcription of the places mentioned in holy writ

There was at that time a diſpute among the Rabbies of Germany about letters of divorce Young people were frequently deſirous of procuring them, and as they were not perfectly acquainted with the antient rites, were guilty of errors In order to prevent this abuſe, it was enacted that none but the received doctors ſhould be privileged to draw up theſe letters, and that all the reſt ſhould be void and null, and it is ſaid that this was the origin of the title of doctor, which Moulin aſſumed But it was probably pride which gave birth to this new degree of honour The Chriſtians preſented the doctors cap with great pomp in their univerſities, and to imitate them, the Jews took this title, and began to confer it with ſome ceremony, whilſt the antique one of Rabbies was deſpiſed The title don was only uſed in Spain, but the doctors were diſtinguiſhed amongſt all the Chriſtians Abravanel, who ſaw that the Germans ordained their diſciples by ſaying, "Morenu," *(you are our doctor,)* was ſurpriſed at this cuſtom, but he found afterwards, that the ſame thing was done in Italy, where this title ſoon came into vogue

The council of Baſil, which extended its juriſdiction far and near, thought it ought not to neglect the Jews who were numerous in this city and in Germany It commanded by a decree, the prelates to chuſe in all places where there were Jews, ſome perſons ſkilled in the languages to preach to them The prelates were obliged to ſend all the Jews of their dioceſes to this ſermon, and heavy puniſhments were decreed againſt thoſe who concealed them or hindered them from receiving inſtruction People at the ſame time were forbid to have any commerce with them at table, or in civil ſociety It was not allowed to have ſervants, nurſes, phyſicians, or farmers of that nation, nor to let them houſes near churches, or in the bodies of cities, and to diſcover them the more eaſily, they were obliged to wear a different habit from the Chriſtians The council alſo condemned thoſe who pledged church books, utenſils, and ornaments, to loſe their money

Regulations were made about thoſe who were converted The new converts by baptiſm obtained the privilege of enjoying their eſtates, except what they had acquired by uſuries, for they obliged them to reſtore the exceſſive intereſts, if the perſons were living, and in caſe of death, as the church was impropriatreſs of the confiſcation of theſe goods, ſhe made a preſent of them to the new converts

The council declared farther, by an edict, the new converts capable of all offices in cities where they were baptiſed It could not, indeed, be aſſured of the ſincerity of thoſe converſions, and it appears that it doubted of them, for it forbad that the new converts ſhould have frequent intercourſe together, as finding, by experience, that they corrupted one another, and weakened their faith They were forbid alſo burying their dead after the Jewiſh way, keeping the ſabbath, and other rites of that nation, which is a ſufficient proof that they had not really renounced them The pariſh-prieſts were ordered to prevent the miſchief, by procuring them good [illegible] among the Chriſtians As the council gave great privileges to new converts, it appointed likewiſe terrible puniſhments for hypocrites for it authorized the prieſts to keep a ſtrict eye over their conduct, to impeach them to the inquiſitors, and to call in the ſecular arm to puniſh them with greater rigour, declaring, that all who protected theſe diſſemblers ſhould be treated as abettors of hereſies, and carrying its authority farther, it annulled all the privileges which might have been given to the Jews, either by popes or emperors The council, upon the whole, was right in ordering the Jews to be inſtructed, and the new converts to be maintained by contribution, but it exceeded the bounds of its power in ſetting itſelf above emperors, and pretending to aboliſh their laws

The decrees of the council of Baſil cauſed no great alteration in Germany It is true Lewis X duke of Bavaria, expelled the Jews out of his dominions, but it was twenty years after and the council laid not this injunction upon ſovereigns, ſo that this prince conſulted not his own intereſts It was vain to repreſent to him that the baniſhment of ſo many opulent people would leſſen his revenues, he ordered them to depart the ſame day and the very ſame hour, from forty cities, and all the towns in his territories he confiſcated their eſtates, and built priſons and other public edifices, in the places which had belonged to them

The princes of Mecklenburgh alſo made a dreadful execution of them in their capital city Thirty Jews were condemned to the fire One of them threw himſelf into the river, to avoid the barbarity of this puniſhment, and, as the women and children were included in this execution, a mother, driven to deſpair, killed, with her own hand, two of her daughters, and a third would have undergone the ſame fate, if the Chriſtians had not taken [illegible] away Two years after they were accuſed, in [illegible] of murdering a Chriſtian, and [illegible] his

tion. They were put to the rack, to force them to confess that they were not only guilty of the crime, but that their nation partook in it.

About five years after the Jews of [illegible] here, who were both numerous and wealthy, were all banished [illegible] the city, and settled in a small town in its neighbourhood, where they built a Synagogue. The citizens had several reasons to their charge, in order to justify the severity of their expulsion; but the true motive seems to have been their wealth, which made them insolent, their numbers, which made them formidable, and their usuries, which [illegible] to debauch their youth, and rendered them at length universally odious.

At the beginning of the sixteenth century they were expelled out of the diocese of Cologne, and Victor a Carben, who renounced Judaism to turn priest, exasperated on the prelate of the bishop, complaining [illegible] he had purged his bishopric from that people of [illegible]. At the same time that he uttered invectives against his nation, he confessed that the Christians [illegible] to others [illegible] them, because they were accustomed to continually [illegible] their interests, and that to convert them, a man had need of a quiver full of arrows. However, he wrote against the Jews, and in this [illegible] these words upon the gates of the church of [illegible] at Cologne: "Victor, formerly a Jew, in the year 1509, wrote four books against the error of the Jews." He was fifty years old when he was baptized, and it was probably the fear of being banished that produced his conversion. We learn from his testimony, that the Jews had suffered in the diocese of Cologne in the beginning of the fifteenth century.

About the time [illegible] flourished, in the neighbourhood of this city, the great R. Simeon, an eloquent preacher and author of the famous book Jalkut, (Pouch), which is a judicious collection of fourteen interpretations of the ancient Jewish doctors on the [illegible] books, as well lost and extant, to be [illegible]. This work was printed at Thessalonica, and afterwards in Italy. A Rabbi, of the family of Gedaliah, who had retired to Jerusalem, composed a long commentary upon it. He [illegible] his labour was lost, because he was not able to [illegible] when Dias Mokato, a rich Spaniard, undertook to defray the expence, and therefore it was printed with Abraham's notes, at Leghorn. The corrector dedicated it to the great duke Ferdinand II. A new Jalkut was afterwards printed at Amsterdam, wherein are collected the literal and mystic interpretations in alphabetical order, whereas Simeon followed the order of the sacred books, and confined himself to the allegorical sense. There is a third, [illegible] of R. Reuben, and is only a collection of notes upon the Pentateuch.

Some years after this transaction, a proselyte, called Pfeffercorn, kindled a terrible war among the learned of this century. Whether it was to acquire a reputation with the party whose profession he had newly embraced, or rather that he had a mind to enrich himself at the cost of his deserted brethren, he [illegible] the emperor Maximilian, that all the Jewish books ought to be burnt, because they were [illegible] fables, lies and blasphemies. He associated with him two Cologne divines, and, amongst others the famous Hochstraten, who afterwards wrote against Luther. He was charged with delivering to seize all the books he condemned, and afterwards oblige the Jews to ransom them at an exorbitant rate. All the devotees engaged in this [illegible], and the emperor himself, prevailed on by the authority of the divines, gave a favourable answer to the request presented to him. However, as this affair made a noise, he was willing to know the opinion of some doctors, and particularly of Capnion, or Reuchlin. This professor had studied the languages under Vessellus. Some say he was under the tuition of John de la Pierre, a German, who was afterwards professor at Paris, and became a Carthusian. But it is certain he was indebted for his first erudition to the professor of Groningen, who was called the Light of the World. The duke of Bavaria, who had a great esteem for Reuchlin, having a very nice affair to manage with Alexander VI. chose him for one of his ministers. He continued a year at Rome, where he perfected his knowledge of the Hebrew under a famous Jew, who flourished at that time, called Abdi Ben Jacob Spuon. The emperor had nominated him to be a triumvir of the league of Suabia, made in the year 1489, to investigate the power of the dukes of Bavaria, and he had executed the office for eleven years. It is no wonder, therefore, that this person, celebrated for his learning, and of importance in the empire, was consulted about the fate of the Talmud, and other Hebrew books.

Reuchlin went not into the opposite extreme of his enemies. He alledged that such books only ought to be burnt, as contained any blasphemies against the Christian religion. But he declared against destroying those which only treated of the tenets, morals, and rites of the Jews. He alledged farther, that the decrees of Germany not being executed wherever the Jews subsisted, it was impossible entirely to suppress the books of [illegible] over the world, whereof one single copy was sufficient for the production of new editions. Good sense required that he should argue in this manner, and extend the argument to [illegible] books that were printed and published. Nevertheless, Reuchlin was highly censured for speaking after this manner, and the divines began to persecute the author of this opinion. The understanding a little Greek was not only sufficient at that time to make a man suspected, and the understanding Hebrew to convict him of heresy, but the design of studying this language was sufficient to [illegible] the resentment of inveterate enemies. Cologne espoused the cause of its divines, and the university of Paris also declared for them. [illegible] was brought before the elector of Mentz, but Reuchlin appearing only by proxy, Hochstraten obtained a sentence, which he caused to be published before the term. Reuchlin appealed to the pope, who committed the [illegible] to judge of the proceeding. Hochstraten, [illegible], was condemned [illegible] costs, [illegible] giving against [illegible] continuing [illegible]. The declaration of the divines of Cologne [illegible]. However, they [illegible] Reuchlin's book to [illegible].

Not satisfied with these [illegible] proceedings, [illegible] published the Letters of Obscure Men. The Jews, who [illegible] to Reuchlin, [illegible] contained a poignant satire against the monks [illegible] were well pleased to see them lashed in a [illegible] vigorous manner, and Reuchlin [illegible] the abuses that had been circulated against him [illegible] revenge would have been more [illegible] died with grief, (as Paul Jovius tells us,) [illegible] professor lived ten years after the publication of these [illegible] letters. Ortuinus Gratius, to whom they were addressed, endeavoured to repel the attack by [illegible] the Lamentations of Obscure Men [illegible] Men. But this satire prevailed over [illegible] at least men of sense [illegible] to look upon Reuchlin [illegible] as an [illegible] of their tenets.

The affair was judged at Rome, where Hochstraten went, fortified with letters from [illegible] considerable sums of money, [illegible] omitted nothing in that court [illegible] to carrying [illegible] cause. He [illegible] the pope [illegible] from his judgement to the council, to reject [illegible] to separate from the church [illegible] Reuchlin [illegible] the Jews he defended were condemned. [illegible] was forced to be content [illegible] the cause [illegible] favour which the pope [illegible] to be condemned, for the judges [illegible] would have pronounced against Hochstraten, [illegible] not been put to it by the pope's order. [illegible] obliged to return with disgrace. Reuchlin's friends [illegible] for him near Nuremberg, where his enemies would have used him ill, if he had not [illegible] of their [illegible].

We are told that Hutten meeting him one day, would have killed him to punish his violent persecutions of the Lutherans, who began to spread in Germany but the [illegible] being [illegible] represented, that it was scandalous to kill [illegible] man, and Hutten being wrought upon, [illegible] his purpose.

P[illegible] a little after, bore the punishment of his [illegible], for being arrested upon some suspicion, he confessed [illegible] as priest for twenty years, without [illegible] received orders [illegible] that he had [illegible] to kill the elector of Brandenburgh, and his brother the archbishop [illegible] Mentz, and that he had voluntarily [illegible] by pretending [illegible] In consequence [illegible] he is said to have [illegible] the most cruel tortures [illegible] concerned.

[illegible] the most [illegible] Luther [illegible] the [illegible] Reuchlin [illegible] Not only [illegible] the languages [illegible] the Jews were no longer [illegible] children [illegible] that [illegible] and the worship of God [illegible] began to be restored. On the other hand [illegible] than [illegible] of [illegible], and [illegible] the writings of the Rabbies, discovered [illegible] and confuted them upon their own [illegible] The [illegible] discovered the [illegible] of the Jews [illegible] We must not [illegible] to [illegible], considera[illegible] due to our divines [illegible] others have followed [illegible] of barbarity, and the others [illegible] they have had their profound [illegible] in this matter, as well as we, so that we cannot [illegible] whether the Jews have gained or lost by the reformation [illegible].

Luther [illegible] with their divinity, and his [illegible] them with that impetuosity of temper that carried him beyond the bounds of moderation. He charged them [illegible] with being cheats, because he had heard [illegible] that a Jew had promised to make him [illegible], but having obliged the impostor to [illegible] upon himself the fraud was discovered [illegible] the Jew [illegible] of the wound that was given him. The greatest [illegible] of their spleen against Luther proceeded from his having hindered some Christian princes from [illegible] them into their dominions. Moreover the reformation produced abundance of doctors in Germany, who, having thoroughly studied the languages, frequently [illegible] with the Jews, and prove to them the truth of the Christian religion.

On the other hand, the Jews, being more closely pressed by the Christians, were obliged to exert themselves [illegible] for their own defence, and it [illegible] that they have produced some learned [illegible] of whom we may [illegible] R. [illegible] He declares that he [illegible] of Germany [illegible] with [illegible] of [illegible] His disciple, who [illegible] compares him to [illegible] his name, and [illegible] children. This produced a book in two parts, one of which may be compared to Esau and the other to Jacob. But this does not inform us who the author was, or at what time he lived. He had frequent conferences with Luther's disciples, and it was against them he composed his Bulwark of Faith. This is a most violent composition, wherein the author [illegible] particular [illegible] of sacred history, and, envious to explode the proofs of it [illegible] all the difficulties he can against it, and presses them with all possible vigour and bitterness, and with the same heat he confutes, or attempts to confute, the objections of Christians against the Jews. The book referred to, intitled by the author, *C[illegible] Emunah*, and, by the Latin translator *M[illegible]*, shews the author to have lived about the beginning of the 17th century. Its editor Joseph, the son of Mordecai, published it after it had remained a long time in [illegible] and was become very scarce. The Portuguese Jews indeed got it translated into Spanish, and dispersed it throughout [illegible] kingdoms. It was [illegible] and it is from thence that the [illegible] brought it into Germany, and having translated it into Latin, inserted it in his *T[illegible]*, or, "[illegible] Darts of Satan."

At the same time was produced [illegible] or Victory, against the Christians. The Jews [illegible] the Christian religion [illegible] it was quoted [illegible] which [illegible] and was [illegible] of the [illegible] the [illegible] century [illegible] wrote about the year 1399. He thought [illegible] Christians would not [illegible] on the people's minds, and there [illegible] judgment [illegible] which taught [illegible] From [illegible] Victory [illegible] is defended with thirty-five arguments, and Christianity attacked with [illegible] objections, [illegible] stated. It is said to be the work [illegible] wrote [illegible] in the [illegible] of their [illegible] age, but they lived since the reformation [illegible] the works of Luther and Calvin.

Besides the Jews who set up in Germany against the reformation, [illegible] appeared in [illegible] called [illegible] or half Jews by way of [illegible] as this. [illegible] one of the [illegible] of this sect, [illegible] that the [illegible] prophet did not respect the Gentiles, but only the Jews, to whom he had been [illegible] the same time [illegible] of Christ, the [illegible] privilege [illegible] their [illegible] ceremonies [illegible] contributing to the worship of God. [illegible] ded that the [illegible] in the decalogue [illegible] was naturally engraven on the hearts of all men. He [illegible] attempts to gain proselytes in Silesia, where [illegible] impossible to [illegible] he went to Poland, where [illegible].

[illegible] Francis David was called a [illegible] because he affected some peculiar [illegible] up prayer and solemn [illegible] was likewise reckoned [illegible] and such were also [illegible] observed the Jewish [illegible] from [illegible] and things strangled, several [illegible] other [illegible].

The Jews pretended to [illegible] since the taking of Jerusalem, but [illegible] did not secure them from being [illegible] expelled them all from thence at the beginning of the fifteenth century. [illegible] themselves in the safe [illegible] for the emperor Ferdinand I [illegible] but granted them the privilege of [illegible]

[illegible] city [illegible] Germany, and ordered that the chief [illegible] Worms should have this preference before all the rest of his nation. They reckon in the catalogue of these princes the famous R. Jakock, of German origin, [illegible] at Worms esteemed by his nation for his learning, [illegible] who had four [illegible] sons who were all presidents of academies, [illegible] of [illegible], and the admiration of [illegible]. One of them taught chiefly at Fribourg, where there was a school and a synagogue, as in most cities of the empire, and particularly at Vienna, where they had erected a magnificent building.

They had in Austria a more famous man than Jakock, which was Solomon [illegible]. He composed the Sea of Solomon, alluding to his name, and called his book a [illegible] [illegible] the [illegible] of the Talmud, and he examined particularly the [illegible] and phrases of it. He died in the year 157[illegible].

[illegible], a native of Germany, which gave him his [illegible], [illegible] a good [illegible], [illegible], and a skilful architect, [illegible] he had acquired [illegible] wealth, and [illegible] a very beautiful [illegible] [illegible] ezer, a German, had [illegible] [illegible]. He left Germany for Poland, where he became head of [illegible] academy, and of the house of [illegible] at Polonia. He intitled two books, one whereof was called the [illegible] of the Lord, and the other, the [illegible] of Doctrine.

Poland abounded [illegible] learned doctors. Herdes taught at C[illegible], [illegible] of [illegible], who came from [illegible]. He was devout, perfect, and [illegible] twenty years, [illegible], he was [illegible] Lewis, born in the [illegible] city, wrote [illegible], [illegible] of the [illegible] empire, and [illegible] a great reputation. At [illegible] a house of [illegible], and [illegible] the Jews. They were [illegible] in [illegible] of Poland, where they had [illegible] privileges. Nevertheless, they sometimes suffered by popular commotions [illegible], their houses were [illegible] on fire at [illegible] and they saw them burnt without being able to extinguish the flames, because they were afraid that the enraged multitude would fall upon them. The [illegible], [illegible], pretended, that a kind of supernatural terror had seized on them, which would not suffer them so [illegible] to draw water, so that all their houses, effects, and books, even that of the law, were reduced to ashes. But, excepting [illegible] popular disorders, learning [illegible] well as traffic [illegible] among them, and their academies were governed by men of great reputation.

Cardinal Commendon, in his way to R[illegible], found likewise, in the province of Ukraine, a number of Jews in [illegible], who [illegible] themselves, as they do in general, by usury, but by a [illegible] and honest commerce. They cultivated their lands, and applied themselves to the study of physic and astrology, and others farmed the customs and carriage of merchandize. They are not only exempt from wearing [illegible] of distinction, but are even allowed to wear swords, [illegible] enjoy the same posts and employments as the natives of the country.

Bohemia cherished many of this nation. We have already observed, that the Jews were settled there in the tenth century, since they rendered [illegible] to the inhabitants against the robbers, and built at that time a synagogue at Prague, this liberty being given them by way of acknowledgment for the [illegible] that had been obtained by their means. In process of time they also erected a college. R. [illegible] was the president, and the first that began to exercise his scholars in controversies like the Christians; but this method was not acceptable to the sages, nor relished by the people in general. The Jews whose system of divinity is [illegible] mystical and [illegible], cannot be reconciled to arguments and syllogisms.

They had also their enemies and persecutors here. A [illegible] general conflagration having destroyed one part of [illegible], the Jews were accused of being the incendiaries, and condemned. Those that escaped the flames were all expelled by Ferdinand, who could no otherwise appease the popular commotion: ten persons only found favour, being allowed the liberty of remaining at Prague. But the incendiaries having been discovered before the end of the year, the Jews were recalled, and settled again in their country.

Another storm fell upon them soon after: for they were suspected of having made prayers at Prague against the Christians. Upon this suspicion they seized all their books, and carried them to Vienna. This loss was an affliction to them, not only on account of their value, which was very considerable, but especially because they were obliged to perform the [illegible] and [illegible], without reading, which subjected them [illegible]. The storm was but short, [illegible] books [illegible] were restored, and perhaps, it was only done [illegible] to redeem them. Ferdinand [illegible] from [illegible] Bohemia, [illegible] Prague, but [illegible] the first [illegible] permitted them to [illegible] of his dominions, and also [illegible] [illegible] Windeiss, who [illegible] of the [illegible], [illegible] them during [illegible]. [illegible] them in the [illegible], [illegible], [illegible] converted many of his [illegible].

They had in Poland [illegible] of their [illegible], [illegible] of the fifteenth century. [illegible] he [illegible] his son, R. Chanan, [illegible] of [illegible]. [illegible] the famous L[illegible] [illegible] from the emperor Rhodolphus [illegible]. He founded a [illegible] academy, called [illegible], [illegible], and [illegible] all the synagogues of Poland.

Judas Bet[illegible], [illegible] de Leo of Prague, was [illegible] [illegible] in the year 157[illegible]. [illegible], [illegible] of Ma[illegible], and [illegible] judge of [illegible]. He [illegible] to Prague [illegible] 157[illegible], when he founded [illegible], in which [illegible]. However, [illegible] go [illegible] to Great Poland, where he [illegible] the end of the [illegible], or the beginning of the [illegible] century. He [illegible] books, among which there is one concerning the [illegible] of Israel, wherein [illegible] the coming of the [illegible] [illegible] the [illegible] of his people [illegible]. Some time before [illegible], [illegible] [illegible] league, who [illegible] commentary [illegible] [illegible] of Jark, and [illegible] the year 154[illegible].

Mardocai Je[illegible], [illegible]. He retired to Poland, [illegible] died in the [illegible] [illegible] one of the [illegible] country [illegible]. [illegible] to know [illegible] method [illegible]. He [illegible] intitled [illegible] the Royal Garment [illegible] borrowed from [illegible], [illegible] from the [illegible] of [illegible] and white, [illegible] garment [illegible] linen [illegible] the Rabbies [illegible] their titles, but [illegible] of the author. He has [illegible] habits, though [illegible] [illegible] contained [illegible]. The first [illegible] habit of purple, in which he treats of [illegible]. The second [illegible] sabbath. The [illegible] of gold, [illegible] courses of [illegible] robe of fine linen and [illegible] ceremonies of marriage, [illegible] of Satan, which [illegible] the [illegible] Je[illegible].

Ganz the Jew [illegible] he composed his Ste[illegible] David [illegible] the creation till [illegible]

We must not confound this work with another Stem of David we have already spoken of, for the one is a dictionary, and this a chronicle The author gives it this title, because it was the first of his works, for he published afterwards the Buckler and Tower of David, one of which treats of arithmetic, and the other of geometry Besides, as his history displays the misery of the Jews, and the power of the Christians, he would hereby oblige his readers to remember the branch of David, and to pray for his manifestation There are three things peculiar in his work 1 That he begins with the creation of the world, and ascends to the first temple and the patriarch, whereas the Jews generally begin with the epocha of the Greeks 2 Though he has often copied the Rabbies of his nation that preceded him, yet he hath been more exact, and corrected their errors 3 He has introduced into his second book several Christian authors, but he is not happy in his choice, and as he departed from the custom of the Jewish doctors, who slight foreign historians, he ought at the same time to have preferred more exact authors, and men of a greater name

They built, at that time, at Prague, a synagogue equal to those of Poland and Jerusalem and one Mordechai [illegible] had liberally contributed to this great edifice, as well as to the relief of the poor of Bohemia and Poland, [illegible] calls him "the Wall and Basis of the School", the [illegible] Sons, the Father of the Poor, the Oak of [illegible] and the Love of his Brethren, and with this [illegible] he ends his chronicle

The [illegible] in Hungary were greatly diminished towards the [illegible] of the [illegible]th century, when the emperor Rodolphus [illegible] in order to oblige them to quit the country [illegible] He at length compelled them to [illegible] of [illegible] denarii per head, which it was [illegible] have ruined them quite nevertheless, a great number of them made shift to maintain themselves [illegible], though a much greater was forced to seek their fortune elsewhere

Moravia had also its synagogues But the Jews suffered a cruel persecution here in the year 1574, for all the professors of their religion were sentenced to the flames, and [illegible] were [illegible] before complaints could be brought to the emperor Maximilian, who at length took compassion on these poor wretches They also suffered greatly in Franconia, for some houses of the city of Bamberg being burnt, the Jews were accused of setting them on fire, and at the same time the people [illegible] their houses, plundered their goods, and indemnified themselves at their cost But, however, there was no one put to death

Some time after they had the same misfortune at Bonn [illegible], the Dutch general, and [illegible] of the fort of [illegible] [illegible] secretly at the head of some troops, had [illegible] at the [illegible] of this city, and, by means of the noise which some [illegible] in the neighbourhood made, [illegible] gate blew it up, and made himself master of the city for the Hollanders He gave the plunder to his [illegible], and the Jews complain that they were particularly [illegible] in that pillage However, this misery was common to them with the rest of the inhabitants, but none were killed

The Jews were afterwards recompensed for these misfortunes, since at the end of the century, they obtained liberty to settle in the duke of Brunswick's territories The princes of this [illegible] had ever before been persuaded that such an establishment would be disadvantageous so that the Jewish merchants were not so much as suffered to cross their lands, and when any one was taken, they plundered him with impunity But their complaints being brought to Henry Julius, duke of Brunswick, he not only granted the Jews liberty of conscience in his territories, but gave them a place in the Lower Saxony, to carry on their commerce, so that there were but few places in all Germany in which they did not traffic at the end of the sixteenth century The present age, however, seems to be the most happy æra they have enjoyed since their dispersion

CHAP XXII

Authority of the Jews in Poland R Solomon's conversion, and theological works Jews at Hamburgh Favoured by Ferdinand III of Bohemia [illegible] between the Christians and Jews of Prague Jews stripped of their privileges in Hungary In high credit at Vienna Banished [illegible] Settled in other parts of the empire Synagogues [illegible] by the French Numerous and dispersed at London [illegible]

THERE is hardly any country in Europe where the Jews enjoy greater liberty, and more inviolable privileges, than in Poland They have their stately synagogues and academies, and their court of judicature is endowed with singular authority, since it is allowed to determine in civil as well as religious cases We are told they have had the singular privilege of coining money, because shekels have been found there with an Hebrew inscription, but as the tomb in which they are said to have been found is rather suspicious, we cannot ground upon it a prerogative usually vested in sovereigns alone

Poland is looked upon as a nursery of learned Rabbies, and the country to which the Jews send their youth to study the Talmud, and the rites of their religion In speaking of the preceding century, we mentioned some Rabbies who were an honour to their nation This kingdom hath produced one, who not only renounced Judaism, but wrote and published thirty-seven demonstrations against it His name was Solomon He had been bound for one of his brethren, and committed to prison, when nothing could have redeemed him but his conversion to Christianity, so that this circumstance, together with the affected style [illegible] in which he wrote, has afforded reason to many to suspect his sincerity However that be, he was an excellent [illegible] well versed in theological matters, and an able assertor of the religion he preached

Hamburgh is called a little Jerusalem The Jews are observed to have been more tractable in that city than elsewhere, for a great number of them were converted, in this century by one Edzas, or Esdras, who made it his business to instruct and confirm them in the Christian faith A divine of that city once asserted, that if these instructions were [illegible] with some violence, they would be more effectual But the senate suppressed his immoderate zeal, which tended only to lessen the number of their citizens, and had already caused some popular commotions

The emperor Ferdinand III granted them great privileges, because, when the city of Prague was besieged by Carolus Gustavus, who was lately declared generalissimo of the armies of Sweden and Germany they defended themselves with a surprizing fidelity and vigour The city was already taken, and the garrison called upon to capitulate, but the conqueror having refused honourable conditions, they withstood many assaults with unshaken fortitude The Jews distinguished themselves in these assaults, and defended their post with a resolution that merited praise and extraordinary privilege

Rabbi Chagim, or Joachim, deceived the Christians of his place by a piece of profound dissimulation [illegible] committing a considerable robbery, he embraced Christianity to wipe off the scandal of his crime, and [illegible] a violent book against his antient brethren He went to Vienna, and introduced himself into the court of Ferdinand, who afforded him his protection Some time after, perceiving his fortune on the decline, with the help of two other Jews, as accomplices, he robbed the [illegible] The criminals were quickly apprehended, and condemned to death Ferdinand Francis Anglesberg (this was

was the name which the convert had taken in his baptism) dissembled till he had lost all hopes of saving his life, but upon the scaffold declared that he never had been a Christian, and that he lived and died a Jew.

In the same place was exhibited an instance of their hatred for the Christians, for one Lazarus, an inhabitant of Prague, understanding his son desired baptism, fell upon him and killed him. He was committed to prison, where, animated by despair, he strangled himself with the assistance of another Jew, who was in the same place. This latter was condemned to be broke upon the wheel.

It appears from various circumstances, that no considerations have been capable of creating a tolerable good understanding between the Christians of Prague and the Jews. On the contrary, they hate one another; and as it must be confessed, the Jews have occasionally been guilty of such enormous deeds as must render them not only suspected, but odious to the Christians, so likewise it must be granted, that the Christians have subjected them to conform to some practices that were inconsistent with their profession, and to [illegible] deceived [illegible] commotions. Nevertheless they are [illegible] in this country, as to [illegible] [illegible] the city of Prague, but [illegible] about strangers, and submit to [illegible] living.

They had enjoyed in Hungary the privilege of farming the revenues, till Ferdinand II took it from them by an edict, notwithstanding which they found means to preserve [illegible], [illegible] Ferdinand III was afterwards obliged to deprive them of it by a new edict, which condemned [illegible] to the loss of their places, who admitted the Jews to any of them, alledging, as the cause, "That they neither [illegible] science or honesty, and are therefore unworthy to enjoy the privileges of Hungary." However [illegible] continued there still, not only under the protection of the grand seignior in those parts under his dominions, but [illegible].

About ten years ago they were in such credit in Vienna, that [illegible] obtained them liberty to build a [illegible] academy, to revive the study of the [illegible] in this country. He had [illegible] a pension for twenty-four persons, who were to read the Talmud every hour, day and night. One relieved another so that the school was always open, and [illegible] a doctor [illegible] this building, however, was scarce finished, when the emperor drove all the Jews from his capital, levelled the synagogue, [illegible] They complain that the superstitious [illegible] the court gave the [illegible] occasioned [illegible] prompted the emperor to banish them, but after the death of this princess they were [illegible] to Vienna. The emperor had a new subject of [illegible] against them in the Turkish war, because they [illegible] the infidels to maintain the siege of Buda, and distinguished themselves by their valour. But this was in [illegible] of fidelity they owed their sovereign, and though this resistance rendered them odious, not only to the people of Germany, but Italy, where they rose against them, yet we cannot condemn them, since they were then subject to the Ottoman empire. Upon the whole, the emperor [illegible] them at Vienna, admits them into affairs of state, and gives honourable titles to those who are employed, or purchase them. The people, indeed, jealous of the riches they heap together, endeavour sometimes to strip them by violent tumults and commotions.

They are numerous and flourishing in Servia, Croatia, Moldavia, Walachia, and in the rich cities of Germany. If they have been expelled Nuremberg, they are spread abroad in the country towns, and have their synagogue at Furt, which is in the neighbourhood.

In the city of Augsburg they had formerly a synagogue and academy, and their doctors and disciples were maintained by the rich merchants of the place. But they have since been banished from it, and must buy the liberty of coming into it at the price of a florin for every hour they stay in it.

It would be tedious to enumerate all the cities where they still subsist without any considerable change in their condition; we shall therefore only attend to those that deserve most notice.

A modern traveller reckons thirty thousand Jews at Frankfort, where they are often plundered, and reduced to the slavery of [illegible] water-carriers, to extinguish the flames when any house is on fire. [illegible] the Jews in several places [illegible] all manner of [illegible] to render them despicable and odious, notwithstanding some learned men have been produced among them.

There [illegible] a famous [illegible] in the middle of the last century, named [illegible] his birth-place, [illegible] de Spira. He published the Gold [illegible] the Holy [illegible]. He composed a volume of [illegible], (Megillath [illegible]) [illegible] commentary upon the works of [illegible] to sound the depths of mysteries [illegible] the difficulties [illegible] in them.

But one of the most [illegible] Germany produced in the last century, was [illegible] Metaphysical Introduction [illegible] a native of Jerusalem, and [illegible] only given him on account of his long abode in that country; for he retired [illegible] end of his life, and was buried at [illegible] alle.

CHAP. XXV.

State of the Jews in Holland. [illegible]

OF all the states of Europe, according to one of their writers, there is not one where the [illegible] more quietly than in Holland. They enrich [illegible] and, through the lenity of the government, [illegible] quisitions without fear. There are two sorts of Jews in Holland, some are Germans, and others come from Portugal and Spain. They [illegible] and hate one another, as if the [illegible] concerned [illegible] tween these two sorts of Jews, [illegible] mans, is the difference [illegible] tugal and Spain, who live in those countries [illegible] in all things with the popish religion [illegible] riching themselves, and [illegible] with more liberty, [illegible].

The Spanish and Portuguese [illegible] part of this nation, retired into Holland to avoid [illegible] cities of the inquisition. [illegible] dera with having [illegible] tries, and [illegible] supply. His name was [illegible] the ten of [illegible] at Antwerp, [illegible] tion not only of [illegible] queen of Hungary, [illegible] Antwerp to Venice, and [illegible] wrote to the [illegible] of Antwerp, intimating, "that [illegible] there continues to [illegible] Catholics, [illegible] signs against the [illegible]

[illegible] is not to give him leisure to think [illegible] in the Netherlands." His letters were read in the [illegible] of Antwerp, and gave great encouragement to [illegible], but [illegible] make good his promise [illegible] afterwards, who turned his arms against [illegible]. It only appears that the Jews [illegible] in the Netherlands than in Spain, since [illegible] a retreat there; but it was forty years after [illegible] of Spain and Portugal began to settle in [illegible] Amsterdam [illegible] occasioned [illegible] in the city, where all things were suspected [illegible]. They [illegible] themselves up, [illegible]. They [illegible] were pursued [illegible] worship; but as they found [illegible] Hebrew books [illegible] law of Moses, they had [illegible] to pray for the prosperity [illegible] to do; and at the same [illegible] synagogue, which they called [illegible] was the name of the [illegible].

[illegible] synagogue, which they called Neve [illegible], the [illegible] of Israel. These synagogues [illegible] a collection of prayers, but [illegible]. The [illegible] was headed by a famous [illegible] from Africa, which [illegible] to [illegible], where he published [illegible] to the destruction of Jerusalem [illegible] who succeeded him censured the [illegible] to [illegible] its hatred. A [illegible] was formed, in which the [illegible] the conduct of David Pardo. It was called [illegible] of Israel.

[illegible] the [illegible] effect of all ecclesiastical separations [illegible], these divisions were accompanied [illegible]. The synagogue of Ben Jacob espoused the [illegible]; but the schism ceased, after it had continued [illegible] about twenty years, and the three synagogues [illegible] one, to which they gave, as to many others, the title of Talmud Thora, that is, the Study or Science of the [illegible].

They have been careful to found schools as well as synagogues, [illegible] is called the Crown of the Law, [illegible] by learned men. But that which [illegible] of this nation, is the great and [illegible] in the year 16[illegible], which has [illegible] admired by all lovers of architecture, [illegible] own preachers, that there [illegible] collection [illegible] of the sermons delivered [illegible].

[illegible] are not [illegible] the only men that have [illegible] it has had also many [illegible] celebrated doctors.

[illegible] one of the most learned and able theologists that [illegible] among the Jews for many ages [illegible], of the family of the Abravanel's [illegible] he was chosen at Amsterdam to [illegible] the Talmud, in which employ he acquired a reputation which drew upon him the jealousy and enmity of the Rabbies, but he despised the calumnies, and continued his application to study. He was not eight and twenty [illegible] published the 1st part of his Conciliator on the [illegible], wherein he endeavoured to reconcile the seeming contradictions of Scripture, by the explications of [illegible] doctors, and his own conjectures. This [illegible], which he finished afterwards, gained him universal [illegible], and, indeed, no Rabbi has written upon this [illegible] with such solid erudition. He composed some [illegible] problems upon the creation. He also wrote [illegible] treatise [illegible] resurrection, in which he undertook to [illegible] immortality of the soul, and its operations, not [illegible] united to the body, but after its separation. As he was head of the synagogue at Amsterdam, he was obliged to study the rites and laws, so that he wrote two [illegible] them, one of which was an abridgment of the [illegible], with this title, "The Treasure of Judgment." The other particularly related to questions concerning marriage, the condition of children, and the division of estates. He also wrote a defence of the Babylonian Talmud, and composed a treatise concerning the Science of the [illegible], and of Rabbinical Philosophy. He translated [illegible] into Spanish verse, made [illegible] Christina's panegyric, and a [illegible] for the prince of Orange. He also formed [illegible] writing the history of his nation, from Josephus to his own time. It seems that he began this work, but could not finish it. Another author formed the same design afterwards.

Bartolocci accused him of having taken the advantage of the civil wars in England, to prevail upon Oliver Cromwell to permit the Jews to settle there. On the other hand a Jewish historian affirms, that C[illegible] parliament [illegible] without [illegible], it was natural for him to endeavour to procure [illegible] settlement to his nation [illegible] of England. However, whether [illegible] invited or not, it is plain he came over to England with that design, and was [illegible] by Cromwell and the parliament, as was [illegible] the Jews, in which he exploded all the calumnies [illegible] his nation, and pleaded their cause [illegible] believe some [illegible] of those times, he obtained much better settlement, and greater privileges, for them, than ever they had enjoyed before in England.

Bartolocci charges him with other frivolous matters, which he represents as crimes, such as [illegible] part with the remonstrants, in order to obtain their friendship and protection, and printing his works without the approbation of the Christian divines; but he has been sufficiently cleared from these imputations. He died at Amsterdam, in the year 16[illegible]2, and left a son, who inherited his press, and employed it in printing some of his father's works.

Men[illegible] had a panegyrist [illegible] in a famous physician, called Zac[illegible], who was born at Lisbon in the year 157[illegible]. His parents, who dissembled their Judaism and made outward profession of popery, sent him to study at Salamanca and Coimbra, from thence he returned and settled in his native place, where he was much esteemed, because he was very charitable to his poor patients, and performed considerable cures [illegible]. He wrote many books, and amongst others an [illegible] of the Principal Physicians, [illegible] to a canon of the cathedral of [illegible], and [illegible] that metropolis. After having dissembled thirty years, he returned to Amsterdam, where [illegible] circumcised [illegible] a Jew, leaving [illegible], which he [illegible] to print. Those he printed were of the physical kind.

[illegible] is a [illegible] of Spain, taught [illegible] at Hamburgh, but he came from thence to Amsterdam. He printed a bible, which was greatly esteemed [illegible]. Mr. Vander Hooght [illegible] on a new edition of this bible, much more exact. The preface of this learned man explains his design and [illegible] of executing it.

A[illegible]s's Treasure of Precepts and Judgments was printed first at Venice, with the approbation of all the [illegible] of that country. The author thought himself obliged to treat on this subject, because the most useful of all books are those that teach the fear of God. The preceding doctors had composed many of them, but the Spanish [illegible] had destroyed great part of these works. Besides, these antient writers composed them in Arabic, which was then better understood. He proves that [illegible] treatise was necessary, because the law without a commentary, is a torch without light; and to render it more useful he joined tradition to the law, and practical [illegible] to speculative truths. He explains [illegible] knowledge of the [illegible] which are not [illegible] in use, that the Jews [illegible] who know them, being convinced of their excellency, [illegible] ardently desire their restoration. The commentary upon each precept is short, and well adapted to explain the Jewish laws.

[illegible] Aboab, who came from Brasil, was not only a [illegible] preacher, but a great casuist. He translated a work, called Iran's Gate of Heaven, from Spanish into Hebrew, from whose version it has since been rendered into Latin. He published a paraphrase upon the Pentateuch, and sung Moses's Triumph in heroic verse.

[illegible] was another learned man, who commented [illegible] the Jerusalem Talmud. He studied a subject that was [illegible] more obscure and intricate, as he undertook to explain the flux and reflux of the sea. He was so perfectly [illegible] master of the Hebrew tongue, that he composed a dictionary, in which he took a more easy method than had been hitherto adopted.

We ought not to forget Spinosa, who made himself famous by the singularity of his tenets. He was born at Amsterdam in 1632. His parents were Portuguese Jews, in good circumstances, but he received nothing but a [illegible] from his father's possessions, and always lived in poverty. He did not [illegible] to follow the law, and imitate the Rabbies, but learnt the trade of polishing glasses, and making spectacles. He compared himself to a serpent that bites [illegible] tail, because he had nothing left at the year's end, though he lived upon milk and gruel. He had learnt Latin of Vanden Ende, who taught then at Amsterdam, and who [illegible], embarked in the Chevalier de Rohan's conspiracy, and was executed. It is pretended it was this person that sowed the first seeds of atheism in Spinosa's mind. But it was Descartes's philosophy which gave him a dislike to the principles of the Rabbies. He did not find in their writings those evident truths built upon demonstrations, which Descartes recommends to his disciples. When he was perceived to neglect the sabbath and synagogue, they attempted, in vain, to retain him by a pension of a thousand livres. By this refusal he incurred so violent an [illegible], that it was resolved to stab him. As he came from the old Portuguese synagogue of Amsterdam, he saw a man with a dagger in his hand, and endeavoured to [illegible] him, and, indeed, the blow only reached his coat, which he kept in memory of this event. Not thinking himself safe in his native country, where the Jews were numerous and potent, he sought a retreat near Leyden, and after [illegible] the Hague. He had the great excommunication [illegible] against him, but he protested against this [illegible] given in his absence, and [illegible] his protestation by a writing in Spanish, addressed to the Rabbies in the synagogue. He published first a geometrical demonstration of Descartes's Principles, afterwards his [illegible], and last produced the Tractatus Theologico Politicus, in which he formed a new system, that makes him much esteemed by those who are called Freethinkers in Holland, Germany, and France, from whom he received several invitations, and large encouragements, but he refused them all, and died at the Hague in 1677, aged forty-four years. He left behind him a sect that has espoused his principles. We cannot tell whether it be numerous, since it is constituted of persons dispersed in different places, who form no body or society.

As Spinosa had many followers and disciples, so also had he many opposers of his own nation, particularly the learned Balthazar Orobio, a Spaniard by birth, and a physician by profession. His parents who professed the Roman religion, taught him betimes to dissemble like themselves. He studied philosophy, and became a metaphysical reader in the university of Salamanca, being a lover of this science, which was then much cultivated. He afterwards became a physician at Seville, where he was seized by the inquisition, because he did not sufficiently conceal his religion to remove all suspicion. At length, tired with dissembling, he came to Amsterdam, was circumcised, and made open profession of Judaism. He practised physic there with great reputation, and assures us, that his pressing occupations did not permit him to apply himself to study as he could wish. When Spinosa's book appeared, he at first despised it on account of its author, but when he received Bredenburgh's answer to it, in which that author agreed with Spinosa in two dangerous positions, he seemed to hesitate about them. Orobio undertook to confute them both, and in the execution of this task proved himself an able metaphysician.

There have been eminent Rabbies in other cities. David Cohen de Lara, [illegible]'s disciple, is compared to Hercules, the conqueror of monsters. He composed [illegible] of David, in which he proves the [illegible] of the Hebrew with the Greek, and [illegible]. [illegible] also the Crown of the Priesthood, which is [illegible] much larger than [illegible], [illegible] were [illegible]. He translated the Beginning of Wisdom out of Hebrew into Spanish [illegible] borrowed [illegible] these words of Solomon, "The Fear of the Lord is the beginning of Wisdom." [illegible] this last work, [illegible] and [illegible] known [illegible] to him.

[illegible] we shall mention [illegible] Leon, famous for his description of Solomon's temple [illegible] he composed at Middleburgh. The [illegible] his birth, because he was [illegible] country, but he left it in pursuit of [illegible] he wanted [illegible] that he might have a clearer idea of the temple of Jerusalem. He built one of wood, upon the plan he had drawn from the [illegible] authors of his nation. He afterwards formed the description of his edifice, which he published first in French, and [illegible]. He [illegible] enlarged this work [illegible] translated it into Hebrew. The learned [illegible] to exact a picture of this ancient edifice, and the duke of Brunswick [illegible] to be translated into Latin, that he might [illegible]. [illegible] Juda added to his first work, a Description of the Tabernacle, a Treatise on Cherubims, and [illegible] of the Psalms. He [illegible] metaphorical passages of the Talmud. He [illegible] that this work cost him a great deal of labour and pains. [illegible] conferences [illegible] some Christian [illegible] tracts were never printed, nor that of the [illegible] offering the Morning and Evening [illegible].

The Jews are no less numerous and [illegible] Hague, where they have also [illegible] those who become wealthy seek a [illegible] retirement. Here they enjoy the greatest prosperity, live in the greatest luxury, and in the [illegible]. Yet such is their happiness under [illegible] government, they enjoy their wealth and grandeur [illegible] jealousy, zeal, and envy of the populace, which [illegible] carry on a considerable [illegible] without being liable to those [illegible], vexatious prosecutions, [illegible], and other difficulties, under which we have [illegible] persecution.

In England they are allowed full liberty of their religion, a full freedom of trade, and the [illegible] their property. They are [illegible] Hebrews [illegible] distinguished into German and Portuguese [illegible] properly into northern and southern [illegible] respective synagogues, chief [illegible] so that they are obliged to [illegible] educated in Germany, or at Amsterdam [illegible] by [illegible] more and [illegible] religion [illegible] careful to instruct them [illegible] whereas the latter, being rich [illegible] are more [illegible] of them cannot so much [illegible] their synagogues, [illegible]

The character of the lower rank, especially such as deal in the pedling mercantile way, is but indifferent

CHAP XXV

Present state of the Jews in all parts of the world R [illegible] account of the [illegible] That of R Menasseh A Jewish [illegible] of the Azores Ten tribes, where [illegible] are ten tribes [illegible] China [illegible] account of [illegible] Present state of the Jews in the East In the Ottoman empire [illegible] of the West [illegible] Great [illegible] Poland [illegible] Protestants [illegible] Jews highly [illegible]

WE have now brought the history of the eastern and western Jews down to the close of the 17th century It remains only that we give our readers an account of their present state in all parts of the world Several eminent writers, both of their nation, and among the Christians have endeavoured to ascertain their number [illegible] whom we shall only select one [illegible], who seem to have been the most successful in their enquiries

R Simon Luzat, who taught at Venice, owns it to be [illegible] to give an exact account of the Jews at present [illegible] into so many places "We cannot (he [illegible]) [illegible] certain intelligence of the ten tribes [illegible] [illegible] carried away, nor is it known where they [illegible] the [illegible] would be sufficiently known [illegible] We know there are abundance [illegible] in the [illegible] of Persia, though they have [illegible] liberty The Turkish empire is their chief [illegible] not only because they have been settled there [illegible] long [illegible], but because many of those banished out of [illegible] There are more of them at Constantinople and Salonichi than in any other place They [illegible] cities, and [illegible] in the empire of the grand seignior A [illegible] number of pilgrims come from all corners of the world to Jerusalem, and considerable sums are sent [illegible] for the benefit of the poor and to keep up the academies There are many of them in the dominions of the emperor of Germany, but they are more numerous in Poland, Lithuania, and Russia Here we have academies and disciples in great numbers, who study our civil and canon laws because we are allowed the privilege of judging in all civil and criminal cases which happen in the [illegible] There are not so many Jews in the Protestant [illegible] which separate from the Roman church yet they treat them with great charity and indulgence in the Low Countries, particularly at Rotterdam, Amsterdam, and Hamburgh, because these merchandizing cities are open to foreigners All the Italian princes receive the Jews countenance, protect them [illegible] maintain their privileges without alteration, and I believe there are not less than twenty-five thousand in this country Fez and Morocco, and the other neighbouring cities which are not subject to the Turks, contain greater numbers because they are not [illegible] from Spain or Portugal, from whence they may retire thither There are other places upon the coast of Africa which are also peopled with Jews, but as we know but little of them, it is hard to fix their number" Thus this Italian Rabbi, who not only since taught at Venice, described the state of his nation, to which let us add the account which Menasses has left us

Menasses observes, that this oracle cannot be applied to the return from the Babylonish captivity, because God did not then recall all the dispersed tribes, nor all the Israelites that were scattered among the nations The deliverance promised is called the second, because the general one from Egypt was before it, whereas the return from Babylon [illegible] respected two tribes, and when the Israelites left Assyria, to pass into the Holy Land, they did not cross the Nile, nor any river of Egypt or Ethiopia, as it was promised they should at the general redemption or the waters of the Nile and Euphrates shall be divided to leave a free passage to the tribes like the waters of the Red Sea, when Israel came out of Egypt

Hence he concludes, that Isaiah intimates the general return of the nation and the different places it shall come from The prophet speaks 1 "Of Assyria and Egypt, because in these two provinces the twelve tribes shall be re-united 2 He mentions Pathros [illegible] we must not understand either Pelusium or [illegible] but the Parthians lying near the Caspian Sea, where many doctors place the river Sabbation, beyond which [illegible] a great number of Jews 3 Cush is Ethiopia And [illegible], here are many tribes in Abyssinia 4 [illegible] is [illegible] Persia or the other side of the Euphrates where we find [illegible] deserts, not inhabited in which one part of the nation is concealed 5 Shinar [illegible] province near Babylon, for Moses has [illegible] ter Babel [illegible] the land of Shinar and [illegible] relates, that Nebuchadnezzar carried the vessels of the temple into the land of Shinar 6 The scripture speaks often of Hamath, and the Chaldee paraphrast who is followed by many interpreters, asserts that this is Antioch There are [illegible] cities of this name, which have been built in divers [illegible] but this is the city of Antioch in [illegible] 7 The Septuagint interpret [illegible] the word Hamath by the east, and [illegible] because Hamath is, perhaps [illegible] the sun or the east So [illegible] speaks there of the Jews, who [illegible] in the East of the Holy Land, that is, in Great Asia, the East Indies and China 8 [illegible] declares that the Israelites shall come from the isles of the [illegible] for [illegible] interpreters have translated it But it ought to be translated the isles of the west, [illegible] the places where the scripture speaks of the four parts of the world, it means the west by the word [illegible], and the prophet, under this expression, includes [illegible] towards the sun-setting, west [illegible] of the Holy Land, that is, the Jews who, [illegible] present, people a certain part of America

"Lastly the prophet [illegible], that God shall bring back the [illegible] of Israel, and he uses a word which signifies [illegible] (excommunicated) [illegible] in reality, the ten tribes [illegible] from the rest, [illegible] places very remote from the Holy Land but are concealed [illegible] extremities of the earth, and [illegible] provinces peopled by the Gentiles, but for the Jews they are dispersed, and God shall gather them together from the [illegible] corners of the earth Because indeed the tribe of Judah is dispersed in different places, [illegible] synagogues in America, it shall return from [illegible] corners of the earth, but there shall be no division or jealousy betwixt these two parts of the nation, between Ephraim and Judah, as says the prophet Ezekiel There shall be but one king and they shall be no more two nations, neither shall they be divided into two kingdoms"

We pretend not to reconcile these two Rabbies, nor to follow them step by step yet the general account they give us of the present condition of the Jews deserves to be considered They do not agree about the fate of the ten tribes, for one says, they have been destroyed long ago, and the other maintains, that they are concealed in America, and in several places where Divine providence has conveyed, and miraculously preserves them till they appear again at the general deliverance, when they shall come from all places they inhabit, and [illegible] in Assyria and Egypt, from whence they shall all [illegible] Jerusalem [illegible] to their rest.

Menasseh supports his opinion upon the people of America's being unknown, and not appearing to have any communication with the rest of the inhabitants. The Spaniards affirm, that, when they came into Peru, they found there a stately edifice, dedicated to the Creator of the Universe, so that as the Indians were idolaters, and as yet had no knowledge of iron tools used in building houses, this structure must be considered as a synagogue erected by the Jews. The Indians also approved this conjecture, since their tradition signifies, that this palace had been built by a bearded nation, more antient than the [illegible]

R. Menasseh likewise quotes an inscription found in the island of St. Michael, one of the Azores, mentioned by [illegible], though somewhat difficult to be [illegible], unless it be by a transposition of letters, yet [illegible] words, appears plainly enough to have [illegible] by the Jews who arrived in this island.

It appears to us that the ten tribes subsist still in the east [illegible] of the places where Salmanassar carried them. We [illegible] conceived, that Salmanassar had placed [illegible] of the Chaborus, which [illegible] the same river the [illegible] a great river [illegible] point but great boats [illegible] which some have [illegible] depending on the [illegible] called Patre, in it [illegible] itself into the Euphrates, and [illegible] Carchemis, since [illegible] a [illegible] of [illegible] the province of Gauzan [illegible] and Stocks. This was the first [illegible] of the tribes. But [illegible] into the [illegible] the [illegible] country [illegible] to bring [illegible] The subsisted there [illegible] of the [illegible] church [illegible] of the [illegible] Though they [illegible] has of [illegible] have those that were there [illegible] great number of Jews are to be found [illegible] We have also [illegible] observing [illegible] other [illegible] different revolutions of that empire, the various tempers of the government, and the [illegible] of that nation which only subsists [illegible] We have therefore reason to conclude that the ten tribes are still in the east, and that they are [illegible], or gone from thence into some remote quarter of the world. They are so blended one tribe with another that they cannot now possibly be distinguished, and [illegible] without a miracle, have happened otherwise during so long a series of ages, and such vicissitudes as they have undergone.

It is therefore reasonable to conclude, that the ten tribes are at present dispersed [illegible] the east, and that [illegible] in America [illegible] so far are they from having kings, and possessing a great extent of land [illegible] to the most [illegible]

Several authors, both Jews and Christians, have likewise affirmed, that the ten tribes were still preserved in China. [illegible] former tells us that there was a synagogue [illegible] 10,000 crowns to [illegible] He [illegible], that they had been settled in this province above five hundred years and that they religiously [illegible] one of the five books of Moses, which are called Sepher Thorah. He could not read Hebrew, having neglected the study of it in his youth, so that he was excluded from the offices and government of the synagogue, which his brother exercised, because he understood the language, but he received the historical parts of the Old Testament, particularly those of Abraham, Joseph and Esther. He added, that there were, in the capital of the province of Chequiam, many synagogues and [illegible] families, for they gave [illegible] because being the posterity of the ten tribes, they [illegible] of the Jews.

Alvarez, who had lived in China [illegible] affirms, that they had been settled there [illegible] 600 [illegible] obtained several privileges on [illegible] to [illegible] were [illegible] numerous in some provinces [illegible] of their [illegible] but [illegible] which they [illegible] volumes [illegible] They prefer [illegible] antient Bible [illegible] Jews, however, are [illegible] and only [illegible] the names of [illegible] very ignorant [illegible] the [illegible] with the [illegible] innocent [illegible]

[illegible] more [illegible] Jews [illegible] synagogue [illegible]

[illegible] into the [illegible]

"[illegible]

"[illegible]

"[illegible]

"[illegible]

"From [illegible]

"[illegible] His [illegible]

"of the [illegible]

[illegible] with him [illegible]

[illegible] formed upon [illegible] in [illegible] the [illegible] of the nation [illegible] and [illegible] found [illegible]

All that we [illegible] the [illegible] of [illegible] China, and [illegible] not the ten tribes [illegible] the [illegible] families of the [illegible] by an [illegible]

Besides, there [illegible] and [illegible] in America [illegible] of India [illegible] remains of the [illegible] of the Euphrates, [illegible] provinces, is [illegible]

In Turkey, Persia, Germany, and [illegible] somewhat more [illegible] public [illegible] princes [illegible] they [illegible] themselves [illegible] their [illegible] government [illegible] million [illegible] they allow [illegible] thousand [illegible]

The Jewish writers divide [illegible] reigns, or rather between two [illegible] Protestants and the Roman Catholics [illegible] that the popes, [illegible] Rome [illegible] protected them [illegible] He was not general of [illegible] but [illegible] instead of protect- [illegible] Nevertheless [illegible] the [illegible] protection, [illegible] requisites rendered them [illegible] their happiness, or [illegible] to the [illegible]

[illegible]

CHAP. [illegible]

[illegible]

[illegible] the prince. [illegible] it is impossible [illegible] the Jews preserved [illegible] theocratical govern- [illegible] their judges [illegible] the judges, those [illegible] that God [illegible] the ephod [illegible] precious stones, [illegible] Urim and Thum- [illegible] The sacrifices [illegible] this people, who [illegible] to borrow [illegible] images and teraphim from other nations. The Jews'

inclination for [illegible] and [illegible] of religion was so violent, [illegible] could not [illegible] but by con- [illegible] of mankind, [illegible] nation, you will find [illegible] Jews [illegible] though [illegible] They are [illegible] Indeed [illegible] ages [illegible] They are not [illegible]

[illegible]

"They [illegible] "among the [illegible] law [illegible] dangerous [illegible]

A [illegible] of [illegible] verts [illegible]

In the [illegible] children [illegible] the prince [illegible] over the children, who [illegible] cities of M[illegible], [illegible] where they were more [illegible] [illegible] the Jews before him, and upon asking whether any would embrace Christianity? [illegible] immediately [illegible] threw themselves at his feet, and desired baptism, and that this example had been followed by forty-[illegible] others. He concluded from thence, that, if the emperor gave his orders to the bishop of Arles, and forced him to do the same thing, many of them might be gained [illegible] the motive was the more forcible, because, if it be [illegible] charity to rescue a man from the jaws of wild beasts that would devour him, it is much greater to deliver [illegible] out of the hands of those who would destroy [illegible].

It appears that this [illegible] made no scruple to baptize Jewish children by forcing them from their fathers, and that the authority of the [illegible] council was not respected in France when [illegible] that contradicted the [illegible] St. [illegible], indeed, that he sent back [illegible] could [illegible] without doing them any violence, but yet he [illegible] could [illegible] knowledge [illegible] the [illegible] and [illegible] to [illegible] bishop of [illegible] to [illegible] enough to show that this bishop [illegible] regarded the law of [illegible], or that of the council of [illegible].

[illegible] more [illegible] than [illegible] that all Jews [illegible] the [illegible] of [illegible] persons, and to [illegible] them to [illegible] the council would [illegible] much [illegible] appointed, unless [illegible] conversion.

[illegible] the [illegible] since the [illegible] no [illegible] the [illegible] instances, [illegible] the following.

Conrad Otton, [illegible] so violently against the synagogue [illegible] that [illegible] "[illegible] and [illegible] the T[illegible], "[illegible] to the [illegible], "they [illegible], "they, in their [illegible], for the [illegible] "what they [illegible], and [illegible], that great [illegible] them [illegible] they [illegible] to believe, or "understood [illegible] the meaning of [illegible]." Nevertheless, this [illegible], so [illegible] by the [illegible] of his brethren, [illegible] his profession in the university of Altorf, and returned to Judaism.

Some years ago [illegible] professor at Vienna, who was thought [illegible] Christianity, for the [illegible] of which he translated the epistle [illegible] to the Hebrews into Hebrew, and rendered [illegible] commentaries upon the [illegible], [illegible] to the synagogue he had left.

In Spain and Portugal [illegible] converts [illegible] Alba, or White Castle, but more by the books he [illegible], which gave him the [illegible] of [illegible] the most ingenious man of his age, left his country [illegible] a [illegible] Rome. But fearing his [illegible] would be severely chastised, he [illegible] to [illegible] apprehensions. Having [illegible] in [illegible] places, he retreated to Thessalonica, where [illegible], he [illegible] the religion he had always [illegible], and disguised under the mask of Christianity.

The Grecian church thought it could not be too precautious in admitting into [illegible] of a [illegible] faith, for we find some marks of its severity in the forms of abjuration, which the Jewish [illegible] were obliged to make. [illegible] two. One is [illegible] in the [illegible] and the other [illegible] Cotelier [illegible] manuscript of the king of France's library. [illegible] last [illegible]

[illegible] larger than the other, because [illegible] fort of pieces [illegible] the first, because [illegible], and we would [illegible] to avoid controversy.

[illegible] the [illegible] converted Jew to own [illegible] he does [illegible] his conversion, [illegible] neither by poverty, [illegible] violence or any human [illegible] make [illegible] of his [illegible] religion [illegible] of the Greeks [illegible] all the Jews [illegible]

[illegible]

[illegible]

[illegible]

[illegible] as it were, congenial with their very nature, a subject [illegible] may afford scope for some [illegible] remarks by [illegible].

[illegible], then, from the corresponding testimony [illegible] sacred and profane, that, from the earliest ages [illegible], unbelief has been the great source of [illegible] that have befallen the Jews. [illegible], has proved, and ever will prove, [illegible] to the human race [illegible]. [illegible] command given [illegible] of all the women [illegible] or their wretched [illegible] partook of their degeneracy, and [illegible], evinced a natural aversion to [illegible]. [illegible] and the [illegible] of the [illegible], the ancient Hebrews were almost perpetually [illegible], and falling into the [illegible] of the [illegible]. Nay, the [illegible] would give occasion for the Divine vengeance [illegible].

[illegible] the Almighty to restrain the impetuous [illegible] the [illegible] few, should [illegible] had [illegible] the earth, Noah, indeed, gave us most [illegible] of his pious gratitude to an all-gracious [illegible] his descendants soon [illegible] in more [illegible], denying obedience to God's [illegible] their [illegible] folly in their [illegible] impracticable attempt of the tower of Babel.

Yet in each succeeding age there appears to have been [illegible] a monument of Divine grace and favour, and a [illegible] example of piety and virtue to cotemporaries, as we find after Noah, there was an Abraham, an Isaac, a Jacob, a Joseph, and at length a Moses, who was honoured with the [illegible] of the friend of God and being the peculiar instrument of conveying the immediate revelation of the Divine will to the people.

A [illegible] view of the most signal events which occurred in the early ages of the Hebrew nation, will afford us a most striking display of the Divine attributes, mercy, and justice, as well as [illegible] effects of human unbelief and impenitence. Disobedience succeeded calamity, and calamity deliverance. Obedience was almost instantaneously rewarded, and disobedience [illegible] instantaneously punished. The power of Omnipotence was exerted, and wonders of mercy and of vengeance were [illegible], yet still, sinful mortals were no sooner freed from the [illegible] they deprecated, than they doubted the [illegible], and presumptuously dared to set Omnipotence at defiance.

In succeeding times the same unbelief, the same impenitence, too generally prevailed, whilst the same [illegible] of the Divine [illegible], and the Divine [illegible] attended them. They had line upon line, and precept upon precept, were never [illegible], yet [illegible] they persisted [illegible], till their kingdom [illegible] were reduced to a [illegible], and they could no longer be considered as a [illegible], but a people dispersed throughout all quarters of the earth, and subject to the vilest ignominy and contempt.

The History of the Jews affords a most important [illegible] to those who call themselves Christians, and a [illegible] example to those who are too wise, or rather too wicked to [illegible] to the Divine will, as [illegible] in the sacred [illegible]. Our first parents [illegible] an equality with their Creator [illegible] presumption [illegible] by [illegible] consummate, and [illegible] to mortality, with its [illegible]. The pride of the human heart has since too frequently prompted it to explore the hidden purposes of Omniscience, and feeble beings have dared to attempt to [illegible] the traces of unerring wisdom. [illegible] experience and sober reflection, will demonstrate the [illegible]. True wisdom will recur to its fountain, [illegible] limits excellence, and beyond its sphere [illegible] are displayed with all lustre in the works of creation and Providence: we cannot turn our eyes or our thoughts on an object, but it impresses us with an idea of the Deity, or, in other words, "all nature cries aloud through all her works there is a God."

To conclude, if the above remarks are admitted, it follows that, as the supreme and ultimate felicity of man consists in a conformity to the Divine will, and as that will is only communicated by Divine revelation, which holds forth competent instructions throughout the whole, it is his highest wisdom and happiness to receive the same with all the deference due to its origin, and to confirm himself and others in the belief and practice of it, by every means which his benevolent Creator hath put in his power.

END OF BOOK II

ILLUSTRATION

OF THE

PREDICTIONS

OF THE

PRINCIPAL PROPHETS

WHOSE NAMES ARE MENTIONED

IN THE WORKS OF

FLAVIUS JOSEPHUS.

INTRODUCTION.

AS, in the course of the work we now offer to the public, prophecies occur, which not only coincide with but corroborate the evidences of, the truth of what is called, by way of eminence, Sacred History in particular, as well as revealed religion in general; we presume that an illustration of the passages particularly alluded to, may be introduced with equal utility and propriety. Many eminent divines and other learned men, unite in opinion, that nothing tends more effectually to confirm serious Christians in their most holy faith, or obviate the gainsayings of infidels, than a display of the time and manner in which events foretold by holy men, in ancient days, have been as remarkable as completely fulfilled.

Those who admit that one all-prevailing mind not only comprehends whatever is present and past, but, with one infinite view, discerns whatever is to happen in future, must readily acknowledge the power of an omnipotent Jehovah, to communicate his will and pleasure to such of his creatures, and in such way and manner [illegible] seem meet to his infinite wisdom. Yet, though it is the sole prerogative of the Almighty, and it has been his pleasure, to appoint and commission certain chosen agents to prophecy things to come, there have not been wanting, in all ages, men disposed to carp, cavil, and impiously avow their incredibility.

But all their efforts combined cannot invalidate demonstrative evidence, or subvert facts founded on the basis of truth. Such as review, with an impartial eye, events recorded in history, both sacred and profane, which, in this instance, throw great light on each other, must discover every truth of authenticity that can be had in points of this kind. They will also find things foretold in plain and explicit terms, though the period of accomplishment was not at those times ascertained. They will also find their completion in ages following, and that in a manner corresponding with the predictions. What further evidence, what more convincing proof can be [illegible]? Nothing surely can withstand them, but a settled obstinacy and hardened infidelity.

The Divine prophecies have been fulfilling in all ages of time: some are past, and others are actually fulfilling at this day, so that we have [illegible] stronger than our progenitors, and are consequently more [illegible], if we reject the oracles of such [illegible] "many righteous men have desired to see those things which ye see, and have not seen them; and to hear those things which ye hear, and have not heard them." Matt. xiii. 17. [illegible] truth, [illegible] of us who live in this latter age [illegible] manifestly, that those who deny the [illegible] of the prophecies contained in the sacred [illegible] have renounced all rational [illegible] or their [illegible], and that they are as grossly [illegible] as they are flagrantly [illegible].

When we [illegible] the particular [illegible] our author, [illegible] in holy writ, [illegible] manner of their relation [illegible] completions, [illegible] [illegible] of our [illegible] [illegible] of [illegible]

CHAP I

[illegible] the future state and co[illegible] of his posterity

WE find in J[illegible]phus, as well the sacred writings, that as soon as the earth began to recover its former state, after the dire effects of the late tremendous deluge, Noah applied himself to the cultivation of the earth, planting of vineyards, gathering and pressing the grapes, and producing a store of wine.

It is further related, that the patriarch, though a pious [illegible] man, having, after an oblation to the bountiful author of every good and perfect gift, drank two [illegible] of the liquor, became intoxicated to a degree [illegible], and laid himself down in a manner that exposed him to shame. His son Ham, seeing the situation [illegible] his [illegible] parent, called his brethren, in derision, to [illegible] what [illegible] could not but should [illegible] the [illegible] filial tenderness. Our [illegible] therefore, the other sons, Shem and [illegible] brought a covering, and veiled the shame of [illegible].

When Noah recovered his senses, and understood what [illegible] upon his other [illegible] good offices they had rendered him, and at [illegible] of Ham, [illegible] prophetic malediction was followed [illegible] with Divine vengeance. Ham [illegible] his own person, escaped the curse from a tender [illegible] Noah to the ties of consanguinity. [illegible] history.

The [illegible] malediction runs thus: "Cursed be "C[illegible]n. A servant of servants shall he be unto his "[illegible] Blessed be the Lord God of Shem, and Ca-"naan shall be his servant. God shall enlarge J[illegible] "and he shall dwell in the tents of Shem, and C[illegible] "[illegible] be his servant." Gen ix 25, 26, 27.

I[illegible] upon due reflection and attention to [illegible] malediction to [illegible] Noah as to other posterity, [illegible] nations by [illegible] respectively [illegible], and [illegible] the Judge of all the earth [illegible], his moral government of the world, his [illegible] virtue and aversion to vice [illegible], and [illegible] for which wise and equitable [illegible] Noah [illegible] a prophetic [illegible] known his will to succeeding generations. [illegible] the word and spirit of [illegible] to individuals or even particular persons [illegible] of them, on the contrary, we must allow them a [illegible] more extensive scope. We must consider [illegible] bodies collected [illegible] whole nations, whereby we shall be enabled to form a right judgment of the Divine superintendance over human affairs, [illegible] the various dispensations of Providence.

On this principle, therefore, we must suppose the curse of servitude [illegible] upon Canaan, as well as the blessing of [illegible] promised to Shem and Japheth, not immediately relating to them personally considered, but as an enlarged and extensive view, comprehending their whole race. So, indeed, as before observed, we must judge of scripture prophecy in general.

The malediction then uttered prophetically by the patriarch Noah, in fact referred to the race of Canaan, from his name called Canaanites, and from whole iniquities the Omniscient Being delegated his antient servant to foretell that curse which was most justly due to their common degeneracy. And it was the evident design of the inspired penman, Moses, in relating the same, to encourage the Hebrews or Israelites in waging a necessary war against an abandoned race, who had renounced all claims to the favour and protection of Heaven, and was therefore doomed to servitude from an early date.

Having thus pointed out the purport and meaning of this prophecy, it now remains that we proceed to display the manner in which it was fully completed.

It is certain the Canaanites were a most wicked and abandoned people, and it was for their great sins that the Almighty was pleased to inflict a most severe punishment not only on them, but their posterity. They were addicted to practise the worst kinds of idolatry. Their religion was bad, and their morals worse, for corrupt religion and corrupt morals usually generate each other. Was not therefore a curse in the nature of things, as well as in the just judgment of God, entailed on such a people and nation as this? It was not for the righteousness of the Israelites that the Lord was pleased to give them the possession of the land of Canaan, but for the wickedness of the people did he drive them out of the country, and he would have driven out the Israelites in like manner had they been guilty of the like abominations. See Levit xviii 24, &c.

The curse pronounced on the descendants of Ham particularly implies servitude and subjection. "Cursed be "Canaan. A servant of servants shall he be unto his "brethren." The descendants, therefore, of Canaan were to be subject to the descendants of Shem and Japheth, and the natural consequence of vice, in communities as well as in single persons, is subjection, slavery, and death.

This part of the prophecy, however, was not fulfilled till several centuries after it was delivered by Noah, when the Israelites, who were the descendants of Shem, under the command of Joshua, invaded the country of the Canaanites, smote above thirty of their kings, took possession of their land, and made the Gibeonites and others servants and tributaries, and the rest were after subdued by Solomon. The Greeks and Romans, who were the descendants of Japheth, not only subdued Syria and Palestine, but also pursued and conquered such of the Canaanites as were any where remaining, as for instance, the Tyrians and Carthaginians, the former of whom were ruined by Alexander and the Grecians, and the latter by Scipio and the Romans. From that period the miserable remainder of these people have been slaves, first to the Saracens, who descended from Shem, and afterwards to the Turks, who descended from Japheth, and under whose dominion great numbers of them [illegible] remain.

Having thus explained the fulfilment of that part of Noah's prophecy [illegible] to the descendants of his son Ham, let us now consider the promises he made to Shem and Japheth. And first: "Blessed be the Lord God of Shem, and Canaan shall be his servant." The wickedness of men proceeded from themselves, but their good from God, and therefore we find the old patriarch, in a strain of devotion, breaketh forth into thanksgiving to God as the author of all good to Shem. God can certainly bestow his particular favours according to his good pleasure, and salvation was to be derived to mankind through Shem and his posterity. By the Lord being called the God of Shem, is plainly intimated, that the Lord would be his God in a particular manner.

The promise made to Japheth was this: "God shall "enlarge Japheth, and he shall dwell in the tents of "Shem, and Canaan shall be his servant." That Japheth was more enlarged than the rest is evident, he having much greater possessions, and a more numerous offspring than either of his brothers. The territories of Japheth's posterity were very large, for besides all Europe, great and extensive as it is, they possessed the lesser Asia, Media, part of Armenia, Iberia, Albania, and those great regions towards the north, which were anciently inhabited by the Scythians, and at [illegible] by the Tartars

[illegible] of Japheth [illegible] enlarged, as well as his [illegible], evidently appears from the 10th chapter of Genesis, wherein we find that Japheth had seven sons, [illegible] Ham [illegible], and Shem only five. The [illegible] "he shall dwell in the tents of Shem," is [illegible] of a double construction, for thereby may be [illegible] at God, or that Japheth, shall dwell in the [illegible] Shem. Those who prefer the former construction, [illegible] on the literal sense of the words in the text [illegible], no other [illegible] to govern the verbs in [illegible] the word God. The whole sentence, [illegible], should run thus, God will enlarge Japheth, [illegible] dwell in the tents of Shem. But [illegible] be taken either way, it is [illegible] been most punctually fulfilled. In the former sense [illegible] literally when [illegible] rested on the ark, and [illegible] the tabernacle [illegible] temple of the Jews. In the [illegible], when the Greeks and Romans, who [illegible] from Japheth, subdued and [illegible] other countries of Asia, belonging to Shem [illegible] when they were more [illegible] that those who were not Israelites by birth became [illegible] by faith.

[illegible] prophecy of Noah is certainly a most extraordinary one [illegible] delivered near four thousand years ago, and yet hath been fulfilling through the several [illegible] to this day. It is both wonderful and [illegible], and is, [illegible], an epitome of the history of the world.

CHAP. II.

Of the prophecies concerning Ishmael, the son of Abraham, by [illegible] Hagar.

AFTER Noah, the next great patriarch we meet with in the Old Testament is the pious Abraham, who was favoured with several Divine revelations. From him two very extraordinary nations descended, namely, the Ishmaelites and [illegible], concerning each of which people there are [illegible] prophecies of the most extraordinary nature.

Ishmael was the son of Abraham, by his handmaid Hagar, who was an Egyptian, and though he was not properly a child of promise, yet he was distinguished by some express predictions, for the comfort and satisfaction of both [illegible].

After Hagar had fled from the face of her mistress Sarah, who had dealt hardly with her, (see Gen. xvi.) the angel of the Lord found her [illegible] the wilderness, and said unto her, "[illegible] submit thyself under her hands." "And the angel of the Lord said unto her, I will multiply "thy seed exceedingly, that it shall not be numbered for "multitude. And the angel of the Lord said unto her, Behold, thou art with child, and shalt bear a son, and shalt "call his name Ishmael, because the Lord hath heard thy "affliction. And he will be a wild man: his hand will be "against every man, and every man's hand against him, "and he shall dwell in the presence of all his brethren."

We find, in the succeeding chapter, that God promised Abraham a son by his wife Sarah, whom he should call Isaac, but notwithstanding this, he still reserved a blessing for Ishmael. "Behold (said he) I have blessed him, and will "make him fruitful, and will multiply him exceedingly: "twelve princes shall he beget: and I will make him a great "nation." After this, when Hagar and Ishmael were sent forth into the wilderness, God said unto Abraham, "And "also of the son of the bond woman will I make a nation, "because he is thy seed." Gen. xxi. 13. And the same is repeated to Hagar, (ver. 18.) "I will make him a great "nation."

Now, if we attend to the particulars mentioned in this prophecy, and trace the course of events which afterwards took place, we shall find the whole strictly fulfilled, and the [illegible] part of it is fulfilling even at this present period. "I will multiply thy seed exceedingly, and it shall not be numbered "for multitude." And [illegible], "Behold, I have blessed "him, and will make him fruitful, and will multiply him "exceedingly." From these two passages it is [illegible] evident, that the prophecy does not [illegible] Ishmael himself, as it does to his descendants, whom it is [illegible] be exceeding numerous, and this part of the prediction was most amply fulfilled.

Hagar, the mother of Ishmael, was an Egyptian, and when he grew to [illegible] of manhood, [illegible] of the same country. In the course of [illegible] children and their [illegible] become so numerous that they formed a considerable body of people, and were [illegible] distinguished for the great [illegible] different parts of Egypt. After [illegible] were greatly multiplied in the [illegible] led to [illegible] Hagar, [illegible] were called [illegible] his son Jethro [illegible], especially the [illegible] a great part of the [illegible] very numerous people.

[illegible] "shall he beget," [illegible] Ishmael, [illegible] "the [illegible]" "twelve princes [illegible] heads of [illegible], or [illegible] tions the [illegible] Melo[illegible] "[illegible] by his Egyptian [illegible] departing [illegible], divided [illegible] were [illegible] kings [illegible] days, [illegible] the Arabians [illegible] had twelve [illegible] names as the [illegible]. At the time of [illegible], the Arabs were governed by what was then called *[illegible]*, and lived in tribes [illegible] as [illegible] by the testimony of [illegible], Maundrel [illegible], and other modern travellers.

"And I will make him a great nation." This part of the prophecy is repeated several times [illegible] the regular [illegible] accomplished in the descendants of [illegible] the great [illegible] several ages, and, [illegible] numbers of them that still inhabit the country, they may be justly called a great nation."

"And he will be a wild man." Ishmael and his posterity were to be wild, fierce [illegible] in the deserts, and not easily [illegible] and whoever has read the accounts given of these people [illegible] know it to be a true [illegible] genuine character [illegible] of Ishmael (Gen. xxi. 20.) that "he [illegible] in the wilderness, and became an archer," and the same [illegible] true of his descendants [illegible] "He dwelt in the wilderness," [illegible] descendants [illegible] the wilderness, and many of them, [illegible] we have both ancient and modern [illegible] agriculture, neither sowing or planting, but living [illegible] by plunder and rapine. "And he became an archer." [illegible] were the archers and mighty men of Kedar, mentioned [illegible] Isaiah chap. [illegible] and such the Arabs have been [illegible] the beginning to the present time. It was very [illegible] they admitted the use of fire arms in their country, and the greater part of them are still strangers to that instrument of defence: for they constantly practice the bow and arrow, and are esteemed the most skilful archers in the universe.

"And he shall dwell in the presence of his brethren," that is shall dwell in tents, as many of the Arabs do at the present time.

If we reflect on this part of the prophecy, we shall, on the first view, think it very extraordinary, that "his hand "should be against every man, and every man's hand a-"gainst him," and yet that he should be able to "dwell in "the presence of all his brethren." But, extraordinary as it was, this also hath been fulfilled, not only in the person of Ishmael, but likewise in his descendants. With respect to Ishmael himself, the sacred historian tells us, that "the "years of the life of Ishmael were an hundred and thirty "and seven years, and he died in the presence of all his "brethren." Gen. xxv. 17, 18. As for his posterity, they [illegible] likewise in the presence of all their brethren, and they still subsist a distinct people, and inhabit the country of their progenitors, notwithstanding the perpetual enmity between them and the rest of mankind.

[illegible] suggested by some, that the reason why these people were never subdued by any other nation is, that their country was never worth the conquering, and that its barrenness [illegible] its preservation; but this is a mistake, for, by all the accounts we have, though the greater part of it be sandy and barren deserts, yet here and there are interspersed beautiful spots, and fruitful vallies. One part of the country was anciently known and distinguished by the name of Arabia the Happy, which appellation it received on account of the natural fertility of the soil, in contrast to the barrenness of the other parts. The whole country of Arabia is, by the oriental writers, generally divided into five provinces, the chief of which is called Yaman, and is thus described by the learned Mr. Sale, in his preface to the Alcoran: "The province of Yaman (says he) has been famous, from all antiquity, for the [illegible] of its climate, its [illegible]. The [illegible] and plenty of [illegible] mountains, for all that part which lie along the Red Sea is a dry [illegible] desert, in some places ten or twelve leagues over, but, in return, bounded by those mountains, which [illegible] well watered, enjoy an almost continual spring, and [illegible] great plenty and variety of fruits, and [illegible] excellent corn, grapes, and spices. The [illegible] more barren than that of Yaman, the greater part [illegible] with dry sands, [illegible] interspersed here and there with some fruitful spots, which receive their greatest advantages from [illegible] water and palm trees."

[illegible] however sterile, or however barren and desolate their country be, yet it was certainly the interest of the neighbouring princes and nations [illegible] to endeavour to root out such a pestilent race of robbers. This, indeed, has several times been attempted, but never accomplished. They have, from first to last, maintained their independency, and, notwithstanding the most powerful efforts have been made to destroy them, they still "dwell in the pre-"sence of all their brethren," and in the presence of all their enemies.

On a judicious and circumspect view of the respective particulars contained in this amazing prophecy, with the astonishing manner in which each article has been fulfilled, we shall easily perceive that the whole, from beginning to end, was guided by the direction of Providence. The sacred historian tells us that these prophecies concerning Ishmael were delivered partly by the angel of the Lord and partly by God himself: and, indeed, who but God, or one enabled and commissioned by him, could describe so particularly the genius and manners, not only of a single person before he was born, but of a whole people, from the first founder of the race to the present time? It was certainly very wonderful, and not to be foreseen by human sagacity or prudence, that a man's whole posterity should so nearly resemble him, and retain the same inclinations, the same [illegible] throughout all ages. The waters of the purest spring or fountain are soon changed [illegible] course, and the farther still they flow, the more they are incorporated and lost in other waters. How are the modern Italians degenerated from the courage and virtues of the old Romans? How are the French and English polished and refined from the barbarism of the ancient Gauls and Britons? In general, men and manners change with the times: but, in all changes and revolutions, the Arabs have continued the same from the beginning. They still remain the same fierce, savage, untractable, unsocial people they were at first, following in every thing their great ancestor, and being entirely different from the rest of their fellow creatures.

The great affinity that still subsists between the present Arabs and their progenitor Ishmael, from whom they descended, will appear evident from the following circumstances. Ishmael was circumcised, and so are his posterity to this day; and as Ishmael was circumcised when he was thirteen years of age, so are the Arabs at the same time. Ishmael was [illegible] who was a concubine, and the Arabs still indulge [illegible] mercenary wives and concubines. He lived in tents in the wilderness, and shifting from place to place, and so do his descendants, even to the present time. He was an archer in the wilderness, and so are they. He was to be the father of twelve princes, or heads of tribes, and [illegible] tribes to this day. He was a wild man, "his hand against every "man, and every man's hand against him;" and they still live in the same state of war, their hand against every man, and every man's hand against them.

If we reflect on these [illegible] circumstances, how wonderful must it appear to us, that the same people should remain the [illegible] for so many ages [illegible] how much more wonderful is it that, with [illegible] enmity against the whole world, [illegible] independent and free people! It cannot be pretended that no attempts were ever made to [illegible] the greatest conquerors of the world have almost all, in their turns, attempted it, and some have been very near effecting it. [illegible] pretended that the drynefs or inaccessibleness of their country has been their preservation; for their country hath been often penetrated, but could never be entirely subdued. [illegible] have found the means of subsistence [illegible] of their powerful invaders ever [illegible] and therefore, the reason of their [illegible] every effort to conquer them, must be imputed to some other cause. This was certainly no less than the Divine interposition, and which will evidently appear if we attend to the following very singular particulars.

Alexander was preparing an expedition against them when [illegible] fever cut him off in the flower of his age. Pompey was in the career of his conquest, when urgent affairs called him elsewhere. Aelius Gallus had penetrated far into the country, when a fatal disease destroyed great numbers of his men, and obliged him to return. Trajan entered their capital city, but was defeated by thunder and lightning, whirlwinds, and other prodigies, and that as often as he renewed his assaults. Severus besieged the same city twice, and was twice repulsed from before it, and the historian Dion (a man of rank and character, though an heathen), himself, ascribes the defeat of these two emperors to the interposition of a Divine power.

In short, if we consider the whole matter in its proper light, we cannot fail being of the same opinion with this heathen historian, for, without a Divine interposition, how could a single nation maintain itself against the enmity of the whole world for any length of time, and much more for near four thousand years together? The peace empires [illegible] them [illegible] are all in their turns, fallen to ruin, while they have continued the ſame from the beginning, and are likely to continue the ſame to the end.

The Arabs are the only people except the Jews who have ſubſiſted as a diſtinct [illegible] the [illegible] and in ſome reſpects th[illegible] reſemble [illegible]er, as will appear by the following compariſons

1 The Arabs, as well as the Jews, are deſcended from Abraham, and both boaſt of their deſcent from that father of the faithful

[illegible] The Arabs as well as the Jews, are circumciſed, and both profeſs to have derived that ceremony from Abraham

3 The Arabs, as well as the Jews, had originally twelve heads of tribes, who were their princes or governors

4 The Arabs, as well as the Jews, marry among themſelves, and in their own tribes.

5 The Arabs as well as the Jews, are ſingular in ſeveral of their cuſtoms, and are ſtanding monuments, to all ages, of the exactneſs of the Divine predictions, and of the [illegible] of [illegible] hiſtory

We have [illegible] more to make on the fulfilment [illegible] contained in the [illegible], and that is, that [illegible] defeat every attempt [illegible] ſpecious light We [illegible] Iſhmael to be d[illegible]ly verified [illegible] we have, as it were, [illegible] truth, which is proving [illegible] "the Moſt High ruleth in "the kingdoms of men" and that his truth, as well as his mercy, "endureth for ever"

CHAP III

Containing [illegible] of the prophecies concerning Jacob and Eſau the ſons of Iſaac

IT having pleaſed the Almighty to diſcloſe unto Abraham the ſtate and condition of his poſterity by Iſhmael who was the ſon of the bond-woman, he was likewiſe pleaſed to predict ſome things of a much more important nature concerning the poſterity of Iſaac, who was the ſon of his wife Sarah This ſon was properly the child of promiſe, and the prophecies relating to him and his family, are much more numerous than thoſe relating to Iſhmael and his deſcendants

Previous to the birth of Iſhmael, the Almighty was pleaſed to make this promiſe to Abraham, "In thee ſhall all families of the earth be bleſſed" Gen xii [illegible] but after the birth of Iſhmael by Hagar, and Iſaac by Sarah, the promiſe was limited to Iſaac "for in Iſaac ſhall thy ſeed be called" Gen xxi 12 And accordingly to Iſaac was the promiſe repeated, "In thy "ſeed ſhall all the nations of the earth be bleſſed," which plainly intimated, that the Saviour of the world was not to come from the family of Iſhmael, but from the deſcendants of Iſaac

The land of Canaan was promiſed to Abraham and his deſcendants four hundred years before they obtained poſſeſſion of it, and it was afterwards promiſed to his ſon Iſaac "Sojourn in this land (ſays the Lord unto Iſaac) "and I will be with thee, and will bleſs thee for unto "thee and unto thy ſeed I will give all theſe countries, "and I will perform the oath which I ſware unto Abra-"ham thy father"

This promiſe was ſtrictly fulfilled ſoon after the death of Moſes, when the Iſraelites got poſſeſſion of the land of Canaan through the aſſiſtance and protection of Joſhua who ſucceeded Moſes in the government of the people In conſequence of that prophecy, they remained in poſſeſſion for ſeveral ages, and afterwards, when, for their ſins and iniquities, they were to be removed from it, their removal alſo was foretold, both the carrying away of the ten tribes, and the captivity of the two remaining tribes for ſeventy years, as likewiſe their final captivity and diſperſion into all nations.

Abraham received a promiſe from God, that his poſterity ſhould be multiplied exceedingly above that of others. "I will make of thee a great nation," and "in bleſ-"ſing I will bleſs thee, and in multiplying I will multi-"ply thy ſeed as the ſtars of heaven, and as the ſand [illegible] upon the ſea-ſhore" See Gen xii 2 xxii 17. [illegible] promiſe was alſo continued to Iſaac "I will [illegible] thy ſeed to multiply as the ſtars of heaven" [illegible] 4

[illegible] to mention the great increaſe of the other poſterity [illegible] Abraham and Iſaac, how ſoon did their deſcendants by Jacob grow up to a mighty nation, and how numerous were they formerly in the land of Canaan? How numerous were they likewiſe in various other parts of the world? and after innumerable ſlaughters and perſecutions which they have undergone, how numerous are they ſtill in their preſent diſperſion among all nations?

Iſaac had two ſons, the one named Jacob, and the other Eſau The deſcendants of theſe ſons did not incorporate themſelves together as one people, but ſeparated into two different nations, and therefore as it had been before ſpecified which of the two, [illegible] of Iſaac, was to be heir to the promiſes made to Abraham, ſo there was a neceſſity now for the ſame diſtinction to be made between Eſau and Jacob, the ſons of Iſaac

This was accordingly done, and that in the moſt ample and clear manner When Rebecca, their mother, had conceived, "the children ſtruggled together within her," Gen xxv 22, and ſhe received the following Divine revelation "Two nations are in thy womb, and two "manner of people ſhall be ſeparated from thy bowels, "and the one people ſhall be ſtronger than the other "people, and the elder ſhall ſerve the younger" Gen xxv 23

The ſame Divine Spirit influenced and directed their father to give his final benediction to the like purpoſe thus did he bleſs Jacob "God give thee of the dew "of heaven and the fatneſs of the earth, and plenty of "corn and wine Let people ſerve thee, and nations "bow down to thee be lord over thy brethren, and let "thy mother's ſons bow down to thee curſed be every "one that curſeth thee, and bleſſed be he that bleſſeth "thee" Gen xxvii 28, 29 And thus did he bleſs Eſau "Behold, thy dwelling ſhall be the fatneſs of "the earth, and of the dew of heaven from above And "by thy ſword ſhalt thou live, and ſhalt ſerve thy bro-"ther and it ſhall come to paſs when thou ſhalt have "the dominion, that thou ſhalt break his yoke from off "thy neck"

But, for greater clearneſs and certainty, a more expreſs revelation was afterwards made to Jacob, and the land of Canaan, a numerous progeny, and the bleſſing of all nations, were promiſed to him in particular "I am "the Lord God of Abraham thy father, and the God of "Iſaac the land whereon thou lieſt to thee will I give "it, and to thy ſeed And thy ſeed ſhall be as the duſt "of the earth, and thou ſhalt ſpread abroad to the weſt, "and to the eaſt, and to the north, and to the ſouth, and "in thee and in thy ſeed ſhall the families of the earth "be bleſſed" Gen xxviii 13 15

This prophecy, as well as thoſe before mentioned, was not to be verified in the perſons of Eſau and Jacob, but in thoſe of their poſterity. Jacob was ſo far from bearing rule over Eſau, that he was forced to fly his country for fear of him He continued abroad ſeveral years, and when he returned, he ſent [illegible] a ſupplicatory meſſage to his brother Eſau, requeſting "that he might find grace in his ſight" [illegible] heard of Eſau's coming to meet him with four hundred men, he "was greatly afraid and diſtreſſed," [illegible] unto the Lord [illegible] "Deliver me, I pray thee, from the "hand of my brother, from the hand of Esau." Gen [illegible] at a magnificent present before him to [illegible] brother [illegible] his lord, and himself his [illegible] "bowed himself to [illegible] seven times until he came near to his brother" [illegible] gracious reception, he [illegible] "I have seen thy face as [illegible] the face of God, and thou wast [illegible]"

[illegible] had no temporal superiority over [illegible] and therefore we must look for the [illegible] of [illegible] descendants [illegible] "two nations" and [illegible] comprehends these [illegible] the [illegible] of Esau and Jacob [illegible] two different people and nations, that [illegible] to that of the younger [illegible] other temporal advantages, [illegible] the elder or [illegible] violence, [illegible] should be subject [illegible] however [illegible] be [illegible] elder should have dominion and [illegible] off [illegible] in all spiritual gifts and [illegible] greatly [illegible] and be the [illegible] the blessing to all nations [illegible] of the prophecy, "Two nations are [illegible]" [illegible] (but as they [illegible] two nations, but [illegible] And [illegible] Edomites ([illegible]), and the Israelites (who [illegible] two very different people [illegible] customs, and religions [illegible] at variance with each [illegible]

[illegible] together with one another." This [illegible] agreement, [illegible] was fully [illegible] of mankind, by their [illegible] nations. Esau was "a [illegible]" [illegible] of the field [illegible] "dwelling in tents," [illegible] Esau slighted his birth [illegible] of which Jacob was [illegible] the profane [illegible] better faith and religion [illegible] their posterity. The [illegible] observers of the Jewish religion [illegible] (whatever they [illegible]) [illegible] the greatest idolaters. [illegible] on other accounts, there [illegible] enmity between the two nations [illegible] the Israelites [illegible] of Egypt [illegible] and the history of the Edomites [illegible] between them and [illegible]

[illegible] one people shall be stronger than the other [illegible] and the elder shall serve the younger." The [illegible] Esau was the elder, and [illegible] the [illegible] two, there having been [illegible] in Edom before there reigned any king over the children of Israel." Gen. xxxvi. 31. But [illegible] entire conquest of the Edomites, [illegible] compelled the rest to become [illegible] and planted garrisons among them [illegible] See 2 Sam. viii. 14 [illegible] being reduced to subjection by David [illegible] continued in a state of servitude for [illegible] years, and, instead of having [illegible] were governed by viceroys, or deputies, appointed by the kings of Judah. In the days of [illegible] the son of Jehoshaphat, they revolted, recovered [illegible] "made a king over themselves." 2 Kings viii. 20. But, after this, they were again reduced by several of the princes of Judah at different periods, and most of their principal places destroyed. Judas Maccabeus attacked and defeated them several times, killing no less than twenty thousand at one time, and upwards of the like number at another. He likewise took their chief city Hebron, and destroyed all the towers and fortresses about it. At length Hyrcanus, the nephew of Judas Maccabeus, took what few cities they had left, and reduced them to the necessity of either embracing the Jewish religion or leaving their country, and seeking new habitations elsewhere. They thought proper to chuse the former, in consequence of which they submitted themselves to be circumcised, became proselytes to the Jewish religion, and were ever after incorporated with those very people whom they had before conquered as their enemies.

It is predicted in one part of this remarkable prophecy, that, in point of situation and other temporal advantages, Esau and Jacob should be much alike. It was said to Jacob "God give thee of the dew of heaven, and of "the fatness of the earth, and plenty of corn and wine." And much the same was said to Esau, "Behold thy "dwelling shall be of the fatness of the earth, and of the "dew of heaven from above." Jacob's [illegible] very fertile [illegible] country, nor was that of Esau [illegible] Mount Seir, and the adjacent country [illegible] first in the possession of the Edomites [illegible] extended themselves farther into Arabia [illegible] southern parts of Judea. [illegible] were situated [illegible] the Edomites [illegible] vantages [illegible] cattle, and [illegible] abundance. [illegible] that the [illegible] bondage [illegible] country in which the Edomites [illegible] abounded with the most [illegible] evidently appears from [illegible] by the [illegible] tories [illegible] "we will not pass [illegible] "yards, [illegible]"

In another part of the prophecy it was predicted [illegible] Esau should [illegible] brother, but [illegible] "by the sword shalt thou live, [illegible]" [illegible] the sword, for he was "a cunning hunter [illegible] the field." He and his posterity [illegible] Mount Seir by force [illegible] pelling from thence the Horites, [illegible] inhabitants. By what means they [illegible] their into Arabia we are not informed, but [illegible] that, upon a jealousy among them, which [illegible] separation, the [illegible] parts of Judea during the Babylonish captivity [illegible] afterwards made that their chief place of residence.

Both before and after this, the Edomites [illegible] continually at war with the Jews [illegible] every occasion were ready to join with their enemies [illegible] after they were subdued by the Jews, they [illegible] the same violent [illegible] by the character given of them by Josephus to the following effect: "They "were (says he) a turbulent and disorderly nation, always "ready for commotions, and [illegible] "least [illegible] who besought them [illegible] "and hastening to battles as it were to a feast." This character, given them by Josephus, appears very just; for, a little before the last siege of Jerusalem, they were at the entreaty of the zealots, to assist them against the priests and people [illegible] together with the zealots, [illegible] ed Ananias, the high-priest, and committed the most unheard of cruelties.

There was, however, to be a time when the elder should have the dominion, and shake off the yoke of the younger. "And it shall come to pass, when thou shalt "have dominion, that thou shalt break thy yoke from [illegible] thy neck." It is not here said or meant that the Idumæans should have dominion over the seed of Jacob, but [illegible] have dominion, as they had when they appointed a king of their own. The whole of this sentence is, in the Jerusalem Targum, thus paraphrased: "And it shall be "when the sons of Jacob attend to the law, and observe the "precepts, they shall impose the yoke of servitude upon "thy neck; but when they shall turn away themselves "from studying the law, and neglect the precepts, behold "thou shalt shake off the yoke of servitude from thy "neck."

It was David who imposed the yoke on the Edomites, (at [illegible] time the Jewish people strictly observed the law) and it was very galling from the first. Towards the latter end of Solomon's reign, Hadad, the Edomite of the blood royal, [illegible] been carried into Egypt in his childhood, returned into his own country, and raised some disturbances; but was not able to recover his throne, his subjects being [illegible] by the garrisons which David had placed among them, [illegible] the reigns of the succeeding princes of Judea [illegible].

[illegible] to the last part of the prophecy, which [illegible], in all spiritual gifts and graces, the younger [illegible] to the elder, and be the happy instrument of conveying the blessing to all nations: "In [illegible] and in thy seed shall all the families of the earth be "blessed." And in order to be received in their full [illegible] expressions, "Let people serve thee, and nations bow down to thee: cursed be every one that "curseth thee, and blessed be he that blesseth thee." The [illegible] was made to Abraham in the name of God: "I will bless them that bless thee, and curse him that curseth "thee." Gen. xii. 3.

Jacob was a man of true religion, and believed the [illegible] of God. The posterity of Jacob [illegible] the true religion, and the worship of one God, while [illegible] were sunk into idolatry. Of the [illegible] was to be born the Saviour of the world. [illegible] and advantage of Jacob, to [illegible] of conveying these spiritual blessings to all [illegible].

[illegible] prophecy, if properly traced from the [illegible] been most strictly fulfilled. [illegible] were several times conquered [illegible] to the Jews, but never the [illegible] Edomites, and the Jews have [illegible], more known in the world, [illegible]. We have, indeed, very [illegible] of the Edomites than what is contained [illegible] which is the same of [illegible] were swallowed up and lost, partly among the Nabathæan Arabs, and partly among the [illegible], the very name of them was abolished and disused.

Thus was fulfilled the prophecies of the other inspired [illegible] Jeremiah xlix. [illegible] &c. Ezekiel xxv. 12, &c. [illegible] Amos i. 11, &c. and lastly, the prophet Obadiah. At this very time we see the Jews subsisting as a distinct people, while the Edomites are no more: and thus [illegible] fulfilled the words of the latter prophet: "For "thy violence against thy brother Jacob, shame shall cover "thee, and thou shalt be cut off for ever." And again, "there shall not be any remaining of the house of Esau, "for the Lord hath spoken it." See Obadiah, ver. 10 and 18.

CHAP. IV.

Containing an account of the prophecies of Jacob relative to [illegible] posterity, but more particularly his son Judah.

WE find two promises in the blessing bestowed upon Jacob, one of which is of a temporal, and the other of a spiritual nature. The first was the promise of the land of Canaan, and the second, the promise of the seed in which all the nations of the earth should be blessed. These promises were first made to Abraham, then repeated to Isaac, and afterwards confirmed to Jacob, who, a short time before his death, bequeathed them to his posterity.

The inheritance of the land of Canaan might be shared and divided among all his sons, but the blessed seed could descend only from one. Accordingly Jacob assigned to each a portion of the former, but [illegible] the latter to the tribe of Judah, and, at the same time, [illegible] the characters and fortunes of the different tribes into which the people were to be divided.

Joseph being the favourite son of Jacob, he adopted his two sons Manasseh and Ephraim for his own, but foretold, that the younger should be the greater of the two. [illegible] prediction was fulfilled in a very ample manner, for the tribe of Ephraim grew to be so numerous and powerful, that it was sometimes put for all the ten tribes of Israel.

Of Reuben, the eldest son of Jacob, it is said, "Unstable as water, thou shalt not excel." Gen. xlix. 4. And [illegible] recorded great or excellent of the tribe of Reuben? In number and power they were inferior to several other tribes.

Of Simeon and Levi it is said, "I will divide them in "Jacob, and scatter them in Israel." And was not this eminently fulfilled in the tribe of Levi, who had no portion or inheritance of their own, but were dispersed among the other tribes? Neither had the tribe of Simeon any inheritance properly of their own, but only [illegible] the midst of the tribe of Judah, from whence [illegible] afterwards went in search of new habitations, and were thereby divided from the rest of their brethren.

Of Zebulun it is said, "He shall dwell at the haven of "the sea, and shall be for an haven of ships." Accordingly, the tribe of Zebulun extended from the sea of Galilee to the Mediterranean, where they had commodious havens for ships.

Of Benjamin it is said, "He shall ravin as a wolf." And [illegible] when they alone waged war against all the other tribes, and overcame them in two battles. See Judges xx.

In like manner Jacob characterizes all the other tribes, and foretels their temporal condition, and the [illegible] as well as the rest. But to Judah [illegible] the spiritual blessing, and delivers it in much the [illegible] of words as it was delivered to him. [illegible] to Jacob, "Let people serve thee, and nations bow down "to thee, be lord over thy brethren, and let thy mother's "sons bow down to thee." Gen. xxvii. 29. And [illegible] Jacob saith to Judah, "Thou art he whom thy brethren "shall praise; thy hand shall be in the neck of thine enemies; thy father's children shall bow down before thee." And it is added, "The sceptre shall not depart from Judah, "nor a lawgiver from between his feet, until Shiloh come, "and unto him shall the gathering of the people be."

There are several things to be attended to in this remarkable prophecy relative to Judah. We are told that Judah's brethren "should praise him," and that his "hand should be in the neck of his enemies." [illegible] was remarkably fulfilled in the local situation of the tribe of Judah, for their being so near their enemies obliged them to be continually on their guard, and as they [illegible] most part, [illegible] may be justly said, that the "hand of Judah was in the neck of his enemies," [illegible] his brethren praised him for standing [illegible] defence. It is also said that "his father's children should bow down "before him," and nothing was ever more literally fulfilled. David, in whom first [illegible] sovereignty was placed, was of the tribe of Judah, and to him all the [illegible] tribes bowed down.

During the time of Joſhua's wars with the Canaanites, the tribe of Judah was more diſtinguiſhed for its valour than the others; and it appears from the book of Judges, that they were always the moſt forward to engage with the common enemy. When it is ſaid, that "the ſceptre ſhall not depart from Judah," it implies, that it ſhould depart from the reſt of the other tribes who ſhould enjoy it. It departed from the tribe of Benjamin on the death of Saul; and it is well known that the ten tribes were carried away captive, and incorporated with other nations, while the tribe of Benjamin preſerved under the protection of Judah.

The expreſſion "until Shiloh come," evidently and incontestably means till the coming of the Meſſiah.

"And unto him ſhall the gathering of the people be." If we underſtand this of Judah, that the other tribes ſhould be gathered to that, it was in ſome meaſure fulfilled by the people going up to Jeruſalem, as they did to Jeruſalem, which was in the tribe of Judah, in order to obtain juſtice in difficult caſes, and to worſhip God in his holy temple.

Upon the diviſions of the kingdoms of Iſrael and Judah, the tribe of Benjamin, and the prieſts and Levites, and ſeveral out of all the other tribes, went over to Judah, and were ſo blended and incorporated together, that they are more than once ſpoken of as one tribe. And it is expreſsly ſaid, (1 Kings xii. 20.) "there was none that followed the houſe of David "but the tribe of Judah only." All the reſt were ſwallowed up in that tribe, and conſidered as parts and members of the ſame.

In like manner, when the Iſraelites were carried away captive into Aſſyria, it is ſaid, "there was none left but the "tribe of Judah only," and yet we know that the tribe of Benjamin, and many of the other tribes, then remained; but they are reckoned as one and the ſame tribe with Judah. Nay, at that very time there was a remnant of Iſrael that eſcaped from the Aſſyrians, and went and adhered to Judah; for we find afterwards that, in the reign of Joſiah, there were ſome of Manaſſeh and Ephraim, and of the remnant of Iſrael, who contributed money towards repairing the temple, as well as Judah and Benjamin (2 Chron. xxxiv. 9). And, at the ſolemn celebration of the paſſover, "many of Iſrael were preſent" as well as "all Judah, and the inhabitants of Jeruſalem." When the people returned from the Babyloniſh captivity, then again ſeveral of the other tribes aſſociated themſelves, and returned with Judah and Benjamin. In ſhort, at ſo many different times, and upon ſuch different occaſions, were the other tribes gathered unto that of Judah, that the latter became the general name of the whole nation, and, after the Babyloniſh captivity, they were no longer called the "people of Iſrael," but the "Jews, or people of Judah."

The government of the tribe of Judah ſubſiſted, in ſome [illegible], from the death of Jacob to the laſt deſtruction of Jeruſalem; but then it was utterly broken and ruined [illegible] the *[illegible]*, and hath been departed [illegible] time to the preſent.

It may not be improper here to add a juſt obſervation made on the ſubject by the learned prelate biſhop Sherlock. "As the tribe of Benjamin (ſays he) annexed itſelf to the tribe of Judah as its head, ſo it ran the ſame fortune with it: they went together into captivity, they returned home together, and were both in being when Shiloh came." This alſo was foretold by Jacob, "Benjamin ſhall raven "as a wolf: in the morning he ſhall devour the prey, and "at night he ſhall divide the ſpoil." The morning and night here can be nothing elſe but the morning and night of the Jewiſh ſtate, for this ſtate is the ſubject of all Jacob's prophecy from one end to the other, and conſequently it is here foretold of Benjamin, that he ſhould continue to the very laſt times of the Jewiſh ſtate. This interpretation is confirmed by Moſes's prophecy; for the prophecy of Moſes, is, in truth, an expoſition of Jacob's. "Benjamin," ſaith Moſes "ſhall dwell in ſafety; the Lord "ſhall cover him all the day long." Deut. xxxiii. 12. What is this "all the day long?" The ſame certainly, as "the morning and night." Does not, therefore, this import a promiſe of a longer continuance to Benjamin than to the other tribes? And was it not moſt exactly fulfilled?

We ſhall only obſerve farther, with reſpect to this prophecy, that the completion of it furniſhes us with an invincible argument, not only that the Meſſiah has come, but that our bleſſed Redeemer is the very perſon. The ſceptre was not to depart from Judah until the Meſſiah ſhould come; but the ſceptre hath long been departed, and conſequently the Meſſiah hath been long come. The ſceptre departed at the final deſtruction of Jeruſalem, and hath been departed now more than ſeventeen centuries, and conſequently the Meſſiah came a little before that period, ſo that prejudice itſelf cannot long make any doubt concerning the reality of the perſon. Every man, therefore, of ſerious reflection, muſt ſay as Simon Peter ſaid to Jeſus, "Lord, "to whom ſhall we go? thou haſt the words of eternal "life. And we believe and are ſure that thou art the "Chriſt, the ſon of the living God." John vi. 68, 69.

CHAP. V.

The Prophecies of Moſes, the great Lawgiver, concerning the Jews.

MOSES, a ſhort time before his death, delivered many prophecies to the Jews, in which he predicted the great bleſſings that would be beſtowed upon them, if they paid a proper attention to the laws he had given them; and, on the contrary, the heavy curſes that would unavoidably fall upon them, if they became refractory and diſobedient to the Divine will. Theſe prophecies are contained in the 28th chapter of Deuteronomy, and the greater part of them to relate to the curſes that ſhould fall on the Jews in caſe of their diſobedience, all which have been ſince moſt ſtrictly fulfilled, as will appear from the following obſervations.

Theſe prophecies commence at the 49th verſe of the beforementioned chapter, in which it is ſaid, "The Lord "ſhall bring a nation againſt thee from far, from the end "of the earth, as ſwift as the eagle that flieth; a nation "whoſe tongue thou ſhalt not underſtand." This was fulfilled in the Chaldeans, who may be juſtly ſaid to have come *from far* in compariſon with the Moabites, Philiſtines and others, who frequently invaded Judea and committed depredations in various parts of the country.

The like deſcription of the Chaldeans is given by the prophet Jeremiah. "Lo, I will bring a nation upon you "from far, O houſe of Iſrael, ſaith the Lord: it is a mighty nation, it is an ancient nation, a nation whoſe language "thou knoweſt not, neither underſtandeſt what they ſay." Jeremiah v. 15. He likewiſe compares the enemies of the Jews to the eagles. "Our perſecutors (ſays he) are ſwifter than the eagles of the heaven: they purſued us upon "the mountains, they laid wait for us in the wilderneſs." Lam. iv. 19.

In the 50th verſe of the 28th chapter of Deuteronomy, the people, who were to be the perſecutors of the Jews, are thus farther characteriſed. "And they ſhall be a nation of fierce countenance, which ſhall not regard the "perſon of the old, nor ſhew favour to the young." Such were the Chaldeans; and the ſacred hiſtorian relates, that, for the wickedneſs of the Jews, God brought "upon them the king of the Chaldees, who ſlew their "young men with the ſword in the houſe of their ſanctuary, and had no compaſſion upon young man or maiden, "old men or him that ſtooped for age; he gave them all "into his hand." 2 Chron. xxxvi. 17.

According to the prophecy of Moſes, the enemies of the Jews were to beſiege and take their cities [illegible]

"[illegible] thee in all thy gates, until thy high and fenced "walls come down wherein thou trustedst throughout "all thy land." This was accordingly fulfilled, [illegible] [illegible], king of Assyria, came up against all the [illegible] cities of Judah, and took them." 2 Kings xviii. 13. "And Nebuchadnezzar, and his captains, took and [illegible] [illegible] the temple, and [illegible] the walls of Jerusalem round about." 2 Kings xxv. 10.

[illegible] likewise [illegible] Josephus [illegible] History of the Jews [illegible] fenced fortified [illegible] destroyed Jerusalem. And the Jews [illegible] that city, many [illegible] to have [illegible] and fenced [illegible] in the open field [illegible] in the strength [illegible] of Jerusalem, [illegible] the former inhabitants of the [illegible] more than [illegible] who shall enter into our habitations?" [illegible] xxi. 13.

[illegible], it need [illegible], and [illegible] [illegible] to [illegible] [illegible], by [illegible]

[illegible]

[illegible] Deut. xxviii. 48. [illegible]

According to [illegible] of the Jews [illegible] "be left few in number, [illegible] the stars of "heaven for multitude." Deut. xxviii. 62. Not to [illegible] [illegible] infinite multitude [illegible] [illegible] been expected to [illegible] the Jews [illegible] misery [illegible] God had not [illegible] numerous posterity, they must, [illegible] have been [illegible]

The prophecy [illegible], that they should be carried into Egypt, [illegible] "And the "Lord shall bring [illegible] again, with ships "and there ye shall be sold unto your enemies for bond-"men [illegible]" [illegible] xxviii. 68. They had indeed, come out [illegible], but now [illegible] to return thither [illegible] had, on their coming out, walked through [illegible] dry land, but now they were to be carried [illegible] They might be carried thither in [illegible] or Sidonian merchants, or by [illegible] in the Mediterranean, and this [illegible] safer way of conveying so many [illegible] them by land.

That this part [illegible] fulfilled, evidently appears from [illegible] the reigns of the two first Ptolemies, many of the Jews [illegible] into Egypt as slaves. And when Jerusalem was taken [illegible] he sent the greater part of those captives, who were [illegible] of seventeen years of age, to the works in Egypt; such as were under that age he sold for slaves, [illegible] little care was taken of them [illegible] perished [illegible] [illegible] who says, that "after their last overthrow [illegible] [illegible] of them were sold [illegible] were transported into Egypt, and [illegible] or famine, or [illegible]"

"And ye shall be [illegible] "thou goest to possess it." Deut. xxviii. 63. [illegible] amply fulfilled when [illegible] captivity [illegible] the king of Assyria, [illegible] planted in their [illegible] were carried [illegible] captives [illegible] besides other captives and [illegible] afterwards, [illegible] the rebellious Jews, [illegible] not so much as to set foot in Jerusalem, but [illegible] the country of [illegible]

[illegible]

[illegible] They [illegible] be called the [illegible]

[illegible] should be [illegible], but [illegible] "A "[illegible] [illegible], I will not [illegible] "them, to [illegible] prophecy [illegible] both of [illegible] confirmed [illegible] that, after so many [illegible] [illegible] or captivity [illegible] terly [illegible] and [illegible]

They were [illegible] to [illegible] "thou [illegible] [illegible] to city, and from country to country In many places they have been banished, recalled, and then banished again

But they were not only to be banished from their own country, and dispersed into various parts throughout the world but likewise, wherever they went, were to be "oppressed and spoiled evermore," and their "houses" and "vineyards," their "oxen" and "asses," to be taken from them Deut xxviii 29 &c That this has been strictly fulfilled, will evidently appear, when we consider the very frequent and great seizures that have been made of their effects in almost all countries How often has heavy fines been laid on them by the princes of the different nations in which they have dwelt? and how often have they been obliged to secure their lives by the forfeiture of their possessions? Of this there have been innumerable instances, and some even in our own country King Henry III of England always laid a heavy tax on the Jews at every low ebb of his fortunes "One Abraham, (says a celebrated writer) who was found a delinquent, was forced to pay seven hundred marks for his redemption Aaron another Jew, protested that the king had taken from him, at times, thirty thousand marks of silver, besides two hundred marks of gold And in like manner he used many others of the Jews" And when they were banished, in the reign of Edward I all their estates were confiscated to the crown

"Their sons and daughters should be given unto another people" Deut xxviii 32 This has been likewise fulfilled, for in several countries but more particularly in Spain and Portugal, the children have been taken from them by order of the government, to be educated in the [illegible]

"And they should be mad for the sight of their eyes "which they should see" Deut xxviii 34 That this part of the prophecy has been most amply fulfilled we have the clearest evidence, for in what madness [illegible] and desperation, have they repeatedly been driven by the cruel [illegible] extortions and oppressions they have undergone at different periods, and in different parts of the world

The prophecy farther tells us, that they "should become an astonishment, a proverb, and a by-word to all "nations" Deut xxviii 37 And do we not [illegible] see this part of the prophecy fulfilled every day? Is not the avarice, usury, and hard-heartedness of a Jew grown proverbial? and are not their persons generally odious among all sorts of people? Mahometans Heathens, and Christians, however they may disagree in other points, yet generally agree in vilifying, abusing, and persecuting the Jews In most places where they are tolerated, they live in a separate quarter by themselves and wear some badge of distinction Their very countenances commonly distinguish them from the rest of mankind, and they are, in all respects, treated as if they were of another species

Lastly, "their plagues should be wonderful, even "great plagues and of long continuance" Deut xxviii 59 And have not their plagues continued upwards of seventeen hundred years? What nation hath suffered so much, and yet continued so long? What nation hath subsisted as a distinct people in their own country so long as these have done in their dispersion into all countries? And what a standing miracle is this exhibited to the view and observation of the whole world!

These astonishing prophecies were delivered upwards of three thousand years ago, and, from the fulfilment of them, which we see every day taking place in the world, are the strongest proofs that can be given of the Divine legation of Moses They are truly, as Moses foretold they would be, "a sign and a wonder for ever More-"over, all these curses shall come upon thee and shall "pursue thee and overtake thee, till thou be destroyed, "because thou hearkenest not unto the voice of the Lord "thy God to keep his commandments and his statutes which he commanded thee and they shall be "upon thee for a sign and for a wonder, and upon thy "seed for ever" Deut. xxviii 45, 46

CHAP VI

The prophecies of Jeremiah, Isaiah, Micah, Ezekiel, and other prophets, relative to the Jews

THE great legislator Moses was not the only person who foretold the punishments to be inflicted on the Jews for their manifold transgressions The like was foretold by many other persons, who received the spirit of inspiration These prophecies were delivered at different periods and were designed to reform the Jews from the wicked course of life to which they were naturally addicted, but as they continued inflexible, the prophecies denounced against them were strictly fulfilled

It was among others of the prophecies foretold that the ten tribes of Israel should be carried away captives by the king of Assyria and that the two remaining tribes of Judah and Benjamin should be made captives by the king of Babylon but with this difference that the two tribes should be restored, and return from their captivity, but the ten tribes should be totally annihilated

The time when the captivity of the two tribes of Judah and Benjamin was to take place, as also that of their restoration, was foretold by the prophet Jeremiah "This "whole land shall be a desolation, and an astonishment, "and these nations shall serve the king of Babylon [illegible] "[illegible] years" Jer xxv 11 And again "thus "saith the Lord, that after seventy years be accomplish-"ed at Babylon, I will visit you and perform my good "word towards you, in causing you to return to this "place" Jer xxix 10

This prophecy was delivered in the fourth year of "Jehoiakim the son of Josiah king of Judah, which was "the first year of Nebuchadnezzar king of Babylon" Jer [illegible] In the same year the prophecy began to take place, for Nebuchadnezzar invaded Judea besieged and took Jerusalem, made Jehoiakim his subject and tributary, and transported the finest children of the royal family, and of the nobility, to Babylon, to be brought up as slaves in his palaces He likewise destroyed the temple carried away the sacred vessels and placed them in the temple of his idol Bel at Babylon Almost the whole of the inhabitants of Judea and Jerusalem were carried into captivity, there being only a few, of very poor and mean condition, left to till and cultivate the land

In this situation they remained for seventy years, when Cyrus, king of Babylon, issued a proclamation for the restoration of the Jews, and for the rebuilding of the temple of Jerusalem In consequence of this the Jews immediately returned to their own country, and dispersed themselves into the respective cities they had formerly inhabited The temple was begun, and carried on with great assiduity, for some time, but by the great interruption they met with from the Samaritans, was not finished till the reign of Darius when all things were again restored to their former state And thus was fulfilled the prophecy of Jeremiah, relative to the two tribes of Judah and Benjamin

The prophecy against the ten tribes of Israel was much more severe than that against the other two The tribe of Ephraim, which was the chief of these, is often put for the whole ten, and it was predicted that "within "threescore and four years shall Ephraim be broken that "it be not a people" Isaiah vii 8 This prophecy was delivered in the first year of Ahaz, king of Judah, when Rezin, king of Syria, and Pekah, king of Israel, formed a conjunction to reduce Jerusalem, and it was to comfort Ahaz and the house of David, in these [illegible] ties and distresses that the prophet Isaiah was commissioned to assure him, that the kings of Syria and [illegible] should remain only the heads of their respective [illegible]

[illegible] should not prevail against Jerusalem, and that, [illegible] and five years, Israel should be so broken that [illegible] no more a people.

The [illegible]ment of this prophecy commenced in the reign [illegible], when Tiglath-pileser took many of the Israelites, [illegible] the Reubenites, and the Gadites, and the half tribe [illegible], and all the land of Naphtali, and carried [illegible] into Assyria, [illegible] them unto Halah, [illegible] Haran, [illegible] 29. [illegible] in the reign [illegible] Samaria, and [illegible] the ten tribes [illegible] Assyria, and put them in Halah, and in Habor [illegible], (the [illegible] places where their brethren [illegible]) [illegible] of the Medes." [illegible] up also against [illegible] the fenced cities of Judah, but his army [illegible] forced to return [illegible] own country, where [illegible] two of his sons [illegible] Kings xix. 19 [illegible]

[illegible] to Assyria and [illegible] reasonable to [illegible] great abundance. But [illegible] found in [illegible] of [illegible] God," [illegible] land," [illegible] Zerubbabel and Ezra [illegible] the main body of the ten tribes [illegible] not return at this [illegible] be supposed to have returned [illegible] "the ten tribes of Israel, [illegible] from the house of David, were [illegible] and never were [illegible] (excepting only the few who [illegible] themselves to [illegible] in the land of their captivity, [illegible] with them [illegible] among whom they were planted, [illegible] in their own land, [illegible] became wholly [illegible], and swallowed up in them, and thence utterly losing their name, their language, and their memorial, were never after spoken of."

But if the whole race of Israel became thus extinct, and perished for ever, it may be asked, how can the numerous prophecies be fulfilled which promise the future conversion and restoration of Israel as well as Judah? The truth [illegible] between these two opinions. Neither [illegible] all return to Jerusalem, nor did all, who remained [illegible], conform with the idolatry of the Gentiles, among whom they lived. But whether they remained, or whether they returned, this prophecy of Isaiah was still fulfilled, the kingdom, the commonwealth, the state of Israel was utterly broken, they no longer subsisted as a distinct people from Judah, they no longer maintained a separate religion, they joined themselves to the Jews from whom they had been unhappily divided, they lost the name of Israel as a name of distinction, and were thenceforth all in common called Jews.

It appears from the book of Esther, that there were great numbers of Jews in all the hundred twenty and seven provinces of the kingdom of Ahasuerus or Artaxerxes Longimanus, king of Persia, and they could not all be the remains of the two tribes of Judah and Benjamin, who had refused to return to Jerusalem with their brethren; they must, at least many of them, have been the descendants of the ten tribes whom the kings of Assyria had carried away captive; but yet they are all spoken of as one and the same people, and all, without distinction, are denominated Jews.

We read, in the Acts of the Apostles, that there were [illegible] Jerusalem to celebrate the feast of Pentecost, [illegible] "and Medes, and Elamites, and the dwellers in Mesopotamia," [illegible] ii. 9. [illegible] wherein the ten tribes had been [illegible] "Jews, devout men, [illegible] nation under heaven." Acts ii. 5. [illegible] of the ten tribes, who [illegible] to Jerusalem, [illegible] the two tribes of Judah and Benjamin, [illegible] They might, perhaps, [illegible] have preserved their genealogies, but they were [illegible] together, and the distinction of tribes and families, is in a great measure, lost among them, and they have [illegible] from the Babylonish captivity to this day, been comprehended under the general name of Jews.

There were many persons of all the ten tribes in being during the time of St Paul's ministry, for he speaks of "the twelve tribes hoping to attain to the promise of God." Acts xxvi. 7. And St James addresses his epistle "to the "twelve tribes which are scattered abroad," [illegible] And there is no doubt but there are [illegible] of the descendants of the ten tribes of Israel still in being, [illegible] with the other Jews, and there is no distinction [illegible] them. The Samaritans indeed, [illegible] pretend to be the descendants of [illegible], but [illegible] derived [illegible] king of Assyria, placed in the country [illegible] carried [illegible] captivity [illegible] the Jews call them [illegible] Cuthites, which was the name of the principal part of [illegible] They [illegible] against them [illegible] aversion to the [illegible]

It may, perhaps, be asked [illegible], what could be the reason that [illegible] the two tribes of Judah and Benjamin, [illegible] the ten tribes of Israel [illegible] in their captivity, and the [illegible] preserved [illegible] ages [illegible] the ten tribes [illegible] from God to the worship of the golden calves at Dan and Bethel, [illegible] in the land of their captivity. The Jews [illegible] not so much for their own sakes, as [illegible] unto their forefathers, namely, [illegible] Judah that the Messiah should come [illegible] to David, that the Messiah should [illegible] family. It was therefore necessary [illegible] of Judah, and the [illegible], to be kept [illegible] Divine dispensation should [illegible] these ends [illegible]

[illegible] as much confounded [illegible] of the rest, [illegible] genealogies is lost among [illegible], [illegible] (Chandler observes) the Jews them[selves] [illegible] in saying, that, when the [illegible] come, it will be part of his office "to [illegible] their [illegible], settle their genealogies, and set [illegible] [illegible]."

[illegible] engage the attention of the most [illegible] on the preservation of the Jews [illegible] the [illegible] periods, [illegible] to extirpate [illegible] all [illegible] [illegible] these events may [illegible] more so by their being [illegible] by the [illegible] of prophecy, as we find [illegible] Jeremiah: "Fear not thou O [illegible] Lord, for I am with thee, [illegible] the nations whither I have [illegible] a full end of thee." [illegible]

[illegible] remarkably [illegible] of the Jews to the present period [illegible] dispersed among all nations, and [illegible] with [illegible] yet they do not live [illegible] according to [illegible] laws, they [illegible] the full exercise of the [illegible] are limited to [illegible] in many ages [illegible] hands [illegible] will not suffer them to [illegible]. No people on the whole face of the earth have [illegible] as they have. The northern [illegible] great multitudes into the more southern [illegible] Europe, but where are they now to be discerned and distinguished? The Gauls went forth in great [illegible] fortunes in foreign parts, but [illegible] of them are now remaining any where? In France, who can separate the race of the ancient Gauls from the various other people, who, from time to time, [illegible]? In Spain, [illegible] the Spaniards and the Goths [illegible] present [illegible] In England, who can [illegible] are derived from the [illegible] from the Romans, or Saxons, or [illegible] Normans? The most ancient and [illegible] to a certain period, and [illegible] community [illegible]. But the Jews can go [illegible] even deduce their pedigree from [illegible]. They may not [illegible] they are descended, but they [illegible] from the rest of [illegible] with which they have [illegible] which they have [illegible], one would think, [illegible] to renounce their original [illegible] and after so many [illegible] still subsist, they [illegible] a supernatural power could have preserved them [illegible] as no other nation upon earth have [illegible].

While we behold, with astonishment, the wise dispensation of Providence, in having protected the Jews even to the present period, we cannot, without equal astonishment, reflect on the circumstance of his having [illegible] utterly to destroy their enemies. The first oppressors of the Jews were the Egyptians, who detained them from their own land, compelled them into captivity, treated them with great cruelty, and kept them for many years in [illegible]. The Assyrians carried away captives the ten tribes of Israel, and the Babylonians afterwards the two remaining tribes of Judah and Benjamin. The Syro-Macedonians, especially Antiochus Epiphanes, cruelly persecuted them [illegible] so that they have [illegible] been [illegible] country [illegible].

And where are now these great [illegible] monarchies which [illegible] subdued and oppressed the people of God? Are they not [illegible], and [illegible] left on the [illegible]? The Egyptians, Assyrians, and Babylonians, were [illegible] by the Persians, and [illegible] the restorers of the Jews, as well as the destroyers of their enemies. The Syro-Macedonians were [illegible] by the Romans, and the Roman [illegible] great [illegible] the Jews [illegible] as a distinct people to this day. [illegible] to this [illegible] survive the victors and [illegible] world [illegible].

[illegible] not only [illegible] of the Jews, [illegible] been their persecutors [illegible] retained, [illegible]

[illegible]

Even to the Jews [illegible] God [illegible]

[illegible]

[illegible] the Chaldeans, [illegible]

[illegible] Gentiles [illegible]

[illegible]

an[illegible] [illegible]editions of [illegible] [illegible] nothing wonderful, but [illegible] it should be [illegible] [illegible]es in th[illegible] [illegible] feeabl[illegible] con-[illegible] [illegible] th[illegible] m[illegible] [illegible] forces, and could be [illegible] [illegible] [illegible] Divine will.

[illegible] of the land of Judea in being forsaken by its [illegible] [illegible], and left desolate and [illegible], is [illegible] some controversy. It is [illegible], to [illegible] could never have been "a land [illegible] [illegible] honey," nor have supplied [illegible] [illegible] it is represented to have [illegible] [illegible] this observation do not see or consider, [illegible] the prophecies are fulfilled.

[illegible] the concurrent testimonies of those who best [illegible] [illegible] the land of Judea was [illegible] a good and fertile country. Both [illegible] and Josephus [illegible] largely in commendation of [illegible] and [illegible] some [illegible], may be allowed [illegible] [illegible] prejudice, [illegible] would hardly have had the [illegible] to [illegible] [illegible] which [illegible] the world could easily [illegible] [illegible] there are even heathen [illegible] [illegible] to [illegible] [illegible] of the [illegible] [illegible] Babylonish captivity, [illegible] [illegible] [illegible] before Strabo, [illegible] [illegible] the country about Jerusalem [illegible] rocky [illegible] [illegible] particularly about [illegible] [illegible] the character of one of the best and most fertile countries. And [illegible] [illegible] [illegible] fruits abound [illegible] [illegible] and palm trees" [illegible] of the land, the[illegible] [illegible] of fruitfulness, [illegible] [illegible] the character [illegible]

[illegible] those [illegible] of the truth of this [illegible] [illegible] of the obser[illegible] [illegible] Mr Maundrell and Dr Shaw, [illegible] ingenious travellers [illegible] [illegible] of these [illegible] [illegible] from [illegible] to B[illegible] [illegible] [illegible] the country dif-"[illegible] quite [illegible] from what it had been, "[illegible] [illegible] most places [illegible] "[illegible] [illegible] At [illegible] "[illegible] [illegible] [illegible] astonished [illegible] "[illegible] [illegible] country [illegible] "[illegible] [illegible] concerning whose great [illegible] "[illegible] [illegible] formed, in their minds, "[illegible] the description given of it in "the word of God [illegible] it almost startles their "faith, [illegible] how it could be possible for a "[illegible] so prodigious a num-"ber [illegible] [illegible] to have been polled in the "[illegible] tribes [illegible], the number given by Joab "(2 Sam [illegible]) [illegible] to no less than thirteen hun-"dred thousand [illegible] besides women and chil-"dren. But [illegible] man, who is not biassed "to [illegible], [illegible] as he passes along, arguments "[illegible] to support his faith against such scruples. For "[illegible] one to observe that the rock[illegible] "[illegible] anciently covered with earth "and cultivated, [illegible] made to contribute to the maintenance "[illegible] no less than if the country had been "[illegible], perhaps much more, forasmuch as "such a mountainous and uneven surface affords a lar[illegible] "[illegible] of ground for cultivation, than this country would "amount to if it were all reduced to a perfect level. For "[illegible] these mountains, their manner was to "gather up the stones, and place them in several lines "[illegible] the sides of the hills, in form of a wall. By such "borders they supported the mould from tumbling or be-"ing washed down, and formed many beds of excellent "soil rising gradually one above another, from the bot-"tom to the top of the mountains. Of this form of cul-"ture you [illegible] footsteps wherever you go on all "the mountains of Palestine. Thus the very rocks were made

"fruitful [illegible] perhaps there [illegible] no [illegible] of ground in "this [illegible] [illegible] not [illegible] [illegible], to the "production of [illegible] thing or [illegible] [illegible] to the "[illegible] of human life [illegible] more "fruitful in the plain countr[illegible] for the pro-"duction of corn or cattle, [illegible] of this "are hills, though [illegible] [illegible] "being [illegible] [illegible] [illegible], "serve very well to [illegible] [illegible], "[illegible] and such [illegible] [illegible] the prin-"cipal [illegible] of [illegible] [illegible] "year. The [illegible] [illegible] well "be [illegible] [illegible] or cor[illegible] "might yet serve for the plantation of vines and olive "trees, which [illegible] [illegible] "other [illegible] of such [illegible] "many [illegible] [illegible] to [illegible] "[illegible] [illegible] might be [illegible] "[illegible] [illegible] "set its [illegible] [illegible] "[illegible] "[illegible] Dr [illegible] "I [illegible] "I [illegible] in many places, [illegible] "[illegible] "[illegible] country [illegible] "[illegible] "[illegible] "the [illegible] [illegible] "[illegible] "including the [illegible] "in [illegible], and [illegible]

In [illegible] Dr [illegible] [illegible] the [illegible] [illegible] "[illegible] [illegible] "the [illegible]

"[illegible] and [illegible], we find that these barren rocks (as [illegible] very rec[illegible] grow[illegible] quantity, in [illegible] the [illegible] a further [illegible] to be made or [illegible]," &c.

[illegible] prophets, Isaiah, and others, not only [illegible] of the country of the Jews, and [illegible] the [illegible] parts of the world, but [illegible] the Messiah, and what [illegible] their reject[illegible] thereof [illegible], but [illegible] from the [illegible] and to [illegible] revealed?" [illegible] St. [illegible] and St. Paul have expressly applied [illegible] Jews of their time. They [illegible] the reason why they would not [illegible] the [illegible] and afflicted condition [illegible] on this account, [illegible] as a temporal [illegible] power and glory.

[illegible] to declare unto [illegible] Gentiles [illegible] "Go [illegible] and tell [illegible] understand not [illegible] Make the heart of this [illegible] and [illegible] their eyes, [illegible] their ears, [illegible] convert, [illegible] 9, &c.

[illegible] to do [illegible] over [illegible] "set over the nations, and over the kingdoms, to root out, and to pull down, and to [illegible], to build, and to plant." [illegible] was authorised to make known the [illegible] decrees of God, and because these events [illegible] consequence of his prophecies. "Make [illegible] people fat" is therefore as much as to say, Denounce my judgments upon his people, that [illegible] and their ears heavy, and [illegible] with their eyes, and hear with [illegible] with their heart, and convert, [illegible] might [illegible] Jews [illegible] Babylonish captivity [illegible] till [illegible] of the New Testament, and be of [illegible]

[illegible] is then informed, that this [illegible] of long duration [illegible] how long? And he answered, until [illegible] without inhabitant, and the houses [illegible] be utterly desolate, and the [illegible] there [illegible] forsaken [illegible] of the land." What [illegible] judgments! Not [illegible] should be [illegible]," but even the single "houses" should be "without man," and not only the "houses" of the [illegible] "without man," but even the country [illegible] "forsaken," and not only the people should be removed out of the "land," but "the Lord" would "remove them far away," and they should not be removed for a short period, but there should be "a great" [illegible] in the midst of the land."

And have we not seen all these particulars exactly fulfilled? Have not the Jews laboured under a spiritual blindness and infatuation in "hearing but not understanding," and "seeing but not perceiving," the Messiah, after the accomplishment of so many prophecies, and after the performance of so many miracles? And in consequence of their refusing to "convert and be healed," have not "their cities been wasted without inhabitant, and their houses without man?" Hath not their "land been utterly desolate?" Have they not been "removed far away," even into the most distant parts of the earth? And hath not their removal or banishment been [illegible] 1700 years duration? Do they not still continue deaf [illegible] blind, unbelieving and obstinate?

When this prophecy was delivered, the Jews gloried in being the peculiar people of God, and [illegible] Jew [illegible] himself have either thought, or [illegible] would, in process of time, become [illegible] for many ages, outcasts [illegible] God? It was more than 750 years before Christ [illegible] prophet [illegible] predicted [illegible] have so long [illegible] been [illegible] vation? [illegible] could they [illegible] unless the spirit of prophecy [illegible] of God?

On the [illegible] are the prophecies concerning the [illegible] of the Gentiles. How could [illegible] an event [illegible] hundreds of years before [illegible] of the Messiah [illegible] "God would give unto [illegible] heathen [illegible] and the uttermost [illegible] earth for his [illegible]" [illegible] ends of the world [illegible] and all the [illegible] of the nations [illegible] him." [illegible] 27. "[illegible] mountain of the Lord's house [illegible] the top of the mountains, [illegible] above the hills, and all [illegible] unto it" [illegible] (which [illegible] "[illegible] from the rising of the sun [illegible] the [illegible] same, my name shall be great among the Gentiles, [illegible] every place incense shall be offered [illegible] pure offering; for my name shall be great among the heathen, saith the Lord of hosts." [illegible]

But the prophet Isaiah is [illegible] upon this as well as other [illegible] 4) [illegible] 60 [illegible] particularly of the [illegible] of the church [illegible] Gentiles. "It is [illegible] thing, that thou [illegible] to raise up the tribes of Jacob [illegible] of Israel. I [illegible] for a light to the Gentiles, that thou mayest be my salvation unto the end of the earth." [illegible] 6. And again, "Arise, [illegible] for thy light is come, and the glory of the Lord is risen upon thee. The Gentiles shall come to thy light, and kings to the brightness of thy rising [illegible] abundance of the sea shall be converted unto thee, the forces of the Gentiles shall come unto thee," &c. [illegible] 1, 2, 3, &c.

The Jews [illegible] these prophecies to the proselytes [illegible] they have [illegible] the [illegible] have been dispersed, but this [illegible] the number of their proselytes [illegible] and [illegible] Neither was their religion [illegible] an universal religion [illegible] all the [illegible] were obliged to repair [illegible] that it was [illegible] could never become the religion of the whole [illegible] There was indeed to be a religion, which [illegible] to be preached in all, and to [illegible] prospect [illegible] this [illegible] on those [illegible] narrow-minded people as the Jews, [illegible] should ever receive a religion [illegible] they most hated and despised? [illegible] Jews should be conquered by [illegible] round them, [illegible] powerful neighbours, than [illegible] the happy instruments of reforming the world, [illegible] ing some of all nations to [illegible] worship of the true God?

The prophet farther intimates, that this revolution (the [illegible] ever happened in the religious world) should [illegible] few people, of low rank and education; "a [illegible] one [illegible] become a thousand, and a small one a strong nation." Isaiah [illegible]

The commission given by our Blessed Saviour to his apostles was, "Go, [illegible] all nations." And who were the persons to whom this commission was given? Was it to those who might have been thought best qualified to carry it into execution; such as the rich, the wise, the mighty of this world? No; they were chiefly a few poor fishermen, of low parentage and education, of no learning or eloquence, of no policy or address, of no worldly credit or authority, despised as Jews by the rest of mankind, and as the meanest and worst of Jews by the Jews themselves. [illegible] were the persons (strange and wonderful as it may appear) who were to contend with the prejudices of all the [illegible], the superstitions of the people, the interests of the [illegible], the vanity of the philosophers, the pride of rulers, [illegible] of Jews, [illegible] of Greeks, and the power of the Roman [illegible].

This great [illegible] only to be brought about by a few persons [illegible], but it was the [illegible] to be [illegible] "I the Lord will hasten it in [illegible] time." Isaiah [illegible]

After the [illegible] of Our Saviour, the number of the disciples together was about "an hundred and twenty," [illegible] the first preaching of St. Peter there [illegible] unto them "about three thousand souls," Acts ii. [illegible] the second [illegible] up the number "about five thousand." Acts iv. [illegible]

Previous to the final destruction of Jerusalem (for about the space of forty years) the gospel had been so spread, that it was preached [illegible] region of the then known world. In the [illegible] Christianity [illegible] of the empire, and, after many [illegible] prevailed, and triumphed over [illegible] idolatry; and still doth [illegible] in the [illegible] parts of the earth. All [illegible] brought about by [illegible] were the [illegible] of the [illegible].

The [illegible] of the gospel could not have been effected by persons so unequal to the task, if the same Divine Saviour who foretold it, had not likewise assisted them in it, according to the [illegible], "I the Lord will hasten it [illegible] as we [illegible] that [illegible] really was [illegible] the Evangelist, "They went forth, and preached every where, the Lord working with them, and confirming the word with signs following." Mark [illegible]

[illegible] the prophecies concerning the Gentiles nor [illegible] have yet received their full and entire completion. [illegible] Saviour hath not yet had "the uttermost parts of the earth for his possession." Psalm [illegible] "All the ends of the earth have not yet turned unto the Lord." [illegible] "All people, nations, and languages" have not yet "served him." Dan. vii. 14. These things have hitherto been only partially, but they will [illegible] be even literally fulfilled. Neither are the Jews yet made "an eternal excellency, a joy of many generations." Isaiah lx. 15. The time is not yet come when "violence shall no more be heard in the land, wasting nor destruction within their borders," ver. 18. God's promises to them [illegible] yet fulfilled to the extent [illegible] "I will take the children of Israel from among the heathen, whither they be gone, and will gather them on every side, and bring them into their own land: And [illegible] dwell in the land that I have given unto Jacob my servant, even they and their children, and their children's children for ever, and my servant David shall be their prince for ever." Ezekiel xxxvii. 21, 25. "Then shall they know that I am the Lord their God, which caused them to be led into captivity among the heathen; but I have gathered them unto their own land, and have left none of them any more there. Neither will I hide my face any more from them: for I have poured out my spirit upon the house of Israel, saith the Lord God." Ezekiel xxxix. 28, 29.

However, what hath already been accomplished [illegible] pledge and earnest of what is yet to [illegible] all imaginable reason to believe [illegible] of the prophecies have been fulfilled, [illegible] will be fulfilled also, that the [illegible] of the nations [illegible] of the earth will be [illegible] the Lord [illegible] for the [illegible] there [illegible] to their [illegible].

I [illegible]

[illegible]

The Jews [illegible]

[illegible]

The [illegible]

[illegible]

It [illegible]

[illegible]

If [illegible]

[illegible]

"natural branches." Rom. xi. 18, 24. But what would he have said, if they had made religion an instrument of faction, and had been for stirring up a persecution against them?

Christians of all denominations should consider and reflect, that it is to the Jews we owe the oracles of God, and the scriptures of the New Testament as well as the Old. We find, that "the glorious company of the apostles," [illegible] "the goodly fellowship of the prophets," were all Jews. We should consider that, "of them, as concerning "the flesh, Christ came," the Saviour of the world; and surely something of kindness and gratitude is due for such infinite obligations.

Though the Jews are now broken off,* yet they are not utterly cast away. "Because of unbelief," as St. Paul argueth, they "were broken off," and thou standest by faith "be not high minded, but fear." Rom. xi. 20. There will be a time when they will be grafted in again, and again become the people of God: for as the apostle proceeds, "I "would not, brethren, that ye should be ignorant of this "mystery, lest ye should be wise in your own conceits, "that blindness in part is happened to Israel, until the fulness of the Gentiles be come in, and so all Israel shall be "saved." Rom. xi. 25, 26.

And what then, it may be asked, is the most likely method to contribute to the conversion of these unhappy people, and which are the most natural means of reconciling them to us and our religion? Is it to be effected by prayer, argument, long-suffering, gentleness and goodness, or by noise, invective, injury, and outrage, the malice of some, and the [illegible] of [illegible]? They certainly cannot be worse now than when they crucified the son of God, and persecuted his apostles. But what saith our Blessed Saviour himself? "Father, forgive them, for they know not what they "do." Luke xxiii. 34. And what saith his apostle St. Paul? "Brethren, my heart's desire and prayer to God for Israel is, "that they might be saved." Rom. x. 1.

In conformity to these blessed examples, our church hath also taught us to pray for them: and how can prayer and persecution consist and agree together? Those who encourage persecution of any kind, are not only pretended friends to the church, but real enemies to religion. All true members of the church, all true protestants, all true Christians, will, as the apostle adviseth, "put away all bitterness and "wrath, and anger, and clamour, and evil speaking, with "all malice." Ephes. iv. 31. And they will all join heart and voice in that excellent collect, "Have mercy upon all "Jews, Turks, Infidels, and Heretics, and take from them "all ignorance, hardness of heart, and contempt of thy "word: and so fetch them home, blessed Lord, to thy flock, "that they may be saved among the remnant of the true "Israelites, and be made one fold under one shepherd, Jesus "Christ Our Lord."

CHAP. VII.

Prophecies concerning the ancient city of Nineveh.

THE first great prophecies contained in the Old Testament are those which more immediately relate to the Jews themselves, who were once the peculiar people of God, and the principal subjects of those prophecies are the various changes and revolutions that were to happen in the Jewish church and state. But the spirit of prophecy is not confined to the Jews alone; there are other subjects occasionally introduced, and for the greater manifestation of Divine Providence, the fate of other nations is also foretold, and more especially those which lay in the neighbourhood of Judea, and had intercourse and connection with the Jews.

It is much to be lamented, that, of these eastern nations, and of these early times, we have no regular histories, but only a few fragments which have escaped the general shipwreck of time. From these, however, we see enough to make us admire the great works of Providence; and from these are clearly shown, that the revolutions of cities and kingdoms hath been such as was long ago foretold by the prophets.

The first prophecies we shall notice on this subject are those relative to the antient city of Nineveh, once the metropolis of the Assyrian empire, and whose inhabitants not only destroyed the kingdom of Israel, but likewise greatly oppressed the kingdom of Judah.

The prophet Isaiah, in denouncing the judgments of God against the Assyrians, says, "O Assyrian, the rod of "mine anger, and the staff in their hand is my indignation." Isaiah x. 3. It was the will of Providence that these people should be employed as the ministers of his wrath, and executioners of his vengeance, against the perverse and obstinate Jews. "I will send him against an hypocritical "nation, and against the people of my wrath will I give "him a charge to take the spoil, and to take the prey, and "to tread them down like the mire in the streets." Isaiah x. 6. But it was far from any intent of the Assyrians to execute the Divine will, or to chastise the vices of [illegible]: they only meant to extend their conquests, and establish their own dominion upon the ruins of others. "Howbeit "he meaneth not so, neither doth his heart think so; but it "is in his heart to destroy, and cut off nations not a few." ver. 7. Wherefore, when they shall have served the purposes of Divine Providence, they shall be severely punished for their pride and ambition, their tyranny and cruelty to their neighbours. "Wherefore it shall come to pass, that, "when the Lord hath performed his whole work upon "mount Zion, and on Jerusalem, I will punish the fruit of "the stout heart of the king of Assyria, and the glory of "his high looks." ver. 12.

There was no prospect of such an event as this while the Assyrians were in the midst of their successes and triumphs; but still the word of the prophet prevailed; [illegible] it was not long after the calamities they brought upon the Jews, the Assyrian empire (properly so called) was overthrown, and Nineveh destroyed.

The city of Nineveh was one of the largest and most antient cities in the world. According to the best chronologers it was built not long after the flood, and very soon after the tower of Babel, by Nimrod; but being afterwards greatly enlarged by Ninus, from him it received its name. It was situated on the banks of the Tigris, and (according to the description given of it by Diodorus Siculus) was, in length, an hundred and fifty stadia; in breadth, ninety; and ten; and in circumference, four hundred and eighty; which, being reduced to our measure, make it at [illegible] one miles long, nine broad, and fifty-four round. How great the number of its inhabitants was, we may learn from "the six score thousand children who could not discern between their right hands and their left." Jonah iv. 11. And, according to a proportionate computation, there must have been in the whole, not less than six hundred thousand persons.

The inhabitants of Nineveh, like those of other great cities abounding in wealth and luxury, became very corrupt in their morals. In consequence of this God was pleased to commission the prophet Jonah to preach unto them the necessity of repentance, as the only means of averting their impending destruction: and such was the success of his preaching that both the king and the people repented, and turned from their evil ways, and thereby, for a time, escaped the executions of the Divine judgments.

But this repentance of the Ninevites, we may reasonably presume, was of no long continuance, for not many years after we find the prophet Nahum foretelling the [illegible] entire destruction of the city. Indeed, the whole of [illegible] prophecy relates to this single event, and the city was accordingly deſtroyed by the Medes and Babylonians, who, joining together, ſubverted the whole Aſſyrian empire.

It is remarkable that the prophet Nahum not only foretold the deſtruction of Nineveh, but likewiſe the manner in which it was to be effected. He foretold that the Aſſyrians would be taken while they were drunken. "For while they be folden together as thorns, and while they are drunken as drunkards, they ſhall be devoured as ſtubble fully dry." Nahum i. 10. And Diodorus Siculus ſays, "It was while the Aſſyrian army were feaſting for their former victories, that thoſe about Arbaces, (the general of the Median forces,) being informed, by ſome deſerters, of the negligence and drunkenneſs in the camp of the enemy, aſſaulted them unexpectedly by night, and falling on them while they were in the utmoſt diſorder, and unprepared, became maſters of the camp, ſlew many of the ſoldiers, and drove the reſt into the city."

The prophet Nahum likewiſe foretells, that "the gates of the rivers ſhall be opened, and the palace ſhall be diſſolved." Nahum ii. 6. And Diodorus tells us, "there was an old prophecy, that Nineveh ſhould not be taken till the river became an enemy to the city; and in the third year of the ſiege the river, being ſwoln with continual rains, overflowed part of the city, and broke down the wall for twenty furlongs: then the king thinking the oracle was fulfilled, and the river become an enemy to the city, built a large funeral pile in the palace, and collecting together all his wealth, and his concubines and eunuchs, burnt himſelf [illegible] them in the palace; and the enemy entered the breach that the waters had made, and took the city."

Thus we find that what the prophet had predicted was literally fulfilled: "With an overflowing flood he will make an utter end of the place thereof." Nahum i. 8. He likewiſe promiſes the enemy much ſpoil of gold and ſilver: "Take ye the ſpoil of ſilver, take the ſpoil of gold, for there is no end to the ſtore, and glory out of all the pleaſant furniture." Nahum ii. 9. And we read in Diodorus Siculus, that Arbaces carried many talents of gold and ſilver to Ecbatana, the royal city belonging to the Medes.

According to the prophecy of Nahum the city was to be deſtroyed partly by water, and partly by fire. "Behold, the gates of thy land ſhall be ſet wide open unto thine enemies: the fire ſhall devour thy bars." Nahum iii. 13. And we find, by Diodorus, that this literally took place; for after the Medes and Babylonians had poſſeſſed themſelves of the city, they ſet fire to it, and reduced the greater part of it to aſhes.

The prophet Nahum was the principal perſon who foretold the total and entire deſtruction of the ancient city of Nineveh. "The Lord (ſaith he) with an over-running flood will make an utter end of the place thereof: he will make an utter end; affliction ſhall not riſe up the ſecond time." Chap. i. 8, 9. Again: "Where is the dwelling of the lions?" (meaning Nineveh, whoſe princes ravaged like lions.) "Behold, I am againſt thee, ſaith the Lord of hoſts, and I will cut off thy prey from the earth, and the voice of thy meſſengers ſhall no more be heard." Chap. ii. 11, 13. And again, "Thy crowned are as the locuſts, and thy captains as the great graſhoppers, which camp in the hedges in the cold day; but when the ſun ariſeth, they flee away, and their place is not known. Thy ſhepherds ſlumber, O king of Aſſyria; thy nobles ſhall dwell in the duſt; thy people is ſcattered upon the mountains, and no man gathereth them: there is no healing of thy bruiſe; thy wound is grievous; all that hear the bruit of thee ſhall clap their hands over thee: for upon whom hath not thy wickedneſs paſſed continually?" Chap. iii. 17, 18, 19.

The prophet Zephaniah likewiſe, in the days of Joſiah, king of Judah, foretold the ſame melancholy event. "The Lord will ſtretch out his hand againſt the north, and deſtroy Aſſyria, and will make Nineveh a deſolation, and dry like a wilderneſs: and flocks ſhall lie down in the midſt of her, all the beaſts of the nations; both the cormorant and bittern ſhall lodge in the upper lintels of it; their voice ſhall ſing in the windows; deſolation ſhall be in the threſholds; for he ſhall uncover the cedar work. This is the rejoicing city that dwelt careleſsly, that ſaid in her heart, I am, and there is none beſide me: how is ſhe become a deſolation, a place for beaſts to lie down in! every one that paſſeth by her ſhall hiſs, and wag his hand." Zeph. ii. 13, &c.

It is not to be wondered at, that when thoſe prophecies were at firſt delivered, the people ſhould think it very unlikely they would ever be fulfilled. What probability, indeed, was there to think that ſo great a city, and which contained ſo many thouſand inhabitants, ſhould ever be totally deſtroyed? And yet ſo totally was it deſtroyed, that even the place where it ſtood is now ſcarcely known.

It has been already obſerved, that Nineveh was taken and deſtroyed by the Medes and Babylonians, and what we may reaſonably ſuppoſe contributed to complete its ruin and devaſtation was, Nebuchadnezzar's ſoon after enlarging and beautifying of Babylon. [illegible] no mention is made of Nineveh by any of the ſacred writers, and the moſt ancient of the profane authors who have occaſion to ſay any thing about it, ſpeak of it as a city that once was great and flouriſhing, but now deſtroyed and deſolate.

The ſame accounts are given of it by all the modern travellers, and particularly by Thevenot, upon whoſe authority Dean Prideaux relates, that "Moſul is ſituated on the weſt ſide of the river Tigris, where was anciently only a ſuburb of the Old Nineveh; for the city itſelf ſtood on the eaſt ſide of the river, where are to be ſeen ſome of its rubbiſh, of great extent, even to this day."

Another modern traveller ſays, "In this country the famous city of Nineveh once ſtood, on the eaſtern bank of the river Tigris, oppoſite to the place where Moſul now ſtands. There is nothing now to be ſeen but heaps of rubbiſh, almoſt a league along the river Tigris, over againſt Moſul, which people imagine to be the ruins of this vaſt city."

Such hath been the fate of this once great city of Nineveh, in the deſtruction of which is moſt amply manifeſted the great truth of the Divine predictions!

CHAP. VII.

Prophecies concerning the city of Babylon.

THE city of Babylon, after the deſtruction of Nineveh, became not only the greateſt and moſt magnificent metropolis in the eaſt, but in the whole world. It is ſaid by ſome to have been originally built by Semiramis, queen of Aſſyria, while others aſſert that it was built by Belus, the ſucceſſor of Nimrod. But whoever was the real founder, we may reaſonably ſuppoſe it received great improvements afterwards, and Nebuchadnezzar in particular enlarged and beautified it to ſuch a degree, that he may in a manner (as Daniel obſerves) be ſaid to have built it: "Is not this (ſays he) great Babylon, that I have built for the houſe of the kingdom, by the might of my power, and for the honour of my majeſty?" Dan. iv. 30. By one means or other Babylon became ſo great and famous a city as to give name to a very large empire. It is called in ſcripture, "the great," "the glory of kingdoms," "the beauty of the Chaldees' excellency," "the praiſe of the whole earth," &c. And its ſtrength, grandeur, walls, temples, and palaces, are deſcribed with ſuch pomp and magnificence by ancient authors, that it muſt deſervedly have been reputed one of the wonders of the world.

"...natural branches." Rom. xi. 19, 24. But what would he ... and ... an influence of faction ... been ... stirring up a persecution against them?

... of all denominations should consider and reflect, that it is to the Jews we owe the oracles of God, and ... the New Testament as well as the Old. We ... that "the glorious company of the apostles," ... the "goodly fellowship of the prophets," were all ... consider that, "of them, as concerning the flesh, Christ came," the Saviour of the world, and ... of kindness and gratitude ... due for such ...

... the Jews are now broken off, yet they are not ... "Because of unbelief," as St. Paul ... "were broken off," and thou standest by faith; "be not high minded, but fear." Rom. xi. 20. ... they will be grafted in again, and again become the people of God: for as the apostle proceeds, "I ... brethren, that ye should be ignorant of this ... lest ye should be wise in your own conceits, ... until the fulness of the Gentiles be come in; and so all Israel shall be saved." Rom. xi. 25, 26.

But what, it may be asked, is the most likely method to contribute to the conversion of these unhappy people? ... the most natural means of reconciling them to ... religion? Is it to be effected by ... argument ... goodness, or by noise ... the malice of terror, and the ... They certainly cannot be worse ... when they crucified the Son of God, and persecuted his ... For what faith our Blessed Saviour himself? "Father, forgive them, for they know not what they do." ... And what faith his apostle St. Paul? "Brethren, my heart's desire and prayer to God for Israel is, that they might be saved." Rom. x. 1.

In conformity to these blessed examples, our church ... to pray for them: and how can prayer and persecution ... together? Those who ... are not only pretended friends ... church, but ... enemies to religion. All true members of the church, all true protestants, all true Christians, ... the apostle ... "put away all bitterness and wrath, and anger, and clamour, and evil speaking, with all malice." ... And they will all join ... that excellent collect, "Have mercy upon all Jews, Turks, Infidels, and Heretics, and take from them all ignorance, hardness of heart, and contempt of thy word: and so fetch them home, blessed Lord, to thy flock, that they may be saved among the remnant of the true Israelites, and be made one fold under one shepherd, Jesus Christ, our Lord."

CHAP. VII.

Prophecies concerning the ancient city of Nineveh.

THE first great prophecies contained in the old Testament are those which more immediately relate to the Jews themselves, who were once the peculiar people of God, and the principal subjects of those prophecies are the various changes and revolutions that were to happen in the Jewish church and state. But the spirit of prophecy is not confined to the Jews alone, there are other subjects occasionally introduced, and for the greater manifestation of Divine Providence, the ... of other nations it also foretold, and ... especially those which lay in the neighbourhood of Judea, and had intercourse and connection with the Jews.

It is much to be lamented, that, of these eastern nations and of these early times, we have no regular histories, but only a few fragments which have escaped the general ... wreck of time. From these, however, we see enough to make us admire the great works of Providence, and from these are clearly shown, that the revolutions of cities and kingdoms hath been such as was long ago foretold by the prophets.

The first prophecies we shall notice on this subject are these relative to the ancient city of Nineveh, once the metropolis of the Assyrian empire, and whose inhabitants not only destroyed the kingdom of Israel, but likewise greatly oppressed the kingdom of Judah.

The prophet Isaiah, in denouncing the judgments of God against the Assyrians, says, "O Assyrian, the rod of mine anger, and the staff in their hand is mine indignation." ... It was the will of Providence that ... should be employed as the ministers of his wrath, ... against the perverse and obstinate Jews. "I will send him against an hypocritical nation, and against the people of my wrath will I give him a charge to take the spoil, and to take the prey, and to tread them down like the mire in the streets." ... But it was far from the intention of the Assyrians to execute the Divine will, or to chastise the vices of ..., they only ... to extend their conquests, ... their own dominion upon the ruins of others. "Howbeit he meaneth not so, neither doth his heart think so, but it is in his heart to destroy, and cut off nations not a few." ... Wherefore, when they shall have ... the purposes of Divine Providence, they shall be ... for their pride and ..., their ... and ... their neighbours. "Wherefore it shall come to pass, that when the Lord hath performed his whole work upon mount Zion and on Jerusalem, I will punish the fruit of the stout heart of the king of Assyria, and the glory of his high looks." ver. 12.

There was no prospect of such an event ... while the Assyrians were in the midst of their successes and ..., but still the word of the prophet prevailed; ... it was not long after the calamities ... brought upon the Jews, the Assyrian empire (properly so called) was overthrown, and Nineveh destroyed.

The city of Nineveh was one of the largest and most ancient cities in the world. According to the best historians it was built not long after the flood, ... after the tower of Babel, by Nimrod, but being ... greatly enlarged by Ninus, from him it received its name. It was situated on the banks of the Tigris, and (according to the description given of it by Diodorus Siculus) ... length, ... and ... and ten, and ... circumference, four hundred and eighty ..., which, being reduced to our measure, ... one miles long, nine broad, ... sixty-four ... great the number of ... inhabitants was, we may ... "the sixscore thousand persons who could not discern between their right hand and their left hand," ... And, according to ... computation, there ... have been, on the whole, not less than six hundred thousand persons.

The inhabitants of Nineveh, like those of other great cities abounding in wealth and luxury, became very corrupt in their morals. In consequence of this, God ... pleased to command the prophet Jonah to preach unto them the necessity of repentance, ... the ... impending destruction ... and ... the success of his preaching, that both the king ... repented and turned from their evil ways, and ... for a time, escaped the executions of the Divine ...

But this repentance of the Ninevites, we may ... presume ... no long continuance, for ... after, we find the prophet Nahum foretelling ... the destruction of the city. Indeed, ... prophecy ... relates to ... single ...

[illegible] def[illegible] by the M[illegible]s and Babylonians, who, [illegible] together, subverted the whole Assyrian empire

It is [illegible] the prophet Nahum not only foretold the [illegible] of Nineveh, but likewise the manner in which it was to be effected He foretold that the Assyrians would be taken while they were drunken "For while they be folden together as thorns, and while they are drunken [illegible] drunkards, they shall be devoured as stubble fully dry" Nahum i 10 And Diodorus Siculus [illegible], "It was while the Assyrian army [illegible] feasting for their [illegible] that those about Arbaces (the general of the Medes [illegible],) being informed by some deserters, of the negligence and drunkenness in the camp of the enemy, [illegible] them unexpectedly by night, and falling on them [illegible] they were in the utmost disorder and unprepared, became masters of the camp, slew many of the [illegible], and drove the rest into the city."

The prophet Nahum likewise foretells, that "the gates of [illegible] shall be opened, and the palace shall be [illegible]" Nahum ii 6 And Diodorus [illegible] "there [illegible] prophecy, that Nineveh should not be [illegible] the river became an enemy to the city, and in the third year of the siege, the river being [illegible] with continual rains, overflowed part of the city, and broke down the wall for [illegible] furlongs; that the king [illegible] the oracle was fulfilled, and the river became an enemy to the city, built a large funeral pile in the palace, and collecting together all his wealth, and his concubines and eunuchs, burnt himself and the [illegible] in the palace, and the enemy entered the breach that the waters had made, and took the city."

Thus we find that what the prophet had predicted was literally fulfilled "With an overflowing flood he will make an utter end of the place thereof" Nahum i 8 He [illegible] the enemy [illegible] gold and silver "Take ye the spoil of silver, take the spoil of gold, for there is no end of the store, [illegible] out of all the [illegible] furniture" Nahum ii [illegible] And [illegible] Diodorus Siculus that Arbaces carried many talents of gold [illegible] to Ecbatana, the royal city belonging to the Medes.

According to the prophecy of Nahum the city was to be destroyed partly by water and partly by fire "Behold the gates of thy land shall be set wide open unto thine enemies, the fire shall devour thy bars" Nahum iii 13 And [illegible] by Diodorus [illegible] took place, for after the Medes and Babylonians had possessed themselves of the city, they set fire to it, and reduced the greater part of it to ashes

The prophet Nahum was the principal person who foretold the total and entire destruction of the ancient city of Nineveh "But with an overrunning flood will he make an utter end of the place thereof, he will make an utter end, affliction shall not rise up the second time" Chap i 8, 9 Again, "Where is the dwelling of the lions?" (meaning Nineveh, [illegible] princes ravaged like lions) "Behold, I am against thee, saith the Lord of hosts, and I will cut off thy prey from the earth and the voice of thy messengers shall no more be heard" Chap ii 11 13 And again "Thy crowned are as the locusts, and thy captains as the great grasshoppers which camp in the hedges in the cold day, but when the sun ariseth they flee away, and their place is not known [illegible] Thy shepherds slumber, O king of Assyria, thy nobles shall dwell in the dust, thy people is scattered upon the mountains, and no man gathereth them [illegible] There is no healing of thy bruise, thy wound is grievous, all that hear the bruit of thee shall clap the hands over thee, for upon whom hath not thy wickedness passed continually?" Chap iii 17, 18 [illegible]

The prophet Zephaniah likewise, in the days of Josiah, king of Judah, foretold the same melancholy event "The Lord will stretch out his hand against the north, and destroy Assyria, and will make Nineveh a desolation, and dry like a wilderness and flocks shall lie down in the midst of her, all the beasts of the nations both the cormorant and bittern shall lodge in the upper lintels of it, their voice shall sing in the windows, desolation shall be in the thresholds, for he shall uncover the [illegible] This is the rejoicing city that dwelt carelessly, that said in her heart, I am, and there is none beside me how is she become a desolation, a place for beasts to lie down in! every one that passeth by her shall hiss and wag his hand" Zeph ii 13 &c

It is not to be wondered at, that when these prophecies were first delivered the people could think it very unlikely they would ever be fulfilled [illegible] to think that so great a city [illegible] which contained so many [illegible] should ever be totally destroyed? And yet [illegible] destroyed, that even the place where it stood is now scarcely known

It has been [illegible] observed, that Nineveh was [illegible] and destroyed by the Medes and Babylonians [illegible] we may reasonably suppose [illegible] to complete [illegible] ruin and devastation [illegible] Nebuchadnezzar [illegible] [illegible] king of Babylon [illegible] [illegible] mention [illegible] of Nineveh [illegible] [illegible] have occasion to say any thing about it [illegible] city that once was great and [illegible] [illegible] and desolate

The same accounts are [illegible] travellers [illegible] [illegible] [illegible] on the west side of the river Tigris [illegible] only a suburb of the Old Nineveh [illegible] on the east side of the river [illegible] its rubbish [illegible]"

Another [illegible] famous city of Nineveh [illegible] [illegible] [illegible] to Mosul, which people [illegible] the city."

Such hath been the [illegible] Nineveh [illegible] [illegible] and the great truths of the Divine oracles !

C H A P. [illegible]III.

P[illegible]

THE [illegible] [illegible] [illegible] [illegible] metropolis of the [illegible] by some [illegible] of Assyria [illegible] the successor of [illegible] B[illegible] founder, was not [illegible] upon it [illegible] improvements [illegible] [illegible] [illegible] he may [illegible] built it [illegible] [illegible] my power, and [illegible] [illegible] By one [illegible] and famous [illegible] [illegible] It is called [illegible] glory, or [illegible] lency [illegible] the whole [illegible] its walls [illegible] [illegible] [illegible] the wonders of the world

It might naturally have been imagined that such a city as this was in no danger of ever being abandoned, much less of its coming to destruction. Such a city as this might surely, with less vanity than any other, boast that it should continue for ever; but, alas! great as it once was, the time did come when all its splendor was laid at an end, and the whole became one continued scene of ruins.

The inhabitants of Babylon were no less enemies to the Jews than those of Nineveh. The one subverted the kingdom of Israel, and the other the kingdom of Judah. It is, therefore, not to be wondered at that there should be several prophecies relative to these two cities, and that the fate of Babylon should be foretold as well as that of Nineveh. "Israel is a scattered sheep, the lions have driven him away; first the king of Assyria hath devoured him, and last this Nebuchadnezzar king of Babylon hath broken his bones. Therefore thus saith the Lord of hosts, the God of Israel, Behold, I will punish the king of Babylon and his land, as I have punished the king of Assyria." Lament. l. 17, 18.

The prophets Isaiah and Jeremiah very plainly, and in a particular manner, foretold the destruction of this great city. They both lived during the declension of the kingdom of Judah. As they predicted the captivity of the Jews, so they likewise foretold the downfall of their enemies; and they speak with such assurance of the event, that they describe a thing future as if it were already past. "Babylon is fallen, is fallen; and all the graven images of her gods he hath broken unto the ground." Isaiah xxi. 9. "Babylon is suddenly fallen and destroyed; howl for her, take balm for her pain, if so be she may be healed." Jeremiah li. 8.

Cyrus, who was the conqueror of Babylon, and transferred the empire of the Babylonians to the Medes and Persians, was particularly foretold by name many years before he was born. Isaiah xliv. 28. xlv. 1. He is honoured with the appellation of the "Lord's anointed," and the Lord is said to "have holden his right hand," and to have "guided him." He was certainly a person of very extraordinary abilities, and was raised up to be the instrument of Providence in executing great and wise purposes.

It was foretold that Cyrus should be a great conqueror, that he should "subdue nations before him, and I will loose the loins of kings to open before him the two-leaved gates; and the gates shall not be shut." Isaiah xlv. [illegible] This was strictly fulfilled, for Cyrus subdued several kings, and took several cities, particularly Sardis and Babylon, and extended his conquests all over Asia, from the river Indus to the Ægean Sea.

It was likewise foretold that Cyrus should find great spoil and treasure among the nations he should conquer. "I will give thee the treasures of darkness, and hidden riches of secret places." Isaiah xlv. 3. And the riches which Cyrus found in his conquests were of prodigious value, as appears from the accounts given us by Pliny. Nor can we wonder at it, when we consider that those parts of Asia, at that time, abounded in wealth and luxury. Babylon had been heaping up treasures many years; and the riches of Crœsus, king of Lydia, whom Cyrus conquered and took prisoner, are, in a manner, become proverbial.

The prophet Jeremiah not only foretells the destruction of the great city of Babylon, but likewise points out the time when it is to be effected. "These nations (says he speaking of the Jews) shall serve the king of Babylon seventy years. And it shall come to pass when seventy years are accomplished, that I will punish the king of Babylon, and that nation saith the Lord." Jer. xxv. 11, 12. This prophecy was delivered, as appears from the first verse of the chapter, "In the fourth year of Jehoiakim the son of Josiah king of Judah, that was the first year of Nebuchadnezzar king of Babylon," from which time there were seventy years to the taking of Babylon, and the restoration of the Jews from captivity. Nebuchadnezzar, after taking Jerusalem, transplanted the Jews to Babylon, in order to strengthen the place: their removal from thence must, therefore, have greatly weakened it; after which it became more and more distressed, till at length it was finally destroyed.

It was foretold that various nations should unite against Babylon. "The noise of a multitude in the mountains, like as of a great people; a tumultuous noise of the kingdoms of nations gathered together; the Lord of hosts mustereth the host of the battle." Isaiah xiii. 4. And particularly it was foretold, that the kingdoms of Ararat, Minni, and Ashchenaz, (that is, the Armenians, Phrygians, and other nations,) should compose part of his army. "Set ye up a standard in the land, blow the trumpet among the nations, prepare the nations against her, call together against her the kingdoms of Ararat, Minni, and Ashchenaz." Jer. li. 27. And accordingly, Cyrus's army consisted of various nations; and among them were those very people whom he had conquered before, and now obliged to attend him in this expedition.

It was foretold that the Babylonians should be terrified, and hide themselves within their walls. "The mighty men of Babylon have forborn to fight, they have remained in their holds, their might hath failed, they became as women." Jer. li. 30. And accordingly, we find that, after a battle or two, the Babylonians never recovered their courage to face the enemy in the field again. They retired within their walls; and the first time that Cyrus came with his army before them, he could not provoke them to venture forth and try the fortune of arms, even though he sent a challenge to their king, to fight with him in single combat. And the last time that he went, he consulted with his officers about the best method of carrying on the siege, "since (saith he) they do not come forth and fight."

It was likewise foretold that the river should be dried up before the city should be taken. This appeared very extraordinary, indeed, the river being more than a furlong broad, and deeper than the height of two men standing one upon another; so that the city was thought to be stronger and better fortified by the river than by the walls. But notwithstanding this, the prophets predicted that the waters should be dried up. See Isaiah xliv. 27. Jer. l. 38. li. 36. And accordingly Cyrus turned the course of the river Euphrates, which ran through the midst of Babylon, and, by means of deep trenches and canals, so drained the waters, that the river became easily fordable for his soldiers to enter the city; and by those means Babylon (which was otherwise impregnable) was taken.

It was foretold that the city should be taken by surprize during the time of a feast. "I have laid a snare for thee, and thou art also taken, O Babylon, and thou wast not aware; thou art found and also caught." Jer. l. 24. "In their heat I will make their feasts, and I will make them drunken, that they may rejoice, and sleep a perpetual sleep, and not wake, saith the Lord." Jer. li. 57. And accordingly the city was taken in the night of a great annual feast, while the inhabitants were dancing, drinking, and revelling, and not having the least suspicion that any immediate danger was at hand.

Such were the very extraordinary circumstances that attended the reduction of Babylon; and how could any man foresee or foretel such singular events, such remarkable circumstances, without revelation and inspiration from God?

If we examine still farther into these mysterious things, we shall see how these and other prophecies have, by degrees, been fulfilled; for in the very nature of th thing, they could not be fulfilled all at once. As the prophets often speak of things to be in future, as if they were already effected, so they speak often of things to be brought about in process of time, as if they were to succeed immediately. The past, present, and to come, are all alike known to infinite wisdom; but it is probable that the intermediate time was not revealed to the minds of the prophets.

The prophet Isaiah addresseth Babylon by the name of a *virgin*, as having never before been taken by an enemy: "Come and sit down in the dust, O virgin daughter of "Babylon, sit on the ground." Isaiah xlvii. 1. And Herodotus saith expressly, that this was the first time Babylon was taken. After this it never more recovered its antient splendor [illegible] it became a tributary city, from [illegible] its own kings, and governing strangers, [illegible] to be governed by strangers, and the seat of empire [illegible] to Shushan, it decayed by degrees, [illegible] at length reduced to utter desolation.

[illegible] told by [illegible], that, when Cyrus had taken [illegible] ordered the outer walls to be pulled down, [illegible] the city [illegible] seemed to him very difficult to be taken [illegible] Xenophon informs us, that Cyrus [illegible] the Babylonians to deliver up all their arms upon [illegible] placed their best horses among his officers, [illegible] upon them, appointed a strong garrison, and compelled the Babylonians to defray the charge, being desirous to keep them poor, as the best means of keeping them obedient.

But notwithstanding these precautions, they rebelled against Darius, and in order to hold out to the last extremity, they took all their women, and each man chose one of them out of his own family whom he liked best, they strangled the rest, that unnecessary mouths might not consume their provisions. And hereby (saith Dean Prideaux) was very signally fulfilled the prophecy of Isaiah against them, in which he foretold, 'That two things should come "to them in a moment, in one day, the loss of children and "widowhood, and that these should come upon them in their "perfection, for the multitude of their sorceries, and the "great abundance of their enchantments." Isaiah xlvii. 9. And in what greater perfection could these calamities come upon them, than when they themselves thus upon themselves became the executioners of them?" They sustained the siege against all the efforts of Darius for twenty months, and at length the city was taken by stratagem. As soon as Darius had made himself master of the place, he ordered three thousand of the principal men to be crucified, and there by fulfilled the prophecies of the cruelty which the Medes and Persians should use towards the Babylonians. Isaiah xiii. 17, 18. Jer. l. 42. He likewise demolished the wall, and took away the gates, by which was remarkably fulfilled the prophecy of Jeremiah: "Thus saith the Lord of hosts, The "broad walls of Babylon shall be utterly broken, and her "high gates shall be burnt with fire." Jer. li. 58.

When Xerxes returned from his unfortunate expedition into Greece, partly out of religious zeal, (being a professed enemy to image worship,) and partly to reimburse himself after his immense expences, he seized upon the treasures, and plundered or destroyed the temples and idols in Babylon, thereby accomplishing the prophecies of Isaiah and Jeremiah: "Babylon is fallen, is fallen, and all the graven "images of her gods he hath broken unto the ground." "Bel boweth down, Nebo stoopeth." Isa. xxi. 9. xlvi. 1. "Babylon is taken, Bel is confounded, Merodach is "broken in pieces." "And I will punish Bel in Babylon, "and I will bring forth out of his mouth that which he "hath swallowed up." Jer. l. 2. li. 44. &c. This part of the prophecy was most literally fulfilled, when the vessels of the house of God, which Nebuchadnezzar had brought from Jerusalem, and placed in the temple of Bel, were restored by order of Cyrus, and carried back to Jerusalem.

After the destruction of Babylon by the Persians, Alexander intended to have made it the seat of his empire, and actually set men at work to rebuild the temple of Belus, to repair the banks of the river, and to bring back the waters into their own channel. But if his designs had taken effect, how could the prophecies have been fulfilled? And what a providence there fore it was, that his designs did not take effect, and that the breaches were never repaired? He met with some difficulties in the work, and death soon after put an end to this and all his other projects, and none of his successors ever attempted it. Seleucia being built a few years after in the neighbourhood, Babylon, in a little time, became *wholly desolate*, Seleucia not only robbing it of its inhabitants, but (according to Pliny) even of its name.

That the prophecies relating to the fate of this antient and once magnificent city, have, in the most perfect manner, been fulfilled, appears from accounts given of it by a variety of authors, both antient and modern. Among the [illegible], Diodorus Siculus describes the buildings as ruined [illegible] decayed in his time, and says, that only a small part of the city was then inhabited, the greatest part within the walls being tilled. Strabo (who wrote not long after [illegible]) says, that one part of the city was destroyed [illegible] and the other by time and the neglect of the Macedonians, and especially after [illegible] had built Seleucia on the Tigris in the neighbourhood of Babylon, and he and his successors [illegible] (saith he) Seleucia is greater than Babylon, and Babylon is much deserted, so that one may [illegible] the poet said of Megalopolis in Arcadia, [illegible] now become a great desert." Pausanias [illegible] [illegible] was reduced to [illegible] the neighbourhood of Seleucia [illegible] Seleucia [illegible] neglected and forsaken, [illegible] [illegible] Jerome (who [illegible] Christ) it was converted into [illegible] within the compass of [illegible] [illegible] "We have learned [illegible] "that [illegible] who now liveth at Jerusalem [illegible] "things are in Persia [illegible] "confined within the circuit of the walls [illegible] after he saith, 'that, excepting the [illegible] "many years, have been repaired [illegible] "beasts, all the space within is [illegible] habitation."

Of later authors the first who [illegible] any thing concerning it is Benjamin of Tudela, a Jew, [illegible] twelfth century. In his itinerary, he says [illegible] Babylon is now laid waste, but some ruins are still [illegible] "of Nebuchadnezzar's palace, and men [illegible] enter [illegible], "on account of the serpents and scorpions which are in the "midst of it." And Texeira, a Portuguese, [illegible] description of his travels from India to Italy [illegible] "great famous city there is nothing but only a very [illegible] "remaining, nor in the whole region is any place less "frequented."

Such are the accounts given us of the state of Babylon by antient authors [illegible] which relation is given [illegible] writers and travellers in modern date. The [illegible] quote of these is [illegible] Rauwolff, a German traveller [illegible] passed that way in the year 1574, [illegible] the ruins of this once [illegible] "village [illegible] "for [illegible]" [illegible] "where people go [illegible] "the celebrated city of Babylon [illegible] "journey [illegible] "try is so [illegible] "be, that [illegible] powerful "city, once the most stately and renowned in all the world, "situated in the pleasant and fruitful country of Shinar, "could have once stood there, if I had not known it by its "[illegible] and many antiquities, of great beauty, which are "still standing hereabout in great desolation [illegible], by the old "bridge which was laid over the Euphrates, whereof there "are some pieces and arches still remaining, built of burnt "brick, and so strong that it is admirable. [illegible] the "village of [illegible] is the hill whereon the castle stood, "and the ruins of its fortification are still visible, though de-"molished and uninhabited. Behind it at a small distance, "stood the tower of Babylon. It is still to be seen, and is "half a league in diameter, but so ruinous, so low, and so "full of venomous creatures, which lodge in holes made "by them in the rubbish, that no one durst approach "nearer to it than within half a league, except during "two months in the winter, when these animals never "stir out of their holes. There is one sort particularly, "which the inhabitants call, in the language of the country, "([illegible] Persian) [illegible], the poison whereof is very "[illegible] they are larger than our lizards."

[illegible] Valerius, ([illegible] Roman) who was at Bagdat [illegible], [illegible] to see the ruins (as they are [illegible]) [illegible] informs us, that, "in the "middle of a [illegible], about a quarter of a "league from the [illegible], in that place, runs "[illegible] buildings like a "[illegible] "together, that one knows not what to make of [illegible] "[illegible] with that pyramid which "[illegible], and it is, in all likelihood, "the tower of Nimrod in Babylon, or Babel, as that place "is still called. There appear no marks of ruins without "the compass of that huge mass, to convince one so great "a city as Babylon had ever stood there: all one discovers, within fifty or sixty paces of it, are only the re-"mains here and there of [illegible] foundations of buildings; "and the country round about it is so flat and level, that "one can hardly believe it should be chosen for the situation "of so great and [illegible] a city as Babylon, or that there "were ever [illegible] buildings on it: but for my part, "I [illegible] so much as there does, con-"sidering it is [illegible] thousand years since that city was "built, and that Diodorus Siculus informs us, it was reduced "almost to nothing in his time."

[illegible] a very celebrated traveler, tells us, that "at the parting of the Tigris, which is but a little way "from Bagdat, there is the foundation of a city, which "seems to have been a large league in compass. There "are some of the walls yet standing, upon which six "[illegible] may go abreast: they are made of burnt brick, "ten feet square, and three thick. The chronicles of the "country say, here stood the antient city of Babylon." [illegible], however, did not think the ruins he saw to be those of Nebuchadnezzar's palace, or of the tower of Babel, as some have supposed they were. He adopts the opinion of the Arabs, and supposes them rather to be the remains of a tower, built by one of their princes for a beacon, to assemble his subjects in time of war, which, in all probability, was the real state of the case.

The observations made by Mr Salmon (in his Modern History) relative to Babylon, are certainly very just and pertinent. "What (says he) is as strange as any thing re-"lated of Babylon is, that we cannot learn with certainty, "either from antient writers, or modern travellers, where "this famous city stood, only in general, that it was situ-"ated in the province of Chaldæa, upon the river Euphra-"tes, considerably above the place where it is united with "the Tigris. Travellers have guessed, from the great ruins "they have discovered in several parts of this country, that "in this or that place Babylon once stood: but when we "come to examine nicely the places they mention, we "only learn that they are certainly wrong, and have "taken the ruins of Seleucia, or some other great town, "for those of Babylon."

The last traveler we shall mention, who takes notice of the ruins of Babylon, is Mr Hanway, who, previous to his giving an account of the siege of Bagdat, by Nadir Shah, prefaces it in these words: "Before we enter upon any "circumstance relating to the siege of Bagdat, it may afford "some light to the subject, to give a short account of this "famous city, in the neighbourhood of which formerly "stood the metropolis of one of the most antient and most "powerful monarchies in the world. The place is gene-"rally called Bagdat, or Bagdad, though some write it, to pre-"serve the antient name of Babylon. The reason of thus "confounding these two cities is, that the Tigris and Eu-"phrates, forming one common stream before they disem-"bogue it to the Persian gulph, are not unfrequently men-"tioned as one and the same river. It is certain that the "present Bagdat is situated on the Tigris, but the antient "Babylon, according to all historians, both sacred and pro-"fane, was on the Euphrates. The ruins of the latter, "which geographical writers place about fifteen leagues to "the south of Bagdat, are now so much effaced, that there "are hardly any vestiges of them to point out the situation. "In the time of the emperor [illegible] there was only a "great park remaining, in which the kings of Persia bred "wild beasts for the amusement of hunting."

How evidently does it appear, from all these accounts, with what great punctuality time hath fulfilled the predictions of the prophets concerning Babylon! When it was converted into a chase for wild beasts to feed and breed there, then were exactly accomplished the words of the prophets, that "the wild beasts of the desert, with the wild "beasts of the island should dwell there, and cry in their "desolate houses." One part of the country was overflowed by the river having been turned out of its course, and never restored to its former channel, and thence became boggy and marshy, so that it might be literally said to be "a "possession for the bittern and pools of water." Isaiah xiv. 23. Another part is described as dry and naked, and barren of every thing, so that thereby was also fulfilled another prophecy, "Her cities are a desolation, a dry land and a "wilderness, a land wherein no man dwelleth, neither doth "any son of man pass thereby." Jer. li. 43. The place thereabout is represented as over-run with serpents, scorpions, and all sorts of venemous and unclean creatures, so that "their houses are full of doleful creatures, and dragons "cry in their pleasant palaces, and Babylon is become "heaps, a dwelling-place for dragons, an astonishment and "an hissing without an inhabitant." [illegible] "neither can the Arabian pitch his tent there, neither can "the shepherds make their folds there." At [illegible] we find that modern travellers cannot now certainly discover the spot of ground whereon this renowned city once was situated, we may very properly say, "How is Babylon become "a [illegible] among the nations! Every purpose of the "Lord shall be performed against Babylon, to make the "land of Babylon a desolation without an inhabitant." [illegible] [illegible] no less true than [illegible], that "the Lord "of hosts hath swept it with the besom of destruction."

Thus have we represented, in the most clear and [illegible] light, the amazing prophecies which are foretold and fulfilled concerning the fate of the once mighty [illegible] of Babylon. How wonderful are such predictions, [illegible] with the events! and what a [illegible] of the truth and divinity of the Holy Scriptures! Well might God represent this as [illegible] of his prescience, and challenge all the other false gods and their votaries to produce the like. "Who hath declared this from ancient "time? have not I the Lord? and there is no God else be-"side me, a just God and a Saviour, there is none beside "me, declaring the end from the beginning, and from "antient times the things that are not yet done, saying

" My counsel shall stand, and I will do all my pleasure " Isaiah xlv 21 xlvi 10 And, indeed, where can we find a similar instance, but in Scripture, from the beginning of the world to the present time?

CHAP IX

Prophecies concerning the city of Tyre

ANOTHER memorable instance of the great truth of prophecy, is that of the destruction of Tyre The inhabitants of this city, as well as those of Nineveh and Babylon, were great enemies to the Jews but it was not altogether on this account that they were punished [illegible] the Divine vengeance, it was owing to their pride and self-sufficiency, both of which were founded on their great riches obtained by traffic, and for which they were more famous than any other nation whatever

The destruction of Tyre was predicted by the prophets many years before it happened, and particularly by Isaiah [illegible] and Ezekiel But it hath been a matter of doubt [illegible] the learned, which of the Tyres [illegible] the [illegible] prophecies, whether Palætyrus, or Old Tyre, that was seated on the continent, or New Tyre, that was built in an island near [illegible] opposite But [illegible] to this, and the most incontested [illegible] observation is, that the prophecies manifestly appertain to both, some expressions being applicable only to the former, and others only to the latter

In one place Tyre is described as " situate at the entry of the sea," Ezek xxvii 3, in others " in the midst of the sea," ver 4 and 25 Sometimes it is [illegible] as besieged " with horses and with chariots " Ezek xxvi, &c and at other times it is expressly called [illegible] island, and the sea, even the strength of the sea " [illegible] xxiii 2 It is said, " By reason of the abundance of his horses their dust shall cover thee thy walls shall shake at the noise of the horsemen, and of the wheels, and of the chariots when he shall enter into thy gates, as men enter into a city wherein is made a breach " Ezek xxvi 10 It is afterwards said, " They shall break down thy walls, and destroy thy pleasant houses and they shall lay thy stones and thy timber, and thy dust in the midst of the water " Ezek xxvi 12 And again " They shall bring thee down to the pit, and thou shalt die the deaths of them that are slain in the midst of the seas " Ezek xxviii 8

It is evident from these expressions, that the insular Tyre, as well as the Tyre on the continent, is included in these prophecies They are both comprehended under the same name, and both spoken of as one and the same city, one part being built on the continent, and the other on an adjoining island

It was usual with the prophets, when they denounced the downfall and desolation of a city or kingdom, to describe, by way of contrast, its then flourishing condition, to show, in a stronger point of view, how Providence changeth the scene, and ordereth and disposeth all events The prophets Isaiah and Ezekiel observe the same method with regard to Tyre Isaiah speaketh of it as a place of great antiquity, " Is this your joyous city, whose antiquity is of antient days " [illegible] xxiii 7 And it is mentioned as a strong place so early as the days of Joshua " The strong city of Tyre " Josh xix 29 Nay, there are even heathen authors who extol the great antiquity of the place The Greek geographer Strabo saith, that, after Sidon, the greatest and most antient city of the Phœnicians was Tyre, which was a rival to Sidon in greatness, and lustre, and antiquity

Antient, however as this city was, it was the " daughter of Sidon," as it is called by the prophet Isaiah xxiii 12 and " the merchants of Sidon, who pass over the sea, replenished it," ver 2 Sidon was the eldest son of Canaan, Gen x 15 and the city of Sidon is mentioned by the patriarch Jacob, Gen xlix 13 In the days of Joshua it was called " Great Sidon " Josh xi 8 And in the days of the Judges, the inhabitants of Laish are said to have " dwelt careless and secure, after the manner of the Sidonians " Judges xviii 7

But though Tyre was the daughter of Sidon, yet the daughter soon equalled, and, in time, excelled the mother, and became the most celebrated place in the world for its trade and navigation, being the seat of commerce, and the center of riches It is therefore called, by the prophet Isaiah " a mart of nations, the crowning city, whose merchants are princes, whose traffickers are the honourable of the earth " Isaiah xxiii 3 8 And Ezekiel (as it were commenting on the words of Isaiah " a mart of nations") recounts the various nations whose commodities were brought to Tyre, and bought and sold by the Tyrians Ezek xxvii

In this wealthy and flourishing condition was Tyre when the prophets foretold its destruction, one of whom [illegible] at least 125 years before it was [illegible] by Nebuchadnezzar An extensive commerce [illegible] plenty soon produced luxury, and pride So it [illegible] with the Tyrians, and for these, and their other vices, as well as for their insults and injuries done to the Jews, the Divine vengeance was denounced against them by the prophets

The prophet Isaiah mentions the pride of the Tyrians as being the principal occasion of their fall " The Lord of hosts (saith he) hath purposed it, to stain the pride of all glory, and to bring into contempt all the honourable of the earth " Isaiah xxiii 9 Ezekiel denounces [illegible] and particularly censures the pride of the king of Tyre, in arrogating to himself divine honours " Because thou hast set thine heart as the heart of God, Behold, therefore I will bring strangers upon thee, the terrible of the nations and they shall draw their swords against the beauty of thy wisdom, and they shall defile thy brightness " Ezek xxviii 6, &c

The prophets Joel and Amos had before denounced [illegible] judgments on the Tyrians for their cruelty to the Jews in general, and in particular for their cruelty to the [illegible] of Israel, and for buying and taking the vessels [illegible] of the temple [illegible] Thus saith the Lord [illegible] " Because ye have taken my silver and my gold, and have carried into your temples my goodly pleasant things the children also of Judah and the children of Jerusalem have ye sold unto the Grecians, that ye might remove them far from their border Behold I will raise them out of the place whither ye have sold them, and will return your recompence upon your own head " Joel iii 5 &c

The prophet Amos likewise [illegible] " Thus saith the Lord, for three transgressions of Tyrus and for four I will not turn away the punishment thereof, because they delivered up the whole captivity to Edom, and remembered not the brotherly covenant " Amos i 9 [illegible]

[illegible] reckons the Tyrians among the [illegible] enemies of the Jews [illegible] " The tabernacles of Edom, and the Ishmaelites, of Moab, and the Hagarenes, Gebal, and Ammon, and Amalek, the Philistines, with the inhabitants of Tyre " Psal lxxxiii [illegible]

Ezekiel also begins his prophecy against the Tyrians with [illegible] that they rejoiced [illegible] were [illegible] over the Jews [illegible] Jerusalem [illegible] " Son of man, because that Tyrus hath said against Jerusalem, Aha, she is broken that was the gates of the people she is turned unto me, I shall be replenished, now she is laid waste " The [illegible]

"[illegible] once the most stately and renowned in all the world, [illegible] the pleasant and fruitful country of [illegible], [illegible] had not known it by [illegible] [illegible] of great beauty, which are [illegible] desolation [illegible], by the old [illegible] was laid over the Euphrates, [illegible] remaining, [illegible] admirable [illegible] [illegible] is the hill whereon the castle stood, [illegible] fortification [illegible] [illegible] and uninhabited [illegible], at a small distance [illegible] tower of Babylon [illegible] is still to be seen, and is [illegible] character, but so ruinous, so low, and so [illegible] venomous creatures, which lodge in holes made [illegible] in the rubbish, that no one durst approach [illegible] to it within half a league, except during two months in the winter, when these animals never [illegible] out of their holes. There is one sort particularly, [illegible] in the language of the country, [illegible] is Persian) [illegible], the poison whereof is very [illegible] [illegible] than our hand."

[illegible], (a [illegible] Roman) who was at Bagdat [illegible] to see the ruins (as they are [illegible] of Babylon, informs us, that, "in the [illegible] [illegible] quarter of a [illegible], in that place, ruins [illegible] [illegible] buildings like a [illegible] [illegible] [illegible] which [illegible] [illegible] [illegible], in Babylon, or Babel, as that place [illegible] [illegible] so many heaps of ruins without [illegible] to convince one so great [illegible] Babylon [illegible] stood there [illegible] one disco-vers, within a few [illegible] paces of it, are only the re-mains [illegible] foundations of buildings [illegible] [illegible] so flat and level, that [illegible] should be chosen for the situation [illegible] Babylon, or that there [illegible] buildings on it; but for my part, [illegible] as [illegible] days, con-[illegible] [illegible] years [illegible] city was [illegible], [illegible] informs us, it was reduced [illegible] [illegible]."

[illegible] traveller, tells us, that "[illegible] [illegible], which is but a little way [illegible] Bagdat, there is the foundation of a city, which [illegible] to have been a large league in compass. There [illegible] of the walls yet standing, upon which six [illegible] go abreast: they are made of burnt brick, [illegible] square, and three thick. The [illegible] of the [illegible] stood the antient city of Babylon." [illegible], however, does not think the ruins he saw to be those of Nebuchadnezzar's palace, or of the tower of Babel, [illegible] they were. He [illegible] the opinion [illegible], and supposes them rather to be the remains of some tower, built by one of their princes for a beacon, to [illegible] his subjects in time of war, which, in all pro-bability, was the [illegible] of the case.

The observations made by Mr Salmon (in his Modern History) relating to Babylon, are certainly very just and [illegible]. "[illegible] as strange as any thing re-lated of Babylon [illegible], that we cannot learn with certainty, "either from antient writers, or modern travellers, where "this famous city stood, only in general, that it was situ-ated in the province of Chaldea, upon the river Eupra-"tes, considerably above the place where it is united with "the Tigris. Travellers have guessed, from the great ruins "they have discovered in several parts of this country, that "in this or that place Babylon once stood: but when we "come to examine nicely the places they mention, we "only learn that they are certainly wrong, and have "taken the ruins of Seleucia, or some other great town, "[illegible] those of Babylon."

The last traveller we shall mention, who takes notice of the ruins of Babylon, is Mr Hanway, who, previous to his giving an account of the siege of Bagdat, by Nadir Shah, prefaceth it in these words: "Before we enter upon "[illegible] circumstance relating to the siege of Bagdat, it may afford [illegible] light to the subject, to give a short account of this "famous city, [illegible] neighbourhood of which formerly "stood the metropolis of one of the most antient and most "powerful monarchies in the world. The place is gene-"rally called [illegible], or Bagdad, though [illegible] pre-"serve the antient name of Babylon. The [illegible] of thus "confounding [illegible] two cities is, that the Tigris and Eu-"phrates, forming one common stream before they [illegible] "[illegible] to the Persian gulph, are not unfrequently men-"tioned as one and the same river. It is certain that the "present Bagdat is situated on the Tigris, but the antient "Babylon, according to all historians, both sacred and pro-"fane, [illegible] on the Euphrates. The ruins of the latter, "[illegible] a place about fifteen leagues "[illegible] of Bagdat, [illegible] now so much effaced, that there "[illegible] hardly any vestiges of them to point out the situation. "In the time of the emperor [illegible] there was only [illegible] "[illegible] remaining, in which the kings of Persia used "[illegible] the amusement of hunting."

How evident [illegible] from [illegible] accounts, [illegible] punctually [illegible] the predic-tions of the prophets concerning Babylon! [illegible] converted [illegible] for wild beasts to feed and [illegible] [illegible], than were exactly accomplished the words of the prophets that "the wild beasts of the desert, with the wild "beasts of the islands should dwell there, [illegible] "desolate houses." [illegible] the country was overflowed by the river [illegible], been turned out of its course [illegible] [illegible] channel, and thence became boggy and marshy, [illegible] might be literally said to be "a "possession for the bittern and pools of water." [illegible] [illegible] the waters, and [illegible] [illegible], so that the [illegible] is also fulfilled [illegible] [illegible], "[illegible] a desolation, a dry land and a [illegible] wilderness, a land wherein no man [illegible], neither doth "any son of man pass thereby" (Jer. li. 43.) The [illegible] [illegible] is over-run with serpents, scor-[illegible], and [illegible] venomous and unclean creatures, so that "their houses are full of doleful creatures, and [illegible] "cry in their pleasant palaces; and Babylon is become "[illegible], a dwelling-place for dragons, an astonishment and "[illegible] without an inhabitant." [illegible] "neither can the Arabian pitch his tent there, neither can "the shepherds make their folds there." [illegible] find that [illegible] cannot [illegible] certainty [illegible] the spot of ground whereon this renowned city once [illegible] [illegible] properly [illegible] How [illegible] [illegible] the [illegible] "[illegible] [illegible] "[illegible] of Babylon [illegible] "[illegible] [illegible] the Lord "[illegible] hath [illegible] with the [illegible]."

Thus have we represented, in the most clear [illegible] light, the [illegible] prophecies [illegible] ful[illegible] concerning the fate of the once [illegible] of Babylon. How wonderful are such predictions [illegible] with the event! [illegible] what a [illegible] the truth and divinity of the Holy Scriptures [illegible] God [illegible] this [illegible] [illegible], and challenge all the other [illegible] to produce the like! "Who hath declared this [illegible] "time? have not I the Lord? and there is no God else be-"side me, a just God and [illegible] "me, declaring the end from the beginning, and from "antient times the things that are not yet done, saying

thus ſaith the Lord God, Behold, I am againſt thee, O Tyrus, and will cauſe many nations to come up againſt thee, as the ſea cauſeth his waves to come up" Ezek xxvi 2 3

These were the circumſtances which occaſioned the prophecies againſt Tyre, and, by carefully conſidering and comparing them together, we ſhall find that they include the following particulars, viz

1 That the city ſhould be taken and deſtroyed by the Chaldeans, or Babylonians

2 That the inhabitants ſhould paſs the Mediterranean into the iſlands and countries adjoining, and even there ſhould not find a quiet ſettlement

3 That the city ſhould be reſtored after ſeventy years, and return to her gain and her merchandiſe

4 That it ſhould be taken and deſtroyed again

5 That the people ſhould, in time, forſake their idolatry, and become converts to the true religion and worſhip of God

6 That the city ſhould be totally deſtroyed, and become a place only for fiſhers to ſpread their nets upon

On a proper examination into theſe reſpective particulars, we ſhall find that they were not only diſtinctly foretold, but likewiſe exactly fulfilled

1 The city ſhould be taken and deſtroyed by the Chaldeans This is expreſsly foretold by the prophet Ezekiel who ſays, "Thus ſaith the Lord God Behold I will bring upon Tyrus Nebuchadnezzar king of Babylon, a king of kings from the north, with horſes and with chariots, and with horſemen, and companies, and much people He ſhall ſlay the people by the ſword, and thy ſtrong garriſons ſhall go down to the ground" Ezek xxvi 7 11 Salmanaſer, king of Aſſyria, had beſieged Tyre without ſucceſs, but Nebuchadnezzar was to prevail The prophet Ezekiel not only foretold the ſiege, but likewiſe mentions it afterwards as a paſt tranſaction, "Son of man Nebuchadnezzar king of Babylon cauſed his army to ſerve a great ſervice againſt Tyrus, every head was made bald, and every ſhoulder was peeled" Ezek xxix 18

Joſephus tells us, that Nebuchadnezzar beſieged Tyre thirteen years when Ithobal was king there, and that he ſubdued all Syria and Phœnicia As the ſiege continued ſo long, the ſoldiers muſt conſequently have endured many hardſhips ſo that thereby we better underſtand the juſtneſs of Ezekiel's expreſſion, that "Nebuchadnezzar cauſed his army to ſerve a great ſervice againſt Tyrus, every head was made bald, and every ſhoulder was peeled" Such light doth profane hiſtory caſt upon ſacred It farther appears, from the Phœnician annals, that the Tyrians received their kings afterwards from Babylon, which plainly evinces that ſome of the blood royal muſt have been carried thither captives The Phœnician annals likewiſe (as is clearly ſhewn by the learned Dr Prideaux) agree exactly with Ezekiel's account of the time and year wherein the city was taken Tyre, therefore, according to the prophecies, was ſubdued and taken by Nebuchadnezzar and the Chaldeans, after which we hear little more of that part of the city which ſtood upon the continent

2 That the inhabitants of Tyre ſhould paſs over the Mediterranean into the iſlands and countries adjoining and even there ſhould find no quiet ſettlement This is plainly ſignified by the prophet Iſaiah "Paſs ye over to Tarſhiſh," (that is, to Tarteſſus, in Spain,) "howl ye inhabitants of the iſle" Iſaiah xxiii 6 And again, "Ariſe, paſs over to Chittim," (that is, the iſlands and countries bordering upon the Mediterranean,) "there alſo ſhalt thou have no reſt" ver 12 What the prophet here delivers by way of advice is to be underſtood as a prediction Ezekiel intimates the ſame thing "The iſles that are in the ſea ſhall be troubled at thy departure" Ezek xxvi 18

The Phœnicians were the beſt navigators of antiquity, and the Tyrians, in particular, were celebrated for their ſhipping and having colonies in different parts of the world In this reſpect Tyre exceeded Sidon ſhe ſent forth colonies into Africa and Spain, and Quintus Curtius ſaith, that her colonies were diffuſed almoſt over the whole world The Tyrians, therefore, having planted colonies at Tarſhiſh, and upon the coaſts of Chittim, it was natural for them, when they were preſſed with dangers and difficulties at home, to fly to their friends and countrymen abroad, for refuge and protection That they really did ſo is aſſerted by St Jerome, whoſe authority is founded on the Aſſyrian hiſtories, which have been ſince loſt "We read (ſays he) in the hiſtories of the Aſſyrians that when the Tyrians were beſieged, after they ſaw no hope of reſiſting the enemy, they went on board their ſhips, and fled to Carthage, or to ſome iſlands of the Ionian and Ægean Sea" And in another place he ſaith, "When the Tyrians ſaw that the works for carrying on the ſiege were perfected, and the foundations of the walls were ſhaken by the battering of the rams, whatſoever precious things in gold, ſilver, clothes, and various kinds of furniture the nobility had, they put them on board their ſhips, and carried them to the iſlands So that the city being taken, Nebuchadnezzar found nothing worthy of his labours"

It muſt certainly have been very mortifying to Nebuchadnezzar, after ſo long and laborious a ſiege, to be diſappointed of the ſpoil of ſuch a city, and therefore Ezekiel was commiſſioned to promiſe the conqueſt of Egypt for his reward "Son of man, Nebuchadnezzar king of Babylon cauſed his army to ſerve a great ſervice againſt Tyrus every head was made bald, and every ſhoulder was peeled yet had he no wages nor his army for Tyrus, for the ſervice that he had ſerved againſt it Therefore thus ſaith the Lord God, Behold I will give the land of Egypt unto Nebuchadnezzar king of Babylon, and he ſhall take her multitude and take her ſpoil and take her prey, and it ſhall be the wages for his army" Ezek xxix 18, 19

But though the Tyrians ſhould paſs over to Tarſhiſh, and to Chittim, yet even there they ſhould find no quiet ſettlement, "there alſo ſhalt thou have no reſt" Megaſthenes, who lived about 300 years before Chriſt and was employed by Seleucus Nicanor in an embaſſy to the king of India, wrote an hiſtory of that country, in which he mentions Nebuchadnezzar as a man of the moſt diſtinguiſhed valour and military prowefs This hiſtorian is quoted by ſeveral antient authors and he is particularly cited by Strabo and Joſephus, for ſaying that Nebuchadnezzar ſurpaſſed Hercules in bravery and great exploits, that he ſubdued great part of Africa and Spain, and that he proceeded as far as the pillars of Hercules

It is reaſonable to ſuppoſe that, after Nebuchadnezzar had ſubdued Tyre and Egypt, he carried his arms farther to the weſtward, and if he proceeded as far as Megaſthenes reports, the Tyrians might well be ſaid to "have no reſt" the conqueror purſuing them from one country to another But beſides this, and after this the Carthaginians, and other colonies of the Tyrians, lived in a very wretched ſtate. Their hiſtory conſiſts of little more than wars and tumults Sicily and Spain Europe and Africa, the land, and their own element the ſea, were theatres of their calamities and miſeries, till at length not only the New, but Old Carthage likewiſe, was utterly deſtroyed As the Carthaginians ſprang from the Tyrians, and the Tyrians from the Sidonians, and Sidon was the firſt born of Canaan, (ſee Gen x 15) ſo the curſe upon Canaan ſeemeth to have purſued them to the moſt diſtant parts of the earth

[illegible] That city should be restored after seventy years, and return to her gain and her merchandise. This circumstance is expressly foretold by the prophet Isaiah: "And it shall "come to pass in that day, that Tyre shall be forgotten "seventy years, according to the days of one king, (or king-"dom, meaning the [illegible] which was to continue "seventy years,) after the end of seventy years shall Tyre "sing as [illegible] Take an harp, go about the city, thou "harlot that hast been forgotten, make sweet melody, sing "many songs, that thou mayest be remembered. And it "shall come to pass after the end of seventy years, that the "Lord will visit Tyre, and she shall turn to her hire, and "shall commit fornication with all the kingdoms of the "world upon the face of the earth." Isaiah xxiii. 15, 16, 17. [illegible] these figurative expressions is, that Tyre [illegible] neglected of traders and merchants for seventy years, as long as the Babylonian empire lasted, and after that she should recover her liberties and her trade, and draw [illegible] of all nations to deal with her, and [illegible] [illegible] of the earth to buy her purples, which were [illegible] and [illegible], and for which Tyre was [illegible] the place in the universe.

The [illegible] for the duration of the Babylonian empire [illegible] seventy years [illegible] long were the nations to groan [illegible] yoke, though these nations were subdued, some sooner and some later than others. "These nations shall serve the king of Babylon seventy "years. [illegible] shall come to pass, when seventy years are "accomplished, [illegible] the king of Babylon, "and that [illegible] for their iniquity, and the "land of the Chaldeans, and will make it perpetual desola-"tions," [illegible] 11, 12. And accordingly, at the end of seventy years, Cyrus and the Persians overturned the Babylonian empire, and [illegible] the conquered nations to their liberties.

Tyre was taken by Nebuchadnezzar [illegible] 32d year of his reign; seventy years [illegible] which time [illegible] come to the 19th of Darius [illegible] appears from history, [illegible] Darius, and the Persians [illegible] and consequently [illegible] [illegible] to their former privileges [illegible] [illegible] with [illegible] Xerxes [illegible] Greece. And [illegible] time of Alexander [illegible] the Tyrians were grown to such power and greatness, that they [illegible] the progress of that [illegible] conqueror longer [illegible] any part of the Persian empire [illegible] to be understood of [illegible] [illegible] city found [illegible] most [illegible] the [illegible] the new city flourished most [illegible] [illegible] celebrated in history.

A[illegible] the city should be [illegible] destroyed again. "Howl "ye [illegible] Isaiah xxiii. 6. "What city "is like Tyrus, like the destroyed in the midst of the sea?" Ezek. xxvii. 32. [illegible] bring thee down to the pit, "and thou shalt die the deaths of them that are slain in the "[illegible]" verse 8. These expressions can imply no less than that the [illegible] should be destroyed as well as that upon the continent, and as the one was accomplished by Nebuchadnezzar, so was the other by Alexander the Great. But the same thing may be inferred more directly from the words of Zechariah, who prophesied in the reign of Darius, (probably Darius Hystaspis) many years after the former destruction of the city, and consequently he must be understood to speak of the latter. His words are these: "And Tyrus did build herself a strong hold, and heaped up "silver as the dust, and fine gold as the mire of the streets. "Behold the Lord will cast her out, and he will smite "her power in the sea, and she shall be devoured with "fire." Zech. ix. 3, 4. Th[illegible] Tyrus did build herself a strong hold is very certain, for her situation was exceeding strong in an island, and, besides the sea to defend her, she was fortified with a wall of 150 feet in heighth and of a proportionable thickness. "She heaped up silver as the [illegible], "and fine gold as the mire of the street," being [illegible] celebrated place in the world for trade and riches, "the mart "of nations," as she is called, conveying the commodities of the east to the west, and of the west to the east. But yet "Behold the Lord will cast her out, and he will smite her "power in the sea, and she shall be devoured with fire." Ezekiel had likewise foretold that the city should be consumed [illegible] fire. "I will bring forth a fire from the midst of "thee, it shall devour thee, and I will bring thee to ashes "upon the earth, in the sight of all them that behold [illegible]." Ezek. xxviii. 18. And accordingly Alexander besieged, and took, and set the city on fire. The ruins of old Tyre contributed much to the taking of the new city; for with the stones, timber, and rubbish of the old city, Alexander made a bank, or causeway, from the continent to the island, thereby literally fulfilling the words of the prophet: "They "shall lay thy stones, and thy timber, and thy dust in the "midst of the water." Ezek. xxvi. 12. Alexander was seven months in completing this work, but the time and labour were well employed, for, by means thereof he was enabled to storm and take the city.

At the time Alexander reduced Tyre, great numbers of the inhabitants, as in the former siege, passed over the Mediterranean to the islands and countries adjoining. Both Diodorus Siculus and Quintus Curtius tell [illegible] that they sent their wives and children to Carthage, and, upon the taking of the place the Sidonians secretly conveyed away fifteen thousand more in their ships. Happy were they who thus escaped, for of those who remained behind, the conqueror slew eight thousand in storming and taking the city, caused two thousand afterwards to be crucified, and thirty thousand he sold for slaves. They had before sold some of the captive Jews, and now it was returned upon them, according to the prediction of Joel: "The children also of Judah, and "the children of Jerusalem have ye sold, [illegible] I [illegible] re-"turn your recompence upon your own head, and will sell "your sons and your daughters." Joel iii. 6, 7, 8.

When the old city was taken, the Tyrians received their kings afterwards from Babylon, but when the new city was conquered by Alexander, the king held the [illegible] by his appointment. The cases are, in many respects, alike, but the city recovered much sooner from the calamities of the last siege than the first. In the space of nineteen years it was able to withstand the fleets and armies of Antigonus, and sustained a siege of fifteen months before it was taken, a plain proof (as Dean Prideaux observes) "of the great advantage of trade: for this city being the grand mart where most of the trade both of the east and west did center, by virtue hereof it was that it soon after revived to its pristine vigour."

[illegible] There should come a time when the Tyrians would forsake their idolatry, and become converts to the true religion and worship of God. The Psalmist is thought [illegible] hinted as much in saying, "The daughter of Tyre shall [illegible] "therewith a gift." Psal. xlv. 12. And again, "The "kings of Tarshish and of the isles shall bring presents." Psal. lxxii. 10. Zechariah, when he foretells the calamities which the Tyrians and neighbouring nations should suffer from Alexander, at the same time predicts their conversion to the true God, "but he that remaineth, even he shall be "for our God." Zech. ix. 7. This prediction is [illegible] expressed by the prophet Isaiah, who says, "And her mer-"chandise and her hire shall be holiness to the Lord: it "shall not be treasured, nor laid up; for her merchandise "shall be for them that dwell before the Lord, to eat suf-"ficiently and for durable clothing." Isaiah xxiii. 18.

The Tyrians were greatly addicted to the worship of Hercules, as he was called by the Greeks, or of Baal as he is denominated in scripture. But in process of time, [illegible] mean is of some Jews and proselytes living and conversing among them, and [illegible] converted to the [illegible] religion, [illegible] multitude of people from the sea coast of Tyre and Sidon [illegible] Christ [illegible] Paul [illegible] came to Tyre [illegible] found disciples [illegible] and prayed [illegible] Acts xxi [illegible]

[illegible] persecution, the Tyrians [illegible] Christianity [illegible] Jews [illegible] the [illegible] they [illegible] for the [illegible] in all [illegible] "And her merchandise [illegible] to [illegible] as well as [illegible] for the [illegible] to the [illegible] at the altar should [illegible] We [illegible] the [illegible] each [illegible]

[illegible] that as Tyre [illegible] the Lord [illegible] it had the [illegible] the [illegible] of [illegible] prophecy, and [illegible]

[illegible] Tyre was to be totally destroyed, and become [illegible] nets upon [illegible] of any city [illegible] condition [illegible] to no [illegible] and [illegible] of Ezekiel [illegible] "Thus saith the Lord God [illegible] Tyrus [illegible] her [illegible] her towers [illegible] her [illegible] like the top of a rock [illegible] the midst of [illegible] for I have spoken it, saith the Lord God" [illegible] And again, "I will make thee [illegible] thou shalt be no more, though thou be sought for, yet shalt thou never be found again," ver. 21.

The prophecies of [illegible] of great [illegible] to most other places, were [illegible] by degrees. Nebuchadnezzar destroyed the old city, and Alexander employed the ruins and rubbish in making his causeway from the continent to the island, which henceforward were joined together. "It is no wonder, therefore, (as bishop Pocock observes) that there are no signs of the ancient city; and, as it is [illegible] the face of [illegible] altered, and the [illegible] many parts [illegible] almost buried in the sand." So that as to this part of the city, the prophecy hath been literally fulfilled: "Thou shalt be built no more, though thou be sought for, yet shalt thou never be found again."

It [illegible] be questioned whether the new city ever arose to that height of power, wealth, and greatness, to which it was exalted in the times of Isaiah and Ezekiel. It received [illegible] blow from Alexander, not only by his taking and burning the city, but much more by his building of Alexandria in Egypt, which, in time, deprived it of much of its trade, and thereby contributed more [illegible] to its ruin. It had then [illegible] afterwards of changing its masters often, being sometimes in the hands of the Ptolemies kings of Egypt, and sometimes of the kings of Syria, till at length it fell under the dominion of the Romans. It was taken by the Saracens about the year of Christ 639, in the reign of Omar, their third emperor. It [illegible] Christians during the time of the holy war, in the year 1124, [illegible] of that name being then king of Jerusalem, and assisted by a fleet of the Venetians. [illegible] Christ it was again taken, in the year 1289, by the Mamalukes of Egypt, [illegible] who sacked and razed this and [illegible] From the Mamalukes it was again taken in the year 1516, by [illegible] the ninth emperor of the Turks, and [illegible] present. But alas! how fallen! how changed from what it was formerly! Instead of being the centre of trade and frequented by the merchants [illegible] is now become [illegible] heap of ruins, a [illegible] of [illegible] poor [illegible] men. So that [illegible] the [illegible] prophecies [illegible] been [illegible] "I will make thee like the top of a rock, thou shalt be a place to spread nets upon."

The description given of the [illegible] present city by Mr. Maundrell, in his journey from Aleppo to Jerusalem, is as follows. "This city [illegible] the [illegible] and [illegible] nothing here but a mere Babel of broken walls, pillars, vaults, &c. there being not so much as one entire house left. Its present inhabitants are only a few poor wretches, harbouring themselves in the vaults, and subsisting chiefly upon fishing, who seem to be preserved in this place by Divine Providence as a visible argument how God has fulfilled his word concerning Tyre," viz. "that it should be as the top of a rock, a place for fishers to dry their nets on."

This account of Mr. Maundrell is corroborated by Mr. Middleton, in his New System of Geography. "This powerful city, says he, [illegible] the capital of Phoenicia, the emporium of commerce, [illegible] of the [illegible] beauty and [illegible] is so [illegible] buried [illegible] the [illegible] only a few very poor people, who [illegible] by fishing."

[illegible] of the once famous city of Tyre, on which [illegible] vengeance was denounced for the [illegible] of its [illegible] and in the [illegible] of which we have [illegible] instance, to [illegible] of the great truth of the Divine predictions, as spoken by the mouths of the prophets.

CHAP. X.

Prophecies concerning Egypt.

EGYPT is one of the most ancient kingdoms in the world, it having been in a very flourishing state even during the days of Abraham, and the inhabitants of it were distinguished for having more wisdom than any other people at that time on the face of the earth. It was (as we may call it) the great academy of the earlier ages. Hither the wits and sages of Greece and other countries repaired, and received their learning at this fountain. It is mentioned to the commendation of Moses, that he "was learned in the wisdom of the Egyptians." Acts vii. 22. And the highest character given of Solomon's wisdom is, that it "excelled the wisdom of all the children of the east country, and all the wisdom of Egypt." 1 Kings iv. 30. But with this wisdom it was early corrupted, and was as much the parent of superstition as it was the mistress of learning, and the one as well as the other, were from thence propagated and diffused over other countries. It was, indeed, the great corrupter of the world, the source of Polytheism and idolatry to [illegible] the [illegible] and [illegible] tern nations, [illegible] such [illegible] not to be equalled by any [illegible]

[illegible] the Israelites [illegible] in Egypt [illegible] [illegible] Egyptians. But still [illegible] were [illegible] into [illegible] common [illegible] occasions [illegible] of Egypt [illegible] for the righteous good [illegible] This [illegible] Egyptians [illegible] with disrespect, but took every advantage [illegible] doing them the greatest [illegible] Solomon, king [illegible] up against Jerusalem [illegible] 1 Kings [illegible] 26. And [illegible] the Israelites [illegible] a broken reed [illegible] it will go into his hand and [illegible] it." [illegible]

[illegible] it is not to be [illegible] should be the subject of several prophecies, [illegible] that the [illegible] revolutions that were to happen in that [illegible] which were to take place from the days of the prophets, and continue to the present time.

The first [illegible] revolution that happened in Egypt (after the prophets [illegible]) was the conquest of it by Nebuchadnezzar [illegible] by Jeremiah [illegible] Ezekiel. [illegible] these two prophets have employed several [illegible] upon this occasion Jeremiah [illegible] Egypt, where he foretold the conquest of Egypt by Nebuchadnezzar, king of Babylon [illegible] entitled, "The word that the Lord spake to Jeremiah the prophet, how Nebuchadnezzar king of Babylon should come and smite the land of Egypt." Jer. xlvi. 13. Ezekiel also declares, "Thus saith the Lord God, I will also make the multitude of Egypt to cease by the hand of Nebuchadnezzar king of Babylon. He and his people with him, the terrible of the nations shall be brought to destroy the land; and they shall draw their swords against Egypt, and fill the land with the slain." Ezekiel xxx. 10, 11. The conquest of this kingdom was promised to Nebuchadnezzar as a reward for his services against Tyre, which, after a long siege, he took and destroyed, but was disappointed of the spoil, as we have already observed in the foregoing chapter.

That this prophecy was strictly fulfilled, appears from the testimonies of Megasthenes and Berosus, two heathen historians, one of whom expressly affirms that Nebuchadnezzar conquered the greatest part of Africa, and the other affirms it in effect, by saying, that, when Nebuchadnezzar heard of the death of his father, having settled his affairs in Egypt, and committed the captives, whom he took there, to the care of some of his friends, to bring them after him, he hasted directly to Babylon.

The testimonies of these two are confirmed by Josephus, who says, that Nebuchadnezzar, having subdued Coelo-Syria, waged war against the Ammonites and Moabites, and having conquered them, he invaded Egypt, slew Pharaoh-Hophra, their king, and appointed another in his stead. This monarch is represented by Ezekiel as an arrogant, impious prince: he calls him "the great dragon (or crocodile) that lieth in the midst of his rivers, which hath said, my river is my own, and I have made it for myself." Ezek. xxix. 4. Agreeable to this Herodotus informs us that he proudly [illegible] boasted of having established his kingdom so [illegible] that it was not in the power of God himself [illegible] of it. [illegible] this presumption he was [illegible] foretold by Jeremiah [illegible] "Thus saith the Lord, Behold, [illegible] Pharaoh-Hophra king of Egypt into the [illegible] enemies, and into the hand of them that [illegible] xliv. 30.

[illegible] the prophet Ezekiel, that the country [illegible] forty years [illegible] people [illegible] into other countries. [illegible] make the [illegible] years, and I will scatter [illegible] disperse them [illegible] countries." Ezek. [illegible] 12. [illegible] that [illegible] continued exactly forty [illegible] doubt but this [illegible] countries [illegible] under the Babylonians [illegible] time of Cyrus. We are assured by Berosus, [illegible] took several captives from Egypt, and [illegible] to Babylon; and from Megasthenes we learn [illegible] and settled [illegible] in Pontus. So [illegible] were "scattered among the nations, and dispersed through the countries;" and the greater [illegible] probably after the dissolution of the Babylonian [illegible] return to their native country.

The [illegible] memorable revolution that happened in Egypt [illegible] the invasion and [illegible] by Cambyses [illegible] of the 29th chapter of the prophet Ezekiel. Some parts, indeed, of this prophecy [illegible] with those of Jeremiah [illegible] conquest of Egypt by Nebuchadnezzar [illegible] as well as several others [illegible] periods. [illegible] Babylonians as well as to Cambyses [illegible] both [illegible] the Egyptians by [illegible] conqueror [illegible] of the Persians [illegible] of the Babylonians.

[illegible] begins the prophecy [illegible] Egypt [illegible] and that [illegible] Egypt should [illegible] "Behold, [illegible] the Lord [illegible] and shall come into Egypt, and the idols of [illegible] shall be moved at his presence, and the [illegible] melt in the midst of it." [illegible] things [illegible] foretold of Nebuchadnezzar by the prophet Jeremiah: "And when he cometh [illegible] smite the land "of Egypt [illegible] And I will kindle a fire in the houses "of the gods of Egypt; and he shall burn them, and 'carry them [illegible] captives He shall break also the 'images of Bethshemesh, that is in the land of Egypt, "and the houses of the gods of the Egyptians shall he burn with fire." Jer xliii 11, &c And again the [illegible] "Thus saith the Lord God, I will [illegible] idols, and I will cause their images to [illegible] of Noph, or Memphis."

[illegible] attempt [illegible] made by Cambyses was upon Pelusium, [illegible] the entrance of Egypt, and he [illegible] by the stratagem of [illegible] before his army a great number of dogs, [illegible] and other [illegible] which being held sacred [illegible] not [illegible] and the town was formed and taken [illegible] resistance He [illegible] laughed at the people [illegible] the [illegible] and burnt [illegible] and [illegible] Ochus too, who was the [illegible] of Persia [illegible] subdued the Egyptians again [illegible] plundered their temples, and [illegible] in [illegible] victories

It was also foretold, by the prophet Isaiah [illegible] should [illegible] with civil wars "I will set the Egyptians against the Egyptians [illegible] against his brother [illegible] city against city, and kingdom against kingdom" Isa xix 2 Egypt [illegible] divided into twelve [illegible] or provinces, [illegible] which presided [illegible] prince, or governor [illegible] kingdom was [illegible] confusion It is, therefore, [illegible] to be wondered at, that [illegible] the Egyptians, [illegible] naturally a cowardly [illegible] "the spirit of Egypt [illegible] fail in the midst thereof," as [illegible] by the prophet, ver 3 and that being [illegible] superstitious people, "they should seek to the [illegible] to the charmers, and to them that have familiar spirits, and to the wizards" But their [illegible] it was their fate to be conquered and oppressed by cruel lords and tyrants "And the Egyptians will I give over into the hand of a cruel lord, and a fierce king shall rule over them, saith the Lord, the Lord of hosts," ver 4 This is a very [illegible] part of the prophecy and may with the greatest [illegible] be applied to the Persians, and [illegible] the former of whom put the yoke [illegible] neck of the Egyptians, and the latter [illegible] Ochus was the cruellest and worst of all the kings of Persia, [illegible] and oppressive to Egypt [illegible] his favourite eunuch, Bagoas, who was an [illegible] in revenge of his injured country, poisoned [illegible] No other [illegible] is wanting to prove that the [illegible] galling and [illegible] to the Egyptians [illegible] frequent revolts and rebellions which [illegible] only served to enslave [illegible] and augment their misery

[illegible] after denouncing these judgments against [illegible] to set forth, in figurative [illegible] the consequences of this subjection and slavery, [illegible] the mourning and lamentation [illegible] and misery, which should be entailed on [illegible] their posterity after which he recounts the [illegible] the folly of the princes [illegible] upon their wisdom, and [illegible] of the people in general [illegible] will plainly [illegible] to any one who attentively peruses the history of that nation, the particulars of which are too considerable to be here admitted It may, however, in general be said, that Egypt would not have become a prey to so many foreign enemies, had it not been for the excessive [illegible] of the people, both in council and in action They had not the courage even to defend themselves They trusted chiefly to their Grecian and other mercenaries, who, instead of defending, [illegible] the first to betray them

The next memorable revolution was effected by Alexander the Great, who subverted the Persian empire in Egypt, as well as in other places, and this event is particularly [illegible] in the same 19th chapter of the [illegible] It is also foretold, that, about the same time, several [illegible] should [illegible] and be converted to the worship of the true God [illegible] In [illegible] the midst [illegible] thereof [illegible]

[illegible] to show that Assyria and [illegible] should be a blessing on [illegible] out [illegible] Assyria, and the Egyptians [illegible] In that day shall [illegible] with Assyria, even [illegible] land [illegible] the Lord [illegible] Blessed [illegible] Egypt my people, and [illegible] mine [illegible]

[illegible] by the prophet, that a great prince from a foreign country, should deliver the Egyptians from [illegible] Persians [illegible] which was [illegible] And who could this be but Alexander who [illegible] the Great, and [illegible] Soter [illegible] to Egypt [illegible] of the country [illegible] the [illegible] and [illegible] [illegible] the God of Israel, [illegible] of Egypt, [illegible] it did happen [illegible]

It [illegible] Nebuchadnezzar had taken Jerusalem, [illegible] them [illegible] Jeremiah the prophet, [illegible] most of his prophecies concerning [illegible] by Nebuchadnezzar From thence the knowledge of God, and some notices of his prophecies might [illegible] be received by the Egyptians [illegible] place [illegible] *[illegible]* which accordingly came to pass [illegible] which the true worship of God was received was *Heliopolis*, the second *Migdol*, or Magdolum, the third, *Tahpanhes*, or Daphne, the fourth, *Noph*, or Memphis, and the fifth, *in the country of Pathros*, or Thebais, all of which are particularly mentioned by the prophet Jeremiah, chap. xliv. 1.

In these cities, at that time, many Jews resided, and though they were, in general, very wicked men, and disobedient to the word of God, yet, no doubt, some good people were mingled among them, who might teach [illegible] the prophecies of Jeremiah, and they [illegible], when they saw them fulfilled, might embrace the [illegible] religion [illegible]. However, is not to be understood of all the inhabitants of those places, but only [illegible] some, [illegible] the expression of "[illegible] cities [illegible] the language "of Canaan, and [illegible] by the Lord of hosts." [illegible] prediction of the prophet [illegible] "[illegible] will I turn to the people a pure language, that [illegible] "may call upon the name of the Lord [illegible] "one consent." Zeph. [illegible] 9.

After Alexander [illegible] had made a conquest of [illegible] he transplanted many of the Jews into his [illegible] city of Alexandria, and allowed them [illegible] privileges and immunities equal to those enjoyed by the [illegible]. [illegible] carried [illegible] of them into Egypt, and [illegible] such indulgences, that many others followed them of their own accord. [illegible], Philadelphus released and ransomed the captive Jews, and in his reign, or his father's, the books of Moses were translated into Greek, and afterwards the other parts of the Old Testament. The third Ptolemy, called Euergetes, having subdued all Syria, did not [illegible] to the gods of Egypt, in acknowledgment of his victory, but going to Jerusalem, offered his oblations to God after the manner of the Jews, and his example, no doubt, was followed by many of his subjects. The sixth Ptolemy, called Philometor, committed the whole management of his kingdom to two Jews, Onias and Dositheus, who were made chief ministers and generals, and had the principal direction of all affairs, [illegible]. This Onias obtained [illegible] to build a temple for the Jews in Egypt, like [illegible] Jerusalem, alleging for the purpose the [illegible] prophecy of Isaiah, that there should "be an altar to the "Lord in the midst of the land of Egypt," and the king and queen, in their edicts, made honourable mention of the law, and cite the prophet Isaiah, and express a dread of sinning against God. The place, chosen for the building of this temple, was in the prefecture of Heliopolis, or "the city of the sun," which place is likewise mentioned in the prophecy. It was built after the model of the temple at Jerusalem, but not so sumptuous and magnificent. Philometer himself was made high-priest; other priests and Levites were appointed for the administration, the Divine service was daily performed there in the same manner as at Jerusalem. By these means "the Egyptians must have known the Lord," and without doubt there must have been many proselytes among them. And of those who came up to the feast of Pentecost, there are particularly mentioned "the dwellers in Egypt, and in the parts of Lybia about Cyrene, Jews and proselytes." Acts ii. 10.

Thus were the Jews settled and encouraged in Egypt, nor were they less favoured by the kings of Syria. Seleucus Nicanor made them free of the cities which he built in Asia and the Lower Syria, and even of Antioch, the [illegible] of his kingdom, and granted the same rights and privileges to them as to the Greeks and Macedonians. Antiochus the Great published several decrees in favour of the Jews, both of those who inhabited Jerusalem, and of those who dwelt in Mesopotamia and Babylon. And thus, by means of the Jews and proselytes dwelling in Egypt and Syria, Israel, Egypt, and Syria, were, in some measure, united in the same worship. But this was more fully accomplished when the inhabitants of these countries became Christians, and were made members of the church of Christ. And it is to be fervently hoped and believed, that the prophecy will still receive its most perfect completion in the latter days, when Mahometanism shall be rooted out, and Christianity shall flourish in these countries, when "the fulness of the Gentiles "shall come in, and all Israel shall be saved."

The state of Egypt, from the days of Nebuchadnezzar to the present period, is predicted, in a most remarkable manner, by the prophet Ezekiel. He foretells that, after the desolation of the land, it "should be a base kingdom. "It shall be the basest of the kingdoms, neither shall it "exalt itself any more above the nations: for I will diminish them, that they shall no more rule over the nations." [illegible] "I will [illegible] the land into "[illegible] the wicked [illegible] I will make the land waste, "[illegible], by the hand of strangers; and "[illegible] no more a prince of the land of Egypt." [illegible]

In order to [illegible] of the fulfilment of [illegible] and make a [illegible] at least that [illegible] Nebuchadnezzar [illegible]

[illegible] he [illegible] crown [illegible] should pay to [illegible] Babylon, [illegible] the country, but [illegible] of [illegible]

[illegible] Cambyses [illegible] him, as [illegible] the [illegible] for him [illegible] the Egyptians [illegible] Darius [illegible]

[illegible] the death of [illegible] Lybia [illegible] and Egypt continued [illegible] part of the [illegible] Darius Nothus [illegible] Amyrtæus, who [illegible] out of [illegible] from Egypt, and made himself master of the [illegible] was succeeded by his son Pausiris, who [illegible] Herodotus, [illegible] the [illegible] by favour of the Persians, from whom [illegible] the Persians had again established [illegible], that the kingdom was not established without [illegible]. It is certain, however, [illegible] much trouble to the [illegible] Romans made several efforts to [illegible], but they proved ineffectual. It [illegible] about 300 years before [illegible], fled [illegible] of the country, and [illegible], [illegible] to Babylon [illegible] to [illegible], and [illegible] been [illegible] of [illegible].

[illegible] into the hands of the [illegible] the Great without [illegible] on his death it fell [illegible] captains, [illegible] and the [illegible] and [illegible] the [illegible] last, [illegible] Strabo [illegible] and many [illegible] Ptolemy, who [illegible] the [illegible] and [illegible] to [illegible] content and [illegible] concerned for [illegible]. The [illegible] the [illegible] that even at [illegible].

[illegible] the descendants of the Macedonians, Egypt fell under the [illegible] of the Romans. [illegible] had, indeed, [illegible] of [illegible] a great [illegible] of the [illegible] after the death of [illegible] province, [illegible] or governor [illegible] however, [illegible] from the reign [illegible] the reign of Omar, [illegible] the command of Amron, made [illegible] formerly called Mem[illegible], now Cairo [illegible], and Alexandria, after [illegible] fourteen months, and had lost [illegible] in the destruction [illegible] was the famous library, founded by the [illegible], and so much enlarged and improved [illegible] the books contained in it amounted to [illegible], all of which were committed to the [illegible]. Before this event, Egypt was frequented by [illegible] foreigners from almost all parts, and it produced [illegible] but afterwards it became more [illegible] into the greatest igno[rance] [illegible] was established there [illegible] the government of the caliphs [illegible] continued till about the year 1250 after Christ.

It was about this time that the Mamelucs usurped the royal authority. Their government began with the Sultan [illegible]beg, in the 648th year of the Hegira, and in the year of Christ 1250, and continued through a series of twenty-four Turkish and twenty-three Circassian Mameluke Sultans, ending with Tumanbai, in the year of Christ 1517. At that time Selim, the [illegible] emperor of the Turks conquered the Mamalucs, hanged their last Sultan [illegible] before the gates of Cairo, and put an end to their government. He caused five hundred of the chief Egyptian families to be transplanted to Constantinople, as well as great numbers of the wives and children of the Mamelucs, besides the Sultan's treasure, and other immense riches, and annexed Egypt to the Ottoman empire, whereof it hath continued [illegible] from that time to this. It is governed by a [illegible], with twenty-four [illegible], or princes, [illegible] the [illegible] to the ordinary direction of public affairs, [illegible] tradition obtaining among the Egyptians, that [illegible] directed by [illegible] shall reign, [illegible] subjected to them. But [illegible] merely a superstitious notion, [illegible] probability, [illegible] derived from [illegible] of [illegible] "Egypt should be [illegible] [illegible]" and [illegible] shall be no more a prince "of the land of Egypt."

[illegible] the events which have taken place in Egypt, and [illegible] of [illegible] of [illegible] prophecy concerning [illegible] great [illegible] and [illegible] the [illegible] that [illegible] and what [illegible] was there [illegible] the Egyptians, [illegible] yoke, and never [illegible] able to recover [illegible] liberties, and have a prince of their own [illegible] but as [illegible] the prophecy [illegible] was delivered, Egypt was conquered by the Babylonians, and after the Babylonians by the Persians, and [illegible] Persians it became [illegible] to the Macedonians, [illegible] to the Romans, and [illegible] to the [illegible] Saracens, and [illegible] to the [illegible] a [illegible] province to the Turkish empire.

We have now [illegible] the cities of Nineveh, Babylon, Tyre, and Egypt, four of the greatest [illegible] (during [illegible] flourishing [illegible]) in the [illegible] were [illegible] to [illegible] the [illegible] to [illegible] persecution of the Jews, the chosen people of God [illegible], [illegible] of these nations were guilty [illegible] others. Egypt, in particular, was so severely threatened for her idolatry, [illegible] and her [illegible] [illegible] have generally been [illegible] nations. Ancient authors describe the [illegible] the [illegible] and [illegible] as [illegible] people, [illegible] and [illegible] the [illegible] of [illegible] Modern authors [illegible] the [illegible] famous [illegible] The people of Egypt (says he generally [illegible]) are [illegible] wicked, [illegible] rogues, [illegible] robbers, [illegible] they will kill a man for [illegible]. Bishop Pocock's character of the [illegible] more favourable, though not so much [illegible] "The natives of Egypt (says he) are now a slothful people, and delight in sitting still, hearing tales, and, [illegible] to have been more fit for the quiet [illegible] sciences. They are also malicious and envious to a [illegible] degree, which keeps them from uniting and [illegible] themselves, and though they are very ignorant, yet they have a natural cunning and artifice, as well as falsehood, and this makes them always ſuſpicious of travellers. The love of money is ſo rooted in them, that nothing is to be done without bribery. They think the greateſt villanies are expiated, when once they have waſhed their hands and feet. Their words paſs for nothing, either in relations, promiſes, or profeſſions of friendſhip, &c."

Such is the ſtate of the Egyptians at the preſent period, [illegible] has been the puniſhment inflicted on them for their manifold ſins and tranſgreſſions, whereby the excellent political aphoriſm of the wiſeſt of kings is fully verified, "righteouſneſs exalteth a nation, but ſin is a reproach "and ruin to any people." Prov. xiv. 34.

CHAP. XII.

The Prophecies of Daniel.

THE firſt prophecy of Daniel, and on which, indeed, all the ſucceeding ones were founded, was his interpretation of Nebuchadnezzar's dream. This monarch, in the ſecond year of his reign, having ſubdued all his enemies, and firmly eſtabliſhed his throne, was thinking "upon his bed what ſhould come to paſs hereafter," what ſhould be the future ſucceſs of his family and kingdom, and whether any, or what families and kingdoms, might [illegible] his own, and, as our waking thoughts generally give ſome tincture to our dreams, he dreamed of ſomething to the ſame purpoſe which aſtoniſhed him, but which he could not rightly underſtand. The dream greatly affected him at the time, but waking in confuſion he had but an imperfect remembrance of it. He therefore called for "the magicians and aſtrologers," and, as abſurdly as imperiouſly, demanded of them, upon pain of certain deſtruction, "to make known unto him both "the dream and the interpretation thereof." They anſwered with great reaſon that no king had ever required ſuch a thing, that it tranſcended all the powers and faculties of man, and that God alone, or only beings like him, could diſcloſe it. "There is not a man upon earth that "can ſhew the king's matter; therefore there is no king, "lord, or ruler, that aſked ſuch things at any magician "or aſtrologer, or Chaldean; and it is a rare thing that the "king requireth, and there is none other that can ſhow "it before the king, except the Gods, whoſe dwelling is "not with fleſh." Dan. ii. 10, 11.

But the pride of [illegible] cannot liſten to reaſon or hear any control. Nebuchadnezzar was ſo incenſed at this reply, that [illegible] the magicians and wiſe men of Babylon to be [illegible] the king "was angry and very furious [illegible] to deſtroy "all the wiſe men of Babylon, [illegible] Daniel and his companions would have been involved in the ſame fate as the reſt, but, by their joint and earneſt prayers to God, "the ſecret was revealed unto Daniel in a night-viſion, "and Daniel bleſſed the God of heaven."

Daniel, having received theſe inſtructions, was deſirous to ſave the lives of the wiſe men of Babylon, who were ſo unjuſtly condemned, as well as his own. He therefore "went into Arioch, the captain of the king's guard, "whom the king had ordered to deſtroy the wiſe men of "Babylon, and ſaid thus unto him, Deſtroy not the "wiſe men of Babylon, bring me in before the king, "and I will ſhow unto the king the interpretation," ver. 12, &c. The captain of the guard immediately introduced him to the king, ſaying, "I have found a man of the "captives of Judah that will make known unto the king "the interpretation," ver. 25. Daniel was far from aſſuming any merit to himſelf; he modeſtly told Nebuchadnezzar, that "this ſecret, which the wiſe men, aſtrologers, magicians, and ſoothſayers could not ſhow unto "the king, was not revealed to him for any wiſdom that "he had more than others; but (ſays he) there is a God "in heaven that revealeth ſecrets, and maketh known "to the king Nebuchadnezzar what ſhall be in the latter "days." Dan. ii. 27, &c. Having ſaid this, Daniel not only told him what he ſaw in his dream, but alſo what he thought within himſelf before his dream. "As "for thee, O king, thy thoughts came into thy mind, "upon thy bed, what ſhould come to paſs hereafter: "and he that revealeth ſecrets maketh known unto thee "what ſhall come to paſs."

Nebuchadnezzar's dream was of "a great image. "This great image, whoſe brightneſs was excellent ſtood "before him, and the form thereof was terrible." It appears, from antient coins, that cities and people were often repreſented by figures of men and women. A great terrible figure was therefore not an improper emblem of human power and dominion; and the various metals of which it was compoſed, not unfitly typified the various kingdoms which ſhould ariſe. It conſiſted of four different metals, gold and ſilver, and braſs and iron with clay; and theſe four metals, according to Daniel's own interpretation, mean ſo many kingdoms; and the order of their ſucceſſion is clearly denoted by the order of the parts, the head and higher parts ſignifying the earlier times, and the lower parts the latter times. From hence it is conjectured by Calvin, the poets drew their fables of the four ages of the world, namely, the golden, the ſilver, the brazen, and the iron age.

Theſe different kingdoms will naturally conſtitute the different heads of our diſcourſe on Daniel's prophecy, and interpretation of Nebuchadnezzar's dream, in the explanation of which we ſhall follow the beſt commentators on the ſubject, but, at the ſame time ſhall not regard any commentator ſo much as the truth of hiſtory, the evidence of reaſon, and the analogy of ſcripture.

"This image's head was of fine gold." (Dan. ii. 32.) which the prophet thus interprets, "Thou art this head "of gold," ver. 38. Thou and thy family, and thy repreſentatives. The Babylonian therefore was the firſt of theſe kingdoms, and it was fitly repreſented by "the "head of fine gold," on account of its great riches; and Babylon, for the ſame reaſon, was called by Iſaiah, "the "golden city." Iſaiah xiv. 4.

Daniel addreſſeth Nebuchadnezzar as a very powerful king. "Thou, O king, art a king of kings," ver. 37. Nebuchadnezzar might, perhaps, think, like ſome of his predeceſſors, that his conqueſts were owing to [illegible] own fortitude and prudence; but the prophet aſſures [illegible] ſucceſſes muſt be primarily imputed to the God of heaven; "For the God of heaven (ſaith he) hath given thee "a kingdom, power, and ſtrength, and glory."

Though almoſt all the antient eaſtern hiſtories are loſt, yet there are ſome fragments preſerved, which ſpeak of this mighty conqueror and his extended empire. Beroſus ſaith, that he held in ſubjection Egypt, Syria, P[illegible], and Arabia, and by his exploits ſurpaſſed all the Chaldeans and Babylonians who reigned before him. Joſephus ſubjoins, that, in the archives of the Phœnicians, there are written things conſonant to thoſe which are ſaid by Beroſus concerning Nebuchadnezzar, namely, that he ſubdued Syria and all Phœnicia. Megaſthenes, in the fourth book of his Indian Hiſtory, endeavours to ſhow throughout, that Nebuchadnezzar exceeded Hercules in fortitude and greatneſs of exploits, and poſitively affirms, that he ſubdued the greateſt part of Lybia and Spain. Strabo likewiſe aſſerts, that this king, among the Chaldeans, was more celebrated than Hercules, and led his army out of Spain into Thrace and Pontus. But his empire, though of great extent, was yet of no long duration, for it ended in his grandſon Belſhazzar, not ſeventy years after the delivery of this prophecy; and this may be the reaſon of Daniel's ſpeaking of him as the only king, "thou art this head of gold, and after thee ſhall riſe, "&c." Dan. ii. 38, 39.

"His breaſt and his arms of ſilver," which Daniel thus interprets: "And after thee ſhall riſe another "kingdom inferior to thee." It is very well known that the kingdom which arofe after the Babylonian was the Medo-Perfian The two hands and the fhoulders fignify that the empires of the Babylonians fhould be diffolved by two kings The two kings were, the kings of the Medes and Perfians, whofe powers were united under Cyrus, who befieged and took Babylon, put an end to that empire, and on its ruins erected the Medo-Perfian, or the Perfian, (as it is more ufually called,) the Perfians having foon gained the afcendency over the Medes

The Perfian empire is faid to be *inferior*, as being *lefs* than the Babylonian, and it is certain that neither Cyrus, or any of his fucceffors, ever carried their arms into Africa or Spain, at leaft as far as Nebuchadnezzar is reported to have done The Perfian empire may likewife be called *inferior* as being *worfe* than the former, for (as Dean Prideaux juftly obferves) the kings of Perfia were certainly "the worft race of men that ever governed an empire" This empire, from its firft eftablifhment by Cyrus, to the death of the laft king, Darius Codomanus, lafted not much above two hundred years And thus far it is agreed by all commentators, that the two firft kingdoms reprefented in Nebuchadnezzar's dream were the Babylonian and the Perfian

"His belly and his thighs of brafs," which is interpreted by Daniel, "And another third kingdom of brafs "which fhall bear rule over all the earth" It is well known that Alexander the Great fubverted the Perfian empire The kingdom, therefore, which fucceeded to the Perfian was the Macedonian, and this kingdom was fitly reprefented by *brafs*, for the Greeks were famous for their brazen armour their ufual epithet being "the brazen coated Greeks" The third kingdom is alfo faid to "bear rule over all the earth" Alexander the Great commanded that he fhould be called "the king of all the "world," not that he really conquered, or nearly conquered, the whole world, but he had confiderable dominions in Europe, Afia and Africa, that is, in all the three parts of the world then known, and Diodorus Siculus and other hiftorians, mention ambaffadors coming from almoft all parts of the world, to congratulate Alexander upon his fucceffes, or to fubmit to his empire

That this third kingdom, therefore, was the Macedonian there is not the leaft doubt "St Jerome faith exprefsly, the third kingdom fignifies Alexander, and the kingdom of the Macedonians, and of the fucceffors of Alexander, which is rightly named brazen faith he, for, among all metals brafs is moft vocal, and tinkles louder, and its found is diffufed far and wide, that it portended not only the fame and power of the kingdom, but alfo the eloquence of the Greek language" After the death of Alexander, the kingdoms of the eaft were divided among his fucceffors, but the whole ftill retained the name of the Macedonian empire, and Juftin reckons Alexander the fame to the Macedonians, as Cyrus was to the Perfians, and Romulus to the Romans

"His legs of iron, his feet part of iron, and part of clay" This is interpreted by Daniel as follows "And "the fourth kingdom fhall be ftrong as iron, forafmuch "as iron breaketh in pieces, and fubdueth all things, "and as iron that breaketh all thefe, fhall it break in "pieces and bruife And whereas thou faweft the feet "and toes, part of potter's clay and part of iron, the "kingdom fhall be divided, but there fhall be in it of "the ftrength of the iron, forafmuch as thou faweft the "iron mixed with miry clay And as the toes of the "feet were part of iron and part of clay, fo the kingdom "fhall be partly ftrong and partly broken And whereas "thou faweft iron mixed with miry clay, they fhall mingle "themfelves with the feed of men, but they fhall not "cleave one to another even as iron is not mixed with "clay" Dan ii 40, &c

This fourth kingdom is defcribed as ftronger than the three preceding As iron breaketh and bruifeth all other metals, fo this was to break and fubdue all the former kingdoms The metal here is different, and confequently the nation was to be different from the preceding The four different metals muft fignify the four different nations, and as the gold fignified the Babylonians, the filver the Perfians and the brafs the Macedonians, fo the iron muft neceffarily denote fome other nation, and that this nation was no other than that of the Romans, will evidently appear from what follows

The Romans fucceeded next to the Macedonians, and therefore, in courfe, were next to be mentioned The Roman empire was ftronger and larger than any of the preceding The Romans brake in pieces, and fubdued, all the former kingdoms Jofephus fays, that, as the two arms of filver denoted the kings of the Medes and Perfians fo we might fay, in like manner, that the two legs of iron fignified the two Roman confuls The iron was "mixed with miry clay, and the Romans were defiled with a mixture of barbarous nations The Roman empire was at length divided into ten leffer kingdoms, anfwered to the ten toes of the image Thefe kingdoms retained much of the old Roman ftrength, and manifefted it upon feveral occafions, fo that the kingdom was partly ftrong and partly broken" They "mingled themfelves with the feed of men" They made marriages and alliances one with another, but no hearty union enfued reafons of ftate are ftronger than thofe founded on the ties of blood and intereft will always avail more than affinity

The Roman empire therefore, is reprefented in a double ftate, firft, with the ftrength of iron, conquering all before it, "his legs of iron," and then weakened and divided by the mixture of barbarous nations, "his feet part of iron, and part of clay" It fubdued Syria, and made the kingdom of the Seleucidæ a Roman province in the year 65 before Chrift It fubdued Egypt and made the kingdom of the Lagidæ a Roman province in the year 30 before Chrift And in the fourth century after Chrift, it began to be torn in pieces by the incurfions of the barbarous nations

St Jerome lived to fee the incurfions of the barbarous nations, and his comment is, "that the fourth kingdom, which plainly belongs to the Romans, is the iron that breaketh and fubdueth all things, but his feet and toes are part of iron, and part of clay, which is moft manifeftly proved at this time for as, in the beginning, nothing was ftronger and harder than the Roman empire fo, in the end of things, nothing is weaker, fince both in civil wars, and againft divers nations, we want the affiftance of other barbarous nations" He hath given the fame interpretation in other parts of his works, and it feemeth that he had been blamed for it, as a reflection upon the government, and therefore he maketh this apology for himfelf "If, (faith he,) in explaining the ftatue, and the difference of his feet and toes, I have interpreted the iron and clay of the Roman kingdom, which the fcripture foretells fhould be firft ftrong and then weak, let them not impute it to me, but to the prophet, for we muft not fo flatter princes, as to neglect the verity of the holy fcriptures, nor is a general difputation an injury to a fingle perfon"

All antient writers, both Jewifh and Chriftian, agree with St Jerome in explaining the fourth kingdom to be the Roman The celebrated Mr Mede, who was as able a judge as any perfon whatever in thefe matters, makes the following very juft obfervation "The Roman empire (fays he) was believed to be the fourth kingdom of Daniel, by the church of Ifrael both before and in Our Saviour's time received by the difciples of the prophets, and the whole Chriftian church, for the firft 300 years, without any known contradiction And I confefs, having fo good a ground in fcripture, it is with me little lefs than an article of faith"

Exclufive of this wonderful image Nebuchadnezzar faw, in his dream, a ftone cut out without hands, "which fmote the image upon his feet that were of iron "and clay, and broke them to pieces: then was the iron, the "clay, the brass, the silver and the gold broken in pieces "together, and became like the chaff of the threshing-"floors, and the wind carried them away, that no place "was found for them; and the stone that smote the image "became a great mountain, and filled the whole earth:" which is thus interpreted and explained by Daniel: "And "in the days of these kings shall the God of heaven set up "a kingdom, which shall never be destroyed; and the king-"dom shall not be left to other people, but it shall break "in pieces, and consume all these kingdoms, and it shall "stand for ever: forasmuch as thou sawest that the stone "was cut out of the mountain without hands, and that it "brake in pieces the iron, the brass, the clay, the silver "and the gold," ver. 44, 45.

By this was evidently meant the kingdom of Christ, which was set up during the days of the last of the before-mentioned kingdoms. The *stone* was totally a very different thing from the *image*, and the kingdom of Christ is totally different from the kingdoms of the world. "The "stone was cut out of the mountain without hands," and was to be "a building of God, a house not made with "hands." This the fathers generally apply to Christ himself, who was miraculously born of a virgin without the concurrence of a man; but it should rather be understood of the kingdom of Christ, which was formed out of the Roman empire, not by number of hands, or strength of armies, but without human means, and the assistance of human causes. This kingdom was "set up by the God of "heaven," and from thence the phrase of "the kingdom "of heaven" came to signify the coming of the Messiah; and so it was used and understood by the Jews, and so it is applied by Our Saviour in the New Testament. Other kingdoms were raised by human ambition, and worldly power; but this was the work not of man, but of God: this was truly, as it is called, "the kingdom of heaven," and "a kingdom not of this world;" its laws, its powers, were all Divine. This kingdom was "never to be de-"stroyed," as the Babylonian, the Persian, and the Macedonian empires have been, and, in a great measure also the Roman. This kingdom was to "break in pieces, and "consume, all the kingdoms," to spread and enlarge itself so that it should comprehend within itself all the former kingdoms. In short, it was to "fill the whole earth," to become universal, and to "stand for ever."

As the fourth kingdom, or the Roman empire, was represented in a two-fold state, first strong and flourishing "with legs of iron," and then weakened and divided, "with feet and toes part of iron and part of clay;" so this fifth kingdom, or the kingdom of Christ, is described likewise in two states, which Mr. Mede very justly distinguishes by the names of "the kingdom of the stone," and "the kingdom of the mountain." The first when "the "stone was cut out of the mountain without hands," that is, the kingdom of Christ was first set up while the Roman empire was in its full strength "with legs of iron." The Roman empire was afterwards divided into ten lesser kingdoms, the remains of which are still subsisting. The image is still standing upon his feet and toes of iron and clay; the kingdom of Christ is still "the stone cut out of "the mountain:" this stone will one day smite the image upon the feet and toes, and destroy it utterly, and will itself "become a great mountain and fill the whole earth;" or in other words, "the kingdoms of this world shall be-"come the kingdoms of our Lord, and of his Christ, and "he shall reign for ever and ever." Rev. xi. 15. We have therefore, seen the kingdom of the *stone*; but we have not yet seen the kingdom of the *mountain*. Some parts of this prophecy still remain to be fulfilled; and from the exact completion of the other parts, there is not the least doubt but that the rest, in due season, will be fully accomplished.

The interpretation of the fifth kingdom is consonant to the sense of all antient writers, both Jews and Christians. Jonathan Ben Uzziel, who made the Chaldee Targum, or paraphrase upon the prophecies, lived a little before Our Saviour. He did not, indeed, make any Chaldee version of Daniel, but he applies his prophecies in his interpretation of those of other prophets. Thus, in a paraphrase upon Habakuk, he speaketh of the four great kingdoms of the earth, that they should, in their turns, be destroyed, and be succeeded by the kingdom of the Messiah. "For the king-dom of Babylon shall not continue, nor exercise dominion over Israel; the kings of Media shall be slain, and the strong men of Greece shall not prosper; the Romans shall be blotted out, nor collect tribute from Jerusalem. Therefore, because of the sign and redemption which thou shalt accomplish for thy Christ, and for the remnant of thy people, they who remain shall praise thee, &c."

Josephus, in speaking of this kingdom, says, "The king-dom of the *stone* shall be the Jews that stumbled at Christ's first coming; but the kingdom of the *mountain*, when manifested, shall beat the feet of the monarchical statue to dust, and leave no remains of the fourth monarchy in its last and degenerate state."

The same opinion was prevalent among the antient Christians, as well as among the Jews. St. Jerome, and all the fathers, who have occasion to comment upon this passage, give the same interpretation; but it will be sufficient here to preserve the testimony of that elegant historian Sulpicius Severus, who, after having given an account of Nebuchadnezzar's dream and all the particulars relating to it, subjoins an exposition of it agreeable to Daniel's interpretation. "The image (says he) is an emblem of the world. The golden head is the empire of the Chaldeans, forasmuch as that was the first and most wealthy. The breast and arms of silver, signify the second kingdom, which was that of the Persians under Cyrus. In the brazen belly the third kingdom is declared to be portended, and that we see fulfilled, forasmuch as the empire, taken from the Persians, was given by Alexander to Macedonia. The iron legs are the fourth kingdom, and that is the Roman, the strongest of all the kingdoms before it. But the feet, part of iron, and part of clay, prefigure the Roman empire to be so divided as that it should never unite again, which is equally fulfilled, forasmuch as the Roman territory is occupied by foreign nations, or rebels: and we see (saith he, and he lived at the beginning of the fifth century) barbarous nations mixed with our armies, cities, and provinces. But in the stone cut without hands, which brake in pieces the gold, the silver, the brass, the iron and the clay, we have a figure of Christ, for he shall reduce this world, in which are the kingdoms of the earth, to nothing, and shall establish a kingdom that will last for ever."

Thus did it please God to reveal unto Daniel, and by Daniel unto Nebuchadnezzar, the great and most [illegible] events of this world: as Daniel said unto Nebuchadnezzar at the time he interpreted his dream, "The great God hath made known to the king what shall come to pass hereafter; and the dream is certain, and the interpretation thereof is sure." Dan. ii. 45. The king having his dream related with such exactness might be better assured of the truth of the interpretation, and of the great events which would follow. And from hence we are enabled in some measure to account for Nebuchadnezzar's prophesying a little before he died. Abydenus wrote the history of the Assyrians. It is not well known in what age he lived, and his history is lost; but there is a fragment of it preserved by Eusebius, wherein it is asserted that Nebuchadnezzar, just before his death, was inspired, and that he prophesied in this manner: "I Nebuchadnezzar foretel unto you, O Babylonians, an imminent calamity, which neither Belus my progenitor, nor queen Beltis can persuade the Fates to avert. A Persian mule shall come assisted by your demons, and impose servitude upon you, whose coadjutor shall be a Mede, the boast of the Assyrians."

This prophecy of Nebuchadnezzar was afterwards thus interpreted Cyrus was the mule he was born of parents of different nations, the mother the better, and the father the meaner, for she was a Mede, and a daughter of the king of the Medes, but he was a Persian, and subject to the Medes If, therefore, any such prophecy was uttered by Nebuchadnezzar a little before his death, if any such oracle was received and believed of Cyrus and the Persians subduing Asia, it may very justly be supposed to have been derived originally from the prophecy of Daniel, which being solemnly delivered to a great king, and published in Chaldea, might come to be generally known in the east, and the truth of it soon evinced by the event that followed

It was likewise from this prophecy of Daniel that the distinction first arose of the four great empires of the world, which hath been followed by most historians and chronologers in their distribution of times As these four empires are the subject of this prophecy, so likewise have they been the subject of the most celebrated writers, both in former and in latter ages The histories of these empires are the best written, and the most read, of any, they are the study of the learned, and the amusement of the polite, they are of use both in schools, and in senates from hence, examples, instructions, laws, and politics are derived for all ages, and very little in comparison is known of other times, or of other nations

It may be observed by some, that there have been empires as great as these, such as those of the Tartars, the Saracens, and the Turks, and it may, perhaps, be thought that they are as well deserving of a place in this succession of kingdoms, and were equally worthy to be made the objects of prophecy, being as eminent for the wisdom of their constitutions, the extent of their dominions, and the length of their duration But these four empires had a particular relation to the church and people of God, who were subjects to each of them in their turns The fate of them was therefore particularly predicted, and we have in them, without the intermixture of others, a line of prophecy (as it may be justly called) from the reign of Nebuchadnezzar to the full and compleat establishment of the kingdom of the Messiah

The great arbiter of kingdoms, and governor of the universe, can reveal as much of their future revolutions as he pleaseth, and he hath revealed enough to manifest his providence, and to confirm the truth of religion What Daniel, therefore, said on the first discovery of these things, may be very justly applied after the completion of so many particulars "Blessed be the name of God for ever and "ever, for wisdom and might are his And he changeth "the times and the seasons he removeth kings, and setteth up kings he giveth wisdom unto the wise, and "knowledge to them that know knowledge He revealeth the deep and secret things he knoweth what "is in the darkness, and the light dwelleth with him. Dan ii 20, &c

CHAP XII

Of Daniel's Vision concerning the Four great Empires

THE last sovereign of the Babylonish empire was Belshazzar, in the first year of whose reign the same things were revealed unto Daniel concerning the four great empires of the world, as had been revealed unto Nebuchadnezzar in the second year of his reign, which was a space of about forty-eight years All the difference between these revelations is, that what was revealed to Nebuchadnezzar in the form of a great image, was represented to Daniel in the shape of great wild beasts, which difference is accounted for by Mr Louth, who says, "this image appeared with a glorious lustre in the imagination of Nebuchadnezzar, whose mind was wholly taken up with admiration of worldly pomp and splendour, whereas the same monarchies were represented to Daniel under the shape of fierce and wild beasts, as being the great supporters of idolatry and tyranny in the world.

In Daniel's vision the first kingdom is represented by a beast, that was "like a lion, and had eagle's wings and I "beheld till the wings thereof were pluckt, and it was lifted "up from the earth, and made to stand upon the feet as a "man, and a man's heart was given to it" Dan vii 4 This is the kingdom of the Babylonians and the king of Babylon is, in like manner, compared to a lion by the prophet Jeremiah "the lion is come up from his thicket, and "the destroyer of the Gentiles is on his way" Jer iv 7 And he is said to fly as an eagle "Behold, he shall fly as "an eagle, and shall spread his wings over Moab," xlviii 40 And he is also compared to an eagle by the prophet Ezekiel "Thus saith the Lord God, A great eagle with "great wings," &c Ezek xvii 3

The lion is the king of beasts, and the eagle the king of birds, and therefore the kingdom of Babylon, which is described as the first and noblest kingdom, and was the kingdom then in being, is said to partake of the nature of both The eagle's wings denote its swiftness and rapidity, and the conquests of Babylon were very rapid, that empire being advanced to its height within a few years by a single person, namely, by the conduct and arms of Nebuchadnezzar It is farther said, that "the wings thereof were "pluckt" Its wings were beginning to be pluckt when Daniel's prophecy was first delivered, for at that time the Medes and Persians were encroaching upon it Belshazzar, the then reigning king, was the last of his race, and in the seventeenth year of his reign Babylon was taken, and the kingdom was transferred to the Medes and Persians

"And it was made to stand upon the feet as a man, and "a man's heart was given to it" The meaning of this passage is supposed to be an allusion to the case of Nebuchadnezzar, when, in his madness, "a beast's heart was given unto him," and, after he was restored to his senses, "a man's heart was given to him" again It evidently appears, that, after the Babylonian empire was subverted, the people became more humane and gentle, their minds were humbled with their ill fortune, and those who vaunted as if they had been more than men, now found themselves to be but men They were, in short, brought to such a sense as the psalmist wishes such persons to have "Put them in fear, O Lord, that the nations may know themselves to be but men" Psalm ix 20

The second kingdom is represented by "another beast "like a bear, and it raised up itself on one side, and it had "three ribs in the mouth of it between the teeth of it and "they said thus unto it, arise, devour much flesh" Dan vii 5 This is the kingdom of the Medes and Persians, and, for their cruelty and greediness after blood, they are compared to a *bear*, which is a savage and voracious animal The learned Bochart recounts several particulars wherein the Persians resembled bears, but the chief likeness consisted in what hath been already mentioned, and this likeness was principally intended by the prophet, as evidently appears from the words of the text itself, "Arise, devour much "flesh"

"And it raised up itself on one side," or, "it raised up one dominion" The Persians were subject to the Medes at the conquest of Babylon, but soon after raised themselves above them

"And it had three ribs in the mouth of it between the "teeth of it" By these are meant the three kingdoms of the Babylonians, Medes, and Persians, which were reduced into one kingdom They might properly be called *ribs*, as the conquest of them much strengthened the Persian empire and they might be said to be between the teeth of "the bear," as they were much grieved and oppressed by the Persians

"And they said thus unto it, arise, devour much flesh" This, as we have before observed, was said to denote the natural cruelty of the Medes and Persians They are also represented as very cruel by the prophet Isaiah, chap xiii 18 Cambyses, Ochus, and other of their princes, were, indeed, more like bears than men Instances of their cruelty abound in almost all the historians who have written of their affairs Ammianus Marcellinus describes them as being proud, cruel, and exercising the power of life and death over slaves and obscure plebeians "They pull off the skin (says he) from men [illegible] by pieces or altogether, and they have abominable laws, by which, for one man's offence, all the neighbourhood is destroyed"

The third kingdom is represented by "another beast like "a leopard, which had on the back of it four wings of a fowl the beast had also four heads, and dominion was given to it" This is the kingdom of the Macedonians or Grecians, who, under the command of Alexander the Great, overcame the Persians, and reigned next after them and it is fitly compared to a leopard on several accounts The leopard is remarkable for its swiftness, and Alexander and the Macedonians were amazingly swift and rapid in their conquests The leopard is a spotted animal, and was therefore a proper emblem (according to Bochart) of the different manners of the nations which Alexander commanded, or (according to Grotius) of the various manners of Alexander himself, who was sometimes merciful, and sometimes cruel, sometimes temperate, and sometimes drunken sometimes abstemious and sometimes incontinent The leopard (as Bochart observes) is of small stature but of great courage, so as not to be afraid to engage with the lion and the largest beasts and so Alexander, a little king, in comparison, of small stature too, and with a small army, dared to attack Darius, whose kingdom extended from the Egean Sea to the Indies

"The beast had upon the back of it four wings of a 'fowl" The Babylonian empire was represented with two wings, but this is represented with four for (as St Jerome says) nothing could be swifter than the victories of Alexander, who ran through all the countries from Illyricum and the Adriatic sea to the Indian Ocean and the river Ganges, not so much fighting, as conquering, and in twelve years subjugated part of Europe, and all Asia to himself

"The beast had also four heads," to denote the four kingdoms into which this same third kingdom should be divided, as it was divided, after the death of Alexander, into four kingdoms, Cassander reigning over Macedon and Greece, Lysimachus over Thrace and Bithynia, Ptolemy over Egypt, and Seleucus over Syria

"And dominion was given to it" This (as St Jerome says) showeth that it was not owing to the fortitude of Alexander, but proceeded from the will of the Lord And, indeed, unless he had been directed, preserved, and assisted by the Supreme Power, how could Alexander, with 30 000 men, have overcome Darius with 600,000, and, in so short a time, have brought all the countries, from Greece as far as to India, into subjection?

The fourth kingdom is represented by a "fourth beast, 'dreadful and terrible, and strong exceedingly, and it had "great iron teeth it devoured, and brake in pieces, and 'stamped the residue with the feet of it, and it was diverse 'from all the beasts that were before" Daniel was particularly desirous to know what this might mean, upon which he was thus answered by the angel, who had explained to him the former part of his vision "The fourth beast shall 'be the fourth kingdom upon the earth, which shall be di- "verse from all kingdoms, and shall devour the whole earth, "and shall tread it down, and break it in pieces." Dan vii 23

This fourth kingdom can be none other than the Roman empire The fourth beast was so great and horrible, that it was not easy to find an adequate name for it, and the Roman empire was "dreadful, and terrible, and strong ex- 'ceedingly," beyond any of the former kingdoms It was "diverse from all kingdoms," not only in its republican form of government, but likewise in strength, and power, and greatness, length of duration, and extent of dominion "It devoured and brake in pieces, and stamped the residue with the feet of it" It reduced Macedon into a Roman province about 168 years, the kingdom of Pergamus about 133 years, Syria about 65 years, and Egypt about 30 years, before Christ And besides the remains of the Macedonian empire, it subdued many other provinces and kingdoms, so that it might very justly be said to 'devour the whole earth, "and to tread it down, and break it in pieces," and it became, in a manner, what the Roman writers delighted to call it, namely, '*The empire of the whole earth*'"

A celebrated Greek writer, who flourished in the reign of Augustus Cæsar, hath a remarkable passage, which is very pertinent towards illustrating the [illegible] of the prophecy, In speaking of the Roman and all former empires, he saith "The Macedonian empire having overthrown the force of the Persians, in greatness, indeed, of [illegible] all the kingdoms which were before it but yet it did not flourish a long time After the death of [illegible] it began to grow worse and worse, and being divided into [illegible] principalities by his successors, it was weakened [illegible], and at last was destroyed by the Romans Notwithstanding its once great power, yet it did not reduce all the earth and sea to its obedience For it did not possess Africa, except that part adjoining to Egypt Nor did it subdue all Europe, but only northwards it proceeded as far as Thrace, and westwards it descended to the Adriatic Sea But the city of Rome ruleth over all the earth, as far as it is inhabited, and commands all the sea, not only that within the Pillars of Hercules, but also the ocean, as far as it is navigable, having first, and alone, of all the most celebrated kingdoms, made the east and west the bounds of its empire and its dominion hath continued not a short time, but longer than that of any other city or kingdom in the world"

Another remarkable property of this fourth beast is, that "it had ten horns" and, according to the angel's interpretation, "the ten horns out of this kingdom are ten kings," or kingdoms, "that shall arise," which was accomplished when the Roman empire was divided into ten different states or kingdoms

But besides these ten horns or kingdoms of the fourth empire, there was to spring up among them another little horn "I considered the horns (saith Daniel) and behold 'there came up among them another little horn, before "whom there were three of the first horns plucked up by the roots" Daniel was eager to know the meaning of this part of the vision, upon which the angel informed him, that as 'the ten horns out of this kingdom are ten kings,' or kingdoms "that shall arise, [illegible] "shall rise after them, and he shall subdue three kings" or kingdoms

We have already seen that the Roman empire was divided into ten horns or kingdoms and [illegible] on a proper examination, find [illegible] dom, answering in all respects, to the character [illegible] The celebrated Machiavel, in his history of Florence [illegible] having shewn how the Roman empire was [illegible] divided by the incursions of the northern nations, [illegible] this time the bishops of Rome began to [illegible] and to exercise greater authority [illegible] done At first the successors of St Peter were [illegible] eminent for their miracles, and the [illegible] and their examples added daily [illegible]

This prophecy of Nebuchadnezzar was afterwards thus interpreted Cyrus was the mule he was born of parents of different nations, the mother the better, and the father the meaner, for ſhe was a Mede, and a daughter of the king of the Medes, but he was a Perſian, and ſubject to the Medes If, therefore, any ſuch prophecy was uttered by Nebuchadnezzar a little before his death, if any ſuch oracle was received and believed of Cyrus and the Perſians ſubduing Aſia, it may very juſtly be ſuppoſed to have been derived originally from the prophecy of Daniel, which being ſolemnly delivered to a great king, and publiſhed in Chaldea, might come to be generally known in the eaſt, and the truth of it ſoon evinced by the event that followed

It was likewiſe from this prophecy of Daniel that the diſtinction firſt aroſe of the four great empires of the world, which hath been followed by moſt hiſtorians and chronologers in their diſtribution of times As theſe four empires are the ſubject of this prophecy, ſo likewiſe have they been the ſubject of the moſt celebrated writers, both in former and in latter ages The hiſtories of theſe empires are the beſt written, and the moſt read, of any, they are the ſtudy of the learned and the amuſement of the polite, they are of uſe both in ſchools, and in ſenates from hence, examples, inſtructions, laws, and politics are derived for all ages and very little in compariſon is known of other times, or of other nations

It may be obſerved by ſome, that there have been empires as great as theſe, ſuch as thoſe of the Tartars, the Saracens, and the Turks, and it may, perhaps, be thought that they are as well deſerving of a place in this ſucceſſion of kingdoms, and were equally worthy to be made the objects of prophecy, being as eminent for the wiſdom of their conſtitutions, the extent of their dominions, and the length of their duration But theſe four empires had a particular relation to the church and people of God, who were ſubjects to each of them in their turns The fate of them was therefore particularly predicted, and we have in them, without the intermixture of others, a line of prophecy (as it may be juſtly called) from the reign of Nebuchadnezzar to the full and compleat eſtabliſhment of the kingdom of the Meſſiah

The great arbiter of kingdoms, and governor of the univerſe, can reveal as much of their future revolutions as he pleaſeth, and he hath revealed enough to manifeſt his providence, and to confirm the truth of religion What Daniel, therefore, ſaid on the firſt diſcovery of theſe things, may be very juſtly applied after the completion of ſo many particulars "Bleſſed be the name of God for ever and "ever, for wiſdom and might are his And he changeth "the times and the ſeaſons he removeth kings, and ſetteth up kings he giveth wiſdom unto the wiſe, and "knowledge to them that know knowledge He re"vealeth the deep and ſecret things he knoweth what "is in the darkneſs, and the light dwelleth with him. Dan ii 20, &c

CHAP XII

Of Daniel's Viſion concerning the Four great Empires

THE laſt ſovereign of the Babyloniſh empire was Belſhazzar, in the firſt year of whoſe reign the ſame things were revealed unto Daniel concerning the four great empires of the world, as had been revealed unto Nebuchadnezzar in the ſecond year of his reign, which was a ſpace of about forty-eight years. All the difference between theſe revelations is, that what was revealed to Nebuchadnezzar in the form of a great image, was repreſented to Daniel in the ſhape of great wild beaſts, which difference is accounted for by Mr. Louth, who ſays, "this image appeared with a glorious luſtre in the imagination of Nebuchadnezzar, whoſe mind was wholly taken up with admiration of worldly pomp and ſplendour, whereas the ſame monarchies were repreſented to Daniel under the ſhape of fierce and wild beaſts, as being the great ſupporters of idolatry and tyranny in the world

In Daniel's viſion the firſt kingdom is repreſented by a beaſt, that was "like a lion, and had eagle's wings and I "beheld till the wings thereof were pluckt, and it was lifted "up from the earth, and made to ſtand upon the feet as a "man, and a man's heart was given to it" Dan vii 4 This is the kingdom of the Babylonians and the king of Babylon is, in like manner, compared to a lion by the prophet Jeremiah "the lion is come up from his thicket, and "the deſtroyer of the Gentiles is on his way" Jer iv 7 And he is ſaid to fly as an eagle "Behold, he ſhall fly as "an eagle, and ſhall ſpread his wings over Moab" xlviii 40 And he is alſo compared to an eagle by the prophet Ezekiel "Thus ſaith the Lord God, A great eagle with "great wings," &c Ezek xvii 3

The lion is the king of beaſts, and the eagle the king of birds, and therefore the kingdom of Babylon, which is deſcribed as the firſt and nobleſt kingdom, and was the kingdom then in being, is ſaid to partake of the nature of both The eagle's wings denote its ſwiftneſs and rapidity, and the conqueſts of Babylon were very rapid, that empire being advanced to its height within a few years by a ſingle perſon, namely, by the conduct and arms of Nebuchadnezzar It is farther ſaid, that "the wings thereof were "pluckt" Its wings were beginning to be pluckt when Daniel's prophecy was firſt delivered, for at that time the Medes and Perſians were encroaching upon it Belſhazzar, the then reigning king, was the laſt of his race, and in the ſeventeenth year of his reign Babylon was taken, and the kingdom was transferred to the Medes and Perſians

"And it was made to ſtand upon the feet as a man, and "a man's heart was given to it" The meaning of this paſſage is ſuppoſed to be an alluſion to the caſe of Nebuchadnezzar, when, in his madneſs, "a beaſt's heart was given unto him," and, after he was reſtored to his ſenſes, "a man's heart was given to him" again It evidently appears, that, after the Babylonian empire was ſubverted, the people became more humane and gentle, their minds were humbled with their ill fortune, and thoſe who vaunted as if they had been more than men, now found themſelves to be but men They were, in ſhort, brought to ſuch a ſenſe as the pſalmiſt wiſhes ſuch perſons to have "Put them in fear, O Lord, that the nations may know themſelves to be but men" Pſalm ix 20

The ſecond kingdom is repreſented by "another beaſt "like a bear, and it raiſed up itſelf on one ſide, and it had "three ribs in the mouth of it between the teeth of it and "they ſaid thus unto it, ariſe, devour much fleſh" Dan vii 5 This is the kingdom of the Medes and Perſians, and, for their cruelty and greedineſs after blood, they are compared to a *bear*, which is a ſavage and voracious animal The learned Bochart recounts ſeveral particulars wherein the Perſians reſembled bears, but the chief likeneſs conſiſted in what hath been already mentioned, and this likeneſs was principally intended by the prophet, as evidently appears from the words of the text itſelf, "Ariſe, devour much "fleſh"

"And it raiſed up itſelf on one ſide," or, "it raiſed up "one dominion" The Perſians were ſubject to the Medes at the conqueſt of Babylon, but ſoon after raiſed themſelves above them

"And it had three ribs in the mouth of it between the "teeth of it" By theſe are meant the three kingdoms of the Babylonians, Medes, and Perſians which were reduced into one kingdom They might properly be called *ribs*, as the conqueſt of them much ſtrengthened the Perſian empire and they might be ſaid to be between the teeth of [illegible], that to obviate or remove the confusionss which were then in the world, many princes turned Christians, and the emperor of Rome being converted among the rest, [illegible] quitting Rome, to hold his residence at Constantinople, the Roman empire began to decline, but the church of Rome augmented fast" He then proceeds to give an account how the Roman empire declined, and the power of the church of Rome increased, first under the Goths, then under the Lombards, and afterwards by calling in of the [illegible].

Here, then, is a little horn springing up among the other ten horns The bishop of Rome was respectable as a bishop long before, but he did not become a *horn* properly (which is an emblem of strength and power) till he became a temporal prince He was to *rise after* the other, that is, *behind* [illegible], so that the ten kings were not aware of the growing up of the little horn, till it had overpowered them "Three "of the first horns (that is, three of the first kings or king-"doms) were to be plucked up by the roots," and to "fall "[illegible]" These three are very fully explained both [illegible] More and Sir Isaac Newton, but, as there is very little [illegible] between them, we shall only quote the words [illegible] "Kings (saith he) are put for kingdoms, and therefore the little horn is a little kingdom It was an horn of the fourth beast, and rooted up three of his first horns, and therefore we are to look for it among the nations of the Latin empire, after the rise of the ten horns In the [illegible] century, by rooting up and subduing the exarchate of Ravenna, the kingdom of the Lombards, and the senate and dukedom of Rome, the bishop acquired Peter's patrimony out of their dominions, and thereby rose up as a temporal prince or king, or horn of the fourth beast" Again, "It was certainly by the victory of the see of Rome over the Greek emperor, the king of Lombardy, and the senate of Rome, that she acquired Peter's patrimony, and rose up to her greatness"—That this explanation of Sir Isaac Newton is justly founded will appear from what follows

First, the exarchate of Ravenna which of right belonged to the Greek emperors, and was the capital of their dominions in Italy, having revolted at the instigation of the pope, was unjustly [illegible] by Astulphus, king of the Lombards, who thereupon thought to make himself master of [illegible] The pope in this exigency, applied for help to Pepin, king of France, who marched into Italy, besieged the Lombards in Pavia, and forced them to surrender the exarchate, and other territories, which were not restored to the Greek emperor, as in justice they ought to have been, but, at the [illegible] of the pope, were given to St Peter and his successors for a perpetual succession Pope Zachary had acknowledged Pepin, usurper of the crown of France, as [illegible] sovereign, and now Pepin, in his turn, bestowed a principality, which was no less properly, upon Pope Stephen II the successor of Zachary, "And so (as Platina says) the name of the exarchate, which had continued from the time of Narses to the taking of Ravenna by Astulphus, [illegible] seventy years, was extinguished" This (according to Sigonius) was effected in the year 755, and henceforward the popes, having become temporal princes, [illegible] no longer date their epistles and bulls by the years of the emperors' reigns, but by the years of their own advancement to the papal chair

Secondly, the kingdom of the Lombards was often troublesome to the pope King Desiderius invaded the territories of pope Adrian I upon which the latter was obliged to have recourse to the king of France, and earnestly invited Charles the Great, the son and successor of Pepin, to come into Italy to his assistance He accordingly went with a great army (being ambitious also himself of enlarging his dominions in Italy) and conquered the Lombards, put an end to their kingdom, and gave great part of their dominions to the pope He not only confirmed the former donations of his father Pepin, but also made an addition of other countries to them, as Corsica, Sardinia, the Sabine territories, the whole track between Lucca and Parma, and that part of Tuscany that belonged to the Lombards and the tables of these donations he not only signed himself, but caused them to be signed by the bishops, abbots, and other great men then present, and laid them so signed upon the altar of St Peter And this was the end of the kingdom of the Lombards, in the 206th year after their possessing Italy, and in the year of Christ 774.

Thirdly, the *state of Rome*, though subject to the popes in things spiritual, was yet, in things temporal, governed by the senate and people, who, after their defection from the eastern emperors, still retained many of their old privileges, and elected both the western emperor and the popes After Charles the Great had overthrown the kingdom of the Lombards, he went again to Rome, and was there, by the pope, bishops, abbots, and people of Rome, chosen Roman patrician, which is the degree of honour and power next to emperor He then settled the affairs of Italy, and permitted the pope to hold under him the dutchy of Rome with other territories but, after a few years, the Romans, desirous to recover their liberty, conspired against pope Leo III accused him of many great crimes, and imprisoned him His accusers were heard on a day appointed before Charles, and a council of French and Italian bishops but the pope, without pleading his own cause, or making any defence, was acquitted, his accusers were slain or banished, and he himself was declared superior to all human judicature And thus the foundation was laid for the absolute authority of the pope over the Romans, which was completed by degrees, and Charles, in return, was chosen emperor of the west However, after the death of Charles the Great, the Romans again conspired against the pope, but Lewis the Pius, the son and successor of Charles, acquitted him again Some time after this pope Leo was taken dangerously ill, which as soon as the Romans, his enemies, knew, they rose again, plundered and burnt his villas, and thence marched to Rome to recover what things had been taken from them by force, but they were repressed by some of the emperor's troops [illegible] same emperor Lewis the Pius, at the request of pope Paschal, confirmed the donations which his father and grandfather had made to the see of Rome Sigonius has recorded the confirmation, and therein are mentioned Rome and its dutchy, containing part of Tuscany and Campania, Ravenna, with the exarchate and Pentapolis, and the other part of Tuscany, and the countries taken from the Lombards and all these are granted to the pope and his successors, that they [illegible] hold them in their own right, principality, and dominions, to the end of the world

These were "the three horns, three of the first horns," which fell before the little horn and the pope hath, in a manner, pointed himself out for the person by wearing the *triple crown* In other respects too the pope fully answers the character of the little horn, so that if [illegible] of application may assure us of the true sense of the prophecy, we can no longer doubt concerning the person He is "a little horn" And the power of the popes was originally very small, and their temporal dominions were little and inconsiderable, in comparison with others of the ten horns

"He shall be diverse from the first" that is, his kingdom shall be of a different nature and constitution [illegible] the power of the pope differs greatly from that of all other princes, he having not only an ecclesiastical, but [illegible] civil and temporal authority

"And behold in this horn were eyes like the eyes of a man" This denotes his cunning and foresight, his looking out and watching all opportunities to promote his own interests and the policy of the Roman hierarchy hath almost passed into a proverb

"He had a mouth speaking very great things" And who hath been more noisy and blustering than the pope, especially in former ages, boasting of his supremacy, thundering out his bulls and anathemas, excommunicating princes, and absolving subjects from their allegiance?

"His look was more stout than his fellows" And the pope assumes a superiority, not only over his fellow bishops, but even over crowned heads, and requires greater honours to be paid to him, than are expected even by kings and emperors themselves

"And he shall speak great words against the Most "High, or, he shall speak great words as the Most High" And has he not set himself up above all laws divine and human arrogating to himself godlike attributes, and titles of *holiness* and *infallibility*, exacting obedience to his ordinances and decrees in preference to, and in open violation of, both reason and scripture?

"And he shall wear out the saints of the Most High" This he has done by wars, massacres, and inquisitions, persecuting and destroying the faithful servants of Christ, and the true worshippers of God, who have protested against his innovations, and refused to comply with the idolatry practised in the Church of Rome

"And he shall think to change times and laws" This he has done by appointing fasts and feasts, canonizing saints, granting pardons and indulgences for sins, instituting new rites of worship, imposing new articles of faith, enjoining new rules of practice, and, in short, reversing, at pleasure, the laws both of God and man

Such is the power of the pope even at this present period, and such is the little horn that was to arise out of the ten horns, or kingdoms, into which the Roman empire was divided

But the four kingdoms represented in Daniel's vision were to be followed by a fifth namely, the kingdom of the Messiah "I beheld (saith Daniel) till the thrones "were cast down and the antient of days did sit, whose "garment was white as snow, and the hair of his head "like the pure wool, his throne was like the fiery flame, "and his wheels as burning fire A fiery stream issued "and came forth from before him, thousand thousands "ministered unto him and ten thousand times ten thou- "sand stood before him the judgment was set and the "books were opened" Dan vii 9 10 These metaphors and figures are taken from the solemnities of earthly judicatories, and particularly of the great Sanhedrim of the Jews where the [illegible] of the consistory sat, with his assessors seated on each side of him, in the form of a semicircle, and the people standing before him and from this was taken the description of the day of judgment as given in the New Testament

"I beheld then, because of the voice of the great words "which the horn spoke, I beheld, even till the beast "was slain and his body destroyed, and given to the "burning flame," ver 11 The beast will be destroyed "because of the great words which the horn spoke," and the destruction of the beast will also be the destruction of the horn, and consequently the horn is a part of the fourth beast or of the Roman empire "As concerning "the rest of the beasts, they had their dominion taken "away yet their lives were prolonged for a season and a "time" When the dominion was taken away from the other beasts, their bodies were not destroyed, for they were suffered to continue still in being but when the dominion shall be taken away from the fourth beast, his body shall be totally destroyed The other kingdoms succeeded each other, but none other earthly kingdom shall succeed to this

"I saw in the night visions, and behold one like the "Son of Man, came in the clouds of heaven, and came "to the antient of days, and they brought him near be- "fore him" Here was evidently displayed the coming of the Messiah From hence "the Son of Man" came to be a known term for Messiah among the Jews From hence it was taken and used so frequently in the gospel Our Saviour intimates himself to be this very Son of Man, "Hereafter (says he) shall ye see the Son of Man "sitting at the right hand of power, and coming in the "clouds of heaven" Matt xxvi 64, 65 And for saying this, he was charged by the high-priest with having "spoken blasphemy"

"And there was given him dominion, and glory and "a kingdom, that all people nations, and languages "should serve him his dominion is an everlasting do- "minion, which shall not pass away, and his kingdom "that which shall not be destroyed" Dan vii 14 All these kingdoms shall in time be destroyed, but the kingdom of the Messiah shall stand for ever And it was in allusion to this part of the prophecy that the angel said of Christ before he was born, "He shall reign over the "house of Jacob for ever, and of his kingdom there shall "be no end" Luke i 33

In what manner these great changes will be effected we cannot pretend to say, as God hath not [illegible] pleased to reveal it unto us We see, however, the remains of the ten horns which arose out of the Roman empire We see the little horn still subsisting, but, it is to be hoped, on the decline, and tending towards a dissolution And [illegible] seeing so many of these particulars accomplished, we can have no reason to doubt but that the rest will [illegible] in due season, be amply fulfilled

If we compare the prophecies of Daniel in interpreting Nebuchadnezzar's dream, with those revealed to Daniel in his vision, and interpreted by the angel, we shall find such a close similarity as must naturally strike us with astonishment What was represented to Nebuchadnezzar in the form of a "great image" was represented [illegible] to Daniel by "four great wild beasts" and the beasts have degenerated as the metals grew worse and worse

"This image's head was of fine gold," and "the "first beast was like a lion with eagle's wings," and [illegible] answer to each other, and both [illegible] the [illegible] then reigning or the kingdom of the Babylonians [illegible] it appeared in splendor and glory to Nebuchadnezzar [illegible] it was then in its flourishing condition [illegible] its [illegible] and its humiliation were shown to Daniel, as it was then drawing near to its fall [illegible]

"The breast and arms of silver, and the [illegible] "like a bear" were designed to represent the second kingdom, or that of the Medes and Persians The "two "arms" are supposed to denote the two [illegible] [illegible] farther particulars were hinted to Daniel, of [illegible] people rising up above the other people, and of the [illegible] of three additional kingdoms [illegible] Nebuchadnezzar [illegible] kingdom was called [illegible] or world [illegible] [illegible] to Daniel [illegible] as described as very [illegible] [illegible] "devour much flesh"

The third kingdom, or that of the [illegible] [illegible] represented by [illegible] [illegible] "the third beast like a leopard, [illegible] four [illegible] of a "fowl" It was said to Nebuchadnezzar [illegible] it shall bear rule over all the earth, [illegible] "dominion was given to it The [illegible] Alexander's four successors [illegible] only signify the two principal of them [illegible] the Seleucidæ and Lagidæ, [illegible] the Syrian and Egyptian kings

"The legs of iron [illegible] the fourth beast [illegible] "iron teeth, [illegible] "in pieces" all other [illegible] devoured and break in pieces" [illegible] both equally proper [illegible] dom of the Roman, which [illegible] further either of the former kingdoms [illegible] too, and the "ten horns," were [illegible]

[illegible] kingdoms, which arose out of the division of the Roman empire [illegible] but all that relates to "the little horn" was [illegible] to Daniel as a person more immediately [illegible] in the fate of the church.

The *stone*, that was "cut out of the mountain with[out hands], and became" itself "a great mountain, and filled the whole earth," is explained to be a kingdom which [shall] prevail over all other kingdoms, and become universal and everlasting. In like manner, "one like the [Son] of man came to the ancient of days," and was advanced to a kingdom, [which] shall prevail likewise over [all other] kingdoms, and become universal and everlasting.

[Such] is the great concord and agreement between these [prophe]cies of Daniel, which, remarkable as they are in [many] [illegible], are not more so, than that they comprehend [illegible] events, and extend through so many ages, [from the] reign of the Babylonians to the consummation [of all] things. They are truly (as Mr. Mede calls them,) "[the sa]cred calendar [illegible], [the] *chain of prophecy*; [illegible] chronology of times measured by the succession of four principal kingdoms, from the beginning of [illegible] of [illegible], until the mystery of God shall be [illegible]."

Daniel was "much troubled, and his countenance [chang]ed in him" [illegible] the calamities that [illegible] brought on [illegible] the horn. "[illegible] matter in his heart." Much more may good [illegible] the [illegible] calamities, and lament [illegible] in the world [illegible] that a time of [illegible] come. The proof of this [illegible] of God, is well [illegible] "The judgment shall sit, and they [illegible] to consume and to de[stroy] [illegible]. And the kingdom, and domi[nion] [illegible] the kingdoms under the whole [heaven] [illegible] to the people of the saints of the [illegible] kingdom is an everlasting kingdom [illegible] shall serve and obey him." Daniel [illegible]

CHAP. XIII.

[illegible] the Rom[an] [illegible]

[illegible] to the four great [illegible] the four great empires of the [illegible] first year of Belshaz[zar] [illegible] In [illegible] of the same king's [illegible], though in a form of [illegible] very great degree, to the [illegible] year of the reign of king [illegible] appeared unto me, even unto me, [illegible] unto me at the first." [illegible] palace of Shushan, and by [illegible] river Ulai, [illegible] as it is called by the [illegible] I saw in a vision, and it [illegible] that I was at Shushan in the [illegible] province of Elam, and I saw in a [illegible] by the river Ulai." Such was the time [illegible] vision, and the vision itself consisted of a [illegible]

[illegible] vision there appeared four beasts, because [illegible] represented, but here are only [illegible] we have a representation of what [illegible] two empires. The first of [illegible] (that is, the Babylonian) is here wholly [illegible], that, at this time, was sufficiently known, [illegible] very near to a conclusion. The second empire, therefore, in the former vision, is the first [illegible], and what was there compared to a bear, is here [pre]figured by a ram. "Then I lifted up mine eyes, and [saw], and behold, there stood before the river a ram which "had two horns, and the two horns were high; but one "was higher than the other, and the higher came up last." Dan. viii. 3. This ram with two horns, according to the explication of the angel Gabriel, was the empire of the Medes and Persians. "The ram which thou sawest "having two horns are the kings (or kingdoms) of Me"dia and Persia," ver. 20.

This empire, therefore, which was formed by the conjunction of the Medes and Persians, and is often called the Medo-Persian, was not unfitly represented by a ram "[with] two horns." Cyrus, the founder of this empire, succeeded to both crowns, and united the kingdoms of Media and Persia. It was a coalition of two very formidable powers, and therefore it is said, that "the two "horns were high; but one," it is added, "was higher "than the other, and the higher came up last." The [illegible] of Media, was the more ancient of the two, and more famous in history. Persia was of little note or account till the time of Cyrus; but under him the Persians gained and preserved the ascendency.

The great exploits of the ram are [illegible] recapitulated by the prophet, who says, "I saw the ram pushing "westward, and northward, and southward; so that no "beasts might stand before him, neither was there any "that could deliver out of his hand; but he did according "to his will, and became great." Dan. viii. [illegible] Cyrus himself the Persians pushed their conquests [illegible] as far as the Ægean sea [illegible] north[ward] they subdued the [illegible] Cappadocians, [illegible] [illegible] and southward they conquered Egypt, [i]f not under Cyrus, yet most certainly under his son Cambyses. In the prophecy there is not any [illegible] of their conquests in the east, the [illegible] of which [illegible] these countries lie very remote, and were of little concern or consequence to them.

The ram was strong and powerful, "so that no beast "might stand before him, neither was there any that could "deliver out of his hand," that is, none of the neighbouring kingdoms were able to contend with the Persians, [illegible] fell under their dominion. "He did according to his will, and became great," and the Persian empire was [illegible] and enlarged to such a degree, that it extended "from India even unto Ethiopia, over an hundred "and seven and twenty provinces." [illegible] seven provinces were added to [illegible] [illegible] in the time of Cyrus. [illegible]

After the ram appears the he-goat. "And as I "was considering (saith Daniel), behold, an he-goat came "from the west on the face of the whole earth, and touched not the ground; and the goat had a notable horn between his eyes." [illegible] thus interpreted by the angel Gabriel. "The rough goat is the king of Grecia, "and the great horn that is between his eyes is the first "king, or kingdom." [illegible] very properly [illegible] type of the Grecian or Macedonian [illegible] [illegible] Macedonians [illegible] about two hundred years [illegible] were known [illegible], or "the goat's people." [illegible] to [illegible] Caranus, [illegible] with [illegible] Greeks to [illegible] in Macedonia, was commanded by the oracle to [take the] goats for his guides to empire, and [illegible] herd of goats flying from a violent storm, [illegible] them to Edessa, and there fixed the seat of [illegible] made the goats his ensign, or standards, [illegible] *Ægeæ*, or "the goats' town," and the people *Ægeadæ*, or "the goat's people," [illegible] the city Ægeæ was the usual burying-place of the [Macedo]nian kings, [illegible] [illegible] son by Roxana [illegible] Alexander [illegible] "or the goat," and [illegible] of Alexander's successors are represented in their coins with goats' horns.

This he-goat "came from the west on the face of the "whole earth," that is, he carried every thing before him in all the three parts of the then known world. "And he touched not the ground." His marches were so swift, and his conquests so rapid, that he might be said, in a manner, to pass over the [illegible] without touching [illegible] the same reason the same empire, [illegible] is likened to a leopard, which [illegible] to denote the [illegible] "a leopard with four wings."

"And the goat had a notable horn between his eyes." This horn, [illegible] the angel, [illegible] king, or kingdom of the Grecians [illegible] erected by Alexander the Great, and [illegible] the same years under his brother Philip Aridæus [illegible] two sons, Alexander Ægus and Hercules. [illegible] of Alexander's [illegible] which is very pertinent to our present [illegible] (which with vision, [illegible] than others [illegible] his enemies [illegible] nights, and sometimes making long marches for several days one after another, as [illegible] of Darius, going near forty miles a day [illegible] that, by the speed of his [illegible] he came upon the enemy before they were aware of him, [illegible] before they could be in a posture to [illegible] This exactly agreeth with the description given of him in the prophecies of Daniel some ages before, [illegible] forth under the similitude of [illegible] four wings; for he was [illegible] as [illegible] expeditions, [illegible] his enemies with that [illegible] of wings. And to [illegible] those prophecies [illegible] from the west with [illegible] Persia, [illegible] touched not the ground. And his actions, [illegible] the former, fully verified [illegible]

In [illegible] vision we [illegible] an account of the Persian [illegible] by the Grecians. "And he came to the ram that had two horns, which I had [illegible] ran unto him in the [illegible] come close unto the ram, [illegible] with [illegible] and there was no [illegible] but he cast him down [illegible] upon him, and there was none that could deliver the ram out of his hand." Dan. viii. 6—

The [illegible] and the Persians [illegible] Xerxes, had poured [illegible] with great [illegible] Greece, [illegible] the Grecians, [illegible] carried the [illegible] into Asia, [illegible] the he-goat invaded the [illegible] that had invaded him.

[illegible] he came to the ram that had two horns, which I [illegible] ran unto him in [illegible] These words strongly point out [illegible] of Darius standing and guarding [illegible] Alexander's on the other [illegible] the Granicus, and running [illegible] fury that can be conceived. [illegible] of Alexander [illegible] of Darius, which was considerably [illegible] his own, but he was [illegible] and thus [illegible] opened [illegible] the conquest of [illegible]

"And I saw him come close unto the ram." He had [illegible] with the king of [illegible] Granicus, in Phrygia, [illegible] Issus, in [illegible] in the plains of Arbela, [illegible]

"And he was moved with choler against him." That [illegible] Persians had exercised towards the Grecians, and for Darius's attempting to corrupt sometimes the soldiers of Alexander to betray [illegible] sometimes his friends to destroy him, so that [illegible] listen to the most advantageous offers of peace, [illegible] determined to pursue the Persian king till he completed his destruction.

"And he smote the ram, and brake his two horns." He subdued Persia and Media, [illegible] the other provinces [illegible] kingdoms of the Persian empire, and [illegible] barbarously [illegible] of Persepolis, the capital of the empire [illegible] was seized, and made a prisoner [illegible] subjects, who not long after [illegible] him.

"And there was no power in the ram to [illegible] him, but he cast him down to the ground, [illegible] upon him." He conquered wherever he went, [illegible] the forces, [illegible] all the [illegible] and cities, [illegible] subverted and ruined the Persian empire.

"And there was none that could deliver the ram out of his hand." Not even the [illegible] of Persia could defend [illegible] of it is amounted to 600,000 [illegible] to 10 or 1,100,000, [illegible] Alexander's was [illegible] Scripture [illegible] the [illegible] by the [illegible]

There is not [illegible] and the [illegible] perhaps, [illegible]

Therefore the he-goat waxed very great, [illegible] was strong, the great horn was broken [illegible] up four notable ones, [illegible] of heaven." [illegible] the angel [illegible] "whereas [illegible] stood up for it, four [illegible] out of the nation, but not in his power." Dan. viii. 22.

The empire of the goat was [illegible] Alexander died [illegible] He was succeeded [illegible] his natural brother Philip Aridæus, and by his own two sons, Alexander Ægus and Hercules; [illegible] they were [illegible] the [illegible] 15 years, [illegible] and the [illegible] reduced to four, [illegible] Seleucus, [illegible] four kingdoms [illegible] the four horns [illegible] "four heads of the leopard [illegible]"

"Four kingdoms shall stand up [illegible] not in his power." They were to be [illegible] Grecks, not of Alexander's [illegible] nation, and [illegible] and dominion, [illegible] ful than an empire [illegible] any of the parts. [illegible] "the four winds of heaven" [illegible] empire, [illegible] Macedon, [illegible] parts, [illegible] and Thrace, [illegible] regions, [illegible] countries, and Seleucus obtained [illegible] vinces. Thus were they divided "toward the four winds of heaven."

As to the former vision, [illegible] the ten horns of the Roman [illegible] described as rising [illegible] empire, [illegible] "which waxed exceeding [illegible] him in all the three parts of the then known world. "And he touched not the ground." His marches were so swift and his conquests so [illegible], that he might be said, in a manner, to pass over the [illegible] without touching [illegible]. For the same reason the same [illegible], in the [illegible] vision, was likened to a *leopard*, which [illegible] the [illegible] animal, and, to denote the [illegible] is [illegible] to "a leopard with four wings."

"And the goat had a notable horn between his eyes." This horn, [illegible] the angel, "[illegible] king," or kingdom of the Grecians [illegible], which was [illegible] by Alexander the Great, and continued in some [illegible] his brother Philip Aridæus, and his two sons, Alexander Ægus and Hercules. [illegible] speaking of the [illegible] of Alexander's [illegible] which is very pertinent to our present [illegible]. "[illegible] (says he) will [illegible] swifter than others [illegible], [illegible] purfuing his enemies [illegible] the [illegible] whole days and nights, and sometimes [illegible] several days one after another, as [illegible] of Darius, going near [illegible] miles a day for eleven days together, so that, by the speed of his [illegible], he came upon the enemy before they were aware of him, and [illegible] them before they could be in a posture to [illegible]. This is exactly agreeable with the description given of him in the prophecies of Daniel some ages before, [illegible] under the similitude of [illegible] four wings [illegible] he was impetuous [illegible] expeditions [illegible] a panther [illegible] came upon his enemies with that speed as [illegible] with a double pair of wings. And to [illegible] of those prophecies, [illegible] coming from the west with [illegible] of Media and Persia, that he seemed [illegible] touch the ground. And his actions, [illegible] as the former, full, [illegible]

In the [illegible] we have an account of the Persian empire [illegible] by the Grecians. "And he came to the ram that had two horns, which I had seen standing [illegible] and ran unto him in the fury of his power. And I saw him come close unto the ram, and he was moved with choler against him, and smote the ram, and brake his two horns, and there was no power in the ram to stand before him, but he cast him down to the ground, and stamped upon him, and there was none that could deliver the ram out of his hand." Dan. viii. 6, 7.

The [illegible] had before [illegible] and the Persians [illegible] reigns of [illegible] Hystaspis and Xerxes, had poured [illegible] with great armies into Greece, but now the Grecians, in their turn, carried their arms into Asia, and the he-goat invaded the ram that had invaded him.

"And he came to the ram that had two horns, which I had seen standing before the river, and ran unto him in the fury of his power." These words strongly paint our [illegible] the army of Darius standing and guarding [illegible], and that of Alexander on the other [illegible], [illegible] the stream, and rushing [illegible] with all the fire and fury that can be conceived. It appeared [illegible] attempt of Alexander to attack the army of Darius, which was considerably [illegible] times the number of his own, but he was [illegible] undertaking, and the success diffused a terror [illegible] name, and opened his way to the conquest of [illegible]

"And I saw him come close unto the ram." He had [illegible] engagement, or set battles, with the king of [illegible], and particularly [illegible] the [illegible] Granicus, in Phrygia, [illegible] of Issus, in [illegible], and in the plains of Arbela, in Assyria.

"And he was moved with choler against him." That is for the cruelties which the Persians had exercised towards the Grecians, and for Darius's attempting to corrupt sometimes the soldiers of Alexander to betray him, and sometimes his friends to destroy him, so that he would not listen to the most advantageous offers of peace, but [illegible] determined to pursue the Persian king till he completed his destruction.

"And he smote the ram, and brake his two horns." He subdued Persia and Media, with the other provinces and kingdoms of the Persian empire, and it is remarkable that in Persia he barbarously sacked and burned the royal [illegible] of Persepolis the capital of the empire, [illegible] Media [illegible] was [illegible], and made a prisoner, [illegible] traitor subjects, who not long afterwards [illegible] him.

"And there was no power in the ram to stand before him, but he cast him down to the ground, and stamped upon him." He conquered wherever he came, routed all the forces, took all the cities and castles, and entirely subverted and ruined the Persian empire.

"And there was none that could deliver the ram out of his hand." Not even the numerous armies of the king of Persia could defend him [illegible] at the battle of Issus amounted to 600,000 [illegible], and [illegible] to 10 or 1,100,000, whereas the whole number of Alexander's was not more than [illegible] thousand [illegible]. So [illegible] is true [illegible] that "the [illegible] by the multitude of an host." Psalm xxxiii. 16.

There is not any thing [illegible] and [illegible] the empire of the goat, [illegible] perhaps, for that reason [illegible] "Therefore the he-goat waxed very great, and when he was strong, the great horn was broken, and for it came up four notable ones, towards the four winds of heaven." Which the angel thus interprets: "[illegible] whereas four stood up for it, four kingdoms shall stand up out of the nation, but not in his power." Dan. viii. 22.

The empire of the goat was in its full strength when Alexander died at Babylon. He was succeeded [illegible] by his natural brother, Philip Aridæus, and by his own two sons, Alexander Ægus and Hercules, but in [illegible], they were all murdered, [illegible] then the first horn or kingdom, was entirely [illegible] being [illegible] the governors [illegible] who had usurped the power, assumed the title of [illegible], and, by the death [illegible] reduced to four, namely, Cassander, Lysimachus, [illegible], and Seleucus, who parted Alexander's dominions [illegible], and divided and settled them into four kingdoms [illegible] four kingdoms are the "four notable horns" [illegible] in the room of the first great horn, [illegible] "four heads of the leopard" in the former [illegible]

"Four kingdoms shall stand up out of the nation, but not in his power." They were to be kingdoms of [illegible] Greeks, not of Alexander's own [illegible] nation, and neither were they to [illegible] and dominion, [illegible] a [illegible] empire divided, [illegible] any of the parts. They were likewise [illegible] "the four winds of heaven," [illegible] empire, [illegible] held Macedon and Greece, [illegible] parts, Lysimachus had Thrace, Bithynia, [illegible] regions, Ptolemy possessed Egypt, [illegible] countries, and Seleucus obtained [illegible] provinces. Thus were they divided "towards the four winds of heaven."

As, in the former vision, a little horn [illegible] the ten horns of the Roman empire [illegible] described as rising [illegible] empire. "And out of one of them came forth a little horn, "which waxed exceeding great, [illegible]

" [illegible] and [illegible] ed." Dan. vii. [illegible] [illegible] can only be applied to the Romans, [illegible] from ſmall [illegible] who firſt ſub- [illegible] of the [illegible] Greece, [illegible] [illegible] [illegible] [illegible] Greece, Aſia, [illegible]

[illegible] and he [illegible] and the [illegible] moſt in [illegible] [illegible] Numb. xxiv. 24 [illegible] the holy people [illegible] to eleven hundred [illegible] of the Jews, [illegible]

[illegible] of the [illegible], is [illegible] to the ground, [illegible] the perſecuting power [illegible] the Jews or towards [illegible] is ſtill " the [illegible] little horn of the he-goat, or [illegible] the weſt, it is the lit- [illegible] fourth empire.

[illegible] the other tyrannical powers, was to [illegible] " he ſhall be broken without [illegible] Nebuchadnezzar's dream was " cut [illegible] without hands," that is, not by hu- [illegible] means, ſo the little horn " ſhall [illegible] hands," that is, not fall by the hand of [illegible] by a ſtroke from heaven. And this agrees [illegible] predictions of the final cataſtrophe [illegible] " The ſtone (that is, the power of Chriſt) [illegible] image upon his feet of iron and clay, and brake " them to pieces." Dan. ii. 34. " I beheld then, becauſe " of the voice of the great words which the horn ſpake; I " beheld even till the beaſt was ſlain, and his body deſtroyed, " and given to the burning flame." Dan. vii. 11. And again, " the judgment ſhall ſit, and they ſhall take away " his dominion, to conſume, and to deſtroy it unto the " end," ver. 26. All which implies, that the dominion of the Romans ſhall finally be deſtroyed with ſome extraordinary manifeſtation of the Divine power.

[illegible] was much affected with the [illegible] which were to befal the church and people of God. " And I Daniel fainted, and was ſick certain days; after- " ward I roſe up, and did the king's buſineſs; and I was " aſtoniſhed at the viſion, but none underſtood it." Dan. viii. 27. [illegible] can [illegible] be [illegible] And, indeed, the [illegible] Romans were [illegible] Nebuchadnezzar [illegible] [illegible] God's [illegible] [illegible] heart [illegible] [illegible] the [illegible] [illegible] " [illegible]

This concern of Daniel, [illegible] and country [illegible] [illegible] spirit, and appears no leſs [illegible] [illegible] [illegible] devoutly pray [illegible] for the pardon and [illegible] of his [illegible] captivity.

[illegible] [illegible] ſeveral illuſtrious examples of it, [illegible] country, are so [illegible] [illegible] [illegible] Chriſtianity [illegible] [illegible] " for the peace of Jeruſalem, they ſhall proſper that love " thee. Peace be within thy walls, and proſperity " within thy palaces. For my brethren and companions' " ſake I will wiſh thee proſperity. Yea, becauſe of the " houſe of the Lord our God, I will ſeek to do thee good." Pſal. cxxii. 6, &c.

CHAP. XIV.

Of the Prophecy of [illegible]

WE have already given an account of the promiſes of Moſes relative to [illegible] and [illegible] ſon that moſt memorable [illegible] great [illegible] [illegible] another prophet to be raiſed like unto himſelf.

At the time [illegible] Moſes [illegible] his people, and the [illegible] promiſes them another prophet. " The Lord thy God " (ſays he) will raiſe up unto thee a prophet from the midſt " of thee, of thy brethren, like unto me; unto him ſhall ye " hearken." Deut. xviii. 15. [illegible] name of God. " I will raiſe them up [illegible] from among " their brethren, like unto thee, [illegible] " to his mouth, and he ſhall ſpeak unto them all that I ſhall " command him," ver. 18. [illegible] next verse, "And it shall come to pass, that whosoever "will not hearken unto [illegible] words which he shall speak "in my name, I will require it of you."

In order to explain the meaning of this amazing prophecy, as well as to point out [illegible] to consider three things.

First, who the prophet [illegible] is here particularly meant.

Secondly, that this pro[illegible] resembled Moses in a much greater degree than any [illegible] A[illegible]

Thirdly, [illegible] still are [illegible] and disfolved [illegible] to this prophet [illegible]

And first we shall consider who the prophet was that is here particularly [illegible] opinion of some that [illegible] is said to have been the "successor of Moses in prophecies." Ecclus. xlvi. [illegible] commanded to hearken unto [illegible] Joshua "According as we [illegible] unto Moses [illegible] "things, so will [illegible] Some [illegible] was Jere[illegible] of [illegible] his [illegible] reckons up [illegible] [illegible] other, and observes [illegible] Moses [illegible] so likewise [illegible] Jeremiah.

[illegible] the prophet [illegible] [illegible] prophets to be [illegible] until [illegible] (says [illegible]) the Jews [illegible] [illegible] [illegible] from [illegible] [illegible] their own, when [illegible] particular occasions.

But notwithstanding [illegible] difference in opinion among [illegible] of the [illegible] yet the very [illegible] contradiction [illegible] [illegible] [illegible] intended [illegible] and ultimate sense of the prophecy [illegible] are many sufficient reasons [illegible] principally [illegible] of a literal and typical [illegible]

[illegible] of the book of Deuteronomy [illegible] refers to [illegible] the notion of Joshua's [illegible] "And Joshua the [illegible] spirit of wisdom, for "[illegible] his hands upon him, and the children "[illegible] unto him, and did as the Lord "[illegible] Moses. And there arose not a prophet "[illegible] like unto Moses, whom the Lord knew "[illegible] In all the signs and the wonders which "[illegible] Lord [illegible] &c." See Deut. xxxiv. 9, &c.

[illegible] this addition was made [illegible] we cannot be certainly told; but [illegible] the death of Moses. The [illegible] "[illegible] not a prophet since in Israel," [illegible] implies that this addition must have been made some time after Joshua succeeded to the government of the [illegible] clearly, that the Jewish church had no [illegible] perpetual succession of the prophets [illegible] [illegible] up like unto Moses. And if we suppose this addition was made [illegible] it is generally believed to have been [illegible] Ezra after the Babylonish captivity, then it is evident, [illegible] all contradiction, that neither Jeremiah [illegible] or the ancient prophets, were esteemed like unto Moses.

Let us consider what are the peculiar marks and characters wherein it is [illegible] that none other prophet [illegible] ever resembled Moses. "There arose not a prophet since in Israel like unto Moses." And which of the prophets ever conversed so frequently, and familiarly, with God? Which of them ever wrought so many and such astonishing miracles? It must be answered, that not any one of all the prophets who succeeded Moses, was ever equal or comparable to him, except the Messiah, the great Saviour and Redeemer of mankind.

It is undeniably evident, from the [illegible] Christ [illegible] of [illegible] [illegible] and Aaron, that [illegible] any prophet in the Jewish church much [illegible] [illegible] jealous of Moses, and [illegible] [illegible] the Lord indeed [illegible] "[illegible]" Numb. [illegible] felt was pleased [illegible] [illegible] there be a prophet [illegible] [illegible] in [illegible] "speak [illegible] "[illegible] "[illegible] mouth to mouth [illegible] dark speeches, and [illegible] the Lord [illegible] "[illegible] my servant Moses."

[illegible] not only [illegible] [illegible] God [illegible] [illegible] prophets [illegible] [illegible] [illegible] [illegible] [illegible] in those [illegible] the [illegible]?

It is, [illegible] [illegible] [illegible] [illegible] represent [illegible] [illegible] God [illegible] and therefore [illegible] a prophet like unto Moses [illegible] to [illegible] his commands [illegible] The prophet, [illegible] here [illegible] but here [illegible] [illegible] and [illegible]

If we take a [illegible] view of [illegible] from the most [illegible] any prophet [illegible] less [illegible] whom the Jews [illegible] like [illegible] death to the coming of the Messiah [illegible] of inspiration [illegible] mention several particulars [illegible] [illegible] indeed, in consequence [illegible] [illegible] of some [illegible] particularly [illegible] coming on the earth [illegible] understood [illegible] only prophet [illegible] or greater, than Moses.

When Our Saviour [illegible] [illegible] acts, than those men [illegible] that should come into the world." John vi. 14. St. Peter and St. Stephen have also directly applyed this prophecy to him, Acts iii. 22, 23. vii. 37. and they may very well be justified for so doing, for he truly answers all the characters [illegible] which are here given of the prophet [illegible] Moses. He had immediate communication with [illegible] and God spake to him *face to face* as he did to Moses. He performed *signs and wonders* as great, or greater than those of Moses. "I will raise them up a prophet," said God; and the people glorified God, saying, "That a great prophet is risen up among us." Luke [illegible] "I will put my words in his mouth," saith God [illegible] the words which thou gavest me," John xvii. 8. "He shall speak [illegible] all that I shall command him," saith God [illegible] I have not spoken of myself, but the Father which sent me, he gave me a commandment, what I should say, and what I should speak. And I know that his commandment is life everlasting [illegible] therefore I speak, even as the Father said unto me, so I speak." John xii. 49, 50.

[illegible] pointed out who the person was [illegible] Moses's prophecy, we are now to take some notice [illegible] likeness between Moses and Christ, [illegible] resembled the former in more particulars than any other person ever did.

[illegible] had [illegible] circumstances wherein they [illegible] Moses [illegible] God's speaking to both [illegible] of both [illegible] *signs and wonders*, or both [illegible] and in these respects none of the ancient [illegible] were like unto Moses. None of them were [illegible] only interpreted and enforced the laws of Moses. None of them performed so many and such great wonders. None of them had such clear communications with God [illegible] visions, and dreams [illegible] Moses and Christ are the only two who perfectly resembled each other in these respects. But, farther [illegible] material part of the prophecy, we shall present [illegible] observations on the subject [illegible] Dr. Jortin, in his "Remarks on Ecclesiastical History."

"Moses," says he, "fled from his country to escape the hands of the kings of Egypt:" so did Christ when his [illegible] afterwards "the Lord said [illegible] return into Egypt, for all [illegible] which sought thy life," Exod. iv. [illegible] the Lord said to Joseph, in almost the same words, "Arise, and take the young child, and go into the land of Israel, for they are dead which sought the young child's life," Matt. ii. 20. pointing him out, as it were, for that prophet who should arise like unto Moses.

[illegible] called the son of Pharaoh's daughter [illegible] to suffer affliction. Christ refused to [illegible] choosing rather to suffer affliction.

[illegible] Stephen, "was learned in all the wisdom of the Egyptians," and Josephus says, that he was [illegible] youth, and had wisdom [illegible] years. St. Luke observes of [illegible] (at times) in wisdom and stature [illegible] with God and man," and his discourse [illegible] with the doctors, when he was but [illegible] were a proof of it.

Moses was not only a law-giver, a prophet, and a [illegible] but a king and a priest: in these [illegible] the resemblance between Moses and Christ was [illegible]

Moses brought darkness over the land: the sun withdrew his light at Christ's crucifixion: and as the darkness which Moses spread over Egypt was followed by the destruction of their first-born, and of Pharaoh and his host: so the darkness at Christ's death was the forerunner of the destruction of the Jews.

Moses foretold the calamities which would befall the nation for their disobedience, so did Christ.

The spirit which was in Moses was conferred [illegible] upon the seventy elders, and they prophesied. Christ conferred miraculous powers upon [illegible] disciples.

Moses was victorious over powerful kings and great nations, so was Christ [illegible] the effects of his religion [illegible] the fall of those who persecuted his cause.

Moses conquered Amalek by holding up both his hands: Christ overcame his and our enemies when his hands were fastened to the cross.

Moses interceded for transgressors, and caused an atonement to be made for them, and stopped the wrath of God, so did Christ.

Moses ratified a covenant between God and the people by sprinkling them with blood: Christ with his own blood.

Moses desired to die for the people, and prayed that God would forgive them, or blot him out of his book: Christ did more, he died for sinners.

Moses instituted the passover, when a lamb was sacrificed, none of whose bones were to be broken, and whose blood protected the people from destruction: Christ is the paschal lamb.

Moses lifted up the serpent, that they who looked upon him might be healed of their mortal wounds: by properly looking up to Christ all will be healed.

All Moses's affection towards the people, all his cares and toils on their account, were repaid by them with ingratitude, murmuring, and rebellion: the same returns the Jews made to Christ for all his benefits.

Moses was insulted by his own family, his brother and sister rebelled against him: there was a time when Christ's own brethren believed not in him.

Moses had a very wicked and perverse generation committed to his care and conduct, and, to enable him to rule them, miraculous powers were given to him, and he used his utmost endeavours to make the people obedient to God, and to save them from ruin, but in vain: in the space of forty years they all fell in the wilderness except two. Christ also was given to a generation not less wicked and perverse, his instructions and miracles were lost upon them, and in about the same space of time, after they had rejected him, they were destroyed.

Moses was very meek above all men that were on the face of the earth, so was Christ.

The people could not enter into the land of promise till Moses was dead: by the death of Christ the kingdom of heaven was opened to believers.

In the death of Moses and Christ there is also a resemblance of some circumstances. Moses died, in one sense, for the iniquities of the people: it was their rebellion which was the occasion of it, which drew down the displeasure of God upon them and upon him. Moses went up, in the sight of the people, to the top of mount Nebo, and there he died, when he was in perfect vigour, when "his eye was not dim, nor his natural force abated." Christ suffered for the sins of men, and was led up, in the presence of the people, to mount Calvary, where he died in the flower of his age, and when he was in his full natural strength.

Neither Moses, or Christ, as far as we can collect from sacred history, were ever sick, or felt any bodily decay or infirmity, which would have rendered them unfit for the toils they underwent, their sufferings were of another kind.

Moses was buried, and no man knew where his body lay: nor could the Jews find the body of Christ.

L[illegible], as Moses, a little before his death, promised "another prophet," so Christ, before his death, promised "another comforter"

Such are the comparisons made by Dr Jortin relative to the great resemblance between Moses and Christ, but the greatest similitude consists in their both being *lawgivers*, which no other prophets ever were. They may resemble each other in many other circumstances, and a fruitful imagination may strike upon a likeness where, in reality, there is none to be found; but as the same excellent writer concludes, "Is this similitude and resemblance in so many things between Moses and Christ the effect of mere chance? Let us search all the records of universal history, and see if we can find a man who was so like to Moses as Christ was, and so like to Christ as Moses was. If we cannot find such an one, then have we found him of whom Moses, in the law, and the prophets, did write, Jesus of Nazareth the Son of God."

We come now to consider the last part of the prophecy, in doing of which it will be no very difficult matter to prove that the people have been, and still are, severely punished for their infidelity and disobedience to this prophecy.

The words in this part of the prophecy are very clear and express: "Unto him ye shall hearken"; "and it shall come to pass, that whosoever will not hearken unto my words which he shall speak in my name, I will require it of him." That is, I will severely punish him for it, or, as the Seventy translate it, "I will take vengeance of him."

This prophecy, as we have clearly proved, evidently relates to Christ. God himself, in a manner, applies to him; for when he was transfigured, there came "a voice out of the cloud, which said, This is my beloved Son in whom I am well pleased; hear ye him." Matt xvii 5. This manifestly alludes to the words of Moses, "unto him ye shall hearken," and clearly points out that Christ alone was the prophet like unto Moses. The apostle St Peter directly applies it unto Our Saviour. "For Moses truly said unto the fathers, A prophet shall the Lord your God raise up unto you of your brethren like unto me; him shall ye hear in all things whatsoever he shall say unto you. And it shall come to pass, that every soul which will not hear that prophet, shall be destroyed from among the people." Acts iii 22, 23.

And hath not this terrible denunciation been fully executed upon the Jews? Was not the complete destruction of that incredulous nation (soon after Christ had finished his ministry among them, and his apostles had likewise preached in vain) the fulfilling of the threat for not hearkening unto him? We may be the more certain of this application as Our Saviour himself not only denounced their utter destruction, but also foretold the signs, the manner, and the circumstances of it with great exactness. Such indeed, of those Jews who believed in his name, by remembering the caution, and following the advice which he had given them, escaped from the general ruin of their country; but the main body either perished in their infidelity, or were carried captives into other nations; and by persisting in the same infidelity, they have ever since been a vagabond, distressed, and a miserable people.

The wise dispensations of Providence are in no respect more amply displayed than in the fulfilment of this part of the prophecy. We must be blind not to see it, and seeing we cannot but admire and adore it. What account can the Jews themselves give of their long captivity, dispersion, and misery? Their former captivity, for the punishment of their wickedness and idolatry, lasted only seventy years, but they have lived in their present dispersion, even though they have not been idolaters, upwards of seventeen hundred

But though they have thus long laboured under these calamities for the enormity of their crimes, yet it is to be hoped that, upon a proper faith and repentance, they will, in time, become objects of the Divine mercy. We shall therefore conclude with the words of the apostle St Paul, "Our hearts desire and prayer to God for Israel is, that they may be saved." Rom x 1.

CHAP XV

Of the Jewish Ritual, or Ceremonial Law

IN the preceding chapters we have given an ample account of the [illegible] prophecies contained in the Old Testament, the greater part of which have already been fulfilled, some are still fulfilling, and, no doubt, the rest will be fulfilled when the appointed time shall arrive. In this chapter we shall take some notice of the [illegible] of the Jews, as also the means whereby they became acquainted with learning and literature.

The constitution of the Mosaic law consisted of three parts, namely,

1 Of political and judicial laws.

2 Of moral precepts, such as the ten commandments.

3 Of rites and ceremonies, such as circumcision, sacrifices, washings, purifications, [illegible], [illegible], &c. and divers [illegible] by the [illegible] and [illegible].

We shall observe, in general, that the design of these [illegible] was to [illegible] religious and moral [illegible] to the people, and the method of them [illegible] [illegible] is in many instances, by hieroglyphics. Thus the government of the world by Divine Providence, this extraordinary interposition in favour of good men, is represented by a ladder standing on the earth, and reaching to heaven, with the angels of God ascending and descending on it to receive and execute orders from God above, who ruleth over all. Gen xxviii 12, 13. In the style of this hieroglyphic Our Lord himself [illegible], "Hereafter shall ye see heaven open, and the angels of God, ascending and descending upon the Son of Man." John i 51.

The exaltation of *Joseph* above the rest of his family, was represented by the hieroglyphic of his sheaf standing upright, and the eleven sheaves of his brethren standing round about, and bowing to it; as also of the sun, and moon, and eleven stars, making obeisance to him. Gen xxxvii 7, 9.

The tribe of Judah is represented by a young lion; *Issachar*, by a strong ass; *Dan*, by a serpent [illegible] [illegible] [illegible]; *Joseph*, by a fruitful bough; *Benjamin*, by a ravening wolf. Gen xlix 9, 14 &c.

A rod or staff, as it is an instrument of [illegible] or beating down, is the hieroglyphic of power, either in correcting, punishing, and ruling [illegible] [illegible] [illegible] [illegible] [illegible] [illegible] [illegible] [illegible] [illegible] the power and authority, [illegible] [illegible] [illegible] the [illegible] of the [illegible] Exod [illegible] [illegible] [illegible] [illegible] [illegible] [illegible] [illegible] [illegible] [illegible] of the [illegible] [illegible] [illegible] [illegible].

A horn [illegible] [illegible] power [illegible] [illegible] 1 Sam ii 10 [illegible] [illegible].

A yoke, [illegible] [illegible] [illegible] [illegible] [illegible] [illegible] [illegible] [illegible] [illegible] [illegible].

8 C

[illegible] in the manner of hieroglyphics, [illegible] to which the Jews were accustomed, [illegible] of the age, which they could [illegible] than abstract reasonings about moral [illegible]

[illegible] therefore, on this account, we [illegible] admit, that [illegible] of their religious institutions [illegible] intended by external representations, [illegible] useful instructors in true religion and [illegible]

[illegible] the prophets and apostles, who were [illegible] with their meaning, we shall find [illegible] of the moral and spiritual intention of [illegible] to believe this was the sense [illegible] of all the rest.

[illegible] were enjoined frequent and various ablutions, [illegible] water, the common use of which is to [illegible] body from all dirt and filth, and to keep it [illegible] representation of purity of [illegible] purged from filth and sin. In this [illegible] to understand it: "Wash me from [illegible]" Psal. li. 2. "Wash me, and I shall [illegible] ver. 7. "Wash you, yourselves, make yourselves clean, put away the evil of your doings." Isa. i. 16.

[illegible] with oil, or ointment, by which the head [illegible] and the countenance exhilarated, had the [illegible] honour, joy, holiness, and inspiration [illegible] Acts x. 38. The priests officiated in garments of fine linen, Exod. xxxix. 27. meaning that the priests should be clothed, or have their minds adorned [illegible]

Burning of incense, whose smoke arising up [illegible] pleasant scent, was an hieroglyphic representation of [illegible] prayer [illegible] Lev. [illegible] 10.

Circumcision had relation to the heart and [illegible] the retrenching the inordinate affections and [illegible] Lev. [illegible] 41. Rom. ii. 29.

The sprinkling of blood, and of the water of separation, (Numb. xix. 13. 19.) was hieroglyphic, and had a moral signification. See Heb. ix. 13, 14. [illegible] As had likewise the muzzled mouth of the ox, Deut. xxv. 4. compared with 1 Cor. ix. 9, 10. 1 [illegible] 17, 18.

Some persons have indulged their fancies more than they ought, and pretended to have found more mysteries in the Hebrew ritual than were really designed; but these instances explained by [illegible], may convince us, that the whole had a spiritual meaning; and as we are taught in the Gospel every thing necessary to faith and practice in the plainest manner, we need not give ourselves much trouble about discovering the meaning of the other rites, which are not explained by the prophets and apostles.

But the affair of sacrifice, so often mentioned in the Old Testament, was a type of Our Blessed Redeemer, who died for our sins, and rose again for our justification.

END OF THE ILLUSTRATION OF THE PREDICTIONS OF THE PRINCIPAL PROPHETS, &c.

A

Geographical and Descriptive

INDEX

OF THE

PRINCIPAL PLACES

MENTIONED IN THE WORKS OF

FLAVIUS JOSEPHUS.

ABARIM, mentioned [illegible] Numbers [illegible] was a long ridge of the moun[illegible] from the tribe of Reuben into the land of [illegible], o[illegible] or the river Arnon, of which the [illegible] Nebo (where Moses died) were a part.

A[illegible], a large fortress, built by A[illegible] during the time of [illegible] persecution of the [illegible] the Maccabees,) on one of the [illegible] the city of David [illegible] which [illegible] and as [illegible] the advantage of [illegible] from the temple. After [illegible] it was demolished by the [illegible] Simon.

A[illegible], mentioned in the Maccabees, as the place where J[illegible] by Jerome to have been [illegible] in the tribe of [illegible].

ADIABENA, [illegible] province of antient Assyria. The whole country has been [illegible] called by the name of this part of it.

ADIDA, the name of the fort recorded in the Maccabees, to be [illegible] up, or built, by Simon, in the region of Sephela [illegible] of Eleutheropolis, in Judea.

ALEXANDRIA, the greatest city in Egypt, was built by Alexander the Great, on the coast of the Egyptian Sea in that part of Africa that is near the mouth of [illegible], where it forms a [illegible] haven, in form of a [illegible]. This city, as founded by Alexander bears his name, and contains his tomb. On its building it, he brought great numbers of Jews thither to [illegible] it, and Ptolemy Soter, after his death, having [illegible] the seat of his government there, was so desirous of [illegible] and adorning it, that, in order to [illegible] it the metropolis of Egypt, he brought thither many of that nation for that purpose, where, having granted them free exercise of their religion, [illegible] the same privileges with the Macedonians [illegible] city [illegible] became a great part of the [illegible] of [illegible] city. We are told that Alexandria [illegible] [illegible] but the emperor A[illegible] [illegible] privileges, but [illegible] [illegible] [illegible] which they [illegible] [illegible] [illegible] [illegible] world, which [illegible] [illegible] [illegible] We have [illegible] [illegible] the old and the new [illegible] into the first none but Turkish vessels [illegible], the later receives vessels from Europe It is [illegible] of Egypt, subject to the Grand Seignior, who [illegible], however, to have a limited authority being often obliged to [illegible] the administration of government to the [illegible] of the petty princes of Egypt

ALEXANDRION, a fortress of Judæa, built by Alexander Jannæus, from whom it had its name It was situated on a high mountain, at the entrance into Judæa, near the [illegible], which was the first place in Judæa on that [illegible] side, and upon the road to Jericho, on the frontiers [illegible] and Benjamin Alexandrion was afterwards the burying place of the Jewish kings, so that, though it was demolished by the Romans, it was rebuilt by Herod

[illegible], a city on the Jordan, built, probably, by Herod, [illegible] of the hot waters for which it was [illegible]

[illegible] by Seleucus, and soon after became, [illegible] ages continued to be, the metropolis of the east, [illegible], the Syrian kings, but afterwards the Roman emperors, [illegible] the usual place of their residence It [illegible] the Orontes, (now called the Hasi,) the place where [illegible] into the Mediterranean, being equally distant from Constantinople and Alexandria, in Egypt Seleucus called it from his father's name, which was Antiochus [illegible] of Syria was afterwards known by the name of Tetrapolis, (i e fourfold city,) being divided, as it were, into four cities, each of them having its proper wall, besides the common one which enclosed them all [illegible] place where it stood was very subject to earthquakes, by which it greatly suffered, and was often in danger of being overwhelmed However, it continued 600 years, till it was taken and utterly destroyed by Bibars, sultan of Egypt [illegible] (it is now [illegible] comparison) a small and contemptible [illegible], known by the name of Anthiochia, and remarkable [illegible] its ruins There is one thing well worth notice with relation to the walls of this city, that within the [illegible] of it, at a certain place there is a space [illegible], and with a gradual and imperceptible ascent, by which loaded carts or waggons may be drawn from the bottom of the wall quite up to the castle They were [illegible] towers strongly built, of which [illegible] number left, every one having a cistern in the middle of it, quite entire to this day It is [illegible] famous for giving the name of Christians to the disciples [illegible] Syria, for being the birth-place of St Luke, the Evangelist, and of Theophilus, he [illegible] surnamed [illegible], and for its celebrated bishop, St Ignatius the Martyr

ANTIPATRIS, a city built, or rather built or repaired, by Herod, and so named in honor of his father Antipater, having been formerly called Capharsalama. It does not stand very far from Jerusalem, in the road to Cæsarea

ANTONIA After Simon had destroyed Mount Acra, (before described), he built fortifications round the mountain on which the temple stood, for the better securing and fortifying it against all future insults from the heathens [illegible] which he built an house, and dwelt there all his life [illegible] house seems to be the same which Hyrcanus [illegible] built into the castle Baris, where he, and all his successors of the Asmonæan family lived and kept their court and here laid up the pontifical stole, or sacred robes of the high-priest &c &c which continued to be done till the time of Herod, who, on being made king of Judæa, having observed the convenience of the place, rebuilt and made it a very strong fortress Instead of Baris, the name it formerly bore, he called it Antonia, thereby complimenting Marcus Antonius, the triumvir, who then governed the eastern provinces of the Roman empire The form of the building was that of a quadrangle, all built on every side, wherein were rooms for all the uses of a palace, and in the middle was a large area for the soldiers to be in, and round it was a stately piazza, or cloister There was a turret near the middle of the north side of the great square of the temple built remarkably high, that from thence might be seen all that was done in the courts within, so that if a tumult should arise in any part of the temple, it might be observed, and soldiers sent down to quell it When Jerusalem fell into the hands of the Romans, they continued keeping a strong garrison in it, and by reason of its immediate influence on the temple, the captain of the garrison is, in scripture, called the Captain of the Temple This fortress was at last invested and taken by the Romans, and destroyed in the [illegible] and total destruction of Jerusalem by Titus and his forces

ARABIA, if we include all those countries which go under that general name, is of very great extent, and has been from early times, divided into three parts, viz Arabia Felix, or happy, to the south, so called from its rich produce, and famous for the queen of Sheba, who came to hear the wisdom of Solomon, of whose [illegible] this fertile country Arabia Petræa, or stony, so called from its capital Petra, as [illegible], but more the [illegible] of the whole division being full of mountains, among which is Mount Sinai, or Horeb, so famous in sacred scripture As Arabia Petræa lies to the [illegible], so still more north, or rather north east, lies the [illegible] division, called, from its natural [illegible], Arabia Deserta Various are the opinions of the learned concerning the origin and name of this country, and it would more tend to perplex than entertain to specify them As to the climate, part of Arabia is under the hottest, viz the torrid zone The air on the north part is extremely hot during the six summer months, the heavens being seldom or ever over-cast with clouds But on the [illegible] much more temperate, being qualified with refreshing dews, which fall almost every night in great abundance The distinct names of the three Arabias sufficiently declare the nature of their soil the northern being extremely barren, and encumbered with huge formidable rocks the other covered with vast mountains of sand But the southern, deservedly stiled the happy is blessed with an excellent soil and extraordinary fertile in many places It abounds with the richest and most valuable commodities, as also with camels [illegible] beasts of singular use for carriage, that seem formed by nature for this dry and sandy soil, which sometimes affords no water for many days travel The country is infested with what are called free-booters, a strange species of [illegible], scarcely deserving the title of human They are [illegible] swarthy complexion, of mean stature, raw-boned, and very swift Their voices are effeminate as well as their [illegible] They have no settled habitation, except their [illegible] the sea-coast, where their cities and towns are more regularly built and inhabited, as well as more [illegible] Those of the inland country rove from place to place, living under tents, which they pitch at night, where their convenience or fancy leads them As we have hitherto [illegible] the worst side of their character, we now ought, in justice, to shew the best, for there are, on the other hand, many of them, especially such as live in towns, that apply themselves to trade and commerce, to arts and sciences, in which they generally excel This is particularly true with regard to the antient Arabians, whose extraordinary performances, in physic, astronomy, and mathematics, shew them to have been men of great genius and application They are, to this day, allowed to be very ingenious, witty, and generous, great admirers of poetry and rhetoric The language of the three Arabias is Arabesk, or corrupt Arabic, which is not only used here, but spoken with some variation of dialect, over great part of the eastern countries The true and antient Arabic is a kind of dialect of the Hebrew, and esteemed, by the learned, very useful for [illegible] the Old Testament Christianity was first preached here by St Paul, and some of his eminent disciples [illegible] received the light of the gospel from the earliest time But in many parts it was much clouded, long before the grand impostor Mahomet, their countryman, appeared, and, upon their being subdued by the Turks, they all embraced his religion, as best suited their depraved inclinations

Aram The name Aram is constantly in Scripture the name of Syria, and the Syrians are called Aramæans in divers places thereof Several authors agree that the people now called Syrians were anciently called Aramæans and Arameans Agreeably hereto, the adjoining countries into which the posterity of Aram might spread took the name, with some other additional names joined to it

Arbela, famed in history for the battle fought near Gaugamela, in its neighbourhood, which last, being but an inconsiderable village, the city Arbela was chosen by historians to give name to that celebrated fight between Darius and Alexander, which proved the decisive stroke for the Persian empire Arbela is by some placed in Persia, but with more truth in Assyria Propria, or Adiabena Its plain is described as being 15 leagues in extent, watered with several rivulets, and producing great variety of fine fruit-trees, and the eminences where the antient cities stood are covered with stately oaks

Armenia Authors differ concerning the origin whence this tract derived its name It was anciently divided into the Greater and Lesser, or Armenia Major and Minor The former was one of the greatest provinces of Asia Minor The soil of this country is very mountainous, yet the hills are here and there interspersed with fruitful and most beautiful dales and vallies. All sorts of grain are very indifferent, and if they had not the conveniency of watering their lands, they would be almost barren What the country produces is almost entirely owing to painful labour, being either watered artfully by hand, or by dug trenches, &c for the refreshing of the fields The cold is so extreme here, that all manner of fruits are more backward than in most of the northern countries The hills are covered with snow the whole year round and sometimes it falls even in the month of June The earth of this country produces an excellent medicine, viz that which, from the name of this country, receives its own surname Bole Armeniac, which was anciently, as well as at present, found in great esteem and was by Galen first introduced into medicine, and used with success in the time of a terrible plague at Rome With respect to the history of the lost of the Armenians, and scarcely with it to form any particular idea of them As to their religion, we are not so much at a loss, for a writer of credit assures us, they worship the same deities with the Medes and Persians, which will be specified hereafter We have likewise no authority for their learning and arts Their language was much the same with that of the Syrians, at least they used the Syriac characters The modern Armenians use two languages, the learned and the vulgar the former (as they say) having no affinity with any other oriental language Though the modern Armenians are now perhaps the greatest traders on the earth yet we find no mention of any commerce carried on by them in antient times Shah Abbas King of Persia, is said to have been the first who commencing the œconomy and indefatigable industry of this people, put them upon trade, and settled a colony of them in Julfa, the famous suburb of Ispahan This place contains at present above 30,000 inhabitants, all Armenians and merchants In the reign of Justinian II the Saracens subdued Armenia, and held it till the irruption of the Turks, who possessed themselves of this country, and called it Turcomania, but the eastern part of it is subject to the Persians at this day Nor was the extirpation of the royal race of Armenia absolutely effected, for we find it had kings again of its own even after such conquests by Saracens, Turks, Tartars, &c And in our own chronicles we find mention of Leo king of Armenia, who, in the reign of Richard II came into England to sue for and against the Turks, who had driven him from his kingdom

Armenia Minor may be described as in most instances similar to Armenia Major, so that it may suffice to observe, that, after a variety of revolutions through a succession of æras, it was, by Vespasian, made a province of the Roman empire, and so continued till the division of the same, when it became subject to the emperors of the east, and, on the decline of their power, it was first subdued by the Persians, and afterwards by the Turks who gave it the name of Ganech, and have held it ever since.

Arnon The brook or torrent of Arnon ran along between the countries of the Ammonites and Moabites, and discharged itself into the Black Sea The river Arnon is supposed to have been the first northern boundary of the Israelites on the other side of Jordan

Ascalon, in Palestine, (or the country of the Philistines) is a great and noble sea-port to the north-ward of Gaza, and known to us still by the same name it bears in Scripture, and in the writings of the ancient Greeks and Romans, by whom it was held in great veneration This city, as well as Gaza, is reckoned into the lot or tribe of Judah, [illegible] them, but not held Its site on cannot be disputed, since it may be said to stand at this day, and has been often visited Ascalon was famous among the antients on many accounts It was the birth-place of Semiramis, the Assyrian empress It is noted for the place where originally produced the kind of onion called the shallot, which is supposed from thence to have derived its name It may seem, at first sight, to be a very odd derivation, but it is observed that the Latin of this plant is Ascalonia, whence the French have their Eschalote which we have curtailed into Shalot It is also famed for its wines, and very remarkable for its great flights of pigeons With respect to the remarkables of Ascalon, we must not forget to mention the cypresses which were said to be admired for the extraordinary growth attributed to Abraham and Isaac This city had, in the first times of Christianity, an episcopal see, and, in the course of the holy wars, it was beautified with a new wall, and many buildings, by King Richard I But it is now dwindled to nothing The Turks call it Scalona, and it is of no note, except for a Turkish garrison kept in it

Ashdod, or Azotus, was a city of the Philistines, to the N E of Ascalon and of extraordinary strength among the antients It stood in a country which produced great plenty of corn Here was the temple of Dagon, and here was he principally worshipped He seems to have been the grand, the most antient, and favourite deity of the Philistines in the art [illegible] the invention of bread-corn or of agriculture as his very name imports, the word Dagon signifying bread-corn It is Ashdod of the Old Testament and Azotus in the New, as well as in the book of the Maccabees It lies near the shore between Gaza and Joppa In the times that Christianity flourished in these parts, it was made an episcopal see, and continued a fair village till the days of St Jerom

Asphaltites, Lake of or the Dead Sea, is called also the Salt Sea Much has been said and supposed of this lake, or (as most will have it) infamous lake, that nothing will sink in it, and that it rose up from the subversion of the vale of Siddim, where once, as is most generally concluded, stood the cities of Sodom and Gomorrah On this account it has been abhorred as the representation of an everlasting monument of the divine judgment to deter man and from the sins committed by those who drew down on them such remarkable vengeance As to this lake's several names, it was called Asphaltites from the quantity of bitumen in and about it It is supposed that great quantities of this combustible fuel are thrown up by this lake, and that it is in great plenty on the shores of it. It resembles pitch and cannot readily be distinguished from it by the sulphureousness of its smell and

[illegible]eceived the light of the gospel from the earliest time But in many parts it was much clouded, long before the grand impostor Mahomet, their countryman, appeared. and, upon their being subdued by the Turks, they all embraced his religion, as best suited their depraved inclinations

Aram The name Aram is constantly in Scripture the name of Syria and the Syrians are called Aramæans in divers places thereof Several authors agree that the people now called Syrians were antiently called Aramæans and Aramæins Agreeably hereto, the adjoining countries into which the posterity of Aram might spread took his name, with some other additional ones joined to it

Arbela, so famed in history for the battle fought near Gaugamela, in its neighbourhood, which last, being [illegible] an inconsiderable village, the city Arbela was chosen by [illegible] to give name to that celebrated fight between Darius and Alexander, which proved the decisive stroke for the Persian empire Arbela is by some placed in Persia, [illegible] with more [illegible] Assyria Propria, or Adiabene Its plain is described as being 15 [illegible] in extent, watered with several rivulets, and producing great variety of fine [illegible], and the [illegible] where the ancient [illegible] stood are covered with stately oaks

Armenia Authors differ concerning the origin whence this track derived its name It was anciently divided into the Greater and Less, or Armenia Major and Minor The former was one of the greatest provinces of Asia Minor The soil of this country is, [illegible], mountainous, yet the hills are here and there interspersed with [illegible] and most beautiful dales and valleys All sorts of grain are very indifferent, and [illegible] they [illegible] the conveniency of watering their lands, they would be almost [illegible] What the country produces is almost entirely owing to painful labour, being either [illegible] by hand, or by digging trenches &c for the [illegible] of the [illegible] The cold is so [illegible] that all [illegible] of fruits are more backward than in most of the northern countries The hills are covered with [illegible] and it sometimes falls even in the month of [illegible] The earth of this country produces an excellent medicine, viz that which from the name of this territory, receives its own surname *Bole Armeniac*, which was anciently, as well as at present, [illegible] and was by Galen [illegible] introduced into medicine, [illegible] success in the time of a terrible plague at Rome We have no [illegible] of the laws of the Armenians, [illegible] to form any particular idea of them As to their religion we are [illegible], for a writer of credit [illegible] us [illegible] the same deities with the Medes and Persians, which will be specified hereafter We have [illegible] no authority for their learning in arts Their language [illegible] much the same with that of the Syrians at least they [illegible] the Syriac characters The modern Armenians [illegible] two languages, the learned and the vulgar the former (as they say) having no affinity with any other oriental language Though the modern Armenians are now perhaps [illegible] greatest traders on the earth yet we find no mention of any commerce carried on by them in antient times [illegible] king of Persia, is said to have been the first who considering the œconomy and indefatigable industry of this people, put them upon trade, and settled a colony of them in Julfa, the famous suburb of Ispahan This place contains at present above 30,000 inhabitants, all Armenians and merchants In the reign of Justinian II the Saracens subdued Armenia, and held it till the irruption of the Turks, who possessed themselves of this country, and called it Turcomania, but the eastern part of it is subject to the Persians at this day Nor was the extirpation of the royal race of Armenia absolutely effected, for we find it had kings again of its own even after such conquests by Saracens, Turks, Tartars, &c And in our own chronicles we find mention of Leo, king of Armenia, who in the reign of Richard II came into England to sue for aid against the Turks, who had driven him from his kingdom

Armenia Minor may be described as in most instances similar to Armenia Major, so that it may suffice to observe, that, after a variety of revolutions through a succession of ages, it was, by Vespasian, made a province of the Roman empire, and so continued till the division of the same, when it became subject to the emperors of the east, and, on the decline of their power, it was first invaded by the Persians, and afterwards by the Turks who gave it the name of Genech, and have held it ever since.

Arnon The brook or torrent of Arnon ran along between the countries of the Ammonites and Moabites, and discharged itself into the Black Sea The river Arnon is supposed to have been the first northern boundary of the Israelites on the other side of Jordan

Ascalon, in Palestine ([illegible] country of the Philistines) is a great and noble [illegible] to the north [illegible] of Gaza, and known to us still by the same name It occurs in Scripture, and in the writings of the antient Greeks and Romans, by whom it was [illegible] This city, as well as Gaza, [illegible] into the lot or tribe of Judah, and [illegible] but not held Its name [illegible] cannot be disputed, since it may be said to stand at this day, and has been often visited Ascalon was famous among [illegible] on [illegible] accounts It was the birth-[illegible] of Semiramis, the Assyrian empress It stood for the [illegible] producing the kind of onion called [illegible] which is supposed from thence to have [illegible] It may seem at first sight to be a very [illegible] derivation, but it is observed that the Latin of this [illegible] is *ascalonia*, whence the French have their *Eschalote*, which we have corrupted into *Shalot* It is also famed for its [illegible] and very remarkable for the great flights of pigeons [illegible] with respect to the remarkables of Ascalon, we must not forget to mention the cypress-[illegible], which [illegible] for the extraordinary [illegible] tributed to Ascalon and Ifaac This city had, in the first times of Christianity, an episcopal see, and in the course of the holy wars, it was beautified with a new wall, and many [illegible] buildings, by king Richard I But it is now dwindled [illegible] to nothing The Turks call it Scalona, [illegible] is [illegible] no more except for a Turkish garrison [illegible]

Ashdod, or Azotus, was a city of the Philistines, [illegible] of Ascalon and of extraordinary strength [illegible] It stood in a country which produced great plenty of corn Here was the temple of Dagon [illegible] worshipped He seems to have been [illegible] great [illegible] and from [illegible] they [illegible] attributed the [illegible] of bread-corn [illegible] culture [illegible], the word Dagon [illegible] This Ashdod of the Old Testament [illegible] Azotus in the New, as well as in the book of the Maccabees It lies near the shore between Gaza and Joppa In the times that Christianity flourished [illegible] it was made an episcopal see, and continued [illegible] till the days of St Jerom.

Asphaltites, Lake or the Dead Sea, is called also the Salt Sea Much has been said [illegible] of this [illegible] or (as most will have it) infamous lake, that [illegible] all [illegible], that it [illegible] the vale of Siddim, where once, as is most [illegible] concluded, stood the cities of Sodom and Gomorrah On this account it has been abhorred and [illegible] an everlasting monument of the [illegible] from [illegible] who [illegible] on them such fierce [illegible] As to this lake's several names it was called [illegible] from [illegible] quantity of [illegible] great quantities of this combustible [illegible] thrown up by this sea, and [illegible] it is in great plenty on the shores of it [illegible] pitch, and cannot readily be distinguished [illegible] it by the sulphureousness of its smell and

tain. It is called the Dead Sea, because it produces no[illegible] [illegible] nothing that has life [illegible] is ex[illegible] [illegible] is called the Salt Sea, as being [illegible] impregnated with salt, in such [illegible] in specific gravity, to be as [illegible] beyond the water [illegible] impossible to [illegible] The same [illegible] the [illegible] an unpleasant bitter [illegible] and this [illegible] we are told of it it pre[illegible] though it [illegible] in its present state, is enclosed on the east and west with exceeding high mountains, on the north, it has the Plain of Jericho, or (the case in both sides of Jordan) the Great Plain properly so called, and on the south it is open, and extends beyond the reach of the eye

B.

BABEL [illegible] the sons of Noah, on their arrival in a [illegible] of Shinar, began to think of build[illegible] [illegible] motive to this undertaking [illegible] second deluge, and to have [illegible] But this enterprize be[illegible] Almighty, they were obliged to [illegible] they had [illegible] it, then [illegible] could not under[illegible] [illegible] the city took [illegible] confusion, whereupon the [illegible] [illegible] name is [illegible]

[illegible] Some authors make queen Semiramis [illegible] Belus the first founder of this renowned city [illegible] most to be depended on [illegible] generally agree, that it was vastly en[illegible] and made the wonder of the world by Nebuchadnezzar. The most famous works were the walls, the city, the temple of Belus, his palace, with the gardens, the banks of the river, and the artificial lake and canals made for the draining of [illegible] the magnificence and expence of which works he much exceeded whatever had been done by any king before him, and, excepting the walls of China, nothing like it hath been since attempted [illegible] a traveller, in [illegible] which he wrote about the middle of the twelfth [illegible] tells us, that he was on the spot where the city of [illegible] stood and [illegible] some ruins of Ne[illegible] [illegible] the [illegible] and [illegible] Another, in [illegible] Italy, tells us that [illegible] there was [illegible] remaining of this [illegible] and that the place on which it stood [illegible] the [illegible] in all that country A [illegible] confirms the accounts of the former, observing, that the village of [illegible] stands in the place where formerly Babylon, the metropolis of Chaldea, stood, that the country is so dry and barren that it cannot be tilled, and so bare, that he should have doubted, very much, whether this potent city, (which was the most famous and [illegible] of the world, situated in the pleasant and fruitful country of Shinar,) stood in that place, if he had not known it by its situation and several antiquities still to be seen in that neighbourhood, particularly the old bridge, which was laid over the Euphrates, whereof there were some arches still remaining, built of burnt brick and wonderfully strong." He adds, that, just before the village of [illegible] the [illegible] stood, and that the ruins of its fortresses were still to be seen and to shew, that [illegible] from the castle stood the tower of Babylon, but [illegible] full of venomous reptiles, that nobody dares come within half a mile of it, except in two of the winter months, when the insects keep within their holes [illegible] shews how fully the predictions of the prophets, relating to this place, have been accomplished It was first called Seleucia Babylonia or Seleucia in the province of Babylon, to distinguish it from several other cities in different provinces bearing the name Seleucia Afterwards it was known by the name of Babylonia, and at length by that of Babylon As [illegible] was drained of its inhabitants by Seleucia, [illegible] Seleucia, in process of time, by Ctesiphon and [illegible] and these again by Bagdat This last city was first built [illegible] same place where Seleucia, or new Babylon stood, which gave rise to the common error, that Bagdat stands on the ruins of old Babylon

With respect to the Babylonian government it was monarchical and despotic, their laws accordingly vague and uncertain, their punishments unfixed, arbitrary, and rigorous to the utmost Their religion was [illegible] idolatry and some at least of their customs (even religious ones) shockingly brutal

BAHURIM This place is remarkable for two circumstances the first as the place where Phaltiel, to whom Saul had given Michal the wife of David, followed her weeping, when Ishbosheth restored her to her first husband The other on account of Shemei's behaviour here towards David, when he fled from his son Absalom It appears from the particulars mentioned as relative to these circumstances that Bahurim was near the mount of Olives and consequently not far from Jerusalem to the east, and situate within the tribe of Benjamin

BARIS Hyrcanus is said to have built the strong tower, or rather castle of Baris, the same which served afterwards for a palace for the Asmonean princes and was some time after re-built, enlarged, and fortified by Herod It is to be noticed, that St Jerome, in his commentary on those sacred books, which were written on the Babylonish captivity, such as those of Daniel, Ezra, Nehemiah, &c observes the word Baris to be of Chaldee extraction peculiar to Palestine, and to signify an house or castle enclosed on every side

BEER-SHEBA In Genesis we learn that Abraham, having entered into a solemn league of friendship with Abimelech, king of the Philistines, to secure his property in a well he had dug, to guard against the outrage of the Philistines, who had taken several wells from him before and to ratify the treaty [illegible] presented the king with seven sheep, &c Then taking seven young sheep, he desired him to accept of them as a token that he had [illegible] well, and that he should from thenceforth [illegible] enjoy it On this occasion this place was called Beer-sheba, or, The Well of the Oath because of the covenant they had sworn there From this Beer, or well, the city, or considerable town in process of time built near it, was called Beer-sheba, which was the utmost bound of the Land of Promise on the south, as Dan was towards the north, whence came the proverb from Dan to Beer-sheba This city was one of those that fell to the tribe of Simeon, but because Simeon had his inheritance in the midst of the tribe of Judah therefore Beer-sheba is also numbered amongst the cities of Judah

BELUS or the Kav-[illegible], as it is called at present, is a river having its sources about four miles to the [illegible] of the head [illegible] Acre, or Ptolemais, in Palestine It is [illegible] for its sands, being not only an excellent material for the making of glass, but also [illegible] the first occasion or hint of [illegible]

BERACHAH [illegible] valley in the wilderness of Tekoa, called the *Valley of Blessing* or [illegible], because of the miraculous rout of the Moabites, Ammonites, and Edomites or inhabitants of Mount Seir, who combined together against Jehoshaphat

BERENICE was a maritime city of Cyrenaica once an archbishopric, and one of the five cities from which the region had the appellation of Pentapolis, situated between the promontory Barcum, towards the greater Syrtis, and the city Arsinoe to the east, from whence it is called. It had its name from queen Berenice, wife of Ptolemy III. Here were the gardens of the Hesperides, so celebrated by the ancients, as also the famous sacred grove. There was another Berenice, in like manner so named by Ptolemy, but also in honour of his queen. It was situated near the Arabian Gulph, and is now called Suaquem.

BERYTUS, [illegible] city of Phoenicia, near mount Libanus, [illegible] called [illegible] Beroe. It had a good port. After having been ruined, it was restored by Augustus Caesar, who made a colony of it, which was called Julia Felix, and enjoyed the Roman right. Agrippa conducted two legions thither, and Herod also granted it many favours. Though it might be, and really was, in [illegible] time, famous on divers accounts, yet it was so for none more than its being one of those three cities where only the law was publicly taught, the other two being Rome and Constantinople. To prove this we may here produce the express declaration of Justinian in these words: "We may command these three volumes, composed by us, "to be delivered only in the royal cities, viz. Rome and "Constantinople, and the fair city of Berytus, (which may "properly be called the nurse of the laws,) as has been "appointed by former princes, and in no other places than "these, which have merited this privilege from our an-"cestors." These words inform us that Justinian's predecessors fixed the number of schools of law to three, but we cannot ascertain the time when it was by them so done. It is now a place of trade and a stage for the caravans that go to and from Grand Cairo.

BETHEL. In Gen. xxviii. we read that Jacob, in his journey to Padan-aram, being overtaken by the night, lay in the open field, with a stone for his pillow. In his sleep he had a dream of a ladder reaching from the earth to heaven, on which angels ascended and descended, while the Almighty encouraged him with a promise of [illegible] his protection, &c. Awaking, surprized and astonished, he cried out, "Surely God is in this place, and I knew it not;" wherefore he gave it the name of Bethel, signifying the House of God. [illegible] plain, therefore, that this was the first time, as well as the occasion, that the place had this name, it being added that it was called Luz at the first, as its former name. This same city was made choice of by Jeroboam for setting up one of his golden calves, whereupon Hosea (alluding to the name given it by Jacob) calls it Bethaven, instead of Bethel, i. e. the *House of Vanity*, instead of the *House of God*. Not that it was the town Bethaven properly so called. Bethel being within the lot of Ephraim, the son of Joseph, belonged to the kingdom of Israel, after the ten tribes revolted from the house of David, and lay in the southern border of that kingdom, not far from Jerusalem. But it was taken from the kingdom of Israel by Abijah, king of Judah, and after that accounted as a part of the kingdom of Judah. Bacchides fortified it in the time of the Maccabees.

BETHLEHEM, the city of David of old, is famous for being the birth-place not only of that renowned king, but of Our Blessed Saviour himself, who, according to the flesh, descended from him. This place was called Ephrath, or Ephratah, sometimes Bethlehem Ephratah, and sometimes Bethlehem Judah, to distinguish it from another Bethlehem, lying in the tribe of Zebulun. It is situated about six or seven miles from Jerusalem to the southward, in the way to Hebron. Bethlehem, though now but thinly inhabited, is seated on a pleasant hill, enjoys an excellent air, and, [illegible] has been much honoured by Christians of all nations, on account of its being the place of Our Blessed Saviour's birth, so it is very [illegible] visited by pilgrims and travellers. It is furnished not only with a convent of the Latins, but also with one of the Greeks, and another of the Armenians, the two latter being contiguous to the former.

BETHORON, mentioned in several places of scripture, was [illegible] towards [illegible] Jerusalem, and between that metropolis and the [illegible]. It is to be noted, that [illegible] express mention of two Bethorons in the Chronicles, where we are told that a woman of the tribe of Ephraim, by name Sherah, built Bethoron the nether and the upper. [illegible] accordingly agreed among writers, that they [illegible] within the bounds of the tribe of Ephraim. But [illegible] in what part of the tribe each lay, some placing [illegible] the upper in the north border of the tribe, whilst others place them nearer one to another, and both in the south border.

BETHSAIDA. Bethsaida, in Hebrew, imports a place of fishing, or else of hunting, and both senses agree [illegible] with the situation of the city, for it lay on the lake of Gennesareth, just at the influx of the river Jordan [illegible] said lake, and so lay very convenient for fishing [illegible] conveniently situated for hunting. [illegible] tribe of Naphtali, a country well stored [illegible] but a village, till Philip the tetrarch [illegible] and appearance of a [illegible] city, [illegible] to which he gave also the name [illegible] to Julia, the daughter of [illegible] eastern shore, and [illegible] been [illegible] from the [illegible] [illegible] ed, [illegible] [illegible] denounced [illegible] upon it, it being reduced [illegible] poor village, or hardly that, consisting [illegible] few poor cottages.

BETHSAN is a city belonging to the [illegible] of Manasseh, on the west of Jordan, and [illegible] the sea of Galilee. It is called Bethshan by the [illegible]. The Canaanites kept possession of it, and it was [illegible] able city in the [illegible] after the [illegible] [illegible] mountain of Gilboa. The Greeks [illegible] Scythopolis, and [illegible] anciently inhabited by the Scythians [illegible] to Herodotus, had, in the reign of [illegible] Egypt and Cyaxares, king of Media, extended [illegible] quests as far as Syria and Palestine. It is [illegible] the eastern [illegible] of [illegible]

BETHSHEMESH, a town belonging to the [illegible] Judah, lay [illegible] the north border, not far [illegible] Kirjath-jearim.

BETHSURA, so called from being [illegible] rock, was a very strong fortress in the time of [illegible]. It was in the tribe of Judah, and had [illegible] fortified by king Rehoboam, being one of [illegible] on the south side of Judah. That [illegible] walls, and other fortifications to [illegible] keep the [illegible] Danites in awe, but the Maccabees added [illegible] as to render the place impregnable. On the top of [illegible] where stood Bethsura, is now the [illegible] and though the adjacent parts are [illegible] they still produce plenty of corn, wine, [illegible]

BEZEC is mentioned, in Judges, as the place where the men of Judah and Simeon [illegible] the Canaanites and Perizzites, and where the [illegible] also Bezec [illegible] his [illegible] scripture as the place where Saul [illegible] the army wherewith he gave the Ammonites a signal overthrow.

BEZETHA was the name given, by king Agrippa, to a new quarter, which, [illegible] would have [illegible] and fortified, [illegible] the city of Jerusalem, the name importing the new city. [illegible] to procure the emperor's leave to surround [illegible] with a strong wall, which if he had obtained, it would have rendered the metropolis absolutely impregnable But the danger of the design being represented to Claudius, orders were sent to Agrippa to desist

BOTRYS, now called Patron and Elpatron, on the coast of Phœnicia, was a very antient town, founded by Ithobold, king of Sidon, and situated near the promontory, called by the antients, Penie, and, by modern pilots, Capo Pagio Under the Christian emperors it became an episcopal see but it has fared so ill since, that there are few traces of its former state remaining, some ruins of churches and two monasteries excepted, the rest consisting of a number of poor cots, inhabited chiefly by fishermen, scarcely deserving to be called a village

C

CÆSAREA This city was raised by Herod, upon a certain place by the sea-side, called Straton's Tower, as being deemed a very commodious tract of ground for that purpose It was completed at an immense charge and was the paragon of elegance and magnificence But the master-piece was the port, which was made as large as the Pyræum, and a safe station against all winds and weathers, not to mention other conveniences It stood in Phœnicia, upon the pass into Egypt between Joppa and Dora, two sea ports, where the south-west wind beats so furiously, that there is no riding in the harbours without being subject to imminent danger Herod therefore, to encounter this difficulty, ordered a mole to be made in form of a half moon, and large enough for a royal navy to ride in This mole was two hundred furlongs in extent one half was designed to break the setting of the sea, and the other half for the foundation of a stone wall, fortified with turrets, calling the largest of them, the Tower of Drusus, from Drusus, the son-in-law of Augustus, who died young In fine nothing was wanting that could contribute to grandeur, safety, or convenience On a mount in the middle stood a temple dedicated to Cæsar, which was of great use to mariners as a sea mark In this temple there were two statues, the one of Rome, the other of Cæsar, and from hence the city took the name of Cæsarea Though it is called Cæsarea in the New Testament, yet it is frequently stiled, by way of distinction from others of the same name, Cæsarea Palestine, as being the metropolis of Palestine, and seat of the Roman proconsul Here it was that St Peter converted Cornelius and his kinsmen, the first fruits of the Gentiles Here lived Philip the apostle Here Paul defended himself against the Jews and their orator Tertullus, and here, in the amphitheatre, it was that Herod Antipas was smitten by an angel, as appears from the Acts of the Apostles As for the times after the New Testament, here was born Eusebius, the learned historian and chronologer, who was bishop of this city in the beginning of the fourth century, and in the reign of Constantine the Great, to whom he made a celebrated oration It was situated between Ptolemais to the north, and Joppa to the south, and was about twenty-six miles to the westward of Jerusalem It was of old inhabited partly by Jews, and partly by idolatrous Greeks, who were perpetually at daggers drawing against each other, and ever hatching some new sedition, till Vespasian took it, and put a Roman colony into it

CÆSAREA PHILIPPI was formerly, by heathen writers, called Paneas, the place where the Jordan had its spring head, which Philip, the brother of Antipas, (Herod) having greatly enlarged and beautified, called it by this new name after his own

CANA of Galilee (so called to distinguish it from Cana, belonging to the tribe of Asher, lying not far from Sidon) mentioned John ii 1 lay within the tribe of Zebulun, not far from Nazareth It was the native, or, at least, dwelling place of Nathaniel, otherwise called Bartholomew; for the Evangelist John expresly stiles him Nathaniel of Cana of Galilee

CANAAN has been successively known by several names, as the Land of Israel, the Land of God, the Holy Land, and simply the Land, also Judea, Palestine, Syria, Cœlo-Syria, Idumea, and Phœnicia It was called the Land of the Hebrews, and sometimes the Land of the Jews It was called the Land of God, as given by him to the posterity of Abraham, and the place of more especial choice It was called the Holy Land, first by the Jews, as solely appropriated to the service of God under their dispensation, and, secondly, by Christians, as was the scene of what was wrought for theirs and the worlds salvation Whence came its appellation of Judea is seemingly plain Judah, being chief of the tribes, communicated its name to the rest, and the kingdom of Judah standing after the dissolution of that of Israel, may have given farther ground for the extensive and general use of this name It was called Palestine, as being a part of that track very early so denominated Though this name properly belonged to no more than what is commonly called the Pentapolis of the Philistines, it had the fortune to spread itself over almost all the neighbouring regions

CAPERNAUM was a city, situated on an eminence by the lake of Genesareth It took its name from an adjoining spring, of great repute for its chrystaline flowing water, which was called by the natives, the Fountain of Capernaum As the excellence of this fountain was probably one inducement to build the town, so there seems to have been another motive for chusing the situation, viz its convenience for a wafting place from Galilee to the other side of the sea

CARMEL (Mount) on the west coast of the Holy Land, at the south-east end of the tribe of Asher, ten miles from Acre, or Ptolemais, is the most remarkable head of land on all the coast Its name Carmel, we are told, was common both to a town and a mountain

CHALCIS, capital of the island of Chalcis in Negropont, stood on the narrowest part of the Euripus, being joined to Bœotia by a bridge, which situation agrees with that of the present city of Negropont It was celebrated by all the antients, as a most magnificent, populous, and wealthy city

CHARRAN, mentioned in Genesis and there called Haran, in memory as it is said, of Haran, the son of Terah, brother of Abraham and father of Lot, was situated in the west or north-west part of Mesopotamia, on a river which runs into the Euphrates It was, with little alteration called Carræ by the Romans

CITIUM, antiently a town in Cyprus, was the birthplace of Zeno the famous stoic

CŒLO-SYRIA Antient geographers differ as to the bounds of what is meant by Cœlo-Syria, but the preference is given to Strabo, who tells us, that Cœlo-Syria was between Libanus and Anti-Libanus which, however the name may be extended was undoubtedly the proper Cœlo-Syria The principal cities are Heliopolis, (now Balbeck,) and Damascus, (now Sham)

COMAGENA, the third division of Syria Propria, was so called from its capital, long since destroyed, after which it was, by the Romans, called Euphratensis, from its situation near the Euphrates It was bounded on the north by Cilicia and the Lesser Armenia, on the west by part of Cilicia, on the south by Cœlo-Syria, and on the east by the Euphrates The principal cities in this province were Samosata, (now Scempsat,) Germanicia, Catamana, Deba, Dolicha, Chaonia, and Chelmadura, of the greater part of which little else is left but the names, and here and there some ruins of monuments, by which one may know where they stood

COPTOS, an ancient city of Thebais, having been the chief residence of the native Egyptians for many ages, since their country has been subjected to a foreign power, and [illegible] received their present name of Copts [illegible] Dioclesian.

CYPRUS [illegible] anciently known by various names. It was called Acamas, from one of its promontories, Amathus, Paphos, and Salamina, from three of its [illegible] cities, Macaria, from the [illegible] of its soil, Æroa, from its copper mines, Cerastis, from its [illegible] hills, Sphecia, [illegible] the Sphecces, and Cerastis [illegible] the many promontories, which, like so many horns, (as the Greek word imports) shoot into the [illegible] Cyprus [illegible] four districts, denominated from [illegible] cities of each, before which cities [illegible] were [illegible] to 800 [illegible] The honey of this island [illegible] much commended, as also the wine, oil, wool, and, above all, the copper. [illegible] the Phœnicians, about two or three generations, according to Sir Isaac Newton's computation, before Minos [illegible] Minor, king of Crete, [illegible] Cyprus [illegible] could not [illegible] of copper, and [illegible] when they began to [illegible] the Mediterranean, (soon [illegible] they used [illegible] great [illegible] They gave [illegible] the [illegible] of the [illegible] Cyrene [illegible] subject to the Ptolemies [illegible] the [illegible] [illegible] It was [illegible] 1194 [illegible] given [illegible] Jerusalem [illegible] generations. The [illegible] in It [illegible] the Turks [illegible] Venetians [illegible] it with [illegible] ance, were [illegible] The [illegible] title of king of Cyprus [illegible] hundred [illegible] out by [illegible] this [illegible] of the [illegible] the Mediterranean, and extends along the north coast of Cilicia, from east to west [illegible] 200 miles. The country was once very fruitful [illegible] though the climate is not very temperate, being excessive hot and sultry in summer, insomuch that [illegible] dries up all the springs, for the [illegible] what rains produce, which happening to fail thirty years successively, during the reign of Constantine the Great, the inhabitants were obliged to abandon the [illegible] for some time. It is likewise much infested with locusts which hover in the air like a cloud, darkening the [illegible] and sometimes devour [illegible] driven into the sea by the [illegible] Considering [illegible] such as the severity of the Turkish government, the country is thinly peopled and [illegible] Yet near the cities, there [illegible] every thing necessary and delightful, [illegible] Here is very good hunting, and [illegible] variety of game. The chief manufactures are cotton and wool, which are the best in all the east. They have [illegible] but not so good in proportion. They have [illegible] great quantities of [illegible] till one of their [illegible] burnt up all the [illegible] The inhabitants have been always branded for an excessive dissoluteness of manners. The men are accounted [illegible] Here we must note, when [illegible] reduced the island, he murdered, or carried off, all the nobility and gentry, and left none but the meaner sort to continue in it, and these are mostly Greeks, [illegible] after the [illegible] but retaining their old customs and religion. [illegible] are interdicted the island on account of a [illegible] in Trajan's reign, in which they massacred 250 000 of the inhabitants. Cyprus has no [illegible] rivers, and the most noted mountain is that called Olympus. Here is a pretty brisk trade between the [illegible] of Europe and Asia, and several European nations have their consuls and factors in the island.

CYRENE, [illegible] Cyrenaica, the metropolis of [illegible] situated at some distance from the sea, [illegible] in [illegible] present [illegible] [illegible] life. [illegible] Greeks, [illegible] Cyrene derived its name from [illegible] Cyre, near which it was situated. [illegible] Cyrenaics [illegible] the philosopher [illegible] Carneades, the philosopher, [illegible] mentioned by St. Luke.

CYRENIAN JEWS. [illegible] Alexander the Great, in [illegible] Egypt, [illegible] [illegible] Jerusalem [illegible] when the Jews [illegible] [illegible] But [illegible] [illegible] they [illegible] [illegible] Strabo [illegible] keep [illegible] [illegible] and in [illegible] their [illegible] [illegible] they [illegible] enjoyed under the Macedonians [illegible] to fill his [illegible] provisions [illegible] Cyrene [illegible] to [illegible] From [illegible] [illegible] of [illegible] (See 2 Maccabees [illegible]) [illegible] were those Cyrenians [illegible] mentioned in the [illegible] [illegible] to death, [illegible] [illegible] the whole [illegible] inhabitants [illegible] were [illegible] though this [illegible] Cyrenaica was [illegible] to [illegible] people.

D

DAGON, Temple of [illegible] tion of his image, [illegible]

DAMASCUS is the capital of [illegible] the part of [illegible] It is the most [illegible] place [illegible] whole world, being generally agreed to [illegible] by Uz, son of Aram, and grandson of Shem, [illegible] Noah [illegible] the birth-place of [illegible] [illegible] Abraham [illegible] [illegible] the kings of Syria [illegible] [illegible] king of [illegible] Rome [illegible] kings of Syria, and [illegible] his dominions to his own [illegible] sequence of which, [illegible]

Coptos, an antient city of Thebais, having been the chief residence of the native Egyptians for many ages since their country has been subjected to a foreign power, and whence they received their present name of Copts. It was ruined by Dioclesian.

Cyprus island was antiently known by various names. It was called Acamas, from one of its promontories; Amathus, Paphos, and Salaminia, from three of its antient cities; Macaria, from the fruitfulness of its soil; Ærosa, from its copper mines; Colinia, from its many hills; Sphecia, from its antient inhabitants the Sphecees; and Cerastis, from the many promontories which, like so many horns, (as the Greek word imports) shoot into the sea. Cyprus was, by antient geographers, divided into four districts, denominated from the chief cities of each, besides which cities, and other less ones, there were no fewer than 800 villages. The honey of this island was much commended, as also the wine, oil, wool, and, above all, the copper. It was first discovered by the Phœnicians, about two or three generations, according to Sir Isaac Newton's computation, before Asterius and Minor, kings of Crete, i. e. about 1000 years before Christ. It was so overgrown with wood that it could not be tilled, and they first cut it down for the melting of copper, and afterwards, when they began to sail without fear on the Mediterranean, (soon after the Trojan war,) they used to build ships even great navies. They gave every man leave to cut down what trees he pleased, and possess all the cleared ground. In time, the inhabitants, invited by the serenity of the soil, [illegible]. The government was, without doubt, monarchical, being governed by no less than nine kings, when Cyrus the Great, by his lieutenants, first conquered it. It afterwards became subject to the Ptolemies of Egypt, from them [illegible] to the Romans [illegible] Constantinople [illegible] perors. It was next conquered by [illegible] A. D. 1194, in his way to the Holy Land, and the [illegible] given by him to Guy of Lusignan, the titular king of Jerusalem, whose posterity reigned in it [illegible] four generations. [illegible] that [illegible] line, seized it in 1420 [illegible] Solyman II claiming it as lord of Egypt [illegible] Famagusta, the strongest [illegible] it. The Venetians defended it with uncommon bravery, but, for want of timely assistance, were forced to surrender, the [illegible] honourable terms. The rest were soon reduced, and it has groaned under the Turkish yoke ever since. The dukes of Savoy claim the title of king of Cyprus [illegible] from Lewis, second husband of Charlotte, [illegible] of James, the 13th king in descent from Guy [illegible], who had been put out by James, her husband's brother. But to the knowledge of this island [illegible] its modern state, [illegible] by far the largest of all those of Asia Minor. [illegible] the bottom of the Mediterranean, and extends along the south coast of Cilicia, from east to west about 150 or 200 miles. The country was once very fruitful, as above hinted, though the climate is not very temperate, being excessive hot and sultry in summer, insomuch that it sometimes dries up all the springs, for there are no springs or rivers, but what rains produce, which happening to fail thirty years successively during the reign of Constantine the Great, the inhabitants were obliged to abandon the island for some time. It is [illegible] much infested with locusts, which hover in the air like clouds during the hot season, and sometimes devour all the corn and fruit, but are often driven into the sea by the winds. On these accounts, as well as the severity of the Turkish government, the country is thinly peopled, and is [illegible] cultivated, in most parts. Yet, near the cities, it not only produces every thing necessary, and delightful, but seems to enjoy a perpetual spring. Here is very good hunting, and a great variety of game. The chief manufactures are cotton and wool, which are the best in all the east. They have likewise silk, but not so good in proportion. They had formerly great quantities of sugar, till one of their bashaws burnt up all the canes. [illegible] inhabitants have been always branded for an excessive dissoluteness of manners. The men are accounted warlike, robust, active, and hospitable. Here we must note, when Solyman reduced the island, he murdered, or carried off, all the nobility and gentry, and left none but the meaner sort to continue in it, and these are mostly Greeks, clad after the Italian manner, but retaining their old customs and religion. Jews are interdicted the island, on account of an attempt they made on it in Trajan's reign, in which they murdered 250,000 of the inhabitants. Cyprus has no considerable rivers, and the most noted mountain is that called Olympus. Here is a pretty brisk trade between the merchants of Europe and Asia, and several European nations have their consuls and factors in the island.

Cyrene, also Cyrenum, or Cyrene, the metropolis of Cyrenaica, stood at some distance from the sea, and not in figure representing a table. It was large and populous, abounding with all the elegancies as well as necessaries of life. This territory produced great numbers of excellent horses, which probably made the Cyreneans, whether natives or Greeks, apply themselves to the study and practice of every thing relating to those animals, more than most others. Cyrene derived its name from the fountain Cyre, near which it was situated. Aristippus, founder of the sect of Cyrenaics, Eratosthenes, the geographer, and Carneades the philosopher, were all natives of Cyrene, as was also Simon mentioned by St Luke.

Cyrenian Jews. Ptolemy, immediately after the death of Alexander the Great, as king of Egypt, with a powerful army, laid siege to Jerusalem in the year of the world 3687, before Christ 317, when the Jews, out of a superstitious notion of violating the sabbath, suffered the city to be taken by storm on that day without resistance. Near 100,000 of them were by him carried away captives into Egypt. But reflecting upon their known loyalty to their former conquerors, and the sacred regard they paid to their oaths, and having taken this city, becoming master of Judea and Samaria, committed the keeping of several garrisons, both there and in Egypt, to them, and having made them swear allegiance, he endowed them with the same privileges they had enjoyed under the Macedonians. Of those whom he carried away, he chose about 30,000 of the stoutest to fill his garrisons; the rest he sent to settle, furnishing them with provisions, others to Libya and Cyrene just spoken of, of which he had made conquest, and annexed it to Egypt, four years before. From these were descended the Cyrenian Jews, among whom was Jason, author of the history of the Maccabees, in five books, [illegible] out of which the second book of the Maccabees is an epitome. (See 2 Macc. ii. 23.) Of the same country were those Cyrenian Jews mentioned in the Acts. This Jewish colony grew in time so numerous, as to have 100,000 of them put to death, for one insurrection, in the time of Vespasian; and yet, in a succeeding reign, they proved strong enough to master the whole province, and massacre 200,000 inhabitants of other nations. Their rage and their cruelty were boundless, so that, through this and other massacres, Cyrenaica was next to quite dispeopled.

D

Dagon, Temple of, see Gaza; and, for a description of his image, see Idol.

Damascus is the capital of the fourth part of Syria. It is the most remarkable place for antiquity now in the whole world, being generally agreed to have been built by Uz, son of Aram, and grandson of Shem, the son of Noah, and was the birth-place of Eliezer, the steward of Abraham. It is famous, in scripture, for being the residence of the kings of Syria 300 years, till Tiglath-pileser, king of Assyria, slew Rezin, the last king of Syria, and added his dominions to his own new empire, in consequence of which, the Syrian kingdom passed to the

Persian and to the Grecian, till the Saracens conquered it, and made this city their royal residence. In this state it continued till Bagdat was built, at which time it was very strong and flourishing. It became afterwards a separate kingdom, under the princes of the Selzucian family, for near 200 years, which ended by the reduction of the city, and death of its last prince, by Halton, the Tartar. Its Hebrew name was Dammesech, and the Turks now call it Scham or Sham. It is situated in a fertile plain, encompassed with hills, and upon the celebrated river Chrysorrhoas (the golden stream,) called by the Syrians, Pharpar, and which encircles the city and its country with all kinds of plenty and pleasure. The emperor Julian stiled it the City of Jupiter, the Eye of the East, and added, that it excelled all others in the magnificence of its temples, temperature of its seasons, excellent fountains, number of [illegible], and fruitfulness of soil. Its territory produces the best corn, wine, and fruits, all the year, which renders the place exceeding pleasant and delightful. The city is of an oblong form, slender towards the middle, and bulges out at both ends, especially that to the north-east. It is computed [illegible] two miles in length, and is so thick set with towers, domes, fine gardens, summer-houses, terraces, &c. that it yields a most noble prospect; and, from the adjacent hills, looks like a stately city in a wood, [illegible] with a most delightful and constant verdure, occasioned by the vast quantity of water with which the river Barrady supplies both town and country. The public buildings bear a much better outside than the private. The chief of all is the great mosque, formerly a Christian church, built by the emperor Heraclius, in honour of Zacharias, father of John Baptist, said to be buried in it. This mosque is reckoned one of the most stately in all Turkey, into which it is death for any but a Mussulman to enter. The city has separate wards for every [illegible], and these are shut up every night by gates, and by a stone and chain every day, to keep off beasts of burthen. In particular here are not less than 20,000 persons employed in making scymeters, sword blades, knives, and other cutlery work, bridles, and divers other things in iron and steel, all which are in great repute for the fine temper which the Barrady water gives the metal. On one side of the city lies a [illegible] which they call the Maidan, or the Green, (*large Pinn ... [illegible]*) which is a spacious grass field, encompassed with gardens, through which runs a branch of the Barrady. On the side of this green is a spacious noble hospital for pilgrims of all religions. The building is surrounded with cloisters, adorned with small cupolas, and a great number of chambers for strangers, who are maintained at the charge of the grand seignior. There is likewise another cloister for the maintenance of poor scholars, with a mosque, and handsome gardens. On another side is a large house, where they bake biscuits for those pilgrims who travel to Mecca, out of which the sultan allows them 200 camels load, and the like quantity of water. Almost in the heart of the city is an high castle, of an oval shape, mostly of square stone, and flanked with fourteen square towers, in which are some cannon. Here are 1,500 janissaries constantly, 500 to guard the city, 500 to escort the caravan to Mecca, and 500 to attend the grand seignior when he goes to Bagdat. The city is governed by a beglerbeg, who has ten sangiacs under him, besides agas, cadis, and other officers. Damascus is the seat of a Greek patriarch, transferred hither from Antioch. It was the birth-place of the celebrated and esteemed St John, thence surnamed Damascenus. All sorts of Christians are allowed churches and their particular ceremonies here. Jews are in great numbers, and have stately synagogues. Other sects make but little figure.

DAMIETTA, or DUMIATA, in Lower Egypt, is situated on one of the east branches of the Nile. This branch and that called the Pelusiac, or utmost eastern, form a kind of small triangular island, on the west angle of which this city is situate. It is one of the most considerable for trade in the whole territory about it, and the most strong in all Egypt. It is reckoned one of the keys of Egypt, is large, though now ill-built, and contains about 25,000 inhabitants. It fell, with the rest of Egypt, under the yoke of the Saracens, who held it till 1218, when the crusaders laid siege to it, and took it the next year, but having held it three years, when the infidels, letting out the water about them, forced them to abandon it. Lewis, (surnamed Saint,) king of France, regained it in the year 1249, but having been taken prisoner about a year after, was forced to restore it for his ransom; [illegible] that the infidels might no more [illegible] such a bone of contention. It soon recovered, and is now a place of great trade, and the [illegible] under the patriarch of Alexandria. Copts and Greeks here settled have each a church, and [illegible] exercise of religion. The town is under the government of an aga, cadi, and [illegible], [illegible] by the bashaw of the province, who exacts [illegible] of their income. The inhabitants are [illegible] employed in their factories, particularly of fine linen cloth of all colours. But they [illegible] [illegible], [illegible] on account of the [illegible], (the chief [illegible] of which in Egypt was hereabout,) that they can scarce let them pass along without insult. Some have confounded Damiata with Old Pelusium, or supposed it to have been reared upon its ruins, but this error has been fully refuted.

DAN, the Tribe of, had their portion of the Land of Promise thus bounded, the Philistines and Judah on the south, Benjamin east, Ephraim, and the half tribe of Manasseh, north, and the Mediterranean west. [illegible] plain and level, but not so fruitful as that of the [illegible], having in most parts less depth of soil, and bordering on the sea [illegible] a range of mountains.

DAN, City of, [illegible] in Genesis and Deuteronomy. It was called also Laish. It was situated at the head of the Jordan, and was [illegible] accounted the utmost [illegible] of the Land of Israel as Beersheba [illegible] the south, [illegible] the expression, "From Dan [illegible]," to denote the whole length of the Holy Land [illegible] north to south. Here it was that Jeroboam placed one of his golden calves. By [illegible] writers it was called Paneas, from the adjoining spring Paneum or Panion. This Dan, with its territory, was given by Augustus to Herod the Great, who left it to Philip his youngest son, together with the tetrarchy of Iturea and Trachonitis, to which it belonged, and he repairing and beautifying it, made it his capital or at least his residence, giving it the name of Cæsarea Philippi, or the Cæsarea of Philip, to [illegible] with Tiberius Cæsar, and to distinguish it from another place of the same name.

DAPHNE, near Antioch. To the account there given of Antioch we may add, that Cæsar Gallus having out of zeal to Christianity erected a Christian church to be built here, the Daphnean Oracle immediately ceased. There were several places of this name besides the foregoing, viz. [illegible] of Egypt, near Pelusium, an island of Ethiopia, also a small region of Thessaly, through which flowed the river Peneus.

DATHEMA is the name of that fortress in the land of Gilead, mentioned in the first book of the Maccabees.

DECAPOLIS, was a canton in Palestine, so called from its [illegible] ten cities, situate some on one and some on the other side Jordan, the capital of which was Scythopolis. It was mostly inhabited by Gentiles.

DELPHOS, or Delphi, was an antient city of antient Phocis, famous for the temple of Apollo, whose oracle was resorted to by all from all parts of Europe, Asia, and Africa. Delphos, among several other cities of Greece and Peloponnesus, contended for being situate in the very middle of the world. It had so convenient a harbour, and was ſo excellently well ſituated, (being rather in the heart of Greece than of the world) that it became in time, a ſeſſions town of all the Grecian ſtates. Here ſat the court of the Amphictyones, choſen out of the prime cities of Greece, and ſo called from Amphictyon firſt founder of this [illegible] court. The time of their [illegible] was in ſpring and autumn. Cauſes of all kinds were brought before them, from all parts of Greece, and their ſentence was deemed definitive. Mention of them is frequently made in hiſtory. Conſidering therefore, the [illegible] concourſe which this court, the oracle, and the games [illegible] in honour of Apollo, brought into the city, we need not wonder at its being one of the moſt opulent of all Greece. As an inſtance of which, it may be noticed, that the gold and ſilver of which the temple was deſpoiled, (the 4th year of the 105th Olympiad) on occaſion of the Grecian holy war, [illegible], amounted to 10,000 talents, i. e. above 1,000,000 Engliſh money. Delphos was [illegible] now Caſtri, in Turkey in Europe, on the ſouth ſide of Mount Parnaſſus, where the town of Caſtri now ſtands. This modern town does not conſiſt of [illegible] 200 [illegible] and thoſe very ill built. It [illegible] vadia, about ten miles from the latter. The number of Turks is very inſignificant, though they have a [illegible] the Greeks have five or ſix churches, and are deemed a very good people, though poor. The little trade they have, conſiſts in cotton and tobacco. Their wine is exceeding good.

DELTA, or the Lower Egypt, reaching from Heptanomis to the Mediterranean Sea, contained not only that part which is compaſſed by the arms of the Nile, and, from its triangular figure, named Delta, but alſo Mareotis and Alexandria, with its dependencies, to the weſt, and Canopus, with ſome other territories towards Arabia, to the eaſt. There are various opinions and conjectures concerning the antient ſtate of this part of the [illegible], but it is [illegible] acknowledged to be the moſt fertile and beſt cultivated land in the whole kingdom of Egypt, containing above [illegible] villages, and yielding grapes and other fruits in abundance [illegible] not bearing [illegible] when the Nile, [illegible] to its uſual height, occaſion [illegible] part.

DIOSPOLIS was antiently [illegible] in Egypt. There was another [illegible] time, vulgarly called [illegible], which [illegible] the Roman general deſtroyed at the [illegible] time, and for the ſame cauſe, [illegible] ſome other adjacent places, [illegible] the frequent revolts of the Jews.

DORA, or Dor, was a maritime town, and conſiderable city, ſtrongly ſituate near Mount Carmel, on the Mediterranean Sea, whence it gave name to the country around it. It was given to the half tribe of Manaſſeh on the [illegible] the weſt ſide of Jordan. Jerome obſerves, that it was [illegible] miles from Tyre, and was gone [illegible] to decay in his time, ſo as to be uninhabited.

DOTHAN, mentioned in Gen. [illegible] was ſeated about twelve miles to the northward of Samaria. In the neighbourhood of it Joſeph was ſold, by his brethren, to the Iſhmaelites.

E

ECBATANA. As there are now no monuments remaining, either of the [illegible] ſaid to have been aſcribed to Daniel, or the proud palace where the monarchs of Aſia went to paſs the ſummer, there is great diſagreement, among our modern travellers, about the place where this ſtately metropolis ſtood. It is the opinion of many writers that Tauris is the ſame with the antient and famous Ecbatana. Our author aſſures us, that the palace built by Daniel was entire in his time, but, at preſent, not even the [illegible] of any magnificent building are to be ſeen either in Tauris, or in that neighbourhood, for, in all the [illegible] there, the materials are only earth, brick, and pebbles, which, in antient times, were never uſed in Media for building of palaces.

ECBATANA, a town in Syria, is remarkable for the death of Cambyſes, King of Perſia, there. This Cambyſes, ſon of Cyrus, is the Ahaſuerus of our bible. While he was in Egypt, having conſulted the oracle of Butus in that country, he was told that he ſhould die at Ecbatana, which he underſtanding of Ecbatana in Media, reſolved to preſerve his life by never going thither, but what he thought to avoid in Media, he found in Syria, for the town where he lay ſick of his mortal wound was of the ſame name, being alſo called Ecbatana.

EDOM. When the antient kingdom of Edom was [illegible] mentioned, it was ſuppoſed to have been bounded on the north by [illegible], and the lake Aſphaltites, on the eaſt by Midian, on the ſouth by the Arabian Gulph, or Red Sea, and on the [illegible] by Amalekites. This tract is very mountainous, and great part of it deſert. It has few or no ſtreams, but [illegible] of water for the uſe of the inhabitants who know where to find them. Corn and wine, nevertheleſs, ſeem to have been anciently in ſome degree of plenty amongſt them. So that Eſau (that is, the poſterity of Eſau, or Edom) may [illegible] have enjoyed the "fatneſs of the earth," according to his father's prophetic bleſſing, Gen. xxvii. 39. though by modern travellers this country is deemed rather [illegible] or Amalekites is by ſome reckoned to have been a part of [illegible] Edom. The cities and moſt remarkable places of [illegible] were, Teman, Dedan, Bozrah, Elath, [illegible] New, the [illegible] name of this kingdom [illegible] Idumea, is [illegible] of the [illegible] name occurs in [illegible] the modern writers, [illegible] Edom, which, long [illegible] impelled [illegible] [illegible] The [illegible] and the [illegible] were [illegible] The [illegible] [illegible] pieces [illegible], the [illegible] [illegible] [illegible] days of King David, who [illegible] were kept [illegible] [illegible] always impatient under the yoke, [illegible] [illegible] opportunity [illegible] They were a [illegible] people, fond of [illegible] [illegible] much delighted in [illegible] pleaſures [illegible]. Concerning their religion [illegible] At firſt they [illegible] and [illegible] as they were [illegible] from [illegible] circumciſion, but, by degrees, they [illegible] [illegible], and [illegible] circumciſion. [illegible] ever, [illegible] with the Jews, and were [illegible] conſidered as one nation with them in [illegible] matters. The Romans [illegible] this country after the reduction of Judea.

It [illegible] the [illegible] diſtrict in the diviſion of Syria. The Turks are now [illegible] of it, though it appears [illegible] that they maintain much, if any, government [illegible], except of the [illegible], to ſecuring the road from Egypt to Judea, where they [illegible] caſtles and villages, as Arſla, [illegible] [illegible] now inhabited by a wild [illegible] kind of Arabs, [illegible] not [illegible], ſo barbarous and rude as ſome repreſent them.

EGYPT, called by its antient inhabitants Chemia, and by the Copts [illegible], according to the general [illegible] from Ham [illegible] Chuſh, the ſon [illegible] Noah [illegible] ſided the [illegible] generally [illegible] [illegible], from whence the Arabs [illegible], which the Greeks write [illegible] [illegible] by ſome, into two parts the Upper and the Lower Egypt, by others into three, the upper, properly ſo called, or Thebais, the middle, or Heptanomis, and the lower, of which the beſt part was the Delta Thebais, now called Al Said, is the moſt ſouthern part of Egypt next to Ethiopia, and is near as large as all the reſt, including the country on both ſides the Nile down to Heptanomis, its laſt cities having been Lycopolis on the weſt, and Antceopolis on the eaſt ſide of the river, which agrees with the preſent extent of Al Said, the moſt northern city of which is Manfalut There were ſo many in this part of Egypt a great number of large and magnificent cities, with temples of ſeveral deities, and tombs of their antient princes Its metropolis, Thebes, called afterwards Diapolis, (the City of Jupiter,) was ſituate on the Nile, and deſervedly reckoned one of the fineſt cities in the world Its 100 gates are mentioned by Homer, whence it had the ſirname of Hecatompylos Its riches were ſo great, that, after it had been plundered by the Perſians, what was found, on [illegible] the remains of the pillage, amounted to above 300 talents of gold, and 2300 of ſilver Who was its founder is uncertain As the name Thebes was formerly given to all Egypt, its great power is [illegible] The Heptanomis was ſo called from the ſeven Nomes, or prefectures, into which it was divided It was full of very large and noble cities, the principal of which was Memphis built by Menes, their firſt king, and, for many ages, capital of the whole kingdom Here alſo was the lake Moeris, the Labyrinths, and the Pyramids The chief cities of the Delta were [illegible], Sais, and Xois, and in later times, Alexandria The climate of Egypt muſt needs be very warm, from its near ſituation to the tropic Though the air is generally dry, yet great dews fall after the ſwelling of the Nile, which continue for ſeveral months In the Delta it ſometimes rains a little in the winter, notwithſtanding what ſome [illegible] to the contrary, and even ſnow, it is ſaid, has been obſerved to fall at Alexandria In Upper Egypt, indeed, towards the cataracts, it rains very ſeldom The firſt ſummer, (for they reckon two,) which is in March, April and May, is the moſt inconvenient and ſickly ſeaſon, becauſe the unequal weather, exceſſive heats, and hot winds, cauſe diſtempers, but in the ſecond, June, July, and Auguſt, and in autumn and winter, the inhabitants breathe a much cooler air, the weather is more conſtant, and it is more delightful living, except from the 7th to the 14th of February, when the cold is ſo ſharp that the rich wear furs The fertility of Egypt, and the excellence of its productions and fruits, were greatly celebrated by the antients, and by Moſes himſelf in the book of Geneſis It was the granary of Old Rome, as it is now of Conſtantinople The moſt plentiful parts of the Delta, and the province now called Al Feyyum For this great fertility the land is indebted to the river Nile The ſources of this celebrated river were unknown to the antients, but they are now well known to be in Ethiopia The annual inundations of this river have been looked on as one of the great wonders of the country Antient writers tell us it begins to riſe in Egypt about the ſummer ſolſtice, and continues ſo to do till after the autumnal equinox, for about 100 days, and then it decreaſes as many, till it retires within its banks, and overflows no more till next year If the river did not riſe to 15 or 16 cubits, the country was not covered with its waters, and dearth enſued This account comes very near to thoſe of modern travellers As this river could not of itſelf overflow the lands every where in the neceſſary proportion, they have cut a vaſt number of canals however, as ſome places are too high to be watered by the canals, they are obliged to raiſe the water to cover them by engines Formerly they made uſe of Archimedes's ſcrew, thence named the Egyptian pump, but now they generally uſe wheels, which carry a rope or chain of earthen pots of about ſeven or eight quarts each, and draw the water from the canals There are beſides a vaſt number of wells, from which the water is drawn in the ſame manner to water the gardens and fruit-trees, ſo that it is no exaggeration of the matter, to ſay there are, in Egypt, above 200,000 oxen daily employed in this ſingle labour, beſides the men who draw water in wicker baſkets, ſo cloſe and well made that not a drop runs through As the land lies perfectly even, they cut their gardens into little ſquare beds, which are all ſurrounded with trenches, which immediately furniſh as much water as is neceſſary, and by theſe means they have the fineſt and moſt fertile gardens in the world Pomegranates, oranges, and ſeveral ſorts of trees, afford a ſhade and coolneſs, that, notwithſtanding the heat of the climate, make it delightful walking The Egyptians have not the laborious taſk of ploughing, digging, or breaking the clods, but when the river has retired, they have no more to do than to mix a little ſand with the earth to abate its ſtrength, after which they ſow with as little pains, and almoſt without charge The paſtures are moſt excellent, the graſs generally growing to the height of the cattle In fine, there is not a more pleaſant ſight in the world than Egypt in two ſeaſons Of the animal productions, the crocodile is the moſt remarkable This amphibious creature is not, indeed, peculiar to the Nile, it being frequent enough in the Ganges, and other large rivers of India With reſpect to vegetable productions, though woods are very rare in Egypt, yet there are ſome foreſts of palm-trees towards the deſerts of Lybia and near Candera, the antient Tentyra, is one of wild dates, whoſe fruit is exceſſive hard, but much admired However, Egypt is not a country proper for trees, but the caſe is different as to plants, which are various, and many of them highly uſeful Amongſt the artificial curioſities of this country are the pyramids, thoſe ſtupendous ſtructures, which were deſervedly reckoned, by the antients, among the wonders of the world The Egyptian Labyrinth, from whence Dædalus is ſuppoſed to have taken the model of that which he afterwards built in Crete, though he therein imitated but the hundredth part of it, was a celebrated ſtructure, and Herodotus, who ſaw it, ſays, that it far ſurpaſſed the report of fame, being, in his judgment, even more admirable than the pyramids But admirable as the Labyrinth was, the lake Moeris, by which it ſtood, is ſaid to be yet more wonderful according to the antients, this lake was much larger than it is now, and one piece in particular, which the water has left, is, indeed, become a dangerous quickſand, wherein men and cattle are ſometimes loſt Later relations aſſure us, it is now above half a league broad, and a day's journey in length, being in circuit above twelve or fifteen leagues And even this is prodigious enough, if we conſider that it was the work of mens hands, as appears from the two pyramids built in the midſt of it, which were ſtanding in the time of Herodotus With reſpect to the government, laws, religion, cuſtoms, &c of the antient Egyptians, we ſhall be as conciſe as poſſible They are ſaid to be the firſt who found out the rules of government, and the art of making life eaſy, and a people happy, the true end of politics Other nations, particularly the Grecians, borrowed the beſt part of thoſe which they eſtabliſhed at home of this nation The crown was hereditary, yet their firſt kings were obliged to conform themſelves to the eſtabliſhed laws of the land, even in their private way of life They could not puniſh any perſon out of paſſion or caprice nor give judgment but as law preſcribed While they thus behaved, they were infinitely dear to their people, the ſtate was flouriſhing, and their extended dominion became exceeding rich and populous, and enabled them to adorn the kingdom with works of inimitable magnificence The king, prieſts, and ſoldiers, made as it were, the three eſtates of the nation The Egyptians were very careful in the adminiſtration of juſtice, formed moſt excellent laws, and minutely attended to the execution of them But as much as the Egyptians ſeemed to excel other nations in the wiſdom of their laws and conſtitutions, they ſurpaſſed them in bigotry and ſuperſtition They are ſaid to have been the firſt who erected idolatrous altars, images, and temples, and the firſt inventors of feſtivals, ceremonies, and tranſactions with the gods by the mediation of others, and to have first given names to the twelve gods They had many deities, of different ranks and orders Those chiefly honoured were Osiris and Isis, by which it is most probable they originally meant the Sun and Moon, whose influences governed and preserve the world Their idolatrous practices became so general at last, that they gave divine honours to several animals, nay, even to some vegetables. We can only hint, that the Egyptians were early famous for many arts and sciences, and particularly so for that called magic To whomsoever the invention may justly be ascribed, it is certain the art was very antient here They had magicians who pretended to the interpretation of dreams, and a way of divining by a cup, in the time of Joseph Gen xliv 5, 15 What were the real grounds of this science is not for us to say. We waive entering upon the Egyptian chronology, in order to present a concise account of the modern state of Egypt This land, though once so populous, and full of noble and opulent cities, is so far decayed and fallen from its pristine splendor, that it hath now very few places deserving to be called cities, either for extent, strength, beauty, or populousness Scarce any are enclosed with walls, and many, formerly celebrated for their wealth and beauty, are now no other than overgrown villages, without ramparts or walls Though Egypt is now by no means so populous as it has formerly been, yet these huge villages, or unwalled towns, are still very numerous, and so near to each other in some parts, that they appear almost contiguous, especially from Cairo to Rosetta, as well as along the canal of Damietta, and much more so in the heart of the Delta Egypt is now inhabited not only by the Copts, or antient natives, but by Arabs, Moors, Turks, Greeks, Jews, Franks, and others The Coptic was the antient language. But the Greek being introduced by Alexander &c continued to be spoken 900 years, till the Greeks were driven out by the Arabs, since which the Arabic hath continued the common language of the country, as they are the most numerous However, they are kept severely under by the Turks, scarce any of them being admitted into offices Both men and women (contrary to the antient Egyptians, who were the most cleanly people in the world) are commonly very nasty, as well as rude and ignorant and as they have not only embraced the doctrine of Mahomet, but are even more zealous observers of it than the Turks, so that has continued the only religion of the country The climate is naturally so excessive hot as to occasion a great variety of diseases, extremely dangerous, and, what is far worse, the plague often rages with such violence as to sweep off many thousands in a year in the whole country

EKRON, situated north-west of Gath, in Palestine, was the most northern of all the five cities which gave name to the five lordships of the Philistines, lay in the north border of Judah, and was consequently a frontier town It was once a place of great wealth and power, and is much spoken of in Scripture, but it faded away to a great degree of obscurity, and though the name, and even very considerable vestiges of what it had once been, subsisted for many ages it happens that no mention is made of it in profane authors It was famous for its idol Baalzebub, called the God of Ekron, which was next in repute and dignity to that of Dagon

ELAH The valley of Elah, or of the Terebinth, lay in the road from Eleutheropolis to Jerusalem Here it was that David slew Goliah As to the height of this gigantic Philistine, according to the English standard, it was twelve feet eight inches, and somewhat better than three tenths His coat of mail weighed 5000 shekels of brass, or upwards of 189 of our pounds troy, and by the same rule the head of his spear, which weighed 600 shekels of iron, exceeded 22 of the same pounds The weight of these, and the other parts of his armour, was not, as we may imagine, too heavy for so huge a person, his strength, doubtless, being in proportion to his stature

ELAM, mentioned in several parts of Scripture, was a kingdom on the river Ulai, to the eastward of the Tigris, It was the Susiana of the Greeks, and lay so opportunely for Nebuchadnezzar, king of Babylon, (who was, according to Jeremiah's prophecy, to subdue it,) that he would have been too great while incompleating its reduction, though, from the prophecy, Elam must have been a great and potent kingdom And it seems to have waged war with the kings of Scythia, beyond the river Cyrus, with various success Chedorlaomer was the first king of Elam, and he extended his conquests over many provinces of Asia

ELATH was a fair and commodious haven on the Arabian Gulph, or Red Sea, adjoining to the South-east part of Idumea, [illegible], or Land of Edom, and, for a long time, was a situation for the shipping which was sent from those parts into the Indies It lies near the [illegible], [illegible] pilgrims take when they go to Mecca [illegible] there were considerable remains of [illegible] This was one of the places whence the [illegible] traded for gold to Ophir It was also a great [illegible] the [illegible]

ELEPHANTINA, island of [illegible] in Upper Egypt It had a [illegible] to have taken its name from [illegible] Romans terminated here [illegible] ters the navigation on [illegible] is pleasant [illegible] [illegible] employed [illegible] last place [illegible] to [illegible]

ELEUTHERUS is [illegible] by geographers set down [illegible] and Phenicia [illegible] the moderns, [illegible] the name [illegible] between Tyre and Sidon, [illegible] the Turks [illegible] but [illegible] The writer of the [illegible] land of Hamath, [illegible] certainly [illegible] years from the [illegible]

ELYMAIS, the [illegible] parts of a province of the [illegible] ratae, lying between the rivers [illegible] and extending from the [illegible] to the Persian Gulph, was famous for a [illegible] Diana, which was [illegible] king, who found it [illegible] is [illegible] the town [illegible] by the [illegible] by their [illegible] from the [illegible] of the Persian [illegible] but [illegible] Antiochus, [illegible] Rome, [illegible] both [illegible] his army in defence of their temple

EMESA, or EMISSA, was a city of Syria Proper, placed by most of the eminent geographers on the Orontes, between Apamea and [illegible] The emperor Heliogabalus was a native of it It made a great figure during the reign of the [illegible], and became a episcopal see under that of Antioch It was [illegible] from the Mahometan Arabs by the crusaders [illegible], and retaken by Saladine about 100 years [illegible] was mastered it about 1258, and [illegible] out of it by the Mussulmen [illegible] length by the Turks It is now called Cemps, and Aman or Hamsa, and is under the [illegible] of Damascus, who keeps a deputy-governor [illegible] It is surrounded by strong walls, with [illegible] and stately towers, at proper distances [illegible] appears to be Roman [illegible] stands the town and [illegible] some fine new churches [illegible] are now turned into mosques [illegible] the place consists in silk of the finest manufacture. The

gods by the [illegible] of others, and to have first given names to the twelve gods. The [illegible] deities, of different ranks [illegible] orders. Those chiefly honoured were Osiris and Isis, by which [illegible] is most probable they originally meant the Sun and Moon, whose influences governed and preserved the world. Their idolatrous practices became so general at last, that they gave divine honours to several animals, [illegible] to [illegible] vegetables. We [illegible], [illegible], that the Egyptians were early famous for many arts and sciences, and particularly so for that called magic. To whomsoever the invention may justly be ascribed, it is certain the art was very ancient here. They had magicians who pretended to the interpretation of dreams, and a way of divining by a cup, in the time of Joseph, Gen. xliv. 5, 15. What were the real grounds of this science is not for us to say. We [illegible] Egyptian chronology, in order to present a concise account of the modern state of Egypt. This land, though once so populous, and full of noble and opulent cities, is so far decayed and fallen from its pristine splendour, that it hath now very few places deserving to be called cities, either for extent, strength, beauty, or populousness. Scarce any are enclosed with walls, and many, formerly celebrated for their wealth and beauty, are now no other than overgrown villages, without ramparts or walls. [illegible] Egypt is now by no means so populous as it has formerly been, yet these huge villages, or unwalled towns, are [illegible] very numerous, and so near to each other in some parts, that they appear almost contiguous, especially from Cairo to Rosetta, as well as along the canal of [illegible], and [illegible] of the Delta. Egypt is now [illegible] by the Copts, or [illegible], Arabs, Moors, Turks, Greeks, Jews, Franks, and others. The Coptic was the [illegible] language. But the Greek [illegible] continued to be spoken 900 years, till the Greeks were driven out by the Arabs, since which the Arabic hath continued the common language of the country, as [illegible]. However, [illegible] kept [illegible] the Turks, [illegible]. Both men and women, contrary to the ancient Egyptians, who were the most [illegible] people in the world, [illegible] commonly very [illegible] ignorant [illegible] only [illegible] the doctrine of [illegible], [illegible] more zealous [illegible] of it than the Turks, so that [illegible] continued [illegible] of the country. [illegible] climate is naturally [illegible] to occasion a great variety of [illegible], and [illegible] is far worse, the plague [illegible] to [illegible] the whole country.

Ekron, situated north-west of [illegible], in [illegible], was the most northern of all the [illegible] which gave name to the five lordships of the Philistines, lay in the northern border of Judah, and was consequently a frontier town. It was once a place of great wealth and power, and is much spoken of in Scripture, but it [illegible] a great degree of obscurity, [illegible] though the name, and [illegible] considerable vestiges of what it had once been, subsisted for many ages, it appears that no mention is made [illegible] of [illegible] authors. It was famous for its [illegible] Baalzebub, called the God of Ekron, which was [illegible] repute and dignity to that of Dagon.

Elah. The valley of Elah, or of the Terebinth, lay in the road from Eleutheropolis to Jerusalem. Here it was that David slew Goliah. As to the height of this gigantic Philistine, according to the English standard, it was twelve feet eight inches, and somewhat better than three tenths. His coat of mail weighed 5000 shekels of brass, or upwards of 189 of our pounds troy, and by the same rule the head of his spear, which weighed 600 shekels of iron, exceeded 22 of the same pounds. The weight of these, and the other parts of his armour, was not, as we may imagine, too heavy for so huge a person, his strength, doubtless, being in proportion to his stature.

Elam, mentioned in several parts of Scripture, was [illegible] kingdom on the river Ulai to the east [illegible] of the Tigris. It was the Susiana of the Greeks, and lay so opportunely for Nebuchadnezzar [illegible] Babylon, (who [illegible] according to Jeremiah's prophecy, to subdue it,) that he could have been [illegible] in completing its [illegible], though, from the prophecy, [illegible] a great and powerful kingdom [illegible] war with the kings of Scythia, [illegible] with various success. Chedorlaomer was the [illegible] king of Elam, and he extended his conquests over many provinces of Asia.

Elath, [illegible] commodious [illegible] the Elanitic Gulph, or Red Sea, belonging to the south [illegible] of Mount Seir, or Land of Edom, [illegible] a situation for the [illegible] into the [illegible]. It [illegible] one of the places whence [illegible] Ophir. It [illegible].

Eleph[illegible] [illegible] Upper Egypt [illegible] Roman [illegible]

Er[illegible] [illegible] [illegible] years from [illegible]

[illegible] Gulph, [illegible] Diu, [illegible] kings, [illegible] is [illegible] from the [illegible] Persian [illegible] and [illegible] in defence of their [illegible].

Emesa or Emissa, [illegible] of Syria [illegible], placed [illegible] most of the [illegible] between [illegible]. The [illegible] Heliogabalus was [illegible] a great [illegible] during the reign of [illegible] and [illegible] of Aurelian. It [illegible] the [illegible] Arabs [illegible] taken by Saladin about [illegible] masters of it about 125[illegible] out of it by the Mamalukes [illegible] longer [illegible] the Turks. It [illegible] Aman or Hims, and is under the [illegible] cus, who keeps [illegible]. It is surrounded by strong [illegible] and stately towers, at [illegible] appears to be Roman [illegible] stands the town [illegible] some [illegible] are now turned into [illegible] the place consists in [illegible].

gardens about it, as well as the neighbouring country, are very fertile and delightful, abounding with fruits of all ſorts, eſpecially, with mulberry trees, to feed ſilk worms with, and theſe are planted in rows of conſiderable length, very regular, and well watered.

EMMA, the ſame as Amatha before deſcribed. The Jews give the name of Hamah, or Hammath, to all places that had ſuch waters; that of Emmaus is the ſame, only ſoftened according to the Greek idiom. We muſt not, therefore, confound this with the following.

EMMAUS, according to St. Luke, was a village about 60 furlongs from Jeruſalem weſt. It was afterwards made a city, and a Roman colony, and called Nicopolis.

ENDOR, mentioned in Scripture as the place of reſidence of a woman that had a familiar ſpirit, and to whom Saul applied to raiſe up Samuel, &c. was a city of the half tribe of Manaſſeh, on the weſt of Jordan.

ENGEDI had anciently the name of Hazezon-tamar. It was a city in the tribe of Judah, not far from the Salt Sea, and in a wilderneſs, or deſolate country. Engedi is noticed for its camphire, or (as others render it) cypreſs; and Jerome tells us it was remarkable for opo-balſamum, ſuppoſed to be the ſame now called Balm of Gilead, and that it was a great town in his days.

EPHESUS, in Ionia, in Aſia Minor, called by the preſent inhabitants Aiaſa olugus, was in former times, the metropolis of all Aſia. Pliny ſtiles it the ornament of all Aſia. Strabo the greateſt and moſt frequented emporium of it. The antient Epheſus was, indeed, very far different from the modern, which is but a ſorry village, inhabited by thirty or forty Greek families, as ignorant as inconſiderable. The antient city ſtood about 50 miles ſouthward of Smyrna, near the mouth of the river Cayſter, and the ſhore of the Icarian Sea, which is a bay of the Ægean; but as it has been ſo often deſtroyed and rebuilt, it is not eaſy to determine the preciſe place. Moſt modern travellers are of opinion, that the antient city ſtood more to the ſouthward than the preſent, which they argue from the ruins that ſtill remain. Epheſus, in antient times, was known by ſeveral names. When in the Roman times it was the metropolis of all Aſia, it acknowledged Lyſimachus for its founder, becauſe that prince, having cauſed the antient city to be entirely demoliſhed, rebuilt, at a vaſt expence, a new one, in a place more convenient, and nearer the temple. This new Epheſus was greatly damaged by an earthquake in the reign of Tiberius, but by him repaired and embelliſhed with ſeveral ſtately buildings, of which there are now but few ruins to be ſeen, and ſcarce any thing worthy of antient Epheſus. The aqueduct, part of which is ſtill ſtanding, is generally believed to have been the work of the Greek emperors. The pillars which ſupport the arches are of fine marble, and higher or lower, as the level of the water required. This aqueduct ſerved to convey water into the city from the ſpring of Halitee, mentioned by Pauſanias. The Cayſter was formerly navigable, and afforded a ſafe place for ſhips to lie in, but is now almoſt choaked up with ſand. But the chief ornament of Epheſus was the ſo much celebrated temple of Diana, built at the common charge of all the ſtates of Aſia, and, for its ſtructure, ſize, and furniture, accounted among the wonders of the world. According to Pliny, an incredible ſpace of time was ſpent in building this wonderful temple by all Aſia. The pillars, which were of marble curiouſly carved, or highly poliſhed, were the works of the moſt famous artiſts of antiquity, and the altar was almoſt wholly the performance of that great maſter Praxiteles. This temple had the privilege of an aſylum, which at firſt extended to a furlong, afterwards enlarged by Mithridates to a bowſhot, and doubled by Mark Anthony, ſo that it took in part of the city. But Tiberius put a ſtop to the many abuſes and diſorders that attended privileges of this kind, and declared that no man, guilty of any wicked or diſhoneſt action, ſhould eſcape juſtice, though he fled to the altar itſelf. All the Ionians reſorted yearly to Epheſus with their wives and children, where they ſolemnized the feſtival of Diana with great pomp and magnificence, making on that occaſion rich offerings to the goddeſs, without forgetting her prieſts. The great Diana of the Epheſians, as ſhe was ſtiled by her blind adorers, was, according to Pliny, but a ſmall ſtatue of ebony, made by one Canetia. As Epheſus was, in the days of heatheniſm, famous for the temple, ſo it was, in the firſt Chriſtian times, adorned with a magnificent church, honoured with the name of St. John's. It is yet ſtanding, and repreſented by a traveller of eminence, as peculiarly ſtriking to a ſtranger, from the loftineſs of its fabric, though now converted into a Turkiſh moſque. Not far from hence was a ſtately laviatory of porphyry, called St. John's Font, the diameter of which was above ſixteen pikes, wherein it is ſaid he baptized great multitudes. The aqueduct on the eaſt ſide appears not very antient, at leaſt it ſeems to have been repaired in latter times, ſome ſtones being reverſed in the walls, and ſeeming as if placed ſo by the ignorant Turks as they came out of, to hand. So now the reliques of the Gentiles, the Chriſtians, and the Turks, are ſubverted and heaped promiſcuouſly together, for the whole town is nothing but a habitation of herdſmen and farmers, in low cottages of dirt, covered on the top with earth, ſheltered from the extremity of the weather by mighty maſſes of ruinous walls, the pride and oſtentation of former days, and the emblem in theſe of the frailty of the world, and the tranſient vanity of human glory. We conclude with obſerving, that the Turks took Epheſus under Mahomet I. the ſon of Bajazet, ſince which it hath remained under them, and that its commerce was tranſported to Smyrna and Scalanova.

EPHRAIM was a tribe. Alſo Ephraim, in which was the wood where Abſalom periſhed on an oak, mentioned in the 2nd book of Samuel, and is undoubtedly to be underſtood not of any wood lying in the tribe of Ephraim on the weſt of Jordan, (for Abſalom, as well as David, were paſſed over Jordan) but of ſome wood lying on the eaſt ſide of Jordan, and ſo named on ſome other account, perhaps, as lying over againſt the tribe of Ephraim.

EPHRATAH, being the ſame city as Bethlehem, ſee that article.

EPHRON is mentioned in the Maccabees, as a great and ſtrong city, lying in the direct way between the land of Gilead and that of Judah.

ETHIOPIA. Several of the antients gave the name of Ethiopians to all perſons either perfectly black, or of a very ſwarthy complexion. The Arabs, therefore, and other Aſiatics, as well as a great number of Africans, fall under this denomination. We find the Africans divided into the weſt, or Heſperian Ethiopians, and the Ethiopians above Egypt to the eaſt of the former. The firſt inhabited that vaſt track called Lybia Interior, but the ſecond were looked upon as the proper Ethiopians. As proper Ethiopia might antiently have been of different extent at different times, its frontiers cannot be preciſely fixed. In Scripture Cuſh, when taken for a country, is always to be underſtood of the proper Ethiopia. The antients imagined the blackneſs of the Ethiopians, Abyſſines, and Abyſſins, to be occaſioned by the intenſe heat of the climate, and therefore ſo named them. As we have not room to ſpecify all the ſeveral Ethiopian nations, as to their characters and cuſtoms, we ſhall only touch on ſome particulars. The Struthophagi (or oſtrich eaters) lived upon oſtriches. They had ſeveral arts and devices to take this their food, though that animal defended itſelf againſt them with ſtones, which it threw out of its feet with great violence. Of the ſkins of theſe creatures they made both garments and coverlids for their beds. The Ichthyophagi (or fiſh eaters) by stopping up the passages of certain caverns on the coast of the Red Sea, part of which they inhabited, with stones, enclosed with numbers of [illegible] and small fishes, which, upon the reflux of the [illegible], were left there as in a net, and served them for food [illegible] devoted [illegible] in their life-time, so they [illegible] on them [illegible] earth, for they [illegible] their dead to the sea shore, where they [illegible] carried them off. The Chelonophagi (or [illegible]-eaters) not only lived upon those fishes, but covered their huts with the shells, and used them also as boats. The Acridophagi (or locust-eaters) [illegible] deep valley in their country, of many [illegible], which they took care to fill with wood, &c. [illegible] when the south wind drove vast numbers of locusts thither, they set the combustibles on fire, and the smoke [illegible] these animals, so infinite in number, that the ground, for leagues, was covered with their bodies, which the people salted [illegible], and lived upon the following year. The Spermatophagi and [illegible]phagi formed two neighbouring cantons, the first feeding on the fruits that fell from the trees in summer, but the rest of the year on a sweet plant, with a stalk, somewhat resembling that of a [illegible], and the latter on the buds and tender shoots of trees. [illegible] people of such [illegible] way, that they skipped from tree to tree [illegible] birds. They always went naked, had wives in common, but quarrelled about their [illegible] habitations, fighting with clubs. Circumcision was a practice among the Ethiopians, as well as Egyptians, from very early antiquity, though which of these first received it [illegible] certainly known. The Ethiopians [illegible] their arrows round their heads, the feathered part of which touched their foreheads, temples, &c. and the other pieces out [illegible] rays, which formed a kind of crown. Their bows were four cubits long, and required so much strength to manage them, that no other people could make use of them. When they came to a general action with the enemy, they [illegible] the air with [illegible] the [illegible] of arrows. They retreated [illegible] the [illegible], discharging their arrows [illegible] with such dexterity, [illegible] while retreating full speed, they dreadfully galled the enemy. Their [illegible] of darts of immense [illegible], which [illegible] vast strength. The Macrobian (or long-lived Ethiopians) fed for the most part, upon roasted flesh, [illegible], and frequently attained to the age of 120 years, which was said to be owing to a rich and fragrant fountain, wherein they frequently bathed themselves. They looked upon [illegible] as the most valuable of metals, and [illegible] esteemed gold, that they secured their common prisoners with golden chains. Diodorus affirms, that they kept the bodies of their relations in their houses, within cases of glass, not thinking it right that the knowledge of the features, and [illegible] of their deceased relations, should be forgotten by their surviving kindred, or concealed from their posterity. This much may suffice concerning the manners, customs, &c. of the divers, and, in some respects, very different nations or tribes of the different Ethiopians. Jupiter Ammon, according to the Greek and Latin authors, seems to have been the principal object of religious worship in Ethiopia. Diodorus says they valued themselves on [illegible] being the first nation that had a religious establishment. In short, from the general account of [illegible] authors, their religion [illegible] from that of the Egyptians, which is not to be wondered at, considering their vicinity to, and intercourse with that people. The country is at present inhabited by people of three different religions, viz. Christians, Mahometans, and Pagans; but the last are most numerous, and are generally the Blacks, as the Mahometans are tawney, possessing the north shore, and those who are called Christians have abundance of Pagan and Jewish rites intermixed, and are but small in number compared with the other two. Ethiopia did not abound in cities and towns of any considerable note. Axume was its metropolis. It is very mountainous, and most of the hills overlook the clouds. In such a region the [illegible] cannot be always alike, and perhaps there is no country in the world where so many different seasons may be found in so small a compass. The Ethiopic, as well as the opposite, coast of the Red Sea, and the islands of this sea, are in summer, intolerably scorched by the sun's rays. However, the air is much more temperate in the mountainous parts. In some provinces the winter is extremely severe, in others as warm as summer in several parts of Europe. They have little or no snow, but frequent and dreadful thunders, that terrify both man and beast, which proceed from the excessive [illegible] of [illegible]. The climate, in general, is very healthy, [illegible] it is still not uncommon for the natives to arrive at 100 years of age. The days and nights in Ethiopia, as lying between the tropic of Cancer and the equator, or equinoctial line, are, for the most part, nearly equal, and the soil in those parts capable of cultivation, is extremely fertile, and produces vast quantities of grain, pulse, and fruit. Metals likewise, particularly gold, minerals, vegetables, and a surprising variety of [illegible], abound here. It is asserted they have sometimes two, sometimes three, [illegible] in a year. They neither [illegible] mow (to make hay) for the cattle, the perpetual heat and continual [illegible] of [illegible] from the mountains, producing grass in great abundance, and covering the fields with a most beautiful verdure through all the different seasons of the year, yet [illegible] is infested with legions of grasshoppers, which cover [illegible], and, in a short time, devour every blade of grass to the very root. Of all the rivers that [illegible] Ethiopia, the [illegible] famous is the Nile, which has its source in [illegible]. The chief [illegible] and [illegible] [illegible], [illegible], and the [illegible] city [illegible], [illegible] upon the Red Sea. The Arabs, [illegible], [illegible] the [illegible] imported fruit, corn, [illegible] [illegible] [illegible], to [illegible] and [illegible], [illegible] [illegible], [illegible], perfumes, ivory, [illegible] [illegible] commodities. The [illegible] the most [illegible] of Ethiopia, [illegible] the [illegible] [illegible]. [illegible] of Africa. [illegible] [illegible]. The [illegible] [illegible], or [illegible] honey, or butter, [illegible] [illegible] Cave, [illegible], [illegible] animals, [illegible] but [illegible]. [illegible] of this country [illegible] food [illegible], [illegible], [illegible] [illegible]. [illegible] flesh [illegible] [illegible] [illegible] for the [illegible], &c.

EZION-GEBER, was a celebrated [illegible] of Solomon [illegible] [illegible] [illegible], [illegible] [illegible], [illegible] places, [illegible] this place, [illegible] [illegible] Elath. [illegible] to [illegible] of the kingdom, [illegible] [illegible] to carry on a trade [illegible] ports of [illegible] and [illegible] Coast, [illegible] [illegible], which they [illegible] Ophir. [illegible] [illegible] prepared to sail to Ophir [illegible] king of Israel [illegible] [illegible]. [illegible], to [illegible] king's [illegible] was therefore [illegible] to [illegible].

G

GADARA, a city of Palestine, in Cælo-Syria, [illegible] on the river [illegible] [illegible] into the [illegible] of Genesareth.

GALAAD, a province of Judea, [illegible] the tribes of [illegible] [illegible]

It [illegible] most [illegible] part of Palestine, extending be-[illegible] great plain of Jezreel, and was bounded north by [illegible], east by the Jordan and the sea of Galilee, [illegible] the river Chison, and west by the Mediterranean. It was divided into [illegible] and low. The former, on the [illegible] Jordan, extending toward the Mac[illegible], the [illegible], and [illegible], was called Galilee of the Gentiles, either [illegible] inhabited [illegible], or intermixed with them. [illegible] was [illegible] the half-tribe of Manasseh. The [illegible] and more fertile, [illegible] the northernmost part, producing excellent corn, wine and [illegible] [illegible] towns [illegible] very populous. The inhabitants [illegible] and very zealous [illegible] [illegible] Capernaum, Chorazin and Bethsaida.

G[illegible] one of the [illegible] cities of the Phi-[illegible] the royal seat [illegible] people, [illegible] carried away to [illegible] [illegible] [illegible] [illegible], [illegible] [illegible] had been [illegible] [illegible] [illegible] [illegible], [illegible] [illegible] the [illegible] of [illegible] city, the [illegible] on the [illegible], are the last on the [illegible] [illegible] [illegible] on [illegible] [illegible] [illegible] strong [illegible] [illegible] [illegible] [illegible] [illegible] Kel[illegible] [illegible] [illegible], Chronicles and [illegible], we find it to have been [illegible] and which [illegible] [illegible] of [illegible] times [illegible] demolished by [illegible] king of Syria [illegible] the various changes it grew to be [illegible] [illegible] time of Christianity, [illegible] [illegible] [illegible] its [illegible]. As to [illegible] [illegible] of the [illegible], [illegible] distinct [illegible] Scripture, the [illegible] inveterate enmity towards the Israelites [illegible], [illegible] says, "one would be [illegible] tempted to [illegible] they were created on purpose to be a thorn [illegible] the sides of those chosen people." [illegible] [illegible] [illegible], for, [illegible] book of Chronicles, [illegible] the men of Gath slew the [illegible] [illegible], because they came down to take away [illegible], and [illegible] their father mourned many days, &c."

GAZA was the most renowned city of the Philistines, [illegible] took away and [illegible] he was carried when he was taken, and [illegible] pulled down the house of [illegible] lord of the Philistines. [illegible] it was [illegible] days [illegible], but, in time, it became con-[illegible] beauty, and extent. [illegible] was situate on [illegible], and [illegible], in the very [illegible] [illegible] of the land of Canaan, upon the [illegible] of the [illegible] to Egypt. In the Hebrew it was called Azzah, [illegible] Syrians, which has been altered into Gaza. [illegible] [illegible] called [illegible] and Minoa [illegible] the [illegible] Gaza [illegible] Empire, was called the [illegible]. In [illegible] was in the lot of Judah, according to the division made by Joshua, but [illegible] it was attempted and [illegible] the Philistines [illegible] it again, and kept it. For the more convenient communication with the sea it had a port, called Majuma, a place of no great account, till Constantine took notice of it and called it Constantia, [illegible] his son Constantius Julian [illegible] the port of Gaza, or [illegible] part of that city. [illegible] no signs it ever [illegible] a commo-dious place for the reception of shipping, but that it was a mere [illegible] for that purpose. Gaza often [illegible] under the [illegible] of war, of which one instance [illegible] in the year of the world 366[illegible], when after a stout [illegible], and great slaughter, it was taken by Alexander the Great. [illegible] was sometimes in a flourishing state, with mighty walls and costly edifices, and sometimes in a dilapidated condition after several vicissitudes, it lay so far neglected, that, in the Acts of the Apostles, it is called desert, that is, such a [illegible] it is now, [illegible] inhabitants, for [illegible] spot can never be called by that appellation ac-cording to the common acceptation of that word [illegible] [illegible] commemorates Gaza with [illegible], whereas [illegible] either forgotten, or omitted, is not worthy a place among the considerable ones of this part of the [illegible]. [illegible] poor place, there are some relics [illegible] having been in a better condition, for [illegible] roofs [illegible] supported with goodly pillars of [illegible] marble [illegible], some curiously carved. On the summit of the hill are the [illegible] of the [illegible] in the earth, and other foundations of [illegible] Majuma, which is the new or present Gaza, retains some monuments of its former grandeur, and is encompassed [illegible] [illegible], producing great plenty of [illegible]. Near this city is a royal castle, flanked with [illegible] towers, [illegible] in good repair. [illegible] it is [illegible], where the [illegible] wives, [illegible] are kept, and a little [illegible] the re-mains of an old Roman castle, the materials of which are remarkably firm and hard.

GENESARETH lake and land. The Lake, called also the Sea of Tiberias, the waters of [illegible], and Sea of Ga-lilee, is supposed to have borrowed its name from the city Cinnereth, on its borders, in the tribe of Naphtali. It has great variety of fish, which, for shape and taste, is not to be found any where else. The Jordan runs through the [illegible] of it. The lake takes its name from the country that surrounds it, which is fruitful and agreeable to admiration. As to the fertility of the soil, no plant comes amiss to it, [illegible] that, it is improved, by the [illegible] industry of the inhabitants, to the highest degree, and, by the climate [illegible] extraordinary [illegible] every thing [illegible], as nuts, palms, figs, and orange-trees, [illegible], though they seem to require different temperature of [illegible]. [illegible] of them. [illegible] a [illegible] [illegible] fountain, called by the natives, Capernaum. The length of the country, along the lake, is thirty furlongs, or [illegible], and the breadth twenty.

GERAR, a place frequently mentioned in the history of Abraham, [illegible] Philistine city, venerable as being the seat of the first kings, but its exact situation is not to be deter-mined. The usual name of the kings thereof seems to have been Abimelech, as Pharaoh was that of the [illegible] Egypt. The kings of Gerar were, in all probability, [illegible] extraction, for the kingdom of Gerar is expressly reckoned within the land of the Philistines.

GESHUR and MAACAH kingdoms. From Joshua xiii. 11, 13, it is evident that the cities Geshur and Maacah, the [illegible] capitals of those two small kingdoms, lay within the borders of the land of Israel, and consequently on the south side of Mount Libanus. That Geshur and Maacah were the capitals of two kingdoms, [illegible] evident from our [illegible] express mention made of the king of Geshur, 2 Sam. [illegible] the king of Maacah, 2 Sam. x. 6. How [illegible] two cities or kingdoms lay, in respect to one another, is not to be determined, but it is certain they both lay in the north part of the half tribe of Manasseh, on the east of Jordan. Geshur was a kingdom before Damascus, and Nicolaus Damascenus writes that Abraham was king ([illegible]) there.

GIBEAH lay to the north of Jerusalem, according to modern geographers, about seven or eight miles, and [illegible] from Gibeon, north-west. It stood on an hill, [illegible] name imports. It is, in Scripture, called Gibeah of Benja-min, as belonging to that tribe, and Gibeah of Saul, as being not only his native place, but the seat of his royal [illegible]. It was here that the [illegible] of the [illegible] is [illegible], the consequence of which is very remarkable, and was very fatal [illegible]. St. Jerome tells us it was totally ruined in his time.

Gibeon, the capital of the ancient Gibeonites, and a city of the Hivites, [illegible] about seven [illegible] north from Jerusalem, and [illegible] properly imports [illegible] Joshua [illegible] that it was a great city, greater than Ai. Eusebius and Jerome tell us, it was [illegible] a king of Gibeon [illegible] to be implied, that, though it [illegible], it was, in reality, as considerable [illegible] other tells us [illegible] going under its own [illegible] considered.

Gihon, [illegible] or fountain [illegible] generally [illegible] to be near [illegible] thereof. It was at this Gihon [illegible] by the especial order of David, was [illegible] Israel, and this is thought to carry in [illegible] that Gihon was a fountain, David [illegible] this fountain for anointing Solomon [illegible] Adonijah, who was at that [illegible] near Ennogel, [illegible] the [illegible] of Rogel, on another side of Jerusalem.

Gilboa, [illegible] mount, lies on the east of the sea of Galilee, being part of the ridge of mountains running from mount Lebanon, [illegible] including the mountainous region called Trachonites. It had its name from the occasion of the heap [illegible] stones by Laban and Jacob, Galeed or Gilead [illegible] *heap of witness* [illegible] the name given to the heap of stones [illegible] the whole mountainous [illegible] was afterwards so called. Hence [illegible] places lying in this tract or country that were [illegible] the name of Gilead [illegible] them, [illegible] Ramoth-Gilead. The word Gilead [illegible] places of Scripture, to denote [illegible] part of the country beyond Jordan, [illegible] tribe of Manasseh, and the tribe of Gad.

Gilgal, [illegible] situated between Jordan [illegible] Jericho. Jerome says [illegible] two miles [illegible] and was held in very great veneration by the [illegible] of the country.

Gischala, [illegible] Galilee, [illegible] was [illegible] John from this place named [illegible], who headed one of the parties of [illegible] who defended Jerusalem [illegible] the Romans, but [illegible] and [illegible] excesses [illegible] brought on [illegible].

Greece. The limits of [illegible] Greece extended from north to south, [illegible] from the [illegible] ridge of mountains which divided it from Macedonia [illegible] from the river Strymon, by which it was parted from Thrace, to the promontory of Tenarus, the utmost southern extent of Peloponnesus, and from east to west [illegible] the Ionian to the Ægean Sea. It contained a great number of kingdoms, all of which have, at one time or other, been governed by kings of their own, whose names we only find occasionally mentioned in the [illegible] the more considerable kingdoms of Argos, Attica, Thebes, and Sparta, of the Argonautic expedition, and of the Trojan war. From the names of [illegible] and Graeco, they were soon changed into those of Achaei and Hellenes, by which they are generally called in ancient authors. It is supposed, and with some [illegible], that Javan, the son of Japhet, and his descendants, were the first who peopled these countries. If we look upon the [illegible] state of Greece with respect to its inhabitants, it appears, even by the confession of their own writers, to have been one continued, uncultivated desert, inhabited by men living indifferently on every [illegible], or root that came in their way, and lying either in the open fields, or at best, sheltering themselves from the inclemencies of the weather, in dens, caves, and hollow trees. Laws they had none, except that of the strongest arm, so that those who were most pleasantly or fruitfully situated, were continually liable to be dispossessed by new invaders. Hence it was that Greece was in a continual fluctuation, the weakest being always sure to be turned out by the strongest. Hence it is also, that whilst other nations, as the Jews, Egyptians, [illegible], and Phœnicians, had improved the useful arts to a very great degree, as [illegible] in their several histories, the Greeks alone seem to have been the only strangers to them, insomuch that one may reasonably question, from Homer's making oxen the standard of the value of things, whether they knew the use of money even in his days. They had no letters till Cadmus brought them [illegible] out of Phœnicia, [illegible] alphabet consisting only of [illegible] teen letters, was not perfected [illegible] to that of twenty-four till many centuries after him. It was from him likewise that they learned [illegible] navigation, and commerce. As to other sciences they continued much longer strangers to them, and it was [illegible] of their great men began to travel into [illegible] kingdoms, that they began to have [illegible] religion was [illegible] (who [illegible]) followed the worship of the Egyptian theology, brought thither first by Cecrops, [illegible] Egyptian [illegible] of the Attic monarchy. This Grecian [illegible] multiplied with a number of deities, [illegible] fabulous [illegible], and [illegible] every [illegible]. To this [illegible] powerful [illegible] of the Grecian nation, [illegible] in some measure, all the [illegible] which the poets [illegible] traction, [illegible] extravagant exploits of those [illegible], who bestowed so much pains [illegible] time to [illegible] and [illegible]. Of this number were [illegible], and many more, some of [illegible] others [illegible] by [illegible] the happy [illegible] for [illegible] and grandeur for which they [illegible] in after ages. Greece (at present called Rumelia [illegible] the Turks) is generally considered [illegible] fertile, [illegible] and [illegible], but has had most of the [illegible] continued destroyed by the barbarous Turks, [illegible] of ignorance introduced into the [illegible] of learning and politeness. Greece, or Rumelia, abounds with fine corn, charming wine, delicious [illegible], and great herds of cattle, [illegible] and venison [illegible].

The Christian religion was planted in this country [illegible] after the death of Our Saviour by St. Paul [illegible], and it flourished here, for many ages, with [illegible] than in the western church, producing [illegible] for the faith, and venerable [illegible] to us the doctrine and discipline of the [illegible] very near to its native purity. But since the Turks [illegible] masters of this country, and made [illegible] state of their religion is very much [illegible] are in their manners much like the Turks [illegible] vetous, perfidious, [illegible] revengeful to the [illegible] degree very superstitious [illegible] deed, are so despised by the [illegible] Greek who ever turns Mahometan [illegible] of Greece is still known to us, being preserved in the writings of their famous [illegible] and poets. But the modern Greek is [illegible] the [illegible] from the [illegible] present [illegible].

II.

[illegible] plainly [illegible] to [illegible]

generally thought that the city of Hamath was the same called by the Greeks Epiphania, the situation of which agrees very well with what is here observed. So that it may be inferred, that the kingdom of Hamath extended itself from the land of Canaan, or more particularly from the kingdom of Rehob, towards the city of Epiphania, northerly, and from the coast of the Mediterranean Sea west, to the kingdom of Damascus (or Syria more particularly called) east. This kingdom is frequently denoted in Scripture by the land of Hamath, and Riblah in the land of Hamath, 2 Kings xxiii. 33. And as the extent of the land of Israel is frequently denoted by this expression, "from Dan unto Beersheba," in Numb. xxxiv. 21. "from the wilderness of Zin unto Rehob," so 1 Kings viii. 65. it is denoted by this expression, "from the entering in of Hamath, unto the river of Egypt;" and, in like manner, in another place, "from the entering in of Hamath, unto the sea of the plain."

Hermitage [illegible], whither David retired, was eventually [illegible] the tribe of Judah by the words of the prophet, [illegible].

Hebron, or Chebron, was a very antient city. Some [illegible] it was built 90 years after the flood, and that it [illegible] of Egypt. It was seated in [illegible], in the south part of Canaan, and is [illegible] on many accounts, but now is almost [illegible]. Near the ruins of this city stands a village, called [illegible], in which is still a handsome church, built by Helena over the cave where the old patriarchs were buried. It is, indeed, turned into a mosque, and held in great esteem by the Turks as well as Christians. Hebron, or [illegible], inconsiderable as it is, is still the capital of a district, called "The territory of the friends of God," consisting of about twenty-five other villages.

[illegible] the place where the Israelites and Syrians engaged in battle, and the latter received a mighty overthrow, is thought to have been the same with Almatna, mentioned by Ptolemy in the reign of Trachonitis.

Heliopolis, i. e. the city of the Sun, was a name given to several Greek cities, and, among the rest to [illegible].

Hermon Mount. There are two of the name mentioned in Scripture. First, the north-east part of Lebanon adjoining to the Holy Land, is distinguished by the name of Mount Hermon, which is consequently mentioned as the northern boundary of the country beyond Jordan, particularly the kingdom of Og, or of the half tribe of Manasseh, east of Jordan. Second, Hermon lies within the land of Canaan, west of the river Jordan, not far from Mount Tabor. This Hermon is, like Libanus, capped with snow, but for nothing so remarkable as for the abundant dews which fall upon and about it. A traveller of note observes, that "he was sufficiently instructed by experience what the holy Psalmist means by the dew of Hermon, as the tents were as wet with it as if it had rained all night."

Herodion. Herod the Great built a stately palace about seven miles from Jerusalem, in the place where he had formerly defeated the Parthians and the Jews of the Asmonean party, when he fled from that city on Antigonus becoming master of it. This, from his own name, he called Herodion. It stood in a very pleasant and strong situation, on the top of a hill, from whence was a prospect of all the country round. From this palace the hill declined all round with an equal and uniform descent, which made a beautiful show, and at the foot of it were soon built such a number of houses, as amounted to the proportion of a considerable city.

Heshbon, the capital of the kingdom of Sihon, appertained to the tribe of Reuben, but stood in the confines of that of Gad, and was remarkable for its excellent fish-pools. After the carrying away of the ten tribes, it was re-possessed by the Moabites, whence, in the prophecies of Isaiah and Jeremiah against Moab, we find frequent mention of it. It had been a Levitical city, and continued a great and noble city till the days of Eusebius and Jerome, being by the Greeks called Esbus.

Hyrcania, a province of Persia, was bounded on the north by the Caspian Sea, on the west by Media, on the south by Parthia, and on the east by Margiana, now called Mazanderan. The capital was called Hyrcania, as well as the province, and is by the moderns denominated Hyrcan. Antient writers agree in representing Hyrcania as a country abounding in wine, wheat, figs, and all other kinds of fruit, but here and there interspersed with meadows and pasture lands, and in some places with the less pleasant prospect of thick woods, abounding with wild beasts almost of every kind. As to its present condition nothing can be more amazing than the wide difference between the accounts given us by persons of credit and capacity, who have had equal opportunities of acquiring a perfect knowledge of the particular they represent.

J

Jabesh-Gilead. That this place lay in Gilead is imported by the name: it joined to the country of the Ammonites. It was still a town in the days of Eusebius and Jerome, six miles from Pella, on a hill in the way to Gerasa. Its inhabitants are remarkable in Scripture for their grateful remembrance of Saul's having raised the siege thereof by the Ammonites.

Jamnia, in Judea, stands a few miles from Joppa on the same coast. It is found in the book of the Maccabees, and placed at about 240 furlongs from Jerusalem. It was an episcopal see, under that of Cæsarea, but it is now in so ruinous a state, that scarce any thing remains worth further notice.

Jericho, in Canaan, about six miles west from the river of Jordan, and 23 almost east of Jerusalem, was the first city that was invaded by the Israelites, after their passage over Jordan, and, by the miraculous fall of its walls, taken, set on fire, and levelled with the ground. The tree from which flowed the famed Balm of Gilead, and other odoriferous trees and [illegible], grew in its vicinity, from the fragrancy of which it is supposed to be named Jericho, which in the original signifies [illegible]. [illegible] Elisha sweetened the waters of the spring that supplied it and the neighbouring countries. Here Herod built a sumptuous palace. It was the dwelling-place of Zaccheus, and honoured with Christ's own presence and miracles. It yielded to none in all Judea but Jerusalem, in the times of the last kings thereof. Besides the palace aforesaid, it was adorned with an hippodrome, an amphitheatre, and other magnificent buildings. But at present, according to modern travellers, it is only a poor village of the Arabs.

Jerusalem. This famous city has been so amply described by our author, together with the various revolutions it underwent, from its foundation to its destruction in the second year of the emperor Vespasian, that a recapitulation of them would be both tedious and unnecessary. We therefore proceed to observe, as to its more modern state, that, in A. D. 136, the emperor Adrian having changed the name of Jerusalem in Ælia Capitolina, after the name (Ælius) of his own family, erected a temple to Jupiter Capitolinus upon the spot where the Jewish temple formerly stood, and planted a Roman colony in the city, whereupon the Jews broke out into a rebellion, took Jerusalem, and massacred all the Romans settled there. But Severus (governor of Britain) being sent against the rebels, retook the city, reduced it to ashes, and plowed up the ground whereon the temple had stood. The emperor and senate of Rome published an edict, forbidding all Jews for ever, upon pain of death, to set foot in Jerusalem, or any place where it might be so much as seen. Even those Jews that embraced Christianity were also [illegible]. This quite delivered the church from the servitude of the law, for, till then, the bishops of Jerusalem had ever been chosen from among the circumcised Christians, who joined the observance of the law to that of the gospel. Adrian, however, next year, ordered Jerusalem, by the name of Elia, to be rebuilt, and peopled, partly by a Roman colony, and partly by such of the neighbouring people as were not Jews. Hence the church at Jerusalem came to be composed only of converted Gentiles, or Christians proper, St Mark being appointed the bishop of the place. Constantine the Great afterwards demolished the heathen temples built by Adrian here, and he and his mother Helena (of British extraction) built sumptuous churches in their stead, and other magnificent structures. A. D. 614, the city was taken by the Persians, and continued in their hands, and those of the Saracens and Mahometans, till the reign of Charlemagne, to whom it was [illegible] by the King of Persia. After his death it was retaken, and held by those infidels till the year 1099, when Godfrey of Bouillon took it from them, and was made its king. A. D. 1187, Saladine, the famed king of Syria and Egypt, made himself master of it, and of all the Holy Land. [illegible] fell into the hands of the Turks, and so it yet continues.

Jerusalem, in its present state, is about three miles in circumference, and lies in 31 deg. 50 min. north lat. and 36 deg. east long. being situated on a rocky mountain. *Dr Busching, in his new system of geography*, says, "The hills which stand about Jerusalem make it appear to be situated, as it were, in an amphitheatre, [illegible] to the eastward. We have no where, as I know of, any distinct view of it, than from the Mount of Olives, which is the least, and, perhaps, the farthest, is, notwithstanding, at so small a distance, that when Our Saviour was there, he might be said almost in a literal sense, *to [illegible]*. There are very few remains of the city, either as it was in Our Saviour's time, or as it was afterwards rebuilt by Adrian, scarce one stone being left upon another. [illegible] the very situation is altered; for Mount Sion, the most eminent part of the Old Jerusalem, is now excluded, and its ditches filled up, whilst the places adjoining to Mount Calvary, where Christ is said to have suffered without the gate, are now almost in the centre of the city." With respect to its present state, the Turks call it Cudsembaric. It is [illegible] inhabited, the walls are weak, and [illegible], the ditch inconsiderable. The gates are six in number, viz. Damascus, St Stephen's, Herods, Sterquilina, Bethlehem, and Mount Sion Gate, beside the Golden Gate, which is shut up, on account of a prophecy which the Turks have among them, that by that gate the Christians are to take Jerusalem. The streets are narrow, and the houses mean. Pilgrims and travellers, who flock from all parts, either through devotion or out of curiosity, are the principal support of the city. A Turkish bashaw resides here, to keep good order, collect the Grand Seignior's revenue, and protect the pilgrims from the insults of the Arabs. No European Christian is allowed to enter the city till the requisite duties are discharged, nor can a stranger safely stay here, without being upon good terms with the [illegible]. The pilgrims' principal object is the church of the Holy Sepulchre, situated upon Mount Calvary. It is 100 paces in length, and 60 in breadth. The workmen were obliged to reduce the hill to a plain area, in order to lay the foundation: but great precaution was used not to alter any part of it where Our Saviour's Passion was concerned. The scene of the Crucifixion is left entire, being about 12 yards square, and stands at this day so much higher than the floor of the church, that it is ascended to by 21 steps. The Holy Sepulchre, which was originally a cave hewn out in the bottom of the rock, may be now compared to a grotto standing above ground, and having the rock cut away, and levelled all round. The walls of the church of the Holy Sepulchre are of stone, and the roof of cedar. The east end encloses Mount Calvary, and the west the Holy Sepulchre: the former is covered with a superb cupola, supported by 16 large columns and open at top. Over the altar there is another fine dome: the nave constitutes the choir, and the sides of the church contain the most remarkable places where the circumstances of Our Saviour's Passion were transacted, together with the tombs of Godfrey and Baldwin, the two first Christian kings of Jerusalem. In the church of the Crucifixion, the hole is shewn where it is said the cross was fixed. The altar has three crosses, richly adorned, on it, [illegible] of immense value, which [illegible] cloister round the sepulchre [illegible]. The Turks, who take care of the church, [illegible] on the north-west side, [illegible] out, the Turks keeping the keys, and [illegible] provisions [illegible] formed at Easter, [illegible] death and resurrection. At [illegible] meet in the chapel of the apparition [illegible] guished, and a sermon preached by one of the [illegible] then each being furnished with a lighted taper, [illegible] procession round the church. They first [illegible] of Flagellation, where an hymn is sung, and a sermon preached; thence they proceed to the Chapel of the Division, to hear another hymn, and another sermon. At the Chapel of the Division of the Garments, to which they go next, an hymn is sung, but no [illegible]. They then proceed to the Chapel of Derision, the altar of which is supported by two pillars, and [illegible] of greyish marble, on which they [illegible] when they crowned him with thorns, and [illegible], saying, "Hail king of the Jews!" Here [illegible]ed, and a fourth hymn is sung. They next enter the higher church, parted from the former only by a curtain, and advancing to the east end, come to the very spot on which Our Redeemer was crucified. This chapel is covered all over with Mosaic work [illegible] are some marble [illegible] designed to shew the very place [illegible] blood [illegible] and [illegible] 12 inches [illegible] sermon [illegible] two friars, who personate Joseph of Arimathea and Nicodemus, [illegible] solemnity to the cross, and take down [illegible] Christ, which they [illegible] sheet, carry it to the [illegible] sermon is then preached in Arabic, and this the ceremony is concluded. On Mount Moriah, in the south part of the city, stands in edifice called Solomon's Temple, which is situated upon the same spot as the ancient temple, but it is uncertain by whom it was erected. The [illegible] part, where the Jewish Sanctum Sanctorum was supposed to have stood, is converted into a Turkish mosque. The priests and other churchmen, are kept miserably poor by the tyranny of the government, and have scarce any subsistence but what they procure by accommodating strangers with food and lodging. The royal sepulchres, without the walls of Jerusalem, are some of the most celebrated curiosities, and the most magnificent remains that imagination can conceive. By whom they were built is uncertain, but they consist of a great number of apartments, most of which are spacious, all cut out of the marble rock. Near Jerusalem is a spot of ground, of 30 yards long, and 50 broad, which is now the burial place of the Armenians. It was formerly called Aceldama, field of Blood, or potter's field, purchased with the price of Judas's treason as a place of interment [illegible] walled round, to prevent the [illegible] between the Christians [illegible]. The most remarkable places around about [illegible] Mounts Olivet, Calvary, and Gilead, the [illegible] Bethlehem, [illegible], and the [illegible] Nebo, Gibeon [illegible]

JOPPA, or Jaffa, as it is at present called, is situated on the Mediterranean coast. It was anciently the principal sea port town to Jerusalem and all Judea, and the place where the cedars of Lebanon, brought in floats from Tyre for building the temple, were landed. It was pleasantly seated on a rock, in a beautiful plain, and situated in 30 deg. 20 min. north latitude, and 35 deg. 3 min. east longitude. Jonah here embarked for Nineveh, and from the history of his being thrown overboard, the fish, or Andromeda was fabricated by the heathen poets, for there is no other, from the . . . of the ... wings, and the whole ...

—— "... Leviathan unwieldy moves,
"And ... the waves ...
"... terribly ...
"... ocean ... supports.
"... the hoary deeps divide,
"... tempest, and ... above a tree."

BROOME.

We cannot help ... the sublime description given by Job of this animal ... which the antients so terrible ... which the moderns have found ... to render it ... to many doubts ...

"His ... with ...
"... clouds of ... from his ... dreadful ... roll,
"As from a furnace, and, ... his ...
"... streams of fire.
"The ... tempest, and the roar of seas,
"... the ocean please.
"Strength ... his ample shoulders sits in state,
"His ... limbs are dreadfully complete.
"... of solid flesh are flow to part.
"As steel his nerves, as adamant his heart.
"... his ... with his ... eyes,
"... their blood ...
"... flames ...
"And black ... ocean ... mud.
"The billows feel him ... his way,
"His hoary footsteps shine along the sea."

The YOUNG's Job.

It was in Joppa, that St. Peter raised Dorcas to life, and received the messengers of Cornelius. Though it was anciently a very magnificent town, and a great commercial port, yet the harbour was never commodious, on account of several rocks, which render the passage into it dangerous. It lay for many ages in ruins, but of late hath been much improved, though it still falls beneath its original splendor. The lower ground towards the sea is covered with good houses, chiefly of stone. The principal commodities are Rama and Jerusalem soap. Rice, and other articles, are brought from Egypt, and exported from hence to various places, which yields the bashaw of Gaza a considerable annual income. ... it is supplied with water from an excellent spring on the west side of the town. The Christians now have no church, except one almost in ruins, and uncovered, but they have several handsome houses appropriated to their use, and for the entertainment of pilgrims. It is at present, on the Mediterranean coast, was the head sea-port town to Jerusalem, and of all Judea, where the timber of Lebanon, brought in floats from Tyre for building the temple, was landed; it being near about thirty miles north-west from Jerusalem, very pleasantly situated on a rock, in a beautiful plain. It is said to have been first built by Japhet, and from him was it named Japho, since moulded into Joppa, and heathen geographers speak of it as very antient. It was famed, in the time of the Maccabees, for the Jews burning the Syrian fleet before it. Its name is now pronounced and written Jaffa, or Japha, and though it hath nothing left of its antient beauty, but its charming prospect, yet its condition ... much amended since Sir Paul Lucas was here in 1707. At present the lower ground towards the sea is covered with good houses, mostly stone, and the town carries on a considerable traffic. Great quantities of rice, and other commodities are brought from Egypt. Ships of burthen can conveniently ride in the road, and on the west side, near the shore, a charming spring of water supplies the town. The Christians have here no church but one, almost ruined and uncovered, but they have commodious houses to entertain pilgrims.

JORDAN (River,) rising from the lake of Phiala, enters the Samachonite lake, whence proceeding, it unites the Sea Tiberias, and thence discharges itself into the Dead Sea. The origin of its name, or names, is somewhat obscure. It being by far the principal stream in those parts, is, by way of eminence, called "the River," the rest in the country being comparatively mere brooks. It is not a little, that, in harvest-time, it is most full, and apt to overflow its banks, contrary to the general nature of rivers, which are fullest in winter, whence it may have been that some have imagined a subterranean communication between this and the Nile. The Jordan, from the account of modern travellers, seems very different from what it was formerly. Its stream is so strong and rapid, that a man cannot stem it by swimming; the dimensions are by no means large, and the water is turbid, the natural consequence of its rapidity. It is very wholesome, and incorrupt ... its ... was formerly fordable in some places, and may still be so. It seems also to have been formerly crossed in boats and ferries.

K

KEILAH is reckoned among the cities of Judah, and it appears from several circumstances, that it was in that part of Judah which adjoined the country of the Philistines.

KIRJATH-JEARIM, very often mentioned in scripture, is expressly reckoned in Joshua among the cities of the tribe of Judah, and said to lay on the north border of that tribe, not far from Bethshemesh. It had its name from Mount Jearim, on or near which it lay.

L.

LIBANUS, or Lebanon, the most considerable mountain in Cœlo-Syria, or between Syria and Palestine, is of prodigious height, as well as extent. The cedars of Lebanon are frequently mentioned in Scripture, the few of which now standing are near a monastery, called Canobine, about ten hours journey from Tripoli. These cedar trees bear leaves much resembling our juniper, and are green all the year; but in the large ones the top spreads itself into a perfect round, whereas the smaller ascends in form of a pyramid, and like the cypress. They bear the usual fruit, which is a kind of large apple, like that of the pine, only smoother, and of a brown colour. Various virtues, and singular uncommon qualities, are attributed to the wood of this tree.

LYDDA lay north, not far off, but somewhat more inland, from Joppa. It was called Diospolis by the Gentiles; but, from the Christians, in the time of the Holy War, it had the name of St. George's, principally from a very erroneous opinion that St. George had there suffered martyrdom, and they also made it, on this mistaken account, an episcopal see.

M

MADIAN is the Modiana of Ptolemy, and Midian, or Madian, of scripture, and was a city of Arabia at present little better than a heap of ruins, situate on the east shore of the Sea At Kolzom, at no great distance from the gulph of Ailah. Most authors agree that the Midianites ought to be looked upon as the descendants of Abraham by Keturah, who was afterwards seen to have coalesced with the Ishmaelites, since Moses names the Ishmaelite merchants, who sold Joseph to Potiphar, in one place Ishmaelites, and in another Midianites.

MAHANAIM (i. e. two camps or hosts) was situated between Mount Gilead and the River Jabbok, [illegible] the confines of the tribe of Gad [illegible] or Manasseh, [illegible] east of Jordan. [illegible] pleasant [illegible] and therefore [illegible] to have been [illegible] for the royal [illegible] of Ishbosheth during [illegible] war between him and David, and for [illegible] seems to have been made choice of for the retiring place of David during the rebellion of Absalom.

MAKKEDAH is reckoned among the cities given to Judah. It [illegible] of the [illegible]

MAON (unto the wilderness of which David [illegible] from [illegible]) was [illegible] to Carmel. Hence it is said of Nabal, 1 Sam. xxv. 2. "There was a man in Maon, whose possessions were in Carmel;" and Nabal, though he [illegible] dwell in Maon, is yet stiled Nabal the Carmelite, from the place where his estate lay.

MARAH. A certain [illegible] informs us, that [illegible] passing from [illegible] to the Mount Sinai, they came into the desert, [illegible] of Marah, where the [illegible] met with [illegible] waters of [illegible] And [illegible] all after [illegible] three [illegible] may [illegible] Coronel, [illegible] of water, [illegible] by [illegible] still continue to be [illegible]

MASSADA, in the tribe of Judah, [illegible] famous fortress [illegible] Judas [illegible] impregnable. It was situated on a high craggy rock inaccessible on all sides but one, and that very steep and difficult. The siege of it by the Romans under Silva, the general of Titus, is one of the most [illegible] events in ancient history. Notwithstanding the height and ruggedness of the rock it stood on, yet, when you had gained the top, you saw an agreeable, flat, fertile country, so spacious as to supply the town with corn, fruit, &c. Herod the Great finding it a place of such strength and importance added new works and fortifications, and [illegible] it had no other supply of water than from the clouds, [illegible] several capacious cisterns [illegible] it, and stored it with a prodigious quantity [illegible] Herod [illegible] place [illegible] Arabia.

MEDIA [illegible] from Media, [illegible] in Scripture [illegible] with their [illegible]

MEGIDDO [illegible] of Manasseh on the west of Jordan, but the Canaanites continued to dwell therein [illegible] Solomon rebuilt it. Here died Ahaziah and Josiah, kings of Judah.

MELITENE, or Melitine, in Lesser Armenia, was a Roman castle, [illegible] which the emperor Trajan made a city, appointing it to be the metropolis of the whole country, whence, in process of time, it became one of the most populous and wealthy cities in the east. It stood on the banks of the Euphrates. The famous thundering legion belonged to this place, being raised and generally quartered here.

MEMPHIS is called in Scripture Moph and Noph, which name is supposed to be derived from Apis-Mophis, according to Sir Isaac Newton, the same person with Menes and Memnon, a prince that either built or fortified it. The chief idol of the Egyptians was here called Apis, which they worshipped in the shape of a bull, and always kept one in his temple. The famous city of Cairo is said to have been built out of its ruins, on the eastern side of the Nile.

MICHMASH, or Michmas, was in the tribe of Benjamin, situate [illegible] from Jerusalem, and between [illegible] and Gibeah. Eusebius says it was very considerable in his time.

MACEDONIA, or more properly Macedon, [illegible] learned to be [illegible] Macedon, by the [illegible] of Chittim. Alexander [illegible] is coming from the [illegible] Perseus [illegible] of Macedonia [illegible] therein [illegible] king of the Chittims. [illegible] this country [illegible] inhabited by various [illegible] was it, for a long succession of ages, distinguished by different appellations. It was very anciently called [illegible] but afterwards the whole country, which the [illegible] called Macedonia, received that denomination [illegible] from [illegible] Macedo, descended from [illegible] according to others, by [illegible] change of [illegible] name of one of its [illegible] into Macedonia. [illegible] with Macedonia [illegible] made at different times, [illegible] Pliny tells us, that not less than 150 [illegible] were [illegible] within its territory, and [illegible] of different [illegible] cities. Its [illegible] situation excellent in respect of [illegible] the earth, the Ægean Sea, [illegible] which [illegible] might have been, [illegible] powerful [illegible] though many noble [illegible] are to be found in that country. [illegible] parts [illegible] In process of time no part of [illegible] peopled, but since it has been in the hands of the Turks, great parts lie uninhabited. [illegible] miles of ground [illegible] with corn, pasture, cattle, [illegible] in some parts, produces wine and oil.

N

NABATHÆA. According to St. Jerome, the country of the Nabathæans [illegible] Red Sea, [illegible] part of Arabia [illegible] of these people were [illegible] of Arabia, Ethiopia, &c. &c.

NAIM, or Nain, according to Eusebius, was a city situated in the plain near Mount Tabor, and within two miles of it. He places it at a small distance from Endor and Scythopolis. [illegible] city so called in Idumea, [illegible] the son of Corias, [illegible] his retreat after he had strongly fortified it.

NAIOTH (to which Samuel retired with David) is situated in Ramah, meaning the district of Ramah, otherwise called Ramathaim-Zophim, the birth-place, and usual residence, of the [illegible] great prophet.

NEAPOLIS, a city of note in Thrace, on the Ægean Sea, between the rivers Strymon and the Nestus, [illegible] signifying only New City. One of the [illegible] was so called.

NICOPOLIS, in Judea. Neapolis, in Armenia Minor, was built by Pompey, in memory of [illegible] over Tigranes the Great, [illegible] Nicopolis Pompeii.

NINEVEH, or Ninus, in Assyria, ([illegible] tradition) is most generally supposed to have been [illegible] Nimrod, [illegible] to be [illegible] Belus. [illegible] is generally thought to be taken from Ninus, the son of Nimrod, and to be a compound [illegible] The Dwelling of Ninus. It was situated on the banks of the Tigris, over against where Mosul now stands, and had increased and grown prodigiously large in the time of Jonas, who prophesied against it, that it was three days journey long, or, as some think, in circumference. It was also so strong, as to be deemed impregnable. However, it was at length taken and destroyed, according to the prophecy of Nahum. What is remarkable that Lucian, in one of his dialogues says, that Ninus (the profane name of Nineveh,) was so utterly destroyed, that there remained no footsteps of it, nor could one tell so much as where once it stood." A new city, it is probable, was quickly built by the Medes, out of the ruins of the old, and called New Nineveh, but this was likewise destroyed by Artyages, the eighth Median king from Arbaces, for its frequent revolts, and to so low a degree was it brought in the time of Cyril, bishop of Alexandria, in the middle of the fifth century, that he tells us there was nothing to be seen of it but great heaps of rubbish. And yet we find a third Nineveh destroyed by the Saracens, as it is supposed, some hundred years after. At a small distance from the ruins of Nineveh is a Turkish mosque.

NISIBIS was once a large, populous, and opulent city, but is at present described as a town in Diarbeker, about 35 miles from the Tigris, and but the shadow of what it once was, though it is still the residence of a Turkish sangiac. It at present is little more than a village, though ancient gates, and the remains of a noble church are yet to be seen. Its territory is fruitful, and, when cultivated, produces corn, wine, and various fruits, the chief business being agriculture. About two miles to the east is a good river, with a very noble stone bridge, and all the way between the town and it, pieces of old walls, and a large arch, whereby it is supposed the city anciently reached quite to that river. Nisibis stands west from the celebrated Ur of the Chaldees, between it and the Tigris.

NOB was a sacerdotal city. By the prophet Nehemiah it is reckoned among the cities of Benjamin. It seems, therefore, to have been added to the priests, and that occasionally, when the ark was at Kirjath-jearim, it being moreover not nominated among those that were assigned to them at first.

NOD, the land of, to which fugitive Cain, under an apprehension that every one who found him would slay him, by divine order, retired, and there in built a city, calling it Enoch, after the name of his son. Where this land of Nod (which word signifies fugitive or wandering) was situate, is thought not quite certain. No remains of the name Nod itself, as a land, are now to be found.

O

OLIVET Mount, or the Mount of Olives, called by the Jews, in their language, the Mount of Unction or the Mount of Olives, or Oil. It was also termed the Mountain of Three Lights, because lighted on the west by the fire of the altar, receiving on the east the light of the sun, and producing much oil, the aliment of light. It stands a sabbath day's journey (i.e. eight furlongs, or one mile) east from Jerusalem, commanding an extensive prospect, as being the loftiest eminence in its neighbourhood. It was once famous for fertility, and was thus described by an author of the 7th century. "Few or no trees are there to be found, except the olive and vine, according to the report of Acculfus, but wheat and barley there flourish in a most kindly manner, for the nature of the soil is quite productive." With respect to the Turks, notwithstanding their pretended veneration for this mount, and its circumstances, it is more than suspected it is not out of real devotion, but for lucre's sake, and to exact money from the popish pilgrims, and travellers of curiosity, for admission to see them.

OPHIR. The acutest, nicest, and most ingenious writers are much at a loss to find out a certain settlement for Ophir. It is by several supposed to be the place whither Solomon sent ships every three years from Ezion-geber to fetch gold. It is opinion some would have supported by several trees, which seem to have been erected here by foreigners, as they have inscriptions in unknown characters. Besides, some say the inhabitants boast of having books proving that the Israelites, in Solomon's time, sailed every third year to these ports to fetch gold.

P

PALESTINE, or Judæa, situated between 31 deg. 30 min and 33 deg 20 min north lat. and from 34 deg. 50 min to 37 deg 15 min east long being bounded by the Mediterranean sea on the west, Syria and Phœnicia on the north, Arabia Deserta on the east, and Arabia Petræa on the south. It is therefore near 200 miles in length, and about 80 in breadth towards the middle, but increases or diminishes 12 or 15 miles in other places. The longest day is about 14 hours 15 minutes. The air of Judæa is the most salubrious and pleasant imaginable, neither heat nor cold are felt in the extreme, but an agreeable serenity diffuses itself throughout the year, which puts the stranger in mind of the golden age,

"The flowers unsown in fields and meadows reign'd,
"And western winds immortal spring maintain'd."

Though the climate of this country is at present the most admirable in the universe, we have no doubt but that, in the early ages of the world, when the pastoral life was the most honourable, and agriculture the most respected employ, it even exceeded its present excellency, by means of the general cultivation of the country. Of the richness and fertility of its soil we have the most authentic testimonies, in particular, that it abounded in corn, wine, oil, honey, pomegranates, dates, figs, citrons, oranges, apples of Paradise, sugar-canes, cotton, hemp, flax, cedars, cypresses, and a great variety of other stately, fragrant, and fruitful trees, balm of Gilead, and other precious drugs, &c. cattle, fowls, fish, game, and other delicacies, as well as necessaries of life. Indeed whoever considers the very small extent of Judæa, will be sensible that nothing but such astonishing fertility could enable it to maintain such a number of inhabitants as resided in it in the time of king David, since they amounted to 6 000 000. The produce of the land not only subsisted this prodigious multitude, but there was a sufficient superfluity to send to Tyre and other places for exportation. Yet the soil was only cultivated six years in seven, as the septennial year was always a time of rest from the labours of agriculture. It is to be observed, that the whole of the country was cultivated, and that woods, parks, waste grounds, &c. were unknown. It is now unhappily inhabited by some of the most indolent people existing, yet Dr Shaw informs us, that, with a little cultivation, it would yield as much as it did in the days of king David and king Solomon.

PALMYRA, as called by the Greeks and Romans, Tadmor in the Wilderness in the Scripture, Palmira and Thadamor by Josephus, Tadmor and Tatmor by the Arabs and Syrians, stood about fifteen miles east of Damascus. The air is exceeding good, but the soil now barren, (though it formerly had perpetual springs, and yielded fruit and corn,) affording nothing green but a few palm-trees in gardens, and some scattered up and down.

Palmyra in the deserts of Arabia, or, as by the Scripture stiled Tadmor in the Wilderness, is a most awful spectacle. "As you approach (*says Dr Bankes, in his System of Geography*) the first object which presents itself is a ruinated castle, on the north side of the city. From it you descry Tadmor, enclosed on the three sides by long ridges of mountains. Southward of it is a vast plain extending far beyond the sight. The city must have been of large extent, from the space now taken up by its ruins, among which live about thirty or forty miserable families in huts of dirt, within a spacious court, which once enclosed a magnificent temple. This court hath a stately high wall of large square stone, adorned with pilasters both within and without, and are about sixty on each side. The beautiful cornices have been beaten down by the Turks. Towards the centre are the remains of a castle, shrouding the fragments of a temple of exquisite beauty, as appears by what is still standing of its entrance, viz. two stones thirty-five feet long, carved with vines and clustres of grapes. In the great court are the remains of two rows of very noble marble pillars, thirty-seven feet high, with capitals finely carved, and the cornices must have been of equal elegance. Fifty-eight of these pillars are entire. There must have been many more, as it appears they went quite round the court, supporting a most spacious double piazza. The walks on the west side of this piazza, which face the front of the temple, seem to have been grand and spacious, and at the end are two niches for statues at length, with pedestals, borders, supporters, canopies, &c. carved with inimitable art. The space within this once beautiful enclosure is (or rather was) encompassed by another row of pillars of a different order, fifty feet high, sixteen of which are yet standing. The temple was ninety feet long, and about forty broad. Its grand entrance, on the west, appears by what remains of it, to have been the most magnificent in the world. Over a door-way, in the remaining walls, you trace a spread-eagle, and here are the fragments of cupids, as well as of eagles, most finely imitating nature, on large stones mouldering on the earth. Nothing of the temple stands but the walls, the window-places of which are narrow at top, but richly adorned with sculpture. In the middle is a cupola, all one solid piece. Leaving this court and temple, your eyes are [illegible] with a great number of pillars of marble, scattered for near a mile. To the north you have a stately obelisk before you consisting of several large stones, besides its capital greatly sculptured. It is more than fifty feet high, and is twelve feet and an half in circumference just above the pedestal, and it is imagined a statue once stood upon it. East and west of it, at the distance of about a quarter of a mile, is [illegible] the obelisk, that seems to have corresponded with the first mentioned, and, according to the fragment of a third, it should seem that there was a continued range of them. On one of them, which is about forty feet high, there is a Greek inscription, commemorating two patriots, and about an hundred paces from it is a large and lofty entrance, leading to a grand piazza, adorned with marble pillars, on most of which there are inscriptions. A little farther onward, to the left, are the remains of a stately pile of remarkable fine marble, twenty-two feet long. On the west side of the piazza are several openings for gates, two of which appear to have been the most superb that ever captivated the human eye, both in point of grandeur of work in general, and the beautiful porphyry pillars with which they were adorned. Eastward of the piazza are a great number of scattered marble pillars, most of which have been deprived of their elegant capitals. A little ruined temple lies mouldering at a short distance, which appears to have been a very curious structure. But of all the venerable remains, none more attract the admiration than the magnificent sepulchres towards the north of the city, extending a mile and more, all which, at a distance, have the appearance of tops of decayed churches, or bastions of ruined fortifications." The magnificent city of Palmyra is mentioned in the Arabic translation of the Chronicles, as subsisting before the days of Solomon. But John of Antioch, surnamed Malela, says, that it was built by Solomon, and on the very spot where his father slew the Philistine chief. He affirms that the city was built in commemoration of that memorable action. We find, in the ninth chapter of the first book of Kings, and the eighth of the second of Chronicles, that Solomon erected a city in a wilderness, and called it Tadmor; that some time afterwards, the Greeks and Romans distinguished it by the name of Palmyra, even while its first name was still retained by the Syrians; and this is confirmed by St. Jerome, who says, that Tadmor and Palmyra are the Syrian and Greek names of the same place; and the country Arabs, even at his time, call it by the former name. In this circumstance they are remarkably particular, preserving the ancient denomination of places through various revolutions. Thus the Acca of the Old Testament is at this day called by the Arabs, Acca, and the Greek name Ptolemais, in which that of Acca was for some time immured, is lost through disuse. Not that human judgment can pretend to advance, however, that Palmyra was actually the work of Solomon; an opinion only can be offered, concurrent with that of the present inhabitants, who say, all these things were done by Solomon the son of David. However such structures as might have been erected by Solomon we will suppose to have been entirely demolished by Nebuchadnezzar, who in his march to the siege of Jerusalem, destroyed this city, as we are assured by John of Antioch. It was afterwards beautifully repaired by Adrian, then destroyed by Antiochus, and rebuilt by Aurelian, and at last totally demolished by the ignorant and bigotted Turks, under whose tyranny the whole country lies waste. The greatest figure Palmyra ever made in history was in the reign of Gallienus, under whose slothful indolence the Roman glory in the east became considerably eclipsed, when Odenathus, joining the emperor's party, collected the remains of the discomfited Romans in Syria, whom he led against Sapor, the Persian monarch, put his army to flight, and advanced with his victorious troops to Ctesiphon, the capital of the empire. On his return from this expedition, his services [illegible] and honoured and revered by the Romans, he was unanimously proclaimed Augustus, and constituted in the empire with Gallienus. Such of the accounts of Odenathus as have reached posterity, serve rather to heighten than gratify the human curiosity. He was a native of [illegible], and of so admirable a position, that he, for a while, held the balance of power between the empire of Persia and Rome. He drove the Goths out of Asia Minor, where they had committed the most violent ravages; and this was a glorious action, in which, it was apprehended he was treacherously slain by Maeonius his kinsman. His son Herodotus, soon afterwards suffered the same fate; nor did Maeonius long survive, being cut to pieces by the soldiers.

The fortune of the beautiful Zenobia, queen of Odenathus, is well worthy the attention of our readers. The vicissitudes which this lady experienced were various and surprising, and her character great and extraordinary, though her memory is tarnished with the suspicion of her having been privy to the deaths of her husband and son. The person of Zenobia was graceful and genteel, her complexion dark brown, her eyes black and sparkling with uncommon lustre, her teeth beautifully white, her countenance sprightly, her air noble, and her voice clear and powerful. Her strength was unusually great. She inured herself much to fatigue, was fond of riding, and would sometimes march on foot at the head of her troops. In council she was circumspect and prudent, in executing bold and determined. She could be open or reserved, mild or severe, as occasion required. She was generous, but not profuse, and observed inviolably the chastest rules of female honour. No woman was better acquainted with history than this accomplished queen. She was mistress of the Greek and Egyptian tongues, as well as the Latin, which she understood [illegible] the former. She boasted herself descended from Ptolemy, and reckoned Cleopatra among her ancestry. That Zenobia attended her husband in the field there is not the least doubt, since the emperor Aurelian praises the highest encomiums on her military prowess. She assumed, after the death of Odenathus, the reins of government in the name of her children, and renouncing all alliance with Rome, attacked, and totally routed the army of

He[illegible], the Roman general, who was ſent [illegible] the Perſians, [illegible] way, eſcaping from [illegible] into [illegible] hands. Since [illegible], while the exigency of public affairs call[illegible] of Claudius nearer home, [illegible] at [illegible] the dominion of Egypt, [illegible] being de[illegible] Ptolemy, and having ſecured a ſtrong part[illegible] there in her [illegible] ſhe ſent thither Zabdas, [illegible] poſſeſſed [illegible] great career, who [illegible] ſerved under Odenathus, and he, defeating the Egyptian [illegible], poſſeſſed himſelf of the province in the name of Zenobia. The Palmyrenes, however, were afterwards [illegible], and nearly driven from their new acquiſitions, [illegible] gallant [illegible] of Probus, the Egyptian prefect, who [illegible] to cut off the retreat of the vanquiſhed, [illegible] his ignorance of the country, they totally defeated his army, and himſelf was taken priſoner, [illegible] he could not outlive, but, dying by his own hand, left Zenobia miſtreſs of Egypt. The progreſs of this heroic queen greatly alarmed Claudius, who being now near the end of the ſecond year of his reign, reſolved to turn his forces [illegible], but was cut off by the [illegible], at Sirmium in Pannonia. He was ſucceeded by Aurelian, who was [illegible], however, ſecured in his power without [illegible], and who, before he thought of relieving the eaſtern empire, reformed the police at Rome, and reduced the Goths, Vandals, and Germans. Theſe great [illegible] being completed, he croſſed the Boſphorus at Byzantium, and having [illegible], Cappadocia, he proceeded to Antioch, of which he poſſeſſed himſelf by ſtratagem. By two battles, one fought here, the other at Emeſa, Aurelian recovered the [illegible] provinces, and forced the queen to ſhelter herſelf within the walls of her capital. Having taken every neceſſary precaution to ſupply his army with proviſions, Aurelian proceeded to Palmyra, not, however, without being conſiderably harraſſed by the Syrian banditti. Arriving at length before the walls of the city, he laid cloſe ſiege to it, and was gallantly [illegible] by the garriſon. Being wearied out with military operations, the emperor had recourſe to negociations, and made ſome offers to Zenobia, which ſhe moſt haughtily rejected, bidding them remember, that [illegible] Cleopatra preferred death to diſhonour. This [illegible] Aurelian, he attacked with redoubled vigour, and the beſieged being at length reduced to the laſt extremity, had no other reſource [illegible] of applying to their allies, the Perſians [illegible], and this reſolution being agreed on, [illegible], Zenobia, [illegible] the city [illegible] into [illegible], and [illegible] the Euphrates [illegible], but was taken [illegible] was about to croſs the Euphrates. Palmyra [illegible] ſurrendered, and the emperor took poſſeſſion. He ſpared the inhabitants, but carried off the beſt part of the [illegible], leaving behind him a garriſon of ſix hundred [illegible], who, ſome years after, were cut off by the [illegible], whom were by the emperor's command, in conſequence of [illegible] were put to death, and the city [illegible]. The emperor, at Emeſa, ſet on foot an enquiry [illegible] Zenobia, and here it was that ſhe ſullied her great character by betraying her beſt friends, among whom was Longinus, by whoſe advice it was that ſhe had rejected the terms of peace which the emperor Aurelian had propoſed: for this he was ordered to be executed, but his miſtreſs was [illegible] to grace a Roman triumph. She afterwards married, and had children, at Conche, on the road from Rome to the antient Tiber, where the emperor aſſigned her ſome lands, and the remains of her villa are at this day to be ſeen. Palmyra was afterwards governed by the Romans, and, from a Latin inſcription ſtill extant, we diſcover that Hierocles was for the fifth time preſident of the provinces, when Diocleſian here erected ſome magnificent edifices. In the year of Chriſt 400 the firſt Illyrian legion was quartered here; but Procopius gives us reaſon to imagine that the place was ſo little regarded as to be ſometimes left without a garriſon. The Roman hiſtory makes no farther mention of Palmyra. According to Benjamin Tudulenſis, there were 2000 Jews among the inhabitants in the twelfth century. We ſhall conclude our account of this once grand and flouriſhing city, with the following extract from an author on the ſubject. "That Palmyra was uſed as a place of ſtrength, is evident from [illegible] which have been made in the caſtle on the hill, and the Temple of the Sun, which muſt have been intended for defence, and are not more than five or ſix hundred years old. The moſt perfect piece of antiquity is a mauſoleum, upwards of ſeventeen hundred years old, with the flooring entire, and an inſcription ſtill legible, informing us that it was built by Jambelicus, ſon of Mocimus, as a burial-place for himſelf and family, in the year 314." See *Barnes's [illegible] Syſtem of Geography*.

PERSIA. The word Perſia is ſuppoſed to be only a corruption of the word Parthia, and that the modern Perſians derive the name from their progenitors the Parthians, the antient inhabitants of the country. The word itſelf implies an horſeman, and the Perſians and Parthians have always been famed for their ſkill in that exerciſe. Perſia includes all thoſe countries which were antiently celebrated and known by the names of Media, Parthia, part of Aſſyria, Armenia, Colchis, Bactria, Iberia, and Suſiana. It is bounded on the north by the Caſpian Sea, which ſeparates it from Ruſſia, and on the north-eaſt by the river Oxus, which divides it from Uſbec Tartary. The north-weſt boundaries are the Dageſtan mountains, and the mountains of Ararat, which divide it from Circaſſian Tartary; and it has the eaſtern boundary, the Indian Ocean, and the Gulphs of Perſia and Ormus, the ſouthern, and Arabia and Turkey the weſtern. The prodigious mountains of Ararat and Caucaſus have long made a diſtinguiſhed figure in hiſtory, [illegible] high that long chain of mountains, known by the name of Taurus, which run quite through the empire, been leſs celebrated. From the diſtracted ſtate of Perſia for many ſucceſſive years, the political diviſion of the provinces cannot be aſcertained, but the moſt remarkable places in the empire are Iſpahan, the metropolis, and reſidence of the ſophi, Schamachie, Ardebil, S[illegible], Caſbin, Rom, Reſchd, Derbent, Schiras, and the cities of Ormus and Gombroon on the Perſian Gulph. Theſe laſt are much on the decline at preſent, though they were formerly places of great commercial conſequence. Moſt of the European nations, particularly the Engliſh, have eſtabliſhed factories at Gombroon, by means of which they carry on a trade with the Perſians, Turks, Tartars, Arabians, Armenians, Banyans, &c. The ſoil of Perſia is in moſt parts very fertile, producing various kinds of grain, cattle of all kinds, game, and plenty of the choiceſt fruits. The Perſian language is ſpoken in common throughout the whole empire, but more correctly in ſome provinces than others. The Turkiſh is the polite or court language, and the Arabic is the learned language, in which all the books on [illegible] ſubjects are written. The ſciences flouriſhed in Perſia long before they did in Europe; but the modern Perſians fall very ſhort of the Europeans in every branch of learning. The grand epocha, by which they date all events, is the Hegira, or flight of Mahomet from Mecca, which took place in the year 622. They reckon twenty-four hours to the day, but do not ſubdivide it into day and night as we do. As they begin their week on Saturday, Friday is their Sabbath. Their year begins at the vernal equinox. [illegible] four and [illegible] years [illegible] in the ſpace of twelve days, becauſe they reckon but twelve moons to their lunar year. The moſt celebrated and ſingular antiquities in Perſia, are the ruins of Perſepolis, formerly a ſuperb city, till it was deſtroyed by Alexander the Great, to oblige the Grecian courtezan Thais. Theſe ruins are about the diſtance of thirty Engliſh miles from the city of Schiras. They are ſituated in a fine plain, which is about 120 miles in length, and only ſix or ſeven in breadth. This plain is overflowed with water ſeveral months in the year, which occaſions it to be ſo exceedingly fertile, particularly in rice, that it is covered with little villages, or hamlets, to the number, as the inhabitants aſſert, of 880 including thoſe which are ſituated in the adjacent mountains. The ruins appear like an amphitheatre, and are ſituated in a kind of ſemicircle, formed by the mo[illegible] the [illegible] of the Per[illegible] [illegible] which [illegible] of Dirm, [illegible] introduce [illegible] Cal[illegible] [illegible] Rom[illegible] [illegible] [illegible] the Royal [illegible] contains [illegible] the [illegible] the [illegible] of which [illegible] Delhi [illegible] which [illegible] 50 le[illegible] in length, [illegible] to have [illegible] from the Caspian to the [illegible] that city [illegible] about 5000 grave-stones, most of which have Arabic inscriptions. [illegible] perhaps, [illegible] kingdom or empire [illegible] revolutions than that of Persia, to recount [illegible] be too extensive to be here admitted. We shall therefore only mention the most recent, which was occasioned by the celebrated [illegible] Kouli Khan, who, in the year 173[illegible], was to exceed [illegible] against the Turks and Tartars, as [illegible] [illegible] open country of Georgia and Armenia. In 173[illegible] he destroyed [illegible] part of the Turkish army at [illegible]. In 1735 the young Shah Abbas (the then emperor) died, when Kouli Khan convened the Persian chiefs [illegible] nobles, [illegible] they [illegible] at liberty to [illegible]. They [illegible] begged him to accept of [illegible], being [illegible] Having [illegible] the throne, he [illegible] the Persians [illegible], destroyed many of the Royal family, and putting [illegible] the nobility, except those [illegible] [illegible] Having [illegible] the Tartars and Russians, [illegible] the territories of the Great Mogul, defeated the [illegible], made himself master of Delhi, the capital of Hindostan, took the Great Mogul himself prisoner, [illegible] to the [illegible], and plundered the empire of [illegible] gold, [illegible] valuables, to the amount of 87,500,000l. sterling, a greater treasure than any other monarch [illegible] possessed. [illegible] he lodged [illegible] [illegible] [illegible] Georgians, [illegible]. He then subdued the Usbeck Tartars and brought their country [illegible] to [illegible] returned to Persia, [illegible] [illegible]. In the year 1741 he [illegible] [illegible] the [illegible] his eldest son [illegible] till the year 1742, when he was brought as a prisoner to his father, who had [illegible] by order of the monarch. The Turks having [illegible] taken up [illegible] [illegible] who [illegible] to be [illegible] younger son of the late emperor Shah [illegible] Kouli Khan [illegible] [illegible] Kouli Khan being informed of this, [illegible] gave orders that [illegible] should be beheaded. [illegible] the year 1745 he [illegible] 1747 he was entirely employed [illegible] rebellions. He [illegible] generally looked upon to be in a state of insanity. His actions were [illegible] blood, and [illegible] scarce [illegible] a gleam of generosity, [illegible] would seem to direct his intentions; but [illegible] the most horrid cruelty at most times predominated. He was, however, on the second of July, 1747, [illegible] by five of the principal officers of his guards [illegible] happened thus: [illegible] his tent about one o'clock in the morning, when one of them stumbling over some of the cords [illegible], Kouli Khan [illegible], started up, [illegible] his [illegible], and with one blow cut off the head of him who was next to him. He then [illegible] on the left shoulder with [illegible], that [illegible] lodged [illegible] and [illegible] thus [illegible] [illegible] When [illegible] rejoiced. They [illegible] his son, and his grandson, [illegible] the blood of [illegible] bloody [illegible] [illegible] [illegible] [illegible] [illegible] Several [illegible] as [illegible] others, [illegible], contending [illegible] the various successes and [illegible] revol[illegible] [illegible] known in Europe, [illegible] least not [illegible], we must conclude [illegible] empire.

PELLA, [illegible] Bucomas or [illegible] Macedonia, was [illegible] at the mouth of the [illegible], [illegible] birth of [illegible] Philip, and his son [illegible] which [illegible] was [illegible] [illegible] it [illegible] made it the capital of Macedonia [illegible] [illegible] [illegible] [illegible] Greece, [illegible] [illegible] [illegible] [illegible]

PELLA, [illegible] Antient [illegible] called [illegible] Belus, [illegible] Pelous [illegible] which [illegible] place [illegible] to have been [illegible] its [illegible] walls.

PENIEL, or Penuel, ([illegible]) [illegible] Jacob, [illegible] wrestling with the angel, [illegible] the brook Jabbok. It became [illegible] Gideon [illegible] down [illegible] had [illegible] It was [illegible] [illegible] [illegible] [illegible] [illegible] [illegible] [illegible] Mount Libanus.

PERGAMOS, or Pergamus, [illegible] of the greatest note [illegible] [illegible] Minor, [illegible] [illegible] kingdom [illegible] year [illegible] [illegible] [illegible] Chris[illegible] [illegible] [illegible] of [illegible] library of 200,000 vol[illegible] parchment was [illegible] [illegible] the [illegible] called Charta Pergamena [illegible] Ptolemy, king of Egypt [illegible] [illegible] [illegible] [illegible] [illegible] [illegible] to [illegible] [illegible] valuable books [illegible] [illegible] that might vie with Alexander's [illegible] library at Alexandria [illegible] here were [illegible] [illegible] [illegible] from [illegible] [illegible] [illegible] native Galen, the [illegible] physician [illegible] [illegible] [illegible] [illegible] Pergamos, [illegible] considerable town [illegible] Pergamo, in Asia Minor, [illegible] the [illegible] Persians, as well as the Christians [illegible] that [illegible] [illegible] [illegible] [illegible] [illegible] [illegible] which falls into the Caicus [illegible] the other [illegible]

Christian church. The antient cathedral was dedicated to St John, but nothing is now left of it, except some of the walls. The Christians here are but two or twelve miserable families, who are allowed a church, but the Turks are said to be between 2 and 3000 souls. On the east side stands the ruins of an antient palace, and [illegible] other antiquities are here; and the [illegible] has a [illegible] of the marble columns, [illegible] a horseback, curiously carved, the remains of [illegible] [illegible] of which six are yet standing, over a throne, and farther south six others, with spacious vaults under them.

PETRA, the capital of Arabia Petræa, seems to have been denominated, by the Hebrews, Selah, (2 Kings, xiv. 7.) both which words are of the same import, viz. Rock, in Greek and Hebrew, Petra being but a translation of Selah. St Jerome intimates, that among the [illegible] it went by the name of Rekem, and that the latter was the same town in the text just quoted, stiled Joktheel. Petra was the chief fortress of the Idumæans, Edomites, or Nabathæans, and derived its name from its rocky situation. It is agreed that it was accessible only by one narrow path, which, with the steepness of the ascent, rendered it almost impregnable. It was seated in a plain full of gardens, but surrounded with rocks, according to Strabo. Pliny says nearly the same, and that the Nabathæans inhabited the city of Petra, situated in a plain watered by a river, and encompassed by inaccessible mountains. A great diversity of opinions in this particular prevails among the moderns; but we shall only observe, that it is [illegible] approved and [illegible], allowed most probable that Er[illegible]n, or Arrakah, a town in a south direction from [illegible] near Caracha, seems to correspond best with the Petra of the antients. There were several other places which had the name of Petra, and particularly one in the third Palestine; but then, as Jerome and Eusebius extend Palestine as far as the Red Sea to Elath, it comprehended Idumæa and Arabia Petræa.

PHASELUS was a tower in Jerusalem, of very great circumference.

PHIALA, Lake, situated not far from the Semechonite Lake, in the Holy Land, is now known to be the true source of the Jordan. That it was so, was long disputed, but the doubt was decided by Philip the Tetrarch, who casting straw or chaff into it, they came out at Panion. The name, which signifies a *phial*, was common to other waters of the same kind. It is situated in the midst of a most delightful country, which is also so well adapted for the carrying on of business, that marts or fairs are held there all the summer by the neighbouring people.

PHILIPPI properly belongs to Thrace, but is by most geographers placed in Macedon, pursuant to the division ever since the time of Philip, the father of Alexander, who having reduced the country between the Strymon (the [illegible] boundary of Macedon) and the Nessus, or Nestus, added it to his hereditary kingdom, whence that tract was ever after looked on as a part of Macedon. It afterwards became a Roman colony. It was situated on a rising ground, abounding with springs, having on the north the several hills, covered with woods; on the south a marsh, which reached to the Ægean Sea; on the east the streights of Symbolon, and on the west a large plain extending to the Strymon. On this plain, the probable boundary between Macedon and Thrace, was the memorable battle between Brutus and Cassius, and Anthony and Octavianus, afterwards Augustus. St Paul preached in this city, converted many, and wrote to them from Rome the epistle we have in the New Testament by such title. To speak of it in its present state, it is situated near the borders of Romania, about 190 miles from Constantinople. The Greeks, we are told, still call it Philippige (Land of Philip). The first thing apparent to travellers is the castle on a mountain, very large, and the walls almost entire. On the several hills, which surround this mountain, stand divers fortresses communicating with the castle, being encompassed with huge walls, which extend into the plain. Within the place are several heaps of free-stones and pieces of marble, but no footsteps of buildings. There are a great number of edifices half demolished. It is natural to suppose here were stately temples of white marble, sumptuous palaces, and magnificent monuments, the broken remains of all which afford beholders a grand idea of antient architecture. This town is still an archbishop's see, but [illegible] it is nothing of its antient splendour, and is very thin peopled.

PTOLEMAIS. Ptolemy makes Ptolemais and Barca in Cyrene, two different cities, placing the former in the inland, the latter on the coast. This Ptolemais is now commonly called Tolmeta.

R

RABBATH, or Rabbah, (a word importing great and populous,) the metropolis of the Ammonites, to distinguish it from the city of Moab, which bore the same name or epithet, was called Rabbah of the children of Ammon. This capital seems to have been distinguished into two parts, Rabbah properly so called, and the City of Waters. Whence these waters were derived to it, whether from the Jabbok, or from exuberant springs in or about it, is not determined. We have some authority to say, it was the most delightful part in the city, and that the king's house stood there; from whence this part may have been stiled the Royal City. This part (before which fell the brave Uriah) Joab took, and then sent to David, who came accordingly with all his forces, and took the other part. Rabbah was also famous for being the place where the great iron bedstead of Og, king of Bashan, was seen. In process of time, the city was called Philadelphia, from Ptolemy Philadelphus, who sumptuously rebuilt it, and for ages was a city of eminence.

RAGABA was a fortress in the territory of the Gerasens, beyond Jordan.

RAPHIA, a city, is placed by Strabo and Livy in Phœnicia, by Ptolemy in Samaria, and by Pliny in Idumæa. But as it stood near Gaza, between it and Rhinocolura, it is by other geographers counted among the [illegible] Palestine. It is particularly famous for the decisive battle between Antiochus, king of Syria, and Ptolemy Euergetes, wherein the former was defeated, forced to withdraw to Antioch, and quit all his conquests.

REPHAIM. The Valley of Rephaim, from a text in Joshua, appears to be near Jerusalem, in the confines at least of Judah and Benjamin. Travellers inform us, that the road from Jerusalem to Bethlehem lies through this valley, famous for being the scene of several victories obtained by David over the Philistines. As to the Rephaims, considered as a nation, race or family, they are mostly placed in Bashan, where reigned Og, the declared last of their race. They were, as the name manifests, men of gigantic stature, that of Og himself being conjectured by the size of his bedstead, &c. In the book of Genesis, the Rephaims are reckoned as one of the ten nations whose land was promised to the seed of Abraham.

RHINOCOLURA was situate near the mouth of the Bisan, (supposed that called in scripture, River of the Wilderness,) and placed by antient geographers sometimes in Syria and sometimes in Egypt, to which last kingdom it once belonged. It is now, we are told, called Pharamia, and was strongly fortified during the holy war, to prevent the Turkish [illegible] coming out of Egypt into Palestine, since which time it is gone to decay, and is an inconsiderable place.

S

SABA in Arabia Felix. The Sabæi seem to have possessed a considerable territory in the S. and best part of this peninsula. It was celebrated amongst the antients for the vast quantity of frankincense it produced. Saba, its metropolis, according to antient geographers, stood upon an hill at no considerable distance from the Red Sea, being a large, opulent and strong city. It was defended by a castle, and, as has been supposed by many learned men, together with the Arab nation in general, the residence of the queen of Sheba. The Arabs assert both the town and district to have been so denominated from Saba, the son of Jexsud, grandson of Joktan, whose name imports *to lead into captivity*, because he was the first who reduced men to a state of servitude. The aforesaid Sheba is said, besides this city of her name, to have built that famous mound which formed the vast reservoir about it, by means whereof, it received all the waters that came down from the mountains, the kings of Yemen did not only supply the inhabitants of Saba and their lands with water, but likewise kept the territories they had subdued in greater awe, for by cutting them off from a communication with it, they could at any time greatly distress them. This building stood like a mountain above the city, and was by the Sabeans esteemed so strong, that they were under no apprehension of its ever failing. Each family had a portion of the water distributed by the aqueducts. But at length a mighty flood broke down the mound by night, while the inhabitants were asleep, and carried away the city with the neighbouring towns and people. This inundation in the Koran, styled, "The inundation of Al-Aren," occasioned so terrible a destruction, that henceforth it became proverbial, thus to express a total dispersion, "They were gone and scattered like Sheba." It is the most received opinion that this catastrophe happened about the time of Alexander the Great.

SAMARIA (or Sebaste) was situated in the tribe of Ephraim 45 miles N. of Jerusalem. It was the capital city of the kingdom, and royal seat of the kings of Israel, till a period was put to that kingdom. Hence Samaria often in the Old Testament denotes the whole kingdom. Samaria, when under king Ahab, was twice besieged by Benhaded, king of Syria, and other confederate princes, which [illegible] armies, and, in the course of the latter siege, reduced to the direst extremities [illegible] however at length, through a [illegible] terror, raised the siege with the utmost precipitation. In the year before Christ 721 Salmanazar, king of Assyria, took the city after three years, and carried away the ten tribes of Israel (or most of them) into captivity, and so put an end to that kingdom after it had stood 254 years divided from that of Judah. The enemy committed the most horrid cruelties on their captives, so that Samaria was reduced almost to an heap of rubbish, and all the land laid waste. This melancholy and fatal end of that kingdom happened in the 6th year of Hezekiah and 9th of Hosea. But Samaria must have been soon repaired, for colonies were then sent either by Salmanazar, or his successor, to re-people the land of Israel, chiefly from Cutha, whence the new inhabitants were called Cutheans. From some religious and other causes there seems a mutual hatred subsisted between the Jews and Samaritans, the former abominating even the name of the latter, and those on their part always [illegible] kindred with them in times of adversity, though forward enough to claim it in time of prosperity. After divers revolutions it was at length taken by Aristobulus, and its region, together with Galilee, and again restored to Judea. Samaria was partly rebuilt by Gabinius, and new called Sebaste by Herod, who put the finishing stroke to it. It was made the metropolis of Palestine Secunda under the Romans, and an archbishopric under the Christians. Herod Agrippa obtained it of the emperor Caligula, and siding with the P[illegible] against the Jews under Vespasian, they at that time avoided the common calamity of the country. But afterwards, taking other measures, they were, together with the rest of the Jews, extirpated out of Palestine by Adrian, and the city has since gone to decay. The melancholy remnants of this once famous city, stand upon a long mount of an oval figure, having, first a fruitful valley, and then a rising hill running about it. The Turks have erected a mosque here, to which they let no Christian [illegible] for a small piece of money.

SAMOSATA, once the capital of Comagena Proper, was situated on the Euphrates, near the confines of Armenia Minor. It was the residence of Antiochus Asiaticus, after Pompey had confined his kingdom to this small province, and stripped him of the rest of Syria. It was the native place of the witty Lucian. It is now called Scempsal, but is only a poor village, surrounded with an heap of ruins of the antient city.

SCYTHOPOLIS. See Bethsan.

SELEUCIA. There were nine cities of this name built by Seleucus, but distinguished by some adjunct, some of the most eminent of which follow. Seleucia on the Tigris, so called from Seleucus Nicanor, its founder, whom [illegible] the metropolis of his empire beyond the Euphrates. Seleucia, surnamed [illegible] or Aspera (an appellation well agreeing with the mountains and [illegible] country of Cilicia, on which it stood,) about twelve miles from the [illegible] on the banks of the Calycadnus. Its bishopric became subject to the patriarch of Constantinople [illegible] centuries. Its modern name is Selefkeh. Seleucia surnamed Pieria, on the north side of the Orontes, now [illegible] called Seluki Jelbe. Seleucia [illegible] Taurum, because it stood on [illegible] Seleucia Ferrea, perhaps [illegible] manufactures, is now [illegible].

SEPPHORIS, a city of Galilee. It stood in the tribe of Zebulun, and was one of the strongest cities in Galilee [illegible] road from Ptolemais. It became in time the metropolis of that province, when the emperor gave it to young Agrippa. The younger Varus, the Roman general [illegible], sold the inhabitants by auction, set fire to the city, and reduced it to ashes. Herod Antipater [illegible] the territory of Galilee for his share of the government, rebuilt it, and surrounded it with strong walls, so that it became one of the best cities in [illegible].

SHILOH in Canaan, where was set up the tabernacle, in which was kept the ark, and where the ark remained till just before the death of Eli. It was situated in the tribe of Ephraim. After the Philistines took the ark, Shiloh [illegible] Jeremiah, [illegible] of Jerusalem, [illegible] would be brought into the [illegible] Jerome [illegible] was nothing [illegible] the days of [illegible].

SICHEM, Sechem, or Shechem. The proper and original name seems to have been Shalem, which [illegible] Sichem and Sichar, [illegible] Sichem, [illegible] Hamor [illegible] [illegible] given to [illegible] the city of [illegible].

SIDON [illegible] to be [illegible]

Judge [illegible] by having [illegible] The [illegible] [illegible] were [illegible] famous for hewing timber, (see 1 Kings [illegible]) and [illegible] Solomon [illegible] his [illegible] to [illegible] temple. They are [illegible] also to have been excellent [illegible] to [illegible] by the Saracens in 9[illegible]6 and recovered, [illegible] red, and [illegible] the Christians [illegible] and was [illegible] [illegible] and [illegible] temple, [illegible] which the [illegible] [illegible] It [illegible] ed [illegible] is [illegible] ted in a [illegible] district, [illegible] town. The [illegible] is [illegible] large, and the public [illegible] in good condition. The haven is large but [illegible] ate, [illegible] and [illegible] all ridge of rocks about a [illegible] of [illegible] Sidon is reckoned to contain about [illegible] The Turks have [illegible], Roman Catholics and Greeks, each a church, and the Maronites a [illegible] carry on a considerable trade. Provisions are very [illegible] and cheap, and [illegible] to [illegible] great numbers into the [illegible] Sidon, by a grant of the [illegible] [illegible]

S[illegible], or Siloam, a fountain in the valley of Jehoshaphat, from which the gardens of it are watered [illegible] the water [illegible] numbers of [illegible] every day wash [illegible] It waters are no [illegible] to be an infallible cure for fevers. Over against this fountain, on the other side of the valley, is the place called [illegible] to have [illegible] wives.

SIN, wilderness of. This wilderness, we are told in [illegible] Sin. Here it was that [illegible] the Israelites manna.

SINAI, [illegible] mount. There are many windings [illegible] between the deserts of Sin [illegible] Sinai [illegible] more than one league broad, [illegible] to the north-west, but closed [illegible] of the [illegible] eminences of the [illegible] on [illegible] the highest [illegible] [illegible] enough for [illegible] There [illegible] convents [illegible] such ridiculous [illegible] [illegible] religious bigots, it cannot be defended [illegible] intelligent reader.

Sodom [illegible] have been the chief of the five cities, [illegible] which [illegible] towards to [illegible] [illegible] [illegible] [illegible] this city derived [illegible]

Solomon's Tower. See Cæsarea.

S[illegible] name of [illegible] That in Exodus [illegible] Israelites [illegible] after their [illegible] geographers of [illegible] places [illegible] the [illegible] Israelites [illegible] known. This Succoth [illegible] be [illegible] that situated [illegible] the river [illegible] between the [illegible] Jabbok, which Jacob called [illegible] [illegible] of Mesopotamia, thought [illegible] been so called in [illegible] booths or tents which the people [illegible]

S[illegible] the Scripture [illegible] (now called [illegible]) was the [illegible] of the [illegible] provinces, [illegible] on the [illegible] of the river [illegible] (by [illegible] called [illegible]) by Memnon, as some [illegible] who was [illegible] the [illegible] in the [illegible] Strabo and Ptolemy [illegible] its walls even with those of Babylon. It [illegible] Memnonica, by Herodotus and others, from Memnon its founder. In Scripture [illegible] the Palace, but [illegible] there was [illegible] city, as [illegible] the profane writers. [illegible] wealth and magnificence [illegible] by Alexander the Great, when [illegible] the [illegible] of Arbela, or [illegible] twenty days after his departure from [illegible], [illegible] had before been delivered up to him. [illegible] kept his great feast 18[illegible] days [illegible] this city [illegible] by the name of Schouster.

T

TARICHEA was a town of Galilee, situate on an eminence by the lake of Genezareth, over against [illegible] It having been besieged by [illegible] both [illegible] and [illegible] made a desperate defence till a dissention happened [illegible] which coming to the ears of the Roman general, it was taken by [illegible]

TARSHISH, son of Javan, settled in the [illegible] part of the [illegible] tract of Asia Minor is very probable, for the name of [illegible] the chief town of Cilicia, is thought to carry [illegible] probable marks of its being [illegible] founded by [illegible] himself, or some of his descendants. It is [illegible] an historian [illegible] that [illegible] was so called from Tarshish, and that Cilicia was originally known by the name of [illegible] Indeed, it is scarcely doubted that this was the [illegible] Tarshish so often mentioned by the prophets on account of its [illegible] Tyre.

T[illegible], in Cilicia as aforesaid, seems to have borrowed its name from Tarshish. It was at first the metropolis of Cilicia, and at [illegible] Constantine's division of Cilicia Prima. It [illegible] the native city of St. Paul (though a Hebrew of the Hebrews, or a Jew born by [illegible] and, [illegible] to Strabo in former times, not inferior, for the [illegible] of philosophy and polite literature, either to Athens [illegible] The inhabitants enjoyed the privileges of Roman citizens according to the Porcian Law, which [illegible] thought proper to claim and use upon several occasions, as is recorded in the Acts. The Tarsians, to ingratiate [illegible] with Julius Cæsar, changed the city's name into Julio[illegible] new, and [illegible] to this day by the Greeks called [illegible] by the Turks Tarsow, and [illegible] It is [illegible] that the [illegible] hardly [illegible]

TAURUS, the greatest mountain of Asia, and hence [illegible] thought the greatest in the world. It runs from west to east under several names, [illegible] large kingdoms and countries [illegible] whence all Asia [illegible] parts, [illegible] the [illegible] and that on the [illegible] It also [illegible] and [illegible] and sends forth many branches under divers [illegible] the north and [illegible]

TABOR Mount, of which [illegible] called Itab[illegible] Judæa, not [illegible] from Nazareth. In the [illegible] century [illegible] is described to [illegible] of wonderful regularity, verdant and [illegible] A [illegible] traveller thus describes [illegible] It has a [illegible] top most fertile and [illegible] of [illegible] The [illegible] trees [illegible] It was [illegible] rounded with walls, trenches, and [illegible] of which [illegible] day.

TIBERIAS. See Genezareth. Herod the tetrarch of Galilee (Antipas) building a city on the north bank of Genezareth, called it Tiberias, in honour of Tiberius, the lake thence took this name [illegible] The city [illegible] spot full of sepulchres; but the great privileges granted by Herod to people for becoming inhabitants, which overcame their scruple of conscience as to pollution by dead bodies, &c. rendered it quickly become one of the principal cities of these parts. It is said to have had in it 13 synagogues and an academy; that here was the last session of the Sanhedrim, or chief council of the Jews, and here the [illegible], or body of the Jewish civil and canon law, was collected.

TIMNAH was first assigned to the tribe of Judah, but afterward to that of Dan. In the days of Eusebius and Jerome, a great town, named Thamnatha, lay in the borders of Diospolis, towards Jerusalem, which is supposed to have been the same with that formerly called Timnah.

TIRZAH is mentioned frequently in the old history, as being long the regal city of the kings of Israel. From an expression in the Canticles, it appears to have been a beautiful and pleasant place to live in; but its situation is not certainly determined.

TRACHONITIS, a region of Judea, which seems to have derived its name from two famous mountains, which Strabo calls Trachones. The greatest part of it had such ridges of rocks and mountains, especially on the sides of Arabia, [illegible] some of them had caverns large enough to lodge 4000 men. It, together with Ituraea, [illegible] in the time of Our Saviour [illegible].

TRIPOLIS in Phoenicia, called Tarablis by the Turks, [illegible] Syria to distinguish it from others, stands [illegible] the same coast with Joppa and Joppa [illegible] Sidon. It has its name from its forming three [illegible] each one furlong distant from the other; one of which belonged to the [illegible], or ancient kingdom of Aradus; the second to the Sidonians, and the third to the Tyrians. It is still divided into the upper and lower town; and is in a flourishing condition, having large population, and strong, adorned with mulberry-tree plantations on the rooms, from which is drawn considerable profit. The walls are strong and fortified with several towers. The castle is the residence of the beglerbeg, and garrisoned by two hundred janizaries. It is strong, situated on an eminence and well stored with cannon. On account of its importance, it is deemed the metropolis of Phoenicia. The haven is rather an open [illegible] than a secure harbour, unless [illegible] [illegible] by two small islands about two leagues from it. There are [illegible] towers, or castles, along the shore, well furnished with artillery. The town contains about 8000 houses, and 60,000 inhabitants, who consist of Turks, Jews, and Christians. [illegible] [illegible] [illegible] the streets [illegible] [illegible] and baths, the country about very [illegible] and [illegible] [illegible] [illegible] the handsome buildings [illegible] [illegible] church, a large and stately edifice. The Christians have some [illegible] [illegible] [illegible] and the Jesuits in handsome college. This city [illegible] the [illegible] being one of the four [illegible] [illegible] Christians had in these parts.

TROGLODYTES. In their manner of life [illegible] part of them only resembled the Lybian [illegible]. They are divided into tribes under one head. A part of them fought with clubs, carrying bucklers made round, and of raw ox hides. Many, however, used bows and arrows.

TYRE, on the coast of Phoenicia Proper, [illegible] Sur. It is commonly called the Daughter of Sidon, and stood about [illegible] furlongs to the south of Sidon. It had two havens, one looking towards Sidon, the other towards Egypt, [illegible] whence it is thought that [illegible] on an island, and the city on the Main were considered as but one city; the common wall was drawn up between them, and part of them might [illegible] be [illegible] contiguous to each other. This famous emporium was never of very great extent, for which reason they built it very lofty, and with more stories, it is said, than the houses at Rome. The buildings, in general, were [illegible] [illegible] magnificent, and above the rest, [illegible] the temples built by King Hiram to Jupiter, Hercules, and Astarte. It is now called Sur, and is a mere babel of broken walls, pillars, vaults, &c. there not being one entire house left. Its present inhabitants are only a few poor wretches, who harbour in vaults, and subsist chiefly by fishing. King Hiram is famed, in sacred history, for maintaining a strict friendship and alliance with King David, presenting him with cedars, and sending him skilful workmen to build his palace. He continued the same affection for his son and successor Solomon, which occasioned an interchange of letters of amity. Tyre was besieged 13 years together by Nebuchadnezzar, who at length [illegible] [illegible], when he put all the [illegible] [illegible] he could find to the sword, and destroyed the [illegible]. But many of the people had, in the [illegible] [illegible] [illegible], with the chief of their effects, to an island at some distance from the shore, where they built New Tyre [illegible] on the island. The city, [illegible] at length [illegible] to Nebuchadnezzar, who appointed [illegible] [illegible] [illegible] [illegible] [illegible] [illegible] [illegible] [illegible] [illegible] Alexander. Tyre was besieged [illegible] [illegible] [illegible] [illegible] [illegible] [illegible] [illegible] [illegible] [illegible] [illegible] [illegible] [illegible] [illegible] [illegible] [illegible] [illegible] [illegible] the [illegible] [illegible] [illegible] [illegible] [illegible] [illegible] [illegible] [illegible] [illegible] [illegible] [illegible] [illegible] [illegible] [illegible] [illegible] [illegible] the city [illegible] [illegible] [illegible] [illegible] [illegible] [illegible] [illegible] [illegible] [illegible] [illegible] [illegible] [illegible] [illegible] [illegible] [illegible] [illegible] Such was the conduct [illegible] [illegible] the great [illegible] [illegible], who fought for [illegible] [illegible] [illegible] [illegible] [illegible] [illegible] [illegible] [illegible] [illegible] [illegible] quarrel [illegible] [illegible] [illegible] [illegible] Pope very justly observes,

> Heroes are much the same [illegible] [illegible]
> From [illegible] [illegible] [illegible] [illegible]
> [illegible] [illegible] [illegible] [illegible] [illegible] to find,
> [illegible] [illegible] [illegible] [illegible] [illegible]
> [illegible] [illegible] [illegible] [illegible] [illegible] [illegible]
> [illegible] [illegible] [illegible] [illegible] [illegible]

[illegible] [illegible] [illegible] [illegible] [illegible] [illegible] peopled [illegible] [illegible] city, [illegible] [illegible] [illegible] [illegible] [illegible] [illegible] [illegible] the [illegible] [illegible] [illegible] [illegible] [illegible] [illegible] be suspected, to prevent the [illegible] from recollecting [illegible] [illegible] [illegible] [illegible] [illegible] [illegible] [illegible] [illegible] [illegible] in time, [illegible] [illegible] [illegible] [illegible] [illegible] [illegible] [illegible] confederate with the Romans, and [illegible] [illegible] [illegible] [illegible] of a Roman city [illegible] [illegible] [illegible] [illegible] in the times of primitive Christianity [illegible] [illegible] the metropolitan see for the province of Phoenicia. In 636 it was conquered by the Saracens, but in [illegible] recovered by the Christians. In 1289 it was finally subdued by the Turks, in whose hands it has [illegible] [illegible] since. Those infidels took it soon after the reduction of Acra, or Acre, while they [illegible] [illegible] [illegible] [illegible] [illegible] [illegible] the Tyrians, [illegible] with the [illegible] [illegible], betook themselves to their [illegible] [illegible] [illegible] abandoned the city [illegible] [illegible] [illegible] [illegible] [illegible] [illegible] [illegible] [illegible] [illegible] [illegible] [illegible] [illegible] [illegible] [illegible] [illegible] [illegible] [illegible] [illegible] [illegible] We must not omit to observe, that the Tyrians [illegible] [illegible] [illegible] [illegible] [illegible] [illegible] purple, which [illegible] [illegible] [illegible] [illegible] [illegible] [illegible] [illegible] [illegible] [illegible] [illegible] [illegible] by eating of the fish called [illegible] [illegible] [illegible] a buccinum [illegible] [illegible] [illegible] by the [illegible] [illegible] [illegible] [illegible] [illegible] [illegible] [illegible] [illegible] [illegible] [illegible] [illegible] [illegible] [illegible] from Pliny [illegible] [illegible] [illegible] [illegible] [illegible] was obtained from [illegible] [illegible] was so much valued in the time of the Roman emperors, on account of its being the imperial colour that only one pound of it cost a thousand Roman denarii, or above thirty pounds sterling

V

VIENNE capital of the province of Viennois, about seven leagues from Lyons, at the foot of a mountain on the Rhone, has been a large, famous city, but now is not above a fourth of what it was, having its two old fortresses demolished The Allobroges are said to have founded it, and it became a colony of the Romans who adorned it with a palace, amphitheatre, and other magnificent works, the ruins whereof are yet seen It was some time the capital of Burgundy The cathedral is a stately pile, as are some other churches and public buildings The inhabitants are expert in manufactures, particularly of plates of iron and steel, paper, &c by mills and engines

UR, of the Chaldees, where Abraham was born, and whence he removed, at the Divine call, to Charran, and so to Canaan The word Ur signifies *fire* The most probable opinion therefore is, that the city might be so denominated from its inhabitants being worshippers of the sun, and of fire, its emblem, and for having temples wherein the sacred fire was kept always burning The Chaldees were famed for it, and carried it, in great pomp, at the head of their armies when they went to battle.

Z

ZEBULON, his lot, or the land of his tribe Jacob, in his prophetic blessing of his son Zebulon, says, that he shall dwell at the haven of the sea, and he shall be for an haven of ships, and his border shall be unto Sidon And so it happened, that tribe's possession being from the Mediterranean, on the west, to the lake of Genezareth, on the east, side.

ZIPH, Wilderness of We find in Joshua a city called Ziph, mentioned together with Carmel and Maon We have also, in the history of David, mention made of Carmel and Maon as adjoining to Ziph So that it is not to be doubted, but in the wilderness where was David, and where was the hill Aschelah, is to be understood Ziph near Carmel and Maon. This is placed, by Jerome, eight miles east from Hebron.

ZOAR The Syriac version reads *Zoan* It was probably the most antient royal seat of the Pharaoh's, for the miracles wrought by Moses and Aaron before one of them, are expresly said, in the Psalms, to be done in the field of *Zoar*

ZOBAH That the country of *Zobah* pertained to the Syrians, is evident from 2 Sam x 6 where we read expresly of the Syrians of Zobah, and, from their being hired by the Ammonites, it appears that Zobah lay in the parts adjoining to the Ammonites. The kingdom of Damascus is looked upon by the learned to have arisen out of that of Zobah, or to be no other than one and the same kingdom which formerly had Zobah, and afterwards Damascus, for its capital city, is the seat of its kings. To the south of *Zobah* lay the land of Ishtob

A

GENERAL INDEX

OF THE

Principal Transactions and Occurrences

RELATED IN THE

WORKS

OF

FLAVIUS JOSEPHUS.

C

D

J

8 M

N

O.

P

Q

R

Y

Z

AN

INDEX

OF THE

Names of the Principal Perſons and Places

MENTIONED IN THE

WORKS

OF

FLAVIUS JOSEPHUS.

DIRECTIONS TO THE BINDER

FOR

Placing the Plates

TO

FLAVIUS JOSEPHUS.

List of Subscribers' Names.

A

DAVID ACKLEY,
Thomas Ackley,
Peter Adams,
Francis Adams,
John Aitken,
Robert Allen,
Rev Richard Allen,
William Allibone,
Lawrence Allwine,
Nicholas Ambruwster,
John Anderson,
Hugh Andrews,
Isaac Andrews,
William Ashby,
William Ashmead
Thomas Ashmoor, *Lamberton*
William Ashton

B

Michael Baker,
John Hilary Baker,
Jacob Baker,
Hilary K Baker,
B. W Ball,
George Barclay
Henry Barrington,
Dr Isaac Bartram, junr
Edward Bartlett,
Thomas Bartleman,
Moses Bartram,
Joseph Beacon, *Trenton.*
Jacob Beckert,
Henry Beck,
William G Bell,
Jacob Belsterling,
John Bender,
Samuel Benge,
William Bethel,
Benjamin Betterton,
Robert Bicknell,
Peter Bicknell,
Thomas Biggs,
James Bigley,
William Black,
Daniel Bœhm,
Frederick Bortfeldt,
Secundo Bosio,
William Bowles,
David Bowers,
Henry Bowles,
William Boyle,
John Brant,
Samuel Brook
David Brooks,
James Brooks,
Richard Brown,
William Brown,
John Brown,
Samuel Browne,
William Brown,
Joseph Brumley, *Tr[illegible]*
Peter Buddy,
William W Bullock,
Philip Burke,
William Buston,
George Buxton

C

Timothy Caldwell,
Charles Campbell,
Gilbert Tennant Carell,
Stephen Carey, *Trenton*
Samuel Carpenter,
Daniel Carteret, junr
Jonathan Carson,
William Chancellor,
E Chandler,
Benjamin Chamberlaine,
George R Chapman,
Benjamin Chew, junr
Dr David Christy,
Neal Christie,
Hugh Christy,
Adam C[illegible]
Samuel Clardy,
Henry Claise,
Abraham Cohen,
John Collard,
Sarah Collins,
Timothy Collins,
Cornelius Comegys,
Joseph Conrade,
Abraham Cook,
William Cook,
Benj Cooper, *Gloucester County*
John Cooper,
John Cope,
John Cotterill,
George Cotte,
Isaac Cox,
Samuel Cox,
James Craft, *Burlington*
G Craft, *Trenton*
Benjamin Crohen,
Dr John Cumming,
Thomas Cumming,
Anthony Cuthbert

D

A J Dallas, Esq
William Dalzell,
William Davidson,
John Davidson,
William Davis
Zephaniah Davis,
Thomas Davis,
John Davis,
Edward Davy,
Jesse Dickerson,
Thomas Dickson
Jacob Dietrick,
Joseph A Dilworth,
Charles Dilworth,
Thomas Dobson, (6 copies)
J H Dobelbower,
Daniel Dolby,
Aaron Donaldson
Joseph Donaldson,
Robert Doughty,
John Douglass,
Dr Samuel Duffield,
John Duffield,
William G Dunn,
Jacob Durang

E

Esther Eastburn,
Adam Eckfelt,
Alexander Edwards,
Samuel Ellicott,
William Ellis,
James Engle,
Charles Erdman,
Lewis Evans, *Trenton*

F

Alexander Fairweather,
Nathaniel Field,
Thomas Fenton,
James Ferguson,
Isaac Ferree, *Lancaster County*
Joseph Fils,
Samuel Fleck *Bucks County*
Christopher Flanagan,
William Forsyth,
William Foudray,
Nathaniel Fowler,
George Fox,
Michael Fox,
Daniel Frazer,
Adam Franks,
John France,
Henry Fraley, *Germantown*
Richard Freeman,
William Fromberger,
Robert Fry

G

James Gamble,
John S Gano, *Kentucky*
Isaac Gano, *Frankfort, (Ken)*
Daniel Gano, *Ditto*
Gilbert Gaw,
Robert Gaw,
John Smith Gardner,
John Gardner
William Gerhard,
Charles Gibbs,
John Gibson,
Jesse Gilbert,
William Giles,
William Gipson,
John Goodman,
George Goddard,
Francis Graham,
William Gray,
Rev Ashbel Green,
William Grum

H.

Philip Habzel,
William Haines,
Abraham Haines,
William Hallowell junr
Martin Harnsted,
Robert Hartel,
Peter Harris,
Robert Harris,
William Harrison,
Benjamin Harper,
Robert Harvey
George Heberton,
Rev F H C Helmuth,
Christian Hemrich, *Bordentown*
Rev Wm Hendel jun *Dauphin County*
Andrew W Henderson,
William Henderson,
Jacob Herman,
Capt William Hess,
John S Hillman,
John Hill,
James Hill,
Jacob Hofner,
William Holderness,
George Honey,
Thomas Hood,
John Hook,
Isaac Hopkins,
J B Horn,
Benjamin Horner,
Aaron Howell, *Trenton*
Ashton Humphreys,
Richard Humphreys,
Dalziel Hunter,
George Hutman,
Nicholas Hybigah

I & J

Philip Jacobs,
Joseph Jacobs,
Robert James,
Francis D Janvier,
Rev William Jessop
Richard Johnson,
John Johnson,
George Ingles,
Henry Ingle,
Thomas Inglish,
Jonathan Insleepe,
Rev Absalom Jones,
Jesse Jones,
John Jones,
Sarah Jones,
Robert Irwin,
Israel Israel,
Joseph Justice,
John Justice

K

John Kean,
Adam Keller,
Peter Keyser,
Daniel King,
George King,
George Kunkle,
George D Kuotr,
Jacob Kurtz,
Jacob Kuhnle

L

David Lake,
John Landon,
[illegible]
George Lauman,
Thomas Lawrence, *Bordentown*
Samuel Leake, *Trenton*
John Leech,
John Lewis,
Aaron Levy,

Joseph Lippincot, [illegible] copies
John Little,
Reese Lloyd
Benjamin Lodet,
John Lodor,
Edward Loder,
Adam Logan,
John Loram, jun
Henry Lot,
Abraham Lott, *New York*
Benjamin Lyndall

M

Samuel Macklin,
George Mallinion,
Thomas Marley,
William Marley,
Jacob Martin,
James Mathers,
James Martin, *Bedford County*,
William Matthews,
Charles Mattis, *New Jersey*
Joseph Mitchell,
Mary M'Allister,
William M'Cully,
Robert M'Koy,
Daniel M Leod,
Nathaniel M'Means,
Daniel M'Arthur,
John Mears, *Cattawessy-Town*
Rev John Meder,
Rev Thomas Menninger,
Barney Meikle, *Reading*,
Robert Merrie,
Edmond Milne, jun
George Millision,
John Mingle,
Thomas Mitchell,
Thomas I Moore,
Thomas Moore,
Elisha Moor,
Richard Morgan,
Abraham Moorhouse,
Anthony Morris,
Alexander Morrison,
Richard Mosley,
Robert C Murray,
Michael Murphy,
Jacob Myrick,
Christopher Myrtelus

N

David Nagle,
David Nelson,
John Nicholson, Esq
John Nicholson, jun.
Richard North,
William North

O

William Ockford,
Hugh Ogden,

P

Thomas Palmore,
John Parker,
[illegible]
Robert Paul,
Robert P[illegible]on,
John P Peckworth,
Joseph Pemberton,
James Pemberton,
James Pentland,
John Phillips,
[illegible] Phipps,
Lewis Phipps
Timothy Pickering, Esq
John Pidgeon,
Samuel Pleasants,
William I Pomeroy *Burlington*
Robert Porter,
James Potter,
Thomas Poultney,
Mrs Powell,
Elizabeth Preston,
John M Price,
Ann Price,
Samuel Prince,
Levi Proctor,
Thomas Pugh

Q

Philip Quarril,
Thomas Quigley

R

Jacob Rabsom,
Nathaniel Raine,
Hon Edmund Randolph,
William Rawle,
George Reese,
Mark Reeve,
Augustus Frederick Reichel,
Rev Charles Reichel, *Nazareth*
Henry Reinholdt,
William Richardson,
Edward Riley,
Dr David Rittenhouse
J Rhea, *Trenton*
Flavel Roan,
James M Robertson,
Jonathan Roberts,
Rev William Rogers,
David Rose, jun
Thomas Ross,
James Rowan,
Martin Row, jun
Edward Rowley,
Daniel Ruff
William Rush,
Benjamin Rush,
Edward Russel.
Anthony Ruston,
Isaac Ryal

S

Elijah Sanders,
Jacob Sch[illegible]ner,
John Schnider,
[illegible] Schell,
Edward Scott
Robert Se[illegible],
John Sears,
Nathan Sellers,
John Sel[illegible],
[illegible] Isaac Salmon,
John [illegible]d,
Archibald [illegible],
Bernard Sheffler,
William Shippen,
Frederick Shinckle, jun
Henry Shriver,
Conrad Shrine, jun
David Shute, *Bordentown*
John Sibley,
Jonas Simonds,
George Simson,
Robert Simson,
David Simmons,
Henry Sims,
John Sims,
John Simpson,
Samuel Sitgreaves, *Easton*,
Joseph Skerrett,
Robert Smithey,
Rev John Smith, *Columbia N. Western Territory*
Uriah Smith,
John Smith,
John Smith, jun
R Smith,
Jacob Smith,
William Smiley,
Joseph Swain,
George H Snider,
John Snider,
Joseph Snowden,
Jacob Souder,
John Springer,
John Sproul,
James Stewart,
James W Stevens,
Aaron Steward,
Joshua Stiles,
Edward Stiles,
Pontius D Stille, *Trenton*
James Stirk,
James Stirling,
Richard Stockton,
Samuel Stock,
John Stokes,
John Street,
John A Summers,
James Sutter,
George Sweetman, *Burlington*
Hugh Sweeny

T

John Thompson,
Joseph Thomas,
David Thum,
Thomas Tomkins,
W[illegible] Townsend,
Frederick Tryon,
Robert Taylor

V

J Van Larburgh, *Borough*
Isaac Van Garden,
James Vaux,
Abraham Vickers,
Amos Vickers,
Henry Voignt,
Sebastian Voight

W

John Waddington,
John Walters,
John Ward,
John Ware,
Isaac Warner,
John Ward,
Charles C Watson,
William Watson,
Patrick Waters,
Thomas Watkins,
Henry Waver,
George Way,
Zephaniah Webster,
Richard Well,
Adam Wever,
Thomas Wharton,
John Wharton,
William Whitesides,
John White,
Jacob Whiteman,
Thomas White,
John Wiggins, *Trenton*
Joseph Will,
John Wilson,
Thomas Wilson,
Achilles Wilson, *Trenton*
James Wilson.
Joseph Wiseman,
Robert Wood,
George Woods,
James Wood,
Benjamin Wolfe,
Hampton Woodruff,
Enoch Wright,
John Wucherer

Y.

David Yerkes,
Archibald Yard

Z

William Zane

List of Subscribers' Names in the City of Baltimore.

A

HUGH AIKEN,
William [illegible],
Michael Aiken

B

PHILIP [illegible]R,
William Bra[illegible]
Michael Bradle[illegible],
Stan[illegible] B[illegible]y,
William Blewford
John Bu[illegible]
William B[illegible]
Alexander Brown
Richard Fer[illegible]
Joseph B[illegible],
John Br[illegible]
William B[illegible]
[illegible],
Peter B[illegible]d,
Richard B[illegible],
[illegible] B[illegible],
John B[illegible],
Gilbert Enger,
William B[illegible]ton,
[illegible] B[illegible]
Joseph B[illegible]ston,
Lawrence B[illegible]
[illegible] Bl[illegible],
[illegible] B[illegible],
R[illegible] B[illegible],
Isaac Baker

C

ROBERT CARI[illegible]
John C[illegible],
[illegible] Cole,
Godlieb Cox
John Cl[illegible],
John Caldwell,
Robert Co[illegible]

D

ROBERT [illegible]EY,
John D[illegible]
John D[illegible],
[illegible],
[illegible] D[illegible],
Thomas D[illegible],
Hugh D[illegible]
[illegible],
[illegible] D[illegible],
William [illegible]
[illegible]
[illegible]
[illegible] D[illegible]
[illegible]
Robert D[illegible]

E

WILLIAM [illegible]
George E[illegible]
James E[illegible]
[illegible],
[illegible]

F

ALEXANDER FURNI[illegible],
[illegible]
[illegible]
Gregory F[illegible],
[illegible]

G

JOHN G[illegible],
[illegible]
[illegible],
[illegible]
[illegible]
[illegible]
[illegible]
[illegible]
[illegible]

H

HUMPHREY COLSTON,
Peter Hoffman,
Thomas Hun[illegible]
John Hog[illegible],
John Herman[illegible]
[illegible] Hall,
Ludwic Herring
[illegible],
Joseph Hook,
Joshua Ha[illegible],
Christopher Hughes,
[illegible] Hall
George Huff[illegible],
[illegible] Hall,
[illegible] Hall, jun

J

CHRISTOPHER JACKSON,
[illegible],
Jacob Jones,
Isaac Jones,
James Johnston,
Richard Jones

K

JOHN KILTY, Esq.
[illegible] Kell,
Christian Keener,
[illegible] Kegler,
John Keener,
George Kraus

L

PETER LEPER
Philip Little,
[illegible],
Peregrine Lloyd,
Jacob [illegible] Le[illegible],
Samuel Lyeth,
Robert Cary Lane,
Jacob Lee,
John Lee, Fell's Point,
John Lee, Pratt [illegible]
Frederick Lauderman
John Lates

M

GEORGE MILLENBERGER
Jonathan Munroe,
William Murphy,
[illegible] Moore,
William Moore,
William M'Cleary,
James M'[illegible],
Jacob Myers, South [illegible]
Jacob Myers, Con[illegible]
Jacob Myers, Baltimore [illegible]
William Muller
John Mackenheimer
Dennis M'Henry
William [illegible]
John Murph[illegible],
George Miller,
Duncan M'Callum
Jacob M[illegible],
Benjamin M'[illegible]
William M'[illegible]
[illegible] M'[illegible],
John M'[illegible],
[illegible]

N

George Na[illegible],
[illegible]

O

Joseph Osburn
[illegible]
[illegible]

P

[illegible]
[illegible]
[illegible]
[illegible]
[illegible]
[illegible]
[illegible]
[illegible] Pe[illegible],
[illegible]
William [illegible]
John P[illegible],
[illegible] Pritchard,
[illegible]

R

RICHARD RA[illegible]
[illegible] R[illegible],
[illegible] Ramsey,
George Ruff,
George Ru[illegible],
Philip Rogers,
Charles Reis,
John Re[illegible]
George P[illegible],
George Redd[illegible],
Enoch Richardson,
John R[illegible],
Jacob Ro[illegible],
[illegible] R[illegible]

S

WILLIAM SMALLWOOD
[illegible] S[illegible],
George [illegible], esq.
Joshua S[illegible]
[illegible],
[illegible] S[illegible]
[illegible] S[illegible],
James S[illegible]
[illegible] S[illegible],
Samuel Sower,
[illegible] Sheppard,
[illegible] S[illegible],
James S[illegible],
[illegible] S[illegible],
[illegible] S[illegible],
Thomas S[illegible],
Jacob S[illegible]
Henry S[illegible],
Christopher Sle[illegible]
Joseph S[illegible],
[illegible] S[illegible],
Job Smith, esq.
William S[illegible]
Thomas S[illegible],
Joseph S[illegible],
[illegible] S[illegible]

T

DANIEL [illegible],
Alexander Thompson,
[illegible] Thompson,
[illegible]
[illegible] Thompson

U

THOMAS U[illegible]
[illegible]
[illegible]

W

[illegible] WILL[illegible]
George W[illegible]
George W[illegible]
[illegible] W[illegible],
John W[illegible]
[illegible],
[illegible]
[illegible]
[illegible]
William W[illegible]
[illegible]

[illegible] Y[illegible]

CPSIA information can be obtained
at www.ICGtesting.com
Printed in the USA
LVHW021050270423
745292LV00022B/95